LITERATURE

LITERATURE

LITERATURE

An Introduction to Fiction,
Poetry, Drama, and Writing

FOURTEENTH EDITION

X. J. Kennedy

Dana Gioia
University of Southern California

Dan Stone

 Pearson

Executive Portfolio Manager: Aron Keesbury
Content Producer: Barbara Cappuccio
Content Developer: Elizabeth Farrell
Portfolio Manager Assistant: Christa Cottone
Senior Product Marketing Manager:
  Michael Coons
Product Marketing Manager: Nicholas Bolt
Content Producer Manager: Ken Volcjak
Managing Editor: Cynthia Cox

Designer: Alisha Webber
Digital Studio Course Producer: Elizabeth Bravo
Full-Service Project Management: Lois Lombardo,
  Cenveo® Publisher Services
Printer/Binder: LSC Communications, Inc.
Cover Printer: Phoenix Color/Hagerstown
Senior Art Director: Cate Barr
Cover Design: Cadence Design Studio
Cover Illustration: Robert Kennedy

Acknowledgments of third party content appear on pages 456, 1056, 1695, 1940–1962, which constitute an extension of this copyright page.

Copyright © 2020, 2016, 2013 by X. J. Kennedy, Dana Goia, and Dan Stone. All Rights Reserved. Printed in the United States of America. This publication is protected by copyright, and permission should be obtained from the publisher prior to any prohibited reproduction, storage in a retrieval system, or transmission in any form or by any means, electronic, mechanical, photocopying, recording, or otherwise. For information regarding permissions, request forms and the appropriate contacts within the Pearson Education Global Rights & Permissions department, please visit www.pearsoned.com/permissions/.

PEARSON, ALWAYS LEARNING, and Revel are exclusive trademarks in the United States and/or other countries owned by Pearson Education, Inc. or its affiliates.

Unless otherwise indicated herein, any third-party trademarks that may appear in this work are the property of their respective owners and any references to third-party trademarks, logos or other trade dress are for demonstrative or descriptive purposes only. Such references are not intended to imply any sponsorship, endorsement, authorization, or promotion of Pearson's products by the owners of such marks, or any relationship between the owner and Pearson Education, Inc. or its affiliates, authors, licensees or distributors.

Library of Congress Cataloging-in-Publication Data
Names: Kennedy, X. J., editor | Gioia, Dana, editor. | Stone, Dan,
  editor.
Title: Literature : an introduction to fiction, poetry, drama, and writing /
  [compiled by] X. J. Kennedy, Dana Gioia, Dan Stone.
Description: Fourteenth edition. Student edition. | Boston : Pearson, [2018]
  | Includes index.
Identifiers: LCCN 2018027019| ISBN 0134668464 (9780134668468) | ISBN
  0134766172 (9780134766171)
Subjects: LCSH: Literature--Collections.
Classification: LCC PN6014 .L58 2018 | DDC 808—dc23
LC record available at https://lccn.loc.gov/2018027019

Rental Edition
ISBN-10: 0-13-466846-4
ISBN-13: 978-0-13-466846-8
Instructor's Review Copy
ISBN-10: 0-13-476617-2
ISBN-13: 978-0-13-476617-1

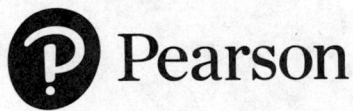 Pearson

CONTENTS

FICTION
TALKING WITH *Amy Tan* 1

1 READING A STORY 5

2 POINT OF VIEW 26

3 CHARACTER 73

4 SETTING 118

7   SYMBOL 223

8   GENRE FICTION 256

9 READING LONG STORIES AND NOVELS 299

10 LATIN AMERICAN FICTION 374

11 CRITICAL CASEBOOK
Flannery O'Connor 398

12 CRITICAL CASEBOOK
Three Stories in Depth   448

13 GALLERY OF INTERNATIONAL VOICES

14 STORIES FOR FURTHER READING 572

POETRY

15 READING A POEM 692

16 LISTENING TO A VOICE 707

17 WORDS 731

18 SAYING AND SUGGESTING 753

19 IMAGERY 766

20 FIGURES OF SPEECH 785

21 SONG 804

25 OPEN FORM 883

28 POETRY AND PERSONAL IDENTITY 942

31 WHAT IS POETRY? 989

32 THREE CRITICAL CASEBOOKS
Emily Dickinson, Langston Hughes, and Robert Frost 992

DRAMA

TALKING WITH *David Ives* 1137

37   CRITICAL CASEBOOK
Sophocles 1196

38 CRITICAL CASEBOOK
Shakespeare 1284

39 THE MODERN THEATER 1481

W RITING 1759

42 WRITING ABOUT LITERATURE 1761

43 WRITING ABOUT A STORY 1783

44 WRITING ABOUT A POEM 1808

45 WRITING ABOUT A PLAY 1830

46 WRITING A RESEARCH PAPER 1841

47 WRITING AS DISCOVERY: KEEPING A JOURNAL 1872

48 WRITING AN ESSAY EXAM 1876

49 CRITICAL APPROACHES TO LITERATURE 1881

GLOSSARY OF LITERARY TERMS 1910

PREFACE

*L*iterature, Fourteenth Edition—the book in your hands—is really four inter-locking volumes sharing one cover. Each of the first three sections is devoted to one of the major literary forms—fiction, poetry, and drama. The fourth section is a comprehensive introduction to critical writing. All together, the book is an attempt to provide the college student with a reasonably compact introduction to the study and appreciation of stories, poems, and plays—as well as practical advice on the sort of writing expected in a college English course.

We assume that appreciation begins in delighted attention to words on a page. Speed reading has its uses; but at times, as Robert Frost said, the person who reads for speed "misses the best part of what a good writer puts into it." Close reading, then, is essential. Still, we do not believe that close reading tells us everything, that it is wrong to read a literary work by any light except that of the work itself. At times we suggest different approaches such as referring to the facts of an author's life, look-ing for myth, or seeing the conventions that typify a kind of writing—noticing, for instance, that an old mansion, cobwebbed and creaking, is the setting for a Gothic horror story.

Although we cannot help having a few convictions about the meanings of sto-ries, poems, and plays, we have tried to step back and give you room to make up your own mind. Here and there, in the wording of a question, our opinions may occasion-ally stick out. If you should notice any, please feel free to ignore them. Be assured that no one interpretation, laid down by authority, is the only right one for any work of literature. Trust your own interpretation—provided that in making it you have looked clearly and carefully at the evidence.

Reading literature often will provide you with a reason to write. Following the fiction, poetry, and drama sections, there are several chapters that give the student-writer some practical advice. It will guide you, step by step, in finding a topic, plan-ning an essay, writing, revising, and putting your paper into finished form. Further, you will find there specific help in writing about fiction, poetry, and drama. There are also short features at the end of most chapters that provide help and perspective on writing about literature. In a few places we have even offered some suggestions about writing your own stories or poems—in case reading the selections in this book inspires you to try your hand at imaginative writing.

A WORD ABOUT CAREERS

Most students agree that to read celebrated writers such as William Faulkner, Emily Dickinson, and William Shakespeare is probably good for the spirit. Most students even take some pleasure in the experience. But many, not planning to teach English and impatient to begin some other career, wonder if the study of literature, however enjoyable, isn't a waste of time—or at least, an annoying obstacle.

This objection may seem reasonable at first glance, but it rests on a shaky assumption. Success in a career does not depend merely on learning the specialized information and skills required to join a profession. In most careers, according to one senior business executive, people often fail not because they don't understand their jobs, but because they don't understand their co-workers, their clients, or their customers. They don't ever see the world from another person's point of view. Their problem is a failure of imagination.

To leap over the wall of self and to look through another's eyes is valuable experience that literature offers. If you are lucky, you may never meet (or have to do business with) anyone exactly like Mrs. Turpin in the story "Revelation," and yet you will learn much about the kind of person she is from Flannery O'Connor's fictional portrait of her. What is it like to be black, a white may wonder? James Baldwin, Toni Morrison, Gwendolyn Brooks, Claude McKay, Langston Hughes, Zora Neale Hurston, Alice Walker, August Wilson, and others have knowledge to impart. What is it like to be a woman? If a man would like to learn, let him read (for a start) Sandra Cisneros, Kate Chopin, Susan Glaspell, Alice Munro, Sylvia Plath, Katherine Anne Porter, Flannery O'Connor, Adrienne Rich, and Amy Tan, and perhaps, too, Henrik Ibsen's A Doll's House and John Steinbeck's "The Chrysanthemums."

Plodding single-mindedly toward careers, some people are like horses wearing blinders. For many, the goals look fixed and predictable. Competent nurses, accountants, and dental technicians seem always in demand. Others may find that in our society some careers, like waves in the sea, will rise or fall unexpectedly. Think how many professions we now take for granted, which a few years ago didn't even exist: genetic engineering, energy conservation, digital editing, and website design. Others that once looked like lifetime meal tickets have been cut back and nearly ruined: shoe repairing, commercial fishing, railroading.

In a perpetually changing society, it may be risky to lock yourself on one track to a career, refusing to consider any other. "We are moving," writes John Naisbitt in *Megatrends*, a study of our changing society, "from the specialist, soon obsolete, to the generalist who can adapt." Perhaps the greatest opportunity in your whole life lies in a career that has yet to be invented. If you do change your career as you go along, you will be like most people. According to a U.S. Bureau of Labor Statistics survey conducted in August 2017, the average American holds nearly twelve jobs between the ages of 18 and 50—often completely changing his or her basic occupation. When for some unforeseen reason you have to make such a change, basic skills—and a knowledge of humanity—may be your most valuable credentials.

Literature has much practical knowledge to offer you. An art of words, it can help you become more sensitive to language—both your own and other people's. It can make you aware of the difference between the word that is exactly right and the word that is merely good enough—Mark Twain calls it "the difference between the lightning and the lightning-bug." Read a fine work of literature alertly, and some of its writer's sensitivity to words may grow on you. A Supreme Court Justice, John Paul Stevens, once remarked that the best preparation for law school is to study poetry. Why? George D. Gopen, an English professor with a law degree, says it may be because "no other discipline so closely replicates the central question asked in the study of legal thinking: Here is a text; in how many ways can it have meaning?"

Many careers today, besides law, call for close reading and clear writing—as well as careful listening and thoughtful speech. Lately, college placement directors have reported more demand for graduates who are good readers and writers. The reason is evident: Employers need people who can handle words. In a survey conducted by Cornell University, business executives were asked to rank in importance the traits they look for when hiring. Leadership was first, but skill in writing and speaking came in fourth, ahead of both managerial and analytical skills. Times change, but to think cogently and to express yourself well will always be among the abilities the world needs.

KEY LITERARY TERMS

Every discipline has its own terminology. This book introduces a large range of critical terms that may help you in both your reading and writing. When these important words and phrases are first defined, they are printed in **boldface**. If you find a critical term anywhere in this book you don't know or don't recall (for example, what is a *carpe diem* poem or a *dramatic question?*), just check the Index of Literary Terms in the back of the book, and you'll see the page where the term is discussed; or look it up in the Glossary of Literary Terms, also at the back of the book.

TEXTS AND DATES

Every effort has been made to supply each selection in its most accurate text and (where necessary) in a lively, faithful translation. For the reader who wishes to know when a work was written, at the right of each title appears the date of its first publication in book form. Parentheses around a date indicate the work's date of composition or first magazine publication, given when it was composed much earlier than when it was first published in book form.

But enough housekeeping—let's enjoy ourselves and read some unforgettable stories, poems, and plays.

X. J. K., D. G., AND D. S.

TO THE INSTRUCTOR

*L*iterature is a book with two major goals. First, it introduces college students to the appreciation and experience of literature in its major forms. Second, the book tries to develop the student's ability to think critically and communicate effectively through writing.

All three editors of this volume are writers. We believe that textbooks should be not only informative and accurate but also lively, accessible, and engaging. In education, it never hurts to have little fun. Our intent has always been to write a book that students will read eagerly and enjoy.

WHAT'S NEW IN THE FOURTEENTH EDITION?

- **Twenty new stories**—including Muriel Spark's "The First Year of My Life," Toni Morrison's "Recitatif," Kelly Link's "The Faery Handbag," Gabriel García Márquez's "The Handsomest Drowned Man in the World," Albert Camus's "The Guest," Nadine Gordimer's "The Defeated," Kazuo Ishiguro's "A Family Supper," and Wells Tower's "Everything Ravaged, Everything Burned," as well as new fables by Aesop and Bidpai.
- **New chapter on international voices in fiction**—presenting powerful stories from Nigeria, Japan, Egypt, India, China, Iran, and elsewhere.
- **Forty-six new poems**—ranging from classic selections by Claude McKay, Emily Dickinson, Robert Hayden, William Carlos Williams, Robert Frost, Langston Hughes, Gertrude Stein, and Walt Whitman to fresh contemporary works by Juan Felipe Herrera, Billy Collins, Rhina P. Espaillat, Aimee Nezhukumatathil, Luis J. Rodriguez, Thao Nguyen, and Hieu Minh Nguyen.
- **New casebook on Edgar Allan Poe's "The Tell-Tale Heart"**—featuring excerpts from Poe's critical writing, photographs of the author, plus insightful and accessible critical excerpts by Poe scholars.
- **Several new plays and dramatic scenes**—providing greater flexibility in studying known favorites, as well as exploring contemporary trends. The new works include David Ives's *Sure Thing*, Sharon E. Cooper's *Mistaken Identity*, Jane Martin's *Beauty*, as well as classics such as Lorraine Hansberry's *A Raisin in the Sun*, and several favorite scenes from Shakespeare's plays.
- **Updated coverage of the 8th edition of the *MLA Handbook***—our concise Reference Guide for MLA Citations has been updated and expanded to reflect the latest MLA guidelines and illustrate a greater variety of online sources.
- **New writing assignments**—new writing ideas have been introduced in many chapters.

Overall, we have tried to create a book to help readers develop sensitivity to language, culture, and identity, to lead them beyond the boundaries of their own selves, and to see the world through the eyes of others. This book is built on the assumption that great literature can enrich and enlarge the lives it touches.

KEY FEATURES

We have revised this edition of *Literature* with the simple aim of introducing useful new features and selections without losing the best-liked material. We have been guided in this effort by scores of instructors and students who use the book in their classrooms. Teaching is a kind of conversation between instructor and student and between reader and text. By revising *Literature*, we try to help keep this conversation fresh by mixing the classic with the new and the familiar with the unexpected.

- **Wide variety of popular and provocative stories, poems, plays, and critical prose**—offers traditional favorites with exciting and sometimes surprising contemporary selections.
  - **73 stories, 20 new selections**—diverse and exciting stories from authors new and old from around the globe.
  - **408 poems, 46 new selections**—great poems, familiar and less well known, mixing classic favorites with engaging contemporary work from a wonderful range of poets.
  - **20 plays, 5 new selections**—a rich array of drama from classical Greek tragedy to Shakespeare to contemporary work by Lorraine Hansberry and David Ives.
  - **121 critical prose pieces, 14 new selections**—extensive selections help students think about different approaches to reading, interpreting, and writing about literature.
- **Talking with Writers**—exclusive conversations between Dana Gioia and celebrated fiction writer Amy Tan, former US Poet Laureate Kay Ryan, and contemporary playwright David Ives offer students an insider's look into the importance of literature and reading in the lives of three modern masters.
- **Ten casebooks on major authors and literary masterpieces**—provide students with a variety of material, including biographies, photographs, critical commentaries, and author statements, to begin an in-depth study of writers and works frequently used for critical analyses or research papers.
  - Flannery O'Connor
  - Emily Dickinson
  - Robert Frost
  - Langston Hughes
  - Sophocles
  - William Shakespeare
  - Edgar Allan Poe's "The Tell-Tale Heart"
  - Charlotte Perkins Gilman's "The Yellow Wallpaper"
  - Alice Walker's "Everyday Use"
  - T. S. Eliot's "The Love Song of J. Alfred Prufrock"
- **Chapters on Latin American Fiction and Poetry in Spanish**—present some of the finest authors of the region, including Sor Juana, Jorge Luis Borges, Octavio Paz, Gabriel García Márquez, Isabel Allende, and Juan Rulfo. These important and unique chapters will not only broaden most students' knowledge of world literature but will also recognize the richness of Spanish language fiction and poetry in the literature of the Americas—a very relevant subject in today's multicultural classrooms. The bilingual selections in poetry will also allow your Spanish-speaking students a chance to bring their native language into their coursework.

■ **Shakespeare, richly illustrated**—production photos of every major scene and character make Shakespeare more accessible to students who have never seen a live production, helping them to visualize the play's action (as well as break up the long blocks of print to make the play's text less intimidating).
  • **Two plays by Shakespeare**—*Othello* and **A Midsummer Night's Dream**— in an illustrated format featuring dozens of production photos.
  • **"Picturing Shakespeare" photo montages**—offer students a pictorial introduction to each Shakespeare play with a visual preview of the key scenes and characters.
  • **Classic Moments from Shakespeare**—a new selection of Shakespeare's most beloved speeches and monologues, with accompanying images.
■ **Terms for Review at the end of every major chapter**—provides students a simple study guide to go over key concepts and terms in each chapter.
■ **Writing Effectively feature in every major chapter** of Fiction, Poetry, and Drama has four elements designed to make the writing process easier, clearer, and less intimidating:
  • **Writers on Writing** personalizes the composition process
  • **Thinking About**_____ discusses the specific topic of the chapter
  • **Checklist** provides a step-by-step approach to composition and critical thinking
  • **Topics for Writing** offers a rich source of ideas for writing a paper.
■ **Writing About Literature**—eight full writing chapters provide comprehensive coverage of the composition and research process, in general and by genre. All chapters have been edited for increased clarity and accessibility. Our chief aim has been to make the information and structure of the writing chapters more visual for today's Internet-oriented students. (We strive to simplify the text but not to dumb it down. Clarity and concision are never out of place in a textbook, but condescension is fatal.)
■ **Student writing**—sixteen sample papers by students, along with annotations, prewriting exercises, and rough drafts, plus a journal entry, provide credible examples of how to write about literature. Includes many samples of student works-in-progress that illustrate the writing process, as well as a step-by-step presentation of the development of a topic, idea generation, and the formulation of a strong thesis and argument. Samples include several types of papers:
  • Argument papers
  • Explication papers
  • Analysis papers
  • Comparison and contrast papers
  • Response paper
  • Research paper
■ **Updated MLA guidelines**—provide students source citation requirements from the eighth edition of the *MLA Handbook* which are incorporated in all sample student papers.
■ **Accessible, easy-to-use format**—section titles and subtitles help web-oriented students navigate easily from topic to topic in every chapter. Additionally, all chapters have been reviewed and updated to include relevant cultural references.
■ **Critical Approaches to Literature, a chapter with 18 prose selections**—provides depth and flexibility for instructors who prefer to incorporate literary theory and

criticism into their introductory courses. Includes two pieces for every major critical school, carefully chosen both to illustrate the major theoretical approaches and to be accessible to beginning students, focusing on literary works found in the present edition (including examinations of work by Elizabeth Bishop and Franz Kafka, and a piece by Camille Paglia on William Blake.

- **Glossary of Literary Terms**—more than 350 terms defined, including those highlighted in boldface throughout the text as well as other important terms. Provides clear and accurate definitions, usually with cross-references to related terms.

FORMAT OPTIONS

Below are format options by which *Literature* is available.

Revel Access Card

The Revel access card is a physical card with a printed access code that is used to redeem access to Revel.

Instant Access

Students can purchase access directly from Pearson to start their subscription immediately.

Print Rental

Students can rent a bound textbook for 180 days from their participating campus bookstore or from Chegg.

Rent to Own

At the end of the rental period, students can choose to own the rented textbook by paying a flat ownership fee.

OTHER EDITIONS

Backpack Edition

There is an even more compact edition of this book, which we have titled *Backpack Literature*, Sixth Edition. This much briefer anthology contains only the most essential selections and writing apparatus, and it is published in a smaller format to create a more travel-friendly book.

SUPPLEMENTS

For Instructors

Make more time for your students with instructor resources that offer effective learning assessments and classroom engagement. Pearson's partnership with educators does not end with the delivery of course materials; Pearson is there with you on the first day of class and beyond. A dedicated team of local Pearson representatives will work with you to not only choose course materials but also integrate them into your class and assess their effectiveness. Our goal is your goal—to improve instruction with each semester.

Pearson offers the following resource to qualified adopters of *Literature*, Fourteenth Edition. This supplement is available to download from the Instructor Resource Center (IRC); please visit the IRC at www.pearson.com/us to register for access.

Instructor's Resource Manual

Create a comprehensive roadmap for teaching classroom, online, or hybrid courses. Designed for new and experienced instructors, the Instructor's Resource Manual includes learning objectives, lecture and discussion suggestions, activities for in or out of class, research activities, participation activities, and suggested readings, series, and films.

THANKS

The collaboration necessary to create this new edition goes far beyond the partnership of its three editors. *Literature: An Introduction to Fiction, Poetry, Drama, and Writing* has once again been revised, corrected, and shaped by wisdom and advice from instructors who actually put it to the test—and also from a number who, in teaching literature, preferred other textbooks to it, but who generously criticized this book anyway and made suggestions for it. Deep thanks to the following individuals:

John Allen, Milwaukee Area Technical College

Alvaro Aleman, University of Florida

Jonathan Alexander, University of Southern Colorado

Ann P. Allen, Salisbury State University

Karla Alwes, SUNY Cortland

Brian Anderson, Central Piedmont Community College

Kimberly Green Angel, Georgia State University

Carmela A. Arnoldt, Glendale Community College

Herman Asarnow, University of Portland

Susan Austin, Johnston Community College

Beverly Bailey, Seminole Community College

Carolyn Baker, San Antonio College

Rosemary Baker, SUNY Morrisville

Lee Barnes, Community College of Southern Nevada, Las Vegas

Sandra Barnhill, South Plains College

Bob Baron, Mesa Community College

Melinda Barth, El Camino Community College

Robin Barrow, University of Iowa

Joseph Bathanti, Mitchell Community College

Judith Baumel, Adelphi University

Anis Bawarski, University of Kansas

Bruce Beckum, Colorado Mountain College

Elaine Bender, El Camino Community College

Pamela Benson, Tarrant County Junior College

Jennifer Black, McLennan Community College

Brian Blackley, North Carolina State University

Debbie Borchers, Pueblo Community College

Alan Braden, Tacoma Community College

Glenda Bryant, South Plains College

Paul Buchanan, Biola University

David Budinger, Broward College

Andrew Burke, University of Georgia

Jolayne Call, Utah Valley State College

Stasia Callan, Monroe Community College

Uzzie T. Cannon, University of North Carolina at Greensboro

Al Capovilla, Folsom Lake Community College

Juliana Cardenas, Grossmont College

Eleanor Carducci, Sussex County Community College

Thomas Carper, University of Southern Maine

Jean W. Cash, James Madison University

Michael Cass, Mercer University

Patricia Cearley, South Plains College

Fred Chancey, Chemeketa Community College

Kitty Chen, Nassau Community College

Edward M. Cifelli, County College of Morris

Marc Cirigliano, Empire State College

Bruce Clary, McPherson College

Maria Clayton, Middle Tennessee State University

Cheryl Clements, Blinn College

Jerry Coats, Tarrant County Community College

Peggy Cole, Arapahoe Community College

Doris Colter, Henry Ford Community College

Dean Cooledge, University of Maryland Eastern Shore

Patricia Connors, University of Memphis

Steve Cooper, California State University, Long Beach

Cynthia Cornell, DePauw University

Ruth Corson, Norwalk Community Technical College, Norwalk

James Finn Cotter, Mount St. Mary College

Dessa Crawford, Delaware Community College

Janis Adams Crowe, Furman University

Allison M. Cummings, University of Wisconsin, Madison

Elizabeth Curtin, Salisbury State University

Hal Daniels, Broward College

Robert Darling, Keuka College

Denise David, Niagara County Community College

Alan Davis, Moorhead State University

Michael Degen, Jesuit College Preparatory School, Dallas

Kathleen De Grave, Pittsburgh State University

Apryl Denny, Viterbo University

Johanna Denzin, Columbia College

Fred Dings, University of South Carolina

Leo Doobad, Stetson University

Stephanie Dowdle, Salt Lake Community College

Dennis Driewald, Laredo Community College

David Driscoll, Benedictine College

John Drury, University of Cincinnati

Tony D'Souza, Shasta College

Denise Dube, Hill College

Victoria Duckworth, Santa Rosa Junior College

Ellen Dugan-Barrette, Brescia University

Dixie Durman, Chapman University

Bill Dynes, University of Indianapolis

Justin Eatmon, Wake Technical Community College

Janet Eber, County College of Morris

Terry Ehret, Santa Rosa Junior College

George Ellenbogen, Bentley College

Peggy Ellsberg, Barnard College

Toni Empringham, El Camino Community College

Lin Enger, Moorhead State University

Alexina Fagan, Virginia Commonwealth University

Lynn Fauth, Oxnard College

Karen Feldman, Seminole State College of Florida

Annie Finch, University of Southern Maine

Katie Fischer, Clarke College

Steven Fischer, Harper College

Susan Fitzgerald, University of Memphis

Juliann Fleenor, Harper College

Richard Flynn, Georgia Southern University

Billy Fontenot, Louisiana State University at Eunice

Deborah Ford, University of Southern Mississippi

Doug Ford, Manatee Community College

James E. Ford, University of Nebraska, Lincoln

Peter Fortunato, Ithaca College

Ray Foster, Scottsdale Community College

Maryanne Garbowsky, County College of Morris

John Gery, University of New Orleans

Mary Frances Gibbons, Richland College

Julie Gibson, Greenville Technical College

Maggie Gordon, University of Mississippi

Joseph Green, Lower Columbia College

William E. Gruber, Emory University

Huey Guagliardo, Louisiana State University

R. S. Gwynn, Lamar University

Steven K. Hale, DeKalb College

Renée Harlow, Southern Connecticut State University

David Harper, Chesapeake College

John Harper, Seminole Community College

Iris Rose Hart, Santa Fe Community College

Karen Hatch, California State University, Chico

Jim Hauser, William Patterson College

Sandra Havriluk, Gwinnett Technical College

Lance Hawvermale, Ranger College

Kevin Hayes, Essex County College

Jennifer Heller, Johnson County Community College

Hal Hellwig, Idaho State University

K. L. Henderson, Northwestern State University

Gillian Hettinger, William Paterson University

Mary Piering Hiltbrand, University of Southern Colorado

Martha Hixon, Middle Tennessee State University

Jan Hodge, Morningside College

David E. Hoffman, Averett University

Sylvia Holladay, Hillsborough Community College

Mary Huffer, Lake-Sumter Community College

Patricia Hymson, Delaware County Community College

Carol Ireland, Joliet Junior College

Jenifer Jackson, Austin Peay State University

Alan Jacobs, Wheaton College

Ann Jagoe, North Central Texas College

Kimberlie Johnson, Seminole Community College

Peter Johnson, Providence College

Ted E. Johnston, El Paso Community College

Jacqueline Jones, Francis Marion University

Mark Jordan, Odessa College

Cris Karmas, Graceland University

Tammy Kearn, Riverside City College

William Kelly, Bristol Community College

Howard Kerner, Polk Community College

Lynn Kerr, Baltimore City Community College

John Kivari, Erie Community College
D. S. Koelling, Northwest College
Damien Kortum, Laramie County Community College
Dennis Kriewald, Laredo Community College
Paul Lake, Arkansas Technical University
Patricia Landy, Laramie County Community College
Susan Lang, Southern Illinois University
Greg LaPointe, Elmira College
Tracy Lassiter, Eastern Arizona College
Helen Lewis, Western Iowa Tech Community College
Sherry Little, San Diego State University
Alfred Guy Litton, Texas Woman's University
Heather Lobban-Viravong, Grinnell College
Karen Locke, Lane Community College
Eric Loring, Scottsdale Community College
Deborah Louvar, Seminole State College
Gerald Luboff, County College of Morris
Susan Popkin Mach, UCLA
Samuel Maio, California State University, San Jose
Jim Martin, Mount Ida College
Paul Marx, University of New Haven
David Mason, Colorado College
Mike Matthews, Tarrant County Junior College
Beth Maxfield, Henderson State University
Janet McCann, Texas A&M University
Susan McClure, Indiana University of Pennsylvania
Kim McCollum-Clark, Millersville University
David McCracken, Texas A&M University
Nellie McCrory, Gaston College
William McGee, Jr., Joliet Junior College
Barbara McGregor, Tarleton State University
Kerri McKeand, Joliet Junior College
Robert McPhillips, Iona College
Jim McWilliams, Dickinson State University
Elizabeth Meador, Wayne Community College
Trista Merrill, Finger Lakes Community College
Brett Mertins, Metropolitan Community College
Bruce Meyer, Laurentian University
Shawn Miller, Francis Marion University
Tom Miller, University of Arizona
Joseph Mills, University of California at Davis
Cindy Milwe, Santa Monica High School
Dorothy Minor, Tulsa Community College
Alan Mitnick, Passaic County Community College
Mary Alice Morgan, Mercer University
Samantha Morgan, University of Tennessee
Bernard Morris, Modesto Junior College

Brian T. Murphy, Burlington Community College
Carrie Myers, Lehigh Carbon Community College
William Myers, University of Colorado at Colorado Springs
Madeleine Mysko, Johns Hopkins University
Jennifer Myskowski, Lehigh Carbon Community College
Kevin Nebergall, Kirkwood Community College
Diorah Nelson, Hillsborough Community College
Eric Nelson, Georgia Southern University
Margaret Nelson Rodriguez, El Paso Community College–Valle Verde Campus
Jeff Newberry, University of West Florida
Marsha Nourse, Dean College
Hillary Nunn, University of Akron
James Obertino, Central Missouri State University
Julia O'Brien, Meredith College
Sally O'Friel, John Carroll University
Elizabeth Oness, Viterbo College
Regina B. Oost, Wesleyan College
Mike Osborne, Central Piedmont Community College
James Ortego II, Troy University–Dothan
Jim Owen, Columbus State University
Jeannette Palmer, Motlow State Community College
Mark Palmer, Tacoma Community College
Paige Paquette, Troy University
Carol Pearson, West Georgia Technical College, Carroll Campus
Dianne Peich, Delaware County Community College
Betty Jo Peters, Morehead State University
Timothy Peters, Boston University
Norm Peterson, County College of Morris
Susan Petit, College of San Mateo
Louis Phillips, School of Visual Arts
Robert Phillips, University of Houston
Jason Pickavance, Salt Lake Community College
Teresa Point, Emory University
Sally Polito, Cape Cod Community College
Deborah Prickett, Jacksonville State University
John Prince, North Carolina Central University
William Provost, University of Georgia
Wyatt Prunty, University of the South, Sewanee
Allen Ramsey, Central Missouri State University
Ron Rash, Tri-County Technical College
Michael W. Raymond, Stetson University
Mary Anne Reiss, Elizabethtown Community College
Barbara Rhodes, Central Missouri State University
Diane Richard-Alludya, Lynn University
Gary Richardson, Mercer University

Jennifer Riske, Northeast Lakeview College

Fred Robbins, Southern Illinois University

Douglas Robillard Jr., University of Arkansas at Pine Bluff

Daniel Robinson, Colorado State University

Dawn Rodrigues, University of Texas, Brownsville

Linda C. Rollins, Motlow State Community College

Mark Rollins, Ohio University

Laura Ross, Seminole Community College

Jude Roy, Madisonville Community College

Lillian Ruiz, Greenfield Community College

M. Runyon, Saddleback College

Mark Sanders, College of the Mainland

Kay Satre, Carroll College

Ben Sattersfield, Mercer University

SueAnn Schatz, University of New Mexico

Roy Scheele, Doane College

Bill Schmidt, Seminole Community College

Beverly Schneller, Millersville University

Meg Schoerke, San Francisco State University

Janet Schwarzkopf, Western Kentucky University

William Scurrah, Pima Community College

Susan Semrow, Northeastern State University

Tom Sexton, University of Alaska, Anchorage

Chenliang Sheng, Northern Kentucky University

Roger Silver, University of Maryland–Asian Division

Josh Simpson, Sullivan University

Phillip Skaar, Texas A&M University

Michael Slaughter, Illinois Central College

Martha K. Smith, University of Southern Indiana

Matthew Snyder, Moreno Valley College

Chrishawn Speller, Seminole State College of Florida

Richard Spiese, California State, Long Beach

Wes Spratlin, Motlow State Community College

Lisa S. Starks, Texas A&M University

John R. Stephenson, Lake Superior State University

Jack Stewart, East Georgia College

Dabney Stuart, Washington and Lee University

David Sudol, Arizona State University

Stan Sulkes, Raymond Walters College

Gerald Sullivan, Savio Preparatory School

Henry Taylor, American University

Jean Tobin, University of Wisconsin Center, Sheboygan County

Linda Travers, University of Massachusetts, Amherst

Tom Treffinger, Greenville Technical College

Michelle Trim, University of New Haven

Pamela Turley, Community College of Allegheny County

Peter Ulisse, Housatonia Community College

Leslie Umschweis, Broward College

Lee Upton, Lafayette College

Rex Veeder, St. Cloud University

Michelle Veenstra, Francis Marion University

Deborah Viles, University of Colorado, Boulder

Melanie Wagner, Lake Sumter State College

Joyce Walker, Southern Illinois University–Carbondale

Sue Walker, University of South Alabama

Irene Ward, Kansas State University

Penelope Warren, Laredo Community College

Barbara Wenner, University of Cincinnati

Terry Witek, Stetson University

Sallie Wolf, Arapahoe Community College

Beth Rapp Young, University of Alabama

William Zander, Fairleigh Dickinson University

Tom Zaniello, Northern Kentucky University

Guanping Zeng, Pensacola Junior College

John Zheng, Mississippi Valley State University

Ongoing thanks go to our friends and colleagues who helped with earlier editions: Michael Palma, who scrupulously examined and updated every chapter of the previous edition; Diane Thiel of the University of New Mexico, who originally helped develop the Latin American poetry chapter; Susan Balée of Temple University, who contributed to the chapter on writing a research paper; April Lindner of Saint Joseph's University in Philadelphia, Pennsylvania, who served as associate editor for the writing sections; Mark Bernier of Blinn College in Brenham, Texas, who helped improve the writing material; Joseph Aimone of Santa Clara University, who helped integrate web-based materials and research techniques; John Swensson of De Anza College, who provided excellent practical suggestions from the classroom; and Neil Aitken of the University of Southern California, who helped update the chapter on writing a research paper.

On the publisher's staff, Aron Keesbury, Rachel Harbour, Tom Stover, Betsy Farrell, and Cynthia Cox made many contributions to the development and revision of the new edition. Thanks to Joseph Croscup for handling the very difficult responsibility of securing hundreds of reprint permissions. Carmen Altes oversaw the art and image production. Lois Lombardo directed the complex job of managing the production of the book in all of its many versions from the manuscript to the final printed form. And lastly, we would like to thank our excellent copyeditor, Stephanie Magean.

Mary Gioia was involved in every stage of planning, editing, and execution. Not only could the book not have been done without her capable hand and careful eye, but her expert guidance made every chapter better.

Past debts that will never be repaid are outstanding to hundreds of instructors named in prefaces past and to the late and dearly missed Dorothy M. Kennedy.

X. J. K., D. G., AND D. S.

ABOUT THE AUTHORS

X. J. KENNEDY, after graduation from Seton Hall and Columbia, became a journalist second class in the Navy ("Actually, I was pretty eighth class"). His poems, some published in the *New Yorker*, were first collected in *Nude Descending a Staircase* (1961). Since then he has published seven more collections, including a volume of new and selected poems in 2007, several widely adopted literature and writing textbooks, and seventeen books for children, including two novels. He has taught at Michigan, North Carolina (Greensboro), California (Irvine), Wellesley, Tufts, and Leeds. Cited in *Bartlett's Familiar Quotations* and reprinted in some 200 anthologies, his verse has brought him a Guggenheim fellowship, a Lamont Award, a Los Angeles Times Book Prize, an award from the American Academy and Institute of Arts and Letters, an Aiken-Taylor prize, and the Award for Poetry for Children from the National Council of Teachers of English. He lives in Peabody, Massachusetts.

DANA GIOIA is a poet, critic, and teacher. Born in Los Angeles of Italian and Mexican ancestry, he attended Stanford and Harvard before taking a detour into business. ("Not many poets have a Stanford MBA, thank goodness!") After years of writing and reading late in the evenings after work, he quit a vice presidency to write and teach. He has published four collections of poetry, *Daily Horoscope* (1986), *The Gods of Winter* (1991), *Interrogations at Noon* (2001), which won the American Book Award, and *Pity the Beautiful* (2012); and three critical volumes, including *Can Poetry Matter?* (1992), an influential study of poetry's place in contemporary America. Gioia has taught at Johns Hopkins, Sarah Lawrence, Wesleyan (Connecticut), Mercer, and Colorado College. From 2003 to 2009 he served as the Chairman of the National Endowment for the Arts. At the NEA he created the largest literary programs in federal history, including Shakespeare in American Communities and Poetry Out Loud, the national high school poetry recitation contest. He also led the campaign to restore active literary reading by creating the Big Read, which helped reverse a quarter century of decline in reading in the United States. He is currently the Judge Widney Professor of Poetry and Public Culture at the University of Southern California.

(The surname Gioia is pronounced JOY-A. As some of you may have already guessed, *gioia* is the Italian word for "joy.")

DAN STONE worked for many years as a program manager and documentary producer at the National Endowment for the Arts, during which time he wrote, recorded, and produced nearly thirty radio documentaries on classic American novels for the Big Read, interviewing more than 200 prominent writers, actors, artists, musicians, and public figures. While at the NEA, Stone helped create Poetry Out Loud, the popular national high school recitation contest, and he produced educational and audio programming for the initiatives Shakespeare in American Communities and NEA Jazz Masters. He studied poetry at Colorado College and received an MFA in fiction from Boston University, and he has taught middle school, high school, and college. With Dana Gioia, Stone edited Penguin's *100 Great Poets of the English Language*. His most recent book, *How Money Became Dangerous*, is about the modern evolution of Wall Street and the financial services industry. He is the founder and editor-in-chief of *Radio Silence*, a magazine of rock 'n' roll and literature. For City Arts & Lectures and NPR, he has conducted lengthy stage conversations with Bruce Springsteen, Patti Smith, George Saunders, and Elvis Costello. Stone owns an establishment near his home in Oakland, California, called North Light, which serves as a bookstore, record store, restaurant, and café.

LITERATURE

LITERATURE

Amy Tan in Chinatown, San Francisco, 1989.

FICTION

TALKING WITH *Amy Tan*

"Life Is Larger Than We Think"
Dana Gioia Interviews Amy Tan

Q: You were born in Oakland to a family in which both parents had come from China. Were you raised bilingually?

AMY TAN: Until the age of five, my parents spoke to me in Chinese or a combination of Chinese and English, but they didn't force me to speak Mandarin. In retrospect, this was sad, because they believed that my chance of doing well in America hinged on my fluency in English. Later, as an adult, I wanted to learn Chinese. Now I make an effort when I am with my sisters, who don't speak English well.

Q: What books do you remember reading early in your childhood?

AMY TAN: I read every fairy tale I could lay my hands on at the public library. It was a wonderful world to escape to. I say "escape" deliberately, because I look back and I feel that my childhood was filled with a lot of tensions in the house, and I was able to go to another place. These stories were also filled with their own kinds of dangers and tensions, but they weren't mine. And they were usually solved in the end. This was something satisfying. You could go through these things and then, suddenly, you would have some kind of ending. I think that every lonely kid loves to escape through stories. And what kids never thought that they were lonely at some point in their life?

Amy Tan with her mother.

Q: Your mother—to put it mildly—did not approve of your ambition to be a writer.

AMY TAN: My mother and father were immigrants and they were practical people. They wanted us to do well in the new country. They didn't want us to be starving artists. Going into the arts was considered a luxury—that was something you did if you were born to wealth. When my mother found out that I had switched from pre-med to English literature, she imagined that I would lead this life of poverty, that this was a dream that couldn't possibly lead to anything. I didn't know what it would lead to. It just occurred to me I could finally make a choice when I was in college. I didn't have to follow what my parents had set out for me from the age of six—to become a doctor.

Q: What did your mother think of *The Joy Luck Club*?

AMY TAN: Well, by the time I wrote *The Joy Luck Club*, she had changed her opinion. I was making a very good living as a business writer, enough to buy a house for her to live in. When you can do that for your parents, they think you're doing fairly well. That was the goal, to become a doctor and be able to make enough money to take care of my mother in her old age. Because I was able to do that as a business writer, she thought it was great. When I decided to write fiction and I said I needed to interview her for stories from her past, she thought that was even better. Then

2

when I got published, and it became a success, she said, "I always knew she was going to be a writer, because she had a wild imagination."

Q: *The Joy Luck Club* is a book of enormous importance, because it brought the complex history of Chinese immigration into the mainstream of American literature. Writing this book, did you have any sense that you were opening up a whole new territory?

AMY TAN: No, I had no idea this was going to be anything but weird stories about a weird family that was unique to us. To think that they would apply to other people who would find similarities to their own families or conflicts was beyond my imagination, and I have a very good imagination.

I wanted to write this book for very personal reasons. One of them, of course, was to learn the craft of writing. The other reason was to understand myself, to figure out who I was. A lot of writers use writing as a way of finding their own personal meaning. I wrote out of total chaos and personal history, which did not seem like something that would ever be used by other people as a way of understanding their lives.

Q: Did you have any literary models in writing your short stories or putting them together as a book? Or did you just do it on intuition?

AMY TAN: I look back, and there were unconscious models—fairy tales, the Bible, especially the cadence of the Bible. There was a book called *Little House in the Big Woods*, by Laura Ingalls Wilder. Wilder wrote this fictional story based on her life as a lonely little girl, moving from place to place. She lived 100 years ago, but that was my life.

The other major influence was my parents. My father wrote sermons and he read them aloud to me, as his test audience. They were not the kind of hell and brimstone sermons. They were stories about himself and his doubts, what he wanted and how he tried to do it.

Then, of course, there was my mother, who told stories as though they were happening right in front of her. She would remember what happened to her in life and act them out in front of me. That's oral storytelling at its best.

Q: Is there anything else that you'd like to say?

AMY TAN: I think reading is really important. It provided for me a refuge, especially during difficult times. It provided me with the notion that I could find an ending that was different from what was happening to me at the time. When you read about the lives of other people, people of different circumstances or similar circumstances, you are part of their lives for that moment. You inhabit their lives, and you feel what they're feeling, and that is compassion.

Life is larger than we think it is. Certain events can happen that we don't understand. We can take it as faith or as superstition or as a fairy tale. The possibilities are wide open as to how we look at them.

It's a wonderful part of life to come to a situation and think that it can offer all kinds of possibilities and you get to choose them. I look at what's happened to me as a published writer, and sometimes I think it's a fairy tale.

H ere is a story, one of the shortest ever written and one of the most difficult to forget:

> A woman is sitting in her old, shuttered house. She knows that she is alone in the whole world; every other thing is dead.
>   The doorbell rings.

In a brief space this small tale of terror, credited to Thomas Bailey Aldrich, makes itself memorable. It sets a promising scene—is this a haunted house?—introduces a character, and places her in a strange and intriguing situation. Although in reading a story that is over so quickly we don't come to know the character well, for a moment we enter her thoughts and begin to share her feelings. Then something amazing happens. The story leaves us to wonder: who or what rang that bell?

Like many richer, longer, more complicated stories, this one, in its few words, engages the imagination. Evidently, how much a story contains and suggests doesn't depend on its size. In the opening chapter of this book, we will look first at other brief stories—examples of three ancient kinds of fiction: a fable, a parable, and a tale—and then at a contemporary short story. We will consider the elements of fiction one after another. By seeing a few short stories broken into their parts, you will come to a keener sense of how a story is put together. Not all stories are short, of course; later in the book, you will find a chapter on reading long stories and novels.

Here follows a wide variety of stories—with many traditional favorites along with some surprising contemporary selections. Among them, may you find at least a few you'll enjoy and care to remember.

1
READING A STORY

When I read a good book . . . I wish that life were
three thousand years long.

—RALPH WALDO EMERSON

What You Will Learn in This Chapter

- To define *fiction*
- To identify the major types of short fiction
- To explain the elements of plot and key narrative techniques
- To identify the protagonist and antagonist in a literary work

After the shipwreck that marooned him on a desert island, Robinson Crusoe, in Daniel Defoe's novel, stood gazing over the water where pieces of cargo from his ship were floating by. Along came "two shoes, not mates." It is the qualification *not mates* that makes the detail memorable. We could well believe that a thing so striking and odd must have been seen, and not invented. But in truth Defoe, like other masters of the art of fiction, had the power to make us believe his imaginings. Borne along by the art of the storyteller, we trust what we are told, even though the story may be sheer fantasy.

THE ART OF FICTION

Fiction (from the Latin *fictio*, "a shaping, a counterfeiting") is a name for stories not entirely factual, but at least partially shaped, made up, imagined. It is true that in some fiction, such as a historical novel, a writer draws on factual information in presenting scenes, events, and characters. But the factual information in a historical novel, unlike that in a history book, is of secondary importance.

Many firsthand accounts of the American Civil War were written by men who had fought in it, but few eyewitnesses give us so keen a sense of actual life on the battlefront as the author of *The Red Badge of Courage*, Stephen Crane, who was born after the war was over. In fiction, the "facts" may or may not be true, and a story is none the worse for their being entirely imaginary. We expect from fiction a sense of how people act, not an authentic chronicle of how, at some past time, a few people acted.

Human beings love stories. We put them everywhere—not only in books, films, and plays, but also in songs, news articles, blogs, social networks, cartoons, and video games. There seems to be a general human curiosity about how other lives, both real and imaginary, take shape and unfold. Some stories provide simple and predictable pleasures according to a conventional plan. Each episode of *CSI* or *New Girl*, for instance, follows a roughly similar structure, so that regular viewers feel comfortably engaged and entertained. But other stories may seek to challenge rather than comfort us, by finding new and exciting ways to tell a tale, or by delving deeper into the mysteries of human nature, or by doing both.

Literary Fiction

Literary fiction calls for close attention. Reading a short story by Ernest Hemingway instead of watching an episode of *Grey's Anatomy* is a little like playing chess rather than checkers. It isn't that Hemingway isn't entertaining. Great literature provides deep and genuine pleasures. But it also requires close attention and skilled engagement from the reader. We are not necessarily led on by the promise of thrills; we do not keep reading mainly to find out what happens next. Indeed, a literary story might even disclose in its opening lines everything that happened, and then spend the rest of its length revealing what that happening meant.

Reading literary fiction is not merely a passive activity, but it is one that demands both attention and insight-lending participation. In return, it offers rewards. In some works of literary fiction, such as Stephen Crane's "The Open Boat" (Chapter 6) and Flannery O'Connor's "Revelation" (Chapter 11), we see more deeply into the minds and hearts of the characters than we ever see into those of our families, our close friends, our lovers—or even ourselves.

TYPES OF SHORT FICTION

Modern literary fiction in English has been dominated by two forms: the novel and the short story. The two have many elements in common. Perhaps we will be able to define the short story more meaningfully if first, for comparison, we consider some related varieties of fiction: the fable, the parable, and the tale. These ancient forms, whose origins date back to the time of word-of-mouth storytelling, are relatively simple in structure; in them we can plainly see elements also found in the short story (and in the novel).

Fable

The **fable** is a brief, typically humorous narrative told to illustrate a moral. The characters in a fable are often animals who embody specific human qualities. An ant, for example, may represent a hardworking type of person, or a lion may represent nobility. But fables can also include human characters. To begin, here is a celebrated Sufi fable, which has been told and retold by many writers, most notably ninth-century Muslim writer Al-Fudhayl bin 'Iyyadh. (Samarra, by the way, is a city sixty miles from Baghdad.)

Sufi Legend

Death Has an Appointment in Samarra   c. 800

Translated by Virgil Abadi

One day in Baghdad a man, a student of Sufi, was sitting in the corner of an inn when he happened to hear two people talking. From their conversation, the man realized that one of the figures was the Angel of Death.

"For the next few weeks," Death told his companion, "I'm gathering people in Baghdad." As he said this, Death looked over at the man in the corner.

Terrified, the man fled from the tavern and tried to plan some way to escape Death. He decided that the best course was to leave Baghdad at once and travel as far away as possible. He hired a fast horse and rode to the town of Samarra.

Meanwhile Death met the man's teacher, who was an old friend. As they talked about various acquaintances, Death asked the Sufi master about his student.

"Where is your disciple?" Death asked.

"He is here in Baghdad, busy with his studies," replied the teacher. "Why do you ask?"

"I was surprised to see him here," Death responded. "I have an appointment to take him next week, but it is over in Samarra."

Elements of Fable

That brief story seems practically all skin and bones; that is, it contains little decoration. For in a fable everything leads directly to the **moral**, or message, sometimes stated at the end (moral: "Haste makes waste"). In "Death Has an Appointment in Samarra" the moral isn't stated outright; it is merely implied. How would you state it in your own words?

You are probably acquainted with some of the fables credited to the Greek slave Aesop (about 620–560 B.C.), whose stories seem designed to teach lessons about human life. Such is the fable of "The Goose That Laid the Golden Eggs," in which the owner of this marvelous creature slaughters her to get at the great treasure that he thinks is inside her, but finds nothing (implied moral: "Be content with what you have"). Another is the fable of "The Tortoise and the Hare" (implied moral: "Slow, steady plodding wins the race"). The characters in a fable may be talking animals (as in many of Aesop's fables), inanimate objects, or people and supernatural beings (as in "Death Has an Appointment in Samarra"). Whoever they may be, these characters are merely sketched, not greatly developed. Evidently, it would not have helped the fable make its point if it had portrayed the teacher, the student, and Death in fuller detail. A more elaborate description of the tavern would not have improved the story. Probably, such a description would strike us as unnecessary and distracting. By its very bareness and simplicity, a fable fixes itself—and its message—in memory.

Aesop

The Fox and the Grapes

6th century B.C.

Translated by V. S. Vernon Jones

Very little is known with certainty about the man called Aesop, but several accounts and many traditions survive from antiquity. According to the Greek historian Herodotus, Aesop was a slave on the island of Samos. He gained great fame from his fables, but he somehow met his death at the hands of the people of Delphi. According to one tradition, Aesop was an ugly and misshapen man who charmed and amused people with his stories. No one knows if Aesop himself wrote down any of his fables, but they circulated widely in ancient Greece and were praised by Plato, Aristotle, and many other authors. His short and witty tales with their incisive morals have remained constantly popular and influenced innumerable later writers.

A hungry fox saw some fine bunches of grapes hanging from a vine that was trained along a high trellis, and did his best to reach them by jumping as high as he could into the air. But it was all in vain, for they were just out of reach: so he gave up trying, and walked away with an air of dignity and unconcern, remarking, "I thought those grapes were ripe, but I see now they are quite sour."

Moral: It is easy to despise what you cannot get.

**Woodcut by William Caxton, from his 1484 edition
of Aesop's fables, the first English translation.**

Questions

1. In fables, the fox is usually clever and frequently successful. Is that the case here?
2. The original Greek word for the fox's description of the grapes is *omphakes*, which more precisely means "unripe." Does the translator's use of the word "sour" add any further level of meaning to the fable?
3. How well does the closing moral fit the fable?

We are so accustomed to the phrase *Aesop's fables* that we might almost start to think the two words inseparable, but in fact there have been fabulists (creators or writers of fables) in virtually every culture throughout recorded history. Here is another fable from many centuries ago, this time from India.

Bidpai

The Camel and His Friends

c. 4th century

Retold in English by Arundhati Khanwalkar

The Panchatantra (Pañca-tantra), a collection of beast fables from India, is attributed to its narrator, a sage named Bidpai, who is a legendary figure about whom almost nothing is known for certain. The Panchatantra, which means the "Five Chapters" in Sanskrit, is based on earlier oral folklore. The collection was composed some time between 100 B.C. and 500 A.D. in a Sanskrit original now lost and is primarily known through an Arabic version of the eighth century and a twelfth-century Hebrew translation, which is the source of most Western versions of the tales. Other translations spread the fables as far as central Europe, Asia, and Indonesia.

Like many collections of fables, the Panchatantra is a frame tale, with an introduction containing verse and aphorisms spoken by an eighty-year-old Brahmin teacher named Vishnusharman, who tells the stories over a period of six months for the edification of three foolish princes named Rich-Power, Fierce-Power, and Endless-Power. The stories are didactic, teaching niti, the wise conduct of life, and artha, practical wisdom that stresses cleverness and self-reliance above more altruistic virtues.

The Lion, the King of the Animals from "The Fables of Bidpai," c.1480 (vellum). Musée Condé, Chantilly, France/The Bridgeman Art Library.

Once a merchant was leading a caravan of heavily-laden camels through a jungle when one of them, overcome by fatigue, collapsed. The merchant decided to leave the camel in the jungle and go on his way. Later, when the camel recovered his strength, he realized that he was alone in a strange jungle. Fortunately there was plenty of grass, and he survived.

One day the king of the jungle, a lion, arrived along with his three friends—a leopard, a fox, and a crow. The king lion wondered what the camel was doing in the jungle! He came near the camel and asked how he, a creature of the desert, had ended up in the hostile jungle. The camel tearfully explained what happened. The lion took pity on him and said, "You have nothing to fear now. Henceforth, you are under my protection and can stay with us." The camel began to live happily in the jungle.

Then one day the lion was wounded in a fight with an elephant. He retired to his cave and stayed there for several days. His friends came to offer their sympathy. They tried to catch prey for the hungry lion but failed. The camel had no problem as he lived on grass while the others were starving.

The fox came up with a plan. He secretly went to the lion and suggested that the camel be sacrificed for the good of the others. The lion got furious, "I can never kill an animal who is under my protection."

The fox humbly said, "But Lord, you have provided us food all the time. If any one of us voluntarily offered himself to save your life, I hope you won't mind!" The hungry lion did not object to that and agreed to take the offer.

5

The fox went back to his companions and said, "Friends, our king is dying of starvation. Let us go and beg him to eat one of us. It is the least we can do for such a noble soul."

So they went to the king and the crow offered his life. The fox interrupted, and said, "You are a small creature, the master's hunger will hardly be appeased by eating you. May I humbly offer my life to satisfy my master's hunger."

The leopard stepped forward and said, "You are no bigger than the crow, it is me whom our master should eat."

The foolish camel thought, "Everyone has offered to lay down their lives for the king, but he has not hurt any one. It is now my turn to offer myself." So he stepped forward and said, "Stand aside friend leopard, the king and you have close family ties. It is me whom the master must eat."

An ominous silence greeted the camel's offer. Then the king gladly said, "I accept your offer, O noble camel." And in no time he was killed by the three rogues, the false friends.

Moral: Be careful in choosing your friends.

Parable

Another traditional form of storytelling is the **parable**. Like a fable, a parable is a brief narrative that delivers a moral, but unlike a fable, its plot is plausibly realistic, and the main characters are human rather than anthropomorphized animals or natural forces. The other key difference is that parables usually possess a more mysterious and suggestive tone. A fable customarily ends by explicitly stating its moral, but parables often present their morals implicitly, and their meanings can be open to several interpretations.

In the Western tradition, the literary conventions of the parable are largely based on the brief stories told by Jesus in his preaching. The forty-three parables recounted in the four Gospels reveal how frequently he used the form to teach. Jesus designed his parables to have two levels of meaning—a literal story that could immediately be understood by the crowds he addressed and a deeper meaning fully comprehended only by his disciples, an inner circle who understood the nature of his ministry. (You can see the richness of interpretations suggested by Jesus's parables by reading and analyzing "The Parable of the Prodigal Son" from St. Luke's Gospel, which appears in Chapter 6.) The parable was also widely used by Eastern philosophers. The Taoist sage Chuang Tzu often portrayed the principles of Tao—which he called the "Way of Nature"—in witty parables such as the following one, traditionally titled "Independence."

Chuang Tzu

Independence   Chou Dynasty (4th century B.C.)

Translated by Herbert Giles

Chuang Chou, usually known as Chuang Tzu (approximately 390–365 B.C.), was one of the great philosophers of the Chou period in China. He was born in the Sung feudal state and received an excellent education. Unlike most educated men, however, Chuang Tzu did not seek public office or political power. Influenced by Taoist philosophy, he believed that individuals should transcend their desire for success and wealth, as well as their fear of failure and poverty. True freedom, he maintained, came from escaping the distractions of worldly affairs. Chuang Tzu's writings have been particularly praised for their combination of humor and wisdom. His parables and stories are classics of Chinese literature.

Chuang Tzu was one day fishing, when the Prince of Ch'u sent two high officials to interview him, saying that his Highness would be glad of Chuang Tzu's assistance in the administration of his government. The latter quietly fished on, and without looking round, replied, "I have heard that in the State of Ch'u there is a sacred tortoise, which has been dead three thousand years, and which the prince keeps packed up in a box on the altar in his ancestral shrine. Now do you think that tortoise would rather be dead and have its remains thus honoured, or be alive and wagging its tail in the mud?" The two officials answered that no doubt it would rather be alive and wagging its tail in the mud; whereupon Chuang Tzu cried out "Begone! I too elect to remain wagging my tail in the mud."

Questions

1. What part of this story is the exposition? How many sentences does Chuang Tzu use to set up the dramatic situation?
2. Why does the protagonist change the subject and mention the sacred tortoise? Why doesn't he answer the request directly and immediately? Does it serve any purpose that Chuang Tzu makes the officials answer a question to which he knows the answer?
3. What does this story tell us about the protagonist Chuang Tzu's personality?

Tale

The name *tale* (from the Old English *talu*, "speech") is sometimes applied to any story, whether short or long, true or fictitious. *Tale* being a more evocative name than *story*, writers sometimes call their stories "tales" as if to imply something handed down from the past. But defined in a more limited sense, a **tale** is a story, usually short, that sets forth strange and wonderful events in more or less bare summary, without detailed character-drawing. "Tale" is pretty much synonymous with "yarn," for it implies a story in which the goal is revelation of the marvelous rather than revelation of character.

In the English folktale "Jack and the Beanstalk," we take away a more vivid impression of the miraculous beanstalk and the giant who dwells at its top than of Jack's mind or personality. Because such venerable stories were told aloud before someone set them down in writing, the storytellers had to limit themselves to brief descriptions. Probably spoken around a fire or hearth, such a tale tends to be less complicated and less closely detailed than a story written for the printed page, whose reader can linger over it. Still, such tales *can* be complicated. It is not merely greater length that makes a short story different from a tale or a fable: one mark of a short story is a fully delineated character.

Types of Tales

Even modern tales favor supernatural or fantastic events: for instance, the **tall tale**, a variety of folk story that recounts the deeds of a superhero (such as the giant lumberjack Paul Bunyan) or of the storyteller. If the storyteller is describing his or her own imaginary experience, the bragging yarn is usually told with a straight face to listeners who take pleasure in scoffing at it. Although the **fairy tale**, set in a world of magic and enchantment, is sometimes the work of a modern author (notably Hans Christian Andersen), well-known examples are those German folktales that probably originated in the Middle Ages, collected by the Brothers Grimm. The label *fairy tale* is something of an English misnomer, for in the Grimm stories, though witches and goblins abound, fairies are a minority.

Jakob and Wilhelm Grimm

Godfather Death   1812 (from oral tradition)

Translated by Dana Gioia

Jakob Grimm (1785–1863) and Wilhelm Grimm (1786–1859), brothers and scholars, were born near Frankfurt am Main, Germany. For most of their lives they worked together—lived together, too, even when in 1825 Wilhelm married. In 1838, as librarians, they began toiling on their Deutsch Wörterbuch, or German dictionary, a vast project that was to outlive them by a century. (It was completed only in 1960.) In 1840 King Friedrich Wilhelm IV appointed both brothers to the Royal Academy of Sciences, and both taught at the University of Berlin for the rest of their days.

The name Grimm is best known to us for that splendid collection of ancient German folk stories we call Grimm's Fairy Tales—in German, Kinder- und Hausmärchen ("Childhood and Household Tales," 1812–1815). This classic

Jakob and Wilhelm Grimm

work spread German children's stories around the world. Many tales we hear early in life were collected by the Grimms: "Hansel and Gretel," "Snow White and the Seven Dwarfs," "Rapunzel," "Tom Thumb," "Little Red Riding Hood," "Rumpelstiltskin." Versions of some of these tales had been written down as early as the sixteenth century, but mainly the brothers relied on the memories of Hessian peasants who recited the stories aloud for them.

A poor man had twelve children and had to work day and night just to give them bread. Now when the thirteenth came into the world, he did not know what to do, so he ran out onto the main highway intending to ask the first one he met to be the child's godfather.

The first person he met was the good Lord God, who knew very well what was weighing on the man's heart. And He said to him, "Poor man, I am sorry for you. I will hold your child at the baptismal font. I will take care of him and fill his days with happiness."

The man asked, "Who are you?"

"I am the good Lord."

"Then I don't want you as godfather. You give to the rich and let the poor starve." 5

The man spoke thus because he did not know how wisely God portions out wealth and poverty. So he turned away from the Lord and went on.

Then the Devil came up to him and said, "What are you looking for? If you take me as your child's sponsor, I will give him gold heaped high and wide and all the joys of this world."

The man asked, "Who are you?"

"I am the Devil."

"Then I don't want you as godfather," said the man. "You trick men and lead them astray." 10

He went on, and bone-thin Death strode up to him and said, "Choose me as godfather."

The man asked, "Who are you?"

"I am Death, who makes all men equal."

Then the man said, "You are the right one. You take the rich and the poor without distinction. You will be the godfather."

Death answered, "I will make your child rich and famous. Whoever has me as a 15 friend shall lack for nothing."

The man said, "The baptism is next Sunday. Be there on time."

Death appeared just as he had promised and stood there as a proper godfather.

When the boy had grown up, his godfather walked in one day and said to come along with him. Death led him out into the woods, showed him an herb, and said, "Now you are going to get your christening present. I am making you a famous doctor. When you are called to a patient, I will always appear to you. If I stand next to the sick person's head, you may speak boldly that you will make him healthy again. Give him some of this herb, and he will recover. But if you see me standing by the sick person's feet, then he is mine. You must say that nothing can be done and that no doctor in the world can save him. But beware of using the herb against my will, or it will turn out badly for you."

It was not long before the young man was the most famous doctor in the whole world. "He needs only to look at the sick person," everyone said, "and then he knows how things stand—whether the patient will get well again or whether he must die." People came from far and wide to bring their sick and gave him so much gold that he quickly became quite rich.

Now it soon happened that the king grew ill, and the doctor was summoned to 20 say whether a recovery was possible. But when he came to the bed, Death was standing at the sick man's feet, and now no herb grown could save him.

"If I cheat Death this one time," thought the doctor, "he will be angry, but since I am his godson, he will turn a blind eye, so I will risk it." He took up the sick man and turned him around so that his head was now where Death stood. Then he gave the king some of the herb. The king recovered and grew healthy again.

But Death then came to the doctor with a dark and angry face and threatened him with his finger. "You have hoodwinked me this time," he said. "And I will forgive you once because you are my godson. But if you try such a thing again, it will be your neck, and I will take you away with me."

Not long after, the king's daughter fell into a serious illness. She was his only child, and he wept day and night until his eyes went blind. He let it be known that whoever saved her from death would become her husband and inherit the crown.

When the doctor came to the sick girl's bed, he saw Death standing at her feet. He should have remembered his godfather's warning, but the princess's great beauty and the happy prospect of becoming her husband so infatuated him that he flung all caution to the wind. He didn't notice that Death stared at him angrily or that he raised his hand and shook his bony fist. The doctor picked up the sick girl and turned her around to place her head where her feet had been. He gave her the herb, and right away her cheeks grew rosy and she stirred again with life.

When Death saw that he had been cheated out of his property a second time, he   25
strode with long steps up to the doctor and said, "It is all over for you. Now it's your turn." Death seized him so firmly with his ice-cold hand that the doctor could not resist. He led him into an underground cavern. There the doctor saw thousands and thousands of candles burning in endless rows. Some were tall, others medium-sized, and others quite small. Every moment some went out and others lit up, so that the tiny flames seemed to jump to and fro in perpetual motion.

"Look," said Death, "these are the life lights of mankind. The tall ones belong to children, the middle-size ones to married people in the prime of life, and the short ones to the very old. But sometimes even children and young people have only a short candle."

"Show me my life light," said the doctor, assuming it would be very tall.

Death pointed to a small stub that seemed about to flicker out.

"Oh, dear godfather!" cried the terrified doctor. "Light a new candle for me. If you love me, do it, so that I may enjoy my life, become king, and marry the beautiful princess."

"That I cannot do," Death replied. "One candle must first go out before a new   30
one is lighted."

"Then put my old one on top of a new candle that will keep burning when the old one goes out," begged the doctor.

Death acted as if he were going to grant the wish and picked up a tall new candle. But because he wanted revenge, he deliberately fumbled in placing the new candle, and the stub toppled over and went out. The doctor immediately dropped to the ground and fell into the hands of Death.

PLOT

Like a fable, the Grimm brothers' tale seems stark in its lack of detail and in the swiftness of its telling. Compared with the fully portrayed characters of many modern stories, the characters of father, son, king, princess, and even Death himself seem hardly more than stick figures. It may have been that to draw ample characters would not have contributed to the storytellers' design; that, indeed, to have done so would have been inartistic. Yet "Godfather Death" is a compelling story. By what methods does it arouse and sustain our interest?

Elements of Plot

Plot sometimes refers simply to the events in a story. In this book, though, **plot** will mean the artistic arrangement of those events. From the opening sentence of "Godfather Death," we watch the unfolding of a **dramatic situation**: a person is involved in some **conflict**. First, this character is a poor man with children to feed, in conflict with the world; very soon, we find him in conflict with God and with the Devil besides. Drama in fiction occurs in any clash of wills, desires, or powers—whether it be a conflict of character against character, character against society, character against some natural force, or, as in "Godfather Death," character against some supernatural entity.

Like any shapely tale, "Godfather Death" has a beginning, a middle, and an end. In fact, it is unusual to find a story so clearly displaying the elements of structure that critics have found in many classic works of fiction and drama. The tale begins with an **exposition**: the opening portion that sets the scene (if any), introduces the main characters, tells us what happened before the story opened, and provides any other background information that we need in order to understand and care about the events to follow. In "Godfather Death," the exposition is brief—all in the opening paragraph. The middle section of the story begins with Death's giving the herb to the boy and his warning not to defy him. This moment introduces a new conflict (a **complication**), and by this time it is clear that the son, and not the father, is to be the central human character of the story.

Protagonist Versus Antagonist

Death's godson is the principal person who strives: the **protagonist** (a better term than **hero**, for it may apply equally well to a central character who is not especially brave or virtuous). The **suspense**, the pleasurable anxiety we feel that heightens our attention to the story, resides in our wondering how it will all turn out. Will the doctor triumph over Death? Even though we suspect, early in the story, that the doctor stands no chance against such a superhuman **antagonist**, we want to see for ourselves the outcome of his defiance.

Crisis and Climax

When the doctor defies his godfather for the first time—when he saves the king—we have a **crisis**, a moment of high tension. The tension is momentarily resolved when Death lets him off. Then an even greater crisis—the turning point in the action—occurs with the doctor's second defiance in restoring the princess to life. In the last section of the story, with the doctor in the underworld, events come to a **climax**, the moment of greatest tension at which the outcome is to be decided, when the terrified doctor begs for a new candle. Will Death grant him one? Will he live, become king, and marry the princess? The outcome or **conclusion**—also called the **resolution** or **dénouement** (French for "the untying of the knot")—quickly follows as Death allows the little candle to go out.

Narrative Techniques

The treatment of plot is one aspect of an author's artistry. Different arrangements of the same material are possible. A writer might decide to tell of the events in chronological order, beginning with the earliest; or he or she might open the story with the last event, then tell what led up to it. Sometimes a writer chooses to skip rapidly over the exposition and begin *in medias res* (Latin for "in the midst of things"), first presenting some exciting or significant moment, then filling in what happened earlier. This method is by no means a modern invention: Homer begins the *Odyssey* with his hero mysteriously late in returning from war and his son searching for him; John Milton's *Paradise Lost* opens with Satan already defeated in his revolt against God. A device useful to writers for filling in what happened earlier is the **flashback** (or **retrospect**), a scene relived in a character's memory. Alternatively, a storyteller can try to incite our anticipation by giving us some **foreshadowing** or indication of events to come. In "Godfather Death" the foreshadowings are apparent in Death's warnings ("But if you try such a thing again, it will be your neck").

THE SHORT STORY

The teller of tales relies heavily on the method of **summary**: terse, general narration. In a **short story**, a form more realistic than the tale and of modern origin, the writer usually presents the main events in greater fullness. Fine writers of short stories, although they may use summary at times (often to give some portion of a story less emphasis), are skilled in rendering a **scene**: a vivid or dramatic moment described in enough detail to create the illusion that the reader is practically there. Avoiding long summary, they try to *show* rather than simply to *tell*, as if following Mark Twain's advice to authors: "Don't say, 'The old lady screamed.' Bring her on and let her scream."

A short story is more than just a sequence of happenings. A finely wrought short story has the richness and conciseness of an excellent lyric poem. Spontaneous and natural as the finished story may seem, the writer has crafted it so artfully that there is meaning in even seemingly casual speeches and apparently trivial details. If we skim it hastily, skipping the descriptive passages, we miss significant parts.

Some literary short stories, unlike commercial fiction in which the main interest is in physical action or conflict, tell of an **epiphany**: some moment of insight, discovery, or revelation by which a character's life, or view of life, is greatly altered. The term, which means "showing forth" in Greek, was first used in Christian theology to signify the manifestation of God's presence in the world. This theological idea was adapted by James Joyce to refer to a heightened moment of secular revelation. (For such moments in fiction, see the stories in this book by Joyce in Chapter 14, John Steinbeck in Chapter 7, and Joyce Carol Oates in Chapter 3.) Other short stories tell of a character initiated into experience or maturity: one such **story of initiation** is William Faulkner's "Barn Burning" (Chapter 5), in which a boy finds it necessary to defy his father and suddenly grows into manhood. Less obviously dramatic, perhaps, than "Godfather Death," such a story may be no less powerful.

The fable and the tale are ancient forms; the short story is of more recent origin. In the nineteenth century, writers of fiction were encouraged by a large, literate audience of middle-class readers who wanted to see their lives reflected in faithful mirrors. Skillfully representing ordinary life, many writers perfected the art of the short story: in Russia, Anton Chekhov, and in America, Nathaniel Hawthorne and Edgar Allan Poe (although the Americans seem less fond of everyday life than of dream and fantasy). It would be false to claim that, in passing from the fable and the tale to the short story, fiction has made triumphant progress; or to claim that, because short stories are modern, they are superior to fables and tales. Fable, tale, and short story are distinct forms, each achieving its own effects. Far from being extinct, fable and tale have enjoyed a resurgence in recent years. Jorge Luis Borges, Italo Calvino, and Gabriel García Márquez have all used fable and folktale to create memorable and very modern fiction. All forms of fiction are powerful in the right authorial hands.

Let's begin with a contemporary short story whose protagonist undergoes an initiation into maturity. To notice the difference between a short story and a tale, you may find it helpful to compare John Updike's "A & P" with "Godfather Death." Although Updike's short story is centuries distant from the Grimm tale in its setting and in its method of telling, you may be reminded of "Godfather Death" in the main character's dramatic situation. To defend a young woman, a young man has to defy his mentor—here, the boss of a supermarket. In so doing, he places himself in jeopardy. Updike has the protagonist tell his own story, amply and with humor. How does it differ from a tale?

John Updike

A & P
1961

John Updike (1932–2009) was born in Reading, Pennsylvania, received his BA from Harvard, and then went to Oxford to study drawing and fine art. In the mid-1950s he worked on the staff of the New Yorker, at times doing errands for the aged James Thurber. Although he left the magazine to become a full-time writer, Updike continued to supply it with memorable stories, witty light verse, and searching reviews. A famously prolific writer, he published more than fifty books. Updike is best known as a hardworking, versatile, highly productive writer of fiction. For his novel The Centaur (1963) he received a National Book Award, and for Rabbit Is Rich (1982) a Pulitzer Prize and an American Book Award. The fourth and last Rabbit Angstrom novel, Rabbit at Rest (1990), won him a second Pulitzer. Updike is one of the few Americans ever to be awarded both the National Medal of Arts (1989) and the National Humanities Medal (2003)—the nation's highest honors in each respective field. His many other books include The Witches of Eastwick *(1984), made into a successful film starring Jack Nicholson,* Terrorist *(2006), and his final novel,* The Widows of Eastwick *(2008).*

John Updike

Almost uniquely among contemporary American writers, Updike moved back and forth successfully among a variety of literary genres: light verse, serious poetry, drama, criticism, children's books, novels, and short stories. But it is perhaps in short fiction that he did his finest work. Many critics agree with the Washington Post's *Jonathan Yardley, who wrote: "It is in his short stories that we find Updike's most assured work, and no doubt it is upon the best of them that his reputation ultimately will rest."*

In walks three girls in nothing but bathing suits. I'm in the third check-out slot, with my back to the door, so I don't see them until they're over by the bread. The one that caught my eye first was the one in the plaid green two-piece. She was a chunky kid, with a good tan and a sweet broad soft-looking can with those two crescents of white just under it, where the sun never seems to hit, at the top of the backs of her legs. I stood there with my hand on a box of HiHo crackers trying to remember if I rang it up or not. I ring it up again and the customer starts giving me hell. She's one of these cash-register-watchers, a witch about fifty with rouge on her cheekbones and no eyebrows, and I know it made her day to trip me up. She'd been watching cash registers for fifty years and probably never seen a mistake before.

By the time I got her feathers smoothed and her goodies into a bag—she gives me a little snort in passing, if she'd been born at the right time they would have burned her over in Salem—by the time I get her on her way the girls had circled around the bread and were coming back, without a pushcart, back my way along the counters, in the aisle between the check-outs and the Special bins. They didn't even have shoes on. There was this chunky one, with the two-piece—it was bright green and the seams on the bra were still sharp and her belly was still pretty pale so

I guessed she just got it (the suit)—there was this one, with one of those chubby berry-faces, the lips all bunched together under her nose, this one, and a tall one, with black hair that hadn't quite frizzed right, and one of these sunburns right across under the eyes, and a chin that was too long—you know, the kind of girl other girls think is very "striking" and "attractive" but never quite makes it, as they very well know, which is why they like her so much—and then the third one, that wasn't quite so tall. She was the queen. She kind of led them, the other two peeking around and making their shoulders round. She didn't look around, not this queen, she just walked straight on slowly, on these long white prima-donna legs. She came down a little hard on her heels, as if she didn't walk in her bare feet that much, putting down her heels and then letting the weight move along to her toes as if she was testing the floor with every step, putting a little deliberate extra action into it. You never know for sure how girls' minds work (do you really think it's a mind in there or just a little buzz like a bee in a glass jar?) but you got the idea she had talked the other two into coming in here with her, and now she was showing them how to do it, walk slow and hold yourself straight.

She had on a kind of dirty-pink—beige maybe, I don't know—bathing suit with a little nubble all over it and, what got me, the straps were down. They were off her shoulders looped loose around the cool tops of her arms, and I guess as a result the suit had slipped a little on her, so all around the top of the cloth there was this shining rim. If it hadn't been there you wouldn't have known there could have been anything whiter than those shoulders. With the straps pushed off, there was nothing between the top of the suit and the top of her head except just *her*, this clean bare plane of the top of her chest down from the shoulder bones like a dented sheet of metal tilted in the light. I mean, it was more than pretty.

She had sort of oaky hair that the sun and salt had bleached, done up in a bun that was unraveling, and a kind of prim face. Walking into the A & P with your straps down, I suppose it's the only kind of face you *can* have. She held her head so high her neck, coming up out of those white shoulders, looked kind of stretched, but I didn't mind. The longer her neck was, the more of her there was.

She must have felt in the corner of her eye me and over my shoulder Stokesie   5 in the second slot watching, but she didn't tip. Not this queen. She kept her eyes moving across the racks, and stopped, and turned so slow it made my stomach rub the inside of my apron, and buzzed to the other two, who kind of huddled against her for relief, and they all three of them went up the cat-and-dog-food-breakfast-cereal-macaroni-rice-raisins-seasonings-spreads-spaghetti-soft-drinks-crackers-and-cookies aisle. From the third slot I look straight up this aisle to the meat counter, and I watched them all the way. The fat one with the tan sort of fumbled with the cookies, but on second thought she put the packages back. The sheep pushing their carts down the aisle—the girls were walking against the usual traffic (not that we have one-way signs or anything)—were pretty hilarious. You could see them, when Queenie's white shoulders dawned on them, kind of jerk, or hop, or hic-cup, but their eyes snapped back to their own baskets and on they pushed. I bet you could set off dynamite in an A & P and the people would by and large keep reaching and checking oatmeal off their lists and muttering "Let me see, there was a third thing, began with A, asparagus, no, ah, yes, applesauce!" or whatever it is they do mutter. But there was no doubt, this jiggled them. A few houseslaves in pin curlers even looked around after pushing their carts past to make sure what they had seen was correct.

You know, it's one thing to have a girl in a bathing suit down on the beach, where what with the glare nobody can look at each other much anyway, and another thing in the cool of the A & P, under the fluorescent lights, against all those stacked packages, with her feet padding along naked over our checkerboard green-and-cream rubber-tile floor.

"Oh Daddy," Stokesie said beside me. "I feel so faint."

"Darling," I said. "Hold me tight." Stokesie's married, with two babies chalked up on his fuselage already, but as far as I can tell that's the only difference. He's twenty-two, and I was nineteen this April.

"Is it done?" he asks, the responsible married man finding his voice. I forgot to say he thinks he's going to be manager some sunny day, maybe in 1990 when it's called the Great Alexandrov and Petrooshki Tea Company or something.

What he meant was, our town is five miles from a beach, with a big summer colony out on the Point, but we're right in the middle of town, and the women generally put on a shirt or shorts or something before they get out of the car into the street. And anyway these are usually women with six children and varicose veins mapping their legs and nobody, including them, could care less. As I say, we're right in the middle of town, and if you stand at our front doors you can see two banks and the Congregational church and the newspaper store and three real-estate offices and about twenty-seven old freeloaders tearing up Central Street because the sewer broke again. It's not as if we're on the Cape; we're north of Boston and there's people in this town haven't seen the ocean for twenty years. The girls had reached the meat counter and were asking McMahon something. He pointed, they pointed, and they shuffled out of sight behind a pyramid of Diet Delight peaches. All that was left for us to see was old McMahon patting his mouth and looking after them sizing up their joints. Poor kids, I began to feel sorry for them, they couldn't help it.

Now here comes the sad part of the story, at least my family says it's sad but I don't think it's sad myself. The store's pretty empty, it being Thursday afternoon, so there was nothing much to do except lean on the register and wait for the girls to show up again. The whole store was like a pinball machine and I didn't know which tunnel they'd come out of. After a while they come around out of the far aisle, around the light bulbs, records at discount of the Caribbean Six or Tony Martin Sings or some such gunk you wonder they waste the wax on, six-packs of candy bars, and plastic toys done up in cellophane that fall apart when a kid looks at them anyway. Around they come, Queenie still leading the way, and holding a little gray jar in her hand. Slots Three through Seven are unmanned and I could see her wondering between Stokes and me, but Stokesie with his usual luck draws an old party in baggy gray pants who stumbles up with four giant cans of pineapple juice (what do these bums *do* with all that pineapple juice? I've often asked myself) so the girls come to me. Queenie puts down the jar and I take it into my fingers icy cold. Kingfish Fancy Herring Snacks in Pure Sour Cream: 49¢. Now her hands are empty, not a ring or a bracelet, bare as God made them, and I wonder where the money's coming from. Still with that prim look she lifts a folded dollar bill out of the hollow at the center of her nubbled pink top. The jar went heavy in my hand. Really, I thought that was so cute.

Then everybody's luck begins to run out. Lengel comes in from haggling with a truck full of cabbages on the lot and is about to scuttle into that door marked MANAGER behind which he hides all day when the girls touch his eye. Lengel's pretty dreary, teaches Sunday school and the rest, but he doesn't miss that much. He comes over and says, "Girls, this isn't the beach."

Queenie blushes, though maybe it's just a brush of sunburn I was noticing for the first time, now that she was so close. "My mother asked me to pick up a jar of herring snacks." Her voice kind of startled me, the way voices do when you see the people first, coming out so flat and dumb yet kind of tony, too, the way it ticked over "pick up" and "snacks." All of a sudden I slid right down her voice into her living room. Her father and the other men were standing around in ice-cream coats and bow ties and the women were in sandals picking up herring snacks on toothpicks off a big plate and they were all holding drinks the color of water with olives and sprigs of mint in them. When my parents have somebody over they get lemonade and if it's a real racy affair Schlitz in tall glasses with "They'll Do It Every Time" cartoons stencilled on.

"That's all right," Lengel said. "But this isn't the beach." His repeating this struck me as funny, as if it had just occurred to him, and he had been thinking all these years the A & P was a great big dune and he was the head lifeguard. He didn't like my smiling—as I say he doesn't miss much—but he concentrates on giving the girls that sad Sunday-school-superintendent stare.

Queenie's blush is no sunburn now, and the plump one in plaid, that I liked bet-   15
ter from the back—a really sweet can—pipes up, "We weren't doing any shopping. We just came in for the one thing."

"That makes no difference," Lengel tells her, and I could see from the way his eyes went that he hadn't noticed she was wearing a two-piece before. "We want you decently dressed when you come in here."

"We *are* decent," Queenie says suddenly, her lower lip pushing, getting sore now that she remembers her place, a place from which the crowd that runs the A & P must look pretty crummy. Fancy Herring Snacks flashed in her very blue eyes.

"Girls, I don't want to argue with you. After this come in here with your shoulders covered. It's our policy." He turns his back. That's policy for you. Policy is what the kingpins want. What the others want is juvenile delinquency.

All this while, the customers had been showing up with their carts but, you know, sheep, seeing a scene, they had all bunched up on Stokesie, who shook open a paper bag as gently as peeling a peach, not wanting to miss a word. I could feel in the silence everybody getting nervous, most of all Lengel, who asks me, "Sammy, have you rung up this purchase?"

I thought and said "No" but it wasn't about that I was thinking. I go through   20
the punches, 4, 9, GROC, TOT—it's more complicated than you think, and after you do it often enough, it begins to make a little song, that you hear words to, in my case "Hello (*bing*) there, you (*gung*) hap-py *pee*-pul (*splat*)!"—the *splat* being the drawer flying out. I uncrease the bill, tenderly as you may imagine, it just having come from between the two smoothest scoops of vanilla I had ever known were there, and pass a half and a penny into her narrow pink palm, and nestle the herrings in a bag and twist its neck and hand it over, all the time thinking.

The girls, and who'd blame them, are in a hurry to get out, so I say "I quit" to Lengel quick enough for them to hear, hoping they'll stop and watch me, their unsuspected hero. They keep right on going, into the electric eye; the door flies open and they flicker across the lot to their car, Queenie and Plaid and Big Tall Goony-Goony (not that as raw material she was so bad), leaving me with Lengel and a kink in his eyebrow.

"Did you say something, Sammy?"

"I said I quit."

"I thought you did."

"You didn't have to embarrass them."

"It was they who were embarrassing us."

I started to say something that came out "Fiddle-de-doo." It's a saying of my grandmother's, and I know she would have been pleased.

"I don't think you know what you're saying," Lengel said.

"I know you don't," I said. "But I do." I pull the bow at the back of my apron and start shrugging it off my shoulders. A couple customers that had been heading for my slot begin to knock against each other, like scared pigs in a chute.

Lengel sighs and begins to look very patient and old and gray. He's been a friend   30
of my parents for years. "Sammy, you don't want to do this to your Mom and Dad," he tells me. It's true, I don't. But it seems to me that once you begin a gesture it's fatal not to go through with it. I fold the apron, "Sammy" stitched in red on the pocket, and put it on the counter, and drop the bow tie on top of it. The bow tie is theirs, if you've ever wondered. "You'll feel this for the rest of your life," Lengel says, and I know that's true, too, but remembering how he made that pretty girl blush makes me so scrunchy inside I punch the No Sale tab and the machine whirs "pee-pul" and the drawer splats out. One advantage to this scene taking place in summer, I can follow this up with a clean exit, there's no fumbling around getting your coat and galoshes, I just saunter into the electric eye in my white shirt that my mother ironed the night before, and the door heaves itself open, and outside the sunshine is skating around on the asphalt.

I look around for my girls, but they're gone, of course. There wasn't anybody but some young married screaming with her children about some candy they didn't get by the door of a powder-blue Falcon station wagon. Looking back in the big windows, over the bags of peat moss and aluminum lawn furniture stacked on the pavement, I could see Lengel in my place in the slot, checking the sheep through. His face was dark gray and his back stiff, as if he'd just had an injection of iron, and my stomach kind of fell as I felt how hard the world was going to be to me hereafter.

Questions

1. Notice how artfully Updike arranges details to set the story in a perfectly ordinary super-market. What details stand out for you as particularly true to life? What does this close attention to detail contribute to the story?

2. How fully does Updike draw the character of Sammy? What traits (admirable or other-wise) does Sammy show? Is he any less a hero for wanting the girls to notice his heroism? To what extent is he more thoroughly and fully portrayed than the doctor in "Godfather Death"?

3. What part of the story seems to be the exposition? (See the definition of *exposition* in the discussion of plot earlier in the chapter.) Of what value to the story is the carefully detailed portrait of Queenie, the leader of the three girls?

4. Where in "A & P" does the dramatic conflict become apparent? What moment in the story brings the crisis? What is the climax of the story?

5. Why exactly does Sammy quit his job?

6. Does anything lead you to *expect* Sammy to make some gesture of sympathy for the three girls? What incident earlier in the story (before Sammy quits) seems a foreshadowing?

7. What do you understand from the conclusion of the story? What does Sammy mean when he acknowledges "how hard the world was going to be . . . hereafter"?

8. What comment does Updike—through Sammy—make on supermarket society?

■ WRITING *effectively*

Wilhelm Grimm on Writing

On the Nature of Fairy Tales   1819

Translated by Dana Gioia

Children's fairy tales are told so that under their pure and gentle light they can awaken and develop the earliest thoughts and virtues in a child's heart. But since their simple poetry and truth pleases everyone, and because they are told and passed on at home, they can also be called household tales. Historical legends usually connect in a straightforward and serious way something unusual and astounding, sometimes even supernatural, with ordinary, familiar, and current things. For this reason they often seem awkward, fierce, and strange. But fairy tales present a world apart in a protected and undisturbed place which never looks beyond itself. Therefore the tale has neither a name nor location, not even a specific home, because it is something common to the entire nation.

● ● ●

All true literature lends itself to multiple interpretations because it has emerged from life itself to which it always returns. It meets us like sunlight wherever we stand. Since it is so grounded, it is easy to draw a lesson from fairy tales and apply it to the present time. This was not their purpose, and with a few exceptions, they were not so conceived, but they develop in this way without human help like good fruit growing out of a healthy flower.

From "On the Nature of Fairy Tales"

THINKING ABOUT PLOT

A day without conflict is pleasant, but a story without conflict is boring. The plot of every short story, novel, or movie derives its energy from conflict. A character desperately wants something he or she can't have, or is frantic to avoid an unpleasant (or deadly) event. In most stories, conflict is established and tension builds, leading to a crisis and, finally, a resolution of some sort. When analyzing a story, be sure to remember these points:

- **Plotting isn't superficial.** Although plot might seem like the most obvious and superficial part of a story, it is an important expressive device. Plot combines with the other elements of fiction—imagery, style, and symbolism, for example—to create an emotional response in the reader: suspense, humor, sadness, excitement, terror.
- **Small events can have large consequences.** In most short stories, plot depends less on large external events than on small occurrences that set off large internal changes in the main character.
- **Action reveals character.** Good stories are a lot like life: the protagonist's true nature is usually revealed not just by what he or she says but also by what he or she does. Stories often show how the protagonist comes to a

personal turning point, or how his or her character is tested or revealed by events.

- **Plot is about cause and effect.** Plot is more than simply a sequence of events ("First A happens, and then B, and then C . . . "). The actions, events, and situations described in most stories are related to each other by more than just accident ("First A happens, which causes B to happen, which makes C all the more surprising, or inevitable, or ironic . . . ").

CHECKLIST: Writing About Plot

☐ What is the story's central conflict?

☐ Who is the protagonist? What does he or she want?

☐ What is at stake for the protagonist in the conflict?

☐ What stands in the way of the protagonist's easily achieving his or her goal?

☐ What are the main events that take place in the story? How does each event relate to the protagonist's struggle?

☐ Where do you find the story's climax, or crisis?

☐ How is the conflict resolved?

☐ Does the protagonist succeed in achieving his or her goals?

☐ What is the impact of success, failure, or a surprising outcome on the protagonist?

TOPICS FOR WRITING ON PLOT

1. Choose and read a story from this collection, and write a brief description of its plot and main characters. Then write at length about how the protagonist is changed or tested by the story's events. What do the main character's actions reveal about his or her personality? Some possible story choices are Updike's "A & P," Alice Walker's "Everyday Use" (Chapter 12), Toni Morrison's "Recitatif" (Chapter 3), and T. C. Boyle's "Greasy Lake" (Chapter 14).

2. Briefly list the events described in "A & P." Now write several paragraphs about the ways in which the story adds up to more than the sum of its events. Why should the reader care about Sammy's thoughts and decisions?

3. How do Sammy's actions in "A & P" reveal his character? In what ways are his thoughts and actions at odds with each other?

4. Write a brief fable modeled on either "Death Has an Appointment in Samarra," "The Fox and the Grapes," or "The Camel and His Friends." Begin with a familiar proverb—"A penny saved is a penny earned" or "Too many cooks spoil the broth"—and invent a story to make the moral convincing.

5. With "Godfather Death" in mind, write a fairy tale set in the present, in a town or city much like your own. After you've completed your fairy tale, write a paragraph explaining what aspects of the fairy tale by the Brothers Grimm you hoped to capture in your story.

6. The Brothers Grimm collected and wrote down many of our best-known fairy tales— "Cinderella," "Snow White and the Seven Dwarfs," and "Little Red Riding Hood," for example. If you have strong childhood recollections of one of these stories—perhaps based on picture books or on the animated Disney versions—find and read the Brothers Grimm version. Are you surprised by the differences? Write a brief essay contrasting the original with your remembered version. What does the original offer that the adaptation does not?

▶ TERMS FOR *review*

Types of Short Fiction

Fable ▶ A brief, often humorous narrative told to illustrate a moral. The characters in fables are traditionally animals whose personality traits symbolize human traits.

Parable ▶ A brief, usually allegorical narrative that teaches a moral. In parables, unlike fables (where the moral is explicitly stated within the narrative), the moral themes are implicit and can often be interpreted in several ways.

Tale ▶ A short narrative without a complex plot. Tales are an ancient form of narrative found in folklore, and traditional tales often contain supernatural elements. A tale differs from a short story by its tendency toward lesser-developed characters and linear plotting.

Tall tale ▶ A humorous short narrative that provides a wildly exaggerated version of events. Originally an oral form, the tall tale usually assumes that its audience knows the narrator is distorting the events. The form is often associated with the American frontier.

Fairy tale, folktale ▶ A traditional form of short narrative folklore, originally transmitted orally, which features supernatural characters such as witches, giants, fairies, or animals with human personality traits. Fairy tales often feature a hero or heroine who strives to achieve some desirable fate—such as marrying royalty or finding great wealth.

Short story ▶ A prose narrative too brief to be published in a separate volume—as novellas and novels frequently are. The short story is usually a focused narrative that presents one or two characters involved in a single compelling action.

Initiation story (also called **coming-of-age story**) ▶ A narrative in which the main character, usually a child or adolescent, undergoes an important experience (or "rite of passage") that prepares him or her for adulthood.

Elements of Plot

Protagonist ▶ The main or central character in a narrative. The protagonist usually initiates the main action of the story, often in conflict with the antagonist.

Antagonist ▶ The most significant character or force that opposes the protagonist in a narrative. The antagonist may be another character, society itself, a force of nature, or even—in some modern literature—conflicting impulses within the protagonist.

Exposition ▶ The opening portion of a narrative. In the exposition, the scene is set, the protagonist is introduced, and the author discloses any other background information necessary for the reader to understand the events that follow.

Conflict ▶ The central struggle between two or more forces in a story. Conflict generally occurs when some person or thing prevents the protagonist from achieving his or her goal. Conflict is the basic material out of which most plots are made.

Complication ▶ The introduction of a significant development in the central conflict between characters (or between a character and his or her situation). Complications may be external (an outside problem that the characters cannot avoid) or internal (a complication that originates in some important aspect of a character's values or personality).

Crisis ▶ The point in a narrative when the crucial action, decision, or realization must take place. From the Greek word *krisis*, meaning "decision."

Climax ▶ The moment of greatest intensity in a story, which almost inevitably occurs toward the end of the work. The climax often takes the form of a decisive confrontation between the protagonist and antagonist.

Conclusion ▶ In plotting, the logical end or outcome of a unified plot, shortly following the climax. Also called **resolution** or **dénouement** ("the untying of the knot"), as in resolving—or untying the knots created by—plot complications earlier in the narrative.

Narrative Techniques

Foreshadowing ▶ An indication of events to come in a narrative. The author may introduce specific words, images, or actions in order to suggest significant later events.

Flashback ▶ A scene relived in a character's memory. Flashbacks may be related by the narrator in a summary, or they may be experienced by the characters themselves. Flashbacks allow the author to include significant events that occurred before the opening of the story.

Epiphany ▶ A moment of profound insight or revelation by which a character's life is greatly altered.

In medias res ▶ A Latin phrase meaning "in the midst of things"; refers to the narrative device of beginning a story midway in the events it depicts (usually at an exciting or significant moment) before explaining the context or preceding actions.

2 POINT OF VIEW

*An author in his book must be like God in his universe,
present everywhere and visible nowhere.*

—GUSTAVE FLAUBERT

What You Will Learn in This Chapter

- To identify the point of view from which a story is told
- To describe different types of narrators
- To explain stream-of-consciousness narration
- To analyze the role of point of view in a story

In the opening lines of *The Adventures of Huckleberry Finn*, Mark Twain takes care to separate himself from the leading character, who is to tell his own story:

> You don't know about me, without you have read a book by the name of *The Adventures of Tom Sawyer*, but that ain't no matter. That book was made by Mr. Mark Twain, and he told the truth, mainly.

Twain wrote the novel, but the **narrator** or speaker is Huck Finn, a fictional character who supposedly tells the story. Of course in *Huckleberry Finn*, the narrator of the story is not the same person as the "real-life" author. In employing Huck as his narrator, Twain selects a special angle of vision: not his own, exactly, but that of a resourceful boy moving through the thick of events, with a mind at times shrewd, at other times innocent. Through Huck's eyes, Twain takes in certain scenes, actions, and characters and—as only Huck's angle of vision could have enabled Twain to do so well—records them memorably.

IDENTIFYING POINT OF VIEW

Narrators come in many forms. Because stories usually are told by someone, almost every story has some kind of narrator. Some theorists reserve the term *narrator* for a character who tells a story in the first person. We use it in a wider sense, to mean a recording consciousness that an author creates, who may or may not be a participant in the events of the story. Real persons can tell stories in a factual way, but when such a story is *written*, the result is usually *nonfiction*: a memoir, a travelogue, an autobiography.

To identify a story's **point of view**, describe the role the narrator plays in the events and any limits placed on his or her knowledge of the events. In a short story, it is usual for the writer to maintain one point of view from beginning to end, but there is nothing to stop him or her from introducing other points of view as well. In his long, panoramic novel *War and Peace*, encompassing the vast drama of Napoleon's invasion of Russia, Leo Tolstoy freely shifts the point of view in and out of the minds of many characters, among them Napoleon himself.

TYPES OF NARRATORS

Theoretically, a great many points of view are possible. One initial way to determine a story's point of view is to identify whether or not the narrator appears as a major or minor character, as a sideline observer, or as an unnamed nonparticipant.

Participant Narrator

When the narrator is cast as a **participant** in the events of the story, he or she is a dramatized character who writes in the first person, who says "I." Such a narrator may be the protagonist (Huck Finn) or may be an **observer**, a minor character standing a little to one side, watching a story unfold that mainly involves other characters. A famous example of a participant narrator occurs in F. Scott Fitzgerald's *The Great Gatsby*. The novel's narrator is not Jay Gatsby, but his neighbor and friend Nick Carraway, who knows only portions of Gatsby's mysterious life.

Nonparticipant Narrator

A narrator who remains a **nonparticipant** does not appear in the story as a character. Viewing the characters, perhaps seeing into the minds of one or more of them, such a narrator refers to them as "he," "she," or "they." In the tale of "Godfather Death," we have a narrator who is not a character in the story at all, someone who is not even named, who stands at a distance from the action while recording what the main characters say and do.

HOW MUCH DOES A NARRATOR KNOW?

The narrator of a story can possess different levels of knowledge about the characters' thoughts, feelings, and actions—from total omniscience to almost total ignorance. Those levels of knowledge can be categorized in the following ways.

All-knowing

The **all-knowing (or omniscient)** narrator sees into the minds of any or all of the characters, moving when necessary from one to another. This is the point of view in "Godfather Death," in which the narrator knows the feelings and motives of the father, of the doctor, and even of Death himself. Since he adds an occasional comment or opinion, this narrator may be said to show **editorial omniscience** (as we can tell from his disapproving remark that the doctor "should have remembered" and his observation that the father did not understand "how wisely God shares out wealth and poverty"). A narrator who shows **impartial omniscience** presents the thoughts and actions of the characters but does not judge them or comment on them.

Limited Omniscience

When a nonparticipating narrator sees events through the eyes of a single character, whether a major character or a minor one, the resulting point of view is sometimes called **limited omniscience or selective omniscience**. The author, of course, selects which character's perspective to see from; the omniscience is his and not the narrator's.

In William Faulkner's "Barn Burning" (Chapter 5), the narrator is almost entirely confined to knowing the thoughts and perceptions of a boy, the central character.

Objective Point of View

In the **objective point of view**, the narrator does not enter the mind of any character but describes events from the outside. Telling us what people say and how their faces look, he or she leaves us to infer their thoughts and feelings. So inconspicuous is the narrator that this point of view has been called "the fly on the wall." Some critics would say that in the objective point of view, the narrator disappears altogether. Crime writer Dashiell Hammett was a master of this technique, as you'll find in his story in Chapter 8.

Unreliable Narrator

In a story told by an **unreliable narrator**, the point of view is that of a person who, we perceive, is deceptive, self-deceptive, deluded, or deranged. Although this narrative device has long been employed by great authors of the past, such as Edgar Allan Poe and Eudora Welty, contemporary writers have been particularly fond of unreliable narrators. For a famous example, consider the demented and unstable condition of Poe's narrator in "The Tell-Tale Heart" (Chapter 12).

Other Narrative Points of View

Besides the common points of view just listed, uncommon points of view are possible. In Jack London's adventure novel *The Call of the Wild*, the story is told from the perspective of its protagonist, a dog.

Also possible, but unusual, is a story written in the second person, "you." This point of view results in a startling directness, as in Jay McInerney's novel *Bright Lights, Big City* (1985), which begins:

> You are not the kind of guy who would be at a place like this at this time of the morning. But here you are, and you cannot say that the terrain is entirely unfamiliar, although the details are fuzzy. You are at a nightclub talking to a girl with a shaved head.

The attitudes and opinions of a narrator aren't necessarily those of the author; in fact, we may notice a lively conflict between what we are told and what, apparently, we are meant to believe. A story may be told by an **innocent narrator** or a **naive narrator**, a character who fails to understand all the implications of the story. One such innocent narrator (despite his sometimes shrewd perceptions) is Huckleberry Finn. Because Huck accepts without question the morality and lawfulness of slavery, he feels guilty about helping Jim, a runaway slave. But, far from condemning Huck for his defiance of the law—"All right, then, I'll *go* to hell," Huck tells himself, deciding against returning Jim to captivity—the author, and the reader along with him, silently applaud.

STREAM OF CONSCIOUSNESS

One popular modern method of writing is called **stream of consciousness**, from a phrase coined by psychologist William James to describe the procession of thoughts passing through the mind. In fiction, the stream of consciousness is a kind of selective omniscience: the presentation of thoughts and sense impressions in a lifelike fashion—not in a sequence arranged by logic, but mingled randomly. When in his novel *Ulysses* James Joyce takes us into the mind of Leopold Bloom, an ordinary Dublin mind well-stocked with trivia and fragments of odd learning, the reader may have an impression not of a smoothly flowing stream but of an ocean of miscellaneous things, all crowded and jostling.

> As he set foot on O'Connell bridge a puffball of smoke plumed up from the parapet. Brewery barge with export stout. England. Sea air sours it, I heard. Be interesting some day to get a pass through Hancock to see the brewery. Regular world in itself. Vats of porter, wonderful. Rats get in too. Drink themselves bloated as big as a collie floating.

Stream-of-consciousness writing usually occurs in relatively short passages, but in the 700-plus-page *Ulysses*, Joyce employs it extensively. Similar in method, an **interior monologue** is an extended presentation of a character's thoughts, not in the seemingly helter-skelter order of a stream of consciousness, but in an arrangement as if the character were speaking out loud to himself, for us to overhear.

Every point of view has limitations. Even **total omniscience**, a knowledge of the minds of all the characters, has its disadvantages. Such a point of view requires high skill to manage, without the storyteller's losing his or her way in a multitude of perspectives. In fact, there are evident advantages in having a narrator not know everything. We are accustomed to seeing the world through one pair of eyes, to having truths gradually occur to us.

By using a particular point of view, an author may artfully withhold information, if need be, rather than immediately present it to us. If, for instance, the suspense in a story depends on our not knowing until the end that the protagonist is a spy, the author would be ill advised to tell the story from the protagonist's point of view. Clearly, the author makes a fundamental decision in selecting, from many possibilities, a story's point of view.

Here is a short story memorable for many reasons, among them its point of view.

William Faulkner

A Rose for Emily
1931

William Faulkner (1897–1962) spent most of his days in Oxford, Mississippi, where he attended the University of Mississippi and where he served as postmaster until angry townspeople ejected him because they had failed to receive mail. During World War I he joined the Royal Canadian Air Force and afterward worked as a feature writer for the New Orleans Times-Picayune. Faulkner's private life was a long struggle to stay solvent: even after fame came to him, he had to write Hollywood scripts and teach at the University of Virginia to support himself. His violent comic novel Sanctuary *(1931) caused a stir and turned a profit, but critics tend most to admire* The Sound and the Fury *(1929), a tale partially told through the eyes of an idiot;* As I Lay Dying *(1930);* Light in August *(1932);* Absalom, Absalom *(1936); and* The Hamlet *(1940).*

William Faulkner

Beginning with Sartoris (1929), *Faulkner in his fiction imagines a Mississippi county named Yoknapatawpha and traces the fortunes of several of its families, including the aristocratic Compsons and Sartorises and the white-trash, dollar-grabbing Snopeses, from the Civil War to the mid-twentieth century. His influence on his fellow Southern writers (and others) has been profound. In 1950 he received the Nobel Prize in Literature. Although we think of Faulkner primarily as a novelist, he wrote nearly a hundred short stories. Forty-two of the best are available in his* Collected Stories (1950; 1995).

I

When Miss Emily Grierson died, our whole town went to her funeral: the men through a sort of respectful affection for a fallen monument, the women mostly out of curiosity to see the inside of her house, which no one save an old manservant—a combined gardener and cook—had seen in at least ten years.

It was a big, squarish frame house that had once been white, decorated with cupolas and spires and scrolled balconies in the heavily lightsome style of the seventies, set on what had once been our most select street. But garages and cotton gins had encroached and obliterated even the august names of that neighborhood; only Miss Emily's house was left, lifting its stubborn and coquettish decay above the cotton wagons and the gasoline pumps—an eyesore among eyesores. And now Miss Emily had gone to join the representatives of those august names where they lay in the cedar-bemused cemetery among the ranked and anonymous graves of Union and Confederate soldiers who fell at the battle of Jefferson.

Alive, Miss Emily had been a tradition, a duty, and a care; a sort of hereditary obligation upon the town, dating from that day in 1894 when Colonel Sartoris, the mayor—he who fathered the edict that no Negro woman should appear on the streets without an apron—remitted her taxes, the dispensation dating from the death of her father on into perpetuity. Not that Miss Emily would have accepted charity. Colonel Sartoris invented an involved tale to the effect that Miss Emily's father had loaned money to the town, which the town, as a matter of business, preferred this way of repaying. Only a man of Colonel Sartoris' generation and thought could have invented it, and only a woman could have believed it.

When the next generation, with its more modern ideas, became mayors and aldermen, this arrangement created some little dissatisfaction. On the first of the year they mailed her a tax notice. February came, and there was no reply. They wrote her a formal letter, asking her to call at the sheriff's office at her convenience. A week later the mayor wrote her himself, offering to call or to send his car for her, and received in reply a note on paper of an archaic shape, in a thin, flowing calligraphy in faded ink, to the effect that she no longer went out at all. The tax notice was also enclosed, without comment.

They called a special meeting of the Board of Aldermen. A deputation waited 5 upon her, knocked at the door through which no visitor had passed since she ceased giving china-painting lessons eight or ten years earlier. They were admitted by the old Negro into a dim hall from which a stairway mounted into still more shadow. It smelled of dust and disuse—a close, dank smell. The Negro led them into the parlor. It was furnished in heavy, leather-covered furniture. When the Negro opened the blinds of one window, they could see that the leather was cracked; and when they sat down, a faint dust rose sluggishly about their thighs, spinning with slow motes in the single sun-ray. On a tarnished gilt easel before the fireplace stood a crayon portrait of Miss Emily's father.

They rose when she entered—a small, fat woman in black, with a thin gold chain descending to her waist and vanishing into her belt, leaning on an ebony cane with a tarnished gold head. Her skeleton was small and spare; perhaps that was why what would have been merely plumpness in another was obesity in her. She looked bloated, like a body long submerged in motionless water, and of that pallid hue. Her eyes, lost in the fatty ridges of her face, looked like two small pieces of coal pressed into a lump of dough as they moved from one face to another while the visitors stated their errand.

She did not ask them to sit. She just stood in the door and listened quietly until the spokesman came to a stumbling halt. Then they could hear the invisible watch ticking at the end of the gold chain.

Her voice was dry and cold. "I have no taxes in Jefferson. Colonel Sartoris explained it to me. Perhaps one of you can gain access to the city records and satisfy yourselves."

"But we have. We are the city authorities, Miss Emily. Didn't you get a notice from the sheriff, signed by him?"

"I received a paper, yes," Miss Emily said. "Perhaps he considers himself the sher- 10 iff . . . I have no taxes in Jefferson."

"But there is nothing on the books to show that, you see. We must go by the—"

"See Colonel Sartoris. I have no taxes in Jefferson."

"But, Miss Emily—"

"See Colonel Sartoris." (Colonel Sartoris had been dead almost ten years.) "I have no taxes in Jefferson. Tobe!" The Negro appeared. "Show these gentlemen out."

II

So she vanquished them, horse and foot, just as she had vanquished their fathers 15 thirty years before about the smell. That was two years after her father's death and a short time after her sweetheart—the one we believed would marry her—had deserted her. After her father's death she went out very little; after her sweetheart went away, people hardly saw her at all. A few of the ladies had the temerity to call, but were not received, and the only sign of life about the place was the Negro man—a young man then—going in and out with a market basket.

"Just as if a man—any man—could keep a kitchen properly," the ladies said; so they were not surprised when the smell developed. It was another link between the gross, teeming world and the high and mighty Griersons.

A neighbor, a woman, complained to the mayor, Judge Stevens, eighty years old.

"But what will you have me do about it, madam?" he said.

"Why, send her word to stop it," the woman said. "Isn't there a law?"

"I'm sure that won't be necessary," Judge Stevens said. "It's probably just a snake 20 or a rat that nigger of hers killed in the yard. I'll speak to him about it."

The next day he received two more complaints, one from a man who came in diffident deprecation. "We really must do something about it, Judge. I'd be the last one in the world to bother Miss Emily, but we've got to do something." That night the Board of Aldermen met—three graybeards and one younger man, a member of the rising generation.

"It's simple enough," he said. "Send her word to have her place cleaned up. Give her a certain time to do it in, and if she don't . . ."

"Dammit, sir," Judge Stevens said, "will you accuse a lady to her face of smelling bad?"

So the next night, after midnight, four men crossed Miss Emily's lawn and slunk about the house like burglars, sniffing along the base of the brickwork and at the cellar openings while one of them performed a regular sowing motion with his hand out of a sack slung from his shoulder. They broke open the cellar door and sprinkled lime there, and in all the outbuildings. As they recrossed the lawn, a window that had been dark was lighted and Miss Emily sat in it, the light behind her, and her upright torso motionless as that of an idol. They crept quietly across the lawn and into the shadow of the locusts that lined the street. After a week or two the smell went away.

That was when people had begun to feel really sorry for her. People in our town,   25 remembering how old lady Wyatt, her great-aunt, had gone completely crazy at last, believed that the Griersons held themselves a little too high for what they really were. None of the young men were quite good enough for Miss Emily and such. We had long thought of them as a tableau, Miss Emily a slender figure in white in the background, her father a spraddled silhouette in the foreground, his back to her and clutching a horsewhip, the two of them framed by the back-flung front door. So when she got to be thirty and was still single, we were not pleased exactly, but vindicated; even with insanity in the family she wouldn't have turned down all of her chances if they had really materialized.

When her father died, it got about that the house was all that was left to her; and in a way, people were glad. At last they could pity Miss Emily. Being left alone, and a pauper, she had become humanized. Now she too would know the old thrill and the old despair of a penny more or less.

The day after his death all the ladies prepared to call at the house and offer con-dolence and aid, as is our custom. Miss Emily met them at the door, dressed as usual and with no trace of grief on her face. She told them that her father was not dead. She did that for three days, with the ministers calling on her, and the doctors, trying to persuade her to let them dispose of the body. Just as they were about to resort to law and force, she broke down, and they buried her father quickly.

We did not say she was crazy then. We believed she had to do that. We remem-bered all the young men her father had driven away, and we knew that with nothing left, she would have to cling to that which had robbed her, as people will.

III

She was sick for a long time. When we saw her again, her hair was cut short, making her look like a girl, with a vague resemblance to those angels in colored church windows—sort of tragic and serene.

The town had just let the contracts for paving the sidewalks, and in the summer   30 after her father's death they began the work. The construction company came with niggers and mules and machinery, and a foreman named Homer Barron, a Yankee—a big, dark, ready man, with a big voice and eyes lighter than his face. The little boys would follow in groups to hear him cuss the niggers, and the niggers singing in time to the rise and fall of picks. Pretty soon he knew everybody in town. Whenever you heard a lot of laughing anywhere about the square, Homer Barron would be in the center of the group. Presently we began to see him and Miss Emily on Sunday after-noons driving in the yellow-wheeled buggy and the matched team of bays from the livery stable.

At first we were glad that Miss Emily would have an interest, because the ladies all said, "Of course a Grierson would not think seriously of a Northerner, a day laborer." But there were still others, older people, who said that even grief could not cause a real lady to forget *noblesse oblige°*—without calling it *noblesse oblige*. They just said, "Poor Emily. Her kinsfolk should come to her." She had some kin in Alabama; but years ago her father had fallen out with them over the estate of old lady Wyatt, the crazy woman, and there was no communication between the two families. They had not even been represented at the funeral.

And as soon as the old people said, "Poor Emily," the whispering began. "Do you suppose it's really so?" they said to one another. "Of course it is. What else could . . ." This behind their hands; rustling of craned silk and satin behind jalousies closed upon the sun of Sunday afternoon as the thin, swift clop-clop-clop of the matched team passed: "Poor Emily."

She carried her head high enough—even when we believed that she was fallen. It was as if she demanded more than ever the recognition of her dignity as the last Grierson; as if it had wanted that touch of earthiness to reaffirm her imperviousness. Like when she bought the rat poison, the arsenic. That was over a year after they had begun to say "Poor Emily," and while the two female cousins were visiting her.

"I want some poison," she said to the druggist. She was over thirty then, still a slight woman, though thinner than usual, with cold, haughty black eyes in a face the flesh of which was strained across the temples and about the eye-sockets as you imagine a lighthouse-keeper's face ought to look. "I want some poison," she said.

"Yes, Miss Emily. What kind? For rats and such? I'd recom—"

"I want the best you have. I don't care what kind."

The druggist named several. "They'll kill anything up to an elephant. But what you want is—"

"Arsenic," Miss Emily said. "Is that a good one?"

"Is . . . arsenic? Yes, ma'am. But what you want—"

"I want arsenic."

The druggist looked down at her. She looked back at him, erect, her face like a strained flag. "Why, of course," the druggist said. "If that's what you want. But the law requires you to tell what you are going to use it for."

Miss Emily just stared at him, her head tilted back in order to look him eye for eye, until he looked away and went and got the arsenic and wrapped it up. The Negro delivery boy brought her the package; the druggist didn't come back. When she opened the package at home there was written on the box, under the skull and bones: "For rats."

IV

So the next day we all said, "She will kill herself"; and we said it would be the best thing. When she had first begun to be seen with Homer Barron, we had said, "She will marry him." Then we said, "She will persuade him yet," because Homer himself had remarked—he liked men, and it was known that he drank with the younger men in the Elks' Club—that he was not a marrying man. Later we said, "Poor Emily," behind the jalousies as they passed on Sunday afternoon in the glittering buggy, Miss Emily with her head high and Homer Barron with his hat cocked and a cigar in his teeth, reins and whip in a yellow glove.

Then some of the ladies began to say that it was a disgrace to the town and a bad example to the young people. The men did not want to interfere, but at last the

noblesse oblige: the obligation of a member of the nobility to behave with honor and dignity.

ladies forced the Baptist minister—Miss Emily's people were Episcopal—to call upon her. He would never divulge what happened during that interview, but he refused to go back again. The next Sunday they again drove about the streets, and the following day the minister's wife wrote to Miss Emily's relations in Alabama.

So she had blood-kin under her roof again and we sat back to watch develop- 45 ments. At first nothing happened. Then we were sure that they were to be married. We learned that Miss Emily had been to the jeweler's and ordered a man's toilet set in silver, with the letters H.B. on each piece. Two days later we learned that she had bought a complete outfit of men's clothing, including a nightshirt, and we said, "They are married." We were really glad. We were glad because the two female cousins were even more Grierson than Miss Emily had ever been.

So we were not surprised when Homer Barron—the streets had been finished some time since—was gone. We were a little disappointed that there was not a public blowing-off, but we believed that he had gone on to prepare for Miss Emily's coming, or to give her a chance to get rid of the cousins. (By that time it was a cabal, and we were all Miss Emily's allies to help circumvent the cousins.) Sure enough, after another week they departed. And, as we had expected all along, within three days Homer Barron was back in town. A neighbor saw the Negro man admit him at the kitchen door at dusk one evening.

And that was the last we saw of Homer Barron. And of Miss Emily for some time. The Negro man went in and out with the market basket, but the front door remained closed. Now and then we would see her at a window for a moment, as the men did that night when they sprinkled the lime, but for almost six months she did not appear on the streets. Then we knew that this was to be expected too; as if that quality of her father which had thwarted her woman's life so many times had been too virulent and too furious to die.

When we next saw Miss Emily, she had grown fat and her hair was turning gray. During the next few years it grew grayer and grayer until it attained an even pepper-and-salt iron-gray, when it ceased turning. Up to the day of her death at seventy-four it was still that vigorous iron-gray, like the hair of an active man.

From that time on her front door remained closed, save for a period of six or seven years, when she was about forty, during which she gave lessons in china-painting. She fitted up a studio in one of the downstairs rooms, where the daughters and granddaughters of Colonel Sartoris' contemporaries were sent to her with the same regularity and in the same spirit that they were sent to church on Sundays with a twenty-five-cent piece for the collection plate. Meanwhile her taxes had been remitted.

Then the newer generation became the backbone and the spirit of the town, and 50 the painting pupils grew up and fell away and did not send their children to her with boxes of color and tedious brushes and pictures cut from the ladies' magazines. The front door closed upon the last one and remained closed for good. When the town got free postal delivery, Miss Emily alone refused to let them fasten the metal numbers above her door and attach a mailbox to it. She would not listen to them.

Daily, monthly, yearly we watched the Negro grow grayer and more stooped, going in and out with the market basket. Each December we sent her a tax notice, which would be returned by the post office a week later, unclaimed. Now and then we would see her in one of the downstairs windows—she had evidently shut up the top floor of the house—like the carven torso of an idol in a niche, looking or not looking at us, we could never tell which. Thus she passed from generation to generation—dear, inescapable, impervious, tranquil, and perverse.

And so she died. Fell ill in the house filled with dust and shadows, with only a doddering Negro man to wait on her. We did not even know she was sick; we had long since given up trying to get any information from the Negro. He talked to no one, probably not even to her, for his voice had grown harsh and rusty, as if from disuse.

She died in one of the downstairs rooms, in a heavy walnut bed with a curtain, her gray head propped on a pillow yellow and moldy with age and lack of sunlight.

V

The Negro met the first of the ladies at the front door and let them in, with their hushed, sibilant voices and their quick, curious glances, and then he disappeared. He walked right through the house and out the back and was not seen again.

The two female cousins came at once. They held the funeral on the second day, with the town coming to look at Miss Emily beneath a mass of bought flowers, with the crayon face of her father musing profoundly above the bier and the ladies sibilant and macabre; and the very old men—some in their brushed Confederate uniforms—on the porch and the lawn, talking of Miss Emily as if she had been a contemporary of theirs, believing that they had danced with her and courted her perhaps, confusing time with its mathematical progression, as the old do, to whom all the past is not a diminishing road but, instead, a huge meadow which no winter ever quite touches, divided from them now by the narrow bottleneck of the most recent decade of years.

Already we knew that there was one room in that region above stairs which no one had seen in forty years, and which would have to be forced. They waited until Miss Emily was decently in the ground before they opened it.

The violence of breaking down the door seemed to fill this room with pervading dust. A thin, acrid pall as of the tomb seemed to lie everywhere upon this room decked and furnished as for a bridal: upon the valance curtains of faded rose color, upon the rose-shaded lights, upon the dressing table, upon the delicate array of crystal and the man's toilet things backed with tarnished silver, silver so tarnished that the monogram was obscured. Among them lay collar and tie, as if they had just been removed, which, lifted, left upon the surface a pale crescent in the dust. Upon a chair hung the suit, carefully folded; beneath it the two mute shoes and the discarded socks.

The man himself lay in the bed.

For a long while we just stood there, looking down at the profound and fleshless grin. The body had apparently once lain in the attitude of an embrace, but now the long sleep that outlasts love, that conquers even the grimace of love, had cuckolded him. What was left of him, rotted beneath what was left of the nightshirt, had become inextricable from the bed in which he lay; and upon him and upon the pillow beside him lay that even coating of the patient and biding dust.

Then we noticed that in the second pillow was the indentation of a head. One of us lifted something from it, and leaning forward, that faint and invisible dust dry and acrid in the nostrils, we saw a long strand of iron-gray hair.

Questions

1. What is meaningful in the final detail that the strand of hair on the second pillow is "iron-gray"?

2. Who is the unnamed narrator? For whom does he (or she?) profess to be speaking?

3. Why does "A Rose for Emily" seem better told from his or her point of view than if it were told (like John Updike's "A & P" in Chapter 1) from the point of view of the main character?

4. What foreshadowings of the discovery of the body of Homer Barron are we given earlier in the story? Share your experience in reading "A Rose for Emily": did the foreshadowings give away the ending for you? Did they heighten your interest?

5. What contrasts does the narrator draw between changing reality and Emily's refusal or inability to recognize change?

6. How do the character and background of Emily Grierson differ from those of Homer Barron? What general observations about the society that Faulkner depicts can be made from his portraits of these two characters and from his account of life in this one Mississippi town?

7. Does the story seem to you totally grim, or do you find any humor in it?

8. What do you infer to be the author's attitude toward Emily Grierson? Is she simply a murderous madwoman? Why do you suppose Faulkner calls his story "A Rose for Emily"?

Muriel Spark

The First Year of My Life

(1975) 1997

Muriel Spark

Born of Scottish-Jewish descent and educated in Edinburgh, Muriel (Sarah Camberg) Spark (1918–2006) lived in Rhodesia (now Zimbabwe) from 1937 to 1944. Returning to England in the last days of World War II, she worked in intelligence for the Foreign Office. After the war, she edited the Poetry Review and began writing poetry and criticism. In her early thirties, Spark won a Christmas-themed short fiction competition sponsored by a London weekly paper, the Observer, for her story "The Seraph and the Zambesi," which she wrote, typed, and mailed off in a single afternoon. That ignited her career as a fiction writer; six years later she published her first novel, The Comforters (1957). Since then, Spark has been a prolific and celebrated novelist. Among her better-known works are The Prime of Miss Jean Brodie (1961), which was heavily revised by other hands into a successful stage play and film; The Abbess of Crewe (1974), a satire that sets a Watergate-style scandal in a convent; and A Far Cry from Kensington (1988), a satiric depiction of London literary life.

Spark also published many short stories throughout her career, gathered in All the Stories of Muriel Spark in 2001. In 1954 she converted to Roman Catholicism and began to explore moral issues in her writing. A New York Times review of her first collection of short fiction, The Go-Away Bird and Other Stories (1958), noted: "Spark communicates her special vision of the universe because she is a master of her craft, combining simple language with subtle construction, and because she has a perception of the reality of evil. Damnation and salvation are facts to her, and so is hocus-pocus. This mixture of mischief and mystery makes her work unique." In 2006 Spark died in Florence, Italy, at age 88, where she had lived for her final three and a half decades with the artist and sculptor Penelope Jardine.

I was born on the first day of the second month of the last year of the First World War, a Friday. Testimony abounds that during the first year of my life I never smiled. I was known as the baby whom nothing and no one could make smile. Everyone who knew me then has told me so. They tried very hard, singing and bouncing me up and down, jumping around, pulling faces. Many times I was told this later by my family and their friends; but, anyway, I knew it at the time.

You will shortly be hearing of that new school of psychology, or maybe you have heard of it already, which after long and far-adventuring research and experiment has established that all of the young of the human species are born omniscient. Babies, in their waking hours, know everything that is going on everywhere in the world; they can tune in to any conversation they choose, switch on to any scene. We have all experienced this power. It is only after the first year that it was brainwashed out of us; for it is demanded of us by our immediate environment that we grow to be of use to it in a practical way. Gradually, our know-all brain-cells are blacked out, although traces remain in some individuals in the form of E.S.P., and in the adults of some primitive tribes.

It is not a new theory. Poets and philosophers, as usual, have been there first. But scientific proof is now ready and to hand. Perhaps the final touches are being put to the new manifesto in some cell at Harvard University. Any day now it will be given to the world, and the world will be convinced.

Let me therefore get my word in first, because I feel pretty sure, now, about the authenticity of my remembrance of things past. My autobiography, as I very well perceived at the time, started in the very worst year that the world had ever seen so far. Apart from being born bedridden and toothless, unable to raise myself on the pillow or utter anything but farmyard squawks or police-siren wails, my bladder and my bowels totally out of control, I was further depressed by the curious behavior of the two-legged mammals around me. There were those black-dressed people, females of the species to which I appeared to belong, saying they had lost their sons. I slept a great deal. Let them go and find their sons. It was like the special pin for my nappies° which my mother or some other hoverer dedicated to my care was always losing. These careless women in black lost their husbands and their brothers. Then they came to visit my mother and clucked and crowed over my cradle. I was not amused.

"Babies never really smile till they're three months old," said my mother. "They're not *supposed* to smile till they're three months old."

My brother, aged six, marched up and down with a toy rifle over his shoulder:

> *The grand old Duke of York*
> *He had ten thousand men;*
> *He marched them up to the top of the hill*
> *And he marched them down again.*
> *And when they were up, they were up.*
> *And when they were down, they were down.*
> *And when they were neither down nor up*
> *They were neither up nor down.*°

"Just listen to him!"
"Look at him with his rifle!"

---

nappies: British word for diapers. *The grand old Duke . . . neither up nor down: a* British nursery rhyme whose lyrics are often evoked to describe futile action.

I was about ten days old when Russia stopped fighting. I tuned in to the Czar,° a prisoner, with the rest of his family, since evidently the country had put him off his throne and there had been a revolution not long before I was born. Everyone was talking about it. I tuned in to the Czar. "Nothing would ever induce me to sign the treaty of Brest-Litovsk,"° he said to his wife. Anyway, nobody had asked him to.

At this point I was sleeping twenty hours a day to get my strength up. And from what I discerned in the other four hours of the day I knew I was going to need it. The Western Front on my frequency was sheer blood, mud, dismembered bodies, blistered crashes, hectic flashes of light in the night skies, explosions, total terror. Since it was plain I had been born into a bad moment in the history of the world, the future bothered me, unable as I was to raise my head from the pillow and as yet only twenty inches long. "I truly wish I were a fox or a bird," D. H. Lawrence was writing to somebody. Dreary old creeping Jesus. I fell asleep. · · · · · · · · · · · · · · · · 10

Red sheets of flame shot across the sky. It was 21st March, the fiftieth day of my life, and the German Spring Offensive° had started before my morning feed. Infinite slaughter. I scowled at the scene, and made an effort to kick out. But the attempt was feeble. Furious, and impatient for some strength, I wailed for my feed. After which I stopped wailing but continued to scowl.

> The grand old Duke of York
> He had ten thousand men . . .

They rocked the cradle. I never heard a sillier song. Over in Berlin and Vienna the people were starving, freezing, striking, rioting and yelling in the streets. In London everyone was bustling to work and muttering that it was time the whole damn business was over.

The big people around me bared their teeth; that meant a smile, it meant they were pleased or amused. They spoke of ration cards for meat and sugar and butter.

"Where will it all end?"

I went to sleep. I woke and tuned into Bernard Shaw° who was telling someone to shut up. I switched over to Joseph Conrad° who, strangely enough, was saying precisely the same thing. I still didn't think it worth a smile, although it was expected of me any day now. I got on to Turkey. Women draped in black huddled and chattered in their harems; yak-yak-yak. This was boring, so I came back to home base.

In and out came and went the women in British black. My mother's brother, dressed in his uniform, came coughing. He had been poison-gassed in the trenches. · · · · · · · 15

Czar: Nicholas II, the last Emperor of Russia, who was imprisoned with his family after the February Revolution of 1917 and executed by the Bolsheviks the following year, as Lenin's new Communist government rose to power.   *treaty of Brest-Litovsk:* an agreement forced on Russia's new government, under military threat from Germany and Austria, that Russia would withdraw from the war and cede territory to Germany and the Ottoman Emprie.   *German Spring Offensive:* After signing the treaty with Russia, Germany shifted a half-million troops from the Russian Front to the Western Theater in spring 1918, launching a large-scale attack in an attempt to win the war before U.S. reinforcements could arrive.   *Bernard Shaw:* Irish playwright and polemicist George Bernard Shaw (1856–1950), who was criticized for denouncing both sides in World War I.   *Joseph Conrad:* Polish-British novelist (1857–1924) whose enduring works include *Heart of Darkness* (1899).

"Tout le monde à la bataille!"° declaimed Marshal Foch° the old swine. He was now Commander-in-Chief of the Allied Forces. My uncle coughed from deep within his lungs, never to recover but destined to return to the Front. His brass buttons gleamed in the firelight. I weighed twelve pounds by now; I stretched and kicked for exercise, seeing that I had a lifetime before me, coping with this crowd. I took six feeds a day and kept most of them down by the time the *Vindictive* was sunk in Ostend harbor,° on which day I kicked with special vigor in my bath.

In France the conscripted soldiers leapfrogged over the dead on the advance and littered the fields with limbs and hands, or drowned in the mud. The strongest men on all fronts were dead before I was born. Now the sentries used bodies for barricades and the fighting men were unhealthy from the start. I checked my toes and fingers, knowing I was going to need them. *The Playboy of the Western World* ° was playing at the Court Theatre in London, but occasionally I beamed over to the House of Commons° which made me drop off gently to sleep. Generally, I preferred the Western Front° where one got the true state of affairs. It was essential to know the worst, blood and explosions and all, for one had to be prepared, as the boy scouts said. Virginia Woolf yawned and reached for her diary. Really, I preferred the Western Front.

In the fifth month of my life I could raise my head from my pillow and hold it up. I could grasp the objects that were held out to me. Some of these things rattled and squawked. I gnawed on them to get my teeth started. "She hasn't smiled yet?" said the dreary old aunties. My mother, on the defensive, said I was probably one of those late smilers. On my wavelength Pablo Picasso was getting married and early in that month of July the Silver Wedding of King George V and Queen Mary was celebrated in joyous pomp at St. Paul's Cathedral. They drove through the streets of London with their children. Twenty-five years of domestic happiness. A lot of fuss and ceremonial handing over of swords went on at the Guildhall° where the King and Queen received a check for £53,000 to dispose of for charity as they thought fit. *Tout le monde à la bataille!* Income tax in England had reached six shillings in the pound. Everyone was talking about the Silver Wedding; yak-yak-yak, and ten days later the Czar and his family, now in Siberia, were invited to descend to a little room in the basement. Crack, crack, went the guns; screams and blood all over the place, and that was the end of the Romanoffs.° I flexed my muscles. "A fine healthy baby," said the doctor; which gave me much satisfaction.

Tout le monde à la bataille!: French for "The whole world to the battle!" *Marshal Foch:* the French general who successfully commanded the Allied forces on the Western Front against the German Spring Offensive. *the* Vindictive *was sunk in Ostend harbor:* a ship strategically sunk in May 1918 to block a Belgian harbor used by the Germans as a submarine base. *The Playboy of the Western World:* a play by Irish playwright John Millington Synge. *House of Commons:* the elected lower house of British Parliament. *Western Front:* zone of battle along Belgium and France where the Germans and Allies clashed. *Guildhall:* a college of music and drama in London. *Romanoffs:* dynasty that ruled Russia from 1613 until the abdication of Nicholas II in 1917. In July 1918, the Romanoff family was executed in the basement, children and all.

Tout le monde à la bataille! That included my gassed uncle. My health had improved to the point where I was able to crawl in my playpen. Bertrand Russell° was still cheerily in prison for writing something seditious about pacifism. Tuning in as usual to the Front Lines it looked as if the Germans were winning all the battles yet losing the war. And so it was. The upper-income people were upset about the income tax at six shillings to the pound. But all women over thirty got the vote. "It seems a long time to wait," said one of my drab old aunts, aged twenty-two. The speeches in the House of Commons always sent me to sleep which was why I missed, at the actual time, a certain oration by Mr. Asquith° following the armistice on 11th November.° Mr. Asquith was a greatly esteemed former prime minister later to be an Earl, and had been ousted by Mr. Lloyd George.° I clearly heard Asquith, in private, refer to Lloyd George as "that damned Welsh goat."

The armistice was signed and I was awake for that. I pulled myself on to my feet with the aid of the bars of my cot. My teeth were coming through very nicely in my opinion, and well worth all the trouble I was put to in bringing them forth. I weighed twenty pounds. On all the world's fighting fronts the men killed in action or dead of wounds numbered 8,538,315 and the warriors wounded and maimed were 21,219,452. With these figures in mind I sat up in my high chair and banged my spoon on the table. One of my mother's black-draped friends recited:

> *I have a rendezvous with Death*
> *At some disputed barricade,*
> *When spring comes back with rustling shade*
> *And apple blossoms fill the air—*
> *I have a rendezvous with Death.*°

Most of the poets, they said, had been killed. The poetry made them dab their eyes with clean white handkerchiefs.   20

Next February on my first birthday, there was a birthday-cake with one candle. Lots of children and their elders. The war had been over two months and twenty-one days. "Why doesn't she smile?" My brother was to blow out the candle. The elders were talking about the war and the political situation. Lloyd George and Asquith, Asquith and Lloyd George. I remembered recently having switched on to Mr. Asquith at a private party where he had been drinking a lot. He was playing cards and when he came to cut the cards he tried to cut a large box of matches by mistake. On another occasion I had seen him putting his arm around a lady's shoulder in a Daimler motor car, and generally behaving towards her in a very friendly fashion. Strangely enough she said, "If you don't stop this nonsense immediately I'll order the chauffeur to stop and I'll get out." Mr. Asquith replied, "And pray, what reason will you give?" Well anyway it was my feeding time.

Bertrand Russell: (1872–1970) British philosopher, mathematician, writer, political activist, and Nobel Laureate.   *Mr. Asquith:* H. H. Asquith (1852–1928), British prime minister from 1908 to 1916.   *armistice on 11th November:* the 1918 agreement between the Allies and Germany that ended the war.   *Mr. Lloyd George:* David Lloyd George (1863–1945), Asquith's war secretary who became prime minister when Asquith resigned, serving from 1916 to 1922.   *I have a rendezvous with Death:* from "I Have a Rendezvous with Death" by American poet Alan Seeger, killed in battle in 1916 at age twenty-eight.

The guests arrived for my birthday. It was so sad, said one of the black widows, so sad about Wilfred Owen who was killed so late in the war, and she quoted from a poem of his:

> What passing-bells for these who die as cattle?
> Only the monstrous anger of the guns.°

The children were squealing and toddling around. One was sick and another wet the floor and stood with his legs apart gaping at the puddle. All was mopped up. I banged my spoon on the table of my high chair.

> But I've a rendezvous with Death
> At midnight in some flaming town;
> When spring trips north again this year,
> And I to my pledged word am true,
> I shall not fail that rendezvous.

More parents and children arrived. One stout man who was warming his behind at the fire, said, "I always think those words of Asquith's after the armistice were so apt..."

They brought the cake close to my high chair for me to see, with the candle shining and flickering above the pink icing. "A pity she never smiles." 25

"She'll smile in time," my mother said, obviously upset.

"What Asquith told the House of Commons just after the war," said that stout gentleman with his backside to the fire, "—so apt, what Asquith said. He said that the war has cleansed and purged the world, by God! I recall his actual words: 'All things have become new. In this great cleansing and purging it has been the privilege of our country to play her part...'"

That did it. I broke into a decided smile and everyone noticed it, convinced that it was provoked by the fact that my brother had blown out the candle on the cake. "She smiled!" my mother exclaimed. And everyone was clucking away about how I was smiling. For good measure I crowed like a demented raven. "My baby's smiling," said my mother.

"It was the candle on her cake," they said.

The cake be damned. Since that time I have grown to smile quite naturally, like any other healthy and house-trained person, but when I really mean a smile, deeply felt from the core, then to all intents and purposes it comes in response to the words uttered in the House of Commons after the First World War by the distinguished, the immaculately dressed and the late Mr. Asquith. 30

Questions

1. Who is the narrator, and what is her special power?
2. Why are the women dressed in black, and what does the narrator seem to think of them and of the relatives who come and go?
3. What is the effect of having an infant narrate a story about war? How would you describe the baby's tone? Comic? Tragic? Passive? Sarcastic? Does she seem to care much about the news and conversations that she reports? Back up your answer with examples. How would the story be different if an adult narrated it?
4. Spark's infant narrator was born on the same day as the author herself—February 1, 1918. Why might she have chosen to have the birthday of her fictional character match her own?
5. Revisit the lyrics for "The Grand Old Duke of York," and reread the footnote. What does Spark intend by including such a nursery rhyme?
6. Why do you think the baby doesn't smile for so long, and what makes her finally smile?

What passing-bells . . . anger of the guns: from "Anthem for Doomed Youth" (see Chapter 24 for the complete poem) by British poet Wilfred Owen (1893–1918), who was killed in action one week before the armistice.

Eudora Welty

A Worn Path   1941

*Eudora Welty (1909–2001) was born in Jackson,
Mississippi, the daughter of an insurance company president. Like William Faulkner, another
Mississippi writer, she stayed close to her roots for
practically all her life, except for short sojourns at the
University of Wisconsin, where she took her B.A.,
and in New York City, where she studied advertising. She lived most of her life in her childhood home
in Jackson, within a stone's throw of the state capi-
tol. Although Welty was a novelist distinguished for
The Robber Bridegroom (1942), Delta Wedding (1946), The Ponder Heart (1954), Losing
Battles (1970), and The Optimist's Daughter
(1972), many critics think her finest work was in
the short-story form. The Collected Stories of
Eudora Welty (1980) gathers the work of more
than forty years. Welty's other books include a*

Eudora Welty

*memoir, One Writer's Beginnings (1984), and The Eye of the Story (1977), a book of
sympathetic criticism on the fiction of other writers, including Willa Cather, Virginia Woolf,
Katherine Anne Porter, and Isak Dinesen. One Time, One Place, a book of photographs
of everyday life that Welty took in Mississippi during the Depression, was republished in a
revised edition in 1996.*

It was December—a bright frozen day in the early morning. Far out in the country there was an old Negro woman with her head tied in a red rag, coming along a
path through the pinewoods. Her name was Phoenix Jackson. She was very old and
small and she walked slowly in the dark pine shadows, moving a little from side to
side in her steps, with the balanced heaviness and lightness of a pendulum in a grandfather clock. She carried a thin, small cane made from an umbrella, and with this she
kept tapping the frozen earth in front of her. This made a grave and persistent noise
in the still air, that seemed meditative like the chirping of a solitary little bird.

She wore a dark striped dress reaching down to her shoe tops, and an equally
longapron of bleached sugar sacks, with a full pocket: all neat and tidy, but every time
she took a step she might have fallen over her shoelaces, which dragged from her
unlaced shoes. She looked straight ahead. Her eyes were blue with age. Her skin had
a pattern all its own of numberless branching wrinkles and as though a whole little
tree stood in the middle of her forehead, but a golden color ran underneath, and the
two knobs of her cheeks were illumined by a yellow burning under the dark. Under
the red rag her hair came down on her neck in the frailest of ringlets, still black, and
with an odor like copper.

Now and then there was a quivering in the thicket. Old Phoenix said, "Out of
my way, all you foxes, owls, beetles, jack rabbits, coons and wild animals! . . . Keep
out from under these feet, little bob-whites. . . . Keep the big wild hogs out of my
path. Don't let none of those come running my direction. I got a long way." Under
her small black-freckled hand her cane, limber as a buggy whip, would switch at the
brush as if to rouse up any hiding things.

On she went. The woods were deep and still. The sun made the pine needles almost too bright to look at, up where the wind rocked. The cones dropped as light as feathers. Down in the hollow was the mourning dove—it was not too late for him.

The path ran up a hill. "Seem like there is chains about my feet, time I get this far," she said, in the voice of argument old people keep to use with themselves. "Something always take a hold of me on this hill—pleads I should stay." 5

After she got to the top she turned and gave a full, severe look behind her where she had come. "Up through pines," she said at length. "Now down through oaks."

Her eyes opened their widest, and she started down gently. But before she got to the bottom of the hill a bush caught her dress.

Her fingers were busy and intent, but her skirts were full and long, so that before she could pull them free in one place they were caught in another. It was not possible to allow the dress to tear. "I in the thorny bush," she said. "Thorns, you doing your appointed work. Never want to let folks pass, no sir. Old eyes thought you was a pretty little *green* bush."

Finally, trembling all over, she stood free, and after a moment dared to stoop for her cane.

"Sun so high!" she cried, leaning back and looking, while the thick tears went over her eyes. "The time getting all gone here." 10

At the foot of this hill was a place where a log was laid across the creek.

"Now comes the trial," said Phoenix.

Putting her right foot out, she mounted the log and shut her eyes. Lifting her skirt, leveling her cane fiercely before her, like a festival figure in some parade, she began to march across. Then she opened her eyes and she was safe on the other side.

"I wasn't as old as I thought," she said.

But she sat down to rest. She spread her skirts on the bank around her and folded her hands over her knees. Up above her was a tree in a pearly cloud of mistletoe. She did not dare to close her eyes, and when a little boy brought her a plate with a slice of marble-cake on it she spoke to him. "That would be acceptable," she said. But when she went to take it there was just her own hand in the air. 15

So she left that tree, and had to go through a barbed-wire fence. There she had to creep and crawl, spreading her knees and stretching her fingers like a baby trying to climb the steps. But she talked loudly to herself: she could not let her dress be torn now, so late in the day, and she could not pay for having her arm or her leg sawed off if she got caught fast where she was.

At last she was safe through the fence and risen up out in the clearing. Big dead trees, like black men with one arm, were standing in the purple stalks of the withered cotton field. There sat a buzzard.

"Who you watching?"

In the furrow she made her way along.

"Glad this not the season for bulls," she said, looking sideways, "and the good Lord made his snakes to curl up and sleep in the winter. A pleasure I don't see no two-headed snake coming around that tree, where it come once. It took a while to get by him, back in the summer." 20

She passed through the old cotton and went into a field of dead corn. It whispered and shook and was taller than her head. "Through the maze now," she said, for there was no path.

Then there was something tall, black, and skinny there, moving before her.

At first she took it for a man. It could have been a man dancing in the field. But she stood still and listened, and it did not make a sound. It was as silent as a ghost.

"Ghost," she said sharply, "who be you the ghost of? For I have heard of nary death close by."

But there was no answer—only the ragged dancing in the wind.   25

She shut her eyes, reached out her hand, and touched a sleeve. She found a coat and inside that an emptiness, cold as ice.

"You scarecrow," she said. Her face lighted. "I ought to be shut up for good," she said with laughter. "My senses is gone. I too old. I the oldest people I ever know. Dance, old scarecrow," she said, "while I dancing with you."

She kicked her foot over the furrow, and with mouth drawn down, shook her head once or twice in a little strutting way. Some husks blew down and whirled in streamers about her skirts.

Then she went on, parting her way from side to side with the cane, through the whispering field. At last she came to the end, to a wagon track where the silver grass blew between the red ruts. The quail were walking around like pullets, seeming all dainty and unseen.

"Walk pretty," she said. "This the easy place. This the easy going."   30

She followed the track, swaying through the quiet bare fields, through the little strings of trees silver in their dead leaves, past cabins silver from weather, with the doors and windows boarded shut, all like old women under a spell sitting there. "I walking in their sleep," she said, nodding her head vigorously.

In a ravine she went where a spring was silently flowing through a hollow log. Old Phoenix bent and drank. "Sweet-gum makes the water sweet," she said, and drank more. "Nobody know who made this well, for it was here when I was born."

The track crossed a swampy part where the moss hung as white as lace from every limb. "Sleep on, alligators, and blow your bubbles." Then the track went into the road.

Deep, deep the road went down between the high green-colored banks. Over-head the live-oaks met, and it was as dark as a cave.

A black dog with a lolling tongue came up out of the weeds by the ditch. She   35
was meditating, and not ready, and when he came at her she only hit him a little with her cane. Over she went in the ditch, like a little puff of milkweed.

Down there, her senses drifted away. A dream visited her, and she reached her hand up, but nothing reached down and gave her a pull. So she lay there and pres-ently went to talking. "Old woman," she said to herself, "that black dog come up out of the weeds to stall you off, and now there he sitting on his fine tail, smiling at you."

A white man finally came along and found her—a hunter, a young man, with his dog on a chain.

"Well, Granny!" he laughed. "What are you doing there?"

"Lying on my back like a June-bug waiting to be turned over, mister," she said, reaching up her hand.

He lifted her up, gave her a swing in the air, and set her down. "Anything bro-   40
ken, Granny?"

"No sir, them old dead weeds is springy enough," said Phoenix, when she had got her breath. "I thank you for your trouble."

"Where do you live, Granny?" he asked, while the two dogs were growling at each other.

"Away back yonder, sir, behind the ridge. You can't even see it from here."

"On your way home?"

"No sir, I going to town."

"Why, that's too far! That's as far as I walk when I come out myself, and I get something for my trouble." He patted the stuffed bag he carried, and there hung down a little closed claw. It was one of the bob-whites, with its beak hooked bitterly to show it was dead. "Now you go on home, Granny!"

"I bound to go to town, mister," said Phoenix. "The time come around."

He gave another laugh, filling the whole landscape. "I know you old colored people! Wouldn't miss going to town to see Santa Claus!"

But something held old Phoenix very still. The deep lines in her face went into a fierce and different radiation. Without warning, she had seen with her own eyes a flashing nickel fall out of the man's pocket onto the ground.

"How old are you, Granny?" he was saying.

"There is no telling, mister," she said, "no telling."

Then she gave a little cry and clapped her hands and said, "Git on away from here, dog! Look! Look at that dog!" She laughed as if in admiration. "He ain't scared of nobody. He a big black dog." She whispered, "Sic him!"

"Watch me get rid of that cur," said the man. "Sic him, Pete! Sic him!"

Phoenix heard the dogs fighting, and heard the man running and throwing sticks. She even heard a gunshot. But she was slowly bending forward by that time, further and further forward, the lids stretched down over her eyes, as if she were doing this in her sleep. Her chin was lowered almost to her knees. The yellow palm of her hand came out from the fold of her apron. Her fingers slid down and along the ground under the piece of money with the grace and care they would have in lifting an egg from under a setting hen. Then she slowly straightened up, she stood erect, and the nickel was in her apron pocket. A bird flew by. Her lips moved. "God watching me the whole time. I come to stealing."

The man came back, and his own dog panted about them. "Well, I scared him off that time," he said, and then he laughed and lifted his gun and pointed it at Phoenix.

She stood straight and faced him.

"Doesn't the gun scare you?" he said, still pointing it.

"No, sir, I seen plenty go off closer by, in my day, and for less than what I done," she said, holding utterly still.

He smiled, and shouldered the gun. "Well, Granny," he said, "you must be a hundred years old, and scared of nothing. I'd give you a dime if I had any money with me. But you take my advice and stay home, and nothing will happen to you."

"I bound to go on my way, mister," said Phoenix. She inclined her head in the red rag. Then they went in different directions, but she could hear the gun shooting again and again over the hill.

She walked on. The shadows hung from the oak trees to the road like curtains. Then she smelled wood-smoke, and smelled the river, and she saw a steeple and the cabins on their steep steps. Dozens of little black children whirled around her. There ahead was Natchez shining. Bells were ringing. She walked on.

In the paved city it was Christmas time. There were red and green electric lights strung and crisscrossed everywhere, and all turned on in the daytime. Old Phoenix would have been lost if she had not distrusted her eyesight and depended on her feet to know where to take her.

She paused quietly on the sidewalk where people were passing by. A lady came along in the crowd, carrying an armful of red-, green- and silver-wrapped presents; she gave off perfume like the red roses in hot summer, and Phoenix stopped her.

"Please, missy, will you lace up my shoe?" She held up her foot.

"What do you want, Grandma?"   65

"See my shoe," said Phoenix. "Do all right for out in the country, but wouldn't look right to go in a big building."

"Stand still then, Grandma," said the lady. She put her packages down on the sidewalk beside her and laced and tied both shoes tightly.

"Can't lace 'em with a cane," said Phoenix, "Thank you, missy. I doesn't mind asking a nice lady to tie up my shoe, when I gets out on the street."

Moving slowly and from side to side, she went into the big building, and into a tower of steps, where she walked up and around and around until her feet knew to stop.

She entered a door, and there she saw nailed up on the wall the document that   70
had been stamped with the gold seal and framed in the gold frame, which matched the dream that was hung up in her head.

"Here I be," she said. There was a fixed and ceremonial stiffness over her body.

"A charity case, I suppose," said an attendant who sat at the desk before her.

But Phoenix only looked above her head. There was sweat on her face, the wrinkles in her skin shone like a bright net.

"Speak up, Grandma," the woman said. "What's your name? We must have your history, you know. Have you been here before? What seems to be the trouble with you?"

Old Phoenix only gave a twitch to her face as if a fly were bothering her.   75

"Are you deaf?" cried the attendant.

But then the nurse came in.

"Oh, that's just old Aunt Phoenix," she said. "She doesn't come for herself—she has a little grandson. She makes these trips just as regular as clockwork. She lives away back off the Old Natchez Trace." She bent down. "Well, Aunt Phoenix, why don't you just take a seat? We won't keep you standing after your long trip." She pointed.

The old woman sat down, bolt upright in the chair.

"Now, how is the boy?" asked the nurse.   80

Old Phoenix did not speak.

"I said, how is the boy?"

But Phoenix only waited and stared straight ahead, her face very solemn and withdrawn into rigidity.

"Is his throat any better?" asked the nurse. "Aunt Phoenix, don't you hear me? Is your grandson's throat any better since the last time you came for the medicine?"

With her hands on her knees, the old woman waited, silent, erect and motion   85
less, just as if she were in armor.

"You mustn't take up our time this way, Aunt Phoenix," the nurse said. "Tell us quickly about your grandson, and get it over. He isn't dead, is he?"

At last there came a flicker and then a flame of comprehension across her face, and she spoke.

"My grandson. It was my memory had left me. There I sat and forgot why I made my long trip."

"Forgot?" The nurse frowned. "After you came so far?"

Then Phoenix was like an old woman begging a dignified forgiveness for waking   90
up frightened in the night. "I never did go to school, I was too old at the Surrender,"

she said in a soft voice. "I'm an old woman without an education. It was my memory fail me. My little grandson, he is just the same, and I forgot it in the coming."

"Throat never heals, does it?" said the nurse, speaking in a loud, sure voice to old Phoenix. By now she had a card with something written on it, a little list. "Yes. Swallowed lye. When was it?—January—two-three years ago—"

Phoenix spoke unasked now. "No, missy, he not dead, he just the same. Every little while his throat begin to close up again, and he not able to swallow. He not get his breath. He not able to help himself. So the time come around, and I go on another trip for the soothing medicine."

"All right. The doctor said as long as you came to get it, you could have it," said the nurse. "But it's an obstinate case."

"My little grandson, he sit up there in the house all wrapped up, waiting by himself," Phoenix went on. "We is the only two left in the world. He suffer and it don't seem to put him back at all. He got a sweet look. He going to last. He wear a little patch quilt and peep out holding his mouth open like a little bird. I remembers so plain now. I not going to forget him again, no, the whole enduring time. I could tell him from all the others in creation."

"All right." The nurse was trying to hush her now. She brought her a bottle of 95 medicine. "Charity," she said, making a check mark in a book.

Old Phoenix held the bottle close to her eyes, and then carefully put it into her pocket.

"I thank you," she said.

"It's Christmas time, Grandma," said the attendant. "Could I give you a few pennies out of my purse?"

"Five pennies is a nickel," said Phoenix stiffly.

"Here's a nickel," said the attendant. 100

Phoenix rose carefully and held out her hand. She received the nickel and then fished the other nickel out of her pocket and laid it beside the new one. She stared at her palm closely, with her head on one side.

Then she gave a tap with her cane on the floor.

"This is what come to me to do," she said. "I going to the store and buy my child a little windmill they sells, made out of paper. He going to find it hard to believe there such a thing in the world. I'll march myself back where he waiting, holding it straight up in this hand."

She lifted her free hand, gave a little nod, turned around, and walked out of the doctor's office. Then her slow step began on the stairs, going down.

Questions

1. What point of view is used in this story? Explain your answer.
2. What is the significance of the old woman being named Phoenix?
3. Welty presents Phoenix's dreams and hallucinations as if they were as real as everything else she encounters. What does this technique contribute to the story's effect?
4. How would you characterize the way Phoenix is viewed and treated by the white people she meets? Does their behavior toward her give you any indication of where the story is set and when it takes place?
5. In paragraph 52, Phoenix laughs at the black dog "as if in admiration." What does she admire about him, and what does this attitude tell us about her?
6. "With her hands on her knees, the old woman waited, silent, erect and motionless, just as if she were in armor" (paragraph 85). Is the comparison at the end of this sentence just a striking visual image, or does it have a larger relevance?

James Baldwin

Sonny's Blues 1957

James Baldwin (1924–1987) was born in Harlem, New York. His father was a Pentecostal minister, and the young Baldwin initially planned to become a clergyman. While still in high school, he preached sermons in a storefront church. At seventeen, however, he left home to live a few miles away in Greenwich Village, where he worked at menial jobs and began publishing articles in Commentary *and the* Nation. *Later he embarked on a series of travels that eventually brought him to France. Baldwin soon regarded France as a second home, a country in which he could avoid the racial discrimination he felt in America. His first novel,* Go Tell It on the Mountain *(1953), which described a single day in the lives of the members of a Harlem church, immediately earned him a position as a leading African American writer. His next two novels,* Giovanni's Room *(1956) and* Another Country *(1962), dealt with homosexual themes and drew criticism from some of his early champions. His collection of essays* Notes of a Native Son *(1955) remains one of the key books of the civil rights movement. His short stories were not collected until* Going to Meet the Man *was published in 1965. Although he spent nearly forty years in France, Baldwin still considered himself an American. He was not an expatriate, he claimed, but a "commuter." He died in St. Paul de Vence, France, and was buried in Ardsley, New York.*

I read about it in the paper, in the subway, on my way to work. I read it, and I couldn't believe it, and I read it again. Then perhaps I just stared at it, at the newsprint spelling out his name, spelling out the story. I stared at it in the swinging lights of the subway car, and in the faces and bodies of the people, and in my own face, trapped in the darkness which roared outside.

It was not to be believed and I kept telling myself that, as I walked from the subway station to the high school. And at the same time I couldn't doubt it. I was scared, scared for Sonny. He became real to me again. A great block of ice got settled in my belly and kept melting there slowly all day long, while I taught my classes algebra. It was a special kind of ice. It kept melting, sending trickles of ice water all up and down my veins, but it never got less. Sometimes it hardened and seemed to expand until I felt my guts were going to come spilling out or that I was going to choke or scream. This would always be at a moment when I was remembering some specific thing Sonny had once said or done.

When he was about as old as the boys in my classes his face had been bright and open, there was a lot of copper in it; and he'd had wonderfully direct brown eyes, and great gentleness and privacy. I wondered what he looked like now. He had been picked up, the evening before, in a raid on an apartment downtown, for peddling and using heroin.

I couldn't believe it: but what I mean by that is that I couldn't find any room for it anywhere inside me. I had kept it outside me for a long time. I hadn't wanted to know. I had had suspicions, but I didn't name them, I kept putting them away. I told myself that Sonny was wild, but he wasn't crazy. And he'd always been a good boy, he hadn't ever turned hard or evil or disrespectful, the way kids can, so quick, so quick, especially in Harlem. I didn't want to believe that I'd ever see my brother going down, coming to nothing, all that light in his face gone out, in the condition I'd already seen so many others. Yet it had happened and here I was, talking about algebra to a lot of boys who might, every one of them for all I knew, be popping off needles every time they went to the head. Maybe it did more for them than algebra could.

I was sure that the first time Sonny had ever had horse,° he couldn't have been   5
much older than these boys were now. These boys, now, were living as we'd been living then, they were growing up with a rush and their heads bumped abruptly against
the low ceiling of their actual possibilities. They were filled with rage. All they really
knew were two darknesses, the darkness of their lives, which was now closing in on
them, and the darkness of the movies, which had blinded them to that other darkness, and in which they now, vindictively, dreamed, at once more together than they
were at any other time, and more alone.

When the last bell rang, the last class ended, I let out my breath. It seemed I'd
been holding it for all that time. My clothes were wet—I may have looked as though
I'd been sitting in a steam bath, all dressed up, all afternoon. I sat alone in the classroom a long time. I listened to the boys outside, downstairs, shouting and cursing and
laughing. Their laughter struck me for perhaps the first time. It was not the joyous
laughter which—God knows why—one associates with children. It was mocking and
insular, its intent to denigrate. It was disenchanted, and in this, also, lay the authority of their curses. Perhaps I was listening to them because I was thinking about my
brother and in them I heard my brother. And myself.

One boy was whistling a tune, at once very complicated and very simple, it seemed
to be pouring out of him as though he were a bird, and it sounded very cool and moving
through all that harsh, bright air, only just holding its own through all those other sounds.

I stood up and walked over to the window and looked down into the courtyard.
It was the beginning of the spring and the sap was rising in the boys. A teacher passed
through them every now and again, quickly, as though he or she couldn't wait to get
out of that courtyard, to get those boys out of their sight and off their minds. I started
collecting my stuff. I thought I'd better get home and talk to Isabel.

The courtyard was almost deserted by the time I got downstairs. I saw this boy
standing in the shadow of a doorway, looking just like Sonny. I almost called his
name. Then I saw that it wasn't Sonny, but somebody we used to know, a boy from
around our block. He'd been Sonny's friend. He'd never been mine, having been
too young for me, and, anyway, I'd never liked him. And now, even though he was
a grown-up man, he still hung around that block, still spent hours on the street corners, was always high and raggy. I used to run into him from time to time and he'd
often work around to asking me for a quarter or fifty cents. He always had some real
good excuse, too, and I always gave it to him, I don't know why.

But now, abruptly, I hated him. I couldn't stand the way he looked at me, partly   10
like a dog, partly like a cunning child. I wanted to ask him what the hell he was
doing in the school courtyard.

He sort of shuffled over to me, and he said, "I see you got the papers. So you
already know about it."

"You mean about Sonny? Yes, I already know about it. How come they didn't get
you?"

He grinned. It made him repulsive and it also brought to mind what he'd looked
like as a kid. "I wasn't there. I stay away from them people."

"Good for you." I offered him a cigarette and I watched him through the smoke.
"You come all the way down here just to tell me about Sonny?"

"That's right." He was sort of shaking his head and his eyes looked strange, as   15
though they were about to cross. The bright sun deadened his damp dark brown

horse: heroin.

skin and it made his eyes look yellow and showed up the dirt in his kinked hair. He smelled funky. I moved a little away from him and I said, "Well, thanks. But I already know about it and I got to get home."

"I'll walk you a little ways," he said. We started walking. There were a couple of kids still loitering in the courtyard and one of them said goodnight to me and looked strangely at the boy beside me.

"What're you going to do?" he asked me. "I mean, about Sonny?"

"Look. I haven't seen Sonny for over a year. I'm not sure I'm going to do anything. Anyway, what the hell *can* I do?"

"That's right," he said quickly, "ain't nothing you can do. Can't much help old Sonny no more, I guess."

It was what I was thinking and so it seemed to me he had no right to say it.   20

"I'm surprised at Sonny, though," he went on—he had a funny way of talking, he looked straight ahead as though he were talking to himself—"I thought Sonny was a smart boy, I thought he was too smart to get hung."

"I guess he thought so too," I said sharply, "and that's how he got hung. And how about you? You're pretty goddamn smart, I bet."

Then he looked directly at me, just for a minute. "I ain't smart," he said. "If I was smart, I'd have reached for a pistol a long time ago."

"Look. Don't tell *me* your sad story, if it was up to me, I'd give you one." Then I felt guilty—guilty, probably, for never having supposed that the poor bastard *had* a story of his own, much less a sad one, and I asked, quickly, "What's going to happen to him now?"

He didn't answer this. He was off by himself some place. "Funny thing," he said,   25
and from his tone we might have been discussing the quickest way to get to Brooklyn, "when I saw the papers this morning, the first thing I asked myself was if I had anything to do with it. I felt sort of responsible."

I began to listen more carefully. The subway station was on the corner, just before us, and I stopped. He stopped, too. We were in front of a bar and he ducked slightly, peering in, but whoever he was looking for didn't seem to be there. The juke box was blasting away with something black and bouncy and I half watched the barmaid as she danced her way from the juke box to her place behind the bar. And I watched her face as she laughingly responded to something someone said to her, still keeping time to the music. When she smiled one saw the little girl, one sensed the doomed, still-struggling woman beneath the battered face of the semiwhore.

"I never *give* Sonny nothing," the boy said finally, "but a long time ago I come to school high and Sonny asked me how it felt." He paused, I couldn't bear to watch him, I watched the barmaid, and I listened to the music which seemed to be causing the pavement to shake. "I told him it felt great." The music stopped, the barmaid paused and watched the juke box until the music began again. "It did."

All this was carrying me some place I didn't want to go. I certainly didn't want to know how it felt. It filled everything, the people, the houses, the music, the dark, quicksilver barmaid, with menace; and this menace was their reality.

"What's going to happen to him now?" I asked again.

"They'll send him away some place and they'll try to cure him." He shook his   30
head. "Maybe he'll even think he's kicked the habit. Then they'll let him loose"—he gestured, throwing his cigarette into the gutter. "That's all."

"What do you mean, that's *all*?"

But I knew what he meant.

"I *mean*, that's *all*." He turned his head and looked at me, pulling down the corners of his mouth. "Don't you know what I mean?" he asked, softly.

"How the hell *would* I know what you mean?" I almost whispered it, I don't know why.

"That's right," he said to the air, "how would *he* know what I mean?" He turned toward me again, patient and calm, and yet I somehow felt him shaking, shaking as though he were going to fall apart. I felt that ice in my guts again, the dread I'd felt all afternoon; and again I watched the barmaid, moving about the bar, washing glasses, and singing. "Listen. They'll let him out and then it'll just start all over again. That's what I mean." 35

"You mean—they'll let him out. And then he'll just start working his way back in again. You mean he'll never kick the habit. Is that what you mean?"

"That's right," he said, cheerfully. "*You* see what I mean."

"Tell me," I said at last, "why does he want to die? He must want to die, he's killing himself, why does he want to die?"

He looked at me in surprise. He licked his lips. "He don't want to die. He wants to live. Don't nobody want to die, ever."

Then I wanted to ask him—too many things. He could not have answered, or if he had, I could not have borne the answers. I started walking. "Well, I guess it's none of my business." 40

"It's going to be rough on old Sonny," he said. We reached the subway station. "This is your station?" he asked. I nodded. I took one step down. "Damn!" he said, suddenly. I looked up at him. He grinned again. "Damn it if I didn't leave all my money home. You ain't got a dollar on you, have you? Just for a couple of days, is all."

All at once something inside gave and threatened to come pouring out of me. I didn't hate him any more. I felt that in another moment I'd start crying like a child.

"Sure," I said. "Don't sweat." I looked in my wallet and didn't have a dollar, I only had a five. "Here," I said. "That hold you?"

He didn't look at it—he didn't want to look at it. A terrible closed look came over his face, as though he were keeping the number on the bill a secret from him and me. "Thanks," he said, and now he was dying to see me go. "Don't worry about Sonny. Maybe I'll write him or something."

"Sure," I said. "You do that. So long."

"Be seeing you," he said. I went on down the steps. 45

And I didn't write Sonny or send him anything for a long time. When I finally did, it was just after my little girl died, he wrote me back a letter which made me feel like a bastard.

Here's what he said:

Dear brother,

You don't know how much I needed to hear from you. I wanted to write you many a time but I dug how much I must have hurt you and so I didn't write. But now I feel like a man who's been trying to climb up out of some deep, real deep and funky hole and just saw the sun up there, outside. I got to get outside.

I can't tell you much about how I got here. I mean I don't know how to tell you. I guess I was afraid of something or I was trying to escape from something and you know I have never been very strong in the head (smile). I'm glad Mama and Daddy are dead and can't see what's happened to their son and I swear if I'd known what I was doing I would never have hurt you so, you and a lot of other fine people who were nice to me and who believed in me.

I don't want you to think it had anything to do with me being a musician. It's more than that. Or maybe less than that. I can't get anything straight in my head down here and I try not to think about what's going to happen to me when I get outside again. Sometime I think I'm going to flip and *never* get outside and sometime I think I'll come straight back. I tell you one thing, though, I'd rather blow my brains out than go through this again. But that's what they all say, so they tell me. If I tell you when I'm coming to New York and if you could meet me, I sure would appreciate it. Give my love to Isabel and the kids and I was sure sorry to hear about little Gracie. I wish I could be like Mama and say the Lord's will be done, but I don't know it seems to me that trouble is the one thing that never does get stopped and I don't know what good it does to blame it on the Lord. But maybe it does some good if you believe it.

Your brother,
Sonny

Then I kept in constant touch with him and I sent him whatever I could and I went to meet him when he came back to New York. When I saw him many things I thought I had forgotten came flooding back to me. This was because I had begun, finally, to wonder about Sonny, about the life that Sonny lived inside. This life, whatever it was, had made him older and thinner and it had deepened the distant stillness in which he had always moved. He looked very unlike my baby brother. Yet, when he smiled, when we shook hands, the baby brother I'd never known looked out from the depths of his private life, like an animal waiting to be coaxed into the light.

"How you been keeping?" he asked me.   50

"All right. And you?"

"Just fine." He was smiling all over his face. "It's good to see you again."

"It's good to see you."

The seven years' difference in our ages lay between us like a chasm: I wondered if these years would ever operate between us as a bridge. I was remembering, and it made it hard to catch my breath, that I had been there when he was born; and I had heard the first words he had ever spoken. When he started to walk, he walked from our mother straight to me. I caught him just before he fell when he took the first steps he ever took in this world.

"How's Isabel?"   55

"Just fine. She's dying to see you."

"And the boys?"

"They're fine, too. They're anxious to see their uncle."

"Oh, come on. You know they don't remember me."

"Are you kidding? Of course they remember you."   60

He grinned again. We got into a taxi. We had a lot to say to each other, far too much to know how to begin.

As the taxi began to move, I asked, "You still want to go to India?"

He laughed. "You still remember that. Hell, no. This place is Indian enough for me."

"It used to belong to them," I said.

And he laughed again. "They damn sure knew what they were doing when they   65
got rid of it."

Years ago, when he was around fourteen, he'd been all hipped on the idea of
going to India. He read books about people sitting on rocks, naked, in all kinds of
weather, but mostly bad, naturally, and walking barefoot through hot coals and arriving at wisdom. I used to say that it sounded to me as though they were getting away
from wisdom as fast as they could. I think he sort of looked down on me for that.

"Do you mind," he asked, "if we have the driver drive alongside the park? On the
west side—I haven't seen the city in so long."

"Of course not," I said. I was afraid that I might sound as though I were humor-
ing him, but I hoped he wouldn't take it that way.

So we drove along, between the green of the park and the stony, lifeless elegance
of hotels and apartment buildings, toward the vivid, killing streets of our childhood.
These streets hadn't changed, though housing projects jutted up out of them now
like rocks in the middle of a boiling sea. Most of the houses in which we had grown
up had vanished, as had the stores from which we had stolen, the basements in which
we had first tried sex, the rooftops from which we had hurled tin cans and bricks.
But houses exactly like the houses of our past yet dominated the landscape, boys
exactly like the boys we once had been found themselves smothering in these houses,
came down into the streets for light and air and found themselves encircled by disaster. Some escaped the trap, most didn't. Those who got out always left something of
themselves behind, as some animals amputate a leg and leave it in the trap. It might
be said, perhaps, that I had escaped, after all, I was a school teacher; or that Sonny
had, he hadn't lived in Harlem for years. Yet, as the cab moved uptown through
streets which seemed, with a rush, to darken with dark people, and as I covertly studied Sonny's face, it came to me that what we both were seeking through our separate
cab windows was that part of ourselves which had been left behind. It's always at the
hour of trouble and confrontation that the missing member aches.

We hit 110th Street and started rolling up Lenox Avenue. And I'd known this   70
avenue all my life, but it seemed to me again, as it had seemed on the day I'd first heard
about Sonny's trouble, filled with a hidden menace which was its very breath of life.

"We almost there," said Sonny.

"Almost." We were both too nervous to say anything more.

We live in a housing project. It hasn't been up long. A few days after it was up
it seemed uninhabitably new, now, of course, it's already rundown. It looks like a
parody of the good, clean, faceless life—God knows the people who live in it do their
best to make it a parody. The beat-looking grass lying around isn't enough to make
their lives green, the hedges will never hold out the streets, and they know it. The
big windows fool no one, they aren't big enough to make space out of no space. They
don't bother with the windows, they watch the TV screen instead. The playground is
most popular with the children who don't play at jacks, or skip rope, or roller skate,
or swing, and they can be found in it after dark. We moved in partly because it's not
too far from where I teach, and partly for the kids; but it's really just like the houses
in which Sonny and I grew up. The same things happen, they'll have the same things
to remember. The moment Sonny and I started into the house I had the feeling that
I was simply bringing him back into the danger he had almost died trying to escape.

Sonny has never been talkative. So I don't know why I was sure he'd be dying
to talk to me when supper was over the first night. Everything went fine, the oldest
boy remembered him, and the youngest boy liked him, and Sonny had remembered

to bring something for each of them; and Isabel, who is really much nicer than I am, more open and giving, had gone to a lot of trouble about dinner and was genuinely glad to see him. And she's always been able to tease Sonny in a way that I haven't. It was nice to see her face so vivid again and to hear her laugh and watch her make Sonny laugh. She wasn't, or, anyway, she didn't seem to be, at all uneasy or embarrassed. She chatted as though there were no subject which had to be avoided and she got Sonny past his first, faint stiffness. And thank God she was there, for I was filled with that icy dread again. Everything I did seemed awkward to me, and everything I said sounded freighted with hidden meaning. I was trying to remember everything I'd heard about dope addiction and I couldn't help watching Sonny for signs. I wasn't doing it out of malice. I was trying to find out something about my brother. I was dying to hear him tell me he was safe.

"Safe!" my father grunted, whenever Mama suggested trying to move to a neighborhood which might be safer for children. "Safe, hell! Ain't no place safe for kids, nor nobody."

He always went on like this, but he wasn't, ever, really as bad as he sounded, not even on weekends, when he got drunk. As a matter of fact, he was always on the lookout for "something a little better," but he died before he found it. He died suddenly, during a drunken weekend in the middle of the war, when Sonny was fifteen. He and Sonny hadn't ever got on too well. And this was partly because Sonny was the apple of his father's eye. It was because he loved Sonny so much and was frightened for him, that he was always fighting with him. It doesn't do any good to fight with Sonny. Sonny just moves back, inside himself, where he can't be reached. But the principal reason that they never hit it off is that they were so much alike. Daddy was big and rough and loud-talking, just the opposite of Sonny, but they both had—that same privacy.

Mama tried to tell me something about this, just after Daddy died. I was home on leave from the army.

This was the last time I ever saw my mother alive. Just the same, this picture gets all mixed up in my mind with pictures I had of her when she was younger. The way I always see her is the way she used to be on a Sunday afternoon, say, when the old folks were talking after the big Sunday dinner. I always see her wearing pale blue. She'd be sitting on the sofa. And my father would be sitting in the easy chair, not far from her. And the living room would be full of church folks and relatives. There they sit, in chairs all around the living room, and the night is creeping up outside, but nobody knows it yet. You can see the darkness growing against the windowpanes and you hear the street noises every now and again, or maybe the jangling beat of a tambourine from one of the churches close by, but it's real quiet in the room. For a moment nobody's talking, but every face looks darkening, like the sky outside. And my mother rocks a little from the waist, and my father's eyes are closed. Everyone is looking at something a child can't see. For a minute they've forgotten the children. Maybe a kid is lying on the rug, half asleep. Maybe somebody's got a kid in his lap and is absent-mindedly stroking the kid's head. Maybe there's a kid, quiet and big-eyed, curled up in a big chair in the corner. The silence, the darkness coming, and the darkness in the faces frightens the child obscurely. He hopes that the hand which strokes his forehead will never stop—will never die. He hopes that there will never come a time when the old folks won't be sitting around the living room, talking about where they've come from, and what they've seen, and what's happened to them and their kinfolk.

But something deep and watchful in the child knows that this is bound to end, is already ending. In a moment someone will get up and turn on the light. Then the old folks will remember the children and they won't talk any more that day. And when light fills the room, the child is filled with darkness. He knows that every time this happens he's moved just a little closer to that darkness outside. The darkness outside is what the old folks have been talking about. It's what they've come from. It's what they endure. The child knows that they won't talk any more because if he knows too much about what's happened to *them,* he'll know too much too soon, about what's going to happen to *him.*

The last time I talked to my mother, I remember I was restless. I wanted to get out and see Isabel. We weren't married then and we had a lot to straighten out between us.

There Mama sat, in black, by the window. She was humming an old church song, *Lord, you brought me from a long ways off.* Sonny was out somewhere. Mama kept watching the streets.

"I don't know," she said, "if I'll ever see you again, after you go off from here. But I hope you'll remember the things I tried to teach you."

"Don't talk like that," I said, and smiled. "You'll be here a long time yet."

She smiled, too, but she said nothing. She was quiet for a long time. And I said, "Mama, don't you worry about nothing. I'll be writing all the time, and you be getting the checks . . ."

"I want to talk to you about your brother," she said, suddenly. "If anything happens to me he ain't going to have nobody to look out for him."

"Mama," I said, "ain't nothing going to happen to you *or* Sonny. Sonny's all right. He's a good boy and he's got good sense."

"It ain't a question of his being a good boy," Mama said, "nor of his having good sense. It ain't only the bad ones, nor yet the dumb ones that gets sucked under." She stopped, looking at me. "Your Daddy once had a brother," she said, and she smiled in a way that made me feel she was in pain. "You didn't never know that, did you?"

"No," I said, "I never knew that," and I watched her face.

"Oh, yes," she said, "your Daddy had a brother." She looked out of the window again. "I know you never saw your Daddy cry. But *I* did—many a time, through all these years."

I asked her, "What happened to his brother? How come nobody's ever talked about him?"

This was the first time I ever saw my mother look old.

"His brother got killed," she said, "when he was just a little younger than you are now. I knew him. He was a fine boy. He was maybe a little full of the devil, but he didn't mean nobody no harm."

Then she stopped and the room was silent, exactly as it had sometimes been on those Sunday afternoons. Mama kept looking out into the streets.

"He used to have a job in the mill," she said, "and, like all young folks, he just liked to perform on Saturday nights. Saturday nights, him and your father would drift around to different places, go to dances and things like that, or just sit around with people they knew, and your father's brother would sing, he had a fine voice, and play along with himself on his guitar. Well, this particular Saturday night, him and your father was coming home from some place, and they were both a little drunk and there was a moon that night, it was bright like day. Your father's brother was feeling kind of good, and he was whistling to himself, and he had his guitar slung over his shoulder. They was coming down a hill and beneath them was a road that turned off from the highway. Well, your father's brother, being always kind of frisky, decided to run down this hill, and he did, with that guitar banging and clanging behind him, and he ran across the road, and he was making water behind a tree. And your father was sort of amused at him and he was still coming down the hill, kind of slow. Then he heard a car motor and that same minute his brother stepped from behind the tree, into the road, in the moonlight. And he started to cross the road. And your father started to run down the hill, he says he don't know why. This car was full of white men. They was all drunk, and when they seen your father's brother they let out a great whoop and holler and they aimed the car straight at him. They was having fun, they just wanted to scare him, the way they do sometimes, you know. But they was drunk. And I guess the boy, being drunk, too, and scared, kind of lost his head. By the time he jumped it was too late. Your father says he heard his brother scream when the car rolled over him, and he heard the wood of that guitar when it give, and he heard them strings go flying, and he heard them white men shouting, and the car kept on a-going and it ain't stopped till this day. And, time your father got down the hill, his brother weren't nothing but blood and pulp."

Tears were gleaming on my mother's face. There wasn't anything I could say.   95

"He never mentioned it," she said, "because I never let him mention it before you children. Your Daddy was like a crazy man that night and for many a night there-after. He says he never in his life seen anything as dark as that road after the lights of that car had gone away. Weren't nothing, weren't nobody on that road, just your Daddy and his brother and that busted guitar. Oh, yes. Your Daddy never did really get right again. Till the day he died he weren't sure but that every white man he saw was the man that killed his brother."

She stopped and took out her handkerchief and dried her eyes and looked at me.

"I ain't telling you all this," she said, "to make you scared or bitter or to make you hate nobody. I'm telling you this because you got a brother. And the world ain't changed."

I guess I didn't want to believe this. I guess she saw this in my face. She turned away from me, toward the window again, searching those streets.

"But I praise my Redeemer," she said at last, "that He called your Daddy home   100 before me. I ain't saying it to throw no flowers at myself, but, I declare, it keeps me from feeling too cast down to know I helped your father get safely through this world. Your father always acted like he was the roughest, strongest man on earth. And everybody took him to be like that. But if he hadn't had *me* there—to see his tears!"

She was crying again. Still, I couldn't move. I said, "Lord, Lord, Mama, I didn't know it was like that."

"Oh, honey," she said, "there's a lot that you don't know. But you are going to find it out." She stood up from the window and came over to me. "You got to hold on to your brother," she said, "and don't let him fall, no matter what it looks like is hap-pening to him and no matter how evil you gets with him. You going to be evil with him many a time. But don't you forget what I told you, you hear?"

"I won't forget," I said. "Don't you worry, I won't forget. I won't let nothing hap-pen to Sonny."

My mother smiled as though she were amused at something she saw in my face. Then, "You may not be able to stop nothing from happening. But you got to let him know you's *there*."

Two days later I was married, and then I was gone. And I had a lot of things on   105 my mind and I pretty well forgot my promise to Mama until I got shipped home on a special furlough for her funeral.

And, after the funeral, with just Sonny and me alone in the empty kitchen, I tried to find out something about him.

"What do you want to do?" I asked him.

"I'm going to be a musician," he said.

For he had graduated, in the time I had been away, from dancing to the juke box to finding out who was playing what, and what they were doing with it, and he had bought himself a set of drums.

"You mean, you want to be a drummer?" I somehow had the feeling that being a   110 drummer might be all right for other people but not for my brother Sonny.

"I don't think," he said, looking at me very gravely, "that I'll ever be a good drummer. But I think I can play a piano."

I frowned. I'd never played the role of the older brother quite so seriously before, had scarcely ever, in fact, *asked* Sonny a damn thing. I sensed myself in the presence of something I didn't really know how to handle, didn't understand. So I made my frown a little deeper as I asked: "What kind of musician do you want to be?"

He grinned. "How many kinds do you think there are?"

"Be *serious*," I said.

He laughed, throwing his head back, and then looked at me. "I *am* serious."   115

"Well, then, for Christ's sake, stop kidding around and answer a serious question. I mean, do you want to be a concert pianist, you want to play classical music and all that, or—or what?" Long before I finished he was laughing again. "For Christ's *sake*, Sonny!"

He sobered, but with difficulty. "I'm sorry. But you sound so—*scared*!" and he was off again.

"Well, you may think it's funny now, baby, but it's not going to be so funny when you have to make your living at it, let me tell you *that*." I was furious because I knew he was laughing at me and I didn't know why.

"No," he said, very sober now, and afraid, perhaps, that he'd hurt me, "I don't want to be a classical pianist. That isn't what interests me. I mean"—he paused, looking hard at me, as though his eyes would help me to understand, and then gestured helplessly, as though perhaps his hand would help—"I mean, I'll have a lot of studying to do, and I'll have to study *everything*, but, I mean, I want to play *with*—jazz musicians." He stopped. "I want to play jazz," he said.

Well, the word had never before sounded as heavy, as real, as it sounded that   120 afternoon in Sonny's mouth. I just looked at him and I was probably frowning a real frown by this time. I simply couldn't see why on earth he'd want to spend his time hanging around nightclubs, clowning around on bandstands, while people pushed each other around a dance floor. It seemed—beneath him, somehow. I had never thought about it before, had never been forced to, but I suppose I had always put jazz musicians in a class with what Daddy called "goodtime people."

"Are you *serious*?"

"Hell, *yes*, I'm serious."

He looked more helpless than ever, and annoyed, and deeply hurt.

I suggested, helpfully: "You mean—like Louis Armstrong?"°

His face closed as though I'd struck him. "No. I'm not talking about none of that   125 old-time, down home crap."

Louis Armstrong: jazz trumpeter and vocalist (1900–1971) born in New Orleans. In the 1950s his music would have been considered conservative by progressive jazz fans.

"Well, look, Sonny, I'm sorry, don't get mad. I just don't altogether get it, that's all. Name somebody—you know, a jazz musician you admire."

"Bird."

"Who?"

"Bird! Charlie Parker!° Don't they teach you nothing in the goddamn army?"

I lit a cigarette. I was surprised and then a little amused to discover that I was   130
trembling. "I've been out of touch," I said. "You'll have to be patient with me. Now. Who's this Parker character?"

"He's just one of the greatest jazz musicians alive," said Sonny, sullenly, his hands in his pockets, his back to me. "Maybe *the* greatest," he added, bitterly, "that's probably why *you* never heard of him."

"All right," I said, "I'm ignorant. I'm sorry. I'll go out and buy all the cat's records right away, all right?"

"It don't," said Sonny, with dignity, "make any difference to me. I don't care what you listen to. Don't do me no favors."

I was beginning to realize that I'd never seen him so upset before. With another part of my mind I was thinking that this would probably turn out to be one of those things kids go through and that I shouldn't make it seem important by pushing it too hard. Still, I didn't think it would do any harm to ask: "Doesn't all this take a lot of time? Can you make a living at it?"

He turned back to me and half leaned, half sat, on the kitchen table. "Every-   135
thing takes time," he said, "and—well, yes, sure, I can make a living at it. But what I don't seem to be able to make you understand is that it's the only thing I want to do."

"Well, Sonny," I said, gently, "you know people can't always do exactly what they *want* to do—"

"*No,* I don't know that," said Sonny, surprising me. "I think people *ought* to do what they want to do, what else are they alive for?"

"You getting to be a big boy," I said desperately, "it's time you started thinking about your future."

"I'm thinking about my future," said Sonny, grimly. "I think about it all the time."

I gave up. I decided, if he didn't change his mind, that we could always talk   140
about it later. "In the meantime," I said, "you got to finish school." We had already decided that he'd have to move in with Isabel and her folks. I knew this wasn't the ideal arrangement because Isabel's folks are inclined to be dicty° and they hadn't especially wanted Isabel to marry me. But I didn't know what else to do. "And we have to get you fixed up at Isabel's."

There was a long silence. He moved from the kitchen table to the window. "That's a terrible idea. You know it yourself."

"Do you have a *better* idea?"

He just walked up and down the kitchen for a minute. He was as tall as I was. He had started to shave. I suddenly had the feeling that I didn't know him at all.

He stopped at the kitchen table and picked up my cigarettes. Looking at me with a kind of mocking, amused defiance, he put one between his lips. "You mind?"

"You smoking already?"   145

Charlie Parker: a jazz saxophonist (1920–1955) who helped create the progressive jazz style called bebop. Parker was a heroin addict who died at an early age.   *dicty:* slang word for stylish, high-class; snobbish.

He lit the cigarette and nodded, watching me through the smoke. "I just wanted to see if I'd have the courage to smoke in front of you." He grinned and blew a great cloud of smoke to the ceiling. "It was easy." He looked at my face. "Come on, now. I bet you was smoking at my age, tell the truth."

I didn't say anything but the truth was on my face, and he laughed. But now there was something very strained in his laugh. "Sure. And I bet that ain't all you was doing."

He was frightening me a little. "Cut the crap," I said. "We already decided that you was going to go and live at Isabel's. Now what's got into you all of a sudden?"

"*You* decided it," he pointed out. "I didn't decide nothing." He stopped in front of me, leaning against the stove, arms loosely folded. "Look, brother. I don't want to stay in Harlem no more, I really don't." He was very earnest. He looked at me, then over toward the kitchen window. There was something in his eyes I'd never seen before, some thoughtfulness, some worry all his own. He rubbed the muscle of one arm. "It's time I was getting out of here."

"Where do you want to go, Sonny?"

"I want to join the army. Or the navy, I don't care. If I say I'm old enough, they'll believe me."

Then I got mad. It was because I was so scared. "You must be crazy. You goddamn fool, what the hell do you want to go and join the *army* for?"

"I just told you. To get out of Harlem."

"Sonny, you haven't even finished *school*. And if you really want to be a musician, how do you expect to study if you're in the *army*?"

He looked at me, trapped, and in anguish. "There's ways. I might be able to work out some kind of deal. Anyway, I'll have the G.I. Bill when I come out."

"*If* you come out." We stared at each other. "Sonny, please. Be reasonable. I know the setup is far from perfect. But we got to do the best we can."

"I ain't learning nothing in school," he said. "Even when I go." He turned away from me and opened the window and threw his cigarette out into the narrow alley. I watched his back. "At least, I ain't learning nothing you'd want me to learn." He slammed the window so hard I thought the glass would fly out, and turned back to me. "And I'm sick of the stink of these garbage cans!"

"Sonny," I said, "I know how you feel. But if you don't finish school now, you're going to be sorry later that you didn't." I grabbed him by the shoulders. "And you only got another year. It ain't so bad. And I'll come back and I swear I'll help you do *whatever* you want to do. Just try to put up with it till I come back. Will you please do that? For me?"

He didn't answer and he wouldn't look at me.

"Sonny. You hear me?"

He pulled away. "I hear you. But you never hear anything I say."

I didn't know what to say to that. He looked out of the window and then back at me. "OK," he said, and sighed. "I'll try."

Then I said, trying to cheer him up a little, "They got a piano at Isabel's. You can practice on it."

And as a matter of fact, it did cheer him up for a minute. "That's right," he said to himself. "I forgot that." His face relaxed a little. But the worry, the thoughtfulness, played on it still, the way shadows play on a face which is staring into the fire.

But I thought I'd never hear the end of that piano. At first, Isabel would write me, saying how nice it was that Sonny was so serious about his music and how, as soon as he came in from school, or wherever he had been when he was supposed to be at school, he went straight to that piano and stayed there until suppertime. And, after supper, he went back to that piano and stayed there until everybody went to bed. He was at the piano all day Saturday and all day Sunday. Then he bought a record player and started playing records. He'd play one record over and over again, all day long sometimes, and he'd improvise along with it on the piano. Or he'd play one section of the record, one chord, one change, one progression, then he'd do it on the piano. Then back to the record. Then back to the piano.

Well, I really don't know how they stood it. Isabel finally confessed that it wasn't like living with a person at all, it was like living with sound. And the sound didn't make any sense to her, didn't make any sense to any of them—naturally. They began, in a way, to be afflicted by this presence that was living in their home. It was as though Sonny were some sort of god, or monster. He moved in an atmosphere which wasn't like theirs at all. They fed him and he ate, he washed himself, he walked in and out of their door; he certainly wasn't nasty or unpleasant or rude, Sonny isn't any of those things; but it was as though he were all wrapped up in some cloud, some fire, some vision all his own; and there wasn't any way to reach him.

At the same time, he wasn't really a man yet, he was still a child, and they had to watch out for him in all kinds of ways. They certainly couldn't throw him out. Neither did they dare to make a great scene about that piano because even they dimly sensed, as I sensed, from so many thousands of miles away, that Sonny was at that piano playing for his life.

But he hadn't been going to school. One day a letter came from the school board and Isabel's mother got it—there had, apparently, been other letters but Sonny had torn them up. This day, when Sonny came in, Isabel's mother showed him the letter and asked where he'd been spending his time. And she finally got it out of him that he'd been down in Greenwich Village, with musicians and other characters, in a white girl's apartment. And this scared her and she started to scream at him and what came up, once she began—though she denies it to this day—was what sacrifices they were making to give Sonny a decent home and how little he appreciated it.

Sonny didn't play the piano that day. By evening, Isabel's mother had calmed down but then there was the old man to deal with, and Isabel herself. Isabel says she did her best to be calm but she broke down and started crying. She says she just watched Sonny's face. She could tell, by watching him, what was happening with him. And what was happening was that they penetrated his cloud, they had reached him. Even if their fingers had been a thousand times more gentle than human fingers ever are, he could hardly help feeling that they had stripped him naked and were spitting on that nakedness. For he also had to see that his presence, that music, which was life or death to him, had been torture for them and that they had endured it, not at all for his sake, but only for mine. And Sonny couldn't take that. He can take it a little better today than he could then but he's still not very good at it and, frankly, I don't know anybody who is.

The silence of the next few days must have been louder than the sound of all the 170 music ever played since time began. One morning, before she went to work, Isabel was in his room for something and she suddenly realized that all of his records were gone. And she knew for certain that he was gone. And he was. He went as far as the navy would carry him. He finally sent me a postcard from some place in Greece and that was the first I knew that Sonny was still alive. I didn't see him any more until we were both back in New York and the war had long been over.

He was a man by then, of course, but I wasn't willing to see it. He came by the house from time to time, but we fought almost every time we met. I didn't like the way he carried himself, loose and dreamlike all the time, and I didn't like his friends, and his music seemed to be merely an excuse for the life he led. It sounded just that weird and disordered.

Then we had a fight, a pretty awful fight, and I didn't see him for months. By and by I looked him up, where he was living, in a furnished room in the Village, and I tried to make it up. But there were lots of people in the room and Sonny just lay on his bed, and he wouldn't come downstairs with me, and he treated these other people as though they were his family and I weren't. So I got mad and then he got mad, and then I told him that he might just as well be dead as live the way he was living. Then he stood up and he told me not to worry about him any more in life, that he *was* dead as far as I was concerned. Then he pushed me to the door and the other people looked on as though nothing were happening, and he slammed the door behind me. I stood in the hallway, staring at the door. I heard somebody laugh in the room and then the tears came to my eyes. I started down the steps, whistling to keep from crying, I kept whistling to myself, *You going to need me, baby, one of these cold, rainy days.*

I read about Sonny's trouble in the spring. Little Grace died in the fall. She was a beautiful little girl. But she only lived a little over two years. She died of polio and she suffered. She had a slight fever for a couple of days, but it didn't seem like anything and we just kept her in bed. And we would certainly have called the doctor, but the fever dropped, she seemed to be all right. So we thought it had just been a cold. Then, one day, she was up, playing, Isabel was in the kitchen fixing lunch for the two boys when they'd come in from school, and she heard Grace fall down in the living room. When you have a lot of children you don't always start running when one of them falls, unless they start screaming or something. And, this time, Grace was quiet. Yet, Isabel says that when she heard that *thump* and then that silence, something happened in her to make her afraid. And she ran to the living room and there was little Grace on the floor, all twisted up, and the reason she hadn't screamed was that she couldn't get her breath. And when she did scream, it was the worst sound, Isabel says, that she'd ever heard in all her life, and she still hears it sometimes in her dreams. Isabel will sometimes wake me up with a low, moaning, strangled sound and I have to be quick to awaken her and hold her to me and where Isabel is weeping against me seems a mortal wound.

I think I may have written Sonny the very day that little Grace was buried. I was sitting in the living room in the dark, by myself, and I suddenly thought of Sonny. My trouble made his real.

One Saturday afternoon, when Sonny had been living with us, or, anyway, been in our house, for nearly two weeks, I found myself wandering aimlessly about the living room, drinking from a can of beer, and trying to work up the courage to search Sonny's room. He was out, he was usually out whenever I was home, and Isabel had taken the children to see their grandparents. Suddenly I was standing still in front of the living room window, watching Seventh Avenue. The idea of searching Sonny's room made me still. I scarcely dared to admit to myself what I'd be searching for. I didn't know what I'd do if I found it. Or if I didn't.

On the sidewalk across from me, near the entrance to a barbecue joint, some people were holding an old-fashioned revival meeting. The barbecue cook, wearing a dirty white apron, his conked hair reddish and metallic in the pale sun, and a

cigarette between his lips, stood in the doorway, watching them. Kids and older people paused in their errands and stood there, along with some older men and a couple
of very tough-looking women who watched everything that happened on the avenue, as though they owned it, or were maybe owned by it. Well, they were watching
this, too. The revival was being carried on by three sisters in black, and a brother. All
they had were their voices and their Bibles and a tambourine. The brother was tes-
tifying and while he testified two of the sisters stood together, seeming to say, amen,
and the third sister walked around with the tambourine outstretched and a couple of
people dropped coins into it. Then the brother's testimony ended and the sister who
had been taking up the collection dumped the coins into her palm and transferred
them to the pocket of her long black robe. Then she raised both hands, striking the
tambourine against the air, and then against one hand, and she started to sing. And
the two other sisters and the brother joined in.

It was strange, suddenly, to watch, though I had been seeing these street meetings all my life. So, of course, had everybody else down there. Yet, they paused and
watched and listened and I stood still at the window. *"Tis the old ship of Zion,"* they
sang, and the sister with the tambourine kept a steady, jangling beat, *"it has rescued
many a thousand!"* Not a soul under the sound of their voices was hearing this song
for the first time, not one of them had been rescued. Nor had they seen much in the
way of rescue work being done around them. Neither did they especially believe in
the holiness of the three sisters and the brother, they knew too much about them,
knew where they lived, and how. The woman with the tambourine, whose voice
dominated the air, whose face was bright with joy, was divided by very little from
the woman who stood watching her, a cigarette between her heavy, chapped lips,
her hair a cuckoo's nest, her face scarred and swollen from many beatings, and her
black eyes glittering like coal. Perhaps they both knew this, which was why, when,
as rarely, they addressed each other, they addressed each other as Sister. As the singing filled the air the watching, listening faces underwent a change, the eyes focusing
on something within; the music seemed to soothe a poison out of them; and time
seemed, nearly, to fall away from the sullen, belligerent, battered faces, as though
they were fleeing back to their first condition, while dreaming of their last. The barbecue cook half shook his head and smiled, and dropped his cigarette and disappeared into his joint. A man fumbled in his pockets for change and stood holding it
in his hand impatiently, as though he had just remembered a pressing appointment
further up the avenue. He looked furious. Then I saw Sonny, standing on the edge of
the crowd. He was carrying a wide, flat notebook with a green cover, and it made him
look, from where I was standing, almost like a schoolboy. The coppery sun brought
out the copper in his skin, he was very faintly smiling, standing very still. Then the
singing stopped, the tambourine turned into a collection plate again. The furious
man dropped in his coins and vanished, so did a couple of the women, and Sonny
dropped some change in the plate, looking directly at the woman with a little smile.
He started across the avenue, toward the house. He has a slow, loping walk, something like the way Harlem hipsters walk, only he's imposed on this his own half-beat.
I had never really noticed it before.

I stayed at the window, both relieved and apprehensive. As Sonny disappeared
from my sight, they began singing again. And they were still singing when his key
turned in the lock.

"Hey," he said.

"Hey, yourself. You want some beer?"

"No. Well, maybe." But he came up to the window and stood beside me, looking out. "What a warm voice," he said.

They were singing *If I could only hear my mother pray again!*

"Yes," I said, "and she can sure beat that tambourine."

"But what a terrible song," he said, and laughed. He dropped his notebook on the sofa and disappeared into the kitchen. "Where's Isabel and the kids?"

"I think they went to see their grandparents. You hungry?"   185

"No." He came back into the living room with his can of beer. "You want to come some place with me tonight?"

I sensed, I don't know how, that I couldn't possibly say no. "Sure. Where?"

He sat down on the sofa and picked up his notebook and started leafing through it. "I'm going to sit in with some fellows in a joint in the Village."

"You mean, you're going to play, tonight?"

"That's right." He took a swallow of his beer and moved back to the window. He   190
gave me a sidelong look. "If you can stand it."

"I'll try," I said.

He smiled to himself and we both watched as the meeting across the way broke up. The three sisters and the brother, heads bowed, were singing *God be with you till we meet again.* The faces around them were very quiet. Then the song ended. The small crowd dispersed. We watched the three women and the lone man walk slowly up the avenue.

"When she was singing before," said Sonny, abruptly, "her voice reminded me for a minute of what heroin feels like sometimes—when it's in your veins. It makes you feel sort of warm and cool at the same time. And distant. And—and sure." He sipped his beer, very deliberately not looking at me. I watched his face. "It makes you feel—in control. Sometimes you've got to have that feeling."

"Do you?" I sat down slowly in the easy chair.

"Sometimes." He went to the sofa and picked up his notebook again. "Some   195
people do."

"In order," I asked, "to play?" And my voice was very ugly, full of contempt and anger.

"Well"—he looked at me with great, troubled eyes, as though, in fact, he hoped his eyes would tell me things he could never otherwise say—"they *think* so. And *if* they think so—!"

"And what do *you* think?" I asked.

He sat on the sofa and put his can of beer on the floor. "I don't know," he said, and I couldn't be sure if he were answering my question or pursuing his thoughts. His face didn't tell me. "It's not so much to *play.* It's to *stand* it, to be able to make it at all. On any level." He frowned and smiled: "In order to keep from shaking to pieces."

"But these friends of yours," I said, "they seem to shake themselves to pieces   200
pretty goddamn fast."

"Maybe." He played with the notebook. And something told me that I should curb my tongue, that Sonny was doing his best to talk, that I should listen. "But of course you only know the ones that've gone to pieces. Some don't—or at least they haven't *yet* and that's just about all *any* of us can say." He paused. "And then there are some who just live, really, in hell, and they know it and they see what's happening and they go right on. I don't know." He sighed, dropped the notebook, folded his arms. "Some guys, you can tell from the way they play, they on something *all* the time. And you can see that, well, it makes something real for them. But of course," he picked up his beer from the floor and sipped it and put the can down again, "they *want* to, too, you've got to see that. Even some of them that say they don't—*some*, not all."

"And what about you?" I asked—I couldn't help it. "What about you? Do *you* want to?"

He stood up and walked to the window and remained silent for a long time. Then he sighed. "Me," he said. Then: "While I was downstairs before, on my way here, listening to that woman sing, it struck me all of a sudden how much suffering she must have had to go through—to sing like that. It's *repulsive* to think you have to suffer that much."

I said: "But there's no way not to suffer—is there, Sonny?"

"I believe not," he said and smiled, "but that's never stopped anyone from try-   205 ing." He looked at me. "Has it?" I realized, with this mocking look, that there stood between us, forever, beyond the power of time or forgiveness, the fact that I had held silence—so long!—when he had needed human speech to help him. He turned back to the window. "No, there's no way not to suffer. But you try all kinds of ways to keep from drowning in it, to keep on top of it, and to make it seem—well, like *you*. Like you did something, all right, and now you're suffering for it. You know?" I said nothing. "Well you know," he said, impatiently, "why *do* people suffer? Maybe it's better to do something to give it a reason, *any* reason."

"But we just agreed," I said, "that there's no way not to suffer. Isn't it better, then, just to—take it?"

"But nobody just takes it," Sonny cried, "that's what I'm telling you! *Everybody* tries not to. You're just hung up on the *way* some people try—it's not *your* way!"

The hair on my face began to itch, my face felt wet. "That's not true," I said, "that's not true. I don't give a damn what other people do, I don't even care how they suffer. I just care how *you* suffer." And he looked at me. "Please believe me," I said, "I don't want to see you—die—trying not to suffer."

"I won't," he said, flatly, "die trying not to suffer. At least, not any faster than anybody else."

"But there's no need," I said, trying to laugh, "is there? in killing yourself."   210

I wanted to say more, but I couldn't. I wanted to talk about will power and how life could be—well, beautiful. I wanted to say that it was all within; but was it? or, rather, wasn't that exactly the trouble? And I wanted to promise that I would never fail him again. But it would all have sounded—empty words and lies.

So I made the promise to myself and prayed that I would keep it.

"It's terrible sometimes, inside," he said, "that's what's the trouble. You walk these streets, black and funky and cold, and there's not really a living ass to talk to, and there's nothing shaking, and there's no way of getting it out—that storm inside. You can't talk it and you can't make love with it, and when you finally try to get with it and play it, you realize *nobody's* listening. So *you've* got to listen. You got to find a way to listen."

And then he walked away from the window and sat on the sofa again, as though all the wind had suddenly been knocked out of him. "Sometimes you'll do *anything* to play, even cut your mother's throat." He laughed and looked at me. "Or your brother's." Then he sobered. "Or your own." Then: "Don't worry. I'm all right now and I think I'll *be* all right. But I can't forget—where I've been. I don't mean just the physical place I've been, I mean where I've *been*. And *what* I've been."

"What have you been, Sonny?" I asked.   215

He smiled—but sat sideways on the sofa, his elbow resting on the back, his fingers playing with his mouth and chin, not looking at me. "I've been something I didn't recognize, didn't know I could be. Didn't know anybody could be." He stopped, looking inward, looking helplessly young, looking old. "I'm not talking about it now because I feel *guilty* or anything like that—maybe it would be better if I did, I don't know. Anyway, I can't really talk about it. Not to you, not to anybody," and now he turned and faced me. "Sometimes, you know, and it was actually when I was most *out* of the world, I felt that I was in it, that I was *with* it, really, and I could play or I didn't really have to *play*, it just came out of me, it was there. And I don't know how I played, thinking about it now, but I know I did awful things, those times, sometimes, to people. Or it wasn't that I *did* anything to them—it was that they weren't real." He picked up the beer can; it was empty; he rolled it between his palms: "And other times—well, I needed a fix, I needed to find a place to lean, I needed to clear a space to *listen*—and I couldn't find it, and I—went crazy, I did terrible things to *me*, I was terrible *for* me." He began pressing the beer can between his hands, I watched the metal begin to give. It glittered, as he played with it, like a knife, and I was afraid he would cut himself, but I said nothing. "Oh well. I can never tell you. I was all by myself at the bottom of something, stinking and sweating and crying and shaking, and I smelled it, you know? *my* stink, and I thought I'd die if I couldn't get away from it and yet, all the same, I knew that everything I was doing was just locking me in with it. And I didn't know," he paused, still flattening the beer can, "I didn't know, I still *don't* know, something kept telling me that maybe it was good to smell your own stink, but I didn't think that *that* was what I'd been trying to do—and—who can stand it?" and he abruptly dropped the ruined beer can, looking at me with a small, still smile, and then rose, walking to the window as though it were the lodestone rock. I watched his face, he watched the avenue. "I couldn't tell you when Mama died—but the reason I wanted to leave Harlem so bad was to get away from drugs. And then, when I ran away, that's what I was running from—really. When I came back, nothing had changed, *I* hadn't changed, I was just—older." And he stopped, drumming with his fingers on the windowpane. The sun had vanished, soon darkness would fall. I watched his face. "It can come again," he said, almost as though speaking to himself. Then he turned to me. "It can come again," he repeated. "I just want you to know that."

"All right," I said, at last. "So it can come again. All right."

He smiled, but the smile was sorrowful. "I had to try to tell you," he said.

"Yes," I said. "I understand that."

"You're my brother," he said, looking straight at me, and not smiling at all.   220

"Yes," I repeated, "yes. I understand that."

He turned back to the window, looking out. "All that hatred down there," he said, "all that hatred and misery and love. It's a wonder it doesn't blow the avenue apart."

We went to the only nightclub on a short, dark street, downtown. We squeezed through the narrow, chattering, jam-packed bar to the entrance of the big room, where the bandstand was. And we stood there for a moment, for the lights were very dim in this room and we couldn't see. Then, "Hello, boy," said a voice and an enormous black man, much older than Sonny or myself, erupted out of all that atmospheric lighting and put an arm around Sonny's shoulder. "I been sitting right here," he said, "waiting for you."

He had a big voice, too, and heads in the darkness turned toward us.

Sonny grinned and pulled a little away, and said, "Creole, this is my brother. I   225
told you about him."

Creole shook my hand. "I'm glad to meet you, son," he said, and it was clear that
he was glad to meet me *there*, for Sonny's sake. And he smiled, "You got a real musician in *your* family," and he took his arm from Sonny's shoulder and slapped him,
lightly, affectionately, with the back of his hand.

"Well. Now I've heard it all," said a voice behind us. This was another musician, and a friend of Sonny's, a coal-black, cheerful-looking man, built close to
the ground. He immediately began confiding to me, at the top of his lungs, the
most terrible things about Sonny, his teeth gleaming like a lighthouse and his laugh
coming up out of him like the beginning of an earthquake. And it turned out that
everyone at the bar knew Sonny, or almost everyone; some were musicians, working there, or nearby, or not working, some were simply hangers-on, and some were
there to hear Sonny play. I was introduced to all of them and they were all very
polite to me. Yet, it was clear that, for them, I was only Sonny's brother. Here, I was
in Sonny's world. Or, rather: his kingdom. Here, it was not even a question that his
veins bore royal blood.

They were going to play soon and Creole installed me, by myself, at a table in a
dark corner. Then I watched them, Creole, and the little black man, and Sonny, and
the others, while they horsed around, standing just below the bandstand. The light
from the bandstand spilled just a little short of them and, watching them laughing
and gesturing and moving about, I had the feeling that they, nevertheless, were being
most careful not to step into that circle of light too suddenly: that if they moved into
the light too suddenly, without thinking, they would perish in flame. Then, while I
watched, one of them, the small, black man, moved into the light and crossed the
bandstand and started fooling around with his drums. Then—being funny and being,
also, extremely ceremonious—Creole took Sonny by the arm and led him to the
piano. A woman's voice called Sonny's name and a few hands started clapping. And
Sonny, also being funny and being ceremonious, and so touched, I think, that he
could have cried, but neither hiding it nor showing it, riding it like a man, grinned,
and put both hands to his heart and bowed from the waist.

Creole then went to the bass fiddle and a lean, very bright-skinned brown man
jumped up on the bandstand and picked up his horn. So there they were, and the
atmosphere on the bandstand and in the room began to change and tighten. Someone stepped up to the microphone and announced them. Then there were all kinds
of murmurs. Some people at the bar shushed others. The waitress ran around, frantically getting in the last orders, guys and chicks got closer to each other, and the lights
on the bandstand, on the quartet, turned to a kind of indigo. Then they all looked
different there. Creole looked about him for the last time, as though he were making
certain that all his chickens were in the coop, and then he—jumped and struck the
fiddle. And there they were.

All I know about music is that not many people ever really hear it. And even   230
then, on the rare occasions when something opens within, and the music enters,
what we mainly hear, or hear corroborated, are personal, private, vanishing evoca-
tions. But the man who creates the music is hearing something else, is dealing with
the roar rising from the void and imposing order on it as it hits the air. What is
evoked in him, then, is of another order, more terrible because it has no words, and
triumphant, too, for that same reason. And his triumph, when he triumphs, is ours. I

just watched Sonny's face. His face was troubled, he was working hard, but he wasn't with it. And I had the feeling that, in a way, everyone on the bandstand was waiting for him, both waiting for him and pushing him along. But as I began to watch Creole, I realized that it was Creole who held them all back. He had them on a short rein. Up there, keeping the beat with his whole body, wailing on the fiddle, with his eyes half closed, he was listening to everything, but he was listening to Sonny. He was having a dialogue with Sonny. He wanted Sonny to leave the shoreline and strike out for the deep water. He was Sonny's witness that deep water and drowning were not the same thing—he had been there, and he knew. And he wanted Sonny to know. He was waiting for Sonny to do the things on the keys which would let Creole know that Sonny was in the water.

And, while Creole listened, Sonny moved, deep within, exactly like someone in torment. I had never before thought of how awful the relationship must be between the musician and his instrument. He has to fill it, this instrument, with the breath of life, his own. He has to make it do what he wants it to do. And a piano is just a piano. It's made out of so much wood and wires and little hammers and big ones, and ivory. While there's only so much you can do with it, the only way to find this out is to try; to try and make it do everything.

And Sonny hadn't been near a piano for over a year. And he wasn't on much better terms with his life, not the life that stretched before him now. He and the piano stammered, started one way, got scared, stopped; started another way, panicked, marked time, started again; then seemed to have found a direction, panicked again, got stuck. And the face I saw on Sonny I'd never seen before. Everything had been burned out of it, and, at the same time, things usually hidden were being burned in, by the fire and fury of the battle which was occurring in him up there.

Yet, watching Creole's face as they neared the end of the first set, I had the feeling that something had happened, something I hadn't heard. Then they finished, there was scattered applause, and then, without an instant's warning, Creole started into something else, it was almost sardonic, it was *Am I Blue*. And, as though he commanded, Sonny began to play. Something began to happen. And Creole let out the reins. The dry, low, black man said something awful on the drums, Creole answered, and the drums talked back. Then the horn insisted, sweet and high, slightly detached perhaps, and Creole listened, commenting now and then, dry, and driving, beautiful and calm and old. Then they all came together again, and Sonny was part of the family again. I could tell this from his face. He seemed to have found, right there beneath his fingers, a damn brand-new piano. It seemed that he couldn't get over it. Then, for awhile, just being happy with Sonny, they seemed to be agreeing with him that brand-new pianos certainly were a gas.

Then Creole stepped forward to remind them that what they were playing was the blues. He hit something in all of them, he hit something in me, myself, and the music tightened and deepened, apprehension began to beat the air. Creole began to tell us what the blues were all about. They were not about anything very new. He and his boys up there were keeping it new, at the risk of ruin, destruction, madness, and death, in order to find new ways to make us listen. For, while the tale of how we suffer, and how we are delighted, and how we may triumph is never new, it always must be heard. There isn't any other tale to tell, it's the only light we've got in all this darkness.

And this tale, according to that face, that body, those strong hands on those strings, 235 has another aspect in every country, and a new depth in every generation. Listen,

Creole seemed to be saying, listen. Now these are Sonny's blues. He made the little black man on the drums know it, and the bright, brown man on the horn. Creole wasn't trying any longer to get Sonny in the water. He was wishing him Godspeed.° Then he stepped back, very slowly, filling the air with the immense suggestion that Sonny speak for himself.

Then they all gathered around Sonny and Sonny played. Every now and again one of them seemed to say, amen. Sonny's fingers filled the air with life, his life. But that life contained so many others. And Sonny went all the way back, he really began with the spare, flat statement of the opening phrase of the song. Then he began to make it his. It was very beautiful because it wasn't hurried and it was no longer a lament. I seemed to hear with what burning he had made it his, with what burning we had yet to make it ours, how we could cease lamenting. Freedom lurked around us and I understood, at last, that he could help us to be free if we would listen, that he would never be free until we did. Yet, there was no battle in his face now. I heard what he had gone through, and would continue to go through until he came to rest in earth. He had made it his: that long line, of which we knew only Mama and Daddy. And he was giving it back, as everything must be given back, so that, passing through death, it can live forever. I saw my mother's face again, and felt, for the first time, how the stones of the road she had walked on must have bruised her feet. I saw the moon-lit road where my father's brother died. And it brought something else back to me, and carried me past it. I saw my little girl again and felt Isabel's tears again, and I felt my own tears begin to rise. And I was yet aware that this was only a moment, that the world waited outside, as hungry as a tiger, and that trouble stretched above us, longer than the sky.

Then it was over. Creole and Sonny let out their breath, both soaking wet, and grinning. There was a lot of applause and some of it was real. In the dark, the girl came by and I asked her to take drinks to the bandstand. There was a long pause, while they talked up there in the indigo light and after awhile I saw the girl put a Scotch and milk on top of the piano for Sonny. He didn't seem to notice it, but just before they started playing again, he sipped from it and looked toward me, and nodded. Then he put it back on top of the piano. For me, then, as they began to play again, it glowed and shook above my brother's head like the very cup of trembling.°

Questions

1. From whose point of view is "Sonny's Blues" told? How do the narrator's values and experiences affect his view of the story?

2. What is the older brother's profession? Does it suggest anything about his personality?

3. How would this story change if it were told by Sonny?

4. What event prompts the narrator to write to his brother?

5. What does the narrator's mother ask him to do for Sonny? Does the older brother keep his promise?

6. The major characters in this story are called Mama, Daddy, and Sonny (the older brother is never named or even nicknamed). How do these names affect our sense of the story?

7. Reread the last four paragraphs and explain the significance of the statement "Now these are Sonny's blues." How has Sonny made this music his own?

wishing him Godspeed: wishing success. *cup of trembling*: image of redemptive suffering from Isaiah 51:15-22—"See, I have taken out of your hand the cup of trembling, the dregs of the cup of My fury; you shall no longer drink it."

■ WRITING *effectively*

James Baldwin on Writing

Race and the African American Writer
1955

I know, in any case, that the most crucial time in my own development came when I was forced to recognize that I was a kind of bastard of the West; when I followed the line of my past I did not find myself in Europe but in Africa. And this meant that in some subtle way, in a really profound way, I brought to Shakespeare, Bach, Rembrandt, to the stones of Paris, to the cathedral at Chartres, and to the Empire State Building, a special attitude. These were not

James Baldwin

really my creations, they did not contain my history; I might search in them in vain forever for any reflection of myself. I was an interloper; this was not my heritage. At the same time I had no other heritage which I could possibly hope to use—I had certainly been unfitted for the jungle or the tribe. I would have to appropriate these white centuries, I would have to make them mine—I would have to accept my special attitude, my special place in this scheme—otherwise I would have no place in *any* scheme. What was the most difficult was the fact that I was forced to admit something I had always hidden from myself, which the American Negro has had to hide from himself as the price of his public progress; that I hated and feared the world. And this meant, not only that I thus gave the world an altogether murderous power over me, but also that in such a self-destroying limbo I could never hope to write.

One writes out of one thing only—one's own experience. Everything depends on how relentlessly one forces from this experience the last drop, sweet or bitter, it can possibly give. This is the only real concern of the artist, to recreate out of the disorder of life that order which is art. The difficulty then, for me, of being a Negro writer was the fact that I was, in effect, prohibited from examining my own experience too closely by the tremendous demands and the very real dangers of my social situation.

I don't think the dilemma outlined above is uncommon. I do think, since writers work in the disastrously explicit medium of language, that it goes a little way towards explaining why, out of the enormous resources of Negro speech and life, and despite the example of Negro music, prose written by Negroes has been generally speaking so pallid and so harsh. I have not written about being a Negro at such length because I expect that to be my only subject, but only because it was the gate I had to unlock before I could hope to write about anything else.

From "Autobiographical Notes"

THINKING ABOUT POINT OF VIEW

When we hear an outlandish piece of news, something that doesn't quite add up, we're well advised, as the saying goes, to consider the source. The same is true when we read a short story.

- ▪ **Consider who is telling the story.** A story's point of view determines how much confidence a reader should have in the events related. A story told from a third-person omniscient point of view generally provides a sense of authority and stability that makes the narrative seem reliable.
- ▪ **Ask why the narrator is telling the story.** The use of a first-person narrator, on the other hand, often suggests a certain bias, especially when the narrator relates events in which he or she has played a part. In such cases the narrator sometimes has an obvious interest in the audience's accepting his or her version of the story as truth.
- ▪ **Think about whether anything important is being left out of the story.** Is something of obvious importance to the situation not being reported? Understanding the limits of a narrator's point of view is key to interpreting what a story says.

CHECKLIST: Writing About Point of View

- ☐ How is the story narrated? Is it told in the third or the first person?
- ☐ If the story is told in the third person, is the point of view omniscient or does it confine itself to what is perceived by a particular character?
- ☐ What is gained by this choice?
- ☐ If the story is told by a first-person narrator, what is the speaker's main reason for telling the story? What does the narrator have to gain by making us believe his or her account?
- ☐ Does the first-person narrator fully understand his or her own motivations? Is there some important aspect of the narrator's character or situation that is being overlooked?
- ☐ Is there anything peculiar about the first-person narrator? Does this peculiarity create any suspicions about the narrator's accuracy or reliability?
- ☐ What does the narrator's perspective add? Would the story seem as memorable if related from another narrative angle?

TOPICS FOR WRITING ON POINT OF VIEW

1. Choose a story from this book and analyze how point of view contributes to the story's overall meaning. Come up with a thesis sentence and back up your argument with specific observations about the text. Incorporate at least three quotations and document them, as explained in Chapter 46. Some stories that might lend themselves well to this assignment are "Sonny's Blues," "Cathedral" (Chapter 3), "The Tell-Tale Heart" (Chapter 12), and "The First Year of My Life."

2. Retell the events in "A & P" (Chapter 1) from the point of view of one of the story's minor characters: Lengel, or Stokesie, or one of the girls. How does the story's emphasis change?

3. Here is another writing exercise to help you sense what a difference point of view makes. Write a short statement from the point of view of William Faulkner's Homer Barron on "My Affair with Miss Emily."

4. Imagine a story such as "A & P" or "A Rose for Emily" told by an omniscient third-person narrator. Write several paragraphs about what would be lost (or gained) by such a change.

5. Choose any tale from "Gallery of International Voices" (Chapter 13) or "Stories for Further Reading" (Chapter 14) and, in a paragraph or two, describe how point of view colors the general meaning. If you like, you may argue that the story might be told more effectively from an alternate point of view.

6. Think back to a confrontation in your own life and describe that event from a point of view contrary to your own. Trying to imagine yourself inside your speaker's personality, present the facts as that person would, as convincingly as you can.

7. With "Sonny's Blues" in mind, write about a family member or friend from your own point of view, allowing, as Baldwin does, an understanding of that person's perspective to slowly develop.

8. Tell the story of a confrontation—biographical or fictional—from the point of view of a minor character peripheral to the central action. You could, for instance, tell the story of a disastrous first date from the point of view of the unlucky waitress who serves the couple dinner.

▶ TERMS FOR *review*

Points of View

Total omniscience ▶ Point of view in which the narrator knows everything about all of the characters and events in a story. A narrator with total omniscience can move freely from one character to another. Generally, a totally omniscient narrative is written in the third person.

Limited or selective omniscience ▶ Point of view in which the narrator sees into the minds of some but not all of the characters. Most typically, limited omniscience sees through the eyes of one major or minor character.

Impartial omniscience ▶ Point of view employed when an omniscient narrator, who presents the thoughts and actions of the characters, does not judge them or comment on them.

Editorial omniscience ▶ Point of view employed when an omniscient narrator goes beyond reporting the thoughts of his characters to make a critical judgment or commentary, revealing the narrator's own thoughts or attitudes.

Objective point of view ▶ Point of view in which the third-person narrator merely reports dialogue and action with little or no interpretation or access to the characters' minds.

Types of Narrators

Omniscient or all-knowing narrator ▶ A narrator who has the ability to move freely through the consciousness of any character. The omniscient narrator also has complete knowledge of all of the external events in a story.

Participant or first-person narrator ▶ A narrator who is a participant in the action. Such a narrator refers to himself or herself as "I" and may be a major or minor character in the story.

Observer ▶ A first-person narrator who is relatively detached from or plays only a minor role in the events described.

Nonparticipant or third-person narrator ▶ A narrator who does not appear in the story as a character but is usually capable of revealing the thoughts and motives of one or more characters.

Innocent or naive narrator ▶ A character who fails to understand all the implications of the story he or she tells. The innocent narrator—often a child or childlike adult—is frequently used by an author to generate irony, sympathy, or pity by creating a gap between what the narrator perceives and what the reader knows.

Unreliable narrator ▶ A narrator who—intentionally or unintentionally—relates events in a subjective or distorted manner. The author usually provides some indication early on in such stories that the narrator is not to be completely trusted.

Narrative Techniques

Interior monologue ▶ An extended presentation of a character's thoughts in a narrative. Usually written in the present tense and printed without quotation marks, an interior monologue reads as if the character were speaking aloud to himself or herself, for the reader to overhear.

Stream of consciousness ▶ A type of modern narration that uses various literary devices, especially interior monologue, in an attempt to duplicate the subjective and associative nature of human consciousness.

3 CHARACTER

Show me a character without anxieties
and I will show you a boring book.

—MARGARET ATWOOD

What You Will Learn in This Chapter

- To define *character*
- To identify types of characters
- To explain motivation and development
- To analyze the role of a character in a story

From popular fiction and drama, both classic and contemporary, we are acquainted with many stereotyped characters. Called **stock characters**, they are often known by an outstanding trait or traits: the *bragging* soldier of Greek and Roman comedy, the Prince *Charming* of fairy tales, the *mad* scientist of horror movies, the *fearlessly reckless* police detective of urban action films, the *brilliant but alcoholic* brain surgeon of medical thrillers on television. Stock characters are especially convenient for writers of commercial fiction: they require little detailed portraiture, for we already know them well. Most writers of the literary story, however, attempt to create characters who strike us not as stereotypes but as unique individuals. While stock characters tend to have single dominant virtues and vices, characters in the finest contemporary short stories tend to have many facets, like people we meet.

A **character**, then, is presumably an imagined person who inhabits a story. Usually we recognize, in the main characters of a story, human personalities that become familiar to us. If the story seems "true to life," we generally find that its characters act in a reasonably consistent manner and that the author has provided them with motivation: sufficient reason to behave as they do. Should a character behave in a sudden and unexpected way, seeming to deny what we have been told about his or her nature or personality, we trust that there was a reason for this behavior and that sooner or later we will discover it.

In good fiction, characters often change or develop. In *A Christmas Carol*, Charles Dickens tells how Ebenezer Scrooge, a tightfisted miser, reforms overnight, suddenly gives to the poor, and endeavors to assist his clerk's struggling family. But Dickens amply demonstrates why Scrooge had such a change of heart: four ghostly visitors—stirring kind memories the old miser had forgotten and also warning him of the probable consequences of his habits—provide the character (and hence the story) with adequate motivation.

CHARACTERIZATION

To borrow the useful terms of English novelist E. M. Forster, characters may seem flat or round, depending on whether a writer sketches or sculpts them. A **flat character** has only one outstanding trait or feature, or at most a few distinguishing marks: for example, the familiar stock character of the mad scientist, with his lust for absolute power and his crazily gleaming eyes. Flat characters, however, need not be stock characters: in all of literature there is probably only one Tiny Tim, though his functions in A *Christmas Carol* are mainly to invoke blessings and to remind others of their Christian duties.

Some writers, such as George R. R. Martin, populate their novels with hosts of characters. Often they distinguish the flat ones by giving each a single odd physical feature or mannerism—a nervous twitch, a piercing gaze, an obsessive fondness for oysters. **Round characters**, however, present us with more facets—that is, their authors portray them in greater depth and in more generous detail. Such a round character may appear to us only as he appears to the other characters in the story. If their views of him differ, we will see him from more than one side. In other stories, we enter a character's mind and come to know him through his own thoughts, feelings, and perceptions.

Character Development

Flat characters tend to stay the same throughout a story, but round characters often change—they learn or become enlightened, they grow or deteriorate. In William Faulkner's "Barn Burning" (Chapter 5), the boy Sarty Snopes, driven to defy his proud and violent father, becomes at the story's end more knowing and more mature. (Some critics call a fixed character **static**; a changing one, **dynamic**.) This is not to damn a flat character as an inferior creation. In most fiction—even the greatest—minor characters tend to be flat instead of round. Why? Rounding them would cost time and space; and so enlarged, they might only distract us from the main characters.

What's in a Name?

"A character, first of all, is the noise of his name," according to novelist William Gass. Names, chosen artfully, can indicate natures. A simple illustration is the completely virtuous Squire Allworthy, the foster father in *Tom Jones* by Henry Fielding. Subtler, perhaps, is the custom of giving a character a name that makes an **allusion**: a reference to some famous person, place, or thing. For his central characters in *Moby-Dick*, Herman Melville chose names from the Old Testament, calling his tragic and domineering Ahab after a biblical tyrant who came to a bad end, and his wandering narrator Ishmael after a biblical outcast. Whether or not it includes such a reference, a good name often reveals the character of the character. Charles Dickens, a vigorous and richly suggestive christener, named a couple of shyster lawyers Dodgson and Fogg (suggesting dodging evasiveness and foglike obfuscation), and named two heartless educators, who grimly drill their schoolchildren in "hard facts," Gradgind and M'Choakumchild.

Hero Versus Antihero

Instead of a hero, many a recent novel has featured an **antihero**: a protagonist conspicuously lacking in one or more of the usual attributes of a traditional **hero**, such as bravery, skill, idealism, or sense of purpose. The antihero is an ordinary, inglorious citizen of the modern world, usually drawn (according to the Irish short story writer Sean O'Faolain) as someone "groping, puzzled, cross, mocking, frustrated, and isolated."

If epic poets once drew their heroes as decisive leaders, embodying their people's highest ideals, antiheroes tend to be loners, without admirable qualities, just barely able to survive. A gulf separates Leopold Bloom, antihero of James Joyce's novel *Ulysses*, from the hero of the Greek *Odyssey*. In Homer's epic, Ulysses wanders the Mediterranean, battling monsters and overcoming enchantments. In Joyce's novel, Bloom wanders the littered streets of Dublin, peddling advertising space.

MOTIVATION

At the heart of most stories is **motivation**—the cause (or causes) of a character's actions. Motivation is what animates a story and justifies the behavior of each character, especially the protagonist, whose motivation usually sets a story in action. In simple narratives, such as a fable or fairy tale, the motivation tends to be straightforward—a prince needs to rescue a princess, a poor boy sets off to find a fortune. In Aesop's famous fable "The Fox and the Grapes" (Chapter 1), the fox is hungry and wants to eat the grapes hanging high above him. That visceral motivation explains every event that follows. In a more sophisticated story, such as Raymond Carver's "Cathedral" (later in this chapter), the motivation is more subtle and complex. Carver's protagonist is a man who reluctantly welcomes a blind visitor into his home. The protagonist doesn't want to meet the man, but he is forced to offer hospitality because his wife has demanded that he be courteous, as proof of his love to her. His motivation is neither pure nor simple, and his mixed feelings both give the story its realistic atmosphere and also lead to the narrative's unexpected climax. Motivation usually reveals a character's psychological traits and values. In a good story the motivation makes the plot feel inevitable, even when it takes a surprising turn.

Tobias Wolff

Bullet in the Brain

1997

Tobias Wolff was born in Birmingham, Alabama, in 1945, the son of an aerospace engineer and a waitress and secretary. Following his parents' divorce, Tobias moved with his mother to Washington State while his older brother, Geoffrey, remained with their father (a pathological liar who was the subject of Geoffrey Wolff's acclaimed memoir The Duke of Deception*). Tobias Wolff's own memoir,* This Boy's Life *(1989), describes, among other things, his tense relationship with his abusive stepfather; it was the basis for the 1993 film starring Robert De Niro and Leonardo DiCaprio. In 1964 Wolff joined the army, where he spent four years, including a year in Vietnam as a Special Forces language expert. This experience is recounted in a second memoir,* In Pharaoh's Army: Memories of the Lost War *(1994). After his military service, he earned a*

Tobias Wolff

bachelor's degree at Oxford University and a master's at Stanford University, where he taught in the creative writing program for twenty years. Wolff is the author of six volumes of fiction: the novella The Barracks Thief (1984, PEN/Faulkner Award), the novel Old School (2003), and four volumes of short stories, most recently Our Story Begins: New and Selected Stories (2008).

Acknowledging Raymond Carver (his onetime faculty colleague at Syracuse University) and Flannery O'Connor as influences, Wolff writes stories that, in the words of one critic, create a "sometimes comic, always compassionate world of ordinary people who suffer twentieth century martyrdoms of growing up, growing old, loving and lacking love, living with parents and lovers and wives and their own weaknesses." Wolff lives in Northern California.

Anders couldn't get to the bank until just before it closed, so of course the line was endless and he got stuck behind two women whose loud, stupid conversation put him in a murderous temper. He was never in the best of tempers anyway, Anders—a book critic known for the weary, elegant savagery with which he dispatched almost everything he reviewed.

With the line still doubled around the rope, one of the bank tellers stuck a "POSITION CLOSED" sign in her window and walked to the back of the bank, where she leaned against a desk and began to pass the time with a man shuffling papers. The women in front of Anders broke off their conversation and watched the teller with hatred. "Oh, that's nice," one of them said. She turned to Anders and added, confident of his accord, "One of those little human touches that keep us coming back for more."

Anders had conceived his own towering hatred of the teller, but he immediately turned it on the presumptuous crybaby in front of him. "Damned unfair," he said, "Tragic, really. If they're not chopping off the wrong leg, or bombing your ancestral village, they're closing their positions."

She stood her ground. "I didn't say it was tragic," she said, "I just think it's a pretty lousy way to treat your customers."

"Unforgivable," Anders said, "Heaven will take note."   5

She sucked in her cheeks but stared past him and said nothing. Anders saw that the other woman, her friend, was looking in the same direction. And then the tellers stopped what they were doing, and the customers slowly turned, and silence came over the bank. Two man wearing black ski masks and blue business suits were standing to the side of the door. One of them had a pistol pressed against the guard's neck. The guard's eyes were closed, and his lips were moving. The other man had a sawed-off shotgun. "Keep your big mouth shut!" the man with the pistol said, though no one had spoken a word. "One of you tellers hits the alarm, you're all dead meat. Got it?"

The tellers nodded.

"Oh, bravo," Anders said. "Dead meat." He turned to the woman in front of him. "Great script, eh? The stern, brass-knuckled poetry of the dangerous classes."

She looked at him with drowning eyes.

The man with the shotgun pushed the guard to his knees. He handed the shot-   10 gun to his partner and yanked the guard's wrists up behind his back and locked them together with a pair of handcuffs. He toppled him onto the floor with a kick between the shoulder blades. Then he took his shotgun back and went over to the security gate at the end of the counter. He was short and heavy and moved with peculiar slowness, even torpor. "Buzz him in," his partner said. The man with the shotgun opened the gate and sauntered along the line of tellers, handing each of them a Hefty bag. When he came to the empty position he looked over at the man with the pistol, who said, "Whose slot is that?"

Anders watched the teller. She put her hand to her throat and turned to the man she'd been talking to. He nodded. "Mine," she said.

"Then get your ugly ass in gear and fill that bag."

"There you go," Anders said to the woman in front of him. "Justice is done."

"Hey! Bright boy! Did I tell you to talk?"

"No," Anders said.   15

"Then shut your trap."

"Did you hear that?" Anders said. "'Bright boy.' Right out of 'The Killers.'"°

"Please be quiet," the woman said.

"Hey, you deaf or what?" The man with the pistol walked over to Anders. He poked the weapon into Anders' gut. "You think I'm playing games?"

"No," Anders said, but the barrel tickled like a stiff finger and he had to fight   20
back the titters. He did this by making himself stare into the man's eyes, which were clearly visible behind the holes in the mask: pale blue and rawly red-rimmed. The man's left eyelid kept twitching. He breathed out a piercing, ammoniac smell that shocked Anders more than anything that had happened, and he was beginning to develop a sense of unease when the man prodded him again with the pistol.

"You like me, bright boy!" he said. "You want to suck my dick!"

"No," Anders said.

"Then stop looking at me."

Anders fixed his gaze on the man's shiny wing-tip shoes.

"Not down there. Up there." He stuck the pistol under Anders' chin and pushed   25
it upwards until Anders was looking at the ceiling.

Anders had never paid much attention to that part of the bank, a pompous old building with marble floors and counters and pillars, and gilt scrollwork over the tellers' cages. The domed ceiling had been decorated with mythological figures whose fleshy, toga-draped ugliness Anders had taken in at a glance years earlier and afterward declined to notice. Now he had no choice but to scrutinize the painter's work. It was even worse than he remembered, and all of it executed with the utmost gravity. The artist had a few tricks up his sleeve and used them again and again—a certain rosy blush on the underside of the clouds, a coy backwards glance on the faces of the cupids and fauns. The ceiling was crowded with various dramas, but the one that caught Anders' eye was Zeus and Europa—portrayed, in this rendition, as a bull ogling a cow from behind a haystack. To make the cow sexy, the painter had canted her hips suggestively and given her long, droopy eyelashes through which she gazed back at the bull with sultry welcome. The bull wore a smirk and his eyebrows were arched. If there'd been a bubble coming out of his mouth, it would have said, "Hubba hubba."

"What's so funny, bright boy?"

"Nothing."

"You think I'm comical? You think I'm some kind of clown?"

"No."   30

"Fuck with me again, you're history. Capiche?"

Anders burst out laughing. He covered his mouth with both hands and said, "I'm sorry, I'm sorry," then snorted helplessly through his fingers and said, "Capiche—oh,

---

"The Killers": a short story by Ernest Hemingway about two gangsters who visit a suburban Chicago diner in search of a prizefighter they have been told to murder. They use the term "bright boy" to condescendingly and aggressively address the other men in the diner.

God—*capiche*," and at that the man with the pistol raised the pistol and shot Anders right in the head.

The bullet smashed Anders' skull and ploughed through his brain and exited behind his right ear, scattering shards of bone into the cerebral cortex, the corpus callosum, back toward the basal ganglia, and down into the thalamus. But before all this occurred, the first appearance of the bullet in the cerebrum set off a crackling chain of iron transports and neuro-transmissions. Because of their peculiar origin these traced a peculiar pattern, flukishly calling into life a summer afternoon some forty years past, and long since lost to memory. After striking the cranium the bullet was moving at 900 feet per second, a pathetically sluggish, glacial pace compared to the synaptic lightning that flashed around it. Once in the brain, that is, the bullet came under the mediation of brain time, which gave Anders plenty of leisure to contemplate the scene that, in a phrase he would have abhorred, "passed before his eyes."

It is worth noting what Anders did not remember, given what he did remember. He did not remember his first lover, Sherry, or what he had most madly loved about her, before it came to irritate him—her unembarrassed carnality, and especially the cordial way she had with his unit, which she called Mr. Mole, as in, "Uh-oh, looks like Mr. Mole wants to play," and, "let's hide Mr. Mole!" Anders did not remember his wife, whom he had also loved before she exhausted him with her predictability, or his daughter, now a sullen professor of economics at Dartmouth. He did not remember standing just outside his daughter's door as she lectured her bear about his naughtiness and described the truly appalling punishment Paws would receive unless he changed his ways. He did not remember a single line of the hundreds of poems he committed to memory in his youth so that he could give himself the shivers at will—not "Silent, upon a peak in Darien," or "My God, I heard this day," or "All my pretty ones? Did you say all? O hell-kite! All?" None of these did he remember; not one. Anders did not remember his dying mother saying of his father, "I should have stabbed him in his sleep."

He did not remember Professor Josephs telling his class how Athenian prisoners in Sicily had been released if they could recite Aeschylus, and then reciting Aeschylus himself, right there, in the Greek. Anders did not remember how his eyes had burned at those sounds. He did not remember the surprise of seeing a college classmate's name on the jacket of a novel not long after they graduated, or the respect he had felt after reading the book. He did not remember the pleasure of giving respect.

35

Nor did Anders remember seeing a woman leap to her death from the building opposite his own just days after his daughter was born. He did not remember shouting, "Lord have mercy!" He did not remember deliberately crashing his father's car into a tree, or having his ribs kicked in by three policemen at an anti-war rally, or waking himself up with laughter. He did not remember when he began to regard the heap of books on his desk with boredom and dread, or when he grew angry at writers for writing them. He did not remember when everything began to remind him of something else.

This is what Anders remembered. Heat. A baseball field. Yellow grass, the whirr of insects, himself leaning against a tree as the boys of the neighborhood gather for a pickup game. He looks on as the others argue the relative genius of Mantle and Mays. They have been worrying this subject all summer, and it has become tedious to Anders; an oppression, like the heat.

Then the last two boys arrive, Coyle and a cousin of his from Mississippi. Anders has never met Coyle's cousin before and will never see him again. He says hi with the rest but takes no further notice of him until they've chosen sides and someone asks the cousin what position he wants to play. "Shortstop," the boy says. "Short's the best position they is." Anders turns and looks at him. He wants to hear Coyle's cousin repeat what he's just said, but he knows better than to ask. The others will think he's being a jerk, ragging the kid for his grammar. But that isn't it, not at all—it's that Anders is strangely roused, elated, by those final two words, their pure unexpectedness and their music. He takes the field in a trance, repeating them to himself.

The bullet is already in the brain; it won't be outrun forever, or charmed to a halt. In the end it will do its work and leave the troubled skull behind, dragging its comet's tail of memory and hope and talent and love into the marble hall of commerce. That can't be helped. But for now Anders can still make time. Time for the shadows to lengthen on the grass, time for the tethered dog to bark at the flying ball, time for the boy in right field to smack his sweat-blackened mitt and softly chant, *They is, They is, They is.*

Questions

1. Describe the character of the adult Anders. Why do you think Wolff chose to make him a book critic?
2. Does Anders seem to experience the robbery as a real-life event? In what ways is his reaction different from the other customers, and why do you suppose that is?
3. Is there anything symbolic about setting the story in a "marble hall of commerce," especially in contrast to the baseball field conjured up in his memory?
4. Considering Anders's occupation as a book critic and the bank robber's reliance on cliché, what might the robber symbolize for Anders? What sort of character is the bank robber—flat, round, or stock?
5. Why did Wolff decide to tell us what Anders did *not* remember?
6. What is the significance of the afternoon that Anders does remember? What do the final words, *They is,* symbolize for him?

Joyce Carol Oates

Where Are You Going, Where Have You Been?   1970

Joyce Carol Oates was born in 1938 into a blue-collar, Catholic family in Lockport, New York. As an under-graduate at Syracuse University, she won a Mademoiselle magazine award for fiction. After graduating with top honors, she took a master's degree in English at the University of Wisconsin and went on to teach at several universities: Detroit, Windsor, and Princeton. A remarkably prolific writer, Oates has produced more than twenty-five collections of stories, including Lovely, Dark, and Deep *(2014), and more than forty novels, including* them *(1969), winner of a National Book Award,* Because It Is Bitter,*

Joyce Carol Oates

and Because It Is My Heart (1990), Blonde *(2000), and, more recently,* A Man Without Shadow *(2016) and* A Book of American Martyrs *(2017). She also writes poetry, plays, and literary criticism.* On Boxing *(1987) is her nonfiction memoir and study of fighters and fighting. Violence and the macabre may inhabit her best stories, but Oates has insisted that these elements in her work are never gratuitous. The 1985 film*

Smooth Talk, *directed by Joyce Chopra, was based on "Where Are You Going, Where Have You Been?"*

For Bob Dylan

Her name was Connie. She was fifteen and she had a quick nervous giggling habit of craning her neck to glance into mirrors, or checking other people's faces to make sure her own was all right. Her mother, who noticed everything and knew everything and who hadn't much reason any longer to look at her own face, always scolded Connie about it. "Stop gawking at yourself, who are you? You think you're so pretty?" she would say. Connie would raise her eyebrows at these familiar complaints and look right through her mother, into a shadowy vision of herself as she was right at that moment: she knew she was pretty and that was everything. Her mother had been pretty once too, if you could believe those old snapshots in the album, but now her looks were gone and that was why she was always after Connie.

"Why don't you keep your room clean like your sister? How've you got your hair fixed—what the hell stinks? Hair spray? You don't see your sister using that junk."

Her sister June was twenty-four and still lived at home. She was a secretary in the high school Connie attended, and if that wasn't bad enough—with her in the same building—she was so plain and chunky and steady that Connie had to hear her praised all the time by her mother and her mother's sisters. June did this, June did that, she saved money and helped clean the house and cooked and Connie couldn't do a thing, her mind was all filled with trashy daydreams. Their father was away at work most of the time and when he came home he wanted supper and he read the newspaper at supper and after supper he went to bed. He didn't bother talking much to them, but around his bent head Connie's mother kept picking at her until Connie wished her mother was dead and she herself was dead and it was all over. "She makes me want to throw up sometimes," she complained to her friends. She had a high, breathless, amused voice which made everything she said sound a little forced, whether it was sincere or not.

There was one good thing: June went places with girl friends of hers, girls who were just as plain and steady as she, and so when Connie wanted to do that her mother had no objections. The father of Connie's best girl friend drove the girls the three miles to town and left them off at a shopping plaza, so that they could walk through the stores or go to a movie, and when he came to pick them up again at eleven he never bothered to ask what they had done.

They must have been familiar sights, walking around that shopping plaza in their shorts and flat ballerina slippers that always scuffed the sidewalk, with charm bracelets jingling on their thin wrists; they would lean together to whisper and laugh secretly if someone passed by who amused or interested them. Connie had long dark blond hair that drew anyone's eye to it, and she wore part of it pulled up on her head and puffed out and the rest of it she let fall down her back. She wore a pull-over jersey blouse that looked one way when she was at home and another way when she was away from home. Everything about her had two sides to it, one for home and one for anywhere that was not home: her walk that could be childlike and bobbing, or languid enough to make anyone think she was hearing music in her head, her mouth which was pale and smirking most of the time, but bright and pink on these evenings out, her laugh

5

which was cynical and drawling at home—"Ha, ha, very funny"—but high-pitched and nervous anywhere else, like the jingling of the charms on her bracelet.

Sometimes they did go shopping or to a movie, but sometimes they went across the highway, ducking fast across the busy road, to a drive-in restaurant where older kids hung out. The restaurant was shaped like a big bottle, though squatter than a real bottle, and on its cap was a revolving figure of a grinning boy who held a hamburger aloft. One night in mid-summer they ran across, breathless with daring, and right away someone leaned out a car window and invited them over, but it was just a boy from high school they didn't like. It made them feel good to be able to ignore him. They went up through the maze of parked and cruising cars to the bright-lit, fly-infested restaurant, their faces pleased and expectant as if they were entering a sacred building that loomed out of the night to give them what haven and what blessing they yearned for. They sat at the counter and crossed their legs at the ankles, their thin shoulders rigid with excitement, and listened to the music that made everything so good: the music was always in the background like music at a church service, it was something to depend upon.

A boy named Eddie came in to talk with them. He sat backwards on his stool, turning himself jerkily around in semi-circles and then stopping and turning again, and after a while he asked Connie if she would like something to eat. She said she did and so she tapped her friend's arm on her way out—her friend pulled her face up into a brave droll look—and Connie said she would meet her at eleven, across the way. "I just hate to leave her like that," Connie said earnestly, but the boy said that she wouldn't be alone for long. So they went out to his car and on the way Connie couldn't help but let her eyes wander over the windshields and faces all around her, her face gleaming with a joy that had nothing to do with Eddie or even this place; it might have been the music. She drew her shoulders up and sucked in her breath with the pure pleasure of being alive, and just at that moment she happened to glance at a face just a few feet from hers. It was a boy with shaggy black hair, in a convertible jalopy painted gold. He stared at her and then his lips widened into a grin. Connie slit her eyes at him and turned away, but she couldn't help glancing back and there he was still watching her. He wagged a finger and laughed and said, "Gonna get you, baby," and Connie turned away again without Eddie noticing anything.

She spent three hours with him, at the restaurant where they ate hamburgers and drank Cokes in wax cups that were always sweating, and then down an alley a mile or so away, and when he left her off at five to eleven only the movie house was still open at the plaza. Her girl friend was there, talking with a boy. When Connie came up the two girls smiled at each other and Connie said, "How was the movie?" and the girl said, "*You* should know." They rode off with the girl's father, sleepy and pleased, and Connie couldn't help but look at the darkened shopping plaza with its big empty parking lot and its signs that were faded and ghostly now, and over at the drive-in restaurant where cars were still circling tirelessly. She couldn't hear the music at this distance.

Next morning June asked her how the movie was and Connie said, "So-so."

She and that girl and occasionally another girl went out several times a week that way, and the rest of the time Connie spent around the house—it was summer vacation—getting in her mother's way and thinking, dreaming, about the boys she met. But all the boys fell back and dissolved into a single face that was not even a face, but an idea, a feeling, mixed up with the urgent insistent pounding of the music and the humid night air of July. Connie's mother kept dragging her back to the daylight by finding things for her to do or saying, suddenly, "What's this about the Pettinger girl?"

And Connie would say nervously, "Oh, her. That dope." She always drew thick clear lines between herself and such girls, and her mother was simple and kindly enough to believe her. Her mother was so simple, Connie thought, that it was maybe cruel to fool her so much. Her mother went scuffling around the house in old bedroom slippers and complained over the telephone to one sister about the other, then the other called up and the two of them complained about the third one. If June's name was mentioned her mother's tone was approving, and if Connie's name was mentioned it was disapproving. This did not really mean she disliked Connie and actually Connie thought that her mother preferred her to June because she was prettier, but the two of them kept up a pretense of exasperation, a sense that they were tugging and struggling over something of little value to either of them. Sometimes, over coffee, they were almost friends, but something would come up—some vexation that was like a fly buzzing suddenly around their heads—and their faces went hard with contempt.

One Sunday Connie got up at eleven—none of them bothered with church— and washed her hair so that it could dry all day long, in the sun. Her parents and sister were going to a barbecue at an aunt's house and Connie said no, she wasn't interested, rolling her eyes to let her mother know just what she thought of it. "Stay home alone then," her mother said sharply. Connie sat out back in a lawn chair and watched them drive away, her father quiet and bald, hunched around so that he could back the car out, her mother with a look that was still angry and not at all softened through the windshield, and in the back seat poor old June all dressed up as if she didn't know what a barbecue was, with all the running yelling kids and the flies. Connie sat with her eyes closed in the sun, dreaming and dazed with the warmth about her as if this were a kind of love, the caresses of love, and her mind slipped over onto thoughts of the boy she had been with the night before and how nice he had been, how sweet it always was, not the way someone like June would suppose but sweet, gentle, the way it was in movies and promised in songs; and when she opened her eyes she hardly knew where she was, the back yard ran off into weeds and a fence-line of trees and behind it the sky was perfectly blue and still. The asbestos "ranch house" that was now three years old startled her—it looked small. She shook her head as if to get awake.

It was too hot. She went inside the house and turned on the radio to drown out the quiet. She sat on the edge of her bed, barefoot, and listened for an hour and a half to a program called XYZ Sunday Jamboree, record after record of hard, fast, shrieking songs she sang along with, interspersed by exclamations from "Bobby King": "An' look here you girls at Napoleon's—Son and Charley want you to pay real close attention to this song coming up!"

And Connie paid close attention herself, bathed in a glow of slow-pulsed joy that seemed to rise mysteriously out of the music itself and lay languidly about the airless little room, breathed in and breathed out with each gentle rise and fall of her chest.

After a while she heard a car coming up the drive. She sat up at once, startled, 15 because it couldn't be her father so soon. The gravel kept crunching all the way in from the road—the driveway was long—and Connie ran to the window. It was a car she didn't know. It was an open jalopy, painted a bright gold that caught the sunlight opaquely. Her heart began to pound and her fingers snatched at her hair, checking it, and she whispered "Christ, Christ," wondering how bad she looked. The car came to a stop at the side door and the horn sounded four short taps as if this were a signal Connie knew.

She went into the kitchen and approached the door slowly, then hung out the screen door, her bare toes curling down off the step. There were two boys in the car and now she recognized the driver: he had shaggy, shabby black hair that looked crazy as a wig and he was grinning at her.

"I ain't late, am I?" he said.

"Who the hell do you think you are?" Connie said.

"Toldja I'd be out, didn't I?"

"I don't even know who you are." 20

She spoke sullenly, careful to show no interest or pleasure, and he spoke in a fast bright monotone. Connie looked past him to the other boy, taking her time. He had fair brown hair, with a lock that fell onto his forehead. His sideburns gave him a fierce, embarrassed look, but so far he hadn't even bothered to glance at her. Both boys wore sunglasses. The driver's glasses were metallic and mirrored everything in miniature.

"You wanta come for a ride?" he said.

Connie smirked and let her hair fall loose over one shoulder.

"Don'tcha like my car? New paint job," he said. "Hey."

"What?" 25

"You're cute."

She pretended to fidget, chasing flies away from the door.

"Don'tcha believe me, or what?" he said.

"Look, I don't even know who you are," Connie said in disgust.

"Hey, Ellie's got a radio, see. Mine's broke down." He lifted his friend's arm and 30 showed her the little transistor the boy was holding, and now Connie began to hear the music. It was the same program that was playing inside the house.

"Bobby King?" she said.

"I listen to him all the time. I think he's great."

"He's kind of great," Connie said reluctantly.

"Listen, that guy's *great*. He knows where the action is."

Connie blushed a little, because the glasses made it impossible for her to see just 35 what this boy was looking at. She couldn't decide if she liked him or if he was just a jerk, and so she dawdled in the doorway and wouldn't come down or go back inside. She said, "What's all that stuff painted on your car?"

"Can'tcha read it?" He opened the door very carefully, as if he was afraid it might fall off. He slid out just as carefully, planting his feet firmly on the ground, the tiny metallic world in his glasses slowing down like gelatine hardening and in the midst of it Connie's bright green blouse. "This here is my name, to begin with," he said. ARNOLD FRIEND was written in tarlike black letters on the side, with a drawing of a round grinning face that reminded Connie of a pumpkin, except it wore sunglasses. "I wanta introduce myself, I'm Arnold Friend and that's my real name and I'm gonna be your friend, honey, and inside the car's Ellie Oscar, he's kinda shy." Ellie brought his transistor radio up to his shoulder and balanced it there. "Now these numbers are a secret code, honey," Arnold Friend explained. He read off the numbers 33, 19, 17 and raised his eyebrows at her to see what she thought of that, but she didn't think much of it. The left rear fender had been smashed and around it was written, on the gleaming gold background: DONE BY CRAZY WOMAN DRIVER. Connie had to laugh at that. Arnold Friend was pleased at her laughter and looked up at her. "Around the other side's a lot more—you wanta come and see them?"

"No."

"Why not?"

"Why should I?"

"Don'tcha wanta see what's on the car? Don'tcha wanta go for a ride?" 40

"I don't know."

"Why not?"

"I got things to do."

"Like what?"

"Things." 45

He laughed as if she had said something funny. He slapped his thighs. He was standing in a strange way, leaning back against the car as if he were balancing himself. He wasn't tall, only an inch or so taller than she would be if she came down to him. Connie liked the way he was dressed, which was the way all of them dressed: tight faded jeans stuffed into black, scuffed boots, a belt that pulled his waist in and showed how lean he was, and a white pull-over shirt that was a little soiled and showed the hard small muscles of his arms and shoulders. He looked as if he probably did hard work, lifting and carrying things. Even his neck looked muscular. And his face was a familiar face, somehow: the jaw and chin and cheeks slightly darkened, because he hadn't shaved for a day or two, and the nose long and hawk-like, sniffing as if she were a treat he was going to gobble up and it was all a joke.

"Connie, you ain't telling the truth. This is your day set aside for a ride with me and you know it," he said, still laughing. The way he straightened and recovered from his fit of laughing showed that it had been all fake.

"How do you know what my name is?" she said suspiciously.

"It's Connie."

"Maybe and maybe not." 50

"I know my Connie," he said, wagging his finger. Now she remembered him even better, back at the restaurant, and her cheeks warmed at the thought of how she sucked in her breath just at the moment she passed him—how she must have looked to him. And he had remembered her. "Ellie and I come out here especially for you," he said. "Ellie can sit in back. How about it?"

"Where?"

"Where what?"

"Where're we going?"

He looked at her. He took off the sunglasses and she saw how pale the skin 55 around his eyes was, like holes that were not in shadow but instead in light. His eyes were chips of broken glass that catch the light in an amiable way. He smiled. It was as if the idea of going for a ride somewhere, to some place, was a new idea to him.

"Just for a ride, Connie sweetheart."

"I never said my name was Connie," she said.

"But I know what it is. I know your name and all about you, lots of things," Arnold Friend said. He had not moved yet but stood still leaning back against the side of his jalopy. "I took a special interest in you, such a pretty girl, and found out all about you like I know your parents and sister are gone somewheres and I know where and how long they're going to be gone, and I know who you were with last night, and your best girl friend's name is Betty. Right?"

He spoke in a simple lilting voice, exactly as if he were reciting the words to a song. His smile assured her that everything was fine. In the car Ellie turned up the volume on his radio and did not bother to look around at them.

"Ellie can sit in the back seat," Arnold Friend said. He indicated his friend with 60 a casual jerk of his chin, as if Ellie did not count and she should not bother with him.

"How'd you find out all that stuff?" Connie said.

"Listen: Betty Schultz and Tony Fitch and Jimmy Pettinger and Nancy Pettinger," he said, in a chant. "Raymond Stanley and Bob Hutter—"

"Do you know all those kids?"

"I know everybody."

"Look, you're kidding. You're not from around here."

"Sure."

"But—how come we never saw you before?"

"Sure you saw me before," he said. He looked down at his boots, as if he were a little offended. "You just don't remember."

"I guess I'd remember you," Connie said.

"Yeah?" He looked up at this, beaming. He was pleased. He began to mark time with the music from Ellie's radio, tapping his fists lightly together. Connie looked away from his smile to the car, which was painted so bright it almost hurt her eyes to look at it. She looked at that name, ARNOLD FRIEND. And up at the front fender was an expression that was familiar—MAN THE FLYING SAUCERS. It was an expression kids had used the year before, but didn't use this year. She looked at it for a while as if the words meant something to her that she did not yet know.

"What're you thinking about? Huh?" Arnold Friend demanded. "Not worried about your hair blowing around in the car, are you?"

"No."

"Think I maybe can't drive good?"

"How do I know?"

"You're a hard girl to handle. How come?" he said. "Don't you know I'm your friend? Didn't you see me put my sign in the air when you walked by?"

"What sign?"

"My sign." And he drew an X in the air, leaning out toward her. They were maybe ten feet apart. After his hand fell back to his side the X was still in the air, almost visible. Connie let the screen door close and stood perfectly still inside it, listening to the music from her radio and the boy's blend together. She stared at Arnold Friend. He stood there so stiffly relaxed, pretending to be relaxed, with one hand idly on the door handle as if he were keeping himself up that way and had no intention of ever moving again. She recognized most things about him, the tight jeans that showed his thighs and buttocks and the greasy leather boots and the tight shirt, and even that slippery friendly smile of his, that sleepy dreamy smile that all the boys used to get across ideas they didn't want to put into words. She recognized all this and also the singsong way he talked, slightly mocking, kidding, but serious and a little melancholy, and she recognized the way he tapped one fist against the other in homage to the perpetual music behind him. But all these things did not come together.

She said suddenly, "Hey, how old are you?"

His smile faded. She could see then that he wasn't a kid, he was much older—thirty, maybe more. At this knowledge her heart began to pound faster.

"That's a crazy thing to ask. Can'tcha see I'm your own age?"

"Like hell you are."

"Or maybe a coupla years older, I'm eighteen."

"Eighteen?" she said doubtfully.

He grinned to reassure her and lines appeared at the corners of his mouth. His teeth were big and white. He grinned so broadly his eyes became slits and she saw how thick the lashes were, thick and black as if painted with a black tarlike material.

65

70

75

80

Then he seemed to become embarrassed, abruptly, and looked over his shoulder at Ellie. "*Him*, he's crazy," he said. "Ain't he a riot, he's a nut, a real character." Ellie was still listening to the music. His sunglasses told nothing about what he was thinking. He wore a bright orange shirt unbuttoned halfway to show his chest, which was a pale, bluish chest and not muscular like Arnold Friend's. His shirt collar was turned up all around and the very tips of the collar pointed out past his chin as if they were protecting him. He was pressing the transistor radio up against his ear and sat there in a kind of daze, right in the sun.

"He's kinda strange," Connie said.   85

"Hey, she says you're kinda strange! Kinda strange!" Arnold Friend cried. He pounded on the car to get Ellie's attention. Ellie turned for the first time and Connie saw with shock that he wasn't a kid either—he had a fair, hairless face, cheeks reddened slightly as if the veins grew too close to the surface of his skin, the face of a forty-year-old baby. Connie felt a wave of dizziness rise in her at this sight and she stared at him as if waiting for something to change the shock of the moment, make it all right again. Ellie's lips kept shaping words, mumbling along with the words blasting in his ear.

"Maybe you two better go away," Connie said faintly.

"What? How come?" Arnold Friend cried. "We come out here to take you for a ride. It's Sunday." He had the voice of the man on the radio now. It was the same voice, Connie thought. "Don'tcha know it's Sunday all day and honey, no matter who you were with last night today you're with Arnold Friend and don't you forget it!—Maybe you better step out here," he said, and this last was in a different voice. It was a little flatter, as if the heat was finally getting to him.

"No. I got things to do."

"Hey."   90

"You two better leave."

"We ain't leaving until you come with us."

"Like hell I am—"

"Connie, don't fool around with me. I mean, I mean, don't fool *around*," he said, shaking his head. He laughed incredulously. He placed his sunglasses on top of his head, carefully, as if he were indeed wearing a wig, and brought the stems down behind his ears. Connie stared at him, another wave of dizziness and fear rising in her so that for a moment he wasn't even in focus but was just a blur, standing there against his gold car, and she had the idea that he had driven up the driveway all right but had come from nowhere before that and belonged nowhere and that everything about him and even about the music that was so familiar to her was only half real.

"If my father comes and sees you—"   95

"He ain't coming. He's at a barbecue."

"How do you know that?"

"Aunt Tillie's. Right now they're—uh—they're drinking. Sitting around," he said vaguely, squinting as if he were staring all the way to town and over to Aunt Tillie's backyard. Then the vision seemed to get clear and he nodded energetically. "Yeah. Sitting around. There's your sister in a blue dress, huh? And high heels, the poor sad bitch—nothing like you, sweetheart! And your mother's helping some fat woman with the corn, they're cleaning the corn—husking the corn—"

"What fat woman?" Connie cried.

"How do I know what fat woman. I don't know every goddam fat woman in the   100
world!" Arnold Friend laughed.

"Oh, that's Mrs. Hornby. . . . Who invited her?" Connie said. She felt a little light-headed. Her breath was coming quickly.

"She's too fat. I don't like them fat. I like them the way you are, honey," he said, smiling sleepily at her. They stared at each other for a while, through the screen door. He said softly, "Now what you're going to do is this: you're going to come out that door. You're going to sit up front with me and Ellie's going to sit in the back, the hell with Ellie, right? This isn't Ellie's date. You're my date. I'm your lover, honey."

"What? You're crazy—"

"Yes, I'm your lover. You don't know what that is but you will," he said. "I know that too. I know all about you. But look: it's real nice and you couldn't ask for nobody better than me, or more polite. I always keep my word. I'll tell you how it is, I'm always nice at first, the first time. I'll hold you so tight you won't think you have to try to get away or pretend anything because you'll know you can't. And I'll come inside you where it's all secret and you'll give in to me and you'll love me—"

"Shut up! You're crazy!" Connie said. She backed away from the door. She put her hands against her ears as if she'd heard something terrible, something not meant for her. "People don't talk like that, you're crazy," she muttered. Her heart was almost too big now for her chest and its pumping made sweat break out all over her. She looked out to see Arnold Friend pause and then take a step toward the porch lurching. He almost fell. But, like a clever drunken man, he managed to catch his balance. He wobbled in his high boots and grabbed hold of one of the porch posts.   105

"Honey?" he said. "You still listening?"

"Get the hell out of here!"

"Be nice, honey. Listen."

"I'm going to call the police—"

He wobbled again and out of the side of his mouth came a fast spat curse, an   110 aside not meant for her to hear. But even this "Christ!" sounded forced. Then he began to smile again. She watched this smile come, awkward as if he were smiling from inside a mask. His whole face was a mask, she thought wildly, tanned down onto his throat but then running out as if he had plastered makeup on his face but had forgotten about his throat.

"Honey—? Listen, here's how it is. I always tell the truth and I promise you this: I ain't coming in that house after you."

"You better not! I'm going to call the police if you—if you don't—"

"Honey," he said, talking right through her voice, "honey, I'm not coming in there but you are coming out here. You know why?"

She was panting. The kitchen looked like a place she had never seen before, some room she had run inside but which wasn't good enough, wasn't going to help her. The kitchen window had never had a curtain, after three years, and there were dishes in the sink for her to do—probably—and if you ran your hand across the table you'd probably feel something sticky there.

"You listening, honey? Hey?"   115

"—going to call the police—"

"Soon as you touch the phone I don't need to keep my promise and can come inside. You won't want that."

She rushed forward and tried to lock the door. Her fingers were shaking. "But why lock it," Arnold Friend said gently, talking right into her face. "It's just a screen door. It's just nothing." One of his boots was at a strange angle, as if his foot wasn't in it. It pointed out to the left, bent at the ankle. "I mean, anybody can break through a screen door and glass and wood and iron or anything else if he needs to, anybody at all and specially Arnold Friend. If the place got lit up with a fire honey you'd come running out into my arms, right into my arms and safe at home—like you knew I was your lover and'd stopped fooling around. I don't mind a nice shy girl but I don't like no fooling around." Part of those words were spoken with a slight rhythmic lilt, and Connie somehow recognized them—the echo of a song from last year, about a girl rushing into her boyfriend's arms and coming home again—

Connie stood barefoot on the linoleum floor, staring at him. "What do you want?" she whispered.

"I want you," he said.   120

"What?"

"Seen you that night and thought, that's the one, yes sir. I never needed to look any more."

"But my father's coming back. He's coming to get me. I had to wash my hair first—" She spoke in a dry, rapid voice, hardly raising it for him to hear.

"No, your daddy is not coming and yes, you had to wash your hair and you washed it for me. It's nice and shining and all for me, I thank you, sweetheart," he said, with a mock bow, but again he almost lost his balance. He had to bend and adjust his boots. Evidently his feet did not go all the way down; the boots must have been stuffed with something so that he would seem taller. Connie stared out at him and behind him Ellie in the car, who seemed to be looking off toward Connie's right, into nothing. This Ellie said, pulling the words out of the air one after another as if he were just discovering them, "You want me to pull out the phone?"

"Shut your mouth and keep it shut," Arnold Friend said, his face red from bend-   125
ing over or maybe from embarrassment because Connie had seen his boots. "This ain't none of your business."

"What—what are you doing? What do you want?" Connie said. "If I call the police they'll get you, they'll arrest you—"

"Promise was not to come in unless you touch that phone, and I'll keep that promise," he said. He resumed his erect position and tried to force his shoulders back. He sounded like a hero in a movie, declaring something important. He spoke too loudly and it was as if he were speaking to someone behind Connie. "I ain't made plans for coming in that house where I don't belong but just for you to come out to me, the way you should. Don't you know who I am?"

"You're crazy," she whispered. She backed away from the door but did not want to go into another part of the house, as if this would give him permission to come through the door. "What do you . . . You're crazy, you . . . ."

"Huh? What're you saying, honey?"

Her eyes darted everywhere in the kitchen. She could not remember what it was,   130
this room.

"This is how it is, honey: you come out and we'll drive away, have a nice ride. But if you don't come out we're gonna wait till your people come home and then they're all going to get it."

"You want that telephone pulled out?" Ellie said. He held the radio away from his ear and grimaced, as if without the radio the air was too much for him.

"I toldja shut up, Ellie," Arnold Friend said, "you're deaf, get a hearing aid, right? Fix yourself up. This little girl's no trouble and's gonna be nice to me, so Ellie keep to yourself, this ain't your date—right? Don't hem in on me. Don't hog. Don't crush. Don't bird dog. Don't trail me," he said in a rapid meaningless voice, as if he were running through all the expressions he'd learned but was no longer sure which one of them was in style, then rushing on to new ones, making them up with his eyes closed, "Don't crawl under my fence, don't squeeze in my chipmunk hole, don't sniff my glue, suck my popsicle, keep your own greasy fingers on yourself!" He shaded his eyes and peered in at Connie, who was backed against the kitchen table. "Don't mind him honey he's just a creep. He's a dope. Right? I'm the boy for you and like I said you come out here nice like a lady and give me your hand, and nobody else gets hurt, I mean, your nice old bald-headed daddy and your mummy and your sister in her high heels. Because listen: why bring them in this?"

"Leave me alone," Connie whispered.

"Hey, you know that old woman down the road, the one with the chickens and stuff—you know her?" 135

"She's dead!"

"Dead? What? You know her?" Arnold Friend said.

"She's dead—"

"Don't you like her?"

"She's dead—she's—she isn't here any more—" 140

"But don't you like her, I mean, you got something against her? Some grudge or something?" Then his voice dipped as if he were conscious of a rudeness. He touched the sunglasses perched on top of his head as if to make sure they were still there. "Now you be a good girl."

"What are you going to do?"

"Just two things, or maybe three," Arnold Friend said. "But I promise it won't last long and you'll like me that way you get to like people you're close to. You will. It's all over for you here, so come on out. You don't want your people in any trouble, do you?"

She turned and bumped against a chair or something, hurting her leg, but she ran into the back room and picked up the telephone. Something roared in her ear, a tiny roaring, and she was so sick with fear that she could do nothing but listen to it—the telephone was clammy and very heavy and her fingers groped down to the dial but were too weak to touch it. She began to scream into the phone, into the roaring. She cried out, she cried for her mother, she felt her breath start jerking back and forth in her lungs as if it were something Arnold Friend were stabbing her with again and again with no tenderness. A noisy sorrowful wailing rose all about her and she was locked inside it the way she was locked inside the house.

After a while she could hear again. She was sitting on the floor with her wet 145 back against the wall.

Arnold Friend was saying from the door, "That's a good girl. Put the phone back."

She kicked the phone away from her.

"No, honey. Pick it up. Put it back right."

She picked it up and put it back. The dial tone stopped.

"That's a good girl. Now come outside." 150

She was hollow with what had been fear, but what was now just an emptiness. All that screaming had blasted it out of her. She sat, one leg cramped under her, and deep inside her brain was something like a pinpoint of light that kept going and would not let her relax. She thought, I'm not going to see my mother again. She thought, I'm not going to sleep in my bed again. Her bright green blouse was all wet.

Arnold Friend said, in a gentle-loud voice that was like a stage voice, "The place where you came from ain't there any more, and where you had in mind to go is cancelled out. This place you are now—inside your daddy's house—is nothing but a cardboard box I can knock down any time. You know that and always did know it. You hear me?"

She thought, I have got to think. I have to know what to do.

"We'll go out to a nice field, out in the country here where it smells so nice and it's sunny," Arnold Friend said. "I'll have my arms around you so you won't need to try to get away and I'll show you what love is like, what it does. The hell with this house! It looks solid all right," he said. He ran a fingernail down the screen and the noise did not make Connie shiver, as it would have the day before. "Now put your hand on your heart, honey. Feel that? That feels solid too but we know better, be nice to me, be sweet like you can because what else is there for a girl like you but to be sweet and pretty and give in?—and get away before her people come back?"

She felt her pounding heart. Her hand seemed to enclose it. She thought for the   155
first time in her life that it was nothing that was hers, that belonged to her, but just a pounding, living thing inside this body that wasn't really hers either.

"You don't want them to get hurt," Arnold Friend went on. "Now get up, honey. Get up all by yourself."

She stood up.

"Now turn this way. That's right. Come over here to me—Ellie, put that away, didn't I tell you? You dope. You miserable creepy dope," Arnold Friend said. His words were not angry but only part of an incantation. The incantation was kindly. "Now come out through the kitchen to me honey and let's see a smile, try it, you're a brave sweet little girl and now they're eating corn and hotdogs cooked to bursting over an outdoor fire, and they don't know one thing about you and never did and honey you're better than them because not a one of them would have done this for you."

Connie felt the linoleum under her feet; it was cool. She brushed her hair back out of her eyes. Arnold Friend let go of the post tentatively and opened his arms for her, his elbows pointing in toward each other and his wrists limp, to show that this was an embarrassed embrace and a little mocking, he didn't want to make her self-conscious.

She put out her hand against the screen. She watched herself push the door   160
slowly open as if she were safe back somewhere in the other doorway, watching this body and this head of long hair moving out into the sunlight where Arnold Friend waited.

"My sweet little blue-eyed girl," he said, in a half-sung sigh that had nothing to do with her brown eyes but was taken up just the same by the vast sunlit reaches of the land behind him and on all sides of him, so much land that Connie had never seen before and did not recognize except to know that she was going to it.

Questions

1. How is Connie characterized in the first few pages of the story, and how is this characterization important in the events that follow?
2. What hints does Oates give us that Arnold Friend is not what he seems? Do you find him funny—or frightening? Why?
3. How does music work in the story? Does music seem to affect the way that Connie acts and thinks?
4. Oates has described Connie's choice at the end as a selfless, almost heroic, choice. Do you agree with this view? How do you interpret her actions at the end of the story?
5. What do you think happens at the end of the story? What are the possible outcomes of the situation? Which ending do you consider most likely and why?

Toni Morrison

Recitatif

1983

Toni Morrison

Toni Morrison (b. 1931) grew up on the banks of Lake Erie, in the Rust Belt town of Lorain, Ohio. She was the first person in her family to attend college, and decades later, after a remarkable career, she became the first African American woman to win the Nobel Prize in Literature. Other high honors include the Pulitzer Prize and American Book Award for her masterpiece novel Beloved *(1987) and the 2012 Presidential Medal of Freedom, the nation's most prestigious civilian award. Morrison was born Chloe Ardella Wofford, the daughter of a welder and a maid. One of four children, she left working-class Lorain to attend Howard University in Washington, D.C., and later earned a master's degree at Cornell. Morrison worked as a professor and as an editor at Random House, publishing* The Bluest Eye *(1970), her first novel, at age thirty-nine, which she wrote while teaching at Howard and raising two children alone. Other novels include* Sula *(1973),* Song of Solomon *(1977),* Jazz *(1992), and* God Help the Child *(2015).*

In a 1993 interview with the Paris Review, *Morrison spoke about why race is central to her artistic identity. She was asked if she wouldn't rather be thought of as a great writer of literature, rather than specifically as an African American writer: "It's very important to me that my work be African-American; if it assimilates into a different or larger pool, so much the better. But I shouldn't be asked to do that. Joyce is not asked to do that. Tolstoy is not. I mean, they can all be Russian, French, Irish, or Catholic, they write out of where they come from, and I do too. It just so happens that that space for me is African American; it could be Catholic, it could be midwestern. I'm those things too, and they are all important."*

My mother danced all night and Roberta's was sick. That's why we were taken to St. Bonny's. People want to put their arms around you when you tell them you were in a shelter, but it really wasn't bad. No big long room with one hundred beds like Bellevue. There were four to a room, and when Roberta and me came, there was a shortage of state kids, so we were the only ones assigned to 406 and could go from bed to bed if we wanted to. And we wanted to, too. We changed beds every night and for the whole four months we were there we never picked one out as our own permanent bed.

It didn't start out that way. The minute I walked in and the Big Bozo introduced us, I got sick to my stomach. It was one thing to be taken out of your own bed early in the morning—it was something else to be stuck in a strange place with a girl from a whole other race. And Mary, that's my mother, she was right. Every now and then she would stop dancing long enough to tell me something important and one of the things she said was that they never washed their hair and they smelled funny. Roberta sure did. Smell funny, I mean. So when the Big Bozo (nobody ever called her Mrs. Itkin, just like nobody ever said St. Bonaventure)—when she said, "Twyla, this is Roberta. Roberta, this is Twyla. Make each other welcome." I said, "My mother won't like you putting me in here."

"Good," said Bozo. "Maybe then she'll come and take you home."

How's that for mean? If Roberta had laughed I would have killed her, but she didn't. She just walked over to the window and stood with her back to us.

"Turn around," said the Bozo. "Don't be rude. Now Twyla. Roberta. When you   5
hear a loud buzzer, that's the call for dinner. Come down to the first floor. Any fights and no movie." And then, just to make sure we knew what we would be missing, *The Wizard of Oz*."

Roberta must have thought I meant that my mother would be mad about my being put in the shelter. Not about rooming with her, because as soon as Bozo left she came over to me and said, "Is your mother sick too?"

"No," I said. "She just likes to dance all night."

"Oh," she nodded her head and I liked the way she understood things so fast. So for the moment it didn't matter that we looked like salt and pepper standing there and that's what the other kids called us sometimes. We were eight years old and got F's all the time. Me because I couldn't remember what I read or what the teacher said. And Roberta because she couldn't read at all and didn't even listen to the teacher. She wasn't good at anything except jacks, at which she was a killer: pow scoop pow scoop pow scoop.

We didn't like each other all that much at first, but nobody else wanted to play with us because we weren't real orphans with beautiful dead parents in the sky. We were dumped. Even the New York City Puerto Ricans and the upstate Indians ignored us. All kinds of kids were in there, black ones, white ones, even two Koreans. The food was good, though. At least I thought so. Roberta hated it and left whole pieces of things on her plate: Spam, Salisbury steak—even jello with fruit cocktail in it, and she didn't care if I ate what she wouldn't. Mary's idea of supper was popcorn and a can of Yoo-Hoo. Hot mashed potatoes and two weenies was like Thanksgiving for me.

It really wasn't bad, St. Bonny's. The big girls on the second floor pushed us   10
around now and then. But that was all. They wore lipstick and eyebrow pencil and wobbled their knees while they watched TV. Fifteen, sixteen, even, some of them were. They were put-out girls, scared runaways most of them. Poor little girls who fought their uncles off but looked tough to us, and mean. God did they look mean. The staff tried to keep them separate from the younger children, but sometimes they caught us watching them in the orchard where they played radios and danced with each other. They'd light out after us and pull our hair or twist our arms. We were scared of them, Roberta and me, but neither of us wanted the other one to know it. So we got a good list of dirty names we could shout back when we ran from them through the orchard. I used to dream a lot and almost always the orchard was there. Two acres, four maybe, of these little apple trees. Hundreds of them. Empty and crooked like beggar women when I first came to St. Bonny's but fat with flowers when I left. I don't know why I dreamt about that orchard so much. Nothing really happened there. Nothing all that important, I mean. Just the big girls dancing and playing the radio. Roberta and me watching. Maggie fell down there once. The kitchen woman with legs like parentheses. And the big girls laughed at her. We should have helped her up, I know, but we were scared of those girls with lipstick and eyebrow pencil. Maggie couldn't talk. The kids said she had her tongue cut out, but I think she was just born that way: mute. She was old and sandy-colored and she worked in the kitchen. I don't know if she was nice or not. I just remember her legs like parentheses and how she rocked when she walked. She worked from early in the

morning till two o'clock, and if she was late, if she had too much cleaning and didn't get out till two-fifteen or so, she'd cut through the orchard so she wouldn't miss her bus and have to wait another hour. She wore this really stupid little hat—a kid's hat with ear flaps—and she wasn't much taller than we were. A really awful little hat. Even for a mute, it was dumb—dressing like a kid and never saying anything at all.

"But what about if somebody tries to kill her?" I used to wonder about that. "Or what if she wants to cry? Can she cry?"

"Sure," Roberta said. "But just tears. No sounds come out."

"She can't scream?"

"Nope. Nothing."

"Can she hear?"   15

"I guess."

"Let's call her," I said. And we did.

"Dummy! Dummy!" She never turned her head.

"Bow legs! Bow legs!" Nothing. She just rocked on, the chin straps of her baby-boy hat swaying from side to side. I think we were wrong. I think she could hear and didn't let on. And it shames me even now to think there was somebody in there after all who heard us call her those names and couldn't tell on us.

We got along all right, Roberta and me. Changed beds every night, got F's in   20 civics and communication skills and gym. The Bozo was disappointed in us, she said. Out of 130 of us state cases, 90 were under twelve. Almost all were real orphans with beautiful dead parents in the sky. We were the only ones dumped and the only ones with F's in three classes including gym. So we got along—what with her leaving whole pieces of things on her plate and being nice about not asking questions.

I think it was the day before Maggie fell down that we found out our mothers were coming to visit us on the same Sunday. We had been at the shelter twenty-eight days (Roberta twenty-eight and a half) and this was their first visit with us. Our mothers would come at ten o'clock in time for chapel, then lunch with us in the teachers' lounge. I thought if my dancing mother met her sick mother it might be good for her. And Roberta thought her sick mother would get a big bang out of a dancing one. We got excited about it and curled each other's hair. After breakfast we sat on the bed watching the road from the window. Roberta's socks were still wet. She washed them the night before and put them on the radiator to dry. They hadn't, but she put them on anyway because their tops were so pretty—scalloped in pink. Each of us had a purple construction-paper basket that we had made in craft class. Mine had a yellow crayon rabbit on it. Roberta's had eggs with wiggly lines of color. Inside were cellophane grass and just the jelly beans because I'd eaten the two marshmallow eggs they gave us. The Big Bozo came herself to get us. Smiling she told us we looked very nice and to come downstairs. We were so surprised by the smile we'd never seen before, neither of us moved.

"Don't you want to see your mommies?"

I stood up first and spilled the jelly beans all over the floor. Bozo's smile disappeared while we scrambled to get the candy up off the floor and put it back in the grass.

She escorted us downstairs to the first floor, where the other girls were lining up to file into the chapel. A bunch of grown-ups stood to one side. Viewers mostly. The old biddies who wanted servants and the fags who wanted company looking for children they might want to adopt. Once in a while a grandmother. Almost never anybody young or anybody whose face wouldn't scare you in the night. Because if any of the real orphans had young relatives they wouldn't be real orphans. I saw Mary right away.

She had on those green slacks I hated and hated even more now because didn't she know we were going to chapel? And that fur jacket with the pocket linings so ripped she had to pull to get her hands out of them. But her face was pretty—like always, and she smiled and waved like she was the little girl looking for her mother—not me.

I walked slowly, trying not to drop the jelly beans and hoping the paper handle   25
would hold. I had to use my last Chiclet because by the time I finished cutting everything out, all the Elmer's was gone. I am left-handed and the scissors never worked for me. It didn't matter, though; I might just as well have chewed the gum. Mary dropped to her knees and grabbed me, mashing the basket, the jelly beans, and the grass into her ratty fur jacket.

"Twyla, baby. Twyla, baby!"

I could have killed her. Already I heard the big girls in the orchard the next time saying, "Twyyyyyla, baby!" But I couldn't stay mad at Mary while she was smiling and hugging me and smelling of Lady Esther dusting powder. I wanted to stay buried in her fur all day.

To tell the truth I forgot about Roberta. Mary and I got in line for the traipse into chapel and I was feeling proud because she looked so beautiful even in those ugly green slacks that made her behind stick out. A pretty mother on earth is better than a beautiful dead one in the sky even if she did leave you all alone to go dancing.

I felt a tap on my shoulder, turned, and saw Roberta smiling. I smiled back, but not too much lest somebody think this visit was the biggest thing that ever happened in my life. Then Roberta said, "Mother, I want you to meet my roommate, Twyla. And that's Twyla's mother."

I looked up it seemed for miles. She was big. Bigger than any man and on her   30
chest was the biggest cross I'd ever seen. I swear it was six inches long each way. And in the crook of her arm was the biggest Bible ever made.

Mary, simple-minded as ever, grinned and tried to yank her hand out of the pocket with the raggedy lining—to shake hands, I guess. Roberta's mother looked down at me and then looked down at Mary too. She didn't say anything, just grabbed Roberta with her Bible-free hand and stepped out of line, walking quickly to the rear of it. Mary was still grinning because she's not too swift when it comes to what's really going on. Then this light bulb goes off in her head and she says "That bitch!" really loud and us almost in the chapel now. Organ music whining; the Bonny Angels singing sweetly. Everybody in the world turned around to look. And Mary would have kept it up—kept calling names if I hadn't squeezed her hand as hard as I could. That helped a little, but she still twitched and crossed and uncrossed her legs all through service. Even groaned a couple of times. Why did I think she would come there and act right? Slacks. No hat like the grandmothers and viewers, and groaning all the while. When we stood for hymns she kept her mouth shut. Wouldn't even look at the words on the page. She actually reached in her purse for a mirror to check her lipstick. All I could think of was that she really needed to be killed. The sermon lasted a year, and I knew the real orphans were looking smug again.

We were supposed to have lunch in the teachers' lounge, but Mary didn't bring anything, so we picked fur and cellophane grass off the mashed jelly beans and ate them. I could have killed her. I sneaked a look at Roberta. Her mother had brought chicken legs and ham sandwiches and oranges and a whole box of chocolate-covered grahams. Roberta drank milk from a thermos while her mother read the Bible to her.

Things are not right. The wrong food is always with the wrong people. Maybe that's why I got into waitress work later—to match up the right people with the right food. Roberta just let those chicken legs sit there, but she did bring a stack of grahams up to me later when the visit was over. I think she was sorry that her mother would not shake my mother's hand. And I liked that and I liked the fact that she didn't say a word about Mary groaning all the way through the service and not bringing any lunch.

Roberta left in May when the apple trees were heavy and white. On her last day we went to the orchard to watch the big girls smoke and dance by the radio. It didn't matter that they said, "Twyyyyyla, baby." We sat on the ground and breathed. Lady Esther. Apple blossoms. I still go soft when I smell one or the other. Roberta was going home. The big cross and the big Bible was coming to get her and she seemed sort of glad and sort of not. I thought I would die in that room of four beds without her and I knew Bozo had plans to move some other dumped kid in there with me. Roberta promised to write every day, which was really sweet of her because she couldn't read a lick so how could she write anybody. I would have drawn pictures and sent them to her but she never gave me her address. Little by little she faded. Her wet socks with the pink scalloped tops and her big serious-looking eyes—that's all I could catch when I tried to bring her to mind.

I was working behind the counter at the Howard Johnson's on the Thruway just   35 before the Kingston exit. Not a bad job. Kind of a long ride from Newburgh,° but okay once I got there. Mine was the second night shift—eleven to seven. Very light until a Greyhound checked in for breakfast around six-thirty. At that hour the sun was all the way clear of the hills behind the restaurant. The place looked better at night—more like shelter—but I loved it when the sun broke in, even if it did show all the cracks in the vinyl and the speckled floor looked dirty no matter what the mop boy did.

It was August and a bus crowd was just unloading. They would stand around a long while: going to the john, and looking at gifts and junk-for- sale machines, reluctant to sit down so soon. Even to eat. I was trying to fill the coffee pots and get them all situated on the electric burners when I saw her. She was sitting in a booth smoking a cigarette with two guys smothered in head and facial hair. Her own hair was so big and wild I could hardly see her face. But the eyes. I would know them anywhere. She had on a powder-blue halter and shorts outfit and earrings the size of bracelets. Talk about lipstick and eyebrow pencil. She made the big girls look like nuns. I couldn't get off the counter until seven o'clock, but I kept watching the booth in case they got up to leave before that. My replacement was on time for a change, so I counted and stacked my receipts as fast as I could and signed off. I walked over to the booth, smiling and wondering if she would remember me. Or even if she wanted to remember me. Maybe she didn't want to be reminded of St. Bonny's or to have anybody know she was ever there. I know I never talked about it to anybody.

I put my hands in my apron pockets and leaned against the back of the booth facing them.

"Roberta? Roberta Fisk?"

She looked up. "Yeah?"

"Twyla."

She squinted for a second and then said, "Wow."   40

"Remember me?"

Newburgh: A city of roughly 30,000 people located sixty miles north of Manhattan along the Hudson River. Newburgh was the site of race riots in the 1960s.

"Sure. Hey. Wow."

"It's been a while," I said, and gave a smile to the two hairy guys.

"Yeah. Wow. You work here?"   45

"Yeah," I said. "I live in Newburgh."

"Newburgh? No kidding?" She laughed then a private laugh that included the guys but only the guys, and they laughed with her. What could I do but laugh too and wonder why I was standing there with my knees showing out from under that uniform. Without looking I could see the blue and white triangle on my head, my hair shapeless in a net, my ankles thick in white oxfords. Nothing could have been less sheer than my stockings. There was this silence that came down right after I laughed. A silence it was her turn to fill up. With introductions, maybe, to her boyfriends or an invitation to sit down and have a Coke. Instead she lit a cigarette off the one she'd just finished and said, "We're on our way to the Coast. He's got an appointment with Hendrix."

She gestured casually toward the boy next to her.

"Hendrix? Fantastic," I said. "Really fantastic. What's she doing now?"

Roberta coughed on her cigarette and the two guys rolled their eyes up at the   50
ceiling.

"Hendrix. Jimi Hendrix, asshole. He's only the biggest—Oh, wow. Forget it."

I was dismissed without anyone saying goodbye, so I thought I would do it for her.

"How's your mother?" I asked.

Her grin cracked her whole face. She swallowed. "Fine," she said. "How's yours?"

"Pretty as a picture," I said and turned away. The backs of my knees were damp. 55
Howard Johnson's really was a dump in the sunlight.

James is as comfortable as a house slipper. He liked my cooking and I liked his big loud family. They have lived in Newburgh all of their lives and talk about it the way people do who have always known a home. His grandmother is a porch swing older than his father and when they talk about streets and avenues and buildings they call them names they no longer have. They still call the A & P° Rico's because it stands on property once a mom and pop store owned by Mr. Rico. And they call the new community college Town Hall because it once was. My mother-in-law puts up jelly and cucumbers and buys butter wrapped in cloth from a dairy. James and his father talk about fishing and baseball and I can see them all together on the Hudson in a raggedy skiff. Half the population of Newburgh is on welfare now, but to my husband's family it was still some upstate paradise of a time long past. A time of ice houses and vegetable wagons, coal furnaces and children weeding gardens. When our son was born my mother-in-law gave me the crib blanket that had been hers.

But the town they remembered had changed. Something quick was in the air. Magnificent old houses, so ruined they had become shelter for squatters and rent risks, were bought and renovated. Smart IBM° people moved out of their suburbs back into the city and put shutters up and herb gardens in their backyards. A brochure came in the mail announcing the opening of a Food Emporium. Gourmet food it said—and listed items the rich IBM crowd would want. It was located in a new mall at the edge of town and I drove out to shop there one day—just to see. It was

A & P: Iconic grocery store chain that ceased operations in 2015 after a century and a half in business.
IBM: One of the first computer and technology companies and still among the most successful.

late in June. After the tulips were gone and the Queen Elizabeth roses were open everywhere. I trailed my cart along the aisle tossing in smoked oysters and Robert's sauce and things I knew would sit in my cupboard for years. Only when I found some Klondike ice cream bars did I feel less guilty about spending James's fireman's salary so foolishly. My father-in-law ate them with the same gusto little Joseph did.

Waiting in the check-out line I heard a voice say, "Twyla!"

The classical music piped over the aisles had affected me and the woman leaning toward me was dressed to kill. Diamonds on her hand, a smart white summer dress. "I'm Mrs. Benson," I said.

"Ho. Ho. The Big Bozo," she sang.   60

For a split second I didn't know what she was talking about. She had a bunch of asparagus and two cartons of fancy water.

"Roberta!"

"Right."

"For heaven's sake. Roberta."   65

"You look great," she said.

"So do you. Where are you? Here? In Newburgh?"

"Yes. Over in Annandale."°

I was opening my mouth to say more when the cashier called my attention to her empty counter.

"Meet you outside." Roberta pointed her finger and went into the express line.

I placed the groceries and kept myself from glancing around to check Roberta's   70
progress. I remembered Howard Johnson's and looking for a chance to speak only to be greeted with a stingy "wow." But she was waiting for me and her huge hair was sleek now, smooth around a small, nicely shaped head. Shoes, dress, everything lovely and summery and rich. I was dying to know what happened to her, how she got from Jimi Hendrix to Annandale, a neighborhood full of doctors and IBM executives. Easy, I thought. Everything is so easy for them. They think they own the world.

"How long," I asked her. "How long have you been here?"

"A year. I got married to a man who lives here. And you, you're married too, right? Benson, you said."

"Yeah. James Benson."

"And is he nice?"

"Oh, is he nice?"   75

"Well, is he?" Roberta's eyes were steady as though she really meant the question and wanted an answer.

"He's wonderful, Roberta. Wonderful."

"So you're happy."

"Very."

"That's good," she said and nodded her head. "I always hoped you'd be happy.   80
Any kids? I know you have kids."

"One. A boy. How about you?"

"Four."

"Four?"

She laughed. "Step kids. He's a widower."

"Oh."   85

Annandale: A more affluent town than Newburgh, forty miles north, Annandale-on-Hudson is home to Bard College.

"Got a minute? Let's have a coffee."

I thought about the Klondikes melting and the inconvenience of going all the way to my car and putting the bags in the trunk. Served me right for buying all that stuff I didn't need. Roberta was ahead of me.

"Put them in my car. It's right here."

And then I saw the dark blue limousine.

"You married a Chinaman?"   90

"No," she laughed. "He's the driver."

"Oh, my. If the Big Bozo could see you now."

We both giggled. Really giggled. Suddenly, in just a pulse beat, twenty years disappeared and all of it came rushing back. The big girls (whom we called gar girls—Roberta's misheard word for the evil stone faces described in a civics class) there dancing in the orchard, the ploppy mashed potatoes, the double weenies, the Spam with pineapple. We went into the coffee shop holding onto one another and I tried to think why we were glad to see each other this time and not before. Once, twelve years ago, we passed like strangers. A black girl and a white girl meeting in a Howard Johnson's on the road and having nothing to say. One in a blue and white triangle waitress hat—the other on her way to see Hendrix. Now we were behaving like sisters separated for much too long. Those four short months were nothing in time. Maybe it was the thing itself. Just being there, together. Two little girls who knew what nobody else in the world knew—how not to ask questions. How to believe what had to be believed. There was politeness in that reluctance and generosity as well. Is your mother sick too? No, she dances all night. Oh—and an understanding nod.

We sat in a booth by the window and fell into recollection like veterans.

"Did you ever learn to read?"   95

"Watch." She picked up the menu. "Special of the day. Cream of corn soup. Entrées. Two dots and a wriggly line. Quiche. Chef salad, scallops..."

I was laughing and applauding when the waitress came up.

"Remember the Easter baskets?"

"And how we tried to *introduce* them?"

"Your mother with that cross like two telephone poles."   100

"And yours with those tight slacks."

We laughed so loudly heads turned and made the laughter harder to suppress.

"What happened to the Jimi Hendrix date?"

Roberta made a blow-out sound with her lips.

"When he died I thought about you."   105

"Oh, you heard about him finally?"

"Finally. Come on, I was a small-town country waitress."

"And I was a small-town country dropout. God, were we wild. I still don't know how I got out of there alive."

"But you did."

"I did. I really did. Now I'm Mrs. Kenneth Norton."   110

"Sounds like a mouthful."

"It is."

"Servants and all?"

Roberta held up two fingers.

"Ow! What does he do?"   115

"Computers and stuff. What do I know?"

"I don't remember a hell of a lot from those days, but Lord, St. Bonny's is as clear as daylight. Remember Maggie? The day she fell down and those gar girls laughed at her?"

Roberta looked up from her salad and stared at me. "Maggie didn't fall," she said.

"Yes, she did. You remember."

"No, Twyla. They knocked her down. Those girls pushed her down and tore her clothes. In the orchard." 120

"I don't—that's not what happened."

"Sure it is. In the orchard. Remember how scared we were?"

"Wait a minute. I don't remember any of that."

"And Bozo was fired."

"You're crazy. She was there when I left. You left before me." 125

"I went back. You weren't there when they fired Bozo."

"What?"

"Twice. Once for a year when I was about ten, another for two months when I was fourteen. That's when I ran away."

"You ran away from St. Bonny's?"

"I had to. What do you want? Me dancing in that orchard?" 130

"Are you sure about Maggie?"

"Of course I'm sure. You've blocked it, Twyla. It happened. Those girls had behavior problems, you know."

"Didn't they, though. But why can't I remember the Maggie thing?"

"Believe me. It happened. And we were there."

"Who did you room with when you went back?" I asked her as if I would know 135 her. The Maggie thing was troubling me.

"Creeps. They tickled themselves in the night."

My ears were itching and I wanted to go home suddenly. This was all very well but she couldn't just comb her hair, wash her face and pretend everything was hunky-dory. After the Howard Johnson's snub. And no apology. Nothing.

"Were you on dope or what that time at Howard Johnson's?" I tried to make my voice sound friendlier than I felt.

"Maybe, a little. I never did drugs much. Why?"

"I don't know; you acted sort of like you didn't want to know me then." 140

"Oh, Twyla, you know how it was in those days: black—white. You know how everything was."

But I didn't know. I thought it was just the opposite. Busloads of blacks and whites came into Howard Johnson's together. They roamed together then: students, musicians, lovers, protesters. You got to see everything at Howard Johnson's and blacks were very friendly with whites in those days. But sitting there with nothing on my plate but two hard tomato wedges wondering about the melting Klondikes it seemed childish remembering the slight. We went to her car, and with the help of the driver, got my stuff into my station wagon.

"We'll keep in touch this time," she said.

"Sure," I said. "Sure. Give me a call."

"I will," she said, and then just as I was sliding behind the wheel, she leaned into 145 the window. "By the way. Your mother. Did she ever stop dancing?"

I shook my head. "No. Never."

Roberta nodded.

"And yours? Did she ever get well?"

She smiled a tiny sad smile. "No. She never did. Look, call me, okay?"

"Okay," I said, but I knew I wouldn't. Roberta had messed up my past somehow   150
with that business about Maggie. I wouldn't forget a thing like that. Would I?

Strife came to us that fall. At least that's what the paper called it. Strife. Racial
strife. The word made me think of a bird—a big shrieking bird out of 1,000,000,000
B.C. Flapping its wings and cawing. Its eye with no lid always bearing down on you.
All day it screeched and at night it slept on the rooftops. It woke you in the morning and from the *Today* show to the eleven o'clock news it kept you an awful company. I couldn't figure it out from one day to the next. I knew I was supposed to feel
something strong, but I didn't know what, and James wasn't any help. Joseph was
on the list of kids to be transferred from the junior high school to another one at
some far-out-of-the-way place and I thought it was a good thing until I heard it was
a bad thing. I mean I didn't know. All the schools seemed dumps to me, and the
fact that one was nicer looking didn't hold much weight. But the papers were full of
it and then the kids began to get jumpy. In August, mind you. Schools weren't even
open yet. I thought Joseph might be frightened to go over there, but he didn't seem
scared so I forgot about it, until I found myself driving along Hudson Street out
there by the school they were trying to integrate and saw a line of women marching. And who do you suppose was in line, big as life, holding a sign in front of her
bigger than her mother's cross? MOTHERS HAVE RIGHTS TOO! it said.

I drove on, and then changed my mind. I circled the block, slowed down, and
honked my horn.

Roberta looked over and when she saw me she waved. I didn't wave back, but I
didn't move either. She handed her sign to another woman and came over to where
I was parked.

"Hi."

"What are you doing?"   155

"Picketing. What's it look like?"

"What for?"

"What do you mean, 'What for?' They want to take my kids and send them out
of the neighborhood. They don't want to go."

"So what if they go to another school? My boy's being bussed too, and I don't
mind. Why should you?"

"It's not about us, Twyla. Me and you. It's about our kids."   160

"What's more *us* than that?"

"Well, it is a free country."

"Not yet, but it will be."

"What the hell does that mean? I'm not doing anything to you."

"You really think that?"   165

"I know it."

"I wonder what made me think you were different."

"I wonder what made me think you were different."

"Look at them," I said. "Just look. Who do they think they are? Swarming all
over the place like they own it. And now they think they can decide where my child
goes to school. Look at them, Roberta. They're Bozos."

Roberta turned around and looked at the women. Almost all of them were stand-   170
ing still now, waiting. Some were even edging toward us. Roberta looked at me out of
some refrigerator behind her eyes. "No, they're not. They're just mothers."

"And what am I? Swiss cheese?"

"I used to curl your hair."

"I hated your hands in my hair."

The women were moving. Our faces looked mean to them of course and they looked as though they could not wait to throw themselves in front of a police car, or better yet, into my car and drag me away by my ankles. Now they surrounded my car and gently, gently began to rock it. I swayed back and forth like a sideways yo-yo. Automatically I reached for Roberta, like the old days in the orchard when they saw us watching them and we had to get out of there, and if one of us fell the other pulled her up and if one of us was caught the other stayed to kick and scratch, and neither would leave the other behind. My arm shot out of the car window but no receiving hand was there. Roberta was looking at me sway from side to side in the car and her face was still. My purse slid from the car seat down under the dashboard. The four policemen who had been drinking Tab in their car finally got the message and strolled over, forcing their way through the women. Quietly, firmly they spoke. "Okay, ladies. Back in line or off the streets."

Some of them went away willingly; others had to be urged away from the car 175
doors and the hood. Roberta didn't move. She was looking steadily at me. I was fumbling to turn on the ignition, which wouldn't catch because the gearshift was still in drive. The seats of the car were a mess because the swaying had thrown my grocery coupons all over it and my purse was sprawled on the floor.

"Maybe I am different now, Twyla. But you're not. You're the same little state kid who kicked a poor old black lady when she was down on the ground. You kicked a black lady and you have the nerve to call me a bigot."

The coupons were everywhere and the guts of my purse were bunched under the dashboard. What was she saying? Black? Maggie wasn't black.

"She wasn't black," I said.

"Like hell she wasn't, and you kicked her. We both did. You kicked a black lady who couldn't even scream."

"Liar!" 180

"You're the liar! Why don't you just go on home and leave us alone, huh?"

She turned away and I skidded away from the curb.

The next morning I went into the garage and cut the side out of the carton our portable TV had come in. It wasn't nearly big enough, but after a while I had a decent sign: red spray-painted letters on a white background—AND SO DO CHILDREN ****. I meant just to go down to the school and tack it up somewhere so those cows on the picket line across the street could see it, but when I got there, some ten or so others had already assembled—protesting the cows across the street. Police permits and everything. I got in line and we strutted in time on our side while Roberta's group strutted on theirs. That first day we were all dignified, pretending the other side didn't exist. The second day there was name calling and finger gestures. But that was about all. People changed signs from time to time, but Roberta never did and neither did I. Actually my sign didn't make sense without Roberta's. "And so do children what?" one of the women on my side asked me. Have rights, I said, as though it was obvious.

Roberta didn't acknowledge my presence in any way and I got to thinking maybe she didn't know I was there. I began to pace myself in the line, jostling people one minute and lagging behind the next, so Roberta and I could reach the end of our respective lines at the same time and there would be a moment in our turn when we would face each other. Still, I couldn't tell whether she saw me and knew my sign was for her. The next day I went early before we were scheduled to assemble. I waited until she got there before I exposed my new creation. As soon as she hoisted her MOTHERS HAVE RIGHTS TOO I began to wave my new one, which said, HOW WOULD YOU KNOW? I know she saw that one, but I had gotten addicted now. My signs got crazier each day, and the women on my side decided that I was a kook. They couldn't make heads or tails out of my brilliant screaming posters.

I brought a painted sign in queenly red with huge black letters that said, IS YOUR   185 MOTHER WELL? Roberta took her lunch break and didn't come back for the rest of the day or any day after. Two days later I stopped going too and couldn't have been missed because nobody understood my signs anyway.

It was a nasty six weeks. Classes were suspended and Joseph didn't go to anybody's school until October. The children—everybody's children—soon got bored with that extended vacation they thought was going to be so great. They looked at TV until their eyes flattened. I spent a couple of mornings tutoring my son, as the other mothers said we should. Twice I opened a text from last year that he had never turned in. Twice he yawned in my face. Other mothers organized living room sessions so the kids would keep up. None of the kids could concentrate so they drifted back to *The Price Is Right* and *The Brady Bunch*. When the school finally opened there were fights once or twice and some sirens roared through the streets every once in a while. There were a lot of photographers from Albany. And just when ABC was about to send up a news crew, the kids settled down like nothing in the world had happened. Joseph hung my HOW WOULD YOU KNOW? sign in his bedroom. I don't know what became of AND SO DO CHILDREN ****. I think my father-in-law cleaned some fish on it. He was always puttering around in our garage. Each of his five children lived in Newburgh and he acted as though he had five extra homes.

I couldn't help looking for Roberta when Joseph graduated from high school, but I didn't see her. It didn't trouble me much what she had said to me in the car. I mean the kicking part. I know I didn't do that, I couldn't do that. But I was puzzled by her telling me Maggie was black. When I thought about it I actually couldn't be certain. She wasn't pitch-black, I knew, or I would have remembered that. What I remember was the kiddie hat, and the semicircle legs. I tried to reassure myself about the race thing for a long time until it dawned on me that the truth was already there, and Roberta knew it. I didn't kick her; I didn't join in with the gar girls and kick that lady, but I sure did want to. We watched and never tried to help her and never called for help. Maggie was my dancing mother. Deaf, I thought, and dumb. Nobody inside. Nobody who would hear you if you cried in the night. Nobody who could tell you anything important that you could use. Rocking, dancing, swaying as she walked. And when the gar girls pushed her down, and started roughhousing, I knew she wouldn't scream, couldn't—just like me—and I was glad about that.

We decided not to have a tree, because Christmas would be at my mother-in-law's house, so why have a tree at both places? Joseph was at SUNY New Paltz° and we had to economize, we said. But at the last minute, I changed my mind. Nothing could be that bad. So I rushed around town looking for a tree, something small but wide. By the time I found a place, it was snowing and very late. I dawdled like it was the most important purchase in the world and the tree man was fed up with me. Finally I chose one and had it tied onto the trunk of the car. I drove away slowly because

SUNY New Paltz: The State University of New York at New Paltz, located twenty miles from Newburgh.

the sand trucks were not out yet and the streets could be murder at the beginning of a snowfall. Downtown the streets were wide and rather empty except for a cluster of people coming out of the Newburgh Hotel. The one hotel in town that wasn't built out of cardboard and Plexiglas. A party, probably. The men huddled in the snow were dressed in tails and the women had on furs. Shiny things glittered from underneath their coats. It made me tired to look at them. Tired, tired, tired. On the next corner was a small diner with loops and loops of paper bells in the window. I stopped the car and went in. Just for a cup of coffee and twenty minutes of peace before I went home and tried to finish everything before Christmas Eve.

"Twyla?"

There she was. In a silvery evening gown and dark fur coat. A man and another woman were with her, the man fumbling for change to put in the cigarette machine. The woman was humming and tapping on the counter with her fingernails. They all looked a little bit drunk.

"Well. It's you."

"How are you?"

I shrugged. "Pretty good. Frazzled. Christmas and all."

"Regular?" called the woman from the counter.

"Fine," Roberta called back and then, "Wait for me in the car." 195

She slipped into the booth beside me. "I have to tell you something, Twyla. I made up my mind if I ever saw you again, I'd tell you."

"I'd just as soon not hear anything, Roberta. It doesn't matter now, anyway."

"No," she said. "Not about that."

"Don't be long," said the woman. She carried two regulars to go and the man peeled his cigarette pack as they left.

"It's about St. Bonny's and Maggie." 200

"Oh, please."

"Listen to me. I really did think she was black. I didn't make that up. I really thought so. But now I can't be sure. I just remember her as old, so old. And because she couldn't talk—well, you know, I thought she was crazy. She'd been brought up in an institution like my mother was and like I thought I would be too. And you were right. We didn't kick her. It was the gar girls. Only them. But, well, I wanted to. I really wanted them to hurt her. I said we did it, too. You and me, but that's not true. And I don't want you to carry that around. It was just that I wanted to do it so bad that day—wanting to is doing it."

Her eyes were watery from the drinks she'd had, I guess. I know it's that way with me. One glass of wine and I start bawling over the littlest thing.

"We were kids, Roberta."

"Yeah. Yeah. I know, just kids." 205

"Eight."

"Eight."

"And lonely."

"Scared, too."

She wiped her cheeks with the heel of her hand and smiled. "Well, that's all I 210 wanted to say."

I nodded and couldn't think of any way to fill the silence that went from the diner past the paper bells on out into the snow. It was heavy now. I thought I'd better wait for the sand trucks before starting home.

"Thanks, Roberta."

"Sure."

"Did I tell you? My mother, she never did stop dancing."

"Yes. You told me. And mine, she never got well." Roberta lifted her hands 215
from the tabletop and covered her face with her palms. When she took them away
she really was crying. "Oh shit, Twyla. Shit, shit, shit. What the hell happened to
Maggie?"

Questions

1. When Twyla and Roberta first meet at St. Bonny's, what unites them?
2. What role do the girls' mothers play in the story? Why does each ask about the other's
    mother throughout the story?
3. Do you know which girl is black and which is white? Do your assumptions about each
    one's race change by the end of the story? What made you form and then reconsider your
    assumptions about each character's race? Cite specific clues and details.
4. Why do you think Morrison would subvert our assumptions about race in that way? What
    does that teach us about ourselves? What does it teach us about race and class in general?
5. Twyla and Roberta encounter each other five separate times during the course of the
    story. Recall those encounters, and describe how their relationship changes. How do the
    characters themselves change?
6. Why do you think Morrison titled the story "Recitatif," a French word that describes a
    moment in an opera or oratorio in which the vocal style resembles ordinary speech?
7. Why is Maggie, the disabled woman who worked at St. Bonaventure's, such an important
    figure in the story? Why is Twyla's memory of the incident with Maggie hazy, and why
    does Roberta invent some of the details of what happened?
8. What do you make of the final scene? Have the women reconciled their differences? Why
    did Morrison close the story with an unanswered question about Maggie?

Raymond Carver

Cathedral   1983

*Raymond Carver (1938–1988) was born in Clatskanie, Oregon. When he was three, his
family moved to Yakima, Washington, where his father worked in a sawmill. In his early
years Carver worked briefly at a lumber mill and at other unskilled jobs, including a stint as
a tulip-picker. Married with two children before he was twenty, he experienced blue-collar
desperation more intimately than most American writers, though he once quipped that, until
he read critics' reactions to his works, he never realized that the characters in his stories
"were so bad off." In 1963 Carver earned a degree from Humboldt State College (now
California State University, Humboldt). He briefly attended the Writers' Workshop of the
University of Iowa, but, needing to support his family, he returned to California, working
for three years as a hospital custodian before finding a job editing textbooks. In 1967 he
met Gordon Lish, the influential editor who would publish several of his stories in Esquire.
Under Lish's demanding tutelage, Carver learned to pare his fiction to the essentials. In
the early 1970s, though plagued with bankruptcies, increasing dependency on alcohol, and
marital problems, he taught at several universities.*

*Carver's publishing career began with a volume of poems, Near Klamath (1968). His
books of short stories include Will You Please Be Quiet, Please? (1977), What We Talk
About When We Talk About Love (1981), Cathedral (1983), and Where I'm Calling From (1988). The compression of language he learned as a poet may in part account
for the lean quality of his prose, often called "minimalist," a term Carver did not like. In
his last decade Carver taught creative writing at Syracuse University and lived with the poet*

Tess Gallagher, whom he married in 1988. He divided his final years between Syracuse and Port Angeles, Washington. Carver's personal victory in 1977 over decades of alcoholism underscored the many professional triumphs of his final decade. He once said, "I'm prouder of that, that I quit drinking, than I am of anything in my life." His reputation as a master craftsman of the contemporary short story was still growing when he died, after a struggle with lung cancer.

This blind man, an old friend of my wife's, he was on his way to spend the night. His wife had died. So he was visiting the dead wife's relatives in Connecticut. He called my wife from his in-laws'. Arrangements were made. He would come by train, a five-hour trip, and my wife would meet him at the station. She hadn't seen him since she worked for him one summer in Seattle ten years ago. But she and the blind man had kept in touch. They made tapes and mailed them back and forth. I wasn't enthusiastic about his visit. He was no one I knew. And his being blind bothered me. My idea of blindness came from the movies. In the movies, the blind moved slowly and never laughed. Sometimes they were led by seeing-eye dogs. A blind man in my house was not something I looked forward to.

That summer in Seattle she had needed a job. She didn't have any money. The man she was going to marry at the end of the summer was in officers' training school. He didn't have any money, either. But she was in love with the guy, and he was in love with her, etc. She'd seen something in the paper: HELP WANTED—*Reading to Blind Man*, and a telephone number. She phoned and went over, was hired on the spot. She'd worked with this blind man all summer. She read stuff to him, case studies, reports, that sort of thing. She helped him organize his little office in the county social-service department. They'd become good friends, my wife and the blind man. How do I know these things? She told me. And she told me something else. On her last day in the office, the blind man asked if he could touch her face. She agreed to this. She told me he touched his fingers to every part of her face, her nose—even her neck! She never forgot it. She even tried to write a poem about it. She was always trying to write a poem. She wrote a poem or two every year, usually after something really important had happened to her.

When we first started going out together, she showed me the poem. In the poem, she recalled his fingers and the way they had moved around over her face. In the poem, she talked about what she had felt at the time, about what went through her mind when the blind man touched her nose and lips. I can remember I didn't think much of the poem. Of course, I didn't tell her that. Maybe I just don't understand poetry. I admit it's not the first thing I reach for when I pick up something to read.

Anyway, this man who'd first enjoyed her favors, the officer-to-be, he'd been her childhood sweetheart. So okay. I'm saying that at the end of the summer she let the blind man run his hands over her face, said good-bye to him, married her childhood etc., who was now a commissioned officer, and she moved away from Seattle. But they'd kept in touch, she and the blind man. She made the first contact after a year or so. She called him up one night from an Air Force base in Alabama. She wanted to talk. They talked. He asked her to send a tape and tell him about her life. She did this. She sent the tape. On the tape, she told the blind man about her husband and about their life together in the military. She told the blind man she loved her husband but she didn't like it where they lived and she didn't like it that he was part of the military-industrial thing. She told the blind man she'd written a poem and he was in it. She told him that she was writing a poem about what it was like to be an

Air Force officer's wife. The poem wasn't finished yet. She was still writing it. The blind man made a tape. He sent her the tape. She made a tape. This went on for years. My wife's officer was posted to one base and then another. She sent tapes from Moody AFB, McGuire, McConnell, and finally Travis, near Sacramento, where one night she got to feeling lonely and cut off from people she kept losing in that moving-around life. She got to feeling she couldn't go it another step. She went in and swallowed all the pills and capsules in the medicine chest and washed them down with a bottle of gin. Then she got into a hot bath and passed out.

But instead of dying, she got sick. She threw up. Her officer—why should he   5
have a name? he was the childhood sweetheart, and what more does he want?—came home from somewhere, found her, and called the ambulance. In time, she put it all on a tape and sent the tape to the blind man. Over the years, she put all kinds of stuff on tapes and sent the tapes off lickety-split. Next to writing a poem every year, I think it was her chief means of recreation. On one tape, she told the blind man she'd decided to live away from her officer for a time. On another tape, she told him about her divorce. She and I began going out, and of course she told her blind man about it. She told him everything, or so it seemed to me. Once she asked me if I'd like to hear the latest tape from the blind man. This was a year ago. I was on the tape, she said. So I said okay, I'd listen to it. I got us drinks and we settled down in the living room. We made ready to listen. First she inserted the tape into the player and adjusted a couple of dials. Then she pushed a lever. The tape squeaked and someone began to talk in this loud voice. She lowered the volume. After a few minutes of harmless chitchat, I heard my own name in the mouth of this stranger, this blind man I didn't even know! And then this: "From all you've said about him, I can only conclude—" But we were interrupted, a knock at the door, something, and we didn't ever get back to the tape. Maybe it was just as well. I'd heard all I wanted to.

Now this same blind man was coming to sleep in my house.

"Maybe I could take him bowling," I said to my wife. She was at the draining board doing scalloped potatoes. She put down the knife she was using and turned around.

"If you love me," she said, "you can do this for me. If you don't love me, okay. But if you had a friend, any friend, and the friend came to visit, I'd make him feel comfortable." She wiped her hands with the dish towel.

"I don't have any blind friends," I said.

"You don't have *any* friends," she said. "Period. Besides," she said, "goddamn it,   10
his wife's just died! Don't you understand that? The man's lost his wife!"

I didn't answer. She'd told me a little about the blind man's wife. Her name was Beulah. Beulah! That's a name for a colored woman.

"Was his wife a Negro?" I asked.

"Are you crazy?" my wife said. "Have you just flipped or something?" She picked up a potato. I saw it hit the floor, then roll under the stove. "What's wrong with you?" she said. "Are you drunk?"

"I'm just asking," I said.

Right then my wife filled me in with more detail than I cared to know. I made a   15
drink and sat at the kitchen table to listen. Pieces of the story began to fall into place.

Beulah had gone to work for the blind man the summer after my wife had stopped working for him. Pretty soon Beulah and the blind man had themselves a church wedding. It was a little wedding—who'd want to go to such a wedding in the first place?—just the two of them, plus the minister and the minister's wife. But it was a church wedding just the same. It was what Beulah had wanted, he'd said. But even then Beulah must have been carrying the cancer in her glands. After they had been inseparable for eight years—my wife's word, *inseparable*—Beulah's health went into a rapid decline. She died in a Seattle hospital room, the blind man sitting beside the bed and holding on to her hand. They'd married, lived and worked together, slept together—had sex, sure—and then the blind man had to bury her. All this without his having ever seen what the goddamned woman looked like. It was beyond my understanding. Hearing this, I felt sorry for the blind man for a little bit. And then I found myself thinking what a pitiful life this woman must have led. Imagine a woman who could never see herself as she was seen in the eyes of her loved one. A woman who could go on day after day and never receive the smallest compliment from her beloved. A woman whose husband could never read the expression on her face, be it misery or something better. Someone who could wear makeup or not—what difference to him? She could, if she wanted, wear green eye-shadow around one eye, a straight pin in her nostril, yellow slacks, and purple shoes, no matter. And then to slip off into death, the blind man's hand on her hand, his blind eyes streaming tears—I'm imagining now—her last thought maybe this: that he never even knew what she looked like, and she on an express to the grave. Robert was left with a small insurance policy and a half of a twenty-peso Mexican coin. The other half of the coin went into the box with her. Pathetic.

So when the time rolled around, my wife went to the depot to pick him up. With nothing to do but wait—sure, I blamed him for that—I was having a drink and watching the TV when I heard the car pull into the drive. I got up from the sofa with my drink and went to the window to have a look.

I saw my wife laughing as she parked the car. I saw her get out of the car and shut the door. She was still wearing a smile. Just amazing. She went around to the other side of the car to where the blind man was already starting to get out. This blind man, feature this, he was wearing a full beard! A beard on a blind man! Too much, I say. The blind man reached into the backseat and dragged out a suitcase. My wife took his arm, shut the car door, and, talking all the way, moved him down the drive and then up the steps to the front porch. I turned off the TV. I finished my drink, rinsed the glass, dried my hands. Then I went to the door.

My wife said, "I want you to meet Robert. Robert, this is my husband. I've told you all about him." She was beaming. She had this blind man by his coat sleeve.

The blind man let go of his suitcase and up came his hand.   20

I took it. He squeezed hard, held my hand, and then he let it go.

"I feel like we've already met," he boomed.

"Likewise," I said. I didn't know what else to say. Then I said, "Welcome. I've heard a lot about you." We began to move then, a little group, from the porch into the living room, my wife guiding him by the arm. The blind man was carrying his suitcase in his other hand. My wife said things like, "To your left here, Robert. That's right. Now watch it, there's a chair. That's it. Sit down right here. This is the sofa. We just bought this sofa two weeks ago."

I started to say something about the old sofa. I'd liked that old sofa. But I didn't say anything. Then I wanted to say something else, small-talk, about the scenic ride along the Hudson. How going *to* New York, you should sit on the right-hand side of the train, and coming *from* New York, the left-hand side.

"Did you have a good train ride?" I said. "Which side of the train did you sit on,   25
by the way?"

"What a question, which side!" my wife said. "What's it matter which side?" she said.

"I just asked," I said.

"Right side," the blind man said. "I hadn't been on a train in nearly forty years. Not since I was a kid. With my folks. That's been a long time. I'd nearly forgotten the sensation. I have winter in my beard now," he said. "So I've been told, anyway. Do I look distinguished, my dear?" the blind man said to my wife.

"You look distinguished, Robert," she said. "Robert," she said. "Robert, it's just so good to see you."

My wife finally took her eyes off the blind man and looked at me. I had the feel- 30 ing she didn't like what she saw. I shrugged.

I've never met, or personally known, anyone who was blind. This blind man was late forties, a heavy-set, balding man with stooped shoulders, as if he carried a great weight there. He wore brown slacks, brown shoes, a light-brown shirt, a tie, a sports coat. Spiffy. He also had this full beard. But he didn't use a cane and he didn't wear dark glasses. I'd always thought dark glasses were a must for the blind. Fact was, I wished he had a pair. At first glance, his eyes looked like anyone else's eyes. But if you looked close, there was something different about them. Too much white in the iris, for one thing, and the pupils seemed to move around in the sockets without his knowing it or being able to stop it. Creepy. As I stared at his face, I saw the left pupil turn in toward his nose while the other made an effort to keep in one place. But it was only an effort, for that eye was on the roam without his knowing it or wanting it to be.

I said, "Let me get you a drink. What's your pleasure? We have a little of every- thing. It's one of our pastimes."

"Bub, I'm a Scotch man myself," he said fast enough in this big voice.

"Right," I said. Bub! "Sure you are. I knew it."

He let his fingers touch his suitcase, which was sitting alongside the sofa. He was 35 taking his bearings. I didn't blame him for that.

"I'll move that up to your room," my wife said.

"No, that's fine," the blind man said loudly. "It can go up when I go up."

"A little water with the Scotch?" I said.

"Very little," he said.

"I knew it," I said. 40

He said, "Just a tad. The Irish actor, Barry Fitzgerald? I'm like that fellow. When I drink water, Fitzgerald said, I drink water. When I drink whiskey, I drink whiskey." My wife laughed. The blind man brought his hand up under his beard. He lifted his beard slowly and let it drop.

I did the drinks, three big glasses of Scotch with a splash of water in each. Then we made ourselves comfortable and talked about Robert's travels. First the long flight from the West Coast to Connecticut, we covered that. Then from Connecticut up here by train. We had another drink concerning that leg of the trip.

I remembered having read somewhere that the blind didn't smoke because, as speculation had it, they couldn't see the smoke they exhaled. I thought I knew that much and that much only about blind people. But this blind man smoked his ciga- rette down to the nubbin and then lit another one. This blind man filled his ashtray and my wife emptied it.

When we sat down at the table for dinner, we had another drink. My wife heaped Robert's plate with cube steak, scalloped potatoes, green beans. I buttered him up two slices of bread. I said, "Here's bread and butter for you." I swallowed some of my drink. "Now let us pray," I said, and the blind man lowered his head. My wife looked at me, her mouth agape. "Pray the phone won't ring and the food doesn't get cold," I said.

We dug in. We ate everything there was to eat on the table. We ate like there 45 was no tomorrow. We didn't talk. We ate. We scarfed. We grazed that table. We were into serious eating. The blind man had right away located his foods, he knew just where everything was on his plate. I watched with admiration as he used his knife and fork on the meat. He'd cut two pieces of meat, fork the meat into his mouth, and then go all out for the scalloped potatoes, the beans next, and then he'd tear off a hunk of buttered bread and eat that. He'd follow this up with a big drink of milk. It didn't seem to bother him to use his fingers once in a while, either.

We finished everything, including half a strawberry pie. For a few moments, we sat as if stunned. Sweat beaded on our faces. Finally, we got up from the table and left the dirty plates. We didn't look back. We took ourselves into the living room and sank into our places again. Robert and my wife sat on the sofa. I took the big chair. We had us two or three more drinks while they talked about the major things that had come to pass for them in the past ten years. For the most part, I just listened. Now and then I joined in. I didn't want him to think I'd left the room, and I didn't want her to think I was feeling left out. They talked of things that had happened to them—to them!—these past ten years. I waited in vain to hear my name on my wife's sweet lips: "And then my dear husband came into my life"—something like that. But I heard nothing of the sort. More talk of Robert. Robert had done a little of everything, it seemed, a regular blind jack-of-all-trades. But most recently he and his wife had had an Amway distributorship, from which, I gathered, they'd earned their living, such as it was. The blind man was also a ham radio operator. He talked in his loud voice about conversations he'd had with fellow operators in Guam, in the Philippines, in Alaska, and even in Tahiti. He said he'd have a lot of friends there if he ever wanted to go visit those places. From time to time, he'd turn his blind face toward me, put his hand under his beard, ask me something. How long had I been in my present position? (Three years.) Did I like my work? (I didn't.) Was I going to stay with it? (What were the options?) Finally, when I thought he was beginning to run down, I got up and turned on the TV.

My wife looked at me with irritation. She was heading toward a boil. Then she looked at the blind man and said, "Robert, do you have a TV?"

The blind man said, "My dear, I have two TVs. I have a color set and a black-and-white thing, an old relic. It's funny, but if I turn the TV on, and I'm always turning it on, I turn on the color set. It's funny, don't you think?"

I didn't know what to say to that. I had absolutely nothing to say to that. No opinion. So I watched the news program and tried to listen to what the announcer was saying.

"This is a color TV," the blind man said. "Don't ask me how, but I can tell." 50

"We traded up a while ago," I said.

The blind man had another taste of his drink. He lifted his beard, sniffed it, and let it fall. He leaned forward on the sofa. He positioned his ashtray on the coffee table, then put the lighter to his cigarette. He leaned back on the sofa and crossed his legs at the ankles.

My wife covered her mouth, and then she yawned. She stretched. She said, "I think I'll go upstairs and put on my robe. I think I'll change into something else. Robert, you make yourself comfortable," she said.

"I'm comfortable," the blind man said.

"I want you to feel comfortable in this house," she said.   55

"I am comfortable," the blind man said.

After she'd left the room, he and I listened to the weather report and then to the sports roundup. By that time, she'd been gone so long I didn't know if she was going to come back. I thought she might have gone to bed. I wished she'd come back downstairs. I didn't want to be left alone with a blind man. I asked him if he wanted another drink, and he said sure. Then I asked if he wanted to smoke some dope with me. I said I'd just rolled a number. I hadn't, but I planned to do so in about two shakes.

"I'll try some with you," he said.

"Damn right," I said. "That's the stuff."

I got our drinks and sat down on the sofa with him. Then I rolled us two fat   60
numbers. I lit one and passed it. I brought it to his fingers. He took it and inhaled.

"Hold it as long as you can," I said. I could tell he didn't know the first thing.

My wife came back downstairs wearing her pink robe and her pink slippers.

"What do I smell?" she said.

"We thought we'd have us some cannabis," I said.

My wife gave me a savage look. Then she looked at the blind man and said,   65
"Robert, I didn't know you smoked."

He said, "I do now, my dear. There's a first time for everything. But I don't feel anything yet."

"This stuff is pretty mellow," I said. "This stuff is mild. It's dope you can reason with," I said. "It doesn't mess you up."

"Not much it doesn't, bub," he said, and laughed.

My wife sat on the sofa between the blind man and me. I passed her the number. She took it and toked and then passed it back to me. "Which way is this going?" she said. Then she said, "I shouldn't be smoking this. I can hardly keep my eyes open as it is. That dinner did me in. I shouldn't have eaten so much."

"It was the strawberry pie," the blind man said. "That's what did it," he said, and   70
he laughed his big laugh. Then he shook his head.

"There's more strawberry pie," I said.

"Do you want some more, Robert?" my wife said.

"Maybe in a little while," he said.

We gave our attention to the TV. My wife yawned again. She said, "Your bed is made up when you feel like going to bed, Robert. I know you must have had a long day. When you're ready to go to bed, say so." She pulled his arm. "Robert?"

He came to and said, "I've had a real nice time. This beats tapes, doesn't it?"   75

I said, "Coming at you," and I put the number between his fingers. He inhaled, held the smoke, and then let it go. It was like he'd been doing it since he was nine years old.

"Thanks, bub," he said. "But I think this is all for me. I think I'm beginning to feel it," he said. He held the burning roach out for my wife.

"Same here," she said. "Ditto. Me, too." She took the roach and passed it to me. "I may just sit here for a while between you two guys with my eyes closed. But don't let me bother you, okay? Either one of you. If it bothers you, say so. Otherwise, I may just sit here with my eyes closed until you're ready to go to bed," she said. "Your bed's made up, Robert, when you're ready. It's right next to our room at the top of the stairs. We'll show you up when you're ready. You wake me up now, you guys, if I fall asleep." She said that and then she closed her eyes and went to sleep.

The news program ended. I got up and changed the channel. I sat back down on the sofa. I wished my wife hadn't pooped out. Her head lay across the back of the sofa, her mouth open. She'd turned so that her robe slipped away from her legs, exposing a juicy thigh. I reached to draw her robe back over her, and it was then that I glanced at the blind man. What the hell! I flipped the robe open again.

"You say when you want some strawberry pie," I said.   80

"I will," he said.

I said, "Are you tired? Do you want me to take you up to your bed? Are you ready to hit the hay?"

"Not yet," he said. "No, I'll stay up with you, bub. If that's all right. I'll stay up until you're ready to turn in. We haven't had a chance to talk. Know what I mean? I feel like me and her monopolized the evening." He lifted his beard and he let it fall. He picked up his cigarettes and his lighter.

"That's all right," I said. Then I said, "I'm glad for the company."

And I guess I was. Every night I smoked dope and stayed up as long as I could   85
before I fell asleep. My wife and I hardly ever went to bed at the same time. When I did go to sleep, I had these dreams. Sometimes I'd wake up from one of them, my heart going crazy.

Something about the church and the Middle Ages was on the TV. Not your run-of-the-mill TV fare. I wanted to watch something else. I turned to the other channels. But there was nothing on them, either. So I turned back to the first channel and apologized.

"Bub, it's all right," the blind man said. "It's fine with me. Whatever you want to watch is okay. I'm always learning something. Learning never ends. It won't hurt me to learn something tonight. I got ears," he said.

We didn't say anything for a time. He was leaning forward with his head turned at me, his right ear aimed in the direction of the set. Very disconcerting. Now and then his eyelids drooped and then they snapped open again. Now and then he put his fingers into his beard and tugged, like he was thinking about something he was hearing on the television.

On the screen, a group of men wearing cowls was being set upon and tormented by men dressed in skeleton costumes and men dressed as devils. The men dressed as devils wore devil masks, horns, and long tails. This pageant was part of a procession. The Englishman who was narrating the thing said it took place in Spain once a year. I tried to explain to the blind man what was happening.

"Skeletons," he said. "I know about skeletons," he said, and he nodded.   90

The TV showed this one cathedral. Then there was a long, slow look at another one. Finally, the picture switched to the famous one in Paris, with its flying buttresses and its spires reaching up to the clouds. The camera pulled away to show the whole of the cathedral rising above the skyline.

There were times when the Englishman who was telling the thing would shut up, would simply let the camera move around the cathedrals. Or else the camera would tour the countryside, men in fields walking behind oxen. I waited as long as I could. Then I felt I had to say something. I said, "They're showing the outside of this cathedral now. Gargoyles. Little statues carved to look like monsters. Now I guess they're in Italy. Yeah, they're in Italy. There's paintings on the walls of this one church."

"Are those fresco paintings, bub?" he asked, and he sipped from his drink.

I reached for my glass. But it was empty. I tried to remember what I could remember. "You're asking me are those frescoes?" I said. "That's a good question. I don't know."

The camera moved to a cathedral outside Lisbon. The differences in the Portuguese cathedral compared with the French and Italian were not that great. But they were there. Mostly the interior stuff. Then something occurred to me, and I said, "Something has occurred to me. Do you have any idea what a cathedral is? What they look like, that is? Do you follow me? If somebody says cathedral to you, do you have any notion what they're talking about? Do you know the difference between that and a Baptist church, say?"

He let the smoke dribble from his mouth. "I know they took hundreds of workers fifty or a hundred years to build," he said. "I just heard the man say that, of course. I know generations of the same families worked on a cathedral. I heard him say that, too. The men who began their life's work on them, they never lived to see the completion of their work. In that wise, bub, they're no different from the rest of us, right?" He laughed. Then his eyelids drooped again. His head nodded. He seemed to be snoozing. Maybe he was imagining himself in Portugal. The TV was showing another cathedral now. This one was in Germany. The Englishman's voice droned on. "Cathedrals," the blind man said. He sat up and rolled his head back and forth. "If you want the truth, bub, that's about all I know. What I just said. What I heard him say. But maybe you could describe one to me? I wish you'd do it. I'd like that. If you want to know, I really don't have a good idea."

I stared hard at the shot of the cathedral on the TV. How could I even begin to describe it? But say my life depended on it. Say my life was being threatened by an insane guy who said I had to do it or else.

I stared some more at the cathedral before the picture flipped off into the countryside. There was no use. I turned to the blind man and said, "To begin with, they're very tall." I was looking around the room for clues. "They reach way up. Up and up. Toward the sky. They're so big, some of them, they have to have these supports. To help hold them up, so to speak. These supports are called buttresses. They remind me of viaducts, for some reason. But maybe you don't know viaducts, either? Sometimes the cathedrals have devils and such carved into the front. Sometimes lords and ladies. Don't ask me why this is," I said.

He was nodding. The whole upper part of his body seemed to be moving back and forth.

"I'm not doing so good, am I?" I said.

He stopped nodding and leaned forward on the edge of the sofa. As he listened to me, he was running his fingers through his beard. I wasn't getting through to him, I could see that. But he waited for me to go on just the same. He nodded, like he was trying to encourage me. I tried to think what else to say. "They're really big," I said. "They're massive. They're built of stone. Marble, too, sometimes. In those olden days, when they built cathedrals, men wanted to be close to God. In those olden days, God was an important part of everyone's life. You could tell this from their cathedral-building. I'm sorry," I said, "but it looks like that's the best I can do for you. I'm just no good at it."

95

100

"That's all right, bub," the blind man said. "Hey, listen. I hope you don't mind my asking you. Can I ask you something? Let me ask you a simple question, yes or no. I'm just curious and there's no offense. You're my host. But let me ask if you are in any way religious? You don't mind my asking?"

I shook my head. He couldn't see that, though. A wink is the same as a nod to a blind man. "I guess I don't believe in it. In anything. Sometimes it's hard. You know what I'm saying?"

"Sure, I do," he said.

"Right," I said.   105

The Englishman was still holding forth. My wife sighed in her sleep. She drew a long breath and went on with her sleeping.

"You'll have to forgive me," I said. "But I can't tell you what a cathedral looks like. It just isn't in me to do it. I can't do any more than I've done."

The blind man sat very still, his head down, as he listened to me.

I said, "The truth is, cathedrals don't mean anything special to me. Nothing. Cathedrals. They're something to look at on late-night TV. That's all they are."

It was then that the blind man cleared his throat. He brought something up. He   110
took a handkerchief from his back pocket. Then he said, "I get it, bub. It's okay. It happens. Don't worry about it," he said. "Hey, listen to me. Will you do me a favor? I got an idea. Why don't you find us some heavy paper? And a pen. We'll do something. We'll draw one together. Get us a pen and some heavy paper. Go on, bub, get the stuff," he said.

So I went upstairs. My legs felt like they didn't have any strength in them. They felt like they did after I'd done some running. In my wife's room I looked around. I found some ballpoints in a little basket on her table. And then I tried to think where to look for the kind of paper he was talking about.

Downstairs, in the kitchen, I found a shopping bag with onion skins in the bottom of the bag. I emptied the bag and shook it. I brought it into the living room and sat down with it near his legs. I moved some things, smoothed the wrinkles from the bag, spread it out on the coffee table.

The blind man got down from the sofa and sat next to me on the carpet.

He ran his fingers over the paper. He went up and down the sides of the paper. The edges, even the edges. He fingered the corners.

"All right," he said. "All right, let's do her."   115

He found my hand, the hand with the pen. He closed his hand over my hand. "Go ahead, bub, draw," he said. "Draw. You'll see. I'll follow along with you. It'll be okay. Just begin now like I'm telling you. You'll see. Draw," the blind man said.

So I began. First I drew a box that looked like a house. It could have been the house I lived in. Then I put a roof on it. At either end of the roof, I drew spires. Crazy.

"Swell," he said. "Terrific. You're doing fine," he said. "Never thought anything like this could happen in your lifetime, did you, bub? Well, it's a strange life, we all know that. Go on now. Keep it up."

I put in windows with arches. I drew flying buttresses. I hung great doors. I couldn't stop. The TV station went off the air. I put down the pen and closed and opened my fingers. The blind man felt around over the paper. He moved the tips of his fingers over the paper, all over what I had drawn, and he nodded.

"Doing fine," the blind man said.   120

I took up the pen again, and he found my hand. I kept at it. I'm no artist. But I kept drawing just the same.

My wife opened up her eyes and gazed at us. She sat up on the sofa, her robe hanging open. She said, "What are you doing? Tell me, I want to know."

I didn't answer her.

The blind man said, "We're drawing a cathedral. Me and him are working on it. Press hard," he said to me. "That's right. That's good," he said. "Sure. You got it, bub, I can tell. You didn't think you could. But you can, can't you? You're cooking with gas now. You know what I'm saying? We're going to really have us something here in a minute. How's the old arm?" he said. "Put some people in there now. What's a cathedral without people?"

My wife said, "What's going on? Robert, what are you doing? What's going on?"   125

"It's all right," he said to her. "Close your eyes now," the blind man said to me.

I did it. I closed them just like he said.

"Are they closed?" he said. "Don't fudge."

"They're closed," I said.

"Keep them that way," he said. He said, "Don't stop now. Draw."   130

So we kept on with it. His fingers rode my fingers as my hand went over the paper. It was like nothing else in my life up to now.

Then he said, "I think that's it. I think you got it," he said. "Take a look. What do you think?"

But I had my eyes closed. I thought I'd keep them that way for a little longer. I thought it was something I ought to do.

"Well?" he said. "Are you looking?"

My eyes were still closed. I was in my house. I knew that. But I didn't feel like I   135 was inside anything.

"It's really something," I said.

Questions

1. What details in "Cathedral" make clear the narrator's initial attitude toward blind people? What hints does the author give about the reasons for this attitude? At what point in the story do the narrator's preconceptions about blind people start to change?

2. For what reason does the wife keep asking Robert if he'd like to go to bed (paragraphs 74–78)? What motivates the narrator to make the same suggestion in paragraph 82? What effect does Robert's reply have on the narrator?

3. What makes the narrator start explaining what he's seeing on television?

4. How does the point of view contribute to the effectiveness of the story?

5. At the end, the narrator has an epiphany. How would you describe it?

6. Would you describe the narrator as an antihero? Use specific details from the story to back up your response.

7. Is the wife a flat or a round character? What about Robert? Support your conclusion about each of them.

8. In a good story, a character doesn't suddenly become a completely different sort of person. Find details early in the story that show the narrator's more sensitive side and thus help to make his development credible and persuasive.

■ WRITING *effectively*

Raymond Carver on Writing

Commonplace but Precise Language   1983

It's possible, in a poem or short story, to write about commonplace things and objects using commonplace but precise language, and to endow those things—a chair, a window curtain, a fork, a stone, a woman's earring—with immense, even startling power. It is possible to write a line of seemingly innocuous dialogue and have it send a chill along the reader's spine—the source of artistic delight, as Nabokov would have it. That's the kind of writing that most interests me. I hate sloppy or haphazard writing whether it flies under the banner of experimentation or else is just clumsily rendered realism. In Isaac Babel's wonderful short story, "Guy de Maupassant," the narrator has this to say about the writing of fiction: "No iron can pierce the heart with such force as a period put just at the right place." This too ought to go on a three-by-five.

Raymond Carver

Evan Connell said once that he knew he was finished with a short story when he found himself going through it and taking out commas and then going through the story again and putting commas back in the same places. I like that way of working on something. I respect that kind of care for what is being done. That's all we have, finally, the words, and they had better be the right ones, with the punctuation in the right places so that they can best say what they are meant to say. If the words are heavy with the writer's own unbridled emotions, or if they are imprecise and inaccurate for some reason—if the words are in any way blurred—the reader's eyes will slide right over them and nothing will be achieved.

From "On Writing"

THINKING ABOUT CHARACTER

Although readers usually consider plot the central element of fiction, writers usually remark that stories begin with characters.

- **Identify the most important character.** The central character is the one who must deal with the plot complications and the primary crisis of the story. The choices made by this character communicate his or her attitudes as well as the story's themes.
- **Consider the ways the characters' personalities and values are communicated.** Note that the way characters speak can immediately reveal important

things about their personalities, beliefs, and behavior. A single line of dialogue can tell the audience a great deal.

■ **Consider how the story's action grows out of its central character.** A story's
action usually grows out of the personality of its protagonist and the situation he or she faces. As novelist Phyllis Bottome observed, "If a writer is true
to his characters, they will give him his plot."

CHECKLIST: Writing About Character

☐ Who is the main character or protagonist of the story?

☐ Make a quick list of the character's physical, mental, moral, or
behavioral traits. Which seem especially significant to the action
of the story?

☐ Does the main character have an antagonist in the story? How do
they differ?

☐ Does the way the protagonist speaks reveal anything about his or
her personality?

☐ If the story is told in the first person, what is revealed about how
the protagonist views his or her surroundings?

☐ What is the character's primary motivation? Does this motivation
seem reasonable to you?

☐ Does the protagonist fully understand his or her motivations?

☐ In what ways is the protagonist changed or tested by the events of
the story?

TOPICS FOR WRITING ON CHARACTER

1. Choose a story with a dynamic protagonist. (See the beginning of this chapter for a discussion of dynamic characters.) Write an essay exploring how that character evolves over
   the course of the story, providing evidence from the story to back up your argument. Some
   good story choices might be Faulkner's "Barn Burning" (Chapter 5), Carver's "Cathedral,"
   Baldwin's "Sonny's Blues" (Chapter 2), and Morrison's "Recitatif."

2. Using a story from this book, write a short essay that explains why a protagonist takes a
   crucial life-changing action. What motivates this character to do something that seems
   bold or surprising? You might consider:
   ■ What motivates the narrator to overcome his instinctive antipathy to the blind
     man in "Cathedral"?
   ■ What motivates the older brother to write to Sonny during his incarceration in
     "Sonny's Blues"?
   ■ Why does Connie go outside at the end of "Where Are You Going, Where Have
     You Been?"

3. Choose a minor character from any of the stories in this book, and write briefly on what
   the story reveals about that person, reading closely for even the smallest of details. Is he or
   she a stock character? Why or why not?

4. Choose a story in which the main character has an obvious antagonist, such as "Cathedral,"
   "Recitatif," or "A & P" (Chapter 1). You can even choose a story with a nonhuman antagonist, such as "The Open Boat" (Chapter 6) or "To Build a Fire" (Chapter 6). What role does
   this second character play in bringing the protagonist to a new awareness of life?

5. Choose a favorite character from a television show you watch regularly. What details are
   provided (either in the show's dialogue or in its visuals) to communicate the personality

of this character? Would you say this person is a stock character or a rounded one? Write a brief essay making a case for your position.

6. Browse through magazines and newspapers to find a picture of a person you can't identify. Cut out the picture. Create a character based on the picture. As many writers do, make a list of characteristics, from the major (her life's ambition) to the minor (his favorite breakfast cereal). As you build your list, make sure your details add up to a rounded character.

▶ TERMS FOR *review*

Characterization ▶ The techniques a writer uses to create, reveal, or develop the characters in a narrative.

Character description ▶ An aspect of characterization through which the author overtly relates either physical or mental traits of a character. This description is almost invariably a sign of what lurks beneath the surface of the character.

Character development ▶ The process by which a character is introduced, advanced, and possibly transformed in a story.

Motivation ▶ What a character in a narrative wants; the reasons an author provides for a character's actions. Motivation can be either explicit (the reasons are specifically stated in a story) or implicit (the reasons are only hinted at or partially revealed).

Flat (or static) character ▶ A term coined by English novelist E. M. Forster to describe a character with only one outstanding trait. Flat characters are rarely the central characters in a narrative and stay the same throughout a story.

Round (or dynamic) character ▶ A term also coined by E. M. Forster to describe a complex character who is presented in depth in a narrative. Round characters are those who change significantly during the course of a narrative or whose full personalities are revealed gradually throughout the story.

Stock character ▶ A common or stereotypical character. Examples of stock characters are the mad scientist, the battle-scarred veteran, and the strong but silent cowboy.

Hero ▶ The central character in a narrative. The term *hero* often implies positive moral attributes.

Antihero ▶ A protagonist who is lacking in one or more of the conventional qualities attributed to a hero. Instead of being dignified, brave, idealistic, or purposeful, for instance, the antihero may be buffoonish, cowardly, self-interested, or weak.

4

SETTING

> *What are the three key rules of real estate?*
> *Location, location, location!*
>
> —AMERICAN BUSINESS PROVERB

What You Will Learn in This Chapter

- To understand and define *setting*
- To identify the elements of setting—including place, time, weather, and atmosphere
- To describe literary modes such as *historical fiction*, *regionalism*, and *naturalism*
- To analyze the role of setting in a story

ELEMENTS OF SETTING

By the **setting** of a story, we mean its time and place. Yet often, in an effective short story, setting may figure as more than mere background or underpinning. It can make things happen. It can prompt characters to act, bring them to realizations, or cause them to reveal their inmost natures.

Place

Of course, the idea of setting includes the physical environment of a story: a house, a street, a city, a landscape, a region. *Where* a story takes place is often called its **locale**. Physical places mattered so greatly to French novelist Honoré de Balzac that sometimes, before writing a story set in a particular town, he would visit that town, select a few houses, and describe them in detail, down to their very smells.

Time

In addition to place, setting may crucially involve the *time* of the story—the hour, year, or century. It might matter greatly that a story takes place at dawn, or on the day of the first moon landing. When we begin to read a historical novel, we are soon made aware that we aren't reading about modern-day life. In *The Scarlet Letter*, nineteenth-century author Nathaniel Hawthorne, by a long introduction and a vivid opening scene at a prison door, prepares us to witness events in the Puritan community of Boston in the seventeenth century. This setting, together with scenes of Puritan times we recall from high school history, helps us understand what happens in the novel. We can appreciate the shocked agitation in town when a woman is accused of adultery: she has given illegitimate birth. Such an event might seem common today, but in the stern, God-fearing New England Puritan community, it was a flagrant defiance of church and state, which were all-powerful (and were all one).

That reader will make no sense of *The Scarlet Letter* who ignores its setting—if it is even possible to ignore the historical setting. The fact that Hawthorne's novel takes place in a time remote from our own leads us to expect different customs and different attitudes. Some critics and teachers regard the setting of a story as its whole society, including the beliefs and assumptions of its characters.

Weather

Besides time and place, setting may also include the weather, which in some stories is a crucial element. Climate seems as substantial as any character in William Faulkner's story "Dry September." After sixty-two rainless days, a long unbroken spell of late-summer heat has frayed every nerve in a small town and caused the main character, a hotheaded white supremacist, to feel more and more irritated. The weather, someone remarks, is "enough to make a man do anything." When a false report circulates that a white woman has been raped by a black man, the rumor, like a match flung into a dry field, ignites rage and provokes a lynching. To fully understand the story we have to recognize its locale, a small town in Mississippi in the 1930s during an infernal heat wave.

Atmosphere

Atmosphere is the dominant mood or feeling that pervades all parts of a literary work. Atmosphere refers to the total effect conveyed by the author's use of language, images, and physical setting. But as the term *atmosphere* suggests, aspects of the physical setting (place, time, and weather) are usually essential elements in achieving the author's intention. In some stories, a writer will seem to draw a setting mainly to evoke atmosphere. In such a story, setting starts us feeling whatever the storyteller would have us feel. In "The Tell-Tale Heart," Poe's having set the action in an old, dark, lantern-lit house greatly contributes to our sense of unease—and so helps the story's effectiveness.

HISTORICAL FICTION

One example of how time can become a major element of setting is in **historical fiction**, where the author tries to recreate a faithful picture of daily life in another time and place. The historical period might be long ago, such as ancient Rome in Robert Graves's novel *I, Claudius* (1934), or it may be more recent, as in the setting of early twentieth-century Britain in Ian McEwan's *Atonement* (2001). Historical fiction sometimes introduces well-known figures from the past. Thornton Wilder's *Ides of March* (1948) includes Julius Caesar and Cleopatra among its many characters. Ron Hansen's *Exiles* (2008) depicts the life of English poet Gerard Manley Hopkins. More often, historical fiction presents imaginary characters in a carefully reconstructed version of a particular period of the past. Part of the pleasure of reading this sort of fiction comes from experiencing the many details of another time, just as films carefully set in a particular historical moment, such as Ridley Scott's *Gladiator* (2000) and James Cameron's *Titanic* (1997), let us see meticulously recreated settings of another time and place.

REGIONALISM

Physical place is especially vital to a **regional writer**, who usually sets stories in one geographic area. Such a writer, often a native of the place, tries to bring it alive for readers who live elsewhere. William Faulkner, a distinguished regional writer, almost always set his novels and stories in his native Mississippi. Kate Chopin became known as a regional writer because she wrote about Louisiana in many of her short stories and in her novel *The Awakening*. Willa Cather, for her novels of frontier Nebraska, is often regarded as another outstanding regionalist (though she also set fiction in Quebec, the Southwest, and, in "Paul's Case" (Chapter 14), Pittsburgh and New York).

There is often something arbitrary, however, about calling an author a regional writer. The label sometimes has a political tinge; it means that the author describes an area outside the political and economic centers of a society. In a sense, we might think of James Joyce as a regional writer, in that all his fiction takes place in the city of Dublin, but instead we usually call him an Irish author.

As such writers show, a place can profoundly affect the character of someone who grew up in it. Willa Cather is fond of portraying strong-minded, independent women, such as the heroine of her novel *My Antonía*, strengthened in part by years of coping with the hardships of life on the wind-lashed prairie.

NATURALISM

Some writers consider the social and economic setting the most important element in the story. They present social environment as the determining factor in human behavior. Their approach is called **naturalism**—fiction of grim realism, in which the writer observes human characters like a scientist observing ants, seeing them as the products and victims of environment and heredity. Naturalism was first consciously developed in fiction in the late nineteenth century by French novelist Émile Zola. Important American naturalists include Jack London, Stephen Crane, and Theodore Dreiser. Dreiser's novel *The Financier* (1912) begins in a city setting. A young boy (who will grow up to be a ruthless industrialist) is watching a battle to the death between a lobster and a squid in a fish-market tank. Dented for the rest of his life by this grim scene, he decides that's exactly the way human society functions.

HOW SETTING CAN HARMONIZE WITH OTHER ELEMENTS OF A STORY

Setting usually operates subtly, and often, setting and character will reveal each other. Recall how Faulkner, at the start of "A Rose for Emily" (Chapter 2), depicts Emily Grierson's house, once handsome but now "an eyesore among eyesores" surrounded by gas stations. Still standing, refusing to yield its old-time horse-and-buggy splendor to the age of the automobile, the house in "its stubborn and coquettish decay" embodies the character of its owner. In John Steinbeck's "The Chrysanthemums" (Chapter 7), the story begins with a fog that has sealed off a valley from the rest of the world—a fog like the lid on a pot. That physical setting helps convey the isolation and loneliness of the protagonist's situation.

But be warned: you'll meet stories in which setting appears hardly to matter. In the Sufi fable "Death Has an Appointment in Samarra" (Chapter 1), all we need to be told about the setting is that it is an inn in Baghdad. In that brief fable, the inevitability of death is the point, not an exotic setting. In this chapter, though, you will meet four fine stories in which setting, for one reason or another, counts greatly. Without it, none of these stories could take place.

Kate Chopin

The Storm (1898)

Kate Chopin (1851–1904) was born Katherine O'Flaherty in St. Louis, the daughter of an Irish immigrant grown wealthy in retailing. On his death, young Kate was raised by her mother's family: aristocratic Creoles, descendants of the French and Spaniards who had colonized Louisiana. She received a convent schooling and at nineteen married Oscar Chopin, a Creole cotton broker from New Orleans. Later, the Chopins lived on a plantation near Cloutierville, Louisiana, a region whose varied people— Creoles, Cajuns, blacks—Kate Chopin was later to write about with loving care in Bayou Folk *(1894) and* A Night in Arcadie *(1897). The shock of her husband's sudden death in 1883, which left her with the raising of six children, seems to have plunged Kate Chopin into writing. She read and admired fine woman writers of her day, such as the Maine realist*

Kate Chopin

Sarah Orne Jewett. She also read Maupassant, Zola, and other new (and scandalous) French naturalist writers. She began to bring into American fiction some of their hard-eyed observation and their passion for telling unpleasant truths. Determined, in defiance of her times, frankly to show the sexual feelings of her characters, Chopin suffered from neglect and censorship. When her major novel, The Awakening, *appeared in 1899, critics were outraged by her candid portrait of a woman who seeks sexual and professional independence. After causing such a literary scandal, Chopin was unable to get her later work published and wrote little more before she died.* The Awakening *and many of her stories had to wait seven decades for a sympathetic audience.*

I

The leaves were so still that even Bibi thought it was going to rain. Bobinôt, who was accustomed to converse on terms of perfect equality with his little son, called the child's attention to certain somber clouds that were rolling with sinister intention from the west, accompanied by a sullen, threatening roar. They were at Friedheimer's store and decided to remain there till the storm had passed. They sat within the door on two empty kegs. Bibi was four years old and looked very wise.

"Mama'll be 'fraid, yes," he suggested with blinking eyes.

"She'll shut the house. Maybe she got Sylvie helpin' her this evenin'," Bobinôt responded reassuringly.

"No; she ent got Sylvie. Sylvie was helpin' her yistiday," piped Bibi.

Bobinôt arose and going across to the counter purchased a can of shrimps, of which Calixta was very fond. Then he returned to his perch on the keg and sat stolidly holding the can of shrimps while the storm burst. It shook the wooden store and seemed to be ripping great furrows in the distant field. Bibi laid his little hand on his father's knee and was not afraid. 5

II

Calixta, at home, felt no uneasiness for their safety. She sat at a side window sewing furiously on a sewing machine. She was greatly occupied and did not notice the approaching storm. But she felt very warm and often stopped to mop her face on which the perspiration gathered in beads. She unfastened her white sacque at the throat. It began to grow dark, and suddenly realizing the situation she got up hurriedly and went about closing windows and doors.

Out on the small front gallery she had hung Bobinôt's Sunday clothes to air and she hastened out to gather them before the rain fell. As she stepped outside, Alcée Laballière rode in at the gate. She had not seen him very often since her marriage, and never alone. She stood there with Bobinôt's coat in her hands, and the big rain drops began to fall. Alcée rode his horse under the shelter of a side projection where the chickens had huddled and there were plows and a harrow piled up in the corner.

"May I come and wait on your gallery till the storm is over, Calixta?" he asked.

"Come 'long in, M'sieur Alcée."

His voice and her own startled her as if from a trance, and she seized Bobinôt's   10
vest. Alcée, mounting to the porch, grabbed the trousers and snatched Bibi's braided jacket that was about to be carried away by a sudden gust of wind. He expressed an intention to remain outside, but it was soon apparent that he might as well have been out in the open: the water beat in upon the boards in driving sheets, and he went inside, closing the door after him. It was even necessary to put something beneath the door to keep the water out.

"My! what a rain! It's good two years sence it rain' like that," exclaimed Calixta as she rolled up a piece of bagging and Alcée helped her to thrust it beneath the crack.

She was a little fuller of figure than five years before when she married; but she had lost nothing of her vivacity. Her blue eyes still retained their melting quality; and her yellow hair, dishevelled by the wind and rain, kinked more stubbornly than ever about her ears and temples.

The rain beat upon the low, shingled roof with a force and clatter that threatened to break an entrance and deluge them there. They were in the dining room—the sitting room—the general utility room. Adjoining was her bed room, with Bibi's couch along side her own. The door stood open, and the room with its white, monumental bed, its closed shutters, looked dim and mysterious.

Alcée flung himself into a rocker and Calixta nervously began to gather up from the floor the lengths of a cotton sheet which she had been sewing.

"If this keeps up, *Dieu sait*° if the levees goin' to stan' it!" she exclaimed.   15

"What have you got to do with the levees?"

"I got enough to do! An' there's Bobinôt with Bibi out in that storm—if he only didn' left Friedheimer's!"

"Let us hope, Calixta, that Bobinôt's got sense enough to come in out of a cyclone."

She went and stood at the window with a greatly disturbed look on her face. She wiped the frame that was clouded with moisture. It was stiflingly hot. Alcée got up and joined her at the window, looking over her shoulder. The rain was coming down in sheets obscuring the view of far-off cabins and enveloping the distant wood in a gray mist. The playing of the lightning was incessant. A bolt struck a tall chinaberry tree at the edge of the field. It filled all visible space with a blinding glare and the crash seemed to invade the very boards they stood upon.

Calixta put her hands to her eyes, and with a cry, staggered backward. Alcée's   20
arm encircled her, and for an instant he drew her close and spasmodically to him.

Dieu sait: God only knows.

"*Bonté!*"° she cried, releasing herself from his encircling arm and retreating from the window, "the house'll go next! If I only knew w'ere Bibi was!" She would not compose herself; she would not be seated. Alcée clasped her shoulders and looked into her face. The contact of her warm, palpitating body when he had unthinkingly drawn her into his arms, had aroused all the old-time infatuation and desire for her flesh.

"Calixta," he said, "don't be frightened. Nothing can happen. The house is too low to be struck, with so many tall trees standing about. There! aren't you going to be quiet? say, aren't you?" He pushed her hair back from her face that was warm and steaming. Her lips were as red and moist as pomegranate seed. Her white neck and a glimpse of her full, firm bosom disturbed him powerfully. As she glanced up at him the fear in her liquid blue eyes had given place to a drowsy gleam that unconsciously betrayed a sensuous desire. He looked down into her eyes and there was nothing for him to do but gather her lips in a kiss. It reminded him of Assumption.°

"Do you remember—in Assumption, Calixta?" he asked in a low voice broken by passion. Oh! she remembered; for in Assumption he had kissed her and kissed and kissed her; until his senses would well nigh fail, and to save her he would resort to a desperate flight. If she was not an immaculate dove in those days, she was still inviolate; a passionate creature whose very defenselessness had made her defense, against which his honor forbade him to prevail. Now—well, now—her lips seemed in a manner free to be tasted, as well as her round, white throat and her whiter breasts.

They did not heed the crashing torrents, and the roar of the elements made her laugh as she lay in his arms. She was a revelation in that dim, mysterious chamber; as white as the couch she lay upon. Her firm, elastic flesh that was knowing for the first time its birthright, was like a creamy lily that the sun invites to contribute its breath and perfume to the undying life of the world.

The generous abundance of her passion, without guile or trickery, was like a   25
white flame which penetrated and found response in depths of his own sensuous nature that had never yet been reached.

When he touched her breasts they gave themselves up in quivering ecstasy, inviting his lips. Her mouth was a fountain of delight. And when he possessed her, they seemed to swoon together at the very borderland of life's mystery.

He stayed cushioned upon her, breathless, dazed, enervated, with his heart beating like a hammer upon her. With one hand she clasped his head, her lips lightly touching his forehead. The other hand stroked with a soothing rhythm his muscular shoulders.

The growl of the thunder was distant and passing away. The rain beat softly upon the shingles, inviting them to drowsiness and sleep. But they dared not yield.

The rain was over; and the sun was turning the glistening green world into a palace of gems. Calixta, on the gallery, watched Alcée ride away. He turned and smiled at her with a beaming face; and she lifted her pretty chin in the air and laughed aloud.

III

Bobinôt and Bibi, trudging home, stopped without at the cistern to make them-   30
selves presentable.

"My! Bibi, w'at will yo' mama say! You ought to be ashame'. You oughtn' put on those good pants. Look at 'em! An' that mud on yo' collar! How you got that mud

---

Bonté!: Heavens!   *Assumption*: a parish west of New Orleans.

on yo' collar, Bibi? I never saw such a boy!" Bibi was the picture of pathetic resignation. Bobinôt was the embodiment of serious solicitude as he strove to remove from his own person and his son's the signs of their tramp over heavy roads and through wet fields. He scraped the mud off Bibi's bare legs and feet with a stick and carefully removed all traces from his heavy brogans. Then, prepared for the worst—the meeting with an overscrupulous housewife, they entered cautiously at the back door.

Calixta was preparing supper. She had set the table and was dripping coffee at the hearth. She sprang up as they came in.

"Oh, Bobinôt! You back! My! but I was uneasy. W'ere you been during the rain? An' Bibi? he ain't wet? he ain't hurt?" She had clasped Bibi and was kissing him effusively. Bobinôt's explanations and apologies which he had been composing all along the way, died on his lips as Calixta felt him to see if he were dry, and seemed to express nothing but satisfaction at their safe return.

"I brought you some shrimps, Calixta," offered Bobinôt, hauling the can from his ample side pocket and laying it on the table.

"Shrimps! Oh, Bobinôt! you too good fo' anything!" and she gave him a smacking kiss on the cheek that resounded. "*J'vous réponds*,° we'll have a feas' to night! umph-umph!"   35

Bobinôt and Bibi began to relax and enjoy themselves, and when the three seated themselves at table they laughed much and so loud that anyone might have heard them as far away as Laballière's.

IV

Alcée Laballière wrote to his wife, Clarisse, that night. It was a loving letter, full of tender solicitude. He told her not to hurry back, but if she and the babies liked it at Biloxi, to stay a month longer. He was getting on nicely; and though he missed them, he was willing to bear the separation a while longer—realizing that their health and pleasure were the first things to be considered.

V

As for Clarisse, she was charmed upon receiving her husband's letter. She and the babies were doing well. The society was agreeable; many of her old friends and acquaintances were at the bay. And the first free breath since her marriage seemed to restore the pleasant liberty of her maiden days. Devoted as she was to her husband, their intimate conjugal life was something which she was more than willing to forego for a while.

So the storm passed and everyone was happy.

Questions

1. Exactly where does Chopin's story take place? How can you tell?
2. What circumstances introduced in Part I turn out to have a profound effect on events in the story?
3. What details in "The Storm" emphasize the fact that Bobinôt loves his wife? What details reveal how imperfectly he comprehends her nature?
4. What general attitudes toward sex, love, and marriage does Chopin imply? Cite evidence to support your answer.
5. What meanings do you find in the title "The Storm"?
6. In the story as a whole, how do setting and plot reinforce each other?

J'vous réponds: Let me tell you.

Jack London

To Build a Fire

1910

Jack London (1876–1916), born in San Francisco, won a large popular audience for his novels of the sea and the Yukon: The Call of the Wild *(1903),* The Sea-Wolf *(1904), and* White Fang *(1906). Like Ernest Hemingway, he was a writer who lived a strenuous and eventful life. In 1893, he marched cross-country in Coxey's Army, an organized protest of the unemployed; in 1897, he took part in the Klondike Gold Rush; and later, as a reporter, he covered the Russo-Japanese War and the Mexican Revolution. Son of an unmarried mother and a father who denied his paternity, London grew up in poverty. At fourteen, he began holding hard jobs: working in a canning factory and a jutemill, serving as a deck hand, pirating oysters in San Francisco Bay. These experiences persuaded him to join the Socialist Labor Party and crusade for workers' rights. In*

Jack London

his political novel The Iron Heel *(1908), London envisions a grim totalitarian America. Like himself, the hero of his novel* Martin Eden *(1909) is a man of brief schooling who gains fame as a writer, works for a cause, loses faith in it, and finds life without meaning. Though endowed with immense physical energy—he wrote fifty volumes—London drank hard, spent fast, and played out early. While his reputation as a novelist may have declined since his own day, some of his short stories have lasted triumphantly.*

Day had broken cold and gray, exceedingly cold and gray, when the man turned aside from the main Yukon trail and climbed the high earth-bank, where a dim and little-travelled trail led eastward through the fat spruce timberland. It was a steep bank, and he paused for breath at the top, excusing the act to himself by looking at his watch. It was nine o'clock. There was no sun nor hint of sun, though there was not a cloud in the sky. It was a clear day, and yet there seemed an intangible pall over the face of things, a subtle gloom that made the day dark, and that was due to the absence of sun. This fact did not worry the man. He was used to the lack of sun. It had been days since he had seen the sun, and he knew that a few more days must pass before that cheerful orb, due south, would just peep above the sky line and dip immediately from view.

The man flung a look back along the way he had come. The Yukon lay a mile wide and hidden under three feet of ice. On top of this ice were as many feet of snow. It was all pure white, rolling in gentle undulations where the ice jams of the freeze-up had formed. North and south, as far as the eye could see, it was unbroken white, save for a dark hairline that curved and twisted from around the spruce-covered island to the south, and that curved and twisted away into the north, where it disappeared behind another spruce-covered island. This dark hairline was the trail—the main trail—that led south five hundred miles to the Chilcoot Pass, Dyea, and salt water; and that led north seventy miles to Dawson, and still on to the north a thousand miles to Nulato, and finally to St. Michael, on Bering Sea, a thousand miles and half a thousand more.

But all this—the mysterious, far-reaching hairline trail, the absence of sun from the sky, the tremendous cold, and the strangeness and weirdness of it all—made no impression on the man. It was not because he was long used to it. He was a newcomer in the land, a *chechaquo*, and this was his first winter. The trouble with him was that he was without imagination. He was quick and alert in the things of life, but only in the things, and not in the significances. Fifty degrees below zero meant eighty-odd degrees of frost. Such fact impressed him as being cold and uncomfortable, and that was all. It did not lead him to meditate upon his frailty as a creature of tempera-ture, and upon man's frailty in general, able only to live within certain narrow limits of heat and cold; and from there on it did not lead him to the conjectural field of immortality and man's place in the universe. Fifty degrees below zero stood for a bite of frost that hurt and that must be guarded against by the use of mittens, ear flaps, warm moccasins, and thick socks. Fifty degrees below zero was to him just precisely fifty degrees below zero. That there should be anything more to it than that was a thought that never entered his head.

As he turned to go on, he spat speculatively. There was a sharp, explosive crackle that startled him. He spat again. And again, in the air, before it could fall to the snow, the spittle crackled. He knew that at fifty below spittle crackled on the snow, but this spittle had crackled in the air. Undoubtedly it was colder than fifty below—how much colder he did not know. But the temperature did not matter. He was bound for the old claim on the left fork of Henderson Creek, where the boys were already. They had come over across the divide from the Indian Creek country, while he had come the roundabout way to take a look at the possibilities of getting out logs in the spring from the islands in the Yukon. He would be in to camp by six o'clock; a bit after dark, it was true, but the boys would be there, a fire would be going, and a hot supper would be ready. As for lunch, he pressed his hand against the protruding bundle under his jacket. It was also under his shirt, wrapped up in a handkerchief and lying against the naked skin. It was the only way to keep the biscuits from freezing. He smiled agree-ably to himself as he thought of those biscuits, each cut open and sopped in bacon grease, and each enclosing a generous slice of fried bacon.

He plunged in among the big spruce trees. The trail was faint. A foot of snow   5
had fallen since the last sled had passed over, and he was glad he was without a sled, travelling light. In fact, he carried nothing but the lunch wrapped in the handker-chief. He was surprised, however, at the cold. It certainly was cold, he concluded, as he rubbed his numb nose and cheekbones with his mittened hand. He was a warm-whiskered man, but the hair on his face did not protect the high cheekbones and the eager nose that thrust itself aggressively into the frosty air.

At the man's heels trotted a dog, a big native husky, the proper wolf dog, gray-coated and without any visible or temperamental difference from its brother, the wild wolf. The animal was depressed by the tremendous cold. It knew that it was no time for travelling. Its instinct told it a truer tale than was told to the man by the man's judgment. In reality, it was not merely colder than fifty below zero; it was colder than sixty below, than seventy below. It was seventy-five below zero. Since the freezing point is thirty-two above zero, it meant that one hundred and seven degrees of frost obtained. The dog did not know anything about thermometers. Possibly in its brain there was no sharp consciousness of a condition of very cold such as was in the man's brain. But the brute had its instinct. It experienced a vague but menacing apprehen-sion that subdued it and made it slink along at the man's heels, and that made it question eagerly every unwonted movement of the man as if expecting him to go into camp or to seek shelter somewhere and build a fire. The dog had learned fire, and it wanted fire, or else to burrow under the snow and cuddle its warmth away from the air.

The frozen moisture of its breathing had settled on its fur in a fine powder of frost, and especially were its jowls, muzzle, and eyelashes whitened by its crystalled breath. The man's red beard and mustache were likewise frosted, but more solidly, the deposit taking the form of ice and increasing with every warm, moist breath he exhaled. Also, the man was chewing tobacco, and the muzzle of ice held his lips so rigidly that he was unable to clear his chin when he expelled the juice. The result was that a crystal beard of the color and solidity of amber was increasing its length on his chin. If he fell down it would shatter itself, like glass, into brittle fragments. But he did not mind the appendage. It was the penalty all tobacco chewers paid in that country, and he had been out before in two cold snaps. They had not been so cold as this, he knew, but by the spirit thermometer at Sixty Mile he knew they had been registered at fifty below and at fifty-five.

He held on through the level stretch of woods for several miles, crossed a wide flat, and dropped down a bank to the frozen bed of a small stream. This was Henderson Creek, and he knew he was ten miles from the forks. He looked at his watch. It was ten o'clock. He was making four miles an hour, and he calculated that he would arrive at the forks at half-past twelve. He decided to celebrate that event by eating his lunch there.

The dog dropped in again at his heels, with a tail drooping discouragement, as the man swung along the creek bed. The furrow of the old sled trail was plainly visible, but a dozen inches of snow covered the marks of the last runners. In a month no man had come up or down that silent creek. The man held steadily on. He was not much given to thinking, and just then particularly he had nothing to think about save that he would eat lunch at the forks and that at six o'clock he would be in camp with the boys. There was nobody to talk to; and, had there been, speech would have been impossible because of the ice muzzle on his mouth. So he continued monotonously to chew tobacco and to increase the length of his amber beard.

Once in a while the thought reiterated itself that it was very cold and that he had never experienced such cold. As he walked along he rubbed his cheekbones and nose with the back of his mittened hand. He did this automatically, now and again changing hands. But, rub as he would, the instant he stopped his cheekbones were numb, and the following instant the end of his nose went numb. He was sure to frost his cheeks; he knew that, and experienced a pang of regret that he had not devised a nose strap of the sort Bud wore in cold snaps. Such a strap passed across the cheeks, as well, and saved them. But it didn't matter much, after all. What were frosted cheeks? A bit painful, that was all; they were never serious.

Empty as the man's mind was of thoughts, he was keenly observant, and he noticed the changes in the creek, the curves and bends and timber jams, and always he sharply noted where he placed his feet. Once, coming around a bend, he shied abruptly, like a startled horse, curved away from the place where he had been walking, and retreated several paces back along the trail. The creek he knew was frozen clear to the bottom—no creek could contain water in that arctic winter—but he knew also that there were springs that bubbled out from the hillsides and ran along under the snow and on top the ice of the creek. He knew that the coldest snaps never froze these springs, and he knew likewise their danger. They were traps. They hid pools of water under the snow that might be three inches deep, or three feet. Sometimes a skin of ice half an inch thick covered them, and in turn was covered by the snow. Sometimes

10

there were alternate layers of water and ice skin, so that when one broke through he kept on breaking through for a while, sometimes wetting himself to the waist.

That was why he had shied in such panic. He had felt the give under his feet and heard the crackle of a snow-hidden ice skin. And to get his feet wet in such a temperature meant trouble and danger. At the very least it meant delay, for he would be forced to stop and build a fire, and under its protection to bare his feet while he dried his socks and moccasins. He stood and studied the creek bed and its banks, and decided that the flow of water came from the right. He reflected awhile, rubbing his nose and cheeks, then skirted to the left, stepping gingerly and testing the footing for each step. Once clear of the danger, he took a fresh chew of tobacco and swung along at his four-mile gait.

In the course of the next two hours he came upon several similar traps. Usually the snow above the hidden pools had a sunken, candied appearance that advertised the danger. Once again, however, he had a close call; and once, suspecting danger, he compelled the dog to go on in front. The dog did not want to go. It hung back until the man shoved it forward, and then it went quickly across the white, unbroken surface. Suddenly it broke through, floundered to one side, and got away to firmer footing. It had wet its fore-feet and legs, and almost immediately the water that clung to it turned to ice. It made quick efforts to lick the ice off its legs, then dropped down in the snow and began to bite out the ice that had formed between the toes. This was a matter of instinct. To permit the ice to remain would mean sore feet. It did not know this. It merely obeyed the mysterious prompting that arose from the deep crypts of its being. But the man knew, having achieved a judgment on the subject, and he removed the mitten from his right hand and helped tear out the ice particles. He did not expose his fingers more than a minute, and was astonished at the swift numbness that smote them. It certainly was cold. He pulled on the mitten hastily, and beat the hand savagely across his chest.

At twelve o'clock the day was at its brightest. Yet the sun was too far south on its winter journey to clear the horizon. The bulge of the earth intervened between it and Henderson Creek, where the man walked under a clear sky at noon and cast no shadow. At half-past twelve, to the minute, he arrived at the forks of the creek. He was pleased at the speed he had made. If he kept it up, he would certainly be with the boys by six. He unbuttoned his jacket and shirt and drew forth his lunch. The action consumed no more than a quarter of a minute, yet in that brief moment the numbness laid hold of the exposed fingers. He did not put the mitten on, but, instead, struck the fingers a dozen sharp smashes against his leg. Then he sat down on a snow-covered log to eat. The sting that followed upon the striking of his fingers against his leg ceased so quickly that he was startled. He had had no chance to take a bite of biscuit. He struck the fingers repeatedly and returned them to the mitten, baring the other hand for the purpose of eating. He tried to take a mouthful, but the ice muzzle prevented. He had forgotten to build a fire and thaw out. He chuckled at his foolishness, and as he chuckled he noted the numbness creeping into the exposed fingers. Also, he noted that the stinging which had first come to his toes when he sat down was already passing away. He wondered whether the toes were warm or numb. He moved them inside the moccasins and decided that they were numb.

He pulled the mitten on hurriedly and stood up. He was a bit frightened. He   15
stamped up and down until the stinging returned into the feet. It certainly was cold, was his thought. That man from Sulphur Creek had spoken the truth when telling how cold it sometimes got in the country. And he had laughed at him at the time! That showed one must not be too sure of things. There was no mistake about it, it

was cold. He strode up and down, stamping his feet and threshing his arms, until reassured by the returning warmth. Then he got out matches and proceeded to make a fire. From the undergrowth, where high water of the previous spring had lodged a supply of seasoned twigs, he got his firewood. Working carefully from a small beginning, he soon had a roaring fire, over which he thawed the ice from his face and in the protection of which he ate his biscuits. For the moment the cold of space was outwitted. The dog took satisfaction in the fire, stretching out close enough for warmth and far enough away to escape being singed.

When the man had finished, he filled his pipe and took his comfortable time over a smoke. Then he pulled on his mittens, settled the ear flaps of his cap firmly about his ears, and took the creek trail up the left fork. The dog was disappointed and yearned back toward the fire. This man did not know cold. Possibly all the generations of his ancestry had been ignorant of cold, of real cold, of cold one hundred and seven degrees below freezing point. But the dog knew; all its ancestry knew, and it had inherited the knowledge. And it knew that it was not good to walk abroad in such fearful cold. It was the time to lie snug in a hole in the snow and wait for a curtain of cloud to be drawn across the face of outer space whence this cold came. On the other hand, there was no keen intimacy between the dog and the man. The one was the toil slave of the other, and the only caresses it had ever received were the caresses of the whip lash and of harsh and menacing throat sounds that threatened the whip lash. So the dog made no effort to communicate its apprehension to the man. It was not concerned in the welfare of the man; it was for its own sake that it yearned back toward the fire. But the man whistled, and spoke to it with the sound of whip lashes, and the dog swung in at the man's heels and followed after.

The man took a chew of tobacco and proceeded to start a new amber beard. Also, his moist breath quickly powdered with white his mustache, eyebrows, and lashes. There did not seem to be so many springs on the left fork of the Henderson, and for half an hour the man saw no signs of any. And then it happened. At a place where there were no signs, where the soft, unbroken snow seemed to advertise solidity beneath, the man broke through. It was not deep. He wet himself halfway to the knees before he floundered out to the firm crust.

He was angry, and cursed his luck aloud. He had hoped to get into camp with the boys at six o'clock, and this would delay him an hour, for he would have to build a fire and dry out his footgear. This was imperative at that low temperature—he knew that much; and he turned aside to the bank, which he climbed. On top, tangled in the underbrush about the trunks of several small spruce trees, was a high-water deposit of dry firewood—sticks and twigs, principally, but also larger portions of seasoned branches and fine, dry, last year's grasses. He threw down several large pieces on top of the snow. This served for a foundation and prevented the young flame from drowning itself in the snow it otherwise would melt. The flame he got by touching a match to a small shred of birch bark that he took from his pocket. This burned even more readily than paper. Placing it on the foundation, he fed the young flame with wisps of dry grass and with the tiniest dry twigs.

He worked slowly and carefully, keenly aware of his danger. Gradually, as the flame grew stronger, he increased the size of the twigs with which he fed it. He squatted in the snow, pulling the twigs out from their entanglement in the brush and feeding directly to the flame. He knew there must be no failure. When it is seventy-five below zero, a man must not fail in his first attempt to build a fire—that is, if his feet are wet. If his feet are dry, and he fails, he can run along the trail for half a mile and restore his circulation. But the circulation of wet and freezing feet cannot be restored by running when it is seventy-five below. No matter how fast he runs, the wet feet will freeze the harder.

All this the man knew. The old-timer on Sulphur Creek had told him about   20
it the previous fall, and now he was appreciating the advice. Already all sensation
had gone out of his feet. To build the fire he had been forced to remove his mittens,
and the fingers had quickly gone numb. His pace of four miles an hour had kept his
heart pumping blood to the surface of his body and to all the extremities. But the
instant he stopped, the action of the pump eased down. The cold of space smote the
unprotected tip of the planet, and he, being on that unprotected tip, received the full
force of the blow. The blood of his body recoiled before it. The blood was alive, like
the dog, and like the dog it wanted to hide away and cover itself up from the fearful cold. So long as he walked four miles an hour, he pumped that blood, willy-nilly,
to the surface; but now it ebbed away and sank down into the recesses of his body.
The extremities were the first to feel its absence. His wet feet froze the faster, and his
exposed fingers numbed the faster, though they had not yet begun to freeze. Nose and
cheeks were already freezing, while the skin of all his body chilled as it lost its blood.

But he was safe. Toes and nose and cheeks would be only touched by the frost, for
the fire was beginning to burn with strength. He was feeding it with twigs the size of
his finger. In another minute he would be able to feed it with branches the size of his
wrist, and then he could remove his wet footgear, and, while it dried, he could keep
his naked feet warm by the fire, rubbing them at first, of course, with snow. The fire
was a success. He was safe. He remembered the advice of the old-timer on Sulphur
Creek, and smiled. The old-timer had been very serious in laying down the law that
no man must travel alone in the Klondike after fifty below. Well, here he was; he
had had the accident; he was alone; and he had saved himself. Those old-timers were
rather womanish, some of them, he thought. All a man had to do was to keep his
head, and he was all right. Any man who was a man could travel alone. But it was
surprising, the rapidity with which his cheeks and nose were freezing. And he had not
thought his fingers could go lifeless in so short a time. Lifeless they were, for he could
scarcely make them move together to grip a twig, and they seemed remote from his
body and from him. When he touched a twig, he had to look and see whether or not
he had hold of it. The wires were pretty well down between him and his finger ends.

All of which counted for little. There was the fire, snapping and crackling and
promising life with every dancing flame. He started to untie his moccasins. They
were coated with ice; the thick German socks were like sheaths of iron halfway to the
knees; and the moccasin strings were like rods of steel all twisted and knotted as by
some conflagration. For a moment he tugged with his numb fingers, then, realizing
the folly of it, he drew his sheath knife.

But before he could cut the strings, it happened. It was his own fault or, rather,
his mistake. He should not have built the fire under the spruce tree. He should have
built it in the open. But it had been easier to pull the twigs from the brush and
drop them directly on the fire. Now the tree under which he had done this carried
a weight of snow on its boughs. No wind had blown for weeks, and each bough was
fully freighted. Each time he had pulled a twig he had communicated a slight agitation to the tree—an imperceptible agitation, so far as he was concerned, but an agitation sufficient to bring about the disaster. High up in the tree one bough capsized
its load of snow. This fell on the boughs beneath, capsizing them. This process continued, spreading out and involving the whole tree. It grew like an avalanche, and it
descended without warning upon the man and the fire, and the fire was blotted out!
Where it had burned was a mantle of fresh and disordered snow.

The man was shocked. It was as though he had just heard his own sentence of death. For a moment he sat and stared at the spot where the fire had been. Then he grew very calm. Perhaps the old-timer on Sulphur Creek was right. If he had only had a trail mate he would have been in no danger now. The trail mate could have built the fire. Well, it was up to him to build the fire over again, and this second time there must be no failure. Even if he succeeded, he would most likely lose some toes. His feet must be badly frozen by now, and there would be some time before the second fire was ready.

Such were his thoughts, but he did not sit and think them. He was busy all the time they were passing through his mind. He made a new foundation for a fire, this time in the open, where no treacherous tree could blot it out. Next he gathered dry grasses and tiny twigs from the high-water flotsam. He could not bring his fingers together to pull them out, but he was able to gather them by the handful. In this way he got many rotten twigs and bits of green moss that were undesirable, but it was the best he could do. He worked methodically, even collecting an armful of the larger branches to be used later when the fire gathered strength. And all the while the dog sat and watched him, a certain yearning wistfulness in its eye, for it looked upon him as the fire provider, and the fire was slow in coming.

When all was ready, the man reached in his pocket for a second piece of birch bark. He knew the bark was there, and, though he could not feel it with his fingers, he could hear its crisp rustling as he fumbled for it. Try as he would, he could not clutch hold of it. And all the time, in his consciousness, was the knowledge that each instant his feet were freezing. This thought tended to put him in a panic, but he fought against it and kept calm. He pulled on his mittens with his teeth, and threshed his arms back and forth, beating his hands with all his might against his sides. He did this sitting down, and he stood up to do it; and all the while the dog sat in the snow, its wolf brush of a tail curled around warmly over its forefeet, its sharp wolf ears pricked forward intently as it watched the man. And the man, as he beat and threshed with his arms and hands, felt a great surge of envy as he regarded the creature that was warm and secure in its natural covering.

After a time he was aware of the first faraway signals of sensation in his beaten fingers. The faint tingling grew stronger till it evolved into a stinging ache that was excruciating, but which the man hailed with satisfaction. He stripped the mitten from his right hand and fetched forth the birch bark. The exposed fingers were quickly going numb again. Next he brought out his bunch of sulphur matches. But the tremendous cold had already driven the life out of his fingers. In his effort to separate one match from the others, the whole bunch fell in the snow. He tried to pick it out of the snow, but failed. The dead fingers could neither touch nor clutch. He was very careful. He drove the thought of his freezing feet, and nose, and cheeks, out of his mind, devoting his whole soul to the matches. He watched, using the sense of vision in place of that of touch, and when he saw his fingers on each side the bunch, he closed them—that is, he willed to close them, for the wires were down, and the fingers did not obey. He pulled the mitten on the right hand, and beat it fiercely against his knee. Then, with both mittened hands, he scooped the bunch of matches, along with much snow, into his lap. Yet he was no better off.

After some manipulation he managed to get the bunch between the heels of his mittened hands. In this fashion he carried it to his mouth. The ice crackled and snapped when by a violent effort he opened his mouth. He drew the lower jaw in, curled the upper lip out of the way, and scraped the bunch with his upper teeth in order to separate a match. He succeeded in getting one, which he dropped on his lap. He was no better off. He could not pick it up. Then he devised a way. He picked it up in his teeth and scratched it on his leg. Twenty times he scratched before he succeeded in lighting it. As it flamed he held it with his teeth to the birch bark. But the burning brimstone went up his nostrils and into his lungs, causing him to cough spasmodically. The match fell into the snow and went out.

The old-timer on Sulphur Creek was right, he thought in the moment of controlled despair that ensued: after fifty below, a man should travel with a partner. He beat his hands, but failed in exciting any sensation. Suddenly he bared both hands, removing the mittens with his teeth. He caught the whole bunch between the heels of his hands. His arm muscles not being frozen enabled him to press the hand heels tightly against the matches. Then he scratched the bunch along his leg. It flared into flame, seventy sulphur matches at once! There was no wind to blow them out. He kept his head to one side to escape the strangling fumes, and held the blazing bunch to the birch bark. As he so held it, he became aware of sensation in his hand. His flesh was burning. He could smell it. Deep down below the surface he could feel it. The sensation developed into pain that grew acute. And still he endured it, holding the flame of the matches clumsily to the bark that would not light readily because his own burning hands were in the way, absorbing most of the flame.

At last, when he could endure no more, he jerked his hands apart. The blazing matches fell sizzling into the snow, but the birch bark was alight. He began laying dry grasses and the tiniest twigs on the flame. He could not pick and choose, for he had to lift the fuel between the heels of his hands. Small pieces of rotten wood and green moss clung to the twigs, and he bit them off as well as he could with his teeth. He cherished the flame carefully and awkwardly. It meant life, and it must not perish. The withdrawal of blood from the surface of his body now made him begin to shiver, and he grew more awkward. A large piece of green moss fell squarely on the little fire. He tried to poke it out with his fingers, but his shivering frame made him poke too far, and he disrupted the nucleus of the little fire, the burning grasses and tiny twigs separating and scattering. He tried to poke them together again, but in spite of the tenseness of the effort, his shivering got away from him, and the twigs were hopelessly scattered. Each twig gushed a puff of smoke and went out. The fire provider had failed. As he looked apathetically about him, his eyes chanced on the dog, sitting across the ruins of the fire from him, in the snow, making restless, hunching movements, slightly lifting one forefoot and then the other, shifting its weight back and forth on them with wistful eagerness.

The sight of the dog put a wild idea into his head. He remembered the tale of the man, caught in the blizzard, who killed a steer and crawled inside the carcass, and so was saved. He would kill the dog and bury his hands in the warm body until the numbness went out of them. Then he could build another fire. He spoke to the dog, calling it to him; but in his voice was a strange note of fear that frightened the animal, who had never known the man to speak in such a way before. Something was the matter, and its suspicious nature sensed danger—it knew not what danger, but somewhere, somehow, in its brain arose an apprehension of the man. It flattened its ears down at the sound of the man's voice, and its restless, hunching movements and the liftings and shiftings of its forefeet became more pronounced; but it would not come to the man. He got on his hands and knees and crawled toward the dog. This unusual posture again excited suspicion, and the animal sidled mincingly away.

The man sat up in the snow for a moment and struggled for calmness. Then he pulled on his mittens, by means of his teeth, and got upon his feet. He glanced down

30

at first in order to assure himself that he was really standing up, for the absence of sensation in his feet left him unrelated to the earth. His erect position in itself started to drive the webs of suspicion from the dog's mind; and when he spoke peremptorily, with the sound of whip lashes in his voice, the dog rendered its customary allegiance and came to him. As it came within reaching distance, the man lost his control. His arms flashed out to the dog, and he experienced genuine surprise when he discovered that his hands could not clutch, that there was neither bend nor feeling in the fingers. He had forgotten for the moment that they were frozen and that they were freezing more and more. All this happened quickly, and before the animal could get away, he encircled its body with his arms. He sat down in the snow, and in this fashion held the dog, while it snarled and whined and struggled.

But it was all he could do, hold its body encircled in his arms and sit there. He realized that he could not kill the dog. There was no way to do it. With his helpless hands he could neither draw nor hold his sheath knife nor throttle the animal. He released it, and it plunged wildly away, with tail between its legs, and still snarling. It halted forty feet away and surveyed him curiously, with ears sharply pricked forward.

The man looked down at his hands in order to locate them, and found them hanging on the ends of his arms. It struck him as curious that one should have to use his eyes in order to find out where his hands were. He began threshing his arms back and forth, beating the mittened hands against his sides. He did this for five minutes, violently, and his heart pumped enough blood up to the surface to put a stop to his shivering. But no sensation was aroused in the hands. He had an impression that they hung like weights on the ends of his arms, but when he tried to run the impression down, he could not find it.

A certain fear of death, dull and oppressive, came to him. This fear quickly   35
became poignant as he realized that it was no longer a mere matter of freezing his fingers and toes, or of losing his hands and feet, but that it was a matter of life and death with the chances against him. This threw him into a panic, and he turned and ran up the creek bed along the old, dim trail. The dog joined in behind and kept up with him. He ran blindly, without intention, in fear such as he had never known in his life. Slowly, as he plowed and floundered through the snow, he began to see things again—the banks of the creek, the old timber jams, the leafless aspens, and the sky. The running made him feel better. He did not shiver. Maybe, if he ran on, his feet would thaw out; and anyway, if he ran far enough, he would reach camp and the boys. Without doubt he would lose some fingers and toes and some of his face; but the boys would take care of him, and save the rest of him when he got there. And at the same time there was another thought in his mind that said he would never get to the camp and the boys; that it was too many miles away, that the freezing had too great a start on him, and that he would soon be stiff and dead. This thought he kept in the background and refused to consider. Sometimes it pushed itself forward and demanded to be heard, but he thrust it back and strove to think of other things.

It struck him as curious that he could run at all on feet so frozen that he could not feel them when they struck the earth and took the weight of his body. He seemed to himself to skim along above the surface, and to have no connection with the earth. Somewhere he had once seen a winged Mercury, and he wondered if Mercury felt as he felt when skimming over the earth.

His theory of running until he reached the camp and the boys had one flaw in it: he lacked the endurance. Several times he stumbled, and finally he tottered, crumpled up, and fell. When he tried to rise, he failed. He must sit and rest, he decided, and next time he would merely walk and keep on going. As he sat and regained his breath, he noted that he was feeling quite warm and comfortable. He was not shivering, and it even seemed that a warm glow had come to his chest and trunk. And yet, when he touched his nose and cheeks, there was no sensation. Running would not thaw them out. Nor would it thaw out his hands and feet. Then the thought came to him that the frozen portions of his body must be extending. He tried to keep this thought down, to forget it, to think of something else; he was aware of the panicky feeling that it caused, and he was afraid of the panic. But the thought asserted itself, and persisted, until it produced a vision of his body totally frozen. This was too much, and he made another wild run along the trail. Once he slowed down to a walk, but the thought of the freezing extending itself made him run again.

And all the time the dog ran with him, at his heels. When he fell down a second time, it curled its tail over its forefeet and sat in front of him, facing him, curiously eager and intent. The warmth and security of the animal angered him, and he cursed it till it flattened down its ears appeasingly. This time the shivering came more quickly upon the man. He was losing in his battle with the frost. It was creeping into his body from all sides. The thought of it drove him on, but he ran no more than a hundred feet, when he staggered and pitched headlong. It was his last panic. When he had recovered his breath and control, he sat up and entertained in his mind the conception of meeting death with dignity. However, the conception did not come to him in such terms. His idea of it was that he had been making a fool of himself, running around like a chicken with its head cut off—such was the simile that occurred to him. Well, he was bound to freeze anyway, and he might as well take it decently. With this new-found peace of mind came the first glimmerings of drowsiness. A good idea, he thought, to sleep off to death. It was like taking an anesthetic. Freezing was not so bad as people thought. There were lots worse ways to die.

He pictured the boys finding his body next day. Suddenly he found himself with them, coming along the trail and looking for himself. And, still with them, he came around a turn in the trail and found himself lying in the snow. He did not belong with himself any more, for even then he was out of himself, standing with the boys and looking at himself in the snow. It certainly was cold, was his thought. When he got back to the States he could tell the folks what real cold was. He drifted on from this to a vision of the old-timer on Sulphur Creek. He could see him quite clearly, warm and comfortable, and smoking a pipe.

"You were right, old hoss; you were right," the man mumbled to the old-timer of Sulphur Creek.   40

Then the man drowsed off into what seemed to him the most comfortable and satisfying sleep he had ever known. The dog sat facing him and waiting. The brief day drew to a close in a long, slow twilight. There were no signs of a fire to be made, and, besides, never in the dog's experience had it known a man to sit like that in the snow and make no fire. As the twilight drew on, its eager yearning for the fire mastered it, and with a great lifting and shifting of forefeet, it whined softly, then flattened its ears down in anticipation of being chidden by the man. But the man remained silent. Later the dog whined loudly. And still later it crept close to the man and caught the scent of death. This made the animal bristle and back away. A little longer it delayed, howling under the stars that leaped and danced and shone brightly in the cold sky. Then it turned and trotted up the trail in the direction of the camp it knew, where were the other food providers and fire providers.

Questions

1. Roughly how much of London's story is devoted to describing the setting? What particular details make it memorable?

2. To what extent does setting determine what happens in this story?

3. From what point of view is London's story told?

4. In "To Build a Fire" the man is never given a name. What is the effect of his being called simply "the man" throughout the story?

5. From the evidence London gives us, what stages are involved in the process of freezing to death? What does the story gain from London's detailed account of the man's experience with each successive stage?

6. What are the most serious mistakes the man makes? To what factors do you attribute these errors?

Ron Carlson

At the Jim Bridger   2002

Ron Carlson (b. 1947) is a writer of the American West. He was born in the town of Logan, Utah, and raised in Salt Lake City, where he attended graduate school, earning a master's in English at the University of Utah. After teaching at Arizona State University for two decades, Carlson now directs the graduate creative writing program at the University of California, Irvine. His fiction frequently evokes the rugged, untamed wilderness of the western United States.

While teaching at an all-boys prep school in Connecticut, Carlson finished his first novel, Betrayed by F. Scott Fitzgerald *(1977), and soon after he began placing stories in top magazines, including the* New Yorker, GQ, Harper's, *and* Esquire, *where "At the Jim Bridger" originally appeared. He has published many novels and story collections, including* Return to Oakpine *(2014),* The Signal *(2010), and* A

Ron Carlson

Kind of Flying: Selected Stories *(2003), as well as a book on craft,* Ron Carlson Writes a Story *(2007). His work has earned numerous awards. The news and opinion website the* Daily Beast *wrote of him: "Ron Carlson is probably the best American writer you've never heard of."*

He parked his truck in the gravel in front of the Jim Bridger Lodge, and when he stepped out into the chilly dark, the dog in the back of the rig next to his was a dog who knew him. A lot of the roughnecks had dogs; you saw them standing in the bed of the four-wheel-drive Fords. It was kind of an outfit: the mud-spattered vehicle, the gear in back, a dog. This was a brown and white Australian shepherd who stood and tagged Donner on the arm with his nose, and when the man turned, the dog eyed him and nodded, or so it seemed. What the dog had done is step up on the wheel well and put his head out to be stroked.

"Scout," Donner said, and with a hand on the dog, he scanned the truck. Donner was four hundred miles from home. He knew the truck, too.

Donner had just come out of the mountains after a week fishing with a woman who was not his wife, and that woman now came around the front of Donner's vehicle. He stopped her. She smiled and came into his arms thinking this was another of his little moments. He'd been talking about a cocktail and a steak at the Jim Bridger for days, building it up, playing the expert the way he did with everything. She was on his turf, and he tried to make each moment a ritual with all of his talking. He had more words than anyone she knew. Around the campfires at night, which he built with too much care, he'd make soup and fry fish and offer her a little of the special brandy in a special glass, measured exactly, and he would talk about what night means and what this food before them would allow them to do and how odd it would be to sit in a chair in the Jim Bridger the night of their wacky end-of-season New Year's Eve party and order the big T-bone steak and eat it with a baked potato, which he would also describe in detail.

It was September and they'd gone in twelve miles, backpacking from the trailhead at Valentine Lake. A quarter mile from his truck, he'd stopped and put a burlap bag of Pacifico bottles in a stream. "We'll be glad to see those on Friday," he told her. "That is my favorite bag in the world; I've pulled it out of twenty creeks, and every time it was full of cold beer."

And that is what they had done today in the late afternoon, their legs sore.   5
They'd walked through the sunny pines for two hours, no speaking, and then he'd stopped and when she caught him, he knelt and pulled the dripping bag and its treasure into the sunlight. They sat on the bank and he opened the bottles with his knife. The cold brown bottles were slippery in their hands, the labels washed off, and they were like two people having their first beer on earth. She put her hand on the wet burlap. It was all as good as he'd said it would be.

They were both changed from the trip in ways they didn't understand. He was fighting a kind of terror that had grown, and now as he ran his hand under Scout's collar and scratched the animal, the feeling rose and tightened his throat.

"I know somebody in here," he said to her.

"I know you do," she said. "Happy New Year." She kissed him. She had given herself over to him sometime at midweek and was not even fighting the love that had taken her.

"No," he said, "really. I know this guy." He indicated the big truck. "I know this dog, Scout."

"Scout?" She'd heard about this dog.   10

"Right," he said. "The dog from the story."

She put both arms around him and asked, "Does this mean we don't get our steak?"

With the euphoric bravado that had infected the whole adventure, he put his cold hand under her sweatshirt and pulled her up and kissed her in front of the dog. Then he took her hand and led her into the big log tavern he'd been talking about for five days. The two windows in front were lined with tiny celebration lights and foil letters read *Happy New Year!* The season always ended this weekend at the Jim Bridger: they pulled the dock up onto the shore of Long Pond behind the place and packed all the patio tables and chairs in a barn off to one side, and celebrated New Year's Eve a hundred and twenty days early.

Inside, there were two little rooms, the small barroom with eight stools and, past a kind of narrow passage, the dining room, which held a scattering of tables, each with a red checked tablecloth, just as he had told her. A dozen trophy heads protruded from the walls, twelve- and fourteen-point deer and over the fireplace a bull elk that would have gone a thousand pounds. There was no one in the bar, though there were oil-field and hunting jackets on every stool, and bottles and glasses standing all along the wooden surface, as if everyone had left suddenly mid-drink. Brenda Lee sang from the jukebox, "Fool Number One." It was full of scratch friction as if coming across the decades to find the room. The dining hall, too, was empty, though there were steak dinners on two of the tables and coats on some of the chairs. Donner sat the woman at a table, and then he saw something through the big back windows. They were flocked with white and gold spray and razored with a loopy script that read *Happy New Year!* Through the words Donner could see a group of people out on the wooden deck looking into Long Pond. "They're all out back," he said. "Some deal out back."

Donner had told the woman the second day of the trip that he had memorized   15
her, her back, the backs of her knees, the scar on her shoulder, her navel, her nipples, how her hair grew, the way she looked immediately after stepping out of her clothes, the way she looked an hour later. But as they opened the plastic menus in the dark little room and he looked across at her beneficent smile, he didn't even know who she was. This had all been accomplished on a rushing wave of what, adrenaline? Lust? Ego? Now that had collapsed and Donner felt ruined and hollow. He felt as if he'd used every gesture, every smile, and he knew that everything he did now was something borrowed.

"There it is," she said, pointing at the menu. She was euphoric. She'd been euphoric for days. "T-bone steak with a baked potato."

"There it is," he said.

The door opened and the conversation noise roared in like a draft and then people followed it in, one and two at a time. Donner saw Rusty right away holding the door for a couple of his buddies, and Donner turned his back and faced the woman until he was sure they had passed through the room and back to the bar.

The waitress was the owner's wife, Kay. Donner knew her name, but she didn't know his. He was here once a year at most. She appeared in a big flannel shirt patterned red and black and a shiny tiara clipped on her head that in rhinestones read *Happy New Year!* and she kept the pencil, as he had described to the woman, behind her ear until she'd heard both their orders and then she wrote it down.

"What was that?" Donner asked her about the people coming in.   20
"Big Jess our bull moose made an appearance across the pond," Kay told him. "He's still over there pulling tall grass off the bottom and eating like there's no tomorrow."

"A moose?" the woman said. "We saw a moose."

"We did," Donner said.

Early the second day, still hiking toward their lake, they had passed through a willow break, and in one of the beaver dams a cow moose was feeding. She was standing to her shoulders in the water, and her huge head would descend and disappear and then emerge in a tremendous splash and her mouth would be full of dark green reeds and she would chew and drip. It thrilled the woman, and she covered her face with her hands. She looked at Donner with a radical amazement, as if her understanding of the world had been reset, and she pulled him over a hillock and dropped her pack. They came together in a way that shocked him, none of it something he could easily describe, not voracious and not tender, but seriously perhaps, and it sobered him and offered the first caution as to the nature of what he was actually doing.

The waitress brought back a bread basket and two plastic flutes of champagne.   25
There was a little stone fireplace and Donner stoked the struggling fire with two fresh
sections of split log. When he sat back down, she said, "So this is New Year's."

"It is."

She scanned the room. "And they'll close the shutters and all be gone tomorrow."

"Right, until May first. But even that is early. The season here doesn't start until June."

Her eyes were on him, and she lifted her glass and held it until he touched it
with his. She was waiting for him to say something, make a toast.

"Moose," he said. "God save the moose."   30

Now he saw her first confusion, and he worried she could read his face. He felt
drained, but he smiled.

"Is that really Scout?" she said. "Isn't that amazing?"

"Yes it is, my dear," he said.

"So, is your friend in here?"

"Yes," he said. "He's sitting at the bar."   35

"Rusty?"

"That's his name," he said. "You remembered."

He didn't want to talk about this, but he would if she wanted, because he realized that he didn't want to talk about anything at all. From the moment the dog had
touched him, everything was all gone. Donner was happy for the fire; if the grate had
been dark, he feared he would have wept.

One year ago in September on Donner's annual fishing trip, he'd gotten trapped
by a surprise snowstorm in the Cascades, and he'd made a bad decision. It was now
his favorite story, though he'd only told it twice, and when he told it, he told it carefully and honestly, owning all of his errors in the event. When he told it, something
in him knitted up taut and he felt centered and ready. He had told the woman who
was not his wife the story over dinner at an Italian restaurant seven months ago, and
it was the story that had kindled all of the rest.

The big mistake Donner made while fishing the year before, larger than going   40
into the mountains late in the year and getting caught by the four-day storm, was
breaking camp late in the afternoon. He should have stayed put, as he had for three
days while the snowfall continued without pause, steady and serious as if trying to put
the year out once and for all.

He had arrived in a thick dusk and set up camp—the tent, the little cook station and grill, the log bench, the clothesline. He always had a clothesline, and on
the clothesline he always hung a thin cotton dish towel bordered by a blue and green
stripe. He woke the first day in the strange quiet and even light and his tent half
in on him. The snow was eight inches deep, and Donner had to dress carefully and
search through the site for his gear. He broke dead limbs and made a small fire; he
was a scrupulous fire maker, and he laid in wood for two days. He made a cup of coffee using the little press his wife had given him, and he brushed a space on the log
and sat down and let the snow gather on his shoulders.

He had the wrong shoes for such weather, but by being prudent and drying them
each time he returned to the fire, he was still able to fish in Native Lake. He was
mindful of the wet rocks and stood with his legs angled on the last two and cast
a series of flies into the blizzard. It was mesmerizing watching the snow in its vast
echelons disappear into the dark water, and he had the rich, high feeling that comes
from being alone in real places. He caught no fish on his flies.

He did, however, take several cutthroat trout on his smallest Mepps spinners, something they could see. These fish he fried slowly in his old pan with olive oil and a little tarragon, and he ate them with his fingers right out of the pan as snow still fell. At night he banked the fire with larger logs, and in the morning snow would cover them all but one small space where smoke would still be working its way into the cold new day.

He fished every year of his life, camping alone or with a partner, because, he said, it pinned everything else in his life in place. He came home tight with the regimen of sleeping on the ground and eating fish, and with a new effulgent appreciation for his house, the roof, the way the doors worked, chairs.

The year of the mistake he'd gone into the mountains under special pressure. 45 Andrew, his fourteen-year-old son, had run away that spring and then come back, and then run off again. It had been a poisonous season of recrimination and fear. He had been a drummer in the school marching band, and then he was just gone and they did not know where.

In twelve years this had been the first snow, and though he wasn't fully unprepared, it vexed him. He wished he had his gaiters. He ate cutthroat trout for three days, drank coffee, and on the fourth day he made his mistake. In the low, even snow light, which was the same at nine A.M. as it was in midafternoon, he decided that he could no longer wait out the snow. Even if it stopped, it would be a week melting in the best of Indian summers. He would hike down halfway to the highway, seven miles, camp there overnight, and then continue down another seven to the highway where the bus had let him off.

He waited and waited, and then for some reason he broke camp late in the fourth day. He should have waited for morning, but he could not. When he pulled the tent and packed it, the little rectangle under it was green as summer, the grass and wildflowers pressed and vivid there like a window onto another world.

He knew he'd made the mistake immediately because of the difficulty locating and keeping the trail. There were yellow blazes hacked into trees at the proper intervals, but the pack trail was impossible to see in the two-foot snow. The rocks tripped him, and he learned in the first mile to simply fall when he stepped on the side of the angled rocks rather than struggle for balance. Game trails confused him and many times he'd follow an elk path and then fifty yards later come face-to-face with a tree the animal would have walked under; he'd have to backtrack in the growing gloom to locate the proper path. He was wet, but moving and warm. When dark took the sky, the snow persisted. He used his flashlight to find the marked trees.

As he had told the story to the woman in the Italian restaurant last February, it lived in him, each word, and he evoked the dark and the night and the snow. He told the next part with complete precision, how he'd followed the trail, breathing into the new night, and suddenly plunged into the huge open meadow. He had forgotten about it. The expanse glowed at him, offering no marker; the trail was lost. He walked into the snowfield for some reason. Was he looking for a clue? He moved slowly now, regretting having left the trees, tramping through the powdered snow. A moment later he came to a rivulet he seemed to remember, the water amber and clear, and he walked right into it and watched the water flow over his boots. He was now somebody else, somebody he was curious about. It was a beautiful night, the snow now tiny dots still wandering, floating all around the man. Habit, he supposed, not a decision, but habit made him walk on into the snow toward the distant trees. He was trying to take care. He looked at his watch, which he was trained to do when confused or lost, but a moment later he couldn't remember what it had said. He looked again, wiping the crystal with his gloved first finger. He swore at the instrument and walked on, each step a kick into the deep drifts, listening to himself cursing. He fell frequently on the uneven ground, and the falling filled his collar with snow and then his ear. Sometimes he'd stay down; he wasn't cold anymore.

He didn't remember getting up, but he was up and in the woods, his pack off, 50 breaking dead limbs from trees, and he was on his knees with his fire kit, starting a fire with a little snarl of twigs, a fire that he nursed into the biggest fire he'd had all week.

As the fire grew in his story, the woman's expression, which was already serious in the restaurant candlelight, grew grave, her eyes on his face, glistening.

His fire worked its way down through the snow to the green forest floor and grew out in a dry circle. He pulled a downed limb over and hung his wet clothing on it piece by piece until he was standing on his towel before the vigorous fire naked, the dots of snow burning on his shoulders. He made some soup and set up his tent while his clothes dried. Hunkered down in the circle of warmth he had created, sipping the steaming tomato soup, he felt as alive as he ever had.

It was about one minute later a dog burst into the bright ring, throwing a splash of snow before putting his iced muzzle onto his paws on the only patch of green grass in this whole world. The dog eyed the naked man. There had been no noise in the arrival, and Donner was sure at first that a coyote had made a mistake, but he stood his ground. When he saw what it was, he said, "Hello, boy," and his voice sounded strange. Donner found the tags and collar frozen, and by the time he'd separated them and read *Scout*, and a Wyoming phone number, he heard a deep voice call from the dark, "Hello, the camp!" When Rusty Patrick stamped into the light, he looked at Donner and pulled his snow-crusted glove off to shake hands. "Well, here's Adam. Is Eve in the tent?"

Donner pulled on his cotton pajama bottoms, which he always took camping. This last week when he erected their camp clothesline and hung up the dish towel, he had also pinned the pajamas to the line and the woman had taken the fabric in her hand and Donner could see her remembering the story.

But in the Italian restaurant last February, when she first heard about the snow 55 camp, the ring of snow, the way it melted, she said, "I want that. I want to have that."

The steaks in the Jim Bridger were big, an end over each side of the huge paper plates, and the baked potatoes were monstrous. The only real silverware was the three-tined fork Kay brought them and pocketknives. It was a trademark of the Bridger to give pocketknives for steaks. They were thick black Forest Master knives with three blades, but the nameplate on each read *Bridger Club*. The woman loved this, and though she didn't look comfortable with the pocketknife, she went at the food with an energy and delectation that Donner envied.

All night long they'd shared the fun of the place, diners getting up and throwing their plates into the fireplace and toasting, "Happy New Year!"

"They're not doing any dishes the last night of the year," Donner had told her.

When she talked now, her mouth was full, chewing, smiling, and Donner knew he had done it double. She was a woman who didn't talk with her mouth full, ever. She was in love and it was his doing. When Kay passed with the bottle, the woman held out her glass for more champagne, and Donner could see her beam. She was beaming.

A three-piece band was setting up in the corner, wiring the keyboard, as Donner 60 and the woman finished their dinner.

"Are you going to speak to him?" she asked Donner. "Do I get to meet Rusty Patrick?"

The second thing Rusty Patrick had said to Donner a year ago in the snow camp was, "I've had a pretty weird month all around." He worked a black revolver from his jacket pocket and showed it to Donner. There were frost starts in the bluing. Rusty hefted the gun and then lobbed it out over the fire into the snow. "I was dead for a while, but I guess I'm back. Do you know how fucking strange it was to see your fire? I came out of the trees and there's this fire. Come on. Whose idea is that?"

After he'd had a cup of soup, he added, "But we're still in plenty of trouble here." His Levi's were frozen in stiff sheets and his boot laces were welded with ice. He kicked and beat at his clothing to peel it off, hanging it to dry. He'd been out to climb Mount Warren and had hit it way too light. Both of his little toes were patched white with crystal frostbite, but he stood by the fire in his damp long underwear and toasted the falling snow with his coffee cup. "People in Sun Valley pay a thousand dollars a day for shit like this."

Donner did not mention the gun when he told the story, and he did not tell the woman or anyone else what happened the night he met Rusty Patrick in the snow camp. As the snow continued, they had another cup of coffee with a lick of whiskey in it, and they decided to walk out in the morning. With two of them, they reasoned, they could take turns breaking trail. They were above eleven thousand feet, and they were still ten miles from the road. Donner had set his tent on the snow, not bothering to kick a clearing for it, and none of the tree wells were large enough for the little two-man spring tent.

He felt odd, wired and wasted, and he understood somewhere deeper than he could reach that when he had seen the dog, he had let go of all the prudence he'd garnered all day. He was tired. Rusty Patrick wanted to talk and did talk for the hour they lay in the tent. Donner felt the snow hardening under them as they settled, and he worried faintly about the cold, but he just lay back and listened. 65

Rusty Patrick had a resonant voice, so even his speaking voice scraped a hard bass note once or twice in every sentence. He was a roughneck driving truck since the oil work had dried up. Now he hauled road gravel all over Wyoming. "They're still blading roads," he said. "That's why there isn't an unbroken windshield in this whole state." At thirty-three, he had never been married, never had a real girl until this last summer when he fell in love with the new dispatcher, a woman named Darlene Youngman who had come west from Pennsylvania. It was the story of this girl that he told Donner.

Rusty Patrick talked in the icy tent, stopping every once in a while to post a question. Donner was awake but not enough to answer, and after a pause, Rusty Patrick would continue. His heart was broken, he said. He used to think that was all bullshit, a broken heart, before this deal. He fell in love with Darlene Youngman and she fell in love with him, and their dating closed in on them until they were spending weekends together at his place in Rawlins or hers in Rock Springs. "I mean, I see now that love is a kind of craziness, right? I was lit up like a refinery at night, blazing, nothing like it. It made everything make sense. My stupid life, the unending wind, the great state of Wyoming. You ever been in love?" Rusty cleaned himself up, his bachelor apartment, his clothing, his truck, and he trimmed his mustache and got out the old Western Wyoming College bulletins that had been in a drawer for six years. He was planning on a career in the Forest Service.

The dog came to the mouth of the tent and looked Donner in the eye. Donner nodded his head and the dog stepped carefully in onto the sleeping bags, finally curling at their knees.

The resonant cadence of Rusty Patrick's voice changed then, or so Donner thought from where he drifted listening. He wanted to drop into sleep, and he could have, but there was something holding him back, some caution, some change in the air and the grip of the snowpack beneath him.

"My boss was a good guy—at least he had been good to me, keeping me on when   70 a lot of men were laid off. His name was Bob Baxter. He took me aside years ago and told me privately to get my big-rig license, and I did what he said, and it saved me. But there was something else. He took an interest in Darlene." The company owner felt fatherly toward the young woman, and in all their hours together in the office, the man talked against Rusty Patrick, warning the woman about a man of his caliber. It was a steady lesson, an onslaught, and she didn't tell Rusty Patrick about it right away. Then one weekend two weeks ago, he'd taken her over to the Western campus at Rock Springs, just driving around with a school map so he wouldn't get lost when he came here next year. He was excited. Their new life was diagrammed before them. He would move in with her and attend classes; he had nine thousand dollars in the bank and he could work part-time in town during the two-year forestry program. Then they'd go together down to Utah State or Colorado State and their lives would really begin. He was thinking about babies and had said as much. He was way in, far gone. That's the way he had said it, "I was far gone. I mean, I'd brought up babies. I'd say anything and I meant it all." They were walking across the windy campus when she stopped and told him quietly that he would never come here. He was surprised by this and asked her why. This is not something you'll do, she told him. Her arms were folded and she went directly to his truck. It was early on a Saturday, so many sweet hours ahead of them, but she sat stone still. When she didn't talk, he didn't talk, and he drove her home. When she walked to her door, he simply backed his rig up and drove home. His ears were ringing. He hadn't talked to her since, but he'd gone in to see his boss. "I went to the office on that Saturday," Rusty whispered. "And Baxter was waiting for me."

Donner could feel Rusty's shoulder; he was crying, speaking sometimes through his teeth. "By then I was like a chunk of stone; it hurt so bad. There is nothing like it. It isn't your heart; it's your heart through every day of your goddamned life. I could understand why a woman like Darlene might want to leave a man like me alone, but I was sure that Bob Baxter. Would not. Have said anything. Against me."

Rusty trembled for a while, breathing as if gathering steam for language. "He told me. He had told her. I was no good. For her. He told me hehadbeen talking. To her since. He had found out we were dating."

Rusty's voice was quieter and the words were spaced oddly, some run together and some repeated shakily and some falling at great intervals. The new cadence woke Donner a level. "It took everything. I had. Not to kill the man," Rusty said. "AndIcouldhavekilledhim with my my my fists. My life was over. I bought the gun. Fourhundredbucks. That was. Tuesday. We've been up above here. Since. Then. In this this this this snow."

The last word had been coughed out and immediately Rusty's breathing changed to a shallow chuffing. It was late but the hard chill pressed in with a new edge; it had stopped snowing. Donner opened his eyes and listened, and he knew that after four days it had stopped snowing. The cold came down now with all the force of the hollow sky. He could feel the frigid air sizing his face, and his feet were aching again.

The story had made him sick. He imagined the big boyish figure of Rusty Patrick confronting an older man he thought of as a father and hearing such news. And the surprise of the surcease of falling snow was like terror, a blank, fearful void that came at Donner's heart. He tried to calm himself, but for the first time in the mountains he was afraid. It was very simple: he wanted to be home. The image of his son in his band uniform took the air from Donner's lungs, the brass buttons on his red wool tunic, his high, proud face under the black beret, his seriousness with the snare drum. He wouldn't even accept any help loading the drums in the car, and when they arrived at school, he went wordlessly into the crowd. And then he disappeared. One night after practice, Donner waited with his wife, and after one A.M., they called the police.

Donner was bumped from sleep by Rusty Patrick shaking beside him. At first Donner thought the other man was sobbing, because he had heard it in his voice earlier, but it persisted, a rippling shudder that wasn't crying. "Hey," Donner had said, but even on an elbow shaking the man, Donner couldn't wake Rusty Patrick. The dog held tight at the bottom of the sleeping bags, his eyes open. The cold was at Donner, blades of it against his exposed neck as he moved up and checked the other man. He ran a hand over Rusty's face and it came away wet, and then cold or no, Donner sat up on his heels and shined the light on his tent mate. The face was gray and smeared with blood from a nosebleed. A delicate fringe of ice rimmed the hair, and Rusty Patrick was shivering in cramping spasms. His chest was wet. Donner was saying, "Come on, come on," as he unzipped their sleeping bags. The other man was damp, cold to the touch, dropping into hypothermia. Both of Donner's hands were bloody and he was getting the blood everywhere as he cut away Rusty's underwear using his sheath knife. Both of the sleeping bags were superior grade, though the zippers wouldn't mesh. Donner was talking the whole time now, saying simply, "Oh now, come on now," and he slipped in with Rusty and wrapped the shell of his own bag over them as tightly as he could. It was what you did. There was no way to take the half hour to rekindle the fire and go that way. Patrick had gone to bed still wet and it had worked into him. Now Donner could feel the cold muscularity of the other man and he held him and moved slowly against him, his hands up and down, the tops of his feet up and down, his face against the side of Rusty Patrick's head. He'd need to bring him up five degrees.

Even dozing, he developed a rhythm, covering the naked body of Rusty Patrick in this embrace, this massage. It wore him down and he felt useless. He woke and renewed his movements. Donner rolled on top of Rusty and in slow degrees as his strength left him, he let his weight descend. The dog moved up to them, and Donner could feel the dog's breath against the side of his face. Rusty's shivering had subsided somewhat, but Donner could still feel the blood warm against his neck.

"Come on, now," he said, whispering, and when that litany lulled him to sleep, he started talking quietly to his son. "You can come home now," he started. "It's not a problem to cross through Indiana and then Nebraska..." and Donner listed the states one at a time in a prayer to his son. He spoke slowly, trying to lay out the fair terms of their rapprochement, so he might again be some part of his life, and in his recitation, he uttered their history, telling at length episodes they'd shared, especially the time they went onto the roof to retrieve the basketball. He'd gone up the ladder and Andrew had followed him onto the flat white surface the shape of Utah. It was littered with odd broken toys and an old volleyball as well as the ball he'd just heaved from the driveway. Each element of this scattered inventory brought a wave of revelation and nostalgia. The blue plastic elephant with three legs was five or six years old, sun-polished on one side, and Donner and Andrew sat on the short rear wall of the roof, looking down at the neighbors' dog, who was swimming in the pool, and they talked about all the toys the elephant had been kindred to, and he asked Donner in real wonder how such a lost thing could get onto the roof. In the late-day shade, they laughed and speculated like two friends for an hour until his wife called them from below.

Donner hugged the freezing man. He trapped Rusty's hands in the warmth between their legs. Their center was warm and Donner moved against it until he felt himself stirred, a reflex he gave in to. Rusty Patrick's breathing had steadied into a rhythmic easy stride cut from time to time with a short shudder. Donner was calling his name now, "Rusty, hey, Rusty." The man beneath him groaned in what might have been acknowledgment and moved, his eyes still shut, and then Donner knew that Rusty had taken him into his hands and they were together that way in the mountain tent.

In the morning Donner saw what he hadn't seen for five days: shadows on the tent, the shocking sunprint of tree limbs on the gray canvas. It warmed to twenty five and then thirty degrees. They took a long time with their morning, boiling water for coffee and oatmeal and then another pan for washing. There was dried blood in their hair and on their faces and necks. The world was a blinding white, the sky blue in tiers to the horizon. They didn't speak, both men packing up carefully and wearing sunglasses against the crushing light. The muted concussions of snow bundles falling from the thawing limbs sounded all around them, and the dog Scout circled in the snow-packed camp space ready to go.

Donner told the woman the rest of the story: the warming, brilliant day in mid-September, and walking out of the mountains with Rusty Patrick and his dog. The dog disappeared right away and then five minutes later came along working two cattle before him like an expert in snow herding. The men stopped to watch this display. Donner took off his jacket and tucked it into his pack. They would walk ten miles downhill on a snow-packed path behind an ever-increasing line of cows which the dog urged and instructed, a kind of rare pleasure that comes once in a lifetime.

In that larger well-lit world with a clear promise of tomorrow and home and hope, Donner thought it might be possible to speak to Rusty Patrick about what had happened, but at each juncture, as they stopped for water or granola bars or just to look the hundred miles east across the snow-patched plains, neither man spoke up except to say, "Some dog," or the like. When they shook hands that evening at the bus station in a town that Donner would never visit again, he thought, I'll never know any of this again, any of it, and I'll never see Rusty Patrick again.

Now in the Jim Bridger, Donner and the woman who was not his wife had thrown their paper plates and steak bones into the fireplace and moved their table to the periphery of the dining room, stacking it upside down on those already there. It was after eleven and people, many wearing gold and silver paper party hats, danced. It was fun for the woman and she held on to Donner's arm happily, pretending every so often to have something to whisper to him and kissing his neck instead. This was all better than he'd described it.

At one point she'd bought an embroidered Jim Bridger cap from the little glass case, a turquoise cap with a moose underneath the name, and she announced it was for Andrew, a present.

80

"I'm not sure that's a good idea," he said.   85

"He likes me; this is a good cap for him," the woman had said. He didn't like her using Andrew's name. His wife's name had come up from time to time in the last days, but it was just a fact, one he was steeled against. When she said his son's name, it just confused him.

One of the band members had a full beard and every third song he'd hoist his accordion and announce, "The New Year's Polka," to which they'd already danced twice. Their waitress, Kay, danced every dance now in the warm wooden-floored room, each with a different young man. The employees were all going home and back to college, and she was dancing with them one by one. Donner heard, through all the talking and the music and the dinner noise, the regular bass beat of Rusty Patrick's deep voice as he spoke to his mates in the other room. After a week of knowing what he was doing or pretending to know, Donner was dislocated and floating, his brave face paper thin.

At a few minutes before the hour, all the men from the bar were herded into the dining room by Kay's husband, the bartender, and Kay herself went around and filled everybody's glass with the champagne they'd been pouring all night. "Kay," her husband said, emerging through the group of men, "evidently the clock in the bar has been five minutes fast for the entire year! Thank God we've made it for the toast."

He was hooted down, and in the ringing laughter, Donner saw Rusty Patrick turn and look into his face. Rusty's expression opened in strange surprise and he came immediately over to where Donner and the woman stood by the stone fireplace.

"No way!" he said, shaking Donner's hand. Then he said it again and clapped   90
Donner in an embrace. He opened his mouth again to say something, which would have been, *What are you doing here?* or *Is it really you?* but with his mouth open, he just hugged Donner hard again.

They were spilling champagne, and Donner could sense the woman at his arm also against him, but he could not speak. The room seemed to be glowing. Donner could only put his arm around Rusty and hug him again, feeling the whiskers against the bones in his face. When they stood back, Rusty asked the woman, "So, you must be his wife?"

She took his arm in their close circle and said no, she was his friend.

"I'm Rusty," he said.

"I know," she said. "I've heard about you." Now she had her hands on both of his forearms. "I've heard the wonderful story."

"One minute!" the bartender called. "Make amends or wait a year! Who needs   95
champagne! Where's my sweetheart!" His wife, Kay, appeared at his back and they kissed. The room was full, everyone shoulder to shoulder.

Rusty Patrick opened his face to Donner in a profound look, plaintive and deep. A basket full of noisemakers suddenly appeared between them, and the men took one each and started blowing the honking whistles until the accordion sounded the countdown: ten … nine … eight. The men's look held. Donner felt a smooth hand on his face and the woman pulled him down, and she kissed him tenderly, keeping her hand there as the minute and the hour and the year lapsed for the people in the Jim Bridger. A shotgun sounded from out on the highway, and paper dots fell into everyone's hair.

Immediately the band fired up and the room sorted itself out, alcoves of people widening until the dancers had some space. It was another version of "The New Year's Polka."

Rusty's buddies all slipped back into the bar, but Rusty Patrick came up to Donner, speaking in his ear. "How's your son?" the man said, his voice full of real concern. "Did he make it home? Did you talk to him?"

Donner could only nod at Rusty then and drop his eyes and step back. The young woman who was not his wife had snugged the turquoise cap onto her head and threaded her hair out the back in a ponytail. "Let's dance!" she called in the thrumming noise. "I haven't danced all year!"

Donner was watching what his body did, and what it did now was push Rusty   100
and the woman together and smile at them. "Go to it!" he said. "This runs a thousand dollars a day in Sun Valley. I'm going to get some air."

The night was ripped, filled, upended with stars sizzling in the deep chill. Donner felt his scalp tighten against the gathering cold, and he blew great plumes into the air. He retrieved his binoculars from his car kit, and when he shut the door, the dog stood in Rusty's truck to be stroked.

"Come on, Scout," Donner said, patting his leg. "Let's go see the moose."

Scout stood two feet on the tailgate and Donner lifted the animal to the ground rather than have him jump. They walked around the side of the old Jim Bridger to the wooden deck over Long Pond. There were two people finishing an argument as he arrived and the woman said to the man, "That's four strikes, Artie, and you damn well know it." They went in, releasing a quick rush of noise.

The binoculars had belonged to Donner's father and they were the best set he'd ever seen. He sighted Big Jess standing well into the trees on the far side. Donner breathed out and held so he could focus. The moose wasn't moving, and Donner couldn't tell if he was looking across at the party.

Certain decisions are made in daylight and certain decisions are made in dark-   105
ness. Winter has its own decisions and summer has its own decisions, as do spring and fall. Donner drew a chestful of the sharp air. He'd made a decision last February with the woman whom he could now see dancing inside the painted window. It was made in the frigid early twilight under low clouds while the car headlamps passing on the highway seemed useless little fires that wouldn't last the night, and that decision to use his story as he had, to show it to her, burn it like a match, had led to this new darkness and the longer night.

Questions

1. Carlson's story bounces between two main settings—the Jim Bridger Lodge and the mountain wilderness nearby. What specific details are memorable about each setting?

2. Both Donner and Rusty Patrick are dealing with difficult situations in their lives—Donner with a runaway son, and Rusty with a broken heart. Why are those backstories important to the present action of the story?

3. When Donner retold his story, why did he omit the details about the gun and about what had occurred between him and Rusty?

4. By the present time of the story, has Donner's son Andrew returned home? What details helped you come to this conclusion?

5. What is the significance of the moose at the Jim Bridger? Why does Carlson choose to end his story with Donner alone outside, watching the moose through binoculars?

6. Reread the final paragraph. Why does Donner seem to regret his "decision to use his story as he had"? What is "this new darkness and the longer night" that Carlson writes of?

7. In what ways is Jack London's "To Build a Fire" evoked in "At the Jim Bridger"? In what ways do the stories differ?

Amy Tan

A Pair of Tickets   1989

Amy Tan was born in Oakland, California, in 1952. Both of her parents were recent Chinese immigrants. Her father was an electrical engineer (as well as a Baptist minister); her mother was a vocational nurse. When her father and older brother both died of brain tumors, the fifteen-year-old Tan moved with her mother and younger brother to Switzerland, where she attended high school. On their return to the United States, Tan attended Linfield College, a Baptist school in Oregon, but she eventually transferred to San Jose State University. At this time Tan and her mother argued about her future. The mother insisted her daughter pursue premedical studies in preparation for becoming a neurosurgeon, but Tan wanted to do something else. For six months the two did not speak to each other. Tan worked for IBM writing computer manuals and also wrote freelance business articles under a pseudonym. In 1987 she and her mother visited China together. This experience, which is reflected in "A Pair of Tickets," deepened Tan's sense of her Chinese American identity. "As soon as my feet touched China," she wrote, "I became Chinese." Soon after, she began writing her first novel, The Joy Luck Club *(1989), which consists of sixteen interrelated stories about a group of Chinese American mothers and their daughters. (The club of the title is a woman's social group.)* The Joy Luck Club *became both a critical success and a best seller, and was made into a movie in 1993. In 1991 Tan published her second novel,* The Kitchen God's Wife. *Her later novels include* The Bonesetter's Daughter *(2001),* Saving Fish from Drowning *(2005), and* The Valley of Amazement *(2013). Tan lives north of San Francisco with her husband.*

The minute our train leaves the Hong Kong border and enters Shenzhen, China, I feel different. I can feel the skin on my forehead tingling, my blood rushing through a new course, my bones aching with a familiar old pain. And I think, My mother was right. I am becoming Chinese.

"Cannot be helped," my mother said when I was fifteen and had vigorously denied that I had any Chinese whatsoever below my skin. I was a sophomore at Galileo High in San Francisco, and all my Caucasian friends agreed: I was about as Chinese as they were. But my mother had studied at a famous nursing school in Shanghai, and she said she knew all about genetics. So there was no doubt in her mind, whether I agreed or not: Once you are born Chinese, you cannot help but feel and think Chinese.

"Someday you will see," said my mother. "It is in your blood, waiting to be let go."

And when she said this, I saw myself transforming like a werewolf, a mutant tag of DNA suddenly triggered, replicating itself insidiously into a *syndrome,*° a cluster of telltale Chinese behaviors, all those things my mother did to embarrass me—haggling with store owners, pecking her mouth with a toothpick in public, being color-blind to the fact that lemon yellow and pale pink are not good combinations for winter clothes.

But today I realize I've never really known what it means to be Chinese. I am thirty-six years old. My mother is dead and I am on a train, carrying with me her dreams of coming home. I am going to China.   5

We are first going to Guangzhou, my seventy-two-year-old father, Canning Woo, and I, where we will visit his aunt, whom he has not seen since he was ten years old. And I don't know whether it's the prospect of seeing his aunt or if it's because

syndrome: a group of symptoms that occur together as the sign of a particular disease or abnormality.

he's back in China, but now he looks like he's a young boy, so innocent and happy I want to button his sweater and pat his head. We are sitting across from each other, separated by a little table with two cold cups of tea. For the first time I can ever remember, my father has tears in his eyes, and all he is seeing out the train window is a sectioned field of yellow, green, and brown, a narrow canal flanking the tracks, low rising hills, and three people in blue jackets riding an ox-driven cart on this early October morning. And I can't help myself. I also have misty eyes, as if I had seen this a long, long time ago, and had almost forgotten.

In less than three hours, we will be in Guangzhou, which my guidebook tells me is how one properly refers to Canton these days. It seems all the cities I have heard of, except Shanghai, have changed their spellings. I think they are saying China has changed in other ways as well. Chungking is Chongqing. And Kweilin is Guilin. I have looked these names up, because after we see my father's aunt in Guangzhou, we will catch a plane to Shanghai, where I will meet my two half-sisters for the first time.

They are my mother's twin daughters from her first marriage, little babies she was forced to abandon on a road as she was fleeing Kweilin for Chungking in 1944. That was all my mother had told me about these daughters, so they had remained babies in my mind, all these years, sitting on the side of a road, listening to bombs whistling in the distance while sucking their patient red thumbs.

And it was only this year that someone found them and wrote with this joyful news. A letter came from Shanghai, addressed to my mother. When I first heard about this, that they were alive, I imagined my identical sisters transforming from little babies into six-year-old girls. In my mind, they were seated next to each other at a table, taking turns with the fountain pen. One would write a neat row of characters: *Dearest Mama. We are alive.* She would brush back her wispy bangs and hand the other sister the pen, and she would write: *Come get us. Please hurry.*

Of course they could not know that my mother had died three months before,   10
suddenly, when a blood vessel in her brain burst. One minute she was talking to my father, complaining about the tenants upstairs, scheming how to evict them under the pretense that relatives from China were moving in. The next minute she was holding her head, her eyes squeezed shut, groping for the sofa, and then crumpling softly to the floor with fluttering hands.

So my father had been the first one to open the letter, a long letter it turned out. And they did call her Mama. They said they always revered her as their true mother. They kept a framed picture of her. They told her about their life, from the time my mother last saw them on the road leaving Kweilin to when they were finally found.

And the letter had broken my father's heart so much—these daughters calling my mother from another life he never knew—that he gave the letter to my mother's old friend Auntie Lindo and asked her to write back and tell my sisters, in the gentlest way possible, that my mother was dead.

But instead Auntie Lindo took the letter to the Joy Luck Club and discussed with Auntie Ying and Auntie An-mei what should be done, because they had known for many years about my mother's search for her twin daughters, her endless hope. Auntie Lindo and the others cried over this double tragedy, of losing my mother three months before, and now again. And so they couldn't help but think of some miracle, some possible way of reviving her from the dead, so my mother could fulfill her dream.

So this is what they wrote to my sisters in Shanghai: "Dearest Daughters, I too have never forgotten you in my memory or in my heart. I never gave up hope that we would see each other again in a joyous reunion. I am only sorry it has been too long.

I want to tell you everything about my life since I last saw you. I want to tell you this when our family comes to see you in China. . . ." They signed it with my mother's name.

It wasn't until all this had been done that they first told me about my sisters, the   15 letter they received, the one they wrote back.

"They'll think she's coming, then," I murmured. And I had imagined my sisters now being ten or eleven, jumping up and down, holding hands, their pigtails bouncing, excited that their mother—*their* mother—was coming, whereas my mother was dead.

"How can you say she is not coming in a letter?" said Auntie Lindo. "She is their mother. She is your mother. You must be the one to tell them. All these years, they have been dreaming of her." And I thought she was right.

But then I started dreaming, too, of my mother and my sisters and how it would be if I arrived in Shanghai. All these years, while they waited to be found, I had lived with my mother and then had lost her. I imagined seeing my sisters at the airport. They would be standing on their tip-toes, looking anxiously, scanning from one dark head to another as we got off the plane. And I would recognize them instantly, their faces with the identical worried look.

"*Jyejye, Jyejye.* Sister, Sister. We are here," I saw myself saying in my poor version of Chinese.

"Where is Mama?" they would say, and look around, still smiling, two flushed   20 and eager faces. "Is she hiding?" And this would have been like my mother, to stand behind just a bit, to tease a little and make people's patience pull a little on their hearts. I would shake my head and tell my sisters she was not hiding.

"Oh, that must be Mama, no?" one of my sisters would whisper excitedly, pointing to another small woman completely engulfed in a tower of presents. And that, too, would have been like my mother, to bring mountains of gifts, food, and toys for children—all bought on sale—shunning thanks, saying the gifts were nothing, and later turning the labels over to show my sisters, "Calvin Klein, 100% wool."

I imagined myself starting to say, "Sisters, I am sorry, I have come alone . . ." and before I could tell them—they could see it in my face—they were wailing, pulling their hair, their lips twisted in pain, as they ran away from me. And then I saw myself getting back on the plane and coming home.

After I had dreamed this scene many times—watching their despair turn from horror into anger—I begged Auntie Lindo to write another letter. And at first she refused.

"How can I say she is dead? I cannot write this," said Auntie Lindo with a stubborn look.

"But it's cruel to have them believe she's coming on the plane," I said. "When   25 they see it's just me, they'll hate me."

"Hate you? Cannot be." She was scowling. "You are their own sister, their only family."

"You don't understand," I protested.

"What I don't understand?" she said.

And I whispered, "They'll think I'm responsible, that she died because I didn't appreciate her."

And Auntie Lindo looked satisfied and sad at the same time, as if this were true   30 and I had finally realized it. She sat down for an hour, and when she stood up she handed me a two-page letter. She had tears in her eyes. I realized that the very thing

I had feared, she had done. So even if she had written the news of my mother's death in English, I wouldn't have had the heart to read it.

"Thank you," I whispered.

The landscape has become gray, filled with low flat cement buildings, old factories, and then tracks and more tracks filled with trains like ours passing by in the opposite direction. I see platforms crowded with people wearing drab Western clothes, with spots of bright colors: little children wearing pink and yellow, red and peach. And there are soldiers in olive green and red, and old ladies in gray tops and pants that stop mid-calf. We are in Guangzhou.

Before the train even comes to a stop, people are bringing down their belongings from above their seats. For a moment there is a dangerous shower of heavy suitcases laden with gifts to relatives, half-broken boxes wrapped in miles of string to keep the contents from spilling out, plastic bags filled with yarn and vegetables and packages of dried mushrooms, and camera cases. And then we are caught in a stream of people rushing, shoving, pushing us along, until we find ourselves in one of a dozen lines waiting to go through customs. I feel as if I were getting on the number 30 Stockton bus in San Francisco. I am in China, I remind myself. And somehow the crowds don't bother me. It feels right. I start pushing too.

I take out the declaration forms and my passport. "Woo," it says at the top, and below that, "June May," who was born in "California, U.S.A.," in 1951. I wonder if the customs people will question whether I'm the same person in the passport photo. In this picture, my chin-length hair is swept back and artfully styled. I am wearing false eyelashes, eye shadow, and lip liner. My cheeks are hollowed out by bronze blusher. But I had not expected the heat in October. And now my hair hangs limp with the humidity. I wear no makeup; in Hong Kong my mascara had melted into dark circles and everything else had felt like layers of grease. So today my face is plain, unadorned except for a thin mist of shiny sweat on my forehead and nose.

Even without makeup, I could never pass for true Chinese. I stand five-foot-six,   35
and my head pokes above the crowd so that I am eye level only with other tourists. My mother once told me my height came from my grandfather, who was a northerner, and may have even had some Mongol blood. "This is what your grandmother once told me," explained my mother. "But now it is too late to ask her. They are all dead, your grandparents, your uncles, and their wives and children, all killed in the war, when a bomb fell on our house. So many generations in one instant."

She had said this so matter-of-factly that I thought she had long since gotten over any grief she had. And then I wondered how she knew they were all dead.

"Maybe they left the house before the bomb fell," I suggested.

"No," said my mother. "Our whole family is gone. It is just you and I."

"But how do you know? Some of them could have escaped."

"Cannot be," said my mother, this time almost angrily. And then her frown was   40
washed over by a puzzled blank look, and she began to talk as if she were trying to remember where she had misplaced something. "I went back to that house. I kept looking up to where the house used to be. And it wasn't a house, just the sky. And below, underneath my feet, were four stories of burnt bricks and wood, all the life of our house. Then off to the side I saw things blown into the yard, nothing valuable. There was a bed someone used to sleep in, really just a metal frame twisted up at one corner. And a book, I don't know what kind, because every page had turned black. And I saw a teacup which was unbroken but filled with ashes. And then I found my doll, with her hands and legs

broken, her hair burned off. . . . When I was a little girl, I had cried for that doll, seeing it all alone in the store window, and my mother had bought it for me. It was an American doll with yellow hair. It could turn its legs and arms. The eyes moved up and down. And when I married and left my family home, I gave the doll to my youngest niece, because she was like me. She cried if that doll was not with her always. Do you see? If she was in the house with that doll, her parents were there, and so everybody was there, waiting together, because that's how our family was."

The woman in the customs booth stares at my documents, then glances at me briefly, and with two quick movements stamps everything and sternly nods me along. And soon my father and I find ourselves in a large area filled with thousands of people and suitcases. I feel lost and my father looks helpless.

"Excuse me," I say to a man who looks like an American. "Can you tell me where I can get a taxi?" He mumbles something that sounds Swedish or Dutch.

"Syau Yen! Syau Yen!" I hear a piercing voice shout from behind me. An old woman in a yellow knit beret is holding up a pink plastic bag filled with wrapped trinkets. I guess she is trying to sell us something. But my father is staring down at this tiny sparrow of a woman, squinting into her eyes. And then his eyes widen, his face opens up and he smiles like a pleased little boy.

"*Aiyi! Aiyi!*" —Auntie Auntie!—he says softly.

"Syau Yen!" coos my great-aunt. I think it's funny she has just called my father 45 "Little Wild Goose." It must be his baby milk name, the name used to discourage ghosts from stealing children.

They clasp each other's hands—they do not hug—and hold on like this, taking turns saying, "Look at you! You are so old. Look how old you've become!" They are both crying openly, laughing at the same time, and I bite my lip, trying not to cry. I'm afraid to feel their joy. Because I am thinking how different our arrival in Shanghai will be tomorrow, how awkward it will feel.

Now Aiyi beams and points to a Polaroid picture of my father. My father had wisely sent pictures when he wrote and said we were coming. See how smart she was, she seems to intone as she compares the picture to my father. In the letter, my father had said we would call her from the hotel once we arrived, so this is a surprise, that they've come to meet us. I wonder if my sisters will be at the airport.

It is only then that I remember the camera. I had meant to take a picture of my father and his aunt the moment they met. It's not too late.

"Here, stand together over here," I say, holding up the Polaroid. The camera flashes and I hand them the snapshot. Aiyi and my father still stand close together, each of them holding a corner of the picture, watching as their images begin to form. They are almost reverentially quiet. Aiyi is only five years older than my father, which makes her around seventy-seven. But she looks ancient, shrunken, a mummified relic. Her thin hair is pure white, her teeth are brown with decay. So much for stories of Chinese women looking young forever, I think to myself.

Now Aiyi is crooning to me: "*Jandale.*" So big already. She looks up at me, at my 50 full height, and then peers into her pink plastic bag—her gifts to us, I have figured out—as if she is wondering what she will give to me, now that I am so old and big. And then she grabs my elbow with her sharp pincerlike grasp and turns me around. A man and woman in their fifties are shaking hands with my father, everybody smiling and saying, "Ah! Ah!" They are Aiyi's oldest son and his wife, and standing next to them are four other people, around my age, and a little girl who's around ten. The introductions go by so fast, all I know is that one of them is Aiyi's grandson, with his wife, and the other is her granddaughter, with her husband. And the little girl is Lili, Aiyi's great-granddaughter.

Aiyi and my father speak the Mandarin dialect from their childhood, but the rest of the family speaks only the Cantonese of their village. I understand only Mandarin but can't speak it that well. So Aiyi and my father gossip unrestrained in Mandarin, exchanging news about people from their old village. And they stop only occasionally to talk to the rest of us, sometimes in Cantonese, sometimes in English.

"Oh, it is as I suspected," says my father, turning to me. "He died last summer." And I already understood this. I just don't know who this person, Li Gong, is. I feel as if I were in the United Nations and the translators had run amok.

"Hello," I say to the little girl. "My name is Jing-mei." But the little girl squirms to look away, causing her parents to laugh with embarrassment. I try to think of Cantonese words I can say to her, stuff I learned from friends in Chinatown, but all I can think of are swear words, terms for bodily functions, and short phrases like "tastes good," "tastes like garbage," and "she's really ugly." And then I have another plan: I hold up the Polaroid camera, beckoning Lili with my finger. She immediately jumps forward, places one hand on her hip in the manner of a fashion model, juts out her chest, and flashes me a toothy smile. As soon as I take the picture she is standing next to me, jumping and giggling every few seconds as she watches herself appear on the greenish film.

By the time we hail taxis for the ride to the hotel, Lili is holding tight onto my hand, pulling me along.

In the taxi, Aiyi talks nonstop, so I have no chance to ask her about the different sights we are passing by.   55

"You wrote and said you would come only for one day," says Aiyi to my father in an agitated tone. "One day! How can you see your family in one day! Toishan is many hours' drive from Guangzhou. And this idea to call us when you arrive. This is nonsense. We have no telephone."

My heart races a little. I wonder if Auntie Lindo told my sisters we would call from the hotel in Shanghai?

Aiyi continues to scold my father. "I was so beside myself, ask my son, almost turned heaven and earth upside down trying to think of a way! So we decided the best was for us to take the bus from Toishan and come into Guangzhou—meet you right from the start."

And now I am holding my breath as the taxi driver dodges between trucks and buses, honking his horn constantly. We seem to be on some sort of long freeway overpass, like a bridge above the city. I can see row after row of apartments, each floor cluttered with laundry hanging out to dry on the balcony. We pass a public bus, with people jammed in so tight their faces are nearly wedged against the window. Then I see the skyline of what must be downtown Guangzhou. From a distance, it looks like a major American city, with high rises and construction going on everywhere. As we slow down in the more congested part of the city, I see scores of little shops, dark inside, lined with counters and shelves. And then there is a building, its front laced with scaffolding made of bamboo poles held together with plastic strips. Men and women are standing on narrow platforms, scraping the sides, working without safety straps or helmets. Oh, would OSHA° have a field day here, I think.

OSHA: Occupational Safety and Health Administration, a U.S. federal agency that regulates and monitors workplace safety conditions.

Aiyi's shrill voice rises up again: "So it is a shame you can't see our village, our   60 house. My sons have been quite successful, selling our vegetables in the free market. We had enough these last few years to build a big house, three stories, all of new brick, big enough for our whole family and then some. And every year, the money is even better. You Americans aren't the only ones who know how to get rich!"

The taxi stops and I assume we've arrived, but then I peer out at what looks like a grander version of the Hyatt Regency. "This is communist China?" I wonder out loud. And then I shake my head toward my father. "This must be the wrong hotel." I quickly pull out our itinerary, travel tickets, and reservations. I had explicitly instructed my travel agent to choose something inexpensive, in the thirty-to-forty-dollar range. I'm sure of this. And there it says on our itinerary: Garden Hotel, Huanshi Dong Lu. Well, our travel agent had better be prepared to eat the extra, that's all I have to say.

The hotel is magnificent. A bellboy complete with uniform and sharp-creased cap jumps forward and begins to carry our bags into the lobby. Inside, the hotel looks like an orgy of shopping arcades and restaurants all encased in granite and glass. And rather than be impressed, I am worried about the expense, as well as the appearance it must give Aiyi, that we rich Americans cannot be without our luxuries even for one night.

But when I step up to the reservation desk, ready to haggle over this booking mistake, it is confirmed. Our rooms are prepaid, thirty-four dollars each. I feel sheepish, and Aiyi and the others seem delighted by our temporary surroundings. Lili is looking wide-eyed at an arcade filled with video games.

Our whole family crowds into one elevator, and the bellboy waves, saying he will meet us on the eighteenth floor. As soon as the elevator door shuts, everybody becomes very quiet, and when the door finally opens again, everybody talks at once in what sounds like relieved voices. I have the feeling Aiyi and the others have never been on such a long elevator ride.

Our rooms are next to each other and are identical. The rugs, drapes, bedspreads   65 are all in shades of taupe. There's a color television with remote-control panels built into the lamp table between the two twin beds. The bathroom has marble walls and floors. I find a built-in wet bar with a small refrigerator stocked with Heineken beer, Coke Classic, and Seven-Up, mini-bottles of Johnnie Walker Red, Bacardi rum, and Smirnoff vodka, and packets of M & M's, honey-roasted cashews, and Cadbury chocolate bars. And again I say out loud, "This is communist China?"

My father comes into my room. "They decided we should just stay here and visit," he says, shrugging his shoulders. "They say, Less trouble that way. More time to talk."

"What about dinner?" I ask. I have been envisioning my first real Chinese feast for many days already, a big banquet with one of those soups steaming out of a carved winter melon, chicken wrapped in clay, Peking duck, the works.

My father walks over and picks up a room service book next to a *Travel & Leisure* magazine. He flips through the pages quickly and then points to the menu. "This is what they want," says my father.

So it's decided. We are going to dine tonight in our rooms, with our family, sharing hamburgers, french fries, and apple pie à la mode.

Aiyi and her family are browsing the shops while we clean up. After a hot ride   70 on the train, I'm eager for a shower and cooler clothes.

The hotel has provided little packets of shampoo which, upon opening, I discover is the consistency and color of hoisin sauce. This is more like it, I think. This is China. And I rub some in my damp hair.

Standing in the shower, I realize this is the first time I've been by myself in what seems like days. But instead of feeling relieved, I feel forlorn. I think about what my mother said, about activating my genes and becoming Chinese. And I wonder what she meant.

Right after my mother died, I asked myself a lot of things, things that couldn't be answered, to force myself to grieve more. It seemed as if I wanted to sustain my grief, to assure myself that I had cared deeply enough.

But now I ask the questions mostly because I want to know the answers. What was that pork stuff she used to make that had the texture of sawdust? What were the names of the uncles who died in Shanghai? What had she dreamt all these years about her other daughters? All the times when she got mad at me, was she really thinking about them? Did she wish I were they? Did she regret that I wasn't?

At one o'clock in the morning, I awake to tapping sounds on the window. I must   75
have dozed off and now I feel my body uncramping itself. I'm sitting on the floor, leaning against one of the twin beds. Lili is lying next to me. The others are asleep, too, sprawled out on the beds and floor. Aiyi is seated at a little table, looking very sleepy. And my father is staring out the window, tapping his fingers on the glass. The last time I listened my father was telling Aiyi about his life since he last saw her. How he had gone to Yenching University, later got a post with a newspaper in Chungking, met my mother there, a young widow. How they later fled together to Shanghai to try to find my mother's family house, but there was nothing there. And then they traveled eventually to Canton and then to Hong Kong, then Haiphong and finally to San Francisco. . . .

"Suyuan didn't tell me she was trying all these years to find her daughters," he is now saying in a quiet voice. "Naturally, I did not discuss her daughters with her. I thought she was ashamed she had left them behind."

"Where did she leave them?" asks Aiyi. "How were they found?"

I am wide awake now. Although I have heard parts of this story from my mother's friends.

"It happened when the Japanese took over Kweilin," says my father.

"Japanese in Kweilin?" says Aiyi. "That was never the case. Couldn't be. The   80
Japanese never came to Kweilin."

"Yes, that is what the newspapers reported. I know this because I was working for the news bureau at the time. The Kuomintang often told us what we could say and could not say. But we knew the Japanese had come into Kwangsi Province. We had sources who told us how they had captured the Wuchang-Canton railway. How they were coming overland, making very fast progress, marching toward the provincial capital."

Aiyi looks astonished. "If people did not know this, how could Suyuan know the Japanese were coming?"

"An officer of the Kuomintang secretly warned her," explains my father. "Suyuan's husband also was an officer and everybody knew that officers and their families would be the first to be killed. So she gathered a few possessions and, in the middle of the night, she picked up her daughters and fled on foot. The babies were not even one year old."

"How could she give up those babies!" sighs Aiyi. "Twin girls. We have never had such luck in our family." And then she yawns again.

"What were they named?" she asks. I listen carefully. I had been planning on   85
using just the familiar "Sister" to address them both. But now I want to know how to pronounce their names.

"They have their father's surname, Wang," says my father. "And their given names are Chwun Yu and Chwun Hwa."

"What do the names mean?" I ask.

"Ah." My father draws imaginary characters on the window. "One means 'Spring Rain,' the other 'Spring Flower,'" he explains in English, "because they born in the spring, and of course rain come before flower, same order these girls are born. Your mother like a poet, don't you think?"

I nod my head. I see Aiyi nod her head forward, too. But it falls forward and stays there. She is breathing deeply, noisily. She is asleep.

"And what does Ma's name mean?" I whisper.

"'Suyuan,'" he says, writing more invisible characters on the glass. "The way she write it in Chinese, it mean 'Long-Cherished Wish.' Quite a fancy name, not so ordinary like flower name. See this first character, it mean something like 'Forever Never Forgotten.' But there is another way to write 'Suyuan.' Sound exactly the same, but the meaning is opposite." His finger creates the brushstrokes of another character. "The first part look the same: 'Never Forgotten.' But the last part add to first part make the whole word mean 'Long-Held Grudge.' Your mother get angry with me, I tell her her name should be Grudge."

My father is looking at me, moist-eyed. "See, I pretty clever, too, hah?"

I nod, wishing I could find some way to comfort him. "And what about my name," I ask, "what does 'Jing-mei' mean?"

"Your name also special," he says. I wonder if any name in Chinese is not something special. "'Jing' like excellent *jing*. Not just good, it's something pure, essential, the best quality. *Jing* is good leftover stuff when you take impurities out of something like gold, or rice, or salt. So what is left—just pure essence. And 'Mei,' this is common *mei*, as in *meimei*, 'younger sister.'"

I think about this. My mother's long-cherished wish. Me, the younger sister who was supposed to be the essence of the others. I feed myself with the old grief, wondering how disappointed my mother must have been. Tiny Aiyi stirs suddenly, her head rolls and then falls back, her mouth opens as if to answer my question. She grunts in her sleep, tucking her body more closely into the chair.

"So why did she abandon those babies on the road?" I need to know, because now I feel abandoned too.

"Long time I wondered this myself," says my father. "But then I read that letter from her daughters in Shanghai now, and I talk to Auntie Lindo, all the others. And then I knew. No shame in what she done. None."

"What happened?"

"Your mother running away—" begins my father.

"No, tell me in Chinese," I interrupt. "Really, I can understand."

He begins to talk, still standing at the window, looking into the night.

After fleeing Kweilin, your mother walked for several days trying to find a main road. Her thought was to catch a ride on a truck or wagon, to catch enough rides until she reached Chungking, where her husband was stationed.

She had sewn money and jewelry into the lining of her dress, enough, she thought, to barter rides all the way. If I am lucky, she thought, I will not have to trade the heavy gold bracelet and jade ring. These were things from her mother, your grandmother.

By the third day, she had traded nothing. The roads were filled with people, everybody running and begging for rides from passing trucks. The trucks rushed by, afraid to stop. So your mother found no rides, only the start of dysentery pains in her stomach.

Her shoulders ached from the two babies swinging from scarf slings. Blisters grew   105
on her palms from holding two leather suitcases. And then the blisters burst and began to bleed. After a while, she left the suitcases behind, keeping only the food and a few clothes. And later she also dropped the bags of wheat flour and rice and kept walking like this for many miles, singing songs to her little girls, until she was delirious with pain and fever.

Finally, there was not one more step left in her body. She didn't have the strength to carry those babies any farther. She slumped to the ground. She knew she would die of her sickness, or perhaps from thirst, from starvation, or from the Japanese, who she was sure were marching right behind her.

She took the babies out of the slings and sat them on the side of the road, then lay down next to them. You babies are so good, she said, so quiet. They smiled back, reaching their chubby hands for her, wanting to be picked up again. And then she knew she could not bear to watch her babies die with her.

She saw a family with three young children in a cart going by. "Take my babies, I beg you," she cried to them. But they stared back with empty eyes and never stopped.

She saw another person pass and called out again. This time a man turned around, and he had such a terrible expression—your mother said it looked like death itself—she shivered and looked away.

When the road grew quiet, she tore open the lining of her dress, and stuffed   110
jewelry under the shirt of one baby and money under the other. She reached into her pocket and drew out the photos of her family, the picture of her father and mother, the picture of herself and her husband on their wedding day. And she wrote on the back of each the names of the babies and this same message: "Please care for these babies with the money and valuables provided. When it is safe to come, if you bring them to Shanghai, 9 Weichang Lu, the Li family will be glad to give you a generous reward. Li Suyuan and Wang Fuchi."

And then she touched each baby's cheek and told her not to cry. She would go down the road to find them some food and would be back. And without looking back, she walked down the road, stumbling and crying, thinking only of this one last hope, that her daughters would be found by a kindhearted person who would care for them. She would not allow herself to imagine anything else.

She did not remember how far she walked, which direction she went, when she fainted, or how she was found. When she awoke, she was in the back of a bouncing truck with several other sick people, all moaning. And she began to scream, thinking she was now on a journey to Buddhist hell. But the face of an American missionary lady bent over her and smiled, talking to her in a soothing language she did not understand. And yet she could somehow understand. She had been saved for no good reason, and it was now too late to go back and save her babies.

When she arrived in Chungking, she learned her husband had died two weeks before. She told me later she laughed when the officers told her this news, she was so delirious with madness and disease. To come so far, to lose so much and to find nothing.

I met her in a hospital. She was lying on a cot, hardly able to move, her dysentery had drained her so thin. I had come in for my foot, my missing toe, which was cut off by a piece of falling rubble. She was talking to herself, mumbling.

"Look at these clothes," she said, and I saw she had on a rather unusual dress for   115
wartime. It was silk satin, quite dirty, but there was no doubt it was a beautiful dress.

"Look at this face," she said, and I saw her dusty face and hollow cheeks, her eyes shining back. "Do you see my foolish hope?"

"I thought I had lost everything, except these two things," she murmured. "And I wondered which I would lose next. Clothes or hope? Hope or clothes?"

"But now, see here, look what is happening," she said, laughing, as if all her prayers had been answered. And she was pulling hair out of her head as easily as one lifts new wheat from wet soil.

It was an old peasant woman who found them. "How could I resist?" the peasant woman later told your sisters when they were older. They were still sitting obediently near where your mother had left them, looking like little fairy queens waiting for their sedan to arrive.

The woman, Mei Ching, and her husband, Mei Han, lived in a stone cave. There 120 were thousands of hidden caves like that in and around Kweilin so secret that the people remained hidden even after the war ended. The Meis would come out of their cave every few days and forage for food supplies left on the road, and sometimes they would see something that they both agreed was a tragedy to leave behind. So one day they took back to their cave a delicately painted set of rice bowls, another day a little footstool with a velvet cushion and two new wedding blankets. And once, it was your sisters.

They were pious people, Muslims, who believed the twin babies were a sign of double luck, and they were sure of this when, later in the evening, they discovered how valuable the babies were. She and her husband had never seen rings and bracelets like those. And while they admired the pictures, knowing the babies came from a good family, neither of them could read or write. It was not until many months later that Mei Ching found someone who could read the writing on the back. By then, she loved these baby girls like her own.

In 1952 Mei Han, the husband, died. The twins were already eight years old, and Mei Ching now decided it was time to find your sisters' true family.

She showed the girls the picture of their mother and told them they had been born into a great family and she would take them back to see their true mother and grandparents. Mei Ching told them about the reward, but she swore she would refuse it. She loved these girls so much, she only wanted them to have what they were entitled to—a better life, a fine house, educated ways. Maybe the family would let her stay on as the girls' amah°. Yes, she was certain they would insist.

Of course, when she found the place at 9 Weichang Lu, in the old French Concession, it was something completely different. It was the site of a factory building, recently constructed, and none of the workers knew what had become of the family whose house had burned down on that spot.

Mei Ching could not have known, of course, that your mother and I, her new 125 husband, had already returned to that same place in 1945 in hopes of finding both her family and her daughters.

Your mother and I stayed in China until 1947. We went to many different cities—back to Kweilin, to Changsha, as far south as Kunming. She was always looking out of one corner of her eye for twin babies, then little girls. Later we went to Hong Kong, and when we finally left in 1949 for the United States, I think she was even looking for them on the boat. But when we arrived, she no longer talked about them. I thought, At last, they have died in her heart.

---

amah: a female servant in East Asia, usually employed as a nanny or nursemaid for children.

When letters could be openly exchanged between China and the United States, she wrote immediately to old friends in Shanghai and Kweilin. I did not know she did this. Auntie Lindo told me. But of course, by then, all the street names had changed. Some people had died, others had moved away. So it took many years to find a contact. And when she did find an old schoolmate's address and wrote asking her to look for her daughters, her friend wrote back and said this was impossible, like looking for a needle on the bottom of the ocean. How did she know her daughters were in Shanghai and not somewhere else in China? The friend, of course, did not ask, How do you know your daughters are still alive?

So her schoolmate did not look. Finding babies lost during the war was a matter of foolish imagination, and she had no time for that.

But every year, your mother wrote to different people. And this last year, I think she got a big idea in her head, to go to China and find them herself. I remember she told me, "Canning, we should go, before it is too late, before we are too old." And I told her we were already too old, it was already too late.

I just thought she wanted to be a tourist! I didn't know she wanted to go and   130
look for her daughters. So when I said it was too late, that must have put a terrible thought in her head that her daughters might be dead. And I think this possibility grew bigger and bigger in her head, until it killed her.

Maybe it was your mother's dead spirit who guided her Shanghai schoolmate to find her daughters. Because after your mother died, the schoolmate saw your sisters, by chance, while shopping for shoes at the Number One Department Store on Nanjing Dong Road. She said it was like a dream, seeing these two women who looked so much alike, moving down the stairs together. There was something about their facial expressions that reminded the schoolmate of your mother.

She quickly walked over to them and called their names, which of course, they did not recognize at first, because Mei Ching had changed their names. But your mother's friend was so sure, she persisted. "Are you not Wang Chwun Yu and Wang Chwun Hwa?" she asked them. And then these double-image women became very excited, because they remembered the names written on the back of an old photo, a photo of a young man and woman they still honored, as their much-loved first parents, who had died and become spirit ghosts still roaming the earth looking for them.

At the airport, I am exhausted. I could not sleep last night. Aiyi had followed me into my room at three in the morning, and she instantly fell asleep on one of the twin beds, snoring with the might of a lumberjack. I lay awake thinking about my mother's story, realizing how much I have never known about her, grieving that my sisters and I had both lost her.

And now at the airport, after shaking hands with everybody, waving good-bye, I think about all the different ways we leave people in this world. Cheerily waving good-bye to some at airports, knowing we'll never see each other again. Leaving others on the side of the road, hoping that we will. Finding my mother in my father's story and saying good-bye before I have a chance to know her better.

Aiyi smiles at me as we wait for our gate to be called. She is so old. I put one   135
arm around her and one around Lili. They are the same size, it seems. And then it's time. As we wave good-bye one more time and enter the waiting area, I get the sense I am going from one funeral to another. In my hand I'm clutching a pair of tickets to Shanghai. In two hours we'll be there.

The plane takes off. I close my eyes. How can I describe to them in my broken Chinese about our mother's life? Where should I begin?

"Wake up, we're here," says my father. And I awake with my heart pounding in my throat. I look out the window and we're already on the runway. It's gray outside.

And now I'm walking down the steps of the plane, onto the tarmac and toward the building. If only, I think, if only my mother had lived long enough to be the one walking toward them. I am so nervous I cannot even feel my feet. I am just moving somehow.

Somebody shouts, "She's arrived!" And then I see her. Her short hair. Her small body. And that same look on her face. She has the back of her hand pressed hard against her mouth. She is crying as though she had gone through a terrible ordeal and were happy it is over.

And I know it's not my mother, yet it is the same look she had when I was five 140 and had disappeared all afternoon, for such a long time, that she was convinced I was dead. And when I miraculously appeared, sleepy-eyed, crawling from underneath my bed, she wept and laughed, biting the back of her hand to make sure it was true.

And now I see her again, two of her, waving, and in one hand there is a photo, the Polaroid I sent them. As soon as I get beyond the gate, we run toward each other, all three of us embracing, all hesitations and expectations forgotten.

"Mama, Mama," we all murmur, as if she is among us.

My sisters look at me, proudly. "*Meimei jandale*," says one sister proudly to the other. "Little Sister has grown up." I look at their faces again and I see no trace of my mother in them. Yet they still look familiar. And now I also see what part of me is Chinese. It is so obvious. It is my family. It is in our blood. After all these years, it can finally be let go.

My sisters and I stand, arms around each other, laughing and wiping the tears from each other's eyes. The flash of the Polaroid goes off and my father hands me the snapshot. My sisters and I watch quietly together, eager to see what develops.

The gray-green surface changes to the bright colors of our three images, sharp- 145 ening and deepening all at once. And although we don't speak, I know we all see it: Together we look like our mother. Her same eyes, her same mouth, open in surprise to see, at last, her long-cherished wish.

Questions

1. How is the external setting of "A Pair of Tickets" essential to what happens internally to the narrator in the course of this story?

2. How does the narrator's view of her father change by seeing him in a different setting?

3. In what ways does the narrator feel at home in China? In what ways does she feel foreign?

4. What do the narrator and her half-sisters have in common? How does this element relate to the theme of the story?

5. In what ways does the story explore specifically Chinese American experiences? In what other ways is the story grounded in universal family issues?

■ WRITING *effectively*

Amy Tan on Writing

Developing a Setting   2006

A lot of people think that all I had to do was take dictation from a relative like my mother, or that I've always known about history in China. Well, when I was growing up, I didn't even know World War II took place in China. That is how ignorant I was of China. My parents didn't talk about it, because these were the McCarthy era days when having any sense of being part of China raised questions as to whether you were a communist. When I began to write these stories, I found it was important for me to get some sense of the history, because it was the history that shaped a lot of what happened to my parents.

Amy Tan

The fact that, in those days, a woman could be taken by force as a concubine, that was a part of the old China, and I had to understand that to understand my family. I did a lot of research; however, the most important parts of the stories for me are what happened to my family. The rape of a woman who is forced to become a concubine and then kills herself, that was the story of my grandmother. She is also the woman in the story called "Scar" who cuts her arm, her piece of flesh, to make a soup for her dying mother, even though her mother had essentially kicked her out of the house when she became disgraced as a concubine. The story about the woman who marries a bad man and practically wants to kill herself to get out of the marriage, that was based on my mother's life. The story about a girl going to China for the first time to meet her sisters, that was a story that I wrote right after going to China to meet my sisters.

A very important layer to everything that I write is this notion of what we believe and why we need to ask questions to find truth. The books may be about mothers and daughters, but they are also about where I found the things that I believe in and why they change over time—notions of faith, fate, luck, curses, destiny, self-determination, accidents. That came from my mother, that need to question the world. The stories are about the conflicts that mothers and daughters have, because they have different beliefs of how they see the world, how it operates, what you need to worry about, what you can control.

From an interview with Dana Gioia

THINKING ABOUT SETTING

The time and place in which a story is set serve as more than mere backdrop. When preparing to write about a story, be sure to consider where and when it is set and what role the setting plays.

- **Ask whether setting helps motivate the plot.** The external pressure of the setting is often the key factor that compels or invites the protagonist into action. Setting can play as large a role as plot and characters do by prompting a protagonist into an action he or she might not otherwise take.
- **Consider whether the external setting suggests the character's inner reality.** A particular setting can create a mood or provide clues to a protagonist's nature. To write about a story's setting, therefore, invites you to study not only the time and place but also their relation to the protagonist. Does the external reality provide a clue to the protagonist's inner reality?
- **Notice whether the setting changes as the plot progresses.** The settings in a story are not static. Characters can move from place to place, and their actions may bring them into significantly different external and internal places.

CHECKLIST: Writing About Setting

- ☐ Where does the story take place?
- ☐ What does the setting suggest about the characters' lives?
- ☐ Are there significant differences in the settings for different characters? What does this suggest about each person?
- ☐ When does the story take place? Is the time of year or time of day significant?
- ☐ Does the weather play a meaningful role in the story's action?
- ☐ What is the protagonist's relationship to the setting?
- ☐ Does the setting of the story in some way compel the protagonist into action?
- ☐ Does the story's time or place suggest something about the character of the protagonist?
- ☐ Does a change in setting during the story suggest some internal change in the protagonist?

TOPICS FOR WRITING ON SETTING

1. Choose a story from this chapter, and explore how character and setting are interrelated. How does the setting of the climax of the story contribute to a change in the character's personal perspective?
2. Write about how setting functions as a kind of character in "To Build a Fire." Do the landscape and weather act as the antagonist in the story's plot?
3. Why does Ron Carlson set "At the Jim Bridger" on a sort of false New Year's Eve? What is the significance of that holiday, in relation to the story?
4. Take any story in this chapter and analyze how the author presents the key setting. Don't pay special attention to the protagonist or other human characters, but focus on the setting that surrounds him or her and how it emerges as a force in the story.
5. Think of a place to which you often return. If possible, go there. Make a list of every physical detail you can think of to describe that place. Then look the list over and write a paragraph on what sort of mood is suggested by it. If you were to describe your emotional connection to the place, which three details would you choose? Why?
6. Choose any story in this book, and pay careful attention to setting as you read it. Write several paragraphs reflecting on the following questions: What details in the story suggest

the time and place in which it is set? Is setting central to the story? If the action were transplanted to some other place and time, how would the story change?

▶ TERMS FOR *review*

Setting ▶ The time and place of a story. The setting may also include the climate and even the social, psychological, or spiritual state of the characters.

Locale ▶ The location where a story takes place.

Atmosphere ▶ The dominant mood or feeling that pervades all or part of a literary work. Atmosphere is the total effect conveyed by the author's use of language, images, and physical setting.

Historical fiction ▶ A type of fiction in which the narrative is set in an earlier time or place, sometimes including well-known figures from the past.

Regionalism ▶ The literary representation of a specific locale that consciously uses the particulars of geography, custom, history, folklore, or speech. In regional narratives, the locale plays a crucial role in the presentation and progression of the story.

Naturalism ▶ A type of fiction in which the characters are presented as products or victims of environment and heredity. Naturalism is considered an extreme form of **realism** (the attempt to reproduce faithfully the surface appearance of life, especially that of ordinary people in everyday situations).

5 TONE AND STYLE

> *Style has no fixed laws; it is changed by the usage of the people, never the same for any length of time.*
>
> —SENECA

What You Will Learn in This Chapter

- To identify the *tone* of a story
- To describe the elements of an author's *style*
- To define *irony* and identify its many forms
- To analyze the tone and style of a story

When the narrator of Joseph Conrad's *Heart of Darkness* comes upon an African outpost littered with abandoned machines and notices "a boiler wallowing in the grass," the exact word *wallowing* conveys an attitude: that there is something swinish about this scene of careless waste. If Conrad had selected a different word than *wallowing*—say, *resting*—his description would have carried less meaning. His example reminds us that not only an author's choice of details may lead us to infer his or her attitude, but also the choice of words, as well as characters, events, and situations.

TONE

Whatever helps us understand the author's attitude is commonly called **tone**. Like a tone of voice, the tone of a story may communicate amusement, anger, affection, sorrow, contempt. It implies the feelings of the author, so far as we can sense them. Those feelings may be similar to feelings expressed by the narrator of the story (or by any character), but sometimes they may be dissimilar, even sharply opposed. The characters in a story may regard an event as sad, but we sense that the author regards it as funny. To understand the tone of a story, then, is to understand some attitude more fundamental to the story than whatever attitudes the characters explicitly declare.

The tone of a story, like a tone of voice, may convey not simply one attitude, but a medley. Reading "A & P" (Chapter 1), we have mingled feelings about Sammy: delight in his wicked comments about other people and his skewering of hypocrisy; irritation at his smugness and condescension; admiration for his readiness to take a stand; sympathy for the pain of his disillusionment. Often the tone of a literary story will be too rich and complicated to sum up in one or two words. But to try to describe the tone of such a story may be a useful way to penetrate to its center and to grasp the whole of it.

163

STYLE

One of the clearest indications of the tone of a story is the **style** in which it is written. In general, style refers to the individual traits or characteristics of a piece of writing: to a writer's particular ways of managing words that we come to recognize as habitual or customary. It includes all the ways in which a writer uses words, imagery, tone, syntax, and figurative language.

A distinctive style marks the work of a fine writer: we can tell his or her work from that of anyone else. From one story to another, however, the writer may fittingly change style; and in some stories, style may be altered meaningfully as the story goes along. In his novel *As I Lay Dying*, William Faulkner changes narrators with every chapter, and he distinguishes the narrators from one another by giving each an individual style or manner of speaking. Though each narrator has his or her own style, the book as a whole demonstrates Faulkner's style as well. For instance, one chapter is written from the point of view of a small boy, Vardaman Bundren, member of a family of poor Mississippi tenant farmers, whose view of a horse in a barn reads like this:

> It is as though the dark were resolving him out of his integrity, into an unrelated scattering of components—snuffings and stampings; smells of cooling flesh and ammoniac hair; an illusion of a co-ordinated whole of splotched hide and strong bones within which, detached and secret and familiar, an *is* different from my *is*.

How can a small boy unaccustomed to libraries use words like *integrity*, *components*, *ammoniac*, *illusion*, and *co-ordinated*? Elsewhere in the story, Vardaman says aloud, with no trace of literacy, "Hit was a-laying right there on the ground." Apparently, in the above description of the horse, it is not the voice of the boy that we are hearing, but something resembling the voice of William Faulkner, elevated and passionate, expressing the boy's thoughts in a style that admits Faulknerian words.

DICTION

Usually, *style* indicates a mode of expression: the language a writer uses. In this sense, the notion of style includes such traits as the length and complexity of sentences, and **diction**, or choice of words: abstract or concrete, bookish ("unrelated scattering of components") or close to speech ("Hit was a-laying right there on the ground"). Involved in the idea of style, too, is any habitual use of imagery, patterns of sound, figures of speech, or other devices.

Several writers of realistic fiction known as **minimalists**—Ann Beattie, Raymond Carver, Bobbie Ann Mason—have written with a flat, laid-back, unemotional tone, in an appropriately bare, unadorned style. Minimalists seem to give nothing but facts drawn from ordinary life, sometimes in picayune detail. Here is a sample passage from Raymond Carver's story "A Small, Good Thing":

> She pulled into the driveway and cut the engine. She closed her eyes and leaned her head against the wheel for a minute. She listened to the ticking sounds the engine made as it began to cool. Then she got out of the car. She could hear the dog barking inside the house. She went to the front door, which was unlocked. She went inside and turned on lights and put on a kettle of water for tea. She opened some dog food and fed Slug on the back porch. The dog ate in hungry little smacks. It kept running into the kitchen to see that she was going to stay.

Explicit feeling and showy language are kept at a minimum here. Notice how Carver's diction relies on everyday words—mostly words of only one or two syllables. Taken out of context, this description may strike you as banal, as if the writer himself were bored; but it works effectively as a part of Carver's entire story. As in all good writing, the style here seems a faithful mirror of what is said. At its best, such writing achieves "a hard-won reduction, a painful stripping away of richness, a baring of bone."[1]

Two Examples of Style: Hemingway Versus Faulkner

To see what style means, compare the stories in this chapter by William Faulkner ("Barn Burning") and by Ernest Hemingway ("A Clean, Well-Lighted Place"). Faulkner frequently falls into a style in which a statement, as soon as it is uttered, is followed by another statement expressing the idea in a more emphatic way. Sentences are interrupted with parenthetical elements (asides, like this) thrust into them unexpectedly. At times, Faulkner writes of seemingly ordinary matters as if giving a speech in a towering passion. Here, from "Barn Burning," is a description of how a boy's father delivers a rug:

> "Don't you want me to help?" he whispered. His father did not answer and now he heard again that stiff foot striking the hollow portico with that wooden and clocklike deliberation, that outrageous overstatement of the weight it carried. The rug, hunched, not flung (the boy could tell that even in the darkness) from his father's shoulder struck the angle of wall and floor with a sound unbelievably loud, thunderous, then the foot again, unhurried and enormous; a light came on in the house and the boy sat, tense, breathing steadily and quietly and just a little fast, though the foot itself did not increase its beat at all, descending the steps now; now the boy could see him.

Faulkner is not merely indulging in language for its own sake. As you will find when you read the whole story, this rug delivery is vital to the story, and so too is the father's profound defiance—indicated by his walk. By devices of style—by *metaphor* and *simile* ("wooden and clocklike"), by exact qualification ("not flung"), by emphatic adjectives ("loud, thunderous")—Faulkner is carefully placing his emphases.

With the words he selects to describe the father's stride, Faulkner directs how we feel toward the man and perhaps also indicates his own wondering but skeptical attitude toward a character whose very footfall is "outrageous" and "enormous." (Fond of long sentences like the last one in the quoted passage, Faulkner remarked that there are sentences that need to be written in the way a circus acrobat pedals a bicycle on a high wire: rapidly, so as not to fall off.)

Hemingway's famous style includes both short sentences and long. His long compound sentences tend to be relatively simple in construction (clause plus clause plus clause), sometimes joined with the use of *and*. He interrupts such a sentence with a dependent clause or a parenthetical element much less frequently than Faulkner does. The effect is like listening to speech:

> In the day time the street was dusty, but at night the dew settled the dust and the old man liked to sit late because he was deaf and now at night it was quiet and he felt the difference.

[1]John Mella, letter in the *New York Times Book Review*, 5 June 1988.

Hemingway is a master of swift, terse dialogue and often casts whole scenes in the form of conversation. As if he were a closemouthed speaker unwilling to let his feelings loose, the narrator of a Hemingway story often addresses us in understatement, implying greater depths of feeling than he puts into words. Read the following story and you will see that its style and tone cannot be separated.

Ernest Hemingway

A Clean, Well-Lighted Place   1933

Ernest Hemingway (1899–1961), born in Oak Park, Illinois, skipped college to become a cub reporter. In World War I, as an eighteen-year-old volunteer ambulance driver in Italy, he was wounded in action. In 1922 he settled in Paris, then aswarm with writers; he later recalled that time in the autobiographical essays of A Moveable Feast *(1964). Hemingway won swift acclaim for his early stories,* In Our Time *(1925), and for his first, perhaps finest, novel,* The Sun Also Rises *(1926), portraying a "lost generation" of postwar American drifters in France and Spain.* For Whom the Bell Tolls *(1940) depicts life during the Spanish Civil War. Hemingway became a celebrity, often photographed as a marlin fisherman or a lion hunter. A fan of bullfighting, he wrote two nonfiction books on the subject:* Death in the Afternoon *(1932) and* The Dangerous Summer *(posthumously published in 1985). After World War II, with his fourth wife, journalist Mary Welsh, he made his home in Cuba, where he wrote* The Old Man and the Sea *(1952). The Nobel Prize in Literature came his way in 1954. In 1961, mentally distressed and physically ailing, he shot himself. Hemingway brought a hard-bitten realism to American fiction. His heroes live dangerously, by personal codes of honor, courage, and endurance. Hemingway's distinctively crisp, unadorned style left American literature permanently changed.*

It was late and every one had left the café except an old man who sat in the shadow the leaves of the tree made against the electric light. In the day time the street was dusty, but at night the dew settled the dust and the old man liked to sit late because he was deaf and now at night it was quiet and he felt the difference. The two waiters inside the café knew that the old man was a little drunk, and while he was a good client they knew that if he became too drunk he would leave without paying, so they kept watch on him.

"Last week he tried to commit suicide," one waiter said.

"Why?"

"He was in despair."

"What about?"

"Nothing."   5

"How do you know it was nothing?"

"He has plenty of money."

They sat together at a table that was close against the wall near the door of the café and looked at the terrace where the tables were all empty except where the old man sat in the shadow of the leaves of the tree that moved slightly in the wind. A girl and a soldier went by in the street. The street light shone on the brass number on his collar. The girl wore no head covering and hurried beside him.

"The guard will pick him up," one waiter said.   10

"What does it matter if he gets what he's after?"

"He had better get off the street now. The guard will get him. They went by five minutes ago."

The old man sitting in the shadow rapped on his saucer with his glass. The younger waiter went over to him.

"What do you want?"

The old man looked at him. "Another brandy," he said.   15

"You'll be drunk," the waiter said. The old man looked at him. The waiter went away.

"He'll stay all night," he said to his colleague. "I'm sleepy now. I never get into bed before three o'clock. He should have killed himself last week."

The waiter took the brandy bottle and another saucer from the counter inside the café and marched out to the old man's table. He put down the saucer and poured the glass full of brandy.

"You should have killed yourself last week," he said to the deaf man. The old man motioned with his finger. "A little more," he said. The waiter poured on into the glass so that the brandy slopped over and ran down the stem into the top saucer of the pile. "Thank you," the old man said. The waiter took the bottle back inside the café. He sat down at the table with his colleague again.

"He's drunk now," he said.   20

"He's drunk every night."°

"What did he want to kill himself for?"

"How should I know?"

"How did he do it?"

"He hung himself with a rope."   25

"Who cut him down?"

"His niece."

"Why did they do it?"

"Fear for his soul."

"How much money has he got?"   30

"He's got plenty."

"He must be eighty years old."

"Anyway I should say he was eighty."°

"I wish he would go home. I never get to bed before three o'clock. What kind of hour is that to go to bed?"

"He stays up because he likes it."   35

"He's lonely. I'm not lonely. I have a wife waiting in bed for me."

"He had a wife once too."

"A wife would be no good to him now."

"You can't tell. He might be better with a wife."

"His niece looks after him."   40

"I know. You said she cut him down."

"I wouldn't want to be that old. An old man is a nasty thing."

"Not always. This old man is clean. He drinks without spilling. Even now, drunk. Look at him."

"I don't want to look at him. I wish he would go home. He has no regard for those who must work."

"He's drunk now," he said. "He's drunk every night": The younger waiter perhaps says both these lines. A device of Hemingway's style is sometimes to have a character pause, then speak again—as often happens in actual speech.   *"He must be eighty years old." "Anyway I should say he was eighty"*: Is this another instance of the same character's speaking twice? Clearly it is the younger waiter who says the next line, "I wish he would go home."

The old man looked from his glass across the square, then over at the waiters.　　45

"Another brandy," he said, pointing to his glass. The waiter who was in a hurry came over.

"Finished," he said, speaking with that omission of syntax stupid people employ when talking to drunken people or foreigners. "No more tonight. Close now."

"Another," said the old man.

"No. Finished." The waiter wiped the edge of the table with a towel and shook his head.

The old man stood up, slowly counted the saucers, took a leather coin purse from　50 his pocket and paid for the drinks, leaving half a peseta tip.

The waiter watched him go down the street, a very old man walking unsteadily but with dignity.

"Why didn't you let him stay and drink?" the unhurried waiter asked. They were putting up the shutters. "It is not half-past two."

"I want to go home to bed."

"What is an hour?"

"More to me than to him."　　55

"An hour is the same."

"You talk like an old man yourself. He can buy a bottle and drink at home."

"It's not the same."

"No, it is not," agreed the waiter with a wife. He did not wish to be unjust. He was only in a hurry.

"And you? You have no fear of going home before the usual hour?"　　60

"Are you trying to insult me?"

"No, hombre, only to make a joke."

"No," the waiter who was in a hurry said, rising from pulling down the metal shutters. "I have confidence. I am all confidence."

"You have youth, confidence, and a job," the older waiter said. "You have everything."

"And what do you lack?"　　65

"Everything but work."

"You have everything I have."

"No. I have never had confidence and I am not young."

"Come on. Stop talking nonsense and lock up."

"I am of those who like to stay late at the café," the older waiter said. "With all　70 those who do not want to go to bed. With all those who need a light for the night."

"I want to go home and into bed."

"We are of two different kinds," the older waiter said. He was not dressed to go home. "It is not only a question of youth and confidence although those things are very beautiful. Each night I am reluctant to close up because there may be some one who needs the café."

"Hombre, there are bodegas° open all night long."

"You do not understand. This is a clean and pleasant café. It is well lighted. The light is very good and also, now, there are shadows of the leaves."

"Good night," said the younger waiter.　　75

"Good night," the other said. Turning off the electric light he continued the conversation with himself. It is the light of course but it is necessary that the place be

bodegas: wineshops.

clean and pleasant. You do not want music. Certainly you do not want music. Nor can you stand before a bar with dignity although that is all that is provided for these hours. What did he fear? It was not fear or dread. It was a nothing that he knew too well. It was all a nothing and a man was nothing too. It was only that and light was all it needed and a certain cleanness and order. Some lived in it and never felt it but he knew it all was nada y pues nada y nada y pues nada.° Our nada who art in nada, nada be thy name thy kingdom nada thy will be nada in nada as it is in nada. Give us this nada our daily nada and nada us our nada as we nada our nadas and nada us not into nada but deliver us from nada; pues nada. Hail nothing full of nothing, nothing is with thee. He smiled and stood before a bar with a shining steam pressure coffee machine.

"What's yours?" asked the barman.

"Nada."

"Otro loco más,"° said the barman and turned away.

"A little cup," said the waiter.   80

The barman poured it for him.

"The light is very bright and pleasant but the bar is unpolished," the waiter said. The barman looked at him but did not answer. It was too late at night for conversation.

"You want another copita?"° the barman asked.

"No, thank you," said the waiter and went out. He disliked bars and bodegas. A   85 clean, well-lighted café was a very different thing. Now, without thinking further, he would go home to his room. He would lie in the bed and finally, with daylight, he would go to sleep. After all, he said to himself, it is probably only insomnia. Many must have it.

Questions

1. What besides insomnia makes the older waiter reluctant to go to bed? Comment especially on his meditation with its *nada* refrain. Why does he understand so well the old man's need for a café? What does the café represent for the two of them?

2. Compare the younger waiter and the older waiter in their attitudes toward the old man. Whose attitude do you take to be closer to that of the author? Even though Hemingway does not editorially state his own feelings, how does he make them clear to us?

3. Point to sentences that establish the style of the story. What is distinctive in them? What repetitions of words or phrases seem particularly effective? Does Hemingway seem to favor a simple or an erudite vocabulary?

4. What is the story's point of view? Discuss its appropriateness.

William Faulkner

Barn Burning   1939

William Faulkner (1897–1962) receives a capsule biography in Chapter 2, page 29, along with his story "A Rose for Emily." "Barn Burning" is among his many contributions to the history of Yoknapatawpha, an imaginary Mississippi county in which the Sartorises and the de Spains are landed aristocrats living by a code of honor, and the Snopeses—most of them—are shiftless ne'er-do-wells.

---

nada y pues . . . nada: nothing and then nothing and nothing and then nothing.   *Otro loco más:* another lunatic.   *copita:* little cup.

The store in which the Justice of the Peace's court was sitting smelled of cheese. The boy, crouched on his nail keg at the back of the crowded room, knew he smelled cheese, and more: from where he sat he could see the ranked shelves close-packed with the solid, squat, dynamic shapes of tin cans whose labels his stomach read, not from the lettering which meant nothing to his mind but from the scarlet devils and the silver curve of fish—this, the cheese which he knew he smelled and the hermetic meat which his intestines believed he smelled coming in intermittent gusts momentary and brief between the other constant one, the smell and sense just a little of fear because mostly of despair and grief, the old fierce pull of blood. He could not see the table where the Justice sat and before which his father and his father's enemy (*our enemy* he thought in that despair: *ourn! mine and hisn both! He's my father!*) stood, but he could hear them, the two of them that is, because his father had said no word yet:

"But what proof have you, Mr. Harris?"

"I told you. The hog got into my corn. I caught it up and sent it back to him. He had no fence that would hold it. I told him so, warned him. The next time I put the hog in my pen. When he came to get it I gave him enough wire to patch up his pen. The next time I put the hog up and kept it. I rode down to his house and saw the wire I gave him still rolled on to the spool in his yard. I told him he could have the hog when he paid me a dollar pound fee. That evening a nigger came with the dollar and got the hog. He was a strange nigger. He said, 'He say to tell you wood and hay kin burn.' I said, 'What?' 'That whut he say to tell you,' the nigger said. 'Wood and hay kin burn.' That night my barn burned. I got the stock out but I lost the barn."

"Where's the nigger? Have you got him?"

"He was a strange nigger, I tell you. I don't know what became of him." 5

"But that's not proof. Don't you see that's not proof?"

"Get that boy up here. He knows." For a moment the boy thought too that the man meant his older brother until Harris said, "Not him. The little one. The boy," and, crouching, small for his age, small and wiry like his father, in patched and faded jeans even too small for him, with straight, uncombed, brown hair and eyes gray and wild as storm scud, he saw the men between himself and the table part and become a lane of grim faces, at the end of which he saw the Justice, a shabby, collarless, graying man in spectacles, beckoning him. He felt no floor under his bare feet; he seemed to walk beneath the palpable weight of the grim turning faces. His father, still in his black Sunday coat donned not for the trial but for the moving, did not even look at him. *He aims for me to lie,* he thought, again with that frantic grief and despair. *And I will have to do hit.*

"What's your name, boy?" the Justice said.

"Colonel Sartoris Snopes," the boy whispered.

"Hey?" the Justice said. "Talk louder. Colonel Sartoris? I reckon anybody named 10 for Colonel Sartoris in this country can't help but tell the truth, can they?" The boy said nothing. *Enemy! Enemy!* he thought; for a moment he could not even see, could not see that the Justice's face was kindly nor discern that his voice was troubled when he spoke to the man named Harris: "Do you want me to question this boy?" But he could hear, and during those subsequent long seconds while there was absolutely no sound in the crowded little room save that of quiet and intent breathing it was as if he had swung outward at the end of a grape vine, over a ravine, and at the top of the swing had been caught in a prolonged instant of mesmerized gravity, weightless in time.

"No!" Harris said violently, explosively. "Damnation! Send him out of here!" Now time, the fluid world, rushed beneath him again, the voices coming to him again through the smell of cheese and sealed meat, the fear and despair and the old grief of blood:

"This case is closed. I can't find against you, Snopes, but I can give you advice. Leave this country and don't come back to it."

His father spoke for the first time, his voice cold and harsh, level, without emphasis: "I aim to. I don't figure to stay in a country among people who . . ." he said something unprintable and vile, addressed to no one.

"That'll do," the Justice said. "Take your wagon and get out of this country before dark. Case dismissed."

His father turned, and he followed the stiff black coat, the wiry figure walking   15
a little stiffly from where a Confederate provost's man's musket ball had taken him in the heel on a stolen horse thirty years ago, followed the two backs now, since his older brother had appeared from somewhere in the crowd, no taller than the father but thicker, chewing tobacco steadily, between the two lines of grim-faced men and out of the store and across the worn gallery and down the sagging steps and among the dogs and half-grown boys in the mild May dust, where as he passed a voice hissed:

"Barn burner!"

Again he could not see, whirling; there was a face in a red haze, moonlike, bigger than the full moon, the owner of it half again his size, he leaping in the red haze toward the face, feeling no blow, feeling no shock when his head struck the earth, scrabbling up and leaping again, feeling no blow this time either and tasting no blood, scrabbling up to see the other boy in full flight and himself already leaping into pursuit as his father's hand jerked him back, the harsh, cold voice speaking above him: "Go get in the wagon."

It stood in a grove of locusts and mulberries across the road. His two hulking sisters in their Sunday dresses and his mother and her sister in calico and sunbonnets were already in it, sitting on and among the sorry residue of the dozen and more movings which even the boy could remember—the battered stove, the broken beds and chairs, the clock inlaid with mother-of-pearl, which would not run, stopped at some fourteen minutes past two o'clock of a dead and forgotten day and time, which had been his mother's dowry. She was crying, though when she saw him she drew her sleeve across her face and began to descend from the wagon. "Get back," the father said.

"He's hurt. I got to get some water and wash his . . ."

"Get back in the wagon," his father said. He got in too, over the tail-gate. His   20
father mounted to the seat where the older brother already sat and struck the gaunt mules two savage blows with the peeled willow, but without heat. It was not even sadistic; it was exactly that same quality which in later years would cause his descendants to over-run the engine before putting a motor car into motion, striking and reining back in the same movement. The wagon went on, the store with its quiet crowd of grimly watching men dropped behind; a curve in the road hid it. *Forever* he thought. *Maybe he's done satisfied now, now that he has* . . . stopping himself, not to say it aloud even to himself. His mother's hand touched his shoulder.

"Does hit hurt?" she said.

"Naw," he said. "Hit don't hurt. Lemme be."

"Can't you wipe some of the blood off before hit dries?"

"I'll wash to-night," he said. "Lemme be, I tell you."

The wagon went on. He did not know where they were going. None of them   25
ever did or ever asked, because it was always somewhere, always a house of sorts waiting for them a day or two days or even three days away. Likely his father had already

arranged to make a crop on another farm before he . . . Again he had to stop himself. He (the father) always did. There was something about his wolflike independence and even courage when the advantage was at least neutral which impressed strangers, as if they got from his latent ravening ferocity not so much a sense of dependability as a feeling that his ferocious conviction in the rightness of his own actions would be of advantage to all whose interest lay with his.

That night they camped, in a grove of oaks and beeches where a spring ran. The nights were still cool and they had a fire against it, of a rail lifted from a nearby fence and cut into lengths—a small fire, neat, niggard almost, a shrewd fire; such fires were his father's habit and custom always, even in freezing weather. Older, the boy might have remarked this and wondered why not a big one; why should not a man who had not only seen the waste and extravagance of war, but who had in his blood an inherent voracious prodigality with material not his own, have burned everything in sight? Then he might have gone a step farther and thought that that was the reason: that niggard blaze was the living fruit of nights passed during those four years in the woods hiding from all men, blue and gray, with his strings of horses (captured horses, he called them). And older still, he might have divined the true reason: that the element of fire spoke to some deep mainspring of his father's being, as the element of steel or of powder spoke to other men, as the one weapon for the preservation of integrity, else breath were not worth the breathing, and hence to be regarded with respect and used with discretion.

But he did not think this now and he had seen those same niggard blazes all his life. He merely ate his supper beside it and was already half asleep over his iron plate when his father called him, and once more he followed the stiff back, the stiff and ruthless limp, up the slope and on to the starlit road where, turning, he could see his father against the stars but without face or depth—a shape black, flat, and bloodless as though cut from tin in the iron folds of the frockcoat which had not been made for him, the voice harsh like tin and without heat like tin:

"You were fixing to tell them. You would have told him." He didn't answer. His father struck him with the flat of his hand on the side of the head, hard but without heat, exactly as he had struck the two mules at the store, exactly as he would strike either of them with any stick in order to kill a horse fly, his voice without heat or anger: "You're getting to be a man. You got to learn. You got to learn to stick to your own blood or you ain't going to have any blood to stick to you. Do you think either of them, any man there this morning, would? Don't you know all they wanted was a chance to get at me because they knew I had them beat? Eh?" Later, twenty years later, he was to tell himself, "If I had said they wanted only truth, justice, he would have hit me again." But now he said nothing. He was not crying. He just stood there. "Answer me," his father said.

"Yes," he whispered. His father turned.

"Get on to bed. We'll be there tomorrow." 30

Tomorrow they were there. In the early afternoon the wagon stopped before a paintless two-room house identical almost with the dozen others it had stopped before even in the boy's ten years, and again, as on the other dozen occasions, his mother and aunt got down and began to unload the wagon, although his two sisters and his father and brother had not moved.

"Likely hit ain't fitten for hawgs," one of the sisters said.

"Nevertheless, fit it will and you'll hog it and like it," his father said. "Get out of them chairs and help your Ma unload."

The two sisters got down, big, bovine, in a flutter of cheap ribbons; one of them drew from the jumbled wagon bed a battered lantern, the other a worn broom. His father handed the reins to the older son and began to climb stiffly over the wheel. "When they get unloaded, take the team to the barn and feed them." Then he said, and at first the boy thought he was still speaking to his brother: "Come with me."

"Me?" he said.   35

"Yes," his father said. "You."

"Abner," his mother said. His father paused and looked back—the harsh level stare beneath the shaggy, graying, irascible brows.

"I reckon I'll have a word with the man that aims to begin to-morrow owning me body and soul for the next eight months."

They went back up the road. A week ago—or before last night, that is—he would have asked where they were going, but not now. His father had struck him before last night but never before had he paused afterward to explain why; it was as if the blow and the following calm, outrageous voice still rang, repercussed, divulging nothing to him save the terrible handicap of being young, the light weight of his few years, just heavy enough to prevent his soaring free of the world as it seemed to be ordered but not heavy enough to keep him footed solid in it, to resist it and try to change the course of its events.

Presently he could see the grove of oaks and cedars and the other flowering trees   40
and shrubs where the house would be, though not the house yet. They walked beside a fence massed with honeysuckle and Cherokee roses and came to a gate swinging open between two brick pillars, and now, beyond a sweep of drive, he saw the house for the first time and at that instant he forgot his father and the terror and despair both, and even when he remembered his father again (who had not stopped) the terror and despair did not return. Because, for all the twelve movings, they had sojourned until now in a poor country, a land of small farms and fields and houses, and he had never seen a house like this before. *Hit's big as a courthouse* he thought quietly, with a surge of peace and joy whose reason he could not have thought into words, being too young for that: *They are safe from him. People whose lives are a part of this peace and dignity are beyond his touch, he no more to them than a buzzing wasp: capable of stinging for a little moment but that's all; the spell of this peace and dignity rendering even the barns and stable and cribs which belong to it impervious to the puny flames he might contrive . . .* this, the peace and joy, ebbing for an instant as he looked again at the stiff black back, the stiff and implacable limp of the figure which was not dwarfed by the house, for the reason that it had never looked big anywhere and which now, against the serene columned backdrop, had more than ever that impervious quality of something cut ruthlessly from tin, depthless, as though, sidewise to the sun, it would cast no shadow. Watching him, the boy remarked the absolutely undeviating course which his father held and saw the stiff foot come squarely down in a pile of fresh droppings where a horse had stood in the drive and which his father could have avoided by a simple change of stride. But it ebbed only a moment, though he could not have thought this into words either, walking on in the spell of the house, which he could even want but without envy, without sorrow, certainly never with that ravening and jealous rage which unknown to him walked in the ironlike black coat before him: *Maybe he will feel it too. Maybe it will even change him now from what maybe he couldn't help but be.*

They crossed the portico. Now he could hear his father's stiff foot as it came down on the boards with clocklike finality, a sound out of all proportion to the displacement of the body it bore and which was not dwarfed either by the white door before it, as though it had attained to a sort of vicious and ravening minimum not to be dwarfed by anything—the flat, wide, black hat, the formal coat of broadcloth which had once been black but which had now that friction-glazed greenish cast of the bodies of old house flies, the lifted sleeve which was too large, the lifted hand like a curled claw. The door opened so promptly that the boy knew the Negro must have been watching them all the time, an old man with neat grizzled hair, in a linen jacket, who stood barring the door with his body, saying, "Wipe yo foots, white man, fo you come in here. Major ain't home nohow."

"Get out of my way, nigger," his father said, without heat too, flinging the door back and the Negro also and entering, his hat still on his head. And now the boy saw the prints of the stiff foot on the doorjamb and saw them appear on the pale rug behind the machinelike deliberation of the foot which seemed to bear (or transmit) twice the weight which the body compassed. The Negro was shouting "Miss Lula! Miss Lula!" somewhere behind them, then the boy, deluged as though by a warm wave by a suave turn of the carpeted stair and a pendant glitter of chandeliers and a mute gleam of gold frames, heard the swift feet and saw her too, a lady—perhaps he had never seen her like before either—in a gray, smooth gown with lace at the throat and an apron tied at the waist and the sleeves turned back, wiping cake or biscuit dough from her hands with a towel as she came up the hall, looking not at his father at all but at the tracks on the blond rug with an expression of incredulous amazement.

"I tried," the Negro cried. "I tole him to . . ."

"Will you please go away?" she said in a shaking voice. "Major de Spain is not at home. Will you please go away?"

His father had not spoken again. He did not speak again. He did not even look at her. He just stood stiff in the center of the rug, in his hat, the shaggy iron-gray brows twitching slightly above the pebble-colored eyes as he appeared to examine the house with brief deliberation. Then with the same deliberation he turned; the boy watched him pivot on the good leg and saw the stiff foot drag around the arc of the turning, leaving a final long and fading smear. His father never looked at it, he never once looked down at the rug. The Negro held the door. It closed behind them, upon the hysteric and indistinguishable woman-wail. His father stopped at the top of the steps and scraped his boot clean on the edge of it. At the gate he stopped again. He stood for a moment, planted stiffly on the stiff foot, looking back at the house. "Pretty and white, ain't it?" he said. "That's sweat. Nigger sweat. Maybe it ain't white enough yet to suit him. Maybe he wants to mix some white sweat with it."

Two hours later the boy was chopping wood behind the house within which his mother and aunt and the two sisters (the mother and aunt, not the two girls, he knew that; even at this distance and muffled by walls the flat loud voices of the two girls emanated an incorrigible idle inertia) were setting up the stove to prepare a meal, when he heard the hooves and saw the linen-clad man on a fine sorrel mare, whom he recognized even before he saw the rolled rug in front of the Negro youth following on a fat bay carriage horse—a suffused, angry face vanishing, still at full gallop, beyond the corner of the house where his father and brother were sitting in the two tilted chairs; and a moment later, almost before he could have put the axe down, he heard the hooves again and watched the sorrel mare go back out of the yard, already galloping again. Then his father began to shout one of the sisters' names, who presently emerged backward from the kitchen door dragging the rolled rug along the ground by one end while the other sister walked behind it.

45

"If you ain't going to tote, go on and set up the wash pot," the first said.

"You, Sarty!" the second shouted. "Set up the wash pot!" His father appeared at the door, framed against that shabbiness, as he had been against that other bland perfection, impervious to either, the mother's anxious face at his shoulder.

"Go on," the father said. "Pick it up." The two sisters stooped, broad, lethargic; stooping, they presented an incredible expanse of pale cloth and a flutter of tawdry ribbons.

"If I thought enough of a rug to have to git hit all the way from France I wouldn't keep hit where folks coming in would have to tromp on hit," the first said. They raised the rug.   50

"Abner," the mother said. "Let me do it."

"You go back and git dinner," his father said. "I'll tend to this."

From the woodpile through the rest of the afternoon the boy watched them, the rug spread flat in the dust beside the bubbling wash pot, the two sisters stooping over it with that profound and lethargic reluctance, while the father stood over them in turn, implacable and grim, driving them though never raising his voice again. He could smell the harsh homemade lye they were using; he saw his mother come to the door once and look toward them with an expression not anxious now but very like despair; he saw his father turn, and he fell to with the axe and saw from the corner of his eye his father raise from the ground a flattish fragment of field stone and examine it and return to the pot, and this time his mother actually spoke: "Abner. Abner. Please don't. Please, Abner."

Then he was done too. It was dusk; the whippoorwills had already begun. He could smell coffee from the room where they would presently eat the cold food remaining from the mid-afternoon meal, though when he entered the house he realized they were having coffee again probably because there was a fire on the hearth, before which the rug now lay spread over the backs of the two chairs. The tracks of his father's foot were gone. Where they had been were now long, water-cloudy scoriations resembling the sporadic course of a lilliputian mowing machine.

It still hung there while they ate the cold food and then went to bed, scattered   55
without order or claim up and down the two rooms, his mother in one bed, where his father would later lie, the older brother in the other, himself, the aunt, and the two sisters on pallets on the floor. But his father was not in bed yet. The last thing the boy remembered was the depthless, harsh silhouette of the hat and coat bending over the rug and it seemed to him that he had not even closed his eyes when the silhouette was standing over him, the fire almost dead behind it, the stiff foot prodding him awake. "Catch up the mule," his father said.

When he returned with the mule his father was standing in the back door, the rolled rug over his shoulder. "Ain't you going to ride?" he said.

"No. Give me your foot."

He bent his knee into his father's hand, the wiry, surprising power flowed smoothly, rising, he rising with it, on to the mule's bare back (they had owned a saddle once; the boy could remember it though not when or where) and with the same effortlessness his father swung the rug up in front of him. Now in the starlight they retraced the afternoon's path, up the dusty road rife with honeysuckle, through the gate and up the black tunnel of the drive to the lightless house, where he sat on the mule and felt the rough warp of the rug drag across his thighs and vanish.

"Don't you want me to help?" he whispered. His father did not answer and now he heard again that stiff foot striking the hollow portico with that wooden and clocklike deliberation, that outrageous overstatement of the weight it carried. The rug, hunched, not flung (the boy could tell that even in the darkness) from his father's shoulder struck the angle of wall and floor with a sound unbelievably loud, thunderous, then the foot again, unhurried and enormous; a light came on in the house and the boy sat, tense, breathing steadily and quietly and just a little fast, though the foot itself did not increase its beat at all, descending the steps now; now the boy could see him.

"Don't you want to ride now?" he whispered. "We kin both ride now," the light   60
within the house altering now, flaring up and sinking. *He's coming down the stairs now,* he thought. He had already ridden the mule up beside the horse block; presently his father was up behind him and he doubled the reins over and slashed the mule across the neck, but before the animal could begin to trot the hard, thin arm came around him, the hard, knotted hand jerking the mule back to a walk.

In the first red rays of the sun they were in the lot, putting plow gear on the mules. This time the sorrel mare was in the lot before he heard it at all, the rider collarless and even bareheaded, trembling, speaking in a shaking voice as the woman in the house had done, his father merely looking up once before stooping again to the hame° he was buckling, so that the man on the mare spoke to his stooping back:

"You must realize you have ruined that rug. Wasn't there anybody here, any of your women . . ." he ceased, shaking, the boy watching him, the older brother leaning now in the stable door, chewing, blinking slowly and steadily at nothing apparently. "It cost a hundred dollars. But you never had a hundred dollars. You never will. So I'm going to charge you twenty bushels of corn against your crop. I'll add it in your contract and when you come to the commissary you can sign it. That won't keep Mrs. de Spain quiet but maybe it will teach you to wipe your feet off before you enter her house again."

Then he was gone. The boy looked at his father, who still had not spoken or even looked up again, who was now adjusting the logger-head in the hame.

"Pap," he said. His father looked at him—the inscrutable face, the shaggy brows beneath where the gray eyes glinted coldly. Suddenly the boy went toward him, fast, stopping as suddenly. "You done the best you could!" he cried. "If he wanted hit done different why didn't he wait and tell you how? He won't git no twenty bushels! He won't git none! We'll gather hit and hide hit! I kin watch . . ."

"Did you put the cutter back in that straight stock like I told you?"   65

"No, sir," he said.

"Then go do it."

That was Wednesday. During the rest of that week he worked steadily, at what was within his scope and some which was beyond it, with an industry that did not need to be driven nor even commanded twice; he had this from his mother, with the difference that some at least of what he did he liked to do, such as splitting wood with the half-size axe which his mother and aunt had earned, or saved money somehow, to present him with at Christmas. In company with the two older women (and on one afternoon, even one of the sisters), he built pens for the shoat and the cow which were a part of his father's contract with the landlord, and one afternoon, his father being absent, gone somewhere on one of the mules, he went to the field.

They were running a middle buster now, his brother holding the plow straight while he handled the reins, and walking beside the straining mule, the rich black soil

---

hame: a curved section of the harness of a draft animal.

shearing cool and damp against his bare ankles, he thought *Maybe this is the end of it. Maybe even that twenty bushels that seems hard to have to pay for just a rug will be a cheap price for him to stop forever and always from being what he used to be*; thinking, dreaming now, so that his brother had to speak sharply to him to mind the mule: *Maybe he even won't collect the twenty bushels. Maybe it will all add up and balance and vanish—corn, rug, fire; the terror and grief; the being pulled two ways like between two teams of horses— gone, done with for ever and ever.*

Then it was Saturday; he looked up from beneath the mule he was harnessing   70 and saw his father in the black coat and hat. "Not that," his father said. "The wagon gear." And then, two hours later, sitting in the wagon bed behind his father and brother on the seat, the wagon accomplished a final curve, and he saw the weath- ered paintless store with its tattered tobacco- and patent-medicine posters and the tethered wagons and saddle animals below the gallery. He mounted the gnawed steps behind his father and brother, and there again was the lane of quiet, watching faces for the three of them to walk through. He saw the man in spectacles sitting at the plank table and he did not need to be told this was a Justice of the Peace; he sent one glare of fierce, exultant, partisan defiance at the man in collar and cravat now, whom he had seen but twice before in his life, and that on a galloping horse, who now wore on his face an expression not of rage but of amazed unbelief which the boy could not have known was at the incredible circumstance of being sued by one of his own ten- ants, and came and stood against his father and cried at the Justice: "He ain't done it! He ain't burnt . . ."

"Go back to the wagon," his father said.

"Burnt?" the Justice said. "Do I understand this rug was burned too?"

"Does anybody here claim it was?" his father said. "Go back to the wagon." But he did not, he merely retreated to the rear of the room, crowded as that other had been, but not to sit down this time, instead, to stand pressing among the motionless bodies, listening to the voices:

"And you claim twenty bushels of corn is too high for the damage you did to the rug?"

"He brought the rug to me and said he wanted the tracks washed out of it. I   75 washed the tracks out and took the rug back to him."

"But you didn't carry the rug back to him in the same condition it was in before you made the tracks on it."

His father did not answer, and now for perhaps half a minute there was no sound at all save that of breathing, the faint, steady suspiration of complete and intent listening.

"You decline to answer that, Mr. Snopes?" Again his father did not answer. "I'm going to find against you, Mr. Snopes. I'm going to find that you were responsible for the injury to Major de Spain's rug and hold you liable for it. But twenty bushels of corn seems a little high for a man in your circumstances to have to pay. Major de Spain claims it cost a hundred dollars. October corn will be worth about fifty cents. I figure that if Major de Spain can stand a ninety-five dollar loss on something he paid cash for, you can stand a five-dollar loss you haven't earned yet. I hold you in damages to Major de Spain to the amount of ten bushels of corn over and above your contract with him, to be paid to him out of your crop at gathering time. Court adjourned."

It had taken no time hardly, the morning was but half begun. He thought they would return home and perhaps back to the field, since they were late, far behind all other farmers. But instead his father passed on behind the wagon, merely indicating with his hand for the older brother to follow with it, and crossed the road toward the blacksmith shop opposite, pressing on after his father, overtaking him, speaking, whispering up at the harsh, calm face beneath the weathered hat: "He won't git no ten bushels either. He won't git one. We'll . . ." until his father glanced for an instant down at him, the face absolutely calm, the grizzled eyebrows tangled above the cold eyes, the voice almost pleasant, almost gentle:

"You think so? Well, we'll wait till October anyway."   80

The matter of the wagon—the setting of a spoke or two and the tightening of the tires—did not take long either, the business of the tires accomplished by driving the wagon into the spring branch behind the shop and letting it stand there, the mules nuzzling into the water from time to time, and the boy on the seat with the idle reins, looking up the slope and through the sooty tunnel of the shed where the slow hammer rang and where his father sat on an upended cypress bolt, easily, either talking or listening, still sitting there when the boy brought the dripping wagon up out of the branch and halted it before the door.

"Take them on to the shade and hitch," his father said. He did so and returned. His father and the smith and a third man squatting on his heels inside the door were talking, about crops and animals; the boy, squatting too in the ammoniac dust and hoof-parings and scales of rust, heard his father tell a long and unhurried story out of the time before the birth of the older brother even when he had been a professional horsetrader. And then his father came up beside him where he stood before a tattered last year's circus poster on the other side of the store, gazing rapt and quiet at the scarlet horses, the incredible poisings and convulsions of tulle and tights and the painted leers of comedians, and said, "It's time to eat."

But not at home. Squatting beside his brother against the front wall, he watched his father emerge from the store and produce from a paper sack a segment of cheese and divide it carefully and deliberately into three with his pocket knife and produce crackers from the same sack. They all three squatted on the gallery and ate, slowly, without talking; then in the store again, they drank from a tin dipper tepid water smelling of the cedar bucket and of living beech trees. And still they did not go home. It was a horse lot this time, a tall rail fence upon and along which men stood and sat and out of which one by one horses were led, to be walked and trotted and then cantered back and forth along the road while the slow swapping and buying went on and the sun began to slant westward, they—the three of them—watching and listening, the older brother with his muddy eyes and his steady, inevitable tobacco, the father commenting now and then on certain of the animals, to no one in particular.

It was after sundown when they reached home. They ate supper by lamplight, then, sitting on the doorstep, the boy watched the night fully accomplish, listening to the whippoorwills and the frogs, when he heard his mother's voice: "Abner! No! No! Oh, God. Oh, God. Abner!" and he rose, whirled, and saw the altered light through the door where a candle stub now burned in a bottle neck on the table and his father, still in the hat and coat, at once formal and burlesque as though dressed carefully for some shabby and ceremonial violence, emptying the reservoir of the lamp back into the five-gallon kerosene can from which it had been filled, while the mother tugged at his arm until he shifted the lamp to the other hand and flung her back, not savagely or viciously, just hard, into the wall, her hands flung out against the wall for balance, her mouth open and in her face the same quality of hopeless despair as had been in her voice. Then his father saw him standing in the door.

"Go to the barn and get that can of oil we were oiling the wagon with," he said. The boy did not move. Then he could speak.   85

"What . . ." he cried. "What are you . . . ."

"Go get that oil," his father said. "Go."

Then he was moving, running, outside the house, toward the stable: this the old habit, the old blood which he had not been permitted to choose for himself, which had been bequeathed him willy nilly and which had run for so long (and who knew where, battening on what of outrage and savagery and lust) before it came to him. *I could keep on*, he thought. *I could run on and on and never look back, never need to see his face again. Only I can't. I can't*, the rusted can in his hand now, the liquid sploshing in it as he ran back to the house and into it, into the sound of his mother's weeping in the next room, and handed the can to his father.

"Ain't you going to even send a nigger?" he cried. "At least you sent a nigger before!"

This time his father didn't strike him. The hand came even faster than the blow   90
had, the same hand which had set the can on the table with almost excruciating care flashing from the can toward him too quick for him to follow it, gripping him by the back of his shirt and on to tiptoe before he had seen it quit the can, the face stooping at him in breathless and frozen ferocity, the cold, dead voice speaking over him to the older brother who leaned against the table, chewing with that steady, curious, sidewise motion of cows:

"Empty the can into the big one and go on. I'll catch up with you."

"Better tie him up to the bedpost," the brother said.

"Do like I told you," the father said. Then the boy was moving, his bunched shirt and the hard, bony hand between his shoulder-blades, his toes just touching the floor, across the room and into the other one, past the sisters sitting with spread heavy thighs in the two chairs over the cold hearth, and to where his mother and aunt sat side by side on the bed, the aunt's arm about his mother's shoulders.

"Hold him," the father said. The aunt made a startled movement. "Not you," the father said. "Lennie. Take hold of him. I want to see you do it." His mother took him by the wrist. "You'll hold him better than that. If he gets loose don't you know what he is going to do? He will go up yonder." He jerked his head toward the road. "Maybe I'd better tie him."

"I'll hold him," his mother whispered.   95

"See you do then." Then his father was gone, the stiff foot heavy and measured upon the boards, ceasing at last.

Then he began to struggle. His mother caught him in both arms, he jerking and wrenching at them. He would be stronger in the end, he knew that. But he had no time to wait for it. "Lemme go!" he cried. "I don't want to have to hit you!"

"Let him go!" the aunt said. "If he don't go, before God, I am going up there myself!"

"Don't you see I can't?" his mother cried. "Sarty! Sarty! No! No! Help me, Lizzie!"

Then he was free. His aunt grasped at him but it was too late. He whirled, run-   100
ning, his mother stumbled forward on to her knees behind him, crying to the nearer sister: "Catch him, Net! Catch him!" But that was too late too, the sister (the sisters were twins, born at the same time, yet either of them now gave the impression

of being, encompassing as much living meat and volume and weight as any other two of the family) not yet having begun to rise from the chair, her head, face, alone merely turned, presenting to him in the flying instant an astonishing expanse of young female features untroubled by any surprise even, wearing only an expression of bovine interest. Then he was out of the room, out of the house, in the mild dust of the starlit road and the heavy rifeness of honeysuckle, the pale ribbon unspooling with terrific slowness under his running feet, reaching the gate at last and turning in, running, his heart and lungs drumming, on up the drive toward the lighted house, the lighted door. He did not knock, he burst in, sobbing for breath, incapable for the moment of speech; he saw the astonished face of the Negro in the linen jacket without knowing when the Negro had appeared.

"De Spain!" he cried, panted. "Where's . . ." then he saw the white man too emerging from a white door down the hall. "Barn!" he cried. "Barn!"

"What?" the white man said. "Barn?"

"Yes!" the boy cried. "Barn!"

"Catch him!" the white man shouted.

But it was too late this time too. The Negro grasped his shirt, but the entire   105
sleeve, rotten with washing, carried away, and he was out that door too and in the drive again, and had actually never ceased to run even while he was screaming into the white man's face.

Behind him the white man was shouting, "My horse! Fetch my horse!" and he thought for an instant of cutting across the park and climbing the fence into the road, but he did not know the park nor how high the vine-massed fence might be and he dared not risk it. So he ran on down the drive, blood and breath roaring; presently he was in the road again though he could not see it. He could not hear either: the galloping mare was almost upon him before he heard her, and even then he held his course, as if the very urgency of his wild grief and need must in a moment more find him wings, waiting until the ultimate instant to hurl himself aside and into the weed-choked roadside ditch as the horse thundered past and on, for an instant in furious silhouette against the stars, the tranquil early summer night sky which, even before the shape of the horse and rider vanished, stained abruptly and violently upward: a long, swirling roar incredible and soundless, blotting the stars, and he springing up and into the road again, running again, knowing it was too late yet still running even after he heard the shot and, an instant later, two shots, pausing now without knowing he had ceased to run, crying, "Pap! Pap!", running again before he knew he had begun to run, stumbling, tripping over something and scrabbling up again without ceasing to run, looking backward over his shoulder at the glare as he got up, running on among the invisible trees, panting, sobbing, "Father! Father!"

At midnight he was sitting on the crest of a hill. He did not know it was midnight and he did not know how far he had come. But there was no glare behind him now and he sat now, his back toward what he had called home for four days anyhow, his face toward the dark woods which he would enter when breath was strong again, small, shaking steadily in the chill darkness, hugging himself into the remainder of his thin, rotten shirt, the grief and despair now no longer terror and fear but just grief and despair. *Father. My father*, he thought. "He was brave!" he cried suddenly, aloud but not loud, no more than a whisper. "He was! He was in the war! He was in Colonel Sartoris' cav'ry!" not knowing that his father had gone to that war a private in the fine old European sense, wearing no uniform, admitting the authority of and giving fidelity to no man or army or flag, going to war as Malbrouck° himself did: for booty—it meant nothing and less than nothing to him if it were enemy booty or his own.

The slow constellations wheeled on. It would be dawn and then sun-up after a while and he would be hungry. But that would be to-morrow and now he was only cold, and walking would cure that. His breathing was easier now and he decided to get up and go on, and then he found that he had been asleep because he knew it was almost dawn, the night almost over. He could tell that from the whippoorwills. They were everywhere now among the dark trees below him, constant and inflectioned and ceaseless, so that, as the instant for giving over to the day birds drew nearer and nearer, there was no interval at all between them. He got up. He was a little stiff, but walking would cure that too as it would the cold, and soon there would be the sun. He went on down the hill, toward the dark woods within which the liquid silver voices of the birds called unceasing—the rapid and urgent beating of the urgent and quiring heart of the late spring night. He did not look back.

Questions

1. After delivering his warning to Major de Spain, the boy Snopes does not actually witness what happens to his father and brother, or what happens to the Major's barn. But what do you assume happens? What evidence is given in the story?
2. What do you understand to be Faulkner's opinion of Abner Snopes? Make a guess, indicating details in the story that convey attitudes.
3. Which adjectives best describe the general tone of the story: *calm, amused, disinterested, scornful, marveling, excited, impassioned*? Point out passages that may be so described. What do you notice about the style in which these passages are written?
4. In tone and style, how does "Barn Burning" compare with Faulkner's story "A Rose for Emily" (Chapter 2)? To what do you attribute any differences?
5. Suppose that, instead of "Barn Burning," Faulkner had written a story told by Abner Snopes in the first person. Why would such a story need a style different from that of "Barn Burning"? (Suggestion: Notice Faulkner's descriptions of Abner Snopes's voice.)
6. Although "Barn Burning" takes place some thirty years after the Civil War, how does the war figure in it?

IRONY

If a friend declares, "Oh, sure, I just *love* to have four papers due on the same day," you detect that the statement contains **irony**. This is **verbal irony**, the most familiar kind, in which we understand the speaker's meaning to be far from the usual meaning of the words—in this case, quite the opposite. (When the irony is found, as here, in a somewhat sour statement tinged with mockery, it is called **sarcasm**.)

Irony, of course, occurs in writing as well as in conversation. When in Isaac Bashevis Singer's story "Gimpel the Fool" the sexton announces, "The wealthy Reb Gimpel invites the congregation to a feast in honor of the birth of a son," the people at the synagogue burst into laughter. They know that Gimpel, in contrast to the sexton's words, is not a wealthy man but a humble baker; that the son is not his own but his wife's lover's; and that the birth brings no honor to anybody. Verbal irony, then, implies a contrast or discrepancy between what is *said* and what is *meant*.

Malbrouck: John Churchill, Duke of Marlborough (1650–1722), English general victorious in the Battle of Blenheim (1704), a triumph that drove the French army out of Germany. The French called him Malbrouck, a name they found easier to pronounce.

Dramatic Irony

There are also times when the speaker, unlike the reader, does not realize the ironic dimension of his or her words; such instances are known as **dramatic irony**. The most famous example occurs in Sophocles's tragic drama *Oedipus the King*, when Oedipus vows to find and punish the murderer of King Laius, unaware that he himself is the man he seeks, and adds: "If by any chance / he proves to be an intimate of our house, / here at my hearth, with my full knowledge, / may the curse I just called down on him strike me!"

Stories often contain other kinds of irony. A situation, for example, can be ironic if it contains some wry contrast or incongruity. In Jack London's "To Build a Fire" (Chapter 4), it is ironic that a freezing man, desperately trying to strike a match to light a fire and save himself, accidentally ignites all his remaining matches.

Irony as Point of View

An entire story may be told from an **ironic point of view**. Whenever we sense a sharp distinction between the narrator of a story and the author, irony is likely to occur—especially when the narrator is telling us something that we are clearly expected to doubt or to interpret very differently. In "A & P," Sammy (who tells his own story) makes many smug and cruel observations about the people around him; but the author makes clear to us that much of his superiority is based on immaturity and lack of self-knowledge. (This irony, by the way, does not negate the fact that Sammy makes some very telling comments about society's superficial values and rigid and judgmental attitudes, comments that Updike seems to endorse and wants us to endorse as well.)

When we read Hemingway's "A Clean, Well-Lighted Place," surely we feel that most of the time the older waiter speaks for the author. Though the waiter gives us a respectful, compassionate view of a lonely old man, and we don't doubt that the view is Hemingway's, still, in the closing lines of the story we are reminded that author and waiter are not identical. Musing on the sleepless night ahead of him, the waiter tries to shrug off his problem—"After all, it is probably only insomnia"—but the reader, who recalls the waiter's bleak view of *nada*, nothingness, knows that it certainly isn't mere insomnia that keeps him awake but a dread of solitude and death. At that crucial moment, Hemingway and the older waiter part company, and we perceive an ironic point of view, and also a verbal irony, "After all, it is probably only insomnia."

Cosmic Irony

Storytellers are sometimes fond of ironic twists of fate—developments that reveal a terrible distance between what people deserve and what they get, between what is and what ought to be. In the novels of Thomas Hardy, some hostile fate keeps playing tricks to thwart the main characters. In *Tess of the D'Urbervilles*, an all-important letter, thrust under a door, by chance slides beneath a carpet and is not received. Such an irony is sometimes called an **irony of fate** or a **cosmic irony**, for it suggests that some malicious fate (or other spirit in the universe) is deliberately frustrating human efforts.

There is an irony of fate in the student's futile attempt to escape Death in the fable "Death Has an Appointment in Samarra," and perhaps in the flaring up of the all-precious matches in "To Build a Fire," as well. To notice an irony gives pleasure. It may move us to laughter, make us feel wonder, or arouse our sympathy. By so involving us, irony—whether in a statement, a situation, an unexpected event, or a point of view—can render a story more likely to strike us, to affect us, and to be remembered.

O. Henry was a master of irony. A famous example can be found in the following story, perhaps the best-known and most-loved of his many tales.

O. Henry (William Sydney Porter)

The Gift of the Magi   1906

O. Henry

William Sydney Porter (1862–1910), known to the world as O. Henry, was born in Greensboro, North Carolina. He began writing in his mid-twenties, contributing humorous sketches to various periodicals. In 1896 he was indicted for embezzlement from the First National Bank of Austin, Texas; he fled to Honduras before his trial but returned when he found that his wife was terminally ill. He was convicted and served three years of a five-year sentence; his guilt or innocence has never been definitively established. Released in 1901, he moved to New York the following year. Already a well-known writer, for the next three years he produced a story every week for the New York World while also contributing tales and sketches to magazines. Beginning with Cabbages and Kings in 1904, his stories were published in nine highly successful collections in the few remaining years of his life, as well as in three posthumously issued volumes. Financial extravagance and alcoholism darkened his last days, culminating in his death from tuberculosis at the age of forty-seven. Ranked during his lifetime with Hawthorne and Poe, O. Henry is more likely now to be invoked in negative terms, for his sentimentality and especially for his reliance on frequently forced trick endings, but the most prestigious annual volume of the best American short fiction is still called The O. Henry Prize Stories, *and the best of his own work is loved by millions of readers.*

One dollar and eighty-seven cents. That was all. And sixty cents of it was in pennies. Pennies saved one and two at a time by bulldozing the grocer and the vegetable man and the butcher until one's cheeks burned with the silent imputation of parsimony that such close dealing implied. Three times Della counted it. One dollar and eighty-seven cents. And the next day would be Christmas.

There was clearly nothing to do but flop down on the shabby little couch and howl. So Della did it. Which instigates the moral reflection that life is made up of sobs, sniffles, and smiles, with sniffles predominating.

While the mistress of the home is gradually subsiding from the first stage to the second, take a look at the home. A furnished flat at $8 per week. It did not exactly beggar description, but it certainly had that word on the lookout for the mendicancy squad.

In the vestibule below was a letter-box into which no letter would go, and an electric button from which no mortal finger could coax a ring. Also appertaining thereunto was a card bearing the name "Mr. James Dillingham Young."

The "Dillingham" had been flung to the breeze during a former period of prosperity when its possessor was being paid $30 per week. Now, when the income was shrunk to $20, the letters of "Dillingham" looked blurred, as though they were thinking seriously of contracting to a modest and unassuming D. But whenever Mr. James Dillingham Young came home and reached his flat above he was called "Jim" and

5

greatly hugged by Mrs. James Dillingham Young, already introduced to you as Della. Which is all very good.

Della finished her cry and attended to her cheeks with the powder rag. She stood by the window and looked out dully at a grey cat walking a grey fence in a grey backyard. Tomorrow would be Christmas Day, and she had only $1.87 with which to buy Jim a present. She had been saving every penny she could for months, with this result. Twenty dollars a week doesn't go far. Expenses had been greater than she had calculated. They always are. Only $1.87 to buy a present for Jim. Her Jim. Many a happy hour she had spent planning for something nice for him. Something fine and rare and sterling—something just a little bit near to being worthy of the honor of being owned by Jim.

There was a pier-glass between the windows of the room. Perhaps you have seen a pier-glass in an $8 flat. A very thin and very agile person may, by observing his reflection in a rapid sequence of longitudinal strips, obtain a fairly accurate conception of his looks. Della, being slender, had mastered the art.

Suddenly she whirled from the window and stood before the glass. Her eyes were shining brilliantly, but her face had lost its color within twenty seconds. Rapidly she pulled down her hair and let it fall to its full length.

Now, there were two possessions of the James Dillingham Youngs in which they both took a mighty pride. One was Jim's gold watch that had been his father's and his grandfather's. The other was Della's hair. Had the Queen of Sheba lived in the flat across the airshaft, Della would have let her hair hang out the window some day to dry just to depreciate Her Majesty's jewels and gifts. Had King Solomon been the janitor, with all his treasures piled up in the basement, Jim would have pulled out his watch every time he passed, just to see him pluck at his beard from envy.

So now Della's beautiful hair fell about her, rippling and shining like a cascade   10
of brown waters. It reached below her knee and made itself almost a garment for her. And then she did it up again nervously and quickly. Once she faltered for a minute and stood still while a tear or two splashed on the worn red carpet.

On went her old brown jacket; on went her old brown hat. With a whirl of skirts and with the brilliant sparkle still in her eyes, she fluttered out the door and down the stairs to the street.

Where she stopped the sign read: "Mme. Sofronie. Hair Goods of All Kinds." One flight up Della ran, and collected herself, panting. Madame, large, too white, chilly, hardly looked the "Sofronie."

"Will you buy my hair?" asked Della.

"I buy hair," said Madame. "Take yer hat off and let's have a sight at the looks of it." Down rippled the brown cascade.   15

"Twenty dollars," said Madame, lifting the mass with a practiced hand.

"Give it to me quick," said Della.

Oh, and the next two hours tripped by on rosy wings. Forget the hashed metaphor. She was ransacking the stores for Jim's present.

She found it at last. It surely had been made for Jim and no one else. There was no other like it in any of the stores, and she had turned all of them inside out. It was a platinum fob chain simple and chaste in design, properly proclaiming its value by substance alone and not by meretricious ornamentation—as all good things should do. It was even worthy of The Watch. As soon as she saw it she knew that it must be Jim's. It was like him. Quietness and value—the description applied to both. Twenty-one dollars they took from her for it, and she hurried home with the 87 cents. With that chain on his watch Jim might be properly anxious about the time in any company. Grand as the watch was, he sometimes looked at it on the sly on account of the old leather strap that he used in place of a chain.

When Della reached home her intoxication gave way a little to prudence and reason. She got out her curling irons and lighted the gas and went to work repairing the ravages made by generosity added to love. Which is always a tremendous task, dear friends—a mammoth task.

Within forty minutes her head was covered with tiny, close-lying curls that made her look wonderfully like a truant schoolboy. She looked at her reflection in the mirror long, carefully, and critically.

"If Jim doesn't kill me," she said to herself, "before he takes a second look at me, he'll say I look like a Coney Island chorus girl. But what could I do—oh! What could I do with a dollar and eighty-seven cents?"

At 7 o'clock the coffee was made and the frying-pan was on the back of the stove hot and ready to cook the chops.

Jim was never late. Della doubled the fob chain in her hand and sat on the corner of the table near the door that he always entered. Then she heard his step on the stair away down on the first flight, and she turned white for just a moment. She had a habit of saying little silent prayers about the simplest everyday things, and now she whispered: "Please God, make him think I am still pretty."

The door opened and Jim stepped in and closed it. He looked thin and very serious. Poor fellow, he was only twenty-two—and to be burdened with a family! He needed a new overcoat and he was without gloves.

Jim stopped inside the door, as immovable as a setter at the scent of quail. His eyes were fixed upon Della, and there was an expression in them that she could not read, and it terrified her. It was not anger, nor surprise, nor disapproval, nor horror, nor any of the sentiments that she had been prepared for. He simply stared at her fixedly with that peculiar expression on his face.

Della wriggled off the table and went for him.

"Jim, darling," she cried, "don't look at me that way. I had my hair cut off and sold because I couldn't have lived through Christmas without giving you a present. It'll grow out again—you won't mind, will you? I just had to do it. My hair grows awfully fast. Say 'Merry Christmas!' Jim, and let's be happy. You don't know what a nice—what a beautiful, nice gift I've got for you."

"You've cut off your hair?" asked Jim, laboriously, as if he had not arrived at that patent fact yet even after the hardest mental labor.

"Cut it off and sold it," said Della. "Don't you like me just as well, anyhow? I'm me without my hair, ain't I?"

Jim looked about the room curiously.

"You say your hair is gone?" he said, with an air almost of idiocy.

"You needn't look for it," said Della. "It's sold, I tell you—sold and gone, too. It's Christmas Eve, boy. Be good to me, for it went for you. Maybe the hairs of my head were numbered," she went on with a sudden serious sweetness, "but nobody could ever count my love for you. Shall I put the chops on, Jim?"

Out of his trance Jim seemed quickly to wake. He enfolded his Della. For ten seconds let us regard with discreet scrutiny some inconsequential object in the other direction. Eight dollars a week or a million a year—what is the difference? A mathematician or a wit would give you the wrong answer. The magi brought valuable gifts, but that was not among them. This dark assertion will be illuminated later on.

Jim drew a package from his overcoat pocket and threw it upon the table. 35

"Don't make any mistake, Dell," he said, "about me. I don't think there's anything in the way of a haircut or a shave or a shampoo that could make me like my girl any less. But if you'll unwrap that package you may see why you had me going a while at first."

White fingers and nimble tore at the string and paper. And then an ecstatic scream of joy; and then, alas! a quick feminine change to hysterical tears and wails, necessitating the immediate employment of all the comforting powers of the lord of the flat.

For there lay The Combs—the set of combs, side and back, that Della had worshipped for long in a Broadway window. Beautiful combs, pure tortoise shell, with jewelled rims—just the shade to wear in the beautiful vanished hair. They were expensive combs, she knew, and her heart had simply craved and yearned over them without the least hope of possession. And now, they were hers, but the tresses that should have adorned the coveted adornments were gone.

But she hugged them to her bosom, and at length she was able to look up with dim eyes and a smile and say: "My hair grows so fast, Jim!"

And then Della leaped up like a little singed cat and cried, "Oh, oh!" 40

Jim had not yet seen his beautiful present. She held it out to him eagerly upon her open palm. The dull precious metal seemed to flash with a reflection of her bright and ardent spirit.

"Isn't it a dandy, Jim? I hunted all over town to find it. You'll have to look at the time a hundred times a day now. Give me your watch. I want to see how it looks on it."

Instead of obeying, Jim tumbled down on the couch and put his hands under the back of his head and smiled.

"Dell," said he, "let's put our Christmas presents away and keep 'em a while. They're too nice to use just at present. I sold the watch to get the money to buy your combs. And now suppose you put the chops on."

The magi, as you know, were wise men—wonderfully wise men—who brought 45 gifts to the Babe in the manger. They invented the art of giving Christmas presents. Being wise, their gifts were no doubt wise ones, possibly bearing the privilege of exchange in case of duplication. And here I have lamely related to you the uneventful chronicle of two foolish children in a flat who most unwisely sacrificed for each other the greatest treasures of their house. But in a last word to the wise of these days let it be said that of all who give gifts these two were the wisest. Of all who give and receive gifts, such as they are wisest. Everywhere they are wisest. They are the magi.

Questions

1. How would you describe the style of this story? Does the author's tone tell you anything about his attitude toward the characters and events of the narrative?

2. What do the details in paragraph 7 tell you about Della and Jim's financial situation?

3. O. Henry tells us that Jim "needed a new overcoat and he was without gloves" (paragraph 25). Why do you think Della didn't buy him these things for Christmas and instead got him a watch chain?

4. "Eight dollars a week or a million a year—what is the difference? A mathematician or a wit would give you the wrong answer" (paragraph 34). What, in your view, is "the wrong answer," and why is it wrong? What might the right answer be?

5. What is ironic about the story's ending? Is this plot twist the most important element of the conclusion? If not, what is?

Margaret Atwood

Happy Endings

1983

Born in Ottawa, Ontario, in 1939, Margaret Eleanor Atwood was the daughter of an entomologist and spent her childhood summers in the forests of northern Quebec, where her father carried out research. Atwood began writing at the age of five and had already seriously entertained thoughts of becoming a professional writer before she finished high school. She graduated from the University of Toronto in 1961 and then got a master's degree from Radcliffe. Atwood initially gained prominence as a poet. Her first full-length collection of poems, The Circle Game (1966), was awarded a Governor General's Award, Canada's most prestigious literary honor, and she has since published nearly twenty volumes of verse. Atwood also began to write fiction seriously in graduate school. Her short stories were first collected in Dancing Girls (1977), followed by numerous additional collections, most recently Stone Mattress (2014).

Margaret Atwood

A dedicated feminist, Atwood's works of fiction explore the complex relations between the sexes, most incisively in The Handmaid's Tale (1985), a futuristic novel about a world in which gender roles are ruthlessly enforced by a society based on religious fundamentalism. (The Handmaid's Tale was adapted as a 2017 award-winning TV series.) In 1986 Atwood was named Woman of the Year by Ms. magazine. Subsequent novels include Cat's Eye (1988), The Robber Bride (1993), The Blind Assassin (2000), MaddAddam (2013), and The Hag-Seed (2016), a modern version of Shakespeare's The Tempest.

John and Mary meet.
What happens next?
If you want a happy ending, try A.

A

John and Mary fall in love and get married. They both have worthwhile and remunerative jobs which they find stimulating and challenging. They buy a charming house. Real estate values go up. Eventually, when they can afford live-in help, they have two children, to whom they are devoted. The children turn out well. John and Mary have a stimulating and challenging sex life and worthwhile friends. They go on fun vacations together. They retire. They both have hobbies which they find stimulating and challenging. Eventually they die. This is the end of the story.

B

Mary falls in love with John but John doesn't fall in love with Mary. He merely uses her body for selfish pleasure and ego gratification of a tepid kind. He comes to her apartment twice a week and she cooks him dinner, you'll notice that he doesn't even consider her worth the price of a dinner out, and after he's eaten the dinner he fucks her and after that he falls asleep, while she does the dishes so he won't think she's

5

untidy, having all those dirty dishes lying around, and puts on fresh lipstick so she'll look good when he wakes up, but when he wakes up he doesn't even notice, he puts on his socks and his shorts and his pants and his shirt and his tie and his shoes, the reverse order from the one in which he took them off. He doesn't take off Mary's clothes, she takes them off herself, she acts as if she's dying for it every time, not because she likes sex exactly, she doesn't, but she wants John to think she does because if they do it often enough surely he'll get used to her, he'll come to depend on her and they will get married, but John goes out the door with hardly so much as a goodnight and three days later he turns up at six o'clock and they do the whole thing over again.

Mary gets run down. Crying is bad for your face, everyone knows that and so does Mary but she can't stop. People at work notice. Her friends tell her John is a rat, a pig, a dog, he isn't good enough for her, but she can't believe it. Inside John, she thinks, is another John, who is much nicer. This other John will emerge like a butterfly from a cocoon, a Jack from a box, a pit from a prune, if the first John is only squeezed enough.

One evening John complains about the food. He has never complained about the food before. Mary is hurt.

Her friends tell her they've seen him in a restaurant with another woman, whose name is Madge. It's not even Madge that finally gets to Mary; it's the restaurant. John has never taken Mary to a restaurant. Mary collects all the sleeping pills and aspirins she can find, and takes them and a half a bottle of sherry. You can see what kind of a woman she is by the fact that it's not even whiskey. She leaves a note for John. She hopes he'll discover her and get her to the hospital in time and repent and then they can get married, but this fails to happen and she dies.

John marries Madge and everything continues as in A.

C

John, who is an older man, falls in love with Mary, and Mary, who is only twenty-two, feels sorry for him because he's worried about his hair falling out. She sleeps with him even though she's not in love with him. She met him at work. She's in love with someone called James, who is twenty-two also and not yet ready to settle down. 10

John on the contrary settled down long ago: this is what is bothering him. John has a steady, respectable job and is getting ahead in his field, but Mary isn't impressed by him, she's impressed by James, who has a motorcycle and a fabulous record collection. But James is often away on his motorcycle, being free. Freedom isn't the same for girls, so in the meantime Mary spends Thursday evenings with John. Thursdays are the only days John can get away.

John is married to a woman called Madge and they have two children, a charming house which they bought just before the real estate values went up, and hobbies which they find stimulating and challenging, when they have the time. John tells Mary how important she is to him, but of course, he can't leave his wife because a commitment is a commitment. He goes on about this more than is necessary and Mary finds it boring, but older men can keep it up longer so on the whole she has a fairly good time.

One day James breezes in on his motorcycle with some top-grade California hybrid and James and Mary get higher than you'd believe possible and they climb into bed. Everything becomes very underwater, but along comes John, who has a key to Mary's apartment. He finds them stoned and entwined. He's hardly in any position to be jealous, considering Madge, but nevertheless he's overcome with despair.

Finally he's middle-aged, in two years he'll be bald as an egg and he can't stand it. He purchases a handgun, saying he needs it for target practice—this is the thin part of the plot, but it can be dealt with later—and shoots the two of them and himself.

Madge, after a suitable period of mourning, marries an understanding man called Fred and everything continues as in A, but under different names.

D

Fred and Madge have no problems. They get along exceptionally well and are   15
good at working out any little difficulties that may arise. But their charming house is by the seashore and one day a giant tidal wave approaches. Real estate values go down. The rest of the story is about what caused the tidal wave and how they escape from it. They do, though thousands drown, but Fred and Madge are virtuous and lucky. Finally on high ground they clasp each other, wet and dripping and grateful, and continue as in A.

E

Yes, but Fred has a bad heart. The rest of the story is about how kind and understanding they both are until Fred dies. Then Madge devotes herself to charity work until the end of A. If you like, it can be "Madge," "cancer," "guilty and confused," and "bird watching."

F

If you think this is all too bourgeois, make John a revolutionary and Mary a counterespionage agent and see how far that gets you. Remember, this is Canada. You'll still end up with A, though in between you may get a lustful brawling saga of passionate involvement, a chronicle of our times, sort of.

You'll have to face it, the endings are the same however you slice it. Don't be deluded by any other endings, they're all fake, either deliberately fake, with malicious intent to deceive, or just motivated by excessive optimism if not by downright sentimentality.

The only authentic ending is the one provided here:

John and Mary die. John and Mary die. John and Mary die.   20

So much for endings. Beginnings are always more fun. True connoisseurs, however, are known to favor the stretch in between, since it's the hardest to do anything with.

That's about all that can be said for plots, which anyway are just one thing after another, a what and a what and a what.

Now try How and Why.

Questions

1. Why does Atwood present the story (or stories) in this manner? What point is she trying to make about the conventions of narrative storytelling?
2. What effect does her method of storytelling have on your understanding of the characters?
3. How would you describe the various possible scenarios for John, Mary, Fred, and Madge?
4. What does "Happy Endings" suggest about love and romance?
5. Despite the dark content, how would you describe Atwood's tone?
6. Is there really a "happy ending" in this story?

▪ WRITING *effectively*

Ernest Hemingway on Writing

The Direct Style   1964

Ernest Hemingway

"When you write," he [Hemingway] said, "your object is to convey every sensation, sight, feeling, emotion, to the reader. So you have to work over what you write. If you use a pencil, you get three different views of it to see if you are getting it across the way you want to. First, when you read it over, then when it is typed, and again in proof. And it keeps it fluid longer so that you can improve it easier."

"How do you ever learn to convey every sensation, sight and feeling to the reader? Just keep working at it for forty-odd years the way you have? Are there any tricks?"

"No. The hardest trade in the world to do is the writing of straight, honest prose about human beings. But there are ways you can train yourself."

"How?"

"When you walk into a room and you get a certain feeling or emotion, remember back until you see exactly what it was that gave you the emotion. Remember what the noises and smells were and what was said. Then write it down, making it clear so the reader will see it too and have the same feeling you had. And watch people, observe, try to put yourself in somebody else's head. If two men argue, don't just think who is right and who is wrong. Think what both their sides are. As a man, you know who is right and who is wrong; you have to judge. As a writer, you should not judge, you should understand."

From "An Afternoon with Hemingway" by Edward Stafford

THINKING ABOUT TONE AND STYLE

If you look around a crowded classroom, you will notice—consciously or not—the styles of your fellow students. The way they dress, talk, and even sit conveys information about their attitudes. A haircut, T-shirt, tattoo, or piece of jewelry all silently say something. Similarly, a writer's style—his or her own distinct voice—can give the reader crucial extra information. To analyze a writer's style, think about:

- **Diction: Consider the flavor of words chosen by the author for a particular story.** In "A Clean, Well-Lighted Place," for example, Hemingway favors simple, unemotional, and descriptive language, whereas in "The Storm" (Chapter 4), Chopin uses extravagant and emotionally charged diction. Each choice reveals something important about the story.

- **Sentence structure: Look for patterns in a story's sentence structure.** Hemingway is famous for his short, clipped sentences, which often repeat certain key words. Faulkner, however, favors complex, elaborate syntax that immerses the reader in the emotion of the narrative.
- **Tone: Try to determine the writer's attitude toward the story he or she is telling.** In "The Gospel According to Mark" (Chapter 10), Borges uses dispassionate restraint to present a central irony, a tragic misunderstanding that will doom his protagonist. Tan's "A Pair of Tickets" (Chapter 4), by contrast, creates a tone of hushed excitement and direct emotional involvement.
- **Organization: Examine the order in which information is presented.** Borges tells his story in a straightforward, chronological manner, which eventually makes it possible for us to appreciate the tale's complex undercurrents. Other stories (for example, Atwood's "Happy Endings") present the narrative's events in more complicated and surprising ways.

CHECKLIST: Writing About Tone and Style

- ☐ Does the writer use word choice in a distinctive way?
- ☐ Is the diction unusual in any way?
- ☐ Does the author tend toward long or short—even fragmented—sentences?
- ☐ How would you characterize the writer's voice? Is it formal or casual? Distant or intimate? Impassioned or restrained?
- ☐ Can the narrator's words be taken at face value? Is there anything ironic about the narrator's voice?
- ☐ How does the writer arrange the material? Is information delivered chronologically, or is the organization more complex?
- ☐ What is the writer's attitude toward the material?

TOPICS FOR WRITING ON TONE AND STYLE

1. Examine a short story with a style you admire. Write an essay in which you analyze the author's approach toward diction, sentence structure, tone, and organization. How do these elements work together to create a certain mood? How does that mood contribute to the story's meaning? If your chosen story has a first-person narrator, how do stylistic choices help to create a sense of that particular character?
2. Write a brief analysis of irony in "The Gift of the Magi" or "The Jilting of Granny Weatherall." What sorts of irony does your story employ?
3. Consider a short story in which the narrator is the central character, perhaps "A & P," "Greasy Lake" (Chapter 14), "Araby" (Chapter 14), or "Cathedral" (Chapter 3), In a brief essay, show how the character of the narrator determines the style of the story. Examine language in particular—words or phrases, slang expressions, figures of speech, local or regional usage.
4. Write a page in which you describe eating a meal in the company of others. Using sensory details, convey a sense of the setting, the quality of the food, and the presence of your dining companions. Now rewrite your paragraph as Ernest Hemingway. Finally, rewrite it as William Faulkner.
5. In a paragraph, describe a city street as seen through the eyes of a college graduate who has just moved to the city to start a new career. Now describe that same street in the

voice of an old woman walking home from the hospital where her husband has just died. Finally, describe the street in the voice of a teenage runaway. In each paragraph, refrain from identifying your character or saying anything about his or her circumstances. Simply present the street as each character would perceive it.

6. Describe the tone and style of Wells Tower's "Everything Ravaged, Everything Burned" (Chapter 14). Does the diction match the setting and characters, or does Tower contrast those elements in a humorous way? Now write a brief tale about a trip or an adventure mimicking the tone and style of "Everything Ravaged, Everything Burned."

▶ TERMS FOR *review*

Tone ▶ The attitude toward a subject conveyed in a literary work. No single stylistic device creates tone; it is the net result of the various elements an author brings to creating the work's feeling and manner.

Style ▶ All the distinctive ways in which an author uses language to create a literary work. An author's style depends on his or her characteristic use of diction, imagery, tone, syntax, and figurative language.

Diction ▶ Word choice or vocabulary. Diction refers to the class of words that an author decides is appropriate to use in a particular work.

Irony ▶ A literary device in which a discrepancy of meaning is masked beneath the surface of the language. Irony is present when a writer says one thing but means something quite the opposite.

Verbal irony ▶ A statement in which the speaker or writer says the opposite of what is really meant. For example, a friend might say, "How graceful!" after you trip clumsily on a stair.

Sarcasm ▶ A conspicuously bitter form of irony in which the ironic statement is designed to hurt or mock its target.

Dramatic irony ▶ Where the reader understands the implication and meaning of a situation and may foresee the oncoming disaster or triumph while the character does not.

Cosmic irony or irony of fate ▶ A type of situational irony that emphasizes the discrepancy between what characters deserve and what they get, between a character's aspirations and the treatment he or she receives at the hands of fate.

6

THEME

To produce a mighty book, you must choose a mighty theme.

—HERMAN MELVILLE

What You Will Learn in This Chapter

- To define *theme*
- To explain the difference between theme and plot *summary*
- To summarize a story's theme in a single sentence
- To analyze the role of a theme in a story

The **theme** of a story is whatever general idea or insight the entire story reveals. In some stories the theme is unmistakable. At the end of Aesop's fable about the council of the mice that can't decide who will take on the dangerous task of hanging a warning bell around the neck of the cat, the theme is stated in the moral: *It is easier to propose a thing than to carry it out.*

In a work of commercial fiction, too, the theme (if any) is usually obvious. Consider a typical detective thriller in which, say, a rookie police officer trained in scientific methods of crime detection sets out to solve a mystery sooner than his or her rival, a veteran sleuth whose only laboratory is carried under his hat. Perhaps the veteran solves the case, leading to the conclusion (and the theme), "The old ways are the best ways after all." Or the story might dramatize the same rivalry but reverse the outcome, having the rookie win, thereby reversing the theme: "The times are changing! Let's shake loose from old-fashioned ways."

PLOT VERSUS THEME

In literary fiction, a theme is seldom so obvious. That is, a theme need not be a moral or a message; it may be what the events add up to, what the story is about. When we come to the end of a finely wrought short story such as Ernest Hemingway's "A Clean, Well-Lighted Place" (Chapter 5), it may be easy to sum up the plot—to say what happens—but it is more difficult to sum up the story's main idea. Hemingway relates the events—how a younger waiter gets rid of an old man and how an older waiter then goes to a coffee bar—but in themselves these events seem relatively slight, though the story as a whole seems large (for its size) and full of meaning. A **summary**, a brief condensation of the main idea or plot of a literary work, may be helpful, but it tends to focus on the surface events of a story. A theme aims for a deeper and more comprehensive statement of its larger meaning.

For the meaning, we must look to other elements in the story besides simply what happens in it. It is clear that Hemingway is most deeply interested in the thoughts and feelings of the older waiter, the character who has more and more to say as the story progresses, until at the end the story is entirely confined to his thoughts and perceptions. What is meaningful in these thoughts and perceptions? The older waiter understands the old man and sympathizes with his need for a clean, well-lighted place. If we say that, we are still talking about what happens in the story, though we have gone beyond merely recording its external events. But a theme is usually stated in *general* words. Another try: "Solitary people who cannot sleep need a cheerful, orderly place where they can drink with dignity." That's a little better. We have indicated, at least, that Hemingway's story is about more than just an old man and a couple of waiters. But what about the older waiter's meditation on *nada*, nothingness? Coming near the end of the story, it is given great emphasis, and probably no good statement of Hemingway's theme can leave it out. Still another try at a thematic statement: "Solitary people need a place of refuge from their terrible awareness that their lives (or, perhaps, human lives) are essentially meaningless." Neither this nor any other statement of the story's theme is unarguably right, but at least the sentence helps the reader to bring into focus one primary idea that Hemingway seems to be driving at.

Moral inferences may be drawn from the story, no doubt, for Hemingway is indirectly giving us advice about properly regarding and sympathizing with the lonely, the uncertain, and the old. But the story doesn't set forth a lesson that we are supposed to put into practice. One could argue that "A Clean, Well-Lighted Place" contains *several* themes, and other statements could be made to include Hemingway's views of love, of communication between people, of dignity. Great short stories, like great symphonies, frequently have more than one theme.

SUMMARIZING THE THEME

In many fine short stories, theme is the center, the moving force, the principle of unity. Clearly, such a theme is something other than the characters or plot of a story. To say that James Joyce's "Araby" (Chapter 14) is a short story about a boy who goes to a bazaar to buy a gift for a young woman, only to arrive too late, is to summarize the plot, not the theme. (The theme *might* be put, "The romantic illusions of a young man are vulnerable to the lessons of reality," or it might be put in any of a hundred other ways.) Although the title of Shirley Jackson's "The Lottery" (Chapter 7), with its hint of the lure of easy riches, may arouse pleasant expectations, which the neutral tone of the narrative does nothing initially to dispel, the theme—the larger realization that the story leaves us with—has to do with the ways in which cruel and insensitive social practices can come to seem like normal and natural ones.

Sometimes you will hear it said that the theme of a story (say, Faulkner's "Barn Burning" in Chapter 5) is "loss of innocence" or that the theme of some other story (Hurston's "Sweat" in Chapter 14, for instance) is "the revolt of the downtrodden." Although such general descriptions of theme in a short phrase can be useful, we suggest that you work to be more specific. Try to sum up the theme in a short sentence that gives a fuller and more vivid sense of whatever truth or insight you think the story reveals. Crafting that sentence, you will find yourself looking closely at the story as you attempt to define its principal meaning.

FINDING THE THEME

You may find it helpful, in making a one-sentence statement of theme, to consider these questions:

1. Look back at the title of the story. From what you have read, what does it indicate?

2. Does the main character change in any way over the course of the story? Does this character arrive at any eventual realization or understanding? Are you left with any realization or understanding you did not have before?
3. Does the author make any general observations about life or human nature? Do the characters make any? (Caution: Characters now and again will utter opinions with which the reader is not necessarily supposed to agree.)
4. Does the story contain any especially curious objects, mysterious flat characters, significant animals, repeated names, song titles, or whatever, that hint at meanings larger than such things ordinarily have? In literary stories, such symbols may point to central themes.
5. When you have worded your statement of theme, have you cast it in general language, not just given a plot summary?
6. Does your statement hold true for the story as a whole, not for just part of it?

In distilling a statement of theme from a rich and complicated story, we have, of course, no more encompassed the whole story than a paleontologist taking a plaster mold of a petrified footprint has captured a living stegosaurus. A writer (other than a fabulist) does not usually set out with theme in hand, determined to make every detail in the story work to demonstrate it. Well then, the skeptical reader may ask, if only *some* stories have themes, if those themes may be hard to sum up, and if readers will probably disagree in their summations, why bother to state themes? Isn't it too much trouble? Surely it is, unless the effort to state a theme ends in pleasure and profit. Trying to sum up the point of a story in our own words is merely one way to make ourselves better aware of whatever we may have understood vaguely and tentatively. Attempted with loving care, such statements may bring into focus our scattered impressions of a rewarding story, may help to clarify and hold fast whatever wisdom the storyteller has offered us.

Stephen Crane

The Open Boat   1897

Stephen Crane (1871–1900) was born in Newark, New Jersey, a Methodist minister's fourteenth and last child. After flunking out of both Lafayette College and Syracuse University, he became a journalist in New York, specializing in the grim lives of the down-and-out, such as the characters of his early self-published novel Maggie: A Girl of the Streets *(1893). Restlessly generating material for stories, Crane trekked to the Southwest, New Orleans, and Mexico. "The Open Boat" is based on personal experience. En route to Havana to report on the Cuban revolution for the* New York Press, *Crane was shipwrecked when the SS Commodore sank in heavy seas east of New Smyrna, Florida, on January 2, 1897. He escaped in a ten-foot lifeboat with the captain and two members of the crew. Later that year, Crane moved into a stately home in England with*

Stephen Crane

Cora Taylor, former madam of a Florida brothel, hobnobbed with literary greats, and lived beyond his means. Hounded by creditors, afflicted by tuberculosis, he died in Germany at twenty-eight. Crane has been called the first writer of American realism. His classic novel The Red Badge of Courage (1895) gives an imagined but convincing account of a young Union soldier's initiation into battle. A handful of his short stories appear immortal. He was also an original poet, writing terse, sardonic poems in open forms, considered radical at the time. In his short life, Crane greatly helped American literature come of age.

A tale intended to be after the fact:
Being the experience of four men from the sunk steamer Commodore

I

None of them knew the color of the sky. Their eyes glanced level, and were fastened upon the waves that swept toward them. These waves were of the hue of slate, save for the tops, which were of foaming white, and all of the men knew the colors of the sea. The horizon narrowed and widened, and dipped and rose, and at all times its edge was jagged with waves that seemed thrust up in points like rocks.

Many a man ought to have a bathtub larger than the boat which here rode upon the sea. These waves were most wrongfully and barbarously abrupt and tall, and each froth-top was a problem in small-boat navigation.

The cook squatted in the bottom, and looked with both eyes at the six inches of gunwale which separated him from the ocean. His sleeves were rolled over his fat forearms, and the two flaps of his unbuttoned vest dangled as he bent to bail out the boat. Often he said, "Gawd! that was a narrow clip." As he remarked it he invariably gazed eastward over the broken sea.

The oiler, steering with one of the two oars in the boat, sometimes raised himself suddenly to keep clear of water that swirled in over the stern. It was a thin little oar, and it seemed often ready to snap.

The correspondent,° pulling at the other oar, watched the waves and wondered   5
why he was there.

The injured captain, lying in the bow, was at this time buried in that profound dejection and indifference which comes, temporarily at least, to even the bravest and most enduring when, willy-nilly, the firm fails, the army loses, the ship goes down. The mind of the master of a vessel is rooted deep in the timbers of her, though he command for a day or a decade; and this captain had on him the stern impression of a scene in the grays of dawn of seven turned faces, and later a stump of a topmast with a white ball on it, that slashed to and fro at the waves, went low and lower, and down. Thereafter there was something strange in his voice. Although steady, it was deep with mourning, and of a quality beyond oration or tears.

"Keep 'er a little more south, Billie," said he.

"A little more south, sir," said the oiler in the stern.

A seat in this boat was not unlike a seat upon a bucking broncho, and by the same token a broncho is not much smaller. The craft pranced and reared and plunged like an animal. As each wave came, and she rose for it, she seemed like a horse making at a fence outrageously high. The manner of her scramble over these walls of

---

correspondent: foreign correspondent, newspaper reporter.

water is a mystic thing, and, moreover, at the top of them were ordinarily these problems in white water, the foam racing down from the summit of each wave requiring a new leap, and a leap from the air. Then, after scornfully bumping a crest, she would slide and race and splash down a long incline, and arrive bobbing and nodding in front of the next menace.

A singular disadvantage of the sea lies in the fact that after successfully surmounting one wave you discover that there is another behind it just as important and just as nervously anxious to do something effective in the way of swamping boats. In a ten-foot dinghy one can get an idea of the resources of the sea in the line of waves that is not probable to the average experience, which is never at sea in a dinghy. As each slaty wall of water approached, it shut all else from the view of the men in the boat, and it was not difficult to imagine that this particular wave was the final outburst of the ocean, the last effort of the grim water. There was a terrible grace in the move of the waves, and they came in silence, save for the snarling of the crests.

In the wan light the faces of the men must have been gray. Their eyes must have glinted in strange ways as they gazed steadily astern. Viewed from a balcony, the whole thing would doubtless have been weirdly picturesque. But the men in the boat had no time to see it, and if they had had leisure, there were other things to occupy their minds. The sun swung steadily up the sky, and they knew it was broad day because the color of the sea changed from slate to emerald green streaked with amber lights, and the foam was like tumbling snow. The process of the breaking day was unknown to them. They were aware only of this effect upon the color of the waves that rolled toward them.

In disjointed sentences the cook and the correspondent argued as to the difference between a life-saving station and a house of refuge. The cook had said: "There's a house of refuge just north of the Mosquito Inlet Light, and as soon as they see us they'll come off in their boat and pick us up."

"As soon as who see us?" said the correspondent.

"The crew," said the cook.

"Houses of refuge don't have crews," said the correspondent. "As I understand them, they are only places where clothes and grub are stored for the benefit of shipwrecked people. They don't carry crews."

"Oh, yes, they do," said the cook.

"No, they don't," said the correspondent.

"Well, we're not there yet, anyhow," said the oiler, in the stern.

"Well," said the cook, "perhaps it's not a house of refuge that I'm thinking of as being near Mosquito Inlet Light; perhaps it's a life-saving station."

"We're not there yet," said the oiler in the stern.

II

As the boat bounced from the top of each wave the wind tore through the hair of the hatless men, and as the craft plopped her stern down again the spray slashed past them. The crest of each of these waves was a hill, from the top of which the men surveyed for a moment a broad tumultuous expanse, shining and wind-riven. It was probably splendid, it was probably glorious, this play of the free sea, wild with lights of emerald and white and amber.

"Bully good thing it's an on-shore wind," said the cook. "If not, where would we be? Wouldn't have a show."

"That's right," said the correspondent.

The busy oiler nodded his assent.

Then the captain, in the bow, chuckled in a way that expressed humor, contempt, 25
tragedy, all in one. "Do you think we've got much of a show now, boys?" said he.

Whereupon the three were silent, save for a trifle of hemming and hawing. To
express any particular optimism at this time they felt to be childish and stupid, but
they all doubtless possessed this sense of the situation in their minds. A young man
thinks doggedly at such times. On the other hand, the ethics of their condition was
decidedly against any open suggestion of hopelessness. So they were silent.

"Oh, well," said the captain, soothing his children, "we'll get ashore all right."

But there was that in his tone which made them think; so the oiler quoth, "Yes!
if this wind holds."

The cook was bailing. "Yes! if we don't catch hell in the surf."

Canton-flannel gulls flew near and far. Sometimes they sat down on the sea, 30
near patches of brown seaweed that rolled over the waves with a movement like
carpets on a line in a gale. The birds sat comfortably in groups, and they were
envied by some in the dinghy, for the wrath of the sea was no more to them than it
was to a covey of prairie chickens a thousand miles inland. Often they came very
close and stared at the men with black bead-like eyes. At these times they were
uncanny and sinister in their unblinking scrutiny, and the men hooted angrily at
them, telling them to be gone. One came, and evidently decided to alight on the
top of the captain's head. The bird flew parallel to the boat and did not circle, but
made short sidelong jumps in the air in chicken-fashion. His black eyes were wistfully fixed upon the captain's head. "Ugly brute," said the oiler to the bird. "You
look as if you were made with a jacknife." The cook and the correspondent swore
darkly at the creature. The captain naturally wished to knock it away with the end
of the heavy painter, but he did not dare do it, because anything resembling an
emphatic gesture would have capsized this freighted boat; and so, with his open
hand, the captain gently and carefully waved the gull away. After it had been discouraged from the pursuit the captain breathed easier on account of his hair, and
others breathed easier because the bird struck their minds at this time as being
somehow gruesome and ominous.

In the meantime the oiler and the correspondent rowed. And also they rowed.
They sat together in the same seat, and each rowed an oar. Then the oiler took both
oars; then the correspondent took both oars; then the oiler; then the correspondent.
They rowed and they rowed. The very ticklish part of the business was when the time
came for the reclining one in the stern to take his turn at the oars. By the very last
star of truth, it is easier to steal eggs from under a hen than it was to change seats in
the dinghy. First the man in the stern slid his hand along the thwart and moved with
care, as if he were of Sèvres.° Then the man in the rowing-seat slid his hand along
the other thwart. It was all done with the most extraordinary care. As the two sidled
past each other, the whole party kept watchful eyes on the coming wave, and the
captain cried: "Look out, now! Steady, there!"

The brown mats of seaweed that appeared from time to time were like islands,
bits of earth. They were travelling, apparently, neither one way nor the other. They
were, to all intents, stationary. They informed the men in the boat that it was making
progress slowly toward the land.

Sèvres: famous porcelain goods made in this suburb of Paris.

The captain, rearing cautiously in the bow after the dinghy soared on a great swell, said that he had seen the lighthouse at Mosquito Inlet. Presently the cook remarked that he had seen it. The correspondent was at the oars then, and for some reason he too wished to look at the lighthouse; but his back was toward the far shore, and the waves were important, and for some time he could not seize an opportunity to turn his head. But at last there came a wave more gentle than the others, and when at the crest of it he swiftly scoured the western horizon.

"See it?" said the captain.

"No," said the correspondent, slowly; "I didn't see anything."   35

"Look again," said the captain. He pointed. "It's exactly in that direction."

At the top of another wave the correspondent did as he was bid, and this time his eyes chanced on a small, still thing on the edge of the swaying horizon. It was precisely like the point of a pin. It took an anxious eye to find a lighthouse so tiny.

"Think we'll make it, Captain?"

"If this wind holds and the boat don't swamp, we can't do much else," said the captain.

The little boat, lifted by each towering sea and splashed viciously by the crests,   40
made progress that in the absence of seaweed was not apparent to those in her. She seemed just a wee thing wallowing, miraculously top up, at the mercy of five oceans. Occasionally a great spread of water, like white flames, swarmed into her.

"Bail her, cook," said the captain, serenely.

"All right, Captain," said the cheerful cook.

III

It would be difficult to describe the subtle brotherhood of men that was here established on the seas. No one said that it was so. No one mentioned it. But it dwelt in the boat, and each man felt it warm him. They were a captain, an oiler, a cook, and a correspondent, and they were friends—friends in a more curiously iron-bound degree than may be common. The hurt captain, lying against the water-jar in the bow, spoke always in a low voice and calmly; but he could never command a more ready and swiftly obedient crew than the motley three of the dinghy. It was more than a mere recognition of what was best for the common safety. There was surely in it a quality that was personal and heartfelt. And after this devotion to the commander of the boat, there was this comradeship, that the correspondent, for instance, who had been taught to be cynical of men, knew even at the time was the best experience of his life. But no one said that it was so. No one mentioned it.

"I wish we had a sail," remarked the captain. "We might try my overcoat on the end of an oar, and give you two boys a chance to rest." So the cook and the correspondent held the mast and spread wide the overcoat; the oiler steered; and the little boat made good way with her new rig. Sometimes the oiler had to scull sharply to keep a sea from breaking into the boat, but otherwise sailing was a success.

Meanwhile the lighthouse had been growing slowly larger. It had now almost   45
assumed color, and appeared like a little gray shadow on the sky. The man at the oars could not be prevented from turning his head rather often to try for a glimpse of this little gray shadow.

At last, from the top of each wave, the men in the tossing boat could see land. Even as the lighthouse was an upright shadow on the sky, this land seemed but a long black shadow on the sea. It certainly was thinner than paper. "We must be about opposite New Smyrna," said the cook, who had coasted this shore often in schooners. "Captain, by the way, I believe they abandoned that life-saving station there about a year ago."

"Did they?" said the captain.

The wind slowly died away. The cook and the correspondent were not now obliged to slave in order to hold high the oar. But the waves continued their old impetuous swooping at the dinghy, and the little craft, no longer under way, struggled woundily over them. The oiler or the correspondent took the oars again.

Shipwrecks are *apropos* of nothing. If men could only train for them and have them occur when the men had reached pink condition, there would be less drowning at sea. Of the four in the dinghy none had slept any time worth mentioning for two days and two nights previous to embarking in the dinghy, and in the excitement of clambering about the deck of a foundering ship they had also forgotten to eat heartily.

For these reasons, and for others, neither the oiler nor the correspondent was   50
fond of rowing at this time. The correspondent wondered ingenuously how in the name of all that was sane could there be people who thought it amusing to row a boat. It was not an amusement; it was a diabolical punishment, and even a genius of mental aberrations could never conclude that it was anything but a horror to the muscles and a crime against the back. He mentioned to the boat in general how the amusement of rowing struck him, and the weary-faced oiler smiled in full sympathy. Previously to the foundering, by the way, the oiler had worked double watch in the engine-room of the ship.

"Take her easy now, boys," said the captain. "Don't spend yourselves. If we have to run a surf you'll need all your strength, because we'll sure have to swim for it. Take your time."

Slowly the land arose from the sea. From a black line it became a line of black and a line of white—trees and sand. Finally the captain said that he could make out a house on the shore. "That's the house of refuge, sure," said the cook. "They'll see us before long, and come out after us."

The distant lighthouse reared high. "The keeper ought to be able to make us out now, if he's looking through a glass," said the captain. "He'll notify the life-saving people."

"None of those other boats could have got ashore to give word of the wreck," said the oiler, in a low voice, "else the life-boat would be out hunting us."

Slowly and beautifully the land loomed out of the sea. The wind came again. It   55
had veered from the northeast to the southeast. Finally a new sound struck the ears of the men in the boat. It was the low thunder of the surf on the shore. "We'll never be able to make the lighthouse now," said the captain. "Swing her head a little more north, Billie."

"A little more north, sir," said the oiler.

Whereupon the little boat turned her nose once more down the wind, and all but the oarsman watched the shore grow. Under the influence of this expansion doubt and direful apprehension were leaving the minds of the men. The management of the boat was still most absorbing, but it could not prevent a quiet cheerfulness. In an hour, perhaps, they would be ashore.

Their backbones had become thoroughly used to balancing in the boat, and they now rode this wild colt of a dinghy like circus men. The correspondent thought that he had been drenched to the skin, but happening to feel in the top pocket of his coat, he found therein eight cigars. Four of them were soaked with seawater; four were perfectly scatheless. After a search, somebody produced three dry matches; and thereupon the four waifs rode impudently in their little boat and, with an assurance of an impending rescue shining in their eyes, puffed at the big cigars, and judged well and ill of all men. Everybody took a drink of water.

IV

"Cook," remarked the captain, "there don't seem to be any signs of life about your house of refuge."

"No," replied the cook. "Funny they don't see us!" 60

A broad stretch of lowly coast lay before the eyes of the men. It was of low dunes topped with dark vegetation. The roar of the surf was plain, and sometimes they could see the white lip of a wave as it spun up the beach. A tiny house was blocked out black upon the sky. Southward, the slim lighthouse lifted its little gray length.

Tide, wind, and waves were swinging the dinghy northward. "Funny they don't see us," said the men.

The surf's roar was here dulled, but its tone was nevertheless thunderous and mighty. As the boat swam over the great rollers the men sat listening to this roar. "We'll swamp sure," said everybody.

It is fair to say here that there was not a life-saving station within twenty miles in either direction; but the men did not know this fact, and in consequence they made dark and opprobrious remarks concerning the eyesight of the nation's life-savers. Four scowling men sat in the dinghy and surpassed records in the invention of epithets.

"Funny they don't see us." 65

The light-heartedness of a former time had completely faded. To their sharpened minds it was easy to conjure pictures of all kinds of incompetency and blindness and, indeed, cowardice. There was the shore of the populous land, and it was bitter and bitter to them that from it came no sign.

"Well," said the captain, ultimately, "I suppose we'll have to make a try for ourselves. If we stay out here too long, we'll none of us have strength left to swim after the boat swamps."

And so the oiler, who was at the oars, turned the boat straight for the shore. There was a sudden tightening of muscles. There was some thinking.

"If we don't all get ashore," said the captain—"if we don't all get ashore, I suppose you fellows know where to send news of my finish?"

They then briefly exchanged some addresses and admonitions. As for the reflec- 70
tions of the men, there was a great deal of rage in them. Perchance they might be formulated thus: "If I am going to be drowned—if I am going to be drowned—if I am going to be drowned, why, in the name of the seven mad gods who rule the sea, was I allowed to come thus far and contemplate sand and trees? Was I brought here merely to have my nose dragged away as I was about to nibble the sacred cheese of life? It is preposterous. If this old ninny-woman, Fate, cannot do better than this, she should be deprived of the management of men's fortunes. She is an old hen who knows not her intention. If she has decided to drown me, why did she not do it in the beginning and save me all this trouble? The whole affair is absurd. . . . But no; she cannot mean to drown me. She dare not drown me. She cannot drown me. Not after all this work." Afterward the man might have had an impulse to shake his fist at the clouds. "Just you drown me, now, and then hear what I call you!"

The billows that came at this time were more formidable. They seemed always just about to break and roll over the little boat in a turmoil of foam. There was a preparatory and long growl in the speech of them. No mind unused to the sea would have concluded that the dinghy could ascend these sheer heights in time. The shore was still afar. The oiler was a wily surfman. "Boys," he said swiftly, "she won't live three minutes more, and we're too far out to swim. Shall I take her to sea again, Captain?"

"Yes; go ahead!" said the captain.

This oiler, by a series of quick miracles and fast and steady oarsmanship, turned the boat in the middle of the surf and took her safely to sea again.

There was a considerable silence as the boat bumped over the furrowed sea to deeper water. Then somebody in gloom spoke: "Well, anyhow, they must have seen us from the shore by now."

The gulls went in slanting flight up the wind toward the gray, desolate east. A 75 squall, marked by dingy clouds and clouds brick-red, like smoke from a burning building, appeared from the southeast.

"What do you think of those life-saving people? Ain't they peaches?"

"Funny they haven't seen us."

"Maybe they think we're out here for sport! Maybe they think we're fishin'. Maybe they think we're damned fools."

It was a long afternoon. A changed tide tried to force them southward, but wind and wave said northward. Far ahead, where coast-line, sea, and sky formed their mighty angle, there were little dots which seemed to indicate a city on the shore.

"St. Augustine?" 80

The captain shook his head. "Too near Mosquito Inlet."

And the oiler rowed, and then the correspondent rowed; then the oiler rowed. It was a weary business. The human back can become the seat of more aches and pains than are registered in books for the composite anatomy of a regiment. It is a limited area, but it can become the theatre of innumerable muscular conflicts, tangles, wrenches, knots, and other comforts.

"Did you ever like to row, Billie?" asked the correspondent.

"No," said the oiler; "hang it!"

When one exchanged the rowing-seat for a place in the bottom of the boat, 85 he suffered a bodily depression that caused him to be careless of everything save an obligation to wiggle one finger. There was cold sea-water swashing to and fro in the boat, and he lay in it. His head, pillowed on a thwart, was within an inch of the swirl of a wave-crest, and sometimes a particularly obstreperous sea came inboard and drenched him once more. But these matters did not annoy him. It is almost certain that if the boat had capsized he would have tumbled comfortably upon the ocean as if he felt sure that it was a great soft mattress.

"Look! There's a man on the shore!"

"Where?"

"There! See 'im? See 'im?"

"Yes, sure! He's walking along."

"Now he's stopped. Look! He's facing us!" 90

"He's waving at us!"

"So he is! By thunder!"

"Ah, now we're all right! Now we're all right! There'll be a boat out here for us in half an hour."

"He's going on. He's running. He's going up to that house there."

The remote beach seemed lower than the sea, and it required a searching glance 95
to discern the little black figure. The captain saw a floating stick, and they rowed to
it. A bath towel was by some weird chance in the boat, and, tying this on the stick,
the captain waved it. The oarsman did not dare turn his head, so he was obliged to
ask questions.

"What's he doing now?"

"He's standing still again. He's looking, I think. . . . There he goes again. Toward
the house. . . . Now he's stopped again."

"Is he waving at us?"

"No, not now; he was, though."

"Look! There comes another man!" 100

"He's running."

"Look at him go, would you!"

"Why, he's on a bicycle. Now he's met the other man. They're both waving at
us. Look!"

"There comes something up the beach."

"What the devil is that thing?" 105

"Why, it looks like a boat."

"Why, certainly, it's a boat."

"No; it's on wheels."

"Yes, so it is. Well, that must be the life-boat. They drag them along shore on a
wagon."

"That's the life-boat, sure." 110

"No, by God, it's—it's an omnibus."

"I tell you it's a life-boat."

"It is not! It's an omnibus. I can see it plain. See? One of these big hotel
omnibuses."

"By thunder, you're right. It's an omnibus, sure as fate. What do you suppose
they are doing with an omnibus? Maybe they are going around collecting the life-
crew, hey?"

"That's it, likely. Look! There's a fellow waving a little black flag. He's standing 115
on the steps of the omnibus. There come those other two fellows. Now they're all
talking together. Look at the fellow with the flag. Maybe he ain't waving it!"

"That ain't a flag, is it? That's his coat. Why, certainly, that's his coat."

"So it is; it's his coat. He's taken it off and is waving it around his head. But
would you look at him swing it!"

"Oh, say, there isn't any life-saving station there. That's just a winter-resort hotel
omnibus that has brought over some of the boarders to see us drown."

"What's that idiot with the coat mean? What's he signalling, anyhow?"

"It looks as if he were trying to tell us to go north. There must be a life-saving 120
station up there."

"No; he thinks we're fishing. Just giving us a merry hand. See? Ah, there, Willie!"

"Well, I wish I could make something out of those signals. What do you suppose
he means?"

"He don't mean anything; he's just playing."

"Well, if he'd just signal us to try the surf again, or to go to sea and wait, or go
north, or go south, or go to hell, there would be some reason in it. But look at him!
He just stands there and keeps his coat revolving like a wheel. The ass!"

"There come more people."   125

"Now there's quite a mob. Look! Isn't that a boat?"

"Where? Oh, I see where you mean. No, that's no boat."

"That fellow is still waving his coat."

"He must think we like to see him do that. Why don't he quit it? It don't mean anything."

"I don't know. I think he is trying to make us go north. It must be that there's a   130
life-saving station there somewhere."

"Say, he ain't tired yet. Look at 'im wave!"

"Wonder how long he can keep that up. He's been revolving his coat ever since he caught sight of us. He's an idiot. Why aren't they getting men to bring a boat out? A fishing boat—one of those big yawls—could come out here all right. Why don't he do something?"

"Oh, it's all right now."

"They'll have a boat out here for us in less than no time, now that they've seen us."

A faint yellow tone came into the sky over the low land. The shadows on the sea   135
slowly deepened. The wind bore coldness with it, and the men began to shiver.

"Holy smoke!" said one, allowing his voice to express his impious mood, "If we keep on monkeying out here! If we've got to flounder out here all night!"

"Oh, we'll never have to stay here all night! Don't you worry. They've seen us now, and it won't be long before they'll come chasing out after us."

The shore grew dusky. The man waving a coat blended gradually into this gloom, and it swallowed in the same manner the omnibus and the group of people. The spray, when it dashed uproariously over the side, made the voyagers shrink and swear like men who were being branded.

"I'd like to catch the chump who waved the coat. I feel like socking him one, just for luck."

"Why? What did he do?"   140

"Oh, nothing, but then he seemed so damned cheerful."

In the meantime the oiler rowed, and then the correspondent rowed, and then the oiler rowed. Gray-faced and bowed forward, they mechanically, turn by turn, plied the leaden oars. The form of the lighthouse had vanished from the southern horizon, but finally a pale star appeared, just lifting from the sea. The streaked saffron in the west passed before the all-merging darkness, and the sea to the east was black. The land had vanished, and was expressed only by the low and drear thunder of the surf.

"If I am going to be drowned—if I am going to be drowned—if I am going to be drowned, why, in the name of the seven mad gods who rule the sea, was I allowed to come thus far and contemplate sand and trees? Was I brought here merely to have my nose dragged away as I was about to nibble the sacred cheese of life?"

The patient captain, drooped over the water-jar, was sometimes obliged to speak to the oarsman.

"Keep her head up! Keep her head up!"   145

"Keep her head, up, sir." The voices were weary and low.

This was surely a quiet evening. All save the oarsman lay heavily and listlessly in the boat's bottom. As for him, his eyes were just capable of noting the tall black waves that swept forward in a most sinister silence, save for an occasional subdued growl of a crest.

The cook's head was on a thwart, and he looked without interest at the water under his nose. He was deep in other scenes. Finally he spoke. "Billie," he murmured, dreamfully, "what kind of pie do you like best?"

V

"Pie!" said the oiler and the correspondent, agitatedly. "Don't talk about those things, blast you!"

"Well," said the cook, "I was just thinking about ham sandwiches, and—"   150

A night on the sea in an open boat is a long night. As darkness settled finally, the shine of the light, lifting from the sea in the south, changed to full gold. On the northern horizon a new light appeared, a small bluish gleam on the edge of the waters. These two lights were the furniture of the world. Otherwise there was nothing but waves.

Two men huddled in the stern, and distances were so magnificent in the dinghy that the rower was enabled to keep his feet partly warm by thrusting them under his companions. Their legs indeed extended far under the rowing-seat until they touched the feet of the captain forward. Sometimes, despite the efforts of the tired oarsman, a wave came piling into the boat, an icy wave of the night, and the chilling water soaked them anew. They would twist their bodies for a moment and groan, and sleep the dead sleep once more, while the water in the boat gurgled about them as the craft rocked.

The plan of the oiler and the correspondent was for one to row until he lost the ability, and then arouse the other from his sea-water couch in the bottom of the boat.

The oiler plied the oars until his head drooped forward and the overpowering sleep blinded him; and he rowed yet afterward. Then he touched a man in the bottom of the boat, and called his name. "Will you spell me for a little while?" he said meekly.

"Sure, Billie," said the correspondent, awaking and dragging himself to a sitting   155 position. They exchanged places carefully, and the oiler, cuddling down in the sea-water at the cook's side, seemed to go to sleep instantly.

The particular violence of the sea had ceased. The waves came without snarling. The obligation of the man at the oars was to keep the boat headed so that the tilt of the roller would not capsize her, and to preserve her from filling when the crests rushed past. The black waves were silent and hard to be seen in the darkness. Often one was almost upon the boat before the oarsman was aware.

In a low voice the correspondent addressed the captain. He was not sure that the captain was awake, although this iron man seemed to be always awake. "Captain, shall I keep her making for that light north, sir?"

The same steady voice answered him. "Yes. Keep it about two points off the port bow."

The cook had tied a life-belt around himself in order to get even the warmth which this clumsy cork contrivance could donate, and he seemed almost stove-like when a rower, whose teeth invariably chattered wildly as soon as he ceased his labor, dropped down to sleep.

The correspondent, as he rowed, looked down at the two men sleeping under-   160 foot. The cook's arm was around the oiler's shoulders, and, with their fragmentary clothing and haggard faces, they were the babes of the sea—a grotesque rendering of the old babes in the wood.

Later he must have grown stupid at his work, for suddenly there was a growling of water, and a crest came with a roar and a swash into the boat, and it was a wonder that it did not set the cook afloat in his life-belt. The cook continued to sleep, but the oiler sat up, blinking his eyes and shaking with the new cold.

"Oh, I'm awful sorry, Billie," said the correspondent, contritely.

"That's all right, old boy," said the oiler, and lay down again and was asleep.

Presently it seemed that even the captain dozed, and the correspondent thought that he was the one man afloat on all the oceans. The wind had a voice as it came over the waves, and it was sadder than the end.

There was a long, loud swishing astern of the boat, and a gleaming trail of phos-   165 phorescence, like blue flame, was furrowed on the black waters. It might have been made by a monstrous knife.

Then there came a stillness, while the correspondent breathed with open mouth and looked at the sea.

Suddenly there was another swish and another long flash of bluish light, and this time it was alongside the boat, and might almost have been reached with an oar. The correspondent saw an enormous fin speed like a shadow through the water, hurling the crystalline spray and leaving the long glowing trail.

The correspondent looked over his shoulder at the captain. His face was hidden, and he seemed to be asleep. He looked at the babes of the sea. They certainly were asleep. So, being bereft of sympathy, he leaned a little way to one side and swore softly into the sea.

But the thing did not then leave the vicinity of the boat. Ahead or astern, on one side or the other, at intervals long or short, fled the long sparkling streak, and there was to be heard the *whirroo* of the dark fin. The speed and power of the thing was greatly to be admired. It cut the water like a gigantic and keen projectile.

The presence of this biding thing did not affect the man with the same horror   170 that it would if he had been a picnicker. He simply looked at the sea dully and swore in an undertone.

Nevertheless, it is true that he did not wish to be alone with the thing. He wished one of his companions to awake by chance and keep him company with it. But the captain hung motionless over the water-jar, and the oiler and the cook in the bottom of the boat were plunged in slumber.

VI

"If I am going to be drowned—if I am going to be drowned—if I am going to be drowned, why, in the name of the seven mad gods who rule the sea, was I allowed to come thus far and contemplate sand and trees?"

During this dismal night, it may be remarked that a man would conclude that it was really the intention of the seven mad gods to drown him, despite the abominable injustice of it. For it was certainly an abominable injustice to drown a man who had worked so hard, so hard. The man felt it would be a crime most unnatural. Other people had drowned at sea since galleys swarmed with painted sails, but still—

When it occurs to a man that nature does not regard him as important, and that she feels she would not maim the universe by disposing of him, he at first wishes to throw bricks at the temple, and he hates deeply the fact that there are no bricks and no temples. Any visible expression of nature would surely be pelleted with his jeers.

Then, if there be no tangible thing to hoot, he feels, perhaps, the desire to confront   175 a personification and indulge in pleas, bowed to one knee, and with hands supplicant, saying, "Yes, but I love myself."

A high cold star on a winter's night is the word he feels that she says to him. Thereafter he knows the pathos of his situation.

The men in the dinghy had not discussed these matters, but each had, no doubt, reflected upon them in silence and according to his mind. There was seldom any expression upon their faces save the general one of complete weariness. Speech was devoted to the business of the boat.

To chime the notes of his emotion, a verse mysteriously entered the correspondent's head. He had even forgotten that he had forgotten this verse, but it suddenly was in his mind.

> A soldier of the Legion lay dying in Algiers;
> There was lack of woman's nursing, there was dearth of woman's tears;
> But a comrade stood beside him, and he took that comrade's hand,
> And he said, "I never more shall see my own, my native land."°

In his childhood the correspondent had been made acquainted with the fact that a soldier of the Legion lay dying in Algiers, but he had never regarded the fact as important. Myriads of his school-fellows had informed him of the soldier's plight, but the dinning had naturally ended by making him perfectly indifferent. He had never considered it his affair that a soldier of the Legion lay dying in Algiers, nor had it appeared to him as a matter for sorrow. It was less to him than the breaking of a pencil's point.

Now, however, it quaintly came to him as a human, living thing. It was no longer merely a picture of a few throes in the breast of a poet, meanwhile drinking tea and warming his feet at the grate; it was an actuality—stern, mournful, and fine.

The correspondent plainly saw the soldier. He lay on the sand with his feet out straight and still. While his pale left hand was upon his chest in an attempt to thwart the going of his life, the blood came between his fingers. In the far Algerian distance, a city of low square forms was set against a sky that was faint with the last sunset hues. The correspondent, plying the oars and dreaming of the slow and slower movements of the lips of the soldier, was moved by a profound and perfectly impersonal comprehension. He was sorry for the soldier of the Legion who lay dying in Algiers.

The thing which had followed the boat and waited had evidently grown bored at the delay. There was no longer to be heard the slash of the cutwater, and there was no longer the flame of the long trail. The light in the north still glimmered, but it was apparently no nearer to the boat. Sometimes the boom of the surf rang in the correspondent's ears, and he turned the craft seaward then and rowed harder. Southward, some one had evidently built a watch-fire on the beach. It was too low and too far to be seen, but it made a shimmering, roseate reflection upon the bluff in back of it, and this could be discerned from the boat. The wind came stronger, and sometimes a wave suddenly raged out like a mountain cat, and there was to be seen the sheen and sparkle of a broken crest.

The captain, in the bow, moved on his water-jar and sat erect. "Pretty long night," he observed to the correspondent. He looked at the shore. "Those life-saving people take their time."

"Did you see that shark playing around?"

"Yes, I saw him. He was a big fellow, all right."

"Wish I had known you were awake."

Later the correspondent spoke into the bottom of the boat.

"Billie!" There was a slow and gradual disentanglement. "Billie, will you spell me?"

"Sure," said the oiler.

A soldier of the Legion . . . native land: The correspondent remembers a Victorian ballad about a German dying in the French Foreign Legion, "Bingen on the Rhine" by Caroline Norton.

As soon as the correspondent touched the cold, comfortable sea-water in the   190
bottom of the boat and had huddled close to the cook's life-belt he was deep in sleep,
despite the fact that his teeth played all the popular airs. This sleep was so good to
him that it was but a moment before he heard a voice call his name in a tone that
demonstrated the last stages of exhaustion. "Will you spell me?"

"Sure, Billie."

The light in the north had mysteriously vanished, but the correspondent took
his course from the wide-awake captain.

Later in the night they took the boat farther out to sea, and the captain directed
the cook to take one oar at the stern and keep the boat facing the seas. He was to call
out if he should hear the thunder of the surf. This plan enabled the oiler and the correspondent to get respite together. "We'll give those boys a chance to get into shape
again," said the captain. They curled down and, after a few preliminary chatterings
and trembles, slept once more the dead sleep. Neither knew they had bequeathed to
the cook the company of another shark, or perhaps the same shark.

As the boat caroused on the waves, spray occasionally bumped over the side and
gave them a fresh soaking, but this had no power to break their repose. The ominous
slash of the wind and the water affected them as it would have affected mummies.

"Boys," said the cook, with the notes of every reluctance in his voice, "she's   195
drifted in pretty close. I guess one of you had better take her to sea again." The correspondent, aroused, heard the crash of the toppled crests.

As he was rowing, the captain gave him some whisky and water, and this steadied the chills out of him. "If I ever get ashore and anybody shows me even a photograph of an oar—"

At last there was a short conversation.

"Billie! . . . Billie, will you spell me?"

"Sure," said the oiler.

VII

When the correspondent again opened his eyes, the sea and sky were each of the   200
gray hue of the dawning. Later, carmine and gold was painted upon the waters. The
morning appeared finally, in its splendor, with a sky of pure blue, and the sunlight
flamed on the tips of the waves.

On the distant dunes were set many little black cottages, and a tall white windmill reared above them. No man, nor dog, nor bicycle appeared on the beach. The
cottages might have formed a deserted village.

The voyagers scanned the shore. A conference was held in the boat. "Well,"
said the captain, "if no help is coming, we might better try a run through the surf
right away. If we stay out here much longer we will be too weak to do anything for
ourselves at all." The others silently acquiesced in this reasoning. The boat was
headed for the beach. The correspondent wondered if none ever ascended the tall
wind-tower, and if they never looked seaward. This tower was a giant, standing with
its back to the plight of the ants. It represented in a degree, to the correspondent,
the serenity of nature amid the struggles of the individual—nature in the wind, and
nature in the vision of men. She did not seem cruel to him then, nor beneficent,
nor treacherous, nor wise. But she was indifferent, flatly indifferent. It is, perhaps,
plausible that a man in this situation, impressed with the unconcern of the universe,
should see the innumerable flaws of life, and have them taste wickedly in his mind,
and wish for another chance. A distinction between right and wrong seems absurdly

clear to him, then, in this new ignorance of the grave-edge, and he understands that if he were given another opportunity he would mend his conduct and his words, and be better and brighter during an introduction or at a tea.

"Now, boys," said the captain, "she is going to swamp sure. All we can do is to work her in as far as possible, and then when she swamps, pile out and scramble for the beach. Keep cool now, and don't jump until she swamps sure."

The oiler took the oars. Over his shoulders he scanned the surf. "Captain," he said, "I think I'd better bring her about and keep her head-on to the seas and back her in."

"All right, Billie," said the captain. "Back her in." The oiler swung the boat   205
then, and, seated in the stern, the cook and the correspondent were obliged to look over their shoulders to contemplate the lonely and indifferent shore.

The monstrous inshore rollers heaved the boat high until the men were again enabled to see the white sheets of water scudding up the slanted beach. "We won't get in very close," said the captain. Each time a man could wrest his attention from the rollers, he turned his glance toward the shore, and in the expression of the eyes during this contemplation there was a singular quality. The correspondent, observing the others, knew that they were not afraid, but the full meaning of their glances was shrouded.

As for himself, he was too tired to grapple fundamentally with the fact. He tried to coerce his mind into thinking of it, but the mind was dominated at this time by the muscles, and the muscles said they did not care. It merely occurred to him that if he should drown it would be a shame.

There were no hurried words, no pallor, no plain agitation. The men simply looked at the shore. "Now, remember to get well clear of the boat when you jump," said the captain.

Seaward the crest of a roller suddenly fell with a thunderous crash, and the long white comber came roaring down upon the boat.

"Steady now," said the captain. The men were silent. They turned their eyes   210
from the shore to the comber and waited. The boat slid up the incline, leaped at the furious top, bounced over it, and swung down the long back of the wave. Some water had been shipped, and the cook bailed it out.

But the next crest crashed also. The tumbling, boiling flood of white water caught the boat and whirled it almost perpendicular. Water swarmed in from all sides. The correspondent had his hands on the gunwale at this time, and when the water entered at that place he swiftly withdrew his fingers, as if he objected to wetting them.

The little boat, drunken with this weight of water, reeled and snuggled deeper into the sea.

"Bail her out, cook! Bail her out!" said the captain.

"All right, Captain," said the cook.

"Now, boys, the next one will do for us sure," said the oiler. "Mind to jump clear   215
of the boat."

The third wave moved forward, huge, furious, implacable. It fairly swallowed the dinghy, and almost simultaneously the men tumbled into the sea. A piece of life-belt had lain in the bottom of the boat, and as the correspondent went overboard he held this to his chest with his left hand.

The January water was icy, and he reflected immediately that it was colder than he had expected to find it off the coast of Florida. This appeared to his dazed mind as a fact important enough to be noted at the time. The coldness of the water was sad; it was tragic. This fact was somehow mixed and confused with his opinion of his own situation, so that it seemed almost a proper reason for tears. The water was cold.

When he came to the surface he was conscious of little but the noisy water. Afterward he saw his companions in the sea. The oiler was ahead in the race. He was swimming strongly and rapidly. Off to the correspondent's left, the cook's great white and corked back bulged out of the water; and in the rear the captain was hanging with his one good hand to the keel of the overturned dinghy.

There is a certain immovable quality to a shore, and the correspondent wondered at it amid the confusion of the sea.

It seemed also very attractive; but the correspondent knew that it was a long journey, and he paddled leisurely. The piece of life-preserver lay under him, and sometimes he whirled down the incline of a wave as if he were on a hand-sled. 220

But finally he arrived at a place in the sea where travel was beset with difficulty. He did not pause swimming to inquire what manner of current had caught him, but there his progress ceased. The shore was set before him like a bit of scenery on a stage, and he looked at it and understood with his eyes each detail of it.

As the cook passed, much farther to the left, the captain was calling to him, "Turn over on your back, cook! Turn over on your back and use the oar."

"All right, sir." The cook turned on his back, and, paddling with an oar, went ahead as if he were a canoe.

Presently the boat also passed to the left of the correspondent, with the captain clinging with one hand to the keel. He would have appeared like a man raising himself to look over a board fence if it were not for the extraordinary gymnastics of the boat. The correspondent marvelled that the captain could still hold to it.

They passed on nearer to shore—the oiler, the cook, the captain—and following them went the water-jar, bouncing gaily over the seas. 225

The correspondent remained in the grip of this strange new enemy—a current. The shore, with its white slope of sand and its green bluff topped with little silent cottages, was spread like a picture before him. It was very near to him then, but he was impressed as one who, in a gallery, looks at a scene from Brittany or Algiers.

He thought: "I am going to drown? Can it be possible? Can it be possible? Can it be possible?" Perhaps an individual must consider his own death to be the final phenomenon of nature.

But later a wave perhaps whirled him out of this small deadly current, for he found suddenly that he could again make progress toward the shore. Later still he was aware that the captain, clinging with one hand to the keel of the dinghy, had his face turned away from the shore and toward him, and was calling his name. "Come to the boat! Come to the boat!"

In his struggle to reach the captain and the boat, he reflected that when one gets properly wearied drowning must really be a comfortable arrangement—a cessation of hostilities accompanied by a large degree of relief; and he was glad of it, for the main thing in his mind for some moments had been horror of the temporary agony. He did not wish to be hurt.

Presently he saw a man running along the shore. He was undressing with most remarkable speed. Coat, trousers, shirt, everything flew magically off him. 230

"Come to the boat!" called the captain.

"All right, Captain." As the correspondent paddled, he saw the captain let himself down to bottom and leave the boat. Then the correspondent performed his one little marvel of the voyage. A large wave caught him and flung him with ease and supreme speed completely over the boat and far beyond it. It struck him even then as an event in gymnastics and a true miracle of the sea. An overturned boat in the surf is not a plaything to a swimming man.

The correspondent arrived in water that reached only to his waist, but his condition did not enable him to stand for more than a moment. Each wave knocked him into a heap, and the undertow pulled at him.

Then he saw the man who had been running and undressing, and undressing and running, come bounding into the water. He dragged ashore the cook, and then waded toward the captain; but the captain waved him away and sent him to the correspondent. He was naked—naked as a tree in winter; but a halo was about his head, and he shone like a saint. He gave a strong pull, and a long drag, and a bully heave at the correspondent's hand. The correspondent, schooled in the minor formulae, said, "Thanks, old man." But suddenly the man cried, "What's that?" He pointed a swift finger. The correspondent said, "Go."

In the shallows, face downward, lay the oiler. His forehead touched sand that was periodically, between each wave, clear of the sea.   235

The correspondent did not know all that transpired afterward. When he achieved safe ground he fell, striking the sand with each particular part of his body. It was as if he had dropped from a roof, but the thud was grateful to him.

It seems that instantly the beach was populated with men with blankets, clothes, and flasks, and women with coffee-pots and all the remedies sacred to their minds. The welcome of the land to the men from the sea was warm and generous; but a still and dripping shape was carried slowly up the beach, and the land's welcome for it could only be the different and sinister hospitality of the grave.

When it came night, the white waves paced to and fro in the moonlight, and the wind brought the sound of the great sea's voice to the men on the shore, and they felt that they could then be interpreters.

Questions

1. In actuality, Crane, the captain of the *Commodore*, and the two crew members spent nearly thirty hours in the open boat. William Higgins, the oiler, was drowned as Crane describes. Does a knowledge of these facts in any way affect your response to the story? Would you admire the story less—or more—if you believed it to be pure fiction?

2. Sum up the personalities of each of the four men in the boat: captain, cook, oiler, and correspondent.

3. What is the point of view of the story?

4. In paragraph 9, we are told that as each wave came, the boat "seemed like a horse making at a fence outrageously high." Point to other vivid similes or figures of speech. What do they contribute to the story's effectiveness?

5. Notice some of the ways in which Crane, as a storyteller conscious of plot, builds suspense. What enemies or obstacles do the men in the boat confront? What is the effect of the episode of the men who wave from the beach (paragraphs 86–141)? What is the climax of the story? (If you need to be refreshed on the meaning of *climax*, see the discussion of plot in Chapter 1.)

6. In paragraph 70 (and again in paragraph 143), the men wonder, "Was I brought here merely to have my nose dragged away as I was about to nibble the sacred cheese of life?" What variety of irony do you find in this quotation?

7. Why does the scrap of verse about the soldier dying in Algiers (paragraph 178) suddenly come to mean so much to the correspondent?

8. What theme in "The Open Boat" seems most important to you? Where is it stated?

9. What secondary themes also enrich the story? See for instance paragraph 43 (the thoughts on comradeship).

10. How do you define *heroism*? Who is a hero in "The Open Boat"?

Sandra Cisneros

Barbie-Q   1991

Sandra Cisneros was born in Chicago in 1954. The child of a Mexican father and a Mexican American mother, she was the only daughter in a family of seven children. She attended Loyola University Chicago and then received a master's degree from the University of Iowa Writers' Workshop. She has instructed high-school dropouts and more recently taught as a visiting writer at numerous universities, including the Universities of California at Irvine and Berkeley and the University of Michigan. Her honors include fellowships from the National Endowment for the Arts and the MacArthur Foundation, an American Book Award, and a 2015 National Medal of Arts. Cisneros's first published work was poetry: Bad Boys *(1980), followed by* My Wicked Wicked Ways *(1987) and* Loose Woman *(1994). Her fiction collections,* The House on Mango Street *(1984) and*

Sandra Cisneros

Woman Hollering Creek *(1991), earned her a broader audience. She has also published a bilingual children's book,* Hairs/Pelitos *(1994), a novel,* Caramelo *(2002), an illustrated fable for adults,* Have You Seen Marie? *(2012), and a collection of autobiographical essays,* A House of My Own *(2015). Cisneros lives in San Antonio, Texas.*

For Licha

Yours is the one with mean eyes and a ponytail. Striped swimsuit, stilettos, sunglasses, and gold hoop earrings. Mine is the one with bubble hair. Red swimsuit, stilettos, pearl earrings, and a wire stand. But that's all we can afford, besides one extra outfit apiece. Yours, "Red Flair," sophisticated A-line coatdress with a Jackie Kennedy pillbox hat, white gloves, handbag, and heels included. Mine, "Solo in the Spotlight," evening elegance in black glitter strapless gown with a puffy skirt at the bottom like a mermaid tail, formal-length gloves, pink chiffon scarf, and mike included. From so much dressing and undressing, the black glitter wears off where her titties stick out. This and a dress invented from an old sock when we cut holes here and here and here, the cuff rolled over for the glamorous, fancy-free, off-the-shoulder look.

Every time the same story. Your Barbie is roommates with my Barbie, and my Barbie's boyfriend comes over and your Barbie steals him, okay? Kiss kiss kiss. Then the two Barbies fight. You dumbbell! He's mine. Oh no he's not, you stinky! Only Ken's invisible, right? Because we don't have money for a stupid-looking boy doll when we'd both rather ask for a new Barbie outfit next Christmas. We have to make do with your mean-eyed Barbie and my bubblehead Barbie and our one outfit apiece not including the sock dress.

Until next Sunday when we are walking through the flea market on Maxwell Street° and *there!* Lying on the street next to some tool bits, and platform shoes with

Maxwell Street: In a historically immigrant Chicago neighborhood, Maxwell Street was the site of a century-old flea market that closed in 1994.

the heels all squashed, and a fluorescent green wicker wastebasket, and aluminum foil, and hubcaps, and a pink shag rug, and windshield wiper blades, and dusty mason jars, and a coffee can full of rusty nails. *There!* Where? Two Mattel boxes. One with the "Career Gal" ensemble, snappy black-and-white business suit, three-quarter-length sleeve jacket with kick-pleated skirt, red sleeveless shell, gloves, pumps, and matching hat included. The other, "Sweet Dreams," dreamy pink-and-white plaid nightgown and matching robe, lace-trimmed slippers, hair-brush and hand mirror included. How much? Please, please, please, please, please, please, please, until they say okay.

On the outside you and me skipping and humming but inside we are doing loopity-loops and pirouetting. Until at the next vendor's stand, next to boxed pies, and bright orange toilet brushes, and rubber gloves, and wrench sets, and bouquets of feather flowers, and glass towel racks, and steel wool, and Alvin and the Chipmunks records, *there!* And *there!* And *there!* And *there!* and *there!* and *there!* and *there!* Bendable Legs Barbie with her new page-boy hairdo. Midge, Barbie's best friend. Ken, Barbie's boyfriend. Skipper, Barbie's little sister. Tutti and Todd, Barbie and Skipper's tiny twin sister and brother. Skipper's friends, Scooter and Ricky. Alan, Ken's buddy. And Francie, Barbie' MOD'ern cousin.

Everybody today selling toys, all of them damaged with water and smelling of smoke. Because a big toy warehouse on Halsted Street burned down yesterday—see there?—the smoke still rising and drifting across the Dan Ryan expressway.° And now there is a big fire sale at Maxwell Street, today only.

So what if we didn't get our new Bendable Legs Barbie and Midge and Ken and Skipper and Tutti and Todd and Scooter and Ricky and Alan and Francie in nice clean boxes and had to buy them on Maxwell Street, all water-soaked and sooty. So what if our Barbies smell like smoke when you hold them up to your nose even after you wash and wash and wash them. And if the prettiest doll, Barbie's MOD'ern cousin Francie with real eyelashes, eyelash brush included, has a left foot that's melted a little—so? If you dress her in her new "Prom Pinks" outfit, satin splendor with matching coat, gold belt, clutch, and hair bow included, so long as you don't lift her dress, right?—who's to know.

Questions

1. What would you guess to be the age of the narrator? What elements of the narration offer clues?
2. Identify places where the narrator seems to have gotten her descriptions from marketing and advertising. Also find language that starkly contrasts the dreamy names and phrases, suggesting a clash of two different worlds.
3. What do we know about the narrator's social class? Why is that important to our understanding of the story?
4. The classic Barbie doll is blond and Caucasian, and she has an unrealistic "idealized" female body. What is significant about the narrator's acceptance of the damaged and deformed dolls? Does the story seem to make a statement about class and privilege in our society?
5. Try to formulate a one-sentence thematic statement of "Barbie-Q," using the guidelines provided earlier in the chapter to assist you.

Dan Ryan expressway: freeway that connects downtown Chicago to the city's South Side neighborhood.

Luke

The Parable of the Prodigal Son   (King James Version, 1611)

Luke (first century) is traditionally considered the author of the Gospel bearing his name and the Acts of the Apostles in the New Testament. A physician who lived in the Greek city of Antioch (now in Syria), Luke accompanied the Apostle Paul on some of his missionary journeys. Luke's elegantly written Gospel includes some of the Bible's most beloved parables, including that of the Good Samaritan and the Prodigal Son.

And he said, A certain man had two sons: And the younger of them said to his father, Father, give me the portion of goods that falleth to me. And he divided unto them his living. And not many days after the younger son gathered all together, and took his journey into a far country, and there wasted his substance with riotous living. And when he had spent all, there arose a mighty famine in that land; and he began to be in want. And he went and joined himself to a citizen of that country; and he sent him into his fields to feed swine. And he would fain have filled his belly with the husks that the swine did eat: and no man gave unto him. And when he came to himself, he said, How many hired servants of my father's have bread enough and to spare, and I perish with hunger! I will arise and go to my father, and will say unto him, Father I have sinned against heaven, and before thee, and am no more worthy to be called thy son; make me as one of thy hired servants. And he arose, and came to his father. But when he was yet a great way off, his father saw him, and had compassion, and ran, and fell on his neck, and kissed him. And the son said unto him, Father I have sinned against heaven, and in thy sight, and am no more worthy to be called thy son. But the father said to his servants, Bring forth the best robe, and put it

The Prodigal Son, woodcut by Gustave Doré, 1865.

on him; and put a ring on his hand, and shoes on his feet: And bring hither the fatted calf, and kill it; and let us eat, and be merry: For this my son was dead, and is alive again; he was lost, and is found. And they began to be merry. Now his elder son was in the field: and he came and drew nigh to the house, he heard music and dancing. And he called one of the servants, and asked what these things meant. And he said unto him, Thy brother is come; and thy father hath killed the fatted calf, because he hath received him safe and sound. And he was angry, and would not go in: therefore came his father out, and entreated him. And he answering said to his father, Lo, these many years do I serve thee, neither transgressed I at any time thy commandment; and yet thou never gavest me a kid, that I might make merry with my friends: But as soon as this thy son was come, which hath devoured thy living with harlots, thou hast killed for him the fatted calf. And he said unto him, Son thou art ever with me, and all that I have is thine. It was meet that we should make merry, and be glad: for this thy brother was dead, and is alive again; and was lost, and is found.

—Luke 15:11-32

Questions

1. This story has traditionally been called "The Parable of the Prodigal Son." What does *prodigal* mean? Which of the two brothers is prodigal?
2. What position does the younger son expect when he returns to his father's house? What does the father give him?
3. When the older brother sees the celebration for his younger brother's return, he grows angry. He makes a very reasonable set of complaints to his father. He has indeed been a loyal and moral son, but what virtue does the older brother lack?
4. Is the father fair to the elder son? Explain your answer.
5. Theologians have discussed this parable's religious significance for two thousand years. What, in your own words, is the human theme of the story?

Kurt Vonnegut Jr.

Harrison Bergeron   1961

Kurt Vonnegut Jr. (1922–2007) was born in Indianapolis. During the Depression his father, a well-to-do architect, had virtually no work, and the family lived in reduced circumstances. Vonnegut attended Cornell University, where he majored in chemistry and was also managing editor of the daily student newspaper. In 1943 he enlisted in the U.S. Army. During the Battle of the Bulge he was captured by German troops and interned as a prisoner of war in Dresden, where he survived the massive Allied firebombing, which killed tens of thousands of people, mostly civilians. (The firebombing of Dresden became the central incident in Vonnegut's best-selling 1969 novel, Slaughterhouse-Five.*) After the war, Vonnegut worked as a reporter and later as a public relations man for General Electric in Schenectady, New York. He quit his job in 1951 to write full-time after publishing several science fiction stories in national magazines. His first novel,* Player Piano, *appeared in 1952, followed by* Sirens of Titan *(1959) and his first best seller,* Cat's Cradle *(1963)—all now considered classics of literary science fiction. Among his many other books are* Mother Night *(1961),* Jailbird *(1979), and a book of biographical essays,* A Man Without a Country *(2005). His short fiction was collected in* Welcome to the Monkey House *(1968) and* Bagombo Snuff Box *(1999). Vonnegut was a singular figure in modern American fiction. An ingenious comic writer, he fused the popular genre of science fiction with the literary tradition of dark satire—a combination splendidly realized in "Harrison Bergeron."*

The year was 2081, and everybody was finally equal. They weren't only equal before God and the law. They were equal every which way. Nobody was smarter than anybody else. Nobody was better looking than anybody else. Nobody was stronger or quicker than anybody else. All this equality was due to the 211th, 212th, and 213th Amendments to the Constitution, and to the unceasing vigilance of agents of the United States Handicapper General.

Some things about living still weren't quite right, though. April, for instance, still drove people crazy by not being springtime. And it was in that clammy month that the H-G men took George and Hazel Bergeron's fourteen-year-old son, Harrison, away.

It was tragic, all right, but George and Hazel couldn't think about it very hard. Hazel had a perfectly average intelligence, which meant she couldn't think about anything except in short bursts. And George, while his intelligence was way above normal, had a little mental handicap radio in his ear. He was required by law to wear it at all times. It was tuned to a government transmitter. Every twenty seconds or so, the transmitter would send out some sharp noise to keep people like George from taking unfair advantage of their brains.

George and Hazel were watching television. There were tears on Hazel's cheeks, but she'd forgotten for the moment what they were about.

On the television screen were ballerinas.   5

A buzzer sounded in George's head. His thoughts fled in panic, like bandits from a burglar alarm.

"That was a real pretty dance, that dance they just did," said Hazel.

"Huh?" said George.

"That dance—it was nice," said Hazel.

"Yup," said George. He tried to think a little about the ballerinas. They weren't   10
really very good—no better than anybody else would have been, anyway. They were burdened with sashweights and bags of birdshot, and their faces were masked, so that no one, seeing a free and graceful gesture or a pretty face, would feel like something the cat drug in. George was toying with the vague notion that maybe dancers shouldn't be handicapped. But he didn't get very far with it before another noise in his ear radio scattered his thoughts.

George winced. So did two out of the eight ballerinas.

Hazel saw him wince. Having no mental handicap herself, she had to ask George what the latest sound had been.

"Sounded like somebody hitting a milk bottle with a ball peen hammer," said George.

"I'd think it would be real interesting, hearing all the different sounds," said Hazel, a little envious. "All the things they think up."

"Um," said George.   15

"Only, if I was Handicapper General, you know what I would do?" said Hazel. Hazel, as a matter of fact, bore a strong resemblance to the Handicapper General, a woman named Diana Moon Glampers. "If I was Diana Moon Glampers," said Hazel, "I'd have chimes on Sunday—just chimes. Kind of in honor of religion."

"I could think, if it was just chimes," said George.

"Well—maybe make 'em real loud," said Hazel. "I think I'd make a good Handicapper General."

"Good as anybody else," said George.

"Who knows better'n I do what normal is?" said Hazel.   20

"Right," said George. He began to think glimmeringly about his abnormal son who was now in jail, about Harrison, but a twenty-one-gun salute in his head stopped that.

"Boy!" said Hazel, "that was a doozy, wasn't it?"

It was such a doozy that George was white and trembling, and tears stood on the rims of his red eyes. Two of the eight ballerinas had collapsed to the studio floor, were holding their temples.

"All of a sudden you look so tired," said Hazel. "Why don't you stretch out on the sofa, so's you can rest your handicap bag on the pillows, honeybunch." She was referring to the forty-seven pounds of birdshot in a canvas bag, which was padlocked around George's neck. "Go on and rest the bag for a little while," she said. "I don't care if you're not equal to me for a while."

George weighed the bag with his hands. "I don't mind it," he said. "I don't notice it any more. It's just a part of me." 25

"You been so tired lately—kind of wore out," said Hazel. "If there was just some way we could make a little hole in the bottom of the bag, and just take out a few of them lead balls. Just a few."

"Two years in prison and two thousand dollars fine for every ball I took out," said George. "I don't call that a bargain."

"If you could just take a few out when you came home from work," said Hazel. "I mean—you don't compete with anybody around here. You just set around."

"If I tried to get away with it," said George, "then other people'd get away with it—and pretty soon we'd be right back to the dark ages again, with everybody competing against everybody else. You wouldn't like that, would you?"

"I'd hate it," said Hazel. 30

"There you are," said George. "The minute people start cheating on laws, what do you think happens to society?"

If Hazel hadn't been able to come up with an answer to this question, George couldn't have supplied one. A siren was going off in his head.

"Reckon it'd fall all apart," said Hazel.

"What would?" said George blankly.

"Society," said Hazel uncertainly. "Wasn't that what you just said?" 35

"Who knows?" said George.

The television program was suddenly interrupted for a news bulletin. It wasn't clear at first as to what the bulletin was about, since the announcer, like all announcers, had a serious speech impediment. For about half a minute, and in a state of high excitement, the announcer tried to say, "Ladies and gentlemen—"

He finally gave up, handed the bulletin to a ballerina to read.

"That's all right—" Hazel said of the announcer, "he tried. That's the big thing. He tried to do the best he could with what God gave him. He should get a nice raise for trying so hard."

"Ladies and gentlemen—" said the ballerina, reading the bulletin. She must 40 have been extraordinarily beautiful, because the mask she wore was hideous. And it was easy to see that she was the strongest and most graceful of all the dancers, for her handicap bags were as big as those worn by two-hundred-pound men.

And she had to apologize at once for her voice, which was a very unfair voice for a woman to use. Her voice was a warm, luminous, timeless melody. "Excuse me—" she said, and she began again, making her voice absolutely uncompetitive.

"Harrison Bergeron, age fourteen," she said in a grackle squawk, "has just escaped from jail, where he was held on suspicion of plotting to overthrow the government. He is a genius and an athlete, is under-handicapped, and should be regarded as extremely dangerous."

A police photograph of Harrison Bergeron was flashed on the screen upside down, then sideways, upside down again, then right side up. The picture showed the full length of Harrison against a background calibrated in feet and inches. He was exactly seven feet tall.

The rest of Harrison's appearance was Halloween and hardware. Nobody had ever borne heavier handicaps. He had outgrown hindrances faster than the H-G men could think them up. Instead of a little ear radio for a mental handicap, he wore a tremendous pair of earphones, and spectacles with thick wavy lenses. The spectacles were intended to make him not only half blind, but to give him whanging headaches besides.

Scrap metal was hung all over him. Ordinarily, there was a certain symmetry, a 45 military neatness to the handicaps issued to strong people, but Harrison looked like a walking junkyard. In the race of life, Harrison carried three hundred pounds.

And to offset his good looks, the H-G men required that he wear at all times a red rubber ball for a nose, keep his eyebrows shaved off, and cover his even white teeth with black caps at snaggle-tooth random.

"If you see this boy," said the ballerina, "do not—I repeat, do not—try to reason with him."

There was the shriek of a door being torn from its hinges.

Screams and barking cries of consternation came from the television set. The photograph of Harrison Bergeron on the screen jumped again and again, as though dancing to the tune of an earthquake.

George Bergeron correctly identified the earthquake, and well he might have— 50 for many was the time his own home had danced to the same crashing tune. "My God—" said George, "that must be Harrison!"

The realization was blasted from his mind instantly by the sound of an automobile collision in his head.

When George could open his eyes again, the photograph of Harrison was gone. A living, breathing Harrison filled the screen.

Clanking, clownish, and huge, Harrison stood in the center of the studio. The knob of the uprooted studio door was still in his hand. Ballerinas, technicians, musicians, and announcers cowered on their knees before him, expecting to die.

"I am the Emperor!" cried Harrison. "Do you hear? I am the Emperor! Everybody must do what I say at once!" He stamped his foot and the studio shook.

"Even as I stand here—" he bellowed, "crippled, hobbled, sickened—I am a greater 55 ruler than any man who ever lived! Now watch me become what I *can* become!"

Harrison tore the straps of his handicap harness like wet tissue paper, tore straps guaranteed to support five thousand pounds.

Harrison's scrap-iron handicaps crashed to the floor.

Harrison thrust his thumbs under the bar of the padlock that secured his head harness. The bar snapped like celery. Harrison smashed his headphones and spectacles against the wall.

He flung away his rubber-ball nose, revealed a man that would have awed Thor, the god of thunder.

"I shall now select my Empress!" he said, looking down on the cowering people. 60 "Let the first woman who dares rise to her feet claim her mate and her throne!"

A moment passed, and then a ballerina arose, swaying like a willow.

Harrison plucked the mental handicap from her ear, snapped off her physical handicaps with marvelous delicacy. Last of all, he removed her mask.

She was blindingly beautiful.

"Now—" said Harrison, taking her hand, "shall we show the people the meaning of the word dance? Music!" he commanded.

The musicians scrambled back into their chairs, and Harrison stripped them of   65
their handicaps, too. "Play your best," he told them, "and I'll make you barons and
dukes and earls."

The music began. It was normal at first—cheap, silly, false. But Harrison snatched
two musicians from their chairs, waved them like batons as he sang the music as he
wanted it played. He slammed them back into their chairs.

The music began again and was much improved.

Harrison and his Empress merely listened to the music for a while—listened
gravely, as though synchronizing their heartbeats with it.

They shifted their weights to their toes.

Harrison placed his big hands on the girl's tiny waist, letting her sense the   70
weightlessness that would soon be hers.

And then, in an explosion of joy and grace, into the air they sprang!

Not only were the laws of the land abandoned, but the law of gravity and the
laws of motion as well.

They reeled, whirled, swiveled, flounced, capered, gamboled, and spun.

They leaped like deer on the moon.

The studio ceiling was thirty feet high, but each leap brought the dancers nearer to it.   75

It became their obvious intention to kiss the ceiling.

They kissed it.

And then, neutralizing gravity with love and pure will, they remained suspended in air inches below the ceiling, and they kissed each other for a long, long
time.

It was then that Diana Moon Glampers, the Handicapper General, came into the
studio with a double-barreled ten-gauge shotgun. She fired twice, and the Emperor
and the Empress were dead before they hit the floor.

Diana Moon Glampers loaded the gun again. She aimed it at the musicians and   80
told them they had ten seconds to get their handicaps back on.

It was then that the Bergerons' television tube burned out.

Hazel turned to comment about the blackout to George. But George had gone
out into the kitchen for a can of beer.

George came back in with the beer, paused while a handicap signal shook him
up. And then he sat down again. "You been crying?" he said to Hazel.

"Yup," she said.

"What about?" he said.   85

"I forget," she said. "Something real sad on television."

"What was it?" he said.

"It's all kind of mixed up in my mind," said Hazel.

"Forget sad things," said George.

"I always do," said Hazel.   90

"That's my girl," said George. He winced. There was the sound of a rivetting gun
in his head.

"Gee—I could tell that one was a doozy," said Hazel.

"You can say that again," said George.

"Gee—" said Hazel, "I could tell that one was a doozy."

Questions

1. What tendencies in present-day American society is Vonnegut satirizing? Does the story
    argue *for* anything? How would you sum up its theme?

2. Is Diana Moon Glampers a "flat" or a "round" character? (If you need to review these terms, see the discussion of character in Chapter 3.) Would you call Vonnegut's characterization of her "realistic"? If not, why doesn't it need to be?

3. From what point of view is the story told? Why is it more effective than if Harrison Bergeron had told his own story in the first person?

4. Two sympathetic critics of Vonnegut's work, Karen and Charles Wood, have said of his stories: "Vonnegut proves repeatedly . . . that men and women remain fundamentally the same, no matter what technology surrounds them." Try applying this comment to "Harrison Bergeron." Do you agree?

5. Stanislaw Lem, Polish author of *Solaris* and other novels, once made this thoughtful criticism of many of his contemporaries among science fiction (SF) writers:

> The revolt against the machine and against civilization, the praise of the "aesthetic" nature of catastrophe, the dead-end course of human civilization—these are their foremost problems, the intellectual content of their works. Such SF is as it were *a priori* vitiated by pessimism, in the sense that anything that may happen will be for the worse. ("The Time-Travel Story and Related Matters of SF Structuring," *Science Fiction Studies 1* [1974], 143–54.)

How might Lem's objection be raised against "Harrison Bergeron"? In your opinion, does it negate the value of Vonnegut's story?

▪ WRITING *effectively*

Kurt Vonnegut Jr. on Writing

The Themes of Science Fiction

1971, 1973

Interviewer: You talked a lot about the difficulties you had when you first began. For instance, I think you gave one of the reasons for using the science fiction form as the fact that you were a professional writer and had to do something which was popular.

Vonnegut: In the beginning I was writing about what concerned me, and what was all around me was machinery. I myself had had some training in engineering and chemistry rather than in the arts and I was working for General Electric in a big factory city, Schenectady. So the first book I wrote was about Schenectady, which is full of machinery and engineers. And I was classified as a science fiction writer. Well, in the past, science fiction writers have been beneath the attention of any serious critic. That is, far

Kurt Vonnegut Jr.

above you are the people dealing with the really important, beautiful issues and using great skills and so forth. It used to be that if you were a science fiction writer you really didn't belong in the arts at all, and other artists wouldn't talk to you. You just had this scruffy little gang of your own.

•••

Interviewer: What attracted you to using the form [of science fiction] yourself?

Vonnegut: . . . I saw a milling machine for cutting the rotors on jet engines, gas turbines. This was a very expensive thing for a machinist to do, to cut what is essentially one of those Brancusi forms. So they had a computer-operated milling machine built to cut the blades, and I was fascinated by that. This was in 1949 and the guys who were working on it were foreseeing all sorts of machines being run by little boxes and punched cards. *Player Piano* was my response to the implications of having everything run by little boxes. The idea of doing that, you know, made sense, perfect sense. To have a little clicking box make all the decisions wasn't a vicious thing to do. But it was too bad for the human beings who got their dignity from their jobs.

Interviewer: So science fiction seemed like the best way to write about your thoughts on the subject.

Vonnegut: There was no avoiding it, since General Electric Company *was* science fiction.

From interviews with Laurie Clancy and David Standish

THINKING ABOUT THEME

A clear, precise statement about a story's theme can serve as a promising thesis for a writing assignment. After you read a short story, you will probably have some vague sense of its theme—the central unifying idea, or the point of the story. How do you hone that vague sense of theme into a sharp and intriguing thesis?

- **Start by making a list of phrases or ideas that suggest the story's possible theme.** If you are discussing Stephen Crane's "The Open Boat," your initial list might look like this:

  camaraderie of people in crisis
  man versus nature
  life-and-death struggle
  blindness of fate
  cruelty of nature
  courage in face of danger
  bravery not enough to overcome nature

- **Choose the most important points and then combine them into a single sentence.** For Crane, you might have circled "man versus nature," "blindness of fate," and "bravery not enough," and your summary might be this:

  The central theme of "The Open Boat" is nature's blindness, cruelty, and indifference to people's fate—even the most courageous individuals.

- **Refine your sentence to capture the story's essence as clearly and specifically as possible.** Remember, your goal is to transcend a mere one-sentence plot summary. How can you clearly express the central theme in a few words? Your refinement might read as follows:

  The theme of "The Open Boat" is nature's indifference to the fate of even the most courageous individuals.

CHECKLIST: Writing About Theme

☐ List as many possible themes as you can.

☐ Circle the two or three most important points and try to combine them into a sentence.

☐ Relate particular details of the story to the theme you have spelled out. Consider plot details, dialogue, setting, point of view, title—any elements that seem especially pertinent.

☐ Check whether all the elements of the story fit your thesis.

☐ Have you missed an important aspect of the story? Or, have you chosen to focus on a secondary idea, overlooking the central one?

☐ If necessary, rework your thesis until it applies to every element in the story.

TOPICS FOR WRITING ON THEME

1. Choose a story that catches your attention, and go through the steps outlined above to develop a strong thesis sentence about the story's theme. Then flesh out your argument into an essay, supporting your thesis with evidence from the text, including quotations. Some good story choices might be "A Clean, Well-Lighted Place" (Chapter 5), "The Chrysanthemums" (Chapter 7), "A Good Man Is Hard to Find" (Chapter 11), and "The Lottery" (Chapter 7).

2. Define the central theme of "Harrison Bergeron." Is Vonnegut's early-1960s vision of the future still relevant today? Why or why not?

3. Write a short parable in the style of Aesop's "The Fox and the Grapes" (Chapter 1), and explicitly state your theme at the end of the story.

4. "To Build a Fire" (Chapter 4), "At the Jim Bridger" (Chapter 4), and "The Open Boat" each address the theme of a human being pitted against indifferent nature. Contrast the stories' approaches to this theme. How do the tones of the stories differ? How do these tonal differences help to communicate theme?

5. What does "Saints" (Chapter 13) have to say about dealing with a broken family? Look particularly at the narrator's relationship to the recurring symbol of the Hindu saint. Back up your response with specific evidence from the story.

6. A recent *Time* magazine article describes a young California woman who distanced herself from her Chinese heritage until reading Amy Tan's *The Joy Luck Club* (which includes "A Pair of Tickets," found in Chapter 4) "turned her into a 'born-again Asian.' It gave her new insights into why her mom was so hard on her and why the ways she showed love—say, through food—were different from those of the families [she] saw on TV, who seemed to say 'I love you' all day long." Have you ever had a similar experience, in which something you read gave you a better understanding of a loved one, or even yourself?

▶ TERMS FOR *review*

Summary ▶ A brief condensation of the main idea or plot of a literary work. A summary is similar to a paraphrase, but less detailed.

Theme ▶ The main idea or larger meaning of a work of literature. A theme may be a message or a moral, but it is more likely to be a central, unifying insight or viewpoint.

7 SYMBOL

> *All you have to do is close your eyes*
> *and wait for the symbols.*
>
> —TENNESSEE WILLIAMS

What You Will Learn in This Chapter

- To recognize and define *literary symbol*
- To define *allegory* and describe its characteristics
- To identify and describe symbolic characters and symbolic acts
- To analyze a symbol's role in a story

In F. Scott Fitzgerald's novel *The Great Gatsby*, a huge pair of bespectacled eyes stares across a wilderness of ash heaps, from a billboard advertising the services of an oculist. Repeatedly entering into the story, the advertisement comes to mean more than simply the availability of eye examinations. Fitzgerald has a character liken it to the eyes of God; he hints that some sad, compassionate spirit is brooding as it watches the passing procession of humanity. Such an object is a **symbol**: in literature, a person, place, or thing that suggests more than its literal meaning.

Symbols generally do not "stand for" any single meaning, nor for anything absolutely definite; they point, they hint, or, as Henry James put it, they cast long shadows. To take a large example: in Herman Melville's *Moby-Dick*, the great white whale of the book's title apparently means more than the literal dictionary-definition meaning of an aquatic mammal. He also suggests more than the devil, to whom some of the characters liken him. The great whale, as the story unfolds, comes to imply an amplitude of meanings, among them the forces of nature and the whole created universe.

ALLEGORY

This indefinite multiplicity of meanings is characteristic of a symbolic story and distinguishes it from an **allegory**, a story in which persons, places, and things form a system of clearly labeled equivalents. In a simple allegory, characters and other elements often stand for abstractions. You will meet such a character in Nathaniel Hawthorne's "Young Goodman Brown" (Chapter 14). This tale's main female character, Faith, represents the religious virtue suggested by her name. Supreme allegories are found in some biblical parables ("The Kingdom of Heaven is like a man who sowed good seed in his field . . . ," Matthew 13:24–30).

A classic allegory is the medieval play *Everyman*, whose hero represents us all, and who, deserted by false friends called Kindred and Goods, faces the judgment of God accompanied only by a faithful friend called Good Deeds. In John Bunyan's seventeenth-century allegory *Pilgrim's Progress*, the protagonist, Christian, struggles along the difficult road toward salvation, meeting along the way persons such as Mr. Worldly Wiseman, who directs him into a more comfortable path (a wrong turn), and the residents of a town called Fair Speech, among them a hypocrite named Mr. Facing-both-ways. Not all allegories are simple: Dante's *Divine Comedy*, written during the Middle Ages, continues to reveal new meanings to careful readers. Allegory was much beloved in the Middle Ages, but in contemporary fiction it is rare. One modern instance is George Orwell's long fable *Animal Farm*, in which (among its double meanings) barnyard animals stand for human victims and totalitarian oppressors.

SYMBOLS

Symbols in fiction are not generally abstract terms such as *love* or *truth*, but are likely to be perceptible objects. In William Faulkner's "A Rose for Emily" (Chapter 2), Miss Emily's invisible watch ticking at the end of a golden chain not only indicates the passage of time, but also suggests that time passes without even being noticed by the watch's owner, and the golden chain carries suggestions of wealth and authority. Objects (and creatures) that seem insignificant in themselves can take on a symbolic importance in the larger context: in Jhumpa Lahiri's "Interpreter of Maladies" (Chapter 14) the piece of gum that Mrs. Das gives Mr. Kapasi—"As soon as Mr. Kapasi put the gum in his mouth a thick sweet liquid burst onto his tongue"—underscores her effect on his slumbering senses.

Often the symbols we meet in fiction are inanimate objects, but other things also may function symbolically. In James Joyce's "Araby" (Chapter 14), the very name of the bazaar, Araby—the poetic name for Arabia—suggests magic, romance, and *The Arabian Nights*; its syllables (the narrator tells us) "cast an Eastern enchantment over me." Even a locale, or a feature of physical topography, can provide rich suggestions. Recall Ernest Hemingway's "A Clean, Well-Lighted Place" (Chapter 5), in which the café is not merely a café, but an island of refuge from night, chaos, loneliness, old age, and impending death.

Symbolic Characters

In some novels and stories, symbolic characters make brief cameo appearances. Such characters often are not well-rounded and fully known, but are seen fleetingly and remain slightly mysterious. Usually such a symbolic character is more a portrait than a person—or somewhat portraitlike, as Faulkner's Miss Emily, who twice appears at a window of her house "like the carven torso of an idol in a niche." Though Faulkner invests Miss Emily with life and vigor, he also clothes her in symbolic hints: she seems almost to personify the vanishing aristocracy of the antebellum South, still maintaining a black servant and being ruthlessly betrayed by a money-making Yankee. Sometimes a part of a character's body or an attribute may convey symbolic meaning: a baleful eye, as in Edgar Allan Poe's "The Tell-Tale Heart" (Chapter 12).

Symbolic Acts

Much as a symbolic whale holds more meaning than an ordinary whale, a **symbolic act** is a gesture with larger significance than usual. For the boy's father in Faulkner's "Barn Burning" (Chapter 5), the act of destroying a barn is no mere act of spite, but an expression of his profound hatred for anything not belonging to him. Faulkner adds that burning a barn reflects the father's memories of the "waste and extravagance of war," and further adds that "the element of fire spoke to some deep mainspring" in his being. A symbolic act, however, doesn't have to be a gesture as large as starting a conflagration. Before setting out in pursuit of the great white whale, Melville's Captain Ahab in *Moby-Dick* deliberately snaps his tobacco pipe and throws it away, as if to suggest (among other things) that he will let no pleasure or pastime distract him from his vengeance.

Why Use Symbols?

Why do writers have to symbolize—why don't they tell us outright? One advantage of a symbol is that it is so compact, and yet so fully laden. Both starkly concrete and slightly mysterious, like Miss Emily's invisible ticking watch, it may impress us with all the force of something beheld in a dream or in a nightmare. The watch suggests, among other things, the slow and invisible passage of time. What this symbol says, it says more fully and more memorably than could be said, perhaps, in a long essay on the subject.

To some extent (it may be claimed), all stories are symbolic. Merely by holding up for our inspection these characters and their actions, the writer lends them *some* special significance. But this is to think of *symbol* in an extremely broad and inclusive way. For the usual purposes of reading a story and understanding it, there is probably little point in looking for symbolism in every word, in every stick or stone, in every striking of a match, in every minor character. Still, to be on the alert for symbols when reading fiction is perhaps wiser than to ignore them. Not to admit that symbolic meanings may be present, or to refuse to think about them, would be another way to misread a story—or to read no further than its outer edges.

RECOGNIZING SYMBOLS

How, then, do you recognize a symbol in fiction when you meet it? Fortunately, the storyteller often gives the symbol particular emphasis. It may be mentioned repeatedly throughout the story; it may even supply the story with a title ("Barn Burning," "A Clean, Well-Lighted Place," "Araby"). At times, a crucial symbol will open a story or end it. Unless an object, act, or character is given some such special emphasis and importance, we may generally feel safe in taking it at face value. Probably it isn't a symbol if it points clearly and unmistakably toward some one meaning, like a whistle in a factory, whose blast at noon means lunch. But an object, an act, or a character is surely symbolic (and almost as surely displays high literary art) if, when we finish the story, we realize that it was that item—that gigantic eye; that clean, well-lighted café; that burning of a barn—which led us to the author's theme, the essential meaning.

John Steinbeck

The Chrysanthemums   1938

*John Steinbeck (1902–1968) was born in Salinas,
California, in the fertile valley he remembers in
"The Chrysanthemums." Off and on, he attended
Stanford University, and then he sojourned in New
York as a reporter and a bricklayer. After years
of struggle to earn his living by fiction, Steinbeck
reached a large audience with* Tortilla Flat *(1935),
a loosely woven novel portraying Mexican Americans
in Monterey with fondness and sympathy. Great
acclaim greeted* The Grapes of Wrath *(1939), the
story of a family of Oklahoma farmers who, ruined
by dust storms in the 1930s, join a mass migration to
California. In 1962 he became the seventh American
to win the Nobel Prize in Literature, but many critics
resisted placing Steinbeck on the same high shelf as*

John Steinbeck

Faulkner *and* Hemingway. *He wrote much, not all good, and yet his best work adds up to
an impressive total. Besides* The Grapes of Wrath, *it includes* In Dubious Battle *(1936),
a novel of an apple-pickers' strike;* Of Mice and Men *(1937), a powerful short novel of
comradeship between a hobo and a man; the short stories in* The Long Valley *(1938), and the
masterful* East of Eden *(1952), the sweeping history of a pair of families in the author's native
Salinas Valley. Throughout the fiction he wrote in his prime, Steinbeck maintains an appealing
sympathy for the poor and downtrodden, the lonely and dispossessed.*

The high grey-flannel fog of winter closed off the Salinas Valley° from the sky
and from all the rest of the world. On every side it sat like a lid on the mountains and
made of the great valley a closed pot. On the broad, level land floor the gang plows
bit deep and left the black earth shining like metal where the shares had cut. On the
foothill ranches across the Salinas River, the yellow stubble fields seemed to be bathed
in pale cold sunshine, but there was no sunshine in the valley now in December. The
thick willow scrub along the river flamed with sharp and positive yellow leaves.

It was a time of quiet and of waiting. The air was cold and tender. A light wind
blew up from the southwest so that the farmers were mildly hopeful of a good rain
before long; but fog and rain do not go together.

Across the river, on Henry Allen's foothill ranch there was little work to be
done, for the hay was cut and stored and the orchards were plowed up to receive the
rain deeply when it should come. The cattle on the higher slopes were becoming
shaggy and rough-coated.

Elisa Allen, working in her flower garden, looked down across the yard and saw
Henry, her husband, talking to two men in business suits. The three of them stood
by the tractor shed, each man with one foot on the side of the little Fordson. They
smoked cigarettes and studied the machine as they talked.

Elisa watched them for a moment and then went back to her work. She was   5
thirty-five. Her face was lean and strong and her eyes were as clear as water. Her
figure looked blocked and heavy in her gardening costume, a man's black hat pulled
low down over her eyes, clodhopper shoes, a figured print dress almost completely

*Salinas Valley: south of San Francisco in Monterey County, a fertile agricultural region just inland from
California's central coast.*

covered by a big corduroy apron with four big pockets to hold the snips, the trowel and scratcher, the seeds and the knife she worked with. She wore heavy leather gloves to protect her hands while she worked.

She was cutting down the old year's chrysanthemum stalks with a pair of short and powerful scissors. She looked down toward the men by the tractor shed now and then. Her face was eager and mature and handsome; even her work with the scissors was over-eager, over-powerful. The chrysanthemum stems seemed too small and easy for her energy.

She brushed a cloud of hair out of her eyes with the back of her glove, and left a smudge of earth on her cheek in doing it. Behind her stood the neat white farm house with red geraniums close-banked around it as high as the windows. It was a hard-swept looking little house with hard-polished windows, and a clean mud-mat on the front steps.

Elisa cast another glance toward the tractor shed. The strangers were getting into their Ford coupe. She took off a glove and put her strong fingers down into the forest of new green chrysanthemum sprouts that were growing around the old roots. She spread the leaves and looked down among the close-growing stems. No aphids were there, no sowbugs or snails or cutworms. Her terrier fingers destroyed such pests before they could get started.

Elisa started at the sound of her husband's voice. He had come near quietly, and he leaned over the wire fence that protected her flower garden from cattle and dogs and chickens.

"At it again," he said. "You've got a strong new crop coming."   10

Elisa straightened her back and pulled on the gardening glove again. "Yes. They'll be strong this coming year." In her tone and on her face there was a little smugness.

"You've got a gift with things," Henry observed. "Some of those yellow chrysanthemums you had this year were ten inches across. I wish you'd work out in the orchard and raise some apples that big."

Her eyes sharpened. "Maybe I could do it, too. I've a gift with things, all right. My mother had it. She could stick anything in the ground and make it grow. She said it was having planters' hands that knew how to do it."

"Well, it sure works with flowers," he said.

"Henry, who were those men you were talking to?"   15

"Why, sure, that's what I came to tell you. They were from the Western Meat Company. I sold those thirty head of three-year-old steers. Got nearly my own price, too."

"Good," she said. "Good for you."

"And I thought," he continued, "I thought how it's Saturday afternoon, and we might go into Salinas for dinner at a restaurant, and then to a picture show—to celebrate, you see."

"Good," she repeated. "Oh, yes. That will be good."

Henry put on his joking tone. "There's fights tonight. How'd you like to go to   20
the fights?"

"Oh, no," she said breathlessly. "No, I wouldn't like fights."

"Just fooling, Elisa. We'll go to a movie. Let's see. It's two now. I'm going to take Scotty and bring down those steers from the hill. It'll take us maybe two hours. We'll go in town about five and have dinner at the Cominos Hotel. Like that?"

"Of course I'll like it. It's good to eat away from home."

"All right, then. I'll go get up a couple of horses."

She said, "I'll have plenty of time to transplant some of these sets, I guess."   25

She heard her husband calling Scotty down by the barn. And a little later she saw the two men ride up the pale yellow hillside in search of the steers.

There was a little square sandy bed kept for rooting the chrysanthemums. With her trowel she turned the soil over and over, and smoothed it and patted it firm. Then she dug ten parallel trenches to receive the sets. Back at the chrysanthemum bed she pulled out the little crisp shoots, trimmed off the leaves of each one with her scissors and laid it on a small orderly pile.

A squeak of wheels and plod of hoofs came from the road. Elisa looked up. The country road ran along the dense bank of willows and cottonwoods that bordered the river, and up this road came a curious vehicle, curiously drawn. It was an old spring-wagon, with a round canvas top on it like the cover of a prairie schooner. It was drawn by an old bay horse and a little grey-and-white burro. A big stubble-bearded man sat between the cover flaps and drove the crawling team. Underneath the wagon, between the hind wheels, a lean and rangy mongrel dog walked sedately. Words were painted on the canvas, in clumsy, crooked letters. "Pots, pans, knives, sisors, lawn mores, Fixed." Two rows of articles, and the triumphantly definitive "Fixed" below. The black paint had run down in little sharp points beneath each letter.

Elisa, squatting on the ground, watched to see the crazy, loose-jointed wagon pass by. But it didn't pass. It turned into the farm road in front of her house, crooked old wheels skirling and squeaking. The rangy dog darted from between the wheels and ran ahead. Instantly the two ranch shepherds flew out at him. Then all three stopped, and with stiff and quivering tails, with taut straight legs, with ambassadorial dignity, they slowly circled, sniffing daintily. The caravan pulled up to Elisa's wire fence and stopped. Now the newcomer dog, feeling out-numbered, lowered his tail and retired under the wagon with raised hackles and bared teeth.

The man on the wagon seat called out, "That's a bad dog in a fight when he gets started."   30

Elisa laughed. "I see he is. How soon does he generally get started?"

The man caught up her laughter and echoed it heartily. "Sometimes not for weeks and weeks," he said. He climbed stiffly down, over the wheel. The horse and the donkey drooped like unwatered flowers.

Elisa saw that he was a very big man. Although his hair and beard were greying, he did not look old. His worn black suit was wrinkled and spotted with grease. The laughter had disappeared from his face and eyes the moment his laughing voice ceased. His eyes were dark, and they were full of the brooding that gets in the eyes of teamsters and of sailors. The calloused hands he rested on the wire fence were cracked, and every crack was a black line. He took off his battered hat.

"I'm off my general road, ma'am," he said. "Does this dirt road cut over across the river to the Los Angeles highway?"

Elisa stood up and shoved the thick scissors in her apron pocket. "Well, yes, it   35 does, but it winds around and then fords the river. I don't think your team could pull through the sand."

He replied with some asperity, "It might surprise you what them beasts can pull through."

"When they get started?" she asked.

He smiled for a second. "Yes. When they get started."

"Well," said Elisa, "I think you'll save time if you go back to the Salinas road and pick up the highway there."

He drew a big finger down the chicken wire and made it sing. "I ain't in any   40 hurry, ma'am. I go from Seattle to San Diego and back every year. Takes all my time. About six months each way. I aim to follow nice weather."

Elisa took off her gloves and stuffed them in the apron pocket with the scissors. She touched the under edge of her man's hat, searching for fugitive hairs. "That sounds like a nice kind of a way to live," she said.

He leaned confidentially over the fence. "Maybe you noticed the writing on my wagon. I mend pots and sharpen knives and scissors. You got any of them things to do?"

"Oh, no," she said quickly. "Nothing like that." Her eyes hardened with resistance.

"Scissors is the worst thing," he explained. "Most people just ruin scissors trying to sharpen 'em, but I know how. I got a special tool. It's a little bobbit kind of thing, and patented. But it sure does the trick."

"No. My scissors are all sharp."

"All right, then. Take a pot," he continued earnestly, "a bent pot, or a pot with a hole. I can make it like new so you don't have to buy no new ones. That's a saving for you."

"No," she said shortly. "I tell you I have nothing like that for you to do."

His face fell to an exaggerated sadness. His voice took on a whining undertone. "I ain't had a thing to do today. Maybe I won't have no supper tonight. You see I'm off my regular road. I know folks on the highway clear from Seattle to San Diego. They save their things for me to sharpen up because they know I do it so good and save them money."

"I'm sorry," Elisa said irritably. "I haven't anything for you to do."

His eyes left her face and fell to searching the ground. They roamed about until they came to the chrysanthemum bed where she had been working. "What's them plants, ma'am?"

The irritation and resistance melted from Elisa's face. "Oh, those are chrysanthemums, giant whites and yellows. I raise them every year, bigger than anybody around here."

"Kind of a long-stemmed flower? Looks like a quick puff of colored smoke?" he asked.

"That's it. What a nice way to describe them."

"They smell kind of nasty till you get used to them," he said.

"It's a good bitter smell," she retorted, "not nasty at all."

He changed his tone quickly. "I like the smell myself."

"I had ten-inch blooms this year," she said.

The man leaned farther over the fence. "Look. I know a lady down the road a piece, has got the nicest garden you ever seen. Got nearly every kind of flower but no chrysanthemums. Last time I was mending a copper-bottom washtub for her (that's a hard job but I do it good), she said to me, 'If you ever run acrost some nice chrysanthemums I wish you'd try to get me a few seeds.' That's what she told me."

Elisa's eyes grew alert and eager. "She couldn't have known much about chrysanthemums. You *can* raise them from seed, but it's much easier to root the little sprouts you see there."

"Oh," he said. "I s'pose I can't take none to her, then."

"Why yes you can," Elisa cried. "I can put some in damp sand, and you can carry them right along with you. They'll take root in the pot if you keep them damp. And then she can transplant them."

"She'd sure like to have some, ma'am. You say they're nice ones?"

"Beautiful," she said. "Oh, beautiful." Her eyes shone. She tore off the battered hat and shook out her dark pretty hair. "I'll put them in a flower pot, and you can take them right with you. Come into the yard."

While the man came through the picket gate Elisa ran excitedly along the geranium-bordered path to the back of the house. And she returned carrying a big red flower pot. The gloves were forgotten now. She kneeled on the ground by the starting bed and dug up the sandy soil with her fingers and scooped it into the bright new flower

pot. Then she picked up the little pile of shoots she had prepared. With her strong
fingers she pressed them in the sand and tamped around them with her knuckles.
The man stood over her. "I'll tell you what to do," she said. "You remember so you
can tell the lady."

"Yes, I'll try to remember." 65

"Well, look. These will take root in about a month. Then she must set them out,
about a foot apart in good rich earth like this, see?" She lifted a handful of dark soil
for him to look at. "They'll grow fast and tall. Now remember this: In July tell her to
cut them down, about eight inches from the ground."

"Before they bloom?" he asked.

"Yes, before they bloom." Her face was tight with eagerness. "They'll grow right
up again. About the last of September the buds will start."

She stopped and seemed perplexed. "It's the budding that takes the most care,"
she said hesitantly. "I don't know how to tell you." She looked deep into his eyes,
searchingly. Her mouth opened a little, and she seemed to be listening. "I'll try to tell
you," she said. "Did you ever hear of planting hands?"

"Can't say I have, ma'am." 70

"Well, I can only tell you what it feels like. It's when you're picking off the buds
you don't want. Everything goes right down into your fingertips. You watch your
fingers work. They do it themselves. You can feel how it is. They pick and pick the
buds. They never make a mistake. They're with the plant. Do you see? Your fingers
and the plant. You can feel that, right up your arm. They know. They never make a
mistake. You can feel it. When you're like that you can't do anything wrong. Do you
see that? Can you understand that?"

She was kneeling on the ground looking up at him. Her breast swelled passionately.

The man's eyes narrowed. He looked away self-consciously. "Maybe I know," he
said. "Sometimes in the night in the wagon there—"

Elisa's voice grew husky. She broke in on him, "I've never lived as you do, but I
know what you mean. When the night is dark—why, the stars are sharp-pointed, and
there's quiet. Why, you rise up and up! Every pointed star gets driven into your body.
It's like that. Hot and sharp and—lovely."

Kneeling there, her hand went out toward his legs in the greasy black trousers. 75
Her hesitant fingers almost touched the cloth. Then her hand dropped to the ground.
She crouched low like a fawning dog.

He said, "It's nice, just like you say. Only when you don't have no dinner, it ain't."

She stood up then, very straight, and her face was ashamed. She held the flower
pot out to him and placed it gently in his arms. "Here. Put it in your wagon, on the
seat, where you can watch it. Maybe I can find something for you to do."

At the back of the house she dug in the can pile and found two old and battered
aluminum saucepans. She carried them back and gave them to him. "Here, maybe
you can fix these."

His manner changed. He became professional. "Good as new I can fix them."
At the back of his wagon he set a little anvil, and out of an oily tool box dug a small
machine hammer. Elisa came through the gate to watch him while he pounded out
the dents in the kettles. His mouth grew sure and knowing. At a difficult part of the
work he sucked his under-lip.

"You sleep right in the wagon?" Elisa asked. 80

"Right in the wagon, ma'am. Rain or shine I'm dry as a cow in there."

"It must be nice," she said. "It must be very nice. I wish women could do such things."

"It ain't the right kind of a life for a woman."

Her upper lip raised a little, showing her teeth. "How do you know? How can you tell?" she said.

"I don't know, ma'am," he protested. "Of course I don't know. Now here's your 85 kettles, done. You don't have to buy no new ones."

"How much?"

"Oh, fifty cents'll do. I keep my prices down and my work good. That's why I have all them satisfied customers up and down the highway."

Elisa brought him a fifty-cent piece from the house and dropped it in his hand. "You might be surprised to have a rival some time. I can sharpen scissors, too. And I can beat the dents out of little pots. I could show you what a woman might do."

He put his hammer back in the oily box and shoved the little anvil out of sight. "It would be a lonely life for a woman, ma'am, and a scarey life, too, with animals creeping under the wagon all night." He climbed over the singletree, steadying himself with a hand on the burro's white rump. He settled himself in the seat, picked up the lines. "Thank you kindly, ma'am," he said. "I'll do like you told me; I'll go back and catch the Salinas road."

"Mind," she called, "if you're long in getting there, keep the sand damp." 90

"Sand, ma'am? . . . Sand? Oh, sure. You mean around the chrysanthemums. Sure I will." He clucked his tongue. The beasts leaned luxuriously into their collars. The mongrel dog took his place between the back wheels. The wagon turned and crawled out the entrance road and back the way it had come, along the river.

Elisa stood in front of her wire fence watching the slow progress of the caravan. Her shoulders were straight, her head thrown back, her eyes half-closed, so that the scene came vaguely into them. Her lips moved silently, forming the words "Good-bye—good-bye." Then she whispered, "That's a bright direction. There's a glowing there." The sound of her whisper startled her. She shook herself free and looked about to see whether anyone had been listening. Only the dogs had heard. They lifted their heads toward her from their sleeping in the dust, and then stretched out their chins and settled asleep again. Elisa turned and ran hurriedly into the house.

In the kitchen she reached behind the stove and felt the water tank. It was full of hot water from the noonday cooking. In the bathroom she tore off her soiled clothes and flung them into the corner. And then she scrubbed herself with a little block of pumice, legs and thighs, loins and chest and arms, until her skin was scratched and red. When she had dried herself she stood in front of a mirror in her bedroom and looked at her body. She tightened her stomach and threw out her chest. She turned and looked over her shoulder at her back.

After a while she began to dress, slowly. She put on her newest underclothing and her nicest stockings and the dress which was the symbol of her prettiness. She worked carefully on her hair, penciled her eyebrows and rouged her lips.

Before she was finished she heard the little thunder of hoofs and the shouts of 95 Henry and his helper as they drove the red steers into the corral. She heard the gate bang shut and set herself for Henry's arrival.

His step sounded on the porch. He entered the house calling, "Elisa, where are you?"

"In my room, dressing. I'm not ready. There's hot water for your bath. Hurry up. It's getting late."

When she heard him splashing in the tub, Elisa laid his dark suit on the bed, and shirt and socks and tie beside it. She stood his polished shoes on the floor beside the bed. Then she went to the porch and sat primly and stiffly down. She looked toward the river road where the willow-line was still yellow with frosted

leaves so that under the high grey fog they seemed a thin band of sunshine. This
was the only color in the grey afternoon. She sat unmoving for a long time. Her
eyes blinked rarely.

Henry came banging out of the door, shoving his tie inside his vest as he came.
Elisa stiffened and her face grew tight. Henry stopped short and looked at her.
"Why—why, Elisa. You look so nice!"

"Nice? You think I look nice? What do you mean by 'nice'?"   100

Henry blundered on. "I don't know. I mean you look different, strong and happy."

"I am strong? Yes, strong. What do you mean 'strong'?"

He looked bewildered. "You're playing some kind of a game," he said helplessly.
"It's a kind of a play. You look strong enough to break a calf over your knee, happy
enough to eat it like a watermelon."

For a second she lost her rigidity. "Henry! Don't talk like that. You didn't know
what you said." She grew complete again. "I'm strong," she boasted. "I never knew
before how strong."

Henry looked down toward the tractor shed, and when he brought his eyes back   105
to her, they were his own again. "I'll get out the car. You can put on your coat while
I'm starting."

Elisa went into the house. She heard him drive to the gate and idle down his
motor, and then she took a long time to put on her hat. She pulled it here and
pressed it there. When Henry turned the motor off she slipped into her coat and
went out.

The little roadster bounced along on the dirt road by the river, raising the birds
and driving the rabbits into the brush. Two cranes flapped heavily over the willow-
line and dropped into the river-bed.

Far ahead on the road Elisa saw a dark speck. She knew.

She tried not to look as they passed it, but her eyes would not obey. She whispered to herself sadly, "He might have thrown them off the road. That wouldn't have
been much trouble, not very much. But he kept the pot," she explained. "He had to
keep the pot. That's why he couldn't get them off the road."

The roadster turned a bend and she saw the caravan ahead. She swung full   110
around toward her husband so she could not see the little covered wagon and the
mismatched team as the car passed them.

In a moment it was over. The thing was done. She did not look back.

She said loudly, to be heard above the motor, "It will be good, tonight, a good
dinner."

"Now you're changed again," Henry complained. He took one hand from the
wheel and patted her knee. "I ought to take you in to dinner oftener. It would be
good for both of us. We get so heavy out on the ranch."

"Henry," she asked, "could we have wine at dinner?"

"Sure we could. Say! That will be fine."   115

She was silent for a while; then she said, "Henry, at those prize fights, do the
men hurt each other very much?"

"Sometimes a little, not often. Why?"

"Well, I've read how they break noses, and blood runs down their chests. I've
read how the fighting gloves get heavy and soggy with blood."

He looked around at her. "What's the matter, Elisa? I didn't know you read
things like that." He brought the car to a stop, then turned to the right over the
Salinas River bridge.

"Do any women ever go to the fights?" she asked.   120

"Oh, sure, some. What's the matter, Elisa? Do you want to go? I don't think you'd like it, but I'll take you if you really want to go."

She relaxed limply in the seat. "Oh, no. No. I don't want to go. I'm sure I don't." Her face was turned away from him. "It will be enough if we can have wine. It will be plenty." She turned up her coat collar so he could not see that she was crying weakly—like an old woman.

Questions

1. When we first meet Elisa Allen in her garden, with what details does Steinbeck delineate her character for us?
2. Elisa works inside a "wire fence that protected her flower garden from cattle and dogs and chickens" (paragraph 9). What does this wire fence suggest?
3. How would you describe Henry and Elisa's marriage? Cite details from the story.
4. With what motive does the traveling salesman take an interest in Elisa's chrysanthemums? What immediate effect does his interest have on Elisa?
5. For what possible purpose does Steinbeck give us such a detailed account of Elisa's preparations for her evening out? Notice her tearing off her soiled clothes and her scrubbing her body with pumice (paragraphs 93–94).
6. Of what significance to Elisa is the sight of the contents of the flower pot discarded in the road? Notice that, as her husband's car overtakes the covered wagon, Elisa turns away; and then Steinbeck adds, "In a moment it was over. The thing was done. She did not look back" (paragraph 111). Explain this passage.
7. How do you interpret Elisa's asking for wine with dinner? How do you account for her new interest in prizefights?
8. In a sentence, try to state this short story's theme.
9. Why are Elisa Allen's chrysanthemums so important to this story? Sum up what you understand them to mean.

Guy de Maupassant

The Necklace   1884

Translated by John Siscoe

Henri René Albert Guy de Maupassant (1850–1893) was born in a rented castle in Normandy. The son of minor aristocrats (the de *in his surname denotes a noble family), Maupassant grew up overshadowed by his parents' unhappy marriage. His mother was a friend of the novelist Gustave Flaubert, who took the teenage boy under his tutelage. "He is my disciple," Flaubert declared, "and I love him like a son." Although Maupassant studied law, the Franco-Prussian war of 1870 inspired him to enlist as a solider. After the war he worked briefly as a minor bureaucrat while continuing to study privately with Flaubert. Finally Maupassant quit his government job and dedicated himself to literature, writing more than three hundred short stories, six novels—most notably* Pierre and Jean *(1888)—and three travel books in the decade before*

Guy de Maupassant

his untimely death. Wealthy and internationally famous from his stories, the hardworking author lived luxuriously. After contracting syphilis (then incurable) in his twenties, Maupassant watched his own health and sanity deteriorate. He died one month before his forty-third birthday.

She was one of those lovely and charming young women born, as if by some quirk of fate, into a family of commoners. She had no dowry, no prospects, no chance to meet a rich and distinguished man who would love, understand, and marry her. So she let herself be married to an insignificant clerk in the Ministry of Education.

She dressed simply, being unable to adorn herself. But she was unhappy, as if she had been denied her rightful place in society. For women recognize neither caste nor lineage; their beauty, grace, and charm serve them instead of birth and family. A natural delicacy, an instinct for elegance, a sparkling wit; these alone define their social status, enabling the daughter of the poor to be the equal of the greatest of ladies.

Believing that she had been born to enjoy every refinement and luxury, she suffered deeply. She suffered from her wretched apartment, from its dingy walls, worn-out chairs, and ugly upholstery. All these things, which another woman of her class wouldn't even have noticed, tormented and infuriated her. The sight of the little Breton girl going about her simple housework aroused in her deep regrets and hopeless dreams. She would imagine gleaming reception rooms rich with oriental draperies, lit by high bronze sconces, with two tall footmen in knee breeches dozing in large armchairs, overcome by the central heating. She would imagine great halls decorated in antique silk, with furniture of fine workmanship displaying priceless bibelots. There were also smaller, more intimate rooms, elegant and perfumed, ideal for five o'clock chats with one's closest friends, men who were well known and much in demand, whose company and attentions all women envied and admired.

When she sat down to dinner, the round table was covered with a cloth that hadn't been cleaned for three days. Across the table her husband, as he lifted the lid of the tureen, exclaimed with delight: "Ah! Good old beef stew! Could there be anything better?" But she was dreaming of refined dinners, of glittering silverware, while on the walls tapestries portrayed people from olden times and exotic birds in the midst of a fairytale forest. She dreamt of exquisite meals served on marvelous china, and of murmured compliments that she would reward with an inscrutable smile, while she tasted the pink flesh of a trout or the wings of a grouse.

She had no fine dresses, no jewels, nothing. Yet luxury was all she cared about; 5 she felt that she had been born for it. She wanted so much to give pleasure, to be envied, to be alluring and admired.

She had one rich friend, a girl she had known in convent school, whom she couldn't bear to visit anymore, because when she returned home she would feel miserable. And she would cry for days on end, from sorrow, regret, despair, and grief.

One evening her husband came home looking very pleased with himself, and holding a large envelope.

"Here's a little something for you."

She immediately tore open the envelope. Inside was a card which read:

"The Minister of Education and Madame Georges Ramponneau request that 10 Monsieur and Madame Loisel would do them the honor of spending the evening with them at the Ministry on Monday, January eighteenth."

Instead of being thrilled, as her husband had hoped, she scornfully tossed the invitation onto the table, muttering:

"What do you want me to do with this?"

"But darling, I thought you'd be pleased. You never go out, and this really is a special occasion. It wasn't easy for me to get that card. Everybody wanted one, there weren't many being handed out, especially to the clerks. You'll see all the important officials there."

She glared at him and said impatiently:

"And what do you expect me to wear?"   15

He hadn't given it a thought. He stammered:

"What about the dress—the one you wear to the theater. It seems perfectly fine to me . . ."

He fell silent, at a loss, struck dumb, as he watched his wife crying. Two large tears slowly trickled down from the corners of her eyes to the corners of her mouth. He blurted out:

"What's wrong? What's the matter?"

But with a supreme effort she had stifled her grief and replied in a calm voice,   20
dabbing at her cheeks:

"It's nothing. But as I haven't a thing to wear, I can't attend this party. Go give your card to a colleague whose wife has a better wardrobe than mine."

He was devastated. He replied:

"Look, Mathilde, how much would a suitable dress cost, one that you could wear on other occasions, something very simple?"

She thought a moment, estimating the costs, and also calculating how much she might ask from this thrifty clerk without risking a cry of horror and immediate rejection.

At last she said hesitantly: 25

"I can't say for certain, but I might be able to find one for four hundred francs."

He blanched a little, since he'd put aside that very sum to buy a rifle so he could go hunting next summer on the Nanterre plain, with some friends who went there on Sundays to shoot larks.

However he said:

"All right. I'll give you four hundred francs. But try to make sure that it's a nice dress."

The day of the ball drew near, and Madame Loisel seemed sad, restless, and wor-   30
ried. And yet her dress was ready. One evening her husband said to her:

"What's the matter with you? You've been acting strange for the past three days."

And she replied:

"I'm upset because I haven't a single piece of jewelry or a gemstone or anything to wear with my dress. I'll look like a pauper. I almost think it would be better if I didn't go."

"What if you wore flowers? They're very chic right now. Ten francs would get you two or three magnificent roses."

She wasn't convinced.   35

"No . . . There's nothing more humiliating than to look poor when you're sur-rounded by rich women."

Then her husband exclaimed:

"Here's what you do: go and look up your friend Madame Forestier and ask her to loan you some of her jewelry. After all, you know each other well enough."

She gave a cry of joy.

"You're right. It didn't occur to me."   40

The next day she paid her friend a visit and explained her problem. Madame Forestier went over to her mirrored wardrobe and took out a large jewelry case. She brought it back, opened it, and said to Madame Loisel:

"You choose, my dear."

First she examined some bracelets, then a pearl necklace, then a finely wrought Venetian cross of gold and gems. She tried on the jewelry in front of the mirror, hesitating, unable to decide which to take and which to leave behind. She kept asking:

"Do you have anything else?"

"I do. Here, take a look yourself. I don't know what would please you."   45

Suddenly she discovered, in a black satin case, a stunning diamond necklace, and her heart began to throb with intense desire. Her hands trembled as she lifted up the necklace. She fastened it around her neck, below the high collar of her dress, and she gazed at her reflection in ecstasy.

Then she asked in a hesitant, anxious voice:

"Would you loan me this, just this?"

"Yes, of course."

She fell on her friend's neck, embraced her passionately, and then fled with her   50
treasure.

The day of the ball arrived: Madame Loisel was a success. She was the loveliest of all; elegant, graceful, smiling, and radiant with joy. All the men looked at her, asked who she was, and wanted to be introduced to her. Every cabinet attaché wanted a waltz with her. The Minister noticed her.

She danced with fervor, with passion, drunk with pleasure, no longer thinking of anything. The triumph of her beauty and the glory of her success enveloped her in a sort of cloud of happiness made up of all the compliments, all the admiring glances, all the awakened desires of this victory so complete and so dear to a woman's heart.

She left around four in the morning. Since midnight her husband had been dozing in a small side room, along with three other gentlemen whose wives had been having a grand time.

He threw over her shoulders the wraps he had brought for the journey home. Humble, everyday things, their shabbiness contrasted with her elegant dress. Sensing this, she wanted to leave at once so as to escape the notice of the other women wrapping themselves in their expensive furs.

Loisel held her back.   55

"Wait here. You'll catch cold outside. I'll go hail a cab."

But she wouldn't listen to him and hurried down the stairs. When they reached the street they didn't see any cabs so they went looking for one, calling out to the coachmen they saw passing in the distance.

Discouraged and shivering, they walked toward the Seine. Finally, on the quay, they found one of those old "sleepwalkers"—cabs that never make their appearance until after dark, as if they were ashamed to show their decrepit selves by day.

It brought them to their building's front door on the Rue de Martyrs, and they made the sad climb up the stairs to their apartment. For her it was all over. And he couldn't help thinking that he'd have to be at his desk by ten o'clock.

Standing in front of the mirror, she pulled the wraps off her shoulders so that   60
she could see herself one more time in all her glory. But suddenly she gave a cry. Her throat was bare: the necklace was gone.

Her husband, already half-undressed, asked:

"What is it?"

She looked at him, panic-stricken:

"I . . . I . . . I don't have Madame Forestier's necklace."

He stood up, bewildered.

"What? . . . How? . . . That's impossible."

And they searched in the folds of the dress, in the folds of the cloak, in the pockets, everywhere. They found nothing.

He asked:

"Are you sure that you still had it when you left the ball?"

"Yes. I touched it, in the vestibule at the Ministry."

"But if you had lost it on the street we would have heard it fall. So it must be in the cab."

"Yes. That makes sense. Did you take down the number?"

"No. You didn't notice it, did you?"

"No."

"They stared at one another, dumbfounded. Finally Loisel started to get dressed.

"I'm going to retrace our steps to see if I can't find it."

And he left. Still in her elegant dress, too nervous to sleep, she sat huddled in her chair, unable to act or to think.

He husband came back around seven o'clock, empty-handed.

That day he filed a report at police headquarters, he placed ads in the newspapers, he inquired at the cab companies; in short he tried everything that had a ghost of a chance.

She waited all day long, still overwhelmed by the weight of the catastrophe.

Loisel returned that evening, his face lined and pale. Nothing had turned up.

"You are going to have to write your friend," he said. "Tell her that you've broken the clasp of her necklace and that you're having it repaired. That will buy us some time."

She wrote as he dictated.

After a week they had lost all hope.

And Loisel, who had aged five years, said:

"We'll have to try to replace the necklace."

The next morning they took the empty case to the jeweler whose name was inside. He consulted his account books.

"I didn't sell such a necklace, Madame. It appears I only provided the case."

So they went from jeweler to jeweler looking for a duplicate necklace, searching their memories, both of them sick with grief and anxiety.

They found, at a store in the Palais-Royal, a diamond necklace that seemed to them almost identical to the original. The price was forty thousand francs. The store would let them have it for thirty-six thousand.

They asked the jeweler to hold it for them for three days. And they reached an agreement that they could return it for a refund of thirty-four thousand francs if they had found the original before the end of February.

Loisel had eighteen thousand francs which his father had left him. He would have to borrow the rest.

And borrow he did, asking now a thousand francs from one, five hundred francs from another, five louis here, three louis there. He signed notes, made reckless promises, struck deals with usurers, with every kind of loan shark. He placed everything he had at risk, signing papers without even knowing if he could fulfill their terms. Haunted by the fear of what lay before him, by the black fate that was about to engulf him, by the prospect of physical hardship and moral agony, he went to the jeweler's and picked up the new necklace, leaving behind on the counter thirty-six thousand francs.

When Madame Loisel brought the necklace to Madame Forestier, the latter said coldly:

"You could have returned it sooner. I might have needed it."   95

She didn't open the case, as her friend feared that she would. If she had noticed the substitution, what would she have thought? What would she have said? Would she have taken her for a thief?

Madame Loisel came to know the wretched life of the poor. Yet she played her part heroically, without faltering. The terrible debt had to be paid. She would pay it. The maid was let go, and they moved from their apartment into a garret, under the eaves.

She came to know the heavy burden of housework and the lowly chores of the kitchen. She scrubbed the dishes, ruining her pink nails scouring the greasy pots and the bottoms of pans. She washed the dirty laundry, the shirts and the cleaning rags, hanging them up on the line to dry. Every morning she would haul the garbage down to the street and carry fresh water back up the stairs, pausing at every landing to catch her breath. Dressed as the poor woman she was, she would scurry from fruit-seller to grocer to butcher, basket on her arm, haggling, arguing, trying to stretch every miserable sou.

Every month they had to pay off some debts, and renew others to pay off later.

Her husband worked evenings balancing a shopkeeper's account books. And he   100
frequently worked nights as well, copying out documents at five sous a page.

And this life lasted for ten years.

When the ten years had come to an end they had paid off everything, including the usurers' fees and the accumulated interest.

Madame Loisel looked old now. She had become the sort of woman often found in poor households: tough, grasping, and coarse. With her hair uncombed, her skirts askew, with red hands, talking in a loud voice, she would wash and scrub the floors. But sometimes, while her husband was at work, she would sit by the window and remember that evening long ago, and that ball where she had been so lovely and so admired.

What might have happened if she hadn't lost that necklace? Who could know? Who could know? Life was so strange, so uncertain: the slightest thing could either ruin you or save you!

One Sunday in the Champs Elysees, while she was taking a walk as a respite   105
from the week's chores, she suddenly noticed a woman walking with a child. It was Madame Forestier: still young, still lovely, still alluring.

Madame Loisel felt moved. Should she speak to her? Yes, she should. And now that she'd paid her debts, she could tell her the whole story. Why not?

She went up to her.

"Hello Jeanne."

The lady, who didn't recognize her, was startled to be addressed so familiarly by a badly dressed stranger.

She stammered: 110

"But . . . Madame . . . I don't know . . . You must be mistaken."

"No. I am Mathilde Loisel."

"Oh! . . . My poor Mathilde, how you've changed!"

"Yes, I've had some hard times since I saw you last, and plenty of misery—and all on account of you."

"Of me? What do you mean?"   115

"I take it you remember the diamond necklace that you let me borrow for the Minister's ball?"

"Yes. So?"

"So I lost it."

"But how? You returned it to me."

"I brought you another that was just like it. And we've spent the last ten years paying for it. You can imagine that it wasn't easy for us, since we had nothing . . . But now, I'm glad to say, it's over and done with at last." 120

Madame Forestier froze.

"You're saying that you bought a diamond necklace to replace mine?"

"Yes. And you never guessed, did you? They were so alike."

And she smiled with a proud and naïve joy.

Madame Forestier, deeply moved, reached out with both of her hands. 125

"Oh, my poor Mathilde! But mine was a fake. It wasn't worth more than five hundred francs."

Questions

1. Why does Mathilde Loisel borrow her friend's diamond necklace for the ball? What do her motivations reveal about her character?

2. Why does Mathilde not admit to her friend that she lost her necklace?

3. How do the Loisels afford the new necklace? What obligations and sacrifices does its purchase involve?

4. The diamond necklace is a symbol whose significance shifts with each turn in the story. What does the necklace represent at the start of the story, when Mathilde attends the ball? What does it represent through the middle of the story, after it is lost? And what does it represent at the end of the story, when the protagonist discovers that the piece of jewelry was not valuable?

5. What is ironic about the story's conclusion? What other ironic elements are present in this story?

Ursula K. Le Guin

The Ones Who Walk Away from Omelas
1975

Ursula Kroeber Le Guin (1929–2018) was born on St. Ursula's Day (October 21) in Berkeley, California, the only daughter and youngest child of Theodora Kroeber, a folklorist, and Alfred Kroeber, a renowned anthropologist. Le Guin attended Radcliffe College and then entered Columbia University to do graduate work in French and Italian literature. While completing her master's, she wrote her first stories. In the early sixties Le Guin began publishing in both science fiction pulp magazines and academic journals. In 1966 her first novel, Rocannon's World, was published as an Ace science fiction paperback original—hardly a respectable format for the debut of one of America's premier writers. In 1968 Le Guin published A Wizard of Earthsea, the first novel in her Earthsea series, now considered a classic of young adult literature.

Ursula K. Le Guin

The next two volumes, The Tombs of Atuan *(1971), which won a Newbery citation, and* The Farthest Shore *(1972), which won a National Book Award, brought Le Guin mainstream acclaim. Le Guin's novels* The Left Hand of Darkness *(1969) and* The Dispossessed *(1974) won both the Hugo and the Nebula awards, science fiction's two most prized honors. Le Guin published more than thirty novels and many volumes of short stories, poetry, and essays. One of her later novels was the Locus Award–winning* Lavinia *(2008). In 2008, Le Guin was awarded the National Book Foundation Medal for Distinguished Contribution to American Letters. She died in 2018 at her long-time home in Portland, Oregon.*

One of the few science fiction writers whose work has earned general critical acclaim, Le Guin belongs most naturally in the company of major novelists of ideas such as Aldous Huxley, George Orwell, and Anthony Burgess, who have used the genre of science fiction to explore the possible consequences of ideological rather than technological change. Le Guin was especially concerned with issues of social justice and equality. In her short stories—including "The Ones Who Walk Away from Omelas"—she created complex imaginary civilizations, envisioned with anthropological authority, and her aim was less to imagine alien cultures than to explore humanity.

With a clamor of bells that set the swallows soaring, the Festival of Summer came to the city Omelas, bright-towered by the sea. The rigging of the boats in harbor sparkled with flags. In the streets between houses with red roofs and painted walls, between old moss-grown gardens and under avenues of trees, past great parks and public buildings, processions moved. Some were decorous: old people in long stiff robes of mauve and grey, grave master workmen, quiet, merry women carrying their babies and chatting as they walked. In other streets the music beat faster, a shimmering of gong and tambourine, and the people went dancing, the procession was a dance. Children dodged in and out, their high calls rising like the swallows' crossing flights over the music and the singing. All the processions wound towards the north side of the city, where on the great water-meadow called the Green Fields boys and girls, naked in the bright air, with mud-stained feet and ankles and long, lithe arms, exercised their restive horses before the race. The horses wore no gear at all but a halter without bit. Their manes were braided with streamers of silver, gold, and green. They flared their nostrils and pranced and boasted to one another; they were vastly excited, the horse being the only animal who has adopted our ceremonies as his own. Far off to the north and west the mountains stood up half encircling Omelas on her bay. The air of morning was so clear that the snow still crowning the Eighteen Peaks burned with white-gold fire across the miles of sunlit air, under the dark blue of the sky. There was just enough wind to make the banners that marked the racecourse snap and flutter now and then. In the silence of the broad green meadows one could hear the music winding through the city streets, farther and nearer and ever approaching, a cheerful faint sweetness of the air that from time to time trembled and gathered together and broke out into the great joyous clanging of the bells.

Joyous! How is one to tell about joy? How describe the citizens of Omelas?

They were not simple folk, you see, though they were happy. But we do not say the words of cheer much any more. All smiles have become archaic. Given a description such as this one tends to make certain assumptions. Given a description such as this one tends to look next for the King, mounted on a splendid stallion and surrounded by his noble knights, or perhaps in a golden litter borne by great-muscled slaves. But there was no king. They did not use swords, or keep slaves. They were not barbarians. I do not know the rules and laws of their society, but I suspect that they were singularly few. As they did without monarchy and slavery, so they also got on without the stock exchange, the advertisement, the secret police, and the bomb. Yet I repeat that these were not simple folk, not dulcet shepherds, noble savages, bland utopians. They were not less complex than us. The trouble is that we have a bad habit, encouraged by pedants and sophisticates, of considering happiness as something rather stupid. Only pain is intellectual, only evil interesting. This is the treason of the artist: a refusal to admit the banality of evil and the terrible boredom of pain. If you can't lick 'em, join 'em. If it hurts, repeat it. But to praise despair is to condemn delight, to embrace violence is to lose hold of everything else. We have almost lost hold; we can no longer describe a happy man, nor make any celebration of joy. How can I tell you about the people of Omelas? They were not naïve and happy children—though their children were, in fact, happy. They were mature, intelligent, passionate adults whose lives were not wretched. O miracle! but I wish I could describe it better. I wish I could convince you. Omelas sounds in my words like a city in a fairy tale, long ago and far away, once upon a time. Perhaps it would be best if you imagined it as your own fancy bids, assuming it will rise to the occasion, for certainly I cannot suit you all. For instance, how about technology? I think that there would be no cars or helicopters in and above the streets; this follows from the fact that the people of Omelas are happy people. Happiness is based on a just discrimination of what is necessary, what is neither necessary nor destructive, and what is destructive. In the middle category, however—that of the unnecessary but undestructive, that of comfort, luxury, exuberance, etc.—they could perfectly well have central heating, subway trains, washing machines, and all kinds of marvelous devices not yet invented here, floating light-sources, fuelless power, a cure for the common cold. Or they could have none of that: it doesn't matter. As you like it. I incline to think that people from towns up and down the coast have been coming in to Omelas during the last days before the Festival on very fast little trains and double-decked trams, and that the train station of Omelas is actually the handsomest building in town, though plainer than the magnificent Farmers' Market. But even granted trains, I fear that Omelas so far strikes some of you as goody-goody. Smiles, bells, parades, horses, bleh. If so, please add an orgy. If an orgy would help, don't hesitate. Let us not, however, have temples from which issue beautiful nude priests and priestesses already half in ecstasy and ready to copulate with any man or woman, lover or stranger, who desires union with the deep godhead of the blood, although that was my first idea. But really it would be better not to have any temples in Omelas—at least, not manned temples. Religion yes, clergy no. Surely the beautiful nudes can just wander about, offering themselves like divine soufflés to the hunger of the needy and the rapture of the flesh. Let them join the processions. Let tambourines be struck above the copulations, and the glory of desire be proclaimed upon the gongs, and (a not unimportant point) let the offspring of these delightful rituals be beloved and looked after by all. One thing I know there is none of in Omelas is guilt. But what else should there be? I thought at first there were no drugs, but that is puritanical. For those who like it, the faint insistent sweetness of *drooz* may perfume the ways of the city, *drooz* which first brings a great lightness and brilliance to the mind and limbs, and then after some hours a dreamy languor, and wonderful visions at last of the very arcana and inmost secrets of the Universe, as well as exciting the pleasure of sex beyond all belief; and it is not habit-forming. For more modest tastes I think there ought to be beer. What else, what else belongs in the joyous city? The sense of victory, surely, the celebration of courage. But as we did without clergy, let us do without soldiers. The joy built upon successful slaughter is not the right kind of joy; it will not do; it is fearful and it is trivial. A boundless and generous contentment, a magnanimous triumph felt not against some outer enemy but in communion with the finest and fairest in the souls of all men everywhere and the splendor of the world's summer: this is what swells the hearts of the people of Omelas, and the victory they celebrate is that of life. I really don't think many of them need to take *drooz*.

Most of the processions have reached the Green Fields by now. A marvelous smell of cooking goes forth from the red and blue tents of the provisioners. The faces of small children are amiably sticky; in the benign grey beard of a man a couple of crumbs of rich pastry are entangled. The youths and girls have mounted their horses and are beginning to group around the starting line of the course. An old woman, small, fat, and laughing, is passing out flowers from a basket, and tall young men wear her flowers in their shining hair. A child of nine or ten sits at the edge of the crowd, alone, playing on a wooden flute. People pause to listen, and they smile, but they do not speak to him, for he never ceases playing and never sees them, his dark eyes wholly rapt in the sweet, thin magic of the tune.

He finishes, and slowly lowers his hands holding the wooden flute.   5

As if that little private silence were the signal, all at once a trumpet sounds from the pavilion near the starting line: imperious, melancholy, piercing. The horses rear on their slender legs, and some of them neigh in answer. Sober-faced, the young riders stroke the horses' necks and soothe them, whispering, "Quiet, quiet, there my beauty, my hope. . . ." They begin to form in rank along the starting line. The crowds along the racecourse are like a field of grass and flowers in the wind. The Festival of Summer has begun.

Do you believe? Do you accept the festival, the city, the joy? No? Then let me describe one more thing.

In a basement under one of the beautiful public buildings of Omelas, or perhaps in the cellar of one of its spacious private homes, there is a room. It has one locked door, and no window. A little light seeps in dustily between cracks in the boards, secondhand from a cobwebbed window somewhere across the cellar. In one corner of the little room a couple of mops, with stiff, clotted, foul-smelling heads, stand near a rusty bucket. The floor is dirt, a little damp to the touch, as cellar dirt usually is. The room is about three paces long and two wide: a mere broom closet or disused tool room. In the room a child is sitting. It could be a boy or a girl. It looks about six, but actually is nearly ten. It is feeble-minded. Perhaps it was born defective, or perhaps it has become imbecile through fear, malnutrition, and neglect. It picks its nose and occasionally fumbles vaguely with its toes or genitals, as it sits hunched in the corner farthest from the bucket and the two mops. It is afraid of the mops. It finds them horrible. It shuts its eyes, but it knows the mops are still standing there; and the door is locked; and nobody will come. The door is always locked; and nobody ever comes, except that sometimes—the child has no understanding of time or interval—sometimes the door rattles terribly and opens, and a person, or several people, are there. One of them may come in and kick the child to make it stand up. The others never come close, but peer in at it with frightened, disgusted eyes. The food bowl and the water jug are hastily filled, the door is locked, the eyes disappear. The people at the door never say anything, but the child, who has not always lived in the tool room, and can remember sunlight and its mother's voice, sometimes speaks. "I will be good," it says. "Please let me out. I will be good!" They never answer. The child used to scream for help at night, and cry a good deal, but now it only makes a kind of whining, "eh-haa, eh-haa," and it speaks less and less often. It is so thin there are no calves to its legs; its belly protrudes; it lives on a half-bowl of corn meal and grease a day. It is naked. Its buttocks and thighs are a mass of festered sores, as it sits in its own excrement continually.

They all know it is there, all the people of Omelas. Some of them have come to see it, others are content merely to know it is there. They all know that it has to be there. Some of them understand why, and some do not, but they all understand that their happiness, the beauty of their city, the tenderness of their friendships, the health of their children, the wisdom of their scholars, the skill of their makers, even the abundance of their harvest and the kindly weathers of their skies, depend wholly on this child's abominable misery.

This is usually explained to children when they are between eight and twelve, whenever they seem capable of understanding; and most of those who come to see the child are young people, though often enough an adult comes, or comes back, to see the child. No matter how well the matter has been explained to them, these young spectators are always shocked and sickened at the sight. They feel disgust, which they had thought themselves superior to. They feel anger, outrage, impotence, despite all the explanations. They would like to do something for the child. But there is nothing they can do. If the child were brought up into the sunlight out of that vile place, if it were cleaned and fed and comforted, that would be a good thing, indeed; but if it were done, in that day and hour all the prosperity and beauty and delight of Omelas would wither and be destroyed. Those are the terms. To exchange all the goodness and grace of every life in Omelas for that single, small improvement: to throw away the happiness of thousands for the chance of the happiness of one: that would be to let guilt within the walls indeed.

The terms are strict and absolute; there may not even be a kind word spoken to the child.

Often the young people go home in tears, or in a tearless rage, when they have seen the child and faced this terrible paradox. They may brood over it for weeks or years. But as time goes on they begin to realize that even if the child could be released, it would not get much good of its freedom: a little vague pleasure of warmth and food, no doubt, but little more. It is too degraded and imbecile to know any real joy. It has been afraid too long ever to be free of fear. Its habits are too uncouth for it to respond to humane treatment. Indeed, after so long it would probably be wretched without walls about it to protect it, and darkness for its eyes, and its own excrement to sit in. Their tears at the bitter injustice dry when they begin to perceive the terrible justice of reality, and to accept it. Yet it is their tears and anger, the trying of their generosity and the acceptance of their helplessness, which are perhaps the true source of the splendor of their lives. Theirs is no vapid, irresponsible happiness. They know that they, like the child, are not free. They know compassion. It is the existence of the child, and their knowledge of its existence, that makes possible the nobility of their architecture, the poignancy of their music, the profundity of their science. It is because of the child that they are so gentle with children. They know that if the wretched one were not there snivelling in the dark, the other one, the flute-player, could make no joyful music as the young riders line up in their beauty for the race in the sunlight of the first morning of summer.

Now do you believe in them? Are they not more credible? But there is one more thing to tell, and this is quite incredible.

At times one of the adolescent girls or boys who go to see the child does not go home to weep or rage, does not, in fact, go home at all. Sometimes also a man or woman much older falls silent for a day or two, and then leaves home. These people go out into the street, and walk down the street alone. They keep walking, and walk straight out of the city of Omelas, through the beautiful gates. They keep walking across the farmlands of Omelas. Each one goes alone, youth or girl, man or woman. Night falls; the traveler must pass down village streets, between the houses with yellow-lit windows, and on out into the darkness of the fields. Each alone, they go west or north, toward the mountains.

They go on. They leave Omelas, they walk ahead into the darkness, and they do not come back. The place they go towards is a place even less imaginable to most of us than the city of happiness. I cannot describe it at all. It is possible that it does not exist. But they seem to know where they are going, the ones who walk away from Omelas.

Questions

1. Does the narrator live in Omelas? What do we know about the narrator's society?
2. What is the narrator's opinion of Omelas? Does the author seem to share that opinion?
3. What is the narrator's attitude toward "the ones who walk away from Omelas"? Would the narrator have been one of those who walked away?
4. How do you account for the narrator's willingness to let readers add anything they like to the story?—"If an orgy would help, don't hesitate" (paragraph 3). Didn't Ursula Le Guin care what her story includes?
5. What is suggested by the locked, dark cellar in which the child sits? What other details in the story are suggestive enough to be called symbolic?
6. Do you find in the story any implied criticism of our own society?

Shirley Jackson

The Lottery
1948

*Shirley Jackson (1919–1965), a native of San Francisco, moved in her teens to Rochester, New York. She started college at the University of Rochester, but had to drop out, stricken by severe depression, a problem that was to recur at intervals throughout her life. Later she graduated from Syracuse University. With her husband, Stanley Edgar Hyman, a literary critic, she settled in Bennington, Vermont, in a sprawling house built in the nineteenth century. There Jackson conscientiously set herself to produce a fixed number of words each day. She wrote novels—*The Road Through the Wall *(1948)—and three psychological thrillers—*Hangsaman *(1951),* The Haunting of Hill House *(1959), and* We Have Always Lived in the Castle *(1962). She wrote light, witty articles for* Good Housekeeping *and other popular magazines about the horrors of housekeeping and rearing four children, collected in* Life Among the Savages *(1953) and* Raising Demons *(1957); but she claimed to have written them only for money. When "The Lottery" appeared in the* New Yorker *in 1948, that issue of the magazine quickly sold out. Her purpose in writing the story, Jackson declared, had been "to shock the story's readers with a graphic demonstration of the pointless violence and general inhumanity in their own lives."*

The morning of June 27th was clear and sunny, with the fresh warmth of a full-summer day; the flowers were blossoming profusely and the grass was richly green. The people of the village began to gather in the square, between the post office and the bank, around ten o'clock; in some towns there were so many people that the lottery took two days and had to be started on June 26th, but in this village, where there were only about three hundred people, the whole lottery took less than two hours, so it could begin at ten o'clock in the morning and still be through in time to allow the villagers to get home for noon dinner.

The children assembled first, of course. School was recently over for the summer, and the feeling of liberty sat uneasily on most of them; they tended to gather together quietly for a while before they broke into boisterous play, and their talk was still of the classroom and the teacher, of books and reprimands. Bobby Martin had already stuffed his pockets full of stones, and the other boys soon followed his example, selecting the smoothest and roundest stones; Bobby and Harry Jones and Dickie Delacroix—the villagers pronounced this name "Dellacroy"—eventually made a great pile of stones in one corner of the square and guarded it against the raids of the other boys. The girls stood aside, talking among themselves, looking over their shoulders at the boys, and the very small children rolled in the dust or clung to the hands of their older brothers or sisters.

Soon the men began to gather, surveying their own children, speaking of planting and rain, tractors and taxes. They stood together, away from the pile of stones in the corner, and their jokes were quiet and they smiled rather than laughed. The women, wearing faded house dresses and sweaters, came shortly after their menfolk. They greeted one another and exchanged bits of gossip as they went to join their husbands. Soon the women, standing by their husbands, began to call to their children, and the children came reluctantly, having to be called four or five times. Bobby Martin ducked under his mother's grasping hand and ran, laughing, back to the pile of stones. His father spoke up sharply, and Bobby came quickly and took his place between his father and his oldest brother.

The lottery was conducted—as were the square dances, the teenage club, the Halloween program—by Mr. Summers, who had time and energy to devote to civic activities. He was a roundfaced, jovial man and he ran the coal business, and people were sorry for him, because he had no children and his wife was a scold. When he arrived in the square, carrying the black wooden box, there was a murmur of conversation among the villagers and he waved and called, "Little late today, folks." The postmaster, Mr. Graves, followed him, carrying a three-legged stool, and the stool was put in the center of the square and Mr. Summers set the black box down on it. The villagers kept their distance, leaving a space between themselves and the stool, and when Mr. Summers said, "Some of you fellows want to give me a hand?" there was a hesitation before two men, Mr. Martin and his oldest son, Baxter, came forward to hold the box steady on the stool while Mr. Summers stirred up the papers inside it.

The original paraphernalia for the lottery had been lost long ago, and the black box now resting on the stool had been put into use even before Old Man Warner, the oldest man in town, was born. Mr. Summers spoke frequently to the villagers about making a new box, but no one liked to upset even as much tradition as was represented by the black box. There was a story that the present box had been made with some pieces of the box that had preceded it, the one that had been constructed when the first people settled down to make a village here. Every year, after the lottery, Mr. Summers began talking again about a new box, but every year the subject was allowed to fade off without anything's being done. The black box grew shabbier each year; by now it was no longer completely black but splintered badly along one side to show the original wood color, and in some places faded or stained.

Mr. Martin and his oldest son, Baxter, held the black box securely on the stool until Mr. Summers had stirred the papers thoroughly with his hand. Because so much of the ritual had been forgotten or discarded, Mr. Summers had been successful in having slips of paper substituted for the chips of wood that had been used for generations. Chips of wood, Mr. Summers had argued, had been all very well when the village was tiny, but now that the population was more than three hundred and likely to keep on growing, it was necessary to use something that would fit more easily into the black box. The night before the lottery, Mr. Summers and Mr. Graves made up the slips of paper and put them in the box, and it was then taken to the safe of Mr. Summers's coal company and locked up until Mr. Summers was ready to take it to the square next morning. The rest of the year, the box was put away, sometimes one place, sometimes

5

another; it had spent one year in Mr. Graves's barn and another year underfoot in the post office, and sometimes it was set on a shelf in the Martin grocery and left there.

There was a great deal of fussing to be done before Mr. Summers declared the lottery open. There were lists to make up—of heads of families, heads of households in each family, members of each household in each family. There was the proper swearing-in of Mr. Summers by the postmaster, as the official of the lottery; at one time, some people remembered, there had been a recital of some sort, performed by the official of the lottery, a perfunctory, tuneless chant that had been rattled off duly each year; some people believed that the official of the lottery used to stand just so when he said or sang it, others believed that he was supposed to walk among the people, but years and years ago this part of the ritual had been allowed to lapse. There had been, also, a ritual salute, which the official of the lottery had had to use in addressing each person who came up to draw from the box, but this also had changed with time, until now it was felt necessary only for the official to speak to each person approaching. Mr. Summers was very good at all this; in his clean white shirt and blue jeans, with one hand resting carelessly on the black box, he seemed very proper and important as he talked interminably to Mr. Graves and the Martins.

Just as Mr. Summers finally left off talking and turned to the assembled villagers, Mrs. Hutchinson came hurriedly along the path to the square, her sweater thrown over her shoulders, and slid into place in the back of the crowd. "Clean forgot what day it was," she said to Mrs. Delacroix, who stood next to her, and they both laughed softly. "Thought my old man was out back stacking wood," Mrs. Hutchinson went on, "and then I looked out the window and the kids were gone, and then I remembered it was the twenty-seventh and came a-running." She dried her hands on her apron, and Mrs. Delacroix said, "You're in time, though. They're still talking away up there."

Mrs. Hutchinson craned her neck to see through the crowd and found her husband and children standing near the front. She tapped Mrs. Delacroix on the arm as a farewell and began to make her way through the crowd. The people separated good-humoredly to let her through; two or three people said, in voices just loud enough to be heard across the crowd, "Here comes your Missus, Hutchinson," and "Bill, she made it after all." Mrs. Hutchinson reached her husband, and Mr. Summers, who had been waiting, said cheerfully, "Thought we were going to have to get on without you, Tessie." Mrs. Hutchinson said, grinning, "Wouldn't have me leave m'dishes in the sink, now would you, Joe?" and soft laughter ran through the crowd as the people stirred back into position after Mrs. Hutchinson's arrival.

"Well, now," Mr. Summers said soberly, "guess we better get started, get this over   10 with, so's we can go back to work. Anybody ain't here?"

"Dunbar," several people said. "Dunbar, Dunbar."

Mr. Summers consulted his list. "Clyde Dunbar," he said. "That's right. He's broke his leg, hasn't he? Who's drawing for him?"

"Me, I guess," a woman said, and Mr. Summers turned to look at her. "Wife draws for her husband," Mr. Summers said. "Don't you have a grown boy to do it for you, Janey?" Although Mr. Summers and everyone else in the village knew the answer perfectly well, it was the business of the official of the lottery to ask such questions formally. Mr. Summers waited with an expression of polite interest while Mrs. Dunbar answered.

"Horace's not but sixteen yet," Mrs. Dunbar said regretfully. "Guess I gotta fill in for the old man this year."

"Right," Mr. Summers said. He made a note on the list he was holding. Then he   15 asked, "Watson boy drawing this year?"

A tall boy in the crowd raised his hand. "Here," he said. "I'm drawing for m'mother and me." He blinked his eyes nervously and ducked his head as several voices in the crowd said things like "Good fellow, Jack," and "Glad to see your mother's got a man to do it."

"Well," Mr. Summers said, "guess that's everyone. Old Man Warner make it?"

"Here," a voice said, and Mr. Summers nodded.

A sudden hush fell on the crowd as Mr. Summers cleared his throat and looked at the list. "All ready?" he called. "Now, I'll read the names—heads of families first—and the men come up and take a paper out of the box. Keep the paper folded in your hand without looking at it until everyone has had a turn. Everything clear?"

The people had done it so many times that they only half listened to the direc-   20
tions; most of them were quiet, wetting their lips, not looking around. Then Mr. Summers raised one hand high and said, "Adams." A man disengaged himself from the crowd and came forward. "Hi, Steve," Mr. Summers said, and Mr. Adams said, "Hi, Joe." They grinned at one another humorlessly and nervously. Then Mr. Adams reached into the black box and took out a folded paper. He held it firmly by one corner as he turned and went hastily back to his place in the crowd, where he stood a little apart from his family, not looking down at his hand.

"Allen," Mr. Summers said. "Anderson.... Bentham."

"Seems like there's no time at all between lotteries any more," Mrs. Delacroix said to Mrs. Graves in the back row. "Seems like we got through with the last one only last week."

"Time sure goes fast," Mrs. Graves said.

"Clark.... Delacroix."

"There goes my old man," Mrs. Delacroix said. She held her breath while her   25
husband went forward.

"Dunbar," Mr. Summers said, and Mrs. Dunbar went steadily to the box while one of the women said, "Go on, Janey," and another said, "There she goes."

"We're next," Mrs. Graves said. She watched while Mr. Graves came around from the side of the box, greeted Mr. Summers gravely, and selected a slip of paper from the box. By now, all through the crowd there were men holding the small folded papers in their large hands, turning them over and over nervously. Mrs. Dunbar and her two sons stood together, Mrs. Dunbar holding the slip of paper.

"Harburt.... Hutchinson."

"Get up there, Bill," Mrs. Hutchinson said, and the people near her laughed.

"Jones."   30

"They do say," Mr. Adams said to Old Man Warner, who stood next to him, "that over in the north village they're talking of giving up the lottery."

Old Man Warner snorted. "Pack of crazy fools," he said. "Listening to the young folks, nothing's good enough for *them*. Next thing you know, they'll be wanting to go back to living in caves, nobody work any more, live *that* way for a while. Used to be a saying about 'Lottery in June, corn be heavy soon.' First thing you know, we'd all be eating stewed chickweed and acorns. There's *always* been a lottery," he added petulantly. "Bad enough to see young Joe Summers up there joking with everybody."

"Some places have already quit lotteries," Mrs. Adams said.

"Nothing but trouble in *that*," Old Man Warner said stoutly. "Pack of young fools."

"Martin." And Bobby Martin watched his father go forward. "Overdyke.... Percy."   35

"I wish they'd hurry," Mrs. Dunbar said to her older son. "I wish they'd hurry."

"They're almost through," her son said.

"You get ready to run tell Dad," Mrs. Dunbar said.

Mr. Summers called his own name and then stepped forward precisely and selected a slip from the box. Then he called, "Warner."

"Seventy-seventh year I been in the lottery," Old Man Warner said as he went   40
through the crowd. "Seventy-seventh time."

"Watson." The tall boy came awkwardly through the crowd. Someone said, "Don't be nervous, Jack," and Mr. Summers said, "Take your time, son."

"Zanini."

After that, there was a long pause, a breathless pause, until Mr. Summers, holding his slip of paper in the air, said, "All right, fellows." For a minute, no one moved, and then all the slips of paper were opened. Suddenly, all the women began to speak at once, saying, "Who is it?" "Who's got it?" "Is it the Dunbars?" "Is it the Watsons?" Then the voices began to say, "It's Hutchinson. It's Bill." "Bill Hutchinson's got it."

"Go tell your father," Mrs. Dunbar said to her older son.

People began to look around to see the Hutchinsons. Bill Hutchinson was   45
standing quiet, staring down at the paper in his hand. Suddenly, Tessie Hutchinson shouted to Mr. Summers, "You didn't give him time enough to take any paper he wanted. I saw you. It wasn't fair!"

"Be a good sport, Tessie," Mrs. Delacroix called, and Mrs. Graves said, "All of us took the same chance."

"Shut up, Tessie," Bill Hutchinson said.

"Well, everyone," Mr. Summers said, "that was done pretty fast, and now we've got to be hurrying a little more to get done in time." He consulted his next list. "Bill," he said, "you draw for the Hutchinson family. You got any other households in the Hutchinsons?"

"There's Don and Eva," Mrs. Hutchinson yelled. "Make them take their chance!"

"Daughters draw with their husbands' families, Tessie," Mr. Summers said gently.   50
"You know that as well as anyone else."

"It wasn't fair," Tessie said.

"I guess not, Joe," Bill Hutchinson said regretfully. "My daughter draws with her husband's family, that's only fair. And I've got no other family except the kids."

"Then, as far as drawing for families is concerned, it's you," Mr. Summers said in explanation, "and as far as drawing for households is concerned, that's you, too. Right?"

"Right," Bill Hutchinson said.

"How many kids, Bill?" Mr. Summers asked formally.   55

"Three," Bill Hutchinson said. "There's Bill, Jr., and Nancy, and little Dave. And Tessie and me."

"All right, then," Mr. Summers said. "Harry, you got their tickets back?"

Mr. Graves nodded and held up the slips of paper. "Put them in the box, then," Mr. Summers directed. "Take Bill's and put it in."

"I think we ought to start over," Mrs. Hutchinson said, as quietly as she could. "I tell you it wasn't *fair*. You didn't give him time enough to choose. *Every*body saw that."

Mr. Graves had selected the five slips and put them in the box, and he dropped all   60
the papers but those onto the ground, where the breeze caught them and lifted them off.

"Listen, everybody," Mrs. Hutchinson was saying to the people around her.

"Ready, Bill?" Mr. Summers asked, and Bill Hutchinson, with one quick glance around at his wife and children, nodded.

"Remember," Mr. Summers said, "take the slips and keep them folded until each person has taken one. Harry, you help little Dave." Mr. Graves took the hand of the little boy, who came willingly with him up to the box. "Take a paper out of the box, Davy," Mr. Summers said. Davy put his hand into the box and laughed. "Take just *one* paper," Mr. Summers said. "Harry, you hold it for him." Mr. Graves took the child's hand and removed the folded paper from the tight fist and held it while little Dave stood next to him and looked up at him wonderingly.

"Nancy next," Mr. Summers said. Nancy was twelve, and her school friends breathed heavily as she went forward, switching her skirt, and took a slip daintily from the box. "Bill, Jr.," Mr. Summers said, and Billy, his face red and his feet over-large, nearly knocked the box over as he got a paper out. "Tessie," Mr. Summers said. She hesitated for a minute, looking around defiantly, and then set her lips and went up to the box. She snatched a paper out and held it behind her.

"Bill," Mr. Summers said, and Bill Hutchinson reached into the box and felt   65
around, bringing his hand out at last with the slip of paper in it.

The crowd was quiet. A girl whispered, "I hope it's not Nancy," and the sound of the whisper reached the edges of the crowd.

"It's not the way it used to be," Old Man Warner said clearly. "People ain't the way they used to be."

"All right," Mr. Summers said. "Open the papers. Harry, you open little Dave's."

Mr. Graves opened the slip of paper and there was a general sigh through the crowd as he held it up and everyone could see that it was blank. Nancy and Bill, Jr., opened theirs at the same time, and both beamed and laughed, turning around to the crowd and holding their slips of paper above their heads.

"Tessie," Mr. Summers said. There was a pause, and then Mr. Summers looked at   70
Bill Hutchinson, and Bill unfolded his paper and showed it. It was blank.

"It's Tessie," Mr. Summers said, and his voice was hushed. "Show us her paper, Bill."

Bill Hutchinson went over to his wife and forced the slip of paper out of her hand. It had a black spot on it, the black spot Mr. Summers had made the night before with the heavy pencil in the coal-company office. Bill Hutchinson held it up, and there was a stir in the crowd.

"All right, folks," Mr. Summers said, "Let's finish quickly."

Although the villagers had forgotten the ritual and lost the original black box, they still remembered to use stones. The pile of stones the boys had made earlier was ready; there were stones on the ground with the blowing scraps of paper that had come out of the box. Mrs. Delacroix selected a stone so large she had to pick it up with both hands and turned to Mrs. Dunbar. "Come on," she said. "Hurry up."

Mrs. Dunbar had small stones in both hands, and she said, gasping for breath, "I   75
can't run at all. You'll have to go ahead and I'll catch up with you."

The children had stones already, and someone gave little Davy Hutchinson a few pebbles.

Tessie Hutchinson was in the center of a cleared space by now, and she held her hands out desperately as the villagers moved in on her. "It isn't fair," she said. A stone hit her on the side of the head.

Old Man Warner was saying, "Come on, come on, everyone." Steve Adams was in the front of the crowd of villagers, with Mrs. Graves beside him.

"It isn't fair, it isn't right," Mrs. Hutchinson screamed, and then they were upon her.

Questions

1. Where do you think "The Lottery" takes place? What purpose do you suppose the writer has in making this setting appear so familiar and ordinary?

2. What details in paragraphs 2 and 3 foreshadow the ending of the story?

3. Take a close look at Jackson's description of the black wooden box (paragraph 5) and of the black spot on the fatal slip of paper (paragraph 72). What do these objects suggest to you? Are there any other symbols in the story?

4. What do you understand to be the writer's own attitude toward the lottery and the stoning? Exactly what in the story makes her attitude clear to us?

5. What do you make of Old Man Warner's saying, "Lottery in June, corn be heavy soon" (paragraph 32)?

6. What do you think Shirley Jackson is driving at? Consider each of the following interpretations and, looking at the story, see if you can find any evidence for it:

> Jackson takes a primitive fertility rite and playfully transfers it to a small town in North America.

> Jackson, writing her story soon after World War II, indirectly expresses her horror at the Holocaust. She assumes that the massacre of the Jews was carried out by unwitting, obedient people, like these villagers.

> Jackson is satirizing our own society, in which men are selected for the army by lottery.

> Jackson is just writing a memorable story that signifies nothing at all.

■ WRITING *effectively*

Shirley Jackson on Writing

Biography of a Story

(1960) 1968

My agent did not care for the story, but—as she said in her note at the time—her job was to sell it, not to like it. She sent it at once to the *New Yorker*, and about a week after the story had been written I received a telephone call from the fiction editor of the *New Yorker*; it was quite clear that he did not really care for the story, either, but the *New Yorker* was going to buy it. He asked for one change—that the date mentioned in the story be changed to coincide with the date of the issue of the magazine in which the story would appear, and I said of course. He then asked, hesitantly, if I had any particular interpretation of my own for the story; Mr. Harold Ross, then the editor of the *New Yorker*, was not altogether sure that he understood the story, and wondered if I

Shirley Jackson

cared to enlarge upon its meaning. I said no. Mr. Ross, he said, thought that the story might be puzzling to some people, and in case anyone telephoned the magazine, as sometimes happened, or wrote in asking about the story, was there anything in particular I wanted them to say? No, I said, nothing in particular; it was just a story I wrote.

I had no more preparation than that. I went on picking up the mail every morning, pushing my daughter up and down the hill in her stroller, anticipating pleasurably the check from the *New Yorker*, and shopping for groceries. The weather stayed nice and it looked as though it was going to be a good summer. Then, on June 28, the *New Yorker* came out with my story.

Things began mildly enough with a note from a friend at the *New Yorker*: "Your story has kicked up quite a fuss around the office," he wrote. I was flattered; it's nice to think that your friends notice what you write. Later that day there was a call from one of the magazine's editors; they had had a couple of people phone in about my story, he said, and was there anything I particularly wanted him to say if there were any more calls? No, I said, nothing particular; anything he chose to say was perfectly all right with me; it was just a story.

I was further puzzled by a cryptic note from another friend: "Heard a man talking about a story of yours on the bus this morning," she wrote. "Very exciting. I wanted to tell him I knew the author, but after I heard what he was saying I decided I'd better not."

One of the most terrifying aspects of publishing stories and books is the realization that they are going to be read, and read by strangers. I had never fully realized this before, although I had of course in my imagination dwelt lovingly upon the thought of millions and millions of people who were going to be uplifted and enriched and delighted by the stories I wrote. It had simply never occurred to me that these millions and millions of people might be so far from being uplifted that they would sit down and write me letters I was downright scared to open; of the three-hundred-odd letters that I received that summer I can count only thirteen that spoke kindly to me, and they were mostly from friends. Even my mother scolded me: "Dad and I did not care at all for your story in the *New Yorker*," she wrote sternly; "it does seem, dear, that this gloomy kind of story is what all you young people think about these days. Why don't you write something to cheer people up?"

By mid-July I had begun to perceive that I was very lucky indeed to be safely in Vermont, where no one in our small town had ever heard of the *New Yorker*, much less read my story. Millions of people, and my mother, had taken a pronounced dislike to me.

The magazine kept no track of telephone calls, but all letters addressed to me care of the magazine were forwarded directly to me for answering, and all letters addressed to the magazine—some of them addressed to Harold Ross personally; these were the most vehement—were answered at the magazine and then the letters were sent to me in great batches, along with carbons of the answers written at the magazine. I have all the letters still, and if they could be considered to give any accurate cross section of the reading public, or the reading public of the *New Yorker*, or even the reading public of one issue of the *New Yorker*, I would stop writing now.

Judging from these letters, people who read stories are gullible, rude, frequently illiterate, and horribly afraid of being laughed at. Many of the writers were positive that the *New Yorker* was going to ridicule them in print; and the most cautious letters were headed, in capital letters: NOT FOR PUBLICATION or PLEASE DO NOT PRINT THIS LETTER, or, at best, THIS LETTER MAY BE PUBLISHED AT YOUR USUAL RATES OF PAYMENT. Anonymous letters, of which there were a few, were destroyed. The *New Yorker* never published any comment of any kind about the story in the magazine, but did issue one publicity release saying that the story had received more mail than any piece of fiction they had ever published; this was after the newspapers had gotten into the act, in midsummer, with a front-page story in the San Francisco *Chronicle* begging to know what the story meant, and a series of columns in New York and Chicago papers pointing out that *New Yorker* subscriptions were being canceled right and left.

Curiously, there are three main themes which dominate the letters of that first summer—three themes which might be identified as bewilderment, speculation, and plain old-fashioned abuse. In the years since then, during which the story has been anthologized, dramatized, televised, and even—in one completely mystifying transformation—made into a ballet, the tenor of letters I receive has changed. I am addressed more politely, as a rule, and the letters largely confine themselves to questions like what does this story mean? The general tone of the early letters, however, was a kind of wide-eyed, shocked innocence. People at first were not so much concerned with what the story meant; what they wanted to know was where these lotteries were held, and whether they could go there and watch.

From *Come Along with Me*

THINKING ABOUT SYMBOLS

One danger in analyzing a story's symbolism is the temptation to read symbolic meaning into *everything*. An image acquires symbolic resonance because it is organically important to the actions and emotions of the story.

- **Consider a symbolic object's relevance to the plot.** What events, characters, and ideas are associated with it? It also helps to remember that some symbols arrive with cultural baggage. Any great white whale that swims into a work of contemporary fiction will inevitably summon up the symbolic associations of Melville's Moby Dick.

- **Ask yourself what the symbol means to the protagonist of your story.** Writers don't simply assign arbitrary meanings to items in their stories; generally, a horse is a horse, and a hammer is just a hammer. Sometimes, though, an object means something more to a character. Think of the flowers in "The Chrysanthemums."

- **Remember: in literature, few symbols are hidden.** Don't go on a symbol hunt. As you read or reread a story, any real symbol will usually find you. If an object appears time and again, or is tied inextricably to the story's events, it is likely to suggest something beyond itself. When an object, an action, or a place has emotional or intellectual power beyond its literal importance, then it is a genuine symbol.

CHECKLIST: Writing About Symbols

- ☐ Which objects, actions, or places seem unusually significant?
- ☐ List the specific objects, people, and ideas with which a particular symbol is associated.
- ☐ Locate the exact place in the story where the symbol links itself to the other thing.
- ☐ Ask whether each symbol comes with ready-made cultural associations.
- ☐ Avoid far-fetched interpretations. Focus first on the literal things, places, and actions in the story.
- ☐ Don't make a symbol mean too much or too little. Don't limit it to one narrow association or claim it summons up many different things.
- ☐ Be specific. Identify the exact place in the story where a symbol takes on a deeper meaning.

SAMPLE STUDENT PAPER

Here is an example of a paper on the symbolism found in Steinbeck's "The Chrysanthemums," written by Samantha L. Brown, a student of Melinda Barth's at El Camino College.

Brown 1

Samantha L. Brown

Professor Barth

English 210

26 Nov. 2019

An Analysis of the Symbolism in Steinbeck's

"The Chrysanthemums"

In a work of literature a symbol is something that suggests more than its surface meaning. In his short story "The Chrysanthemums," John Steinbeck uses the flowers of the title for both realistic and symbolic purposes. On the realistic level, the chrysanthemums advance the plot because they are the basis for the story's central action. They also help define the character of Elisa, provide a greater understanding of the setting, and play a vital part in revealing the story's theme.

The chrysanthemums provide the reader with insight into Elisa. When we first see her, she is in her flower garden working with her chrysanthemums. She is putting a great deal of energy into the relatively simple job of tending to the flowers. Elisa and her husband, Henry, have no children. They do not appear to have a very intense or passionate relationship. He praises her skill at growing flowers but says that he wishes she would work in the orchard and grow larger apples for him. His interests are practical and financial. The beauty of the flowers, which also symbolizes her beauty as a woman, is not important to him.

"The Chrysanthemums" is set in rural Monterey, California, in the 1930s. The ranch where Elisa and Henry live is in an isolated area. The flower garden is isolated from the rest of the ranch. The reader sees that Elisa is unhappy and frustrated, emotionally isolated from her husband and the life of their ranch. The flower garden is also surrounded by a wire fence, which symbolizes Elisa's feelings of being fenced in. She shows such feelings later in the story when she envies the free and easy life of the tinker and wishes that women could live that way.

The symbolic significance of the chrysanthemums is especially brought out in Elisa's conversation with the tinker. At first she resists his attempts to

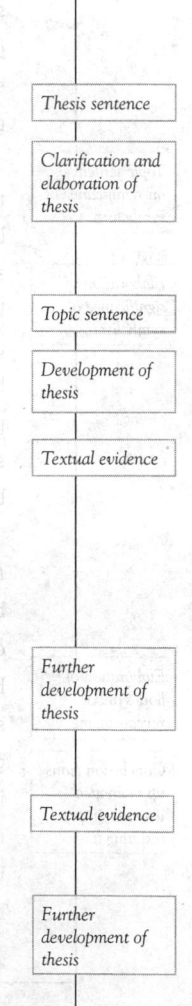

Thesis sentence

Clarification and elaboration of thesis

Topic sentence

Development of thesis

Textual evidence

Further development of thesis

Textual evidence

Further development of thesis

repair something for her, but then she responds to him because he admires her flowers. When he describes them in a poetic-sounding way, she feels she has met someone like herself that she can share an emotional bond with. The feelings he arouses in her are passionate—even sexual, as we see when she stops herself from reaching out and touching his pants. This is also shown after he leaves, when she takes off her mannish gardening clothes, bathes, and looks at her body in the mirror.

Textual evidence

The last and most painful symbolic use of the flowers comes toward the end of the story, when Elisa and her husband are driving into town for their evening out. Even before she can see it clearly, she knows that the speck by the side of the road is the chrysanthemum sprouts she gave the tinker to give to the (probably fictitious) woman he told her about. This is so upsetting to her that she turns around toward her husband so as not to see the tinker again as the car passes his wagon.

Topic sentence announces culmination of thesis

If we read the story only on the surface level, we won't be able to understand why Elisa is so upset. So a cunning traveler has manipulated her love of flowers to soften her up into giving him some work. Maybe he made a fool of her, but it's in the middle of the Depression, and he has to eat, too. What's the big deal? Only when we understand the symbolic importance of the chrysanthemums do we understand why this is so painful for her. She had felt that someone understood her, maybe even felt that life was richer in possibilities than it had seemed. This illusion is shattered, however, when she sees the plant sprouts. The discarded, dying plants symbolize her diminished life, her failure to find anyone who can understand her needs and feelings.

Topic sentence on significance of symbolism

Elaboration of significance of symbolism

The chrysanthemums are vital to Steinbeck's presentation of the theme. At the beginning, Elisa is presented as a strong woman, strong enough to break the back of a calf. At the end, she is seen huddled like an old woman, crying weakly. The newly revealed Elisa is not the strong woman that she or her husband thought she was. It wasn't until she saw the discarded plant sprouts that she felt the sting of her rejection and isolation. Until that moment, her gardening had protected—or at least distracted—her from her loneliness, isolation, and feelings of inadequacy. Finally, the theme emerges from our understanding of this woman and the importance of her chrysanthemums. Understanding Steinbeck's symbolism, therefore, is essential to understanding how the story works.

Elaboration of how symbol reveals theme

Conclusion sums up main idea without simply restating it

TOPICS FOR WRITING ON SYMBOLS

1. From the stories in this book, choose one with a strong central symbol. Explain how the symbol helps to communicate the story's meaning, citing specific moments in the text.
2. Choose a story from this chapter. Describe your experience of reading that story and of encountering its symbols. At what point did the main symbol's meaning become clear? What in the story indicated the larger importance of that symbol?
3. From any story in this book, select an object, or place, or action that seems clearly symbolic. How do you know? Now select an object, place, or action from the same story that clearly seems to signify no more than itself. How can you tell?
4. Analyze the symbolism in a story from "Gallery of International Voices" (Chapter 13) or "Stories for Further Reading" (Chapter 14). Some good choices might be "Dead Men's Path," "Saints," "Greasy Lake," and "The Story of an Hour." Choose a symbol that recurs over the course of the story, and look closely at each appearance it makes. How does the story's use of the symbol evolve?
5. In an essay of 600 to 800 words, compare and contrast the symbolic use of the scapegoat in "The Lottery" and "The Ones Who Walk Away from Omelas."

▶ TERMS FOR *review*

Symbol ▶ A person, place, or thing in a narrative that suggests meanings beyond its literal sense. Symbol is related to allegory, but it works more complexly. A symbol often contains multiple meanings and associations.

Conventional symbol ▶ A literary symbol that has a conventional or customary meaning for most readers—for example, a black cat crossing a path or a young bride in a white dress.

Symbolic act ▶ An action whose significance goes well beyond its literal meaning. In literature, symbolic acts often involve some conscious or unconscious ritual element such as rebirth, purification, forgiveness, vengeance, or initiation.

Allegory ▶ A narrative in which the literal events (persons, places, and things) consistently point to a parallel sequence of symbolic equivalents. This narrative strategy is often used to dramatize abstract ideas, historical events, religious systems, or political issues. An allegory has two levels of meaning: a literal level that tells a surface story and a symbolic level in which the abstract ideas unfold.

GENRE FICTION

*I have never listened to anyone who criticized my taste
in space travel, sideshows, or gorillas. When this occurs,
I pack up my dinosaurs and leave the room.*

—RAY BRADBURY

What You Will Learn in This Chapter

- To define *genre fiction*
- To explain the difference between the romantic and realistic modes
  of fiction
- To identify the major types of genre fiction
- To analyze the role of genre in shaping a story

Some of the most memorable characters in literature and popular culture—Dracula, Tarzan, Gandalf, Sherlock Holmes—come from the wide range of imaginative writing known as **genre fiction**. That broad label encompasses a variety of literary modes, including science fiction, fantasy, horror, detective stories, westerns, ghost stories, and countless other offshoots. As described in Chapter 9, the novel (as well as short stories that are considered "literary fiction") is primarily defined as a realistic form, intended to evoke the experience of actual life. Genre fiction, by contrast, tries to conjure up the excitement of adventure, surprise, romantic love, and fantasy.

While some types of genre fiction, such as J. R. R. Tolkien's *The Lord of the Rings*, invent entire worlds populated by fantastic beings and supernatural powers, other works, such as Ray Bradbury's *Fahrenheit 451*, offer a more familiar and believable setting. Bradbury's science fiction classic shares many of the qualities and approaches we find in realistic fiction. Although Bradbury's novel takes place in a future, dystopian society in which books are burned and freethinking squashed, his characters are just as complex and dynamic as the characters who populate realistic novels—they struggle and make mistakes, they grieve and change, fail and triumph. Furthermore, *Fahrenheit 451*'s themes of oppression, censorship, and rebellion have remained relevant and poignant to many cultures—including our own. While genre fiction might, in large or small ways, stray from what we experience as real life, these powerfully imaginative and appealing literary forms still have a special gift for helping us recognize and understand truths about our past, our future, our society, and ourselves.

ROMANCE VERSUS REALISM

There are two major modes of telling stories: realism and romance. Realism tries to create a sense of the everyday world in which we all live. By contrast, romance appeals to the world of our imagination and our desires—both what we long for and what we fear. Genre fiction comes out of the tradition known as **romance**, a highly inventive literary mode that employs exotic adventure, surprise, and wish fulfillment, in contrast to the more realistic depictions of character and action that we associate with traditional literary modes. Jonathan Swift's *Gulliver's Travels* (1726) is a classic example of a romance. In this marvel-filled account of Lemuel Gulliver's voyages among pygmies, giants, civilized horses, and noxious humanoid swine, Swift does not seem primarily to care if we find his story credible. Though he arrays the adventures of Gulliver in painstaking detail, Swift neither attempts nor achieves a convincing illusion of real life.

You surely recognize the word *romance* to have connotations of starry-eyed love. There is even a popular fictional genre called "romance" which depicts passionate love affairs. That is how the term is most commonly used today, but the word had a different meaning when it was first employed to describe literature. The word *romance* originated in the Middle Ages, steming from the Latin word *Romanicus*, meaning "in the Roman style." During those times, authors used the term to describe stories about the adventures of kings, knights, and aristocratic ladies. The term *romance* took on additional meanings over the centuries, but one important characteristic has remained: its approachability and popularity with a broad audience.

Modern works of romance, emerging in the nineteenth century, were epitomized by adventure novels such as Sir Walter Scott's *Ivanhoe*, which presented the symbolic quests and idealized characters of those earlier, chivalric tales in slightly more realistic terms. (The romantic tradition continues today, especially in motion pictures, as evident in such blockbuster franchises as *Stars Wars* and James Bond.) The ever-broadening category of genre fiction later came to include mystery, science fiction, and fantasy, as well as the more contemporary subgenres of splatterpunk, workplace fiction, superhero, and even space opera, to name only a few.

It is particularly interesting to see the rare occasions when authors deliberately stray across the boundary between the novelistic and romantic methods. In Franz Kafka's *The Metamorphosis* (Chapter 9), for example, the story begins with a fantastic premise—Gregor Samsa wakes up one morning to discover himself turned into a giant insect. This bizarre transformation would seem the very stuff of romance, but after the first sentence Kafka tells the story in the most matter-of-fact and realistic way. The stunning quality of Kafka's masterpiece comes from his novelistic manner of telling his seemingly unrealistic tale.

WHAT IS GENRE?

When applied to fiction, the word **genre**—French for *kind* or *type*—refers to a conventional combination of form and subject matter. Each sort of genre fiction employs common structures and techniques. A person reading a traditional detective story, for instance, would expect to find a certain type of narrative with a particular kind of protagonist. In Arthur Conan Doyle's "The Adventure of the Speckled Band," Sherlock Holmes is hired by a young woman to investigate the death of her sister, who perished under mysterious circumstances in the family's country manor. Holmes pokes around, following leads and hunches, and finally he holds an all-night stakeout in the eerie mansion, which provides him with the final clues to be able to solve the crime. This is a classic form for a detective story—a distressed client comes seeking help, and a brilliant but eccentric protagonist unravels the mystery, using instinct, experience, talent, and intelligence. There is often a twist in the plot and, finally, a satisfying resolution. These rules are general, of course, and are often bent slightly, as such rules should be.

COMMON TYPES OF GENRE FICTION

Science Fiction

Rockets, robots, time machines, and ray-guns. Everyone recognizes the elements of science fiction, one of the most popular genres in literature, film, and television. Essentially, **science fiction** offers a narrative that presents some technological innovation (such as time travel) or scientific assumption (alien races) and then logically develops a story from that imaginary premise. Such stories are frequently set in the future or on other planets. Science-fiction writers often use these fantastic situations to comment on the real world. Robert A. Heinlein defined science fiction as "realistic speculation about possible future events, based solidly on adequate knowledge of the real world, past and present, and on a thorough understanding of the nature and significance of the scientific method." Science fiction was developed in the late nineteenth and early twentieth centuries by authors such as Jules Verne and H. G. Wells, and it has steadily grown in popularity as real-world science and technology have made contemporary life more complex and dynamic. Classics of modern science fiction include George Orwell's *Nineteen Eighty-Four*, Anthony Burgess's *A Clockwork Orange*, Frank Herbert's *Dune*, and Orson Scott Card's *Ender's Game*.

Fantasy

Fantasy is the oldest form of romance. While science fiction explores the implications of technological innovation, fantasy is usually unconcerned with realism or technology. Fantasy allows anything to be possible—magic, dragons, unicorns, giants. It expresses the fears and desires of the human imagination without being required to explain them in logical terms. Fantasy has grown from ancient myths, legends, and classic fairy tales into a modern mode of storytelling. Fantasy writers often invent alternate worlds, such as Middle-Earth in J. R. R. Tolkien's *The Lord of the Rings* trilogy; Earthsea, featured in Ursula K. Le Guin's works; or the three continents of George R. R. Martin's *A Song of Ice and Fire* series. Sometimes fantasy writers even set their magical tales in hidden corners of the real world, as in J. K. Rowling's *Harry Potter* novels and Neil Gaiman's *Neverwhere*.

Detective Fiction

Detective fiction and **mystery fiction** usually present a protagonist who solves a puzzling crime (most often a murder) by using observation, deduction, and intuition to find the culprit. The protagonist may be a police detective, but more often it is a private eye (such as Raymond Chandler's Philip Marlowe), a consultant

Dashiell Hammett's famous 1930 detective novel *The Maltese Falcon* was adapted into a classic film starring Humphrey Bogart.

(Doyle's Sherlock Holmes), or an amateur bystander (such as Agatha Christie's Miss Marple). Classic detectives display great analytical powers to notice and connect clues that other characters miss. The detective story was first invented by Edgar Allan Poe and quickly became an internationally beloved genre. Early British mysteries such as the works of Doyle and Christie or the Father Brown stories of G. K. Chesterton tended to prize clever plots, brilliant detectives, and satiric characters with little overt violence. The American "hard-boiled" school, as exemplified by Chandler, Dashiell Hammett, and Ross Macdonald, presented flawed, rough-edged detectives and graphic violence in a corrupt, urban setting. The detective story continues as a popular international genre as exemplified by the success of the Swedish author Stieg Larsson's ultra-hard-boiled *Girl with the Dragon Tattoo* in his Millennium trilogy.

Horror

Horror fiction attempts to frighten the reader through the use of suspense, shock, and fear. It often places its protagonist in a mysteriously uncomfortable situation that gradually becomes more terrifying as the story progresses. Some horror fiction is populated by werewolves, vampires, and ghosts, while some is more realistically terrifying. Edgar Allan Poe first perfected the horror genre by creating evocatively written tales carefully designed to create the single effect of psychological terror, as in "The Tell-Tale Heart" (Chapter 12). Poe's approach was adopted and developed by later writers, most notably H. P. Lovecraft. Other examples of horror fiction include Mary Shelley's *Frankenstein*, Bram Stoker's *Dracula*, and the novels of modern masters such as Stephen King, Clive Barker, and Anne Rice.

A cover from *Weird Tales*, the pulp magazine where H. P. Lovecraft published many of his horror stories.

GENRE AND POPULAR CULTURE

Despite its immense appeal to readers young and old and its frequent use for film and television adaptations, genre fiction was long marginalized by academia and the literary establishment. Early on it was condescendingly known as ***pulp fiction***, in reference to the inexpensive wood-pulp paper used by genre magazines throughout the twentieth century. These publications were also called "penny dreadfuls" and "dime novels," slights aimed at their affordable pricing and meant to suggest that the material between the covers was likewise cheap. But genre fiction's continuous, broad appeal demonstrates that one of literature's most important rewards is pleasure, as its throngs of dedicated readers surely agree. Many important writers such as Poe, Lovecraft, Bradbury, and Le Guin have been attracted by the imaginative freedom of genre fiction. At its best, genre fiction fulfills Robert Frost's definition of a poem, that it "begins in delight and ends in wisdom."

The great popular appeal of genre fiction is perhaps most apparent in its domination of film and television. The many police procedurals that have filled prime-time TV—*NCIS*, *The Mentalist*, *Elementary*, *Dexter*—are direct descendants of classic detective fiction. If you were to consult a current list of the fifty highest-grossing films of all time, you would find that forty-eight of them are science fiction or fantasy. It should suffice to say, genre fiction has captured the modern imagination. The critical establishment has finally come around to recognizing what audiences have long known—that this entertaining, imaginative, intelligent, and often prophetic art commands our attention and respect.

Ray Bradbury

A Sound of Thunder   1953

Raymond Douglas Bradbury (1920–2012) was born in Waukegan, Illinois, a small Midwestern town he has frequently evoked in his fiction. His mother was a Swedish immigrant and his father an electrical lineman. In 1934, Bradbury's unemployed father moved the family from the Depression-ravaged Midwest to Los Angeles, where Ray entered high school. The teenaged Bradbury soon discovered science fiction and began publishing stories in his high school magazine. Unable to afford college, he took odd jobs while making his way as a writer. By 1941 he was publishing fiction in commercial magazines and very quickly developed a personal style that was strikingly unlike the conventional science fiction of the era. His stories were quietly poetic, evocatively detailed, overtly symbolic, and often suffused with nostalgia. Bradbury's first collection, Dark Carnival *(1947), made a modest impression, but his 1950 cycle of stories about mankind's doomed colonization of Mars,* The Martian Chronicles, *was immediately recognized as a classic of science fiction. The success of* The Martian Chronicles *made Bradbury the first American science-fiction writer to cross over into the mainstream literary market. His novels became both critical and popular successes, especially* Fahrenheit 451 *(1953),* Dandelion Wine *(1957), and* Something Wicked This Way Comes *(1962), but he was best known for his short stories, which were collected in volumes such as* The Illustrated Man *(1951),* The Golden Apples of the Sun *(1953),* A Medicine for Melancholy *(1959), and* I Sing the Body Electric! *(1969). Bradbury's literary vision has also been disseminated through film, television, and theater. Although at his best an elegant stylist, Bradbury was perhaps primarily a mythmaker. His science fiction and fantasy narratives have given contemporary readers the stories, situations, images, and symbols necessary to a complex, and rapidly changing, technology-driven society. Bradbury received many honors, including the National Medal of Arts in 2004 and a lifetime Pulitzer Prize in 2007. He died in Los Angeles, where he had lived for his entire adult life, at age ninety-one.*

The sign on the wall seemed to quaver under a film of sliding warm water. Eckels felt his eyelids blink over his stare, and the sign burned in this momentary darkness:

TIME SAFARI, INC.

SAFARIS TO ANY YEAR IN THE

PAST.

YOU NAME THE ANIMAL.

WE TAKE YOU THERE.

YOU SHOOT IT.

A warm phlegm gathered in Eckels' throat; he swallowed and pushed it down. The muscles around his mouth formed a smile as he put his hand slowly out upon the air, and in that hand waved a check for ten thousand dollars to the man behind the desk.

"Does this safari guarantee I come back alive?"

"We guarantee nothing," said the official, "except the dinosaurs." He turned. "This is Mr. Travis, your Safari Guide in the Past. He'll tell you what and where to shoot. If he says no shooting, no shooting. If you disobey instructions, there's a stiff penalty of another ten thousand dollars, plus possible government action, on your return."

Eckels glanced across the vast office at a mass and tangle, a snaking and humming of wires and steel boxes, at an aurora that flickered now orange, now silver, now blue. 5

There was a sound like a gigantic bonfire burning all of Time, all the years and all the parchment calendars, all the hours piled high and set aflame.

A touch of the hand and this burning would, on the instant, beautifully reverse itself. Eckels remembered the wording in the advertisements to the letter. Out of chars and ashes, out of dust and coals, like golden salamanders, the old years, the green years, might leap; roses sweeten the air, white hair turn Irish-black, wrinkles vanish; all, everything fly back to seed, flee death, rush down to their beginnings, suns rise in western skies and set in glorious easts, moons eat themselves opposite to the custom, all and everything cupping one in another like Chinese boxes, rabbits into hats, all and everything returning to the fresh death, the seed death, the green death, to the time before the beginning. A touch of a hand might do it, the merest touch of a hand.

"Unbelievable." Eckels breathed, the light of the Machine on his thin face. "A real Time Machine." He shook his head. "Makes you think, If the election had gone badly yesterday, I might be here now running away from the results. Thank God Keith won. He'll make a fine President of the United States."

"Yes," said the man behind the desk. "We're lucky. If Deutscher had gotten in, we'd have the worst kind of dictatorship. There's an anti everything man for you, a militarist, anti-Christ, anti-human, anti-intellectual. People called us up, you know, joking but not joking. Said if Deutscher became President they wanted to go live in 1492. Of course it's not our business to conduct Escapes, but to form Safaris. Anyway, Keith's President now. All you got to worry about is—"

"Shooting my dinosaur," Eckels finished it for him.

"A *Tyrannosaurus rex*. The Tyrant Lizard, the most incredible monster in history. Sign this release. Anything happens to you, we're not responsible. Those dinosaurs are hungry."

Eckels flushed angrily. "Trying to scare me!"

"Frankly, yes. We don't want anyone going who'll panic at the first shot. Six Safari leaders were killed last year, and a dozen hunters. We're here to give you the severest thrill a *real* hunter ever asked for. Traveling you back sixty million years to bag the biggest game in all of Time. Your personal check's still there. Tear it up."

Mr. Eckels looked at the check. His fingers twitched.

"Good luck," said the man behind the desk. "Mr. Travis, he's all yours."

They moved silently across the room, taking their guns with them, toward the Machine, toward the silver metal and the roaring light.

First a day and then a night and then a day and then a night, then it was day-night-day-night-day. A week, a month, a year, a decade! A.D. 2055. A.D. 2019. 1999! 1957! Gone! The Machine roared.

They put on their oxygen helmets and tested the intercoms.

Eckels swayed on the padded seat, his face pale, his jaw stiff. He felt the trembling in his arms and he looked down and found his hands tight on the new rifle. There were four other men in the Machine. Travis, the Safari Leader, his assistant, Lesperance, and two other hunters, Billings and Kramer. They sat looking at each other, and the years blazed around them.

"Can these guns get a dinosaur cold?" Eckels felt his mouth saying.

"If you hit them right," said Travis on the helmet radio. "Some dinosaurs have two brains, one in the head, another far down the spinal column. We stay away from those. That's stretching luck. Put your first two shots into the eyes, if you can, blind them, and go back into the brain."

The Machine howled. Time was a film run backward. Suns fled and ten million moons fled after them. "Think," said Eckels. "Every hunter that ever lived would envy us today. This makes Africa seem like Illinois."

The Machine slowed; its scream fell to a murmur. The Machine stopped.

The sun stopped in the sky.

The fog that had enveloped the Machine blew away and they were in an old time, a very old time indeed, three hunters and two Safari Heads with their blue metal guns across their knees.

"Christ isn't born yet," said Travis. "Moses has not gone to the mountain to talk with God. The Pyramids are still in the earth, waiting to be cut out and put up. *Remember* that. Alexander, Caesar, Napoleon, Hitler—none of them exists."

The man nodded.

"That"—Mr. Travis pointed—"is the jungle of sixty million two thousand and fifty-five years before President Keith."

He indicated a metal path that struck off into green wilderness, over streaming swamp, among giant ferns and palms.

"And that," he said, "is the Path, laid by Time Safari for your use. It floats six inches above the earth. Doesn't touch so much as one grass blade, flower, or tree. It's an anti-gravity metal. Its purpose is to keep you from touching this world of the past in any way. Stay on the Path. Don't go off it. I repeat. *Don't go off.* For *any* reason! If you fall off, there's a penalty. And don't shoot any animal we don't okay."

"Why?" asked Eckels.

They sat in the ancient wilderness. Far birds' cries blew on a wind, and the smell of tar and an old salt sea, moist grasses, and flowers the color of blood.

"We don't want to change the Future. We don't belong here in the Past. The government doesn't *like* us here. We have to pay big graft to keep our franchise. A Time Machine is finicky business. Not knowing it, we might kill an important animal, a small bird, a roach, a flower even, thus destroying an important link in a growing species."

"That's not clear," said Eckels.

"All right," Travis continued, "say we accidentally kill one mouse here. That means all the future families of this one particular mouse are destroyed, right?"

"Right."

"And all the families of the families of the families of that one mouse! With a stamp of your foot, you annihilate first one, then a dozen, then a thousand, a million, a billion possible mice!"

"So they're dead," said Eckels. "So what?"

"So what?" Travis snorted quietly. "Well, what about the foxes that'll need those mice to survive? For want of ten mice, a fox dies. For want of ten foxes a lion starves. For want of a lion, all manner of insects, vultures, infinite billions of life forms are thrown into chaos and destruction. Eventually it all boils down to this: fifty-nine million years later, a caveman, one of a dozen on the *entire world*, goes hunting wild boar or saber-toothed tiger for food. But you, friend, have stepped on all the tigers in that region. By stepping on *one* single mouse. So the caveman starves. And the caveman, please note, is not just *any* expendable man, no! He is an *entire future nation*. From his loins would have sprung ten sons. From their loins one hundred sons, and thus onward to a civilization. Destroy this one man, and you destroy a race, a people, an entire history of life. It is comparable to slaying some of Adam's grandchildren. The stomp of your foot, on one mouse, could start an earthquake, the effects of which could shake our earth and destinies down through Time, to their very foundations. With the death of that one caveman, a billion others yet unborn are throttled in the womb. Perhaps Rome never rises on its seven hills. Perhaps Europe is forever a dark forest, and only Asia waxes healthy and teeming. Step on a mouse and you crush the Pyramids. Step on a mouse and you leave your print, like a Grand Canyon, across Eternity. Queen Elizabeth might never be born, Washington might not cross the Delaware, there might never be a United States at all. So be careful. Stay on the Path. *Never* step off!"

"I see," said Eckels. "Then it wouldn't pay for us even to touch the *grass*?"

"Correct. Crushing certain plants could add up infinitesimally. A little error 40 here would multiply in sixty million years, all out of proportion. Of course maybe our theory is wrong. Maybe Time *can't* be changed by us. Or maybe it can be changed only in little subtle ways. A dead mouse here makes an insect imbalance there, a population disproportion later, a bad harvest further on, a depression, mass starvation, and finally, a change in *social* temperament in far-flung countries. Something much more subtle, like that. Perhaps only a soft breath, a whisper, a hair, pollen on the air, such a slight, slight change that unless you looked close you wouldn't see it. Who knows? Who really can say he knows? We don't know. We're guessing. But until we do know for certain whether our messing around in Time *can* make a big roar or a little rustle in history, we're being careful. This Machine, this Path, your clothing and bodies, were sterilized, as you know, before the journey. We wear these oxygen helmets so we can't introduce our bacteria into an ancient atmosphere."

"How do we know which animals to shoot?"

"They're marked with red paint," said Travis. "Today, before our journey, we sent Lesperance here back with the Machine. He came to this particular era and followed certain animals."

"Studying them?"

"Right," said Lesperance. "I track them through their entire existence, noting which of them lives longest. Very few. How many times they mate. Not often. Life's short. When I find one that's going to die when a tree falls on him, or one that drowns in a tar pit, I note the exact hour, minute, and second. I shoot a paint bomb. It leaves a red patch on his side. We can't miss it. Then I correlate our arrival in the Past so that we meet the Monster not more than two minutes before he would have died anyway. This way, we kill only animals with no future, that are never going to mate again. You see how *careful* we are?"

"But if you came back this morning in Time," said Eckels eagerly, you must've 45 bumped into *us*, our Safari! How did it turn out? Was it successful? Did all of us get through—alive?"

Travis and Lesperance gave each other a look.

"That'd be a paradox," said the latter. "Time doesn't permit that sort of mess—a man meeting himself. When such occasions threaten, Time steps aside. Like an airplane hitting an air pocket. You felt the Machine jump just before we stopped? That was us passing ourselves on the way back to the Future. We saw nothing. There's no way of telling *if* this expedition was a success, *if* we got our monster, or whether all of us—meaning *you*, Mr. Eckels—got out alive."

Eckels smiled palely.

"Cut that," said Travis sharply. "Everyone on his feet!"

They were ready to leave the Machine. 50

The jungle was high and the jungle was broad and the jungle was the entire world forever and forever. Sounds like music and sounds like flying tents filled the sky, and those were pterodactyls soaring with cavernous gray wings, gigantic bats of delirium and night fever.

Eckels, balanced on the narrow Path, aimed his rifle playfully.

"Stop that!" said Travis. "Don't even aim for fun, blast you! If your guns should go off—"

Eckels flushed. "Where's our *Tyrannosaurus?*"

Lesperance checked his wristwatch. "Up ahead. We'll bisect his trail in sixty seconds. Look for the red paint! Don't shoot till we give the word. Stay on the Path. *Stay on the Path!*"

They moved forward in the wind of morning.

"Strange," murmured Eckels. "Up ahead, sixty million years, Election Day over. Keith made President. Everyone celebrating. And here we are, a million years lost, and they don't exist. The things we worried about for months, a lifetime, not even born or thought of yet."

"Safety catches off, everyone!" ordered Travis. "You, first shot, Eckels. Second, Billings, Third, Kramer."

"I've hunted tiger, wild boar, buffalo, elephant, but now, this is *it*," said Eckels. "I'm shaking like a kid."

"Ah," said Travis.

Everyone stopped.

Travis raised his hand. "Ahead," he whispered. "In the mist. There he is. There's His Royal Majesty now."

The jungle was wide and full of twitterings, rustlings, murmurs, and sighs.

Suddenly it all ceased, as if someone had shut a door.

Silence.

A sound of thunder.

Out of the mist, one hundred yards away, came *Tyrannosaurus rex.*

"It," whispered Eckels. "It . . ."

"Sh!"

It came on great oiled, resilient, striding legs. It towered thirty feet above half of the trees, a great evil god, folding its delicate watchmaker's claws close to its oily reptilian chest. Each lower leg was a piston, a thousand pounds of white bone, sunk in thick ropes of muscle, sheathed over in a gleam of pebbled skin like the mail of a terrible warrior. Each thigh was a ton of meat, ivory, and steel mesh. And from the great breathing cage of the upper body those two delicate arms dangled out front, arms with hands which might pick up and examine men like toys, while the snake neck coiled. And the head itself, a ton of sculptured stone, lifted easily upon the sky. Its mouth gaped, exposing a fence of teeth like daggers. Its eyes rolled, ostrich eggs, empty of all expression save hunger. It closed its mouth in a death grin. It ran, its pelvic bones crushing aside trees and bushes, its taloned feet clawing damp earth, leaving prints six inches deep wherever it settled its weight.

It ran with a gliding ballet step, far too poised and balanced for its ten tons. It moved into a sunlit area warily, its beautifully reptilian hands feeling the air.

"Why, why," Eckels twitched his mouth. "It could reach up and grab the moon."

"Sh!" Travis jerked angrily. "He hasn't seen us yet."

"It can't be killed," Eckels pronounced this verdict quietly, as if there could be no argument. He had weighed the evidence and this was his considered opinion. The rifle in his hands seemed a cap gun. "We were fools to come. This is impossible."

"Shut up!" hissed Travis.

"Nightmare."

"Turn around," commanded Travis. "Walk quietly to the Machine. We'll remit half your fee."

Marginal line numbers: 55, 60, 65, 70, 75

"I didn't realize it would be this *big*," said Eckels. "I miscalculated, that's all. And now I want out."

"It *sees* us!"

"There's the red paint on its chest!"   80

The Tyrant Lizard raised itself. Its armored flesh glittered like a thousand green coins. The coins, crusted with slime, steamed. In the slime, tiny insects wriggled, so that the entire body seemed to twitch and undulate, even while the monster itself did not move. It exhaled. The stink of raw flesh blew down the wilderness.

"Get me out of here," said Eckels. "It was never like this before. I was always sure I'd come through alive. I had good guides, good safaris, and safety. This time, I figured wrong. I've met my match and admit it. This is too much for me to get hold of."

"Don't run," said Lesperance. "Turn around. Hide in the Machine."

"Yes." Eckels seemed to be numb. He looked at his feet as if trying to make them move. He gave a grunt of helplessness.

"Eckels!"   85

He took a few steps, blinking, shuffling.

"Not *that* way!"

The Monster, at the first motion, lunged forward with a terrible scream. It covered one hundred yards in six seconds. The rifles jerked up and blazed fire. A windstorm from the beast's mouth engulfed them in the stench of slime and old blood. The Monster roared, teeth glittering with sun.

Eckels, not looking back, walked blindly to the edge of the Path, his gun limp in his arms, stepped off the Path, and walked, not knowing it, in the jungle. His feet sank into green moss. His legs moved him, and he felt alone and remote from the events behind.

The rifles cracked again. Their sound was lost in shriek and lizard thunder. The   90
great level of the reptile's tail swung up, lashed sideways. Trees exploded in clouds of leaf and branch. The Monster twitched its jeweler's hands down to fondle at the men, to twist them in half, to crush them like berries, to cram them into its teeth and its screaming throat. Its boulderstone eyes leveled with the men. They saw themselves mirrored. They fired at the metallic eyelids and the blazing black iris.

Like a stone idol, like a mountain avalanche, *Tyrannosaurus* fell. Thundering, it clutched trees, pulled them with it. It wrenched and tore the metal Path. The men flung themselves back and away. The body hit, ten tons of cold flesh and stone. The guns fired. The Monster lashed its armored tail, twitched its snake jaws, and lay still. A fount of blood spurted from its throat. Somewhere inside, a sac of fluids burst. Sickening gushes drenched the hunters. They stood, red and glistening.

The thunder faded.

The jungle was silent. After the avalanche, a green peace. After the nightmare, morning.

Billings and Kramer sat on the pathway and threw up. Travis and Lesperance stood with smoking rifles, cursing steadily.

In the Time Machine, on his face, Eckels lay shivering. He had found his way   95
back to the Path, climbed into the Machine.

Travis came walking, glanced at Eckels, took cotton gauze from a metal box, and returned to the others, who were sitting on the Path.

"Clean up."

They wiped the blood from their helmets. They began to curse too. The Monster lay, a hill of solid flesh. Within, you could hear the sighs and murmurs as the furthest chambers of it died, the organs malfunctioning, liquids running a final instant from pocket to sac to spleen, everything shutting off, closing up forever. It was like standing by a wrecked locomotive or a steam shovel at quitting time, all valves being released or levered tight. Bones cracked; the tonnage of its own flesh, off balance, dead weight, snapped the delicate forearms, caught underneath. The meat settled, quivering.

Another cracking sound. Overhead, a gigantic tree branch broke from its heavy mooring, fell. It crashed upon the dead beast with finality.

"There." Lesperance checked his watch. "Right on time. That's the giant tree 100 that was scheduled to fall and kill this animal originally." He glanced at the two hunters. "You want the trophy picture?"

"What?"

"We can't take a trophy back to the Future. The body has to stay right here where it would have died originally, so the insects, birds, and bacteria can get at it, as they were intended to. Everything in balance. The body stays. But we *can* take a picture of you standing near it."

The two men tried to think, but gave up, shaking their heads.

They let themselves be led along the metal Path. They sank wearily into the Machine cushions. They gazed back at the ruined Monster, the stagnating mound, where already strange reptilian birds and golden insects were busy at the steaming armor. A sound on the floor of the Time Machine stiffened them. Eckels sat there, shivering.

"I'm sorry," he said at last. 105

"Get up!" cried Travis.

Eckels got up.

"Go out on that Path alone," said Travis. He had his rifle pointed, "You're not coming back in the Machine. We're leaving you here!"

Lesperance seized Travis's arm. "Wait—"

"Stay out of this!" Travis shook his hand away. "This fool nearly killed us. But 110 it isn't *that* so much, no. It's his *shoes!* Look at them! He ran off the Path. That *ruins* us! We'll forfeit! Thousands of dollars of insurance! We guarantee no one leaves the Path. He left it. Oh, the fool! I'll have to report to the government. They might revoke our license to travel. Who knows *what* he's done to Time, to History!"

"Take it easy, all he did was kick up some dirt."

"How do we *know?*" cried Travis. "We don't know anything! It's all a mystery! Get out of here, Eckels!"

Eckels fumbled his shirt. "I'll pay anything. A hundred thousand dollars!"

Travis glared at Eckels' checkbook and spat. "Go out there. The Monster's next to the Path. Stick your arms up to your elbows in his mouth. Then you can come back with us."

"That's unreasonable!" 115

"The Monster's dead, you idiot. The bullets! The bullets can't be left behind. They don't belong in the Past; they might change anything. Here's my knife. Dig them out!"

The jungle was alive again, full of the old tremorings and bird cries. Eckels turned slowly to regard the primeval garbage dump, that hill of nightmares and terror. After a long time, like a sleepwalker he shuffled out along the Path.

He returned, shuddering, five minutes later, his arms soaked and red to the elbows. He held out his hands. Each held a number of steel bullets. Then he fell. He lay where he fell, not moving.

"You didn't have to make him do that," said Lesperance.

"Didn't I? It's too early to tell." Travis nudged the still body. "He'll live. Next 120
time he won't go hunting game like this. Okay." He jerked his thumb wearily at
Lesperance. "Switch on. Let's go home."

1492. 1776. 1812.

They cleaned their hands and faces. They changed their caking shirts and pants.
Eckels was up and around again, not speaking. Travis glared at him for a full ten
minutes.

"Don't look at me," cried Eckels. "I haven't done anything."

"Who can tell?"

"Just ran off the Path, that's all, a little mud on my shoes—what do you want me 125
to do—get down and pray?"

"We might need it. I'm warning you, Eckels, I might kill you yet. I've got my gun
ready."

"I'm innocent. I've done nothing!"

1999. 2000. 2055.

The Machine stopped.

"Get out," said Travis. 130

The room was there as they had left it. But not the same as they had left it. The
same man sat behind the same desk. But the same man did not quite sit behind the
same desk. Travis looked around swiftly. "Everything okay here?" he snapped.

"Fine. Welcome home!"

Travis did not relax. He seemed to be looking through the one high window.

"Okay, Eckels, get out. Don't ever come back." Eckels could not move.

"You heard me," said Travis. "What're you *staring* at?" 135

Eckels stood smelling of the air, and there was a thing to the air, a chemical taint
so subtle, so slight, that only a faint cry of his subliminal senses warned him it was
there. The colors, white, gray, blue, orange, in the wall, in the furniture, in the sky
beyond the window, were . . . were. . . . And there was a *feel*. His flesh twitched. His
hands twitched. He stood drinking the oddness with the pores of his body. Somewhere, someone must have been screaming one of those whistles that only a dog
can hear. His body screamed silence in return. Beyond this room, beyond this wall,
beyond this man who was not quite the same man seated at this desk that was not
quite the same desk . . . lay an entire world of streets and people. What sort of world
it was now, there was no telling. He could feel them moving there, beyond the walls,
almost, like so many chess pieces blown in a dry wind. . . .

But the immediate thing was the sign painted on the office wall, the same sign
he had read earlier today on first entering. Somehow, the sign had changed:

TYME SEFARI INC.

SEFARIS TU ANY YEER EN THE

PAST.

YU NAIM THE ANIMALL.

WEE TAEKYUTHAIR.

YU SHOOT ITT.

Eckels felt himself fall into a chair. He fumbled crazily at the thick slime on his boots.
He held up a clod of dirt, trembling, "No, it *can't* be. Not a *little* thing like that. No!"

Embedded in the mud, glistening green and gold and black, was a butterfly, very
beautiful and very dead.

"Not a little thing like *that*! Not a butterfly!" cried Eckels. 140

It fell to the floor, an exquisite thing, a small thing that could upset balances and knock down a line of small dominoes and then big dominoes and then gigantic dominoes, all down the years across Time. Eckels' mind whirled. It *couldn't* change things. Killing one butterfly couldn't be *that* important! Could it?

His face was cold. His mouth trembled, asking: "Who—who won the presidential election yesterday?"

The man behind the desk laughed. "You joking? You know very well. Deutscher, of course! Who else? Not that fool weakling Keith. We got an iron man now, a man with guts!" The official stopped. "What's wrong?"

Eckels moaned. He dropped to his knees. He scrabbled at the golden butterfly with shaking fingers. "Can't we," he pleaded to the world, to himself, to the officials, to the Machine, "can't we take it *back*, can't we *make* it alive again? Can't we start over? Can't we—"

He did not move. Eyes shut, he waited, shivering. He heard Travis breathe 145 loud in the room; he heard Travis shift his rifle, click the safety catch, and raise the weapon.

There was a sound of thunder.

Questions

1. What are the two main settings of Bradbury's story? What is unusual about both settings?
2. How does the plot of the story depend on the setting? Would it be possible to tell this story in different settings?
3. Why does the government not approve of time travel? How does Time Safari Inc. deal with governmental obstacles?
4. When Eckels returns to the altered present, when does he first sense that something has changed?
5. In what specific ways has the present been changed by the trip?
6. What happens in the last three paragraphs of the story?

Kelly Link

The Faery Handbag   2005

The work of Kelly Link (b. 1969) is difficult to categorize. At times, her smart and playful stories incorporate elements of fantasy, magic realism, and horror, yet they also toe the line of realism, often leaving the reader on uncertain ground. One certainty, however, is that her fiction is always a pleasure to read. Born in Miami, Florida, Link's parents instilled in her an early appreciation of imaginative literature. She told NPR in 2015: "My dad read me all of Tolkien when I was in kindergarten. My mom read me all of C. S. Lewis. And then when once I learned to read—I was a little bit slow—I would just go to the library and sort of work my way through the shelves." Link has published four collections of stories: Stranger Things Happen *(2001),* Magic for Beginners *(2005),*

Kelly Link

Pretty Monsters (2008), *and* Get in Trouble (2015), *which was a finalist for the Pulitzer Prize, a rarity for a book that some critics might dismiss as genre fiction. Her work has earned several honors, including both Hugo and Nebula awards for "The Faery Handbag," as well as a grant from the National Endowment for the Arts. In addition to her achievements as an author, Link has taught at several universities. With her husband, writer Gavin Grant, she operates Small Beer Press in Northampton, Massachusetts, which publishes fantasy and literary fiction. The couple also edits the zine* Lady Churchill's Rosebud Wristlet.

I used to go to thrift stores with my friends. We'd take the train into Boston, and go to The Garment District, which is this huge vintage clothing warehouse. Everything is arranged by color, and somehow that makes all of the clothes beautiful. It's kind of like if you went through the wardrobe in the Narnia books, only instead of finding Aslan and the White Witch and horrible Eustace, you found this magic clothing world—instead of talking animals, there were feather boas and wedding dresses and bowling shoes, and paisley shirts and Doc Martens and everything hung up on racks so that first you have black dresses, all together, like the world's largest indoor funeral, and then blue dresses—all the blues you can imagine—and then red dresses and so on. Pink reds and orangey reds and purple reds and exit-light reds and candy reds. Sometimes I would close my eyes and Natasha and Natalie and Jake would drag me over to a rack, and rub a dress against my hand. "Guess what color this is."

We had this theory that you could learn how to tell, just by feeling, what color something was. For example, if you're sitting on a lawn, you can tell what color green the grass is, with your eyes closed, depending on how silky-rubbery it feels. With clothing, stretchy velvet stuff always feels red when your eyes are closed, even if it's not red. Natasha was always best at guessing colors, but Natasha is also best at cheating at games and not getting caught.

One time we were looking through kids' T-shirts and we found a Muppets T-shirt that had belonged to Natalie in third grade. We knew it belonged to her, because it still had her name inside, where her mother had written it in permanent marker when Natalie went to summer camp. Jake bought it back for her, because he was the only one who had money that weekend. He was the only one who had a job.

Maybe you're wondering what a guy like Jake is doing in The Garment District with a bunch of girls. The thing about Jake is that he always has a good time, no matter what he's doing. He likes everything, and he likes everyone, but he likes me best of all. Wherever he is now, I bet he's having a great time and wondering when I'm going to show up. I'm always running late. But he knows that.

We had this theory that things have life cycles, the way that people do. The   5
life cycle of wedding dresses and feather boas and T-shirts and shoes and handbags involves The Garment District. If clothes are good, or even if they're bad in an interesting way, The Garment District is where they go when they die. You can tell that they're dead, because of the way that they smell. When you buy them, and wash them, and start wearing them again, and they start to smell like you, that's when they reincarnate. But the point is, if you're looking for a particular thing, you just have to keep looking for it. You have to look hard.

Down in the basement at The Garment District they sell clothing and beat-up suitcases and teacups by the pound. You can get eight pounds' worth of prom dresses—a slinky black dress, a poufy lavender dress, a swirly pink dress, a silvery, starry lamé dress so fine you could pass it through a key ring—for eight dollars. I go there every week, hunting for Grandmother Zofia's faery handbag.

The faery handbag: It's huge and black and kind of hairy. Even when your eyes are closed, it feels black. As black as black ever gets, like if you touch it, your hand might get stuck in it, like tar or black quicksand or when you stretch out your hand at night, to turn on a light, but all you feel is darkness.

Fairies live inside it. I know what that sounds like, but it's true.

Grandmother Zofia said it was a family heirloom. She said that it was over two hundred years old. She said that when she died, I had to look after it. Be its guardian. She said that it would be my responsibility.

I said that it didn't look that old, and that they didn't have handbags two hun- 10 dred years ago, but that just made her cross. She said, "So then tell me, Genevieve, darling, where do you think old ladies used to put their reading glasses and their heart medicine and their knitting needles?"

I know that no one is going to believe any of this. That's okay. If I thought you would, then I couldn't tell you. Promise me that you won't believe a word. That's what Zofia used to say to me when she told me stories. At the funeral, my mother said, half-laughing and half-crying, that her mother was the world's best liar. I think she thought maybe Zofia wasn't really dead. But I went up to Zofia's coffin, and I looked her right in the eyes. They were closed. The funeral parlor had made her up with blue eyeshadow, and blue eyeliner. She looked like she was going to be a news anchor on Fox television, instead of dead. It was creepy and it made me even sadder than I already was. But I didn't let that distract me.

"Okay, Zofia," I whispered. "I know you're dead, but this is important. You know exactly how important this is. Where's the handbag? What did you do with it? How do I find it? What am I supposed to do now?"

Of course, she didn't say a word. She just lay there, this little smile on her face, as if she thought the whole thing—death, blue eyeshadow, Jake, the handbag, faeries, Scrabble, Baldeziwurlekistan, all of it—was a joke. She always did have a weird sense of humor. That's why she and Jake got along so well.

I grew up in a house next door to the house where my mother lived when she was a little girl. Her mother, Zofia Swink, my grandmother, babysat me while my mother and father were at work.

Zofia never looked like a grandmother. She had long black hair, which she 15 plaited up in spiky towers. She had large blue eyes. She was taller than my father. She looked like a spy or ballerina or a lady pirate or a rock star. She acted like one too. For example, she never drove anywhere. She rode a bike. It drove my mother crazy. "Why can't you act your age?" she'd say, and Zofia would just laugh.

Zofia and I played Scrabble all the time. Zofia always won, even though her English wasn't all that great, because we'd decided that she was allowed to use Baldeziwurleki vocabulary. Baldeziwurlekistan is where Zofia was born, over two hundred years ago. That's what Zofia said. (My grandmother claimed to be over two hundred years old. Or maybe even older. Sometimes she claimed that she'd even met Genghis Khan. He was much shorter than her. I probably don't have time to tell that story.) Baldeziwurlekistan is also an incredibly valuable word in Scrabble points, even though it doesn't exactly fit on the board. Zofia put it down the first time we played. I was feeling pretty good because I'd gotten forty-one points for *zippery* on my turn.

Zofia kept rearranging her letters on her tray. Then she looked over at me, as if daring me to stop her, and put down *eziwurlekistan*, after *bald*. She used *delicious*, *zippery*, *wishes*, *kismet*, and *needle*, and made *to* into *toe*. *Baldeziwurlekistan* went all the way across the board and then trailed off down the right-hand side.

I started laughing.

"I used up all my letters," Zofia said. She licked her pencil and started adding up points.

"That's not a word," I said. "*Baldeziwurlekistan* is not a word. Besides, you can't do that. You can't put an eighteen-letter word on a board that's fifteen squares across." 20

"Why not? It's a country," Zofia said. "It's where I was born, little darling."

"Challenge," I said. I went and got the dictionary and looked it up. "There's no such place."

"Of course there isn't nowadays," Zofia said. "It wasn't a very big place, even when it was a place. But you've heard of Samarkand, and Uzbekistan and the Silk Road and Genghis Khan. Haven't I told you about meeting Genghis Khan?"

I looked up Samarkand. "Okay," I said. "Samarkand is a real place. A real word. But Baldeziwurlekistan isn't."

"They call it something else now," Zofia said. "But I think it's important to remem- 25 ber where we come from. I think it's only fair that I get to use Baldeziwurleki words. Your English is so much better than me. Promise me something, mouthful of dumpling, a small, small thing. You'll remember its real name. Baldeziwurlekistan. Now when I add it up, I get three hundred and sixty-eight points. Could that be right?"

If you called the faery handbag by its right name, it would be something like *orzipanikanikcz*, which means the "bag of skin where the world lives," only Zofia never spelled that word the same way twice. She said you had to spell it a little differently each time. You never wanted to spell it exactly the right way, because that would be dangerous.

I called it the faery handbag because I put *faery* down on the Scrabble board once. Zofia said that you spelled it with an *i*, not an *e*. She looked it up in the dictionary, and lost a turn.

Zofia said that in Baldeziwurlekistan they used a board and tiles for divination, prognostication, and sometimes even just for fun. She said it was a little like playing Scrabble. That's probably why she turned out to be so good at Scrabble. The Baldeziwurlekistanians used their tiles and board to communicate with the people who lived under the hill. The people who lived under the hill knew the future. The Baldeziwurlekistanians gave them fermented milk and honey, and the young women of the village used to go and lie out on the hill and sleep under the stars. Apparently the people under the hill were pretty cute. The important thing was that you never went down into the hill and spent the night there, no matter how cute the guy from under the hill was. If you did, even if you only spent a single night under the hill, when you came out again, a hundred years might have passed. "Remember that," Zofia said to me. "It doesn't matter how cute a guy is. If he wants you to come back to his place, it isn't a good idea. It's okay to fool around, but don't spend the night."

Every once in a while, a woman from under the hill would marry a man from the village, even though it never ended well. The problem was that the women under the hill were terrible cooks. They couldn't get used to the way time worked in the village, which meant that supper always got burnt, or else it wasn't cooked long enough. But they couldn't stand to be criticized. It hurt their feelings. If their village husband complained, or even if he looked like he wanted to complain, that was it. The woman from under the hill went back to her home, and even if her husband went and begged and pleaded and apologized, it might be three years or thirty years or a few generations before she came back out.

Even the best, happiest marriages between the Baldeziwurlekistanians and the people under the hill fell apart when the children got old enough to complain about dinner. But everyone in the village had some hill blood in them.

"It's in you," Zofia said, and kissed me on the nose. "Passed down from my grandmother and her mother. It's why we're so beautiful."

When Zofia was nineteen, the shaman-priestess in her village threw the tiles and discovered that something bad was going to happen. A raiding party was coming. There was no point in fighting them. They would burn down everyone's houses and take the young men and women for slaves. And it was even worse than that. There was going to be an earthquake as well, which was bad news because usually, when raiders showed up, the village went down under the hill for a night and when they came out again, the raiders would have been gone for months or decades or even a hundred years. But this earthquake was going to split the hill right open.

The people under the hill were in trouble. Their home would be destroyed, and they would be doomed to roam the face of the earth, weeping and lamenting their fate until the sun blew out and the sky cracked and the seas boiled and the people dried up and turned to dust and blew away. So the shaman-priestess went and divined some more, and the people under the hill told her to kill a black dog and skin it and use the skin to make a purse big enough to hold a chicken, an egg, and a cooking pot. So she did, and then the people under the hill made the inside of the purse big enough to hold all of the village and all of the people under the hill and mountains and forests and seas and rivers and lakes and orchards and a sky and stars and spirits and fabulous monsters and sirens and dragons and dryads and mermaids and beasties and all the little gods that the Baldeziwurlekistanians and the people under the hill worshipped.

"Your purse is made out of dog skin?" I said. "That's disgusting!"

"Little dear pet," Zofia said, looking wistful. "Dog is delicious. To Baldeziwurlekistanians, dog is a delicacy."

Before the raiding party arrived, the village packed up all of their belongings and moved into the handbag. The clasp was made out of bone. If you opened it one way, then it was just a purse big enough to hold a chicken and an egg and a clay cooking pot, or else a pair of reading glasses and a library book and a pillbox. If you opened the clasp another way, then you found yourself in a little boat floating at the mouth of a river. On either side of you was forest, where the Baldeziwurlekistanian villagers and the people under the hill made their new settlement.

If you opened the handbag the wrong way, though, you found yourself in a dark land that smelled like blood. That's where the guardian of the purse (the dog whose skin had been sewn into a purse) lived. The guardian had no skin. Its howl made blood come out of your ears and nose. It tore apart anyone who turned the clasp in the opposite direction and opened the purse in the wrong way.

"Here is the wrong way to open the handbag," Zofia said. She twisted the clasp, showing me how she did it. She opened the mouth of the purse, but not very wide and held it up to me. "Go ahead, darling, and listen for a second."

I put my head near the handbag, but not too near. I didn't hear anything. "I don't hear anything," I said.

"The poor dog is probably asleep," Zofia said. "Even nightmares have to sleep now and then."   40

After he got expelled, everybody at school called Jake Houdini instead of Jake. Everybody except for me. I'll explain why, but you have to be patient. It's hard work telling everything in the right order.

Jake is smarter and also taller than most of our teachers. Not quite as tall as me. We've known each other since third grade. Jake has always been in love with me. He says he was in love with me even before third grade, even before we ever met. It took me a while to fall in love with Jake.

In third grade, Jake knew everything already, except how to make friends. He used to follow me around all day long. It made me so mad that I kicked him in the knee. When that didn't work, I threw his backpack out of the window of the school bus. That didn't work either, but the next year Jake took some tests and the school decided that he could skip fourth and fifth grade. Even I felt sorry for Jake then. Sixth grade didn't work out. When the sixth graders wouldn't stop flushing his head down the toilet, he went out and caught a skunk and set it loose in the boys' locker room.

The school was going to suspend him for the rest of the year, but instead Jake took two years off while his mother home-schooled him. He learned Latin and Hebrew and Greek, how to write sestinas, how to make sushi, how to play bridge, and even how to knit. He learned fencing and ballroom dancing. He worked in a soup kitchen and made a Super 8 movie about Civil War re-enactors who play extreme croquet in full costume instead of firing off cannons. He started learning how to play guitar. He even wrote a novel. I've never read it—he says it was awful.

When he came back two years later, because his mother had cancer for the first   45
time, the school put him back with our year, in seventh grade. He was still way too smart, but he was finally smart enough to figure out how to fit in. Plus he was good at soccer and he was yummy. Did I mention that he played guitar? Every girl in school had a crush on Jake, but he used to come home after school with me and play Scrabble with Zofia and ask her about Baldeziwurlekistan.

Jake's mom was named Cynthia. She collected ceramic frogs and knock-knock jokes. When we were in ninth grade, she had cancer again. When she died, Jake smashed all of her frogs. That was the first funeral I ever went to. A few months later, Jake's father asked Jake's fencing teacher out on a date. They got married right after the school expelled Jake for his AP project on Houdini. That was the first wedding I ever went to. Jake and I stole a bottle of wine and drank it, and I threw up in the swimming pool at the country club. Jake threw up all over my shoes.

So, anyway, the village and the people under the hill lived happily every after for a few weeks in the handbag, which they had tied around a rock in a dry well which the people under the hill had determined would survive the earthquake. But some of the Baldeziwurlekistanians wanted to come out again and see what was going on in the world. Zofia was one of them. It had been summer when they went into the bag, but when they came out again, and climbed out of the well, snow was falling and their village was ruins and crumbly old rubble. They walked through the snow, Zofia carrying the handbag, until they came to another village, one that they'd never seen before. Everyone in that village was packing up their belongings and leaving, which gave Zofia and her friends a bad feeling. It seemed to be just the same as when they went into the handbag.

They followed the refugees, who seemed to know where they were going, and finally everyone came to a city. Zofia had ever seen such a place. There were trains and electric lights and movie theaters, and there were people shooting each other. Bombs were falling. A war going on. Most of the villagers decided to climb right back inside the handbag, but Zofia volunteered to stay in the world and look after the handbag. She had fallen in love with movies and silk stockings and with a young man, a Russian deserter.

Zofia and the Russian deserter married and had many adventures and finally came to America, where my mother was born. Now and then Zofia would consult the tiles and talk to the people who lived in the handbag and they would tell her how best to avoid trouble and how she and her husband could make some money. Every now and then one of the Baldeziwurlekistanians or one of the people from under the hill came out of the handbag and wanted to go grocery shopping, or to a movie or an amusement park to ride on roller coasters, or to the library.

The more advice Zofia gave her husband, the more money they made. Her hus- 50
band became curious about Zofia's handbag, because he could see that there was something odd about it, but Zofia told him to mind his own business. He began to spy on Zofia, and saw that strange men and women were coming in and out of the house. He became convinced that either Zofia was a spy for the Communists, or maybe that she was having affairs. They fought and he drank more and more, and finally he threw away her divination tiles. "Russians make bad husbands," Zofia told me. Finally, one night while Zofia was sleeping, her husband opened the bone clasp and climbed inside the handbag.

"I thought he'd left me," Zofia said. "For almost twenty years I thought he'd left me and your mother and taken off for California. Not that I minded. I was tired of being married and cooking dinners and cleaning house for someone else. It's better to cook what I want to eat, and clean up when I decide to clean up. It was harder on your mother, not having a father. That was the part that I minded most."

"Then it turned out that he hadn't run away after all. He spent one night in the handbag and came out again twenty years later, exactly as handsome as I remembered, and enough time had passed that I had forgiven him all the quarrels. We made up and it was all very romantic and then when we had another fight the next morning, he went and kissed your mother, who had slept right through his visit, on the cheek, and then he climbed right back inside the handbag. I didn't see him again for another twenty years. The last time he showed up, we went to see *Star Wars* and he liked it so much that he went back inside the handbag to tell everyone else about it. In a couple of years they'll all show up and want to see it on video and all of the sequels too."

"Tell them not to bother with the prequels," I said.

The thing about Zofia and libraries is that she's always losing library books. She says that she hasn't lost them, and in fact that they aren't even overdue, really. It's just that even one week inside the faery handbag is a lot longer in library-world time. So what is she supposed to do about it? The librarians all hate Zofia. She's banned from using any of the branches in our area. When I was eight, she got me to go to the library for her and check out biographies and science books and some Georgette Heyer romance novels. My mother was livid when she found out, but it was too late. Zofia had already misplaced most of them.

It's really hard to write about somebody as if they're really dead. I still think   55
Zofia must be sitting in her living room, in her house, watching some old horror movie, dropping popcorn into her handbag. She's waiting for me to come over and play Scrabble.

Nobody is ever going to return those library books now.

My mother used to come home from work and roll her eyes. "Have you been telling them your fairy stories?" she'd say. "Genevieve, your grandmother is a horrible liar."
Zofia would fold up the Scrabble board and shrug at me and Jake. "I'm a wonderful liar," she'd say. "I'm the best liar in the world. Promise me you won't believe a single word."
But she wouldn't tell the story of the faery handbag to Jake. Only the old Baldeziwurlekistanian folktales and fairy tales about the people under the hill. She told him about how she and her husband made it all the way across Europe, hiding in haystacks and in barns. What she told me was how once, when her husband went off to find food, a farmer found her hiding in his chicken coop and tried to rape her. But she opened up the faery handbag in the way she showed me, and the dog came out and ate the farmer and all his chickens too.
She was teaching Jake and me how to curse in Baldeziwurleki. I also know how   60
to say I love you, but I'm not going to ever say it to anyone again, except to Jake, when I find him.
When I was eight, I believed everything Zofia told me. By the time I was thirteen, I didn't believe a single word. When I was fifteen, I saw a man come out of her house and get on Zofia's three-speed bicycle and ride down the street. He wore funny clothes. He was a lot younger than my mother and father, and even though I'd never seen him before, he was familiar. I followed him on my bike, all the way to the grocery store. I waited just past the checkout lanes while he bought peanut butter, Jack Daniel's, half a dozen instant cameras, and at least sixty packs of Reese's Peanut Butter Cups, three bags of Hershey's Kisses, a handful of Milky Way bars, and other stuff from the rack of checkout candy. While the checkout clerk was helping him bag up all of that chocolate, he looked up and saw me. "Genevieve?" he said. "That's your name, right?"
I turned and ran out of the store. He grabbed up the bags and ran after me. I don't even think he got his change back. I was still running away, and then one of the straps on my flip-flops popped out of the sole, the way they do, and that made me really angry so I just stopped. I turned around.
"Who are you?" I said.
But I already knew. He looked like he could have been my mom's younger brother. He was really cute. I could see why Zofia had fallen in love with him.
His name was Rustan. Zofia told my parents that he was an expert in Baldezi-   65
wurlekistanian folklore who would be staying with her for a few days. She brought

him over for dinner. Jake was there too, and I could tell that Jake knew something was up. Everybody except my dad knew something was going on.

"You mean Baldeziwurlekistan is a real place?" my mother asked Rustan. "My mother is telling the truth?"

I could see that Rustan was having a hard time with that one. He obviously wanted to say that his wife was a horrible liar, but then where would he be? Then he couldn't be the person that he was supposed to be.

There were probably a lot of things that he wanted to say. What he said was, "This is really good pizza."

Rustan took a lot of pictures at dinner. The next day I went with him to get the pictures developed. He'd brought back some film with him, with pictures he'd taken inside the faery handbag, but those didn't come out well. Maybe the film was too old. We got doubles of the pictures from dinner so that I could have some too. There's a great picture of Jake, sitting outside on the porch. He's laughing, and he has his hand up to his mouth, like he's going to catch the laugh. I have that picture up on my computer, and also up on my wall over my bed.

I bought a Cadbury Creme Egg for Rustan. Then we shook hands and he kissed me once on each cheek. "Give one of those kisses to your mother," he said, and I thought about how the next time I saw him, I might be Zofia's age, and he would only be a few days older. The next time I saw him, Zofia would be dead. Jake and I might have kids. That was too weird. 70

I know Rustan tried to get Zofia to go with him, to live in the handbag, but she wouldn't.

"It makes me dizzy in there," she used to tell me. "And they don't have movie theaters. And I have to look after your mother and you. Maybe when you're old enough to look after the handbag, I'll poke my head inside, just long enough for a little visit."

I didn't fall in love with Jake because he was smart. I'm pretty smart myself. I know that smart doesn't mean nice, or even mean that you have a lot of common sense. Look at all the trouble smart people get themselves into.

I didn't fall in love with Jake because he could make maki rolls and had a black belt in fencing, or whatever it is that you get if you're good in fencing. I didn't fall in love with Jake because he plays guitar. He's a better soccer player than he is a guitar player.

Those were the reasons why I went out on a date with Jake. That, and because he asked me. He asked if I wanted to go see a movie, and I asked if I could bring my grandmother and Natalie and Natasha. He said sure and so all five of us sat and watched *Bring It On* and every once in a while Zofia dropped a couple of Milk Duds or some popcorn into her purse. I don't know if she was feeding the dog, or if she'd opened the purse the right way, and was throwing food at her husband. 75

I fell in love with Jake because he told stupid knock-knock jokes to Natalie, and told Natasha that he liked her jeans. I fell in love with Jake when he took me and Zofia home. He walked her up to her front door and then he walked me up to mine. I fell in love with Jake when he didn't try to kiss me. The thing is, I was nervous about the whole kissing thing. Most guys think that they're better at it than they really are. Not that I think I'm a real genius at kissing either, but I don't think kissing should be a competitive sport. It isn't tennis.

Natalie and Natasha and I used to practice kissing with each other. Just for practice. We got pretty good at it. We could see why kissing was supposed to be fun.

But Jake didn't try to kiss me. Instead he just gave me this really big hug. He put his face in my hair and he sighed. We stood there like that, and then finally I said, "What are you doing?"

"I just wanted to smell your hair," he said.

"Oh," I said. That made me feel weird, but in a good way. I stuck my nose in his 80 hair, which is brown and curly. I smelled it. We stood there and smelled each other's hair, and I felt so good. I felt so happy.

Jake said into my hair, "Do you know that actor John Cusack?"

I said, "Yeah. One of Zofia's favorite movies is *Better Off Dead*. We watch it all the time."

"So he likes to go up to women and smell their armpits."

"Gross!" I said. "That's such a lie! What are you doing now? That tickles."

"I'm smelling your ear," Jake said. 85

Jake's hair smelled like iced tea with honey in it, after all the ice has melted.

Kissing Jake is like kissing Natalie or Natasha, except that it isn't just for fun. It feels like something there isn't a word for in Scrabble.

The deal with Houdini is that Jake got interested in him during Advanced Placement American History. He and I were both put in tenth-grade history. We were doing biography projects. I was studying Joseph McCarthy. My grandmother had all sorts of stories about McCarthy. She hated him for what he did to Hollywood.

Jake didn't turn in his project—instead he told everyone in our AP class except for Mr. Streep (we call him Meryl) to meet him at the gym on Saturday. When we showed up, Jake reenacted one of Houdini's escapes with a laundry bag, handcuffs, a gym locker, bicycle chains, and the school's swimming pool. It took him three and a half minutes to get free, and this guy named Roger took a bunch of photos and then put the photos online. One of the photos ended up in *The Boston Globe*, and Jake got expelled. The really ironic thing was that while his mom was in the hospital, Jake had applied to MIT. He did it for his mom. He thought that way she'd have to stay alive. She was so excited about MIT. A couple of days after he'd been expelled, right after the wedding, while his dad and the fencing instructor were in Bermuda, he got an acceptance letter in the mail and a phone call from this guy in the admissions office who explained why they had to withdraw the acceptance.

My mother wanted to know why I let Jake wrap himself up in bicycle chains and 90 then watched while Peter and Michael pushed him into the deep end of the school pool. I said that Jake had a backup plan. Ten more seconds and we were all going to jump into the pool and open the locker and get him out of there. I was crying when I said that. Even before he got in the locker, I knew how stupid Jake was being. Afterwards, he promised me that he'd never do anything like that again.

That was when I told him about Zofia's husband, Rustan, and about Zofia's handbag. How stupid am I?

So I guess you can figure out what happened next. The problem is that Jake believed me about the handbag. We spent a lot of time over at Zofia's, playing Scrabble.

Zofia never let the faery handbag out of her sight. She even took it with her when she went to the bathroom. I think she even slept with it under her pillow.

I didn't tell her that I'd said anything to Jake. I wouldn't ever have told anybody else about it. Not Natasha. Not even Natalie, who is the most responsible person in all of the world. Now, of course, if the handbag turns up and Jake still hasn't come back, I'll have to tell Natalie. Somebody has to keep an eye on the stupid thing while I go find Jake.

What worries me is that maybe one of the Baldeziwurlekistanians or one of the people under the hill or maybe even Rustan popped out of the handbag to run an errand and got worried when Zofia wasn't there. Maybe they'll come looking for her and bring it back. Maybe they know I'm supposed to look after it now. Or maybe they took it and hid it somewhere. Maybe someone turned it in at the lost-and-found at the library and that stupid librarian called the FBI. Maybe scientists at the Pentagon are examining the handbag right now. Testing it. If Jake comes out, they'll think he's a spy or a superweapon or an alien or something. They're not going to just let him go.

Everyone thinks Jake ran away, except for my mother, who is convinced that he was trying out another Houdini escape and is probably lying at the bottom of a lake somewhere. She hasn't said that to me, but I can see her thinking it. She keeps making cookies for me.

What happened is that Jake said, "Can I see that for just a second?"

He said it so casually that I think he caught Zofia off guard. She was reaching into the purse for her wallet. We were standing in the lobby of the movie theater on a Monday morning. Jake was behind the snack counter. He'd gotten a job there. He was wearing this stupid red paper hat and some kind of apron bib thing. He was supposed to ask us if we wanted to supersize our drinks.

He reached over the counter and took Zofia's handbag right out of her hand. He closed it and then he opened it again. I think he opened it the right way. I don't think he ended up in the dark place. He said to me and Zofia, "I'll be right back." And then he wasn't there anymore. It was just me and Zofia and the handbag, lying there on the counter where he'd dropped it.

If I'd been fast enough, I think I could have followed him. But Zofia had been guardian of the faery handbag for a lot longer. She snatched the bag back and glared at me. "He's a very bad boy," she said. She was absolutely furious. "You're better off without him, Genevieve, I think."

"Give me the handbag," I said. "I have to go get him."

"It isn't a toy, Genevieve," she said. "It isn't a game. This isn't Scrabble. He comes back when he comes back. If he comes back."

"Give me the handbag," I said. "Or I'll take it from you."

She held the handbag up high over her head, so that I couldn't reach it. I hate people who are taller than me. "What are you going to do now," Zofia said. "Are you going to knock me down? Are you going to steal the handbag? Are you going to go away and leave me here to explain to your parents where you've gone? Are you going to say good-bye to your friends? When you come out again, they will have gone to college. They'll have jobs and babies and houses and they won't even recognize you. Your mother will be an old woman and I will be dead."

"I don't care," I said. I sat down on the sticky red carpet in the lobby and started to cry. Someone wearing a little metal name tag came over and asked if we were okay. His name was MISSY. Or maybe he was wearing someone else's tag.

95

100

"We're fine," Zofia said. "My granddaughter has the flu." 105

She took my hand and pulled me up. She put her arm around me and we walked out of the theater. We never even got to see the stupid movie. We never even got to see another movie together. I don't ever want to go see another movie. The problem is, I don't want to see unhappy endings. And I don't know if I believe in the happy ones.

"I have a plan," Zofia said. "I will go find Jake. You will stay here and look after the handbag."

"You won't come back either," I said. I cried even harder. "Or if you do, I'll be like a hundred years old and Jake will still be sixteen."

"Everything will be okay," Zofia said. I wish I could tell you how beautiful she looked right then. It didn't matter if she was lying or if she actually knew that everything was going to be okay. The important thing was how she looked when she said it. She said, with absolute certainty, or maybe with all the skill of a very skillful liar, "My plan will work. First we go to the library, though. One of the people under the hill just brought back an Agatha Christie mystery, and I need to return it."

"We're going to the library?" I said. "Why don't we just go home and play Scrab- 110 ble for a while." You probably think I was just being sarcastic here, and I was being sarcastic. But Zofia gave me a sharp look. She knew that if I was being sarcastic that my brain was working again. She knew that I knew she was stalling for time. She knew that I was coming up with my own plan, which was a lot like Zofia's plan, except that I was the one who went into the handbag. *How* was the part I was working on.

"We could do that," she said. "Remember, when you don't know what to do, it never hurts to play Scrabble. It's like reading the I Ching or tea leaves."

"Can we please just hurry?" I said.

Zofia just looked at me. "Genevieve, we have plenty of time. If you're going to look after the handbag, you have to remember that. You have to be patient. Can you be patient?"

"I can try," I told her. I'm trying, Zofia. I'm trying really hard. But it isn't fair. Jake is off having adventures and talking to talking animals, and who knows, learning how to fly and some beautiful three-thousand-year-old girl from under the hill is teaching him how to speak fluent Baldeziwurleki. I bet she lives in a house that runs around on chicken legs, and she tells Jake that she'd love to hear him play something on the guitar. Maybe you'll kiss her, Jake, because she's put a spell on you. But whatever you do, don't go up into her house. Don't fall asleep in her bed. Come back soon, Jake, and bring the handbag with you.

I hate those movies, those books, where some guy gets to go off and have adven- 115 tures and meanwhile the girl has to stay home and wait. I'm a feminist. I subscribe to *Bust* magazine, and I watch *Buffy* reruns. I don't believe in that kind of shit.

We hadn't been in the library for five minutes before Zofia picked up a biography of Carl Sagan and dropped it in her purse. She was definitely stalling for time. She was trying to come up with a plan that would counteract the plan that she knew I was planning. I wondered what she thought I was planning. It was probably much better than anything I'd come up with.

"Don't do that!" I said.

"Don't worry," Zofia said. "Nobody was watching."

"I don't care if nobody saw! What if Jake's sitting there in the boat, or what if he was coming back and you just dropped it on his head!"

"It doesn't work that way," Zofia said. Then she said, "It would serve him right, anyway." 120

That was when the librarian came up to us. She had a name tag on as well. I was so sick of people and their stupid name tags. I'm not even going to tell you what her name was. "I saw that," the librarian said.

"Saw what?" Zofia said. She smiled down at the librarian, like she was Queen of the Library, and the librarian was a petitioner.

The librarian stared hard at her. "I know you," she said, almost sounding awed, like she was a weekend bird-watcher who had just seen Bigfoot. "We have your picture on the office wall. You're Ms. Swink. You aren't allowed to check out books here."

"That's ridiculous," Zofia said. She was at least two feet taller than the librarian. I felt a bit sorry for the librarian. After all, Zofia had just stolen a seven-day book. She probably wouldn't return it for a hundred years. My mother has always made it clear that it's my job to protect other people from Zofia. I guess I was Zofia's guardian before I became the guardian of the handbag.

The librarian reached up and grabbed Zofia's handbag. She was small but she was 125 strong. She jerked the handbag and Zofia stumbled and fell back against a work desk. I couldn't believe it. Everyone except for me was getting a look at Zofia's handbag. What kind of guardian was I going to be?

"Genevieve," Zofia said. She held my hand very tightly, and I looked at her. She looked wobbly and pale. She said, "I feel very bad about all of this. Tell your mother I said so."

Then she said one last thing, but I think it was in Baldeziwurleki.

The librarian said, "I saw you put a book in here. Right here." She opened the handbag and peered inside. Out of the handbag came a long, lonely, ferocious, utterly hopeless scream of rage. I don't ever want to hear that noise again. Everyone in the library looked up. The librarian made a choking noise and threw Zofia's handbag away from her. A little trickle of blood came out of her nose and a drop fell on the floor. What I thought at first was that it was just plain luck that the handbag was closed when it landed. Later on I was trying to figure out what Zofia said. My Baldeziwurleki isn't very good, but I think she was saying something like "Figures. Stupid librarian. I have to go take care of that damn dog." So maybe that's what happened. Maybe Zofia sent part of herself in there with the skinless dog. Maybe she fought it and won and closed the handbag. Maybe she made friends with it. I mean, she used to feed it popcorn at the movies. Maybe she's still in there.

What happened in the library was Zofia sighed a little and closed her eyes. I helped her sit down in a chair, but I don't think she was really there any more. I rode with her in the ambulance, when the ambulance finally showed up, and I swear I didn't even think about the handbag until my mother showed up. I didn't say a word. I just left her there in the hospital with Zofia, who was on a respirator, and I ran all the way back to the library. But it was closed. So I ran all the way back again, to the hospital, but you already know what happened, right? Zofia died. I hate writing that. My tall, funny, beautiful, book-stealing, Scrabble-playing, story-telling grandmother died.

But you never met her. You're probably wondering about the handbag. What   130
happened to it. I put up signs all over town, like Zofia's handbag was some kind of
lost dog, but nobody ever called.

So that's the story so far. Not that I expect you to believe any of it. Last night
Natalie and Natasha came over and we played Scrabble. They don't really like
Scrabble, but they feel like it's their job to cheer me up. I won. After they went
home, I flipped all the tiles upside-down and then I started picking them up in groups
of seven. I tried to ask a question, but it was hard to pick just one. The words I
got weren't so great either, so I decided that they weren't English words. They were
Baldeziwurleki words.

Once I decided that, everything became perfectly clear. First I put down *kirif*
which means "happy news," and then I got a *b*, an *o*, an *l*, an *e*, another *i*, an *s*, and a
z. So then I could make *kirif* into *bolekirifisz*, which could mean "the happy result of a
combination of diligent effort and patience."

I would find the faery handbag. The tiles said so. I would work the clasp and go
into the handbag and have my own adventures and would rescue Jake. Hardly any
time would have gone by before we came back out of the handbag. Maybe I'd even
make friends with that poor dog and get to say goodbye, for real, to Zofia. Rustan
would show up again and be really sorry that he'd missed Zofia's funeral and this time
he would be brave enough to tell my mother the whole story. He would tell her that
he was her father. Not that she would believe him. Not that you should believe this
story. Promise me that you won't believe a word.

Questions

1. Is "The Faery Handbag" a work of fantasy, or is it a story about a wacky grandmother who
   has a fondness for telling tall tales? Did your answer to this question change by the end of
   the story?
2. What is the importance of Scrabble in the story, particularly with the revised rules that
   Genevieve and Zofia use? Look back especially at when Genevieve first encounters the
   word *Baldeziwurlekistan* during a game of Scrabble (paragraph 17). Does it seem to be a
   real word, or do you get the impression that Zofia is inventing it?
3. The middle of the story describes a war that Zofia experienced in Europe. She talks of
   "hiding in haystacks and in barns" and of nearly being raped by a farmer, before the dog
   in the handbag saved her. What war is she describing? Do you expect that Zofia and her
   husband really had pleasant adventures during the war, as she relays to Genevieve and
   Jake, or do you think they may have endured something terrible?
4. What are the complicated emotional reasons why Jake reenacts one of Houdini's escapes?
   Later, when Jake allegedly disappears into the handbag, that's another sort of escape—and
   one very similar to that of Zofia's husband Rustan. What do you make of those parallels?
5. In paragraph 106, Genevieve says this of movies: "The problem is, I don't want to see
   unhappy endings. And I don't know if I believe in the happy ones." Could she be talking
   about more than just movies here?
6. Reread the description in the final scene of Genevieve creating Baldeziwurleki words from
   randomly selected tiles. How does that description reflect back on the Baldeziwurleki words
   and stories we encounter throughout "The Faery Handbag"?
7. Zofia's faery handbag seems to be the repository of an entire mythology of fantastic stories.
   When Zofia tells Genevieve that she will one day be responsible for taking care of the
   handbag, what do you think she might be referring to, besides the physical handbag? What
   responsibility is Zofia passing down to her granddaughter? Does the final line, "Promise
   me that you won't believe a word," offer a clue, especially considering that Zofia used to
   say the same line when she would tell stories? What, then, might the handbag represent?

H. P. Lovecraft

The Outsider

(1926) 1939

Howard Phillips Lovecraft (1890–1937) was born in Providence, Rhode Island. When Lovecraft was a young boy, his father, who suffered from syphilis, was committed to a mental institution where he would remain until his death. His mother died in the same institution some twenty years later. Raised in his maternal grandfather's home, Lovecraft received sporadic schooling due to poor health and breakdowns. However, he read voraciously and was especially fascinated with astronomy and the works of Edgar Allan Poe. Lovecraft spent most of his life in Rhode Island, with the exception of two years in Brooklyn during a failed marriage. In his late twenties he began writing stories and poems that were first published in the genre magazine Weird Tales.

H. P. Lovecraft

Lovecraft's horror stories are filled with supernatural beings and mythic themes. His style, which often employs archaic language, is famously ornate and extravagant. His legacy is the Cthulhu Mythos, a collection of stories based around the mythical priest Cthulhu and the ancient tome Necronomicon.

Lovecraft died at age forty-seven, penniless and unknown to the mainstream. He had never published a volume of his own fiction. After his death, his fans strove to keep his work alive by collecting it into books. His vein of supernatural horror has only increased in popularity, with many of his stories now adapted as films, TV shows, video games, and graphic novels. His terror-filled imagination has been an influence on such writers as Clive Barker, Neil Gaiman, and Stephen King.

> That night the Baron dreamt of many a woe;
> And all his warrior-guests, with shade and form
> Of witch, and demon, and large coffin-worm,
> Were long be-nightmared.
>
> —JOHN KEATS

Unhappy is he to whom the memories of childhood bring only fear and sadness. Wretched is he who looks back upon lone hours in vast and dismal chambers with brown hangings and maddening rows of antique books, or upon awed watches in twilight groves of grotesque, gigantic, and vine-encumbered trees that silently wave twisted branches far aloft. Such a lot the gods gave to me—to me, the dazed, the disappointed; the barren, the broken. And yet I am strangely content, and cling desperately to those sere memories, when my mind momentarily threatens to reach beyond to *the other*.

I know not where I was born, save that the castle was infinitely old and infinitely horrible; full of dark passages and having high ceilings where the eye could find only cobwebs and shadows. The stones in the crumbling corridors seemed always hideously damp, and there was an accursed smell everywhere, as of the piled-up corpses of dead generations. It was never light, so that I used sometimes to light candles and gaze steadily at them for relief; nor was there any sun outdoors, since the terrible trees grew high above the topmost accessible tower. There was one black tower which reached above the trees into the unknown outer sky, but that was partly ruined and could not be ascended save by a well-nigh impossible climb up the sheer wall, stone by stone.

I must have lived years in this place, but I cannot measure the time. Beings must have cared for my needs, yet I cannot recall any person except myself; or anything alive but the noiseless rats and bats and spiders. I think that whoever nursed me must have been shockingly aged, since my first conception of a living person was that of something mockingly like myself, yet distorted, shrivelled, and decaying like the castle. To me there was nothing grotesque in the bones and skeletons that strowed some of the stone crypts deep down among the foundations. I fantastically associated these things with every-day events, and thought them more natural than the coloured pictures of living beings which I found in many of the mouldy books. From such books I learned all that I know. No teacher urged or guided me, and I do not recall hearing any human voice in all those years—not even my own; for although I had read of speech, I had never thought to try to speak aloud. My aspect was a matter equally unthought of, for there were no mirrors in the castle, and I merely regarded myself by instinct as akin to the youthful figures I saw drawn and painted in the books. I felt conscious of youth because I remembered so little.

Outside, across the putrid moat and under the dark mute trees, I would often lie and dream for hours about what I read in the books; and would longingly picture myself amidst gay crowds in the sunny world beyond the endless forest. Once I tried to escape from the forest, but as I went farther from the castle the shade grew denser and the air more filled with brooding fear; so that I ran frantically back lest I lose my way in a labyrinth of nighted silence.

So through endless twilights I dreamed and waited, though I knew not what I 5 waited for. Then in the shadowy solitude my longing for light grew so frantic that I could rest no more, and I lifted entreating hands to the single black ruined tower that reached above the forest into the unknown outer sky. And at last I resolved to scale that tower, fall though I might; since it were better to glimpse the sky and perish, than to live without ever beholding day.

In the dank twilight I climbed the worn and aged stone stairs till I reached the level where they ceased, and thereafter clung perilously to small footholds leading upward. Ghastly and terrible was that dead, stairless cylinder of rock; black, ruined, and deserted, and sinister with startled bats whose wings made no noise. But more ghastly and terrible still was the slowness of my progress; for climb as I might, the darkness overhead grew no thinner, and a new chill as of haunted and venerable mould assailed me. I shivered as I wondered why I did not reach the light, and would have looked down had I dared. I fancied that night had come suddenly upon me, and vainly groped with one free hand for a window embrasure, that I might peer out and above, and try to judge the height I had attained.

All at once, after an infinity of awesome, sightless crawling up that concave and desperate precipice, I felt my head touch a solid thing, and I knew I must have gained the roof, or at least some kind of floor. In the darkness I raised my free hand and tested the barrier, finding it stone and immovable. Then came a deadly circuit of the tower, clinging to whatever holds the slimy wall could give; till finally my testing hand found the barrier yielding, and I turned upward again, pushing the slab or door with my head as I used both hands in my fearful ascent. There was no light revealed above, and as my hands went higher I knew that my climb was for the nonce ended; since the slab was the trap-door of an aperture leading to a level stone surface of greater circumference than the lower tower, no doubt the floor of some lofty and capacious observation chamber.

I crawled through carefully, and tried to prevent the heavy slab from falling back into place; but failed in the latter attempt. As I lay exhausted on the stone floor I heard the eerie echoes of its fall, but hoped when necessary to pry it open again.

Believing I was now at a prodigious height, far above the accursed branches of the wood, I dragged myself up from the floor and fumbled about for windows, that I might look for the first time upon the sky, and the moon and stars of which I had read. But on every hand I was disappointed; since all that I found were vast shelves of marble, bearing odious oblong boxes of disturbing size. More and more I reflected, and wondered what hoary secrets might abide in this high apartment so many aeons cut off from the castle below. Then unexpectedly my hands came upon a doorway, where hung a portal of stone, rough with strange chiselling. Trying it, I found it locked; but with a supreme burst of strength I overcame all obstacles and dragged it open inward. As I did so there came to me the purest ecstasy I have ever known; for shining tranquilly through an ornate grating of iron, and down a short stone passageway of steps that ascended from the newly found doorway, was the radiant full moon, which I had never before seen save in dreams and in vague visions I dared not call memories.

Fancying now that I had attained the very pinnacle of the castle, I commenced to rush up the few steps beyond the door; but the sudden veiling of the moon by a cloud caused me to stumble, and I felt my way more slowly in the dark. It was still very dark when I reached the grating—which I tried carefully and found unlocked, but which I did not open for fear of falling from the amazing height to which I had climbed. Then the moon came out.

Most daemoniacal of all shocks is that of the abysmally unexpected and grotesquely unbelievable. Nothing I had before undergone could compare in terror with what I now saw; with the bizarre marvels that sight implied. The sight itself was as simple as it was stupefying, for it was merely this: instead of a dizzying prospect of treetops seen from a lofty eminence, there stretched around me on a level through the grating nothing less than *the solid ground*, decked and diversified by marble slabs and columns, and overshadowed by an ancient stone church, whose ruined spire gleamed spectrally in the moonlight.

Half unconscious, I opened the grating and staggered out upon the white gravel path that stretched away in two directions. My mind, stunned and chaotic as it was, still held the frantic craving for light; and not even the fantastic wonder which had happened could stay my course. I neither knew nor cared whether my experience was insanity, dreaming, or magic; but was determined to gaze on brilliance and gaiety at any cost. I knew not who I was or what I was, or what my surroundings might be; though as I continued to stumble along I became conscious of a kind of fearsome latent memory that made my progress not wholly fortuitous. I passed under an arch out of that region of slabs and columns, and wandered through the open country; sometimes following the visible road, but sometimes leaving it curiously to tread across meadows where only occasional ruins bespoke the ancient presence of a forgotten road. Once I swam across a swift river where crumbling, mossy masonry told of a bridge long vanished.

Over two hours must have passed before I reached what seemed to be my goal, a venerable ivied castle in a thickly wooded park; maddeningly familiar, yet full of perplexing strangeness to me. I saw that the moat was filled in, and that some of the well-known towers were demolished; whilst new wings existed to confuse the beholder. But what I observed with chief interest and delight were the open windows—gorgeously ablaze with light and sending forth sound of the gayest revelry. Advancing to one of these I looked in and saw an oddly dressed company, indeed;

making merry, and speaking brightly to one another. I had never, seemingly, heard human speech before; and could guess only vaguely what was said. Some of the faces seemed to hold expressions that brought up incredibly remote recollections; others were utterly alien.

I now stepped through the low window into the brilliantly lighted room, step-ping as I did so from my single bright moment of hope to my blackest convulsion of despair and realisation. The nightmare was quick to come; for as I entered, there occurred immediately one of the most terrifying demonstrations I had ever con-ceived. Scarcely had I crossed the sill when there descended upon the whole com-pany a sudden and unheralded fear of hideous intensity, distorting every face and evoking the most horrible screams from nearly every throat. Flight was universal, and in the clamour and panic several fell in a swoon and were dragged away by their madly fleeing companions. Many covered their eyes with their hands, and plunged blindly and awkwardly in their race to escape; overturning furniture and stumbling against the walls before they managed to reach one of the many doors.

The cries were shocking; and as I stood in the brilliant apartment alone and dazed, listening to their vanishing echoes, I trembled at the thought of what might be lurking near me unseen. At a casual inspection the room seemed deserted, but when I moved toward one of the alcoves I thought I detected a presence there—a hint of motion beyond the golden-arched doorway leading to another and somewhat similar room. As I approached the arch I began to perceive the presence more clearly; and then, with the first and last sound I ever uttered—a ghastly ululation that revolted me almost as poignantly as its noxious cause—I beheld in full, frightful vividness the inconceivable, indescribable, and unmentionable monstrosity which had by its simple appearance changed a merry company to a herd of delirious fugitives.

I cannot even hint what it was like, for it was a compound of all that is unclean,   15
uncanny, unwelcome, abnormal, and detestable. It was the ghoulish shade of decay, antiquity, and desolation; the putrid, dripping eidolon of unwholesome revelation; the awful baring of that which the merciful earth should always hide. God knows it was not of this world—or no longer of this world—yet to my horror I saw in its eaten-away and bone-revealing outlines a leering, abhorrent travesty on the human shape; and in its mouldy, disintegrating apparel an unspeakable quality that chilled me even more.

I was almost paralysed, but not too much so to make a feeble effort toward flight; a backward stumble which failed to break the spell in which the nameless, voiceless monster held me. My eyes, bewitched by the glassy orbs which stared loathsomely into them, refused to close; though they were mercifully blurred, and shewed the ter-rible object but indistinctly after the first shock. I tried to raise my hand to shut out the sight, yet so stunned were my nerves that my arm could not fully obey my will. The attempt, however, was enough to disturb my balance; so that I had to stagger forward several steps to avoid falling. As I did so I became suddenly and agonisingly aware of the *nearness* of the carrion thing, whose hideous hollow breathing I half fancied I could hear. Nearly mad, I found myself yet able to throw out a hand to ward off the foetid apparition which pressed so close; when in one cataclysmic second of cosmic nightmarishness and hellish accident *my fingers touched the rotting outstretched paw of the monster beneath the golden arch.*

I did not shriek, but all the fiendish ghouls that ride the night-wind shrieked for me as in that same second there crashed down upon my mind a single and fleeting avalanche of soul-annihilating memory. I knew in that second all that had been; I remembered beyond the frightful castle and the trees, and recognised the altered edifice in which I now stood; I recognised, most terrible of all, the unholy abomination that stood leering before me as I withdrew my sullied fingers from its own.

But in the cosmos there is balm as well as bitterness, and that balm is nepenthe. In the supreme horror of that second I forgot what had horrified me, and the burst of black memory vanished in a chaos of echoing images. In a dream I fled from that haunted and accursed pile, and ran swiftly and silently in the moonlight. When I returned to the churchyard place of marble and went down the steps I found the stone trap-door immovable; but I was not sorry, for I had hated the antique castle and the trees. Now I ride with the mocking and friendly ghouls on the night-wind, and play by day amongst the catacombs of Nephren-Ka in the sealed and unknown valley of Hadoth by the Nile. I know that light is not for me, save that of the moon over the rock tombs of Neb, nor any gaiety save the unnamed feasts of Nitokris beneath the Great Pyramid; yet in my new wildness and freedom I almost welcome the bitterness of alienage.

For although nepenthe has calmed me, I know always that I am an outsider; a stranger in this century and among those who are still men. This I have known ever since I stretched out my fingers to the abomination within that great gilded frame; stretched out my fingers and touched *a cold and unyielding surface of polished glass*.

Questions

1. Paraphrase the story. What is revealed in the final sentence?
2. How would you describe the tone Lovecraft uses? Does he rely heavily on adjectives, or is his writing more spare, like Hemingway's? Find some examples.
3. Describe the story's setting.
4. Does the narrator seem at the end of the story to have accepted his lot? Do you find the tone hopeful or forlorn?

Dashiell Hammett

One Hour

(1924) 1945

Samuel Dashiell Hammett (1894–1961) grew up in Baltimore and Philadelphia. At age thirteen he dropped out of school and worked menial jobs, including as a railroad laborer and stevedore, to help support his family. As a young man he took up detective work with the Pinkerton Agency, laying the foundation for his future success as a genre-defining writer. Hammett enlisted in the Army and served as a sergeant in the Motor Ambulance Corps in World War I, during which he contracted tuberculosis. After the war, he moved to San Francisco. His health was too poor to continue detective work, so Hammett tried his hand at writing. With his stark prose, his dark depictions of urban America, and his likable, tough-guy heroes,

Dashiell Hammett

Hammett mastered the hard-boiled detective story. He created the immortal characters of the Continental Op, Sam Spade of The Maltese Falcon *(1930), and Nick and Nora Charles of* The Thin Man *(1934).*

Hammett later moved to Hollywood where he enjoyed great success from his novels and from screenwriting for the movies. He hobnobbed with high society and carried on a longtime love affair with playwright Lillian Hellman. Later in life, Hammett was involved with left-wing politics and was called to testify before the House Un-American Activities Committee. He refused to give up any names and was imprisoned for five months for contempt of Congress. Hammett was blacklisted by Hollywood.

Hammett spent the final years of his life as a recluse in a cottage in Westchester County, New York. In 1961 he died of lung cancer.

I

"This is Mr. Chrostwaite," Vance Richmond said.

Chrostwaite, wedged between the arms of one of the attorney's large chairs, grunted what was perhaps meant for an acknowledgment of the introduction. I grunted back at him, and found myself a chair.

He was a big balloon of a man—this Chrostwaite—in a green plaid suit that didn't make him look any smaller than he was. His tie was a gaudy thing, mostly of yellow, with a big diamond set in the center of it, and there were more stones on his pudgy hands. Spongy fat blurred his features, making it impossible for his round purplish face to even hold any other expression than the discontented hoggishness that was habitual to it. He reeked of gin.

"Mr. Chrostwaite is the Pacific Coast agent for the Mutual Fire Extinguisher Manufacturing Company," Vance Richmond began, as soon as I had got myself seated. "His office is on Kearny Street, near California. Yesterday, at about two forty-five in the afternoon, he went to his office, leaving his machine—a Hudson touring car—standing in front, with the engine running. Then minutes later, he came out. The car was gone."

I looked at Chrostwaite. He was looking at his fat knees, showing not the least   5
interest in what his attorney was saying. I looked quickly back at Vance Richmond; his clean gray face and lean figure were downright beautiful beside his bloated client.

"A man named Newhouse," the lawyer was saying, "who was the proprietor of a printing establishment on California Street, just around the corner from Mr. Chrostwaite's office, was run down and killed by Mr. Chrostwaite's car at the corner of Clay and Kearny Streets, five minutes after Mr. Chrostwaite had left the car to go into his office. The police found the car shortly afterward, only a block away from the scene of the accident—on Montgomery near Clay.

"The thing is fairly obvious. Someone stole the car immediately after Mr. Chrostwaite left it; and in driving rapidly away, ran down Newhouse; and then, in fright, abandoned the car. But here is Mr. Chrostwaite's position; three nights ago, while driving perhaps a little recklessly out—"

"Drunk," Chrostwaite said, not looking up from his plaid knees; and though his voice was hoarse, husky—it was the hoarseness of a whisky-burned throat—there was no emotion in his voice.

"While driving perhaps a little recklessly out Van Ness Avenue," Vance Richmond went on, ignoring the interruption, "Mr. Chrostwaite knocked a pedestrian down. The man wasn't badly hurt, and he is being compensated very generously for his injuries. But we are to appear in court next Monday to face a charge of reckless driving, and I am afraid that this accident of yesterday, in which the printer was killed, may hurt us.

"No one thinks that Mr. Chrostwaite was in his car when it killed the printer—   10
we have a world of evidence that he wasn't. But I am afraid that the printer's death may be made a weapon against us when we appear on the Van Ness Avenue charge.

Being an attorney, I know just how much capital the prosecuting attorney—if he so chooses—can make out of the really insignificant fact that the same car that knocked down the man on Van Ness Avenue killed another man yesterday. And, being an attorney, I know how likely the prosecuting attorney is to so choose. And he can handle it in such a way that we will be given little or no opportunity to tell our side.

"The worst that can happen, of course, is that, instead of the usual fine, Mr. Chrostwaite will be sent to the city jail for thirty or sixty days. That is bad enough, however, and that is what we wish to—"

Chrostwaite spoke again, still regarding his knees.

"Damned nuisance!" he said.

"That is what we wish to avoid," the attorney continued. "We are willing to pay a stiff fine, and expect to, for the accident on Van Ness Avenue was clearly Mr. Chrostwaite's fault. But we—"

"Drunk as a lord!" Chrostwaite said.

"But we don't want to have this other accident, with which we had nothing to do, given a false weight in connection with the slighter accident. What we want then, is to find the man or men who stole the car and ran down John Newhouse. If they are apprehended before we go to court, we won't be in danger of suffering for their act. Think you can find them before Monday?"

"I'll try," I promised; "though it isn't—"

The human balloon interrupted me by heaving himself to his feet, fumbling with his fat jeweled fingers for his watch.

"Three o'clock," he said. "Got a game of golf for three-thirty." He picked up his hat and gloves from the desk. "Find 'em, will you? Damned nuisance going to jail!"

And he waddled out.

II

From the attorney's office, I went down to the Hall of Justice, and, after hunting around a few minutes, found a policeman who had arrived at the corner of Clay and Kearny Streets a few seconds after Newhouse had been knocked down.

"I was just leaving the Hall when I seen a bus scoot around the corner at Clay Street," this patrolman—a big sandy-haired man named Coffee—told me. "Then I seen people gathering around, so I went up there and found this John Newhouse stretched out. He was already dead. Half a dozen people had seen him hit, and one of 'em had got the license number of the car that done it. We found the car standing empty just around the corner on Montgomery Street, pointing north. There was two fellows in the car when it hit Newhouse, but nobody saw what they looked like. Nobody was in it when we found it."

"In what direction was Newhouse walking?"

"North along Kearny Street, and he was about three-quarters across Clay when he was knocked. The car was coming north on Kearny, too, and turned east on Clay. It mightn't have been all the fault of the fellows in the car—according to them that seen the accident. Newhouse was walking across the street looking at a piece of paper in his hand. I found a piece of foreign money—paper money—in his hand, and I guess that's what he was looking at. The lieutenant tells me it was Dutch money—a hundred-florin note, he says."

"Found out anything about the men in the car?"

"Nothing! We lined up everybody we could find in the neighborhood of California and Kearny Streets—where the car was stolen from—and around Clay and Montgomery Streets—where it was left at. But nobody remembered seeing the fellows getting in it or getting out of it. The man that owns the car wasn't driving it—it was stole all right, I guess. At first I thought maybe there was something shady about the accident. This John Newhouse had a two or three-day-old black eye on him. But we run that out and found that he had an attack of heart trouble or something a couple days ago, and fell, fetching his eye up against a chair. He'd been home sick for three days—just left his house half an hour or so before the accident."

"Where'd he live?

"On Sacramento Street—way out. I got his address here somewhere."

He turned over the pages of a grimy memoranda book, and I got the dead man's house number, and the names and addresses of the witnesses to the accident that Coffee had questioned.

That exhausted the policeman's information, so I left him.   30

III

My next play was to canvass the vicinity of where the car had been stolen and where it had been deserted, and then interview the witnesses. The fact that the police had fruitlessly gone over this ground made it unlikely that I would find anything of value; but I couldn't skip these things on that account. Ninety-nine per cent of detective work is a patient collecting of details—and your details must be got as nearly first-hand as possible, regardless of who else has worked the territory before you.

Before starting on this angle, however, I decided to run around to the dead man's printing establishment—only three blocks from the Hall of Justice—and see if any of his employees had heard anything that might help me.

Newhouse's establishment occupied the ground floor of a small building on California, between Kearny and Montgomery. A small office was partitioned off in front, with a connecting doorway leading to the pressroom in the rear.

The only occupant of the small office, when I came in from the street, was a short, stocky, worried-looking blond man of forty or thereabouts, who sat at the desk in his shirt-sleeves, checking off figures in a ledger against others on a batch of papers before him.

I introduced myself, telling him that I was a Continental Detective Agency   35 operative, interested in Newhouse's death. He told me his name was Ben Soules, and that he was Newhouse's foreman. We shook hands, and then he waved me to a chair across the desk, pushed back the papers and book upon which he had been working, and scratched his head disgustedly with the pencil in his hand.

"This is awful!" he said. "What with one thing and another, we're heels over head in work, and I got to fool with these books that I don't know anything at all about, and—"

He broke off to pick up the telephone, which had jingled.

"Yes. . . . This is Soules. . . . We're working on them now. . . . I'll give 'em to you by Monday noon at the least. . . . I know! I know! But the boss's death set us back. Explain that to Mr. Chrostwaite. And . . . And I'll promise you that we'll give them to you Monday morning, sure!"

Soules slapped the receiver irritably on its hook and looked at me.

"You'd think that since it was his own car that killed the boss, he'd have decency   40 enough not to squawk over the delay!"

"Chrostwaite?"

"Yes—that was one of his clerks. We're printing some leaflets for him—promised to have 'em ready yesterday—but between the boss's death and having a couple new hands to break in, we're behind with everything. I've been here eight years, and this is the first time we ever fell down on an order—and every damned customer is yelling his head off. If we were like most printers they'd be used to waiting; but we've been too good to them. But this Chrostwaite! You'd think he'd have some decency, seeing that his car killed the boss!"

I nodded sympathetically, slid a cigar across the desk, and waited until it was burning in Soules's mouth before I asked:

"You said something about having a couple new hands to break in. How come?"

"Yes. Mr. Newhouse fired two of our printers last week—Fincher and Keys. He 45 found that they belonged to the I.W.W.,° so he gave them their time."

"Any trouble with them or anything against them except that they were Wobblies?"

"No—they were pretty good workers."

"Any trouble with them after he fired them?" I asked.

"No real trouble, though they were pretty hot. They made red speeches all over the place before they left."

"Remember what day that was?" 50

"Wednesday of last week, I think. Yes, Wednesday, because I hired two new men on Thursday."

"How many men do you work?"

"Three, besides myself."

"Was Mr. Newhouse sick very often?"

"Not sick enough to stay away very often, though every now and then his heart 55 would go back on him, and he'd have to stay in bed for a week or ten days. He wasn't what you could call real well at any time. He never did anything but the office work—I run the shop."

"When was he taken sick this last time?"

"Mrs. Newhouse called up Tuesday morning and said he had had another spell, and wouldn't be down for a few days. He came in yesterday—which was Thursday— for about ten minutes in the afternoon, and said he would be back on the job this morning. He was killed just after he left."

"How did he look—very sick?"

"Not so bad. He never looked well, of course, but I couldn't see much difference from usual yesterday. This last spell hadn't been as bad as most, I reckon—he was usually laid up for a week or more."

"Did he say where he was going when he left? The reason I ask is that, living out 60 on Sacramento Street, he would naturally have taken a car at that street if he had been going home, whereas he was run down on Clay Street."

"He said he was going up to Portsmouth Square to sit in the sun for half an hour or so. He had been cooped up indoors for two or three days, he said, and he wanted some sunshine before he went back home."

"He had a piece of foreign money in his hand when he was hit. Know anything about it?"

"Yes. He got it here. One of our customers—a man named Van Pelt—came in to pay for some work we had done yesterday afternoon while the boss was here. When Van Pelt pulled out his wallet to pay his bill, this piece of Holland money—I don't know what you call it—was among the bills. I think he said it was worth something

I.W.W.: The Industrial Workers of the World, also known as the Wobblies, is an international labor union.

like thirty-eight dollars. Anyway, the boss took it, giving Van Pelt his change. The
boss said he wanted to show the Holland money to his boys—and he could have it
changed back into American money later."

"Who is this Van Pelt?"

"He's a Hollander—is planning to open a tobacco importing business here in a   65
month or two. I don't know much about him outside of that."

"Where's his home, or office?"

"His office is on Bush Street, near Sansome."

"Did he know that Newhouse had been sick?"

"I don't think so. The boss didn't look much different from usual."

"What's this Van Pelt's full name?"   70

"Hendrik Van Pelt."

"What does he look like?"

Before Soules could answer, three evenly spaced buzzes sounded above the rattle
and whirring of the presses in the back of the shop.

I slid the muzzle of my gun—I had been holding it in my lap for five minutes—
far enough over the edge of the desk for Ben Soules to see it.

"Put both of your hands on top of the desk," I said.   75

He put them there.

The pressroom door was directly behind him, so that, facing him across the desk,
I could look over his shoulder at it. His stocky body served to screen my gun from the
view of whoever came through the door, in response to Soules's signal.

I didn't have long to wait.

Three men—black with ink—came to the door, and through it into the little
office. They strolled in careless and casual, laughing and joking to one another.

But one of them licked his lips as he stepped through the door. Another's eyes   80
showed white circles all around the irises. The third was the best actor—but he held
his shoulders a trifle too stiffly to fit his otherwise careless carriage.

"Stop right there!" I barked at them when the last one was inside the office—
and I brought my gun up where they could see it.

They stopped as if they had all been mounted on the same pair of legs.

I kicked my chair back, and stood up.

I didn't like my position at all. The office was entirely too small for me. I had
a gun, true enough, and whatever weapons may have been distributed among these
other men were out of sight. But these four men were too close to me; and a gun
isn't a thing of miracles. It's a mechanical contraption that is capable of just so much
and no more.

If these men decided to jump me, I could down just one of them before the other   85
three were upon me. I knew it, and they knew it.

"Put your hands up," I ordered, "and turn around!"

None of them moved to obey. One of the inked men grinned wickedly; Soules
shook his head slowly; the other two stood and looked at me.

I was more or less stumped. You can't shoot a man just because he refuses to obey
an order—even if he is a criminal. If they had turned around for me, I could have
lined them up against the wall, and, being behind them, have held them safe while I
used the telephone.

But that hadn't worked.

My next thought was to back across the office to the street door, keeping them   90
covered, and then either stand in the door and yell for help, or take them into

the street, where I could handle them. But I put that thought away as quickly as it came to me.

These four men were going to jump me—there was no doubt of that. All that was needed was a spark of any sort to explode them into action. They were standing stiff-legged and tense, waiting for some move on my part. If I took a step backward— the battle would be on.

We were close enough for any of the four to have reached out and touched me. One of them I could shoot before I was smothered—one out of four. That meant that each of them had only one chance out of four of being the victim—low enough odds for any but the most cowardly of men.

I grinned what was supposed to be a confident grin—because I was up against it hard—and reached for the telephone: I had to do something! Then I cursed myself! I had merely changed the signal for the onslaught. It would come now when I picked up the receiver.

But I couldn't back down again—that, too, would be a signal—I had to go through with it.

The perspiration trickled across my temples from under my hat as I drew the 95 phone closer with my left hand.

The street door opened! An exclamation of surprise came from behind me.

I spoke rapidly, without taking my eyes from the four men in front of me.

"Quick! The phone! The police!"

With the arrival of this unknown person—one of Newhouse's customers, probably—I figured I had the edge again. Even if he took no active part beyond calling the police in, the enemy would have to split to take care of him—and that would give me a chance to pot at least two of them before I was knocked over. Two out of four— each of them had an even chance of being dropped—which *is* enough to give even a nervy man cause for thinking a bit before he jumps.

"Hurry!" I urged the newcomer. 100

"Yes! Yes!" he said—and in the blurred sound of the "s" there was evidence of foreign birth.

Keyed up as I was, I didn't need any more warning than that.

I threw myself sidewise—a blind tumbling away from the spot where I stood. But I wasn't quite quick enough.

The blow that came from behind didn't hit me fairly, but I got enough of it to fold up my legs as if the knees were hinged with paper—and I slammed into a heap on the floor. . . .

Something dark crashed toward me. I caught it with both hands. It may have 105 been a foot kicking at my face. I wrung it as a washerwoman wrings a towel.

Down my spine ran jar after jar. Perhaps somebody was beating me over the head. I don't know. My head wasn't alive. The blow that had knocked me down had numbed me all over. My eyes were no good. Shadows swam to and fro in front of them—that was all. I struck, gouged, tore at the shadows. Sometimes I found nothing. Sometimes I found things that felt like parts of bodies. Then I would hammer at them, tear at them. My gun was gone.

My hearing was no better than my sight—or not so good. There wasn't a sound in the world. I moved in a silence that was more complete than any silence I had ever known. I was a ghost fighting ghosts.

I found presently that my feet were under me again, though some squirming thing was on my back, and kept me from standing upright: A hot, damp thing like a hand was across my face.

I put my teeth into it. I snapped my head back as far as it would go. Maybe it smashed into the face it was meant for. I don't know. Anyhow the squirming thing was no longer on my back.

Dimly I realized that I was being buffeted about by blows that I was too numb to feel. Ceaselessly, with head and shoulders and elbows and fists and knees and feet, I struck at the shadows that were around me. . . . 110

Suddenly I could see again—not clearly—but the shadows were taking on colors; and my ears came back a little, so that grunts and growls and curses and the impact of blows sounded in them. My straining gaze rested upon a brass cuspidor six inches or so in front of my eyes. I knew then that I was down on the floor again.

As I twisted about to hurl a foot into a soft body above me, something that was like a burn, but wasn't a burn, ran down one leg—a knife. The sting of it brought consciousness back into me with a rush.

I grabbed the brass cuspidor and used it to club a way to my feet—to club a clear space in front of me. Men were hurling themselves upon me. I swung the cuspidor high and flung it over their heads through the frosted glass door into California Street.

Then we fought some more.

But you can't throw a brass cuspidor through a glass door into California Street 115 between Montgomery and Kearny without attracting attention—it's too near the heart of daytime San Francisco. So presently—when I was on the floor again with six or eight hundred pounds of flesh hammering my face into the boards—we were pulled apart, and I was dug out of the bottom of the pile by a squad of policemen.

Big sandy-haired Coffee was one of them, but it took a lot of arguing to convince him that I was the Continental operative who had talked to him a little while before.

"Man! Man!" he said, when I finally convinced him. "Them lads sure—God!—have worked you over! You got a face like a wet geranium!"

I didn't laugh. It wasn't funny.

I looked out of the one eye which was working just now at the five men lined up across the office—Soules, the three inky printers, and the man with the blurred "s," who had started the slaughter by tapping me on the back of the head.

He was a rather tall man of thirty or so, with a round ruddy face that wore a few 120 bruises now. He had been, apparently, rather well-dressed in expensive black clothing, but he was torn and ragged now. I knew who he was without asking—Hendrik Van Pelt.

"Well, man, what's the answer?" Coffee was asking me.

By holding one side of my jaw firmly with one hand I found that I could talk without too much pain.

"This is the crowd that ran down Newhouse," I said, "and it wasn't an accident. I wouldn't mind having a few more of the details myself, but I was jumped before I got around to all of them. Newhouse had a hundred-florin note in his hand when he was run down, and he was walking in the direction of police headquarters—was only half a block away from the Hall of Justice.

"Soules tells me that Newhouse said he was going up to Portsmouth Square to sit in the sun. But Soules didn't seem to know that Newhouse was wearing a black eye—the one you told me you had investigated. If Soules didn't see the shiner, then it's a good bet that Soules didn't see Newhouse's face that day!

"Newhouse was walking from his printing shop toward police headquarters with 125 a piece of foreign paper money in his hand—remember that!

"He had frequent spells of sickness, which, according to friend Soules, always before kept him at home for a week or ten days at a time. This time he was laid up for only two and a half days.

"Soules tells me that the shop is three days behind with its orders, and he says that's the first time in eight years they've ever been behind. He blames Newhouse's death—which only happened yesterday. Apparently, Newhouse's previous sick spells never delayed things—why should this last spell?

"Two printers were fired last week, and two new ones hired the very next day—pretty quick work. The car with which Newhouse was run down was taken from just around the corner, and was deserted within quick walking distance of the shop. It was left facing north, which is pretty good evidence that its occupants went south after they got out. Ordinary car thieves wouldn't have circled back in the direction from which they came.

"Here's my guess: This Van Pelt is a Dutchman, and he had some plates for phony hundred-florin notes. He hunted around until he found a printer who would go in with him. He found Soules, the foreman of a shop whose proprietor was now and then at home for a week or more at a time with a bad heart. One of the printers under Soules was willing to go in with them. Maybe the other two turned the offer down. Maybe Soules didn't ask them at all. Anyhow, they were discharged, and two friends of Soules were given their places.

"Our friends then got everything ready, and waited for Newhouse's heart to flop 130 again. It did—Monday night. As soon as his wife called up next morning and said he was sick, these birds started running off their counterfeits. That's why they fell behind with their regular work. But this spell of Newhouse's was lighter than usual. He was up and moving around within two days, and yesterday afternoon he came down here for a few minutes.

"He must have walked in while all of our friends were extremely busy in some far corner. He must have spotted some of the phony money, immediately sized up the situation, grabbed one bill to show the police, and started out for police headquarters—no doubt thinking he had not been seen by our friends here.

"They must have got a glimpse of him as he was leaving, however. Two of them followed him out. They couldn't, afoot, safely knock him over within a block or two of the Hall of Justice. But, turning the corner, they found Chrostwaite's car standing there with idling engine. That solved their getaway problem. They got in the car and went on after Newhouse. I suppose the original plan was to shoot him—but he crossed Clay Street with his eyes fastened upon the phony money in his hand. That gave them a golden chance. They piled the car into him. It was sure death, they knew—his bum heart would finish the job if the actual collision didn't kill him. Then they deserted the car and came back here.

"There are a lot of loose ends to be gathered in—but this pipe-dream I've just told you fits in with all the facts we know—and I'll bet a month's salary I'm not far off anywhere. There ought be a three-day crop of Dutch notes cached somewhere! You people—"

I suppose I'd have gone on talking forever—in the giddy, head-swimming intoxication of utter exhaustion that filled me—if the big sandy-haired patrolman hadn't shut me off by putting a big hand across my mouth.

"Be quiet, man," he said, lifting me out the chair, and spreading me flat on my 135 back on the desk. "I'll have an ambulance here in a second for you."

The office was swirling around in front of my one open eye—the yellow ceiling swung down toward me, rose again, disappeared, came back in odd shapes. I turned my head to one side to avoid it, and my glance rested upon the white dial of a spinning clock.

Presently the dial came to rest, and I read it—four o'clock.

I remembered that Chrostwaite had broken up our conference in Vance Richmond's office at three, and I had started to work.

"One full hour!" I tried to tell Coffee before I went to sleep.

The police wound up the job while I was lying on my back in bed. In Van Pelt's 140 office on Bush Street they found a great bale of hundred-florin notes. Van Pelt, they learned, had a considerable reputation in Europe as a high-class counterfeiter. One of the printers came through, stating that Van Pelt and Soules were the two who followed Newhouse out of the shop, and killed him.

Questions

1. Notice how Hammett describes Chrostwaite early in the story. What details, behavior, and physical attributes help develop his characterization?
2. In the tense moments leading up to the fight, how can you tell that this isn't the narrator's first rumble?
3. The narrator describes the fight and his condition afterward with little emotion. What effect does that have on how we perceive the narrator?
4. The story takes place in the time span of a single hour. How does Hammett achieve such suspense and speed of narration? What elements of storytelling does he leave out that another writer might have included?

■ WRITING *effectively*

Ray Bradbury on Writing

Falling in Love at the Library   (2005) 2013

Interviewer: Do you have memories of your early childhood reading?

Bradbury: Oh, sure. The library was the most exciting place in the world. Every Monday evening, starting when I was about seven years old, my brother and I would run to the library—not walk, *run* to the library. Especially in autumn, going to the library, you're accompanied by leaves. So the wind blows you along the street, and you and the leaves go to the library. And the air smells good, and you're alive and electric. You get into the library, and there's that wonderful ambience. To sit in the center of the room, and all the stacks of all your lovers and all your loved ones surround you—they impinge on you. You feel them, but you don't feel them. Because Edgar Allan Poe is up there watching you, and Jules Verne is up there accompanying you.

Ray Bradbury

Interviewer: Where did you grow up?

Bradbury: Waukegan, Illinois.

Interviewer: And you moved to Los Angeles when you were how old?

Bradbury: When I was fourteen. It was the middle of the Depression, and my dad was out of work for years, and we finally moved to California because we hoped my dad would find work. And thank god we did. It was the perfect time—I just turned fourteen; puberty was upon me; I was falling in love with Marlene Dietrich; it was time to move.

Interviewer: Where did you go to high school?

Bradbury: L.A. High School. And that was my education—I just graduated from high school and that was it. Then I went to the library and stayed there and educated myself for ten years. I graduated from the library when I was twenty-seven. The head of a university heard about this—oh, about twenty years ago I was lecturing up the coast—and at the end of my lecture he came up with a diploma for me, and he graduated me from the library. Which is a beautiful thing to do.

• • •

Interviewer: What advice would you give to young people who would like to be writers?

Bradbury: Fall in love and stay in love. Go to the library and never come out. Just wander through and pull books off the shelf and open them up. And someday you're gonna open a book and there you are looking at yourself. It's a mirror image—it could be Melville, it could be Poe, Hawthorne, Shakespeare, Robert Frost, who knows. The more you read, the more you want. Find out what you love, and do it with all your heart.

2005 Interview with Dana Gioia
First Published in *Radio Silence*, 2013

TOPICS FOR WRITING ABOUT "A SOUND OF THUNDER"

1. "A Sound of Thunder" provided the origin of a scientific chaos theory commonly known as the "butterfly effect," in which a tiny change in one time and place can have massive consequences later on. Write a brief essay explaining how that idea is exemplified in the story. Use specific examples.
2. Write about how the two imaginary settings (near future and distant past) contribute to the larger meaning of the story. (You could possibly discuss how two settings create possibilities to dramatize ideas more powerfully than a single setting might.)
3. "A Sound of Thunder" is not a realistic story, but it nevertheless conveys a pertinent message about humanity's relation to the natural world. How would you summarize that message?

TOPICS FOR WRITING ABOUT "THE FAERY HANDBAG"

1. Considering that someone can vanish into the faery handbag and then reappear years later unchanged, while those left behind continue to age, write a short essay making an argument that the handbag could be interpreted as a symbol for death. Cite examples from the text.
2. Kelly Link is a master of writing stories that blur the line between fantasy and reality. As if you were a courtroom lawyer and the magical elements of "The Faery Handbag" were

on trial, write a closing statement arguing for the believability of Zofia's stories. Then write the counterargument, claiming that Zofia's stories were nothing more than colorful fictions. Build each case using evidence from the text.

3. Write your own short story that blurs the line between fantasy and reality, structuring it in a way that will leave the believability of the story in question.

TOPICS FOR WRITING ABOUT "THE OUTSIDER"

1. Describe the setting of "The Outsider" and how it contributes to the story's effect. Would this story have been as effective in a different setting?

2. Is this simply a story about a monstrous creature, or might the narrator's experience be seen as more universal? In what ways does Lovecraft's story suggest lessons about real life?

3. Write your own horror story in the elaborate, gothic style of Lovecraft.

TOPICS FOR WRITING ABOUT "ONE HOUR"

1. Detectives are often described as following their own complex moral code. For example, Chrostwaite doesn't seem to be a very good guy, yet our detective takes his case and does indeed bring the real criminals to justice. Write a short essay about this detective's moral code, using evidence from the text.

2. Point out sentences that typify Hammett's style. Is his language complex or accessible? Write an essay comparing Hammett's style to that of another writer in this book.

3. Consider the elements, pacing, and characterization that help make a good detective story, and then write your own.

▶ TERMS FOR *review*

Romance ▶ A narrative mode that stresses exotic adventure and idealized emotion rather than realistic depiction of character and action. Romance presents the world as we wish (or fear) it would be rather than the complex way it really is.

Genre ▶ A conventional combination of literary form and subject matter usually aimed at creating a certain effect on the reader.

Genre fiction ▶ A general category of fiction that encompasses a variety of romantic narrative forms, including science fiction, fantasy, horror, detective, mystery, western, and many other varieties of popular literature.

Science fiction ▶ A popular genre that presents a technological innovation (such as time travel) or scientific assumption (alien races) and then logically develops a story from that imaginary premise.

Fantasy ▶ A narrative that depicts events, characters, or places that do not exist in the real world. The oldest form of romance, fantasy expresses the fears and desires of the human imagination without being required to explain them in logical terms.

Detective fiction, mystery fiction ▶ A narrative that presents a protagonist who solves a puzzling crime (most often a murder) by using observation, deduction, and intuition to find the culprit.

Horror fiction ▶ A literary genre that attempts to frighten the reader through the use of suspense, shock, and fear. It often places its protagonist in a mysteriously uncomfortable situation that gradually becomes more terrifying as the story progresses.

9

READING LONG STORIES AND NOVELS

The novel is the one bright book of life.

—D. H. LAWRENCE

What You Will Learn in This Chapter

- To describe the nature and origins of the *novel*
- To define *novella*
- To explain how novels and novellas are different from short stories
- To identify various types of novels

Among the forms of imaginative literature in our language, the novel has been the favorite of both writers and readers for more than two hundred years. Broadly defined, a **novel** is a book-length fictional story in prose, whose author tries to create the sense that while we read, we experience actual life. This sense of actuality, also found in artful short stories, may be the quality that sets the novel apart from other long prose narratives.

ORIGINS OF THE NOVEL

Unlike other major literary forms—drama, lyric, ballad, and epic—the novel is a relative newcomer. Originally, the drama in ancient Greece came alive only when actors performed it; the epic or heroic poem (from the classic *Iliad* through the Old English *Beowulf*), only when a bard sang or chanted it. But the English novel came to maturity in literate times, in the eighteenth century, and by its nature was something different: a story to be communicated silently in printed books, at whatever moment and at whatever pace (whether quickly or slowly and meditatively) the reader desired.

Some definitions of the novel would more strictly define the form. "The Novel is a picture of real life and manners, and of the time in which it was written," declared Clara Reeve in 1785. By so specifying that the novel depicts life in the present day, the critic was probably observing the derivation of the word *novel*. Akin to the French word for "news" (*nouvelles*), it comes from the Italian *novella* ("something new and small"), a term applied to a newly made story taking place in recent times, and not a traditional story taking place long ago.

Novels and Journalism

Since both the novel and journalism try to capture the fabric of everyday life, there has long been a close relationship between the two literary forms. Many novelists, among them Ernest Hemingway, Stephen Crane, and Jack London, began their writing careers as cub reporters. Ambrose Bierce was the most influential newspaper satirist of his day.

The two modes of writing, however, remain different. "Literature is the art of writing something that will be read twice," commented critic and novelist Cyril Connolly, "journalism what will be grasped at once." Journalism greatly influences how novelists depict the world around them. Stephen Crane's "The Open Boat" (Chapter 6) began as a newspaper account of his actual experiences in a small rowboat after the sinking of the *Commodore* in 1897. A journalist might have been content with such a gripping first-person story of surviving a shipwreck, but a great fiction writer has the gift of turning personal bad luck into art, and Crane eventually created a masterpiece of fiction based on fact.

NOVELISTIC METHODS

Many early novels were told in the form of letters. Sometimes these **epistolary novels** contained letters by only one character; often they contained letters exchanged by several of the characters in the book. By casting his novel *Pamela* (1740) into the form of personal letters, Samuel Richardson helped give the story the appearance of being not invented but discovered from real documents. Alice Walker's *The Color Purple* (1982) is a more recent epistolary novel, though some of the letters that tell the story are addressed to God.

Another method favored by novelists is to write as though setting down a memoir or an autobiography. Daniel Defoe, whose skill in feigning such memoirs was phenomenal, succeeded in writing the supposedly true confessions of a woman retired from a life of crime, *Moll Flanders* (1722), and in maintaining a vivid truthfulness:

> Going through Aldersgate Street, there was a pretty little child who had been at a dancing-school, and was going home all alone: and my prompter, like a true devil, set me upon this innocent creature. I talked to it, and it prattled to me again, and I took it by the hand and led it along till I came to a paved alley that goes into Bartholomew Close, and I led it in there. The child said that was not its way home. I said, "Yes, my dear, it is; I'll show you the way home." The child had a little necklace on of gold beads, and I had my eye upon that, and in the dark of the alley I stooped, pretending to mend the child's clog that was loose, and took off her necklace, and the child never felt it, and so led the child on again. Here, I say, the devil put me upon killing the child in the dark alley, that it might not cry, but the very thought frighted me so that I was ready to drop down; but I turned the child about and bade it go back again. . . . The last affair left no great concern upon me, for as I did the poor child no harm, I only said to myself, I had given the parents a just reproof for their negligence in leaving the poor little lamb to come home by itself, and it would teach them to take more care of it another time.

What could sound more like the voice of an experienced child-robber than this manner of excusing her crime, and even justifying it?

Some novelists place great emphasis on research and notetaking. Research alone, however, is not enough to produce a novel. A novel grows to completion only through the slow mental process of creation, selection, and arrangement. But raw facts can sometimes provide a beginning. Many novels started when the author read some arresting episode in a newspaper or magazine. Theodore Dreiser's impressive study of a murder, *An American Tragedy* (1925), for example, was inspired by a journalist's account of a real-life case.

Nonfiction Novels

In the 1960s there was a great deal of talk about the **nonfiction novel**, in which the author presents actual people and events in story form. The vogue of the nonfiction novel was created by Truman Capote's *In Cold Blood* (1966), which depicts an actual multiple murder and the resulting trial in Kansas. Capote traveled to the scene of the crime and interviewed all of the principal parties, including the murderers. More recently, John Berendt's darkly comic 1994 account of the upper class and under class of Savannah, Georgia, *Midnight in the Garden of Good and Evil* (which also centers on a murder and the subsequent trial), revived interest in the form.

Perhaps the name "nonfiction novel" (Capote's term for it) is newer than the form. In the past, writers of autobiography have cast their memoirs into what looks like novel form: Richard Wright in *Black Boy* (1945), William Burroughs in *Junkie* (1953). Derived from his reporting, John Hersey's *Hiroshima* (1946) reconstructs the lives of six survivors of the atom bomb as if they were fictional. In reading such works we may nearly forget we are reading literal truth, so well do the techniques of the novel lend an air of immediacy to remembered facts.

Historical Novels

A familiar kind of fiction that claims a basis in fact is the **historical novel**, a detailed reconstruction of life in another time, perhaps in another place. In some historical novels the author attempts a faithful picture of daily life in another era, as does Robert Graves in *I, Claudius* (1934), a novel of patrician Rome. More often, history is a backdrop for an exciting story of love and heroic adventure. Nathaniel Hawthorne's *The Scarlet Letter* (set in Puritan Boston) and Stephen Crane's *The Red Badge of Courage* (set on the battlefields of the Civil War) are historical novels in that their authors lived considerably later than the scenes and events that they depicted, and strove for truthfulness, by imaginative means.

Other Types of Novels

Another kind of novel is the *Bildungsroman* (German for a "novel of growth and development"), sometimes called the **apprenticeship novel** after its classic example, *Wilhelm Meister's Apprenticeship* (1796) by Johann Wolfgang von Goethe. This is the type of novel in which a youth struggles toward maturity, seeking, perhaps, some consistent worldview or philosophy of life. Sometimes the apprenticeship novel is evidently derived from the author's recollection of his own early life: James Joyce's *A Portrait of the Artist as a Young Man* (1916) and Tobias Wolff's *Old School* (2003).

Picaresques

In a **picaresque** (another famous category), a likable scoundrel wanders through adventures, living by his wits, duping the straight citizenry. The name comes from Spanish: *pícaro*, "rascal" or "rogue." The classic picaresque novel is the anonymous Spanish *Life of Lazarillo de Tormes* (1554), imitated by many English writers, among them Henry Fielding in his story of a London thief and racketeer, *Jonathan Wild* (1743). Mark Twain's *Adventures of Huckleberry Finn* (1885) owes something to the tradition; like early picaresque novels, it is told in episodes rather than in one all-unifying plot and is narrated in the first person by a hero at odds with respectable society ("dismal regular and decent," Huck Finn calls it). In Twain's novel, however, the traveling swindlers who claim to be a duke and a dauphin are much more typical rogues of picaresque fiction than Huck himself, an honest innocent.

Short Novels and Novellas

The term **short novel** (or **novella**) mainly describes the size of a narrative; it refers to a narrative midway in length between a short story and a novel. (E. M. Forster once said that a novel should be at least 50,000 words in length, and most editors and publishers would agree with that definition.)

Many writers, such as Thomas Mann, Henry James, Joseph Conrad, and Willa Cather, favored the novella as a perfect medium between the necessary compression of the short story and the potential sprawl of the novel. When the term **novelette** is used, it usually refers (often condescendingly) to a short novel written for a popular magazine, especially in such genres as science fiction, romance, the western, and horror.

READING NOVELS

Trying to perceive a novel as a whole, we may find it helpful to look for the same elements that we have noticed in reading short stories. By asking ourselves leading questions, we may be drawn more deeply into the novel's world, and may come to recognize and appreciate the techniques of the novelist. Does the novel have themes, or an overall theme? Who is its main character? What is the author's kind of narrative voice? How would we describe the tone, style, and use of irony? Why is this novel written from one point of view rather than from another?

If the novel in question is large and thickly populated, it may help to read it with a pencil and take brief notes. Forced to put the novel aside and later return to it, we may find that the notes refresh the memory. Once our reading of a novel is finished and we prepare to discuss it or write about it, it may be a good idea to browse through it again, rereading brief portions. This method of overall browsing may also help when first approaching a bulky and difficult novel. Just as an explorer mapping unfamiliar territory may find it best to begin by taking an aerial view of it, so too the reader approaching an exceptionally thick and demanding novel may wish, at the start, to look for its general shape. There is, of course, no shortcut to novel reading, and probably the best method is to settle in comfort and read the book through: with your own eyes, not with the borrowed glasses of literary criticism.

The Future of the Novel

The death of the novel has been frequently announced. Competition from television, films, video games, and the internet, some critics claim, will overwhelm the habit of reading; the public is lazy and will follow the easiest route available for entertainment. But in England and America television and films have been sending people back in vast numbers to the books they dramatize. Jane Austen has never lacked readers, but films such as *Pride and Prejudice*, *Emma*, *Persuasion*, and *Sense and Sensibility* (not to mention *Clueless*, a teenage version of *Emma* set in Beverly Hills, or *Bride and Prejudice*, a singing and dancing Bollywood treatment set in modern-day India) made her one of the world's best-selling novelists. Stylish adaptations of Philip K. Dick's offbeat science fiction, including *Blade Runner*, *Total Recall*, *Minority*

Report, and *The Man in the High Castle*, have created a cult for his once neglected work. Sometimes Hollywood even helps bring a good book into print. No one would publish Thomas M. Disch's sophisticated children's novella *The Brave Little Toaster* until Walt Disney turned it into an animated film. A major publisher then not only rushed it into print, but commissioned a sequel.

Meanwhile, each year new novels by the hundreds continue to appear, their authors wistfully looking for a public. Some of these books reach a mass audience. To forecast the end of the novel seems risky, for the novel exercises the imagination of the beholder. At any hour, at a touch of the hand, it opens and begins to speak.

Leo Tolstoy

The Death of Ivan Ilych

1886

Translated by Constance Garnett
Edited by Theodore Stromberg

The complex and contradictory Leo Nikolaevich Tolstoy (1828–1910) is generally considered the greatest Russian novelist. Born on his aristocratic family's country estate where he would spend much of his life, Yasnaya Polyana, in central Russia, he was orphaned at nine and raised by aunts. In 1851 Tolstoy joined the army and fought in the Caucasus. It was there that he completed his first book, Childhood (1852), a lyrical memoir. A decade later he wed Sonya Bers, an intellectual middle-class woman. Initially happy, the marriage was undermined by the sex-obsessed and guilt-ridden Tolstoy, who engaged in many infidelities. Despite its problems, the union produced thirteen children. At Yasnaya Polyana, Tolstoy wrote his two greatest novels, the multi-volume War and Peace *(1863–1869), which*

Leo Tolstoy

depicts the lives of five aristocratic Russian families during the Napoleonic Wars, and Anna Karenina *(1877), which tells the tragic story of a woman led by romantic illusions into a destructive adulterous liaison. As Tolstoy grew older, he became infatuated with early Christianity and formulated his own version of Christ's teachings, stressing simplicity, love, nonviolence, and community property. Excommunicated by the Orthodox Church, the count, who now dressed in peasant clothing, preached his "Christian anarchism" to the Russian intelligentsia in streams of books and pamphlets. Upset by his ruined marriage and his inability to renounce his personal wealth, the eighty-two-year-old Tolstoy fled home one night, planning to enter a monastery. He died of pneumonia a few days later in a provincial railway station.*

Tolstoy is one of the great masters of European Realism. Much of his fiction examines a tragic predicament of human existence—the difficult search for truth and justice in a world of limited knowledge and ethical imperfection. Tolstoy resolutely believed in the moral development of humanity, but was also painfully aware of the obstacles to genuine progress. His gripping novella The Death of Ivan Ilych *dramatizes Tolstoy's central spiritual concerns. His antiheroic Everyman faces death with the horrifying realization that he has not lived a correct or meaningful life.*

I

Inside the great building of the Law Courts, during the recess in the hearing of the Melvinsky case, the members of the Judicial Council and the Public Prosecutor were gathered together in the private room of Ivan Egorovich Shebek, and the conversation turned upon the celebrated Krasovsky case. Fyodor Vasilievich hotly maintained that the case was not in the jurisdiction of the court. Ivan Egorovich stood up for a different view; but from the first Peter Ivanovich, who had not entered into the discussion, took no interest in it, but was looking through the newspapers which had just been brought in.

"Gentlemen!" he said, "Ivan Ilych is dead!"

"You don't say so!"

"Here, read it," he said to Fyodor Vasilievich, handing him the paper, still damp from the press. Within a black margin was printed: "Praskovya Fyodorovna Golovina, with heartfelt affliction, informs friends and relatives of the decease of her beloved husband, member of the Court of Justice, Ivan Ilych Golovin, who passed away on the 4th of February, 1882. The funeral will take place on Friday at one o'clock."

Ivan Ilych was a colleague of the gentlemen present, and all liked him. It was   5
some weeks now since he had taken ill; his illness had been said to be incurable. His post had been kept open for him, but it had been thought that in case of his death Alexyeev might receive his appointment, and either Vinnikov or Shtabel would succeed to Alexyeev's. So, on hearing of Ivan Ilych's death, the first thought of each of the gentlemen in the room was of the effect this death might have on the transfer or promotion of themselves or their friends.

"Now I am sure of getting Shtabel's place or Vinnikov's," thought Fyodor Vasilievich. "It was promised me long ago, and the promotion means eight hundred rubles additional income, besides the grants for office expenses."

"Now I should petition for my brother-in-law to be transferred from Kaluga," thought Peter Ivanovich. "My wife will be very glad. She won't be able to say now that I've never done anything for her family."

"I thought somehow that he'd never get up from his bed again," Peter Ivanovich said aloud. "I'm sorry!"

"But what was it exactly that was wrong with him?"

"The doctors could not decide. That's to say, they did decide, but differently.   10
When I saw him last, I thought he would get over it."

"Well, I positively haven't called there ever since the holidays. I've kept meaning to go."

"Had he any property?"

"I think there's something, very small, of his wife's. But something quite trifling."

"Yes, we will have to go and call, but they live such a terribly long way off."

"A long way from you, you mean. Everything's a long way from your place."   15

"There, he can never forgive me for living on the other side of the river," said Peter Ivanovich, smiling at Shebek. And they began to talk of the great distances between different parts of the town, and went back into the court.

Besides the reflections upon the changes and promotions likely to ensue from Ilych's death, the very fact of the death of an intimate acquaintance excited in everyone who heard of it, as such a fact always does, a feeling of relief that "it is he that is dead, and not I."

"Only think! He is dead, but here am I all right," each one thought or felt. The more intimate acquaintances, the so-called friends of Ivan Ilych, could not help thinking, too, that now they had the exceedingly tiresome social duties to perform of going to the funeral service and paying the widow a visit of condolence.

The most intimately acquainted with their late colleague were Fyodor Vasilievich and Peter Ivanovich. Peter Ivanovich had been a comrade of his at the School of Jurisprudence, and considered himself under obligation to Ivan Ilych.

Telling his wife at dinner of the news of Ivan Ilych's death and his reflections as to the possibility of getting her brother transferred into their circuit, Peter Ivanovich, without lying down for his usual nap, put on his frockcoat and drove to Ivan Ilych's. 20

At the entrance before Ivan Ilych's flat stood a carriage and two hired cabs. Downstairs in the entry near the hat-stand there was leaning against the wall a coffin-lid with tassels and braiding freshly rubbed up with pipe clay. Two ladies were taking off their cloaks. One of them he knew, the sister of Ivan Ilych; the other was a lady he did not know. Peter Ivanovich's colleague, Schwartz, was coming down; and from the top stair, seeing who it was coming in, he stopped and winked at him, as though to say: "Ivan Ilych has made a mess of it; it's a very different matter with you and me."

Schwartz, with his English whiskers and slender figure, had, as always, an air of elegant solemnity; and this solemnity, always such a contrast to Schwartz's playful character, had a special piquancy here. So thought Peter Ivanovich.

Peter Ivanovich allowed the ladies to precede him, and slowly followed them upstairs. Schwartz had not come down, but was waiting at the top, and Peter Ivanovich knew what for; he obviously wanted to arrange where their game of bridge would be that evening. The ladies went up to the widow's room; while Schwartz, with his lips tightly and gravely shut, but amusement in his eyes, with a twitch of his eyebrows motioned Peter Ivanovich to the right, to the room where the dead man lay.

Peter Ivanovich went in, as people always do on such occasions, in uncertainty as to what he would have to do. One thing he felt sure of—that crossing oneself never comes amiss at such times. As to whether it was necessary to bow down while doing so, he did not feel quite sure, and so chose a middle course. On entering the room he began crossing himself, and made a slight sort of bow. So far as the movements of his hands and head permitted him, he glanced while doing so about the room. Two young men, one a high school boy, nephews probably, were going out of the room, crossing themselves. An old lady was standing motionless; and a lady, with her eyebrows queerly lifted, was saying something to her in a whisper. A deacon in a frockcoat, resolute and hearty, was reading something aloud with an expression that precluded all possibility of contradiction. A young peasant who used to wait at table, Gerasim, walking with light footsteps in front of Peter Ivanovich, was sprinkling something on the floor. Seeing this, Peter Ivanovich was at once aware of the faint odor of the decomposing corpse.

On his last visit to Ivan Ilych, Peter Ivanovich had seen this peasant in his room; 25 he was performing the duties of a sick-nurse, and Ivan Ilych liked him particularly.

Peter Ivanovich continued crossing himself and bowing in a direction intermediate between the coffin, the deacon, and the holy icons on the table in the corner. Then when this action of making the sign of the cross with his hand seemed to him to have been unduly prolonged, he stood still and began to scrutinize the dead man.

The dead man lay, as dead men always do lie, in a peculiarly heavy dead way, his stiffened limbs sunk in the cushions of the coffin, and his head bent back forever on the pillow. His yellow waxen forehead with bald spots on the sunken temples was thrust up, in a way dead men always are, and his nose stood out sharply as if it

were squeezed on the upper lip. He was much changed, even thinner since Peter Ivanovich had seen him, but his face—as always with the dead—was more handsome,
and, above all, more impressive than when he was alive. On the face was an expression that said what had to be done, was in fact done, and rightly done. Besides this,
there was too in that expression a reproach or a warning for the living. This reminder
seemed to Peter Ivanovich uncalled for, or, at least, to have nothing to do with him.
He felt something unpleasant and so Peter Ivanovich once more crossed himself hurriedly, and, as it struck him, perhaps too hurriedly, not quite in accordance with the
proprieties, turned and went to the door.

Schwartz was waiting for him in the adjoining room, standing with his legs apart
and both hands behind his back playing with his top hat. A single glance at the
playful, sleek, and elegant figure of Schwartz revived Peter Ivanovich. He felt that
Schwartz was above it all, and would not give way to depressing influences. The mere
sight of him said plainly: the incident of the service over the body of Ivan Ilych cannot possibly constitute a sufficient ground for recognizing the business of the session
suspended—in other words, in no way can it hinder us from shuffling and cutting a
pack of cards this evening, while the footman sets four unsanctified candles on the
table for us; in fact, there is no ground for supposing that this incident could prevent
us from spending the evening agreeably. He said as much indeed to Peter Ivanovich
as he came out, proposing that the party should meet at Fyodor Vasilievich's. But
apparently it was Peter Ivanovich's destiny not to play bridge that evening. Praskovya Fyodorovna, a short, fat woman who, in spite of all efforts in a contrary direction, was steadily broader from her shoulders downwards, all in black, with lace on
her head and her eyebrows as queerly arched as the lady standing beside the coffin,
came out of her own apartments with some other ladies, and conducting them to the
dead man's room, said: "The service will take place immediately; come in."

Schwartz, making an indefinite bow, stood still, obviously neither accepting
nor declining this invitation. Praskovya Fyodorovna, recognizing Peter Ivanovich,
sighed, went right up to him, took his hand, and said, "I know that you were a true
friend of Ivan Ilych's . . ." and looked at him, expecting from him the suitable action
in response to these words. Peter Ivanovich knew that, just as before he had to cross
himself, now what he had to do was to press her hand, to sigh and to say, "Ah, I was
indeed!" And he did so. And as he did so, he felt that the desired result had been
attained; that he was touched, and she was touched.

"Come, since it's not begun yet, I have something I want to say to you," said the   30
widow. "Give me your arm."

Peter Ivanovich gave her his arm, and they moved towards the inner rooms,
passing Schwartz, who winked gloomily at Peter Ivanovich.

"So much for our bridge! Don't complain if we find another partner. You can
make a fifth when you do get away," said his humorous glance.

Peter Ivanovich sighed still more deeply and despondently, and Praskovya
Fyodorovna pressed his hand gratefully. Going into her drawing room, which was
upholstered with pink cretonne and lighted by a dismal-looking lamp, they sat down
at the table, she on a sofa and Peter Ivanovich on a low ottoman with deranged
springs which yielded spasmodically under his weight. Praskovya Fyodorovna was
about to warn him to sit on another seat, but felt such a recommendation out of
keeping with her position, and changed her mind. Sitting down on the ottoman,
Peter Ivanovich remembered how Ivan Ilych had arranged this drawing room, and
had consulted him about this very pink cretonne with green leaves. Seating herself

on the sofa, and pushing by the table (the whole drawing room was crowded with fur-niture and things), the widow caught the lace of her black shawl in the carving of the table. Peter Ivanovich got up to disentangle it for her; and the ottoman, freed from his weight, began bobbing up spasmodically under him. The widow began unhook-ing her shawl herself, and Peter Ivanovich again sat down, suppressing the mutinous ottoman springs under him. But the widow could not quite free herself, and Peter Ivanovich rose again, and again the ottoman became mutinous and popped up with a positive snap. When this was all over, she took out a clean cambric° handkerchief and began weeping. Peter Ivanovich had been chilled off by the incident with the lace shawl and the struggle with the ottoman springs, and he sat looking sullen. This awkward position was cut short by the entrance of Sokolov, Ivan Ilych's butler, who came in to announce that the place in the cemetery fixed on by Praskovya Fyodoro-vna would cost two hundred rubles. She left off weeping, and with the air of a victim, glancing at Peter Ivanovich, said in French that it was very terrible for her. Peter Ivanovich made a silent gesture signifying his unhesitating conviction that it must indeed be so.

"Please, smoke," she said in a magnanimous, and at the same time, crushed voice, and she began discussing with Sokolov the question of the price of the site for the grave.

Peter Ivanovich, lighting a cigarette, listened to her very substantial inquiries   35
as to the various prices of sites and her decision as to the one to be selected. Having settled on the site for the grave, she made arrangements also about the choristers. Sokolov went away.

"I see to everything myself," she said to Peter Ivanovich, moving to one side the albums that lay on the table; and noticing that the table was in danger from the cigarette-ash, she promptly passed him an ash-tray and said: "I consider it an affecta-tion to pretend that my grief prevents me from looking after practical matters. On the contrary, if anything could—not console me . . . but distract me, it is seeing after everything for him." She took out her handkerchief again, as though preparing to weep; and suddenly, as though struggling with herself, she shook herself, and began speaking calmly: "But I've business to talk about with you."

Peter Ivanovich bowed, carefully keeping in check the springs of the ottoman, which had at once begun quivering under him.

"The last few days his sufferings were awful."

"Did he suffer very much?" asked Peter Ivanovich.

"Oh, awfully! For the last moments, hours indeed, he never left off screaming.   40
For three days and nights in succession he screamed incessantly. It was insufferable. I can't understand how I bore it; one could hear it through three closed doors. Ah, what I suffered!"

"And was he really conscious?" asked Peter Ivanovich.

"Yes," she whispered, "up to the last minute. He said good-bye to us a quarter of an hour before his death, and asked Volodya to be taken away too."

The thought of the sufferings of a man he had known so intimately, at first as a light-hearted child, a schoolboy, then grown up as a colleague, suddenly horrified Peter Ivanovich, in spite of the unpleasant consciousness of his own and this wom-an's hypocrisy. He saw again that forehead, the nose that seemed to be squeezing the lip, and he felt frightened for himself.

---

cambric: linen or cotton fabric, usually plain and white.

"Three days and nights of awful suffering and death. Why, that may at once, any minute, come upon me too," he thought, and he felt for an instant terrified. But immediately, he could not himself have said how, there came to his support the customary reflection that this had happened to Ivan Ilych and not to him, and that to him this must not and could not happen; that in thinking thus he was giving way to depression, which was not the right thing to do, as was evident from Schwartz's expression of face. And making these reflections, Peter Ivanovich felt reassured, and began with interest inquiring about the details of Ivan Ilych's end, as though death were a mischance peculiar to Ivan Ilych, but not at all incidental to himself.

After various observations about the details of the truly awful physical sufferings 45 endured by Ivan Ilych (these details Peter Ivanovich learned only through the effect Ivan Ilych's agonies had had on the nerves of Praskovya Fyodorovna), the widow apparently thought it time to get to business.

"Ah, Peter Ivanovich, how hard it is, how awfully, awfully hard!" and she began to cry again.

Peter Ivanovich sighed, and waited for her to blow her nose. When she had done so, he said, "Indeed it is," and again she began to talk, and brought out what was evidently the business she wished to discuss with him; that business consisted in the inquiry as to how on the occasion of her husband's death she was to obtain a grant from the government. She made a show of asking Peter Ivanovich's advice about a pension. But he perceived that she knew already, to the minutest details, what he did not know himself, indeed, everything that could be got out of the government on the ground of this death; but that what she wanted to find out was, whether there were not any means of obtaining a little more? Peter Ivanovich tried to imagine such means; but after pondering a little, and out of politeness abusing the government for its stinginess, he said that he believed that it was impossible to obtain more. Then she sighed and began unmistakably looking about for an excuse for getting rid of her visitor. He perceived this, put out his cigarette, got up, pressed her hand, and went out into the passage.

In the dining room, where the clock stood that Ivan Ilych had been so delighted at buying, Peter Ivanovich met the priest and several people he knew who had come to the service for the dead, and saw too Ivan Ilych's daughter, a handsome young lady. She was all in black. Her very slender figure looked even slenderer than usual. She had a gloomy, determined, almost wrathful expression. She bowed to Peter Ivanovich as though he were to blame in some way. Behind the daughter, with the same offended air on his face, stood a rich young man, whom Peter Ivanovich knew too, an examining magistrate, the young lady's fiancé, as he had heard. He bowed dejectedly to him, and would have gone on into the dead man's room, when from the staircase there appeared the figure of the son, the high school boy, extraordinarily like Ivan Ilych. He was the young Ivan Ilych all over again, as Peter Ivanovich remembered him at school. His eyes were red with crying, and had that look often seen in unclean boys of thirteen or fourteen. The boy, seeing Peter Ivanovich, scowled morosely and bashfully. Peter Ivanovich nodded to him and went into the dead man's room. The service for the dead began—candles, groans, incense, tears, sobs. Peter Ivanovich stood frowning, staring at his feet in front of him. He did not once glance at the dead man, and right through to the end did not once give way to depressing influences, and was one of the first to walk out. In the hall there was no one. Gerasim, the young peasant, darted out of the dead man's room, tossed over with his strong hand all the fur cloaks to find Peter Ivanovich's, and gave it him.

"Well, Gerasim, my boy?" said Peter Ivanovich, so as to say something. "A sad business, isn't it?"

"It's God's will. We shall come to the same," said Gerasim, showing his white, even, peasant teeth in a smile, and, like a man in a rush of extra work, he briskly opened the door, called up the coachman, saw Peter Ivanovich into the carriage, and darted back to the steps as though thinking to himself what he had to do next.

Peter Ivanovich had a special pleasure in the fresh air after the smell of incense, of the corpse, and of carbolic acid.

"Where to?" asked the coachman.

"It's not too late. I'll still go round to Fyodor Vasilievich."

And Peter Ivanovich drove there. And he did, in fact, find them just finishing the first rubber, so that he came just at the right time to take a hand.

II

The previous history of Ivan Ilych was the simplest, the most ordinary, and the most awful.

Ivan Ilych died at the age of forty-five, a member of the Judicial Council. He was the son of an official, whose career in Petersburg through various ministries and departments had been such as leads people into that position in which, though it is distinctly obvious that they are unfit to perform any kind of real duty, they yet cannot, owing to their long past service and their official rank, be dismissed; and they therefore receive a specially created fictitious post, and by no means fictitious thousands—from six to ten thousand rubles—on which they go on living till extreme old age.

Such was the Privy Councilor and superfluous member of various superfluous institutions, Ilya Efimovich Golovin.

He had three sons, of whom Ivan Ilych was the second. The eldest son's career was exactly like his father's, only in a different department, and he was by now close upon that stage in the service in which the same sinecure would be reached. The third son was the unsuccessful one. He had in various positions always made a mess of things, and was now employed in the railway department. And his father and his brothers, and still more their wives, did not merely dislike meeting him, but avoided, except in extreme necessity, recollecting his existence. His sister had married Baron Greff, a Petersburg official of the same stamp as his father-in-law. Ivan Ilych was *le phénix de la famille*,° as people said. He was not so frigid and precise as the eldest son, nor so wild as the youngest. He was the happy mean between them—a shrewd, lively, pleasant, and well-bred man. He had been educated with his younger brother at the School of Jurisprudence. The younger brother had not finished the school course, but was expelled when in the fifth class. Ivan Ilych completed the course successfully. At school he was just the same as he was later on all his life—an intelligent fellow, highly good-humored and sociable, but strict in doing what he considered to be his duty. His duty he considered whatever was so considered by those persons who were set in authority over him. He was not a toady as a boy, nor later on as a grown-up person; but from his earliest years he was attracted, as a fly to the light, to persons of good standing in the world, assimilated their manners and their views of life, and established friendly relations with them. All the enthusiasms of childhood and youth passed, leaving no great traces in him; he gave way to sensuality and to vanity, and

le phénix de la famille: French for "the prize of the family."

latterly when in the higher classes at school to liberalism, but always keeping within certain limits which were unfailingly marked out for him by his instincts.

At school he had committed actions which had struck him beforehand as great vileness, and gave him a feeling of loathing for himself at the very time he was committing them. But later on, perceiving that such actions were committed also by men of good position, and were not regarded by them as base, he was able, not to regard them as good, but to forget about them completely, and was never mortified by recollections of them.

Leaving the School of Jurisprudence in the tenth class, and receiving from his father a sum of money for his outfit, Ivan Ilych ordered his clothes at Sharmer's, hung on his watch-chain a medallion inscribed *respice finem*,° said good-bye to the prince who was the patron of his school, had a farewell dinner with his comrades at Donon's, and with all his new fashionable belongings—traveling trunk, linen, suits of clothes, shaving and grooming equipment, and traveling blanket, all ordered and purchased at the very best shops—set off to take the post of secretary on special commissions for the governor of a province, a post which had been obtained for him by his father. 60

In the province Ivan Ilych soon made himself a position as easy and agreeable as his position had been in the School of Jurisprudence. He did his work, made his career, and at the same time led a life of well-bred social gaiety. Occasionally he visited various districts on official duty, behaved with dignity both with his superiors and his inferiors; and with exactitude and an incorruptible honesty of which he could not help feeling proud, performed the duties with which he was entrusted, principally having to do with the dissenters.°

When engaged in official work he was, in spite of his youth and taste for frivolous amusements, exceedingly reserved, official, and even severe. But in social life he was often amusing and witty, and always good-natured, well bred, and *bon enfant*,° as was said of him by his chief and his chief's wife, with whom he was like one of the family.

In the province there was, too, a connection with one of the ladies who obtruded their charms on the stylish young lawyer. There was a dressmaker, too, and there were drinking bouts with smart officers visiting the neighborhood, and visits to a certain outlying street after supper; there was a rather cringing obsequiousness in his behavior, too, with his chief, and even his chief's wife. But all this was accompanied with such a tone of the highest breeding, that it could not be called by harsh names; it all came under the rubric of the French saying, "*Il faut que la jeunesse se passe*."° Everything was done with clean hands, in clean shirts, with French phrases, and, what was of most importance, in the highest society, and consequently with the approval of people of rank.

Such was Ivan Ilych's career for five years, and then came a change in his official life. New methods of judicial procedure were established; new men were wanted to carry them out. And Ivan Ilych became such a new man. Ivan Ilych was offered the post of examining magistrate, and he accepted it in spite of the fact that this post was in another province, and he would have to break off all the ties he had formed and form new ones. Ivan Ilych's friends met together to see him off, had their photographs taken in a group, presented him with a silver cigarette case, and he set off to his new post.

As an examining magistrate, Ivan Ilych was as *comme il faut*,° as well bred, as adroit in keeping official duties apart from private life, and as successful in gaining 65

respice finem: Latin for "Think of the end (of your life)." *dissenters*: dissenters from the Orthodox Church. *bon enfant*: French for "a well-behaved child." *"Il faut que la jeunesse se passe"*: "Youth doesn't last." *comme il faut*: "as required," rule-abiding.

universal respect, as he had been as secretary of private commissions. The duties of his new office were in themselves of far greater interest and attractiveness to Ivan Ilych. In his former post it had been pleasant to pass in his smart uniform from Sharmer's through the crowd of petitioners and officials waiting timorously and envying him, and to march with his easy swagger straight into the governor's private room, there to sit down with him to tea and cigarettes. But the persons directly subject to his authority were few. The only such persons were the district police superintendents and the dissenters, when he was serving on special commissions. And he liked treating such persons affably, almost like comrades; liked to make them feel that he, able to annihilate them, was behaving in this simple, friendly way with them. But such people were then few in number. Now as an examining magistrate Ivan Ilych felt that everyone—everyone without exception—the most dignified, the most self-satisfied people, all were in his hands, and that he had but to write certain words on a sheet of paper with a printed heading, and this dignified self-satisfied person would be brought before him in the capacity of a defendant or a witness; and if he did not care to make him sit down, he would have to stand up before him and answer his questions. Ivan Ilych never abused his authority; on the contrary, he tried to soften the expression of it. But the consciousness of this power and the possibility of softening its effect constituted for him the chief interest and attractiveness of his new position. In the work itself, in the preliminary inquiries, that is, Ivan Ilych very rapidly acquired the art of setting aside every consideration irrelevant to the official aspect of the case, and of reducing every case, however complex, to that form in which it could in a purely external fashion be put on paper, completely excluding his personal view of the matter, and what was of paramount importance, observing all the necessary formalities. All this work was new. And he was one of the first men who put into practical working the reforms in judicial procedure enacted in 1864.°

On settling in the new town in his position as examining magistrate, Ivan Ilych made new acquaintances, formed new ties, took up a new line, and adopted a rather different attitude. He took up an attitude of somewhat dignified aloofness towards the provincial authorities, while he picked out the best circle among the legal gentlemen and wealthy gentry living in the town, and adopted a tone of slight dissatisfaction with the government, moderate liberalism, and lofty civic virtue. With this, while making no change in the elegance of his grooming, Ivan Ilych in his new office gave up shaving, and left his beard free to grow as it liked.

Ivan Ilych's existence in the new town proved to be very agreeable; the society which took the line of opposition to the governor was friendly and good; his income was larger, and he found a source of increased enjoyment in bridge, at which he began to play at this time; and having a faculty for playing cards good-humoredly, and being rapid and exact in his calculations, he was as a rule on the winning side.

After living two years in the new town, Ivan Ilych met his future wife. Praskovya Fyodorovna Mikhel was the most attractive, clever, and brilliant girl in the set in which Ivan Ilych moved. Among other amusements and recreations after his labors as a magistrate, Ivan Ilych started a light, playful flirtation with Praskovya Fyodorovna.

When he was an assistant secretary, Ivan Ilych had danced as a rule; as an examining magistrate he danced only as an exception. He danced now as if under protest, as though to show "that though I am serving in the new reformed legal code, and am

---

reforms in judicial procedure enacted in 1864: The emancipation of the serfs in 1861 was followed by a reform of judicial proceedings.

of the fifth class in official rank, still if it comes to a question of dancing, in that line too I can do better than others." In this spirit he danced now and then towards the end of the evening with Praskovya Fyodorovna, and it was principally during these dances that he won her heart. She fell in love with him. Ivan Ilych had no clearly defined intention of marrying; but when the girl fell in love with him, he put the question to himself: "After all, why not get married?" he said to himself.

The young lady, Praskovya Fyodorovna, was of good family, nice-looking. There was a little bit of property. Ivan Ilych might have reckoned on a more brilliant match, but this was a good match. Ivan Ilych had his salary; she, he hoped, would have as much of her own. It was a good family; she was a sweet, pretty, and perfectly *comme il faut* young woman. To say that Ivan Ilych got married because he fell in love with his wife and found in her sympathy with his views of life, would be as incorrect as to say that he got married because the people of his world approved of the match. Ivan Ilych was influenced by both considerations; he was doing what was agreeable to himself in securing such a wife, and at the same time doing what persons of higher standing looked upon as the correct thing. 70

And so Ivan Ilych got married.

The process itself of getting married and the early period of married life, with the conjugal caresses, the new furniture, the new china, the new house linen, all up to the time of his wife's pregnancy, went off very well; so that Ivan Ilych had begun to think that not only would marriage not break up that kind of frivolous, agreeable, light-hearted life, always decorous and always approved by society, which he regarded as the normal life, it would even increase its agreeableness. But at that point, in the early months of his wife's pregnancy, there came in a new element, unexpected, unpleasant, tiresome and unseemly, which could never have been anticipated, and from which there was no escape.

His wife, without any kind of reason, it seemed to Ivan Ilych, *de gaieté de coeur,*° as he expressed it, began to disturb the agreeableness and decorum of their life. She began without any sort of justification to be jealous, exacting in her demands on his attention, squabbled over everything, and treated him to the coarsest and most unpleasant scenes.

At first Ivan Ilych hoped to escape from the unpleasantness of this position by taking up the same frivolous and well-bred line that had served him well on other occasions of difficulty. He endeavored to ignore his wife's ill-humor, went on living light-heartedly and agreeably as before, invited friends to play cards, tried to get away himself to the club or to his friends. But his wife began on one occasion with such energy, abusing him in such coarse language, and so obstinately persisted in her abuse of him every time he failed in carrying out her demands, obviously having made up her mind firmly to persist till he gave way, that is, stayed at home and was as dull as she was, that Ivan Ilych took alarm. He perceived that matrimony, at least with his wife, was not invariably conducive to the pleasures and proprieties of life; but, on the contrary, often destructive of them, and that it was therefore essential to erect some barrier to protect himself from these disturbances. And Ivan Ilych began to look about for such means of protecting himself. His official duties were the only thing that impressed Praskovya Fyodorovna, and Ivan Ilych began to use his official position and the duties arising from it in his struggle with his wife to fence off his own independent world apart.

de gaieté de coeur: "from pure whim."

With the birth of the baby, the attempts at nursing it, and the various unsuccess- 75
ful experiments with foods, with the illnesses, real and imaginary, of the infant and
its mother, in which Ivan Ilych was expected to sympathize, though he never had
the slightest idea about them, the need for him to fence off a world apart for himself
outside his family life became still more imperative.

As his wife grew more irritable and exacting, so did Ivan Ilych more and more
transfer the center of gravity of his life to his official work. He became fonder and
fonder of official life, and more ambitious than he had been.

Very quickly, not more than a year after his wedding, Ivan Ilych had become
aware that conjugal life, though providing certain comforts, was in reality a very
intricate and difficult business towards which one must, if one is to do one's duty, that
is, lead the decorous life approved by society, work out for oneself a definite line, just
as in government service.

And such a line Ivan Ilych established for himself in his married life. He
expected from his home life only those comforts—of dinner at home, of housekeeper
and bed—which it could give him, and, above all, that perfect propriety in external
observances required by public opinion. For the rest, he looked for good-humored
pleasantness, and if he found it he was very thankful. If he met with antagonism and
querulousness, he promptly retreated into the separate world he had shut off for himself in his official life, and there he found solace.

Ivan Ilych was prized as a good official, and three years later he was made Assistant Public Prosecutor. The new duties of this position, their dignity, the possibility of bringing anyone to trial and putting anyone in prison, the publicity of the
speeches and the success Ivan Ilych had in that part of his work—all this made his
official work still more attractive to him.

More children were born. His wife became steadily more querulous and ill- 80
tempered, but the line Ivan Ilych had adopted for himself in home life put him
almost out of reach of her grumbling.

After seven years of service in the same town, Ivan Ilych was transferred to
another province with the post of Public Prosecutor. They moved, money was short,
and his wife did not like the place they had moved to. The salary was indeed a little
higher than before, but their expenses were larger, and besides, a couple of children
died, so home life consequently became even less agreeable for Ivan Ilych.

For every mischance that occurred in their new place of residence, Praskovya
Fyodorovna blamed her husband. The greater number of subjects of conversation
between husband and wife, especially the education of the children, led to questions
which were associated with previous quarrels, and quarrels were ready to break out
at every instant. There remained only those rare periods of being in love which did
indeed come upon them, but never lasted long. These were the islands at which they
put in for a time, but they soon set off again upon the ocean of concealed hostility,
that was made manifest in their aloofness from one another. This aloofness might
have distressed Ivan Ilych if he had believed that this ought not to be so, but by now
he regarded this position as perfectly normal, and it was indeed the goal towards
which he worked in his home life. His aim was to make himself more and more free
from the unpleasant aspects of domestic life and to render them harmless and decorous. And he attained this aim by spending less and less time with his family; and
when he was forced to be at home, he endeavored to secure his tranquility by the
presence of outsiders. The great thing for Ivan Ilych was having his office. In the official world all the interest of life was concentrated for him. And this interest absorbed

him. The sense of his own power, the consciousness of being able to ruin anyone he wanted to ruin, even the external dignity of his office, when he made his entry into the court or met subordinate officials, his success in the eyes of his superiors and his subordinates, and, above all, his masterly handling of cases, of which he was conscious—all this delighted him and, together with chats with his colleagues, dining out, and whist, filled his life. So that, on the whole, Ivan Ilych's life still went on in the way he thought it should go—agreeably and decorously.

So he lived for another seven years. His eldest daughter was already sixteen, another child had died, and there was left only one other, a boy at the High School, a subject of dissension. Ivan Ilych wanted to send him to the School of Jurisprudence, while Praskovya Fyodorovna to spite him sent him to the High School. The daughter had been educated at home, and had turned out well; the boy also did fairly well at his lessons.

III

Such was Ivan Ilych's life for seventeen years after his marriage. He had been Public Prosecutor by now for a long while, and had refused several appointments offered him, looking out for a more desirable post, when there occurred an unexpected incident which utterly destroyed his peace of mind. Ivan Ilych had been expecting to be appointed presiding judge in a university town, but a certain Goppe somehow stole a march on him and secured the appointment. Ivan Ilych took offence, began upbraiding him, and quarreled with him and with his own superiors. A coolness was felt towards him, and on the next appointment that was made, he was again passed over.

This was in the year 1880. That year was the most painful one in Ivan Ilych's life. 85 During that year it became evident on the one hand that his pay was insufficient for his expenses; on the other hand, that he had been forgotten by everyone, and that what seemed to him the most monstrous, the crudest injustice, appeared to other people as a quite commonplace fact. Even his father felt no obligation to assist him. He felt that everyone had deserted him, and that everyone regarded his position with an income of 3,500 rubles as quite normal and even fortunate. He alone, with a sense of the injustice done him, the everlasting nagging of his wife, and the debts he had begun to accumulate living beyond his means, knew that his position was far from being normal.

The summer of that year, to cut down his expenses, he took a holiday and went with his wife to spend the summer in the country at her brother's.

In the country, with no official duties to occupy him, Ivan Ilych was for the first time a prey not to simple boredom, but to intolerable depression; and he made up his mind that things could not go on like that, and that it was absolutely necessary to take some decisive steps.

After a sleepless night spent walking up and down the terrace, Ivan Ilych determined to go to Petersburg to take active steps to get transferred to some other department, so as to revenge himself on the people who had not known how to appreciate him.

The next day, in spite of all the efforts of his wife and his mother-in-law to dissuade him, he set off to Petersburg. He went with a single object before him—to obtain a post with an income of 5,000 rubles. He was ready to be satisfied with a post in any department, of any tendency, with any kind of work. All he wanted was a post with five thousand, in the executive department, the banks, the railways, the Empress Marya's Institutions,° even in the customs duties—what was essential was

Empress Marya's Institutions: orphanages.

five thousand, and to get out of the department in which they had failed to appreciate his value.

And, behold, this quest of Ivan Ilych's was crowned with wonderful, unexpected success. At Kursk, an acquaintance named F. S. Ilyin got into the same first-class carriage and told him of a telegram just received by the governor of Kursk, announcing a change about to take place in the ministry—Peter Ivanovich was to be superseded by Ivan Semyonovich.

The proposed change, apart from its significance for Russia, had special significance for Ivan Ilych from the fact that by bringing to the front a new person, Peter Petrovich, and obviously, therefore, his friend Zachar Ivanovich, it was in the highest degree favorable to Ivan Ilych's own plans. Zachar Ivanovich was a friend and schoolfellow of Ivan Ilych's.

In Moscow the news was confirmed. On arriving at Petersburg, Ivan Ilych looked up Zachar Ivanovich, and received a definite promise of an appointment in his former department of Justice.

A week later he telegraphed to his wife: "Zachar Miller's place. At first report I receive appointment.'"

Thanks to these changes, Ivan Ilych unexpectedly obtained, in the same department as before, an appointment which placed him two stages higher than his former colleagues, and gave him an income of five thousand rubles, together with the official allowance of three thousand five hundred for traveling expenses. All his ill humor with his former enemies and the whole department was forgotten, and Ivan Ilych was completely happy.

He went back to the country more light-hearted and good-tempered than he had been for a very long while. Praskovya Fyodorovna was in better spirits, too, and peace was patched up between them. Ivan Ilych described what respect everyone had shown him in Petersburg; how all those who had been his enemies had been put to shame, and were now cringing before him; how envious they were of his appointment, and still more of the high favor in which he stood at Petersburg.

Praskovya Fyodorovna listened to this, and pretended to believe it, and did not contradict him in anything, but confined herself to making plans for her new arrangements in the town to which they would be moving. And Ivan Ilych saw with delight that these plans were his plans; that they were agreed; and that his life after this disturbing hitch in its progress was about to regain its true, normal character of light-hearted agreeableness and propriety.

Ivan Ilych had come back to the country for a short stay only. He had to enter upon the duties of his new office on the 10th of September; and besides, he needed some time to settle in a new place, to move all his belongings from the other province, to purchase and order many things in addition; in short, to arrange things as settled in his own mind, and almost exactly as what Praskovya Fyodorovna too had decided upon.

And now when everything was so successfully arranged, and when he and his wife were agreed in their aim, and were, besides, so little together, they got on with one another as they had not got on together since the early years of their married life. Ivan Ilych had thought of taking his family away with him at once; but his sister and his brother-in-law, who had suddenly become extremely cordial and intimate with him and his family, were so pressing in urging them to stay that he set off alone.

Ivan Ilych started off, and the light-hearted temper produced by his success, and his good understanding with his wife, one thing backing up another, did not

90

95

desert him all the time. He found a charming set of apartments, the very thing both husband and wife had dreamed of. Spacious, lofty reception rooms in the old style, a comfortable, dignified-looking study for him, rooms for his wife and daughter, a schoolroom for his son, everything as though planned especially for them. Ivan Ilych himself looked after the furnishing of them, chose the wallpapers, bought furniture, by preference antique furniture, which had a peculiar *comme il faut* style to his mind, and it all progressed and progressed, and really attained the ideal he had set before himself. When he had half finished arranging the house, his arrangement surpassed his own expectations. He saw the *comme il faut* character, elegant and free from vulgarity, that the whole would have when it was all ready. As he fell asleep he pictured to himself the reception room, as it would be. Looking at the drawing room, not yet finished, he could see the hearth, the screen, the *étagère,*° and the little chairs dotted here and there, the plates and dishes on the wall, and the bronzes as they would be when they were all put in their places. He was delighted with the thought of how he would impress Praskovya and Lizanka, who shared his taste in this line. They would never expect anything like it. He was particularly successful in coming across and buying cheap old pieces of furniture, which gave a peculiarly aristocratic air to the whole. In his letters he purposely disparaged everything so as to surprise them. All this so absorbed him that the duties of his new office, though he was so fond of his official work, interested him less than he had expected. During sittings of the court he had moments of inattention; he pondered the question which sort of cornices to have on the window blinds, straight or fluted. He was so interested in this business that he often set to work with his own hands, moved a piece of furniture, or hung up curtains himself. One day he went up a ladder to show a workman, who did not understand, how he wanted some hangings draped, made a false step and slipped; but, like a strong and nimble person, he clung on, and only knocked his side against the corner of a frame. The bruised place ached, but it soon passed off. Ivan Ilych felt all this time particularly good-humored and well. He wrote: "I feel fifteen years younger." He thought his house furnishing would be finished in September, but it dragged on to the middle of October. But then the effect was charming; not only he said so, but everyone who saw it told him so too.

In reality, it was all just what is commonly seen in the houses of people who are   100 not exactly wealthy but want to look like wealthy people, and so succeed only in being like one another—hangings, dark wood, flowers, rugs and bronzes, everything dark and highly polished, everything that all people of a certain class have so as to be like all people of a certain class. And in his case it was all so like that it made no impression at all; but it all seemed to him somehow special. When he met his family at the railway station and brought them to his newly furnished rooms, all lighted up in readiness, and a footman in a white tie opened the door into an entry decorated with flowers, and then they walked into the drawing room and the study, uttering cries of delight, he was very happy, conducted them everywhere, eagerly drinking in their praises, and beaming with satisfaction. The same evening, while they talked about various things at tea, Praskovya Fyodorovna inquired about his fall, and he laughed and showed them how he had gone flying, and how he had frightened the upholsterer.

"It is as well I'm something of an athlete. Another man might have been killed, and I got nothing worse than a blow here; when it's touched it hurts, but it's going off already; nothing but a bruise."

étagère: piece of furniture featuring open shelves to display trinkets and collectibles.

And they began to live in their new abode, which, as is always the case, when they had got thoroughly settled in they found to be short just one room, and with their new income, which, as always, was only a little—some five hundred rubles—too little, but everything went very well.

Things went particularly well at first, before everything was quite finally arranged, and there was still something to do to the place—something to buy, something to order, something to move, something to make fit. Though there were indeed several disputes between husband and wife, both were so well satisfied, and there was so much to do, that it all went off without serious quarrels. When there was nothing left to arrange, it became a little dull, and something seemed to be lacking, but by then they were making acquaintances and forming habits, and life was filled up again.

Ivan Ilych, after spending the morning in the court, returned home to dinner, and at first he was generally in a good humor, although this was apt to be upset a little, and precisely on account of the new abode. Every spot on the tablecloth, on the hangings, the string of a window blind broken, irritated him. He had devoted so much trouble to the arrangement of the rooms that any disturbance of their order distressed him. But, on the whole, the life of Ivan Ilych ran its course as, according to his conviction, life ought to do—easily, agreeably, and decorously.

He got up at nine, drank his coffee, read the newspaper, then put on his official uniform, and went to the court. There the routine of the daily work was already mapped out for him, and he stepped into it at once. People with petitions, inquiries in the office, the office itself, the sittings—public and preliminary. In all this the necessary thing was to exclude everything with the sap of life in it, which always disturbs the regular course of official business, not to admit any sort of relations with people except the official relations; the motive of all intercourse had to be simply the official motive, and the intercourse itself to be only official. A man would come, for instance, anxious for certain information. Ivan Ilych, not being the functionary on duty, would have nothing whatever to do with such a man. But if this man's relation to him as a member of the court is such as can be formulated on official stamped paper—within the limits of such a relation Ivan Ilych would do everything, positively everything he could, and in doing so would observe the semblance of friendly human relations, that is, the courtesies of social life. But where the official relation ended, there everything else stopped too. This art of keeping the official aspect of things apart from his real life, Ivan Ilych possessed in the highest degree; and through long practice and natural aptitude, he had brought it to such a pitch of perfection that he even permitted himself at times, like a skilled specialist as if in jest, to let the human and official relations mingle. He allowed himself this liberty just because he felt he had the power at any moment if he wished it to take up the purely official line again and to drop the human relation. This thing was not simply easy, agreeable, and decorous; in Ivan Ilych's hands it attained a positively artistic character. In the intervals of business he smoked, drank tea, chatted a little about politics, a little about public affairs, a little about cards, but most of all about appointments in the service. And tired, but feeling like some artist who has skillfully played his part in the performance, one of the first violins in the orchestra, he returned home. At home his daughter and her mother had been paying calls somewhere, or else someone had been calling on them; the son had been at school, had been preparing his lessons with his teachers, and duly learning correctly what was taught at the High School. Everything was as it should be. After dinner, if there were no visitors, Ivan Ilych sometimes read some book about

which people were talking, and in the evening sat down to work, that is, read official papers, compared them with the laws, sorted depositions, and put them under
the laws. This he found neither tiresome nor entertaining. It was tiresome when he
might have been playing bridge; but if there were no bridge going on, it was anyway
better than sitting alone or with his wife. Ivan Ilych's pleasures were little dinners, to
which he invited ladies and gentlemen of good social position, and such methods of
passing the time with them as were usual with such persons, so that his drawing room
might be like all other drawing rooms.

Once they even gave a party—a dance. And Ivan Ilych enjoyed it, and everything was very successful, except that it led to a violent quarrel with his wife over
the tarts and sweetmeats. Praskovya Fyodorovna had her own plan; while Ivan Ilych
insisted on getting everything from an expensive pastry-cook, and ordered a great
many tarts, and the quarrel was because these tarts were left over and the pastry-
cook's bill came to forty-five rubles. The quarrel was a violent and unpleasant one, so
much so that Praskovya Fyodorovna called him, "Fool, imbecile." And he clutched at
his head, and in his anger made some allusion to a divorce.

But the party itself was enjoyable. There were all the best people, and Ivan Ilych
danced with Princess Trufonov, the sister of the distinguished founder of the charitable association called "Bear my Burden."

His official pleasures lay in the gratification of his pride; his social pleasures lay
in the gratification of his vanity. But Ivan Ilych's most real pleasure was the pleasure
of playing bridge. He admitted to himself that after all, after whatever unpleasant
incidents there had been in his life, the pleasure which burned like a candle before
all others was sitting with good players, and not noisy partners, at bridge; and, of
course, a four-hand game (playing with five was never a success, though one pretends
to like it particularly), and with good cards, to play a shrewd, serious game, then supper and a glass of wine. And after bridge, especially after winning some small stakes
(winning large sums was unpleasant), Ivan Ilych went to bed in a particularly happy
frame of mind.

So they lived. They moved in the very best circle, and were visited by people of
consequence and young people. In their views about their circle of acquaintances,
the husband, the wife, and the daughter were in complete accord; and without any
expressed agreement on the subject, they all acted alike in dropping and shaking off
various friends and relations, shabby persons who swooped down upon them in their
drawing room with Japanese plates on the walls, and pressed their civilities on them.
Soon these shabby persons ceased fluttering about them, and none but the very best
society was seen at the Golovins'.

Young men began to pay attention to Lizanka; and Petrishchev, an examining   110
magistrate, the son of Dmitry Ivanovich Petrishchev and sole heir of his fortune,
began to be so attentive to Lizanka, that Ivan Ilych had raised the question with his
wife whether it would not be as well to arrange a sleigh ride for them, or to get up
some theatricals.

So they lived. And everything went on in this way without change, and everything was very pleasant.

IV

All were in good health. One could not use the word ill-health in connection
with the symptoms Ivan Ilych sometimes complained of, namely, a queer taste in his
mouth and a sort of uncomfortable feeling on the left side of his stomach.

But it came to pass that this uncomfortable feeling kept increasing, and became not exactly a pain, but a continual sense of pressure in his side accompanied by an irritable temper. This irritability, continually growing and growing, began at last to mar the agreeable easiness and decorum that had reigned in the Golovin household. Quarrels between the husband and wife became more and more frequent, and soon all the easiness and amenity of life had fallen away, and mere propriety was maintained with difficulty. Scenes again became more frequent. Again there were islands in the sea of contention—and but few of these—where the husband and wife could meet without an outbreak. And Praskovya Fyodorovna said now, not without grounds, that her husband had a trying temper. With her characteristic exaggeration, she said he had always had this awful temper, and she had needed all her sweetness to put up with it for twenty years. It was true that it was now he who began the quarrels. His gusts of temper always broke out just before dinner, and often just as he was beginning to eat, at the soup. He would notice that some piece of the china had been chipped, or that the food was not nice, or that his son put his elbow on the table, or his daughter's hair was not arranged as he liked it. And whatever it was, he laid the blame on Praskovya Fyodorovna. Praskovya Fyodorovna had at first retorted in the same strain, and said all sorts of horrid things to him; but on two occasions, just at the beginning of dinner, he had flown into such a frenzy that she perceived that it was due to physical derangement, and was brought on by taking food, and she controlled herself; she did not reply, but simply made haste to get dinner over. Praskovya Fyodorovna gave great credit to herself for this exercise of self-control. Making up her mind that her husband had a fearful temper, and made her life miserable, she began to feel sorry for herself. And the more she felt sorry for herself, the more she hated her husband. She began to wish he were dead; yet could not wish it, because then there would be no income. And this exasperated her against him even more. She considered herself dreadfully unfortunate, precisely because even his death could not save her, and she felt irritated and concealed it, and this hidden irritation on her side increased his irritability.

After one violent scene, in which Ivan Ilych had been particularly unjust, and after which he had said in explanation that he certainly was irritable, but that it was due to illness, she said that if he were ill he ought to take steps, and insisted on his going to see a celebrated doctor.

He went. Everything was as he had expected; everything was as it always is. The waiting and the assumption of dignity, that professional dignity he knew so well, exactly as he assumed it himself in court, and the sounding and listening and questions that called for answers that were foregone conclusions and obviously superfluous, and the significant air that seemed to insinuate: you leave it all to us, and we will arrange everything, for us it is certain and incontestable how to arrange everything, everything in one way for every man of every sort. It was exactly the same as in his court of justice. The doctor put on for him exactly the same air as he put on in dealing with a man brought up for judgment.

The doctor said that this-and-that proves that you have such-and-such a thing wrong inside you; but if that is not confirmed by analysis of this-and-that, then we must assume this-and-that. If we assume this-and-that, then—and so on. To Ivan Ilych there was only one question of consequence, "Was his condition dangerous or not?" But the doctor ignored that irrelevant inquiry. From the doctor's point of view this was a side issue, not the subject under consideration; the only real question was the balance of probabilities between a floating kidney, chronic catarrh, and

115

appendicitis. It was not a question of the life of Ivan Ilych, but the question between the floating kidney and the intestinal appendix. And this question, as it seemed to Ivan Ilych, the doctor solved in a brilliant manner in favor of the appendix, with the reservation that a urine analysis might give a fresh clue, and that then the aspect of the case would be altered. All this was point-for-point identical with what Ivan Ilych had himself done in brilliant fashion a thousand times over in dealing with some man on trial. Just as brilliantly, the doctor made his summing-up and triumphantly, gaily even, glanced over his spectacles at the prisoner in the dock. From the doctor's summing-up Ivan Ilych deduced the conclusion—that things looked bad, and that he, the doctor, and most likely everyone else, did not care, but that things looked bad for him. And this conclusion impressed Ivan Ilych morbidly, arousing in him a great feeling of pity for himself and great anger against this doctor who seemed unconcerned about a matter of such importance.

But he said nothing of that. He got up, and, laying the fee on the table, he said with a sigh, "We sick people probably often ask inconvenient questions. Tell me, is this generally a dangerous illness or not?"

The doctor glanced severely at him with one eye through his spectacles, as though to say: "Prisoner at the bar, if you will not keep within the limits of the questions allowed you, I shall be compelled to take measures for your removal from the precincts of the court."

"I have told you what I thought necessary and suitable already," said the doctor; "the analysis will show anything further." And the doctor bowed him out.

Ivan Ilych went out slowly and dejectedly, got into his sleigh, and drove home.   120 All the way home he was incessantly going over all the doctor had said, trying to translate all the complicated, obscure, scientific phrases into simple language, and to read in them an answer to the question, "Is it bad—is it very bad, or nothing much as yet?" And it seemed to him that the upshot of all the doctor had said was that it was very bad. Everything seemed dismal to Ivan Ilych in the streets. The cabmen were dismal, the houses were dismal, the people passing, and the shops were dismal. This ache, this dull gnawing ache, that never ceased for a second, seemed, when connected with the doctor's obscure utterances, to have gained a new, more serious significance. With a new sense of misery Ivan Ilych kept watch on it now.

He reached home and began to tell his wife about it. His wife listened; but in the middle of his account his daughter came in with her hat on, ready to go out with her mother. Reluctantly she half sat down to listen to these tedious details, but she could not stand it for long, and her mother did not hear his story to the end.

"Well, I'm very glad," said his wife; "now you must be sure and take the medicine regularly. Give me the prescription; I'll send Gerasim to the chemist's!" And she went to get ready to go out.

He had not taken a breath while she was in the room, and he heaved a deep sigh when she was gone.

"Well," he said, "maybe it really is nothing as yet."

He began to take the medicine, to carry out the doctor's directions, which were   125 changed after the urine analysis. But it was just at this point that some confusion arose, either in the analysis or in what ought to have followed from it. The doctor himself, of course, could not be blamed for it, but it turned out that things had not gone as the doctor had told him. Either he had forgotten or told a lie, or was hiding something from him. But Ivan Ilych still went on just as exactly carrying out the doctor's direction, and in doing so he found comfort at first.

From the time of his visit to the doctor Ivan Ilych's principal occupation became the exact observance of the doctor's prescriptions as regards to hygiene and medicine and the careful observation of his ailment in all the functions of his organism. Ivan Ilych's principal interest came to be people's ailments and people's health. When anything was said in his presence about sick people, about deaths and recoveries, especially in the case of an illness resembling his own, he listened, trying to conceal his excitement, asked questions, and applied what he heard to his own trouble.

The ache did not grow less; but Ivan Ilych made great efforts to force himself to believe that he was better. And he succeeded in deceiving himself so long as nothing happened to disturb him. But as soon as he had a mischance, some unpleasant words with his wife, a failure in his official work, an unlucky hand at bridge, he was at once acutely aware of his illness. In former days he had borne with such mishaps, hoping soon to retrieve the mistake, to make a struggle, to reach success later, to have a lucky hand. But now he was cast down by every mischance and reduced to despair. He would say to himself: "Here I'm only just beginning to get better, and the medicine has begun to take effect, and now this mischance or disappointment." And he was furious against the mischance or the people who were causing him the disappointment and killing him, and he felt that this fury was killing him, but could not check it. One would have thought that it should have been clear to him that this exasperation against circumstances and people was aggravating his disease, and that therefore he ought not to pay attention to the unpleasant incidents. But his reasoning took quite the opposite direction. He said that he needed peace, and was on the watch for everything that disturbed his peace, and at the slightest disturbance of it he flew into a rage. What made his position worse was that he read medical books and consulted doctors. He got worse so gradually that he might have deceived himself, comparing one day with another, the difference was so slight. But when he consulted the doctors, then it seemed to him that he was getting worse, and very rapidly so indeed. And in spite of this, he was continually consulting the doctors.

That month he called on another celebrated doctor. The second celebrity said almost the same as the first, but put his questions differently; and the interview with this celebrity only redoubled the doubts and terrors of Ivan Ilych. A friend of a friend of his, a very good doctor, diagnosed the disease quite differently; and in spite of the fact that he guaranteed recovery, by his questions and his suppositions he confused Ivan Ilych even more and strengthened his suspicions. A homeopath gave yet another diagnosis of the complaint, and prescribed medicine, which Ivan Ilych took secretly for a week; but after a week of the homeopathic medicine he felt no relief, and losing faith both in the other doctor's treatment and in this, he fell into even deeper depression. One day a lady of his acquaintance talked to him of the miraculous healings wrought by holy icons. Ivan Ilych caught himself listening attentively and believing in the reality of the accounts. This incident alarmed him. "Can I have degenerated to such a point of intellectual feebleness?" he said to himself. "Nonsense! It's all rubbish. I must not give way to nervous fears, but fixing on one doctor, adhere strictly to his treatment. That's what I will do. Now it's settled. I won't think about it, but till next summer I will stick to the treatment, and then I shall see. Now I'll put a stop to this wavering!" It was easy to say this, but impossible to carry it out. The pain in his side was always dragging at him, seeming to grow more acute and ever more incessant; it seemed to him that the taste in his mouth was queerer, and there was a loathsome smell even from his breath, and his appetite and strength kept dwindling. There was no deceiving himself; something terrible, new, and so important that nothing more important had ever been in Ivan Ilych's life, was taking place in him, and he alone knew of it. All about him did not or would not understand, and believed that everything in the world was going on as before. This was what tortured Ivan Ilych more than anything. Those of his own household, most of all his wife and daughter, who were absorbed in a perfect whirl of visits, did not, he saw, comprehend it at all, and were annoyed that he was so depressed and exacting, as though he were to blame for it. Though they tried indeed to disguise it, he saw he was a nuisance to them; but that his wife had taken up a definite line of her own in regard to his illness, and stuck to it regardless of what he might say and do. This line was expressed thus: "You know," she would say to acquaintances, "Ivan Ilych cannot, like all other simple-hearted folks, keep to the treatment prescribed him. One day he'll take his drops and eat what he's ordered and go to bed in good time; the next day, if I don't see to it, he'll suddenly forget to take his medicine, eat sturgeon (which is forbidden by the doctors), yes, and sit up at bridge till past midnight."

"Why, when did I do that?" Ivan Ilych asked in vexation one day at Peter Ivanovich's.

"Why, yesterday, with Shebek." 130

"It makes no difference. I couldn't sleep for pain."

"Well, it doesn't matter what you do it for, only you'll never get well like that, and you make us wretched."

Praskovya Fyodorovna's external attitude to her husband's illness, openly expressed to others and to himself, was that Ivan Ilych was to blame in the matter of his illness, and that the whole illness was another injury he was inflicting on his wife. Ivan Ilych felt that the expression of this dropped from her unconsciously, but that made it no easier for him.

In his official life, too, Ivan Ilych noticed, or fancied he noticed, a strange attitude toward him. At one time it seemed to him that people were looking inquisitively at him, as a man who would shortly have to vacate his position; at another time his friends would suddenly begin chaffing him in a friendly way over his nervous fears, as though that awful and horrible, unheard-of thing that was going on within him, incessantly gnawing at him, and irresistibly dragging him away somewhere, was the most agreeable subject for joking. Schwartz especially, with his jocoseness, his liveliness, and his *comme il faut* tone, exasperated Ivan Ilych by reminding him of himself ten years ago.

Friends came sometimes to play cards. They sat down to the card table; they 135 shuffled and dealt the new cards. Diamonds were led and followed by diamonds, the seven. His partner said, "Can't trump," and played the two of diamonds. What then? Why, delightful, capital, it should have been—he had a trump hand. And suddenly Ivan Ilych feels that gnawing ache, that taste in his mouth, and it strikes him as something grotesque that with that he could be glad of a trump hand.

He looks at Mikhail Mikhailovich, his partner, how he taps on the table with his red hand, and affably and indulgently abstains from snatching up the trick, and pushes the cards towards Ivan Ilych so as to give him the pleasure of taking them up, without any trouble, without even stretching out his hand. "What, does he suppose that I'm so weak that I can't stretch out my hand?" thinks Ivan Ilych, and he forgets the trumps, and trumps his partner's cards, and plays his trump hand without making three tricks; and what's the most awful thing of all is that he sees how upset Mikhail Mikhailovich is about it, while he doesn't care a bit, and it's awful for him to think why he doesn't care.

They all see that he's in pain, and say to him, "We can stop if you're tired. You go and lie down." Lie down? No, he's not in the least tired; they will play the rubber. All are gloomy and silent. Ivan Ilych feels that it is he who has brought this gloom upon them, and he cannot disperse it. They have supper, and the party breaks up, and Ivan Ilych is left alone with the consciousness that his life is poisoned for him and poisons the life of others, and that this poison is not losing its force, but is continually penetrating more and more deeply into his whole existence.

And with the consciousness of this, and with the physical pain in addition, and the terror in addition to that, he must lie in his bed, often not able to sleep for pain the greater part of the night; and in the morning he must get up again, dress, go to the law court, speak, write, or, if he does not go out, stay at home for all the four-and-twenty hours of the day and night, of which each one is a torture. And he had to live thus on the edge of the precipice alone, without one man who would understand and feel for him.

V

In this way one month, then a second, passed by. Just before the New Year his brother-in-law arrived in town to visit them. Ivan Ilych was at the court when he arrived. Praskovya Fyodorovna had gone out shopping. Coming home and going into his study, he found his brother-in-law there, a healthy, florid man, unpacking his trunk. He raised his head, hearing Ivan Ilych's step, and for a second stared at him without a word. That stare told Ivan Ilych everything. His brother-in-law opened his mouth to utter an "Oh!" of surprise, but checked himself. That confirmed it all.

"What! Have I changed?"   140

"Yes, there is a change."

And all Ivan Ilych's efforts to draw him into talking of his appearance his brother-in-law met with obstinate silence. Praskovya Fyodorovna came in; the brother-in-law went to see her. Ivan Ilych locked his door, and began gazing at himself in the mirror, first full face, then in profile. He took up his photograph, taken with his wife, and compared the portrait with what he saw in the mirror. The change was immense. Then he bared his arm to the elbow, looked at it, pulled the sleeve down again, sat down on an ottoman, and felt blacker than night.

"I mustn't, I mustn't," he said to himself, jumped up, went to the table, opened some official paper, tried to read it, but could not. He opened the door, went into the drawing room. The door into the drawing room was closed. He went up to it on tiptoe and listened.

"No, you're exaggerating," Praskovya Fyodorovna was saying.

"Exaggerating? You can't see it. Why, he's a dead man. Look at his eyes—there's 145 no light in them. But what's wrong with him?"

"No one can tell. Nikolaevich" (that was another doctor) "said something, but I don't know. Leshchetitsky" (this was the celebrated doctor) "said the opposite."

Ivan Ilych walked away, went to his own room, lay down, and fell to musing. A kidney—a floating kidney. He remembered all the doctors had told him, how it had been detached, and how it was loose; and by an effort of imagination he tried to catch that kidney and to stop it, to strengthen it. So little was needed, it seemed to him. No, I'll go again to Peter Ivanovich (this was the friend who had a friend who was a doctor). He rang, ordered the horse to be put in the carriage, and got ready to go out.

"Where are you off to, Jean?" asked his wife with a peculiarly melancholy and exceptionally kind expression.

This exceptionally kind expression exasperated him. He looked darkly at her. "I must see Peter Ivanovich." 150

He went to the friend who had a friend who was a doctor. And together they went to the doctor's. He found him in, and had a long conversation with him.

Reviewing the anatomical and physiological details of what, according to the doctor's view, was taking place within him, he understood it all. It was just one thing—a little thing wrong with the intestinal appendix. It might all come right. Only strengthen one sluggish organ, and decrease the undue activity of another, and absorption would take place, and all would be set right. He was a little late for dinner. He ate his dinner, talked cheerfully, but it was a long while before he could go to his own room to work. At last he went to his study, and at once sat down to work. He read his legal documents and did his work, but the consciousness never left him of having a matter of importance very near to his heart which he had put off, but would look into later. When he had finished his work, he remembered that the matter near his heart was thinking about the intestinal appendix. But he did not give himself up to it; he went into the drawing room for tea. There were visitors; and there was talking, playing on the piano, and singing; there was the young examining magistrate, the desirable match for his daughter. Ivan Ilych spent the evening, as Praskovya Fyodorovna observed, in better spirits than any of them; but he never forgot for an instant that he had the important matter of the intestinal appendix put off for consideration later. At eleven o'clock he said good night and went to his own room. He had slept alone since his illness in a little room adjoining his study. He went in, undressed, and took up a novel of Zola, but did not read it; instead he fell to thinking. And in his imagination the desired recovery of the intestinal appendix had taken place. There had been absorption, rejection, re-establishment of the regular action.

"Why, it's all simply that," he said to himself. "One only wants to assist nature." He remembered the medicine, got up, took it, lay down on his back, watching for the medicine to act beneficially and overcome the pain. "It's only to take it regularly and avoid injurious influences; why, already I feel rather better, much better." He began to feel his side; it was not painful to the touch. "Yes, I don't feel it—really, much better already." He put out the candle and lay on his side. "The appendix is getting better, absorption." Suddenly he felt the familiar, old, dull, gnawing ache, persistent, quiet, in earnest. In his mouth the same familiar loathsome taste. His heart sank, his brain felt dim, misty. "My God, my God!" he said, "again, again, and it will never cease." And suddenly the whole thing rose before him in quite a different aspect. "Intestinal appendix! Kidney!" he said to himself. "It's not a question of the appendix, not a question of the kidney, but of life and . . . death. Yes, life has been and now it's going, going away, and I cannot stop it. Yes. Why deceive myself? Isn't it obvious to everyone, except me, that I'm dying, and it's only a question of weeks, of days—at once perhaps. There was light, and now there is darkness. I was here, and now I am going! Where?" A cold chill ran over him, his breath stopped. He heard nothing but the throbbing of his heart.

"I shall be no more, then what will there be? There'll be nothing. Where then shall I be when I'm no more? Can this be dying? No; I don't want to!" He jumped up, tried to light the candle; and fumbling with trembling hands, he dropped the candle and the candlestick on the floor and fell back again on the pillow.

"Why trouble? It doesn't matter," he said to himself, staring with open eyes into 155 the darkness. "Death. Yes, death. And they—all of them—don't understand, and don't want to understand, and feel no pity. Now they are playing." (He heard through the closed doors the far-away sounds of a song and the accompaniment.) "They don't care, but they will die too. Fools! Me sooner and them later; but it will be the same for them. And they are merry. The beasts!"

Anger stifled him. And he was agonizingly, insufferably miserable. "It cannot be that all men always have been doomed to this awful horror!" He raised himself.

"There is something wrong in it; I must be calm, I must think it all over from the beginning." And then he began to consider. "Yes, the beginning of my illness. I knocked my side, and I was just the same, that day and the days after; it ached a little, then more, then doctors, then depression, misery, and again doctors; and I've gone on getting closer and closer to the abyss. Strength growing less. Nearer and nearer. And here I am, waiting away, no light in my eyes. I think of how to cure the appendix, but this is death. Can it be death?" Again a horror came over him; gasping for breath, he bent over, began feeling for the matches, and knocked his elbow against the bedside table. It was in his way and hurt him; he felt furious with it, in his anger knocked against it more violently, and upset it. And in despair, breathless, he fell back on his spine waiting for death to come that instant.

The visitors were leaving at that time. Praskovya Fyodorovna was seeing them out. She heard something fall, and came in.

"What is it?"

"Nothing. I dropped something by accident."   160

She went out, brought a candle. He was lying, breathing hard and fast, like a man who has run a mile, and staring with fixed eyes at her.

"What is it, Jean?"

"No—nothing, I say. I dropped something."—"Why speak? She won't understand," he thought.

She certainly did not understand. She picked up the candle, lit it for him, and went out hastily. She had to say good-bye to a departing guest. When she came back, he was lying in the same position on his back, looking upwards.

"How are you—worse?"   165

"Yes."

She shook her head, sat down.

"Do you know what, Jean? I wonder if we hadn't better send for Leshchetitsky to see you here?"

This meant calling in the celebrated doctor, regardless of expense. He smiled malignantly, and said no. She sat a moment longer, went up to him, and kissed him on the forehead.

He hated her with all the force of his soul when she was kissing him, and had to   170
make an effort not to push her away.

"Good night. Please God, you'll sleep."

"Yes."

VI

Ivan Ilych saw that he was dying, and was in continual despair.

At the bottom of his heart Ivan Ilych knew that he was dying; but so far from growing used to this idea, he simply did not grasp it—he was utterly unable to grasp it.

The example of the syllogism that he had learned in Kiesewetter's logic—Caius   175
is a man, men are mortal, therefore Caius is mortal—had seemed to him all his life correct only as regards Caius, but not at all in regard to himself. In that case it was a question of Caius, a man, an abstract man, and it was perfectly true, but he was not Caius, and was not an abstract man; he had always been a creature quite, quite

different from all others; he had been little Vanya with a mamma and papa, and Mitya and Volodya, with playthings and a coachman and a nurse; afterwards with Katenka, with all the joys and griefs and ecstasies of childhood, boyhood, and youth. What did Caius know of the smell of the leather ball Vanya had been so fond of? Had Caius kissed his mother's hand like that? Caius had not heard the silk rustle of his mother's skirts. He had not made a riot at school over the pudding. Had Caius been in love like that? Could Caius preside over the sittings of the court?

And Caius certainly was mortal, and it was right for him to die; but for me, little Vanya, Ivan Ilych, with all my feelings and ideas—for me it's a different matter. And it cannot be that I ought to die. That would be too awful.

Such was his feeling.

"If I had to die like Caius, I should have known it was so, some inner voice would have told me so. But there was nothing of the sort in me. And I and all my friends, we felt that it was not at all the same as with Caius. And now here it is!" he said to himself. "It can't be! It can't be, but it is! How is it? How's one to understand it?" And he could not conceive it, and tried to drive away this idea as false, incorrect, and morbid, and to supplant it with other, correct, healthy ideas. But this idea, not as an idea merely, but as it were an actual fact, came back again and stood confronting him.

And to replace this thought he called up other thoughts, one after another, in the hope of finding support in them. He tried to get back into former trains of thought, which in the old days had screened off the thought of death. But, strange to say, all that had in the old days covered up, obliterated the sense of death, could now not produce the same effect. Ivan Ilych now spent the greater part of his time in these efforts to restore his old trains of thought which had shut off death. At one time he would say to himself, "I'll put myself into my official work; why, I used to live in it." And he would go to the law courts, banishing every doubt. He would enter into conversation with his colleagues, and would sit carelessly, as his old habit was, scanning the crowd below dreamily, and with both his wasted hands he would lean on the arms of the oak armchair just as he always did; and bending over to a colleague, pass the papers to him and whisper to him, then suddenly dropping his eyes and sitting up straight, he would pronounce the familiar words that opened the proceedings. But suddenly in the middle, the pain in his side, utterly regardless of the stage he had reached in his conduct of the case, began its work. It riveted Ivan Ilych's attention. He drove away the thought of it, but it still did its work, and then It came and stood confronting him and looked at him, and he felt turned to stone, and the light died away in his eyes, and he began to ask himself again, "Can it be that It is the only truth?" And his colleagues and his subordinates saw with surprise and distress that he, the brilliant, subtle judge, was losing the thread of his speech, was making blunders. He shook himself, tried to regain his self-control, and got somehow to the end of the sitting, and went home with the painful sense that his judicial labors could not as of old hide him from what he wanted to hide; that he could not by means of his official work escape from It. And the worst of it was that It drew him to itself not for him to do anything in particular, but simply for him to look at It straight in the face, to look at It and, doing nothing, suffer unspeakably.

And to save himself from this, Ivan Ilych sought amusements, other screens, and these screens he found, and for a little while they did seem to save him; but soon again they were not so much broken down as let the light through, as though It pierced through everything, and there was nothing that could shut It off.

Sometimes during those days he would go into the drawing room he had furnished, that drawing room where he had fallen, for which—how bitterly ludicrous it was for him to think of it!—for the decoration of which he had sacrificed his life, for he knew that it was that bruise that had started his illness. He went in and saw that the polished table had been scratched by something. He looked for the cause, and found it in the bronze clasps of the album, which had been twisted on one side. He took up the album, a costly one, which he had himself arranged with loving care, and was vexed at the carelessness of his daughter and her friends. Here a page was torn, here the photographs had been shifted out of their places. He carefully put it back in order and bent the clasp back. Then the idea occurred to him to move all of these albums to another corner where the flowers stood. He called the footman; but his daughter or his wife came to help him. They did not agree with him, contradicted him; he argued, got angry. But all that was very well, since he did not think of It; It was not in sight.

But then his wife would say, as he moved something himself, "Do let the servants do it, you'll hurt yourself again," and all at once It peeped through the screen; he caught a glimpse of it. He caught a glimpse of It, but still he hoped it would disappear. Involuntarily though, he kept focusing attention on his side; there it is just the same, aching still, and now he cannot forget it, and It is staring openly at him from behind the flowers. What's the use of it all?

"And it's the fact that here, at that curtain, as if I had been storming a fort, I lost my life. Is it possible? How awful and how silly! It cannot be! It cannot be, and it is."

He went into his own room, lay down, and was again alone with It. Face to face with It, and nothing to be done with it. Nothing but to look at It and shiver.

VII

How it came to pass during the third month of Ivan Ilych's illness, it would be impossible to say, for it happened little by little, imperceptibly, but it had come to pass that his wife and his daughter and his son and their servants and their acquaintances, and the doctors, and, most of all, he himself—all were aware that all interest in him for other people consisted now in the question of how soon he would leave his place empty, free the living from the constraint of his presence, and be set free himself from his sufferings.

He slept less and less; they gave him opium, and began to inject morphine. But this did not relieve him. The dull pain he experienced in the half-asleep condition at first only relieved him as a change, but then it became as bad, or even more agonizing, than the open pain.

He had special things to eat prepared for him according to the doctors' orders; but these dishes became more and more distasteful, more and more revolting to him.

Special arrangements, too, had to be made for his other physical needs, and this was a continual misery to him. Misery from the uncleanliness, the unseemliness, and the stench, from the feeling of another person having to assist in it.

But just from this most unpleasant side of his illness there came comfort to Ivan Ilych. There always came into his room on these occasions to clear up for him the peasant who waited at table, Gerasim. Gerasim was a clean, fresh, young peasant, who had grown stout and hearty on the good fare in town. Always cheerful and bright. At first the sight of this lad, always cleanly dressed in the Russian style, engaged in this revolting task, embarrassed Ivan Ilych.

One day, getting up from the commode, too weak to pull up his trousers, he   190
dropped onto a soft low chair and looked with horror at his bare, powerless thighs,
with the muscles so sharply standing out on them.

Then Gerasim came in, with light, strong steps, in his thick boots, diffusing a
pleasant smell of tar, and bringing in the freshness of the winter air. Wearing a clean
apron and a clean cotton shirt, with his sleeves tucked up on his strong, bare young
arms, without looking at Ivan Ilych, obviously trying to check the radiant happiness
in his face so as not to hurt the sick man, he went up to the commode.

"Gerasim," said Ivan Ilych faintly.

Gerasim started, clearly afraid that he had done something amiss, and with a
rapid movement turned his fresh, good-natured, simple young face, just beginning to
be downy with the first growth of beard.

"Yes, your honor."

"I'm afraid this is very disagreeable for you. You must excuse me. I can't help it."   195

"Why, upon my word, sir!" And Gerasim's eyes beamed, and he showed his white
young teeth in a smile. "What's a little trouble? It's a case of illness with you, sir."

And with his deft, strong arms he performed his habitual task, and went out,
stepping lightly. And five minutes later, treading just as lightly, he came back.
Ivan Ilych was still sitting in the same way in the armchair.

"Gerasim," he said, when the latter had replaced the commode, now clean,
"please help me; come here." Gerasim went up to him. "Lift me up. It's difficult for
me alone, and I've sent Dmitry away."

Gerasim went up to him; as lightly as he stepped he put his strong arms round   200
him, deftly and gently lifted and supported him, and with the other hand pulled up
his trousers. He would have set him down again, but Ivan Ilych asked him to carry
him to the sofa. Gerasim, without effort, carefully not squeezing him, led him, almost
carrying him, to the sofa, and settled him there.

"Thank you; how neatly and well . . . you do everything."

Gerasim smiled again, and would have gone away. But Ivan Ilych felt his presence such a comfort that he was reluctant to let him go.

"Oh, move that chair near me, please. No, that one, under my legs. I feel easier
when my legs are higher."

Gerasim picked up the chair, and without letting it knock, set it gently down
on the ground just at the right place, and lifted Ivan Ilych's legs onto it. It seemed to
Ivan Ilych that he was easier when Gerasim lifted his legs higher.

"I'm better when my legs are higher," said Ivan Ilych. "Put that cushion under   205
me."

Gerasim did so. Again he lifted his legs to put the cushion under them. Again it
seemed to Ivan Ilych that he was easier at that moment when Gerasim held his legs
raised. When he laid them down again, he felt worse.

"Gerasim," he said to him, "are you busy just now?"

"Not at all, sir," said Gerasim, who had learned among the town-bred servants
how to speak to gentry.

"What have you left to do?"

"Why, what have I to do? I've done everything, there's only the wood to chop   210
for tomorrow."

"Then hold my legs up like that—can you?"

"To be sure, I can." Gerasim lifted the legs up. And it seemed to Ivan Ilych that
in that position he did not feel the pain at all.

"But how about the wood?"

"Don't you trouble about that, sir. We shall have time enough."

Ivan Ilych made Gerasim sit and hold his legs, and began to talk to him. And, strange to say, he fancied he felt better while Gerasim had hold of his legs. 215

From that time forward Ivan Ilych would sometimes call Gerasim, and get him to hold his legs on his shoulders, and he liked talking with him. Gerasim did this easily, readily, simply, and with a good nature that touched Ivan Ilych. Health, strength, and heartiness in all other people were offensive to Ivan Ilych; but the strength and heartiness of Gerasim did not mortify him, but soothed him.

Ivan Ilych's great misery was due to the deception that for some reason or other everyone kept up with him—that he was simply ill, and not dying, and that he need only keep quiet and follow the doctor's orders, and then some great change for the better would be the result. He knew that whatever they might do, there would be no result except more agonizing sufferings and death. And he was made miserable by this lie, made miserable at their refusing to acknowledge what they all knew and he knew, by their persisting in lying over him about his awful position, and in forcing him too to take part in this lie. Lying, lying, this lying carried on over him to the eve of his death, and destined to bring that terrible, solemn act of his death down to the level of all their visits, their curtains, their sturgeons for dinner—this was a horrible agony for Ivan Ilych. And, strange to say, many times when they had been going through the regular performance over him, he had been within a hair's-breadth of screaming at them: "Cease your lying! You know, and I know, that I'm dying; so do, at least, stop lying!" But he had never had the spirit to do this. The terrible, awful act of his dying was, he saw, by all those about him, brought down to the level of a casual, unpleasant, and to some extent indecorous, incident (somewhat as they would behave with a person who might enter a drawing room smelling unpleasant). It was brought down to this level by that very decorum to which he had been enslaved all his life. He saw that no one felt for him, because no one would even grasp his position. Gerasim was the only person who recognized the position, and felt sorry for him. And that was why Ivan Ilych was only at ease with Gerasim. He felt comforted when Gerasim sometimes supported his legs for whole nights at a stretch, and would not go away to bed, saying, "Don't you worry yourself, Ivan Ilych, I'll get sleep enough," or when suddenly dropping into the familiar peasant forms of speech, he added: "If thou weren't sick 'twould be another thing, but as 'tis, 'twould be strange if I didn't wait on thee." Gerasim alone did not lie; everything showed clearly that he alone understood what it meant, and saw no necessity to disguise it, and simply felt sorry for his sick, wasting master. He even said this once straight out, when Ivan Ilych was sending him away. "We shall all die. So what's a little trouble?" he said, meaning to express that he did not complain of taking this trouble for a dying man, and he hoped that for him too someone would be willing to take the same trouble when his time came.

Apart from this deception, or because of it, what made the greatest misery for Ivan Ilych was that no one felt for him as he would have liked them to feel for him. At certain moments, after prolonged suffering, Ivan Ilych, ashamed as he would have been to own it, longed more than anything for someone to feel sorry for him, as for a sick child. He longed to be petted, kissed, and wept over, as children are petted and comforted. He knew that he was an important member of the law courts, that he had a beard turning grey, and that therefore it was impossible. But still he longed for it. And in his relations with Gerasim there was something approaching that. And that was why being with Gerasim was a comfort to him. Ivan Ilych longs to weep, longs to be petted and wept over, and then there comes in a colleague, Shebek; and instead of weeping and being petted, Ivan Ilych puts on his serious, severe, earnest face, and from mere inertia gives his views on the effect of the last decision in the Court of Appeals, and obstinately insists upon them. This falsity around him and within him did more than anything to poison Ivan Ilych's last days.

VIII

It was morning. All that made it morning for Ivan Ilych was that Gerasim had gone away, and Peter the footman had come in; he had put out the candles, opened one of the curtains, and begun surreptitiously to straighten up the room. Whether it was morning or evening, Friday or Sunday, it all made no difference; it was always just the same thing. Gnawing, agonizing pain never ceasing for an instant; the hopeless sense of life always ebbing away, but still not yet gone; always swooping down on him that fearful, hated death, which was the only reality, and always the same falsity. What were days, or weeks, or hours of the day to him?

"Will you have tea, sir?" 220

"He wants things done in their regular order. In the morning the family should have tea," he thought, and only said—"No."

"Would you care to move onto the sofa?"

"He wants to make the room tidy, and I'm in his way. I'm uncleanness, disorder," he thought, and only said—

"No, leave me alone."

The servant still moved busily about his work. Ivan Ilych stretched out his hand. 225 Peter went up to offer his services.

"What can I get you?"

"My watch."

Peter got out the watch, which lay just under his hand, and gave it him.

"Half-past eight. Are they up?"

"Not yet, sir. Vladimir Ivanovich" (that was his son) "has gone to school, and 230 Praskovya Fyodorovna gave orders that she was to be waked if you asked for her. Shall I send word?"

"No, no need." "Should I try some tea?" he thought. "Yes, tea . . . bring it."

Peter was on his way out. Ivan Ilych felt frightened of being left alone. "How to keep him? Oh, the medicine." "Peter, give me my medicine. Oh well, maybe medicine may still do some good." He took the spoon, drank it. "No, it does no good. It's all rubbish, deception," he decided, as soon as he tasted the familiar, mawkish, hopeless taste. "No, I can't believe it now. But the pain, why this pain; if it would only cease for a minute." And he groaned. Peter turned round. "No, go on. Bring the tea."

Peter went away. Ivan Ilych, left alone, moaned, not so much from the pain, awful as it was, as from misery. Always the same thing again and again, all these endless days and nights. If it would only be quicker. Quicker to what? Death, darkness. No, no. Anything better than death!

When Peter came in with the tea on a tray, Ivan Ilych stared for some time absent-mindedly at him, not grasping who he was and what he wanted. Peter was disconcerted by this stare. And when he showed he was disconcerted, Ivan Ilych came to himself.

"Oh yes," he said, "tea, good, set it down. Only help me wash and put on a clean 235 shirt."

And Ivan Ilych began his washing. He washed his hands slowly, and then his face, cleaned his teeth, combed his hair, and looked in the mirror. He felt frightened at what he saw, especially at the way his hair clung limply to his pale forehead.

When his shirt was being changed, he knew he would be still more terrified if he glanced at his body, and he avoided looking at himself. But at last it was all over. He put on his dressing gown, covered himself with a blanket, and sat in the armchair to drink his tea. For one moment he felt refreshed; but as soon as he began to drink the tea, again there was the same taste, the same pain. He forced himself to finish it, and lay down, stretching out his legs. He lay down and dismissed Peter.

Always the same. A gleam of hope flashes for a moment, then again the sea of despair roars about him and always pain, always pain, always heartache, and always the same thing. Alone it is awfully dreary; he longs to call someone, but he knows beforehand that with others present it will be worse. "Morphine again—only to forget again. I'll tell him, the doctor, that he must think of something else. It can't go on; it can't go on like this."

One hour, two hours pass like this. Then there is a ring at the front door. The doctor, perhaps. Yes, it is the doctor, fresh, hearty, fat, and cheerful, wearing that expression that seems to say, "You there are in a panic about something, but we'll soon set things right for you." The doctor is aware that this expression is hardly fitting here, but he has put it on once and for all, and can't take it off, like a man who has put on a frockcoat to pay a round of calls.

In a hearty, reassuring manner the doctor rubs his hands.   240

"I'm cold. It's a sharp frost. Just let me warm myself," he says with an expression, as though it's only a matter of waiting a little till he's warm, and as soon as he's warm he'll set everything right.

"Well, now, how are you?"

Ivan Ilych feels that the doctor would like to say, "How's the little trouble?" but that he feels that he can't talk like that, and says, "How did you pass the night?"

Ivan Ilych looks at the doctor with an expression that asks—"Is it possible you're never ashamed of lying?" But the doctor does not care to understand this look. And Ivan Ilych says—"It's always just as awful. The pain never leaves me, never ceases. If only there were something!"

"Ah, you're all like that, all sick people say that. Come, now I do believe I'm   245
thawed; even Praskovya Fyodorovna, who's so particular, could find no fault with my temperature. Well, now I can say good morning." And the doctor shakes hands.

And dropping his former levity, the doctor, with a serious face, proceeds to examine the patient, feeling his pulse, to take his temperature, and then the tappings and soundings begin.

Ivan Ilych knows positively and indubitably that it's all nonsense and empty deception; but when the doctor, kneeling down, stretches over him, putting his ear first higher, then lower, and goes through various gymnastic evolutions over him with a serious face, Ivan Ilych is affected by this, as he used sometimes to be affected by the speeches of the lawyers in court, though he was perfectly well aware that they were telling lies and why they were telling lies.

The doctor, kneeling on the sofa, was still sounding him, when there was the rustle of Praskovya Fyodorovna's silk dress in the doorway, and she was heard scolding Peter for not letting her know that the doctor had come.

She comes in, kisses her husband, and at once begins to explain that she has been up a long while, and that it was only through a misunderstanding that she was not there when the doctor came.

Ivan Ilych looks at her, scans her all over, and resents the whiteness and plump- 250
ness, the cleanness of her hands and neck, the glossiness of her hair, and the gleam
full of life in her eyes. With all the force of his soul he hates her. And when she
touches him it makes him suffer from the thrill of hatred he feels for her.

Her attitude towards him and his illness is still the same. Just as the doctor had
taken up a certain line with the patient which he was not now able to drop, so she
too had taken up a line with him—that he was not doing something he ought to do,
and was himself to blame, and she was lovingly reproaching him for his neglect, and
now she could not get out of this attitude.

"Why, you know, he won't listen to me; he doesn't take his medicine at the right
times. And what's worse still, he insists on lying in a position that surely must be bad
for him—with his legs in the air."

She described how he made Gerasim hold his legs up.

The doctor smiled with kindly condescension that said, "Oh well, it can't be
helped, these sick people do take up such foolish fancies; but we must forgive them."

When the examination was over, the doctor looked at his watch, and then 255
Praskovya Fyodorovna informed Ivan Ilych that it must, of course, be as he liked, but
she had sent today for a celebrated doctor, and that he would examine him, and have
a consultation with Mikhail Danilovich (that was the name of their regular doctor).

"Don't oppose it now, please. This I'm doing entirely for my own sake," she said
ironically, letting it be understood that she was doing it all for his sake, and was
only saying this to give him no right to refuse her request. He lay silent, knitting his
brows. He felt that he was hemmed in by such a web of falsity that it was hard to disentangle anything from it.

Everything she did for him was entirely for her own sake, and she told him she
was doing for her own sake what she actually *was* doing for her own sake, as if that
was something so incredible that he would take it as meaning the opposite.

At half-past eleven the celebrated doctor came. Again came the sounding,
and then grave conversation in his presence and in the other room about the kidney and the appendix, and questions and answers, with such an air of significance,
that again, instead of the real question of life and death, which was now the only
one that confronted him, the question that came up was of the kidney and the
appendix, which were doing something not as they should, and were for that reason being attacked by Mikhail Danilovich and the celebrated doctor, and forced to
mend their ways.

The celebrated doctor took leave of him with a serious, but not a hopeless face.
And to the timid question that Ivan Ilych addressed to him while he lifted his eyes,
shining with terror and hope, up towards him, "Was there a chance of recovery?" He
answered that he could not answer for it, but that there was a chance. The look of
hope with which Ivan Ilych watched the doctor depart was so piteous that, seeing it,
Praskovya Fyodorovna positively burst into tears, as she went out of the door to hand
the celebrated doctor his fee in the next room.

The gleam of hope kindled by the doctor's assurance did not last long. Again the 260
same room, the same pictures, the curtains, the wallpaper, the medicine bottles, and
ever the same, his aching suffering body. And Ivan Ilych began to moan; they gave
him injections, and he sank into oblivion.

When he woke up it was getting dark; they brought him his dinner. He forced
himself to eat some broth; and again everything was the same, and again the coming
night.

After dinner at seven o'clock, Praskovya Fyodorovna came into his room, dressed as though to go to a soiree, with her full bosom laced in tight, and traces of powder on her face. She had in the morning mentioned to him that they were going to the theater. Sarah Bernhardt° was visiting the town, and they had a box, which he had insisted on their taking. By now he had forgotten about it, and her smart attire was an offence to him. But he concealed this feeling when he recollected that he had himself insisted on their taking a box and going, because it was an aesthetic pleasure, beneficial and instructive for the children.

Praskovya Fyodorovna came in satisfied with herself, but yet with something of a guilty air. She sat down, asked how he was, as he saw, simply for the sake of asking, and not for the sake of learning anything, knowing indeed that there was nothing to learn, and began telling him how absolutely necessary it was; how she would not have gone for anything, but the box had been taken, and Ellen, and their daughter, and Petrishchev (the examining lawyer, their daughter's suitor) were going, and that it was out of the question to let them go alone. But that she would have liked much better to stay with him. If only he would be sure to follow the doctor's orders while she was away.

"Oh, and Fyodor Dmitryevich Petrishchev" (the suitor) "would like to come in. May he? And Liza?"

"Yes, let them come in."

The daughter entered, in full dress, her fresh young body bare, while his body made him suffer so. But she made a show of it; she was strong, healthy, obviously in love, and impatient of the illness, suffering, and death that hindered her happiness.

Fyodor Dmitryevich came in too in evening dress, his hair curled *a la Capoul,*° with his long sinewy neck tightly fenced round by a white collar, with his vast expanse of white chest and strong thighs displayed in narrow black trousers, with one white glove and his opera hat in his hand.

Behind him crept in unnoticed his high school son in his new uniform, poor fellow, in gloves, and with that awful blue ring under his eyes that Ivan Ilych knew the meaning of.

He always felt sorry for his son. And pitiable indeed was his scared face of sympathetic suffering. Except Gerasim, Ivan Ilych fancied that Volodya was the only one who understood and was sorry.

They all sat down; again they asked how he was. A silence followed. Liza asked her mother about the opera-glasses. An altercation ensued between the mother and daughter about who had taken it, and where it had been put. It turned into an unpleasant squabble.

Fyodor Dmitryevich asked Ivan Ilych whether he had seen Sarah Bernhardt. Ivan Ilych could not at first catch the question, but then he said, "No, have you seen her before?"

"Yes, in *Adrienne Lecouvreur.*°"

Praskovya Fyodorovna commented that she was particularly good in that part. The daughter made some reply. A conversation sprang up about the art and naturalness of her acting, that conversation that is continually repeated and always the same.

265

270

Sarah Bernhardt: Perhaps the most famous actress of the nineteenth century, Bernhardt (1844–1923) toured widely in Europe and the United States. *a la Capoul:* imitating the hairdo of Victor Capoul, a contemporary French singer. *Adrienne Lecouvreur:* French tragic play by Eugène Scribe.

In the middle of the conversation Fyodor Dmitryevich glanced at Ivan Ilych and relapsed into silence. The others looked at him and became mute too. Ivan Ilych was staring with glittering eyes straight before him, obviously furious with them. This had to be set right, but it could not anyhow be set right. This silence had somehow to be broken. No one would venture to break it, and they all began to feel alarmed that the decorous deception was somehow breaking down, and the facts would be exposed to all. Liza was the first to pluck up courage. She broke the silence. She tried to cover up what they were all feeling, but inadvertently she betrayed it.

"Well, if we are going, it's time to start," she said, glancing at her watch, a gift from   275
her father; and with a scarcely perceptible and meaningful smile at the young man, referring to something only known to themselves, she got up with a rustle of her skirts.

They all got up, said good-bye, and went away.

When they were gone, Ivan Ilych fancied he felt better; there was no falsity— that had gone away with them, but the pain remained. That continual pain, that continual terror, made nothing harder, nothing easier. It was always worse.

Again came minute after minute, hour after hour, still the same and still no end, and ever more terrible the inevitable end.

"Yes, send Gerasim," he said in response to Peter's question.

IX

Late at night his wife came back. She came in on tiptoe, but he heard her,   280
opened his eyes, and made haste to close them again. She wanted to send Gerasim away and sit up with him herself instead. He opened his eyes and said, "No, go away."

"Are you in great pain?"

"Always the same."

"Take some opium."

He agreed, and drank it. She went away.

Till three o'clock he slept a miserable sleep. It seemed to him that he and his   285
pain were being thrust somewhere into a narrow, deep, black sack, and they kept pushing him further and further in, and still could not thrust him to the bottom. And this operation was awful to him, and was accompanied with agony. And he was afraid, and yet wanted to fall into it, but struggled against it and yet tried to get into it. And all of a sudden he slipped and fell and woke up. Gerasim, still the same, is sitting at the foot of the bed half-dozing peacefully, patient. And he is lying with his wasted legs clad in stockings, raised on Gerasim's shoulders, the same candle burning in the alcove, and the same interminable pain.

"Go away, Gerasim," he whispered.

"It's all right, sir. I'll stay a bit longer."

"No, go away."

He took his legs down, lay sideways on his arm, and he felt very sorry for himself. He only waited till Gerasim had gone away into the next room; he could restrain himself no longer, and cried like a child. He cried at his own helplessness, at his awful loneliness, at the cruelty of people, at the cruelty of God, at the absence of God.

"Why hast Thou done all this? What brought me to this? Why, why torture me   290
so horribly?"

He did not expect an answer, and wept indeed that there was and could be no answer. The pain grew more acute again, but he did not stir, did not call.

He said to himself, "Come, more then; come, strike me! But what for? What have I done to Thee? What for?"

Then he was still, ceased weeping, held his breath, and was all attention; he listened, as it were, not to a voice uttering sounds, but to the voice of his soul, to the current of thoughts that rose up within him.

"What is it you want?" was the first clear idea he was able to put into words that he grasped.

"What? Not to suffer, to live," he answered.   295

And again he was utterly plunged into attention so intense that even the pain did not distract him.

"To live? Live how?" the voice of his soul was asking.

"Why, live as I used to live before—happily and pleasantly."

"As you used to live before—happily and pleasantly?" queried the voice.

And he began going over in his imagination the best moments of his pleasant   300
life. But, strange to say, all these best moments of his pleasant life seemed now not at all what they had seemed then. All—except the first memories of childhood—there, in his childhood there had been something really pleasant in which one could have lived if it had come back. But the creature who had this pleasant experience was no more; it was like a memory of someone else.

As soon as he reached the beginning of what had resulted in him, all that had seemed joys to him then now melted away before his eyes and were transformed into something trivial, and often disgusting.

And the further he went from childhood, the nearer to the actual present, the more worthless and uncertain were the joys. It began with life at the School of Jurisprudence. Then there had still been something genuinely good; then there had been gaiety; then there had been friendship; then there had been hopes. But in the higher classes these good moments were already becoming rarer. Later on, during the first period of his official life at the governor's, good moments appeared; but it was all mixed, and less and less of it was good. And further on even less was good, and the further he went the less good there was. His marriage . . . a mere accident, then as the disillusion of it and the smell of his wife's breath and the sensuality, the hypocrisy! And that deadly official life, and anxiety about money, and so for one year, and two, and ten, and twenty, and always the same thing. And the further he went, the more deadly it became. "As though I had been going steadily downhill, imagining that I was going uphill. So it was in fact. In public opinion I was going uphill, and steadily as I got up it, life was ebbing away from me. . . . And now the work's done, there's only death."

"But what is this? What for? It cannot be! It cannot be that life has been so senseless, so loathsome. And if it really was so loathsome and senseless, then why die, and die in agony? There's something wrong."

"Can it be I have not lived as one ought?" suddenly came into his head. "But how not, when I've done everything as it should be done?" he said, and at once dismissed this only solution of all the enigma of life and death as something utterly out of the question.

"What do you want now? To live? Live how? Live as you live at the courts when   305
the usher booms out: 'The judge is coming!' . . . The judge is coming, the judge is coming," he repeated to himself. "Here he is, the judge! But I'm not to blame!" he shrieked in fury. "What's it for?" And he left off crying, and turning with his face to the wall, fell to pondering always the same question, "What is it for, why all this horror?" But however much he pondered, he could not find an answer. And whenever the idea struck him, as it often did, that it all came of his never having lived as he ought, he thought of all the correctness of his life and dismissed this strange idea.

X

Another fortnight passed. Ivan Ilych could not now get up from the sofa. He did not like lying in bed, and lay on the sofa. And lying almost all the time facing the wall, in loneliness he suffered all the inexplicable agonies, and in loneliness pondered always that inexplicable question, "What is it? Can it be true that it's death?"

And an inner voice answered, "Yes, it is true." "Why these agonies?" and a voice answered, "For no reason." Beyond and besides this there was nothing.

From the very beginning of his illness, ever since Ivan Ilych first went to the doctor's, his life had been split into two contradictory moods, which were continually alternating—one was despair and the anticipation of an uncomprehended and awful death; the other was hope and an absorbed watching over the actual condition of his body. First there was nothing confronting him but a kidney or intestine which had temporarily declined to perform its duties, then there was nothing but unknown awful death, which there was no escaping.

These two moods had alternated from the very beginning of the illness; but the further the illness progressed, the more doubtful and fantastic became the conception of the kidney, and the more real the sense of approaching death.

He had but to reflect on what he had been three months before and what he was now, to reflect how steadily he had been going downhill, for every possibility of hope to be shattered.   310

Of late, in the loneliness in which he found himself, lying with his face to the back of the sofa, a loneliness in the middle of a populous town surrounded by numerous acquaintances and his family, a loneliness that could not be more complete anywhere—not at the bottom of the sea, not deep down in the earth—of late in this fearful loneliness Ivan Ilych had lived only in imagination in the past. One by one the pictures of his past rose up before him. It always began from what was nearest in time and went back to the most remote, to childhood, and rested there. If Ivan Ilych thought of the stewed prunes that had been offered him for dinner that day, his mind went back to the damp, wrinkled French plum of his childhood, of its peculiar taste and the flow of saliva when the stone was sucked; and along with this memory of a taste, there rose up a whole series of memories of that period—his nurse, his brother, his playthings. "I mustn't think of that . . . it's too painful," Ivan Ilych said to himself, and he brought himself back to the present, to the button on the back of the sofa and the creases in the morocco.° "Morocco is expensive, and doesn't wear well; there was a quarrel over it. But that morocco was different, and the quarrel was different too the time we tore father's portfolio and were punished, and mamma bought us the tarts." And again his mind rested on his childhood, and again it was painful, and he tried to drive it away and think of something else.

And again at that point, together with that chain of associations, quite another chain of memories came into his heart, of how his illness had progressed and become more acute. It was the same there, the further back the more life there had been. There had been both more that was good in life and more of life itself. And the two began to melt into one. "Just as the pain goes on getting worse and worse, so has my whole life gone on getting worse and worse," he thought. One light spot was there at the back, at the beginning of life, and then it kept getting blacker and blacker, and going faster and faster. "In inverse ratio to the square of the distance from death," thought Ivan Ilych. And the image of a stone falling downwards with increasing

_____

morocco: a type of fine leather made from goatskin.

velocity sank into his soul. Life, a series of increasing sufferings, falls more and more swiftly to the end—the most fearful of all sufferings. "I am falling." He shuddered, shifted himself, would have resisted, but he knew beforehand that he could not resist; and again, with eyes weary with gazing at it, but unable not to gaze at what was before him, he stared at the back of the sofa and waited, waited expecting that fearful fall and shock and dissolution.

"Resistance is impossible," he said to himself. "But if one could at least comprehend what it's for. Even that's impossible. It could be explained if one were to say that I hadn't lived as I ought. But that can't be alleged," he said to himself, thinking of all the regularity, correctness, and propriety of his life. "That really can't be admitted," he said to himself, his lips smiling ironically as though someone could see his smile and be deceived by it. "No explanation! Agony, death . . . What for?"

XI

So passed a fortnight. During that fortnight an event occurred that had been desired by Ivan Ilych and his wife. Petrishchev made a formal proposal. This took place in the evening. Next day Praskovya Fyodorovna went in to her husband, wondering in her mind how to inform him of Fyodor Dmitryevich's proposal, but that night there had been a change for the worse in Ivan Ilych. Praskovya Fyodorovna found him on the same sofa, but in a different position. He was lying on his face, groaning, and staring straight before him with a fixed gaze.

She began talking of remedies. He turned his stare on her. She did not finish what she had begun saying; such hatred of her in particular was expressed in that stare. 315

"For Christ's sake, let me die in peace," he said.

She would have gone away, but at that moment the daughter came in and went up to say good morning to him. He looked at his daughter just as at his wife, and to her inquiries about how he was, he told her dryly that they would soon all be rid of him. Both were silent, sat a little while, and went out.

"How are we to blame?" said Liza to her mother. "As though we had done it! I'm sorry for papa, but why punish us?"

At the usual hour the doctor came. Ivan Ilych answered, "Yes, no," never taking his exasperated stare from him, and towards the end he said, "Why, you know that you can do nothing, so let me be."

"We can relieve your suffering," said the doctor. 320

"Even that you can't do; let me be."

The doctor went into the drawing room and told Praskovya Fyodorovna that it was very serious, and that the only resource left them was opium to relieve his sufferings, which must be terrible.

The doctor said his physical sufferings were terrible, and that was true; but even more terrible than his physical sufferings were his mental sufferings, and in that lay his chief misery.

His mental sufferings were due to the fact that during that night, as he looked at the sleepy, good-natured, broad-cheeked face of Gerasim, the thought had suddenly come into his head, "What if in reality all my life, my conscious life, has been not the right thing?"

The thought struck him that what he had regarded before as an utter impos- 325 sibility, that he had spent his life not as he ought, might be the truth. It struck him that those scarcely detected impulses of struggle within him against what was considered good by persons of higher position, scarcely detected impulses which he had dismissed, that *they* might be the real thing, and everything else might not be the right thing. And his official work, and his ordering of his daily life and of his family, and these social and official interests—all that might not be the right thing. He tried to defend it all to himself. And suddenly he felt all the weakness of what he was defending. And it was useless to defend it.

"But if it's so," he said to himself, "and I am leaving life—with the consciousness that I have lost all that was given me, and there's no correcting it, then what?"

He lay on his back and began going over his whole life entirely anew. When he saw the footman in the morning, then his wife, then his daughter, then the doctor, every movement they made, every word they uttered, confirmed for him the terrible truth that had been revealed to him in the night. In them he saw himself, saw all in which he had lived, and saw distinctly that it was all not the right thing; it was a horrible, vast deception that concealed both life and death. This consciousness intensified his physical agonies, multiplied them tenfold. He groaned and tossed from side to side and pulled at the covering over him. It seemed to him that it was stifling him and weighing him down. And for that he hated them.

They gave him a big dose of opium; he sank into unconsciousness; but at dinner-time the same thing began again. He drove them all away, and tossed from side to side.

His wife came to him and said,

"Jean, darling, do this for my sake, for me. It can't do any harm, and it often does   330
good. Why, it's nothing. And often healthy people—"

He opened his eyes wide.

"What? Take communion? What for? No. Besides . . ."

She began to cry.

"Yes, my dear? I'll send for our priest, he's so nice."

"All right, very well," he said.   335

When the priest came and took his confession, he was softened, felt as it were a relief from his doubts, and consequently from his sufferings, and there came a moment of hope. He began once more thinking of the intestinal appendix and the possibility of curing it. He took the sacrament with tears in his eyes.

When they laid him down again after the sacrament for a minute, he felt comfortable, and again the hope of life sprang up. He began to think about the operation which had been suggested to him. "To live, I want to live," he said to himself.

His wife came in to congratulate him; she uttered the customary words and added—

"It's quite true, isn't it, that you're better?"

Without looking at her, he said, "Yes."   340

Her dress, her figure, the expression of her face, the tone of her voice—all told him the same: "Not the right thing. All that in which you lived and are living is lying, deceit, hiding life and death away from you." And as soon as he had formed that thought, hatred sprang up in him, and with that hatred agonizing physical sufferings, and with these sufferings the sense of inevitable, approaching ruin. Something new was happening; there were twisting and shooting pains, and a tightness in his breathing.

The expression of his face as he uttered that "Yes" was terrible. After uttering that "Yes," looking her straight in the face, he turned face down, with a rapidity extraordinary in his weakness, and shrieked—

"Go away, go away, let me be!"

XII

From that moment there began the screaming that never ceased for three days, and was so awful that through two closed doors one could not hear it without horror. At the moment when he answered his wife he grasped that he had fallen, that there was no return, that the end had come, quite the end, while his doubt was still unsolved, and still remained doubt.

"Oh! Oo—h! Oh!" he screamed in varying intonations. He had begun scream- 345 ing, "I don't want to!" and so had gone on screaming the same vowel sound—Ooh!

All those three days, during which time did not exist for him, he was struggling in that black sack into which he was being thrust by an unseen resistless force. He struggled as the man condemned to death struggles in the hands of the executioner, knowing that he cannot save himself. And every moment he felt that in spite of all his efforts to struggle against it, he was getting nearer and nearer to what terrified him. He felt that his agony was due both to his being thrust into this black hole and still more to his not being able to get right into it. What hindered him from getting into it was the claim that his life had been good. That justification of his life held him fast and would not let him get forward, and it caused him the most agony of all.

All at once some force struck him in the chest, in the side, and stifled his breathing more than ever; he rolled forward into the hole, and there at the end was some sort of light. It had happened with him, as it had sometimes happened to him in a railway carriage, when he had thought he was going forward while he was going back, and all of a sudden recognized his real direction.

"Yes, it has all not been the right thing," he said to himself, "but that's no matter." He could, he could do the right thing. "What is the right thing?" he asked himself, and suddenly he became quiet.

This was at the end of the third day, two hours before his death. At that very moment the schoolboy had stealthily crept into his father's room and gone up to his bedside. The dying man was screaming and waving his arms. His hand fell on the schoolboy's head. The boy snatched it, pressed it to his lips, and burst into tears.

At that very moment Ivan Ilych had fallen into the hole, and caught sight of the 350 light, and it was revealed to him that his life had not been what it ought to have been, but that that it could still be set right. He asked himself, "What is the right thing?"— and became quiet, listening. Then he felt someone was kissing his hand. He opened his eyes and glanced at his son. He felt sorry for him. His wife went up to him. He glanced at her. She was gazing at him with open mouth, the tears unwiped streaming over her nose and cheeks, a look of despair on her face. He felt sorry for her.

"Yes, I'm making them miserable," he thought. "They're sorry, but it will be better for them when I die." He would have said this, but had not the strength to utter it. "Besides, why speak, I must act," he thought. With a glance to his wife he pointed to his son and said—"Take him away . . . sorry for him. . . . and you too . . ." He tried to say "forgive me," but said "forgo" . . . and too weak to correct himself, shook his hand, knowing that He whose understanding mattered would understand.

And all at once it became clear to him that what had tortured him and would not leave him was suddenly dropping away all at once on both sides and on ten sides and on all sides. He was sorry for them, must act so that they might not suffer. Set them free and free himself of those agonies. "How right and how simple!" he thought. "And the pain?" he asked himself. "Where's it gone? Eh, where are you, pain?"

He began to watch for it.

"Yes, here it is. Well what of it, let the pain be."

"And death. Where is it?"   355

He looked for his old accustomed terror of death, and did not find it. "Where is it? What death?" There was no terror, because there was no death.

In the place of death there was light.

"So this is it!" he suddenly exclaimed aloud. "What joy!"

To him all this passed in a single instant, and the meaning of that instant did not change. For those present his agony lasted another two hours. There was a rattle in his throat, a twitching in his wasted body. Then the rattle and the gasping came at longer and longer intervals.

"It is finished!" someone said over him.   360

He caught those words and repeated them in his soul.

"Death is finished," he said to himself. "It is no more."

He drew in a breath, stopped midway in the breath, stretched and died.

Questions

1. Sum up the reactions of Ivan Ilych's colleagues to the news of his death. What is implied in Tolstoy's calling them "so-called friends"?

2. What comic elements do you find in the account of the wake that Peter Ivanovich attends?

3. In Tolstoy's description of the corpse and its expression (paragraph 27), what details seem especially revealing and meaningful?

4. Do you think Tolstoy would have improved the story if he had placed the events in chronological order? What would be lost if the opening scene of Ivan Ilych's colleagues at the law courts and the wake scene were to be given last?

5. Would you call Ivan Ilych, when we first meet him, a religious man? Sum up his goals in life, his values, and his attitudes.

6. By what "virtues" and abilities does Ivan Ilych rise through the ranks? While he continues to succeed in his career, what happens to his marriage?

7. "Every spot on the tablecloth, on the hangings, the string of a window blind broken, irritated him. He had devoted so much trouble to the arrangement of the rooms that any disturbance of their order distressed him" (paragraph 104). What do you make of this passage? What is its tone? Does the narrator sympathize with Ivan's attachment to his possessions?

8. Consider the account of Ivan Ilych's routine in paragraph 105 ("He got up at nine . . ."). What elements of a full life, what higher satisfactions, does this routine omit?

9. What caused Ivan Ilych's illness? How would it probably be diagnosed today? What is the narrator's attitude toward Ivan Ilych's doctors?

10. In what successive stages does Tolstoy depict Ivan Ilych's growing isolation as his progressive illness sets him more and more apart?

11. What are we apparently supposed to admire in the character and conduct of the servant Gerasim?

12. What do you understand from the statement that Ivan's justification of his life "held him fast and would not let him get forward, and it caused him the most agony of all" (paragraph 346)?

13. What is memorable in the character of Ivan Ilych's schoolboy son? Why is he crucial to the story? (Suggestion: Look closely at paragraphs 349–350.)

14. What realization allows Ivan Ilych to triumph over pain? Why does he die peacefully?

15. The writer Henri Troyat has said that through the story of Ivan Ilych we imagine what our own deaths will be. Is it possible to identify with an aging, selfish, worldly, nineteenth-century Russian judge?

Franz Kafka

The Metamorphosis   1915

Translated by John Siscoe

Franz Kafka (1883–1924) was born into a German-speaking Jewish family in Prague, Czechoslovakia (then part of the Austro-Hungarian empire). He was the only surviving son of a domineering, successful father. After earning a law degree, Kafka worked as a claims investigator for the state accident insurance company. He worked on his stories at night, especially during his frequent bouts of insomnia. He never married, and lived mostly with his parents. Kafka was such a careful and self-conscious writer that he found it difficult to finish his work and send it out for publication. During his lifetime he published only a few thin volumes of short fiction, most notably The Metamorphosis *(1915) and* In the Penal Colony *(1919). He never finished to his own satisfaction any of his three novels (all published posthumously):* The*

Franz Kafka

Trial *(1925),* The Castle *(1926), and* Amerika *(1927). As Kafka was dying of tuberculosis, he begged his friend and literary executor Max Brod to burn his uncompleted manuscripts. Brod pondered this request but fortunately didn't obey. Kafka's two major novels,* The Trial *and* The Castle, *both depict huge, remote, bumbling, irresponsible bureaucracies in whose power the individual feels helpless and blind. Kafka's works appear startlingly prophetic to readers looking back on them in the later light of Stalinism, World War II, and the Holocaust. His haunting vision of an alienated modern world led the poet W. H. Auden to remark at midcentury, "Had one to name the author who comes nearest to bearing the same kind of relation to our age as Dante, Shakespeare, and Goethe bore to theirs, Kafka is the first one would think of."* The Metamorphosis, *which arguably has the most famous opening sentence in twentieth-century literature, shows Kafka's dreamlike fiction at its most brilliant and most disturbing.*

I

When Gregor Samsa awoke one morning from troubled dreams, he found himself transformed in his bed into a monstrous insect. He was lying on his back, which was hard, as if plated in armor, and when he lifted his head slightly he could see his belly: rounded, brown, and divided into stiff arched segments; on top of it the blanket, about to slip off altogether, still barely clinging. His many legs, which seemed pathetically thin when compared to the rest of his body, flickered helplessly before his eyes.

"What's happened to me?" he thought. It was no dream. His room, a normal though somewhat small human bedroom, lay quietly within its four familiar walls. Above the table on which his unpacked fabric samples were spread—Samsa was a traveling salesman—hung the picture he had recently cut out of an illustrated magazine and had set in a lovely gilt frame. It showed a lady wearing a fur hat and a fur stole, sitting upright, and thrusting out to the viewer a thick fur muff, into which her whole forearm had disappeared.

Gregor's glance then fell on the window, and the overcast sky—one could hear raindrops drumming on the tin sheeting of the windowsill—made him feel profoundly sad. "What if I went back to sleep for a while and forgot all this nonsense," he thought. But that wasn't to be, for he was used to sleeping on his right side and in his present state was unable to get into that position. No matter how hard he threw himself to his right, he would immediately roll onto his back again. He must have tried a hundred times, shutting his eyes so as not to see his wriggling legs, not stopping until he began to feel in his side a slight dull pain that he had never felt before.

"My God," he thought, "what an exhausting job I've chosen! Always on the go, day in and day out. There are far more worries on the road than at the office, what with the constant travel, the nuisance of making your train connections, the wretched meals eaten at odd hours, and the casual acquaintances you meet only in passing, never to see again, never to become intimate friends. To hell with it all!" He felt a slight itch on the surface of his belly. Slowly he shoved himself on his back closer to the bedpost so that he could lift his head more easily. He found the place where it itched. It was covered with small white spots he did not understand. He started to touch it with one of his legs, but pulled back immediately, for the contact sent a cold shiver through him.

He slid back down to his former position. "Getting up this early," he thought, "would turn anyone into an idiot. A man needs his sleep. Other salesmen live like harem women. For example, when I get back to the hotel in the morning to write up the sales I've made, these gentlemen are sitting down to breakfast. If I tried that with my director, I'd be fired on the spot. Actually, that might not be such a bad idea. If I didn't have to curb my tongue because of my parents, I'd have given notice long ago. I'd have gone up to the director and told him from the bottom of my heart exactly what I thought. That would have knocked him from his desk! It's an odd way to run things, this sitting high at a desk and talking down to employees, especially when, since the director is hard of hearing, they have to approach so near. Well, there's hope yet; as soon as I've saved enough money to pay back what my parents owe him—that should take another five or six years—I'll go do it for sure. Then, I'll cut myself completely free. Right now, though, I'd better get up, as my train leaves at five."

He looked at the alarm clock ticking on top of the chest of drawers. "God Almighty!" he thought. It was half past six and the hands were quietly moving forward, it was later than half past, it was nearly a quarter to seven. Hadn't the alarm clock gone off? You could see from the bed that it had been correctly set for four o'clock; of course it must have gone off. Yes, but could he really have slept peacefully through that ear-splitting racket? Well, if he hadn't slept peacefully, he'd slept deeply all the same. But what was he to do now? The next train left at seven, to make it he would have to rush like mad, and his samples weren't even packed, and he himself wasn't feeling particularly spry or alert. And even if he were to make the train, there would be no avoiding a scene with the director. The office messenger would've been waiting for the five o'clock train and would've long since reported his not showing up. The messenger, dim-witted and lacking a will of his own, was a tool of the director. Well, what if he were to call in sick? But that would look embarrassing and suspicious since in his five years with the firm Gregor had not been sick once. The director himself was sure to come over with the health insurance doctor, would upbraid his parents for their son's laziness, and would cut short all excuses by deferring to the doctor, who believed that everyone in the world was a perfectly healthy layabout. And really, would he be so wrong in this case? Apart from a drowsiness that

5

was hard to account for after such a long sleep, Gregor really felt quite well, and in fact was exceptionally hungry.

As he was thinking all this at top speed, without being able to make up his mind to get out of bed—the alarm clock had just struck a quarter to seven—a cautious tap sounded on the door behind his head. "Gregor," said a voice—it was his mother—"it's a quarter to seven. Don't you have a train to catch?" That gentle voice! Gregor was shocked when he heard his own voice answering hers; unmistakably his own voice, true, but mixed in with it, like an undertone, a miserable squeaking that allowed the words to be clearly heard only for a moment before rising up, reverberating, to drown out their meaning, so that no one could be sure if he had heard them correctly. Gregor wanted to answer fully and give a complete explanation, but under the circumstances he merely said, "Yes, yes, thank you, Mother, I'm just getting up." Through the wooden door between them the change in Gregor's voice was probably not obvious, for his mother, quietly accepting his words, shuffled away. However, this brief exchange had made the rest of the family aware that Gregor, surprisingly, was still in the house, and already at one of the side doors his father was knocking, softly, yet with his fist. "Gregor, Gregor," he called, "what's the matter?" Before long he called once more in a deeper voice, "Gregor? Gregor?" From the other side door came the sound of his sister's voice, gentle and plaintive. "Gregor, aren't you feeling well? Is there anything I can get you?" Gregor answered the two of them at the same time: "I'm almost ready." He tried hard to keep his voice from sounding strange by enunciating the words with great care, and by inserting long pauses between the words. His father went back to his breakfast but his sister whispered, "Gregor, please, open the door." But Gregor had no intention of opening the door, and was thankful for having formed, while traveling, the prudent habit of keeping all his doors locked at night, even at home.

What he wanted to do now was to get up quietly and calmly, to get dressed, and above all to eat his breakfast. Only then would he think about what to do next, for he understood that mulling things over in bed would lead him nowhere. He remembered how often in the past he had felt some small pain in bed, perhaps caused by lying in an uncomfortable position, which as soon as he had gotten up had proven to be purely imaginary, and he looked forward to seeing how this morning's fancies would gradually fade and disappear. As for the change in his voice, he hadn't the slightest doubt that it was nothing more than the first sign of a severe cold, an occupational hazard of traveling salesmen.

Throwing off the blanket was easy enough; he had only to puff himself up a little and it slipped right off. But the next part was difficult, especially as he was so unusually wide. He would have needed arms and legs to lift himself up; instead he had only these numerous little legs that never stopped moving and over which he had no control at all. As soon as he tried to bend one of them it would straighten itself out, and if he finally succeeded in making it do as he wished, all the others, as if set free, would waggle about in a high degree of painful agitation. "But what's the point of lying uselessly in bed?" Gregor said to himself.

He thought that he might start by easing the lower part of his body out of bed first, but this lower part, which incidentally he hadn't yet seen and of which he couldn't form a clear picture, turned out to be very difficult to budge—it went so slowly. When finally, almost in a frenzy, he gathered his strength and pushed forward desperately, he miscalculated his direction and bumped sharply against the post at the foot of the bed, and the searing pain he felt told him that, for right now at least, it was exactly this lower part of his body that was perhaps the most tender.

10

So he tried getting the top part of his body out first, and cautiously turned his head towards the side of the bed. This proved easy enough, and eventually, despite its breadth and weight the bulk of his body slowly followed the turning of his head. But when he finally got his head out over the edge of the bed he felt too afraid to go any farther, for if he were to let himself fall from this position only a miracle would prevent him from hurting his head. And it was precisely now, at all costs, that he must not lose consciousness; he would be better off staying in bed.

But when after repeating his efforts he lay, sighing, in his former position, and once more watched his little legs struggling with one another more furiously than ever, if that were possible, and saw no way of bringing calm and order into this mindless confusion, he again told himself that it was impossible to stay in bed and that the wisest course would be to stake everything on the hope, however slight, of getting away from the bed. At the same time he didn't forget to remind himself that the calmest of calm reflection was much better than frantic resolutions. During this time he kept his eyes fixed as firmly as possible on the window, but unfortunately the morning fog, which shrouded even the other side of the narrow street, gave him little comfort and cheer. "Already seven o'clock," he said to himself when the alarm clock chimed again, "already seven and still such a thick fog." And for some time he lay still, breathing quietly, as if in the hope that utter stillness would bring all things back to how they really and normally were.

But then he said to himself: "I must make sure that I'm out of bed before it strikes a quarter past seven. Anyway, by then someone from work will have come to check on me, since the office opens before seven." And he immediately set the whole length of his body rocking with a rhythmic motion in order to swing out of bed. If he tumbled out this way he could prevent his head from being injured by keeping it tilted upward as he fell. His back seemed to be hard; the fall onto the carpet would probably not hurt it. His greatest worry was the thought of the loud crash he was bound to make; it would probably cause anxiety, if not outright fear, on the other side of the doors. Yet he had to take the chance.

When Gregor was already half out of bed—his new technique made it more of a game than a struggle, since all he had to do was to edge himself across by rocking back and forth—it struck him how simple it would be if he could get someone to help him. Two strong people—he thought of his father and the maid—would be more than enough. All they would have to do would be to slip their arms under his curved back, lift him out of bed, bend down with their burden, and then wait patiently while he flipped himself right side up onto the floor, where, one might hope, his little legs would acquire some purpose. Well then, aside from the fact that the doors were locked, wouldn't it be a good idea to call for help? In spite of his misery, he could not help smiling at the thought.

He had reached the point where, if he rocked any harder, he was in danger of   15
losing his balance, and very soon he would have to commit himself, because in five minutes it would be a quarter past seven—when the doorbell rang. "It's someone from the office," he said to himself, and almost froze, while his little legs danced even faster. For a moment everything remained quiet. "They won't open the door," Gregor said to himself, clutching at an absurd sort of hope. But then, of course, the maid, as usual, went with her firm tread to the door and opened it. Gregor had only to hear the visitor's first word of greeting to know at once who it was—the office manager himself. Why was Gregor condemned to work for a firm where the most insignificant failure to appear instantly provoked the deepest suspicion? Were the employees, one

and all, nothing but scoundrels? Wasn't there among them one man who was true and loyal, who if, one morning, he were to waste an hour or so of the firm's time, would become so conscience-stricken as to be driven out of his mind and actually rendered incapable of leaving his bed? Wouldn't it have been enough to send an office boy to ask—that is, if such prying were necessary at all? Did the office manager have to come in person, and thus demonstrate to an entire family of innocent people that he was the only one wise enough to properly investigate this suspicious affair? And it was more from the anxiety caused by these thoughts than by any act of will that Gregor swung himself out of bed with all his might. There was a loud thump, but not really a crash. The carpet broke his fall somewhat, and his back too was more elastic than he had thought, so there was only a muffled thud that was relatively unobtrusive. However, he had not lifted his head carefully enough and had banged it; he twisted it and rubbed it against the carpet in frustration and pain.

"Something fell down in there," said the office manager in the room on the left. Gregor tried to imagine whether something like what had happened to him today might one day happen to the office manager; really, one had to admit that it was possible. But as if in a blunt reply to this question the office manager took several determined steps in the next room and his patent leather boots creaked. From the room on the right his sister was whispering to let him know what was going on: "Gregor, the office manager is here." "I know," said Gregor to himself, but he didn't dare speak loudly enough for his sister to hear him.

"Gregor," his father now said from the room on the left, "the office manager is here and he wants to know why you weren't on the early train. We don't know what to tell him. Besides, he wants to speak to you in person. So please open the door. I'm sure he'll be kind enough to excuse any untidiness in your room." "Good morning, Mr. Samsa," the manager was calling out amiably. "He isn't feeling well," said his mother to the manager, while his father was still speaking at the door. "He's not well, sir, believe me. Why else would Gregor miss his train? The boy thinks of nothing but his work. It nearly drives me to distraction the way he never goes out in the evening; he's been here the last eight days, and every single evening he's stayed at home. He just sits here at the table with us quietly reading the newspapers or looking over train schedules. The only enjoyment he gets is when he's working away with his fretsaw.° For example, he spent two or three evenings cutting out a little picture frame, you'd be surprised at how pretty it is, it's hanging in his room, you'll see it in a minute as soon as Gregor opens the door. By the way, I'm glad you've come, sir, we would've never have gotten him to unlock the door by ourselves, he's so stubborn; and I'm sure he's sick, even though he wouldn't admit it this morning." "I'm coming right now," said Gregor, slowly and carefully and not moving an inch for fear of missing a single word of the conversation. "I can't imagine any other explanation, madam," said the office manager, "I hope it's nothing serious. But on the other hand businessmen such as ourselves—fortunately or unfortunately—very often have to ignore any minor indisposition, since the demands of business come first." "So, can the office manager come in now?" asked Gregor's father impatiently, once more knocking on the door. "No," said Gregor. In the room on the left there was an embarrassed silence; in the room on the right his sister began to sob.

But why didn't his sister go and join the others? Probably because she had just gotten out of bed and hadn't even begun to dress yet. Then why was she crying?

---

fretsaw: saw with a long, narrow, fine-toothed blade, for cutting thin wooden boards or metal plates into patterns.

Because he was in danger of losing his job, and because the director would start once again dunning his parents for the money they owed him? Yet surely these were matters one didn't need to worry about just now. Gregor was still here, and hadn't the slightest intention of deserting the family. True, at the moment he was lying on the carpet, and no one aware of his condition could seriously expect him to let the office manager in. But this minor discourtesy, for which in good time an appropriate excuse could easily be found, was unlikely to result in Gregor's being fired on the spot. And it seemed to Gregor far more sensible for them now to leave him in peace than to bother him with their tears and entreaties. But the uncertainty that preyed upon them excused their behavior.

"Mr. Samsa," the office manager now called in a louder voice, "what's the matter with you? You've barricaded yourself in your room, giving only yes or no answers, causing your parents a great deal of needless grief and neglecting—I mention this only in passing—neglecting your business responsibilities to an unbelievable degree. I am speaking now in the name of your parents and of your director, and I beg you in all seriousness to give me a complete explanation at once. I'm amazed at you, simply amazed. I took you for a calm and reliable person, and now all at once you seem determined to make a ridiculous spectacle of yourself. Earlier this morning the director did suggest to me a possible explanation for your disappearance—I'm referring to the sums of cash that were recently entrusted to you—but I practically swore on my solemn word of honor that this could not be. However, now when I see how incredibly stubborn you are, I no longer have the slightest desire to defend you. And your position with the firm is by no means secure. I came intending to tell you all this in private, but since you're so pointlessly wasting my time I don't see why your parents shouldn't hear it as well. For some time now your work has left much to be desired. We are aware, of course, that this is not the prime season for doing business; but a season for doing no business at all—that, Mr. Samsa, does not and must not exist."

"But sir," Gregor called out distractedly, forgetting everything else in his excitement, "I'm on the verge of opening the door right now. A slight indisposition, a dizzy spell, has prevented me from getting up. I'm still in bed. But I'm feeling better already. I'm getting up now. Please be patient for just a moment. It seems I'm not quite as well as I thought. But really I'm all right. Something like this can come on so suddenly! Only last night I was feeling fine, as my parents can tell you, or actually I did have a slight premonition. I must have shown some sign of it. Oh, why didn't I report it to the office! But one always thinks one can get better without having to stay at home. Please, sir, have mercy on my parents! None of what you've just accused me of has any basis in fact; no one has even spoken a word to me about it. Perhaps you haven't seen the latest orders I've sent in. Anyway, I can still make the eight o'clock train. Don't let me keep you, sir, I'll be showing up at the office very soon. Please be kind enough to inform them, and convey my best wishes to the director."

And while hurriedly blurting all this out, hardly knowing what he was saying, Gregor had reached the chest of drawers easily enough, perhaps because of the practice he had already gotten in bed, and was now trying to use it to lift himself upright. For he actually wanted to open the door, actually intended to show himself, and to talk with the manager; he was eager to find out what the others, who now wanted to see him so much, would say at the sight of him. If they recoiled in horror then he would take no further responsibility and could remain peaceably where he was. But if they took it all in stride then he too had no reason to be upset, and, if he hurried, could even get to the station by eight. The first few times, he slipped down the polished surface of the chest, but finally with one last heave he stood upright. He no longer paid attention to the burning pains in his abdomen, no matter how they hurt. Then, allowing himself to fall against the backrest of a nearby chair, he clung to its edges with his little legs. Now he was once more in control of himself; he fell silent, and was able to hear what the manager was saying.

"Did you understand a single word?" the office manager was asking his parents. "He's not trying to make fools of us, is he?" "My God," cried his mother, already in tears, "maybe he's seriously ill and we're tormenting him. Grete! Grete!" she shouted then. "Mother?" called his sister from the other side. They were calling to each other across Gregor's room. "You must go to the doctor at once. Gregor is sick. Go get the doctor now. Did you hear how Gregor was speaking?" "That was the voice of an animal," said the manager in a tone that was noticeably restrained compared to his mother's shrillness. "Anna! Anna!" his father shouted through the hall to the kitchen, clapping his hands, "get a locksmith and hurry!" And the two girls, their skirts rustling, were already running down the hall—how could his sister have gotten dressed so quickly?—and were pulling the front door open. There was no sound of its being shut; evidently they had left it standing open, as is the custom in houses stricken by some great sorrow.

But Gregor now felt much calmer. Though the words he spoke were apparently no longer understandable, they seemed clear enough to him, even clearer than before, perhaps because his hearing had grown accustomed to their sound. In any case, people were now convinced that something was wrong with him, and were ready to help him. The confidence and assurance with which these first measures had been taken comforted him. He felt himself being drawn back into the human circle and hoped for marvelous and astonishing results from both doctor and locksmith, without really drawing a distinction between them. To ready his voice for the crucial discussion that was now almost upon him, to make it sound as clear as possible, he coughed slightly, as quietly as he could, since for all he knew it might sound different from human coughing. Meanwhile in the next room there was utter silence. Perhaps his parents and the manager were sitting at the table, whispering; perhaps they were, all of them, leaning against the door, listening.

Gregor slowly advanced on the door, pushing the chair in front of him. Then he let go of it, grabbed onto the door for support—the pads at the end of his little legs were somewhat sticky—and, leaning against it, rested for a moment after his efforts. Then he started to turn the key in the lock with his mouth. Unfortunately, he didn't really have any teeth—how was he going to grip the key?—but to make up for that he clearly had very powerful jaws; with their help he was in fact able to start turning the key, paying no attention to the fact that he was surely hurting them somehow, for a brown liquid poured out of his mouth, flowed over the key, and dripped onto the floor. "Listen," said the manager on the other side of the door, "he's turning the key." This was a great encouragement to Gregor, but they should all have been cheering him on, his mother and his father too. "Come on, Gregor," they should have been shouting, "keep at it, hold on to that key!" And, imagining that they were all intently following his efforts, he grimly clamped his jaws on the key with all his might. As the key continued to turn he danced around the lock, holding himself by his mouth alone, either hanging onto the key or pressing down on it with the full weight of his body, as the situation required. The sharper sound of the lock as it finally snapped free woke Gregor up completely. With a sigh of relief he said to himself, "So I didn't need the locksmith after all," and he pressed his head down on the handle to open one wing of the double door.

Because he had to pull the wing in towards him, even when it stood wide open   25
he remained hidden from view. He had to edge slowly around this wing and to do
it very carefully or he would fall flat on his back as he made his entrance. He was
still busy carrying out this maneuver, with no time to notice anything else, when he
heard the manager give a loud "Oh!"—it sounded like a gust of wind—and now he
could see him, standing closest to the door, his hand over his open mouth, slowly
backing away as if propelled by the relentless pressure of some invisible force. His
mother—in spite of the manager's presence, she was standing there with her hair
still unpinned and sticking out in all directions—first folded her hands and looked at
Gregor's father, then took two steps forward and sank to the floor, her skirts billowing
out all around her and her face completely buried in her breast. His father, glowering, clenched his fist, as if he intended to drive Gregor back into his room; then he
looked around the living room with uncertainty, covered his eyes with his hands, and
wept so hard his great chest shook.

Now Gregor made no attempt to enter the living room, but leaned against the
locked wing of the double door, so that only half of his body was visible, with his
head above it cocked to one side, peering at the others. Meanwhile the daylight had
grown much brighter; across the street one could clearly see a section of the endless, dark gray building opposite—it was a hospital—with a row of uniform windows
starkly punctuating its facade. The rain was still falling, but only in large, visibly separate drops that looked as though they were being flung, one by one, onto the earth.
On the table the breakfast dishes were set out in lavish profusion, for breakfast was
the most important meal of the day for Gregor's father, who lingered over it for hours
while reading various newspapers. Hanging on the opposite wall was a photograph of
Gregor from his army days, showing him as a lieutenant, with his hand on his sword
and his carefree smile demanding respect for his bearing and his rank. The door to
the hall stood open, and as the front door was open too, one could see the landing
beyond and the top of the stairs going down.

"Well," said Gregor, who was perfectly aware that he was the only one who had
kept his composure, "I'll go now and get dressed, pack up my samples, and be on my
way. You will, you will let me go, won't you? You can see, sir, that I'm not stubborn
and I'm willing to work; the life of a traveling salesman is hard, but I couldn't live
without it. Where are you going, sir? To the office? You are? Will you give an honest
report about all this? A man may be temporarily unable to work, but that's just the
time to remember the service he has rendered in the past, and to bear in mind that
later on, when the present problem has been resolved, he is sure to work with even
more energy and diligence than before. As you know very well, I am deeply obligated
to the director. At the same time, I'm responsible for my parents and my sister. I'm
in a tight spot right now, but I'll get out of it. Don't make things more difficult for
me than they already are. Stand up for me at the office! People don't like traveling
salesmen, I know. They think they make scads of money and lead lives of luxury. And
there's no compelling reason for them to revise this prejudice. But you, sir, have a
better understanding of things than the rest of the staff, a better understanding, if I
may say so, than even the director himself, who, since he is the owner, can be easily
swayed against an employee. You also know very well that a traveling salesman, who
is away from the office for most of the year, can so easily fall victim to gossip and
bad luck and groundless accusations, against which he is powerless to defend himself
since he knows nothing about them until, returning home exhausted from his journeys, he suffers personally from evil consequences that can no longer be traced back

to their origins. Sir, please don't go away without giving me some word to show that you think that I'm at least partly right!"

But the office manager had turned away at Gregor's first words, and was looking at him now over one twitching shoulder, his mouth agape. And during Gregor's speech he didn't stand still for even a moment, but without once taking his eyes off him kept edging towards the door, yet very slowly, as if there were some secret injunction against his leaving the room. He was already in the hall, and from the suddenness with which he took his last step out of the living room, one might have thought he had burned the sole of his foot. But once in the hall, he stretched out his right hand as far as possible in the direction of the staircase, as if some supernatural rescuer awaited him there.

Gregor realized that he could not let the manager leave in this frame of mind, or his position with the firm would be in extreme jeopardy. His parents were incapable of clearly grasping this; over the years they had come to believe that Gregor was set for life with this firm, and besides they were now so preoccupied with their immediate problems that they had lost the ability to foresee events. But Gregor had this ability. The manager must be overtaken, calmed, swayed, and finally convinced; the future of Gregor and of his family depended on it! If only his sister were here—she was perceptive; she had already begun to cry while Gregor was still lying calmly on his back. And surely the manager, that ladies' man, would've listened to her; she would've shut the door behind them and in the hall talked him out of his fright. But his sister wasn't there, and he would have to handle this himself. And forgetting that he had no idea what his powers of movement were, and forgetting as well that once again his words would possibly, even probably, be misunderstood, he let go of the door, pushed his way through the opening, and started towards the manager, who by now was on the landing, clinging in a ridiculous manner to the banister with both hands. But as Gregor reached out for support, he immediately fell down with a little cry onto his numerous legs. The moment this happened he felt, for the first time that morning, a sense of physical well-being. His little legs had solid ground under them, and, he noticed with joy, they were at his command, and were even eager to carry him in whatever direction he might desire; and he already felt sure that the final recovery from all his misery was at hand. But at that very moment, as he lay on the floor rocking with suppressed motion, not far from his mother and just opposite her, she, who had seemed so completely overwhelmed, leapt to her feet, stretched her arms out wide, spread her fingers, and cried, "Help! For God's sake, help!" She then craned her neck forward as if to see Gregor better, but at the same time, inconsistently, backed away from him. Forgetting that the table with all its dishes was behind her, she sat down on it, and, as if in a daze when she bumped into it, seemed utterly unaware that the large coffee pot next to her had tipped over and was pouring out a flood of coffee onto the carpet.

"Mother, Mother," said Gregor gently, looking up at her. For the moment he had completely forgotten the office manager; on the other hand, he couldn't resist snapping his jaws a few times at the sight of the streaming coffee. This made his mother scream again; she ran from the table and into the outstretched arms of his father, who came rushing to her. But Gregor had no time now for his parents. The manager had already reached the staircase; with his chin on the banister railing, he was looking back for the last time. Gregor darted forward, to be as sure as possible of catching up with him, but the manager must have guessed his intention, for he sprinted down several steps and disappeared. He was still yelling "Oohh!" and the sound echoed throughout the stairwell.

30

Unfortunately the manager's escape seemed to make his father, who until now had seemed reasonably calm, lose all sense of proportion. Instead of running after the man himself, or at least not interfering with Gregor's pursuit, he grabbed with his right hand the manager's cane, which he had left behind, together with his hat and overcoat, on the chair; with his left hand he snatched up a large newspaper from the table. He began stamping his feet and waving the cane and newspaper in order to drive Gregor back into his room. Nothing Gregor said made any difference, indeed, nothing he said was even understood. No matter how humbly he lowered his head his father only stamped the louder. Behind his father his mother, despite the cold, had flung open a window and was leaning far outside it, her face in her hands. A strong breeze from the street blew across the room to the stairwell, the window curtains billowed inwards, the newspapers fluttered on the table, stray pages skittered across the floor. His father, hissing like a savage, mercilessly drove him back. But as Gregor had had no practice in walking backwards, it was a very slow process. If he had been given a chance to turn around then he would've gotten back into his room at once, but he was afraid that the length of time it would take him to turn around would exasperate his father and that at any moment the cane in his father's hand might deal him a fatal blow on his back or his head. In the end, though, he had no choice, for he noticed to his horror that while moving backwards he couldn't even keep a straight course. And so, looking back anxiously, he began turning around as quickly as possible, which in reality was very slowly. Perhaps his father divined his good intentions, for he did not interfere, and even helped to direct the maneuver from afar with the tip of his cane. If only he would stop that unbearable hissing! It made Gregor completely lose his concentration. He had turned himself almost all the way around when, confused by this hissing, he made a mistake and started turning back the wrong way. But when at last he'd succeeded in getting his head in front of the doorway, he found that his body was too wide to make it through. Of course his father, in the state he was in, couldn't even begin to consider opening the other wing of the door to let Gregor in. His mind was on one thing only: to drive Gregor back into his room as quickly as possible. He would never have permitted the complicated preparations necessary for Gregor to haul himself upright and in that way perhaps slip through. Instead, making even more noise, he urged Gregor forward as if the way were clear. To Gregor the noise behind him no longer sounded like the voice of merely one father; this really wasn't a joke, and Gregor squeezed himself into the doorway, heedless of the consequences. One side of his body lifted up, he was pitched at an angle in the doorway; the other side was scraped raw, ugly blotches stained the white door. Soon he was stuck fast and couldn't have moved any further by himself. On one side his little legs hung trembling in the air, while those on the other were painfully crushed against the floor—when, from behind, his father gave him a hard blow that was truly a deliverance, and bleeding profusely, he flew far into his room. Behind him the door was slammed shut with the cane, and then at last everything was still.

II

It was already dusk when Gregor awoke from a deep, almost comatose sleep. Surely, even if he hadn't been disturbed he would've soon awakened by himself, since he'd rested and slept long enough; yet it seemed to him that he'd been awakened by the sound of hurried steps and the furtive closing of the hallway door. The light from the electric streetlamps cast pale streaks here and there on the ceiling and the upper part of the furniture, but down below, where Gregor was, it was dark. Groping awkwardly with the feelers which he was only now beginning to appreciate, he slowly pushed himself over to the door to see what had been going on there. His left side felt as if it were one long, painfully tightening scar, and he was actually limping on his two rows of legs. One little leg, moreover, had been badly hurt during the morning's events—it was nearly miraculous that only one had been hurt—and it trailed along lifelessly.

Only when he reached the door did he realize what had impelled him forward— the smell of something to eat. For there stood a bowl full of fresh milk, in which floated small slices of white bread. He could almost have laughed for joy, since he was even hungrier now than he'd been during the morning, and he immediately dipped his head into the milk, almost up to his eyes. But he soon drew it back in disappointment; not only did he find it difficult to eat because of the soreness in his left side— and he was capable of eating only if his whole gasping body cooperated—but also because he didn't like the milk at all, although it had once been his favorite drink, which, no doubt, was why his sister had brought it in. In fact, he turned away from the bowl almost in disgust, and crawled back to the middle of the room.

In the living room, as Gregor could see through the crack in the door, the gaslight had been lit. But while this was the hour when his father would usually be reading the afternoon paper in a loud voice to his mother and sometimes to his sister as well, now there wasn't a sound to be heard. Well, perhaps this custom of reading aloud, which his sister was always telling him about or mentioning in her letters, had recently been discontinued. Still, though the apartment was completely silent, it was scarcely deserted. "What a quiet life the family's been leading," said Gregor to himself, and, staring fixedly into the darkness, he felt a genuine pride at having been able to provide his parents and his sister with such a life in such a nice apartment. But what if all this calm, prosperity, and contentment were to end in horror? So as not to give in to such thoughts, Gregor set himself in motion, and he crawled up and down the room.

Once during the long evening first one of the side doors and then the other was opened a crack and then quickly shut. Someone, it seemed, had wanted to come in but then had thought better of it. Gregor now stationed himself so as to somehow get the hesitant visitor to come in or at least to find out who it might be. But the door did not open again and he waited in vain. That morning when the doors had been locked, everyone had wanted to come in, but now after he'd unlocked one of the doors himself—and the others had evidently been unlocked during the day—nobody came in, and the keys, too, were now on the outside.

It was late at night before the light was put out in the living room, and it was easy for Gregor to tell that his parents and sister had stayed up all the while, since he could plainly hear the three of them as they tiptoed away. As it was obvious that no one would be visiting Gregor before morning, he had plenty of time in which to contemplate, undisturbed, how best to rearrange his life. But the open, high-ceilinged room in which he was forced to lie flat on the floor filled him with a dread which he couldn't account for—since it was, after all, the room he had lived in for the past five years. Almost unthinkingly, and not without a faint sense of shame, he scurried under the couch. There, although his back was slightly cramped and he could no longer raise his head, he immediately felt very much at home, and his only regret was that his body was too wide to fit completely under the couch.

There he spent the rest of the night, now in a doze from which hunger pangs kept awakening him with a start, now preoccupied with worries and vague hopes, all of which, however, led to the same conclusion: that for the time being he must remain calm and, by being patient and showing every consideration, try to help his family bear the burdens that his present condition had placed upon them.

Early the next morning—the night was barely over—Gregor got an opportunity to test the strength of his newly-made resolutions, because his sister, who was almost fully dressed, opened the hallway door and looked in expectantly. She didn't see him at first, but when she spotted him underneath the couch—well, my God, he had to be somewhere, he couldn't just fly away—she was so surprised that she lost her self-control and slammed the door shut again. But, as if she felt sorry for her behavior, she opened it again right away and tiptoed in, as if she were in the presence of someone who was very ill, or who was a stranger. Gregor had moved his head forward almost to the edge of the couch and was watching her. Would she notice that he'd let the milk sit there, and not from lack of hunger, and would she bring him some other food that was more to his taste? If she wasn't going to do it on her own, he'd sooner starve than call her attention to it, although in fact he was feeling a tremendous urge to dash out from under the couch, fling himself at his sister's feet, and beg her for something good to eat. But his sister immediately noticed to her astonishment that the bowl was still full, with only a little milk spilt around it. She picked up the bowl at once—not, it's true, with her bare hands but using a rag—and carried it out. Gregor was extremely curious to find out what she would bring in its place, and he speculated at length as to what it might be. But he never would have guessed what his sister, in the goodness of her heart, actually did. She brought him a wide range of choices, all spread out on an old newspaper. There were old, half-rotten vegetables; bones left over from dinner, covered with a congealed white sauce; some raisins and almonds; a piece of cheese which Gregor two days ago had declared inedible; a slice of plain bread, a slice of bread and butter, and a slice with butter and salt. In addition to all this she replaced the bowl, now evidently reserved for Gregor, filled this time with water. And out of a sense of delicacy, since she knew that Gregor wouldn't eat in front of her, she left in a hurry, even turning the key in the lock in order that Gregor might know that he was free to make himself as comfortable as possible. Gregor's legs whirred as they propelled him toward the food. Besides, his wounds must have healed completely, for he no longer felt handicapped, which amazed him. He thought of how, a month ago, he'd cut his finger slightly with his knife and how only the day before yesterday that little wound had still hurt. "Am I less sensitive now?" he wondered, greedily sucking on the cheese, to which, above all the other dishes, he was immediately and strongly attracted. Tears of joy welled up in his eyes as he devoured the cheese, the vegetables, and the sauce. The fresh foods, on the other hand, were not to his liking; in fact, he couldn't stand to smell them and he actually dragged the food he wanted to eat a little way off. He'd long since finished eating, and was merely lying lazily in the same spot, when his sister began to slowly turn the key in the lock as a signal for him to withdraw. He got up at once, although he'd almost fallen asleep, and scurried back under the couch. But it took a great deal of self-control for him to remain under the couch even for the brief time his sister was in the room, for his heavy meal had swollen his body to some extent and he could scarcely breathe in that confined space. Between little fits of suffocation he stared with slightly bulging eyes as his unsuspecting sister took a broom and swept away not only the scraps of what he'd eaten, but also the food that he'd left untouched—as if these too were no longer any good—and hurriedly dumped everything into a bucket, which she covered with a wooden lid and carried away. She'd hardly turned her back before Gregor came out from under the couch to stretch and puff himself out.

So this was how Gregor was fed each day, once in the morning when his parents and the maid were still asleep, and again after the family's midday meal, while his parents took another brief nap and his sister could send the maid away on some errand or other. His parents didn't want Gregor to starve any more than his sister did, but perhaps for them to be directly involved in his feeding was more than they could bear, or perhaps his sister wanted to shield them even from what might prove to be no more than a minor discomfort, for they were surely suffering enough as it was.

Gregor was unable to discover what excuses had served to get rid of the doctor   40 and the locksmith that first morning. Since the others couldn't understand what he said it never occurred to them, not even to his sister, that he could understand them, so when his sister was in the room, he had to be satisfied with occasionally hearing her sighs and her appeals to the saints. Only later, after she began to get used to the situation—of course she could never become completely used to it—would Gregor sometimes hear a remark that was intended to be friendly or could be so interpreted. "He really liked it today," she'd say when Gregor had polished off a good portion, and when the opposite was the case, which began to happen more and more often, she'd say almost sadly, "Once again, he didn't touch a thing."

But while Gregor wasn't able to get any news directly, he could overhear a considerable amount from the adjoining rooms, and as soon as he would hear the sound of voices he would immediately run to the appropriate door and press his whole body against it. In the early days especially, there wasn't a conversation that didn't in some way, if only indirectly, refer to him. For two whole days, at every meal, the family discussed what they should do, and they kept on doing so between meals as well, for at least two members of the family were now always at home, probably because nobody wanted to be in the apartment alone, and it would be unthinkable to leave it empty. Furthermore, on the very first day the cook—it wasn't completely clear how much she knew of what had happened—had on her knees begged Gregor's mother to dismiss her immediately, and when she said her goodbyes a quarter of an hour later, she thanked them for her dismissal with tears in her eyes, as if this had been the greatest favor ever bestowed on her in the house, and without having to be asked she made a solemn vow never to breathe a word of this to anyone.

So now his sister, together with his mother, had to do all the cooking as well, though in fact this wasn't too much of a chore, since the family ate practically nothing. Gregor kept hearing them vainly urging one another to eat, without receiving any reply except "No thanks, I've had enough," or some similar remark. They didn't seem to drink anything, either. His sister would often ask his father if he'd like some beer, and would gladly offer to go out and get it herself. When he wouldn't respond she'd say, in order to remove any hesitation on his part, that she could always send the janitor's wife, but at that point the father would finally utter an emphatic "No" and that would be the end of the matter.

It was on the very first day that his father gave a full account, to both mother and sister, of the family's financial situation and prospects. Every now and then he would get up from the table and take a receipt or notebook from out of the small safe he'd salvaged from the collapse of his business five years before. He could be heard opening the complicated lock and then securing it again after taking out whatever he'd been looking for. The account that his father gave, or at least part of it, was the first encouraging news that Gregor had heard since being imprisoned. He'd always had the impression that his father had failed to save a penny from the ruin of his business; at least his father had never told him otherwise, and Gregor, for that matter, had never asked him about it. At that time Gregor's only concern had been to do his utmost to make the family forget as quickly as possible the business failure that had plunged them all into a state of total despair. And so he had set to work with tremendous zeal, and had risen almost overnight from junior clerk to become a traveling salesman, which naturally opened up completely new financial opportunities so that in no time at all his success was instantly translated, by way of commissions, into hard cash, which could be laid out on the table under the eyes of his astonished and delighted family. Those had been wonderful times, and they had never returned, at least not with the same glory, even though later on Gregor had been earning enough to pay the entire family's expenses, and in fact had been doing so. They'd simply gotten used to it, both family and Gregor; they had gratefully accepted the money, and he had given it gladly, but no special warmth went with it. Gregor had remained close only to his sister, and it was his secret plan that she, who unlike Gregor loved music and could play the violin with deep feeling, should next year attend the Conservatory, despite the expense which, great as it was, would have to be met in some way. During Gregor's brief stays in the city the subject of the Conservatory would often come up in his conversations with his sister, but always only as a beautiful dream that wasn't meant to come true. His parents weren't happy to hear even these innocent remarks, but Gregor's ideas on the subject were firm and he had intended to make a solemn announcement on Christmas Eve.

Such were the thoughts, so futile in his present condition, that ran through his mind as he stood there, pressed against the door, listening. Sometimes he would grow so thoroughly weary that he couldn't listen any more and would carelessly let his head bump against the door, and though he'd pull it back immediately, even the slight noise he'd made would be heard in the next room, causing everyone to fall silent. "What's he up to now?" his father would say after a pause, obviously looking at the door, and only then would the interrupted conversation gradually be resumed.

Gregor now learned with considerable thoroughness—for his father tended to   45
repeat his explanations several times, partly because he hadn't dealt with these matters in a long time, and partly because his mother didn't understand everything the first time through—that despite their catastrophic ruin a certain amount of capital, a very small amount, it's true, had survived intact from the old days, and thanks to the interest being untouched had even increased slightly. And what was more, the money which Gregor had been bringing home every month—he'd kept only a small sum for himself—hadn't been completely spent and had grown into a tidy sum. Gregor nodded eagerly behind his door, delighted to hear of this unexpected foresight and thrift. Of course he might have been able to use this extra money to pay off more of his father's debt to the director, and thus have brought nearer the day when he could quit his current job, but, given the present circumstances, things were better the way his father had arranged them.

Now the sum of this money wasn't nearly large enough for the family to live off the interest; the principal might support them for a year, or two at the most, but that was all. So this was really only a sum that was not to be touched, but saved instead for emergencies. As for money to live on—that would have to be earned. Though Gregor's father was indeed still healthy, nevertheless he was an old man who hadn't worked for five years and one from whom not too much should be expected in any case. During those five years, the first ones of leisure in his hard-working but unsuccessful life, he had put on a lot of weight and consequently had grown somewhat sluggish. And as for Gregor's elderly mother, was she supposed to start bringing in money, burdened as she was by her asthma which made it a strain for her to even walk across the apartment and which kept her gasping for breath every other day on the couch by the open window? Or should his sister go to work instead—she who though seventeen was still a child and one moreover whom it would be cruel to deprive of the life she'd led up until now, a life of wearing pretty clothes, sleeping late, helping around the house, enjoying a few modest pleasures, and above all playing the violin? At first, whenever their conversation turned to the need to earn money, Gregor would let go of the door and fling himself down on the cool leather couch which stood beside it, for he felt hot with grief and shame.

Often he would lie there all night long, not sleeping a wink, scratching at the leather couch for hours. Or, undaunted by the great effort it required, he would push the chair over to the window. Then he would crawl up to the sill and, propped up by the chair, would lean against the pane, apparently inspired by some memory of the sense of freedom that gazing out a window used to give him. For in truth objects only a short distance away were now, each day, becoming more indistinct; the hospital across the street, which he used to curse because he could see it all too clearly, was now completely outside his field of vision, and if he hadn't known for a fact that he lived on Charlotte Street—a quiet but nevertheless urban street—he could have imagined that he was looking out his window at a wasteland where gray sky and gray earth had indistinguishably merged as one. His observant sister needed only to notice twice that the armchair had been moved to the window. From then on, whenever she cleaned the room, she carefully placed the chair back by the window, and even began leaving the inner casement open.

If only Gregor had been able to speak to his sister and thank her for everything she'd had to do for him, he could have borne her kindnesses more easily, but as it was they were painful to him. Of course his sister tried her best to ease the general embarrassment, and naturally as time passed she grew better and better at it. But Gregor too, over time, gained a clearer sense of what was involved. Even the way in which she entered the room was a torture to him. No sooner had she stepped in when—not even pausing to shut the door, despite the care she normally would take in sparing others the sight of Gregor's room—she would run straight over to the window and tear it open with impatient fingers, almost as if she were suffocating, and she would remain for some time by the window, even in the coldest weather, breathing deeply. Twice a day she would terrify Gregor with all this noise and rushing around. He would cower under the couch the entire time, knowing full well that she surely would have spared him this if only she could have stood being in the room with him with the windows closed.

Once, about a month after Gregor's metamorphosis—so there was really no particular reason for his sister to be upset by his appearance—she came in earlier than usual and caught Gregor as he gazed out the window, terrifying in his stillness. It wouldn't have surprised Gregor if she'd decided not to come in, since his position prevented her from opening the window right away, but not only did she not come in, she actually jumped back and shut the door—a stranger might have thought that Gregor had been planning to ambush her and bite her. Of course he immediately hid under the couch, but he had to wait until noon before she came back, and this time she seemed much more nervous than usual. In this way he came to realize that the sight of him disgusted her, and likely would always disgust her, and that she probably had to steel herself not to run away at the sight of even the tiny portion of his body that stuck out from under the couch. So, one day, to spare her even this, he carried the bedsheet on his back over to the couch—it took him four hours—and spread it so that he was completely covered and his sister wouldn't be able to see him even if she bent down. If she felt this sheet wasn't necessary then of course she could remove it, since obviously Gregor wasn't shutting himself away so completely in order to amuse himself. But she left the sheet alone, and Gregor even thought that he caught a look of gratitude when he cautiously lifted the sheet a little with his head in order to see how his sister was taking to this new arrangement.

During the first two weeks, his parents couldn't bring themselves to come in to see him, and he frequently heard them remarking how much they appreciated his sister's efforts, whereas previously they'd often been annoyed with her for being, in their eyes, somewhat useless. But now both father and mother had fallen into the habit of waiting outside Gregor's door while his sister cleaned up the room, and as soon as she emerged she would have to tell them every detail of the room's condition, what Gregor had eaten, how he'd behaved this time, and whether he'd perhaps shown a little improvement. It wasn't long before his mother began to want to visit Gregor, but his father and sister were at first able to dissuade her by rational arguments to which Gregor listened with great care, and with which he thoroughly agreed. But as time went by she had to be restrained by force, and when she cried out "Let me go to Gregor, he's my unhappy boy! Don't you understand that I have to go to him?" Gregor began to think that it might be a good idea if his mother did come in after all, not every day, naturally, but, say, once a week. She was really a much more capable person than his sister, who, for all her courage, was still only a child and had perhaps taken on such a difficult task only out of a childish impulsiveness.

Gregor's wish to see his mother was soon fulfilled. During the day Gregor didn't want to show himself at the window, if only out of consideration for his parents. But his few square meters of floor gave him little room to crawl around in, he found it hard to lie still even at night, and eating soon ceased to give him any pleasure. So in order to distract himself he fell into the habit of crawling all over the walls and the ceiling. He especially enjoyed hanging from the ceiling; it was completely different from lying on the floor. He could breathe more freely, a faint pulsing coursed through his body, and in his state of almost giddy absentmindedness up there, Gregor would sometimes, to his surprise, lose his grip and tumble onto the floor. But now, of course, since he had much better control over his body, even such a great fall didn't hurt him. His sister noticed right away the new pastime Gregor had discovered for himself—he'd left sticky traces where he'd been crawling—and so she got it into her head to provide Gregor with as much room as possible to crawl around in by removing all the furniture that was in the way—especially the chest of drawers and the desk. But she couldn't manage this by herself; she didn't dare ask her father for help; the maid wouldn't be of any use, for while this girl, who was around sixteen, was brave enough to stay on after the cook had left, she'd asked to be allowed to always keep the kitchen door locked, opening it only when specifically asked to do so. This left his sister with no choice but, one day when her father was out, to ask her mother for help. And indeed, her mother followed her with joyful, excited cries, although she fell silent when they reached the door to Gregor's room. Naturally his sister first made sure that everything in the room was as it should be; only then did she let her mother come in. Gregor had hurriedly pulled his sheet even lower and had folded it more tightly and it really did look as if it had been casually tossed over the couch. This time Gregor also refrained from peeking out from under the sheet; he denied himself the pleasure of seeing his mother for now and was simply glad that

50

she'd come after all. "Come on in, he's nowhere in sight," said his sister, apparently leading his mother in by the hand. Now Gregor could hear the two delicate women moving the heavy chest of drawers away from its place, his sister stubbornly insisting on doing the hardest work, ignoring the warnings of her mother, who was afraid her daughter would overstrain herself. The work took a very long time. After struggling for over a quarter of an hour, his mother suggested that they might leave the chest where it was; in the first place, it was just too heavy, they'd never be done before his father came home and they'd have to leave it in the middle of the room, blocking Gregor's movements in every direction; in the second place, it wasn't at all certain that they were doing Gregor a favor in removing the furniture. It seemed to her that the opposite was true, the sight of the bare walls broke her heart; and why shouldn't Gregor feel the same since he'd been used to this furniture for so long and would feel abandoned in the empty room? "And wouldn't it look as if," his mother concluded very softly—in fact, she'd been almost whispering the entire time, as if she wanted to prevent Gregor, whose exact whereabouts she didn't know, from hearing the sound of her voice (she was convinced that he couldn't understand her words)—"as if by removing his furniture we were telling him that we'd given up all hope of his getting better, and were callously leaving him to his own devices? I think the best course would be to try to keep the room exactly the way it was, so that when Gregor does come back to us he'll find everything the same, making it easier for him to forget what has happened in the meantime."

When he heard his mother's words, Gregor realized that, over the past two months, the lack of having anyone to converse with, together with the monotonous life within the family, must have befuddled his mind; there wasn't any other way he could explain to himself how he could have ever seriously wanted his room cleared out. Did he really want this warm room of his, so comfortably furnished with family heirlooms, transformed into a lair where he'd be perfectly free to crawl around in every direction, but only at the cost of simultaneously forgetting his human past, swiftly and utterly? Just now he'd been on the brink of forgetting, and only his mother's voice, which he hadn't heard for so long, had brought him back. Nothing should be removed; everything must stay. He couldn't do without the furniture's soothing influence on his state of mind, and if the furniture were to impede his senselessly crawling around, that wouldn't be a loss but rather a great advantage.

But unfortunately his sister thought otherwise. She'd become accustomed, and not without some justification, to assuming the role of the acknowledged expert whenever she and her parents discussed Gregor's affairs; so her mother's advice was enough for her to insist now not merely on her original plan of moving the chest and the desk, but on the removal of every bit of furniture except for the indispensable couch. Her resolve, to be sure, didn't stem merely from childish stubbornness or from the self-confidence she had recently and unexpectedly gained at such great cost. For in fact she'd noticed that while Gregor needed plenty of room to crawl around in, on the other hand, as far as she could tell, he never used the furniture at all. Perhaps too, the sentimental enthusiasm of girls her age, which they indulge themselves in at every opportunity, now tempted Grete to make Gregor's situation all the more terrifying so that she might be able to do more for him. No one but Grete would ever be likely to enter a room where Gregor ruled the bare walls all alone.

And so she refused to give in to her mother, who in any case, from the sheer anxiety caused by being in Gregor's room, seemed unsure of herself. She soon fell silent and began as best she could to help her daughter remove the chest of drawers. Well, if he must, then Gregor could do without the chest, but the desk had to stay. And no sooner had the two women, groaning and squeezing, gotten the chest out of the room than Gregor poked his head out from under the couch to see how he might intervene as tactfully as possible. But unfortunately it was his mother who came back first, leaving Grete in the next room, gripping the chest with her arms and rocking it back and forth without, of course, being able to budge it from the spot. His mother wasn't used to the sight of him—it might make her sick; so Gregor, frightened, scuttled backwards to the far end of the couch, but he couldn't prevent the front of the sheet from stirring slightly. That was enough to catch his mother's attention. She stopped, stood still for a moment, and then went back to Grete.

Gregor kept telling himself that nothing unusual was happening, that only a few pieces of furniture were being moved around. But he soon had to admit that all this coming and going of the two women, their little calls to one another, the scraping of the furniture across the floor, affected him as if it were some gigantic commotion rushing in on him from every side, and though he tucked in his head and legs and pressed his body against the floor, he had to accept the fact that he wouldn't be able to stand it much longer. They were cleaning out his room, taking away from him everything that he loved; already they'd carried off his chest, where he kept his fretsaw and his other tools; now they were trying to pry his writing desk loose—it was practically embedded in the floor—the same desk where he'd always done his homework when he'd been a student at business school, in high school, and even in elementary school. He really no longer had any time left in which to weigh the good intentions of these two women whose existence, for that matter, he'd almost forgotten, since they were so exhausted by now that they worked in silence, the only sound being that of their weary, plodding steps.

And so, while the women were in the next room, leaning against the desk and trying to catch their breath, he broke out, changing his direction four times—since he really didn't know what to rescue first—when he saw, hanging conspicuously on the otherwise bare wall, the picture of the lady all dressed in furs. He quickly crawled up to it and pressed himself against the glass, which held him fast, soothing his hot belly. Now that Gregor completely covered it, this picture at least wasn't about to be carried away by anyone. He turned his head towards the living room door, so that he could watch the women when they returned.

They hadn't taken much of a rest and were already coming back. Grete had put her arm around her mother and was almost carrying her. "Well, what should we take next?" said Grete, looking around. And then her eyes met Gregor's, looking down at her from the wall. Probably only because her mother was there, she kept her composure, bent her head down to her mother to prevent her from glancing around, and said, though in a hollow, quavering voice: "Come on, let's go back to the living room for a minute." To Gregor, her intentions were obvious: she wanted to get his mother to safety and then chase him down from the wall. Well, just let her try! He clung to his picture and he wasn't going to give it up. He'd rather fly at Grete's face.

But Grete's words had made her mother even more anxious; she stepped aside, glimpsed the huge brown blotch on the flowered wallpaper, and before she fully understood that what she was looking at was Gregor, she cried out, "Oh God, oh God!" in a hoarse scream of a voice, and, as if giving up completely, fell with outstretched arms across the couch, and lay there without moving. "You! Gregor!" cried his sister, raising her fist and glaring at him. These were the first words she had addressed directly to him since his metamorphosis. She ran into the next room to get some spirits to revive her mother from her faint. Gregor also wanted to help—he could rescue the picture another time—but he was stuck to the glass and had to tear himself free. He then scuttled into the next room as if to give some advice, as he used to, to his sister. Instead, he had to stand behind her uselessly while she rummaged among various little bottles. When she turned around she was startled, a bottle fell to the floor, a splinter of glass struck Gregor in the face, some sort of corrosive medicine splashed on him, and Grete, without further delay, grabbing as many of the little bottles as she could carry, ran inside with them to her mother, and slammed the door shut behind her with her foot. Now Gregor was cut off from his mother, who was perhaps near death because of him. He didn't dare open the door for fear of scaring his sister, who had to remain with his mother. There wasn't anything for him to do but wait; and so, tormented by guilt and anxiety, he began crawling. He crawled over everything, walls, furniture, and ceiling, until finally, in despair, the room beginning to spin around him, he collapsed onto the middle of the large table.

A short time passed; Gregor lay there stupefied. Everything was quiet around him; perhaps that was a good sign. Then the doorbell rang. The maid, of course, stayed locked up in her kitchen, so Grete had to answer the door. His father was back. "What's happened?" were his first words. Grete's expression must've told him everything. Her answers came in muffled tones—she was obviously burying her face in her father's chest. "Mother fainted, but she's better now. Gregor's broken loose." "I knew it," her father said. "I told you this would happen, but you women refuse to listen." It was clear to Gregor that his father had put the worst construction on Grete's all too brief account and had assumed that Gregor was guilty of some violent act. That meant that he must calm his father down, since he had neither the time nor the ability to explain things to him. So he fled to the door of his room and pressed himself against it in order that his father might see, as soon as he entered the living room, that Gregor had every intention of returning immediately to his own room and there was no need to force him back. All they had to do was to open the door and he would disappear at once.

But his father wasn't in the mood to notice such subtleties; "Ah!" he roared as he entered, in a voice that sounded at once furious and gleeful. Gregor turned his head from the door and lifted it towards his father. He really hadn't imagined that his father would look the way he did standing before him now; true, Gregor had become too absorbed lately by his new habit of crawling to bother about whatever else might be going on in the apartment, and he should have anticipated that there would be some changes. And yet, and yet, could this really be his father? Was this the same man who used to lie sunk in bed, exhausted, whenever Gregor would set out on one of his business trips; who would greet him upon his return in the evening while sitting in his bathrobe in the armchair; who was hardly capable of getting to his feet, and to show his joy could only lift up his arms; and who, on those rare times when the whole family went out for a walk—on the occasional Sunday or on a legal holiday—used to painfully shuffle along between Gregor and his mother, who were slow walkers themselves, and yet he was always slightly slower than they, wrapped up in his old overcoat, carefully planting his crook-handled cane before him with every step, and almost invariably stopping and gathering his escort around him whenever he wanted to say something? Now, however, he held himself very erect, dressed up in a closely-fitting blue uniform with gold buttons, of the kind worn by bank messengers. His heavy chin thrust out over the stiff collar of his jacket; his black eyes stared, sharp and bright, from under his bushy eyebrows; his white hair,

60

once so rumpled, was combed flat, it gleamed, and the part was meticulously exact. He tossed his cap—which bore a gold monogram, probably that of some bank—in an arc across the room so that it landed on the couch, and with his hands in his pockets, the tails of his uniform's long jacket flung back, his face grim, he went after Gregor. He probably didn't know himself what he was going to do, but he lifted his feet unusually high, and Gregor was amazed at the immense size of the soles of his boots. However, Gregor didn't dwell on these reflections, for he had known from the very first day of his new life that his father considered only the strictest measures to be appropriate in dealing with him. So he ran ahead of his father, stopped when he stood still, and scurried on again when he made the slightest move. In this way they circled the room several times without anything decisive happening; in fact, their movements, because of their slow tempo, did not suggest those of a chase. So Gregor kept to the floor for the time being, especially since he was afraid that his father might consider any flight to the walls or ceiling to be particularly offensive. All the same, Gregor had to admit that he wouldn't be able to keep up even this pace for long, since whenever his father took a single step, Gregor had to perform an entire series of movements. He was beginning to get winded, since even in his former life his lungs had never been strong. As he kept staggering on like this, so weary he could barely keep his eyes open, since he was saving all his strength for running; not even thinking, dazed as he was, that there might be any other way to escape than by running; having almost forgotten that he was free to use the walls, though against these walls, admittedly, were placed bits of intricately carved furniture, bristling with spikes and sharp corners—suddenly something sailed overhead, hit the floor nearby, and rolled right in front of him. It was an apple; at once a second one came flying after it. Gregor stopped, petrified with fear; it was useless to keep on running, for his father had decided to bombard him. He had filled his pockets with the fruit from the bowl on the sideboard and now he was throwing one apple after another, for now at least without bothering to take good aim. These little red apples, colliding with one another, rolled around on the floor as if electrified. One weakly-thrown apple grazed Gregor's back, rolling off without causing harm. But another one that came flying immediately afterwards actually imbedded itself in Gregor's back. Gregor wanted to drag himself onward, as if this shocking and unbelievable pain might disappear if he could only keep moving, but he felt as if he were nailed to the spot, and he splayed himself out in the utter confusion of his senses. With his last glance he saw the door of his room burst open, and his mother, wearing only her chemise—his sister had removed her dress to help her breathe after she'd fainted—rush out, followed by his screaming sister. He saw his mother run toward his father, her loosened underskirts slipping one by one onto the floor. Stumbling over her skirts she flung herself upon his father, embraced him, was as one with him—but now Gregor's sight grew dim—and with her arms clasped around his father's neck, begged for Gregor's life.

III

Gregor's serious wound, which made him suffer for over a month—the apple remained imbedded in his flesh as a visible reminder, no one having the courage to remove it—seemed to have persuaded even his father that Gregor, despite his present pathetic and disgusting shape, was a member of the family who shouldn't be treated as an enemy. On the contrary, familial duty required them to swallow their disgust and to endure him, to endure him and nothing more.

And though his wound probably had caused Gregor to suffer a permanent loss of mobility, and though it now took him, as if he were some disabled war veteran, many a long minute to creep across his room—crawling above ground level was out of the question—yet in return for this deterioration of his condition he was granted a compensation which satisfied him completely: each day around dusk the living room door—which he was in the habit of watching closely for an hour or two ahead of time—was opened, and lying in the darkness of his room, invisible from the living room, he could see the whole family sitting at the table lit by the lamp and could listen to their conversation as if by general consent, instead of the way he'd done before.

True, these were no longer the lively conversations of old, those upon which Gregor had mused somewhat wistfully as he'd settled wearily into his damp bed in some tiny hotel room. Things were now very quiet for the most part. Soon after dinner his father would fall asleep in his armchair, while his mother and sister would admonish each other to be quiet; his mother, bending forward under the light, would sew fine lingerie for a fashion store; his sister, who had found work as a salesgirl, would study shorthand and French in the evenings, hoping to obtain a better job in the future. Sometimes his father would wake up, as if he hadn't the slightest idea that he'd been asleep, and would say to his mother, "Look how long you've been sewing again today!" and then would fall back to sleep, while his mother and sister would exchange weary smiles.

With a kind of perverse obstinacy his father refused to take off his messenger's uniform even in the apartment; while his robe hung unused on the clothes hook, he would sleep fully dressed in his chair, as if he were always ready for duty and were waiting even here for the voice of his superior. As a result his uniform, which hadn't been new in the first place, began to get dirty in spite of all his mother and sister could do to care for it, and Gregor would often spend entire evenings gazing at this garment covered with stains and with its constantly polished buttons gleaming, in which the old man would sit, upright and uncomfortable, yet peacefully asleep.

As soon as the clock would strike ten, his mother would try to awaken his father with soft words of encouragement and then persuade him to go to bed, for this wasn't any place in which to get a decent night's sleep, and his father badly needed his rest, since he had to be at work at six in the morning. But with the stubbornness that had possessed him ever since he'd become a bank messenger he would insist on staying at the table a little while longer, though he invariably would fall asleep again, and then it was only with the greatest difficulty that he could be persuaded to trade his chair for bed. No matter how much mother and sister would urge him on with little admonishments, he'd keep shaking his head for a good fifteen minutes, his eyes closed, and wouldn't get up. Gregor's mother would tug at his sleeve, whisper sweet words into his ear; and his sister would leave her homework to help her mother, but it was all useless. He only sank deeper into his armchair. Not until the two women would lift him up by the arms would he open his eyes, look now at one, now at the other, and usually say, "What a life. So this is the peace of my old age." And leaning on the two women he would get up laboriously, as if he were his own greatest burden, and would allow the women to lead him to the door, where, waving them aside, he continued on his own, while Gregor's mother abandoned her sewing and his sister her pen so that they might run after his father and continue to look after him.

Who in this overworked and exhausted family had time to worry about Gregor any more than was absolutely necessary? Their resources grew more limited; the maid was now dismissed after all; a gigantic bony cleaning woman with white hair

65

fluttering about her head came in the mornings and evenings to do the roughest work; Gregor's mother took care of everything else, in addition to her sewing. It even happened that certain pieces of family jewelry, which his mother and sister had worn with such pleasure at parties and celebrations in days gone by, were sold, as Gregor found out one evening by listening to a general discussion of the prices they'd gone for. But their greatest complaint was that they couldn't give up the apartment, which was too big for their current needs, since no one could figure out how they would move Gregor. But Gregor understood clearly enough that it wasn't simply consideration for him which prevented them moving, since he could have easily been transported in a suitable crate equipped with a few air holes. The main reason preventing them from moving was their utter despair and the feeling that they had been struck by a misfortune far greater than any that had ever visited their friends and relatives. What the world demands of the poor they did to the utmost: his father fetched breakfast for the bank's minor officials, his mother sacrificed herself for the underwear of strangers, his sister ran back and forth behind the counters at the beck and call of customers; but they lacked the strength for anything beyond this. And the wound in Gregor's back began to ache once more when his mother and sister, after putting his father to bed, returned to the room, ignored their work, and sat huddled together cheek to cheek, and his mother said, "Close that door, Grete," so that Gregor was back in the dark, while in the next room the women wept together or simply stared at the table with dry eyes.

Gregor spent the days and nights almost entirely without sleep. Sometimes he imagined that the next time the door opened he would once again assume control of the family's affairs, as he'd done in the old days. Now, after a long absence, there reappeared in his thoughts the director and the manager, the salesmen and the apprentices, the remarkably stupid errand runner, two or three friends from other firms, a chambermaid at one of the provincial hotels—a sweet, fleeting memory—a cashier at a hat store whom he'd courted earnestly but too slowly—they all came to him mixed up with strangers and with people whom he'd already forgotten. But instead of helping him and his family they were all unapproachable, and he was glad when they faded away. At other times he was in no mood to worry about his family; he was utterly filled with rage at how badly he was being treated, and although he couldn't imagine anything that might tempt his appetite, he nevertheless tried to think up ways of getting into the pantry to take what was rightfully his, even if he wasn't hungry. No longer bothering to consider what Gregor might like as a treat, his sister, before she hurried off to work in the morning and after lunch, would shove any sort of food into Gregor's room with her foot. In the evening, regardless of whether the food had been picked at, or—as was more often the case—left completely untouched, she would sweep it out with a swish of the broom. Nowadays she would clean the room in the evening, and she couldn't have done it any faster. Streaks of grime ran along the walls, balls of dust and dirt lay here and there on the floor. At first, whenever his sister would come in, Gregor would station himself in some corner that was particularly objectionable, as if his presence there might serve as a reproach to her. But he probably could have remained there for weeks without her mending her ways; she obviously could see the dirt as clearly as he could, but she'd made up her mind to leave it. At the same time she made certain—with a touchiness that was completely new to her and which indeed was infecting the entire family—that the cleaning of Gregor's room was to remain her prerogative. On one occasion Gregor's mother had subjected his room to a thorough cleaning, which she managed to accomplish only with the aid of several buckets of water—all this dampness being a further annoyance to Gregor, who lay flat, unhappy, and motionless on the couch. But his mother's punishment was not long in coming. For that evening, as soon as Gregor's sister noticed the difference in his room, she ran, deeply insulted, into the living room, and without regard for his mother's uplifted, beseeching hands, burst into a fit of tears. Both parents—the father, naturally, had been startled out of his armchair—at first looked on with helpless amazement, and then they joined in, the father on his right side blaming the mother: she shouldn't have interfered with the sister's cleaning of the room, while on his left side yelling at the sister that she'd never be allowed to clean Gregor's room again. The mother was trying to drag the father, who was half out of his mind, into their bedroom while the sister, shaking with sobs, pounded the table with her little fists, and Gregor hissed loudly with rage because not one of them had thought to close the door and spare him this scene and this commotion.

But even if his sister, worn out by her job at the store, had gotten tired of taking care of Gregor as she once had, it wasn't really necessary for his mother to take her place so that Gregor wouldn't be neglected. For now the cleaning woman was there. This ancient widow, whose powerful bony frame had no doubt helped her through the hard times in her long life, wasn't at all repelled by Gregor. Without being the least bit inquisitive, she had once, by chance, opened the door to Gregor's room and at the sight of Gregor—who, taken completely by surprise, began running back and forth although no one was chasing him—stood there in amazement, her hands folded over her belly. From then on, morning and evening, she never failed to open his door a crack and peek in on him. At first she also would call him to her, using phrases she probably meant to be friendly, such as "Come on over here, you old dung beetle!" or "Just look at that old dung beetle!" Gregor wouldn't respond to such forms of address, but would remain motionless where he was as if the door had never been opened. If only this cleaning woman, instead of pointlessly disturbing him whenever she felt like it, had been given orders to clean his room every day! Once, early in the morning, when a heavy rain, perhaps a sign of the already approaching spring, was beating against the window panes, Gregor became so exasperated when the cleaning woman started in with her phrases that he made as if to attack her, though, of course, in a slow and feeble manner. But instead of being frightened, the cleaning woman simply picked up a chair by the door and, lifting it high in the air, stood there with her mouth wide open. Obviously she didn't plan on shutting it until the chair in her hands had first come crashing down on Gregor's back. "So you're not going through with it?" she asked as Gregor turned back while she calmly set the chair down again in the corner.

By now Gregor was eating next to nothing. Only when he happened to pass by the food set out for him would he take a bite, hold it in his mouth for hours, and then spit most of it out again. At first he imagined that it was his anguish at the state of his room that kept him from eating, but it was those very changes to which he had quickly become accustomed. The family had fallen into the habit of using the room to store things for which there wasn't any place anywhere else, and there were many of these things now, since one room in the apartment had been rented to three boarders. These serious gentlemen—all three of them had full beards, as Gregor once noted, peering through a crack in the door—had a passion for neatness, not only in their room but since they were now settled in as boarders, throughout the entire apartment, and especially in the kitchen. They couldn't abide useless, let alone dirty, junk. Besides, they'd brought most of their own household goods along with them. This meant that many objects were now superfluous, which, while clearly without any resale value, couldn't just be thrown out either. All these things ended up in Gregor's room, and so did the ash bucket and the garbage can from the kitchen. Anything that wasn't being used at the moment was simply tossed into Gregor's room by the cleaning woman, who was always in a tremendous hurry. Fortunately, Gregor generally saw only the object in question and the hand that held it. Perhaps the cleaning woman intended to come back for these things when she had the time, or perhaps she planned on throwing them all out, but in fact there they remained, wherever they'd happened to land, except for Gregor's disturbing them as he squeezed his way through the junk pile. At first he did so simply because he was forced to, since there wasn't any other space to crawl in, but later he took a growing pleasure in these rambles even though they left him dead tired and so sad that he would lie motionless for hours. Since the boarders would sometimes have their dinner at home in the shared living room, on those evenings the door between that room and Gregor's would remain shut. But Gregor didn't experience the door's not being open as a hardship; in fact there had been evenings when he'd ignored the open door and had lain, unnoticed by the family, in the darkest corners of his room. But one time the cleaning woman left the door slightly ajar, and it remained ajar when the boarders came in that evening and the lamp was lit. They sat down at the head of the table, where Gregor, his mother and his father had sat in the old days; they unfolded their napkins, and picked up their knives and forks. At once his mother appeared at the kitchen door carrying a platter of meat and right behind her came his sister carrying a platter piled high with potatoes. The steaming food gave off a thick vapor. The platters were set down in front of the boarders, who bent over them as if to examine them before eating, and in fact the one sitting in the middle, who was apparently looked up to as an authority by the other two, cut into a piece of meat while it was still on the platter, evidently to determine if it was tender enough or whether perhaps it should be sent back to the kitchen. He was satisfied, and both mother and daughter, who'd been watching anxiously, breathed a sigh of relief and began to smile.

The family itself ate in the kitchen. Even so, before going to the kitchen his   70 father came into the living room, bowed once and, cap in hand, walked around the table. The boarders all rose together and mumbled something into their beards. When they were once more alone, they ate in almost complete silence. It seemed strange to Gregor that, out of all the noises produced by eating, he distinctly heard the sound of their teeth chewing; it was as if he were being told you needed teeth in order to eat and that even with the most wonderful toothless jaws, you wouldn't be able to accomplish a thing. "Yes, I'm hungry enough," Gregor told himself sadly, "but not for those things. How well these boarders feed themselves, while I waste away."

That very evening—during this whole time Gregor couldn't once remember hearing the violin—the sound of violin playing came from the kitchen. The boarders had already finished their dinner, the one in the middle had pulled out a newspaper, handed one sheet each to the other two, and now they were leaning back, reading and smoking. When the violin began to play, they noticed it, stood up, and tiptoed to the hall doorway where they stood together in a tight group. They must have been heard in the kitchen for his father called, "Does the playing bother you, gentlemen? We can stop it at once." "On the contrary," said the gentleman in the middle, "wouldn't the young lady like to come and play in here where it's much more roomy and comfortable?" "Why, certainly," called Gregor's father, as if he were the violinist. Soon his father came in carrying the music stand, his mother the sheet music, and his sister the violin. His sister calmly got everything ready for playing; his parents—who had never rented out rooms before and so were overly polite to the boarders—didn't even dare to sit down in their own chairs. His father leaned against the door, slipping his right hand between the buttons of his uniform's jacket, which he'd kept buttoned up; but his mother was offered a chair by one of the gentlemen, and, leaving it where he happened to have placed it, she sat off to one side, in the corner.

His sister began to play; his father and mother, on either side, closely followed the movements of her hands. Gregor, attracted by the playing, had moved a little farther forward and already had his head in the living room. He was hardly surprised that recently he'd shown so little concern for others, although in the past he'd taken pride in being considerate. Now more than ever he had good reason to remain hidden, since he was completely covered with the dust that lay everywhere in his room and was stirred up by the slightest movement. Moreover, threads, hairs, and scraps of food clung to his back and sides, his indifference to everything was much too great for him to have gotten onto his back and rubbed himself clean against the carpet, as he had once done several times a day. And despite his condition he wasn't ashamed to edge his way a little further across the spotless living room floor.

To be sure, no one took any notice of him. The family was completely absorbed by the violin-playing. The boarders, however, who had at first placed themselves, their hands in their pockets, much too close to the music stand—close enough for every one of them to have followed the score, which surely must have flustered his sister—soon retreated to the window, muttering to one another, with their heads lowered. And there they remained while his father watched them anxiously. It seemed all too obvious that they had been disappointed in their hopes of hearing good or entertaining violin-playing; they had had enough of the entire performance, and it was only out of politeness that they continued to let their peace be disturbed. It was especially obvious, by the way they blew their smoke out of their mouths and noses—it floated upwards to the ceiling—just how ill at ease they were. And yet his sister was playing so beautifully. Her face was inclined to one side, and her sad eyes carefully followed the notes of the music. Gregor crawled forward a little farther, keeping his head close to the floor so that their eyes might possibly meet. Was he an animal, that music could move him so? He felt that he was being shown the way to an unknown nourishment he yearned for. He was determined to press on until he reached his sister, to tug at her skirt, and to let her know in this way that she should bring her violin into his room, for no one here would honor her playing as he would. He would never let her out of his room again, at least not for as long as he lived; at last his horrifying appearance would be useful; he would be at every door of his room at once, hissing and spitting at the attackers. His sister, however, wouldn't be forced to remain with him, she would do so of her own free will. She would sit beside him on the couch, leaning towards him and listening as he confided that he had firmly intended to send her to the Conservatory, and if the misfortune hadn't intervened, he would've announced this to everyone last Christmas—for hadn't Christmas come and gone by now?—without paying the slightest attention to any objection. After this declaration his sister would be so moved that she would burst into tears, and Gregor would lift himself up to her shoulder and kiss her on her neck, which, since she had started her job, she had kept bare, without ribbon or collar.

"Mr. Samsa!" cried the middle gentleman to Gregor's father, and without wasting another word pointed with his index finger at Gregor, who was slowly advancing. The violin stopped, the middle gentleman, shaking his head, smiled first at his friends and then looked at Gregor again. Instead of driving Gregor away, his father seemed to think it more important to soothe the boarders, although they weren't upset at all and appeared to consider Gregor more entertaining than the violin-playing. His father rushed over to them and with outstretched arms tried to herd them back into their room and at the same time block their view of Gregor with his body. Now they actually got a little angry—it wasn't clear whether this was due to his father's behavior or to their dawning realization that they had had all along, without knowing it, a next-door neighbor like Gregor. They demanded explanations from his father, raised their own arms now as well, tugged nervously at their beards, and only slowly backed away toward their room. Meanwhile his sister had managed to overcome the bewildered state into which she'd fallen when her playing had been so abruptly interrupted, and after some moments spent holding the violin and bow in her slackly dangling hands and staring at the score as if she were still playing, she suddenly pulled herself together, placed her instrument on her mother's lap—she was still sitting in her chair with her lungs heaving, gasping for breath—and ran into the next room, which the boarders, under pressure from her father, were ever more swiftly approaching. One could see pillows and blankets flying high in the air and then neatly arranging themselves under his sister's practical hands. Before the gentlemen had even reached their room, she had finished making the beds and had slipped out.

Once again a perverse stubbornness seemed to grip Gregor's father, to the extent that he forgot to pay his tenants the respect still due them. He kept on pushing and shoving until the middle gentleman, who was already standing in the room's doorway, brought him up short with a thunderous stamp of his foot. "I hereby declare," he said, raising his hand and looking around for Gregor's mother and sister as well, "that considering the disgusting conditions prevailing in this apartment and in this family"—here he suddenly spat on the floor—"I'm giving immediate notice. Naturally I'm not going to pay a penny for the time I've spent here; on the contrary, I shall be seriously considering bringing some sort of action against you with claims that—I assure you—will be very easy to substantiate." He stopped speaking and stared ahead of him, as if expecting something. And indeed his two friends chimed right in, saying "We're giving immediate notice too." Whereupon he grabbed the doorknob and slammed the door shut with a crash.

Gregor's father, groping his way and staggering forward, collapsed into his armchair; it looked as if he were stretching himself out for his usual evening nap, but his heavily drooping head, looking as if it had lost all means of support, showed that he was anything but asleep. All this time Gregor had lain quietly right where the boarders had first seen him. His disappointment over the failure of his plan, and perhaps also the weakness caused by eating so little for so long, made movement an impossibility. He feared with some degree of certainty that at the very next moment the whole catastrophe would fall on his head, and he waited. He wasn't even startled when the violin slipped from his mother's trembling fingers and fell off her lap with a reverberating clatter.

"Dear parents," said his sister, pounding the table with her hand by way of preamble, "we can't go on like this. Maybe you don't realize it, but I do. I refuse to utter my brother's name in the presence of this monster, and so all I have to say is: we've got to try to get rid of it. We've done everything humanly possible to take care of it and put up with it; I don't think anyone can blame us in the least."

"She's absolutely right," said his father to himself. His mother, still trying to catch her breath, with a wild look in her eyes, began to cough, her cupped hand muffling the sound.

His sister rushed over to his mother and held her forehead. His father seemed to have been led to more definite thoughts by Grete's words; he was sitting up straight and toying with his messenger's cap, which lay on the table among the dishes left over from the boarders' dinner. From time to time he would glance over at Gregor's motionless form.

"We must try to get rid of it," said his sister, speaking only to her father since her mother's coughing was such that she was incapable of hearing a word. "It will be the death of you both. I can see it coming. People who have to work as hard as we do can't stand this constant torture at home. I can't stand it anymore either." And she burst out sobbing so violently that her tears ran down onto her mother's face, where she wiped them away mechanically with her hand.

"But, my child," said her father with compassion and remarkable understanding, "what should we do?"

Gregor's sister could only shrug her shoulders as a sign of the helplessness that had overcome her while she wept, in contrast to her earlier self-confidence.

"If he could understand us," said her father tentatively; Gregor's sister, through her tears, shook her hand violently to indicate how impossible that was.

"If he could understand us," repeated her father, closing his eyes so as to take in his daughter's belief that this was impossible, "then perhaps we might be able to reach some agreement with him, but the way things are——"

"He's got to go," cried Gregor's sister, "it's the only way, Father. You just have to get rid of the idea that this is Gregor. Our real misfortune is having believed it for so long. But how can it be Gregor? If it were, he would've realized a long time ago that it's impossible for human beings to live with a creature like that, and he would've left of his own accord. Then we would've lost a brother, but we'd have been able to go on living and honor his memory. But the way things are, this animal persecutes us, drives away our boarders, obviously it wants to take over the whole apartment and make us sleep in the gutter. Look, Father," she suddenly screamed, "he's at it again!" And in a panic which Gregor found incomprehensible his sister abandoned his mother, and actually pushing herself from the chair as if she would rather sacrifice her mother than remain near Gregor, she rushed behind her father, who, startled by this behavior, got up as well, half raising his arms in front of Grete as if to protect her.

Gregor hadn't the slightest desire to frighten anyone, least of all his sister. He had merely started to turn around in order to go back to his room, a procedure which admittedly looked strange, since in his weakened condition he had to use his head to help him in this difficult maneuver, several times raising it and then knocking it against the floor. He stopped and looked around. His good intentions seemed to have been understood; the panic had only been temporary. Now, silent and sad, they all looked at him. His mother lay in her armchair with her legs outstretched and pressed together, her eyes almost closed from exhaustion. His father and sister sat side by side, and his sister had put her arm around her father's neck.

"Now maybe they'll let me turn around," thought Gregor, resuming his efforts. He couldn't stop panting from the strain, and he also had to rest from time to time. At least no one harassed him and he was left alone. When he had finished turning around, he immediately began to crawl back in a straight line. He was amazed at the distance between him and his room and couldn't understand how, weak as he was, he'd covered the same stretch of ground only a little while ago almost without being aware of it. Completely intent on crawling rapidly, he scarcely noticed that neither a word nor an exclamation came from his family to interrupt his progress.

Only when he reached the doorway did he turn his head; not all the way, for he felt his neck growing stiff, but enough to see that behind him all was as before except that his sister had gotten to her feet. His last glimpse was of his mother, who by now was fast asleep.

He was barely inside the room before the door was slammed shut, bolted, and locked. Gregor was so frightened by the sudden noise behind him that his little legs collapsed underneath him. It was his sister who had been in such a hurry. She'd been standing there, ready and waiting, and then had sprung swiftly forward, before Gregor had even heard her coming. "At last!" she cried to her parents as she turned the key in the lock.

"And now?" Gregor asked himself, looking around in the darkness. He soon discovered that he was no longer able to move. This didn't surprise him; rather it seemed to him strange that until now he'd actually been able to propel himself with these thin little legs. In other respects he felt relatively comfortable. It was true that his entire body ached, but the pain seemed to him to be growing fainter and fainter and soon would go away altogether. The rotten apple in his back and the inflamed area around it, completely covered with fine dust, hardly bothered him anymore. He recalled his family with deep emotion and love. His own belief that he must disappear was, if anything, even firmer than his sister's. He remained in this state of empty and peaceful reflection until the tower clock struck three in the morning. He could still just sense the general brightening outside his window. Then, involuntarily, his head sank all the way down, and from his nostrils came his last feeble breath.

Early that morning, when the cleaning woman appeared—out of sheer energy and impatience she always slammed all the doors, no matter how often she'd been asked not to, so hard that sleep was no longer possible anywhere in the apartment once she'd arrived—she didn't notice anything peculiar when she paid Gregor her usual brief visit. She thought that he was lying there so still on purpose, pretending that his feelings were hurt; she considered him to be very clever. As she happened to be holding a long broom, she tried to tickle Gregor with it from the doorway. When this too had no effect, she became annoyed and jabbed it into Gregor a little, and it was only when she shoved him from his place without meeting resistance that she began to take notice. Quickly realizing how things stood, she opened her eyes wide, gave a soft whistle, and without wasting any time she tore open the bedroom door and yelled at the top of her lungs into the darkness: "Come and look, it's had it, it's lying there, dead and done for." 90

Mr. and Mrs. Samsa sat up in their marriage bed, trying to absorb the shock the cleaning woman had given them and yet at first unable to comprehend the meaning of her words. Then they quickly climbed out of bed, Mr. Samsa on one side, Mrs. Samsa on the other. Mr. Samsa threw a blanket over his shoulders, Mrs. Samsa wore only her nightgown; dressed in this fashion they entered Gregor's room. Meanwhile the door to the living room, where Grete had been sleeping since the boarders' arrival, opened as well. Grete was fully dressed, as if she'd never gone to bed, and the pallor of her face seemed to confirm this. "Dead?" asked Mrs. Samsa and looked inquiring at the cleaning woman, although she could have checked for herself, or guessed at the truth without having to investigate. "That's for sure," said the cleaning woman, and to prove it she pushed Gregor's corpse a good way to one side with her broom. Mrs. Samsa made a move as if to stop her, then let it go. "Well," said Mr. Samsa, "now thanks be to God." He crossed himself, and the three women followed his example. Grete, who never took her eyes off the corpse, said, "Just look how thin he was. It's been a long time since he's eaten anything. The food came out just as it was when it came in." Indeed, Gregor's body was completely flat and dry; this was only now obvious because the body was no longer raised on its little legs and nothing else distracted the eye.

"Come to our room with us for a little while, Grete," said Mrs. Samsa with a sad smile, and Grete, not without a look back at the corpse, followed her parents into the bedroom. The cleaning woman shut the door and opened the windows wide. Although it was early in the morning, there was a certain mildness in the fresh air. After all, these were the last days of March.

The three boarders came out of their rooms and looked around in amazement for their breakfast; they had been forgotten. "Where's our breakfast?" the middle gentleman asked the cleaning woman in a sour tone. But she put her finger to her lips, and then quickly and quietly beckoned to the gentlemen to enter Gregor's room. So they did, and, with their hands in the pockets of their somewhat threadbare jackets, they stood in a circle around Gregor's corpse in the now sunlit room.

At that point the bedroom door opened and Mr. Samsa, wearing his uniform, appeared with his wife on one arm and his daughter on the other. They all looked a little tearful; from time to time Grete would press her face against her father's sleeve.

"Leave my home at once," Mr. Samsa told the three gentlemen, pointing to the   95
door without letting go of the women. "What do you mean?" said the middle gentleman, who, somewhat taken aback, smiled a sugary smile. The other two held their hands behind their backs, and kept rubbing them together as if cheerfully anticipating a major argument which they were bound to win. "I mean just what I say," replied Mr. Samsa, and advanced in a line with his two companions directly on the middle boarder. At first this gentleman stood still, looking at the floor as if the thoughts inside his head were arranging themselves in a new pattern. "Well, so we'll be off," he then said, looking up at Mr. Samsa as if, suddenly overcome with humility, he was asking permission for even this decision. Mr. Samsa, his eyes glowering, merely gave him a few brief nods. With that the gentleman, taking long strides, actually set off in the direction of the hall; his two friends, who had been listening for some time with their hands quite still, now went hopping right along after him, as if they were afraid that Mr. Samsa might reach the hall before them and cut them off from their leader. Once in the hall the three of them took their hats from the coat rack, pulled their canes from the umbrella stand, bowed silently, and left the apartment. Impelled by a suspicion that would turn out to be utterly groundless, Mr. Samsa led the two women out onto the landing; leaning against the banister railing they watched the three gentlemen as they marched slowly but steadily down the long staircase, disappearing at every floor when the staircase made a turn and then after a few moments reappearing once again. The lower they descended the more the Samsas' interest in them waned; and when a butcher's boy with a basket on his head came proudly up the stairs towards the gentlemen and then swept on past them, Mr. Samsa and the women quickly left the banister and, as if relieved, returned to the apartment.

They decided to spend this day resting and going for a walk; not only did they deserve this break from work, they absolutely needed it. And so they sat down at the table to write their three letters excusing themselves, Mr. Samsa to the bank manager, Mrs. Samsa to her employer, and Grete to the store's owner. While they were writing, the cleaning woman came by to say that she was leaving now, since her morning's work was done. At first the three letter writers merely nodded without looking up, but when the cleaning woman made no move to go, they looked up at her, annoyed. "Well?" asked Mr. Samsa. The cleaning woman stood in the doorway, smiling as if she had some wonderful news for the family, news she wasn't about to share until they came right out and asked her to. The little ostrich feathers in her hat, which stood up nearly straight in the air and which had irritated Mr. Samsa the entire time she had worked for them, swayed gently in every direction. "What can we do for you?" asked Mrs. Samsa, whom the cleaning woman respected the most. "Well," the cleaning woman replied, with such good-humored laughter that she had to pause before continuing, "you don't have to worry about getting rid of that thing in the next room. It's already been taken care of." Mrs. Samsa and Grete bent over their letters as if they intended to keep on writing; Mr. Samsa, who realized that the cleaning woman was about to go into the details, stopped her firmly with an outstretched hand. Seeing that she wasn't going to be allowed to tell her story, she suddenly remembered that she was in a great hurry; clearly insulted, she called out, "Bye, everybody," whirled around wildly, and left the apartment with a terrible slamming of doors.

"She'll be dismissed tonight," said Mr. Samsa, but without getting a reply from his wife or his daughter, for the cleaning woman seemed to have ruined their tenuous peace of mind. They got up, went to the window, and remained there holding each other tightly. Mr. Samsa turned around in his chair toward them and watched them quietly for some time. Then he called out, "Come on now, come over here. Let those old troubles alone. And have a little consideration for me, too." The two women promptly obeyed him, hurried over to him, caressed him, and quickly finished their letters.

Then all three of them left the apartment together, something they hadn't done in months, and took a streetcar out to the open country on the outskirts of the city. Their car, which they had all to themselves, was completely bathed in warm sunlight. Leaning comfortably back in their seats they discussed their prospects for the future, which on closer inspection seemed to be not so bad, since all three of them had jobs which—though they'd never asked one another about them in any detail—were in each case very advantageous and promising. Of course the greatest immediate improvement in their situation would quickly come about when they found a new apartment, one that was smaller, cheaper, and in every way easier to maintain than their current one, which Gregor had chosen for them. As they were talking on in this way, it occurred to both Mr. and Mrs. Samsa, almost simultaneously, as they watched their daughter become more and more vivacious, that in spite of all the recent troubles that had turned her cheeks pale, she had blossomed into a pretty and shapely girl. Growing quieter now, communicating almost unconsciously through glances, they reflected that soon it would be time to find her a good husband. And it was as if in confirmation of their new dreams and good intentions that at the end of their ride their daughter got up first and stretched her young body.

Questions

1. What was Gregor's occupation before his transformation? How did he come to his particular job? What kept him working for his firm?

2. When Gregor wakes to discover he has become a gigantic insect, he is mostly intent on the practical implications of his metamorphosis—how to get out of bed, how to get to his job, and so on. He never wonders why or how he has been changed. What does this odd reaction suggest about Gregor?

3. When Gregor's parents first see the gigantic insect (paragraph 25), do they recognize it as their son? What do their initial reactions suggest about their attitude toward their son?

4. How does each family member react to Gregor after his transformation? How do their reactions differ from one another? What do they have in common?

5. What things about Gregor have been changed? What seems to have remained the same? List specific qualities.

6. *The Metamorphosis* takes place almost entirely in the Samsa family apartment. How does the story's setting shape its themes?

7. Which family member first decides that the family must "get rid of" the insect? What rationale is given? In what specific ways does the family's decision affect Gregor?

8. How does the family react to Gregor's death?

9. Does Grete change in the course of the story? If so, how does she change?

10. In what ways is Gregor's metamorphosis symbolic?

■ WRITING *effectively*

Franz Kafka on Writing

Gustav Janouch Discussing *The Metamorphosis*   c. 1920

My friend Alfred Kämpf . . . admired Kafka's story *The Metamorphosis*. He described the author as "a new, more profound and therefore more significant Edgar Allan Poe."

During a walk with Franz Kafka on the Altstädter Ring° I told him about this new admirer of his, but aroused neither interest nor understanding. On the contrary, Kafka's expression showed that any discussion of his book was distasteful to him. I, however, was filled with a zeal for discoveries, and so I was tactless.

"The hero of the story is called Samsa," I said. "It sounds like a cryptogram for Kafka. Five letters in each word. The S in the word Samsa has the same position as the K in the word Kafka. The A . . ."

Kafka interrupted me.

"It is not a cryptogram. Samsa is not merely Kafka, and nothing else. *The Metamorphosis* is not a confession, although it is—in a certain sense—an indiscretion."

"I know nothing about that."

"Is it perhaps delicate and discreet to talk about the bugs in one's own family?"

"It isn't usual in good society."

"You see what bad manners I have."

Kafka smiled. He wished to dismiss the subject. But I did not wish to.

"It seems to me that the distinction between good and bad manners hardly applies here," I said. "*The Metamorphosis* is a terrible dream, a terrible conception."

Kafka stood still.

"The dream reveals the reality, which conception lags behind. That is the horror of life—the terror of art. But now I must go home."

From *Conversations with Kafka* by Gustav Janouch

Altstädter Ring: a major street in Prague.

THINKING ABOUT LONG STORIES AND NOVELS

Writing about a long story or novella may seem overwhelming. There can seem to be so much to analyze and consider. You may despair of being able to master the material and discuss it coherently, but if you focus your attention on some central concerns, you will be surprised at how easily you can develop and express your responses to the work.

- **Be aware that characters in a longer narrative often have more complex personalities**. In a short story, characters are often presented in terms of two or three basic personality traits. But in a long story or novella, characters are usually drawn with more depth and shading—and sometimes even contradictory elements—to their personalities. In reading a long story, you should be alert to all the different aspects of a character's nature.

- **Consider that a longer narrative allows for more development**. Often the intention of a short story is to reveal a personality or a situation as it is, much in the manner of showing a snapshot or drawing back a curtain. But a longer story requires movement and development to sustain the reader's interest. As you read, notice the—often subtle—changes that may take place in the protagonist as he or she initiates or otherwise experiences the events of the narrative.

- **Review the work**. As a long story or novella unfolds, your recollections of the earlier parts of the text may be pushed aside as new events and situations occur. A first-rate work of fiction will yield a wealth of interconnections of language, images, actions, and ideas. After you finish reading the work, by going through the text again you may often see much more in the story than you did the first time around.

CHECKLIST: Writing About Long Stories and Novels

- ☐ What is the protagonist's situation at the beginning of the work?
- ☐ What is the protagonist's main objective at the beginning?
- ☐ What changes take place in the protagonist's situation as the narrative proceeds?
- ☐ How does the protagonist react to these changes? How does his or her response to stress reveal the protagonist's basic nature?
- ☐ Who are the story's other important characters, and what are their relationships to the protagonist?
- ☐ Can anyone be described as an antagonist?
- ☐ Compare and contrast the beginning of the story with its conclusion.
- ☐ Don't try to put everything in your essay. Focus on the main points and be selective in the choice of textual details.
- ☐ Try to put your ideas in some logical order.
- ☐ Outline the main points of your argument to see clearly what is relevant to that argument and what is not.

TOPICS FOR WRITING ON LONG STORIES AND NOVELS

1. What do Ivan Ilych and Gregor Samsa have in common? In what ways are their lives and deaths dissimilar?

2. Choose a thematic concern of either *The Death of Ivan Ilych* or *The Metamorphosis*; some possibilities are work, romantic love, and the family. Develop a thesis about what your story has to say on your chosen theme. Now choose three key moments from the story to back up your argument. Make your case in a medium-length paper (600 to 1,000 words); be sure to quote as needed from the text.

3. In one carefully thought-out paragraph, sum up what you believe Tolstoy is saying in *The Death of Ivan Ilych*.

4. Compare Tolstoy's short novel with another story of spiritual awakening: Flannery O'Connor's "Revelation" or "A Good Man Is Hard to Find" (both in Chapter 11). In each, what brings about the enlightenment of the central character?

5. Is *The Metamorphosis* a horror story? What elements does Kafka's story share with horror fiction or films you have known? How does *The Metamorphosis* differ?

6. Compare and contrast Gregor Samsa's relationships with the people in his life to Miss Emily's relationships with those around her in "A Rose for Emily" (Chapter 2).

7. Explore how Gregor Samsa's metamorphosis into a giant insect is symbolic of his earlier life and relations with his family. (For a discussion of literary symbols, see Chapter 7, "Symbol.")

8. Write a metamorphosis story of your own. Imagine a character who turns overnight into something quite other than himself or herself. As you describe that character's struggles, try for a mix of tragedy and grotesque comedy, as found in *The Metamorphosis*.

▶ TERMS FOR *review*

Novel ▶ An extended work of fictional prose narrative. The term *novel* usually implies a book-length narrative.

Epistolary novel ▶ Novel in which the story is told by way of letters written by one or more of the characters. This form often lends an authenticity to the story, an illusion that the author may have discovered these letters, even though they are a product of the author's imagination.

Nonfiction novel ▶ A genre in which actual events are presented as a novel-length story, using the techniques of fiction.

Historical fiction ▶ A type of fiction in which the narrative is set in an earlier time. In historical fiction, the author often attempts to recreate a faithful picture of daily life during the period. While it may depict real historical figures, more often it places imaginary characters in a carefully reconstructed version of a particular era.

Bildungsroman ▶ German for "novel of growth and development." Sometimes called an **apprenticeship novel**, this genre depicts a youth who struggles toward maturity and the forming of a worldview or philosophy of life.

Picaresque ▶ A type of narrative, usually a novel, that presents the life of a likable scoundrel at odds with respectable society. The narrator of a picaresque was originally a *pícaro* (Spanish for "rascal" or "rogue") who recounts his or her adventures tricking the rich and gullible. This type of narrative rarely has a tightly constructed plot, and the episodes or adventures follow in a loose chronological order.

Novella ▶ In modern terms, a prose narrative longer than a short story but shorter than a novel. Unlike a short story, a novella is long enough to be published independently as a brief book.

10 LATIN AMERICAN FICTION

Writing is nothing more than a guided dream.

—JORGE LUIS BORGES

What You Will Learn in This Chapter

- To describe the important contributions of Latin American fiction to world literature
- To explain the origins and characteristics of *El Boom*
- To define *magic realism*
- To analyze the elements of magic realism in a story

Before the middle of the twentieth century, Latin America produced a number of highly talented novelists, but their work had relatively little impact outside their region, and often little impact beyond their own individual nations. For the most part, these novels fit into the tradition of realism that dominated European literature in the late nineteenth century and often pursued a social agenda, emphasizing the economic and geographical characteristics that were unique to the writer's own country. One author whose work crossed national borders was the Guatemalan novelist Miguel Ángel Asturias (1899–1974), who is credited with introducing some of the techniques of Modernism into Latin American fiction. He would go on to win the Nobel Prize in Literature in 1967.

But even Asturias felt that Latin American literature, while powerful, remained provincial. In a 1970 interview he said, "To believe that we Latin Americans are going to teach Europeans to reflect, to philosophize, to write egocentric or psychological novels, to believe that we are already a mature enough society to produce a Proust or a Goethe—that would be daydreaming and self-deception." His remarks exemplified the marginality still felt by most Latin American writers of his generation.

EL BOOM

Asturias underestimated the growing influence and appeal of Latin American literature. By 1970 Latin American fiction had begun to capture international attention. A new generation of fiction writers had emerged who had been profoundly influenced by the great Modernists of American, British, and European literature. In their hands, formal literary style relaxed to incorporate common speech, sudden shifts of tone, and extravagant wordplay. Characterization became more complex and multilayered; instead of straightforward, realist narrative there were now often fractured time sequences and fantastic events. These young writers were the catalysts of an explosion of creativity—commonly referred to as *El Boom*—that transformed Latin America into one of the centers of modern world fiction.

One of the pioneering figures of the movement was the Mexican writer Carlos Fuentes; Chilean novelist José Donoso would later write of Fuentes's 1959 novel *Where the Air Is Clear*: "Reading it was a cataclysm for me. Until then, I had been governed by a paralyzing good taste, and for me, the politics and forces giving shape to our history were matters of hometown gossip on the level of friendly phone calls, never on the level of myths, invasions, or idolatries." Other writers prominently associated with the Boom were Julio Cortázar of Argentina, whose experimental novel *Hopscotch* (1963) attracted widespread international attention, and Mario Vargas Llosa of Peru, who also achieved an international reputation with *The Time of the Hero* (1963) and *Aunt Julia and the Scriptwriter* (1977). But its best-known and most influential figure is the Colombian novelist Gabriel García Márquez, whose *One Hundred Years of Solitude* (1967) is the defining text both of *El Boom* and of the genre known as *magic realism*.

MAGIC REALISM

Magic realism, or **magical realism** (*el realismo magical*), was a term coined in 1949 by the Cuban novelist Alejo Carpentier to describe the matter-of-fact combination of the fantastic and everyday in Latin American fiction. Magic realism has now become the standard name for a major trend in contemporary fiction that stretches from Latin American works such as García Márquez's *One Hundred Years of Solitude* and Octavio Paz's "My Life with the Wave" to *norteamericana* novels such as Mark Helprin's *Winter's Tale* (1983) and Asian works such as Salman Rushdie's *Midnight's Children* (1981). In all cases the term refers to the tendency among contemporary fiction writers to mix the magical and mundane in an overall context of realistic narration.

If the term *magic realism* is relatively new, what it describes has been around since the early development of the novel and short story as modern literary forms. One already sees the key elements of magic realism in *Gulliver's Travels* (1726), which factually narrates the fabulous adventures of an English surgeon. Likewise Nikolai Gogol's short story "The Nose" (1842), in which a minor Czarist bureaucrat's nose takes off to pursue its own career in St. Petersburg, fulfills virtually every requirement of this purportedly contemporary style. One finds similar precedents in Charles Dickens, Honoré de Balzac, Fyodor Dostoyevsky, Guy de Maupassant, Franz Kafka, and others. Seen from a historical perspective, therefore, magic realism is a vital contemporary manifestation of a venerable fictive impulse.

The possibilities of storytelling will always hover between the opposing poles of realism and romance. Until recently most English-language critics almost exclusively favored the realist mode—their emphasis reflected what F. R. Leavis called the "Great Tradition" of the psychological and social realist novel. This tradition encompassed Jane Austen, George Eliot, Henry James, Edith Wharton, Joseph Conrad, Virginia Woolf, D. H. Lawrence, Willa Cather, and early James Joyce. These British and American critics would hardly have imagined that a radically different kind of fiction was being developed beyond their ken in places like Argentina, Colombia, and Peru. By the time García Márquez and his fellow members of *El Boom* in Latin American fiction came to maturity, the reemergence of the fantastic heritage in fiction seemed nearly as revolutionary as the region's politics.

García Márquez and Borges

As a young law student, García Márquez read Kafka's *The Metamorphosis*. It proved a decisive encounter, and the influence is not hard to observe in the early stories, which so often present bizarre incidents unfolding in ordinary circumstances. If Kafka reinvented the animal fable by placing it in the everyday modern world, García Márquez reset it in the unfamiliar landscape of his poverty-stricken homeland. If Kafka made spiritual issues more mysterious by surrounding them with bureaucratic procedure, his Colombian follower changed our perception of Latin America by insisting that in this New World visionary romanticism was merely reportage. García Márquez also had another crucial mentor closer at hand—the Argentine master, Jorge Luis Borges.

Only thirty years García Márquez's senior, Borges had quietly redrawn the imaginative boundaries of Latin American fiction, though his work appeared only sporadically in English translation until the early 1960s. Almost single-handedly he had rehabilitated the fantastic tale for literary fiction. Significantly, Borges expressed his sophisticated fictions in popular rather than experimental forms—the fable, the detective story, the supernatural tale, the gaucho legend. Intellectually and temperamentally, Borges was a true citizen of the world; both bookish and playful by nature, he was widely read in European literature and was influenced by an impressive range of writers, including—among many others—Cervantes, Poe, Kafka, and Robert Louis Stevenson. Possessed of an essentially ironic sensibility, he was also strongly influenced by the late-nineteenth-century Symbolist movement—both of which tendencies can be found in "The Gospel According to Mark." He was the first great postmodernist storyteller, and he found an eager apprentice in García Márquez, who developed these innovative notions in different and usually more expansive forms.

AFTER *EL BOOM*

One of the most frequently raised criticisms of *El Boom* was its heavily male emphasis, in terms of both the authors themselves and the characters in their novels. More recent years have seen the emergence of important female authors, including the Chilean Isabel Allende (her story, "Revenge," can be found in this chapter), a writer in the tradition of magical realism whose novel *The House of the Spirits* (1982) was an international best seller, and the Mexican Inés Arredondo, whose subtle and moving short stories—of which "The Shunammite" (Chapter 13) is a remarkable example—explore the psychology of women and their place in society. In the wake of *El Boom*, Latin American literature is notably richer, deeper, and more diverse than ever before.

Jorge Luis Borges

The Gospel According to Mark   1970

Translated by Andrew Hurley

Jorge Luis Borges (1899–1986), an outstanding modern writer of Latin America, was born in Buenos Aires into a family prominent in Argentine history. His father, with whom he had a very close relationship, was a lawyer and teacher. Borges grew up bilingual, learning English from his English grandmother and receiving his early education from an English tutor. In later years, he would translate work by Poe, Melville, Whitman, Faulkner, and others into Spanish. Caught in Europe by the outbreak of World War I, Borges lived in

Switzerland—where he learned French and taught himself German—and later Spain, where he joined the Ultraists, a group of experimental poets who renounced realism. On returning to Argentina, he edited a poetry magazine printed in the form of a poster and affixed to city walls. In his early writings, Borges favored the style of Criollismo (regionalism), but by the mid-1930s he had begun to take a more cosmopolitan and internationalist approach; in this same period, his principal literary mode began to shift from poetry to fiction. In 1946, for his opposition to the regime of Colonel Juan Perón, Borges was forced to resign his post as a librarian and was mockingly offered a job as a chicken inspector. In 1955, after Perón was deposed, Borges became director of the National Library and professor of English literature at the University of Buenos Aires. A sufferer since childhood from poor eyesight, Borges eventually went blind. His eye problems may have encouraged him to work mainly in short, highly crafted forms: stories, essays, fables, and lyric poems full of elaborate music. His short stories, in Ficciones (1944), El hacedor (1960; translated as Dreamtigers, 1964), and Labyrinths (1962), have been admired worldwide.

The incident took place on the Los Alamos ranch, south of the small town of Junín, in late March of 1928. Its protagonist was a medical student named Baltasar Espinosa. We might define him for the moment as a Buenos Aires youth much like many others, with no traits worthier of note than the gift for public speaking that had won him more than one prize at the English school° in Ramos Mejía and an almost unlimited goodness. He didn't like to argue; he preferred that his interlocutor rather than he himself be right. And though he found the chance twists and turns of gambling interesting, he was a poor gambler, because he didn't like to win. He was intelligent and open to learning, but he was lazy; at thirty-three he had not yet completed the last requirements for his degree. (The work he still owed, incidentally, was for his favorite class.) His father, like all the gentlemen of his day a freethinker,° had instructed Espinosa in the doctrines of Herbert Spencer,° but once, before he set off on a trip to Montevideo, his mother had asked him to say the Lord's Prayer every night and make the sign of the cross, and never in all the years that followed did he break that promise. He did not lack courage; one morning, with more indifference than wrath, he had traded two or three blows with some of his classmates that were trying to force him to join a strike at the university. He abounded in debatable habits and opinions, out of a spirit of acquiescence: his country mattered less to him than the danger that people in other countries might think the Argentines still wore feathers; he venerated France but had contempt for the French; he had little respect for Americans but took pride in the fact that there were skyscrapers in Buenos Aires; he thought that the gauchos° of the plains were better horsemen than the gauchos of the mountains. When his cousin Daniel invited him to spend the summer at Los Alamos, he immediately accepted—not because he liked the country but out of a natural desire to please, and because he could find no good reason for saying no.

The main house at the ranch was large and a bit run-down; the quarters for the foreman, a man named Gutre, stood nearby. There were three members of the Gutre family: the father, the son (who was singularly rough and unpolished), and a girl of uncertain paternity. They were tall, strong, and bony, with reddish hair and Indian features. They rarely spoke. The foreman's wife had died years before.

English school: a prep school that emphasized English (well-to-do Argentines of this era wanted their children to learn English).   freethinker: person who rejects traditional beliefs, especially religious dogma, in favor of rational inquiry.   Herbert Spencer: a British philosopher (1820–1903) who championed the theory of evolution.   gauchos: South American cowboys.

In the country, Espinosa came to learn things he hadn't known, had never even suspected; for example, that when you're approaching a house there's no reason to gallop and that nobody goes out on a horse unless there's a job to be done. As the summer wore on, he learned to distinguish birds by their call.

Within a few days, Daniel had to go to Buenos Aires to close a deal on some livestock. At the most, he said, the trip would take a week. Espinosa, who was already a little tired of his cousin's *bonnes fortunes* and his indefatigable interest in the vagaries of men's tailoring, stayed behind on the ranch with his textbooks. The heat was oppressive, and not even nightfall brought relief. Then one morning toward dawn, he was awakened by thunder. Wind lashed the casuarina trees. Espinosa heard the first drops of rain and gave thanks to God. Suddenly the wind blew cold. That afternoon, the Salado overflowed.

The next morning, as he stood on the porch looking out over the flooded plains, Baltasar Espinosa realized that the metaphor equating the pampas with the sea was not, at least that morning, an altogether false one, though Hudson° had noted that the sea seems the grander of the two because we view it not from horseback or our own height, but from the deck of a ship. The rain did not let up; the Gutres, helped (or hindered) by the city dweller, saved a good part of the livestock, though many animals were drowned. There were four roads leading to the ranch; all were under water. On the third day, when a leaking roof threatened the foreman's house, Espinosa gave the Gutres a room at the back of the main house, alongside the toolshed. The move brought Espinosa and the Gutres closer, and they began to eat together in the large dining room. Conversation was not easy; the Gutres, who knew so much about things in the country, did not know how to explain them. One night Espinosa asked them if people still remembered anything about the Indian raids, back when the military command for the frontier had been in Junín. They told him they did, but they would have given the same answer if he had asked them about the day Charles I° had been beheaded. Espinosa recalled that his father used to say that all the cases of longevity that occur in the country are the result of either poor memory or a vague notion of dates—gauchos quite often know neither the year they were born in nor the name of the man that fathered them.

In the entire house, the only reading material to be found were several copies of a farming magazine, a manual of veterinary medicine, a deluxe edition of the romantic verse drama *Tabaré*, a copy of *The History of the Shorthorn in Argentina*, several erotic and detective stories, and a recent novel that Espinosa had not read—*Don Segundo Sombra*, by Ricardo Güiraldes. In order to put some life into the inevitable after-dinner attempt at conversation, Espinosa read a couple of chapters of the novel to the Gutres, who did not know how to read or write. Unfortunately, the foreman had been a cattle drover himself, and he could not be interested in the adventures of another such a one. It was easy work, he said; they always carried along a pack mule with everything they might need. If he had not been a cattle drover, he announced, he'd never have seen Lake Gómez, or the Bragado River, or even the Núñez ranch, in Chacabuco. . . .

In the kitchen there was a guitar; before the incident I am narrating, the laborers would sit in a circle and someone would pick up the guitar and strum it, though never managing actually to play it. That was called "giving it a strum."

Hudson: W. H. Hudson was an English naturalist and author (1841–1922) who wrote extensively about South America.   *Charles I:* King of England, beheaded in 1649.

Espinosa, who was letting his beard grow out, would stop before the mirror to look at his changed face; he smiled to think that he'd soon be boring the fellows in Buenos Aires with his stories about the Salado overrunning its banks. Curiously, he missed places in the city he never went, and would never go: a street corner on Cabrera where a mailbox stood; two cement lions on a porch on Calle Jujuy a few blocks from the Plaza del Once; a tile-floored corner grocery-store-and-bar (whose location he couldn't quite remember). As for his father and his brothers, by now Daniel would have told them that he had been isolated—the word was etymologically precise—by the floodwaters.

Exploring the house still cut off by the high water, he came upon a Bible printed in English. On its last pages the Guthries (for that was their real name) had kept their family history. They had come originally from Inverness° and had arrived in the New World—doubtlessly as peasant laborers—in the early nineteenth century; they had intermarried with Indians. The chronicle came to an end in the eighteen-seventies; they no longer knew how to write. Within a few generations they had forgotten their English; by the time Espinosa met them, even Spanish gave them some difficulty. They had no faith, though in their veins, alongside the superstitions of the pampas, there still ran a dim current of the Calvinist's harsh fanaticism. Espinosa mentioned his find to them, but they hardly seemed to hear him.

He leafed through the book, and his fingers opened it to the first verses of the   10
Gospel According to St. Mark. To try his hand at translating, and perhaps to see if they might understand a little of it, he decided that that would be the text he read the Gutres after dinner. He was surprised that they listened first attentively and then with mute fascination. The presence of gold letters on the binding may have given it increased authority. "It's in their blood," he thought. It also occurred to him that throughout history, humankind has told two stories: the story of a lost ship sailing the Mediterranean seas in quest of a beloved isle, and the story of a god who allows himself to be crucified on Golgotha. He recalled his elocution classes in Ramos Mejía, and he rose to his feet to preach the parables.

In the following days, the Gutres would wolf down the spitted beef and canned sardines in order to arrive sooner at the Gospel.

The girl had a little lamb; it was her pet, and she prettied it with a sky blue ribbon. One day it cut itself on a piece of barbed wire; to stanch the blood, the Gutres were about to put spiderwebs on the wound, but Espinosa treated it with pills. The gratitude awakened by that cure amazed him. At first, he had not trusted the Gutres and had hidden away in one of his books the two hundred forty pesos he'd brought; now, with Daniel gone, he had taken the master's place and begun to give timid orders, which were immediately followed. The Gutres would trail him through the rooms and along the hallway, as though they were lost. As he read, he noticed that they would sweep away the crumbs he had left on the table. One afternoon, he surprised them as they were discussing him in brief, respectful words. When he came to the end of the Gospel According to St. Mark, he started to read another of the three remaining gospels, but the father asked him to reread the one he'd just finished, so they could understand it better. Espinosa felt they were like children, who prefer repetition to variety or novelty. One night he dreamed of the Flood (which is not surprising) and was awakened by the hammering of the building of the Ark, but he told himself it was thunder. And in fact the rain, which had

Inverness: a county in Scotland.

let up for a while, had begun again; it was very cold. The Gutres told him the rain had broken through the roof of the toolshed; when they got the beams repaired, they said, they'd show him where. He was no longer a stranger, a foreigner, and they all treated him with respect; he was almost spoiled. None of them liked coffee, but there was always a little cup for him, with spoonfuls of sugar stirred in.

That second storm took place on a Tuesday. Thursday night there was a soft knock on his door; because of his doubts about the Gutres he always locked it. He got up and opened the door; it was the girl. In the darkness he couldn't see her, but he could tell by her footsteps that she was barefoot, and afterward, in the bed, that she was naked—that in fact she had come from the back of the house that way. She did not embrace him, or speak a word; she lay down beside him and she was shivering. It was the first time she had lain with a man. When she left, she did not kiss him; Espinosa realized that he didn't even know her name. Impelled by some sentiment he did not attempt to understand, he swore that when he returned to Buenos Aires, he'd tell no one of the incident.

The next day began like all the others, except that the father spoke to Espinosa to ask whether Christ had allowed himself to be killed in order to save all mankind. Espinosa, who was a freethinker like his father but felt obliged to defend what he had read them, paused.

"Yes," he finally replied. "To save all mankind from hell."   15

"What *is* hell?" Gutre then asked him.

"A place underground where souls will burn in fire forever."

"And those that drove the nails will also be saved?"

"Yes," replied Espinosa, whose theology was a bit shaky. (He had worried that the foreman wanted to have a word with him about what had happened last night with his daughter.)

After lunch they asked him to read the last chapters again.   20

Espinosa had a long siesta that afternoon, although it was a light sleep, interrupted by persistent hammering and vague premonitions. Toward evening he got up and went out into the hall.

"The water's going down," he said, as though thinking out loud. "It won't be long now."

"Not long now," repeated Gutre, like an echo.

The three of them had followed him. Kneeling on the floor, they asked his blessing. Then they cursed him, spat on him, and drove him to the back of the house. The girl was weeping. Espinosa realized what awaited him on the other side of the door. When they opened it, he saw the sky. A bird screamed; *it's a goldfinch*, Espinosa thought. There was no roof on the shed; they had torn down the roof beams to build the Cross.

Questions

1. What is about to happen to Baltasar Espinosa at the end of this story?
2. How old is Espinosa? What is ironic about his age?
3. What is the background of the Gutre family? How did they come to own an English Bible? Why is it ironic that they own this book?
4. The narrator claims that the protagonist, Espinosa, has only two noteworthy qualities: an almost unlimited kindness and a capacity for public speaking. How do these qualities become important in the story?
5. When Espinosa begins reading the Gospel of Saint Mark to the Gutres, what changes in their behavior does he notice?

6. What other action does Espinosa perform that earns the Gutres's gratitude?
7. Reread the last paragraph. Why is it ironic that the Gutres ask Espinosa's blessing and the daughter weeps?
8. Why do the Gutres kill Espinosa? What do they hope to gain?
9. Is the significance of Espinosa's death entirely ironic? Or does he resemble Christ in any important respect?

Gabriel García Márquez

The Handsomest Drowned Man in the World   1968

Translated by Gregory Rabassa

Gabriel García Márquez

Gabriel García Márquez (1928–2014), among the most eminent Latin American writers, was born in Aracataca, a Caribbean port in Colombia, one of sixteen children of an impoverished telegraph operator. For a time he studied law in Bogotá; later he then became a newspaper reporter. Although he never joined the Communist Party, García Márquez outspokenly advocated many left-wing proposals for reform. In 1954, despairing of any prospect for political change, he left Colombia to live in Mexico City. Though at nineteen he had already completed a book of short stories, La hojarasca (Leaf Storm), *he waited until 1955 to publish it. Soon he began to build a towering reputation among readers of Spanish. His celebrated novel* Cien años de soledad *(1967), published in English as* One Hundred Years of Solitude *(1969), traces the history of a Colombian family through six generations. Called by Chilean poet Pablo Neruda "the greatest revelation in the Spanish language since Don Quixote," the book has sold more than thirty million copies in thirty-five languages. In 1982 García Márquez was awarded the Nobel Prize in Literature. His fiction, rich in myth and invention, has reminded American readers of the work of William Faulkner, another explorer of his native ground; indeed, García Márquez called Faulkner "my master." His later novels include* Love in the Time of Cholera *(1988),* The General in His Labyrinth *(1990),* Of Love and Other Demons *(1995), and* Memories of My Melancholy Whores *(2005). His* Collected Stories *was published in 1994.* Living to Tell the Tale *(2003), the first volume of an autobiographical trilogy, traces the author's life up to the beginning of his journalistic career, and offers many insights into the sources and techniques of his works of fiction. García Márquez died in Mexico City in 2014. In a note of mourning after the author's death, the president of his native country called him "the greatest Colombian of all time."*

A Tale for Children

The first children who saw the dark and slinky bulge approaching through the sea let themselves think it was an empty ship. Then they saw it had no flags or masts and they thought it was a whale. But when it washed up on the beach, they removed the clumps of seaweed, the jellyfish tentacles, and the remains of fish and flotsam, and only then did they see that it was a drowned man.

They had been playing with him all afternoon, burying him in the sand and digging him up again, when someone chanced to see them and spread the alarm in the village. The men who carried him to the nearest house noticed that he weighed more than any dead man they had ever known, almost as much as a horse, and they said to each other that maybe he'd been floating too long and the water had got into his bones. When they laid him on the floor they said he'd been taller than all the other men because there was barely enough room for him in the house, but they thought that maybe the ability to keep on growing after death was part of the nature of certain drowned men. He had the smell of the sea about him and only his shape gave one to suppose that it was the corpse of a human being, because the skin was covered with a crust of mud and scales.

They did not even have to clean off his face to know that the dead man was a stranger. The village was made up of only twenty-odd wooden houses that had stone courtyards with no flowers and which were spread about on the end of a desertlike cape. There was so little land that mothers always went about with the fear that the wind would carry off their children and the few dead that the years had caused among them had to be thrown off the cliffs. But the sea was calm and bountiful and all the men fit into seven boats. So when they found the drowned man they simply had to look at one another to see that they were all there. That night they did not go out to work at sea. While the men went to find out if anyone was missing in neighboring villages, the women stayed behind to care for the drowned man. They took the mud off with grass swabs, they removed the underwater stones entangled in his hair, and they scraped the crust off with tools used for scaling fish. As they were doing that they noticed that the vegetation on him came from faraway oceans and deep water and that his clothes were in tatters, as if he had sailed through labyrinths of coral. They noticed too that he bore his death with pride, for he did not have the lonely look of other drowned men who came out of the sea or that haggard, needy look of men who drowned in rivers. But only when they finished cleaning him off did they become aware of the kind of man he was and it left them breathless. Not only was he the tallest, strongest, most virile, and best built man they had ever seen, but even though they were looking at him there was no room for him in their imagination.

They could not find a bed in the village large enough to lay him on nor was there a table solid enough to use for his wake. The tallest men's holiday pants would not fit him, nor the fattest ones' Sunday shirts, nor the shoes of the one with the biggest feet. Fascinated by his huge size and his beauty, the women then decided to make him some pants from a large piece of sail and a shirt from some bridal brabant linen so that he could continue through his death with dignity. As they sewed, sitting in a circle and gazing at the corpse between stitches, it seemed to them that the wind had never been so steady nor the sea so restless as on that night and they supposed that the change had something to do with the dead man. They thought that if that magnificent man had lived in the village, his house would have had the widest doors, the highest ceiling, and the strongest floor, his bedstead would have been made from a midship frame held together by iron bolts, and his wife would have been the happiest woman. They thought that he would have had so much authority that he could have drawn fish out of the sea simply by calling their names and that he would have put so much work into his land that springs would have burst forth from among the rocks so that he would have been able to plant flowers on the cliffs. They secretly compared him to their own men, thinking that for all their lives theirs were incapable of doing what he could do in one night, and they ended up dismissing them deep in their hearts as the weakest, meanest, and most useless creatures on earth. They were wandering through the maze of fantasy when the oldest woman, who as the oldest had looked upon the drowned man with more compassion than passion, sighed:

"He has the face of someone called Esteban."

It was true. Most of them had only to take another look at him to see that he could not have any other name. The more stubborn among them, who were the youngest, still lived for a few hours with the illusion that when they put his clothes on and he lay among the flowers in patent leather shoes his name might be Lautaro. But it was a vain illusion. There had not been enough canvas, the poorly cut and worse sewn pants were too tight, and the hidden strength of his heart popped the buttons on his shirt. After midnight the whistling of the wind died down and the sea fell into its Wednesday drowsiness. The silence put an end to any last doubts: he was Esteban. The women who had dressed him, who had combed his hair, had cut his nails and shaved him were unable to hold back a shudder of pity when they had to resign themselves to his being dragged along the ground. It was then that they understood how unhappy he must have been with that huge body since it bothered him even after death. They could see him in life, condemned to going through doors sideways, cracking his head on crossbeams, remaining on his feet during visits, not knowing what to do with his soft, pink, sea lion hands while the lady of the house looked for her most resistant chair and begged him, frightened to death, sit here, Esteban, please, and he, leaning against the wall, smiling, don't bother, ma'am, I'm fine where I am, his heels raw and his back roasted from having done the same thing so many times whenever he paid a visit, don't bother, ma'am, I'm fine where I am, just to avoid the embarrassment of breaking up the chair, and never knowing perhaps that the ones who said don't go, Esteban, at least wait till the coffee's ready, were the ones who later on would whisper the big boob finally left, how nice, the handsome fool has gone. That was what the women were thinking beside the body a little before dawn. Later, when they covered his face with a handkerchief so that the light would not bother him, he looked so forever dead, so defenseless, so much like their men that the first furrows of tears opened in their hearts. It was one of the younger ones who began the weeping. The others, coming to, went from sighs to wails, and the more they sobbed the more they felt like weeping, because the drowned man was becoming all the more Esteban for them, and so they wept so much, for he was the most destitute, most peaceful, and most obliging man on earth, poor Esteban. So when the men returned with the news that the drowned man was not from the neighboring villages either, the women felt an opening of jubilation in the midst of their tears.

"Praise the Lord," they sighed, "he's ours!"

The men thought the fuss was only womanish frivolity. Fatigued because of the difficult nighttime inquiries, all they wanted was to get rid of the bother of the newcomer once and for all before the sun grew strong on that arid, windless day. They improvised a litter with the remains of foremasts and gaffs, tying it together with rigging so that it would bear the weight of the body until they reached the cliffs. They wanted to tie the anchor from a cargo ship to him so that he would sink easily into the deepest waves, where fish are blind and divers die of nostalgia, and bad currents would not bring him back to shore, as had happened with other bodies. But the more they hurried, the more the women thought of ways to waste time. They walked about like startled hens, pecking with the sea charms on their breasts, some interfering on one side to put a scapular of the good wind on the drowned man, some on the other side to put a wrist compass on him, and after a great deal of *get away from there, woman, stay out of the way, look, you almost made me fall on top of the dead man*, the men began to feel mistrust in their livers and started grumbling about why so many main-altar decorations for a stranger, because no matter how many nails and holy-water jars he had on him, the sharks would chew him all the same, but the women kept piling on their junk relics, running back and forth, stumbling, while they released in sighs what they did not in tears, so that the men finally exploded with *since when has there ever been such a fuss over a drifting corpse, a drowned nobody, a piece of cold Wednesday meat*. One of the women, mortified by so much lack of care, then removed the handkerchief from the dead man's face and the men were left breathless too.

He was Esteban. It was not necessary to repeat it for them to recognize him. If they had been told Sir Walter Raleigh,° even they might have been impressed with his gringo accent, the macaw on his shoulder, his cannibal-killing blunderbuss, but there could be only one Esteban in the world and there he was, stretched out like a sperm whale, shoeless, wearing the pants of an undersized child, and with those stony nails that had to be cut with a knife. They only had to take the handkerchief off his face to see that he was ashamed, that it was not his fault that he was so big or so heavy or so handsome, and if he had known that this was going to happen, he would have looked for a more discreet place to drown in, seriously, I even would have tied the anchor off a galleon around my neck and staggered off a cliff like someone who doesn't like things in order not to be upsetting people now with this Wednesday dead body, as you people say, in order not to be bothering anyone with this filthy piece of cold meat that doesn't have anything to do with me. There was so much truth in his manner that even the most mistrustful men, the ones who felt the bitterness of endless nights at sea fearing that their women would tire of dreaming about them and begin to dream of drowned men, even they and others who were harder still shuddered in the marrow of their bones at Esteban's sincerity.

That was how they came to hold the most splendid funeral they could conceive   10
of for an abandoned drowned man. Some women who had gone to get flowers in the neighboring villages returned with other women who could not believe what they had been told, and those women went back for more flowers when they saw the dead man, and they brought more and more until there were so many flowers and so many people that it was hard to walk about. At the final moment it pained them to return him to the waters as an orphan and they chose a father and mother from among the best people, and aunts and uncles and cousins, so that through him all the inhabitants of the village became kinsmen. Some sailors who heard weeping from a distance went off course and people heard of one who had himself tied to the mainmast, remembering ancient fables about sirens. While they fought for the privilege of carrying him on their shoulders along the steep escarpment by the cliffs, men and women became aware for the first time of the desolation of their streets, the dryness of their courtyards, the narrowness of their dreams as they faced the splendor and beauty of their drowned man. They let him go without an anchor so that he could come back if he wished and whenever he wished, and they all held their breath for the fraction of centuries the body took to fall into the abyss. They did not need to look at one another to realize that they were no longer all present, that they would never be. But they also knew that everything would be different from then on, that their houses would have wider doors, higher ceilings, and stronger floors so that Esteban's memory could

Sir Walter Raleigh: Elizabethan explorer and statesman (1552–1618).

go everywhere without bumping into beams and so that no one in the future would dare whisper the big boob finally died, too bad, the handsome fool has finally died, because they were going to paint their house fronts gay colors to make Esteban's memory eternal and they were going to break their backs digging for springs among the stones and planting flowers on the cliffs so that in future years at dawn the passengers on great liners would awaken, suffocated by the smell of gardens on the high seas, and the captain would have to come down from the bridge in his dress uniform, with his astrolabe, his pole star, and his row of war medals and, pointing to the promontory of roses on the horizon, he would say in fourteen languages, look there, where the wind is so peaceful now that it's gone to sleep beneath the beds, over there, where the sun's so bright that the sunflowers don't know which way to turn, yes, that's Esteban's village.

Questions

1. What is unusual about the drowned man? Why is it important that the man is a complete stranger?
2. What was life like in the village before the man washed ashore? Cite examples from the text.
3. What is symbolic about the drowned man's great size and the villagers' difficulty in accommodating him?
4. How does the drowned man's beauty affect the women? How are their feelings about the village and their men revealed, or transformed, by the stranger's arrival?
5. How do the men react to Esteban in paragraph 8? How does their reaction change when the handkerchief is pulled away and they see his face?
6. By the end, how has the drowned man altered the village and its inhabitants? Does the story make a statement about the power of myth?

Isabel Allende

Revenge   1989

Translated by Margaret Sayers Peden

Isabel Allende was born in 1942 in Lima, Peru; her father, Tomás, was a Chilean diplomat and cousin of Salvador Allende, who would be elected president of Chile in 1970. When Isabel was only three years old, her parents' marriage ended, and she and her two siblings returned to Chile with their mother to live with their grandfather. In 1953 her mother married another Chilean diplomat, and the family spent the next five years in Bolivia and Beirut, Lebanon. After completing her high school education in Chile, Isabel worked for a United Nations organization in Santiago and later as a magazine and television journalist. She and her family left Chile in 1975 because of the political situation following the coup that overthrew the Allende government in 1973. They spent the next thirteen years in Venezuela, where she continued to work as a journalist and writer.

Isabel Allende

In 1981, upon learning that her ninety-nine-year-old grandfather was dying, Allende begin to write him a letter, which evolved into her first novel, The House of the Spirits *(1982), which became an international best seller. Her later novels include* Eva Luna *(1988),* Daughter of Fortune *(1999),* Maya's Notebook *(2013),* The Japanese Lover *(2015), and* In the Midst of Winter *(2017). She has also published* The Stories of Eva Luna *(1991), a collection of short fiction that includes "Revenge";* Paula *(1995), an autobiography and family history begun during her daughter's ultimately fatal illness;* Aphrodite: A Memoir of the Senses *(1997), a paean to pleasure in all its manifestations; and* Island Beneath the Sea *(2010), a historical novel about a mulatto girl who is sold as a slave in eighteenth-century Santo Domingo. Her novels, written in a lyrical style and blending fantasy and legend with family and social history, have made her one of the most prominent practitioners of magical realism. Her books have been translated into more than twenty languages and have sold millions of copies worldwide. In 2010 Allende was awarded Chile's National Literature Prize. Barack Obama awarded her the Presidential Medal of Freedom in 2014. She lives with her husband in Marin County, California.*

On the radiant day that Dulce Rosa Orellano was crowned with the jasmine of the Queen of Carnival, the mothers of the other candidates had grumbled that the competition was rigged, that the title had been given to her only because she was the daughter of Senator Anselmo Orellano, the most powerful man in all the province. They admitted that the girl had charm and that she could play the piano and dance like no one else, but other girls who had sought the same prize were much more beautiful. They watched her standing there on the dais in her organza dress and flower crown, waving to the crowd, and cursed her under their breath. That was why some were not at all unhappy when several months later misfortune fell upon the house of the Orellanos, sowing so much death and calamity that it took twenty-five years to reap it.

On the night of the queen's election, there was a dance at Santa Teresa's Mayoral Hall, and young men flocked from miles around to meet Dulce Rosa. She was so happy, and danced so gracefully, that many of them did not perceive that in truth she was not the most beautiful, and when they returned home they told everyone they had never seen a face like hers. And so she had won undeserved fame as a beauty, and no later assertion would ever disprove it. Exaggerated descriptions of her translucent skin and crystal-clear eyes circulated from mouth to mouth, and every teller added some bit from his own fancy. Poets in remote towns composed sonnets to a hypothetical maiden by the name of Dulce Rosa.

The rumor of the beauty flowering in the home of Senator Orellano eventually reached the ears of Tadeo Céspedes, who never dreamed he would meet her, because at no time in his life had he had time to learn verses or look at women. His sole preoccupation was the civil war. From the time he had first shaved his mustache, he had carried a weapon in his hand, and for years now he had lived amid the roar of gunpowder. He had forgotten his mother's kisses, even the music of the mass. He did not always have cause to fight, because during brief periods of truce there were no adversaries within reach of his troops; even in those times of forced peace, however, he lived the life of a corsair. He was a man habituated to violence. He crisscrossed the country fighting visible enemies, when there were such, and shadows, when he had to invent them, and he would have continued forever had his party not won the presidential election. Overnight he passed from hiding out to prominence, and lost all pretexts for shooting up the countryside.

Tadeo Céspedes's last mission was a punitive raid against Santa Teresa. With a hundred and twenty men he rode into town by night to make an example of the town and to wipe out the leaders of enemy factions. His troops shot out the windows of public buildings; they battered down the church door and rode right up to the high altar, in the process running down Padre Clemente, who stood in their way, then clattered on toward Senator Orellano's villa rising proudly on the crown of the hill.

After unleashing the dogs and locking his daughter in the farthest room of the   5 farthest patio, the Senator, backed by a dozen loyal servants, prepared to make his stand against Tadeo Céspedes. In that moment, as at so many other times of his life, he lamented not having male descendants who could take up weapons with him and defend the honor of his house. He felt very old, but he had no time to dwell on such thoughts, because on the slopes of the hill he saw the awesome glimmer of a hundred and twenty torches spreading fear in the night. In silence he handed out the last store of ammunition. Everything had been said, and each man knew that before the dawn he must die like a man at his post.

"The last person will take the key to the room where my daughter is hidden and do what must be done," the Senator said at the sound of the first shots.

All those men had been with him when Dulce Rosa was born; they had held her on their knees when she could barely walk; they had told her ghost stories on winter afternoons, listened to her practice the piano, and wildly applauded on the day of her coronation as Queen of Carnival. Her father could die in peace, because the girl would never be taken alive by Tadeo Céspedes. The only possibility Senator Orellano had not considered was that despite his fierceness in the fighting he would be the last to die. He watched his friends fall one after another and recognized when it was futile to continue to resist. He had a bullet in his belly and his sight was clouding over; he could barely make out the shadows climbing the high walls of his property, but he was conscious enough to drag himself to the third patio. The dogs recognized his scent through layers of sweat, blood, and sorrow and opened a path to let him pass. He put the key in the lock, pushed open the heavy door, and through the mist blurring his eyes saw Dulce Rosa waiting for him. She was wearing the organza dress she had worn at Carnival, and the flowers of her crown adorned her hair.

"It's time, daughter, " the Senator said, cocking his pistol as a pool of blood formed about his feet.

"Don't kill me, Father," Dulce Rosa replied in a firm voice. "Let me live to avenge you, and myself."

Senator Anselmo Orellano studied the face of his fifteen-year-old daughter and   10 imagined what Tadeo Céspedes would do to her, but there was unflinching fortitude in Dulce Rosa's clear eyes, and he knew she would survive and punish his executioner. The girl sat back down on the bed, and he sat beside her, gun pointed toward the door.

With the last howls of the dying dogs, the wooden bar yielded, the bolt flew off the door, and the first men burst in to the room. The Senator managed to fire off six shots before he lost consciousness. Tadeo Céspedes thought he must be dreaming when he saw the angel in a jasmine crown holding a dying old man in her arms while her white dress slowly turned red, but he could not summon enough pity for a second glance: he was drunk with violence and bone weary from hours of fighting. "The woman is mine," he said, before his men set hands on her.

Friday dawned to a leaden sky stained by the glare of fire. Silence lay heavy on the hilltop. The last moans had faded when Dulce Rosa struggled to her feet and walked to the garden fountain; the day before it had been surrounded by magnolia blossoms, but now it was a bubbling pool in the midst of rubble. Her dress hung in shreds; she removed it slowly and stood naked. She sank into the cold water. The sun appeared through the birch trees and Dulce Rosa watched the water turn pink as she washed away the blood from between her legs and that of her father, crusted in her long hair. Once she was clean and calm and had dried her tears, she returned to the ruined house, looked for something to cover her nakedness, pulled a linen sheet from the clothespress, and went outside to look for her father's remains. The marauders had tied him by the feet and then galloped up and down the hill, dragging his body until it was nothing but pitiable, battered flesh, but guided by love his daughter unerringly recognized him. She wrapped his remains in the sheet and sat beside him to watch the day brighten. That was how her neighbors from Santa Teresa had found her when they dared climb the hill to the Orellanos' villa. They helped Dulce Rosa bury the dead and extinguished the last coals of the fires; then they begged her to go live with her godmother in another town where no one would know her story. When she refused, the townspeople formed crews to rebuild the house and gave her six fierce dogs to defend herself.

From the instant they had borne away her still-living father and Tadeo Céspedes closed the door and unbuckled his leather belt, Dulce Rosa had lived for revenge. That memory caused her sleepless nights and consumed her days, but it never completely stilled her laughter or diminished her good nature. Her reputation as a beauty continued to grow; musicians wandered the byways giving her magnified charms, until they had made of her a living legend. She rose every morning at four to oversee the work in the fields and the household; to ride over her property; to buy and sell, haggling like a Syrian; to breed stock and cultivate magnolias and jasmine in her gardens. When dusk fell, she would remove her riding trousers, boots, and pistol, and dress in exquisite gowns shipped from the capital in trunks perfumed with aromatic herbs. As night fell, her visitors would arrive to find her playing the piano, while servants prepared trays of pastries and glasses of cool drinks. At first, people wondered why she was not in the sanatorium in a straitjacket, or a novice with the Carmelite nuns, but as there were frequent parties in the Orellano villa, with time people stopped talking about the tragedy and erased the murdered Senator from their memories. A few gentlemen of good name and sizeable fortune were able to overlook the stigma of rape and, drawn by Dulce Rosa's sensitivity and reputation as a beauty, propose marriage. She rejected them all, because her one mission in this world was revenge.

Neither could Tadeo Céspedes rid himself of the memory of that fatal night. The sweeping tide of the slaughter and the excitement of the rape evaporated as he was riding back to the capital to make his report of the havoc he had wrought on his foray. He thought of the girl in the ball gown and crown of sweet jasmine who had suffered him in silence in that dark room suffused with the smell of gunpowder. He saw her again, as he had left her, sprawled on the floor, half-naked in her bloodied rags, sunk in the compassionate sleep of unconsciousness; that was how he was to see her for the rest of his life at the moment of falling asleep. Peace, governing, and power turned Céspedes into a composed and hard-working man. With the passing of time, memories of the civil war faded, and people began to address him as *don* Tadeo. He bought a hacienda on the far side of the mountains, dedicated himself to administering justice, and was elected mayor. If it had not been for the tireless ghost of Dulce Rosa Orellano, he might have achieved a measure of happiness, but all the women he met along his path, all the women he took in his arms in search of consolation, all the loves he pursued through the years—all had the face of the Queen of Carnival. To add to his torment, from time to time he heard her name in the verses of wandering poets, making it impossible to eradicate her from his heart. The image of the young girl grew within him, filled him completely, until the day came when he could bear no more. He was sitting at the head of a long banquet table, celebrating his fifty-seventh birthday, surrounded by friends and colleagues, when he thought he saw a naked girl lying on the tablecloth among the jasmine blossoms, and he realized that this nightmare would not leave him in peace, not even after death. He pounded the table with a fist that made the china tremble, and asked for his hat and his cane.

"Where are you going, _don_ Tadeo?" his Chief Administrator asked.   15

"To atone for an old injury," he replied, and left without bidding anyone goodbye.

He did not have to go in search of Dulce Rosa, because he had always known he would find her in the house of her misfortune, and it was there he drove. By then, good highways had been built across the country, and distances seemed much shorter. The landscape had changed in twenty-five years, but as he turned the last comer of the hill, the Orellano villa appeared, just as he remembered seeing it before his band stormed the hill. There stood the solid walls of river rock he had destroyed with charges of dynamite; there were the dark wood beams he had set fire to; there the trees from which he had strung the bodies of the Senator's men; there the patio where he had massacred the dogs. He stopped his car a hundred meters from the door; he could go no farther, he felt as if his heart was exploding in his chest. He was about to turn and drive back where he had come from, when from among the rosebushes emerged a figure enveloped in a swirl of skirts. He shivered, hoping with all his might that she would not recognize him. In the soft light of evening he watched Dulce Rosa Orellano float toward him along the garden path. He saw her hair, her bright face, the harmony of her movements, the fluttering dress, and he felt as if he were suspended in a dream he had been dreaming for twenty-five years.

"You've come at last, Tadeo Céspedes," she said when she saw him. She was not deceived by the black mayor's suit or the gray hair of a gentleman; his corsair's hands were unchanged.

"You have pursued me relentlessly. I have never been able to love anyone but you," he whispered in a voice hoarse with shame.

Dulce Rosa Orellano breathed a sigh of satisfaction. She had called him in her   20 mind night and day all those years, and finally he had come. It was her hour. But she looked into his eyes and could not find any trace of the executioner, only welling tears. She searched deep in her own heart for the hatred she had nurtured and could not find it. She evoked the moment when she had asked her father to sacrifice her and let her live to collect a debt; she relived the rough embrace of the man she had so often cursed and the early morning when she had wrapped her father's pitiful remains in a linen sheet. She reviewed the perfect plan of her revenge, but she did not find the expected happiness. To the contrary, she felt profoundly sad. Tadeo Céspedes took her hand and softly kissed her palm, wetting it with his tears. She realized then, to her horror, that from having thought of him so long, from having savored his punishment before the fact, her emotions had made a complete circle and she had come to love him.

In the days that followed, both lifted the floodgates on the love they had never released, and for the first time in their unhappy fates allowed another being close to them. They strolled through the gardens, talking about themselves, not avoiding the fatal night that had twisted the course of their lives. At dusk Dulce Rosa would play the piano as Tadeo Céspedes smoked, and as he listened he felt his bones grow weak and happiness enfold him like a blanket, erasing all his old nightmares. After dinner he would drive back to Santa Teresa, where no one remembered any longer the old horror story. He took rooms in the best hotel and there made plans for their wedding. He wanted a celebration with all possible fanfare, extravagance, and enthusiasm, a fiesta in which the whole town would participate. He had discovered love at an age when other men lose hope, and that discovery had restored the vigor of his youth. He wanted to surround Dulce Rosa with love and beauty, to lavish on her all the pleasures money could buy, to see whether in her later years he could compensate for the harm he had done her as a young girl. Occasionally he would be overcome by panic. He would search her face for signs of rancor, but found only the light of shared love and was reassured. A happy month went by in this way.

Two days before the wedding, when the tables for the wedding party were being set up in the garden, the fowls and hogs were being slaughtered for the feast, and the flowers being cut to decorate the house, Dulce Rosa Orellano tried on her wedding dress. She gazed at herself in the mirror, so like the day of her coronation as Queen of Carnival that she could not go on deceiving her own heart. She knew she would never be able to carry out the revenge she had planned, because she was in love with the assassin, but neither could she silence the Senator's ghost. She dismissed the seamstress, picked up the scissors, and walked to the room in the third patio that had been empty so many years.

Tadeo Céspedes looked for her everywhere, calling her frantically. The barking of the dogs led him to the far end of the house. With the help of the gardeners he kicked down the bolted door and rushed into the room, where once he had seen an angel crowned with jasmine blossoms. He found Dulce Rosa just as she was in his dreams every night of his life, in the same bloody organza dress, and he knew he would live to be ninety and pay for his guilt with the memory of the only woman who had ever touched his heart.

Questions

1. What are the circumstances that lead Tadeo Céspedes and his band of men to attack the Orellano house?

2. Allende points out that, at the Carnival, Dulce Rosa "had won undeserved fame as a beauty." Why didn't Allende simply make Dulce Rosa a beauty to match the legend that was built up by poets and songwriters over the decades? Why make her imperfect?

3. In what ways has Allende evoked a fairytale-like tone in "Revenge," and what is the effect of that tone on your experience of reading the story?

4. Three times during "Revenge"—at the opening Carnival, on the night of her rape, and just before her wedding to *don* Tadeo—Dulce Rosa is wearing a white organza dress. What is the significance of the dress and crown of jasmine?

5. How does the character of Tadeo Céspedes change from when he is a young man to when he is old? Did your feelings about him evolve?

Juan Rulfo

Tell Them Not to Kill Me!   1953

Translated by Ilan Stavans

Juan Rulfo

Born in the rural Mexican state of Jalisco, Juan Rulfo (1917–1986) experienced war firsthand. From 1926 to 1929, western Mexico underwent a backlash to the Mexican Revolution, known as the Cristero Rebellion. During the violence, Rulfo's father was assassinated and his mother died of a heart attack. Rulfo's uncles also perished in the Rebellion, and the boy was sent to live with his grandmother and later to various boarding schools. When he came of age, Rulfo aspired to attend the University of Guadalajara, but the college was closed due to strikes, so he moved to Mexico City, attended literary lectures, traveled widely, and began to write. Rulfo produced only two books during his lifetime, yet he is remembered as one of the most influential mid-century Latin American authors. El Llano en Llamas (1953; translated as The Burning Plain, *1967) is a collection of short stories that centers on the violence of the Mexican countryside. His ambitious, slim novel,* Pedro Páramo *(1955), was massively influential for emerging authors of magic realism. Jorge Luis Borges considered* Pedro Páramo, *which portrays a town populated by ghosts, one of the greatest works of literature in any language. Rulfo won the National Literature Prize in 1970 and the Príncipe de Asturias Prize for literature in 1983. For more than two decades he served as an editor for the National Indigenous Institute in Mexico City. He died of lung cancer at age sixty-eight.*

"Tell them not to kill me, Justino! Go on, go and tell them that. For pity's sake. Just tell them that. Tell them to not do it out of pity."

"I can't. There's a *sargento* over there who doesn't want to hear anything about you."

"Make him listen. Find a way and tell him I've been frightened enough. Tell him for God's sake."

"It doesn't have anything to do with being frightened. It looks like they're really going to kill you. And I don't want to go back there."

"Go one more time. Just one more time, to see what you can do."   5

"No. I don't feel like going. If I do that, they'll know I'm your son. And, if I go to them that much, in the end they'll know who I am and they'll end up shooting me as well. Better to leave things as they are."

"Come on, Justino. Tell them to have a little pity on me. Just tell them that."

Justino clenched his teeth and shook his head saying:

"No."

For a long time he continued shaking his head.   10

"Tell the *sargento* to let you see the *coronel*. And tell him how old I am. How I'm not worth very much. What will he gain by killing me? Nothing. After all, he must have a soul. Tell him to do it for the salvation of his blessed soul."

Justino got up from the pile of rocks on which he was sitting and walked toward the corral gate. Then he turned around and said:

"Okay, I'll go. But if they shoot me, too, who'll take care of my wife and children?"

"Providence, Justino. Providence will take care of them. Just take a minute and go over there and see what you can do for me. That's what it'll take."

They had brought him at daybreak. And now the morning was well along and he was still there, tied to a post, waiting. He couldn't sit still. He had tried to sleep for a while so he would calm down, but sleep had escaped him. His hunger had fled, as well. He didn't feel like doing anything. Just staying alive. Now that he knew for sure he was going to be killed, he had been overwhelmed by such an intense desire to live, as only a man who had recently been resuscitated can be.

Who would have thought that that old business would come back to haunt him, so rancid, so deeply buried, he had always thought. That business of when he had to kill Don Lupe. No, not just like that, as those from Alima wanted him to admit, but because he had his own reasons. He remembered:

Don Lupe Terreros, owner of Puerta de Piedra, and his compadre to boot. Whom he, Juvencio Nava, had to kill for one reason; for being the owner of Puerta de Piedra and who, in spite of being his compadre, had refused pasture to his animals.

At first, he did nothing out of duty. But then, when the drought came along, when he saw how one after another of his animals died of hunger and his compadre Don Lupe still refused to let them have the grass in his fields, that's when he broke the fence and drove his herd of skinny animals to the pasture so they could eat their fill. And Don Lupe hadn't liked that, and he ordered the fence mended so he, Juvencio Nava, had to break open a hole again. In that way, by day the hole was mended and by night it was opened again, while the stock stayed there, always near the fence, always waiting; that stock of his that before had only smelled the grass without being able to taste it.

And he and Don Lupe argued and argued without ever reaching an agreement.

Until one time Don Lupe said to him:

"Look, Juvencio, if you put one more of your animals in my pasture again, I'll kill it."

And he answered:

"Look, Don Lupe, it's not my fault that the animals fend for themselves. They're innocent. You kill them and we'll see what happens."

"And he killed one of my yearlings.

"This happened thirty-five years ago, around March, because in April I was already in the mountains, fleeing the warrant. The ten cows I gave the judge did me no good, nor did the bond I paid on my house to get out of jail. And they still paid themselves out of what was left so they wouldn't keep after me, but they kept after me all the same. That's why I came to live with my son on this other little piece of land I had named Palo de Venado. And my son grew up and married my daughter-in-law Ignacia and has already had eight children. In other words, that business is already old and should have been forgotten by now. But it's clear it hasn't been.

"I figured that with about a hundred pesos everything would be fine. The late Don Lupe left only a wife and two little boys, who were still on all fours. And the widow died, too, of grief, apparently, soon after. And the boys were taken away to live with relatives. So there was nothing to fear from them.

"But other people considered that I was still under warrant and awaiting trial so they could keep on stealing from me. Any time someone came to the town, I was told:

"'Some strangers are in town, Juvencio.'

"And I would head for the hills, hiding among the madrone thickets and eating only wild grasses all day long. Sometimes, in the middle of the night, I would have to come out, as if dogs were after me. I spent my entire life that way. It wasn't a year or two. It was my whole life."

And now they had come for him, when he was no longer expecting anyone, 30 confident that people had forgotten him, believing that he would at least spend his remaining days in tranquility. "At least that," he thought, "I'll end up with that because I'm old. They'll leave me in peace."

He had given himself over fully to that hope. That's why it was hard for him to imagine he would die that way, suddenly, at this stage of his life, after fighting so hard to liberate himself from death; after spending his best years running from pillar to post, dragged along by fear and when his body had ended up as a dried-out carcass, leathery from the bad days in which he needed to hide from everyone.

Hadn't he even gone so far that his wife left him, as well? That day when he woke up to the news she had left him it didn't even enter his head to go out looking for her. He let her go without even trying to find out anything, whom she had left with or where, as long as he didn't have to go down to the village. He let her go the way he had let everything else go, without bothering to put up a fight. The only thing left was to take care of his life, which he would protect no matter what. He couldn't let them kill him. He couldn't. Even less so now.

But that's why they had brought him from over yonder, from Palo de Venado. They didn't even need to tie him up for him to follow them. He walked on his own, handcuffed solely by fear. They realized he couldn't run with that old body, with those skinny legs like dried-out ropes, cramped up by the fear of dying. That's why he went along. To die. That's what they told him.

That's when he knew. He started to feel an itch in his stomach, which would come to him suddenly whenever he would see death nearby, bringing out the fear in his eyes and making his mouth swell up with that sour water he hadn't wanted to swallow. And that thing that made his feet heavy while his head turned soft and his heart pounded with all its might against his ribs. No, he couldn't get used to the idea that they were going to kill him.

There had to be some sort of hope. Someplace there had to be some sort of hope. 35 Maybe they had made a mistake. Maybe they were looking for a different Juvencio Nava and not this Juvencio Nava.

He walked with the men in silence, his arms at his sides. The predawn was dark, without stars. The wind blew slowly, carrying dried earth with it and bringing something else, full of that odor, like urine, that road dust has.

As his eyes, squinty with the years, went along, they stared at the ground here, under his feet, despite the darkness. His entire life was there in that earth. Sixty years of living on it, of grasping it tightly in his hands, of having tested it the way one tests the flavor of meat. For a long time he had been crumbling it with his eyes, savoring each piece as if it were his last, almost knowing it would be his last.

Then, as if trying to say something, he would look at the men next to him. He was going to tell them to set him free, to let him go: "I haven't hurt anyone, muchachos," he was about to say to them, but he said nothing. "I'll tell them a bit later," he thought. He would only look at them. He could almost imagine they were his friends; but he didn't want to do that. They weren't. He didn't know who they were. He would watch them leaning to the side and bending down from time to time to see where the road was leading.

He had seen them for the first time in the gray of the evening, in that dusky hour when everything looks scorched. They had crossed the furrows stepping on tender young corn. That's why he had come down: to tell them the corn was just beginning to grow there. But they didn't stop.

He had seen them in time. He had always been lucky to see everything in time. He could have hidden, walking a few hours in the hills until they left and he could go back down. After all, there was no way the corn crop would come to anything anyway. It was already past the time for rain, but no rain had come and the corn was beginning to wither. Soon it would all be dry.

So it wasn't even worth having come down; having put himself among those men as if in a hole, never to get out again.

And now he was right next to them, suppressing the desire to tell them to let him go. He couldn't see their faces; he could only see shapes closing in and then moving away from him. So when he actually began to talk, he didn't know if they had heard him. He said:

"I've never hurt anybody," is what he said. But nothing changed. Not one of the shapes appeared to pay attention. The faces didn't turn around to look at him. They remained the same, as if they were asleep.

Then he thought he had nothing more to say, that he needed to seek hope somewhere else. He again dropped his arms and went by the first houses in the village in the middle of those four men obscured by the black color of night.

"*Mi coronel,* here's the man."

They had stopped before the opening of the doorway. With his hat in his hand out of respect, he waited for someone to come out. But only the voice came out:

"What man?" it asked.

"The one from Pablo de Venado, *mi coronel.* The one you ordered us to bring in."

"Ask him if he has ever lived in Alima," the voice inside said.

"Hey, you! Have you ever lived in Alima?" repeated the *sargento* in front of him.

"Yes. Tell the *coronel* that's exactly where I'm from. And I've lived there until recently."

"Ask him if he knew one Guadalupe Terreros."

"He wants to know if you knew one Guadalupe Terreros."

"Don Lupe? Yes. Tell him I knew him. He's dead."

Then the tone of the inside voice changed:

"I know he's dead," it said. And it continued talking as if it were talking with someone there, on the other side of the reed wall.

"Guadalupe Terreros was my father. When I grew up and went out looking for him, people told me he was dead. It's a bit difficult growing up knowing that the thing you can grab on to to make roots for yourself is dead. That's what happened to us.

"Then I found out he had been killed with a machete and with a cattle prod stuck in his stomach. They told me that he spent more than two days alone and that when they found him, lying in an arroyo, he was still in agony, asking people to take care of his family.

"With time, one apparently forgets all that. One tries to forget. What one can't forget is finding out that the person who did it is still alive, feeding his rotten soul

40

45

50

55

with the illusion of eternal life. I couldn't forgive that man, though I don't know him; but the fact that he has placed himself where I know he is makes me want to finish him off. I can't forgive him his still being alive. He shouldn't have been born in the first place."

From here, from the outside, you could hear what he said clearly. Then he ordered:

"Take him away and tie him up for a while, so that he suffers, and then shoot him!"

"Look at me, *coronel*," he asked. "I'm not worth anything. It won't take long for me to die all by myself, crippled by old age. Don't kill me . . . !"

"Take him away!" the voice inside said again.

" . . . I've already paid for this, *coronel*. I've paid for it many times over. Everything was taken away from me. They punished me in many different ways. I've spent over forty years hiding like a leper, with the constant fear that I'd be killed at any moment. I don't deserve to die like this, *coronel*. Let me be, at least, so that God may forgive me. Don't kill me! Tell them not to kill me!"

There he was, as if they had been beating him, slapping his hat against the earth. Screaming.

The voice inside said immediately:

"Tie him up and give him something to drink until he gets so drunk that the shots won't hurt."

Now, finally, he was calm. He was curled up at the foot of the post. His son Justino had come and his son Justino had gone and had come back and now he was back again.

He slung him on top of the donkey. He cinched him up tight against the rigging so he wouldn't fall on the way. He put a sack over his head so he wouldn't give a bad impression. And then he prodded the donkey and they hurriedly left, in order to reach Palo de Venado still with time to arrange a wake for the dead man.

"Your daughter-in-law and grandkids will miss you," he was telling him. "They'll see your face and think it's not you. They'll think coyotes gnawed on you when they see you with that face full of holes, so many more gunshots than they needed."

Questions

1. From what point of view is the story told? Do you feel pity for Juvencio Nava?
2. Describe the setting of the story. What details about the Mexican countryside and its system of justice give you a clearer understanding of this time and place?
3. When you learn that Don Lupe "had been killed with a machete and with a cattle prod stuck in his stomach," how does that change your feelings about Juvencio?
4. The final section begins this way: "Now, finally, he was calm." While that short statement does not reveal that Juvencio is dead, what other information is packed in those simple five words?
5. Why might Rulfo have ended the story by reminding us that the old man has left behind children and grandchildren?

■ WRITING *effectively*

Jorge Luis Borges on Writing

On Storytelling   1976

Interviewer: I find it curious that all the writers you seem to admire the most, Borges, are writers who have what I would call very strong narrative gifts, the gift of telling a story—and I rather suspect from listening to you talk about your own stories, that this is what you are primarily interested in—and yet I think that your reputation and your appeal is more intellectual than it is narrative, more symbolic than narrative.

Jorge Luis Borges: I wish I had the gift of storytelling. I wish I was Scheherazade. But I'm not. But still I must do the best I can. There's nothing wrong about storytelling. The literature we have of storytelling—the epic, a good story—

Jorge Luis Borges

why should we be ashamed of that? Especially in my country, where people seem especially fond of words, of coining words, of weaving and interweaving them. I am interested in the story, in the fact of wanting to know what will happen next. I think plots are important; besides plots are also symbols; the plot is a way of conveying something. But perhaps I am more interested in the plot than in what is conveyed by it. I think I'm keenly aware of, let us say, the beauty of words; I'm quite sensitive to word-music. You, Yates, remarked today that my mind, my memory, is full of words and quotations, and that those I can remember because I like those poems.

From "A Colloquy with Jorge Luis Borges" by Donald Yates

TOPICS FOR WRITING ABOUT "THE GOSPEL ACCORDING TO MARK"

1. The long opening paragraph of "The Gospel According to Mark" tells a great deal about the background and personality of Baltasar Espinosa. Write a brief essay in which you consider how the character traits described there foreshadow the story's events.

2. Have you ever been involved in a misunderstanding that was caused by excessive literal-mindedness, your own or someone else's? Write a description of the incident, including how it was resolved, if at all.

3. What larger point do you think Borges is making about his protagonist's final fate, especially in light of Espinosa's attitudes toward religious belief? Back up your conclusions with references to the text.

TOPICS FOR WRITING ABOUT "THE HANDSOMEST DROWNED MAN IN THE WORLD"

1. García Márquez is a master of magic realism, a literary mode in which magical and mundane elements are combined. Write a short essay examining which elements in this story are in the magical dimension, which in the realistic, and what the effect is of mixing the two.
2. Why do you think García Márquez dedicated the story as "A Tale for Children"? Reread the final paragraph to see if it offers any clues.
3. Write an essay in which you discuss what you understand the meaning of the story to be. Refer as specifically as possible to the text of the story to back up your arguments.

TOPICS FOR WRITING ABOUT "REVENGE"

1. Does "Revenge" seem particularly Latin American? How so? Write your own simple tale of revenge, set anywhere you like, paying particular attention to the landscape, the traditions, and the cultural signifiers that help shape your setting.
2. In the end, does Dulce Rosa get her revenge? Can you make an argument that her final act is a more effective form of revenge than if she had killed Tadeo Céspedes?
3. When Dulce Rosa and Tadeo Céspedes finally meet again, twenty-five years after their first terrible encounter, neither of them have the expected emotional reaction. Write a brief psychological analysis of each character, examining how they changed and why.

TOPICS FOR WRITING ABOUT "TELL THEM NOT TO KILL ME!"

1. If this story was told from another character's point of view—the Colonel's, for instance, or Justino's—do you expect you would feel differently about what happens? Why is that? How is point of view effective at eliciting our sympathies?
2. Are you surprised by Justino's reaction to his father's pleas for help? Can you justify his refusal to involve himself too deeply in this grim affair? What does the final section of the story teach us about Justino? Use examples from the text to back up your conclusions.
3. Look back at the biographical details presented here about Juan Rulfo. Do you think "Tell Them Not to Kill Me!" may have been inspired by true events? Research the Cristero Rebellion and present a portrait of rural Mexico at the time Rulfo's story takes place.

▶ TERMS FOR *review*

Magic (or magical) realism ▶ A type of contemporary narrative in which the magical and the mundane are mixed in an overall context of realistic storytelling; the term was originally used to describe the matter-of-fact combination of the fantastic and the everyday in Latin American fiction.

El Boom ▶ An explosion of creativity in the 1960s—marked by stylistic extravagance, complex characterization, fractured time sequences, and fantastic events—that transformed Latin America into one of the centers of modern world fiction.

11 CRITICAL CASEBOOK
Flannery O'Connor

What You Will Learn in This Chapter

- To understand the work of Flannery O'Connor within its biographical, critical, and cultural contexts

Flannery O'Connor

The main concern of the fiction writer is with mystery as it is incarnated in real life.

—FLANNERY O'CONNOR

FLANNERY O'CONNOR

Mary Flannery O'Connor (1925–1964) was born in Savannah, Georgia, but spent most of her life in the small town of Milledgeville. While attending Georgia State College for Women, she won a local reputation for her fledgling stories and satiric cartoons. After graduating in 1945, she went on to study at the University of Iowa, where she earned an MFA in 1947. Diagnosed in 1950 with disseminated lupus, the same incurable illness that had killed her father, O'Connor returned home and spent the last decade of her life living with her mother in Milledgeville. Back on the family dairy farm, she wrote, maintained an extensive literary correspondence, raised peacocks, and underwent medical treatment. When her illness occasionally went into a period of remission, she made trips to lecture and read her stories to college audiences. Her health declined rapidly after surgery early in 1964 for an unrelated complaint. She died at thirty-nine.

O'Connor is unusual among modern American writers in the depth of her Christian vision. A devout Roman Catholic, she attended mass daily while growing up and living in the largely Protestant South. As a latter-day satirist in the manner of Jonathan Swift, O'Connor levels the eye of an uncompromising moralist on the violence and spiritual disorder of the modern world, focusing on what she calls "the action of grace in territory held largely by the devil." She is sometimes called a "Southern Gothic" writer because of her fascination with grotesque incidents and characters. Throughout her career she depicted the South as a troubled region in which the social, racial, and religious status quo that had existed since before the Civil War was coming to a violent end. Despite the inherent seriousness of her religious and social themes, O'Connor's mordant and frequently outrageous humor is everywhere apparent. Her combination of profound vision and dark comedy is the distinguishing characteristic of her literary sensibilities.

O'Connor's published work includes two short novels, Wise Blood *(1952) and* The Violent Bear It Away *(1960), and two collections of short stories,* A Good Man Is Hard to Find *(1955) and* Everything That Rises Must Converge, *published posthumously in 1965. A collection of essays and miscellaneous prose,* Mystery and Manners *(1969), and her selected letters,* The Habit of Being *(1979), reveal an innate cheerfulness and engaging personal warmth that are not always apparent in her fiction.* The Complete Stories of Flannery O'Connor *was posthumously awarded the National Book Award in 1971.*

STORIES

A Good Man Is Hard to Find   1955

The grandmother didn't want to go to Florida. She wanted to visit some of her connections in east Tennessee and she was seizing at every chance to change Bailey's mind. Bailey was the son she lived with, her only boy. He was sitting on the edge of his chair at the table, bent over the orange sports section of the *Journal.* "Now look here, Bailey," she said, "see here, read this," and she stood with one hand on her thin hip and the other rattling the newspaper at his bald head. "Here this fellow that calls himself The Misfit is aloose from the Federal Pen and headed toward Florida and you read here what it says he did to these people. Just you read it. I wouldn't take my children in any direction with a criminal like that aloose in it. I couldn't answer to my conscience if I did."

Bailey didn't look up from his reading so she wheeled around then and faced the children's mother, a young woman in slacks, whose face was as broad and innocent as a cabbage and was tied around with a green head-kerchief that had two points on the top like rabbit's ears. She was sitting on the sofa, feeding the baby his apricots out of a jar. "The children have been to Florida before," the old lady said. "You all ought to take them somewhere else for a change so they would see different parts of the world and be broad. They never have been to east Tennessee."

The children's mother didn't seem to hear her but the eight-year-old boy, John Wesley, a stocky child with glasses, said, "If you don't want to go to Florida, why dontcha stay at home?" He and the little girl, June Star, were reading the funny papers on the floor.

"She wouldn't stay at home to be queen for a day," June Star said without raising her yellow head.

"Yes and what would you do if this fellow, The Misfit, caught you?" the grand-   5
mother said.

"I'd smack his face," John Wesley said.

"She wouldn't stay at home for a million bucks," June Star said. "Afraid she'd miss something. She has to go everywhere we go."

"All right, Miss," the grandmother said. "Just remember that the next time you want me to curl your hair."

June Star said her hair was naturally curly.

The next morning the grandmother was the first one in the car, ready to go. She   10
had her big black valise that looked like the head of a hippopotamus in one corner, and underneath it she was hiding a basket with Pitty Sing, the cat, in it. She didn't intend for the cat to be left alone in the house for three days because he would miss her too much and she was afraid he might brush against one of the gas burners and accidentally asphyxiate himself. Her son, Bailey, didn't like to arrive at a motel with a cat.

She sat in the middle of the back seat with John Wesley and June Star on either side of her. Bailey and the children's mother and the baby sat in front and they left Atlanta at eight forty-five with the mileage on the car at 55890. The grandmother wrote this down because she thought it would be interesting to say how many miles they had been when they got back. It took them twenty minutes to reach the outskirts of the city.

The old lady settled herself comfortably, removing her white cotton gloves and putting them up with her purse on the shelf in front of the back window. The children's mother still had on slacks and still had her hair tied up in a green kerchief, but the grandmother had on a navy blue straw sailor hat with a bunch of white violets on the brim and a navy blue dress with a small white dot in the print. Her collars and cuffs were white organdy trimmed with lace and at her neckline she had pinned a purple spray of cloth violets containing a sachet. In case of an accident, anyone seeing her dead on the highway would know at once that she was a lady.

She said she thought it was going to be a good day for driving, neither too hot nor too cold, and she cautioned Bailey that the speed limit was fifty-five miles an hour and that the patrolmen hid themselves behind billboards and small clumps of trees and sped out after you before you had a chance to slow down. She pointed out interesting details of the scenery: Stone Mountain; the blue granite that in some places came up to both sides of the highway; the brilliant red clay banks slightly streaked with purple; and the various crops that made rows of green lace-work on the ground. The trees were full of silver-white sunlight and the meanest of them sparkled. The children were reading comic magazines and their mother had gone back to sleep.

"Let's go through Georgia fast so we won't have to look at it much," John Wesley said.

"If I were a little boy," said the grandmother, "I wouldn't talk about my native state that way. Tennessee has the mountains and Georgia has the hills." 15

"Tennessee is just a hillbilly dumping ground," John Wesley said, "and Georgia is a lousy state too."

"You said it," June Star said.

"In my time," said the grandmother, folding her thin veined fingers, "children were more respectful of their native states and their parents and everything else. People did right then. Oh look at the cute little pickaninny!" she said and pointed to a Negro child standing in the door of a shack. "Wouldn't that make a picture, now?" she asked and they all turned and looked at the little Negro out of the back window. He waved.

"He didn't have any britches on," June Star said.

"He probably didn't have any," the grandmother explained. "Little niggers in the 20 country don't have things like we do. If I could paint, I'd paint that picture," she said.

The children exchanged comic books.

The grandmother offered to hold the baby and the children's mother passed him over the front seat to her. She set him on her knee and bounced him and told him about the things they were passing. She rolled her eyes and screwed up her mouth and stuck her leathery thin face into his smooth bland one. Occasionally he gave her a faraway smile. They passed a large cotton field with five or six graves fenced in the middle of it, like a small island. "Look at the graveyard!" the grandmother said, pointing it out. "That was the old family burying ground. That belonged to the plantation."

"Where's the plantation?" John Wesley asked.

"Gone With the Wind," said the grandmother. "Ha. Ha."

When the children finished all the comic books they had brought, they opened 25 the lunch and ate it. The grandmother ate a peanut butter sandwich and an olive and would not let the children throw the box and the paper napkins out the window. When there was nothing else to do they played a game by choosing a cloud and making the other two guess what shape it suggested. John Wesley took one the shape of a cow and June Star guessed a cow and John Wesley said, no, an automobile, and June Star said he didn't play fair, and they began to slap each other over the grandmother.

The grandmother said she would tell them a story if they would keep quiet. When she told a story, she rolled her eyes and waved her head and was very dramatic. She said once when she was a maiden lady she had been courted by a Mr. Edgar Atkins Teagarden from Jasper, Georgia. She said he was a very good-looking man and a gentleman and that he brought her a watermelon every Saturday afternoon with his initials cut in it, E. A. T. Well, one Saturday, she said, Mr. Teagarden brought the watermelon and there was nobody at home and he left it on the front porch and returned in his buggy to Jasper, but she never got the watermelon, she said, because a nigger boy ate it when he saw the initials, E. A. T.! This story tickled John Wesley's funny bone and he giggled and giggled but June Star didn't think it was any good. She said she wouldn't marry a man that just brought her a watermelon on Saturday. The grandmother said she would have done well to marry Mr. Teagarden because he was a gentleman and had bought Coca-Cola stock when it first came out and that he had died only a few years ago, a very wealthy man.

They stopped at The Tower for barbecued sandwiches. The Tower was a part stucco and part wood filling station and dance hall set in a clearing outside of Timothy. A fat man named Red Sammy Butts ran it and there were signs stuck here and there on the building and for miles up and down the highway saying, TRY RED SAMMY'S FAMOUS BARBECUE. NONE LIKE FAMOUS RED SAMMY'S! RED SAM! THE FAT BOY WITH THE HAPPY LAUGH. A VETERAN! RED SAMMY'S YOUR MAN!

Red Sammy was lying on the bare ground outside The Tower with his head under a truck while a gray monkey about a foot high, chained to a small chinaberry tree, chattered nearby. The monkey sprang back into the tree and got on the highest limb as soon as he saw the children jump out of the car and run toward him.

Inside, The Tower was a long dark room with a counter at one end and tables at the other and dancing space in the middle. They all sat down at a board table next to the nickelodeon and Red Sam's wife, a tall burnt-brown woman with hair and eyes lighter than her skin, came and took their order. The children's mother put a dime in the machine and played "The Tennessee Waltz," and the grandmother said that tune always made her want to dance. She asked Bailey if he would like to dance but he only glared at her. He didn't have a naturally sunny disposition like she did and trips made him nervous. The grandmother's brown eyes were very bright. She swayed her head from side to side and pretended she was dancing in her chair. June Star said play something she could tap to so the children's mother put in another dime and played a fast number and June Star stepped out onto the dance floor and did her tap routine.

"Ain't she cute?" Red Sam's wife said, leaning over the counter. "Would you like to come be my little girl?"   30

"No I certainly wouldn't," June Star said. "I wouldn't live in a broken-down place like this for a million bucks!" and she ran back to the table.

"Ain't she cute?" the woman repeated, stretching her mouth politely.

"Aren't you ashamed?" hissed the grandmother.

Red Sam came in and told his wife to quit lounging on the counter and hurry up with these people's order. His khaki trousers reached just to his hip bones and his stomach hung over them like a sack of meal swaying under his shirt. He came over and sat down at a table nearby and let out a combination sigh and yodel. "You can't win," he said. "You can't win," and he wiped his sweating red face off with a gray handkerchief. "These days you don't know who to trust," he said. "Ain't that the truth?"

"People are certainly not nice like they used to be," said the grandmother.   35

"Two fellers come in here last week," Red Sammy said, "driving a Chrysler. It was a old beat-up car but it was a good one and these boys looked all right to me. Said they worked at the mill and you know I let them fellers charge the gas they bought? Now why did I do that?"

"Because you're a good man!" the grandmother said at once.

"Yes'm, I suppose so," Red Sam said as if he were struck with this answer.

His wife brought the orders, carrying the five plates all at once without a tray, two in each hand and one balanced on her arm. "It isn't a soul in this green world of God's that you can trust," she said. "And I don't count nobody out of that, not nobody," she repeated, looking at Red Sammy.

"Did you read about that criminal, The Misfit, that's escaped?" asked the   40 grandmother.

"I wouldn't be a bit surprised if he didn't attact this place right here," said the woman. "If he hears about it being here, I wouldn't be none surprised to see him. If he hears it's two cent in the cash register, I wouldn't be a-tall surprised if he . . ."

"That'll do," Red Sam said. "Go bring these people their Co'-Colas," and the woman went off to get the rest of the order.

"A good man is hard to find," Red Sammy said. "Everything is getting terrible. I remember the day you could go off and leave your screen door unlatched. Not no more."

He and the grandmother discussed better times. The old lady said that in her opinion Europe was entirely to blame for the way things were now. She said the way Europe acted you would think we were made of money and Red Sam said it was no use talking about it, she was exactly right. The children ran outside into the white sunlight and looked at the monkey in the lacy chinaberry tree. He was busy catching fleas on himself and biting each one carefully between his teeth as if it were a delicacy.

They drove off again into the hot afternoon. The grandmother took cat naps and   45
woke up every five minutes with her own snoring. Outside of Toombsboro she woke up and recalled an old plantation that she had visited in this neighborhood once when she was a young lady. She said the house had six white columns across the front and that there was an avenue of oaks leading up to it and two little wooden trellis arbors on either side in front where you sat down with your suitor after a stroll in the garden. She recalled exactly which road to turn off to get to it. She knew that Bailey would not be willing to lose any time looking at an old house, but the more she talked about it, the more she wanted to see it once again and find out if the little twin arbors were still standing. "There was a secret panel in this house," she said craftily, not telling the truth but wishing that she were, "and the story went that all the family silver was hidden in it when Sherman° came through but it was never found . . ."

"Hey!" John Wesley said. "Let's go see it! We'll find it! We'll poke all the woodwork and find it! Who lives there? Where do you turn off at? Hey, Pop, can't we turn off there?"

"We never have seen a house with a secret panel!" June Star shrieked. "Let's go to the house with the secret panel! Hey Pop, can't we go see the house with the secret panel!"

"It's not far from here, I know," the grandmother said. "It wouldn't take over twenty minutes."

Bailey was looking straight ahead. His jaw was as rigid as a horseshoe. "No," he said.

The children began to yell and scream that they wanted to see the house with   50
the secret panel. John Wesley kicked the back of the front seat and June Star hung over her mother's shoulder and whined desperately into her ear that they never had any fun even on their vacation, that they could never do what THEY wanted to do. The baby began to scream and John Wesley kicked the back of the seat so hard that his father could feel the blows in his kidney.

"All right!" he shouted and drew the car to a stop at the side of the road. "Will you all shut up? Will you all just shut up for one second? If you don't shut up, we won't go anywhere."

"It would be very educational for them," the grandmother murmured.

"All right," Bailey said, "but get this: this is the only time we're going to stop for anything like this. This is the one and only time."

"The dirt road that you have to turn down is about a mile back," the grandmother directed. "I marked it when we passed."

"A dirt road," Bailey groaned.   55

After they had turned around and were headed toward the dirt road, the grandmother recalled other points about the house, the beautiful glass over the front doorway and the candle-lamp in the hall. John Wesley said that the secret panel was probably in the fireplace.

"You can't go inside this house," Bailey said. "You don't know who lives there."

"While you all talk to the people in front, I'll run around behind and get in a window," John Wesley suggested.

"We'll all stay in the car," his mother said.

They turned onto the dirt road and the car raced roughly along in a swirl of pink   60
dust. The grandmother recalled the times when there were no paved roads and thirty miles was a day's journey. The dirt road was hilly and there were sudden washes in it and sharp curves on dangerous embankments. All at once they would be on a hill, looking down over the blue tops of trees for miles around, then the next minute, they would be in a red depression with the dust-coated trees looking down on them.

"This place had better turn up in a minute," Bailey said, "or I'm going to turn around."

The road looked as if no one had traveled on it for months.

"It's not much farther," the grandmother said and just as she said it, a horrible thought came to her. The thought was so embarrassing that she turned red in the face and her eyes dilated and her feet jumped up, upsetting her valise in the corner. The instant the valise moved, the newspaper top she had over the basket under it rose with a snarl and Pitty Sing, the cat, sprang onto Bailey's shoulder.

The children were thrown to the floor and their mother, clutching the baby, was thrown out the door onto the ground; the old lady was thrown into the front seat. The car turned over once and landed right-side-up in a gulch off the side of the road. Bailey remained in the driver's seat with the cat—gray-striped with a broad white face and an orange nose—clinging to his neck like a caterpillar.

As soon as the children saw they could move their arms and legs, they scrambled   65
out of the car, shouting, "We've had an ACCIDENT!" The grandmother was curled up under the dashboard, hoping she was injured so that Bailey's wrath would not come down on her all at once. The horrible thought she had had before the accident was that the house she had remembered so vividly was not in Georgia but in Tennessee.

Bailey removed the cat from his neck with both hands and flung it out the window against the side of a pine tree. Then he got out of the car and started looking for the children's mother. She was sitting against the side of the red gutted ditch, holding the screaming baby, but she only had a cut down her face and a broken shoulder. "We've had an ACCIDENT!" the children screamed in a frenzy of delight.

"But nobody's killed," June Star said with disappointment as the grandmother limped out of the car, her hat still pinned to her head but the broken front brim standing up at a jaunty angle and the violet spray hanging off the side. They all sat down in the ditch, except the children, to recover from the shock. They were all shaking.

"Maybe a car will come along," said the children's mother hoarsely.

"I believe I have injured an organ," said the grandmother, pressing her side, but no one answered her. Bailey's teeth were clattering. He had on a yellow sport shirt with bright blue parrots designed in it and his face was as yellow as the shirt. The grandmother decided that she would not mention that the house was in Tennessee.

The road was about ten feet above and they could see only the tops of the trees on the other side of it. Behind the ditch they were sitting in there were more woods, tall and dark and deep. In a few minutes they saw a car some distance away on top of a hill, coming slowly as if the occupants were watching them. The grandmother stood up and waved both her arms dramatically to attract their attention. The car continued to come on slowly, disappeared around a bend and appeared again, moving even slower, on top of the hill they had gone over. It was a big black battered hearse-like automobile. There were three men in it.

It came to a stop just over them and for some minutes, the driver looked down with a steady expressionless gaze to where they were sitting, and didn't speak. Then he turned his head and muttered something to the other two and they got out. One was a fat boy in black trousers and a red sweat shirt with a silver stallion embossed on the front of it. He moved around on the right side of them and stood staring, his mouth partly open in a kind of loose grin. The other had on khaki pants and a blue striped coat and a gray hat pulled down very low, hiding most of his face. He came around slowly on the left side. Neither spoke.

The driver got out of the car and stood by the side of it, looking down at them. He was an older man than the other two. His hair was just beginning to gray and he wore silver-rimmed spectacles that gave him a scholarly look. He had a long creased face and didn't have on any shirt or undershirt. He had on blue jeans that were too tight for him and was holding a black hat and a gun. The two boys also had guns.

"We've had an ACCIDENT!" the children screamed.

The grandmother had the peculiar feeling that the bespectacled man was someone she knew. His face was as familiar to her as if she had known him all her life but she could not recall who he was. He moved away from the car and began to come down the embankment, placing his feet carefully so that he wouldn't slip. He had on tan and white shoes and no socks, and his ankles were red and thin. "Good afternoon," he said. "I see you all had you a little spill."

"We turned over twice!" said the grandmother.

"Oncet," he corrected. "We seen it happen. Try their car and see will it run, Hiram," he said quietly to the boy with the gray hat.

"What you got that gun for?" John Wesley asked. "Whatcha gonna do with that gun?"

"Lady," the man said to the children's mother, "would you mind calling them children to sit down by you? Children make me nervous. I want all you all to sit down right together there where you're at."

"What are you telling US what to do for?" June Star asked.

Behind them the line of woods gaped like a dark open mouth. "Come here," said their mother.

"Look here now," Bailey began suddenly, "we're in a predicament! We're in . . ."

The grandmother shrieked. She scrambled to her feet and stood staring. "You're The Misfit!" she said. "I recognized you at once!"

"Yes'm," the man said, smiling slightly as if he were pleased in spite of himself to be known, "but it would have been better for all of you, lady, if you hadn't of reckernized me."

Bailey turned his head sharply and said something to his mother that shocked even the children. The old lady began to cry and The Misfit reddened.

"Lady," he said, "don't you get upset. Sometimes a man says things he don't mean. I don't reckon he meant to talk to you thataway."

"You wouldn't shoot a lady, would you?" the grandmother said and removed a clean handkerchief from her cuff and began to slap at her eyes with it.

The Misfit pointed the toe of his shoe into the ground and made a little hole and then covered it up again. "I would hate to have to," he said.

"Listen," the grandmother almost screamed, "I know you're a good man. You don't look a bit like you have common blood. I know you must come from nice people!"

"Yes mam," he said, "finest people in the world." When he smiled he showed a row of strong white teeth. "God never made a finer woman than my mother and my daddy's heart was pure gold," he said. The boy with the red sweat shirt had come around behind them and was standing with his gun at his hip. The Misfit squatted down on the ground. "Watch them children, Bobby Lee," he said. "You know they make me nervous." He looked at the six of them huddled together in front of him and he seemed to be embarrassed as if he couldn't think of anything to say. "Ain't a cloud in the sky," he remarked, looking up at it. "Don't see no sun but don't see no cloud neither."

"Yes, it's a beautiful day," said the grandmother. "Listen," she said, "you shouldn't   90 call yourself The Misfit because I know you're a good man at heart. I can just look at you and tell."

"Hush!" Bailey yelled. "Hush! Everybody shut up and let me handle this!" He was squatting in the position of a runner about to sprint forward but he didn't move.

"I pre-chate that, lady," The Misfit said and drew a little circle in the ground with the butt of his gun.

"It'll take a half a hour to fix this here car," Hiram called, looking over the raised hood of it.

"Well, first you and Bobby Lee get him and that little boy to step over yonder with you," The Misfit said, pointing to Bailey and John Wesley. "The boys want to ast you something," he said to Bailey. "Would you mind stepping back in them woods there with them?"

"Listen," Bailey began, "we're in a terrible predicament! Nobody realizes what   95 this is," and his voice cracked. His eyes were as blue and intense as the parrots in his shirt and he remained perfectly still.

The grandmother reached up to adjust her hat brim as if she were going to the woods with him but it came off in her hand. She stood staring at it and after a second she let it fall on the ground. Hiram pulled Bailey up by the arm as if he were assisting an old man. John Wesley caught hold of his father's hand and Bobby Lee followed. They went off toward the woods and just as they reached the dark edge, Bailey turned and supporting himself against a gray naked pine trunk, he shouted, "I'll be back in a minute, Mamma, wait on me!"

"Come back this instant!" his mother shrilled but they all disappeared into the woods.

"Bailey Boy!" the grandmother called in a tragic voice but she found she was looking at The Misfit squatting on the ground in front of her. "I just know you're a good man," she said desperately. "You're not a bit common!"

"Nome, I ain't a good man," The Misfit said after a second as if he had considered her statement carefully, "but I ain't the worst in the world neither. My daddy said I was a different breed of dog from my brothers and sisters. 'You know,' Daddy said, 'it's some that can live their whole life out without asking about it and it's others has to know why it is, and this boy is one of the latters. He's going to be into everything!'" He put on his black hat and looked up suddenly and then away deep into the woods as if he were embarrassed again. "I'm sorry I don't have on a shirt before you ladies," he said, hunching his shoulders slightly. "We buried our clothes that we had on when we escaped and we're just making do until we can get better. We borrowed these from some folks we met," he explained.

"That's perfectly all right," the grandmother said. "Maybe Bailey has an extra   100 shirt in his suitcase."

"I'll look and see terrectly," The Misfit said.

"Where are they taking him?" the children's mother screamed.

"Daddy was a card himself," The Misfit said. "You couldn't put anything over on him. He never got in trouble with the Authorities though. Just had the knack of handling them."

"You could be honest too if you'd only try," said the grandmother. "Think how wonderful it would be to settle down and live a comfortable life and not have to think about somebody chasing you all the time."

The Misfit kept scratching in the ground with the butt of his gun as if he were   105 thinking about it. "Yes'm, somebody is always after you," he murmured.

The grandmother noticed how thin his shoulder blades were just behind his hat because she was standing up looking down on him. "Do you ever pray?" she asked.

He shook his head. All she saw was the black hat wiggle between his shoulder blades. "Nome," he said.

There was a pistol shot from the woods, followed closely by another. Then silence. The old lady's head jerked around. She could hear the wind move through the tree tops like a long satisfied insuck of breath. "Bailey Boy!" she called.

"I was a gospel singer for a while," The Misfit said. "I been most everything. Been in the arm service, both land and sea, at home and abroad, been twict married, been an undertaker, been with the railroads, plowed Mother Earth, been in a tornado, seen a man burnt alive oncet," and he looked up at the children's mother and the little girl who were sitting close together, their faces white and their eyes glassy; "I even seen a woman flogged," he said.

"Pray, pray," the grandmother began, "pray, pray . . ."   110

"I never was a bad boy that I remember of," The Misfit said in an almost dreamy voice, "but somewheres along the line I done something wrong and got sent to the penitentiary. I was buried alive," and he looked up and held her attention to him by a steady stare.

"That's when you should have started to pray," she said. "What did you do to get sent to the penitentiary that first time?"

"Turn to the right, it was a wall," The Misfit said, looking up again at the cloudless sky. "Turn to the left, it was a wall. Look up it was a ceiling, look down it was a floor. I forget what I done, lady. I set there and set there, trying to remember what it was I done and I ain't recalled it to this day. Oncet in a while, I would think it was coming to me, but it never come."

"Maybe they put you in by mistake," the old lady said vaguely.

"Nome," he said. "It wasn't no mistake. They had the papers on me."   115

"You must have stolen something," she said.

The Misfit sneered slightly. "Nobody had nothing I wanted," he said. "It was a head-doctor at the penitentiary said what I had done was kill my daddy but I known that for a lie. My daddy died in nineteen ought nineteen of the epidemic flu and I never had a thing to do with it. He was buried in the Mount Hopewell Baptist churchyard and you can go there and see for yourself."

"If you would pray," the old lady said, "Jesus would help you."

"That's right," The Misfit said.

"Well then, why don't you pray?" she asked trembling with delight suddenly.   120

"I don't want no hep," he said. "I'm doing all right by myself."

Bobby Lee and Hiram came ambling back from the woods. Bobby Lee was dragging a yellow shirt with bright blue parrots in it.

"Thow me that shirt, Bobby Lee," The Misfit said. The shirt came flying at him and landed on his shoulder and he put it on. The grandmother couldn't name what the shirt reminded her of. "No, lady," The Misfit said while he was buttoning it up, "I found out the crime don't matter. You can do one thing or you can do another, kill a man or take a tire off his car, because sooner or later you're going to forget what it was you done and just be punished for it."

The children's mother had begun to make heaving noises as if she couldn't get her breath. "Lady," he asked, "would you and that little girl like to step off yonder with Bobby Lee and Hiram and join your husband?"

"Yes, thank you," the mother said faintly. Her left arm dangled helplessly and   125
she was holding the baby, who had gone to sleep, in the other. "Hep that lady up, Hiram," The Misfit said as she struggled to climb out of the ditch, "and Bobby Lee, you hold onto that little girl's hand."

"I don't want to hold hands with him," June Star said. "He reminds me of a pig."

The fat boy blushed and laughed and caught her by the arm and pulled her off into the woods after Hiram and her mother.

Alone with The Misfit, the grandmother found that she had lost her voice. There was not a cloud in the sky nor any sun. There was nothing around her but woods. She wanted to tell him that he must pray. She opened and closed her mouth several times before anything came out. Finally she found herself saying, "Jesus. Jesus," meaning, Jesus will help you, but the way she was saying it, it sounded as if she might be cursing.

"Yes'm," The Misfit said as if he agreed. "Jesus thown everything off balance. It was the same case with Him as with me except He hadn't committed any crime and they could prove I had committed one because they had the papers on me. Of course," he said, "they never shown me my papers. That's why I sign myself now. I said long ago, you get you a signature and sign everything you do and keep a copy of it. Then you'll know what you done and you can hold up the crime to the punishment and see do they match and in the end you'll have something to prove you ain't been treated right. I call myself The Misfit," he said, "because I can't make what all I done wrong fit what all I gone through in punishment."

There was a piercing scream from the woods, followed closely by a pistol report.   130
"Does it seem right to you, lady, that one is punished a heap and another ain't punished at all?"

"Jesus!" the old lady cried. "You've got good blood! I know you wouldn't shoot a lady! I know you come from nice people! Pray! Jesus, you ought not to shoot a lady. I'll give you all the money I've got!"

"Lady," The Misfit said, looking beyond her far into the woods, "there never was a body that give the undertaker a tip."

There were two more pistol reports and the grandmother raised her head like a parched old turkey hen crying for water and called, "Bailey Boy, Bailey Boy!" as if her heart would break.

"Jesus was the only One that ever raised the dead," The Misfit continued, "and He shouldn't have done it. He thown everything off balance. If He did what He said, then it's nothing for you to do but thow away everything and follow Him, and if He didn't, then it's nothing for you to do but enjoy the few minutes you got left the best way you can—by killing somebody or burning down his house or doing some other meanness to him. No pleasure but meanness," he said and his voice had become almost a snarl.

"Maybe He didn't raise the dead," the old lady mumbled, not knowing what she 135
was saying and feeling so dizzy that she sank down in the ditch with her legs twisted under her.

"I wasn't there so I can't say He didn't," The Misfit said. "I wisht I had of been there," he said, hitting the ground with his fist. "It ain't right I wasn't there because if I had of been there I would of known. Listen lady," he said in a high voice, "if I had of been there I would of known and I wouldn't be like I am now." His voice seemed about to crack and the grandmother's head cleared for an instant. She saw the man's face twisted close to her own as if he were going to cry and she murmured, "Why you're one of my babies. You're one of my own children!" She reached out and touched him on the shoulder. The Misfit sprang back as if a snake had bitten him and shot her three times through the chest. Then he put his gun down on the ground and took off his glasses and began to clean them.

Hiram and Bobby Lee returned from the woods and stood over the ditch, looking down at the grandmother who half sat and half lay in a puddle of blood with her legs crossed under her like a child's and her face smiling up at the cloudless sky.

Without his glasses, The Misfit's eyes were red-rimmed and pale and defenseless-looking. "Take her off and thow her where you thown the others," he said, picking up the cat that was rubbing itself against his leg.

"She was a talker, wasn't she?" Bobby Lee said, sliding down the ditch with a yodel.

"She would of been a good woman," The Misfit said, "if it had been somebody 140
there to shoot her every minute of her life."

"Some fun!" Bobby Lee said.

"Shut up, Bobby Lee," The Misfit said. "It's no real pleasure in life."

Questions

1. How early in the story does O'Connor foreshadow what will happen in the end? What further hints does she give us along the way? How does the scene at Red Sammy's Barbecue advance the story toward its conclusion?

2. When we first meet the grandmother, what kind of person is she? What do her various remarks reveal about her? Does she remain a static character, or does she change in any way as the story goes on?

3. When the grandmother's head clears for an instant (paragraph 136), what does she suddenly understand? Reread this passage carefully and prepare to discuss what it means.

4. What do we learn from the conversation between The Misfit and the grandmother while the others go out to the woods? How would you describe The Misfit's outlook on the world? Compare it with the author's, from whatever you know about Flannery O'Connor and from the story itself.

5. How would you respond to a reader who complained, "The title of this story is just an obvious platitude"?

Revelation

1965

The doctor's waiting room, which was very small, was almost full when the Turpins entered and Mrs. Turpin, who was very large, made it look even smaller by her presence. She stood looming at the head of the magazine table set in the center of it, a living demonstration that the room was inadequate and ridiculous. Her little bright black eyes took in all the patients as she sized up the seating situation. There was one vacant chair and a place on a sofa occupied by a blond child in a dirty blue romper who should have been told to move over and make room for the lady. He was five or six, but Mrs. Turpin saw at once that no one was going to tell him to move over. He was slumped down in the seat, his arms idle at his sides and his eyes idle in his head; his nose ran unchecked.

Mrs. Turpin put a firm hand on Claud's shoulder and said in a voice that included anyone who wanted to listen, "Claud, you sit in that chair there," and gave him a push down into the vacant one. Claud was florid and bald and sturdy, somewhat shorter than Mrs. Turpin, but he sat down as if he were accustomed to doing what she told him to.

Mrs. Turpin remained standing. The only man in the room besides Claud was a lean stringy old fellow with a rusty hand spread out on each knee, whose eyes were closed as if he were asleep or dead or pretending to be so as not to get up and offer her his seat. Her gaze settled agreeably on a well-dressed grey-haired lady whose eyes met hers and whose expression said: if that child belonged to me, he would have some manners and move over—there's plenty of room there for you and him too.

Claud looked up with a sigh and made as if to rise.

"Sit down," Mrs. Turpin said. "You know you're not supposed to stand on that leg. He has an ulcer on his leg," she explained.   5

Claud lifted his foot onto the magazine table and rolled his trouser leg up to reveal a purple swelling on a plump marble-white calf.

"My!" the pleasant lady said. "How did you do that?"

"A cow kicked him," Mrs. Turpin said.

"Goodness!" said the lady.

Claud rolled his trouser leg down.   10

"Maybe the little boy would move over," the lady suggested, but the child did not stir.

"Somebody will be leaving in a minute," Mrs. Turpin said. She could not understand why a doctor—with as much money as they made charging five dollars a day to just stick their head in the hospital door and look at you—couldn't afford a decent-sized waiting room. This one was hardly bigger than a garage. The table was cluttered with limp-looking magazines and at one end of it there was a big green glass ash tray full of cigaret butts and cotton wads with little blood spots on them. If she had had anything to do with the running of the place, that would have been emptied every so often. There were no chairs against the wall at the head of the room. It had a rectangular-shaped panel in it that permitted a view of the office where the nurse came and went and the secretary listened to the radio. A plastic fern in a gold pot sat in the opening and trailed its fronds down almost to the floor. The radio was softly playing gospel music.

Just then the inner door opened and a nurse with the highest stack of yellow hair Mrs. Turpin had ever seen put her face in the crack and called for the next patient. The woman sitting beside Claud grasped the two arms of her chair and hoisted herself up; she pulled her dress free from her legs and lumbered through the door where the nurse had disappeared.

Mrs. Turpin eased into the vacant chair, which held her tight as a corset. "I wish I could reduce," she said, and rolled her eyes and gave a comic sigh.

"Oh, *you* aren't fat," the stylish lady said.

"Ooooo I am too," Mrs. Turpin said. "Claud he eats all he wants to and never weighs over one hundred and seventy-five pounds, but me I just look at something good to eat and I gain some weight," and her stomach and shoulders shook with laughter. "You can eat all you want to, can't you, Claud?" she asked, turning to him.

Claud only grinned.

"Well, as long as you have such a good disposition," the stylish lady said, "I don't think it makes a bit of difference what size you are. You just can't beat a good disposition."

Next to her was a fat girl of eighteen or nineteen, scowling into a thick blue book which Mrs. Turpin saw was entitled *Human Development*. The girl raised her head and directed her scowl at Mrs. Turpin as if she did not like her looks. She appeared annoyed that anyone should speak while she tried to read. The poor girl's face was blue with acne and Mrs. Turpin thought how pitiful it was to have a face like that at that age. She gave the girl a friendly smile but the girl only scowled the harder. Mrs. Turpin herself was fat but she had always had good skin, and, though she was forty-seven years old, there was not a wrinkle in her face except around her eyes from laughing too much.

Next to the ugly girl was the child, still in exactly the same position, and next to him was a thin leathery old woman in a cotton print dress. She and Claud had three sacks of chicken feed in their pump house that was in the same print. She had seen from the first that the child belonged with the old woman. She could tell by the way they sat—kind of vacant and white-trashy, as if they would sit there until Doomsday if nobody called and told them to get up. And at right angles but next to the well-dressed pleasant lady was a lank-faced woman who was certainly the child's mother. She had on a yellow sweat shirt and wine-colored slacks, both gritty-looking, and the rims of her lips were stained with snuff. Her dirty yellow hair was tied behind with a little piece of red paper ribbon. Worse than niggers any day, Mrs. Turpin thought.

The gospel hymn playing was, "When I looked up and He looked down," and Mrs. Turpin, who knew it, supplied the last line mentally, "And wona these days I know I'll we-eara crown."

Without appearing to, Mrs. Turpin always noticed people's feet. The well-dressed lady had on red and grey suede shoes to match her dress. Mrs. Turpin had on her good black patent leather pumps. The ugly girl had on Girl Scout shoes and heavy socks. The old woman had on tennis shoes and the white-trashy mother had on what appeared to be bedroom slippers, black straw with gold braid threaded through them—exactly what you would have expected her to have on.

Sometimes at night when she couldn't go to sleep, Mrs. Turpin would occupy herself with the question of who she would have chosen to be if she couldn't have been herself. If Jesus had said to her before he made her, "There's only two places available for you. You can either be a nigger or white-trash," what would she have said? "Please, Jesus, please," she would have said, "just let me wait until there's another place available," and he would have said, "No, you have to go right now and I have only those two places so make up your mind." She would have wiggled and squirmed and begged and pleaded but it would have been no use and finally she would have said, "All right, make me a nigger then—but that don't mean a trashy one." And he would have made her a neat clean respectable Negro woman, herself but black.

Next to the child's mother was a red-headed youngish woman, reading one of the magazines and working a piece of chewing gum, hell for leather, as Claud would say. Mrs. Turpin could not see the woman's feet. She was not white-trash, just common. Sometimes Mrs. Turpin occupied herself at night naming the classes of people. On the bottom of the heap were most colored people, not the kind she would have been if she had been one, but most of them; then next to them—not above, just away from—were the white-trash; then above them were the home-owners, and above them the home-and-land owners, to which she and Claud belonged. Above she and Claud were people with a lot of money and much bigger houses and much more land. But here the complexity of it would begin to bear in on her, for some of the people with a lot of money were common and ought to be below she and Claud and some of the people who had good blood had lost their money and had to rent and then there were colored people who owned their homes and land as well. There was a colored dentist in town who had two red Lincolns and a swimming pool and a farm with registered white-face cattle on it. Usually by the time she had fallen asleep all the classes of people were moiling and roiling around in her head, and she would dream they were all crammed in together in a box car, being ridden off to be put in a gas oven.

"That's a beautiful clock," she said and nodded to her right. It was a big wall   25
clock, the face encased in a brass sunburst.

"Yes, it's very pretty," the stylish lady said agreeably. "And right on the dot too," she added, glancing at her watch.

The ugly girl beside her cast an eye upward at the clock, smirked, then looked directly at Mrs. Turpin and smirked again. Then she returned her eyes to her book. She was obviously the lady's daughter because, although they didn't look anything alike as to disposition, they both had the same shape of face and the same blue eyes. On the lady they sparkled pleasantly but in the girl's seared face they appeared alternately to smolder and to blaze.

What if Jesus had said, "All right, you can be white-trash or a nigger or ugly"!

Mrs. Turpin felt an awful pity for the girl, though she thought it was one thing to be ugly and another to act ugly.

The woman with the snuff-stained lips turned around in her chair and looked up   30
at the clock. Then she turned back and appeared to look a little to the side of Mrs. Turpin. There was a cast in one of her eyes. "You want to know wher you can get you one of themther clocks?" she asked in a loud voice.

"No, I already have a nice clock," Mrs. Turpin said. Once somebody like her got a leg in the conversation, she would be all over it.

"You can get you one with green stamps," the woman said. "That's most likely wher he got hisn. Save you up enough, you can get you most anythang. I got me some joo'ry."

Ought to have got you a wash rag and some soap, Mrs. Turpin thought.

"I get contour sheets with mine," the pleasant lady said.

The daughter slammed her book shut. She looked straight in front of her, directly   35
through Mrs. Turpin and on through the yellow curtain and the plate glass window which made the wall behind her. The girl's eyes seemed lit all of a sudden with a peculiar light, an unnatural light like night road signs give. Mrs. Turpin turned her head to see if there was anything going on outside that she should see, but she could not see anything. Figures passing cast only a pale shadow through the curtain. There was no reason the girl should single her out for her ugly looks.

"Miss Finley," the nurse said, cracking the door. The gum-chewing woman got up and passed in front of her and Claud and went into the office. She had on red high-heeled shoes.

Directly across the table, the ugly girl's eyes were fixed on Mrs. Turpin as if she had some very special reason for disliking her.

"This is wonderful weather, isn't it?" the girl's mother said.

"It's good weather for cotton if you can get the niggers to pick it," Mrs. Turpin said, "but niggers don't want to pick cotton any more. You can't get the white folks to pick it and now you can't get the niggers—because they got to be right up there with the white folks."

"They gonna *try* anyways," the white-trash woman said, leaning forward. 40

"Do you have one of those cotton-picking machines?" the pleasant lady asked.

"No," Mrs. Turpin said, "they leave half the cotton in the field. We don't have much cotton anyway. If you want to make it farming now, you have to have a little of everything. We got a couple of acres of cotton and a few hogs and chickens and just enough white-face that Claud can look after them himself."

"One thang I don't want," the white-trash woman said, wiping her mouth with the back of her hands. "Hogs. Nasty stinking things, a-gruntin and a-rootin all over the place."

Mrs. Turpin gave her the merest edge of her attention. "Our hogs are not dirty and they don't stink," she said. "They're cleaner than some children I've seen. Their feet never touch the ground. We have a pig-parlor—that's where you raise them on concrete," she explained to the pleasant lady, "and Claud scoots them down with the hose every afternoon and washes off the floor." Cleaner by far than that child right there, she thought. Poor nasty little thing. He had not moved except to put the thumb of his dirty hand into his mouth.

The woman turned her face away from Mrs. Turpin. "I know I wouldn't scoot 45 down no hog with no hose," she said to the wall.

You wouldn't have no hog to scoot down, Mrs. Turpin said to herself.

"A-gruntin and a-rootin and a-groanin," the woman muttered.

"We got a little of everything," Mrs. Turpin said to the pleasant lady. "It's no use in having more than you can handle yourself with help like it is. We found enough niggers to pick our cotton this year but Claud he has to go after them and take them home again in the evening. They can't walk that half a mile. No they can't. I tell you," she said and laughed merrily, "I sure am tired of buttering up niggers, but you got to love em if you want em to work for you. When they come in the morning, I run out and I say, 'Hi yawl this morning?' and when Claud drives them off to the field I just wave to beat the band and they just wave back." And she waved her hand rapidly to illustrate.

"Like you read out of the same book," the lady said, showing she understood perfectly.

"Child, yes," Mrs. Turpin said. "And when they come in from the field, I run out 50 with a bucket of icewater. That's the way it's going to be from now on," she said. "You may as well face it."

"One thang I know," the white-trash woman said. "Two thangs I ain't going to do: love no niggers or scoot down no hog with no hose." And she let out a bark of contempt.

The look that Mrs. Turpin and the pleasant lady exchanged indicated they both understood that you had to *have* certain things before you could *know* certain things. But every time Mrs. Turpin exchanged a look with the lady, she was aware that the ugly girl's peculiar eyes were still on her, and she had trouble bringing her attention back to the conversation.

"When you got something," she said, "you got to look after it." And when you ain't got a thing but breath and britches, she added to herself, you can afford to come to town every morning and just sit on the Court House coping and spit.

A grotesque revolving shadow passed across the curtain behind her and was thrown palely on the opposite wall. Then a bicycle clattered down against the outside of the building. The door opened and a colored boy glided in with a tray from the drug store. It had two large red and white paper cups on it with tops on them. He was a tall, very black boy in discolored white pants and a green nylon shirt. He was chewing gum slowly, as if to music. He set the tray down in the office opening next to the fern and stuck his head through to look for the secretary. She was not in there. He rested his arms on the ledge and waited, his narrow bottom stuck out, swaying slowly to the left and right. He raised a hand over his head and scratched the base of his skull.

"You see that button there, boy?" Mrs. Turpin said. "You can punch that and   55
she'll come. She's probably in the back somewhere."

"Is thas right?" the boy said agreeably, as if he had never seen the button before. He leaned to the right and put his finger on it. "She sometime out," he said and twisted around to face his audience, his elbows behind him on the counter. The nurse appeared and he twisted back again. She handed him a dollar and he rooted in his pocket and made the change and counted it out to her. She gave him fifteen cents for a tip and he went out with the empty tray. The heavy door swung to slowly and closed at length with the sound of suction. For a moment no one spoke.

"They ought to send all them niggers back to Africa," the white-trash woman said. "That's wher they come from in the first place."

"Oh, I couldn't do without my good colored friends," the pleasant lady said.

"There's a heap of things worse than a nigger," Mrs. Turpin agreed. "It's all kinds of them just like it's all kinds of us."

"Yes, and it takes all kinds to make the world go round," the lady said in her   60
musical voice.

As she said it, the raw-complexioned girl snapped her teeth together. Her lower lip turned downwards and inside out, revealing the pale pink inside of her mouth. After a second it rolled back up. It was the ugliest face Mrs. Turpin had ever seen any-one make and for a moment she was certain that the girl had made it at her. She was looking at her as if she had known and disliked her all her life—all of Mrs. Turpin's life, it seemed too, not just all the girl's life. Why, girl, I don't even know you, Mrs. Turpin said silently.

She forced her attention back to the discussion. "It wouldn't be practical to send them back to Africa," she said. "They wouldn't want to go. They got it too good here."

"Wouldn't be what they wanted—if I had anythang to do with it," the woman said.

"It wouldn't be a way in the world you could get all the niggers back over there," Mrs. Turpin said. "They'd be hiding out and lying down and turning sick on you and wailing and hollering and raring and pitching. It wouldn't be a way in the world to get them over there."

"They got over here," the trashy woman said. "Get back like they got over."   65

"It wasn't so many of them then," Mrs. Turpin explained.

The woman looked at Mrs. Turpin as if here was an idiot indeed but Mrs. Turpin was not bothered by the look, considering where it came from.

"Nooo," she said, "they're going to stay here where they can go to New York and marry white folks and improve their color. That's what they all want to do, every one of them, improve their color."

"You know what comes of that, don't you?" Claud asked.

"No, Claud, what?" Mrs. Turpin said.

Claud's eyes twinkled. "White-faced niggers," he said with never a smile. 70

Everybody in the office laughed except the white-trash and the ugly girl. The girl gripped the book in her lap with white fingers. The trashy woman looked around her from face to face as if she thought they were all idiots. The old woman in the feed sack dress continued to gaze expressionless across the floor at the hightop shoes of the man opposite her, the one who had been pretending to be asleep when the Turpins came in. He was laughing heartily, his hands still spread out on his knees. The child had fallen to the side and was lying now almost face down in the old woman's lap.

While they recovered from their laughter, the nasal chorus on the radio kept the room from silence.

> "You go to blank blank
> And I'll go to mine
> But we'll all blank along
> To-geth-ther,
> And all along the blank
> We'll hep eachother out
> Smile-ling in any kind of
> Weath-ther!"

Mrs. Turpin didn't catch every word but she caught enough to agree with the 75 spirit of the song and it turned her thoughts sober. To help anybody out that needed it was her philosophy of life. She never spared herself when she found somebody in need, whether they were white or black, trash or decent. And of all she had to be thankful for, she was most thankful that this was so. If Jesus had said, "You can be high society and have all the money you want and be thin and svelte-like, but you can't be a good woman with it," she would have had to say, "Well don't make me that then. Make me a good woman and it don't matter what else, how fat or how ugly or how poor!" Her heart rose. He had not made her a nigger or white-trash or ugly! He had made her herself and given her a little of everything. Jesus, thank you! she said. Thank you thank you thank you! Whenever she counted her blessings she felt as buoyant as if she weighed one hundred and twenty-five pounds instead of one hundred and eighty.

"What's wrong with your little boy?" the pleasant lady asked the white-trashy woman.

"He has a ulcer," the woman said proudly. "He ain't give me a minute's peace since he was born. Him and her are just alike," she said, nodding at the old woman, who was running her leathery fingers through the child's pale hair. "Look like I can't get nothing down them two but Co' Cola and candy."

That's all you try to get down em, Mrs. Turpin said to herself. Too lazy to light the fire. There was nothing you could tell her about people like them that she didn't know already. And it was not just that they didn't have anything. Because if you gave them everything, in two weeks it would all be broken or filthy or they would have chopped it up for lightwood. She knew all this from her own experience. Help them you must, but help them you couldn't.

All at once the ugly girl turned her lips inside out again. Her eyes were fixed like two drills on Mrs. Turpin. This time there was no mistaking that there was something urgent behind them.

Girl, Mrs. Turpin exclaimed silently, I haven't done a thing to you! The girl   80
might be confusing her with somebody else. There was no need to sit by and let herself be intimidated. "You must be in college," she said boldly, looking directly at the girl. "I see you reading a book there."

The girl continued to stare and pointedly did not answer.

Her mother blushed at this rudeness. "The lady asked you a question, Mary Grace," she said under her breath.

"I have ears," Mary Grace said.

The poor mother blushed again. "Mary Grace goes to Wellesley College," she explained. She twisted one of the buttons on her dress. "In Massachusetts," she added with a grimace. "And in the summer she just keeps right on studying. Just reads all the time, a real book worm. She's done real well at Wellesley; she's taking English and Math and History and Psychology and Social Studies," she rattled on, "and I think it's too much. I think she ought to get out and have fun."

The girl looked as if she would like to hurl them all through the plate glass   85
window.

"Way up north," Mrs. Turpin murmured and thought, well, it hasn't done much for her manners.

"I'd almost rather to have him sick," the white-trash woman said, wrenching the attention back to herself. "He's so mean when he ain't. Look like some children just take natural to meanness. It's some gets bad when they get sick but he was the opposite. Took sick and turned good. He don't give me no trouble now. It's me waitin to see the doctor," she said.

If I was going to send anybody back to Africa, Mrs. Turpin thought, it would be your kind, woman. "Yes, indeed," she said aloud, but looking up at the ceiling, "it's a heap of things worse than a nigger." And dirtier than a hog, she added to herself.

"I think people with bad dispositions are more to be pitied than anyone on earth," the pleasant lady said in a voice that was decidedly thin.

"I thank the Lord he has blessed me with a good one," Mrs. Turpin said. "The   90
day has never dawned that I couldn't find something to laugh at."

"Not since she married me anyways," Claud said with a comical straight face.

Everybody laughed except the girl and the white-trash.

Mrs. Turpin's stomach shook. "He's such a caution," she said, "that I can't help but laugh at him."

The girl made a loud ugly noise through her teeth.

Her mother's mouth grew thin and straight. "I think the worst thing in the   95
world," she said, "is an ungrateful person. To have everything and not appreciate it. I know a girl," she said, "who has parents who would give her anything, a little brother who loves her dearly, who is getting a good education, who wears the best clothes, but who can never say a kind word to anyone, who never smiles, who just criticizes and complains all day long."

"Is she too old to paddle?" Claud asked.

The girl's face was almost purple.

"Yes," the lady said, "I'm afraid there's nothing to do but leave her to her folly. Some day she'll wake up and it'll be too late."

"It never hurt anyone to smile," Mrs. Turpin said. "It just makes you feel better all over."

"Of course," the lady said sadly, "but there are just some people you can't tell   100
anything to. They can't take criticism."

"If it's one thing I am," Mrs. Turpin said with feeling, "it's grateful. When I think who all I could have been besides myself and what all I got, a little of everything, and a good disposition besides, I just feel like shouting, 'Thank you, Jesus, for making everything the way it is!' It could have been different!" For one thing, somebody else could have got Claud. At the thought of this, she was flooded with gratitude and a terrible pang of joy ran through her. "Oh thank you, Jesus, Jesus, thank you!" she cried aloud.

The book struck her directly over her left eye. It struck almost at the same instant that she realized the girl was about to hurl it. Before she could utter a sound, the raw face came crashing across the table toward her, howling. The girl's fingers sank like clamps into the soft flesh of her neck. She heard the mother cry out and Claud shout, "Whoa!" There was an instant when she was certain that she was about to be in an earthquake.

All at once her vision narrowed and she saw everything as if it were happening in a small room far away, or as if she were looking at it through the wrong end of a telescope. Claud's face crumpled and fell out of sight. The nurse ran in, then out, then in again. Then the gangling figure of the doctor rushed out of the inner door. Magazines flew this way and that as the table turned over. The girl fell with a thud and Mrs. Turpin's vision suddenly reversed itself and she saw everything large instead of small. The eyes of the white-trashy woman were staring hugely at the floor. There the girl, held down on one side by the nurse and on the other by her mother, was wrenching and turning in their grasp. The doctor was kneeling astride her, trying to hold her arm down. He managed after a second to sink a long needle into it.

Mrs. Turpin felt entirely hollow except for her heart which swung from side to side as if it were agitated in a great empty drum of flesh.

"Somebody that's not busy call for the ambulance," the doctor said in the off-   105
hand voice young doctors adopt for terrible occasions.

Mrs. Turpin could not have moved a finger. The old man who had been sitting next to her skipped nimbly into the office and made the call, for the secretary still seemed to be gone.

"Claud!" Mrs. Turpin called.

He was not in his chair. She knew she must jump up and find him but she felt like some one trying to catch a train in a dream, when everything moves in slow motion and the faster you try to run the slower you go.

"Here I am," a suffocated voice, very unlike Claud's, said.

He was doubled up in the corner on the floor, pale as paper, holding his leg. She   110
wanted to get up and go to him but she could not move. Instead, her gaze was drawn slowly downward to the churning face on the floor, which she could see over the doctor's shoulder.

The girl's eyes stopped rolling and focused on her. They seemed a much lighter blue than before, as if a door that had been tightly closed behind them was now open to admit light and air.

Mrs. Turpin's head cleared and her power of motion returned. She leaned forward until she was looking directly into the fierce brilliant eyes. There was no doubt in her mind that the girl did know her, knew her in some intense and personal way, beyond time and place and condition. "What you got to say to me?" she asked hoarsely and held her breath, waiting, as for a revelation.

The girl raised her head. Her gaze locked with Mrs. Turpin's. "Go back to hell where you came from, you old wart hog," she whispered. Her voice was low but clear. Her eyes burned for a moment as if she saw with pleasure that her message had struck its target.

Mrs. Turpin sank back in her chair.

After a moment the girl's eyes closed and she turned her head wearily to the side. 115

The doctor rose and handed the nurse the empty syringe. He leaned over and put both hands for a moment on the mother's shoulders, which were shaking. She was sitting on the floor, her lips pressed together, holding Mary Grace's hand in her lap. The girl's fingers were gripped like a baby's around her thumb. "Go on to the hospital," he said. "I'll call and make the arrangements."

"Now let's see that neck," he said in a jovial voice to Mrs. Turpin. He began to inspect her neck with his first two fingers. Two little moon-shaped lines like pink fish bones were indented over her windpipe. There was the beginning of an angry red swelling above her eye. His fingers passed over this also.

"Lea' me be," she said thickly and shook him off. "See about Claud. She kicked him."

"I'll see about him in a minute," he said and felt her pulse. He was a thin grey-haired man, given to pleasantries. "Go home and have yourself a vacation the rest of the day," he said and patted her on the shoulder.

Quit your pattin me, Mrs. Turpin growled to herself. 120

"And put an ice pack over that eye," he said. Then he went and squatted down beside Claud and looked at his leg. After a moment he pulled him up and Claud limped after him into the office.

Until the ambulance came, the only sounds in the room were the tremulous moans of the girl's mother, who continued to sit on the floor. The white-trash woman did not take her eyes off the girl. Mrs. Turpin looked straight ahead at nothing. Presently the ambulance drew up, a long dark shadow, behind the curtain. The attendants came in and set the stretcher down beside the girl and lifted her expertly onto it and carried her out. The nurse helped the mother gather up her things. The shadow of the ambulance moved silently away and the nurse came back in the office.

"That ther girl is going to be a lunatic, ain't she?" the white-trash woman asked the nurse, but the nurse kept on to the back and never answered her.

"Yes, she's going to be a lunatic," the white-trash woman said to the rest of them.

"Po' critter," the old woman murmured. The child's face was still in her lap. His 125 eyes looked idly out over her knees. He had not moved during the disturbance except to draw one leg up under him.

"I thank Gawd," the white-trash woman said fervently, "I ain't a lunatic."

Claud came limping out and the Turpins went home.

As their pick-up truck turned into their own dirt road and made the crest of the hill, Mrs. Turpin gripped the window ledge and looked out suspiciously. The land sloped gracefully down through a field dotted with lavender weeds and at the start of the rise their small yellow frame house, with its little flower beds spread out around it like a fancy apron, sat primly in its accustomed place between two giant hickory trees. She would not have been startled to see a burnt wound between two blackened chimneys.

Neither of them felt like eating so they put on their house clothes and lowered the shade in the bedroom and lay down, Claud with his leg on a pillow and herself with a damp washcloth over her eye. The instant she was flat on her back, the image of a razor-backed hog with warts on its face and horns coming out behind its ears snorted into her head. She moaned, a low quiet moan.

"I am not," she said tearfully, "a wart hog. From hell." But the denial had no 130 force. The girl's eyes and her words, even the tone of her voice, low but clear, directed only to her, brooked no repudiation. She had been singled out for the message, though there was trash in the room to whom it might justly have been applied. The full force of this fact struck her only now. There was a woman there who was neglecting her own child but she had been overlooked. The message had been given to Ruby Turpin, a respectable, hard-working, church-going woman. The tears dried. Her eyes began to burn instead with wrath.

She rose on her elbow and the washcloth fell into her hand. Claud was lying on his back, snoring. She wanted to tell him what the girl had said. At the same time, she did not wish to put the image of herself as a wart hog from hell into his mind.

"Hey, Claud," she muttered and pushed his shoulder.

Claud opened one pale baby blue eye.

She looked into it warily. He did not think about anything. He just went his way.

"Wha, whasit?" he said and closed the eye again. 135

"Nothing," she said. "Does your leg pain you?"

"Hurts like hell," Claud said.

"It'll quit terreckly," she said and lay back down. In a moment Claud was snoring again. For the rest of the afternoon they lay there. Claud slept. She scowled at the ceiling. Occasionally she raised her fist and made a small stabbing motion over her chest as if she was defending her innocence to invisible guests who were like the comforters of Job, reasonable-seeming but wrong.

About five-thirty Claud stirred. "Got to go after those niggers," he sighed, not moving.

She was looking straight up as if there were unintelligible handwriting on the ceil- 140 ing. The protuberance over her eye had turned a greenish-blue. "Listen here," she said.

"What?"

"Kiss me."

Claud leaned over and kissed her loudly on the mouth. He pinched her side and their hands interlocked. Her expression of ferocious concentration did not change. Claud got up, groaning and growling, and limped off. She continued to study the ceiling.

She did not get up until she heard the pick-up truck coming back with the Negroes. Then she rose and thrust her feet in her brown oxfords, which she did not bother to lace, and stumped out onto the back porch and got her red plastic bucket. She emptied a tray of ice cubes into it and filled it half full of water and went out into the back yard. Every afternoon after Claud brought the hands in, one of the boys helped him put out hay and the rest waited in the back of the truck until he was ready to take them home. The truck was parked in the shade under one of the hickory trees.

"Hi yawl this evening?" Mrs. Turpin asked grimly, appearing with the bucket and 145 the dipper. There were three women and a boy in the truck.

"Us doin nicely," the oldest woman said. "Hi you doin?" and her gaze stuck immediately on the dark lump on Mrs. Turpin's forehead. "You done fell down, ain't you?"

she asked in a solicitous voice. The old woman was dark and almost toothless. She had on an old felt hat of Claud's set back on her head. The other two women were younger and lighter and they both had new bright green sun hats. One of them had hers on her head; the other had taken hers off and the boy was grinning beneath it.

Mrs. Turpin set the bucket down on the floor of the truck. "Yawl hep yourselves," she said. She looked around to make sure Claud had gone. "No. I didn't fall down," she said, folding her arms. "It was something worse than that."

"Ain't nothing bad happen to you!" the old woman said. She said it as if they all knew Mrs. Turpin was protected in some special way by Divine Providence. "You just had you a little fall."

"We were in town at the doctor's office for where the cow kicked Mr. Turpin," Mrs. Turpin said in a flat tone that indicated they could leave off their foolishness. "And there was this girl there. A big fat girl with her face all broke out. I could look at that girl and tell she was peculiar but I couldn't tell how. And me and her mama were just talking and going along and all of a sudden WHAM! She throws this big book she was reading at me and . . ."

"Naw!" the old woman cried out. 150

"And then she jumps over the table and commences to choke me."

"Naw!" they all exclaimed, "naw!"

"Hi come she do that?" the old woman asked. "What ail her?"

Mrs. Turpin only glared in front of her.

"Somethin ail her," the old woman said. 155

"They carried her off in an ambulance," Mrs. Turpin continued, "but before she went she was rolling on the floor and they were trying to hold her down to give her a shot and she said something to me." She paused. "You know what she said to me?"

"What she say?" they asked.

"She said," Mrs. Turpin began, and stopped, her face very dark and heavy. The sun was getting whiter and whiter, blanching the sky overhead so that the leaves of the hickory tree were black in the face of it. She could not bring forth the words. "Something real ugly," she muttered.

"She sho shouldn't said nothin ugly to you," the old woman said. "You so sweet. You the sweetest lady I know."

"She pretty too," the one with the hat on said. 160

"And stout," the other one said. "I never knowed no sweeter white lady."

"That's the truth befo' Jesus," the old woman said. "Amen! You des as sweet and pretty as you can be."

Mrs. Turpin knew just exactly how much Negro flattery was worth and it added to her rage. "She said," she began again and finished this time with a fierce rush of breath, "that I was an old wart hog from hell."

There was an astounded silence.

"Where she at?" the youngest woman cried in a piercing voice. 165

"Lemme see her. I'll kill her!"

"I'll kill her with you!" the other one cried.

"She b'long in the sylum," the old woman said emphatically. "You the sweetest white lady I know."

"She pretty too," the other two said. "Stout as she can be and sweet. Jesus satisfied with her!"

"Deed he is," the old woman declared. 170

Idiots! Mrs. Turpin growled to herself. You could never say anything intelligent to a nigger. You could talk at them but not with them. "Yawl ain't drunk your water," she said shortly. "Leave the bucket in the truck when you're finished with it. I got more to do than just stand around and pass the time of day," and she moved off and into the house.

She stood for a moment in the middle of the kitchen. The dark protuberance over her eye looked like a miniature tornado cloud which might any moment sweep across the horizon of her brow. Her lower lip protruded dangerously. She squared her massive shoulders. Then she marched into the front of the house and out the side door and started down the road to the pig parlor. She had the look of a woman going single-handed, weaponless, into battle.

The sun was a deep yellow now like a harvest moon and was riding westward very fast over the far tree line as if it meant to reach the hogs before she did. The road was rutted and she kicked several good-sized stones out of her path as she strode along. The pig parlor was on a little knoll at the end of a lane that ran off from the side of the barn. It was a square of concrete as large as a small room, with a board fence about four feet high around it. The concrete floor sloped slightly so that the hog wash could drain off into a trench where it was carried to the field for fertilizer. Claud was standing on the outside, on the edge of the concrete, hanging onto the top board, hosing down the floor inside. The hose was connected to the faucet of a water trough nearby.

Mrs. Turpin climbed up beside him and glowered down at the hogs inside. There were seven long-snouted bristly shoats in it—tan with liver-colored spots—and an old sow a few weeks off from farrowing. She was lying on her side grunting. The shoats were running about shaking themselves like idiot children, their little slit pig eyes searching the floor for anything left. She had read that pigs were the most intelligent animal. She doubted it. They were supposed to be smarter than dogs. There had even been a pig astronaut. He had performed his assignment perfectly but died of a heart attack afterwards because they left him in his electric suit, sitting upright throughout his examination when naturally a hog should be on all fours.

A-gruntin and a-rootin and a-groanin.   175

"Gimme that hose," she said, yanking it away from Claud. "Go on and carry them niggers home and then get off that leg."

"You look like you might have swallowed a mad dog," Claud observed, but he got down and limped off. He paid no attention to her humors.

Until he was out of earshot, Mrs. Turpin stood on the side of the pen, holding the hose and pointing the stream of water at the hind quarters of any shoat that looked as if it might try to lie down. When he had had time to get over the hill, she turned her head slightly and her wrathful eyes scanned the path. He was nowhere in sight. She turned back again and seemed to gather herself up. Her shoulders rose and she drew in her breath.

"What do you send me a message like that for?" she said in a low fierce voice, barely above a whisper but with the force of a shout in its concentrated fury. "How am I a hog and me both? How am I saved and from hell too?" Her free fist was knotted and with the other she gripped the hose, blindly pointing the stream of water in and out of the eye of the old sow whose outraged squeal she did not hear.

The pig parlor commanded a view of the back pasture where their twenty beef   180
cows were gathered around the hay-bales Claud and the boy had put out. The freshly cut pasture sloped down to the highway. Across it was their cotton field and beyond that a dark green dusty wood which they owned as well. The sun was behind the wood, very red, looking over the paling of trees like a farmer inspecting his own hogs.

"Why me?" she rumbled. "It's no trash around here, black or white, that I haven't given to. And break my back to the bone every day working. And do for the church."

She appeared to be the right size woman to command the arena before her. "How am I a hog?" she demanded. "Exactly how am I like them?" and she jabbed the stream of water at the shoats. "There was plenty of trash there. It didn't have to be me."

"If you like trash better, go get yourself some trash then," she railed. "You could have made me trash. Or a nigger. If trash is what you wanted why didn't you make me trash?" She shook her fist with the hose in it and a watery snake appeared momentarily in the air. "I could quit working and take it easy and be filthy," she growled. "Lounge about the sidewalks all day drinking root beer. Dip snuff and spit in every puddle and have it all over my face. I could be nasty."

"Or you could have made me a nigger. It's too late for me to be a nigger," she said with deep sarcasm, "but I could act like one. Lay down in the middle of the road and stop traffic. Roll on the ground."

In the deepening light everything was taking on a mysterious hue. The pasture 185 was growing a peculiar glassy green and the streak of highway had turned lavender. She braced herself for a final assault and this time her voice rolled out over the pasture. "Go on," she yelled, "call me a hog! Call me a hog again. From hell. Call me a wart hog from hell. Put that bottom rail on top. There'll still be a top and bottom!"

A garbled echo returned to her.

A final surge of fury shook her and she roared, "Who do you think you are?"

The color of everything, field and crimson sky, burned for a moment with a transparent intensity. The question carried over the pasture and across the highway and the cotton field and returned to her clearly like an answer from beyond the wood.

She opened her mouth but no sound came out of it.

A tiny truck, Claud's, appeared on the highway, heading rapidly out of sight. Its 190 gears scraped thinly. It looked like a child's toy. At any moment a bigger truck might smash into it and scatter Claud's and the niggers' brains all over the road.

Mrs. Turpin stood there, her gaze fixed on the highway, all her muscles rigid, until in five or six minutes the truck reappeared, returning. She waited until it had had time to turn into their own road. Then like a monumental statue coming to life, she bent her head slowly and gazed, as if through the very heart of mystery, down into the pig parlor at the hogs. They had settled all in one corner around the old sow who was grunting softly. A red glow suffused them. They appeared to pant with a secret life.

Until the sun slipped finally behind the tree line, Mrs. Turpin remained there with her gaze bent to them as if she were absorbing some abysmal life-giving knowledge. At last she lifted her head. There was only a purple streak in the sky, cutting through a field of crimson and leading, like an extension of the highway, into the descending dusk. She raised her hands from the side of the pen in a gesture hieratic and profound. A visionary light settled in her eyes. She saw the streak as a vast swinging bridge extending upward from the earth through a field of living fire. Upon it a vast horde of souls were rumbling toward heaven. There were whole companies of white-trash, clean for the first time in their lives, and bands of black niggers in white robes, and battalions of freaks and lunatics shouting and clapping and leaping like frogs. And bringing up the end of the procession was a tribe of people whom she recognized at once as those who, like herself and Claud, had always had a little of everything and the God-given wit to use it right. She leaned forward to observe them closer. They were marching behind the others with great dignity, accountable as they had always been for good order and common sense and respectable behavior. They alone were on key. Yet she could see by their shocked and altered faces that even their virtues were being burned away. She lowered her hands and gripped the rail of the hog pen, her eyes small but fixed unblinkingly on what lay ahead. In a moment the vision faded but she remained where she was, immobile.

At length she got down and turned off the faucet and made her slow way on the darkening path to the house. In the woods around her the invisible cricket choruses had struck up, but what she heard were the voices of the souls climbing upward into the starry field and shouting hallelujah.

Questions

1. How does Mrs. Turpin see herself before Mary Grace calls her a wart hog?

2. What is the narrator's attitude toward Mrs. Turpin in the beginning of the story? How can you tell? Does this attitude change or stay the same, at the end?

3. Describe the relationship between Mary Grace and her mother. What annoying platitudes does the mother mouth? Which of Mrs. Turpin's opinions seem to anger Mary Grace?

4. Sketch the plot of the story. What moment or event do you take to be the crisis, or turning point? What is the climax? What is the conclusion?

5. What do you infer from Mrs. Turpin's conversation with the black farm workers? Is she their friend? Why does she now find their flattery unacceptable ("Jesus satisfied with her")?

6. When, near the end of the story, Mrs. Turpin roars "Who do you think you are?" an echo "returned to her clearly like an answer from beyond the wood" (paragraph 188). Explain.

7. What is the final revelation given to Mrs. Turpin? (To state it is to state the theme of the story.) What new attitude does the revelation impart? (How is Mrs. Turpin left with a new vision of humanity?)

8. Other stories in this book contain revelations: "Young Goodman Brown" (Chapter 14), "The Gospel According to Mark" (Chapter 10). Try to sum up the supernatural revelation made to the central character in each story. Is the revelation the same as a statement of the story's main theme?

Parker's Back[1]   1965

Parker's wife was sitting on the front porch floor, snapping beans. Parker was sitting on the step, some distance away, watching her sullenly. She was plain, plain. The skin on her face was thin and drawn as tight as the skin on an onion and her eyes were gray and sharp like the points of two icepicks. Parker understood why he had married her—he couldn't have got her any other way—but he couldn't understand why he stayed with her now. She was pregnant and pregnant women were not his favorite kind. Nevertheless, he stayed as if she had him conjured. He was puzzled and ashamed of himself.

The house they rented sat alone save for a single tall pecan tree on a high embankment overlooking a highway. At intervals a car would shoot past below and his wife's eyes would swerve suspiciously after the sound of it and then come back to rest on the newspaper full of beans in her lap. One of the things she did not approve of was automobiles. In addition to her other bad qualities, she was forever sniffing up sin. She did not smoke or dip, drink whiskey, use bad language or paint her face, and God knew some paint would have improved it, Parker thought. Her being against color, it was the more remarkable she had married him. Sometimes he supposed that she had married him because she meant to save him. At other times he had a suspicion that she actually liked everything she said she didn't. He could account for her one way or another; it was himself he could not understand.

[1] "Parker's Back" was the last story Flannery O'Connor wrote, published the year after her death.

She turned her head in his direction and said, "It's no reason you can't work for a man. It don't have to be a woman."

"Aw shut your mouth for a change," Parker muttered.

If he had been certain she was jealous of the woman he worked for he would have been pleased but more likely she was concerned with the sin that would result if he and the woman took a liking to each other. He had told her that the woman was a hefty young blonde; in fact she was nearly seventy years old and too dried up to have an interest in anything except getting as much work out of him as she could. Not that an old woman didn't sometimes get an interest in a young man, particularly if he was as attractive as Parker felt he was, but this old woman looked at him the same way she looked at her old tractor—as if she had to put up with it because it was all she had. The tractor had broken down the second day Parker was on it and she had set him at once to cutting bushes, saying out of the side of her mouth to the nigger, "Everything he touches, he breaks." She also asked him to wear his shirt when he worked; Parker had removed it even though the day was not sultry; he put it back on reluctantly.

This ugly woman Parker married was his first wife. He had had other women but he had planned never to get himself tied up legally. He had first seen her one morning when his truck broke down on the highway. He had managed to pull it off the road into a neatly swept yard on which sat a peeling two-room house. He got out and opened the hood of the truck and began to study the motor. Parker had an extra sense that told him when there was a woman nearby watching him. After he had leaned over the motor a few minutes, his neck began to prickle. He cast his eye over the empty yard and porch of the house. A woman he could not see was either nearby beyond a clump of honeysuckle or in the house, watching him out the window.

Suddenly Parker began to jump up and down and fling his hand about as if he had mashed it in the machinery. He doubled over and held his hand close to his chest. "God dammit!" he hollered, "Jesus Christ in hell! Jesus God Almighty damm! God dammit to hell!" he went on, flinging out the same few oaths over and over as loud as he could.

Without warning a terrible bristly claw slammed the side of his face and he fell backwards on the hood of the truck. "You don't talk no filth here!" a voice close to him shrilled.

Parker's vision was so blurred that for an instant he thought he had been attacked by some creature from above, a giant hawk-eyed angel wielding a hoary weapon. As his sight cleared, he saw before him a tall raw-boned girl with a broom.

"I hurt my hand," he said. "I HURT my hand." He was so incensed that he forgot that he hadn't hurt his hand. "My hand may be broke," he growled although his voice was still unsteady.

"Lemme see it," the girl demanded.

Parker stuck out his hand and she came closer and looked at it. There was no mark on the palm and she took the hand and turned it over. Her own hand was dry and hot and rough and Parker felt himself jolted back to life by her touch. He looked more closely at her. I don't want nothing to do with this one, he thought.

The girl's sharp eyes peered at the back of the stubby reddish hand she held. There emblazoned in red and blue was a tattooed eagle perched on a cannon. Parker's sleeve was rolled to the elbow. Above the eagle a serpent was coiled about a shield and in the spaces between the eagle and the serpent there were hearts, some with arrows through them. Above the serpent there was a spread hand of cards. Every space on the skin of Parker's arm, from wrist to elbow, was covered in some loud design. The girl

5

10

gazed at this with an almost stupefied smile of shock, as if she had accidentally grasped a poisonous snake; she dropped the hand.

"I got most of my other ones in foreign parts," Parker said. "These here I mostly got in the United States. I got my first one when I was only fifteen year old."

"Don't tell me," the girl said, "I don't like it. I ain't got any use for it."   15

"You ought to see the ones you can't see," Parker said and winked.

Two circles of red appeared like apples on the girl's cheeks and softened her appearance. Parker was intrigued. He did not for a minute think that she didn't like the tattoos. He had never yet met a woman who was not attracted to them.

Parker was fourteen when he saw a man in a fair, tattooed from head to foot. Except for his loins which were girded with a panther hide, the man's skin was patterned in what seemed from Parker's distance—he was near the back of the tent, standing on a bench—a single intricate design of brilliant color. The man, who was small and sturdy, moved about on the platform, flexing his muscles so that the arabesque of men and beasts and flowers on his skin appeared to have a subtle motion of its own. Parker was filled with emotion, lifted up as some people are when the flag passes. He was a boy whose mouth habitually hung open. He was heavy and earnest, as ordinary as a loaf of bread. When the show was over, he had remained standing on the bench, staring where the tattooed man had been, until the tent was almost empty.

Parker had never before felt the least motion of wonder in himself. Until he saw the man at the fair, it did not enter his head that there was anything out of the ordinary about the fact that he existed. Even then it did not enter his head, but a peculiar unease settled in him. It was as if a blind boy had been turned so gently in a different direction that he did not know his destination had been changed.

He had his first tattoo some time after—the eagle perched on the cannon. It was   20 done by a local artist. It hurt very little, just enough to make it appear to Parker to be worth doing. This was peculiar too for before he had thought that only what did not hurt was worth doing. The next year he quit school because he was sixteen and could. He went to the trade school for a while, then he quit the trade school and worked for six months in a garage. The only reason he worked at all was to pay for more tattoos. His mother worked in a laundry and could support him, but she would not pay for any tattoo except her name on a heart, which he had put on, grumbling. However, her name was Betty Jean and nobody had to know it was his mother. He found out that the tattoos were attractive to the kind of girls he liked but who had never liked him before. He began to drink beer and get in fights. His mother wept over what was becoming of him. One night she dragged him off to a revival with her, not telling him where they were going. When he saw the big lighted church, he jerked out of her grasp and ran. The next day he lied about his age and joined the navy.

Parker was large for the tight sailor's pants but the silly white cap, sitting low on his forehead, made his face by contrast look thoughtful and almost intense. After a month or two in the navy, his mouth ceased to hang open. His features hardened into the features of a man. He stayed in the navy five years and seemed a natural part of the grey mechanical ship, except for his eyes, which were the same pale slate-color as the ocean and reflected the immense spaces around him as if they were a microcosm of the mysterious sea. In port Parker wandered about comparing the run-down places he was in to Birmingham, Alabama. Everywhere he went he picked up more tattoos.

He had stopped having lifeless ones like anchors and crossed rifles. He had a tiger and a panther on each shoulder, a cobra coiled about a torch on his chest, hawks on his thighs, Elizabeth II and Philip over where his stomach and liver were respectively.

He did not care much what the subject was so long as it was colorful; on his abdomen he had a few obscenities but only because that seemed the proper place for them. Parker would be satisfied with each tattoo about a month, then something about it that had attracted him would wear off. Whenever a decent-sized mirror was available, he would get in front of it and study his overall look. The effect was not of one intricate arabesque of colors but of something haphazard and botched. A huge dissatisfaction would come over him and he would go off and find another tattooist and have another space filled up. The front of Parker was almost completely covered but there were no tattoos on his back. He had no desire for one anywhere he could not readily see it himself. As the space on the front of him for tattoos decreased, his dissatisfaction grew and became general.

After one of his furloughs, he didn't go back to the navy but remained away without official leave, drunk, in a rooming house in a city he did not know. His dissatisfaction, from being chronic and latent, had suddenly become acute and raged in him. It was as if the panther and the lion and the serpents and the eagles and the hawks had penetrated his skin and lived inside him in a raging warfare. The navy caught up with him, put him in the brig for nine months and then gave him a dishonorable discharge.

After that Parker decided that country air was the only kind fit to breathe. He rented the shack on the embankment and bought the old truck and took various jobs which he kept as long as it suited him. At the time he met his future wife, he was buying apples by the bushel and selling them for the same price by the pound to isolated homesteaders on back country roads.

"All that there," the woman said, pointing to his arm, "is no better than what a 25 fool Indian would do. It's a heap of vanity." She seemed to have found the word she wanted. "Vanity of vanities," she said.

Well what the hell do I care what she thinks of it? Parker asked himself, but he was plainly bewildered. "I reckon you like one of these better than another anyway," he said, dallying until he thought of something that would impress her. He thrust the arm back at her. "Which you like best?"

"None of them," she said, "but the chicken is not as bad as the rest."

"What chicken?" Parker almost yelled.

She pointed to the eagle.

"That's an eagle," Parker said. "What fool would waste their time having a 30 chicken put on themself?"

"What fool would have any of it?" the girl said and turned away. She went slowly back to the house and left him there to get going. Parker remained for almost five minutes, looking agape at the dark door she had entered.

The next day he returned with a bushel of apples. He was not one to be outdone by anything that looked like her. He liked women with meat on them, so you didn't feel their muscles, much less their old bones. When he arrived, she was sitting on the top step and the yard was full of children, all as thin and poor as herself; Parker remembered it was Saturday. He hated to be making up to a woman when there were children around, but it was fortunate he had brought the bushel of apples off the truck. As the children approached him to see what he carried, he gave each child an apple and told it to get lost; in that way he cleared out the whole crowd.

The girl did nothing to acknowledge his presence. He might have been a stray pig or goat that had wandered into the yard and she too tired to take up the broom and send it off. He set the bushel of apples down next to her on the step. He sat down on a lower step.

"Hep yourself," he said, nodding at the basket; then he lapsed into silence.

She took an apple quickly as if the basket might disappear if she didn't make   35
haste. Hungry people made Parker nervous. He had always had plenty to eat himself. He grew very uncomfortable. He reasoned he had nothing to say so why should
he say it? He could not think now why he had come or why he didn't go before he
wasted another bushel of apples on the crowd of children. He supposed they were her
brothers and sisters.

She chewed the apple slowly but with a kind of relish of concentration, bent
slightly but looking out ahead. The view from the porch stretched off across a long
incline studded with iron weed and across the highway to a vast vista of hills and one
small mountain. Long views depressed Parker. You look out into space like that and
you begin to feel as if someone were after you, the navy or the government or religion.

"Who them children belong to, you?" he said at length.

"I ain't married yet," she said. "They belong to momma." She said it as if it were
only a matter of time before she would be married.

Who in God's name would marry her? Parker thought.

A large barefooted woman with a wide gap-toothed face appeared in the door   40
behind Parker. She had apparently been there for several minutes.

"Good evening," Parker said.

The woman crossed the porch and picked up what was left of the bushel of
apples. "We thank you," she said and returned with it into the house.

"That your old woman?" Parker muttered.

The girl nodded. Parker knew a lot of sharp things he could have said like "You
got my sympathy," but he was gloomily silent. He just sat there, looking at the view.
He thought he must be coming down with something.

"If I pick up some peaches tomorrow I'll bring you some," he said.   45

"I'll be much obliged to you," the girl said.

Parker had no intention of taking any basket of peaches back there but the next
day he found himself doing it. He and the girl had almost nothing to say to each
other. One thing he did say was, "I ain't got any tattoo on my back."

"What you got on it?" the girl said.

"My shirt," Parker said. "Haw."

"Haw, haw," the girl said politely.   50

Parker thought he was losing his mind. He could not believe for a minute that he
was attracted to a woman like this. She showed not the least interest in anything but
what he brought until he appeared the third time with two cantaloups. "What's your
name?" she asked.

"O. E. Parker," he said.

"What does the O. E. stand for?"

"You can just call me O. E.," Parker said. "Or Parker. Don't nobody call me by
my name."

"What's it stand for?" she persisted.   55

"Never mind," Parker said. "What's yours?"

"I'll tell you when you tell me what them letters are the short of," she said. There
was just a hint of flirtatiousness in her tone and it went rapidly to Parker's head. He
had never revealed the name to any man or woman, only to the files of the navy
and the government, and it was on his baptismal record which he got at the age of
a month; his mother was a Methodist. When the name leaked out of the navy files,
Parker narrowly missed killing the man who used it.

"You'll go blab it around," he said.

"I'll swear I'll never tell nobody," she said. "On God's holy word I swear it."

Parker sat for a few minutes in silence. Then he reached for the girl's neck, drew   60
her ear close to his mouth and revealed the name in a low voice.

"Obadiah," she whispered. Her face slowly brightened as if the name came as a
sign to her. "Obadiah," she said.

The name still stank in Parker's estimation.

"Obadiah Elihue," she said in a reverent voice.

"If you call me that aloud, I'll bust your head open," Parker said. "What's yours?"

"Sarah Ruth Cates," she said.   65

"Glad to meet you, Sarah Ruth," Parker said.

Sarah Ruth's father was a Straight Gospel preacher but he was away, spreading
it in Florida. Her mother did not seem to mind his attention to the girl so long as he
brought a basket of something with him when he came. As for Sarah Ruth herself, it
was plain to Parker after he had visited three times that she was crazy about him. She
liked him even though she insisted that pictures on the skin were vanity of vanities
and even after hearing him curse, and even after she had asked him if he was saved
and he had replied that he didn't see it was anything in particular to save him from.
After that, inspired, Parker had said, "I'd be saved enough if you was to kiss me."

She scowled. "That ain't being saved," she said.

Not long after that she agreed to take a ride in his truck. Parker parked it on a
deserted road and suggested to her that they lie down together in the back of it.

"Not until after we're married," she said—just like that.   70

"Oh that ain't necessary," Parker said and as he reached for her, she thrust him
away with such force that the door of the truck came off and he found himself flat on
his back on the ground. He made up his mind then and there to have nothing further
to do with her.

They were married in the County Ordinary's office because Sarah Ruth thought
churches were idolatrous. Parker had no opinion about that one way or the other.
The Ordinary's office was lined with cardboard file boxes and record books with dusty
yellow slips of paper hanging on out of them. The Ordinary was an old woman with
red hair who had held office for forty years and looked as dusty as her books. She
married them from behind the iron-grill of a stand-up desk and when she finished,
she said with a flourish, "Three dollars and fifty cents and till death do you part!" and
yanked some forms out of a machine.

Marriage did not change Sarah Ruth a jot and it made Parker gloomier than ever.
Every morning he decided he had had enough and would not return that night; every
night he returned. Whenever Parker couldn't stand the way he felt, he would have
another tattoo, but the only surface left on him now was his back. To see a tattoo
on his own back he would have to get two mirrors and stand between them in just
the correct position and this seemed to Parker a good way to make an idiot of himself. Sarah Ruth who, if she had had better sense, could have enjoyed a tattoo on his
back, would not even look at the ones he had elsewhere. When he attempted to point
out especial details of them, she would shut her eyes tight and turn her back as well.
Except in total darkness, she preferred Parker dressed and with his sleeves rolled down.

"At the judgement seat of God, Jesus is going to say to you, 'What you been
doing all your life besides have pictures drawn all over you?'" she said.

"You don't fool me none," Parker said, "you're just afraid that hefty girl I work   75
for'll like me so much she'll say, 'Come on, Mr. Parker, let's you and me . . .'"

"You're tempting sin," she said, "and at the judgement seat of God you'll have to answer for that too. You ought to go back to selling the fruits of the earth."

Parker did nothing much when he was at home but listen to what the judgement seat of God would be like for him if he didn't change his ways. When he could, he broke in with tales of the hefty girl he worked for. "'Mr. Parker,'" he said she said, "'I hired you for your brains.'" (She had added, "So why don't you use them?")

"And you should have seen her face the first time she saw me without my shirt," he said. "'Mr. Parker,' she said, 'you're a walking panner-rammer!'" This had, in fact, been her remark but it had been delivered out of one side of her mouth.

Dissatisfaction began to grow so great in Parker that there was no containing it outside of a tattoo. It had to be his back. There was no help for it. A dim half-formed inspiration began to work in his mind. He visualized having a tattoo put there that Sarah Ruth would not be able to resist—a religious subject. He thought of an open book with HOLY BIBLE tattooed under it and an actual verse printed on the page. This seemed just the thing for a while; then he began to hear her say, "Ain't I already got a real Bible? What you think I want to read the same verse over and over for when I can read it all?" He needed something better even than the Bible! He thought about it so much that he began to lose sleep. He was already losing flesh—Sarah Ruth just threw food in the pot and let it boil. Not knowing for certain why he continued to stay with a woman who was both ugly and pregnant and no cook made him generally nervous and irritable, and he developed a little tic in the side of his face.

Once or twice he found himself turning around abruptly as if someone were trailing him. He had had a granddaddy who had ended in the state mental hospital, although not until he was seventy-five, but as urgent as it might be for him to get a tattoo, it was just as urgent that he get exactly the right one to bring Sarah Ruth to heel. As he continued to worry over it, his eyes took on a hollow preoccupied expression. The old woman he worked for told him that if he couldn't keep his mind on what he was doing, she knew where she could find a fourteen-year-old colored boy who could. Parker was too preoccupied even to be offended. At any time previous, he would have left her then and there, saying drily, "Well, you go ahead on and get him then."

Two or three mornings later he was baling hay with the old woman's sorry baler and her broken down tractor in a large field, cleared save for one enormous old tree standing in the middle of it. The old woman was the kind who would not cut down a large old tree because it was a large old tree. She had pointed it out to Parker as if he didn't have eyes and told him to be careful not to hit it as the machine picked up hay near it. Parker began at the outside of the field and made circles inward toward it. He had to get off the tractor every now and then and untangle the baling cord or kick a rock out of the way. The old woman had told him to carry the rocks to the edge of the field, which he did when she was there watching. When he thought he could make it, he ran over them. As he circled the field his mind was on a suitable design for his back. The sun, the size of a golf ball, began to switch regularly from in front to behind him, but he appeared to see it both places as if he had eyes in the back of his head. All at once he saw the tree reaching out to grasp him. A ferocious thud propelled him into the air, and he heard himself yelling in an unbelievably loud voice, "GOD ABOVE!"

He landed on his back while the tractor crashed upside down into the tree and burst into flame. The first thing Parker saw were his shoes, quickly being eaten by the fire; one was caught under the tractor, the other was some distance away, burning by itself. He was not in them. He could feel the hot breath of the burning tree on his face. He scrambled backwards, still sitting, his eyes cavernous, and if he had known how to cross himself he would have done it.

His truck was on a dirt road at the edge of the field. He moved toward it, still sitting, still backwards, but faster and faster; halfway to it he got up and began a kind of forward-bent run from which he collapsed on his knees twice. His legs felt like two old rusted rain gutters. He reached the truck finally and took off in it, zigzagging up the road. He drove past his house on the embankment and straight for the city, fifty miles distant.

Parker did not allow himself to think on the way to the city. He only knew that there had been a great change in his life, a leap forward into a worse unknown, and that there was nothing he could do about it. It was for all intents accomplished.

The artist had two large cluttered rooms over a chiropodist's office on a back street. Parker, still barefooted, burst silently in on him at a little after three in the afternoon. The artist, who was about Parker's own age—twenty-eight—but thin and bald, was behind a small drawing table, tracing a design in green ink. He looked up with an annoyed glance and did not seem to recognize Parker in the hollow-eyed creature before him. 85

"Let me see the book you got with all the pictures of God in it," Parker said breathlessly. "The religious one."

The artist continued to look at him with his intellectual, superior stare. "I don't put tattoos on drunks," he said.

"You know me!" Parker cried indignantly. "I'm O. E. Parker! You done work for me before and I always paid!"

The artist looked at him another moment as if he were not altogether sure. "You've fallen off some," he said. "You must have been in jail."

"Married," Parker said. 90

"Oh," said the artist. With the aid of mirrors the artist had tattooed on the top of his head a miniature owl, perfect in every detail. It was about the size of a half-dollar and served him as a show piece. There were cheaper artists in town but Parker had never wanted anything but the best. The artist went over to a cabinet at the back of the room and began to look over some art books. "Who are you interested in?" he said, "saints, angels, Christs or what?"

"God," Parker said.

"Father, Son or Spirit?"

"Just God," Parker said impatiently. "Christ. I don't care. Just so it's God."

The artist returned with a book. He moved some papers off another table and put the book down on it and told Parker to sit down and see what he liked. "The up-to-date ones are in the back," he said. 95

Parker sat down with the book and wet his thumb. He began to go through it, beginning at the back where the up-to-date pictures were. Some of them he recognized—The Good Shepherd, Forbid Them Not, The Smiling Jesus, Jesus the Physician's Friend, but he kept turning rapidly backwards and the pictures became less and less reassuring. One showed a gaunt green dead face streaked with blood. One was yellow with sagging purple eyes. Parker's heart began to beat faster and faster until it appeared to be roaring inside him like a great generator. He flipped the pages quickly, feeling that when he reached the one ordained, a sign would come. He continued to flip through until he had almost reached the front of the book. On one of the pages a pair of eyes glanced at him swiftly. Parker sped on, then stopped. His heart too appeared to cut off; there was absolute silence. It said as plainly as if silence were a language itself, GO BACK.

Parker returned to the picture—the haloed head of a flat stern Byzantine Christ with all-demanding eyes. He sat there trembling; his heart began slowly to beat again as if it were being brought to life by a subtle power.

"You found what you want?" the artist asked.

Parker's throat was too dry to speak. He got up and thrust the book at the artist, opened at the picture.

"That'll cost you plenty," the artist said. "You don't want all those little blocks though, just the outline and some better features." 100

"Just like it is," Parker said, "just like it is or nothing."

"It's your funeral," the artist said, "but I don't do that kind of work for nothing."

"How much?" Parker asked.

"It'll take maybe two days work."

"How much?" Parker said. 105

"On time or cash?" the artist asked. Parker's other jobs had been on time, but he had paid.

"Ten down and ten for every day it takes," the artist said.

Parker drew ten dollar bills out of his wallet; he had three left in.

"You come back in the morning," the artist said, putting the money in his own pocket. "First I'll have to trace that out of the book."

"No no!" Parker said. "Trace it now or gimme my money back," and his eyes 110 blared as if he were ready for a fight.

The artist agreed. Any one stupid enough to want a Christ on his back, he reasoned, would be just as likely as not to change his mind the next minute, but once the work was begun he could hardly do so.

While he worked on the tracing, he told Parker to go wash his back at the sink with the special soap he used there. Parker did it and returned to pace back and forth across the room, nervously flexing his shoulders. He wanted to go look at the picture again but at the same time he did not want to. The artist got up finally and had Parker lie down on the table. He swabbed his back with ethyl chloride and then began to outline the head on it with his iodine pencil. Another hour passed before he took up his electric instrument. Parker felt no particular pain. In Japan he had had a tattoo of the Buddha done on his upper arm with ivory needles; in Burma, a little brown root of a man had made a peacock on each of his knees using thin pointed sticks, two feet long; amateurs had worked on him with pins and soot. Parker was usually so relaxed and easy under the hand of the artist that he often went to sleep, but this time he remained awake, every muscle taut.

At midnight the artist said he was ready to quit. He propped one mirror, four feet square, on a table by the wall and took a smaller mirror off the lavatory wall and put it in Parker's hands. Parker stood with his back to the one on the table and moved the other until he saw a flashing burst of color reflected from his back. It was almost completely covered with little red and blue and ivory and saffron squares; from them he made out the lineaments of the face—a mouth, the beginning of heavy brows, a straight nose, but the face was empty; the eyes had not yet been put in. The impression for the moment was almost as if the artist had tricked him and done the Physician's Friend.

"It don't have eyes," Parker cried out.

"That'll come," the artist said, "in due time. We have another day to go on it 115 yet."

Parker spent the night on a cot at the Haven of Light Christian Mission. He found these the best places to stay in the city because they were free and included a meal of sorts. He got the last available cot and because he was still barefooted, he accepted a pair of second-hand shoes which, in his confusion, he put on to go to bed; he was still shocked from all that had happened to him. All night he lay awake in the long dormitory of cots with lumpy figures on them. The only light was from a phosphorescent cross glowing at the end of the room. The tree reached out to grasp him again, then burst into flame; the shoe burned quietly by itself; the eyes in the book said to him distinctly GO BACK and at the same time did not utter a sound. He wished that he were not in this city, not in this Haven of Light Mission, not in a bed by himself. He longed miserably for Sarah Ruth. Her sharp tongue and icepick eyes were the only comfort he could bring to mind. He decided he was losing it. Her eyes appeared soft and dilatory compared with the eyes in the book, for even though he could not summon up the exact look of those eyes, he could still feel their penetration. He felt as though, under their gaze, he was as transparent as the wing of a fly.

The tattooist had told him not to come until ten in the morning, but when he arrived at that hour, Parker was sitting in the dark hallway on the floor, waiting for him. He had decided upon getting up that, once the tattoo was on him, he would not look at it, that all his sensations of the day and night before were those of a crazy man and that he would return to doing things according to his own sound judgement.

The artist began where he left off. "One thing I want to know," he said presently as he worked over Parker's back, "why do you want this on you? Have you gone and got religion? Are you saved?" he asked in a mocking voice.

Parker's throat felt salty and dry. "Naw," he said, "I ain't got no use for none of that. A man can't save his self from whatever it is he don't deserve none of my sympathy." These words seemed to leave his mouth like wraiths and to evaporate at once as if he had never uttered them.

"Then why . . ." 120

"I married this woman that's saved," Parker said. "I never should have done it. I ought to leave her. She's done gone and got pregnant."

"That's too bad," the artist said. "Then it's her making you have this tattoo."

"Naw," Parker said, "she don't know nothing about it. It's a surprise for her."

"You think she'll like it and lay off you a while?"

"She can't hep herself," Parker said. "She can't say she don't like the looks of 125 God." He decided he had told the artist enough of his business. Artists were all right in their place but he didn't like them poking their noses into the affairs of regular people. "I didn't get no sleep last night," he said. "I think I'll get some now."

That closed the mouth of the artist but it did not bring him any sleep. He lay there, imagining how Sarah Ruth would be struck speechless by the face on his back and every now and then this would be interrupted by a vision of the tree of fire and his empty shoe burning beneath it.

The artist worked steadily until nearly four o'clock, not stopping to have lunch, hardly pausing with the electric instrument except to wipe the dripping dye off Parker's back as he went along. Finally he finished. "You can get up and look at it now," he said.

Parker sat up but he remained on the edge of the table.

The artist was pleased with his work and wanted Parker to look at it at once. Instead Parker continued to sit on the edge of the table, bent forward slightly but with a vacant look. "What ails you?" the artist said. "Go look at it."

"Ain't nothing ail me," Parker said in a sudden belligerent voice. "That tattoo   130 ain't going nowhere. It'll be there when I get there." He reached for his shirt and began gingerly to put it on.

The artist took him roughly by the arm and propelled him between the two mirrors. "Now *look*," he said, angry at having his work ignored.

Parker looked, turned white and moved away. The eyes in the reflected face continued to look at him—still, straight, all-demanding, enclosed in silence.

"It was your idea, remember," the artist said. "I would have advised something else."

Parker said nothing. He put on his shirt and went out the door while the artist shouted, "I'll expect all of my money!"

Parker headed toward a package shop on the corner. He bought a pint of whiskey   135 and took it into a nearby alley and drank it all in five minutes. Then he moved on to a pool hall nearby which he frequented when he came to the city. It was a well-lighted barn-like place with a bar up one side and gambling machines on the other and pool tables in the back. As soon as Parker entered, a large man in a red and black checkered shirt hailed him by slapping him on the back and yelling, "Yeyyyyyy boy! O. E. Parker!"

Parker was not yet ready to be struck on the back. "Lay off," he said, "I got a fresh tattoo there."

"What you got this time?" the man asked and then yelled to a few at the machines. "O. E.'s got him another tattoo."

"Nothing special this time," Parker said and slunk over to a machine that was not being used.

"Come on," the big man said, "let's have a look at O. E.'s tattoo," and while Parker squirmed in their hands, they pulled up his shirt. Parker felt all the hands drop away instantly and his shirt fell again like a veil over the face. There was a silence in the pool room which seemed to Parker to grow from the circle around him until it extended to the foundations under the building and upward through the beams in the roof.

Finally some one said, "Christ!" Then they all broke into noise at once. Parker   140 turned around, an uncertain grin on his face.

"Leave it to O. E.!" the man in the checkered shirt said. "That boy's a real card!"

"Maybe he's gone and got religion," some one yelled.

"Not on your life," Parker said.

"O. E.'s got religion and is witnessing for Jesus, ain't you, O. E.?" a little man with a piece of cigar in his mouth said wryly. "An o-riginal way to do it if I ever saw one."

"Leave it to Parker to think of a new one!" the fat man said.   145

"Yyeeeeeeyyyyyyy boy!" someone yelled and they all began to whistle and curse in compliment until Parker said, "Aaa shut up."

"What'd you do it for?" somebody asked.

"For laughs," Parker said. "What's it to you?"

"Why ain't you laughing then?" somebody yelled. Parker lunged into the midst of them and like a whirlwind on a summer's day there began a fight that raged amid overturned tables and swinging fists until two of them grabbed him and ran to the door with him and threw him out. Then a calm descended on the pool hall as nerve shattering as if the long barn-like room were the ship from which Jonah had been cast into the sea.

Parker sat for a long time on the ground in the alley behind the pool hall, exam-   150 ining his soul. He saw it as a spider web of facts and lies that was not at all important to him but which appeared to be necessary in spite of his opinion. The eyes that were now forever on his back were eyes to be obeyed. He was as certain of it as he had ever been of anything. Throughout his life, grumbling and sometimes cursing, often afraid, once in rapture, Parker had obeyed whatever instinct of this kind had come to him—in rapture when his spirit had lifted at the sight of the tattooed man at the fair, afraid when he had joined the navy, grumbling when he had married Sarah Ruth.

The thought of her brought him slowly to his feet. She would know what he had to do. She would clear up the rest of it, and she would at least be pleased. It seemed to him that, all along, that was what he wanted, to please her. His truck was still parked in front of the building where the artist had his place, but it was not far away. He got in it and drove out of the city and into the country night. His head was almost clear of liquor and he observed that his dissatisfaction was gone, but he felt not quite like himself. It was as if he were himself but a stranger to himself, driving into a new country though everything he saw was familiar to him, even at night.

He arrived finally at the house on the embankment, pulled the truck under the pecan tree and got out. He made as much noise as possible to assert that he was still in charge here, that his leaving her for a night without word meant nothing except it was the way he did things. He slammed the car door, stamped up the two steps and across the porch and rattled the door knob. It did not respond to his touch. "Sarah Ruth!" he yelled, "let me in."

There was no lock on the door and she had evidently placed the back of a chair against the knob. He began to beat on the door and rattle the knob at the same time.

He heard the bed springs screak and bent down and put his head to the keyhole, but it was stopped up with paper. "Let me in!" he hollered, bamming on the door again. "What you got me locked out for?"

A sharp voice close to the door said, "Who's there?"   155

"Me," Parker said, "O. E."

He waited a moment.

"Me," he said impatiently, "O. E."

Still no sound from inside.

He tried once more. "O. E.," he said, bamming the door two or three more times.   160 "O. E. Parker. You know me."

There was a silence. Then the voice said slowly, "I don't know no O. E."

"Quit fooling," Parker pleaded. "You ain't got any business doing me this way. It's me, old O. E., I'm back. You ain't afraid of me."

"Who's there?" the same unfeeling voice said.

Parker turned his head as if he expected someone behind him to give him the answer. The sky had lightened slightly and there were two or three streaks of yellow floating above the horizon. Then as he stood there, a tree of light burst over the skyline.

Parker fell back against the door as if he had been pinned there by a lance.   165

"Who's there?" the voice from inside said and there was a quality about it now that seemed final. The knob rattled and the voice said peremptorily, "Who's there, I ast you?"

Parker bent down and put his mouth near the stuffed keyhole. "Obadiah," he whispered and all at once he felt the light pouring through him, turning his spider web soul into a perfect arabesque of colors, a garden of trees and birds and beasts.

"Obadiah Elihue!" he whispered.

The door opened and he stumbled in. Sarah Ruth loomed there, hands on her hips. She began at once, "That was no hefty blonde woman you was working for and you'll have to pay her every penny on her tractor you busted up. She don't keep insurance on it. She came here and her and me had us a long talk and I . . ."

Trembling, Parker set about lighting the kerosene lamp.   170

"What's the matter with you, wasting that kerosene this near daylight?" she demanded. "I ain't got to look at you."

A yellow glow enveloped them. Parker put the match down and began to unbutton his shirt.

"And you ain't going to have none of me this near morning," she said.

"Shut your mouth," he said quietly. "Look at this and then I don't want to hear no more out of you." He removed the shirt and turned his back to her.

"Another picture," Sarah Ruth growled. "I might have known you was off after   175
putting some more trash on yourself."

Parker's knees went hollow under him. He wheeled around and cried, "Look at it! Don't just say that! *Look* at it!"

"I done looked," she said.

"Don't you know who it is?" he cried in anguish.

"No, who is it?" Sarah Ruth said. "It ain't anybody I know."

"It's him," Parker said.   180

"Him who?"

"God!" Parker cried.

"God? God don't look like that!"

"What do you know how he looks?" Parker moaned. "You ain't seen him."

"He don't *look*," Sarah Ruth said. "He's a spirit. No man shall see his face."   185

"Aw listen," Parker groaned, "this is just a picture of him."

"Idolatry!" Sarah Ruth screamed. "Idolatry! Enflaming yourself with idols under every green tree! I can put up with lies and vanity but I don't want no idolator in this house!" and she grabbed up the broom and began to thrash him across the shoulders with it.

Parker was too stunned to resist. He sat there and let her beat him until she had nearly knocked him senseless and large welts had formed on the face of the tattooed Christ. Then he staggered up and made for the door.

She stamped the broom two or three times on the floor and went to the window and shook it out to get the taint of him off it. Still gripping it, she looked toward the pecan tree and her eyes hardened still more. There he was—who called himself Obadiah Elihue—leaning against the tree, crying like a baby.

Questions

1. Why, in your judgment, did Parker marry Sarah Ruth? Why did she marry him?

2. At the end of the second paragraph, the narrator says of Parker and Sarah Ruth: "He could account for her one way or another; it was himself he could not understand." How accurate is each part of this assumption?

3. What does Parker's employer think of him? How valid is her estimation?

4. What is the basis of Parker's fascination with tattooing? What kinds of feelings usually prompt him to get a new tattoo?

5. "Long views depressed Parker. You look out into space like that and you begin to feel as if someone were after you, the navy or the government or religion" (paragraph 36). What insights does this statement give us into Parker's character—and, consequently, into his behavior?

6. What motivates Parker to get the tattoo on his back? How does he expect Sarah Ruth to respond to it?

7. While waiting for the artist to finish the "God" tattoo, Parker feels that "his sensations of the day and night before were those of a crazy man and that he would return to doing things according to his own sound judgement" (paragraph 117). How much self-awareness does this observation demonstrate?

8. When the artist asks him if he's "gone and got religion," Parker says, "I ain't got no use for none of that. A man can't save his self from whatever it is he don't deserve none of my sympathy" (paragraph 119). What does this attitude illustrate about Parker's personality? By his own standard, how much of his own sympathy does he deserve?

9. Why does Sarah Ruth refuse to recognize Parker by his initials? What is the significance of his whispering his name through the keyhole, and what effect does doing so have on him?

FLANNERY O'CONNOR ON WRITING

Insights into "A Good Man Is Hard to Find"   1963

A story really isn't any good unless it successfully resists paraphrase, unless it hangs on and expands in the mind. Properly, you analyze to enjoy, but it's equally true that to analyze with any discrimination, you have to have enjoyed already, and I think that the best reason to hear a story read is that it should stimulate that primary enjoyment.

I don't have any pretensions to being an Aeschylus or Sophocles and providing you in this story with a cathartic experience out of your mythic background, though this story I'm going to read certainly calls up a good deal of the South's mythic background, and it should elicit from you a degree of pity and terror, even though its way of being serious is a comic one. I do think, though, that like the Greeks you should know what is going to happen in this story so that any element of suspense in it will be transferred from its surface to its interior.

I would be most happy if you had already read it, happier still if you knew it well, but since experience has taught me to keep my expectations along these lines modest, I'll tell you that this is the story of a family of six which, on its way driving to Florida, gets wiped out by an escaped convict who calls himself the Misfit. The family is made up of the Grandmother and her son, Bailey, and his children, John Wesley and June Star and the baby, and there is also the cat and the children's mother. The cat is named Pitty Sing, and the Grandmother is taking him with them, hidden in a basket.

Now I think it behooves me to try to establish with you the basis on which reason operates in this story. Much of my fiction takes its character from a reasonable use of the unreasonable, though the reasonableness of my use of it may not always be apparent. The assumptions that underlie this use of it, however, are those of the central Christian mysteries. These are assumptions to which a large part of the modern audience takes exception. About this I can only say that there are perhaps other ways than my own in which this story could be read, but none other by which it could have been written. Belief, in my own case anyway, is the engine that makes perception operate.

Flannery O'Connor and her *Self-Portrait with Pheasant Cock*, 1962.

The heroine of this story, the Grandmother, is in the most significant position life offers the Christian. She is facing death. And to all appearances she, like the rest of us, is not too well prepared for it. She would like to see the event postponed. Indefinitely.

I've talked to a number of teachers who use this story in class and who tell their students that the Grandmother is evil, that in fact, she's a witch, even down to the cat. One of these teachers told me that his students, and particularly his Southern students, resisted this interpretation with a certain bemused vigor, and he didn't understand why. I had to tell him that they resisted it because they all had grandmothers or great-aunts just like her at home, and they knew, from personal experience, that the old lady lacked comprehension, but that she had a good heart. The Southerner is usually tolerant of those weaknesses that proceed from innocence, and he knows that a taste for self-preservation can be readily combined with the missionary spirit.

This same teacher was telling his students that morally the Misfit was several cuts above the Grandmother. He had a really sentimental attachment to the Misfit. But then a prophet gone wrong is almost always more interesting than your grandmother, and you have to let people take their pleasures where they find them.

It is true that the old lady is a hypocritical old soul; her wits are no match for the Misfit's, nor is her capacity for grace equal to his; yet I think the unprejudiced reader will feel that the Grandmother has a special kind of triumph in this story which instinctively we do not allow to someone altogether bad.

I often ask myself what makes a story work, and what makes it hold up as a story, and I have decided that it is probably some action, some gesture of a character that is unlike any other in the story, one which indicates where the real heart of the story lies. This would have to be an action or a gesture which was both totally right and totally unexpected; it would have to be one that was both in character and beyond character; it would have to suggest both the world and eternity. The action or gesture I'm talking about would have to be on the anagogical level, that is, the level which has to do with the Divine life and our participation in it. It would be a gesture that transcended any neat allegory that might have been intended or any pat moral categories a reader could make. It would be a gesture which somehow made contact with mystery.

There is a point in this story where such a gesture occurs. The Grandmother is at last alone, facing the Misfit. Her head clears for an instant and she realizes, even in her limited way, that she is responsible for the man before her and joined to him by ties of kinship which have their roots deep in the mystery she has been merely prattling about so far. And at this point, she does the right thing, she makes the right gesture.

I find that students are often puzzled by what she says and does here, but I think myself that if I took out this gesture and what she says with it, I would have no story. What was left would not be worth your attention. Our age not only does not have a very sharp eye for the almost imperceptible intrusions of grace, it no longer has much feeling for the nature of the violences which precede and follow them. The devil's greatest wile, Baudelaire has said, is to convince us that he does not exist.

I suppose the reasons for the use of so much violence in modern fiction will differ with each writer who uses it, but in my own stories I have found that violence is strangely capable of returning my characters to reality and preparing them to accept their moment of grace. Their heads are so hard that almost nothing else will do the work. This idea, that reality is something to which we must be returned at considerable cost, is one which is seldom understood by the casual reader, but it is one which is implicit in the Christian view of the world.

I don't want to equate the Misfit with the devil. I prefer to think that, however unlikely this may seem, the old lady's gesture, like the mustard-seed, will grow to be a great crow-filled tree in the Misfit's heart, and will be enough of a pain to him there to turn him into the prophet he was meant to become. But that's another story.

This story has been called grotesque, but I prefer to call it literal. A good story is literal in the same sense that a child's drawing is literal. When a child draws, he doesn't intend to distort but to set down exactly what he sees, and as his gaze is direct, he sees the lines that create motion. Now the lines of motion that interest the writer are usually invisible. They are lines of spiritual motion. And in this story you should be on the lookout for such things as the action of grace in the Grandmother's soul, and not for the dead bodies.

We hear many complaints about the prevalence of violence in modern fiction, and it is always assumed that this violence is a bad thing and meant to be an end in itself. With the serious writer, violence is never an end in itself. It is the extreme situation that best reveals what we are essentially, and I believe these are times when writers are more interested in what we are essentially than in the tenor of our daily lives. Violence is a force which can be used for good or evil, and among other things taken by it is the kingdom of heaven. But regardless of what can be taken by it, the man in the violent situation reveals those qualities least dispensable in his personality, those qualities which are all he will have to take into eternity with him; and since the characters in this story are all on the verge of eternity, it is appropriate to think of what they take with them. In any case, I hope that if you consider these points in connection with the story, you will come to see it as something more than an account of a family murdered on the way to Florida.

From "On Her Own Work"

Flannery O'Connor sitting on the steps of her home in Milledgeville, Georgia, September 22, 1959.

On Her Catholic Faith   1955

I write the way I do because (not though) I am a Catholic. This is a fact and nothing covers it like the bald statement. However, I am a Catholic peculiarly possessed of the modern consciousness, the thing Jung describes as unhistorical, solitary, and guilty. To possess this within the Church is to bear a burden, the necessary burden for the conscious Catholic. It's to feel the contemporary situation at the ultimate level. I think that the Church is the only thing that is going to make the terrible world we are coming to endurable; the only thing that makes the Church endurable is that it is somehow the body of Christ and that on this we are fed. It seems to be a fact that you suffer as much from the Church as for it but if you believe in the divinity of Christ, you have to cherish the world at the same time that you struggle to endure it. This may explain the lack of bitterness in the stories.

From a letter (July 20, 1955) in *The Habit of Being*

CRITICS ON FLANNERY O'CONNOR

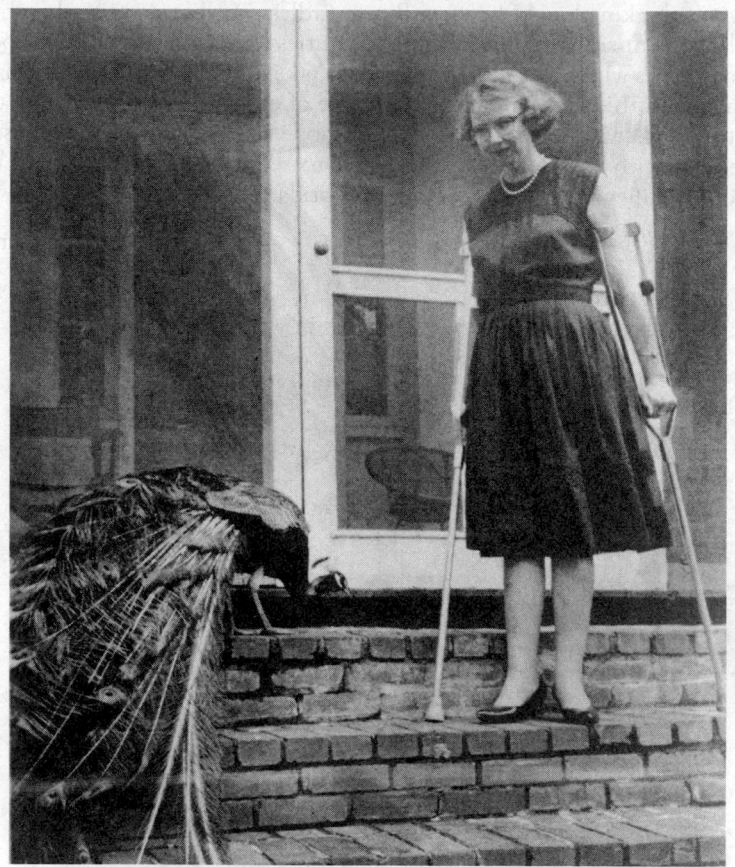

Flannery O'Connor, c. 1962, at her mother's Georgia farm where she raised peacocks.

Benjamin Percy (b. 1979)

There Will Be Blood: Violence in Flannery O'Connor's Fiction   2016

The darkhearted godmother of literary fiction, Flannery O'Connor, when discussing her use of violence in "A Good Man Is Hard to Find," had this to say:

> We hear many complaints about the prevalence of violence in modern fiction, and it is always assumed that this violence is a bad thing and meant to be an end in itself. With the serious writer, violence is never an end in itself. It is the extreme situation that best reveals what we are essentially, and I believe these are times when writers are more interested in what we are essentially than in the tenor of our daily lives. Violence is a force which can be used for good or evil, and among other things taken by it is the kingdom of heaven. But regardless of what can be taken by it, the man in the violent situation reveals those qualities least dispensable in his personality, those qualities which are all he will have to take into eternity with him.

O'Connor uses violence to unmask, to strip a character to his core. The Misfit from "A Good Man Is Hard to Find" is not "the man in the violent situation": he *is* that situation. He is the agent of violence that O'Connor uses to reveal her characters, to peel back their layers and expose what's beneath. He goes on to challenge every tenet of the grandmother's belief system as her family—son, daughter-in-law, granddaughter, and grandson—are led off-scene and into the woods to be executed. The ditch is the stage and the audience remains with the faithful sociopath and faithless old woman while they discuss, among other things, Christ. Pistol shots echo from woods that "gaped like a dark open mouth." The grandmother won't enter this forest, and neither will the reader, but the family members are marched off to be serially devoured. The effect is akin to a countdown, a bomb ticking. When the father is ushered away with the son, the reader thinks, *They'll kill the men, but surely not the women.* Until, of course, they very politely pull the mother to her feet and walk her away as well. The grandmother voices precisely what the reader is thinking: You wouldn't shoot a lady, would you? The Misfit can reply only that he'd hate to have to.

Interestingly, the shooting of the grandmother is not rendered obscene. And yet the reader doesn't exactly *see* it. O'Connor chooses here to tell the violence rather than to show it: "She reached out and touched him on the shoulder. The Misfit sprang back as if a snake had bitten him and shot her three times through the chest." O'Connor doesn't display the violence. Instead, she shows the results: "the grandmother who half sat and half lay in a puddle of blood with her legs crossed under her like a child's and her face smiling up at the cloudless sky." The carnage O'Connor reveals is a savage, zero-sum redemption, and the grandmother's reward for recognizing (re-cog-nizing = re-think-ing) the Misfit as "one of [her] own children" is tranquility and peace: the Misfit's violence returns her to a posture of innocence, like a child's.

Now imagine that O'Connor hadn't led the family into the woods. Imagine if instead she had allowed the Misfit to execute them publicly, if she had detailed the father's skull opening up, the bits of brain decorating the grass. If the mother had clutched her boy, rocking his corpse and crying out even as blood filled her lungs. Or imagine that Joyce Carol Oates—who uses a similar technique at the end of "Where Are You Going, Where Have You Been?" [Chapter 3]—had taken us out of the house, into that car with the grinning pumpkin painted on it, up the driveway, and down the road to the field where young Connie would be held down, raped, and strangled to death.

The stories would not resonate as they do. Why? As the stories are written, they invite the audience backstage—into the dark—where imagination takes over and the reader becomes a kind of writer, inventing the violence, and in doing so the story becomes their own and they carry it with them like a red-veined tumor.

And the technique suits the purpose of their stories. O'Connor and Oates are both concerned with the ordinariness of evil. Bad guys don't necessarily wear a black mask and carry a red light saber, nor do they howl at the moon or sleep in dirt-filled coffins. The Misfit talks like a deranged philosophy professor, but otherwise his "hair was beginning to go gray and he wore silver-rimmed spectacles that gave him a scholarly look." In Oates's story, Arnold Friend has "shaggy black hair" and dresses like any other teenage boy: in "tight faded jeans stuffed into black, scuffed boots, a belt that pulled his waist in and showed how lean he was." The villains of their stories look like people you might pass in the cereal aisle at the grocery store. Evil is banal. And the point is emphasized through the use of the obscene: when the violence occurs offstage, the reader creates it and becomes a perpetrator. Goethe famously said, "There is no crime of which I do not deem myself capable," and O'Connor and Oates imply the same is true of us. You are a molester. I am a murderer. We have, each and every one of us, bodies in the basements of our minds.

From *Thrill Me*

J. O. Tate (b. 1943)

A Good Source Is Not So Hard to Find: The Real Life Misfit   1980

The mounting evidence of O'Connor's use of items from the Milledgeville and Atlanta newspapers will interest those who realize that these sources, in and of themselves, have nothing to do with the Gothic, the grotesque, the American Romance tradition, Southwestern humor, Southern literature, adolescent aggression, the New Hermeneutics, the anxiety of influence, structuralism, pentecostal Gnosticism, medieval theology, Christian humanism, existentialism, or the Roman Catholic Church.

I. On "The Misfit" as Name and Word

The text of an Atlanta *Constitution* article of November 6, 1952, p. 29, identifies for us the source of a celebrated sobriquet. This newspaper reference was reprinted in *The Flannery O'Connor Bulletin*, Volume III, Autumn 1974. The headline says enough: "'The Misfit' Robs Office, Escapes With $150." Flannery O'Connor took a forgotten criminal's alias and used it for larger purposes: *her* Misfit was out of place in a grander way than the original. But we should not forget O'Connor's credentials as "a literalist of the imagination." There is always "a little lower layer." She meant to mock pop psychology by exploiting the original Misfit's exploitation of a sociopsychological "excuse" for aberrant behavior. But even a little lower: the original meaning of the word "misfit" has to do with clothing. We should not fail, therefore, to note that The Misfit's "borrowed" blue jeans are too tight. He leaves the story, of course, wearing Bailey's shirt.

II. On the Identity and Destiny of the Original Misfit

By November 15, 1952, The Misfit had been apprehended; he had also advanced himself to page three of the Atlanta *Journal*. The Misfit was a twenty-five-year old named James C. Yancey. He "was found to be of unsound mind" and committed to the state mental hospital at—Milledgeville. Where else?

III. On The Misfit's Notoriety, Peregrinations, Good Manners, Eye-glasses, Companions, and Mental Hygiene

The original Misfit was, as criminals go, small potatoes. He was an unambitious thief, no more. O'Connor took nothing from him but his imposing signature. But it just so happens that there was another well-publicized criminal aloose in Tennessee and Georgia just before the time that O'Connor appropriated the Misfit's name. This other hold-up artist had four important qualities in common with *her* Misfit. First, he inspired a certain amount of terror through several states. Second, he had, or claimed to have, a certain *politesse*. Third, he wore spectacles. Fourth, he had two accomplices, in more than one account.

James Francis ("Three-Gun") Hill, the sinister celebrity of the front pages, much more closely resembles the object of the grandmother's warnings than the original

Misfit. Various articles tell of "a fantastic record of 26 kidnappings in four states, as many robberies, 10 car thefts, and a climactic freeing of four Florida convicts from a prison gang—all in two kaleidoscopic weeks." He had advanced "from an obscure hoodlum to top billing as a public enemy" (The Atlanta *Constitution*, November 1, p. 1). Such headlines as the grandmother had in mind screamed of Hill (though not in the sports section that Bailey was reading): "Maniac's Gang Terrorizes Hills" (*Constitution*, October 24, p. 2, from Sparta, Tenn.); "Search for Kidnap-Robbery Trio Centers in Atlanta and Vicinity" (October 25, p. 1, from Atlanta); "Chattanooga Is Focal Point for Manhunt" (October 27, p. 26); "2nd of Terror Gang Seized In Florida/Pal Said Still In Atlanta Area" (October 29, p. 32); "Self-Styled 3-Gun Maniac Frees 4 Road Gang Convicts at Gunpoint" (October 31, p. 1, from Bartow, Florida). It is quite clear that O'Connor, imagining through the grandmother's point of view, was, like the newspapers, assuming an Atlanta locale and orientation. The southward trip was in the same direction as Hill's last run.

The article of October 24 gives us a bit of color: "A fantastic band of highwaymen, led by a self-styled 'maniac' who laughed weirdly while he looted his victims, spread terror through the Cumberland hills today. . . . [The leader] boasted that he had escaped from the Utah State Prison and 'killed two people' . . . 'They call me a three-gun maniac, and brother, they got the picture straight,' the head bandit was quoted by victims." The October 31 article hints at the rustic setting of O'Connor's story: "The escapees and Hill . . . drove up a dead-end road and abandoned the car. They fled into thick woods on foot. . . ."

The *Constitution* of November 1 speaks of Hill on the front page as "the bespectacled, shrunken-cheeked highwayman." A later article gives us, as it gave O'Connor, a clue to her Misfit's respectful modes of address ("Good afternoon . . . I pre-chate that, lady . . . Nome . . . I'm sorry I don't have on a shirt before you ladies . . . Yes'm . . ."): We read of the trial of "Accused kidnapper, James Francis (Three-Gun) Hill, who says he's a 'gentleman-bandit' because 'I didn't cuss in front of ladies. . . .'" This Associated Press wire story from Chattanooga was on page 26 of the November 13 Atlanta *Journal*.

The *Constitution* of the same date says "Hearing Delayed for 'Maniac' Hill and 2 Cronies," and goes on to mention "James Francis Hill, self-styled 'three-gun maniac.'" We may observe that both Yancey and Hill were referred to in the newspapers as "self-styled," an arresting phrase perhaps to an author attuned to extravagances of self. I think we may also recognize here the genesis of Hiram and Bobby Lee.

The result of Hill's plea of guilty was perhaps not as forthright as his intention: "'Maniac' Hill Is Adjudged Incompetent" (*Constitution*, November 18). Like Yancey, The Misfit, Hill was sent to a mental institution—in Tennessee, this time. (His cronies were sentenced to jail.) The diagnosis of both Yancey and Hill as mentally ill may have suggested O'Connor's Misfit's experiences with the "head-doctor."

IV. On the Misfit, Memory, and Guilt

The fictional Misfit was not easily freudened: he knew perfectly well that he had not killed his daddy. Yet he insisted there was no balance between guilt and punishment—if memory served.

The issues of accuracy of memory, consciousness of guilt, and conscience were also raised in an odd "human-interest" story that was published in those same days when O'Connor was gathering so much material from the newspapers. The Misfit's claim that he was punished for crimes he did not remember may have been inspired by this account of a man who was *not* punished for a crime he *did* remember—but remembered wrongly.

The *Journal* of November 5, 1952 carried the article, written from Brookhaven, New York, on page 12: "'Murder' Didn't Happen, House Painter Free." Louis Roberts had shot a policeman in 1928; he assumed he had killed him. Over twenty years later, his conscience finally forced him to confess. When his tale was investigated, it was discovered that the policeman had survived after all. There was no prosecution for, as an authority was quoted as saying, "His conscience has punished him enough."

From "A Good Source Is Not So Hard to Find"

Louise S. Cowan (1916–2015)

The Character of Mrs. Turpin in "Revelation"   2005

O'Connor held that serious writers cannot produce their works simply from their own ideas and conscious convictions; rather, if they are to produce anything of value, they must submit to a larger body of customs and manners of which they are a part. "As far as the creation of a body of fiction is concerned," she writes, "the social is superior to the purely personal." The writer whose themes are religious particularly needs a region where the themes find a response in the life of the people. "What the Southern Catholic writer is apt to find when he descends within his imagination is not Catholic life but the life of his region in which he is both native and alien." For O'Connor, then, the South presented the region to which she could devote her genius. It was out of step with the rest of the nation, since it was still largely agrarian, retaining in the early twentieth century traces in it of an older worldview. Further, as she saw, it still had a "folk," both white and black, who maintained an outlook fundamentally religious. It was likely to be from these groups that the prophetic figures in her fiction could emerge. In the South the general conception of man is still, O'Connor maintained, theological:

> The Bible is known by the ignorant as well as the educated and it is always the *mythos* which the poor hold in common that is most valuable to the fiction writer. When the poor hold sacred history in common, they have ties to the universal and the holy which allows the meaning of their every action to be heightened and seen under the aspect of eternity.

• • •

"Revelation"

The short story "Revelation," which won first prize in the 1964 O. Henry Awards, is one of O'Connor's last-written pieces and one of her most accomplished. It is about her familiar theme of Pharisaism;° and the epiphany with which it ends is no less devastating for occurring while the protagonist, Mrs. Turpin, is hosing down one of her prize hogs.

O'Connor's favorite target is the respectable, moral person who has lived a good and sensible life. The main character in "Revelation," Ruby Turpin, is such a figure, innocently falling into the pattern of self-satisfaction that finally assumes God himself must be impressed with her virtue. It is a mistake, however, to construe

Pharisaism: hypocritical self-righteousness.

O'Connor's keen portrayals as pitiless. Her pharisaical characters are unaware of their self-love; they conduct themselves with kindness and courtesy, as good decent people should do. Mrs. Turpin in "Revelation" is such a naively self-righteous person, convinced that her righteousness makes her a special friend of Jesus. One of O'Connor's worries about the story "Revelation," as a matter of fact, was that people would think she was disapproving of Mrs. Turpin. "You got to be a very big woman to shout at the Lord across a hog pen," she wrote in a letter to a friend.

Ruby Turpin is one of O'Connor's masterpieces. Essentially good-hearted, she is blind to her own pride and self-satisfaction. She passes judgment on everyone she meets, sometimes occupying herself with naming over the classes of people. "On the bottom of the heap were most colored people . . . then next to them, not above, just away from—were the white trash, then above them the home-owners, and above them the home-and-land owners to which she and Claud belonged." She naively congratulates herself on having been born as who she is, a good respectable white woman who, with her husband, makes do with what they have and takes care of their property. But there are people who own more property—and people over them, and some of them are not morally good; so Mrs. Turpin's neat little scale of measurement becomes blurry and leaves her puzzled.

The crucial event in Ruby Turpin's life begins in a doctor's office. . . . She has been singled out, she knows, for a message. And, afterwards, the more she thinks about it in her isolation (for she can't bring herself to ask her husband about it; and the black servants who work for her merely flatter her), the more the incident seems to have some sort of divine import. "The message had been given to Ruby Turpin, a respectable, hard-working, church-going woman." Angry, she makes her way to the hogpen; and as she is watering down a white sow she begins her questioning of God that turns into a challenge: "Go on, call me a hog! Call me a hog again. From hell. Call me a wart hog from hell." And finally the blasphemous, "Who do you think you are?"

It is this direct challenge to the Almighty that produces the real revelation for Ruby Turpin. And in the vision that she receives, the question she had always stumbled over—the complexity of categorizing the classes of people—is answered, with a revelation at once grotesque and sublime.

From "Passing by the Dragon: Flannery O'Connor's Art of Revelation"

Damian J. Ference (b. 1976)

No Vague Believer   2012

In "Parker's Back," O. E. Parker longs for a tattoo that will finally satisfy him, a tattoo that will complete him. He has been collecting tattoos his whole adult life, and his back is the only space left on his body without ink. After crashing his tractor into a tree and having a private revelation, he speedily drives to town to the tattoo parlor and tells the tattoo artist that he wants to see "the book you got with all the pictures of God in it." When the artist asks Parker to be more specific, "What are you interested in? Saints, angels, Christs or what?" Parker responds, "God." The artist wants him to be more precise, "Father, Son or Spirit?" "Just God," Parker said impatiently. "Christ. I don't care. Just so it's God." (Note that once again, O'Connor uses a violation of the second commandment to point to God's specificity, particularly in Christ.)

The tattoo artist hands Parker the book containing a wide variety of pictures of Jesus Christ and invites him to page through it. The artist tells him, "The up-to-date ones are in the back." The up-to-date images of Jesus represent the Jesus of vague belief — watered-down and soft: "The Good Shepherd, Forbid Them Not, The Smiling Jesus, Jesus the Physician's Friend." (Think of "Buddy Christ" from the movie *Dogma*.) As Parker makes his way from the back of the book to the front, the images of Jesus become less reassuring, more demanding, more orthodox, and I would argue, more specific:

> Parker returned to the picture—the haloed head of a flat stern Byzantine Christ with all demanding eyes. He sat there trembling; his heart began slowly to beat again as if it were being brought to life by a subtle power.
>
> "You found what you want?" the artist asked.
>
> Parker's throat was too dry to speak. He got up and thrust the book at the artist, opened at the picture.
>
> "That'll cost you plenty," the artist said. "You don't want all those little blocks though, just the outline and some better features."
>
> "Just like it is," Parker said, "just like it is or nothing."
>
> "It's your funeral," the artist said, "but I don't do that kind of work for nothing."

In the image of the Byzantine Christ, Parker finds the Christ of specific belief, and he knows that he must accept him as he is, as the Son of God and Savior of the world. It is not for Parker to make Christ less than he is, that is, to diminish his divinity and his specificity in order to make him more palatable. And Parker also knows that accepting Christ as he is will cost him plenty—it will cost him his life. The tattoo artist offers, "It's your funeral," as a way of pointing to the reality that specific belief in Christ calls for a death to self.

From "No Vague Believer: The Specificity of the Person
of Christ According to Flannery O'Connor and Benedict XVI"

Lucinda Williams (b. 1953)

Meeting Flannery O'Connor   2014

My dad, when he was a younger writer, always had a mentor. Flannery O'Connor was one. We lived in Macon, Georgia, and she was in Milledgeville. So my dad took me. I can't remember if my brother and sister went or not, and this is what's so beautiful about the story: O'Connor—unlike me—was very disciplined. She had a certain time that she would write. She would get up at eight in the morning and write till three in the afternoon, and if the shades were down, that meant she was writing and you couldn't come in. We showed up, well, she was still writing, so we had to sit out on the front porch until she was done. And she raised peacocks; my memory is of chasing her peacocks around the yard.

When I was about fifteen and sixteen I discovered her writing and read everything I could get my hands on, which wasn't that much. I read everything, and I also devoured Eudora Welty's stuff. But for me, Flannery O'Connor was to writing what Robert Johnson was to blues. That might be the best way to say it. There was something about her stuff that was just a little more crooked, a little more weird, a little more out-there.

From "Where the Spirit Meets the Bone"
First Published in *Radio Silence*, 2014

■ WRITING *effectively*

TOPICS FOR WRITING ON FLANNERY O'CONNOR

1. Read three stories by Flannery O'Connor or by any of the writers who appear in this book. Identify a theme or idea common to all three stories. Write an essay describing how your chosen author treats this theme. Support your argument with evidence from all three stories.

2. Compare and contrast a pair of characters from two different stories who feel conceptually related. Good choices might be Sarah Ruth from "Parker's Back," Mary Grace or Mrs. Turpin from "Revelation," and the grandmother in "A Good Man Is Hard to Find." Do these characters play similar roles in their respective stories?

3. All three stories are about revelations of one kind or another. How do these three revelations relate to each other? Back up your argument with evidence from the three stories.

4. In the excerpt from "On Her Own Work," O'Connor writes:

   > I often ask myself what makes a story work, and what makes it hold up as a story, and I have decided that it is probably some action, some gesture of a character that is unlike any other in the story, one which indicates where the real heart of the story lies. This would have to be an action or a gesture which was both totally right and totally unexpected; it would have to be one that was both in character and beyond character; it would have to suggest both the world and eternity. . . . It would be a gesture which somehow made contact with mystery.

   While O'Connor is speaking specifically about "A Good Man Is Hard to Find," her words can be applied to her other stories. Choose a gesture from "Revelation" or "Parker's Back" that fits this description and explain your choice.

5. "In most good stories it is the character's personality that creates the action of the story," O'Connor declares in her essay "Writing Short Stories." "If you start with a real personality, a real character, then something is bound to happen." Discuss this statement as it applies to one or more of the O'Connor stories you have read. Do O'Connor's characters seem to you to be real people, or do you see them as mere vessels for the author's religious views?

6. In 750 to 1,000 words, comment on O'Connor's use of humor. How does comedy help her say what she has to say?

12 CRITICAL CASEBOOK
Three Stories in Depth

Edgar Allan Poe ▪ *The Tell-Tale Heart*

Charlotte Perkins Gilman ▪ *The Yellow Wallpaper*

Alice Walker ▪ *Everyday Use*

What You Will Learn in This Chapter

- ▪ To understand three classic stories within their biographical, critical, and cultural contexts

EDGAR ALLAN POE

Edgar Poe was born in Boston in January 1809, the second son of actors Eliza and David Poe. Edgar inherited his family's legacy of artistic talent, financial instability, and social inferiority (actors were not considered respectable in the nineteenth century), as well as his father's problems with alcohol. David Poe abandoned his family after the birth of Edgar's little sister, Rosalie, and Eliza died of tuberculosis in a Richmond, Virginia, boardinghouse before Edgar turned three. He was taken in by the wealthy John and Frances Allan of Richmond, whose name he added to his own. Allan educated Poe at first-rate schools, where he excelled in all subjects. But he grew into a moody adolescent, and his relationship with his foster father deteriorated.

Edgar Allan Poe

Poe's first year at the University of Virginia was marked by scholastic success, alcoholic binges, and gambling debts. Disgraced, he fled to Boston and joined the army under the name Edgar Perry. He performed well as an enlisted man and published his first collection of poetry, Tamerlane and Other Poems, *at age eighteen. After an abortive stint at West Point led to a final break with Allan, Poe embarked on a full-time literary career. A respected critic and editor, he sharply improved both the content and circulation of every magazine with which he was associated. But, morbidly sensitive to criticism, paranoid and belligerent when drunk, he left or was fired from every post he held. Poorly paid as both an editor and a writer, he earned almost nothing from the works that made him famous, such as "The Fall of the House of Usher" and "The Raven."*

After the break with his foster family, Poe rediscovered his own. From 1831, he lived with his father's widowed sister, Maria Clemm, and her daughter, Virginia. In 1836 Poe married this thirteen-year-old first cousin. These women provided him with much-needed emotional stability. However, like his mother, Poe's wife died of tuberculosis at age twenty-four, her demise doubtless hastened by poverty. Afterward, Poe's life came apart; his drinking intensified, as did his self-destructive tendencies. In October 1849 he died in mysterious circumstances, a few days after being found sick and incoherent on a Baltimore street.

The Tell-Tale Heart   (1843) 1850

True!—nervous—very, very dreadfully nervous I had been and am; but why *will* you say that I am mad? The disease had sharpened my senses—not destroyed—not dulled them. Above all was the sense of hearing acute. I heard all things in the heaven and in the earth. I heard many things in hell. How, then, am I mad? Hearken! and observe how healthily—how calmly, I can tell you the whole story.

It is impossible to say how first the idea entered my brain; but once conceived, it haunted me day and night. Object there was none. Passion there was none. I loved the old man. He had never wronged me. He had never given me insult. For his gold I had no desire. I think it was his eye! yes, it was this! One of his eyes resembled that of a vulture—a pale blue eye, with a film over it. Whenever it fell upon me, my blood ran cold; and so by degrees—very gradually—I made up my mind to take the life of the old man, and thus rid myself of the eye forever.

Now this is the point. You fancy me mad. Madmen know nothing. But you should have seen *me*. You should have seen how wisely I proceeded—with what caution—with what foresight—with what dissimulation I went to work! I was never kinder to the old man than during the whole week before I killed him. And every night, about midnight, I turned the latch of his door and opened it—oh, so gently! And then, when I had made an opening sufficient for my head, I put in a dark lantern, all closed, closed, so that no light shone out, and then I thrust in my head. Oh, you would have laughed to see how cunningly I thrust it in! I moved it slowly—very, very slowly, so that I might not disturb the old man's sleep. It took me an hour to place my whole head within the opening so far that I could see him as he lay upon his bed. Ha!—would a madman have been so wise as this? And then, when my head was well in the room, I undid the lantern cautiously—oh, so cautiously—cautiously (for the hinges creaked)—I undid it just so much that a single thin ray fell upon the vulture eye. And this I did for seven long nights—every night just at midnight—but I found the eye always closed; and so it was impossible to do the work; for it was not the old man who vexed me, but his Evil Eye. And every morning, when the day broke, I went boldly into the chamber, and spoke courageously to him, calling him by name in a hearty tone, and inquiring how he had passed the night. So you see he would have been a very profound old man, indeed, to suspect that every night, just at twelve, I looked in upon him while he slept.

Upon the eighth night I was more than usually cautious in opening the door. A watch's minute hand moves more quickly than did mine. Never before that night had I *felt* the extent of my own powers—of my sagacity. I could scarcely contain my feelings of triumph. To think that there I was, opening the door, little by little, and he not even to dream of my secret deeds or thoughts. I fairly chuckled at the idea; and perhaps he heard me; for he moved on the bed suddenly, as if startled. Now you may think that I drew back—but no. His room was as black as pitch with the thick

FROM THE TERRIFYING PAGES of EDGAR ALLAN POE!

RUE MORGUE

"He had the pale blue eyes of a vulture ...so horrible, it chilled the very marrow in my bones!"

EDGAR ALLAN POE'S

THE TELL-TALE HEART

"THE BEAT OF HIS DEATHLESS HEART ...RIPPED INTO MY TORTURED BRAIN."

LAURENCE PAYNE · ADRIENNE CORRI · DERMOT WALSH   A Brigadier Release

Poster for 1960 film *The Tell-Tale Heart*.

darkness (for the shutters were close fastened, through fear of robbers), and so I knew that he could not see the opening of the door, and I kept pushing it on steadily, steadily.

I had my head in, and was about to open the lantern, when my thumb slipped upon the tin fastening, and the old man sprang up in the bed, crying out—"Who's there?"   5

I kept quite still and said nothing. For a whole hour I did not move a muscle, and in the meantime I did not hear him lie down. He was still sitting up in the bed, listening;— just as I have done, night after night, hearkening to the death watches° in the wall.

Presently I heard a slight groan, and I knew it was the groan of mortal terror. It was not a groan of pain or of grief—oh, no!—it was the low stifled sound that arises from the bottom of the soul when overcharged with awe. I knew the sound very well. Many a night, just at midnight, when all the world slept, it has welled up from my own bosom, deepening, with its dreadful echo, the terrors that distracted me. I say I knew it well. I knew what the old man felt, and pitied him, although I chuckled at heart. I knew that he had been lying awake ever since the first slight noise, when he had turned in the bed. His fears had been ever since growing upon him. He had been trying to fancy them causeless, but could not. He had been saying to himself—"It is nothing but the wind in the chimney—it is only a mouse crossing the floor," or "it is merely a cricket which has made a single chirp." Yes, he had been trying to comfort himself with these suppositions; but he had found all in vain. *All in vain*; because Death, in approaching him, had stalked with his black shadow before him, and enveloped the victim. And it was the mournful influence of the unperceived shadow that caused him to feel—although he neither saw nor heard—to *feel* the presence of my head within the room.

death watches: beetles that infest timbers. Their clicking sound was thought to be an omen of death.

When I had waited a long time, very patiently, without hearing him lie down, I resolved to open a little—a very, very little crevice in the lantern. So I opened it—you cannot imagine how stealthily, stealthily—until, at length, a single dim ray, like the thread of the spider, shot from out of the crevice and fell upon the vulture eye.

It was open—wide, wide open—and I grew furious as I gazed upon it. I saw it with perfect distinctness—all a dull blue, with a hideous veil over it that chilled the very marrow in my bones; but I could see nothing else of the old man's face or person: for I had directed the ray as if by instinct, precisely upon the damned spot.

And now have I not told you that what you mistake for madness is but over-acuteness of the senses?—now, I say, there came to my ears a low, dull, quick sound, such as a watch makes when enveloped in cotton. I knew *that* sound well, too. It was the beating of the old man's heart. It increased my fury, as the beating of a drum stimulates the soldier into courage.

But even yet I refrained and kept still. I scarcely breathed. I held the lantern motion-less. I tried how steadily I could maintain the ray upon the eye. Meantime the hellish tattoo of the heart increased. It grew quicker and quicker, and louder and louder every instant. The old man's terror *must* have been extreme! It grew louder, I say, louder every moment!—do you mark me well? I have told you that I am nervous: so I am. And now at the dead hour of the night, amid the dreadful silence of that old house, so strange a noise as this excited me to uncontrollable terror. Yet, for some minutes longer I refrained and stood still. But the beating grew louder, louder! I thought the heart must burst. And now a new anxiety seized me—the sound would be heard by a neighbor! The old man's hour had come! With a loud yell, I threw open the lantern and leaped into the room. He shrieked once—once only. In an instant I dragged him to the floor, and pulled the heavy bed over him. I then smiled gaily, to find the deed so far done. But, for many minutes, the heart beat on with a muffled sound. This, however, did not vex me; it would not be heard through the wall. At length it ceased. The old man was dead. I removed the bed and examined the corpse. Yes, he was stone, stone dead. I placed my hand upon the heart and held it there many minutes.

If still you think me mad, you will think so no longer when I describe the wise precau-tions I took for the concealment of the body. The night waned, and I worked hastily, but in silence. First of all I dismembered the corpse. I cut off the head and the arms and the legs.

I then took up three planks from the flooring of the chamber, and deposited all between the scantlings. I then replaced the boards so cleverly, so cunningly, that no human eye—not even *his*—could have detected anything wrong. There was nothing to wash out—no stain of any kind—no blood-spot whatever. I had been too wary for that. A tub had caught all—ha! ha!

When I had made an end of these labors, it was four o'clock—still dark as mid-night. As the bell sounded the hour, there came a knocking at the street door. I went down to open it with a light heart,—for what had I *now* to fear? There entered three men, who introduced themselves, with perfect suavity, as officers of the police. A shriek had been heard by a neighbor during the night; suspicion of foul play had been aroused, information had been lodged at the police office, and they (the officers) had been deputed to search the premises.

I smiled,—for *what* had I to fear? I bade the gentlemen welcome. The shriek, I said, was my own in a dream. The old man, I mentioned, was absent in the country. I took my visitors all over the house. I bade them search—search *well*. I led them, at length, to *his* chamber. I showed them his treasures, secure, undisturbed. In the enthusiasm of my confidence, I brought chairs into the room, and desired them *here* to rest from their

10

15

fatigues, while I myself, in the wild audacity of my perfect triumph, placed my own seat upon the very spot beneath which reposed the corpse of the victim.

The officers were satisfied. My *manner* had convinced them. I was singularly at ease. They sat, and while I answered cheerily, they chatted of familiar things. But, ere long, I felt myself getting pale and wished them gone. My head ached, and I fancied a ringing in my ears: but still they sat and still chatted. The ringing became more distinct:—it continued and became more distinct: I talked more freely to get rid of the feeling: but it continued and gained definitiveness—until, at length, I found that the noise was *not* within my ears.

No doubt I now grew *very* pale:—but I talked more fluently, and with a heightened voice. Yet the sound increased—and what could I do? It was a *low, dull, quick sound—much such a sound as a watch makes when enveloped in cotton.* I gasped for breath—and yet the officers heard it not. I talked more quickly—more vehemently; but the noise steadily increased. I arose and argued about trifles, in a high key and with violent gesticulations; but the noise steadily increased. Why *would* they not be gone? I paced the floor to and fro with heavy strides, as if excited to fury by the observations of the men—but the noise steadily increased. Oh God! what *could* I do? I foamed—I raved—I swore! I swung the chair upon which I had been sitting, and grated it upon the boards, but the noise arose over all and continually increased. It grew louder—louder—*louder!* And still the men chatted pleasantly, and smiled. Was it possible they heard not? Almighty God!—no, no! They heard!—they suspected!—they *knew!*—they were making a mockery of my horror!—this I thought, and this I think. But anything was better than this agony! Anything was more tolerable than this derision! I could bear those hypocritical smiles no longer! I felt that I must scream or die!—and now—again!—hark! louder! louder! louder! *louder!*—

"Villains!" I shrieked, "dissemble no more! I admit the deed!—tear up the planks!—here, here!—it is the beating of his hideous heart!"

Questions

1. From what point of view is Poe's story told? Why is this point of view particularly effective for "The Tell-Tale Heart"?
2. Point to details in the story that identify its speaker as an unreliable narrator.
3. What do we know about the old man in the story? What motivates the narrator to kill him?
4. In spite of all his precautions, the narrator does not commit the perfect crime. What trips him up?
5. How do you account for the police officers' chatting calmly with the murderer instead of reacting to the sound that stirs the murderer into a frenzy?
6. See the student essays on this story in the chapter "Writing About a Story" (Chapter 43). What do they point out that enlarges your own appreciation of Poe's art?

EDGAR ALLAN POE ON WRITING

On Imagination   1849

The *pure Imagination* chooses, from *either Beauty or Deformity,* only the most combinable things hitherto uncombined; the compound, as a general rule, partaking, in character, of beauty, or sublimity, in the ratio of the respective beauty or sublimity of the things combined—which are themselves still to be considered as atomic—that is to say, as previous combinations. But, as often analogously happens in physical chemistry, so not infrequently does it occur in this chemistry of the intellect, that the admixture of two elements results in a something that has nothing of the qualities of one of them, or even nothing of the qualities of either. . . . Thus, the range of Imagination is unlimited. Its materials extend throughout the universe. Even out of deformities it fabricates that *Beauty* which is at once its sole object and its inevitable test. But, in general, the richness or force of the matters combined; the facility for discovering combinable novelties worth combining; and, especially the absolute "chemical combination" of the completed mass—are the particulars to be regarded in our estimate of Imagination. It is this thorough harmony of an imaginative work which so often causes it to be undervalued by the thoughtless, through the character of *obviousness* which is superinduced. We are apt to find ourselves asking *why* it is that these combinations have never been imagined before.

From "Marginalia," *Southern Literary Messenger*

The Philosophy of Composition   1846

Nothing is more clear than that every plot, worth the name, must be elaborated to its denouement before anything be attempted with the pen. It is only with the denouement constantly in view that we can give a plot its indispensable air of consequence, or causation, by making the incidents, and especially the tone at all points, tend to the development of the intention.

There is a radical error, I think, in the usual mode of constructing a story. Either history affords a thesis—or one is suggested by an incident of the day—or, at best, the author

Edgar Allan Poe by John Sherffius.

sets himself to work in the combination of striking events to form merely the basis of his narrative—designing, generally, to fill in with description, dialogue, or autorial comment, whatever crevices of fact, or action, may, from page to page, render themselves apparent.

I prefer commencing with the consideration of an effect. Keeping originality always in view—for he is false to himself who ventures to dispense with so obvious and so easily attainable a source of interest—I say to myself, in the first place, "Of the innumerable effects, or impressions, of which the heart, the intellect, or (more generally) the soul is susceptible, what one shall I, on the present occasion, select?" Having chosen a novel, first, and secondly a vivid effect, I consider whether it can be best wrought by incident or tone—whether by ordinary incidents and peculiar tone, or the converse, or by peculiarity both of incident and tone—afterward looking about me (or rather within) for such combinations of event, or tone, as shall best aid me in the construction of the effect.

From "The Philosophy of Composition"

CRITICS ON "THE TELL-TALE HEART"

Daniel Hoffman (1923–2013)

The Father-Figure in "The Tell-Tale Heart"   1972

There are no parents in the tales of Edgar Poe, nary a Mum nor a Dad. Instead all is symbol. And what does this total repression of both sonhood and parenthood signify but that to acknowledge such relationships is to venture into territory too dangerous, too terrifying, for specificity. Desire and hatred are alike insatiable and unallayed. But the terrible war of superego upon the id, the endless battle between conscience and impulse, the unsleeping enmity of the self and its Imp of the Perverse—these struggles are enacted and reenacted in Poe's work, but always in disguise.

Take "The Tell-Tale Heart," surely one of his nearly perfect tales. It's only four pages long, a triumph of the art of economy:

> How, then, am I mad? Hearken! and observe how healthily—how calmly I can tell you the whole story.

When a narrator commences in *this* vein, we know him to be mad already. But we also know his author to be sane. For with such precision to portray the methodicalness of a madman is the work not of a madman but of a man who truly understands what it is to be mad. Artistic control is the warrant of auctorial sanity. It is axiomatic in the psychiatric practice of our century that self-knowledge is a necessary condition for the therapeutic process. Never using the language of the modern diagnostician—which was unavailable to him in the first place, and which in any case he didn't need—Poe demonstrates the extent of his self-knowledge in his manipulation of symbolic objects and actions toward ends which his tales embody.

The events are few, the action brief. "I" (in the story) believes himself sane because he is so calm, so methodical, so fully aware and in control of his purpose. Of course his knowledge of that purpose is limited, while his recital thereof endows the reader with a greater knowledge than his own. "The disease," he says right at the start, "had sharpened my senses. . . . Above all was the sense of hearing acute. I heard all things in the heavens and in the earth. I heard many things in hell." Now of whom can this be said but a

Illustration of the Edgar Allan Poe cottage, now a museum, in the Bronx, New York. Poe lived here from 1846–49.

delusional person? At the same time, mad as he is, this narrator is *the hero of sensibility*. His heightened senses bring close both heaven and hell.

His plot is motiveless. "Object there was none. Passion there was none. I loved the old man. He had never wronged me. He had never given me insult. For his gold I had no desire." The crime he is about to commit will be all the more terrible because apparently gratuitous. But let us not be lulled by this narrator's lack of admitted motive. He may have a motive—one which he cannot admit, even to himself.

Nowhere does this narrator explain what relationship, if any, exists between him and the possessor of the Evil Eye. We do, however, learn from his tale that he and the old man live under the same roof—apparently alone together, for there's no evidence of anyone else's being in the house. Is the young man the old man's servant? Odd that he would not say so. Perhaps the youth is the old man's son. Quite natural that he should not say so. "I loved the old man. He had never wronged me. . . . I was never kinder to the old man than during the whole week before I killed him." Such the aggressive revulsion caused by the old man's Evil Eye!

What can this be all about? The Evil Eye is a belief as old and as dire as any in man's superstitious memory, and it usually signifies the attribution to another of a power wished for by the self. In this particular case there are other vibrations emanating from the vulture-like eye of the benign old man. Insofar as we have warrant—which I think we do—to take him as a father-figure, his Eye becomes the all-seeing surveillance of the child by the father, even by The Father. This surveillance is of course the origin of the child's conscience, the inculcation into his soul of the paternal principles of right and wrong. As such, the old man's eye becomes a ray to be feared. For if the boy deviates ever so little from the strict paths of rectitude, *it will find him out*.

Could he but rid himself of its all-seeing scrutiny, he would then be free of his subjection to time.

All the more so if the father-figure in this tale be, in one of his aspects, a Father-Figure. As, to an infant, his own natural father doubtless is. As, to the baby Eddie, his foster-father may have been. Perhaps he had even a subliminal memory of his natural father, who so early deserted him, eye and all, to the hard knocks experience held in store. So, the evil in that Evil Eye is likely a mingling of the stern reproaches of conscience with the reminder of his own subjection to time, age, and death.

From *Poe Poe Poe Poe Poe Poe Poe*

Scott Peeples   (b.1963)

"The Tell-Tale Heart" as a Love Story   1998

It might seem strange to classify "The Tell-Tale Heart" and "The Black Cat," two of
Poe's infamous "tales of terror," as love stories. Certainly neither treats love as a goal
or an answer to its main character's problems; rather, love itself is the problem. "I
loved the old man," the narrator of "The Tell-Tale Heart" explains early in the story,
and yet he kills him. Does he kill him *even though* he loves him, or *because* he
loves him? The narrator does not divulge his legal relationship to the old man—he
could be his landlord, his uncle, a friend—but most readers seem to agree with Daniel
Hoffman's claim that he is a "father figure" if not literally his father. The narrator
knows him very well, or at least believes he does, for he identifies the old man's
thoughts as his own, even as he awaits his opportunity to kill him:

> Presently I heard a slight groan, and I knew it was the groan of mortal
> terror. . . . it was the low stifled sound that arises from the bottom of the soul
> when overcharged with awe. I knew the sound very well. Many a night, just at
> midnight, when all the world slept, it has welled up from my own bosom, deep-
> ening, with its dreadful echo, the terrors that distracted me. I say I knew it well. I
> knew what the old man felt, and pitied him, although I chuckled at heart.

The ability to duplicate the thought processes of another person becomes a valuable
skill for Monsieur Dupin in Poe's detective tales, but here the narrator's knowledge of
what the old man thinks and feels is not so much an ability as the inevitable result of
their intimacy. Here is a rather commonplace instance of doubling: he feels the old
man in himself, as sons often feel the presence of their fathers.

The narrator kills the old man, he says, because of his Evil Eye. Superstitions and
folklore notwithstanding, this explanation is proof of what almost every reader intuits
from the story's opening: the narrator is insane. But the story invites us to find a method
to the narrator's madness, to locate the logic beneath the insanity. After all, the narrator fulfills his promise to tell the story "healthily" and "calmly" (at least until the last
two paragraphs), and he does have the presence of mind to engineer the perfect crime,
although he lacks the self-restraint to keep quiet about it. The keys to his mad logic are
two obsessions: although he names the Evil Eye as his motive, he is equally obsessed with
time-keeping. He makes a point of looking in on the old man "just at twelve" and notes
that "[i]t took me an hour to place my whole head within the opening," and that on
the fatal eighth night, "[a] watch's minute hand moves more quickly than did mine."
Twice he compares the sound that haunts him—the beating of a heart—to the sound "a
watch makes when enveloped in cotton." On the night of the murder, he believes that
the old man is "listening;—just as I have done, night after night, hearkening to the death
watches in the wall." This last detail is particularly ripe with implications. The "death
watch" is an insect that, as part of its mating ritual, rhythmically strikes its head against
the wood to which it has attached itself. The name emphasizes the double meaning of
watch: both a timepiece (enveloped in cotton) and a period of watching, specifically
anticipating death—precisely what the narrator, and perhaps the old man, is doing. And
although love is probably not a component of the mating practices of bugs, the human
association between love and mating makes the death watch an uncanny figure for the
narrator's relationship with the old man: he loves him but wishes for his death.

From Peeples. *Edgar Allan Poe Revisited*, 1e. © 1999 Gale, a part of Cengage, Inc.
Reprinted by permission. http://www.cengage.com/permissions.

Charles Baudelaire   (1821–1867)

Poe's Characters   1856

Translated by Joan F. Mele

The characters in Poe, or rather the character in Poe, the man with extremely acute faculties, the man with relaxed nerves, the man whose patient and ardent will hurls defiance at difficulties, he whose gaze is fixed as straight as a sword on objects which increase in importance as he stares at them—this man is Poe himself. And his women, all luminous and sickly, dying of strange diseases and speaking with a voice which is like music, they too are Poe; or at least, through their strange aspirations, through their knowledge, through their incurable melancholy, they strongly share the nature of their creator. As for his ideal woman, she is revealed in different portraits scattered through his scant collection of poems, portraits, or rather ways of feeling beauty, which the temperament of the author joins together and blends in a vague but sensible unity, and in which exists perhaps more delicately than elsewhere that insatiable love of the Beautiful, which is his great title, that is to say the summation of his claims on the affection and admiration of poets.

From preface to *Histoires Extraordinaires*

CHARLOTTE PERKINS GILMAN

Charlotte Perkins Gilman (1860–1935) was born in Hartford, Connecticut. Her father was the writer Frederick Beecher Perkins (a nephew of reformer-novelist Harriet Beecher Stowe, author of Uncle Tom's Cabin, *and abolitionist minister Henry Ward Beecher), but he abandoned the family shortly after his daughter's birth. Raised in meager surroundings, the young Gilman adopted her intellectual Beecher aunts as role models. Because she and her mother moved from one relation to another, Gilman's early education was neglected—at fifteen, she had had only four years of schooling. In 1878 she studied commercial art at the Rhode Island School of Design. In 1884 she married Walter Stetson, an artist. After the birth of her one daughter, she experienced a severe depression. The rest cure her doctor prescribed became the basis of her most famous*

Charlotte Perkins Gilman

story, "The Yellow Wallpaper." This tale combines standard elements of Gothic fiction (the isolated country mansion, the brooding atmosphere of the room, the aloof but dominating husband) with the fresh clarity of Gilman's feminist perspective. Gilman's first marriage ended in an amicable divorce. A celebrated essayist and public speaker, she became an important early figure in American feminism. Her study Women and Economics *(1898) stressed the importance of both sexes having a place in the working world. Her feminist-Utopian novel* Herland *(1915) describes a thriving nation of women without men. In 1900 Gilman married a second time—this time, more happily—to her cousin George Houghton Gilman. Following his sudden death in 1934, Gilman discovered she had inoperable breast cancer. After finishing her autobiography, she killed herself with chloroform in Pasadena, California.*

The Yellow Wallpaper   1892

It is very seldom that mere ordinary people like John and myself secure ancestral halls for the summer.

A colonial mansion, a hereditary estate, I would say a haunted house and reach the height of romantic felicity—but that would be asking too much of fate!

Still I will proudly declare that there is something queer about it.

Else, why should it be let so cheaply? And why have stood so long untenanted?

John laughs at me, of course, but one expects that in marriage.   5

John is practical in the extreme. He has no patience with faith, an intense horror of superstition, and he scoffs openly at any talk of things not to be felt and seen and put down in figures.

John is a physician, and *perhaps*—(I would not say it to a living soul, of course, but this is dead paper and a great relief to my mind)—*perhaps* that is one reason I do not get well faster.

You see he does not believe I am sick!

And what can one do?

If a physician of high standing, and one's own husband, assures friends and relatives   10
that there is really nothing the matter with one but temporary nervous depression—a slight hysterical tendency—what is one to do?

My brother is also a physician, and also of high standing, and he says the same thing.

So I take phosphates or phosphites—whichever it is—and tonics, and journeys, and air, and exercise, and am absolutely forbidden to "work" until I am well again.

Personally, I disagree with their ideas.

Personally, I believe that congenial work, with excitement and change, would do me good.

But what is one to do?   15

I did write for a while in spite of them; but it *does* exhaust me a good deal—having to be so sly about it, or else meet with heavy opposition.

I sometimes fancy that in my condition if I had less opposition and more society and stimulus—but John says the very worst thing I can do is to think about my condition, and I confess it always makes me feel bad.

So I will let it alone and talk about the house.

The most beautiful place! It is quite alone, standing well back from the road, quite three miles from the village. It makes me think of English places that you read about, for there are hedges and walls and gates that lock, and lots of separate little houses for the gardeners and people.

There is a *delicious* garden! I never saw such a garden—large and shady, full of   20
box-bordered paths, and lined with long grape-covered arbors with seats under them.

There were greenhouses, too, but they are all broken now.

There was some legal trouble, I believe, something about the heirs and co-heirs; anyhow, the place has been empty for years.

That spoils my ghostliness, I am afraid, but I don't care—there is something strange about the house—I can feel it.

I even said so to John one moonlight evening, but he said what I felt was a *draught*, and shut the window.

I get unreasonably angry with John sometimes. I'm sure I never used to be so   25
sensitive. I think it is due to this nervous condition.

But John says if I feel so, I shall neglect proper self-control; so I take pains to control myself—before him, at least, and that makes me very tired.

I don't like our room a bit. I wanted one downstairs that opened on the piazza and had roses all over the window, and such pretty old-fashioned chintz hangings! But John would not hear of it.

He said there was only one window and not room for two beds, and no near room for him if he took another.

He is very careful and loving, and hardly lets me stir without special direction.

I have a schedule prescription for each hour in the day; he takes all care from 30 me, and so I feel basely ungrateful not to value it more.

He said we came here solely on my account, that I was to have perfect rest and all the air I could get. "Your exercise depends on your strength, my dear," said he, "and your food somewhat on your appetite; but air you can absorb all the time." So we took the nursery at the top of the house.

It is a big, airy room, the whole floor nearly, with windows that look all ways, and air and sunshine galore. It was a nursery first and then playroom and gymnasium, I should judge; for the windows are barred for little children, and there are rings and things in the walls.

The paint and paper look as if a boys' school had used it. It is stripped off—the paper—in great patches all around the head of my bed, about as far as I can reach, and in a great place on the other side of the room low down. I never saw a worse paper in my life.

One of those sprawling flamboyant patterns committing every artistic sin.

It is dull enough to confuse the eye in following, pronounced enough to con- 35 stantly irritate and provoke study, and when you follow the lame uncertain curves for a little distance they suddenly commit suicide—plunge off at outrageous angles, destroy themselves in unheard of contradictions.

The color is repellent, almost revolting; a smouldering unclean yellow, strangely faded by the slow-turning sunlight.

It is a dull yet lurid orange in some places, a sickly sulphur tint in others.

No wonder the children hated it! I should hate it myself if I had to live in this room long.

There comes John, and I must put this away—he hates to have me write a word.

We have been here two weeks, and I haven't felt like writing before, since that 40 first day.

I am sitting by the window now, up in this atrocious nursery, and there is nothing to hinder my writing as much as I please, save lack of strength.

John is away all day, and even some nights when his cases are serious.

I am glad my case is not serious!

But these nervous troubles are dreadfully depressing.

John does not know how much I really suffer. He knows there is no *reason* to suf- 45 fer, and that satisfies him.

Of course it is only nervousness. It does weigh on me so not to do my duty in any way!

I meant to be such a help to John, such a real rest and comfort, and here I am a comparative burden already!

Nobody would believe what an effort it is to do what little I am able—to dress and entertain, and order things.

It is fortunate Mary is so good with the baby. Such a dear baby!

And yet I *cannot* be with him, it makes me so nervous. 50

I suppose John never was nervous in his life. He laughs at me so about this wallpaper!

At first he meant to repaper the room, but afterward he said that I was letting it get the better of me, and that nothing was worse for a nervous patient than to give way to such fancies.

He said that after the wallpaper was changed it would be the heavy bedstead, and then the barred windows, and then that gate at the head of the stairs, and so on.

"You know the place is doing you good," he said, "and really, dear, I don't care to renovate the house just for a three months' rental."

"Then do let us go downstairs," I said, "there are such pretty rooms there." 55

Then he took me in his arms and called me a blessed little goose, and said he would go down cellar, if I wished, and have it whitewashed into the bargain.

But he is right enough about the beds and windows and things.

It is as airy and comfortable a room as any one need wish, and, of course, I would not be so silly as to make him uncomfortable just for a whim.

I'm really getting quite fond of the big room, all but that horrid paper.

Out of one window I can see the garden, those mysterious deep-shaded arbors, 60 the riotous old-fashioned flowers, and bushes and gnarly trees.

Out of another I get a lovely view of the bay and a little private wharf belonging to the estate. There is a beautiful shaded lane that runs down there from the house. I always fancy I see people walking in these numerous paths and arbors, but John has cautioned me not to give way to fancy in the least. He says that with my imaginative power and habit of story-making, a nervous weakness like mine is sure to lead to all manner of excited fancies, and that I ought to use my will and good sense to check the tendency. So I try.

I think sometimes that if I were only well enough to write a little it would relieve the press of ideas and rest me.

But I find I get pretty tired when I try.

It is so discouraging not to have any advice and companionship about my work. When I get really well, John says we will ask Cousin Henry and Julia down for a long visit; but he says he would as soon put fireworks in my pillow-case as to let me have those stimulating people about now.

I wish I could get well faster. 65

But I must not think about that. This paper looks to me as if it *knew* what a vicious influence it had!

There is a recurrent spot where the pattern lolls like a broken neck and two bulbous eyes stare at you upside down.

I get positively angry with the impertinence of it and the everlastingness. Up and down and sideways they crawl, and those absurd unblinking eyes are everywhere. There is one place where two breadths didn't match, and the eyes go all up and down the line, one a little higher than the other.

I never saw so much expression in an inanimate thing before, and we all know how much expression they have! I used to lie awake as a child and get more entertainment and terror out of blank walls and plain furniture than most children could find in a toy-store.

I remember what a kindly wink the knobs of our big, old bureau used to have, 70 and there was one chair that always seemed like a strong friend.

I used to feel that if any of the other things looked too fierce I could always hop into that chair and be safe.

The furniture in this room is no worse than inharmonious, however, for we had to bring it all from downstairs. I suppose when this was used as a playroom they had to take the nursery things out, and no wonder! I never saw such ravages as the children have made here.

The wallpaper, as I said before, is torn off in spots, and it sticketh closer than a brother°—they must have had perseverance as well as hatred.

Then the floor is scratched and gouged and splintered, the plaster itself is dug out here and there, and this great heavy bed, which is all we found in the room, looks as if it had been through the wars.

But I don't mind it a bit—only the paper.

There comes John's sister. Such a dear girl as she is, and so careful of me! I must not let her find me writing.

She is a perfect and enthusiastic housekeeper, and hopes for no better profession. I verily believe she thinks it is the writing which made me sick!

But I can write when she is out, and see her a long way off from these windows.

There is one that commands the road, a lovely shaded winding road, and one that just looks off over the country. A lovely country, too, full of great elms and velvet meadows.

This wallpaper has a kind of sub-pattern in a different shade, a particularly irritating one, for you can only see it in certain lights, and not clearly then.

But in the places where it isn't faded and where the sun is just so—I can see a strange, provoking, formless sort of figure, that seems to skulk about behind that silly and conspicuous front design.

There's sister on the stairs!

Well, the Fourth of July is over! The people are all gone and I am tired out. John thought it might do me good to see a little company, so we just had Mother and Nellie and the children down for a week.

Of course I didn't do a thing. Jennie sees to everything now.

But it tired me all the same.

John says if I don't pick up faster he shall send me to Weir Mitchell° in the fall.

But I don't want to go there at all. I had a friend who was in his hands once, and she says he is just like John and my brother, only more so!

Besides, it is such an undertaking to go so far.

I don't feel as if it was worthwhile to turn my hand over for anything, and I'm getting dreadfully fretful and querulous.

I cry at nothing, and cry most of the time.

Of course I don't when John is here, or anybody else, but when I am alone.

And I am alone a good deal just now. John is kept in town very often by serious cases, and Jennie is good and lets me alone when I want her to.

So I walk a little in the garden or down that lovely lane, sit on the porch under the roses, and lie down up here a good deal.

I'm getting really fond of the room in spite of the wallpaper. Perhaps *because* of the wallpaper.

It dwells in my mind so!

I lie here on this great immovable bed—it is nailed down, I believe—and follow that pattern about by the hour. It is as good as gymnastics, I assure you. I start, we'll say, at the bottom, down in the corner over there where it has not been touched, and

---

it sticketh . . . brother: From Proverbs 18:24: "There is a friend that sticketh closer than a brother." *Weir Mitchell:* (1829–1914): famed nerve specialist who actually treated the author, Charlotte Perkins Gilman, for nervous prostration with his well-known "rest cure." (The cure was not successful.) Also the author of *Diseases of the Nervous System, Especially of Women* (1881).

I determine for the thousandth time that I *will* follow that pointless pattern to some sort of a conclusion.

I know a little of the principle of design, and I know this thing was not arranged on any laws of radiation,° or alternation, or repetition, or symmetry, or anything else that I ever heard of.

It is repeated, of course, by the breadths, but not otherwise.

Looked at in one way, each breadth stands alone, the bloated curves and flourishes—a kind of "debased Romanesque" with *delirium tremens*—go waddling up and down in isolated columns of fatuity.

But, on the other hand, they connect diagonally, and the sprawling outlines run off in great slanting waves of optic horror, like a lot of wallowing sea-weeds in full chase.   100

The whole thing goes horizontally, too, at least it seems so, and I exhaust myself trying to distinguish the order of its going in that direction.

They have used a horizontal breadth for a frieze, and that adds wonderfully to the confusion.

There is one end of the room where it is almost intact, and there, when the crosslights fade and the low sun shines directly upon it, I can almost fancy radiation after all—the interminable grotesques seem to form around a common centre and rush off in headlong plunges of equal distraction.

It makes me tired to follow it. I will take a nap I guess.

I don't know why I should write this.   105
I don't want to.
I don't feel able.
And I know John would think it absurd. But I *must* say what I feel and think in some way—it is such a relief!
But the effort is getting to be greater than the relief.
Half the time now I am awfully lazy, and lie down ever so much.   110
John says I mustn't lose my strength, and has me take cod liver oil and lots of tonics and things, to say nothing of ale and wine and rare meat.

Dear John! He loves me very dearly, and hates to have me sick. I tried to have a real earnest reasonable talk with him the other day, and tell him how I wish he would let me go and make a visit to Cousin Henry and Julia.

But he said I wasn't able to go, nor able to stand it after I got there; and I did not make out a very good case for myself, for I was crying before I had finished.

It is getting to be a great effort for me to think straight. Just this nervous weakness I suppose.

And dear John gathered me up in his arms, and just carried me upstairs and laid   115
me on the bed, and sat by me and read to me till it tired my head.

He said I was his darling and his comfort and all he had, and that I must take care of myself for his sake, and keep well.

He says no one but myself can help me out of it, that I must use my will and self-control and not let any silly fancies run away with me.

There's one comfort, the baby is well and happy, and does not have to occupy this nursery with the horrid wallpaper.

---

laws of radiation: a principle of design in which all elements are arranged in some circular pattern around a center.

If we had not used it, that blessed child would have! What a fortunate escape! Why, I wouldn't have a child of mine, an impressionable little thing, live in such a room for worlds.

I never thought of it before, but it is lucky that John kept me here after all, I can 120 stand it so much easier than a baby, you see.

Of course I never mention it to them any more—I am too wise—but I keep watch of it all the same.

There are things in that paper that nobody knows but me, or ever will.

Behind that outside pattern the dim shapes get clearer every day.

It is always the same shape, only very numerous.

And it is like a woman stooping down and creeping about behind that pattern. I 125 don't like it a bit. I wonder—I begin to think—I wish John would take me away from here!

It is so hard to talk with John about my case, because he is so wise, and because he loves me so.

But I tried it last night.

It was moonlight. The moon shines in all around just as the sun does.

I hate to see it sometimes, it creeps so slowly, and always comes in by one window or another.

John was asleep and I hated to waken him, so I kept still and watched the moon- 130 light on that undulating wallpaper till I felt creepy.

The faint figure behind seemed to shake the pattern, just as if she wanted to get out.

I got up softly and went to feel and see if the paper *did* move, and when I came back John was awake.

"What is it, little girl?" he said. "Don't go walking about like that—you'll get cold."

I thought it was a good time to talk, so I told him that I really was not gaining here, and that I wished he would take me away.

"Why, darling!" said he, "our lease will be up in three weeks, and I can't see how 135 to leave before.

"The repairs are not done at home, and I cannot possibly leave town just now. Of course if you were in any danger, I could and would, but you really are better, dear, whether you can see it or not. I am a doctor, dear, and I know. You are gaining flesh and color, your appetite is better, I feel really much easier about you."

"I don't weigh a bit more," said I, "nor as much; and my appetite may be better in the evening when you are here, but it is worse in the morning when you are away!"

"Bless her little heart!" said he with a big hug, "she shall be as sick as she pleases! But now let's improve the shining hours by going to sleep, and talk about it in the morning!"

"And you won't go away?" I asked gloomily.

"Why, how can I, dear? It is only three weeks more and then we will take a nice 140 little trip of a few days while Jennie is getting the house ready. Really, dear, you are better!"

"Better in body perhaps—" I began, and stopped short, for he sat up straight and looked at me with such a stern, reproachful look that I could not say another word.

"My darling," said he, "I beg of you, for my sake and for our child's sake, as well as for your own, that you will never for one instant let that idea enter your mind!

There is nothing so dangerous, so fascinating, to a temperament like yours. It is a false and foolish fancy. Can you not trust me as a physician when I tell you so?"

So of course I said no more on that score, and we went to sleep before long. He thought I was asleep first, but I wasn't, and lay there for hours trying to decide whether that front pattern and the back pattern really did move together or separately.

On a pattern like this, by daylight, there is a lack of sequence, a defiance of law, that is a constant irritant to a normal mind.

The color is hideous enough, and unreliable enough, and infuriating enough, but   145
the pattern is torturing.

You think you have mastered it, but just as you get well underway in following, it turns a back-somersault and there you are. It slaps you in the face, knocks you down, and tramples upon you. It is like a bad dream.

The outside pattern is a florid arabesque,° reminding one of a fungus. If you can imagine a toadstool in joints, an interminable string of toadstools, budding and sprouting in endless convolutions—why, that is something like it.

That is, sometimes!

There is one marked peculiarity about this paper, a thing nobody seems to notice but myself, and that is that it changes as the light changes.

When the sun shoots in through the east window—I always watch for that first   150
long, straight ray—it changes so quickly that I never can quite believe it.

That is why I watch it always.

By moonlight—the moon shines in all night when there is a moon—I wouldn't know it was the same paper.

At night in any kind of light, in twilight, candlelight, lamplight, and worst of all by moonlight, it becomes bars! The outside pattern, I mean, and the woman behind it is as plain as can be.

I didn't realize for a long time what the thing was that showed behind, that dim sub-pattern, but now I am quite sure it is a woman.

By daylight she is subdued, quiet. I fancy it is the pattern that keeps her so still. It   155
is so puzzling. It keeps me quiet by the hour.

I lie down ever so much now. John says it is good for me, and to sleep all I can.

Indeed he started the habit by making me lie down for an hour after each meal.

It is a very bad habit, I am convinced, for you see I don't sleep.

And that cultivates deceit, for I don't tell them I'm awake—O, no!

The fact is I am getting a little afraid of John.   160

He seems very queer sometimes, and even Jennie has an inexplicable look.

It strikes me occasionally, just as a scientific hypothesis, that perhaps it is the paper!

I have watched John when he did not know I was looking, and come into the room suddenly on the most innocent excuses, and I've caught him several times *looking at the paper*! And Jennie too. I caught Jennie with her hand on it once.

She didn't know I was in the room, and when I asked her in a quiet, a very quiet voice, with the most restrained manner possible, what she was doing with the paper—she turned around as if she had been caught stealing, and looked quite angry—asked me why I should frighten her so!

---

arabesque: a type of ornamental style (Arabic in origin) that uses flowers, foliage, fruit, or other figures to create an intricate pattern of interlocking shapes and lines.

Then she said that the paper stained everything it touched, that she had found   165
yellow smooches° on all my clothes and John's, and she wished we would be more
careful!

Did not that sound innocent? But I know she was studying that pattern, and I am
determined that nobody shall find it out but myself!

Life is very much more exciting now than it used to be. You see I have something
more to expect, to look forward to, to watch. I really do eat better, and am more quiet
than I was.

John is so pleased to see me improve! He laughed a little the other day, and said
I seemed to be flourishing in spite of my wallpaper.

I turned it off with a laugh. I had no intention of telling him it was *because* of the
wallpaper—he would make fun of me. He might even want to take me away.

I don't want to leave now until I have found it out. There is a week more, and I   170
think that will be enough.

I'm feeling ever so much better! I don't sleep much at night, for it is so interesting to watch developments; but I sleep a good deal in the daytime.

In the daytime it is tiresome and perplexing.

There are always new shoots on the fungus, and new shades of yellow all over it.
I cannot keep count of them, though I have tried conscientiously.

It is the strangest yellow, that wallpaper! It makes me think of all the yellow
things I ever saw—not beautiful ones like buttercups, but old foul, bad yellow things.

But there is something else about that paper—the smell! I noticed it the moment   175
we came into the room, but with so much air and sun it was not bad. Now we have had
a week of fog and rain, and whether the windows are open or not, the smell is here.

It creeps all over the house.

I find it hovering in the dining-room, skulking in the parlor, hiding in the hall,
lying in wait for me on the stairs.

It gets into my hair.

Even when I go to ride, if I turn my head suddenly and surprise it—there is that
smell!

Such a peculiar odor, too! I have spent hours in trying to analyze it, to find what   180
it smelled like.

It is not bad—at first—and very gentle, but quite the subtlest, most enduring
odor I ever met.

In this damp weather it is awful. I wake up in the night and find it hanging over me.

It used to disturb me at first. I thought seriously of burning the house—to reach
the smell.

But now I am used to it. The only thing I can think of that it is like is the *color* of
the paper! A yellow smell.

There is a very funny mark on this wall, low down, near the mopboard. A streak   185
that runs round the room. It goes behind every piece of furniture, except the bed, a
long, straight, even *smooch*, as if it had been rubbed over and over.

I wonder how it was done and who did it, and what they did it for. Round and
round and round—round and round and round—it makes me dizzy!

---

smooches: smudges or smears.

*

I really have discovered something at last.

Through watching so much at night, when it changes so, I have finally found out. The front pattern *does* move—and no wonder! The woman behind shakes it!

Sometimes I think there are a great many women behind, and sometimes only   190
one, and she crawls around fast, and her crawling shakes it all over.

Then in the very bright spots she keeps still, and in the very shady spots she just takes hold of the bars and shakes them hard.

And she is all the time trying to climb through. But nobody could climb through that pattern—it strangles so; I think that is why it has so many heads.

They get through, and then the pattern strangles them off and turns them upside down, and makes their eyes white!

If those heads were covered or taken off it would not be half so bad.

I think that woman gets out in the daytime!   195

And I'll tell you why—privately—I've seen her!

I can see her out of every one of my windows!

It is the same woman, I know, for she is always creeping, and most women do not creep by daylight.

I see her in that long shaded lane, creeping up and down. I see her in those dark grape arbors, creeping all round the garden.

I see her on that long road under the trees, creeping along, and when a carriage   200
comes she hides under the blackberry vines.

I don't blame her a bit. It must be very humiliating to be caught creeping by daylight!

I always lock the door when I creep by daylight. I can't do it at night, for I know John would suspect something at once.

And John is so queer now, that I don't want to irritate him. I wish he would take another room! Besides, I don't want anybody to get that woman out at night but myself.

I often wonder if I could see her out of all the windows at once.

But, turn as fast as I can, I can only see out of one at one time.   205

And though I always see her, she *may* be able to creep faster than I can turn!

I have watched her sometimes away off in the open country, creeping as fast as a cloud shadow in a high wind.

If only that top pattern could be gotten off from the under one! I mean to try it, little by little.

I have found out another funny thing, but I shan't tell it this time! It does not do to trust people too much.

There are only two more days to get this paper off, and I believe John is begin-   210
ning to notice. I don't like the look in his eyes.

And I heard him ask Jennie a lot of professional questions about me. She had a very good report to give.

She said I slept a good deal in the daytime.

John knows I don't sleep very well at night, for all I'm so quiet!

He asked me all sorts of questions, too, and pretended to be very loving and kind.

As if I couldn't see through him!   215

Still, I don't wonder he acts so, sleeping under this paper for three months.

It only interests me, but I feel sure John and Jennie are affected by it.

*

Hurrah! This is the last day, but it is enough. John had to stay in town over night, and won't be out until this evening.

Jennie wanted to sleep with me—the sly thing—but I told her I should undoubtedly rest better for a night all alone.

That was clever, for really I wasn't alone a bit! As soon as it was moonlight 220
and that poor thing began to crawl and shake the pattern, I got up and ran to help her.

I pulled and she shook, I shook and she pulled, and before morning we had peeled off yards of that paper.

A strip about as high as my head and half around the room.

And then when the sun came and that awful pattern began to laugh at me, I declared I would finish it to-day!

We go away to-morrow, and they are moving all my furniture down again to leave things as they were before.

Jennie looked at the wall in amazement, but I told her merrily that I did it out of 225
pure spite at the vicious thing.

She laughed and said she wouldn't mind doing it herself, but I must not get tired.

How she betrayed herself that time!

But I am here, and no person touches this paper but me—not *alive*!

She tried to get me out of the room—it was too patent! But I said it was so quiet and empty and clean now that I believed I would lie down again and sleep all I could; and not to wake me even for dinner—I would call when I woke.

So now she is gone, and the servants are gone, and the things are gone, and 230
there is nothing left but that great bedstead nailed down, with the canvas mattress we found on it.

We shall sleep downstairs to-night, and take the boat home to-morrow.

I quite enjoy the room, now it is bare again.

How those children did tear about here!

This bedstead is fairly gnawed!

But I must get to work. 235

I have locked the door and thrown the key down into the front path.

I don't want to go out, and I don't want to have anybody come in, till John comes.

I want to astonish him.

I've got a rope up here that even Jennie did not find. If that woman does get out, and tries to get away, I can tie her!

But I forgot I could not reach far without anything to stand on! 240

This bed will *not* move!

I tried to lift and push it until I was lame, and then I got so angry I bit off a little piece at one corner—but it hurt my teeth.

Then I peeled off all the paper I could reach standing on the floor. It sticks horribly and the pattern just enjoys it! All those strangled heads and bulbous eyes and waddling fungus growths just shriek with derision!

I am getting angry enough to do something desperate. To jump out of the window would be admirable exercise, but the bars are too strong even to try.

Besides, I wouldn't do it. Of course not. I know well enough that a step like that 245
is improper and might be misconstrued.

I don't like to *look* out of the windows even—there are so many of those creeping women, and they creep so fast.

I wonder if they all come out of that wallpaper as I did!

But I am securely fastened now by my well-hidden rope—you don't get *me* out in the road there!

I suppose I shall have to get back behind the pattern when it comes night, and that is hard!

It is so pleasant to be out in this great room and creep around as I please!   250

I don't want to go outside. I won't, even if Jennie asks me to.

For outside you have to creep on the ground, and everything is green instead of yellow.

But here I can creep smoothly on the floor, and my shoulder just fits in that long smooch around the wall, so I cannot lose my way.

Why, there's John at the door!

It is no use, young man, you can't open it!   255

How he does call and pound!

Now he's crying for an axe.

It would be a shame to break down that beautiful door!

"John, dear!" said I in the gentlest voice, "the key is down by the front steps, under a plantain leaf!"

That silenced him for a few moments.   260

Then he said—very quietly indeed—"Open the door, my darling!"

"I can't," said I. "The key is down by the front door under a plantain leaf!"

And then I said it again, several times, very gently and slowly, and said it so often that he had to go and see, and he got it of course, and came in. He stopped short by the door.

"What is the matter?" he cried. "For God's sake, what are you doing!"

I kept on creeping just the same, but I looked at him over my shoulder.   265

"I've got out at last," said I, "in spite of you and Jane! And I've pulled off most of the paper, so you can't put me back!"

Now why should that man have fainted? But he did, and right across my path by the wall, so that I had to creep over him every time!

Questions

1. Several times at the beginning of the story, the narrator says such things as "What is one to do?" and "What can one do?" What do these comments refer to? What, if anything, do they suggest about women's roles at the time the story was written?

2. The narrator says, "I get unreasonably angry with John sometimes" (paragraph 25). How unreasonable is her anger at him? What does the fact that she feels it is unreasonable say about her?

3. What do her changing feelings about the wallpaper tell us about her condition?

4. "It is so hard to talk with John about my case, because he is so wise, and because he loves me so" (paragraph 126). His wisdom is, to say the least, open to question, but what about his love? Do you think he suffers merely from a failure of perception, or is there a failure of affection as well? Explain your response.

5. Where precisely in the story do you think it becomes clear that she has begun to hallucinate?

6. What does the woman behind the wallpaper represent? Why does the narrator come to identify with her?

7. How ill does the narrator seem at the beginning of the story? How ill does she seem at the end? How do you account for the change in her condition?

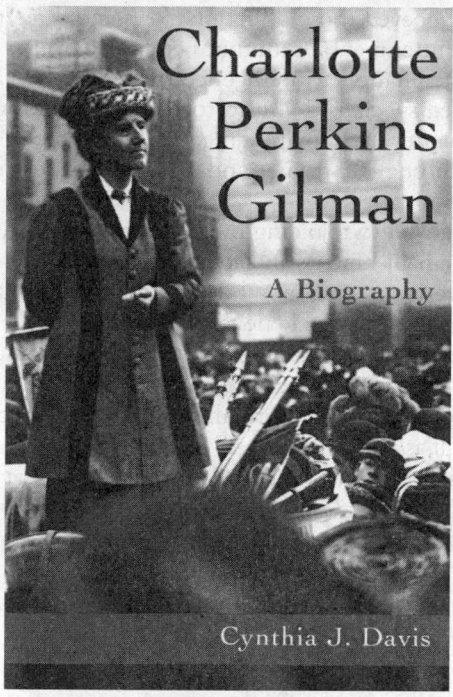

Charlotte
Perkins
Gilman

A Biography

Cynthia J. Davis

Cover of 2010 biography of Gilman.

CHARLOTTE PERKINS GILMAN ON WRITING

Why I Wrote "The Yellow Wallpaper"   1913

Many and many a reader has asked that. When the story first came out, in the *New England Magazine* about 1891, a Boston physician made protest in *The Transcript*. Such a story ought not to be written, he said; it was enough to drive anyone mad to read it.

Another physician, in Kansas I think, wrote to say that it was the best description of incipient insanity he had ever seen, and—begging my pardon—had I been there?

Now the story of the story is this: For many years I suffered from a severe and continuous nervous breakdown tending to melancholia—and beyond. During about the third year of this trouble I went, in devout faith and some faint stir of hope, to a noted specialist in nervous diseases, the best known in the country. This wise man put me to bed and applied the rest cure, to which a still-good physique responded so promptly that he concluded there was nothing much the matter with me, and sent me home with solemn advice to "live as domestic a life as far as possible," to "have but two hours' intellectual life a day," and "never to touch pen, brush, or pencil again" as long as I lived. This was in 1887.

I went home and obeyed those directions for some three months, and came so near the borderline of utter mental ruin that I could see over.

Then, using the remnants of intelligence that remained, and helped by a wise friend, I cast the noted specialist's advice to the winds and went to work again—work, the normal life of every human being; work, in which is joy and growth and service, without which one is a pauper and a parasite—ultimately recovering some measure of power.

Being naturally moved to rejoicing by this narrow escape, I wrote "The Yellow Wallpaper," with its embellishments and additions, to carry out the ideal (I never had hallucinations or objections to my mural decorations) and sent a copy to the physician who so nearly drove me mad. He never acknowledged it.

The little book is valued by alienists and as a good specimen of one kind of literature. It has, to my knowledge, saved one woman from a similar fate—so terrifying her family that they let her out into normal activity and she recovered.

But the best result is this. Many years later I was told that the great specialist had admitted to friends of his that he had altered his treatment of neurasthenia since reading "The Yellow Wallpaper."

It was not intended to drive people crazy, but to save people from being driven crazy, and it worked.

From *The Forerunner*, October 1913

The Nervous Breakdown of Women   1916

[A]s a hindrance they [women] have to meet something which men have never met—the cold and cruel opposition of the other sex. In every step of their long upward path men have had women with them, never against them. In hardship, in privation, in danger, in the last test of religious martyrdom, in the pains and terrors of warfare, in rebellions and revolutions, men have had women with them. Individual women have no doubt been a hindrance to individual men, and the economic dependence of women is a drag upon men's freedom of action; but at no step of man's difficult advance has he had to meet the scorn, the neglect, the open vilification of massed womanhood.

No one has seemed to notice the cost of this great artificial barrier to the advance of woman, the effect upon her nervous system of opposition and abuse from the quarter where nature and tradition had taught her to expect aid and comfort. She has had to keep pace with him in meeting the demands of our swiftly changing times. She has had to meet the additional demands of her own even more swiftly changing conditions. And she has had to do this in the face not only of the organized opposition of the other sex, entrenched in secure possession of all the advantageous positions of church and state, buttressed by law and custom, fully trained and experienced, and holding all the ammunition—the "sinews of war"—the whole money power of the world; but besides this her slow, difficult, conscientious efforts to make the changes she knew were right, or which were forced upon her by conditions, have too often cost her man's love, respect and good will.

This is a heavy price to pay for progress.

We should be more than gentle with the many women who cannot yet meet it.

We should be more than grateful for those strong men who are more human than male, who can feel, think and act above the limitations of their sex, and who have helped women in their difficult advance.

Also we should deeply honor those great women of the last century, who met all demands, paid every exaction, faced all opposition and made the way easier for us now.

But we should not be surprised at the "nervous breakdown" of some women, nor attribute it to weakness.

Only the measureless strength of the mother sex could have enabled women to survive the sufferings of yesterday and to meet the exactions of today.

— From *The Forerunner*, July–August 1916

CRITICS ON "THE YELLOW WALLPAPER"

Juliann Fleenor (b. 1942)

Gender and Pathology in "The Yellow Wallpaper"   1983

Although it is not generally known, Gilman wrote at least two other Gothic stories around the same time as "The Yellow Wallpaper." All three were published in the *New England Magazine*. At the time that "The Rocking Chair" and "The Giant Wistaria" were written, Gilman and her young daughter, Katherine, were living in the warmth of Pasadena, separated from her husband, Charles Walter Stetson. Gilman later noted in her papers: "'The Yellow Wallpaper' was written in two days, with the thermometer at one hundred and three in Pasadena, Ca." Her husband was living on the east coast, and, perhaps coincidentally, all three stories appear to be set in a nameless eastern setting, one urban and two rural. All three display similar themes, and all three are evidence that the conflict, central to Gilman's Gothic fiction and later to her autobiography, was a conflict with the mother, with motherhood, and with creation.

In all three stories women are confined within the home; it is their prison, their insane asylum, even their tomb. A sense of the female isolation which Gilman felt, of exclusion from the public world of work and of men, is contained in the anecdote

Aric Cushing as John, Juliet Landau as Charlotte, and Dale Dickey as Jennie in 2012 film *The Yellow Wallpaper*.

related by Zona Gale in her introduction to Gilman's autobiography. After watching the approach of several locomotives to a train platform in a small town in Wisconsin, Gilman said, "'All that, . . . and women have no part in it. Everything done by men, working together, while women worked on alone within their four walls!'" Female exclusion, women denied the opportunity to work, or their imprisonment behind four walls, led to madness. Her image, interestingly, does not suggest a female subculture of women working together; Gilman was working against her own culture's definition of women, and her primary antagonists were women like her own mother.

Diseased maternity is explicit in Gilman's third Gothic story. The yellow wallpaper symbolizes more than confinement, victimization, and the inability to write. It suggests a disease within the female self. When the narrator peels the wallpaper off, "It sticks horribly and the pattern just enjoys it! All those strangled heads and bulbous eyes and waddling fungus growths just shriek with derision." This passage describes more than the peeling of wallpaper: the "strangled heads and bulbous eyes and waddling fungus" imply something strange and terrible about birth and death conjoined, about female procreation, and about female physiology. Nature is perverted here, too. The narrator thinks of "old, foul, bad yellow things." The smell "creeps all over the house." She finds it "hovering in the dining-room, skulking in the parlor, hiding in the hall, lying in wait for me on the stairs." Finally, "it gets into my hair."

The paper stains the house in a way that suggests the effect of afterbirth. The house, specifically this room, becomes more than a symbol of a repressive society; it represents the physical self of the narrator as well. She is disgusted, perhaps awed, perhaps frightened of her own bodily processes. The story establishes a sense of fear and disgust, the skin crawls and grows clammy with the sense of physiological fear that Ellen Moers refers to as the Female Gothic.

My contention is that one of the major themes in the story, punishment for becoming a mother (as well as punishment for being female), is supported by the absence of the child. The child is taken away from the mother, almost in punishment, as was the child in "The Giant Wistaria." This differs from Gilman's experience; she had been told to keep her child with her at all times. In both the story and in Gilman's life, a breakdown occurs directly after the birth of a child. The narrator is confined as if she had committed a crime. Maternity—the creation of a child—is combined with writing—the creation of writing—in a way that suggests they are interrelated and perhaps symbiotic, as are the strange toadstools behind the wallpaper.

The pathological nature of both experiences is not surprising, given the treatment Gilman received, and given the fact that maternity reduced women to mothers and not writers. Childbirth has long been a rite of passage for women. But the question is, where does that passage lead? Becoming a mother leads to a child-like state. The narrator becomes the absent child.

From "The Gothic Prism"

Sandra M. Gilbert (b. 1936) and Susan Gubar (b. 1944)

Imprisonment and Escape: The Psychology of Confinement   1979

["The Yellow Wallpaper" is a] striking story of female confinement and escape, a paradigmatic tale which (like *Jane Eyre*) seems to tell *the* story that all literary women would tell if they could speak their "speechless woe." "The Yellow Wallpaper," which Gilman herself called "a description of a case of nervous breakdown," recounts in the first person the experiences of a woman who is evidently suffering from a severe postpartum psychosis. Her husband, a censorious and paternalistic physician, is treating her according to methods by which S. Weir Mitchell, a famous "nerve specialist," treated Gilman herself for a similar problem. He has confined her to a large garret room in an "ancestral hall" he has rented, and he has forbidden her to touch pen to paper until she is well again, for he feels, says the narrator, "that with my imaginative power and habit of story-making, a nervous weakness like mine is sure to lead to all manner of excited fancies, and that I ought to use my will and good sense to check the tendency."

The cure, of course, is worse than the disease, for the sick woman's mental condition deteriorates rapidly. "I think sometimes that if I were only well enough to write a little it would relieve the press of ideas and rest me," she remarks, but literally confined in a room she thinks is a one-time nursery because it has "rings and things" in the walls, she is literally locked away from creativity. The "rings and things," although reminiscent of children's gymnastic equipment, are really the paraphernalia of confinement, like the gate at the head of the stairs, instruments that definitively indicate her imprisonment. Even more tormenting, however, is the room's wallpaper: a sulfurous yellow paper, torn off in spots, and patterned with "lame uncertain curves" that "plunge off at outrageous angles" and "destroy themselves in unheard-of contradictions." Ancient, smoldering, "unclean" as the oppressive structures of the society in which she finds herself, this paper surrounds the narrator like an inexplicable text, censorious and overwhelming as her physician husband, haunting as the "hereditary estate" in which she is trying to survive. Inevitably she studies its suicidal implications— and inevitably, because of her "imaginative power and habit of story-making," she revises it, projecting her own passion for escape into its otherwise incomprehensible hieroglyphics. "This wallpaper," she decides, at a key point in her story,

> has a kind of sub-pattern in a different shade, a particularly irritating one, for you can only see it in certain lights, and not clearly then.
> But in the places where it isn't faded and where the sun is just so—I can see a strange, provoking, formless sort of figure that seems to skulk about behind that silly and conspicuous front design.

As time passes, this figure concealed behind what corresponds (in terms of what we have been discussing) to the facade of the patriarchal text becomes clearer and clearer. By moonlight the pattern of the wallpaper "becomes bars! The outside pattern I mean, and the woman behind it is as plain as can be." And eventually, as the narrator sinks more deeply into what the world calls madness, the terrifying implications of both the paper and the figure imprisoned behind the paper begin to permeate—that is, to *haunt*—the rented ancestral mansion in which she and her husband are immured. The "yellow smell" of the paper "creeps all over the house," drenching every room in its subtle aroma of decay. And the woman creeps too—through the house, in the house, and out of the house, in the garden and "on that long road under the trees." Sometimes, indeed, the narrator confesses, "I think there are a great many women" both behind the paper and creeping in the garden,

> and sometimes only one, and she crawls around fast, and her crawling shakes [the paper] all over. . . . And she is all the time trying to climb through. But nobody could climb through that pattern—it strangles so; I think that is why it has so many heads.

Eventually it becomes obvious to both reader and narrator that the figure creeping through and behind the wallpaper is both the narrator and the narrator's double. By the end of the story, moreover, the narrator has enabled this double to escape from her textual/architectural confinement: "I pulled and she shook, I shook and she pulled, and before morning we had peeled off yards of that paper." Is the message of the tale's conclusion mere madness? Certainly the righteous Doctor John—whose name links him to the anti-hero of Charlotte Bronte's *Villette*—has been temporarily defeated, or at least momentarily stunned. "Now why should that man have fainted?" the narrator ironically asks as she creeps around her attic. But John's unmasculine swoon of surprise is the least of the triumphs Gilman imagines for her madwoman. More significant are the madwoman's own imaginings and creations, mirages of health and freedom with which her author endows her like a fairy godmother showering gold on a sleeping heroine. The woman from behind the wallpaper creeps away, for instance, creeps fast and far on the long road, in broad daylight. "I have watched her sometimes away off in the open country," says the narrator, "creeping as fast as a cloud shadow in a high wind."

Indistinct and yet rapid, barely perceptible but inexorable, the progress of that cloud shadow is not unlike the progress of nineteenth-century literary women out of the texts defined by patriarchal poetics into the open spaces of their own authority. That such an escape from the numb world behind the patterned walls of the text was a flight from disease into health was quite clear to Gilman herself. When "The Yellow Wallpaper" was published she sent it to Weir Mitchell, whose strictures had kept her from attempting the pen during her own breakdown, thereby aggravating her illness, and she was delighted to learn, years later, that "he had changed his treatment of nervous prostration since reading" her story. "If that is a fact," she declared, "I have not lived in vain."

From *The Madwoman in the Attic*

Elizabeth Ammons (b. 1943)

Biographical Echoes in "The Yellow Wallpaper"   1991

"The Yellow Wallpaper" probably had deep roots in Gilman's childhood. In her autobiography, the account she gives of her growing up focuses on the misery of her mother, a woman who adored her husband and loved having babies, only to have her husband leave and her babies grow up. Deserted, Gilman's mother—in the daughter's telling—grew bitter and fiercely repressed, deciding not to show any affection for her daughter in order to toughen the child. Life, as Gilman's mother had come to know it, brought women terrible disappointment and denial. Only in the dead of night would she allow herself to hug her daughter.

As a story about her mother, the early portions of Gilman's autobiography construct a family drama in which sexual desire in a woman leads to babies and death. (According to Gilman, her mother was warned that one more pregnancy would kill her, at which point the father left the family.) On the other hand, denial of sexual desire, the celibate life that Mary Fitch Perkins knew when her husband left, resulted in furious repression and frustration. Either way, female sexual desire, motherhood, and masculine power were bitterly entangled for Gilman's mother, who even after years of separation and rejection remained her husband's prisoner, calling for him on her deathbed. Looked at from the child's point of view, Charlotte Perkins Gilman clearly both admired and hated her father. Frederick Beecher Perkins's power over his wife was so strong that she had to stamp out all that was free and physical and warm in herself, and try to do the same to her daughter. In a sense the woman on her knees at the end of "The Yellow Wallpaper," the prisoner of a charming man and an ugly empty domestic life that she cannot escape, is Gilman's mother as the child experienced her while growing up—humiliated, angry, crushed.

• • •

The drama of patriarchal control in "The Yellow Wallpaper" is the same one that Charlotte Perkins Gilman felt as a child, saw in her mother's life, and then experienced again herself as a young wife and mother. The story is not limited to just one stage of her life as a woman, but applies potentially to all stages, from childhood to old age. It is not, moreover, simply a story about the desire for escape from male control. It is also a story about the desire to escape to a female world, a desire to unite with the mother, indeed with all women creeping and struggling in growing numbers, through the paper, behind the wall.

From *Conflicting Stories: American Women Writers*
at the Turn into the Twentieth Century

ALICE WALKER

Alice Walker, a leading black writer and social activist, was born in 1944 in Eatonton, Georgia, the youngest of eight children. Her father, a sharecropper and dairy farmer, earned about $300 a year; her mother helped by working as a maid. Both entertained their children by telling stories. When Alice Walker was eight, she was accidentally struck by a pellet from a brother's BB gun. She lost the sight of her right eye because the Walkers had no car to rush her to the hospital. Later she attended Spelman College in Atlanta and finished college at Sarah Lawrence College on a scholarship. While working for the civil rights movement in Mississippi, she met a young lawyer, Melvyn Leventhal. In 1967 they settled in Jackson, Mississippi, the first legally married interracial couple in town. After much racial harassment, they returned to New York in 1974, later divorcing.

Alice Walker

First known as a poet, Walker has published nine books of verse. She has edited a collection of the work of the then-neglected writer Zora Neale Hurston, written a study of Langston Hughes, and published many volumes of nonfiction, including the essay collection In Search of Our Mothers' Gardens: Womanist Prose *(1983). (By womanist she means "black feminist.") But the largest part of Walker's reading audience knows her fiction: four story collections, including* In Love and Trouble *(1973), from which "Everyday Use" is taken, and her many novels. Her best-known novel,* The Color Purple *(1982), won both a Pulitzer Prize and National Book Award and*

was made into a film by Steven Spielberg in 1985. Recent novels include By the Light
of My Father's Smile *(1998) and* Now Is the Time to Open Your Heart *(2004).*
Walker lives in Northern California.

Everyday Use   1973

for your grandmama

I will wait for her in the yard that Maggie and I made so clean and wavy yesterday afternoon. A yard like this is more comfortable than most people know. It is not
just a yard. It is like an extended living room. When the hard clay is swept clean as
a floor and the fine sand around the edges lined with tiny, irregular grooves, anyone
can come and sit and look up into the elm tree and wait for the breezes that never
come inside the house.

Maggie will be nervous until after her sister goes: she will stand hopelessly in corners, homely and ashamed of the burn scars down her arms and legs, eyeing her sister
with a mixture of envy and awe. She thinks her sister has held life always in the palm
of one hand, that "no" is a word the world never learned to say to her.

You've no doubt seen those TV shows where the child who has "made it" is
confronted, as a surprise, by her own mother and father, tottering in weakly from
backstage. (A pleasant surprise, of course: What would they do if parent and child
came on the show only to curse out and insult each other?) On TV mother and child
embrace and smile into each other's faces. Sometimes the mother and father weep,
the child wraps them in her arms and leans across the table to tell how she would not
have made it without their help. I have seen these programs.°

Sometimes I dream a dream in which Dee and I are suddenly brought together
on a TV program of this sort. Out of a dark and soft-seated limousine I am ushered
into a bright room filled with many people. There I meet a smiling, gray, sporty man
like Johnny Carson who shakes my hand and tells me what a fine girl I have. Then
we are on the stage and Dee is embracing me with tears in her eyes. She pins on my
dress a large orchid, even though she has told me once that she thinks orchids are
tacky flowers.

In real life I am a large, big-boned woman with rough, man-working hands. In   5
the winter I wear flannel nightgowns to bed and overalls during the day. I can kill
and clean a hog as mercilessly as a man. My fat keeps me hot in zero weather. I
can work outside all day, breaking ice to get water for washing. I can eat pork liver
cooked over the open fire minutes after it comes steaming from the hog. One winter
I knocked a bull calf straight in the brain between the eyes with a sledge hammer and
had the meat hung up to chill before nightfall. But of course all this does not show on
television. I am the way my daughter would want me to be: a hundred pounds lighter,
my skin like an uncooked barley pancake. My hair glistens in the hot bright lights.
Johnny Carson has much to do to keep up with my quick and witty tongue.

But that is a mistake. I know even before I wake up. Who ever knew a Johnson
with a quick tongue? Who can even imagine me looking a strange white man in the
eye? It seems to me I have talked to them always with one foot raised in flight, with

---

these programs: On the NBC television show *This Is Your Life,* people were publicly and often tearfully
reunited with friends, relatives, and teachers they had not seen in years.

my head turned in whichever way is farthest from them. Dee, though. She would always look anyone in the eye. Hesitation was no part of her nature.

"How do I look, Mama?" Maggie says, showing just enough of her thin body enveloped in pink skirt and red blouse for me to know she's there, almost hidden by the door.

"Come out into the yard," I say.

Have you ever seen a lame animal, perhaps a dog run over by some careless person rich enough to own a car, sidle up to someone who is ignorant enough to be kind to him? That is the way my Maggie walks. She has been like this, chin on chest, eyes on ground, feet in shuffle, ever since the fire that burned the other house to the ground.

Dee is lighter than Maggie, with nicer hair and a fuller figure. She's a woman 10 now, though sometimes I forget. How long ago was it that the other house burned? Ten, twelve years? Sometimes I can still hear the flames and feel Maggie's arms sticking to me, her hair smoking and her dress falling off her in little black papery flakes. Her eyes seemed stretched open, blazed open by the flames reflected in them. And Dee. I see her standing off under the sweet gum tree she used to dig gum out of; a look of concentration on her face as she watched the last dingy gray board of the house fall in toward the red-hot brick chimney. Why don't you do a dance around the ashes? I'd wanted to ask her. She had hated the house that much.

I used to think she hated Maggie, too. But that was before we raised the money, the church and me, to send her to Augusta to school. She used to read to us without pity; forcing words, lies, other folks' habits, whole lives upon us two, sitting trapped and ignorant underneath her voice. She washed us in a river of make-believe, burned us with a lot of knowledge we didn't necessarily need to know. Pressed us to her with the serious way she read, to shove us away at just the moment, like dimwits, we seemed about to understand.

Dee wanted nice things. A yellow organdy dress to wear to her graduation from high school; black pumps to match a green suit she'd made from an old suit somebody gave me. She was determined to stare down any disaster in her efforts. Her eyelids would not flicker for minutes at a time. Often I fought off the temptation to shake her. At sixteen she had a style of her own: and knew what style was.

I never had an education myself. After second grade the school was closed down. Don't ask me why: in 1927 colored asked fewer questions than they do now. Sometimes Maggie reads to me. She stumbles along good-naturedly but can't see well. She knows she is not bright. Like good looks and money, quickness passed her by. She will marry John Thomas (who has mossy teeth in an earnest face) and then I'll be free to sit here and I guess just sing church songs to myself. Although I never was a good singer. Never could carry a tune. I was always better at a man's job. I used to love to milk till I was hoofed in the side in '49. Cows are soothing and slow and don't bother you, unless you try to milk them the wrong way.

I have deliberately turned my back on the house. It is three rooms, just like the one that burned, except the roof is tin; they don't make shingle roofs any more. There are no real windows, just some holes cut in the sides, like the portholes in a ship, but not round and not square, with rawhide holding the shutters up on the outside. This house is in a pasture, too, like the other one. No doubt when Dee sees it she will want to tear it down. She wrote me once that no matter where we "choose" to live, she will manage to come see us. But she will never bring her friends. Maggie and I thought about this and Maggie asked me, "Mama, when did Dee ever *have* any friends?"

She had a few. Furtive boys in pink shirts hanging about on washday after school. 15 Nervous girls who never laughed. Impressed with her they worshiped the well-turned phrase, the cute shape, the scalding humor that erupted like bubbles in lye. She read to them.

When she was courting Jimmy T she didn't have much time to pay to us, but turned all her faultfinding power on him. He *flew* to marry a cheap city girl from a family of ignorant flashy people. She hardly had time to recompose herself.

When she comes I will meet—but there they are!

Maggie attempts to make a dash for the house, in her shuffling way, but I stay her with my hand. "Come back here," I say. And she stops and tries to dig a well in the sand with her toe.

It is hard to see them clearly through the strong sun. But even the first glimpse of leg out of the car tells me it is Dee. Her feet were always neat-looking, as if God himself had shaped them with a certain style. From the other side of the car comes a short, stocky man. Hair is all over his head a foot long and hanging from his chin like a kinky mule tail. I hear Maggie suck in her breath. "Uhnnnh," is what it sounds like. Like when you see the wriggling end of a snake just in front of your foot on the road. "Uhnnnh."

Dee next. A dress down to the ground, in this hot weather. A dress so loud it hurts 20 my eyes. There are yellows and oranges enough to throw back the light of the sun. I feel my whole face warming from the heat waves it throws out. Earrings, too, gold and hanging down to her shoulders. Bracelets dangling and making noises when she moves her arm up to shake the folds of the dress out of her armpits. The dress is loose and flows, and as she walks closer, I like it. I hear Maggie go "Uhnnnh" again. It is her sister's hair. It stands straight up like the wool on a sheep. It is black as night and around the edges are two long pigtails that rope about like small lizards disappearing behind her ears.

"Wa-su-zo-Tean-o!"° she says, coming on in that gliding way the dress makes her move. The short stocky fellow with the hair to his navel is all grinning and he follows up with "Asalamalakim,° my mother and sister!" He moves to hug Maggie but she falls back, right up against the back of my chair. I feel her trembling there and when I look up I see the perspiration falling off her chin.

"Don't get up," says Dee. Since I am stout it takes something of a push. You can see me trying to move a second or two before I make it. She turns, showing white heels through her sandals, and goes back to the car. Out she peeks next with a Polaroid. She stoops down quickly and lines up picture after picture of me sitting there in front of the house with Maggie cowering behind me. She never takes a shot without making sure the house is included. When a cow comes nibbling around the edge of the yard she snaps it and me and Maggie *and* the house. Then she puts the Polaroid in the back seat of the car, and comes up and kisses me on the forehead.

Meanwhile Asalamalakim is going through the motions with Maggie's hand. Maggie's hand is as limp as a fish, and probably as cold, despite the sweat, and she keeps trying to pull it back. It looks like Asalamalakim wants to shake hands but wants to do it fancy. Or maybe he don't know how people shake hands. Anyhow, he soon gives up on Maggie.

"Well," I say. "Dee."

Wa-su-zo-Tean-o!: salutation in Swahili, an African language. Notice that Dee has to sound it out, syllable by syllable.   *Asalamalakim*: salutation in Arabic: "Peace be upon you."

"No, Mama," she says. "Not 'Dee,' Wangero Leewanika Kemanjo!"   25
"What happened to 'Dee'?" I wanted to know.
"She's dead," Wangero said. "I couldn't bear it any longer, being named after the people who oppress me."
"You know as well as me you was named after your aunt Dicie," I said. Dicie is my sister. She named Dee. We called her "Big Dee" after Dee was born.
"But who was *she* named after?" asked Wangero.
"I guess after Grandma Dee," I said.   30
"And who was she named after?" asked Wangero.
"Her mother," I said, and saw Wangero was getting tired. "That's about as far back as I can trace it," I said. Though, in fact, I probably could have carried it back beyond the Civil War through the branches.
"Well," said Asalamalakim, "there you are."
"Uhnnnh," I heard Maggie say.
"There I was not," I said, "before 'Dicie' cropped up in our family, so why should   35
I try to trace it that far back?"
He just stood there grinning, looking down on me like somebody inspecting a Model A car.° Every once in a while he and Wangero sent eye signals over my head.
"How do you pronounce this name?" I asked.
"You don't have to call me by it if you don't want to," said Wangero.
"Why shouldn't I?" I asked. "If that's what you want us to call you, we'll call you."
"I know it might sound awkward at first," said Wangero.   40
"I'll get used to it," I said. "Ream it out again."
Well, soon we got the name out of the way. Asalamalakim had a name twice as long and three times as hard. After I tripped over it two or three times he told me to just call him Hakim-a-barber. I wanted to ask him was he a barber, but I didn't really think he was, so I didn't ask.
"You must belong to those beef-cattle peoples down the road," I said. They said "Asalamalakim" when they met you, too, but they didn't shake hands. Always too busy: feeding the cattle, fixing the fences, putting up salt-lick shelters, throwing down hay. When the white folks poisoned some of the herd the men stayed up all night with rifles in their hands. I walked a mile and a half just to see the sight.
Hakim-a-barber said, "I accept some of their doctrines, but farming and raising cattle is not my style." (They didn't tell me, and I didn't ask, whether Wangero (Dee) had really gone and married him.)
We sat down to eat and right away he said he didn't eat collards and pork was   45
unclean. Wangero, though, went on through the chitlins and corn bread, the greens and everything else. She talked a blue streak over the sweet potatoes. Everything delighted her. Even the fact that we still used the benches her daddy made for the table when we couldn't afford to buy chairs.
"Oh, Mama!" she cried. Then turned to Hakim-a-barber. "I never knew how lovely these benches are. You can feel the rump prints," she said, running her hands underneath her and along the bench. Then she gave a sigh and her hand closed over Grandma Dee's butter dish. "That's it!" she said. "I knew there was something I wanted to ask you if I could have." She jumped up from the table and went over in the corner where the churn stood, the milk in it clabber° by now. She looked at the churn and looked at it.

Model A car: popular low-priced automobile introduced by the Ford Motor Company in 1927.   *clabber:* sour milk or buttermilk.

"This churn top is what I need," she said. "Didn't Uncle Buddy whittle it out of a tree you all used to have?"

"Yes," I said.

"Uh huh," she said happily. "And I want the dasher, too."

"Uncle Buddy whittle that, too?" asked the barber.   50

Dee (Wangero) looked up at me.

"Aunt Dee's first husband whittled the dash," said Maggie so low you almost couldn't hear her. "His name was Henry, but they called him Stash."

"Maggie's brain is like an elephant's," Wangero said, laughing. "I can use the churn top as a centerpiece for the alcove table," she said, sliding a plate over the churn, "and I'll think of something artistic to do with the dasher."

When she finished wrapping the dasher the handle stuck out. I took it for a moment in my hands. You didn't even have to look close to see where hands pushing the dasher up and down to make butter had left a kind of sink in the wood. In fact, there were a lot of small sinks; you could see where thumbs and fingers had sunk into the wood. It was beautiful light yellow wood, from a tree that grew in the yard where Big Dee and Stash had lived.

After dinner Dee (Wangero) went to the trunk at the foot of my bed and started   55
rifling through it. Maggie hung back in the kitchen over the dishpan. Out came Wangero with two quilts. They had been pieced by Grandma Dee and then Big Dee and me had hung them on the quilt frames on the front porch and quilted them. One was in the Lone Star pattern. The other was Walk Around the Mountain. In both of them were scraps of dresses Grandma Dee had worn fifty and more years ago. Bits and pieces of Grandpa Jarrell's paisley shirts. And one teeny faded blue piece, about the size of a penny matchbox, that was from Great Grandpa Ezra's uniform that he wore in the Civil War.

"Mama," Wangero said sweet as a bird. "Can I have these old quilts?"

I heard something fall in the kitchen, and a minute later the kitchen door slammed.

"Why don't you take one or two of the others?" I asked. "These old things was just done by me and Big Dee from some tops your grandma pieced before she died."

"No," said Wangero. "I don't want those. They are stitched around the borders by machine."   60

"That'll make them last better," I said.

"That's not the point," said Wangero. "These are all pieces of dresses Grandma used to wear. She did all this stitching by hand. Imagine!" She held the quilts securely in her arms, stroking them.

"Some of the pieces, like those lavender ones, come from old clothes her mother handed down to her," I said, moving up to touch the quilts. Dee (Wangero) moved back just enough so that I couldn't reach the quilts. They already belonged to her.

"Imagine!" she breathed again, clutching them closely to her bosom.

"The truth is," I said, "I promised to give them quilts to Maggie, for when she marries John Thomas."

She gasped like a bee had stung her.   65

"Maggie can't appreciate these quilts!" she said. "She'd probably be backward enough to put them to everyday use."

"I reckon she would," I said. "God knows I been saving 'em for long enough with nobody using 'em. I hope she will!" I didn't want to bring up how I had offered Dee (Wangero) a quilt when she went away to college. Then she had told me they were old-fashioned, out of style.

"But they're *priceless*!" she was saying now, furiously; for she has a temper. "Maggie would put them on the bed and in five years they'd be in rags. Less than that!"

"She can always make some more," I said. "Maggie knows how to quilt."

Dee (Wangero) looked at me with hatred. "You just will not understand. The   70
point is these quilts, *these* quilts!"

"Well," I said, stumped. "What would *you* do with them?"

"Hang them," she said. As if that was the only thing you *could* do with quilts.

Maggie by now was standing in the door. I could almost hear the sound her feet
made as they scraped over each other.

"She can have them, Mama," she said, like somebody used to never winning
anything, or having anything reserved for her. "I can 'member Grandma Dee without
the quilts."

I looked at her hard. She had filled her bottom lip with checkerberry snuff and it   75
gave her face a kind of dopey, hangdog look. It was Grandma Dee and Big Dee who
taught her how to quilt herself. She stood there with her scarred hands hidden in the
folds of her skirt. She looked at her sister with something like fear but she wasn't mad
at her. This was Maggie's portion. This was the way she knew God to work.

When I looked at her like that something hit me in the top of my head and
ran down to the soles of my feet. Just like when I'm in church and the spirit of God
touches me and I get happy and shout. I did something I never had done before:
hugged Maggie to me, then dragged her on into the room, snatched the quilts out of
Miss Wangero's hands and dumped them into Maggie's lap. Maggie just sat there on
my bed with her mouth open.

"Take one or two of the others," I said to Dee.

But she turned without a word and went out to Hakim-a-barber.

"You just don't understand," she said, as Maggie and I came out to the car.

"What don't I understand?" I wanted to know.   80

"Your heritage," she said. And then she turned to Maggie, kissed her, and said,
"You ought to try to make something of yourself, too, Maggie. It's really a new day for
us. But from the way you and Mama still live you'd never know it."

She put on some sunglasses that hid everything above the tip of her nose and her
chin.

Maggie smiled; maybe at the sunglasses. But a real smile, not scared. After we
watched the car dust settle I asked Maggie to bring me a dip of snuff. And then the
two of us sat there just enjoying, until it was time to go in the house and go to bed.

Questions

1. What is the basic conflict in "Everyday Use"?
2. What is the tone of Walker's story? By what means does the author communicate it?
3. From whose point of view is "Everyday Use" told? What does the story gain from
   being told from this point of view—instead of, say, from the point of view of Dee
   (Wangero)?
4. What does the narrator of the story feel toward Dee? What seems to be Dee's present attitude toward her mother and sister?
5. What do you take to be the author's attitude toward each of her characters? How does she
   convey it?
6. What levels of meaning do you find in the story's title?
7. Contrast Dee's attitude toward her heritage with the attitudes of her mother and sister.
   How much truth is there in Dee's accusation that her mother and sister don't understand
   their heritage?
8. Does the knowledge that "Everyday Use" was written by a black writer in any way influence your reactions to it? Explain.

ALICE WALKER ON WRITING

The Black Woman Writer in America   1973

Interview by John O'Brien

Alice Walker

Interviewer: Why do you think that the black woman writer has been so ignored in America? Does she have even more difficulty than the black male writer, who perhaps has just begun to gain recognition?

Walker: There are two reasons why the black woman writer is not taken as seriously as the black male writer. One is that she's a woman. Critics seem unusually ill-equipped to intelligently discuss and analyze the works of black women. Generally, they do not even make the attempt; they prefer, rather, to talk about the lives of black women writers, not about what they write. And, since black women writers are not—it would seem—very likable—until recently they were the least willing worshipers of male supremacy—comments about them tend to be cruel.

In Nathan Huggins's very readable book, *Harlem Renaissance*, he hardly refers to Zora Neale Hurston's work, except negatively. He quotes from Wallace Thurman's novel, *Infants of the Spring*, at length, giving us the words of a character, "Sweetie Mae Carr," who is allegedly based on Zora Neale Hurston. "Sweetie Mae" is a writer noted more "for her ribald wit and personal effervescence than for any actual literary work. She was a great favorite among those whites who went in for Negro prodigies." Mr. Huggins goes on for several pages, never quoting Zora Neale Hurston herself, but rather the opinions of others about her character. He does say that she was "a master of dialect," but adds that "Her greatest weakness was carelessness or indifference to her art."

Having taught Zora Neale Hurston, and of course, having read her work myself, I am stunned. Personally, I do not care if Zora Hurston was fond of her white women friends. When she was a child in Florida, working for nickels and dimes, two white women helped her escape. Perhaps this explains it. But even if it doesn't, so what? Her work, far from being done carelessly, is done (especially in *Their Eyes Were Watching God*) almost too perfectly. She took the trouble to capture the beauty of rural black expression. She saw poetry where other writers merely saw failure to cope with English. She was so at ease with her blackness it never occurred to her that she should act one way among blacks and another among whites (as her more sophisticated black critics apparently did).

It seems to me that black writing has suffered, because even black critics have assumed that a book that deals with the relationships between members of a black family—or between a man and a woman—is less important than one that has white people as a primary antagonist. The consequence of this is that many of our books by "major" writers (always male) tell us little about the culture, history, or future, imagination, fantasies, etc., of black people, and a lot about isolated (often improbable) or limited encounters with a nonspecific white world. Where is the book, by an American black person (aside from *Cane*), that equals Elechi Amadi's *The Concubine*, for example? A book that exposes the *subconscious* of a people, because the people's dreams, imaginings, rituals, legends, etc., are known to be important, are known to contain the accumulated collective reality of the people themselves. Or, in *The Radiance of the King*, the white person is shown to be the outsider he is, because the culture he enters into in Africa *itself* [expels] him. Without malice, but as nature expels what does not suit. The white man is mysterious, a force to be reckoned with, but he is not glorified to such an extent that the Africans turn their attention away from themselves and their own imagination and culture. Which is what often happens with "protest literature." The superficial becomes— for a time—the deepest reality, and replaces the still waters of the collective subconscious.

When my own novel was published, a leading black monthly admitted (the editor did) that the book itself was never read; but the magazine ran an item stating that a *white* reviewer had praised the book (which was, in itself, an indication that the book was no good—such went the logic) and then hinted that the reviewer had liked my book because of my life-style. When I wrote to the editor to complain, he wrote me a small sermon on the importance of my "image," of what is "good" for others to see. Needless to say, what others "see" of me is the least of my worries, and I assumed that "others" are intelligent enough to recover from whatever shocks my presence might cause.

Women writers are supposed to be intimidated by male disapprobation. What they write is not important enough to be read. How they live, however, their "image," they owe to the race. Read the reason Zora Neale Hurston gave for giving up her writing. See what "image" the Negro press gave her, innocent as she was. I no longer read articles or reviews unless they are totally about the work. I trust that someday a generation of men and women will arise who will forgive me for such wrong as I do not agree I do, and will read my work because it is a true account of my feelings, my perceptions, and my imagination, and because it will reveal something to them of their own selves. They will also be free to toss it—and me—out of a high window. They can do what they like.

From *Interviews with Black Writers*

Reflections on Writing and Women's Lives (mid-1990s) 2004

Interview by William R. Ferris

If you think of the early stories, it's true that the women end badly, but it's because they belong to the generation of my mother and grandmother, when they were suspended because they had nowhere to go. All of them couldn't be Bessie Smith or Billie Holiday, so they ended up doing all kinds of destructive things. Most of that generation didn't have any fame or glory. But notice that all of those women are much older than I am. They exist in an historical place that is removed from my generation of women. . . . I wrote about these women in *In Search of Our Mothers' Gardens*. The women who have not had anything, have been, almost of necessity, self-destructive. They've just been driven insane. And the ones who have managed have been the ones who could focus their enormous energies on art forms that were not necessarily recognized as art forms—on quilting, on flowers, on making things. It's a very human need, to make things, to create. To think that women didn't need that—that by having a baby you fulfill your whole function—is absurd and demeaning.

From Southern Cultures

CRITICS ON "EVERYDAY USE"

Barbara T. Christian (1943–2000)

"Everyday Use" and the Black Power Movement   1994

"Everyday Use" is, in part, Alice Walker's response to the concept of heritage as articulated by the black movements of the 1960s. In that period, many African Americans, disappointed by the failure of integration, gravitated to the philosophy of cultural nationalism as the means to achieve liberation. In contrast to the veneration of Western ideas and ideals by many integrationists of the 1950s, Black Power ideologues emphasized the African cultural past as the true heritage of African Americans. The acknowledgment and appreciation of that heritage, which had too often been denigrated by African Americans themselves as well as by Euro-Americans, was a major tenet of the revolutionary movements of the period. Many blacks affirmed their African roots by changing their "slave names" to African names, and by wearing Afro styles and African clothing. Yet, ideologues of the period also lambasted older African Americans, opposing them to the lofty mythical models of the ancient past. These older men and women, they claimed, had become Uncle Toms and Aunt Jemimas who displayed little awareness of their culture and who, as a result of their slave past, had internalized the white man's view of blacks. So while these 1960s ideologues extolled an unknown ancient history, they denigrated the known and recent past. The tendency to idealize an ancient African past while ignoring the recent African American past still persists in the Afrocentric movements of the 1990s.

In contrast to that tendency, Walker's "Everyday Use" is dedicated to "your grandmama." And the story is told by a woman many African Americans would recognize as their grandmama, that supposedly backward Southern ancestor the cultural nationalists of the North probably visited during the summers of their youth and probably considered behind the times. Walker stresses those physical qualities which suggest such a person, qualities often demeaned by cultural nationalists. For this grandmama, like the stereotypical mammy of slavery, is "a large big-boned woman with rough, man-working hands," who wears "flannel nightgowns to bed and overalls during the day," and whose "fat keeps [her] hot in zero weather." Nor is this grandmama politically conscious according to the fashion of the day; she never had an education after the second grade, she knows nothing about African names, and she eats pork. In having the grandmama tell this story, Walker gives voice to an entire maternal ancestry often silenced by the political rhetoric of the period. Indeed, Walker tells us in "In Search of Our Mothers' Gardens" that her writing is part of her mother's legacy to her, that many of her stories are based on stories *her* mother told her. Thus, Walker's writing is her way of breaking silences and stereotypes about her grandmothers', mothers', sisters' lives. In effect, her work is a literary continuation of a distinctly oral tradition in which African American women have been and still are pivotal participants.

Alice Walker is well aware of the restrictions of the African American Southern past, for she is the eighth child of Georgia sharecroppers. Born in 1944, she grew up during the period when, as she put it, apartheid existed in America. For in the 1940s and 1950s, when segregation was the law of the South, opportunities for economic and social advancement were legally denied to Southern blacks. Walker was fortunate to come to adulthood during the social and political movements of the late fifties and sixties. Of her siblings, only she, and a slightly older sister, Molly, were able even to imagine the possibility of moving beyond the poverty of their parents. It is unlikely that Alice Walker would have been able to go to college—first at Spelman, the African American women's college in Atlanta, and then at Sarah Lawrence, the white women's college near New York City—if it had not been for the changes that came about as a result of the Civil Rights Movement. Nor is it likely that she, a Southern black woman from a poor family, would have been able to become the writer that she did without the changes resulting from the ferment of the Black and Women's Movements of the 1960s and early 1970s.

While Walker was a participant in these movements, she was also one of their most astute critics. As a Southerner, she was aware of the ways in which black Southern culture was often thought of as backward by predominantly Northern Black Power ideologues, even as they proclaimed their love for black people. She was also acutely aware of the ways in which women were oppressed within the Black Power Movement itself, even as the very culture its participants revered was so often passed on by women. Walker had also visited Africa during her junior year of college and had personally experienced the gap between the Black Power advocates' idealization of Africa and the reality of the African societies she visited.

• • •

Names are extremely important in African and African American culture as a means of indicating a person's spirit. During the 1960s Walker criticized the tendency among some African Americans to give up the names their parents gave them—names which embodied the history of their recent past—for African names that did not relate to a single person they knew. Hence the mother in "Everyday Use" is amazed that Dee would give up her name for the name Wangero. For Dee was the name of her great-grandmother, a woman who had kept her family together against great odds. Wangero might have sounded authentically African but it had no relationship to a person she knew, nor to the personal history that had sustained her.

• • •

In "Everyday Use," by contrasting a sister who has the opportunity to go to college with a sister who stays at home, Walker reminds us of the challenges that contemporary African American women face as they discover what it means to be truly educated. The same concern appears in many of her works. For example, in "For My Sister Molly Who in the Fifties," she explores the conflicts that can result from an education that takes a woman away from her cultural source. Like Molly, Dee/Wangero in "Everyday Use" is embarrassed by her folk. She has been to the North, wears an Afro, and knows the correct political rhetoric of the 1960s, but she has little regard for her relatives who have helped to create that heritage. Thus, she does not know how to quilt and can only conceive of her family's quilts as priceless artifacts, as things, which she intends to hang on her wall as a means of demonstrating to others that she has "heritage." On the other hand, Maggie, the supposedly uneducated sister, who has been nowhere beyond the supposedly uneducated black South, loves and understands her family and can appreciate its history. She knows how to quilt

Lyne Odums as Mama and Rachel Luttrell as Dee in the 2003 film of *Everyday Use*.

and would put the precious quilts to "everyday use," which is precisely what, Walker suggests, one needs to do with one's heritage. For Maggie, the quilts are an embodiment of the spirit her folks have passed on to her.

From introduction to *Everyday Use*

Mary Helen Washington

"Everyday Use" as a Portrait of the Artist   1994

In 1994 Rutgers University Press brought out a collection of critical essays on Walker's "Everyday Use" in its Women Writers: Texts and Contexts series. The book reprinted an earlier essay by Mary Helen Washington on Walker's work, along with an addendum she entitled "A Postscript to My 1979 Essay on Alice Walker." This excerpt comes from that 1994 postscript.

One of the most interesting and glaring omissions of my earlier Walker essay is Walker's statement in the 1973 interview (which took place in her home in Jackson, Mississippi) of the way she sees the story "Everyday Use" as a reflection of her own struggles as an artist, an admission that suggests that female conflicts over art are not so easily resolved as they are in "A Sudden Trip Home . . ."° In "Everyday Use" (published in 1973) all three women characters are artists: Mama, as the narrator, tells her own story; Maggie is the quiltmaker, the creator of art for "everyday use"; Dee, the photographer and collector of art, has designed her jewelry, dress, and hair so deliberately and self-consciously that she

---

"*A Sudden Trip Home* . . .": "A Sudden Trip Home in the Spring," a later Walker story about a black college student returning home from the north to Georgia for her father's funeral.

appears in the story as a self-creation. Walker says in the interview that she thinks of these three characters as herself split into three parts:

> I really see that story as almost about one person, the old woman and two daughters being one person. The one who stays and sustains—this is the older woman—who has on the one hand a daughter who is the same way, who stays and abides and loves, plus the part of them—*the autonomous person*, the part of them that also wants to go out into the world to see change and be changed. . . . I do in fact have an African name that was given to me, and I love it and use it when I want to, and I love my Kenyan gowns and my Ugandan gowns—the whole bit—it's a part of me. But, on the other hand, my parents and grandparents were part of it, and they take precedence.[1]

Walker is most closely aligned in the story with the "bad daughter," Dee, "this autonomous person," the one who goes out in the world and returns with African clothes and an African name. Like Dee, Walker leaves the community, appropriating the oral tradition in order to turn it into a written artifact, which will no longer be available for "everyday use" by its originators. Everywhere in the story the fears and self-doubts of the woman artist are revealed. The narrator-mother remains hostile to Dee and partial to the homely daughter, Maggie, setting up the opposition between the two daughters that Walker says mirrors her own internal struggles.

● ● ●

The oppositions in "Everyday Use," between mother and daughters and sisters, between art for everyday use and art for art's sake, between insider and outsider, certainly capture [a] sense of contradiction and conflict. The story ends with Mama choosing Maggie and rejecting Dee, but Dee, who represents Walker herself as the artist who returns home, at least imaginatively, in order to collect the material for her art, certainly cannot be repressed. In this story, as in her essays, Walker shows that the quiltmaker, who has female precursors and female guidance, has an easier relationship with her art than the "deviant" female who finds herself outside of acceptable boundaries. Unlike quiltmaking and garden making and even blues singing, which are part of women's traditions, the writing of fiction is still done under the shadow of men, without female authority. The self-assurance of "A Sudden Trip Home in the Spring" is acquired through an alliance with that male authority. "Everyday Use" tells a different, more threatening tale of the woman writer's fears, of the difficulty of reconciling home and art, particularly when the distance from home has been enlarged by education, by life among the "gentlefolk," and by literary recognition.

From "A Postscript to My 1979 Essay on Alice Walker"

Houston A. Baker (b. 1943) *and* Charlotte Pierce-Baker (b. 1943)

Stylish vs. Sacred in "Everyday Use"   1985

The Johnson women, who populate the generations represented in Walker's short story "Everyday Use," are inhabitants of southern cabins who have always worked with "scraps" and seen what they could make of them. The result of their labor has

[1]Mary Helen Washington, "Interview with Alice Walker," June 1973, *Black-Eyed Susans: Classic Stories By and About Black Women* (Garden City: Doubleday, 1975).

been a succession of mothers and daughters surviving the ignominies of Jim Crow life and passing on ancestral blessings to descendants. The guardians of the Johnson homestead when the story commences are the mother—"a large, big-boned woman with rough, man-working hands"—and her daughter Maggie, who has remained with her "chin on chest, eyes on ground, feet in shuffle, ever since the fire that burned the other house to the ground" ten or twelve years ago. The mood at the story's beginning is one of ritualistic "waiting": "I will wait for her in the yard that Maggie and I made so clean and wavy yesterday afternoon." The subject awaited is the other daughter, Dee. Not only has the yard (as ritual ground) been prepared for the arrival of a goddess, but the sensibilities and costumes of Maggie and her mother have been appropriately attuned for the occasion. The mother daydreams of television shows where parents and children are suddenly—and pleasantly—reunited, banal shows where chatty hosts oversee tearful reunions. In her fantasy, she weighs a hundred pounds less, is several shades brighter in complexion, and possesses a devastatingly quick tongue. She returns abruptly to real life meditation, reflecting on her own heroic, agrarian accomplishments in slaughtering hogs and cattle and preparing their meat for winter nourishment. She is a robust provider who has gone to the people of her church and raised money to send her light-complexioned, lithe-figured, and ever-dissatisfied daughter Dee to college. Today, as she waits in the purified yard, she notes the stark differences between Maggie and Dee and recalls how the "last dingy gray board of the house [fell] in toward the red-hot brick chimney" when her former domicile burned. Maggie was scarred horribly by the fire, but Dee, who had hated the house with an intense fury, stood "off under the sweet gum tree . . . a look of concentration on her face." A scarred and dull Maggie, who has been kept at home and confined to everyday offices, has but one reaction to the fiery and vivacious arrival of her sister: "I hear Maggie suck in her breath. 'Uhnnnh,' is what it sounds like. Like when you see the wriggling end of a snake just in front of your foot on the road. 'Uhnnnh.'"

Indeed, the question raised by Dee's energetic arrival is whether there are words adequate to her flair, her brightness, her intense colorfulness of style which veritably blocks the sun. She wears "a dress so loud it hurts my eyes. There are yellows and oranges enough to throw back the light of the sun. I feel my whole face warming from the heat waves it throws out." Dee is both serpent and fire introduced with bursting esprit into the calm pasture that contains the Johnsons' tin-roofed, three-room, windowless shack and grazing cows. She has joined the radical, black nationalists of the 1960s and 1970s, changing her name from Dee to Wangero and cultivating a suddenly fashionable, or stylish, interest in what she passionately describes as her "heritage." If there is one quality that Dee (Wangero) possesses in abundance, it is "style": "At sixteen she had a style of her own: and knew what style was."

But in her stylishness, Dee is not an example of the indigenous rapping and styling out of Afro-America. Rather, she is manipulated by the style-makers, the fashion designers whose semiotics the French writer Roland Barthes has so aptly characterized. "Style" for Dee is the latest vogue—the most recent fantasy perpetuated by American media. When she left for college, her mother had tried to give her a quilt whose making began with her grandmother Dee, but the bright daughter felt such patched coverings were "old-fashioned and out of style." She has returned at the commencement of "Everyday Use," however, as one who now purports to know the value of the work of black women as holy patchers.

The dramatic conflict of the story surrounds the definition of holiness. The ritual purification of earth and expectant atmosphere akin to that of Beckett's famous drama ("I will wait for her in the yard that Maggie and I made so clean and wavy yesterday afternoon.") prepare us for the narrator's epiphanic experience at the story's conclusion.

Near the end of "Everyday Use," the mother (who is the tale's narrator) realizes that Dee (a.k.a. Wangero) is a *fantasy* child, a perpetrator and victim of: "words, lies, other folks's habits." The energetic daughter is as frivolously careless of other people's lives as the fiery conflagration that she had watched ten years previously. Assured by the makers of American fashion that "black" is currently "beautiful," she has conformed her own "style" to that notion. Hers is a trendy "blackness" cultivated as "art" and costume. She wears "a dress down to the ground . . . bracelets dangling and making noises when she moves her arm up to shake the folds of the dress out of her armpits." And she says of quilts she has removed from a trunk at the foot of her mother's bed: "Maggie can't appreciate these quilts! She'd probably be backward enough to put them to everyday use." "Art" is, thus, juxtaposed with "everyday use" in Walker's short story, and the fire goddess Dee, who has achieved literacy only to burn "us with a lot of knowledge we didn't necessarily need to know," is revealed as a perpetuator of institutional theories of aesthetics.

● ● ●

Quilts designed for everyday use, pieced wholes defying symmetry and pattern, are signs of the scarred generations of women who have always been alien to a world of literate words and stylish fantasies. The crafted fabric of Walker's story is the very weave of blues and jazz traditions in the Afro-American community, daringly improvisational modes that confront breaks in the continuity of melody (or theme) by riffing. The asymmetrical quilts of southern black women are like the off-centered stomping of the jazz solo or the innovative musical showmanship of the blues interlude. They

Lone Star quilt pattern: "Out came Wangero with two quilts. . . . One was in the Lone Star pattern" (paragraph 55).

speak a world in which the deceptively shuffling Maggie is capable of a quick change into goddess, an unlikely holy figure whose dues are paid in full. Dee's anger at her mother is occasioned principally by the mother's insistence that paid dues make Maggie a more likely bearer of sacredness, tradition, and true value than the "brighter" sister. "You just don't understand," she says to her mother. Her assessment is surely correct where institutional theories and systems of "art" are concerned. The mother's cognition contains no categories for framed art. The mother works according to an entirely different scale of use and value, finally assigning proper weight to the virtues of Maggie and to the ancestral importance of the pieced quilts that she has kept out of use for so many years. Smarting, perhaps, from Dee's designation of the quilts as "old-fashioned," the mother has buried the covers away in a trunk. At the end of Walker's story, however, she has become aware of her own mistaken value judgments, and she pays homage that is due to Maggie. The unlikely daughter is a *griot*° of the vernacular who remembers actors and events in a distinctively black "historical" drama.

Before Dee departs, she "put on some sunglasses that hid everything above the tip of her nose and her chin." Maggie smiles at the crude symbolism implicit in this act, for she has always known that her sister saw "through a glass darkly." But it is the mother's conferral of an ancestral blessing (signaled by her deposit of the quilts in Maggie's lap) that constitutes the occasion for the daughter's first "real smile." Maggie knows that it is only communal recognition by elders of the tribe that confers ancestral privileges on succeeding generations. The mother's holy recognition of the scarred daughter's sacred status as quilter is the best gift of a hard-pressed womankind to the fragmented goddess of the present.

At the conclusion of "Everyday Use," which is surely a fitting precursor to *The Color Purple*, with its sewing protagonist and its scenes of sisterly quilting, Maggie and her mother relax in the ritual yard after the dust of Dee's departing car has settled. They dip snuff in the manner of African confreres sharing cola nuts. The moment is past when a putatively "new" generation has confronted scenes of black, everyday life. A change has taken place, but it is a change best described by Amiri Baraka's designation for Afro-American music's various styles and discontinuities. The change in Walker's story is the "changing same." What has been reaffirmed at the story's conclusion is the value of the quiltmaker's motion and strategy in the precincts of a continuously undemocratic South.

From "Patches: Quilts and Community in Alice Walker's 'Everyday Use'"

■ WRITING *effectively*

TOPICS FOR WRITING ABOUT "THE TELL-TALE HEART"

1. In his essay "The Tale and Its Effect," Edgar Allan Poe claims that an author's very first sentence must bring out the effect he's trying to produce on the reader, otherwise "he has failed in his first step." Consider the first sentence of "The Tell-Tale Heart" and judge the author by his own criteria.

---

griot: African storyteller, guardian of the people's history [authors' note].

2. Poe never knew his real father and had a conflicted relationship with his foster father, John Allan. Although the relationship between the narrator and the old man is never explicitly defined, how do you think Poe feels about the relationship of fathers and sons, based on this story?

3. Poe was one of the first Southern writers to employ the "grotesque"—a combination of horror and humor—in his stories. He has many followers in this genre, most notably Flannery O'Connor, who claimed that Poe's short stories were a major influence on her own writing. Track down a couple other Poe stories—"The Cask of Amontillado" and "The Fall of the House of Usher" are good choices—and, along with "The Tell-Tale Heart," consider them as examples of the grotesque. Compare Poe's tales to the three O'Connor stories in Chapter 11. Do you see any evidence in O'Connor's work that she was influenced by Poe's stories?

4. If someone said that Poe's stories were just simple shockers of no literary value, how would you defend Poe's artistry? Draw examples from at least two Poe stories to support your points. (His stories will be easy to find, as they are in public domain.)

TOPICS FOR WRITING ABOUT "THE YELLOW WALLPAPER"

1. "The Yellow Wallpaper" is cast in the form of the journal written by its central character. Consider how the use of this narrative device enriches—or impoverishes—the story.

2. Thomas L. Erskine and Connie L. Richards have written of "the aesthetic problem with much of Gilman's literary work; often her sociopolitical agenda overwhelms the characters, who become one-dimensional mouthpieces for different ideas. Propaganda all too often threatens art." Discuss whether or not you think these concerns apply to "The Yellow Wallpaper."

3. Think of a contemporary issue that involves women's feelings of being confined or thwarted by the male power structure. Then write a brief treatment of that issue in the style of "The Yellow Wallpaper."

4. Discuss the larger implications of the conclusion of "The Yellow Wallpaper." In the end, has the narrator triumphed by escaping her oppression, or has she been crushed by it?

TOPICS FOR WRITING ABOUT "EVERYDAY USE"

1. Write a brief version of the encounter in "Everyday Use" from Dee's point of view. Is it possible to present a nonironic affirmation of her values over those of her mother and sister? Why or why not?

2. Have you grown apart from a friend or relative with whom you once had a close relationship? Imagine an encounter with that person, and write a first-person description of it from the other person's point of view.

3. Alice Walker has suggested that one of her principal intentions in her writing is "nurturing and healing the reader." Is "nurturing and healing" one of the primary aims of "Everyday Use"?

4. How does the use of a first-person narrator function in "Everyday Use"? Are there places in which the reader is expected to understand more than the narrator does, or is everything that she says and sees to be accepted at face value?

13   GALLERY OF INTERNATIONAL VOICES

I haven't been everywhere, but it's on my list.

—SUSAN SONTAG

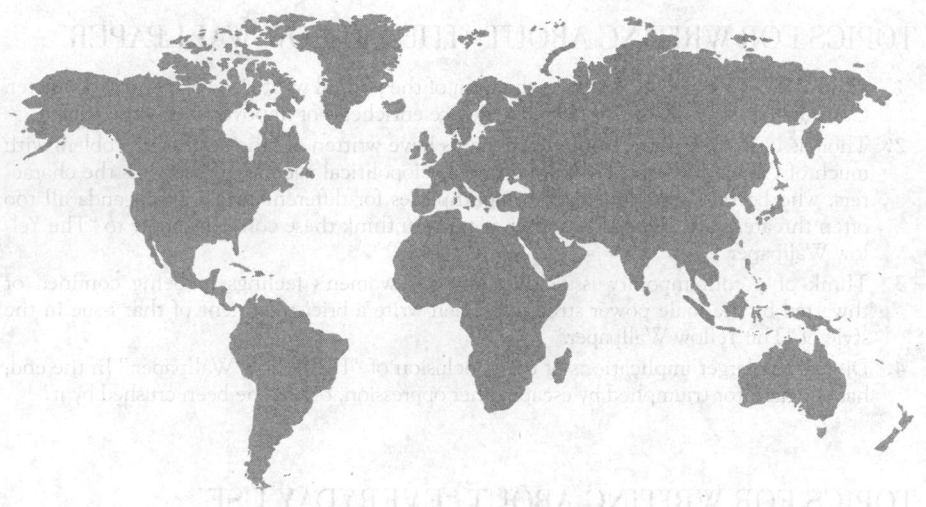

Stories from Around the World

Chinua Achebe—*Nigeria*

Tahmima Anam—*Bangladesh*

Inés Arredondo—*Mexico*

Albert Camus—*Algeria/France*

Nadine Gordimer—*South Africa*

Kazuo Ishiguro—*Japan*

Ha Jin—*China*

Jamaica Kincaid—*Antigua*

Naguib Mahfouz—*Egypt*

Bharati Mukherjee—*India*

Alice Munro—*Canada*

Marjane Satrapi—*Iran*

Note: Elsewhere in the Fiction section are stories from Argentina, Chile, Columbia, Czech Republic, England, France, Germany, Greece, Ireland, New Zealand, Russia, and Syria.

NIGERIA

Chinua Achebe

Dead Men's Path

(1953) 1972

Chinua Achebe (1930–2013) was born in Ogidi, a village in eastern Nigeria. His father was a missionary schoolteacher, and Achebe had a devout Christian up-bringing. A member of the Ibo tribe, the future writer grew up speaking Igbo, but at the age of eight, he began learning English. He went abroad to study at London University but returned to Africa to complete his BA at the University College of Ibadan in 1953. Achebe worked for years in Nigerian radio. Shortly after Nigeria's independence from Great Britain in 1963, civil war broke out, and the nation split in two. Achebe left his job to join the Ministry of Information for Biafra, the new country created from eastern Nigeria. It was not until 1970 that the bloody civil war ended. Approximately one million Ibos lay dead from war, disease, and starvation as the defeated Biafrans reunited with Nigeria. Achebe was often considered Africa's premier novelist. His novels included Things

Chinua Achebe

Fall Apart *(1958),* No Longer at Ease *(1962),* A Man of the People *(1966), and* Anthills of the Savannah *(1987). His short stories were collected in* Girls at War *(1972). He also published poetry, children's stories, and several volumes of essays, the last of which is* Home and Exile *(2000). In 1990 Achebe suffered massive injuries in a car accident outside Lagos that left him paralyzed from the waist down. Following the accident, he taught at Bard College in upstate New York for almost nineteen years. In 1999 he visited Nigeria again after a deliberate nine-year absence to protest government dictatorship, and his homecoming became a national event. In 2007 he was awarded the second Man Booker International Prize for his lifetime contribution to world literature. He died at age 82.*

Michael Obi's hopes were fulfilled much earlier than he had expected. He was appointed headmaster of Ndume Central School in January 1949. It had always been an unprogressive school, so the Mission authorities decided to send a young and energetic man to run it. Obi accepted this responsibility with enthusiasm. He had many wonderful ideas and this was an opportunity to put them into practice. He had had sound secondary school education which designated him a "pivotal teacher" in the official records and set him apart from the other headmasters in the mission field. He was outspoken in his condemnation of the narrow views of these older and often less-educated ones.

"We shall make a good job of it, shan't we?" he asked his young wife when they first heard the joyful news of his promotion.

"We shall do our best," she replied. "We shall have such beautiful gardens and everything will be just *modern* and delightful . . ." In their two years of married life she had become completely infected by his passion for "modern methods" and his denigration of "these old and superannuated people in the teaching field who would be better employed as traders in the Onitsha market." She began to see herself already as the admired wife of the young headmaster, the queen of the school.

The wives of the other teachers would envy her position. She would set the fashion in everything . . . Then, suddenly, it occurred to her that there might not be other wives. Wavering between hope and fear, she asked her husband, looking anxiously at him.

"All our colleagues are young and unmarried," he said with enthusiasm which for   5 once she did not share. "Which is a good thing," he continued.

"Why?"

"Why? They will give all their time and energy to the school."

Nancy was downcast. For a few minutes she became skeptical about the new school; but it was only for a few minutes. Her little personal misfortune could not blind her to her husband's happy prospects. She looked at him as he sat folded up in a chair. He was stoop-shouldered and looked frail. But he sometimes surprised people with sudden bursts of physical energy. In his present posture, however, all his bodily strength seemed to have retired behind his deep-set eyes, giving them an extraordinary power of penetration. He was only twenty-six, but looked thirty or more. On the whole, he was not unhandsome.

"A penny for your thoughts, Mike," said Nancy after a while, imitating the woman's magazine she read.

"I was thinking what a grand opportunity we've got at last to show these people   10 how a school should be run."

Ndume School was backward in every sense of the word. Mr. Obi put his whole life into the work, and his wife hers too. He had two aims. A high standard of teaching was insisted upon, and the school compound was to be turned into a place of beauty. Nancy's dream-gardens came to life with the coming of the rains, and blossomed. Beautiful hibiscus and allamanda hedges in brilliant red and yellow marked out the carefully tended school compound from the rank neighborhood bushes.

One evening as Obi was admiring his work he was scandalized to see an old woman from the village hobble right across the compound, through a marigold flower-bed and the hedges. On going up there he found faint signs of an almost disused path from the village across the school compound to the bush on the other side.

"It amazes me," said Obi to one of his teachers who had been three years in the school, "that you people allowed the villagers to make use of this footpath. It is simply incredible." He shook his head.

"The path," said the teacher apologetically, "appears to be very important to them. Although it is hardly used, it connects the village shrine with their place of burial."

"And what has that got to do with the school?" asked the headmaster.   15

"Well, I don't know," replied the other with a shrug of the shoulders. "But I remember there was a big row some time ago when we attempted to close it."

"That was some time ago. But it will not be used now," said Obi as he walked away. "What will the Government Education Officer think of this when he comes to inspect the school next week? The villagers might, for all I know, decide to use the schoolroom for a pagan ritual during the inspection."

Heavy sticks were planted closely across the path at the two places where it entered and left the school premises. These were further strengthened with barbed wire.

Three days later the village priest of *Ani* called on the headmaster. He was an old man and walked with a slight stoop. He carried a stout walking-stick which he usually tapped on the floor, by way of emphasis, each time he made a new point in his argument.

"I have heard," he said after the usual exchange of cordialities, "that our ances-   20 tral footpath has recently been closed . . ."

"Yes," replied Mr. Obi. "We cannot allow people to make a highway of our school compound."

"Look here, my son," said the priest bringing down his walking-stick, "this path was here before you were born and before your father was born. The whole life of this village depends on it. Our dead relatives depart by it and our ancestors visit us by it. But most important, it is the path of children coming in to be born . . ."

Mr. Obi listened with a satisfied smile on his face.

"The whole purpose of our school," he said finally, "is to eradicate just such beliefs as that. Dead men do not require footpaths. The whole idea is just fantastic. Our duty is to teach your children to laugh at such ideas."

"What you say may be true," replied the priest, "but we follow the practices of   25 our fathers. If you reopen the path we shall have nothing to quarrel about. What I always say is: let the hawk perch and let the eagle perch." He rose to go.

"I am sorry," said the young headmaster. "But the school compound cannot be a thoroughfare. It is against our regulations. I would suggest your constructing another path, skirting our premises. We can even get our boys to help in building it. I don't suppose the ancestors will find the little detour too burdensome."

"I have no more words to say," said the old priest, already outside.

Two days later a young woman in the village died in childbed. A diviner was immediately consulted and he prescribed heavy sacrifices to propitiate ancestors insulted by the fence.

Obi woke up next morning among the ruins of his work. The beautiful hedges were torn up not just near the path but right round the school, the flowers trampled to death and one of the school buildings pulled down . . . . That day, the white Supervisor came to inspect the school and wrote a nasty report on the state of the premises but more seriously about the "tribal-war situation developing between the school and the village, arising in part from the misguided zeal of the new headmaster."

 # BANGLADESH

Tahmima Anam

Garments   2015

Born in 1975 in Dhaka, Bangladesh, Tahmima Anam comes from a family of newspaper publishers, editors, and journalists. Her grandfather, Abul Mansur Ahmed, was a prominent politician, satirist, novelist, and journalist; her uncle was a journalist and editor of the Bangladesh Times; *and her father, Mahfuz Anam, served as editor and publisher of the* Daily Star, *the premier English-language newspaper in Bangladesh. As a result of the political volatility of her home nation, her grandfather was imprisoned for his work, and her father has endured threats and dozens of lawsuits for publishing criticisms of the Bangladeshi government. Tahmima was educated in a handful of international cities, including Paris, New York, and Bangkok, due to her father's work*

Tahmima Anam

with UNESCO, yet her parents insisted that she speak Bengali at home and steeped their daughter in the poetry of Nobel Laureate Rabindranath Tagore. Anam came to the United States to attend college at Mount Holyoke, then completed a PhD in anthropology at Harvard. Her first novel, The Golden Age *(2007), portrayed the fictional Haque family during the Bangladeshi Liberation War—the bloody 1971 conflict that earned Bangladesh its independence from Pakistan and in which both her parents were freedom fighters. For that novel and its follow-up,* The Good Muslim *(2011)—the second book of what would become her Bengal Trilogy—Anam interviewed hundreds of fighters. In 2016 she published* The Bones of Grace, *completing the series that depicted three generations of the Haque family. Anam is a* New York Times *Contributing Opinion Writer and lives in London with her husband, an American inventor. "Garments"—which was inspired by the Rana Plaza factory collapse in 2013, in which 1,129 workers were killed—was included in the* Best American Short Stories 2016 *anthology and shortlisted for the BBC National Short Story Award.*

One day Mala lowers her mask and says to Jesmin, my boyfriend wants to marry you. Jesmin is six shirts behind so she doesn't look up. After the bell, Mala explains. For months now she's been telling the girls, ya, any day now me and Dulal are going to the Kazi. They don't believe her, they know her boyfriend works in an air-conditioned shop. No way he was going to marry a garments girl. Now she has a scheme and when Jesmin hears it, she thinks, it's not so bad.

Two days later Mala's sweating like it's July. He wants one more. Three wives. We have to find a girl. After the bell they look down the row of sewing machines and try to choose. Mala knows all the unmarried girls, which one needs a room, which one has hungry relatives, which one borrowed money against her wage and can't work enough overtime to pay it off. They squint down the line and consider Fatima, Keya, Komola, but for some reason or other they reject them all. There's a new girl at the end of the row, but when Mala takes a break and limps over to the toilet she comes back and says the girl has a milky eye.

There's a new order for panties. Jesmin picks up the sample. She's never seen a panty like it before. It's thick, with double seams on the front, back, and around the buttocks. The leg is just cut off without a stitch. Mala, she says, what's this? Mala says, the foreign ladies use them to hold in their fat and they call them Thanks. Thanks? Yep. Because they look so good, in the mirror they say to the panties, Thanks. Jesmin and Mala pull down their masks and trade a laugh when the morning supervisor, Jamal, isn't looking.

Jesmin decides it won't be so bad to share a husband. She doesn't have dreams of a love marriage, and if they have to divide the sex that's fine with her, and if he wants something, like he wants his rice the way his mother makes it, maybe one of them will know how to do it. Walking home as she did every evening with all the other factory workers, a line two girls thick and a mile long, snaking out of Tongi and all the way to Uttara, she spots a new girl. Sometimes Jesmin looks in front and behind her at that line, all the ribbons flapping and the song of sandals on the pavement, and she feels a swell in her chest. She catches up to the girl. Her name's Ruby. She's dark, but pretty. Small white teeth and filmy eyes. She's new and eager to make friends. I'm coming two, three hours from my village every morning, she complains. I know, Jesmin says. Finding a place to live is why I'm doing this.

The year Jesmin came to Dhaka she said to her father, ask Nasir chacha to give you   5
his daughter's mobile contact. Nasir chacha's daughter Kulsum had a job in garments. Her father nodded, said she will help you. Her mother, drying mustard in front of their hut, put her face in the crook of her arm. Go, go, she said. I don't want to see you again.

Jesmin left without looking back, knowing that, once, her mother had another dream for her, that she would marry and be treated like a queen, that all the village would tell her what a good forehead she had. But that was before Amin, before the punishing hut.

Kulsum did help her. Put in a good word when she heard they were looking. She has a place, a room in Korail she shares with her kid and her in-laws. Her husband works in foreign so she lets Jesmin sleep on the floor. She takes half of Jesmin's pay every month. You're lucky, she tells her, I didn't ask for the money up front. But now her husband's coming back and Jesmin has to find somewhere else. She has another relative, a cousin's cousin, but he lives all the way out in Mogbajar and Jesmin doesn't like the way he looks at her. There's a shanty not far from the factory and she heard there were rooms going, but when she went to look, the landlord said, I can't have so many girls in my building. What building? Just a row of tin, paper between the walls, sharing an outside tap. But still he told her he wasn't sure, had to think about it. If you had a husband, he said, that would be a different story.

When Jesmin joined the line, she started as Mala's helper. She tied her knots and clipped the threads from her shirt buttons. The Rana strike was over and Mala's leg was broken and the bosses had their eye on her, always waiting to see if she'd make more trouble. Even now, Jamal gives her a look every time she walks by, waiting to see if she takes too long in the toilet. They would have got rid of her a long time ago if her hands weren't so good, always first in the line, seams straight as blades of grass, five, seven pieces ahead of everyone.

To make the Thanks you have to stretch the fabric tight against your left arm while running the stitch. Then you fold it, stretch again, run the stitch back up, till the whole thing is hard and tight. Jesmin trims the leg and takes a piece home. She pulls it up over her leg. Her thigh bulges in front and behind it. She doesn't understand. Maybe the legs of foreign ladies are different.

Jesmin and Mala know a foreign lady, Miss Bridgey. She came to the factory and asked them a few questions and wrote down what they said. How many minutes for lunch? Where is the toilet? If there's a fire, what will you do? In the morning before she came, Jamal lined everyone up. There's an inspector coming, he said. You want to make a good impression. Jamal liked to ask a question and supply the answer. Are we proud of the factory? Yes we are! What do we think of Sunny Textiles? We love SunnyTex! That day they opened all the windows and did the fire drill ten times. Then Miss Bridgey showed up and Jesmin could see the laugh behind Jamal's face. He thought it would be a man in a suit, and there was this little yellow-haired girl. Nothing to worry. Aren't we lucky? Yes we are.

When Miss Bridgey comes back Jesmin is going to ask her about the Thanks. But right now they have to explain the whole thing to Ruby. Mala's doing all the talking. We marry him, and that way we can tell people we are married. We give him a place to stay, we give him food, we give him all the things a wife gives. If he wants sex, we give him sex. When she mentions the sex, Jesmin feels her legs filling up with water. Why don't we get our own husbands? Ruby asks. She's green, she doesn't know. Ruby looks like she's going to cry. Then she bites her full lip with a line of those perfect little teeth and she says, okay, I'll do it.

When Jesmin was born, her mother took a piece of coal and drew a big black mark behind her ear. Jesmin went to school and learned the letters and the sums before any of the other children. The teacher, Amin, always asked her to sing the national anthem on Victory Day and stand first in the parade. Amin said she should go to secondary. He said, meet me after school. He taught her sums and a, b, c. He put his hand over her hand on the chalk.

10

Miss Bridgey comes a few days later and she takes Jesmin aside. I'm worried about the factory, she says. Has it always been this bad? Jesmin looks around. She takes in the fans in the ceiling, bars on the windows, rows and rows of girls bent over their machines. It's the same, she says. Always like this. This place good. This place okay. We love SunnyTex! But why, she asks Miss Bridgey, do the ladies in your country wear this? She holds up the Thanks. Miss Bridgey takes it from her hand, turns it around, then she laughs and laughs. Jesmin, you know how expensive these are?

On the wedding day Dulal comes to the factory. He's wearing a red shirt under the gray sleeveless sweater they made last year when the SunnyTex bosses decided to expand into knitwear. Jesmin and Mala and Ruby stand in front of him, and he looks at them with his head tilted to the side. Take a look at my prince! Mala says. He's got a narrow face and small black eyes and hair that sticks to his forehead. Now it's time to get married so they set off on two rickshaws, him and Mala in the front, Jesmin and Ruby following behind. They are all wearing red saris like brides do, except nobody's family has showed up to feed them sweets or paint their feet.

Jesmin watches the back of Mala and Dulal. She knows that Mala's brother died in Rana. That Mala had held up his photo for seven weeks, hoping he would come out from under the cement. That she was at the strike, shouting her brother's name. That her mother kept writing from the village asking for money, so Mala had to turn around and go back to the line. Mala's face was cracked, like a broken eggshell, until she found Dulal. Now she comes to the factory, works like magic, tells her jokes, does her overtime as if it never happened, but Jesmin knows that once you die like that, on the street or in the factory, your life isn't your life anymore.

This morning Jesmin went to the shanty to talk to the landlord. I'm getting married.   15
Can I stay? He looked at her with one side of his face. Married? Show me the groom. I'll bring him next week, she said. He took one more drag and threw his cigarette into the drain and Jesmin thought for sure he was going to say no, but then he turned to her and said, what, I don't get any sweets? Then he slapped her on the back, and she shrank, but it was a friendly slap, as if she was a man, or his daughter. Next she went to Kulsum. I found a husband. Good, she said, you're getting old. Now I don't have to worry about you.

Jesmin sees marriage as a remedy. If you are a girl you have many problems, but all of them can be fixed if you have a husband. In the factory, if Jamal puts you in ironing, which is the easiest job, or if he says, take a few extra minutes for lunch, you can finish after hours and get overtime, you can say, but my husband is waiting, and then you won't have to feel his breath like a spider on your shoulder later that night when the current goes out and you're still in the factory finishing up a sleeve. Everything is better if you're married. Jesmin is giving Ruby all this good advice as their rickshaw passes the Mohakhali flyover° but the girl's eyes are somewhere else. Bet she had some other idea about her life. Jesmin puts her arm around Ruby's shoulder and notices she smells very nice, like the biscuit factory she passes on the way to SunnyTex.

Jesmin is the only one who can sign her name on the wedding register. The others dip their thumbs into ink and press them into the big book. The kazi° takes their money and gives them a piece of paper that has all their names on it. Jesmin reads it out loud to the others.

After, Dulal wants to stop at a chotpoti° stall. Three men, friends of his, are waiting there. They look at the brides, up and down, and then they stick their elbows into Dulal's side and Dulal smiles like he's just opened a drawer full of cash.

Mohakhali flyover: a highway overpass in a neighborhood of Dhaka, Bangladesh.   *kazi:* Bengali word for judge.   *chotpoti:* popular street food in Bangladesh consisting of spicy cooked vegetables.

Who's first? they ask him. The old one, he replies, not bothering to whisper it. Then that one, he says, pointing to Jesmin. Next week Kulsum said she would let Jesmin string a blanket across and take half the bed. Her in-laws will be on the other half and she'll take the kid and sleep on the floor. Best for last, eh? his friend says. Dulal looks at Ruby like he's seeing her for the first time and he says, yeah, she's the cream.

The friends take off and then it's just the brides and groom. They sit on four stools along the pavement. Jesmin feels the winter air on her neck. Where's your village? Dulal asks, but before she can tell him, she hears Ruby's voice saying, Kurigram. Something in the sound of her voice makes Jesmin think maybe Ruby wants to be the favorite wife. She notices now that Ruby has tied a ribbon in her hair. They finish their plates and Mala holds hands with Dulal and they take off in the direction of her place. Jesmin and Ruby are taking the bus to Kulsum's. Ruby's giving Kulsum some of her pay so she can stay there too, just until they find her somewhere else.

Jesmin wants to say something to mark the fact that they are all married now.   20 She can't think of anything so she asks Ruby if it gets cold in her village. Yes, she says, in winter sometimes people die. I'm from the south, Jesmin tells her, it's not so bad but still in winter, it bites. They hug their arms now as the sun sets. I wonder what they're doing, Ruby says. Do you think he's nice? He looks nice.

They're doing what people do, she tells Ruby, at night when no one is looking. They arrive at Kulsum's. She can share your blanket, Kulsum says, throwing a look at Ruby until Ruby takes the money out of her bag. They warm some leftover rice on the stove Kulsum shares with two other families at the back of the building. The gas is low and it takes half an hour to heat the rice, then they crush a few chilies into it. I have three younger sisters, Ruby says, even though Jesmin hasn't asked about her family. Where are they? Home and hungry, she says, and Jesmin gets a picture in her mind of three dark-skinned girls with perfect teeth, shivering together in the northern cold. What about you? Ruby asks. A snake took my brother, Jesmin says, remembering his face, gray and swollen, before they threw it in the ground. Hai Allah! Ruby rubs her hand up and down Jesmin's back. His forehead was unlucky, Jesmin says, pretending it wasn't so bad, like this wasn't the reason everything started to go sour, her parents with nothing to look forward to, just a daughter whose head was a curse and the hope that next year's rice would come up without a fight.

It's freezing on the floor. Jesmin is glad for Ruby's back spreading the warm into their blanket. You are kind, Ruby mumbles as she falls asleep, and Jesmin can see her breathing, her shoulders moving up and down. She lies awake for a long time imagining Mala with their husband. The watery feeling returns to her legs. Ruby shifts, moves closer, and her biscuit smell clouds up around them. Jesmin takes a strand of Ruby's hair and puts it into her mouth.

When she gets to SunnyTex the next morning Mala is already at her machine with her head down. Jesmin tries to catch her eye but she won't look up, and when they break for lunch she disappears and Jesmin doesn't see her until it's too late. Finally it's the end of the day and Mala is hurrying along in the going-home line. What d'you want? She squints as if she's looking from far away and when Jesmin asks her what the wedding night was like, she says, it wasn't so bad. That's all? You'll find out for yourself, don't let me go and spoil it, and then her face bends into a smile. She won't say anything else.

After their shift is over Jesmin tells Ruby, let's go to a shop. I don't have any money, Ruby says. Don't worry, we'll just look. They walk to the sandal shop at the end of the street. They stare at the wall of sandals. Ruby takes Jesmin's hand and squeezes her fingers. It's so nice she can almost feel the sandals on her feet.

The week is over and finally it's Jesmin's turn. She scrubs her face till Kulsum   25 scolds her for taking too long at the tap. She wears a red shalwar kameez. Ruby wants to do her hair. She makes a braid that begins at the top of Jesmin's head and runs all the way down her back. Her fingers move quickly and Jesmin feels a shiver that starts at her neck and disappears into her kameez. Ruby reaches back and takes the clip out of her own hair and puts it into Jesmin's. She feels it tense her hair together.

All day while they're sewing buttons onto check shirts, Jesmin can feel the clip pulling at her scalp. Mala, she says, I'm feeling scared. At first Mala looks like she's going to tell her something, but her eyes go back to her sewing machine and she says, all brides are scared. Don't worry, I tested him out for you. Equipment is working tip-top.

After work Dulal is standing outside the SunnyTex gate. He puts his finger under her chin and stares into her face like he's examining a leg of goat. His breathing is ragged and his cheeks are shining. She notices how dirty his shirt is under the sweater and she starts to wonder what sort of a man would want three wives all at once. She shakes her head to knock the thoughts out of it. She has a husband, that's what matters. The road unfolds in front of them as they walk home, his hand molded onto her waist. Kulsum is wearing lipstick and she tells her kid, look, your khalu has come to visit, give him foot-salaam, and her kid kneels in front of Dulal and touches his sandal. In the kitchen they pass around the food. Jesmin puts rice on Dulal's plate, and the bigger piece of meat. Kulsum gets a piece too and the rest of them do with gravy. She's given him the mora from under the bed so he sits taller than everyone else. The gravy is watery but Jesmin watches Kulsum's kid run his tongue all across his plate. She thinks about Ruby. It's Thursday and she's gone home on the bus to spend the weekend with her brothers. Jesmin fingers the clip, still standing stiff on the side of her head.

Now it's time and they lie down together. The blanket is strung across but Jesmin can see the outline of Kulsum's mother-in-law, her elbow jutting into their side of the bed. Dulal turns his face to the wall and says, scratch my back. He squirms out of his shirt and she runs her fingers up and down his back and soon her nails are clogged with dirt. He takes her hand and pulls it over to the front of his body, and then he takes out his thing. His hand is over her hand, and she thinks of Amin and the chalk and the village, fog in the winter and the new season's molasses and everything smelling clean, the dung drying against the walls of her father's hut. Her arm is getting sore and Dulal's breath is slow and steady, his thing soft as a mouse. She thinks maybe he's fallen asleep but then he turns around and she feels the weight of him pressing down on her. He drags down her kameez and tries to push the mouse in. After a few minutes he gives up and turns back around. Scratch my back, he says, irritated, and finally he falls asleep with her hand trapped under his elbow.

The next day is Friday and Dulal says he's going to spend it with his sister, who lives in Uttara. Jesmin was hoping they could go to the market and look at the shops, but he leaves before she can ask. She takes the bus to Mohakhali. Mala's neighbor looks Jesmin up and down and says to her, so your friend is married now. Look at her, like a queen she is. Mala's wearing bright orange lipstick and acting like something good has happened to her. She's talking on her mobile and Jesmin waits for her to finish. Then she asks, is it supposed to be like that?

Mala looks up from the bed. You couldn't do it?   30

What, what was I supposed to do?

She grabs an arm. Did he put it in?

No.

She curses under her breath. But I told him you would be the one.

The one to what?   35

The one to cure his, you know, not being able to.

Jesmin struggles to understand. You told me his equipment was tip-top.

Mala shrinks from her. It occurs to Jesmin that she never asked the right question, the one that has been on everyone's mind. Why does a guy working in a shop, who doesn't get his hands dirty all day, want a garments girl, especially a broken one like Mala? Jesmin stares at her until Mala can't hold her eye anymore. Mala looks down at her hands. I paid him, she says.

You paid him?

Then he started asking for more, more money, and I didn't have it, so I told him   40
you and Ruby would fix him. That's the only way he would stay.

She's got her head in her hands and she's crying. She rubs her broken leg, and Jesmin thinks of Rana, and Mala's brother, and her own brother, and she decides there's nothing to be done now but try and fix Dulal's problem, because now that they were married to him, his bad was their bad.

What next?

Try again, try everything. Mala hands her the tube of lipstick. Here, take this.

That night Jesmin asks Kulsum for a few sprays from the bottle of scent she keeps in a box under the bed and Kulsum takes it out reluctantly, eyeing her while she pats some of it onto her neck. Jesmin draws thick lines across her eyelids and smears the lipstick on hard. Dulal cleans his plate and goes outside to gargle into the drain. She stands with him at the edge of the drain and after he rinses and spits, he looks up at the night. There's all kinds of noise coming from the compound, kids screaming, dogs, a radio, but up there it looks quiet. Maybe Dulal's looking for a bit of quiet too. Fog's coming, she says. She asks about his sister. Alhamdulillah,° he tells her, but doesn't say, I will take you to meet her. I hate winter, he says instead, makes my bones tired.

Winter makes her think of the sesame her mother had planted, years ago when she   45
was a baby. The harvest was for selling, but after the first season the price at the market wasn't worth the water and the effort, so she gave it up. But still the branches came up, twisted and pointy every year, tearing the feet off anyone who dared walk across the field. Only Amin knew how to tread between the bushes, his feet unscarred, the soles of his feet always so soft. Jesmin ran them across her cheeks and it was like his palm was touching her, or the tip of his penis, rather than the underside of his big toe, that's how delicate his feet were. I'm only here to talk, he said, telling her the story of Laila and Majnu.° From Amin she learned what it was to be swallowed by a man, like a snake swallowing a rat, whole and without effort. He pressed his feet against her face, showing her the difference between a schoolteacher and a farmer's daughter, and she licked the salt between his toes, and when she asked when they would get married, he laughed as if she had told him the funniest joke in the world. And then his wife went to the Salish, and the Salish decided she had tempted Amin, and they said, leave the village. But not before you are punished. And into the punishing hut she went, and when she came out, she looked exactly like she was meant to look, ugly and broken. Like a rat swallowed by a snake. Just like Mala looked after they told her the search was over and she would never see her brother again. Now Jesmin is wondering if something happened to Dulal that made him feel like the rest of them, like a small animal in a big, spiteful world.

Maybe that's why, she offers, speaking softly into the dark. He turns to her. What did you say?

Maybe that's why, you know, it's not—it's not your fault.

He comes close. His breath is eggy. That's when, out of nowhere, one side of her face explodes. When she opens her eyes she's on the ground and everyone is standing

---

Alhamdulillah: an Arabic phrase meaning "Praise be to God."   *Laila and Majnu:* an ancient, well-known, Arabic love story.

over her, Kulsum, her kid, her in-laws, and Dulal. The kid tugs at her kameez and she stands up, brushes herself off. No one says anything. Jesmin can taste lipstick and blood where she's bitten herself.

In the morning Jamal takes one look at her and runs her to the back of the line. You look like a bat, he says, you should've stayed home. What if that inspector comes nosing around? Her eye is swollen so she has to change the thread on the machine with her head tilted to one side. Ruby's back from her village and when she sees Jesmin she starts to cry. Don't worry, Jesmin says, it's nothing. She takes a toilet break, borrows a compact from Mala and looks at herself. One side of her face is swallowing the other. When she comes out Ruby's holding a chocbar. She presses it against Jesmin's cheek and they wait for it to melt, then they tear open a corner and take turns pouring the ice cream into their mouths.

They go home. Dulal isn't there. Now look what you did, Kulsum says. They wait   50
until the mosquitoes come in and finally everyone eats. When the kerosene lamp comes on and she's about to bed on the floor with Ruby, Dulal bursts in and demands food. She makes him a plate and watches him belch. The food's cold, he says. After, it's the same, lying there facing his back, holding his small, lifeless thing, except this time Ruby's on the floor next to Kulsum and her kid. Scratch my head, Dulal mutters. He falls asleep, and later, in the night, she hears him cry out, a sharp, bleating sound. She thinks she must have dreamed it because in the moonlight his face is as mean as ever.

On the day of Ruby's turn, she looks so small. When she's cut too much thread off her machine, Jamal scolds her and she spends the rest of the day with her head down. But after lunch she goes into the toilet and when she comes out she's got a new sari on and the ribbon is twisted into her hair like a thread of happy running all around the back of her head. Dulal comes to the gate and when he sees Ruby his face is as bright as money. Ruby says something to Dulal and he laughs. Jesmin watches them leave together, holding hands, her heart breaking against her ribs.

Jesmin covers her ears against the sound of laughter.

In the punishing hut, the Salish gathered. The oldest one said, take off your dress. When her clothes were on the ground he said, walk. They sat in a circle and threw words like rotten fruit. She's nothing but a piece of trash. Amin said: her pussy stinks like a dead eel. She is the child of pigs. She's a slut. She's the shit of pigs. Walk, walk. Move your hands. You want to cover it now? Where was your shame when you seduced a married man? Get out now. Get out and don't come back. Afterward, they laughed.

Jesmin covers her ears against the sound of laughter.

It's Friday. She packs her things and says goodbye to Kulsum. The kid wraps   55
his legs around her waist and bites into her shoulder. She hands money to the land-lord and he waves her to the room. There's a kerosene lamp in one corner, and a cot pushed up against another. Last year's calendar is tacked to the wall. The roof is leaking and there's a large puddle on the floor. She sees her face in the pool of water. She sees her eyes and the shape of her head and Ruby's clip in her hair. She opens her trunk and finds the pair of Thanks she stole from the factory. She holds it up. It makes the silhouette of a piece of woman. She pulls the door shut and the room darkens. She takes off her sandals, her shalwar. She lies on the floor, the damp and the dirt under her back, and drags the Thanks over her legs. When she stands up she straddles the pool of water and casts her eyes over her reflection. There is a body encased, legs and hips and buttocks. The body is hers but it is far away, unreachable. She looks at herself and hears the sound of laughter, but this time it is not the laughter of the Salish, but the laughter of the piece of herself that is closed. She knows now that Ruby will fix Dulal, that she will parade with him in the factory, spreading her small-toothed smile among the spools of thread that

hang above their heads, and that Dulal will take Ruby to his air-conditioned shop, and her sisters will no longer be hungry, and Jesmin will be here, joined by the laughter of her own legs, no longer the girl of the punishing hut, but a garments girl with a room and a closed-up body that belongs only to herself.

The door opens. Jesmin turns to the smell of biscuits.

MEXICO

Inés Arredondo

The Shunammite   1965

Translated by Alberto Manguel

Inés Arredondo (1928–1989) was born in Culi-acán, the capital and largest city of the state of Sinaloa, Mexico, the daughter of a doctor. In 1947 she enrolled in the National Autonomous University of Mexico, but in the following year experienced a spiritual and emotional crisis that brought her close to suicide. In 1953 she married the writer Tomas Segovia; the union, which produced three children, was troubled, leading to separation in 1962 and divorce three years later. In 1972 she married Car-los Ruiz Sanchez, a physician. Throughout her adult life, financial necessity caused Arredondo to work at a variety of jobs—librarian, editor, translator, and professor. Because of spinal problems she was forced to undergo five operations and was ultimately con-fined to a wheelchair. Beginning in 1965, she pub-lished several small volumes of short fiction, which

Inés Arredondo

brought her several awards and established her reputation as a major writer. "The Shunam-mite" was filmed, with a screenplay by Arredondo, as a segment in a 1965 Mexican movie called Amor Amor Amor and was the basis for a 1991 opera by Marcela Rodríguez. Under-ground River and Other Stories (1996) presents twelve of her stories in English translation.

> *So they sought for a fair damsel throughout all the coasts of Israel,*
> *and found Abishag, a Shunammite,° and brought her to the king.*
> *And the damsel was very fair, and cherished the king,*
> *and ministered to him; but the king knew her not.*
>
> —1 KINGS 1:3–4

The summer had been a fiery furnace. The last summer of my youth.

Abishag, a Shunammite: Among the tasks Abishag was called upon to perform for the dying King David was to lie with him and warm him with her body, yet there was no sexual contact between them. A Shunam-mite was someone from the town of Shunem in ancient Palestine.

Tense, concentrated in the arrogance that precedes combustion, the city shone in a dry and dazzling light. I stood in the very midst of the light, dressed in mourning, proud, feeding the flames with my blonde hair, alone. Men's sly glances slid over my body without soiling it, and my haughty modesty forced them to barely nod at me, full of respect. I was certain of having the power to dominate passions, to purify anything in the scorching air that surrounded but did not singe me.

Nothing changed when I received the telegram; the sadness it brought me did not affect in the least my feelings towards the world. My uncle Apolonio was dying at the age of seventy-odd years and wanted to see me. I had lived as a daughter in his house for many years and I sincerely felt pain at the thought of his inevitable death. All this was perfectly normal, and not a single omen, not a single shiver made me suspect anything. Quickly I made arrangements for the journey, in the very same untouchable midst of the motionless summer.

I arrived at the village during the hour of siesta.

Walking down the empty streets with my small suitcase, I fell to daydream- 5
ing, in that dusky zone between reality and time, born of the excessive heat. I was not remembering; I was almost reliving things as they had been. "Look, Licha, the *amapas*° are blooming again." The clear voice, almost childish. "I want you to get yourself a dress like that of Margarita Ibarra to wear on the sixteenth." I could hear her, feel her walking by my side, her shoulders bent a little forwards, light in spite of her plumpness, happy and old. I carried on walking in the company of my aunt Panchita, my mother's sister. "Well, my dear, if you *really* don't like Pepe . . . but he's such a *nice* boy." Yes, she had used those exact words, here, in front of Tichi Valen-zuela's window, with her gay smile, innocent and impish. I walked a little further, where the paving stones seemed to fade away in the haze, and when the bells rang, heavy and real, ending the siesta and announcing the Rosary, I opened my eyes and gave the village a good, long look: it was not the same. The *amapas* had not bloomed and I was crying, in my mourning dress, at the door of my uncle's house.

The front gate was open, as always, and at the end of the courtyard rose the bou-gainvillea. As always: but not the same. I dried my tears, and felt that I was not arriv-ing: I was leaving. Everything looked motionless, pinioned in my memory, and the heat and the silence seemed to wither it all. My footsteps echoed with a new sound, and María came out to greet me.

"Why didn't you let us know? We'd have sent . . ."

We went straight into the sick man's room. As I entered, I felt cold. Silence and gloom preceded death.

"Luisa, is that you?"

The dear voice was dying out and would soon be silent for ever. 10

"I'm here, uncle."

"God be praised! I won't die alone."

"Don't say that; you'll soon be much better."

He smiled sadly; he knew I was lying but he did not want to make me cry.

"Yes, my daughter. Yes. Now have a rest, make yourself at home and then come 15
and keep me company. I'll try to sleep a little."

Shriveled, wizened, toothless, lost in the immense bed and floating senselessly in whatever was left of his life, he was painful to be with, like something superfluous, out of place, like so many others at the point of death. Stepping out of the overheated passageway, one would take a deep breath, instinctively, hungry for light and air.

---

amapa: a small tree that is covered, when in bloom, by masses of yellow, pink, or purple tubular flowers.

I began to nurse him and I felt happy doing it. This house was *my* house, and in the morning, while tidying up, I would sing long-forgotten songs. The peace that surrounded me came perhaps from the fact that my uncle no longer awaited death as something imminent and terrible, but instead let himself be carried by the passing days towards a more or less distant or nearby future, with the unconscious tenderness of a child. He would go over his past life with great pleasure and enjoy imagining that he was bequeathing me his images, as grandparents do with their children.

"Bring me that small chest, there, in the large wardrobe. Yes, that one. The key is underneath the mat, next to Saint Anthony. Bring the key as well."

And his sunken eyes would shine once again at the sight of all his treasures.

"Look: this necklace—I gave it to your aunt for our tenth wedding anniver-   20
sary. I bought it in Mazatlán from a Polish jeweler who told me God-knows-what story about an Austrian princess, and asked an impossible price for it. I brought it back hidden in my pistol-holder and didn't sleep a wink in the stagecoach—I was so afraid someone would steal it!"

The light of dusk made the young, living stones glitter in his calloused hands.

"This ring, so old, belonged to my mother; look carefully at the miniature in the other room and you'll see her wearing it. Cousin Begoña would mutter behind her back that a sweetheart of hers . . . "

The ladies in the portraits would move their lips and speak, once again, would breathe again—all these ladies he had seen, he had touched. I would picture them in my mind and understand the meaning of these jewels.

"Have I told you about the time we traveled to Europe, in 1908, before the Revolution?° You had to take a ship to Colima. And in Venice your aunt Panchita fell in love with a certain pair of earrings. They were much too expensive, and I told her so. 'They are fit for a queen.' Next day I bought them for her. You just can't imagine what it was like because all this took place long, long before you were born, in 1908, in Venice, when your aunt was so young, so . . . "

"Uncle, you're getting tired, you should rest."   25

"You're right, I'm tired. Leave me a while and take the small chest to your room. It's yours."

"But, uncle . . . "

"It's all yours, that's all! I trust I can give away whatever I want!"

His voice broke into a sob: the illusion was vanishing and he found himself again on the point of dying, of saying goodbye to the things he had loved. He turned to the wall and I left with the box in my hands, not knowing what to do.

On other occasions he would tell me about "the year of the famine," or "the year   30
of the yellow corn," or "the year of the plague," and very old tales of murderers and ghosts. Once he even tried to sing a *corrido*° from his youth, but it shattered in his jagged voice. He was leaving me his life, and he was happy.

The doctor said that yes, he could see some recovery, but that we were not to raise our hopes, there was no cure, it was merely a matter of a few days more or less.

One afternoon of menacing dark clouds, when I was bringing in the clothes hanging out to dry in the courtyard, I heard María cry out. I stood still, listening to her cry as if it were a peal of thunder, the first of the storm to come. Then silence,

the Revolution: The Mexican Revolution, which toppled the dictator Porfirio Díaz and led to a decade of political unrest and civil war, began in 1910.   *corrido:* a kind of narrative ballad; *corridos* were originally about romantic love, but at the time of the Revolution they were frequently political in nature.

and I was left alone in the courtyard, motionless. A bee buzzed by and the rain did
not fall. No one knows as well as I do how awful a foreboding can be, a premonition
hanging above a head turned towards the sky.

"Lichita, he's dying! He's gasping for air!"

"Go get the doctor . . . No! I'll go. But call doña Clara to stay with you till I'm back."

"And the priest, fetch the priest."   35

I ran, I ran away from that unbearable moment, blunt and asphyxiating. I ran,
hurried back, entered the house, made coffee; I greeted the relatives who began to
arrive dressed in half-mourning; I ordered candles; I asked for a few holy relics; I kept
on feverishly trying to fulfill my only obligation at the time, to be with my uncle. I
asked the doctor: he had given him an injection, so as not to leave anything untried,
but he knew it was useless. I saw the priest arrive with the Eucharist, even then I
lacked the courage to enter. I knew I would regret it afterwards. "Thank God, now I
won't die alone"—but I couldn't. I covered my face with my hands and prayed.

The priest came and touched my shoulder. I thought that all was over and I
shivered.

"He's calling you. Come in."

I don't know how I reached the door. Night had fallen and the room, lit by a bedside lamp, seemed enormous. The furniture, larger than life, looked black, and a strange
clogging atmosphere hung about the bed. Trembling, I felt I was inhaling death.

"Stand next to him," said the priest.   40

I obeyed, moving towards the foot of the bed, unable to look even at the sheets.

"Your uncle's wish, unless you say otherwise, is to marry you *in articulo mortis*,° so
that you may inherit his possessions. Do you accept?"

I stifled a cry of horror. I opened my eyes wide enough to let in the whole terrible
room. "Why does he want to drag me into his grave?" I felt death touching my skin.

"Luisa . . . "

It was uncle Apolonio. Now I had to look at him. He could barely mouth the words,   45
his jaw seemed slack and he spoke moving his face like that of a ventriloquist's doll.

"Please."

And he fell silent with exhaustion.

I could take no more. I left the room. That was not my uncle, it did not even look
like him. Leave everything to me, yes, but not only his possessions, his stories, his life. I
didn't want it, his life, his death. I didn't want it. When I opened my eyes I was standing
once again in the courtyard and the sky was still overcast. I breathed in deeply, painfully.

"Already?" the relatives drew near to ask, seeing me so distraught.

I shook my head. Behind me, the priest explained.   50

"Don Apolonio wants to marry her with his last breath, so that she may inherit him."

"And you won't?" the old servant asked anxiously. "Don't be silly, no one
deserves it more than you. You were a daughter to them, and you have worked very
hard looking after him. If you don't marry him, the cousins in Mexico City will leave
you without a cent. Don't be silly!"

"It's a fine gesture on his part."

"And afterwards you'll be left a rich widow, as untouched as you are now." A
young cousin laughed nervously.

"It's a considerable fortune, and I, as your uncle several times removed, would   55
advise you to . . . "

---

in articulo mortis: "at the point of death." Such marriages were allowed to take place without the usual formalities and were considered binding even if, as here, the dying party subsequently recovered.

"If you think about it, not accepting shows a lack of both charity and humility."

"That's true, that's absolutely true."

I did not want to give an old man his last pleasure, a pleasure I should, after all, be thankful for, because my youthful body, of which I felt so proud, had not dwelt in any of the regions of death. I was overcome by nausea. That was my last clear thought that night. I woke from a kind of hypnotic slumber as they forced me to hold his hand covered in cold sweat. I felt nauseous again, but said "yes."

I remember vaguely that they hovered over me all the time, talking all at once, taking me over there, bringing me over here, making me sign, making me answer. The taste of that night—a taste that has stayed with me for the rest of my life—was that of an evil ring-around-the-rosies turning vertiginously around me, while everyone laughed and sang grotesquely

This is the way the widow is wed,
The widow is wed, the widow is wed

while I stood, a slave, in the middle. Something inside me hurt, and I could not lift my eyes.

When I came to my senses, all was over, and on my hand shone the braided ring   60
which I had seen so many times on my aunt Panchita's finger: there had been no time for anything else.

The guests began to leave.

"If you need me, don't hesitate to call. In the meantime give him these drops every six hours."

"May God bless you and give you strength."

"Happy honeymoon," whispered the young cousin in my ear, with a nasty laugh.

I returned to the sickbed. "Nothing has changed, nothing has changed." My fear   65
certainly had not changed. I convinced María to stay and help me look after uncle Apolonio. I only calmed down once I saw dawn was breaking. It had started to rain, but without thunder or lightning, very still.

It kept on drizzling that day and the next, and the day after. Four days of anguish. Nobody came to visit, nobody other than the doctor and the priest. On days like these no one goes out, everyone stays indoors and waits for life to start again. These are the days of the spirit, sacred days.

If at least the sick man had needed plenty of attention my hours would have seemed shorter, but there was little that could be done for him.

On the fourth night María went to bed in a room close by, and I stayed alone with the dying man. I was listening to the monotonous rain and praying unconsciously, half asleep and unafraid, waiting. My fingers stopped turning the rosary, and as I held the beads I could feel through my fingertips a peculiar warmth, a warmth both alien and intimate, the warmth we leave in things and which is returned to us transformed, a comrade, a brother foreshadowing the warmth of others, a warmth both unknown and recollected, never quite grasped and yet inhabiting the core of my bones. Softly, deliciously, my nerves relaxed, my fingers felt light, I fell asleep.

I must have slept many hours: it was dawn when I woke up. I knew because the lights had been switched off and the electric plant stops working at two in the morning. The room, barely lit by an oil lamp at the feet of the Holy Virgin on the chest of drawers, made me think of the wedding night, my wedding night. It was so long ago, an empty eternity.

From the depth of the gloomy darkness don Apolonio's broken and tired breath- 70
ing reached me. There he still was, not the man himself, simply the persistent and
incomprehensible shred that hangs on, with no goal, with no apparent motive. Death
is frightening, but life mingled with death, soaked in death, is horrible in a way that
owes little to either life or death. Silence, corruption of the flesh, the stench, the
monstrous transformation, the final vanishing act, all this is painful, but it reaches
a climax and then gives way, dissolves into the earth, into memory, into history. But
not this: this arrangement worked out between life and death—echoed in the useless
exhaling and inhaling—could carry on forever. I would hear him trying to clear his
anaesthetized throat and it occurred to me that air was not entering that body, or
rather, that it was not a human body breathing the air: it was a machine, puffing and
panting, stopping in a curious game, a game to kill time without end. That thing was
no human being: it was somebody playing with huffs and snores. And the horror of
it all won me over: I began to breathe to the rhythm of his panting; to inhale, stop
suddenly, choke, breathe, choke again, unable to control myself, until I realized I had
been deceived by what I thought was the sense of the game. What I really felt was
the pain and shortness of breath of an animal in pain. But I kept on, on, until there
was one single breathing, one single inhuman breath, one single agony. I felt calmer,
terrified but calmer: I had lifted the barrier, I could let myself go and simply wait for
the common end. It seemed to me that by abandoning myself, by giving myself up
unconditionally, the end would happen quickly, would not be allowed to continue. It
would have fulfilled its purpose and its persistent search in the world.

Not a hint of farewell, not a glimmer of pity towards me. I carried on the mortal
game for a long, long while, from someplace where time had ceased to matter.

The shared breathing became less agitated, more peaceful, but also weaker. I
seemed to be drifting back. I felt so tired I could barely move, exhaustion nestling in
forever inside my body. I opened my eyes. Nothing had changed.

No: far away, in the shadows, is a rose. Alone, unique, alive. There it is, cut out
against the darkness, clear as day, with its fleshy, luminous petals, shining. I look at
it and my hand moves and I remember its touch and the simple act of putting it in a
vase. I looked at it then, but I only understand it now. I stir, I blink, and the rose is
still there, in full bloom, identical to itself.

I breathe freely, with my own breath. I pray, I remember, I doze off, and the
untouched rose mounts guard over the dawning light and my secret. Death and hope
suffer change.

And now day begins to break and in the clean sky I see that at last the days of 75
rain are over. I stay at the window a long time, watching everything change in the
sun. A strong ray enters and the suffering seems a lie. Unjustified bliss fills my lungs
and unwittingly I smile. I turn to the rose as if to an accomplice but I can't find it: the
sun has withered it.

Clear days came again, and maddening heat. The people went to work, and sang,
but don Apolonio would not die; in fact he seemed to get better. I kept on looking
after him, but no longer in a cheerful mood—my eyes downcast, I turned the guilt I
felt into hard work. My wish, now clearly, was that it all end, that he die. The fear,
the horror I felt looking at him, at his touch, his voice, were unjustified because the
link between us was not real, could never be real, and yet he felt like a dead weight
upon me. Through politeness and shame I wanted to get rid of it.

Yes, don Apolonio was visibly improving. Even the doctor was surprised and
offered no explanation.

On the very first morning I sat him up among the pillows, I noticed that certain look in my uncle's eyes. The heat was stifling and I had to lift him all by myself. Once I had propped him up I noticed: the old man was staring as if dazed at my heaving chest, his face distorted and his trembling hands unconsciously moving towards me. I drew back instinctively and turned my head away.

"Please close the blinds, it's too hot."

His almost dead body was growing warm.   80

"Come here, Luisa, sit by my side. Come."

"Yes, uncle." I sat, my knees drawn up, at the foot of the bed, without looking at him.

"Polo, you must call me Polo, after all we are closer relatives now." There was mockery in the tone of his voice.

"Yes, uncle."

"Polo, Polo." His voice was again sweet and soft. "You'll have a lot to forgive me.   85
I'm old and sick, and a man in my condition is like a child."

"Yes."

"Let's see. Try saying, 'Yes, Polo.'"

"Yes, Polo."

The name on my lips seemed to me an aberration, made me nauseated.

Polo got better, but became fussy and irritable. I realized he was fighting to be the   90
man he once had been, and yet the resurrected self was not the same, but another.

"Luisa, bring me . . . Luisa, give me . . . Luisa, plump up my pillows . . . pour me some water . . . prop up my leg . . ."

He wanted me to be there all day long, always by his side, seeing to his needs, touching him. And the fixed look and distorted face kept coming back, more and more frequently, growing over his features like a mask.

"Pick up my book. It fell underneath the bed, on this side."

I kneeled and stuck my head and almost half my body underneath the bed, and had to stretch my arm as far as it would go, to reach it. At first I thought it had been my own movements, or maybe the bedclothes, but once I had the book in my hand and was shuffling to get out, I froze, stunned by what I had long foreseen, even expected: the outburst, the scream, the thunder. A rage never before felt raced through me when the realization of what was happening reached my consciousness, when his shaking hand, taking advantage of my amazement, became surer and heavier, and enjoyed itself, adventuring with no restraints, feeling and exploring my thighs—a fleshless hand glued to my skin, fingering my body with delight, a dead hand searching impatiently between my legs, a bodyless hand.

I rose as quickly as I could, my face burning with shame and determination, but   95
when I saw him I forgot myself and entered like an automaton into the nightmare. Polo was laughing softly through his toothless mouth. And then, suddenly serious, with a coolness that terrified me, he said:

"What? Aren't you my wife before God and men? Come here, I'm cold, heat my bed. But first take off your dress, you don't want to get it creased."

What followed, I know, is my story, my life, but I can barely remember it; like a disgusting dream I can't even tell whether it was long or short. Only one thought kept me sane during the early days: "This can't go on, it can't go on." I imagined that God would not allow it, would prevent it in some way or another. He, personally, God, would interfere. Death, once dreaded, seemed my only hope. Not Apolonio's— he was a demon of death—but mine, the just and necessary death for my corrupted flesh. But nothing happened. Everything stayed on, suspended in time, without future. Then, one morning, taking nothing with me, I left.

It was useless. Three days later they let me know that my husband was dying, and they called me back. I went to see the father confessor and told him my story.

"What keeps him alive is lust, the most horrible of all sins. This isn't life, Father, it's death. Let him die!"

"He would die in despair. I can't allow it."   100

"And I?"

"I understand, but if you don't go to him, it would be like murder. Try not to arouse him, pray to the Blessed Virgin, and keep your mind on your duties."

I went back. And lust drew him out of the grave once more.

Fighting, endlessly fighting, I managed, after several years, to overcome my hatred, and finally, at the very end, I even conquered the beast: Apolonio died in peace, sweetly, his old self again.

But I was not able to go back to who I was. Now wickedness, malice, shine in the   105
eyes of the men who look at me, and I feel I have become an occasion of sin for all, I, the vilest of harlots. Alone, a sinner, totally engulfed by the never-ending flames of this cruel summer which surrounds us all, like an army of ants.

ALGERIA/FRANCE

Albert Camus

The Guest   1957

Translated by Justin O'Brien

Albert Camus (1913–1960) was born in Mondovi, Algeria (then a French colony), the son of a farm worker who was killed in the first months of World War I. Camus's mother, an illiterate Spanish house-cleaner, supported the family, which included two children, a grandmother, and a disabled uncle. Camus studied philosophy at the University of Algiers, but his plans for an academic career were sidetracked by recurring attacks of tuberculosis. In the period before World War II, he briefly joined the Algerian Communist Party and established a theater that produced plays for working-class audiences. During the Nazi occupation of France, Camus, who had worked as a journalist in Algiers, came to Paris, where he edited a Resistance newspaper called Combat. His first novel, The Stranger, *was published in 1942, the same year as his philosophi-*

Albert Camus

cal essay on suicide, The Myth of Sisyphus. *Along with Jean-Paul Sartre and Simone de Beauvoir, Camus became a leader of the brilliant literary generation that arose from the French defeat in 1940 and the subsequent loss of its colonial empire. Camus's name became forever linked with existentialism, and his writings reflected the sense of the "absurd" that character- ized intellectual life in a Europe whose traditional values were destroyed during the war. Other important works included the novel* The Plague *(1947), a philosophical essay titled* The Rebel *(1951), and his only collection of short fiction,* Exile and the Kingdom *(1957).*

"The Guest" takes place in Algeria during the waning years of French control, when even the most fundamentally decent of civil servants is forced to share the blame for what is perceived as a callous example of colonial injustice. As critic English Showalter Jr. noted, "If there is a villain in 'The Guest,' it is the same one as in the other stories, not a person or a society, but the universe itself. That is the truly silent, completely passive and indifferent element in every story." Camus, who loved his Algerian homeland but once stated, "Yes, I have a native land: the French language," lived to witness the terrorism that swept Algeria and France in the 1950s but died before Algerian independence was proclaimed in 1962. Camus was awarded the Nobel Prize in Literature in 1957. Three years later he was killed in an automobile accident at age forty-six.

The schoolmaster was watching the two men climb toward him. One was on horseback, the other on foot. They had not yet tackled the abrupt rise leading to the schoolhouse built on the hillside. They were toiling onward, making slow progress in the snow, among the stones, on the vast expanse of the high, deserted plateau. From time to time the horse stumbled. Without hearing anything yet, he could see the breath issuing from the horse's nostrils. One of the men, at least, knew the region. They were following the trail although it had disappeared days ago under a layer of dirty white snow. The schoolmaster calculated that it would take them half an hour to get onto the hill. It was cold; he went back into the school to get a sweater.

He crossed the empty, frigid classroom. On the blackboard the four rivers of France, drawn with four different colored chalks, had been flowing toward their estu- aries for the past three days. Snow had suddenly fallen in mid-October after eight months of drought without the transition of rain, and the twenty pupils, more or less, who lived in the villages scattered over the plateau had stopped coming. With fair weather they would return. Daru now heated only the single room that was his lodg- ing, adjoining the classroom and giving also on to the plateau to the east. Like the class windows, his window looked to the south too. On that side the school was a few kilometers from the point where the plateau began to slope toward the south. In clear weather could be seen the purple mass of the mountain range where the gap opened on to the desert.

Somewhat warmed, Daru returned to the window from which he had first seen the two men. They were no longer visible. Hence they must have tackled the rise. The sky was not so dark, for the snow had stopped falling during the night. The morning had opened with a dirty light which had scarcely become brighter as the ceiling of clouds lifted. At two in the afternoon it seemed as if the day were merely beginning. But still this was better than those three days when the thick snow was falling amidst unbroken darkness with little gusts of wind that rattled the double door of the classroom. Then Daru had spent long hours in his room, leaving it only to go to the shed and feed the chickens or get some coal. Fortunately the delivery truck from Tadjid, the nearest village to the north, had brought his supplies two days before the blizzard. It would return in forty-eight hours.

Besides, he had enough to resist a siege, for the little room was cluttered with bags of wheat that the administration left as a stock to distribute to those of his pupils whose families had suffered from the drought. Actually they had all been victims because they were all poor. Every day Daru would distribute a ration to the children. They had missed it, he knew, during these bad days. Possibly one of the fathers or big brothers would come this afternoon and he could supply them with grain. It was just a matter of carrying them over to the next harvest. Now shiploads of wheat were arriving from France and the worst was over. But it would be hard to forget that poverty, that army of ragged ghosts wandering in the sunlight, the plateaus burned to a cinder month after month, the earth shriveled up little by little, literally scorched, every stone bursting into dust under one's foot. The sheep had died then by thousands and even a few men, here and there, sometimes without anyone's knowing.

In contrast with such poverty, he who lived almost like a monk in his remote   5 schoolhouse, nonetheless satisfied with the little he had and with the rough life, had felt like a lord with his whitewashed walls, his narrow couch, his unpainted shelves, his well, and his weekly provision of water and food. And suddenly this snow, without warning, without the foretaste of rain. This is the way the region was, cruel to live in, even without men—who didn't help matters either. But Daru had been born here. Everywhere else, he felt exiled.

He stepped on to the terrace in front of the schoolhouse. The two men were now halfway up the slope. He recognized the horseman as Balducci, the old gendarme° he had known for a long time. Balducci was holding on the end of a rope an Arab who was walking behind him with hands bound and head lowered. The gendarme waved a greeting to which Daru did not reply, lost as he was in contemplation of the Arab dressed in a faded blue jellaba,° his feet in sandals but covered with socks of heavy raw wool, his head surmounted by a narrow, short chèche.° They were approaching. Balducci was holding back his horse in order not to hurt the Arab, and the group was advancing slowly.

Within earshot, Balducci shouted: "One hour to do the three kilometers from El Ameur!" Daru did not answer. Short and square in his thick sweater, he watched them climb. Not once had the Arab raised his head. "Hello," said Daru when they got up onto the terrace. "Come in and warm up." Balducci painfully got down from his horse without letting go of the rope. From under his bristling mustache he smiled at the schoolmaster. His little dark eyes, deep-set under a tanned forehead, and his mouth surrounded with wrinkles made him look attentive and studious. Daru took the bridle, led the horse to the shed, and came back to the two men, who were now waiting for him in the school. He led them into his room. "I am going to heat up the classroom," he said. "We'll be more comfortable there."

When he entered the room again, Balducci was on the couch. He had undone the rope tying him to the Arab, who had squatted near the stove. His hands still bound, the chèche pushed back on his head, he was looking toward the window. At first Daru noticed only his huge lips, fat, smooth, almost Negroid; yet his nose was straight, his eyes were dark and full of fever. The chèche revealed an obstinate forehead and, under the weathered skin now rather discolored by the cold, the whole face had a restless and rebellious look that struck Daru when the Arab, turning his face toward him, looked him straight in the eyes. "Go into the other room," said the schoolmaster, "and I'll make you some mint tea." "Thanks," Balducci said. "What a nuisance! How I long for retirement." And addressing his prisoner in Arabic: "Come on, you." The Arab got up and, slowly, holding his bound wrists in front of him, went into the classroom.

With the tea, Daru brought a chair. But Balducci was already enthroned on the nearest pupil's desk and the Arab had squatted against the teacher's platform facing

gendarme: policeman.   jellaba: hooded cloak worn in North Africa.   chèche: cap.

the stove, which stood between the desk and the window. When he held out the glass of tea to the prisoner, Daru hesitated at the sight of his bound hands. "He might perhaps be untied." "Certainly," said Balducci. "That was for the journey." He started to get to his feet. But Daru, setting the glass on the floor, had knelt beside the Arab. Without saying anything, the Arab watched him with his feverish eyes. Once his hands were free, he rubbed his swollen wrists against each other, took the glass of tea, and sucked up the burning liquid in swift little sips.

"Good," said Daru. "And where are you headed for?"   10

Balducci withdrew his mustache from the tea. "Here, my boy."

"Odd pupils! And you're spending the night?"

"No. I'm going back to El Ameur. And you will deliver this fellow to Tinguit. He is expected at police headquarters."

Balducci was looking at Daru with a friendly little smile.

"What's this story?" asked the schoolmaster. "Are you pulling my leg?"   15

"No, my boy. Those are the orders."

"The orders? I'm not . . ." Daru hesitated, not wanting to hurt the old Corsican. "I mean, that's not my job."

"What! What's the meaning of that? In wartime people do all kinds of jobs."

"Then I'll wait for the declaration of war!"

Balducci nodded.   20

"OK. But the orders exist and they concern you too. Things are brewing, it appears. There is talk of a forthcoming revolt. We are mobilized, in a way."

Daru still had his obstinate look.

"Listen, my boy," Balducci said. "I like you and you must understand. There's only a dozen of us at El Ameur to patrol throughout the whole territory of a small department and I must get back in a hurry. I was told to hand this man over to you and return without delay. He couldn't be kept there. His village was beginning to stir; they wanted to take him back. You must take him to Tinguit tomorrow before the day is over. Twenty kilometers shouldn't worry a husky fellow like you. After that, all will be over. You'll come back to your pupils and your comfortable life."

Behind the wall the horse could be heard snorting and pawing the earth. Daru was looking out the window. Decidedly, the weather was clearing and the light was increasing over the snowy plateau. When all the snow was melted, the sun would take over again and once more would burn the fields of stone. For days, still, the unchanging sky would shed its dry light on the solitary expanse where nothing had any connection with man.

"After all," he said, turning around toward Balducci, "what did he do?" And,   25
before the gendarme had opened his mouth, he asked: "Does he speak French?"

"No, not a word. We had been looking for him for a month, but they were hiding him. He killed his cousin."

"Is he against us?"

"I don't think so. But you can never be sure."

"Why did he kill?"

"A family squabble, I think. One owed the other grain, it seems. It's not all clear.   30
In short, he killed his cousin with a billhook. You know, like a sheep, *kreezk!*"

Balducci made the gesture of drawing a blade across his throat and the Arab, his attention attracted, watched him with a sort of anxiety. Daru felt a sudden wrath against the man, against all men with their rotten spite, their tireless hates, their blood lust.

But the kettle was singing on the stove. He served Balducci more tea, hesitated, then served the Arab again, who, a second time, drank avidly. His raised arms made the jellaba fall open and the schoolmaster saw his thin, muscular chest.

"Thanks, my boy," Balducci said. "And now, I'm off."

He got up and went toward the Arab, taking a small rope from his pocket.

"What are you doing?" Daru asked dryly.   35

Balducci, disconcerted, showed him the rope.

"Don't bother."

The old gendarme hesitated. "It's up to you. Of course, you are armed?"

"I have my shotgun."

"Where?"   40

"In the trunk."

"You ought to have it near your bed."

"Why? I have nothing to fear."

"You're mad. If there's an uprising, no one is safe; we're all in the same boat."

"I'll defend myself. I'll have time to see them coming."   45

Balducci began to laugh, then suddenly the mustache covered the white teeth.

"You'll have time? OK. That's just what I was saying. You have always been a little cracked. That's why I like you, my son was like that."

At the same time he took out his revolver and put it on the desk.

"Keep it; I don't need two weapons from here to El Ameur."

The revolver shone against the black paint of the table. When the gendarme   50
turned toward him, the schoolmaster caught the smell of leather and horseflesh.

"Listen, Balducci," Daru said suddenly, "every bit of this disgusts me, and most of all your fellow here. But I won't hand him over. Fight, yes, if I have to. But not that."

The old gendarme stood in front of him and looked at him severely.

"You're being a fool," he said slowly. "I don't like it either. You don't get used to putting a rope on a man even after years of it, and you're even ashamed—yes, ashamed. But you can't let them have their way."

"I won't hand him over," Daru said again.

"It's an order, my boy, and I repeat it."   55

"That's right. Repeat to them what I've said to you: I won't hand him over."

Balducci made a visible effort to reflect. He looked at the Arab and at Daru. At last he decided.

"No, I won't tell them anything. If you want to drop us, go ahead; I'll not denounce you. I have an order to deliver the prisoner and I'm doing so. And now you'll just sign this paper for me."

"There's no need. I'll not deny that you left him with me."

"Don't be mean with me. I know you'll tell the truth. You're from hereabouts and   60
you are a man. But you must sign, that's the rule."

Daru opened his drawer, took out a little square bottle of purple ink, the red wooden penholder with the "sergeant-major" pen he used for making models of penmanship, and signed. The gendarme carefully folded the paper and put it into his wallet. Then he moved toward the door.

"I'll see you off," Daru said.

"No," said Balducci. "There's no use being polite. You insulted me."

He looked at the Arab, motionless in the same spot, sniffed peevishly, and turned away toward the door. "Good-bye, son," he said. The door shut behind him. Balducci appeared suddenly outside the window and then disappeared. His footsteps were muffled by the snow. The horse stirred on the other side of the wall and several chickens fluttered in fright. A moment later Balducci reappeared outside the window leading the horse by the bridle. He walked toward the little rise without turning round and disappeared from sight with the horse following him. A big stone could be heard bouncing down. Daru walked back toward the prisoner, who, without stirring, never took his eyes off him. "Wait," the schoolmaster said in Arabic and went toward the bedroom. As he was going through the door, he had a second thought, went to the desk, took the revolver, and stuck it in his pocket. Then, without looking back, he went into his room.

For some time he lay on his couch watching the sky gradually close over, listening   65
to the silence. It was this silence that had seemed painful to him during the first days
here, after the war. He had requested a post in the little town at the base of the foothills
separating the upper plateaus from the desert. There, rocky walls, green and black to
the north, pink and lavender to the south, marked the frontier of eternal summer. He
had been named to a post farther north, on the plateau itself. In the beginning, the solitude and the silence had been hard for him on these wastelands peopled only by stones.
Occasionally, furrows suggested cultivation, but they had been dug to uncover a certain
kind of stone good for building. The only plowing here was to harvest rocks. Elsewhere
a thin layer of soil accumulated in the hollows would be scraped out to enrich paltry
village gardens. This is the way it was: bare rock covered three-quarters of the region.
Towns sprang up, flourished, then disappeared; men came by, loved one another or
fought bitterly, then died. No one in this desert, neither he nor his guest, mattered.
And yet, outside this desert neither of them, Daru knew, could have really lived.

When he got up, no noise came from the classroom. He was amazed at the unmixed joy he derived from the mere thought that the Arab might have fled and that he would be alone with no decision to make. But the prisoner was there. He had merely stretched out between the stove and the desk. With eyes open, he was staring at the ceiling. In that position, his thick lips were particularly noticeable, giving him a pouting look. "Come," said Daru. The Arab got up and followed him. In the bedroom, the schoolmaster pointed to a chair near the table under the window. The Arab sat down without taking his eyes off Daru.

"Are you hungry?"

"Yes," the prisoner said.

Daru set the table for two. He took flour and oil, shaped a cake in a frying-pan, and lighted the little stove that functioned on bottled gas. While the cake was cooking, he went out to the shed to get cheese, eggs, dates, and condensed milk. When the cake was done he set it on the window sill to cool, heated some condensed milk diluted with water, and beat up the eggs into an omelet. In one of his motions he knocked against the revolver stuck in his right pocket. He set the bowl down, went into the classroom, and put the revolver in his desk drawer. When he came back to the room, night was falling. He put on the light and served the Arab. "Eat," he said. The Arab took a piece of the cake, lifted it eagerly to his mouth, and stopped short.

"And you?" he asked.   70

"After you. I'll eat too."

The thick lips opened slightly. The Arab hesitated, then bit into the cake determinedly.

The meal over, the Arab looked at the schoolmaster. "Are you the judge?"

"No, I'm simply keeping you until tomorrow."

"Why do you eat with me?"   75

"I'm hungry."

The Arab fell silent. Daru got up and went out. He brought back a folding bed from the shed, set it up between the table and the stove, at right angles to his own bed. From a large suitcase which, upright in a corner, served as a shelf for papers, he took two blankets and arranged them on the camp bed. Then he stopped, felt useless, and sat down on his bed. There was nothing more to do or to get ready. He had to look at this man. He looked at him, therefore, trying to imagine his face bursting with rage. He couldn't do so. He could see nothing but the dark yet shining eyes and the animal mouth.

"Why did you kill him?" he asked in a voice whose hostile tone surprised him.

The Arab looked away.

"He ran away. I ran after him." 80

He raised his eyes to Daru again and they were full of a sort of woeful interrogation. "Now what will they do to me?"

"Are you afraid?"

He stiffened, turning his eyes away.

"Are you sorry?"

The Arab stared at him open-mouthed. Obviously he did not understand. Daru's 85 annoyance was growing. At the same time he felt awkward and self-conscious with his big body wedged between the two beds.

"Lie down there," he said impatiently. "That's your bed."

The Arab didn't move. He called to Daru:

"Tell me!"

The schoolmaster looked at him.

"Is the gendarme coming back tomorrow?" 90

"I don't know."

"Are you coming with us?"

"I don't know. Why?"

The prisoner got up and stretched out on top of the blankets, his feet toward the window. The light from the electric bulb shone straight into his eyes and he closed them at once.

"Why?" Daru repeated, standing beside the bed. 95

The Arab opened his eyes under the blinding light and looked at him, trying not to blink.

"Come with us," he said.

In the middle of the night, Daru was still not asleep. He had gone to bed after undressing completely; he generally slept naked. But when he suddenly realized that he had nothing on, he hesitated. He felt vulnerable and the temptation came to him to put on his clothes again. Then he shrugged his shoulders; after all, he wasn't a child and, if need be, he could break his adversary in two. From his bed he could observe him, lying on his back, still motionless with his eyes closed under the harsh light. When Daru turned out the light, the darkness seemed to coagulate all of a sudden. Little by little, the night came back to life in the window where the starless sky was stirring gently. The schoolmaster soon made out the body lying at his feet. The Arab still did not move, but his eyes seemed open. A light wind was prowling around the schoolhouse. Perhaps it would drive away the clouds and the sun would reappear.

During the night the wind increased. The hens fluttered a little and then were silent. The Arab turned over on his side with his back to Daru, who thought he heard him moan. Then he listened for his guest's breathing, become heavier and more regular. He listened to that breath so close to him and mused without being able to go to sleep. In this room where he had been sleeping alone for a year, this presence bothered him. But it bothered him also by imposing on him a sort of brotherhood he knew well but refused to accept in the present circumstances. Men who share the same rooms, soldiers or prisoners, develop a strange alliance as if, having cast off their armor with their clothing, they fraternized every evening, over and above their differences, in the ancient community of dream and fatigue. But Daru shook himself; he didn't like such musings, and it was essential to sleep.

A little later, however, when the Arab stirred slightly, the schoolmaster was still not asleep. When the prisoner made a second move, he stiffened, on the alert. The Arab was lifting himself slowly on his arms with almost the motion of a sleepwalker. Seated upright in bed, he waited motionless without turning his head toward Daru, as if he were listening attentively. Daru did not stir; it had just occurred to him that the revolver was still in the drawer of his desk. It was better to act at once. Yet he continued to observe the prisoner, who, with the same slithery motion, put his feet on the ground, waited again, then began to stand up slowly. Daru was about to call out to him when the Arab began to walk, in a quite natural but extraordinarily silent way. He was heading toward the door at the end of the room that opened into the shed. He lifted the latch with precaution and went out, pushing the door behind him but without shutting it. Daru had not stirred. "He is running away," he merely thought. "Good riddance!" Yet he listened attentively. The hens were not fluttering; the guest must be on the plateau. A faint sound of water reached him, and he didn't know what it was until the Arab again stood framed in the doorway, closed the door carefully, and came back to bed without a sound. Then Daru turned his back on him and fell asleep. Still later he seemed, from the depths of his sleep, to hear furtive steps around the schoolhouse. "I'm dreaming! I'm dreaming!" he repeated to himself. And he went on sleeping.

When he awoke, the sky was clear; the loose window let in a cold, pure air. The Arab was asleep, hunched up under the blankets now, his mouth open, utterly relaxed. But when Daru shook him, he started dreadfully, staring at Daru with wild eyes as if he had never seen him and such a frightened expression that the schoolmaster stepped back. "Don't be afraid. It's me. You must eat." The Arab nodded his head and said yes. Calm had returned to his face, but his expression was vacant and listless.

The coffee was ready. They drank it seated together on the folding bed as they munched their pieces of the cake. Then Daru led the Arab under the shed and showed him the tap where he washed. He went back into the room, folded the blankets and the bed, made his own bed and put the room in order. Then he went through the classroom and out on to the terrace. The sun was already rising in the blue sky; a soft, bright light was bathing the deserted plateau. On the ridge the snow was melting in spots. The stones were about to reappear. Crouched on the edge of the plateau, the schoolmaster looked at the deserted expanse. He thought of Balducci. He had hurt him, for he had sent him off in a way as if he didn't want to be associated with him. He could still hear the gendarme's farewell and, without knowing why, he felt strangely empty and vulnerable. At that moment, from the other side of the schoolhouse, the prisoner coughed. Daru listened to him almost despite himself and then, furious, threw a pebble that whistled through the air before sinking into the snow. That man's stupid crime revolted him, but to hand him over was contrary to honor. Merely thinking of it made him smart with humiliation. And he cursed at one and the same time his own people who had sent him this Arab and the Arab too who had dared to kill and not managed to get away. Daru got up, walked in a circle on the terrace, waited motionless, and then went back into the schoolhouse.

The Arab, leaning over the cement floor of the shed, was washing his teeth with two fingers. Daru looked at him and said: "Come." He went back into the room ahead of the prisoner. He slipped a hunting-jacket on over his sweater and put on walking-shoes. Standing, he waited until the Arab had put on his *chèche* and sandals. They went into the classroom and the schoolmaster pointed to the exit, saying: "Go ahead." The fellow didn't budge. "I'm coming," said Daru. The Arab went out. Daru went back into the room and made a package of pieces of rusk, dates, and sugar. In the classroom, before going out, he hesitated a second in front of his desk, then crossed the threshold and locked the door. "That's the way," he said. He started toward the east, followed by the prisoner. But, a short distance from the schoolhouse, he thought he heard a slight sound behind them. He retraced his steps and examined the surroundings of the house; there was no one there. The Arab watched him without seeming to understand. "Come on," said Daru.

They walked for an hour and rested beside a sharp peak of limestone. The snow was melting faster and faster and the sun was drinking up the puddles at once, rapidly cleaning the plateau, which gradually dried and vibrated like the air itself. When they resumed walking, the ground rang under their feet. From time to time a bird rent the space in front of them with a joyful cry. Daru breathed in deeply the fresh morning light. He felt a sort of rapture before the vast familiar expanse, now almost entirely yellow under its dome of blue sky. They walked an hour or more, descending toward the south. They reached a level height made up of crumbly rocks. From there on, the plateau sloped down, eastward toward a low plain where there were a few spindly trees and, to the south, toward outcroppings of rock that gave the landscape a chaotic look.

Daru surveyed the two directions. There was nothing but the sky on the hori- 105 zon. Not a man could be seen. He turned toward the Arab, who was looking at him blankly. Daru held out the package to him. "Take it," he said. "There are dates, bread, and sugar. You can hold out for two days. Here are a thousand francs too." The Arab took the package and the money but kept his full hands at chest level as if he didn't know what to do with what was being given him. "Now look," the schoolmaster said as he pointed in the direction of the east, "there's the way to Tinguit. You have a two-hour walk. At Tinguit you'll find the administration and the police. They are expecting you." The Arab looked toward the east, still holding the package and the money against his chest. Daru took his elbow and turned him rather roughly toward the south. At the foot of the height on which they stood could be seen a faint path. "That's the trail across the plateau. In a day's walk from here you'll find pasture-lands and the first nomads. They'll take you in and shelter you according to their law." The Arab had now turned toward Daru and a sort of panic was visible in his expression. "Listen," he said. Daru shook his head: "No, be quiet. Now I'm leaving you." He turned his back on him, took two long steps in the direction of the school, looking hesitantly at the motionless Arab, and started off again. For a few minutes he heard nothing but his own step resounding on the cold ground and did not turn his head. A moment later, however, he turned around. The Arab was still there on the edge of the hill, his arms hanging now, and he was looking at the schoolmaster. Daru felt something rise in his throat. But he swore with impatience, waved vaguely, and started off again. He had already gone some distance when he again stopped and looked. There was no longer anyone on the hill.

Daru hesitated. The sun was now rather high in the sky and was beginning to beat down on his head. The schoolmaster retraced his steps, at first somewhat uncertainly, then with decision. When he reached the little hill, he was bathed in sweat.

He climbed it as fast as he could and stopped, out of breath, at the top. The rock-fields to the south stood out sharply against the blue sky, but on the plain to the east a steamy heat was already rising. And in that slight haze, Daru, with heavy heart made out the Arab walking slowly on the road to prison.

A little later, standing before the window of the classroom, the schoolmaster was watching the clear light bathing the whole surface of the plateau but he hardly saw it. Behind him on the blackboard, among the winding French rivers, sprawled the clumsily chalked-up words he had just read: "You handed over our brother. You will pay for this." Daru looked at the sky, the plateau, and, beyond, the invisible lands stretching all the way to the sea. In this vast landscape he had loved so much, he was alone.

SOUTH AFRICA

Nadine Gordimer

The Defeated

1952

Nadine Gordimer (1923–2014) was born in Springs, a small gold-mining town near Johannesburg, South Africa. Her father, a Lithuanian Jewish immigrant, was a watchmaker. Her mother was an English-woman who founded a daycare center in the local black township. Gordimer attended convent school until age ten, when her mother pulled her from school, mistakenly concerned that the girl's health was weak. Isolated from other children, Gordimer immersed herself in reading and writing fiction, first as a way to keep herself company. She started publishing stories locally at fifteen, then left home for the University of Witwatersrand, flourishing in what which she described as the "nursery bohemia" of college life.

Nadine Gordimer

She began collecting her short fiction with Face to Face *(1949) and* The Soft Voice of the Serpent *(1952). Her first novel,* The Lying Days, *appeared in 1953. Gordimer was quickly recognized as a writer of international stature. Her strong moral sense and independent-minded politics were criticized by both the Right and the Left. A vocal opponent of South Africa's apartheid policy, three of her books were banned in her native land. Her novels include* A Guest of Honour *(1970),* Burger's Daughter *(1979),* A Sport of Nature *(1987),* My Son's Story *(1990), and* The House Gun *(1998). In 1986 Gordimer won the Hudson Review's Bennett Award for lifetime achievement. In 1991 she received the Nobel Prize in Literature. Her critical and at times personal book on craft,* Writing and Being, *appeared in 1994. Although Gordimer published fifteen novels, the short story remained a central form throughout her career. As novelist Salman Rushdie noted, her fiction "makes its point and creates its resonances not by any exaggeration or flashiness, but by the scrupulous depiction of what all Nadine Gordimer's readers will instantly recognize as the unvarnished truth." Gordimer died in Johannesburg at age 90.*

My mother did not want me to go near the Concession stores° because they smelled, and were dirty, and the natives spat tuberculosis germs into the dust. She said it was no place for little girls.

But I used to go down there sometimes, in the afternoon, when static four o'clock held the houses of our Mine, and the sun washed over them like the waves of the sea over sand castles. I felt that life was going on down there at the Concession stores: noise, and movement and—yes, bad smells, even—and so I would wander down the naked road, with the hot sun uncomfortably drying the membrane inside my nose, seeing the irregular line of narrow white shops lying away ahead like a jumble of shoe boxes.

The signs of life that I craved were very soon evident: rich and careless of its vitality, it overflowed from the crowded pavement of the stores, and the surrounding veld° was littered with sucked-out oranges and tatters of dirty paper, and worn into the shabby barrenness peculiar to earth much trampled upon by the feet of men. A fat, one-legged native, with the patient detachment of the businessman who knows himself indispensable, sat on the bald veld beside the path that led from the Compound, his stock of walking sticks standing up, handles tied together, points splayed out fanwise, his pyramids of bright, thin-skinned oranges waiting. Sometimes he had mealies° as well—those big, hard, full-grown ears with rows of yellowish tombstones instead of little pearly teeth—and a brazier° made from a paraffin tin to roast them by. Propped against the chipped pillars of the pavement, there were always other vendors, making their small way in lucky beans, herbs, bracelets beaten from copper wire, knitted caps in wonderful colors—blooming like great hairy petunias, or bursting suns, from the needles of old, old native women—and, of course, oranges. Everywhere there were oranges; the pushing, ambling crowds filling the pavement ate them as they stared at the windows, the gossips, sitting with their blankets drawn close and their feet in the gutter, sucked at them, the Concession store cats sniffed at the skins where they lay, hollow-cheeked, discarded in every doorway.

Quite often I had to flick the white pith from where it had landed, on my shoe or even my dress, spat negligently by some absorbed orange-eater contemplating a shirt through breath-smudged plate glass. The wild, wondering, dirty men came up from the darkness of the mine and they lay themselves out to the sun on the veld, and to their mouths they put the round fruit of the sun; and it was the expression of their need.

I would saunter along the shop windows amongst them, and for me there was a quickening of glamour about the place: the air was thicker with their incense-like body smell, and the sudden rank shock of their stronger sweat, as a bare armpit lifted over my head. The clamor of their voices—always shouting, but so merry, so angry!—and the size of their laughter, and the open-mouthed startle with which they greeted every fresh sight: I felt vaguely the spell of the books I had read, returning; markets in Persia, bazaars in Cairo . . . Nevertheless, I was careful not to let them brush too closely past me, lest some unnamable *something* crawl from their dusty blankets or torn cotton trousers on to my clean self, and I did not like the way they spat, with that terrible gurgle in the throat, into the gutter, or, worse still, blew their noses loudly between finger and thumb, and flung the excrement horribly to the air.

5

Concession stores: stores authorized by the mining company or local government.   *veld:* a South African word for sparsely wooded grassland.   *mealies:* a South African term for Indian corn.   *brazier:* metal pan for holding burning coals.

And neither did I like the heavy, sickening, greasy carrion-breath that poured from the mouth of the Hotela la Bantu, where the natives hunched intent at zinc-topped forms, eating steaming no-color chunks of horror that bore no relation to meat as I knew it. The down on my arms prickled in revulsion from the pulpy entrails hanging in dreadful enticement at the window, and the blood-embroidered sawdust spilling out of the doorway.

I know that I wondered how the storekeepers' wives, who sat on soap boxes outside the doorways of the shops on either side of the eating-house, could stand the breath of that maw.° How they could sit, like lizards in the sun; and all the time they breathed in the breath of the eating-house: took it deep into the recesses of their beings, whilst my throat closed against it in disgust.

It was down there one burning afternoon that I met Mrs. Saiyetovitz. She was one of the storekeepers' wives, and I had seen her many times before, sitting before the deep, blanket-hung cave of her husband's store, where a pile of tinsel-covered wooden trunks shimmered and flashed a pink or green eye out of the gloom into the outside—wearing her creased alpaca apron, her fat insteps leaning over her down-at-heel shoes. Sometimes she knitted, and sometimes she just sat. On this day there was a small girl hanging about her, drawing on the shopwindow with a sticky forefinger. When the child turned to look at me, I recognized her as one of the girls from "our school"; a girl from my class, as a matter of fact, called Miriam Saiyetovitz. Yes, that was her name: I remembered it because it was ugly—I was always sorry for girls with ugly names.

Miriam was a tousled, black-haired little girl, who wore a red bow in her hair. Now she recognized me, and we stood looking at one another; all at once the spare line of the name "Miriam Saiyetovitz," that was like the scrolled pattern of an iron gate with only the sky behind it, shifted its perspective in my mind, so that now between the cold curly M's and the implacable A's of that gate's framework, I saw a house, a complication of buildings and flowers and figures walking, where before there was nothing but the sky. Miriam Saiyetovitz—and this: behind her name and her school self, the hot and buzzing world of the stores. And I smiled at her, very friendly.

So she knew we had decided to recognize one another and she sauntered over to 10
talk to me. I stood with her in the doorway of her father's store, and I, too, wrote my name and drew cats composed of two capital O's and a sausage tail, with the point of my hot and sticky finger on the window. Of course, she did not exactly introduce me to her mother—children never do introduce their mothers; they merely let it be known, by referring to the woman in question off-hand, in the course of play, or going up to speak to her in such a way that the relationship becomes obvious. Miriam went up to her mother and said diffidently: "Ma, I know this girl from school—she's in class with me, can we have some red lemonade?"

And the woman lifted her head from where she sat, wide-legged, so that you couldn't help seeing the knee-elastic of her striped pink silk bloomers, holding over the cotton tops of her stockings and said, peering, "Take it! Take it! Go, have it!"

Because I did not then know her, I thought that she was angry, she spoke with such impatience; but soon I knew that it was only her eager generosity that made her fling permission almost fiercely at Miriam whenever the child made some request. Mrs. Saiyetovitz's glance wavered over to me, but she did not seem to be seeing me very clearly: indeed, she could not, for her small, pale, pale eyes narrowed into her

---

maw: the throat or jaws of an animal, especially of a carnivore.

big, simple, heavy face were half-blind, and she had always to peer at everything, and never quite see.

I saw that she was very ugly.

Ugly, with the blunt ugliness of a toad; the ugliness of seeming not entirely at home in any element—as if the earth were the wrong place, too heavy and magnetic for a creature already so blunt; and the water would be no better: too subtle and contour-swayed for a creature so graceless. And yet her ugliness was without repellence. When I grew older I often wondered why; she should have been repellent, one should have turned from her, but one did not. She was only ugly. She had the short, stunted yet heavy bones of generations of oppression in the ghettos of Europe; breasts, stomach, hips crowded sadly, no height, wide strong shoulders and a round back. Her head settled right down between her shoulders without even the grace of a neck, and her dun flat hair was cut at the level of her ears. Her features were not essentially Semitic; there was nothing so *definite* as that about her: she had no distinction whatever.

Miriam reappeared from the shades of the store, carrying two bottles of red lem- 15
onade. A Shangaan emerged at the same time, clutching a newspaper parcel and puzzling over his handful of change, not looking where he was going. Miriam swept past him, the dusty African with his odd, troglodyte unsureness, and his hair plastered into savage whorls with red clay. With one swift movement she knocked the tin caps off the bottles against the scratched frame of the shopwindow, and handed my lemonade to me. "Where did you get it so quickly?" I asked, surprised. She jerked her head back toward the store: "In the kitchen," she said—and applied herself to the bottle.

And so I knew that the Saiyetovitzes lived there, behind the Concession store.

Saturday afternoons were the busiest. Mrs. Saiyetovitz's box stood vacant outside and she helped her husband in the shop. Saturday afternoon was usually my afternoon for going down there, too; my mother and father went out to golf, and I was left with the tick of the clock, the purring monologue of our cat, and the doves gurgling in the empty garden.

On Saturdays every doorway was crowded; a continual shifting stream snaked up and down the pavements; flies tangled overhead, the air smelled hotter, and from the doorway of every store the high, wailing blare and repetition of native songs, played on the gramophone, swung out upon the air and met in discord with the tune of the record being played next door.

Miriam's mother's brother was the proprietor of the Hotela la Bantu, and another uncle had the bicycle shop two doors down. Sometimes she had a message to deliver at the bicycle shop, and I would go in with her. Spare wheels hung across the ceiling, there was a battered wooden counter with a pile of puncture repair outfits, a sewing machine or two for sale, and, in the window, bells and pumps and mascots cut out of tin, painted yellow and red for the adornment of handle bars. We were invariably offered a lemonade by the uncle, and we invariably accepted. At home I was not allowed to drink lemonades unlimited; they might "spoil my dinner"; but Miriam drank them whenever she pleased.

Wriggling in and out amongst the gray-dusty bodies of the natives—their silky 20
brown skin dies in the damp fug° underground: after a few months down the mine, it reflects only weariness—Miriam looked with her own calm, quick self-possession

---

fug: a bad smell, especially from a poorly ventilated area.

upon the setting in which she found herself. Like someone sitting in a swarm of ants; and letting them swarm, letting them crawl all over and about her. Not lifting a hand to flick them off. Not crying out against them in disgust; nor explaining, saying, well, I *like* ants. Just sitting there and letting them swarm, and looking out of herself as if to say: What ants? What ants are you talking about? I giggled and shuddered in excitement at the sight of the dried bats and cobwebby snakeskins rotting in the bleary little window of the medicine shop, but Miriam tugged at my dress and said, "Oh, come on—" I exclaimed at the purple and red shirts lying amongst the dead flies in the wonderful confusion of Saiyetovitz's store window, but Miriam was telling me about her music exam in September, and only frowned at the interruption. I was approaching the confusion of adolescence, and sometimes an uncomfortable, terrible, fascinating curiosity—like a headless worm which lay shamefully hidden in the earth of my soul—crawled out into my consciousness at the sight of the animal obviousness of the natives' male bodies in their scanty covering; but the flash of my guilt at these moments met no answer in Miriam, although she was the same age as I.

If the sight of a boy interrupting his conversation to step out a yard or two onto the veld to relieve himself filled me with embarrassment and real disgust, so that I wanted to go and look at flowers—it seemed that Miriam did not see.

It was quite a long time before she took me into her father's store.

For months it remained a vague, dark, dust-moted world beyond the blanket-hung doorway, into which she was swallowed up and appeared again, whilst I waited outside, with the boys who looked and looked and looked at the windows. Then one day, as she was entering, she paused, and said suddenly and calmly: "Aren't you coming . . . ?" Without a word, I followed her in.

It was cool in the store; and the coolness was a surprise. Out of the sun-baked pavement—and into the store that was cool, like a cellar! Light danced only furtively along the folds of the blankets that hung from the ceiling: crackling silent and secret little fires in the curly woolen furze. The blankets were dark somber hangings, in proud colors, bold and primal. They hung like dark stalactites in the cave, still and heavy, communing only their own colors back to themselves. They brooded over the shop; and over Mr. Saiyetovitz there beneath, treading the worn cement with his disgruntled, dispossessed air of doing his best, but . . . I had glimpsed him before. He lurked within the depths of his store like a beast in its lair, and now and then I had seen the glimmer of his pale, pasty face with the wide upper lip under which the lower closed glumly and puffily.

John Saiyetovitz (his name wasn't John at all, really—it was Yanka, but when   25
he arrived at Cape Town, long ago, the Immigration authorities were tired of attempting to understand and spell the unfamiliar names of the immigrants pouring off the boat, and by the time they'd got the "Saiyetovitz" spelt right, they couldn't be bothered puzzling over the "Yanka," so they scrawled "John" on his papers, and John he was)—John Saiyetovitz was a gentle man, with an almost hangdog gentleness, but when he was trading with the natives, strange blasts of power seemed to blow up in his soul. Africans are the slowest buyers in the world; to them, buying is a ritual, a slow and solemn undertaking. They must go carefully; they nervously scent pitfalls on every side. And confronted with a selection of different kinds of the one thing they want, they are as confused as a child before a plate of pastries; fingering, hesitating, this or that . . . ? On a busy Saturday they must be allowed to stand about the shop endlessly, looking up and about, pausing to shake their heads

and give a profound "ow!"; sauntering off; going to press their noses against the window again; coming back. And Mr. Saiyetovitz—always the same, unshaven and collarless—lugging a blanket down from the shelves, flinging it upon the counter—and another, and then another, and standing, arms hanging, sullen and smoldering before the blank-faced purchaser. The boy with his helpless stance, and his eyes rolling up in the agony of decision, filling the shop with the sickly odor of his anxious sweat, and clutching his precious guitar.

Waiting, waiting.

And then Mr. Saiyetovitz swooping away in a gesture of rage and denial; don't care, sick-to-death. And the boy anxious, edging forward to feel the cloth again, and the whole business starting up all over again; more blankets, different colors, down from the shelf and hooked from the ceiling—stalactites crumpled to woolen heaps to wonder over. Mr. Saiyetovitz throwing them down, moving in jerks of rage now, and then roughly bullying the boy into a decision. Shouting at him, bundling his purchase into his arms, snatching the money, gesturing him cowed out of the store.

Mr. Saiyetovitz treated the natives honestly, but with bad grace. He forced them to feel their ignorance, their inadequacy, and their submission to the white man's world of money. He spiritually maltreated them, and bitterly drove his nail into the coffin of their confidence.

With me, he was shy, he smiled widely and his hand went to the stud swinging loose at the neck of his half-buttoned shirt, and drew as if in apology over the stubbled landscape of his jaw. He always called me "little girl" and he liked to talk to me in the way that he thought children like to be talked to, but I found it very difficult to make a show of reply, because his English was so broken and fragmentary. So I used to stand there, and say yes, Mr. Saiyetovitz, and smile back and say thank you! to anything that sounded like a question, because the question usually was did I want a lemonade?, and of course, I usually did.

The first time Miriam ever came to my home was the day of my birthday party.   30

Our relationship at school had continued unchanged, just as before; she had her friends and I had mine, but outside of school there was the curious plane of intimacy on which we had, as it were, surprised one another wandering, and so which was shared peculiarly by us.

I had put Miriam's name down on my guest list; she was invited; and she came. She wore a blue taffeta dress which Mrs. Saiyetovitz had made for her (on the old Singer on the counter in the shop, I guessed) and it was quite nice if a bit too frilly. My home was pretty and well-furnished and full of flowers and personal touches of my mother's hands; there was space, and everything shone. Miriam did not open her eyes at it; I saw her finger a bowl of baby-skinned pink roses in the passing, but all afternoon she looked out indifferently as she did at home.

The following Saturday at the store we were discussing the party. Miriam was telling Mrs. Saiyetovitz about my presents, and I was standing by in a pleasurable embarrassment at my own importance.

"Well, please God, Miri," said Mrs. Saiyetovitz at the finish, "you'll also have a party for your birday in April . . . Ve'll be in d'house, and everyting'll be nice, just like you want."—They were leaving the rooms behind the shop—the mournful green plush curtains glooming the archway between the bedroom and the living room; the tarnished samovar; the black beetles in the little kitchen; Miriam's old black piano with the candlesticks, wheezing in the drafty passage; the damp puddly yard piled with empty packing-cases and eggshells and banana skins; the hovering smell of fish frying. They were going to live in a little house in the township nearby.

But when April came, Miriam took ten of her friends to the Saturday afternoon bioscope in celebration of her birthday. "And to Costas Café afterwards for ice cream," she stated to her mother, looking out over her head. I think Mrs. Saiyetovitz was disappointed about the party, but she reasoned then, as always, that as her daughter went to school and was educated and could speak English, whilst she herself knew nothing, wasn't clever at all, the little daughter must know best what was right and what was *nice*.

I know now what of course I did not know then: that Miriam Saiyetovitz and I were intelligent little girls into whose brains there never had, and never would, come the freak and wonderful flash that is brilliance. Ours were alabaster intellects: clear, perfect, light; no streaks of dark, unknown granite splitting to reveal secret veins of brightness, like thin gold, between stratum and stratum. We were fitted to be good schoolteachers, secretaries, organizers; we did everything well, nothing badly, and nothing remarkably. But to the Saiyetovitzes, Miriam's brain blazed like the sun, warming their humbleness.

In the year-by-year passage through school, our classmates thinned out one by one; the way seedlings come up in a bunch to a certain stage in their development, and then by some inexplicable process of natural selection, one or two continue to grow and branch up into the air, whilst the others wither or remain small and weedy. The other girls left to go and learn shorthand-and-typewriting: weeded out by the necessity of earning a living. Or moved, and went to other schools: transplanted to some ground of their own. Miriam and I remained, growing straight and steadily . . .

During our matriculation year a sense of wonder and impending change came upon us both; the excitement of coming to an end that is also a beginning. We felt this in one another, and so were drawn together in new earnestness. Miriam came to study with me in the garden at my house, and oftener than ever, I slipped down to the Concession stores to exchange a book or discuss work with her. For although they now had a house, the Saiyetovitzes still lived, in the wider sense of the word, at the store. When Miriam and I discussed our schoolwork, the Saiyetovitzes crept about, very quiet, talking to one another only in hoarse, respectful whispers.

It was during this year, when the wonder of our own capacity to learn was reaching out and catching into light like a veld fire within us, that we began to talk of the University. And, all at once, we talked of nothing else. I spoke to my father of it, and he was agreeable, although my mother thought a girl could do better with her time. But so long as my father was willing to send me, I knew I should go. Ah yes, said Miriam. She liked my father very much; I knew that. In fact she said to me once—it was a strange thing to say, and almost emotionally, she said it, and at a strange time, because we were on the bus going into the town to buy a new winter coat which she had wanted very badly and talked about longingly for days, and her father had just given her the money to get it—she said to me: You know, I think your father's just right—I mean, if you had to choose somebody, a certain kind of person for a father, well, your father'd be just the kind you'd want.

When she broached the subject of University to her parents, they were agreeable for her to go, too. Indeed, they wanted her to go almost more than she herself did. But they worried a great deal about the money side of it; every time I went down to the store there'd be a discussion of ways and means, Saiyetovitz slowly munching his bread and garlic polony lunch, and worrying. Miriam didn't worry about it;

they'll find the money, she said. She was a tall girl, now, with beautiful breasts, and a large, dark-featured face that had a certain capable elegance, although her father's glum mouth was unmistakable and on her upper lip faint dark down foreshadowed a heavy middle age. Her parents were peasants; but she was the powerful young Jewess. Beside her, I felt pale in my Scotch gingery-fairness: lightly drawn upon the mind's eye, whilst she was painted in oils.

We both matriculated; not so well as we thought we should, but well enough; and we went to the University. And there too, we did well enough. We had both decided upon the same course: teaching. In the end, it had seemed the only thing to do. Neither of us had any particular bent.

It must have been a hard struggle for the Saiyetovitzes to keep Miriam at the University, buy her clothes, and pay for her board and lodging in Johannesburg. There is a great deal of money to be made out of native trade concessions purchased from the government; and it doesn't require education or trained commercial astuteness to make it—in fact, trading of this sort seems to flourish in response to something very different: what is needed is instinctive peasant craftiness such as can only be found in the uneducated, in those who have scratched up their own resources. Storekeepers with this quality of peasant craft made money all about Mr. Saiyetovitz, bought houses and motor cars and banded their wives' retired hands with diamonds in mark of their new idleness. But Mr. Saiyetovitz was a peasant without the peasant's craft; without that flaw in his simplicity that might have given him checks and deeds of transfer to sign, even if he were unable to read the print on the documents . . . Without this craft, the peasant has only one thing left to him: hard work, dirty work, with the sweet, sickly body-smell of the black men about him all day. Saiyetovitz made no money: only worked hard and long, standing in his damp shirt amidst the clamor of the stores and the death-smell from the eating-house always in his nose.

Meanwhile, Miriam fined down into a lady. She developed a half-bored, half-intolerant shrug of the shoulders in place of the childish sharpness that had been filed jagged by the rub-rub of rough life and harsh contrasts. She became soft-voiced, where she had been loud and gay. She watched and conformed; and soon took on the attitude of liberal-mindedness that sets the doors of the mind slackly open, so that any idea may walk in and out again, leaving very little impression: she could appreciate Bach and Stravinsky, and spend a long evening listening to swing music in the dark of somebody's flat.

Race and creed had never meant very much to Miriam and me, but at the University she sifted naturally towards the young Jews who were passing easily and enthusiastically, with their people's extraordinary aptitude for creative and scientific work, through Medical School. They liked her; she was invited to their homes for tennis parties, swimming on Sundays, and dances, and she seemed as unimpressed by the luxury of their ten-thousand-pound houses as she had been by the contrast of our clean, pleasant little home, long ago, when she herself was living behind the Concession store.

She usually spent part of the vacations with friends in Johannesburg; I missed   45
her—wandering about the Mine on my own, out of touch, now, with the girls I had left behind in the backwater of the small town. During the second half of one July vacation—she had spent the first two weeks in Johannesburg—she asked me if she could come and spend Sunday at my home, and in the afternoon, one of the medical students arrived at our house in his small car. He had come from Johannesburg;

Miriam had evidently told him she would be with us. I gathered her parents did not know of the young man's visit, and I did not speak of it before them.

So the four years of our training passed. Miriam Saiyetovitz and I had dropped like two leaves, side by side into the same current, and been carried downstream together: now the current met a swirl of dead logs, reeds, and the force of other waters, and broke up, divided its drive and its one direction. The leaves floated clear; divergent from one another. Miriam got a teaching post in Johannesburg, but I was sent to a small school in the Northern Transvaal.° We met seldom during the first six months of our adult life: Miriam went to Cape Town during the vacation, and I flew to Rhodesia with the first profits of my independence. Then came the war, and I, glad to escape so soon the profession I had once anticipated with such enthusiasm, joined the nursing service and went away for the long, strange interlude of four years. Whilst I was with a field hospital in Italy, I heard that Miriam had married—a Doctor Somebody-or-other; my informant wasn't sure of the name. I guessed it must be one of the boys whom she had known as students. I sent a cable of congratulation, to the Saiyetovitzes' address.

And then, one day, I came back to the small mining town and found it there, the same, like a face that has been waiting a long time. My Mother, and my Dad, the big wheels of the shaft turning, the trees folding their wings about the Mine houses; and our house, with the green, square lawn and the cat watching the doves. For the first few weeks I faltered about the old life, feeling my way in a dream so like the old reality that it hurt.

There was a feel about an afternoon that made my limbs tingle with familiarity … What … ? And then, lying on our lawn under the hot sky, I knew: just the sort of glaring summer afternoon that used to send me down to the Concession stores, feeling isolated in the heat. Instantly, I thought of the Saiyetovitzes, and I wanted to go and see them, see if they were still there; what Miriam was doing; where she was, now.

Down at the stores it was the same as ever, only dirtier, smaller, more chipped and smeared—the way reality often is in contrast with the image carried long in the mind. As I stepped so strangely on that old pocked pavement, with the skeleton cats and the orange peel and the gobs of spit, my heart tightened with the thought of the Saiyetovitzes. I was in a kind of excitement to see the store again. And there it was; and excitement sank out at the evidence of the monotony of "things." Blankets swung a little in the doorway. Flies crawled amongst the shirts and shoes posed in the window, the hot, wet, sickening fatty smell came over from the eating-house. I met it with the old revulsion: it was like breathing inside someone's stomach. And in the store, amongst the wicked glitter of the tin trunks, beneath the secret whispering of the blankets, the old Saiyetovitzes sat glumly, with patience, waiting … As animals wait in a cage; for nothing.

In their delight at seeing me again, I saw that they were older, sadder; that they had somehow given themselves into the weight of their own humbleness, they were without a pinnacle on which to fix their eyes. Whatever place it was that they looked upon now, it was flat.

Mr. Saiyetovitz's mouth had creased in further to the dead folds of his chin; his hair straggled to the rims of his ears. As he spoke to me, I noticed that his hands lay,

50

Northern Transvaal: the northeastern region of South Africa.

with a curious helpless indifference, curled on the counter. Mrs. Saiyetovitz shuffled off at once to the back of the shop to make a cup of tea for me, and carried it in, slopping over into the saucer. She was uglier than ever, now, her back hunched up to meet her head, her old thick legs spiraled in crêpe bandages because of varicose veins. And blinder too, I could see: that enquiring look of the blind or deaf smiling unsure at you from her face.

The talk turned almost at once to Miriam, and as they answered my questions about her, I saw them go inert. Yes, she was married; had married a doctor—a flicker of pride in the old man at this. She lived in Johannesburg. Her husband was doing very well. There was a photograph of her home, in one of the more expensive suburbs; a large, white modern house, with flower borders and a fishpond. And there was Miri's little boy, sitting on his swing; and a studio portrait of him, taken with his mother.

There was the face of Miriam Saiyetovitz, confident, carefully made-up and framed in a good hairdresser's version of her dark hair, smiling queenly over the face of her child. One hand lay on the child's shoulder, a smooth hand, wearing large, plain, expensive diamond rings. Her bosom was proud and rounded now—a little too heavy, a little overripe in the climate of ease.

I could see in her face that she had forgotten a lot of things.

When his wife had gone into the back of the shop to refill my teacup, old Saiye- 55
tovitz went silent, looking at the hand that lay before him on the counter, the fingers twitching a little under the gaze.

It doesn't come out like you think, he said, it doesn't come out like you think.

He looked up at me with a comforting smile.

And then he told me that they had seen Miriam's little boy only three times since he was born. Miriam they saw hardly at all; her husband never. Once or twice a year she came out from Johannesburg to visit them, staying an hour on a Sunday afternoon, and then driving herself back to town again. She had not invited her parents to her home at any time; they had been there only once, on the occasion of the birth of their grandson.

Mrs. Saiyetovitz came back into the store: she seemed to know of what we had been speaking. She sat down on a shot-purple tin trunk, and folded her arms over her breast. Ah yes, she breathed, ah yes. . . .

I stood there in Miriam' s guilt before the Saiyetovitzes, and they were silent, in 60
the accusation of the humble.

But in a little while a Swazi° in a tobacco-colored blanket sauntered dreamily into the shop, and Mr. Saiyetovitz rose heavy with defeat.

Through the eddy of dust in the lonely interior and the wavering fear round the head of the native and the bright hot dance of the jazz blankets and the dreadful submission of Mrs. Saiyetovitz's conquered voice in my ear, I heard his voice strike like a snake at my faith: angry and browbeating, sullen and final, lashing weakness at the weak.

Mr. Saiyetovitz and the native.

Defeated, and without understanding in their defeat.

Swazi: one of the largest Bantu tribes of southeastern Africa.

JAPAN

Kazuo Ishiguro

A Family Supper   1982

*Born in Nagasaki, Japan, in 1954, Kazuo Ishiguro
moved to England while still a child. He completed
his education there, graduating from the University of Kent and then receiving an MA in creative
writing from the University of East Anglia. In his
late teens he had the unusual job of grouse-beating
for the Queen Mother at Balmoral Castle in Scotland, but after university went on to hone his skill
for cultural observation more directly, as a social
worker, first in Scotland and later in West London.
Ishiguro became a full-time writer in 1983, following the successful reception of his debut novel,
A Pale View of Hills (1982). The book won
the Royal Society of Literature's Winifred Holtby
Award for the best first novel of the year, and it
was soon translated into more than ten languages.
Ishiguro's second novel,* An Artist of the Float-
ing World *(1986), received the Whitbread Book of the Year Award (Britain's largest cash
prize for literature), but his greatest success came with* The Remains of the Day, *which in
1989 won Great Britain's most prestigious literary award, the Booker Prize, and was made
into an Academy Award-winning film in 1993, from a screenplay by Ishiguro, who has
also written the scripts for the films* The Saddest Music in the World *(2003) and* The
White Countess *(2005). His more recent novels are* The Unconsoled *(1995),* When
We Were Orphans *(2000),* Never Let Me Go *(2005), and* The Buried Giant *(2015).*

Kazuo Ishiguro

    *Ishiguro is not a prolific writer. He has written only seven novels in more than three
decades, along with a handful of short stories, most notably "A Family Supper," which like* An
Artist of the Floating World, *is set in his home country. "I had very strong emotional relationships in Japan that were broken at a formative age," he has commented. "There's this other
life I might have had." Ishiguro won the Nobel Prize in Literature in 2017. He lives in London.*

    Fugu is a fish caught off the Pacific shores of Japan. The fish has held a special
significance for me ever since my mother died through eating one. The poison resides
in the sexual glands of the fish, inside two fragile bags. When preparing the fish,
these bags must be removed with caution, for any clumsiness will result in the poison
leaking into the veins. Regrettably, it is not easy to tell whether or not this operation
has been carried out successfully. The proof is, as it were, in the eating.

    Fugu poisoning is hideously painful and almost always fatal. If the fish has been
eaten during the evening, the victim is usually overtaken by pain during his sleep.
He rolls about in agony for a few hours and is dead by morning. The fish became
extremely popular in Japan after the war. Until stricter regulations were imposed,
it was all the rage to perform the hazardous gutting operation in one's own kitchen,
then to invite neighbors and friends round for the feast.

At the time of my mother's death, I was living in California. My relationship with my parents had become somewhat strained around that period, and consequently I did not learn of the circumstances surrounding her death until I returned to Tokyo two years later. Apparently, my mother had always refused to eat fugu, but on this particular occasion she had made an exception, having been invited by an old schoolfriend whom she was anxious not to offend. It was my father who supplied me with the details as we drove from the airport to his home in the Kamakura district. When we finally arrived, it was nearing the end of a sunny autumn day.

"Did you eat on the plane?" my father asked. We were sitting on the tatami floor of his tea-room.

"They gave me a light snack."

"You must be hungry. We'll eat as soon as Kikuko arrives."

My father was a formidable-looking man with a large stony jaw and furious black eyebrows. I think now in retrospect that he much resembled Chou En-lai, although he would not have cherished such a comparison, being particularly proud of the pure samurai blood that ran in the family. His general presence was not one which encouraged relaxed conversation; neither were things helped much by his odd way of stating each remark as if it were the concluding one. In fact, as I sat opposite him that afternoon, a boyhood memory came back to me of the time he had struck me several times around the head for "chattering like an old woman." Inevitably, our conversation since my arrival at the airport had been punctuated by long pauses.

"I'm sorry to hear about the firm," I said when neither of us had spoken for some time. He nodded gravely.

"In fact the story didn't end there," he said. "After the firm's collapse, Watanabe killed himself. He didn't wish to live with the disgrace."

"I see."

"We were partners for seventeen years. A man of principle and honor. I respected him very much."

"Will you go into business again?" I said.

"I am—in retirement. I'm too old to involve myself in new ventures now. Business these days has become so different. Dealing with foreigners. Doing things their way. I don't understand how we've come to this. Neither did Watanabe." He sighed. "A fine man. A man of principle."

The tea-room looked out over the garden. From where I sat I could make out the ancient well which as a child I had believed haunted. It was just visible now through the thick foliage. The sun had sunk low and much of the garden had fallen into shadow.

"I'm glad in any case that you've decided to come back," my father said. "More than a short visit, I hope."

"I'm not sure what my plans will be."

"I for one am prepared to forget the past. Your mother too was always ready to welcome you back—upset as she was by your behavior."

"I appreciate your sympathy. As I say, I'm not sure what my plans are."

"I've come to believe now that there were no evil intentions in your mind," my father continued. "You were swayed by certain—influences. Like so many others."

"Perhaps we should forget it, as you suggest."

"As you will. More tea?"

Just then, a girl's voice came echoing through the house.

"At last." My father rose to his feet. "Kikuko has arrived."

Despite our difference in years, my sister and I had always been close. Seeing me again seemed to make her excessively excited and for a while she did nothing but giggle nervously. But she calmed down somewhat when my father started to question her about Osaka and the university. She answered him with short formal replies. She in turn asked me a few questions, but she seemed inhibited by the fear that her questions might lead to awkward topics. After a while, the conversation had become even sparser than prior to Kikuko's arrival. Then my father stood up, saying: "I must attend to supper. Please excuse me for being burdened down by such matters. Kikuko will look after you."

My sister relaxed quite visibly once he had left the room. Within a few minutes, she was chatting freely about her friends in Osaka and about her classes at university. Then quite suddenly she decided we should walk in the garden and went striding out onto the veranda. We put on some straw sandals that had been left along the veranda rail and stepped out into the garden. The daylight had almost gone.

"I've been dying for a smoke for the last half-hour," she said, lighting a cigarette.

"Then why didn't you smoke?"

She made a furtive gesture back toward the house, then grinned mischievously.

"Oh I see," I said.

"Guess what? I've got a boyfriend now."

"Oh yes?"

"Except I'm wondering what to do. I haven't made up my mind yet."

"Quite understandable."

"You see, he's making plans to go to America. He wants me to go with him as soon as I finish studying."

"I see. And you want to go to America?"

"If we go, we're going to hitch-hike." Kikuko waved a thumb in front of my face. "People say it's dangerous, but I've done it in Osaka and it's fine."

"I see. So what is it you're unsure about?"

We were following a narrow path that wound through the shrubs and finished by the old well. As we walked, Kikuko persisted in taking unnecessarily theatrical puffs on her cigarette.

"Well. I've got lots of friends now in Osaka. I like it there. I'm not sure I want to leave them all behind just yet. And Suichi—I like him, but I'm not sure I want to spend so much time with him. Do you understand?"

"Oh perfectly."

She grinned again, then skipped on ahead of me until she reached the well. "Do you remember," she said, as I came walking up to her, "how you used to say this well was haunted?"

"Yes, I remember."

We both peered over the side.

"Mother always told me it was the old woman from the vegetable store you'd seen that night," she said. "But I never believed her and never came out here alone."

"Mother used to tell me that too. She even told me once the old woman had confessed to being the ghost. Apparently she'd been taking a short cut through our garden. I imagine she had some trouble clambering over these walls."

Kikuko gave a giggle. She then turned her back to the well, casting her gaze about the garden.

"Mother never really blamed you, you know," she said, in a new voice. I remained silent. "She always used to say to me how it was their fault, hers and Father's, for not bringing you up correctly. She used to tell me how much more careful they'd been with me, and that's why I was so good." She looked up and the mischievous grin had returned to her face. "Poor Mother," she said.

"Yes. Poor Mother."

"Are you going back to California?"

"I don't know. I'll have to see."   50

"What happened to—to her? To Vicki?"

"That's all finished with," I said. "There's nothing much left for me now in California."

"Do you think I ought to go there?"

"Why not? I don't know. You'll probably like it." I glanced toward the house. "Perhaps we'd better go in soon. Father might need a hand with the supper."

But my sister was once more peering down into the well. "I can't see any ghosts,"   55 she said. Her voice echoed a little.

"Is Father very upset about his firm collapsing?"

"Don't know. You can never tell with Father." Then suddenly she straightened up and turned to me. "Did he tell you about old Watanabe? What he did?"

"I heard he committed suicide."

"Well, that wasn't all. He took his whole family with him. His wife and his two little girls."

"Oh, yes?"   60

"Those two beautiful little girls. He turned on the gas while they were all asleep. Then he cut his stomach with a meat knife."

"Yes, Father was just telling me how Watanabe was a man of principle."

"Sick." My sister turned back to the well.

"Careful. You'll fall right in."

"I can't see any ghost," she said. "You were lying to me all that time."   65

"But I never said it lived down the well."

"Where is it, then?"

We both looked around at the trees and shrubs. The light in the garden had grown very dim. Eventually I pointed to a small clearing some ten yards away.

"Just there I saw it. Just there."

We stared at the spot.   70

"What did it look like?"

"I couldn't see very well. It was dark."

"But you must have seen something."

"It was an old woman. She was just standing there, watching me."

We kept staring at the spot as if mesmerized.   75

"She was wearing a white kimono," I said. "Some of her hair had come undone. It was blowing around a little."

Kikuko pushed her elbow against my arm. "Oh be quiet. You're trying to frighten me all over again." She trod on the remains of her cigarette, then for a brief moment stood regarding it with a perplexed expression. She kicked some pine needles over it, then once more displayed her grin. "Let's see if supper's ready," she said.

We found my father in the kitchen. He gave us a quick glance, then carried on with what he was doing.

"Father's become quite a chef since he's had to manage on his own," Kikuko said with a laugh. He turned and looked at my sister coldly.

"Hardly a skill I'm proud of," he said. "Kikuko, come here and help."   80

For some moments my sister did not move. Then she stepped forward and took an apron hanging from a drawer.

"Just these vegetables need cooking now," he said to her. "The rest just needs watching." Then he looked up and regarded me strangely for some seconds. "I expect you want to look around the house," he said eventually. He put down the chopsticks he had been holding. "It's a long time since you've seen it."

As we left the kitchen I glanced back toward Kikuko, but her back was turned.

"She's a good girl," my father said quietly.

I followed my father from room to room. I had forgotten how large the   85 house was. A panel would slide open and another room would appear. But the rooms were all startlingly empty. In one of the rooms the lights did not come on, and we stared at the stark walls and tatami in the pale light that came from the windows.

"This house is too large for a man to live in alone," my father said. "I don't have much use for most of these rooms now."

But eventually my father opened the door to a room packed full of books and papers. There were flowers in vases and pictures on the walls. Then I noticed something on a low table in the corner of the room. I came nearer and saw it was a plastic model of a battleship, the kind constructed by children. It had been placed on some newspaper; scattered around it were assorted pieces of grey plastic.

My father gave a laugh. He came up to the table and picked up the model.

"Since the firm folded," he said, "I have a little more time on my hands." He laughed again, rather strangely. For a moment his face looked almost gentle. "A little more time."

"That seems odd," I said. "You were always so busy."   90

"Too busy perhaps." He looked at me with a small smile. "Perhaps I should have been a more attentive father."

I laughed. He went on contemplating his battleship. Then he looked up. "I hadn't meant to tell you this, but perhaps it's best that I do. It's my belief that your mother's death was no accident. She had many worries. And some disappointments."

We both gazed at the plastic battleship.

"Surely," I said eventually, "my mother didn't expect me to live here for ever."

"Obviously you don't see. You don't see how it is for some parents. Not only must   95 they lose their children, they must lose them to things they don't understand." He spun the battleship in his fingers. "These little gunboats here could have been better glued, don't you think?"

"Perhaps. I think it looks fine."

"During the war I spent some time on a ship rather like this. But my ambition was always the air force. I figured it like this. If your ship was struck by the enemy, all you could do was struggle in the water hoping for a lifeline. But in an aeroplane—well—there was always the final weapon." He put the model back onto the table. "I don't suppose you believe in war."

"Not particularly."

He cast an eye around the room. "Supper should be ready by now," he said. "You must be hungry."

Supper was waiting in a dimly lit room next to the kitchen. The only source of   100 light was a big lantern that hung over the table, casting the rest of the room into shadow. We bowed to each other before starting the meal.

There was little conversation. When I made some polite comment about the food, Kikuko giggled a little. Her earlier nervousness seemed to have returned to her. My father did not speak for several minutes. Finally he said:

"It must feel strange for you, being back in Japan."

"Yes, it is a little strange."

"Already, perhaps, you regret leaving America."

"A little. Not so much. I didn't leave behind much. Just some empty rooms."   105

"I see."

I glanced across the table. My father's face looked stony and forbidding in the half-light. We ate on in silence.

Then my eye caught something at the back of the room. At first I continued eating, then my hands became still. The others noticed and looked at me. I went on gazing into the darkness past my father's shoulder.

"Who is that? In that photograph there?"

"Which photograph?" My father turned slightly, trying to follow my gaze.   110

"The lowest one. The old woman in the white kimono."

My father put down his chopsticks. He looked first at the photograph, then at me.

"Your mother." His voice had become very hard. "Can't you recognize your own mother?"

"My mother. You see, it's dark. I can't see it very well."

No one spoke for a few seconds, then Kikuko rose to her feet. She took the   115
photograph down from the wall, came back to the table and gave it to me.

"She looks a lot older," I said.

"It was taken shortly before her death," said my father.

"It was the dark. I couldn't see very well."

I looked up and noticed my father holding out a hand. I gave him the photograph. He looked at it intently, then held it toward Kikuko. Obediently, my sister rose to her feet once more and returned the picture to the wall.

There was a large pot left unopened at the center of the table. When Kikuko had   120
seated herself again, my father reached forward and lifted the lid. A cloud of steam rose up and curled toward the lantern. He pushed the pot a little toward me.

"You must be hungry," he said. One side of his face had fallen into shadow.

"Thank you." I reached forward with my chopsticks. The steam was almost scalding. "What is it?"

"Fish."

"It smells very good."

In amidst soup were strips of fish that had curled almost into balls. I picked one   125
out and brought it to my bowl.

"Help yourself. There's plenty."

"Thank you." I took a little more, then pushed the pot toward my father. I watched him take several pieces to his bowl. Then we both watched as Kikuko served herself.

My father bowed slightly. "You must be hungry," he said again. He took some fish to his mouth and started to eat. Then I too chose a piece and put it in my mouth. It felt soft, quite fleshy against my tongue.

"Very good," I said. "What is it?"

"Just fish."   130

"It's very good."

The three of us ate on in silence. Several minutes went by.

"Some more?"

"Is there enough?"

"There's plenty for all of us." My father lifted the lid and once more steam rose   135
up. We all reached forward and helped ourselves.

"Here," I said to my father, "you have the last piece."

"Thank you."

When we had finished the meal, my father stretched out his arms and yawned
with an air of satisfaction. "Kikuko," he said. "Prepare a pot of tea, please."

My sister looked at him, then left the room without comment. My father stood
up.

"Let's retire to the other room. It's rather warm in here."   140

I got to my feet and followed him into the tea-room. The large sliding windows
had been left open, bringing in a breeze from the garden. For a while we sat in silence.

"Father," I said, finally.

"Yes?"

"Kikuko tells me Watanabe-San took his whole family with him."

My father lowered his eyes and nodded. For some moments he seemed deep in   145
thought. "Watanabe was very devoted to his work." He said at last. "The collapse of
the firm was a great blow to him. I fear it must have weakened his judgment."

"You think what he did—it was a mistake?"

"Why, of course. Do you see it otherwise?"

"No, no. Of course not."

"There are other things besides work."

"Yes."   150

We fell silent again. The sound of locusts came in from the garden. I looked out
into the darkness. The well was no longer visible.

"What do you think you will do now?" my father asked. "Will you stay in Japan
for a while?"

"To be honest, I hadn't thought that far ahead."

"If you wish to stay here, I mean here in this house, you would be very welcome.
That is, if you don't mind living with an old man."

"Thank you. I'll have to think about it."   155

I gazed out once more into the darkness.

"But of course," said my father, "this house is so dreary now. You'll no doubt
return to America before long."

"Perhaps. I don't know yet."

"No doubt you will."

For some time my father seemed to be studying the back of his hands. Then he   160
looked up and sighed.

"Kikuko is due to complete her studies next spring," he said. "Perhaps she will
want to come home then. She's a good girl."

"Perhaps she will."

"Things will improve then."

"Yes, I'm sure they will."

We fell silent once more, waiting for Kikuko to bring the tea.   165

CHINA

Ha Jin

Saboteur   2000

Ha Jin is the pen name of Xuefei Jin, who was born in Liaoning, China, in 1956. The son of military doctors, Jin grew up during the turbulent Cultural Revolution, a ten-year upheaval initiated by the Communist Party in 1966 to transform China into a Marxist workers' society by destroying all remnants of the nation's ancient past. During this period many schools and universities were closed and intellectuals were required to work in proletarian jobs. Jin taught himself English by listening to the radio. At fourteen, he joined the People's Liberation Army, where he remained for nearly six years, and he later worked as a telegraph operator for a railroad company. He then attended Heilongjiang University, where in 1981 he received a BA in English. After earning an MA in American literature from Shangdong University in 1984, Jin traveled to the United States to work on a

Ha Jin

PhD at Brandeis University. He intended to return to China, but the Communist Party's violent suppression of the student movement in 1989 made him decide to stay in the United States and write only in English. "It's such a brutal government," he commented. "I was very angry, and I decided not to return to China." "Writing in English became my means of survival," he remarked, "of spending or wasting my life, of retrieving losses, mine, and those of others." Jin has published both poetry and fiction, including the novels Waiting (1999, National Book Award), War Trash (2004, PEN/Faulkner Award), A Free Life (2007), Nanjing Requiem (2011), and The Boat Rocker (2016). His first volume of short fiction, Ocean of Words (1996), was drawn from his experience in the People's Liberation Army and won the PEN/Hemingway Award. He teaches creative writing at Boston University.

Mr. Chiu and his bride were having lunch in the square before Muji Train Station. On the table between them were two bottles of soda spewing out brown foam and two paper boxes of rice and sautéed cucumber and pork. "Let's eat," he said to her, and broke the connected ends of the chopsticks. He picked up a slice of streaky pork and put it into his mouth. As he was chewing, a few crinkles appeared on his thin jaw.

To his right, at another table, two railroad policemen were drinking tea and laughing; it seemed that the stout, middle-aged man was telling a joke to his young comrade, who was tall and of athletic build. Now and again they would steal a glance at Mr. Chiu's table.

The air smelled of rotten melon. A few flies kept buzzing above the couple's lunch. Hundreds of people were rushing around to get on the platform or to catch buses to downtown. Food and fruit vendors were crying for customers in lazy voices. About a dozen young women, representing the local hotels, held up placards which displayed the daily prices and words as large as a palm, like FREE MEALS,

AIR-CONDITIONING, and ON THE RIVER. In the center of the square stood a concrete statue of Chairman Mao, at whose feet peasants were napping, their backs on the warm granite and their faces toward the sunny sky. A flock of pigeons perched on the Chairman's raised hand and forearm.

The rice and cucumber tasted good, and Mr. Chiu was eating unhurriedly. His sallow face showed exhaustion. He was glad that the honeymoon was finally over and that he and his bride were heading back for Harbin. During the two weeks' vacation, he had been worried about his liver, because three months ago he had suffered from acute hepatitis; he was afraid he might have a relapse. But he had had no severe symptoms, despite his liver being still big and tender. On the whole he was pleased with his health, which could endure even the strain of a honeymoon; indeed, he was on the course of recovery. He looked at his bride, who took off her wire glasses, kneading the root of her nose with her fingertips. Beads of sweat coated her pale cheeks.

"Are you all right, sweetheart?" he asked.   5

"I have a headache. I didn't sleep well last night."

"Take an aspirin, will you?"

"It's not that serious. Tomorrow is Sunday and I can sleep in. Don't worry."

As they were talking, the stout policeman at the next table stood up and threw a bowl of tea in their direction. Both Mr. Chiu's and his bride's sandals were wet instantly.

"Hooligan!" she said in a low voice.   10

Mr. Chiu got to his feet and said out loud, "Comrade Policeman, why did you do this?" He stretched out his right foot to show the wet sandal.

"Do what?" the stout man asked huskily, glaring at Mr. Chiu while the young fellow was whistling.

"See, you dumped tea on our feet."

"You're lying. You wet your shoes yourself."

"Comrade Policemen, your duty is to keep order, but you purposely tortured us   15
common citizens. Why violate the law you are supposed to enforce?" As Mr. Chiu was speaking, dozens of people began gathering around.

With a wave of his hand, the man said to the young fellow, "Let's get hold of him!"

They grabbed Mr. Chiu and clamped handcuffs around his wrists. He cried, "You can't do this to me. This is utterly unreasonable."

"Shut up!" The man pulled out his pistol. "You can use your tongue at our headquarters."

The young fellow added, "You're a saboteur, you know that? You're disrupting public order."

The bride was too petrified to say anything coherent. She was a recent college   20
graduate, had majored in fine arts, and had never seen the police make an arrest. All she could say was, "Oh, please, please!"

The policemen were pulling Mr. Chiu, but he refused to go with them, holding the corner of the table and shouting, "We have a train to catch. We already bought the tickets."

The stout man punched him in the chest. "Shut up. Let your ticket expire." With the pistol butt he chopped Mr. Chiu's hands, which at once released the table. Together the two men were dragging him away to the police station.

Realizing he had to go with them, Mr. Chiu turned his head and shouted to his bride, "Don't wait for me here. Take the train. If I'm not back by tomorrow morning, send someone over to get me out."

She nodded, covering her sobbing mouth with her palm.

After removing his belt, they locked Mr. Chiu into a cell in the back of the Rail-   25
road Police Station. The single window in the room was blocked by six steel bars; it
faced a spacious yard, in which stood a few pines. Beyond the trees, two swings hung
from an iron frame, swaying gently in the breeze. Somewhere in the building a cleaver
was chopping rhythmically. There must be a kitchen upstairs, Mr. Chiu thought.

He was too exhausted to worry about what they would do to him, so he lay down on
the narrow bed and shut his eyes. He wasn't afraid. The Cultural Revolution was over
already, and recently the Party had been propagating the idea that all citizens were equal
before the law. The police ought to be a law-abiding model for common people. As long
as he remained coolheaded and reasoned with them, they probably wouldn't harm him.

Late in the afternoon he was taken to the Interrogation Bureau on the second
floor. On his way there, in the stairwell, he ran into the middle-aged policeman who
had manhandled him. The man grinned, rolling his bulgy eyes and pointing his fingers at him as if firing a pistol. Egg of a tortoise! Mr. Chiu cursed mentally.

The moment he sat down in the office, he burped, his palm shielding his mouth.
In front of him, across a long desk, sat the chief of the bureau and a donkey-faced
man. On the glass desktop was a folder containing information on his case. He felt
it bizarre that in just a matter of hours they had accumulated a small pile of writing
about him. On second thought he began to wonder whether they had kept a file on
him all the time. How could this have happened? He lived and worked in Harbin,
more than three hundred miles away, and this was his first time in Muji City.

The chief of the bureau was a thin, bald man who looked serene and intelligent.
His slim hands handled the written pages in the folder in the manner of a lecturing
scholar. To Mr. Chiu's left sat a young scribe, with a clipboard on his knee and a black
fountain pen in his hand.

"Your name?" the chief asked, apparently reading out the question from a form.   30

"Chiu Maguang."

"Age?"

"Thirty-four."

"Profession?"

"Lecturer."   35

"Work unit?"

"Harbin University."

"Political status?"

"Communist Party member."

The chief put down the paper and began to speak. "Your crime is sabotage,   40
although it hasn't induced serious consequences yet. Because you are a Party member,
you should be punished more. You have failed to be a model for the masses and you—"

"Excuse me, sir," Mr. Chiu cut him off.

"What?"

"I didn't do anything. Your men are the saboteurs of our social order. They threw
hot tea on my feet and on my wife's feet. Logically speaking, you should criticize
them, if not punish them."

"That statement is groundless. You have no witness. Why should I believe you?"
the chief said matter-of-factly.

"This is my evidence." He raised his right hand. "Your man hit my fingers with   45
a pistol."

"That doesn't prove how your feet got wet. Besides, you could have hurt your fingers yourself."

"But I am telling the truth!" Anger flared up in Mr. Chiu. "Your police station owes me an apology. My train ticket has expired, my new leather sandals are ruined, and I am late for a conference in the provincial capital. You must compensate me for the damage and losses. Don't mistake me for a common citizen who would tremble when you sneeze. I'm a scholar, a philosopher, and an expert in dialectical material-ism. If necessary, we will argue about this in *The Northeastern Daily*, or we will go to the highest People's Court in Beijing. Tell me, what's your name?" He got carried away with his harangue, which was by no means trivial and had worked to his advan-tage on numerous occasions.

"Stop bluffing us," the donkey-faced man broke in. "We have seen a lot of your kind. We can easily prove you are guilty. Here are some of the statements given by eyewitnesses." He pushed a few sheets of paper toward Mr. Chiu.

Mr. Chiu was dazed to see the different handwritings, which all stated that he had shouted in the square to attract attention and refused to obey the police. One of the wit-nesses had identified herself as a purchasing agent from a shipyard in Shanghai. Some-thing stirred in Mr. Chiu's stomach, a pain rising to his rib. He gave out a faint moan.

"Now you have to admit you are guilty," the chief said. "Although it's a seri-ous crime, we won't punish you severely, provided you write out a self-criticism and promise that you won't disrupt the public order again. In other words, your release will depend on your attitude toward this crime." 50

"You're daydreaming," Mr. Chiu cried. "I won't write a word, because I'm inno-cent. I demand that you provide me with a letter of apology so I can explain to my university why I'm late."

Both the interrogators smiled contemptuously. "Well, we've never done that," said the chief, taking a puff of his cigarette.

"Then make this a precedent."

"That's unnecessary. We are pretty certain that you will comply with our wishes." The chief blew a column of smoke toward Mr. Chiu's face.

At the tilt of the chief's head, two guards stepped forward and grabbed the crimi-nal by the arms. Mr. Chiu meanwhile went on saying, "I shall report you to the Pro-vincial Administration. You'll have to pay for this! You are worse than the Japanese military police." 55

They dragged him out of the room.

After dinner, which consisted of a bowl of millet porridge, a corn bun, and a piece of pickled turnip, Mr. Chiu began to have a fever, shaking with a chill and sweating profusely. He knew that the fire of anger had gotten into his liver and that he was probably having a relapse. No medicine was available, because his brief-case had been left with his bride. At home it would have been time for him to sit in front of their color TV, drinking jasmine tea and watching the evening news. It was so lonesome in here. The orange bulb above the single bed was the only source of light, which enabled the guards to keep him under surveillance at night. A moment ago he had asked them for a newspaper or a magazine to read, but they turned him down.

Through the small opening on the door noises came in. It seemed that the police on duty were playing cards or chess in a nearby office; shouts and laughter could be heard now and then. Meanwhile, an accordion kept coughing from a remote corner in the building. Looking at the ballpoint and the letter paper left for him by the guards when they took him back from the Interrogation Bureau, Mr. Chiu remembered the old saying, "When a scholar runs into soldiers, the more he argues, the muddier his point becomes." How ridiculous this whole thing was. He ruffled his thick hair with his fingers.

He felt miserable, massaging his stomach continually. To tell the truth, he was more upset than frightened, because he would have to catch up with his work once he was back home—a paper that was due at the printers next week, and two dozen books he ought to read for the courses he was going to teach in the fall.

A human shadow flitted across the opening. Mr. Chiu rushed to the door and shouted through the hole, "Comrade Guard, Comrade Guard!"   60

"What do you want?" a voice rasped.

"I want you to inform your leaders that I'm very sick. I have heart disease and hepatitis. I may die here if you keep me like this without medication."

"No leader is on duty on the weekend. You have to wait till Monday."

"What? You mean I'll stay in here tomorrow?"

"Yes."   65

"Your station will be held responsible if anything happens to me."

"We know that. Take it easy, you won't die."

It seemed illogical that Mr. Chiu slept quite well that night, though the light above his head had been on all the time and the straw mattress was hard and infested with fleas. He was afraid of ticks, mosquitoes, cockroaches—any kind of insect but fleas and bedbugs. Once, in the countryside, where his school's faculty and staff had helped the peasants harvest crops for a week, his colleagues had joked about his flesh, which they said must have tasted nonhuman to fleas. Except for him, they were all afflicted with hundreds of bites.

More amazing now, he didn't miss his bride a lot. He even enjoyed sleeping alone, perhaps because the honeymoon had tired him out and he needed more rest.

The backyard was quiet on Sunday morning. Pale sunlight streamed through the   70
pine branches. A few sparrows were jumping on the ground, catching caterpillars and ladybugs. Holding the steel bars, Mr. Chiu inhaled the morning air, which smelled meaty. There must have been an eatery or a cooked-meat stand nearby. He reminded himself that he should take this detention with ease. A sentence that Chairman Mao had written to a hospitalized friend rose in his mind: "Since you are already in here, you may as well stay and make the best of it."

His desire for peace of mind originated in his fear that his hepatitis might get worse. He tried to remain unperturbed. However, he was sure that his liver was swelling up, since the fever still persisted. For a whole day he lay in bed, thinking about his paper on the nature of contradictions. Time and again he was overwhelmed by anger, cursing aloud, "A bunch of thugs!" He swore that once he was out, he would write an article about this experience. He had better find out some of the policemen's names.

It turned out to be a restful day for the most part; he was certain that his university would send somebody to his rescue. All he should do now was remain calm and wait patiently. Sooner or later the police would have to release him, although they had no idea that he might refuse to leave unless they wrote him an apology. Damn those hoodlums, they had ordered more than they could eat!

When he woke up on Monday morning, it was already light. Somewhere a man was moaning; the sound came from the backyard. After a long yawn, and kicking off the tattered blanket, Mr. Chiu climbed out of bed and went to the window. In the middle of the yard, a young man was fastened to a pine, his wrists handcuffed around the trunk from behind. He was wriggling and swearing loudly, but there was no sight of anyone else in the yard. He looked familiar to Mr. Chiu.

Mr. Chiu squinted his eyes to see who it was. To his astonishment, he recognized the man, who was Fenjin, a recent graduate from the Law Department at Harbin University. Two years ago Mr. Chiu had taught a course in Marxist materialism, in which Fenjin had enrolled. Now, how on earth had this young devil landed here?

Then it dawned on him that Fenjin must have been sent over by his bride. What 75
a stupid woman! A bookworm, who only knew how to read foreign novels! He had expected that she would contact the school's Security Section, which would for sure send a cadre here. Fenjin held no official position; he merely worked in a private law firm that had just two lawyers; in fact, they had little business except for some detective work for men and women who suspected their spouses of having extramarital affairs. Mr. Chiu was overcome with a wave of nausea.

Should he call out to let his student know he was nearby? He decided not to, because he didn't know what had happened. Fenjin must have quarreled with the police to incur such a punishment. Yet this could never have occurred if Fenjin hadn't come to his rescue. So no matter what, Mr. Chiu had to do something. But what could he do?

It was going to be a scorcher. He could see purple steam shimmering and rising from the ground among the pines. Poor devil, he thought, as he raised a bowl of corn glue to his mouth, sipped, and took a bite of a piece of salted celery.

When a guard came to collect the bowl and the chopsticks, Mr. Chiu asked him what had happened to the man in the backyard. "He called our boss 'bandit,'" the guard said. "He claimed he was a lawyer or something. An arrogant son of a rabbit."

Now it was obvious to Mr. Chiu that he had to do something to help his rescuer. Before he could figure out a way, a scream broke out in the backyard. He rushed to the window and saw a tall policeman standing before Fenjin, an iron bucket on the ground. It was the same young fellow who had arrested Mr. Chiu in the square two days before. The man pinched Fenjin's nose, then raised his hand, which stayed in the air for a few seconds, then slapped the lawyer across the face. As Fenjin was groaning, the man lifted up the bucket and poured water on his head.

"This will keep you from getting sunstroke, boy. I'll give you some more every 80
hour," the man said loudly.

Fenjin kept his eyes shut, yet his wry face showed that he was struggling to hold back from cursing the policeman, or, more likely, that he was sobbing in silence. He sneezed, then raised his face and shouted, "Let me go take a piss."

"Oh, yeah?" the man bawled. "Pee in your pants."

Still Mr. Chiu didn't make any noise, gripping the steel bars with both hands, his fingers white. The policeman turned and glanced at the cell's window; his pistol, partly holstered, glittered in the sun. With a snort he spat his cigarette butt to the ground and stamped it into the dust.

Then the door opened and the guards motioned Mr. Chiu to come out. Again they took him upstairs to the Interrogation Bureau.

The same men were in the office, though this time the scribe was sitting there 85
empty-handed. At the sight of Mr. Chiu the chief said, "Ah, here you are. Please be seated."

After Mr. Chiu sat down, the chief waved a white silk fan and said to him, "You may have seen your lawyer. He's a young man without manners, so our director had him taught a crash course in the backyard."

"It's illegal to do that. Aren't you afraid to appear in a newspaper?"

"No, we are not, not even on TV. What else can you do? We are not afraid of any story you make up. We call it fiction. What we do care about is that you cooperate with us. That is to say, you must admit your crime."

"What if I refuse to cooperate?"

"Then your lawyer will continue his education in the sunshine."   90

A swoon swayed Mr. Chiu, and he held the arms of the chair to steady himself. A numb pain stung him in the upper stomach and nauseated him, and his head was throbbing. He was sure that the hepatitis was finally attacking him. Anger was flaming up in his chest; his throat was tight and clogged.

The chief resumed, "As a matter of fact, you don't even have to write out your self-criticism. We have your crime described clearly here. All we need is your signature."

Holding back his rage, Mr. Chiu said, "Let me look at that."

With a smirk the donkey-faced man handed him a sheet which carried these words:

I hereby admit that on July 13 I disrupted public order at Muji Train Station, and that I refused to listen to reason when the railroad police issued their warning. Thus I myself am responsible for my arrest. After two days' detention, I have realized the reactionary nature of my crime. From now on, I shall continue to educate myself with all my effort and shall never commit this kind of crime again.

A voice started screaming in Mr. Chiu's ears, "Lie, lie!" But he shook his head   95
and forced the voice away. He asked the chief, "If I sign this, will you release both my lawyer and me?"

"Of course, we'll do that." The chief was drumming his fingers on the blue folder—their file on him.

Mr. Chiu signed his name and put his thumbprint under his signature.

"Now you are free to go," the chief said with a smile, and handed him a piece of paper to wipe his thumb with.

Mr. Chiu was so sick that he couldn't stand up from the chair at first try. Then he doubled his effort and rose to his feet. He staggered out of the building to meet his lawyer in the backyard, having forgotten to ask for his belt back. In his chest he felt as though there were a bomb. If he were able to, he would have razed the entire police station and eliminated all their families. Though he knew he could do nothing like that, he made up his mind to do something.

"I'm sorry about this torture, Fenjin," Mr. Chiu said when they met.   100

"It doesn't matter. They are savages." The lawyer brushed a patch of dirt off his jacket with trembling fingers. Water was still dribbling from the bottoms of his trouser legs.

"Let's go now," the teacher said.

The moment they came out of the police station, Mr. Chiu caught sight of a tea stand. He grabbed Fenjin's arm and walked over to the old woman at the table. "Two bowls of black tea," he said and handed her a one-yuan note.

After the first bowl, they each had another one. Then they set out for the train station. But before they walked fifty yards, Mr. Chiu insisted on eating a bowl of tree-ear soup at a food stand. Fenjin agreed. He told his teacher, "You mustn't treat me like a guest."

"No, I want to eat something myself."

As if dying of hunger, Mr. Chiu dragged his lawyer from restaurant to restaurant near the police station, but at each place he ordered no more than two bowls of food. Fenjin wondered why his teacher wouldn't stay at one place and eat his fill.

Mr. Chiu bought noodles, wonton, eight-grain porridge, and chicken soup, respectively, at four restaurants. While eating, he kept saying through his teeth, "If only I could kill all the bastards!" At the last place he merely took a few sips of the soup without tasting the chicken cubes and mushrooms.

Fenjin was baffled by his teacher, who looked ferocious and muttered to himself mysteriously, and whose jaundiced face was covered with dark puckers. For the first time Fenjin thought of Mr. Chiu as an ugly man.

Within a month over eight hundred people contracted acute hepatitis in Muji. Six died of the disease, including two children. Nobody knew how the epidemic had started.

ANTIGUA

Jamaica Kincaid

Girl

1983

Jamaica Kincaid was born Elaine Potter Rich-ardson in 1949 in St. John's, capital of the West Indian island nation of Antigua and Barbuda (she adopted the name Jamaica Kincaid in 1973 because of her family's disapproval of her writing). In 1965 she was sent to Westchester County, New York, to work as an au pair (or "servant," as she prefers to describe it). She attended Franconia College in New Hampshire, but did not complete a degree. Kincaid worked as a staff writer for the New Yorker for nearly twenty years; Talk Stories (2001) is a collection of seventy-seven short pieces that she wrote for the magazine. She won wide attention for At the Bottom of the River (1983), the volume of her stories that includes "Girl." In 1985 she published Annie John, an interlocking cycle of short stories about growing

Jamaica Kincaid

up in Antigua. Lucy (1990) was her first novel; it was followed by The Autobiography of My Mother (1996) and Mr. Potter (2002), novels inspired by the lives of her parents. Kincaid is also the author of A Small Place (1988), a memoir of her homeland and meditation on the destructiveness of colonialism, and My Brother (1997), a reminiscence of her brother Devon, who died of AIDS at thirty-three. Her recent works include a travel book titled Among Flowers: A Walk in the Himalaya (2005) and a novel, See Now Then (2013). A naturalized US citizen, Kincaid has said of her adopted country: "It's given me a place to be myself—but myself as I was formed somewhere else."

Wash the white clothes on Monday and put them on the stone heap; wash the color clothes on Tuesday and put them on the clothesline to dry; don't walk barehead in the hot sun; cook pumpkin fritters in very hot sweet oil; soak your little cloths right after you take them off; when buying cotton to make yourself a nice blouse, be sure that it doesn't have gum on it, because that way it won't hold up well after a wash; soak salt fish overnight before you cook it; is it true that you sing benna° in Sunday school?; always eat your food in such a way that it won't turn someone else's stomach; on Sundays try to walk like a lady and not like the slut you are so bent on becoming; don't sing benna in Sunday school; you mustn't speak to wharf-rat boys, not even to give directions; don't eat fruits on the street—flies will follow you; *but I don't sing benna on Sundays at all and never in Sunday school*; this is how to sew on a button; this is how to make a buttonhole for the button you have just sewed on; this is how to hem a dress when you see the hem coming down and so to prevent yourself from looking like the slut I know you are so bent on becoming; this is how you iron your father's khaki shirt so that it doesn't have a crease; this is how you iron your father's khaki pants so that they don't have a crease; this is how you grow okra—far from the house, because okra tree harbors red ants; when you are growing dasheen, make sure it gets plenty of water or else it makes your throat itch when you are eating it; this is how you sweep a corner; this is how you sweep a whole house; this is how you sweep a yard; this is how you smile to someone you don't like too much; this is how you smile to someone you don't like at all; this is how you smile to someone you like completely; this is how you set a table for tea; this is how you set a table for dinner; this is how you set a table for dinner with an important guest; this is how you set a table for lunch; this is how you set a table for breakfast; this is how to behave in the presence of men who don't know you very well, and this way they won't recognize immediately the slut I have warned you against becoming; be sure to wash every day, even if it is with your own spit; don't squat down to play marbles—you are not a boy, you know; don't pick people's flowers—you might catch something; don't throw stones at blackbirds, because it might not be a blackbird at all; this is how to make a bread pudding; this is how to make doukona°; this is how to make pepper pot; this is how to make a good medicine for a cold; this is how to make a good medicine to throw away a child before it even becomes a child; this is how to catch a fish; this is how to throw back a fish you don't like, and that way something bad won't fall on you; this is how to bully a man; this is how a man bullies you; this is how to love a man, and if this doesn't work there are other ways, and if they don't work don't feel too bad about giving up; this is how to spit up in the air if you feel like it, and this is how to move quick so that it doesn't fall on you; this is how to make ends meet; always squeeze bread to make sure it's fresh; *but what if the baker won't let me feel the bread?*; you mean to say that after all you are really going to be the kind of woman who the baker won't let near the bread?

---

benna: Kincaid defined this word, for two editors who inquired, as meaning "songs of the sort your parents didn't want you to sing, at first calypso and later rock and roll" (quoted by Sylvan Barnet and Marcia Stubbs, *The Little Brown Reader*, 2nd ed. [Boston: Little, 1980] 74). doukona: a pudding made from sweet potato, coconut, and spices.

EGYPT

Naguib Mahfouz

The Lawsuit   1989

Translated by Denys Johnson-Davies

Naguib Mahfouz (1911–2006) was born in Cairo, Egypt, where he spent his entire life and which served as the setting for his thirty-four novels and fourteen collections of short stories. His father was a civil servant, a path that Mahfouz himself would follow, spending most of his career in the Ministry of Culture. Mahfouz graduated from Cairo University in 1934 with a degree in philosophy but abandoned his postgraduate studies to pursue writing, concentrating so intently on this goal that he even deferred marriage until 1943. Prose fiction was a relatively new genre in Arabic literature, and Mahfouz—who had read and admired many Western novelists, including Melville, Dostoevsky, Balzac, and Camus—was enormously influential in modernizing its language, techniques, and subject

Naguib Mahfouz

matter. He planned a sequence of novels telling the entire history of Egypt, but after writing three novels set in the time of the Pharaohs he abandoned this project in favor of contemporary settings. Among his most important works are The Cairo Trilogy *(which includes* Palace Walk, Palace of Desire, Sugar Street, *1956–1957), depicting three generations of a middle-class Cairo family, and* Children of Gebelawi *(1959), an allegorical treatment of the development of Judaism, Christianity, and Islam. Considered blasphemous, this novel has not been published in the Arabic world, except in Lebanon. Mahfouz further alienated Islamic fundamentalists through his condemnation of the fatwa against Salman Rushdie for* The Satanic Verses *in 1989. Although Mahfouz regarded Rushdie's novel as offensive, he supported the author's freedom of expression. As a result of defending Rushdie, Mahfouz was stabbed in the neck by an Islamic fundamentalist. He recovered, but was left with permanent nerve damage that impaired his ability to write. In 1988 Mahfouz became the first Arabic writer to win the Nobel Prize in Literature. Though the award had little effect on his modest lifestyle, it had an immense impact on his literary fortunes: previously almost unknown outside the Arab world, he became a widely translated author with an international reputation.*

I found myself suddenly the subject of a lawsuit. My father's widow was demanding maintenance. Awakened from the depths of time, the past with its memories had invaded me. After reading the petition I exclaimed, "When did she go broke? Has she in her turn been robbed?"

"This woman robbed us and deprived us of our legal rights," I said to my lawyer.

I felt a strong desire to see her, not through any temptation to gloat over her but in order to see what effects time had had upon her. Today, like me, she was in her forties. Had her beauty withstood the passage of time? Was it holding out against poverty?

If the lawsuit was not genuine, would she have stretched out a demanding hand to one of her enemies? On the other hand, if it was specious, why had she not stretched out her hand before? What a ravishing beauty she had been!

"My father married her," I told the lawyer, "when he was in his middle fifties and she a girl of twenty." A semiliterate, old-fashioned contractor, he did not deal with banks but stored his profits away in a large cupboard in his bedroom. We were happy about this so long as we were a single family. The announcement of the new marriage was like a bomb exploding among us—my mother, my elder brother, and myself, as well as my sisters in their various homes. The top floor was given over to my father, the bride, and the cupboard. We were struck dumb by her youth and beauty. My mother said in a quavering voice choked with weeping, "What a catastrophe! We'll end up without a bean."

My elder brother was illiterate and mentally retarded. He was without work, but   5
considered himself a landowner. He flared up in a rage, declaring, "I'll defend myself to the very death."

Some of our relatives advised us to consult a lawyer, but my father threatened my mother with divorce if we were to entertain any such move. "I'm not gullible or an idiot, and no one's rights will be lost."

I was the one least affected by the disaster, partly because of my youth and partly because I was the only one in the family who wanted to study, hoping to enter the engineering college. Yet even so, I did not miss the significance of the facts—my father's age and that of his beautiful bride, and the fortune under threat. By way of smoothing things over, I would say, "I have confidence in my father."

"If we say nothing," my brother would say, "we'll find the cupboard empty."

I shared his fears but affected outwardly what I did not feel inwardly. All the time I felt that our oasis, which had appeared so tranquil, was being subjected to a wild wind and that on the horizon black clouds were gathering. My mother took refuge in silent anxiety, with each new day giving her warning of a bad outcome. As for my elder brother, he would brave the lion in his lair, pleading with his father. "I am the first-born, uneducated as you can see, and without means of support, so give me my share."

"Do you want to inherit from me while I'm still alive? It's a disgrace for you to   10
doubt me—no one's rights will be lost." But my brother would not calm down and would pester my father whenever they met. He would hurl threats at him from behind his back, and my mother would say that she was more worried about my brother than she was about the fortune.

For my part, I wondered whether my father, that capable master of his trade, the man who was such a meticulous accountant despite his illiteracy, would meet defeat at the hands of a pretty girl. Yet, without doubt, he was changing, slipping down little by little each day. He would take himself off to the Turkish baths twice a month, would clip his beard and trim his mustache every week, and would strut about in new clothes. Finally he took to dyeing his hair. Precious gifts embellished the bride's neck, bosom, and arms. Now there was a Chevrolet and a chauffeur waiting in front of our house.

My brother became more and more angry. "Where did he get her from?" he would say to me. Was it so impossible that she might get hold of the key and find her way to opening the cupboard? Would she not take from him something to secure her future? Did she not have the power to make him happy or to turn his life into one of misery and turmoil as she wished?

Arguments would develop between my brother and my father that would go beyond the bounds of propriety. My father would grow angry and spit in my brother's face. In an explosive outburst, my brother seized hold of a table lamp and hurled it at

his father, drawing blood. Seeing the blood, my brother was scared, but even so persevered in his attempts to do Father in, with the cook and the chauffeur intervening.
My father insisted on informing the police, and my brother was taken off to court and
from there to prison, where he died after a year.

"How did she find the courage to bring her case?" I asked the lawyer.

"Necessity has its own rules." 15

In the midst of our alarm and our mourning for my brother, my mother and I
heard the noise of something striking the floor above us. We hurried upstairs and
found ourselves standing aghast over my father's body. As is usual in such circumstances, we asked ourselves again and again what could have happened, but no
amount of questioning can bring back the dead. It seems that he had had a paralyzing
stroke a whole day before his death without our knowing.

We waited till he had been buried and the rites of mourning were over, and
then the family gathered together. My sisters, their husbands, and their husbands'
parents were there, and the lawyer was present as well. We asked about the key to the
cupboard, and the young widow answered quite simply that she knew nothing about
it. Sometimes the mind boggles at the sheer brazenness of lying. But what could be
done? We then came across the key, and the cupboard finally divulged its secrets,
exhibiting to us with profound mockery a bundle of notes that did not exceed five
thousand pounds. "Then where is the man's fortune?" everyone called out.

All eyes were fixed on the beautiful widow, who answered defiantly. We had
recourse to the police, and there were investigations and searches. As my mother
had predicted, we came out of it all "without a bean." The beautiful widow went off
to her parents' house, and the curtain was brought down upon her and the inheritance. My mother died. I got a job, married, and achieved a notable success. I became
oblivious of the past until the lawsuit brought me back to it.

"It's really the height of irony," I said to the lawyer, "that I should be required to
pay maintenance to that woman."

His voice came to me from between the files on his desk. "The old story does on 20
the face of it appear worthy of being put forward, but what's the point of unearthing
it when we have no evidence against her?"

"Even if the old story may not be open for discussion, it's a good starting point,
whose effect should not be underrated."

"On the contrary, we would be providing the woman's lawyer with the chance to
take the offensive and to attract sympathy for her."

"Sympathy?"

"Steady now. Let's think about it a bit objectively. An old man hoards his wealth
in a cupboard in his bedroom. He then buys himself a beautiful girl of twenty when
he's a man of fifty-five. Such and such happens to his family and such and such to
his beautiful wife. Fine, who was to blame?" He was silent for a while, scowling, then
continued. "Let's look at it from your side. You're a man who's earning and has a family, and the cost of living is unbearably high, and so on and so forth. . . . Let's content
ourselves by settling on a reasonable sum for maintenance."

"Too bad!" I muttered. "She robbed us; then there was the death of my brother 25
and my mother's distress."

"I'm sorry about that, but she's as much a victim as you are. Even the fortune she
made off with brought her to disaster. And now here she is begging."

Prompted by casual curiosity, I said, "It's as though you know something about
her."

He shook his head with diplomatic vagueness. "A woman who couldn't have children, she was married and divorced several times when she was in her prime. In middle age she fell in love with a student, who, in his turn, robbed her and went off."

He did not divulge the sources of his information, but I surmised the logical progression of events. I experienced a feeling of gratification, which a sense of decency prevented me from showing.

On the day of the court session, I was again seized by a mysterious desire to set eyes on her. I recognized her as she waited in front of the lawyers' room. I knew her by conjecture before actually recognizing her, for the beauty that had made away with our fortune and ruined us had completely vanished. She was fat, excessively and unacceptably so, and the charming freshness had leaked away from her face. What little beauty was left seemed insipid. A veneer of perpetual dejection acted like a screen between her and other people. Without giving the matter any thought, I went up to her, inclined my head in greeting, and said, "I remember you. . . perhaps you remember me?"   30

At first she gazed at me in surprise, then in confusion. She returned the greeting with a gesture of her covered head. "I'm sorry to cause you trouble," she said, as though apologizing, "but I am forced to do so."

I forgot what I wanted to say. In fact words failed me, and I felt an inner peace. "Don't worry—let the Lord do as He wills." I quietly moved away as I said to myself, "Why not? Even a farce must continue right to the final act."

INDIA

Bharati Mukherjee

Saints   1985

Bharati Mukherjee

Bharati Mukherjee (1940–2017) spent her earliest years in Calcutta, raised in a large family compound of nearly fifty relatives, which was financially supported by her father, the proprietor of a thriving pharmaceutical company. When Mukherjee was eight, the family traveled abroad, and she received her education for three years in England and Switzerland. Upon return to Calcutta, Mukherjee was placed in a Roman Catholic school run by Irish nuns. She later studied English at the University of Calcutta and earned a master's degree from the University of Baroda. In the early 1960s, she came to the United States to study in the prestigious writing program at the University of Iowa. Mukherjee wrote eight novels, including The Tiger's Daughter *(1971),* Jasmine *(1989),* Desirable Daughters *(2002), and* Miss New India *(2011), as well as a memoir and three books of nonfiction. A short story collection,* The Middleman and Other Stories *(1988), won the National Book Critics Circle Award. Mukherjee taught at several universities in Canada and the United States, most notably the University of California at Berkeley, where she joined the English department in 1989. Although India was Mukherjee's home country into adulthood, she had intimate, firsthand knowledge of the immigrant experience—moving from India to Europe to America to Canada and back to America. The challenge of immigrant life—which she called "the epic narrative of this millennium"—was the primary subject of her strongest fiction. In a Boston Globe interview upon the publication of* The Holder of the World *(1993; a retelling of Hawthorne's* The Scarlet Letter*), Mukherjee said: "While I have changed in my 30 years in this country, it has also had to change because of the hundreds of thousands of people like me, forcing the culture, moment by moment, into something new. I am looking for that new, constantly evolving thing."*

"And one more thing," Mom says. "Your father can't take you this August."

I can tell from the way she fusses with the placemats that she is interested in my reaction. The placemats are made of pinkish linen and I can see a couple of ironing marks, like shiny little arches. Wayne is coming for dinner. Wayne Latta is her new friend. It's the first time she's having him over with others, but that's not why she's nervous.

"That's okay," I tell her. "Tran and I have plans for the summer."

Mom rolls up the spray-starched napkins and knots them until they look like nesting birds on each dinner plate. "It isn't that he's really busy," she says. She gives me one of her I-know-you-are-hurting, son, looks. "I don't see why he can't take you. He says he has a conference to go to in Hong Kong at the end of July, so he might as well do China in August."

"It's okay. Really," I say. It's true, I am okay. At fifteen I'm too old to be a pawn   5
between them, and too young to get caught in problems of my own. I'm in a state of grace. I want to get to my room in this state of grace before it disintegrates, and start a new game of "Geopolitique 1990" on the Apple II-Plus Dad gave me last Christmas.

"Can you get the flower holders, Shawn?" Mom asks.

I take a wide, flat cardboard box out of the buffet.

She lifts eight tiny glass holders out of the box, and lines them up in the center of the table. She hasn't used them since things started going bad between Dad and her. When things blew up, they sold the big house in New Jersey and Mom and I moved to this college town in upstate New York. Mom works in the Admissions Office. Wayne calls it a college for rich bitches who were too dumb to get into Bennington or Barnard.

"Get me a pitcher of water and the flowers," Mom says.

In a dented aluminum pot in the kitchen sink, eight yellow rosebuds are soak-   10
ing up water. Granules of sugar are whitish and still sludgy in the bottom of the pot. Mom's a believer; she's read somewhere that sugar in lukewarm water keeps cut flowers fresh. I move the pot to one side and fill a quart-sized measuring cup with lukewarm water. I know her routines.

It's going to be an anxious evening for Mom. She's set out extra goblets for spritzers on a tray lined with paper towels. Index cards typed up with recipes for dips and sauces are stacked on the windowsill. She shouldn't do sauces, nothing that requires last-minute frying and stirring. She's the flustery type, and she's only setting herself up for failure.

"What happened to the water, Shawn?"

It's a Pizza Hut night for me, definitely. I know what she's going through with Wayne. He's not at all like Dad, the good Dr. Manny Patel, who soothes crazies at Creedmore all day. Nights he's a playboy and slum landlord, Mom says.

Mom says, "Your father will call you tomorrow, he said. He wants to talk to you himself. He wants to know what you want this Christmas."

This is only the first Thursday in November. Dad's planning ahead is a joke with us. Foresight is what got him out of Delhi to New York. "Could I have become a psychiatrist and a near-millionaire if I hadn't planned well ahead?" Dad used to tell Mom in the medium-bad days.

Mom thinks making a million is a vicious, selfish aim. But Dad's really very generous. He sends money to relatives and to Indian orphanages. He's generous but practical. He says he doesn't want to send me stuff—cashmere sweaters and Ultrasuede jackets, the stuff he likes—that'll end up in basement cedar closets.

"I'll be late tomorrow," I remind Mom. "Fridays I have my chess club."

Actually, Tran and I and a bunch of other guys from the chess club play four afternoons a week. Thursdays we don't play because Tran has Debate Workshop.

"You know what I want, Mom. You can tell him."

I ask for computer games, video cassettes, nothing major. So twice a year Dad sends big checks. Dad's real generous with me. It makes him feel the big benefactor, Mom says, whenever a check comes in the mail. But that's only because things went really bad two years ago. They sent me away to boarding school, but they still couldn't work things out between them.

At five, Wayne comes into our driveway in his blue Toyota pickup. The wheels squeal and rock in the deep, snowy ruts. Wayne has a cord of firewood in the back of the truck. Mom paid him for the firewood yesterday and for the time he put in picking up the cord from some French guy in Ballston Spa. Wayne's a writer; meantime he works as a janitor in the college. A "mopologist" is what he calls himself. It's so corny, but every time Wayne uses that word, Mom gives him a tinkly, supportive laugh. Janitors are more caring than shrinks, the laugh seems to say.

We hear Wayne on the back porch, cursing as he drops an armload of logs. For all his muscles, he's a clumsy man. But then Mom could never have gotten Dad to carry the logs himself. Dad would have had them delivered or done without them.

Mom takes five-dollar bills out of the buffet drawer and counts out thirty dollars. "For the wine, would you give it to him? I couldn't do a production all by myself on a weeknight."

"Why do a production at all?"

She stiffens. "I'm not ashamed of Wayne," she says. "Wayne is who he is.

Wayne finally comes into the dining room. I slip him the money: it's more than he expected. "I got some beer too, Mila." Mom's name is Camille but he calls her Mila. That's a hard thing to get used to. He drops my rucksack on the floor, turns the chair around and straddles it. There are five other chairs around the table and two folding chairs brought up from the basement for tonight. Under Wayne's muscular thighs, the dining room chair looks rickety, absurdly elegant. Red longjohns show through the knee rips of his blue jeans. He keeps his red knit cap on. But he's not as tough as he looks. He keeps the cap on because he's sensitive about his bald, baby-pink head.

"Hey, Shawn," he says to me. "Still baking the competition?"

It's Wayne's usual joke about my playing competitive chess. Our school team has T-shirts that we paid for by working the concession stands on basketball nights last winter. Tran plays varsity first board, I play third. Now we need chess cheerleaders, Wayne kids me. "Hey, hey, push that pawn! Dee-fense, dee-fense. King's Indian dee-fense!" Wayne isn't a bad sort, not for around here. Last year we went for trout out on the Battenkill. The day with Wayne wasn't bad, given our complicated situation. I went back to the creek with Tran a week later, but it was different. Tran's idea of fishing is throwing a net across the river, tossing in a stick of dynamite, then pulling it up.

"You'll like Milos and Verna," Mom tells Wayne. "They're both painters in the Art Department. From Yugoslavia, but I think they're hoping to stay in the States."

From the soft, nervous look she's giving Wayne, I know it isn't the Yugoslavs she's thinking of right at the moment. Wayne grabs her throat in his thick hairy hands. She lifts her face. Then she glances at me in a quick guilty way as if she's already given away too much.

I know about feelings. I've got a secret life, too.

"D'you have enough for a pizza?" Mom asks me. She's moved away from Wayne.

Yeah, I have enough.

From the Pizza Hut, Tran and I go back to Tran's place. Tran's sixteen and he owns a noisy used Plymouth. It's two-tone, white and aquamarine. I like the colors. Tran's a genuine boatperson. When he was younger, the English teacher made him tell the class about having to hide from pirates and having to chew on raw fish just to stay alive. Women on his boat hid any valuable stuff they had in their vaginas. "That's enough, Tran, thank you," the teacher said. Now he never mentions his cruise to America.

We skid to a stop inside the Indian Lookout Point Trailer Park where he lives with his mother in a flash of aqua. The lights are on in Tran's mobile home. Tran's mother's muddy Chevy and his stepfather's Dodge Ram are angle-parked. Tran's real father got left behind in Saigon.

"I don't know," Tran says. He doesn't cut the engine. We sit in the warm, dark car. "Maybe we ought to go on to your place. He never gets home this early."

It's minus ten outside, maybe worse with the wind-chill factor. I open the car door softly. The car light on Tran's face makes his face look ochre-dingy, mottled with pimples.

"Mom's entertaining tonight," I warn him. The snow is slippery cold under my Adidas. I pick my way through icy patches to the trailer, and look in a little front window.

Tran's mom is at the kitchen sink, washing a glass. She's still wearing her wool coat and plaid scarf. Her face has an odd puffy quiver. There are no signs of physical violence, but someone's sure been hurt. Tran's stepfather (he didn't, and can't, adopt Tran until some agency can locate Tran's real father, and get his consent) is sitting hunched forward in a rocker, and drinking Miller Lite.

Like Tran, I've learned to discount homey scenes.

"That's okay," Tran says. He's calling out from the car. His sad face is in the opened window. "Your place is bigger."

It makes sense, but I can't move away from his little window.

"I can show you a move that'll bake Sato," he says. "I mean really bake his ass."

We both hate Sato but Sato isn't smart enough to wince under our hate or even smart enough to know when his ass has really been baked.

"Okay." There's that new killer chess move, and a new Peter Gabriel for us to listen to. Tran's chess rating is just under 1900. Farelli's is higher, but Farelli is more than arrogant. He's so arrogant he dropped off the team. He goes down to Manhattan instead and hustles games in Times Square or in the chess clubs. Tran's a little guilty about playing first board; he knows he owes it to Farelli's vanity. The difference between Farelli and Tran is about the same as between Tran and me. Farelli wants to charge the club four-fifty an hour for tutoring. He's the only real American in the club. The rest of us have names like Sato, Chin, Duoc, Cho and Prasad.

My name's Patel, Shawn Patel. Mom took back her maiden name, Belliveau, when we moved out of Upper Montclair. We're supposed to be out of Dad's reach here, except for checks.

A week after Mom's dinner party, Tran and I are coming out of an arcade on Upper Broadway Street when we see Wayne walking our way. Upper Broadway's short and squat. The storefronts have shallow doorways you can't hide in. Wayne is with the Yugoslav woman, the painter who doesn't intend to go back to her country. They aren't holding hands or anything, they aren't even touching shoulders, but I can tell they want to do things. The Yugoslav has both her hands in the pockets of her duffle coat. A toggle at her throat is missing and the loop has nothing to weigh it down. The Yugoslav has red cheeks. With her red cheeks, her button nose and her long, loose hair, she looks very young. Maybe it's a trick of afternoon light or of European make-up, but she looks too young to be a friend of Mom's.

Wayne wants to hug her. I can tell from the way he arches his upper body inside his coat. He wants to sneak his hand into her pocket, pull out her fist, swing hands on Upper Broadway and be stared at by everyone.

I pull Tran back inside the arcade.

"I got to get to Houston," Tran says. We're playing "Joust," his favorite game, but his slight body is twisted in misery.

"It'll work out," I tell him. Wanting to go to Houston has to do with his mother   50
and stepfather. Things always go bad between parents. "You can't leave in the middle of the semester. It doesn't make sense."

"What does?"

Tran has an older brother in Houston, in engineering school. Tran thinks his mother will come up with the bus fare south. She works at Grand Union, and weekends she waitresses. "My luck's got to change," he says.

Luck has nothing to do with anything, I want to say. You're out of the clutch of pirates now. No safe hiding places.

Wayne and his painter make us spend too many tokens on this Joust machine.

Mom's in the eating nook of the kitchen, reading a book on English gardens   55
when I come in the back door. She's wearing a long skirt made of quilted fabric and a matching jacket. The quilting makes her look fat, and ridiculous.

She catches my grin. "It's warm, don't knock it," she says of her skirt. These upstate houses are drafty. Then she pulls her feet up under her and wriggles her raised knees gracelessly under the long skirt. "And I love the color on me."

I bleed. Mom should have had a daughter. Two women could have consoled each other. I can only think of Wayne, how even now he's slipping the loops over Serbian toggles. It's a complicated feeling. I bleed because I'm disloyal.

"Your father's sent a present by UPS," she says. She doesn't look up from the illustration of a formal garden of a lord. A garden with a stiff, bristly hedged maze to excite desire and contain it. "I put the package on your desk upstairs. It looks like a book."

She means to say, Dad's presents are always impersonal.

Actually it's two books that Dad has sent me this time. The thick, heavy one is   60
an art book, reproductions of Moghul paintings that Dad loves. Even India was once an empire-building nation. The other is a thin book with bad binding put out by a religious printing house in Madras. The little book is about a Hindu saint who had visions. Dad has sent me a book about visions.

May this book bring you as much happiness as it did me when I was your age, Dad's inscription reads. Then a p.s. *The saint died of throat cancer and was briefly treated by your great-uncle, the cancer specialist in Calcutta.*

Forty pages into the book, the saint describes a vision. "I see the Divine Mother in all things." He sees Her in ants, dogs, flowers, the latrine bowls in the temple. He keeps falling into trances as he goes for walks or as he says his prayers. In this perfect state, sometimes the saint kicks his disciples. He eats garbage thrown out by temple cooks for cows and pariah dogs.

"Did I kick you?" the saint asks when he comes out of his trance. "Kick, kick," beg the disciples as they push each other to get near enough for a saintly touch.

My father, healer of derangements, slum landlord with income properties on two continents, believer of visions, pleasure-taker where none seems present, is a mystery.

Downstairs Mom is dialing Wayne's number. In the whir of the telephone dial, I   65
read the new rhythms of her agony. Wayne will not answer his phone tonight. Wayne is in bed with his naked Yugoslav.

It's my turn to call. I slip my bony finger into the dial's fingerholes. "Want to ball?" I whisper into the mouthpiece. My throat is raspy from the fullness of desire.

"What?" It's a girlish voice at the other end. "What did you say?"

The girl giggles. "You dumb pervert." She leaves it to me to hang up first.

The next night, a Friday night, Tran and I come down from my room to get Mountain Dew out of the fridge. Mom and Wayne are making out in the kitchen. He has her jammed up against the eating nook's wall. There are Indian paintings on that wall. She kept the paintings and gave Dad the statues and framed batiks. Wayne holds Mom's head against dusty glass, behind which an emperor in Moghul battledress is leading his army out of the capital. Wayne's got his knee high up Mom's quilted skirt. The knee presses in, hard. I see love's monstrous force bloat her face. Wayne has her head in his grasp. Her orange hair tufts out between his knuckles, and its orange mist covers the bygone emperor and his soldiers.

Tran's used to living in small, usurped spaces. He drops a shy, civil little cough,   70
and right away Wayne lets go of Mom's hair. But his knee is still raised, still pressing into her skirt.

"Get outta here, guys," he says. He looks pleased, he sounds good-natured. "You got better things to do. Go push your pawns."

"Tell her about the painter," I say. My voice is even, not emotional.

"What're you talking about? What's the matter with you?"

Tran says, "Let's get the soda, Shawn." He picks up the six-pack and two glasses and pushes me toward the stairwell.

Upstairs, Tran and I take turns dialing the town's other insomniacs. "Do you   75
have soft breasts?" I ask. I really want to know. "Yes," one of them confesses. "Very soft and very white and I'm so lonely tonight. Do you want to touch?"

Tran reads aloud an episode from the life of the Hindu saint. Reaching the state of perfection while strolling along the Ganges one day, the saint fell and broke his arm. The saint had been thinking of his love for the young boy followers who lived in the temple. He had been thinking of his love for them—love as for a sweetheart, he says—when he slipped into a trance and stumbled. Love and pain: in the saint's mind there is no separation.

Trans makes the last of our calls for the night. "You bitch," he says as he shakes his thin body in a parody of undulation. To me he says, "Mother won't come through with the bus fare to Houston."

Tonight Tran wants to sleep over in my room. Tomorrow we'll find a way to raise the bus fare.

I want to tell him things, to console him. Bad luck and good luck even out over a lifetime. Cancer can ravage an ecstatic saint. Things pass. I don't remember Dad in any intimate way except that he embarrassed me when he came to pick me up from my old boarding school. The overstated black Mercedes, the hugging and kissing in such a foreign way.

A little before midnight, Tran's moan startles me awake. He must be dreaming of   80
fathers, pirates, saints and Houston. For me the worst isn't dreams. It's having to get out of the house at night and walk around. At midnight I float like a ghost through other people's gardens. I peer into other boys' bedrooms, I become somebody else's son.

Tonight I'm more restless than other nights. I look for an Indian name in the phone book. The directory in our upstate town is thin; it caves against my eager arms. The first name I spot is Batliwalla. Meaning perhaps bottle-walla, a dealer in bottles in the ancestral long-ago. Batliwalla, Jamshed S., M.D.

I dress in the dark for a night of cold roaming. It'll be a night of walking in a state of perfect grace. For disguise, I choose Mom's red cloth coat from the hall cupboard and her large red wool beret into which she has stuck a pheasant feather. She keeps five more feathers, like a bouquet, in a candy jar. The feathers are from Wayne the hunter. Wayne's promised to put a pheasant on our table for Thanksgiving dinner. I can taste its hard, stringy birdflesh and pellets of buckshot.

Like the Hindu saint, I walk my world in boots and a trance. But in this upstate town the only body of water is an icy creek, not the Ganges.

The Batliwallas have no curtains on their back windows. I look into a back bedroom that glows from a bedside lamp. A kid in pajamas is sitting up in bed, a book in his hands. He's a little kid, a junior high kid, or maybe a studious dwarf. The dwarfkid rocks back and forth under his bedclothes. He seems to be learning something, maybe a poem, by heart. He's the conqueror of alien syllables. His fleshy, brown lips purse and pout ferociously. His tiny head in its helmet of glossy black hair bumps, bumps, bumps the bed's white vinyl headboard. The dwarfkid's eyes are screwed tightly shut, and his long eyelashes look like tiny troughs for ghosts to drink out of. Wanting good grades, the dwarfkid studies into the night. He rocks, he shouts, he bumps his head. I can't hear the words, but I want to reach out to a fellow saint.

When I get home, the back porch is dark but the kitchen light is on. I sit on the   85
stack of firewood and look in. I'm not cold, or sleepy. Wayne and Mom are fighting in the kitchen, literally slugging each other. I had Wayne figured wrong. He isn't the sly operator after all. He's opened up my Mom's upper lip. It's blood Mom is washing off.

"Get out," Mom screams at him. This time I can make out all the words. I feel like a god, overseeing lives.

The faucet is running as it had done the day there were yellow rosebuds in a kitchen pot. Steam from the hot, running water frizzes Mom's hair. She looks old. "Get out of my house."

"I'm getting out." Wayne says. But he doesn't leave. First he lights a cigarette, something Mom doesn't permit. Then he flops down on one of the two kitchen stools, props his work boots on the other and starts to adjust the laces. "I wouldn't stay if you begged me."

"Get out, out!" Mom's still screaming as I turn my house key in the lock. She might as well know it all. "Do me a favor, get out. Lace your goddamn boots in your goddamn truck. Please get out."

I move through the bright kitchen into the dark dining room, and wait for the   90
lovers to finish.

In a while Wayne leaves. He doesn't slam the door. He doesn't toss the key on
the floor. The pickup's low beams dance on frozen bushes.

"My god, Shawn! " Mom has switched on a wall light in the dining room. She's
staring at me, she's really looking at me. Finally. "My god, what have you done to
your face, poor baby."

Her fingers scrape at the muck on my face, the cheek-blush, lipstick, eyeshadow.
Her bruised mouth is on my hair. I can feel her warm, wet sobs, but I don't hurt. I am
in a trance in the middle of a November night. I can't hurt for me, for Dad, I can't
hurt for anyone in the world. I feel so strong, so much a potentate in battledress.

How wondrous to be a visionary. If I were to touch someone now, I'd be touching god.

CANADA

Alice Munro

Wild Swans   1978

Alice Munro (b. 1931), one of the most widely
admired contemporary writers, was born to a
schoolteacher mother and a father who was a fox
and mink farmer. She has spent most of her life in
Wingham, in southwestern Ontario, Canada; its
small-town people figure in many of her stories. For
two years, she attended the University of Western
Ontario, while waiting tables and picking tobacco
on the side, but she dropped out at twenty, after
her first marriage. The mother of three daughters,
Munro is a particularly sensitive explorer of the rela-
tions between parents and children, yet she ranges
widely in choosing her themes. She has published
more than a dozen remarkable collections of short
fiction, including Dance of the Happy Shades
(1968), The Beggar Maid *(1982),* The Love of

Alice Munro

a Good Woman *(1998),* Too Much Happiness *(2009), and* Dear Life *(2012). Three of*
her books have won Canada's prestigious Governor General's Literary Award; in the United
States she has won the National Book Critics Circle Award. In 2009 she was awarded the
Man Booker International Prize and in 2013 became the first Canadian to win the Nobel
Prize in Literature. Called a "master of the short story" by the Nobel committee, Munro has
declared her preference for short fiction over novels, saying that she aims "to write the story
that will zero in and give you intense, but not connected, moments of experience."

Flo said to watch for White Slavers. She said this was how they operated: an old
woman, a motherly or grandmotherly sort, made friends while riding beside you on a

bus or train. She offered you candy, which was drugged. Pretty soon you began to droop and mumble, were in no condition to speak for yourself. Oh, help, the woman said, my daughter (granddaughter) is sick, please somebody help me get her off so that she can recover in the fresh air. Up stepped a polite gentleman, pretending to be a stranger, offering assistance. Together, at the next stop, they hustled you off the train or bus, and that was the last the ordinary world ever saw of you. They kept you a prisoner in the White Slave place (to which you had been transported drugged and bound so you wouldn't even know where you were), until such time as you were thoroughly degraded and in despair, your insides torn up by drunken men and invested with vile disease, your mind destroyed by drugs, your hair and teeth fallen out. It took about three years for you to get to this state. You wouldn't want to go home then; maybe couldn't remember home, or find your way if you did. So they let you out on the streets.

Flo took ten dollars and put it in a little cloth bag, which she sewed to the strap of Rose's slip. Another thing likely to happen was that Rose would get her purse stolen.

Watch out, Flo said as well, for people dressed up as ministers. They were the worst. That disguise was commonly adopted by White Slavers, as well as those after your money.

Rose said she didn't see how she could tell which ones were disguised.

Flo had worked in Toronto once. She had worked as a waitress in a coffee   5
shop in Union Station. That was how she knew all she knew. She never saw sunlight, in those days, except on her days off. But she saw plenty else. She saw a man cut another man's stomach with a knife, just pull out his shirt and do a tidy cut, as if it was a watermelon not a stomach. The stomach's owner just sat looking down surprised, with no time to protest. Flo implied that that was nothing, in Toronto. She saw two bad women (that was what Flo called whores, running the two words together, like badminton) get into a fight, and a man laughed at them, other men stopped and laughed and egged them on, and they had their fists full of each other's hair. At last the police came and took them away, still howling and yelping.

She saw a child die of a fit too. Its face was black as ink.

"Well, I'm not scared," said Rose provokingly. "There's the police, anyway."

"Oh, them! They'd be the first ones to diddle you!"

She did not believe anything Flo said on the subject of sex. Consider the undertaker.

A little bald man, very neatly dressed, would come into the store sometimes and   10
speak to Flo with a placating expression.

"I only wanted a bag of candy. And maybe a few packages of gum. And one or two chocolate bars. Could you go to the trouble of wrapping them?"

Flo in her mock-deferential tone would assure him that she could. She wrapped them in heavy-duty white paper, so they were something like presents. He took his time with the selection, humming and chatting, then dawdled for a while. He might ask how Flo was feeling. And how Rose was, if she was there.

"You look pale. Young girls need fresh air." To Flo he would say, "You work too hard. You've worked hard all your life."

"No rest for the wicked," Flo would say agreeably.

When he went out she hurried to the window. There it was—the old black   15
hearse with its purple curtains.

"He'll be after them today!" Flo would say as the hearse rolled away at a gentle pace, almost a funeral pace. The little man had been an undertaker, but he was retired now. The hearse was retired too. His sons had taken over the undertaking and bought a new one. He drove the old hearse all over the country, looking for women. So Flo said. Rose could not believe it. Flo said he gave them the gum and the candy. Rose said he probably ate them himself. Flo said he had been seen, he had been heard. In mild weather he drove with the windows down, singing, to himself or to somebody out of sight in the back.

"Her brow is like the snowdrift
Her throat is like the swan..."

Flo imitated him singing. Gently overtaking some woman walking on a back road, or resting at a country crossroads. All compliments and courtesy and chocolate bars, offering a ride. Of course every woman who reported being asked said she had turned him down. He never pestered anybody, drove politely on. He called in at houses, and if the husband was home he seemed to like just as well as anything to sit and chat. Wives said that was all he ever did anyway but Flo did not believe it.

"Some women are taken in," she said. "A number." She liked to speculate on what the hearse was like inside. Plush. Plush on the walls and the roof and the floor. Soft purple, the color of the curtains, the color of dark lilacs.

All nonsense, Rose thought. Who could believe it, of a man that age?

Rose was going to Toronto on the train for the first time by herself. She had been once before, but that was with Flo, long before her father died. They took along their own sandwiches and bought milk from the vendor on the train. It was sour. Sour chocolate milk. Rose kept taking tiny sips, unwilling to admit that something so much desired could fail her. Flo sniffed it, then hunted up and down the train until she found the old man in his red jacket, with no teeth and the tray hanging around his neck. She invited him to sample the chocolate milk. She invited people nearby to smell it. He let her have some ginger ale for nothing. It was slightly warm.

"I let him know," Flo said, looking around after he had left. "You have to let them know."   20

A woman agreed with her but most people looked out the window. Rose drank the warm ginger ale. Either that, or the scene with the vendor, or the conversation Flo and the agreeing woman now got into about where they came from, why they were going to Toronto, and Rose's morning constipation which was why she was lacking color, or the small amount of chocolate milk she had got inside her, caused her to throw up in the train toilet. All day long she was afraid people in Toronto could smell vomit on her coat.

This time Flo started the trip off by saying, "Keep an eye on her, she's never been away from home before!" to the conductor, then looking around and laughing, to show that was jokingly meant. Then she had to get off. It seemed the conductor had no more need for jokes than Rose had, and no intention of keeping an eye on anybody. He never spoke to Rose except to ask for her ticket. She had a window seat, and was soon extraordinarily happy. She felt Flo receding, West Hanratty flying away from her, her own wearying self discarded as easily as everything else. She loved the towns less and less known. A woman was standing at her back door in her nightgown, not caring if everybody on the train saw her. They were travelling south, out of the snowbelt, into an earlier spring, a tenderer sort of landscape. People could grow peach trees in their back yards.

Rose collected in her mind the things she had to look for in Toronto. First, things for Flo. Special stockings for her varicose veins. A special kind of cement for sticking handles on pots. And a full set of dominoes.

For herself Rose wanted to buy hair-remover to put on her arms and legs, and if possible an arrangement of inflatable cushions, supposed to reduce your hips and thighs. She thought they probably had hairremover in the drugstore in Hanratty, but the woman in there was a friend of Flo's and told everything. She told Flo who bought hair dye and slimming medicine and French safes. As for the cushion business, you could send away for it but there was sure to be a comment at the Post Office, and Flo knew people there as well. She also planned to buy some bangles, and an angora sweater. She had great hopes of silver bangles and powder-blue angora. She thought they could transform her, make her calm and slender and take the frizz out of her hair, dry her underarms and turn her complexion to pearl.

The money for these things, as well as the money for the trip, came from a   25
prize Rose had won, for writing an essay called "Art and Science in the World of Tomorrow." To her surprise, Flo asked if she could read it, and while she was reading it, she remarked that they must have thought they had to give Rose the prize for swallowing the dictionary. Then she said shyly, "It's very interesting."

She would have to spend the night at Cela McKinney's. Cela McKinney was her father's cousin. She had married a hotel manager and thought she had gone up in the world. But the hotel manager came home one day and sat down on the dining-room floor between two chairs and said, "I am never going to leave this house again." Nothing unusual had happened, he had just decided not to go out of the house again, and he didn't, until he died. That had made Cela McKinney odd and nervous. She locked her doors at eight o'clock. She was also very stingy. Supper was usually oatmeal porridge, with raisins. Her house was dark and narrow and smelled like a bank.

The train was filling up. At Brantford a man asked if she would mind if he sat down beside her.

"It's cooler out than you'd think," he said. He offered her part of his newspaper. She said no thanks.

Then, lest he think her rude, she said it really was cooler. She went on looking out the window at the spring morning. There was no snow left, down here. The trees and bushes seemed to have a paler bark than they did at home. Even the sunlight looked different. It was as different from home, here, as the coast of the Mediterranean would be, or the valleys of California.

"Filthy windows, you'd think they'd take more care," the man said. "Do you   30
travel much by train?"

She said no.

Water was lying in the fields. He nodded at it and said there was a lot this year.

"Heavy snows."

She noticed his saying "snows," a poetic-sounding word. Anyone at home would have said "snow."

"I had an unusual experience the other day. I was driving out in the country. In   35
fact, I was on my way to see one of my parishioners, a lady with a heart condition—"

She looked quickly at his collar. He was wearing an ordinary shirt and tie and a dark-blue suit.

"Oh, yes," he said. "I'm a United Church minister. But I don't always wear my uniform. I wear it for preaching in. I'm off duty today.

"Well, as I said, I was driving through the country and I saw some Canada geese down on a pond, and I took another look, and there were some swans down with them. A whole great flock of swans. What a lovely sight they were. They would be on their spring migration, I expect, heading up North. What a spectacle. I never saw anything like it."

Rose was unable to think appreciatively of the wild swans because she was afraid he was going to lead the conversation from them to Nature in general and then to God, the way a minister would feel obliged to do. But he did not, he stopped with the swans.

"A very fine sight. You would have enjoyed them."   40

He was between fifty and sixty years old, Rose thought. He was short, and energetic-looking, with a square ruddy face and bright waves of gray hair combed straight up from his forehead. When she realized he was not going to mention God she felt she ought to show her gratitude.

She said they must have been lovely.

"It wasn't even a regular pond, it was only some water lying in a field. It was just luck the water was lying there and they came down and I came driving by at the right time. Just luck. They come in at the east end of Lake Erie, I think. But I never was lucky enough to see them before."

She turned by degrees to the window, and he returned to his paper. She remained slightly smiling, so as not to seem rude, not to seem to be rejecting conversation altogether. The morning really was cool, and she had taken down her coat off the hook where she put it when she first got on the train; she had spread it over herself, like a lap robe. She had set her purse on the floor when the minister sat down, to give him room. He took the sections of the paper apart, shaking and rustling them in a leisurely, rather showy way. He seemed to her the sort of person who does everything in a showy way. A ministerial way. He brushed aside the sections he didn't want at the moment. A corner of newspaper touched her leg, just at the edge of her coat.

She thought for some time that it was the paper. Then she said to herself, What   45
if it is a hand? That was the kind of thing she could imagine. She would sometimes look at men's hands, at the fuzz on their forearms, their concentrating profiles. She would think about everything they could do. Even the stupid ones. For instance the driver-salesman who brought the bread to Flo's store. The ripeness and confidence of manner, the settled mixture of ease and alertness with which he handled the bread truck. A fold of mature belly over the belt did not displease her. Another time she had her eye on the French teacher at school. Not a Frenchman at all, really, his name was McLaren, but Rose thought teaching French had rubbed off on him, made him look like one. Quick and sallow; sharp shoulders; hooked nose and sad eyes. She saw him lapping and coiling his way through slow pleasures, a perfect autocrat of indulgences. She had a considerable longing to be somebody's object. Pounded, pleasured, reduced, exhausted.

But what if it was a hand? What if it really was a hand? She shifted slightly, moved as much as she could toward the window. Her imagination seemed to have created this reality, a reality she was not prepared for at all. She found it alarming. She was concentrating on that leg, that bit of skin with the stocking over it. She could not bring herself to look. Was there a pressure, or was there not? She shifted again. Her legs had been, and remained, tightly closed. It was. It was a hand. It was a hand's pressure.

Please don't. That was what she tried to say. She shaped the words in her mind, tried them out, then couldn't get them past her lips. Why was that? The embarrassment, was it, the fear that people might hear? People were all around them, the seats were full.

It was not only that.

She did manage to look at him, not raising her head but turning it cautiously. He had tilted his seat back and closed his eyes. There was his dark-blue suit sleeve, disappearing under the newspaper. He had arranged the paper so that it overlapped Rose's coat. His hand was underneath, simply resting, as if flung out in sleep.

Now, Rose could have shifted the newspaper and removed her coat. If he was   50
not asleep, he would have been obliged to draw back his hand. If he was asleep, if he did not draw it back, she could have whispered *Excuse me* and set his hand firmly on his own knee. This solution, so obvious and foolproof, did not occur to her. And she would have to wonder, Why not? The minister's hand was not, or not yet, at all welcome to her. It made her feel uncomfortable, resentful, slightly disgusted, trapped, and wary. But she could not take charge of it, to reject it. She could not insist that it was there, when he seemed to be insisting that it was not. How could she declare him responsible, when he lay there so harmless and trusting, resting himself before his busy day, with such a pleased and healthy face? A man older than her father would be, if he were living, a man used to deference, an appreciator of Nature, delighter in wild swans. If she did say *Please don't* she was sure he would ignore her, as if overlooking some silliness or impoliteness on her part. She knew that as soon as she said it she would hope he had not heard.

But there was more to it than that. Curiosity. More constant, more imperious, than any lust. A lust in itself, that will make you draw back and wait, wait too long, risk almost anything, just to see what will happen. *To see what will happen.*

The hand began, over the next several miles, the most delicate, the most timid, pressures and investigations. Not asleep. Or if he was, his hand wasn't. She did feel disgust. She felt a faint, wandering nausea. She thought of flesh: lumps of flesh, pink snouts, fat tongues, blunt fingers, all on their way trotting and creeping and lolling and rubbing, looking for their comfort. She thought of cats in heat rubbing themselves along the top of board fences, yowling with their miserable complaint. It was pitiful, infantile, this itching and shoving and squeezing. Spongy tissues, inflamed membranes, tormented nerve-ends, shameful smells; humiliation.

All that was starting. His hand, that she wouldn't ever have wanted to hold, that she wouldn't have squeezed back, his stubborn patient hand was able, after all, to get the ferns to rustle and the streams to flow, to waken a sly luxuriance.

Nevertheless, she would rather not. She would still rather not. Please remove this, she said out the window. Stop it, please, she said to the stumps and barns. The hand moved up her leg past the top of her stocking to her bare skin, had moved higher, under her suspender, reached her underpants and the lower part of her belly. Her legs were still crossed, pinched together. While her legs stayed crossed she could lay claim to innocence, she had not admitted anything. She could still believe that she would stop this in a minute. Nothing was going to happen, nothing more. Her legs were never going to open.

But they were. They were. As the train crossed the Niagara Escarpment above   55
Dundas, as they looked down at the preglacial valley, the silver-wooded rubble of little hills, as they came sliding down to the shores of Lake Ontario, she would make this slow, and silent, and definite declaration, perhaps disappointing as much as

satisfying the hand's owner. He would not lift his eyelids, his face would not alter, his fingers would not hesitate, but would go powerfully and discreetly to work. Invasion, and welcome, and sunlight flashing far and wide on the lake water; miles of bare orchards stirring round Burlington.

This was disgrace, this was beggary. But what harm in that, we say to ourselves at such moments, what harm in anything, the worse the better, as we ride the cold wave of greed, of greedy assent. A stranger's hand, or root vegetables or humble kitchen tools that people tell jokes about; the world is tumbling with innocent-seeming objects ready to declare themselves, slippery and obliging. She was careful of her breathing. She could not believe this. Victim and accomplice she was borne past Glassco's Jams and Marmalades, past the big pulsating pipes of oil refineries. They glided into suburbs where bedsheets, and towels used to wipe up intimate stains, flapped leeringly on the clotheslines, where even the children seemed to be frolicking lewdly in the schoolyards, and the very truck drivers stopped at the railway crossings must be thrusting their thumbs gleefully into curled hands. Such cunning antics now, such popular visions. The gates and towers of the Exhibition Grounds came into view, the painted domes and pillars floated marvelously against her eyelids' rosy sky. Then flew apart in celebration. You could have had such a flock of birds, wild swans, even, wakened under one big dome together, exploding from it, taking to the sky.

She bit the edge of her tongue. Very soon the conductor passed through the train, to stir the travellers, warn them back to life.

In the darkness under the station the United Church minister, refreshed, opened his eyes and got his paper folded together, then asked if she would like some help with her coat. His gallantry was self-satisfied, dismissive. No, said Rose, with a sore tongue. He hurried out of the train ahead of her. She did not see him in the station. She never saw him again in her life. But he remained on call, so to speak, for years and years, ready to slip into place at a critical moment, without even any regard, later on, for husband or lovers. What recommended him? She could never understand it. His simplicity, his arrogance, his perversely appealing lack of handsomeness, even of ordinary grown-up masculinity? When he stood up she saw that he was shorter even than she had thought, that his face was pink and shiny, that there was something crude and pushy and childish about him.

Was he a minister, really, or was that only what he said? Flo had mentioned people who were not ministers, dressed up as if they were. Not real ministers dressed as if they were not. Or, stranger still, men who were not real ministers pretending to be real but dressed as if they were not. But that she had come as close as she had, to what could happen, was an unwelcome thing. Rose walked through Union Station feeling the little bag with the ten dollars rubbing at her, knew she would feel it all day long, rubbing its reminder against her skin.

She couldn't stop getting Flo's messages, even with that. She remembered, because she was in Union Station, that there was a girl named Mavis working here, in the gift shop, when Flo was working in the coffee shop. Mavis had warts on her eyelids that looked like they were going to turn into sties but they didn't, they went away. Maybe she had them removed, Flo didn't ask. She was very good-looking, without them. There was a movie star in those days she looked a lot like. The movie star's name was Frances Farmer.

Frances Farmer. Rose had never heard of her.

That was the name. And Mavis went and bought herself a big hat that dipped over one eye and a dress entirely made of lace. She went off for the weekend to Georgian Bay, to a resort up there. She booked herself in under the name of Florence Farmer. To give everybody the idea she was really the other one, Frances Farmer, but calling herself Florence because she was on holiday and didn't want to be recognized. She had a little cigarette holder that was black and mother-of-pearl. She could have been arrested, Flo said. For the *nerve*.

Rose almost went over to the gift shop, to see if Mavis was still there and if she could recognize her. She thought it would be an especially fine thing to manage a transformation like that. To dare it; to get away with it, to enter on preposterous adventures in your own, but newly named, skin.

IRAN

Marjane Satrapi

Kim Wilde   2000

Marjane Satrapi

Marjane Satrapi (b. 1969) won wide acclaim for her autobiographical graphic novel, Persepolis (2000), which portrayed her childhood in Tehran after the Iranian Revolution of 1979. As depicted in Persepolis and its subsequent volumes, the revolution formed the Islamic Republic of Iran, in which women's rights were largely revoked and freedom of speech suppressed. Satrapi's parents were politically active—her father, an engineer, and her mother, a clothing designer, had supported the overthrow of the monarchy, but they were distressed by the Islamic fundamentalists that rose to power. Much of the early story told in Persepolis concerns Satrapi's uncle Anoosh, with whom she was very close, and his imprisonment and execution at the hands of the government. "Kim Wilde" takes place a year after Anoosh was killed and buried in an unmarked prison grave. Satrapi, an adolescent at the time of Anoosh's execution, was deeply affected by the event. After several run-ins with the Iranian authorities for misbehavior and violating the new modesty codes, Satrapi was sent by her parents, who were concerned for their daughter's safety, to boarding school in Austria. The sequel to Persepolis concerns that experience. Satrapi has spent most of her adult life in France. Along with the four volumes of Persepolis—which was adapted into a 2007 Oscar-nominated film that Satrapi co-wrote and co-directed—her other works include the graphic novel Chicken with Plums (2004) and an illustrated fairy tale, The Sigh (2011).

KIM WILDE

A YEAR AFTER MY UNCLE DIED, THE BORDERS WERE REOPENED. MY PARENTS RAN TO GET PASSPORTS.

LOOK AT THE LAST PAGE: "IT IS STRICTLY FORBIDDEN TO TRAVEL IN OCCUPIED PALESTINE WITH THIS DOCUMENT."

MY GOD. JUST LOOK AT ME IN THIS PICTURE, WITH THE SCARF ON MY HEAD.

CAN I SEE?

SHE SURE DIDN'T LOOK VERY HAPPY. IN FACT, SHE WAS UNRECOGNIZABLE.

NAME: CHALKH TAJI
DATE OF BIRTH 12·03·1947
IRAN

AS SOON AS I GET MY PASSPORT, WE'LL GO ON A BIG TRIP!

WELL, ACTUALLY...

WE WANT TO SPEND SOME TIME TOGETHER, JUST THE TWO OF US, FOR A FEW DAYS.

WHERE?

TURKEY.

BAH...TURKEY'S FOR THE BIRDS. ONLY UNCOOL PEOPLE GO TO TURKEY. IF YOU'RE TAKING A TRIP, WHY NOT GO TO EUROPE OR THE UNITED STATES?!...

IF YOU WANT US TO BRING YOU BACK SOME PRESENTS, JUST ASK.

WHAT CAN YOU BRING ME BACK FROM TURKEY? SHISH-KEBABS?

LISTEN MARJI, WHERE DO YOU THINK ALL THE HIP STUFF YOU LIKE COMES FROM?

DURING THE WAR, THERE WERE NO IMPORTS FROM THE WEST.

A DENIM JACKET, CHOCOLATE, A POSTER, NO, TWO POSTERS. ONE OF KIM WILDE AND ONE OF IRON MAIDEN.

IRON MAIDEN? THOSE FOUR BRUTES?

THEY'RE NOT BRUTES. I REALLY LIKE WHAT THEY DO.

YOU LIKE THAT?

I LOVE IT.

SEE, MOM?

SHE TORE OUT THE LINING.

THEN, SHE PLACED THE TWO POSTERS BEHIND IT...

...AND THEN SEWED IT BACK IN.

I PUT MY POSTERS UP IN MY ROOM.

IRON MAIDEN

KIM WILDE

I PUT MY 1983 NIKES ON ...

... AND MY DENIM JACKET WITH THE MICHAEL JACKSON BUTTON, AND OF COURSE, MY HEADSCARF.

SO WHAT DO YOU THINK?

NICE! VERY CUTE!

OK, I'M GOING OUT.

WHERE?

TO BUY SOME TAPES.

WHERE?

NOT FAR. ON GANDHI AVENUE.

BE BACK IN AN HOUR!

I'LL BE BACK IN TWO HOURS.

FOR AN IRANIAN MOTHER, MY MOM WAS VERY PERMISSIVE. I ONLY KNEW TWO OR THREE OTHER GIRLS WHO COULD GO OUT ALONE AT THIRTEEN.

FOR A YEAR NOW, THE FOOD SHORTAGE HAD BEEN RESOLVED BY THE GROWTH OF THE BLACK MARKET. HOWEVER, FINDING TAPES WAS A LITTLE MORE COMPLICATED. ON GANDHI AVENUE YOU COULD FIND THEM SOMETIMES.

THEY WERE GUARDIANS OF THE REVOLUTION, THE WOMEN'S BRANCH. THIS GROUP HAD BEEN ADDED IN 1982, TO ARREST WOMEN WHO WERE IMPROPERLY VEILED. (LIKE ME, FOR EXAMPLE.)

AT THE COMMITTEE, THEY DIDN'T HAVE TO INFORM MY PARENTS. THEY COULD DETAIN ME FOR HOURS, OR FOR DAYS. I COULD BE WHIPPED. IN SHORT, ANYTHING COULD HAPPEN TO ME. IT WAS TIME FOR ACTION.

I'M SORRY MA'AM! I'LL NEVER DO IT AGAIN...

GET IN THE CAR!

MA'AM, MY MOTHER'S DEAD. MY STEPMOTHER IS REALLY CRUEL AND IF I DON'T GO HOME RIGHT AWAY, SHE'LL KILL ME...

SHE'LL BURN ME WITH THE CLOTHES IRON!

SHE'LL MAKE MY FATHER PUT ME IN AN ORPHANAGE

MAYBE SHE BELIEVED ME, MAYBE SHE JUST PRETENDED TO. BUT, MIRACULOUSLY, SHE LET ME GO.

BACK HOME...

MARJI! WHAT HAPPENED? HAVE YOU BEEN CRYING?

NO MOM. I'M JUST TIRED. I'M GOING TO MY ROOM.

THERE WAS NO WAY I COULD TELL THE TRUTH. SHE NEVER WOULD HAVE LET ME GO OUT ALONE AGAIN.

I GOT OFF PRETTY EASY, CONSIDERING. THE GUARDIANS OF THE REVOLUTION DIDN'T FIND MY TAPES.

♫ WE'RE THE KIDS IN AMERICA WHOAO ♫

TO EACH HIS OWN WAY OF CALMING DOWN.

STORIES FOR
FURTHER READING

*The novel tends to tell us everything, whereas the short
story tells us only one thing and that intensely.*

—V. S. PRITCHETT

Sherman Alexie

This Is What It Means to Say Phoenix, Arizona   1993

Sherman Alexie

*Sherman Alexie was born in 1966 on the Spokane
Indian Reservation in Wellpinit, Washington.
Hydrocephalic at birth, he underwent surgery at
the age of six months. At first he was expected not
to survive; when that prognosis proved wrong,
it was predicted, again wrongly, that he would be
severely mentally disabled. Alexie attended Gon-
zaga University in Spokane and graduated from
Washington State University with a degree in
American studies. His first book, a collection of
poems called* The Business of Fancydancing,
*appeared in 1991, and he has published pro-
lifically since then, averaging a book a year. He is the author of several volumes of
poetry as well as five collections of stories—*The Lone Ranger and Tonto Fistfight in Heaven *(1993),* The Toughest Indian in the World *(2000),* Ten Little
Indians *(2003),* War Dances *(2009), which won the PEN/Faulkner Award, and*
Blasphemy *(2012)—and three novels—*Reservation Blues *(1995),* Indian Killer
(1996), Flight *(2007), and the semi-autobiographical novel depicting his adolescent
years,* The Absolutely True Diary of a Part-Time Indian *(2007), which won a
National Book Award. A memoir of his childhood,* You Don't Have to Say You
Love Me, *appeared in 2017. In addition to his writing, Alexie won the World Heavy-
weight Poetry Bout competition an unprecedented four consecutive times (1998–
2001); he has appeared on television discussion programs hosted by Bill Maher, Bill
Moyers, and Jim Lehrer (a 1998 "Dialogue on Race" whose participants also included
President Bill Clinton); he has performed frequently as a stand-up comedian; and he
co-produced and wrote the 1998 feature film* Smoke Signals, *based on "This Is What
It Means to Say Phoenix, Arizona." Alexie lives with his wife and two sons in Seattle,
Washington.*

Just after Victor lost his job at the BIA,° he also found out that his father had died of a heart attack in Phoenix, Arizona. Victor hadn't seen his father in a few years, only talked to him on the telephone once or twice, but there still was a genetic pain, which was soon to be pain as real and immediate as a broken bone.

Victor didn't have any money. Who does have money on a reservation, except the cigarette and fireworks salespeople? His father had a savings account waiting to be claimed, but Victor needed to find a way to get to Phoenix. Victor's mother was just as poor as he was, and the rest of his family didn't have any use at all for him. So Victor called the Tribal Council.

"Listen," Victor said. "My father just died. I need some money to get to Phoenix to make arrangements."

"Now, Victor," the council said. "You know we're having a difficult time financially."

"But I thought the council had special funds set aside for stuff like this." 5

"Now, Victor, we do have some money available for the proper return of tribal members' bodies. But I don't think we have enough to bring your father all the way back from Phoenix."

"Well," Victor said. "It ain't going to cost all that much. He had to be cremated. Things were kind of ugly. He died of a heart attack in his trailer and nobody found him for a week. It was really hot, too. You get the picture."

"Now, Victor, we're sorry for your loss and the circumstances. But we can really only afford to give you one hundred dollars."

"That's not even enough for a plane ticket."

"Well, you might consider driving down to Phoenix." 10

"I don't have a car. Besides, I was going to drive my father's pickup back up here."

"Now, Victor," the council said. "We're sure there is somebody who could drive you to Phoenix. Or is there somebody who could lend you the rest of the money?"

"You know there ain't nobody around with that kind of money."

"Well, we're sorry, Victor, but that's the best we can do."

Victor accepted the Tribal Council's offer. What else could he do? So he 15 signed the proper papers, picked up his check, and walked over to the Trading Post to cash it.

While Victor stood in line, he watched Thomas Builds-the-Fire standing near the magazine rack, talking to himself. Like he always did. Thomas was a storyteller that nobody wanted to listen to. That's like being a dentist in a town where everybody has false teeth.

Victor and Thomas Builds-the-Fire were the same age, had grown up and played in the dirt together. Ever since Victor could remember, it was Thomas who always had something to say.

Once, when they were seven years old, when Victor's father still lived with the family, Thomas closed his eyes and told Victor this story: "Your father's heart is weak. He is afraid of his own family. He is afraid of you. Late at night he sits in the dark. Watches the television until there's nothing but that white noise. Sometimes he feels like he wants to buy a motorcycle and ride away. He wants to run and hide. He doesn't want to be found."

Thomas Builds-the-Fire had known that Victor's father was going to leave, knew it before anyone. Now Victor stood in the Trading Post with a one-hundred-dollar

BIA: Bureau of Indian Affairs, a federal agency responsible for management of Indian lands and concerns.

check in his hand, wondering if Thomas knew that Victor's father was dead, if he knew what was going to happen next.

Just then Thomas looked at Victor, smiled, and walked over to him.   20

"Victor, I'm sorry about your father," Thomas said.

"How did you know about it?" Victor asked.

"I heard it on the wind. I heard it from the birds. I felt it in the sunlight. Also, your mother was just in here crying."

"Oh," Victor said and looked around the Trading Post. All the other Indians stared, surprised that Victor was even talking to Thomas. Nobody talked to Thomas anymore because he told the same damn stories over and over again. Victor was embarrassed, but he thought that Thomas might be able to help him. Victor felt a sudden need for tradition.

"I can lend you the money you need," Thomas said suddenly. "But you have to   25
take me with you."

"I can't take your money," Victor said. "I mean, I haven't hardly talked to you in years. We're not really friends anymore."

"I didn't say we were friends. I said you had to take me with you."

"Let me think about it."

Victor went home with his one hundred dollars and sat at the kitchen table. He held his head in his hands and thought about Thomas Builds-the-Fire, remembered little details, tears and scars, the bicycle they shared for a summer, so many stories.

Thomas Builds-the-Fire sat on the bicycle, waited in Victor's yard. He was ten   30
years old and skinny. His hair was dirty because it was the Fourth of July.

"Victor," Thomas yelled. "Hurry up. We're going to miss the fireworks."

After a few minutes, Victor ran out of his house, jumped the porch railing, and landed gracefully on the sidewalk.

"And the judges award him a 9.95, the highest score of the summer," Thomas said, clapped, laughed.

"That was perfect, cousin," Victor said. "And it's my turn to ride the bike."

Thomas gave up the bike and they headed for the fairgrounds. It was nearly dark   35
and the fireworks were about to start.

"You know," Thomas said. "It's strange how us Indians celebrate the Fourth of July. It ain't like it was *our* independence everybody was fighting for."

"You think about things too much," Victor said. "It's just supposed to be fun. Maybe Junior will be there."

"Which Junior? Everybody on this reservation is named Junior."

And they both laughed.

The fireworks were small, hardly more than a few bottle rockets and a fountain.   40
But it was enough for two Indian boys. Years later, they would need much more.

Afterwards, sitting in the dark, fighting off mosquitoes, Victor turned to Thomas Builds-the-Fire.

"Hey," Victor said. "Tell me a story."

Thomas closed his eyes and told this story: "There were these two Indian boys who wanted to be warriors. But it was too late to be warriors in the old way. All the horses were gone. So the two Indian boys stole a car and drove to the city. They parked the stolen car in front of the police station and then hitchhiked back home to the reservation. When they got back, all their friends cheered and their parents' eyes shone with pride. *You were very brave*, everybody said to the two Indian boys. *Very brave.*"

"Ya-hey," Victor said. "That's a good one. I wish I could be a warrior."

"Me, too," Thomas said.   45

They went home together in the dark, Thomas on the bike now, Victor on foot. They walked through shadows and light from streetlamps.

"We've come a long ways," Thomas said. "We have outdoor lighting."

"All I need is the stars," Victor said. "And besides, you still think about things too much."

They separated then, each headed for home, both laughing all the way.

Victor sat at his kitchen table. He counted his one hundred dollars again and   50
again. He knew he needed more to make it to Phoenix and back. He knew he needed Thomas Builds-the-Fire. So he put his money in his wallet and opened the front door to find Thomas on the porch.

"Ya-hey, Victor," Thomas said. "I knew you'd call me."

Thomas walked into the living room and sat down on Victor's favorite chair.

"I've got some money saved up," Thomas said. "It's enough to get us down there, but you have to get us back."

"I've got this hundred dollars," Victor said. "And my dad had a savings account I'm going to claim."

"How much in your dad's account?"   55

"Enough. A few hundred."

"Sounds good. When we leaving?"

When they were fifteen and had long since stopped being friends, Victor and Thomas got into a fistfight. That is, Victor was really drunk and beat Thomas up for no reason at all. All the other Indian boys stood around and watched it happen. Junior was there and so were Lester, Seymour, and a lot of others. The beating might have gone on until Thomas was dead if Norma Many Horses hadn't come along and stopped it.

"Hey, you boys," Norma yelled and jumped out of her car. "Leave him alone."

If it had been someone else, even another man, the Indian boys would've just   60
ignored the warnings. But Norma was a warrior. She was powerful. She could have picked up any two of the boys and smashed their skulls together. But worse than that, she would have dragged them all over to some tipi and made them listen to some elder tell a dusty old story.

The Indian boys scattered, and Norma walked over to Thomas and picked him up.

"Hey, little man, are you okay?" she asked.

Thomas gave her a thumbs up.

"Why they always picking on you?"

Thomas shook his head, closed his eyes, but no stories came to him, no words or   65
music. He just wanted to go home, to lie in his bed and let his dreams tell his stories for him.

Thomas Builds-the-Fire and Victor sat next to each other in the airplane, coach section. A tiny white woman had the window seat. She was busy twisting her body into pretzels. She was flexible.

"I have to ask," Thomas said, and Victor closed his eyes in embarrassment.

"Don't," Victor said.

"Excuse me, miss," Thomas asked. "Are you a gymnast or something?"

"There's no something about it," she said. "I was first alternate on the 1980   70
Olympic team."

"Really?" Thomas asked.

"Really."

"I mean, you used to be a world-class athlete?" Thomas asked.

"My husband still thinks I am."

Thomas Builds-the-Fire smiled. She was a mental gymnast, too. She pulled her   75
leg straight up against her body so that she could've kissed her kneecap.

"I wish I could do that," Thomas said.

Victor was ready to jump out of the plane. Thomas, that crazy Indian storyteller
with ratty old braids and broken teeth, was flirting with a beautiful Olympic gymnast.
Nobody back home on the reservation would ever believe it.

"Well," the gymnast said. "It's easy. Try it."

Thomas grabbed at his leg and tried to pull it up into the same position as the
gymnast. He couldn't even come close, which made Victor and the gymnast laugh.

"Hey," she asked. "You two are Indian, right?"   80

"Full-blood," Victor said.

"Not me," Thomas said. "I'm half magician on my mother's side and half clown
on my father's."

They all laughed.

"What are your names?" she asked.

"Victor and Thomas."   85

"Mine is Cathy. Pleased to meet you all."

The three of them talked for the duration of the flight. Cathy the gymnast
complained about the government, how they screwed the 1980 Olympic team by
boycotting.°

"Sounds like you all got a lot in common with Indians," Thomas said.

Nobody laughed.

After the plane landed in Phoenix and they had all found their way to the termi-   90
nal, Cathy the gymnast smiled and waved good-bye.

"She was really nice," Thomas said.

"Yeah, but everybody talks to everybody on airplanes," Victor said. "It's too bad
we can't always be that way."

"You always used to tell me I think too much," Thomas said. "Now it sounds like
you do."

"Maybe I caught it from you."

"Yeah."   95

Thomas and Victor rode in a taxi to the trailer where Victor's father died.

"Listen," Victor said as they stopped in front of the trailer. "I never told you I was
sorry for beating you up that time."

"Oh, it was nothing. We were just kids and you were drunk."

"Yeah, but I'm still sorry."

"That's all right."   100

___

they screwed the 1980 Olympic team by boycotting: in an international movement led by the United States at
the direction of President Jimmy Carter, some sixty nations boycotted the 1980 Summer Olympic Games
in Moscow as a protest against the Soviet invasion of Afghanistan in December 1979.

Victor paid for the taxi and the two of them stood in the hot Phoenix summer. They could smell the trailer.

"This ain't going to be nice," Victor said. "You don't have to go in."

"You're going to need help."

Victor walked to the front door and opened it. The stink rolled out and made them both gag. Victor's father had lain in that trailer for a week in hundred-degree temperatures before anyone found him. And the only reason anyone found him was because of the smell. They needed dental records to identify him. That's exactly what the coroner said. They needed dental records.

"Oh, man," Victor said. "I don't know if I can do this."   105

"Well, then don't."

"But there might be something valuable in there."

"I thought his money was in the bank."

"It is. I was talking about pictures and letters and stuff like that."

"Oh," Thomas said as he held his breath and followed Victor into the trailer.   110

When Victor was twelve, he stepped into an underground wasp nest. His foot was caught in the hole, and no matter how hard he struggled, Victor couldn't pull free. He might have died there, stung a thousand times, if Thomas Builds-the-Fire had not come by.

"Run," Thomas yelled and pulled Victor's foot from the hole. They ran then, hard as they ever had, faster than Billy Mills, faster than Jim Thorpe,° faster than the wasps could fly.

Victor and Thomas ran until they couldn't breathe, ran until it was cold and dark outside, ran until they were lost and it took hours to find their way home. All the way back, Victor counted his stings.

"Seven," Victor said. "My lucky number."

Victor didn't find much to keep in the trailer. Only a photo album and a stereo.   115
Everything else had that smell stuck in it or was useless anyway.

"I guess this is all," Victor said. "It ain't much."

"Better than nothing," Thomas said.

"Yeah, and I do have the pickup."

"Yeah," Thomas said. "It's in good shape."

"Dad was good about that stuff."   120

"Yeah, I remember your dad."

"Really?" Victor asked. "What do you remember?"

Thomas Builds-the-Fire closed his eyes and told this story: "I remember when I had this dream that told me to go to Spokane, to stand by the Falls in the middle of the city and wait for a sign. I knew I had to go there but I didn't have a car. Didn't have a license. I was only thirteen. So I walked all the way, took me all day, and I finally made it to the Falls. I stood there for an hour waiting. Then your dad came walking up. *What the hell are you doing here?* he asked me. I said, *Waiting for a vision.* Then your father said,

---

Billy Mills . . . Jim Thorpe: William Mervin "Billy" Mills (born 1938), a member of the Sioux tribe, won a gold medal in the 10,000-meter run at the 1964 Summer Olympic Games in Tokyo, Japan. Jacobus Franciscus "Jim" Thorpe (1888–1953), of the Sac and Fox tribe, is widely regarded as one of the greatest American athletes of the twentieth century; he won gold medals in the pentathlon and decathlon at the 1912 Summer Olympic Games in Stockholm, Sweden. He also played professional football, baseball, and basketball.

All you're going to get here is mugged. So he drove me over to Denny's, bought me dinner, and then drove me home to the reservation. For a long time I was mad because I thought my dreams had lied to me. But they didn't. Your dad was my vision. *Take care of each other* is what my dreams were saying. *Take care of each other.*"

Victor was quiet for a long time. He searched his mind for memories of his father, found the good ones, found a few bad ones, added it all up, and smiled.

"My father never told me about finding you in Spokane," Victor said.   125

"He said he wouldn't tell anybody. Didn't want me to get in trouble. But he said I had to watch out for you as part of the deal."

"Really?"

"Really. Your father said you would need the help. He was right."

"That's why you came down here with me, isn't it?" Victor asked.

"I came because of your father."   130

Victor and Thomas climbed into the pickup, drove over to the bank, and claimed the three hundred dollars in the savings account.

Thomas Builds-the-Fire could fly.

Once, he jumped off the roof of the tribal school and flapped his arms like a crazy eagle. And he flew. For a second, he hovered, suspended above all the other Indian boys who were too smart or too scared to jump.

"He's flying," Junior yelled, and Seymour was busy looking for the trick wires or mirrors. But it was real. As real as the dirt when Thomas lost altitude and crashed to the ground.

He broke his arm in two places.   135

"He broke his wing," Victor chanted, and the other Indian boys joined in, made it a tribal song.

"He broke his wing, he broke his wing, he broke his wing," all the Indian boys chanted as they ran off, flapping their wings, wishing they could fly, too. They hated Thomas for his courage, his brief moment as a bird. Everybody has dreams about flying. Thomas flew.

One of his dreams came true for just a second, just enough to make it real.

Victor's father, his ashes, fit in one wooden box with enough left over to fill a cardboard box.

"He always was a big man," Thomas said.   140

Victor carried part of his father and Thomas carried the rest out to the pickup. They set him down carefully behind the seats, put a cowboy hat on the wooden box and a Dodgers cap on the cardboard box. That's the way it was supposed to be.

"Ready to head back home," Victor asked.

"It's going to be a long drive."

"Yeah, take a couple days, maybe."

"We can take turns," Thomas said.   145

"Okay," Victor said, but they didn't take turns. Victor drove for sixteen hours straight north, made it halfway up Nevada toward home before he finally pulled over.

"Hey, Thomas," Victor said. "You got to drive for a while."

"Okay."

Thomas Builds-the-Fire slid behind the wheel and started off down the road. All through Nevada, Thomas and Victor had been amazed at the lack of animal life, at the absence of water, of movement.

"Where is everything?" Victor had asked more than once. 150

Now when Thomas was finally driving they saw the first animal, maybe the only animal in Nevada. It was a long-eared jackrabbit.

"Look," Victor yelled. "It's alive."

Thomas and Victor were busy congratulating themselves on their discovery when the jackrabbit darted out into the road and under the wheels of the pickup.

"Stop the goddamn car," Victor yelled, and Thomas did stop, backed the pickup to the dead jackrabbit.

"Oh, man, he's dead," Victor said as he looked at the squashed animal. 155

"Really dead."

"The only thing alive in this whole state and we just killed it."

"I don't know," Thomas said. "I think it was suicide."

Victor looked around the desert, sniffed the air, felt the emptiness and loneliness, and nodded his head.

"Yeah," Victor said. "It had to be suicide." 160

"I can't believe this," Thomas said. "You drive for a thousand miles and there ain't even any bugs smashed on the windshield. I drive for ten seconds and kill the only living thing in Nevada."

"Yeah," Victor said. "Maybe I should drive."

"Maybe you should."

Thomas Builds-the-Fire walked through the corridors of the tribal school by himself. Nobody wanted to be anywhere near him because of all those stories. Story after story.

Thomas closed his eyes and this story came to him: "We are all given one thing 165 by which our lives are measured, one determination. Mine are the stories which can change or not change the world. It doesn't matter which as long as I continue to tell the stories. My father, he died on Okinawa in World War II, died fighting for this country, which had tried to kill him for years. My mother, she died giving birth to me, died while I was still inside her. She pushed me out into the world with her last breath. I have no brothers or sisters. I have only my stories which came to me before I even had the words to speak. I learned a thousand stories before I took my first thousand steps. They are all I have. It's all I can do."

Thomas Builds-the-Fire told his stories to all those who would stop and listen. He kept telling them long after people had stopped listening.

Victor and Thomas made it back to the reservation just as the sun was rising. It was the beginning of a new day on earth, but the same old shit on the reservation.

"Good morning," Thomas said.

"Good morning."

The tribe was waking up, ready for work, eating breakfast, reading the newspa- 170 per, just like everybody else does. Willene LeBret was out in her garden wearing a bathrobe. She waved when Thomas and Victor drove by.

"Crazy Indians made it," she said to herself and went back to her roses.

Victor stopped the pickup in front of Thomas Builds-the-Fire's HUD house.° They both yawned, stretched a little, shook dust from their bodies.

HUD house: housing subsidized by the U.S. Department of Housing and Urban Development.

"I'm tired," Victor said.

"Of everything," Thomas added.

They both searched for words to end the journey. Victor needed to thank   175
Thomas for his help, for the money, and make the promise to pay it all back.

"Don't worry about the money," Thomas said. "It don't make any difference
anyhow."

"Probably not, enit?"°

"Nope."

Victor knew that Thomas would remain the crazy storyteller who talked
to dogs and cars, who listened to the wind and pine trees. Victor knew that he
couldn't really be friends with Thomas, even after all that had happened. It was
cruel but it was real. As real as the ashes, as Victor's father, sitting behind the
seats.

"I know how it is," Thomas said. "I know you ain't going to treat me any   180
better than you did before. I know your friends would give you too much shit
about it."

Victor was ashamed of himself. Whatever happened to the tribal ties, the sense
of community? The only real thing he shared with anybody was a bottle and broken
dreams. He owed Thomas something, anything.

"Listen," Victor said and handed Thomas the cardboard box which contained
half of his father. "I want you to have this."

Thomas took the ashes and smiled, closed his eyes, and told this story: "I'm going
to travel to Spokane Falls one last time and toss these ashes into the water. And your
father will rise like a salmon, leap over the bridge, over me, and find his way home. It
will be beautiful. His teeth will shine like silver, like a rainbow. He will rise, Victor,
he will rise."

Victor smiled.

"I was planning on doing the same thing with my half," Victor said. "But I   185
didn't imagine my father looking anything like a salmon. I thought it'd be like
cleaning the attic or something. Like letting things go after they've stopped having
any use."

"Nothing stops, cousin," Thomas said. "Nothing stops."

Thomas Builds-the-Fire got out of the pickup and walked up his driveway. Victor
started the pickup and began the drive home.

"Wait," Thomas yelled suddenly from his porch. "I just got to ask one favor."

Victor stopped the pickup, leaned out the window, and shouted back. "What do
you want?"

"Just one time when I'm telling a story somewhere, why don't you stop and lis-   190
ten?" Thomas asked.

"Just once?"

"Just once."

Victor waved his arms to let Thomas know that the deal was good. It was
a fair trade, and that was all Victor had ever wanted from his whole life. So Victor
drove his father's pickup toward home while Thomas went into his house,
closed the door behind him, and heard a new story come to him in the silence
afterwards.

---

enit: slang for "isn't it," used primarily by Native Americans and British people.

T. Coraghessan Boyle

Greasy Lake

1985

T. Coraghessan Boyle (the T. stands for Tom) was born in 1948 in Peekskill, New York, the son of Irish immigrants. He grew up, he recalls, "as a sort of pampered punk" who did not read a book until he was eighteen. After a brief period as a high school teacher, he studied in the University of Iowa Writers' Workshop, submitting a collection of stories for his Phd. His stories in Esquire, Paris Review, *the* Atlantic, *and other magazines quickly won him notice for their outrageous macabre humor and bizarre inventiveness. Boyle has published many volumes of short stories, including* Greasy Lake *(1985),* T. C. Boyle Stories *(1998), and* Tooth and Claw *(2005). He has also published more than a dozen novels that are quite unlike anything else in contemporary American fiction. The sub-*

T. Coraghessan Boyle

jects of some Boyle novels reveal his wide-ranging and idiosyncratic interests. Budding Prospects *(1984) is a picaresque romp among adventurous marijuana growers.* East Is East *(1990) is a half-serious, half-comic story of a Japanese fugitive in an American writers' colony.* The Road to Wellville *(1993) takes place in 1907 in a sanitarium run by Dr. John Harvey Kellogg of corn flakes fame, with cameo appearances by Henry Ford, Thomas Edison, and Harvey Firestone. A recent novel—his sixteenth—is* The Terranauts *(2016). Boyle is Distinguished Professor of English at University of Southern California.*

> *It's about a mile down on the dark side of Route 88.*
>
> —BRUCE SPRINGSTEEN

There was a time when courtesy and winning ways went out of style, when it was good to be bad, when you cultivated decadence like a taste. We were all dangerous characters then. We wore torn-up leather jackets, slouched around with toothpicks in our mouths, sniffed glue and ether and what somebody claimed was cocaine. When we wheeled our parents' whining station wagons out onto the street we left a patch of rubber half a block long. We drank gin and grape juice, Tango, Thunderbird, and Bali Hai. We were nineteen. We were bad. We read André Gide° and struck elaborate poses to show that we didn't give a shit about anything. At night, we went up to Greasy Lake.

Through the center of town, up the strip, past the housing developments and shopping malls, street lights giving way to the thin streaming illumination of the headlights, trees crowding the asphalt in a black unbroken wall: that was the way out to Greasy Lake. The Indians had called it Wakan, a reference to the clarity of

---

André Gide: controversial French writer (1869–1951) whose novels, including *The Counterfeiters* and *Lafcadio's Adventures,* often show individuals in conflict with accepted morality.

its waters. Now it was fetid and murky, the mud banks glittering with broken glass and strewn with beer cans and the charred remains of bonfires. There was a single ravaged island a hundred yards from shore, so stripped of vegetation it looked as if the air force had strafed it. We went up to the lake because everyone went there, because we wanted to snuff the rich scent of possibility on the breeze, watch a girl take off her clothes and plunge into the festering murk, drink beer, smoke pot, howl at the stars, savor the incongruous full-throated roar of rock and roll against the primeval susurrus of frogs and crickets. This was nature.

I was there one night, late, in the company of two dangerous characters. Digby wore a gold star in his right ear and allowed his father to pay his tuition at Cornell; Jeff was thinking of quitting school to become a painter/musician/head-shop proprietor. They were both expert in the social graces, quick with a sneer, able to manage a Ford with lousy shocks over a rutted and gutted blacktop road at eighty-five while rolling a joint as compact as a Tootsie Roll Pop stick. They could lounge against a bank of booming speakers and trade "man"s with the best of them or roll out across the dance floor as if their joints worked on bearings. They were slick and quick and they wore their mirror shades at breakfast and dinner, in the shower, in closets and caves. In short, they were bad.

I drove. Digby pounded the dashboard and shouted along with Toots & the Maytals while Jeff hung his head out the window and streaked the side of my mother's Bel Air with vomit. It was early June, the air soft as a hand on your cheek, the third night of summer vacation. The first two nights we'd been out till dawn, looking for something we never found. On this, the third night, we'd cruised the strip sixty-seven times, been in and out of every bar and club we could think of in a twenty-mile radius, stopped twice for bucket chicken and forty-cent hamburgers, debated going to a party at the house of a girl Jeff's sister knew, and chucked two dozen raw eggs at mailboxes and hitchhikers. It was 2:00 A.M.; the bars were closing. There was nothing to do but take a bottle of lemon-flavored gin up to Greasy Lake.

The taillights of a single car winked at us as we swung into the dirt lot with its   5
tufts of weed and washboard corrugations; '57 Chevy, mint, metallic blue. On the far side of the lot, like the exoskeleton of some gaunt chrome insect, a chopper leaned against its kickstand. And that was it for excitement: some junkie halfwit biker and a car freak pumping his girlfriend. Whatever it was we were looking for, we weren't about to find it at Greasy Lake. Not that night.

But then all of a sudden Digby was fighting for the wheel. "Hey, that's Tony Lovett's car! Hey!" he shouted, while I stabbed at the brake pedal and the Bel Air nosed up to the gleaming bumper of the parked Chevy. Digby leaned on the horn, laughing, and instructed me to put my brights on. I flicked on the brights. This was hilarious. A joke. Tony would experience premature withdrawal and expect to be confronted by grim-looking state troopers with flashlights. We hit the horn, strobed the lights, and then jumped out of the car to press our witty faces to Tony's windows; for all we knew we might even catch a glimpse of some little fox's tit, and then we could slap backs with red-faced Tony, roughhouse a little, and go on to new heights of adventure and daring.

The first mistake, the one that opened the whole floodgate, was losing my grip on the keys. In the excitement, leaping from the car with the gin in one hand and a roach clip in the other, I spilled them in the grass—in the dark, rank, mysterious nighttime grass of Greasy Lake. This was a tactical error, as damaging and irreversible in its way as Westmoreland's decision to dig in at Khe Sanh.° I felt it like a jab of intuition, and I stopped there by the open door, peering vaguely into the night that puddled up round my feet.

The second mistake—and this was inextricably bound up with the first—was identifying the car as Tony Lovett's. Even before the very bad character in greasy jeans and engineer boots ripped out of the driver's door, I began to realize that this chrome blue was much lighter than the robin's-egg of Tony's car, and that Tony's car didn't have rear-mounted speakers. Judging from their expressions, Digby and Jeff were privately groping toward the same inevitable and unsettling conclusion as I was.

In any case, there was no reasoning with this bad greasy character—clearly he was a man of action. The first lusty Rockette° kick of his steel-toed boot caught me under the chin, chipped my favorite tooth, and left me sprawled in the dirt. Like a fool, I'd gone down on one knee to comb the stiff hacked grass for the keys, my mind making connections in the most dragged-out, testudineous way, knowing that things had gone wrong, that I was in a lot of trouble, and that the lost ignition key was my grail and my salvation. The three or four succeeding blows were mainly absorbed by my right buttock and the tough piece of bone at the base of my spine.

Meanwhile, Digby vaulted the kissing bumpers and delivered a savage kung-fu   10 blow to the greasy character's collarbone. Digby had just finished a course in martial arts for phys-ed credit and had spent the better part of the past two nights telling us apocryphal tales of Bruce Lee types and of the raw power invested in lightning blows shot from coiled wrists, ankles, and elbows. The greasy character was unimpressed. He merely backed off a step, his face like a Toltec mask, and laid Digby out with a single whistling roundhouse blow . . . but by now Jeff had got into the act, and I was beginning to extricate myself from the dirt, a tinny compound of shock, rage, and impotence wadded in my throat.

Jeff was on the guy's back, biting at his ear. Digby was on the ground, cursing. I went for the tire iron I kept under the driver's seat. I kept it there because bad characters always keep tire irons under the driver's seat, for just such an occasion as this. Never mind that I hadn't been involved in a fight since sixth grade, when a kid with a sleepy eye and two streams of mucus depending from his nostrils hit me in the knee with a Louisville slugger,° never mind that I'd touched the tire iron exactly twice before, to change tires: it was there. And I went for it.

I was terrified. Blood was beating in my ears, my hands were shaking, my heart turning over like a dirtbike in the wrong gear. My antagonist was shirtless, and a single cord of muscle flashed across his chest as he bent forward to peel Jeff from his back like a wet overcoat. "Motherfucker," he spat, over and over, and I was aware in that instant that all four of us—Digby, Jeff, and myself included—were chanting "motherfucker, motherfucker," as if it were a battle cry. (What happened next? the detective asks the murderer from beneath the turned-down brim of his porkpie hat. I don't know, the murderer says, something came over me. Exactly.)

Westmoreland's decision . . . Khe Sanh: General William C. Westmoreland commanded U.S. troops in Vietnam (1964–1968). In late 1967 the North Vietnamese and Viet Cong forces attacked Khe Sanh (or Khesanh) with a show of strength, causing Westmoreland to expend great effort to defend a plateau of relatively little tactical importance.   *Rockette:* member of a dance troupe in the stage show at Radio City Music Hall, New York; the dancers are famous for their ability to kick fast and high with wonderful coordination.   *Louisville slugger:* a brand of baseball bat.

Digby poked the flat of his hand in the bad character's face and I came at him like a kamikaze, mindless, raging, stung with humiliation—the whole thing, from the initial boot in the chin to this murderous primal instant involving no more than sixty hyperventilating, gland-flooding seconds—I came at him and brought the tire iron down across his ear. The effect was instantaneous, astonishing. He was a stunt man and this was Hollywood, he was a big grimacing toothy balloon and I was a man with a straight pin. He collapsed. Wet his pants. Went loose in his boots.

A single second, big as a zeppelin, floated by. We were standing over him in a circle, gritting our teeth, jerking our necks, our limbs and hands and feet twitching with glandular discharges. No one said anything. We just stared down at the guy, the car freak, the lover, the bad greasy character laid low. Digby looked at me; so did Jeff. I was still holding the tire iron, a tuft of hair clinging to the crook like dandelion fluff, like down. Rattled, I dropped it in the dirt, already envisioning the headlines, the pitted faces of the police inquisitors, the gleam of handcuffs, clank of bars, the big black shadows rising from the back of the cell . . . when suddenly a raw torn shriek cut through me like all the juice in all the electric chairs in the country.

It was the fox. She was short, barefoot, dressed in panties and a man's shirt.   15 "Animals!" she screamed, running at us with her fists clenched and wisps of blow-dried hair in her face. There was a silver chain round her ankle, and her toenails flashed in the glare of the headlights. I think it was the toenails that did it. Sure, the gin and the cannabis and even the Kentucky Fried may have had a hand in it, but it was the sight of those flaming toes that set us off—the toad emerging from the loaf in *Virgin Spring*,° lipstick smeared on a child; she was already tainted. We were on her like Bergman's deranged brothers—see no evil, hear none, speak none—panting, wheezing, tearing at her clothes, grabbing for flesh. We were bad characters, and we were scared and hot and three steps over the line—anything could have happened.

It didn't.

Before we could pin her to the hood of the car, our eyes masked with lust and greed and the purest primal badness, a pair of headlights swung into the lot. There we were, dirty, bloody, guilty, dissociated from humanity and civilization, the first of the Ur-crimes behind us, the second in progress, shreds of nylon panty and spandex brassiere dangling from our fingers, our flies open, lips licked—there we were, caught in the spotlight. Nailed.

We bolted. First for the car, and then, realizing we had no way of starting it, for the woods. I thought nothing. I thought escape. The headlights came at me like accusing fingers. I was gone.

Ram-bam-bam, across the parking lot, past the chopper and into the feculent undergrowth at the lake's edge, insects flying up in my face, weeds whipping, frogs and snakes and red-eyed turtles splashing off into the night: I was already ankle-deep in muck and tepid water and still going strong. Behind me, the girl's screams rose in intensity, disconsolate, incriminating, the screams of the Sabine women,° the Christian martyrs, Anne Frank° dragged from the garret. I kept going, pursued by those cries, imagining cops and bloodhounds. The water was up to my knees when I realized

---

Virgin Spring: film about a rape by Swedish director Ingmar Bergman (1960).   *Sabine women:* members of an ancient tribe in Italy, according to legend, forcibly carried off by the early Romans under Romulus to be their wives. The incident is depicted in a famous painting, *The Rape of the Sabine Women*, by seventeenth-century French artist Nicolas Poussin.   *Anne Frank:* German Jewish girl (1929–1945) whose diary written during the Nazi occupation of the Netherlands later became world-famous. She hid with her family in a secret attic in Amsterdam, but was caught by the Gestapo and sent to the concentration camp at Belsen, where she died.

what I was doing: I was going to swim for it. Swim the breadth of Greasy Lake and hide myself in the thick clot of woods on the far side. They'd never find me there.

I was breathing in sobs, in gasps. The water lapped at my waist as I looked out over the moon-burnished ripples, the mats of algae that clung to the surface like scabs. Digby and Jeff had vanished. I paused. Listened. The girl was quieter now, screams tapering to sobs, but there were male voices, angry, excited, and the high-pitched ticking of the second car's engine. I waded deeper, stealthy, hunted, the ooze sucking at my sneakers. As I was about to take the plunge—at the very instant I dropped my shoulder for the first slashing stroke—I blundered into something. Something unspeakable, obscene, something soft, wet, moss-grown. A patch of weed? A log? When I reached out to touch it, it gave like a rubber duck, it gave like flesh.

In one of those nasty little epiphanies for which we are prepared by films and TV and childhood visits to the funeral home to ponder the shrunken painted forms of dead grandparents, I understood what it was that bobbed there so inadmissibly in the dark. Understood, and stumbled back in horror and revulsion, my mind yanked in six different directions (I was nineteen, a mere child, an infant, and here in the space of five minutes I'd struck down one greasy character and blundered into the waterlogged carcass of a second), thinking, The keys, the keys, why did I have to go and lose the keys? I stumbled back, but the muck took hold of my feet—a sneaker snagged, balance lost—and suddenly I was pitching face forward into the buoyant black mass, throwing out my hands in desperation while simultaneously conjuring the image of reeking frogs and muskrats revolving in slicks of their own deliquescing juices. AAAAArrrgh! I shot from the water like a torpedo, the dead man rotating to expose a mossy beard and eyes cold as the moon. I must have shouted out, thrashing around in the weeds, because the voices behind me suddenly became animated.

"What was that?"

"It's them, it's them: they tried to, tried to . . . *rape* me!" Sobs.

A man's voice, flat Midwestern accent. "You sons a bitches, we'll kill you!"

Frogs, crickets.

Then another voice, harsh, *r*-less, Lower East Side: "Motherfucker!" I recognized the verbal virtuosity of the bad greasy character in the engineer boots. Tooth chipped, sneakers gone, coated in mud and slime and worse, crouching breathless in the weeds waiting to have my ass thoroughly and definitively kicked and fresh from the hideous stinking embrace of a three-days-dead-corpse, I suddenly felt a rush of joy and vindication: the son of a bitch was alive! Just as quickly, my bowels turned to ice. "Come on out of there, you pansy mothers!" the bad greasy character was screaming. He shouted curses till he was out of breath.

The crickets started up again, then the frogs. I held my breath. All at once there was a sound in the reeds, a swishing, a splash: thunk-a-thunk. They were throwing rocks. The frogs fell silent. I cradled my head. Swish, swish, thunk-a-thunk. A wedge of feldspar the size of a cue ball glanced off my knee. I bit my finger.

It was then that they turned to the car. I heard a door slam, a curse, and then the sound of the headlights shattering—almost a good-natured sound, celebratory, like corks popping from the necks of bottles. This was succeeded by the dull booming of the fenders, metal on metal, and then the icy crash of the windshield. I inched forward, elbows and knees, my belly pressed to the muck, thinking of guerrillas and commandos and *The Naked and the Dead*.° I parted the weeds and squinted the length of the parking lot.

The Naked and the Dead: 1948 novel by Norman Mailer, about US Army life in World War II.

The second car—it was a Trans-Am—was still running, its high beams washing the scene in a lurid stagy light. Tire iron flailing, the greasy bad character was laying into the side of my mother's Bel Air like an avenging demon, his shadow riding up the trunks of the trees. Whomp. Whomp. Whomp-whomp. The other two guys— blond types, in fraternity jackets—were helping out with tree branches and skull-sized boulders. One of them was gathering up bottles, rocks, muck, candy wrappers, used condoms, poptops, and other refuse and pitching it through the window on the driver's side. I could see the fox, a white bulb behind the windshield of the '57 Chevy. "Bobbie," she whined over the thumping, "come on." The greasy character paused a moment, took one good swipe at the left taillight, and then heaved the tire iron halfway across the lake. Then he fired up the '57 and was gone.

Blond head nodded at blond head. One said something to the other, too low for   30 me to catch. They were no doubt thinking that in helping to annihilate my mother's car they'd committed a fairly rash act, and thinking too that there were three bad characters connected with that very car watching them from the woods. Perhaps other possibilities occurred to them as well—police, jail cells, justices of the peace, reparations, lawyers, irate parents, fraternal censure. Whatever they were thinking, they suddenly dropped branches, bottles, and rocks and sprang for their car in unison, as if they'd choreographed it. Five seconds. That's all it took. The engine shrieked, the tires squealed, a cloud of dust rose from the rutted lot and then settled back on darkness.

I don't know how long I lay there, the bad breath of decay all around me, my jacket heavy as a bear, the primordial ooze subtly reconstituting itself to accommodate my upper thighs and testicles. My jaws ached, my knee throbbed, my coccyx was on fire. I contemplated suicide, wondered if I'd need bridgework, scraped the recesses of my brain for some sort of excuse to give my parents—a tree had fallen on the car, I was blinded by a bread truck, hit and run, vandals had got to it while we were playing chess at Digby's. Then I thought of the dead man. He was probably the only person on the planet worse off than I was. I thought about him, fog on the lake, insects chirring eerily, and felt the tug of fear, felt the darkness opening up inside me like a set of jaws. Who was he, I wondered, this victim of time and circumstance bobbing sorrowfully in the lake at my back. The owner of the chopper, no doubt, a bad older character come to this. Shot during a murky drug deal, drowned while drunkenly frolicking in the lake. Another headline. My car was wrecked; he was dead.

When the eastern half of the sky went from black to cobalt and the trees began to separate themselves from the shadows, I pushed myself up from the mud and stepped out into the open. By now the birds had begun to take over for the crickets, and dew lay slick on the leaves. There was a smell in the air, raw and sweet at the same time, the smell of the sun firing buds and opening blossoms. I contemplated the car. It lay there like a wreck along the highway, like a steel sculpture left over from a vanished civilization. Everything was still. This was nature.

I was circling the car, as dazed and bedraggled as the sole survivor of an air blitz, when Digby and Jeff emerged from the trees behind me. Digby's face was cross-hatched with smears of dirt; Jeff's jacket was gone and his shirt was torn across the shoulder. They slouched across the lot, looking sheepish, and silently came up beside me to gape at the ravaged automobile. No one said a word. After a while Jeff swung open the driver's door and began to scoop the broken glass and garbage off the seat. I looked at Digby. He shrugged. "At least they didn't slash the tires," he said.

It was true: the tires were intact. There was no windshield, the headlights were staved in, and the body looked as if it had been sledge-hammered for a quarter a shot at the county fair, but the tires were inflated to regulation pressure. The car was drivable. In silence, all three of us bent to scrape the mud and shattered glass from the interior. I said nothing about the biker. When we were finished, I reached in my pocket for the keys, experienced a nasty stab of recollection, cursed myself, and turned to search the grass. I spotted them almost immediately, no more than five feet from the open door, glinting like jewels in the first tapering shaft of sunlight. There was no reason to get philosophical about it: I eased into the seat and turned the engine over.

It was at that precise moment that the silver Mustang with the flame decals   35
rumbled into the lot. All three of us froze; then Digby and Jeff slid into the car and slammed the door. We watched as the Mustang rocked and bobbed across the ruts and finally jerked to a halt beside the forlorn chopper at the far end of the lot. "Let's go," Digby said. I hesitated, the Bel Air wheezing beneath me.

Two girls emerged from the Mustang. Tight jeans, stiletto heels, hair like frozen fur. They bent over the motorcycle, paced back and forth aimlessly, glanced once or twice at us, and then ambled over to where the reeds sprang up in a green fence round the perimeter of the lake. One of them cupped her hands to her mouth. "Al," she called. "Hey, Al!"

"Come on," Digby hissed. "Let's get out of here."

But it was too late. The second girl was picking her way across the lot, unsteady on her heels, looking up at us and then away. She was older—twenty-five or -six— and as she came closer we could see there was something wrong with her: she was stoned or drunk, lurching now and waving her arms for balance. I gripped the steering wheel as if it were the ejection lever of a flaming jet, and Digby spat out my name, twice, terse and impatient.

"Hi," the girl said.

We looked at her like zombies, like war veterans, like deaf-and-dumb pencil   40
peddlers.

She smiled, her lips cracked and dry. "Listen," she said, bending from the waist to look in the window, "you guys seen Al?" Her pupils were pinpoints, her eyes glass. She jerked her neck. "That's his bike over there—Al's. You seen him?"

Al. I didn't know what to say. I wanted to get out of the car and retch, I wanted to go home to my parents' house and crawl into bed. Digby poked me in the ribs. "We haven't seen anybody," I said.

The girl seemed to consider this, reaching out a slim veiny arm to brace herself against the car. "No matter," she said, slurring the t's, "he'll turn up." And then, as if she'd just taken stock of the whole scene—the ravaged car and our battered faces, the desolation of the place—she said: "Hey, you guys look like some pretty bad characters—been fightin', huh?" We stared straight ahead, rigid as catatonics. She was fumbling in her pocket and muttering something. Finally she held out a handful of tablets in glassine wrappers: "Hey, you want to party, you want to do some of these with me and Sarah?"

I just looked at her. I thought I was going to cry. Digby broke the silence. "No, thanks," he said, leaning over me. "Some other time."

I put the car in gear and it inched forward with a groan, shaking off pellets of   45
glass like an old dog shedding water after a bath, heaving over the ruts on its worn springs, creeping toward the highway. There was a sheen of sun on the lake. I looked back. The girl was still standing there, watching us, her shoulders slumped, hand outstretched.

Willa Cather

Paul's Case   1905

*Willa Cather (1873–1947) was born in Gore,
Virginia, but at nine moved to Webster County,
Nebraska, where pioneer sod houses still clung to
the windswept plains. There, mainly in the town
of Red Cloud, she grew up among Scandinavians,
Czechs, Bohemians, and other immigrant settlers,
for whom she felt a quick kinship: they too had been
displaced from their childhood homes. After graduation from the University of Nebraska, Cather went
east to spend ten years in Pittsburgh, where the
story "Paul's Case" opens. (When she wrote the
story, she was a high school teacher of Latin and
English and a music critic for a newspaper.) Then,
because her early stories had attracted notice, New
York beckoned. A job on the staff of McClure's
led to her becoming managing editor of that popular magazine. Her early novels of Nebraska won*

Willa Cather

*immense popularity: O Pioneers! (1913), My Ántonia (1918), and A Lost Lady
(1923). In her later novels Cather explores other regions of the North American past: in
Death Comes for the Archbishop (1927), frontier New Mexico; in Shadows on the
Rock (1931), seventeenth-century Quebec. She does not romanticize the rugged lives of
farm people on the plains, nor glamorize village life. Often, as in The Song of the Lark
(1915), the story of a Colorado girl who becomes an opera singer, she depicts a small town
as stifling. With remarkable skill, she may tell a story from a man's point of view, but her
favorite characters are likely to be women of strong will who triumph over obstacles.*

It was Paul's afternoon to appear before the faculty of the Pittsburgh High School
to account for his various misdemeanors. He had been suspended a week ago, and his
father had called at the Principal's office and confessed his perplexity about his son.
Paul entered the faculty room suave and smiling. His clothes were a trifle outgrown
and the tan velvet on the collar of his open overcoat was frayed and worn; but for
all that there was something of the dandy about him, and he wore an opal pin in his
neatly knotted black four-in-hand, and a red carnation in his buttonhole. This latter
adornment the faculty somehow felt was not properly significant of the contrite spirit
befitting a boy under the ban of suspension.

Paul was tall for his age and very thin, with high, cramped shoulders and a narrow chest. His eyes were remarkable for a certain hysterical brilliancy and he continually used them in a conscious, theatrical sort of way, peculiarly offensive in a boy.
The pupils were abnormally large, as though he were addicted to belladonna, but
there was a glassy glitter about them which that drug does not produce.

When questioned by the Principal as to why he was there, Paul stated, politely
enough, that he wanted to come back to school. This was a lie, but Paul was quite
accustomed to lying; found it, indeed, indispensable for overcoming friction. His
teachers were asked to state their respective charges against him, which they did with
such a rancor and aggrievedness as evinced that this was not a usual case. Disorder
and impertinence were among the offenses named, yet each of his instructors felt

that it was scarcely possible to put into words the real cause of the trouble, which lay in a sort of hysterically defiant manner of the boy's; in the contempt which they all knew he felt for them, and which he seemingly made not the least effort to conceal. Once, when he had been making a synopsis of a paragraph at the blackboard, his English teacher had stepped to his side and attempted to guide his hand. Paul had started back with a shudder and thrust his hands violently behind him. The astonished woman could scarcely have been more hurt and embarrassed had he struck at her. The insult was so involuntary and definitely personal as to be unforgettable. In one way and another, he had made all his teachers, men and women alike, conscious of the same feeling of physical aversion. In one class he habitually sat with his hand shading his eyes; in another he always looked out of the window during the recitation; in another he made a running commentary on the lecture, with humorous intention.

His teachers felt this afternoon that his whole attitude was symbolized by his shrug and his flippantly red carnation flower, and they fell upon him without mercy, his English teacher leading the pack. He stood through it smiling, his pale lips parted over his white teeth. (His lips were continually twitching, and he had a habit of raising his eyebrows that was contemptuous and irritating to the last degree.) Older boys than Paul had broken down and shed tears under that baptism of fire, but his set smile did not once desert him, and his only sign of discomfort was the nervous trembling of the fingers that toyed with the buttons of his overcoat, and an occasional jerking of the other hand that held his hat. Paul was always smiling, always glancing about him, seeming to feel that people might be watching him and trying to detect something. This conscious expression, since it was as far as possible from boyish mirthfulness, was usually attributed to insolence or "smartness."

As the inquisition proceeded, one of his instructors repeated an impertinent   5
remark of the boy's, and the Principal asked him whether he thought that a courteous speech to have made a woman. Paul shrugged his shoulders slightly and his eyebrows twitched.

"I don't know," he replied. "I didn't mean to be polite or impolite, either. I guess it's a sort of way I have of saying things regardless."

The Principal, who was a sympathetic man, asked him whether he didn't think that a way it would be well to get rid of. Paul grinned and said he guessed so. When he was told that he could go, he bowed gracefully and went out. His bow was but a repetition of the scandalous red carnation.

His teachers were in despair, and his drawing master voiced the feeling of them all when he declared there was something about the boy which none of them understood. He added: "I don't really believe that smile of his comes altogether from insolence; there's something sort of haunted about it. The boy is not strong, for one thing. I happen to know that he was born in Colorado, only a few months before his mother died out there of a long illness. There is something wrong about the fellow."

The drawing master had come to realize that, in looking at Paul, one saw only his white teeth and the forced animation of his eyes. One warm afternoon the boy had gone to sleep at his drawing-board, and his master had noted with amazement what a white, blue-veined face it was; drawn and wrinkled like an old man's about the eyes, the lips twitching even in his sleep, and stiff with a nervous tension that drew them back from his teeth.

His teachers left the building dissatisfied and unhappy; humiliated to have felt so   10
vindictive toward a mere boy, to have uttered this feeling in cutting terms, and to have

set each other on, as it were, in the gruesome game of intemperate reproach. Some of them remembered having seen a miserable street cat set at bay by a ring of tormentors.

As for Paul, he ran down the hill whistling the Soldiers' Chorus from *Faust*,° looking wildly behind him now and then to see whether some of his teachers were not there to writhe under his light-heartedness. As it was now late in the afternoon and Paul was on duty that evening as usher at Carnegie Hall,° he decided that he would not go home to supper. When he reached the concert hall the doors were not yet open and, as it was chilly outside, he decided to go up into the picture gallery—always deserted at this hour—where there were some of Raffaelli's° gay studies of Paris streets and an airy blue Venetian scene or two that always exhilarated him. He was delighted to find no one in the gallery but the old guard, who sat in one corner, a newspaper on his knee, a black patch over one eye and the other closed. Paul possessed himself of the place and walked confidently up and down, whistling under his breath. After a while he sat down before a blue Rico° and lost himself. When he bethought him to look at his watch, it was after seven o'clock, and he rose with a start and ran downstairs, making a face at Augustus, peering out from the cast-room,° and an evil gesture at the Venus of Milo as he passed her on the stairway.

When Paul reached the ushers' dressing-room half-a-dozen boys were there already, and he began excitedly to tumble into his uniform. It was one of the few that at all approached fitting, and Paul thought it very becoming—though he knew that the tight, straight coat accentuated his narrow chest, about which he was exceedingly sensitive. He was always considerably excited while he dressed, twanging all over to the tuning of the strings and the preliminary flourishes of the horns in the music-room; but tonight he seemed quite beside himself, and he teased and plagued the boys until, telling him that he was crazy, they put him down on the floor and sat on him.

Somewhat calmed by his suppression, Paul dashed out to the front of the house to seat the early comers. He was a model usher; gracious and smiling he ran up and down the aisles; nothing was too much trouble for him; he carried messages and brought programmes as though it were his greatest pleasure in life, and all the people in his section thought him a charming boy, feeling that he remembered and admired them. As the house filled, he grew more and more vivacious and animated, and the color came to his cheeks and lips. It was very much as though this were a great reception and Paul were the host. Just as the musicians came out to take their places, his English teacher arrived with checks for the seats which a prominent manufacturer had taken for the season. She betrayed some embarrassment when she handed Paul the tickets, and a hauteur° which subsequently made her feel very foolish. Paul was startled for a moment, and had the feeling of wanting to put her out; what business had she here among all these fine people and gay colors? He looked her over and decided that she was not appropriately dressed and must be a fool to sit downstairs in such togs. The tickets had probably been sent her out of kindness, he reflected as he put down a seat for her, and she had about as much right to sit there as he had.

Faust: tragic grand opera (1859) by French composer Charles Gounod.   *Carnegie Hall:* concert hall endowed by Pittsburgh steel manufacturer Andrew Carnegie, not to be confused with the better-known Carnegie Hall in New York City.   *Raffaelli:* Jean-Francois Raffaelli (1850–1921), painter and graphic artist, native and lifelong resident of Paris, attained great popularity for his paintings and drawings of that city.   *Rico:* (flourished 1500–1550), painter of the Byzantine school, a native of Crete.   *Augustus . . . cast-room:* Paul mocks a plaster cast of the Vatican Museum's famous statue of the first Roman emperor (63 B.C.–A.D. 14), whom an unknown sculptor posed sternly pointing an index finger at his beholders. *hauteur:* haughtiness.

When the symphony began Paul sank into one of the rear seats with a long sigh of relief, and lost himself as he had done before the Rico. It was not that symphonies, as such, meant anything in particular to Paul, but the first sigh of the instruments seemed to free some hilarious and potent spirit within him; something that struggled there like the Genius° in the bottle found by the Arab fisherman. He felt a sudden zest of life; the lights danced before his eyes and the concert hall blazed into unimaginable splendor. When the soprano soloist came on, Paul forgot even the nastiness of his teacher's being there and gave himself up to the peculiar stimulus such personages always had for him. The soloist chanced to be a German woman, by no means in her first youth, and the mother of many children; but she wore an elaborate gown and a tiara, and above all she had that indefinable air of achievement, that world-shine upon her, which, in Paul's eyes, made her a veritable queen of Romance.

After a concert was over Paul was always irritable and wretched until he got to   15
sleep, and tonight he was even more than usually restless. He had the feeling of not being able to let down, of its being impossible to give up this delicious excitement which was the only thing that could be called living at all. During the last number he withdrew and, after hastily changing his clothes in the dressing-room, slipped out to the side door where the soprano's carriage stood. Here he began pacing rapidly up and down the walk, waiting to see her come out.

Over yonder the Schenley, in its vacant stretch, loomed big and square through the fine rain, the windows of its twelve stories glowing like those of a lighted cardboard house under a Christmas tree. All the actors and singers of the better class stayed there when they were in the city, and a number of the big manufacturers of the place lived there in the winter. Paul had often hung about the hotel, watching the people go in and out, longing to enter and leave schoolmasters and dull care behind him forever.

At last the singer came out, accompanied by the conductor, who helped her into her carriage and closed the door with a cordial *auf wiedersehen*° which set Paul to wondering whether she were not an old sweetheart of his. Paul followed the carriage over to the hotel, walking so rapidly as not to be far from the entrance when the singer alighted and disappeared behind the swinging glass doors that were opened by a negro in a tall hat and a long coat. In the moment that the door was ajar it seemed to Paul that he, too, entered. He seemed to feel himself go after her up the steps, into the warm, lighted building, into an exotic, a tropical world of shiny, glistening surfaces and basking ease. He reflected upon the mysterious dishes that were brought into the dining-room, the green bottles in buckets of ice, as he had seen them in the supper party pictures of the *Sunday World* supplement. A quick gust of wind brought the rain down with sudden vehemence, and Paul was startled to find that he was still outside in the slush of the gravel driveway; that his boots were letting in the water and his scanty overcoat was clinging wet about him; that the lights in front of the concert hall were out, and that the rain was driving in sheets between him and the orange glow of the windows above him. There it was, what he wanted—tangibly before him, like the fairy world of a Christmas pantomime, but mocking spirits stood guard at the doors, and, as the rain beat in his face, Paul wondered whether he were destined always to shiver in the black night outside, looking up at it.

He turned and walked reluctantly toward the car tracks. The end had to come sometime; his father in his night-clothes at the top of the stairs, explanations that did

---

Genius: genie in a tale from *The Arabian Nights*.   *auf wiedersehen:* German equivalent of *au revoir*, or "here's to seeing you again."

not explain, hastily improvised fictions that were forever tripping him up, his upstairs room and its horrible yellow wall-paper, the creaking bureau with the greasy plush collar-box, and over his painted wooden bed the pictures of George Washington and John Calvin,° and the framed motto, "Feed my Lambs," which had been worked in red worsted by his mother.

Half an hour later, Paul alighted from his car and went slowly down one of the side streets off the main thoroughfare. It was a highly respectable street, where all the houses were exactly alike, and where businessmen of moderate means begot and reared large families of children, all of whom went to Sabbath-school and learned the shorter catechism, and were interested in arithmetic; all of whom were as exactly alike as their homes, and of a piece with the monotony in which they lived. Paul never went up Cordelia Street without a shudder of loathing. His home was next to the house of the Cumberland° minister. He approached it tonight with the nerveless sense of defeat, the hopeless feeling of sinking back forever into ugliness and commonness that he had always had when he came home. The moment he turned into Cordelia Street he felt the waters close above his head. After each of these orgies of living, he experienced all the physical depression which follows a debauch; the loathing of respectable beds, of common food, of a house penetrated by kitchen odors; a shuddering repulsion for the flavorless, colorless mass of every-day existence; a morbid desire for cool things and soft lights and fresh flowers.

The nearer he approached the house, the more absolutely unequal Paul felt to   20
the sight of it all; his ugly sleeping chamber; the cold bathroom with the grimy zinc tub, the cracked mirror, the dripping spigots; his father, at the top of the stairs, his hairy legs sticking out from his night-shirt, his feet thrust into carpet slippers. He was so much later than usual that there would certainly be inquiries and reproaches. Paul stopped short before the door. He felt that he could not be accosted by his father tonight; that he could not toss again on that miserable bed. He would not go in. He would tell his father that he had no car fare, and it was raining so hard he had gone home with one of the boys and stayed all night.

Meanwhile, he was wet and cold. He went around to the back of the house and tried one of the basement windows, found it open, raised it cautiously, and scrambled down the cellar wall to the floor. There he stood, holding his breath, terrified by the noise he had made, but the floor above him was silent, and there was no creak on the stairs. He found a soap-box, and carried it over to the soft ring of light that streamed from the furnace door, and sat down. He was horribly afraid of rats, so he did not try to sleep, but sat looking distrustfully at the dark, still terrified lest he might have awakened his father. In such reactions, after one of the experiences which made days and nights out of the dreary blanks of the calendar, when his senses were deadened, Paul's head was always singularly clear. Suppose his father had heard him getting in at the window and had come down and shot him for a burglar? Then, again, suppose his father had come down, pistol in hand, and he had cried out in time to save himself, and his father had been horrified to think how nearly he had killed him? Then, again, suppose a day should come when his father would remember that night, and wish there had been no warning cry to stay his hand? With this last supposition Paul entertained himself until daybreak.

John Calvin: French Protestant theologian of the Reformation (1509–1564) whose teachings are the basis of Presbyterianism.   *Cumberland:* The minister, a Cumberland Presbyterian, belongs to a frontier denomination that had splintered away from the Presbyterian Church and whose ministers were ordained after a briefer training.

    The following Sunday was fine; the sodden November chill was broken by the last flash of autumnal summer. In the morning Paul had to go to church and Sabbath-school, as always. On seasonable Sunday afternoons the burghers of Cordelia Street always sat out on their front "stoops," and talked to their neighbors on the next stoop, or called to those across the street in neighborly fashion. The men usually sat on gay cushions placed upon the steps that led down to the sidewalk, while the women, in their Sunday "waists," sat in rockers on the cramped porches, pretending to be greatly at their ease. The children played in the streets; there were so many of them that the place resembled the recreation grounds of a kindergarten. The men on the steps—all in their shirt sleeves, their vests unbuttoned—sat with their legs well apart, their stomachs comfortably protruding, and talked of the prices of things, or told anecdotes of the sagacity of their various chiefs and overlords. They occasionally looked over the multitude of squabbling children, listened affectionately to their high-pitched, nasal voices, smiling to see their own proclivities reproduced in their offspring, and interspersed their legends of the iron kings with remarks about their sons' progress at school, their grades in arithmetic, and the amounts they had saved in their toy banks.

    On this last Sunday of November, Paul sat all the afternoon on the lowest step of his "stoop," staring into the street, while his sisters, in their rockers, were talking to the minister's daughters next door about how many shirt-waists they had made in the last week, and how many waffles some one had eaten at the last church sup-per. When the weather was warm, and his father was in a particularly jovial frame of mind, the girls made lemonade, which was always brought out in a red-glass pitcher, ornamented with forget-me-nots in blue enamel. This the girls thought very fine, and the neighbors always joked about the suspicious color of the pitcher.

    Today Paul's father sat on the top step, talking to a young man who shifted a restless baby from knee to knee. He happened to be the young man who was daily held up to Paul as a model, and after whom it was his father's dearest hope that he would pattern. This young man was of a ruddy complexion, with a compressed, red mouth, and faded, near-sighted eyes, over which he wore thick spectacles, with gold bows that curved about his ears. He was clerk to one of the magnates of a great steel corporation, and was looked upon in Cordelia Street as a young man with a future. There was a story that, some five years ago—he was now barely twenty-six—he had been a trifle dissipated but in order to curb his appetites and save the loss of time and strength that a sowing of wild oats might have entailed, he had taken his chief's advice oft reiterated to his employees, and at twenty-one had married the first woman whom he could persuade to share his fortunes. She happened to be an angu-lar school-mistress, much older than he, who also wore thick glasses, and who had now borne him four children, all near-sighted, like herself.

    The young man was relating how his chief, now cruising in the Mediterranean,   25
kept in touch with all the details of the business, arranging his office hours on his yacht just as though he were at home, and "knocking off work enough to keep two stenographers busy." His father told, in turn, the plan his corporation was consider-ing, of putting in an electric railway plant at Cairo. Paul snapped his teeth; he had an awful apprehension that they might spoil it all before he got there. Yet he rather liked to hear these legends of the iron kings, that were told and retold on Sundays and holidays; these stories of palaces in Venice, yachts on the Mediterranean, and high play at Monte Carlo appealed to his fancy, and he was interested in the tri-umphs of these cash boys who had become famous, though he had no mind for the cash-boy stage.

After supper was over, and he had helped to dry the dishes, Paul nervously asked his father whether he could go to George's to get some help in his geometry, and still more nervously asked for car fare. This latter request he had to repeat, as his father, on principle, did not like to hear requests for money, whether much or little. He asked Paul whether he could not go to some boy who lived nearer, and told him that he ought not to leave his school work until Sunday; but he gave him the dime. He was not a poor man, but he had a worthy ambition to come up in the world. His only reason for allowing Paul to usher was, that he thought a boy ought to be earning a little.

Paul bounded upstairs, scrubbed the greasy odor of the dish-water from his hands with the ill-smelling soap he hated, and then shook over his fingers a few drops of violet water from the bottle he kept hidden in his drawer. He left the house with his geometry conspicuously under his arm, and the moment he got out of Cordelia Street and boarded a downtown car, he shook off the lethargy of two deadening days, and began to live again.

The leading juvenile of the permanent stock company which played at one of the downtown theatres was an acquaintance of Paul's, and the boy had been invited to drop in at the Sunday-night rehearsals whenever he could. For more than a year Paul had spent every available moment loitering about Charley Edwards's dressing-room. He had won a place among Edwards's following not only because the young actor, who could not afford to employ a dresser, often found him useful, but because he recognized in Paul something akin to what churchmen term "vocation."

It was at the theatre and at Carnegie Hall that Paul really lived; the rest was but a sleep and a forgetting. This was Paul's fairy tale, and it had for him all the allurement of a secret love. The moment he inhaled the gassy, painty, dusty odor behind the scenes, he breathed like a prisoner set free, and felt within him the possibility of doing or saying splendid, brilliant, poetic things. The moment the cracked orchestra beat out the overture from *Martha*,° or jerked at the serenade from *Rigoletto*,° all stupid and ugly things slid from him, and his senses were deliciously, yet delicately fired.

Perhaps it was because, in Paul's world, the natural nearly always wore the guise   30
of ugliness, that a certain element of artificiality seemed to him necessary in beauty. Perhaps it was because his experience of life elsewhere was so full of Sabbath-school picnics, petty economies, wholesome advice as to how to succeed in life, and the unescapable odors of cooking, that he found this existence so alluring, these smartly-clad men and women so attractive, that he was so moved by these starry apple orchards that bloomed perennially under the limelight.

It would be difficult to put it strongly enough how convincingly the stage entrance of that theatre was for Paul the actual portal of Romance. Certainly none of the company ever suspected it, least of all Charley Edwards. It was very like the old stories that used to float about London of fabulously rich Jews, who had subterranean halls there, with palms, and fountains, and soft lamps and richly apparelled women who never saw the disenchanting light of London day. So, in the midst of that smoke-palled city, enamored of figures and grimy toil, Paul had his secret temple, his wishing carpet, his bit of blue-and-white Mediterranean shore bathed in perpetual sunshine.

Several of Paul's teachers had a theory that his imagination had been perverted by garish fiction, but the truth was that he scarcely ever read at all. The books at

Martha: grand opera about romance among English aristocrats (1847) by German composer Friedrich von Flotow.   *Rigoletto:* tragic grand opera (1851) by Italian composer Giuseppe Verdi.

home were not such as would either tempt or corrupt a youthful mind, and as for reading the novels that some of his friends urged upon him—well, he got what he wanted much more quickly from music; any sort of music, from an orchestra to a barrel organ. He needed only the spark, the indescribable thrill that made his imagination master of his senses, and he could make plots and pictures enough of his own. It was equally true that he was not stage struck—not, at any rate, in the usual acceptation of that expression. He had no desire to become an actor, any more than he had to become a musician. He felt no necessity to do any of these things; what he wanted was to see, to be in the atmosphere, float on the wave of it, to be carried out, blue league after blue league, away from everything.

After a night behind the scenes, Paul found the school-room more than ever repulsive; the bare floors and naked walls; the prosy men who never wore frock coats, or violets in their buttonholes; the women with their dull gowns, shrill voices, and pitiful seriousness about prepositions that govern the dative. He could not bear to have the other pupils think, for a moment, that he took these people seriously; he must convey to them that he considered it all trivial, and was there only by way of a jest, anyway. He had autographed pictures of all the members of the stock company which he showed his classmates, telling them the most incredible stories of his familiarity with these people, of his acquaintance with the soloists who came to Carnegie Hall, his suppers with them and the flowers he sent them. When these stories lost their effect, and his audience grew listless, he became desperate and would bid all the boys good-bye, announcing that he was going to travel for a while; going to Naples, to Venice, to Egypt. Then, next Monday, he would slip back, conscious and nervously smiling; his sister was ill, and he should have to defer his voyage until spring.

Matters went steadily worse with Paul at school. In the itch to let his instructors know how heartily he despised them and their homilies, and how thoroughly he was appreciated elsewhere, he mentioned once or twice that he had no time to fool with theorems; adding—with a twitch of the eyebrows and a touch of that nervous bravado which so perplexed them—that he was helping the people down at the stock company; they were old friends of his.

The upshot of the matter was that the Principal went to Paul's father, and Paul   35
was taken out of school and put to work. The manager at Carnegie Hall was told to get another usher in his stead; the door-keeper at the theatre was warned not to admit him to the house; and Charley Edwards remorsefully promised the boy's father not to see him again.

The members of the stock company were vastly amused when some of Paul's stories reached them—especially the women. They were hardworking women, most of them supporting indigent husbands or brothers, and they laughed rather bitterly at having stirred the boy to such fervid and florid inventions. They agreed with the faculty and with his father that Paul's was a bad case.

The east-bound train was ploughing through a January snow-storm; the dull dawn was beginning to show gray when the engine whistled a mile out of Newark. Paul started up from the seat where he had lain curled in uneasy slumber, rubbed the breath-misted window glass with his hand, and peered out. The snow was whirling in curling eddies above the white bottom lands, and the drifts lay already deep in the fields and along the fences, while here and there the long dead grass and dried weed stalks protruded black above it. Lights shone from the scattered houses, and a gang of laborers who stood beside the track waved their lanterns.

Paul had slept very little, and he felt grimy and uncomfortable. He had made the all-night journey in a day coach, partly because he was ashamed, dressed as he was, to go into a Pullman, and partly because he was afraid of being seen there by some Pittsburgh business man, who might have noticed him in Denny & Carson's office. When the whistle awoke him, he clutched quickly at his breast pocket, glancing about him with an uncertain smile. But the little, clay-bespattered Italians were still sleeping, the slatternly women across the aisle were in open-mouthed oblivion, and even the crumby, crying babies were for the nonce stilled. Paul settled back to struggle with his impatience as best as he could.

When he arrived at the Jersey City station, he hurried through his breakfast, manifestly ill at ease and keeping a sharp eye about him. After he reached the Twenty-third Street station,° he consulted a cabman, and had himself driven to a men's furnishing establishment that was just opening for the day. He spent upward of two hours there, buying with endless reconsidering and great care. His new street suit he put on in the fitting-room; the frock coat and dress clothes he had bundled into the cab with his linen. Then he drove to a hatter's and a shoe house. His next errand was at Tiffany's, where he selected his silver and a new scarf-pin. He would not wait to have his silver marked, he said. Lastly, he stopped at a trunk shop on Broadway, and had his purchases packed into various travelling bags.

It was a little after one-o'clock when he drove up to the Waldorf, and after settling with the cabman, went into the office. He registered from Washington; said his mother and father had been abroad, and that he had come down to await the arrival of their steamer. He told his story plausibly and had no trouble, since he volunteered to pay for them in advance, in engaging his rooms; a sleeping-room, sitting-room and bath.   40

Not once, but a hundred times Paul had planned this entry into New York. He had gone over every detail of it with Charley Edwards, and in his scrap book at home there were pages of description about New York hotels, cut from the Sunday papers. When he was shown to his sitting-room on the eighth floor, he saw at a glance that everything was as it should be; there was but one detail in his mental picture that the place did not realize, so he rang for the bell boy and sent him down for flowers. He moved about nervously until the boy returned, putting away his new linen and fingering it delightedly as he did so. When the flowers came, he put them hastily into water, and then tumbled into a hot bath. Presently he came out of his white bath-room, resplendent in his new silk underwear, and playing with the tassels of his red robe. The snow was whirling so fiercely outside his windows that he could scarcely see across the street, but within the air was deliciously soft and fragrant. He put the violets and jonquils on the taboret beside the couch, and threw himself down, with a long sigh, covering himself with a Roman blanket. He was thoroughly tired; he had been in such haste, he had stood up to such a strain, covered so much ground in the last twenty-four hours, that he wanted to think how it had all come about. Lulled by the sound of the wind, the warm air, and the cool fragrance of the flowers, he sank into deep, drowsy retrospection.

It had been wonderfully simple; when they had shut him out of the theatre and concert hall, when they had taken away his bone, the whole thing was virtually determined. The rest was a mere matter of opportunity. The only thing that at all surprised him was his own courage—for he realized well enough that he had always been tormented by fear, a sort of apprehensive dread that, of late years, as the meshes of the lies he had told closed about him, had been pulling the muscles of his body

Twenty-third Street station: The scene is now New York City.

tighter and tighter. Until now, he could not remember the time when he had not been dreading something. Even when he was a little boy, it was always there—behind him, or before, or on either side. There had always been the shadowed corner, the dark place into which he dared not look, but from which something seemed always to be watching him—and Paul had done things that were not pretty to watch, he knew.

But now he had a curious sense of relief, as though he had at last thrown down the gauntlet to the thing in the corner.

Yet it was but a day since he had been sulking in the traces; but yesterday afternoon that he had been sent to the bank with Denny & Carson's deposit, as usual—but this time he was instructed to leave the book to be balanced. There was above two thousand dollars in checks, and nearly a thousand in the bank notes which he had taken from the book and quietly transferred to his pocket. At the bank he had made out a new deposit slip. His nerves had been steady enough to permit of his returning to the office, where he had finished his work and asked for a full day's holiday tomorrow, Saturday, giving a perfectly reasonable pretext. The bank book, he knew, would not be returned before Monday or Tuesday, and his father would be out of town for the next week. From the time he slipped the bank notes into his pocket until he boarded the night train for New York, he had not known a moment's hesitation. It was not the first time Paul had steered through treacherous waters.

How astonishingly easy it had all been; here he was, the thing done; and this time there would be no awakening, no figure at the top of the stairs. He watched the snow flakes whirling by his window until he fell asleep.   45

When he awoke, it was three o'clock in the afternoon. He bounded up with a start; half of one of his precious days gone already! He spent more than an hour in dressing, watching every stage of his toilet carefully in the mirror. Everything was quite perfect; he was exactly the kind of boy he had always wanted to be.

When he went downstairs, Paul took a carriage and drove up Fifth Avenue toward the Park. The snow had somewhat abated; carriages and tradesmen's wagons were hurrying soundlessly to and fro in the winter twilight; boys in woollen mufflers were shovelling off the doorsteps; the avenue stages made fine spots of color against the white street. Here and there on the corners were stands, with whole flower gardens blooming under glass cases, against the sides of which the snow flakes stuck and melted; violets, roses, carnations, lilies of the valley—somewhat vastly more lovely and alluring that they blossomed thus unnaturally in the snow. The Park itself was a wonderful stage winter-piece.

When he returned, the pause of the twilight had ceased, and the tune of the streets had changed. The snow was falling faster, lights streamed from the hotels that reared their dozen stories fearlessly up into the storm, defying the raging Atlantic winds. A long, black stream of carriages poured down the avenue, intersected here and there by other streams, tending horizontally. There were a score of cabs about the entrance of his hotel, and his driver had to wait. Boys in livery were running in and out of the awning stretched across the sidewalk, up and down the red velvet carpet laid from the door to the street. Above, about, within it all was the rumble and roar, the hurry and toss of thousands of human beings as hot for pleasure as himself, and on every side of him towered the glaring affirmation of the omnipotence of wealth.

The boy set his teeth and drew his shoulders together in a spasm of realization: the plot of all dramas, the text of all romances, the nerve-stuff of all sensations was whirling about him like the snow flakes. He burnt like a faggot in a tempest.

When Paul went down to dinner, the music of the orchestra came floating up the elevator shaft to greet him. His head whirled as he stepped into the thronged   50 corridor, and he sank back into one of the chairs against the wall to get his breath. The lights, the chatter, the perfumes, the bewildering medley of color—he had, for a moment, the feeling of not being able to stand it. But only for a moment; these were his own people, he told himself. He went slowly about the corridors, through the writing-rooms, smoking-rooms, reception-rooms, as though he were exploring the chambers of an enchanted palace, built and peopled for him alone.

When he reached the dining-room he sat down at a table near a window. The flowers, the white linen, the many-colored wine glasses, the gay toilettes of the women, the low popping of corks, the undulating repetitions of the *Blue Danube* from the orchestra, all flooded Paul's dream with bewildering radiance. When the roseate tinge of his champagne was added—that cold, precious, bubbling stuff that creamed and foamed in his glass—Paul wondered that there were honest men in the world at all. This was what all the world was fighting for, he reflected; this was what all the struggle was about. He doubted the reality of his past. Had he ever known a place called Cordelia Street, a place where fagged-looking businessmen got on the early car; mere rivets in a machine they seemed to Paul—sickening men, with combings of children's hair always hanging to their coats, and the smell of cooking in their clothes. Cordelia Street—Ah! that belonged to another time and country; had he not always been thus, had he not sat here night after night, from as far back as he could remember, looking pensively over just such shimmering textures, and slowly twirling the stem of a glass like this one between his thumb and middle finger? He rather thought he had.

He was not in the least abashed or lonely. He had no especial desire to meet or to know any of these people; all he demanded was the right to look on and conjecture, to watch the pageant. The mere stage properties were all he contended for. Nor was he lonely later in the evening, in his loge at the Metropolitan. He was now entirely rid of his nervous misgivings, of his forced aggressiveness, of the imperative desire to show himself different from his surroundings. He felt now that his surroundings explained him. Nobody questioned the purple; he had only to wear it passively. He had only to glance down at his attire to reassure himself that here it would be impossible for anyone to humiliate him.

He found it hard to leave his beautiful sitting-room to go to bed that night, and sat long watching the raging storm from his turret window. When he went to sleep it was with the lights turned on in his bedroom; partly because of his old timidity, and partly so that, if he should wake in the night, there would be no wretched moment of doubt, no horrible suspicion of yellow wall-paper, or of Washington and Calvin above his bed.

Sunday morning the city was practically snow-bound. Paul breakfasted late, and in the afternoon he fell in with a wild San Francisco boy, a freshman at Yale, who said he had run down for a "little flyer" over Sunday. The young man offered to show Paul the night side of the town, and the two boys went out together after dinner, not returning to the hotel until seven o'clock the next morning. They had started out in the confiding warmth of a champagne friendship, but their parting in the elevator was singularly cool. The freshman pulled himself together to make his train, and Paul went to bed. He awoke at two o'clock in the afternoon, very thirsty and dizzy, and rang for ice-water, coffee, and the Pittsburgh papers.

On the part of the hotel management, Paul excited no suspicion. There was this to be said for him, that he wore his spoils with dignity and in no way made himself conspicuous. Even under the glow of his wine he was never boisterous, though he

55

found the stuff like a magician's wand for wonder-building. His chief greediness lay in his ears and eyes, and his excesses were not offensive ones. His dearest pleasures were the gray winter twilights in his sitting-room; his quiet enjoyment of his flowers, his clothes, his wide divan, his cigarette, and his sense of power. He could not remember a time when he had felt so at peace with himself. The mere release from the necessity of petty lying, lying every day and every day, restored his self-respect. He had never lied for pleasure, even at school; but to be noticed and admired, to assert his difference from other Cordelia Street boys; and he felt a good deal more manly, more honest, even, now that he had no need for boastful pretensions, now that he could, as his actor friends used to say, "dress the part." It was characteristic that remorse did not occur to him. His golden days went by without a shadow, and he made each as perfect as he could.

On the eighth day after his arrival in New York, he found the whole affair exploited in the Pittsburgh papers, exploited with a wealth of detail which indicated that local news of a sensational nature was at a low ebb. The firm of Denny & Carson announced that the boy's father had refunded the full amount of the theft, and that they had no intention of prosecuting. The Cumberland minister had been interviewed, and expressed his hope of yet reclaiming the motherless lad, and his Sabbath-school teacher declared that she would spare no effort to that end. The rumor had reached Pittsburgh that the boy had been seen in a New York hotel, and his father had gone East to find him and bring him home.

Paul had just come in to dress for dinner; he sank into a chair, weak to the knees, and clasped his head in his hands. It was to be worse than jail, even; the tepid waters of Cordelia Street were to close over him finally and forever. The gray monotony stretched before him in hopeless, unrelieved years; Sabbath-school, Young People's Meeting, the yellow-papered room, the damp dish-towels; it all rushed back upon him with a sickening vividness. He had the old feeling that the orchestra had suddenly stopped, the sinking sensation that the play was over. The sweat broke out on his face, and he sprang to his feet, looked about him with his white, conscious smile, and winked at himself in the mirror. With something of the old childish belief in miracles with which he had so often gone to class, all his lessons unlearned, Paul dressed and dashed whistling down the corridor to the elevator.

He had no sooner entered the dining-room and caught the measure of the music than his remembrance was lightened by his old elastic power of claiming the moment, mounting with it, and finding it all sufficient. The glare and glitter about him, the mere scenic accessories had again, and for the last time, their old potency. He would show himself that he was game, he would finish the thing splendidly. He doubted, more than ever, the existence of Cordelia Street, and for the first time he drank his wine recklessly. Was he not, after all, one of those fortunate beings born to the purple, was he not still himself and in his own place? He drummed a nervous accompaniment to the Pagliacci music and looked about him, telling himself over and over that it had paid.

He reflected drowsily, to the swell of the music and the chill sweetness of his wine, that he might have done it more wisely. He might have caught an outbound steamer and been well out of their clutches before now. But the other side of the world had seemed too far away and too uncertain then; he could not have waited for it; his need had been too sharp. If he had to choose over again, he would do the same thing tomorrow. He looked affectionately about the dining-room, now gilded with a soft mist. Ah, it had paid indeed!

Paul was awakened next morning by a painful throbbing in his head and feet. He   60
had thrown himself across the bed without undressing, and had slept with his shoes
on. His limbs and hands were lead heavy, and his tongue and throat were parched
and burnt. There came upon him one of those fateful attacks of clear-headedness that
never occurred except when he was physically exhausted and his nerves hung loose.
He lay still and closed his eyes and let the tide of things wash over him.

His father was in New York; "stopping at some joint or other," he told himself.
The memory of successive summers on the front stoop fell upon him like a weight of
black water. He had not a hundred dollars left; and he knew now, more than ever,
that money was everything, the wall that stood between all he loathed and all he
wanted. The thing was winding itself up; he had thought of that on his first glorious day in New York, and had even provided a way to snap the thread. It lay on his
dressing-table now; he had got it out last night when he came blindly up from dinner,
but the shiny metal hurt his eyes, and he disliked the looks of it.

He rose and moved about with a painful effort, succumbing now and again to
attacks of nausea. It was the old depression exaggerated; all the world had become
Cordelia Street. Yet somehow he was not afraid of anything, was absolutely calm;
perhaps because he had looked into the dark corner at last and knew. It was bad
enough, what he saw there, but somehow not so bad as his long fear of it had been.
He saw everything clearly now. He had a feeling that he had made the best of it, that
he had lived the sort of life he was meant to live, and for half an hour he sat staring
at the revolver. But he told himself that was not the way, so he went downstairs and
took a cab to the ferry.

When Paul arrived at Newark, he got off the train and took another cab, directing the driver to follow the Pennsylvania tracks out of the town. The snow lay heavy
on the roadways and had drifted deep in the open fields. Only here and there the
dead grass or dried weed stalks projected, singularly black, above it. Once well into
the country, Paul dismissed the carriage and walked, floundering along the tracks, his
mind a medley of irrelevant things. He seemed to hold in his brain an actual picture
of everything he had seen that morning. He remembered every feature of both his
drivers, of the toothless old woman from whom he had bought the red flowers in his
coat, the agent from whom he had got his ticket, and all of his fellow-passengers on
the ferry. His mind, unable to cope with vital matters near at hand, worked feverishly
and deftly at sorting and grouping these images. They made for him a part of the
ugliness of the world, of the ache in his head, and the bitter burning on his tongue.
He stooped and put a handful of snow into his mouth as he walked, but that, too,
seemed hot. When he reached a little hillside, where the tracks ran through a cut
some twenty feet below him, he stopped and sat down.

The carnations in his coat were drooping with the cold, he noticed; their red
glory all over. It occurred to him that all the flowers he had seen in the glass cases
that first night must have gone the same way, long before this. It was only one splendid breath they had, in spite of their brave mockery at the winter outside the glass;
and it was a losing game in the end, it seemed, this revolt against the homilies by
which the world is run. Paul took one of the blossoms carefully from his coat and
scooped a little hole in the snow, where he covered it up. Then he dozed a while,
from his weak condition, seemingly insensible to the cold.

The sound of an approaching train awoke him, and he started to his feet, remem-   65
bering only his resolution, and afraid lest he should be too late. He stood watching
the approaching locomotive, his teeth chattering, his lips drawn away from them in

a frightened smile; once or twice he glanced nervously sidewise, as though he were being watched. When the right moment came, he jumped. As he fell, the folly of his haste occurred to him with merciless clearness, the vastness of what he had left undone. There flashed through his brain, clearer than ever before, the blue of Adriatic water, the yellow of Algerian sands.

He felt something strike his chest, and that his body was being thrown swiftly through the air, on and on, immeasurably far and fast, while his limbs were gently relaxed. Then, because the picture making mechanism was crushed, the disturbing visions flashed into black, and Paul dropped back into the immense design of things.

Kate Chopin

The Story of an Hour
1894

Kate Chopin (1851–1904) demonstrates again, as in "The Storm" in Chapter 4, her ability to write short stories of compressed intensity. For a brief biography and a portrait see page 121.

Knowing that Mrs. Mallard was afflicted with a heart trouble, great care was taken to break to her as gently as possible the news of her husband's death.

It was her sister Josephine who told her, in broken sentences; veiled hints that revealed in half concealing. Her husband's friend Richards was there, too, near her. It was he who had been in the newspaper office when intelligence of the railroad disaster was received, with Brently Mallard's name leading the list of "killed." He had only taken the time to assure himself of its truth by a second telegram, and had hastened to forestall any less careful, less tender friend in bearing the sad message.

She did not hear the story as many women have heard the same, with a paralyzed inability to accept its significance. She wept at once, with sudden, wild abandonment, in her sister's arms. When the storm of grief had spent itself she went away to her room alone. She would have no one follow her.

There stood, facing the open window, a comfortable, roomy armchair. Into this she sank, pressed down by a physical exhaustion that haunted her body and seemed to reach into her soul.

She could see in the open square before her house the tops of trees that were all aquiver with the new spring life. The delicious breath of rain was in the air. In the street below a peddler was crying his wares. The notes of a distant song which some one was singing reached her faintly, and countless sparrows were twittering in the eaves.

There were patches of blue sky showing here and there through the clouds that had met and piled one above the other in the west facing her window.

She sat with her head thrown back upon the cushion of the chair, quite motionless, except when a sob came up into her throat and shook her, as a child who has cried itself to sleep continues to sob in its dreams.

She was young, with a fair, calm face, whose lines bespoke repression and even a certain strength. But now there was a dull stare in her eyes, whose gaze was fixed away off yonder on one of those patches of blue sky. It was not a glance of reflection, but rather indicated a suspension of intelligent thought.

There was something coming to her and she was waiting for it, fearfully. What was it? She did not know; it was too subtle and elusive to name. But she felt it, creeping out of the sky, reaching toward her through the sounds, the scents, the color that filled the air.

Now her bosom rose and fell tumultuously. She was beginning to recognize this thing that was approaching to possess her, and she was striving to beat it back with her will—as powerless as her two white slender hands would have been. 10

When she abandoned herself a little whispered word escaped her slightly parted lips. She said it over and over under her breath: "free, free, free!" The vacant stare and the look of terror that had followed it went from her eyes. They stayed keen and bright. Her pulses beat fast, and the coursing blood warmed and relaxed every inch of her body.

She did not stop to ask if it were or were not a monstrous joy that held her. A clear and exalted perception enabled her to dismiss the suggestion as trivial.

She knew that she would weep again when she saw the kind, tender hands folded in death; the face that had never looked save with love upon her, fixed and gray and dead. But she saw beyond that bitter moment a long procession of years to come that would belong to her absolutely. And she opened and spread her arms out to them in welcome.

There would be no one to live for her during those coming years; she would live for herself. There would be no powerful will bending hers in that blind persistence with which men and women believe they have a right to impose a private will upon a fellow-creature. A kind intention or a cruel intention made the act seem no less a crime as she looked upon it in that brief moment of illumination.

And yet she had loved him—sometimes. Often she had not. What did it matter! 15 What could love, the unsolved mystery, count for in face of this possession of self-assertion which she suddenly recognized as the strongest impulse of her being!

"Free! Body and soul free!" she kept whispering.

Josephine was kneeling before the closed door with her lips to the keyhole, imploring for admission. "Louise, open the door! I beg; open the door—you will make yourself ill. What are you doing, Louise? For heaven's sake open the door."

"Go away. I am not making myself ill." No; she was drinking in a very elixir of life through that open window.

Her fancy was running riot along those days ahead of her. Spring days, and summer days, and all sorts of days that would be her own. She breathed a quick prayer that life might be long. It was only yesterday she had thought with a shudder that life might be long.

She arose at length and opened the door to her sister's importunities. There was 20 a feverish triumph in her eyes, and she carried herself unwittingly like a goddess of Victory. She clasped her sister's waist, and together they descended the stairs. Richards stood waiting for them at the bottom.

Some one was opening the front door with a latchkey. It was Brently Mallard who entered, a little travel-stained, composedly carrying his grip-sack and umbrella. He had been far from the scene of the accident, and did not even know there had been one. He stood amazed at Josephine's piercing cry; at Richards' quick motion to screen him from the view of his wife.

But Richards was too late.

When the doctors came they said she had died of heart disease—of joy that kills.

Neil Gaiman

How to Talk to Girls at Parties   2006

Neil Gaiman was born in Hampshire, England, in 1960 to a father who worked for a chain of grocery stores and a mother who was a pharmacist. When still a young boy, his parents quit their jobs, moved the family, and joined the Church of Scientology, for which his father became a public relations official. Gaiman has stated that he practices neither Scientology nor Judaism, his family's other religion, although that odd combination of fantasy and tradition pervades his writing. He did not attend university, but instead began a prolific career in literature—initially as a writer of graphic novels. Early on, Gaiman worked as a journalist and book reviewer on his way to becoming one of the most successful living writers of several imaginative

Neil Gaiman

genres, including literary fiction, fantasy, and comic books. He has also written horror, children's literature, and screenplays for television and film. "How to Talk to Girls at Parties" was adapted into a film by John Cameron Mitchell in 2018. Gaiman launched to fame with the publication of The Sandman *(1989–1996), a series that became one of DC Comic's bestselling titles in their storied history, even surpassing the sales of such classics as* Superman *and* Batman.

Gaiman started reading at age four and was soon immersed in the works of C. S. Lewis, J. R. R. Tolkien, Ursula K. Le Guin, Edgar Allan Poe, Lewis Carroll, and others. His writing is full of allusion; the depth and diversity of his literary accomplishments were influenced by spending countless hours in the library throughout his childhood. "I wouldn't be who I am without libraries," he has said. "I was the sort of kid who devoured books, and my happiest times as a boy were when I persuaded my parents to drop me off in the local library on their way to work, and I spent the day there." Gaiman has three children from his first marriage. He lives near Minneapolis and is married to the musician Amanda Palmer.

"Come on," said Vic. "It'll be great."

"No, it won't," I said, although I'd lost this fight hours ago, and I knew it.

"It'll be brilliant," said Vic, for the hundredth time. "Girls! Girls! Girls!" He grinned with white teeth.

We both attended an all-boys' school in south London. While it would be a lie to say that we had no experience with girls—Vic seemed to have had many girlfriends, while I had kissed three of my sister's friends—it would, I think, be perfectly true to say that we both chiefly spoke to, interacted with, and only truly understood, other boys. Well, I did, anyway. It's hard to speak for someone else, and I've not seen Vic for thirty years. I'm not sure that I would know what to say to him now if I did.

We were walking the backstreets that used to twine in a grimy maze behind East   5
Croydon station—a friend had told Vic about a party, and Vic was determined to go whether I liked it or not, and I didn't. But my parents were away that week at a conference, and I was Vic's guest at his house, so I was trailing along beside him.

"It'll be the same as it always is," I said. "After an hour you'll be off somewhere snogging the prettiest girl at the party, and I'll be in the kitchen listening to somebody's mum going on about politics or poetry or something."

"You just have to talk to them," he said. "I think it's probably that road at the end here." He gestured cheerfully, swinging the bag with the bottle in it.

"Don't you know?"

"Alison gave me directions and I wrote them on a bit of paper, but I left it on the hall table. S'okay. I can find it."

"How?" Hope welled slowly up inside me.   10

"We walk down the road," he said, as if speaking to an idiot child. "And we look for the party. Easy."

I looked, but saw no party: just narrow houses with rusting cars or bikes in their concreted front gardens; and the dusty glass fronts of newsagents, which smelled of alien spices and sold everything from birthday cards and secondhand comics to the kind of magazines that were so pornographic that they were sold already sealed in plastic bags. I had been there when Vic had slipped one of those magazines beneath his sweater, but the owner caught him on the pavement outside and made him give it back.

We reached the end of the road and turned into a narrow street of terraced houses. Everything looked very still and empty in the Summer's evening. "It's all right for you," I said. "They fancy you. You don't actually have to talk to them." It was true: one urchin grin from Vic and he could have his pick of the room.

"Nah. S'not like that. You've just got to talk."

The times I had kissed my sister's friends I had not spoken to them. They had   15
been around while my sister was off doing something elsewhere, and they had drifted into my orbit, and so I had kissed them. I do not remember any talking. I did not know what to say to girls, and I told him so.

"They're just girls," said Vic. "They don't come from another planet."

As we followed the curve of the road around, my hopes that the party would prove unfindable began to fade: a low pulsing noise, music muffled by walls and doors, could be heard from a house up ahead. It was eight in the evening, not that early if you aren't yet sixteen, and we weren't. Not quite.

I had parents who liked to know where I was, but I don't think Vic's parents cared that much. He was the youngest of five boys. That in itself seemed magical to me: I merely had two sisters, both younger than I was, and I felt both unique and lonely. I had wanted a brother as far back as I could remember. When I turned thirteen, I stopped wishing on falling stars or first stars, but back when I did, a brother was what I had wished for.

We went up the garden path, crazy paving leading us past a hedge and a solitary rosebush to a pebble-dashed facade. We rang the doorbell, and the door was opened by a girl. I could not have told you how old she was, which was one of the things about girls I had begun to hate: when you start out as kids you're just boys and girls, going through time at the same speed, and you're all five, or seven, or eleven, together. And then one day there's a lurch and the girls just sort of sprint off into the future ahead of you, and they know all about everything, and they have periods and breasts and makeup and God-only-knew-what-else—for I certainly didn't. The diagrams in biology textbooks were no substitute for being, in a very real sense, young adults. And the girls of our age were.

Vic and I weren't young adults, and I was beginning to suspect that even when   20
I started needing to shave every day, instead of once every couple of weeks, I would still be way behind.

The girl said, "Hello?"

Vic said, "We're friends of Alison's." We had met Alison, all freckles and orange hair and a wicked smile, in Hamburg, on a German exchange. The exchange organizers had sent some girls with us, from a local girls' school, to balance the sexes. The girls, our age, more or less, were raucous and funny, and had more or less adult boyfriends with cars and jobs and motorbikes and—in the case of one girl with crooked teeth and a raccoon coat, who spoke to me about it sadly at the end of a party in Hamburg, in, of course, the kitchen—a wife and kids.

"She isn't here," said the girl at the door. "No Alison."

"Not to worry," said Vic, with an easy grin. "I'm Vic. This is Enn." A beat, and then the girl smiled back at him. Vic had a bottle of white wine in a plastic bag, removed from his parents' kitchen cabinet. "Where should I put this, then?"

She stood out of the way, letting us enter. "There's a kitchen in the back," she said. "Put it on the table there, with the other bottles." She had golden, wavy hair, and she was very beautiful. The hall was dim in the twilight, but I could see that she was beautiful.   25

"What's your name, then?" said Vic.

She told him it was Stella, and he grinned his crooked white grin and told her that that had to be the prettiest name he had ever heard. Smooth bastard. And what was worse was that he said it like he meant it.

Vic headed back to drop off the wine in the kitchen, and I looked into the front room, where the music was coming from. There were people dancing in there. Stella walked in, and she started to dance, swaying to the music all alone, and I watched her.

This was during the early days of punk. On our own record players we would play the Adverts and the Jam, the Stranglers and the Clash and the Sex Pistols. At other people's parties you'd hear ELO or 10cc or even Roxy Music. Maybe some Bowie, if you were lucky. During the German exchange, the only LP that we had all been able to agree on was Neil Young's *Harvest*, and his song "Heart of Gold" had threaded through the trip like a refrain: *I crossed the ocean for a heart of gold. . . .*

The music playing in that front room wasn't anything I recognized.   30

It sounded a bit like a German electronic pop group called Kraftwerk, and a bit like an LP I'd been given for my last birthday, of strange sounds made by the BBC Radiophonic Workshop. The music had a beat, though, and the half-dozen girls in that room were moving gently to it, although I only looked at Stella. She shone.

Vic pushed past me, into the room. He was holding a can of lager. "There's booze back in the kitchen," he told me. He wandered over to Stella and he began to talk to her. I couldn't hear what they were saying over the music, but I knew that there was no room for me in that conversation.

I didn't like beer, not back then. I went off to see if there was something I wanted to drink. On the kitchen table stood a large bottle of Coca-Cola, and I poured myself a plastic tumblerful, and I didn't dare say anything to the pair of girls who were talking in the underlit kitchen. They were animated and utterly lovely. Each of them had very black skin and glossy hair and movie star clothes, and their accents were foreign, and each of them was out of my league.

I wandered, Coke in hand.

The house was deeper than it looked, larger and more complex than the two-up   35
two-down model I had imagined. The rooms were underlit—I doubt there was a bulb of more than 40 watts in the building—and each room I went into was inhabited: in my memory, inhabited only by girls. I did not go upstairs.

A girl was the only occupant of the conservatory. Her hair was so fair it was white, and long, and straight, and she sat at the glass-topped table, her hands clasped together, staring at the garden outside, and the gathering dusk. She seemed wistful.

"Do you mind if I sit here?" I asked, gesturing with my cup. She shook her head, and then followed it up with a shrug, to indicate that it was all the same to her. I sat down.

Vic walked past the conservatory door. He was talking to Stella, but he looked in at me, sitting at the table, wrapped in shyness and awkwardness, and he opened and closed his hand in a parody of a speaking mouth. Talk. Right.

"Are you from around here?" I asked the girl.

She shook her head. She wore a low-cut silvery top, and I tried not to stare at the swell of her breasts.   40

I said, "What's your name? I'm Enn."

"Wain's Wain," she said, or something that sounded like it. "I'm a second."

"That's uh. That's a different name."

She fixed me with huge, liquid eyes. "It indicates that my progenitor was also Wain, and that I am obliged to report back to her. I may not breed."

"Ah. Well. Bit early for that anyway, isn't it?"   45

She unclasped her hands, raised them above the table, spread her fingers. "You see?" The little finger on her left hand was crooked, and it bifurcated at the top, splitting into two smaller fingertips. A minor deformity. "When I was finished a decision was needed. Would I be retained, or eliminated? I was fortunate that the decision was with me. Now, I travel, while my more perfect sisters remain at home in stasis. They were firsts. I am a second.

"Soon I must return to Wain, and tell her all I have seen. All my impressions of this place of yours."

"I don't actually live in Croydon," I said. "I don't come from here." I wondered if she was American. I had no idea what she was talking about.

"As you say," she agreed, "neither of us comes from here." She folded her six-fingered left hand beneath her right, as if tucking it out of sight. "I had expected it to be bigger, and cleaner, and more colorful. But still, it is a jewel."

She yawned, covered her mouth with her right hand, only for a moment, before   50
it was back on the table again. "I grow weary of the journeying, and I wish sometimes that it would end. On a street in Rio at Carnival, I saw them on a bridge, golden and tall and insect-eyed and winged, and elated I almost ran to greet them, before I saw that they were only people in costumes. I said to Hola Colt, 'Why do they try so hard to look like us?' and Hola Colt replied, 'Because they hate themselves, all shades of pink and brown, and so small.' It is what I experience, even me, and I am not grown. It is like a world of children, or of elves." Then she smiled, and said, "It was a good thing they could not any of them see Hola Colt."

"Um," I said, "do you want to dance?"

She shook her head immediately. "It is not permitted," she said. "I can do nothing that might cause damage to property. I am Wain's."

"Would you like something to drink, then?"

"Water," she said.

I went back to the kitchen and poured myself another Coke, and filled a cup   55
with water from the tap. From the kitchen back to the hall, and from there into the conservatory, but now it was quite empty.

I wondered if the girl had gone to the toilet, and if she might change her mind about dancing later. I walked back to the front room and stared in. The place was filling up. There were more girls dancing, and several lads I didn't know, who looked a few years older than me and Vic. The lads and the girls all kept their distance, but Vic was holding Stella's hand as they danced, and when the song ended he put an arm around her, casually, almost proprietorially, to make sure that nobody else cut in.

I wondered if the girl I had been talking to in the conservatory was now upstairs, as she did not appear to be on the ground floor.

I walked into the living room, which was across the hall from the room where the people were dancing, and I sat down on the sofa. There was a girl sitting there already. She had dark hair, cut short and spiky, and a nervous manner.

Talk, I thought. "Um, this mug of water's going spare," I told her, "if you want it?"

She nodded, and reached out her hand and took the mug, extremely carefully, 60 as if she were unused to taking things, as if she could trust neither her vision nor her hands.

"I love being a tourist," she said, and smiled hesitantly. She had a gap between her two front teeth, and she sipped the tap water as if she were an adult sipping a fine wine. "The last tour, we went to sun, and we swam in sunfire pools with the whales. We heard their histories and we shivered in the chill of the outer places, then we swam deepward where the heat churned and comforted us.

"I wanted to go back. This time, I wanted it. There was so much I had not seen. Instead we came to world. Do you like it?"

"Like what?"

She gestured vaguely to the room—the sofa, the armchairs, the curtains, the unused gas fire.

"It's all right, I suppose." 65

"I told them I did not wish to visit world," she said. "My parent-teacher was unimpressed. 'You will have much to learn,' it told me. I said, 'I could learn more in sun, again. Or in the deeps. Jessa spun webs between galaxies. I want to do that.'

"But there was no reasoning with it, and I came to world. Parent-teacher engulfed me, and I was here, embodied in a decaying lump of meat hanging on a frame of calcium. As I incarnated I felt things deep inside me, fluttering and pumping and squishing. It was my first experience with pushing air through the mouth, vibrating the vocal cords on the way, and I used it to tell parent-teacher that I wished that I would die, which it acknowledged was the inevitable exit strategy from world."

There were black worry beads wrapped around her wrist, and she fiddled with them as she spoke. "But knowledge is there, in the meat," she said, "and I am resolved to learn from it."

We were sitting close at the center of the sofa now. I decided I should put an arm around her, but casually. I would extend my arm along the back of the sofa and eventually sort of creep it down, almost imperceptibly, until it was touching her. She said, "The thing with the liquid in the eyes, when the world blurs. Nobody told me, and I still do not understand. I have touched the folds of the Whisper and pulsed and flown with the tachyon swans, and I still do not understand."

She wasn't the prettiest girl there, but she seemed nice enough, and she was a 70 girl, anyway. I let my arm slide down a little, tentatively, so that it made contact with her back, and she did not tell me to take it away.

Vic called to me then, from the doorway. He was standing with his arm around Stella, protectively, waving at me. I tried to let him know, by shaking my head, that I was onto something, but he called my name and, reluctantly, I got up from the sofa and walked over to the door. "What?"

"Er. Look. The party," said Vic, apologetically. "It's not the one I thought it was. I've been talking to Stella and I figured it out. Well, she sort of explained it to me. We're at a different party."

"Christ. Are we in trouble? Do we have to go?"

Stella shook her head. He leaned down and kissed her, gently, on the lips. "You're just happy to have me here, aren't you darlin'?"

"You know I am," she told him.   75

He looked from her back to me, and he smiled his white smile: roguish, lovable, a little bit Artful Dodger, a little bit wide-boy Prince Charming. "Don't worry. They're all tourists here anyway. It's a foreign exchange thing, innit? Like when we all went to Germany."

"It is?"

"Enn. You got to talk to them. And that means you got to listen to them, too. You understand?"

"I did. I already talked to a couple of them."

"You getting anywhere?"   80

"I was till you called me over."

"Sorry about that. Look, I just wanted to fill you in. Right?"

And he patted my arm and he walked away with Stella. Then, together, the two of them went up the stairs.

Understand me, all the girls at that party, in the twilight, were lovely; they all had perfect faces but, more important than that, they had whatever strangeness of proportion, of oddness or humanity it is that makes a beauty something more than a shop window dummy.

Stella was the most lovely of any of them, but she, of course, was Vic's, and they   85
were going upstairs together, and that was just how things would always be.

There were several people now sitting on the sofa, talking to the gap-toothed girl. Someone told a joke, and they all laughed. I would have had to push my way in there to sit next to her again, and it didn't look like she was expecting me back, or cared that I had gone, so I wandered out into the hall. I glanced in at the dancers, and found myself wondering where the music was coming from. I couldn't see a record player or speakers.

From the hall I walked back to the kitchen.

Kitchens are good at parties. You never need an excuse to be there, and, on the good side, at this party I couldn't see any signs of someone's mum. I inspected the various bottles and cans on the kitchen table, then I poured a half an inch of Pernod into the bottom of my plastic cup, which I filled to the top with Coke. I dropped in a couple of ice cubes and took a sip, relishing the sweet-shop tang of the drink.

"What's that you're drinking?" A girl's voice.

"It's Pernod," I told her. "It tastes like aniseed balls, only it's alcoholic." I didn't   90
say that I only tried it because I'd heard someone in the crowd ask for a Pernod on a live Velvet Underground LP.

"Can I have one?" I poured another Pernod, topped it off with Coke, passed it to her. Her hair was a coppery auburn, and it tumbled around her head in ringlets. It's not a hair style you see much now, but you saw it a lot back then.

"What's your name?" I asked.

"Triolet," she said.

"Pretty name," I told her, although I wasn't sure that it was. She was pretty, though.

"It's a verse form," she said, proudly. "Like me."   95

"You're a poem?"

She smiled, and looked down and away, perhaps bashfully. Her profile was almost flat—a perfect Grecian nose that came down from her forehead in a straight line. We did Antigone in the school theater the previous year. I was the messenger who brings Creon the news of Antigone's death. We wore half-masks that made us look like that. I thought of that play, looking at her face, in the kitchen, and I thought of Barry Smith's drawings of women in the Conan comics: five years later I would have thought of the Pre-Raphaelites, of Jane Morris and Lizzie Siddall. But I was only fifteen then.

"You're a poem?" I repeated.

She chewed her lower lip. "If you want. I am a poem, or I am a pattern, or a race of people whose world was swallowed by the sea."

"Isn't it hard to be three things at the same time?"   100

"What's your name?"

"Enn."

"So you are Enn," she said. "And you are a male. And you are a biped. Is it hard to be three things at the same time?"

"But they aren't different things. I mean, they aren't contradictory." It was a word I had read many times but never said aloud before that night, and I put the stresses in the wrong places. Contradictory.

She wore a thin dress made of a white, silky fabric. Her eyes were a pale green,   105
a color that would now make me think of tinted contact lenses; but this was thirty years ago; things were different then. I remember wondering about Vic and Stella, upstairs. By now, I was sure that they were in one of the bedrooms, and I envied Vic so much it almost hurt.

Still, I was talking to this girl, even if we were talking nonsense, even if her name wasn't really Triolet (my generation had not been given hippie names: all the Rainbows and the Sunshines and the Moons, they were only six, seven, eight years old back then). She said, "We knew that it would soon be over, and so we put it all into a poem, to tell the universe who we were, and why we were here, and what we said and did and thought and dreamed and yearned for. We wrapped our dreams in words and patterned the words so that they would live forever, unforgettable. Then we sent the poem as a pattern of flux, to wait in the heart of a star, beaming out its message in pulses and bursts and fuzzes across the electromagnetic spectrum, until the time when, on worlds a thousand sun systems distant, the pattern would be decoded and read, and it would become a poem once again."

"And then what happened?"

She looked at me with her green eyes, and it was as if she stared out at me from her own Antigone half-mask; but as if her pale green eyes were just a different, deeper, part of the mask. "You cannot hear a poem without it changing you," she told me. "They heard it, and it colonized them. It inherited them and it inhabited them, its rhythms becoming part of the way that they thought; its images permanently transmuting their metaphors; its verses, its outlook, its aspirations becoming their lives. Within a generation their children would be born already knowing the poem, and, sooner rather than later, as these things go, there were no more children born. There was no need for them, not any longer. There was only a poem, which took flesh and walked and spread itself across the vastness of the known."

I edged closer to her, so I could feel my leg pressing against hers.

She seemed to welcome it: she put her hand on my arm, affectionately, and I felt   110
a smile spreading across my face.

"There are places that we are welcomed," said Triolet, "and places where we are regarded as a noxious weed, or as a disease, something immediately to be quarantined and eliminated. But where does contagion end and art begin?"

"I don't know," I said, still smiling. I could hear the unfamiliar music as it pulsed and scattered and boomed in the front room.

She leaned into me then and—I suppose it was a kiss. . . . I suppose. She pressed her lips to my lips, anyway, and then, satisfied, she pulled back, as if she had now marked me as her own.

"Would you like to hear it?" she asked, and I nodded, unsure what she was offering me, but certain that I needed anything she was willing to give me.

She began to whisper something in my ear. It's the strangest thing about poetry—   115
you can tell it's poetry, even if you don't speak the language. You can hear Homer's Greek without understanding a word, and you still know it's poetry. I've heard Polish poetry, and Inuit poetry, and I knew what it was without knowing. Her whisper was like that. I didn't know the language, but her words washed through me, perfect, and in my mind's eye I saw towers of glass and diamond; and people with eyes of the palest green; and, unstoppable, beneath every syllable, I could feel the relentless advance of the ocean.

Perhaps I kissed her properly. I don't remember. I know I wanted to.

And then Vic was shaking me violently. "Come on!" he was shouting. "Quickly. Come on!"

In my head I began to come back from a thousand miles away.

"Idiot. Come on. Just get a move on," he said, and he swore at me. There was fury in his voice.

For the first time that evening I recognized one of the songs being played in the front   120
room. A sad saxophone wail followed by a cascade of liquid chords, a man's voice singing cut-up lyrics about the sons of the silent age.° I wanted to stay and hear the song.

She said, "I am not finished. There is yet more of me."

"Sorry love," said Vic, but he wasn't smiling any longer. "There'll be another time," and he grabbed me by the elbow and he twisted and pulled, forcing me from the room. I did not resist. I knew from experience that Vic could beat the stuffing out me if he got it into his head to do so. He wouldn't do it unless he was upset or angry, but he was angry now.

Out into the front hall. As Vic pulled open the door, I looked back one last time, over my shoulder, hoping to see Triolet in the doorway to the kitchen, but she was not there. I saw Stella, though, at the top of the stairs. She was staring down at Vic, and I saw her face.

This all happened thirty years ago. I have forgotten much, and I will forget more, and in the end I will forget everything; yet, if I have any certainty of life beyond death, it is all wrapped up not in psalms or hymns, but in this one thing alone: I cannot believe that I will ever forget that moment, or forget the expression on Stella's face as she watched Vic hurrying away from her. Even in death I shall remember that.

---

sons of the silent age: "Sons of the Silent Age" is a song by David Bowie from his 1977 album *Heroes,* the second of three dark, minimalist records that were known as the "Berlin Trilogy."

Her clothes were in disarray, and there was makeup smudged across her face, and   125
her eyes—

You wouldn't want to make a universe angry. I bet an angry universe would look
at you with eyes like that.

We ran then, me and Vic, away from the party and the tourists and the twilight,
ran as if a lightning storm was on our heels, a mad helter-skelter dash down the confusion of streets, threading through the maze, and we did not look back, and we did
not stop until we could not breathe; and then we stopped and panted, unable to run
any longer. We were in pain. I held on to a wall, and Vic threw up, hard and long,
into the gutter.

He wiped his mouth.

"She wasn't a—" He stopped.

He shook his head.   130

Then he said, "You know . . . I think there's a thing. When you've gone as far
as you dare. And if you go any further, you wouldn't be you anymore? You'd be the
person who'd done that? The places you just can't go. . . . I think that happened to
me tonight."

I thought I knew what he was saying. "Screw her, you mean?" I said.

He rammed a knuckle hard against my temple, and twisted it violently. I wondered if I was going to have to fight him—and lose—but after a moment he lowered
his hand and moved away from me, making a low, gulping noise.

I looked at him curiously, and I realized that he was crying: his face was scarlet; snot and tears ran down his cheeks. Vic was sobbing in the street, as unselfcon-
sciously and heartbreakingly as a little boy.

He walked away from me then, shoulders heaving, and he hurried down the road   135
so he was in front of me and I could no longer see his face. I wondered what had
occurred in that upstairs room to make him behave like that, to scare him so, and I
could not even begin to guess.

The streetlights came on, one by one; Vic stumbled on ahead, while I trudged
down the street behind him in the dusk, my feet treading out the measure of a poem
that, try as I might, I could not properly remember and would never be able to repeat.

Nathaniel Hawthorne

*Nathaniel Hawthorne (1804–1864) was born
in the clipper-ship seaport of Salem, Massachusetts, son of a merchant captain (who died when
the future novelist was only four years old) and
great-great-grandson of a magistrate involved in
the notorious Salem witchcraft trials. Hawthorne
takes a keen interest in New England's sin-and-
brimstone Puritan past in many of his stories,
especially "Young Goodman Brown," and in the
classic novel* The Scarlet Letter *(1850), his deepest exploration of his major themes of conscience,
sin, and guilt. In 1825 Hawthorne graduated from
Bowdoin College; one of his classmates—and his
lifelong best friend—was Franklin Pierce, who
in 1852 would be elected president of the United*

Nathaniel Hawthorne

States. After college, Hawthorne lived at home and trained to be a writer. His first novel, Fanshawe (1828), begun while he was still an undergraduate, was published anonymously and at his own expense. During this period, Hawthorne also experienced great difficulty in trying to publish his short fiction, both in magazines and in book form, until the appearance of Twice-Told Tales (1837). In 1841, he was appointed to a position in the Boston Custom House; in the following year he married Sophia Peabody. The newlyweds settled in the Old Manse in Concord, Massachusetts. Three more novels followed: The House of the Seven Gables (1851, the story of a family curse, tinged with nightmarish humor), The Blithedale Romance (1852, drawn from his short, irritating stay at a Utopian commune, Brook Farm), and The Marble Faun (1860, inspired by a stay in Italy). When Franklin Pierce ran for president, Hawthorne wrote his campaign biography. After taking office, Pierce appointed his old friend American consul at Liverpool, England. Depressed by ill health and the terrible toll of the Civil War, Hawthorne died suddenly while on a tour with Pierce of New Hampshire's White Mountains. With his contemporary Edgar Allan Poe, Hawthorne transformed the American short story from popular magazine filler into a major literary form.

Young Goodman Brown   (1835) 1846

Young Goodman° Brown came forth, at sunset, into the street of Salem village,° but put his head back, after crossing the threshold, to exchange a parting kiss with his young wife. And Faith, as the wife was aptly named, thrust her own pretty head into the street, letting the wind play with the pink ribbons of her cap, while she called to Goodman Brown.

"Dearest heart," whispered she, softly and rather sadly, when her lips were close to his ear, "pray thee, put off your journey until sunrise, and sleep in your own bed to-night. A lone woman is troubled with such dreams and such thoughts, that she's afraid of herself, sometimes. Pray, tarry with me this night, dear husband, of all nights in the year!"

"My love and my Faith," replied young Goodman Brown, "of all nights in the year, this one night must I tarry away from thee. My journey, as thou callest it, forth and back again, must needs be done 'twixt now and sunrise. What, my sweet, pretty wife, dost thou doubt me already, and we but three months married!"

"Then, God bless you!" said Faith, with the pink ribbons, "and may you find all well, when you come back."

"Amen!" cried Goodman Brown. "Say thy prayers, dear Faith, and go to bed at   5
dusk, and no harm will come to thee."

So they parted; and the young man pursued his way, until, being about to turn the corner by the meeting-house, he looked back, and saw the head of Faith still peeping after him, with a melancholy air, in spite of her pink ribbons.

"Poor little Faith!" thought he, for his heart smote him. "What a wretch am I, to leave her on such an errand! She talks of dreams, too. Methought, as she spoke, there was trouble in her face, as if a dream had warned her what work is to be done tonight. But, no, no! 'twould kill her to think it. Well; she's a blessed angel on earth; and after this one night, I'll cling to her skirts and follow her to Heaven."

Goodman: title given by Puritans to a male head of a household; a farmer or other ordinary citizen. Salem village: in England's Massachusetts Bay Colony.

With this excellent resolve for the future, Goodman Brown felt himself justified in making more haste on his present evil purpose. He had taken a dreary road, darkened by all the gloomiest trees of the forest, which barely stood aside to let the narrow path creep through, and closed immediately behind. It was all as lonely as could be; and there is this peculiarity in such a solitude, that the traveller knows not who may be concealed by the innumerable trunks and the thick boughs overhead; so that, with lonely footsteps, he may yet be passing through an unseen multitude.

"There may be a devilish Indian behind every tree," said Goodman Brown, to himself; and he glanced fearfully behind him, as he added, "What if the devil himself should be at my very elbow!"

His head being turned back, he passed a crook of the road, and looking forward   10
again, beheld the figure of a man, in grave and decent attire, seated at the foot of an old tree. He arose, at Goodman Brown's approach, and walked onward, side by side with him.

"You are late, Goodman Brown," said he. "The clock of the Old South was striking as I came through Boston; and that is full fifteen minutes agone."°

"Faith kept me back awhile," replied the young man, with a tremor in his voice, caused by the sudden appearance of his companion, though not wholly unexpected.

It was now deep dusk in the forest, and deepest in that part of it where these two were journeying. As nearly as could be discerned, the second traveller was about fifty years old, apparently in the same rank of life as Goodman Brown, and bearing a considerable resemblance to him, though perhaps more in expression than features. Still, they might have been taken for father and son. And yet, though the elder person was as simply clad as the younger, and as simple in manner too, he had an indescribable air of one who knew the world, and would not have felt abashed at the governor's dinner-table, or in King William's court,° were it possible that his affairs should call him thither. But the only thing about him, that could be fixed upon as remarkable, was his staff, which bore the likeness of a great black snake, so curiously wrought, that it might almost be seen to twist and wriggle itself, like a living serpent. This, of course, must have been an ocular deception, assisted by the uncertain light.

"Come, Goodman Brown!" cried his fellow-traveller, "this is dull pace for the beginning of a journey. Take my staff, if you are so soon weary."

"Friend," said the other, exchanging his slow pace for a full stop, "having kept   15
covenant by meeting thee here, it is my purpose now to return whence I came. I have scruples, touching the matter thou wot'st° of."

"Sayest thou so?" replied he of the serpent, smiling apart. "Let us walk on, nevertheless, reasoning as we go, and if I convince thee not, thou shalt turn back. We are but a little way in the forest, yet."

"Too far, too far!" exclaimed the goodman, unconsciously resuming his walk. "My father never went into the woods on such an errand, nor his father before him. We have been a race of honest men and good Christians, since the days of the martyrs.° And shall I be the first of the name of Brown, that ever took this path, and kept—"

---

full fifteen minutes agone: Apparently this mystery man has traveled in a flash from Boston's Old South Church all the way to the woods beyond Salem—as the crow flies, a good sixteen miles. *King William's court:* back in England, where William III reigned from 1689 to 1702. *wot'st:* know. *days of the martyrs:* a time when many forebears of the New England Puritans had given their lives for religious convictions—when Mary I (Mary Tudor, nicknamed "Bloody Mary"), queen of England from 1553 to 1558, briefly reestablished the Roman Catholic Church in England and launched a campaign of persecution against Protestants.

"Such company, thou wouldst say," observed the elder person, interpreting his pause. "Well said, Goodman Brown! I have been as well acquainted with your family as with ever a one among the Puritans; and that's no trifle to say. I helped your grandfather, the constable, when he lashed the Quaker woman so smartly through the streets of Salem. And it was I that brought your father a pitch-pine knot, kindled at my own hearth, to set fire to an Indian village, in King Philip's war.° They were my good friends, both; and many a pleasant walk have we had along this path, and returned merrily after midnight. I would fain be friends with you, for their sake."

"If it be as thou sayest," replied Goodman Brown, "I marvel they never spoke of these matters. Or, verily, I marvel not, seeing that the least rumor of the sort would have driven them from New England. We are a people of prayer, and good works, to boot, and abide no such wickedness."

"Wickedness or not," said the traveller with the twisted staff, "I have a very general acquaintance here in New England. The deacons of many a church have drunk the communion wine with me; the selectmen, of divers towns, make me their chairman; and a majority of the Great and General Court are firm supporters of my interest. The governor and I, too—but these are state-secrets."   20

"Can this be so!" cried Goodman Brown, with a stare of amazement at his undisturbed companion. "Howbeit, I have nothing to do with the governor and council; they have their own ways, and are no rule for a simple husbandman, like me. But, were I to go on with thee, how should I meet the eye of that good old man, our minister, at Salem village? Oh, his voice would make me tremble, both Sabbath-day and lecture-day!"°

Thus far, the elder traveller had listened with due gravity, but now burst into a fit of irrepressible mirth, shaking himself so violently, that his snake-like staff actually seemed to wriggle in sympathy.

"Ha! ha! ha!" shouted he, again and again; then composing himself, "Well, go on, Goodman Brown, go on; but pray thee, don't kill me with laughing!"

"Well, then, to end the matter at once," said Goodman Brown, considerably nettled, "there is my wife, Faith. It would break her dear little heart; and I'd rather break my own!"

"Nay, if that be the case," answered the other, "e'en go thy ways, Goodman Brown. I would not, for twenty old women like the one hobbling before us, that Faith should come to any harm."   25

As he spoke, he pointed his staff at a female figure on the path, in whom Goodman Brown recognized a very pious and exemplary dame, who had taught him his catechism, in youth, and was still his moral and spiritual adviser, jointly with the minister and Deacon Gookin.

"A marvel, truly, that Goody° Hoyse should be so far in the wilderness, at nightfall!" said he. "But, with your leave, friend, I shall take a cut through the woods, until we have left this Christian woman behind. Being a stranger to you, she might ask whom I was consorting with, and whither I was going."

King Philip's war: Metacomet, or King Philip (as the English called him), chief of the Wampanoag Indians, had led a bitter, widespread uprising of several New England tribes (1675–1678). Metacomet died in the war, as did one out of every ten white male colonists.   *lecture-day:* a weekday when everyone had to go to church to hear a sermon or Bible-reading.   *Goody:* short for Goodwife, title for a married woman of ordinary station. In his story, Hawthorne borrows from history the names of two "Goodys"—Goody Cloyse and Goody Cory—and one unmarried woman, Martha Carrier. In 1692 Hawthorne's great-great-grandfather John Hathorne, a judge in the Salem witchcraft trials, had condemned all three to be hanged.

"Be it so," said his fellow-traveller. "Betake you to the woods, and let me keep the path."

Accordingly, the young man turned aside, but took care to watch his companion, who advanced softly along the road, until he had come within a staff's length of the old dame. She, meanwhile, was making the best of her way, with singular speed for so aged a woman, and mumbling some indistinct words, a prayer, doubtless, as she went. The traveller put forth his staff, and touched her withered neck with what seemed the serpent's tail.

"The devil!" screamed the pious old lady.   30

"Then Goody Cloyse knows her old friend?" observed the traveller, confronting her, and leaning on his writhing stick.

"Ah, forsooth, and is it your worship, indeed?" cried the good dame. "Yea, truly is it, and in the very image of my old gossip,° Goodman Brown, the grandfather of the silly fellow that now is. But—would your worship believe it?—my broomstick hath strangely disappeared, stolen, as I suspect, by that unhanged witch, Goody Cory, and that, too, when I was all anointed with the juice of smallage and cinquefoil and wolfs bane—"°

"Mingled with fine wheat and the fat of a new-born babe," said the shape of old Goodman Brown.

"Ah, your worship knows the receipt,"° cried the old lady, cackling aloud. "So, as I was saying, being all ready for the meeting, and no horse to ride on, I made up my mind to foot it; for they tell me, there is a nice young man to be taken into communion to-night. But now your good worship will lend me your arm, and we shall be there in a twinkling."

"That can hardly be," answered her friend. "I may not spare you my arm, Goody   35
Cloyse, but here is my staff, if you will."

So saying, he threw it down at her feet, where, perhaps, it assumed life, being one of the rods which its owner had formerly lent to the Egyptian Magi.° Of this fact, however, Goodman Brown could not take cognizance. He had cast up his eyes in astonishment, and looking down again, beheld neither Goody Cloyse nor the serpentine staff, but his fellow-traveller alone, who waited for him as calmly as if nothing had happened.

"That old woman taught me my catechism!" said the young man; and there was a world of meaning in this simple comment.

They continued to walk onward, while the elder traveller exhorted his companion to make good speed and persevere in the path, discoursing so aptly, that his arguments seemed rather to spring up in the bosom of his auditor, than to be suggested by himself. As they went, he plucked a branch of maple, to serve for a walking-stick, and began to strip it of the twigs and little boughs, which were wet with evening dew. The moment his fingers touched them, they became strangely withered and dried up, as with a week's sunshine. Thus the pair proceeded, at a good free pace, until suddenly, in a gloomy hollow of the road, Goodman Brown sat himself down on the stump of a tree, and refused to go any farther.

---

gossip: friend or kinsman. *smallage and cinquefoil and wolf's bane:* wild plants—here, ingredients for a witch's brew. *receipt:* recipe. *Egyptian Magi:* In the Bible, Pharaoh's wise men and sorcerers who by their magical powers changed their rods into live serpents. (This incident, part of the story of Moses and Aaron, is related in Exodus 7:8–12.)

"Friend," said he, stubbornly, "my mind is made up. Not another step will I budge on this errand. What if a wretched old woman do choose to go to the devil, when I thought she was going to Heaven! Is that any reason why I should quit my dear Faith, and go after her?"

"You will think better of this, by-and-by," said his acquaintance, composedly. 40 "Sit here and rest yourself awhile; and when you feel like moving again, there is my staff to help you along."

Without more words, he threw his companion the maple stick, and was as speedily out of sight, as if he had vanished into the deepening gloom. The young man sat a few moments, by the road-side, applauding himself greatly, and thinking with how clear a conscience he should meet the minister, in his morning-walk, nor shrink from the eye of good old Deacon Gookin. And what calm sleep would be his, that very night, which was to have been spent so wickedly, but purely and sweetly now, in the arms of Faith! Amidst these pleasant and praiseworthy meditations, Goodman Brown heard the tramp of horses along the road, and deemed it advisable to conceal himself within the verge of the forest, conscious of the guilty purpose that had brought him thither, though now so happily turned from it.

On came the hoof-tramps and the voices of the riders, two grave old voices, conversing soberly as they drew near. These mingled sounds appeared to pass along the road, within a few yards of the young man's hiding-place; but owing, doubtless, to the depth of the gloom, at that particular spot, neither the travellers nor their steeds were visible. Though their figures brushed the small boughs by the way-side, it could not be seen that they intercepted, even for a moment, the faint gleam from the strip of bright sky, athwart which they must have passed. Goodman Brown alternately crouched and stood on tip-toe, pulling aside the branches, and thrusting forth his head as far as he durst, without discerning so much as a shadow. It vexed him the more, because he could have sworn, were such a thing possible, that he recognized the voices of the minister and Deacon Gookin, jogging along quietly, as they were wont to do, when bound to some ordination or ecclesiastical council. While yet within hearing, one of the riders stopped to pluck a switch.

"Of the two, reverend Sir," said the voice like the deacon's, "I had rather miss an ordination-dinner than to-night's meeting. They tell me that some of our community are to be here from Falmouth and beyond, and others from Connecticut and Rhode Island; besides several of the Indian powows,° who, after their fashion, know almost as much deviltry as the best of us. Moreover, there is a goodly young woman to be taken into communion."

"Mighty well, Deacon Gookin!" replied the solemn old tones of the minister. "Spur up, or we shall be late. Nothing can be done, you know, until I get on the ground."

The hoofs clattered again, and the voices, talking so strangely in the empty air, 45 passed on through the forest, where no church had ever been gathered, nor solitary Christian prayed. Whither, then, could these holy men be journeying, so deep into the heathen wilderness? Young Goodman Brown caught hold of a tree, for support, being ready to sink down on the ground, faint and overburdened with the heavy sickness of his heart. He looked up to the sky, doubting whether there really was a Heaven above him. Yet, there was the blue arch, and the stars brightening in it.

"With Heaven above, and Faith below, I will yet stand firm against the devil!" cried Goodman Brown.

powows: Indian priests or medicine men.

While he still gazed upward, into the deep arch of the firmament, and had lifted his hands to pray, a cloud, though no wind was stirring, hurried across the zenith, and hid the brightening stars. The blue sky was still visible, except directly over-head, where this black mass of cloud was sweeping swiftly northward. Aloft in the air, as if from the depths of the cloud, came a confused and doubtful sound of voices. Once, the listener fancied that he could distinguish the accents of town's-people of his own, men and women, both pious and ungodly, many of whom he had met at the communion-table, and had seen others rioting at the tavern. The next moment, so indistinct were the sounds, he doubted whether he had heard aught but the murmur of the old forest, whispering without a wind. Then came a stronger swell of those familiar tones, heard daily in the sunshine, at Salem village, but never, until now, from a cloud of night. There was one voice, of a young woman, uttering lamenta-tions, yet with an uncertain sorrow, and entreating for some favor, which, perhaps, it would grieve her to obtain. And all the unseen multitude, both saints and sinners, seemed to encourage her onward.

"Faith!" shouted Goodman Brown, in a voice of agony and desperation; and the echoes of the forest mocked him, crying—"Faith! Faith!" as if bewildered wretches were seeking her, all through the wilderness.

The cry of grief, rage, and terror, was yet piercing the night, when the unhappy husband held his breath for a response. There was a scream, drowned immediately in a louder murmur of voices, fading into far-off laughter, as the dark cloud swept away, leaving the clear and silent sky above Goodman Brown. But something flut-tered lightly down through the air, and caught on the branch of a tree. The young man seized it, and beheld a pink ribbon.

"My Faith is gone!" cried he, after one stupefied moment. "There is no good on earth; and sin is but a name. Come, devil! for to thee is this world given."   50

And maddened with despair, so that he laughed loud and long, did Goodman Brown grasp his staff and set forth again, at such a rate, that he seemed to fly along the forest-path, rather than to walk or run. The road grew wilder and drearier, and more faintly traced, and vanished at length, leaving him in the heart of the dark wil-derness, still rushing onward, with the instinct that guides mortal man to evil. The whole forest was peopled with frightful sounds; the creaking of the trees, the howling of wild beasts, and the yell of Indians; while, sometimes, the wind tolled like a distant church-bell, and sometimes gave a broad roar around the traveller, as if all Nature were laughing him to scorn. But he was himself the chief horror of the scene, and shrank not from its other horrors.

"Ha! ha! ha!" roared Goodman Brown, when the wind laughed at him. "Let us hear which will laugh loudest! Think not to frighten me with your deviltry! Come witch, come wizard, come Indian powow, come devil himself! and here comes Good-man Brown. You may as well fear him as he fear you!"

In truth, all through the haunted forest, there could be nothing more frightful than the figure of Goodman Brown. On he flew, among the black pines, brandishing his staff with frenzied gestures, now giving vent to an inspiration of horrid blasphemy, and now shouting forth such laughter, as set all the echoes of the forest laughing like demons around him. The fiend in his own shape is less hideous, than when he rages in the breast of man. Thus sped the demoniac on his course, until, quivering among the trees, he saw a red light before him, as when the felled trunks and branches of a clearing have been set on fire, and throw up their lurid blaze against the sky, at the hour of midnight. He paused, in a lull of the tempest that had driven him onward, and heard the swell of what seemed a hymn, rolling solemnly from a distance, with the weight of many voices. He knew the tune; it was a familiar one in the choir of the village meeting-house. The verse died heavily away, and was lengthened by a chorus, not of human voices, but of all the sounds of the benighted wilderness, pealing in awful harmony together. Goodman Brown cried out; and his cry was lost to his own ear, by its unison with the cry of the desert.

In the interval of silence, he stole forward, until the light glared full upon his eyes. At one extremity of an open space, hemmed in by the dark wall of the forest, arose a rock, bearing some rude, natural resemblance either to an altar or a pulpit, and surrounded by four blazing pines, their tops aflame, their stems untouched, like candles at an evening meeting. The mass of foliage, that had overgrown the summit of the rock, was all on fire, blazing high into the night, and fitfully illuminating the whole field. Each pendent twig and leafy festoon was in a blaze. As the red light arose and fell, a numerous congregation alternately shone forth, then disappeared in shadow, and again grew, as it were, out of the darkness, peopling the heart of the solitary woods at once.

"A grave and dark-clad company!" quoth Goodman Brown. 55

In truth, they were such. Among them, quivering to-and-fro, between gloom and splendor, appeared faces that would be seen, next day, at the council-board of the province, and others which, Sabbath after Sabbath, looked devoutly heavenward, and benignantly over the crowded pews, from the holiest pulpits in the land. Some affirm that the lady of the governor was there. At least, there were high dames well known to her, and wives of honored husbands, and widows, a great multitude, and ancient maidens, all of excellent repute, and fair young girls, who trembled, lest their mothers should espy them. Either the sudden gleams of light, flashing over the obscure field, bedazzled Goodman Brown, or he recognized a score of the church-members of Salem village, famous for their especial sanctity. Good old Deacon Gookin had arrived, and waited at the skirts of that venerable saint, his revered pastor. But, irreverently consorting with these grave, reputable, and pious people, these elders of the church, these chaste dames and dewy virgins, there were men of dissolute lives and women of spotted fame, wretches given over to all mean and filthy vice, and suspected even of horrid crimes. It was strange to see, that the good shrank not from the wicked, nor were the sinners abashed by the saints. Scattered, also, among their pale-faced enemies, were the Indian priests, or powows, who had often scared their native forest with more hideous incantations than any known to English witchcraft.

"But, where is Faith?" thought Goodman Brown; and, as hope came into his heart, he trembled.

Another verse of the hymn arose, a slow and mournful strain, such as the pious love, but joined to words which expressed all that our nature can conceive of sin, and darkly hinted at far more. Unfathomable to mere mortals is the lore of fiends. Verse after verse was sung, and still the chorus of the desert swelled between, like the deepest tone of a mighty organ. And, with the final peal of that dreadful anthem, there came a sound, as if the roaring wind, the rushing streams, the howling beasts, and every other voice of the unconverted wilderness, were mingling and according with the voice of guilty man, in homage to the prince of all. The four blazing pines threw up a loftier flame, and obscurely discovered shapes and visages of horror on the smoke-wreaths, above the impious assembly. At the same moment, the fire on the rock shot redly forth, and formed a glowing arch above its base, where now appeared a figure. With reverence be it spoken, the figure bore no slight similitude, both in garb and manner, to some grave divine of the New England churches.

"Bring forth the converts!" cried a voice, that echoed through the field and rolled into the forest.

At the word, Goodman Brown stepped forth from the shadow of the trees, and approached the congregation, with whom he felt a loathful brotherhood, by the sympathy of all that was wicked in his heart. He could have well nigh sworn, that the shape of his own dead father beckoned him to advance, looking downward from a smoke-wreath, while a woman, with dim features of despair, threw out her hand to warn him back. Was it his mother? But he had no power to retreat one step, nor to resist, even in thought, when the minister and good old Deacon Gookin seized his arms, and led him to the blazing rock. Thither came also the slender form of a veiled female, led between Goody Cloyse, that pious teacher of the catechism, and Martha Carrier, who had received the devil's promise to be queen of hell. A rampant hag was she! And there stood the proselytes,° beneath the canopy of fire.

"Welcome, my children," said the dark figure, "to the communion of your race! Ye have found, thus young, your nature and your destiny. My children, look behind you!"

They turned; and flashing forth, as it were, in a sheet of flame, the fiend-worshippers were seen; the smile of welcome gleamed darkly on every visage.

"There," resumed the sable form, "are all whom ye have reverenced from youth. Ye deemed them holier than yourselves, and shrank from your own sin, contrasting it with their lives of righteousness, and prayerful aspirations heavenward. Yet, here are they all, in my worshipping assembly! This night it shall be granted you to know their secret deeds; how hoary-bearded elders of the church have whispered wanton words to the young maids of their households; how many a woman, eager for widow's weeds, has given her husband a drink at bedtime, and let him sleep his last sleep in her bosom; how beardless youths have made haste to inherit their fathers' wealth; and how fair damsels—blush not, sweet ones!—have dug little graves in the garden, and bidden me, the sole guest, to an infant's funeral. By the sympathy of your human hearts for sin, ye shall scent out all the places—whether in church, bedchamber, street, field, or forest—where crime has been committed, and shall exult to behold the whole earth one stain of guilt, one mighty bloodspot. Far more than this! It shall be yours to penetrate, in every bosom, the deep mystery of sin, the fountain of all wicked arts, and which inexhaustibly supplies more evil impulses than human power—than my power, at its utmost!—can make manifest in deeds. And now, my children, look upon each other."

They did so; and, by the blaze of the hell-kindled torches, the wretched man beheld his Faith, and the wife her husband, trembling before that unhallowed altar.

"Lo! there ye stand, my children," said the figure, in a deep and solemn tone, almost sad, with its despairing awfulness, as if his once angelic nature could yet mourn for our miserable race. "Depending upon one another's hearts, ye had still hoped, that virtue were not all a dream. Now are ye undeceived! Evil is the nature of mankind. Evil must be your only happiness. Welcome, again, my children, to the communion of your race!"

"Welcome!" repeated the fiend-worshippers, in one cry of despair and triumph.

And there they stood, the only pair, as it seemed, who were yet hesitating on the verge of wickedness, in this dark world. A basin was hollowed, naturally, in the rock. Did it contain water, reddened by the lurid light? or was it blood? or, perchance, a

60

65

---

proselytes: new converts.

liquid flame? Herein did the Shape of Evil dip his hand, and prepare to lay the mark of baptism upon their foreheads, that they might be partakers of the mystery of sin, more conscious of the secret guilt of others, both in deed and thought, than they could now be of their own. The husband cast one look at his pale wife, and Faith at him. What polluted wretches would the next glance show them to each other, shuddering alike at what they disclosed and what they saw!

"Faith! Faith!" cried the husband. "Look up to Heaven, and resist the Wicked one!"

Whether Faith obeyed, he knew not. Hardly had he spoken, when he found himself amid calm night and solitude, listening to a roar of the wind, which died heavily away through the forest. He staggered against the rock and felt it chill and damp, while a hanging twig, that had been all on fire, besprinkled his cheek with the coldest dew.

The next morning, young Goodman Brown came slowly into the street of Salem   70 village, staring around him like a bewildered man. The good old minister was taking a walk along the grave-yard, to get an appetite for breakfast and meditate his sermon, and bestowed a blessing, as he passed, on Goodman Brown. He shrank from the venerable saint, as if to avoid an anathema.° Old Deacon Goodkin was at domestic worship, and the holy words of his prayer were heard through the open window. "What God doth the wizard pray to?" quoth Goodman Brown. Goody Cloyse, that excellent old Christian, stood in the early sunshine, at her own lattice, catechizing a little girl, who had brought her a pint of morning's milk. Goodman Brown snatched away the child, as from the grasp of the fiend himself. Turning the corner by the meeting-house, he spied the head of Faith, with the pink ribbons, gazing anxiously forth, and bursting into such joy at sight of him, that she skipt along the street, and almost kissed her husband before the whole village. But, Goodman Brown looked sternly and sadly into her face, and passed on without a greeting.

Had Goodman Brown fallen asleep in the forest, and only dreamed a wild dream of a witch-meeting?

Be it so, if you will. But, alas! it was a dream of evil omen for young Goodman Brown. A stern, a sad, a darkly meditative, a distrustful, if not a desperate man, did he become, from the night of that fearful dream. On the Sabbath-day, when the congregation were singing a holy psalm, he could not listen, because an anthem of sin rushed loudly upon his ear, and drowned all the blessed strain. When the minister spoke from the pulpit, with power and fervid eloquence, and, with his hand on the open Bible, of the sacred truths of our religion, and of saint-like lives and triumphant deaths, and of future bliss or misery unutterable, then did Goodman Brown turn pale, dreading, lest the roof should thunder down upon the gray blasphemer and his hearers. Often, awakening suddenly at midnight, he shrank from the bosom of Faith, and at morning or even-tide, when the family knelt down at prayer, he scowled, and muttered to himself, and gazed sternly at his wife, and turned away. And when he had lived long, and was borne to his grave, a hoary corpse, followed by Faith, an aged woman, and children and grandchildren, a goodly procession, besides neighbors, not a few, they carved no hopeful verse upon his tombstone; for his dying hour was gloom.

---

anathema: an official curse, a decree that casts communicants out of a church and bans them from receiving the sacraments.

Zora Neale Hurston

Sweat

1926

Zora Neale Hurston (1901?–1960) was born in Eatonville, Florida, but no record of her actual date of birth exists (best guesses range from 1891 to 1901). Hurston was one of eight children. Her father, a carpenter and Baptist preacher, was also the three-term mayor of Eatonville, the first all-black town incorporated in the United States. When Hurston's mother died in 1912, the father moved the children from one relative to another. Consequently, Hurston never finished grammar school, although in 1918 she began taking classes at Howard University, paying her way through school by working as a manicurist and maid. While at Howard, she published her first story. In early 1925 she moved to New York, arriving with "$1.50, no job, no friends, and a lot of hope." She

Zora Neale Hurston

soon became an important member of the Harlem Renaissance, a group of young black artists (including Langston Hughes, Countee Cullen, Jean Toomer, and Claude McKay) who sought "spiritual emancipation" for African Americans by exploring black heritage and identity in the arts. Hurston eventually became, according to critic Laura Zaidman, "the most prolific black American woman writer of her time." In 1925 she became the first African American student at Barnard College, where she completed a BA in anthropology. Hurston's most famous story, "Sweat," appeared in the only issue of Fire!!, a 1926 avant-garde Harlem Renaissance magazine edited by Hurston, Hughes, and Wallace Thurman. This powerful story of an unhappy marriage turned murderous was particularly noteworthy for having the characters speak in the black country dialect of Hurston's native Florida. Hurston achieved only modest success during her lifetime, despite the publication of her memorable novel Their Eyes Were Watching God (1937) and her many contributions to the study of African American folklore. She died, poor and neglected, in a Florida welfare home and was buried in an unmarked grave. In 1973 novelist Alice Walker erected a gravestone for her carved with the words:

Zora Neale Hurston
"A Genius of the South"
1901–1960
Novelist, Folklorist
Anthropologist

I

It was eleven o'clock of a Spring night in Florida. It was Sunday. Any other night, Delia Jones would have been in bed for two hours by this time. But she was a washwoman, and Monday morning meant a great deal to her. So she collected the soiled clothes on Saturday when she returned the clean things. Sunday night after church, she sorted and put the white things to soak. It saved her almost a half-day's start. A great hamper in the bedroom held the clothes that she brought home. It was so much neater than a number of bundles lying around.

She squatted on the kitchen floor beside the great pile of clothes, sorting them into small heaps according to color, and humming a song in a mournful key, but wondering through it all where Sykes, her husband, had gone with her horse and buckboard.°

Just then something long, round, limp, and black fell upon her shoulders and slithered to the floor beside her. A great terror took hold of her. It softened her knees and dried her mouth so that it was a full minute before she could cry out or move. Then she saw that it was the big bull whip her husband liked to carry when he drove.

She lifted her eyes to the door and saw him standing there bent over with laughter at her fright. She screamed at him.

"Sykes, what you throw dat whip on me like dat? You know it would skeer me— looks just like a snake, an' you knows how skeered Ah is of snakes." 5

"Course Ah knowed it! That's how come Ah done it." He slapped his leg with his hand and almost rolled on the ground in his mirth. "If you such a big fool dat you got to have a fit over a earth worm or a string, Ah don't keer how bad Ah skeer you."

"You ain't got no business doing it. Gawd knows it's a sin. Some day Ah'm goin- tuh drop dead from some of yo' foolishness. 'Nother thing, where you been wid mah rig? Ah feeds dat pony. He ain't fuh you to be drivin' wid no bull whip."

"You sho' is one aggravatin' nigger woman!" he declared and stepped into the room. She resumed her work and did not answer him at once. "Ah done tole you time and again to keep them white folks' clothes outa dis house."

He picked up the whip and glared at her. Delia went on with her work. She went out into the yard and returned with a galvanized tub and set it on the wash-bench. She saw that Sykes had kicked all of the clothes together again, and now stood in her way truculently, his whole manner hoping, *praying*, for an argument. But she walked calmly around him and commenced to re-sort the things.

"Next time, Ah'm gointer kick 'em outdoors," he threatened as he struck a match along the leg of his corduroy breeches. 10

Delia never looked up from her work, and her thin, stooped shoulders sagged further.

"Ah ain't for no fuss t'night Sykes. Ah just come from taking sacrament at the church house."

He snorted scornfully. "Yeah, you just come from de church house on a Sunday night, but heah you is gone to work on them clothes. You ain't nothing but a hypocrite. One of them amen-corner Christians—sing, whoop, and shout, then come home and wash white folks' clothes on the Sabbath."

He stepped roughly upon the whitest pile of things, kicking them helter-skelter as he crossed the room. His wife gave a little scream of dismay, and quickly gathered them together again.

"Sykes, you quit grindin' dirt into these clothes! How can Ah git through by Sat'day if Ah don't start on Sunday?" 15

"Ah don't keer if you never git through. Anyhow, Ah done promised Gawd and a couple of other men, Ah ain't gointer have it in mah house. Don't gimme no lip neither, else Ah'll throw 'em out and put mah fist up side yo' head to boot."

Delia's habitual meekness seemed to slip from her shoulders like a blown scarf. She was on her feet; her poor little body, her bare knuckly hands bravely defying the strapping hulk before her.

buckboard: a four-wheeled open carriage with the seat resting on a spring platform.

"Looka heah, Sykes, you done gone too fur. Ah been married to you fur fifteen years, and Ah been takin' in washin' fur fifteen years. Sweat, sweat, sweat! Work and sweat, cry and sweat, pray and sweat!"

"What's that got to do with me?" he asked brutally.

"What's it got to do with you, Sykes? Mah tub of suds is filled yo' belly with vittles more times than yo' hands is filled it. Mah sweat is done paid for this house and Ah reckon Ah kin keep on sweatin' in it."   20

She seized the iron skillet from the stove and struck a defensive pose, which act surprised him greatly, coming from her. It cowed him and he did not strike her as he usually did.

"Naw you won't," she panted, "that ole snaggle-toothed black woman you runnin' with ain't comin' heah to pile up on *mah* sweat and blood. You ain't paid for nothin' on this place, and Ah'm gointer stay right heah till Ah'm toted out foot foremost."

"Well, you better quit gittin' me riled up, else they'll be totin' you out sooner than you expect. Ah'm so tired of you Ah don't know whut to do. Gawd! How Ah hates skinny wimmen!"

A little awed by this new Delia, he sidled out of the door and slammed the back gate after him. He did not say where he had gone, but she knew too well. She knew very well that he would not return until nearly daybreak also. Her work over, she went on to bed but not to sleep at once. Things had come to a pretty pass!

She lay awake, gazing upon the debris that cluttered their matrimonial trail.   25 Not an image left standing along the way. Anything like flowers had long ago been drowned in the salty stream that had been pressed from her heart. Her tears, her sweat, her blood. She had brought love to the union and he had brought a longing after the flesh. Two months after the wedding, he had given her the first brutal beating. She had the memory of his numerous trips to Orlando with all of his wages when he had returned to her penniless, even before the first year had passed. She was young and soft then, but now she thought of her knotty, muscled limbs, her harsh knuckly hands, and drew herself up into an unhappy little ball in the middle of the big feather bed. Too late now to hope for love, even if it were not Bertha it would be someone else. This case differed from the others only in that she was bolder than the others. Too late for everything except her little home. She had built it for her old days, and planted one by one the trees and flowers there. It was lovely to her, lovely.

Somehow, before sleep came, she found herself saying aloud: "Oh well, whatever goes over the Devil's back, is got to come under his belly. Sometime or ruther, Sykes, like everybody else, is gointer reap his sowing." After that she was able to build a spiritual earthworks° against her husband. His shells could no longer reach her. AMEN. She went to sleep and slept until he announced his presence in bed by kicking her feet and rudely snatching the covers away.

"Gimme some kivah heah, an' git yo' damn foots over on yo' own side! Ah oughter mash you in yo' mouf fuh drawing dat skillet on me."

Delia went clear to the rail without answering him. A triumphant indifference to all that he was or did.

II

The week was full of work for Delia as all other weeks, and Saturday found her behind her little pony, collecting and delivering clothes.

spiritual earthworks: earthworks are military fortifications made of earth; here Hurston uses it metaphorically to mean Delia's emotional defenses.

It was a hot, hot day near the end of July. The village men on Joe Clarke's porch   30
even chewed cane listlessly. They did not hurl the cane-knots as usual. They let them
dribble over the edge of the porch. Even conversation had collapsed under the heat.

"Heah come Delia Jones," Jim Merchant said, as the shaggy pony came 'round
the bend of the road toward them. The rusty buckboard was heaped with baskets of
crisp, clean laundry.

"Yep," Joe Lindsay agreed. "Hot or col', rain or shine, jes'ez reg'lar ez de weeks
roll roun' Delia carries 'em an' fetches 'em on Sat'day."

"She better if she wanter eat," said Moss. "Syke Jones ain't wuth de shot an' powder hit would tek tuh kill 'im. Not to *huh* he ain't."

"He sho' ain't," Walter Thomas chimed in. "It's too bad, too, cause she wuz a
right pretty li'l trick when he got huh. Ah'd uh mah'ied huh mahself if he hadnter
beat me to it."

Delia nodded briefly at the men as she drove past.   35

"Too much knockin' will ruin *any* 'oman. He done beat huh 'nough tuh kill three
women, let 'lone change they looks," said Elijah Moseley. "How Syke kin stommuck
dat big black greasy Mogul he's layin' roun' wid, gits me. Ah swear dat eight-rock
couldn't kiss a sardine can Ah done thowed out de back do' 'way las' yeah."

"Aw, she's fat, thass how come. He's allus been crazy 'bout fat women," put in
Merchant. "He'd a' been tied up wid one long time ago if he could a' found one tuh
have him. Did Ah tell yuh 'bout him come sidlin' roun' *mah* wife—bringin' her a
basket uh peecans outa his yard fuh a present? Yessir, mah wife! She tol' him tuh
take 'em right straight back home, 'cause Delia works so hard ovah dat washtub she
reckon everything on de place taste lak sweat an' soapsuds. Ah jus' wisht Ah'd a'
caught 'im 'roun' dere! Ah'd a' made his hips ketch on fiah down dat shell road."

"Ah know he done it, too. Ah sees 'im grinnin' at every 'oman dat passes,"
Walter Thomas said. "But even so, he useter eat some mighty big hunks uh humble
pie tuh git dat li'l 'oman he got. She wuz ez pritty ez a speckled pup! Dat wuz fifteen
years ago. He useter be so skeered uh losin' huh, she could make him do some parts of
a husband's duty. Dey never wuz de same in de mind."

"There oughter be a law about him," said Lindsay. "He ain't fit tuh carry guts tuh
a bear."

Clarke spoke for the first time. "Tain't no law on earth dat kin make a man be   40
decent if it ain't in 'im. There's plenty men dat takes a wife lak dey do a joint uh
sugarcane. It's round, juicy, an' sweet when dey gits it. But dey squeeze an' grind,
squeeze an' grind an' wring tell dey wring every drop uh pleasure dat's in 'em out.
When dey's satisfied dat dey is wrung dry, dey treats 'em jes' lak dey do a cane-chew.
Dey thows 'em away. Dey knows whut dey is doin' while dey is at it, an' hates their-
selves fuh it but they keeps on hangin' after huh tell she's empty. Den dey hates huh
fuh bein' a cane-chew an' in de way."

"We oughter take Syke an' dat stray 'oman uh his'n down in Lake Howell swamp
an' lay on de rawhide till they cain't say Lawd a' mussy. He allus wuz uh ovahbearin
niggah, but since dat white 'oman from up north done teached 'im how to run a automobile, he done got too biggety to live—an' we oughter kill 'im," Old Man Anderson
advised.

A grunt of approval went around the porch. But the heat was melting their civic
virtue and Elijah Moseley began to bait Joe Clarke.

"Come on, Joe, git a melon outa dere an' slice it up for yo' customers. We'se all
sufferin' wid de heat. De bear's done got *me*!"

"Thass right, Joe, a watermelon is jes' whut Ah needs tuh cure de eppizudicks," Walter Thomas joined forces with Moseley. "Come on dere, Joe. We all is steady customers an' you ain't set us up in a long time. Ah chooses dat long, bowlegged Floridy favorite."

"A god, an' be dough. You all gimme twenty cents and slice away," Clarke retorted. "Ah needs a col' slice m'self. Heah, everybody chip in. Ah'll lend y'all mah meat knife."

The money was all quickly subscribed and the huge melon brought forth. At that moment, Sykes and Bertha arrived. A determined silence fell on the porch and the melon was put away again.

Merchant snapped down the blade of his jackknife and moved toward the store door.

"Come on in, Joe, an' gimme a slab uh sow belly an' uh pound uh coffee—almost fuhgot 'twas Sat'day. Got to git on home." Most of the men left also.

Just then Delia drove past on her way home, as Sykes was ordering magnificently for Bertha. It pleased him for Delia to see.

"Git whutsoever yo' heart desires, Honey. Wait a minute, Joe. Give huh two bottles uh strawberry soda-water, uh quart parched ground-peas, an' a block uh chewin' gum."

With all this they left the store, with Sykes reminding Bertha that this was his town and she could have it if she wanted it.

The men returned soon after they left, and held their watermelon feast.

"Where did Syke Jones git da 'oman from nohow?" Lindsay asked.

"Ovah Apopka. Guess dey musta been cleanin' out de town when she lef'. She don't look lak a thing but a hunk uh liver wid hair on it."

"Well, she sho' kin squall," Dave Carter contributed. "When she gits ready tuh laff, she jes' opens huh mouf an' latches it back tuh de las' notch. No ole granpa alligator down in Lake Bell ain't got nothin' on huh."

III

Bertha had been in town three months now. Sykes was still paying her room-rent at Della Lewis'—the only house in town that would have taken her in. Sykes took her frequently to Winter Park to "stomps." He still assured her that he was the swellest man in the state.

"Sho' you kin have dat li'l ole house soon's Ah git dat 'oman outadere. Everything b'longs tuh me an' you sho' kin have it. Ah sho' 'bominates uh skinny 'oman. Lawdy, you sho' is got one portly shape on you! You kin git *anything* you wants. Dis is *mah* town an' you sho' kin have it."

Delia's work-worn knees crawled over the earth in Gethsemane° and up the rocks of Calvary° many, many times during these months. She avoided the villagers and meeting places in her efforts to be blind and deaf. But Bertha nullified this to a degree, by coming to Delia's house to call Sykes out to her at the gate.

Delia and Sykes fought all the time now with no peaceful interludes. They slept and ate in silence. Two or three times Delia had attempted a timid friendliness, but she was repulsed each time. It was plain that the breaches must remain agape.

Gethsemane: the garden outside Jerusalem that was the scene of Jesus's agony and arrest (see Matthew 26:36–57); hence, a scene of great suffering. Calvary: the hill outside Jerusalem where Jesus was crucified.

The sun had burned July to August. The heat streamed down like a million hot   60
arrows, smiting all things living upon the earth. Grass withered, leaves browned,
snakes went blind in shedding, and men and dogs went mad. Dog days!

Delia came home one day and found Sykes there before her. She wondered, but
started to go on into the house without speaking, even though he was standing in
the kitchen door and she must either stoop under his arm or ask him to move. He
made no room for her. She noticed a soap box beside the steps, but paid no particular
attention to it, knowing that he must have brought it there. As she was stooping to
pass under his outstretched arm, he suddenly pushed her backward, laughingly.

"Look in de box dere, Delia, Ah done brung yuh somethin'!"

She nearly fell upon the box in her stumbling, and when she saw what it held,
she all but fainted outright.

"Syke! Syke, mah Gawd! You take dat rattlesnake 'way from heah! You *gottuh*.
Oh, Jesus, have mussy!"

"Ah ain't got tuh do nuthin' uh de kin'—fact is Ah ain't got tuh do nothin' but   65
die. Tain't no use uh you puttin' on airs makin' out lak you skeered uh dat snake—
he's gointer stay right heah tell he die. He wouldn't bite me cause Ah knows how tuh
handle 'im. Nohow he wouldn't risk breakin' out his fangs 'gin yo skinny laigs."

"Naw, now Syke, don't keep dat thing 'round tryin' tuh skeer me tuh death. You
knows Ah'm even feared uh earth worms. Thass de biggest snake Ah evah did see.
Kill 'im, Syke, please."

"Doan ast me tuh do nothin' fuh yuh. Goin' 'round tryin' tuh be so damn asterperious.° Naw, Ah ain't gonna kill it. Ah think uh damn sight mo' uh him dan you!
Dat's a nice snake an' anybody doan lak 'im kin jes' hit de grit."

The village soon heard that Sykes had the snake, and came to see and ask
questions.

"How de hen-fire did you ketch dat six-foot rattler, Syke?" Thomas asked.

"He's full uh frogs so he cain't hardly move, thass how Ah eased up on 'im. But   70
Ah'm a snake charmer an' knows how tuh handle 'em. Shux, dat ain't nothin'. Ah
could ketch one eve'y day if Ah so wanted tuh."

"Whut he needs is a heavy hick'ry club leaned real heavy on his head. Dat's de
bes' way tuh charm a rattlesnake."

"Naw, Walt, y'all jes' don't understand dese diamon' backs lak Ah do," said Sykes
in a superior tone of voice.

The village agreed with Walter, but the snake stayed on. His box remained by
the kitchen door with its screen wire covering. Two or three days later it had digested
its meal of frogs and literally came to life. It rattled at every movement in the kitchen
or the yard. One day as Delia came down the kitchen steps she saw his chalky-white
fangs curved like scimitars hung in the wire meshes. This time she did not run away
with averted eyes as usual. She stood for a long time in the doorway in a red fury that
grew bloodier for every second that she regarded the creature that was her torment.

That night she broached the subject as soon as Sykes sat down to the table.

"Syke, Ah wants you tuh take dat snake 'way fum heah. You done starved me   75
an' Ah put up widcher, you done beat me an Ah took dat, but you done kilt all mah
insides bringin' dat varmint heah."

Sykes poured out a saucer full of coffee and drank it deliberately before he
answered her.

---

asterperious: haughty.

"A whole lot Ah keer 'bout how you feels inside uh out. Dat snake ain't goin' no damn wheah till Ah gits ready fuh 'im tuh go. So fur as beatin' is concerned, yuh ain't took near all dat you gointer take ef yuh stay 'round *me*."

Delia pushed back her plate and got up from the table. "Ah hates you, Sykes," she said calmly. "Ah hates you tuh de same degree dat Ah useter love yuh. Ah done took an' took till mah belly is full up tuh mah neck. Dat's de reason Ah got mah letter fum de church an' moved mah membership tuh Woodbridge—so Ah don't haftuh take no sacrament wid yuh. Ah don't wantuh see yuh 'round me atall. Lay 'round wid dat 'oman all yuh wants tuh, but gwan 'way fum me an' mah house. Ah hates yuh lak uh suck-egg dog."

Sykes almost let the huge wad of corn bread and collard greens he was chewing fall out of his mouth in amazement. He had a hard time whipping himself up to the proper fury to try to answer Delia.

"Well, Ah'm glad you does hate me. Ah'm sho' tiahed uh you hangin' ontuh   80
me. Ah don't want yuh. Look at yuh stringey ole neck! Yo' rawbony laigs an' arms is enough tuh cut uh man tuh death. You looks jes' lak de devvul's doll-baby tuh *me*. You cain't hate me no worse dan Ah hates you. Ah been hatin' *you* fuh years."

"Yo' ole black hide don't look lak nothin' tuh me, but uh passle uh wrinkled up rubber, wid yo' big ole yeahs flappin' on each side lak uh paih uh buzzard wings. Don't think Ah'm gointuh be run 'way fum mah house neither. Ah'm goin' tuh de white folks 'bout *you*, mah young man, de very nex' time you lay yo' han's on me. Mah cup is done run ovah." Delia said this with no signs of fear and Sykes departed from the house, threatening her, but made not the slightest move to carry out any of them.

That night he did not return at all, and the next day being Sunday, Delia was glad she did not have to quarrel before she hitched up her pony and drove the four miles to Woodbridge.

She stayed to the night service—"love feast"—which was very warm and full of spirit. In the emotional winds her domestic trials were borne far and wide so that she sang as she drove homeward,

Jurden water,° black an' col
Chills de body, not de soul
An' Ah wantah cross Jurden in uh calm time.

She came from the barn to the kitchen door and stopped.

"Whut's de mattah, ol' Satan, you ain't kickin' up yo' racket?" She addressed   85
the snake's box. Complete silence. She went on into the house with a new hope in its birth struggles. Perhaps her threat to go to the white folks had frightened Sykes! Perhaps he was sorry! Fifteen years of misery and suppression had brought Delia to the place where she would hope *anything* that looked towards a way over or through her wall of inhibitions.

She felt in the match-safe behind the stove at once for a match. There was only one there.

"Dat niggah wouldn't fetch nothin' heah tuh save his rotten neck, but he kin run thew whut Ah brings quick enough. Now he done toted off nigh on tuh haff uh box uh matches. He done had dat 'oman heah in mah house, too."

Jurden water: black Southern dialect for the River Jordan, which represents the last boundary before entering heaven. It comes from the Old Testament, when the Jews had to cross the Jordan River to reach the Promised Land.

Nobody but a woman could tell how she knew this even before she struck the match. But she did and it put her into a new fury.

Presently she brought in the tubs to put the white things to soak. This time she decided she need not bring the hamper out of the bedroom; she would go in there and do the sorting. She picked up the pot-bellied lamp and went in. The room was small and the hamper stood hard by the foot of the white iron bed. She could sit and reach through the bedposts—resting as she worked.

"*Ah wantah cross Jurden in uh calm time.*" She was singing again. The mood of the   90 "love feast" had returned. She threw back the lid of the basket almost gaily. Then, moved by both horror and terror, she sprang back toward the door. *There lay the snake in the basket!* He moved sluggishly at first, but even as she turned round and round, jumped up and down in an insanity of fear, he began to stir vigorously. She saw him pouring his awful beauty from the basket upon the bed, then she seized the lamp and ran as fast as she could to the kitchen. The wind from the open door blew out the light and the darkness added to her terror. She sped to the darkness of the yard, slamming the door after her before she thought to set down the lamp. She did not feel safe even on the ground, so she climbed up in the hay barn.

There for an hour or more she lay sprawled upon the hay a gibbering wreck.

Finally she grew quiet, and after that came coherent thought. With this stalked through her a cold, bloody rage. Hours of this. A period of introspection, a space of retrospection, then a mixture of both. Out of this an awful calm.

"Well, Ah done de bes' Ah could. If things ain't right, Gawd knows tain't mah fault."

She went to sleep—a twitch sleep—and woke up to a faint gray sky. There was a loud hollow sound below. She peered out. Sykes was at the wood-pile, demolishing a wire-covered box.

He hurried to the kitchen door, but hung outside there some minutes before he   95 entered, and stood some minutes more inside before he closed it after him.

The gray in the sky was spreading. Delia descended without fear now, and crouched beneath the low bedroom window. The drawn shade shut out the dawn, shut in the night. But the thin walls held back no sound.

"Dat ol' scratch° is woke up now!" She mused at the tremendous whirr inside, which every woodsman knows, is one of the sound illusions. The rattler is a ventriloquist. His whirr sounds to the right, to the left, straight ahead, behind, close under foot—everywhere but where it is. Woe to him who guesses wrong unless he is prepared to hold up his end of the argument! Sometimes he strikes without rattling at all.

Inside, Sykes heard nothing until he knocked a pot lid off the stove while trying to reach the match-safe in the dark. He had emptied his pockets at Bertha's.

The snake seemed to wake up under the stove and Sykes made a quick leap into the bedroom. In spite of the gin he had had, his head was clearing now.

"Mah Gawd!" he chattered, "ef Ah could on'y strack uh light!"

The rattling ceased for a moment as he stood paralyzed. He waited. It seemed   100 that the snake waited also.

"Oh, fuh de light! Ah thought he'd be too sick"—Sykes was muttering to himself when the whirr began again, closer, right underfoot this time. Long before this, Sykes' ability to think had been flattened down to primitive instinct and he leaped—onto the bed.

scratch: a folk expression for the devil.

Outside Delia heard a cry that might have come from a maddened chimpanzee, a stricken gorilla. All the terror, all the horror, all the rage that man possibly could express, without a recognizable human sound.

A tremendous stir inside there, another series of animal screams, the intermittent whirr of the reptile. The shade torn violently down from the window, letting in the red dawn, a huge brown hand seizing the window stick, great dull blows upon the wooden floor punctuating the gibberish of sound long after the rattle of the snake had abruptly subsided. All this Delia could see and hear from her place beneath the window, and it made her ill. She crept over to the four-o'clocks and stretched herself on the cool earth to recover.

She lay there. "Delia, Delia!" She could hear Sykes calling in a most despairing tone as one who expected no answer. The sun crept on up, and he called. Delia could not move—her legs had gone flabby. She never moved, he called, and the sun kept rising. 105

"Mah Gawd!" She heard him moan, "Mah Gawd fum Heben!" She heard him stumbling about and got up from her flower-bed. The sun was growing warm. As she approached the door she heard him call out hopefully, "Delia, is dat you Ah heah?"

She saw him on his hands and knees as soon as she reached the door. He crept an inch or two toward her—all that he was able, and she saw his horribly swollen neck and his one open eye shining with hope. A surge of pity too strong to support bore her away from that eye that must, could not, fail to see the tubs. He would see the lamp. Orlando with its doctors was too far. She could scarcely reach the chinaberry tree, where she waited in the growing heat while inside she knew the cold river was creeping up and up to extinguish that eye which must know by now that she knew.

James Joyce

Araby

1914

James Joyce (1882–1941) quit Ireland at twenty to spend his mature life in voluntary exile on the continent, writing of nothing but Dublin, where he was born. In Trieste, Zurich, and Paris, he supported his family with difficulty, sometimes teaching in Berlitz language schools, until his writing won him fame and wealthy patrons. At first Joyce had trouble getting his work printed and circulated. Publication of Dubliners *(1914), the collection of stories that includes "Araby," was delayed seven years because its prospective Irish publisher feared libel suits. (The book depicts local citizens, some of them recognizable, and views Dubliners mostly as a thwarted, self-deceived lot.) A Portrait of the Artist as a Young Man (1916), a novel of thinly veiled autobiography, recounts a young intellectual's breaking away from country, church, and*

James Joyce

home. *Joyce's immense comic novel* Ulysses *(1922), a parody of the* Odyssey, *spans eighteen hours in the life of a wandering Jew, a Dublin seller of advertising. Frank about sex but untitillating, the book was banned at one time by the US Post Office. Joyce's later work stepped up its demands on readers. The challenging* Finnegans Wake *(1939), if read aloud, sounds as though a learned comic poet were sleep-talking, jumbling several languages. Joyce was an innovator whose bold experiments showed other writers many possibilities in fiction that had not earlier been imagined.*

North Richmond Street, being blind,° was a quiet street except at the hour when the Christian Brothers' School set the boys free. An uninhabited house of two stories stood at the blind end, detached from its neighbors in a square ground. The other houses of the street, conscious of decent lives within them, gazed at one another with brown imperturbable faces.

The former tenant of our house, a priest, had died in the back drawing-room. Air, musty from having been long enclosed, hung in all the rooms, and the waste room behind the kitchen was littered with old useless papers. Among these I found a few paper-covered books, the pages of which were curled and damp: *The Abbot*, by Walter Scott, *The Devout Communicant* and *The Memoirs of Vidocq*.° I liked the last best because its leaves were yellow. The wild garden behind the house contained a central apple-tree and a few straggling bushes under one of which I found the late tenant's rusty bicycle-pump. He had been a very charitable priest: in his will he had left all his money to institutions and the furniture of his house to his sister.

When the short days of winter came dusk fell before we had well eaten our dinners. When we met in the street the houses had grown somber. The space of sky above us was the color of ever-changing violet and towards it the lamps of the street lifted their feeble lanterns. The cold air stung us and we played till our bodies glowed. Our shouts echoed in the silent street. The career of our play brought us through the dark muddy lanes behind the houses where we ran the gauntlet of the rough tribes from the cottages, to the back doors of the dark dripping gardens where odors arose from the ashpits, to the dark odorous stables where a coachman smoothed and combed the horse or shook music from the buckled harness. When we returned to the street light from the kitchen windows had filled the areas. If my uncle was seen turning the corner we hid in the shadow until we had seen him safely housed. Or if Mangan's sister° came out on the doorstep to call her brother in to his tea we watched her from our shadow peer up and down the street. We waited to see whether she would remain or go in and, if she remained, we left our shadow and walked up to Mangan's steps resignedly. She was waiting for us, her figure defined by the light from the half-opened door. Her brother always teased her before he obeyed and I stood by the railings looking at her. Her dress swung as she moved her body and the soft rope of her hair tossed from side to side.

Every morning I lay on the floor in the front parlor watching her door. The blind was pulled down within an inch of the sash so that I could not be seen. When she came out on the doorstep my heart leaped. I ran to the hall, seized my books and followed her. I kept her brown figure always in my eye and, when we came near the point at which our ways diverged, I quickened my pace and passed her. This happened morning after morning. I had never spoken to her, except for a few casual words, and yet her name was like a summons to all my foolish blood.

being blind: being a dead-end street.   *The Abbot . . . Vidocq*: a popular historical romance (1820); a book of pious meditations by an eighteenth-century English Franciscan, Pacificus Baker; and the autobiography of François-Jules Vidocq (1775–1857), a criminal who later turned detective.   *Mangan's sister*: an actual young woman in this story, but the phrase recalls Irish poet James Clarence Mangan (1803–1849) and his best-known poem, "Dark Rosaleen," which personifies Ireland as a beautiful woman for whom the poet yearns.

Her image accompanied me even in places the most hostile to romance. On   5
Saturday evenings when my aunt went marketing I had to go to carry some of the
parcels. We walked through the flaring streets, jostled by drunken men and bargain-
ing women, amid the curses of laborers, the shrill litanies of shopboys who stood on
guard by the barrels of pigs' cheeks, the nasal chanting of street-singers, who sang a
come-all-you about O'Donovan Rossa,° or a ballad about the troubles in our native
land. These noises converged in a single sensation of life for me: I imagined that
I bore my chalice safely through a throng of foes. Her name sprang to my lips at
moments in strange prayers and praises which I myself did not understand. My eyes
were often full of tears (I could not tell why) and at times a flood from my heart
seemed to pour itself out into my bosom. I thought little of the future. I did not know
whether I would ever speak to her or not or, if I spoke to her, how I could tell her of
my confused adoration. But my body was like a harp and her words and gestures were
like fingers running upon the wires.

One evening I went into the back drawing-room in which the priest had died.
It was a dark rainy evening and there was no sound in the house. Through one of
the broken panes I heard the rain impinge upon the earth, the fine incessant needles
of water playing in the sodden beds. Some distant lamp or lighted window gleamed
below me. I was thankful that I could see so little. All my senses seemed to desire to
veil themselves and, feeling that I was about to slip from them, I pressed the palms of
my hands together until they trembled, murmuring: *O love! O love!* many times.

At last she spoke to me. When she addressed the first words to me I was so confused that I did not know what to answer. She asked me was I going to *Araby.* I forget
whether I answered yes or no. It would be a splendid bazaar, she said; she would love
to go.

—And why can't you? I asked.

While she spoke she turned a silver bracelet round and round her wrist. She
could not go, she said, because there would be a retreat that week in her convent.°
Her brother and two other boys were fighting for their caps and I was alone at the
railings. She held one of the spikes, bowing her head towards me. The light from the
lamp opposite our door caught the white curve of her neck, lit up her hair that rested
there and, falling, lit up the hand upon the railing. It fell over one side of her dress
and caught the white border of a petticoat, just visible as she stood at ease.

—It's well for you, she said.   10

—If I go, I said, I will bring you something.

What innumerable follies laid waste my waking and sleeping thoughts after
that evening! I wished to annihilate the tedious intervening days. I chafed against
the work of school. At night in my bedroom and by day in the classroom her
image came between me and the page I strove to read. The syllables of the word
Araby were called to me through the silence in which my soul luxuriated and cast
an Eastern enchantment over me. I asked for leave to go to the bazaar on Saturday night. My aunt was surprised and hoped it was not some Freemason° affair.

---

come-all-you about O'Donovan Rossa: the street singers earned their living by singing timely songs that usually began, "Come all you gallant Irishmen / And listen to my song." Their subject, also called Dynamite
Rossa, was a popular hero jailed by the British for advocating violent rebellion. *a retreat . . . in her convent:* a week devoted to religious observances more intense than usual, at the convent school Miss Mangan
attends; probably she will have to listen to a number of hellfire sermons. *Freemason:* Catholics in Ireland
viewed the Masonic order as a Protestant conspiracy against them.

I answered few questions in class. I watched my master's face pass from amiability to sternness; he hoped I was not beginning to idle. I could not call my wandering thoughts together. I had hardly any patience with the serious work of life which, now that it stood between me and my desire, seemed to me child's play, ugly monotonous child's play.

On Saturday morning I reminded my uncle that I wished to go to the bazaar in the evening. He was fussing at the hallstand, looking for the hatbrush, and answered me curtly:

—Yes, boy, I know.

As he was in the hall I could not go into the front parlor and lie at the window. 15 I left the house in bad humor and walked slowly towards the school. The air was pitilessly raw and already my heart misgave me.

When I came home to dinner my uncle had not yet been home. Still it was early. I sat staring at the clock for some time and, when its ticking began to irritate me, I left the room. I mounted the staircase and gained the upper part of the house. The high cold empty gloomy rooms liberated me and I went from room to room singing. From the front window I saw my companions playing below in the street. Their cries reached me weakened and indistinct and, leaning my forehead against the cool glass, I looked over at the dark house where she lived. I may have stood there for an hour, seeing nothing but the brown-clad figure cast by my imagination, touched discreetly by the lamplight at the curved neck, at the hand upon the railings and at the border below the dress.

When I came downstairs again I found Mrs. Mercer sitting at the fire. She was an old garrulous woman, a pawnbroker's widow, who collected used stamps for some pious purpose. I had to endure the gossip of the tea-table. The meal was prolonged beyond an hour and still my uncle did not come. Mrs. Mercer stood up to go: she was sorry she couldn't wait any longer, but it was after eight o'clock and she did not like to be out late, as the night air was bad for her. When she had gone I began to walk up and down the room, clenching my fists. My aunt said:

—I'm afraid you may put off your bazaar for this night of Our Lord.

At nine o'clock I heard my uncle's latchkey in the halldoor. I heard him talking to himself and heard the hallstand rocking when it had received the weight of his overcoat. I could interpret these signs. When he was midway through his dinner I asked him to give me the money to go to the bazaar. He had forgotten.

—The people are in bed and after their first sleep now, he said.   20

I did not smile. My aunt said to him energetically:

—Can't you give him the money and let him go? You've kept him late enough as it is.

My uncle said he was very sorry he had forgotten. He said he believed in the old saying: *All work and no play makes Jack a dull boy*. He asked me where I was going and, when I had told him a second time he asked me did I know *The Arab's Farewell to His Steed*.° When I left the kitchen he was about to recite the opening lines of the piece to my aunt.

The Arab's Farewell to His Steed: This sentimental ballad by a popular poet, Caroline Norton (1808–1877), tells the story of a nomad of the desert who, in a fit of greed, sells his beloved horse, then regrets the loss, flings away the gold he had received, and takes back his horse. Notice the echo of "Araby" in the song title.

I held a florin tightly in my hands as I strode down Buckingham Street towards the station. The sight of the streets thronged with buyers and glaring with gas recalled to me the purpose of my journey. I took my seat in a third-class carriage of a deserted train. After an intolerable delay the train moved out of the station slowly. It crept onward among ruinous houses and over the twinkling river. At Westland Row Station a crowd of people pressed to the carriage doors; but the porters moved them back, saying that it was a special train for the bazaar. I remained alone in the bare carriage. In a few minutes the train drew up beside an improvised wooden platform. I passed out on to the road and saw by the lighted dial of a clock that it was ten minutes to ten. In front of me was a large building which displayed the magical name.

I could not find any sixpenny entrance and, fearing that the bazaar would be   25
closed, I passed in quickly through a turnstile, handing a shilling to a weary-looking man. I found myself in a big hall girdled at half its height by a gallery. Nearly all the stalls were closed and the greater part of the hall was in darkness. I recognized a silence like that which pervades a church after a service. I walked into the center of the bazaar timidly. A few people were gathered about the stalls which were still open. Before a curtain, over which the words *Café Chantant*° were written in colored lamps, two men were counting money on a salver.° I listened to the fall of the coins.

Remembering with difficulty why I had come I went over to one of the stalls and examined porcelain vases and flowered tea-sets. At the door of the stall a young lady was talking and laughing with two young gentlemen. I remarked their English accents and listened vaguely to their conversation.

—O, I never said such a thing!

—O, but you did!

—O, but I didn't!

—Didn't she say that?   30

—Yes. I heard her.

—O, there's a . . . fib!

Observing me the young lady came over and asked me did I wish to buy anything. The tone of her voice was not encouraging; she seemed to have spoken to me out of a sense of duty. I looked humbly at the great jars that stood like eastern guards at either side of the dark entrance to the stall and murmured:

—No, thank you.

The young lady changed the position of one of the vases and went back to the   35
two young men. They began to talk of the same subject. Once or twice the young lady glanced at me over her shoulder.

I lingered before her stall, though I knew my stay was useless, to make my interest in her wares seem the more real. Then I turned away slowly and walked down the middle of the bazaar. I allowed the two pennies to fall against the sixpence in my pocket. I heard a voice call from one end of the gallery that the light was out. The upper part of the hall was now completely dark.

Gazing up into the darkness I saw myself as a creature driven and derided by vanity; and my eyes burned with anguish and anger.

Café Chantant: name for a Paris nightspot featuring topical songs.   *salver*: a tray like that used in serving Holy Communion.

Jhumpa Lahiri

Interpreter of Maladies

1999

Jhumpa Lahiri

Jhumpa Lahiri was born in London in 1967 and grew up in Rhode Island. Her father, a librarian, and her mother, a teacher, had emigrated from their native India, to which Lahiri has made a number of extended visits. After writing a great deal of fiction as a child and teenager, she wrote none at all during her college years. She graduated from Barnard College with a BA in English literature, and after all her graduate school applications had been rejected, she went to work as a research assistant for a nonprofit organization. She began staying late after work to use her office computer to write short stories, on the strength of which she was accepted into the creative writing program at Boston University. Earning an MA in creative writing, Lahiri stayed on to complete an MA in English, an MA in comparative literature and the arts, and a PhD in Renaissance studies. "In the process," she has said, "it became clear to me that I was not meant to be a scholar. It was something I did out of a sense of duty and practicality, but it was never something I loved." Lahiri's first book of stories, Interpreter of Maladies, was published in 1999 to excellent reviews and won the Pulitzer Prize for fiction. Its title story was also selected for both an O. Henry Award and publication in The Best American Short Stories. Her first novel, The Namesake (2003), was made into a film (2006) directed by Mira Nair. Her second collection of stories, Unaccustomed Earth (2008), also received glowing reviews and debuted at the top of the New York Times best-seller list. In 2013 she published the novel The Lowland. More recently, Lahiri moved her family to Rome and began writing only in Italian, which she explores in her 2016 book In Other Words (translated from Italian). President Obama awarded her a National Humanities Medal in 2014. Lahiri has taught creative writing at her alma mater Boston University and at Princeton University and the Rhode Island School of Design.

At the tea stall Mr. and Mrs. Das bickered about who should take Tina to the toilet. Eventually Mrs. Das relented when Mr. Das pointed out that he had given the girl her bath the night before. In the rearview mirror Mr. Kapasi watched as Mrs. Das emerged slowly from his bulky white Ambassador, dragging her shaved, largely bare legs across the back seat. She did not hold the little girl's hand as they walked to the rest room.

They were on their way to see the Sun Temple at Konarak. It was a dry, bright Saturday, the mid-July heat tempered by a steady ocean breeze, ideal weather for sightseeing. Ordinarily Mr. Kapasi would not have stopped so soon along the way, but less than five minutes after he'd picked up the family that morning in front of Hotel Sandy Villa, the little girl had complained. The first thing Mr. Kapasi had noticed when he saw Mr. and Mrs. Das, standing with their children under the portico of the hotel, was that they were very young, perhaps not even thirty. In addition to Tina they had two boys, Ronny and Bobby, who appeared very close in age and had teeth covered in a network of flashing silver wires. The family looked Indian but dressed as foreigners did, the children in stiff, brightly colored clothing and caps with translucent visors. Mr. Kapasi was accustomed to foreign tourists; he was assigned to them regularly because he could speak English. Yesterday he had driven an elderly couple from Scotland, both with spotted faces and fluffy white hair so thin it exposed their sunburnt scalps. In comparison, the tanned, youthful faces of Mr. and Mrs. Das were all the more striking. When he'd introduced himself, Mr. Kapasi had pressed his palms together in greeting, but Mr. Das squeezed hands like an American so that Mr. Kapasi felt it in his elbow. Mrs. Das, for her part, had flexed one side of her mouth, smiling dutifully at Mr. Kapasi, without displaying any interest in him.

As they waited at the tea stall, Ronny, who looked like the older of the two boys, clambered suddenly out of the back seat, intrigued by a goat tied to a stake in the ground.

"Don't touch it," Mr. Das said. He glanced up from his paperback tour book, which said "INDIA" in yellow letters and looked as if it had been published abroad. His voice, somehow tentative and a little shrill, sounded as though it had not yet settled into maturity.

"I want to give it a piece of gum," the boy called back as he trotted ahead.   5

Mr. Das stepped out of the car and stretched his legs by squatting briefly to the ground. A clean-shaven man, he looked exactly like a magnified version of Ronny. He had a sapphire blue visor, and was dressed in shorts, sneakers, and a T-shirt. The camera slung around his neck, with an impressive telephoto lens and numerous buttons and markings, was the only complicated thing he wore. He frowned, watching as Ronny rushed toward the goat, but appeared to have no intention of intervening. "Bobby, make sure that your brother doesn't do anything stupid."

"I don't feel like it," Bobby said, not moving. He was sitting in the front seat beside Mr. Kapasi, studying a picture of the elephant god taped to the glove compartment.

"No need to worry," Mr. Kapasi said. "They are quite tame." Mr. Kapasi was forty-six years old, with receding hair that had gone completely silver, but his butterscotch complexion and his unlined brow, which he treated in spare moments to dabs of lotus-oil balm, made it easy to imagine what he must have looked like at an earlier age. He wore gray trousers and a matching jacket-style shirt, tapered at the waist, with short sleeves and a large pointed collar, made of a thin but durable synthetic material. He had specified both the cut and the fabric to his tailor—it was his preferred uniform for giving tours because it did not get crushed during his long hours behind the wheel. Through the windshield he watched as Ronny circled around the goat, touched it quickly on its side, then trotted back to the car.

"You left India as a child?" Mr. Kapasi asked when Mr. Das had settled once again into the passenger seat.

"Oh, Mina and I were both born in America," Mr. Das announced with an air of   10
sudden confidence. "Born and raised. Our parents live here now, in Assansol.° They retired. We visit them every couple years." He turned to watch as the little girl ran toward the car, the wide purple bows of her sundress flopping on her narrow brown shoulders. She was holding to her chest a doll with yellow hair that looked as if it had been chopped, as a punitive measure, with a pair of dull scissors. "This is Tina's first trip to India, isn't it, Tina?"

"I don't have to go to the bathroom anymore," Tina announced.

Assansol: a city in the state of West Bengal in northeastern India.

"Where's Mina?" Mr. Das asked.

Mr. Kapasi found it strange that Mr. Das should refer to his wife by her first name when speaking to the little girl. Tina pointed to where Mrs. Das was purchasing something from one of the shirtless men who worked at the tea stall. Mr. Kapasi heard one of the shirtless men sing a phrase from a popular Hindi love song as Mrs. Das walked back to the car, but she did not appear to understand the words of the song, for she did not express irritation, or embarrassment, or react in any other way to the man's declarations.

He observed her. She wore a red-and-white-checkered skirt that stopped above her knees, slip-on shoes with a square wooden heel, and a close-fitting blouse styled like a man's undershirt. The blouse was decorated at chest-level with a calico appliqué in the shape of a strawberry. She was a short woman, with small hands like paws, her frosty pink fingernails painted to match her lips, and was slightly plump in her figure. Her hair, shorn only a little longer than her husband's, was parted far to one side. She was wearing large dark brown sunglasses with a pinkish tint to them, and carried a big straw bag, almost as big as her torso, shaped like a bowl, with a water bottle poking out of it. She walked slowly, carrying some puffed rice tossed with peanuts and chili peppers in a large packet made from newspapers. Mr. Kapasi turned to Mr. Das.

"Where in America do you live?"   15

"New Brunswick, New Jersey."

"Next to New York?"

"Exactly. I teach middle school there."

"What subject?"

"Science. In fact, every year I take my students on a trip to the Museum of Natu-   20
ral History in New York City. In a way we have a lot in common, you could say, you and I. How long have you been a tour guide, Mr. Kapasi?"

"Five years."

Mrs. Das reached the car. "How long's the trip?" she asked, shutting the door.

"About two and a half hours," Mr. Kapasi replied.

At this Mrs. Das gave an impatient sigh, as if she had been traveling her whole life without pause. She fanned herself with a folded Bombay film magazine written in English.

"I thought that the Sun Temple is only eighteen miles north of Puri," Mr. Das   25
said, tapping on the tour book.

"The roads to Konarak are poor. Actually it is a distance of fifty-two miles," Mr. Kapasi explained.

Mr. Das nodded, readjusting the camera strap where it had begun to chafe the back of his neck.

Before starting the ignition, Mr. Kapasi reached back to make sure the cranklike locks on the inside of each of the back doors were secured. As soon as the car began to move the little girl began to play with the lock on her side, clicking it with some effort forward and backward, but Mrs. Das said nothing to stop her. She sat a bit slouched at one end of the back seat, not offering her puffed rice to anyone. Ronny and Tina sat on either side of her, both snapping bright green gum.

"Look," Bobby said as the car began to gather speed. He pointed with his finger to the tall trees that lined the road. "Look."

"Monkeys!" Ronny shrieked. "Wow!"   30

They were seated in groups along the branches, with shining black faces, silver bodies, horizontal eyebrows, and crested heads. Their long gray tails dangled like a series of ropes among the leaves. A few scratched themselves with black leathery hands, or swung their feet, staring as the car passed.

"We call them the hanuman," Mr. Kapasi said. "They are quite common in the area."

As soon as he spoke, one of the monkeys leaped into the middle of the road, causing Mr. Kapasi to brake suddenly. Another bounced onto the hood of the car, then sprang away. Mr. Kapasi beeped his horn. The children began to get excited, sucking in their breath and covering their faces partly with their hands. They had never seen monkeys outside of a zoo, Mr. Das explained. He asked Mr. Kapasi to stop the car so that he could take a picture.

While Mr. Das adjusted his telephoto lens, Mrs. Das reached into her straw bag and pulled out a bottle of colorless nail polish, which she proceeded to stroke on the tip of her index finger.

The little girl stuck out a hand. "Mine too. Mommy, do mine too."   35

"Leave me alone," Mrs. Das said, blowing on her nail and turning her body slightly. "You're making me mess up."

The little girl occupied herself by buttoning and unbuttoning a pinafore on the doll's plastic body.

"All set," Mr. Das said, replacing the lens cap.

The car rattled considerably as it raced along the dusty road, causing them all to pop up from their seats every now and then, but Mrs. Das continued to polish her nails. Mr. Kapasi eased up on the accelerator, hoping to produce a smoother ride. When he reached for the gearshift the boy in front accommodated him by swinging his hairless knees out of the way. Mr. Kapasi noted that this boy was slightly paler than the other children. "Daddy, why is the driver sitting on the wrong side in this car, too?" the boy asked.

"They all do that here, dummy," Ronny said.   40

"Don't call your brother a dummy," Mr. Das said. He turned to Mr. Kapasi. "In America, you know . . . . it confuses them."

"Oh yes, I am well aware," Mr. Kapasi said. As delicately as he could, he shifted gears again, accelerating as they approached a hill in the road. "I see it on *Dallas*,° the steering wheels are on the left-hand side."

"What's *Dallas*?" Tina asked, banging her now naked doll on the seat behind Mr. Kapasi.

"It went off the air," Mr. Das explained. "It's a television show."

They were all like siblings, Mr. Kapasi thought as they passed a row of date trees.   45
Mr. and Mrs. Das behaved like an older brother and sister, not parents. It seemed that they were in charge of the children only for the day; it was hard to believe they were regularly responsible for anything other than themselves. Mr. Das tapped on his lens cap, and his tour book, dragging his thumbnail occasionally across the pages so that they made a scraping sound. Mrs. Das continued to polish her nails. She had still not removed her sunglasses. Every now and then Tina renewed her plea that she wanted her nails done, too, and so at one point Mrs. Das flicked a drop of polish on the little girl's finger before depositing the bottle back inside her straw bag.

"Isn't this an air-conditioned car?" she asked, still blowing on her hand. The window on Tina's side was broken and could not be rolled down.

Dallas: extremely popular 1980s television drama centered on the professional and romantic affairs of unscrupulous oil baron J. R. Ewing and his family.

"Quit complaining," Mr. Das said. "It isn't so hot."

"I told you to get a car with air-conditioning," Mrs. Das continued. "Why do you do this, Raj, just to save a few stupid rupees. What are you saving us, fifty cents?"

Their accents sounded just like the ones Mr. Kapasi heard on American television programs, though not like the ones on *Dallas*.

"Doesn't it get tiresome, Mr. Kapasi, showing people the same thing every day?"   50
Mr. Das asked, rolling down his own window all the way. "Hey, do you mind stopping the car. I just want to get a shot of this guy."

Mr. Kapasi pulled over to the side of the road as Mr. Das took a picture of a bare-foot man, his head wrapped in a dirty turban, seated on top of a cart of grain sacks pulled by a pair of bullocks.° Both the man and the bullocks were emaciated. In the back seat Mrs. Das gazed out another window, at the sky, where nearly transparent clouds passed quickly in front of one another.

"I look forward to it, actually," Mr. Kapasi said as they continued on their way. "The Sun Temple is one of my favorite places. In that way it is a reward for me. I give tours on Fridays and Saturdays only. I have another job during the week."

"Oh? Where?" Mr. Das asked.

"I work in a doctor's office."

"You're a doctor?"   55

"I am not a doctor. I work with one. As an interpreter."

"What does a doctor need an interpreter for?"

"He has a number of Gujarati patients. My father was Gujarati, but many people do not speak Gujarati in this area, including the doctor. And so the doctor asked me to work in his office, interpreting what the patients say."

"Interesting. I've never heard of anything like that," Mr. Das said.

Mr. Kapasi shrugged. "It is a job like any other."   60

"But so romantic," Mrs. Das said dreamily, breaking her extended silence. She lifted her pinkish brown sunglasses and arranged them on top of her head like a tiara. For the first time, her eyes met Mr. Kapasi's in the rearview mirror: pale, a bit small, their gaze fixed but drowsy.

Mr. Das craned to look at her. "What's so romantic about it?"

"I don't know. Something." She shrugged, knitting her brows together for an instant. "Would you like a piece of gum, Mr. Kapasi?" she asked brightly. She reached into her straw bag and handed him a small square wrapped in green-and-white-striped paper. As soon as Mr. Kapasi put the gum in his mouth a thick sweet liquid burst onto his tongue.

"Tell us more about your job, Mr. Kapasi," Mrs. Das said.

"What would you like to know, madame?"   65

"I don't know," she shrugged, munching on some puffed rice and licking the mustard oil from the corners of her mouth. "Tell us a typical situation." She settled back in her seat, her head tilted in a patch of sun, and closed her eyes. "I want to picture what happens."

"Very well. The other day a man came in with a pain in his throat."

"Did he smoke cigarettes?"

"No. It was very curious. He complained that he felt as if there were long pieces of straw stuck in his throat. When I told the doctor he was able to prescribe the proper medication."

bullocks: young or castrated bulls; steers.

"That's so neat."   70

"Yes," Mr. Kapasi agreed after some hesitation.

"So these patients are totally dependent on you," Mrs. Das said. She spoke slowly, as if she were thinking aloud. "In a way, more dependent on you than the doctor."

"How do you mean? How could it be?"

"Well, for example, you could tell the doctor that the pain felt like a burning, not straw. The patient would never know what you had told the doctor, and the doctor wouldn't know that you had told the wrong thing. It's a big responsibility."

"Yes, a big responsibility you have there, Mr. Kapasi," Mr. Das agreed.   75

Mr. Kapasi had never thought of his job in such complimentary terms. To him it was a thankless occupation. He found nothing noble in interpreting people's maladies, assiduously translating the symptoms of so many swollen bones, countless cramps of bellies and bowels, spots on people's palms that changed color, shape, or size. The doctor, nearly half his age, had an affinity for bell-bottom trousers and made humorless jokes about the Congress party.° Together they worked in a stale little infirmary where Mr. Kapasi's smartly tailored clothes clung to him in the heat, in spite of the blackened blades of a ceiling fan churning over their heads.

The job was a sign of his failings. In his youth he'd been a devoted scholar of foreign languages, the owner of an impressive collection of dictionaries. He had dreamed of being an interpreter for diplomats and dignitaries, resolving conflicts between people and nations, settling disputes of which he alone could understand both sides. He was a self-educated man. In a series of notebooks, in the evenings before his parents settled his marriage, he had listed the common etymologies of words, and at one point in his life he was confident that he could converse, if given the opportunity, in English, French, Russian, Portuguese, and Italian, not to mention Hindi, Bengali, Orissi, and Gujarati. Now only a handful of European phrases remained in his memory, scattered words for things like saucers and chairs. English was the only non-Indian language he spoke fluently anymore. Mr. Kapasi knew it was not a remarkable talent. Sometimes he feared that his children knew better English than he did, just from watching television. Still, it came in handy for the tours.

He had taken the job as an interpreter after his first son, at the age of seven, contracted typhoid—that was how he had first made the acquaintance of the doctor. At the time Mr. Kapasi had been teaching English in a grammar school, and he bartered his skills as an interpreter to pay the increasingly exorbitant medical bills. In the end the boy had died one evening in his mother's arms, his limbs burning with fever, but then there was the funeral to pay for, and the other children who were born soon enough, and the newer, bigger house, and the good schools and tutors, and the fine shoes and the television, and the countless other ways he tried to console his wife and to keep her from crying in her sleep, and so when the doctor offered to pay him twice as much as he earned at the grammar school, he accepted. Mr. Kapasi knew that his wife had little regard for his career as an interpreter. He knew it reminded her of the son she'd lost, and that she resented the other lives he helped, in his own small way, to save. If ever she referred to his position, she used the phrase "doctor's assistant," as if the process of interpretation were equal to taking someone's temperature, or changing a bedpan. She never asked him about the patients who came to the doctor's office, or said that his job was a big responsibility.

the Congress party: India's governing party for five decades after independence in 1947, widely perceived as corrupt.

For this reason it flattered Mr. Kapasi that Mrs. Das was so intrigued by his job. Unlike his wife, she had reminded him of its intellectual challenges. She had also used the word "romantic." She did not behave in a romantic way toward her husband, and yet she had used the word to describe him. He wondered if Mr. and Mrs. Das were a bad match, just as he and his wife were. Perhaps they, too, had little in common apart from three children and a decade of their lives. The signs he recognized from his own marriage were there—the bickering, the indifference, the protracted silences. Her sudden interest in him, an interest she did not express in either her husband or her children, was mildly intoxicating. When Mr. Kapasi thought once again about how she had said "romantic," the feeling of intoxication grew.

He began to check his reflection in the rearview mirror as he drove, feeling grateful that he had chosen the gray suit that morning and not the brown one, which tended to sag a little in the knees. From time to time he glanced through the mirror at Mrs. Das. In addition to glancing at her face he glanced at the strawberry between her breasts, and the golden brown hollow in her throat. He decided to tell Mrs. Das about another patient, and another: the young woman who had complained of a sensation of raindrops in her spine, the gentleman whose birthmark had begun to sprout hairs. Mrs. Das listened attentively, stroking her hair with a small plastic brush that resembled an oval bed of nails, asking more questions, for yet another example. The children were quiet, intent on spotting more monkeys in the trees, and Mr. Das was absorbed by his tour book, so it seemed like a private conversation between Mr. Kapasi and Mrs. Das. In this manner the next half hour passed, and when they stopped for lunch at a roadside restaurant that sold fritters and omelette sandwiches, usually something Mr. Kapasi looked forward to on his tours so that he could sit in peace and enjoy some hot tea, he was disappointed. As the Das family settled together under a magenta umbrella fringed with white and orange tassels, and placed their orders with one of the waiters who marched about in tricornered caps, Mr. Kapasi reluctantly headed toward a neighboring table.

"Mr. Kapasi, wait. There's room here," Mrs. Das called out. She gathered Tina onto her lap, insisting that he accompany them. And so, together, they had bottled mango juice and sandwiches and plates of onions and potatoes deep-fried in graham-flour batter. After finishing two omelette sandwiches Mr. Das took more pictures of the group as they ate.

"How much longer?" he asked Mr. Kapasi as he paused to load a new roll of film in the camera.

"About half an hour more."

By now the children had gotten up from the table to look at more monkeys perched in a nearby tree, so there was a considerable space between Mrs. Das and Mr. Kapasi. Mr. Das placed the camera to his face and squeezed one eye shut, his tongue exposed at one corner of his mouth. "This looks funny. Mina, you need to lean in closer to Mr. Kapasi."

She did. He could smell a scent on her skin, like a mixture of whiskey and rose-water. He worried suddenly that she could smell his perspiration, which he knew had collected beneath the synthetic material of his shirt. He polished off his mango juice in one gulp and smoothed his silver hair with his hands. A bit of the juice dripped onto his chin. He wondered if Mrs. Das had noticed.

She had not. "What's your address, Mr. Kapasi?" she inquired, fishing for something inside her straw bag.

"You would like my address?"

80

85

"So we can send you copies," she said. "Of the pictures." She handed him a scrap of paper which she had hastily ripped from a page of her film magazine. The blank portion was limited, for the narrow strip was crowded by lines of text and a tiny picture of a hero and heroine embracing under a eucalyptus tree.

The paper curled as Mr. Kapasi wrote his address in clear, careful letters. She would write to him, asking about his days interpreting at the doctor's office, and he would respond eloquently, choosing only the most entertaining anecdotes, ones that would make her laugh out loud as she read them in her house in New Jersey. In time she would reveal the disappointment of her marriage, and he his. In this way their friendship would grow, and flourish. He would possess a picture of the two of them, eating fried onions under a magenta umbrella, which he would keep, he decided, safely tucked between the pages of his Russian grammar. As his mind raced, Mr. Kapasi experienced a mild and pleasant shock. It was similar to a feeling he used to experience long ago when, after months of translating with the aid of a dictionary, he would finally read a passage from a French novel, or an Italian sonnet, and understand the words, one after another, unencumbered by his own efforts. In those moments Mr. Kapasi used to believe that all was right with the world, that all struggles were rewarded, that all of life's mistakes made sense in the end. The promise that he would hear from Mrs. Das now filled him with the same belief.

When he finished writing his address Mr. Kapasi handed her the paper, but as 90 soon as he did so he worried that he had either misspelled his name, or accidentally reversed the numbers of his postal code. He dreaded the possibility of a lost letter, the photograph never reaching him, hovering somewhere in Orissa,° close but ultimately unattainable. He thought of asking for the slip of paper again, just to make sure he had written his address accurately, but Mrs. Das had already dropped it into the jumble of her bag.

They reached Konarak at two-thirty. The temple, made of sandstone, was a massive pyramid-like structure in the shape of a chariot. It was dedicated to the great master of life, the sun, which struck three sides of the edifice as it made its journey each day across the sky. Twenty-four giant wheels were carved on the north and south sides of the plinth. The whole thing was drawn by a team of seven horses, speeding as if through the heavens. As they approached, Mr. Kapasi explained that the temple had been built between A.D. 1243 and 1255, with the efforts of twelve hundred artisans, by the great ruler of the Ganga dynasty, King Narasimhadeva the First, to commemorate his victory against the Muslim army.

"It says the temple occupies about a hundred and seventy acres of land," Mr. Das said, reading from his book.

"It's like a desert," Ronny said, his eyes wandering across the sand that stretched on all sides beyond the temple.

"The Chandrabhaga River once flowed one mile north of here. It is dry now," Mr. Kapasi said, turning off the engine.

They got out and walked toward the temple, posing first for pictures by the pair 95 of lions that flanked the steps. Mr. Kapasi led them next to one of the wheels of the chariot, higher than any human being, nine feet in diameter.

"'The wheels are supposed to symbolize the wheel of life,'" Mr. Das read. "'They depict the cycle of creation, preservation, and achievement of realization.' Cool." He

Orissa: a state on the southwest border of West Bengal.

turned the page of his book. "'Each wheel is divided into eight thick and thin spokes, dividing the day into eight equal parts. The rims are carved with designs of birds and animals, whereas the medallions in the spokes are carved with women in luxurious poses, largely erotic in nature.'"

What he referred to were the countless friezes of entwined naked bodies, making love in various positions, women clinging to the necks of men, their knees wrapped eternally around their lovers' thighs. In addition to these were assorted scenes from daily life, of hunting and trading, of deer being killed with bows and arrows and marching warriors holding swords in their hands.

It was no longer possible to enter the temple, for it had filled with rubble years ago, but they admired the exterior, as did all the tourists Mr. Kapasi brought there, slowly strolling along each of its sides. Mr. Das trailed behind, taking pictures. The children ran ahead, pointing to figures of naked people, intrigued in particular by the Nagamithunas, the half-human, half-serpentine couples who were said, Mr. Kapasi told them, to live in the deepest waters of the sea. Mr. Kapasi was pleased that they liked the temple, pleased especially that it appealed to Mrs. Das. She stopped every three or four paces, staring silently at the carved lovers, and the processions of elephants, and the topless female musicians beating on two-sided drums.

Though Mr. Kapasi had been to the temple countless times, it occurred to him, as he, too, gazed at the topless women, that he had never seen his own wife fully naked. Even when they had made love she kept the panels of her blouse hooked together, the string of her petticoat knotted around her waist. He had never admired the backs of his wife's legs the way he now admired those of Mrs. Das, walking as if for his benefit alone. He had, of course, seen plenty of bare limbs before, belonging to the American and European ladies who took his tours. But Mrs. Das was different. Unlike the other women, who had an interest only in the temple, and kept their noses buried in a guidebook, or their eyes behind the lens of a camera, Mrs. Das had taken an interest in him.

Mr. Kapasi was anxious to be alone with her, to continue their private conver- 100 sation, yet he felt nervous to walk at her side. She was lost behind her sunglasses, ignoring her husband's requests that she pose for another picture, walking past her children as if they were strangers. Worried that he might disturb her, Mr. Kapasi walked ahead, to admire, as he always did, the three life-sized bronze avatars of Surya, the sun god, each emerging from its own niche on the temple facade to greet the sun at dawn, noon, and evening. They wore elaborate headdresses, their languid, elongated eyes closed, their bare chests draped with carved chains and amulets. Hibiscus petals, offerings from previous visitors, were strewn at their gray-green feet. The last statue, on the northern wall of the temple, was Mr. Kapasi's favorite. This Surya had a tired expression, weary after a hard day of work, sitting astride a horse with folded legs. Even his horse's eyes were drowsy. Around his body were smaller sculptures of women in pairs, their hips thrust to one side.

"Who's that?" Mrs. Das asked. He was startled to see that she was standing beside him.

"He is the Astachala-Surya," Mr. Kapasi said. "The setting sun."

"So in a couple of hours the sun will set right here?" She slipped a foot out of one of her square-heeled shoes, rubbed her toes on the back of her other leg.

"That is correct."

She raised her sunglasses for a moment, then put them back on again. "Neat." 105

Mr. Kapasi was not certain exactly what the word suggested, but he had a feeling it was a favorable response. He hoped that Mrs. Das had understood Surya's beauty, his power. Perhaps they would discuss it further in their letters. He would explain things to her, things about India, and she would explain things to him about America. In its own way this correspondence would fulfill his dream, of serving as an interpreter between nations. He looked at her straw bag, delighted that his address lay nestled among its contents. When he pictured her so many thousands of miles away he plummeted, so much so that he had an overwhelming urge to wrap his arms around her, to freeze with her, even for an instant, in an embrace witnessed by his favorite Surya. But Mrs. Das had already started walking.

"When do you return to America?" he asked, trying to sound placid.

"In ten days."

He calculated: A week to settle in, a week to develop the pictures, a few days to compose her letter, two weeks to get to India by air. According to his schedule, allowing room for delays, he would hear from Mrs. Das in approximately six weeks' time.

The family was silent as Mr. Kapasi drove them back, a little past four-thirty, 110 to Hotel Sandy Villa. The children had bought miniature granite versions of the chariot's wheels at a souvenir stand, and they turned them round in their hands. Mr. Das continued to read his book. Mrs. Das untangled Tina's hair with her brush and divided it into two little ponytails.

Mr. Kapasi was beginning to dread the thought of dropping them off. He was not prepared to begin his six-week wait to hear from Mrs. Das. As he stole glances at her in the rearview mirror, wrapping elastic bands around Tina's hair, he wondered how he might make the tour last a little longer. Ordinarily he sped back to Puri using a shortcut, eager to return home, scrub his feet and hands with sandalwood soap, and enjoy the evening newspaper and a cup of tea that his wife would serve him in silence. The thought of that silence, something to which he'd long been resigned, now oppressed him. It was then that he suggested visiting the hills at Udayagiri and Khandagiri, where a number of monastic dwellings were hewn out of the ground, facing one another across a defile. It was some miles away, but well worth seeing, Mr. Kapasi told them.

"Oh yeah, there's something mentioned about it in this book," Mr. Das said. "Built by a Jain° king or something."

"Shall we go then?" Mr. Kapasi asked. He paused at a turn in the road. "It's to the left."

Mr. Das turned to look at Mrs. Das. Both of them shrugged.

"Left, left," the children chanted. 115

Mr. Kapasi turned the wheel, almost delirious with relief. He did not know what he would do or say to Mrs. Das once they arrived at the hills. Perhaps he would tell her what a pleasing smile she had. Perhaps he would compliment her strawberry shirt, which he found irresistibly becoming. Perhaps, when Mr. Das was busy taking a picture, he would take her hand.

He did not have to worry. When they got to the hills, divided by a steep path thick with trees, Mrs. Das refused to get out of the car. All along the path, dozens of monkeys were seated on stones, as well as on the branches of the trees. Their hind legs were stretched out in front and raised to shoulder level, their arms resting on their knees.

Jain: an adherent of Jainism, a dualistic, ascetic religion founded in the sixth century B.C. in revolt against the Hindu caste system.

"My legs are tired," she said, sinking low in her seat. "I'll stay here."

"Why did you have to wear those stupid shoes?" Mr. Das said. "You won't be in the pictures."

"Pretend I'm there."   120

"But we could use one of these pictures for our Christmas card this year. We didn't get one of all five of us at the Sun Temple. Mr. Kapasi could take it."

"I'm not coming. Anyway, those monkeys give me the creeps."

"But they're harmless," Mr. Das said. He turned to Mr. Kapasi. "Aren't they?"

"They are more hungry than dangerous," Mr. Kapasi said. "Do not provoke them with food, and they will not bother you."

Mr. Das headed up the defile with the children, the boys at his side, the little   125
girl on his shoulders. Mr. Kapasi watched as they crossed paths with a Japanese man and woman, the only other tourists there, who paused for a final photograph, then stepped into a nearby car and drove away. As the car disappeared out of view some of the monkeys called out, emitting soft whooping sounds, and then walked on their flat black hands and feet up the path. At one point a group of them formed a little ring around Mr. Das and the children. Tina screamed in delight. Ronny ran in circles around his father. Bobby bent down and picked up a fat stick on the ground. When he extended it, one of the monkeys approached him and snatched it, then briefly beat the ground.

"I'll join them," Mr. Kapasi said, unlocking the door on his side. "There is much to explain about the caves."

"No. Stay a minute," Mrs. Das said. She got out of the back seat and slipped in beside Mr. Kapasi. "Raj has his dumb book anyway." Together, through the windshield, Mrs. Das and Mr. Kapasi watched as Bobby and the monkey passed the stick back and forth between them.

"A brave little boy," Mr. Kapasi commented.

"It's not so surprising," Mrs. Das said.

"No?"   130

"He's not his."

"I beg your pardon?"

"Raj's. He's not Raj's son."

Mr. Kapasi felt a prickle on his skin. He reached into his shirt pocket for the small tin of lotus-oil balm he carried with him at all times, and applied it to three spots on his forehead. He knew that Mrs. Das was watching him, but he did not turn to face her. Instead he watched as the figures of Mr. Das and the children grew smaller, climbing up the steep path, pausing every now and then for a picture, surrounded by a growing number of monkeys.

"Are you surprised?" The way she put it made him choose his words with care.   135

"It's not the type of thing one assumes," Mr. Kapasi replied slowly. He put the tin of lotus-oil balm back in his pocket.

"No, of course not. And no one knows, of course. No one at all. I've kept it a secret for eight whole years." She looked at Mr. Kapasi, tilting her chin as if to gain a fresh perspective. "But now I've told you."

Mr. Kapasi nodded. He felt suddenly parched, and his forehead was warm and slightly numb from the balm. He considered asking Mrs. Das for a sip of water, then decided against it.

"We met when we were very young," she said. She reached into her straw bag in search of something, then pulled out a packet of puffed rice. "Want some?"

"No, thank you."

She put a fistful in her mouth, sank into the seat a little, and looked away from Mr. Kapasi, out the window on her side of the car. "We married when we were still in college. We were in high school when he proposed. We went to the same college, of course. Back then we couldn't stand the thought of being separated, not for a day, not for a minute. Our parents were best friends who lived in the same town. My entire life I saw him every weekend, either at our house or theirs. We were sent upstairs to play together while our parents joked about our marriage. Imagine! They never caught us at anything, though in a way I think it was all more or less a setup. The things we did those Friday and Saturday nights, while our parents sat downstairs drinking tea . . . I could tell you stories, Mr. Kapasi."

As a result of spending all her time in college with Raj, she continued, she did not make many close friends. There was no one to confide in about him at the end of a difficult day, or to share a passing thought or a worry. Her parents now lived on the other side of the world, but she had never been very close to them, anyway. After marrying so young she was overwhelmed by it all, having a child so quickly, and nursing, and warming up bottles of milk and testing their temperature against her wrist while Raj was at work, dressed in sweaters and corduroy pants, teaching his students about rocks and dinosaurs. Raj never looked cross or harried, or plump as she had become after the first baby.

Always tired, she declined invitations from her one or two college girlfriends, to have lunch or shop in Manhattan. Eventually the friends stopped calling her, so that she was left at home all day with the baby, surrounded by toys that made her trip when she walked or wince when she sat, always cross and tired. Only occasionally did they go out after Ronny was born, and even more rarely did they entertain. Raj didn't mind; he looked forward to coming home from teaching and watching television and bouncing Ronny on his knee. She had been outraged when Raj told her that a Punjabi° friend, someone whom she had once met but did not remember, would be staying with them for a week for some job interviews in the New Brunswick area.

Bobby was conceived in the afternoon, on a sofa littered with rubber teething toys, after the friend learned that a London pharmaceutical company had hired him, while Ronny cried to be freed from his playpen. She made no protest when the friend touched the small of her back as she was about to make a pot of coffee, then pulled her against his crisp navy suit. He made love to her swiftly, in silence, with an expertise she had never known, without the meaningful expressions and smiles Raj always insisted on afterward. The next day Raj drove the friend to JFK. He was married now, to a Punjabi girl, and they lived in London still, and every year they exchanged Christmas cards with Raj and Mina, each couple tucking photos of their families into the envelopes. He did not know that he was Bobby's father. He never would.

"I beg your pardon, Mrs. Das, but why have you told me this information?" Mr. Kapasi asked when she had finally finished speaking, and had turned to face him once again.

"For God's sake, stop calling me Mrs. Das. I'm twenty-eight. You probably have children my age."

"Not quite." It disturbed Mr. Kapasi to learn that she thought of him as a parent. The feeling he had had toward her, that had made him check his reflection in the rearview mirror as they drove, evaporated a little.

Punjabi: a native of Punjab, a state in northwest India.

"I told you because of your talents." She put the packet of puffed rice back into her bag without folding over the top.

"I don't understand," Mr. Kapasi said.

"Don't you see? For eight years I haven't been able to express this to anybody,   150
not to friends, certainly not to Raj. He doesn't even suspect it. He thinks I'm still in love with him. Well, don't you have anything to say?"

"About what?"

"About what I've just told you. About my secret, and about how terrible it makes me feel. I feel terrible looking at my children, and at Raj, always terrible. I have terrible urges, Mr. Kapasi, to throw things away. One day I had the urge to throw everything I own out the window, the television, the children, everything. Don't you think it's unhealthy?"

He was silent.

"Mr. Kapasi, don't you have anything to say? I thought that was your job."

"My job is to give tours, Mrs. Das."   155

"Not that. Your other job. As an interpreter."

"But we do not face a language barrier. What need is there for an interpreter?"

"That's not what I mean. I would never have told you otherwise. Don't you realize what it means for me to tell you?"

"What does it mean?"

"It means that I'm tired of feeling so terrible all the time. Eight years, Mr. Kapasi,   160
I've been in pain eight years. I was hoping you could help me feel better, say the right thing. Suggest some kind of remedy."

He looked at her, in her red plaid skirt and strawberry T-shirt, a woman not yet thirty, who loved neither her husband nor her children, who had already fallen out of love with life. Her confession depressed him, depressed him all the more when he thought of Mr. Das at the top of the path, Tina clinging to his shoulders, taking pictures of ancient monastic cells cut into the hills to show his students in America, unsuspecting and unaware that one of his sons was not his own. Mr. Kapasi felt insulted that Mrs. Das should ask him to interpret her common, trivial little secret. She did not resemble the patients in the doctor's office, those who came glassy-eyed and desperate, unable to sleep or breathe or urinate with ease, unable, above all, to give words to their pains. Still, Mr. Kapasi believed it was his duty to assist Mrs. Das. Perhaps he ought to tell her to confess the truth to Mr. Das. He would explain that honesty was the best policy. Honesty, surely, would help her feel better, as she'd put it. Perhaps he would offer to preside over the discussion, as a mediator. He decided to begin with the most obvious question, to get to the heart of the matter, and so he asked, "Is it really pain you feel, Mrs. Das, or is it guilt?"

She turned to him and glared, mustard oil thick on her frosty pink lips. She opened her mouth to say something, but as she glared at Mr. Kapasi some certain knowledge seemed to pass before her eyes, and she stopped. It crushed him; he knew at that moment that he was not even important enough to be properly insulted. She opened the car door and began walking up the path, wobbling a little on her square wooden heels, reaching into her straw bag to eat handfuls of puffed rice. It fell through her fingers, leaving a zigzagging trail, causing a monkey to leap down from a tree and devour the little white grains. In search of more, the monkey began to follow Mrs. Das. Others joined him, so that she was soon being followed by about half a dozen of them, their velvety tails dragging behind.

Mr. Kapasi stepped out of the car. He wanted to holler, to alert her in some way, but he worried that if she knew they were behind her, she would grow nervous. Perhaps she would lose her balance. Perhaps they would pull at her bag or her hair. He began to jog up the path, taking a fallen branch in his hand to scare away the monkeys. Mrs. Das continued walking, oblivious, trailing grains of puffed rice. Near the top of the incline, before a group of cells fronted by a row of squat stone pillars, Mr. Das was kneeling on the ground focusing the lens of his camera. The children stood under the arcade, now hiding, now emerging from view.

"Wait for me," Mrs. Das called out. "I'm coming."

Tina jumped up and down. "Here comes Mommy!"   165

"Great," Mr. Das said without looking up. "Just in time. We'll get Mr. Kapasi to take a picture of the five of us."

Mr. Kapasi quickened his pace, waving his branch so that the monkeys scampered away, distracted, in another direction.

"Where's Bobby?" Mrs. Das asked when she stopped.

Mr. Das looked up from the camera. "I don't know. Ronny, where's Bobby?"

Ronny shrugged, "I thought he was right here."   170

"Where is he?" Mrs. Das repeated sharply. "What's wrong with all of you?"

They began calling his name, wandering up and down the path a bit. Because they were calling, they did not initially hear the boy's screams. When they found him, a little farther down the path under a tree, he was surrounded by a group of monkeys, over a dozen of them, pulling at his T-shirt with their long black fingers. The puffed rice Mrs. Das had spilled was scattered at his feet, raked over by the monkeys' hands. The boy was silent, his body frozen, swift tears running down his startled face. His bare legs were dusty and red with welts from where one of the monkeys struck him repeatedly with the stick he had given to it earlier.

"Daddy, the monkey's hurting Bobby," Tina said.

Mr. Das wiped his palms on the front of his shorts. In his nervousness he accidentally pressed the shutter on his camera; the whirring noise of the advancing film excited the monkeys, and the one with the stick began to beat Bobby more intently. "What are we supposed to do? What if they start attacking?"

"Mr. Kapasi," Mrs. Das shrieked, noticing him standing to one side. "Do some- 175
thing, for God's sake, do something!"

Mr. Kapasi took his branch and shooed them away, hissing at the ones that remained, stomping his feet to scare them. The animals retreated slowly, with a measured gait, obedient but unintimidated. Mr. Kapasi gathered Bobby in his arms and brought him back to where his parents and siblings were standing. As he carried him he was tempted to whisper a secret into the boy's ear. But Bobby was stunned, and shivering with fright, his legs bleeding slightly where the stick had broken the skin. When Mr. Kapasi delivered him to his parents, Mr. Das brushed some dirt off the boy's T-shirt and put the visor on him the right way. Mrs. Das reached into her straw bag to find a bandage which she taped over the cut on his knee. Ronny offered his brother a fresh piece of gum. "He's fine. Just a little scared, right, Bobby?" Mr. Das said, patting the top of his head.

"God, let's get out of here," Mrs. Das said. She folded her arms across the strawberry on her chest. "This place gives me the creeps."

"Yeah. Back to the hotel, definitely," Mr. Das agreed.

"Poor Bobby," Mrs. Das said. "Come here a second. Let Mommy fix your hair." Again she reached into her straw bag, this time for her hairbrush, and began to run it around the edges of the translucent visor. When she whipped out the hairbrush, the slip of paper with Mr. Kapasi's address on it fluttered away in the wind. No one but Mr. Kapasi noticed. He watched as it rose, carried higher and higher by the breeze, into the trees where the monkeys now sat, solemnly observing the scene below. Mr. Kapasi observed it too, knowing that this was the picture of the Das family he would preserve forever in his mind.

Katherine Mansfield

Miss Brill   1922

Katherine Mansfield Beauchamp (1888–1923), was born into a sedate Victorian family in New Zealand, the daughter of a successful businessman. At fifteen, she emigrated to England to attend school and did not ever permanently return Down Under. In 1918, after a time of wild-oat sowing in bohemian London, she married the journalist and critic John Middleton Murry. All at once, Mansfield found herself struggling to define her sexual identity, to earn a living by her pen, to endure World War I (in which her brother was killed in action), and to survive the ravages of tuberculosis. She died at thirty-four, in France, at a spiritualist commune where she had sought to regain her health. Mansfield wrote no novels, but during her brief career concentrated on the short story, in which she has few peers. Bliss *(1920) and* The*

Katherine Mansfield

Garden-Party and Other Stories (1922) were greeted with an acclaim that has continued; her collected short stories were published in 1937. Some of her stories celebrate life, others wryly poke fun at it. Many reveal, in ordinary lives, small incidents that open like doorways into significances.

   Although it was so brilliantly fine—the blue sky powdered with gold and great spots of light like white wine splashed over the Jardins Publiques—Miss Brill was glad that she had decided on her fur. The air was motionless, but when you opened your mouth there was just a faint chill, like a chill from a glass of iced water before you sip, and now and again a leaf came drifting—from nowhere, from the sky. Miss Brill put up her hand and touched her fur. Dear little thing! It was nice to feel it again. She had taken it out of its box that afternoon, shaken out the moth-powder, given it a good brush, and rubbed the life back into the dim little eyes. "What has been happening to me?" said the sad little eyes. Oh, how sweet it was to see them snap at her again from the red eiderdown! . . . But the nose, which was of some black composition, wasn't at all firm. It must have had a knock, somehow. Never mind—a little dab of black sealing-wax when the time came—when it was absolutely necessary. . . . Little rogue! Yes, she really felt like that about it. Little rogue biting its tail just by her left ear. She could have taken it off and laid it on her lap and stroked it. She felt a tingling in her hands and arms, but that came from walking, she supposed. And when she breathed, something light and sad—no, not sad, exactly—something gentle seemed to move in her bosom.

There were a number of people out this afternoon, far more than last Sunday. And the band sounded louder and gayer. That was because the Season had begun. For although the band played all year round on Sundays, out of season it was never the same. It was like some one playing with only the family to listen; it didn't care how it played if there weren't any strangers present. Wasn't the conductor wearing a new coat, too? She was sure it was new. He scraped with his foot and flapped his arms like a rooster about to crow, and the bandsmen sitting in the green rotunda blew out their cheeks and glared at the music. Now there came a little "flutey" bit—very pretty!—a little chain of bright drops. She was sure it would be repeated. It was; she lifted her head and smiled.

Only two people shared her "special" seat: a fine old man in a velvet coat, his hands clasped over a huge carved walking-stick, and a big old woman, sitting upright, with a roll of knitting on her embroidered apron. They did not speak. This was disappointing, for Miss Brill always looked forward to the conversation. She had become really quite expert, she thought, at listening as though she didn't listen, at sitting in other people's lives just for a minute while they talked round her.

She glanced, sideways, at the old couple. Perhaps they would go soon. Last Sunday, too, hadn't been as interesting as usual. An Englishman and his wife, he wearing a dreadful Panama hat and she button boots. And she'd gone on the whole time about how she ought to wear spectacles; she knew she needed them; but that it was no good getting any; they'd be sure to break and they'd never keep on. And he'd been so patient. He'd suggested everything—gold rims, the kind that curved round your ears, little pads inside the bridge. No, nothing would please her. "They'll always be sliding down my nose!" Miss Brill wanted to shake her.

The old people sat on the bench, still as statues. Never mind, there was always   5 the crowd to watch. To and fro, in front of the flower-beds and the band rotunda, the couples and groups paraded, stopped to talk, to greet, to buy a handful of flowers from the old beggar who had his tray fixed to the railings. Little children ran among them, swooping and laughing; little boys with big white silk bows under their chins, little girls, little French dolls, dressed up in velvet and lace. And sometimes a tiny staggerer came suddenly rocking into the open from under the trees, stopped, stared, as suddenly sat down "flop," until its small high-stepping mother, like a young hen, rushed scolding to its rescue. Other people sat on the benches and green chairs, but they were nearly always the same, Sunday after Sunday, and—Miss Brill had often noticed—there was something funny about nearly all of them. They were odd, silent, nearly all old, and from the way they stared they looked as though they'd just come from dark little rooms or even—even cupboards!

Behind the rotunda the slender trees with yellow leaves down drooping, and through them just a line of sea, and beyond the blue sky with gold-veined clouds.

Tum-tum-tum tiddle-um! tiddle-um! turn tiddley-um turn ta! blew the band.

Two young girls in red came by and two young soldiers in blue met them, and they laughed and paired and went off arm-in-arm. Two peasant women with funny straw hats passed, gravely, leading beautiful smoke-colored donkeys. A cold, pale nun hurried by. A beautiful woman came along and dropped her bunch of violets, and a little boy ran after to hand them to her, and she took them and threw them away as if they'd been poisoned. Dear me! Miss Brill didn't know whether to admire that or not! And now an ermine toque and a gentleman in grey met just in front of her. He was tall, stiff, dignified, and she was wearing the ermine toque she'd bought when her hair was yellow. Now everything, her hair, her face, even her eyes, was the same color as the shabby ermine, and her hand, in its cleaned glove, lifted to dab her lips, was a tiny yellowish paw. Oh, she was so pleased to see him—delighted! She rather thought they were going to meet that afternoon. She described where she'd been—everywhere, here, there, along by the sea. The day was so charming—didn't he agree? And wouldn't he, perhaps? . . . But he shook his head, lighted a cigarette, slowly breathed a great deep puff into her face, and, even while she was still talking and laughing, flicked the match away and walked on. The ermine toque was alone; she smiled more brightly than ever. But even the band seemed to know what she was feeling and played more softly, played tenderly, and the drum beat, "The Brute! The Brute!" over and over. What would she do? What was going to happen now? But as Miss Brill wondered, the ermine toque turned, raised her hand as though she'd seen some one else, much nicer, just over there, and pattered away. And the band changed again and played more quickly, more gaily than ever, and the old couple on Miss Brill's seat got up and marched away, and such a funny old man with long whiskers hobbled along in time to the music and was nearly knocked over by four girls walking abreast.

Oh, how fascinating it was! How she enjoyed it! How she loved sitting here, watching it all! It was like a play. It was exactly like a play. Who could believe the sky at the back wasn't painted? But it wasn't till a little brown dog trotted on solemn and then slowly trotted off, like a little "theatre" dog, a little dog that had been drugged, that Miss Brill discovered what it was that made it so exciting. They were all on the stage. They weren't only the audience, not only looking on; they were acting. Even she had a part and came every Sunday. No doubt somebody would have noticed if she hadn't been there; she was part of the performance after all. How strange she'd never thought of it like that before! And yet it explained why she made such a point of starting from home at just the same time each week—so as not to be late for the performance—and it also explained why she had quite a queer, shy feeling at telling her English pupils how she spent her Sunday afternoons. No wonder! Miss Brill nearly laughed out loud. She was on the stage. She thought of the old invalid gentleman to whom she read the newspaper four afternoons a week while he slept in the garden. She had got quite used to the frail head on the cotton pillow, the hollowed eyes, the open mouth and the high pinched nose. If he'd been dead she mightn't have noticed for weeks; she wouldn't have minded. But suddenly he knew he was having the paper read to him by an actress! "An actress!" The old head lifted; two points of light quivered in the old eyes. "An actress—are ye?" And Miss Brill smoothed the newspaper as though it were the manuscript of her part and said gently: "Yes, I have been an actress for a long time."

The band had been having a rest. Now they started again. And what they played was warm, sunny, yet there was just a faint chill—a something, what was it?—not sadness—no, not sadness—a something that made you want to sing. The tune lifted, lifted, the light shone; and it seemed to Miss Brill that in another moment all of them, all the whole company, would begin singing. The young ones, the laughing ones who were moving together, they would begin, and the men's voices, very resolute and brave, would join them. And then she too, she too, and the others on the benches—they would come in with a kind of accompaniment—something low, that scarcely rose or fell, something so beautiful—moving . . . And Miss Brill's eyes filled with tears and she looked smiling at all the other members of the company. Yes, we understand, we understand, she thought—though what they understood she didn't know.

Just at that moment a boy and a girl came and sat down where the old couple had been. They were beautifully dressed; they were in love. The hero and heroine, of course, just arrived from his father's yacht. And still soundlessly singing, still with that trembling smile, Miss Brill prepared to listen.

"No, not now," said the girl. "Not here, I can't."

"But why? Because of that stupid old thing at the end there?" asked the boy. "Why does she come here at all—who wants her? Why doesn't she keep her silly old mug at home?"

"It's her fu-fur which is so funny," giggled the girl. "It's exactly like a fried whiting."

"Ah, be off with you!" said the boy in an angry whisper. Then: "Tell me, my petite cherie—"   15

"No, not here," said the girl. "Not yet."

On her way home she usually bought a slice of honeycake at the baker's. It was her Sunday treat. Sometimes there was an almond in her slice, sometimes not. It made a great difference. If there was an almond it was like carrying home a tiny present—a surprise—something that might very well not have been there. She hurried on the almond Sundays and struck the match for the kettle in quite a dashing way.

But today she passed the baker's boy, climbed the stairs, went into the little dark room—her room like a cupboard—and sat down on the red eiderdown. She sat there for a long time. The box that the fur came out of was on the bed. She unclasped the necklet quickly; quickly, without looking, laid it inside. But when she put the lid on she thought she heard something crying.

Tim O'Brien

The Things They Carried   1990

Tim O'Brien was born in Austin, Minnesota, in 1946. Immediately after graduating summa cum laude from Macalester College in 1968, he was drafted into the US Army. Serving as an infantry-man in Vietnam, O'Brien attained the rank of sergeant and was awarded a Purple Heart after being wounded by shrapnel. Upon his discharge in 1970, he began graduate work at Harvard. In 1973 he published If I Die in a Combat Zone, Box Me Up and Ship Me Home, *a mixture of memoir and fiction about his wartime experiences. His 1978 novel* Going After Cacciato *won the National Book Award, and is considered by some critics to be the best book of American fiction about the Vietnam War. "The Things They Carried" was first published in* Esquire *in 1986, and later became the title piece in a book of interlocking short*

Tim O'Brien

stories published in 1990. His other novels include The Nuclear Age *(1985),* In the Lake of the Woods *(1994),* Tomcat in Love *(1998), and* July, July *(2002). O'Brien currently teaches at Texas State University–San Marcos.*

First Lieutenant Jimmy Cross carried letters from a girl named Martha, a junior at Mount Sebastian College in New Jersey. They were not love letters, but Lieutenant Cross was hoping, so he kept them folded in plastic at the bottom of his rucksack. In the late afternoon, after a day's march, he would dig his foxhole, wash his hands under a canteen, unwrap the letters, hold them with the tips of his fingers, and spend the last hour of light pretending. He would imagine romantic camping trips into the White Mountains in New Hampshire. He would sometimes taste the envelope flaps, knowing her tongue had been there. More than anything, he wanted Martha to love him as he loved her, but the letters were mostly chatty, elusive on the matter of love. She was a virgin, he was almost sure. She was an English major at Mount Sebastian, and she wrote beautifully about her professors and roommates and midterm exams, about her respect for Chaucer and her great affection for Virginia Woolf. She often quoted lines of poetry; she never mentioned the war, except to say, Jimmy, take care of yourself. The letters weighed 10 ounces. They were signed Love, Martha, but Lieutenant Cross understood that Love was only a way of signing and did not mean what he sometimes pretended it meant. At dusk, he would carefully return the letters to his rucksack. Slowly, a bit distracted, he would get up and move among his men, checking the perimeter; then at full dark he would return to his hole and watch the night and wonder if Martha was a virgin.

The things they carried were largely determined by necessity. Among the necessities or near-necessities were P-38 can openers, pocket knives, heat tabs, wristwatches, dog tags, mosquito repellent, chewing gum, candy, cigarettes, salt tablets, packets of Kool-Aid, lighters, matches, sewing kits, Military Payment Certificates, C rations, and two or three canteens of water. Together, these items weighed between 15 and 20 pounds, depending upon a man's habits or rate of metabolism. Henry Dobbins, who was a big man, carried extra rations; he was especially fond of canned peaches in heavy syrup over pound cake. Dave Jensen, who practiced field hygiene, carried a toothbrush, dental floss, and several hotel-sized bars of soap he'd stolen on R&R° in Sydney, Australia. Ted Lavender, who was scared, carried tranquilizers until he was shot in the head outside the village of Than Khe in mid-April. By necessity, and because it was SOP,° they all carried steel helmets that weighed 5 pounds including the liner and camouflage cover. They carried the standard fatigue jackets and trousers. Very few carried underwear. On their feet they carried jungle boots—2.1 pounds—and Dave Jensen carried three pairs of socks and a can of Dr. Scholl's foot powder as a precaution against trench foot. Until he was shot, Ted Lavender carried six or seven ounces of premium dope, which for him was a necessity. Mitchell Sanders, the RTO,° carried condoms. Norman Bowker carried a diary. Rat Kiley carried comic books. Kiowa, a devout Baptist, carried an illustrated New Testament that had been presented to him by his father, who taught Sunday school in Oklahoma City, Oklahoma. As a hedge against bad times, however, Kiowa also carried his grandmother's distrust of the white man, his grandfather's old hunting hatchet. Necessity dictated. Because the land was mined and booby-trapped, it was SOP for each man to carry a steel-centered, nylon-covered flak jacket, which weighed 6.7 pounds, but which on hot days seemed much heavier. Because you could die so quickly, each man carried at least one large compress bandage, usually in the helmet band for easy access. Because the nights were cold, and because the monsoons were wet, each

R&R: the military abbreviation for "rest and relaxation," a brief vacation from active service.　SOP: standard operating procedure.　RTO: radio and telephone operator.

carried a green plastic poncho that could be used as a raincoat or groundsheet or makeshift tent. With its quilted liner, the poncho weighed almost two pounds, but it was worth every ounce. In April, for instance, when Ted Lavender was shot, they used his poncho to wrap him up, then to carry him across the paddy, then to lift him into the chopper that took him away.

They were called legs or grunts.

To carry something was to hump it, as when Lieutenant Jimmy Cross humped his love for Martha up the hills and through the swamps. In its intransitive form, to hump meant to walk, or to march, but it implied burdens far beyond the intransitive.

Almost everyone humped photographs. In his wallet, Lieutenant Cross carried two photographs of Martha. The first was a Kodacolor snapshot signed Love, though he knew better. She stood against a brick wall. Her eyes were gray and neutral, her lips slightly open as she stared straight-on at the camera. At night, sometimes, Lieutenant Cross wondered who had taken the picture, because he knew she had boyfriends, because he loved her so much, and because he could see the shadow of the picture-taker spreading out against the brick wall. The second photograph had been clipped from the 1968 Mount Sebastian yearbook. It was an action shot—women's volleyball—and Martha was bent horizontal to the floor, reaching, the palms of her hands in sharp focus, the tongue taut, the expression frank and competitive. There was no visible sweat. She wore white gym shorts. Her legs, he thought, were almost certainly the legs of a virgin, dry and without hair, the left knee cocked and carrying her entire weight, which was just over one hundred pounds. Lieutenant Cross remembered touching that left knee. A dark theater, he remembered, and the movie was *Bonnie and Clyde*, and Martha wore a tweed skirt, and during the final scene, when he touched her knee, she turned and looked at him in a sad, sober way that made him pull his hand back, but he would always remember the feel of the tweed skirt and the knee beneath it and the sound of the gunfire that killed Bonnie and Clyde, how embarrassing it was, how slow and oppressive. He remembered kissing her good night at the dorm door. Right then, he thought, he should've done something brave. He should've carried her up the stairs to her room and tied her to the bed and touched that left knee all night long. He should've risked it. Whenever he looked at the photographs, he thought of new things he should've done.

What they carried was partly a function of rank, partly of field specialty.

As a first lieutenant and platoon leader, Jimmy Cross carried a compass, maps, code books, binoculars, and a .45-caliber pistol that weighed 2.9 pounds fully loaded. He carried a strobe light and the responsibility for the lives of his men.

As an RTO, Mitchell Sanders carried the PRC-25 radio, a killer, 26 pounds with its battery.

As a medic, Rat Kiley carried a canvas satchel filled with morphine and plasma and malaria tablets and surgical tape and comic books and all the things a medic must carry, including M&M's for especially bad wounds, for a total weight of nearly 20 pounds.

As a big man, therefore a machine gunner, Henry Dobbins carried the M-60, which weighed 23 pounds unloaded, but which was almost always loaded. In addition, Dobbins carried between 10 and 15 pounds of ammunition draped in belts across his chest and shoulders.

As PFCs or Spec 4s, most of them were common grunts and carried the standard M-16 gas-operated assault rifle. The weapon weighed 7.5 pounds unloaded, 8.2

pounds with its full 20-round magazine. Depending on numerous factors, such as topography and psychology, the riflemen carried anywhere from 12 to 20 magazines, usually in cloth bandoliers, adding on another 8.4 pounds at minimum, 14 pounds at maximum. When it was available, they also carried M-16 maintenance gear— rods and steel brushes and swabs and tubes of LSA oil—all of which weighed about a pound. Among the grunts, some carried the M-79 grenade launcher, 5.9 pounds unloaded, a reasonably light weapon except for the ammunition, which was heavy. A single round weighed 10 ounces. The typical load was 25 rounds. But Ted Lavender, who was scared, carried 34 rounds when he was shot and killed outside Than Khe, and he went down under an exceptional burden, more than 20 pounds of ammunition, plus the flak jacket and helmet and rations and water and toilet paper and tranquilizers and all the rest, plus the unweighed fear. He was dead weight. There was no twitching or flopping. Kiowa, who saw it happen, said it was like watching a rock fall, or a big sandbag or something—just boom, then down—not like the movies where the dead guy rolls around and does fancy spins and goes ass over teakettle—not like that, Kiowa said, the poor bastard just flat-fuck fell. Boom. Down. Nothing else. It was a bright morning in mid-April. Lieutenant Cross felt the pain. He blamed himself. They stripped off Lavender's canteens and ammo, all the heavy things, and Rat Kiley said the obvious, the guy's dead, and Mitchell Sanders used his radio to report one U.S. KIA° and to request a chopper. Then they wrapped Lavender in his poncho. They carried him out to a dry paddy, established security, and sat smoking the dead man's dope until the chopper came. Lieutenant Cross kept to himself. He pictured Martha's smooth young face, thinking he loved her more than anything, more than his men, and now Ted Lavender was dead because he loved her so much and could not stop thinking about her. When the dustoff arrived, they carried Lavender aboard. Afterward they burned Than Khe. They marched until dusk, then dug their holes, and that night Kiowa kept explaining how you had to be there, how fast it was, how the poor guy just dropped like so much concrete. Boom-down, he said. Like cement.

In addition to the three standard weapons—the M-60, M-16, and M-79—they carried whatever presented itself, or whatever seemed appropriate as a means of killing or staying alive. They carried catch-as-catch-can. At various times, in various situations, they carried M-14s and CAR-15s and Swedish Ks and grease guns and captured AK-47s and Chi-Coms and RPGs and Simonov carbines and black market Uzis and .38-caliber Smith & Wesson handguns and 66 mm LAWs and shotguns and silencers and blackjacks and bayonets and C-4 plastic explosives. Lee Strunk carried a slingshot; a weapon of last resort, he called it. Mitchell Sanders carried brass knuckles. Kiowa carried his grandfather's feathered hatchet. Every third or fourth man carried a Claymore antipersonnel mine—3.5 pounds with its firing device. They all carried fragmentation grenades—14 ounces each. They all carried at least one M-18 colored smoke grenade—24 ounces. Some carried CS or tear gas grenades. Some carried white phosphorus grenades. They carried all they could bear, and then some, including a silent awe for the terrible power of the things they carried.

In the first week of April, before Lavender died, Lieutenant Jimmy Cross received a good-luck charm from Martha. It was a simple pebble, an ounce at most. Smooth to the touch, it was a milky white color with flecks of orange and violet,

KIA: killed in action.

oval-shaped, like a miniature egg. In the accompanying letter, Martha wrote that she had found the pebble on the Jersey shoreline, precisely where the land touched water at high tide, where things came together but also separated. It was this separate-but-together quality, she wrote, that had inspired her to pick up the pebble and to carry it in her breast pocket for several days, where it seemed weightless, and then to send it through the mail, by air, as a token of her truest feelings for him. Lieutenant Cross found this romantic. But he wondered what her truest feelings were, exactly, and what she meant by separate-but-together. He wondered how the tides and waves had come into play on that afternoon along the Jersey shoreline when Martha saw the pebble and bent down to rescue it from geology. He imagined bare feet. Martha was a poet, with the poet's sensibilities, and her feet would be brown and bare, the toenails unpainted, the eyes chilly and somber like the ocean in March, and though it was painful, he wondered who had been with her that afternoon. He imagined a pair of shadows moving along the strip of sand where things came together but also separated. It was phantom jealousy, he knew, but he couldn't help himself. He loved her so much. On the march, through the hot days of early April, he carried the pebble in his mouth, turning it with his tongue, tasting sea salt and moisture. His mind wandered. He had difficulty keeping his attention on the war. On occasion he would yell at his men to spread out the column, to keep their eyes open, but then he would slip away into daydreams, just pretending, walking barefoot along the Jersey shore, with Martha, carrying nothing. He would feel himself rising. Sun and waves and gentle winds, all love and lightness.

What they carried varied by mission.

When a mission took them to the mountains, they carried mosquito netting, machetes, canvas tarps, and extra bug juice.

If a mission seemed especially hazardous, or if it involved a place they knew to be bad, they carried everything they could. In certain heavily mined AOs,° where the land was dense with Toe Poppers and Bouncing Betties, they took turns humping a 28-pound mine detector. With its headphones and big sensing plate, the equipment was a stress on the lower back and shoulders, awkward to handle, often useless because of the shrapnel in the earth, but they carried it anyway, partly for safety, partly for the illusion of safety.

On ambush, or other night missions, they carried peculiar little odds and ends. Kiowa always took along his New Testament and a pair of moccasins for silence. Dave Jensen carried night-sight vitamins high in carotene. Lee Strunk carried his slingshot; ammo, he claimed, would never be a problem. Rat Kiley carried brandy and M&M's candy. Until he was shot, Ted Lavender carried the starlight scope, which weighed 6.3 pounds with its aluminum carrying case. Henry Dobbins carried his girlfriend's pantyhose wrapped around his neck as a comforter. They all carried ghosts. When dark came, they would move out single file across the meadows and paddies to their ambush coordinates, where they would quietly set up the Claymores and lie down and spend the night waiting.

Other missions were more complicated and required special equipment. In mid-April, it was their mission to search out and destroy the elaborate tunnel complexes in the Than Khe area south of Chu Lai. To blow the tunnels, they carried one-pound blocks of pentrite high explosives, four blocks to a man, 68 pounds in all. They

15

AOs: areas of operation.

carried wiring, detonators, and battery-powered clackers. Dave Jensen carried ear-plugs. Most often, before blowing the tunnels, they were ordered by higher command to search them, which was considered bad news, but by and large they just shrugged and carried out orders. Because he was a big man, Henry Dobbins was excused from tunnel duty. The others would draw numbers. Before Lavender died there were 17 men in the platoon, and whoever drew the number 17 would strip off his gear and crawl in headfirst with a flashlight and Lieutenant Cross's .45-caliber pistol. The rest of them would fan out as security. They would sit down or kneel, not facing the hole, listening to the ground beneath them, imagining cobwebs and ghosts, whatever was down there—the tunnel walls squeezing in—how the flashlight seemed impossibly heavy in the hand and how it was tunnel vision in the very strictest sense, compression in all ways, even time, and how you had to wiggle in—ass and elbows—a swallowed-up feeling—and how you found yourself worrying about odd things: Will your flashlight go dead? Do rats carry rabies? If you screamed, how far would the sound carry? Would your buddies hear it? Would they have the courage to drag you out? In some respects, though not many, the waiting was worse than the tunnel itself. Imagination was a killer.

On April 16, when Lee Strunk drew the number 17, he laughed and muttered something and went down quickly. The morning was hot and very still. Not good, Kiowa said. He looked at the tunnel opening, then out across a dry paddy toward the village of Than Khe. Nothing moved. No clouds or birds or people. As they waited, the men smoked and drank Kool-Aid, not talking much, feeling sympathy for Lee Strunk but also feeling the luck of the draw. You win some, you lose some, said Mitchell Sanders, and sometimes you settle for a rain check. It was a tired line and no one laughed.

Henry Dobbins ate a tropical chocolate bar. Ted Lavender popped a tranquilizer 20 and went off to pee.

After five minutes, Lieutenant Jimmy Cross moved to the tunnel, leaned down, and examined the darkness. Trouble, he thought—a cave-in maybe. And then suddenly, without willing it, he was thinking about Martha. The stresses and fractures, the quick collapse, the two of them buried alive under all that weight. Dense, crushing love. Kneeling, watching the hole, he tried to concentrate on Lee Strunk and the war, all the dangers, but his love was too much for him, he felt paralyzed, he wanted to sleep inside her lungs and breathe her blood and be smothered. He wanted her to be a virgin and not a virgin, all at once. He wanted to know her. Intimate secrets: Why poetry? Why so sad? Why that grayness in her eyes? Why so alone? Not lonely, just alone—riding her bike across campus or sitting off by herself in the cafeteria—even dancing, she danced alone—and it was the aloneness that filled him with love. He remembered telling her that one evening. How she nodded and looked away. And how, later, when he kissed her, she received the kiss without returning it, her eyes wide open, not afraid, not a virgin's eyes, just flat and uninvolved.

Lieutenant Cross gazed at the tunnel. But he was not there. He was buried with Martha under the white sand at the Jersey shore. They were pressed together, and the pebble in his mouth was her tongue. He was smiling. Vaguely, he was aware of how quiet the day was, the sullen paddies, yet he could not bring himself to worry about matters of security. He was beyond that. He was just a kid at war, in love. He was twenty-four years old. He couldn't help it.

A few moments later Lee Strunk crawled out of the tunnel. He came up grinning, filthy but alive. Lieutenant Cross nodded and closed his eyes while the others clapped Strunk on the back and made jokes about rising from the dead.

Worms, Rat Kiley said. Right out of the grave. Fuckin' zombie.

The men laughed. They all felt great relief.   25

Spook city, said Mitchell Sanders.

Lee Strunk made a funny ghost sound, a kind of moaning, yet very happy, and right then, when Strunk made that high happy moaning sound, when he went *Ahhooooo*, right then Ted Lavender was shot in the head on his way back from peeing. He lay with his mouth open. The teeth were broken. There was a swollen black bruise under his left eye. The cheekbone was gone. Oh shit, Rat Kiley said, the guy's dead. The guy's dead, he kept saying, which seemed profound—the guy's dead. I mean really.

The things they carried were determined to some extent by superstition. Lieutenant Cross carried his good-luck pebble. Dave Jensen carried a rabbit's foot. Norman Bowker, otherwise a very gentle person, carried a thumb that had been presented to him as a gift by Mitchell Sanders. The thumb was dark brown, rubbery to the touch, and weighed four ounces at most. It had been cut from a VC corpse, a boy of fifteen or sixteen. They'd found him at the bottom of an irrigation ditch, badly burned, flies in his mouth and eyes. The boy wore black shorts and sandals. At the time of his death he had been carrying a pouch of rice, a rifle, and three magazines of ammunition.

You want my opinion, Mitchell Sanders said, there's a definite moral here.

He put his hand on the dead boy's wrist. He was quiet for a time, as if counting   30
a pulse, then he patted the stomach, almost affectionately, and used Kiowa's hunting hatchet to remove the thumb.

Henry Dobbins asked what the moral was.

Moral?

You know. *Moral.*

Sanders wrapped the thumb in toilet paper and handed it across to Norman Bowker. There was no blood. Smiling, he kicked the boy's head, watched the flies scatter, and said, It's like with that old TV show—Paladin. Have gun, will travel.

Henry Dobbins thought about it.   35

Yeah, well, he finally said. I don't see no moral.

There it *is*, man.

Fuck off.

They carried USO stationery and pencils and pens. They carried Sterno, safety pins, trip flares, signal flares, spools of wire, razor blades, chewing tobacco, liberated joss sticks and statuettes of the smiling Buddha, candles, grease pencils, *The Stars and Stripes*, fingernail clippers, Psy Ops leaflets, bush hats, bolos, and much more. Twice a week, when the resupply choppers came in, they carried hot chow in green mermite cans and large canvas bags filled with iced beer and soda pop. They carried plastic water containers, each with a two-gallon capacity. Mitchell Sanders carried a set of starched tiger fatigues for special occasions. Henry Dobbins carried Black Flag insecticide. Dave Jensen carried empty sandbags that could be filled at night for added protection. Lee Strunk carried tanning lotion. Some things they carried in common. Taking turns, they carried the big PRC-77 scrambler radio, which weighed 30 pounds with its battery. They shared the weight of memory. They took up what others could no longer bear. Often, they carried each other, the wounded or weak. They carried infections. They carried chess sets, basketballs, Vietnamese-English dictionaries, insignia of rank, Bronze Stars and Purple Hearts, plastic cards imprinted with the

Code of Conduct. They carried diseases, among them malaria and dysentery. They carried lice and ringworm and leeches and paddy algae and various rots and molds. They carried the land itself—Vietnam, the place, the soil—a powdery orange-red dust that covered their boots and fatigues and faces. They carried the sky. The whole atmosphere, they carried it, the humidity, the monsoons, the stink of fungus and decay, all of it, they carried gravity. They moved like mules. By daylight they took sniper fire, at night they were mortared, but it was not battle, it was just the endless march, village to village, without purpose, nothing won or lost. They marched for the sake of the march. They plodded along slowly, dumbly, leaning forward against the heat, unthinking, all blood and bone, simple grunts, soldiering with their legs, toiling up the hills and down into the paddies and across the rivers and up again and down, just humping, one step and then the next and then another, but no volition, no will, because it was automatic, it was anatomy, and the war was entirely a matter of posture and carriage, the hump was everything, a kind of inertia, a kind of emptiness, a dullness of desire and intellect and conscience and hope and human sensibility. Their principles were in their feet. Their calculations were biological. They had no sense of strategy or mission. They searched the villages without knowing what to look for, not caring, kicking over jars of rice, frisking children and old men, blowing tunnels, sometimes setting fires and sometimes not, then forming up and moving on to the next village, then other villages, where it would always be the same. They carried their own lives. The pressures were enormous. In the heat of early afternoon, they would remove their helmets and flak jackets, walking bare, which was dangerous but which helped ease the strain. They would often discard things along the route of march. Purely for comfort, they would throw away rations, blow their Claymores and grenades, no matter, because by nightfall the resupply choppers would arrive with more of the same, then a day or two later still more, fresh watermelons and crates of ammunition and sunglasses and woolen sweaters—the resources were stunning—sparklers for the Fourth of July, colored eggs for Easter—it was the great American war chest—the fruits of science, the smokestacks, the canneries, the arsenals at Hartford, the Minnesota forests, the machine shops, the vast fields of corn and wheat—they carried like freight trains; they carried it on their backs and shoulders—and for all the ambiguities of Vietnam, all the mysteries and unknowns, there was at least the single abiding certainty that they would never be at a loss for things to carry.

After the chopper took Lavender away, Lieutenant Jimmy Cross led his men into   40
the village of Than Khe. They burned everything. They shot chickens and dogs, they trashed the village well, they called in artillery and watched the wreckage, then they marched for several hours through the hot afternoon, and then at dusk, while Kiowa explained how Lavender died, Lieutenant Cross found himself trembling.

He tried not to cry. With his entrenching tool, which weighed five pounds, he began digging a hole in the earth.

He felt shame. He hated himself. He had loved Martha more than his men, and as a consequence Lavender was now dead, and this was something he would have to carry like a stone in his stomach for the rest of the war.

All he could do was dig. He used his entrenching tool like an ax, slashing, feeling both love and hate, and then later, when it was full dark, he sat at the bottom of his foxhole and wept. It went on for a long while. In part, he was grieving for Ted Lavender, but mostly it was for Martha, and for himself, because she belonged to another world, which was not quite real, and because she was a junior at Mount

Sebastian College in New Jersey, a poet and a virgin and uninvolved, and because he realized she did not love him and never would.

Like cement, Kiowa whispered in the dark. I swear to God—boom, down. Not a word.

I've heard this, said Norman Bowker. 45

A pisser, you know? Still zipping himself up. Zapped while zipping.

All right, fine. That's enough.

Yeah, but you had to see it, the guy just—

I *heard*, man. Cement. So why not shut the fuck *up*?

Kiowa shook his head sadly and glanced over at the hole where Lieutenant 50 Jimmy Cross sat watching the night. The air was thick and wet. A warm dense fog had settled over the paddies and there was the stillness that precedes rain.

After a time Kiowa sighed.

One thing for sure, he said. The lieutenant's in some deep hurt. I mean that crying jag—the way he was carrying on—it wasn't fake or anything, it was real heavyduty hurt. The man cares.

Sure, Norman Bowker said.

Say what you want, the man does care.

We all got problems. 55

Not Lavender.

No, I guess not, Bowker said. Do me a favor, though.

Shut up?

That's a smart Indian. Shut up.

Shrugging, Kiowa pulled off his boots. He wanted to say more, just to lighten up 60 his sleep, but instead he opened his New Testament and arranged it beneath his head as a pillow. The fog made things seem hollow and unattached. He tried not to think about Ted Lavender, but then he was thinking how fast it was, no drama, down and dead, and how it was hard to feel anything except surprise. It seemed unchristian. He wished he could find some great sadness, or even anger, but the emotion wasn't there and he couldn't make it happen. Mostly he felt pleased to be alive. He liked the smell of the New Testament under his cheek, the leather and ink and paper and glue, whatever the chemicals were. He liked hearing the sounds of night. Even his fatigue, it felt fine, the stiff muscles and the prickly awareness of his own body, a floating feeling. He enjoyed not being dead. Lying there, Kiowa admired Lieutenant Jimmy Cross's capacity for grief. He wanted to share the man's pain, he wanted to care as Jimmy Cross cared. And yet when he closed his eyes, all he could think was Boom-down, and all he could feel was the pleasure of having his boots off and the fog curling in around him and the damp soil and the Bible smells and the plush comfort of night.

After a moment Norman Bowker sat up in the dark.

What the hell, he said. You want to talk, *talk*. Tell it to me.

Forget it.

No, man, go on. One thing I hate, it's a silent Indian.

For the most part they carried themselves with poise, a kind of dignity. Now and 65 then, however, there were times of panic, when they squealed or wanted to squeal but couldn't, when they twitched and made moaning sounds and covered their heads and said Dear Jesus and flopped around on the earth and fired their weapons blindly and cringed and sobbed and begged for the noise to stop and went wild and made stupid promises to themselves and to God and to their mothers and fathers, hoping not to die. In different ways, it happened to all of them. Afterward, when the firing ended, they would blink and peek up. They would touch their bodies, feeling shame, then quickly hiding it. They would force themselves to stand. As if in slow motion, frame by frame, the world would take on the old logic—absolute silence, then the wind, then sunlight, then voices. It was the burden of being alive. Awkwardly, the men would reassemble themselves, first in private, then in groups, becoming soldiers again. They would repair the leaks in their eyes. They would check for casualties, call in dustoffs, light cigarettes, try to smile, clear their throats and spit and begin cleaning their weapons. After a time someone would shake his head and say, No lie, I almost shit my pants, and someone else would laugh, which meant it was bad, yes, but the guy had obviously not shit his pants, it wasn't that bad, and in any case nobody would ever do such a thing and then go ahead and talk about it. They would squint into the dense, oppressive sunlight. For a few moments, perhaps, they would fall silent, lighting a joint and tracking its passage from man to man, inhaling, holding in the humiliation. Scary stuff, one of them might say. But then someone else would grin or flick his eyebrows and say, Roger-dodger, almost cut me a new asshole, *almost*.

There were numerous such poses. Some carried themselves with a sort of wistful resignation, others with pride or stiff soldierly discipline or good humor or macho zeal. They were afraid of dying but they were even more afraid to show it.

They found jokes to tell.

They used a hard vocabulary to contain the terrible softness. *Greased*, they'd say. *Offed, lit up, zapped while zipping*. It wasn't cruelty, just stage presence. They were actors. When someone died, it wasn't quite dying, because in a curious way it seemed scripted, and because they had their lines mostly memorized, irony mixed with tragedy, and because they called it by other names, as if to encyst and destroy the reality of death itself. They kicked corpses. They cut off thumbs. They talked grunt lingo. They told stories about Ted Lavender's supply of tranquilizers, how the poor guy didn't feel a thing, how incredibly tranquil he was.

There's a moral here, said Mitchell Sanders.

They were waiting for Lavender's chopper, smoking the dead man's dope.   70

The moral's pretty obvious, Sanders said, and winked. Stay away from drugs. No joke, they'll ruin your day every time.

Cute, said Henry Dobbins.

Mind blower, get it? Talk about wiggy. Nothing left, just blood and brains.

They made themselves laugh.

There it is, they'd say. Over and over—there it is, my friend, there it is—as if the   75 repetition itself were an act of poise, a balance between crazy and almost crazy, knowing without going, there it is, which meant be cool, let it ride, because Oh yeah, man, you can't change what can't be changed, there it is, there it absolutely and positively and fucking well *is*.

They were tough.

They carried all the emotional baggage of men who might die. Grief, terror, love, longing—these were intangibles, but the intangibles had their own mass and specific gravity, they had tangible weight. They carried shameful memories. They carried the common secret of cowardice barely restrained, the instinct to run or freeze or hide, and in many respects this was the heaviest burden of all, for it could never be put down, it required perfect balance and perfect posture. They carried their reputations. They carried the soldier's greatest fear, which was the fear of blushing. Men killed, and died, because they were embarrassed not to. It was what had brought them to the war in the first place, nothing positive, no dreams of glory or honor, just to avoid the blush of dishonor. They died so as not to die of embarrassment. They crawled into tunnels and walked point and advanced under fire. Each morning, despite the unknowns, they made their legs move. They endured. They kept humping. They did not submit to the obvious alternative, which was simply to close the eyes and fall. So easy, really. Go limp and tumble to the ground and let the muscles unwind and not speak and not budge until your buddies picked you up and lifted you into the chopper that would roar and dip its nose and carry you off to the world. A mere matter of falling, yet no one ever fell. It was not courage, exactly; the object was not valor. Rather, they were too frightened to be cowards.

By and large they carried these things inside, maintaining the masks of composure. They sneered at sick call. They spoke bitterly about guys who had found release by shooting off their own toes or fingers. Pussies, they'd say. Candy-asses. It was fierce, mocking talk, with only a trace of envy or awe, but even so the image played itself out behind their eyes.

They imagined the muzzle against flesh. So easy: squeeze the trigger and blow away a toe. They imagined it. They imagined the quick, sweet pain, then the evacuation to Japan, then a hospital with warm beds and cute geisha nurses.

And they dreamed of freedom birds.

80

At night, on guard, staring into the dark, they were carried away by jumbo jets. They felt the rush of takeoff. *Gone!* they yelled. And then velocity—wings and engines—a smiling stewardess—but it was more than a plane, it was a real bird, a big sleek silver bird with feathers and talons and high screeching. They were flying. The weights fell off; there was nothing to bear. They laughed and held on tight, feeling the cold slap of wind and altitude, soaring, thinking *It's over, I'm gone!*—they were naked, they were light and free—it was all lightness, bright and fast and buoyant, light as light, a helium buzz in the brain, a giddy bubbling in the lungs as they were taken up over the clouds and the war, beyond duty, beyond gravity and mortification and global entanglements—*Sin loi!*° they yelled. *I'm sorry, mother-fuckers, but I'm out of it, I'm goofed, I'm on a space cruise, I'm gone!*—and it was a restful, unencumbered sensation, just riding the light waves, sailing that big silver freedom bird over the mountains and oceans, over America, over the farms and great sleeping cities and cemeteries and highways and the golden arches of McDonald's, it was flight, a kind of fleeing, a kind of falling, falling higher and higher, spinning off the edge of the earth and beyond the sun and through the vast, silent vacuum where there were no burdens and where everything weighed exactly nothing—*Gone!* they screamed. *I'm sorry but I'm gone!*—and so at night, not quite dreaming, they gave themselves over to lightness, they were carried, they were purely borne.

On the morning after Ted Lavender died, First Lieutenant Jimmy Cross crouched at the bottom of his foxhole and burned Martha's letters. Then he burned the two photographs. There was a steady rain falling, which made it difficult, but he used heat tabs and Sterno to build a small fire, screening it with his body, holding the photographs over the tight blue flame with the tips of his fingers.

Sin loi: Vietnamese for "sorry."

He realized it was only a gesture. Stupid, he thought. Sentimental, too, but mostly just stupid.

Lavender was dead. You couldn't burn the blame.

Besides, the letters were in his head. And even now, without photographs, Lieutenant Cross could see Martha playing volleyball in her white gym shorts and yellow T-shirt. He could see her moving in the rain. 85

When the fire died out, Lieutenant Cross pulled his poncho over his shoulders and ate breakfast from a can.

There was no great mystery, he decided.

In those burned letters Martha had never mentioned the war, except to say, Jimmy, take care of yourself. She wasn't involved. She signed the letters Love, but it wasn't love, and all the fine lines and technicalities did not matter. Virginity was no longer an issue. He hated her. Yes, he did. He hated her. Love, too, but it was a hard, hating kind of love.

The morning came up wet and blurry. Everything seemed part of everything else, the fog and Martha and the deepening rain.

He was a soldier, after all. 90

Half smiling, Lieutenant Jimmy Cross took out his maps. He shook his head hard, as if to clear it, then bent forward and began planning the day's march. In ten minutes, or maybe twenty, he would rouse the men and they would pack up and head west, where the maps showed the country to be green and inviting. They would do what they had always done. The rain might add some weight, but otherwise it would be one more day layered upon all the other days.

He was realistic about it. There was that new hardness in his stomach. He loved her but he hated her.

No more fantasies, he told himself.

Henceforth, when he thought about Martha, it would be only to think that she belonged elsewhere. He would shut down the daydreams. This was not Mount Sebastian, it was another world, where there were no pretty poems or midterm exams, a place where men died because of carelessness and gross stupidity. Kiowa was right. Boom-down, and you were dead, never partly dead.

Briefly, in the rain, Lieutenant Cross saw Martha's gray eyes gazing back at him. 95

He understood.

It was very sad, he thought. The things men carried inside. The things men did or felt they had to do.

He almost nodded at her, but didn't.

Instead he went back to his maps. He was now determined to perform his duties firmly and without negligence. It wouldn't help Lavender, he knew that, but from this point on he would comport himself as an officer. He would dispose of his good-luck pebble. Swallow it, maybe, or use Lee Strunk's slingshot, or just drop it along the trail. On the march he would impose strict field discipline. He would be careful to send out flank security, to prevent straggling or bunching up, to keep his troops moving at the proper pace and at the proper interval. He would insist on clean weapons. He would confiscate the remainder of Lavender's dope. Later in the day, perhaps, he would call the men together and speak to them plainly. He would accept the blame for what had happened to Ted Lavender. He would be a man about it. He would look them in the eyes, keeping his chin level, and he would issue the new SOPs in a calm, impersonal tone of voice, a lieutenant's voice, leaving no room for argument or discussion. Commencing immediately, he'd tell them, they would no longer abandon equipment along the route of march. They would police up their acts. They would get their shit together, and keep it together, and maintain it neatly and in good working order.

He would not tolerate laxity. He would show strength, distancing himself.　　100

Among the men there would be grumbling, of course, and maybe worse, because their days would seem longer and their loads heavier, but Lieutenant Jimmy Cross reminded himself that his obligation was not to be loved but to lead. He would dispense with love; it was not now a factor. And if anyone quarreled or complained, he would simply tighten his lips and arrange his shoulders in the correct command posture. He might give a curt little nod. Or he might not. He might just shrug and say, Carry on, then they would saddle up and form into a column and move out toward the villages west of Than Khe.

Daniel Orozco

Orientation　　　　　　　　　　　　　　　　　　　　　　　　　　(1994) 2011

Daniel Orozco was born in 1957 and raised in San Francisco, California, the son of Nicaraguan immigrants. He attended Stanford University where he earned a BA in communications. In his twenties he worked as an office assistant, a depressing experience he later satirized in his short story "Orientation." In an interview for the alumni newsletter of the Iowa Writers' Workshop, where Orozco was a visiting professor in 2013, he described "Orientation" as "a kind of disorientation. It is set in an office, the most mundane and safest of work environments, and so the challenge was in how to make that place dangerous—perhaps literally, but mostly emotionally. So, these are the jobs that can kill you: longshoreman, fireman, and these office jobs that I'm writing about, which kill you in a different way." Orozco studied creative writing at San

Daniel Orozco

Francisco State University, and then at thirty he enrolled at the University of Washington to earn an MFA Soon after his short stories began appearing in journals, he was awarded the prestigious Jones Fellowship in Fiction at Stanford. In 2003 he began teaching fiction writing at the University of Idaho, and in 2006 was awarded a literature fellowship by the National Endowment for the Arts. His collection of short stories, Orientation, *appeared in 2011. Orozco won the Whiting Writers' Award that year.*

Those are the offices and these are the cubicles. That's my cubicle there, and this is your cubicle. This is your phone. Never answer your phone. Let the Voicemail System answer it. This is your Voicemail System Manual. There are no personal phone calls allowed. We do, however, allow for emergencies. If you must make an emergency phone call, ask your supervisor first. If you can't find your supervisor, ask Phillip Spiers, who sits over there. He'll check with Clarissa Nicks, who sits over there. If you make an emergency phone call without asking, you may be let go.

These are your in- and out-boxes. All the forms in your in-box must be logged in by the date shown in the upper-left-hand corner, initialed by you in the upper-right-hand corner, and distributed to the Processing Analyst whose name is numerically coded in the lower-left-hand corner. The lower-right-hand corner is left blank. Here's your Processing Analyst Numerical Code Index. And here's your Forms Processing Procedures Manual.

You must pace your work. What do I mean? I'm glad you asked that. We pace our work according to the eight-hour workday. If you have twelve hours of work in your in-box, for example, you must compress that work into the eight-hour day. If you have one hour of work in your in-box, you must expand that work to fill the eight-hour day. That was a good question. Feel free to ask questions. Ask too many questions, however, and you may be let go.

That is our receptionist. She is a temp. We go through receptionists here. They quit with alarming frequency. Be polite and civil to the temps. Learn their names, and invite them to lunch occasionally. But don't get close to them, as it only makes it more difficult when they leave. And they always leave. You can be sure of that.

The men's room is over there. The women's room is over there. John LaFoun-   5
taine, who sits over there, uses the women's room occasionally. He says it is accidental. We know better, but we let it pass. John LaFountaine is harmless, his forays into
the forbidden territory of the women's room simply a benign thrill, a faint flip on the
dull, flat line of his life.

Russell Nash, who sits in the cubicle to your left, is in love with Amanda Pierce,
who sits in the cubicle to your right. They ride the same bus together after work. For
Amanda Pierce, it is just a tedious bus ride made less tedious by the idle nattering of
Russell Nash. But for Russell Nash, it is the highlight of his day. It is the highlight
of his life. Russell Nash has put on forty pounds and grows fatter with each passing month, nibbling on chips and cookies while peeking glumly over the partitions
at Amanda Pierce and gorging himself at home on cold pizza and ice cream while
watching adult videos on TV.

Amanda Pierce, in the cubicle to your right, has a six-year-old son named Jamie,
who is autistic. Her cubicle is plastered from top to bottom with the boy's crayon
artwork—sheet after sheet of precisely drawn concentric circles and ellipses, in
black and yellow. She rotates them every other Friday. Be sure to comment on them.
Amanda Pierce also has a husband, who is a lawyer. He subjects her to an escalating
array of painful and humiliating sex games, to which Amanda Pierce reluctantly sub-
mits. She comes to work exhausted and freshly wounded each morning, wincing from
the abrasions on her breasts, or the bruises on her abdomen, or the second-degree
burns on the backs of her thighs.

But we're not supposed to know any of this. Do not let on. If you let on, you may
be let go.

Amanda Pierce, who tolerates Russell Nash, is in love with Albert Bosch, whose
office is over there. Albert Bosch, who only dimly registers Amanda Pierce's existence, has eyes only for Ellie Tapper, who sits over there. Ellie Tapper, who hates
Albert Bosch, would walk through fire for Curtis Lance. But Curtis Lance hates Ellie
Tapper. Isn't the world a funny place? Not in the ha-ha sense, of course.

Anika Bloom sits in that cubicle. Last year, while reviewing quarterly reports in   10
a meeting with Barry Hacker, Anika Bloom's left palm began to bleed. She fell into
a trance, stared into her hand, and told Barry Hacker when and how his wife would
die. We laughed it off. She was, after all, a new employee. But Barry Hacker's wife
is dead. So unless you want to know exactly when and how you'll die, never talk to
Anika Bloom.

Colin Heavey sits in that cubicle over there. He was new once, just like you. We warned him about Anika Bloom. But at last year's Christmas Potluck he felt sorry for her when he saw that no one was talking to her. Colin Heavey brought her a drink. He hasn't been himself since. Colin Heavey is doomed. There's nothing he can do about it, and we are powerless to help him. Stay away from Colin Heavey. Never give any of your work to him. If he asks to do something, tell him you have to check with me. If he asks again, tell him I haven't gotten back to you.

This is the fire exit. There are several on this floor, and they are marked accordingly. We have a Floor Evacuation Review every three months, and an Escape Route Quiz once a month. We have our Biannual Fire Drill twice a year, and our Annual Earthquake Drill once a year. These are precautions only. These things never happen.

For your information, we have a comprehensive health plan. Any catastrophic illness, any unforeseen tragedy, is completely covered. All dependents are completely covered. Larry Bagdikian, who sits over there, has six daughters. If anything were to happen to any of his girls, or to all of them, if all six were to simultaneously fall victim to illness or injury—stricken with a hideous degenerative muscle disease or some rare toxic blood disorder, sprayed with semi-automatic gunfire while on a class field trip, or attacked in their bunk beds by some prowling nocturnal lunatic—if any of this were to pass, Larry's girls would all be taken care of. Larry Bagdikian would not have to pay one dime. He would have nothing to worry about.

We also have a generous vacation and sick leave policy. We have an excellent disability insurance plan. We have a stable and profitable pension fund. We get group discounts for the symphony, and block seating at the ballpark. We get commuter ticket books for the bridge. We have direct deposit. We are all members of Costco.

This is our kitchenette. And this, this is our Mr. Coffee. We have a coffee pool, into which we each pay two dollars a week for coffee, filters, sugar, and Coffee-Mate. If you prefer Cremora or half-and-half to Coffee-Mate, there is a special pool for three dollars a week. If you prefer Sweet'N Low to sugar, there is a special pool for two-fifty a week. We do not do decaf. You are allowed to join the coffee pool of your choice, but you are not allowed to touch the Mr. Coffee.

This is the microwave oven. You are allowed to *heat* food in the microwave oven. You are not, however, allowed to *cook* food in the microwave oven.

We get one hour for lunch. We also get one fifteen-minute break in the morning, and one fifteen-minute break in the afternoon. Always take your breaks. If you skip a break, it is gone forever. For your information, your break is a privilege, not a right. If you abuse the break policy, we are authorized to rescind your breaks. Lunch, however, is a right, not a privilege. If you abuse the lunch policy, our hands will be tied, and we will be forced to look the other way. We will not enjoy that.

This is the refrigerator. You may put your lunch in it. Barry Hacker, who sits over there, steals food from this refrigerator. His petty theft is an outlet for his grief. Last New Year's Eve, while kissing his wife, a blood vessel burst in her brain. Barry Hacker's wife was two months pregnant at the time, and lingered in a coma for half a year before she died. It was a tragic loss for Barry Hacker. He hasn't been himself since. Barry Hacker's wife was a beautiful woman. She was also completely covered. Barry Hacker did not have to pay one dime. But his dead wife haunts him. She haunts all of us. We have seen her, reflected in the monitors of our computers, moving past our cubicles. We have seen the dim shadow of her face in our photocopies. She pencils herself in in the receptionist's appointment book with the notation "To see Barry Hacker." She has left messages in the receptionist's Voicemail box, messages garbled by the electronic chirrups and buzzes in the phone line, her voice echoing from an immense distance within the ambient hum. But the voice is hers. And beneath the voice, beneath the tidal whoosh of static and hiss, the gurgling and crying of a baby can be heard.

In any case, if you bring a lunch, put a little something extra in the bag for Barry Hacker. We have four Barrys in this office. Isn't that a coincidence?

This is Matthew Payne's office. He is our Unit Manager, and his door is always   20
closed. We have never seen him, and you will never see him. But he is there. You can be sure of that. He is all around us.

This is the Custodian's Closet. You have no business in the Custodian's Closet.

And this, this is our Supplies Cabinet. If you need supplies, see Curtis Lance. He will log you in on the Supplies Cabinet Authorization Log, then give you a Supplies Authorization Slip. Present your pink copy of the Supplies Authorization Slip to Ellie Tapper. She will log you in on the Supplies Cabinet Key Log, then give you the key. Because the Supplies Cabinet is located outside the Unit Manager's office, you must be very quiet. Gather your supplies quietly. The Supplies Cabinet is divided into four sections. Section One contains letterhead stationery, blank paper and envelopes, memo pads and notepads, and so on. Section Two contains pens and pencils and typewriter and printer ribbons, and the like. In Section Three we have erasers, correction fluids, transparent tapes, glue sticks, et cetera. And in Section Four we have paper clips and pushpins and scissors and razor blades. And here are the spare blades for the shredder. Do not touch the shredder, which is located over there. The shredder is of no concern to you.

Gwendolyn Stich sits in that office there. She is crazy about penguins and collects penguin knickknacks: penguin posters and coffee mugs and stationery, penguin stuffed animals, penguin jewelry, penguin sweaters and T-shirts and socks. She has a pair of penguin fuzzy slippers she wears when working late at the office. She has a tape cassette of penguin sounds, which she listens to for relaxation. Her favorite colors are black and white. She has personalized license plates that read PEN GWEN. Every morning, she passes through all the cubicles to wish each of us a *good* morning. She brings Danish on Wednesdays for Hump Day morning break, and doughnuts on Fridays for TGIF afternoon break. She organizes the Annual Christmas Potluck and is in charge of the Birthday List. Gwendolyn Stich's door is always open to all of us. She will always lend an ear and put in a good word for you; she will always give you a hand, or the shirt off her back, or a shoulder to cry on. Because her door is always open, she hides and cries in a stall in the women's room. And John LaFountaine—who, enthralled when a woman enters, sits quietly in his stall with his knees to his chest— John LaFountaine has heard her vomiting in there. We have come upon Gwendolyn Stich huddled in the stairwell, shivering in the updraft, sipping a Diet Mr. Pibb and hugging her knees. She does not let any of this interfere with her work. If it interfered with her work, she might have to be let go.

Kevin Howard sits in that cubicle over there. He is a serial killer, the one they call the Carpet Cutter, responsible for the mutilations across town. We're not supposed to know that, so do not let on. Don't worry. His compulsion inflicts itself on strangers only, and the routine established is elaborate and unwavering. The victim must be a white male, a young adult no older than thirty, heavyset, with dark hair and eyes, and the like. The victim must be chosen at random, before sunset, from a public place; the victim is followed home and must put up a struggle; et cetera. The carnage inflicted is precise: the angle and direction of the incisions, the layering of skin and muscle tissue, the rearrangement of visceral organs, and so on. Kevin Howard does not let any of this interfere with his work. He is, in fact, our fastest typist. He types as if he were on fire. He has a secret crush on Gwendolyn Stich and leaves a red-foil-wrapped Hershey's Kiss on her desk every afternoon. But he hates Anika Bloom and keeps well away from her. In his presence, she has uncontrollable fits of shaking and trembling. Her left palm does not stop bleeding.

In any case, when Kevin Howard gets caught, act surprised. Say that he seemed   25
like a nice person, a bit of a loner, perhaps, but always quiet and polite.

This is the photocopier room. And this, this is our view. It faces southwest. West is down there, toward the water. North is back there. Because we are on the seventeenth floor, we are afforded a magnificent view. Isn't it beautiful? It overlooks the park, where the tops of those trees are. You can see a segment of the bay between those two buildings over there. You can see the sun set in the gap between those two buildings over there. You can see this building reflected in the glass panels of that building across the way. There. See? That's you, waving. And look there. There's Anika Bloom in the kitchenette, waving back.

Enjoy this view while photocopying. If you have problems with the photocopier, see Russell Nash. If you have any questions, ask your supervisor. If you can't find your supervisor, ask Phillip Spiers. He sits over there. He'll check with Clarissa Nicks. She sits over there. If you can't find them, feel free to ask me. That's my cubicle. I sit in there.

George Saunders

Puppy   2013

George Saunders was born in 1958 in Amarillo, Texas, and grew up in suburban Chicago. Early on, he planned for a career in geophysical engineering, getting his degree from the Colorado School of Mines and landing a job in the oil fields of Sumatra. During his time in the Indonesian jungle, he fell ill and returned home to Texas, where he worked a variety of jobs—doorman, roofer, store clerk, and slaughterhouse worker—and began to write fiction in earnest. He was accepted to the graduate creative writing program at Syracuse University, where he studied under Tobias Wolff and met his future wife, fellow student Paula Redick. After graduation, Saunders worked as a technical writer at a pharmaceutical company and an environmental engineering firm, experiences he would later satirize in his stories. "In the end," he told WAG

George Saunders

Magazine, "the two interests dovetailed: the tech writing I was doing influenced both style and subject. And any claim I might make to 'originality' in my fiction is really just the result of this odd background: basically, just me working inefficiently, with flawed tools, in a mode I don't have sufficient background to really understand. Like if you put a welder to designing dresses." Saunders published his first collection, CivilWarLand in Bad Decline (1996), to much praise. He joined the creative writing faculty at Syracuse, where he still teaches today. His other volumes of short stories include Pastoralia (2000), In Persuasion

Nation (2006), and Tenth of December (2013). *Saunders published his first novel in 2017,* Lincoln in the Bardo, *which imagines Abraham Lincoln coping with the death of his son, a book that Saunders has described as "ostensibly historical [yet] more like a sci-fi story than anything I've ever done before." His highly inventive fiction, which often blurs genres, has been widely admired by readers, critics, and other writers. He has earned several National Magazine Awards, a MacArthur "Genius Grant," a Guggenheim Fellowship, and the Story Prize for* Tenth of December, *in which "Puppy" appeared.*

Twice already Marie had pointed out the brilliance of the autumnal sun on the perfect field of corn, because the brilliance of the autumnal sun on the perfect field of corn put her in mind of a haunted house—not a haunted house she had ever actually seen but the mythical one that sometimes appeared in her mind (with adjacent graveyard and cat on a fence) whenever she saw the brilliance of the autumnal sun on the perfect etc. etc.—and she wanted to make sure that, if the kids had a corresponding mythical haunted house that appeared in their minds whenever they saw the brilliance of the etc. etc., it would come up now, so that they could all experience it together, like friends, like college friends on a road trip, sans pot, ha ha ha!

But no. When she, a third time, said, "Wow, guys, check that out," Abbie said, "Okay, Mom, we get it, it's corn," and Josh said, "Not now, Mom, I'm Leavening my Loaves," which was fine with her; she had no problem with that, Noble Baker being preferable to Bra Stuffer, the game he'd asked for.

Well, who could say? Maybe they didn't even have any mythical vignettes in their heads. Or maybe the mythical vignettes they had in their heads were totally different from the ones she had in her head. Which was the beauty of it, because, after all, they were their own little people! You were just a caretaker. They didn't have to feel what *you* felt; they just had to be supported in feeling what *they* felt.

Still, wow, that cornfield was such a classic.

"Whenever I see a field like that, guys?" she said. "I somehow think of a haunted house!"   5

"Slicing Knife! Slicing Knife!" Josh shouted. "You nimrod machine! I chose that!"

Speaking of Halloween, she remembered last year, when their cornstalk column had tipped their shopping cart over. Gosh, how they'd laughed at that! Oh, family laughter was golden; she'd had none of that in her childhood, Dad being so dour and Mom so ashamed. If Mom and Dad's cart had tipped, Dad would have given the cart a despairing kick and Mom would have stridden purposefully away to reapply her lipstick, distancing herself from Dad, while she, Marie, would have nervously taken that horrid plastic Army man she'd named Brady into her mouth.

Well, in this family laughter was encouraged! Last night, when Josh had goosed her with his Game Boy, she'd shot a spray of toothpaste across the mirror and they'd all cracked up, rolling around on the floor with Goochie, and Josh had said, such nostalgia in his voice, "Mom, remember when Goochie was a puppy?" Which was when Abbie had burst into tears, because, being only five, she had no memory of Goochie as a puppy.

Hence this Family Mission. And as far as Robert? Oh, God bless Robert! There was a man. He would have no problem whatsoever with this Family Mission. She loved the way he had of saying "Ho HO!" whenever she brought home something new and unexpected.

"Ho HO!" Robert had said, coming home to find the iguana. "Ho HO!" he had   10
said, coming home to find the ferret trying to get into the iguana cage. "We appear to
be the happy operators of a menagerie!"

She loved him for his playfulness—you could bring home a hippo you'd put on a
credit card (both the ferret and the iguana had gone on credit cards) and he'd just say
"Ho HO!" and ask what the creature ate and what hours it slept and what the heck
they were going to name the little bugger.

In the backseat, Josh made the *git-git-git* sound he always made when his
Baker was in Baking Mode, trying to get his Loaves into the oven while fighting
off various Hungry Denizens, such as a Fox with a distended stomach; such as a fey
Robin that would improbably carry the Loaf away, speared on its beak, whenever
it had succeeded in dropping a Clonking Rock on your Baker—all of which Marie
had learned over the summer by studying the Noble Baker manual while Josh was
asleep.

And it had helped, it really had. Josh was less withdrawn lately, and when she
came up behind him now while he was playing and said, like, "Wow, honey, I didn't
know you could do Pumpernickel," or "Sweetie, try Serrated Blade, it cuts quicker.
Try it while doing Latch the Window," he would reach back with his noncontrolling
hand and swat at her affectionately, and yesterday they'd shared a good laugh when
he'd accidentally knocked off her glasses.

So her mother could go right ahead and claim that she was spoiling the kids.
These were not spoiled kids. These were *well-loved* kids. At least she'd never left one
of them standing in a blizzard for two hours after a junior-high dance. At least she'd
never drunkenly snapped at one of them, "I hardly consider you college material." At
least she'd never locked one of them in a closet (a closet!) while entertaining a literal
ditchdigger in the parlor.

Oh, God, what a beautiful world! The autumn colors, that glinting river, that   15
lead-colored cloud pointing down like a rounded arrow at that half-remodeled
McDonald's standing above I-90 like a castle.

This time would be different, she was sure of it. The kids would care for this pet
themselves, since a puppy wasn't scaly and didn't bite. ("Ho HO!" Robert had said
the first time the iguana bit him. "I see you have an opinion on the matter!")

Thank you, Lord, she thought, as the Lexus flew through the cornfield. You have
given me so much: struggles and the strength to overcome them; grace, and new
chances every day to spread that grace around. And in her mind she sang out, as she
sometimes did when feeling that the world was good and she had at last found her
place in it, "Ho HO, ho HO!"

Callie pulled back the blind.

Yes. Awesome. It was still solved so *perfect*.

There was plenty for him to do back there. A yard could be a whole world. Like   20
her yard when she was a kid had been a whole world. From the three holes in her
wood fence she'd been able to see Exxon (Hole One) and Accident Corner (Hole
Two), and Hole Three was actually two holes that if you lined them up right your
eyes would do this weird crossing thing and you could play Oh My God I Am So
High by staggering away with your eyes crossed, going, "Peace, man, peace."

When Bo got older, it would be different. Then he'd need his freedom. But now
he just needed not to get killed. Once they'd found him way over on Testament. And
that was across I-90. How had he crossed I-90? She knew how. Darted. That's how he

crossed streets. Once a total stranger had called them from Hightown Plaza. Even Dr. Brile had said it: "Callie, this boy is going to end up dead if you don't get this under control. Is he taking the medications?"

Well, he was and he wasn't. The meds made him grind his teeth and his fist would suddenly pound down. He'd broken plates that way, and once a glass tabletop and got four stitches in his wrist.

Today he didn't need the meds because he was safe in the yard, because she'd fixed it so *perfect*.

He was out there practicing pitching by filling his Yankees helmet with pebbles and winging them at the tree.

He looked up and saw her and did the thing where he blew a kiss.   25

Sweet little man.

Now all she had to worry about was the pup. She hoped the lady who'd called would actually show up. It was a nice pup. White, with brown around one eye. Cute. If the lady showed up, she'd definitely want it. And if she took it, Jimmy was off the hook. He'd hated doing it that time with the kittens. But if no one took the pup he'd do it. He'd have to. Because his feeling was, when you said you were going to do a thing and didn't do it, that was how kids got into drugs. Plus he'd been raised on a farm, or near a farm anyways, and anybody raised on a farm knew you had to do what you had to do in terms of sick animals or extra animals—the pup being not sick, just extra.

That time with the kittens, Brianna and Jessi had called him a murderer, getting Bo all worked up, and Jimmy had yelled, "Look, you kids, I was raised on a farm and you got to do what you got to do!" Then he'd cried in bed, saying how the kittens had mewed in the bag all the way to the pond, and how he wished he'd never been raised on a farm, and she'd almost said, "You mean near a farm" (his dad had run a car wash outside Cortland), but sometimes when she got too smart-assed he would do this hard pinching thing on her arm while waltzing her around the bedroom, as if the place where he was pinching were like her handle, going, "I'm not sure I totally heard what you just said."

So, that time after the kittens, she'd only said, "Oh, honey, you did what you had to do."

And he'd said, "I guess I did, but it's sure not easy raising kids the right way."   30

And then, because she hadn't made his life harder by being a smart-ass, they had lain there making plans, like why not sell this place and move to Arizona and buy a car wash, why not buy the kids Hooked on Phonics, why not plant tomatoes, and then they'd got to wrestling around and (she had no idea why she remembered this) he had done this thing of, while holding her close, bursting this sudden laugh/despair-snort into her hair, like a sneeze, or like he was about to start crying.

Which had made her feel special, him trusting her with that.

So what she'd love, for tonight? Was getting the pup sold, putting the kids to bed early, and then, Jimmy seeing her as all organized in terms of the pup, they could mess around and afterward lie there making plans, and he could do that laugh/snort thing in her hair again.

Why that laugh/snort meant so much to her she had no freaking idea. It was just one of the weird things about the Wonder That Was Her, ha ha ha.

Outside, Bo hopped to his feet, suddenly curious, because (here we go) the lady   35
who'd called had just pulled up?

Yep, and in a nice car, too, which meant too bad she'd put "Cheap" in the ad.

Abbie squealed, "I love it, Mommy, I want it!" as the puppy looked up dimly from its shoebox and the lady of the house went trudging away and one-two-three-four plucked up four *dog turds* from the rug.

Well, wow, what a super field trip for the kids, Marie thought, ha ha (the filth, the mildew smell, the dry aquarium holding the single encyclopedia volume, the pasta pot on the bookshelf with an inflatable candy cane inexplicably sticking out of it), and although some might have been disgusted (by the spare tire on the *dining-room table*, by the way the glum mother dog, the presumed in-house pooper, was now dragging her rear over the pile of clothing in the corner, in a sitting position, splay-legged, moronic look of pleasure on her face), Marie realized (resisting the urge to rush to the sink and wash her hands, in part because the sink had a *basketball* in it) that what this really was, was deeply sad.

Please do not touch anything, please do not touch, she said to Josh and Abbie, but just in her head, wanting to give the children a chance to observe her being demo-cratic and accepting, and afterward they could all wash up at the half-remodeled McDonald's, as long as they just please please kept their hands out of their mouths, and God forbid they should rub their eyes.

The phone rang, and the lady of the house plodded into the kitchen, placing the daintily held, paper-towel-wrapped turds *on the counter.* 40

"Mommy, I want it," Abbie said.

"I will definitely walk him like twice a day," Josh said.

"Don't say 'like,'" Marie said.

"I will definitely walk him twice a day," Josh said.

Okay, then, all right, they would adopt a white-trash dog. Ha ha. They could name it Zeke, buy it a little corncob pipe and a straw hat. She imagined the puppy, having crapped on the rug, looking up at her, going, *Cain't hep it.* But no. Had she come from a perfect place? Everything was transmutable. She imagined the puppy grown up, entertaining some friends, speaking to them in a British accent: *My family of origin was, um, rather not, shall we say, of the most respectable . . .* 45

Ha ha, wow, the mind was amazing, always cranking out these—

Marie stepped to the window and, anthropologically pulling the blind aside, was shocked, so shocked that she dropped the blind and shook her head, as if trying to wake herself, shocked to see a young boy, just a few years younger than Josh, har-nessed and chained to a tree, via some sort of doohickey by which—she pulled the blind back again, sure she could not have seen what she thought she had—

When the boy ran, the chain spooled out. He was running now, looking back at her, showing off. When he reached the end of the chain, it jerked and he dropped as if shot.

He rose to a sitting position, railed against the chain, whipped it back and forth, crawled to a bowl of water, and, lifting it to his lips, took a drink: a drink *from a dog's bowl.*

Josh joined her at the window. 50

She let him look.

He should know that the world was not all lessons and iguanas and Nintendo. It was also this muddy simple boy tethered like an animal.

She remembered coming out of the closet to find her mother's scattered linge-rie and the ditchdigger's metal hanger full of orange flags. She remembered waiting outside the junior high in the bitter cold, the snow falling harder, as she counted over and over to two hundred, promising herself each time that when she reached two hundred she would begin the long walk back—

God, she would have killed for just one righteous adult to confront her mother, shake her, and say, "You idiot, this is your child, your child you're—"

"So what were you guys thinking of naming him?" the woman said, coming out of the kitchen.   55

The cruelty and ignorance just radiated from her fat face, with its little smear of lipstick.

"I'm afraid we won't be taking him after all," Marie said coldly.

Such an uproar from Abbie! But Josh—she would have to praise him later, maybe buy him the Italian Loaves Expansion Pak—hissed something to Abbie, and then they were moving out through the trashed kitchen (past some kind of *crank-shaft* on a cookie sheet, past a partial red pepper afloat *in a can of green paint*) while the lady of the house scuttled after them, saying, wait, wait, they could have it free, please take it—she really wanted them to have it.

No, Marie said, it would not be possible for them to take it at this time, her feeling being that one really shouldn't possess something if one wasn't up to properly caring for it.

"Oh," the woman said, slumping in the doorway, the scrambling pup on one shoulder.   60

Out in the Lexus, Abbie began to cry softly, saying, "Really, that was the perfect pup for me."

And it was a nice pup, but Marie was not going to contribute to a situation like this in even the smallest way.

Simply was not going to do it.

The boy came to the fence. If only she could say to him, with a single look, *Life will not necessarily always be like this. Your life could suddenly blossom into something wonderful. It can happen. It happened to me.*

But secret looks, looks that conveyed a world of meaning with their subtle blah blah blah—that was all bullshit. What was not bullshit was a call to Child Welfare, where she knew Linda Berling, a very no-nonsense lady who would snatch this poor kid away so fast it would make that fat mother's thick head spin.   65

Callie shouted, "Bo, back in a sec!," and, swiping the corn out of the way with her non-pup arm, walked until there was nothing but corn and sky.

It was so small it didn't move when she set it down, just sniffed and tumped over.

Well, what did it matter, drowned in a bag or starved in the corn? This way Jimmy wouldn't have to do it. He had enough to worry about. The boy she'd first met with hair to his waist was now this old man shrunk with worry. As far as the money, she had sixty hidden away. She'd give him twenty of that and go, "The people who bought the pup were super-nice."

Don't look back, don't look back, she said in her head as she raced away through the corn.

Then she was walking along Teallback Road like a sportwalker, like some lady who walked every night to get slim, except that she was nowhere near slim, she knew that, and she also knew that when sportwalking you did not wear jeans and unlaced hiking boots. Ha ha. She wasn't stupid. She just made bad choices. She remembered Sister Lynette saying, "Callie, you are bright enough but you incline toward that which does   70 not benefit you." *Yep, well, Sister, you got that right,* she said to the nun in her mind. But what the hell. What the heck. When things got easier moneywise, she'd get some decent tennis shoes and start walking and get slim. And start night school. Slimmer. Maybe medical technology. She was never going to be really slim. But Jimmy liked her the way she was. And she liked him the way he was. Which maybe that's what love was: liking someone how he was and doing things to help him get even better.

Like right now she was helping Jimmy by making his life easier by killing something so he—no. All she was doing was walking, walking away from—

What had she just said? That had been good. *Love was liking someone how he was and doing things to help him get even better.*

Like Bo wasn't perfect, but she loved him how he was and tried to help him get better. If they could keep him safe, maybe he'd mellow out as he got older. If he mellowed out, maybe he could someday have a family. Like there he was now in the yard, sitting quietly, looking at flowers. Tapping with his bat, happy enough. He looked up, waved the bat at her, gave her that smile. Yesterday he'd been stuck in the house, all miserable. He'd ended the day screaming in bed, so frustrated. Today he was looking at flowers. Who was it that thought up that idea, the idea that had made today better than yesterday? Who loved him enough to think that up? Who loved him more than anyone else in the world loved him?

Her.

She did.

Wells Tower

Everything Ravaged, Everything Burned

2009

Wells Tower was born in 1973 in Vancouver, British Columbia, although his family moved to rural North Carolina when Wells was young. Starting in his late teens, he played guitar and sang in a Chapel Hill–based punk band called Hellbender, which continued for six years, even as Tower attended Wesleyan University in Connecticut. There he majored in anthropology and sociology—an unsurprising course of study for the author of a Viking tale as inventive as "Everything Ravaged, Everything Burned." Tower's first taste of the literary world was at the now-defunct DoubleTake magazine. "I just went over and gave them my resume and pleaded with them to give me any sort of job," Tower told the Observer. *"They gave me a job as night manager, which entailed going over there and locking up and watering the plants. From there I started writing some of their press releases." Soon*

Wells Tower

Tower was freelancing for the Washington Post Magazine *and has continued to write journalism for publications such as the* New Yorker, Harper's, GQ, *and the* New York Times. *After Tower got an MFA in fiction at Columbia University, he mailed the first two short stories he had completed to the* Paris Review *and soon received a phone call from renowned editor George Plimpton. Tower would win the magazine's Plimpton*

Discovery Prize, as well as two Pushcarts, for the stories that would make up his first collection, Everything Ravaged, Everything Burned, *published in 2009 to rave reviews. Writer David Sedaris claimed that the book "seems to have reinvented the English language. . . . What an exciting story collection it is, unlike anything I've ever come across." Tower, who has stated that the intention of his fiction "is always to get at the weird, dark marrow of human experience," is working on a novel. He splits his time between Chapel Hill, North Carolina, and Brooklyn, New York.*

Just as we were all getting back into the mainland domestic groove, somebody started in with dragons and crop blights from across the North Sea. We all knew who it was. A turncoat Norwegian monk named Naddod had been big medicine on the dragon-and-blight circuit for the last decade or so, and was known to bring heavy ordnance for whoever could lay out some silver. Scuttlebutt had it that Naddod was operating out of a monastery on Lindisfarne, whose people we'd troubled on a pillage-and-consternation tour through Northumbria after Corn Harvesting Month last fall. Now bitter winds were screaming in from the west, searing the land and ripping the grass from the soil. Salmon were turning up spattered with sores, and grasshoppers clung to the wheat in rapacious buzzing bunches.

I tried to put these things out of my mind. We'd been away three long months harrying the Hibernian shores, and now I was back with Pila, my common-law, and thinking that home was very close to paradise in these endless summer days. We'd built our house together, Pila and me. It was a fine little wattle-and-daub cabin on a pretty bit of plain where a wide blue fjord stabbed into the land. On summer evenings my young wife and I would sit out front, high on potato wine, and watch the sun stitch its orange skirt across the horizon. At times such as these, you get a good, humble feeling, like the gods made this place, this moment, first and concocted you as an afterthought just to be there to enjoy it.

I was doing a lot of enjoying and relishing and laying around the rack with Pila, though I knew what it meant when I heard those flint-edged winds howling past the house. Some individuals three weeks' boat ride off were messing up our summer and would probably need their asses whipped over it.

Of course, Djarf Fairhair had his stinger out even before his wife spotted those dragons winging it inland from the coast. He was boss on our ship and a fool for warfare. His appetite for action was so terrifying and infectious, he'd once riled up a gang of Frankish slaves and led them south to afflict and maim their own countrymen. He'd gotten in four days of decent sacking when the slaves began to see the situation for what it was and underwent a sudden change of attitude. Djarf had been fighting his way up the Rhine Valley, making steady progress through a half-assed citizens' militia of children and farmers, when the slaves closed in behind him. People who were there say he turned absolutely feral and began berserking with a pair of broadaxes, chewing through the lines like corn kernels on a cob, and that when the axes broke, he took up someone's severed leg and used it as a club, so horrifying those gentle provincials that they fell back and gave him wide berth to the ship.

Djarf was from Hedeby-Slesvig up the Sli fjord, a foul and rocky locality whose people take a worrisome pleasure in the gruesome sides of life. They have a habit down there if they don't like a child's looks when he slides from the womb,   5

they pitch him into the deep and wait for the next one. Djarf himself was supposedly a colicky baby, and it was only the beneficence of the tides and his own
vicious tenacity that got him to the far beach when his father tried to wash him
from the world.

He'd been campaigning for payback ever since. I guess I was with him on a
search-and-destroy tour against Louis the Pious, and with my own eyes watched him
climb up over the soldiers' backs and stride across their shoulders, scything skulls as
he went. On that same trip, we ran low on food, and it was Djarf who decided to
throw our own dead on the fire and have at last night's mutton when their stomachs
burst. He'd been the only one of us to dig in, apart from a deranged Arab along as
a spell-buster. He reached right in there, scooping out chewed-up victuals with a
shank of pine bark. "Greenhorns," he called us, the firelight twitching on his face.
"Food's food. If these boys hadn't gotten their threads snipped, they'd tell you the
same thing."

So Djarf, whose wife was a sour, carp-mouthed thing and little argument for staying home, was agitating to hop back in the ship and go straighten things out in Northumbria. My buddy Gnut, who lived just over the stony moraine our wheat field
backed up on, came down the hill one day and admitted that he, too, was giving it
some thought. Like me, he wasn't big on warrioring. He was just crazy for boat. He'd
have rowed from his shack to his shithouse if somebody would invent a ship whose
prow could cut sod. His wife had passed years ago, dead from bad milk, and now that
she was gone, the part of Gnut that felt peaceful in a place that didn't move beneath
him had sickened and died as well.

Pila saw him coming down the hill and scowled. "Don't need to guess what he'll
be wanting," she said, and headed back indoors. Gnut ambled down over the hum-
mocky earth and stopped at the pair of stump chairs Pila and I had put up on the hill
where the view was so fine. From there, the fjord shone like poured silver, and sometimes you could spot a seal poking his head up through the waves.

Gnut's wool coat was stiff with filth and his long hair so heavy and unclean that
even the raw wind was having a hard time getting it to move. He had a good crust of
snot going in his mustache, not a pleasant thing to look at, but then, he had no one
around to find it disagreeable. He tore a sprig of heather from the ground and chewed
at its sweet roots.

"Djarf get at you yet?" he asked.   10

"No, not yet, but I'm not worried he'll forget."

He took the sprig from his teeth and briefly jammed it into his ear before tossing
it away. "You gonna go?"

"Not until I hear the particulars, I won't."

"You can bet I'm going. A hydra flew in last night and ran off Rolf Hierdal's
sheep. We can't be putting up with this shit. It comes down to pride, is what it comes
down to."

"Hell, Gnut, when'd you get to be such a gung-ho motherfucker? I don't recall   15
you being so proud and thin-skinned before Astrud went off to her good place. Anyhow, Lindisfarne is probably sacked-out already. If you don't recall, we pillaged the
tar out of those people on the last swing through, and I doubt they've come up with
much in the meantime to justify a trip."

I wished Gnut would go ahead and own up to the fact that his life out here was
making him lonely and miserable instead of laying on with this warrior-man routine.

I could tell just to look at him that most days he was thinking of walking into the water and not bothering to turn back. It wasn't combat he was after. He wanted back on the boat among company.

Not that I was all that averse to a job myself, speaking in the abstract, but I was needing more sweet time with Pila. I cared more for that girl than even she probably knew, and I was hoping to get in some thorough lovemaking before the Haycutting Month was under way and see if I couldn't make us a little monkey.

But the days wore on and the weather worsened. Pila watched it closely, and the sadness welled up in her, as it often did when I'd be leaving. She cussed me on some days, and others she'd hold me to her and weep. And late one evening, far toward dawn, the hail started. It came suddenly, with the rasping sound a ship makes when its keel scrapes stone. We hunkered down in the sheepskins, and I whispered soothing things to Pila, trying to drown out the clatter.

The sun was not yet full up in the sky when Djarf came and knocked. I rose and stepped across the floor, which was damp with cold dew. Djarf stood in the doorway wearing a mail jacket and shield and breathing like he'd jogged the whole way over. He chucked a handful of hail at my feet. "Today's the day," he said with a wild grin. "We got to get it on."

Sure, I could have told him thanks anyway, but once you back down from one job, you're lucky if they'll even let you put in for a flat-fee trade escort. I had to think long-term, me and Pila, and any little jits we might produce. Still, she didn't like to hear it. When I got back in bed, she tucked the covers over her face, hoping I'd think she was angry instead of crying.

The clouds were spilling out low across the sky when we shoved off. Thirty of us on board, Gnut rowing with me at the bow and behind us a lot of other men I'd been in some shit with before. Some of their families came down to watch us go. Ørl Stender fucked up the cadence waving to his son, who stood on the beach waving back. He was a tiny one, not four or five, standing there with no pants on, holding a baby pig on a hide leash. Some of the others on board weren't a whole lot older, rash and violent children, so innocent about the world they would just as soon stick a knife in you as shake your hand.

Gnut was overjoyed. He laughed and sang and put a lot of muscle into the oar, me just holding my hands on it to keep up appearances. I was missing Pila already. I watched the beach for her and her bright red hair. She hadn't come down to see me off, too mad and sad about me leaving to get up out of bed. But I looked for her anyway, the land scooting away with every jerk of the oars. If Gnut knew I was hurting, he didn't say so. He nudged me and joked, and kept up a steady flow of dull, merry chatter, as though this whole thing was a private vacation the two of us had cooked up together.

Djarf stood at his spot in the bow, the blood in his cheeks. His high spirits were wearying. Slesvigers will burst into song with no provocation whatever, their affinity for music roughly on a par with the wretchedness of their singing. He screeched out a cadence ballad that lasted hours, and his gang of young hockchoppers howled along with him and gave no one any peace.

Three days out, the sun punched through the dirty clouds and put a steely shimmer on the sea. It cooked the brine out of our clothes and got everybody dry and happy. I couldn't help but think that if Naddod was really as serious as we thought he was, this crossing would be a fine opportunity to call up a typhoon and drown us all like cats. But the weather held, and the seas stayed drowsy and low.

20

*

We had less light in the evenings out here than at home, and it was a little easier   25
sleeping in the open boat without an all-night sun. Gnut and I slept where we rowed,
working around each other to get comfy on the bench. I woke up once in the middle
of the night and found Gnut dead asleep, muttering and slobbering and holding me
in a rough embrace. I tried to peel him off, but he was large, and his hard arms stayed
on me tight as if they'd grown there. I poked him and yelled at him, but the big man
would not be roused, so I just tried to work up a little slack to where he wasn't hurting my ribs, and I drifted back to sleep.

Later, I told him what had happened. "That's a lot of horseshit," he said, his
broad face going red.

"I wish it was," I said. "But I've got bruises I could show you. Hey, if I ever come
around asking to be your sweetheart, do me a favor and remind me about last night."

He was all upset. "Go to hell, Harald. You're not funny. Nobody thinks you're
funny."

"I'm sorry," I said. "Guess you haven't had a whole lot of practice lately having a
body beside you at night."

He rested on the oar a second. "So what if I haven't."   30

Thanks to the easy wind bellying our sails, we crossed fast and sighted the island
six days early. One of the hockchoppers spotted it first, and when he did, he let
everyone know it by cutting loose with a long, obnoxious battle howl. He drew his
sword and swung it in figure eights above his head, causing the men around him to
scatter under the gunwales. This boy was a nasty item, with a face like a buzzard's, his
cheeks showing more boils than beard. I'd seen him around at home. He had three
blackened, chopped-off thumbs reefed to his belt.

Haakon Gokstad glanced up from his seat in the stern and shot the boy a baleful
look. Haakon had been on more raids and runs than the bunch of us put together. He
was old and achy and worked the rudder, partly because he could read the tides by
how the blood moved through his hands, and also because those old arms were poor
for pulling oars. "Put your ass on that bench, young man," Haakon said to the boy.
"We got twelve hours' work between here and there."

The boy colored. He let his sword arm hang. He looked at his friends to see if
he'd been humiliated in front of them and, if he had, what he needed to do about it.
The whole boat was looking over him. Even Djarf paused in his song. The other kid
on his bench whispered something and scooted over. The boy sat and took the oar.
The rowing and the chatter started up again.

You could say that those people on Lindisfarne were fools, living out there
on a tiny island without high cliffs or decent natural defenses, and so close to us
and also the Swedes and the Norwegians, how we saw it, we couldn't afford *not*
to come by and sack every now and again. But when we came into the bright
little bay, a quiet fell over all of us. Even the hockchoppers quit grab-assing and
looked. The place was wild with fields of purple thistle, and when the wind blew,
it twitched and rolled, like the hide of some fantastic animal shrugging in its
sleep. Wildflowers spurted on the hills in fat red gouts. Apple trees lined the
shore, and there was something sorrowful in how they hung so low with fruit.
We could see a man making his way toward a clump of white-walled cottages, his
donkey loping along behind him with a load. On the far hill, I could make out
the silhouette of the monastery, which still lacked a roof from when we'd burned

it last. It was a lovely place, and I hoped there would still be something left to enjoy after we got off the ship and wrecked it up.

We gathered on the beach, and already Djarf was in a lather. He did a few deep   35
knee bends, got down in front of all of us and ran through some poses, cracking his bones and drawing out the knots in his muscles. Then he closed his eyes and said a silent prayer. His eyes were still closed when a man in a long robe appeared, picking his way down through the thistle.

Haakon Gokstad had a finger stuck in his mouth where one of his teeth had come out. He removed the finger and spat through the hole. He nodded up the hill at the figure heading our way, "My, that sumbitch has got some brass," he said.

The man walked straight to Djarf. He stood before him and removed his hood. His hair lay thin on his scalp and had probably been blond before it went white. He was old, with lines on his face that could have been drawn with a dagger point.

"Naddod," Djarf said, dipping his head slightly. "Suppose you've been expecting us."

"I certainly have not," Naddod said. He brought his hand up to the rude wooden cross that hung from his neck. "And I won't sport with you and pretend the surprise is entirely a pleasant one. Frankly, there isn't much left here worth pirating, so, yes, it's a bit of a puzzle."

"Uh-huh," said Djarf. "Can't tell us anything about a hailstorm, or locusts and   40
shit, or a bunch of damn dragons coming around and scaring the piss out of everybody's wife. You don't know nothing about any of that."

Naddod held his palms up and smiled piteously. "No, I'm very sorry, I don't. We did send a monkey pox down to the Spanish garrison at Much Wenlock, but honestly, nothing your way."

Djarf's tone changed, and his voice got loud and amiable. "Huh. Well, that's something." He turned to us and held up his hands. "Hey, boys, hate to break it to you, but it sounds like somebody fucked something up here. Old Naddod says it wasn't him, and as soon as he tells me just who in the hell it was behind the inconveniences we been having, we'll get back under way."

"Right." Naddod was uneasy, and I could see a chill run through him. "If you're passing through Mercia, I know they've just gotten hold of this man Aethelrik. Supposed to be a very tough customer. You know, that was his leprosy outbreak last year in—"

Djarf was grinning and nodding, but Naddod looked suddenly ill.

Djarf kept a small knife in his belt, and in the way other men smoked a pipe   45
or chewed seeds, Djarf liked to strop that little knife. It was sharpened down to a little fingernail of blade. You could shave a fairy's ass with that thing. And while Naddod was talking, Djarf had pulled out his knife and drawn it neatly down the priest's belly. At the sight of blood washing over the white seashells, everybody pressed forward, hollering and whipping their swords around. Djarf was overcome with crazed elation, and he hopped up and down, yelling for everybody to be quiet and watch him.

Naddod was not dead. His insides had pretty much spilled out, but he was still breathing. Not crying out or anything, though, which you had to give him credit for. Djarf hunkered and flipped Naddod onto his stomach and rested a foot in the small of his back.

Gnut was right beside me. He sighed and put his hand over his eyes. "Oh, Lord, he doing a blood eagle?"

"Yeah," I said. "Looks that way."

Djarf raised his palm for quiet. "Now I know most of the old-timers have seen one of these, but it might be a new one on some of you young men." The hockchoppers tittered. "This thing is what we call a blood *eagle*, and if you'll just sit tight a second you can see—well, it's a pretty wild effect."

The men stepped back to give Djarf room to work. He placed the point of his sword to one side of Naddod's spine. He leaned into it and worked the steel in gingerly, delicately crunching through one rib at a time until he'd made an incision about a foot long. He paused to wipe sweat from his brow, and made a parallel cut on the other side of the backbone. Then he knelt and put his hands into the cuts. He fumbled around in there a second, and then drew Naddod's lungs out through the slits. As Naddod huffed and gasped, the lungs flapped, looking sort of like a pair of wings. I had to turn away myself. It was very grisly stuff.

The young men roared, and Djarf stood there, conducting the applause. Then, at his command, they all broke out their sieging tackle and swarmed up the hill.

Only Gnut and Haakon and Ørl Stender and me didn't go. Ørl watched the others flock up toward the monastery, and when he was sure no one was looking back, he went to where Naddod lay dying, and struck him hard on the skull with the back of a hatchet. We were all relieved to see those lungs stop quivering. Ørl sighed and blessed himself. He said a funerary prayer, the gist of which was that he didn't know what this man's god was all about, but he was sorry that his humble servant had gotten sent up early, and on a bullshit pretext, too. He said he didn't know the man, but that he probably deserved something better the next time around.

"Cross all that water for this damn stupidity, and a flock of sheep to shave at home," Haakon grumbled.

Gnut smiled and squinted up at the sky. "My God, it's a fine day. Let's go up the hill and see if we can't scratch up a bite to eat."

We hiked to the little settlement on the hill. Some ways over, where the monastery was, the young men were on a real binge. They'd dragged out a half-dozen monks, hanged them from a tree, and then set the tree on fire.

Our hands were stiff and raw from the row over, and we paused at a well in the center of the village to wet our palms and have a drink. We were surprised to see the kid with the thumbs in his belt bust forth from a stand of ash trees, yanking some poor half-dead citizen along behind him. He walked over to where we were standing and let his victim collapse in the dusty boulevard.

"This is nice," he said to us. "You'd make good chieftains, standing around like this, watching other people work."

"Why, you little turd," Haakon said, and backhanded the boy across the mouth. The fellow lying there in the dust looked up and chuckled. The boy flushed. He plucked a dagger from his hip scabbard and stabbed Haakon in the stomach. There was a still moment. Haakon gazed down at the ruby stain spreading across his tunic. He looked greatly vexed.

As the young man realized what he'd done, his features fretted up like a child trying to pout his way out of a spanking. He was still looking that way when Haakon cleaved his head across the eyebrows with one crisp stroke.

Haakon cleaned his sword and looked again at his stomach. "Sumbitch," he said, probing the wound with his pinky. "It's deep. I believe I'm in a fix."

"Nonsense," said Gnut. "Just need to lay you down and stitch you up."

Ørl, who was softhearted, went over to the man the youngster had left. He propped him up against the well and gave him the bucket to sip at.

Across the road, an old dried-up farmer had come out of his house. He stared off at the smoke from the monastery rolling down across the bay. He nodded at us. We walked over.

"Hello," he said.

I told him good day.   65

He squinted at my face. "Something wrong?" I asked him.

"Apologies," he said. "Just thought I recognized you, is all."

"Could be. I was through here last fall."

"Uh-huh," he said. "Now, that was a hot one. Don't know why you'd want to come back. You got everything that was worth a damn on the last going-over."

"Yeah, well, we're having a hard time figuring it ourselves. Came to see your man   70
Naddod. Wrong guy, looks like, but he got gotten anyway, sorry to say."

The man sighed. "Doesn't harelip me any. We all had to tithe in to cover his retainer. Do just as well without him, I expect. So what are you doing, any looting?"

"Why? You got anything to loot?"

"Me? Oh, no. Got a decent cookstove, but I can't see you toting that back on the ship."

"Don't suppose you've got a coin hoard or anything buried out back?"

"Jeezum crow, I wish I did have. Coin hoard, I'd really turn things around for   75
myself."

"Yeah, well, I don't suppose you'd own up if you did."

He laughed. "You got that right, my friend. But I suppose you got to kill me or believe me, and either way, you get nothing out of the deal." He pointed at Haakon, who was leaning on Gnut and looking pretty spent. "Looks like your friend's got a problem. Unless you'd like to watch him die, why don't you bring him inside? Got a daughter who's hell's own seamstress."

The man, who was called Bruce, had a cozy little place. We all filed in. His daughter was standing by the stove. She gave a nervous little cry when we came through the door. She had a head full of thick black hair, and a thin face, pale as sugar—a pretty girl. So pretty, in fact, that you didn't notice right off that she was missing an arm. We all balked and had a good stare at her. But Gnut, you could tell, was truly smitten. The way he looked, blanched and wide-eyed, he could have been facing a wild dog instead of a good-looking woman. He rucked his hands through his hair and tried to lick the crust off his lips. Then he nodded and uttered a solemn "Hullo."

"Mary," Bruce said, "this man has developed a hole in his stomach. I said we'd help fix him up."

Mary looked at Haakon. "Aha," she said. She lifted his tunic and surveyed the   80
wound. "Water," she said to Ørl, who was looking on. Gnut eyed him jealously as he left for the well. Then Gnut cleared his throat. "I'd like to pitch in," he said. Mary directed him to a little sack of onions in the corner and told him to chop. Bruce got a fire going in the stove. Mary set the water on and shook in some dry porridge. Haakon, who had grown rather waxen, crawled up on the table and lay still. "I don't feel like no porridge," he said.

"Don't worry about that," Bruce said. "The porridge is just for the onions to ride in on."

Gnut kept an eye on Mary as he bent over a small table and overdid it on the onions. He chopped and chopped, and when he'd chopped all they had, he started chopping the chopped-up ones over again. Finally, Mary looked over and told him, "That's fine, thank you," and Gnut laid the knife down.

When the porridge was cooked, Mary threw in a few handfuls of onion and took the concoction over to Haakon. He regarded her warily, but when she held the wooden spoon out to him, he opened his mouth like a baby bird. He chewed and swallowed. "Doesn't taste very good," he said, but he kept eating anyway.

A minute passed, and then a peculiar thing occurred. Mary lifted Haakon's tunic again, put her face to the wound, and sniffed at it. She paused a second and then did it again.

"What in the world is this?" I asked.   85

"Gotta do this with a wound like that," Bruce said. "See if he's got the porridge illness."

"He doesn't have any porridge illness," I said. "At least, he didn't before now. What he's got is a stab hole in his stomach. Now stitch the man up."

"Won't do any good if you smell onions coming out of that hole. Means he's got the porridge illness and he's done for."

Haakon looked up. "Talking about a pierced bowel? Can't believe it's as bad as all that."

Mary had another sniff. The wound didn't smell like onions. She cleaned Haa- 90
kon with hot water and stitched the hole to a tight pucker.

Haakon fingered the stitches, and, satisfied, passed out. The five of us stood around, and no one could think of anything to say.

"So," Gnut said in an offhand way. "Were you born like that?"

"Like what?" Mary said.

"Without both arms, I mean. Is that how you came out?"

"Sir, that's fine a thing to ask my daughter," Bruce said. "It was your people that 95
did it to her."

Gnut said, "Oh." And then he said it again, and then really no one could think of anything to say.

Then Mary spoke. "It wasn't you who did it," she said. "But the man who did, I think I'd like to kill him."

Gnut told her that if she would please let him know who it was, he'd consider it a favor if she'd let him intervene on her behalf.

I said, "I would like a drink. Ørl, what have you got in that wineskin?"

He said nothing. The skin hung from his shoulder, and he put his hands on it 100
protectively.

"I asked what have you got to drink."

"Little bit of root brandy, for your information, Harald. But it's got to last me the way back. I can't be damp and not have something to take the chill off."

Gnut was glad to have something to raise his voice about. "Ørl, you're a sonofabitch. We been three weeks on the water for nothing, Haakon is maybe gonna die, and you can't even see your way to splash a little taste around. Now, that is the worst, the lowest thing I've ever heard."

So Ørl opened up his wineskin, and we all had a dose. It was sweet and potent and we drank and laughed and carried on. Haakon came to. His ordeal had put him in a mawkish bent of mind, and he raised a toast to his pretty surgeon, and to the splendid day, and how much it pleased him that he'd get to see the end of it. Bruce and Mary loosened up and we all talked like old friends. Mary told a lewd story about an apothecary who lived down the road. She was having a good time and did not seem to mind how close Gnut was standing. No one looking in on us would have known we were the reason this girl was missing an arm, and also the reason, probably, that nobody asked where Bruce's wife had gone.

It was not long before we heard somebody causing a commotion at the well. Me   105
and Gnut and Ørl stepped outside. Djarf had stripped to his waist, and his face and arms and pants looked about how you'd figure. He was hauling up buckets of cold water, dumping it over his head, and shrieking with delight. The blood ran off him pink and watery. He saw us and came over.

"Hoo," he said, shaking water from his hair. He jogged in place for a minute, shivered, and then straightened up. "Mercy, that was a spree. Not much loot to speak of, but a hell of a goddamn spree." He massaged his thighs and spat a few times. Then he said, "So, you do much killing?"

"Nah," I said. "Haakon killed that little what's-his-name lying over there, but no, we've just been sort of taking it easy."

"Hm. What about in there?" he asked, indicating Bruce's cottage. "Who lives there? You kill them?"

"No, we didn't," Ørl said. "They helped put Haakon back together and every-thing. Seem like good folks."

"Nobody's killing them," Gnut said.   110

"So everybody's back at the monastery, then?" I asked.

"Well, most of them. Those young men had a disagreement over some damn thing and fell to cutting each other. Gonna make for a tough row out of here. Pray for wind, I guess."

Brown smoke was heavy in the sky, and I could hear dim sounds of people screaming.

"So here's the deal," Djarf said. "We bivouac here tonight, and if the weather holds, we shoot down to Mercia tomorrow and see if we can't sort things out with this fucker Aethelrik."

"I don't know," Ørl said.   115

"No deal," I said. "This thing was a goose chase as it is. I got a wife at home and wheat straw to bale. I'll be damned if I'll row you to Mercia."

Djarf clenched his jaw. He looked at Gnut. "You, too?"

Gnut nodded.

"Serious? Mutiny?"

"No," Gnut said. "We're just saying we—"   120

"Call it what it is, motherfucker," Djarf barked. "You sons of bitches are mutiniz-ing my operation?"

"Look, Djarf," I said. "Nobody's doing anything to anybody. We just need to head on back."

He yelled and snorted. Then he ran at us with his sword raised high, and Gnut had to slip behind him quickly and put a bear hug on him. I went over and clamped one hand over Djarf's mouth and pinched his nose shut with the other, and after a while he started to cool down.

We let him go. He stood there huffing and eyeing us, and we kept our knives and things out, and finally he put the sword back and composed himself.

"Okay, sure, I read you," he said. "Fair enough. We go back. Oh, I should have 125
told you, Olaffssen found a stash of beef shells somewhere. He's gonna cook those up
for everybody who's left. Ought to be tasty." He turned and humped it back toward
the bay.

Gnut didn't come down to the feast. He said he needed to stay at Bruce and
Mary's to look after Haakon. Bullshit, of course, seeing as Haakon made it down the
hill by himself and crammed his tender stomach with about nine tough steaks. When
the dusk started going black and still no Gnut, I legged it back up to Bruce's to see
about him. Gnut was sitting on a hollow log outside the cottage, flicking gravel into
the weeds.

She's coming with me," he said.

"Mary?"

He nodded gravely. "I'm taking her home with me to be my wife. She's in there
talking it over with Bruce."

"This a voluntary thing, or an abduction-type deal?" 130

Gnut looked off toward the bay as though he hadn't heard the question. "She's
coming with me."

I mulled it over. "You sure this is such a hot idea, bringing her back to live among
our people, all things considering?"

He grew quiet. "Any man that touches her, or says anything unkind, it will really
be something different, what I'll do to him."

We sat a minute and watched the sparks rising from the bonfire on the beach.
The warm evening wind carried smells of blossoms and wood smoke, and I was overcome with calm.

We walked into Bruce's, where only a single suet candle was going. Mary stood 135
by the window with her one arm across her chest. Bruce was worked up. When we
came in, he moved to block the door. "You get out of my house," he said. "You just
can't take her, what little I've got."

Gnut did not look happy, but he shouldered past and knocked Bruce on his ass. I
went and put a hand on the old farmer, who was quaking with rage.

Mary did not hold her hand out to Gnut. But she didn't protest when he put his
arm around her and moved her toward the door. The look she gave her father was a
wretched thing, but still she went easy. With just one arm like that, what could she
do? What other man would have her?

Their backs were to us when Bruce grabbed up an awl from the table and made
for Gnut. I stepped in front of him and broke a chair on his face, but still he kept
coming, scrabbling at my sword, trying to snatch up something he could use to keep
his daughter from going away. I had to hold him steady and run my knife into his
cheek. I held it there like a horse's bit, and then he didn't want to move. When I
got up off him he was crying quietly. As I was leaving, he threw something at me and
knocked the candle out.

And you might think it was a good thing, that Gnut had found a woman who
would let him love her, and if she didn't exactly love him back, at least she would,
in time, get to feeling something for him that wasn't so far from it. But what would
you say about that crossing, when the winds went slack and it was five long weeks
before we finally fetched up home? Gnut didn't hardly say a word to anybody, just
held Mary close to him, trying to keep her soothed and safe from all of us, his friends.

He wouldn't look me in the face, stricken as he was by the awful fear that comes with getting hold of something you can't afford to lose.

After that trip, things changed. It seemed to me that all of us were leaving the 140 high and easy time of life and heading into deeper waters. Not long after we got back, Djarf had a worm crawl up a hole in his foot and had to give up raiding. Gnut and Mary turned to homesteading full-time, and I saw less of him. Just catching up over a jar turned into a hassle you had to plan two weeks in advance. And when we did get together, he would laugh and jaw with me a little bit, but you could see he had his mind on other things. He'd gotten what he wanted, but he didn't seem too happy about it, just worried all the time.

It didn't make much sense to me then, what Gnut was going through, but after Pila and me had our little twins, and we put a family together, I got an understanding of how terrible love can be. You wish you hated those people, your wife and children, because you know the things the world will do to them, because you have done some of those things yourself. It's crazy-making, yet you cling to them with everything and close your eyes against the rest of it. But still you wake up late at night and lie there listening for the creak and splash of oars, the clank of steel, the sounds of men rowing toward your home.

Virginia Woolf

A Haunted House   1921

Adeline Virginia Stephen Woolf (1882–1941) was born in London, the daughter of Sir Leslie Stephen, an influential critic and editor of the voluminous Dictionary of National Biography. *Virginia and her sister Vanessa (later Vanessa Bell) were largely self-educated in their father's extensive library while—in a distinction not lost on them—their brothers were sent to college. After their father's death in 1904, Virginia and Vanessa moved to Bloomsbury, a bohemian London neighborhood, and became the center of the "Bloomsbury Group" of progressive artists and intellectuals. Always in frail health, Virginia experienced episodes of mental disturbance. In 1912 she married Leonard Woolf, a journalist and novelist. In 1917 as therapy, they set up a hand-press in their home and started the Hogarth*

Virginia Woolf

Press, which became one of the most celebrated small presses of the century. In addition to Woolf's books, it issued works by T. S. Eliot, Katherine Mansfield, Robinson Jeffers, Edwin Arlington Robinson, and Sigmund Freud. Woolf's first novel was The Voyage Out *(1915); though realistic in technique, it foreshadowed the psychological depth and poetic force of her late work. In innovative novels such as* Mrs. Dalloway *(1925) and* To the Lighthouse *(1927), Woolf became one of the central Modernist writers in English and a pioneer of stream-of-consciousness narration, which portrays the random flow of thoughts and feelings through a character's mind. Her critical essays are collected in* The Common Reader *(1925, second series 1932); her long essay* A Room of One's Own*

(1929) is a feminist classic. After several nervous breakdowns, Woolf, fearing for her sanity, drowned herself in 1941.

Whatever hour you woke there was a door shutting. From room to room they went, hand in hand, lifting here, opening there, making sure—a ghostly couple.

"Here we left it," she said. And he added, "Oh, but here too!" "It's upstairs," she murmured. "And in the garden," he whispered. "Quietly," they said, "or we shall wake them."

But it wasn't that you woke us. Oh, no. "They're looking for it; they're drawing the curtain," one might say, and so read on a page or two. "Now they've found it," one would be certain, stopping the pencil on the margin. And then, tired of reading, one might rise and see for oneself, the house all empty, the doors standing open, only the wood pigeons bubbling with content and the hum of the threshing machine sounding from the farm. "What did I come in here for? What did I want to find?" My hands were empty. "Perhaps it's upstairs then?" The apples were in the loft. And so down again, the garden still as ever, only the book had slipped into the grass.

But they had found it in the drawing room. Not that one could ever see them. The window panes reflected apples, reflected roses; all the leaves were green in the glass. If they moved in the drawing room, the apple only turned its yellow side. Yet, the moment after, if the door was opened, spread about the floor, hung upon the walls, pendant from the ceiling—what? My hands were empty. The shadow of a thrush crossed the carpet; from the deepest wells of silence the wood pigeon drew its bubble of sound. "Safe, safe, safe," the pulse of the house beat softly. "The treasure buried; the room . . ." the pulse stopped short. Oh, was that the buried treasure?

A moment later the light had faded. Out in the garden then? But the trees spun darkness for a wandering beam of sun. So fine, so rare, coolly sunk beneath the surface the beam I sought always burnt behind the glass. Death was the glass; death was between us; coming to the woman first, hundreds of years ago, leaving the house, sealing all the windows; the rooms were darkened. He left it, left her, went North, went East, saw the stars turned in the Southern sky; sought the house, found it dropped beneath the Downs. "Safe, safe, safe," the pulse of the house beat gladly. "The Treasure yours." 5

The wind roars up the avenue. Trees stoop and bend this way and that. Moonbeams splash and spill wildly in the rain. But the beam of the lamp falls straight from the window. The candle burns stiff and still. Wandering through the house, opening the windows, whispering not to wake us, the ghostly couple seek their joy.

"Here we slept" she says. And he adds, "Kisses without number." "Waking in the morning—" "Silver between the trees—" "Upstairs—" "In the garden—" "When summer came—" "In winter snowtime—" The doors go shutting far in the distance, gently knocking like the pulse of a heart.

Nearer they come; cease at the doorway. The wind falls, the rain slides silver down the glass. Our eyes darken; we hear no steps beside us; we see no lady spread her ghostly cloak. His hands shield the lantern. "Look," he breathes. "Sound asleep. Love upon their lips."

Stooping, holding their silver lamp above us, long they look and deeply. Long they pause. The wind drives straightly; the flame stoops slightly. Wild beams of moonlight cross both floor and wall, and, meeting, stain the faces bent; the faces pondering; the faces that search the sleepers and seek their hidden joy.

"Safe, safe, safe," the heart of the house beats proudly. "Long years—" he sighs. 10 "Again you found me." "Here," she murmurs, "sleeping; in the garden reading; laughing, rolling apples in the loft. Here we left our treasure—" Stooping, their light lifts the lids upon my eyes. "Safe! safe! safe!" the pulse of the house beats wildly. Waking, I cry "Oh, is this *your* buried treasure? The light in the heart."

Kay Ryan, US Poet Laureate, 2008–2010.

POETRY

TALKING WITH *Kay Ryan*

"Language That Lasts"
Dana Gioia Interviews Former US Poet Laureate Kay Ryan

Q: When did you start writing poetry?

KAY RYAN: In a way I'd say I started writing poetry when I started collecting language, which was as soon as I could. I loved hearing a new word or phrase, and I had a private game of trying to say things differently than I'd said them before. I remember when I was quite advanced in this language study, in ninth grade, I went on a summer trip with my friend and her parents down to Texas. I was sitting there quietly in the small hot living room of my friend's aunt, listening to the adult conversation. Someone said something irritated along the lines of, "Tracy totaled Teddy's Toronado, and Tyler tattled it to Tina!" and I just burst out laughing: that accidental string of T's nobody else seemed to notice. Language brought me constant, secret pleasure, and it was free; I could have as much as I wanted, which is nice if you're poor.

As to writing-writing, I fooled around with writing poetry during high school and college and even after I'd become a community college teacher, trying to keep it at arm's length because I didn't want to be exposed the way poetry makes you exposed. I wanted to stay superficial. But by the time I was thirty I could see that poetry was eating away at my mind anyhow. Why not accept it and try to get really good at it? So, either I started writing poetry at three or thirty.

Q: Did poetry play much of a part in your childhood?

KAY RYAN: I guess the short answer would be no. But my mother had one lovely poem about a dead kitten that she liked to say. I always enjoyed feeling tender and sad when she did; it was a kind of intimacy with a mother who wasn't very intimate. And my mother's mother liked to recite poems when she came to visit. They made me feel very serious, and that is a lovely feeling for a child: "Life is real! Life is earnest! / And the grave is not its goal; / Dust thou art, to dust returnest, / Was not spoken of the soul!" My grandmother grew up in a time when people really memorized poetry for pleasure, and I loved hearing it.

My only other contact with poetry—but it was an important one—was in sixth grade. My enlightened teacher, Mrs. Kimball, at Roosevelt Elementary School in Bakersfield, California, had us do "choral reading," meaning the whole class memorized poems and stood up on the stage like a chorus at assemblies and recited them with great gusto. So I got a chance, like my grandmother, to memorize poetry for pleasure and have the pleasure of saying it aloud.

Q: Whom do you write for?

KAY RYAN: This is a devilish question. I'll answer it in parts.

First, when I write a poem I'm completely occupied with trying to net some elusive fish; I'm desperate to get the net (made of words) knotted in such a way that it will catch this desired fish (a half-formed idea, a wisp of a feeling). I'm not thinking of anything but that; I'm not thinking of me, I'm not thinking of you.

But then later, after I've finished writing the poem and have let it sit for days or months and look back to see if there's a fish in the net after all (many times, I'm sorry to say, there is no fish), I begin thinking of you. Have I put the necessary connections in the poem, or are some of them still in my head? Have I shaped the lines so they will present the reader with the most pleasure in discovering the secret rhymes? Have I removed self-indulgences? Because a poem, by its nature, must please others. If it doesn't, it can't last; and if it doesn't last it wasn't a poem, because poems are language that lasts.

Q: What gives you pleasure in writing?

KAY RYAN: People have dreams where they begin noticing that their house is lots bigger than they knew; they realize there is a maze of rooms behind the ones they've been occupying. The dreamer (I've had this dream) doesn't know why she hasn't noticed this before, because it's fascinating.

Writing a poem is like this; I go back behind my usual mind and find places I didn't know about, places that only the activity of writing a poem can let me into.

Q: Who are your favorite poets?

Kay Ryan with Dana Gioia

KAY RYAN: My favorite American poets are Emily Dickinson and Robert Frost. British favorites include John Donne, Gerard Manley Hopkins, Philip Larkin, and Stevie Smith. Favorites in other languages are Fernando Pessoa and Constantine Cavafy.

Q: Did a poem ever change your life?

KAY RYAN: A dream poem might have. When I was around ten, I dreamed that a piece of white paper was blowing around and I was chasing it. I knew it had the most beautiful poem in the world written on it. I couldn't catch it.

I never forgot that dream, although at the time I wasn't even thinking of trying to write poetry. Still, maybe some deep part of me was busy at it even then. I'm still trying to catch that piece of paper.

Q: What is the purpose of poetry? Why do people need poetry?

KAY RYAN: The secret, long-term purpose of poetry is to create more space between everything. Poetry is the main engine of the expanding universe. You yourself will have noticed how reading a poem that really strikes you (that will be one in twenty-five, if you're lucky; a poem can be great and still not strike *you*) makes you feel freer and less burdened, even if it's about death. You feel fresher, more awake. This proves my point; your atoms have been subtly distanced from each other, like a breeze is blowing through your DNA. That's poetry loosening you.

What is poetry? Pressed for an answer, Robert Frost made a classic reply: "Poetry is the kind of thing poets write." In all likelihood, Frost was trying not merely to evade the question but to chide his questioner into thinking for himself. A trouble with definitions is that they may stop thought. If Frost had said, "Poetry is a rhythmical composition of words expressing an attitude, designed to surprise and delight, and to arouse an emotional response," the questioner might have settled back in his chair, content to have learned the truth about poetry. He would have learned nothing, or not so much as he might learn by continuing to wonder.

The nature of poetry eludes simple definitions. (In this respect it is rather like jazz. Asked after one of his concerts "What is jazz?," Louis Armstrong replied, "Man, if you gotta ask, you'll never know.") Definitions will be of little help at first, if we are to know poetry and respond to it. We have to go to it willing to see and hear. For this reason, you are asked in reading this book not to be in any hurry to decide what poetry is, but instead to study poems and to let them grow in your mind.

Confronted with an introduction to poetry, you may be wondering "Who needs it?" and you may well be right. It's unlikely that you have avoided meeting poetry before; and perhaps you already have a friendship, or at least a fair acquaintance, with some of the greatest English-speaking poets of all time. What this book provides is an introduction to the *study* of poetry. It tries to help you look at a poem closely, to offer you a wider and more accurate vocabulary with which to express what poems say to you. It will suggest ways to judge for yourself the poems you read. It may set forth some poems new to you.

A frequent objection is that poetry ought not to be studied at all. In this view, a poem is either a series of gorgeous noises to be funneled into one ear and out the other without being allowed to trouble the mind, or an experience so holy that to analyze it in a classroom is as cruel and mechanical as dissecting a hummingbird. To the first view, it might be countered that a good poem has something to say that is well worth listening to. To the second view, it might be argued that poems are much less perishable than hummingbirds, and luckily, we can study them in flight. The risk of a poem's dying from observation is not nearly so great as the risk of not really seeing it at all. It is doubtful that any excellent poem has ever vanished from human memory because people have read it too closely.

That poetry matters to the people who write it has been shown unmistakably by the ordeal of Soviet poet Irina Ratushinskaya. Sentenced to prison for three and a half years, she was given paper and pencil only twice a month to write letters to her husband and her parents and was not allowed to write anything else. Nevertheless, Ratushinskaya composed more than two hundred poems in her cell, engraving them with a burnt match in a bar of soap, then memorizing the lines. "I would read the poem and read it," she said, "until it was committed to memory—then with one washing of my hands, it would be gone."

Good poetry is something that readers can care about. In fact, an ancient persuasion of humankind is that the hearing of a poem, as well as the making of a poem, can be a religious act. Poetry, in speech and song, was part of classic Greek drama, which for playwright, actor, and spectator alike was a holy-day ceremony. The Greeks' belief that a poet writes a poem only by supernatural assistance is clear from the invocations to the Muse that begin the *Iliad* and the *Odyssey* and from the opinion of Socrates (in Plato's *Ion*) that a poet has no powers of invention until divinely inspired. Among the ancient Celts, poets were regarded as magicians and priests, and whoever insulted one of them might expect to receive a curse in rime potent enough to afflict him with boils and to curdle the milk of his cows. Such identifications between the poet and the magician are less common these days, although we know that poetry is involved in the primitive white magic of children, who warn against a hex while jumping along a sidewalk: "Step on a crack, / Break your mother's back." To read a poem, we have to be willing to offer it responses *besides* a logical understanding. Whether we attribute the effect of a poem to a divine spirit or to the reactions of our glands and cortexes, we have to take the reading of poetry seriously (not solemnly), if only because—as some of the poems in this book may demonstrate—few other efforts can repay us so generously, both in wisdom and in joy.

Here is a poem one of the editors wrote for the first edition of this book.

To the Muse

Give me leave, Muse, in plain view to array
Your shift and bodice by the light of day.
I would have brought an epic. Be not vexed
Instead to grace a niggling schoolroom text;
Let down your sanction, help me to oblige
Those who would lead fresh devots to your liege,
And at your altar, grant that in a flash
Readers and I know incense from dead ash.

—X. J. K.

691

15 READING A POEM

Every good poem begins as the poet's but ends as the reader's.

—MILLER WILLIAMS

What You Will Learn in This Chapter

- To *paraphrase* a poem
- To recognize and define *lyric poetry*
- To define the other major kinds of poetry—*narrative, dramatic, didactic*
- To define and differentiate *subject* and *theme*

How do you read a poem? The literal-minded might say, "Just let your eye light on it"; but there is more to poetry than meets the eye. What Shakespeare called "the mind's eye" also plays a part. Many readers who have no trouble understanding and enjoying prose find poetry difficult. This is to be expected. At first glance, a poem usually will make some sense and give some pleasure, but it may not yield everything at once. Poetry is not to be galloped over like the daily news: a poem differs from most prose in that it is to be read slowly, carefully, and attentively. Not all poems are difficult, of course, and some can be understood and enjoyed on first encounter. But good poems yield more if read twice; and the best poems—after ten, twenty, or a hundred readings—still go on yielding.

POETRY OR VERSE

Approaching a thing written in lines and surrounded with white space, we need not expect it to be a poem just because it is verse. (Any composition in lines of more or less regular rhythm, often ending in rimes, is **verse**.) Here, for instance, is a specimen of verse that few will call poetry:

Thirty days hath September,
April, June, and November;
All the rest have thirty-one
Excepting February alone,
To which we twenty-eight assign
Till leap year makes it twenty-nine.

To a higher degree than that classic memory-tickler, poetry appeals to the mind and arouses feelings. Poetry may state facts, but, more important, it makes imaginative statements that we may value even if its facts are incorrect. Coleridge's error in placing a star within the horns of the crescent moon in "The Rime of the Ancient Mariner" does not stop the passage from being good poetry, though it is faulty astronomy. According to poet Gerard Manley Hopkins, poetry is "to be heard for its own sake and interest even over and above its interest of meaning." There are other elements in a poem besides plain prose sense: sounds, images, rhythms, figures of speech. These may strike us and please us even before we ask, "But what does it all mean?"

This is a truth not readily grasped by anyone who regards a poem as a kind of puzzle written in secret code with a message slyly concealed. The effect of a poem (our whole mental and emotional response to it) consists of much more than simply a message. By its musical qualities, by its suggestions, it can work on the reader's unconscious. T. S. Eliot put it well when he said in *The Use of Poetry and the Use of Criticism* that the prose sense of a poem is chiefly useful in keeping the reader's mind "diverted and quiet, while the poem does its work upon him." Eliot went on to liken the meaning of a poem to the bit of meat a burglar brings along to throw to the family dog. What is the work of a poem? To touch us, to stir us, to make us glad, and possibly even to tell us something.

HOW TO READ A POEM

How to set about reading a poem? Here are a few suggestions. To begin with, read the poem once straight through, with no particular expectations; read open-mindedly. Let yourself experience whatever you find, without worrying just yet about the large general and important ideas the poem contains (if indeed it contains any). Don't dwell on a troublesome word or difficult passage—just push on. Some of the difficulties may seem smaller when you read the poem for a second time; at least, they will have become parts of a whole for you.

On the second reading, read for the exact sense of all the words; if there are words you don't understand, look them up in a dictionary. Dwell on any difficult parts as long as you need to.

If you read the poem silently, sound its words in your mind. Better still, read the poem aloud, or listen to someone else reading it. You may discover meanings you didn't perceive in it before. To decide how to speak a poem can be an excellent method of getting to understand it.

PARAPHRASE

Try to **paraphrase** the poem as a whole, or perhaps just the more difficult lines. In paraphrasing, we put into our own words what we understand the poem to say, restating ideas that seem essential, coming out and stating what the poem may only suggest. This may sound like a heartless thing to do to a poem, but good poems can stand it. In fact, to compare a poem to its paraphrase is a good way to see the distance between poetry and prose.

In making a paraphrase, we generally work through a poem or a passage line by line. The statement that results may take as many words as the original, if not more. A paraphrase, then, is ampler than a **summary**, a brief condensation of gist, main idea, or story. (Click the "Info" button on your TV remote control, and you'll get a movie summary such as: "Scientist seeks revenge by creating giant man-eating cockroaches.") Here is a poem worth considering line by line. The poet writes of an island in a lake in the west of Ireland, in a region where he spent many summers as a boy.

William Butler Yeats (1865–1939)

The Lake Isle of Innisfree 1892

I will arise and go now, and go to Innisfree,
And a small cabin build there, of clay and wattles made:
Nine bean-rows will I have there, a hive for the honey-bee,
And live alone in the bee-loud glade.

And I shall have some peace there, for peace comes dropping slow, 5
Dropping from the veils of the morning to where the cricket sings;
There midnight's all a glimmer, and noon a purple glow,
And evening full of the linnet's wings.

I will arise and go now, for always night and day
I hear lake water lapping with low sounds by the shore; 10
While I stand on the roadway, or on the pavements gray,
I hear it in the deep heart's core.

Though relatively simple, this poem is far from simple-minded. We need to absorb it slowly and thoughtfully. At the start, for most of us, it raises problems: what are *wattles*, from which the speaker's dream-cabin is to be made? We might guess, but in this case it will help to consult a dictionary: they are "poles interwoven with sticks or branches, formerly used in building as frameworks to support walls or roofs." Evidently, this getaway house will be built in an old-fashioned way: it won't be a prefabricated log cabin or A-frame house, nothing modern or citified. The phrase *bee-loud glade* certainly isn't commonplace language, but right away, we can understand it, at least partially: it's a place loud with bees. What is a *glade*? Experience might tell us that it is an open space in woods, but if that word stops us, we can look it up. Although the *linnet* doesn't live in North America, it is a creature with wings—a songbird of the finch family, adds the dictionary. But even if we don't make a special trip to the dictionary to find *linnet*, we probably recognize that the word means "bird," and so the line makes sense to us.

A paraphrase of the whole poem might go something like this (in language easier to forget than that of the original): "I'm going to get up now, go to Innisfree, build a cabin, plant beans, keep bees, and live peacefully by myself amid nature and beautiful light. I want to because I can't forget the sound of that lake water. When I'm in the city, a gray and dingy place, I seem to hear it deep inside me."

These dull remarks, roughly faithful to what Yeats is saying, seem a long way from poetry. Nevertheless, they make certain things clear. For one, they spell out what the poet merely hints at in his choice of the word *gray*: that he finds the city dull and depressing. He stresses the word; instead of saying *gray pavements*, in the usual word order, he turns the phrase around and makes *gray* stand at the end of the line, where it rimes with *day* and so takes extra emphasis. The grayness of the city therefore seems important to the poem, and the paraphrase tries to make its meaning obvious.

Theme and Subject

Whenever you paraphrase, you stick your neck out. You affirm what the poem gives you to understand. And making a paraphrase can help you see the central thought of the poem, its **theme**. The theme isn't the same as the **subject**, which is the main topic, whatever the poem is "about." In Yeats's poem, the subject is the lake isle of Innisfree, or a wish to retreat to it. But the theme is, "I yearn for an ideal place where I will find perfect peace and happiness."

Themes can be stated variously, depending on what you believe matters most in the poem. Taking a different view of the poem, placing more weight on the speaker's wish to escape the city, you might instead state the theme: "This city is getting me down—I want to get back to nature." But after taking a second look at that statement, you might want to sharpen it. After all, this Innisfree seems a special, particular place, where the natural world means more to the poet than just any old trees and birds he might see in a park. Perhaps a stronger statement of theme, one closer to what matters most in the poem, might be: "I want to quit the city for my heaven on earth." That, of course, is saying in an obvious way what Yeats says more subtly, more memorably.

Limits of Paraphrase

A paraphrase never tells *all* that a poem contains, nor will every reader agree that a particular paraphrase is accurate. We all make our own interpretations, and sometimes the total meaning of a poem evades even the poet who wrote it. Asked to explain a passage in one of his poems, Robert Browning replied that when he had written the poem, only God and he knew what it meant; but "Now, only God knows." Still, to analyze a poem *as if* we could be certain of its meaning is, in general, more fruitful than to proceed as if no certainty could ever be had. A useful question might be, "What can we understand from the poem's very words?"

All of us bring personal associations to the poems we read. "The Lake Isle of Innisfree" might give you special pleasure if you have ever vacationed on a small island or on the shore of a lake. Such associations are inevitable, even to be welcomed, as long as they don't interfere with our reading the words on the page. We need to distinguish irrelevant responses from those the poem calls for. The reader who can't stand "The Lake Isle of Innisfree" because she is afraid of bees isn't reading a poem by Yeats, but one of her own invention.

Now and again we meet a poem—perhaps startling and memorable—into which the method of paraphrase won't take us far. Some portion of any deep poem resists explanation, but certain poems resist it almost entirely. Many poems by religious mystics seem closer to dream than waking. So do poems that purport to record drug experiences, such as Coleridge's "Kubla Khan" (Chapter 34). So do nonsense poems, translations of primitive folk songs, and surreal poems. Such poetry may move us and give pleasure (although not, perhaps, the pleasure of intellectual understanding). We do it no harm by trying to paraphrase it, though we may fail. Whether logically clear or strangely opaque, good poems appeal to the intelligence and do not shrink from it.

So far, we have taken for granted that poetry differs from prose; yet all our strategies for reading poetry—plowing straight on through and then going back, isolating difficulties, trying to paraphrase, reading aloud, using a dictionary—are no different from those we might employ in unraveling a complicated piece of prose. Poetry, after all, is similar to prose in most respects. At the very least, it is written in the same language. Like prose, poetry shares knowledge with us. It tells us, for instance, of a beautiful island in Lake Gill, County Sligo, Ireland, and of how one man feels about it.

LYRIC POETRY

Originally, as its Greek name suggests, a *lyric* was a poem sung to the music of a lyre. This earlier meaning—a poem made for singing—is still current today, when we use *lyrics* to mean the words of a popular song. But the kind of printed poem we now call a *lyric* is usually something else, as over the past five hundred years the nature of lyric poetry has changed greatly. Ever since the invention of the printing press in the fifteenth century, poets have written less often for singers, more often for readers. In general, this tendency has made lyric poems contain less word-music and (since they can be pondered on a page) more thought—and perhaps more complicated feelings.

What Is a Lyric Poem?

Here is a rough definition of a **lyric poem** as it is written today: a short poem expressing the thoughts and feelings of a single speaker. Often a poet will write a lyric in the first person ("I will arise and go now, and go to Innisfree"), but not always. A lyric can also be in the first person plural, as in Paul Laurence Dunbar's "We Wear the Mask" (Chapter 24). Or, a lyric might describe an object or recall an experience without the speaker's ever bringing himself or herself into it. (For an example of such a lyric, one in which the poet refrains from saying "I," see Theodore Roethke's "Root Cellar" or Gerard Manley Hopkins's "Pied Beauty," both found in Chapter 19.)

Perhaps because, rightly or wrongly, some people still think of lyrics as lyre-strummings, they expect a lyric to be an outburst of feeling, somewhat resembling a song, at least containing musical elements such as rime, rhythm, or sound effects. Such expectations are fulfilled in "The Lake Isle of Innisfree," that impassioned lyric full of language rich in sound. Many contemporary poets, however, write short poems in which they voice opinions or complicated feelings—poems that no reader would dream of trying to sing.

But in the sense in which we use it, *lyric* will usually apply to a kind of poem you can easily recognize. Here, for instance, are two lyrics. They differ sharply in subject and theme, but they have traits in common: both are short, and (as you will find) both set forth one speaker's definite, unmistakable feelings.

Robert Hayden (1913–1980)

Those Winter Sundays   1962

Sundays too my father got up early
and put his clothes on in the blueblack cold,
then with cracked hands that ached
from labor in the weekday weather made
banked fires blaze. No one ever thanked him.   5

I'd wake and hear the cold splintering, breaking.
When the rooms were warm, he'd call,
and slowly I would rise and dress,
fearing the chronic angers of that house,

Speaking indifferently to him,   10
who had driven out the cold
and polished my good shoes as well.
What did I know, what did I know
of love's austere and lonely offices?

Questions

1. Jot down a brief paraphrase of this poem. In your paraphrase, clearly show what the speaker finds himself remembering.
2. What are the speaker's various feelings? What do you understand from the words "chronic angers" and "austere"?
3. With what specific details does the poem make the past seem real?
4. What is the subject of Hayden's poem? How would you state its theme?

Adrienne Rich (1929–2012)

Aunt Jennifer's Tigers   1951

Aunt Jennifer's tigers prance across a screen,
Bright topaz denizens of a world of green.
They do not fear the men beneath the tree;
They pace in sleek chivalric certainty.

Aunt Jennifer's fingers fluttering through her wool   5
Find even the ivory needle hard to pull.
The massive weight of Uncle's wedding band
Sits heavily upon Aunt Jennifer's hand.

When Aunt is dead, her terrified hands will lie
Still ringed with ordeals she was mastered by.   10
The tigers in the panel that she made
Will go on prancing, proud and unafraid.

Compare

"Aunt Jennifer's Tigers" with Adrienne Rich's critical comments on the poem included in the "Writing Effectively" section at the end of this chapter.

NARRATIVE POETRY

Although a lyric sometimes relates an incident, or like "Those Winter Sundays" draws a scene, it does not usually relate a series of events. That happens in a **narrative poem**, one whose main purpose is to tell a story.

Narrative poetry dates back to the Babylonian *Epic of Gilgamesh* (composed before 2000 B.C.) and Homer's epics the *Iliad* and the *Odyssey* (composed before 700 B.C.). The **epic**, which is a long narrative form often tracing the adventures of a legendary or mythic hero, may well have originated much earlier. In England and Scotland, storytelling poems, such as *Beowulf*, have long been popular; in the late Middle Ages, **ballads**—or storytelling songs—circulated widely. Some, such as "Sir Patrick Spence" and "Bonny Barbara Allan," survive in our day, and folksingers sometimes perform them.

The art of narrative poetry invites the skills of a writer of fiction: the ability to draw characters and settings, to engage attention, to shape a plot. Needless to say, it calls for all the skills of a poet as well. In the English language today, lyrics seem more plentiful than other kinds of poetry. Although there has recently been a revival of interest in writing narrative poems, they have a far smaller audience than the readership enjoyed by long verse narratives in the nineteenth century, such as Henry Wadsworth Longfellow's *Evangeline* and Alfred, Lord Tennyson's *Idylls of the King*.

Here are two narrative poems: one medieval, one modern. How would you paraphrase the stories they tell? How do they hold your attention on their stories?

Anonymous (traditional Scottish ballad)

Sir Patrick Spence

The king sits in Dumferling toune,
   Drinking the blude-reid wine:
"O whar will I get guid sailor
   To sail this schip of mine?"

Up and spak an eldern knicht,°   *knight*   5
   Sat at the kings richt kne:
"Sir Patrick Spence is the best sailor
   That sails upon the se."

The king has written a braid letter,
   And signed it wi' his hand,   10
And sent it to Sir Patrick Spence,
   Was walking on the sand.

The first line that Sir Patrick red,
   A loud lauch lauchèd he;
The next line that Sir Patrick red,   15
   The teir blinded his ee.

"O wha° is this has don this deid,   *who*
   This ill deid don to me,
To send me out this time o' the yeir,
   To sail upon the se!   20

"Mak haste, mak haste, my mirry men all,
   Our guid schip sails the morne."
"O say na sae,° my master deir,   *so*
   For I feir a deadlie storme.

"Late late yestreen I saw the new moone,   25
   Wi' the auld moone in hir arme,
And I feir, I feir, my deir master,
   That we will cum to harme."

O our Scots nobles wer richt laith°   *loath*
   To weet° their cork-heild schoone,°   *wet; shoes* 30
Bot lang owre° a' the play wer playd,   *long before*
   Their hats they swam aboone.°   *above (their heads)*

O lang, lang may their ladies sit,
   Wi' their fans into their hand,
Or ere° they se Sir Patrick Spence   *before*   35
   Cum sailing to the land.

O lang, lang may the ladies stand,
   Wi' their gold kems° in their hair,   *combs*
Waiting for their ain° deir lords,   *own*
   For they'll se thame na mair.   40

Haf owre,° haf owre to Aberdour,   *halfway over*
   It's fiftie fadom deip,
And thair lies guid Sir Patrick Spence,
   Wi' the Scots lords at his feit.

SIR PATRICK SPENCE. *9 braid:* Broad, but broad in what sense? The poet could have meant *plain-spoken, official,* or *on wide paper.*

Questions

1. That the king drinks "blude-reid wine" (line 2)—what meaning do you find in that detail? What does it hint at or foreshadow? (If the phrase "blude-reid" is confusing, trying saying it aloud, and your ear may pick up its meaning.)
2. What do you make of this king and his motives for sending Spence and the Scots lords into an impending storm? Is he a fool, is he cruel and inconsiderate, is he deliberately trying to drown Sir Patrick and his crew, or is it impossible for us to know? Let your answer rely on the poem alone, not on anything you read into it.
3. Comment on this ballad's methods of storytelling. Is the story told too briefly for us to care what happens to Spence and his men, or are there any means by which the poet makes us feel compassion for them? Do you resent the lack of a detailed account of the shipwreck?
4. Lines 25–28—the new moon with the old moon in her arm—have been much admired as poetry. In what way does this stanza also contribute to the story of the poem?

Robert Frost (1874–1963)

"Out, Out—"   1916

The buzz-saw snarled and rattled in the yard
And made dust and dropped stove-length sticks of wood,
Sweet-scented stuff when the breeze drew across it.
And from there those that lifted eyes could count
Five mountain ranges one behind the other   5
Under the sunset far into Vermont.
And the saw snarled and rattled, snarled and rattled,
As it ran light, or had to bear a load.
And nothing happened: day was all but done.
Call it a day, I wish they might have said   10
To please the boy by giving him the half hour
That a boy counts so much when saved from work.
His sister stood beside them in her apron
To tell them "Supper." At the word, the saw,
As if to prove saws knew what supper meant,   15
Leaped out at the boy's hand, or seemed to leap—
He must have given the hand. However it was,
Neither refused the meeting. But the hand!
The boy's first outcry was a rueful laugh,
As he swung toward them holding up the hand   20
Half in appeal, but half as if to keep

The life from spilling. Then the boy saw all—
Since he was old enough to know, big boy
Doing a man's work, though a child at heart—
He saw all spoiled. "Don't let him cut my hand off—   25
The doctor, when he comes. Don't let him, sister!"
So. But the hand was gone already.
The doctor put him in the dark of ether.
He lay and puffed his lips out with his breath.
And then—the watcher at his pulse took fright.   30
No one believed. They listened at his heart.
Little—less—nothing!—and that ended it.
No more to build on there. And they, since they
Were not the one dead, turned to their affairs.

"Out, Out—." The title of this poem echoes the words of Shakespeare's Macbeth on receiving news that his queen is dead: "Out, out, brief candle! / Life's but a walking shadow, a poor player / That struts and frets his hour upon the stage / And then is heard no more. It is a tale / Told by an idiot, full of sound and fury, / Signifying nothing" (*Macbeth* 5.5.23–28).

Questions

1. How does Frost make the buzz-saw appear sinister? How does he make it seem, in another way, like a friend?

2. What do you make of the people who surround the boy—the "they" of the poem? Who might they be? Do they seem to you concerned and compassionate, cruel, indifferent, or what?

3. What does Frost's reference to *Macbeth* contribute to your understanding of "'Out, Out—'"? How would you state the theme of Frost's poem?

4. Set this poem beside "Sir Patrick Spence." How does "'Out, Out—'" resemble or differ from that medieval folk ballad in subject? How is Frost's poem similar or different in its way of telling a story?

DRAMATIC POETRY

A third kind of poetry is **dramatic poetry**, which presents the voice of an imaginary character (or characters) speaking directly, without any additional narration by the author.

A dramatic poem, according to T. S. Eliot, does not consist of "what the poet would say in his own person, but only what he can say within the limits of one imaginary character addressing another imaginary character." Strictly speaking, the term *dramatic poetry* describes any verse written for the stage (and until a few centuries ago most playwrights, like Shakespeare and Molière, wrote their plays mainly in verse).

Dramatic Monologue

The term *dramatic poetry* most often refers to the **dramatic monologue**, a poem written as a speech made by a character (other than the author) at some decisive moment. A dramatic monologue is usually addressed by the speaker to some other character who remains silent. If the listener replies, the poem becomes a dialogue (such as Thomas Hardy's "The Ruined Maid" in Chapter 17) in which the story unfolds in the conversation between two speakers.

The Victorian poet Robert Browning, who developed the form of the dramatic monologue, liked to put words in the mouths of characters who were conspicuously nasty, weak, reckless, or crazy: see, for instance, Browning's "Soliloquy of the Spanish Cloister" (Chapter 34), in which the speaker is an obsessively proud and jealous monk. The dramatic monologue has been a popular form among American poets, including Edwin Arlington Robinson, Robert Frost, Ezra Pound, Randall Jarrell, Sylvia Plath, and David Mason. The most famous dramatic monologue ever written is probably Browning's "My Last Duchess," in which the poet conjures up a Renaissance Italian duke whose words reveal much more about himself than the aristocratic speaker intends.

Robert Browning (1812–1889)

My Last Duchess   1842

Ferrara

That's my last Duchess painted on the wall,
Looking as if she were alive. I call
That piece a wonder, now: Frà Pandolf's hands
Worked busily a day, and there she stands.
Will't please you sit and look at her? I said   5
"Frà Pandolf" by design, for never read
Strangers like you that pictured countenance,
The depth and passion of its earnest glance,
But to myself they turned (since none puts by
The curtain I have drawn for you, but I)   10
And seemed as they would ask me, if they durst,
How such a glance came there; so, not the first
Are you to turn and ask thus. Sir, 'twas not
Her husband's presence only, called that spot
Of joy into the Duchess' cheek: perhaps   15
Frà Pandolf chanced to say, "Her mantle laps
Over my lady's wrist too much," or "Paint
Must never hope to reproduce the faint
Half-flush that dies along her throat": such stuff
Was courtesy, she thought, and cause enough   20
For calling up that spot of joy. She had
A heart—how shall I say?—too soon made glad,
Too easily impressed; she liked whate'er
She looked on, and her looks went everywhere.
Sir, 'twas all one! My favor at her breast,   25
The dropping of the daylight in the West,
The bough of cherries some officious fool
Broke in the orchard for her, the white mule
She rode with round the terrace—all and each
Would draw from her alike the approving speech,   30
Or blush, at least. She thanked men,—good! but thanked
Somehow—I know not how—as if she ranked
My gift of a nine-hundred-years-old name
With anybody's gift. Who'd stoop to blame
This sort of trifling? Even had you skill   35

In speech—(which I have not)—to make your will
Quite clear to such an one, and say, "Just this
Or that in you disgusts me; here you miss,
Or there exceed the mark"—and if she let
Herself be lessoned so, nor plainly set   40
Her wits to yours, forsooth, and made excuse,
—E'en then would be some stooping; and I choose
Never to stoop. Oh sir, she smiled, no doubt,
Whene'er I passed her; but who passed without
Much the same smile? This grew; I gave commands;   45
Then all smiles stopped together. There she stands
As if alive. Will't please you rise? We'll meet
The company below, then. I repeat,
The Count your master's known munificence
Is ample warrant that no just pretense   50
Of mine for dowry will be disallowed;
Though his fair daughter's self, as I avowed
At starting, is my object. Nay, we'll go
Together down, sir. Notice Neptune, though,
Taming a sea-horse, thought a rarity,   55
Which Claus of Innsbruck cast in bronze for me!

MY LAST DUCHESS. Ferrara, a city in northern Italy, is the scene. Browning may have modeled his
speaker after Alonzo, Duke of Ferrara (1533–1598). 3 *Frà Pandolf* and 56 *Claus of Innsbruck:* names
of fictitious artists.

Questions

1. Whom is the Duke addressing? What is this person's business in Ferrara?
2. What is the Duke's opinion of his last Duchess's personality? Do we see her character differently?
3. If the Duke was unhappy with the Duchess's behavior, why didn't he make his displeasure known? Cite a specific passage to explain his reticence.
4. How much do we know about the fate of the last Duchess? Would it help our understanding of the poem to know more?
5. Does Browning imply any connection between the Duke's art collection and his attitude toward his wife?

DIDACTIC POETRY

More fashionable in former times was a fourth variety of poetry, **didactic poetry:** poetry or verse written to state a message or teach a body of knowledge. In a lyric, a speaker may express sadness; in a didactic poem, he or she may explain that sadness is inherent in life. Poems that impart a body of knowledge, such as Ovid's *Art of Love* and Lucretius's *On the Nature of Things*, are didactic. Such instructive poetry was favored especially by classical Latin poets and by English poets of the eighteenth century. In *The Fleece* (1757), John Dyer celebrated the British woolen industry and included practical advice on raising sheep:

In cold stiff soils the bleaters oft complain
Of gouty ails, by shepherds termed the halt:
Those let the neighboring fold or ready crook
Detain, and pour into their cloven feet
Corrosive drugs, deep-searching arsenic,
Dry alum, verdigris, or vitriol keen.

One might agree with Dr. Johnson's comment on Dyer's effort: "The subject, Sir, cannot be made poetical." But it may be argued that the subject of didactic poetry does not make it any less poetical. Good poems, it seems, can be written about anything under the sun. Like Dyer, John Milton described sick sheep in "Lycidas," a poem few readers have thought unpoetic:

The hungry sheep look up, and are not fed,
But, swoll'n with wind and the rank mist they draw,
Rot inwardly, and foul contagion spread . . .

What makes Milton's lines better poetry than Dyer's is, among other things, a difference in attitude. Sick sheep to Dyer mean the loss of a few shillings and pence; to Milton, whose sheep stand for English Christendom, they mean a moral catastrophe.

■ WRITING *effectively*

Adrienne Rich on Writing

Recalling "Aunt Jennifer's Tigers"   1971

I know that my style was formed first by male poets: by the men I was reading as an undergraduate—Frost, Dylan Thomas, Donne, Auden, MacNeice, Stevens, Yeats. What I chiefly learned from them was craft. But poems are like dreams: in them you put what you don't know you know. Looking back at poems I wrote before I was 21, I'm startled because beneath the conscious craft are glimpses of the split I even then experienced between the girl who wrote poems, who defined herself in writing poems, and the girl who was to define herself by her relationships with men. "Aunt Jennifer's Tigers," written while I was a student, looks with deliberate detachment at this split. In writing this poem, composed and appar-

Adrienne Rich

ently cool as it is, I thought I was creating a portrait of an imaginary woman. But this woman suffers from the opposition of her imagination, worked out in tapestry, and her life-style, "ringed with ordeals she was mastered by." It was important to me that Aunt Jennifer was a person as distinct from myself as possible—distanced by the formalism of the poem, by its objective, observant tone—even by putting the woman in a different generation.

In those years formalism was part of the strategy—like asbestos gloves, it allowed me to handle materials I couldn't pick up bare-handed.

From "When We Dead Awaken: Writing as Re-Vision"

THINKING ABOUT PARAPHRASING

A poet takes pains to choose each word of a poem for both its sound and its exact shade of meaning. Since a poem's full effect is so completely wedded to its precise wording, some would say that no poem can be truly paraphrased. But even though it represents an imperfect approximation of the real thing, a paraphrase can be useful to write and read. It can clearly map out a poem's key images, actions, and ideas. A map is no substitute for a landscape, but a good map often helps us find our way through the landscape without getting lost.

William Stafford (1914–1993)

Ask Me   1975

Some time when the river is ice ask me
mistakes I have made. Ask me whether
what I have done is my life. Others
have come in their slow way into
my thought, and some have tried to help   5
or to hurt—ask me what difference
their strongest love or hate has made.

I will listen to what you say.
You and I can turn and look
at the silent river and wait. We know   10
the current is there, hidden; and there
are comings and goings from miles away
that hold the stillness exactly before us.
What the river says, that is what I say.

William Stafford (1914–1993)

A Paraphrase of "Ask Me"   1977

I think my poem can be paraphrased—and that any poem can be paraphrased. But every pass through the material, using other words, would have to be achieved at certain costs, either in momentum, or nuance, or dangerously explicit (and therefore misleading in tone) adjustments. I'll try one such pass through the poem:

> When it's quiet and cold and we have some chance to interchange without
> hurry, confront me if you like with a challenge about whether I think I have
> made mistakes in my life—and ask me, if you want to, whether to me my
> life is actually the sequence of events or exploits others would see. Well,

those others tag along in my living, and some of them in fact have played significant roles in the narrative run of my world; they have intended either helping or hurting (but by implication in the way I am saying this you will know that neither effort is conclusive). So—ask me how important their good or bad intentions have been (both intentions get a drastic *leveling* judgment from this cool stating of it all). You, too, will be entering that realm of maybe-help-maybe-hurt, by entering that far into my life by asking this serious question—so: I will stay still and consider. Out there will be the world confronting us both; we will both know we are surrounded by mystery, tremendous things that do not reveal themselves to us. That river, that world—and our lives—all share the depth and stillness of much more significance than our talk, or intentions. There is a steadiness and somehow a solace in knowing that what is around us so greatly surpasses our human concerns.

From "Ask Me"

CHECKLIST: Writing a Paraphrase

☐ **Read the poem closely.** It is important to read it more than once to understand it well.

☐ **Go through it line by line.** Don't skip lines or stanzas or any key details. In your own words, what does each line say?

☐ **Write your paraphrase as prose.**

☐ **State the poem's literal meaning.** Don't worry about deeper meanings.

☐ **Reread your statement to see if you have missed anything important.** Check to see if you have captured the overall significance of the poem along with the details.

TOPICS FOR WRITING ON PARAPHRASING

1. Paraphrase any short poem from Chapter 34, "Poems for Further Reading." Be sure to do a careful line-by-line reading. Include the most vital points and details, and state the poem's main thought or theme without quoting any original passage.

2. In a paragraph, contrast William Stafford's poem with his paraphrase. What does the poem offer that the paraphrase does not? What, then, is the value of the paraphrase?

3. Write a two-page paraphrase of the events described in "'Out, Out—.'" Then take your paraphrase further: summarize the poem's message in a single sentence.

▶ **TERMS FOR** *review*

Analytic Terms

Verse ▶ This term has two major meanings. It refers to any single line of poetry or to any composition written in separate lines of more or less regular rhythm, in contrast to prose.

Paraphrase ▶ The restatement in one's own words of what one understands a poem to say or suggest. A paraphrase is similar to a summary, although not as brief or simple.

Summary ▶ A brief condensation of the main idea or plot of a work. A summary is similar to a paraphrase, but less detailed.

Subject ▶ The main topic of a work, whatever the work is "about."

Theme ▶ A generally recurring subject or idea noticeably evident in a literary work. Not all subjects in a work can be considered themes, only the central one(s).

Types of Poetry

Lyric poem ▶ A short poem expressing the thoughts and feelings of a single speaker. Often written in the first person, it traditionally has a songlike immediacy and emotional force.

Narrative poem ▶ A poem that tells a story. **Epics** and **ballads** are two common forms of narrative poetry.

Dramatic monologue ▶ A poem written as a speech made by a character at some decisive moment. The speaker is usually addressing a silent listener.

Didactic poem ▶ A poem intended to teach a moral lesson or impart a body of knowledge.

16

LISTENING TO A VOICE

Irony is that little pinch of salt
which alone makes the dish palatable.

—JOHANN WOLFGANG VON GOETHE

What You Will Learn in This Chapter

- To identify the speaker in a poem
- To understand and characterize the *tone* of a poem
- To define *irony* in its major forms
- To analyze the role of a *persona* in a poem

TONE

In old Western movies, when one hombre taunts another, it is customary for the second to drawl, "Smile when you say that, pardner" or "Mister, I don't like your tone of voice." Sometimes in reading a poem, although we can neither see a face nor hear a voice, we can infer the poet's attitude from other evidence.

Like tone of voice, **tone** in literature often conveys an attitude toward the person addressed. Like the manner of a person, the manner of a poem may be friendly or belligerent toward its reader, condescending or respectful. Again like tone of voice, the tone of a poem may tell us how the speaker feels about himself or herself: cocksure or humble, sad or glad. But usually when we ask "What is the tone of a poem?" we mean "What attitude does the poet take toward a theme or a subject?" Is the poet being affectionate, hostile, earnest, playful, sarcastic, or what? We may never be able to know, of course, the poet's personal feelings. All we need know is how to feel when we read the poem.

Strictly speaking, tone isn't an attitude; it is whatever in the poem makes an attitude clear to us: the choice of certain words instead of others, the picking out of certain details. In A. E. Housman's "Loveliest of trees" (Chapter 34), for example, the poet communicates his admiration for a cherry tree's beauty by singling out its white blossoms for attention; had he wanted to show his dislike for the tree, he might have concentrated on its broken branches, birdlime, or snails. To perceive the tone of a poem rightly, we need to read the poem carefully, paying attention to whatever suggestions we find in it.

Theodore Roethke (1908–1963)

My Papa's Waltz   1948

The whiskey on your breath
Could make a small boy dizzy;
But I hung on like death:
Such waltzing was not easy.

We romped until the pans 5
Slid from the kitchen shelf;
My mother's countenance
Could not unfrown itself.

The hand that held my wrist
Was battered on one knuckle; 10
At every step you missed
My right ear scraped a buckle.

You beat time on my head
With a palm caked hard by dirt,
Then waltzed me off to bed 15
Still clinging to your shirt.

What is the tone of this poem? Most readers find the speaker's attitude toward his father critical, but nonetheless affectionate. They take this recollection of childhood to be an odd but happy one. Other readers, however, concentrate on other details, such as the father's rough manners and drunkenness. One reader has written that "Roethke expresses his resentment for his father, a drunken brute with dirty hands and whiskey breath who carelessly hurt the child's ear and manhandled him." Although this reader accurately noticed some of the events in the poem and perceived that there was something desperate in the son's hanging onto the father "like death," he simplifies the tone of the poem and so misses its humorous side.

While "My Papa's Waltz" contains the dark elements of manhandling and drunkenness, the tone remains grotesquely comic. The rollicking rhythms of the poem underscore Roethke's complex humor—half loving and half censuring of the unwashed, intoxicated father. The humor is further reinforced by playful rimes such as *dizzy* and *easy*, *knuckle* and *buckle*, as well as the joyful suggestions of the words *waltz*, *waltzing*, and *romped*. The scene itself is comic, with kitchen pans falling because of the father's roughhousing while the mother looks on unamused. However much the speaker satirizes the overly rambunctious father, he does not have the boy identify with the soberly disapproving mother. Not all comedy is comfortable and reassuring. Certainly, this small boy's family life has its frightening side, but the last line suggests the boy is *still clinging* to his father with persistent if also complicated love.

Satiric Poetry

"My Papa's Waltz," though it includes lifelike details that aren't pretty, has a tone relatively easy to recognize. So does **satiric poetry**, a kind of comic poetry that generally conveys a message. Usually its tone is one of detached amusement, withering contempt, and implied superiority. In a satiric poem, the poet ridicules some person or persons (or perhaps some type of human behavior), examining the victim by the light of certain principles and implying that the reader, too, ought to feel contempt for the victim.

Stephen Crane (1871–1900)

The Wayfarer 1899

The wayfarer,
Perceiving the pathway to truth,
Was struck with astonishment.

It was thickly grown with weeds.
"Ha," he said,   5
"I see that none has passed here
In a long time."
Later he saw that each weed
Was a singular knife.
"Well," he mumbled at last,   10
"Doubtless there are other roads."

Questions

1. What is Crane's message?
2. How would you characterize the tone of this poem? Disillusioned? Amused?

A Spectrum of Tones

In some poems the poet's attitude may be plain enough, while in other poems attitudes may be so mingled that it is hard to describe them tersely without doing injustice to the poem. Does Andrew Marvell in "To His Coy Mistress" (Chapter 34) take a serious or playful attitude toward the fact that he and his lady are destined to be food for worms? No one-word answer will suffice. And what of T. S. Eliot's "The Love Song of J. Alfred Prufrock" (Chapter 33)? In his attitude toward his redemption-seeking hero who wades with trousers rolled, Eliot is seriously funny. Such a mingled tone may be seen in the following poem by the wife of a governor of the Massachusetts Bay Colony and the earliest American poet of note. Anne Bradstreet's first book, *The Tenth Muse Lately Sprung Up in America* (1650), had been published in England without her consent. She wrote these lines to preface a second edition.

Anne Bradstreet   (1612?–1672)

The Author to Her Book   1678

Thou ill-formed offspring of my feeble brain,
Who after birth did'st by my side remain,
Till snatched from thence by friends, less wise than true,
Who thee abroad exposed to public view;
Made thee in rags, halting, to the press to trudge,   5
Where errors were not lessened, all may judge.
At thy return my blushing was not small,
My rambling brat (in print) should mother call;
I cast thee by as one unfit for light,
Thy visage was so irksome in my sight;   10
Yet being mine own, at length affection would
Thy blemishes amend, if so I could:
I washed thy face, but more defects I saw,
And rubbing off a spot, still made a flaw.
I stretched thy joints to make thee even feet,   15
Yet still thou run'st more hobbling than is meet;
In better dress to trim thee was my mind,

But nought save homespun cloth in the house I find.
In this array, 'mongst vulgars may'st thou roam;
In critics' hands beware thou dost not come;   20
And take thy way where yet thou are not known.
If for thy Father asked, say thou had'st none;
And for thy Mother, she alas is poor,
Which caused her thus to send thee out of door.

In the author's comparison of her book to an illegitimate ragamuffin, we may be struck by the details of scrubbing and dressing a child: details that might well occur to a mother who had scrubbed and dressed many. As she might feel toward such a child, so she feels toward her book. She starts by deploring it, but, as the poem goes on, cannot deny it her affection. Humor enters (as in the pun in line 15). She must dress the creature in *homespun cloth*, something both crude and serviceable. By the end of her poem, Bradstreet seems to regard her book-child with tenderness, amusement, and a certain indulgent awareness of its faults. To read this poem is to sense its mingling of several attitudes. A poet can be merry and in earnest at the same time.

Rhina Espaillat (b. 1932)

Bilingual/*Bilingüe*   1998

My father liked them separate, one there,
one here (*allá y aquí*), as if aware

that words might cut in two his daughter's heart
(*el corazón*) and lock the alien part

to what he was—his memory, his name   5
(*su nombre*)—with a key he could not claim.

"English outside this door, Spanish inside,"
he said, "*y basta*." But who can divide

the world, the word (*mundo y palabra*) from
any child? I knew how to be dumb   10

and stubborn (*testaruda*); late, in bed,
I hoarded secret syllables I read

until my tongue (*mi lengua*) learned to run
where his stumbled. And still the heart was one.

I like to think he knew that, even when,   15
proud (*orgulloso*) of his daughter's pen,

he stood outside *mis versos*, half in fear
of words he loved but wanted not to hear.

Questions

1. Espaillat's poem is full of Spanish words and phrases. (Even the title is given in both languages.) What does the Spanish add to the poem? Could we remove the phrases without changing the poem?
2. How does the father want to divide his daughter's world, at least in terms of language? Does his request suggest any other divisions he hopes to enforce in her life?
3. How does the daughter respond to her father's request to leave English outside their home?
4. "And still the heart was one," states the speaker of the poem. Should we take her statement at face value or do we sense a cost to her bilingual existence? Agree or disagree with the daughter's statement, but state the reasons for your opinion.

Franz Wright (1953–2015)

Alcohol   1989

You do look a little ill.

But we can do something about that, now.

Can't we.

The fact is you're a shocking wreck.

Do you hear me.   5

You aren't all alone.

And you could use some help today, packing in the dark, boarding buses
    north, putting the seat back and grinning with terror flowing over your
    legs through your fingers and hair . . .

I was always waiting, always here.

Know anyone else who can say that?

My advice to you is think of her for what she is: one more name cut in the   10
    scar of your tongue.

What was it you said, "To rather be harmed than harm is not abject."

Please.

Can we be leaving now.

We like bus trips, remember. Together

we could watch these winter fields slip past, and never care again,   15

think of it.

I don't have to be anywhere.

Questions

1. Who or what is the speaker in the poem? Who is being addressed?
2. Does the poem provide clues toward a backstory, a conflict, or a situation?
3. What is the effect of the unusual spacing and the often ungrammatical punctuation?

Gwendolyn Brooks (1917–2000)

Speech to the Young. Speech to the Progress-Toward.   1970/1987

(Among them Nora and Henry III)

Say to them,
say to the down-keepers,
the sun-slappers,
the self-soilers,
the harmony-hushers,   5
"Even if you are not ready for day
it cannot always be night."
You will be right.
For that is the hard home-run.
                                                                10
Live not for battles won.
Live not for the-end-of-the-song.
Live in the along.

SPEECH TO THE YOUNG. SPEECH TO THE PROGRESS-TOWARD. *Nora and Henry III:* Brooks's two
children, Nora (b. 1951) and Henry III (b. 1940).

Questions

1. This poem was the concluding text in Brooks's 1970 chapbook *Family Pictures.* In what
   sense, then, is this a poem about family relationships?
2. Explain, in the context of the poem, the epithets in lines 2–5.
3. Why is the attitude affirmed in the poem described as "hard" (line 9)?
4. How would you paraphrase the theme of this poem?

Weldon Kees (1914–1955)

For My Daughter   1940

Looking into my daughter's eyes I read
Beneath the innocence of morning flesh
Concealed, hintings of death she does not heed.
Coldest of winds have blown this hair, and mesh
Of seaweed snarled these miniatures of hands;   5
The night's slow poison, tolerant and bland,
Has moved her blood. Parched years that I have seen
That may be hers appear: foul, lingering
Death in certain war, the slim legs green.
Or, fed on hate, she relishes the sting   10
Of others' agony; perhaps the cruel
Bride of a syphilitic or a fool.
These speculations sour in the sun.
I have no daughter. I desire none.

Questions

1. How does the last line of this sonnet affect the meaning of the poem?
2. "For My Daughter" was first published in 1940. What considerations might a potential
   American parent have felt at that time? Are these historical concerns mirrored in the poem?

3. Donald Justice has said that "Kees is one of the bitterest poets in history." Is bitterness the only attitude the speaker reveals in this poem?

THE SPEAKER IN THE POEM

The tone of a poem, we said, is like tone of voice in that both communicate feelings. Still, this comparison raises a question: when we read a poem, whose "voice" speaks to us?

"The poet's" is one possible answer; and in the case of many a poem that answer may be right. Reading Anne Bradstreet's "The Author to Her Book," we can be reasonably sure that the poet speaks of her very own book, and of her own experiences. In order to read a poem, we seldom need to read a poet's biography; but in truth there are certain poems whose full effect depends upon our knowing at least a fact or two of the poet's life. Here is one such poem.

Natasha Trethewey (b. 1966)

White Lies   2000

The lies I could tell,
when I was growing up
light-bright, near-white,
high-yellow, red-boned
in a black place,   5
were just white lies.

I could easily tell the white folks
that we lived uptown,
not in that pink and green
shanty-fied shotgun section   10
along the tracks. I could act
like my homemade dresses
came straight out the window
of Maison Blanche. I could even
keep quiet, quiet as kept,   15
like the time a white girl said
(squeezing my hand), *Now
we have three of us in this class.*

But I paid for it every time
Mama found out.   20
She laid her hands on me,
then washed out my mouth
with Ivory soap. *This
is to purify,* she said,
and cleanse your lying tongue.   25
Believing her, I swallowed suds
thinking they'd work
from the inside out.

Through its pattern of vivid color imagery, Trethewey's poem tells of a black child light enough to "pass for white" in a society that was still extremely race-sensitive. But knowing the author's family background gives us a deeper insight into the levels of meaning in the poem. Trethewey was born in Mississippi in 1966, at a time when her parents' interracial marriage was a criminal act in that state. On her birth certificate, her mother's race was given as "colored"; in the box intended to record the race of her father—who was white and had been born in Nova Scotia—appeared the word "Canadian" (although her parents divorced before she began grade school, she remained extremely close to both of them). Trethewey has said of her birth certificate: "Something is left out of the official record that way. The irony isn't lost on me. Even in documenting myself as a person there is a little fiction." "White Lies" succeeds admirably on its own, but these biographical details allow us to read it as an even more complex meditation on issues of racial definition and personal identity in America.

Persona

Most of us can tell the difference between a person we meet in life and a person we meet in a work of art. And yet, in reading poems, we are liable to temptation. When the poet says "I," we may want to assume that he or she is making a personal statement. But reflect: do all poems have to be personal? Here is a brief poem inscribed on the tombstone of an infant in Burial Hill Cemetery, Plymouth, Massachusetts:

> Since I have been so quickly done for,
> I wonder what I was begun for.

We do not know who wrote those lines, but it is clear that the poet was not a short-lived infant writing from personal experience. In some poems, the speaker is obviously a **persona**, or fictitious character: not the poet, but the poet's creation. As a grown man, William Blake, a skilled professional engraver, wrote a poem in the voice of a boy, an illiterate chimney sweeper. (The poem appears later in this chapter.)

Let's consider a poem spoken not by a poet, but by a persona—in this case a mysterious one. Edwin Arlington Robinson's "Luke Havergal" is a dramatic monologue, but the identity of the speaker is never clearly stated. In 1905, upon first reading the poem in Robinson's *The Children of the Night* (1897), President Theodore Roosevelt was so moved that he wrote an essay about the book that made the author famous. Roosevelt, however, admitted that he found the musically seductive poem difficult. "I am not sure I understand 'Luke Havergal,'" he wrote, "but I am entirely sure I like it." Possibly what most puzzled our twenty-sixth president was who was speaking in the poem. How much does Robinson let us know about the voice and the person it addresses?

Edwin Arlington Robinson (1869–1935)

Luke Havergal   1897

Go to the western gate, Luke Havergal,
There where the vines cling crimson on the wall,
And in the twilight wait for what will come.
The leaves will whisper there of her, and some,

Like flying words, will strike you as they fall;   5
But go, and if you listen she will call.
Go to the western gate, Luke Havergal—
Luke Havergal.

No, there is not a dawn in eastern skies
To rift the fiery night that's in your eyes;   10
But there, where western glooms are gathering,
The dark will end the dark, if anything:
God slays Himself with every leaf that flies,
And hell is more than half of paradise.
No, there is not a dawn in eastern skies—   15
In eastern skies.

Out of a grave I come to tell you this,
Out of a grave I come to quench the kiss
That flames upon your forehead with a glow
That blinds you to the way that you must go.   20
Yes, there is yet one way to where she is,
Bitter, but one that faith may never miss.
Out of a grave I come to tell you this—
To tell you this.

There is the western gate, Luke Havergal,   25
There are the crimson leaves upon the wall.
Go, for the winds are tearing them away,—
Nor think to riddle the dead words they say,
Nor any more to feel them as they fall;
But go, and if you trust her she will call.   30
There is the western gate, Luke Havergal—
Luke Havergal.

Questions

1. Who is the speaker of the poem? What specific details does the author reveal about the speaker?
2. What does the speaker ask Luke Havergal to do?
3. What do you understand "the western gate" to be?
4. Would you advise Luke Havergal to follow the speaker's advice? Why or why not?

No literary law decrees that the speaker in a poem even has to be human. Good poems have been uttered by clouds, pebbles, clocks, and animals. Here is a comic poem spoken by man's best friend, a dog.

Anonymous

Dog Haiku   2001

Today I sniffed
Many dog behinds—I celebrate
By kissing your face.

                                   *

I sound the alarm!
Garbage man—come to kill us all—   5
Look! Look! Look! Look! Look!

                                   *

How do I love thee?
The ways are numberless as
My hairs on the rug.

                                   *

I sound the alarm!
Paper boy—come to kill us all—   10
Look! Look! Look! Look! Look!

                                   *

I am your best friend,
Now, always, and especially
When you are eating.   15

Questions

1. Who is the "I" in the poem? Who is the "you"?
2. Do you recognize the allusion in lines 7–9?
3. What elements create the humorous effect of the poem?

A Classic Poem and Its Source

In a famous definition, William Wordsworth calls poetry "the spontaneous overflow of powerful feelings . . . recollected in tranquillity." But in the case of the following poem, Wordsworth's feelings weren't all his; they didn't just overflow spontaneously; and the process of tranquil recollection had to go on for years.

William Wordsworth (1770–1850)

I Wandered Lonely as a Cloud   (1807) 1815

I wandered lonely as a cloud
That floats on high o'er vales and hills,
When all at once I saw a crowd,
A host, of golden daffodils,
Beside the lake, beneath the trees,   5
Fluttering and dancing in the breeze.

Continuous as the stars that shine
And twinkle on the milky way,
They stretched in never-ending line
Along the margin of a bay: 10
Ten thousand saw I at a glance,
Tossing their heads in sprightly dance.

The waves beside them danced; but they
Out-did the sparkling waves in glee;
A poet could not but be gay,   15
In such a jocund company;
I gazed—and gazed—but little thought
What wealth the show to me had brought:

For oft, when on my couch I lie
In vacant or in pensive mood,   20
They flash upon that inward eye
Which is the bliss of solitude;
And then my heart with pleasure fills,
And dances with the daffodils.

Between the first printing of the poem in 1807 and the version of 1815 given here, Wordsworth made several deliberate improvements. He changed *dancing* to *golden* in line 4, *Along* to *Beside* in line 5, *Ten thousand* to *Fluttering and* in line 6, and *laughing* to *jocund* in line 16, and he added a whole stanza (the second). In fact, the writing of the poem was unspontaneous enough for Wordsworth, at a loss for lines 21–22, to take them from his wife, Mary. It is likely that the experience of daffodil-watching was not entirely his to begin with but was derived in part from the recollections his sister, Dorothy Wordsworth, had set down in her journal on April 15, 1802, two years before he first drafted his poem.

Dorothy Wordsworth   (1771–1855)

Journal Entry   1802

When we were in the woods beyond Gowbarrow Park we saw a few daffodils close to the water-side. We fancied that the lake had floated the seeds ashore, and that the little colony had so sprung up. But as we went along there were more and yet more; and at last, under the boughs of the trees, we saw that there was a long belt of them along the shore, about the breadth of a country turnpike road. I never saw daffodils so beautiful. They grew among the mossy stones about and about them; some rested their heads upon these stones as on a pillow for weariness; and the rest tossed and reeled and danced, and seemed as if they verily laughed with the wind, that blew upon them over the Lake; they looked so gay, ever glancing, ever changing. This wind blew directly over the Lake to them. There was here and there a little knot, and a few stragglers a few yards higher up; but they were so few as not to disturb the simplicity, unity, and life of that one busy highway.

Notice that Wordsworth's poem echoes a few of his sister's observations. Weaving poetry out of their mutual memories, Wordsworth has offered the experience as if it were altogether his own, made himself lonely, and left Dorothy out. The point is not that Wordsworth is a liar or a plagiarist but that, like any other good poet, he has transformed ordinary life into art. A process of interpreting, shaping, and ordering had to intervene between the experience of looking at daffodils and the finished poem.

The Art of Imagination

We need not deny that a poet's experience can contribute to a poem or that the emotion in the poem can indeed be the poet's. Still, to write a good poem one has to do more than live and feel. Writing poetry takes skill and imagination—qualities that extensive travel and wide experience do not necessarily give. Emily Dickinson seldom strayed from her family's house and grounds in Amherst, Massachusetts, yet her rimed life studies of a snake, a bee, and a hummingbird contain more poetry than we find in any firsthand description (so far) of the surface of the moon.

Karen An-hwei Lee (b. 1973)

Rainfall   2002

I wonder what is seen when it is raining. In the streets, the birds flying up—I hear them; and the children running; the leaves shivering, turning up lighter sides; rain skirting the curbs, rushing through open gutters, washed under, to the open sea; the long legs of a bird flying up, the tumult of rain closing, the sky's heart roving, and great cool light ensuing.

Questions

1. From the details the poet chooses, what do you suppose are her feelings about rain?
2. How would you describe the tone of the poem?
3. What is the effect of the poem being set as one long line, rather than being split into short lines and stanzas? Does it alter the cadence with which you read it?

William Carlos Williams (1883–1963)

The Red Wheelbarrow   1923

so much depends
upon

a red wheel
barrow

glazed with rain   5
water

beside the white
chickens

Experiment: Reading With and Without Biography

1. Write a paragraph summing up your initial reactions to "The Red Wheelbarrow."
2. Now write a second paragraph with the benefit of this snippet of biographical information: Inspiration for this poem apparently came to Dr. Williams as he was gazing from the window of a house where one of his patients, a small girl, lay suspended between life and death.[1] How does this information affect your reading of the poem?

IRONY

To see a distinction between the poet and the words of a fictitious character—between Robert Browning and "My Last Duchess"—is to be aware of **irony**: a manner of speaking that implies a discrepancy. If the mask says one thing and we sense that

---

[1]This account, from the director of the public library in Williams's native Rutherford, New Jersey, is given by Geri M. Rhodes in "The Paterson Metaphor in William Carlos Williams's *Paterson*," master's thesis, Tufts University, 1965.

the writer is in fact saying something else, the writer has adopted an **ironic point of view**. No finer illustration exists in English than Jonathan Swift's "A Modest Proposal," an essay in which Swift speaks as an earnest, humorless citizen who sets forth his reasonable plan to aid the Irish poor. The plan is so monstrous no sane reader can assent to it: the poor are to sell their children as meat for the tables of their landlords. From behind his false face, Swift is actually recommending not cannibalism but love and Christian charity.

A poem is often made complicated and more interesting by another kind of irony. **Verbal irony** occurs whenever words say one thing but mean something else, usually the opposite. The word *love* means *hate* here: "I just *love* to stay home and scroll through Instagram on a Saturday night!"

Sarcasm

When verbal irony is conspicuously bitter, heavy-handed, and mocking, it is defined as **sarcasm**: "Oh, he's the biggest spender in the world, all right!" (The sarcasm, if that statement were spoken, would be underscored by the speaker's tone of voice.) A famous instance of sarcasm occurs in Shakespeare's *Julius Caesar* in Mark Antony's oration over the body of the slain Caesar: "Brutus is an honorable man." Antony repeats this line until the enraged populace begins shouting exactly what he means to call Brutus and the other conspirators: traitors, villains, murderers. We had best be alert for irony on the printed page, for if we miss it, our interpretations of a poem may go wild.

Robert Creeley (1926–2005)

Oh No   1959

If you wander far enough
you will come to it
and when you get there
they will give you a place to sit

for yourself only, in a nice chair,   5
and all your friends will be there
with smiles on their faces
and they will likewise all have places.

This poem is rich in verbal irony. The title helps point out that between the speaker's words and attitude lie deep differences. In line 2, what is *it*? Old age? The wandering suggests a conventional metaphor: the journey of life. Is *it* literally a rest home for "senior citizens," or perhaps some naïve popular concept of heaven (such as we meet in comic strips: harps, angels with hoops for halos) in which the saved all sit around in a ring, smugly congratulating one another? We can't be sure, but the speaker's attitude toward this final sitting-place is definite. It is a place for the selfish, as we infer from the phrase *for yourself only*. And *smiles on their faces* may hint that the smiles are unchanging and forced. There is a difference between saying "They had smiles on their faces" and "They smiled": the latter suggests that the smiles came from within. The word *nice* is to be regarded with distrust. If we see through this speaker, as Creeley implies we can, we realize that, while pretending to be sweet-talking us into a seat, actually he is revealing the horror of a little hell. And the title is the poet's reaction to it (or the speaker's unironic, straightforward one): "Oh no! Not *that*!"

Dramatic Irony

Dramatic irony, like verbal irony, contains an element of contrast, but it usually refers to a situation in a play wherein a character whose knowledge is limited says, does, or encounters something of greater significance than he or she knows. We, the spectators, realize the meaning of this speech or action, for the playwright has afforded us superior knowledge. In Sophocles's *Oedipus the King*, when Oedipus vows to punish whoever has brought down a plague upon the city of Thebes, we know—as he does not—that the man he would punish is himself. The situation of Oedipus also contains **cosmic irony**, or **irony of fate**: some Fate with a grim sense of humor seems cruelly to trick a human being. Cosmic irony clearly exists in poems in which fate or the Fates are personified and seen as hostile, as in Thomas Hardy's "The Convergence of the Twain" (Chapter 34); and it may be said to occur also in Robinson's "Richard Cory" (Chapter 21). Obviously it is a twist of fate for the most envied man in town to kill himself.

To sum up: the effect of irony depends on the reader's noticing some incongruity or discrepancy between two things. In *verbal irony*, there is a contrast between the speaker's words and meaning; in an *ironic point of view*, between the writer's attitude and what is spoken by a fictitious character; in *dramatic irony*, between the limited knowledge of a character and the fuller knowledge of the reader or spectator; in *cosmic irony*, between a character's position or aspiration and the treatment he or she receives at the hands of Fate. Although, in the work of an inept poet, irony can be crude and obvious sarcasm, it is invaluable to a poet of more complicated mind, who imagines more than one perspective.

W. H. Auden (1907–1973)

The Unknown Citizen   1940

> (To JS/07/M/378
> *This Marble Monument Is Erected by the State*)

He was found by the Bureau of Statistics to be
One against whom there was no official complaint,
And all the reports on his conduct agree
That, in the modern sense of an old-fashioned word, he was a saint,
For in everything he did he served the Greater Community.   5
Except for the War till the day he retired
He worked in a factory and never got fired,
But satisfied his employers, Fudge Motors Inc.
Yet he wasn't a scab or odd in his views,
For his Union reports that he paid his dues,   10
(Our report on his Union shows it was sound)
And our Social Psychology workers found
That he was popular with his mates and liked a drink.
The Press are convinced that he bought a paper every day
And that his reactions to advertisements were normal in every way.   15
Policies taken out in his name prove that he was fully insured,
And his Health-card shows he was once in hospital but left it cured.
Both Producers Research and High-Grade Living declare
He was fully sensible to the advantages of the Installment Plan
And had everything necessary to the Modern Man,   20

A phonograph, a radio, a car and a frigidaire.
Our researchers into Public Opinion are content
That he held the proper opinions for the time of year;
When there was peace, he was for peace; when there was war, he went.
He was married and added five children to the population,   25
Which our Eugenist says was the right number for a parent of his generation,
And our teachers report that he never interfered with their education.
Was he free? Was he happy? The question is absurd:
Had anything been wrong, we should certainly have heard.

Questions

1. Read the two-line epitaph at the beginning of the poem as carefully as you read what follows. How does the epitaph help establish the voice by which the rest of the poem is spoken?
2. Who is speaking?
3. What ironic discrepancies do you find between the speaker's attitude toward the subject and that of the poet himself? By what is the poet's attitude made clear?
4. In the phrase "The Unknown Soldier" (of which "The Unknown Citizen" reminds us), what does the word *unknown* mean? What does it mean in the title of Auden's poem?
5. What tendencies in our civilization does Auden satirize?
6. How would you expect the speaker to define a Modern Man, if an iPod, a radio, a car, and a refrigerator are "everything" a Modern Man needs?

Sharon Olds (b. 1942)

Rite of Passage   1983

As the guests arrive at my son's party
they gather in the living room—
short men, men in first grade
with smooth jaws and chins.
Hands in pockets, they stand around   5
jostling, jockeying for place, small fights
breaking out and calming. One says to another
How old are you? Six. I'm seven. So?
They eye each other, seeing themselves
tiny in the other's pupils. They clear their   10
throats a lot, a room of small bankers,
they fold their arms and frown. *I could beat you
up*, a seven says to a six,
the dark cake, round and heavy as a
turret, behind them on the table. My son,   15
freckles like specks of nutmeg on his cheeks,
chest narrow as the balsa keel of a
model boat, long hands
cool and thin as the day they guided him
out of me, speaks up as a host   20
for the sake of the group.
We could easily kill a two-year-old,
he says in his clear voice. The other

men agree, they clear their throats
like Generals, they relax and get down to   25
playing war, celebrating my son's life.

Questions

1. What is ironic about the way the speaker describes the first-grade boys at her son's birthday party?
2. What other irony does the author underscore in the last two lines?
3. Does this mother sentimentalize her own son by seeing him as better than the other boys?

Exercise: Detecting Irony

Point out the kinds of irony that occur in "The Workbox."

Thomas Hardy (1840–1928)

The Workbox   1914

"See, here's the workbox, little wife,
    That I made of polished oak."
He was a joiner,° of village life;   *carpenter*
    She came of borough folk.
He holds the present up to her   5
    As with a smile she nears
And answers to the profferer,
    "'Twill last all my sewing years!"

"I warrant it will. And longer too.
    'Tis a scantling that I got   10
Off poor John Wayward's coffin, who
    Died of they knew not what.

"The shingled pattern that seems to cease
    Against your box's rim
Continues right on in the piece   15
    That's underground with him.

"And while I worked it made me think
    Of timber's varied doom:
One inch where people eat and drink,
    The next inch in a tomb.   20

"But why do you look so white, my dear,
    And turn aside your face?
You knew not that good lad, I fear,
    Though he came from your native place?"

"How could I know that good young man,   25
    Though he came from my native town,
When he must have left far earlier than
    I was a woman grown?"

"Ah, no. I should have understood!
   It shocked you that I gave   30
To you one end of a piece of wood
   Whose other is in a grave?"

"Don't, dear, despise my intellect,
   Mere accidental things
Of that sort never have effect   35
   On my imaginings."

Yet still her lips were limp and wan,
   Her face still held aside,
As if she had known not only John,
   But known of what he died.   40

Sarah N. Cleghorn (1876–1959)

The Golf Links   1917

The golf links lie so near the mill
   That almost every day
The laboring children can look out
   And see the men at play.

Questions

1. Is this brief poem satiric? Does it contain any verbal irony or is the poet making a matter-of-fact statement in words that mean just what they say?
2. What other kind of irony is present in the poem?
3. Sarah N. Cleghorn's poem dates from before the enactment of legislation against child labor. Is it still a good poem, or is it hopelessly dated?
4. Would you call this poem lyric, narrative, or didactic?

Edna St. Vincent Millay (1892–1950)

Second Fig   1920

Safe upon the solid rock the ugly houses stand:
Come and see my shining palace built upon the sand!

Question

Do you think the author is making fun of the speaker's attitude or agreeing with it?

FOR REVIEW AND FURTHER STUDY

William Blake (1757–1827)

The Chimney Sweeper   1789

When my mother died I was very young,
And my father sold me while yet my tongue
Could scarcely cry "'weep! 'weep! 'weep! 'weep!"
So your chimneys I sweep, and in soot I sleep.

There's little Tom Dacre, who cried when his head,   5
That curled like a lamb's back, was shaved: so I said
"Hush, Tom! never mind it, for when your head's bare
You know that the soot cannot spoil your white hair."

And so he was quiet, and that very night,
As Tom was a-sleeping, he had such a sight!   10
That thousands of sweepers, Dick, Joe, Ned, and Jack,
Were all of them locked up in coffins of black.

And by came an Angel who had a bright key,
And he opened the coffins and set them all free;
Then down a green plain leaping, laughing, they run,   15
And wash in a river, and shine in the sun.

Then naked and white, all their bags left behind,
They rise upon clouds and sport in the wind;
And the Angel told Tom, if he'd be a good boy,
He'd have God for his father, and never want° joy.   *lack* 20

And so Tom awoke; and we rose in the dark,
And got with our bags and our brushes to work.
Though the morning was cold, Tom was happy and warm;
So if all do their duty they need not fear harm.

Questions

1. What does Blake's poem reveal about conditions of life in the London of his day?
2. What does this poem have in common with "The Golf Links"?
3. Sum up your impressions of the speaker's character. What does he say and do that displays it to us?
4. What pun do you find in line 3? Is its effect comic or serious?
5. In Tom Dacre's dream (lines 11–20), what wishes come true? Do you understand them to be the wishes of the chimney sweepers, of the poet, or of both?
6. In the last line, what is ironic in the speaker's assurance that the dutiful "need not fear harm"? What irony is there in his urging all to "do their duty"? (Who have failed in their duty to him?)
7. What is the tone of Blake's poem? Angry? Hopeful? Sorrowful? Compassionate? (Don't feel obliged to sum it up in a single word.)

Exercise: Telling Tone

Here are two radically different poems on a similar subject. Try stating the theme of each poem in your own words. How is the tone (the speaker's attitude) different in the two poems?

Richard Lovelace (1618–1658)

To Lucasta   1649

On Going to the Wars

Tell me not, Sweet, I am unkind
    That from the nunnery
Of thy chaste breast and quiet mind,
    To war and arms I fly.

True, a new mistress now I chase,   5
    The first foe in the field;
And with a stronger faith embrace
    A sword, a horse, a shield.

Yet this inconstancy is such
    As you too shall adore;   10
I could not love thee, Dear, so much,
    Loved I not Honor more.

Wilfred Owen (1893–1918)

Dulce et Decorum Est   1920

Bent double, like old beggars under sacks,
Knock-kneed, coughing like hags, we cursed through sludge,
Till on the haunting flares we turned our backs
And towards our distant rest began to trudge.
Men marched asleep. Many had lost their boots   5
But limped on, blood-shod. All went lame; all blind;
Drunk with fatigue; deaf even to the hoots
Of tired, outstripped Five-Nines that dropped behind.

Gas! Gas! Quick, boys!—An ecstasy of fumbling,
Fitting the clumsy helmets just in time;   10
But someone still was yelling out and stumbling,
And flound'ring like a man in fire or lime . . .
Dim, through the misty panes and thick green light,
As under a green sea, I saw him drowning.

In all my dreams, before my helpless sight,   15
He plunges at me, guttering, choking, drowning.

If in some smothering dreams you too could pace
Behind the wagon that we flung him in,
And watch the white eyes writhing in his face,
His hanging face, like a devil's sick of sin;   20
If you could hear, at every jolt, the blood
Come gargling from the froth-corrupted lungs,
Obscene as cancer, bitter as the cud
Of vile, incurable sores on innocent tongues,—
My friend, you would not tell with such high zest   25
To children ardent for some desperate glory,
The old Lie: Dulce et decorum est
Pro patria mori.

DULCE ET DECORUM EST. Owen's title is the beginning of the famous Latin quotation from the
Roman poet Horace with which he ends this poem: "*Dulce et decorum est pro patria mori.*" It is translated as "It is sweet and proper to die for your country." 8 *Five-Nines:* German howitzers often used to
shoot poison gas shells. 17 *you too:* Some manuscript versions of this poem carry the dedication "To
Jessie Pope" (a writer of patriotic verse) or "To a certain Poetess."

■ WRITING *effectively*

Wilfred Owen on Writing

War Poetry   (1917?)

Wilfred Owen was only twenty-one years old when World War I broke out in 1914. Twice wounded in battle, he was rapidly promoted and eventually became a company commander. The shocking violence of modern war summoned up his poetic genius, and in a two-year period he grew from a negligible minor poet into the most important English-language poet of World War I. Owen, however, did not live to see his talent recognized. He was killed one week before the end of the war; he was twenty-five years old. Owen published only four poems during his lifetime. Shortly before his death he drafted a few lines of prose for the preface of a book of poems.

Wilfred Owen

This book is not about heroes. English poetry is not yet fit to speak of them.

Nor is it about deeds, or lands, nor anything about glory, honor, might, majesty, dominion, or power, except War.

Above all I am not concerned with Poetry.

My subject is War, and the pity of War.

The Poetry is in the pity.

Yet these elegies are to this generation in no sense consolatory. They may be to the next. All a poet can do today is warn. That is why the true Poets must be truthful.

From Collected Poems

THINKING ABOUT TONE

To understand the tone of a poem, we need to listen to the words, as we might listen to an actual conversation. The key is to hear not only *what* is being said but also *how* it is being said. Does the speaker sound noticeably surprised, angry, nostalgic, or tender? Begin with an obvious but often overlooked question: who is speaking? Don't assume that every poem is spoken by its author.

- **Look for the ways—large and small—in which the speaker reveals aspects of his or her character.** Attitudes may be revealed directly or indirectly. Often, emotions must be intuited. The details a poet chooses to convey can reveal much about a speaker's stance toward his or her subject matter.
- **Consider also how the speaker addresses the listener.** Again, listen to the sound of the poem as you would listen to the sound of someone's voice—is it shrill, or soothing, or sarcastic?

- Look for an obvious difference between the speaker's attitude and your own honest reaction toward what is happening in the poem. If the gap between the two responses is wide, the poem may be taken as ironic.
- Remember that many poets strive toward understatement, writing matter-of-factly about occasions of intense sorrow, horror, or joy. In poems, as in conversation, understatement can be a powerful tool, more convincing—and often more moving—than hyperbole.

CHECKLIST: Writing About Tone

☐ Who is speaking the poem?

☐ Is the narrator's voice close to the poet's, or is it the voice of a fictional or historical person?

☐ How does the speaker address the listener?

☐ Does the poem directly reveal an emotion or attitude?

☐ Does it indirectly reveal any attitudes or emotions?

☐ Does your reaction to what is happening in the poem differ widely from that of the speaker? If so, what does that difference suggest? Is the poem in some way ironic?

☐ What adjectives would best describe the poem's tone?

TOPICS FOR WRITING ON TONE

1. Describe the tone of W. H. Auden's "The Unknown Citizen," quoting as necessary to back up your argument. How does the poem's tone contribute to its meaning?

2. Write an analysis of Thomas Hardy's "The Workbox," focusing on what the poem leaves unsaid.

3. In an essay of 250 to 500 words, compare and contrast the tone of two poems on a similar subject. You might examine how Walt Whitman and Emily Dickinson treat the subject of locomotives, or how Richard Lovelace and Wilfred Owen write about war. (For advice on writing about poetry by the method of comparison and contrast, see Chapter 44, "Writing About a Poem.")

4. Write a poem of your own in which the speaker's attitude toward the subject is revealed not by what the poem says but by the tone in which it is said. William Blake's "The Chimney Sweeper," W. H. Auden's "The Unknown Citizen," and Sharon Olds's "Rite of Passage" provide good models.

5. Look closely at any poem in this chapter. Going through it line by line, make a list of the sensory details the poem provides. Now write briefly about how those details combine to create a particular tone. Two choices are Wilfred Owen's "Dulce et Decorum Est" and Sharon Olds's "Rite of Passage."

6. Choose a poem from this chapter, and analyze its speaker's attitude toward the poem's main subject. Examine the author's choice of specific words and images to create the particular tone used to convey the speaker's attitudes. (Possible subjects include Wilfred Owen's attitude toward war in "Dulce et Decorum Est," the tone and imagery of Weldon Kees's "For My Daughter," and Anne Bradstreet's attitude toward her own poetry in "The Author to Her Book.")

SAMPLE STUDENT PAPER

Here is a paper on the tone of Theodore Roethke's "My Papa's Waltz," written by a student of Karen Locke's at Lane Community College in Eugene, Oregon.

Kim Larsen

Professor Locke

English 110

16 January 2019

Title gives sense of the paper's focus

Name of author and work

Thesis sentence

Topic sentence on title's significance

Topic sentence on word choice

Paragraph focuses on first stanza

Textual evidence

Key word defined

Word Choice, Tone, and Point of View in Roethke's

"My Papa's Waltz"

Some readers may find Theodore Roethke's "My Papa's Waltz" a reminiscence of a happy childhood scene. I believe, however, that the poem depicts a more painful and complicated series of emotions. By examining the choice of words that Roethke uses to convey the tone of his scene, I will demonstrate that beneath the seemingly comic situation of the poem is a darker story. The true point of view of "My Papa's Waltz" is that of a resentful adult reliving his fear of a domineering parent.

The first clue that the dance may not have been a mutually enjoyable experience is in the title itself. The author did not title the poem "Our Waltz" or "Waltzing with My Papa," either of which would set an initial tone for readers to expect a shared, loving sentiment. It does not even have a neutral title, such as "The Waltz." The title specifically implies that the waltz was exclusively the father's. Since a waltz normally involves two people, it can be reasoned that the father dances his waltz without regard for his young partner.

Examining each stanza of the poem offers numerous examples where the choice of words sustains the tone implied in the title. The first line, "The whiskey on your breath," conjures up an olfactory image that most would find unpleasant. The small boy finds it so overpowering he is made "dizzy." This stanza contains the only simile in the poem, "I hung on like death" (line 3), which creates a ghastly and stark visual image. There are many choices of similes to portray hanging on: a vine, an infant, an animal cub, all of which would have illustrated a lighthearted romp. The choice of "death" was purposefully used to convey an intended image. The first stanza ends by stating the "waltzing was not easy." The definitions of *easy*, as found in *Merriam-Webster's Online Dictionary*, include "free from pain, annoyance or anxiety," and "not difficult to endure or undergo" ("Easy"). Obviously the speaker did not find those qualities in the waltz.

Further evidence of this harsh and oppressive scene is brought to mind by reckless disregard for "the pans / Slid from the kitchen shelf" (5–6), which the reader can almost hear crashing on the floor in loud cacophony, and the "mother's countenance," which "[c]ould not unfrown itself" (7, 8). If this were only a silly, playful romp between father and son, even a stern, fastidious mother might be expected to at least make an unsuccessful attempt to suppress a grin. Instead, the reader gets a visual image of a silent, unhappy woman, afraid, probably because of past experience, to interfere in the domestic destruction around her. Once more, this detail suggests a domineering father who controls the family.

The third stanza relates the father's "battered" hand holding the boy's wrist. The tactile image of holding a wrist suggests dragging or forcing an unwilling person, not holding hands, as would be expected with a mutual dance partner. Further disregard for the son's feelings is displayed by the lines "At every step you missed / My right ear scraped a buckle" (11–12). In each missed step, probably due to his drunkenness, the father causes the boy physical pain.

The tone continues in the final stanza as the speaker recalls "You beat time on my head / With a palm caked hard by dirt" (13–14). The visual and tactile image of a dirt-hardened hand beating on a child's head as if it were a drum is distinctly unpleasant. The last lines, "Then waltzed me off to bed / Still clinging to your shirt" (15–16), are the most ambiguous in the poem. It can be reasoned, as X. J. Kennedy and Dana Gioia do, that the lines suggest "the boy is *still clinging* to his father with persistent if also complicated love" (708). On the other hand, if one notices the earlier dark images, the conclusion could describe a boy clinging out of fear, the physical fear of being dropped by one who is drunk and the emotional fear of not being loved and nurtured as a child needs to be by his father.

(It can also be argued)that the poem's rollicking rhythm contributes to a sense of fun, and in truth, the poem can be read in that fashion. On the other hand, it can be read in such a way as to de-emphasize the rhythm, as the author himself does in his recording of "My Papa's Waltz" (Roethke, *Poets.org*). The joyful, rollicking rhythm can be seen as ironic. By reminding readers of a waltzing tempo, it is highlighting the discrepancy between what a waltz should be and the bleak, frightening picture painted in the words.

While "My Papa's Waltz" can be read as a roughhouse comedy, by examining Roethke's title and choice of words closely to interpret the meaning of their images and sounds, it is also plausible to hear an entirely different tone. I believe "My Papa's Waltz" employs the voice of an embittered adult remembering a harsh scene in which both he and his mother were powerless in the presence of a drunk and domineering father.

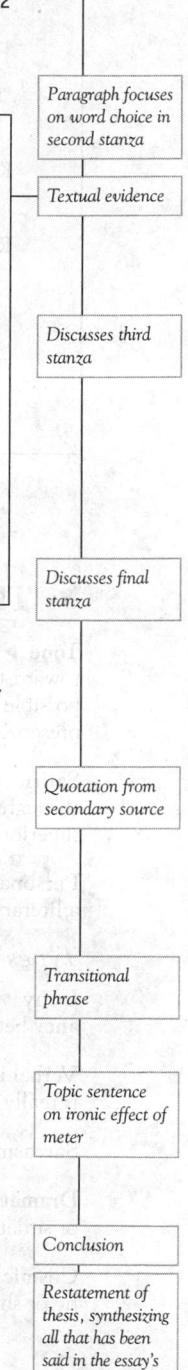

Paragraph focuses on word choice in second stanza

Textual evidence

Discusses third stanza

Discusses final stanza

Quotation from secondary source

Transitional phrase

Topic sentence on ironic effect of meter

Conclusion

Restatement of thesis, synthesizing all that has been said in the essay's body.

Larsen 3

Works Cited

"Easy." *Merriam-Webster Dictionary,* 2019, www.merriam-webster.com/
    dictionary/easy.

Kennedy, X. J., et al., editors. *Literature: An Introduction to Fiction, Poetry, Drama,
    and Writing.* 14th ed., Pearson, 2020, p. 708.

Roethke, Theodore. "My Papa's Waltz." *Literature: An Introduction to Fiction,
    Poetry, Drama, and Writing,* edited by X. J. Kennedy et al., 14th ed., Pearson,
    2020, p. 707.

---. "My Papa's Waltz." *Poets.org.,* audio clip, Academy of American Poets,
    www.poets.org/poetsorg/poem-my-papas-waltz-audio-only.

▶ TERMS FOR *review*

Tone ▶ The mood or manner of expression of a literary work, which conveys an attitude toward the work's subject, which may be playful, sarcastic, ironic, sad, solemn, or any other possible attitude. Tone helps to establish the reader's relationship to the characters or ideas presented in the work.

Satiric poetry ▶ Poetry that blends criticism with humor to convey a message, usually through the use of irony and a tone of detached amusement, withering contempt, and implied superiority.

Persona ▶ Latin for "mask." A fictitious character created by an author to be the speaker of a literary work.

Types of Irony

Irony ▶ In language, a discrepancy between what is said and what is meant. In life, a discrepancy between what is expected and what occurs.

Verbal irony ▶ A mode of expression in which the speaker or writer says the opposite of what is really meant, such as saying "Great story!" in response to a boring, pointless anecdote.

Sarcasm ▶ A style of bitter irony intended to hurt or mock its target.

Dramatic irony ▶ A situation in which the larger implications of a character's words, actions, or situation are unrealized by that character but seen by the author and the reader or audience.

Cosmic irony ▶ The contrast between a character's position or aspiration and the treatment he or she receives at the hands of a seemingly hostile fate; also called **irony of fate**.

17

WORDS

*We all write poems; it is simply that poets
are the ones who write in words.*

—JOHN FOWLES

What You Will Learn in This Chapter

- To define *diction*
- To recognize and define the standard *levels of diction*
- To recognize and explain *allusions* in a poem
- To analyze the role of diction in a poem

LITERAL MEANING: WHAT A POEM SAYS FIRST

Although successful as a painter, Edgar Degas found poetry discouragingly hard to write. To his friend, the poet Stéphane Mallarmé, he complained, "What a business! My whole day gone on a blasted sonnet, without getting an inch further . . . and it isn't ideas I'm short of . . . I'm full of them, I've got too many. . . ."

"But Degas," said Mallarmé, "you can't make a poem with ideas—you make it with *words*!"

Like the celebrated painter, some people assume that all it takes to make a poem is a bright idea. Poems state ideas, to be sure, and sometimes the ideas are invaluable; and yet the most impressive idea in the world will not make a poem, unless its words are selected and arranged with loving art. Some poets take great pains to find the right word. Unable to fill a two-syllable gap in an unfinished line that went, "The seal's wide_____gaze toward Paradise," Hart Crane paged through an unabridged dictionary. When he reached S, he found the object of his quest in *spindrift*: "spray skimmed from the sea by a strong wind." The word is exact and memorable.

In reading a poem, some people assume that its words can be skipped over rapidly, and they try to leap at once to the poem's general theme. It is as if they fear being thought clods unless they can find huge ideas in the poem (whether or not there are any). Such readers often ignore the literal meanings of words: the ordinary, matter-of-fact sense to be found in a dictionary. (In Chapter 18, "Saying and Suggesting," words possess not only dictionary meanings—denotations—but also many associations and suggestions—connotations.) Consider the following poem and see what you make of it.

William Carlos Williams (1883–1963)

This Is Just to Say   1934

I have eaten
the plums
that were in
the icebox

and which   5
you were probably
saving
for breakfast

Forgive me
they were delicious   10
so sweet
and so cold

    Some readers distrust a poem so simple and candid. They think, "What's wrong with me? There has to be more to it than this!" But poems seldom are puzzles in need of solutions. We can begin by accepting the poet's statements, without suspecting the poet of trying to hoodwink us. On later reflection, of course, we might possibly decide that the poet is playfully teasing or being ironic; but Williams gives us no reason to think that. There seems no need to look beyond the literal sense of his words, no profit in speculating that the plums symbolize worldly joys and that the icebox stands for the universe. Clearly, a reader who held such a grand theory would have overlooked (in eagerness to find a significant idea) the plain truth that the poet makes clear to us: that ice-cold plums are a joy to taste.

    To be sure, Williams's small poem is simpler than most poems are; and yet in reading any poem, no matter how complicated, you will do well to reach slowly and reluctantly for a theory to explain it by. To find the general theme of a poem, you first need to pay attention to its words. Yeats's "The Lake Isle of Innisfree" (Chapter 15), is a poem that makes a statement—crudely summed up, "I yearn to leave the city and retreat to a place of ideal peace and happiness." And yet before we can realize this theme, we have to notice details: nine bean rows, a glade loud with bees, "lake water lapping with low sounds by the shore," the gray of a pavement. These details and not some abstract remark make clear what the poem is saying: that the city is drab, while the island hideaway is sublimely beautiful.

DICTION

If a poem says *daffodils* instead of *plant life*, or, *diaper years* instead of *infancy*, we call its **diction**, or choice of words, **concrete** rather than **abstract**. Concrete words refer to what we can immediately perceive with our senses: *dog, actor, chemical,* or particular individuals who belong to those general classes: *Bonzo the fox terrier, Ryan Gosling, hydrogen sulfate*. Abstract words express ideas or concepts: *love, time, truth*. In abstracting, we leave out some characteristics found in each individual, and instead observe a quality common to many. The word *beauty*, for instance, denotes what may be observed in numerous persons, places, and things.

    Ezra Pound gave a famous piece of advice to his fellow poets: "Go in fear of abstractions." This is not to say that a poet cannot employ abstract words, nor that all poems have to be about physical things. Much of T. S. Eliot's *Four Quartets* is concerned with time, eternity, history, language, reality, and other things that cannot be physically handled. But Eliot, however high he may soar for a larger view, keeps returning to earth. He makes us aware of *things*.

Here is a famous poem that groups together some very specific things: certain ships and their cargoes.

John Masefield (1878–1967)

Cargoes   1902

Quinquireme of Nineveh from distant Ophir,
Rowing home to haven in sunny Palestine,
With a cargo of ivory,
And apes and peacocks,
Sandalwood, cedarwood, and sweet white wine.   5

Stately Spanish galleon coming from the Isthmus,
Dipping through the Tropics by the palm-green shores,
With a cargo of diamonds,
Emeralds, amethysts,
Topazes, and cinnamon, and gold moidores.   10

Dirty British coaster with a salt-caked smoke stack,
Butting through the Channel in the mad March days,
With a cargo of Tyne coal,
Road-rails, pig-lead,
Firewood, iron-ware, and cheap tin trays.

CARGOES. 1 *Quinquireme*: ancient Assyrian vessel propelled by sails and oars. *Nineveh*: capital of ancient Assyrian empire. *Ophir*: a vanished place, possibly in Arabia; according to the Bible, King Solomon sent expeditions there for its celebrated pure gold, and also for ivory, apes, peacocks, and other luxury items. (See I Kings 9–10.) 10 *Moidores*: Portuguese coins. 13 *Tyne*: a river in Scotland.

Questions

1. Does this poem use elevated language or everyday words?
2. Pick out some examples of unusual words in this poem.

Robert Graves (1895–1985)

Down, Wanton, Down!   1933

Down, wanton, down! Have you no shame
That at the whisper of Love's name,
Or Beauty's, presto! up you raise
Your angry head and stand at gaze?

Poor bombard-captain, sworn to reach   5
The ravelin and effect a breach—
Indifferent what you storm or why,
So be that in the breach you die!

Love may be blind, but Love at least
Knows what is man and what mere beast;   10
Or Beauty wayward, but requires
More delicacy from her squires.

Tell me, my witless, whose one boast
Could be your staunchness at the post,
When were you made a man of parts   15
To think fine and profess the arts?

Will many-gifted Beauty come
Bowing to your bald rule of thumb,
Or Love swear loyalty to your crown?
Be gone, have done! Down, wanton, down!   20

DOWN, WANTON, DOWN! 5 *bombard-captain:* officer in charge of a bombard, an early type of cannon that hurled stones. 6 *ravelin:* fortification with two faces that meet in a protruding angle. *effect a breach:* break an opening through (a fortification). 15 *man of parts:* man of talent or ability.

Questions

1. How do you define a "wanton"?
2. What wanton does the poet address?
3. Explain the comparison drawn in the second stanza.
4. In line 14, how many meanings do you find in "staunchness at the post"?
5. Explain any other puns you find in lines 15–19.
6. Do you take this to be a cynical poem making fun of Love and Beauty, or is Graves making fun of stupid, animal lust?

John Donne (1572–1631)

Batter my heart, three-personed God, for You   (about 1610)

Batter my heart, three-personed God, for You
As yet but knock, breathe, shine, and seek to mend.
That I may rise and stand, o'erthrow me, and bend
Your force to break, blow, burn, and make me new.
I, like an usurped town to another due,   5
Labor to admit You, but Oh! to no end.
Reason, Your viceroy in me, me should defend,
But is captived, and proves weak or untrue.
Yet dearly I love You, and would be lovèd fain,
But am betrothed unto Your enemy;   10
Divorce me, untie or break that knot again;
Take me to You, imprison me, for I,
Except You enthrall me, never shall be free,
Nor ever chaste, except You ravish me.

Questions

1. In the last line of this sonnet, to what does Donne compare the onslaught of God's love? Do you think the poem is weakened by the poet's comparing a spiritual experience to something so grossly carnal? Discuss.
2. Explain the seeming contradiction in the last line: in what sense can a ravished person be "chaste"? Explain the seeming contradictions in lines 3–4 and 12–13: how can a

person thrown down and destroyed be enabled to "rise and stand"; an imprisoned person be "free"?

3. In lines 5–6 the speaker compares himself to a "usurped town" trying to throw off its conqueror by admitting an army of liberation. Who is the "usurper" in this comparison?
4. Explain the comparison of "Reason" to a "viceroy" (lines 7–8).
5. Sum up in your own words the message of Donne's poem. In stating its theme, did you have to read the poem for literal meanings, figurative comparisons, or both?

THE VALUE OF A DICTIONARY

Use the dictionary. It's better than the critics.

—ELIZABETH BISHOP TO HER STUDENTS

If a poet troubles to seek out the best words available, the least we can do is to find out what the words mean. The dictionary is a firm ally in reading poems; if the poems are more than a century old, it is indispensable. Meanings change. When the Elizabethan poet George Gascoigne wrote, "O Abraham's brats, O brood of blessed seed," the word *brats* implied neither irritation nor contempt. When in the seventeenth century Andrew Marvell imagined two lovers' "vegetable love," he referred to a vegetative or growing love, not one resembling a lettuce. And when Queen Anne, in a famous anecdote, called the just-completed Saint Paul's Cathedral "awful, artificial, and amusing," its architect, Sir Christopher Wren, was overwhelmed with joy and gratitude, for what she had told him was that it was awe-inspiring, artful, and stimulating to contemplate (or *muse* upon).

In reading poetry, there is nothing to be done about the inevitable tendency of language to change except to watch out for it. If you suspect that a word has shifted in meaning over the years, most standard desk dictionaries will be helpful, an unabridged dictionary more helpful still, and most helpful of all the *Oxford English Dictionary (OED)*, which gives, for each definition, successive examples of the word's written use through the past thousand years. You need not feel a grim obligation to keep interrupting a poem in order to rummage in the dictionary; but if the poem is worth reading very closely, you may wish for any aid you can find.

"Every word which is used to express a moral or intellectual fact," said Emerson in his study *Nature*, "if traced to its root, is found to be borrowed from some material appearance. *Right* means straight; *wrong* means twisted. *Spirit* primarily means wind; *transgression*, the crossing of a line; *supercilious*, the raising of an eyebrow." Browse in a dictionary and you will discover such original concretenesses. These are revealed in your dictionary's etymologies, or brief notes on the derivation of words, given in most dictionaries near the beginning of an entry on a word; in some dictionaries, at the end of the entry. Look up *squirrel*, for instance, and you will find it comes from two Greek words meaning "shadow-tail." For another example of a common word that originally contained a poetic metaphor, look up the origin of *daisy*.

Experiment: Use the Dictionary to Read Longfellow's "Aftermath"

The following short poem seems very simple and straightforward, but much of its total effect depends on the reader knowing the literal meanings of several words. The most crucial word is in the title—"aftermath." Most readers today will assume that they know what that word means, but in this poem Longfellow uses it in both its current sense and its original, more literal meaning. Read the poem twice—first without a dictionary, then a second time after looking up the meanings of "aftermath," "fledged," "rowen," and "mead." How does knowing the exact meanings of these words add to both your literal and critical reading of the poem?

Henry Wadsworth Longfellow (1807–1882)

Aftermath   1873

When the summer fields are mown,
When the birds are fledged and flown,
   And the dry leaves strew the path;
With the falling of the snow,
With the cawing of the crow,   5
   Once again the fields we mow
And gather in the aftermath.

Not the sweet, new grass with flowers
In this harvesting of ours;
   Not the upland clover bloom;   10
But the rowen mixed with weeds,
Tangled tufts from marsh and meads,
Where the poppy drops its seeds
   In the silence and the gloom.

Questions

1. How do the etymology and meaning of "aftermath" help explain this poem? (Look the word up in your dictionary.)
2. What is the meaning of "fledged" (line 2) and "rowen" (line 11)?
3. Once you understand the literal meaning of the poem, do you think that Longfellow intended any further significance to it?

Allusion

An **allusion** is an indirect reference to any person, place, or thing—fictitious, historical, or actual. Sometimes, to understand an allusion in a poem, we have to find out something we didn't know before. But usually the poet asks of us only common knowledge. When, in his poem "To Helen" (Chapter 27), Edgar Allan Poe refers to "the glory that was Greece / And the grandeur that was Rome," he assumes that we have heard of those places. He also expects that we will understand his allusion to the cultural achievements of those ancient nations and perhaps even catch the subtle contrast between those two similar words *glory* and *grandeur*, with its suggestion that, for all its merits, Roman civilization was also more pompous than Greek.

Allusions not only enrich the meaning of a poem, they also save space. In "The Love Song of J. Alfred Prufrock" (Chapter 33), T. S. Eliot, by giving a brief introductory quotation from the speech of a damned soul in Dante's *Inferno*, is able to suggest that his poem will be the confession of a soul in torment, who sees no chance of escape and who feels the need to confide in someone, yet trusts that his secrets will be kept safe.

Often in reading a poem, you will meet a name you don't recognize, on which the meaning of a line (or perhaps a whole poem) seems to depend. In this book, most such unfamiliar references and allusions are glossed or footnoted, but when you venture out on your own in reading poems, you may find yourself needlessly perplexed unless you look up such names, the way you look up any other words. Unless the name is one that the poet made up, you will probably find it in one of the larger desk dictionaries, such as *Merriam-Webster's Collegiate Dictionary* or the *American Heritage Dictionary*. If you don't solve your problem there, try an online search of the word or phrase, as some allusions are quotations from other poems.

Exercise: Catching Allusions

From your knowledge, supplemented by a dictionary or other reference work if need be, explain the allusions in the following poems.

Samuel Menashe (1925–2011)

Bread   1985

Thy will be done
By crust and crumb
And loaves left over
The sea is swollen
With the bread I throw   5
Upon the water

Questions

1. Can you identify the two allusions Menashe uses in this poem? (Hint: The first allusion occurs in line 1; the second in lines 5–6).
2. Paraphrase the content of the poem in a few sentences.
3. How do you think these references add meaning to this very short poem?

Carl Sandburg (1878–1967)

Grass   1918

Pile the bodies high at Austerlitz and Waterloo.
Shovel them under and let me work—
　　I am the grass; I cover all.

And pile them high at Gettysburg
And pile them high at Ypres and Verdun.   5
Shovel them under and let me work.
Two years, ten years, and passengers ask the conductor:
　　What place is this?
　　Where are we now?

　　I am the grass.   10
　　Let me work.

Questions

1. What do the five proper nouns in Sandburg's poem have in common?
2. How much does the reader need to understand about the allusions in "Grass" to appreciate their importance to the literal meaning of the poem?

J. V. Cunningham (1911–1985)

Friend, on this scaffold Thomas More lies dead   1960

Friend, on this scaffold Thomas More lies dead
Who would not cut the Body from the Head.

WORD CHOICE AND WORD ORDER

Even if Samuel Johnson's famous *Dictionary* of 1755 had been as thick as Webster's unabridged, an eighteenth-century poet searching through it for words would have had a narrower choice. For in English literature of the neoclassical period, many poets subscribed to a belief in **poetic diction**: "A system of words," said Dr. Johnson, "refined from the grossness of domestic use." The system admitted into a serious poem only certain words and subjects, excluding others as violations of **decorum** (propriety). Accordingly, such common words as *rat*, *cheese*, *big*, *sneeze*, and *elbow*, although admissible to satire, were thought inconsistent with the loftiness of tragedy, epic, ode, and elegy. Dr. Johnson's biographer, James Boswell, tells how a poet writing an epic reconsidered the word "rats" and instead wrote "the whiskered vermin race." Johnson himself objected to Lady Macbeth's allusion to her "keen knife," saying that "we do not immediately conceive that any crime of importance is to be committed with a knife; or who does not, at last, from the long habit of connecting a knife with sordid offices, feel aversion rather than terror?"

Anglo-Saxon Versus Latinate Diction

When Wordsworth, in his Preface to *Lyrical Ballads*, asserted that "the language really spoken by men," especially by humble rustics, is plainer and more emphatic, and conveys "elementary feelings . . . in a state of greater simplicity," he was, in effect, advocating a new poetic diction. Wordsworth's ideas invited freshness into English poetry and, by admitting words that neoclassical poets would have called "low" ("His poor old *ankles* swell"), helped rid poets of the fear of being thought foolish for mentioning a commonplace.

This theory of the superiority of rural diction was, as Coleridge pointed out, hard to adhere to, and, in practice, Wordsworth was occasionally to write a language as Latinate and citified as these lines on yew trees:

> Huge trunks!—and each particular trunk a growth
> Of intertwisted fibers serpentine
> Up-coiling, and inveterately convolved . . .

Language so Latinate sounds pedantic to us, especially the phrase *inveterately convolved*. In fact, some poets, notably Gerard Manley Hopkins, have subscribed to the view that English words derived from Anglo-Saxon (Old English) have more force and flavor than their Latin equivalents. *Kingly*, one may feel, has more power than *regal*. One argument for this view is that so many words of Old English origin—*man*, *wife*, *child*, *house*, *eat*, *drink*, *sleep*—are basic to our living speech. Yet Latinate diction is not necessarily elevated. We use Latinate words every day, such as *station*, *office*, *order*, and *human*. None of these terms seem "inveterately convolved." Word choice is a subtle and flexible art.

Levels of Diction

When E. E. Cummings begins a poem, "mr youse needn't be so spry / concernin questions arty," we recognize another kind of diction available to poetry: **low diction** (or **vulgate**, speech not much affected by schooling). Handbooks of grammar sometimes distinguish various **levels of diction**. A sort of ladder is imagined, on whose rungs words, phrases, and sentences may be ranked in an ascending order of formality, from the curses of an illiterate thug to the commencement-day address of a doctor of divinity. These levels range from vulgate through **colloquial** (the casual conversation or informal writing of literate people) and **middle diction** (or **general English**, most literate speech and writing, more studied than colloquial but not pretentious), up to **high diction** (or **formal English**, the impersonal language of educated persons, usually only written, possibly spoken on dignified occasions). Recently, however, lexicographers have been shunning such labels. The designation *colloquial* was expelled from *Webster's Third New International Dictionary* on the grounds that "it is impossible to know whether a word out of context is colloquial or not" and that the diction of Americans nowadays is more fluid than the labels suggest. Aware that we are being unscientific, you may find the labels useful. They may help roughly to describe what happens when, as in the following poem, a poet shifts from one level of usage to another.

Robert Herrick (1591–1674)

Upon Julia's Clothes   1648

Whenas in silks my Julia goes,
Then, then, methinks, how sweetly flows
That liquefaction of her clothes.

Next, when I cast mine eyes and see
That brave vibration each way free,   5
O how that glittering taketh me!

UPON JULIA'S CLOTHES. 3 *liquefaction*: becoming fluid, turning to liquid. 5 *brave*: Herrick uses *brave* in its original sense, meaning excellent or fine.

Even in so short a poem as "Upon Julia's Clothes," we see how a sudden shift in the level of diction can produce a surprising and memorable effect. One word in each stanza—*liquefaction* in the first, *vibration* in the second—stands out from the standard, but not extravagant, language that surrounds it. Try to imagine the entire poem being written in such formal English, in mostly unfamiliar words of several syllables each: the result, in all likelihood, would be merely an oddity, and a turgid one at that. But by using such terms sparingly, Herrick allows them to take on a greater strength and significance through their contrast with the words that surround it. It is *liquefaction* in particular that strikes the reader: like a great catch by an outfielder, it impresses both for its appropriateness in the situation and for its sheer beauty as a demonstration of superior skill. Once we have read the poem, we realize that the effect would be severely compromised, if not ruined, by the substitution of any other word in its place.

Dialect

At present, most poetry in English avoids elaborate literary expressions such as "fleecy care" in favor of more colloquial language. In many English-speaking areas, such as Scotland, there has even been a movement to write poems in regional dialects. (A **dialect** is a particular variety of language spoken by an identifiable regional group or social class of persons.) Dialect poets frequently try to capture the freshness and authenticity of the language spoken in their immediate locale.

Sentence Structure

Not only the poet's choice of words makes a poem seem more formal, or less, but also the way the words are arranged into sentences. Compare these lines

Jack and Jill went up the hill
To fetch a pail of water.
Jack fell down and broke his crown
And Jill came tumbling after.

with Milton's account of a more significant downfall:

Earth trembled from her entrails, as again
In pangs, and Nature gave a second groan;
Sky loured and, muttering thunder, some sad drops
Wept at completing of the mortal sin
Original; while Adam took no thought,
Eating his fill, nor Eve to iterate
Her former trespass feared, the more to soothe
Him with her loved society, that now
As with new wine intoxicated both
They swim in mirth, and fancy that they feel
Divinity within them breeding wings
Wherewith to scorn the Earth.

Not all the words in Milton's lines are bookish: indeed, many of them can be found
in nursery rimes. What helps, besides diction, to distinguish this account of the biblical fall from "Jack and Jill" is that Milton's nonstop sentence seems further removed
from usual speech in its length (83 words), in its complexity (subordinate clauses),
and in its word order ("with new wine intoxicated both" rather than "both intoxicated with new wine"). Should we think less (or more) highly of Milton for choosing
a style so elaborate and formal? No judgment need be passed: both Mother Goose
and the author of *Paradise Lost* use language appropriate to their purposes.

Coleridge offered "homely definitions of prose and poetry; that is, *prose*: words in
their best order; *poetry*: the best words in the best order." If all goes well, a poet may
fasten the right word into the right place, and the result may be—as T. S. Eliot said in
"Little Gidding"—a "complete consort dancing together."

Kay Ryan (b. 1945)

Blandeur   2000

If it please God,
let less happen.
Even out Earth's
rondure, flatten
Eiger, blanden   5
the Grand Canyon.
Make valleys
slightly higher,
widen fissures
to arable land,   10
remand your
terrible glaciers
and silence
their calving,
halving or doubling   15

all geographical features
toward the mean.
Unlean against our hearts.
Withdraw your grandeur
from these parts.   20

BLANDEUR. 4 *rondure:* an elegant curvature. 5 *Eiger:* a mountain in the Alps. 11 *remand:* send back;
often a legal term meaning to send back to a lower court. 14 *calving:* when a small glacier splits from
a larger one; often an agricultural term for when a cow births a calf.

Questions

1. The title of Ryan's poem is a word that she invented. What do you think it means?
   Explain the reasoning behind your theory.
2. Where else does Ryan use a different form of this new word?
3. What other unusual but real words does the author use?

Thomas Hardy (1840–1928)

The Ruined Maid   1901

"O 'Melia, my dear, this does everything crown!
Who could have supposed I should meet you in Town?
And whence such fair garments, such prosperi-ty?"—
"O didn't you know I'd been ruined?" said she.

—"You left us in tatters, without shoes or socks,   5
Tired of digging potatoes, and spudding up docks;°   *spading up dockweed*
And now you've gay bracelets and bright feathers three!"
"Yes: that's how we dress when we're ruined," said she.

—"At home in the barton° you said 'thee' and 'thou,'   *farmyard*
And 'thik oon,' and 'theäs oon,' and 't'other'; but now   10
Your talking quite fits 'ee for high compa-ny!"—
"Some polish is gained with one's ruin," said she.

—"Your hands were like paws then, your face blue and bleak
But now I'm bewitched by your delicate cheek,
And your little gloves fit as on any la-dy!"—   15
"We never do work when we're ruined," said she.

—"You used to call home-life a hag-ridden dream,
And you'd sigh, and you'd sock;° but at present you seem   *groan*
To know not of megrims° or melancho-ly!"—   *blues*
"True. One's pretty lively when ruined," said she.   20

—"I wish I had feathers, a fine sweeping gown,
And a delicate face, and could strut about Town!"—
"My dear—a raw country girl, such as you be,
Cannot quite expect that. You ain't ruined," said she.

Questions

1. Where does this dialogue take place? Who are the two speakers?
2. Comment on Hardy's use of the word *ruined.* What is the conventional meaning of the
   word when applied to a woman? As 'Melia applies it to herself, what is its meaning?

3. Sum up the attitude of each speaker toward the other. What details of the new 'Melia does the first speaker most dwell on? Would you expect Hardy to be so impressed by all these details, or is there, between his view of the characters and their view of themselves, any hint of an ironic discrepancy?

4. In losing her country dialect ("thik oon" and "theäs oon" for "this one" and "that one"), 'Melia is presumed to have gained in sophistication. What does Hardy suggest by her "ain't" in the last line?

Richard Eberhart (1904–2005)

The Fury of Aerial Bombardment   1947

You would think the fury of aerial bombardment
Would rouse God to relent; the infinite spaces
Are still silent. He looks on shock-pried faces.
History, even, does not know what is meant.

You would feel that after so many centuries   5
God would give man to repent; yet he can kill
As Cain could, but with multitudinous will,
No farther advanced than in his ancient furies.

Was man made stupid to see his own stupidity?
Is God by definition indifferent, beyond us all?   10
Is the eternal truth man's fighting soul
Wherein the Beast ravens in its own avidity?

Of Van Wettering I speak, and Averill,
Names on a list, whose faces I do not recall
But they are gone to early death, who late in school   15
Distinguished the belt feed lever from the belt holding pawl.

Questions

1. As a naval officer during World War II, Richard Eberhart was assigned for a time as an instructor in a gunnery school. How has this experience apparently contributed to the diction of his poem?

2. In his *Life of John Dryden*, complaining about a description of a sea fight Dryden had filled with nautical language, Samuel Johnson argued that technical terms should be excluded from poetry. Is this criticism applicable to Eberhart's last line? Can a word succeed for us in a poem, even though we may not be able to define it? (For more evidence, see also the technical terms in Henry Reed's "Naming of Parts," Chapter 34.)

3. Some readers have found a contrast in tone between the first three stanzas of this poem and the last stanza. How would you describe this contrast? What does diction contribute to it?

Julie Larios (b. 1949)

What Bee Did   2006

Bee not only buzzed.
When swatted at, Bee deviled,
Bee smirched. And when fuddled,
like many of us, Bee labored, Bee reaved.
He behaved as well as any Bee can have.   5

Bee never lied. Bee never lated.
And despite the fact Bee took, Bee also stowed.
In love, Bee seiged. Bee seeched.
Bee moaned, Bee sighed himself,
Bee gat with his Beloved.   10

And because Bee tokened summer
(the one season we all, like Bee, must lieve)
Bee also dazzled.

Questions

1. Can you identify the play on words or running joke in this poem? It may help to read the poem aloud.
2. Even when some of the words aren't used in their common or correct forms, does the poem instill them with new meaning and surprising humor? Point out some examples.

Wendy Cope (b. 1945)

Lonely Hearts   1986

Can someone make my simple wish come true?
Male biker seeks female for touring fun.
Do you live in North London? Is it you?

Gay vegetarian whose friends are few,
I'm into music, Shakespeare and the sun.   5
Can someone make my simple wish come true?

Executive in search of something new—
Perhaps bisexual woman, arty, young.
Do you live in North London? Is it you?

Successful, straight and solvent? I am too—   10
Attractive Jewish lady with a son.
Can someone make my simple wish come true?

I'm Libran, inexperienced and blue—
Need slim non-smoker, under twenty-one.
Do you live in North London? Is it you?   15

Please write (with photo) to Box 152.
Who knows where it may lead once we've begun?
Can someone make my simple wish come true?
Do you live in North London? Is it you?

LONELY HEARTS. This poem has a double form: the rhetorical, a series of "lonely heart" personal ads from a newspaper, and metrical, a **villanelle**, a fixed form developed by French courtly poets in imitation of Italian folk song. For other villanelles, see Elizabeth Bishop's "One Art" (Chapter 30) and Dylan Thomas's "Do not go gentle into that good night" (Chapter 24). In the villanelle, the first and the third lines are repeated in a set pattern throughout the poem.

Questions

1. What sort of language does Wendy Cope borrow for this poem?
2. The form of the villanelle requires that the poet end each stanza with one of two repeating lines. What special use does the author make of these mandatory repetitions?

3. How many speakers are there in the poem? Does the author's voice ever enter or is the entire poem spoken by individuals in personal ads?

4. The poem seems to begin satirically. Does the poem ever move beyond the critical, mocking tone typical of satire?

FOR REVIEW AND FURTHER STUDY

Sarah Cortez (b. 1950)

Adam   2016

What song is being sung
by your bones? The pink
ache of sunrise? The small
birds' hollow worries? Sighs
that cannot affix themselves
to your wealth of ruffled flowers?   5

Both my feet prickle
with the humming
from your tibia and pelvis,
collarbone, and metatarsals
strung like dominoes   10
who love a careful distance
but find their meaning
only in collapse
and closeness, followed
by stacking in a lidded box.   15

ADAM. This is an example of an **ekphrastic poem**—a poem created in response to a visual image such as a painting or photograph.

Questions

1. "Adam" was included in an anthology of poems inspired by roadside crosses in Texas. Does that change your understanding of the poem?
2. Why does the poem meditate on bones?
3. What is the "lidded box" in the final line?
4. What elements in Dan Streck's photograph do you see reflected in the poem?

Adam Ayala by Dan Streck.

E. E. Cummings (1894–1962)

anyone lived in a pretty how town   1940

anyone lived in a pretty how town
(with up so floating many bells down)
spring summer autumn winter
he sang his didn't he danced his did.

Women and men (both little and small)   5
cared for anyone not at all
they sowed their isn't they reaped their same
sun moon stars rain

children guessed (but only a few
and down they forgot as up they grew   10
autumn winter spring summer)
that noone loved him more by more

when by now and tree by leaf
she laughed his joy she cried his grief
bird by snow and stir by still   15
anyone's any was all to her

someones married their everyones
laughed their cryings and did their dance
(sleep wake hope and then) they
said their nevers they slept their dream   20

stars rain sun moon
(and only the snow can begin to explain
how children are apt to forget to remember
with up so floating many bells down)

one day anyone died i guess   25
(and noone stooped to kiss his face)
busy folk buried them side by side
little by little and was by was

all by all and deep by deep
and more by more they dream their sleep   30
noone and anyone earth by april
wish by spirit and if by yes.

Women and men (both dong and ding)
summer autumn winter spring
reaped their sowing and went their came   35
sun moon stars rain

Questions

1. Summarize the story told in this poem. Who are the characters?
2. Rearrange the words in the two opening lines into the order you would expect them usually to follow. What effect does Cummings obtain by his unconventional word order?

3. Another of Cummings's strategies is to use one part of speech as if it were another; for instance, in line 4, *didn't* and *did* ordinarily are verbs, but here they are used as nouns. What other words in the poem perform functions other than their expected ones?

Exercise: Different Kinds of English

Read the following poems and see what kinds of diction and word order you find in them. Which poems are least formal in their language and which most formal? Is there any use of low diction? Any dialect? What does each poem achieve that its own kind of English makes possible?

Anonymous (American oral verse)

Carnation Milk   (about 1900?)

Carnation Milk is the best in the land;
Here I sit with a can in my hand—
No tits to pull, no hay to pitch,
You just punch a hole in the son of a bitch.

CARNATION MILK. "This quatrain is imagined as the caption under a picture of a rugged-looking cowboy seated upon a bale of hay," notes William Harmon in his *Oxford Book of American Light Verse* (New York: Oxford UP, 1979). Possibly the first to print this work was David Ogilvy (1911–1999), who quotes it in his *Confessions of an Advertising Man* (New York: Atheneum, 1963).

Gina Valdés (b. 1943)

English con Salsa   1993

Welcome to ESL 100, English Surely Latinized,
inglés con chile y cilantro, English as American
as Benito Juárez. Welcome, muchachos from Xochicalco,
learn the language of dólares and dolores, of kings
and queens, of Donald Duck and Batman. Holy Toluca!   5
In four months you'll be speaking like George Washington,
in four weeks you can ask, More coffee? In two months
you can say, May I take your order? In one year you
can ask for a raise, cool as the Tuxpan River.

Welcome, muchachas from Teocaltiche, in this class   10
we speak English refrito, English con sal y limón,
English thick as mango juice, English poured from
a clay jug, English tuned like a requinto from Uruapan,
English lighted by Oaxacan dawns, English spiked
with mezcal from Mitla, English with a red cactus   15
flower blooming in its heart.

Welcome, welcome, amigos del sur, bring your Zapotec
tongues, your Nahuatl tones, your patience of pyramids,
your red suns and golden moons, your guardian angels,
your duendes, your patron saints, Santa Tristeza,   20
Santa Alegría, Santo Todolopuede. We will sprinkle
holy water on pronouns, make the sign of the cross
on past participles, jump like fish from Lake Pátzcuaro
on gerunds, pour tequila from Jalisco on future perfects,
say shoes and shit, grab a cool verb and a pollo loco   25
and dance on the walls like chapulines.

When a teacher from La Jolla or a cowboy from Santee
asks you, Do you speak English? You'll answer, Sí,
yes, simón, of course, I love English!
                              And you'll hum
A Mixtec chant that touches la tierra and the heavens.   30

ENGLISH CON SALSA. 3 *Benito Juárez:* Mexican statesman (1806–1872), president of Mexico in the
1860s and 1870s.

William Wordsworth (1770–1850)

My heart leaps up when I behold   1807

My heart leaps up when I behold
   A rainbow in the sky:
So was it when my life began;
So is it now I am a man;
So be it when I shall grow old,   5
   Or let me die!
The Child is father of the Man;
And I could wish my days to be
Bound each to each by natural piety.

William Wordsworth (1770–1850)

Mutability   1822

From low to high doth dissolution climb,
And sink from high to low, along a scale
Of awful notes, whose concord shall not fail;
A musical but melancholy chime,
Which they can hear who meddle not with crime,   5
Nor avarice, nor over-anxious care.
Truth fails not; but her outward forms that bear
The longest date do melt like frosty rime,°   *frozen dew*
That in the morning whitened hill and plain
And is no more; drop like the tower sublime   10

Of yesterday, which royally did wear
His crown of weeds, but could not even sustain
Some casual shout that broke the silent air,
Or the unimaginable touch of Time.

Lewis Carroll
[*Charles Lutwidge Dodgson*] (1832–1898)

Jabberwocky   1871

'Twas brillig, and the slithy toves
   Did gyre and gimble in the wabe:
All mimsy were the borogoves,
   And the mome raths outgrabe.

"Beware the Jabberwock, my son!   5
   The jaws that bite, the claws that catch!
Beware the Jubjub bird, and shun
   The frumious Bandersnatch!"

He took his vorpal sword in hand:
   Long time the manxome foe he sought—   10
So rested he by the Tumtum tree
   And stood awhile in thought.

And, as in uffish thought he stood,
   The Jabberwock, with eyes of flame,
Came whiffling through the tulgey wood,   15
   And burbled as it came!

**The Jabberwock,
as illustrated
by John Tenniel, 1872.**

One, two! One, two! And through and through
   The vorpal blade went snicker-snack!
He left it dead, and with its head
   He went galumphing back.   20

"And hast thou slain the Jabberwock?
   Come to my arms, my beamish boy!
O frabjous day! Callooh! Callay!"
   He chortled in his joy.

'Twas brillig, and the slithy toves   25
   Did gyre and gimble in the wabe:
All mimsy were the borogoves,
   And the mome raths outgrabe.

JABBERWOCKY. Fussy about pronunciation, Carroll in his preface to *The Hunting of the Snark* declares:
"The first 'o' in 'borogoves' is pronounced like the 'o' in 'borrow.' I have heard people try to give it
the sound of the 'o' in 'worry.' Such is Human Perversity." *Toves*, he adds, rimes with *groves*.

Questions

  1. Look up *chortled* (line 24) in your dictionary and find out its definition and origin.
  2. In *Through the Looking Glass*, Alice seeks the aid of Humpty Dumpty to decipher the
      meaning of this nonsense poem. "*Brillig*," he explains, "means four o'clock in the

afternoon—the time when you begin *broiling* things for dinner." Does "brillig" sound like any other familiar word?

3. *"Slithy,"* the explanation goes on, "means 'lithe and slimy.' 'Lithe' is the same as 'active.' You see it's like a portmanteau—there are two meanings packed up into one word." "Mimsy" is supposed to pack together both "flimsy" and "miserable." In the rest of the poem, what other portmanteau—or packed suitcase—words can you find?

■ WRITING *effectively*

Lewis Carroll on Writing

Humpty Dumpty Explicates "Jabberwocky"   1871

"You seem very clever at explaining words, Sir," said Alice. "Would you kindly tell me the meaning of the poem called 'Jabberwocky'?"

"Let's hear it," said Humpty Dumpty. "I can explain all the poems that ever were invented—and a good many that haven't been invented just yet."

This sounded very hopeful, so Alice repeated the first verse:—

Lewis Carroll

"'Twas brillig, and the slithy toves
  Did gyre and gimble in the wabe:
All mimsy were the borogoves,
  And the mome raths outgrabe."

"That's enough to begin with," Humpty Dumpty interrupted: "there are plenty of hard words there. 'Brillig' means four o'clock in the afternoon—the time when you begin *broiling* things for dinner."

"That'll do very well," said Alice. "And 'slithy'?"

"Well, 'slithy' means 'lithe and slimy.' 'Lithe' is the same as 'active.' You see it's like a portmanteau—there are two meanings packed up into one word."

"I see it now," Alice remarked thoughtfully. "And what are 'toves'?"

"Well, 'toves' are something like badgers—they're something like lizards—and they're something like corkscrews."

"They must be very curious-looking creatures."

"They are that," said Humpty Dumpty, "also they make their nests under sundials—also they live on cheese."

"And what's to 'gyre' and to 'gimble'?"

"To 'gyre' is to go round and round like a gyroscope. To 'gimble' is to make holes like a gimlet."

"And 'the wabe' is the grass-plot round a sun-dial, I suppose?" said Alice, surprised at her own ingenuity.

"Of course it is. It's called '*wabe*,' you know, because it goes a long way before it, and a long way behind it."

"And a long way beyond it on each side," Alice added.

"Exactly so. Well, then, '*mimsy*' is 'flimsy and miserable' (there's another portmanteau for you). And a '*borogove*' is a thin shabby-looking bird with its feathers sticking out all round—something like a live mop."

"And then '*mome raths*'?" said Alice. "I'm afraid I'm giving you a great deal of trouble."

"Well, a '*rath*' is a sort of green pig: but '*mome*' I'm not certain about. I think it's short for 'from home'—meaning that they'd lost their way, you know."

"And what does '*outgrabe*' mean?"

"Well, '*outgribing*' is something between bellowing and whistling, with a kind of sneeze in the middle: however, you'll hear it done, maybe—down in the wood yonder—and, when you've once heard it, you'll be *quite* content. Who's been repeating all that hard stuff to you?"

"I read it in a book," said Alice.

From Through the Looking Glass

HUMPTY DUMPTY EXPLICATES "JABBERWOCKY." This celebrated passage is the origin of the term **portmanteau word**, an artificial word that combines parts of other words to express some combination of their qualities. (*Brunch*, for example, is a meal that combines aspects of both breakfast and lunch.) A portmanteau is a large suitcase that opens up into two separate compartments.

THINKING ABOUT DICTION

Although a poem may contain images and ideas, it is made up of words. Language is the medium of poetry, and a poem's diction—its exact wording—is the chief source of its power. Writers labor to shape each word and phrase to create particular effects. Poets choose words for their meanings, their associations, and even their sounds. Changing a single word may ruin a poem's effect, just as changing one letter or number in an online password makes all the other characters useless.

- **As you prepare to write about a poem, ask yourself if some particular word or combination of words gives you particular pleasure or especially intrigues you.** Don't worry yet about why the word or words impress you. Don't even worry about the meaning. Just underline the words in your book.

- **Try to determine what about the word or phrase commanded your attention.** Maybe a word strikes you as being unexpected but just right. A phrase might seem especially musical or it might call forth a vivid picture in your imagination.

- **Consider your underlined words and phrases in the context of the poem.** How does each relate to the words around it? What does it add to the poem?

- **Think about the poem as a whole.** What sort of language does it rely on? Many poems favor the plain, straightforward language people use in everyday conversation, but others reach for more elegant diction. Choices such as these contribute to the poem's distinctive flavor, as well as to its ultimate meaning.

CHECKLIST: Writing About Diction

☐ As you read, underline words or phrases that appeal to you or seem especially significant.

☐ What is it about each underlined word or phrase that appeals to you?

☐ How does the word or phrase relate to the other lines? What does it contribute to the poem's effect?

☐ How does the sound of a word you've chosen add to the poem's mood?

☐ What would be lost if synonyms were substituted for your favorite words?

☐ What sort of diction does the poem use? Conversational? Lofty? Monosyllabic? Polysyllabic? Concrete? Abstract?

☐ How does diction contribute to the poem's flavor and meaning?

TOPICS FOR WRITING ON WORD CHOICE

1. Find two poems in this book that use very different sorts of diction to address similar subjects. You might choose one with formal and elegant language and another with very down-to-earth or slangy word choices. Some good pairings include John Milton's "When I consider how my light is spent" and Seamus Heaney's "Digging" (both in Chapter 34); Dylan Thomas's "Do not go gentle into that good night" (Chapter 24) and Ted Kooser's "Carrie" (Chapter 26); and William Shakespeare's "When, in disgrace with Fortune and men's eyes" (Chapter 34); and Jane Kenyon's "The Suitor" (Chapter 20). In a short essay (750 to 1000 words), discuss how the difference in diction affects the tones of the two poems.

2. Browse through Chapter 34, "Poems for Further Reading," for a poem that catches your interest. Within that poem, find a word or phrase that particularly intrigues you. Write a paragraph on what the word or phrase adds to the poem, including how it shades the meaning and contributes to the overall effect.

3. Choose a brief poem from this chapter. Type the poem out, substituting synonyms for each of its nouns and verbs, using a thesaurus if necessary. Next, write a one-page analysis of the difference in feel and meaning between the original and your creation.

4. Choose a poem that strikes you as particularly inventive or unusual in its language, such as E. E. Cummings's "anyone lived in a pretty how town," Wendy Cope's "Lonely Hearts," or Gerard Manley Hopkins's "The Windhover" (Chapter 34), and write a brief analysis of it. Concentrate on the diction of the poem and word order. For what possible purposes does the poet depart from standard English or incorporate unusual vocabulary?

5. Writers are notorious word junkies who often jot down interesting words they stumble across in daily life. Over the course of a day, keep a list of any intriguing words you encounter in your reading, music listening, or television viewing. Even street signs and advertisements can supply surprising words. After twenty-four hours of list-keeping, choose your five favorites. Write a five line poem, incorporating your five words, letting them take you where they will. Then write a page-long description of the process. What appealed to you in the words you chose? What did you learn about the process of composing a poem?

▶ TERMS FOR *review*

Diction and Allusion

Diction ▶ Word choice or vocabulary. *Diction* refers to the class of words that an author chooses as appropriate for a particular work.

Concrete diction ▶ Words that specifically name or describe things or persons. *Concrete diction* refers to what we can immediately perceive with our senses.

Abstract diction ▶ Words that express general ideas or concepts.

Poetic diction ▶ Strictly speaking, *poetic diction* means any language deemed suitable for verse, but the term generally refers to elevated language intended for poetry rather than common use.

Allusion ▶ A brief, sometimes indirect, reference in a text to a person, place, or thing. Allusions imply a common body of knowledge between reader and writer and act as a literary shorthand to enrich the meaning of a text.

Levels of Diction

Low diction (or **vulgate**) ▶ The language of the common people. Not necessarily containing foul or inappropriate language, it refers simply to unschooled, everyday speech. The term *vulgate* comes from the Latin word *vulgus*, meaning "mob" or "common people."

Colloquial English ▶ The casual or informal but correct language of ordinary native speakers. Conversational in tone, it may include contractions, slang, and shifts in grammar, vocabulary, and diction.

Middle diction (or **general English**) ▶ The ordinary speech of educated native speakers. Most literate speech and writing is in middle diction, which is more educated than **colloquial English**, yet not as elevated as **high diction**.

High diction (or **formal English**) ▶ The heightened, impersonal language of educated persons, usually only written, although possibly spoken on dignified occasions.

Dialect ▶ A particular variety of language spoken by an identifiable regional group or social class.

18 SAYING AND SUGGESTING

*To name an object is to take away three-fourths
of the pleasure given by a poem. . . .
to suggest it, that is the ideal.*

—STÉPHANE MALLARMÉ

What You Will Learn in This Chapter

- To understand and define *denotation*
- To understand and define *connotation*
- To explain the difference between what words say and suggest in a poem
- To analyze the role of *suggestion* in a poem

The goal of scientists—according to Bishop Thomas Sprat, who lived in the seventeenth century—was to write so clearly that they might bring "all things as near the mathematical plainness" as possible. Such an effort would seem bound to fail, because words, unlike numbers, are ambiguous indicators. Although it may have troubled Bishop Sprat, the tendency of a word to have multiplicity of meaning rather than mathematical plainness opens broad avenues to poetry.

DENOTATION AND CONNOTATION

Every word has at least one **denotation**: a dictionary definition, also known as a **literal meaning**. But the English language has many a common word with so many denotations that a reader may need to think twice to see what it means in a specific context. The noun *field*, for instance, can denote an expanse of land, a sports arena, the scene of a battle, part of a flag, a profession, and a number system in mathematics. Further, the word can be used as a verb ("he fielded a grounder") or an adjective ("field trip," "field glasses").

A word also has **connotations**: overtones or suggestions of additional meaning that it gains from all the contexts in which we have met it in the past. **Suggestion** is the power of a word to imply unspoken associations, in addition to its literal meaning. Suggestion is one of the greatest powers of poetry. The word *skeleton*, according to a dictionary, denotes "the bony framework of a human being or other vertebrate animal, which supports the flesh and protects the organs." But by its associations, the word can rouse thoughts of war, of disease and death, of Halloween, or of one's plans to go to medical school. Think, too, of the difference between "Old Doc Jones" and "Theodore E. Jones, M.D." In the mind's eye, the former appears in his shirtsleeves; the latter has a gold nameplate on his door.

That some words denote the same thing but have sharply different connotations is pointed out in this anonymous Victorian jingle:

Here's a little ditty that you really ought to know:
Horses "sweat" and men "perspire," but ladies only "glow."

The power of suggestion is inherent in all language. For example, the terms *druggist*, *pharmacist*, and *apothecary* all denote the same occupation, but apothecaries lay claim to special distinction, known as makers of potions and mysterious cures.

Poets aren't the only people who care about the connotations of language. Advertisers know that connotations make money. Nowadays many automobile dealers advertise their secondhand cars not as "used" but as "pre-owned," as if fearing that "used car" would connote an old heap with soiled upholstery and mysterious engine troubles. "Pre-owned," however, suggests that the previous owner has kindly taken the trouble of breaking in the car for you. Not long ago prune-packers, alarmed by a slump in sales, sponsored a survey to determine the connotations of prunes in the public consciousness. Asked, "What do you think of when you hear the word *prunes*?" most people replied, "dried up," "wrinkled," or "constipated." Dismayed, the packers hired an advertising agency to create a new image for prunes, in hopes of inducing new connotations. Soon, advertisements began to show prunes in brightly colored settings, in the company of bikinied bathing beauties.

In imaginative writing, connotations are as crucial as they are in advertising. Consider this sentence: "A new brand of journalism is being born, or spawned" (Dwight Macdonald writing in the *New York Review of Books*). The last word, by its associations with fish and crustaceans, suggests that this new journalism is scarcely the product of human beings.

William Blake was a master at choosing words loaded with connotation, as in this classic poem.

William Blake (1757–1827)

London   1794

I wander through each chartered street,
Near where the chartered Thames does flow,
And mark in every face I meet
Marks of weakness, marks of woe.

In every cry of every man,   5
In every infant's cry of fear,
In every voice, in every ban,
The mind-forged manacles I hear.

How the chimney-sweeper's cry
Every black'ning church appalls   10
And the hapless soldier's sigh
Runs in blood down palace walls.

But most through midnight streets I hear
How the youthful harlot's curse
Blasts the new-born infant's tear   15
And blights with plagues the marriage hearse.

Here are only a few of the possible meanings of four of Blake's words:

- *chartered* (lines 1, 2)

  Denotations: Established by a charter (a written grant or a certificate of incorporation); leased or hired.

  Connotations: Defined, limited, restricted, channeled, mapped, bound by law; bought and sold (like a slave or an inanimate object); Magna Carta; charters given to crown colonies by the King.

  Other words in the poem with similar connotations: Ban, which can denote (1) a legal prohibition; (2) a churchman's curse or malediction; (3) in medieval times, an order summoning a king's vassals to fight for him. *Manacles,* or shackles, restrain movement. *Chimney-sweeper, soldier,* and *harlot* are all hirelings.

  Interpretation of the lines: The street has had mapped out for it the direction in which it must go; the Thames has had laid down to it the course it must follow. Street and river ｟ channeled, imprisoned, enslaved (like every inhabitant of London).

- *black'ning* (line 10)

  Denotation: Becoming black.

  Connotations: The darkening of something once light, the defilement of something once clean, the deepening of guilt, the gathering of darkness at the approach of night.

  Other words in the poem with similar connotations: Objects becoming marked or smudged (*marks of weakness, marks of woe* in the faces of passersby; bloodied walls of a palace; marriage blighted with plagues); the word *appalls* (denoting not only "to overcome with horror" but "to make pale" and also "to cast a pall or shroud over"); *midnight streets.*

  Interpretation of the line: Literally, every London church grows black from soot and hires a chimney-sweeper (a small boy) to help clean it. But Blake suggests too that by profiting from the suffering of the child laborer, the church is soiling its original purity.

- *Blasts, blights* (lines 15, 16)

  Denotations: Both *blast* and *blight* mean "to cause to wither" or "to ruin and destroy." Both are terms from horticulture. Frost *blasts* a bud and kills it; disease *blights* a growing plant.

  Connotations: Sickness and death; gardens shriveled and dying; gusts of wind and the ravages of insects; things blown to pieces or rotted and warped.

  Other words in the poem with similar connotations: Faces marked with weakness and woe; the child becomes a chimney-sweep; the soldier killed by war; blackening church and bloodied palace; young girl turned harlot; wedding carriage transformed into a hearse.

  Interpretation of the lines: Literally, the harlot spreads the plague of syphilis, which, carried into marriage, can cause a baby to be born blind. In a larger and more meaningful sense, Blake sees the prostitution of even one young girl corrupting the entire institution of matrimony and endangering every child.

Some of these connotations are more to the point than others; the reader of a poem nearly always has the problem of distinguishing relevant associations from irrelevant ones. We need to read a poem in its entirety and, when a word leaves us in doubt, look for other things in the poem to corroborate or refute what we think it means. Relatively simple and direct in its statement, Blake's account of his stroll through the city at night becomes an indictment of a whole social and religious order. The indictment could hardly be this effective if it were "mathematically plain," its every word restricted to one denotation clearly spelled out.

Wallace Stevens (1879–1955)

Disillusionment of Ten O'Clock   1923

The houses are haunted
By white night-gowns.
None are green,
Or purple with green rings,
Or green with yellow rings,   5
Or yellow with blue rings.
None of them are strange,
With socks of lace
And beaded ceintures.
People are not going   10
To dream of baboons and periwinkles.
Only, here and there, an old sailor,
Drunk and asleep in his boots,
Catches tigers
In red weather.   15

Questions

1. What are "beaded ceintures"? What does the phrase suggest?
2. What contrast does Stevens draw between the people who live in these houses and the old sailor? What do the connotations of "white night-gowns" and "sailor" add to this contrast?
3. What is lacking in these people who wear white night-gowns? Why should the poet's view of them be a "disillusionment"?

E. E. Cummings (1894–1962)

next to of course god america i   1926

"next to of course god america i
love you land of the pilgrims' and so forth oh
say can you see by the dawn's early my
country 'tis of centuries come and go
and are no more what of it we should worry   5
in every language even deafanddumb
thy sons acclaim your glorious name by gorry
by jingo by gee by gosh by gum
why talk of beauty what could be more beaut-
iful than these heroic happy dead   10
who rushed like lions to the roaring slaughter

they did not stop to think they died instead
then shall the voice of liberty be mute?"

He spoke. And drank rapidly a glass of water

Questions

1. How many allusions in this poem can you identify? What do all the sources of those allusions have in common?
2. Look up the origin of "jingo" (line 8). Is it used here as more than just a mindless exclamation?
3. Beyond what is actually said, what do the rhetoric of the first thirteen lines and the description in the last one suggest about the author's intentions in this poem?

Maria Hummel (b. 1973)

The Tree   2013
which was

in equal parts
earth and sky

is now in equal parts

house and fire   5

Questions

1. Although the poet doesn't directly say it, what is suggested in the last two lines?
2. Is the diction of the poem simple or complex? Might the simplicity be misleading? Is there more suggested here than we find on the surface?

Timothy Steele (b. 1948)

Epitaph   1979
Here lies Sir Tact, a diplomatic fellow
Whose silence was not golden, but just yellow.

Questions

1. To what famous saying does the poet allude?
2. What are the connotations of "golden"? Of "yellow"?

Hieu Minh Nguyen (b. 1991)

Arranged   2014

my grandmother tells me you are very pretty
your smile not of a girl but of a package
teeth straight and perfectly arranged
like each petal in a bride's bouquet

your smile not of a girl but of a package   5
you are presented to me as a trophy
like each petal in a bride's bouquet
a haunting hiding underneath a veil

you are presented to me as a trophy
in my sheets there's a continent between us   10
a haunting hiding underneath a veil
we will sleep in separate beds

in my sheets there's a continent between us
wedding photos hang in the walk-in closet
we will sleep in separate beds   15
make a habit out of undressing in the bathroom

wedding photos hang in the walk-in closet
teeth straight and perfectly arranged
make a habit out of undressing in the bathroom
my grandmother tells me you are very pretty   20

Questions

1. What is the dictionary definition of "arranged," as used in first and last stanzas of the poem? Does the word take on another meaning when you look more closely at the poem?

2. The form of "Arranged" is a **pantoum**, a Malayan poetic form that was adopted by the French and then made its way into English. Study the line repetitions in the poem. Can you determine the pattern? How does the use of this form enhance the meaning of the poem?

Diane Thiel (b. 1967)

The Minefield   2000

He was running with his friend from town to town.
They were somewhere between Prague and Dresden.
He was fourteen. His friend was faster
and knew a shortcut through the fields they could take.
He said there was lettuce growing in one of them,   5
and they hadn't eaten all day. His friend ran a few lengths ahead,
like a wild rabbit across the grass,
turned his head, looked back once,
and his body was scattered across the field.

My father told us this, one night,   10
and then continued eating dinner.

He brought them with him—the minefields.
He carried them underneath his good intentions.
He gave them to us—in the volume of his anger,
in the bruises we covered up with sleeves.   15
In the way he threw anything against the wall—
a radio, that wasn't even ours,
a melon, once, opened like a head.
In the way we still expect, years later and continents away,
that anything might explode at any time,   20
and we would have to run on alone

with a vision like that
only seconds behind.

Questions

1. In the opening lines of the poem, a seemingly small decision—to take a shortcut and find something to eat—leads to a horrifying result. What does this suggest about the poem's larger view of what life is like?
2. The speaker tells the story of the minefield before letting us know that the other boy was her father. What is the effect of this narrative strategy?
3. How does the image of the melon reinforce the poem's intentions?

H.D. [Hilda Doolittle] (1886–1961)

Sea Rose   1916

Rose, harsh rose,
marred and with stint of petals,
meagre flower, thin,
sparse of leaf,

more precious   5
than a wet rose
single on a stem—
you are caught in the drift.

Stunted, with small leaf,
you are flung on the sand,   10
you are lifted
in the crisp sand
that drives in the wind.

Can the spice-rose
drip such acrid fragrance   15
hardened in a leaf?

Po Chü-i (772–846)

The Cranes   830

The western wind has blown but a few days;
Yet the first leaf already flies from the bough.
On the drying paths I walk in my thin shoes;
In the first cold I have donned my quilted coat.
Through shallow ditches the floods are clearing away;   5
Through sparse bamboos trickles a slanting light.
In the early dusk, down an alley of green moss,
The garden-boy is leading the cranes home.

—Translated by Arthur Waley

Alfred, Lord Tennyson (1809–1892)

Tears, Idle Tears   1847

Tears, idle tears, I know not what they mean,
Tears from the depth of some divine despair
Rise in the heart, and gather to the eyes,
In looking on the happy Autumn-fields,
And thinking of the days that are no more.   5

Fresh as the first beam glittering on a sail,
That brings our friends up from the underworld,
Sad as the last which reddens over one
That sinks with all we love below the verge;
So sad, so fresh, the days that are no more.   10

Ah, sad and strange as in dark summer dawns
The earliest pipe of half-awakened birds
To dying ears, when unto dying eyes
The casement slowly grows a glimmering square;
So sad, so strange, the days that are no more.   15

Dear as remembered kisses after death,
And sweet as those by hopeless fancy feigned
On lips that are for others; deep as love,
Deep as first love, and wild with all regret;
O Death in Life, the days that are no more.   20

Question

Why is the speaker crying?

Anne-Marie Thompson (b. 1982)

Audiation   2008

for a future love

It will be clear, it will be like a tune
we heard as children, or have always known,
that echoes in our ears one later noon
and makes us feel, somehow, much less alone.
We will not sing, or hum, make it too real,   5
but think the line, and cast it from the keel.

* * *

It will be summer, it will be mid-June,
when children's voices try to hold the light
a little longer still—*too soon*. Too soon,
at eight o'clock, to turn in for the night,   10
we'll both decide on separate whims to turn
back from our doors and watch the last glints burn.

It will be warm, it will be slightly damp
after the long rains from the day before.
We'll watch the water underneath a lamp   15
begin to spark and wink toward something more
than concrete, something more than empty stair
to linger on, toward something in the air.

It will be sudden, it will be a gust
of wind that blows some bit of nothing—paper—   20
out of my hand. And you, thinking it must
be a great prize, will start a hopeless caper
up the street, returning empty-handed
to where I stand and wait, as if we'd planned it.

AUDIATION. A cognitive process by which the brain gives meaning to musical sound. *Audiation* is
similar to imagination for the auditory sense.

Rebecca Foust (b. 1957)

What You Work For   2010

Heft and hank of rope, halyard
clank of ringing chain

dragged link by gunnel-clunking link
and hand-over-hand hauled in

until at end, sudden greased release   5
of anchor weight

and you fall back, stunned by what
your dragging work has yoked

you to. Has brought
aboard to share your boat.   10

Richard Wilbur (1921–2017)

Love Calls Us to the Things of This World   1956

   The eyes open to a cry of pulleys,
And spirited from sleep, the astounded soul
Hangs for a moment bodiless and simple
As false dawn.
            Outside the open window
The morning air is all awash with angels.   5

   Some are in bed-sheets, some are in blouses,
Some are in smocks: but truly there they are.
Now they are rising together in calm swells
Of halcyon feeling, filling whatever they wear
With the deep joy of their impersonal breathing;   10

Now they are flying in place, conveying
The terrible speed of their omnipresence, moving
And staying like white water; and now of a sudden
They swoon down into so rapt a quiet
That nobody seems to be there.
                 The soul shrinks   15

From all that it is about to remember,
From the punctual rape of every blessèd day,
And cries,
          "Oh, let there be nothing on earth but laundry,
Nothing but rosy hands in the rising steam
And clear dances done in the sight of heaven."   20

Yet, as the sun acknowledges
With a warm look the world's hunks and colors,
The soul descends once more in bitter love
To accept the waking body, saying now
In a changed voice as the man yawns and rises,   25
   "Bring them down from their ruddy gallows;
Let there be clean linen for the backs of thieves;
Let lovers go fresh and sweet to be undone,
And the heaviest nuns walk in a pure floating
Of dark habits,
               keeping their difficult balance."   30

LOVE CALLS US TO THE THINGS OF THIS WORLD. Wilbur once said that his title was taken from St. Augustine, but in a later interview he admitted that neither he nor any critic has ever been able to locate the quotation. Whatever its source, however, the title establishes the poem's central idea that love allows us to return from the divine world of the spirit to the imperfect world of our everyday lives.

Questions

1. What are the "angels" in line 5? Why does this metaphor seem appropriate to the situation?
2. What is "the punctual rape of every blessèd day"? Who is being raped? Who or what commits the rape? Why would Wilbur choose this particular word with all its violent associations?
3. Whom or what does the soul love in line 23, and why is that love bitter?
4. Is it merely obesity that make the nuns' balance "difficult" in the two final lines of the poem? What other "balance" does Wilbur's poem suggest?
5. The soul has two speeches in the poem. How do they differ in tone and imagery?
6. The spiritual world is traditionally considered invisible. What concrete images does Wilbur use to express its special character?

■WRITING *effectively*

Richard Wilbur on Writing

Concerning "Love Calls Us to the Things of This World"   1966

If I understand this poem rightly, it has a free and organic rhythm: that is to say, its movement arises naturally from the emotion and from the objects and actions depicted. At the same time, the lines are metrical and disposed in stanzas. The subject matter is both exalted and vulgar. There is, I should think, sufficient description to satisfy an Imagist, but there is also a certain amount of statement; my hope is that the statement seems to grow inevitably out of the situation described. The language of the poem is at one moment elevated and at the next colloquial or slangy: for example, the imposing word "omnipresence" occurs not far from the undignified word "hunks." A critic would find in this poem certain patterns of sound, but those patterns of sound do not constitute an abstract music; they are meant,

Richard Wilbur

at any rate, to be inseparable from what is being said, a subordinate aspect of the poem's meaning.

The title of the poem is a quotation from St. Augustine: "Love Calls Us to the Things of This World." You must imagine the poem as occurring at perhaps seven-thirty in the morning; the scene is a bedroom high up in a city apartment building; outside the bedroom window, the first laundry of the day is being yanked across the sky and one has been awakened by the squeaking pulleys of the laundry line.

From "On My Own Work"

THINKING ABOUT DENOTATION AND CONNOTATION

People often convey their feelings indirectly, through body language, facial expression, tone of voice, and other ways. Similarly, the imagery, tone, and diction of a poem can suggest a message so clearly that it doesn't need to be stated outright.

- **Pay careful attention to what a poem suggests.** Jot down a few key observations both about what the poem says directly and what you might want to know but aren't told. What important details are you left to infer for yourself?
- **Establish what the poem actually says.** When journalists write a news story, they usually try to cover the "five W's" in the opening paragraph—who, what, when, where, and why. These questions are worthwhile ones to ask about a poem:

Who? Who is the speaker or central figure of the poem? (In William Blake's "London," for instance, the speaker is also the protagonist who witnesses the hellish horror of the city.) If the poem seems to be addressed not simply to the reader but to a more specific listener, identify that listener as well.

What? What objects or events are being seen or presented? Does the poem ever suddenly change its subject? (In Wallace Stevens's "Disillusionment of Ten O'Clock," for example, there are essentially two scenes—one dull and proper, the other wild and disreputable. What does that obvious shift suggest about Stevens's meaning?)

When? When does the poem take place? If a poet explicitly states a time of day or a season of the year, it is likely that the *when* of the poem is important. (The fact that Stevens's poem takes place at 10 P.M. and not 2 A.M. tells us a great deal about the people it describes.)

Where? Where is the poem set? Often the setting suggests something important, or plays a role in setting the mood.

Why? If the poem describes a dramatic action but does not provide an overt reason for the occurrence, perhaps the reader is meant to draw his or her own conclusions on the subject. (Tennyson's "Tears, Idle Tears" becomes more evocative by not being explicit about why the speaker weeps.)

■ **Remember, it is almost as important to know what a poem does not tell us as to know what it does.**

CHECKLIST: Writing About What a Poem Says and Suggests

☐ Who speaks the words of the poem? Is it a voice close to the poet's own? A fictional character? A real person?

☐ Who is the poem's central figure?

☐ To whom—if anyone—is the poem addressed?

☐ What objects or events are depicted?

☐ When does the poem take place? Is that timing significant in any way?

☐ Where does the action of the poem take place?

☐ Why does the action of the poem take place? Is there some significant motivation?

☐ Does the poem leave any of the above information out? If so, what does that lack of information reveal about the poem's intentions?

TOPICS FOR WRITING ON DENOTATION AND CONNOTATION

1. Search a poem of your own choosing for the answers to the "five W's"—*Who? What? When? Where? Why?* Indicate, with details, which of the questions are explicitly answered by the poem and which are left unaddressed.

2. Look closely at the central image of Richard Wilbur's "Love Calls Us to the Things of This World." Why does such an ordinary sight cause such intense feelings in the poem's speaker? Give evidence from the poem to back up your theory.

3. What do the various images in Tennyson's "Tears, Idle Tears" suggest about the speaker's reasons for weeping? Address each image, and explain what the images add up to.

4. The title of Anne-Marie Thompson's "Audiation" is a somewhat obscure term defined as "a cognitive process by which the brain gives meaning to musical sound." How does that definition harmonize with the content of the poem?

5. Paraphrase the literal content of H.D.'s "Sea Rose," then analyze how her word choice suggests additional meanings.

6. Browse through a newspaper or magazine for an advertisement that tries to surround a product with an aura. A new car, for instance, might be described in terms of some powerful jungle cat ("purring power, ready to spring"). Clip or photocopy the ad and circle words in it that seem especially suggestive. Then, in an accompanying essay, unfold the suggestions in these words and try to explain the ad's appeal. What differences can you see between how poetry and advertising copy use connotative language?

▶ TERMS FOR *review*

Denotation ▶ The literal, dictionary meaning of a word.

Connotation ▶ An association or additional meaning that a word, image, or phrase may carry, apart from its literal denotation or dictionary definition. A word may pick up connotations from the uses to which it has been put in the past.

Suggestion ▶ The power of a word to imply unspoken associations, in addition to its literal meaning.

Pantoum ▶ A Malayan poetic form that was adopted by the French and then made its way into English, which consists of interlocking quatrains. In a pantoum, the second and fourth lines of a stanza become the first and third lines of the succeeding stanza.

19

IMAGERY

*It is better to present one image in a lifetime
than to produce voluminous works.*

—EZRA POUND

What You Will Learn in This Chapter

- To define *imagery*
- To differentiate and explain the major types of imagery
- To recognize and describe *haiku* as a literary form
- To analyze the role of imagery in a poem

Ezra Pound (1885–1972)

In a Station of the Metro
1916

The apparition of these faces in the crowd;
Petals on a wet, black bough.

Pound said he wrote this poem to convey an experience: emerging one day from a train in the Paris subway (*Métro*), he beheld "suddenly a beautiful face, and then another and another." Originally he had described his impression in a poem thirty lines long. In this final version, each line contains an image, which, like a picture, may take the place of a thousand words.

Though the term **image** suggests a thing seen, when speaking of images in poetry, we generally mean *a word or sequence of words that refers to any sensory experience.* Often this experience is a sight (**visual imagery**, as in Pound's poem), but it may be a sound (**auditory imagery**) or a touch (**tactile imagery**, such as a perception of roughness or smoothness). It may be an odor or a taste or perhaps a bodily sensation such as pain, the prickling of gooseflesh, the quenching of thirst, or—as in the following brief poem—the perception of something cold.

Taniguchi Buson (1716–1783)

The piercing chill I feel
(about 1760)

The piercing chill I feel:
  my dead wife's comb, in our bedroom,
    under my heel . . .

—*Translated by Harold G. Henderson*

As in this **haiku** (in Japanese, a poem typically of three lines and seventeen syllables), an image can convey a flash of understanding. Had he wished, the poet might have spoken of the dead woman, of the contrast between her death and his memory of her, of his feelings toward death in general. But such a discussion would be quite different from the poem he actually wrote. Striking his bare foot against the comb, now cold and motionless but associated with the living wife (perhaps worn in her hair), the widower feels a shock as if he had touched the woman's corpse. A literal, physical sense of death is conveyed; the abstraction "death" is understood through the senses. To render the abstract in concrete terms is what poets often try to do; in this attempt, an image can be valuable.

IMAGERY

An image may occur in a single word, a phrase, a sentence, or, as in this case, an entire short poem. To speak of the **imagery** of a poem—all its images taken together—is often more useful than to speak of separate images. To divide Buson's haiku into five images—*chill, wife, comb, bedroom, heel*—is possible, for any noun that refers to a visible object or a sensation is an image, but this is to draw distinctions that in themselves mean little and to disassemble a single experience.

Does an image cause a reader to experience a sense impression? Not quite. Reading the word *petals*, no one literally sees petals; but the occasion is given for imagining them. The image asks to be seen with the mind's eye. And although "In a Station of the Metro" records what Ezra Pound saw, it is of course not necessary for a poet actually to have lived through a sensory experience in order to write of it. Keats may never have seen a newly discovered planet through a telescope, despite the image in his sonnet "On first looking into Chapman's Homer."

It is tempting to think of imagery as mere decoration, particularly when we read Keats, who fills his poems with an abundance of sights, sounds, odors, and tastes. But a successful image is not just a dab of paint or a flashy bauble. When Keats opens "The Eve of St. Agnes" with what have been called the coldest lines in literature, he evokes by a series of images a setting and a mood:

> St. Agnes' eve—Ah, bitter chill it was!
> The owl, for all his feathers, was a-cold;
> The hare limped trembling through the frozen grass,
> And silent was the flock in woolly fold:
> Numb were the Beadsman's fingers, while he told
> His rosary, and while his frosted breath,
> Like pious incense from a censer old,
> Seemed taking flight for heaven, without a death . . .

T. S. Eliot (1888–1965)

The winter evening settles down   1917

The winter evening settles down
With smell of steaks in passageways.
Six o'clock.
The burnt-out ends of smoky days.
And now a gusty shower wraps   5
The grimy scraps
Of withered leaves about your feet
And newspapers from vacant lots;
The showers beat
On broken blinds and chimney-pots,   10
And at the corner of the street
A lonely cab-horse steams and stamps.

And then the lighting of the lamps.

Questions

1. What mood is evoked by the images in Eliot's poem?
2. What kind of city neighborhood has the poet chosen to describe? How can you tell?

Theodore Roethke (1908–1963)

Root Cellar   1948

Nothing would sleep in that cellar, dank as a ditch,
Bulbs broke out of boxes hunting for chinks in the dark,
Shoots dangled and drooped,
Lolling obscenely from mildewed crates,
Hung down long yellow evil necks, like tropical snakes.   5
And what a congress of stinks!—
Roots ripe as old bait,
Pulpy stems, rank, silo-rich,
Leaf-mold, manure, lime, piled against slippery planks.
Nothing would give up life: 10
Even the dirt kept breathing a small breath.

Questions

1. As a boy growing up in Saginaw, Michigan, Theodore Roethke spent much of his time
   in a large commercial greenhouse run by his family. What details in his poem show more
   than a passing acquaintance with growing things?
2. What varieties of image does "Root Cellar" contain? Point out examples.
3. What do you understand to be Roethke's attitude toward the root cellar? Does he view it
   as a disgusting chamber of horrors? Pay special attention to the last two lines.

Elizabeth Bishop (1911–1979)

The Fish   1946

I caught a tremendous fish
and held him beside the boat
half out of water, with my hook
fast in a corner of his mouth.
He didn't fight.   5
He hadn't fought at all.
He hung a grunting weight,
battered and venerable
and homely. Here and there
his brown skin hung in strips   10
like ancient wallpaper,
and its pattern of darker brown
was like wallpaper:
shapes like full-blown roses
stained and lost through age.   15
He was speckled with barnacles,
fine rosettes of lime,
and infested
with tiny white sea-lice,
and underneath two or three   20
rags of green weed hung down.
While his gills were breathing in
the terrible oxygen
—the frightening gills,
fresh and crisp with blood,   25
that can cut so badly—
I thought of the coarse white flesh
packed in like feathers,
the big bones and the little bones,
the dramatic reds and blacks   30
of his shiny entrails,
and the pink swim-bladder
like a big peony.
I looked into his eyes
which were far larger than mine   35
but shallower, and yellowed,
the irises backed and packed
with tarnished tinfoil
seen through the lenses
of old scratched isinglass.   40
They shifted a little, but not
to return my stare.
—It was more like the tipping
of an object toward the light.
I admired his sullen face,   45

the mechanism of his jaw,
and then I saw
that from his lower lip
—if you could call it a lip—
grim, wet, and weaponlike,   50
hung five old pieces of fish-line,
or four and a wire leader
with the swivel still attached,
with all their five big hooks
grown firmly in his mouth.   55
A green line, frayed at the end
where he broke it, two heavier lines,
and a fine black thread
still crimped from the strain and snap
when it broke and he got away.   60
Like medals with their ribbons
frayed and wavering,
a five-haired beard of wisdom
trailing from his aching jaw.
I stared and stared   65
and victory filled up
the little rented boat,
from the pool of bilge
where oil had spread a rainbow
around the rusted engine   70
to the bailer rusted orange,
the sun-cracked thwarts,
the oarlocks on their strings,
the gunnels—until everything
was rainbow, rainbow, rainbow!   75
And I let the fish go.

Questions

1. How many abstract words does this poem contain? What proportion of the poem is imagery?
2. What is the speaker's attitude toward the fish? Comment in particular on lines 61–64.
3. What attitude do the images of the rainbow of oil (line 69), the orange bailer (bailing bucket, line 71), and the "sun-cracked thwarts" (line 72) convey? Does the poet expect us to feel mournful because the boat is in such sorry condition?
4. What is meant by "rainbow, rainbow, rainbow"?
5. How do these images prepare us for the conclusion? Why does the speaker let the fish go?

Emily Dickinson (1830–1886)

A Route of Evanescence   (about 1879)

A Route of Evanescence
With a revolving Wheel –
A Resonance of Emerald –
A Rush of Cochineal° –

                                                           red dye

And every Blossom on the Bush   5
Adjusts its tumbled Head –
The mail from Tunis, probably,
An easy Morning's Ride –

A ROUTE OF EVANESCENCE. Dickinson titled this poem "A Humming-bird" in an 1880 letter to a friend.
1 *Evanescence:* ornithologist's term for the luminous sheen of certain birds' feathers. 7 *Tunis:* capital
city of Tunisia, North Africa.

Question

What is the subject of this poem? How can you tell?

Jean Toomer (1894–1967)

Reapers   1923

Black reapers with the sound of steel on stones
Are sharpening scythes. I see them place the hones
In their hip-pockets as a thing that's done,
And start their silent swinging, one by one.
Black horses drive a mower through the weeds,   5
And there, a field rat, startled, squealing bleeds,
His belly close to ground. I see the blade,
Blood-stained, continue cutting weeds and shade.

Questions

1. Imagine the scene Toomer describes. What details most vividly strike the mind's eye?
2. What kind of image is "silent swinging"?
3. Read the poem aloud. Notice especially the effect of the words "sound of steel on stones"
   and "field rat, startled, squealing bleeds." What interesting sounds are present in the very
   words that contain these images?
4. What feelings do you get from this poem as a whole? Besides appealing to our auditory
   and visual imagination, what do the images contribute?

Gerard Manley Hopkins (1844–1889)

Pied Beauty   (1877)

Glory be to God for dappled things—
    For skies of couple-color as a brinded° cow;   streaked
        For rose-moles all in stipple° upon trout that swim;   speckled or dotted
Fresh-firecoal chestnut-falls; finches' wings;
    Landscape plotted and pieced—fold, fallow, and plow;   5
        And áll trádes, their gear and tackle and trim.°   equipment

All things counter, original, spare, strange;
    Whatever is fickle, freckled (who knows how?)
        With swift, slow; sweet, sour; adazzle, dim;
He fathers-forth whose beauty is past change: 10
                    Praise him.

Questions

1. What does the word "pied" mean? (Hint: what does a Pied Piper look like?)
2. According to Hopkins, what do "skies," "cow," "trout," "ripe chestnuts," "finches' wings," and "landscapes" all have in common? What landscapes can the poet have in mind? (Have you ever seen any "dappled" landscape while looking down from an airplane, or from a mountain or high hill?)
3. What do you make of line 6? What can carpenters' saws and ditch-diggers' spades possibly have in common with the dappled things in lines 2–4?
4. Does Hopkins refer only to visual contrasts? What other kinds of variation interest him?
5. Try to state in your own words the theme of this poem. How essential to our understanding of this theme are Hopkins's images?

ABOUT HAIKU

Arakida Moritake (1473–1549)

The falling flower

The falling flower
I saw drift back to the branch
Was a butterfly.

—Translated by Babette Deutsch

Haiku means "beginning-verse" in Japanese—perhaps because the form may have originated in a game. Players, given a haiku, were supposed to extend its three lines into a longer poem. Haiku (the word can also be plural) consist mainly of imagery, but, as we saw in Buson's lines about the cold comb, their imagery is not always only pictorial; it can involve any of the five senses. Haiku are so short that they depend on imagery to trigger associations and responses in the reader. A haiku in Japanese is rimeless; its seventeen syllables are traditionally arranged in three lines, usually following a pattern of five, seven, and five syllables. English haiku frequently ignore such a pattern, being rimed or unrimed as the poet prefers. What English haiku do try to preserve is the powerful way Japanese haiku capture the intensity of a particular moment, usually by linking two concrete images. There is little room for abstract thoughts or general observations. The following attempt, though containing seventeen syllables, is far from haiku in spirit:

Now that our love is gone
I feel within my soul
a nagging distress.

Unlike the author of those lines, haiku poets look out upon a literal world, seldom looking inward to *discuss* their feelings. Japanese haiku tend to be seasonal in subject, but because they are so highly compressed, they usually only *imply* a season: a blossom indicates spring; a crow on a branch, autumn; snow, winter. Not just pretty little sketches of nature (as some Westerners think), haiku assume a view of the universe in which observer and nature are not separated.

Haiku emerged in sixteenth-century Japan and soon developed into a deeply esteemed form. Even today, Japanese soldiers, stockbrokers, scientists, schoolchildren, and the emperor himself (who abdicated in 2017, possibly to dedicate more time to poetry) still find occasion to pen haiku. Soon after the form first captured the attention of Western poets at the end of the nineteenth century, it became immensely influential for modern poets, such as Ezra Pound, William Carlos Williams, and H.D., as a model for the kind of verse they wanted to write—concise, direct, and imagistic.

The Japanese consider the poems of the "Three Masters"—Basho, Buson, and Issa—to be the pinnacle of the classical haiku. Each poet had his own personality: Basho, the ascetic seeker of Zen enlightenment; Buson, the worldly artist; Issa, the sensitive master of wit and pathos. Here are liberal translations of poems from each of the "Three Masters."

Matsuo Basho (1644–1694)

Heat-lightning streak

Heat-lightning streak—
through darkness pierces
the heron's shriek.

> —*Translated by X. J. Kennedy*

In the old stone pool

In the old stone pool
a frogjump:
splishhhhh.

> —*Translated by X. J. Kennedy*

Taniguchi Buson (1716–1783)

On the one-ton temple bell

On the one-ton temple bell
a moonmoth, folded into sleep,
sits still.

> —*Translated by X. J. Kennedy*

Moonrise on mudflats

Moonrise on mudflats,
the line of water and sky
blurred by a bullfrog

> —*Translated by Michael Stillman*

Kobayashi Issa (1763–1827)

only one guy

only one guy and
only one fly trying to
make the guest room do.

> —*Translated by Cid Corman*

Cricket

Cricket, be
careful! I'm rolling
over!

> —*Translated by Robert Bly*

HAIKU FROM JAPANESE INTERNMENT CAMPS

Japanese immigrants brought the tradition of haiku-writing to the United States, often forming local clubs to pursue their shared literary interests. During World War II, when Japanese Americans were unjustly considered "enemy aliens" and confined to federal internment camps, these poets continued to write in their bleak new surroundings. Today these haiku provide a vivid picture of the deprivations suffered by the poets, their families, and their fellow internees.

Suiko Matsushita

Rain shower from mountain

Rain shower from mountain
quietly soaking
barbed wire fence

> —Translated by Violet Kazue
> de Cristoforo

Cosmos in bloom

Cosmos in bloom
as if no war
were taking place

> —Translated by Violet Kazue
> de Cristoforo

Hakuro Wada

Even the croaking of frogs

Even the croaking of frogs
comes from outside the barbed wire fence
this is our life

> —Translated by Violet Kazue
> de Cristoforo

Neiji Ozawa

The war—this year

The war—this year
New Year midnight bell
ringing in the desert

> —Translated by Violet Kazue
> de Cristoforo

CONTEMPORARY HAIKU

If you care to try your hand at haiku-writing, here are a few suggestions: make every word matter; use few adjectives; shun needless conjunctions; set your poem in the present. ("Haiku," said Basho, "is simply what is happening in this place at this moment.") Like many writers of haiku, you may wish to confine your poem to what can be seen, heard, smelled, tasted, or touched. Mere sensory reports, however, will be meaningless unless they make the reader feel something.

Here are six more recent haiku written in English. (Don't expect them all to observe a strict arrangement of seventeen syllables, however.) Haiku, in any language, is an art of few words but many suggestions. A haiku starts us thinking and telling.

Nick Virgilio (1928–1989)

The Old Neighborhood

the old neighborhood
falling to the wrecking ball:
names in the sidewalk

Yone Noguchi (1875–1947)

Oh, How Cool   1920

Oh, how cool—
The sound of the bell
That leaves the bell itself.

Penny Harter (b. 1940)

broken bowl

broken bowl
the pieces
still rocking.

Adelle Foley (1940–2016)

Learning to Shave (Father Teaching Son)

   A nick on the jaw
The razor's edge of manhood
   Along the bloodline.

Jennifer Brutschy (b. 1960)

Born Again

Born Again
she speaks excitedly
of death.

Garry Gay (b. 1951)

Hole in the ozone

Hole in the ozone
My bald spot . . .
sunburned

FOR REVIEW AND FURTHER STUDY

John Keats (1795–1821)

Bright star, would I were steadfast as thou art   (1819)

Bright star, would I were steadfast as thou art—
   Not in lone splendor hung aloft the night,
And watching, with eternal lids apart,
   Like Nature's patient, sleepless Eremite,°   *hermit*
The moving waters at their priestlike task   5
   Of pure ablution round earth's human shores,
Or gazing on the new soft-fallen mask
   Of snow upon the mountains and the moors—
No—yet still steadfast, still unchangeable,
   Pillowed upon my fair love's ripening breast,   10
To feel for ever its soft swell and fall,
   Awake for ever in a sweet unrest,
Still, still to hear her tender-taken breath,
And so live ever—or else swoon to death.

Questions

1. Stars are conventional symbols for love and a loved one. (Love, Shakespeare tells us in a sonnet, "is the star to every wandering bark.") In this sonnet, why is it not possible for the star to have this meaning? How does Keats use it?
2. What seems concrete and particular in the speaker's observations?
3. Suppose Keats had said "slow and easy" instead of "tender-taken" in line 13. What would have been lost?

Experiment: Writing with Images

Taking the following poems as examples from which to start rather than as models to be slavishly copied, try to compose a brief poem that consists largely of imagery.

Walt Whitman (1819–1892)

The Runner   1867

On a flat road runs the well-train'd runner,
He is lean and sinewy with muscular legs,
He is thinly clothed, he leans forward as he runs,
With lightly closed fists and arms partially rais'd.

H.D. [*Hilda Doolittle*] (1886–1961)

Heat   1916

O wind, rend open the heat,
cut apart the heat,
rend it to tatters.

Fruit cannot drop
through this thick air—   5
fruit cannot fall into heat
that presses up and blunts
the points of pears
and rounds the grapes.

Cut the heat—   10
plough through it,
turning it on either side
of your path.

William Carlos Williams (1883–1963)

El Hombre   1917

It's a strange courage
you give me ancient star:

Shine alone in the sunrise
toward which you lend no part!

Billy Collins (b. 1941)

Embrace   1988

You know the parlor trick.
Wrap your arms around your own body
and from the back it looks like
someone is embracing you,
her hands grasping your shirt,   5
her fingernails teasing your neck.

From the front it is another story.
You never looked so alone,
your crossed elbows and screwy grin.
You could be waiting for a tailor   10
to fit you for a straitjacket,
one that would hold you really tight.

Robert Bly (b. 1926)

Driving to Town Late to Mail a Letter   1962

It is a cold and snowy night. The main street is deserted.
The only things moving are swirls of snow.
As I lift the mailbox door, I feel its cold iron.
There is a privacy I love in this snowy night.
Driving around, I will waste more time.   5

Chana Bloch (b. 1940)

Tired Sex   1998

We're trying to strike a match in a matchbook
that has lain all winter under the woodpile:
damp sulphur
on sodden cardboard.
I catch myself yawning. Through the window   5
I watch that sparrow the cat
keeps batting around.

Like turning the pages of a book the teacher assigned—

You ought to read it, she said.
It's great literature.   10

Gary Snyder (b. 1930)

Mid-August at Sourdough Mountain Lookout   1959

Down valley a smoke haze
Three days heat, after five days rain
Pitch glows on the fir-cones
Across rocks and meadows
Swarms of new flies.   5

I cannot remember things I once read
A few friends, but they are in cities.
Drinking cold snow-water from a tin cup
Looking down for miles
Through high still air.   10

MID-AUGUST AT SOURDOUGH MOUNTAIN LOOKOUT. *Sourdough Mountain:* in the state of Washington, where the poet's job at the time was to watch for forest fires.

Angela Alaimo O'Donnell (b. 1960)

Tattoo   2007

> *Queequeg himself in his own proper person was a*
> *riddle to unfold, a wondrous work in one volume.*
> —*Moby Dick*

Aureola of vaccination, small sun.
Stippled freckles burnt deep by Spain.

The bite of escalator steps, right knee.
The scalpel's ounce of flesh, right breast.

Lines of longitude etched along the belly   5
By swell and swell and swell of child.

Wrinkled forehead, crinkled brow of poor sight.
Neat print of crow's feet at each eye.

The moles doled out at birth.
The stiff lip of strong-limbed women.   10

These marks, too, hieroglyphic,
A language of eternity and once.

Story inscribed on warm parchment
That breathes and beats beneath life's needle.

Stevie Smith (1902–1971)

Not Waving but Drowning   1957

Nobody heard him, the dead man,
But still he lay moaning:
I was much further out than you thought
And not waving but drowning.

Poor chap, he always loved larking   5
And now he's dead
It must have been too cold for him his heart gave way,
They said.

Oh, no no no, it was too cold always
(Still the dead one lay moaning)   10
I was much too far out all my life
And not waving but drowning.

■ WRITING *effectively*

Ezra Pound on Writing

The Image   1913

An "Image" is that which presents an intellectual and emotional complex in an instant
of time. I use the term "complex" rather in the
technical sense employed by the newer psychologists, such as Hart, though we might not
agree absolutely in our application.

Ezra Pound

It is the presentation of such a "complex"
instantaneously which gives that sense of sudden liberation; that sense of freedom from time
limits and space limits; that sense of sudden
growth, which we experience in the presence of
the greatest works of art.

It is better to present one Image in a lifetime than to produce voluminous works.

All this, however, some may consider open
to debate. The immediate necessity is to tabu-
late A LIST OF DON'TS for those beginning to
write verses. I can not put all of them into Mosaic negative.

• • •

Use no superfluous word, no adjective which does not reveal something.

Don't use such an expression as "dim lands *of peace*." It dulls the image. It mixes
an abstraction with the concrete. It comes from the writer's not realizing that the
natural object is always the *adequate* symbol.

Go in fear of abstractions. Do not retell in mediocre verse what has already been
done in good prose. Don't think any intelligent person is going to be deceived when
you try to shirk all the difficulties of the unspeakably difficult art of good prose by
chopping your composition into line lengths.

From "A Few Don'ts"

THINKING ABOUT IMAGERY

Images are powerful things—thus the old saw, "A picture is worth a thousand words."
A poem, however, must build its pictures from words. By taking note of its imagery,
and watching how the nature of those images evolves from start to finish, you can go
a long way toward a better understanding of the poem. The following steps can help:

- **Make a short list of the poem's key images.** Be sure to write them down
  in the order they appear, because the sequence can be as important as the
  images themselves.
- **Take the poem's title into account.** A title often points the way to important insights.

- **Remember: not all images are visual.** Images can draw on any or all of the five senses.
- **Jot down key adjectives or other qualifying words.**
- **Go back through your list and take notes about what moods or attitudes are suggested by each image.** What do you notice about the movement from the first image to the last?

Example: **Robert Bly's "Driving to Town Late to Mail a Letter"**

Let's try this method on a short poem. An initial list of images in Bly's "Driving to Town Late to Mail a Letter" might look like this:

> cold and snowy night
> deserted main street
> mailbox door—cold iron
> snowy night (speaker loves its privacy)
> speaker drives around (to waste time)

Bly's title also contains several crucial images. Let's add them to the top of the list:

> driving (to town)
> late night
> a letter (to be mailed)

Looking over our list, we see how the images provide an outline of the poem's story. We also see how Bly begins the poem without providing an initial sense of how his speaker feels about the situation. Is driving to town late on a snowy evening a positive, negative, or neutral experience? By noting where (in line 4) the speaker reveals a subjective response to an image ("There is a privacy I love in this snowy night"), we begin to grasp the poem's overall emotional structure. We might also note on our list how the poem begins and ends with the same image (driving), but uses it for different effects. At the beginning, the speaker is driving for the practical purpose of mailing a letter, but at the end, he drives purely for pleasure.

Simply by noting the images from start to finish, we have already worked out a rough essay outline—all on a single sheet of paper or a few inches of computer screen.

CHECKLIST: Writing About Imagery

☐ List a poem's key images, in the order in which they appear.

☐ What does the poem's title suggest?

☐ Remember, images can draw on all five senses—not just the visual.

☐ List key adjectives or other qualifying words.

☐ What emotions or attitudes are suggested by each image?

☐ Does the mood of the imagery change from start to finish?

☐ What is suggested by the movement from one image to the next? Remember that the order or sequence of images is almost as important as the images themselves.

TOPICS FOR WRITING ON IMAGERY

1. Apply the steps listed in "Checklist: Writing About Imagery" to one of the poems in this chapter. Stevie Smith's "Not Waving but Drowning," John Keats's "Bright star, would I were steadfast as thou art," Billy Collins's "Embrace," and Jean Toomer's "Reapers" would each make a good subject. Make a brief list of images, and jot down notes on what the images suggest. Now write a two-page description of this process—what it revealed about the poem itself and about reading poetry in general.

2. Choose a small, easily overlooked object in your home that has special significance to you. Write a paragraph-long, excruciatingly detailed description of the item, putting at least four senses into play. Without making any direct statements about the item's importance to you, try to let the imagery convey the mood you associate with it. Bring your paragraph to class, exchange it with a partner, and see if he or she can identify the mood you were trying to convey.

3. Reread the section on haiku in this chapter. Write three or four haiku of your own and a brief prose account of your experience in writing them. Did anything about the process surprise you?

4. Examining any poem in this chapter, demonstrate how its imagery helps communicate its general theme. Be specific in noting how each key image contributes to the poem's total effect. Feel free to consult criticism on the poem but make sure to credit any observation you borrow from a critical source.

SAMPLE STUDENT PAPER

Here is a paper on the imagery in Elizabeth Bishop's "The Fish," written by a student of Mark Bernier's at Blinn College in Brenham, Texas.

Woods 1

Becki Woods

Professor Bernier

English 220

23 February 2019

Faded Beauty: Bishop's Use of Imagery in "The Fish"

Upon first reading, Elizabeth Bishop's "The Fish" appears to be a simple fishing tale. A close investigation of the imagery in Bishop's highly detailed description, however, reveals a different sort of poem. The real theme of Bishop's poem is a compassion and respect for the fish's lifelong struggle to survive. By carefully and effectively describing the captured fish, his reaction to being caught, and the symbols of his past struggles to stay alive, Bishop creates, through her images of beauty, victory, and survival, something more than a simple tale.

The first four lines of the poem are quite ordinary and factual:

I caught a tremendous fish

and held him beside the boat

half out of water, with my hook

fast in a corner of his mouth. (lines 1–4)

First sentence gives name of author and work

Thesis sentence

Topic sentence

Woods 2

Except for *tremendous*, Bishop's persona uses no exaggerations—unlike most fishing stories—to set up the situation of catching the fish. The detailed description begins as the speaker recounts the event further, noticing something signally important about the captive fish: "He didn't fight" (5). At this point the poem begins to seem unusual: most fish stories are about how ferociously the prey resists being captured. The speaker also notes that the "battered and venerable / and homely" fish offered no resistance to being caught (8–9). The image of the submissive attitude of the fish is essential to the theme of the poem. It is his "utter passivity [that] makes [the persona's] detailed scrutiny possible" (McNally 192).

Once the image of the passive fish has been established, the speaker begins an examination of the fish itself, noting that "Here and there / his brown skin hung in strips / like ancient wallpaper" (9–11). By comparing the fish's skin to wallpaper, the persona creates, as Sybil Estess argues, "implicit suggestions of both artistry and decay" (713). Images of peeling wallpaper are instantly brought to mind. The comparison of the fish's skin and wallpaper, though "helpful in conveying an accurate notion of the fish's color to anyone with memories of Victorian parlors and their yellowed wallpaper . . . is," according to Nancy McNally, "even more useful in evoking the associations of deterioration which usually surround such memories" (192). The fish's faded beauty has been hinted at in the comparison, thereby setting up the detailed imagery that soon follows:

> He was speckled with barnacles,
>
> fine rosettes of lime,
>
> and infested
>
> with tiny white sea-lice,
>
> and underneath two or three
>
> rags of green weed hung down. (16–21)

The persona sees the fish as he is; the infestations and faults are not left out of the description. Yet, at the same time, the fisher "express[es] what [he/she] has sensed of the character of the fish" (Estess 714).

Bishop's persona notices "shapes like full-blown roses / stained and lost through age" on the fish's skin (14–15). The persona's perception of the fish's beauty is revealed along with a recognition of its faded beauty, which is best shown in the description of the fish's being speckled with barnacles and spotted with lime. However, the fisher observes these spots and sees them as rosettes—as objects of beauty, not just ugly brown spots. These images contribute to the persona's recognition of beauty's having become faded beauty.

The poem next turns to a description of the fish's gills. The imagery in "While his gills were breathing in / the terrible oxygen" (22–23) leads "to the very

Sidebar annotations:

Quotations from secondary source

Topic sentence

Essay moves systematically through poem, from start to finish

Textual evidence, mix of long and short quotations

Transitional phrase begins topic sentence

structure of the creature" that is now dying (Hopkins 201). The descriptions of the fish's interior beauty—"the coarse white flesh / packed in like feathers," the colors "of his shiny entrails," and his "pink swim-bladder / like a big peony"—are reminders of the life that seems about to end (27–28, 31–33).

The composite image of the fish's essential beauty—his being alive—is developed further in the description of the five fish hooks that the captive, living fish carries in his lip:

> grim, wet, and weaponlike,
>
> hung five old pieces of fish-line,
>
> . . . .
>
> with all their five big hooks
>
> grown firmly in his mouth. (50–51, 54–55)

As if fascinated by them, the persona, observing how the lines must have been broken during struggles to escape, sees the hooks as "medals with their ribbons / frayed and wavering, / a five-haired beard of wisdom / trailing from his aching jaw" (61–64), and the fisher becomes enthralled by re-created images of the fish's fighting desperately for his life on at least five separate occasions—and winning. Crale Hopkins suggests that "[i]n its capability not only for mere existence, but for action, escaping from previous anglers, the fish shares the speaker's humanity" (202), thus revealing the fisher's deepening understanding of how he or she must now act. The persona has "all along," notes Estess, "describe[d] the fish not just with great detail but with an imaginative empathy for the aquatic creature. In her more-than-objective description, [the fisher] relates what [he/she] has seen to be both the pride and poverty of the fish" (715). It is at this point that the narrator of this fishing tale has a moment of clarity. Realizing the fish's history and the glory the fish has achieved in escaping previous hookings, the speaker sees everything become "rainbow, rainbow, rainbow!" (75)—and then unexpectedly lets the fish go.

Bishop's "The Fish" begins by describing an event that might easily be a conventional story's climax: "I caught a tremendous fish" (1). The poem, however, develops into a highly detailed account of a fisher noticing both the age and the faded beauty of the captive and his present beauty and past glory as well. The fishing tale is not simply a recounting of a capture; it is a gradually unfolding epiphany in which the speaker sees the fish in an entirely new light. The intensity of this encounter between an apparently experienced fisher in a rented boat and a battle-hardened fish is delivered through the poet's skillful use of imagery. It is through the description of the capture of an aged fish that Bishop offers her audience her theme of compassion derived from a respect for the struggle for survival.

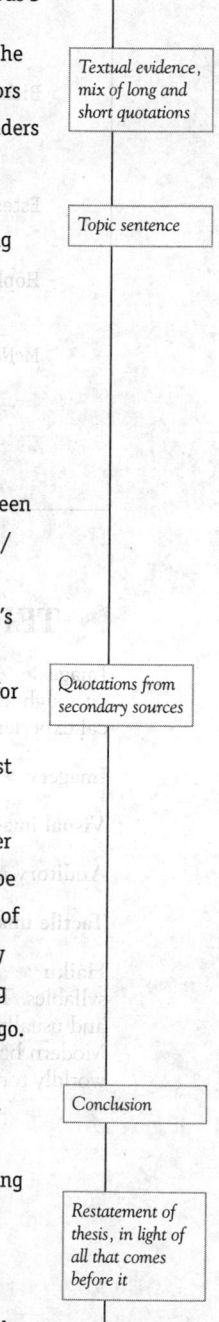

Textual evidence, mix of long and short quotations

Topic sentence

Quotations from secondary sources

Conclusion

Restatement of thesis, in light of all that comes before it

Woods 4

Works Cited

Bishop, Elizabeth. "The Fish." *Literature: An Introduction to Fiction, Poetry, Drama, and Writing*, edited by X. J. Kennedy et al., 14th ed., Pearson, 2020, pp. 769–70.

Estess, Sybil P. "Elizabeth Bishop: The Delicate Art of Map Making." *Southern Review*, vol. 13, no. 4, Autumn 1977, pp. 705–27.

Hopkins, Crale D. "Inspiration as Theme: Art and Nature in the Poetry of Elizabeth Bishop." *Arizona Quarterly*, vol. 32, 1976, pp. 200–02.

McNally, Nancy L. "Elizabeth Bishop: The Discipline of Description." *Twentieth Century Literature*, vol. 11, no. 4, Jan. 1966, pp. 189–201. *JSTOR*, doi: 10.2307/440842.

▶ TERMS FOR *review*

Image ▶ A word or series of words that refers to any sensory experience (usually sight, although also sound, smell, touch, or taste). An image is a direct or literal recreation of physical experience and adds immediacy to literary language.

Imagery ▶ The collective set of images in a poem or other literary work.

Visual imagery ▶ Imagery that refers to the sense of sight or presents something one may see.

Auditory imagery ▶ Imagery that refers to the sense of hearing.

Tactile imagery ▶ Imagery that refers to the sense of touch.

Haiku ▶ A Japanese verse form that typically has three unrhymed lines of five, seven, and five syllables. Traditional haiku are often serious and spiritual in tone, relying mostly on imagery, and usually set (often by implication instead of direct statement) in one of the four seasons. Modern haiku in English sometimes ignore strict syllable count and may have a more playful, worldly tone.

20 FIGURES OF SPEECH

All slang is metaphor, and all metaphor is poetry.
—G. K. CHESTERTON

What You Will Learn in This Chapter

- To define *simile*
- To define *metaphor*
- To recognize the major figures of speech
- To analyze the role of figurative speech in a poem

WHY SPEAK FIGURATIVELY?

"I will speak daggers to her, but use none," says Hamlet, preparing to confront his mother. His statement makes sense only because we realize that *daggers* is to be taken two ways: literally (denoting sharp, pointed weapons) and nonliterally (referring to something that can be used *like* weapons—namely, words). Reading poetry, we often meet comparisons between two things whose similarity we have never noticed before. When Marianne Moore observes that a fir tree has "an emerald turkey-foot at the top," the result is a pleasure that poetry richly affords: the sudden recognition of likenesses.

A treetop like a turkey-foot, words like daggers—such comparisons are called **figures of speech**. A figure of speech occurs whenever a speaker or writer, for the sake of freshness or emphasis, departs from the usual denotations, or literal definitions, of words. Certainly, when Hamlet says he will speak daggers, no one expects him to release pointed weapons from his lips, for *daggers* is not to be read solely for its denotation. Its connotations, or suggested meanings—sharp, stabbing, piercing, wounding—also come to mind, and we see ways in which words and daggers might work alike.

Figures of speech are not devices to state what is demonstrably untrue. Indeed they often state truths that more literal language cannot communicate; they call attention to such truths; they lend them emphasis.

Alfred, Lord Tennyson (1809–1892)

The Eagle

1851

He clasps the crag with crooked hands;
Close to the sun in lonely lands,
Ringed with the azure world, he stands.

The wrinkled sea beneath him crawls;
He watches from his mountain walls,   5
And like a thunderbolt he falls.

This brief poem is rich in figurative language. In the first line, the phrase *crooked hands* may surprise us. An eagle does not have hands, we might protest; but the objection would be a quibble, for evidently Tennyson is indicating exactly how an eagle clasps a crag, in the way that human fingers clasp a thing. By implication, too, the eagle is a person. *Close to the sun*, if taken literally, is an absurd exaggeration, the sun being a mean distance of 93 million miles from the earth. For the eagle to be closer to it by the altitude of a mountain is so minor as to be insignificant. But figuratively, Tennyson conveys that the eagle stands above the clouds, perhaps silhouetted against the sun, and for the moment belongs to the heavens rather than to the land and sea. The word *ringed* makes a circle of the whole world's horizons and suggests that we see the world from the eagle's height; the *wrinkled sea* becomes an aged, sluggish animal; *mountain walls*, possibly literal, also suggests a fort or castle; and finally the eagle itself is likened to a thunderbolt in speed and in power, perhaps also in that its beak is—like our abstract conception of a lightning bolt—pointed. How much of the poem can be taken literally? Only *he clasps the crag, he stands, he watches, he falls*. The rest is made of figures of speech. The result is that, reading Tennyson's poem, we gain a bird's-eye view of sun, sea, and land—and even of bird. Like imagery, figurative language refers us to the physical world.

William Shakespeare (1564–1616)

Shall I compare thee to a summer's day? (Sonnet 18)   1609

Shall I compare thee to a summer's day?
Thou art more lovely and more temperate.
Rough winds do shake the darling buds of May,
And summer's lease hath all too short a date.
Sometime too hot the eye of heaven shines,   5
And often is his gold complexion dimmed;
And every fair° from fair sometimes declines,   *fair one*
By chance, or nature's changing course, untrimmed:
But thy eternal summer shall not fade,
Nor lose possession of that fair thou ow'st,°   *ownest, have*   10
Nor shall death brag thou wand'rest in his shade,
When in eternal lines to time thou grow'st.
    So long as men can breathe or eyes can see,
    So long lives this, and this gives life to thee.

Howard Moss (1922–1987)

Shall I Compare Thee to a Summer's Day?   1976

Who says you're like one of the dog days?
You're nicer. And better.
Even in May, the weather can be gray,
And a summer sub-let doesn't last forever.

Sometimes the sun's too hot; 5
Sometimes it is not.
Who can stay young forever?
People break their necks or just drop dead!
But you? Never!
If there's just one condensed reader left 10
Who can figure out the abridged alphabet,
  After you're dead and gone,
  In this poem you'll live on!

SHALL I COMPARE THEE TO A SUMMER'S DAY? (Moss). 1 *dog days:* the hottest days of summer. The ancient Romans believed that the Dog-star, Sirius, added heat to summer months.

Questions

1. In Howard Moss's streamlined version of Shakespeare, from a series called "Modified Sonnets (Dedicated to adapters, abridgers, digesters, and condensers everywhere)," to what extent does the poet use figurative language? In Shakespeare's original sonnet, how high a proportion of Shakespeare's language is figurative?

2. Compare some of Moss's lines to the corresponding lines in Shakespeare's sonnet. Why is "Even in May, the weather can be gray" less interesting than the original? In the lines on the sun (5–6 in both versions), what has Moss's modification deliberately left out? Why is Shakespeare's seeing death as a braggart memorable? Why aren't you greatly impressed by Moss's last two lines?

3. Can you explain Shakespeare's play on the word "untrimmed" (line 8)? Evidently the word can mean "divested of trimmings," but what other suggestions do you find in it?

4. How would you answer someone who argued, "Maybe Moss's language isn't as good as Shakespeare's, but the meaning is still there. What's wrong with putting Shakespeare into up-to-date words that can be understood by everybody?"

METAPHOR AND SIMILE

  Life, like a dome of many-colored glass,
  Stains the white radiance of Eternity.

The first of these lines (from Shelley's "Adonais") is a **simile**: a comparison of two things, indicated by some connective, usually *like, as, than,* or a verb such as *resembles.* A simile expresses a similarity. Still, for a simile to exist, the things compared have to be dissimilar in kind. It is no simile to say "Your fingers are like mine"; it is a literal observation. But to say "Your fingers are like sausages" is to use a simile. Omit the connective—say "Your fingers are sausages"—and the result is a **metaphor**, a statement that one thing *is* something else, which, in a literal sense, it is not. In the second of Shelley's lines, it is *assumed* that Eternity is light or radiance, and we have an **implied metaphor**, one that uses neither a connective nor the verb *to be.* Here are examples:

Oh, my love is like a red, red rose. *Simile*
Oh, my love resembles a red, red rose. *Simile*
Oh, my love is redder than a rose. *Simile*
Oh, my love is a red, red rose. *Metaphor*
Oh, my love has red petals and sharp thorns. *Implied metaphor*
Oh, I placed my love into a long-stem vase
  and I bandaged my bleeding thumb. *Implied metaphor*

Often you can tell a metaphor from a simile by much more than just the presence or absence of a connective. In general, a simile refers to only one characteristic that two things have in common, while a metaphor is not plainly limited in the number of resemblances it may indicate. To use the simile "He eats like a pig" is to compare man and animal in one respect: eating habits. But to say "He's a pig" is to use a metaphor that might also involve comparisons of appearance and morality.

The Usefulness of Metaphors

For scientists as well as poets, the making of metaphors is customary. In 1933 George Lemaitre, the Belgian priest and physicist credited with the big bang theory of the origin of the universe, conceived of a primal atom that existed before anything else, which expanded and produced everything. And so, he remarked, making a wonderful metaphor, the evolution of the cosmos as it is today "can be compared to a display of fireworks that has just ended." As astrophysicist and novelist Alan Lightman has noted, we can't help envisioning scientific discoveries in terms of things we know from daily life—spinning balls, waves in water, pendulums, weights on springs. "We have no other choice," Lightman reasons. "We cannot avoid forming mental pictures when we try to grasp the meaning of our equations, and how can we picture what we have not seen?"[1] In science as well as in poetry, it would seem, metaphors are necessary instruments of understanding.

Mixed Metaphors

In everyday speech, simile and metaphor occur frequently. We use metaphors ("She's a doll") and similes ("The tickets are selling like hotcakes") without being fully conscious of them. If, however, we are aware that words possess literal meanings as well as figurative ones, we should avoid using what are called **mixed metaphors** and not follow the example of the writer who advised, "Water the spark of knowledge and it will bear fruit," or the speaker who urged, "To get ahead, keep your nose to the grindstone, your shoulder to the wheel, your ear to the ground, and your eye on the ball." Perhaps the unintended humor of these statements comes from our seeing that the writer, busy stringing together stale metaphors, was not aware that they had any physical reference.

Unlike a writer who thoughtlessly mixes metaphors, a good poet can intentionally join together incongruous things and still keep the reader's respect. In his ballad "Thirty Bob a Week," John Davidson has a British workingman tell how it feels to try to support a large family on small wages:

> It's a naked child against a hungry wolf;
>   It's playing bowls upon a splitting wreck;
> It's walking on a string across a gulf
>   With millstones fore-and-aft about your neck;
> But the thing is daily done by many and many a one;
>   And we fall, face forward, fighting, on the deck.

Like the man with his nose to the grindstone, Davidson's wage earner is in an absurd fix; but his balancing act seems far from merely nonsensical. Each one of the poet's comparisons—of workingman to child, to bowler, to tightrope walker, and to

[1]"Physicists' Use of Metaphor," *The American Scholar* (Winter 1989), 99.

seaman—offers suggestions of a similar kind. All help us see (and imagine) the workingman's hard life: a brave and unyielding struggle against impossible odds.

Poetry and Metaphor

A poem may make a series of comparisons, like Davidson's, or the whole poem may be one extended comparison:

Emily Dickinson (1830–1886)

My Life had stood – a Loaded Gun   (about 1863)

My Life had stood – a Loaded Gun –
In Corners – till a Day
The Owner passed – identified –
And carried Me away –

And now We roam in Sovereign Woods –   5
And now We hunt the Doe –
And every time I speak for Him –
The Mountains straight reply –

And do I smile, such cordial light
Upon the Valley glow –   10
It is as a Vesuvian face
Had let its pleasure through –

And when at Night – Our good Day done –
I guard My Master's Head –
'Tis better than the Eider-Duck's   15
Deep Pillow – to have shared –

To foe of His – I'm deadly foe –
None stir the second time –
On whom I lay a Yellow Eye –
Or an emphatic Thumb –   20

Though I than He – may longer live
He longer must – than I –
For I have but the power to kill,
Without – the power to die –

How much life metaphors can bring to poetry may be seen by comparing two poems by Tennyson and Blake.

Alfred, Lord Tennyson (1809–1892)

Flower in the Crannied Wall   1869

Flower in the crannied wall,
I pluck you out of the crannies,
I hold you here, root and all, in my hand,

Little flower—but *if* I could understand
What you are, root and all, and all in all,   5
I should know what God and man is.

How many metaphors does this poem contain? None. Compare it with a briefer poem on a similar theme: the quatrain that begins Blake's "Auguries of Innocence." (We follow here the opinion of W. B. Yeats, who, in editing Blake's poems, thought the lines, each with its own metaphor, deserved to be printed separately.)

William Blake (1757–1827)

To see a world in a grain of sand   (about 1803)

To see a world in a grain of sand
And a heaven in a wild flower,
Hold infinity in the palm of your hand
And eternity in an hour.

Set beside Blake's poem, Tennyson's—short though it is—seems lengthy. What contributes to the richness of "To see a world in a grain of sand" is Blake's use of a metaphor in every line. And every metaphor is loaded with suggestion. Our world does indeed resemble a grain of sand: in being round, in being stony, in being one of a myriad (the suggestions go on and on). Like Blake's grain of sand, a metaphor holds much within a small circumference.

Sylvia Plath (1932–1963)

Metaphors   1960

I'm a riddle in nine syllables,
An elephant, a ponderous house,
A melon strolling on two tendrils.
O red fruit, ivory, fine timbers!
This loaf's big with its yeasty rising.   5
Money's new-minted in this fat purse.
I'm a means, a stage, a cow in calf.
I've eaten a bag of green apples,
Boarded the train there's no getting off.

Questions

1. To what central fact do all the metaphors in this poem refer?
2. In the first line, what has the speaker in common with a riddle? Why does she say she has *nine* syllables? What patterns using the number nine do you find in the poem?

N. Scott Momaday (b. 1934)

Simile   1974

What did we say to each other
that now we are as the deer
who walk in single file
with heads high

with ears forward
with eyes watchful
with hooves always placed on firm ground
in whose limbs there is latent flight   5

Questions

1. Momaday never tells us what was said. Does this omission keep us from understanding the comparison?
2. The comparison is extended with each detail adding some new twist. Explain the implications of the last line.

Experiment: Likening

Write a poem that follows the method of N. Scott Momaday's "Simile," consisting of one long comparison between two objects. Possible subjects might include talking to a loved one long-distance; how you feel going to a weekend job; being on a diet; not being noticed by someone you love; winning a lottery.

Emily Dickinson   (1830–1886)

It dropped so low – in my Regard   (about 1863)

It dropped so low – in my Regard –
I heard it hit the Ground –
And go to pieces on the Stones
At bottom of my Mind –

Yet blamed the Fate that flung it – *less*   5
Than I denounced Myself,
For entertaining Plated Wares
Upon my Silver Shelf –

Questions

1. What is "it"? What two things are compared?
2. How much of the poem develops and amplifies this comparison?

Jill Alexander Essbaum   (b. 1971)

The Heart   2007

Four simple chambers.
A thousand complicated doors.

One of them is yours.

Questions

1. Which line contains a figure of speech?
2. Is that figure a metaphor or a simile? Explain.

Craig Raine (b. 1944)

A Martian Sends a Postcard Home   1979

Caxtons are mechanical birds with many wings
and some are treasured for their markings—

they cause the eyes to melt
or the body to shriek without pain.

I have never seen one fly, but   5
sometimes they perch on the hand.

Mist is when the sky is tired of flight
and rests its soft machine on ground:

then the world is dim and bookish
like engravings under tissue paper.   10

Rain is when the earth is television.
It has the property of making colors darker.

Model T is a room with the lock inside—
a key is turned to free the world

for movement, so quick there is a film   15
to watch for anything missed.

But time is tied to the wrist
or kept in a box, ticking with impatience.

In homes, a haunted apparatus sleeps,
that snores when you pick it up.   20

If the ghost cries, they carry it
to their lips and soothe it to sleep

with sounds. And yet, they wake it up
deliberately, by tickling with a finger.

Only the young are allowed to suffer   25
openly. Adults go to a punishment room

with water but nothing to eat.
They lock the door and suffer the noises

alone. No one is exempt
and everyone's pain has a different smell.   30

At night, when all the colors die,
they hide in pairs

and read about themselves—
in color, with their eyelids shut.

A Martian Sends a Postcard Home. The title of this poem literally describes its contents. A Martian briefly describes everyday objects and activities on earth, but the visitor sees them all from an alien perspective. The Martian/author lacks a complete vocabulary and sometimes describes general categories of things with a proper noun (as in "Model T" in line 13). 1 *Caxtons*: Books, since William Caxton (c. 1422–1491) was the first person to print books in England.

Question

Can you recognize *everything* the Martian describes and translate it back into Earth-based English?

Cody Walker (b. 1967)

I'm Like   2016

I'm like a twenty-inch Fatbike: extra-tired.
I'm like milk from the Third Reich: expired.
I'm like a word deleted from *Leaves of Grass*.
I'm like a bird homing in on a sheet of glass.
I'm like a gnome transported to the dreary present.   5
I'm like a Roman laborer or a wounded pheasant.
I'm like the neighbor you watch till he lowers his light.
I'm like a kid with a light saber and a Diet Sprite.
I'm like the guy at Kroger who left his wallet in the car.
I'm like a Geiger counter. I'm like the devil's cigar.   10

Question

Describe what each simile adds to the poem. What is the accumulative effect?

Exercise: What Is Similar?

Each of these quotations contains a simile or a metaphor. In each of these figures of speech, what two things are being compared? Try to state exactly what you understand the two things to have in common: the most striking similarity or similarities that the poet sees.

1.   All the world's a stage,
      And all the men and women merely players:
      They have their exits and their entrances,
      And one man in his time plays many parts,
      His acts being seven ages.
            —William Shakespeare, *As You Like It*

2. When the hounds of spring are on winter's traces . . .
            —Algernon Charles Swinburne, "Atalanta in Calydon"

3. Art is long, and Time is fleeting,
      And our hearts, though stout and brave,
    Still, like muffled drums, are beating
      Funeral marches to the grave.
            —Henry Wadsworth Longfellow, "A Psalm of Life"

4. "Hope" is the thing with feathers –
     That perches in the soul –
     And sings the tune without the words –
     And never stops – at all –
              —Emily Dickinson, an untitled poem

5. Why should I let the toad *work*
         Squat on my life?
     Can't I use my wit as a pitchfork
         And drive the brute off?
              —Philip Larkin, "Toads"

6. I wear my patience like a light-green dress
     and wear it thin.
              —Emily Grosholz, "Remembering the Ardèche"

7. a laugh maybe, like glasses on a shelf
     suddenly found by the sun . . .
              —Beth Gylys, "Briefly"

8. Spring stirs Gossamer Beynon schoolmistress like a spoon.
              —Dylan Thomas, *Under Milk Wood*

OTHER FIGURES OF SPEECH

When Shakespeare asks, in a sonnet,

> O! how shall summer's honey breath hold out
> Against the wrackful siege of batt'ring days,

it might seem at first that he mixes metaphors. How can a *breath* confront the battering ram of an invading army? But it is summer's breath and, by giving it to summer, Shakespeare makes the season seem human. It is as if the fragrance of summer were the breath within a person's body, and winter were the onslaught of old age.

Personification

Such is Shakespeare's instance of **personification**: a figure of speech in which a thing, an animal, or an abstract term (*truth*, *nature*) is made human. A personification extends throughout this short poem.

James Stephens (1882–1950)

The Wind   1915

The wind stood up, and gave a shout;
He whistled on his fingers, and

Kicked the withered leaves about,
And thumped the branches with his hand,

And said he'd kill, and kill, and kill;   5
And so he will! And so he will!

The wind is a wild man, and evidently it is not just any autumn breeze but a hurricane or at least a stiff gale.

Apostrophe

Hand in hand with personification often goes **apostrophe**: a way of addressing someone or something invisible or not ordinarily spoken to. In an apostrophe, a poet (in these examples Wordsworth) may address an inanimate object ("Spade! with which Wilkinson hath tilled his lands"), some dead or absent person ("Milton! thou shouldst be living at this hour"), an abstract thing ("Return, Delights!"), or a spirit ("Thou Soul that art the eternity of thought"). More often than not, the poet uses apostrophe to announce a lofty and serious tone. An "O" may even be put in front of it ("O moon!") since, according to W. D. Snodgrass, every poet has a right to do so at least once in a lifetime. But apostrophe doesn't have to be highfalutin. It is a means of giving life to the inanimate. It is a way of giving body to the intangible, a way of speaking to it person to person, as in the words of a moving American spiritual: "Death, ain't you got no shame?"

Robinson Jeffers (1887–1962)

Hands   1929

Inside a cave in a narrow canyon near Tassajara
The vault of rock is painted with hands,
A multitude of hands in the twilight, a cloud of men's palms,
    no more,
No other picture. There's no one to say
Whether the brown shy quiet people who are dead intended   5
Religion or magic, or made their tracings
In the idleness of art; but over the division of years these careful
Signs-manual are now like a sealed message
Saying: "Look: we also were human; we had hands, not paws.
    All hail
You people with the cleverer hands, our supplanters   10
In the beautiful country; enjoy her a season, her beauty, and
    come down
And be supplanted; for you also are human."

Question

Can you identify examples of personification and apostrophe in "Hands"?

Overstatement and Understatement

Most of us, from time to time, emphasize a point with a statement containing exaggeration: "Faster than greased lightning"; "I've told him a thousand times." We speak, then, not literal truth but use a figure of speech called **overstatement** (or **hyperbole**). Poets too, being fond of emphasis, often exaggerate for effect. Instances are Marvell's profession of a love that should grow "Vaster than empires, and more slow" and John Burgon's description of Petra: "A rose-red city, half as old as Time." Overstatement can be used also for humorous purposes, as in a fat woman's boast (from a blues song): "Every time I shake, some skinny gal loses her home."[2] The opposite

[2]Quoted by Amiri Baraka [LeRoi Jones] in *Blues People* (New York: Morrow, 1963), 92.

is **understatement**, implying more than is said. Mark Twain in *Life on the Mississippi* recalls how, as an apprentice steamboat-pilot asleep when supposed to be on watch, he was roused by the pilot and sent clambering to the pilot house: "Mr. Bixby was close behind, commenting." Another example is Robert Frost's line "One could do worse than be a swinger of birches"—the conclusion of a poem that has suggested that to swing on a birch tree is one of the most deeply satisfying activities in the world.

Metonymy and Synecdoche

In **metonymy**, the name of a thing is substituted for that of another closely associated with it. For instance, we say "The White House decided" and mean that the president did. When John Dyer writes in "Grongar Hill,"

> A little rule, a little sway,
> A sun beam in a winter's day,
> Is all the proud and mighty have
> Between the cradle and the grave,

we recognize that *cradle* and *grave* signify birth and death. A kind of metonymy, **synecdoche** is the use of a part of a thing to stand for the whole of it or vice versa. We say "She lent a hand," and mean that she lent her entire presence. Similarly, Milton in "Lycidas" refers to greedy clergymen as "blind mouths."

Paradox

Paradox occurs in a statement that at first strikes us as self-contradictory but that on reflection makes some sense. "The peasant," said G. K. Chesterton, "lives in a larger world than the globe-trotter." Here, two different meanings of *larger* are contrasted: "greater in spiritual values" versus "greater in miles." Some paradoxical statements, however, are much more than plays on words. In a moving sonnet, the blind John Milton tells how one night he dreamed he could see his dead wife. The poem ends in a paradox:

> But oh, as to embrace me she inclined,
> I waked, she fled, and day brought back my night.

Pun

Asked to tell the difference between men and women, Samuel Johnson replied, "I can't conceive, madam, can you?" The great dictionary-maker was using a figure of speech known to classical rhetoricians as *paronomasia*, better known to us as a **pun** or play on words. How does a pun operate? Usually with humorous intent, it reminds us of another word (or other words) of similar or identical sound but of very different denotation. Although puns at their worst can be mere piddling quibbles, at best they can sharply point to surprising but genuine resemblances. The name of a dentist's country estate, Tooth Acres, is accurate: aching teeth paid for the property. In his novel *Moby-Dick*, Herman Melville takes up questions about whales that had puzzled scientists: for instance, are the whale's spoutings water or gaseous vapor? When Melville speaks pointedly of the great whale "sprinkling and mistifying the gardens of the deep," we catch his pun and conclude that the creature both mistifies and mystifies at once.

In poetry, a pun may be facetious, as in Thomas Hood's ballad of "Faithless Nelly Gray":

> Ben Battle was a soldier bold,
>   And used to war's alarms;
> But a cannon-ball took off his legs,
>   So he laid down his arms!

Or it may be serious, as in these lines on war by E. E. Cummings:

> the bigness of cannon
> is skilful,

(*is skilful* becoming *is kill-ful* when read aloud), or perhaps, as in Shakespeare's song in *Cymbeline*, "Fear no more the heat o' th' sun," both facetious and serious at once:

> Golden lads and girls all must,
> As chimney-sweepers, come to dust.

Poets often make puns on images, thereby combining the sensory force of imagery with the verbal pleasure of wordplay. Find and explain the punning images in these two poems.

Aurora Stewart   (b. 1998)

Word Play   (2014)

Been piecing things together lately,
And frankly,
I'm puzzled.

George Herbert   (1593–1633)

The Pulley   1633

> When God at first made man,
> Having a glass of blessings standing by—
> Let us (said he) pour on him all we can;
> Let the world's riches, which dispersèd lie,
>   Contract into a span.   5
>
> So strength first made a way,
> Then beauty flowed, then wisdom, honor, pleasure:
> When almost all was out, God made a stay,
> Perceiving that, alone of all His treasure,
>   Rest in the bottom lay.   10
>
> For if I should (said he)
> Bestow this jewel also on My creature,
> He would adore My gifts instead of Me,
> And rest in Nature, not the God of Nature:
>   So both should losers be.   15
>
> Yet let him keep the rest,
> But keep them with repining restlessness;
> Let him be rich and weary, that at least,
> If goodness lead him not, yet weariness
>   May toss him to My breast.   20

Questions

1. What different senses of the word *rest* does Herbert bring into this poem?
2. How do God's words in line 16, "Yet let him keep the rest," seem paradoxical?
3. What do you feel to be the tone of Herbert's poem? Does the punning make the poem seem comic?
4. Why is the poem called "The Pulley"? What is its implied metaphor?

To sum up: even though figures of speech are not to be taken *only* literally, they refer us to a tangible world. By *personifying* an eagle, Tennyson reminds us that the bird and humankind have certain characteristics in common. Through *metonymy*, a poet can focus our attention on a particular detail in a larger object; through *hyperbole* and *understatement*, make us see the physical actuality in back of words. *Pun* and *paradox* cause us to realize this actuality, too, and probably surprise us enjoyably at the same time. Through *apostrophe*, the poet animates the inanimate and asks it to listen—speaks directly to an immediate god or to the revivified dead. Put to such uses, figures of speech have power. They are more than just ways of playing with words.

Dana Gioia (b. 1950)

Money   1991

> *Money is a kind of poetry.*
> —Wallace Stevens

Money, the long green,
cash, stash, rhino, jack
or just plain dough.

Chock it up, fork it over,
shell it out. Watch it   5
burn holes through pockets.

To be made of it! To have it
to burn! Greenbacks, double eagles,
megabucks and Ginnie Maes.

It greases the palm, feathers a nest,   10
holds heads above water,
makes both ends meet.

Money breeds money.
Gathering interest, compounding daily.
Always in circulation.   15

Money. You don't know where it's been,
but you put it where your mouth is.
And it talks.

Question

What figures of speech can you identify in this poem?

Carl Sandburg (1878–1967)

Fog   1916

The fog comes
on little cat feet.

It sits looking
over harbor and city
on silent haunches   5
and then moves on.

Questions

1. What figure of speech does this poem use?
2. Which specific feline qualities does the speaker impute to the fog?

FOR REVIEW AND FURTHER STUDY

Exercise: Figures of Speech

Identify the central figure of speech in each of the following short poems.

Jane Kenyon (1947–1995)

The Suitor   1978

We lie back to back. Curtains
lift and fall,
like the chest of someone sleeping.
Wind moves the leaves of the box elder;
they show their light undersides,   5
turning all at once
like a school of fish.
Suddenly I understand that I am happy.
For months this feeling
has been coming closer, stopping   10
for short visits, like a timid suitor.

Robert Frost (1874–1963)

A Patch of Old Snow   1916

There's a patch of old snow in a corner
    That I should have guessed
Was a blow-away paper the rain
    Had brought to rest.

It is speckled with grime as if   5
    Small print overspread it,
The news of a day I've forgotten—
    If I ever read it.

Kay Ryan (b. 1945)

Turtle   1994

Who would be a turtle who could help it?
A barely mobile hard roll, a four-oared helmet,
she can ill afford the chances she must take
in rowing toward the grasses that she eats.
Her track is graceless, like dragging   5
a packing case places, and almost any slope
defeats her modest hopes. Even being practical,
she's often stuck up to the axle on her way
to something edible. With everything optimal,
she skirts the ditch which would convert   10
her shell into a serving dish. She lives
below luck-level, never imagining some lottery
will change her load of pottery to wings.
Her only levity is patience,
the sport of truly chastened things.   15

Emily Brontë (1818–1848)

Love and Friendship   (1839)

Love is like the wild rose-briar;
Friendship like the holly-tree—
The holly is dark when the rose-briar blooms
But which will bloom most constantly?

The wild rose-briar is sweet in spring,   5
Its summer blossoms scent the air;
Yet wait till winter comes again
And who will call the wild-briar fair?

Then scorn the silly rose-wreath now
And deck thee with the holly's sheen,   10
That when December blights thy brow
He still may leave thy garland green.

■ WRITING *effectively*

Robert Frost on Writing

The Importance of Poetic Metaphor 1930

I do not think anybody ever knows the discreet use of metaphors, his own and other people's, the discreet handling of metaphor, unless he has been properly educated in poetry.

Poetry begins in trivial metaphors, pretty metaphors, "grace" metaphors, and goes on to the profoundest thinking that we have. Poetry provides the one permissible way of saying one thing and meaning another. People say, "Why don't you say what you mean?" We never do that, do we, being all of us too much poets. We like to talk in parables and in hints and in indirections— whether from diffidence or some other instinct.

I have wanted in late years to go further and further in making metaphor the whole of thinking. I find someone now and then to agree with me that all thinking, except mathematical think-

Robert Frost

ing, is metaphorical, or all thinking except scientific thinking. The mathematical might be difficult for me to bring in, but the scientific is easy enough.

• • •

What I am pointing out is that unless you are at home in the metaphor, unless you have had your proper poetical education in the metaphor, you are not safe anywhere. Because you are not at ease with figurative values: you don't know the metaphor in its strength and its weakness. You don't know how far you may expect to ride it and when it may break down with you. You are not safe in science; you are not safe in history.

From "Education by Poetry"

THINKING ABOUT METAPHORS

Metaphors are more than mere decoration. Sometimes, for example, they help us envision an unfamiliar thing more clearly by comparing it with another, more familiar item. A metaphor can reveal interesting aspects of both items. Usually we can see the main point of a good metaphor immediately, but in interpreting a poem, the practical issue sometimes arises of how far to extend a comparison.

- **To write effectively about a metaphorical poem, start by considering the general scope of its key metaphor.** In what ways, for instance, do the characters resemble deer in N. Scott Momaday's "Simile"?

- **Before you begin to write, clarify which aspects of the comparison are true and which are false.** While the characters in Momaday's poem may resemble alert, anxious deer in their emotional response to their conflict, they probably don't actually have hooves and forward-pointing ears.

- **Make a list of metaphors and key images in the poem.** Then draw lines to connect the ones that seem to be related.
- **Notice whether there are obvious connections among all the metaphors or similes in a poem.** Perhaps all of them are threatening, or inviting, or nocturnal, or exaggerated. Such similarities, if they occur, will almost certainly be significant.

CHECKLIST: Writing About Metaphors

- ☐ Underline a poem's key comparisons. Look for both similes and metaphors.
- ☐ How are the two things being compared alike?
- ☐ In what ways are the two things unlike each other?
- ☐ Do the metaphors or similes in the poem have anything in common?
- ☐ If so, what does that commonality suggest?

TOPICS FOR WRITING ON FIGURES OF SPEECH

1. In a brief essay of approximately 500 words, analyze the figures of speech to be found in any poem in this chapter. To what effect does the poem employ metaphors, similes, hyperbole, overstatement, paradox, or any other figure of speech?

2. Examine the extended implied metaphor that constitutes John Donne's "The Flea" (Chapter 34). Paraphrase the poem's argument. In your opinion, does the use of metaphor strengthen the speaker's case?

3. Whip up some similes of your own. Choose someone likely to be unfamiliar to your classmates—your brother or your best friend from home, for example. Write a paragraph in which you use multiple metaphors and similes to communicate a sense of what that person looks, sounds, and acts like. Come up with at least one figure of speech in each sentence.

4. Write a paragraph on any topic, tossing in as many hyperbolic statements as possible. Then write another version, changing all your exaggeration to understatement. In one last paragraph, sum up what this experience taught you about figurative language.

5. Rewrite a short poem rich in figurative language: for example, William Shakespeare's "Shall I compare thee to a summer's day?" or Sylvia Plath's "Metaphors." Taking for your model Howard Moss's deliberately bepiddling version of Shakespeare's poem, use language as flat and unsuggestive as possible. Eliminate every figure of speech. (Ignore any rime or rhythm in the original.) Then, in a paragraph, indicate lines in your revised version that seem glaringly worsened. In conclusion, sum up what your barbaric rewrite tells you about the nature of poetry.

▶ TERMS FOR *review*

Simile and Metaphor

Simile ▶ A comparison of two things, indicated by some connective, usually *like*, *as*, or *than*, or a verb such as *resembles*. A simile usually compares two things that initially seem unlike but are shown to have a significant resemblance. "Cool as a cucumber" and "My love is like a red, red rose" are examples of similes.

Metaphor ▶ A statement that one thing *is* something else, which, in a literal sense, it is not. A metaphor creates a close association between the two entities and underscores some important similarity between them. An example of metaphor is "Simon is a pig."

Implied metaphor ▶ A metaphor that uses neither connectives nor the verb *to be*. If we say "John crowed over his victory," we imply metaphorically that John is a rooster but do not say so specifically.

Mixed metaphor ▶ The (usually unintentional) combining of two or more incompatible metaphors, resulting in ridiculousness or nonsense. For example, "Mary was such a tower of strength that she breezed her way through all the work." ("Towers" do not "breeze.")

Other Figures of Speech

Personification ▶ The endowing of a thing, an animal, or an abstract term with human characteristics. Personification dramatizes the nonhuman world in tangibly human terms.

Apostrophe ▶ A direct address to someone or something. In an apostrophe, a speaker may address an inanimate object, a dead or absent person, an abstract thing, or a spirit.

Overstatement ▶ Also called **hyperbole**. Exaggeration used to emphasize a point.

Understatement ▶ An ironic figure of speech that deliberately describes something in a way that is less than the case.

Metonymy ▶ Figure of speech in which the name of a thing is substituted for that of another closely associated with it. For instance, we might say "the White House decided" when we mean that the president did.

Synecdoche ▶ The use of a significant part of a thing to stand for the whole of it, or vice versa. Saying *wheels* for *car* is an example of synecdoche.

Paradox ▶ A statement that at first strikes one as self-contradictory, but that on reflection reveals some deeper sense. Paradox is often achieved by a play on words.

Pun ▶ A play on words, usually for humorous effect, in which one word is substituted for another of similar or identical sound but of very different meaning.

21

SONG

> To sing is to be.
>
> —RAINER MARIA RILKE

What You Will Learn in This Chapter

- To define *stanza* and *refrain*
- To recognize and describe the *ballad stanza*
- To define *blues* and *rap*
- To analyze the musical structures of a poem

SINGING AND SAYING

Most poems are more memorable than ordinary speech, and when music is combined with poetry, the result can be more memorable still. The differences between speech, poetry, and song may appear if we consider, first of all, this fragment of an imaginary conversation between two lovers:

> Let's not drink; let's just sit here and look at each other. Or put a kiss inside my goblet and I won't want anything to drink.

The sound of the words is not yet especially interesting. Here is another try, by Ben Jonson:

> Drink to me only with thine eyes,
>   And I will pledge with mine;
> Or leave a kiss but in the cup,
>   And I'll not look for wine.

In these opening lines from Jonson's poem "To Celia," the improvement is noticeable. These lines are poetry; their language has become special. For one thing, the lines rime (with an additional rime sound on *thine*). There is interest, too, in the proximity of the words *kiss* and *cup*: the repetition (or alliteration) of the k sound. The rhythm of the lines has become regular; generally every other word (or syllable) is stressed:

> DRINK to me ON-ly WITH thine EYES,
>   And I will PLEDGE with MINE;
> Or LEAVE a KISS but IN the CUP,
>   And I'LL not LOOK for WINE.

All these devices of sound and rhythm, together with metaphor, produce a pleasing effect—more pleasing than the effect of "Let's not drink; let's just look at each other." But the words became more pleasing still when later set to music:

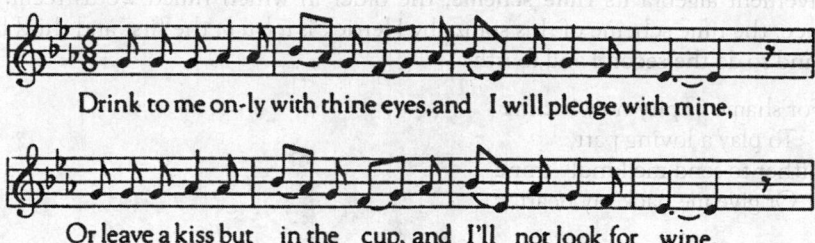

Drink to me on-ly with thine eyes, and I will pledge with mine,

Or leave a kiss but in the cup, and I'll not look for wine.

In this memorable form, the poem is still alive today.

Ben Jonson (1573?–1637)

To Celia 1616

Drink to me only with thine eyes,
   And I will pledge with mine;
Or leave a kiss but in the cup,
   And I'll not look for wine.
The thirst that from the soul doth rise   5
   Doth ask a drink divine;
But might I of Jove's nectar sup,
   I would not change for thine.

I sent thee late a rosy wreath,
   Not so much honoring thee   10
As giving it a hope that there
   It could not withered be.
But thou thereon didst only breathe,
   And sent'st it back to me;
Since when it grows, and smells, I swear,   15
   Not of itself but thee.

A compliment to a lady has rarely been put in language more graceful, more rich with interesting sounds. Other figures of speech besides metaphor make the praise unforgettable: for example, the hyperbolic tributes to the power of the lady's sweet breath, which can start picked roses growing again, and her kisses, which even surpass the nectar of the gods.

Stanza

"To Celia" falls into stanzas—as do many poems that resemble songs. A **stanza** (Italian for "stopping-place" or "room") is a group of lines whose pattern is often repeated throughout the poem. Most songs have more than one stanza. When printed, the stanzas of songs and poems usually are set off from one another by space. When sung, stanzas of songs are indicated by a pause or by the introduction of a refrain, or chorus (a line or lines repeated). The word **verse**, which strictly refers to one line of a poem, is sometimes loosely used to mean a whole stanza: "All join in and sing the second verse!" In speaking of a stanza, whether sung or read, it is customary to indicate by a convenient algebra its **rime scheme**, the order in which rimed words recur. For instance, the rime scheme of this stanza by Herrick is *a b a b*; the first and third lines rime and so do the second and fourth:

> For shame or pity now incline
> 　To play a loving part,
> Either to send me kindly thine
> 　Or give me back my heart.

Refrain

Refrains are words, phrases, or lines repeated at intervals in a song or songlike poem. A refrain usually follows immediately after a stanza, and when it does, it is sometimes called a **terminal refrain**. Sometimes we also hear an **internal refrain**: one that appears within a stanza, generally in a position that stays fixed throughout a poem. James Weldon Johnson uses a blues-based stanza with both an internal refrain and a terminal refrain in "Sence You Went Away":

James Weldon Johnson (1871–1938)

Sence You Went Away　　　　　　　　　　　　　　　　　　　1917

Seems lak to me de stars don't shine so bright,
Seems lak to me de sun done loss his light,
Seems lak to me der's nothin' goin' right,
　　　Sence you went away.

Seems lak to me de sky ain't half so blue,　　　　　　　　　　　5
Seems lak to me dat ev'ything wants you,
Seems lak to me I don't know what to do,
　　　Sence you went away.

Seems lak to me dat ev'ything is wrong,
Seems lak to me de day's jes twice ez long,　　　　　　　　　　10
Seems lak to me de bird's forgot his song,
　　　Sence you went away.

Seems lak to me I jes can't he'p but sigh,
Seems lak to me ma th'oat keeps gittin' dry,
Seems lak to me a tear stays in ma eye,　　　　　　　　　　　15
　　　Sence you went away.

We usually meet poems as words on a page, but songs we generally first encounter as sounds in the air. Consequently, songs tend to be written in language simple enough to be understood on first hearing. But some contemporary songwriters have created songs that require listeners to pay close and repeated attention to their words. Beginning in the 1960s with performers such as Bob Dylan, Leonard Cohen, Joni Mitchell, and Frank Zappa, some pop songwriters crafted deliberately challenging songs. More recently, St. Vincent, Kendrick Lamar, Sturgill Simpson, and Conor Oberst have written complex lyrics, often full of strange, dreamlike imagery. Anyone who feels that literary criticism is solely an academic enterprise should listen to high school and college students discuss the lyrics of their favorite songs.

Madrigals

Many familiar poems began life as songs, but today, their tunes forgotten, they survive only in poetry anthologies. Shakespeare studded his plays with songs, and many of his contemporaries wrote verses to fit existing tunes. Some poets were themselves musicians (such as Thomas Campion), and composed both words and music. In Shakespeare's day, **madrigals**, short secular songs for three or more voices arranged in counterpoint, enjoyed great popularity. A madrigal is usually short, often just one stanza, and rarely exceeds twelve or thirteen lines. Elizabethans loved to sing, and a person was considered a dolt if he or she could not join in a three-part song. Here is madrigal from one of Shakespeare's comedies—a love song performed by the clown in *Twelfth Night*.

William Shakespeare (1564–1616)

O mistress mine (about 1602)

O mistress mine, where are you roaming?
O, stay and hear! your true love's coming,
    That can sing both high and low:
Trip no further, pretty sweeting;
Journeys end in lovers meeting— 5
    Every wise man's son doth know.
What is love? 'Tis not hereafter;
Present mirth hath present laughter;
    What's to come is still unsure:
In delay there lies no plenty; 10
Then, come kiss me, sweet and twenty,
    Youth's a stuff will not endure.

Some poets who were not composers printed their work in madrigal books for others to set to music. In the seventeenth century, however, poetry and song seem to have fallen away from each other. By the end of the century, much new poetry was written to be printed and silently read. Poets who wrote popular songs—such as Thomas D'Urfey, compiler of the collection *Pills to Purge Melancholy*—were considered somewhat disreputable. With the notable exceptions of John Gay, who took existing popular tunes for *The Beggar's Opera*, and Robert Burns, who rewrote folk songs or provided completely new words for them, few important English poets since Campion have been first-rate songwriters.

Occasionally, a poet has learned a thing or two from music. "But for the opera I could never have written *Leaves of Grass*," said Walt Whitman, who loved the Italian art form for its expansiveness. Samuel Coleridge, Thomas Hardy, and W. H. Auden learned from folk ballads. Langston Hughes and Gwendolyn Brooks borrowed from blues, jazz, and boogie-woogie. T. S. Eliot patterned his thematically repetitive *Four Quartets* after the structure of a quartet in classical music. "Poetry," said Ezra Pound, "begins to atrophy when it gets too far from music." Still, even in the twentieth century, the poet was more often a corrector of printer's proofs than a tunesmith or performer.

From Troubadours to Rock Stars

You may not know that when rock stars go on tour today, they are following the venerable tradition of the **troubadours**, traveling poets of the late Middle Ages who would sing their poems to audiences. There are, of course, differences. Despite winning the 2016 Nobel Prize in Literature, Bob Dylan has publicly denied that he is a poet, and Paul Simon once told an interviewer, "If you want poetry, read Wallace Stevens." Nevertheless, many rock and folk lyrics have the verbal intensity of poetry. Few rock lyrics, however, can be judged independent of their musical accompaniment. Songwriters rarely create their lyrics to be read on the page by themselves. A song joins words and music; a great song joins them inseparably.

Although the words of a great song do not necessarily stand on their own without their music, they are not invalidated as lyrics. If the words seem rich and interesting in themselves, our enjoyment is only increased. Like most poems and songs of the past, most current songs will likely end up in the trash can of time. And yet, certain memorable rimed and rhythmic lines may live on, especially if they are expressed in stirring music and have been given wide exposure.

Exercise: Comparing Poem and Song

Compare the following poem by Edwin Arlington Robinson and a popular song lyric based on it. Notice what Paul Simon had to do to Robinson's original poem in order to make it into a song, and how Simon altered Robinson's conception.

Edwin Arlington Robinson (1869–1935)

Richard Cory   1897

Whenever Richard Cory went down town,
We people on the pavement looked at him:
He was a gentleman from sole to crown,
Clean favored, and imperially slim.

And he was always quietly arrayed,   5
And he was always human when he talked;
But still he fluttered pulses when he said,
"Good-morning," and he glittered when he walked.

And he was rich—yes, richer than a king—
And admirably schooled in every grace: 10
In fine,° we thought that he was everything   *in short*
To make us wish that we were in his place.

So on we worked, and waited for the light,
And went without the meat, and cursed the bread;
And Richard Cory, one calm summer night,   15
Went home and put a bullet through his head.

Paul Simon (b. 1941)

Richard Cory

1966

With Apologies to E. A. Robinson

They say that Richard Cory owns
One half of this whole town,
With political connections
To spread his wealth around.
Born into Society,   5
A banker's only child,
He had everything a man could want:
Power, grace and style.

Refrain:

But I, I work in his factory
And I curse the life I'm livin'   10
And I curse my poverty
And I wish that I could be
Oh I wish that I could be
Oh I wish that I could be
Richard Cory.   15

The papers print his picture
Almost everywhere he goes:
Richard Cory at the opera,
Richard Cory at a show.
And the rumor of his parties   20
And the orgies on his yacht—
Oh he surely must be happy
With everything he's got.   *(Refrain.)*

He freely gave to charity,
He had the common touch,   25
And they were grateful for his patronage,
And they thanked him very much,
So my mind was filled with wonder
When the evening headlines read:
"Richard Cory went home last night   30
And put a bullet through his head."   *(Refrain.)*

RICHARD CORY by Paul Simon. If possible, listen to the ballad sung by Simon and Garfunkel on *Sounds of Silence* (Sony, 2001), © 1966 by Paul Simon. Used by permission.

BALLADS

Any narrative song, such as Paul Simon's "Richard Cory," may be called a **ballad**. In English, some of the most famous ballads are **folk ballads**, loosely defined as anonymous story-songs transmitted orally before they were ever written down. Sir Walter Scott, a pioneer collector of Scottish folk ballads, drew the ire of an old woman whose songs he had transcribed: "They were made for singing and no' for reading, but ye ha'e broken the charm now and they'll never be sung mair." The old singer had a point. Print freezes songs and tends to hold them fast to a single version. If Scott and others had not written them down, however, many would have been lost.

In his monumental work *The English and Scottish Popular Ballads* (1882–1898), the American scholar Francis J. Child winnowed out 305 folk ballads he considered authentic—that is, creations of illiterate or semiliterate people who had preserved them orally. Child, who worked by insight as well as by learning, did such a good job of telling the difference between folk ballads and other kinds that later scholars have added only about a dozen ballads to his count. Often called **Child ballads**, his texts include "Lord Randall," "Sir Patrick Spence," and many others still on the lips of singers. Here is one of the best-known Child ballads.

Anonymous (traditional Scottish ballad)

Bonny Barbara Allan

It was in and about the Martinmas time,
    When the green leaves were afalling,
That Sir John Graeme, in the West Country,
    Fell in love with Barbara Allan.

He sent his men down through the town,   5
    To the place where she was dwelling;
"O haste and come to my master dear,
    Gin° ye be Barbara Allan."   *if*

O hooly,° hooly rose she up,   *slowly*
    To the place where he was lying,   10
And when she drew the curtain by:
    "Young man, I think you're dying."

"O it's I'm sick, and very, very sick,
    And 'tis a' for Barbara Allan."—
"O the better for me ye's never be,   15
    Tho your heart's blood were aspilling.

"O dinna ye mind,° young man," said she,   *don't you remember*
    "When ye was in the tavern adrinking,
That ye made the health° gae round and round,   *toasts*
    And slighted Barbara Allan?"   20

He turned his face unto the wall,
    And death was with him dealing:
"Adieu, adieu, my dear friends all,
    And be kind to Barbara Allan."

And slowly, slowly raise she up,   25
    And slowly, slowly left him,
And sighing said she could not stay,
    Since death of life had reft him.

She had not gane a mile but twa,
  When she heard the dead-bell ringing,   30
And every jow° that the dead-bell geid,°   *stroke, gave*
  It cried, "Woe to Barbara Allan!"

"O mother, mother, make my bed!
  O make it saft and narrow!
Since my love died for me today,   35
  I'll die for him tomorrow."

BONNY BARBARA ALLAN. 1 *Martinmas:* Saint Martin's Day, November 11.

Questions

1. In any line does the Scottish dialect cause difficulty? If so, try reading the line aloud.
2. Without ever coming out and explicitly calling Barbara hard-hearted, this ballad reveals that she is. In which stanza and by what means is her cruelty demonstrated?
3. At what point does Barbara evidently have a change of heart? Again, how does the poem dramatize this change without explicitly talking about it?
4. In many American versions of this ballad, noble knight John Graeme becomes an ordinary citizen. The gist of the story is the same, but at the end are these additional stanzas, incorporated from a different ballad:

   They buried Willie in the old churchyard
     And Barbara in the choir;
   And out of his grave grew a red, red rose,
     And out of hers a briar.

   They grew and grew to the steeple top
     Till they could grow no higher;
   And there they locked in a true love's knot,
     The red rose round the briar.

   Do you think this appendage heightens or weakens the final impact of the story? Can the American ending be defended as an integral part of a new song? Explain.
5. Paraphrase lines 9, 15–16, 22, and 25–28. By putting these lines into prose, what has been lost?

As you can see from "Bonny Barbara Allan," in a traditional English or Scottish folk ballad the storyteller speaks of the lives and feelings of others. Even if the pronoun "I" occurs, it rarely has much personality. Characters often exchange dialogue, but no one character speaks all the way through. Events move rapidly, perhaps because some of the dull transitional stanzas have been forgotten. The events themselves, as ballad scholar Albert B. Friedman has said, are frequently "the stuff of tabloid journalism—sensational tales of lust, revenge and domestic crime. Unwed mothers slay their newborn babes; lovers unwilling to marry their pregnant mistresses brutally murder the poor women, for which, without fail, they are justly punished."[1] There are also many ballads of the supernatural and of gallant knights ("Sir Patrick Spence"), and there are a few humorous ballads, usually about unhappy marriages.

[1]Introduction to *The Viking Book of Folk Ballads of the English-Speaking World*, ed. Albert B. Friedman (New York: Viking, 1956).

Ballad Stanza

One favorite pattern of ballad-makers is the so-called **ballad stanza**, four lines rimed *a b c b*, tending to fall into 8, 6, 8, and 6 syllables:

> Clerk Saunders and Maid Margaret
>   Walked owre yon garden green,
> And deep and heavy was the love
>   That fell thir twa between.°   *between those two*

Though not the only possible stanza for a ballad, this easily singable quatrain has continued to attract poets since the Middle Ages. Close kin to the ballad stanza is **common meter**, a stanza found in hymns such as "Amazing Grace," by the eighteenth-century English hymnist John Newton:

> Amazing grace! how sweet the sound
>   That saved a wretch like me!
> I once was lost, but now am found,
>   Was blind, but now I see.

Notice that its pattern is that of the ballad stanza except for its *two* pairs of rimes. That all its lines rime is probably a sign of more literate artistry than we usually hear in folk ballads. Another sign of schoolteachers' influence is that Newton's rimes are exact. (Rimes in folk ballads are often rough-and-ready, as if made by ear, rather than polished and exact, as if the riming words had been matched for their similar spellings. In "Barbara Allan," for instance, the hard-hearted lover's name rimes with *afalling, dwelling, aspilling, dealing,* and even with *ringing* and *adrinking.*) That so many hymns were written in common meter may have been due to convenience. If a congregation didn't know the tune to a hymn in common meter, they readily could sing its words to the tune of another such hymn they knew.

Literary Ballads

Literary ballads, not meant for singing, are written by sophisticated poets for book-educated readers who enjoy being reminded of folk ballads. Literary ballads imitate certain features of folk ballads: they may tell of dramatic conflicts or of mortals who encounter the supernatural; they may use conventional figures of speech or ballad stanzas. Well-known poems of this kind include Keats's "La Belle Dame sans Merci" (Chapter 27), Coleridge's "Rime of the Ancient Mariner," and (more recently) Dudley Randall's "Ballad of Birmingham."

Dudley Randall (1914–2000)

Ballad of Birmingham   1966

> (*On the Bombing of a Church in*
> *Birmingham, Alabama, 1963*)

"Mother dear, may I go downtown
Instead of out to play,
And march the streets of Birmingham
In a Freedom March today?"

"No, baby, no, you may not go,   5
For the dogs are fierce and wild,
And clubs and hoses, guns and jails
Aren't good for a little child."

"But, mother, I won't be alone.
Other children will go with me,   10
And march the streets of Birmingham
To make our country free."

"No, baby, no, you may not go,
For I fear those guns will fire.
But you may go to church instead   15
And sing in the children's choir."

She has combed and brushed her night-dark hair,
And bathed rose petal sweet,
And drawn white gloves on her small brown hands,
And white shoes on her feet.   20

The mother smiled to know her child
Was in the sacred place,
But that smile was the last smile
To come upon her face.

For when she heard the explosion,   25
Her eyes grew wet and wild.
She raced through the streets of Birmingham
Calling for her child.

She clawed through bits of glass and brick,
Then lifted out a shoe.   30
"O here's the shoe my baby wore,
But, baby, where are you?"

Questions

1. This poem, about a dynamite blast set off in an African American church by a racial terrorist (later convicted), delivers a message without preaching. How would you sum up this message, its implied theme?

2. What is ironic in the mother's denying her child permission to take part in a protest march?

3. How does this modern poem resemble a traditional ballad?

Exercise: Seeing the Traits of Ballads

Read the Child ballads "Lord Randall" (Chapter 34) and "Sir Patrick Spence" (Chapter 15). With these ballads in mind, consider these modern poems:

W. H. Auden, "As I Walked Out One Evening" (Chapter 34)
Edwin Arlington Robinson, "Luke Havergal" (Chapter 16)

What characteristics of folk ballads do you find in them? In what ways do these modern poets depart from the traditions of folk ballads of the Middle Ages?

BLUES

Among the many song forms to have shaped the way poetry is written in English, no recent form has been more influential than the **blues**. Originally a type of folk music developed by black slaves in the South, blues songs have both a distinctive form and tone. They traditionally consist of three-line stanzas in which the first two identical lines are followed by a concluding riming third line:

> Trouble, trouble, I've had it all my days
> Trouble, trouble, I've had it all my days
> It seems that trouble's going to follow me to my grave

Early blues lyrics almost always spoke of some sadness, pain, or deprivation— often the loss of a loved one. The melancholy tone of the lyrics, however, is not only world-weary but also world-wise. The blues expound the hard-won wisdom of bitter life experience. They frequently create their special mood through down-to-earth, even gritty, imagery drawn from everyday life. Although blues reach back into the nineteenth century, they were not widely known outside African American communities before 1920, when the first commercial recordings appeared. Their influence on both music and song from that time on was rapid and extensive. By 1930 James Weldon Johnson could declare, "It is from the blues that all that may be called American music derives its most distinctive characteristic." Blues have not only become an enduring category of popular music, but they have also helped shape virtually all the major styles of contemporary pop—jazz, rap, rock, gospel, country, and, of course, rhythm and blues.

The style and structure of blues have also influenced modern poets. Not only have African American writers such as Langston Hughes, Sterling A. Brown, Etheridge Knight, Kevin Young, and Sonia Sanchez written blues poems, but white poets as dissimilar as W. H. Auden, Elizabeth Bishop, Donald Justice, and Sandra McPherson have employed the form. The classic touchstones of the blues, however, remain the early singers, such as Robert Johnson, Ma Rainey, Blind Lemon Jefferson, Charley Patton, and Bessie Smith, "the Empress of the Blues." Any form that has fascinated Bishop and Auden as well as B. B. King, Mick Jagger, Amy Winehouse, and Tom Waits surely deserves special notice.

The blues remind us of how closely related song and poetry will always be. Here are the lyrics of one of Bessie Smith's earliest songs, based on traditional folk blues, followed by a more contemporary poem by Ishmael Reed that employs a classic blues form.

Bessie Smith (1898?–1937)
with Clarence Williams (1898–1965)

Jailhouse Blues   1923

Thirty days in jail with my back turned to the wall.
Thirty days in jail with my back turned to the wall.
Look here, Mister Jailkeeper, put another gal in my stall.

I don't mind bein' in jail but I got to stay there so long.
I don't mind bein' in jail but I got to stay there so long.   5
Well, ev'ry friend I had has done shook hands and gone.

You better stop your man from ticklin' me under my chin.
You better stop your man from ticklin' me under my chin.
'Cause if he keep on ticklin' I'm sure gonna take him in.

Good mornin' blues, blues how do you do?   10
Good mornin' blues, blues how do you do?
Well, I just come here to have a few words with you.

Ishmael Reed (b. 1938)

Oakland Blues   1988

Well it's six o'clock in Oakland
and the sun is full of wine
I say, it's six o'clock in Oakland
and the sun is red with wine
We buried you this morning, baby   5
in the shadow of a vine

Well, they told you of the sickness
almost eighteen months ago
Yes, they told you of the sickness
almost eighteen months ago   10
You went down fighting, daddy. Yes
You fought Death toe to toe

O, the egrets fly over Lake Merritt
and the blackbirds roost in trees
O, the egrets fly over Lake Merritt   15
and the blackbirds roost in trees
Without you little papa
what O, what will become of me

O, it's hard to come home, baby
To a house that's still and stark   20
O, it's hard to come home, baby
To a house that's still and stark
All I hear is myself
thinking
and footsteps in the dark   25

RAP AND PERFORMANCE POETRY

One of the most interesting musical and literary developments of the 1980s was the
emergence of **rap**, a form of popular music in which words are recited to a rhythmic
beat. It differs from mainstream popular music in several ways, but, most interestingly in literary terms, rap lyrics are spoken rather than sung. In that sense, rap is a
form of popular poetry as well as popular music. Rap has branched off into countless
subgenres and regional styles, but in its most common early forms, the lead performer
would talk or recite, often at top speed, long, rhythmic, four-stress lines that ended
in rimes.

Although today many rap singers and groups use electronic or sampled backgrounds, rap began on city streets in the game of "signifying," in which two poets aimed improvised insults at each other, sometimes accompanying their rimes with a rhythm made by clapping, stomping, or beat-boxing, in which the sounds of drums and other instruments are imitated by the human voice. This sort of improvised rapping, usually alternating back and forth between performers, is called **freestyling**. A highly creative form of street poetry, this is how many rappers first hone their talents.

Rap developed so quickly that it now uses a variety of metrical forms. It is interesting to look at the underlying beat of hip-hop lyrics. Rap is typically rich in rime and usually is composed in couplets. Here you'll see a recent example that mixes full rime with assonance and alliteration. San Bernadino poet/MC Tanjint (Tristan Acker) wrote "Hope for the City" in response to the December 2015 shootings in his hometown that left fourteen people dead. Here are four lines from Tanjint's rap:

Our families had to travel from the urban hard scrabble.

Now we dabble between the shadows of the sunlight and the candles.

This for the neighbors and nephews because the spirit ain't left you.

We go from Mars then to Neptune to seek a space that accepts you.

Rap is not written in the standard meters of English literary verse, but its basic measures do come out of the English tradition. The characteristic four-stress, accentual line of "Hope for the City" resembles the most common meter for spoken popular poetry in English from Anglo-Saxon verse and the folk ballads to the work of Robert W. Service and Rudyard Kipling.

What is a woman that you forsake her,

And the hearth-fire and the home-acre,

To go with the old grey Widow-maker?

She has no house to lay a guest in—

But one chill bed for all to rest in,

That the pale suns and the stray bergs nest in?

—"Harp Song of the Dane Women," Rudyard Kipling, 1906

Rap deliberately makes use of stress-meter's ability to stretch and contract in syllable count. Like jazz, rap sets a flexible syncopated rhythm against a fixed metrical beat, turning a traditional English folk meter into something distinctively African American. By hitting the beat hard while exploiting other elements of word music, rappers play interesting and elaborate games with the total rhythm of their lines.

Related to rap, but delivered without musical accompaniment, **performance poetry** is made to be recited for a live audience. Harkening back to ancient Greece, when poets met head-to-head in competition and were featured alongside the athletes of the early Olympic Games, **poetry slams** are now widespread and well-attended events in which performers are scored by a panel of judges who ultimately declare a victor. Slam poetry is often political, confessional, and humorous in subject and style. A construction worker named Marc Smith is credited with having introduced the concept of slam at a Chicago jazz club in the mid-1980s. The first annual National Poetry Slam took place in 1990, and the events have only become more

numerous and popular since. Some examples of performance poetry follow here. Try
reading them aloud, as they were intended.

Patricia Smith (b. 1955)

Hip-hop Ghazel   2012

Gotta love us brown girls, munching on fat, swinging blue hips,
decked out in shells and splashes, Lawdie, bringing them woo hips.

As the jukebox teases, watch my sistas throat the heartbreak,
inhaling bassline, cracking backbone and singing thru hips.

Like something boneless, we glide silent, seeping 'tween floorboards,   5
wrapping around the hims, and *ooh wee*, clinging like glue hips.

Engines grinding, rotating, smokin', gotta pull back some.
Natural minds are lost at the mere sight of ringing true hips.

Gotta love us girls, just struttin' down Manhattan streets
killing the menfolk with a dose of that stinging view. Hips.   10

Crying 'bout getting old—Patricia, you need to get up off
what God gave you. Say a prayer and start slinging. Cue hips.

Taylor Mali (b. 1965)

Totally like whatever, you know?   2002

In case you hadn't noticed,
it has somehow become uncool
to sound like you know what you're talking about?
Or believe strongly in what you're saying?
Invisible question marks and parenthetical (you know?)'s   5
have been attaching themselves to the ends of our sentences?
Even when those sentences aren't, like, questions? You know?

Declarative sentences—so-called
because they used to, like, DECLARE things to be true, okay,
as opposed to other things are, like, totally, you know, not—   10
have been infected by a totally hip
and tragically cool interrogative tone? You know?
Like, don't think I'm uncool just because I've noticed this;
this is just like the word on the street, you know?
It's like what I've heard?   15
I have nothing personally invested in my own opinions, okay?
I'm just inviting you to join me in my uncertainty?
What has happened to our conviction?
Where are the limbs out on which we once walked?
Have they been, like, chopped down   20
with the rest of the rain forest?
Or do we have, like, nothing to say?
Has society become so, like, totally . . .
I mean absolutely . . . You know?

That we've just gotten to the point where it's just, like . . .   25
whatever!

And so actually our disarticulation . . . ness
is just a clever sort of . . . thing
to disguise the fact that we've become
the most aggressively inarticulate generation   30
to come along since . . .
you know, a long, long time ago!

I entreat you, I implore you, I exhort you,
I challenge you: To speak with conviction.

To say what you believe in a manner that bespeaks   35
the determination with which you believe it.
Because contrary to the wisdom of the bumper sticker,
it is not enough these days to simply QUESTION AUTHORITY.
You have to speak with it, too.

Franny Choi (b. 1989)

Choi Jeong Min   2016

For my parents, Choi Inyeong & Nam Songeun

In the first grade, I asked my mother permission
to go by Frances at school. At seven years old,

I already knew the exhaustion of hearing my name
butchered by hammerhead tongues. Already knew

to let my salty gook name drag behind me   5
in the sand, safely out of sight. In fourth grade

I wanted to be a writer & worried
about how to escape my surname—Choi

is nothing if not Korean, if not garlic breath,
if not seaweed & sesame & food stamps   10

during the lean years—could I go by F.J.C.? Could I be
paper thin & raceless? Dust jacket & coffee stain,

boneless rumor smoldering behind the curtain
& speaking through an ink-stained puppet?

My father ran through all his possible rechristenings—   15
Ian, Isaac, Ivan—& we laughed at each one,

knowing his accent would always give him away.
You can hear the pride in my mother's voice

when she answers the phone *this is Grace*. & it is
some kind of strange grace she's spun herself,   20

some lightning made of chainmail. Grace is not
her pseudonym, though everyone in my family is a poet.

These are the shields for the names we speak in the dark
to remember our darkness. Savage death rites

we still practice in the new world. Myths we whisper   25
to each other to keep warm. My Korean name

is the star my mother cooks into the jjigae
to follow home when I am lost, which is always

in this gray country, this violent foster home
whose streets are paved with shame, this factory yard   30

riddled with bullies ready to steal your skin
& sell it back to your mother for profit,

land where they stuff our throats with soil
& accuse us of gluttony when we learn to swallow.

I confess. I am greedy. I think I deserve to be seen   35
for what I am: a boundless, burning wick.

A perfect chord. I confess: If someone has looked
at my crooked spine and called it elmwood,

I've accepted. If someone has loved me more
for my gook name, for my saint name,   40

for my good vocabulary & bad joints,
I've welcomed them into this house.

I've cooked them each a meal with a star singing
at the bottom of the bowl, a secret ingredient

to follow home when we are lost: 45
sunflower oil, blood sausage, a name

given by a dead grandfather who eventually
forgot everything he'd touched. I promise:

I'll never stop stealing back what's mine.
I promise: I won't forget again.   50

FOR REVIEW AND FURTHER STUDY

Thao & The Get Down Stay Down [Thao Nguyen] (b. 1984)

Meticulous Bird   2016

I don't know who's getting any
I don't know who's giving
What a, what a pity
Such a pretty city bears no children

I don't see them on the runway   5
They bus them in on Sundays
The visitors are meeting
To decide if you can come stay

Why deny?

I chase a stone-cold thief   10
With a regular grab
I find the scene of the crime
I take my body back

I resent the invention
Listen, listen, pay attention   15
I know the science of the fiction
Of conviction of the henchmen

I am here for the masterminds
They told us that you sold us
Oh my oh my oh my god   20
We didn't know you'd get ferocious

Oh my oh my oh my god
You didn't know I'd get ferocious

Why deny?

Grow my hair so long to wrap around you   25
You've been starving for air ever since I found you

You had a dalliance with valiance
A violence to vow against
Not what I dream, not what I dreamt
Not what I mean, not how I meant   30

We ate like birds
Seeds and things
Hunting only for seasoning

I planned on no problems to punctuate my stay
Now I perch above you   35
Meticulous bird of prey

Why deny?

I find the scene of the crime
I take my body back
Grow my hair so long to wrap around you   40
You've been starving for air ever since I found you

Question

If possible, find and listen to "Meticulous Bird." The song walks the line between hip-hop and rock. How does Nguyen make use of repetition and internal rime? Point out examples and discuss their effect.

Father John Misty [Joshua Tillman] (b. 1981)

Bored in the USA   2015

How many people rise and say,
"My brain's so awfully glad to be here for yet another mindless day
Now I've got all morning to obsessively accrue
A small nation of meaningful objects and they've got to represent me, too
By this afternoon I'll live in debt   5
By tomorrow be replaced by children"?

How many people rise and think,
"Oh good, the stranger's body's still here, our arrangement hasn't changed
Now I've got a lifetime to consider all the ways
I've grown more disappointing to you as my beauty warps and fades   10
And I suspect you feel the same
When I was young I dreamt of a passionate obligation to a roommate"?

Is this the part where I get all I ever wanted?
Who said that?
Can I get my money back?   15

Just a little bored in the USA
Oh, just a little bored in the USA
Save me, White Jesus
Bored in the USA

They gave me a useless education   20
And a subprime loan on a craftsman home
Keep my prescriptions filled
And now I can't get off
But I can kind of deal
With being   25

Bored in the USA
Oh, just a little
Bored in the USA
Save me, President Jesus
I'm bored in the USA   30
How did it happen?
Bored in the USA

Questions

1. Track down Bruce Springsteen's classic 1984 song "Born in the USA," and compare the
   lyrics with those by Father John Misty. In what ways are the songs similar and in what
   ways do they differ? What does Misty's song say about his generation compared with the
   generational concerns voiced by Springsteen's song?
2. Where do you find examples of sarcasm and irony?

St. Vincent [Annie Clark] (b. 1982)

Severed Crossed Fingers   2014

When your calling ain't calling back to you
I'll be side-stage mouthing lines for you
Humiliated by age, terrified of youth
I got hope but my hope isn't helping you

Spitting our guts from their gears   5
Draining our spleen over years
Find my severed crossed fingers in the rubble there

Wake up puddle-eyed
Sleeping in a suit
The truth is ugly   10
Well, I feel ugly too
We'll be heroes on every barstool
Seeing double beats not seeing one of you

Spitting our guts from their gears
Draining our spleen over years   15
Find my severed crossed fingers in the rubble there
Well, you stole the heart right out my chest
Changed the words that I know best
Find my severed crossed fingers in the rubble there

Bob Dylan (b. 1941)

The Times They Are a-Changin'   1963

Come gather 'round people
Wherever you roam
And admit that the waters
Around you have grown
And accept it that soon   5
You'll be drenched to the bone.
If your time to you
Is worth savin'
Then you better start swimmin'
Or you'll sink like a stone   10
For the times they are a-changin'.

Come writers and critics
Who prophesize with your pen
And keep your eyes wide
The chance won't come again   15
And don't speak too soon
For the wheel's still in spin

And there's no tellin' who
That it's namin'.
For the loser now   20
Will be later to win
For the times they are a-changin'.

Come senators, congressmen
Please heed the call
Don't stand in the doorway   25
Don't block up the hall
For he that gets hurt
Will be he who has stalled
There's a battle outside
And it is ragin'.   30
It'll soon shake your windows
And rattle your walls
For the times they are a-changin'.

Come mothers and fathers
Throughout the land   35
And don't criticize
What you can't understand
Your sons and your daughters
Are beyond your command
Your old road is   40
Rapidly agin'.
Please get out of the new one
If you can't lend your hand
For the times they are a-changin'.

The line it is drawn   45
The curse it is cast
The slow one now
Will later be fast
As the present now
Will later be past   50
The order is
Rapidly fadin'.
And the first one now
Will later be last
For the times they are a-changin'.   55

Questions

1. What features does Dylan keep constant from stanza to stanza? What changes?
2. Who is addressed at the start of each stanza? How do those people affect what is said later in the same stanza?
3. Could the stanzas be sung in a different order without greatly changing the impact of the song? Or would any change undercut the structure of the song?
4. Do the words of this song work well on the page? Or is something essential lost when the music is taken away? Choose and defend one point of view.

■ WRITING *effectively*

Bob Dylan on Writing

Rhythm, Rime, and Songwriting from the Outside   1991

Paul Zollo: People have an idea of your songs freely flowing out from you, but that song ["Isis"] and many others of yours are so well-crafted; it has an ABAB rhyme scheme, which is like something Byron would do, interlocking every line—

Dylan: Oh, yeah. Oh, yeah. Oh, sure. If you've heard a lot of free verse, if you've been raised on free verse, William Carlos Williams, E.E. Cummings, those kind of people who wrote free verse, your ear is not going to be trained for things to sound that way. Of course, for me it's no secret that all my stuff is rhythmically oriented that way.

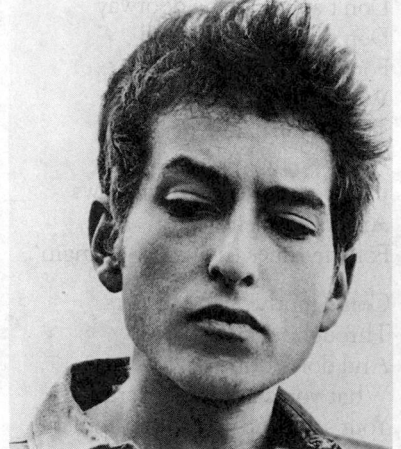

Bob Dylan

Like a Byron line° would be something as simple as: "What is it ye buy so dear / With your pain and with your fear?" Now that's a Byron line, but that could have been one of my lines.

Up until a certain time, maybe in the twenties, that's the way poetry was. It was that way. It was simple and easy to remember, and always in rhythm. It had a rhythm whether the music was there or not.

Zollo: Is rhyming fun for you?

Dylan: Well, it can be, but, you know, it's a game. . . . It gives you a thrill to rhyme something you might think, well, that's never been rhymed before.

But then again, people have taken rhyming now, it doesn't have to be exact anymore. Nobody's going to care if you rhyme "represent" with "ferment." Nobody's gonna care.

Zollo: That was the result of a lot of people of your generation for whom the craft elements of songwriting didn't seem to matter as much. But in your songs the craft is always there, along with the poetry and the energy—

Dylan: My sense of rhyme used to be more involved in my songwriting than it is. . . . Still staying in the unconscious frame of mind, you can pull yourself out and throw up two rhymes first and work it back. You get the rhymes first and work it back and then see if you can make it make sense in another kind of way. You can still stay in

---

Byron line: Dylan attributes the lines to Lord Byron, while they are actually from Percy Bysshe Shelley's poem "Men of England." Byron (1788–1824) and Shelley (1792–1822) were both key figures of Romantic poetry.

the unconscious frame of mind to pull it off, which is the state of mind you have to be in anyway.

Zollo: So sometimes you work backwards, like that?

Dylan: Oh, yeah. Yeah, a lot of times. That's the only way you're going to finish something. That's not uncommon, though.

• • •

Zollo: You said your songs are responsive. Does life have to be in turmoil for songs to come?

Dylan: Well, to me, when you need them, they appear. Your life doesn't have to be in turmoil to write a song like that, but you need to be outside of it. That's why a lot of people, me myself included, write songs when one form or another of society has rejected you. So that you can truly write about it from the outside. Someone who's never been out there can only imagine it as anything, really.

Zollo: Outside of life itself?

Dylan: No. Outside of the situation you find yourself in.

From Songwriters on Songwriting

THINKING ABOUT POETRY AND SONG

Poetry and song were originally one art, and even today the two forms remain closely related. We celebrate the sounds of a poem by praising its "music" just as we compliment a great song lyric by calling it "poetic." And yet a very simple distinction separates the two arts: in a song the lyrics combine with music to create a collaborative work, whereas in a poem the author must create all the effects by words alone.

- **To analyze song lyrics as poetry, separate the words temporarily from their music.**
- **Write out the lyrics and read them without the music playing in the background.** This can help you see how the words hold up on the page. While some lyrics stand well on their own, you may find that the song's power resides mostly in its music, or in the combination of words and music.

Remember, if you find yourself disappointed by the lyrics separated from their music, that song is no less powerful as a song just because the words don't stand on their own as poetry. A song, after all, *is* meant to be sung.

CHECKLIST: Writing About Song Lyrics

☐ Listen to the song and jot down the three or four moments that affect you most powerfully.

☐ Transcribe all of the lyrics onto the page. (Or find the lyrics on the Internet and print them out.)

☐ Compare the moments you remembered with the transcribed lyrics.

☐ Are the lyrics as moving without the music?

☐ Notice the form. Are there stanzas? A refrain? A rime scheme?

☐ What accounts for the song's power? Its music alone? Its lyrics? Its blend of words and music?

TOPICS FOR WRITING ON SONG

1. Write a short paper (750–1000 words) in which you analyze the lyrics of a favorite song. Discuss what the words alone provide and what they lack in re-creating the total power of the original song. The purpose of the paper is not to justify the song you have chosen as great poetry (though it may perhaps qualify); rather, it is to examine which parts of the song's power come solely from the words and which come from the music or performance. (Don't forget to provide your instructor with an accurate transcription of the song lyrics.)

2. Compare and contrast Edward Arlington Robinson's "Richard Cory" with Paul Simon's song of the same name. What changes did Simon make to the original? Why do you suppose he chose to make them? How did he alter Robinson's story and its characters?

3. Compare and contrast the folk ballad "Lord Randall" (Chapter 34) with the literary ballad "La Belle Dame sans Merci" by John Keats (Chapter 27).

4. Think of several recent popular songs. Can you think of any that qualify as ballads? Type out the lyrics of a narrative song you know well, and write a brief analysis of what those lyrics have in common with "Ballad of Birmingham" or "Bonny Barbara Allan."

5. What gives you the blues? Choose one of the blues songs in this chapter as a model, and write your own lyrics about a sad subject of your choice.

▶ TERMS FOR *review*

Components of Songs and Formal Poems

Stanza ▶ From the Italian, meaning "stopping-place" or "room." A recurring pattern of two or more lines of verse, poetry's equivalent to the paragraph in prose. The stanza is the basic organizational principle of most formal poetry.

Rime scheme ▶ Any recurrent pattern of rime within an individual poem. A rime scheme is usually described by using lowercase letters to represent each end rime—*a* for the first rime, *b* for the second, and so on—in the order in which the rimed words occur. The rime scheme of a stanza of common meter, for example, would be notated *a b a b*.

Refrain ▶ A word, phrase, line, or stanza repeated at intervals in a song or poem. The repeated chorus of a song is a refrain.

Ballads

Ballad ▶ Traditionally, a song that tells a story. Ballads are characteristically compressed, dramatic, and objective in their narrative style.

Folk ballads ▶ Anonymous narrative songs, usually in ballad meter. They were originally created for oral performance, often resulting in many versions of a single ballad.

Ballad stanza ▶ The most common pattern for a ballad, consisting of four lines rimed *a b c b*, in which the first and third lines have four metrical feet (usually eight syllables) and the second and fourth lines have three feet (usually six syllables). **Common meter**, often used in hymns, is a variation rimed *a b a b*.

Literary ballad ▶ A ballad not meant for singing, written by a sophisticated poet for educated readers, rather than arising from the anonymous oral tradition.

Other Kinds of Songs

Blues ▶ A type of folk music originally developed by African Americans in the South, often about some pain or loss. Blues lyrics traditionally consist of three-line stanzas in which two identical lines are followed by a third, riming line. The influence of the blues is fundamental in virtually all styles of contemporary pop—jazz, rap, rock, gospel, country, and rhythm and blues.

Rap ▶ A popular style of music that emerged in the 1980s in which lyrics are spoken or chanted over a steady beat, usually sampled or prerecorded. Rap lyrics are almost always rimed and very rhythmic, syncopating a heavy metrical beat in a manner similar to jazz.

Freestyle rap ▶ A form of improvised rap, often alternating verses back and forth between performers.

Performance poetry ▶ A type of oral poetry that is intended to be performed for an audience.

Poetry slam ▶ A competition made popular in the 1990s in which poets perform for a live audience and are scored by judges.

22

SOUND

The sound must seem an echo to the sense.

—ALEXANDER POPE

What You Will Learn in This Chapter

- To recognize and define *alliteration* and *assonance*
- To differentiate and define *euphony*, *cacophony*, and *onomatopoeia*
- To recognize and define the major types of *rime*
- To analyze the role of sound in a poem

SOUND AS MEANING

Isak Dinesen, in a memoir of her life on a plantation in East Africa, tells how some Kikuyu tribesmen reacted to their first hearing of rimed verse:

> The Natives, who have a strong sense of rhythm, know nothing of verse, or at least did not know anything before the times of the schools, where they were taught hymns. One evening out in the maize-field, where we had been harvesting maize, breaking off the cobs and throwing them on to the ox-carts, to amuse myself, I spoke to the field laborers, who were mostly quite young, in Swahili verse. There was no sense in the verse, it was made for the sake of the rime—"Ngumbe na-penda chumbe, Malaya-mbaya. Wakamba na-kula mamba." The oxen like salt—whores are bad,—The Wakamba do eat snakes. It caught the interest of the boys, they formed a ring round me. They were quick to understand that the meaning in poetry is of no consequence, and they did not question the thesis of the verse, but waited eagerly for the rime, and laughed at it when it came. I tried to make them themselves find the rime and finish the poem when I had begun it, but they could not, or would not, do that, and turned away their heads. As they had become used to the idea of poetry, they begged: "Speak again. Speak like rain." Why they should feel verse to be like rain I do not know. It must have been, however, an expression of applause, since in Africa rain is always longed for and welcomed.[1]

What the tribesmen had discovered is that poetry, like music, appeals to the ear. However limited it may be in comparison with the sound of an orchestra—or a tribal drummer—the sound of words in itself gives pleasure. However, we might doubt Isak

---

[1] Isak Dinesen, *Out of Africa* (New York: Random, 1972).

Dinesen's assumption that "meaning in poetry is of no consequence." "Hey nonny-nonny" and such nonsense has a place in song lyrics and other poems, and we might take pleasure in hearing rimes in Swahili; but most good poetry has meaningful sound as well as musical sound. Certainly the words of a song have an effect different from that of wordless music: they go along with their music and, by making statements, add more meaning. In the response of the Kikuyu tribesmen, there may have been not only the pleasure of hearing sounds but also the agreeable surprise of finding that things not usually associated had been brought together.

Euphony and Cacophony

More powerful when in the company of meaning, not apart from it, the sounds of consonants and vowels can contribute greatly to a poem's effect. The sound of *s*, which can suggest the swishing of water, has rarely been used more accurately than in Surrey's line "Calm is the sea, the waves work less and less." When, in a poem, the sound of words working together with meaning pleases mind and ear, the effect is **euphony**, as in the following lines from Tennyson's "Come down, O maid":

> Myriads of rivulets hurrying through the lawn,
> The moan of doves in immemorial elms,
> And murmuring of innumerable bees.

Its opposite is **cacophony**: a harsh, discordant effect. It too is chosen for the sake of meaning. We hear it in Milton's scornful reference in "Lycidas" to corrupt clergymen whose songs "Grate on their scrannel pipes of wretched straw." (Read that line and one of Tennyson's aloud and see which requires lips, teeth, and tongue to do more work.) But note that although Milton's line is harsh in sound, the line (when we meet it in his poem) is pleasing because it is artful. In a famous passage from his *Essay on Criticism*, Pope has illustrated both euphony and cacophony. (Given here as Pope printed it, the passage relies heavily on italics and capital letters for particular emphasis. If you read these lines aloud, dwelling a little longer or harder on the italicized words, you will find that Pope has given you very good directions for a meaningful reading.)

Alexander Pope (1688–1744)

True Ease in Writing comes from Art, not Chance   1711

True Ease in Writing comes from Art, not Chance,
As those move easiest who have learned to dance.
'Tis not enough no Harshness gives Offence,
The *Sound* must seem an *Echo* to the *Sense*.
Soft is the Strain when *Zephyr*° gently blows,   *the west wind*   5
And the *smooth Stream* in *smoother Numbers*° flows;   *metrical rhythm*
But when loud Surges lash the sounding Shore,
The *hoarse, rough Verse* should like the *Torrent* roar.
When *Ajax* strives, some Rock's vast Weight to throw,
The Line too *labors*, and the Words move *slow*;   10
Not so, when swift *Camilla* scours the Plain,
Flies o'er th' unbending Corn, and skims along the Main.°   *expanse (of sea)*
Hear how *Timotheus*' varied Lays surprise,

And bid Alternate Passions fall and rise!
While, at each Change, the Son of *Lybian Jove*   15
Now *burns* with Glory, and then *melts* with Love;
Now his *fierce Eyes* with *sparkling Fury* glow;
Now *Sighs* steal out, and *Tears begin to flow*:
Persians and *Greeks* like *Turns of Nature* found,
And the *World's Victor* stood subdued by *Sound!*   20
The Pow'rs of Music all our Hearts allow;
And what *Timotheus* was, is *Dryden* now.

TRUE EASE IN WRITING COMES FROM ART, NOT CHANCE (*An Essay on Criticism*, lines 362–383).
9 *Ajax*: Greek hero, almost a superman, who in Homer's account of the siege of Troy hurls an enormous rock that momentarily flattens Hector, the Trojan prince (*Iliad* VII, 268–272). 11 *Camilla*: a kind of Amazon or warrior woman of the Volcians, whose speed and lightness of step are praised by the Roman poet Virgil: "She could have skimmed across an unmown grainfield / Without so much as bruising one tender blade; / She could have sped across an ocean's surge / Without so much as wetting her quicksilver soles" (*Aeneid* VII, 808–811). 13 *Timotheus*: favorite musician of Alexander the Great. In "Alexander's Feast, or The Power of Music," John Dryden imagines him: "Timotheus, placed on high / Amid the tuneful choir, / With flying fingers touched the lyre: / The trembling notes ascend the sky, / And heavenly joys inspire." 15 *Son of Lybian Jove*: name for Alexander. A Libyan oracle had declared the king to be the son of the god Zeus Ammon.

Notice the pleasing effect of all the *s* sounds in the lines about the west wind and the stream, and in another meaningful place, the effect of the consonants in *Ajax strives*, a phrase that makes our lips work almost as hard as Ajax throwing the rock.

Is sound identical with meaning in lines such as these? Not quite. In the passage from Tennyson, for instance, the cooing of doves is not *exactly* a moan. As John Crowe Ransom pointed out, the sound would be almost the same but the meaning entirely different in "The murdering of innumerable beeves." While it is true that the consonant sound *sl-* will often begin a word that conveys ideas of wetness and smoothness—*slick, slimy, slippery, slush*—we are so used to hearing it in words that convey nothing of the kind—*slave, slow, sledgehammer*—that it is doubtful whether, all by itself, the sound communicates anything definite. The most beautiful phrase in the English language, according to Dorothy Parker, is *cellar door*. Another wit once nominated, as our most euphonious word, not *sunrise* or *silvery* but *syphilis*.

Onomatopoeia

Relating sound more closely to meaning, the device called **onomatopoeia** is an attempt to represent a thing or action by a word that imitates the sound associated with it: *zoom, whiz, crash, bang, ding-dong, pitter-patter, yakety-yak*. Onomatopoeia is often effective in poetry, as in Emily Dickinson's line about the fly with its "uncertain stumbling Buzz," in which the nasal sounds *n, m, ng* and the sibilants *c, s* help make a droning buzz.

Like the Kikuyu tribesmen, others who care for poetry have discovered in the sound of words something of the refreshment of cool rain. Dylan Thomas, describing how he began to write poetry, said that from early childhood words were to him "as the notes of bells, the sounds of musical instruments, the noises of wind, sea, and rain, the rattle of milk carts, the clopping of hooves on cobbles, the fingering of branches on the window pane, might be to someone, deaf from birth, who has miraculously found his hearing."[2] For readers, too, the sound of words can have a magical spell, most powerful when it points to meaning.

[2]"Notes on the Art of Poetry," *Modern Poetics*, ed. James Scully (New York: McGraw-Hill, 1965).

William Butler Yeats (1865–1939)

Who Goes with Fergus?   1892

Who will go drive with Fergus now,
And pierce the deep wood's woven shade,
And dance upon the level shore?
Young man, lift up your russet brow,
And lift your tender eyelids, maid,   5
And brood on hopes and fear no more.

And no more turn aside and brood
Upon love's bitter mystery;
For Fergus rules the brazen cars,°   *chariots*
And rules the shadows of the wood,   10
And the white breast of the dim sea
And all dishevelled wandering stars.

Who Goes with Fergus? *Fergus*: Irish king who gave up his throne to be a wandering poet.

Questions

1. In what lines do you find euphony?
2. In what line do you find cacophony?
3. How do the sounds of these lines stress what is said in them?

Exercise: Listening to Meaning

Read aloud the following brief poems. In the sounds of which particular words are meanings
well captured? In which of the following three poems do you find onomatopoeia?

Edgar Allan Poe (1809–1849)

from Ulalume   1847

The skies they were ashen and sober;
   The leaves they were crispéd and sere—
   The leaves they were withering and sere;
It was night, in the lonesome October
   Of my most immemorial year;   5
It was hard by the dim lake of Auber,
   In the misty mid region of Weir—
It was down by the dank tarn of Auber,
   In the ghoul-haunted woodland of Weir.

William Wordsworth (1770–1850)

A Slumber Did My Spirit Seal   1800

A slumber did my spirit seal;
   I had no human fears—
She seemed a thing that could not feel
   The touch of earthly years.

No motion has she now, no force;   5
    She neither hears nor sees;
Rolled round in earth's diurnal course,
    With rocks, and stones, and trees.

Aphra Behn   (1640?–1689)

When maidens are young   1687

When maidens are young, and in their spring,
Of pleasure, of pleasure let 'em take their full swing,
    Full swing, full swing,
And love, and dance, and play, and sing,
For Silvia, believe it, when youth is done,   5
There's nought but hum-drum, hum-drum, hum-drum,
There's nought but hum-drum, hum-drum, hum-drum.

ALLITERATION AND ASSONANCE

Listening to a symphony in which themes are repeated throughout each movement, we enjoy both their recurrence and their variation. We take similar pleasure in the repetition of a phrase or a single chord. Something like this pleasure is afforded us frequently in poetry.

Analogies between poetry and wordless music, it is true, tend to break down when carried far, since poetry—to mention a single difference—has words with literal meanings. But like musical compositions, poems have patterns of sounds. Among such patterns long popular in English poetry is **alliteration**, which has been defined as a succession of similar sounds. Alliteration occurs in the repetition of the same consonant sound at the beginning of successive words—"round and round the rugged rocks the ragged rascal ran," or in this delightful stanza by Witter Bynner, written a century ago as part of an elaborate literary hoax:

> If I were only dafter
>   I might be making hymns
> To the liquor of your laughter
>   And the lacquer of your limbs.

Or it may occur inside the words, as in Milton's description of the gates of Hell:

>   On a sudden open fly
> With impetuous recoil and jarring sound
> The infernal doors, and on their hinges grate
> Harsh thunder, that the lowest bottom shook
> Of Erebus.

Bynner's stanza exemplifies **initial alliteration**, while Milton's lines contain **internal alliteration** or **hidden alliteration**. We recognize alliteration by sound, not by spelling: *know* and *nail* alliterate, *know* and *key* do not. In a line by E. E. Cummings, "colossal hoax of clocks and calendars," the sound of *x* within *hoax* alliterates with the *cks* in clocks. Incidentally, the letter *r* does not always lend itself to cacophony: elsewhere in *Paradise Lost* Milton says that

> Heaven opened wide
> Her ever-during gates, harmonious sound
> On golden hinges moving . . .

By itself, a letter-sound has no particular meaning. This is a truth forgotten by people who would attribute the effectiveness of Milton's lines on the Heavenly Gates to, say, "the mellow *o*'s and liquid *l* of *harmonious* and *golden*." Mellow *o*'s and liquid *l*'s occur also in the phrase *moldy cold oatmeal*, which may have a quite different effect. Meaning depends on larger units of language than letters of the alphabet.

Poetry formerly contained more alliteration than it usually contains today. In Old English verse, each line was held together by alliteration, a basic pattern still evident in the fourteenth century, as in the following description of the world as a "fair field" in *Piers Plowman*:

> A *f*eir *f*eld *f*ul of *f*olk *f*ond I ther bi-twene,
> Of alle *m*aner of *m*en, the *m*ene and the riche . . .

Most poets nowadays save alliteration for special occasions. They may use it to give emphasis, as Edward Lear does: "*F*ar and *f*ew, *f*ar and *f*ew, / Are the *l*ands where the Jumblies *l*ive." Alliteration can also point out the relationship between two things placed side by side, as in Pope's line on things of little worth: "The courtier's *p*romises, and sick man's *p*rayers." Alliteration can be a powerful aid to memory. It is hard to forget such tongue twisters as "Peter Piper picked a peck of pickled peppers" or common expressions such as "green as grass" and "tried and true."

As we have seen, to repeat the sound of a consonant is to produce alliteration, but to repeat the sound of a *vowel* is to produce **assonance**. Like alliteration, assonance may occur either initially—"*a*ll the *a*wful *au*guries"—or internally—Edmund Spenser's "Her goodly *eyes* like sapphires shining bright, / Her forehead *i*vory white . . ." —and it can help make common phrases unforgettable: "eager beaver," "holy smoke." Like alliteration, it slows the reader down and focuses attention.

Frances Cornford (1886–1960)

The Watch   1910

I wakened on my hot, hard bed,
Upon the pillow lay my head;
Beneath the pillow I could hear
My little watch was ticking clear.
I thought the throbbing of it went   5
Like my continual discontent;
I thought it said in every tick:
I am so sick, so sick, so sick;
O Death, come quick, come quick, come quick,
Come quick, come quick, come quick, come quick.   10

Questions

1. Read the poem aloud, and identify examples of internal alliteration.
2. What do the hard *ck* sounds at the end of the poem resemble, and how does that fit with the poem's theme and subject?

James Joyce (1882–1941)

All day I hear   1907

All day I hear the noise of waters
   Making moan,
Sad as the sea-bird is, when going
   Forth alone,
He hears the winds cry to the waters'   5
   Monotone.

The grey winds, the cold winds are blowing
   Where I go.
I hear the noise of many waters
   Far below.   10
All day, all night, I hear them flowing
   To and fro.

Questions

1. Find three instances of alliteration in the first stanza. Do any of them serve to reinforce meaning?
2. There is a great deal of assonance throughout the poem on a single vowel sound. What sound is it, and what effect is achieved by its repetition?

Experiment: Reading for Assonance

Try reading aloud as rapidly as possible the following poem by Tennyson. From the difficulties you encounter, you may be able to sense the slowing effect of assonance. Then read the poem aloud a second time, with consideration.

Alfred, Lord Tennyson (1809–1892)

The splendor falls on castle walls   1847

The splendor falls on castle walls
   And snowy summits old in story:
The long light shakes across the lakes,
   And the wild cataract leaps in glory.
Blow, bugle, blow, set the wild echoes flying,   5
Blow, bugle; answer, echoes, dying, dying, dying.

   O hark, O hear! how thin and clear,
     And thinner, clearer, farther going!
   O sweet and far from cliff and scar°   *jutting rock*
     The horns of Elfland faintly blowing!   10
Blow, let us hear the purple glens replying:
Blow, bugle; answer, echoes, dying, dying, dying.

   O love, they die in yon rich sky,
     They faint on hill or field or river:
   Our echoes roll from soul to soul,   15
     And grow for ever and for ever.
Blow, bugle, blow, set the wild echoes flying,
And answer, echoes, answer, dying, dying, dying.

RIME

Isak Dinesen's tribesmen, to whom rime was a new phenomenon, recognized at once that rimed language is special language. So do we, for, although much English poetry is unrimed, rime is one means of setting poetry apart from ordinary conversation and bringing it closer to music. A **rime** (or **rhyme**), defined most narrowly, occurs when two or more words or phrases contain an identical or similar vowel sound, usually accented, and the consonant sounds (if any) that follow the vowel sound are identical: *hay* and *sleigh*, *prairie schooner* and *piano tuner*. These examples demonstrate that rime depends not on spelling but on sound.

Excellent rimes surprise. It is all very well that a reader may anticipate which vowel sound is coming next, for patterns of rime give pleasure by satisfying expectations; but riming becomes dull clunking if, at the end of each line, the reader can predict the word that will end the next. Hearing many a jukebox song for the first time, a listener can do so: *charms* lead to *arms*, *skies above* to *love*. As Alexander Pope observes of the habits of dull rimesters,

> Where'er you find "the cooling western breeze,"
> In the next line it "whispers through the trees";
> If crystal streams "with pleasing murmurs creep,"
> The reader's threatened (not in vain) with "sleep" . . .

But who, given the opening line of this poem, could predict the comic lines that follow?

William Cole (1919–2000)

On my boat on Lake Cayuga   1985

On my boat on Lake Cayuga
I have a horn that goes "Ay-oogah!"
I'm not the modern sort of creep
Who has a horn that goes "beep beep."

Robert Herrick, in a more subtle poem, made good use of rime to indicate a startling contrast:

> Then while time serves, and we are but decaying,
> Come, my Corinna, come, let's go a-Maying.

Though good rimes seem fresh, not all will startle us, and probably few will call to mind things so unlike as *May* and *decay*, *Cayuga* and *Ay-oogah*. Some masters of rime often link words that, taken out of context, might seem common and unevocative. Here are the opening lines of Rachel Hadas's poem "Three Silences," which describe an infant feeding at a mother's breast:

> Of all the times when not to speak is best,
> mother's and infant's is the easiest,
> the milky mouth still warm against her breast.

Hadas's rimes are not memorable in themselves, and yet these lines are—at least in part because they rime so well. The quiet echo of sound at the end of each line reinforces the intimate tone of the mother's moment with her child. Poetic invention may be driven home without rime, but sometimes it is rime that rings the doorbell.

Some rimes wear thin from too much use. Rimes such as *moon, June, croon* seem leaden and would need an extremely powerful context to ring true. *Death, breath* is a rime that poets have used with wearisome frequency; another is *birth, earth, mirth*. And yet we cannot exclude these from the diction of poetry, for they might be the very words a poet would need in order to say something new and original.

Types of Rime

To have an **exact rime**, sounds following the vowel sound have to be the same: *red* and *bread, wealthily* and *stealthily, walk to her* and *talk to her*. If final consonant sounds are the same but the vowel sounds are different, the result is **slant rime**, also called **near rime**, **off rime,** or **imperfect rime**: *sun* riming with *bone, moon, rain, green, gone, thin*. By not satisfying the reader's expectation of an exact chime, but instead giving a clunk, a slant rime can help a poet say some things in a particular way. It works especially well for disappointed letdowns, negations, and denials, as in Blake's couplet:

> He who the ox to wrath has moved
> Shall never be by woman loved.

Many poets have admired the unexpected and arresting effects of slant rime. One of the first poets to explore the possibilities of riming consonants in a consistent way was Wilfred Owen, an English soldier in World War I, who wrote his best poems in the thirteen months before he was killed in action. Seeking a poetic language strong enough to describe the harsh reality of modern war, Owen experimented with matching consonant sounds in striking ways, here in an excerpt from "Strange Meeting":

> Now men will go content with what we spoiled,
> Or, discontent, boil bloody, and be spilled.
> They will be swift with swiftness of the tigress.
> None will break ranks, though nations trek from progress.
> Courage was mine, and I had mystery,
> Wisdom was mine, and I had mastery:
> To miss the march of this retreating world
> Into vain citadels that are not walled.

Consonance, a kind of slant rime, occurs when the rimed words or phrases have the same beginning and ending consonant sounds but a different vowel, as in *chitter* and *chatter*. Owen rimes *spoiled* and *spilled* in this way. Consonance is used in a traditional nonsense poem, "The Cutty Wren": "'O where are you going?' says *Milder* to *Malder*." (W. H. Auden wrote a variation on it that begins, "'O where are you going?' said *reader* to *rider*," thus keeping the consonance.)

End rime, as its name indicates, comes at the ends of lines; **internal rime** within them. Most rime tends to be end rime. Few recent poets have used internal rime so heavily as Wallace Stevens in the beginning of "Bantams in Pine-Woods": "Chieftain Iffucan of Azcan in caftan / Of tan with henna hackles, halt!" (lines also heavy on alliteration). A poet may employ both end rime and internal rime in the same poem, as in Robert Burns's satiric ballad "The Kirk's Alarm":

> Orthodox, Orthodox, wha believe in John Knox,
>   Let me sound an alarm to your conscience:
> A heretic blast has been blawn i' the wast,°   *west*
>   That "what is not sense must be nonsense."

Masculine rime is a rime of one-syllable words (*jail, bail*) or (in words of more than one syllable) stressed final syllables: *di-VORCE, re-MORSE,* or *horse, re-MORSE.* **Feminine rime** is a rime of two or more syllables, with stress on a syllable other than the last: *TUR-tle, FER-tile,* or (to take an example from Byron) *in-tel-LECT-u-al, hen-PECKED you all.* Often it lends itself to comic verse, but it can occasionally be valuable to serious poems, as in Wordsworth's "Resolution and Independence":

> We Poets in our youth begin in gladness;
> But thereof come in the end despondency and madness.

Artfully used, feminine rime can give a poem a heightened musical effect for the simple reason that it offers the listener twice as many riming syllables in each line. In the wrong hands, however, that sonic abundance can make a bad poem twice as painful to endure. Serious poems containing feminine rimes of three syllables have been attempted, notably by Thomas Hood in "The Bridge of Sighs":

> Take her up tenderly,
> Lift her with care;
> Fashioned so slenderly,
> Young, and so fair!

But the pattern is hard to sustain without lapsing into unintended comedy, as in the same poem:

> Still, for all slips of hers,
> One of Eve's family—
> Wipe those poor lips of hers,
> Oozing so clammily.

It works better when the comedy is intentional.

Hilaire Belloc (1870–1953)

The Hippopotamus   1896

I shoot the Hippopotamus
    with bullets made of platinum,
Because if I use leaden ones
    his hide is sure to flatten 'em.

Bob Kaufman (1925–1986)

No More Jazz at Alcatraz (1967)

No More Jazz
at Alcatraz
No more piano
for Lucky Luciano
No more trombone   5
for Al Capone
No More Jazz
at Alcatraz
No more cello
for Frank Costello   10
No more screeching of the
Seagulls
As they line up for
Chow
No More Jazz   15
at Alcatraz

No More Jazz at Alcatraz. *Alcatraz*: maximum security federal prison on an island in the San Francisco Bay, closed down in 1963; now a popular tourist attraction. The prison once had an all-inmate jazz band. 4, 6, 10 *Lucky Luciano, Al Capone, Frank Costello*: famous Mafia gangsters.

Questions

1. What is unusual about Kaufman's rimes?
2. The poem describes one of the harshest prisons in American history. What is surprising about the poem's mood? How does the poet achieve that effect?

In **eye rime**, spellings look alike but pronunciations differ—*rough* and *dough*, *idea* and *flea*, *Venus* and *menus*. Strictly speaking, eye rime is not rime at all.

Rime in American poetry suffered a significant fall from favor in the early 1960s. A new generation of poets took for models the open forms of Whitman, Pound, and William Carlos Williams. By the 1980s, however, some young poets began to use rime and meter again in their work. Often called the **New Formalists**, these poets include Julia Alvarez, Dana Gioia, R. S. Gwynn, Marilyn Nelson, A. E. Stallings, and Timothy Steele. Often combining traditional form with contemporary subjects, such as pop music, movies, and television, these writers led the way for a general revival of poetic form. At present almost any style appears in American poetry, from free verse and prose poems to sonnets and haiku. American poetry is now as diverse as the nation's population.

David Barber (b. 1960)

Aria 2013

What if it were possible to vanquish
All this shame with a wash of varnish
Instead of wishing the stain would vanish?

What if you gave it a glossy finish?
What if there were a way to burnish 5
All this foolishness, all the anguish?

What if you gave yourself leave to ravish
All these ravages with famished relish?
What if this were your way to flourish?

What if the self you love to punish— 10
Knavish, peevish, wolfish, sheepish—
Were all slicked up in something lavish?

Why so squeamish? Why make a fetish
Out of everything you must relinquish?
Why not embellish what you can't abolish? 15

What would be left if you couldn't brandish
All the slavishness you've failed to banish?
What would you be without this gibberish?

What if the true worth of the varnish
Were to replenish your resolve to vanquish 20
Every vain wish before you vanish?

Gerard Manley Hopkins (1844–1889)

God's Grandeur (1877)

The world is charged with the grandeur of God.
  It will flame out, like shining from shook foil;
  It gathers to a greatness, like the ooze of oil
Crushed. Why do men then now not reck his rod?
Generations have trod, have trod, have trod; 5
  And all is seared with trade; bleared, smeared with toil;
  And wears man's smudge and shares man's smell: the soil
Is bare now, nor can foot feel, being shod.

And for all this, nature is never spent;
  There lives the dearest freshness deep down things; 10
And though the last lights off the black West went
  Oh, morning, at the brown brink eastward, springs—
Because the Holy Ghost over the bent
  World broods with warm breast and with ah! bright wings.

GOD'S GRANDEUR. 1 *charged:* as though with electricity. 3–4 *It gathers . . . Crushed:* The grandeur of God will rise and be manifest, as oil rises and collects from crushed olives or grain. 4 *reck his rod:* heed His law. 10 *deep down things:* Tightly packing the poem, Hopkins omits the preposition *in* or *within* before *things.* 11 *last lights . . . went:* When in 1534 Henry VIII broke ties with the Roman Catholic Church and created the Church of England.

Questions

1. In a letter Hopkins explained "shook foil" (line 2): "I mean foil in its sense of leaf or tinsel. . . . Shaken goldfoil gives off broad glares like sheet lightning and also, and this is true of nothing else, owing to its zigzag dints and creasings and network of small many cornered facets, a sort of fork lightning too." What do you think he meant by the phrase "ooze of oil" (line 3)? Would you call this phrase an example of alliteration?

2. What instances of internal rime does the poem contain? How would you describe their effects?

3. Point out some of the poet's uses of alliteration and assonance. Do you believe that Hopkins perhaps goes too far in his heavy use of devices of sound, or would you defend his practice?

4. Why do you suppose Hopkins, in the last two lines, says "over the bent / World" instead of (as we might expect) *bent over the world*? How can the world be bent? Can you make any sense out of this wording, or is Hopkins just trying to get his rime scheme to work out?

HOW TO READ A POEM ALOUD

There is no better way to understand a poem than to read it aloud. Developing skill at reading poems aloud will not only deepen your understanding of literature, but it will also improve your ability to speak in public.

Before trying to read a poem aloud to other people, understand its meaning as thoroughly as possible. If you know what the poet is saying and the poet's attitude toward it, you will be able to find an appropriate tone of voice and to give each part of the poem a proper emphasis.

Except in the most informal situations and in some class exercises, read a poem to yourself before trying it on an audience. No actor goes before the footlights without first having studied the script, and the language of poems usually demands even more consideration than the language of most contemporary plays. Prepare your reading in advance. Check pronunciations you are not sure of. Underline words that should be emphasized.

Read more slowly than you normally would. Keep in mind that you are saying something to somebody. Don't race through the poem as if you are eager to get it over with.

Don't lapse into singsong. A poem may have a definite swing, but swing should never be exaggerated at the cost of sense. If you understand what the poem is saying and speak the poem as if you do, the temptation to fall into such a mechanical intonation should not occur. Observe the punctuation, making slight pauses for commas and longer pauses for full stops (periods, question marks, exclamation points).

If the poem is rimed, don't raise your voice and make the rimes stand out unnaturally. They should receive no more volume than other words in the poem, though a faint pause at the end of each line will call the listener's attention to them.

If, in first listening to a poem, you don't take in all its meaning, don't be discouraged. With more practice in listening, your attention span and your ability to understand poems read aloud will increase. Incidentally, following the text of poems in a book while hearing them read aloud may increase your comprehension, but it may not necessarily help you to *listen*. At least some of the time, close your book and let your ears make the poems welcome. That way, their sounds may better work for you.

Exercise: **Reading for Sound and Meaning**

Read these brief poems aloud. What devices of sound do you find in each of them? Try to explain what sound contributes to the total effect of the poem and how it reinforces what the poet is saying.

Michael Stillman (b. 1940)

In Memoriam John Coltrane   1972

Listen to the coal
rolling, rolling through the cold
   steady rain, wheel on

  wheel, listen to the
turning of the wheels this night   5
   black as coal dust, steel

  on steel, listen to
these cars carry coal, listen
   to the coal train roll.

IN MEMORIAM JOHN COLTRANE. John Coltrane (1926–1967) was a saxophonist whose originality, passion, and technical wizardry have had a deep influence on the history of modern jazz.

William Shakespeare (1564–1616)

When daisies pied and violets blue   1598

When daisies pied and violets blue
  And lady-smocks all silver-white
And cuckoo-buds° of yellow hue   *buttercups*
  Do paint the meadows with delight,
The cuckoo then, on every tree,   5
Mocks married men; for thus sings he,
             "Cuckoo,
Cuckoo, cuckoo!"—O word of fear,
Unpleasing to a married ear!

When shepherds pipe on oaten straws,
  And merry larks are ploughmen's clocks,   10
When turtles tread,° and rooks, and daws,   *turtledoves mate*
  And maidens bleach their summer smocks,
The cuckoo then, on every tree,
Mocks married men; for thus sings he,   15
             "Cuckoo,
Cuckoo, cuckoo!"—O word of fear,
Unpleasing to a married ear!

WHEN DAISIES PIED AND VIOLETS BLUE. This song and "When icicles hang by the wall" conclude the play *Love's Labor's Lost.* 2 *lady-smocks*: also named cuckoo-flowers. 8 O *word of fear*: because it sounds like *cuckold*, a man whose wife has deceived him.

T. S. Eliot (1888–1965)

Virginia   1934

Red river, red river,
Slow flow heat is silence
No will is still as a river
Still. Will heat move
Only through the mocking-bird   5
Heard once? Still hills
Wait. Gates wait. Purple trees,
White trees, wait, wait,
Delay, decay. Living, living,
Never moving. Ever moving   10
Iron thoughts came with me
And go with me:
Red river, river, river.

VIRGINIA. This poem is one of a series entitled "Landscapes."

■ WRITING *effectively*

T. S. Eliot on Writing

The Music of Poetry   1942

I would remind you, first, that the music of
poetry is not something which exists apart from
the meaning. Otherwise, we could have poetry of
great musical beauty which made no sense, and I
have never come across such poetry. The apparent exceptions only show a difference of degree:
there are poems in which we are moved by the
music and take the sense for granted, just as
there are poems in which we attend to the sense
and are moved by the music without noticing
it. Take an apparently extreme example—the
nonsense verse of Edward Lear. His non-sense is
not vacuity of sense: it is a parody of sense, and
that is the sense of it.

T. S. Eliot

• • •

So, while poetry attempts to convey something beyond what can be conveyed in prose
rhythms, it remains, all the same, one person talking to another; and this is just as true
if you sing it, for singing is another way of talking. The immediacy of poetry to conversation is not a matter on which we can lay down exact laws. Every revolution in poetry
is apt to be, and sometimes to announce itself to be, a return to common speech . . . .

It would be a mistake, however, to assume that all poetry ought to be melodious, or that melody is more than one of the components of the music of words. Some poetry is meant to be sung; most poetry, in modern times, is meant to be spoken— and there are many other things to be spoken of besides the murmur of innumerable bees or the moan of doves in immemorial elms. Dissonance, even cacophony, has its place: just as, in a poem of any length, there must be transitions between passages of greater and less intensity, to give a rhythm of fluctuating emotion essential to the musical structure of the whole; and the passages of less intensity will be, in relation to the level on which the total poem operates, prosaic—so that, in the sense implied by that context, it may be said that no poet can write a poem of amplitude unless he is a master of the prosaic.

From "The Music of Poetry"

THINKING ABOUT A POEM'S SOUND

A poem's music—the distinct way it sounds—is an important element of its effect and a large part of what separates it from prose. Describing a poem's sound can be tricky, though. Critics often disagree about the sonic effects of particular poems. Cataloguing every auditory element of a poem would be a huge, unwieldy job. The easiest way to write about sound is to focus your discussion. Concentrate on a single, clearly defined sonic element that strikes you as especially noteworthy. Simply try to understand how that element helps communicate the poem's main theme.

- **You might examine, for example, how certain features (such as rime, rhythm, meter, or alliteration) add force to the literal meaning of each line.** Or, for an ironic poem, you might look at how those same elements undercut and change the surface meaning of the poem.
- **Keep in mind that for a detailed analysis of this sort, it often helps to choose a short poem.** If you want to write about a longer poem, focus on a short passage that strikes you as especially rich in sonic effects.
- **Let your data build up before you force any conclusions about the poem's auditory effects.** As your list grows, a pattern should emerge, and ideas will probably occur to you that were not apparent earlier.

CHECKLIST: Writing About a Poem's Sound

- ☐ List the main auditory elements you find in the poem.
- ☐ Look for rime, meter, alliteration, assonance, euphony, cacophony, repetition, onomatopoeia.
- ☐ Is there a pattern in your list? Is the poem particularly heavy in alliteration or repetition, for example?
- ☐ Limit your discussion to one or two clearly defined sonic effects.
- ☐ How do your chosen effects help communicate the poem's main theme?
- ☐ How does the sound of the words add to the poem's mood?

TOPICS FOR WRITING ON SOUND

1. Choose a brief poem from this chapter or Chapter 34 and examine how one or two elements of sound work throughout the poem to strengthen its meaning. Before you write, review the elements of sound described in this chapter. Back up your argument with specific quotations from the poem.

2. In a 500-word essay, explore how wordplay contributes to the mood and meaning of T. S. Eliot's "Virginia."

3. Silently read Sylvia Plath's "Daddy" or Dylan Thomas's "Fern Hill" (Chapter 34). Then read the poem aloud, to yourself or to a friend. Now write a brief essay examining what you perceived about the poem from reading it aloud that you hadn't noticed before.

4. Consider the verbal music of Michael Stillman's "In Memoriam John Coltrane" (or a selection from Chapter 34). Read the poem both silently and aloud, listening for sonic effects. Describe how the poem's line breaks and sound underscore its meaning.

▶ TERMS FOR *review*

Sound Effects

Alliteration ▶ The repetition of a consonant sound in a line of verse or prose. Alliteration can be used at the beginning of words (**initial alliteration** as in "cool cats") or internally on stressed syllables (**internal alliteration** as in "I met a traveler from an antique land.").

Assonance ▶ The repetition of two or more vowel sounds in successive words, which creates a kind of rime. Like alliteration, the assonance may occur initially ("all the *awful auguries*") or internally ("white lilacs").

Cacophony ▶ A harsh, discordant sound often mirroring the meaning of the context in which it is used. The opposite of cacophony is **euphony**.

Euphony ▶ The harmonious effect when the sounds of the words connect with the meaning in a way pleasing to the ear and mind. The opposite of euphony is **cacophony**.

Onomatopoeia ▶ An attempt to represent a thing or action by a word that imitates the sound associated with it.

Rime

Rime (rhyme) ▶ Two or more words that contain an identical or similar vowel sound, usually accented, with following consonant sounds (if any) identical as well (*woo* and *stew*). An **exact rime** is a full rime in which the sounds following the initial letters of the words are identical in sound (*follow* and *hollow*).

Consonance ▶ Also called **slant rime**. A kind of rime in which the linked words share similar consonant sounds but have different vowel sounds, as in *reason* and *raisin*, *mink* and *monk*. Sometimes only the final consonant sound is identical, as in *fame* and *room*.

End rime ▶ Rime that occurs at the ends of lines, rather than within them. End rime is the most common kind of rime in English-language poetry.

Internal rime ▶ Rime that occurs within a line of poetry, as opposed to **end rime**.

Masculine rime ▶ Either a rime of one-syllable words (*fox* and *socks*) or—in polysyllabic words—a rime on the stressed final syllables (con-*trive* and sur-*vive*).

Feminine rime ▶ A rime of two or more syllables with stress on a syllable other than the last (*tur*-tle and *fer*-tile).

Eye rime ▶ A "false" rime in which the spelling of the words is alike, but the pronunciations differ (*daughter* and *laughter*).

23

RHYTHM

I would define, in brief, the Poetry of words as
the Rhythmical Creation of Beauty.

—EDGAR ALLAN POE

What You Will Learn in This Chapter

- To define *rhythm* and *stress*
- To define *prosody* and *scansion*
- To recognize and define the four major English meters
- To analyze the role of rhythm in a poem

STRESSES AND PAUSES

Rhythms affect us powerfully. We are lulled by a hammock's sway, awakened by an alarm clock's repeated yammer. Long after we come home from a beach, the rising and falling of waves and tides continue in memory. How powerfully the rhythms of poetry also move us may be felt in folk songs of railroad workers and chain gangs whose words were chanted in time to the lifting and dropping of a sledgehammer, and in verse that marching soldiers shout, putting a stress on every word that coincides with a footfall:

> Your LEFT! TWO! THREE! FOUR!
> Your LEFT! TWO! THREE! FOUR!
> You LEFT your WIFE and TWEN-ty-one KIDS
> And you LEFT! TWO! THREE! FOUR!
> You'll NEV-er get HOME to-NIGHT!

A rhythm is produced by a series of recurrences: the returns and departures of the seasons, the repetitions of an engine's stroke, the beats of the heart. A rhythm may be produced by the recurrence of a sound (the throb of a drum, a telephone's busy signal), but rhythm and sound are not identical. A totally deaf person at a parade can sense rhythm from the motions of the marchers' arms and feet, from the shaking of the pavement as they tramp. Rhythms inhere in the motions of the moon and stars, even though when they move, we hear no sound.

Rhythm

In poetry, several kinds of recurrent *sound* are possible, including (as described in Chapter 22) rime, alliteration, and assonance. But most often when we speak of the **rhythm** of a poem, we mean the recurrence of stresses and pauses in it. When we hear a poem read aloud, stresses and pauses are, of course, part of its sound. It is possible to be aware of rhythms in poems read silently, too.

Stresses

A **stress** (or **accent**) is a greater amount of force given to one syllable in speaking than is given to another. We favor a stressed syllable with a little more breath and emphasis, with the result that it comes out slightly louder, higher in pitch, or longer in duration than other syllables. In this manner we place a stress on the first syllable of words such as *eagle*, *impact*, *open*, and *statue*, and on the second syllable in *cigar*, *mystique*, *precise*, and *until*.

Each word in English carries at least one stress, except (usually) for the articles *a*, *an*, and *the*, the conjunction *and*, and one-syllable prepositions: *at*, *by*, *for*, *from*, *of*, *to*, *with*. One word by itself is seldom long enough for us to notice a rhythm in it. Usually a sequence of at least a few words is needed for stresses to establish their pattern: a line, a passage, a whole poem.

Strong rhythms may be seen in most Mother Goose rimes, to which children have been responding for hundreds of years. This rime is for an adult to chant while bouncing a child up and down on a knee:

> Here goes my lord
> A trot, a trot, a trot, a trot!
> Here goes my lady
> A canter, a canter, a canter, a canter!
> Here goes my young master
> Jockey-hitch, jockey-hitch, jockey-hitch, jockey-hitch!
> Here goes my young miss
> An amble, an amble, an amble, an amble!
> The footman lags behind to tipple ale and wine
> And goes gallop, a gallop, a gallop, to make up his time.

More than one rhythm occurs in these lines, as the make-believe horse changes pace. How do these rhythms differ? From one line to the next, the interval between stresses lengthens or grows shorter. In "a TROT a TROT a TROT a TROT," the stress falls on every other syllable. But in the middle of the line "A CAN-ter a CAN-ter a CAN-ter a CAN-ter," the stress falls on every third syllable. When stresses recur at fixed intervals as in these lines, the result is called a **meter**.

STRESS AND MEANING

Stresses embody meanings. Whenever two or more fall side by side, words gain in emphasis. Consider these hard-hitting lines from John Donne, in which accent marks have been placed, dictionary-fashion, to indicate the stressed syllables:

> Bat·ter my heart, three·per·soned God, for You
> As yet but knock, breathe, shine, and seek to mend.
> That I may rise and stand, o'er·throw me, and bend
> Your force to break, blow, burn, and make me new.

When unstressed syllables (or **slack syllables**) recur in pairs, the result is a rhythm that trips and bounces, as in Robert Service's rollicking line:

A bunch of the boys were whoop·ing it up in the Ma·la·mute sa·loon . . .

or in Edgar Allan Poe's lines—also light but meant to be serious:

For the moon nev·er beams, with·out bring·ing me dreams
Of the beau·ti·ful An·na·bel Lee.

Apart from the words that convey it, the rhythm of a poem has no meaning. There are no essentially sad rhythms, nor any essentially happy ones. But some rhythms enforce certain meanings better than others do. The bouncing rhythm of Service's line seems fitting for an account of a merry night in a Klondike saloon; but it may be distracting when encountered in Poe's wistful elegy.

The special power of poetry comes from allowing us to hear simultaneously every level of meaning in language—denotation and connotation, image and idea, abstract content and physical sound. Since sound stress is one of the ways that the English language most clearly communicates meaning, any regular rhythmic pattern will affect the poem's effect. Poets learn to use rhythms that reinforce the meaning and the tone of a poem. As film directors know, any movie scene's effect can change dramatically if different background music accompanies the images. Master of the suspense film Alfred Hitchcock, for instance, could fill an ordinary scene with tension or terror just by playing nervous, grating music underneath it.

Exercise: Get with the Beat

Describe how the strong rhythm in these passages helps establish the tone and meaning of the poem.

1. I couldn't be cooler, I come from Missoula,
   And I rope and I chew and I ride.
   But I'm a heroin dealer, and I drive a four-wheeler
   With stereo speakers inside.
   My ol' lady Phoebe's out rippin' off C.B.'s
   From the rigs at the Wagon Wheel Bar,
   Near a Montana truck stop and a shit-outta-luck stop
   For a trucker who's driven too far.
   —Greg Keeler, from "There Ain't No Such Thing as a
   Montana Cowboy" (a song lyric)

2. Oh newsprint moonprint Marilyn!
   Rub ink from a finger
   to make your beauty mark.
   —Rachel Eisler, from "Marilyn's Nocturne" (a poem
   about a newspaper photograph of Marilyn Monroe)

Pauses

Rhythms in poetry are due not only to stresses but also to pauses. "Every nice ear," observed Alexander Pope, "must, I believe, have observed that in any smooth English verse of ten syllables, there is naturally a pause either at the fourth, fifth, or sixth syllable." Such a light but definite pause within a line is called a **cesura** (or **caesura**), Latin for "a cutting." More liberally than Pope, we apply the name to a pause in a line of any length, after any word in the line. In studying a poem, we indicate a cesura by double vertical lines (‖). A cesura often occurs at a punctuation mark, but there can be a cesura even if no punctuation is present. Sometimes you will find it at the end of a phrase or clause or, as in these lines by William Blake, after an internal rime:

> And priests in black gowns ‖ were walking their rounds
> And binding with briars ‖ my joys and desires.

Lines of ten or twelve syllables (as Pope knew) tend to have just one cesura, though sometimes there are more, as in John Webster's line from *The Duchess of Malfi*:

> Cover her face: ‖ mine eyes dazzle: ‖ she died young.

Line Endings

Pauses also tend to recur at more prominent places—namely, after each line. At the end of a verse (from *versus*, Latin for "a turning"), the reader's eye, before turning to go on to the next line, makes a pause, however brief. If a line ends in a full pause—usually indicated by some mark of punctuation—we call it **end-stopped**. All the lines in this passage from Christopher Marlowe's *Doctor Faustus* (in which Faustus addresses the apparition of Helen of Troy) are end-stopped:

> Was this the face that launch'd a thousand ships,
> And burnt the topless towers of Ilium?
> Sweet Helen, make me immortal with a kiss.
> Her lips suck forth my soul: see, where it flies!
> Come, Helen, come, give me my soul again.
> Here will I dwell, for heaven is in these lips,
> And all is dross that is not Helena.

A line that does not end in punctuation and that therefore is read with only a slight pause after it is called a **run-on line**. Because a run-on line gives us only part of a phrase, clause, or sentence, we have to read on to the line or lines following, in order to complete a thought. All these lines from Robert Browning's "My Last Duchess" (Chapter 15) are run-on lines:

> Sir, 'twas not
> Her husband's presence only, called that spot
> Of joy into the Duchess' cheek: perhaps
> Frà Pandolf chanced to say "Her mantle laps
> Over my lady's wrist too much," or "Paint
> Must never hope to reproduce the faint
> Half-flush that dies along her throat": such stuff
> Was courtesy, she thought . . .

A passage in run-on lines has a rhythm different from that of a passage like Marlowe's in end-stopped lines. When emphatic pauses occur in the quotation from Browning, they fall within a line rather than at the end of one. Marlowe's and Browning's passages are in lines of the same meter (iambic) and the same length (ten syllables). What makes the big difference in their rhythms is the running on, or lack of it.

To sum up: rhythm is recurrence. In poems, it is made of stresses and pauses. The poet can produce it by doing any of several things: making the intervals between stresses fixed or varied, long or short; indicating pauses (cesuras) within lines; end-stopping lines or running them over; writing in short or long lines. Rhythm in itself cannot convey meaning. And yet if a poet's words have meaning, their rhythm must be one with it.

Gwendolyn Brooks (1917–2000)

We Real Cool
1960

> The Pool Players.
> Seven at the Golden Shovel.

We real cool. We
Left school. We

Lurk late. We
Strike straight. We

Sing sin. We   5
Thin gin. We

Jazz June. We
Die soon.

Question

Read the poem aloud and describe its rhythms. By what techniques are they produced?

George Gordon, Lord Byron (1788–1824)

So, We'll Go No More a-Roving
1830

So, we'll go no more a-roving
    So late into the night,
Though the heart be still as loving,
    And the moon be still as bright.

For the sword outwears its sheath,   5
    And the soul wears out the breast,
And the heart must pause to breathe,
    And love itself have rest.

Though the night was made for loving,
    And the day returns too soon,   10
Yet we'll go no more a-roving
    By the light of the moon.

Questions

1. How would you describe this poem's rhythm?
2. Paraphrase the poem. Is it hopeful, joyous, or sad? Does the rhythm create an effect counter to the subject matter?

Alfred, Lord Tennyson (1809–1892)

Break, Break, Break   (1834)

Break, break, break,
   On thy cold gray stones, O Sea!
And I would that my tongue could utter
   The thoughts that arise in me.

O well for the fisherman's boy,   5
   That he shouts with his sister at play!
O well for the sailor lad,
   That he sings in his boat on the bay!

And the stately ships go on
   To their haven under the hill;   10
But O for the touch of a vanish'd hand,
   And the sound of a voice that is still!

Break, break, break,
   At the foot of thy crags, O Sea!
But the tender grace of a day that is dead   15
   Will never come back to me.

Questions

1. Read the first line aloud. What effect does it create at the beginning of the poem?
2. Is there a regular rhythmic pattern in this poem? If so, how would you describe it?
3. The speaker claims that his or her thoughts are impossible to utter. Using evidence from the poem, can you describe the speaker's thoughts and feelings?

Dorothy Parker (1893–1967)

Résumé   1926

Razors pain you;
Rivers are damp;
Acids stain you;
And drugs cause cramp.
Guns aren't lawful;   5
Nooses give;
Gas smells awful;
You might as well live.

Questions

1. Which of the following words might be used to describe the rhythm of this poem, and which might not—*flowing, jaunty, mournful, tender, abrupt*?
2. Is this light verse or a serious poem? Can it be both?

METER

Meter is the rhythmic pattern of stresses in verse. To enjoy the rhythms of a poem, no special knowledge of meter is necessary. All you need do is pay attention to stresses and where they fall, and you will perceive the basic pattern, if there is any. There is nothing occult about the study of meter. Most people find they can master its essentials in no more time than it takes to learn a new video game. If you take the time, you will then have the pleasure of knowing what is happening in the rhythms of many a fine poem, and pleasurable knowledge may even deepen your insight into poetry. The study of metrical structures in poetry is called **prosody**.

Scansion

To make ourselves aware of a meter, we need only listen to a poem, or sound its words to ourselves. If we care to work out exactly what a poet is doing, we *scan* a line or a poem by indicating the stresses in it. **Scansion**, the art of so doing, is not just a matter of pointing to syllables; it is also a matter of listening to a poem and making sense of it. To scan a poem is one way to indicate how to read it aloud; in order to see where stresses fall, you have to see the places where the poet wishes to put emphasis. That is why, when scanning a poem, you may find yourself suddenly understanding it.

The idea in scanning a poem is not to reproduce the sound of a human voice. To scan a poem, rather, is to make a diagram of the stresses (and absences of stress) to show its rhythmical shape, its musical beat. Various marks are used in scansion; in this book we use ′ for a stressed syllable and ‿ for an unstressed syllable.

Types of Meter

There are four common accentual-syllabic meters in English: iambic, anapestic, trochaic, and dactylic. Each is named for its basic **foot** (usually a unit of two or three syllables that contains one strong stress) or building block.

1. **Iambic**—the most common meter in English poetry. An iambic line is made up primarily of **iambs**, an unstressed syllable followed by a stressed syllable, ‿ ′. Many writers, such as Robert Frost, feel iambs most easily capture the natural rhythms of our speech.

   But soft, | what light | through yon | der win | dow breaks?
   —*William Shakespeare*

   When I | have fears | that I | may cease | to be
   —*John Keats*

   Had we | but world | e·nough | and time,
   This coy | ness, la | dy, were | no crime
   —*Andrew Marvell*

   My life | had stood – | a load | ed Gun
   —*Emily Dickinson*

2. **Anapestic**—a galloping meter. The anapestic line is made up primarily of **anapests**, two unstressed syllables followed by a stressed syllable, ˘ ˘ ´. Anapestic meter resembles iambic but contains an extra unstressed syllable. Totally anapestic lines often roll with such speed that poets sometimes slow them down by substituting an iambic foot (as Poe does in "Annabel Lee").

> ˘ ˘ ´ | ˘ ˘ ´ | ˘ ˘ ´ | ˘ ˘ ´
> The As·syr | ian came down | like the wolf | on the fold,
>
> ˘ ˘ ´ | ˘ ˘ ´ | ˘ ˘ ´ | ˘ ˘ ´
> And his co | horts were gleam | ing in pur | ple and gold.
>
> ˘ ˘ ´ | ˘ ˘ ´ | ˘ ˘ ´ | ˘ ˘ ´
> And the sheen | of their spears | was like stars | on the sea,
>
> ˘ ˘ ´ | ˘ ˘ ´ | ˘ ˘ ´ | ˘ ˘ ´
> When the blue | wave rolls night | ly on deep | Gal· i ·lee.
> —*Lord Byron*

> ˘ ´ | ˘ ´ | ˘ ˘ ´ | ˘ ´ | ˘ ˘ ´
> Now this | is the Law | of the Jun | gle—as old | and as true
>
> ˘ ˘ ´
> | as the sky;
>
> ˘ ˘ ´ | ˘ ˘ ´ | ˘ ˘ ´ | ˘ ˘ ´ | ˘ ˘ ´
> And the Wolf | that shall keep | it may pros | per, | but the Wolf
>
> ˘ ˘ ´ | ˘ ˘ ´
> | that shall break | it must die.
> —*Rudyard Kipling*

> ˘ ˘ ´ | ˘ ˘ ´ | ˘ ˘ ´ | ˘ ´
> It was ma | ny and ma | ny a year | a go,
>
> ˘ ˘ ´ | ˘ ˘ ´ | ˘ ´
> In a king | dom by | the sea,
>
> ˘ ˘ ´ | ˘ ˘ ´ | ˘ ´ | ˘ ´
> That a maid | en there lived | whom you | may know
>
> ˘ ˘ ´ | ˘ ´ | ˘ ˘ ´
> By the name | of An | na·bel Lee.
> —*Edgar Allan Poe*

3. **Trochaic**—often associated with songs, chants, and magic spells in English. The trochaic line is made up primarily of **trochees**, a stressed syllable followed by an unstressed syllable, ´ ˘. Trochees make a strong, emphatic meter that is often very mnemonic—that is, "helping, or meant to help, the memory." Shakespeare and Blake used trochaic meter to exploit its magical associations. Notice how Blake drops the unstressed syllable at the end of his lines from "The Tyger." (The location of a missing syllable in a metrical foot is usually marked with a caret sign, ˅.)

> ´ ˘ | ´ ˘ | ´ ˘ | ´ ˘
> Dou·ble, | dou·ble, | toil and | trou·ble,
>
> ´ ˘ | ´ ˘ | ´ ˘ | ´ ˘
> Fi·re | burn and | caul·dron | bub·ble.
> —*William Shakespeare*

´ ˘   ´ ˘   ´ ˘   ´   ˘
Ty·ger! | Ty·ger! | burn·ing | bright

´ ˘   ´ ˘   ´ ˘   ´   ˘
In the | for·ests | of the | night
—*William Blake*

´ ˘   ´ ˘   ´ ˘   ´ ˘
Go and | catch a | fall·ing | star
—*John Donne*

4. **Dactylic**—a less common meter for English poetry, with a gently rolling meter. The dactylic line is made up primarily of **dactyls**, one stressed syllable followed by two unstressed syllables, ´ ˘ ˘. The dactylic meter is more often found in classical languages such as Greek or Latin. Used carefully, dactylic meter can sound stately, as in Longfellow's *Evangeline*.

´ ˘ ˘   ´ ˘ ˘   ´ ˘ ˘   ´ ˘ ˘   ´ ˘ ˘
This is the | for·est pri | me·val. The | mur·mur·ing | pines and the

´   ´
| hem·lock
—*Henry Wadsworth Longfellow*

But it also easily becomes a prancing, propulsive measure and is often used in comic verse.

´ ˘ ˘   ´ ˘ ˘   ´   ˘ ˘   ´   ˘
Puss·y·cat, | puss·y·cat, | where have you | been?
—*Mother Goose*

Poets often drop the unstressed syllables at the end of a dactylic line (noting the omission with a caret sign, ˘).

´ ˘ ˘   ´   ˘ ˘
Take her up | ten·der·ly,

´ ˘ ˘   ´   ˘
Lift her with | care;

´ ˘ ˘   ´   ˘ ˘
Fash·ioned so | slen·der·ly,

´   ˘ ˘   ´ ˘
Young, and so | fair!
—*Thomas Hood*

In the twentieth century, the bouncing meters—anapestic and dactylic—were used more often for comic verse than for serious poetry. Called feet, though they contain no unaccented syllables, are the **monosyllabic foot** (´) and the **spondee** (´´). Meters are not ordinarily made up of them; if one were, it would be like the steady impact of nails being hammered into a board—no pleasure to hear or to dance to. But inserted now and then, they can lend emphasis and variety to a meter, as Yeats well knew when he broke up the predominantly iambic rhythm of "Who Goes with Fergus?" (Chapter 22) with a line in which two spondees occur.

˘ ˘   ´   ´ ˘ ˘   ´ ´
And the white breast of the dim sea.

The Poetic Line

Meters are classified also by line lengths: *trochaic monometer*, for instance, is a line one trochee long, as in this anonymous brief comment on microbes:

> Adam
> Had 'em.

A frequently used meter is **iambic pentameter**: a line of five iambs, a meter especially familiar because it occurs in heroic couplets, sonnets, and blank verse (such as Shakespeare's plays and Milton's *Paradise Lost*).

Line Lengths

Here are the commonly used names for line lengths:

monometer	one foot
dimeter	two feet
trimeter	three feet
tetrameter	four feet
pentameter	five feet
hexameter	six feet
heptameter	seven feet
octameter	eight feet

Lines of more than eight feet are possible but are rare. They tend to break up into shorter lengths in the listening ear.

When Yeats chose the spondees *white breast* and *dim sea*, he was doing what poets who write in meter do frequently for variety—using a foot other than the expected one. Often such a substitution will be made at the very beginning of a line, as in the third line of this passage from Christopher Marlowe's *Tragical History of Doctor Faustus*:

> Was this | the face | that launched | a thou | sand ships
> And burnt | the top | less tow'rs | of Il | i·um?
> Sweet Hel | en, make | me im·mor | tal with | a kiss.

How, we might wonder, can that last line be called iambic at all? But it is, just as a waltz that includes an extra step or two, or leaves a few steps out, remains a waltz. In the preceding lines the basic iambic pentameter is established, and though in the third line the regularity strays, it does not altogether disappear. It continues for a while to run on in the reader's mind, where (if the poet does not stay away from it for too long) the meter will be when the poem comes back to it.

Because meter is orderly and the rhythms of living speech are unruly, poets can play one against the other, in a sort of counterpoint. Robert Frost, a master at pitting a line of iambs against a very natural-sounding and irregular sentence, declared, "I am never more pleased than when I can get these into strained relation. I like to drag and break the intonation across the meter as waves first comb and then break stumbling on the shingle."[1]

---

[1]Letter to John Cournos in 1914, in *Selected Letters of Robert Frost*, ed. Lawrance Thompson (New York: Holt, 1964) 128.

Although in good poetry we seldom meet a very long passage of absolute metrical regularity, we sometimes find (in a line or so) a monotonous rhythm that is effective. Words fall meaningfully in Macbeth's famous statement of world-weariness: "Tomorrow and tomorrow and tomorrow . . ." and in the opening lines of Thomas Gray's "Elegy Written in a Country Churchyard":

The cur·few tolls the knell of part·ing day,
The low· ing herd wind slow·ly o'er the lea,
The plow·man home·ward plods his wear·y way,
And leaves the world to dark·ness and to me.

Although certain unstressed syllables in these lines seem to call for more emphasis than others—you might, for instance, care to throw a little more weight on the second syllable of *curfew* in the opening line—we can still say that the lines are notably iambic. Their almost unvarying rhythm seems just right to convey the tolling of a bell and the weary setting down of one foot after the other.

Accentual Meter

Besides iambic, anapestic, trochaic, and dactylic, English poets have another valuable meter, which is commonly found in spoken or sung forms of poetry, such as the ballad and rap music. It is **accentual meter**, in which the poet does not write in feet but instead counts stresses, typically having the same number of stresses in each line. The poet may place them anywhere in the line and may include practically any number of unstressed syllables. In "Christabel," for instance, Coleridge keeps four stresses to a line, though the first line has only eight syllables and the last line has eleven:

There is not wind e·nough to twirl
The one red leaf, the last of its clan,
That dan·ces as of·ten as dance it can,
Hang·ing so light, and hang·ing so high,
On the top-most twig that looks up at the sky.

The history of accentual meter is long and honorable. Old English poetry was written in a kind of accentual meter. Many later poets, from the authors of Mother Goose rimes to Gerard Manley Hopkins, have sometimes found accentual meters congenial. Recently, accentual meter has enjoyed huge popularity through rap music, which often employs a four-stress line (see Chapter 21 for further discussion of rap).

Meter has seen a great return to popularity in the past many years. Most contemporary poets now explore the rhythmic possibilities of regular meter in their work, following the examples of major poets from Shakespeare through Yeats, who fashioned their work by it. To enjoy metrical poetry—even to write it—you do not have to slice lines into feet; yet you *do* need to recognize when a meter is present in a line, and when the line departs from it. Meter can remind us of body rhythms such as breathing, walking, the beating of the heart. In an effective metrical poem, these rhythms cannot be separated from what the poet is saying—or, in the words of an old jazz song of Duke Ellington's, "It don't mean a thing if it ain't got that swing."

Exercise: Meaningful Variation

At what place or places in each of these passages does the poet depart from basic iambic meter? How does each departure help underscore the meaning?

1. Shadwell alone, of all my sons, is he
   Who stands confirmed in full stupidity.
   The rest to some faint meaning make pretense,
   But Shadwell never deviates into sense.
   —John Dryden, "Mac Flecknoe" (speech of Flecknoe, prince of
   Nonsense, referring to Thomas Shadwell, poet and playwright)

2. A needless Alexandrine ends the song
   That, like a wounded snake, drags its slow length along.
   —Alexander Pope, An Essay on Criticism

3. Roll on, thou deep and dark blue Ocean—roll!
   Ten thousand fleets sweep over thee in vain;
   Man marks the earth with ruin—his control
   Stops with the shore; upon the watery plain
   The wrecks are all thy deed, nor doth remain
   A shadow of man's ravage, save his own,
   When, for a moment, like a drop of rain,
   He sinks into thy depths with bubbling groan,
   Without a grave, unknell'd, uncoffin'd, and unknown.
   —George Gordon, Lord Byron, Childe Harold's Pilgrimage

4. Deer walk upon our mountains, and the quail
   Whistle about us their spontaneous cries;
   Sweet berries ripen in the wilderness;
   And, in the isolation of the sky,
   At evening, casual flocks of pigeons make
   Ambiguous undulations as they sink,
   Downward to darkness, on extended wings.
   —Wallace Stevens, "Sunday Morning"

Exercise: Recognizing Rhythms

Which of the following poems contain predominant meters? Which poems are not wholly metrical, but are metrical in certain lines? Point out any such lines. What reasons do you see, in such places, for the poet's seeking a metrical effect?

Edna St. Vincent Millay (1892–1950)

Counting-out Rhyme   1928

Silver bark of beech, and sallow
Bark of yellow birch and yellow
  Twig of willow.

Stripe of green in moosewood maple,
Color seen in leaf of apple, 5
  Bark of popple.

Wood of popple pale as moonbeam,
Wood of oak for yoke and barn-beam,
  Wood of hornbeam.

Silver bark of beech, and hollow 10
Stem of elder, tall and yellow
  Twig of willow.

Edith Sitwell (1887–1964)

Mariner Man 1918

"What are you staring at, mariner man,
Wrinkled as sea-sand and old as the sea?"
"Those trains will run over their tails, if they can,
Snorting and sporting like porpoises! Flee
The burly, the whirligig wheels of the train, 5
As round as the world and as large again,
Running half the way over to Babylon, down
Through fields of clover to gay Troy town—
A-puffing their smoke as grey as the curl
On my forehead as wrinkled as sands of the sea!— 10
But what can that matter to you, my girl?
(And what can that matter to me?)"

A. E. Housman (1859–1936)

When I was one-and-twenty 1896

When I was one-and-twenty
  I heard a wise man say,
"Give crowns and pounds and guineas
  But not your heart away;
Give pearls away and rubies 5
  But keep your fancy free."
But I was one-and-twenty,
  No use to talk to me.

When I was one-and-twenty
  I heard him say again, 10
"The heart out of the bosom
  Was never given in vain;
'Tis paid with sighs a plenty
  And sold for endless rue."
And I am two-and-twenty, 15
  And oh, 'tis true, 'tis true.

William Carlos Williams (1883–1963)

Smell!   1917

Oh strong-ridged and deeply hollowed
nose of mine! what will you not be smelling?
What tactless asses we are, you and I, boney nose,
always indiscriminate, always unashamed,
and now it is the souring flowers of the bedraggled   5
poplars: a festering pulp on the wet earth
beneath them. With what deep thirst
we quicken our desires
to that rank odor of a passing springtime!
Can you not be decent? Can you not reserve your ardors   10
for something less unlovely? What girl will care
for us, do you think, if we continue in these ways?
Must you taste everything? Must you know everything?
Must you have a part in everything?

Walt Whitman (1819–1892)

Beat! Beat! Drums!   (1861)

Beat! beat! drums!—blow! bugles! blow!
Through the windows—through doors—burst like a ruthless force,
Into the solemn church, and scatter the congregation,
Into the school where the scholar is studying;
Leave not the bridegroom quiet—no happiness must he have now with   5
      his bride,
Nor the peaceful farmer any peace, ploughing his field or gathering his grain,
So fierce you whirr and pound you drums—so shrill you bugles blow.

Beat! beat! drums!—blow! bugles! blow!
Over the traffic of cities—over the rumble of wheels in the streets;
Are beds prepared for sleepers at night in the houses? no sleepers must   10
      sleep in those beds,
No bargainers' bargains by day—no brokers or speculators—would they
      continue?
Would the talkers be talking? would the singer attempt to sing?
Would the lawyer rise in the court to state his case before the judge?
Then rattle quicker, heavier drums—you bugles wilder blow.

Beat! beat! drums!—blow! bugles! blow!   15
Make no parley—stop for no expostulation,
Mind not the timid—mind not the weeper or prayer,
Mind not the old man beseeching the young man,
Let not the child's voice be heard, nor the mother's entreaties,
Make even the trestles to shake the dead where they lie awaiting the   20
      hearses,
So strong you thump O terrible drums—so loud you bugles blow.

■ WRITING *effectively*

Gwendolyn Brooks on Writing

Hearing "We Real Cool" 1969

Interviewer: How about the seven pool players in the poem "We Real Cool"?

Brooks: They have no pretensions to any glamor. They are supposedly dropouts, or at least they're in the poolroom when they should be possibly in school, since they're probably young enough or at least those I saw were when I looked in a poolroom, and they . . . . First of all, let me tell you how that's supposed to be said, because there's a reason why I set it out as I did. These are people who are essentially saying, "Kilroy is here. We *are*." But they're a little uncertain of the strength of their identity. The "We"—you're supposed to stop after the "We" and think about *validity*; of course, there's no way for you to tell whether it should be said softly or not, I suppose, but I say it rather softly because I want to represent their basic uncertainty, which they don't bother to question every day, of course.

Gwendolyn Brooks

Interviewer: Are you saying that the form of this poem, then, was determined by the colloquial rhythm you were trying to catch?

Brooks: No, determined by my feelings about these boys, these young men.

From "An Interview with Gwendolyn Brooks" by George Stavros

THINKING ABOUT RHYTHM

When we read casually, we don't need to think very hard about a poem's rhythm. We *feel* it as we read, even if we aren't consciously paying attention to matters such as iambs or anapests. When analyzing a poem, though, it helps to have a clear sense of how the rhythm works, and the best way to reach that understanding is through scansion. A scansion gives us a picture of the poem's most important sound patterns. Scanning a poem can seem a bit intimidating at first, but it really isn't all that difficult.

- **Read the poem aloud, marking the stressed syllables as you go.**
- **If you're having a hard time hearing the stresses, read the line a few different ways.** Try to detect which way seems most like natural speech.

Example: **Tennyson's "Break, Break, Break"**

A simple scansion of the opening of Tennyson's poem might look like this:

  Break, break, break   (3 syllables)

  On thy cold gray stones, O Sea!   (7 syllables, rime)

  And I would that my tongue could utter   (9 syllables)

  The thoughts that arise in me.   (7 syllables, rime)

By now some basic organizing principles of the poem have become clear. The lines are rimed *a b c b*, but they contain an irregular number of syllables. The number of strong stresses, however, seems to be constant, at least in the opening stanza.

Now that you have a visual diagram of the poem's sound, the rhythm will be much easier to write about. This diagram will also lead you to a richer understanding of how the poet's artistry reinforces the poem's meaning. The three sharp syllables of the first line give the reader an immediate sense of the depth and intensity of the speaker's feelings. The sudden burst of syllables in the third line underscores the rush of passion that wells up in his breast and outstrips his ability to give voice to it. And the rhythm of the last two lines—the rising intensity of the third line followed by the ebb of the fourth—subtly suggests the effect of the surging and receding of the waves.

CHECKLIST: Scanning a Poem

☐ Read the poem aloud.

☐ Mark the main speech stresses. When in doubt, read the line aloud several different ways. Which way seems most natural?

☐ Are there rimes? Indicate where they occur.

☐ How many syllables are there in each line?

☐ Do any other recurring sound patterns strike you?

☐ Does the poem set up a reliable pattern and then diverge from it? If so, how does that irregularity underscore the line's meaning?

TOPICS FOR WRITING ON RHYTHM

1. Scan the rhythm of a passage from any poem in this chapter, following the guidelines listed above. Discuss how the poem uses rhythm to create certain key effects. Be sure that your scansion shows all the elements you've chosen to discuss.

2. With a classmate, take turns reading a poem from this chapter out loud to each other. Now write briefly on what you learned about the poem's rhythm by speaking and hearing it.

3. How do rhythm and other kinds of sonic effects (alliteration and consonance, for example) combine to make meaning in Edna St. Vincent Millay's "Counting-out Rhyme"?

4. Scan a stanza of Walt Whitman's "Beat! Beat! Drums!" What do you notice about the poem's rhythms? How do the rhythms underscore the poem's meaning?

5. Scan two poems, one in free verse, and the other in regular meter. For a free verse poem you might pick William Carlos Williams's "Smell!" (in this chapter) or Hart Crane's "My Grandmother's Love Letters" (Chapter 34); for a poem in regular meter you could go with one of the poems in this chapter, for example, A. E. Housman's "When I was one-and-twenty" or Lord Byron's "So We'll Go No More a-Roving." Now write about the experience. Do you detect any particular strengths offered by regular meter? How about by free verse?

▶ **TERMS FOR** *review*

Pattern and Structure

Rhythm ▶ The recurring pattern of stresses and pauses in a poem. A fixed rhythm in a poem is called **meter**.

Stress ▶ An emphasis, or **accent**, placed on a syllable in speech. An unstressed syllable in a line of verse is called a **slack syllable**.

Cesura or caesura ▶ A light but definite pause within a line of verse. Cesuras often appear near the middle of a line, but their placement may be varied for rhythmic effect.

Run-on line ▶ A line of verse that does not end in punctuation but carries on grammatically to the next line. The use of run-on lines is called *enjambment*.

End-stopped line ▶ A line of verse that ends in a full pause, often indicated by a mark of punctuation.

Meter

Prosody ▶ The study of metrical structures in poetry.

Scansion ▶ A practice used to describe rhythmic patterns in a poem by separating the metrical feet, counting the syllables, marking the accents, and indicating the cesuras.

Foot ▶ The basic unit of measurement in metrical poetry. Each separate meter is identified by the pattern and order of stressed and unstressed syllables in its foot.

Iamb ▶ A metrical foot in verse in which an unaccented syllable is followed by an accented one (⏑ ′). The iambic measure is the most common one used in English poetry.

Iambic pentameter ▶ The most common meter in English verse, five iambic feet per line. Many fixed forms, such as the sonnet and heroic couplets, employ iambic pentameter.

Anapest ▶ A metrical foot in verse in which two unstressed syllables are followed by a stressed syllable (⏑ ⏑ ′).

Trochee ▶ A metrical foot in which a stressed syllable is followed by an unstressed one (′ ⏑).

Dactyl ▶ A metrical foot in which one stressed syllable is followed by two unstressed ones (′ ⏑ ⏑). Dactylic meter is less common in English than in classical Greek and Latin.

Spondee ▶ A metrical foot of verse consisting of two stressed syllables (′ ′).

Accentual meter ▶ Verse meter based on the number of stresses per line, not the number of syllables.

24   CLOSED FORM

Anybody can write the first line of a poem,
but it is a very difficult task to make
the second line rhyme with the first.

—MARK TWAIN

What You Will Learn in This Chapter

- To define *form* as a literary concept
- To describe and differentiate *closed* and *open forms*
- To recognize and describe the two major *sonnet* forms, Italian and English
- To analyze the role of form in a poem

Form, as a general idea, is the design of a thing as a whole, the configuration of all its parts. No poem can escape having some kind of form, whether its lines are as various in length as a tree's branches or all in hexameter. To put this point in another way: if you were to listen to a poem read aloud in a language unknown to you, or if you saw the poem printed in that foreign language, whatever in the poem you could see or hear would be the form of it.

Writing in **closed form**, a poet follows (or finds) some sort of pattern, such as that of a sonnet with its rime scheme and its fourteen lines of iambic pentameter. On a page, poems in closed form tend to look regular and symmetrical, often falling into stanzas that indicate groups of rimes. Along with William Butler Yeats, who held that a successful poem will "come shut with a click, like a closing box," the poet who writes in closed form apparently strives for a kind of perfection—seeking, perhaps, to lodge words so securely in place that no word can be budged without a worsening. For the sake of meaning, though, a competent poet often will depart from a symmetrical pattern. As Robert Frost observed, there is satisfaction to be found in things not mechanically regular: "We enjoy the straight crookedness of a good walking stick."

The poet who writes in **open form** usually seeks no final click. Often, such a poet views the writing of a poem as a process, rather than a quest for an absolute. Free to use white space for emphasis, able to shorten or lengthen lines as the sense seems to require, the poet lets the poem discover its shape as it goes along, moving as water flows downhill, adjusting to its terrain, engulfing obstacles. (Open form provides the focus of Chapter 25.)

Most poetry of the past is in closed form, exhibiting at least a pattern of rime or meter, but since the early 1960s the majority of American poets have preferred forms that stay open. Lately, the situation has been changing yet again, with closed form reappearing in much recent poetry. Whatever the fashion of the moment, the reader who seeks a wide understanding of poetry of both the present and the past will need to know both the closed and open varieties.

THE VALUE OF FORM

Closed form gives some poems a valuable advantage: it makes them more easily memorable. The **epic** poems of nations—long narratives tracing the adventures of popular heroes: the Greek *Iliad* and *Odyssey*, the French *Song of Roland*, the Spanish *Cid*—tend to occur in patterns of fairly consistent line length or number of stresses because these works were sometimes transmitted orally. Sung to the music of a lyre or chanted to a drumbeat, they may have been easier to memorize because of their patterns. If a singer forgot something, the song would have a noticeable hole in it, so rime or fixed meter probably helped prevent an epic from deteriorating when passed along from one singer to another. It is no coincidence that so many English play-wrights of Shakespeare's day favored iambic pentameter. Companies of actors, often called on to perform a different play each day, could count on a fixed line length to aid their burdened memories.

Some poets complain that closed form is a straitjacket, a limit to free expression. Other poets, however, feel that, like fires held fast in a narrow space, thoughts stated in a tightly binding form may take on a heightened intensity. "Limitation makes for power," according to one contemporary practitioner of closed form, Richard Wilbur; "the strength of the genie comes of his being confined in a bottle." Compelled by some strict pattern to arrange and rearrange words, delete, and exchange them, poets must focus on them the keenest attention. Often they stand a chance of discovering words more meaningful than the ones they started out with. And at times, in obedience to a rime scheme, the poet may be surprised by saying something quite unexpected.

FORMAL PATTERNS

The best-known line-by-line pattern for a poem in English is **blank verse**: unrimed iambic pentameter. Most portions of Shakespeare's plays are in blank verse, and so are Milton's *Paradise Lost*, Tennyson's "Ulysses" (Chapter 27), certain dramatic monologues of Browning and Frost, and thousands of other poems. Here are some lines of blank verse that begin Robert Frost's "Mending Wall":

> Something there is that doesn't love a wall,
> That sends the frozen-ground-swell under it,
> And spills the upper boulders in the sun;
> And makes gaps even two can pass abreast.

The Couplet

The **couplet** is a two-line stanza, usually rimed. Its lines often tend to be equal in length, whether short or long. Here are examples from two wintery poems:

> Blow,
> Snow!

> As I in hoary winter's night stood shivering in the snow,
> Surprised I was with sudden heat which made my heart to glow.

Actually, any pair of rimed lines that contains a complete thought is called a couplet, even if it is not a stanza, such as the couplet that ends a sonnet by Shakespeare. Unlike other stanzas, couplets are often printed solid; one couplet is not separated from the next by white space. This practice is usual in writing the **heroic couplet**—or **closed couplet**—two rimed lines of iambic pentameter, with the first ending in a light pause and the second more heavily end-stopped. George Crabbe, in *The Parish Register*, described a shotgun wedding:

> Next at our altar stood a luckless pair,
> Brought by strong passions and a warrant there:
> By long rent cloak, hung loosely, strove the bride,
> From every eye, what all perceived, to hide;
> While the boy bridegroom, shuffling in his pace,
> Now hid awhile and then exposed his face.
> As shame alternately with anger strove
> The brain confused with muddy ale to move,
> In haste and stammering he performed his part,
> And looked the rage that rankled in his heart.

Though employed by Chaucer, the heroic couplet was named from its later use by Dryden and others in poems, translations of classical epics, and verse plays of epic heroes. It continued in favor through most of the eighteenth century. Much of our pleasure in reading good heroic couplets comes from the seemingly easy precision with which a skilled poet unites statements and strict pattern.

The Tercet

A **tercet** is a group of three lines. If rimed, they usually keep to one rime sound, as in this anonymous English children's jingle:

> Julius Caesar,
> The Roman geezer,
> Squashed his wife with a lemon-squeezer.

(That, by the way, is a great demonstration of surprising and unpredictable rimes.) *Terza rima*, the form Dante employs in *The Divine Comedy*, is made of tercets linked together by the rime scheme *a b a, b c b, c d c, d e d, e f e*, and so on. Harder to do in English than in Italian—with its greater resources of riming words—the form nevertheless was managed by Shelley in "Ode to the West Wind" (with the aid of some slant rimes):

> Make me thy lyre, even as the forest is:
> What if my leaves are falling like its own!
> The tumult of thy mighty harmonies

> Will take from both a deep, autumnal tone,
> Sweet though in sadness. Be thou, Spirit fierce,
> My spirit! Be thou me, impetuous one!

The Quatrain

The workhorse of English poetry is the **quatrain**, a stanza consisting of four lines. Quatrains are used in rimed poems more often than any other form.

Ernest Dowson (1867–1900)

Days of wine and roses 1896

> *Vitae summa brevis spem nos vetat incohare longam*

They are not long, the weeping and the laughter,
   Love and desire and hate:
I think they have no portion in us after
   We pass the gate.

They are not long, the days of wine and roses: 5
   Out of a misty dream
Our path emerges for a while, then closes
   Within a dream.

DAYS OF WINE AND ROSES. The epigraph, from Horace's *Odes* Book 1, 4, translates as "the brief sum of life forbids us the hope of enduring long."

Question

What elements of sound and rhythm are consistent between the two stanzas?

Quatrains come in many line lengths, and sometimes contain lines of varying length. Most often, poets rime the second and fourth lines of quatrains, as in the ballad stanza (Chapter 21), but the rimes can occur in any combination the poet chooses. Here are two quatrains from Tennyson's long, elegiac poem *In Memoriam*. The poem's form—quatrains of iambic tetrameter with the unusual rime scheme *a b b a*—became so celebrated that this pattern is now called the "*In Memoriam* stanza":

> Be near me when my light is low,
>   When the blood creeps, and the nerves prick
>   And tingle; and the heart is sick,
> And all the wheels of Being slow.
>
> Be near me when the sensuous frame
>   Is rack'd with pangs that conquer trust;
>   And Time, a maniac scattering dust,
> And Life, a Fury slinging flame.

Longer and more complicated stanzas are, of course, possible, but couplet, tercet, and quatrain have been called the building blocks of our poetry because most longer stanzas are made up of them. What short stanzas does John Donne mortar together to make the longer stanza of his "Song"?

John Donne (1572–1631)

Song 1633

Go and catch a falling star,
   Get with child a mandrake root,
Tell me where all past years are,
   Or who cleft the Devil's foot,

Teach me to hear mermaids singing,   5
   Or to keep off envy's stinging,
      And find
      What wind
Serves to advance an honest mind.

If thou be'st borne to strange sights,   10
   Things invisible to see,
Ride ten thousand days and nights,
   Till age snow white hairs on thee,
Thou, when thou return'st, wilt tell me
   All strange wonders that befell thee,   15
      And swear
      Nowhere
Lives a woman true, and fair.

If thou findst one, let me know,
   Such a pilgrimage were sweet—   20
Yet do not, I would not go,
   Though at next door we might meet;
Though she were true, when you met her,
   And last, till you write your letter,
      Yet she   25
      Will be
False, ere I come, to two, or three.

Syllabic Verse

Recently in vogue is a form known as **syllabic verse**, in which the poet establishes a pattern of a certain number of syllables to a line. Either rimed or rimeless but usually stanzaic, syllabic verse has been hailed as a way for poets to escape "the tyranny of the iamb" and discover less conventional rhythms, since, if they take as their line length an *odd* number of syllables, then iambs, being feet of *two* syllables, cannot fit perfectly into it. A well-known syllabic poem is Dylan Thomas's "Fern Hill" (Chapter 34). Notice its shape on the page, count the syllables in its lines, and you'll discover its perfect symmetry.

Other Patterns

Poets who write in demanding forms seem to enjoy taking on an arbitrary task for the fun of it, as ballet dancers do, or weight lifters. Much of our pleasure in reading such poems comes from watching words fall into a shape. It is the pleasure of seeing any hard thing done skillfully—a leap executed in a dance, a basketball swished through a basket. Still, to be excellent, a poem needs more than skill; and to enjoy a poem it isn't always necessary for the reader to be aware of the skill that went into it. Unknowingly, the editors of the *New Yorker* once printed an **acrostic**—a poem in which the initial letter of each line, read downward, spells out a word or words—that named (and insulted) a well-known anthologist. In the Old Testament book of Lamentations, profoundly moving songs tell of the sufferings of the Jews after the destruction of Jerusalem. Four of the songs are written as an alphabetical acrostic, each line beginning with a letter of the Hebrew alphabet in sequential order.

However ingenious, such sublime poetry cannot be dismissed as merely witty; nor can it be charged that a poet who writes in such a form does not express deep feeling. The following poem, while not an acrostic, plays with the alphabet in an inventive way.

Thomas M. Disch (1940–2008)

Zewhyexary   1981

Z is the Zenith from which we decline,
While Y is your Yelp as you're twisting your spine.
X is for Xmas; the alternative
Is an X-ray that gives you just one year to live.
So three cheers for Santa, and onward to W.   5
W's Worry, but don't let it trouble you:
W easily might have been Worse.
V, unavoidably, has to be Verse.
U is Uncertainty. T is a Trial
At which every objection is met with denial.   10
S is a Sentence of "Guilty as Charged."
R is a Russian whose nose is enlarged
By inveterate drinking, while Q is the Quiet
That falls on a neighborhood after a riot.
P is a Pauper with nary a hope   15
Of lining his pockets or learning to cope.
O is an Organ transplanted in vain,
While N is the Number of "Enemies Slain":
Three thousand three hundred and seventy-three.
If no one else wants it, could M be for Me?   20
No, M is reserved for a mad Millionaire,
And L is his Likewise, and goes to his heir.
K is a Kick in the seat of your pants,
And J is the Jury whose gross ignorance
Guaranteed the debacle referred to above.   25
I's the Inevitability of
Continued inflation and runaway crime,
So draw out your savings and have a good time.
H is your Heart at the moment it breaks,
And G is the Guile it initially takes   30
To pretend to believe that it someday will heal.
F is the strange Fascination we feel
For whatever's Evil—Yes, Evil is E—
And D is our Dread at the sight of a C,
Which is Corpse, as you've surely foreseen. B is Bone.   35
A could be anything. A is unknown.

Questions

1. How would you describe Disch's invented form?
2. Is there a plot to the poem, or an atmosphere that is evoked?

THE SONNET

When we speak of "traditional verse forms," we usually mean **fixed forms**. If written in a fixed form, a poem inherits from other poems certain familiar elements of structure: an unvarying number of lines, say, or a stanza pattern. In addition, it may display certain **conventions**: expected features such as themes, subjects, attitudes, or figures of speech. In medieval folk ballads a "milk-white steed" is a conventional figure of speech; and if its rider be a cruel and beautiful witch who kidnaps mortals, she is a conventional character.

In the poetry of western Europe and America, the **sonnet** is the fixed form that has attracted for the longest time the largest number of noteworthy practitioners. Originally an Italian form (*sonetto*: "little song"), the sonnet owes much of its prestige to Petrarch (1304–1374), who wrote in it of his love for the unattainable Laura. So great was the vogue for sonnets in England at the end of the sixteenth century that a gentleman might have been thought a boor if he couldn't turn out a decent one. Not content to adopt merely the sonnet's fourteen-line pattern, English poets also tried on its conventional mask of the tormented lover. They borrowed some of Petrarch's similes (a lover's heart, for instance, is like a storm-tossed boat) and invented others.

Soon after English poets imported the sonnet in the sixteenth century, they worked out their own rime scheme—one easier for them to follow than Petrarch's, which calls for a greater number of riming words than English can readily provide. (It's a popular though exaggerated belief that in Italian, practically everything rimes.) In the following **English sonnet**, sometimes called a **Shakespearean sonnet**, the rimes cohere in four clusters: *a b a b, c d c d, e f e f, g g*. Because a rime scheme tends to shape the poet's statements to it, the English sonnet has three places where the procession of thought is likely to turn in another direction. Within its form, a poet may pursue one idea throughout the three quatrains and then in the couplet end with a surprise.

William Shakespeare   (1564–1616)

Let me not to the marriage of true minds (Sonnet 116)   1609

Let me not to the marriage of true minds
Admit impediments; love is not love
Which alters when it alteration finds,
Or bends with the remover to remove.
O, no, it is an ever-fixèd mark   5
That looks on tempests and is never shaken;
It is the star to every wand'ring bark,
Whose worth's unknown, although his height be taken.
Love's not Time's fool, though rosy lips and cheeks
Within his bending sickle's compass° come;   *range*   10
Love alters not with his° brief hours and weeks,   *Time's*
But bears° it out even to the edge of doom.   *endures*
    If this be error and upon me proved,
    I never writ, nor no man ever loved.

LET ME NOT TO THE MARRIAGE OF TRUE MINDS. 5 *ever-fixèd mark*: a sea-mark like a beacon or a lighthouse that provides mariners with safe bearings. 7 *the star*: presumably the North Star, which gave sailors the most dependable bearing at sea. 12 *edge of doom*: either the brink of death or—taken more generally—Judgment Day.

Michael Drayton (1563–1631)

Since there's no help, come let us kiss and part   1619

Since there's no help, come let us kiss and part;
Nay, I have done, you get no more of me,
And I am glad, yea, glad with all my heart,
That thus so cleanly I myself can free;
Shake hands for ever, cancel all our vows,   5
And when we meet at any time again,
Be it not seen in either of our brows
That we one jot of former love retain.
Now at the last gasp of Love's latest breath,
When, his pulse failing, Passion speechless lies,   10
When Faith is kneeling by his bed of death,
And Innocence is closing up his eyes,
   Now if thou wouldst, when all have given him over,
   From death to life thou mightst him yet recover.

Less frequently met in English poetry, the **Italian sonnet**, or **Petrarchan sonnet**, follows the rime scheme *a b b a a b b a* in its first eight lines, called the **octave**, and then adds new rime sounds in the last six lines, called the **sestet**. The sestet may rime *c d c d c d, c d e c d e, c d c c d c*, or in almost any other variation that doesn't end in a couplet. This organization into two parts sometimes helps arrange the poet's thoughts. In the octave, the poet may state a problem, and then, in the sestet, may offer a resolution. A lover, for example, may lament all octave long that a loved one is neglectful, then in line 9 begin to foresee some outcome: the speaker will die, or accept unhappiness, or trust that the beloved will have a change of heart.

Edna St. Vincent Millay (1892–1950)

What lips my lips have kissed, and where, and why   1923

What lips my lips have kissed, and where, and why,
I have forgotten, and what arms have lain
Under my head till morning; but the rain
Is full of ghosts tonight, that tap and sigh
Upon the glass and listen for reply,   5
And in my heart there stirs a quiet pain
For unremembered lads that not again
Will turn to me at midnight with a cry.
Thus in the winter stands the lonely tree,
Nor knows what birds have vanished one by one,   10
Yet knows its boughs more silent than before:
I cannot say what loves have come and gone,
I only know that summer sang in me
A little while, that in me sings no more.

In this Italian sonnet, the turn of thought comes at the traditional point—the beginning of the ninth line. Many English-speaking poets, however, feel free to vary its placement. In John Milton's commanding sonnet on his blindness ("When I consider how my light is spent" in Chapter 34), the turn comes midway through line 8, and no one has ever thought the worse of it for bending the rules.

"The sonnet," quipped poet-critic Robert Bly, "is where old professors go to die." And certainly in the hands of an unskilled practitioner, the form can seem moribund. Considering the impressive number of powerful sonnets by modern poets such as Yeats, Frost, Auden, Millay, Cummings, Kees, and Heaney, however, the form hardly appears to be exhausted. No law compels sonnets to adopt an exalted tone or confines them to an Elizabethan vocabulary. To see some of the surprising shapes contemporary sonnets take, read this selection of six recent examples, followed by a much-admired sonnet from World War I.

Kim Addonizio (b. 1954)

First Poem for You   1994

I like to touch your tattoos in complete
darkness, when I can't see them. I'm sure of
where they are, know by heart the neat
lines of lightning pulsing just above
your nipple, can find, as if by instinct, the blue   5
swirls of water on your shoulder where a serpent
twists, facing a dragon. When I pull you
to me, taking you until we're spent
and quiet on the sheets, I love to kiss
the pictures in your skin. They'll last until   10
you're seared to ashes; whatever persists
or turns to pain between us, they will still
be there. Such permanence is terrifying.
So I touch them in the dark; but touch them, trying.

Questions

1. What is the speaker of this poem "sure of"? What, by implication, is she not sure of?
2. Why do you think the speaker feels that "Such permanence is terrifying"?
3. What, in your view, is she "trying" to do in the poem's last line?

Luis J. Rodríguez (b. 1954)

Praise to Shoes   2016

Praise to shoes on a homeless winter night
Praise to mothers who nurture without men
Praise to the bottom in a drug-mad flight
Praise to the poet who shatters with a pen
Praise to vibrant children in a static world   5
Praise to dreamers in cash-only exchanges
Praise to the tattered flag of justice, unfurled
Praise to our nation's depth, breadth, and ranges
Praise to a restoring earth with global warming
Praise to large spirits even in cages   10
Praise to the new alignments now forming
Praise to anger with eyes, not blind rages
        There is much to praise, if we are to last
        The big within the small, the small in the vast.

Questions

1. The poem is a sonnet, but how else would you describe its form? How does the final couplet operate differently from the first twelve lines?
2. Examine the rime scheme. Does it follow English or Italian rules?

A. E. Stallings (b. 1968)

Sine Qua Non   2002

Your absence, father, is nothing. It is naught—
The factor by which nothing will multiply,
The gap of a dropped stitch, the needle's eye
Weeping its black thread. It is the spot
Blindly spreading behind the looking glass.   5
It is the startled silences that come
When the refrigerator stops its hum,
And crickets pause to let the winter pass.

Your absence, father, is nothing—for it is
Omega's long last O, memory's elision,   10
The fraction of impossible division,
The element I move through, emptiness,
The void stars hang in, the interstice of lace,
The zero that still holds the sum in place.

SINE QUA NON. *Sine qua non* is Latin, meaning literally "without which not." Used to describe something that is indispensable, an essential part, a prerequisite.

Questions

1. "Nothing" is a key concept in this poem. As used here, does it have its customary connotations of meaninglessness and unimportance? Explain.
2. In "Writing Effectively" (at the end of the chapter), A. E. Stallings says that when she was young, she felt "that formal verse could not be contemporary, lacked spontaneity, had no room for the intimate." Discuss whether "Sine Qua Non" demonstrates the short-sightedness of that view.

Amit Majmudar (b. 1979)

Rites to Allay the Dead   2009

It is never enough to close their door.
You have to calm the ripples where they last slept.
The sandals that remember where they stepped
Out of the world must be picked up off the floor,
Their pictures not just folded to face the wood   5
But slid from the frames and snipped like credit cards.
Open the windows to air out the dark.
Closed blinds attract them, stopped clocks, cooling food.

They'll lick the doorstep like the cat come round,
Remembering you when they remember hunger.   10
They'll try to billow through their onetime sleeves
And point to your heart as in a lost and found.
The dead will know it, if you love much longer,
And whistle you near through the shuddering leaves.

Questions

1. To whom does the "they" in this poem refer?
2. Is there a change in this sonnet from the octave to the sestet?
3. What do the dead seem to want from the living?

R. S. Gwynn (b. 1948)

Shakespearean Sonnet   2002

With a first line taken from the TV listings

A man is haunted by his father's ghost.
Boy meets girl while feuding families fight.
A Scottish king is murdered by his host.
Two couples get lost on a summer night.
A hunchback slaughters all who block his way.   5
A ruler's rivals plot against his life.
A fat man and a prince make rebels pay.
A noble Moor has doubts about his wife.
An English king decides to conquer France.
A duke finds out his best friend is a she.   10
A forest sets the scene for this romance.
An old man and his daughters disagree.
A Roman leader makes a big mistake.
A sexy queen is bitten by a snake.

Questions

1. Explain the play on words in the title.
2. How many of the texts described in this sonnet can you identify?
3. Does this poem intend merely to amuse, or does it have a larger point?

Sherman Alexie (b. 1966)

The Facebook Sonnet   (2011)

Welcome to the endless high-school
Reunion. Welcome to past friends
And lovers, however kind or cruel.
Let's undervalue and unmend

The present. Why can't we pretend   5
Every stage of life is the same?
Let's exhume, resume, and extend
Childhood. Let's play all the games

That occupy the young. Let fame
And shame intertwine. Let one's search   10
For God become public domain.
Let church.com become our church.

Let's sign up, sign in, and confess
Here at the altar of loneliness.

Questions

1. How would you paraphrase this poem? What are the speaker's objections to social media?
2. Read the poem aloud, pausing slightly at the line endings. What is the rhythmic effect of the run-on lines?

Wilfred Owen (1893–1918)

Anthem for Doomed Youth   (1917)

What passing-bells for these who die as cattle?
   Only the monstrous anger of the guns.
Only the stuttering rifles' rapid rattle
   Can patter out their hasty orisons.
No mockeries now for them; no prayers nor bells,   5
   Nor any voice of mourning save the choirs,—
The shrill, demented choirs of wailing shells;
   And bugles calling for them from sad shires.°   *counties*

What candles may be held to speed them all?
   Not in the hands of boys, but in their eyes   10
   Shall shine the holy glimmers of good-byes.
The pallor of girls' brows shall be their pall;
Their flowers the tenderness of patient minds,
And each slow dusk a drawing-down of blinds.

Questions

1. Who are "these who die as cattle" (line 1), and what is the speaker asking? What implicit comparison does the entire poem turn upon? (Hint: What is meant by "passing-bells"?)
2. Why would the speaker consider traditional funeral rites to be "mockeries" (line 5) under these circumstances?
3. Do you detect any shift in tone between the first eight lines and the last six? How appropriate is the tone of each part of the poem to what is being said there?

THE EPIGRAM

Oscar Wilde said that a cynic is "a man who knows the price of everything and the value of nothing." Such a terse, pointed statement is called an epigram. In poetry, however, an **epigram** is a form: "A short poem ending in a witty or ingenious turn of thought, to which the rest of the composition is intended to lead up" (according to the *Oxford English Dictionary*). Often it is a malicious gibe with an unexpected stinger in the final line—perhaps in the very last word.

Sir John Harrington   (1561?–1612)

Of Treason   1618

Treason doth never prosper; what's the reason?
For if it prosper, none dare call it treason.

William Blake   (1757–1827)

To H——   (1805)

Thy Friendship oft has made my heart to ache
Do be my Enemy—for Friendship's sake.

Langston Hughes   (1901–1967)

Two Somewhat Different Epigrams   1957

I

Oh, God of dust and rainbows, help us see
That without dust the rainbow would not be.

II

I look with awe upon the human race
And God, who sometimes spits right in its face.

John Frederick Nims   (1913–1999)

Contemplation   1967

"I'm Mark's alone!" you swore. Given cause to doubt you,
I think less of you, dear. But more about you.

Anonymous

Epitaph on a dentist

Stranger, approach this spot with gravity;
John Brown is filling his last cavity.

Hilaire Belloc   (1870–1953)

Fatigue   1923

I'm tired of Love: I'm still more tired of Rhyme.
But Money gives me pleasure all the time.

Wendy Cope   (b. 1945)

Variation on Belloc's "Fatigue"   1992

I hardly ever tire of love or rhyme—
That's why I'm poor and have a rotten time.

Wendy Videlock (b. 1961)

If Not for the Dark 2013

If not for the dark,
no
spark.

Limerick

In English the only other fixed form to rival the sonnet and the epigram in favor is the **limerick**: five anapestic lines usually riming *a a b b a*. The limerick was made popular by Edward Lear (1812–1888), English painter and author of such nonsense poems as "The Owl and the Pussycat." Here is a sample, attributed to President Woodrow Wilson (1856–1924):

> I sat next to the Duchess at tea;
> It was just as I feared it would be:
> Her rumblings abdominal
> Were truly phenomenal
> And everyone thought it was me!

OTHER FORMS

There are many other verse forms used in English. The classical Persian poet Omar Khayyam was the master of the *rubai*, a four-line stanza usually rimed *a a b a*. This Persian form was introduced into English by Edward FitzGerald (1809–1883) in his hugely popular translation, *The Rubaiyat of Omar Khayyam* (*rubaiyat* is the plural of *rubai*). In FitzGerald's Victorian version, Omar Khayyam became one of the most frequently quoted poets in English. Here are four famous *rubaiyat*.

Omar Khayyam (1048–1131)

Rubaiyat (about 1100)

VII

Come, fill the Cup, and in the fire of Spring
Your Winter-garment of Repentance fling:
  The Bird of Time has but a little way
To flutter—and the Bird is on the Wing.

XII

A Book of Verses underneath the Bough,
A Jug of Wine, a Loaf of Bread—and Thou
  Beside me singing in the Wilderness—
Oh, Wilderness were Paradise enow!°   *enough*

LXXI

The Moving Finger writes; and, having writ,
Moves on: nor all your Piety nor Wit
  Shall lure it back to cancel half a Line,
Nor all your Tears wash out a Word of it.

XCIX

Ah Love! could you and I with Him conspire
To grasp this sorry Scheme of Things entire,
    Would not we shatter it to bits—and then
Re-mold it nearer to the Heart's Desire!

—Translated by Edward FitzGerald

English has borrowed fixed forms from an astonishing variety of sources. The haiku (Chapter 19) and tanka originated in Japan. Other borrowed forms include the ghazal (Arabic), pantoum (Malay), and sapphics (Greek). Even blank verse, which seems as English as the royal family, began as an attempt by Elizabethan poets to copy an Italian eleven-syllable line. To conclude this chapter, here are poems in four widely used closed forms—the villanelle, triolet, rondeau, and sestina. Their patterns, which are sometimes called "French forms," have been particularly fascinating to English-language poets because they do not merely require the repetition of rime sounds; instead, they demand more elaborate echoing, involving the repetition of either full words or whole lines of verse. Sometimes difficult to master, these forms can create a powerful musical effect unlike ordinary riming.

Dylan Thomas (1914–1953)

Do not go gentle into that good night   1952

Do not go gentle into that good night,
Old age should burn and rave at close of day;
Rage, rage against the dying of the light.
Though wise men at their end know dark is right,
Because their words had forked no lightning they   5
Do not go gentle into that good night.

Good men, the last wave by, crying how bright
Their frail deeds might have danced in a green bay,
Rage, rage against the dying of the light.

Wild men who caught and sang the sun in flight,   10
And learn, too late, they grieved it on its way,
Do not go gentle into that good night.

Grave men, near death, who see with blinding sight
Blind eyes could blaze like meteors and be gay,
Rage, rage against the dying of the light.   15

And you, my father, there on the sad height,
Curse, bless, me now with your fierce tears, I pray,
Do not go gentle into that good night.
Rage, rage against the dying of the light.

Questions

1. "Do not go gentle into that good night" is a **villanelle**: a fixed form originated by French courtly poets of the Middle Ages. What are its rules?

2. Whom does the poem address? What is the speaker saying?
3. Villanelles are sometimes criticized as elaborate exercises in trivial wordplay. How would you defend Thomas's poem against this charge?

Robert Bridges (1844–1930)

Triolet   1890

When first we met we did not guess
That Love would prove so hard a master;
Of more than common friendliness
When first we met we did not guess.
Who could foretell this sore distress,   5
This irretrievable disaster
When first we met?—We did not guess
That Love would prove so hard a master.

TRIOLET. The **triolet** is a short lyric form borrowed from the French; its two opening lines are repeated according to a set pattern, as Bridges's poem illustrates. The triolet is often used for light verse, but Bridges's poem demonstrates how it can carry heavier emotional loads, if used with sufficient skill.

Question

How do the first two lines of "Triolet" change in meaning when they reappear at the end of the poem?

Paul Laurence Dunbar (1872–1906)

We Wear the Mask   1895

We wear the mask that grins and lies,
It hides our cheeks and shades our eyes,—
This debt we pay to human guile;
With torn and bleeding hearts we smile,
And mouth with myriad subtleties.   5

Why should the world be over-wise,
In counting all our tears and sighs?
Nay, let them only see us, while
    We wear the mask.

We smile, but, O great Christ, our cries   10
To thee from tortured souls arise.
We sing, but oh the clay is vile
Beneath our feet, and long the mile;
But let the world dream otherwise,
    We wear the mask!   15

Question

"We Wear the Mask" uses another French form, the **rondeau**, a cousin to the triolet. Where do you find patterns of repetition, and how is that repetition effective at expressing the poem's theme?

Elizabeth Bishop (1911–1979)

Sestina   1965

September rain falls on the house.
In the failing light, the old grandmother
sits in the kitchen with the child
beside the Little Marvel Stove,
reading the jokes from the almanac,   5
laughing and talking to hide her tears.

She thinks that her equinoctial tears
and the rain that beats on the roof of the house
were both foretold by the almanac,
but only known to a grandmother.   10
The iron kettle sings on the stove.
She cuts some bread and says to the child,

It's time for tea now; but the child
is watching the teakettle's small hard tears
dance like mad on the hot black stove,   15
the way the rain must dance on the house.
Tidying up, the old grandmother
hangs up the clever almanac

on its string. Birdlike, the almanac
hovers half open above the child,   20
hovers above the old grandmother
and her teacup full of dark brown tears.
She shivers and says she thinks the house
feels chilly, and puts more wood in the stove.

It was to be, says the Marvel Stove.   25
I know what I know, says the almanac.
With crayons the child draws a rigid house
and a winding pathway. Then the child
puts in a man with buttons like tears
and shows it proudly to the grandmother.   30

But secretly, while the grandmother
busies herself about the stove,
the little moons fall down like tears
from between the pages of the almanac
into the flower bed the child   35
has carefully placed in the front of the house.

Time to plant tears, says the almanac.
The grandmother sings to the marvellous stove
and the child draws another inscrutable house.

SESTINA. As its title indicates, this poem is written in the trickiest of medieval fixed forms, that of the **sestina** (or "song of sixes"), said to have been invented in Provence in the thirteenth century by the troubadour poet Arnaut Daniel. In six six-line stanzas, the poet repeats six end-words (in a prescribed order) and then reintroduces the six repeated words (in any order) in a closing **envoy** of three lines.

Elizabeth Bishop strictly follows the troubadour rules for the order in which the end-words recur. (If you'd like, you can figure out the formula: in the first stanza, the six words are arranged A B C D E F; in the second, F A E B D C; and so on.)

Questions

1. A perceptive comment from a student: "Something seems to be going on here that the child doesn't understand. Maybe some terrible loss has happened." Test this guess by reading the poem closely.
2. In the "little moons" that fall from the almanac (line 33), does the poem introduce dream or fantasy, or do you take these to be small round pieces of paper?
3. What is the tone of this poem—the speaker's apparent attitude toward the scene described?
4. In an essay, "The Sestina," in *A Local Habitation* (U of Michigan P, 1985), John Frederick Nims defends the form against an obvious complaint against it:

> A shallow view of the sestina might suggest that the poet writes a stanza, and then is stuck with six words which he has to juggle into the required positions through five more stanzas and an envoy—to the great detriment of what passion and sincerity would have him say. But in a good sestina the poet has six words, six images, six ideas so urgently in his mind that he cannot get away from them; he wants to test them in all possible combinations and come to a conclusion about their relationship.

How well does this description of a good sestina fit Bishop's "Sestina"?

■ WRITING *effectively*

A. E. Stallings on Writing

On Form and Artifice   2000

Is form artificial? Of course it is. I am all for the artificial. I am reminded of an anecdote. A lovely girl, with natural blonde hair, but of a rather dark, rather dingy shade, complains to a friend. She has wanted for a long time to get it highlighted, which she thinks will brighten her appearance, but with the qualms and vanity of a natural blonde, scruples about the artificiality of having her hair colored. At which point her friend laughs and declares, "Honey, the point is to *look* natural. Not to *be* natural."

It seems an obvious point for art. Art is effective and direct because of its use of artifice, not simply because the artist has something sincere or important to communicate. Anyone who has written a letter of condolence should

A. E. Stallings

be able to sympathize. When a close friend has lost a loved one, what can one say? "I cannot imagine your loss" "words cannot begin to" "our thoughts and prayers are with you" etc. That these phrases are threadbare does not make them less sincere. Phrases become threadbare *because* they are sincere.

I had several revelations about the nature of poetry in a college Latin class on Catullus. I was shocked by how *modern*, how *contemporary* the poems seemed. And it was a revelation to see how a poet could at one and the same time be a supreme formal architect of verse, and write poems that seemed utterly spontaneous, candid, and confessional, with room for the sublime, the learned, the colloquial, and the frankly obscene.

I suppose at some point I had somehow imbibed the opposite notion, a notion still held by many, that formal verse could not be contemporary, lacked spontaneity, had no room for the intimate. At that time I did not see much formal work getting published: I wanted to publish, and therefore struggled in free verse. I did not have much luck. Eventually I gave up, wrote what I really wanted to write, which rhymed and scanned, and, oddly, *then* I had some success in publishing. Which leads to yet another little adage of mine, which is, don't write what you *know* (I think this is better fitted for prose writers), write what you *like*, the sort of stuff you actually enjoy reading, fashionable or not.

From "Crooked Roads Without Improvement: Some Thoughts on Formal Verse"

THINKING ABOUT A SONNET

A poem's form is closely tied to its meaning. This is especially true of the sonnet, a form whose rules dictate not only the sound of a poem but also, to a certain extent, its sense. A sonnet traditionally looks at a single theme, but reverses its stance on the subject somewhere along the way. One possible definition of the sonnet might be a fourteen-line poem divided into two unequal parts. Traditionally, Italian sonnets divide their parts into an octave (the first eight lines) and a sestet (the last six), while English sonnets are more lopsided, with a final couplet balanced against three preceding quatrains. The moment when a sonnet changes its direction is commonly called "the turn."

- **Identifying the moment when the poem "turns" helps in understanding both its theme and its structure.** In a Shakespearean sonnet, the turn usually—but not always—comes in the final couplet. In modern sonnets, the turn is often less overt.
- **To find that moment, study the poem's opening.** Latch on to the mood and manner of the opening lines. Is the feeling joyful or sad, loving or angry?
- **Read the poem from this opening perspective until you feel it tug strongly in another direction.** Sometimes the second part of a sonnet will directly contradict the opening. More often it explains, augments, or qualifies the opening.

CHECKLIST: Writing About a Sonnet

- ☐ Read the poem carefully.
- ☐ What is the mood of its opening lines?
- ☐ At what line do you feel a shift in the poem's mood?
- ☐ What is the tone after the sonnet's turn away from its opening direction?
- ☐ What do the two alternative points of view add up to?
- ☐ How does the poem reconcile its contrasting sections?

TOPICS FOR WRITING ON CLOSED FORM

1. Examine a sonnet from anywhere in this book. Explain how its two parts combine to create a total effect neither part could achieve alone. Be sure to identify the turning point. Paraphrase what each of the poem's two sections says and describe how the poem as a whole reconciles the two contrasting parts. (In addition to the sonnets in this chapter, you might consider the following from Chapter 34: Elizabeth Barrett Browning's "How Do I Love Thee?"; Gerard Manley Hopkins's "The Windhover"; John Keats's "When I have fears that I may cease to be"; John Milton's "When I consider how my light is spent"; William Shakespeare's "When in disgrace with Fortune and men's eyes"; or William Wordsworth's "Composed upon Westminster Bridge.")

2. Select a poem from Chapter 34 that incorporates rime. Write a paragraph describing how the rime scheme helps to advance the poem's meaning.

3. Write ten lines of blank verse on a topic of your own choice. Then write about the experience. What aspects of writing in regular meter did you find most challenging? What did you learn about reading blank verse from trying your hand at writing it?

4. Write a *rubai* of your own on any topic. Some possible subjects include: what you plan to do next weekend to relax; advice to a friend to stop worrying; an invitation to a loved one; a four-line *carpe diem* ode. Reread Khayyam's *rubaiyat* for inspiration.

5. Discuss the use of form in Robert Bridges's "Triolet." What is the effect of so many repeated lines in so brief a poem?

6. Compare Dylan Thomas's "Do not go gentle into that good night" with Wendy Cope's "Lonely Hearts" (Chapter 17). How can the same form be used to create such different kinds of poems?

7. William Carlos Williams, in an interview, delivered this blast:

    > Forcing twentieth-century America into a sonnet—gosh, how I hate sonnets—is like putting a crab into a square box. You've got to cut his legs off to make him fit. When you get through, you don't have a crab any more.

    In a two-page essay, defend the modern American sonnet against Williams's charge. Or instead, open fire on it, using Williams's view for ammunition. Some sonnets to consider: Sherman Alexie's "The Facebook Sonnet"; Kim Addonizio's "First Poem for You"; and R. S. Gwynn's "Shakespearean Sonnet."

8. Write a sestina and see what you find out by doing so. (Even if you fail in the attempt, you just might learn something interesting.) To start, pick six words you think are worth repeating six times. This elaborate pattern gives you much help: as John Ashbery has pointed out, writing a sestina is "like riding downhill on a bicycle and having the pedals push your feet." Here is some encouragement from a poet and critic, John Heath-Stubbs: "I have never read a sestina that seemed to me a total failure."

▶ TERMS FOR *review*

Form

Form ▶ In a general sense, form is the means by which a literary work expresses its content. In poetry, form is usually used to describe the design of a poem.

Fixed form ▶ A traditional verse form requiring certain predetermined elements of structure—for example, a stanza pattern, set meter, or predetermined line length.

Closed form ▶ A generic term that describes poetry written in a pattern of meter, rime, lines, or stanzas. A closed form adheres to a set structure.

Open form ▶ Verse that has no set scheme—no regular meter, rime, or stanzaic pattern. Open form has also been called **free verse**.

Blank verse ▶ Verse that contains five iambic feet per line (iambic pentameter) and is not rimed. ("Blank" means unrimed.)

Couplet ▶ A two-line stanza in poetry, usually rimed and with lines of roughly equal length.

Closed couplet ▶ Two rimed lines of iambic pentameter that usually contain an independent and complete thought or statement. Also called **heroic couplet**.

Quatrain ▶ A stanza consisting of four lines, it is the most common stanza form used in English-language poetry.

Epic ▶ A long narrative poem tracing the adventures of a popular hero. Epic poems are usually written in a consistent form and meter throughout.

Epigram ▶ A very short comic poem, often turning at the end with some sharp wit or unexpected stinger.

Rubai ▶ An ancient Persian stanza form (**rubaiyat** is the plural) consisting of four lines, usually rimed *a a b a*.

The Sonnet

Sonnet ▶ A fixed form of fourteen lines, traditionally written in iambic pentameter and rimed throughout.

Italian sonnet ▶ Also called **Petrarchan sonnet**, it rimes the **octave** (first eight lines) *a b b a a b b a*; the **sestet** (last six lines) may follow any rime pattern, as long as it does not end in a couplet. The poem traditionally turns, or shifts in mood or tone, after the octave.

English sonnet ▶ Also called **Shakespearean sonnet**, it has the following rime scheme organized into three quatrains and a concluding couplet: *a b a b c d c d e f e f g g*. The poem may turn—that is, shift in mood or tone—between any of the rime clusters.

25

All poetry is experimental poetry.

—WALLACE STEVENS

What You Will Learn in This Chapter

- To recognize and describe *free verse* and *open form*
- To define *prose poetry*
- To define *concrete poetry*
- To analyze the role of free verse in shaping the meaning of a poem

Writing in **open form**, a poet seeks to discover a fresh and individual arrangement for words in every poem. Such a poem, generally speaking, has neither a rime scheme nor a basic meter informing the whole of it. Doing without those powerful (some would say hypnotic) elements, the poet who writes in open form relies on other means to engage and sustain the reader's attention. Novice poets often think that open form looks easy, not nearly so hard as riming everything; but in truth, formally open poems are easy to write only if written carelessly. To compose lines with keen awareness of open form's demands, and of its infinite possibilities, calls for skill: at least as much as that needed to write in meter and rime, if not more. Should the poet succeed, then the discovered arrangement will seem exactly right for what the poem is saying.

Denise Levertov (1923–1997)

Ancient Stairway

1999

Footsteps like water hollow
the broad curves of stone
ascending, descending
century by century.
Who can say if the last   5
to climb these stairs
will be journeying
downward or upward?

Open form, in this brief poem, affords Denise Levertov certain advantages. Able to break off a line at whatever point she likes (a privilege not available to the poet writing, say, a conventional sonnet, who has to break off each line after its tenth syllable), she selects her pauses artfully. Line breaks lend emphasis: a word or phrase at the end of a line takes a little more stress (and receives a little more attention), because the ending of the line compels the reader to make a slight pause, if only for the brief moment it takes to sling back one's eyes and fix them on the line following. Slight pauses, then, follow the words and phrases *hollow/stone/descending/century/last/ stairs/journeying/upward*—all these being elements that apparently the poet wishes to call to our attention. (The pause after a line break also casts a little more weight on the *first* word or phrase of each succeeding line.)

Levertov makes the most of white space—another means of calling attention to things, as any good picture-framer knows. She has greater control over the shape of the poem, its look on the page, than would be allowed by the demands of meter; she uses that control to stack on top of one another lines that appear much like the steps of a staircase. The opening line with its quick stresses might suggest to us the feet passing over the steps. From there, Levertov slows the rhythm to the heavy beats of lines 3–4, which could communicate a sense of repeated trudging up and down the stairs (in a particularly effective touch, all four of the stressed syllables in these two lines make the same sound), a sense that is reinforced by the poem's last line, which echoes the rhythm of line 3. In all likelihood, we perceive these effects instinctively, not consciously (which may also be the way the author created them), but no matter how we apprehend them, they serve to deepen our understanding of and pleasure in the text.

FREE VERSE

Poetry in open form can also be called **free verse** (from the French **vers libre**), suggesting a kind of verse liberated from the shackles of rime and meter. "Writing free verse," said Robert Frost, who wasn't interested in it, "is like playing tennis with the net down." And yet, as Denise Levertov and many other poets demonstrate, high scores can be made in such an unconventional game, provided it doesn't straggle all over the court. For a successful poem in open form, the term *free verse* seems inaccurate. "Being an art form," said William Carlos Williams, "verse cannot be 'free' in the sense of having *no* limitations or guiding principles."[1] Various substitute names have been suggested: organic poetry, composition by field, raw (as opposed to cooked) poetry, open form poetry. "But what does it matter what you call it?" remark the editors of a 1969 anthology called *Naked Poetry*. "The best poems of the last thirty years don't rhyme (usually) and don't move on feet of more or less equal duration (usually). That nondescription moves toward the only technical principle they all have in common."[2]

Projective Verse

Yet many poems in open form have much more in common than absences and lacks. One positive principle has been Ezra Pound's famous suggestion that poets "compose in the sequence of the musical phrase, not in the sequence of the metronome"—good advice, perhaps, even for poets who write inside fixed forms. In Charles Olson's influential theory of **projective verse**, poets compose by listening to their own breathing. On paper, they indicate the rhythms of a poem by using a little white space or a lot, a slight indentation or a deep one, depending on whether a short pause or a long one is intended. Words can be grouped in clusters on the page (usually no more words than

---

[1]"Free Verse," *Princeton Encyclopedia of Poetry and Poetics*, 2nd ed., 1975.
[2]Stephen Berg and Robert Mezey, eds., foreword, *Naked Poetry: Recent American Poetry in Open Forms* (Indianapolis: Bobbs, 1969).

a lungful of air can accommodate). Heavy cesuras are sometimes shown by breaking a line in two and lowering the second part of it.

Free Verse Lines

To the poet working in open form, no less than to the poet writing a sonnet, line length can be valuable. Walt Whitman, who loved to expand vast sentences for line after line, knew well that an impressive rhythm can accumulate if the poet will keep long lines approximately the same length, causing a pause to recur at about the same interval after every line. Sometimes, too, Whitman repeats the same words at each line's opening. An instance is the masterly sixth section of "When Lilacs Last in the Dooryard Bloom'd," an elegy for Abraham Lincoln:

> Coffin that passes through lanes and streets,
> Through day and night with the great cloud darkening the land,
> With the pomp of the inloop'd flags with the cities draped in black,
> With the show of the States themselves as of crape-veil'd women
>   standing,
> With processions long and winding and the flambeaus of the night,
> With the countless torches lit, with the silent sea of faces and the
>   unbared heads,
> With the waiting depot, the arriving coffin, and the somber faces,
> With dirges through the night, with the thousand voices rising
>   strong and solemn,
> With all the mournful voices of the dirges pour'd around the coffin,
> The dim-lit churches and the shuddering organs—where amid
>   these you journey,
> With the tolling tolling bells' perpetual clang,
> Here, coffin that slowly passes,
> I give you my sprig of lilac.

There is music in such solemn, operatic arias. Whitman's lines echo another model: the Hebrew **psalms**, or sacred songs, as translated in the King James Version of the Bible. In Psalm 150, repetition also occurs inside of lines:

> Praise ye the Lord. Praise God in his sanctuary: praise him in the
>   firmament of his power.
> Praise him for his mighty acts: praise him according to his excellent
>   greatness.
> Praise him with the sound of the trumpet: praise him with the
>   psaltery and harp.
> Praise him with the timbrel and dance: praise him with stringed
>   instruments and organs.
> Praise him upon the loud cymbals: praise him upon the high
>   sounding cymbals.
> Let every thing that hath breath praise the Lord. Praise ye the Lord.

Whitman was a more deliberate craftsman than he let his readers think, and to anyone interested in writing in open form, his work will repay close study. He knew that repetitions of any kind often make memorable rhythms, as in this passage from "Song of Myself," with every line ending on an *-ing* word (a stressed syllable followed by an unstressed syllable):

Here and there with dimes on the eyes walking,
To feed the greed of the belly the brains liberally spooning,
Tickets buying, taking, selling, but in to the feast never once going,
Many sweating, ploughing, thrashing, and then the chaff for
  payment receiving,
A few idly owning, and they the wheat continually claiming.

Much more than simply repetition, of course, went into the music of those lines—the internal rime *feed*, *greed*, the use of assonance, the trochees that begin the third and fourth lines, whether or not they were calculated.

Sound and Rhythm in Free Verse

In many classics of open form poetry, sound and rhythm are positive forces. When speaking a poem in open form, you often may find that it makes a difference for the better if you pause at the end of each line. Why do the pauses matter? Open form poetry usually has no meter to lend it rhythm. *Some* lines in an open form poem, as we have seen in Whitman's "dimes on the eyes" passage, do fall into metrical feet; sometimes the whole poem does. Usually lacking meter's aid, however, open form, in order to have more and more noticeable rhythms, has need of all the recurring pauses it can get.

Some poems, to be sure, seem more widely open in form than others. A poet may wish to avoid the rigidity and predictability of fixed line lengths and stanzaic forms but still wish to hold a poem together through a strong rhythmic impulse and even a discernible metrical emphasis. A poet may employ rime, but have the rimes recur at various intervals, or perhaps rime lines of varying lengths. In a 1917 essay called "Reflections on *Vers Libre*," T. S. Eliot famously observed, "No *vers* is *libre* for the man who wants to do a good job."

At the moment, much exciting new poetry is being written in both open form and closed. A number of poets have taken up rime and meter and are writing sonnets, epigrams, and poems in rimed stanzas. Meanwhile, many younger poets continue to explore a wide range of open forms from conventional and conversational free verse to wildly challenging experimental styles. The contemporary American determination to play every possible trick that both written and spoken language allows is at least partially inspired by the early Modernist master E. E. Cummings, the smiling godfather of poetic experimentalists everywhere.

E. E. Cummings (1894–1962)

Buffalo Bill 's   1923

Buffalo Bill 's
defunct
          who used to
          ride a watersmooth-silver
                              stallion   5
and break onetwothreefourfive pigeonsjustlikethat
                              Jesus

he was a handsome man
                    and what i want to know is
how do you like your blueeyed boy   10
Mister Death

Question

Cummings's poem would look like this if given conventional punctuation and set as prose:

> Buffalo Bill's defunct, who used to ride a water-smooth silver stallion and break one, two, three, four, five pigeons just like that. Jesus, he was a handsome man. And what I want to know is: "How do you like your blue-eyed boy, Mister Death?"

By what characteristics is this still recognizable as poetry? What has been lost?

W. S. Merwin (b. 1927)

For the Anniversary of My Death   1967

Every year without knowing it I have passed the day
When the last fires will wave to me
And the silence will set out
Tireless traveler
Like the beam of a lightless star   5

Then I will no longer
Find myself in life as in a strange garment
Surprised at the earth
And the love of one woman
And the shamelessness of men   10
As today writing after three days of rain
Hearing the wren sing and the falling cease
And bowing not knowing to what

Questions

1. Read the poem aloud. Try pausing for a fraction of a second at the end of every line. Is there a justification for each line break?
2. The poem is divided into two asymmetrical sections. Does this formal division reflect some change or difference of meaning between the two sections?

Ezra Pound (1885–1972)

Salutation   1916

O generation of the thoroughly smug
      and thoroughly uncomfortable,
I have seen fishermen picnicking in the sun,
I have seen them with untidy families,
I have seen their smiles full of teeth   5
      and heard ungainly laughter.
And I am happier than you are,
And they were happier than I am;
And the fish swim in the lake
      and do not even own clothing.   10

Questions

1. What organizational devices does this poem use?
2. Why are lines 2, 6, and 10 indented and without initial capital letters?
3. What is the point of the poem's last two lines?

The Kermess or *Peasant Dance* by Pieter Brueghel the Elder (1520?–1569).

William Carlos Williams   (1883–1963)

The Dance   1944

In Brueghel's great picture, The Kermess,
the dancers go round, they go round and
around, the squeal and the blare and the
tweedle of bagpipes, a bugle and fiddles
tipping their bellies (round as the thick-   5
sided glasses whose wash they impound)
their hips and their bellies off balance
to turn them. Kicking and rolling about
the Fair Grounds, swinging their butts, those
shanks must be sound to bear up under such   10
rollicking measures, prance as they dance
in Brueghel's great picture, The Kermess.

THE DANCE. 1 *Brueghel*: Flemish painter known for his scenes of peasant activities. *The Kermess*: painting of a celebration on the feast day of a local patron saint.

Questions

1. Scan this poem and try to describe the effect of its rhythms.
2. Williams, widely admired for his free verse, insisted for many years that what he sought was a form not in the least bit free. What effect does he achieve by ending lines on such weak words as the articles "and" and "the"? By splitting "thick- / sided"? By splitting a prepositional phrase with the break at the end of line 8? By using line breaks to split "those" and "such" from what they modify? What do you think he is trying to convey?
3. Is there any point in his making line 12 a repetition of the opening line?
4. Look at the reproduction of Brueghel's painting *The Kermess* (also called *Peasant Dance*). Aware that the rhythms of dancers, the rhythms of a painting, and the rhythms of a poem are not all the same, can you put in your own words what Brueghel's dancing figures have in common with Williams's descriptions of them?
5. Compare "The Dance" with another poem that refers to a Brueghel painting: W. H. Auden's "Musée des Beaux Arts" (Chapter 34). What seems to be each poet's main concern: to convey in words a sense of the painting, or to visualize the painting in order to state some theme?

Stephen Crane (1871–1900)

The Heart   1895

In the desert
I saw a creature, naked, bestial,
Who, squatting upon the ground,
Held his heart in his hands,
And ate of it.   5
I said, "Is it good, friend?"
"It is bitter—bitter," he answered;
"But I like it
Because it is bitter,
And because it is my heart."   10

Walt Whitman (1819–1892)

I Hear America Singing   1860

I hear America singing, the varied carols I hear,
Those of mechanics, each one singing his as it should be blithe and strong,
The carpenter singing his as he measures his plank or beam,
The mason singing his as he makes ready for work, or leaves off work,
The boatman singing what belongs to him in his boat, the deckhand   5
    singing on the steamboat deck,
The shoemaker singing as he sits on his bench, the hatter singing as he stands,
The wood-cutter's song, the ploughboy's on his way in the morning, or at
    noon intermission or at sundown,
The delicious singing of the mother, or of the young wife at work, or of the
    girl sewing or washing,
Each singing what belongs to him or her and to none else,
The day what belongs to the day—at night the party of young fellows,   10
    robust, friendly,
Singing with open mouths their strong melodious songs.

Questions: Crane Versus Whitman

The following nit-picking questions are intended to help you see exactly what makes these two open form poems by Crane and Whitman so different in their music.

1. After reading Whitman's poem aloud, how would you describe its rhythm? In what way, and to what effect, does he use repetition?
2. How would you describe the rhythm of Crane's poem, and how is that rhythm determined by the shorter lines and more frequent punctuation?
3. Point out words in Whitman's poem that seem musical. Is "melodious," the word found in Whitman's final line, an apt description of "I Hear America Singing"?
4. Do you find many melodious words in "The Heart"? Is Crane's poem necessarily an inferior poem for having less music?

Analyzing Line Breaks

Wallace Stevens's lineation in "Thirteen Ways of Looking at a Blackbird" allows us not only to see but also to savor the connections between the poem's ideas and images. Consider section II of the poem:

> I was of three minds,
> Like a tree
> In which there are three blackbirds.

On a purely semantic level, these lines may mean the same as the prose statement, "I was of three minds, like a tree in which there are three blackbirds," but Stevens's choice of line breaks adds special emphasis at several points. Each of these three lines isolates and presents a separate image (the speaker, the tree, and the blackbirds). The placement of *three* in the opening and closing lines helps us feel the similar nature of the two statements. The short middle line allows us to see the image of the tree before we fully understand why it is parallel to the divided mind—thus adding a touch of suspense that the prose version of this statement just can't supply. Ending each line with a key noun and image also gives the poem a concrete feel not altogether evident in the prose.

Wallace Stevens (1879–1955)

Thirteen Ways of Looking at a Blackbird   1923

I

Among twenty snowy mountains,
The only moving thing
Was the eye of the blackbird.

II

I was of three minds,
Like a tree
In which there are three blackbirds.   5

III

The blackbird whirled in the autumn winds.
It was a small part of the pantomime.

IV

A man and a woman
Are one.   10
A man and a woman and a blackbird
Are one.

V

I do not know which to prefer,
The beauty of inflections
Or the beauty of innuendoes,
The blackbird whistling
Or just after.

VI

Icicles filled the long window
With barbaric glass.
The shadow of the blackbird
Crossed it, to and fro.
The mood
Traced in the shadow
An indecipherable cause.

VII

O thin men of Haddam,
Why do you imagine golden birds?
Do you not see how the blackbird
Walks around the feet
Of the women about you?

VIII

I know noble accents
And lucid, inescapable rhythms;
But I know, too,
That the blackbird is involved
In what I know.

IX

When the blackbird flew out of sight,
It marked the edge
Of one of many circles.

X

At the sight of blackbirds
Flying in a green light,
Even the bawds of euphony
Would cry out sharply.

15

20

25

30

35

40

XI

He rode over Connecticut
In a glass coach.
Once, a fear pierced him,
In that he mistook
The shadow of his equipage   45
For blackbirds.

XII

The river is moving.
The blackbird must be flying.

XIII

It was evening all afternoon.
It was snowing   50
And it was going to snow.
The blackbird sat
In the cedar-limbs.

THIRTEEN WAYS OF LOOKING AT A BLACKBIRD. 25 *Haddam:* This biblical-sounding name is that of a town in Connecticut.

Questions

1. What is the speaker's attitude toward the men of Haddam? What attitude toward this world does he suggest they lack? What is implied by calling them "thin" (line 25)?

2. What do the landscapes of winter contribute to the poem's effectiveness? If Stevens had chosen images of summer lawns, what would have been lost?

3. In which sections of the poem does Stevens suggest that a unity exists between human being and blackbird, between blackbird and the entire natural world? Can we say that Stevens "philosophizes"? What role does imagery play in Stevens's statement of his ideas?

4. What sense can you make of Part X? Make an enlightened guess.

5. Consider any one of the thirteen parts. What patterns of sound and rhythm do you find in it? What kind of structure does it have?

6. If the thirteen parts were arranged in some different order, would the poem be just as good? Or can you find a justification for its beginning with Part I and ending with Part XIII?

7. Does the poem seem an arbitrary combination of thirteen separate poems? Or is there any reason to call it a whole?

PROSE POETRY

No law requires a poet to split thoughts into verse lines. Charles Baudelaire, Rainer Maria Rilke, Jorge Luis Borges, Alexander Solzhenitsyn, T. S. Eliot, and many others have written **prose poems**, in which, without caring that eye appeal and some of the rhythm of a line structure may be lost, the poet prints words in a block like a prose paragraph. To some, the term "prose poetry" is as oxymoronic as "jumbo shrimp" or "plastic glasses," if not a flat-out contradiction in terms. Yet prose poems exist. Here are two by twentieth-century American poets. As you read them, ask yourself: Are they prose poems, or very short pieces of prose? If they are poetry, what features distinguish them from prose? If they should be considered prose, what essential features of poetry do they lack?

Charles Simic (b. 1939)

The Magic Study of Happiness   1992

In the smallest theater in the world the bread crumbs speak. It's a mystery play on the subject of a lost paradise. Once there was a kitchen with a table on which a few crumbs were left. Through the window you could see your young mother by the fence talking to a neighbor. She was cold and kept hugging her thin dress tighter and tighter. The clouds in the sky sailed on as she threw her head back   5
to laugh.

Where the words can't go any further—there's the hard table. The crumbs are watching you as you in turn watch them. The unknown in you and the unknown in them attract each other. The two unknowns are like illicit lovers when they're exceedingly and unaccountably happy.   10

Questions

1. What is the effect of the phrases "the smallest theater in the world" and "mystery play"?
2. How do you interpret "Where the words can't go any further—there's the hard table"?
3. What is the significance of the simile in the last sentence?

Gertrude Stein (1874–1946)

Nothing Elegant   1914

A charm a single charm is doubtful. If the red is rose and there is a gate surrounding it, if inside is let in and there places change then certainly something is upright. It is earnest.

Questions

1. Try to paraphrase the poem. Despite the lack of conventional punctuation and sentence structure, does the poem convey meaning?
2. How would the effect of this poem change by breaking it into lines?

VISUAL POETRY

Let's look at a famous poem with a distinctive visible shape. In the seventeenth century, a few ingenious poets trimmed their lines into the silhouettes of altars and crosses, pillars and pyramids. Here is one. Is it anything more than a demonstration of ingenuity?

George Herbert (1593–1633)

Easter Wings   1633

Lord, who createdst man in wealth and store,
Though foolishly he lost the same,
Decaying more and more
Till he became
Most poor;
With thee
Oh, let me rise
As larks, harmoniously,
And sing this day thy victories;
Then shall the fall further the flight in me.

My tender age in sorrow did begin;
And still with sicknesses and shame
Thou didst so punish sin,
That I became
Most thin.
With thee
Let me combine,
And feel this day thy victory;
For if I imp my wing on thine,
Affliction shall advance the flight in me.

(In the next-to-last line, *imp* is a term from falconry meaning to repair the wing of an injured bird by grafting feathers onto it.)

If we see the poem merely as a picture, we will have to admit that Herbert's word design does not go far. It renders with difficulty shapes that a sketcher's pencil could set down in a flash, with more detail and accuracy. Was Herbert's effort wasted? It might have been, were there not more to his poem than meets the eye. The mind, too, is engaged by the visual pattern, by the realization that the words *most thin* are given emphasis by their narrow form. Here, visual pattern points out meaning. Heard aloud, too, "Easter Wings" gives further pleasure. Its rimes and rhythm are perceptible.

Ever since George Herbert's day, poets have continued to experiment with the looks of printed poetry. Notable efforts to entertain the eye are Lewis Carroll's rimed mouse's tail in *Alice in Wonderland* and the *Calligrammes* of Guillaume Apollinaire, who arranged words in the shapes of a necktie, of the Eiffel Tower, of spears of falling rain. Here is a bird-shaped poem of more recent inspiration than Herbert's. What does its visual form have to do with what the poet is saying?

John Hollander (1929–2013)

Swan and Shadow   1969

```
                        Dusk
                      Above the
                    water hang the
                        loud
                        flies
                        Here
                        O so
                        gray
                        then
              What                A pale signal will appear
              When                Soon before its shadow fades
              Where               Here in this pool of opened eye
              In us         No Upon us As at the very edges
                  of where we take shape in the dark air
                    this object bares its image awakening
                      ripples of recognition that will
                        brush darkness up into light
         even after this bird this hour both drift by atop the perfect sad instant now
                        already passing out of sight
                      toward yet-untroubled reflection
                    this image bears its object darkening
                  into memorial shades Scattered bits of
              light        No of water Or something across
              water              Breaking up No Being regathered
              soon                Yet by then a swan will have
              gone                Yet out of mind into what
                      vast
                      pale
                      hush
                      of a
                      place
                      past
                  sudden dark as
                    if a swan
                       sang
```

A whole poem doesn't need to be such a verbal silhouette, of course, for its appearance on the page to seem meaningful. In some lines from a longer poem, William Carlos Williams conveyed the way an energetic bellhop runs downstairs:

```
    ta tuck a
            ta tuck a
                    ta tuck a
                            ta tuck a
                                    ta tuck a
```

This is not only good onomatopoeia and an accurate description of a rhythm; the steplike appearance of the lines goes together with their meaning.

At least some of our pleasure in silently reading a poem derives from the way it looks on the page. A poem in an open form can engage the eye with snowfields of white space and thickets of close-set words. A poem in stanzas can please us by its visual symmetry. And, far from being merely decorative, the visual devices of a poem can be meaningful, too. White space—as poets who work in open forms demonstrate—can indicate pauses. If white space entirely surrounds a word or phrase or line, then that portion of the poem obviously takes special emphasis. Typographical devices such as capital letters and italics also can lay stress upon words. In most traditional poems, a capital letter at the beginning of each new line helps indicate the importance the poet places on line divisions, whose regular intervals make a rhythm out of pauses. And the poet may be trying to show us that certain lines rime by indenting them.

Some contemporary poets have taken advantage of the computer's ability to mix words and images. They use visual images as integral parts of their poems to explore possibilities beyond traditional prosody. Ezra Pound did similar things in his modernist epic, *The Cantos*, by incorporating Chinese ideograms, musical notations, and marginal notes into the text of the poem.

CONCRETE POETRY

In recent decades, a movement called **concrete poetry** has traveled far and wide. Though practitioners of the art disagree over its definition, what most concretists seem to do is make designs out of letters and words. Some concrete poets wield typography like a brush dipped in paint, using such techniques as blow-up, montage, and superimposed elements (the same words printed many times on top of the same impression, so that the result is blurriness). They may even keep words in a usual order, perhaps employing white space as freely as any writer of open form verse. (More freely sometimes—Aram Saroyan has a concrete poem that consists of a page blank except for the word *oxygen*.)

Admittedly, some concrete poems mean less than meets the eye. Like other structures of language, however, concrete poems evidently can have the effect of poetry, if written by poets. Whether or not it ought to be dubbed poetry, this art can do what poems traditionally have done: use language in delightful ways that reveal meanings to us.

Dorthi Charles (b. 1963)

Concrete Cat   1971

Questions

1. What does this writer indicate by capitalizing the *a* in "ear"? The *y* in "eye"? The *u* in "mouth"? By using spaces between the letters in the word "tail"?
2. Why is the word "mouse" upside down?
3. What possible pun might be seen in the cat's middle stripe?
4. What is the tone of "Concrete Cat"? How is it made evident?
5. Do these words seem chosen for their connotations or only for their denotations? Would you call this work of art a poem?

Experiment: Do It Yourself

Make a concrete poem of your own. If you need inspiration, pick some familiar object or animal and try to find words that look like it. For more ideas, study the typography of a magazine or newspaper; cut out interesting letters and numerals and try pasting them into arrangements. What (if anything) do your experiments tell you about familiar letters and words?

FOR REVIEW AND FURTHER STUDY

Exercise: Seeing the Logic of Open Form Verse

Read the following poems in open form silently to yourself, noticing what each poet does with white space, repetitions, line breaks, and indentations. Then read the poems aloud, trying to indicate by slight pauses where lines end and also pausing slightly at any space inside a line. Can you see any reasons for the poet's placing his or her words in this arrangement rather than in a prose paragraph? Do any of these poets seem also to care about visual effect? (As with other kinds of poetry, there may not be any obvious logical reason for everything that happens in these poems.)

Carole Satyamurti (b. 1939)

I Shall Paint My Nails Red   1990

Because a bit of color is a public service.

Because I am proud of my hands.

Because it will remind me I'm a woman.

Because I will look like a survivor.

Because I can admire them in traffic jams.   5

Because my daughter will say ugh.

Because my lover will be surprised.

Because it is quicker than dyeing my hair.

Because it is a ten-minute moratorium.

Because it is reversible.   10

Question

"I Shall Paint My Nails Red" is written in free verse, but the poem has several organizing principles. How many can you discover?

E. E. Cummings (1894–1962)

in Just-   1923

in Just-
spring   when the world is mud-
luscious the little
lame balloonman

whistles   far   and wee   5

and eddieandbill come
running from marbles and
piracies and it's
spring

when the world is puddle-wonderful   10

the queer
old balloonman whistles
far   and   wee
and bettyandisbel come dancing

from hop-scotch and jump-rope and   15

it's
spring
and
    the

        goat-footed   20

balloonMan   whistles
far
and
wee

Francisco X. Alarcón (1954–2016)

Frontera	Border	2003
ninguna	no	
frontera	border	
podrá	can ever	
separanos	separate us	

Question

How would the meaning of this short poem change if you dropped one of the languages?

Naomi Shihab Nye (b. 1952)

The Traveling Onion   1986

> It is believed that the onion originally came from India. In Egypt it was an object
> of worship—why I haven't been able to find out. From Egypt the onion entered
> Greece and on to Italy, thence into all of Europe.
>
> —Better Living Cookbook

When I think how far the onion has traveled
just to enter my stew today, I could kneel and praise
all small forgotten miracles,
crackly paper peeling on the drainboard,
pearly layers in smooth agreement,   5
the way the knife enters onion
and onion falls apart on the chopping block,
a history revealed.

And I would never scold the onion
for causing tears.   10
It is right that tears fall for something small and forgotten.
How at meal, we sit to eat,
commenting on texture of meat or herbal aroma
but never on the translucence of onion,
now limp, now divided,   15
or its traditionally honorable career:
For the sake of others,
disappear.

Question

Where do you find regular patterns or examples of rime in this open form poem? Are they
obvious or subtle?

■ WRITING *effectively*

Walt Whitman on Writing

The Poetry of the Future   1882

The poetry of the future, (a phrase open to sharp criticism, and not satisfactory to
me, but significant, and I will use it)—the poetry of the future aims at the free expression of emotion, (which means far, far more than appears at first,) and to arouse and
initiate, more than to define or finish. Like all modern tendencies, it has direct or
indirect reference continually to the reader, to you or me, to the central identity of
everything, the mighty Ego. (Byron's was a vehement dash, with plenty of impatient

democracy, but lurid and introverted amid all its magnetism; not at all the fitting, lasting song of a grand, secure, free, sunny race.) It is more akin, likewise, to outside life and landscape, (returning mainly to the antique feeling,) real sun and gale, and woods and shores—to the elements themselves—not sitting at ease in parlor or library listening to a good tale of them, told in good rhyme. Character, a feature far above style or polish—a feature not absent at any time, but now first brought to the fore—gives predominant stamp to advancing poetry. . . .

Walt Whitman

Is there not even now, indeed, an evolution, a departure from the masters? Venerable and unsurpassable after their kind as are the old works, and always unspeakably precious as studies, (for Americans more than any other people,) is it too much to say that by the shifted combinations of the modern mind the whole underlying theory of first-class verse has changed?

From "Poetry To-day in America—Shakspere—The Future"

THINKING ABOUT FREE VERSE

"That's not poetry! It's just chopped-up prose." So runs one old-fashioned complaint about free verse. Such criticism may be true of inept poems, but in the best free verse the line endings transform language in ways beyond the possibilities of prose. A line break implies a slight pause so that the last word of each line receives special emphasis. The last word in a line is meant to linger, however briefly, in the listener's ear. With practice and attention, you can easily develop a better sense of how a poem's line breaks operate.

- **Note whether the breaks tend to come at the end of sentences or phrases, or in the middle of an idea.** An abundance of breaks in mid-thought can create a tumbling, headlong effect, forcing your eye to speed down the page. Conversely, lines that tend to break at the end of a full idea can give a more stately rhythm to a poem.

- **Determine whether the lines tend to be all brief, all long, or a mix.** A very short line forces us to pay special attention to its every word, no matter how small.

- **Ask yourself how the poet's choices about line breaks help to reinforce the poem's meaning.** Can you identify any example of a line break affecting the meaning of a phrase or sentence?

CHECKLIST: Writing About Line Breaks

☐ Reread a poem, paying attention to where its lines end.
☐ Do the breaks tend to come at the end of the sentences or phrases?
☐ Do they tend to come in the middle of an idea?
☐ Do the lines tend to be long? Short? A mix of both?
☐ Is the poem broken into stanzas? Are they long? Short? A mix of both?
☐ What mood is created by the breaks?
☐ How do line breaks and stanza breaks reinforce the poem's meaning as a whole?

TOPICS FOR WRITING ON OPEN FORM

1. Retype a free verse poem as prose, adding conventional punctuation and capitalization if necessary. Then compare and contrast the prose version with the poem itself. How do the two texts differ in tone, rhythm, emphasis, and effect? How do they remain similar? Use any poem from this chapter or any of the following from Chapter 34: W. H. Auden's "Musée des Beaux Arts"; Robert Lowell's "Skunk Hour"; Ezra Pound's "The River-Merchant's Wife: A Letter"; or William Carlos Williams's "Queen-Anne's-Lace."

2. Write a 500-word essay on how the line breaks and white space (or lack thereof) in E. E. Cummings's "Buffalo Bill 's" contribute to the poem's effect.

3. Read aloud William Carlos Williams's "The Dance." Examine how the poem's line breaks and sonic effects underscore the poem's meaning.

4. Imagine Charles Simic's "The Magic Study of Happiness" broken into free-verse lines. What are the benefits of the prose-poem form to this particular text?

5. Compare any poem in this chapter with a poem in rime and meter. Discuss several key features that they have in common despite their apparent differences in style. Features it might be useful to compare include imagery, tone, figures of speech, and word choice.

6. Write an imitation of Wallace Stevens's "Thirteen Ways of Looking at a Blackbird." Come up with thirteen ways of looking at your car, a can opener, a housecat—or any object that intrigues you. Choose your line breaks carefully, to recreate some of the mood of the original. You might also have a look at Aaron Abeyta's parody "thirteen ways of looking at a tortilla" in Chapter 34.

▶ TERMS FOR *review*

Open form ▶ Poems that have neither a rime scheme nor a basic meter are in open form. Open form has also been called **free verse**.

Free verse ▶ From the French *vers libre*. Free verse is poetry whose lines follow no consistent meter. It may be rimed but usually is not. In the last hundred years, free verse has become a common practice.

Prose poetry ▶ Poetic language printed in prose paragraphs but displaying the careful attention to sound, imagery, and figurative language characteristic of poetry.

Concrete poetry ▶ A visual poetry composed exclusively for the page in which a picture or image is made of printed letters and words. Concrete poetry attempts to blur the line between language and visual objects, usually relying on puns and cleverness.

26

SYMBOL

A symbol is like a rock dropped into a pool:
it sends out ripples in all directions,
and the ripples are in motion.

—JOHN CIARDI

What You Will Learn in This Chapter

- To recognize and define a *poetic symbol*
- To identify and define *symbolic actions*
- To describe *allegory* and its characteristics
- To analyze the role of a symbol in a poem

The national flag is supposed to stir our patriotic feelings. When a black cat crosses his path, a superstitious man shivers, foreseeing bad luck. To each of these, by custom, our society expects a standard response. A flag, a black cat crossing one's path—each is a **symbol**: a visible object or action that suggests some further meaning in addition to itself. In literature, a symbol might be the word *flag* or the words *a black cat crossed his path* or every description of flag or cat in an entire novel, story, play, or poem.

A flag and the crossing of a black cat may be called **conventional symbols**, since they can have a conventional or customary effect on us. Conventional symbols are also part of the language of poetry, as we know when we meet the red rose, emblem of love, in a lyric, or the Christian cross in the devotional poems of George Herbert. More often, however, symbols in literature have no conventional, long-established meaning, but particular meanings of their own. In Melville's novel *Moby-Dick*, to take a rich example, whatever we associate with the great white whale is *not* attached unmistakably to white whales by custom. Though Melville tells us that men have long regarded whales with awe and relates Moby Dick to the celebrated fish that swallowed Jonah, the reader's response is to one particular whale, the creature of Herman Melville. Only the experience of reading the novel in its entirety can give Moby Dick his particular meaning.

THE MEANINGS OF A SYMBOL

As Eudora Welty has observed, it is a good thing Melville made Moby Dick a whale, a creature large enough to contain all that critics have found in him. A symbol in literature, if not conventional, has more than just one meaning. In "The Raven," by Edgar Allan Poe, the appearance of a strange black bird in the narrator's study is sinister; and indeed, if we take the poem seriously, we may even respond with a sympathetic shiver of dread. Does the bird mean death, fate, melancholy, the loss of a loved one, knowledge in the service of evil? All of these, perhaps. Like any well-chosen symbol, Poe's raven sets off within the reader an unending train of feelings and associations.

We miss the value of a symbol, however, if we think it can mean absolutely anything we wish. If a poet has any control over our reactions, the poem will guide our responses in a certain direction.

T. S. Eliot (1888–1965)

The *Boston Evening Transcript*   1917

The readers of the *Boston Evening Transcript*
Sway in the wind like a field of ripe corn.

When evening quickens faintly in the street,
Wakening the appetites of life in some
And to others bringing the *Boston Evening Transcript*,   5
I mount the steps and ring the bell, turning
Wearily, as one would turn to nod good-bye to La Rochefoucauld,
If the street were time and he at the end of the street,
And I say, "Cousin Harriet, here is the *Boston Evening Transcript*."

The newspaper, whose name Eliot purposely repeats so monotonously, indicates what this poem is about. Now defunct, the *Transcript* covered in detail the slightest activity of Boston's leading families and was noted for the great length of its obituaries. Eliot, then, uses the newspaper as a symbol for an existence of boredom, fatigue ("Wearily"), petty and unvarying routine (since an evening newspaper, like night, arrives on schedule). The *Transcript* evokes a way of life without zest or passion, for, opposed to people who read it, Eliot sets people who do not: those whose desires revive, not expire, when the working day is through. Suggestions abound in the ironic comparison of the *Transcript*'s readers to a cornfield late in summer. To mention only a few: the readers sway because they are sleepy; they vegetate; they are drying up; each makes a rattling sound when turning a page. It is not necessary that we know the remote and similarly disillusioned friend to whom the speaker might nod: La Rochefoucauld, for example, whose cynical *Maxims* entertained Parisian society under Louis XIV. We understand that the nod is symbolic of an immense weariness of spirit. We know nothing about Cousin Harriet, whom the speaker addresses, but imagine from the greeting she inspires that she is probably a bore.

If Eliot wishes to say that certain Bostonians lead lives of sterile boredom, why does he couch his meaning in symbols? Why doesn't he tell us directly what he means? These questions imply two assumptions not necessarily true: first, that Eliot has a message to impart; second, that he is concealing it. We have reason to think that Eliot did not usually have a message in mind when beginning a poem, for as he once told a critic: "The conscious problems with which one is concerned in the actual writing are more those of a quasi-musical nature . . . than of a conscious exposition of ideas." Poets sometimes discover what they have to say while in the act of saying it. And it may be that in his *Transcript* poem, Eliot is saying exactly what he means. By communicating his meaning through symbols instead of statements, he may be choosing the only kind of language appropriate to an idea of great subtlety and complexity. (The paraphrase "Certain Bostonians are bored" hardly begins to describe the poem in all its possible meanings.) And by his use of symbolism, Eliot affords us the pleasure of finding our own entrances to his poem.

This power of suggestion that a symbol contains is, perhaps, its greatest advantage. Sometimes, as in the following poem by Emily Dickinson, a symbol will lead us from a visible object to something too vast to be perceived.

Emily Dickinson (1830–1886)

The Lightning is a yellow Fork (about 1870)

The Lightning is a yellow Fork
From Tables in the sky
By inadvertent fingers dropt
The awful Cutlery

Of mansions never quite disclosed 5
And never quite concealed
The Apparatus of the Dark
To ignorance revealed.

If the lightning is a fork, then whose are the fingers that drop it, the table from which it slips, the household to which it belongs? The poem implies this question without giving an answer. An obvious answer is "God," but can we be sure? We wonder, too, about these partially lighted mansions: if our vision were clearer, what would we behold?

THE SYMBOLIST MOVEMENT

The often complex and indirect way in which symbols communicate their meanings led to a group of nineteenth-century French poets being dubbed **Symbolists**. (This elegant moniker was their second name; their early critics had originally condemned them as the "decadent" poets.) Eventually becoming an international literary movement, the Symbolists began with poets such as Charles Baudelaire, Arthur Rimbaud, Paul Verlaine, and Stéphane Mallarmé. Influenced by sources as diverse as Edgar Allan Poe, Neo-Platonic philosophy, Roman Catholic ritual, and drugs, they tried to write poetry that resembled music. They avoided direct statement and exposition for powerful evocation and suggestion. Symbolists also considered the poet as a seer who could look beyond the mundane aspects of the everyday world to capture visions of a higher and frequently occult reality. Their poems were often musical, evocative, and mysterious. Many critics consider the Symbolist Movement the beginning of Modernist literature, and both its poetry and theory had a major impact on later writers such as Yeats, Eliot, and Pound. But in this chapter when we speak of symbolism (with a small s) we mean an element in certain poems, not Symbolism, a specific literary movement.

IDENTIFYING SYMBOLS

You might wonder, "But how am I supposed to know a symbol when I see one?" The best approach is to read poems closely, taking comfort in the likelihood that it is better not to notice symbols at all than to find significance in every literal stone and huge meanings in every thing. In looking for the symbols in a poem, pick out all the references to concrete objects—newspapers, black cats, twisted pins. Consider these with special care. Notice any that the poet emphasizes by detailed description, by repetition, or by placing them at the very beginning or end of the poem. Ask: What is the poem about; what does it add up to? If, when the poem is paraphrased, the paraphrase depends primarily on the meaning of certain concrete objects, these richly suggestive objects may be the symbols.

There are some things a literary symbol usually is *not*. A symbol is not an abstraction. Such terms as *truth*, *death*, *love*, and *justice* cannot work as symbols (unless personified, as in the traditional figure of Justice holding a scale). Most often, a symbol is something we can see in the mind's eye: a newspaper, a lightning bolt, a gesture of nodding good-bye.

In narratives, a well-developed character who speaks much dialogue and is not the least bit mysterious is usually not a symbol. But watch out for an executioner in a black hood; a character, named for a biblical prophet, who does little but utter a prophecy; a trio of old women who resemble the Three Fates. (It has been argued, with good reason, that Milton's fully rounded character of Satan in *Paradise Lost* is a symbol embodying evil and human pride, but a narrower definition of symbol is more frequently useful.) A symbol *may* be a part of a person's body (the baleful eye of the murder victim in Poe's story "The Tell-Tale Heart") or a look, a voice, or a mannerism.

A symbol usually is not the second term of a metaphor. In the line "The Lightning is a yellow Fork," the symbol is the lightning, not the fork.

Sometimes a symbol addresses a sense other than sight: in William Faulkner's tale "A Rose for Emily" (Chapter 2), the odor of decay that surrounds the house of the last survivor of a town's leading family suggests not only physical dissolution but also the decay of a social order. A symbol is a special kind of image, for it exceeds the usual image in the richness of its connotations. The dead wife's cold comb in the haiku of Buson (Chapter 19) works symbolically, suggesting among other things the chill of the grave, the contrast between the living and the dead.

Symbolic Action

Holding a narrower definition than that used in this book, some readers of poetry prefer to say that a symbol is always a concrete object, never an act. They would deny the label "symbol" to Ahab's breaking his tobacco pipe before setting out to pursue Moby Dick (suggesting, perhaps, his determination to allow no pleasure to distract him from the chase) or to any large motion (such as Ahab's whole quest). This distinction, while confining, does have the merit of sparing one from seeing all motion to be possibly symbolic. Some would call Ahab's gesture not a symbol but a **symbolic act**.

To sum up: a symbol radiates hints or casts long shadows (to use Henry James's metaphor). We are unable to say it "stands for" or "represents" a meaning. It evokes, it suggests, it manifests. It demands no single necessary interpretation, such as the interpretation a driver gives to a red traffic light. Rather, like Emily Dickinson's lightning bolt, it points toward an indefinite meaning, which may lie in part beyond the reach of words.

Thomas Hardy (1840–1928)

Neutral Tones   1898

We stood by a pond that winter day,
And the sun was white, as though chidden of° God,   *rebuked by*
And a few leaves lay on the starving sod;
  —They had fallen from an ash, and were gray.

Your eyes on me were as eyes that rove   5
Over tedious riddles of years ago;
And some words played between us to and fro
    On which lost the more by our love.

The smile on your mouth was the deadest thing
Alive enough to have strength to die;   10
And a grin of bitterness swept thereby
    Like an ominous bird a-wing. . . .

Since then, keen lessons that love deceives,
And wrings with wrong, have shaped to me
Your face, and the God-curst sun, and a tree,   15
    And a pond edged with grayish leaves.

Questions

1. Sum up the story told in this poem. In lines 1–12, what is the dramatic situation? What
   has happened in the interval between the experience related in these lines and the reflection in the last stanza?
2. What meanings do you find in the title?
3. Explain in your own words the metaphor in line 2.
4. What connotations appropriate to this poem does the "ash" (line 4) have that *oak* or *maple*
   would lack?
5. What visible objects in the poem function symbolically? What actions or gestures?

ALLEGORY

If we read of a ship, its captain, its sailors, and the rough seas, and we realize we are
reading about a commonwealth and how its rulers and workers keep it going even in
difficult times, then we are reading an **allegory**. Closely akin to symbolism, allegory is a
description—usually narrative—in which persons, places, and things are employed in
a continuous and consistent system of equivalents. In an allegory an object has a single additional significance, one largely determined by convention. When an allegory
appears in a work, it usually has a one-to-one relationship to an abstract entity, recognizable to readers and audiences familiar with the cultural context of the work.

Although more strictly limited in its suggestions than symbolism, allegory need
not be thought inferior. Few poems continue to interest readers more than Dante's
allegorical *Divine Comedy*. Sublime evidence of the appeal of allegory may be found
in Jesus's use of the **parable**: a brief narrative—usually allegorical but sometimes
not—that teaches a moral.

Matthew

The Parable of the Good Seed   (King James Version, 1611)

The kingdom of heaven is likened unto a man which sowed good seed in
    his field:
But while men slept, his enemy came and sowed tares among the wheat,
    and went his way.

But when the blade was sprung up, and brought forth fruit, then appeared
    the tares also.
So the servants of the householder came and said unto him, Sir, didst not
    thou sow good seed in thy field? From whence then hath it tares?
He said unto them, An enemy hath done this. The servants said unto him,   5
    Wilt thou then that we go and gather them up?
But he said, Nay; lest while ye gather up the tares, ye root up also the
    wheat with them.
Let both grow together until the harvest: and in the time of harvest I will
    say to the reapers, Gather ye together first the tares, and bind them in
    bundles to burn them: but gather the wheat into my barn.

—Matthew 13:24–30

THE PARABLE OF THE GOOD SEED. 2 *tares:* harmful weeds.

Jesus explains this parable to his disciples, saying that the sower is the Son of man,
the field is the world, the good seed are the children of the Kingdom, the tares are
the children of the wicked one, the enemy is the devil, the harvest is the end of the
world, the reapers are angels. "As therefore the tares are gathered and burned in the
fire; so shall it be in the end of this world" (Matthew 13:36–42).

    Usually, as in this parable, the meanings of an allegory are plainly labeled or
thinly disguised. An allegory, when carefully built, is systematic. It makes one principal comparison, the working out of whose details may lead to further comparisons,
then still further comparisons.

George Herbert (1593–1633)

Redemption 1633

Having been tenant long to a rich Lord,
   Not thriving, I resolved to be bold,
   And make a suit unto him, to afford
A new small-rented lease, and cancel th' old.

In Heaven at his manor I him sought: 5
   They told me there, that he was lately gone
   About some land, which he had dearly bought
Long since on earth, to take possession.

I straight returned, and knowing his great birth,
   Sought him accordingly in great resorts;   10
   In cities, theaters, gardens, parks, and courts:
At length I heard a ragged noise and mirth

   Of thieves and murderers: there I him espied,
   Who straight, *Your suit is granted,* said, and died.

Questions

1. In this allegory, what equivalents does Herbert give each of these terms: "tenant," "Lord,"
   "not thriving," "suit," "new lease," "old lease," "manor," "land," "dearly bought," "take
   possession," "his great birth"?
2. What scene is depicted in the last three lines?

An object in an allegory is like a bird whose cage is clearly lettered with its identity—"RAVEN, *Corvus corax*; habitat of specimen, Maine." A symbol, by contrast, is a bird with piercing eyes that mysteriously appears one evening in your library. It is there; you can touch it. But what does it mean? You look at it. It continues to look at you.

Edwin Markham   (1852–1940)

Outwitted   1914

He drew a circle that shut me out—
Heretic, rebel, a thing to flout.
But Love and I had the wit to win:
We drew a circle that took him in!

Questions

What does a circle symbolize in this poem? Does it represent the same thing both times it is mentioned?

Suji Kwock Kim   (b. 1968)

Occupation   2003

The soldiers
are hard at work
building a house.
They hammer
bodies into the earth   5
like nails,
they paint the walls
with blood.
Inside the doors
stay shut, locked   10
as eyes of stone.
Inside the stairs
feel slippery,
all flights go down.
There is no floor: 15
only a roof,
where ash is falling—
dark snow,
human snow,
thickly, mutely   20
falling.
Come, they say.
This house will
last forever.
You must occupy it.   25
And you, and you—

Come, they say.
There is room
for everyone.   30

Questions

1. What materials do the soldiers use to build the house?
2. What is unusual about the interior of the house?
3. How is the ash unusual?
4. The title contains a pun. Find and explain it.
5. What does the soldiers' house seem to symbolize?

Whether an object in literature is a symbol, part of an allegory, or no such thing at all, it has at least one sure meaning. Moby Dick is first a whale, and the *Boston Evening Transcript* is a newspaper. Besides deriving a multitude of intangible suggestions from the title symbol in Eliot's long poem *The Waste Land*, its readers cannot fail to carry away a sense of the land's physical appearance: a river choked with sandwich papers and cigarette ends, London Bridge "under the brown fog of a winter dawn." The most vital element of a literary work may pass us by, unless, before seeking further depths in a thing, we look to the thing itself.

Frank O'Hara (1926–1966)

To the Harbormaster   1957

I wanted to be sure to reach you;
though my ship was on the way it got caught
in some moorings. I am always tying up
and then deciding to depart. In storms and
at sunset, with the metallic coils of the tide   5
around my fathomless arms, I am unable
to understand the forms of my vanity
or I am hard alee with my Polish rudder
in my hand and the sun sinking. To
you I offer my hull and the tattered cordage   10
of my will. The terrible channels where
the wind drives me against the brown lips
of the reeds are not all behind me. Yet
I trust the sanity of my vessel; and
if it sinks, it may well be in answer   15
to the reasoning of the eternal voices,
the waves which have kept me from reaching you.

To the Harbormaster. 8 *alee*: the side of a ship protected from the wind.

Questions

1. Unpack the symbols in "To the Harbormaster." If the poem isn't about an actual seagoing vessel, what is it about? What are some clues that the poem might not literally be about sailing?
2. To whom does the title refer?
3. How would you describe the tone of the poem? Despairing? Hopeful?

Antonio Machado (1875–1939)

Proverbios y Cantares (XXIX) 1912	Traveler 2011
Caminante, son tus huellas	Traveler, your footsteps are
el camino, y nada más;	the road, there's nothing more;
caminante, no hay camino,	traveler, there is no road,
se hace camino al andar.	the road is made by walking.
Al andar se hace camino,	Walking makes the road, 5
y al volver la vista atrás	and if you turn around,
se ve la senda que nunca	you only see the path
se ha de volver a pisar.	you cannot walk again.
Caminante, no hay camino	Traveler, there is no road,
sino estelas en la mar.	only a track of foam upon the sea. 10

— *Translated by Michael Ortiz*

Question

Compare Machado's poem with Robert Frost's famous "The Road Not Taken" (Chapter 32). In what ways does Machado's use of the road as a symbol resemble Frost's use? In what ways does it differ?

Christina Rossetti (1830–1894)

Up-Hill   1862

Does the road wind up-hill all the way?
　Yes, to the very end.
Will the day's journey take the whole long day?
　From morn to night, my friend.

But is there for the night a resting-place?   5
　A roof for when the slow dark hours begin.
May not the darkness hide it from my face?
　You cannot miss that inn.

Shall I meet other wayfarers at night?
　Those who have gone before.   10
Then must I knock, or call when just in sight?
　They will not keep you standing at that door.

Shall I find comfort, travel-sore and weak?
　Of labor you shall find the sum.
Will there be beds for me and all who seek?   15
　Yea, beds for all who come.

Questions

1. In reading this poem, at what line did you realize that the poet is building an allegory?
2. For what does each thing stand?
3. What does the title of the poem suggest to you?
4. Recast the meaning of line 14, a knotty line, in your own words.
5. Discuss the possible identities of the two speakers—the apprehensive traveler and the character with all the answers. Are they specific individuals? Allegorical figures?
6. Compare "Up-Hill" with Robert Creeley's "Oh No" (Chapter 16). What striking similarities do you find in these two dissimilar poems?

FOR REVIEW AND FURTHER STUDY

Exercise: **Symbol Hunting**

After you have read each of the following poems, decide which description best suits each one:

1. The poem has a central symbol.
2. The poem contains no symbolism, but it should be taken literally.

William Carlos Williams (1883–1963)

Winter Trees   1921

All the complicated details
of the attiring and
the disattiring are completed!
A liquid moon
moves gently among   5
the long branches.
Thus having prepared their buds
against a sure winter
the wise trees
stand sleeping in the cold.   10

Ted Kooser (b. 1939)

Carrie   1979

"There's never an end to dust
and dusting," my aunt would say
as her rag, like a thunderhead,
scudded across the yellow oak
of her little house. There she lived   5
seventy years with a ball
of compulsion closed in her fist,
and an elbow that creaked and popped
like a branch in a storm. Now dust
is her hands and dust her heart.   10
There's never an end to it.

Mary Oliver (b. 1935)

Wild Geese   1986

You do not have to be good.
You do not have to walk on your knees
for a hundred miles through the desert, repenting.
You only have to let the soft animal of your body
    love what it loves.
Tell me about despair, yours, and I will tell you mine.   5
Meanwhile the world goes on.
Meanwhile the sun and the clear pebbles of the rain
are moving across the landscapes,

over the prairies and the deep trees,
the mountains and the rivers.   10
Meanwhile the wild geese, high in the clean blue air,
are heading home again.
Whoever you are, no matter how lonely,
the world offers itself to your imagination,
calls to you like the wild geese, harsh and exciting—   15
over and over announcing your place
in the family of things.

Questions

1. Is this poem addressed to a specific person?
2. What is meant by "good" in the first line?
3. What do the wild geese symbolize? What is the significance of the use of the term "wild"?
4. What other adjectives are used to describe the phenomena of nature? What thematic purpose is served by this characterization of the natural world?

William Blake (1757–1827)

The Tyger   1794

Tyger! Tyger! burning bright
In the forests of the night,
What immortal hand or eye
Could frame thy fearful symmetry?

In what distant deeps or skies   5
Burnt the fire of thine eyes?
On what wings dare he aspire?
What the hand dare seize the fire?

And what shoulder, and what art,
Could twist the sinews of thy heart?   10
And when thy heart began to beat,
What dread hand? and what dread feet?

What the hammer? what the chain?
In what furnace was thy brain?
What the anvil? what dread grasp   15
Dare its deadly terrors clasp?

When the stars threw down their spears,
And watered heaven with their tears,
Did he smile his work to see?
Did he who made the Lamb make thee?   20

Tyger! Tyger! burning bright
In the forests of the night,
What immortal hand or eye
Dare frame thy fearful symmetry?

Illuminated manuscript of William Blake's "The Tyger."

Karen Holden (b. 1955)

Bats in a Box   2010

Strange and beautiful, the bats
cling to the corrugated corner, dead to day

This tiny tribe of sleepers and I, somnambulist
travel from house to woods in quiet camaraderie

I carry them the way I would anything precious   5
hands held out in astonishment and cupped as if

cradling water or the world, as if this moment
is the gift I was waiting for all along.

Tami Haaland (b. 1960)

Lipstick   2001

I wonder how they do it, those women
who can slip lipstick over lips without

looking, after they've finished a meal
or when they ride in cars. Satin Claret
or Plum or Twig or Pecan. I can't stay   5
inside the lines, late comer to lipstick
that I am, and sometimes get messy
even in front of a mirror. But these
women know where lips end and plain
skin begins, probably know how to put   10
their hair in a knot with a single pin.

Questions

1. How does the speaker use lipstick differently from the way "those women" do?
2. Why do the other women know how to apply lipstick more accurately? What does this
   knowledge suggest about the difference between them and the speaker?
3. What does lipstick seem to suggest in the poem? Support your ideas with specific examples from the poem.

Lorine Niedecker (1903–1970)

Popcorn-can cover   (about 1959)

Popcorn-can cover
screwed to the wall
over a hole
        so the cold
can't mouse in   5

Wallace Stevens (1879–1955)

The Snow Man   1923

One must have a mind of winter
To regard the frost and the boughs
Of the pine-trees crusted with snow;

And have been cold a long time
To behold the junipers shagged with ice,   5
The spruces rough in the distant glitter

Of the January sun; and not to think
Of any misery in the sound of the wind,
In the sound of a few leaves,

Which is the sound of the land   10
Full of the same wind
That is blowing in the same bare place

For the listener, who listens in the snow,
And, nothing himself, beholds
Nothing that is not there and the nothing that is.   15

Wallace Stevens (1879–1955)

Anecdote of the Jar   1923

I placed a jar in Tennessee,
And round it was, upon a hill.
It made the slovenly wilderness
Surround that hill.

The wilderness rose up to it,   5
And sprawled around, no longer wild.
The jar was round upon the ground
And tall and of a port in air.

It took dominion everywhere.
The jar was gray and bare.   10
It did not give of bird or bush,
Like nothing else in Tennessee.

■ WRITING *effectively*

William Butler Yeats on Writing

Poetic Symbols   1903

Any one who has any experience of any mystical state of the soul knows how there float up in
the mind profound symbols, whose meaning, if
indeed they do not delude one into the dream
that they are meaningless, one does not perhaps understand for years. Nor I think has any
one, who has known that experience with any
constancy, failed to find some day, in some old
book or on some old monument, a strange or
intricate image, that had floated up before him,
and to grow perhaps dizzy with the sudden conviction that our little memories are but a part
of some great memory that renews the world
and men's thoughts age after age, and that our
thoughts are not, as we suppose, the deep, but a
little foam upon the deep.

William Butler Yeats

• • •

It is only by ancient symbols, by symbols that have numberless meanings beside
the one or two the writer lays an emphasis upon, or the half-score he knows of, that
any highly subjective art can escape from the barrenness and shallowness of a too conscious arrangement, into the abundance and depth of nature. The poet of essences and
pure ideas must seek in the half-lights that glimmer from symbol to symbol as if to the
ends of the earth, all that the epic and dramatic poet finds of mystery and shadow in
the accidental circumstances of life.

From "The Philosophy of Shelley's Poetry"

THINKING ABOUT SYMBOLS

A symbol, to use poet John Drury's concise definition, is "an image that radiates meanings." While images in a poem can and should be read as what they literally are, images often do double duty, suggesting deeper meanings. Exactly what those meanings are, however, often differs from poem to poem.

Some symbols have been used so often and effectively over time that a traditional reading of them has developed. At times a poet clearly adopts an image's traditional symbolic meaning. Some poems, however, deliberately play against a symbol's conventional associations.

- **To determine the meaning (or meanings) of a symbol, start by asking if it has traditional associations.** If so, consider whether the symbol is being used in the expected way or if the poet is playing with those associations.
- **Consider the symbol's relationship to the rest of the poem.** Let context be your guide. The image might have a unique meaning to the poem's speaker.
- **Consider the emotions that the image evokes.** If the image recurs in the poem, pay attention to how it changes from one appearance to the next.
- **Keep in mind that not everything is a symbol.** If an image doesn't appear to radiate meanings above and beyond its literal sense, don't feel you have failed as a critic. As Sigmund Freud once said about symbol-hunting, "Sometimes a cigar is just a cigar."

CHECKLIST: Writing About Symbols

☐ Is the symbol a traditional one?

☐ If so, is it being used in the expected way? Or is the poet playing with its associations?

☐ What does the image seem to mean to the poem's speaker?

☐ What emotions are evoked by the image?

☐ If an image recurs in a poem, how does it change from one appearance to the next?

☐ Does the image radiate meaning beyond its literal sense? If not, it might not be intended as a symbol.

TOPICS FOR WRITING ON SYMBOLISM

1. Do an in-depth analysis of the symbolism in a poem of your choice from Chapter 34, "Poems for Further Reading." Some likely choices would be W. H. Auden's "As I Walked Out One Evening," Robert Lowell's "Skunk Hour," Sylvia Plath's "Daddy," and Adrienne Rich's "Living in Sin."

2. Compare and contrast the use of roads as symbols in Christina Rossetti's "Up-Hill" and Robert Frost's "The Road Not Taken" (Chapter 32). What does the use of this image suggest in each poem?

3. Discuss "The Snow Man" and "Anecdote of the Jar" in terms of Wallace Stevens's use of symbolism to portray the relationship between humanity and nature.

4. Write an explication of any poem from this chapter, paying careful attention to its symbols. Some good choices are Tami Haaland's "Lipstick," Thomas Hardy's "Neutral Tones,"

and Christina Rossetti's "Up-Hill." For a further description of poetic explication, see Chapter 44, "Writing About a Poem."

5. Take a relatively simple, straightforward poem, such as William Carlos Williams's "This Is Just to Say" (Chapter 17), and write a burlesque critical interpretation of it. Claim to discover symbols that the poem doesn't contain. While running wild with your "reading into" the poem, don't invent anything that you can't somehow support from the text of the poem itself. At the end of your burlesque, sum up in a paragraph what this exercise taught you about how to read poems, or how not to.

▶ TERMS FOR *review*

Symbol ▶ A person, place, or thing in a narrative that suggests meanings beyond its literal sense. Symbol is related to *allegory*, but it works more complexly. A symbol bears multiple suggestions and associations. It is unique to the work, not common to a culture.

Allegory ▶ A description—often a narrative—in which the literal events (persons, places, and things) consistently point to a parallel sequence of ideas, values, or other recognizable abstractions. An allegory has two levels of meaning: a literal level that tells a surface story and a symbolic level in which the abstractions unfold.

Symbolic act ▶ An action whose significance goes well beyond its literal meaning. In literature, symbolic acts often involve a primal or unconscious ritual element such as rebirth, purification, forgiveness, vengeance, or initiation.

Conventional symbols ▶ Symbols that, because of their frequent use, have acquired a standard significance. They may range from complex metaphysical images such as those of Christian saints in Gothic art to social customs such as a young bride in a white dress. They are conventional symbols because they carry recognizable meanings and suggestions.

27

MYTH

Myth does not mean something untrue,
but a concentration of truth.

—DORIS LESSING

What You Will Learn in This Chapter

- To define *myth* and *mythology*
- To recognize and describe an *archetype*
- To describe personal myth
- To analyze the role of myth and archetype in a poem

Poets have long been fond of retelling **myths**, narrowly defined as traditional stories about the exploits of immortal beings. Such stories taken collectively may also be called myth or **mythology**.

Our use of the term *myth* in discussing poetry, then, differs from its use in expressions such as "the myth of communism" and "the myth of democracy." In these examples, *myth* is used broadly to represent any idea people believe in, whether true or false. In the following discussion, *myth* will mean a kind of story—either from ancient or modern sources—whose actions implicitly symbolize some profound truth about human or natural existence.

THE SUBJECTS AND USES OF MYTH

Traditional myths tell us stories of gods or heroes—their battles, their lives, their loves, and often their suffering—all on a scale of magnificence larger than our life. These exciting stories usually reveal part of a culture's worldview. Myths often try to explain universal natural phenomena, like the phases of the moon or the turning of the seasons.

Modern psychologists, such as Sigmund Freud and Carl Jung, have been fascinated by myth and legend, since they believe these stories symbolically enact deep truths about human nature. Our myths, psychologists insist, express our wishes, dreams, and nightmares. Whether or not we believe myths, we recognize their psychological power. Even in the first century B.C., the Roman poet Ovid did not believe in the literal truth of the legends he so suavely retold; he confessed, "I prate of ancient poets' monstrous lies."

Yet it is characteristic of a myth that it *can* be believed. Throughout history, myths have accompanied religious doctrines and rituals. They have helped sanction or recall the reasons for religious observances. A sublime instance is the New

Testament account of the Last Supper. Because of its record of the words of Jesus, "Do this in remembrance of Me," Christians have continued to re-enact the offering and partaking of the body and blood of their Lord, under the appearances of bread and wine. It is essential to recall that, just because a myth narrates the acts of a god, we do not necessarily mean by the term a false or fictitious narrative. When we speak of "the myth of Islam" or "the Christian myth," we do so without implying either belief or disbelief.

Myths can also help sanction customs and institutions other than religious ones. Some myths seem designed to divert and regale, not to sanction anything. Such may be the story of the sculptor Pygmalion, who fell in love with the statue he had carved of a beautiful woman; so exquisite was his work, so deep was his feeling, that Aphrodite, the goddess of Love, brought the statue to life. And yet perhaps the story goes deeper than mere diversion: perhaps it is a way of saying that works of art achieve a reality of their own, that love can transform or animate its object.

Poets have many coherent mythologies on which to draw; perhaps those most frequently consulted by British and American poets are the classical, the Christian, the Norse, the Native American, and the folktales of the American frontier (embodying the deeds of superhuman characters such as Paul Bunyan). Some poets have taken inspiration from other myths as well: T. S. Eliot's *The Waste Land*, for example, is enriched by allusions to Buddhism and to pagan vegetation cults.

A tour through any good art museum will demonstrate how thoroughly myth pervades the painting and sculpture of nearly every civilization. In literature, one evidence of its continuing value to recent poets and storytellers is how frequently ancient myths are retold. Even in modern society, writers often turn to myth when they try to tell stories of deep significance. Mythic structures still touch a powerful and primal part of the human imagination. William Faulkner's story "The Bear" recalls tales of Indian totem animals; James Joyce's *Ulysses* transposes the *Odyssey* to modern Dublin (and the Coen brothers' film *O Brother, Where Art Thou?* reimagines Homer's epic in Depression-era Mississippi); Rita Dove's play *The Darker Face of the Earth* recasts the story of Oedipus in the slave-era South; Bernard Shaw retells the story of Pygmalion in his popular Edwardian social comedy *Pygmalion*, later the basis of the hit musical *My Fair Lady*. Popular interest in such works may testify to the profound appeal myths continue to hold for us. Like other varieties of poetry, myth is a kind of knowledge, not at odds with scientific knowledge but existing in addition to it.

Robert Frost (1874–1963)

Nothing Gold Can Stay   1923

Nature's first green is gold,
Her hardest hue to hold.
Her early leaf's a flower;
But only so an hour.
Then leaf subsides to leaf.   5
So Eden sank to grief,
So dawn goes down to day.
Nothing gold can stay.

Questions

1. To what myth does this poem allude? Does Frost sound as though he believes in the myth or as though he rejects it?
2. When Frost says, "Nature's first green is gold," he is describing how many leaves first appear as tiny yellow buds and blossoms. But what else does this line imply?
3. What would happen to the poem's meaning if line 6 were omitted?

William Wordsworth (1770–1850)

The world is too much with us   1807

The world is too much with us; late and soon,
Getting and spending, we lay waste our powers:
Little we see in Nature that is ours;
We have given our hearts away, a sordid boon!
This Sea that bares her bosom to the moon;   5
The winds that will be howling at all hours,
And are up-gathered now like sleeping flowers;
For this, for everything, we are out of tune;
It moves us not.—Great God! I'd rather be
A Pagan suckled in a creed outworn;   10
So might I, standing on this pleasant lea,
Have glimpses that would make me less forlorn;
Have sight of Proteus rising from the sea;
Or hear old Triton blow his wreathèd horn.

Questions

1. What condition does the speaker complain of in this sonnet? To what does he attribute this condition?
2. How does this situation affect him personally?

H.D. [Hilda Doolittle] (1886–1961)

Helen   1924

All Greece hates
the still eyes in the white face,
the lustre as of olives
where she stands,
and the white hands.   5

All Greece reviles
the wan face when she smiles,
hating it deeper still
when it grows wan and white,
remembering past enchantments   10
and past ills.

Greece sees, unmoved,
God's daughter, born of love,
the beauty of cool feet
and slenderest knees,   15
could love indeed the maid,
only if she were laid,
white ash amid funereal cypresses.

HELEN. In Greek mythology, Helen, most beautiful of all women, was the daughter of a mortal, Leda, by the god Zeus. Her abduction set off the long and devastating Trojan War. While married to Menelaus, king of the Greek city-state of Sparta, Helen was carried off by Paris, prince of Troy. Menelaus and his brother, Agamemnon, raised an army, besieged Troy for ten years, and eventually recaptured her. One episode of the Trojan War is related in the *Iliad*, Homer's epic poem, composed before 700 B.C.

Questions

1. At what point in the Troy narrative does this poem appear to be set?
2. What connotations does the color white usually possess? Does it have those same associations here?

Edgar Allan Poe (1809–1849)

To Helen   1831

Helen, thy beauty is to me
  Like those Nicéan barks of yore,
That gently, o'er a perfumed sea,
  The weary, way-worn wanderer bore
  To his own native shore.   5

On desperate seas long wont to roam,
  Thy hyacinth hair, thy classic face,
Thy Naiad airs have brought me home
  To the glory that was Greece
And the grandeur that was Rome.   10

Lo! in yon brilliant window-niche
  How statue-like I see thee stand,
  The agate lamp within thy hand!
Ah! Psyche, from the regions which
  Are Holy-Land!   15

To Helen. 1 *Helen*: Helen of Troy, in legend the most beautiful woman in the world. 2 *Nicéan barks*: boats from Nicea, an ancient trading city in Asia Minor. 7 *Naiad*: in classical mythology, a nymph of a lake or river. 14 *Psyche*: the beautiful mortal woman who was Cupid's lover.

Questions

1. Why does Poe invoke the name of Helen to address his beloved?
2. Compare Poe's Helen with H.D.'s in her poem "Helen." How do the two versions of the mythic woman differ?

ARCHETYPE

An important concept in understanding myth is the **archetype**, a basic image, character, situation, or symbol that appears so often in literature and legend that it evokes a deep universal response. (The Greek root of *archetype* means "original pattern.") The term was borrowed by literary critics from the writings of the Swiss psychologist Carl Jung, a serious scholar of myth and religion, who formulated a theory of the "collective unconscious," a set of primal memories common to the entire human race. Archetypal patterns emerged, he speculated, in prerational thought and often reflect key primordial experiences such as birth, growth, sexual awakening, family, generational struggle, and death, as well as primal elements such as fire, sun, moon, blood, and water. Jung also believed that these situations, images, and figures had actually been genetically coded into the human brain and are passed down to successive generations, but no one has ever been able to prove a biological base for the undeniable phenomenon of similar characters, stories, and symbols appearing across widely separated and diverse cultures.

Whatever their origin, archetypal images do seem verbally coded in most myths, legends, and traditional tales. One sees enough recurring patterns and figures from Greek myth to *Star Wars*, from Hindu epic to Marvel superhero comics, to strongly suggest that there is some common psychic force at work. Typical archetypal figures include the trickster, the cruel stepmother, the rebellious young man, the beautiful but destructive woman, and the stupid youngest son who succeeds through simple goodness. Any one of these figures can be traced from culture to culture. The trickster, for instance, appears in American Indian coyote tales, Norse myths about the fire god Loki, Marx Brothers films, and *Batman* comic books and movies featuring the Joker.

Archetypal myths are the basic conventions of human storytelling, which we learn without necessarily being aware of the process. The patterns we absorb in our first nursery rhymes and fairy tales, as mythological critic Northrop Frye has demonstrated, underlie—though often very subtly—the most sophisticated poems and novels. One powerful archetype seen across many cultures is the demon-goddess who immobilizes men by locking them into a deathly trance or—in the most primitive forms of the myth—turning them to stone. Here are two modern versions of this ancient myth.

Louise Bogan (1897–1970)

Medusa   1923

I had come to the house, in a cave of trees,
Facing a sheer sky.
Everything moved,—a bell hung ready to strike,
Sun and reflection wheeled by.

When the bare eyes were before me   5
And the hissing hair,
Held up at a window, seen through a door.
The stiff bald eyes, the serpents on the forehead
Formed in the air.

This is a dead scene forever now.   10
Nothing will ever stir.
The end will never brighten it more than this,
Nor the rain blur.

The water will always fall, and will not fall,
And the tipped bell make no sound.   15
The grass will always be growing for hay
Deep on the ground.

And I shall stand here like a shadow
Under the great balanced day,
My eyes on the yellow dust, that was lifting in the wind,   20
And does not drift away.

MEDUSA. One of the Gorgons of Greek mythology. Hideously ugly with snakes for hair, Medusa turned those who looked upon her face into stone.

Questions

1. Who is the speaker of the poem?
2. Why are the first two stanzas spoken in the past tense while the final three are mainly in the future tense?
3. What is the speaker's attitude toward Medusa? Is there anything surprising about his or her reaction to being transformed into stone?
4. Does Bogan merely dramatize an incident from classical mythology, or does the poem suggest other interpretations as well?

John Keats (1795–1821)

La Belle Dame sans Merci   1819

I

O what can ail thee, knight at arms,
    Alone and palely loitering?
The sedge has wither'd from the lake,
    And no birds sing.

II

O what can ail thee, knight at arms,   5
    So haggard and so woe-begone?
The squirrel's granary is full,
    And the harvest's done.

III

I see a lily on thy brow
    With anguish moist and fever dew,   10
And on thy cheeks a fading rose
    Fast withereth too.

IV

I met a lady in the meads,
    Full beautiful, a fairy's child;
Her hair was long, her foot was light,
    And her eyes were wild.   15

V

I made a garland for her head,
    And bracelets too, and fragrant zone;
She look'd at me as she did love,
    And made sweet moan.   20

VI

I set her on my pacing steed,
    And nothing else saw all day long,
For sidelong would she bend, and sing
    A fairy's song.

VII

She found me roots of relish sweet,   25
    And honey wild, and manna dew,
And sure in language strange she said—
    I love thee true.

VIII

She took me to her elfin grot,
    And there she wept, and sigh'd full sore,   30
And there I shut her wild wild eyes
    With kisses four.

IX

And there she lulled me asleep,
    And there I dream'd—Ah! woe betide!
The latest dream I ever dream'd   35
    On the cold hill's side.

X

I saw pale kings, and princes too,
    Pale warriors, death pale were they all;
They cried—"La belle dame sans merci
    Hath thee in thrall!"   40

XI

I saw their starv'd lips in the gloam
    With horrid warning gaped wide,
And I awoke and found me here
    On the cold hill's side.

XII

And this is why I sojourn here,   45
   Alone and palely loitering,
Though the sedge is wither'd from the lake,
   And no birds sing.

LA BELLE DAME SANS MERCI. The title is French for "the beautiful woman without mercy." Keats borrowed the title from a fifteenth-century French poem.

Questions

1. What time of year is suggested by the details of the first two stanzas? What is the significance of the season in the larger context of the poem?
2. How many speakers are there? Where does the change of speaker occur?
3. What details throughout the text tell us that *la belle dame* is no ordinary woman?
4. Why do you think the poet chose to imitate the form of the folk ballad in this poem?

PERSONAL MYTH

Sometimes poets have been inspired to make up myths of their own, to embody their own visions of life. "I must create a system or be enslaved by another man's," said William Blake, who in his "prophetic books" peopled the cosmos with supernatural beings having names such as Los, Urizen, and Vala (side by side with recognizable figures from the Old and New Testaments). This kind of system-making probably has advantages and drawbacks. T. S. Eliot, in his essay on Blake, wishes that the author of *The Four Zoas* had accepted traditional myths, and he compares Blake's thinking to a piece of homemade furniture whose construction diverted valuable energy from the writing of poems. Others have found Blake's untraditional cosmos an achievement—notably William Butler Yeats, himself the creator of an elaborate personal mythology. Although we need not know all of Yeats's mythology to enjoy his poems, to know of its existence can make a few great poems deeper for us and less difficult.

William Butler Yeats   (1865–1939)

The Second Coming   1921

Turning and turning in the widening gyre°   *spiral*
The falcon cannot hear the falconer;
Things fall apart; the center cannot hold;
Mere anarchy is loosed upon the world,
The blood-dimmed tide is loosed, and everywhere   5
The ceremony of innocence is drowned;
The best lack all conviction, while the worst
Are full of passionate intensity.

Surely some revelation is at hand;
Surely the Second Coming is at hand.   10
The Second Coming! Hardly are those words out
When a vast image out of *Spiritus Mundi*
Troubles my sight: somewhere in sands of the desert
A shape with lion body and the head of a man,
A gaze blank and pitiless as the sun,   15

Is moving its slow thighs, while all about it
Reel shadows of the indignant desert birds.
The darkness drops again; but now I know
That twenty centuries of stony sleep
Were vexed to nightmare by a rocking cradle,   20
And what rough beast, its hour come round at last,
Slouches towards Bethlehem to be born?

What kind of Second Coming does Yeats expect? Evidently it is not to be a
Christian one. Yeats saw human history as governed by the turning of a Great Wheel,
whose phases influence events and determine human personalities—rather like
the signs of the Zodiac in astrology. Every two thousand years comes a horrendous
moment: the Wheel completes a turn; one civilization ends and another begins. In
1919 when Yeats wrote "The Second Coming," his Ireland was in the midst of turmoil
and bloodshed; the Western Hemisphere had been severely shaken by World War I
and the Russian Revolution. A new millennium seemed imminent. What sphinx-
like, savage deity would next appear on earth, with birds proclaiming it angrily? Yeats
imagines it emerging from *Spiritus Mundi*, Soul of the World, a collective unconscious
from which a human being (since the individual soul touches it) receives dreams,
nightmares, and memories.

Diane Thiel (b. 1967)

Memento Mori in Middle School   2000

When I was twelve, I chose Dante's *Inferno*
in gifted class—an oral presentation
with visual aids. My brother, *il miglior fabbro*,

said he would draw the tortures. We used ten
red posterboards. That day, for school, I dressed   5
in pilgrim black, left earlier to hang them

around the class. The students were impressed.
The teacher, too. She acted quite amused
and peered too long at all the punishments.

We knew by reputation she was cruel.   10
The class could see a hint of twisted forms
and asked to be allowed to round the room

as I went through my final presentation.
We passed the first one, full of poets cut
out of a special issue of *Horizon*.   15

The class thought these were such a boring set,
they probably deserved their tedious fates.
They liked the next, though—bodies blown about,

the lovers kept outside the tinfoil gates.
We had a new boy in our class named Paolo   20
and when I noted Paolo's wind-blown state

and pointed out Francesca, people howled.
I knew that more than one of us not-so-
covertly liked him. It seemed like hours

before we moved on to the gluttons, though,   25
where they could hold the cool fistfuls of slime
I brought from home. An extra touch. It sold

in canisters at toy stores at the time.
The students recognized the River Styx,
the logo of a favorite band of mine.   30

We moved downriver to the town of Dis,
which someone loudly re-named Dis and Dat.
And for the looming harpies and the furies,

who shrieked and tore things up, I had clipped out
the shrillest, most deserving teacher's heads   35
from our school paper, then thought better of it.

At the wood of suicides, we quieted.
Though no one in the room would say a word,
I know we couldn't help but think of Fred.

His name was in the news, though we had heard   40
he might have just been playing with the gun.
We moved on quickly by that huge, dark bird

and rode the flying monster, Geryon,
to reach the counselors, each wicked face,
again, I had resisted pasting in.   45

To represent the ice in that last place,
where Satan chewed the traitors' frozen heads,
my mother had insisted that I take

an ice-chest full of popsicles—to end
my gruesome project on a lighter note.   50
"It *is* a comedy, isn't it," she said.

She hadn't read the poem, or seen our art,
but asked me what had happened to the sweet,
angelic poems I once read and wrote.

The class, though, was delighted by the treat,   55
and at the last round, they all pushed to choose
their colors quickly, so they wouldn't melt.

The bell rang. Everyone ran out of school,
as always, yelling at the top of their lungs,
The *Inferno* fast forgotten, but their howls   60

showed off their darkened red and purple tongues.

MEMENTO MORI IN MIDDLE SCHOOL. *Memento Mori:* Latin for "Remember you must die," the phrase now means any reminder of human mortality and the need to lead a virtuous life. 1 *Dante's Inferno:* The late medieval epic poem by the Italian poet Dante Alighieri describes a Christian soul's journey through hell. (*Inferno* means "hell" in Italian.) 3 *il miglior fabbro:* the better craftsman—Dante's term for fellow poet Arnaut Daniel, which T. S. Eliot later famously quoted to praise Ezra Pound. 15 Horizon: a magazine of art and culture. 20–23 *Paolo . . . Francesca:* two lovers in Dante's *Inferno* who have been damned for their adultery. 29 *River Styx:* the river that flows around hell to mark its boundary. 31 *Dis:* the main city of hell named after its ruler, Dis (Pluto). 43 *Geryon:* a mythical monster Dante places in his *Inferno.*

MYTH AND POPULAR CULTURE

If one can find myths in an art museum, one can also find them abundantly in popular culture. Movies and comic books, for example, are full of myths in modern guise. What is Superman, if not a mythic hero who has adapted himself to modern urban life? Marvel Comics even made the Norse thunder god, Thor, into a superhero, although they initially obliged him, like Clark Kent, to get a job. We also see myths retold on the technicolor screen. Sometimes Hollywood presents the traditional story directly, as in Walt Disney's *Cinderella*; more often the ancient tales acquire contemporary settings, as in another celluloid Cinderella story, *Pretty Woman.* (See how Anne Sexton has retold the Cinderella story from a feminist perspective, later in this chapter, and try to track down a recording of Dana Dane's Brooklyn housing-project version of the fairy tale done from a masculine perspective in his 1980s underground rap hit "Cinderfella Dana Dane.") George Lucas's *Star Wars* series borrowed the structure of medieval quest legends. In quest stories, young knights pursued their destiny, often by seeking the Holy Grail, the cup Christ used at the Last Supper; in *Star Wars*, Luke Skywalker searched for his own parentage and identity, but his interstellar quest brought him to a surprisingly similar cast of knights, monsters, princesses, and wizards. Medieval Grail romances, which influenced Eliot's *The Waste Land* and J. R. R. Tolkien's *The Lord of the Rings* trilogy, also shaped films such as *The Matrix.* Science fiction commonly uses myth to original effect. Extraterrestrial visitors usually appear as either munificent mythic gods or nightmarish demons. Steven Spielberg's *E.T.*, for example, revealed a gentle, Christ-like alien recognized by innocent children, but persecuted by adults. E.T. even healed the sick, fell into a deathlike coma, and was resurrected.

It hardly matters whether an audience recognizes the literal source of a myth; the viewers intuitively understand the structure of the story and feel its deep imaginative resonance. That is why poets retell these myths; they are powerful sources of collective psychic energy, waiting to be tapped.

Aimee Nezhukumatathil (b. 1974)

What I Learned from the Incredible Hulk   2003

When it comes to clothes, make
an allowance for the unexpected.
Be sure the spare in the trunk
of your station wagon with wood paneling

isn't in need of repair. A simple jean jacket   5
says *Hey, if you aren't trying to smuggle*
rare Incan coins through this peaceful
little town and kidnap the local orphan,

I can be one heck of a mellow kinda guy.
But no matter how angry a man gets, a smile   10
and a soft stroke on his bicep can work
wonders. I learned that male chests

also have nipples, warm and established—
green doesn't always mean envy.
It's the meadows full of clover   15
and chicory the Hulk seeks for rest, a return

to normal. And sometimes, a woman
gets to go with him, her tiny hands
correcting his rumpled hair, the cuts
in his hand. Green is the space between   20

water and sun, cover for a quiet man,
each rib shuttling drops of liquid light.

Questions

1. What is the joke of lines 1 and 2?
2. How is the color green used in the poem?
3. In what way does the poem cast the Incredible Hulk as a mythic hero of popular culture? Does the poet assume that her audience has a shared knowledge of the character and history of the Hulk?
4. How might this poem be different if a man had written it?
5. Describe the tone of the first nine lines. How does that tone shift in line ten, and how would you describe the second half of the poem?

Why do poets retell myths? Why don't they just make up their own stories? First, using myth allows poets to be concise. By alluding to stories that their audiences know, they can draw on powerful associations with just a few words. If someone describes an acquaintance, "He thinks he's James Bond," that one allusion speaks volumes. Likewise, when Robert Frost inserts the single line "So Eden sank to grief" in "Nothing Gold Can Stay," those five words summon up a wealth of associations. They tie the perishable quality of spring's beauty to the equally transient nature of human youth. They also suggest that everything in the human world is subject to time's ravages, that perfection is impossible for us to maintain, just as it was for Adam and Eve.

Second, poets know that many stories fall into familiar mythic patterns, and that the most powerful stories of human existence tend to be the same, generation after generation. Sometimes using an old story allows a writer to describe a new situation in a fresh and surprising way.

FOR REVIEW AND FURTHER STUDY

A. E. Stallings (b. 1968)

First Love: A Quiz   2006

He came up to me:
    a. in his souped-up Camaro
    b. to talk to my skinny best friend
    c. and bumped my glass of wine so I wore the ferrous stain on my sleeve
    d. from the ground, in a lead chariot drawn by a team of stallions black as   5
       crude oil and breathing sulfur; at his heart, he sported a tiny golden arrow

He offered me:
    a. a ride
    b. dinner and a movie, with a wink at the cliché
    c. an excuse not to go back alone to the apartment with its sink of dirty
       knives
    d. a narcissus with a hundred dazzling petals that breathed a sweetness as   10
       cloying as decay

I went with him because:
    a. even his friends told me to beware
    b. I had nothing to lose except my virginity
    c. he placed his hand in the small of my back and I felt the tread of
       honeybees
    d. he was my uncle, the one who lived in the half-finished basement, and   15
       he took me by the hair

The place he took me to:
    a. was dark as my shut eyes
    b. and where I ate bitter seed and became ripe
    c. and from which my mother would never take me wholly back, though
       she wept and walked the earth and made the bearded ears of barley
       wither on their stalks and the blasted flowers drop from their sepals
    d. is called by some men hell and others love   20
    e. all of the above

FIRST LOVE: A QUIZ. Stallings's poem alludes to the classical myth of Persephone. A beautiful young goddess, the daughter of Zeus and Demeter, she was abducted by Hades, the ruler of the Underworld (and the brother of Zeus). Her mother Demeter, the goddess of agriculture, became so grief-stricken that plants stopped growing. Eventually, Persephone was permitted to spend six months on the earth each year, which allows spring and summer to return, before descending again to Hades, which brings back winter.

Questions

1. How does Stallings adapt a classical myth of abduction and rape into a contemporary story? Give specific examples.
2. In each option, does the speaker see the man as dangerous? If so, why does she go with him?
3. What is your interpretation of the last line?

Alfred, Lord Tennyson (1809–1892)

Ulysses   (1833)

It little profits that an idle king,
By this still hearth, among these barren crags,
Matched with an agèd wife, I mete and dole°   *measure and dispense*
Unequal laws unto a savage race
That hoard, and sleep, and feed, and know not me.   5

I cannot rest from travel; I will drink
Life to the lees.° All times I have enjoyed   *to the bottom, the dregs*
Greatly, have suffered greatly, both with those
That loved me, and alone; on shore, and when
Through scudding drifts the rainy Hyades   10
Vexed the dim sea. I am become a name;
For always roaming with a hungry heart
Much have I seen and known—cities of men
And manners, climates, councils, governments,
Myself not least, but honored of them all—   15
And drunk delight of battle with my peers,
Far on the ringing plains of windy Troy.
I am a part of all that I have met;
Yet all experience is an arch wherethrough
Gleams that untraveled world whose margin fades   20
Forever and forever when I move.
How dull it is to pause, to make an end,
To rust unburnished, not to shine in use!
As though to breathe were life! Life piled on life
Were all too little, and of one to me   25
Little remains; but every hour is saved
From that eternal silence, something more,
A bringer of new things; and vile it were
For some three suns to store and hoard myself,
And this grey spirit yearning in desire   30
To follow knowledge like a sinking star,
Beyond the utmost bound of human thought.

　　This is my son, mine own Telemachus,
To whom I leave the scepter and the isle—
Well-loved of me, discerning to fulfill   35
This labor, by slow prudence to make mild
A rugged people, and through soft degrees
Subdue them to the useful and the good.
Most blameless is he, centered in the sphere
Of common duties, decent not to fail   40
In offices of tenderness, and pay
Meet adoration to my household gods,
When I am gone. He works his work, I mine.

There lies the port; the vessel puffs her sail;
There gloom the dark, broad seas. My mariners,   45
Souls that have toiled, and wrought, and thought with me—
That ever with a frolic welcome took
The thunder and the sunshine, and opposed
Free hearts, free foreheads—you and I are old;
Old age hath yet his honor and his toil.   50
Death closes all; but something ere the end,
Some work of noble note, may yet be done,
Not unbecoming men that strove with Gods.
The lights begin to twinkle from the rocks;
The long day wanes; the slow moon climbs; the deep   55
Moans round with many voices. Come, my friends,
'Tis not too late to seek a newer world.
Push off, and sitting well in order smite
The sounding furrows; for my purpose holds
To sail beyond the sunset, and the baths   60
Of all the western stars, until I die.
It may be that the gulfs will wash us down;
It may be we shall touch the Happy Isles,
And see the great Achilles, whom we knew.
Though much is taken, much abides; and though   65
We are not now that strength which in old days
Moved earth and heaven, that which we are, we are—
One equal temper of heroic hearts,
Made weak by time and fate, but strong in will
To strive, to seek, to find, and not to yield.   70

ULYSSES. Known as Odysseus in Greek, Ulysses was the king of Ithaca and a hero of the Trojan War.
His ten-year journey home was portrayed in Homer's epic poem the *Odyssey*. 10 *Hyades*: daughters
of Atlas, who were transformed into a group of stars. Their rising with the sun was thought to be a
sign of rain. 33 *Telemachus*: son of Ulysses and Prince of Ithaca. 63 *Happy Isles*: Elysium, a paradise
believed to be attainable by sailing west. 64 *Achilles*: also a hero of the Trojan War, a great warrior
whose only vulnerability was found on a single spot on his heel.

Questions

1. Who is the speaker of this poem? What details tell us so?
2. What does the speaker mean by "'Tis not too late to seek a newer world" (line 57)?
3. What do you know, or what can you find out, about Ulysses's life that may shed light on what is said here?

Anne Sexton (1928–1974)

Cinderella   1971

You always read about it:
the plumber with twelve children
who wins the Irish Sweepstakes.
From toilets to riches.
That story.   5

Or the nursemaid,
some luscious sweet from Denmark
who captures the oldest son's heart.
From diapers to Dior.
That story.   10

Or a milkman who serves the wealthy,
eggs, cream, butter, yogurt, milk,
the white truck like an ambulance
who goes into real estate
and makes a pile.   15
From homogenized to martinis at lunch.

Or the charwoman
who is on the bus when it cracks up
and collects enough from the insurance.
From mops to Bonwit Teller.   20
That story.

Once
the wife of a rich man was on her deathbed
and she said to her daughter Cinderella:
Be devout. Be good. Then I will smile   25
down from heaven in the seam of a cloud.
The man took another wife who had
two daughters, pretty enough
but with hearts like blackjacks.
Cinderella was their maid.   30
She slept on the sooty hearth each night
and walked around looking like Al Jolson.
Her father brought presents home from town,
jewels and gowns for the other women
but the twig of a tree for Cinderella.   35
She planted that twig on her mother's grave
and it grew to a tree where a white dove sat.
Whenever she wished for anything the dove
would drop it like an egg upon the ground.
The bird is important, my dears, so heed him.   40

Next came the ball, as you all know.
It was a marriage market.
The prince was looking for a wife.
All but Cinderella were preparing
and gussying up for the big event.   45
Cinderella begged to go too.
Her stepmother threw a dish of lentils
into the cinders and said: Pick them
up in an hour and you shall go.
The white dove brought all his friends;   50
all the warm wings of the fatherland came,
and picked up the lentils in a jiffy.
No, Cinderella, said the stepmother,

you have no clothes and cannot dance.
That's the way with stepmothers.   55

Cinderella went to the tree at the grave
and cried forth like a gospel singer:
Mama! Mama! My turtledove,
send me to the prince's ball!
The bird dropped down a golden dress   60
and delicate little gold slippers.
Rather a large package for a simple bird.
So she went. Which is no surprise.
Her stepmother and sisters didn't
recognize her without her cinder face   65
and the prince took her hand on the spot
and danced with no other the whole day.

As nightfall came she thought she'd better
get home. The prince walked her home
and she disappeared into the pigeon house   70
and although the prince took an axe and broke
it open she was gone. Back to her cinders.

These events repeated themselves for three days.
However on the third day the prince
covered the palace steps with cobbler's wax   75
and Cinderella's gold shoe stuck upon it.
Now he would find whom the shoe fit
and find his strange dancing girl for keeps.
He went to their house and the two sisters
were delighted because they had lovely feet.   80
The eldest went into a room to try the slipper on
but her big toe got in the way so she simply
sliced it off and put on the slipper.
The prince rode away with her until the white dove
told him to look at the blood pouring forth.   85
That is the way with amputations.
They just don't heal up like a wish.
The other sister cut off her heel
but the blood told as blood will.
The prince was getting tired.   90
He began to feel like a shoe salesman.
But he gave it one last try.
This time Cinderella fit into the shoe
like a love letter into its envelope.

At the wedding ceremony   95
the two sisters came to curry favor
and the white dove pecked their eyes out.
Two hollow spots were left
like soup spoons.

Cinderella and the prince   100
lived, they say, happily ever after,
like two dolls in a museum case
never bothered by diapers or dust,
never arguing over the timing of an egg,
never telling the same story twice,   105
never getting a middle-aged spread,
their darling smiles pasted on for eternity.
Regular Bobbsey Twins.
That story.

CINDERELLA. 32 *Al Jolson:* Extremely popular American entertainer (1886–1950) who frequently
performed in blackface.

Questions

1. Most of Sexton's "Cinderella" straightforwardly retells a version of the famous fairy tale.
   But in the beginning and ending of the poem, how does Sexton change the story?
2. How does Sexton's refrain of "That story" alter the meaning of the episodes it describes?
   What is the tone of this poem (the poet's attitude toward her material)?
3. What does Sexton's final stanza suggest about the way fairy tales usually end?

■ WRITING *effectively*

Diane Thiel on Writing

The Map of Myth   2014

As a writer I often see myth as a map. Every
myth is a story that offers some guidance
through a part of the human experience. When
I unfold the archetypal tale and reflect on its
message, I feel inspired by the possibilities of
traveling through that landscape—known and
unknown, familiar and yet foreign.

I find tapping into myth to be useful in
all forms of writing but particularly in writing
poetry, perhaps because poetry is a more compressed form. Having a backdrop that can be
recognized by others can allow us to more fully
enter and elucidate aspects that are most relevant to our own experiences. We can sometimes reflect in a more compressed way, with
the potency of archetype surrounding the
experience. Myth and poetic form feel con-

Diane Thiel

nected on many levels, and both can be valuable as guides that help us tap into the
subconscious.

I have been attracted to myth from my early years. The fairy tales I heard in German as a child as well as myths from other cultures have found new dimensions in my poetry. Sometimes a poem brings together this childhood attraction to mythology and a later reflection on its significance. In one of my poems, "Memento Mori in Middle School," I wrote about an odd memory from childhood, where I was already reinventing myth. When I chose to do a middle school project on Dante's *Inferno*, complete with circles of hell pasted on the walls, a dark wood of suicides, and the icy popsicles and howling at the end, I was already following a map of stories, while adding personal and contemporary dimensions.

Despite the humorous elements of the poem, the story is a kind of *memento mori*, a recognition of our mortality. The archetypes in Dante's epic had found their way into my childhood project as well as my later poem. Myth and form also came together in the writing of the poem. Using Dante's *terza rima* (albeit somewhat loosely rhymed) helped the poem come into being. Dante took a journey of human failings, guided by ancient motifs and a form he invented. When I am inspired by myth, I embark on a journey through a landscape that offers many possibilities. As I chart my own course, I am often surprised by the places I find myself traveling.

THINKING ABOUT MYTH

Of the many myths conjured by the poets in these pages, you may know some by heart, some only vaguely, and others not at all. When reading a poem inspired by myth, there's no way around it: your understanding will be more precise if you know the mythic story the poem refers to. With the vast resources available on line, it's never hard to find a description of a myth, whether traditional or contemporary. While different versions of most myths exist, what usually remains fixed is the tale's basic pattern. A familiarity with that narrative is a key to the meaning—both intellectual and emotional—of any poem that makes reference to mythology.

- **Start with the underlying pattern of the narrative in question.** Does the basic shape of the poem's story seem familiar? Does it have some recognizable source in myth or legend? Even if the poem has no obvious narrative line, does it call to mind other stories?
- **Notice what new details the poem has added, and what it inevitably leaves out.** The difference between the poem and the source material will reveal something about the author's attitude toward the original, and may give you a sense of his or her intentions in reworking the original myth.
- **Read the section "Mythological Criticism" in Chapter 49.** A quick sense of how critics analyze myth in literature will help you approach a poem with mythological allusions.

CHECKLIST: Writing About Myth

- ☐ Does the poem have a recognizable source in myth or legend?
- ☐ What new details has the poet added to the original myth?
- ☐ What do these details reveal about the poet's attitude toward the source material?

☐ Have important elements of the original been discarded? What does their absence suggest about the author's primary focus?

☐ Does the poem rely heavily on its mythic imagery? Or is myth tangential to the poem's theme?

☐ How do mythic echoes underscore the poem's meaning?

TOPICS FOR WRITING ON MYTH

1. Anne Sexton's "Cinderella" freely mixes period detail and slang from twentieth-century American life with elements from the original fairy tale. (You can read the original in Charles Perrault's *Mother Goose Tales*.) Write an analysis of the effect of all this anachronistic mixing and matching. Be sure to look up any period details you don't recognize.

2. Provide an explication of Louise Bogan's "Medusa." For tips on poetic explication, refer to Chapter 44, "Writing About a Poem."

3. Write an essay of approximately 750 words discussing A. E. Stallings's "First Love: A Quiz." How does the poet combine modern circumstances and mythological allusions to suggest personal meaning for the reader?

4. You're probably familiar with an urban legend or two—near-fantastical stories passed on from one person to another, with the suggestion that they really happened to a friend of a friend of the person who told you the tale. Retell an urban myth in free-verse form. If you don't know any urban myths, an internet search engine can lead you to scores of them.

5. Compare and contrast H.D.'s portrait of Helen of Troy in "Helen" with Edgar Allan Poe's version in "To Helen." In what ways are the treatments similar? In what significant ways do they differ?

6. Retell a famous myth or fairy tale to reflect your personal worldview.

7. Provide a close reading of any poem from this book that uses a traditional myth or legend. In the course of your analysis, demonstrate how the author borrows or changes certain details of the myth to emphasize his or her meaning. In addition to the poems in this chapter, some selections to consider include T. S. Eliot's "Journey of the Magi" and William Butler Yeats's "The Magi" (Chapter 34).

SAMPLE STUDENT PAPER

Here is an example of an essay on this assignment written by Heather Burke when she was a sophomore at Wesleyan University in Middletown, Connecticut.

Burke 1

Heather Burke

Professor Greene

English 150

18 January 2019

The Bonds Between Love and Hatred in H.D.'s "Helen"

> *Title sets tone and draws reader in*
>
> *Thesis sentence*

    In her poem "Helen," H.D. examines the close connection between the emotions of love and hatred as embodied in the figure of Helen of Troy. Helen was the cause of the long and bloody Trojan War, and her homecoming is tainted by the memory of the suffering this war caused. As in many Imagist poems, the title is essential to the poem's meaning; it gives the reader both a specific mythic context and a particular subject.

> *Necessary background*

Without the title, it would be virtually impossible to understand the poem fully since Helen's name appears nowhere else in the text. The reader familiar with Greek myth knows that Helen, who was the wife of Menelaus, ran away with Paris. Their adultery provoked the Trojan War, which lasted for ten years and resulted in the destruction of Troy.

> *Topic sentence on poem's focus*

    What is unusual about the poem is H.D.'s perspective on Helen of Troy. The poem refuses to romanticize Helen's story, but its stark new version is easy for a reader to accept. After suffering so much for the sake of one adulterous woman, how could the Greeks not resent her? Rather than idealizing the situation, H.D. describes the enmity which defiles Helen's homecoming and explores the irony of the hatred which "All Greece" feels for her.

> *Topic sentence on tone and theme*

    The opening line of the poem sets its tone and introduces its central theme— hatred. Helen's beauty required thousands of men to face death in battle, but it cannot assuage the emotional aftermath of the war. Even though Helen is described as "God's daughter, born of love" (line 13), all she inspires now is resentment, and the poem explores the ways in which these two emotions are closely related.

> *Topic sentence on specific image*

    In the first stanza, the poet uses the color white, as well as the radiance or luster connected with it, in her description of Helen, and this color will be associated with her throughout the poem:

> the still eyes in the white face,
>
> the lustre as of olives
>
> where she stands,
>
> and the white hands. (2–5)

Burke 2

As one of the foundations of agriculture and civilization, the olive was a crucial symbol in Greek culture. Helen's beauty is compared to the "lustre" of this olive. This word presumably refers to the radiance or light which the whiteness of her face reflects, but Helen's identification with this fruit also has an ironic connotation. The olive branch is a traditional symbol of peace, but the woman it is compared to was the cause of a bitter war.

Exploration of specific image

The majority of the imagery in the poem is connected with the color white. H.D. uses white to describe Helen's skin; white would have been seen as the appropriate color for a rich and beautiful woman's skin in pre-twentieth century poetry. This color also has several connotations, all of which operate simultaneously in the poem. The color white has a connection to Helen's paternity; her immortal father Zeus took the form of a white swan when he made love to her mortal mother Leda. At the same time, whiteness suggests a certain chilliness, as with snow or frost. In the third stanza, H.D. makes this suggestion explicit with her use of the phrase "the beauty of cool feet" (14). This image also suggests the barrenness connected with such frigidity. In this sense, it is a very accurate representation of Helen, because in the *Odyssey* Homer tells us that "the gods had never after granted Helen / a child to bring into the sunlit world / after the first, rose-lipped Hermione" (4.13–15). Helen is returned to her rightful husband, but after her adulterous actions, she is unable to bear him any more children. She is a woman who is renowned for exciting passion in legions of men, but that passion is now sterile.

Topic sentence (further analysis of imagery)

Another traditional connotation of the color white is purity, but this comparison only accentuates Helen's sexual transgressions; she is hardly pure. H.D. emphasizes her lasciviousness through the use of irony. In the third stanza, she refers to Helen as a "maid." A maid is a virgin, but Helen is most definitely not virginal in any sense. In the following line, the poet rhymes "maid" with the word "laid," which refers to the placement of Helen's body on the funeral pyre. This particular word, however, deliberately emphasized by the rhyme, also carries slangy associations with the act of sexual intercourse. This connotation presents another ironic contrast with the word "maid."

Topic sentence (further analysis of specific image)

The first line of the second stanza is almost identical to that of the first, and again we are reminded of the intense animosity that Helen's presence inspires. This hatred is now made more explicit. The word *revile* is defined by the *American Heritage College Dictionary* as "to denounce with abusive language" ("Revile"). Helen is a queen, but she is subjected to the insults of her subjects as well as the rest of Greece.

Topic sentence on effect of poem's form

Key word defined

Burke 3

*Topic sentence/
textual analysis*

Helen's homecoming is not joyous, but a time of exile and penance. The war is over, but no one, especially Helen, can forget the past. Her memories seem to cause her wanness, which the dictionary defines as "indicating weariness, illness, or unhappiness" ("Wan"). Her face now ". . . grows wan and white, / remembering past enchantments / and past ills" (9–11). The enchantment she remembers is that of Aphrodite, the goddess who lured her from her home and husband to Paris's bed. The "ills" which Helen remembers can be seen as both her sexual offenses and the human losses sustained in the Trojan War. The use of the word *ills* works in conjunction with the word *wan* to demonstrate Helen's spiritual sickness; she is plagued by regret.

*Topic sentence/
textual analysis*

As the opening of the third stanza shows, the woman who was famous for her beauty and perfection now leaves Greece "unmoved." This opening may not echo the sharpness of those of the first two stanzas, but it picks up on the theme of Helen as a devalued prize. In the eyes of the Greeks, she is not the beauty who called two armies to battle but merely an unfaithful wife for whom many died needlessly.

Conclusion

The final lines of the poem reveal the one condition which could turn the people's hatred into love again. They "could love indeed the maid, / only if she were laid, / white ash amid funereal cypresses" (16–18). The Greeks can only forgive Helen once her body has been burned on the funeral pyre. These disturbing lines illustrate the destructive power of hatred; it can only be conquered by death. These lines also reveal the final significance of the color white. It suggests Helen's death. As Helen's face is pale and white in life, so her ashes will be in death. The flames of the funeral pyre are the only way to purify the flesh that was tainted by the figurative flames of passion. Death is the only way to restore Helen's beauty and make it immortal. While she is alive, her beauty is only a reminder of lost fathers, sons, and brothers. The people of Greece can only despise her while she is living, but they can love and revere the memory of her beauty once she is dead.

*More complex and
specific restate-
ment of thesis*

Burke 4

Works Cited

H.D. "Helen." *Literature: An Introduction to Fiction, Poetry, Drama, and Writing*, edited by X. J. Kennedy et al., 14th ed., Pearson, 2020, p. 920.

Homer. *The Odyssey*. Translated by Robert Fitzgerald, Noonday Press, 1998.

"Revile." *American Heritage College Dictionary*, 4th ed., 2002.

"Wan." *American Heritage College Dictionary*, 4th ed., 2002.

▶ TERMS FOR *review*

Myth ▶ A traditional narrative of anonymous authorship that arises out of a culture's oral tradition. The characters in traditional myths are often gods or heroic figures engaged in significant actions and decisions. Myth is usually differentiated from *legend*, which has a specific historical base.

Mythology ▶ The body of myths belonging to a particular culture.

Archetype ▶ A recurring symbol, character, landscape, or event found in myth and literature across different cultures and eras, one that appears so often that it evokes a universal response.

28 POETRY AND PERSONAL IDENTITY

All literature is, finally, autobiographical.

—JORGE LUIS BORGES

What You Will Learn in This Chapter

- To define *confessional poetry*
- To describe and define *identity poetics*
- To explain the influence of gender and sexual identity in shaping a poem
- To analyze the role of personal identity in a poem

Only a naive reader assumes that all poems directly reflect the personal experience of their authors. That would be like believing that a TV sitcom actually describes the real family life of its cast. As you will recall if you read "The Speaker in the Poem" (Chapter 16), poets often speak in voices other than their own. These voices may be borrowed or imaginary. Stevie Smith appropriates the voice of a dead swimmer in her poem "Not Waving but Drowning" (Chapter 19), and Alfred, Lord Tennyson borrows the voice of an ancient Greek hero in "Ulysses" (Chapter 27). Some poets also try to give their personal poems a universal feeling. Edna St. Vincent Millay's emotion-charged sonnet "Well, I Have Lost You; and I Lost You Fairly" describes the end of a difficult love affair with a younger man, but she dramatizes the situation in such a way that it seems deliberately independent of any particular time and place. Even her lover remains shadowy and nameless. No one has ever been able to identify the characters in Shakespeare's sonnets as actual people, but that fact does not diminish our pleasure in them as poems.

And yet there are times when poets try to speak openly in their own voices. What could be a more natural subject for a poet than examining his or her own life? The autobiographical elements in a poem may be indirect, as in Wilfred Owen's "Anthem for Doomed Youth" (Chapter 24), which is clearly drawn from its author's battle experience in World War I, although it never refers to his own participation, or they may form the central subject, as in Sylvia Plath's "Lady Lazarus" (see below), which discusses her suicide attempts. In either case, the poem's autobiographical stance affects a reader's response.

Although we respond to a poem's formal elements, we also cannot help reacting to what we know about its human origins. Reading Plath's chilling exploration of her death wish while knowing that within a few months the poet would kill herself, we receive an extra jolt of emotion. In a good autobiographical poem, that shock of veracity adds to the poem's power. In an unsuccessful poem, the autobiographical facts become a substitute for emotions not credibly conveyed by the words themselves.

CONFESSIONAL POETRY

One literary movement, **Confessional poetry**, has made frank self-definition its main purpose. As the name implies, Confessional poetry renders personal experience as candidly as possible, even sharing confidences that may violate social conventions or propriety. Confessional poets sometimes shock their readers with admissions of experiences so intimate and painful—adultery, family violence, suicide attempts—that most people would try to suppress them, or at least not proclaim them to the world.

Some confessional poets, such as Anne Sexton, W. D. Snodgrass, and Robert Lowell, underwent psychoanalysis, and at times their poems sound like patients telling their analysts every detail of their personal lives. For this reason, confessional poems run the danger of being more interesting to their authors than to their readers. But when a poet successfully frames his or her personal experience so that the reader can feel an extreme emotion from the inside, the result can be powerful. Here is a chilling poem that takes us within the troubled psyche of a poet who contemplates suicide.

Sylvia Plath (1932–1963)

Lady Lazarus (1962) 1965

I have done it again.
One year in every ten
I manage it—

A sort of walking miracle, my skin
Bright as a Nazi lampshade,   5
My right foot

A paperweight,
My face a featureless, fine
Jew linen.

Peel off the napkin   10
O my enemy.
Do I terrify?—

The nose, the eye pits, the full set of teeth?
The sour breath
Will vanish in a day.   15

Soon, soon the flesh
The grave cave ate will be
At home on me

And I a smiling woman.
I am only thirty.   20
And like the cat I have nine times to die.

This is Number Three.
What a trash
To annihilate each decade.

What a million filaments.   25
The peanut-crunching crowd
Shoves in to see

Them unwrap me hand and foot—
The big strip tease.
Gentleman, ladies   30

These are my hands
My knees.
I may be skin and bone,

Nevertheless, I am the same, identical woman.
The first time it happened I was ten.   35
It was an accident.

The second time I meant
To last it out and not come back at all.
I rocked shut

As a seashell.   40
They had to call and call
And pick the worms off me like sticky pearls.

Dying
Is an art, like everything else.
I do it exceptionally well.   45

I do it so it feels like hell.
I do it so it feels real.
I guess you could say I've a call.

It's easy enough to do it in a cell.
It's easy enough to do it and stay put.   50
It's the theatrical

Comeback in broad day
To the same place, the same face, the same brute
Amused shout:

"A miracle!"   55
That knocks me out.
There is a charge

For the eyeing of my scars, there is a charge
For the hearing of my heart—
It really goes.   60

And there is a charge, a very large charge,
For the word or a touch
Or a bit of blood

Or a piece of my hair or my clothes.
So, so, Herr Doktor.   65
So, Herr Enemy.

I am your opus,°   *work, work of art*
I am your valuable,
The pure gold baby

That melts to a shriek.   70
I turn and burn.
Do not think I underestimate your great concern.

Ash, ash—
You poke and stir.
Flesh, bone, there is nothing there—   75

A cake of soap,
A wedding ring,
A gold filling,

Herr God, Herr Lucifer
Beware   80
Beware.

Out of the ash
I rise with my red hair
And I eat men like air.

Questions

1. Although the poem is openly autobiographical, Plath uses certain symbols to represent herself (Lady Lazarus, a Jew murdered in a concentration camp, a cat with nine lives, and so on). What do these symbols tell us about Plath's attitude toward herself and the world around her?

2. In her biography of Plath, *Bitter Fame*, the poet Anne Stevenson says that this poem penetrates "the furthest reaches of disdain and rage . . . bereft of all 'normal' human feelings." What do you think Stevenson means? Does anything in the poem strike you as particularly chilling?

3. The speaker in "Lady Lazarus" says, "Dying / Is an art, like everything else" (lines 43–44). What sense do you make of this metaphor?

4. Does the ending of "Lady Lazarus" imply that the speaker assumes that she will outlive her suicide attempts? Set forth your final understanding of the poem.

Not all autobiographical poetry needs to shock the reader, as Plath overtly does in "Lady Lazarus." Poets can also try to share the special moments that illuminate their day-to-day lives, as Elizabeth Bishop does in "Filling Station" (Chapter 34), when she describes a roadside gas station whose shabby bric-a-brac she sees as symbols of love. But when poets attempt to place their own lives under scrutiny, they face certain difficulties. Honest, thorough self-examination isn't as easy as it might seem. It is one thing to examine oneself in the mirror; it is quite another to sketch accurately what one sees there. Even if we have the skill to describe ourselves in words (or in paint) so that a stranger would recognize the self-portrait, there is the challenge of honesty. Drawing or writing our own self-portrait, most of us yield, often unconsciously, to the temptation of making ourselves a little nobler or better-looking than we really are. The best self-portraits, like Rembrandt's unflattering self-examinations, are usually critical. No one enjoys watching someone else preen in front of a dressing mirror, unless the intention is satiric.

IDENTITY POETICS

Autobiographical poetry requires a hunger for honest self-examination. Many poets find that, in order to understand themselves and who they are, they must scrutinize more than the self in isolation. Other forces may shape their identities: ethnic background, family, race, gender, sexual orientation, religion, economic status, and age. Aware of these elements, many recent poets have written memorable personal poems. Dominican-born Rhina Espaillat addresses these concerns in the following poem, which examines the complexities of the immigrant identity in America.

Rhina Espaillat (b. 1932)

Bra   1998

What a good fit! But the label says Honduras:
Alas, I am Union forever, yes, both breasts
and the heart between them committed to U.S. labor.

But such a splendid fit! And the label tells me
the woman who made it, bronze as the breasts now in it,   5
speaks the language I dream in; I count in Spanish

the pesos she made stitching this breast-divider:
will they go for her son's tuition, her daughter's wedding?
The thought is a lovely fit, but oh, the label!

And oh, those pesos that may be pennies, and hard-earned.   10
Was it son or daughter who made this, unschooled, unwedded?
How old? Fourteen? Ten? That fear is a tight fit.

If only the heart could be worn like the breast, divided,
nosing in two directions for news of the wide world,
sniffing here and there for justice, for mercy.   15

How burdened every choice is with politics, guilt,
expensive with duty, heavy as breasts in need of
this perfect fit whose label says Honduras.

Questions

1. Paraphrase the poem. How would you describe the speaker's conflicting feelings in "Bra"?
2. Why do you think Espaillat selected a bra as the item on which to center the poem? Would the poem have a different effect if it were about socks?
3. Does the poem arrive at an easy conclusion in the last two stanzas, or is the matter of the bra—and the speaker's feelings about it—left unresolved? What does that suggest about the difficulty of balancing one's origins with allegiance to one's adopted country?

CULTURE, RACE, AND ETHNICITY

One of the personal issues Rhina Espaillat addresses in "Bra," and even more directly in "Bilingual/*Bilingüe*" (Chapter 16), is her dual identity as Dominican and American. The daughter of immigrants, she was born in the Dominican Republic but came to America at the age of seven and grew up in New York. Consequently,

self-definition for her has meant resolving the claims of two potentially contradictory cultures, as well as dealing, on a more immediate level, with the conflicting
demands of family love and loyalty, on the one hand, and personal growth and fulfillment, on the other. As she demonstrates in "Bilingual/*Bilingüe*," as much as she loves
her father and wishes to honor him, she cannot be held back from what she is and
what she needs to become, and "I hoarded secret syllables I read // until my tongue
(*mi lengua*) learned to run / where his stumbled." Here Espaillat touches on the central issue facing the autobiographical poet—using *words* to embody experience. The
tongue must "learn to run," even if where it runs, for an immigrant poet, is away from
the language of one's parents.

American poetry is rich in immigrant cultures, as shown in the work of both first-
generation writers such as Francisco X. Alarcón and John Ciardi and foreign-born
authors such as Joseph Brodsky (Russia), Nina Cassian (Romania), Claude McKay
(Jamaica), Eamon Grennan (Ireland), Thom Gunn (England), Shirley Geok-lin Lim
(Malaysia), Emanuel di Pasquale (Italy), José Emilio Pacheco (Mexico), Herberto
Padilla (Cuba), and Derek Walcott (St. Lucia). Some literary immigrants, such as
the late Russian novelist and poet Vladimir Nabokov, make the difficult transition to
writing in English. Others, such as Cassian and Pacheco, continue to write in their
native languages. A few, such as Brodsky, write bilingually. Such texts often remind
us of the multicultural nature of American poetry. Here is a poem by one literary
immigrant that raises some important issues of personal identity.

Claude McKay (1889–1948)

America   1922

Although she feeds me bread of bitterness,
And sinks into my throat her tiger's tooth,
Stealing my breath of life, I will confess
I love this cultured hell that tests my youth!
Her vigor flows like tides into my blood,   5
Giving me strength erect against her hate.
Her bigness sweeps my being like a flood.
Yet, as a rebel fronts a king in state,
I stand within her walls with not a shred
Of terror, malice, not a word of jeer.   10
Darkly I gaze into the days ahead,
And see her might and granite wonders there,
Beneath the touch of Time's unerring hand,
Like priceless treasures sinking in the sand.

Questions

1. Is "America" written in a personal or public voice? What specific elements seem personal?
   What elements seem public?
2. McKay was a black immigrant from Jamaica, but he mentions neither his race nor
   national origin in the poem. Is his background important to understanding "America"?
3. "America" is written in a traditional form. Can you identify it? How does the poem's form
   contribute to its impact?

Claude McKay's "America" raises the question of how an author's race and ethnic identity influence the poetry he or she writes. In the 1920s, for instance, there was an ongoing discussion among black poets as to whether their poetry should deal specifically with the African American experience. Did black poetry exist apart from the rest of American poetry or was it, as Robert Hayden would later suggest, "shaped over some three centuries by social, moral, and literary forces essentially American"? Should black authors primarily address a black audience or should they try to engage a broader literary public? Should black poetry focus on specifically black subjects, forms, and idioms or should it rely mainly on the traditions of English literature? Black poets divided into two camps. Claude McKay and Countee Cullen were among the writers who favored universal themes. (Cullen, for example, insisted he be called a "poet," not a "Negro poet.") Langston Hughes and Jean Toomer were among the "new" poets who felt that black poetry must reflect racial themes. They believed, as James Weldon Johnson had once said, that race was "perforce the thing that the American Negro Poet knows best." Writers on both sides of the debate produced excellent poems, but their work has a very different character.

The debate between ethnicity and universality has echoed among American writers of every racial and religious minority. Today, we find the same issues being discussed by Arab, Asian, Hispanic, Italian, Jewish, and Native American authors. There is no one correct answer to the questions of identity, for individual artists need the freedom to pursue their own imaginative vision. But considering the issues of race and ethnicity does help a poet think through the artist's sometimes conflicting responsibilities between group and personal identity. Even in poets who have pursued their individual vision, we often see how unmistakably they write from their racial, social, and cultural background. Sometimes a poet's ethnic background becomes part of his or her private mythology. In "Riding into California," Shirley Geok-lin Lim describes the dizzy mixture of alienation and acceptance an Asian immigrant might experience arriving in Southern California.

Shirley Geok-lin Lim (b. 1944)

Riding into California   1998

If you come to a land with no ancestors
to bless you, you have to be your own
ancestor. The veterans in the mobile home
park don't want to be there. It isn't easy.
Oil rigs litter the land like giant frozen birds.   5
Ghosts welcome us to a new life, and
an immigrant without home ghosts
cannot believe the land is real. So you're
grateful for familiarity, and Bruce Lee
becomes your hero. Coming into Fullerton,   10
everyone waiting at the station is white.
The good thing about being Chinese on Amtrak
is no one sits next to you. The bad thing is
you sit alone all the way to Irvine.

RIDING INTO CALIFORNIA. *9 Bruce Lee:* Bruce Lee (1940–1973) was a martial arts and film star from Hong Kong.

Questions

1. What does the speaker find familiar in California?
2. Why does the speaker long for ancestors and ghosts in California? What does this wish tell us about the speaker's identity?

Francisco X. Alarcón (1954–2016)

The X in My Name   1993

the poor
signature
of my illiterate
and peasant
self   5
giving away
all rights
in a deceiving
contract for life

Question

What does the speaker imply the X in his name signifies?

Sometimes a single word announces a new sort of voice, as in Judith Ortiz Cofer's "Quinceañera." The title is a Spanish noun for which there is no one-word English equivalent. That one word signals that we will be hearing a new voice.

Judith Ortiz Cofer (1952–2016)

Quinceañera   1987

My dolls have been put away like dead
children in a chest I will carry
with me when I marry.
I reach under my skirt to feel
a satin slip bought for this day. It is soft   5
as the inside of my thighs. My hair
has been nailed back with my mother's
black hairpins to my skull. Her hands
stretched my eyes open as she twisted
braids into a tight circle at the nape   10
of my neck. I am to wash my own clothes
and sheets from this day on, as if
the fluids of my body were poison, as if
the little trickle of blood I believe
travels from my heart to the world were   15
shameful. Is not the blood of saints and
men in battle beautiful? Do Christ's hands
not bleed into your eyes from His cross?

At night I hear myself growing and wake
to find my hands drifting of their own will   20
to soothe skin stretched tight
over my bones.
I am wound like the guts of a clock,
waiting for each hour to release me.

QUINCEAÑERA. The title refers to a fifteen-year-old girl's coming-out party in Latin cultures.

Questions

1. What items and actions are associated with the speaker's new life? What items are put away?
2. What is the speaker waiting to release in the final two lines?
3. If the poem's title were changed to "Fifteen-Year-Old Girl," what would the poem lose in meaning?

Sherman Alexie   (b. 1966)

The Powwow at the End of the World   1996

I am told by many of you that I must forgive and so I shall
after an Indian woman puts her shoulder to the Grand Coulee Dam
and topples it. I am told by many of you that I must forgive
and so I shall after the floodwaters burst each successive dam
downriver from the Grand Coulee. I am told by many of you   5
that I must forgive and so I shall after the floodwaters find
their way to the mouth of the Columbia River as it enters the Pacific
and causes all of it to rise. I am told by many of you that I must forgive
and so I shall after the first drop of floodwater is swallowed by that salmon
waiting in the Pacific. I am told by many of you that I must forgive and   10
  so I shall
after that salmon swims upstream, through the mouth of the Columbia
and then past the flooded cities, broken dams and abandoned reactors
of Hanford. I am told by many of you that I must forgive and so I shall
after that salmon swims through the mouth of the Spokane River
as it meets the Columbia, then upstream, until it arrives   15
in the shallows of a secret bay on the reservation where I wait alone.
I am told by many of you that I must forgive and so I shall after
that salmon leaps into the night air above the water, throws
a lightning bolt at the brush near my feet, and starts the fire
which will lead all of the lost Indians home. I am told   20
by many of you that I must forgive and so I shall
after we Indians have gathered around the fire with that salmon
who has three stories it must tell before sunrise: one story will teach us
how to pray; another story will make us laugh for hours;
the third story will give us reason to dance. I am told by many   25
of you that I must forgive and so I shall when I am dancing
with my tribe during the powwow at the end of the world.

Questions

1. Who, in your opinion, is the "you" of the poem's refrain?
2. What is it that the speaker is told he "must forgive"?
3. The tone of the poem is not overtly angry or bitter. Does that make its statement more effective or less so, in your judgment? Explain.

Yusef Komunyakaa (b. 1947)

Facing It   1988

My black face fades,
hiding inside the black granite.
I said I wouldn't,
dammit: No tears.
I'm stone. I'm flesh.   5
My clouded reflection eyes me
like a bird of prey, the profile of night
slanted against morning. I turn
this way—the stone lets me go.
I turn that way—I'm inside   10
the Vietnam Veterans Memorial
again, depending on the light
to make a difference.
I go down the 58,022 names,
half-expecting to find   15
my own in letters like smoke.
I touch the name Andrew Johnson;
I see the booby trap's white flash.
Names shimmer on a woman's blouse
but when she walks away   20
the names stay on the wall.
Brushstrokes flash, a red bird's
wings cutting across my stare.
The sky. A plane in the sky.
A white vet's image floats   25
closer to me, then his pale eyes
look through mine. I'm a window.
He's lost his right arm
inside the stone. In the black mirror
a woman's trying to erase names: 30
No, she's brushing a boy's hair.

Questions

1. How does the title of "Facing It" relate to the poem? Does it have more than one meaning?
2. The narrator describes the people around him by their reflections on the polished granite rather than by looking at them directly. What does this indirect way of scrutinizing contribute to the poem?
3. This poem comes out of the life experience of a black Vietnam veteran. Is Komunyakaa's writing closer to McKay's "universal" method or to Toomer's "ethnic" style?

GENDER

In her celebrated study *You Just Don't Understand: Women and Men in Conversation* (1990), Georgetown University linguist Deborah Tannen explored how men and women use language differently. Tannen compared many everyday conversations between husbands and wives to "cross-cultural communications," as if people from separate worlds lived under the same roof. While analyzing the divergent ways in which women and men converse, Tannen carefully emphasizes that neither linguistic style is superior, only that they are different.

While it would be simplistic to assume that all poems reveal the sex of their authors, many poems do become both richer and clearer when we examine their gender assumptions. Theodore Roethke's "My Papa's Waltz" (Chapter 16) is hardly a macho poem, but it does reflect the complicated mix of love, authority, and violent horseplay that exists in many father-son relationships. By contrast, Sylvia Plath's "Metaphors" (Chapter 20), which describes her own pregnancy through a series of images, deals with an experience that, by biological definition, only a woman can know firsthand. Feminist criticism has shown us how gender influences literary texts in subtler ways. (See Chapter 49, "Critical Approaches to Literature," for a discussion of gender theory.) The central insight of feminist criticism seems inarguable—our gender does often influence how we speak, write, and interpret language. But that insight need not be intimidating. It can also invite us to bring our whole life experience, as women or men, to reading a poem. It reminds us that poetry, the act of using language with the greatest clarity and specificity, is a means to see the world through the eyes of the opposite sex. Or, it can demonstrate how deeply sexual orientation affects an individual's worldview. Sometimes the messages we get from this exchange are unsettling, but at least they may move us into better understanding the diversity of human behavior.

Anne Stevenson (b. 1933)

The Victory   1969

I thought you were my victory
though you cut me like a knife
when I brought you out of my body
into your life.

Tiny antagonist, gory,   5
blue as a bruise. The stains
of your cloud of glory
bled from my veins.

How can you dare, blind thing,
blank insect eyes?   10
You barb the air. You sting
with bladed cries.

Snail. Scary knot of desires.
Hungry snarl. Small son.
Why do I have to love you?   15
How have you won?

Questions

1. Newborn babies are often described as "little angels" or "bundles of joy." How does the speaker of "The Victory" describe her son?
2. Why does the speaker describe the child as an "antagonist"?
3. Why is the infant compared to a knife in both lines 2 and 12?
4. Why is the poem titled "The Victory"?

Jenny Factor (b. 1969)

Rubyfruit   2002

You kissed my mouth as if it were my sex
before you kissed me everywhere, before
that night in Rubyfruit's, my glasses off,
the room elided, darkness stretched, a blur
zip-studded by red pinlights, hemmed and held   5
a cloth we had no future written on.
Around us, well-dressed women stirred the darkness
as they walked. The bar's cold black streak streamed
past willows, necks swayed in to sup and speak.
I learned the map of textures on your cheek.   10
Benched near the place where others knit limbs, lives,
my body's affirmation—a surprise
to our established friendship. You confessed—
amazing humming of my flesh's yes.

Questions

1. Can you identify the form of "Rubyfruit"? How does the poem's form add a layer of meaning?
2. What details in the poem hint at the speaker's sexual identity?

Exercise: "Autumn Begins in Martins Ferry, Ohio" and "Women"

Rewrite either of the following poems from the perspective of the opposite sex. Then evaluate in what ways the new poem has changed the original's meaning and in what ways the original poem comes through more or less unaltered.

James Wright (1927–1980)

Autumn Begins in Martins Ferry, Ohio   1963

In the Shreve High football stadium,
I think of Polacks nursing long beers in Tiltonsville,
And gray faces of Negroes in the blast furnace at Benwood,
And the ruptured night watchman of Wheeling Steel,
Dreaming of heroes.   5

All the proud fathers are ashamed to go home.
Their women cluck like starved pullets,
Dying for love.

Therefore,
Their sons grow suicidally beautiful   10
At the beginning of October,
And gallop terribly against each other's bodies.

Adrienne Rich (1929–2012)

Women   1968

My three sisters are sitting
on rocks of black obsidian.
For the first time, in this light, I can see who they are.

My first sister is sewing her costume for the procession.
She is going as the Transparent Lady   5
and all her nerves will be visible.

My second sister is also sewing,
at the seam over her heart which has never healed entirely.
At last, she hopes, this tightness in her chest will ease.

My third sister is gazing   10
at a dark-red crust spreading westward far out on the sea.
Her stockings are torn but she is beautiful.

FOR REVIEW AND FURTHER STUDY

Brian Turner (b. 1967)

The Hurt Locker   2005

Nothing but the hurt left here.
Nothing but bullets and pain
and the bled-out slumping
and all the *fucks* and *goddamns*
and *Jesus Christs* of the wounded.   5
Nothing left here but the hurt.

Believe it when you see it.
Believe it when a twelve-year-old
rolls a grenade into the room.
Or when a sniper punches a hole   10
deep into someone's skull.
Believe it when four men
step from a taxicab in Mosul
to shower the street in brass
and fire. Open the hurt locker   15
and see what there is of knives
and teeth. Open the hurt locker and learn
how rough men come hunting for souls.

THE HURT LOCKER. Turner's title, based on military slang he learned in Iraq, is said to have inspired
the title of the 2009 Academy Award–winning film *The Hurt Locker*. 13 *Mosul:* city in northern Iraq.

Questions

1. Who seems to be the speaker of the poem? What clues does the speaker give about his or her background?
2. Where do the memories surfacing in the poem take place?
3. How would you explain the title metaphor? What is a "hurt locker"?
4. Based on this poem, how would you say the experience of combat seems to affect personal identity?

Philip Larkin (1922–1985)

Aubade   1977

I work all day, and get half-drunk at night.
Waking at four to soundless dark, I stare.
In time the curtain-edges will grow light.
Till then I see what's really always there:
Unresting death, a whole day nearer now,   5

Making all thought impossible but how
And where and when I shall myself die.
Arid interrogation: yet the dread
Of dying, and being dead,
Flashes afresh to hold and horrify.   10

The mind blanks at the glare. Not in remorse
—The good not done, the love not given, time
Torn off unused—nor wretchedly because
An only life can take so long to climb
Clear of its wrong beginnings, and may never;   15
But at the total emptiness for ever,
The sure extinction that we travel to
And shall be lost in always. Not to be here,
Not to be anywhere,
And soon; nothing more terrible, nothing more true.   20

This is a special way of being afraid
No trick dispels. Religion used to try,
That vast moth-eaten musical brocade
Created to pretend we never die,
And specious stuff that says *No rational being*   25
Can fear a thing it will not feel, not seeing
That this is what we fear—no sight, no sound,
No touch or taste or smell, nothing to think with,
Nothing to love or link with,
The anaesthetic from which none come round.   30

And so it stays just on the edge of vision,
A small unfocused blur, a standing chill
That slows each impulse down to indecision.
Most things may never happen: this one will,
And realisation of it rages out   35
In furnace-fear when we are caught without
People or drink. Courage is no good:

It means not scaring others. Being brave
Lets no one off the grave.
Death is no different whined at than withstood.   40

Slowly light strengthens, and the room takes shape.
It stands plain as a wardrobe, what we know,
Have always known, know that we can't escape,
Yet can't accept. One side will have to go.
Meanwhile telephones crouch, getting ready to ring   45
In locked-up offices, and all the uncaring
Intricate rented world begins to rouse.
The sky is white as clay, with no sun.
Work has to be done.
Postmen like doctors go from house to house.   50

Questions

1. Is "Aubade" a confessional poem? If so, what social taboo does it violate?
2. What embarrassing facts about the narrator does the poem reveal? Do these confessions lead us to trust or distrust him?
3. The narrator says that "Courage is no good" (line 37). How might he defend this statement?
4. Would a twenty-year-old reader respond differently to this poem than a seventy-year-old one? Would a devout Christian respond differently to the poem than an atheist?

■ WRITING *effectively*

Rhina P. Espaillat on Writing

Being a Bilingual Writer   1998

Recent interest in the phenomenon known as "Spanglish" has led me to reexamine my own experience as a writer who works chiefly in her second language, and especially to recall my father's inflexible rule against the mixing of languages. In fact, no English was allowed in that midtown Manhattan apartment that became home after my arrival in New York in 1939. My father read the daily paper in English, taught himself to follow disturbing events in Europe through the medium of English-language radio, and even taught me to read the daily comic strips, in an effort to speed my learning of the language he knew I would need. But that necessary language was banished from family conversation: it was the medium of the outer world,

Rhina P. Espaillat

beyond the door; inside, among ourselves, only Spanish was permitted, and it had to be pure, grammatical, unadulterated Spanish.

At the age of seven, however, nothing seems more important than communicating with classmates and neighborhood children. For my mother, too, the new language was a way out of isolation, a means to deal with the larger world and with those American women for whom she sewed. But my father, a political exile waiting for changes in our native country, had different priorities: he lived in the hope of return, and believed that the new home, the new speech, were temporary. His theory was simple: if it could be said at all, it could be said best in the language of those authors whose words were the core of his education. But his insistence on pure Spanish made it difficult, sometimes impossible, to bring home and share the jokes of friends, puns, pop lyrics, and other staples of seven-year-old conversation. Table talk sometimes ended with tears or sullen silence.

And yet, despite the friction it caused from time to time, my native language was also a source of comfort—the reading that I loved, intimacy within the family, and a peculiar auditory delight best described as echoes in the mind. I learned early to relish words as counters in a game that could turn suddenly serious without losing the quality of play, and to value their sound as a meaning behind their meaning.

Nostalgia, a confusion of identity, the fear that if the native language is lost the self will somehow be altered forever: all are part of the subtle flavor of immigrant life, as well as the awareness that one owes gratitude to strangers for acts of communication that used to be simple and once imposed no such debt.

Memory, folklore, and food all become part of the receding landscape that language sets out to preserve. Guilt, too, adds to the mix, the suspicion that to love the second language too much is to betray those ancestors who spoke the first and could not communicate with us in the vocabulary of our education, our new thoughts. And finally, a sense of grievance and loss may spur hostility toward the new language and those who speak it, as if the common speech of the perceived majority could weld together a disparate population into a huge, monolithic, and threatening Other. That Other is then assigned traits and habits that preclude sympathy and mold "Us" into a unity whose cohesiveness gives comfort.

Luckily, there is another side to bilingualism: curiosity about the Other may be as natural and pervasive as group loyalty. If it weren't, travel, foreign residence, and intermarriage would be less common than they are. For some bilingual writers, the Other—and the language he speaks—are appealing. Some acknowledge and celebrate the tendency of languages to borrow from each other and produce something different in the process.

From Afterword to Where Horizons Go

THINKING ABOUT POETIC VOICE AND IDENTITY

Every writer strives to find his or her own voice, that distinct mix of subject matter and style that can make an author's work as instantly recognizable as a friend's voice on the phone. Poetic voice reflects matters of style—characteristic tone, word choice, figures of speech, and rhythms—as well as characteristic themes and subjects. Finding an authentic voice has long been a central issue among minority and female poets. In exploring their subjects, which often lie outside the existing poetic traditions, these writers sometimes need to find innovative forms of expression.

- **You will often find it illuminating to consider the author's personal identity when writing about voice in poetry.** Does the poem present any personal details of the author's life or background?
- **Consider whether the poem's subject matter is directly or indirectly shaped by race, gender, age, ethnicity, social class, sexual orientation, or religious beliefs.** If so, how is the viewpoint reflected in the poem's formal aspects (images, tone, metaphors, and so on)?
- **Read the section "Gender Criticism" Chapter 49.** Although that section discusses only one aspect of identity, the general principles it explores relate to the broader question of how an author's life experience may influence the kinds of poetry he or she creates.

CHECKLIST: Writing About Voice and Personal Identity

- ☐ Is the poem's subject matter shaped by an aspect of the poet's identity?
- ☐ Does the poem address issues related to race, gender, social class, ethnicity, sexual orientation, age, or religious beliefs?
- ☐ Does personal identity reveal itself directly or indirectly in the poem's voice or content?
- ☐ If so, *how* does the voice reflect identity? Does it appear in the poem's diction, imagery, tone, metaphors, or sound?

TOPICS FOR WRITING ON PERSONAL IDENTITY

1. Analyze any poem from this chapter from the perspective of its author's race, gender, ethnicity, age, or religious beliefs. Take into account the poem's style—its approach to tone, word choice, figures of speech, and rhythm—as well as its content. You may find it helpful to look at some biographical information on the poem's author, but focus your comments on the information provided by the poem itself.
2. Find another poem in Chapter 34 in which the poet, like Rhina Espaillat, considers his or her own family. In a paragraph or two, describe what the poem reveals about the author.
3. Write an explication of Adrienne Rich's "Women." What argument does the poem seem to be making?
4. Write a brief analysis (750 to 1,000 words) on how color imagery contributes to meaning in Yusef Komunyakaa's "Facing It."
5. Write an imitation of Shirley Geok-lin Lim's "Riding into California," about coming to terms with a place—a state, city, or neighborhood—in which you have lived and felt like an outsider.
6. Write about the personal identity of men and boys as explored in James Wright's "Autumn Begins in Martins Ferry, Ohio."
7. Compare Philip Larkin's "Aubade" with another poem about old age and death, such as William Butler Yeats's "Sailing to Byzantium" (Chapter 30) or Dylan Thomas's "Do not go gentle into that good night" (Chapter 24).

▶ TERMS FOR *review*

Confessional poetry ▶ A poetic genre emerging in the 1950s and 1960s primarily concerned with autobiography and the unexpurgated exposure of the poet's personal life. Notable practioners included Robert Lowell, Sylvia Plath, and Anne Sexton.

Identity poetics ▶ An approach to writing poetry that scrutinizes the forces that help shape the poet's identity, which may include ethnic background, family, race, gender, sexual orientation, religion, economic status, and age.

29

POETRY IN SPANISH
Literature of Latin America

Poetry belongs to all epochs: it is man's natural form of expression.

—OCTAVIO PAZ

What You Will Learn in This Chapter

- To describe the important contributions of Latin American poets to world literature
- To define *Surrealism*
- To describe the works of Sor Juana, Neruda, Borges, and Paz in their cultural context
- To analyze the elements of Surrealism in a poem

Most Americans experience poetry in only one language—English. Because English is a world language, with its native speakers spread across every continent, it is easy for us to underestimate the significance of poetry written in other tongues. Why is it important to experience poetry in a different language or in translation? It matters because such poetry represents and illuminates a different cultural experience. Exposure to different cultures enriches our perspectives and challenges our assumptions; it also helps us to understand our own culture better.

Latin American poetry is particularly relevant to the English speaker in the United States or Canada because of the long interconnected history of the Americas. Spanish is also an important world language, spoken by almost 400 million people and the primary language in more than twenty countries. The vast spread of Spanish has created an enormous and prominent body of literature, an international tradition in which Latin America has gradually replaced Spain as the center. Poetry occupies a very significant place in Latin American culture—a more public place than in the United States. Poetry even forms an important part of the popular culture in Latin America, where the average person is able to name his or her favorite poets and can often recite some of their works from memory.

The tradition of Latin American poetry is long and rich. Many poets and scholars consider Sor Juana, a Catholic nun who lived in Mexico during the seventeenth century, to be the mother of Latin American poetry. Mexico's Nobel Laureate poet, Octavio Paz, acknowledges this lineage in his critical work on Sor Juana, *Traps of Faith* (1988), a quintessential book about her life and work. Sor Juana's writing was groundbreaking, not just in the context of Latin American poetry, but truly in the context of world literature, as she was the first writer in Latin America (and one of very few in her era) to address the rights of women to study and write. Her poems are also harbingers of important tendencies in Latin American poetry because of their heightened lyricism.

This lyrical quality finds new form and vitality in the works of the most widely known poets of Latin America—including César Vallejo, Pablo Neruda, Jorge Luis Borges, and Octavio Paz. Each of these poets addresses questions of cultural and personal identity in his work. Events of the twentieth century had great impact on both the subject matter and style of Latin American poets. The Spanish Civil War (1936–1939) sent many poets who had been living in Europe back to the Americas, conscious of the political and social values being tried and tested in Europe at the time.

Latin American poetry, particularly in the twentieth century, has been marked by a recognition of the region as a unique blending of different cultures, European and indigenous, among others. It has also been marked by a variety of artistic and political movements, of which Surrealism is perhaps the most influential. The works of artists such as Mexican painter Frida Kahlo coincided with a body of new writing that emphasized a blurring of fantasy and reality. Some writers, such as Vallejo, became best known for their Surrealist writing, while other poets, such as Neruda and Paz, incorporated some elements of the movement into their styles.

Three Latin American poets were awarded the Nobel Prize in Literature in the twentieth century: Paz, Neruda, and Gabriela Mistral. (Borges, to the astonishment of many readers and critics, never won the award, though he captured nearly every other major international literary honor.) The importance of Spanish as a global language and in literature is reflected in the recognition of the stature of Latin American writers in the world. Even when decidedly political, Latin American poetry is known for its focus on the personal experience. One does not love one's country as a symbol, José Emilio Pacheco claims; rather, one loves its people, its mountains, and three or four of its rivers.

Sor Juana

Sor Juana Inés de la Cruz is said to have been born in Nepantla, Mexico, somewhere between 1648 and 1651. In 1667, she entered the convent of the "barefoot Carmelites," so named because of the austere way of life they adopted, either going barefoot or wearing rope sandals. In 1691 she wrote her famous Reply, *the first document in the Americas to argue for a woman's right to study and to write. She stated that she chose the convent life because it offered her more possibilities for engaging in intellectual pursuits than marriage at that time would allow. The Church responded by demanding she give up writing, and she renewed her vows to the Church, signing documents in her own blood. Sor Juana died during a devastating plague in 1695, after having given aid to a great number of the ill.*

Portrait of Sor Juana Inés de la Cruz
(by unknown Mexican artist, eighteenth century)

Presente en que el Cariño Hace Regalo la Llaneza 1689	A Simple Gift Made Rich by Affection 2004
Lysi: a tus manos divinas	Lysi, I give to your divine hand
doy castañas espinosas,	these chestnuts in their thorny guise
porque donde sobran rosas	because where velvet roses rise,
no pueden faltar espinas.	thorns also grow unchecked, unplanned.
Si a su aspereza te inclinas	If you're inclined toward their barbed brand 5
y con eso el gusto engañas,	and with this choice, betray your taste,
perdona las malas mañas	forgive the ill-bred lack of taste
de quien tal regalo te hizo;	of one who sends you such a missive—
perdona, pues que un erizo	Forgive me, only this husk can give
sólo puede dar castañas.	the chestnut, in its thorns embraced. 10

—*Translated by Diane Thiel*

Questions

1. How would you relate the title to the content of the poem?
2. Why does the speaker reject a gift of roses? Why does she fear that her gift may be rejected by its recipient?
3. How does the chestnut function as a metaphor? What does the thorny husk seem to represent? What does the chestnut represent?

Pablo Neruda

Pablo Neruda was born Neftali Ricardo Reyes Basoalto in 1904 in Parral, southern Chile. His mother died a month later, a fact which is said to have affected Neruda's choice of imagery throughout his life's work. He began writing poems as a child despite his family's disapproval, which led him to adopt the "working class" pen name Pablo Neruda. His early book Twenty Love Poems and a Song of Despair *(1924), published when Neruda was only nineteen years old, received vast attention, and he decided to devote himself to writing poetry.*

Neruda served in a long line of diplomatic positions. He lived several years in Spain and chronicled the Spanish Civil War. He journeyed home to Chile in 1938, then served as consul to Mexico, and returned again to Chile in 1943.

Pablo Neruda

When the Chilean government moved to the right, Neruda, who was a communist, went into hiding.

In 1952, when the Chilean government ceased its persecution of leftist writers, Neruda returned to his native land and in 1970 was nominated for the presidency of Chile, but he ultimately declined the run for the position. He was awarded the Nobel Prize in Literature in 1971. Neruda died in Santiago in 1973.

Pablo Neruda

Muchos Somos 1958	**We Are Many** 1967

De tantos hombres que soy,
  que somos,
no puedo encontrar a ninguno:
se me pierden bajo la ropa,
se fueron a otra ciudad.

Cuando todo está preparado
para mostrarme inteligente
el tonto que llevo escondido
se toma la palabra en mi boca.

Otras veces me duermo en medio
de la sociedad distinguida
y cuando busco en mí al valiente,
un cobarde que no conozco
corre a tomar con mi esqueleto
mil deliciosas precauciones.

Cuando arde una casa estimada
en vez del bombero que llamo
se precipita el incendiario
y ése soy yo. No tengo arreglo.
Qué debo hacer para escogerme?
Cómo puedo rehabilitarme?

Todos los libros que leo
celebran héroes refulgentes
siempre seguros de sí mismos:
me muero de envidia por ellos,
y en los filmes de vientos y balas
me quedo envidiando al jinete,
me quedo admirando al caballo.

Pero cuando pido al intrépido
me sale el viejo perezoso,
y así yo no sé quién soy,
no sé cuántos soy o seremos.
Me gustaría tocar un timbre
y sacar el mí verdadero
porque si yo me necesito
no debo desaparecerme.

Of the many men who I am, who
  we are,
I can't find a single one;   5
they disappear among my clothes,
they've left for another city.

When everything seems to be set   5
to show me off as intelligent,
the fool I always keep hidden
takes over all that I say.

At other times, I'm asleep
among distinguished people,   10
and when I look for my brave self,
a coward unknown to me
rushes to cover my skeleton
with a thousand fine excuses.

When a decent house catches fire,   15
instead of the fireman I summon,
an arsonist bursts on the scene,
and that's me. What can I do?
What can I do to distinguish myself?
How can I pull myself together?   20

All the books I read
are full of dazzling heroes,
always sure of themselves.
I die with envy of them;
and in films full of wind and bullets,   25
I goggle at the cowboys,
I even admire the horses.

But when I call for a hero,
out comes my lazy old self;
so I never know who I am,   30
nor how many I am or will be.
I'd love to be able to touch a bell
and summon the real me,
because if I really need myself,
I mustn't disappear.   35

Mientras escribo estoy ausente	While I am writing, I'm far away;
y cuando vuelvo ya he partido:	and when I come back, I've gone.
voy a ver si a las otras gentes	I would like to know if others
les pasa lo que a mí me pasa,	go through the same things that I do,
si son tantos como soy yo,	have as many selves as I have, 40
si se parecen a sí mismos	and see themselves similarly;
y cuando lo haya averiguado	and when I've exhausted this problem,
voy a aprender tan bien las cosas	I'm going to study so hard
que para explicar mis problemas	that when I explain myself,
les hablaré de geografía.	I'll be talking geography. 45

—*Translated by Alastair Reid*

Questions

1. In line 26, Reid translates Neruda's phrase "me quedo envidiando al jinete" as "I goggle at the cowboys." What does Reid gain or lose with that version? (In Spanish, *jinete* means *horseman* or *rider* but not specifically *cowboy*, which is *vaquero* or even—thanks to Hollywood—*cowboy*.) Neruda once told Reid, "Alastair, don't just translate my poems. I want you to improve them." Is this line an improvement?

2. How many men are represented by the speaker of the poem? What seems to be their relationship to one another?

Jorge Luis Borges

Jorge Luis Borges

Jorge Luis Borges (1899–1986), a blind librarian who became one of the most important writers ever to emerge from Latin America, was born in Buenos Aires. Borges's Protestant father and Catholic mother reflected Argentina's diverse background; their ancestry included Spanish, English, Italian, Portuguese, and Indian blood. In his youth, Borges lived in Switzerland and later Spain. On returning to Argentina in 1921, he edited a poetry magazine printed in the form of a poster and affixed to city walls. In 1937, to help support his mother and dying father, the thirty-seven-year-old Borges (who still lived at home) got his first job as an assistant librarian.

During this decisive period, Borges encountered political trouble. For his opposition to the regime of Colonel Juan Perón, Borges was forced in 1946 to resign his post as a librarian and was mockingly offered a job as a chicken inspector. In 1955, after Perón was deposed, Borges became director of the National Library and a professor of English literature at the University of Buenos Aires. Suffering from poor eyesight since childhood, Borges eventually went blind. Probably the most influential short story writer of the last half-century, Borges considered himself first and foremost a poet.

Jorge Luis Borges

On his blindness 1985	On His Blindness 1994
Al cabo de los años me rodea	In the fullness of the years, like it or not,
una terca neblina luminosa	a luminous mist surrounds me, unvarying,
que reduce las cosas a una cosa	that breaks things down into a single thing,
sin forma ni color. Casi a una idea.	colorless, formless. Almost into a thought.
La vasta noche elemental y el día	The elemental, vast night and the day 5
lleno de gente son esa neblina	teeming with people have become that fog
de luz dudosa y fiel que no declina	of constant, tentative light that does not flag,
y que acecha en el alba. Yo querría	and lies in wait at dawn. I longed to see
ver una cara alguna vez. Ignoro	just once a human face. Unknown to me
la inexplorada enciclopedia, el goce	the closed encyclopedia, the sweet play 10
de libros que mi mano reconoce,	in volumes I can do no more than hold,
las altas aves y las lunas de oro.	the tiny soaring birds, the moons of gold.
A los otros les queda el universo;	Others have the world, for better or worse;
a mi penumbra, el hábito del verso.	I have this half-dark, and the toil of verse.

—Translated by Robert Mezey

Questions

1. Borges's Spanish original has an English title. Why would he use English? (Hint: Look at John Milton's poem in Chapter 34.)
2. What is the form of the poem?
3. What images and metaphors does Borges use to describe his blindness?

Octavio Paz

Octavio Paz

Octavio Paz, the only Mexican author to win the Nobel Prize in Literature, was born in Mexico City in 1914. Paz once commented that he came from "a typical Mexican family" because it combined European and indigenous ancestors. "Impoverished by the revolution and civil war," his family lived in his grandfather's huge, crumbling house in Mixoac, a suburb of Mexico City, where they abandoned rooms one by one as the roof collapsed. His grandfather had a library containing more than six thousand books in which the young author immersed himself. Joining his father in exile, the young Paz lived for two years in Los Angeles, and later went to Spain to fight in the Spanish Civil War. In the highly political world of Latin American letters, Paz refused to adopt the political opinions of the two extremes—military dictatorship or Marxist revolution—but worked toward democracy, "the mystery of freedom," as he called it in an early poem.

In 1945 Paz became a diplomat, spending years in San Francisco, New York, Geneva, and Delhi. In 1968 he resigned his post as ambassador to India in protest of the Mexican government's massacre of student demonstrators shortly before the Mexico City Olympic games. Paz then taught abroad at several universities, but he always returned to Mexico City, where he died in 1998.

Con los ojos cerrados	1968	With eyes closed	1986

Con los ojos cerrados
te iluminas por dentro
eres la piedra ciega

Noche a noche te labro
con los ojos cerrados
eres la piedra franca

Nos volvemos inmensos
sólo por conocernos
con los ojos cerrados

With eyes closed
you light up within
you are blind stone

Night after night I carve you
with eyes closed   5
you are frank stone

We have become enormous
just knowing each other
with eyes closed

               —*Translated by Eliot Weinberger*

Question

How does the refrain contribute to the musical quality of "With eyes closed"?

SURREALISM IN LATIN AMERICAN POETRY

Surrealism was one of the great artistic revolutions of the twentieth century. It first arose in the mockingly named "Dada" movement during World War I. (*Dada* is the French children's word for "rocking horse.") Dadaism announced itself as the radical rejection of the insanity perpetrated by the self-proclaimed "rational" world of the turbulent modern era. The approach was an attempt to shock the world out of its terrible self-destructive traditions. "The only way for Dada to continue," proclaimed poet André Breton, "is for it to cease to exist." Sure enough, the movement soon fell apart through its own excesses of energy, irreverence, and absurdism.

In 1922 **Surrealism** emerged as the successor to Dada, first as a literary movement, soon to spread to the visual arts. Surrealism also sought to free art from the bounds of rationality, promoting the creation of fantastic, dreamlike works that reflected the unconscious mind. Breton's famous "Manifesto of Surrealism" (1924) launched a movement that continues to influence a great number of writers and artists around the world.

Surrealism emphasized spontaneity rather than craft as the essential element in literary creation. Not all Surrealist art, however, was spontaneous. Breton, for instance, spent six months on a poem of thirty words, in order to achieve what looked like spontaneity. And many Surrealist visual artists would do several versions of the same "automatic drawing" in pursuit of the effect of immediacy.

The early Surrealists showed as much genius for absurd humor as for art, and their works often tried to shock and amuse. Marcel Duchamp once exhibited a huge printed reproduction of the *Mona Lisa* on which he had painted a large mustache. Louis Aragon's poem "Suicide" consisted only of the letters of the alphabet, and Breton once published a poem made up of names and numbers copied from the telephone directory. Is it any wonder that the Surrealist motto was "The approval of the public must be shunned at all cost"?

Surrealism's greatest international literary influence was on Latin American poetry. In the early twentieth century, Latin America was much influenced by French culture, and literary innovations in Paris were quickly imported to Mexico City, Buenos Aires, and other New World capitals. In Latin America, however, Surrealism lost much of the playfulness it exhibited in Europe, and the movement often took on a darker and more explicitly political quality. According to Octavio Paz, many poets, such as himself, César Vallejo, and Pablo Neruda, adopted Surrealist processes, and their creative developments often coincided with the movement, although their work is not usually considered "Surrealist."

Surrealism also had a powerful effect on Latin American art. A tradition of Surrealist painting emerged parallel to the movement in literature. One of the best known Surrealist painters is the Mexican artist Frida Kahlo, whose work often created dreamlike visions of the human body, especially her own. In *The Two Fridas*, for example, she presents a frightening image of the body's interior exposed and mirrored. Kahlo's paintings are simultaneously personal and political—surrealistically portraying her own trauma as well as the schism in her native country.

Frida Kahlo (1907–1954) beside her painting, *The Two Fridas*, c. 1939.

César Vallejo (1892–1938)

La cólera que quiebra al hombre en niños   (1937) 1939

La cólera que quiebra al hombre en niños,
que quiebra al niño en pájaros iguales,
y al pájaro, después, en huevecillos;
la cólera del pobre
tiene un aceite contra dos vinagres.   5

La cólera que el árbol quiebra en hojas,
a la hoja en botones desiguales
y al botón, en ranuras telescópicas;
la cólera del pobre
tiene dos ríos contra muchos mares.   10

La cólera que quiebra al bien en dudas,
a la duda, en tres arcos semejantes
y al arco, luego, en tumbas imprevistas;
la cólera del pobre
tiene un acero contra dos puñales.   15

La cólera que quiebra el alma en cuerpos,
al cuerpo en órganos desemejantes
y al órgano, en octavos pensamientos;
la cólera del pobre
tiene un fuego central contra dos cráteres.   20

The anger that breaks the man into children   2017

The anger that breaks the man into children,
that breaks the child into equal birds,
and the bird, after, into little eggs;
the anger of the poor
has one oil against two vinegars.   5

The anger that breaks the tree into leaves,
the leaf into unequal buds
and the bud into telescopic grooves;
the anger of the poor
has two rivers against many seas.   10

The anger that breaks the good into doubts,
the doubt into three similar arcs
and the arc, then, into unforeseen tombs;
the anger of the poor
has one steel against two daggers.   15

The anger that breaks the soul into bodies,
the body into dissimilar organs
and the organ into eighths of thoughts;
the anger of the poor
has one central fire against two craters.   20

—*Translated by Kimberly Gooden*

CONTEMPORARY MEXICAN POETRY

José Emilio Pacheco (1939–2014)

Alta Traición   1969

No amo mi Patria. Su fulgor abstracto
es inasible.
Pero (aunque suene mal) daría la vida
por diez lugares suyos, cierta gente,
puertos, bosques de pinos, fortalezas,   5
una ciudad deshecha, gris, monstruosa,
varias figuras de su historia,
montañas
(y tres o cuatro ríos)

High Treason   1978

I do not love my country. Its abstract lustre
is beyond my grasp.
But (although it sounds bad) I would give my life
for ten places in it, for certain people,
seaports, pinewoods, fortresses,   5
a run-down city, gray, grotesque,
various figures from its history,
mountains
(and three or four rivers).

—*Translated by Alastair Reid*

■ WRITING *effectively*

Alastair Reid on Writing (1926–2014)

Translating Neruda   1996

Translating someone's work, poetry in particular, has something about it akin to
being possessed, haunted. Translating a poem means not only reading it deeply and
deciphering it, but clambering about backstage among the props and the scaffolding.
I found I could no longer read a poem of Neruda's simply as words on a page without
hearing behind them that languid, caressing voice. Most important to me in translating these two writers [Neruda and Borges] was the sound of their voices in my memory, for it very much helped in finding the English appropriate to those voices. I found
that if I learned poems of Neruda's by heart I could replay them at odd moments, on
buses, at wakeful times in the night, until, at a certain point, the translation would

somehow set. The voice was the clue: I felt that all Neruda's poems were fundamentally vocative—spoken poems, poems of direct address—and that Neruda's voice was in a sense the instrument for which he wrote. He once made a tape for me, reading pieces of different poems, in different tones and rhythms. I played it over so many times that I can hear it in my head at will. Two lines of his I used to repeat like a Zen koan, for they seemed to apply particularly to translating:

> in this net it's not just the strings that count
> but also the air that escapes through the meshes.

He often wrote of himself as having many selves, just as he had left behind him several very different poetic manners and voices.

From "Neruda and Borges"

TOPICS FOR WRITING ON SPANISH POETRY

1. Compare the two love poems in this chapter—Sor Juana's "A Simple Gift Made Rich by Affection" and Octavio Paz's "With eyes closed." Analyze each poem's presentation of the beloved and contrast it to the presentation in the other poem.

2. Consider the surreal effects in César Vallejo's "The anger that breaks the man into children," as well as in Frida Kahlo's painting *The Two Fridas*.

3. Consider the way personal and political themes merge in José Emilio Pacheco's "High Treason" or César Vallejo's "The anger that breaks the man into children."

4. Compare Jorge Luis Borges's sonnet "On his blindness" with John Milton's sonnet "When I consider how my light is spent" in Chapter 34 (from which Borges drew his title). How do their reactions to their disability differ? Are they similar in any significant ways?

30 CELEBRATING EXCELLENCE

Poetry is life distilled.

—GWENDOLYN BROOKS

What You Will Learn in This Chapter

- To describe the challenges of evaluating a poem
- To define *sentimentality*
- To recognize and define *literary conventions*
- To understand the role of evaluation in analyzing a poem

Why do we call some poems "bad"? We are not talking about their moral implications. Rather, we mean that, for one or more of many possible reasons, the poem has failed to move us or to engage our sympathies. Instead, it has made us doubt that the poet is in control of language and vision; perhaps it has aroused our antipathies or unwittingly appealed to our sense of the comic, though the poet is serious. Some poems can be said to succeed despite burdensome faults. But in general such faults are symptoms of a deeper malady: some weakness in a poem's basic conception or in the poet's competence.

THE EFFECT A POEM MAKES

Nearly always, a bad poem reveals only a dim and distorted awareness of its probable effect on its audience. Perhaps the sound of words may clash with what a poem is saying, as in the jarring last word of this opening line of a tender lyric (author unknown, quoted by Richard Wilbur): "Come into the tent, my love, and close the flap." A bad poem usually overshoots or falls short of its mark by the poet's thinking too little or too much.

In a poem that has a rime scheme or a set line length, when all is well, pattern and structure move inseparably with the rest of the poem, the way a tiger's skin and bones move with the tiger. But sometimes, in a poem that fails, the poet evidently has had difficulty in fitting the statements into a formal pattern. English poets have long felt free to invert word order for a special effect (Milton: "ye myrtles brown"). This change of normal word order, usually done for purposes of meter or rime, is called **poetic inversion**. The poet having trouble keeping to a rime scheme may invert words for no apparent reason but convenience. Needing a rime for *barge* may lead to ending a line with *a police dog large* instead of *a large police dog*. Another sign of trouble is a profusion of adjectives. If a line of iambic pentameter reads "Her lovely skin, like dear sweet white old silk," we suspect the poet of stuffing the line to make it long enough.

Even Great Poets Stumble

Even great poets write awful poems, and after their deaths, their worst efforts are collected with their masterpieces with no consumer warning labels to inform the reader. Some lines in the canon of celebrated bards make us wonder, "How could they have written this?" Wordsworth, Shelley, Whitman, and Browning are among the great whose failures can be painful, and sometimes even an excellent poem will have a bad spot in it. To be unwilling to read them, though, would be as ill advised as to refuse to see Venice just because the Grand Canal is said to contain impurities. The seasoned reader of poetry thinks no less of Tennyson for having written the lines "Form, Form, Riflemen Form! . . . // Look to your butts, and take good aims!" The collected works of a duller poet may contain no such lines of unconscious double meaning, but neither do they contain any poem as good as "Ulysses." If the duller poet never had a spectacular failure, it may be because of a failure to take risks. "In poetry," said Pierre de Ronsard, "the greatest vice is mediocrity."

How Poems Can Fail

Often, inept poems fall into familiar categories. At one extreme is the poem written entirely in conventional diction, dimly echoing Shakespeare, Wordsworth, and the Bible, but garbling them. Couched in a rhythm that ticks along like a metronome, this kind of poem shows no sign that its author has ever taken a hard look at anything that can be tasted, handled, or felt. It employs loosely and thoughtlessly the most abstract of words: *love, beauty, life, death, time, eternity*. Littered with old-fashioned contractions (*'tis, o'er, where'er*), it may end in a simple preachment or platitude. George Orwell's complaint against much contemporary writing (not only poetry) is applicable: "As soon as certain topics are raised"—and one thinks of such standard topics for poetry as spring, a first kiss, and stars—"the concrete melts into the abstract and no one seems able to think of turns of speech that are not hackneyed."

At the opposite extreme is the poem that displays no acquaintance with poetry of the past but manages, instead, to fabricate its own clichés. Slightly paraphrased, a manuscript once submitted to the *Paris Review* began:

> Vile
>
>   rottenflush
>
>   o   —screaming—   ooze
>
>   f CORPSEBLOOD!!
>
> STRANGLE my
>
>   *eyes. . .*
>
>   HELL's
>
>   O, ghastly   stench**!!!

At most, such a work has only a private value. The writer has vented personal frustrations upon words, instead of kicking stray dogs. In its way, "Vile Rottenflush" is as self-indulgent as the oldfangled "first kiss in spring" kind of poem. "I dislike," said John Livingston Lowes, "poems that black your eyes, or put up their mouths to be kissed."

Comparing Poems

As jewelers tell which of two diamonds is fine by seeing which scratches the other, two poems may be tested by comparing them. This method works only on poems similar in length and kind: an epigram cannot be held up to test an epic. Most poems we meet are neither sheer trash nor obvious masterpieces. Because good diamonds to be proven need softer ones to scratch, in this chapter you will find a few clear-cut gems and a few clinkers.

Anonymous (English)

O Moon, when I gaze on thy beautiful face   (about 1900)

O Moon, when I gaze on thy beautiful face,
Careering along through the boundaries of space,
The thought has often come into my mind
If I ever shall see thy glorious behind.

O MOON. Sir Edmund Gosse, the English critic (1849–1928), offered this quatrain as the work of his servant, but there is reason to suspect him of having written it.

Questions

1. To what fact of astronomy does the last line refer?
2. Which words seem chosen with too little awareness of their denotations and connotations?
3. Even if you did not know that these lines probably were deliberately bad, how would you argue with someone who maintained that the opening "O" in the poem was admirable as a bit of concrete poetry?

Emily Dickinson (1830–1886)

Safe in their Alabaster Chambers   (1861 version)

Safe in their Alabaster Chambers –
Untouched by Morning
And untouched by Noon –
Lie the meek members of the Resurrection –
Rafter of Satin – and Roof of Stone!   5

Grand go the Years – in the Crescent – above them –
Worlds scoop their Arcs –
And Firmaments – row –
Diadems – drop – and Doges – surrender –
Soundless as dots – on a Disc of Snow –   10

Question

How does this poem compare in success with other poems of Emily Dickinson that you know? Justify your opinion by pointing to some of this poem's particulars.

Exercise: Five Terrible Moments in Poetry

Here is a small anthology of bad moments in poetry. For what reasons does each selection fail? In which passages do you attribute the failure

to inappropriate sound or diction?
to awkward word order?
to inaccurate metaphor?
to forced rime?
to monotonous rhythm?
to simple-mindedness or excessive ingenuity?

1. From *Purely Original Verse* (1891) by J. Gordon Coogler (1865–1901), of Columbia, South Carolina:

   > Alas for the South, her books have grown fewer—
   > She never was much given to literature.

2. From *Dolce Far Niente* by the American poet Francis Saltus Saltus, who flourished in the 1890s:

   > Her laugh is like sunshine, full of glee,
   > And her sweet breath smells like fresh-made tea.

3. From "The Abbey Mason" by Thomas Hardy:

   > When longer yet dank death had wormed
   > The brain wherein the style had germed
   >
   > From Gloucester church it flew afar—
   > The style called Perpendicular.—
   >
   > To Winton and to Westminster
   > It ranged, and grew still beautifuller . . .

4. A metaphor from "The Crucible of Life" by the once-popular American newspaper poet Edgar A. Guest:

   > Sacred and sweet is the joy that must come
   > From the furnace of life when you've poured off the scum.

5. From an elegy for Queen Victoria by one of her subjects:

   > Dust to dust, and ashes to ashes,
   > Into the tomb the Great Queen dashes.

SENTIMENTALITY

Sentimentality is a failure of writers who seem to feel a great emotion but who fail to give us sufficient grounds for sharing it. The emotion may be an anger greater than its object seems to call for, as in these lines by Ali Hilmi to a girl who caused scandal (the exact nature of her act never being specified):

> The gossip in each hall
> Will curse your name . . .
> Go! better cast yourself right down the falls!

The sentimental poet is especially prone to tenderness. Great tears fill his eyes at a glimpse of an aged grandmother sitting by a hearth. For all the poet knows, she may be the manager of a casino in Las Vegas who would be startled to find herself an object of pity, but the sentimentalist doesn't care to know about the woman herself. She is a general excuse for feeling maudlin. Any other conventional object will serve as well: a faded valentine, the strains of an old song, a baby's cast-off pacifier. An instance of such emotional self-indulgence is "The Old Oaken Bucket," by Samuel Woodworth, a stanza of which goes:

> How sweet from the green mossy brim to receive it,
>   As, poised on the curb, it inclined to my lips!
> Not a full-flushing goblet could tempt me to leave it,
>   Tho' filled with the nectar that Jupiter sips.
> And now, far removed from the loved habitation,
>   The tear of regret will intrusively swell,
> As fancy reverts to my father's plantation,
>   And sighs for the bucket which hangs in the well.

The staleness of the phrasing and imagery (Jove's nectar, *tear of regret*) suggests that the speaker is not even seeing the actual physical bucket, and the tripping meter of the lines is inappropriate to an expression of tearful regret. Perhaps the poet's nostalgia is genuine. Indeed, as Keith Waldrop has put it, "a bad poem is always sincere."

RECOGNIZING EXCELLENCE

How can we tell an excellent poem from any other? With poetry, explaining excellence is harder than explaining failure (so often due to familiar kinds of imprecision and sentimentality). A bad poem tends to be stereotyped, an excellent poem unique. In judging either, we can have no absolute specifications. A poem is not like an electric toaster that an inspector can test using a check-off list. It has to be judged on the basis of what it is trying to be and how well it succeeds in the effort.

To judge a poem, we first have to understand it. At least, we need to understand it *almost* all the way; to be sure, there are poems such as Hopkins's "The Windhover" (Chapter 34) which most readers probably would call excellent even though their meaning are still being debated. Although it is a good idea to give a poem at least a couple of considerate readings before judging it, sometimes our first encounter starts turning into an act of evaluation. Moving along into the poem, becoming more deeply involved in it, we may begin forming an opinion. In general, the more a poem contains for us to understand, the more rewarding we are likely to find it. Difficult poems can be pretentious and incoherent; still, there is something to be said for the poem complicated enough to leave us something to discover on our fifteenth reading (unlike most limericks, which yield their all at a look). Here is such a poem, one not readily fathomed and exhausted.

William Butler Yeats (1865–1939)

Sailing to Byzantium   1927

I

That is no country for old men. The young
In one another's arms, birds in the trees
—Those dying generations—at their song,
The salmon-falls, the mackerel-crowded seas,
Fish, flesh, or fowl, commend all summer long   5
Whatever is begotten, born, and dies.
Caught in that sensual music all neglect
Monuments of unaging intellect.

II

An aged man is but a paltry thing,
A tattered coat upon a stick, unless   10
Soul clap its hands and sing, and louder sing
For every tatter in its mortal dress,
Nor is there singing school but studying
Monuments of its own magnificence;
And therefore I have sailed the seas and come   15
To the holy city of Byzantium.

III

O sages standing in God's holy fire
As in the gold mosaic of a wall,
Come from the holy fire, perne in a gyre,°   *spin down a spiral*
And be the singing-masters of my soul.   20
Consume my heart away; sick with desire
And fastened to a dying animal
It knows not what it is; and gather me
Into the artifice of eternity.

IV

Once out of nature I shall never take   25
My bodily form from any natural thing,
But such a form as Grecian goldsmiths make
Of hammered gold and gold enameling
To keep a drowsy Emperor awake;
Or set upon a golden bough to sing   30
To lords and ladies of Byzantium
Of what is past, or passing, or to come.

SAILING TO BYZANTIUM. Byzantium was the capital of the Byzantine Empire, the city now called Istanbul. Yeats means, though, not merely the physical city. Byzantium is also a name for his conception of paradise. 1 *no country for old men:* a line that provided the title for Cormac McCarthy's masterful 2005 novel and for the Coen brothers' 2007 Academy Award-winning film adaptation.

Though *salmon-falls* (line 4) suggests Yeats's native Ireland, the poem, as we find out in line 25, is about escaping from the entire natural world. If the poet desires this escape, then probably the *country* of the opening line is no political nation but the cycle of birth and death in which human beings are trapped; and, indeed, the poet says his heart is "fastened to a dying animal." Imaginary landscapes, it would seem, are merging with the historical Byzantium. Lines 17–18 refer to mosaic images, adornments of the Byzantine cathedral of St. Sophia, in which the figures of saints are inlaid against backgrounds of gold. The clockwork bird of the last stanza is also a reference to something actual. Yeats noted: "I have read somewhere that in the Emperor's palace at Byzantium was a tree made of gold and silver, and artificial birds that sang." This description of the role the poet would seek—that of a changeless, immortal singer—directs us back to the earlier references to music and singing. Taken all together, they point toward the central metaphor of the poem: the craft of poetry can be a kind of singing. One kind of everlasting monument is a great poem.

To study masterpieces of poetry is the only "singing school"—the only way to learn to write a poem.

Yeats's poem makes us aware of relationships between what a person can imagine and the physical world. There is the statement that a human heart is bound to the body that perishes, and yet it is possible to see consciousness for a moment independent of flesh, to sing with joy at the very fact that the body is crumbling away. Much of the power of Yeats's poem comes from the physical terms with which he states the ancient quarrel between body and spirit, body being a "tattered coat upon a stick."

Yeats's poem has the three qualities essential to beauty, according to the definition of Thomas Aquinas: wholeness, harmony, and radiance. The poem is all one; its parts move in peace with one another; it shines with emotional intensity. There is an orderly progression going on in it: from the speaker's statement of his discontent with the world of "sensual music" to his statement that he is quitting this world, to his prayer that the sages will take him in, and his vision of future immortality. And the images of the poem relate to one another—*dying generations* (line 3), *dying animal* (line 22), and the undying golden bird (lines 27–32)—to mention just one series of related things.

"Sailing to Byzantium" has a theme that matters to us. What human being does not long, at times, to transcend timid, imperfect flesh, to live in a state of absolute joy, unperishing? Being human, perhaps we too are stirred by Yeats's prayer: "Consume my heart away; sick with desire / And fastened to a dying animal. . . ." If it is true that in poetry, as Ezra Pound declared, "only emotion endures," then Yeats's poem ought to endure.

Most excellent poems, it might be argued, contain significant themes, as does "Sailing to Byzantium." But the presence of such a theme is not enough to render a poem excellent. No theme alone makes an excellent poem, but rather how well the theme is stated.

Exercise: Two Poems to Compare

Here are two poems with a similar theme. Which contains more qualities of excellent poetry? Decide whether the other is bad or whether it may be praised for achieving something different.

Arthur Guiterman (1871–1943)

On the Vanity of Earthly Greatness   1936

The tusks that clashed in mighty brawls
Of mastodons, are billiard balls.

The sword of Charlemagne the Just
Is ferric oxide, known as rust.

The grizzly bear whose potent hug   5
Was feared by all, is now a rug.

Great Caesar's bust is on the shelf,
And I don't feel so well myself.

Percy Bysshe Shelley (1792–1822)

Ozymandias   1819

I met a traveler from an antique land
Who said: Two vast and trunkless legs of stone
Stand in the desert. . . . Near them, on the sand,
Half sunk, a shattered visage lies, whose frown,
And wrinkled lip, and sneer of cold command,   5
Tell that its sculptor well those passions read
Which yet survive, stamped on these lifeless things,
The hand that mocked° them, and the heart that fed: *imitated*
And on the pedestal these words appear:
"My name is Ozymandias, king of kings: 10
Look on my works, ye Mighty, and despair!"
Nothing beside remains. Round the decay
Of that colossal wreck, boundless and bare
The lone and level sands stretch far away.

There is no predictable pattern for poetic excellence. A reader needs to remain
open to surprise and innovation. Remember, too, that a superb poem is not necessarily an uplifting one—full of noble sentiments and inspiring ideas. Some powerful
poems deal with difficult and even unpleasant subjects. What matters is the compelling quality of the presentation, the evocative power of the language, and the depth
of feeling and perception achieved by the total work.

Robert Hayden (1913–1980)

Frederick Douglass   1947

When it is finally ours, this freedom, this liberty, this beautiful
and terrible thing, needful to man as air,
usable as earth; when it belongs at last to all,
when it is truly instinct, brain matter, diastole, systole,
reflex action; when it is finally won; when it is more   5
than the gaudy mumbo jumbo of politicians:
this man, this Douglass, this former slave, this Negro
beaten to his knees, exiled, visioning a world
where none is lonely, none hunted, alien,
this man, superb in love and logic, this man   10
shall be remembered. Oh, not with statues' rhetoric,
not with legends and poems and wreaths of bronze alone,
but with the lives grown out of his life, the lives
fleshing his dream of the beautiful, needful thing.

FREDERICK DOUGLASS. Frederick Douglass (1818–1895), a freed slave, became the most influential
African American abolitionist in America and later an eloquent advocate for civil rights for eman-
cipated slaves.

Questions

1. What is unusual about the sentence structure of this poem?
2. What is the "it" repeatedly invoked in the poem?
3. When will this "it" be realized?

A **convention**, in literature, is any established feature or technique that is commonly understood by both authors and readers. A convention is something generally agreed on to be appropriate for customary uses, such as the sonnet form for a love poem or the opening "Once upon a time" for a fairy tale. Sometimes poets use conventions in an innovative way, stretching the rules for new expressive ends. Here Elizabeth Bishop takes the form of the villanelle and bends the rules to give her poem a heartbreaking effect.

Elizabeth Bishop (1911–1979)

One Art   1976

The art of losing isn't hard to master;
so many things seem filled with the intent
to be lost that their loss is no disaster.

Lose something every day. Accept the fluster
of lost door keys, the hour badly spent.   5
The art of losing isn't hard to master.

Then practice losing farther, losing faster:
places, and names, and where it was you meant
to travel. None of these will bring disaster.

I lost my mother's watch. And look! my last, or   10
next-to-last, of three loved houses went.
The art of losing isn't hard to master.

I lost two cities, lovely ones. And, vaster,
some realms I owned, two rivers, a continent.
I miss them, but it wasn't a disaster.   15

—Even losing you (the joking voice, a gesture
I love) I shan't have lied. It's evident
the art of losing's not too hard to master
though it may look like (*Write* it!) like disaster.

Questions

1. What things has the speaker lost? Put together a complete list in the order she reveals them. What does the list suggest about her experience with loss?
2. Bishop varies the repeated lines that end with the word "disaster." Look only at those lines: what do they suggest about the story being unfolded in the poem?
3. What effect does the parenthetical comment in the poem's last line create? Would the poem be different if it were omitted?
4. Compare this poem to other villanelles in this book, such as Dylan Thomas's "Do not go gentle into that good night" (Chapter 24) and Wendy Cope's "Lonely Hearts" (Chapter 17). In what ways does Bishop bend the rules of the form?

The best lyric poetry has the strange ability to seem both intensely personal and almost universal in its significance. In "Ode to a Nightingale" the English Romantic John Keats gave sublime expression to the complex and contradictory impulses of human desire and imagination. Vacillating between joy and melancholy, hope and despair, Keats recognized how such warring emotions lie at the heart of human experience. Originating in classical Greek and Latin literature, the **ode** is a special, exalted type of lyric poem, usually addressing a single subject in a stately and formal style. Odes have no set form; each one establishes its own stanza structure, sometimes very complex. The object is to create powerfully rhapsodic music. Keats's perpetually astonishing "Ode to a Nightingale," published less than a year before the poet's untimely death at twenty-five, is imbued with a sense of human suffering and mortality amid the enduring beauty of nature and art.

John Keats (1795–1821)

Ode to a Nightingale   1820

I

My heart aches, and a drowsy numbness pains
   My sense, as though of hemlock I had drunk,
Or emptied some dull opiate to the drains
   One minute past, and Lethe-wards had sunk:
'Tis not through envy of thy happy lot,   5
   But being too happy in thine happiness,—
     That thou, light-winged Dryad of the trees,
      In some melodious plot
   Of beechen green, and shadows numberless,
     Singest of summer in full-throated ease.   10

II

O, for a draught of vintage! that hath been
   Cool'd a long age in the deep-delved earth,
Tasting of Flora and the country green,
   Dance, and Provençal song, and sunburnt mirth!
O for a beaker full of the warm South,   15
   Full of the true, the blushful Hippocrene,
     With beaded bubbles winking at the brim,
      And purple-stained mouth;
   That I might drink, and leave the world unseen,
     And with thee fade away into the forest dim: 20

III

Fade far away, dissolve, and quite forget
   What thou among the leaves hast never known,
The weariness, the fever, and the fret
   Here, where men sit and hear each other groan;
Where palsy shakes a few, sad, last gray hairs,   25
   Where youth grows pale, and specter-thin, and dies;
     Where but to think is to be full of sorrow
      And leaden-eyed despairs,
   Where Beauty cannot keep her lustrous eyes,
     Or new Love pine at them beyond to-morrow.   30

IV

Away! away! for I will fly to thee,
    Not charioted by Bacchus and his pards,
But on the viewless wings of Poesy,
    Though the dull brain perplexes and retards:
Already with thee! tender is the night,   35
    And haply the Queen-Moon is on her throne,
        Cluster'd around by all her starry Fays;
            But here there is no light,
Save what from heaven is with the breezes blown
        Through verdurous glooms and winding mossy ways.   40

V

I cannot see what flowers are at my feet,
    Nor what soft incense hangs upon the boughs,
But, in embalmed darkness, guess each sweet
    Wherewith the seasonable month endows
The grass, the thicket, and the fruit-tree wild;   45
    White hawthorn, and the pastoral eglantine;
        Fast fading violets cover'd up in leaves;
            And mid-May's eldest child,
The coming musk-rose, full of dewy wine,
        The murmurous haunt of flies on summer eves.   50

VI

Darkling I listen; and, for many a time
    I have been half in love with easeful Death,
Call'd him soft names in many a mused rhyme,
    To take into the air my quiet breath;
Now more than ever seems it rich to die,   55
    To cease upon the midnight with no pain,
        While thou art pouring forth thy soul abroad
            In such an ecstasy!
Still wouldst thou sing, and I have ears in vain—
        To thy high requiem become a sod.   60

VII

Thou wast not born for death, immortal Bird!
    No hungry generations tread thee down;
The voice I hear this passing night was heard
    In ancient days by emperor and clown:
Perhaps the self-same song that found a path   65
    Through the sad heart of Ruth, when, sick for home,
        She stood in tears amid the alien corn;
            The same that oft-times hath
Charm'd magic casements, opening on the foam
        Of perilous seas, in faery lands forlorn.   70

VIII

Forlorn! the very word is like a bell
　To toll me back from thee to my sole self!
Adieu! the fancy cannot cheat so well
　As she is fam'd to do, deceiving elf.
Adieu! adieu! thy plaintive anthem fades 　　　　　　　　　75
　　Past the near meadows, over the still stream,
　　　Up the hill-side; and now 'tis buried deep
　　　　In the next valley-glades:
　　Was it a vision, or a waking dream?
　　Fled is that music:—Do I wake or sleep? 　　　　　　　80

ODE TO A NIGHTINGALE. 4 *Lethe-wards*: towards Lethe, the river of oblivion in Hades, the classical Underworld; dead souls drank the waters of Lethe to forget their past lives. 7 *Dryad*: wood nymph. 13 *Flora*: the classical goddess of flowers and spring. 16 *Hippocrene*: the sacred fountain of the Muses, whose waters have the power to inspire poetry. 32 *pards*: leopards, the animals who pull the chariot of Bacchus, the god of wine. 66–67 *Ruth . . . alien corn*: In the Old Testament, Ruth is a Moabite widow who gleans grain from the Israelite Boaz's field.

Questions

1. In the opening stanza to what things does the speaker compare the effect of the nightingale's song?
2. Why does the speaker desire wine in stanza II?
3. What are the worldly troubles and sorrows the speaker wishes to escape? (Cite specific lines.)
4. Why can't the speaker (in stanza V) see the flowers at his feet or in the branches above him?
5. What specifically is the attraction the speaker feels for death? (Cite specific lines.)
6. How could the nightingale singing in the poem be the same voice heard in the ancient world? What point is Keats making about the permanence of nature?
7. By the time Keats wrote this poem, he knew he would die young from tuberculosis. Do you see any evidence of this knowledge in the text of the poem?
8. What is your favorite line or lines from the ode? The choice is, of course, personal, but give your reasons, if possible, for your choice.

Excellent poetry might be easier to recognize if each poet had a fixed position on the slopes of Mount Parnassus, but, from one century to the next, the reputations of some poets have taken humiliating slides, or made impressive clambers. We decide for ourselves which poems to call excellent, but readers of the future may reverse our opinions.

In a sense, all readers of poetry are constantly reexamining the judgments of the past by choosing those poems they care to go on reading. In the end, we have to admit that the critical principles set forth in this chapter are all very well for admiring excellent poetry we already know, but they cannot be carried like a yardstick in the hand, to go out looking for it. As Ezra Pound said in his *ABC of Reading*, "A classic is classic not because it conforms to certain structural rules, or fits certain definitions (of which its author had quite probably never heard). It is classic because of a certain eternal and irrepressible freshness."

A great poem shocks us into another order of perception. It points beyond language to something still more essential. It ushers us into an experience so moving and true that we feel (to quote King Lear) "cut to the brain." In bad or indifferent poetry, words are all there is.

Exercise: Reevaluating Popular Classics

In this exercise you will read two of the most popular American poems of the nineteenth century: Emma Lazarus's "The New Colossus" and Edgar Allan Poe's "Annabel Lee." In their time, not only were these poems considered classics by serious critics, but thousands of ordinary readers knew them by heart. Recently, however, they have fallen out of critical favor. You will also read Walt Whitman's "O Captain! My Captain!," which, while still somewhat popular with modern readers, enjoyed a higher esteem a century ago than it does today.

Your assignment is to read these poems carefully and make your own personal, tentative evaluation of each poem's merit. Here are some questions you might ask yourself as you consider them.

- Do these poems engage your sympathies? Do they stir you and touch your feelings?
- What, if anything, might make them memorable? Do they have any vivid images? Any metaphors, understatement, overstatement, or other figures of speech? Do these poems appeal to the ear?
- Do the poems exhibit any wild incompetence? Do you find any forced rimes, inappropriate words, or other unintentionally comic features? Can the poems be accused of sentimentality, or do you trust the poet to report honest feelings?
- How well does the poet seem in control of language? Does the poet's language reflect in any detail the physical world we know?
- Do these poems seem entirely drawn from other poetry of the past, or do you have a sense that the poet is thinking and feeling on her (or his) own? Does the poet show any evidence of having read other poets' poetry?
- What is the poet trying to do in each poem? How successful, in your opinion, is the attempt?

Try setting these poems next to similar poems you know and admire. (You might try comparing Emma Lazarus's "The New Colossus" to Percy Bysshe Shelley's "Ozymandias," found in this chapter; both are sonnets, and their subjects have interesting similarities and contrasts. Or compare Edgar Allan Poe's "Annabel Lee" with A. E. Housman's "To an Athlete Dying Young" (Chapter 34). Or read Walt Whitman's "O Captain! My Captain!" next to other works by Whitman, and consider in what ways this poem is uncharacteristic of his works.

Are these poems sufficiently rich and interesting to repay more than one reading? Do you think that these poems still deserve to be considered classics? Or do they no longer speak powerfully to a contemporary audience?

Walt Whitman (1819–1892)

O Captain! My Captain!   1865

O Captain! my Captain! our fearful trip is done,
The ship has weather'd every rack, the prize we sought is won,
The port is near, the bells I hear, the people all exulting,
While follow eyes the steady keel, the vessel grim and daring;
    But O heart! heart! heart!   5
      O the bleeding drops of red,
        Where on the deck my Captain lies,
          Fallen cold and dead.

O Captain! my Captain! rise up and hear the bells;
Rise up—for you the flag is flung—for you the bugle trills,   10
For you bouquets and ribbon'd wreaths—for you the shores a-crowding,
For you they call, the swaying mass, their eager faces turning;
    Here Captain! dear father!
      This arm beneath your head!
        It is some dream that on the deck,   15
          You've fallen cold and dead.

My Captain does not answer, his lips are pale and still,
My father does not feel my arm, he has no pulse nor will,
The ship is anchor'd safe and sound, its voyage closed and done,
From fearful trip the victor ship comes in with object won;   20
    Exult O shores, and ring O bells!
      But I with mournful tread,
        Walk the deck my Captain lies,
          Fallen cold and dead.

O CAPTAIN! MY CAPTAIN! Written soon after the death of Abraham Lincoln, this was, in Whitman's lifetime, by far the most popular of his poems.

Emma Lazarus (1849–1887)

The New Colossus   (1883) 1888

Not like the brazen giant of Greek fame,
With conquering limbs astride from land to land;
Here at our sea-washed, sunset gates shall stand
A mighty woman with a torch, whose flame
Is the imprisoned lightning, and her name   5
Mother of Exiles. From her beacon-hand
Glows world-wide welcome; her mild eyes command
The air-bridged harbor that twin cities frame.
"Keep, ancient lands, your storied pomp!" cries she
With silent lips. "Give me your tired, your poor,   10
Your huddled masses yearning to breathe free,
The wretched refuse of your teeming shore.
Send these, the homeless, tempest-tost to me,
I lift my lamp beside the golden door!"

THE NEW COLOSSUS. In 1883, a committee was formed to raise funds to build a pedestal for what would be the largest statue in the world, "Liberty Enlightening the World" by Fréderic-Auguste Bartholdi, which was a gift from the French people to celebrate America's centennial. American authors were asked to donate manuscripts for a fund-raising auction. The young poet Emma Lazarus sent in this sonnet composed for the occasion. When President Grover Cleveland unveiled the Statue of Liberty in October 1886, Lazarus's sonnet was read at the ceremony. In 1903, the poem was carved on the statue's pedestal. The reference in the opening line to "the brazen giant of Greek fame" is to the famous Colossus of Rhodes, a huge bronze statue that once stood in the harbor on the Aegean island of Rhodes. Built to commemorate a military victory, it was one of the so-called Seven Wonders of the World.

Edgar Allan Poe (1809–1849)

Annabel Lee   1849

It was many and many a year ago,
    In a kingdom by the sea,
That a maiden there lived whom you may know
    By the name of Annabel Lee;
And this maiden she lived with no other thought   5
    Than to love and be loved by me.

I was a child and *she* was a child,
    In this kingdom by the sea,
But we loved with a love that was more than love—
    I and my Annabel Lee—   10
With a love that the wingéd seraphs of Heaven
    Coveted her and me.

And this was the reason that, long ago,
    In this kingdom by the sea,
A wind blew out of a cloud, chilling   15
    My beautiful Annabel Lee;
So that her highborn kinsmen came
    And bore her away from me,
To shut her up in a sepulchre
    In this kingdom by the sea.   20

The angels, not half so happy in Heaven,
    Went envying her and me:—
Yes!—that was the reason (as all men know,
    In this kingdom by the sea)
That the wind came out of the cloud by night,   25
    Chilling and killing my Annabel Lee.

But our love it was stronger by far than the love
    Of those who were older than we—
    Of many far wiser than we—
And neither the angels in Heaven above,   30
    Nor the demons down under the sea,
Can ever dissever my soul from the soul
    Of the beautiful Annabel Lee:—

For the moon never beams, without bringing me dreams
    Of the beautiful Annabel Lee;   35
And the stars never rise, but I feel the bright eyes
    Of the beautiful Annabel Lee:
And so, all the night-tide, I lie down by the side
Of my darling—my darling—my life and my bride,
    In the sepulchre there by the sea—   40
    In her tomb by the sounding sea.

■ WRITING *effectively*

Edgar Allan Poe on Writing

A Long Poem Does Not Exist   1848

I hold that a long poem does not exist. I maintain that the phrase, "a long poem," is simply a flat contradiction in terms.

I need scarcely observe that a poem deserves its title only inasmuch as it excites, by elevating the soul. The value of the poem is in the ratio of this elevating excitement. But all excitements are, through a psychal necessity, transient. That degree of excitement which would entitle a poem to be so called at all, cannot be sustained throughout a composition of any great length. After the lapse of half an hour, at the very utmost, it flags—fails—a revulsion ensues—and then the poem is, in effect, and in fact, no longer such.

From "The Poetic Principle"

Edgar Allan Poe

THINKING ABOUT EVALUATING A POEM

Evaluating a poem begins with personal taste. Though your first impressions may become part of your ultimate judgment, they should usually end up being no more than a departure point. The question isn't merely whether a work pleases or moves you, but how well it manages the literary tasks it sets out to perform. A good critic is willing both to admire a strong poem that he or she doesn't like and to admit that a personal favorite might not really stand up to close scrutiny. Whatever your final opinion, the goal is to nourish your personal response with careful critical examination so that your evaluation will grow into an informed judgment.

■ **In evaluating a poem, first try to understand your own subjective response.**
Admit to yourself whether the poem delights, moves, bores, or annoys you.

- **Try to determine what the poem seems designed to make you think and feel.** If a poem is written within a genre, then you need to weigh the work against the generic expectations it sets up.
- **Consider how well it fulfills these expectations.** An epigram usually seeks to be witty and concise. If it proves tiresome and verbose, it can be fairly said to fail.
- **Focus on specific elements in the poem.** How well do its language, imagery, symbols, and figures of speech communicate its meanings? Are the metaphors or similes effective? Is the imagery fresh and precise? Is the language vague or verbose? Does the poem ever fall into clichés or platitudes?

CHECKLIST: Writing an Evaluation

- ☐ What is your subjective response to the poem?
- ☐ Highlight or underline moments that call up a strong reaction. Why do you think those passages elicit such a response?
- ☐ What task does the poem set for itself?
- ☐ Does it belong to some identifiable form or genre?
- ☐ If so, what are the expectations for that genre? How well does the poem fulfill the expectations it creates?
- ☐ How do its specific elements work to communicate meaning (e.g., language, imagery, symbols, figures of speech, rhythm, sound, rime)?
- ☐ Reread the poem. Does it seem better or worse than it did initially?

TOPICS FOR WRITING ON EVALUATING A POEM

1. Look at a short poem to which you have a strong initial response—either positive or negative. Write an essay in which you begin by stating your response, then work through the steps outlined above. Does the poem succeed in fulfilling the task it sets for itself? Back up your opinion with specifics. Finally, state whether the process has changed your impression of the poem. Why or why not?

2. Choose a short poem that you admire from anywhere in this book. Write a brief essay defending the poem's excellence. Be specific in describing its particular strengths.

3. Write a brief evaluation of "The New Colossus" by Emma Lazarus, "O Captain! My Captain!" by Walt Whitman, or "Annabel Lee" by Edgar Allan Poe. In what ways is the poem successful? In what ways is it unsuccessful?

4. Find a poem you admire in this book and wreck it. First, type the poem as is into a computer. Then go through it, substituting clichés and overly vague language for moments that are vivid and precise. Replace understatement with overstatement, restraint with sentimentality. Keep making changes until you've turned a perfectly good poem into a disaster. Now write a brief explanation of your choices.

▶ **TERMS FOR** *review*

Poetic inversion ▶ The inversion of normal word order, usually done for purposes of meter and/or rime.

Sentimentality ▶ A term negatively applied to a literary work that tries to convey great feeling but fails to give the reader sufficient grounds for sharing it. Sentimentality involves an emotion that is excessive in relation to its cause, as opposed to *sentiment*, which connotes one proper to its cause.

Convention ▶ Any established feature or technique in literature that is commonly understood by both authors and readers. A convention is something generally agreed on to be appropriate for customary uses, such as the sonnet form for a love poem or the opening "Once upon a time" for a fairy tale.

Ode ▶ A special, exalted type of lyric poem, usually addressing a single subject in a stately and formal style.

31 WHAT IS POETRY?

Poetry is a way of taking life by the throat.

—ROBERT FROST

What You Will Learn in This Chapter

■ To appreciate the diverse ways in which poetry has been defined

By now, perhaps, you have formed your own idea of what poetry is, whether or not you can easily define it. Robert Frost made a try at a definition: "A poem is an idea caught in the act of dawning." Just in case further efforts at definition may be useful, here are a few memorable ones (including, for a second look, some given earlier):

things that are true expressed in words that are beautiful.
>   —*Dante*

the art of uniting pleasure with truth by calling imagination to the
>   help of reason.
>   —*Samuel Johnson*

the best words in the best order.
>   —*Samuel Taylor Coleridge*

the spontaneous overflow of powerful feelings.
>   —*William Wordsworth*

emotion put into measure.
>   —*Thomas Hardy*

If I feel physically as if the top of my head were taken off, I know *that* is poetry.
>   —*Emily Dickinson*

speech framed . . . to be heard for its own sake and interest even over and
>   above its interest of meaning.
>   —*Gerard Manley Hopkins*

a way of remembering what it would impoverish us to forget.
>   —*Robert Frost*

a revelation in words by means of the words.
>   —*Wallace Stevens*

Poetry is prose bewitched.
    —*Mina Loy*

not the assertion that something is true, but the making of that truth
    more fully real to us.
    —*T. S. Eliot*

the clear expression of mixed feelings.
    —*W. H. Auden*

an angel with a gun in its hand . . .
    —*José Garcia Villa*

the language in which man explores his own amazement.
    —*Christopher Fry*

hundreds of things coming together at the right moment.
    —*Elizabeth Bishop*

Poetry is a sound art.
    —*Joy Harjo*

Reduced to its simplest and most essential form, the poem is a song.
    Song is neither discourse nor explanation.
    —*Octavio Paz*

During the writing of a poem the various elements of a poet's being
    are in communion with each other, and heightened.
    —*Denise Levertov*

Poems come out of wonder, not out of knowing.
    —*Lucille Clifton*

Poetry is always the cat concert under the window of the room in
    which the official version of reality is being written.
    —*Charles Simic*

A poem differs from most prose in several ways. For one, both writer and reader tend to regard it differently. The poet's attitude is something like this: I offer this piece of writing to be read not as prose but as a poem—that is, more perceptively, thoughtfully, and creatively, with more attention to sounds and connotations. This is a great deal to expect, but in return, the reader, too, has a right to certain expectations.

Approaching the poem in the anticipation of out-of-the-ordinary knowledge and pleasure, the reader assumes that the poem may use certain enjoyable devices not commonly found in prose: rime, alliteration, meter, and rhythms—definite, various, or emphatic. (The poet may not *always* decide to use these things.) The reader expects the poet to make greater use, perhaps, of resources of meaning such as figurative language, allusion, symbol, and imagery. As readers of prose, we might seek no more than meaning: no more than what could be paraphrased without serious loss. Meeting any figurative language or graceful turns of word order, we think them pleasant extras. But in poetry all these "extras" matter as much as the paraphrasable content, if not more. For, when we finish reading a good poem, we cannot explain precisely to ourselves what we have experienced—without repeating, word for word, the language of the poem itself. Archibald MacLeish makes this point memorably in "Ars Poetica":

> A poem should not mean
> But be.

"Poetry is to prose as dancing is to walking," remarked Paul Valéry. It is doubtful, however, that anyone can draw an immovable boundary between poetry and prose. Certain prose needs only to be arranged in lines to be seen as poetry—especially prose that conveys strong emotion in vivid, physical imagery and in terse, figurative, rhythmical language. Even in translation the words of Chief Joseph of the Nez Perce tribe, at the moment of his surrender to the US Army in 1877, still move us and are memorable:

> Hear me, my warriors, my heart is sick and sad:
> Our chiefs are killed,
> The old men all are dead,
> It is cold and we have no blankets.
> The little children freeze to death.
>
> Hear me, my warriors, my heart is sick and sad:
> From where the sun now stands I will fight no more forever.

It may be that a poem can point beyond words to something still more essential. Language has its limits, and probably Edgar Allan Poe was the only poet ever to claim he could always find words for whatever he wished to express. For, of all a human being can experience and imagine, words say only part. "Human speech," said Flaubert, who strove after the best of it, "is like a cracked kettle on which we hammer out tunes to make bears dance, when what we long for is the compassion of the stars."

Like Yeats's chestnut tree in "Among School Children" (which, when asked whether it is leaf, blossom, or trunk, has no answer), a poem is to be seen not as a confederation of form, rime, image, metaphor, tone, and theme, but as a whole. We study a poem one element at a time because the intellect best comprehends what it can separate. But only our total attention, involving the participation of our blood and marrow, can see all elements in a poem fused, all dancing together. Yeats knew how to make poems and how to read them:

> God guard me from those thoughts men think
> In the mind alone;
> He that sings a lasting song
> Thinks in a marrow-bone.

Throughout this book, we have been working on the assumption that the patient and conscious explication of poems will sharpen unconscious perceptions. We can only hope that it will; the final test lies in whether you care to go on by yourself, reading other poems, finding in them pleasure and enlightenment. Pedagogy must have a stop; so too must the viewing of poems as if their elements fell into chapters. For the total experience of reading a poem surpasses the mind's categories. The wind in the grass, says a proverb, cannot be taken into the house.

32

THREE CRITICAL CASEBOOKS

Emily Dickinson, Langston Hughes, and Robert Frost

What You Will Learn in This Chapter

- To understand three major poets in their biographical, critical, and cultural contexts

Emily Dickinson

Langston Hughes

Robert Frost

EMILY DICKINSON

Emily Dickinson (1830–1886) spent nearly all her life in her family home in Amherst, Massachusetts. Her father, Edward Dickinson, was a prominent lawyer who ranked as Amherst's leading citizen. (He even served a term in the US Congress.) Dickinson attended one year of college at Mount Holyoke Female Seminary in South Hadley. She proved to be a good student, but, suffering from homesickness and poor health, she did not return for the second year. This brief period of study and a few trips to Boston, Philadelphia, and Washington, DC, were the only occasions she left home in her fifty-five-year life. As time passed, Dickinson became more reclusive. She stopped attending church (and refused to endorse the orthodox Congregationalist creed). She also spent increasing time alone in her room—often writing poems. Dickinson never married, but she had a significant romantic relationship with at least one unidentified man. Although scholars have suggested several likely candidates, the historical object of Dickinson's affections will likely never be known. What survives unmistakably, however, is the intensely passionate poetry written out of these private circumstances. By the end of her life, Dickinson had become a locally famous recluse; she rarely left home. She would greet visitors from her own upstairs room, clearly heard but never seen. When she died in 1886, she was buried, according to her own instructions, within sight of the family home. Although Dickinson composed 1,789 known poems, only a handful were published in her lifetime. She often, however, sent copies of poems to friends in letters, but only after her death would the full extent of her writings become known, when a cache of manuscripts was discovered in a trunk in the homestead attic—handwritten little booklets of poems sewn together by the poet with needle and thread. From 1890 until the mid-twentieth century, nine posthumous collections of her poems were published by friends and relatives, some of whom rewrote her work and changed her idiosyncratic punctuation to make it more conventional. Thomas H. Johnson's three-volume edition, Poems (1955), established a more accurate text. In relatively few and simple forms clearly indebted to the hymns she heard in church, Dickinson succeeded in being a true visionary and a poet of colossal originality.

POEMS

Wild Nights – Wild Nights!   (about 1861)

Wild Nights – Wild Nights!
Were I with thee
Wild Nights should be
Our luxury!

Futile – the Winds –
To a Heart in port –   5
Done with the Compass –
Done with the Chart!

Rowing in Eden –
Ah, the Sea!   10
Might I but moor – Tonight –
In Thee!

"Hope" is the thing with feathers

(about 1861)

"Hope" is the thing with feathers –
That perches in the soul –
And sings the tune without the words –
And never stops – at all –

And sweetest – in the Gale – is heard –   5
And sore must be the storm –
That could abash the little Bird
That kept so many warm –

I've heard it in the chillest land –
And on the strangest Sea –   10

Yet, never, in Extremity,
It asked a crumb – of Me.

I felt a Funeral, in my Brain

(about 1861)

I felt a Funeral, in my Brain,
And Mourners to and fro
Kept treading – treading – till it seemed
That Sense was breaking through –

And when they all were seated,   5
A Service, like a Drum –
Kept beating – beating – till I thought
My Mind was going numb –

And then I heard them lift a Box
And creak across my Soul   10
With those same Boots of Lead, again,
Then Space – began to toll,

As all the Heavens were a Bell,
And Being, but an Ear,
And I, and Silence, some strange Race   15
Wrecked, solitary, here –

And Then a Plank in Reason, broke,
And I dropped down, and down –
And hit a World, at every plunge,
And Finished knowing – then –   20

I'm Nobody! Who are you?

(about 1861)

I'm Nobody! Who are you?
Are you – Nobody – Too?
Then there's a pair of us?
Don't tell! they'd advertise – you know!

How dreary – to be – Somebody!   5
How public – like a Frog –
To tell one's name – the livelong June –
To an admiring Bog!

The Soul selects her own Society

(about 1862)

The Soul selects her own Society –
Then – shuts the Door –
To her divine Majority –
Present no more –

Unmoved – she notes the Chariots – pausing –   5
At her low Gate –
Unmoved – an Emperor be kneeling
Upon her Mat –

I've known her – from an ample nation –
Choose One –   10
Then – close the Valves of her attention –
Like Stone –

Some keep the Sabbath going to Church

(about 1862) Published 1864

Some keep the Sabbath going to Church –
I keep it, staying at Home –
With a Bobolink for a Chorister –
And an Orchard, for a Dome –

Some keep the Sabbath in Surplice –   5
I just wear my Wings –
And instead of tolling the Bell, for Church,
Our little Sexton – sings.

God preaches, a noted Clergyman –
And the sermon is never long,   10
So instead of getting to Heaven, at last –
I'm going, all along.

Much Madness is divinest Sense

(about 1862)

Much Madness is divinest Sense –
To a discerning Eye –
Much Sense – the starkest Madness –
'Tis the Majority
In this, as All, prevail –   5
Assent – and you are sane –
Demur – you're straightway dangerous –
And handled with a Chain –

This is my letter to the World

(about 1862)

This is my letter to the World
That never wrote to Me –
The simple News that Nature told –
With tender Majesty

Her Message is committed   5
To Hands I cannot see –
For love of Her – Sweet – countrymen –
Judge tenderly – of Me

I heard a Fly buzz – when I died   (about 1862)

I heard a Fly buzz – when I died –
The Stillness in the Room
Was like the Stillness in the Air –
Between the Heaves of Storm –

The Eyes around – had wrung them dry –   5
And Breaths were gathering firm
For that last Onset – when the King
Be witnessed – in the Room –

I willed my Keepsakes – Signed away
What portion of me be   10
Assignable – and then it was
There interposed a Fly –

With Blue – uncertain stumbling Buzz –
Between the light – and me –
And then the Windows failed – and then   15
I could not see to see –

I started Early – Took my Dog   (about 1862)

I started Early – Took my Dog –
And visited the Sea –
The Mermaids in the Basement
Came out to look at me –

And Frigates – in the Upper Floor   5
Extended Hempen Hands –
Presuming Me to be a Mouse –
Aground – upon the Sands –

But no Man moved Me – till the Tide
Went past my simple Shoe –   10
And past my Apron – and my Belt
And past my Bodice – too –

And made as He would eat me up –
As wholly as a Dew
Upon a Dandelion's Sleeve –   15
And then – I started – too –

And He – He followed – close behind –
I felt His Silver Heel
Upon my Ankle – Then my Shoes
Would overflow with Pearl –   20

Until We met the Solid Town –
No One He seemed to know –
And bowing – with a Mighty look –
At me – The Sea withdrew –

I dwell in Possibility   (about 1862)

I dwell in Possibility –
A fairer House than Prose –
More numerous of Windows –
Superior – for Doors –

Of Chambers as the Cedars –   5
Impregnable of Eye –
And for an Everlasting Roof
The Gambrels of the Sky –

Of Visitors – the fairest –
For Occupation – This –   10
The spreading wide my narrow Hands
To gather Paradise –

Because I could not stop for Death   (about 1863)

Because I could not stop for Death –
He kindly stopped for me –
The Carriage held but just Ourselves –
And Immortality.

We slowly drove – He knew no haste   5
And I had put away
My labor and my leisure too,
For His Civility –

We passed the School, where Children strove
At Recess – in the Ring –   10
We passed the Fields of Gazing Grain –
We passed the Setting Sun –

Or rather – He passed Us –
The Dews drew quivering and chill –
For only Gossamer, my Gown –   15
My Tippet° – only Tulle –   *cape*

We paused before a House that seemed
A Swelling of the Ground –
The Roof was scarcely visible –
The Cornice – in the Ground –   20

Since then – 'tis Centuries – and yet
Feels shorter than the Day
I first surmised the Horses' Heads
Were toward Eternity –

Tell all the Truth but tell it slant   (about 1868)

Tell all the Truth but tell it slant –
Success in Circuit lies
Too bright for our infirm Delight
The Truth's superb surprise
As Lightning to the Children eased   5
With explanation kind
The Truth must dazzle gradually
Or every man be blind –

Compare

Other poems by Emily Dickinson that are found in this book:

> Safe in their Alabaster Chambers (Chapter 30)
> It dropped so low – in my Regard (Chapter 20)
> The Lightning is a yellow Fork (Chapter 26)
> My Life had stood – a Loaded Gun (Chapter 20)
> A Route of Evanescence (Chapter 19)

EMILY DICKINSON ON WRITING

Recognizing Poetry   (1870)

If I read a book [and] it makes my whole body
so cold no fire ever can warm me I know *that*
is poetry. If I feel physically as if the top of
my head were taken off, I know *that* is poetry.
These are the only ways I know it. Is there any
other way.

How do most people live without any
thoughts. There are many people in the world
(you must have noticed them in the street).
How do they live. How do they get strength to
put on their clothes in the morning.

When I lost the use of my Eyes it was a
comfort to think there were so few real *books*
that I could easily find some one to read me all
of them.

Truth is such a *rare* thing it is delightful to
tell it.

I find ecstasy in living – the mere sense of
living is joy enough.

**Emily Dickinson by John
Sherffius**

From a conversation with Thomas Wentworth Higginson

The Dickinson house in Amherst, Massachusetts, where the poet was born and spent most of her life.

Self-Description°   (25 April 1862)

Mr. Higginson,

Your kindness claimed earlier gratitude – but I was ill – and write today, from my pillow.

Thank you for the surgery – it was not so painful as I supposed. I bring you others – as you ask – though they might not differ –

While my thought is undressed – I can make the distinction, but when I put them in the Gown – they look alike, and numb.

You asked how old I was? I made no verse – but one or two – until this winter – Sir –

I had a terror – since September – I could tell to none – and so I sing, as the Boy does by the Burying Ground – because I am afraid – You inquire my Books – For Poets – I have Keats – and Mr and Mrs Browning. For Prose – Mr Ruskin – Sir Thomas Browne – and the Revelations.° I went to school – but in your manner of the phrase – had no education. When a little Girl, I had a friend, who taught me Immortality – but venturing too near, himself – he never returned – Soon after, my Tutor, died – and for several years, my Lexicon – was my only companion – Then I found one more – but he was not contented I be his scholar – so he left the Land.

You ask of my Companions[.] Hills – Sir – and the Sundown – and a Dog – large as myself, that my Father bought me – They are better than Beings – because they know – but do not tell – and the noise in the Pool, at Noon – excels my Piano. I have a Brother and Sister – My Mother does not care for thought – and Father, too busy with his Briefs° – to notice what we do – He buys me many Books – but begs me not

---

Self-Description: Emily Dickinson's letter was written to Thomas Wentworth Higginson, a noted writer. Dickinson had read his article of advice to young writers in the *Atlantic Monthly.* She sent him four poems and a letter asking if her verse was "alive." When he responded with comments and suggestions (the "surgery" Dickinson mentions in the second paragraph), she wrote him this letter about herself.

Mr Ruskin . . . Revelations: in listing her favorite prose authors Dickinson chose John Ruskin (1819–1900), an English art critic and essayist; Sir Thomas Browne (1605–1682), a doctor and philosopher with a magnificent prose style; and the final book of the New Testament. *Briefs:* legal papers (her father was a lawyer).

to read them – because he fears they joggle the Mind. They are religious – except me – and address an Eclipse, every morning – whom they call their "Father." But I fear my story fatigues you – I would like to learn – Could you tell me how to grow – or is it unconveyed – like Melody – or Witchcraft?

You speak of Mr Whitman – I never read his Book° – but was told that he was disgraceful –

I read Miss Prescott's "Circumstance,"° but it followed me, in the Dark – so I avoided her –

Two Editors of Journals came to my Father's House, this winter – and asked me for my Mind – and when I asked them "Why," they said I was penurious – and they, would use it for the World –

I could not weigh myself – Myself –

My size felt small – to me – I read your Chapters in the Atlantic – and experienced honor for you – I was sure you would not reject a confiding question –

Is this – Sir – what you asked me to tell you?

Your friend,
E – Dickinson

From The Letters of Emily Dickinson

CRITICS ON EMILY DICKINSON

Thomas Wentworth Higginson (1823–1911)

Meeting Emily Dickinson   1870

A large county lawyer's house, brown brick, with great trees & a garden—I sent up my card. A parlor dark & cool & stiffish, a few books & engravings & an open piano . . . .

A step like a pattering child's in entry & in glided a little plain woman with two smooth bands of reddish hair & a face a little like Belle Dove's; not plainer—with no good feature—in a very plain & exquisitely clean white piqué & a blue net worsted shawl. She came to me with two day lilies which she put in a sort of childlike way into my hand & said "These are my introduction" in a soft frightened breathless childlike voice—& added under her breath Forgive me if I am frightened; I never see strangers & hardly know what I say—but she talked soon & thenceforward continuously—& deferentially—sometimes stopping to ask me to talk instead of her—but readily recommencing . . . thoroughly ingenuous & simple . . . & saying many things which you would have thought foolish & I wise—& some things you wd. hv. liked. I add a few over the page. . . .

"Women talk; men are silent; that is why I dread women."

"My father only reads on Sunday—he reads *lonely* & *rigorous* books."

"If I read a book [and] it makes my whole body so cold no fire ever can warm me I know *that* is poetry. If I feel physically as if the top of my head were taken off, I know *that* is poetry. These are the only ways I know it. Is there any other way."

• • •

I asked if she never felt want of employment, never going off the place & never seeing any visitor "I never thought of conceiving that I could ever have the slightest

Whitman . . . book: Leaves of Grass (1855) by Walt Whitman was considered an improper book for women at this time because of the volume's sexual candor. *Miss Prescott's "Circumstance":* a story, also published in the *Atlantic Monthly*, that was full of violence.

approach to such a want in all future time" (& added) "I feel that I have not expressed myself strongly enough."

She makes all the bread for her father only likes hers & says "& people must have puddings" this *very* dreamily, as if they were comets—so she makes them.

• • •

E D again

"Could you tell me what home is"

"I never had a mother. I suppose a mother is one to whom you hurry when you are troubled."

"I never knew how to tell time by the clock till I was 15. My father thought he had taught me but I did not understand & I was afraid to say I did not & afraid to ask any one else lest he should know."

Her father was not severe I should think but remote. He did not wish them to read anything but the Bible. One day her brother brought home Kavanagh° hid it under the piano cover & made signs to her & they read it: her father at last found it & was displeased. Perhaps it was before this that a student of his was amazed that they had never heard of Mrs. [Lydia Maria] Child° & used to bring them books & hide in a bush by the door. They were then little things in short dresses with their feet on the rungs of the chair. After the first book she thought in ecstasy "This then is a book! And there are more of them!"

"Is it oblivion or absorption when things pass from our minds?"

Major Hunt interested her more than any man she ever saw. She remembered two things he said—that her great dog "understood gravitation" & when he said he should come again "in a year. If I say a shorter time it will be longer."

When I said I would come again *some time* she said "Say in a long time, that will be nearer. Some time is nothing."

After long disuse of her eyes she read Shakespeare & thought why is any other book needed.

I never was with any one who drained my nerve power so much. Without touching her, she drew from me. I am glad not to live near her. She often thought me *tired* & seemed very thoughtful of others.

From a letter to his wife, August 16–17, 1870

Thomas H. Johnson (1902–1985)

The Discovery of Emily Dickinson's Manuscripts   1955

Shortly after Emily Dickinson's death on May fifteenth, 1886, her sister Lavinia discovered a locked box in which Emily had placed her poems. Lavinia's amazement seems to have been genuine. Though the sisters had lived intimately together under the same roof all their lives, and though Lavinia had always been aware that her sister wrote poems, she had not the faintest concept of the great number of them. The story of Lavinia's willingness to spare them because she found no instructions specifying that they be destroyed, and her search for an editor and a publisher to give them to the world, has already been told in some detail.

Kavanagh: Kavanagh: A Tale (1849), an utterly innocuous work of fiction by the poet Henry Wadsworth Longfellow.   *Mrs. [Lydia Maria] Child*: anti-slavery writer and author (1802–1880) of didactic novels.

Lavinia first consulted the two people most interested in Emily's poetry, her sister-in-law Susan Dickinson, and Mrs. Todd. David Peck Todd, a graduate of Amherst College in 1875, returned to Amherst with his young bride in 1881 as director of the college observatory and soon became professor of Astronomy and Navigation. These were the months shortly before Mrs. Edward Dickinson's death, when neighbors were especially thoughtful. Mrs. Todd endeared herself to Emily and Lavinia by small but understanding attentions, in return for which Emily sent Mrs. Todd copies of her poems. At first approach neither Susan Dickinson nor Mrs. Todd felt qualified for the editorial task which they both were hesitant to undertake. Mrs. Todd says of Lavinia's discovery: "She showed me the manuscripts and there were over sixty little 'volumes,' each composed of four or five sheets of note paper tied together with twine. In this box she discovered eight or nine hundred poems tied up in this way."

• • •

As the story can be reconstructed, at some time during the year 1858 Emily Dickinson began assembling her poems into packets. Always in ink, they are gatherings of four, five, or six sheets of letter paper usually folded once but sometimes single. They are loosely held together by thread looped through them at the spine at two points equidistant from the top and bottom. When opened up they may be read like a small book, a fact that explains why Emily's sister Lavinia, when she discovered them after Emily's death, referred to them as "volumes." All of the packet poems are either fair copies or semifinal drafts, and they constitute two-thirds of the entire body of her poetry.

For the most part the poems in a given packet seem to have been written and assembled as a unit. Since rough drafts of packet poems are almost totally lacking, one concludes that they were systematically discarded. If the poems were in fact composed at the time the copies were made, as the evidence now seems to point, one concludes that nearly two-thirds of her poems were created in the brief span of eight years, centering on her early thirties. Her interest in the packet method of assembling the verses thus coincides with the years of fullest productivity. In 1858 she gathered some fifty poems into packets. There are nearly one hundred so transcribed in 1859, some sixty-five in 1860, and in 1861 more than eighty. By 1862 the creative drive must have been almost frightening; during that year she transcribed into packets no fewer than three hundred and sixty-six poems, the greater part of them complete and final texts.

Whether this incredible number was in fact composed in that year or represents a transcription of earlier worksheet drafts can never be established by direct evidence. But the pattern established during the preceding four years reveals a gathering momentum, and the quality of tenseness and prosodic skill uniformly present in the poems of 1861–1862 bears scant likeness to the conventionality of theme and treatment in the poems of 1858–1859. Excepting a half dozen occasional verses written in the early fifties, there is not a single scrap of poetry that can be dated earlier than 1858.

From *The Poems of Emily Dickinson*

Richard Wilbur (1921–2017)

The Three Privations of Emily Dickinson   1959

Emily Dickinson never lets us forget for very long that in some respects life gave her short measure; and indeed it is possible to see the greater part of her poetry as an effort to cope with her sense of privation. I think that for her there were three major privations: she was deprived of an orthodox and steady religious faith; she was deprived of love; she was deprived of literary recognition.

At the age of seventeen, after a series of revival meetings at Mount Holyoke Seminary, Emily Dickinson found that she must refuse to become a professing Christian. To some modern minds this may seem to have been a sensible and necessary step; and surely it was a step toward becoming such a poet as she became. But for her, no pleasure in her own integrity could then eradicate the feeling that she had betrayed a deficiency, a want of grace. In her letters to Abiah Root she tells of the enhancing effect of conversion on her fellow-students, and says of herself in a famous passage:

> I am one of the lingering bad ones, and so do I slink away, and pause and ponder, and ponder and pause, and do work without knowing why, not surely for this brief world, and more sure it is not for heaven, and I ask what this message *means* that they ask for so very eagerly: *you* know of this depth and fulness, will you try to tell me about it?

There is humor in that, and stubbornness, and a bit of characteristic lurking pride: but there is also an anguished sense of having separated herself, through some dry incapacity, from spiritual community, from purpose, and from magnitude of life. As a child of evangelical Amherst, she inevitably thought of purposive, heroic life as requiring a vigorous faith. Out of such a thought she later wrote:

> The abdication of Belief
> Makes the Behavior small –
> Better an ignis fatuus
> Than no illume at all –

That hers *was* a species of religious personality goes without saying; but by her refusal of such ideas as original sin, redemption, hell, and election, she made it impossible for herself—as Whicher observed—"to share the religious life of her generation." She became an unsteady congregation of one.

Her second privation, the privation of love, is one with which her poems and her biographies have made us exceedingly familiar, though some biographical facts remain conjectural. She had the good fortune, at least once, to bestow her heart on another; but she seems to have found her life, in great part, a history of loneliness, separation, and bereavement.

As for literary fame, some will deny that Emily Dickinson ever greatly desired it, and certainly there is evidence, mostly from her latter years, to support such a view. She *did* write that "Publication is the auction / Of the mind of man." And she *did* say to Helen Hunt Jackson, "How can you print a piece of your soul?" But earlier, in 1861, she had frankly expressed to Sue Dickinson the hope that "sometime" she might make her kinfolk proud of her. The truth is, I think, that Emily Dickinson knew she was good, and began her career with a normal appetite for recognition. I think that she later came, with some reason, to despair of being understood or properly valued, and so directed against her hopes of fame what was by then a well-developed disposition to renounce. That she wrote a good number of poems about fame supports my view: the subjects to which a poet returns are those which vex him.

What did Emily Dickinson do, as a poet, with her sense of privation? One thing she quite often did was to pose as the laureate and attorney of the empty-handed, and question God about the economy of His creation. Why, she asked, is a fatherly God so sparing of His presence? Why is there never a sign that prayers are heard? Why does

Nature tell us no comforting news of its Maker? Why do some receive a whole loaf, while others must starve on a crumb? Where is the benevolence in shipwreck and earthquake? By asking such questions as these, she turned complaint into critique, and used her own sufferings as experiential evidence about the nature of the deity. The God who emerges from these poems is a God who does not answer, an unrevealed God whom one cannot confidently approach through Nature or through doctrine.

From "Sumptuous Destitution"

Cynthia Griffin Wolff (b. 1935)

Dickinson and Death   1993

(A Reading of "Because I could not stop for Death")

Modern readers are apt to comment upon the frequency with which Dickinson returns to this subject of death—"How morbid," people say. Perhaps. But if Dickinson was morbid, so was everyone else in her culture. Poe's aestheticizing of death (along with the proliferation of Gothic fiction and poetry) reflects a pervasive real-world concern: in mid-nineteenth-century America death rates were high. It was a truism that men had three wives (two of them having predeceased the spouse); infant mortality was so common that parents often gave several of their children the same name so that at least one "John" or "Lavinia" might survive to adulthood; rapid urbanization had intensified the threat of certain diseases—cholera, typhoid, and tuberculosis.

Poe and the Gothic tradition were one response to society's anxiety about death. Another came from the pulpit: mid-nineteenth-century sermons took death as their almost constant subject. Somewhat later in the century, preachers would embrace a doctrine of consolation: God would be figured as a loving parent—almost motherly—who had prepared a home in heaven for us all, and ministers would tell the members of their congregation that they need not be apprehensive. However, stern traces of Puritanism still tinctured the religious discourse of Dickinson's young womanhood, and members of the Amherst congregation were regularly exhorted with blood-stirring urgency to reflect upon the imminence of their own demise. Repeatedly, then, in attempting to comprehend Dickinson's work, a reader must return to the fundamental tenets of Protestant Christianity, for her poetry echoes the Bible more often than any other single work or author.

In part this preoccupation with the doctrines of her day reflected a more general concern with the essential questions of human existence they addressed. In a letter to Higginson she once said, "To live is so startling, it leaves but little room for other occupations." And to her friend Mrs. Holland she wrote, "All this and more, though *is* there more? More than Love and Death? Then tell me its name." The religious thought and language of the culture was important to her poetry because it comprised the semiotic system that her society employed to discuss the mysteries of life and death. If she wished to contemplate these, what other language was there to employ?

In part, however, conventional Christianity—especially the latter-day Puritanism of Dickinson's New England—represented for Dickinson an ultimate expression of patriarchal power. Rebelling against its rule, upbraiding a "Father" in Heaven who required absolute "faith" from his followers, but gave no discernible response, became a way of attacking the very essence of unjust authority, especially male authority.

• • •

It is true that the stern doctrines of New England Protestantism offered hope for a life after death; yet in Dickinson's estimation, the trope that was used for this "salvation" revealed some of the most repellent features of God's power, for the invitation to accept "faith" had been issued in the context of a courtship with a macabre, sexual component. It was promised that those who had faith would be carried to Heaven by the "Bridegroom" Christ. "Blessed are they which are called unto the marriage supper of the Lamb" (Revelation 19:9). Nor did it escape Dickinson's notice that the perverse prurience of Poe's notions was essentially similar to this Christian idea of Christ's "love" for a "bride" which promised a reunion that must be "consummated" through death. Thus the poem that is, perhaps, the apotheosis of that distinctive Dickinson voice, "the speaking dead," offers an astonishing combination: this conventional promise of Christianity suffused with the tonalities of the Gothic tradition.

[*Wolff quotes the entire text of "Because I could not stop for Death."*]

The speaker is a beautiful woman (already dead!), and like some spectral Cinderella, she is dressed to go to a ball: "For only Gossamer, my Gown – / My Tippet – only Tulle –." Her escort recalls both the lover of Poe's configuration and the "Bridegroom" that had been promised in the Bible: "We slowly drove – He knew no haste / And I had put away / My labor and my leisure too, / For His Civility –". Their "Carriage" hovers in some surrealistic state that is exterior to both time and place: they are no longer earth-bound, not quite dead (or at least still possessed of consciousness), but they have not yet achieved the celebration that awaits them, the "marriage supper of the Lamb."

Yet the ultimate implication of this work turns precisely upon the poet's capacity to explode the finite temporal boundaries that generally define our existence, for there is a third member of the party—also exterior to time and location—and that is "Immortality." *True* immortality, the verse suggests, comes neither from the confabulations of a male lover nor from God's intangible Heaven. Irrefutable "Immortality" resides in the work of art itself, the creation of an empowered woman poet that continues to captivate readers more than one hundred years after her death. And this much-read, often-cited poem stands as patent proof upon the page of its own argument!

From "Emily Dickinson"

LANGSTON HUGHES

Langston Hughes

Langston Hughes was born in Joplin, Missouri, in 1901. After his parents separated, he and his mother often lived a life of itinerant poverty, mostly in Kansas. Hughes attended high school in Cleveland, where as a senior he wrote "The Negro Speaks of Rivers." Reluctantly supported by his father, he attended Columbia University for a year before withdrawing. After a series of menial jobs, Hughes became a merchant seaman in 1923 and visited the ports of West Africa. He lived in Paris, Genoa, and Rome, before returning to the United States. The publication of The Weary Blues (1926) earned him immediate fame, which he solidified a few months later with his pioneering essay "The Negro Artist and the Racial Mountain." In 1926 he entered Lincoln University in Pennsylvania, from which he graduated in 1929. By then Hughes was one of the central figures of the Harlem Renaissance, the flowering of African American arts and literature in New York City's Harlem neighborhood in the 1920s. A strikingly versatile author, Hughes worked in the modes of fiction, drama, translation, criticism, opera libretti, memoir, cinema, and songwriting, as well as poetry. He became a tireless promoter of African American culture, crisscrossing the United States on speaking tours, as well as compiling twenty-eight anthologies of African American folklore and poetry. His newspaper columns, which often reported conversations with an imaginary Harlem friend named Jesse B. Semple, nicknamed "Simple," attracted large following. During the 1930s Hughes became involved in radical politics and traveled to the Soviet Union, but after World War II he gradually shifted to mainstream progressive politics. In his last years he became a spokesman for the moderate wing of the civil rights movement. He died in Harlem in 1967. His ashes are buried at the New York Public Library's Shomburg Center for Research in Black Culture.

POEMS

The Negro Speaks of Rivers (1921) 1926

I've known rivers:
I've known rivers ancient as the world and older than the flow of human
    blood in human veins.

My soul has grown deep like the rivers.

I bathed in the Euphrates when dawns were young.
I built my hut near the Congo and it lulled me to sleep.
I looked upon the Nile and raised the pyramids above it.   5
I heard the singing of the Mississippi when Abe Lincoln went down to New
    Orleans, and I've seen its muddy bosom turn all golden in the sunset.

I've known rivers:
Ancient, dusky rivers.

My soul has grown deep like the rivers.   10

The Negro   1922

I am a Negro:
    Black as the night is black,
    Black like the depths of my Africa.

I've been a slave:
    Caesar told me to keep his door-steps clean.   5
    I brushed the boots of Washington.

I've been a worker:
    Under my hand the pyramids arose.
    I made mortar for the Woolworth Building.

I've been a singer: 10
    All the way from Africa to Georgia I carried my sorrow songs.
    I made ragtime.

I've been a victim:
    The Belgians cut off my hands in the Congo.
    They lynch me now in Texas.   15

I am a Negro:
    Black as the night is black,
    Black like the depths of my Africa.

My People   1922

Dream-singers,
Story-tellers,
Dancers,
Loud laughers in the hands of Fate—
    My People.   5
Dish-washers,
Elevator-boys,
Ladies' maids,
Crap-shooters,
Cooks,   10
Waiters,
Jazzers,
Nurses of babies,
Loaders of ships,
Porters,   15
Hairdressers,
Comedians in vaudeville
And band-men in circuses—
Dream-singers all,
Story-tellers all.   20
    Dancers—
God! What dancers!
Singers—

God! What singers!
Singers and dancers   25
Dancers and laughers.
Laughers?
Yes, laughers . . . laughers . . . laughers—
Loud-mouthed laughers in the hands
    Of Fate.   30

Song for a Banjo Dance   1922

Shake your brown feet, honey,
Shake your brown feet, chil',
Shake your brown feet, honey,
Shake 'em swift and wil'—
    Get way back, honey,   5
    Do that low-down step.
    Get on over, darling,
        Now! Step out
        With your left.
Shake your brown feet, honey,   10
Shake 'em, honey chil'.

Sun's going down this evening—
Might never rise no mo'.
The sun's going down this very night—
Might never rise no mo'—   15
So dance with swift feet, honey,
    (The banjo's sobbing low),
Dance with swift feet, honey—
Might never dance no mo'.

Shake your brown feet, Liza,   20
Shake 'em, Liza, chil',
Shake your brown feet, Liza,
    (The music's soft and wil').
Shake your brown feet, Liza,
    (The banjo's sobbing low),   25
The sun's going down this very night—
Might never rise no mo'.

Mother to Son   (1922) 1932

Well, son, I'll tell you:
Life for me ain't been no crystal stair.
It's had tacks in it,
And splinters,
And boards torn up,   5
And places with no carpet on the floor—
Bare.
But all the time
I'se been a-climbin' on,

And reachin' landin's,   10
And turnin' corners,
And sometimes goin' in the dark
Where there ain't been no light.
So boy, don't you turn back.
Don't you set down on the steps   15
'Cause you finds it's kinder hard.
Don't you fall now—
For I'se still goin', honey,
I'se still climbin',
And life for me ain't been no crystal stair.   20

I, Too   1926

I, too, sing America.

I am the darker brother.
They send me to eat in the kitchen
When company comes,
But I laugh,   5
And eat well,
And grow strong.

Tomorrow,
I'll be at the table
When company comes.   10
Nobody'll dare
Say to me,
"Eat in the kitchen,"
Then.

Besides,   15
They'll see how beautiful I am
And be ashamed—

I, too, am America.

Cross   1926

My old man's a white old man
And my old mother's black.
If ever I cursed my white old man
I take my curses back.

If ever I cursed my black old mother   5
And wished she were in hell,
I'm sorry for that evil wish
And now I wish her well.

My old man died in a fine big house.
My ma died in a shack.   10
I wonder where I'm going to die,
Being neither white nor black?

Song for a Dark Girl   1927

Way Down South in Dixie
  (Break the heart of me)
They hung my black young lover
  To a cross roads tree.

Way Down South in Dixie
  (Bruised body high in air)   5
I asked the white Lord Jesus
  What was the use of prayer.

Way Down South in Dixie
  (Break the heart of me)
Love is a naked shadow   10
  On a gnarled and naked tree.

Prayer   (1931) 1947

Gather up
In the arms of your pity
The sick, the depraved,
The desperate, the tired,
All the scum   5
Of our weary city
Gather up
In the arms of your pity.
Gather up
In the arms of your love—   10
Those who expect
No love from above.

Theme for English B   1951

The instructor said,

> Go home and write
> a page tonight.
> And let that page come out of you—
> Then, it will be true.   5

I wonder if it's that simple?
I am twenty-two, colored, born in Winston-Salem.
I went to school there, then Durham, then here
to this college on the hill above Harlem.
I am the only colored student in my class.   10
The steps from the hill lead down into Harlem,
through a park, then I cross St. Nicholas,
Eighth Avenue, Seventh, and I come to the Y,

the Harlem Branch Y, where I take the elevator
up to my room, sit down, and write this page: 15

It's not easy to know what is true for you or me
at twenty-two, my age. But I guess I'm what
I feel and see and hear, Harlem, I hear you:
hear you, hear me—we two—you, me, talk on this page.
(I hear New York, too.) Me—who?   20
Well, I like to eat, sleep, drink, and be in love.
I like to work, read, learn, and understand life.
I like a pipe for a Christmas present,
or records—Bessie, bop, or Bach.
I guess being colored doesn't make me *not* like   25
the same things other folks like who are other races.
So will my page be colored that I write?
Being me, it will not be white.
But it will be
a part of you, instructor.   30
You are white—
yet a part of me, as I am a part of you.
That's American.
Sometimes perhaps you don't want to be a part of me.
Nor do I often want to be a part of you.   35
But we are, that's true!
As I learn from you,
I guess you learn from me—
although you're older—and white—
and somewhat more free.   40

This is my page for English B.

THEME FOR ENGLISH B. 9 *college on the hill above Harlem:* Columbia University, where Hughes was briefly a student. (Note, however, that this poem is not autobiographical. The young speaker is a character invented by the middle-aged author.) 24 *Bessie:* Bessie Smith (1898?–1937) was a popular blues singer often called the "Empress of the Blues."

Nightmare Boogie   1951

I had a dream
and I could see
a million faces
black as me!
A nightmare dream: 5
Quicker than light
All them faces
Turned dead white!
Boogie-woogie,
Rolling bass,   10
Whirling treble
Of cat-gut lace.

Harlem [Dream Deferred]   1951

What happens to a dream deferred?

> Does it dry up
> like a raisin in the sun?
> Or fester like a sore—
> And then run?   5
> Does it stink like rotten meat?
> Or crust and sugar over—
> like a syrupy sweet?

> Maybe it just sags
> like a heavy load.   10

> *Or does it explode?*

HARLEM. This famous poem appeared under two titles in the author's lifetime. Both titles appear above.

Homecoming   1959

I went back in the alley
And I opened up my door.
All her clothes was gone:
She wasn't home no more.

I pulled back the covers,   5
I made down the bed.
A *whole* lot of room
Was the only thing I had.

Compare

Another poem by Langston Hughes that is found in this book:

Two Somewhat Different Epigrams (Chapter 24)

LANGSTON HUGHES ON WRITING

Langston Hughes, c. 1945.

The Negro Artist and the Racial Mountain   1926

Most of my own poems are racial in theme and treatment, derived from the life I know. In many of them I try to grasp and hold some of the meanings and rhythms of jazz. I am as sincere as I know how to be in these poems and yet after every reading I answer questions like these from my own people: Do you think Negroes should always write about Negroes? I wish you wouldn't read some of your poems to white folks. How do you find anything interesting in a place like a cabaret? Why do you write about black people? You aren't black. What makes you do so many jazz poems?

But jazz to me is one of the inherent expressions of Negro life in America; the eternal tom-tom beating in the Negro soul— the tom-tom of revolt against weariness in a white world, a world of subway trains, and work, work, work; the tom-tom of joy and laughter, and pain swallowed in a smile. Yet the Philadelphia clubwoman is ashamed to say that her race created it and she does not like me to write about it. The old subconscious "white is best" runs through her mind. Years of study under white teachers, a lifetime of white books, pictures, and papers, and white manners, morals, and Puritan standards made her dislike the spirituals. And now she turns up her nose at jazz and all its manifestations—likewise almost everything else distinctly racial. She doesn't care for the Winold Reiss portraits of Negroes because they are "too Negro." She does not want a true picture of herself from anybody. She wants the artist to flatter her, to make the white world believe that all Negroes are as smug and as near white in soul as she wants to be. But, to my mind, it is the duty of the younger Negro artist, if he accepts any duties at all from outsiders, to change through the force of his art that old whispering "I want to be white," hidden in the aspirations of his people, to "Why should I want to be white? I am a Negro—and beautiful."

So I am ashamed for the black poet who says, "I want to be a poet, not a Negro poet," as though his own racial world were not as interesting as any other world. I am ashamed, too, for the colored artist who runs from the painting of Negro faces to the painting of sunsets after the manner of the academicians because he fears the strange un-whiteness of his own features. An artist must be free to choose what he does, certainly, but he must also never be afraid to do what he might choose.

From "The Negro Artist and the Racial Mountain"

Compare

Hughes's comments on the African American artist with Darryl Pinckney's critical observations on Langston Hughes's public identity as a black poet, later in this chapter.

The Harlem Renaissance   1940

White people began to come to Harlem in droves. For several years they packed the expensive Cotton Club on Lenox Avenue. But I was never there, because the Cotton Club was a Jim Crow club for gangsters and monied whites. They were not cordial to Negro patronage, unless you were a celebrity like Bojangles.° So Harlem Negroes did not like the Cotton Club and never appreciated its Jim Crow policy in the very heart of their dark community. Nor did ordinary Negroes like the growing influx of whites toward Harlem after sundown, flooding the little cabarets and bars where formerly only colored people laughed and sang, and where now the strangers were given the best ringside tables to sit and stare at the Negro customers—like amusing animals in a zoo.

The Negroes said: "We can't go downtown and sit and stare at you in your clubs. You won't even let us in your clubs." But they didn't say it out loud—for Negroes are practically never rude to white people. So thousands of whites came to Harlem night after night, thinking the Negroes loved to have them there, and firmly believing that all Harlemites left their houses at sundown to sing and dance in cabarets, because most of the whites saw nothing but the cabarets, not the houses.

Some of the owners of Harlem clubs, delighted at the flood of white patronage, made the grievous error of barring their own race, after the manner of the famous Cotton Club. But most of these quickly lost business and folded up, because they failed to realize that a large part of the Harlem attraction for downtown New Yorkers lay in simply watching the colored customers amuse themselves. And the smaller clubs, of course, had no big floor shows or a name band like the Cotton Club, where Duke Ellington usually held forth, so, without black patronage, they were not amusing at all.

Some of the small clubs, however, had people like Gladys Bentley, who was something worth discovering in those days, before she got famous, acquired an accompanist, specially written material, and conscious vulgarity. But for two or three amazing years, Miss Bentley sat, and played a big piano all night long, literally all

---

Bojangles: Bill "Bojangles" Robinson (1876–1949), dancer.

Lenox Avenue, Harlem, during the Harlem Renaissance.

night, without stopping—singing songs like "The St. James Infirmary," from ten in the evening until dawn, with scarcely a break between the notes, sliding from one song to another, with a powerful and continuous underbeat of jungle rhythm. Miss Bentley was an amazing exhibition of musical energy—a large, dark, masculine lady, whose feet pounded the floor while her fingers pounded the keyboard—a perfect piece of African sculpture, animated by her own rhythm.

But when the place where she played became too well known, she began to sing with an accompanist, became a star, moved to a larger place, then downtown, and is now in Hollywood. The old magic of the woman and the piano and the night and the rhythm being one is gone. But everything goes, one way or another. The '20s are gone and lots of fine things in Harlem night life have disappeared like snow in the sun—since it became utterly commercial, planned for the downtown tourist trade, and therefore dull.

The lindy-hoppers at the Savoy even began to practice acrobatic routines, and to do absurd things for the entertainment of the whites, that probably never would have entered their heads to attempt merely for their own effortless amusement. Some of the lindy-hoppers had cards printed with their names on them and became dance professors teaching the tourists. Then Harlem nights became show nights for the Nordics.

Some critics say that that is what happened to certain Negro writers, too—that they ceased to write to amuse themselves and began to write to amuse and entertain white people, and in so doing distorted and overcolored their material, and left out a great many things they thought would offend their American brothers of a lighter complexion. Maybe—since Negroes have writer-racketeers, as has any other race. But I have known almost all of them, and most of the good ones have tried to be honest, write honestly, and express their world as they saw it.

From *The Big Sea*

CRITICS ON LANGSTON HUGHES

Arnold Rampersad (b. 1941)

Hughes as an Experimentalist

1991

From his first publication of verse in the *Crisis*, Hughes had reflected his admiration for Sandburg and Whitman by experimenting with free verse as opposed to committing himself conservatively to rhyme. Even when he employed rhyme in his verse, as he often did, Hughes composed with relative casualness—unlike other major black poets of the day, such as Countee Cullen and Claude McKay, with their highly wrought stanzas. He seemed to prefer, as Whitman and Sandburg had preferred, to write lines that captured the cadences of common American speech, with his ear always especially attuned to the variety of black American language. This last aspect was only a token of his emotional and aesthetic involvement in black American culture, which he increasingly saw as his prime source of inspiration, even as he regarded black Americans ("Loud laughers in the hands of Fate— / My People") as his only indispensable audience.

Early poems captured some of the sights and sounds of ecstatic black church worship ("Glory! Hallelujah!"), but Hughes's greatest technical accomplishment as a poet was in his fusing of the rhythms of blues and jazz with traditional poetry. This technique, which he employed his entire life, surfaced in his art around 1923 with the landmark poem "The Weary Blues," in which the persona recalls hearing a blues singer and piano player ("Sweet Blues! / Coming from a black man's soul") performing in what most likely is a speakeasy in Harlem. The persona recalls the plaintive verse intoned by the singer ("Ain't got nobody in all this world, / Ain't got nobody but ma self.") but finally surrenders to the mystery and magic of the blues singer's art. In the process, Hughes had taken an indigenous African American art form, perhaps the most vivid and commanding of all, and preserved its authenticity even as he formally enshrined it in the midst of a poem in traditional European form.

"The Weary Blues," a work virtually unprecedented in American poetry in its blending of black and white rhythms and forms, won Hughes the first prize for poetry in May 1925 in the epochal literary contest sponsored by *Opportunity* magazine, which marked the first high point of the Harlem Renaissance. The work also confirmed his leadership, along with Countee Cullen, of all the younger poets of the burgeoning movement. For Hughes, it was only the first step in his poetical tribute to blues and jazz. By the time of his second volume of verse, *Fine Clothes to the Jew* (1927), he was writing blues poems without either apology or framing devices taken from the traditional world of poetry. He was also delving into the basic subject matters of the blues—love and raw sexuality, deep sorrow and sudden violence, poverty and heartbreak. These subjects, treated with sympathy for the poor and dispossessed, and without false piety, made him easily the most controversial black poet of his time.

From "Langston Hughes"

Rita Dove (b. 1952)
and Marilyn Nelson (b. 1946)

The Voices in Langston Hughes   1998

Affectionately known for most of his life as "The Poet Laureate of Harlem," Langston Hughes was born in Missouri and raised in the Midwest, moving to Harlem only as a young man. There he discovered his spiritual home, in Harlem's heart of Blackness finding both his vocation—"to explain and illuminate the Negro condition in America"—and the proletarian voice of most of his best work. If Johnson° was the Renaissance man of the Harlem Renaissance, Hughes was its greatest man of letters; he saw through publication more than a dozen collections of poems, ten plays, two novels, several collections of short fiction, one historical study, two autobiographical works, several anthologies, and many books for children. His essay, "The Negro Artist and the Racial Mountain," provided a personal credo and statement of direction for the poets of his generation, who, he says, "intend to express our individual dark-skinned selves without fear or shame . . . We know we are beautiful. And ugly too." His forthright commitment to the Negro people led him to explore with great authenticity the frustrated dreams of the Black masses and to experiment with diction, rhythm, and musical forms.

Hughes was ever quick to confess the influences of Whitman and Sandburg on his work, and his best poetry also reflects the influence of Sherwood Anderson's *Winesburg, Ohio*. Like these poets, Hughes collected individual voices; his work is a notebook of life-studies. In his best poems Hughes the man remains masked; his voices are the voices of the Negro race as a whole, or of individual Negro speakers. "The Negro Speaks of Rivers," a widely anthologized poem from his first book, *The Weary Blues* (1926), is a case in point. Here Hughes is visible only as spokesman for the race as he proclaims "I bathed in the Euphrates when dawns were young. / I built my hut near the Congo and it lulled me to sleep." Poems frequently present anonymous Black personae, each of whom shares a painful heritage and an ironic pride. As one humorous character announces:

> I do cooking,
> Day's work, too!
> Alberta K. Johnson—
> *Madam* to you.

Hughes took poetry out of what Cullen called "the dark tower"—which was, and even during the Harlem Renaissance, ivy-covered and distant—and took it directly to the people. His blues and jazz experiments described and addressed an audience for which music was a central experience; he became a spokesman for their troubles, as in "Po' Boy Blues":

> When I was home de
> Sunshine seemed like gold.
> When I was home de
> Sunshine seemed like gold.
> Since I come up North de
> Whole damn world's turned cold.

Johnson: James Weldon Johnson, a leading poet of the Harlem Renaissance.

American democracy appears frequently in Hughes's work as the unfulfilled but potentially realizable dream of the Negro, who says in "Let America Be America Again":

O, yes,
I say it plain,
America never was America to me
And yet I swear this oath—
America will be!

There are many fine poems in the Hughes canon, but the strongest single work is *Montage of a Dream Deferred* (1951), a collection of sketches, captured voices, and individual lives unified by the jazzlike improvisations on the central theme of "a dream deferred." Like many of his individual poems, this work is intended for performance: think of it as a Harlem *Under Milk Wood.*° Hughes moves rapidly from one voice or scene to the next; from the person in "Blues in Dawn" who says "I don't dare start thinking in the morning," to, in "Dime," a snatch of conversation: "Chile, these steps is hard to climb. / Grandma, lend me a dime."

The moods of the poems are as varied as their voices, for Hughes includes the daylight hours as well as the night. There are the bitter jump-rope rhymes of disillusioned children, the naive exclamations of young lovers, the gossip of friends. A college freshman writes in his "Theme for English B": "I guess being colored doesn't make me *not* like / the same things other folks like who are other races." A jaded woman offers in "Advice" the observation that "birthing is hard / and dying is mean," and advises youth to "get yourself / a little loving / in between." "Hope" is a miniature vignette in which a dying man asks for fish, and "His wife looked it up in her dream book / and played it." The changing voices, moods, and rhythms of this collection are, as Hughes wrote in a preface, "Like be-bop . . . marked by conflicting change, sudden nuances. . . ." We are reminded throughout that we should be hearing the poem as music; as boogie-woogie, as blues, as bass, as saxophone. Against the eighty-odd dreams collected here, the refrain insists that these frustrated dreams are potentially dangerous:

What happens to a dream deferred?

Does it dry up
like a raisin in the sun?
Or fester like a sore—
And then run?
Does it stink like rotten meat?
Or crust and sugar over—
like a syrupy sweet?

Maybe it just sags
like a heavy load.

Or does it explode?

More than any other Black poet, Langston Hughes spoke for the Negro people. Most of those after him have emulated his ascent of the Racial Mountain, his

Under Milk Wood: a 1954 radio play by Dylan Thomas which features the voices and thoughts of the inhabitants of a small Welsh fishing town.

painfully joyous declaration of pride and commonality. His work offers white readers a glimpse into the social and the personal lives of Black America; Black readers recognize a proud affirmation of self.

From "A Black Rainbow: Modern Afro-American Poetry"

Darryl Pinckney (b. 1953)

Black Identity in Langston Hughes

1989

Fierce identification with the sorrows and pleasures of the poor black—"I myself belong to that class"—propelled Hughes toward the voice of the black Everyman. He made a distinction between his lyric and his social poetry, the private and the public. In the best of his social poetry he turned himself into a transmitter of messages and made the "I" a collective "I":

> I've known rivers:
> I've known rivers ancient as the world and older than the flow
> of human blood in human veins.
>
> My soul has grown deep like the rivers.
>
> I bathed in the Euphrates when dawns were young.
> I built my hut near the Congo and it lulled me to sleep.
> I looked upon the Nile and raised the pyramids above it.
> I heard the singing of the Mississippi when Abe Lincoln went down to
> New Orleans, and I've seen its muddy bosom turn all golden in the
> sunset.

("The Negro Speaks of Rivers")

The medium conveys a singleness of intention: to make the black known. The straightforward, declarative style doesn't call attention to itself. Nothing distracts from forceful statement, as if the shadowy characters Sandburg wrote about in, say, "When Mammy Hums" had at last their chance to come forward and testify. Poems like "Aunt Sue's Stories" reflect the folk ideal of black women as repositories of racial lore. The story told in dramatic monologues like "The Negro Mother" or "Mother to Son" is one of survival—life "ain't been no crystal stair." The emphasis is on the capacity of black people to endure, which is why Hughes's social poetry, though not strictly protest writing, indicts white America, even taunts it with the steady belief that blacks will overcome simply by "keeping on":

> I, too, sing America.
>
> I am the darker brother.
> They send me to eat in the kitchen
> When company comes,
> But I laugh,
> And eat well,
> And grow strong.

("I, Too")

Whites were not the only ones who could be made uneasy by Hughes's attempts to boldly connect past and future. The use of "black" and the invocation of Africa were defiant gestures back in the days when many blacks described themselves as brown. When Hughes answered Sandburg's "Nigger" ("I am the nigger, / Singer of Songs . . . ") with "I am a Negro, / Black as the night is black, / Black like the depths of my Africa" ("Negro") he challenged the black middle class with his absorption in slave heritage.

From "Suitcase in Harlem"

Peter Townsend (b. 1948)

Langston Hughes and Jazz

2000

Hughes's engagement with jazz was close and long-lived, from his "Weary Blues" of 1926 up to the time of his death in 1967. Jazz crops naturally out of the landscape of Hughes's poetry, which is largely that of the black communities of Harlem and Chicago, and it remains fluid in its significance. Hughes's earliest references to jazz, in poems like "Jazzonia" and "Jazz Band in a Parisian Cabaret," acknowledge the exoticism which was customary in the presentation of jazz in the 1920s, and the novelty which the music still possessed for Hughes himself:

Langston Hughes, 1954.

In a Harlem cabaret
Six long-headed jazzers play.
A dancing girl whose eyes are bold
Lifts high a dress of silken gold.

("Jazzonia")

This novelty is compounded by a further level of exoticism for the white visitors to the black cabarets who figure frequently in Hughes's jazz world. "Jazz Band in a Parisian Cabaret," for instance, has the band

Play it for the lords and ladies,
For the dukes and counts,
For the whores and gigolos,
For the American millionaires,

and "Harlem Night Club" pictures "dark brown girls / In blond men's arms." In Hughes's more politically barbed poetry of the 1930s these comments on white voyeurism harden into his attitude in "Visitors to the Black Belt":

You can say
Jazz on the South Side—
To me it's hell
On the South Side.

At the same time, jazz is one of the threads that make up the fabric of urban life in the "Harlem Renaissance" period. In a poem entitled "Heart of Harlem" Hughes places jazz musicians such as Earl Hines and Billie Holiday alongside individuals of the stature of Adam Clayton Powell, Joe Louis and W. E. B. Du Bois. Hughes's continuous awareness of the place of jazz in his community enables him to record its scenes and its changes across the decades. "Lincoln Theatre," a poem published in a collection in 1949, gives a memorably exact rendering of the sort of Swing Era performance, in a Harlem theater, that was discussed [earlier]:

The movies end. The lights flash gaily on.
The band down in the pit bursts into jazz.
The crowd applauds a plump brown-skin bleached blonde
Who sings the troubles every woman has.

Hughes responded with particular sympathy to jazz of the bebop period, which he saw as having great political significance. *Montage of a Dream Deferred*, published in 1951, is one of Hughes's most substantial sequences of poems, and it is shot through with references to jazz. His editorial note to the sequence explains the stylistic influence of bebop on its composition:

This poem on contemporary Harlem, like be-bop, is marked by conflicting changes, sudden nuances, sharp and impudent interjections, broken rhythms, and passages sometimes in the manner of the jam session, sometimes the popular song, punctuated by the riffs, runs, breaks, and distortions of the music of a community in transition.

As Hughes made clear in other places, he heard bebop as an expression of a dissident spirit within the younger black community:

> Little cullud boys with fears,
> frantic, kick their draftee years
> into flatted fifths and flatter beers . . .

and "Dream Boogie" resounds with suggestions, threatening or impudent, that well up in the music, the "boogie-woogie rumble":

> Listen to it closely:
> Ain't you heard
> something underneath . . .

Bebop affected the forms of Hughes's poetry at the higher architectural levels, dictating the structural rhythm of longer works like "Dream Deferred," but otherwise he employed a small range of simple verse forms that originate in earlier styles of black music. A particular favourite was a two-stress line rhymed in quatrains, derived from spirituals, and he also frequently used a looser form drawn from the 12-bar blues. The first of these Hughes was able to use with remarkable flexibility, considering its brevity. The form is often used for aphoristic effect, as in "Motto":

> I play it cool
> And dig all jive.
> That's the reason
> I stay alive.

or in "Sliver," a comment on the form itself:

> A cheap little tune
> To cheap little rhymes
> Can cut a man's
> Throat sometimes.

What is even more remarkable is the naturalness of its effect in these diverse contexts. Hughes makes the form serve the purposes of narrative and description just as flexibly as that of comment. It gives Hughes's verse its idiomatic flavor, so that even where the subject is not jazz or even music, the verse is still permeated with the qualities of black musical culture.

From *Jazz in American Culture*

ROBERT FROST

Robert Frost

Despite his indelible association with New England, Robert Lee Frost (1874–1963) was born in San Francisco, California. After his father's death in 1885, his mother moved the family to Lawrence, Massachusetts. Frost never finished college, though over the course of his life he would be the recipient of many honorary degrees from the most prestigious universities in the United States and Britain. He married Elinor White in December 1895, and their first child was born in September 1896; his death, from cholera, in July 1900, was the first of many family tragedies that Frost would endure. Between 1899 and 1907, the couple had five more children—another son and four daughters, the last of whom lived for only three days. Frost moved his family to England in August 1912, hoping to find the literary success that had eluded him in his own country. With surprising ease, he had a pair of manuscripts accepted by a London publisher, and returned to America early in 1915 as the author of two highly regarded books of verse. The first of these, A Boy's Will (1913), is a young man's book. North of Boston (1914), much more substantial in power and originality, is often considered his finest collection. This book and his next two, Mountain Interval (1916) and New Hampshire (1923), contain the core of his achievement, in the two modes that he made his own—subtle, concentrated lyric poems of understated but brilliant technical accomplishment, and longer narratives, often dramatizing the hard life of rural northern New England a century ago. The speaker in Frost's poems is usually careful and often sly, meditating on and distilling the essence of many years of observation and experience. The poet's rhetoric is measured and precise as he strives to catch the rhythms of ordinary speech—in his own phrase, "the sound of sense." After many years of accumulating fame and honors, including an unprecedented four Pulitzer Prizes, the capstone of Frost's public career was his appearance at John F. Kennedy's presidential inauguration in January 1961. Kennedy also sent him to the Soviet Union as a cultural envoy in 1962, not long before Frost's death in a Boston hospital on January 29, 1963, eight weeks short of his eighty-ninth birthday. To the broad public, Frost often seemed like a front-porch philosopher dispensing consolation and old-fashioned country wisdom, but behind this stereotype he was a tragic poet, whose deepest note is one of inevitable human isolation. In a life more painful than most, he struggled heroically with his inner and outer demons, and out of that struggle he produced what many consider the greatest body of work by any American poet of the twentieth century.

POEMS

Mowing   1913

There was never a sound beside the wood but one,
And that was my long scythe whispering to the ground.
What was it it whispered? I knew not well myself;
Perhaps it was something about the heat of the sun,

Something, perhaps, about the lack of sound—   5
And that was why it whispered and did not speak.
It was no dream of the gift of idle hours,
Or easy gold at the hand of fay or elf:
Anything more than the truth would have seemed too weak
To the earnest love that laid the swale in rows,   10
Not without feeble-pointed spikes of flowers
(Pale orchises), and scared a bright green snake.
The fact is the sweetest dream that labor knows.
My long scythe whispered and left the hay to make.

My November Guest   1915

My Sorrow, when she's here with me,
    Thinks these dark days of autumn rain
Are beautiful as days can be;
She loves the bare, the withered tree;
    She walks the sodden pasture lane.   5

Her pleasure will not let me stay.
    She talks and I am fain to list:
She's glad the birds are gone away,
She's glad her simple worsted gray
    Is silver now with clinging mist.   10

The desolate, deserted trees,
    The faded earth, the heavy sky,
The beauties she so truly sees,
She thinks I have no eye for these,
    And vexes me for reason why.   15

Not yesterday I learned to know
    The love of bare November days
Before the coming of the snow,
But it were vain to tell her so,
    And they are better for her praise.   20

Mending Wall   1914

Something there is that doesn't love a wall,
That sends the frozen-ground-swell under it,
And spills the upper boulders in the sun;
And makes gaps even two can pass abreast.
The work of hunters is another thing: 5
I have come after them and made repair
Where they have left not one stone on a stone,
But they would have the rabbit out of hiding,
To please the yelping dogs. The gaps I mean,
No one has seen them made or heard them made,   10
But at spring mending-time we find them there.
I let my neighbor know beyond the hill;
And on a day we meet to walk the line

And set the wall between us once again.
We keep the wall between us as we go.   15
To each the boulders that have fallen to each.
And some are loaves and some so nearly balls
We have to use a spell to make them balance:
"Stay where you are until our backs are turned!"
We wear our fingers rough with handling them.   20
Oh, just another kind of outdoor game,
One on a side. It comes to little more:
There where it is we do not need the wall:
He is all pine and I am apple orchard.
My apple trees will never get across   25
And eat the cones under his pines, I tell him.
He only says, "Good fences make good neighbors."
Spring is the mischief in me, and I wonder
If I could put a notion in his head:
"*Why* do they make good neighbors? Isn't it   30
Where there are cows? But here there are no cows.
Before I built a wall I'd ask to know
What I was walling in or walling out,
And to whom I was like to give offence.
Something there is that doesn't love a wall,   35
That wants it down." I could say "Elves" to him,
But it's not elves exactly, and I'd rather
He said it for himself. I see him there
Bringing a stone grasped firmly by the top
In each hand, like an old-stone savage armed.   40
He moves in darkness as it seems to me,
Not of woods only and the shade of trees.
He will not go behind his father's saying,
And he likes having thought of it so well
He says again, "Good fences make good neighbors."   45

After Apple-Picking   1914

My long two-pointed ladder's sticking through a tree
Toward heaven still,
And there's a barrel that I didn't fill
Beside it, and there may be two or three
Apples I didn't pick upon some bough.   5
But I am done with apple-picking now.
Essence of winter sleep is on the night,
The scent of apples: I am drowsing off.
I cannot rub the strangeness from my sight
I got from looking through a pane of glass   10
I skimmed this morning from the drinking trough
And held against the world of hoary grass.
It melted, and I let it fall and break.
But I was well
Upon my way to sleep before it fell,   15

And I could tell
What form my dreaming was about to take.
Magnified apples appear and disappear,
Stem end and blossom end,
And every fleck of russet showing clear.   20
My instep arch not only keeps the ache,
It keeps the pressure of a ladder-round.
I feel the ladder sway as the boughs bend.
And I keep hearing from the cellar bin
The rumbling sound   25
Of load on load of apples coming in.
For I have had too much
Of apple-picking: I am overtired
Of the great harvest I myself desired.
There were ten thousand thousand fruit to touch, 30
Cherish in hand, lift down, and not let fall.
For all
That struck the earth,
No matter if not bruised or spiked with stubble,
Went surely to the cider-apple heap   35
As of no worth.
One can see what will trouble
This sleep of mine, whatever sleep it is.
Were he not gone,
The woodchuck could say whether it's like his   40
Long sleep, as I describe its coming on,
Or just some human sleep.

The Road Not Taken   1916

Two roads diverged in a yellow wood,
And sorry I could not travel both
And be one traveler, long I stood
And looked down one as far as I could
To where it bent in the undergrowth;   5

Then took the other, as just as fair,
And having perhaps the better claim,
Because it was grassy and wanted wear;
Though as for that the passing there
Had worn them really about the same,   10

And both that morning equally lay
In leaves no step had trodden black.
Oh, I kept the first for another day!
Yet knowing how way leads on to way,
I doubted if I should ever come back.   15

I shall be telling this with a sigh
Somewhere ages and ages hence:
Two roads diverged in a wood, and I—

I took the one less traveled by,
And that has made all the difference.   20

Birches   1916

When I see birches bend to left and right
Across the lines of straighter darker trees,
I like to think some boy's been swinging them.
But swinging doesn't bend them down to stay
As ice-storms do. Often you must have seen them   5
Loaded with ice a sunny winter morning
After a rain. They click upon themselves
As the breeze rises, and turn many-colored
As the stir cracks and crazes their enamel.
Soon the sun's warmth makes them shed crystal shells   10
Shattering and avalanching on the snow-crust—
Such heaps of broken glass to sweep away
You'd think the inner dome of heaven had fallen.
They are dragged to the withered bracken by the load,
And they seem not to break; though once they are bowed   15
So low for long, they never right themselves:
You may see their trunks arching in the woods
Years afterwards, trailing their leaves on the ground
Like girls on hands and knees that throw their hair
Before them over their heads to dry in the sun.   20
But I was going to say when Truth broke in
With all her matter-of-fact about the ice-storm
I should prefer to have some boy bend them
As he went out and in to fetch the cows—
Some boy too far from town to learn baseball,   25
Whose only play was what he found himself,
Summer or winter, and could play alone.
One by one he subdued his father's trees
By riding them down over and over again
Until he took the stiffness out of them,   30
And not one but hung limp, not one was left
For him to conquer. He learned all there was
To learn about not launching out too soon
And so not carrying the tree away
Clear to the ground. He always kept his poise   35
To the top branches, climbing carefully
With the same pains you use to fill a cup
Up to the brim, and even above the brim.
Then he flung outward, feet first, with a swish,
Kicking his way down through the air to the ground.   40
So was I once myself a swinger of birches.
And so I dream of going back to be.
It's when I'm weary of considerations,
And life is too much like a pathless wood
Where your face burns and tickles with the cobwebs   45

Broken across it, and one eye is weeping
From a twig's having lashed across it open.
I'd like to get away from earth awhile
And then come back to it and begin over.
May no fate willfully misunderstand me   50
And half grant what I wish and snatch me away
Not to return. Earth's the right place for love:
I don't know where it's likely to go better.
I'd like to go by climbing a birch tree,
And climb black branches up a snow-white trunk   55
Toward heaven, till the tree could bear no more,
But dipped its top and set me down again.
That would be good both going and coming back.
One could do worse than be a swinger of birches.

Design   (1922) 1936

I found a dimpled spider, fat and white,
On a white heal-all, holding up a moth
Like a white piece of rigid satin cloth—
Assorted characters of death and blight
Mixed ready to begin the morning right,   5
Like the ingredients of a witches' broth—
A snow-drop spider, a flower like a froth,
And dead wings carried like a paper kite.

What had that flower to do with being white,
The wayside blue and innocent heal-all?   10
What brought the kindred spider to that height,
Then steered the white moth thither in the night?
What but design of darkness to appall?—
If design govern in a thing so small.

Stopping by Woods on a Snowy Evening   1923

Whose woods these are I think I know.
His house is in the village though;
He will not see me stopping here
To watch his woods fill up with snow.

My little horse must think it queer   5
To stop without a farmhouse near
Between the woods and frozen lake
The darkest evening of the year.

He gives his harness bells a shake
To ask if there is some mistake.   10
The only other sound's the sweep
Of easy wind and downy flake.

The woods are lovely, dark and deep,
But I have promises to keep,
And miles to go before I sleep,   15
And miles to go before I sleep.

Fire and Ice   1923

Some say the world will end in fire,
Some say in ice.
From what I've tasted of desire
I hold with those who favor fire.
But if it had to perish twice,   5
I think I know enough of hate
To say that for destruction ice
Is also great
And would suffice.

Acquainted with the Night   1928

I have been one acquainted with the night.
I have walked out in rain—and back in rain.
I have outwalked the furthest city light.

I have looked down the saddest city lane.
I have passed by the watchman on his beat   5
And dropped my eyes, unwilling to explain.

I have stood still and stopped the sound of feet
When far away an interrupted cry
Came over houses from another street,

But not to call me back or say good-by;   10
And further still at an unearthly height,
One luminary clock against the sky

Proclaimed the time was neither wrong nor right.
I have been one acquainted with the night.

Desert Places   1936

Snow falling and night falling fast, oh, fast
In a field I looked into going past,
And the ground almost covered smooth in snow,
But a few weeds and stubble showing last.

The woods around it have it—it is theirs.   5
All animals are smothered in their lairs.
I am too absent-spirited to count;
The loneliness includes me unawares.

And lonely as it is that loneliness
Will be more lonely ere it will be less—   10
A blanker whiteness of benighted snow
With no expression, nothing to express.

They cannot scare me with their empty spaces
Between stars—on stars where no human race is.
I have it in me so much nearer home   15
To scare myself with my own desert places.

Home Burial   1914

He saw her from the bottom of the stairs
Before she saw him. She was starting down,
Looking back over her shoulder at some fear.
She took a doubtful step and then undid it
To raise herself and look again. He spoke   5
Advancing toward her: "What is it you see
From up there always—for I want to know."
She turned and sank upon her skirts at that,
And her face changed from terrified to dull.
He said to gain time: "What is it you see,"   10
Mounting until she cowered under him.
"I will find out now—you must tell me, dear."
She, in her place, refused him any help
With the least stiffening of her neck and silence.
She let him look, sure that he wouldn't see,   15
Blind creature; and awhile he didn't see.
But at last he murmured, "Oh," and again, "Oh."

"What is it—what?" she said.

                            "Just that I see."

"You don't," she challenged. "Tell me what it is."

"The wonder is I didn't see at once.   20
I never noticed it from here before.
I must be wonted to it—that's the reason.
The little graveyard where my people are!
So small the window frames the whole of it.
Not so much larger than a bedroom, is it?   25
There are three stones of slate and one of marble,
Broad-shouldered little slabs there in the sunlight
On the sidehill. We haven't to mind *those*.
But I understand: it is not the stones,
But the child's mound—"

                            "Don't, don't, don't, don't," she cried.   30

She withdrew shrinking from beneath his arm
That rested on the banister, and slid downstairs;
And turned on him with such a daunting look,

He said twice over before he knew himself:
"Can't a man speak of his own child he's lost?"   35

"Not you! Oh, where's my hat? Oh, I don't need it!
I must get out of here. I must get air.
I don't know rightly whether any man can."

"Amy! Don't go to someone else this time.
Listen to me. I won't come down the stairs."   40
He sat and fixed his chin between his fists.
"There's something I should like to ask you, dear."

"You don't know how to ask it."

                              "Help me, then."

Her fingers moved the latch for all reply.

"My words are nearly always an offense.   45
I don't know how to speak of anything
So as to please you. But I might be taught
I should suppose. I can't say I see how.
A man must partly give up being a man
With women-folk. We could have some arrangement   50
By which I'd bind myself to keep hands off
Anything special you're a-mind to name.
Though I don't like such things 'twixt those that love.
Two that don't love can't live together without them.
But two that do can't live together with them."   55
She moved the latch a little. "Don't—don't go.
Don't carry it to someone else this time.
Tell me about it if it's something human.
Let me into your grief. I'm not so much
Unlike other folks as your standing there   60
Apart would make me out. Give me my chance.
I do think, though, you overdo it a little.
What was it brought you up to think it the thing
To take your mother-loss of a first child
So inconsolably—in the face of love.   65
You'd think his memory might be satisfied—"

"There you go sneering now!"

                           "I'm not, I'm not!
You make me angry. I'll come down to you.
God, what a woman! And it's come to this,
A man can't speak of his own child that's dead."   70

"You can't because you don't know how to speak.
If you had any feelings, you that dug
With your own hand—how could you?—his little grave;
I saw you from that very window there,
Making the gravel leap and leap in air,   75
Leap up, like that, like that, and land so lightly

And roll back down the mound beside the hole.
I thought, Who is that man? I didn't know you.
And I crept down the stairs and up the stairs
To look again, and still your spade kept lifting.   80
Then you came in. I heard your rumbling voice
Out in the kitchen, and I don't know why,
But I went near to see with my own eyes.
You could sit there with the stains on your shoes
Of the fresh earth from your own baby's grave   85
And talk about your everyday concerns.
You had stood the spade up against the wall
Outside there in the entry, for I saw it."

"I shall laugh the worst laugh I ever laughed.
I'm cursed. God, if I don't believe I'm cursed."   90

"I can repeat the very words you were saying.
'Three foggy mornings and one rainy day
Will rot the best birch fence a man can build.'
Think of it, talk like that at such a time!
What had how long it takes a birch to rot   95
To do with what was in the darkened parlor?
You *couldn't* care! The nearest friends can go
With anyone to death, comes so far short
They might as well not try to go at all.
No, from the time when one is sick to death,   100
One is alone, and he dies more alone.
Friends make pretense of following to the grave,
But before one is in it, their minds are turned
And making the best of their way back to life
And living people, and things they understand.   105
But the world's evil. I won't have grief so
If I can change it. Oh, I won't, I won't!"

"There, you have said it all and you feel better.
You won't go now. You're crying. Close the door.
The heart's gone out of it: why keep it up.   110
Amy! There's someone coming down the road!"

"*You*—oh, you think the talk is all. I must go—
Somewhere out of this house. How can I make you—"

"If—you—do!" She was opening the door wider.
"Where do you mean to go? First tell me that.   115
I'll follow and bring you back by force. I *will!*—"

Compare

Other poems by Robert Frost that are found in this book:

ROBERT FROST ON WRITING

Robert Frost with students.

The Sound of Sense   1913

I am possibly the only person going who works on any but a worn out theory (principle I had better say) of versification. You see the great successes in recent poetry
have been made on the assumption that the music of words was a matter of harmon-
ised vowels and consonants. Both Swinburne and Tennyson arrived largely at effects
in assonation. But they were on the wrong track or at any rate on a short track. They
went the length of it. Anyone else who goes that way must go after them. And that's
where most are going. I alone of English writers have consciously set myself to make
music out of what I may call the sound of sense. Now it is possible to have sense without the sound of sense (as in much prose that is supposed to pass muster but makes
very dull reading) and the sound of sense without sense (as in Alice in Wonderland
which makes anything but dull reading). The best place to get the abstract sound of
sense is from voices behind a door that cuts off the words. Ask yourself how these
sentences would sound without the words in which they are embodied:

> You mean to tell me you can't read?
> I said no such thing.
> Well read then.
> You're not my teacher.

He says it's too late.
Oh, say!
Damn an Ingersoll watch anyway.

One–two–three—go!
No good! Come back—come back.
Haslam go down there and make those kids get out of the track.

Those sounds are summoned by the audile imagination and they must be positive, strong, and definitely and unmistakeably indicated by the context. The reader must be at no loss to give his voice the posture proper to the sentence. The simple declarative sentence used in making a plain statement is one sound. But Lord love ye it mustn't be worked to death. It is against the law of nature that whole poems should be written in it. If they are written they won't be read. The sound of sense, then. You get that. It is the abstract vitality of our speech. It is pure sound—pure form. One who concerns himself with it more than the subject is an artist. But remember we are still talking merely of the raw material of poetry. An ear and an appetite for these sounds of sense is the first qualification of a writer, be it of prose or verse.

From a letter to John Bartlett

The Figure a Poem Makes   1939

Scholars and artists thrown together are often annoyed at the puzzle of where they differ. Both work from knowledge; but I suspect they differ most importantly in the way their knowledge is come by. Scholars get theirs with conscientious thoroughness along projected lines of logic; poets theirs cavalierly and as it happens in and out of books. They stick to nothing deliberately, but let what will stick to them like burrs where they walk in the fields. No acquirement is on assignment, or even self-assignment. Knowledge of the second kind is much more available in the wild free ways of wit and art. A schoolboy may be defined as one who can tell you what he knows in the order in which he learned it. The artist must value himself as he snatches a thing from some previous order in time and space into a new order with not so much as a ligature clinging to it of the old place where it was organic.

More than once I should have lost my soul to radicalism if it had been the originality it was mistaken for by its young converts. Originality and initiative are what I ask for my country. For myself the originality need be no more than the freshness of a poem run in the way I have described: from delight to wisdom. The figure is the same as for love. Like a piece of ice on a hot stove the poem must ride on its own melting. A poem may be worked over once it is in being, but may not be worried into being. Its most precious quality will remain its having run itself and carried away the poet with it. Read it a hundred times: it will forever keep its freshness as a metal keeps its fragrance. It can never lose its sense of a meaning that once unfolded by surprise as it went.

From the Preface to Frost's *Collected Poems*

"There Are Two Types of Realist": 1920
An Interview with Robert Frost

Mr. Frost is at once a believer in realism and symbolism. His bent for realism is readily enough recognized by the reader of any Frost poem, but the other side is by no means generally known. This is how Mr. Frost put it, in a discussion of realism: "There are two types of realist—the one who offers a good deal of dirt with his potato, to show that it is a real one, and the one who is satisfied with the potato brushed clean. I'm inclined to be the second kind. . . . To me, the thing that art does for life is to strip it to form."

If it were possible to read *North of Boston*,° and not get the feeling of a personality deeply committed to reality in language, subject matter and spirit, one would get it quickly in a conversation with Mr. Frost. He is instinctively distrustful of anything not genuinely rooted in earth, and with a deep placid voice that may or may not carry a touch of irony—you are always free to guess for yourself—has brought many an ecstatic conversationalist back to common sense abruptly. He has a particularly strong aversion for high flown language, so often mistaken for the substance of poetry.

The suggestion has often been made that the famous poem "Mending Wall," with its flavor of symbolism in the powerful line, "Something there is that does not love a wall," is an expression of international spirit, an allegorical appeal for the breaking up of national barriers. But this literal-minded interpretation is not the symbolism of Robert Frost, which has not only made him the poet of New England, but has made New England the substance of universal poetry. His answer to the ingenious explanation of "Mending Wall" was: "No, I wasn't arguing for internationalism or anything else. If I was thinking of anything beyond the matter of the moment, I suppose it must have been of life the cell-builder. That's all life is: cell-walls it builds only to break them down itself. I don't happen to be an internationalist myself . . . Not that it matters at all, but just in the interest of keeping things separate."

"Keeping things separate" is something of a philosophy in itself, with Mr. Frost. "You can't mix things to your taste till you have unscrambled them from their original chaotic mixture and held them separate long enough to learn their values," he told me.

From an interview with Joseph Anthony

North of Boston: Frost's second book of poems, published in 1914.

CRITICS ON ROBERT FROST

Frost recites a poem at the presidential inauguration of John F. Kennedy in 1961.

Katherine Kearns

On "Mending Wall"   2000

One begins over time to apprehend this poem more and more intimately. In growing old with it, making it one's own, it seems to get under the skin and into the bones. The poem sitting on the page becomes the objective correlative of some internal process of making and undoing and mending and coming undone; and this respiration comes to feel both physical and existential. The wall, like Frost's houses, gradually becomes more than merely a wall and more than merely a metaphor. Laid across a physical landscape already dense with metaphorical bodies, it seems sinewy, muscular. The wall holds things together by keeping things apart—and of course the formal and the prosodic structure seeks to include the poem itself in this willed order. But it is itself vulnerable to random force and must suffer interventions by whatever comes along—dogs, hunters, frost, gravity, and, standing in for a world of ontological possibilities that cannot be named, "Elves," but not elves exactly. This poem is encrypted with evidence of itself as lyric poem, one that rides on the "frozen groundswell" of Frost's invention: the stones may be the same stones, it seems to say, and the hands that build the wall back up may be the same hands, but the wall never becomes the same wall it was before, even if it looks precisely the same as before. This mending-wall poem tells Frost's lyric secret: that the "same" formal manifestations of his lyricism are produced, not from a stable self but from a series of strangers, alienated forms who perpetually contest the fiction of an intact, single human soul and who also dispute the fiction of its masculinity.

From "Frost on the Doorstep and Lyricism at the Millennium"

Ezra Pound (1885–1972)

An Honest Writer   1914

Mr. Frost is an honest writer, writing from himself, from his own knowledge and emotion; not simply picking up the manner which magazines are accepting at the moment, and applying it to topics in vogue. He is quite consciously and definitely putting New England rural life into verse. He is not using themes that anybody could have cribbed out of Ovid.

There are only two passions in art; there are only love and hate—with endless modifications. Frost has been honestly fond of the New England people, I dare say with spells of irritation. He has given their life honestly and seriously. He has never turned aside to make fun of it. He has taken their tragedy as tragedy, their stubbornness as stubbornness. I know more of farm life than I did before I had read his poems. That means I know more of "Life."

Mr. Frost has dared to write, and for the most part with success, in the natural speech of New England; in natural spoken speech, which is very different from the "natural" speech of the newspapers, and of many professors. His poetry is a bit slow, but you aren't held up every five minutes by the feeling that you are listening to a fool; so perhaps you read it just as easily and quickly as you might read the verse of some of the sillier and more "vivacious" writers.

● ● ●

Mr. Frost has humor, but he is not its victim. *The Code* has a pervasive humor, the humor of things as they are, not that of an author trying to be funny, or trying to "bring out" the ludicrous phase of some incident or character because he dares not rely on sheer presentation. There is nothing more nauseating to the developed mind than that sort of local buffoonery which the advertisements call "racy"—the village wit presenting some village joke which is worn out everywhere else. It is a great comfort to find someone who tries to give life, the life of the rural district, as a whole, evenly, and not merely as a hook to hang jokes on. The easiest thing to see about a man is an eccentric or worn-out garment, and one is godforsakenly tired of the post-Bret-Hartian, post-Mark-Twainian humorist.

Mr. Frost's work is not "accomplished," but it is the work of a man who will make neither concessions nor pretenses. He will perform no monkey-tricks. His stuff sticks in your head—not his words, nor his phrases, nor his cadences, but his subject matter. You do not confuse one of his poems with another in your memory. His book is a contribution to American literature, the sort of sound work that will develop into very interesting literature if persevered in.

From a review in *Poetry* magazine, December 1914

Rhina P. Espaillat (b. 1932)

Translating Frost into Spanish   2014

The one thing everybody knows about translation—because it's repeated so often and with such authority—is that it's impossible. But people who love to read and are curious about books produced by cultures other than their own know a second thing: that translation may be impossible, but it's also essential. Without the long history of this universally disparaged art, there would be none of the intellectual and aesthetic cultural crossbreeding that gave us Homer, the Hebrew Bible, Virgil and Dante, to name only a few of the texts without which our literature would be unrecognizable. Clearly our view of the world and of ourselves as a species depends, in large measure, on what authors distant in space and time have left us in all the world's languages.

Those of us who spend most of our lives thinking in two or more languages know still another thing about translation, and it's this: whatever else it may be, translation is also inevitable. Human curiosity about the thoughts and experiences of others demands it, as it demands gossip, because somewhere in the human psyche lives the suspicion that we are, wherever and whenever we live, a network of neighbors, at the very least, and probably more than that, as geneticists are learning. It is tantalizing to encounter the family secrets of gods and men, civilizing to discover our similarities, and crucial to learn our differences.

● ● ●

What is insurmountable—and this is what renders the ideal translation ultimately impossible—is the peculiar unity that exists in every successful poem between what is said and the manner of its saying. For example, there is no substitute, in other words in another language, for the effect of these precise words from "After Apple-Picking":

> . . . I am overtired
> Of the great harvest I myself desired.

The combination of regret, fatigue, utter simplicity, backward-looking gratitude, loss perceived if unexpressed, and barely-hinted-at relief is perfectly captured by the rhyming words that seem inevitable and yet strain against each other, by the rich associations of "harvest," and by the stately pace of the language that suggests both rue and ripeness. What to do with insights that word themselves so flawlessly that it seems almost wrong to diminish them by dressing them in words other than those they wear so well?

Even the best translation is, by necessity, "a diminished thing," but how else make the original at least partly accessible to a foreign reader? Diminished or not, great poems should—and do—belong to everyone, but only translation makes it possible for foreign-language readers to claim what is and ought to be theirs. I think the work of the translator is to give those readers as full and accurate an impression as possible of the original unavailable to them—its sense, sound, imagery and tone—without pretending that he has done, or can do, the admittedly impossible.

From the introduction to her translations of Frost

Dana Gioia (b. 1950)

Robert Frost's Dramatic Narratives   2013

The fourth category of Frost's narrative work is both the largest and most original. These poems were so innovative in style and structure that even a hundred years later there is no conventional name for Frost's verse form, which I shall call the dramatic narrative. Written in conversational blank verse (with the sole exception of "Blueberries," which is in rhymed anapestic couplets), the dramatic narratives combine direct dialogue with minimalist narration usually in the omniscient third person. The dialogue predominates and the narration is strictly descriptive, never offering any overt authorial interpretation of the characters or situations. The narration sets the

In 1974, the U.S. Postal Service issued a commemorative stamp to celebrate the 100th anniversary of Robert Frost's birth.

scene as well as describes the characters' actions when they are not speaking, just as stage directions would in a realist play. Here is a characteristic example of the narration's role from "Home Burial":

> "Don't, don't, don't, don't," she cried.
>
> She withdrew shrinking from beneath his arm
> That rested on the banister, and slid downstairs;
> And turned on him with such a daunting look,
> He said twice over before he knew himself:
> "Can't a man speak of his own child he's lost?"
>
> (*Collected Poems, Prose, and Plays*, 56)

The dramatic narrative is Frost's characteristic form, and it accounts for over two thirds of his narrative verse—twenty-two of the thirty-two narratives in the four key books. The form reads so naturally that it is easy to miss Frost's extraordinary inventiveness. In literature when an experimental form entirely succeeds, as for example Thornton Wilder's *Our Town*, critics often forget how innovative it was. So has it been with *North of Boston*. Frost, a failed playwright and short story writer, had learned essential things about telling stories in his struggles with prose and brought those lessons into his poetry with transformative effect.

• • •

The first notable aspect of the dramatic narratives is their lack of traditional poetic musicality. They are, with the exception of "Blueberries," all written in blank verse. Unrhymed, with no stanzaic patterns, they eschew the word music and auditory patterns of repetition typical of Browning or Tennyson. There is the steady metrical beat of iambic pentameter, but rather than overlay it with conventional lyric effects, Frost counterpoints it with "the sound of sense." This famous concept, which Frost explained to John Bartlett in 1913, refers to the vital spoken sound of English syntax, "[t]he simple declarative sentence used in making a plain statement" (*CPPP* 664-65). Of course, English-language poets had been contrasting metrical and speech patterns since Elizabethan blank verse. What makes Frost's method distinctive is that he eliminates most of the other poetic devices to make the counterpoint between syntax and meter more audible. The result is a poetic language very close to everyday spoken English but slightly heightened by the iambic beat.

The effect is further intensified by the plain diction of the poems. As Frost bragged, they employ "language absolutely unliterary" (*Selected Letters* 102). Frost never condescends to his characters; the country people who inhabit the poems speak plainly but clearly and usually with genuine insight. Since the dramatic narratives consist mostly of dialogue, the realistic use of rural vernacular gives the poems the texture of short plays. Frost's form and diction also underscore an important quality of his characters—their initial reticence. His characters often have difficulty in adequately expressing their thoughts and feelings. They are also often reluctant to reveal their fears and desires without being questioned or challenged. Only as the poems progress do the characters begin to explain themselves adequately. In the process they often say the wrong thing. As the desperate husband in "Home Burial" tells his angry and grief-stricken wife:

> My words are nearly always an offense.
> I don't know how to speak of anything
> So as to please you. But I might be taught
> I should suppose. I can't say I see how. (*CPPP* 56–57)

Most significantly, the dramatic narratives consist mostly of dialogue usually spoken in a single location—like one-act plays framed by stage directions. The narrative line moves forward dialectically as the characters, usually only two or three figures, converse, argue, cajole, rebuke, and confide. The plot and the dramatic situation are nearly always inseparable—the grieving couple arguing in "Home Burial" or the husband and his terrified wife in "The Fear." Frost's focus is mostly on the inner lives of the characters. What would constitute the plot line in a conventional narrative is often left unresolved. Frost's dramatic narratives mostly just end rather than conclude. The dialogue in "The Mountain" ends in mid-sentence when the farmer moves out of earshot. "The Housekeeper" stops when the old woman insults the hapless middle-aged farmer whose wife ran off, "Who wants to hear your news, you—dreadful fool?" (*CPPP* 89). The reader never learns the news. "The Fear" ends as the terrified woman cries for her husband, but he doesn't answer.

> ["]You understand that we have to be careful.
> This is a very, very lonely place.
> Joel!" She spoke as if she couldn't turn.
> The swinging lantern lengthened to the ground,
> It touched, it struck, it clattered and went out. (*CPPP* 92)

From "Robert Frost and the Modern Narrative"

■ WRITING *effectively*

TOPICS FOR WRITING ABOUT EMILY DICKINSON

1. Focusing on one or two poems, demonstrate how Dickinson's idiosyncratic capitalization and punctuation add special impact to her work.

2. How do the poems by Dickinson in this chapter and elsewhere in the book illustrate her statement (in "Recognizing Poetry") that "I find ecstasy in living—the mere sense of living is joy enough"?

3. In her work, Dickinson frequently adopts the stance of an outsider or nonconformist. Discuss this point through detailed examination of at least two of her poems. What does she seem to find uncongenial about going along with the crowd?

4. Emily Dickinson is perhaps as famous for her reclusiveness as she is for her poetry. Discuss this element of her personality as it is reflected in at least three of the poems in this casebook. Do the poems suggest any reason—or reasons—for this tendency?

TOPICS FOR WRITING ABOUT LANGSTON HUGHES

1. Compare and contrast the use of first-person voices in two poems by Langston Hughes (such as "I, Too" and "Theme for English B," or "Mother to Son" and "The Negro Speaks of Rivers"). In what ways does the speaker's "I" differ in each poem and in what ways is it similar?

2. Discussing a single poem by Hughes, examine how musical forms (such as jazz, blues, or popular song) help shape the effect of the work.

3. Analyzing "Theme for English B" and "I, Too" as well as the excerpts from Hughes's essays in this casebook, discuss the poet's vision of racial identity and integration in American society. What specific obstacles and opportunities does Hughes envision? What stereotypes and prejudices need to be overcome? (Cite from the text to present Hughes's opinion rather than expounding your own views.)

4. Write your own "Theme for English B," using autobiographical details and personal tastes to express both your sense of yourself and your relationship to your community.

TOPICS FOR WRITING ABOUT ROBERT FROST

1. "The Road Not Taken," "Fire and Ice," and "Stopping by Woods on a Snowy Evening" all involve the making of a choice. What are the alternative options in each poem? What choice is made in each poem, and why?

2. Based on the poems in this casebook, would you say that Frost is an optimist, a pessimist, or neither? Explain.

3. Pick a favorite poem by Frost and write a parody, or humorous imitation of it. Remember that it is easier to parody a poem you really love.

4. Robert Frost claimed he tried to make poetry out of the "sound of sense." He wrote that English sentences often contain an abstract sound that helps communicate their meaning. After reading the excerpt "The Sound of Sense" (earlier in this chapter), can you see how it throws any light on one of his poems? In two or three paragraphs, discuss how Frost uses the "simple declarative sentence" as a distinctive rhythmic feature in his poetry.

33 CRITICAL CASEBOOK
T. S. Eliot's "The Love Song of J. Alfred Prufrock"

What You Will Learn in This Chapter

■ To understand T. S. Eliot's classic poem in its biographical, critical, and cultural context

T. S. Eliot around 1910.

> *Yeats and Pound achieved modernity;*
> *Eliot was modern from the start.*
>
> —LOUISE BOGAN

T. S. ELIOT

Thomas Stearns Eliot was born on September 26, 1888, in St. Louis, Missouri. Both his father, a brick manufacturer, and mother were descended from families that had emigrated from England to Massachusetts in the seventeenth century. Entering Harvard on his eighteenth birthday, he earned a BA in 1909 and an MA in English literature in 1910. After a year in Paris, he returned to Harvard, where he undertook graduate studies in philosophy and also served as a teaching assistant. Awarded a traveling fellowship, he intended to study in Germany, but the outbreak of World War I in August 1914 forced him to leave the country after only several weeks. He then went to London, England, which would be his home for the remaining fifty years of his life.

T. S. Eliot in his early twenties

In September 1914, Eliot met fellow poet Ezra Pound, who would be a great influence on his work and his literary career. In June 1915, Eliot married Vivienne Haigh-Wood after an acquaintance of two months. (The marriage was troubled from the start. He would separate from Vivienne in 1933; she was subsequently institutionalized and died in a nursing home in 1947.) The year 1915 also saw Eliot's first major publication, when "The Love Song of J. Alfred Prufrock" appeared in the June issue of Poetry. *It became the central piece of his first collection,* Prufrock and Other Observations *(1917). During this period, he taught school briefly and worked in Lloyds Bank for several years. He secured permanent employment when he joined the publishing firm of Faber and Gwyer (later Faber and Faber) in 1925.*

Eliot became one of the best-known and most controversial poets of his time with the publication of The Waste Land *(1922). Conservative critics denounced it as impenetrable and incoherent; readers of more advanced tastes responded at once to the poem's depiction of a sordid society, empty of spiritual values, in the wake of World War I. Through the* Criterion, *a journal that he founded in 1922, and through his essays and volumes of literary and social criticism, Eliot came to exert immense influence as a molder of opinion.*

Religious themes became increasingly important to his poetry, from "Journey of the Magi" (1927), through Ash-Wednesday *(1930), to* Murder in the Cathedral *(1935), which dealt with the death of St. Thomas à Becket, and was the first of his several full-length verse dramas. Others included* The Family Reunion *(1939) and* The Cocktail Party *(1949), which became a remarkable popular success, estimated to have been seen by more than a million and a half people in Eliot's lifetime. Another of his works reached many more millions, at least indirectly: the light-verse pieces of* Old Possum's Book of Practical Cats *(1939) later became the basis of the record-breaking Broadway musical* Cats *(1982). Eliot's last major work of nondramatic poetry was* Four Quartets *(1943). In 1948, he was awarded the Nobel Prize in Literature.*

In January 1957, Eliot married Valerie Fletcher, his secretary at Faber and Faber. After several years of declining health, he died of emphysema at his home in London on January 4, 1965.

The Love Song of J. Alfred Prufrock   1917

> S'io credessi che mia risposta fosse
> a persona che mai tornasse al mondo,
> questa fiamma staria senza più scosse.
> Ma per ciò che giammai di questo fondo
> non tornò vivo alcun, s'i'odo il vero,
> senza tema d'infamia ti rispondo.

Let us go then, you and I,
When the evening is spread out against the sky
Like a patient etherized upon a table;
Let us go, through certain half-deserted streets,
The muttering retreats   5
Of restless nights in one-night cheap hotels
And sawdust restaurants with oyster-shells:
Streets that follow like a tedious argument
Of insidious intent
To lead you to an overwhelming question . . .   10
Oh, do not ask, "What is it?"
Let us go and make our visit.

In the room the women come and go
Talking of Michelangelo.

The yellow fog that rubs its back upon the window-panes,   15
The yellow smoke that rubs its muzzle on the window-panes,
Licked its tongue into the corners of the evening,
Lingered upon the pools that stand in drains,
Let fall upon its back the soot that falls from chimneys,
Slipped by the terrace, made a sudden leap,   20
And seeing that it was a soft October night,
Curled once about the house, and fell asleep.

And indeed there will be time
For the yellow smoke that slides along the street
Rubbing its back upon the window-panes;   25
There will be time, there will be time
To prepare a face to meet the faces that you meet;
There will be time to murder and create,
And time for all the works and days of hands
That lift and drop a question on your plate;   30
Time for you and time for me,
And time yet for a hundred indecisions,
And for a hundred visions and revisions,
Before the taking of a toast and tea.

In the room the women come and go   35
Talking of Michelangelo.

And indeed there will be time
To wonder, "Do I dare?" and, "Do I dare?"
Time to turn back and descend the stair,
With a bald spot in the middle of my hair—   40
(They will say: "How his hair is growing thin!")
My morning coat, my collar mounting firmly to the chin,
My necktie rich and modest, but asserted by a simple pin—
(They will say: "But how his arms and legs are thin!")
Do I dare   45
Disturb the universe?
In a minute there is time
For decisions and revisions which a minute will reverse.

For I have known them all already, known them all—
Have known the evenings, mornings, afternoons,   50
I have measured out my life with coffee spoons;
I know the voices dying with a dying fall
Beneath the music from a farther room.
      So how should I presume?

And I have known the eyes already, known them all—   55
The eyes that fix you in a formulated phrase,
And when I am formulated, sprawling on a pin,
When I am pinned and wriggling on the wall,
Then how should I begin
To spit out all the butt-ends of my days and ways?   60
      And how should I presume?

And I have known the arms already, known them all—
Arms that are braceleted and white and bare
(But in the lamplight, downed with light brown hair!)
Is it perfume from a dress   65
That makes me so digress?
Arms that lie along a table, or wrap about a shawl.
      And should I then presume?
      And how should I begin?

          .   .   .   .   .

Shall I say, I have gone at dusk through narrow streets   70
And watched the smoke that rises from the pipes
Of lonely men in shirt-sleeves, leaning out of windows? . . .

I should have been a pair of ragged claws
Scuttling across the floors of silent seas.

          .   .   .   .   .

And the afternoon, the evening, sleeps so peacefully!   75
Smoothed by long fingers,
Asleep . . . tired . . . or it malingers,
Stretched on the floor, here beside you and me.
Should I, after tea and cakes and ices,
Have the strength to force the moment to its crisis?   80
But though I have wept and fasted, wept and prayed,

Though I have seen my head (grown slightly bald) brought in upon a platter,
I am no prophet—and here's no great matter;
I have seen the moment of my greatness flicker,
And I have seen the eternal Footman hold my coat, and snicker,   85
And in short, I was afraid.

And would it have been worth it, after all,
After the cups, the marmalade, the tea,
Among the porcelain, among some talk of you and me,
Would it have been worth while,   90
To have bitten off the matter with a smile,
To have squeezed the universe into a ball
To roll it toward some overwhelming question,
To say: "I am Lazarus, come from the dead,
Come back to tell you all, I shall tell you all"—   95
If one, settling a pillow by her head,
   Should say: "That is not what I meant at all.
   That is not it, at all."

And would it have been worth it, after all,
Would it have been worth while,   100
After the sunsets and the dooryards and the sprinkled streets,
After the novels, after the teacups, after the skirts that trail along the floor—
And this, and so much more?—
It is impossible to say just what I mean!
But as if a magic lantern threw the nerves in patterns on a screen: 105
Would it have been worth while
If one, settling a pillow or throwing off a shawl,
And turning toward the window, should say:
   "That is not it at all,
   That is not what I meant, at all."   110

   . . . . . .

No! I am not Prince Hamlet, nor was meant to be;
Am an attendant lord, one that will do
To swell a progress, start a scene or two,
Advise the prince; no doubt, an easy tool,
Deferential, glad to be of use,   115
Politic, cautious, and meticulous;
Full of high sentence, but a bit obtuse;
At times, indeed, almost ridiculous—
Almost, at times, the Fool.

I grow old . . . I grow old . . .   120
I shall wear the bottoms of my trousers rolled.

Shall I part my hair behind? Do I dare to eat a peach?
I shall wear white flannel trousers, and walk upon the beach.
I have heard the mermaids singing, each to each.

I do not think that they will sing to me.   125

I have seen them riding seaward on the waves
Combing the white hair of the waves blown back
When the wind blows the water white and black.

We have lingered in the chambers of the sea
By sea-girls wreathed with seaweed red and brown   130
Till human voices wake us, and we drown.

THE LOVE SONG OF J. ALFRED PRUFROCK. The epigraph, from Dante's *Inferno*, is the speech of one dead and damned, who thinks that his hearer also is going to remain in Hell. Count Guido da Montefeltro, whose sin has been to give false counsel after a corrupt prelate had offered him prior absolution and whose punishment is to be wrapped in a constantly burning flame, offers to tell Dante his story:

> If I thought my answer were to someone who
>   might see the world again, then there would be
>   no more stirrings of this flame. Since it is true
> that no one leaves these depths of misery
>   alive, from all that I have heard reported,
> I answer you without fear of infamy.

(Translation by Michael Palma from: Dante Alighieri, *Inferno: A New Verse Translation* [New York: Norton, 2002].) 29 *works and days:* title of a poem by Hesiod (eighth century B.C.), depicting his life as a hardworking Greek farmer and exhorting his brother to be like him. 82 *head . . . platter:* like that of John the Baptist, prophet and praiser of chastity, whom King Herod beheaded at the demand of Herodias, his unlawfully wedded wife (see Mark 6:17–28). 92–93 *squeezed . . . To roll it:* an echo from Marvell's "To His Coy Mistress," lines 41–42. 94 *Lazarus:* probably the Lazarus whom Jesus called forth from the tomb (John 11:1–44), but possibly the beggar seen in Heaven by the rich man in Hell (Luke 16:19–25). 105 *magic lantern:* an early type of projector used to display still pictures from transparent slides.

Questions

1. What expectations are created by the title of the poem? Are those expectations fulfilled by the text?

2. John Berryman wrote of line 3, "With this line, modern poetry begins." What do you think he meant?

3. It has been said that Prufrock suffers from a "morbid self-consciousness." How many references can you find in the poem to back up that statement?

4. In the total context of the poem, is the sense of lines 47–48 reassuring or disturbing? Explain your choice.

5. How do lines 70–72 relate to the questions that Prufrock raises in the three preceding stanzas (lines 49–69)?

6. What is the effect of riming "ices" and "crisis" (lines 79–80)? Can you find similar instances elsewhere in the poem?

7. Is the situation in the poem presented statically, or is there discernible development as the poem proceeds? Defend your answer with references to the text.

8. What, finally, is your attitude toward Prufrock—identification, sympathy, contempt, or something more complicated?

PUBLISHING "PRUFROCK"

Ezra Pound, living in London, was the foreign correspondent for Chicago-based *Poetry* magazine from its beginnings in 1912. Tireless in his efforts to promote writers he believed in, Pound made it his mission to champion poets who were doing new and original work in contrast to what he saw as the dullness and sterility of mainstream verse. His literary enthusiasms differed sharply from the more conservative values of Harriet Monroe, *Poetry*'s founder and editor, and the two clashed frequently. Pound's first mention to Harriet Monroe of T. S. Eliot came in a letter of September 22, 1914:

> An American called Eliot called this P.M. I think he has some sense tho' he has not yet sent me any verse.

Eliot sent Pound "The Love Song of J. Alfred Prufrock" shortly thereafter, and on September 30 Pound wrote to Monroe:

> I was jolly well right about Eliot. He has sent in the best poem I have yet had or seen from an American. PRAY GOD IT BE NOT A SINGLE AND UNIQUE SUCCESS. He has taken it back to get it ready for the press and you shall have it in a few days.
>
> He is the only American I know of who has made what I can call adequate preparation for writing. He has actually trained himself *and* modernized himself *on his own*. The rest of the *promising young* have done one or the other but never both (most of the swine have done neither). It is such a comfort to meet a man and not have to tell him to wash his face, wipe his feet, and remember the date (1914) on the calendar.

Objecting to her request for revisions to make the poem more accessible, Pound wrote on November 9, 1914:

> No, most emphatically I will not ask Eliot to write down to any audience whatsoever. . . . Neither will I send you Eliot's address in order that he may be insulted.

Despite Pound's vigorous advocacy, Monroe continued to object to certain passages and delayed printing the poem, leading Pound to write on January 31, 1915:

> Now as to Eliot: "Mr. Prufrock" does not "go off at the end." It is a portrait of failure, or of a character which fails, and it would be false art to make it end on a note of triumph. I dislike the paragraph about Hamlet, but it is an early and cherished bit and T.E. won't give it up, and as it is the only portion of the poem that most readers will like at first reading, I don't see that it will do much harm.
>
> For the rest: a portrait satire on futility can't end by turning that quintessence of futility, Mr. P., into a reformed character breathing out fire and ozone. . . .
>
> I assure you it is better, "more unique," than the other poems of Eliot which I have seen. Also that he is quite *intelligent* (an adjective which is seldom in my mouth).

"Prufrock" finally appeared in the June 1915 issue of *Poetry*. Writing to Monroe on December 1, Pound explained his insistence on her printing it before other, less experimental pieces by Eliot:

As to T.S.E. the "Prufrock" is more individual and unusual than the "Portrait of a Lady"! I chose it of the two as I wanted his first poem to be published to be a poem that would at once differentiate him from everyone else, in the public mind.

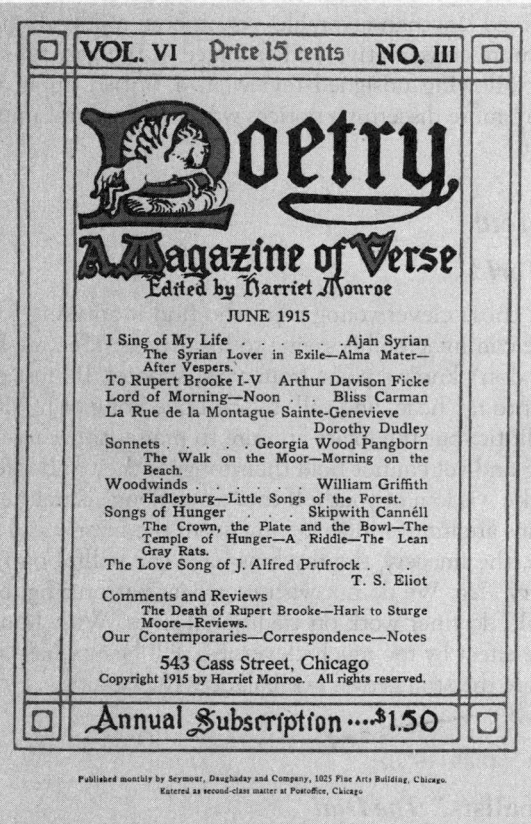

Cover of *Poetry*, June 1915.

Pound continued zealously to promote Eliot, sending Monroe other Eliot poems and lobbying, without success, for "Prufrock" to receive the prize for the best work published in *Poetry* that year.

While Eliot was preoccupied with marital and financial concerns in late 1916 and early 1917, it was Pound who gathered together twelve of Eliot's poems. Along with "Prufrock," the collection included a number of other pieces that Pound had placed in American and British journals, such as "Portrait of a Lady," "Preludes," "Rhapsody on a Windy Night," and "The *Boston Evening Transcript*." He approached his own publisher, Elkin Matthews, with the manuscript, but Matthews demanded an advance guarantee against poor sales. Pound then turned to Harriet Shaw Weaver, one of the editors of the journal *The Egoist*, with the proposal that he would cover the printing costs if she would allow the book to appear under the Egoist imprint. She agreed to these terms, and *Prufrock and Other Observations* was published in July 1917 in an edition of 500 copies.

THE REVIEWERS ON *PRUFROCK*

For a pamphlet of twelve poems by an almost totally unknown writer, *Prufrock and Other Observations* received a considerable amount of press attention, even when one subtracts everything written by Ezra Pound. Below are excerpts from some of the notices of Eliot's collection. Given the experimental nature of his work, it is not surprising that it received less than favorable—or, at best, mildly dismissive—responses from some of the more conservative outlets aimed at the general reading public (as illustrated by the following unsigned review in a British publication). Balancing these reactions were more discerning notices written by several important American and British writers.

Unsigned Review

from *Literary World*   July 5, 1917

Mr. Eliot is one of those clever young men who find it amusing to pull the leg of a sober reviewer. We can imagine his saying to his friends: "See me have a lark out of the old fogies who don't know a poem from a pea-shooter. I'll just put down the first thing that comes into my head, and call it 'The Love Song of J. Alfred Prufrock.' Of course it will be idiotic; but the fogies are sure to praise it, because when they don't understand a thing and yet cannot hold their tongues they find safety in praise." . . . Mr. Eliot has not the wisdom of youth. If the "Love Song" is neither witty nor amusing, the other poems are interesting experiments in the bizarre and violent. The subjects of the poems, the imagery, the rhythms have the willful outlandishness of the young revolutionary idea. We do not wish to appear patronizing, but we are certain that Mr. Eliot could do finer work on traditional lines. With him it seems to be a case of missing the effect by too much cleverness. All beauty has in it an element of strangeness, but here the strangeness overbalances the beauty.

Conrad Aiken (1889–1973)

from "Divers Realists," *The Dial*   November 8, 1917

Mr. Eliot gives us, in the first person, the reactions of an individual to a situation for which to a large extent his own character is responsible. . . . [I]t will puzzle many, it will delight a few. Mr. Eliot writes pungently and sharply, with an eye for unexpected and vivid details, and, particularly in the two longer poems and in the "Rhapsody on a Windy Night," he shows himself to be an exceptionally acute technician. Such free rhyme as this, with irregular line lengths, is difficult to write well, and Mr. Eliot does it well enough to make one wonder whether such a form is not what the adorers of free verse will eventually have to come to. In the rest of Mr. Eliot's volume one finds the piquant and the trivial in about equal proportions.

Babette Deutsch (1895–1982)

from "Another Impressionist," *The New Republic*   February 16, 1918

The language has the extraordinary quality of common words uncommonly used. Less formal than prose, more nervous than metrical verse, the rhythms are suggestive of program music of an intimate sort. This effect is emphasized by the use of rhyme. It recurs, often internally, with an echoing charm that is heightened by its irregularity. But Mr. Eliot . . . is so clever a technician that the rhymes are subordinated to afford an unconsidered pleasure.

Marianne Moore (1887–1972)

from "A Note on T. S. Eliot's Book," *Poetry*   April 1918

It might be advisable for Mr. Eliot to publish a fangless edition of *Prufrock and Other Observations* for the gentle reader who likes his literature, like breakfast coffee or grapefruit, sweetened. . . .

But Eliot deals with life, with beings and things who live and move almost nakedly before his individual mind's eye—in the darkness, in the early sunlight, and in the fog. Whatever one may feel about sweetness in literature, there is also the word honesty, and this man is a faithful friend of the objects he portrays; altogether unlike the sentimentalist who really stabs them treacherously in the back while pretending affection.

Eliot began working as an editor at the publishing house Faber & Gwyer in 1925.

T. S. ELIOT ON WRITING

Poetry and Emotion   1920

It is not in his personal emotions, the emotions provoked by particular events in his life, that the poet is in any way remarkable or interesting. His particular emotions may be simple, or crude, or flat. The emotion in his poetry will be a very complex thing, but not with the complexity of the emotions of people who have very complex or unusual emotions in life. One error, in fact, of eccentricity in poetry is to seek for new human emotions to express; and in this search for novelty in the wrong place it discovers the perverse. The business of the poet is not to find new emotions, but to use the ordinary ones and, in working them up into poetry, to express feelings which are not in actual emotions at all. And emotions which he has never experienced will serve his turn as well as those familiar to him. Consequently, we must believe that "emotion recollected in tranquility"° is an inexact formula. For it is neither emotion, nor recollection, nor, without distortion of meaning, tranquility. It is a concentration, and a new thing resulting from the concentration, of a very great number of experiences which to the practical and active person would not seem to be experiences at all; it is a concentration which does not happen consciously or of deliberation. These experiences are not "recollected," and they finally unite in an atmosphere which is "tranquil" only in that it is a passive attending upon the event. Of course this is not quite the whole story. There is a great deal, in the writing of poetry, which must be conscious and deliberate. In fact, the bad poet is usually unconscious where he ought to be conscious, and conscious where he ought to be unconscious. Both errors tend to make him "personal." Poetry is not a turning loose of emotion, but an escape from emotion; it is not the expression of personality, but an escape from personality. But, of course, only those who have personality and emotions know what it means to want to escape from these things.

From "Tradition and the Individual Talent"

The Objective Correlative   1920

The only way of expressing emotion in the form of art is by finding an "objective correlative"; in other words, a set of objects, a situation, a chain of events which shall be the formula of that *particular* emotion; such that when the external facts, which must terminate in sensory experience, are given, the emotion is immediately evoked. If you examine any of Shakespeare's more successful tragedies, you will find this exact equivalence; you will find that the state of mind of Lady Macbeth walking in her sleep has been communicated to you by a skillful accumulation of imagined sensory impressions; the words of Macbeth on hearing of his wife's death strike us as if, given the sequence of events, these words were automatically released by the last event in the series. The artistic "inevitability" lies in this complete adequacy of the external to the emotion.

From "Hamlet and His Problems"

"emotion recollected in tranquility": Eliot is alluding to William Wordsworth's famous statement in his 1800 Preface to *Lyrical Ballads*: "I have said that Poetry is the spontaneous overflow of powerful feelings: it takes its origin from emotion recollected in tranquility."

Free Verse and the Ghost of Meter (1917)

It is assumed that *vers libre* exists. It is assumed that *vers libre* is a school; that it consists of certain theories; that its group or groups of theorists will either revolutionise or demoralise poetry if their attack upon the iambic pentameter meets with any success. *Vers libre* does not exist, and it is time that this preposterous fiction followed the *élan vital*° into oblivion.

When a theory of art passes it is usually found that a groat's° worth of art has been bought with a million of advertisement. The theory which sold the wares may be quite false, or it may be confused and incapable of elucidation, or it may never have existed. A mythical revolution will have taken place and produced a few works of art which perhaps would be even better if still less of the revolutionary theories clung to them. In modern society such revolutions are almost inevitable. An artist happens upon a method, perhaps quite unreflectingly, which is new in the sense that it is essentially different from that of the second-rate people about him, and different in everything but essentials from that of any of his great predecessors. The novelty meets with neglect; neglect provokes attack; and attack demands a theory. In an ideal state of society one might imagine the good New growing naturally out of the good Old, without the need for polemic and theory; this would be a society with a living tradition. In a sluggish society, as actual societies are, tradition is ever lapsing into superstition, and the violent stimulus of novelty is required. This is bad for the artist and his school, who may become circumscribed by their theory and narrowed by their polemic; but the artist can always console himself for his errors in his old age by considering that if he had not fought nothing would have been accomplished.

Vers libre has not even the excuse of a polemic; it is a battle-cry of freedom, and there is no freedom in art. And as the so-called *vers libre* which is good is anything but "free," it can better be defended under some other label. Particular types of *vers libre* may be supported on the choice of content, or on the method of handling the content. I am aware that many writers of *vers libre* have introduced such innovations, and that the novelty of their choice and manipulation of material is confused—if not in their own minds, in the minds of many of their readers—with the novelty of the form. But I am not here concerned with imagism, which is a theory about the use of material; I am only concerned with the theory of the verse-form in which imagism is cast. If *vers libre* is a genuine verse-form it will have a positive definition. And I can define it only in negatives: (1) absence of pattern, (2) absence of rhyme, (3) absence of meter.

The third of these qualities is easily disposed of. What sort of a line that would be which would not scan at all I cannot say. Even in the popular American magazines, whose verse columns are now largely given over to *vers libre*, the lines are usually explicable in terms of prosody. Any line can be divided into feet and accents. The simpler meters are a repetition of one combination, perhaps a long and a short, or a short and a long syllable, five times repeated. There is, however, no reason why, within the single line, there should be any repetition; why there should not be lines (as there are) divisible only into feet of different types. How can the grammatical

---

élan vital: life force, an antiquated biological theory.   *groat:* an old British coin worth four pennies.

exercise of scansion make a line of this sort more intelligible? Only by isolating elements which occur in other lines, and the sole purpose of doing this is the production of a similar effect elsewhere. But repetition of effect is a question of pattern.

• • •

The most interesting verse which has yet been written in our language has been done either by taking a very simple form, like the iambic pentameter, and constantly withdrawing from it, or taking no form at all, and constantly approximating to a very simple one. It is this contrast between fixity and flux, this unperceived evasion of monotony, which is the very life of verse.

• • •

We may therefore formulate as follows: the ghost of some simple meter should lurk behind the arras in even the "freest" verse; to advance menacingly as we doze, and withdraw as we rouse. Or, freedom is only truly freedom when it appears against the background of an artificial limitation.

From "Reflections on *Vers Libre*"

Poet T. S. Eliot teaching a class.

CRITICS ON "PRUFROCK"

Christopher Ricks (b. 1933)

What's in a Name? 1988

Then, back in 1917, before ever you entered upon reading a line of poetry by Mr. T. S. Eliot, you would have been met by the title of the first poem in this, his first book of poems: "The Love Song of J. Alfred Prufrock." At once the crystalline air is thick with incitements to prejudice. For we are immediately invited, or incited, to think and to feel our way through a prejudicial sequence. First, as often with prejudice, comes a concession: that of course a man cannot be blamed for being called Prufrock. Second, that nevertheless the name does have comical possibilities, given not only the play of "frock" against "pru"—prudent, prudish, prurient—but also the suggestive contrariety between splitting the name there, at *pru* and *frock*, as against splitting it as *proof* and *rock*. And, third, that therefore a man in these circumstances might be well advised to call himself John A. Prufrock or J. A. Prufrock, rather than to risk the roll, the rise, the carol, the creation of "J. Alfred Prufrock.". . . And then we are further invited to think and to feel that should Mr. Prufrock, as is his right, plump for J. Alfred Prufrock, he must not then expect the words "The Love Song of" to sit happily in his immediate vicinity. The tax returns of J. Alfred Prufrock, fine, but a love song does not harmonize with the rotund name, with how he has chosen to think of himself, to sound himself. He has, after all, chosen to issue his name in a form which is not only formal but unspeakable: no one, not even the most pompous self-regarder, could ever introduce himself as, or be addressed as, J. Alfred Prufrock. He has adopted a form for his name which is powerfully appropriate to a certain kind of page but not to the voice, and which is therefore for ever inimical to the thought of love's intimacy. "I'm in love." "Who's the lucky man?" "J. Alfred Prufrock." Inconceivable.

But then life often involves these choices and these sacrifices; if you want to cut a public figure and to wax ceremonious and to live on the business page or the title page, you may have to relinquish the more intimate happinesses. And all of this is unobtrusively at work before ever we have arrived at a word of the poem.

Unjust, of course, these incitements. What's in a name? Yet even with something like a name, which is usually given and not chosen, we manage to exercise choices, to adopt a style which becomes our man, or, if we are Prufrock, to wear our name with a difference. Then a name starts to become so mingled with its owner as to call in question which is doing the owning.

"The Love Song of J. Alfred Prufrock": even while the title tempts us—not necessarily improperly—to suspect things about the man, it raises the question of whether we are entitled to do so. Can we deduce much from so localized a thing as how a man chooses to cast his name? Can we deduce anything? But then can we imagine that one either could or should refrain from doing any deducing? Straws in the wind are often all that we have to go on. "And should I have the right to smile?": the question ends the succeeding poem, "Portrait of a Lady," but it is a question that haunts the whole book.

As so often with prejudice, one kind of categorizing melts into another. For the teasing speculation as to what sort of man names himself in such a way, especially given "Prufrock" as his climax, merges itself in the class question, not just what class of man but what social class. Calling oneself J. Alfred Prufrock has an air of prerogative and privilege. The class presumption in turn brings a whole culture and society with it.

From T. S. Eliot and Prejudice

Philip R. Headings (1922–1982)

The Pronouns in the Poem: "One," "You," and "I"   1982

"One"

The "one"° of the poem presents no great problems. She seems to be a feminine counterpart of either "you" or "I," frequenting the same Boston teas, expressing on occasion dissatisfactions with the unfulfilling, conventionalized life of that whole milieu. Her awarenesses may parallel theirs, though "I" is not sure. He probably does not even have a particular lady in mind; if he had, he would likely have used "she" instead of "one." This is not to deny the sexual component in his Love Song; it is rather to say that he is open to various possibilities in that regard—to whatever lady demonstrates the qualities requisite to become his Lady, his Beatrice.°

"You" and "I"

The "you" and "I" of the first line present greater difficulties. Critics have commonly interpreted them as referring to two parts of Prufrock, carrying on a conversation with himself. This interpretation now seems to me both too clever and much simpler than the actual situation in the poem. . . .

Sometime before 1949 Eliot wrote to Kristian Smidt:

> As for THE LOVE SONG OF J. ALFRED PRUFROCK anything I say now must be somewhat conjectural, as it was written so long ago that my memory may deceive me; but I am prepared to assert that the "you" in THE LOVE SONG is merely some friend or companion, *presumably of the male sex*, whom *the speaker* is at that moment addressing . . . [italics mine].

Having finally carefully compared "Prufrock" to Dante's *Inferno* and read dozens of critiques of the poem, I now see no reason to dissent from Eliot's straightforward statement. In fact, I see no other way of interpreting the poem that will fit all its complexities. Old Possum's° delightful sense of humor is apparent in that phrase "presumably of the male sex" and in "the speaker"; he knew very well that he himself, allegorically projected to the age of thirty-five, or a persona very like that projection, was the "friend or companion," the Dante-figure of the poem. The "I" who addresses him is an unidentified friend.

"You" and "I" are probably close friends and confidants who have attended such teas together, though perhaps they have only discussed them.

Though the presence of "you" is crucial to Eliot's Dantean intent, "Prufrock" is a dramatic monologue, not a dialogue. It parallels monologues of Shakespeare's Polonius, Dante's Pilgrim, Guido, and Ulysses. The only functions of the "you" are to elicit confidences, set the Dantean tone, indicate Prufrock's equivalence with Guido in the poem's epigraph, listen to the "I," and write the poem—bring back the story.

From Headings. T S Eliot Rev, 1e. © 1982 Gale, a part of Cengage, Inc.
Reproduced by permission. http://www.cengage.com/permissions.

"one": The "one" of lines 96–98, "If one, settling a pillow by her head / Should say: 'That is not what I meant at all. / That is not it, at all.'"   *Beatrice*: Beatrice Portinari (1266–1290), Dante's inspiration in *The New Life* and *The Divine Comedy*.   *Old Possum*: Eliot's playful nickname for himself, used in the title *Old Possum's Book of Practical Cats* (1939).

Maud Ellmann (b. 1954)

Will There Be Time? 1987

. . . Prufrock is etherized by *time*. This is the time that separates desire from fulfill-ment, motive from execution, thought from speech: in Eliot's words, "the awful sepa-ration between potential passion and any actualization possible in life." Time defers.

The way that time defers is through revision. Time itself becomes the object of revision, for the whole poem agonizes over writing time. The incessant repetition of "There will be time" is itself a way of losing time, as Nancy K. Gish[1] suggests; but also a way of gaining it, to prolong the re-editions of desire. "Stretched . . . beside you and me," time deflects Prufrock's ardor from his lover. But in this process time itself becomes the object of desire, in the form of the voluptuary sweetness of the evening. Indeed, Prufrock addresses time so constantly, in every tone of envy, rage, pain, impa-tience, longing, humor, flattery, seduction, that he can only really be in love with time.

Revisionary time: because revision has no present tense, and neither does "The Love Song." Instead, the poem hesitates between anticipation and regret for missed appointments with the self, the other or the muse. It begins in the future tense ("there will be time . . ." [23ff]); shifts into the perfect ("For I have known . . ." [49ff]); and finally subsides into the past conditional, the tense of wishful thinking: "I should have been . . ." (73). Because presence would mean speech, apocalypse, Prufrock only pauses in the present tense to say what he is not—"No! I am not Prince Hamlet" (a disavowal that conjures up the effigy that it denies, since Hamlet is the very spirit of theatricality). The poem concludes dreaming the future, faithful if only to its hope-less passion for postponement: "Till human voices wake us, and we drown." Prufrock feels the need to speak as a proof of his identity and as a rock to give him anchorage: yet speech would also mean his end, for voices are waters in which Prufrocks drown.

Through time, all Prufrock's aims have turned awry. His passion and his speech have lost themselves in detours, never to achieve satiety. Love becomes desire—tormenting, inexhaustible—while speech and revelation have surrendered to writing and revision, to the digressions which prolong his dalliance with time. Time is the greatest fetish of them all, the mother of all fetishes, since it is through time that all aims turn aside to revel in rehearsals, detours, transferences. What Prufrock longs for is a talking cure because, like Freud, he thinks that speech alone can transform repeti-tion into memory. What talking remedies is *writing*: for his illness lies in his obsessive re-editions of the text of love. But Prufrock's very histrionics show he is condemned to reenactment, to forget what he repeats in a script that restlessly obliterates its history. It is by remembering the past that the subject can establish his identity, but only by forgetting it can he accede to his desire. Refusing to declare his love, or pop the over-whelming question, Prufrock renounces the position of the speaking subject, but he instigates the drama of revision in its stead. And it is by refusing sexual relation that he conjures up the theater of desire. The love song Prufrock could not *sing* has been *writing* itself all the time, and the love that could not speak its name has been roving among all the fetishes his rhetoric has liberated to desire. We had the love song, even if we missed the meaning.

From *The Poetics of Impersonality: T. S. Eliot and Ezra Pound*

---

[1]Nancy K. Gish, *Time in the Poetry of T. S. Eliot* (London: Macmillan, 1981) 15–16.

Burton Raffel (1928-2015)

"Indeterminacy" in Eliot's Poetry   1982

Perhaps the most difficult aspect of "Prufrock," and a continuing difficulty in all of Eliot's poetry to the end of his life, is what might be called its "indeterminacy." That is, Eliot is constantly making two basic and exceedingly important kinds of assumptions as to his readership: (1) that his readers can and do understand his allusions, his references to people and to literary works, and in time to other things as well; and (2) that his readers can readily reconstruct an entire skeleton, as it were, though presented only with, say, a metatarsal bone or a chunk of a skull. Eliot's allusions are not much of a problem in "Prufrock," though they become a matter of some importance later on in his work. Let me therefore focus briefly on the second variety of "indeterminacy."

Perhaps the most famous example in "Prufrock" is the couplet toward the end, "I grow old . . . I grow old . . . / I shall wear the bottoms of my trousers rolled" (120–21). We can read, in the ingenious pages of Eliot's many scholarly explicators, that this refers to "stylish trousers with cuffs." Over-ingenuity can create, and in the past it has, fantastic and profound (but also profoundly irrelevant) significance for such minor matters. And it is true that Eliot has not troubled to give us all the information we need. But is it true that he has not given us *enough* information (as in other and later poems I think he sometimes has not)? We know that Prufrock is a socialite; we have heard him tell us, proudly, of "My morning coat, my collar mounting firmly to the chin, / My necktie rich and modest, but asserted by a simple pin—" (42–43). Just after the lines at issue he worries, "Shall I part my hair behind?" and goes on to proclaim that he will "wear white flannel trousers, and walk upon the beach" (123). And with so full a presentation of Prufrock's sartorial nature, do we really need more details about his trouser cuffs? Or, to put it differently, is it not enough to leave some minor indeterminacies, when the main outlines are so firmly sketched in? . . .

The poet needs, of course, to draw a fine but basic line between confusing and illuminating the reader. Indeterminacy can be bewildering if not kept under control. Even in "Prufrock," readers have for years been troubled by the "overwhelming question," which is never expressly formulated. It is one thing, such readers have argued, to shock us into comprehension with indeterminate metaphors like, "I have measured out my life with coffee spoons," metaphors which we do not and cannot take literally but which forcefully oblige us to see the intense triviality of Prufrock's well-bred existence. But how, they insist, are we to deal with what seems much more specific—an "overwhelming question"—yet is in the end only infuriatingly obscure? One response to such objections might be that we simply do not need to know. The fact that Prufrock never asks an "overwhelming" question, that he is not, indeed, capable of asking it, is arguably enough information. But I think it is not difficult, using the larger context of the poem as a whole, to see that the overwhelming question which Prufrock "dares not ask [is]: What is the meaning of this life? He realizes the sterile monotony of his 'works and days,' and he senses that a more fruitful and meaningful life must exist."[2] If this is not precise enough, I do not know what is. Nor is it drawn from external (or esoteric) sources: the poem itself gives us all we need, if we read it closely enough.

From *T. S. Eliot*

[2]Quoted from Nancy Duvall Hargrove, *Landscape as Symbol in the Poetry of T. S. Eliot* (Jackson: UP Mississippi, 1978) 48.

■ WRITING *effectively*

TOPICS FOR WRITING

1. "The Love Song of J. Alfred Prufrock" is very firmly grounded in upper-class society in the early twentieth century. Is the poem of purely historical value, opening a window on a society and a set of values that no longer exist, or are the attitudes and concerns that it expresses still relevant today?

2. In the excerpt entitled "Poetry and Emotion," Eliot says: "There is a great deal, in the writing of poetry, which must be conscious and deliberate. . . . Poetry is not a turning loose of emotion, but an escape from emotion; it is not the expression of personality, but an escape from personality." Discuss this statement, in terms of both its own meaning and its application to "The Love Song of J. Alfred Prufrock."

3. "The Love Song of J. Alfred Prufrock" features a speaker who expresses fear or ambivalence about love. What are the speaker's fears? Are there any sound reasons for his romantic uncertainty?

4. Eliot's poem mentions several famous cultural names—Michelangelo, John the Baptist, Lazarus, and Hamlet (as well as his epigraph from Dante's *Inferno*). What do these allusions tell the reader about Prufrock and his social environment? Would Eliot's poem be more accessible without them or would it be less effective?

5. Write your own version of the poem by substituting for Michelangelo, morning coats, coffee spoons, and other specific references in the text. The idea is not to parody Eliot or spoof the poem, but instead to do something more challenging—to come up with "objective correlatives" appropriate to contemporary society and culture, just as Eliot found them for his time and place.

34   POEMS FOR FURTHER READING

Aaron Abeyta (b. 1971)

thirteen ways of looking at a tortilla   2001

Aaron Abeyta

i.

among twenty different tortillas
the only thing moving
was the mouth of the niño

ii.

i was of three cultures
like a tortilla
for which there are three bolios   5

iii.

the tortilla grew on the wooden table
it was a small part of the earth

iv.

a house and a tortilla
are one   10
a man a woman and a tortilla
are one

v.

i do not know which to prefer
the beauty of the red wall
or the beauty of the green wall   15
the tortilla fresh
or just after

vi.

tortillas filled the small kitchen
with ancient shadows
the shadow of Maclovia   20
cooking long ago
the tortilla
rolled from the shadow
the innate roundness

vii.

o thin viejos of chimayo   25
why do you imagine biscuits
do you not see how the tortilla
lives with the hands
of the women about you

viii.

i know soft corn   30
and beautiful inescapable sopapillas
but i know too
that the tortilla
has taught me what I know

ix.

when the tortilla is gone   35
it marks the end
of one of many tortillas

x.

at the sight of tortillas
browning on a black comal°   *flat griddle pan*
even the pachucos of española   40
would cry out sharply

xi.

he rode over new mexico
in a pearl low rider
once he got a flat
in that he mistook   45
the shadow of his spare
for a tortilla

xii.

the abuelitas are moving
the tortilla must be baking

xiii.

it was cinco de mayo all year
it was warm   50
and it was going to get warmer
the tortilla sat
on the frijolito plate

Compare

"thirteen ways of looking at a tortilla" with "Thirteen Ways of Looking at a Blackbird" by
Wallace Stevens (Chapter 25).

Julia Alvarez (b. 1950)

By Accident   2004

Sometimes I think I became the woman
I am by accident, nothing prepared
the way, not a dramatic, wayward aunt,
or moody mother who read *Middlemarch*,
or godmother who whispered, "You can be   5
whatever you want!" and by doing so
performed the god-like function of breathing
grit into me. Even my own sisters
were more concerned with hairdryers and boys
than with the poems I recited ad nauseum   10

in our shared bedrooms when the lights were out.
"You're making me sick!" my sisters would say
as I ranted on, Whitman's "Song of Myself"
not the best lullaby, I now admit,
or Chaucer in Middle English which caused   15
many a nightmare fight. "Mami!" they'd called,
"She's doing it again!" Slap of slippers
in the hall, door clicks, and lights snapped on.
"Why can't you be considerate for once?"
"I am," I pleaded, "these are sounds, sweet airs   20

that give delight and—" "Keep it to yourself!"
my mother said, which more than anything
anyone in my childhood advised
turned me to this paper solitude
where I both keep things secret and broadcast   25
my heart for all the world to read. And so,
through many drafts, I became the woman
I kept to myself as I lay awake
in that dark bedroom with the lonesome sound
of their soft breathing as my sisters slept.   30

Julia Alvarez

Compare

"By Accident" with "One Art" by Elizabeth Bishop (Chapter 30).

Anonymous (traditional Scottish ballad)

Lord Randall

"O where ha you been, Lord Randal, my son?
And where ha you been, my handsome young man?"
"I ha been at the greenwood; mother, mak my bed soon,
For I'm wearied wi hunting, and fain wad lie down."

"An wha° met ye there, Lord Randal, my son?   who   5
An wha met you there, my handsome young man?"
"O I met wi my true-love; mother, mak my bed soon,
For I'm wearied wi hunting, and fain wad lie down."

"And what did she give you, Lord Randal, my son?
And what did she give you, my handsome young man?"   10
"Eels fried in a pan; mother, mak my bed soon,
For I'm wearied wi hunting, and fain wad lie down."

"And wha gat° your leavins,° Lord Randal, my son?   got; leftovers
And wha gat your leavins, my handsome young man?"
"My hawks and my hounds; mother, mak my bed soon,   15
For I'm wearied wi hunting, and fain wad lie down."

"And what becam of them, Lord Randal, my son?
And what becam of them, my handsome young man?"
"They stretched their legs out an died; mother, mak my bed soon,
For I'm wearied wi hunting, and fain wad lie down."   20

"O I fear you are poisoned, Lord Randal, my son!
I fear you are poisoned, my handsome young man!"
"O yes, I am poisoned; mother, mak my bed soon,
For I'm sick at the heart, and I fain wad lie down."

"What d' ye leave to your mother, Lord Randal, my son?   25
What d' ye leave to your mother, my handsome young man?"
"Four and twenty milk kye;° mother, mak my bed soon,   cows
For I'm sick at the heart, and I fain wad lie down."

"What d' ye leave to your sister, Lord Randal, my son?
What d' ye leave to your sister, my handsome young man?"   30
"My gold and my silver; mother, mak my bed soon,
For I'm sick at the heart, and I fain wad lie down."

"What d' ye leave to your brother, Lord Randal, my son?
What d' ye leave to your brother, my handsome young man?"
"My house and my lands; mother, mak my bed soon,   35
For I'm sick at the heart, and I fain wad lie down."

"What d' ye leave to your true-love, Lord Randal, my son?
What d' ye leave to your true-love, my handsome young man?"
"I leave her hell and fire; mother, mak my bed soon,
For I'm sick at the heart, and I fain wad lie down."   40

Compare

"Lord Randall" with "Ballad of Birmingham" by Dudley Randall (Chapter 21).

Anonymous (Navajo mountain chant)

Last Words of the Prophet

Farewell, younger brother!
From the holy places the gods come for me.
You will never see me again; but when the showers pass and the
    thunder peals,
"There," you will say, "is the voice of my elder brother."
And when the harvest comes, of the beautiful birds and grasshoppers   5
    you will say,
"There is the ordering of my elder brother!"

—*Translated by Washington Matthews*

Compare

"Last Words of the Prophet" with "A Slumber Did My Spirit Seal" by William Wordsworth
(Chapter 22).

Matthew Arnold (1822–1888)

Dover Beach   1867

The sea is calm to-night.
The tide is full, the moon lies fair
Upon the straits; on the French coast the light
Gleams and is gone; the cliffs of England stand,
Glimmering and vast, out in the tranquil bay.   5
Come to the window, sweet is the night-air!
Only, from the long line of spray
Where the sea meets the moon-blanched land,
Listen! you hear the grating roar
Of pebbles which the waves draw back, and fling,   10
At their return, up the high strand,
Begin, and cease, and then again begin,
With tremulous cadence slow, and bring
The eternal note of sadness in.

Sophocles long ago   15
Heard it on the Aegean, and it brought
Into his mind the turbid ebb and flow
Of human misery; we
Find also in the sound a thought,
Hearing it by this distant northern sea.   20

The Sea of Faith
Was once, too, at the full, and round earth's shore

Lay like the folds of a bright girdle furled.
But now I only hear
Its melancholy, long, withdrawing roar,   25
Retreating, to the breath
Of the night-wind, down the vast edges drear
And naked shingles° of the world.   *gravel beaches*

Ah, love, let us be true
To one another! for the world, which seems   30
To lie before us like a land of dreams,
So various, so beautiful, so new,
Hath really neither joy, nor love, nor light,
Nor certitude, nor peace, nor help for pain;
And we are here as on a darkling° plain   *darkened or darkening* 35
Swept with confused alarms of struggle and flight,
Where ignorant armies clash by night.

Compare
"Dover Beach" with "Hap" by Thomas Hardy (in this chapter).

John Ashbery   (1927–2017)

At North Farm   1984

Somewhere someone is traveling furiously toward you,
At incredible speed, traveling day and night,
Through blizzards and desert heat, across torrents, through narrow passes.
But will he know where to find you,
Recognize you when he sees you,   5
Give you the thing he has for you?

Hardly anything grows here,
Yet the granaries are bursting with meal,
The sacks of meal piled to the rafters.
The streams run with sweetness, fattening fish;   10
Birds darken the sky. Is it enough
That the dish of milk is set out at night,
That we think of him sometimes,
Sometimes and always, with mixed feelings?

Compare
"At North Farm" with "Up-Hill" by Christina Rossetti (Chapter 26).

W. H. Auden (1907–1973)

As I Walked Out One Evening 1940

As I walked out one evening,
    Walking down Bristol Street,
The crowds upon the pavement
    Were fields of harvest wheat.

And down by the brimming river   5
    I heard a lover sing
Under an arch of the railway:
    "Love has no ending.

"I'll love you, dear, I'll love you
    Till China and Africa meet,   10
And the river jumps over the mountain
    And the salmon sing in the street,

"I'll love you till the ocean
    Is folded and hung up to dry
And the seven stars go squawking   15
    Like geese about the sky.

"The years shall run like rabbits,
    For in my arms I hold
The Flower of the Ages,
    And the first love of the world."   20

But all the clocks in the city
    Began to whirr and chime:
"O let not Time deceive you,
    You cannot conquer Time.

"In the burrows of the Nightmare   25
    Where Justice naked is,
Time watches from the shadow
    And coughs when you would kiss.

"In headaches and in worry
    Vaguely life leaks away,   30
And Time will have his fancy
    To-morrow or to-day.

"Into many a green valley
   Drifts the appalling snow;
Time breaks the threaded dances   35
   And the diver's brilliant bow.

"O plunge your hands in water,
   Plunge them in up to the wrist;
Stare, stare in the basin
   And wonder what you've missed.   40

"The glacier knocks in the cupboard,
   The desert sighs in the bed,
And the crack in the tea-cup opens
   A lane to the land of the dead.

"Where the beggars raffle the banknotes   45
   And the Giant is enchanting to Jack,
And the Lily-white Boy is a Roarer,
   And Jill goes down on her back.

"O look, look in the mirror,
   O look in your distress;   50
Life remains a blessing
   Although you cannot bless.

"O stand, stand at the window
   As the tears scald and start;
You shall love your crooked neighbor   55
   With your crooked heart."

It was late, late in the evening,
   The lovers they were gone;
The clocks had ceased their chiming,
   And the deep river ran on.   60

Compare

"As I Walked Out One Evening" with "Dover Beach" by Matthew Arnold (in this chapter)
and "anyone lived in a pretty how town" by E. E. Cummings (Chapter 17).

W. H. Auden (1907–1973)

Musée des Beaux Arts   1940

About suffering they were never wrong,
The Old Masters: how well they understood
Its human position; how it takes place
While someone else is eating or opening a window or just walking dully along;
How, when the aged are reverently, passionately waiting   5
For the miraculous birth, there always must be
Children who did not specially want it to happen, skating
On a pond at the edge of the wood:
They never forgot

The Fall of Icarus by Pieter Brueghel the Elder (1520?–1569).

That even the dreadful martyrdom must run its course   10
Anyhow in a corner, some untidy spot
Where the dogs go on with their doggy life and the torturer's horse
Scratches its innocent behind on a tree.

In Brueghel's *Icarus*, for instance: how everything turns away
Quite leisurely from the disaster; the ploughman may   15
Have heard the splash, the forsaken cry,
But for him it was not an important failure; the sun shone
As it had to on the white legs disappearing into the green
Water; and the expensive delicate ship that must have seen
Something amazing, a boy falling out of the sky,   20
Had somewhere to get to and sailed calmly on.

Compare

"Musée des Beaux Arts" with "The Dance" by William Carlos Williams (Chapter 25) and the
painting by Pieter Brueghel to which each poem refers.

Jimmy Santiago Baca (b. 1952)

Spliced Wire   1982

I filled your house with light.
There was warmth in all the corners
of the house. My words I gave you
like soft warm toast in early morning.
I brewed your tongue   5
to a rich dark coffee, and drank

my fill. I turned on the music for you,
playing notes along the crest
of your heart, like birds,
eagles, ravens, owls on rim of red canyon.   10

I brought reception clear to you,
and made the phone ring at your request,
from Paris or South America,
you could talk to any of the people,
as my words gave them life,   15
from a child in a boat with his father,
to a prisoner in a concentration camp,
all at your bedside.

And then you turned away, wanted
a larger mansion. I said no. I left you.   20
The plug pulled out, the house blinked out,
into a quiet darkness, swallowing wind,
collecting autumn leaves like stamps
between its old boards where they stick.

You say, or carry the thought with you   25
to comfort you, that faraway somewhere,
lightning knocked down all the power lines.
But no my love, it was I,
pulling the plug. Others will come, plug in,
but often the lights will dim weakly   30
in storms, the music stop to a drawl,
the warmth shredded by cold drafts.

Compare

"Spliced Wire" with "First Poem for You" by Kim Addonizio (Chapter 24).

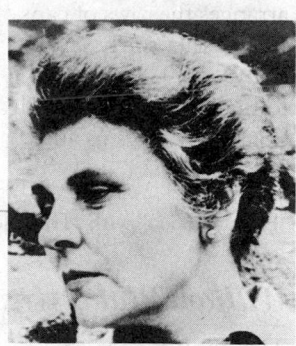

Elizabeth Bishop (1911–1979)

Filling Station   1965

Oh, but it is dirty!
—this little filling station,
oil-soaked, oil-permeated
to a disturbing, over-all
black translucency.   5
Be careful with that match!

Elizabeth Bishop

Father wears a dirty,
oil-soaked monkey suit
that cuts him under the arms,
and several quick and saucy
and greasy sons assist him
(it's a family filling station),
all quite thoroughly dirty.

Do they live in the station?
It has a cement porch
behind the pumps, and on it
a set of crushed and grease-
impregnated wickerwork;
on the wicker sofa
a dirty dog, quite comfy.

Some comic books provide
the only note of color—
of certain color. They lie
upon a big dim doily
draping a taboret°   *stool*   25
(part of the set), beside
a big hirsute begonia.

Why the extraneous plant?
Why the taboret?
Why, oh why, the doily?   30
(Embroidered in daisy stitch
with marguerites, I think,
and heavy with gray crochet.)

Somebody embroidered the doily.
Somebody waters the plant,   35
or oils it, maybe. Somebody
arranges the rows of cans
so that they softly say:
ESSO—SO—SO—SO
to high-strung automobiles.   40
Somebody loves us all.

Compare
"Filling Station" with "The splendor falls on castle walls" by Alfred, Lord Tennyson (Chapter 22).

William Blake (1757–1827)

The Sick Rose   1794

O Rose, thou art sick.
The invisible worm,
That flies in the night
In the howling storm:

10

15

20

Has found out thy bed   5
Of crimson joy:
And his dark secret love
Does thy life destroy.

Compare
"The Sick Rose" with "Go, Lovely Rose" by Edmund Waller (in this chapter).

Gwendolyn Brooks (1917–2000)

the mother   1945

Abortions will not let you forget.
You remember the children you got that you did not get,
The damp small pulps with a little or with no hair,
The singers and workers that never handled the air.
You will never neglect or beat   5
Them, or silence or buy with a sweet.
You will never wind up the sucking-thumb
Or scuttle off ghosts that come.
You will never leave them, controlling your luscious sigh,
Return for a snack of them, with gobbling mother-eye.   10

I have heard in the voices of the wind the voices of my dim killed children.
I have contracted. I have eased
My dim dears at the breasts they could never suck.
I have said, Sweets, if I sinned, if I seized
Your luck   15
And your lives from your unfinished reach,
If I stole your births and your names,
Your straight baby tears and your games,
Your stilted or lovely loves, your tumults, your marriages, aches, and your deaths,
If I poisoned the beginnings of your breaths,   20
Believe that even in my deliberateness I was not deliberate.
Though why should I whine,
Whine that the crime was other than mine?—
Since anyhow you are dead.
Or rather, or instead,   25
You were never made.
But that too, I am afraid,
Is faulty: oh, what shall I say, how is the truth to be said?
You were born, you had body, you died.
It is just that you never giggled or planned or cried.   30

Believe me, I loved you all.
Believe me, I knew you, though faintly, and I loved, I loved you
All.

Compare
"the mother" with "Metaphors" by Sylvia Plath (Chapter 20).

Gwendolyn Brooks

Gwendolyn Brooks (1917–2000)

the rites for Cousin Vit   1949

Carried her unprotesting out the door.
Kicked back the casket-stand. But it can't hold her,
That stuff and satin aiming to enfold her,
The lid's contrition nor the bolts before.
Oh oh. Too much. Too much. Even now, surmise,   5
She rises in the sunshine. There she goes,
Back to the bars she knew and the repose
In love-rooms and the things in people's eyes.
Too vital and too squeaking. Must emerge.
Even now she does the snake-hips with a hiss,   10
Slops the bad wine across her shantung, talks
Of pregnancy, guitars and bridgework, walks
In parks or alleys, comes haply on the verge
Of happiness, haply hysterics. Is.

Compare

"the rites for Cousin Vit" with "Do not go gentle into that good night" by Dylan Thomas
(Chapter 24).

Elizabeth Barrett Browning (1806–1861)

How Do I Love Thee? Let Me Count the Ways   1850

How do I love thee? Let me count the ways.
I love thee to the depth and breadth and height
My soul can reach, when feeling out of sight
For the ends of Being and ideal Grace.
I love thee to the level of every day's   5
Most quiet need, by sun and candle-light.
I love thee freely, as men strive for Right;
I love thee purely, as they turn from Praise.
I love thee with the passion put to use
In my old griefs, and with my childhood's faith.   10
I love thee with a love I seemed to lose
With my lost saints,—I love thee with the breath,
Smiles, tears, of all my life!—and, if God choose,
I shall but love thee better after death.

Compare

"How Do I Love Thee?" with "What lips my lips have kissed" by Edna St. Vincent Millay
(Chapter 24).

Robert Browning (1812–1889)

Soliloquy of the Spanish Cloister   1842

Gr-r-r—there go, my heart's abhorrence!
   Water your damned flower-pots, do!
If hate killed men, Brother Lawrence,
   God's blood, would not mine kill you!
What? your myrtle-bush wants trimming?   5
   Oh, that rose has prior claims—
Needs its leaden vase filled brimming?
   Hell dry you up with its flames!

At the meal we sit together;
   Salve tibi!° I must hear   *Hail to thee!*   10
Wise talk of the kind of weather,
   Sort of season, time of year:
Not a plenteous cork-crop: scarcely
   Dare we hope oak-galls, I doubt:
What's the Latin name for "parsley"?   15
   What's the Greek name for Swine's Snout?

Whew! We'll have our platter burnished,
   Laid with care on our own shelf!
With a fire-new spoon we're furnished,
   And a goblet for ourself,   20
Rinsed like something sacrificial
   Ere 'tis fit to touch our chaps°—   *lower jaw*
Marked with L. for our initial!
   (He-he! There his lily snaps!)

Saint, forsooth! While brown Dolores   25
   Squats outside the Convent bank
With Sanchicha, telling stories,
   Steeping tresses in the tank,
Blue-black, lustrous, thick like horsehairs,
   —Can't I see his dead eye glow,   30
Bright as 'twere a Barbary corsair's?
   (That is, if he'd let it show!)

When he finishes refection,
   Knife and fork he never lays
Cross-wise, to my recollection,   35
   As I do, in Jesu's praise.
I the Trinity illustrate,
   Drinking watered orange-pulp—
In three sips the Arian frustrate;
   While he drains his at one gulp!   40

Oh, those melons! if he's able
  We're to have a feast; so nice!
One goes to the Abbot's table,
  All of us get each a slice.
How go on your flowers? None double?   45
  Not one fruit-sort can you spy?
Strange!—And I, too, at such trouble,
  Keep them close-nipped on the sly!

There's a great text in Galatians,
  Once you trip on it, entails   50
Twenty-nine distinct damnations,
  One sure, if another fails:
If I trip him just a-dying,
  Sure of heaven as sure can be,
Spin him round and send him flying   55
  Off to hell, a Manichee?

Or, my scrofulous French novel
  On grey paper with blunt type!
Simply glance at it, you grovel
  Hand and foot in Belial's gripe: 60
If I double down its pages
  At the woeful sixteenth print,
When he gathers his greengages,
  Ope a sieve and slip it in't?

Or, there's Satan!—one might venture   65
  Pledge one's soul to him, yet leave
Such a flaw in the indenture
  As he'd miss till, past retrieve,
Blasted lay that rose-acacia
  We're so proud of! Hy, Zy, Hine. . . .   70
'St, there's Vespers! *Plena gratia*
  Ave, Virgo!° Gr-r-r—you swine!   *Hail, Virgin, full of grace!*

SOLILOQUY OF THE SPANISH CLOISTER. 3 *Brother Lawrence*: one of the speaker's fellow monks. 31 *Barbary corsair*: a pirate operating off the Barbary Coast of Africa. 39 *Arian*: a follower of Arius, a heretic who denied the doctrine of the Trinity. 49 *a Great text in Galatians*: a difficult verse in this book of the Bible. Brother Lawrence will be damned as a heretic if he wrongly interprets it. 56 *Manichee*: another kind of heretic, one who (after the Persian philosopher Mani) sees in the world a constant struggle between good and evil, neither able to win. 60 *Belial*: here, not specifically Satan but (as used in the Old Testament) a name for wickedness. 70 *Hy, Zy, Hine*: possibly the sound of a bell to announce evening devotions.

Compare

"Soliloquy of the Spanish Cloister" with "The Magi" by William Butler Yeats (in this chapter).

Charles Bukowski (1920–1994)

Dostoevsky   1997

Charles Bukowski

against the wall, the firing squad ready.
then he got a reprieve.
suppose they had shot Dostoevsky?
before he wrote all that?
I suppose it wouldn't have   5
mattered
not directly.
there are billions of people who have
never read him and never
will.   10
but as a young man I know that he
got me through the factories,
past the whores,
lifted me high through the night
and put me down   15
in a better
place.
even while in the bar
drinking with the other
derelicts,   20
I was glad they gave Dostoevsky a
reprieve,
it gave me one,
allowed me to look directly at those
rancid faces   25
in my world,
death pointing its finger,
I held fast,
an immaculate drunk
sharing the stinking dark with   30
my
brothers.

DOSTOEVSKY. The Russian novelist Fyodor Dostoevsky (1821–1880), author of *Crime and Punishment*
and *The Brothers Karamazov*, was arrested in 1849 in a czarist crackdown on liberal organizations and
sentenced to death. It was not until the members of the firing squad had aimed their rifles and were
awaiting the order to fire that he was informed that his sentence had been commuted to four years of
hard labor in Siberia.

Compare

"Dostoevsky" with "When to the sessions of sweet silent thought" by William Shakespeare (in
this chapter).

Geoffrey Chaucer (1340?–1400)

Merciless Beauty

(late 14th century)

Your ÿen° two wol slee° me sodenly;   eyes; slay
I may the beautee of hem° not sustene,°   them; resist
So woundeth hit thourghout my herte kene.

And but° your word wol helen° hastily   unless; heal
My hertes wounde, while that hit is grene,°   new   5
    Your ÿen two wol slee me sodenly;
    I may the beautee of hem not sustene.

Upon my trouthe° I sey you feithfully   word
That ye ben of my lyf and deeth the quene;
For with my deeth the trouthe° shal be sene.   truth 10
    Your ÿen two wol slee me sodenly;
    I may the beautee of hem not sustene,
    So woundeth it thourghout my herte kene.

MERCILESS BEAUTY. This poem is one of a group of three roundels, collectively titled "Merciles Beaute." A **roundel** (or **rondel**) is an English form consisting of 11 lines in 3 stanzas rimed with a refrain. 3 *So woundeth . . . kene:* "So deeply does it wound me through the heart."

Compare

"Merciless Beauty" with "My mistress' eyes are nothing like the sun" by William Shakespeare (in this chapter).

G. K. Chesterton (1874–1936)

The Donkey

1900

When fishes flew and forests walked
    And figs grew upon thorn,
Some moment when the moon was blood
    Then surely I was born;

With monstrous head and sickening cry   5
    And ears like errant wings,
The devil's walking parody
    On all four-footed things.

The tattered outlaw of the earth,
    Of ancient crooked will;   10
Strave, scourge, deride me: I am dumb,
    I keep my secret still.

Fools! For I also had my hour;
    One far fierce hour and sweet:
There was a shout about my ears,   15
    And palms before my feet.

THE DONKEY. For more details of the donkey's hour of triumph see Matthew 21:1–8.

Compare

"The Donkey" with "The Tyger" by William Blake (Chapter 26).

John Ciardi   (1916–1986)

Most Like an Arch This Marriage   1958

Most like an arch—an entrance which upholds
and shores the stone-crush up the air like lace.
Mass made idea, and idea held in place.
A lock in time. Inside half-heaven unfolds.

Most like an arch—two weaknesses that lean   5
into a strength. Two fallings become firm.
Two joined abeyances become a term
naming the fact that teaches fact to mean.

Not quite that? Not much less. World as it is,
what's strong and separate falters. All I do   10
at piling stone on stone apart from you
is roofless around nothing. Till we kiss

I am no more than upright and unset.
It is by falling in and in we make
the all-bearing point, for one another's sake,   15
in faultless failing, raised by our own weight.

Compare

"Most Like an Arch This Marriage" with "Let me not to the marriage of true minds" by William Shakespeare (Chapter 24).

Samuel Taylor Coleridge   (1772–1834)

Kubla Khan   (1797–1798)

   Or, a Vision in a Dream. A Fragment.

In Xanadu did Kubla Khan
A stately pleasure-dome decree:
Where Alph, the sacred river, ran
Through caverns measureless to man
  Down to a sunless sea.   5
So twice five miles of fertile ground
With walls and towers were girdled round:
And here were gardens bright with sinuous rills,
Where blossomed many an incense-bearing tree;
And here were forests ancient as the hills,   10
Enfolding sunny spots of greenery.

But oh! that deep romantic chasm which slanted
Down the green hill athwart a cedarn cover!
A savage place! as holy and enchanted
As e'er beneath a waning moon was haunted   15

By woman wailing for her demon-lover!
And from this chasm, with ceaseless turmoil seething,
As if this earth in fast thick pants were breathing,
A mighty fountain momently was forced: 20
Amid whose swift half-intermitted burst
Huge fragments vaulted like rebounding hail,
Or chaffy grain beneath the thresher's flail:
And 'mid these dancing rocks at once and ever
It flung up momently the sacred river.
Five miles meandering with a mazy motion   25
Through wood and dale the sacred river ran,
Then reached the caverns measureless to man,
And sank in tumult to a lifeless ocean:
And 'mid this tumult Kubla heard from far
Ancestral voices prophesying war!   30
    The shadow of the dome of pleasure
    Floated midway on the waves;
    Where was heard the mingled measure
    From the fountain and the caves.
It was a miracle of rare device,   35
A sunny pleasure-dome with caves of ice!

    A damsel with a dulcimer
    In a vision once I saw:
    It was an Abyssinian maid,
    And on her dulcimer she played,   40
    Singing of Mount Abora.
    Could I revive within me
    Her symphony and song,
    To such a deep delight 'twould win me,
That with music loud and long,   45
I would build that dome in air,
That sunny dome! those caves of ice!
And all who heard should see them there,
And all should cry, Beware! Beware!
His flashing eyes, his floating hair!   50
Weave a circle round him thrice,
And close your eyes with holy dread,
For he on honey-dew hath fed,
And drunk the milk of Paradise.

KUBLA KHAN. There was an actual Kublai Khan, a thirteenth-century Mongol emperor, and a
Chinese city of Xanadu; but Coleridge's dream vision also borrows from travelers' descriptions of
such other exotic places as Abyssinia and America. 51 *circle:* a magic circle drawn to keep away
evil spirits.

Compare

"Kubla Khan" with "The Second Coming" by William Butler Yeats (Chapter 27).

Billy Collins

Billy Collins (b. 1941)

Introduction to Poetry   1988

I ask them to take a poem
and hold it up to the light
like a color slide

or press an ear against its hive.

I say drop a mouse into a poem   5
and watch him probe his way out,

or walk inside the poem's room
and feel the walls for a light switch.

I want them to waterski
across the surface of a poem   10
waving at the author's name on the shore.

But all they want to do
is tie the poem to a chair with rope
and torture a confession out of it.

They begin beating it with a hose   15
to find out what it really means.

Compare

"Introduction to Poetry" with "I'm Like" by Cody Walker (Chapter 20).

Hart Crane (1899–1932)

My Grandmother's Love Letters   1926

There are no stars tonight
But those of memory.
Yet how much room for memory there is
In the loose girdle of soft rain.

There is even room enough   5
For the letters of my mother's mother,
Elizabeth,
That have been pressed so long
Into a corner of the roof
That they are brown and soft,   10
And liable to melt as snow.

Over the greatness of such space
Steps must be gentle.
It is all hung by an invisible white hair.
It trembles as birch limbs webbing the air.   15

And I ask myself:

"Are your fingers long enough to play
Old keys that are but echoes:
Is the silence strong enough
To carry back the music to its source   20
And back to you again
As though to her?"

Yet I would lead my grandmother by the hand
Through much of what she would not understand;
And so I stumble. And the rain continues on the roof   25
With such a sound of gently pitying laughter.

Compare

"My Grandmother's Love Letters" with "When You Are Old" by William Butler Yeats (in this chapter).

E. E. Cummings (1894–1962)

somewhere i have never   1931
travelled,gladly beyond

somewhere i have never travelled,gladly beyond
any experience,your eyes have their silence:
in your most frail gesture are things which enclose me,
or which i cannot touch because they are too near

E. E. Cummings

your slightest look easily will unclose me 5
though i have closed myself as fingers,
you open always petal by petal myself as Spring opens
(touching skilfully,mysteriously)her first rose

or if your wish be to close me,i and
my life will shut very beautifully,suddenly, 10
as when the heart of this flower imagines
the snow carefully everywhere descending;

nothing which we are to perceive in this world equals
the power of your intense fragility:whose texture
compels me with the colour of its countries, 15
rendering death and forever with each breathing

(i do not know what it is about you that closes
and opens;only something in me understands
the voice of your eyes is deeper than all roses)
nobody,not even the rain,has such small hands 20

Compare

"somewhere i have never travelled,gladly beyond" with "Merciless Beauty" by Geoffrey Chaucer
(in this chapter).

Marisa de los Santos (b. 1966)

Perfect Dress   2000

It's here in a student's journal, a blue confession
in smudged, erasable ink: "I can't stop hoping
I'll wake up, suddenly beautiful," and isn't it strange
how we want it, despite all we know? To be at last

Marisa de los Santos

the girl in the photograph, cobalt-eyed, hair puddling 5
like cognac, or the one stretched at the ocean's edge,
curved and light-drenched, more like a beach than
the beach. I confess I have longed to stalk runways,

leggy, otherworldly as a mantis, to balance a head
like a Fabergé egg on the longest, most elegant neck. 10
Today in the checkout line, I saw a magazine
claiming to know "How to Find the Perfect Dress

for that Perfect Evening," and I felt the old pull, flare
of the pilgrim's twin flames, desire and faith. At fifteen,
I spent weeks at the search. Going from store to store,   15
hands thirsty for shine, I reached for polyester satin,

machine-made lace, petunia- and Easter egg-colored,
brilliant and flammable. Nothing *haute* about this
couture but my hopes for it, as I tugged it on
and waited for my one, true body to emerge.   20

(Picture the angel inside uncut marble, articulation
of wings and robes poised in expectation of release.)
What I wanted was ordinary miracle, the falling away
of everything wrong. Silly maybe or maybe

I was right, that there's no limit to the ways eternity   25
suggests itself, that one day I'll slip into it, say
floor-length plum charmeuse. Someone will murmur,
"She is sublime," will be precisely right, and I will step,

with incandescent shoulders, into my perfect evening.

PERFECT DRESS. 10 *Fabergé*: Peter Carl Fabergé (1846–1920) was a Russian jeweler renowned for his
elaborately decorated, golden, jeweled eggs.

Compare
"Perfect Dress" with "Cinderella" by Anne Sexton (Chapter 27).

John Donne (1572–1631)

Death be not proud   (about 1610)

Death be not proud, though some have callèd thee
Mighty and dreadful, for thou art not so;
For those whom thou think'st thou dost overthrow
Die not, poor death, nor yet canst thou kill me.
From rest and sleep, which but thy pictures be,   5
Much pleasure, then from thee much more must flow,
And soonest our best men with thee do go,
Rest of their bones, and soul's delivery.
Thou art slave to fate, chance, kings, and desperate men,
And dost with poison, war, and sickness dwell,   10
And poppy, or charms can make us sleep as well,
And better than thy stroke; why swell'st thou then?
One short sleep past, we wake eternally,
And death shall be no more; death, thou shalt die.

Compare
Compare Donne's personification of Death in "Death be not proud" with Emily Dickinson's in
"Because I could not stop for Death" (Chapter 32).

John Donne (1572–1631)

The Flea   1633

Mark but this flea, and mark in this
How little that which thou deny'st me is;
It sucked me first, and now sucks thee,
And in this flea our two bloods mingled be;
Thou know'st that this cannot be said   5
A sin, nor shame, nor loss of maidenhead,
    Yet this enjoys before it woo,
      And pampered swells with one blood made of two,
    And this, alas, is more than we would do.

Oh stay, three lives in one flea spare,   10
Where we almost, yea more than married are.
This flea is you and I, and this
Our marriage bed, and marriage temple is;
Though parents grudge, and you, we're met
And cloistered in these living walls of jet.   15
    Though use° make you apt to kill me,   *custom*
    Let not to that, self-murder added be,
    And sacrilege, three sins in killing three.

Cruel and sudden, hast thou since
Purpled thy nail in blood of innocence?   20
Wherein could this flea guilty be,
Except in that drop which it sucked from thee?
Yet thou triumph'st, and say'st that thou
Find'st not thyself, nor me, the weaker now;
    'Tis true; then learn how false, fears be;   25
    Just so much honor, when thou yield'st to me,
    Will waste, as this flea's death took life from thee.

Compare

"The Flea" with "To His Coy Mistress" by Andrew Marvell (in this chapter).

John Donne (1572–1631)

A Valediction: Forbidding Mourning   (1611)

As virtuous men pass mildly away,
    And whisper to their souls to go,
Whilst some of their sad friends do say
    The breath goes now, and some say no:

So let us melt, and make no noise,   5
    No tear-floods, nor sigh-tempests move;
'Twere profanation of our joys
    To tell the laity° our love.   *common people*

Moving of th' earth° brings harms and fears;   *earthquake*
    Men reckon what it did and meant;   10
But trepidation of the spheres,
    Though greater far, is innocent.°   *harmless*

Dull sublunary lovers' love
    (Whose soul is sense) cannot admit
Absence, because it doth remove   15
    Those things which elemented° it.   *constituted*

But we, by a love so much refined
    That ourselves know not what it is,
Inter-assurèd of the mind,
    Care less, eyes, lips, and hands to miss.   20

Our two souls, therefore, which are one,
    Though I must go, endure not yet
A breach, but an expansión,
    Like gold to airy thinness beat.

If they be two, they are two so   25
    As stiff twin compasses are two:
Thy soul, the fixed foot, makes no show
    To move, but doth, if th' other do.

And though it in the center sit,
    Yet when the other far doth roam,   30
It leans and harkens after it,
    And grows erect as that comes home.

Such wilt thou be to me, who must,
    Like th' other foot, obliquely run;
Thy firmness makes my circle just,°   *perfect* 35
    And makes me end where I begun.

A VALEDICTION: FORBIDDING MOURNING. According to Donne's biographer Izaak Walton, Donne's wife received this poem as a gift before the poet departed on a journey to France. 11 *spheres*: in Ptolemaic astronomy, the concentric spheres surrounding the earth. The trepidation or motion of the ninth sphere was thought to change the date of the equinox. 19 *Inter-assurèd of the mind:* each sure in mind that the other is faithful. 24 *gold to airy thinness:* gold is so malleable that, if beaten to the thickness of gold leaf (1/250,000 of one inch), one ounce of gold would cover 250 square feet.

Compare
"A Valediction: Forbidding Mourning" with "To Lucasta" by Richard Lovelace (Chapter 16).

T. S. Eliot (1888–1965)

Journey of the Magi   1927

"A cold coming we had of it,
Just the worst time of the year
For a journey, and such a long journey:
The ways deep and the weather sharp,
The very dead of winter."   5

And the camels galled, sore-footed, refractory,
Lying down in the melting snow.
There were times we regretted
The summer palaces on slopes, the terraces,
And the silken girls bringing sherbet.   10
Then the camel men cursing and grumbling
And running away, and wanting their liquor and women,
And the night-fires going out, and the lack of shelters,
And the cities hostile and the towns unfriendly
And the villages dirty and charging high prices: 15
A hard time we had of it.
At the end we preferred to travel all night,
Sleeping in snatches,
With the voices singing in our ears, saying
That this was all folly.   20

Then at dawn we came down to a temperate valley,
Wet, below the snow line, smelling of vegetation;
With a running stream and a water-mill beating the darkness,
And three trees on the low sky,
And an old white horse galloped away in the meadow.   25
Then we came to a tavern with vine-leaves over the lintel,
Six hands at an open door dicing for pieces of silver,
And feet kicking the empty wine-skins.
But there was no information, and so we continued
And arrived at evening, not a moment too soon   30
Finding the place; it was (you may say) satisfactory.

All this was a long time ago, I remember,
And I would do it again, but set down
This set down
This: were we led all that way for   35
Birth or Death? There was a Birth, certainly,
We had evidence and no doubt. I had seen birth and death,
But had thought they were different; this Birth was
Hard and bitter agony for us, like Death, our death.
We returned to our places, these Kingdoms,   40
But no longer at ease here, in the old dispensation,
With an alien people clutching their gods.
I should be glad of another death.

JOURNEY OF THE MAGI. The story of the Magi, the three wise men who traveled to Bethlehem to behold the baby Jesus, is told in Matthew 2:1–12. That the three were kings is a later tradition. 1–5 *A cold coming . . . winter:* Eliot quotes with slight changes from a sermon preached on Christmas Day, 1622, by Bishop Lancelot Andrewes. 24 *three trees:* foreshadowing the three crosses on Calvary (see Luke 23:32–33). 25 *white horse:* perhaps the steed that carried the conquering Christ in the vision of St. John the Divine (Revelation 19:11–16). 41 *old dispensation:* older, pagan religion about to be displaced by Christianity.

Compare

"Journey of the Magi" with "The Magi" by William Butler Yeats (in this chapter).

Allen Ginsberg (1926–1997)

A Supermarket in California   1956

What thoughts I have of you tonight, Walt Whitman, for I walked down the sidestreets under the trees with a headache self-conscious looking at the full moon.

Allen Ginsberg

In my hungry fatigue, and shopping for images, I went into the neon fruit supermarket, dreaming of your enumerations!

What peaches and what penumbras! Whole families shopping at night! Aisles full of husbands! Wives in the avocados, babies in the tomatoes!— and you, García Lorca, what were you doing down by the watermelons?

I saw you, Walt Whitman, childless, lonely old grubber, poking among the meats in the refrigerator and eyeing the grocery boys.

I heard you asking questions of each: Who killed the pork chops? What   5
price bananas? Are you my Angel?

I wandered in and out of the brilliant stacks of cans following you, and followed in my imagination by the store detective.

We strode down the open corridors together in our solitary fancy tasting artichokes, possessing every frozen delicacy, and never passing the cashier.

Where are we going, Walt Whitman? The doors close in an hour. Which way does your beard point tonight?

(I touch your book and dream of our odyssey in the supermarket and feel absurd.)

Will we walk all night through solitary streets? The trees add shade to   10
shade, lights out in the houses, we'll both be lonely.

Will we stroll dreaming of the lost America of love past blue automobiles in driveways, home to our silent cottage?

Ah, dear father, graybeard, lonely old courage-teacher, what America did you have when Charon quit poling his ferry and you got out on a smoking bank and stood watching the boat disappear on the black waters of Lethe?

A SUPERMARKET IN CALIFORNIA. 2 *enumerations:* many of Whitman's poems contain lists of observed details. 3 *García Lorca:* modern Spanish poet who wrote an "Ode to Walt Whitman" in his book-length sequence *Poet in New York.* 12 *Charon . . . Lethe:* Is the poet confusing two underworld rivers? Charon, in Greek and Roman mythology, is the boatman who ferries the souls of the dead across the river Styx. The river Lethe also flows through Hades, and a drink of its waters makes the dead lose their painful memories of loved ones they have left behind.

Compare

"A Supermarket in California" with Walt Whitman's "I Hear America Singing" (Chapter 25).

Thomas Hardy (1840–1928)

The Convergence of the Twain   1912

Lines on the Loss of the "Titanic"

I

In a solitude of the sea
Deep from human vanity,
And the Pride of Life that planned her, stilly couches she.

II

Steel chambers, late the pyres
Of her salamandrine fires,
Cold currents thrid,° and turn to rhythmic tidal lyres.   5   *thread*

III

Over the mirrors meant
To glass the opulent
The sea-worm crawls—grotesque, slimed, dumb, indifferent.

IV

Jewels in joy designed   10
To ravish the sensuous mind
Lie lightless, all their sparkles bleared and black and blind.

V

Dim moon-eyed fishes near
Gaze at the gilded gear
And query: "What does this vaingloriousness down here?" . . .   15

VI

Well: while was fashioning
This creature of cleaving wing,
The Immanent Will that stirs and urges everything

VII

Prepared a sinister mate
For her—so gaily great—   20
A Shape of Ice, for the time far and dissociate.

VIII

And as the smart ship grew
In stature, grace, and hue,
In shadowy silent distance grew the Iceberg too.

IX

Alien they seemed to be: 25
No mortal eye could see
The intimate welding of their later history,

X

Or sign that they were bent
By paths coincident
On being anon twin halves of one august event,   30

XI

Till the Spinner of the Years
Said "Now!" And each one hears,
And consummation comes, and jars two hemispheres.

THE CONVERGENCE OF THE TWAIN. The luxury liner *Titanic*, supposedly unsinkable, went down in 1912 after striking an iceberg on its first Atlantic voyage. 5 *salamandrine*: like the salamander, a lizard that supposedly thrives in fires, or like a spirit of the same name that inhabits fire (according to alchemists).

Compare

"The Convergence of the Twain" with "Thirteen Ways of Looking at a Blackbird" by Wallace Stevens (Chapter 25).

Thomas Hardy (1840–1928)

Hap   (1866)

If but some vengeful god would call to me
From up the sky, and laugh: "Thou suffering thing,
Know that thy sorrow is my ecstasy,
That thy love's loss is my hate's profiting!"

Then would I bear it, clench myself, and die,   5
Steeled by the sense of ire unmerited;
Half-eased in that a Powerfuller than I
Had willed and meted me the tears I shed.

But not so. How arrives it joy lies slain,
And why unblooms the best hope ever sown?   10
—Crass Casualty obstructs the sun and rain,
And dicing Time for gladness casts a moan. . . .
These purblind Doomsters had as readily strown
Blisses about my pilgrimage as pain.

Compare

"Hap" with "The Facebook Sonnet" by Sherman Alexie (Chapter 24).

Seamus Heaney (1939–2013)

Digging   1966

Between my finger and my thumb
The squat pen rests; snug as a gun.

Under my window, a clean rasping sound
When the spade sinks into gravelly ground:
My father, digging. I look down   5

Till his straining rump among the flowerbeds
Bends low, comes up twenty years away
Stooping in rhythm through potato drills
Where he was digging.

The coarse boot nestled on the lug, the shaft   10
Against the inside knee was levered firmly.
He rooted out tall tops, buried the bright edge deep
To scatter new potatoes that we picked
Loving their cool hardness in our hands.

By God, the old man could handle a spade.   15
Just like his old man.

My grandfather cut more turf in a day
Than any other man on Toner's bog.
Once I carried him milk in a bottle
Corked sloppily with paper. He straightened up   20
To drink it, then fell to right away
Nicking and slicing neatly, heaving sods
Over his shoulder, going down and down
For the good turf. Digging.

The cold smell of potato mould, the squelch and slap   25
Of soggy peat, the curt cuts of an edge
Through living roots awaken in my head.
But I've no spade to follow men like them.

Between my finger and my thumb
The squat pen rests.   30
I'll dig with it.

Compare

"Digging" with "Speech to the Young. Speech to the Progress-Toward." by Gwendolyn Brooks
(Chapter 16).

William Ernest Henley (1849–1903)

Invictus   1875

Out of the night that covers me,
    Black as the pit from pole to pole,
I thank whatever gods may be
    For my unconquerable soul.

In the fell clutch of circumstance   5
    I have not winced nor cried aloud.
Under the bludgeonings of chance
    My head is bloody, but unbowed.

Beyond this place of wrath and tears
  Looms but the Horror of the shade,   10
And yet the menace of the years
  Finds and shall find me unafraid.

It matters not how strait the gate,
  How charged with punishments the scroll,
I am the master of my fate,   15
  I am the captain of my soul.

Compare

"Invictus" with "Dulce et Decorum Est" by Wilfred Owen (Chapter 16).

Juan Felipe Herrera (b. 1948)

El Ángel de la Guarda   1999

I should have visited more often.
I should have taken the sour pudding they offered.
I should have danced that lousy beggar shuffle.
I should have painted their rooms in a brighter color.
I should have put a window in there, for the daughters.   5
I should have provided a decent mountain for a view.
I should have nudged them a little closer to the sky.
I should have guessed they would never come out to wave.
I should have cleaned up that mole, the abyss, in the back.
I should have touched them, thass it, it comes to me now.   10
I should have touched them.

Compare

"El Ángel de la Guarda" with "I'm Like" by Cody Walker (Chapter 20).

Linocut by Artemio Rodríguez

George Herbert (1593–1633)

Love   1633

Love bade me welcome; yet my soul drew back,
        Guilty of dust and sin.
But quick-eyed Love, observing me grow slack
        From my first entrance in,
Drew nearer to me, sweetly questioning   5
        If I lacked anything.

"A guest," I answered, "worthy to be here";
        Love said, "You shall be he."
"I, the unkind, ungrateful? Ah, my dear,
        I cannot look on Thee."   10
Love took my hand, and smiling did reply,
        "Who made the eyes but I?"

"Truth, Lord, but I have marred them; let my shame
        Go where it doth deserve."
"And know you not," says Love, "who bore the blame?"   15
        "My dear, then I will serve."
"You must sit down," says Love, "and taste My meat."
        So I did sit and eat.

Compare

"Love" with "Batter my heart, three-personed God" by John Donne (Chapter 17).

Robert Herrick (1591–1674)

To the Virgins, to Make Much of Time   1648

Gather ye rose-buds while ye may,
    Old Time is still a-flying;
And this same flower that smiles today,
    Tomorrow will be dying.

The glorious lamp of heaven, the sun,   5
    The higher he's a-getting,
The sooner will his race be run,
    And nearer he's to setting.

That age is best which is the first,
    When youth and blood are warmer;   10
But being spent, the worse, and worst
    Times still succeed the former.

Then be not coy, but use your time,
    And while ye may, go marry;
For having lost but once your prime,   15
    You may for ever tarry.

Compare

"To the Virgins, to Make Much of Time" with "To His Coy Mistress" by Andrew Marvell and
"Go, Lovely Rose" by Edmund Waller (both in this chapter).

Gerard Manley Hopkins (1844–1889)

Spring and Fall   (1880)

To a young child

Gerard Manley Hopkins

Márgarét, áre you gríeving
Over Goldengrove unleaving?°   shedding its leaves
Leáves, líke the things of man, you
With your fresh thoughts care for, can you?
Áh! ás the heart grows older   5
It will come to such sights colder
By and by, nor spare a sigh
Though worlds of wanwood leafmeal lie;
And yet you wíll weep and know why.
Now no matter, child, the name: 10
Sórrow's spríngs áre the same.
Nor mouth had, no nor mind, expressed
What heart heard of, ghost° guessed: spirit
It ís the blight man was born for,
It is Margaret you mourn for.   15

Compare

"Spring and Fall" with "Aftermath" by Henry Wadsworth Longfellow (Chapter 17).

Gerard Manley Hopkins (1844–1889)

The Windhover   (1877)

To Christ Our Lord

I caught this morning morning's minion, king-
   dom of daylight's dauphin, dapple-dawn-drawn Falcon, in his riding
   Of the rolling level underneath him steady air, and striding
High there, how he rung upon the rein of a wimpling wing
In his ecstasy! then off, off forth on swing,   5
   As a skate's heel sweeps smooth on a bow-bend: the hurl and gliding
   Rebuffed the big wind. My heart in hiding
Stirred for a bird, —the achieve of, the mastery of the thing!

Brute beauty and valor and act, oh, air, pride, plume, here
   Buckle! AND the fire that breaks from thee then, a billion   10
Times told lovelier, more dangerous, O my chevalier!

No wonder of it: shéer plód makes plough down sillion°   *furrow*
Shine, and blue-bleak embers, ah my dear,
    Fall, gall themselves, and gash gold-vermilion.

THE WINDHOVER. A windhover is a kestrel, or small falcon, so called because it can hover upon the wind. 4 *rung . . . wing:* A horse is "rung upon the rein" when its trainer holds the end of a long rein and has the horse circle him. The possible meanings of *wimpling* include: (1) curving; (2) pleated, arranged in many little folds one on top of another; (3) rippling or undulating like the surface of a flowing stream.

Compare

"The Windhover" with "Batter my heart, three-personed God" by John Donne (Chapter 17).

A. E. Housman (1859–1936)

Loveliest of trees, the cherry now   1896

Loveliest of trees, the cherry now
Is hung with bloom along the bough,
And stands about the woodland ride°   *path*
Wearing white for Eastertide.

Now, of my threescore years and ten,
Twenty will not come again,   5
And take from seventy springs a score,
It only leaves me fifty more.

And since to look at things in bloom
Fifty springs are little room,   10
About the woodlands I will go
To see the cherry hung with snow.

Compare

"Loveliest of trees, the cherry now" with "To the Virgins, to Make Much of Time" by Robert Herrick and "Spring and Fall" by Gerard Manley Hopkins (both in this chapter).

A. E. Housman (1859–1936)

To an Athlete Dying Young   1896

The time you won your town the race
We chaired you through the market-place;
Man and boy stood cheering by,
And home we brought you shoulder-high.

To-day, the road all runners come,   5
Shoulder-high we bring you home,
And set you at your threshold down,
Townsman of a stiller town.

Smart lad, to slip betimes away
From fields where glory does not stay   10
And early though the laurel grows
It withers quicker than the rose.

Eyes the shady night has shut
Cannot see the record cut,
And silence sounds no worse than cheers   15
After earth has stopped the ears:

Now you will not swell the rout
Of lads that wore their honors out,
Runners whom renown outran
And the name died before the man.   20

So set, before its echoes fade,
The fleet foot on the sill of shade,
And hold to the low lintel up
The still-defended challenge-cup.

And round that early-laureled head   25
Will flock to gaze the strengthless dead,
And find unwithered on its curls
The garland briefer than a girl's.

Compare

"To an Athlete Dying Young" with "Autumn Begins in Martins Ferry, Ohio" by James Wright
(Chapter 28).

Randall Jarrell (1914–1965)

The Death of the Ball Turret Gunner   1945

From my mother's sleep I fell into the State,
And I hunched in its belly till my wet fur froze.
Six miles from earth, loosed from its dream of life,
I woke to black flak and the nightmare fighters.
When I died they washed me out of the turret with a hose.   5

THE DEATH OF THE BALL TURRET GUNNER. Jarrell has written: "A ball turret was a plexiglass sphere
set into the belly of a B-17 or B-24, and inhabited by two .50 caliber machine-guns and one man, a
short small man. When this gunner tracked with his machine-guns a fighter attacking his bomber
from below, he revolved with the turret; hunched upside-down in his little sphere, he looked like the
fetus in the womb. The fighters which attacked him were armed with cannon firing explosive shells.
The hose was a steam hose."

Compare

"The Death of the Ball Turret Gunner" with "Dulce et Decorum Est" by Wilfred Owen
(Chapter 16).

Robinson Jeffers (1887–1962)

Fire on the Hills   1932

Robinson Jeffers

The deer were bounding like blown leaves
Under the smoke in front the roaring wave of the
    brushfire;
I thought of the smaller lives that were caught.
Beauty is not always lovely; the fire was beautiful, the terror
Of the deer was beautiful; and when I returned   5
Down the back slopes after the fire had gone by, an eagle
Was perched on the jag of a burnt pine,
Insolent and gorged, cloaked in the folded storms of his shoulders.
He had come from far off for the good hunting
With fire for his beater to drive the game; the sky was merciless   10
Blue, and the hills merciless black,
The sombre-feathered great bird sleepily merciless between them.
I thought, painfully, but the whole mind,
The destruction that brings an eagle from heaven is better than mercy.

Compare

"Fire on the Hills" with "Wild Geese" by Mary Oliver (Chapter 26).

Ha Jin (b. 1956)

Missed Time   (2000)

My notebook has remained blank for months
thanks to the light you shower
around me. I have no use
for my pen, which lies
languorously without grief.   5

Nothing is better than to live
a storyless life that needs
no writing for meaning—
when I am gone, let others say
they lost a happy man,   10
though no one can tell how happy I was.

Compare

"Missed Time" with "somewhere i have never travelled,gladly beyond" by E. E. Cummings (in this chapter).

Ben Jonson (1573?–1637)

On My First Son   (1603)

Farewell, thou child of my right hand, and joy.
My sin was too much hope of thee, loved boy;
Seven years thou wert lent to me, and I thee pay,
Exacted by thy fate, on the just day.
Oh, could I lose all father° now. For why   *fatherhood*   5
Will man lament the state he should envy´—
To have so soon 'scaped world's and flesh's rage,
And, if no other misery, yet age?
Rest in soft peace, and asked, say, "Here doth lie
Ben Jonson his best piece of poetry,"   10
For whose sake henceforth all his vows be such
As what he loves may never like° too much.   *thrive*

ON MY FIRST SON. 1 *child of my right hand:* Jonson's son was named Benjamin; this phrase translates
the Hebrew name. 4 *the just day:* the very day. The boy had died on his seventh birthday. 10 *poetry:*
Jonson uses the word *poetry* here reflecting its Greek root *poiesis*, which means *creation.*

Compare

"On My First Son" with "'Out, Out—'" by Robert Frost (Chapter 15).

Donald Justice (1925–2004)

On the Death of Friends in Childhood   1960

We shall not ever meet them bearded in heaven,
Nor sunning themselves among the bald of hell;
If anywhere, in the deserted schoolyard at twilight,
Forming a ring, perhaps, or joining hands
In games whose very names we have forgotten.   5
Come, memory, let us seek them there in the shadows.

Compare

"On the Death of Friends in Childhood" with "To an Athlete Dying Young" by A. E. Housman
(in this chapter).

John Keats

John Keats (1795–1821)

Ode on a Grecian Urn   1820

I

Thou still unravished bride of quietness,
   Thou foster-child of silence and slow time,
Sylvan historian, who canst thus express
   A flowery tale more sweetly than our rhyme:
What leaf-fringed legend haunts about thy shape   5
   Of deities or mortals, or of both,
      In Tempe or the dales of Arcady?
   What men or gods are these? What maidens loth?
What mad pursuit? What struggle to escape?
      What pipes and timbrels? What wild ecstasy?   10

II

Heard melodies are sweet, but those unheard
   Are sweeter; therefore, ye soft pipes, play on;
Not to the sensual° ear, but, more endeared,   *physical*
   Pipe to the spirit ditties of no tone:
Fair youth, beneath the trees, thou canst not leave   15
   Thy song, nor ever can those trees be bare;
      Bold Lover, never, never canst thou kiss,
Though winning near the goal—yet, do not grieve;
      She cannot fade, though thou hast not thy bliss,
   For ever wilt thou love, and she be fair!   20

III

Ah, happy, happy boughs! that cannot shed
   Your leaves, nor ever bid the Spring adieu;
And, happy melodist, unwearièd,
   For ever piping songs for ever new;
More happy love! more happy, happy love!   25
   For ever warm and still to be enjoyed,
      For ever panting, and for ever young;
All breathing human passion far above,
   That leaves a heart high-sorrowful and cloyed,
      A burning forehead, and a parching tongue.   30

IV

Who are these coming to the sacrifice?
   To what green altar, O mysterious priest,
Lead'st thou that heifer lowing at the skies,
   And all her silken flanks with garlands drest?
What little town by river or sea shore,   35
   Or mountain-built with peaceful citadel,

Is emptied of this folk, this pious morn?
And, little town, thy streets for evermore
    Will silent be; and not a soul to tell
        Why thou art desolate, can e'er return.   40

V

O Attic shape! Fair attitude! with brede°   *design*
    Of marble men and maidens overwrought,
With forest branches and the trodden weed;
    Thou, silent form, dost tease us out of thought
As doth eternity: Cold Pastoral!   45
    When old age shall this generation waste,
        Thou shalt remain, in midst of other woe
    Than ours, a friend to man, to whom thou say'st,
Beauty is truth, truth beauty,—that is all
        Ye know on earth, and all ye need to know.   50

ODE ON A GRECIAN URN. 7 *Tempe, dales of Arcady:* valleys in Greece. 41 *Attic:* Athenian, possessing
a classical simplicity and grace. 49–50: If Keats had put the urn's words in quotation marks, critics
might have been spared much ink. Does the urn say just "beauty is truth, truth beauty," or does its
statement take in the whole of the last two lines?

Compare

"Ode on a Grecian Urn" with "Musée des Beaux Arts" by W. H. Auden (in this chapter).

John Keats (1795–1821)

When I have fears that I may cease to be   (1818)

When I have fears that I may cease to be
    Before my pen has gleaned my teeming brain,
Before high-pilèd books, in charact'ry,°   *written language*
    Hold like rich garners° the full-ripened grain;   *storehouses*
When I behold, upon the night's starred face,   5
    Huge cloudy symbols of a high romance,
And think that I may never live to trace
    Their shadows with the magic hand of chance;
And when I feel, fair creature of an hour,
    That I shall never look upon thee more,   10
Never have relish in the fairy° power   *supernatural*
    Of unreflecting love;—then on the shore
Of the wide world I stand alone, and think
Till love and fame to nothingness do sink.

WHEN I HAVE FEARS THAT I MAY CEASE TO BE. 12 *unreflecting:* thoughtless and spontaneous, rather
than deliberate.

Compare

"When I have fears that I may cease to be" with Philip Larkin's "Aubade" (Chapter 28).

Ted Kooser (b. 1939)

Abandoned Farmhouse   1969

He was a big man, says the size of his shoes
on a pile of broken dishes by the house;
a tall man too, says the length of the bed
in an upstairs room; and a good, God-fearing man,
says the Bible with a broken back   5
on the floor below the window, dusty with sun;
but not a man for farming, say the fields
cluttered with boulders and the leaky barn.

A woman lived with him, says the bedroom wall
papered with lilacs and the kitchen shelves   10
covered with oilcloth, and they had a child,
says the sandbox made from a tractor tire.
Money was scarce, say the jars of plum preserves
and canned tomatoes sealed in the cellar hole.
And the winters cold, say the rags in the window frames.   15
It was lonely here, says the narrow country road.

Something went wrong, says the empty house
in the weed-choked yard. Stones in the fields
say he was not a farmer; the still-sealed jars
in the cellar say she left in a nervous haste.   20
And the child? Its toys are strewn in the yard
like branches after a storm—a rubber cow,
a rusty tractor with a broken plow,
a doll in overalls. Something went wrong, they say.

Compare

"Abandoned Farmhouse" with "Home is so Sad" by Philip Larkin (below).

Philip Larkin (1922–1985)

Home is so Sad   1964

Home is so sad. It stays as it was left,
Shaped to the comfort of the last to go
As if to win them back. Instead, bereft
Of anyone to please, it withers so,
Having no heart to put aside the theft   5

Philip Larkin

And turn again to what it started as,
A joyous shot at how things ought to be,
Long fallen wide. You can see how it was:
Look at the pictures and the cutlery.
The music in the piano stool. That vase.   10

Compare

"Home is so Sad" with "Piano" by D. H. Lawrence (in this chapter).

Philip Larkin (1922–1985)

Poetry of Departures   1955

Sometimes you hear, fifth-hand,
As epitaph:
He chucked up everything
And just cleared off,
And always the voice will sound   5
Certain you approve
This audacious, purifying,
Elemental move.

And they are right, I think.
We all hate home   10
And having to be there:
I detest my room,
Its specially-chosen junk,
The good books, the good bed,
And my life, in perfect order: 15
So to hear it said

He walked out on the whole crowd
Leaves me flushed and stirred,
Like *Then she undid her dress*
Or *Take that you bastard;*   20
Surely I can, if he did?
And that helps me stay
Sober and industrious.
But I'd go today,

Yes, swagger the nut-strewn roads,   25
Crouch in the fo'c'sle
Stubbly with goodness, if
It weren't so artificial,
Such a deliberate step backwards
To create an object: 30
Books; china; a life
Reprehensibly perfect.

POETRY OF DEPARTURES. 26 *fo'c'sle*: nautical term, short for *forecastle*, the front upper deck of a sailing ship.

Compare

"Poetry of Departures" with "Miniver Cheevy" by Edwin Arlington Robinson (in this chapter).

D. H. Lawrence   (1885–1930)

Piano   1918

Softly, in the dusk, a woman is singing to me;
Taking me back down the vista of years, till I see
A child sitting under the piano, in the boom of the tingling strings
And pressing the small, poised feet of a mother who smiles as she sings.

In spite of myself, the insidious mastery of song   5
Betrays me back, till the heart of me weeps to belong
To the old Sunday evenings at home, with winter outside
And hymns in the cozy parlor, the tinkling piano our guide.

So now it is vain for the singer to burst into clamor
With the great black piano appassionato. The glamour   10
Of childish days is upon me, my manhood is cast
Down in the flood of remembrance, I weep like a child for the past.

Compare

"Piano" with "Fern Hill" by Dylan Thomas (in this chapter).

Li-Young Lee

Li-Young Lee   (b. 1957)

Night Mirror   2001

Li-Young, don't feel lonely
when you look up
into great night and find
yourself the far face peering
hugely out from between
a star and a star. All that space   5
the nighthawk plunges through,
homing, all that distance beyond embrace,
what is it but your own infinity.

And don't be afraid   10
when, eyes closed, you look inside you
and find night is both
the silence tolling after stars
and the final word
that founds all beginning, find night,   15

abyss and shuttle,
a finished cloth
frayed by the years, then gathered
in the songs and games
mothers teach their children.   20

Look again
and find yourself changed
and changing, now the bewildered honey
fallen into your own hands,
now the immaculate fruit born of hunger.   25
Now the unequaled perfume of your dying.
And time? Time is the salty wake
of your stunned entrance upon
no name.

Compare

"Night Mirror" with "Drinking Alone by Moonlight" by Li Po (this chapter) and "Quinceañera"
by Judith Ortiz Cofer (Chapter 28).

Denise Levertov (1923–1997)

O Taste and See   1964

The world is
not with us enough.
O taste and see

the subway Bible poster said,
meaning **The Lord**, meaning   5
if anything all that lives
to the imagination's tongue,

grief, mercy, language,
tangerine, weather, to
breathe them, bite,   10
savor, chew, swallow, transform

into our flesh our
deaths, crossing the street, plum, quince,
living in the orchard and being

hungry, and plucking   15
the fruit.

Compare

"O Taste and See" with "Bread" by Samuel Menashe (Chapter 17).

Li Po (701–762)

Drinking Alone by Moonlight

(about 750) 1919

A cup of wine, under the flowering trees;
I drink alone, for no friend is near.
Raising my cup I beckon the bright moon,
For he, with my shadow, will make three men.
The moon, alas, is no drinker of wine;   5
Listless, my shadow creeps about at my side.
Yet with the moon as friend and the shadow as slave
I must make merry before the Spring is spent.
To the songs I sing the moon flickers her beams;
In the dance I weave my shadow tangles and breaks.   10
While we were sober, three shared the fun;
Now we are drunk, each goes his way.
May we long share our odd, inanimate feast,
And meet at last on the Cloudy River of the sky.

—Translated by Arthur Waley

DRINKING ALONE BY MOONLIGHT. 14 *the Cloudy River of the sky:* the Milky Way.

Compare

"Drinking Alone by Moonlight" with "I Wandered Lonely as a Cloud" by William Wordsworth
(Chapter 16).

Shirley Geok-lin Lim (b. 1944)

Learning to love America

1998

because it has no pure products

because the Pacific Ocean sweeps along the coastline
because the water of the ocean is cold
and because land is better than ocean

Shirley Geok-lin Lim

because I say we rather than they   5

because I live in California
I have eaten fresh artichokes
and jacarandas bloom in April and May

because my senses have caught up with my body
my breath with the air it swallows   10
my hunger with my mouth

because I walk barefoot in my house

because I have nursed my son at my breast
because he is a strong American boy
because I have seen his eyes redden when he is asked who he is   15
because he answers I don't know

because to have a son is to have a country
because my son will bury me here
because countries are in our blood and we bleed them

because it is late and too late to change my mind   20
because it is time.

LEARNING TO LOVE AMERICA. 1 *pure products*: an allusion to poem XVIII of *Spring and All* (1923) by
William Carlos Williams, which begins: "The pure products of America / go crazy—."

Compare
"Learning to love America" with "I Hear America Singing" by Walt Whitman (Chapter 25).

Robert Lowell (1917–1977)

Skunk Hour   1959

> For Elizabeth Bishop

Nautilus Island's hermit
heiress still lives through winter in her Spartan cottage;
her sheep still graze above the sea.
Her son's a bishop. Her farmer
is first selectman in our village;   5
she's in her dotage.

Thirsting for
the hierarchic privacy
of Queen Victoria's century,
she buys up all   10
the eyesores facing her shore,
and lets them fall.

The season's ill—
we've lost our summer millionaire,
who seemed to leap from an L. L. Bean   15
catalogue. His nine-knot yawl
was auctioned off to lobstermen.
A red fox stain covers Blue Hill.

And now our fairy
decorator brightens his shop for fall;   20
his fishnet's filled with orange cork,
orange, his cobbler's bench and awl;
there is no money in his work,
he'd rather marry.

One dark night,   25
my Tudor Ford climbed the hill's skull;
I watched for love-cars. Lights turned down,
they lay together, hull to hull,
where the graveyard shelves on the town. . . .
My mind's not right.   30

A car radio bleats,
"Love, O careless Love. . . ." I hear
my ill-spirit sob in each blood cell,
as if my hand were at its throat. . . .
I myself am hell;   35
nobody's here—

only skunks, that search
in the moonlight for a bite to eat.
They march on their soles up Main Street:
white stripes, moonstruck eyes' red fire   40
under the chalk-dry and spar spire
of the Trinitarian Church.

I stand on top
of our back steps and breathe the rich air—
a mother skunk with her column of kittens swills the garbage pail.   45
She jabs her wedge-head in a cup
of sour cream, drops her ostrich tail,
and will not scare.

Compare
"Skunk Hour" with "Desert Places" by Robert Frost (Chapter 32).

Andrew Marvell (1621–1678)

To His Coy Mistress   1681

Had we but world enough, and time,	
This coyness,° Lady, were no crime.	*modesty, reluctance*
We would sit down, and think which way	
To walk, and pass our long love's day.	
Thou by the Indian Ganges' side	5
Should'st rubies find; I by the tide	
Of Humber would complain.° I would	*sing sad songs*
Love you ten years before the Flood,	
And you should, if you please, refuse	
Till the Conversion of the Jews.	10
My vegetable° love should grow	*vegetative, flourishing*
Vaster than empires, and more slow.	
An hundred years should go to praise	
Thine eyes, and on thy forehead gaze,	
Two hundred to adore each breast,	15
But thirty thousand to the rest.	

An age at least to every part,
And the last age should show your heart.
For, Lady, you deserve this state,°   *pomp, ceremony*
Nor would I love at lower rate.   20
    But at my back I always hear
Time's wingèd chariot hurrying near,
And yonder all before us lie
Deserts of vast eternity.
Thy beauty shall no more be found,   25
Nor, in thy marble vault, shall sound
My echoing song; then worms shall try
That long preserved virginity,
And your quaint honor turn to dust,
And into ashes all my lust.   30
The grave's a fine and private place,
But none, I think, do there embrace.
    Now therefore, while the youthful hue
Sits on thy skin like morning glew°   *glow*
And while thy willing soul transpires   35
At every pore with instant° fires,   *eager*
Now let us sport us while we may;
And now, like amorous birds of prey,
Rather at once our time devour,
Than languish in his slow-chapped° power.   *slow-jawed*   40
Let us roll all our strength, and all
Our sweetness, up into one ball
And tear our pleasures with rough strife,
Thorough° the iron gates of life.   *through*
Thus, though we cannot make our sun   45
Stand still, yet we will make him run.

To His Coy Mistress. 7 *Humber:* a river that flows by Marvell's town of Hull (on the side of the
world opposite from the Ganges). 10 *conversion of the Jews:* an event that, according to St. John the
Divine, is to take place just before the end of the world. 35 *transpires:* exudes, as a membrane lets
fluid or vapor pass through it.

Compare

"To His Coy Mistress" with "To the Virgins, to Make Much of Time" by Robert Herrick (in
this chapter).

David Mason (b. 1954)

Song of the Powers   1996

Mine, said the stone,
mine is the hour.
I crush the scissors,
such is my power.
Stronger than wishes,   5
my power, alone.

Mine, said the paper,
mine are the words
that smother the stone
with imagined birds,
reams of them, flown   10
from the mind of the shaper.

Mine, said the scissors,
mine all the knives
gashing through paper's
ethereal lives;   15
nothing's so proper
as tattering wishes.

As stone crushes scissors,
as paper snuffs stone
and scissors cut paper,   20
all end alone.
So heap up your paper
and scissor your wishes
and uproot the stone
from the top of the hill.   25
They all end alone
as you will, you will.

SONG OF THE POWERS. The three key images of this poem are drawn from the children's game of
Scissors, Paper, Stone (also called Rock, Paper, Scissors). In this game each object has a specific
power: Scissors cuts paper, paper covers stone, and stone crushes scissors.

Compare

"Song of the Powers" with "Résumé" by Dorothy Parker (Chapter 23).

Claude McKay (1889–1948)

If We Must Die   1922

If we must die, let it not be like hogs
Hunted and penned in an inglorious spot,
While round us bark the mad and hungry dogs,
Making their mock at our accursèd lot.
If we must die, O let us nobly die,   5
So that our precious blood may not be shed
In vain; then even the monsters we defy
Shall be constrained to honor us though dead!
O kinsmen! we must meet the common foe!
Though far outnumbered let us show us brave,   10

Claude McKay

And for their thousand blows deal one death-blow!
What though before us lies the open grave?
Like men we'll face the murderous, cowardly pack,
Pressed to the wall, dying, but fighting back!

Compare

"If We Must Die" with "Anthem for Doomed Youth" by Wilfred Owen (Chapter 24).

Edna St. Vincent Millay (1892–1950)

Recuerdo   1920

We were very tired, we were very merry—
We had gone back and forth all night on the ferry.
It was bare and bright, and smelled like a stable—
But we looked into a fire, we leaned across a table,
We lay on a hill-top underneath the moon;   5
And the whistles kept blowing, and the dawn came soon.

Edna St. Vincent Millay

We were very tired, we were very merry—
We had gone back and forth all night on the ferry;
And you ate an apple, and I ate a pear,
From a dozen of each we had bought somewhere;   10
And the sky went wan, and the wind came cold,
And the sun rose dripping, a bucketful of gold.

We were very tired, we were very merry,
We had gone back and forth all night on the ferry.
We hailed, "Good morrow, mother!" to a shawl-covered head,   15
And bought a morning paper, which neither of us read;
And she wept, "God bless you!" for the apples and pears,
And we gave her all our money but our subway fares.

RECUERDO. The Spanish title means "a recollection" or "a memory."

Compare

"Recuerdo" with "To the Virgins, to Make Much of Time" by Robert Herrick (in this chapter).

John Milton (1608–1674)

When I consider how my light is spent   (1655?)

When I consider how my light is spent,
  Ere half my days in this dark world and wide,
    And that one talent which is death to hide
    Lodged with me useless, though my soul more bent
To serve therewith my Maker, and present   5
  My true account, lest He returning chide;
  "Doth God exact day-labor, light denied?"
  I fondly° ask. But Patience, to prevent   *foolishly*

That murmur, soon replies, "God doth not need
   Either man's work or his own gifts. Who best   10
   Bear his mild yoke, they serve him best. His state
Is kingly: thousands at his bidding speed,
   And post o'er land and ocean without rest;
   They also serve who only stand and wait."

WHEN I CONSIDER HOW MY LIGHT IS SPENT. 1 *my light is spent*: Milton had become blind. 3 *that one talent*: For Jesus' parable of the talents (measures of money), see Matthew 25:14–30.

Compare

"When I consider how my light is spent" with "On His Blindness" by Jorge Luis Borges (Chapter 29).

Marianne Moore (1887–1972)

Poetry   1921

I too, dislike it: there are things that are important beyond all this fiddle.
   Reading it, however, with a perfect contempt for it, one discovers
                that there is in
it after all, a place for the genuine.
   Hands that can grasp, eyes
      that can dilate, hair that can rise   5
         if it must, these things are important not because a

high sounding interpretation can be put upon them but because they are
   useful; when they become so derivative as to become
                unintelligible, the
same thing may be said for all of us—that we
   do not admire what   10
      we cannot understand. The bat,
        holding on upside down or in quest of something to

eat, elephants pushing, a wild horse taking a roll, a tireless wolf under
   a tree, the immovable critic twinkling his skin like a horse that
                feels a flea, the base-
ball fan, the statistician—case after case   15
      could be cited did
      one wish it; nor is it valid
        to discriminate against "business documents and

school-books"; all these phenomena are important. One must make a
                distinction
however: when dragged into prominence by half poets, the result   20
        is not poetry,
   nor till the autocrats among us can be
      "literalists of
      the imagination"—above
        insolence and triviality and can present

for inspection, imaginary gardens with real toads in them, shall we have   25
  it. In the meantime, if you demand on one hand, in defiance of
        their opinion—
  the raw material of poetry in
    all its rawness and
    that which is, on the other hand,
       genuine then you are interested in poetry.   30

Compare

Compare "Poetry" with "A little Learning is a dang'rous Thing" by Alexander Pope (in this chapter).

Harryette Mullen (b. 1953)

Dim Lady   2002

My honeybunch's peepers are nothing like neon. Today's special at
Red Lobster is redder than her kisser. If Liquid Paper is white, her racks
are institutional beige. If her mop were Slinkys, dishwater Slinkys would
grow on her noggin. I have seen tablecloths in Shakey's Pizza Parlors, red
and white, but no such picnic colors do I see in her mug. And in some   5
minty-fresh mouthwashes there is more sweetness than in the garlic breeze
my main squeeze wheezes. I love to hear her rap, yet I'm aware that Muzak
has a hipper beat. I don't know any Marilyn Monroes. My ball and chain is
plain from head to toe. And yet, by gosh, my scrumptious Twinkie has as
much sex appeal for me as any lanky model or platinum movie idol who's   10
hyped beyond belief.

Compare

"Dim Lady" with "My mistress' eyes are nothing like the sun" by William Shakespeare (in this chapter).

Marilyn Nelson

Marilyn Nelson (b. 1946)

A Strange Beautiful Woman   1985

A strange beautiful woman
met me in the mirror
the other night.
Hey,
I said,   5
What you doing here?
She asked me
the same thing.

Compare

Compare "A Strange Beautiful Woman" with "Embrace" by Billy Collins (Chapter 19).

Lorine Niedecker (1903–1970)

Sorrow Moves in Wide Waves   (about 1950)

Sorrow moves in wide waves,
    it passes, lets us be.
It uses us, we use it,
    it's blind while we see.

Consciousness is illimitable,   5
    too good to forsake
tho what we feel be misery
    and we know will break.

          *

Old Mother turns blue and from us,
    "Don't let my head drop to the earth.   10
I'm blind and deaf." Death from the heart,
    a thimble in her purse.

"It's a long day since last night.
    Give me space. I need
floors. Wash the floors, Lorine!   15
    Wash clothes! Weed!"

Compare

Compare "Sorrow Moves in Wide Waves" with "One Art" by Elizabeth Bishop (Chapter 30).

Yone Noguchi (1875–1947)

Japanese Hokku   1920

1

Suppose the stars
Fall and break?—do they ever sound
Like my own love song?

12

Leaves blown,
Birds flown away.

I wander in and out the Hall of Autumn.

16

Are the fallen stars
Returning up the sky?—
The dews on the grass.

Yone Noguchi

48

It is too late to hear a nightingale?
Tut, tut, tut, . . . some bird sings,—
That's quite enough, my friend.

61

Like a cobweb hung upon the tree,
A prey to wind and sunlight!
Who will say that we are safe and strong?

Compare

"Japanese Hokku" to the haiku in Chapter 19.

Sylvia Plath (1932–1963)

Sylvia Plath

Daddy   (1962) 1965

You do not do, you do not do
Any more, black shoe
In which I have lived like a foot
For thirty years, poor and white,
Barely daring to breathe or Achoo.   5

Daddy, I have had to kill you.
You died before I had time—
Marble-heavy, a bag full of God,
Ghastly statue with one grey toe
Big as a Frisco seal   10

And a head in the freakish Atlantic
Where it pours bean green over blue
In the waters off beautiful Nauset.
I used to pray to recover you.
Ach, du.   15

In the German tongue, in the Polish town
Scraped flat by the roller
Of wars, wars, wars.
But the name of the town is common.
My Polack friend   20

Says there are a dozen or two.
So I never could tell where you
Put your foot, your root,
I never could talk to you.
The tongue stuck in my jaw.   25

It stuck in a barb wire snare.
Ich, ich, ich, ich,
I could hardly speak.
I thought every German was you.
And the language obscene   30

An engine, an engine
Chuffing me off like a Jew.
A Jew to Dachau, Auschwitz, Belsen.
I began to talk like a Jew.
I think I may well be a Jew.   35

The snows of the Tyrol, the clear beer of Vienna
Are not very pure or true.
With my gypsy ancestress and my weird luck
And my Taroc pack and my Taroc pack
I may be a bit of a Jew.   40

I have always been scared of *you*,
With your Luftwaffe, your gobbledygoo.
And your neat moustache
And your Aryan eye, bright blue.
Panzer-man, panzer-man, O You—   45

Not God but a swastika
So black no sky could squeak through.
Every woman adores a Fascist,
The boot in the face, the brute
Brute heart of a brute like you.   50

You stand at the blackboard, daddy,
In the picture I have of you,
A cleft in your chin instead of your foot
But no less a devil for that, no not
Any less the black man who   55

Bit my pretty red heart in two.
I was ten when they buried you.
At twenty I tried to die
And get back, back, back to you.
I thought even the bones would do.   60

But they pulled me out of the sack,
And they stuck me together with glue.
And then I knew what to do.
I made a model of you,
A man in black with a Meinkampf look   65

And a love of the rack and the screw.
And I said I do, I do.
So daddy, I'm finally through.
The black telephone's off at the root,
The voices just can't worm through.   70

If I've killed one man, I've killed two—
The vampire who said he was you
And drank my blood for a year,
Seven years, if you want to know.
Daddy, you can lie back now.   75

There's a stake in your fat black heart
And the villagers never liked you.
They are dancing and stamping on you.
They always *knew* it was you.
Daddy, daddy, you bastard, I'm through.   80

DADDY. 15 *Ach, du*: Oh, you. 27 *Ich, ich, ich, ich*: I, I, I, I. 51 *blackboard*: Otto Plath had been a professor of biology at Boston University. 65 *Meinkampf*: Adolf Hitler titled his autobiography *Mein Kampf*
("My Struggle").

Introducing this poem in a reading, Sylvia Plath remarked:

> The poem is spoken by a girl with an Electra complex. Her father died while she thought he
> was God. Her case is complicated by the fact that her father was also a Nazi and her mother
> very possibly part Jewish. In the daughter the two strains marry and paralyze each other—she
> has to act out the awful little allegory before she is free of it. (Quoted by A. Alvarez, *Beyond All
> This Fiddle* [New York: Random, 1968].)

In some details "Daddy" is autobiography: the poet's father, Otto Plath, a German, had come to the
United States from Grabow, Poland. He died following the amputation of a gangrened foot and leg
when Sylvia was eight years old. Politically, Otto Plath was a Republican, not a Nazi, but was apparently a somewhat domineering head of the household. (See the recollections of the poet's mother,
Aurelia Schober Plath, in her edition of *Letters Home* by Sylvia Plath [New York: Harper, 1975].)

Compare
"Daddy" with "My Papa's Waltz" by Theodore Roethke (Chapter 16).

Alexander Pope (1688–1744)

A little Learning is a dang'rous Thing (from *An Essay on Criticism*)   1711

A *little Learning* is a dang'rous Thing;
Drink deep, or taste not the *Pierian* Spring:
There *shallow Draughts* intoxicate the Brain,
And drinking *largely* sobers us again.
Fir'd at first Sight with what the *Muse* imparts,   5
In *fearless Youth* we tempt the Heights of Arts,
While from the bounded *Level* of our Mind,
Short Views we take, nor see the *Lengths behind*,
But *more advanc'd*, behold with strange Surprize
New, distant Scenes of *endless* Science rise!   10
So pleas'd at first, the towring *Alps* we try,
Mount o'er the Vales, and seem to tread the Sky;
Th' Eternal Snows appear already past,
And the first *Clouds* and *Mountains* seem the last:
But *those attain'd*, we tremble to survey   15
The growing Labours of the lengthen'd Way,

Th' *increasing* Prospect *tires* our wandring Eyes,
Hills peep o'er Hills, and *Alps* on *Alps* arise!

A LITTLE LEARNING IS A DANG'ROUS THING. 2 *Pierian Spring*: the spring of the Muses.

Compare

"A little Learning is a dang'rous Thing" with "Speech to the Young. Speech to the Progress-Toward." by Gwendolyn Brooks (Chapter 16).

Ezra Pound (1885–1972)

The River–Merchant's Wife: A Letter   1915

While my hair was still cut straight across my forehead
I played about the front gate, pulling flowers.
You came by on bamboo stilts, playing horse,
You walked about my seat, playing with blue plums.
And we went on living in the village of Chokan: 5
Two small people, without dislike or suspicion.

At fourteen I married My Lord you.
I never laughed, being bashful.
Lowering my head, I looked at the wall.
Called to, a thousand times, I never looked back.   10

At fifteen I stopped scowling,
I desired my dust to be mingled with yours
Forever and forever and forever.
Why should I climb the look out?

At sixteen you departed,   15
You went into far Ku-to-yen, by the river of swirling eddies,
And you have been gone five months.
The monkeys make sorrowful noise overhead.

You dragged your feet when you went out.
By the gate now, the moss is grown, the different mosses,   20
Too deep to clear them away!
The leaves fall early this autumn, in wind.
The paired butterflies are already yellow with August
Over the grass in the West garden;
They hurt me. I grow older.   25
If you are coming down through the narrows of the river Kiang,
Please let me know beforehand,
And I will come out to meet you
                    As far as Cho-fu-sa.

THE RIVER-MERCHANT'S WIFE: A LETTER. A free translation from the Chinese poet Li Po (eighth century).

Compare

"The River-Merchant's Wife: A Letter" with "A Valediction: Forbidding Mourning" by John Donne (in this chapter).

Henry Reed (1914–1986)

Naming of Parts   1946

Today we have naming of parts. Yesterday,
We had daily cleaning. And tomorrow morning,
We shall have what to do after firing. But today,
Today we have naming of parts. Japonica
Glistens like coral in all of the neighboring gardens,   5
        And today we have naming of parts.

This is the lower sling swivel. And this
Is the upper sling swivel, whose use you will see,
When you are given your slings. And this is the piling swivel,
Which in your case you have not got. The branches   10
Hold in the gardens their silent, eloquent gestures,
        Which in our case we have not got.

This is the safety-catch, which is always released
With an easy flick of the thumb. And please do not let me
See anyone using his finger. You can do it quite easy   15
If you have any strength in your thumb. The blossoms
Are fragile and motionless, never letting anyone see
        Any of them using their finger.

And this you can see is the bolt. The purpose of this
Is to open the breech, as you see. We can slide it   20
Rapidly backwards and forwards: we call this
Easing the spring. And rapidly backwards and forwards
The early bees are assaulting and fumbling the flowers:
        They call it easing the Spring.

They call it easing the Spring: it is perfectly easy   25
If you have any strength in your thumb: like the bolt,
And the breech, and the cocking-piece, and the point of balance,
Which in our case we have not got; and the almond-blossom
Silent in all of the gardens and the bees going backwards and forwards,
        For today we have naming of parts.   30

Compare
"Naming of Parts" with "The Fury of Aerial Bombardment" by Richard Eberhart (Chapter 17).

Adrienne Rich

Adrienne Rich (1929–2012)

Living in Sin   1955

She had thought the studio would keep itself;
no dust upon the furniture of love.
Half heresy, to wish the taps less vocal,
the panes relieved of grime. A plate of pears,
a piano with a Persian shawl, a cat   5
stalking the picturesque amusing mouse
had risen at his urging.
Not that at five each separate stair would writhe
under the milkman's tramp; that morning light
so coldly would delineate the scraps   10
of last night's cheese and three sepulchral bottles;
that on the kitchen shelf among the saucers
a pair of beetle-eyes would fix her own—
envoy from some village in the moldings . . .
Meanwhile, he, with a yawn,   15
sounded a dozen notes upon the keyboard,
declared it out of tune, shrugged at the mirror,
rubbed at his beard, went out for cigarettes;
while she, jeered by the minor demons,
pulled back the sheets and made the bed and found   20
a towel to dust the table-top,
and let the coffee-pot boil over on the stove.
By evening she was back in love again,
though not so wholly but throughout the night
she woke sometimes to feel the daylight coming   25
like a relentless milkman up the stairs.

Compare

"Living in Sin" with "Let me not to the marriage of true minds" by William Shakespeare
(Chapter 24).

Edwin Arlington Robinson (1869–1935)

Miniver Cheevy   1910

Miniver Cheevy, child of scorn,
    Grew lean while he assailed the seasons;
He wept that he was ever born,
    And he had reasons.

Miniver loved the days of old   5
    When swords were bright and steeds were prancing;
The vision of a warrior bold
    Would set him dancing.

Miniver sighed for what was not,
    And dreamed, and rested from his labors;   10
He dreamed of Thebes and Camelot,
    And Priam's neighbors.

Miniver mourned the ripe renown
    That made so many a name so fragrant;
He mourned Romance, now on the town,   15
    And Art, a vagrant.

Miniver loved the Medici,
    Albeit he had never seen one;
He would have sinned incessantly
    Could he have been one.   20

Miniver cursed the commonplace
    And eyed a khaki suit with loathing;
He missed the medieval grace
    Of iron clothing.

Miniver scorned the gold he sought,   25
    But sore annoyed was he without it;
Miniver thought, and thought, and thought,
    And thought about it.

Miniver Cheevy, born too late,
    Scratched his head and kept on thinking;   30
Miniver coughed, and called it fate,
    And kept on drinking.

MINIVER CHEEVY. 11 *Thebes:* a city in ancient Greece and the setting of many famous Greek myths; *Camelot:* the legendary site of King Arthur's Court. 12 *Priam:* the last king of Troy; his "neighbors" would have included Helen of Troy, Aeneas, and other famous figures. 17 *the Medici:* the ruling family of Florence during the high Renaissance, the Medici were renowned patrons of the arts.

Compare

"Miniver Cheevy" with "Ulysses" by Alfred, Lord Tennyson (Chapter 27).

Christina Rossetti (1830–1894)

Song   (1848) 1862

When I am dead, my dearest,
   Sing no sad songs for me;
Plant thou no roses at my head,
   Nor shady cypress tree:
Be the green grass above me   5
   With showers and dewdrops wet;
And if thou wilt, remember,
   And if thou wilt, forget.
I shall not see the shadows,
   I shall not feel the rain;   10
I shall not hear the nightingale
   Sing on, as if in pain:
And dreaming through the twilight
   That doth not rise nor set,
Haply I may remember,   15
   And haply may forget.

Compare

"Song" with "When I have fears that I may cease to be" by John Keats (in this chapter).

Kay Ryan (b. 1945)

That Will to Divest   2000

Action creates
a taste
for itself.
Meaning: once
you've swept   5
the shelves
of spoons
and plates
you kept
for guests,   10
it gets harder
not to also
simplify the larder,
not to dismiss
rooms, not to   15
divest yourself
of all the chairs
but one, not
to test what
singleness can bear,   20
once you've begun.

Compare

"That Will to Divest" with "Drinking Alone by Moonlight" by Li Po (in this chapter).

William Shakespeare (1564–1616)

When, in disgrace with
Fortune and men's eyes (Sonnet 29)   1609

When, in disgrace with Fortune and men's eyes,
I all alone beweep my outcast state,
And trouble deaf heaven with my bootless° cries,   *futile*
And look upon myself and curse my fate,
Wishing me like to one more rich in hope,   5
Featured like him, like him with friends possessed,
Desiring this man's art, and that man's scope,
With what I most enjoy contented least,
Yet in these thoughts myself almost despising,
Haply° I think on thee, and then my state,   *luckily*   10
Like to the lark at break of day arising
From sullen earth, sings hymns at heaven's gate;
  For thy sweet love rememb'red such wealth brings
  That then I scorn to change my state with kings.

Compare

"When, in disgrace with Fortune and men's eyes" with "When I have fears that I may cease to be" by John Keats (in this chapter).

William Shakespeare (1564–1616)

When to the sessions of sweet silent thought (Sonnet 30)   1609

When to the sessions of sweet silent thought
I summon up remembrance of things past,
I sigh the lack of many a thing I sought,
And with old woes new wail my dear time's waste:
Then can I drown an eye, unused to flow,   5
For precious friends hid in death's dateless night,
And weep afresh love's long since cancelled woe,
And moan the expense of many a vanished sight;
Then can I grieve at grievances foregone,
And heavily from woe to woe tell o'er   10
The sad account of fore-bemoanèd moan,
Which I new pay as if not paid before.
  But if the while I think on thee, dear friend,
  All losses are restored, and sorrows end.

Compare

"When to the sessions of sweet silent thought" with "Dostoevsky" by Charles Bukowski (in this chapter).

William Shakespeare (1564–1616)

My mistress' eyes are nothing like the sun (Sonnet 130)   1609

My mistress' eyes are nothing like the sun;
Coral is far more red than her lips' red;
If snow be white, why then her breasts are dun;
If hairs be wires, black wires grow on her head.
I have seen roses damasked, red and white,   5
But no such roses see I in her cheeks;
And in some perfumes is there more delight
Than in the breath that from my mistress reeks.
I love to hear her speak, yet well I know
That music hath a far more pleasing sound;   10
I grant I never saw a goddess go:
My mistress, when she walks, treads on the ground.
   And yet, by heaven, I think my love as rare
   As any she° belied with false compare.   *woman*

Compare

"My mistress' eyes are nothing like the sun" with "Shall I Compare Thee to a Summer's Day?"
by Howard Moss (Chapter 20).

Charles Simic (b. 1938)

Butcher Shop   1967

Sometimes walking late at night
I stop before a closed butcher shop.
There is a single light in the store
Like the light in which the convict digs his tunnel.

An apron hangs on the hook: 5
The blood on it smeared into a map
Of the great continents of blood,
The great rivers and oceans of blood.

There are knives that glitter like altars
In a dark church   10
Where they bring the cripple and the imbecile
To be healed.

There is a wooden block where bones are broken,
Scraped clean—a river dried to its bed
Where I am fed,   15
Where deep in the night I hear a voice.

Charles Simic

Compare

"Butcher Shop" with "Fire on the Hills" by Robinson Jeffers (in this chapter).

Christopher Smart (1722–1771)

For I will consider my Cat Jeoffry   (1759–1763)

For I will consider my Cat Jeoffry.
For he is the servant of the Living God, duly and daily serving him.
For at the first glance of the glory of God in the East he worships in his way.
For is this done by wreathing his body seven times round with elegant
    quickness.
For then he leaps up to catch the musk,° which is the blessing of God   *catnip* 5
    upon his prayer.
For he rolls upon prank to work it in.
For having done duty and received blessing he begins to consider himself.
For this he performs in ten degrees.
For first he looks upon his fore-paws to see if they are clean.
For secondly he kicks up behind to clear away there.   10
For thirdly he works it upon stretch° with the fore-paws   *he works his muscles, stretching*
    extended.
For fourthly he sharpens his paws by wood.
For fifthly he washes himself.
For sixthly he rolls upon wash.
For seventhly he fleas himself, that he may not be interrupted   15
    upon the beat.°   *his patrol*
For eighthly he rubs himself against a post.
For ninthly he looks up for his instructions.
For tenthly he goes in quest of food.
For having considered God and himself he will consider his neighbor.
For if he meets another cat he will kiss her in kindness.   20
For when he takes his prey he plays with it to give it a chance.
For one mouse in seven escapes by his dallying.
For when his day's work is done his business more properly begins.
For he keeps the Lord's watch in the night against the Adversary.
For he counteracts the powers of darkness by his electrical skin   25
    and glaring eyes.
For he counteracts the Devil, who is death, by brisking about the life.
For in his morning orisons° he loves the sun and the sun loves him.   *prayers*
For he is of the tribe of Tiger.
For the Cherub Cat is a term of the Angel Tiger.
For he has the subtlety and hissing of a serpent, which in goodness he   30
    suppresses.
For he will not do destruction if he is well-fed, neither will he spit without
    provocation.
For he purrs in thankfulness when God tells him he's a good Cat.
For he is an instrument for the children to learn benevolence upon.
For every house is incomplete without him, and a blessing is lacking in the
    spirit.
For the Lord commanded Moses concerning the cats at the departure of the   35
    Children of Israel from Egypt.
For every family had one cat at least in the bag.

For the English cats are the best in Europe.

For he is the cleanest in the use of his fore-paws of any quadruped.

For the dexterity of his defense is an instance of the love of God to him
    exceedingly.

For he is the quickest to his mark of any creature.   40

For he is tenacious of his point.

For he is a mixture of gravity and waggery.

For he knows that God is his Savior.

For there is nothing sweeter than his peace when at rest.

For there is nothing brisker than his life when in motion.   45

For he is of the Lord's poor, and so indeed is he called by benevolence
    perpetually—Poor Jeoffry! poor Jeoffry! the rat has bit thy throat.

For I bless the name of the Lord Jesus that Jeoffry is better.

For the divine spirit comes about his body to sustain it in complete cat.

For his tongue is exceeding pure so that it has in purity what it wants in
    music.

For he is docile and can learn certain things.   50

For he can sit up with gravity which is patience upon approbation.

For he can fetch and carry, which is patience in employment.

For he can jump over a stick which is patience upon proof positive.

For he can spraggle upon waggle at the word of command.

For he can jump from an eminence into his master's bosom.   55

For he can catch the cork and toss it again.

For he is hated by the hypocrite and miser.

For the former is afraid of detection.

For the latter refuses the charge.

For he camels his back to bear the first notion of business.   60

For he is good to think on, if a man would express himself neatly.

For he made a great figure in Egypt for his signal services.

For he killed the Icneumon-rat, very pernicious by land.

For his ears are so acute that they sting again.

For from this proceeds the passing quickness of his attention.   65

For by stroking of him I have found out electricity.

For I perceived God's light about him both wax and fire.

For the electrical fire is the spiritual substance which God sends from
    heaven to sustain the bodies both of man and beast.

For God has blessed him in the variety of his movements.

For, though he cannot fly, he is an excellent clamberer.   70

For his motions upon the face of the earth are more than any other quadruped.

For he can tread to all the measures upon the music.

For he can swim for life.

For he can creep.

For I will consider my Cat Jeoffry. This is a self-contained extract from Smart's long poem *Jubilate Agno* (Rejoice in the Lamb). 35 *For the Lord commanded Moses concerning the cats:* No such command is mentioned in Scripture. 54 *spraggle upon waggle:* W. F. Stead, in his edition of Smart's poem, suggests that this means Jeoffry will sprawl when his master waggles a finger or a stick. 59 *the charge:* perhaps the cost of feeding a cat.

Compare

"For I will consider my Cat Jeoffry" with "The Tyger" by William Blake (Chapter 26).

Cathy Song (b. 1955)

Cathy Song

Stamp Collecting   1988

The poorest countries
have the prettiest stamps
as if impracticality were a major export
shipped with the bananas, T-shirts, and coconuts.
Take Tonga, where the tourists,   5
expecting a dramatic waterfall replete with birdcalls,
are taken to see the island's peculiar mystery:
hanging bats with collapsible wings
like black umbrellas swing upside down from fruit trees.
The Tongan stamp is a fruit.   10
The banana stamp is scalloped like a butter-varnished seashell.
The pineapple resembles a volcano, a spout of green on top,
and the papaya, a tarnished goat skull.

They look impressive,
these stamps of countries without a thing to sell   15
except for what is scraped, uprooted and hulled
from their mule-scratched hills.
They believe in postcards,
in portraits of progress: the new dam;
a team of young native doctors   20
wearing stethoscopes like exotic ornaments;
the recently constructed "Facultad de Medicina,"
a building as lack-lustre as an American motel.

The stamps of others are predictable.
Lucky is the country that possesses indigenous beauty.   25
Say a tiger or a queen.
The Japanese can display to the world
their blossoms: a spray of pink on green.
Like pollen, they drift, airborne.
But pity the country that is bleak and stark.   30

Beauty and whimsy are discouraged as indiscreet.
Unbreakable as their climate, a monument of ice,
they issue serious statements, commemorating
factories, tramways and aeroplanes;

athletes marbled into statues.   35
They turn their noses upon the world, these countries,
and offer this: an unrelenting procession
of a grim, historic profile.

Compare

"Stamp Collecting" with "Autumn Begins in Martins Ferry, Ohio" by James Wright (Chapter 28).

Wallace Stevens (1879–1955)

Wallace Stevens

The Emperor of Ice-Cream   1923

Call the roller of big cigars,
The muscular one, and bid him whip
In kitchen cups concupiscent curds.
Let the wenches dawdle in such dress
As they are used to wear, and let the boys   5
Bring flowers in last month's newspapers.
Let be be finale of seem.
The only emperor is the emperor of ice-cream.

Take from the dresser of deal,
Lacking the three glass knobs, that sheet   10
On which she embroidered fantails once
And spread it so as to cover her face.
If her horny feet protrude, they come
To show how cold she is, and dumb.
Let the lamp affix its beam.   15
The only emperor is the emperor of ice-cream.

THE EMPEROR OF ICE-CREAM. 9 *deal:* fir or pine wood used to make cheap furniture.

Compare

"The Emperor of Ice-Cream" with "A Slumber Did My Spirit Seal" by William Wordsworth
(Chapter 22).

Jonathan Swift (1667–1745)

A Description of the Morning   1711

Now hardly here and there a hackney-coach,°   *horse-drawn cab*
Appearing, showed the ruddy morn's approach.
Now Betty from her master's bed had flown
And softly stole to discompose her own.
The slipshod 'prentice from his master's door   5
Had pared the dirt, and sprinkled round the floor.
Now Moll had whirled her mop with dextrous airs,
Prepared to scrub the entry and the stairs.
The youth with broomy stumps began to trace
The kennel°-edge, where wheels had worn the place.   *gutter* 10
The smallcoal man was heard with cadence deep
Till drowned in shriller notes of chimney-sweep.
Duns° at his lordship's gate began to meet,   *bill-collectors*
And Brickdust Moll had screamed through half a street.
The turnkey° now his flock returning sees,   *jailkeeper* 15

Duly let out a-nights to steal for fees;
The watchful bailiffs° take their silent stands;   constables
And schoolboys lag with satchels in their hands.

A Description of the Morning. *9 youth with broomy stumps:* a young man sweeping the gutter's
edge with worn-out brooms, looking for old nails fallen from wagonwheels, which were valuable. 14
Brickdust Moll: woman selling brickdust to be used for scouring.

Compare

"A Description of the Morning" with "London" by William Blake (Chapter 18).

Dylan Thomas (1914–1953)

Fern Hill   1946

Now as I was young and easy under the apple boughs
About the lilting house and happy as the grass was
    green,
        The night above the dingle° starry,   *wooded valley*   **Dylan Thomas**
           Time let me hail and climb
        Golden in the heydays of his eyes,   5
And honored among wagons I was prince of the apple towns
And once below a time I lordly had the trees and leaves
           Trail with daisies and barley
        Down the rivers of the windfall light.

And as I was green and carefree, famous among the barns   10
About the happy yard and singing as the farm was home,
        In the sun that is young once only,
           Time let me play and be
        Golden in the mercy of his means,
And green and golden I was huntsman and herdsman, the calves   15
Sang to my horn, the foxes on the hills barked clear and cold,
           And the sabbath rang slowly
        In the pebbles of the holy streams.

All the sun long it was running, it was lovely, the hay
Fields high as the house, the tunes from the chimneys, it was air 20
        And playing, lovely and watery
          And fire green as grass.
        And nightly under the simple stars
As I rode to sleep the owls were bearing the farm away,
All the moon long I heard, blessed among stables, the nightjars   25
           Flying with the ricks, and the horses
              Flashing into the dark.

And then to awake, and the farm, like a wanderer white
With the dew, come back, the cock on his shoulder: it was all
        Shining, it was Adam and maiden,   30
            The sky gathered again
        And the sun grew round that very day.
So it must have been after the birth of the simple light
In the first, spinning place, the spellbound horses walking warm
        Out of the whinnying green stable   35
            On to the fields of praise.

And honored among foxes and pheasants by the gay house
Under the new made clouds and happy as the heart was long,
        In the sun born over and over,
            I ran my heedless ways,   40
            My wishes raced through the house high hay
And nothing I cared, at my sky blue trades, that time allows
In all his tuneful turning so few and such morning songs
        Before the children green and golden
            Follow him out of grace,   45

Nothing I cared, in the lamb white days, that time would take me
Up to the swallow thronged loft by the shadow of my hand,
        In the moon that is always rising,
            Nor that riding to sleep
I should hear him fly with the high fields   50
And wake to the farm forever fled from the childless land.
Oh as I was young and easy in the mercy of his means,
            Time held me green and dying
        Though I sang in my chains like the sea.

Compare

"Fern Hill" with "in Just-" by E. E. Cummings (Chapter 25) and "The world is too much with
us" by William Wordsworth (Chapter 27).

Amy Uyematsu (b. 1947)

Deliberate   1992

Amy Uyematsu

So by sixteen we move in packs
learn to strut and slide
in deliberate lowdown rhythm
talk in a syn/co/pa/ted beat
because we want so bad   5
to be cool, never to be mistaken
for white, even when we leave
these rowdier L.A. streets—

remember how we paint our eyes
like gangsters 10
flash our legs in nylons
sassy black high heels
or two inch zippered boots
stack them by the door at night
next to Daddy's muddy gardening shoes. 15

Compare
"Deliberate" with "Fern Hill" by Dylan Thomas (in this chapter).

Derek Walcott (1930–2017)

Sea Grapes 1976

That sail which leans on light,
tired of islands,
a schooner beating up the Caribbean

for home, could be Odysseus,
home-bound on the Aegean; 5
that father and husband's

longing, under gnarled sour grapes, is
like the adulterer hearing Nausicaa's name
in every gull's outcry.

This brings nobody peace. The ancient war 10
between obsession and responsibility
will never finish and has been the same

for the sea-wanderer or the one on shore
now wriggling on his sandals to walk home,
since Troy sighed its last flame, 15

and the blind giant's boulder heaved the trough
from whose groundswell the great hexameters come
to the conclusions of exhausted surf.

The classics can console. But not enough.

SEA GRAPES. 4 *Odysseus:* Legendary king of Ithaca, the hero of Homer's *Odyssey.* 5 *Aegean:* Odysseus sailed over the Aegean Sea to return home after the Trojan War. 8 *Nausicaa:* beautiful young daughter of King Alcinous of Phaeacia, with whom Odysseus took refuge during his voyage home. 16 *blind giant:* allusion to the one-eyed cyclops whom Odysseus outwitted and blinded in order to avoid being eaten. 17 *hexameters:* dactylic hexameter is the meter in which Homer's *Odyssey* (as well as most classical epics) is written.

Compare
"Sea Grapes" with "Ulysses" by Alfred, Lord Tennyson (Chapter 27).

Edmund Waller (1606–1687)

Go, Lovely Rose   1645

Go, lovely rose,
Tell her that wastes her time and me
   That now she knows,
When I resemble° her to thee,   *compare*
How sweet and fair she seems to be.   5

   Tell her that's young
And shuns to have her graces spied,
   That hadst thou sprung
In deserts where no men abide,
Thou must have uncommended died.   10

   Small is the worth
Of beauty from the light retired:
   Bid her come forth,
Suffer herself to be desired,
And not blush so to be admired.   15

   Then die, that she
The common fate of all things rare
   May read in thee:
How small a part of time they share
That are so wondrous sweet and fair.   20

Compare

"Go, Lovely Rose" with "To the Virgins, to Make Much of Time" by Robert Herrick and "To His Coy Mistress" by Andrew Marvell (both in this chapter).

Walt Whitman (1819–1892)

When I Heard the Learn'd Astronomer   1867, 1881

When I heard the learn'd astronomer,
When the proofs, the figures, were ranged in columns before me,
When I was shown the charts and diagrams, to add, divide, and measure
   them,
When I sitting heard the astronomer where he lectured with much applause
   in the lecture-room,
How soon unaccountable I became tired and sick,   5
Till rising and gliding out I wander'd off by myself,
In the mystical moist night-air, and from time to time,
Look'd up in perfect silence at the stars.

Compare

"When I Heard the Learn'd Astronomer" with "The Soul selects her own Society" by Emily Dickinson (Chapter 32).

Walt Whitman

Walt Whitman (1819–1892)

from **Song of the Open Road**   1856, 1881

Allons! the road is before us!
It is safe—I have tried it—my own feet have tried it
well—be not detain'd!

Let the paper remain on the desk unwritten, and the
    book on the shelf unopen'd!
Let the tools remain in the workshop! let the money remain unearn'd!
Let the school stand! mind not the cry of the teacher!   5
Let the preacher preach in his pulpit! let the lawyer plead in the court, and
the judge expound the law.

Camerado, I give you my hand!
I give you my love more precious than money,
I give you myself before preaching or law;
Will you give me yourself? will you come travel with me?   10
Shall we stick by each other as long as we live?

SONG OF THE OPEN ROAD. This is part 15 of Whitman's long poem. 1 *Allons!*: French for "Come on!"
or "Let's go!"

Compare

"Song of the Open Road" with "Luke Havergal" by Edwin Arlington Robinson (Chapter 16).

Walt Whitman (1819–1892)

To a Stranger   1856, 1881

Passing stranger! you do not know how longingly I look upon you,
You must be he I was seeking, or she I was seeking, (it comes to me as of a
    dream,)
I have somewhere surely lived a life of joy with you,
All is recall'd as we flit by each other, fluid, affectionate, chaste, matured,
You grew up with me, were a boy with me or a girl with me,   5
I ate with you and slept with you, your body has become not yours only nor
    left my body mine only,
You give me the pleasure of your eyes, face, flesh, as we pass, you take of my
    beard, breast, hands, in return,
I am not to speak to you, I am to think of you when I sit alone or wake at
    night alone,
I am to wait, I do not doubt I am to meet you again,
I am to see to it that I do not lose you.   10

Compare

"To a Stranger" with "A Supermarket in California" by Allen Ginsberg (this chapter).

William Carlos Williams (1883–1963)

William Carlos Williams

The Widow's Lament in Springtime   1921

Sorrow is my own yard
where the new grass
flames as it has flamed
often before but not
with the cold fire   5
that closes round me this year.

Thirtyfive years
I lived with my husband.
The plumtree is white today
with masses of flowers.   10

Masses of flowers
load the cherry branches
and color some bushes
yellow and some red
but the grief in my heart   15

is stronger than they
for though they were my joy
formerly, today I notice them
and turn away forgetting.
Today my son told me   20

that in the meadows,
at the edge of the heavy woods
in the distance, he saw
trees of white flowers.
I feel that I would like   25

to go there
and fall into those flowers
and sink into the marsh near them.

Compare

"The Widow's Lament in Springtime" with "The River-Merchant's Wife: A Letter" by Ezra
Pound (this chapter).

William Carlos Williams (1883–1963)

Queen-Anne's-Lace   1921

Her body is not so white as
anemone petals nor so smooth—nor
so remote a thing. It is a field
of the wild carrot taking
the field by force; the grass   5
does not raise above it.
Here is no question of whiteness,
white as can be, with a purple mole
at the center of each flower.
Each flower is a hand's span   10
of her whiteness. Wherever
his hand has lain there is
a tiny purple blemish. Each part
is a blossom under his touch
to which the fibers of her being   15
stem one by one, each to its end,
until the whole field is a
white desire, empty, a single stem,
a cluster, flower by flower,
a pious wish to whiteness gone over—   20
or nothing.

Compare

"Queen-Anne's-Lace" with "Go, Lovely Rose" by Edmund Waller (in this chapter).

William Wordsworth (1770–1850)

Composed upon Westminster Bridge   1807

Earth has not anything to show more fair:
Dull would he be of soul who could pass by
A sight so touching in its majesty:
This City now doth, like a garment, wear
The beauty of the morning; silent, bare,   5
Ships, towers, domes, theaters, and temples lie
Open unto the fields, and to the sky;
All bright and glittering in the smokeless air.
Never did sun more beautifully steep
In his first splendor, valley, rock, or hill;   10
Ne'er saw I, never felt, a calm so deep!
The river glideth at his own sweet will:
Dear God! the very houses seem asleep;
And all that mighty heart is lying still!

Compare

"Composed upon Westminster Bridge" with "London" by William Blake (Chapter 18).

Mary Sidney Wroth (1587–1653?)

In this strange labyrinth   1621

In this strange labyrinth how shall I turn?
Ways are on all sides while the way I miss:
If to the right hand, there in love I burn;
Let me go forward, therein danger is;
If to the left, suspicion hinders bliss,   5
Let me turn back, shame cries I ought return
Nor faint though crosses with my fortunes kiss.
Stand still is harder, although sure to mourn;
Thus let me take the right, or left hand way;
Go forward, or stand still, or back retire;   10
I must these doubts endure without allay
Or help, but travail find for my best hire;
Yet that which most my troubled sense doth move
Is to leave all, and take the thread of love.

IN THIS STRANGE LABYRINTH. This sonnet comes from Wroth's *Urania* (1621), the first significant
sonnet sequence by a woman. Wroth was the niece of Sir Philip Sidney and of the Countess of
Pembroke as well as a distant relation of Sir Walter Ralegh. The *Labyrinth* of the title was the maze
built by Minos to trap the young men and women sacrificed to the Minotaur. King Minos's daughter
Ariadne saved her beloved Theseus by giving him a skein of thread to guide his way through the
Labyrinth. (See the final line of the sonnet.)

Compare

"In this strange labyrinth" with Shakespeare's "Let me not to the marriage of true minds"
(Chapter 24).

Sir Thomas Wyatt (1503?–1542)

They flee from me that sometime did me sekë   (about 1535)

They flee from me that sometime did me sekë
　　With naked fotë° stalking in my chamber.   *foot*
I have seen them gentle, tame and mekë
　　That now are wild, and do not remember
　　That sometime they put themself in danger   5
To take bread at my hand; and now they range
Busily seeking with a continual change.

Thankèd be fortune, it hath been otherwise
　　Twenty times better; but once in speciàll,
In thin array, after a pleasant guise,   10
　　When her loose gown from her shoulders did fall,
　　And she me caught in her armës long and small,
Therëwith all sweetly did me kiss,
And softly said, *Dear heart, how like you this?*

It was no dremë: I lay broadë waking.   15
　　But all is turned thorough° my gentleness   *through*
Into a strangë fashion of forsaking;

And I have leave to go of her goodness,
And she also to use newfangleness.°   *to seek novelty*
But since that I so kindëly am served   20
I would fain knowë what she hath deserved.

THEY FLEE FROM ME THAT SOMETIME DID ME SEKË. Some latter-day critics have called Sir Thomas
Wyatt a careless poet because some of his lines appear faltering and metrically inconsistent; others
have thought he knew what he was doing. It is uncertain whether the final *e*'s in English spelling
were still pronounced in Wyatt's day as they were in Chaucer's, but if they were, perhaps Wyatt has
been unjustly blamed. In this text, spellings have been modernized except in words where the final
e would make a difference in rhythm. To sense how it matters, try reading the poem aloud leaving
out the *e*'s and then putting them in wherever indicated. Sound them like the *a* in *sofa*. 20 *kindëly*:
according to my kind (or hers), that is, as befits the nature of man (or woman). Perhaps there is also
irony here, and the word means "unkindly."

Compare

"They flee from me that sometime did me sekë" with "When, in disgrace with Fortune and
men's eyes" by William Shakespeare (in this chapter).

William Butler Yeats (1865–1939)

When You Are Old   1893

William Butler Yeats

When you are old and grey and full of sleep,
And nodding by the fire, take down this book,
And slowly read, and dream of the soft look
Your eyes had once, and of their shadows deep;

How many loved your moments of glad grace,   5
And loved your beauty with love false or true,
But one man loved the pilgrim soul in you,
And loved the sorrows of your changing face;

And bending down beside the glowing bars,
Murmur, a little sadly, how Love fled   10
And paced upon the mountains overhead
And hid his face amid a crowd of stars.

Compare

"When You Are Old" with "Shall I compare thee to a summer's day?" by William Shakespeare
(Chapter 20).

William Butler Yeats (1865–1939)

He wishes for the Cloths of Heaven   1899

Had I the heavens' embroidered cloths,
Enwrought with golden and silver light,
The blue and the dim and the dark cloths
Of night and light and the half light,
I would spread the cloths under your feet: 5
But I, being poor, have only my dreams;
I have spread my dreams under your feet;
Tread softly because you tread on my dreams.

Compare

"He wishes for the Cloths of Heaven" with "When You Are Old" by William Butler Yeats
(above).

William Butler Yeats (1865–1939)

The Magi   1914

Now as at all times I can see in the mind's eye,
In their stiff, painted clothes, the pale unsatisfied ones
Appear and disappear in the blue depth of the sky
With all their ancient faces like rain-beaten stones,
And all their helms of silver hovering side by side,   5
And all their eyes still fixed, hoping to find once more,
Being by Calvary's turbulence unsatisfied,
The uncontrollable mystery on the bestial floor.

Compare

"The Magi" with "Journey of the Magi" by T. S. Eliot (in this chapter).

Playwright David Ives.

DRAMA

TALKING WITH *David Ives*

"Comedy is just tragedy without the sentimentality."
Dana Gioia Interviews David Ives

Q: When did you first become interested in theater?

DAVID IVES: I played The Wolf opposite drop-dead-sexy Amy Skeehan in our third-grade production of "Little Red Riding Hood" at St. Mary Magdalene School in South Chicago. Basically it was all over after that. The show was so successful Amy and I took it on tour to the fourth and fifth grades. By then I had learned the Great Lesson of Theater, which is: *theater is a great way to hang out with girls.* It may be why Shakespeare became both an actor and a playwright: *more girls.*

Q: When did you discover that you could make people laugh?

DAVID IVES: There's some debate about this. An aunt of mine, a few years ago, said to me, "You're just like you were as a boy. Such a happy, funny child." I reported this to my mother, who said without a pause: "I wouldn't say that." She didn't seem to want to explain. One of my old high-school classmates recently mentioned that I was funny in high school. I only remember reading Russian novels about suicide in high school. Maybe I was funny between novels, but they were pretty thick.

Q: Tell us about your first play.

DAVID IVES: I wrote my first play when I was nine. It was about gangsters and had lots of gunfire and a girl I based on Amy Skeehan. I wrote my second play in high school. It was about Russian-like people talking about suicide a lot. My third play was at college and was The Worst Play Ever Written. From there, I had nowhere to go but up. My next play got produced, and suddenly I was a real live playwright. I've been faking it ever since.

Q: When you see one of your plays onstage, how different is it from what you imagined while writing it?

DAVID IVES: It's always better than I imagined it, unless it's worse.

Q: You are the master of the short comic play. What drew you to this unconventional form?

DAVID IVES: Probably a shorter and shorter attention span, like everybody else. Also, my wife Martha is on the short side and I am very drawn to her, so it is only a short (so to speak) way to short plays. I'm fond in general of the concise, the compact, the jeweled, the specific, and perfect as opposed to the verbose, the bloated, the baggy, and general. A good rock-and-roll song can be three or four minutes long and when it's over, if it's been made right and played right, you feel like you've gotten into a barfight, had a love affair, and ridden a convertible down Pacific Coast One on the most beautiful day of the year, all in three minutes. Imagine what you can do with a ten- or fifteen-minute play. You can make an audience feel like they've done all those things, plus they've gotten married, had kids, died, and went to heaven. There they are, breathless just inside the pearly gates with their heads still spinning, and only ten minutes have passed. As far as I'm concerned, all plays, short or long,

should aspire to the conditions of rock-and-roll, whose purpose is to make us aware of our mortality and the fact that we had better get with it before the song ends. Not a bad rule of thumb for art as a whole.

Q: Who are your favorite comic writers and comedians?

DAVID IVES: Nothing depresses me like comedians. Maybe it's because people who try to make me laugh instantly put me in a really bad mood. I once shot a man in Tucson and spent 38 years in the penitentiary because he tried to tell me a joke that started "A priest, a minister, and a rabbi walk into a bar. . . ." As for funny playwrights, Joe Orton and Noel Coward and Chris Durang do it for me because they're not just trying to be funny. They have a vision of life that happens to be comic. They've also got *style*, which is the outward and visible sign of having a vision of life.

Q: Why do people need comedy?

DAVID IVES: Comedy is important for three reasons. First, it's funny. Second, it makes us laugh. Third, it's easier to get a girl to go see a comedy than, let's say, *Hamlet*. Fourth, it shows us what frigging idiots we can be under the right circumstances. As Wendell Berry once said, "It is not from ourselves that we will learn to be better." Watching idiots cavort around onstage is one possible way to do that. First, of course, you have to be interested in being better.

Q: Comedy seems to get less critical respect than tragedy. Does that seem fair to you?

DAVID IVES: Nothing seems fair to me. That's why I write comedy. If you've ever met a critic you'll understand why they give more respect to sadder plays: because critics are the saddest dogs you'll ever meet. The fact is, comedy is much harder to do—to write, to act—than drama, the same way it's harder to look at life and say, *Okay*, than it is to mope around thinking about Russian roulette all the time. But let's get one thing clear: Comedy is not jokes. It certainly isn't sitcoms, which to me are about as funny as a sack of dead kittens. I'm talking about real comedy—human comedy, which is to say comedy that thinks and feels. I'm talking about *Twelfth Night*, or *The Marriage of Bette and Boo*, or *The Importance of Being Earnest*, where there's truth and sadness mixed in with the joy, just as there is in life. Theater *is* life, and it fails when it settles for merely being funny, the same way life is not enough when it settles for just being funny. In the end, comedy is just tragedy without the sentimentality. Dostoyevsky, anyone?

Drama is life with the dull bits left out.

—ALFRED HITCHCOCK

U nlike a short story or a novel, a **play** is a work of storytelling in which actors represent the characters. A play also differs from a work of fiction in another essential way: it is addressed not to readers but to spectators.

To be part of an audience in a theater is an experience far different from reading a story in solitude. As the house lights dim and the curtain rises, we become members of a community. The responses of people around us affect our own responses. We, too, contribute to the community's response whenever we laugh, sigh, applaud, murmur in surprise, or catch our breath in excitement. In contrast, when we watch a movie by ourselves in our living room—say, a slapstick comedy—we probably laugh less often than if we were watching the same film in a theater, surrounded by a roaring crowd. On the other hand, no one is spilling popcorn down the backs of our necks. Each kind of theatrical experience, to be sure, has its advantages.

A theater of live actors has another advantage: a sensitive give-and-take between actors and audience. (Such rapport, of course, depends on the skill of the actors and the perceptiveness of the audience.) Although professional actors may try to give a first-rate performance on all occasions, it is natural for them to feel more keenly inspired by a lively, appreciative audience than by a lethargic one. As veteran playgoers well know, something unique and wonderful can happen when good actors and a good audience respond to each other.

In another sense, a play is more than actors and audience. Like a short story or a poem, a play is a work of art made of words. Watching a play, of course, we don't notice the playwright standing between us and the characters. If the play is absorbing, it flows before our eyes. In a silent reading, the usual play consists mainly of **dialogue**, exchanges of speech, punctuated by stage directions. In performance, though, stage directions vanish. And although the thoughtful efforts of perhaps a hundred people—actors, director, producer, stage designer, costumer, makeup artist, technicians—may have gone into a production, a successful play makes us forget its artifice. We may even forget that the play is literature, for its gestures, facial expressions, bodily stances, lighting, and special effects are as much a part of it as the playwright's written words. Even though words are not all there is to a living play, they are its bones. And the whole play, the finished production, is the total of whatever takes place on stage.

There is an aspect of theater related to both religious ritual and civic festival—a mixture of church service and rock concert. These are occasions when people gather for the special communal experiences of being reawakened emotionally and spiritually and celebrating their complex identities. Twice in the history of Europe, drama has sprung forth as a part of worship. In ancient Greece, plays were performed on feast days of Dionysus; in the Christian Middle Ages, a play was introduced as an adjunct to the Easter mass with the enactment of the meeting between the three Marys and the angel at Jesus's empty tomb. Evidently, something in drama remains constant over the years—something as old, perhaps, as the deepest desires and highest aspirations of humanity.

35 READING A PLAY

*I regard the theatre as the greatest of all art forms,
the most immediate way in which a human being can share
with another the sense of what it is to be a human being.*

—OSCAR WILDE

What You Will Learn in This Chapter

- To define the play as a literary form
- To identify and describe theatrical conventions
- To recognize and describe the elements of a play
- To analyze a play

Most plays are written not to be read in books but to be performed. Finding plays in a literature anthology, the student may well ask: Isn't there something wrong with the idea of reading plays on the printed page? Isn't that a perversion of their nature?

True, plays are meant to be seen on stage, but equally true, reading a play may afford advantages. One is that it is better to know some masterpieces by reading them than never to know them at all. Even if you live in a large city with many theaters, even if you attend a college with many theatrical productions, to succeed in your lifetime in witnessing, say, all the plays of Shakespeare might well be impossible. In print, they are as near to hand as a book on a shelf, ready to be enacted (if you like) on the stage of the mind.

INTERPRETING PLAYS

After all, a play is literature before it comes alive in a theater, and it might be argued that when we read an unfamiliar play, we meet it in the same form in which it first appears to its actors and its director. If a play is rich and complex or if it dates from the remote past and contains difficulties of language and allusion, to read it on the page enables us to study it at our leisure and return to the parts that demand greater scrutiny.

But even if a play may be seen in a theater, sometimes to read it in print may be our way of knowing it as the author wrote it in its entirety. Far from regarding Shakespeare's words as holy writ, producers of *Hamlet*, *King Lear*, *Othello*, and other masterpieces often shorten or even leave out whole speeches and scenes. Besides, the nature of the play, as far as you can tell from a stage production, may depend on decisions of the director. In one production Othello may dress as a Renaissance Moor, in another as a modern general. Every actor who plays Iago in *Othello* makes his own interpretation of this knotty character. Some see Iago as a figure of pure evil; others, as a madman; still others, as a suffering human being consumed by hatred, jealousy, and pride. What do you think Shakespeare meant? You can always read the play and decide for yourself.

If every stage production of a play is a fresh interpretation, so, too, is every reader's reading of it. Some readers, when silently reading a play to themselves, try to visualize a stage, imagining the characters in costume and under lights. If such a reader is an actor or a director and is reading the play with an eye toward staging it, then he or she may try to imagine every detail of a possible production, even shades of makeup and the loudness of sound effects. But the nonprofessional reader, who regards the play as literature, need not attempt such exhaustive imagining. Although some readers find it enjoyable to imagine the play taking place on a stage, others prefer to imagine the people and events that the play brings vividly to mind. Sympathetically following the tangled life of Nora in *A Doll's House* by Henrik Ibsen (Chapter 39), we forget that we are reading printed stage directions and instead feel ourselves in the presence of human conflict. Thus regarded, a play becomes a form of storytelling, and the playwright's instructions to the actors and the director become a conventional mode of narrative that we accept much as we accept the methods of a novel or short story.

THEATRICAL CONVENTIONS

Most plays, whether seen in a theater or in print, employ some **conventions**: customary methods of presenting an action, usual and recognizable devices that an audience is willing to accept. In reading a great play from the past, such as *Oedipus the King* (Chapter 37) or *Othello* (Chapter 38), it will help if we know some of the conventions of the classical Greek theater or the Elizabethan theater. When in *Oedipus the King* we encounter a character called the Chorus, it may be useful to be aware that this is a group of citizens who stand to one side of the action, conversing with the principal character and commenting. In *Othello*, when the sinister Iago, left on stage alone, begins to speak (at the end of Act I, Scene iii), we recognize the conventional device of a **soliloquy**, a monologue in which we seem to overhear the character's inmost thoughts uttered aloud. Another such device is the **aside**, in which a character addresses the audience directly, unheard by the other characters on stage, as when the villain in a melodrama chortles, "Heh! Heh! Now she's in my power!" Like conventions in poetry, such familiar methods of staging a narrative afford us a happy shock of recognition. Often, as in these examples, they are ways of making clear to us exactly what the playwright would have us know.

ELEMENTS OF A PLAY

When we read a play on the printed page and find ourselves swept forward by the motion of its story, we need not wonder how—and from what ingredients—the playwright put it together. Still, to analyze the structure of a play is one way to understand and appreciate a playwright's art. Analysis is complicated, however, because in an excellent play the elements (including plot, theme, and characters) do not stand in isolation. Often, deeds clearly follow from the kinds of people the characters are, and from those deeds it is left to the reader to infer the **theme** of the play—the general point or truth about human beings that may be drawn from it. Perhaps the most meaningful way to study the elements of a play (and certainly the most enjoyable) is to consider a play in its entirety.

Here is a short, famous one-act play worth reading for the boldness of its elements—and for its own sake. *Trifles* tells the story of a murder. As you will discover, the "trifles" mentioned in its title are not of trifling stature. In reading the play, you will probably find yourself imagining what you might see on stage if you were in a theater. You may also want to imagine what took place in the lives of the characters before the curtain rose. All this imagining may sound like a tall order, but don't worry. Just read the play for enjoyment the first time through, and then we will consider what makes it effective.

Susan Glaspell

Trifles   1916

Susan Glaspell (1876–1948) grew up in her native Davenport, Iowa, daughter of a grain dealer. After four years at Drake University and a job as a reporter in Des Moines, she settled in New York's Greenwich Village. In 1915, with her husband, George Cram Cook, a theatrical director, she founded the Provincetown Players, the first influential noncommercial theater troupe in America. During the summers of 1915 and 1916, in a makeshift playhouse on a Cape Cod pier, the Players staged the earliest plays of Eugene O'Neill and works by John Reed, Edna St. Vincent Millay, and Glaspell herself. Transplanting the company to New York in the fall of 1916, Glaspell and Cook renamed it the Playwrights' Theater. Glaspell wrote several still-remembered plays, among them a pioneering work of feminist drama, The Verge *(1921), and the Pulitzer Prize-winning* Alison's House *(1930), about the family of a reclusive poet reminiscent of Emily Dickinson who, after her death, squabble over the right to publish her poems. First widely known for her fiction set in Iowa, Glaspell wrote ten novels, including* Fidelity *(1915) and* The Morning Is Near Us *(1939). Shortly after writing the play* Trifles, *she rewrote it as a short story, "A Jury of Her Peers."*

CHARACTERS

George Henderson, county attorney
Henry Peters, sheriff
Lewis Hale, a neighboring farmer
Mrs. Peters
Mrs. Hale

SCENE. *The kitchen in the now abandoned farmhouse of John Wright, a gloomy kitchen, and left without having been put in order—unwashed pans under the sink, a loaf of bread outside the breadbox, a dish towel on the table—other signs of incompleted work. At the rear the outer door opens and the Sheriff comes in followed by the County Attorney and Hale. The Sheriff and Hale are men in middle life, the County Attorney is a young man; all are much bundled up and go at once to the stove. They are followed by two women—the Sheriff's wife first; she is a slight wiry woman, a thin nervous face. Mrs. Hale is larger and would ordinarily be called more comfortable looking, but she is disturbed now and looks fearfully about as she enters. The women have come in slowly, and stand close together near the door.*

County Attorney (*rubbing his hands*): This feels good. Come up to the fire, ladies.
Mrs. Peters (*after taking a step forward*): I'm not—cold.
Sheriff (*unbuttoning his overcoat and stepping away from the stove as if to mark the beginning of official business*): Now, Mr. Hale, before we move things about, you explain to Mr. Henderson just what you saw when you came here yesterday morning.

County Attorney: By the way, has anything been moved? Are things just as you left them yesterday?

Sheriff (looking about): It's just the same. When it dropped below zero last night I thought I'd better send Frank out this morning to make a fire for us—no use getting pneumonia with a big case on, but I told him not to touch anything except the stove—and you know Frank.

County Attorney: Somebody should have been left here yesterday.

Sheriff: Oh—yesterday. When I had to send Frank to Morris Center for that man who went crazy—I want you to know I had my hands full yesterday, I knew you could get back from Omaha by today and as long as I went over everything here myself—

County Attorney: Well, Mr. Hale, tell just what happened when you came here yesterday morning.

Hale: Harry and I had started to town with a load of potatoes. We came along the road from my place and as I got here I said, "I'm going to see if I can't get John Wright to go in with me on a party telephone." I spoke to Wright about it once before and he put me off, saying folks talked too much anyway, and all he asked was peace and quiet—I guess you know about how much he talked himself; but I thought maybe if I went to the house and talked about it before his wife, though I said to Harry that I didn't know as what his wife wanted made much difference to John—

County Attorney: Let's talk about that later, Mr. Hale. I do want to talk about that, but tell now just what happened when you got to the house.

Hale: I didn't hear or see anything; I knocked at the door, and still it was all quiet inside. I knew they must be up, it was past eight o'clock. So I knocked again, and I thought I heard somebody say, "Come in." I wasn't sure, I'm not sure yet, but I opened the door—this door (*indicating the door by which the two women are still standing*) and there in that rocker—(*pointing to it*) sat Mrs. Wright.

(*They all look at the rocker.*)

County Attorney: What—was she doing?

Hale: She was rockin' back and forth. She had her apron in her hand and was kind of—pleating it.

County Attorney: And how did she—look?

Hale: Well, she looked queer.

County Attorney: How do you mean—queer?

Hale: Well, as if she didn't know what she was going to do next. And kind of done up.

County Attorney: How did she seem to feel about your coming?

Hale: Why, I don't think she minded—one way or other. She didn't pay much attention. I said, "How do, Mrs. Wright, it's cold, ain't it?" And she said, "Is it?"—and went on kind of pleating at her apron. Well, I was surprised; she didn't ask me to come up to the stove, or to set down, but just sat there, not even looking at me, so I said, "I want to see John." And then she—laughed. I guess you would call it a laugh. I thought of Harry and the team outside, so I said a little sharp: "Can't I see John?" "No," she says, kind o' dull like. "Ain't he home?" says I. "Yes," says she, "he's home." "Then why can't I see him?" I asked her, out of patience. "'Cause he's dead," says she. "*Dead?*" says I. She just nodded her head, not getting a bit excited, but rockin' back and forth. "Why—where is he?" says I, not knowing what to say. She just pointed upstairs—like that. (*Himself pointing to the room*

Original 1916 production of *Trifles* at the Wharf Theater in Provincetown, Massachusetts.

above.) I got up, with the idea of going up there. I walked from there to here—then I says, "Why, what did he die of?" "He died of a rope round his neck," says she, and just went on pleatin' at her apron. Well, I went out and called Harry. I thought I might—need help. We went upstairs and there he was lyin'—

County Attorney: I think I'd rather have you go into that upstairs, where you can point it all out. Just go on now with the rest of the story.

Hale: Well, my first thought was to get that rope off. It looked . . . (*stops, his face twitches*) . . . but Harry, he went up to him, and he said, "No, he's dead all right, and we'd better not touch anything." So we went back down stairs. She was still sitting that same way. "Has anybody been notified?" I asked. "No," says she, unconcerned. "Who did this, Mrs. Wright?" said Harry. He said it businesslike—and she stopped pleatin' of her apron. "I don't know," she says. "You don't *know*?" says Harry. "No," says she. "Weren't you sleepin' in the bed with him?" says Harry. "Yes," says she, "but I was on the inside." "Somebody slipped a rope round his neck and strangled him and you didn't wake up?" says Harry. "I didn't wake up," she said after him. We must 'a looked as if we didn't see how that could be, for after a minute she said, "I sleep sound." Harry was going to ask her more questions but I said maybe we ought to let her tell her story first to the coroner, or the sheriff, so Harry went fast as he could to Rivers' place, where there's a telephone.

County Attorney: And what did Mrs. Wright do when she knew that you had gone for the coroner?

Hale: She moved from that chair to this one over here (*pointing to a small chair in the corner*) and just sat there with her hands held together and looking down. I got a feeling that I ought to make some conversation, so I said I had come in to see if John wanted to put in a telephone, and at that she started to laugh, and then she stopped and looked at me—scared. (*The County Attorney, who has had his notebook out, makes a note.*) I dunno, maybe it wasn't scared. I wouldn't like to say it was. Soon Harry got back, and then Dr. Lloyd came, and you, Mr. Peters, and so I guess that's all I know that you don't.

County Attorney (looking around): I guess we'll go upstairs first—and then out to the barn and around there. *(To the Sheriff)* You're convinced that there was nothing important here—nothing that would point to any motive.

Sheriff: Nothing here but kitchen things.

(The County Attorney, after again looking around the kitchen, opens the door of a cupboard closet. He gets up on a chair and looks on a shelf. Pulls his hand away, sticky.)

County Attorney: Here's a nice mess.

(The women draw nearer.)

Mrs. Peters (to the other woman): Oh, her fruit; it did freeze. *(To the County Attorney)* She worried about that when it turned so cold. She said the fire'd go out and her jars would break.

Sheriff: Well, can you beat the women! Held for murder and worryin' about her preserves.

County Attorney: I guess before we're through she may have something more serious than preserves to worry about.

Hale: Well, women are used to worrying over trifles.

(The two women move a little closer together.)

County Attorney (with the gallantry of a young politician): And yet, for all their worries, what would we do without the ladies? *(The women do not unbend. He goes to the sink, takes a dipperful of water from the pail and pouring it into a basin, washes his hands. Starts to wipe them on the roller towel, turns it for a cleaner place.)* Dirty towels! *(Kicks his foot against the pans under the sink.)* Not much of a housekeeper, would you say, ladies?

Mrs. Hale (stiffly): There's a great deal of work to be done on a farm.

County Attorney: To be sure. And yet *(with a little bow to her)* I know there are some Dickson County farmhouses which do not have such roller towels.

(He gives it a pull to expose its full length again.)

Mrs. Hale: Those towels get dirty awful quick. Men's hands aren't always as clean as they might be.

County Attorney: Ah, loyal to your sex, I see. But you and Mrs. Wright were neighbors. I suppose you were friends, too.

Mrs. Hale (shaking her head): I've not seen much of her of late years. I've not been in this house—it's more than a year.

County Attorney: And why was that? You didn't like her?

Mrs. Hale: I liked her all well enough. Farmers' wives have their hands full, Mr. Henderson. And then—

County Attorney: Yes—?

Mrs. Hale (looking about): It never seemed a very cheerful place.

County Attorney: No—it's not cheerful. I shouldn't say she had the home-making instinct.

Mrs. Hale: Well, I don't know as Wright had, either.

County Attorney: You mean that they didn't get on very well?

Mrs. Hale: No, I don't mean anything. But I don't think a place'd be any cheerfuller for John Wright's being in it.

County Attorney: I'd like to talk more of that a little later. I want to get the lay of things upstairs now.

(*He goes to the left, where three steps lead to a stair door.*)

Sheriff: I suppose anything Mrs. Peters does'll be all right. She was to take in some clothes for her, you know, and a few little things. We left in such a hurry yesterday.

County Attorney: Yes, but I would like to see what you take, Mrs. Peters, and keep an eye out for anything that might be of use to us.

Mrs. Peters: Yes, Mr. Henderson.

(*The women listen to the men's steps on the stairs, then look about the kitchen.*)

Mrs. Hale: I'd hate to have men coming into my kitchen, snooping around and criticizing.

(*She arranges the pans under sink which the County Attorney had shoved out of place.*)

Mrs. Peters: Of course it's no more than their duty.

Mrs. Hale: Duty's all right, but I guess that deputy sheriff that came out to make the fire might have got a little of this on. (*Gives the roller towel a pull.*) Wish I'd thought of that sooner. Seems mean to talk about her for not having things slicked up when she had to come away in such a hurry.

Mrs. Peters (*who has gone to a small table in the left rear corner of the room, and lifted one end of a towel that covers a pan*): She had bread set.

(*Stands still.*)

Mrs. Hale (*eyes fixed on a loaf of bread beside the breadbox, which is on a low shelf at the other side of the room; moves slowly toward it*): She was going to put this in there. (*Picks up loaf, then abruptly drops it. In a manner of returning to familiar things.*) It's a shame about her fruit. I wonder if it's all gone. (*Gets up on the chair and looks.*) I think there's some here that's all right, Mrs. Peters. Yes—here; (*holding it toward the window*) this is cherries, too. (*Looking again.*) I declare I believe that's the only one. (*Gets down, bottle in her hand. Goes to the sink and wipes it off on the outside.*) She'll feel awful bad after all her hard work in the hot weather. I remember the afternoon I put up my cherries last summer.

(*She puts the bottle on the big kitchen table, center of the room. With a sigh, is about to sit down in the rocking-chair. Before she is seated realizes what chair it is; with a slow look at it, steps back. The chair which she has touched rocks back and forth.*)

Mrs. Peters: Well, I must get those things from the front room closet. (*She goes to the door at the right, but after looking into the other room, steps back.*) You coming with me, Mrs. Hale? You could help me carry them.

(*They go in the other room; reappear, Mrs. Peters carrying a dress and skirt, Mrs. Hale following with a pair of shoes.*)

Mrs. Peters: My, it's cold in there.

(*She puts the clothes on the big table, and hurries to the stove.*)

Mrs. Hale (*examining her skirt*): Wright was close. I think maybe that's why she kept so much to herself. She didn't even belong to the Ladies Aid. I suppose she felt she couldn't do her part, and then you don't enjoy things when you feel shabby. She used to wear pretty clothes and be lively, when she was Minnie Foster, one of the town girls singing in the choir. But that—oh, that was thirty years ago. This all you was to take in?

Mrs. Peters: She said she wanted an apron. Funny thing to want, for there isn't much to get you dirty in jail, goodness knows. But I suppose just to make her feel more natural. She said they was in the top drawer in this cupboard. Yes, here. And then her little shawl that always hung behind the door. (*Opens stair door and looks.*) Yes, here it is.

(*Quickly shuts door leading upstairs.*)

Mrs. Hale (abruptly moving toward her): Mrs. Peters?

Mrs. Peters: Yes, Mrs. Hale?

Mrs. Hale: Do you think she did it?

Mrs. Peters (in a frightened voice): Oh, I don't know.

Mrs. Hale: Well, I don't think she did. Asking for an apron and her little shawl. Worrying about her fruit.

Mrs. Peters (starts to speak, glances up, where footsteps are heard in the room above; in a low voice): Mr. Peters says it looks bad for her. Mr. Henderson is awful sarcastic in a speech and he'll make fun of her sayin' she didn't wake up.

Mrs. Hale: Well, I guess John Wright didn't wake when they was slipping that rope under his neck.

Mrs. Peters: No, it's strange. It must have been done awful crafty and still. They say it was such a—funny way to kill a man, rigging it all up like that.

Mrs. Hale: That's just what Mr. Hale said. There was a gun in the house. He says that's what he can't understand.

Mrs. Peters: Mr. Henderson said coming out that what was needed for the case was a motive; something to show anger, or—sudden feeling.

Mrs. Hale (who is standing by the table): Well, I don't see any signs of anger around here. (*She puts her hand on the dish towel which lies on the table, stands looking down at table, one half of which is clean, the other half messy.*) It's wiped to here. (*Makes a move as if to finish work, then turns and looks at loaf of bread outside the breadbox. Drops towel. In that voice of coming back to familiar things.*) Wonder how they are finding things upstairs. I hope she had it a little more red-up° there. You know, it seems kind of *sneaking*. Locking her up in town and then coming out here and trying to get her own house to turn against her!

Mrs. Peters: But Mrs. Hale, the law is the law.

Mrs. Hale: I s'pose 'tis. (*Unbuttoning her coat.*) Better loosen up your things, Mrs. Peters. You won't feel them when you go out.

(*Mrs. Peters takes off her fur tippet, goes to hang it on hook at back of room, stands looking at the under part of the small corner table.*)

Mrs. Peters: She was piecing a quilt.

(*She brings the large sewing basket and they look at the bright pieces.*)

---

red-up: (slang) readied up, ready to be seen.

Mrs. *Hale:* It's a log cabin pattern. Pretty, isn't it? I wonder if she was goin' to quilt it or just knot it?

(Footsteps have been heard coming down the stairs. The Sheriff enters followed by Hale and the County Attorney.)

Sheriff: They wonder if she was going to quilt it or just knot it!

(The men laugh; the women look abashed.)

County Attorney *(rubbing his hands over the stove):* Frank's fire didn't do much up there, did it? Well, let's go out to the barn and get that cleared up.

(The men go outside.)

Mrs. *Hale (resentfully):* I don't know as there's anything so strange, our takin' up our time with little things while we're waiting for them to get the evidence. *(She sits down at the big table smoothing out a block with decision.)* I don't see as it's anything to laugh about.

Mrs. *Peters (apologetically):* Of course they've got awful important things on their minds.

(Pulls up a chair and joins Mrs. Hale at the table.)

Mrs. *Hale (examining another block):* Mrs. Peters, look at this one. Here, this is the one she was working on, and look at the sewing! All the rest of it has been so nice and even. And look at this! It's all over the place! Why, it looks as if she didn't know what she was about!

(After she has said this they look at each, then start to glance back at the door. After an instant Mrs. Hale has pulled at a knot and ripped the sewing.)

Mrs. *Peters:* Oh, what are you doing, Mrs. Hale?

Mrs. *Hale (mildly):* Just pulling out a stitch or two that's not sewed very good. *(Threading a needle.)* Bad sewing always made me fidgety.

Mrs. *Peters (nervously):* I don't think we ought to touch things.

Mrs. *Hale:* I'll just finish up this end. *(Suddenly stopping and leaning forward.)* Mrs. Peters?

Mrs. *Peters:* Yes, Mrs. Hale?

Mrs. *Hale:* What do you suppose she was so nervous about?

Mrs. *Peters:* Oh—I don't know. I don't know as she was nervous. I sometimes sew awful queer when I'm just tired. *(Mrs. Hale starts to say something, looks at Mrs. Peters, then goes on sewing.)* Well, I must get these things wrapped up. They may be through sooner than we think. *(Putting apron and other things together.)* I wonder where I can find a piece of paper, and string.

Mrs. *Hale:* In that cupboard, maybe.

Mrs. *Peters (looking in cupboard):* Why, here's a birdcage. *(Holds it up.)* Did she have a bird, Mrs. Hale?

Mrs. *Hale:* Why, I don't know whether she did or not—I've not been here for so long. There was a man around last year selling canaries cheap, but I don't know as she took one; maybe she did. She used to sing real pretty herself.

Mrs. *Peters (glancing around):* Seems funny to think of a bird here. But she must have had one, or why would she have a cage? I wonder what happened to it.

Mrs. *Hale:* I s'pose maybe the cat got it.

Mrs. Peters: No, she didn't have a cat. She's got that feeling some people have about cats—being afraid of them. My cat got in her room and she was real upset and asked me to take it out.

Mrs. Hale: My sister Bessie was like that. Queer, ain't it?

Mrs. Peters (examining the cage): Why, look at this door. It's broke. One hinge is pulled apart.

Mrs. Hale (looking too): Looks as if someone must have been rough with it.

Mrs. Peters: Why, yes.

(She brings the cage forward and puts it on the table.)

Mrs. Hale: I wish if they're going to find any evidence they'd be about it. I don't like this place.

Mrs. Peters: But I'm awful glad you came with me, Mrs. Hale. It would be lonesome for me sitting here alone.

Mrs. Hale: It would, wouldn't it? *(Dropping her sewing.)* But I tell you what I do wish, Mrs. Peters. I wish I had come over sometimes when *she* was here. I—*(looking around the room)*—wish I had.

Mrs. Peters: But of course you were awful busy, Mrs. Hale—your house and your children.

Mrs. Hale: I could've come. I stayed away because it weren't cheerful—and that's why I ought to have come. I—I've never liked this place. Maybe because it's down in a hollow and you don't see the road. I dunno what it is but it's a lonesome place and always was. I wish I had come over to see Minnie Foster sometimes. I can see now—

(Shakes her head.)

Mrs. Peters: Well, you mustn't reproach yourself, Mrs. Hale. Somehow we just don't see how it is with other folks until—something comes up.

Mrs. Hale: Not having children makes less work—but it makes a quiet house, and Wright out to work all day, and no company when he did come in. Did you know John Wright, Mrs. Peters?

Mrs. Peters: Not to know him; I've seen him in town. They say he was a good man.

Mrs. Hale: Yes—good; he didn't drink, and kept his word as well as most, I guess, and paid his debts. But he was a hard man, Mrs. Peters. Just to pass the time of day with him—*(shivers)*. Like a raw wind that gets to the bone. *(Pauses, her eye falling on the cage.)* I should think she would'a wanted a bird. But what do you suppose went with it?

Mrs. Peters: I don't know, unless it got sick and died.

(She reaches over and swings the broken door, swings it again. Both women watch it.)

Mrs. Hale: You weren't raised round here, were you? *(Mrs. Peters shakes her head.)* You didn't know—her?

Mrs. Peters: Not till they brought her yesterday.

Mrs. Hale: She—come to think of it, she was kind of like a bird herself—real sweet and pretty, but kind of timid and—fluttery. How—she—did—change. *(Silence; then as if struck by a happy thought and relieved to get back to everyday things.)* Tell you what, Mrs. Peters, why don't you take the quilt in with you? It might take up her mind.

Mrs. Peters: Why, I think that's a real nice idea, Mrs. Hale. There couldn't possibly be any objection to it, could there? Now, just what would I take? I wonder if her patches are in here—and her things.

(They look in the sewing basket.)

Mrs. Hale: Here's some red. I expect this has got sewing things in it. *(Brings out a fancy box.)* What a pretty box. Looks like something somebody would give you. Maybe her scissors are in here. *(Opens box. Suddenly puts her hand to her nose.)* Why—*(Mrs. Peters bends nearer, then turns her face away.)* There's something wrapped up in this piece of silk.
Mrs. Peters: Why, this isn't her scissors.
Mrs. Hale (lifting the silk): Oh, Mrs. Peters—it's—

(Mrs. Peters bends closer.)

Mrs. Peters: It's the bird.
Mrs. Hale (jumping up): But, Mrs. Peters—look at it! Its neck! Look at its neck! It's all—other side *to*.
Mrs. Peters: Somebody—wrung—its—neck.

(Their eyes meet. A look of growing comprehension, of horror. Steps are heard outside. Mrs. Hale slips box under quilt pieces, and sinks into her chair. Enter Sheriff and County Attorney. Mrs. Peters rises.)

County Attorney (as one turning from serious things to little pleasantries): Well, ladies, have you decided whether she was going to quilt it or knot it?
Mrs. Peters: We think she was going to—knot it.
County Attorney: Well, that's interesting, I'm sure. *(Seeing the birdcage.)* Has the bird flown?
Mrs. Hale (putting more quilt pieces over the box): We think the—cat got it.
County Attorney (preoccupied): Is there a cat?

(Mrs. Hale glances in a quick covert way at Mrs. Peters.)

Mrs. Peters: Well, not *now*. They're superstitious, you know. They leave.
County Attorney (to Sheriff Peters, continuing an interrupted conversation): No sign at all of anyone having come from the outside. Their own rope. Now let's go up again and go over it piece by piece. *(They start upstairs.)* It would have to have been someone who knew just the—

(Mrs. Peters sits down. The two women sit there not looking at one another, but as if peering into something and at the same time holding back. When they talk now it is in the manner of feeling their way over strange ground, as if afraid of what they are saying, but as if they cannot help saying it.)

Mrs. Hale: She liked the bird. She was going to bury it in that pretty box.
Mrs. Peters (in a whisper): When I was a girl—my kitten—there was a boy took a hatchet, and before my eyes—and before I could get there—*(covers her face an instant)*. If they hadn't held me back I would have—*(catches herself, looks upstairs where steps are heard, falters weakly)*—hurt him.
Mrs. Hale (with a slow look around her): I wonder how it would seem never to have had any children around. *(Pause.)* No, Wright wouldn't like the bird—a thing that sang. She used to sing. He killed that, too.

Mrs. *Peters* (*moving uneasily*): We don't know who killed the bird.

Mrs. *Hale:* I knew John Wright.

Mrs. *Peters:* It was an awful thing was done in this house that night, Mrs. Hale. Killing a man while he slept, slipping a rope around his neck that choked the life out of him.

Mrs. *Hale:* His neck. Choked the life out of him.

(*Her hand goes out and rests on the birdcage.*)

Mrs. *Peters* (*with rising voice*): We don't know who killed him. We don't *know.*

Mrs. *Hale* (*her own feeling not interrupted*): If there'd been years and years of nothing, then a bird to sing to you, it would be awful—still, after the bird was still.

Mrs. *Peters* (*something within her speaking*): I know what stillness is. When we homesteaded in Dakota, and my first baby died—after he was two years old, and me with no other then—

Mrs. *Hale* (*moving*): How soon do you suppose they'll be through looking for the evidence?

Mrs. *Peters:* I know what stillness is. (*Pulling herself back.*) The law has got to punish crime, Mrs. Hale.

Mrs. *Hale* (*not as if answering that*): I wish you'd seen Minnie Foster when she wore a white dress with blue ribbons and stood up there in the choir and sang. (*A look around the room.*) Oh, I *wish* I'd come over here once in a while! That was a crime! That was a crime! Who's going to punish that?

Mrs. *Peters* (*looking upstairs*): We mustn't—take on.

Mrs. *Hale:* I might have known she needed help! I know how things can be—for women. I tell you, it's queer, Mrs. Peters. We live close together and we live far apart. We all go through the same things—it's all just a different kind of the same thing. (*Brushes her eyes; noticing the bottle of fruit, reaches out for it.*) If I was you I wouldn't tell her her fruit was gone. Tell her it *ain't.* Tell her it's all right. Take this in to prove it to her. She—she may never know whether it was broke or not.

Mrs. *Peters* (*takes the bottle, looks about for something to wrap it in; takes petticoat from the clothes brought from the other room, very nervously begins winding this around the bottle; in a false voice*): My, it's a good thing the men couldn't hear us. Wouldn't they just laugh! Getting all stirred up over a little thing like a—dead canary. As if that could have anything to do with—with—wouldn't they *laugh!*

(*The men are heard coming down stairs.*)

Mrs. *Hale* (*under her breath*): Maybe they would—maybe they wouldn't.

County Attorney: No, Peters, it's all perfectly clear except a reason for doing it. But you know juries when it comes to women. If there was some definite thing. Something to show—something to make a story about—a thing that would connect up with this strange way of doing it—

(*The women's eyes meet for an instant. Enter Hale from outer door.*)

Hale: Well, I've got the team around. Pretty cold out there.

County Attorney: I'm going to stay here a while by myself. (*To the Sheriff*) You can send Frank out for me, can't you? I want to go over everything. I'm not satisfied that we can't do better.

Sheriff: Do you want to see what Mrs. Peters is going to take in?

(*The County Attorney goes to the table, picks up the apron, laughs.*)

County Attorney: Oh, I guess they're not very dangerous things the ladies have picked out. (*Moves a few things about, disturbing the quilt pieces which cover the box. Steps back.*) No, Mrs. Peters doesn't need supervising. For that matter, a sheriff's wife is married to the law. Ever think of it that way, Mrs. Peters?

Mrs. Peters: Not—just that way.

Sheriff (chuckling): Married to the law. (*Moves toward the other room.*) I just want you to come in here a minute, George. We ought to take a look at these windows.

County Attorney (scoffingly): Oh, windows!

Sheriff: We'll be right out, Mr. Hale.

(*Hale goes outside. The Sheriff follows the County Attorney into the other room. Then Mrs. Hale rises, hands tight together, looking intensely at Mrs. Peters, whose eyes make a slow turn, finally meeting Mrs. Hale's. A moment Mrs. Hale holds her, then her own eyes point the way to where the box is concealed. Suddenly Mrs. Peters throws back quilt pieces and tries to put the box in the bag she is wearing. It is too big. She opens box, starts to take bird out, cannot touch it, goes to pieces, stands there helpless. Sound of a knob turning in the other room. Mrs. Hale snatches the box and puts it in the pocket of her big coat. Enter County Attorney and Sheriff.*)

County Attorney (facetiously): Well, Henry, at least we found out that she was not going to quilt it. She was going to—what is it you call it, ladies?

Mrs. Hale (her hand against her pocket): We call it—knot it, Mr. Henderson.

CURTAIN

Questions

1. What attitudes toward women do the Sheriff and the County Attorney express? How do Mrs. Hale and Mrs. Peters react to these sentiments?
2. Why does the County Attorney care so much about discovering a motive for the killing?
3. What does Glaspell show us about the position of women in this early twentieth-century community?
4. What do we learn about the married life of the Wrights? By what means is this knowledge revealed to us?
5. What is the setting of this play, and how does it help us to understand Mrs. Wright's deed?
6. What do you infer from the wildly stitched block in Minnie's quilt? Why does Mrs. Hale rip out the crazy stitches?
7. What is so suggestive in the ruined birdcage and the dead canary wrapped in silk? What do these objects have to do with Minnie Foster Wright? What similarity do you notice between the way the canary died and John Wright's own death?
8. What thoughts and memories confirm Mrs. Peters and Mrs. Hale in their decision to help Minnie beat the murder rap?
9. In what places does Mrs. Peters show that she is trying to be a loyal, law-abiding sheriff's wife? How do she and Mrs. Hale differ in background and temperament?
10. What ironies does the play contain? Comment on Mrs. Hale's closing speech: "We call it—knot it, Mr. Henderson." Why is that little hesitation before "knot it" such a meaningful pause?
11. Point out some moments in the play when the playwright conveys much to the audience without needing dialogue.

12. How would you sum up the play's major theme?

13. How does this play, first produced in 1916, show its age? In what ways does it seem still remarkably new?

14. "*Trifles* is a lousy mystery. All the action took place before the curtain went up. Almost in the beginning, on the third page, we find out 'who done it.' So there isn't really much reason for us to sit through the rest of the play." Discuss this view.

ANALYZING *TRIFLES*

Some plays endure, perhaps because (among other reasons) actors take pleasure in performing them. *Trifles* is such a play, a showcase for the skills of its two principals. While the men importantly bumble about, trying to discover a motive, Mrs. Peters and Mrs. Hale solve the case right under their dull noses. The two players in these leading roles face a challenging task: to show both characters growing onstage before us. Discovering a secret that binds them, the two women must realize painful truths in their own lives, become aware of all they have in common with Minnie Wright, and gradually resolve to side with the accused against the men. That *Trifles* has enjoyed a revival of attention may reflect its evident feminist views, its convincing portrait of two women forced reluctantly to arrive at a moral judgment and to make a defiant move.

Conflict

Some critics say that the essence of drama is **conflict**, the central struggle between two or more forces in a play. Evidently, Glaspell's play is rich in this essential, even though its most violent conflict—the war between John and Minnie Wright—takes place before the play begins. Right away, when the menfolk barge through the door into the warm room, letting the women trail in after them; right away, when the sheriff makes fun of Minnie for worrying about "trifles" and the county attorney (that slick politician) starts crudely trying to flatter the "ladies," we sense a conflict between officious, self-important men and the women they expect to wait on them. What is the play's *theme*? Surely the title points to it: women, who men say worry over trifles, can find large meanings in those little things.

Plot

Like a carefully constructed traditional short story, *Trifles* has a **plot**, a term sometimes taken to mean whatever happens in a story, but more exactly referring to the unique arrangement of events that the author has made. (For more about plot in a story, see Chapter 1.) If Glaspell had elected to tell the story of John and Minnie Wright in chronological order, the sequence in which events took place in time, she might have written a much longer play, opening perhaps with a scene of Minnie's buying her canary and John's cold complaint, "That damned bird keeps twittering all day long!" She might have included scenes showing John strangling the canary and swearing when it beaks him; the Wrights in their loveless bed while Minnie knots her noose; and farmer Hale's entrance after the murder, with Minnie rocking. Only at the end would she have shown us what happened after the crime. That arrangement of events would have made for a quite different play than the short, tight one Glaspell wrote. By telling of events in retrospect, by having the women detectives piece together what happened, Glaspell leads us to focus not only on the murder but,

more importantly, on the developing bond between the two women and their growing compassion for the accused.

Subplot

Tightly packed, the one-act *Trifles* contains a single plot: the story of how two women
discover evidence that might hang another woman and then hide it. Some plays,
usually longer ones, may be more complicated. They may contain a **double plot** (or
subplot), a secondary arrangement of incidents, involving not the protagonist but
someone less important. In Henrik Ibsen's *A Doll's House*, the main plot involves a
woman and her husband; they are joined by a second couple, whose fortunes we also
follow with interest and whose futures pose different questions.

Protagonist

If *Trifles* may be said to have a **protagonist**, a leading character—a word we usually
save for the primary figure of a larger and more eventful play such as *Othello* (Chapter
38)—then you would call the two women dual protagonists. They act in unison to
make the plot unfold. Or you could argue that Mrs. Hale—because she destroys the
wild stitching in the quilt, because she finds the dead canary, because she invents a
cat to catch the bird (thus deceiving the county attorney), and because in the end
when Mrs. Peters helplessly "goes to pieces" it is she who takes the initiative and
seizes the evidence—deserves to be called the protagonist. More than anyone else in
the play, you could claim, the more decisive Mrs. Hale makes things happen.

Exposition

A vital part of most plays is an **exposition**, the part in which we first meet the characters, learn what happened before the curtain rose, and find out what is happening
now. For a one-act play, *Trifles* has a fairly long exposition, extending from the opening of the kitchen door through the end of farmer Hale's story. Clearly, this substantial exposition is necessary to set the situation and to fill in the facts of the crime. By
comparison, Shakespeare's far longer *Tragedy of Richard III* begins almost abruptly,
with its protagonist, a duke who yearns to be king, summing up history in an opening
speech and revealing his evil character: "And therefore, since I cannot prove a lover
. . . I am determinèd to prove a villain." But Glaspell, too, knows her craft. In the
exposition, we are given a **foreshadowing**—a hint of what is to come—in Hale's dry
remark, "I didn't know as what his wife wanted made much difference to John." The
remark announces the play's theme that men often ignore women's feelings, and it
hints at Minnie Wright's motive, later to be revealed. The county attorney, failing to
pick up a valuable clue, tables the discussion. (Still another foreshadowing occurs in
Mrs. Hale's ripping out the wild, panicky stitches in Minnie's quilt. In the end, Mrs.
Hale will make a similar final move to conceal the evidence.)

Dramatic Question

With the county attorney's speech to the sheriff, "You're convinced that there was
nothing important here—nothing that would point to any motive," we begin to
understand what he seeks. As he will make even clearer later, the attorney needs
a motive in order to convict the accused wife of murder in the first degree. Will
Minnie's motive in killing her husband be discovered? Through the first two-thirds
of *Trifles*, this is the play's **dramatic question**. Whether or not we state such a question in our minds (and it is doubtful that we do), our interest quickens as we sense

that here is a problem to be solved, an uncertainty to be cleared up. When Mrs. Hale and Mrs. Peters find the dead canary with the twisted neck, the question is answered. We know that Minnie killed John to repay him for his act of gross cruelty. The playwright, however, now raises a *new* dramatic question. Having discovered Minnie's motive, will the women reveal it to the lawmen? Alternatively (if you care to phrase the new question differently), what will they do with the incriminating evidence? We keep reading, or stay clamped to our theater seats, because we want that question answered. We share the women's secret now, and we want to see what they will do with it.

Climax

Step by step, *Trifles* builds to a **climax**: a moment, usually coming late in a play, when tension reaches its greatest height. At such a moment, we sense that the play's dramatic question (or its final dramatic question, if the writer has posed more than one) is about to be answered. In *Trifles* this climax occurs when Mrs. Peters finds herself torn between her desire to save Minnie and her duty to the law. "It was an awful thing was done in this house that night," she reminds herself in one speech, suggesting that Minnie deserves to be punished; then in the next speech she insists, "We don't know who killed him. We don't *know*." Shortly after that, in one speech she voices two warring attitudes. Remembering the loss of her first child, she sympathizes with Minnie: "I know what stillness is." But in her next breath she recalls once more her duty to be a loyal sheriff's wife: "The law has got to punish crime, Mrs. Hale." For a moment, she is placed in conflict with Mrs. Hale, who knew Minnie personally. The two now stand on the edge of a fateful brink. Which way will they decide?

You will sometimes hear climax used in a different sense to mean any **crisis**— that is, a moment of tension when one or another outcome is possible. What crisis means will be easy to remember if you think of a crisis in medicine: the turning point in an illness when it becomes clear that a patient will either die or recover. In talking about plays, you will probably find both crisis and climax useful. You can say that a play has more than one crisis, perhaps several. In such a play, the last and most decisive crisis is the climax. A play has only one climax.

Resolution and Dénouement

From this moment of climax, the play, like its protagonist (or if you like, protagonists), will make a final move. Mrs. Peters takes her stand. Mrs. Hale, too, decides. She owes Minnie something to make up for her own "crime"—her failure to visit the desperate woman. The plot now charges ahead to its outcome or **resolution**, also called the **conclusion** or **dénouement** (French for "untying of a knot"). The two women act: they scoop up the damaging evidence. Seconds before the very end, Glaspell heightens the **suspense**, our enjoyable anxiety, by making Mrs. Peters fumble with the incriminating box as the sheriff and the county attorney draw near. Mrs. Hale's swift grab for the evidence saves the day and presumably saves Minnie's life. The sound of the doorknob turning in the next room, as the lawmen return, is a small but effective bit of **stage business**—any nonverbal action that engages the attention of an audience. Earlier, when Mrs. Hale almost sits down in Minnie's place, the empty chair that ominously starts rocking is another brilliant piece of stage business. Not only does it give us something interesting to watch, but it also gives us something to think about.

Rising and Falling Action

The German critic Gustav Freytag maintained that events in a plot can be arranged in the outline of a pyramid. In his influential view, a play begins with a **rising action**, that part of the narrative (including the exposition) in which events start moving toward a climax. After the climax, the story tapers off in a **falling action**—that is, the subsequent events, including a resolution. In a tragedy, this falling action usually is recognizable: the protagonist's fortunes proceed downhill to an inevitable end.

Some plays indeed have demonstrable pyramids. In *Trifles*, we might claim that in the first two-thirds of the play a rising action builds in intensity. It proceeds through each main incident: the finding of the crazily stitched quilt, Mrs. Hale's ripping out the evidence, the discovery of the birdcage, then of the bird itself, and Mrs. Hale's concealing it. At the climax, the peak of the pyramid, the two women seem about to clash as Mrs. Peters wavers uncertainly. The action then falls to a swift resolution. If you outlined that pyramid on paper, however, it would look lopsided—a long rise and a short, steep fall. The pyramid metaphor seems more meaningfully to fit longer plays, among them some classic tragedies, such as *Oedipus the King*. Nevertheless, in most other plays, it is hard to find a symmetrical pyramid. (For a demonstration of another, quite different way to outline *Trifles*, see "Writing a Card Report" in Chapter 45.)

Unity of Time, Place, and Action

Because its action occurs all at one time and in one place, *Trifles* happens to observe the **unities**, certain principles of good drama laid down by Italian literary critics in the sixteenth century. Interpreting the theories of Aristotle as binding laws, these critics set down three basic principles: a good play, they maintained, should display unity of *action*, unity of *time*, and unity of *place*. In practical terms, this theory maintained that a play must represent a single series of interrelated actions that take place within twenty-four hours in a single location. Furthermore, they insisted, to have true unity of action, a play had to be entirely serious or entirely funny. Mixing tragic and comic elements was not allowed. That Glaspell consciously strove to obey those critics is doubtful, and certainly many great plays, such as Shakespeare's *Othello*, defy such arbitrary rules. Still, it is at least arguable that some of the power of *Trifles* (or Sophocles's *Oedipus the King*) comes from the intensity of the playwright's concentration on what happens in one place, in one short expanse of time.

Symbols in Drama

Brief though it is, *Trifles* has main elements you will find in much longer, more complicated plays. It even has **symbols** (Chapter 7), things that hint at large meanings—for example, the broken birdcage and the dead canary, both suggesting the music and the joy that John Wright stifled in Minnie and the terrible stillness that followed his killing the one thing she loved. Perhaps the lone remaining jar of cherries, too, radiates suggestions: it is the one bright, cheerful thing poor Minnie has to show for a whole summer of toil. Plays can also contain symbolic characters (generally flat ones such as a prophet who croaks, "Beware the ides of March"), symbolic settings, and symbolic gestures. Symbols in drama may be as big as a house—the home in Ibsen's *A Doll's House*, for instance—or they may appear to be trifles. In Glaspell's rich art, such trifles aren't trifling at all.

■ WRITING *effectively*

Susan Glaspell on Writing

Creating *Trifles*   1927

We went to the theater, and for the most part we came away wishing we had gone somewhere else. Those were the days when Broadway flourished almost unchallenged. Plays, like magazine stories, were patterned. They might be pretty good within themselves, seldom did they open out to—where it surprised or thrilled your spirit to follow. They didn't ask much of *you*, those plays. Having paid for your seat, the thing was all done for you, and your mind came out where it went in, only tireder. An audience, Jig° said, had imagination. What was this "Broadway," which could make a thing as interesting as life into a thing as dull as a Broadway play?

Susan Glaspell

There was a meeting at the Liberal Club— Eddie Goodman, Phil Moeller, Ida Rauh, the Boni brothers, exciting talk about starting a theater.

• • •

He [Jig] wrote a letter to the people who had seen the plays, asking if they cared to become associate members of the Provincetown Players. The purpose was to give American playwrights of sincere purpose a chance to work out their ideas in freedom, to give all who worked with the plays their opportunity as artists. Were they interested in this? One dollar for the three remaining bills.

The response paid for seats and stage, and for sets. A production need not cost a lot of money, Jig would say. The most expensive set at the Wharf Theater° cost thirteen dollars. There were sets at the Provincetown Playhouse which cost little more. . . .

"Now, Susan," he [Jig] said to me, briskly, "I have announced a play of yours for the next bill."

"But I have no play!"

"Then you will have to sit down to-morrow and begin one."

I protested. I did not know how to write a play. I had never "studied it."

"Nonsense," said Jig. "You've got a stage, haven't you?"

So I went out on the wharf, sat alone on one of our wooden benches without a back, and looked a long time at that bare little stage. After a time the stage became a

---

Jig: the nickname of George Cram Cook (1873–1924), Glaspell's husband, who was the central founder and director of the Provincetown Players, perhaps the most influential theater company in the history of American drama.   *Wharf Theater:* the makeshift theater that Cook created from an old fish-house at the end of a Provincetown wharf.

kitchen—a kitchen there all by itself. I saw just where the stove was, the table, and the steps going upstairs. Then the door at the back opened, and people all bundled up came in—two or three men, I wasn't sure which, but sure enough about the two women, who hung back, reluctant to enter that kitchen. When I was a newspaper reporter out in Iowa, I was sent down-state to do a murder trial, and I never forgot going into the kitchen of a woman locked up in town. I had meant to do it as a short story, but the stage took it for its own, so I hurried in from the wharf to write down what I had seen. Whenever I got stuck, I would run across the street to the old wharf, sit in that leaning little theater under which the sea sounded, until the play was ready to continue. Sometimes things written in my room would not form on the stage, and I must go home and cross them out. "What playwrights need is a stage," said Jig, "their own stage."

Ten days after the director said he had announced my play, there was a reading at Mary Heaton Vorse's. I was late to the meeting, home revising the play. But when I got there the crowd liked "Trifles," and voted to put it in rehearsal next day.

From *The Road to the Temple*

THINKING ABOUT A PLAY

A good play almost always presents a conflict. Conflict creates suspense and keeps an audience from meandering out to the lobby refreshment stand. Without it, a play would be static and, most likely, dull. When a character intensely desires something but some obstacle—perhaps another character—stands in the way, the result is dramatic tension. To understand a play, it is essential to understand the basic conflicts motivating the plot.

- **Identify the play's protagonist.** Who is the central character of the play? What motivates this character? What does this character want most to achieve or avoid? Is this goal reasonable or does it reflect some delusion on the part of the protagonist?
- **Identify the antagonist.** Who prevents the main character from achieving his or her goal? Is the opposition conscious or accidental? What motivates this character to oppose the protagonist?
- **Identify the central dramatic conflict.** What does the struggle between the protagonist and antagonist focus on? Is it another person, a possession, an action, some sort of recognition, or honor?
- **How does the conflict influence the action of the play?** The central conflict usually fuels the plot, causing characters to do and say all sorts of things they might not otherwise undertake. What series of later events does the central conflict set in motion?

CHECKLIST: Writing About a Play

☐ List the play's three or four main characters. Jot down what each character wants most at the play's beginning.

☐ Which of these characters is the protagonist?

☐ What stands in the way of the protagonist achieving his or her goal?

☐ How do the other characters' motivations fit into the central conflict? Identify any double plots or subplots.

☐ What are the play's main events? How does each relate to the protagonist's struggle?

☐ Where do you find the play's climax?

☐ How is the conflict resolved? What qualities in the protagonist's character bring about the play's outcome?

☐ Does the protagonist achieve his or her goal? How does success or failure affect the protagonist?

TOPICS FOR WRITING ON *TRIFLES*

1. Write a brief essay on the role gender differences play in Susan Glaspell's *Trifles*.
2. Write an analysis of the exposition—how the scene is set, characters introduced, and background information communicated—in *Trifles*.
3. Describe the significance of setting in *Trifles*.
4. Imagine you are a lawyer hired to defend Minnie Wright. Present your closing argument to the jury.
5. Watch any hour-long television drama. Write about the main conflict that drives the story. What motivates the protagonist? What stands in his or her way? How do each of the drama's main events relate to the protagonist's struggle? How is the conflict resolved? Is the show's outcome connected to the protagonist's character, or do events just happen to him or her? Do you believe the script is well written? Why or why not?
6. Select any short play, and write a brief essay identifying the protagonist, central conflict, and dramatic question.

SAMPLE STUDENT PAPER

Here is a paper by Tara Mazzucca, a student of Beverly Schneller at Millersville University, that examines and compares the protagonists and dramatic questions of two short plays by Susan Glaspell.

Mazzucca 1

Tara Mazzucca

Professor Schneller

English 102

29 January 2019

Outside *Trifles*

Susan Glaspell was one of America's first feminist playwrights. A founder of the non-commercial Provincetown Players, she used this experimental company to present plays that realistically explored the lives of women. I would like to examine and compare two of Glaspell's early one-act plays, *Trifles* (1916) and *The Outside* (1917). I will discuss how they present women who are forced to survive in a world where men make most of the rules.

Both plays focus on female protagonists, and both realistically present the emotional hardships these women endure in their daily lives. Both plays have contemporary settings; they take place in the early twentieth century. Both plays present women who are isolated from society—Mrs. Wright in *Trifles* and the two protagonists of *The Outside*. And in both plays a pair of female characters work together to solve the central dramatic question.

In *Trifles* Glaspell ironically places two wives, one married to a farmer and the other to the sheriff, at the scene of a mysterious murder case. The play takes place entirely in familiar territory for women in the early 1900s—a kitchen. The kitchen becomes a symbol for the game of hot and cold that the characters unwittingly play. In the kitchen where it is hot, the women find all the clues necessary to solve the case. Meanwhile the men search the rest of the cold house and find nothing to suggest a motive for the crime.

The two wives soon recognize the story behind the murder by observing small details in the house. They see clues in what the men pass over as mere trifles. When the women mention the ruined fruit preserves in the kitchen, Mr. Hale dismisses the potential importance of housekeeping details and comments, "Well, women are used to worrying over trifles" (1146). The two women, however, understand that small things can affect a person deeply.

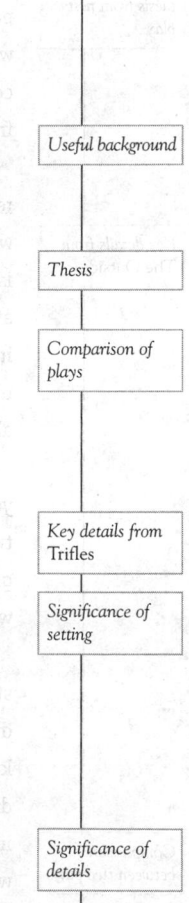

Useful background

Thesis

Comparison of plays

Key details from Trifles

Significance of setting

Significance of details

More details

The two women also recognize the importance of singing in Mrs. Wright's life. Singing was something she was known for when she was younger, only to have it taken away from her when she married John Wright. Doing housework alone all day in silence, Mrs. Wright became a different person. The stress of loneliness and depression finally got to Mrs. Wright. She bought a canary for company and enjoyment. She loved the singing bird, but her husband killed it. In desperation the woman decided to live without her husband.

Examination of thesis from first play

Mrs. Hale and Mrs. Peters instinctively understand Mrs. Wright's worries. Their perspective gives them an advantage over their male counterparts. The women must work together, because if they did not, each would break under the pressure of the cold treatment they receive from their husbands—break like the glass jars of canned fruit Mrs. Wright stores away in her cabinet.

Key details from The Outside

The plot of *The Outside* is relatively simple. The widowed Mrs. Patrick lives in a remote building that was once a life-saving station. Mrs. Patrick employs another widow, Allie Mayo, to help her with housekeeping. They lead lives of almost total isolation. One day three life-savers bring in the body of a drowned sailor and attempt unsuccessfully to revive him. Mrs. Patrick is furious that they have used her house as a rescue station and demands that they leave. Her behavior so upsets the usually silent Allie that the servant confronts Mrs. Patrick with a passionate speech about the futility of renouncing life.

Allie also keeps to herself from grief. As a girl, she was talkative, but after her young husband vanished at sea, she resolved never to say an unnecessary word. Now twenty years later, she is notorious for her silence. The two women share a common grief of having lost the husbands they loved. Losing a husband changed each woman. Allie chose silence. Mrs. Patrick left society.

When the men bring the drowned young man into the former life-saving station, the incident upsets Mrs. Patrick, and she explodes with anger. This incident disturbs Allie in a different way. She realizes how isolated they have become. She knows that if they do not change, they will die without anyone caring. Deeply disturbed, Allie breaks her silence and argues with her employer. Mrs. Patrick

Comparison between two plays

initially resists Allie's remarks because she still has not come to terms with life without her husband. Allie resembles Mrs. Wright in *Trifles*. Both women keep quiet for years and do what they're told, until they reach a breaking point. A critical event forces each of them to take dramatic action. Allie violently argues with her employer; Mrs. Wright decides to murder her husband.

Mrs. Hale and Mrs. Peters resemble Mrs. Patrick from *The Outside*. Throughout the play Mrs. Hale and Mrs. Peters try to understand why Mrs. Wright killed her husband. In the end, they recognize that their lives have much in common with that of the murderer. Their actions show their confusion about their own values. They do things that hinder the sheriff's investigation to protect an oppressed woman. First, Mrs. Hale rips out Mrs. Wright's erratic stitching so the men will not notice her nervous condition. Second, Mrs. Peters, who is—ironically—the sheriff's wife, hides the strangled bird from her husband and the other men. The women see a new side of Mrs. Wright's marriage and sympathize with her pathetic situation. By the end of *The Outside* Mrs. Patrick also sees a new side of Allie. Allie's outburst forces Mrs. Patrick to consider changing her life and reconsider her ideas.

Comparison continued

Mrs. Patrick of *The Outside* and Mrs. Wright of *Trifles* are also alike because they are now isolated from the world they used to enjoy. One stopped living because of a harsh husband, the other because of a dead husband. Mrs. Hale and Allie also resemble one another because they both waited too late to understand the depression of their neighbor or living companion. In *Trifles*, Mrs. Hale decides to help her neighbor even though it means protecting a criminal. Allie speaks truthfully even though it might jeopardize her job. In the end, the actions Allie and Mrs. Hale take are helpful. The men never find a motive for the murder. Mrs. Patrick finally considers changing her way of life in *The Outside*. In the end each woman has found something new inside of her.

Topic sentence— comparison

Mrs. Hale and Mrs. Peters both realize the secret they must keep to protect Mrs. Wright. They also realize the injustices women go through to be accepted in society. Mrs. Hale says:

Topic sentence/ textual analysis

> I might have known she needed help! I know how things can be—for women. I tell you, it's queer, Mrs. Peters. We live close together and we live far apart. We all go through the same things—it's all just a different kind of the same thing. (1152)

In *The Outside*, the women don't feel socially oppressed by men, but they cannot define their lives except in relation to their husbands. When they become widows, they lose their reason to live. Allie realizes that their grief has gone too far. She finds her voice to say that life must be lived. Mrs. Patrick listens enough to feel uncertainty about her life of loneliness and isolation. Each play deals with death and its effects on the survivors.

Topic sentence/textual analysis

Mazzucca 4

Contrast

Conclusion

Restatement of thesis

A major difference between the two plays is found in the way the central female characters treat one another. In *Trifles* the women work together to solve the mystery, but in *The Outside* the women clash and refuse to help one another. Glaspell did not have only one idealized image of female behavior. She realized that different women behave differently. Each play presents different ways women in the early twentieth century used to survive in a man's world. Trapped in the trifles of everyday life, many women felt as if they were living on the outside of the world.

Mazzucca 5

Works Cited

Glaspell, Susan. *The Outside*. 1917. *Project Gutenberg,* www.gutenberg.org/
   files/10623/10623-h/10623-h.htm#THE_OUTSIDE.

---. *Trifles*. 1916. *Literature: An Introduction to Fiction, Poetry, Drama, and Writing,*
   edited by X. J. Kennedy et al., 14th ed., Pearson, 2020, pp. 1143–53.

▶ TERMS FOR *review*

To review definitions of the elements of plot (**protagonist, antagonist, exposition, conflict, complication, crisis, climax,** and **conclusion**), see Chapter 1, "Terms for Review" on pages 24 and 25.

Double plot (also called **subplot**) ▶ A second story or plotline that is complete and interesting in its own right, often doubling or inverting the main plot.

Unities ▶ Unity of time, place, and action, the three formal qualities recommended by Renaissance critics to give a theatrical plot cohesion and integrity. According to this theory, a play should depict the causes and effects of a single action unfolding in one day in one place.

Soliloquy ▶ In drama, a speech by a character alone onstage in which he or she utters his or her thoughts aloud.

Aside ▶ A speech that a character addresses directly to the audience, unheard by the other characters on stage, as when the villain in a melodrama chortles: "Heh! Heh! Now she's in my power!"

Stage business ▶ Nonverbal action that engages the attention of an audience.

36

TRAGEDY AND COMEDY

Show me a hero and I will write you a tragedy.

— F. SCOTT FITZGERALD

What You Will Learn in This Chapter

- To define *tragedy* as a dramatic mode
- To define *comedy* as a dramatic mode
- To explain the difference between tragedy and comedy
- To understand and describe the various levels and kinds of comedy

In 1770, Horace Walpole wrote, "the world is a comedy to those that think, a tragedy to those that feel." All of us, of course, both think and feel, and all of us have moments when we stand back and laugh, whether ruefully or with glee, at life's absurdities, just as we all have times when our hearts are broken by its pains and losses. Thus, the modes of tragedy and comedy, diametrically opposed to one another though they are, do not demand that we choose between them: both of them speak to something deep and real within us, and each of them has its own truth to tell about the infinitely complex experience of living in this world.

TRAGEDY

By **tragedy** we mean a play that portrays a serious conflict between human beings and some superior, overwhelming force. It ends sorrowfully and disastrously, and this outcome seems inevitable. Few spectators of *Oedipus the King* (Chapter 37) wonder how the play will turn out or wish for a happy ending. "In a tragedy," French playwright Jean Anouilh has remarked, "nothing is in doubt and everyone's destiny is known. . . . Tragedy is restful, and the reason is that hope, that foul, deceitful thing, has no part in it. There isn't any hope. You're trapped. The whole sky has fallen on you, and all you can do about it is shout."[1]

Many of our ideas of tragedy (from the Greek *tragoidia*, "goat song," referring to the goatskin dress of the performers) go back to ancient Athens; the plays of the Greek dramatists Sophocles, Aeschylus, and Euripides exemplify the art of tragedy. In the fourth century B.C., the philosopher Aristotle described Sophocles's *Oedipus the King* and other tragedies he had seen, analyzing their elements and trying to account for their power over our emotions. Aristotle's observations will make more sense after you read *Oedipus the King*, so we will save our principal discussion of them for

---

[1]Anouilh, Jean, "Preface," *Antigone*, trans. Lewis Galantière (New York: Random, 1946) 24.

Chapter 37. But for now, to understand something of the nature of tragedy, let us take a brief overview of the subject.

One of the oldest and most durable of literary genres, tragedy is also one of the simplest—the protagonist undergoes a reversal of fortune, from good to bad, ending in catastrophe. However simple, though, tragedy can be one of the most complex genres to explain satisfactorily, with almost every principal point of its definition open to differing and often hotly debated interpretations. It is a fluid and adaptive genre, and for every one of its defining points, we can cite a tragic masterpiece that fails to observe that particular convention. Its fluidity and adaptability can also be shown by the way in which the classical tragic pattern is played out in pure form in such unlikely places as Orson Welles's film *Citizen Kane* (1941) and Chinua Achebe's great novel *Things Fall Apart* (1958): in each of these works, a man of high position and character—one a multimillionaire newspaper publisher, the other a late nineteenth-century African warrior—moves inexorably to destruction, impelled by his rigidity and self-righteousness. Even a movie such as *King Kong*—despite its oversized and hirsute protagonist—exemplifies some of the principles of tragedy.

To gain a clearer understanding of what tragedy is, let us first take a moment to talk about what it is not. Consider the kinds of events that customarily bring the term "tragedy" to mind: the death of a child, a fire that destroys a family's home and possessions, the killing of innocent people by a deranged shooter, and so on. What all of these unfortunate instances have in common, obviously, is that they involve the infliction of great and irreversible suffering. But what they also share is the sense that the sufferers are innocent, that they have done nothing to cause or to deserve their fate. This is what we usually describe as a tragedy in real life, but tragedy in a literary or dramatic context has a different meaning: most theorists take their lead from Aristotle (see Chapter 37 for a fuller discussion of several of the points raised here) in maintaining that the protagonist's reversal of fortune is brought about through some error or weakness on his part, generally referred to as his **tragic flaw**.

Despite this weakness, the hero is traditionally a person of nobility, of both social rank and personality. Just as the suffering of totally innocent people stirs us to sympathetic sorrow rather than a tragic response, so too the destruction of a purely evil figure, a tyrant or a murderer with no redeeming qualities, would inspire only feelings of relief and satisfaction—hardly the emotions that tragedy seeks to stimulate. In most tragedies, the catastrophe entails not only the loss of outward fortune—things such as reputation, power, and life itself, which even the basest villain may possess and then be deprived of—but also the erosion of the protagonist's moral character and greatness of spirit.

Tragic Style

In keeping with this emphasis on nobility of spirit, tragedies are customarily written in an elevated style, one characterized by dignity and seriousness. In the Middle Ages, just as *tragedy* meant a work written in a high style in which the central character went from good fortune to bad, *comedy* indicated just the opposite, a work written in a low or common style, in which the protagonist moved from adverse circumstances to happy ones—hence Dante's great triptych of hell, purgatory, and heaven, written in everyday Italian rather than scholarly Latin, is known as *The Divine Comedy*, despite the relative absence of humor, let alone hilarity, in its pages. The tragic view of life, clearly, presupposes that in the end we will prove unequal to the challenges we must face, while the comic outlook asserts a view of human possibility in which our common sense and resilience—or pure dumb luck—will enable us to win out.

Tragedy's complexity can be seen also in the response that, according to Aristotle, it seeks to arouse in the viewer: pity and fear. By its very nature, pity distances the one who pities from the object of that pity, since we can feel sorry only for those whom we perceive to be worse off than ourselves. When we watch or read a tragedy, moved as we may be, we observe the downfall of the protagonist with a certain detachment; "better him than me" may be a rather crude way of putting it, but perhaps not an entirely incorrect one. Fear, on the other hand, usually involves an immediate anxiety about our own well-being. Even as we regard the hero's destruction from the safety of a better place, we are made to feel our own vulnerability in the face of life's dangers and instability, because we see that neither position nor virtue can protect even the great from ruin.

The following is a scene from Christopher Marlowe's classic Elizabethan tragedy *Doctor Faustus*. Based on an anonymous pamphlet published in Germany in 1587 and translated into English shortly thereafter, this celebrated play tells the story of an elderly professor who feels that he has wasted his life in fruitless inquiry. Chafing at the limits of human understanding, he makes a pact with the devil to gain forbidden knowledge and power. The scene presented here is the decisive turning point of the play, in which Faustus seals the satanic bargain that will damn him. Stimulated by his thirst for knowledge and experience, spurred on by his pride to assume that the divinely ordained limits of human experience no longer apply to him, he rushes to embrace his own undoing. Marlowe dramatizes Faustus's situation by bringing a good angel and a fallen angel (i.e., a demon) to whisper conflicting advice in this pivotal scene. (This good angel versus bad angel device has proved popular for centuries. We still see it today in everything from TV commercials to cartoons such as *The Simpsons*.) Notice the dignified and often gorgeous language Marlowe employs to create the serious mood necessary for tragedy.

Christopher Marlowe

Scene from Doctor Faustus[2]

(about 1588)

Edited by Sylvan Barnet

*Christopher Marlowe was born in Canterbury, England, in February 1564, about ten weeks before William Shakespeare. Marlowe, the son of a prosperous shoemaker, received a BA from Cambridge University in 1584 and a MA in 1587, after which he settled in London. The rest of his short life was marked by rumor, secrecy, and violence, including suspicions that he was a secret agent for Queen Elizabeth's government and allegations against him of blasphemy and atheism—no small matter in light of the political instability and religious controversies of the times. Peripherally implicated in several violent deaths, he met his own end in May 1593 when he was stabbed above the right eye during a tavern brawl, under circumstances that have never been fully explained. Brief and crowded as his life was, he wrote a number of intense, powerful, and highly influential tragedies—*Tamburlaine the Great, Parts 1 and 2 (1587), Doctor Faustus (1588), The Jew of Malta (1589), Edward the Second (c. 1592), The Massacre at Paris (1593), and Dido, Queen of Carthage (c. 1593, with Thomas Nashe). He is also the author of the lyric poem "The Passionate Shepherd to His Love," with its universally known first line: "Come live with me and be my love."*

---

[2]This scene is from the 1616 text, or "B-Text," published as *The Tragicall History of the Life and Death of Doctor Faustus*. Modernizations have been made in spelling and punctuation.

Doctor Faustus with the Bad Angel and the Good Angel, from the Utah Shakespeare Festival's 2005 production.

DRAMATIS PERSONAE

Doctor Faustus
Good Angel
Bad Angel
Mephistophilis, a devil

ACT II

SCENE I

    (*Enter Faustus in his study.*)

Faustus: Now, Faustus, must thou needs be damned;
    Canst thou not be saved!
    What boots° it then to think on God or heaven?
    Away with such vain fancies, and despair—
    Despair in God and trust in Belzebub!   5
    Now go not backward Faustus; be resolute!
    Why waver'st thou? O something soundeth in mine ear,
    "Abjure this magic, turn to God again."
    Ay, and Faustus will turn to God again.
    To God? He loves thee not.   10

3 *boots:* avails.

The god thou serv'st is thine own appetite
Wherein is fixed the love of Belzebub!
To him I'll build an altar and a church,
And offer lukewarm blood of newborn babes!

(Enter the two Angels.)

Bad Angel: Go forward, Faustus, in that famous art.   15
Good Angel: Sweet Faustus, leave that execrable art.
Faustus: Contrition, prayer, repentance? What of these?
Good Angel: O, they are means to bring thee unto heaven.
Bad Angel: Rather illusions, fruits of lunacy,
    That make men foolish that do use them most.   20
Good Angel: Sweet Faustus, think of heaven and heavenly things.
Bad Angel: No, Faustus, think of honor and of wealth.

                                                    (Exeunt Angels.)

Faustus: Wealth!
    Why, the signory of Emden° shall be mine!
    When Mephistophilis shall stand by me   25
    What power can hurt me? Faustus, thou art safe.
    Cast no more doubts! Mephistophilis, come,
    And bring glad tidings from great Lucifer.
    Is't not midnight? Come Mephistophilis,
    Veni, veni, Mephostophile!°   30

(Enter Mephistophilis.)

    Now tell me, what saith Lucifer thy lord?
Mephistophilis: That I shall wait on Faustus whilst he lives,
    So he will buy my service with his soul.
Faustus: Already Faustus hath hazarded that for thee.
Mephistophilis: But now thou must bequeath it solemnly   35
    And write a deed of gift with thine own blood,
    For that security craves Lucifer.
    If thou deny it I must back to hell.
Faustus: Stay Mephistophilis and tell me,
    What good will my soul do thy lord?   40
Mephistophilis: Enlarge his kingdom.
Faustus: Is that the reason why he tempts us thus?
Mephistophilis: *Solamen miseris socios habuisse doloris.*°
Faustus: Why, have you any pain that torture other?°
Mephistophilis: As great as have the human souls of men.   45
    But tell me, Faustus, shall I have thy soul—
    And I will be thy slave and wait on thee
    And give thee more than thou hast wit to ask?
Faustus: Ay Mephistophilis, I'll give it him.°

---

24 *signory of Emden:* lordship of the rich German port at the mouth of the Ems.   30 *Veni, veni, Mephostophile!*:
Come, come, Mephistophilis (Latin).   43 *Solamen . . . doloris:* Misery loves company (Latin).   44 *other:* others.
49 *him:* i.e., to Lucifer.

Mephistophilis: Then, Faustus, stab thy arm courageously,   50
 And bind thy soul, that at some certain day
 Great Lucifer may claim it as his own.
 And then be thou as great as Lucifer!
Faustus: Lo, Mephistophilis: for love of thee
 Faustus hath cut his arm, and with his proper° blood   55
 Assures° his soul to be great Lucifer's,
 Chief Lord and Regent of perpetual night.
 View here this blood that trickles from mine arm,
 And let it be propitious for my wish.
Mephistophilis: But, Faustus,   60
 Write it in manner of a deed of gift.
Faustus: Ay, so I do—But Mephistophilis,
 My blood congeals and I can write no more.
Mephistophilis: I'll fetch thee fire to dissolve it straight.

                                                                                        (*Exit.*)

Faustus: What might the staying of my blood portend?   65
 Is it unwilling I should write this bill?°
 Why streams it not that I may write afresh:
 "Faustus gives to thee his soul"? O there it stayed.
 Why should'st thou not? Is not thy soul thine own?
 Then write again: "Faustus gives to thee his soul."   70

(*Enter Mephistophilis, with the chafer° of fire.*)

Mephistophilis: See, Faustus, here is fire. Set it° on.
Faustus: So, now the blood begins to clear again.
 Now will I make an end immediately.
Mephistophilis (aside): What will not I do to obtain his soul!
Faustus: Consummatum est!° This bill is ended: 75
 And Faustus hath bequeathed his soul to Lucifer.
 —But what is this inscription on mine arm?
 Homo fuge!° Whither should I fly?
 If unto God, He'll throw me down to hell.
 My senses are deceived; here's nothing writ.   80
 O yes, I see it plain! Even here is writ
 Homo fuge! Yet shall not Faustus fly!
Mephistophilis (aside): I'll fetch him somewhat° to delight his mind.
                                                                    (*Exit Mephistophilis.*)

(*Enter Devils, giving crowns and rich apparel to Faustus. They dance and then depart.*)

(*Enter Mephistophilis.*)

Faustus: What means this show? Speak, Mephistophilis.
Mephistophilis: Nothing, Faustus, but to delight thy mind,   85
 And let thee see what magic can perform.
Faustus: But may I raise such spirits when I please?

55 *proper:* own.   56 *Assures:* conveys by contract.   66 *bill:* contract.   70 *s.d. chafer:* portable grate.   71 *it:* i.e.,
the receptacle containing the congealed blood.   75 *Consummatum est:* It is finished. (Latin: a blasphemous
repetition of Christ's words on the Cross; see John 19:30.)   78 *Homo fuge:* fly, man (Latin).   83 *somewhat:*
something.

Mephistophilis: Ay, Faustus, and do greater things than these.
Faustus: Then, Mephistophilis, receive this scroll,
    A deed of gift of body and of soul: 90
    But yet conditionally that thou perform
    All covenants and articles between us both.
Mephistophilis: Faustus, I swear by hell and Lucifer
    To effect all promises between us both.
Faustus: Then hear me read it, Mephistophilis: 95

"On these conditions following:

First, that Faustus may be a spirit° in form and substance.

Secondly, that Mephistophilis shall be his servant, and be by him commanded.

Thirdly, that Mephistophilis shall do for him and bring him whatsoever.

Fourthly, that he shall be in his chamber or house invisible.   100

Lastly, that he shall appear to the said John Faustus, at all times, in what shape and form soever he please.

I, John Faustus of Wittenberg, Doctor, by these presents, do give both body and soul to Lucifer, Prince of the East, and his minister Mephistophilis, and furthermore grant unto them that, four and twenty years being expired, and these arti- 105 cles written being inviolate,° full power to fetch or carry the said John Faustus, body and soul, flesh, blood, into their habitation wheresoever.

                                 By me John Faustus."

Mephistophilis: Speak, Faustus, do you deliver this as your deed?
Faustus: Ay, take it, and the devil give thee good of it!   110
Mephistophilis: So, now Faustus, ask me what thou wilt.
Faustus: First, I will question with thee about hell.
    Tell me, where is the place that men call hell?
Mephistophilis: Under the heavens.
Faustus: Ay, so are all things else, but whereabouts?   115
Mephistophilis: Within the bowels of these elements,
    Where we are tortured, and remain forever.
    Hell hath no limits, nor is circumscribed,
    In one self place, but where we are is hell,
    And where hell is there must we ever be.   120
    And to be short, when all the world dissolves,
    And every creature shall be purified,
    All places shall be hell that is not heaven!
Faustus: I think hell's a fable.
Mephistophilis: Ay, think so still—till experience change thy mind.   125
Faustus: Why, dost thou think that Faustus shall be damned?
Mephistophilis: Ay, of necessity, for here's the scroll
    In which thou hast given thy soul to Lucifer.

97 *spirit:* evil spirit, devil. (But to see Faustus as transformed now into a devil deprived of freedom to repent is to deprive the remainder of the play of much of its meaning.)   106 *inviolate:* unviolated.

Faustus: Ay, and body too; but what of that?
  Think'st thou that Faustus is so fond° to imagine,   130
  That after this life there is any pain?
  No, these are trifles, and mere old wives' tales.
Mephistophilis: But I am an instance to prove the contrary,
  For I tell thee I am damned, and now in hell!
Faustus: Nay, and this be hell, I'll willingly be damned—   135
  What, sleeping, eating, walking, and disputing?
  But leaving this, let me have a wife,
  The fairest maid in Germany,
  For I am wanton and lascivious,
  And cannot live without a wife.   140
Mephistophilis: Well, Faustus, thou shalt have a wife.

(*He fetches in a woman devil.*)

Faustus: What sight is this?
Mephistophilis: Now, Faustus, wilt thou have a wife?
Faustus: Here's a hot whore indeed! No, I'll no wife.
Mephistophilis: Marriage is but a ceremonial toy,°   145

                                                    (*Exit she-devil.*)

  And if thou lov'st me, think no more of it.
  I'll cull thee out° the fairest courtesans
  And bring them every morning to thy bed.
  She whom thine eye shall like, thy heart shall have,
  Were she as chaste as was Penelope,°   150
  As wise as Saba,° or as beautiful
  As was bright Lucifer before his fall.
  Here, take this book and peruse it well.
  The iterating° of these lines brings gold;
  The framing° of this circle on the ground   155
  Brings thunder, whirlwinds, storm, and lightning;
  Pronounce this thrice devoutly to thyself,
  And men in harness° shall appear to thee,
  Ready to execute what thou command'st.
Faustus: Thanks, Mephistophilis, for this sweet book.   160
  This will I keep as chary as my life.

                                                    (*Exeunt.*)

Questions

1. What specifically motivates Faustus to make his satanic compact? Cite the text to back up your response.
2. How does his behavior constitute a compromise of his nobility?
3. "Is not thy soul thine own?" Faustus asks rhetorically (line 69). Discuss the implications of this statement in terms of the larger thematic concerns of the work.
4. Does Faustus inspire your pity and fear in this scene? Why or why not?

---

130 *fond:* foolish.   145 *toy:* trifle.   147 *cull thee out:* select for you.   150 *Penelope:* wife of Ulysses, famed for her fidelity.   151 *Saba:* the Queen of Sheba.   154 *iterating:* repetition.   155 *framing:* drawing.   158 *harness:* armor.

Traditional masks of comedy and tragedy.

COMEDY

The best-known traditional emblem of drama—a pair of masks, one sorrowful (representing tragedy) and one smiling (representing comedy)—suggests that tragedy and comedy, although opposites, are close relatives. Often, comedy shows people getting into trouble through error or weakness; in this respect it is akin to tragedy. An important difference between comedy and tragedy lies in the attitude toward human failing that is expected of us. When a main character in a comedy suffers from overweening pride, as does Oedipus, or if he fails to recognize that his bride-to-be is actually his mother, we laugh—something we would never do in watching a competent performance of *Oedipus the King*.

Comedy, from the Greek *komos*, "a revel," is thought to have originated in festivities to celebrate spring, ritual performances in praise of Dionysus, god of fertility and wine. In drama, comedy may be broadly defined as whatever makes us laugh. A comedy may be a name for one entire play, or we may say that there is comedy in only part of a play—as in a comic character or a comic situation.

Theories of Comedy

Many theories have been propounded to explain why we laugh; most of these notions fall into a few familiar types. One school, exemplified by French philosopher Henri Bergson, sees laughter as a form of ridicule, implying a feeling of disinterested superiority; all jokes are *on* somebody. Bergson suggests that laughter springs from situations in which we sense a conflict between some mechanical or rigid pattern of behavior and our sense of a more natural or "organic" kind of behavior that is possible. An example occurs in Buster Keaton's comic film *The Boat*. Having launched a little boat that springs a leak, Keaton rigidly goes down with it, with frozen face. (The more natural and organic thing to do would be to swim for shore.)

Other thinkers view laughter as our response to expectations fulfilled or to expectations set up but then suddenly frustrated. Some hold it to be the expression of our delight in seeing our suppressed urges acted out (as when a comedian hurls an egg at a pompous stuffed shirt); some, to be our defensive reaction to a painful and disturbing truth.

Satiric Comedy

Derisive humor is basic to **satiric comedy**, in which human weakness or folly is ridiculed from a vantage point of supposedly enlightened superiority. Satiric comedy may be coolly malicious and gently biting, but it tends to be critical of people, their manners, and their morals. It is at least as old as the comedies of Aristophanes, who thrived in the fifth century B.C. In *Lysistrata*, the satirist shows how the women of two warring cities speedily halt a war by agreeing to deny themselves to their husbands. (The satirist's target is men so proud that they go to war rather than make the slightest concession.)

High Comedy

Comedy is often divided into two varieties—"high" and "low." **High comedy** relies more on wit and wordplay than on physical action for its humor. It tries to address the audience's intelligence by pointing out the pretension and hypocrisy of human behavior. High comedy also generally avoids derisive humor. Jokes about physical appearance would, for example, be avoided. One technique it employs to appeal to a sophisticated, verbal audience is use of the **epigram**, a brief and witty statement that memorably expresses some truth, large or small. Oscar Wilde's plays such as *The Importance of Being Earnest* (1895) and *Lady Windermere's Fan* (1892) sparkle with such brilliant epigrams as: "I can resist everything except temptation"; "Experience is the name everyone gives to their mistakes"; "There is only one thing in the world worse than being talked about, and that is not being talked about."

A type of high comedy is the **comedy of manners**, a witty satire set in elite or fashionable society. Popular since the seventeenth-century Restoration period, splendid comedies of manners continue to be written to this day. Bernard Shaw's *Pygmalion* (1913), which eventually became the musical *My Fair Lady*, contrasts life in the streets of London with that in aristocratic drawing rooms. Contemporary playwrights such as Tom Stoppard, Michael Frayn, Tina Howe, and John Guare have all created memorable comedies of manners.

Low Comedy

Low comedy explores the opposite extreme of humor. It places greater emphasis on physical action and visual gags, and its verbal jokes do not require much intellect to appreciate (as in Groucho Marx's pithy put-down to his brother Chico, "You have the brain of a five-year-old, and I bet he was glad to get rid of it!"). Low comedy does not avoid derisive humor; rather, it revels in making fun of whatever will get a good laugh. Drunkenness, stupidity, lust, senility, trickery, insult, and clumsiness are inexhaustible staples of this style of comedy. Although it is all too easy for critics to dismiss low comedy, like high comedy it serves a valuable purpose in satirizing human failings. Shakespeare indulged in coarse humor in some of his noblest plays. Low comedy is usually the preferred style of popular culture, and it has inspired many incisive satires on modern life—from the classic films of W. C. Fields and the Marx Brothers to the weekly TV antics of Matt Groening's *The Simpsons* or Zooey Deschanel's *New Girl*.

Low comedy includes several distinct types. One is the **burlesque**, a broadly humorous parody or travesty of another play or kind of play. (In the United States, *burlesque* is something else: a once-popular form of variety show featuring stripteases interspersed with bits of ribald low comedy.) Another valuable type of low comedy is the **farce**, a broadly humorous play whose action is usually fast-moving and improbable. The farce is a descendant of the Italian **commedia dell'arte** ("artistic comedy") of the late Renaissance, a kind of theater developed by comedians who traveled from town to town, regaling crowds at country fairs and in marketplaces. This popular art featured familiar stock characters in masks or whiteface: Harlequin, a clown; Columbine, his peppery sweetheart; and Pantaloon, a doddering duffer. Lately making a comeback, the more modern farces of French playwright Georges Feydeau (1862–1921) are practically all plot, with only the flattest of characters, mindless ninnies who play frantic games of hide-and-seek in order to deceive their spouses. **Slapstick comedy** (such as that of the Three Stooges) is a kind of farce. Featuring pratfalls, pie-throwing, fisticuffs, and other violent action, it takes its name from a circus clown's prop—a bat with two boards that loudly clap together when one clown swats another.

Romantic Comedy

Romantic comedy, another traditional sort of comedy, is subtler. Its main characters are generally lovers, and its plot unfolds their ultimately successful strivings to be united. Unlike satiric comedy, romantic comedy portrays its characters not with withering contempt but with kindly indulgence. It may take place in the everyday world, or perhaps in some never-never land, such as the forest of Arden in Shakespeare's *As You Like It*. Romantic comedy is also a popular staple of Hollywood, which depicts two people undergoing humorous mishaps on their way to falling in love. The characters often suffer humiliation and discomfort along the way, but these moments are funny rather than sad, and the characters are rewarded in the end by true love.

Here is an example of high comedy—a scene from the first act of Oscar Wilde's classic play, *The Importance of Being Earnest*. Following that is *Sure Thing*, a short contemporary comedy by David Ives, one of America's most ingenious playwrights, as well as a twist on the romantic comedy genre by Sharon E. Cooper.

Oscar Wilde

Scene from The Importance of Being Earnest: Lady Bracknell Interviews Her Daughter's Suitor   1895

Oscar Fingal O'Flahertie Wills Wilde (1854–1900) was born in Ireland to a mother who wrote revolutionary poetry and a philandering father who was an eye and ear surgeon. Wilde was a top student at Trinity College in Dublin and then Magdalen College in Oxford. After settling in London, Wilde married Constance Lloyd and promptly had two sons. Soon after, he entered his years of great productivity. He published two volumes of fairy tales and his sole novel, The Picture of Dorian Gray *(1891), which critics derided for its homosexual undertones. However, it was Wilde's plays that marked him as one of the great writers of England's late-Victorian era. He wrote a string of successes that started with* Lady Windermere's Fan *(1892) and culminated with his masterpiece,* The Importance of Being Earnest *(1895). His comedies focused on high society, the stratum in which Wilde was famously popular. It was said that he was London's "most sought-after dinner guest" and was known for his boundless wit and his many epigrams, such as "Work is the curse of the drinking classes." In 1895 Wilde endured a very public and humiliating legal battle over accusations of "gross indecency" with men, and he was sentenced to two years of hard labor, which devastated him as an artist. Upon his release, Wilde wandered Europe under the name Sebastian Melmoth. Three years later he died of meningitis in Paris, with barely a penny to his name.*

A 2008 production of *The Importance of Being Earnest*, by the Vaudeville Theatre of London.

CHARACTERS

Lady Bracknell, mother of Gwendolen Fairfax
Jack, the suitor

SCENE. *Morning-room in Algernon's flat in Half-Moon Street. The room is luxuriously and artistically furnished. The sound of a piano is heard in the adjoining room.*

[The following is an excerpt from Act I, Scene 1 of the play.]

Lady Bracknell (sitting down): You can take a seat, Mr. Worthing.

> (*Looks in her pocket for note-book and pencil.*)

Jack: Thank you, Lady Bracknell, I prefer standing.
Lady Bracknell (pencil and note-book in hand): I feel bound to tell you that you are not down on my list of eligible young men, although I have the same list as the dear Duchess of Bolton has. We work together, in fact. However, I am quite ready to enter your name, should your answers be what a really affectionate mother requires. Do you smoke?
Jack: Well, yes, I must admit I smoke.
Lady Bracknell: I am glad to hear it. A man should always have an occupation of some kind. There are far too many idle men in London as it is. How old are you?
Jack: Twenty-nine.
Lady Bracknell: A very good age to be married at. I have always been of opinion that a man who desires to get married should know either everything or nothing. Which do you know?

Jack (after some hesitation): I know nothing, Lady Bracknell.

Lady Bracknell: I am pleased to hear it. I do not approve of anything that tampers with natural ignorance. Ignorance is like a delicate exotic fruit; touch it and the bloom is gone. The whole theory of modern education is radically unsound. Fortunately in England, at any rate, education produces no effect whatsoever. If it did, it would prove a serious danger to the upper classes, and probably lead to acts of violence in Grosvenor Square. What is your income?

Jack: Between seven and eight thousand a year.

Lady Bracknell (makes a note in her book): In land, or in investments?

Jack: In investments, chiefly.

Lady Bracknell: That is satisfactory. What between the duties expected of one during one's lifetime, and the duties exacted from one after one's death, land has ceased to be either a profit or a pleasure. It gives one position, and prevents one from keeping it up. That's all that can be said about land.

Jack: I have a country house with some land, of course, attached to it, about fifteen hundred acres, I believe; but I don't depend on that for my real income. In fact, as far as I can make out, the poachers are the only people who make anything out of it.

Lady Bracknell: A country house! How many bedrooms? Well, that point can be cleared up afterwards. You have a town house, I hope? A girl with a simple, unspoiled nature, like Gwendolen, could hardly be expected to reside in the country.

Jack: Well, I own a house in Belgrave Square, but it is let by the year to Lady Bloxham. Of course, I can get it back whenever I like, at six months' notice.

Lady Bracknell: Lady Bloxham? I don't know her.

Jack: Oh, she goes about very little. She is a lady considerably advanced in years.

Lady Bracknell: Ah, nowadays that is no guarantee of respectability of character. What number in Belgrave Square?

Jack: 149.

Lady Bracknell (shaking her head): The unfashionable side. I thought there was something. However, that could easily be altered.

Jack: Do you mean the fashion, or the side?

Lady Bracknell (sternly): Both, if necessary, I presume. What are your politics?

Jack: Well, I am afraid I really have none. I am a Liberal Unionist.

Lady Bracknell: Oh, they count as Tories. They dine with us. Or come in the evening, at any rate. Now to minor matters. Are your parents living?

Jack: I have lost both my parents.

Lady Bracknell: To lose one parent, Mr. Worthing, may be regarded as a misfortune; to lose both looks like carelessness. Who was your father? He was evidently a man of some wealth. Was he born in what the Radical papers call the purple of commerce, or did he rise from the ranks of the aristocracy?

Jack: I am afraid I really don't know. The fact is, Lady Bracknell, I said I had lost my parents. It would be nearer the truth to say that my parents seem to have lost me . . . I don't actually know who I am by birth. I was . . . well, I was found.

Lady Bracknell: Found!

Jack: The late Mr. Thomas Cardew, an old gentleman of a very charitable and kindly disposition, found me, and gave me the name of Worthing, because he happened to have a first-class ticket for Worthing in his pocket at the time. Worthing is a place in Sussex. It is a seaside resort.

Lady Bracknell: Where did the charitable gentleman who had a first-class ticket for this seaside resort find you?

Jack (gravely): In a hand-bag.

Lady Bracknell: A hand-bag?

Jack (very seriously): Yes, Lady Bracknell. I was in a hand-bag—a somewhat large, black leather hand-bag, with handles to it—an ordinary hand-bag in fact.

Lady Bracknell: In what locality did this Mr. James, or Thomas, Cardew come across this ordinary hand-bag?

Jack: In the cloak-room at Victoria Station. It was given to him in mistake for his own.

Lady Bracknell: The cloak-room at Victoria Station?

Jack: Yes. The Brighton line.

Lady Bracknell: The line is immaterial. Mr. Worthing, I confess I feel somewhat bewildered by what you have just told me. To be born, or at any rate bred, in a hand-bag, whether it had handles or not, seems to me to display a contempt for the ordinary decencies of family life that reminds one of the worst excesses of the French Revolution. And I presume you know what that unfortunate movement led to? As for the particular locality in which the hand-bag was found, a cloak-room at a railway station might serve to conceal a social indiscretion—has probably, indeed, been used for that purpose before now—but it could hardly be regarded as an assured basis for a recognised position in good society.

Jack: May I ask you then what you would advise me to do? I need hardly say I would do anything in the world to ensure Gwendolen's happiness.

Lady Bracknell: I would strongly advise you, Mr. Worthing, to try and acquire some relations as soon as possible, and to make a definite effort to produce at any rate one parent, of either sex, before the season is quite over.

Jack: Well, I don't see how I could possibly manage to do that. I can produce the hand-bag at any moment. It is in my dressing-room at home. I really think that should satisfy you, Lady Bracknell.

Lady Bracknell: Me, sir! What has it to do with me? You can hardly imagine that I and Lord Bracknell would dream of allowing our only daughter—a girl brought up with the utmost care—to marry into a cloak-room, and form an alliance with a parcel? Good morning, Mr. Worthing!

(Lady Bracknell sweeps out in majestic indignation.)

Questions

1. How would you characterize Lady Bracknell? What are her chief concerns in interviewing her daughter's suitor? Find examples from the text to support your argument.
2. Describe Jack's tone. Does he seem amused with Lady Bracknell, nervous about the interview, or genuinely eager to please her?
3. Would you call this passage high comedy or low? Explain the reasons for your choice.

David Ives

Sure Thing   1988

David Ives (b. 1950) grew up on the South Side of Chicago. He attended Catholic schools before entering Northwestern University. Later Ives studied at the Yale Drama School—"a blissful time for me," he recalls, "in spite of the fact that there is slush on the ground in New Haven 238 days a year." Ives received his first professional production in Los Angeles at the age of twenty-one "at America's smallest, and possibly worst theater, in a storefront that had a pillar dead center in the middle of the stage." He continued writing for the theater while working as an editor at Foreign Affairs, and gradually achieved a reputation in theatrical circles for his wildly original and brilliantly written short comic plays. His public breakthrough came in 1993 with the New York staging of All in the Timing, which presented six short comedies. This production earned ecstatic reviews and a busy box office, and in the 1995–1996 season, All in the Timing was the most widely performed play in America (except for the works of Shakespeare). His second group of one-act comedies, Mere Mortals (1997), was produced with great success in New York City, followed by Lives of the Saints, a third group of one-act plays. Ives's full-length plays Don Juan in Chicago (1995), Ancient History (1996), The Red Address (1997), and Polish Joke (2000) are collected in the volume Polish Joke and Other Plays (2004). A talented adapter, Ives was chosen to rework a newly discovered play by Mark Twain, Is He Dead?, which had a successful run on Broadway in 2007. His most recent plays are Venus in Fur (2010), which was the most-produced play in the country in 2013–2014, and a number of translations and adaptations of French theater, including Pierre Corneille's comedy The Liar (2010) and Molière's The Misanthrope, which Ives titled The School For Lies (2011). He also writes short stories and screenplays for both motion pictures and television. Ives lives in New York City.

CHARACTERS

Betty
Bill

SCENE. *A café. Betty, a woman in her late twenties, is reading at a café table. An empty chair is opposite her. Bill, same age, enters.*

Bill: Excuse me. Is this chair taken?
Betty: Excuse me?
Bill: Is this taken?
Betty: Yes it is.
Bill: Oh. Sorry.
Betty: Sure thing.

 (*A bell rings softly.*)

Bill: Excuse me. Is this chair taken?
Betty: Excuse me?
Bill: Is this taken?
Betty: No, but I'm expecting somebody in a minute.
Bill: Oh. Thanks anyway.
Betty: Sure thing.

 (*A bell rings softly.*)

2003 Off-Broadway production of *Sure Thing* by Primary Stages.

Bill: Excuse me. Is this chair taken?

Betty: No, but I'm expecting somebody very shortly.

Bill: Would you mind if I sit here till he or she or it comes?

Betty (glances at her watch): They do seem to be pretty late. . . .

Bill: You never know who you might be turning down.

Betty: Sorry. Nice try, though.

Bill: Sure thing.

    (*Bell.*)

    Is this seat taken?

Betty: No it's not.

Bill: Would you mind if I sit here?

Betty: Yes I would.

Bill: Oh.

    (*Bell.*)

    Is this chair taken?

Betty: No it's not.

Bill: Would you mind if I sit here?

Betty: No. Go ahead.

Bill: Thanks. (*He sits. She continues reading.*) Everyplace else seems to be taken.

Betty: Mm-hm.

Bill: Great place.

Betty: Mm-hm.

Bill: What's the book?

Betty: I just wanted to read in quiet, if you don't mind.
Bill: No. Sure thing.

(*Bell.*)

Everyplace else seems to be taken.
Betty: Mm-hm.
Bill: Great place for reading.
Betty: Yes, I like it.
Bill: What's the book?
Betty: *The Sound and the Fury.*
Bill: Oh. Hemingway.

(*Bell.*)

What's the book?
Betty: *The Sound and the Fury.*
Bill: Oh. Faulkner.
Betty: Have you read it?
Bill: Not . . . actually. I've sure read *about* it, though. It's supposed to be great.
Betty: It is great.
Bill: I hear it's great. (*Small pause.*) Waiter?

(*Bell.*)

What's the book?
Betty: *The Sound and the Fury.*
Bill: Oh. Faulkner.
Betty: Have you read it?
Bill: I'm a Mets fan, myself.

(*Bell.*)

Betty: Have you read it?
Bill: Yeah, I read it in college.
Betty: Where was college?
Bill: I went to Oral Roberts University.

(*Bell.*)

Betty: Where was college?
Bill: I was lying. I never really went to college. I just like to party.

(*Bell.*)

Betty: Where was college?
Bill: Harvard.
Betty: Do you like Faulkner?
Bill: I love Faulkner. I spent a whole winter reading him once.
Betty: I've just started.
Bill: I was so excited after ten pages that I went out and bought everything else he
wrote. One of the greatest reading experiences of my life. I mean, all that incred-
ible psychological understanding. Page after page of gorgeous prose. His pro-
found grasp of the mystery of time and human existence. The smells of the earth
. . . What do you think?

Betty: I think it's pretty boring.

(*Bell.*)

Bill: What's the book?
Betty: The Sound and the Fury.
Bill: Oh! Faulkner!
Betty: Do you like Faulkner?
Bill: I love Faulkner.
Betty: He's incredible.
Bill: I spent a whole winter reading him once.
Betty: I was so excited after ten pages that I went out and bought everything else he wrote.
Bill: All that incredible psychological understanding.
Betty: And the prose is so gorgeous.
Bill: And the way he's grasped the mystery of time—
Betty: —and human existence. I can't believe I've waited this long to read him.
Bill: You never know. You might not have liked him before.
Betty: That's true.
Bill: You might not have been ready for him. You have to hit these things at the right moment or it's no good.
Betty: That's happened to me.
Bill: It's all in the timing. (*Small pause.*) My name's Bill, by the way.
Betty: I'm Betty.
Bill: Hi.
Betty: Hi. (*Small pause.*)
Bill: Yes I thought reading Faulkner was . . . a great experience.
Betty: Yes. (*Small pause.*)
Bill: The Sound and the Fury. . . . (*Another small pause.*)
Betty: Well. Onwards and upwards. (*She goes back to her book.*)
Bill: Waiter—?

(*Bell.*)

You have to hit these things at the right moment or it's no good.
Betty: That's happened to me.
Bill: It's all in the timing. My name's Bill, by the way.
Betty: I'm Betty.
Bill: Hi.
Betty: Hi.
Bill: Do you come in here a lot?
Betty: Actually I'm just in town for two days from Pakistan.
Bill: Oh. Pakistan.

(*Bell.*)

My name's Bill, by the way.
Betty: I'm Betty.
Bill: Hi.
Betty: Hi.
Bill: Do you come in here a lot?

Betty: Every once in a while. Do you?
Bill: Not so much anymore. Not as much as I used to. Before my nervous breakdown.

(*Bell.*)

Do you come in here a lot?
Betty: Why are you asking?
Bill: Just interested.
Betty: Are you really interested, or do you just want to pick me up?
Bill: No, I'm really interested.
Betty: Why would you be interested in whether I come in here a lot?
Bill: I'm just . . . getting acquainted.
Betty: Maybe you're only interested for the sake of making small talk long enough to ask me back to your place to listen to some music, or because you've just rented this great tape for your VCR, or because you've got some terrific unknown Django Reinhardt record, only all you really want to do is fuck—which you won't do very well—after which you'll go into the bathroom and pee very loudly, then pad into the kitchen and get yourself a beer from the refrigerator without asking me whether I'd like anything, and then you'll proceed to lie back down beside me and confess that you've got a girlfriend named Stephanie who's away at medical school in Belgium for a year, and that you've been involved with her—*off and on*—in what you'll call a very "intricate" relationship, for the past *seven YEARS*. None of which *interests* me, mister!
Bill: Okay.

(*Bell.*)

Do you come in here a lot?
Betty: Every other day, I think.
Bill: I come in here quite a lot and I don't remember seeing you.
Betty: I guess we must be on different schedules.
Bill: Missed connections.
Betty: Yes. Different time zones.
Bill: Amazing how you can live right next door to somebody in this town and never even know it.
Betty: I know.
Bill: City life.
Betty: It's crazy.
Bill: We probably pass each other in the street every day. Right in front of this place, probably.
Betty: Yep.
Bill (looks around): Well the waiters here sure seem to be in some different time zone. I can't seem to locate one anywhere. . . . Waiter! (*He looks back.*) So what do you—(*He sees that she's gone back to her book.*)
Betty: I beg pardon?
Bill: Nothing. Sorry.

(*Bell.*)

Betty: I guess we must be on different schedules.
Bill: Missed connections.

Betty: Yes. Different time zones.

Bill: Amazing how you can live right next door to somebody in this town and never even know it.

Betty: I know.

Bill: City life.

Betty: It's crazy.

Bill: You weren't waiting for somebody when I came in, were you?

Betty: Actually I was.

Bill: Oh. Boyfriend?

Betty: Sort of.

Bill: What's a sort-of boyfriend?

Betty: My husband.

Bill: Ah-ha.

(*Bell.*)

You weren't waiting for somebody when I came in, were you?

Betty: Actually I was.

Bill: Oh. Boyfriend?

Betty: Sort of.

Bill: What's a sort-of boyfriend?

Betty: We were meeting here to break up.

Bill: Mm-hm . . .

(*Bell.*)

What's a sort-of boyfriend?

Betty: My lover. Here she comes right now!

(*Bell.*)

Bill: You weren't waiting for somebody when I came in, were you?

Betty: No, just reading.

Bill: Sort of a sad occupation for a Friday night, isn't it? Reading here, all by yourself?

Betty: Do you think so?

Bill: Well sure. I mean, what's a good-looking woman like you doing out alone on a Friday night?

Betty: Trying to keep away from lines like that.

Bill: No, listen—

(*Bell.*)

You weren't waiting for somebody when I came in, were you?

Betty: No, just reading.

Bill: Sort of a sad occupation for a Friday night, isn't it? Reading here all by yourself?

Betty: I guess it is, in a way.

Bill: What's a good-looking woman like you doing out alone on a Friday night anyway? No offense, but . . .

Betty: I'm out alone on a Friday night for the first time in a very long time.

Bill: Oh.

Betty: You see, I just recently ended a relationship.

Bill: Oh.

Betty: Of rather long standing.

Bill: I'm sorry. (*Small pause.*) Well listen, since reading by yourself is such a sad occupation for a Friday night, would you like to go elsewhere?

Betty: No . . .

Bill: Do something else?

Betty: No thanks.

Bill: I was headed out to the movies in a while anyway.

Betty: I don't think so.

Bill: Big chance to let Faulkner catch his breath. All those long sentences get him pretty tired.

Betty: Thanks anyway.

Bill: Okay.

Betty: I appreciate the invitation.

Bill: Sure thing.

(*Bell.*)

You weren't waiting for somebody when I came in, were you?

Betty: No, just reading.

Bill: Sort of a sad occupation for a Friday night, isn't it? Reading here all by yourself?

Betty: I guess I was trying to think of it as existentially romantic. You know—cappuccino, great literature, rainy night . . .

Bill: That only works in Paris. We *could* hop the late plane to Paris. Get on a Concorde. Find a café . . .

Betty: I'm a little short on plane fare tonight.

Bill: Darn it, so am I.

Betty: To tell you the truth, I was headed to the movies after I finished this section. Would you like to come along? Since you can't locate a waiter?

Bill: That's a very nice offer, but . . .

Betty: Uh-huh. Girlfriend?

Bill: Two, actually. One of them's pregnant, and Stephanie—

(*Bell.*)

Betty: Girlfriend?

Bill: No, I don't have a girlfriend. Not if you mean the castrating bitch I dumped last night.

(*Bell.*)

Betty: Girlfriend?

Bill: Sort of. Sort of.

Betty: What's a sort-of girlfriend?

Bill: My mother.

(*Bell.*)

I just ended a relationship, actually.

Betty: Oh.

Bill: Of rather long standing.

Betty: I'm sorry to hear it.

Bill: This is my first night out alone in a long time. I feel a little bit at sea, to tell you the truth.

Betty: So you didn't stop to talk because you're a Moonie, or you have some weird political affiliation—?

Bill: Nope. Straight-down-the-ticket Republican.

(*Bell.*)

Straight-down-the-ticket Democrat.

(*Bell.*)

Can I tell you something about politics?

(*Bell.*)

I like to think of myself as a citizen of the universe.

(*Bell.*)

I'm unaffiliated.

Betty: That's a relief. So am I.

Bill: I vote my beliefs.

Betty: Labels are not important.

Bill: Labels are not important, exactly. Take me, for example. I mean, what does it matter if I had a two-point at—

(*Bell.*)

three-point at—

(*Bell.*)

four-point at college? Or if I did come from Pittsburgh—

(*Bell.*)

Cleveland—

(*Bell.*)

Westchester County?

Betty: Sure.

Bill: I believe that a man is what he is.

(*Bell.*)

A person is what he is.

(*Bell.*)

A person is . . . what they are.

Betty: I think so too.

Bill: So what if I admire Trotsky?

(*Bell.*)

So what if I once had a total-body liposuction?

(*Bell.*)

So what if I don't have a penis?

(*Bell.*)

So what if I spent a year in the Peace Corps? I was acting on my convictions.
Betty: Sure.
Bill: You just can't hang a sign on a person.
Betty: Absolutely. I'll bet you're a Scorpio.

(*Many bells ring.*)

Listen, I was headed to the movies after I finished this section. Would you like to come along?
Bill: That sounds like fun. What's playing?
Betty: A couple of the really early Woody Allen movies.
Bill: Oh.
Betty: You don't like Woody Allen?
Bill: Sure. I like Woody Allen.
Betty: But you're not crazy about Woody Allen.
Bill: Those early ones kind of get on my nerves.
Betty: Uh-huh.

(*Bell.*)

Bill: Y'know I was headed to the—
Betty (*simultaneously*): I was thinking about—
Bill: I'm sorry.
Betty: No, go ahead.
Bill: I was going to say that I was headed to the movies in a little while, and . . .
Betty: So was I.
Bill: The Woody Allen festival?
Betty: Just up the street.
Bill: Do you like the early ones?
Betty: I think anybody who doesn't ought to be run off the planet.
Bill: How many times have you seen Bananas?
Betty: Eight times.
Bill: Twelve. So are you still interested? (*Long pause.*)
Betty: Do you like Entenmann's crumb cake . . . ?
Bill: Last night I went out at two in the morning to get one. Did you have an Etch-a-Sketch as a child?
Betty: Yes! And do you like Brussels sprouts? (*Pause.*)
Bill: No, I think they're disgusting.
Betty: They *are* disgusting!
Bill: Do you still believe in marriage in spite of current sentiments against it?
Betty: Yes.
Bill: And children?
Betty: Three of them.
Bill: Two girls and a boy.
Betty: Harvard, Vassar, and Brown.
Bill: And will you love me?

Betty: Yes.
Bill: And cherish me forever?
Betty: Yes.
Bill: Do you still want to go to the movies?
Betty: Sure thing.
Bill and Betty (together): Waiter!

BLACKOUT

Questions

1. Ives originally planned to set *Sure Thing* at a bus stop. What does its current setting in a café suggest about the characters?
2. What happens on stage when the bell rings?
3. Who is the protagonist? What does the protagonist want?
4. Does the play have a dramatic question?
5. When does the climax of the play occur?
6. Is *Sure Thing* a romantic comedy or a farce? (See earlier in this chapter for a discussion of these types of comedy.)
7. "*Sure Thing* was not a funny play because it isn't realistic. Conversations just don't happen this way." Discuss that opinion. Do you agree or disagree?

Sharon E. Cooper

Mistaken Identity   2004

The plays of Sharon E. Cooper (b. 1975) have been produced in the United States and abroad. Her work has won awards and been included in several annual editions of The Best Ten-Minute Plays. *Cooper's production credits include the plays* Painting Seventeen, Occupied, Lifeline, The Cooking King, *and* The Match. *Besides writing for theater and film, she works as a teacher and yoga instructor in New York City.* Mistaken Identity *premiered at the Open Space Arts Center in Reistertown, Maryland, in July 2004.*

Sharon E. Cooper

CHARACTERS

Kali Patel, 29. Single lesbian Hindu of Indian heritage; social worker who works as much as possible; lives in Leicester, England.

Steve Dodd, 32. Single straight guy, desperate to marry, raised Baptist but attends church only on Christmas and Easter; studying abroad for his final year.

SETTING. *The Castle, a pub in Kirby Muxlowe in Leicester, England.*

TIME. *The present.*

Lights up on Steve and Kali in a busy pub on their first date. They are in the middle of dinner.

Steve: You must get tired of fish and chips all the time. Why do y'all call them "chips"? When they're french fries, I mean. And you ever notice when people swear, they say, "Excuse my French." Not me. Nope. I have nothing against the French.

Kali: Right, well, I'm not French, Steve, now am I?

Steve: I just didn't want you to think I was prejudiced against the French or *anyone else.* . . . They're like your neighbors, the French. And your neighbors are like my neighbors. And like a good neighbor, State Farm is there. Have you heard that commercial?

Kali: What? No. Steve—

Steve: It's for insurance. Y'all must not play it here. (*Pause.*) So I know that you all do the "arranged marriage thing." Rashid and I had a long talk about it. Of course, Rashid and I wanted you to approve, too, Kali.

Kali: How twenty-first century of you and my brother. Steve . . .

Kali: I'm gay.   / *Steve:* Will you marry me?

Kali: Come again?   / *Steve:* What?

Kali: How could you ask me to . . .   / *Steve:* Well, I can't believe this.

Kali: Bloody hell, stop talking while I'm talking . . .   / *Steve:* This is very strange.

Kali: So—what?

Steve: This new information is, well, new, and changes things, I guess.

Kali: You guess? What the hell is wrong with you? I'm sorry, Steve, you just happened to show up at the end of a very long line of a lot of very bad dates. You know, movies where the bloke negotiates holding your hand while you're just trying to eat popcorn; running across De Montfort University in the pouring rain; dropping a bowling ball on the bloke's pizza.

Steve: You had me until the bowling ball. Kali, this doesn't make sense. I invite you out on a lovely date. We eat fish and chips—when I would rather be eating a burger or lasagna—

Kali: Steve, I'm sorry.

Steve: I figured we would have a nice long traditional wedding with the colorful tents. All of my family would be there. We're more of the Christmas/Easter Christians, so we'd do your religion and I would wear—

Kali (overlapping): You don't know anything about my people. What are you—

Steve (overlapping): Ooohhh, yes, I do. I saw *Monsoon Wedding*. And the director's cut! And I saw *Bend It Like Beckham* like three times. Three times. Unbelievable!

Kali: Yes, this makes loads of sense at the end of the day. I am a lesbian who has to date every Hindu bloke in England until her brother gets so desperate that he sets her up with a cowboy—

Steve: I take offense to that.

Kali (overlapping): But I should feel sorry for *you* because *you* watched *two*, count them, *two* movies about Indian people in your entire life and ordered fish when there are hamburgers on the menu! Forgive *me* for being so insensitive.

Steve: I ordered fish because I wanted you to like me. And I'm sure I've seen other Asian movies. Like all those fighting movies. You know, the ones where women are jumping through the air—

Kali: Aaahhh! Do you see how all of this is a moot point now?

Steve: I'm confused. Let's review.

Kali: Please, no, bloody hell, let's not review. Let's get the waiter. Haven't you had enough?

(*She gets up. He follows.*)

Steve (overlapping): Why is your brother setting up his *lesbian* sister—

Kali (overlapping): Will you please keep your voice down?

Steve (overlapping): —up on dates for marriage and tricking well-meaning men— specifically me—into proposing to her? I'm here to finish my business degree, but I wasn't born yesterday. So I took a few years off and changed careers a few times, was a fireman—

Kali (overlapping): What does that have to do with anything?

Steve: And I'm thirty-two years old, but that doesn't mean—

Kali: Mate, are you going to keep on and on?

Steve: Why did your brother put me through this? This isn't one of those new reality shows: "Big Brothers Set Up Their Lesbian Sisters." Is there a camera under the table? (*He looks.*) Let's talk about this. (*He sits back down.*) I'm a good listener. Go ahead. (*Pause.*) I'm listening. (*Pause.*) You have to say something if you want this to continue as what we call in America a conversation.

Kali: Are you done?

Steve: Go ahead.

(*She sits.*)

Kali: I guess I was hoping you wouldn't tell Rashid.

Steve: He doesn't know?

Kali: You are finishing your bachelor's degree, is that right?

Steve: If you're so "bloody" smart, I'm wondering why you would tell me, a man that is friends with your brother and sits next to him twice a week in eight A.M. classes—why would you tell *me* you're a lesbian and *not* your brother?

Kali: Maybe for the same reason you would ask a woman you've never met before to marry you.

Steve: Your brother made it sound like it would be easy. I've been looking for that.

Kali (overlapping): Look, you seem very nice, you do.

Steve: I am very nice.

Kali: And at the end of the day, I hope you find someone you like.

Steve: I like how you say "at the end of the day" and I like how you say "bloke" and "mate." It's so endearing. And you're beautiful and small and your hair falls on your back so.

Kali: Steve, being a lesbian is not negotiable. And don't start with how sexy it would be to be with me or to watch me and another woman—

Steve (overlapping): Kali, I didn't say any of that.

Kali: You didn't have to. Up until a few minutes ago, you thought I was a quiet, sub- servient Asian toy for sale from her brother. Steve, go get a doll. She can travel with you to America whenever you want. In the meantime, I'll continue to be a loud, abrasive (*Whispering.*) lesbian while my brother sets me up with every bloke on the street—and they don't even have to be Hindu anymore! Do you have any idea what that's like? (*Pause.*) How would you know?

Steve: You're right. I wouldn't.

Kali: Steve, why did you want to be with me? I mean, before.

Steve: I figured that we would have visited my family in the winter when it's so cold here. I would have been willing to stay here when I'm done with school and we would get a nice little place by the—

Kali: Steve, we hadn't even shared dessert yet.

Steve: Don't blame me for all of this. Five minutes ago, we were on a date.

Kali: We're just two people in a pub.

Steve: Kali, do you remember the last time someone—man woman, I don't care—had their hand down the small of your back or leaned into you like it didn't matter where you ended and they began?

Kali: Yes, I do remember that. And that was strangely poetic.

Steve: You don't have to sound so surprised. Anyway, I remember that feeling. Three years ago, at a Fourth of July celebration—you know, that's the holiday—

Kali: Yes, Steve, I know the holiday.

Steve: She was the only woman I ever really loved. I knew it was ending. Could taste it. I just held her as the fireworks went off and the dust got in our skin. Figured I would hold on, hoping that would keep me for a while. You know how they say babies will die if they're left alone too long. Always wondered if it's true for bigger people, too. Like how long would we last? . . . She left with her Pilates mat and Snoopy slippers a few days later. I bet it hasn't been three years for you.

Kali: No, it hasn't. But you wouldn't want to hear about that.

Steve: Why not?

Kali: Come on, Steve, I'm not here for your fantasies—

Steve: This thing where you assume you know what I'm thinking—it's gettin' old.

Kali: I'm . . . sorry. I do have a woman in my life, Michele—She's a teacher for people that are deaf. We've been together for seven months. The longest we were away from each other was this one time for three weeks. She was at a retreat where they weren't allowed to talk—you know, total immersion. So she would call and I would say, "Is it beautiful there, love?" and she would hit a couple of buttons. Sometimes she would leave me messages: "beep, beep, beep beep beep beep." It didn't matter that she didn't say anything . . . But I can't take her home for Diwali.

Steve: What's that?

Kali: It's a festival of lights where—

Steve: You mean like Hanukkah.

Kali: No, like Diwali. It's a New Year's celebration where we remember ancestors, family, and friends. And reflect back and look to the future.

Steve: It sounds nice. You know, my mother has been asking me for grandchildren since I turned twenty-seven. Every year at Christmas, it's the same: "I can't wait to hang another stocking for my grandchildren, if I ever get to have them."

Kali: Now, imagine that same conversation, well, not about Christmas, and what if you could never give that to them—could never bring someone home for any holiday for the rest of your life?

Steve: Then why don't you just tell them the truth?

Kali: I can't say, Mum, Daddy, Rashid, I've chosen women over men—it's not a hamburger over fish. You just don't know how they'll react. I'd run the risk of not being allowed to see my nieces. I'm so exhausted from hiding, I can barely breathe.

Steve: So stop hiding.

Kali: Have you been listening to what I've been saying?

Steve: Have you?

Kali: Are you going to tell my brother?

Steve: Do you want me to?

Kali: I don't know.

Steve: I've never thought about that thing that you said.

Kali: Which thing would that be?

Steve: The one where maybe you can't see your nieces 'cause you're gay. That must suck.

Kali: Yes, well, thanks for trying to make me feel better.

Steve: Listen, you get to decide what you tell your family and when. As far as I'm concerned, I'll tell Rashid tomorrow that we're getting married. Or I can tell him you're a lesbian, and if he doesn't let you be with his kids anymore, I'll punch him in the face. That was me kidding.

Kali: You're funny. (*Pause.*) Maybe I told you because somewhere deep down, I do want him to know. But I don't know if I can take the risk.

Steve: You don't have to rush.

Kali: I just wish it could be more simple. Like, why can't what I want be part of the whole picket-fence thing? That's pretty ridiculous, huh?

Steve: We're all looking for that. My grandparents met before World War II, dated for seven days in a row, and my grandfather asked my grandmother to go with him to Louisiana, where he'd be stationed. She said, "Is that a proposal?" And he said, "Of course it is." And they've been together ever since. And I just want that, too. Huh—asking you to marry me on a first date! You must think I'm pretty desperate, huh?

Kali: Not any more than the rest of us . . . Oh, hell, do you want to have some dessert?

Steve: Oh, hell, sure. You know, we're going to share dessert.

Kali: Hey, mate, no one said anything about sharing.

Steve: I would go home with you for Diwali. I mean, as friends. If you ever wanted one around. You're a nice girl, Kali. I mean woman, mate, bloke. I mean—

Kali: Sssshhhh. Let's just get some dessert.

(*Lights fade as they motion for the waiter. Blackout.*)

Questions

1. What is the central tension between the two characters? What does each character want?
2. In what ways does their conversation shift in focus and subject as the play proceeds?
3. Would you consider *Mistaken Identity* to be a romantic comedy, according to the definition at the end of this chapter? If so, what is the happy ending for Steve and Kali?

◼ WRITING *effectively*

David Ives on Writing

On the One-Act Play   2006

Moss Hart said that you never really learn how to write a play, you only learn how to write *this* play. That is as true of one-acts as of two-, three-, four- or five-acts. To my mind the challenge of the one-act may be even greater than the challenge of larger and necessarily messier plays, in the same way that the sonnet with only fourteen lines remains the ever-attempted Everest of poetry. For what the one-act demands is a kind of concentrated perfection. "A play," said Lorca, "is a poem standing up," and I can't think of a better description of a one-act.

David Ives

The long play, like the symphony, luxuriates in development and recapitulation. The one-act has no time for them. Develop the story and you start to look overly melodramatic, forcing too much event into too little time. Develop the characters and you look like you're not doing them justice. (In fact you start to look like you want to write a larger play.) Develop your theme and you start to sound like one of those guys at a party trying to explain all of particle theory between two grabs at the canapés. Recapitulate and you're dead.

A one-act masterpiece like Pinter's *The Dumb Waiter* would be tedious and attenuated if stretched over two hours. It says all it needs to say—and that's volumes—in a quarter of that, then stops. *Death of a Salesman* as a one-act would look either like a character study or a short story transcribed for the stage. A full-length is a four-ton, cast-steel, Richard Serra ellipse that you can walk around in; a one-act, a piece of string draped by Richard Tuttle on a gallery wall. Not a ride on the *Titanic*, but a single suitcase left floating in the middle of a theatrical sea.

So what does a one-act like, if not development and recapitulation?

Compression, obviously. Think of a one-act and chances are good you're thinking of something short and sharp, a punch in the nose, the rug pulled out from under you, over before you know it—as if an actor had turned a camera on the audience and flashed a picture. A good one-act should leave you blinking. Think of a one-act and chances are also good you're picturing something like a small, bare, black-box stage with just a park bench, or a table and chair, or a bus-stop sign. One or two people. Minimal props. There is something necessarily stripped-down about the mere staging of one-acts, and this goes to the heart of the nature of one-acts themselves. They are *elemental*.

From *The Dramatist*

THINKING ABOUT COMEDY

If you have ever tried to explain a punch line to an uncomprehending friend, you know how hard it can be to convey the essence of humor. Too much explanation makes any joke fizzle out fast. We don't often stop to analyze why a joke strikes us as funny. It simply makes us laugh. For this reason, writing about comedy can be challenging.

- **What makes the play amusing?** Is there a central gag or situation (such as mistaken identity) that creates comic potential in every scene? Note that the central gag is often visual (such as a disguise), something that the audience constantly sees but is not equally apparent in the written text.
- **What is the flavor of the humor?** Is the comedy high or low? Is it verbal or visual, or both? Is there mostly slapstick action or clever wordplay? Is it a romantic comedy in which love plays a central role? A play often mixes types of comedy, but usually one style predominates. A farce may have a few moments of intellectual wit, but it will mostly keep silly jokes and pratfalls coming fast and furiously.
- **How do the personalities of the main characters intensify the humor?** Even when comedy arises out of a situation, character is likely to play an important role. In A *Midsummer Night's Dream* (Chapter 38), for example, the fairy queen Titania is bewitched into falling in love with the weaver Bottom, whose head has been transformed into that of an ass. The situation is funny in its own right, but the humor is intensified by the personalities involved, the proud fairy queen pursuing the lowly and foolish tradesman. Humor often may be found in the unexpected, a twist on the normal and the logical.

CHECKLIST: Writing About Comedy

- ☐ What kind of comedy is the play? Romantic? Slapstick? Satire? How can you tell?
- ☐ Which style of comedy prevails? Is there more emphasis on high comedy or low? More emphasis on verbal humor or physical comedy?
- ☐ Focus on a key comic moment. Does the comedy grow out of situation? Character? A mix of both?
- ☐ How does the play end? In a wedding or romance? A reconciliation? Mutual understanding?

TOPICS FOR WRITING ABOUT TRAGEDY

1. According to Oscar Wilde, "In this world there are only two tragedies: one is not getting what one wants, and the other is getting it." Write an essay in which you discuss this statement in its application to the scene from *Doctor Faustus*.

2. Imagine that Faustus, after his death, has sought forgiveness and salvation with the claim, "The Devil tricked me. I didn't know what I was doing." Write a "judicial opinion" setting forth the grounds for the denial of his plea.

TOPICS FOR WRITING ABOUT COMEDY

1. What or who is being satirized in *Sure Thing*? How true or incisive do you find this satire? Why?
2. "*Sure Thing* isn't good drama because it doesn't have a plot or conflict." Write a two-page response to that complaint.
3. Write about a recent romantic comedy film. How does its plot fulfill the notion of comedy? Or if it was meant to be funny but fell short, what was lacking?
4. Write your own version of Oscar Wilde's scene, set in the present day, in which a young man is interviewed by his girlfriend's mother. Use Wilde's scene for your model, drawing forth the personalities of each character through their words and reactions.
5. Reread either the scene from *The Importance of Being Earnest*, *Sure Thing*, or *Mistaken Identity*, and write a brief analysis of what makes the selection amusing or humorous. Provide details to back up your argument. Consult the "Comedy" section of this chapter for more information on specific types of humor.

▶ TERMS FOR *review*

Dramatic Genres

Tragedy ▶ A play that portrays a serious conflict between human beings and some superior, overwhelming force. It ends sorrowfully and disastrously, an outcome that seems inevitable.

Comedy ▶ A literary work aimed at amusing an audience. In traditional comedy, the protagonist often faces obstacles and complications that threaten disaster but are overturned at the last moment to produce a happy ending.

Kinds of Comedy

High comedy ▶ A comic genre evoking thoughtful laughter from an audience in response to the play's depiction of the folly, pretense, and hypocrisy of human behavior.

Satiric comedy ▶ A genre using derisive humor to ridicule human weakness and folly or attack political injustices and incompetence. Satiric comedy often focuses on ridiculing overly serious characters who resist the festive mood of comedy.

Comedy of manners ▶ A realistic form of high comic drama. It deals with the social relations and romantic intrigues of sophisticated upper-class men and women, whose verbal fencing and witty repartee produce the principal comic effects.

Romantic comedy ▶ A form of comic drama in which the plot focuses on one or more pairs of young lovers who overcome difficulties to achieve a happy ending (usually marriage).

Low comedy ▶ A comic style arousing laughter through jokes, slapstick antics, sight gags, boisterous clowning, and vulgar humor.

Burlesque ▶ A broadly humorous parody or travesty of another play or kind of play.

Farce ▶ A broadly humorous play whose action is usually fast-moving and improbable.

Slapstick comedy ▶ A kind of farce featuring pratfalls, pie-throwing, fisticuffs, and other violent action. It takes its name from a circus clown's prop—a bat with two boards that loudly clap together when one clown swats another.

37 CRITICAL CASEBOOK
Sophocles

What You Will Learn in This Chapter

- To understand the plays of Sophocles in their biographical, critical, and cultural context

Oedipus with chorus in Tyrone Guthrie's 1957 film
Oedipus Rex.

None but a poet can write a tragedy.

—EDITH HAMILTON

THE THEATER OF SOPHOCLES

For the citizens of Athens in the fifth century B.C., theater was both a religious and a civic occasion. Plays were presented only twice a year at religious festivals, both associated with Dionysus, the god of wine and crops. In January there was the Lenaea, the festival of the winepress, when plays, especially comedies, were performed. But the major theatrical event of the year came in March at the Great Dionysia, a city-wide celebration that included sacrifices, prize ceremonies, and spectacular processions as well as three days of drama.

Each day at dawn a different author presented a trilogy of tragic plays—three interrelated dramas that portrayed an important mythic or legendary event. Each intense tragic trilogy was followed by a **satyr play**, an obscene parody of a mythic story, performed with the chorus dressed as satyrs, unruly mythic attendants of Dionysus who were half goat or horse and half human.

The Greeks loved competition and believed it fostered excellence. Even theater was a competitive event—not unlike the Olympic games. A panel of five judges voted each year at the Great Dionysia for the best dramatic presentation, and a substantial cash prize was given to the winning poet-playwright (all plays were written in verse). Any aspiring writer who has ever lost a literary contest may be comforted to learn that Sophocles, who triumphed in the competition twenty-four times, seems not to have won the annual prize for *Oedipus the King*. Although this play ultimately proved to be the most celebrated Greek tragedy ever written, it lost the award to a revival of a popular trilogy by Aeschylus, who had recently died.

Staging

Seated in the open air in a hillside amphitheater, as many as 17,000 spectators could watch a performance that must have somewhat resembled an opera or musical. The audience was arranged in rows, with the Athenian governing council and young military cadets seated in the middle sections. Priests, priestesses, and foreign dignitaries were given special places of honor in the front rows. The performance space they watched was divided into two parts—the **orchestra**, a level circular "dancing space" (at the base of the amphitheater), and a slightly raised stage built in front of the *skene* or stage house, originally a canvas or wooden hut for costume changes.

The actors spoke and performed primarily on the stage, and the chorus sang and danced in the orchestra. The *skene* served as a general set or backdrop—the exterior of a palace, a temple, a cave, or a military tent, depending on the action of the play. The *skene* had a large door at its center that served as the major entrance for principal characters. When opened wide, the door could be used to frame a striking tableau, as when the body of Eurydice is displayed at the end of Sophocles's play *Antigone*. The *skene* supported a hook and pulley by which actors who played gods could be lowered or lifted—hence the Latin phrase **deus ex machina** ("god out of the machine") for any means of bringing a play quickly to a resolution.

What did the actors look like? They wore **masks** (*personae*, the source of our word *person*, "a thing through which sound comes"): some of these masks had exaggerated mouthpieces, possibly designed to project speech across the open air. Certainly, the masks, each of which covered an actor's entire head, helped spectators far away recognize the chief characters. The masks often represented certain conventional types of characters: the old king, the young soldier, the shepherd, the beautiful girl (women's

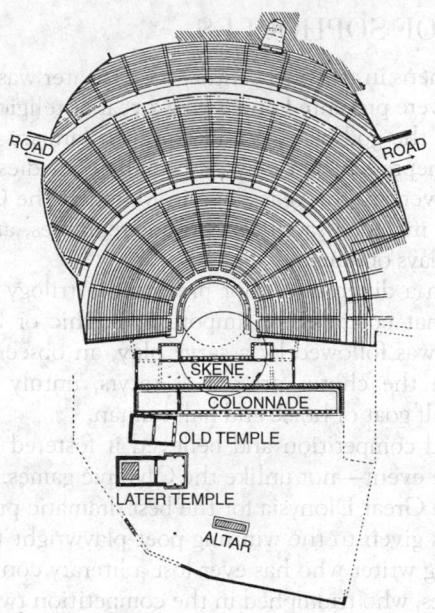

The Theater of Dionysus in Athens during the time of Sophocles; a modern drawing based on scholarly guesswork.
From R. C. Flickinger, *The Greek Theater and Its Drama* (1918).

parts were played by male actors). Perhaps in order to gain in both increased dignity and visibility, actors in the Greek theater eventually came to wear **cothurni**, high, thick-soled elevator shoes that made them appear taller than ordinary men. All this equipment must have given the actors a slightly inhuman yet very imposing appearance, but we may infer that the spectators accepted such conventions as easily as opera lovers accept an opera's special artifice or today's football fans hardly notice the elaborate helmets, shoulderpads, gloves, and often brightly colored uniforms worn by their favorite teams.

Dramatic Structure

By Sophocles's time, the tragedy had a conventional structure understood by most of the citizens sitting in the audience. No more than three actors were allowed on stage at any one time, along with a chorus of fifteen (the number was fixed by Sophocles himself). The actors' spoken monologue and dialogue alternated with the chorus's singing and dancing. Each tragedy began with a **prologue**, a preparatory scene. In *Oedipus the King*, for example, the play begins with Oedipus asking the suppliants why they have come and the priest telling him about the plague ravaging Thebes. Next came the *párodos*, the song for the entrance of the chorus. Then the action was enacted in **episodes**, like the acts or scenes in modern plays; the episodes were separated by danced choral songs or **odes**. Finally, there was a closing *éxodos*, the last scene, in which the characters and chorus concluded the action and departed.

A modern reconstruction of a classical Athenian theater. Note that the chorus performs in the circular orchestra while the actors stand on the raised stage behind.

THE CIVIC ROLE OF GREEK DRAMA

Athenian drama was supported and financed by the state. Administration of the Great Dionysia fell to the head civil magistrate. He annually appointed three wealthy citizens to serve as *choregoi*, or producers, for the competing plays. Each producer had to equip the chorus and rent the rehearsal space in which the poet-playwright would prepare the new work for the festival. The state covered the expenses of the theater, actors, and prizes (which went to author, actors, and *choregos* alike). Theater tickets were distributed free to citizens, which meant that every registered Athenian, even the poorest, could participate. The playwrights therefore addressed themselves to every element of the Athenian democracy. Only the size of the amphitheater limited the attendance. Holding between 14,000 and 17,000 spectators, it could accommodate slightly less than half of Athens's 40,000 citizens.

Greek theater was directed at the moral and political education of the community. The poet's role was the improvement of the *polis* or city-state (made up of a town and its surrounding countryside). Greek city-states traditionally sponsored public contests between *rhapsodes* (professional poetry performers) reciting stories from Homer's epics, the *Iliad* and *Odyssey*. As Greek society developed and urbanized, however, the competitive and individualized heroism of the Homeric epics had to be tempered with the values of cooperation and compromise necessary to a democracy. Civic theater provided the ideal medium to address these cultural needs.

Tragedy and Empathy

As a public art form, tragedy was not simply a stage for political propaganda to promote the status quo. Nor was it exclusively a celebration of idealized heroes nobly enduring the blows of harsh circumstance and misfortune. Tragedy often enabled its audience to reflect on personal values that might be in conflict with civic ideals, on the claims of minorities that it neglected or excluded from public life, or on its own irrational prejudices toward the foreign or the unknown. Frequently a play challenged its audience to feel sympathy for a vanquished enemy (as in Euripides's *Trojan Women*, the greatest antiwar play of the period, which dramatizes the horrible fate of captured women). Some plays explored the problems facing members of the politically powerless groups that made up nearly three-fourths of the Athenian population—women, children, resident aliens, and slaves. A largely male audience also frequently watched male performers enact stories of the power and anger of women, such as Euripides's *Medea*, which made their tragic violence understandable (if not entirely pardonable) to an audience not particularly disposed to treat them sympathetically. Other plays such as Sophocles's *Oedipus the King* or Euripides's *Herakles* depicted powerful men undone by misfortune, their own bad judgment, or hubris, and thrown into defeat and exile.

Such tragic stories required performers and audience members to put themselves in the places of persons quite unlike themselves, in situations that might engulf any unlucky citizen—war, political upheaval, betrayal, domestic crisis. The release of the powerful emotions of pity and fear through a carefully crafted plot in the orderly context of highly conventionalized performance accounts for the paradox of tragic drama—how a viewer takes aesthetic pleasure in witnessing the sufferings of others.

ARISTOTLE'S CONCEPT OF TRAGEDY

> *Tragedy is an imitation of an action of high importance, complete and of some amplitude; in language enhanced by distinct and varying beauties; acted not narrated; by means of pity and fear effecting its purgation of these emotions.*

—ARISTOTLE, *POETICS*, CHAPTER VI

Aristotle's famous definition of tragedy, constructed in the fourth century B.C., is the testimony of one who probably saw many classical tragedies performed. In making his observations, Aristotle does not seem to be laying down laws for what a tragedy ought to be. More likely, he is drawing—from tragedies he has seen or read—a general description of them.

Tragic Hero

Aristotle observes that the protagonist, the hero or chief character of a tragedy, is a person of "high estate," apparently a king or queen or other member of a royal family. In thus being as keenly interested as are contemporary dramatists in the private lives of the powerful, Greek dramatists need not be accused of snobbery. It is the nature of tragedy that the protagonist must fall from power and from happiness; his high estate gives him a place of dignity to fall from and perhaps makes his fall seem all the more a calamity in that it involves an entire nation or people. Nor is the protagonist extraordinary merely by his position in society. Oedipus is not only a king but also a noble soul who suffers profoundly and who employs splendid eloquence to express his suffering.

The tragic hero, however, is not a superman; he is fallible. The hero's downfall is the result, as Aristotle said, of his **hamartia**: his error or transgression or (as some translators would have it) his flaw or weakness of character. The notion that a tragic hero has such a **tragic flaw** has often been attributed to Aristotle, but it is by no means clear that Aristotle meant just that. According to this interpretation, every tragic hero has some fatal weakness, some moral Achilles's heel, that brings him to a bad end. In some classical tragedies, his transgression is a weakness the Greeks called **hubris**—extreme pride, leading to overconfidence.

Whatever Aristotle had in mind, however, many later critics find value in the idea of the tragic flaw. In this view, the downfall of a hero follows from his very nature. Whatever view we take—whether we find the hero's sufferings due to a flaw of character or to an error of judgment—we will probably find that his downfall results from acts for which he himself is responsible. In a Greek tragedy, the hero is a character amply capable of making choices—capable, too, of accepting the consequences.

Katharsis

It may be useful to take another look at Aristotle's definition of *tragedy*, with which we began. By **purgation** (or **katharsis**), did the ancient theorist mean that after witnessing a tragedy we feel relief, having released our pent-up emotions? Or did he mean that our feelings are purified, refined into something more ennobling? Scholars continue to argue. Whatever his exact meaning, clearly Aristotle implies that after witnessing a tragedy we feel better, not worse—not depressed, but somehow elated. We take a kind of pleasure in the spectacle of a noble man being brought down, but surely this pleasure is a legitimate one. Part of that catharsis may also be based in our feeling of the "rightness" or accuracy of what we have just witnessed. The terrible but undeniable truth of the tragic vision of life is that blind overreaching and the destruction of hopes and dreams are very much a part of what really happens in the world.

Recognition and Reversal

Aristotle, in describing the workings of this inexorable force in *Oedipus the King*, uses terms that later critics have found valuable. One is **recognition**, or discovery (*anagnorisis*): the revelation of some fact not known before or some person's true identity. Oedipus makes such a discovery: he recognizes that he himself was the child whom his mother had given over to be destroyed. Such a recognition also occurs in Shakespeare's *Macbeth* when Macduff reveals himself to have been "from his mother's womb / Untimely ripped," thus disclosing a double meaning in the witches' prophecy that Macbeth could be harmed by "none of woman born," and sweeping aside Macbeth's last shred of belief that he is infallible. Modern critics have taken the term to mean also the terrible enlightenment that accompanies such a recognition with the protagonist's consequent awareness of his role in his own undoing. "To see things plain—that is *anagnorisis*," Clifford Leech observes, "It is what tragedy ultimately is about: the realization of the unthinkable."

Having made his discovery, Oedipus suffers a reversal in his fortunes; he goes off into exile, blinded and dethroned. Such a fall from happiness seems intrinsic to tragedy, but we should know that Aristotle has a more particular meaning for his term **reversal** (*peripeteia*, anglicized as **peripety**). He means an action that turns out to have the opposite effect from the one its doer had intended. One of his illustrations of such an ironic reversal is from *Oedipus the King*. The first messenger intends to cheer Oedipus with the partially good news that, contrary to the prophecy that Oedipus would kill his father, his father has died of old age. The reversal is in the fact that, when the messenger further reveals that old Polybus was Oedipus's father only by adoption, the king, instead of having his fears allayed, is stirred to new dread.

We are not altogether sorry, perhaps, to see an arrogant man such as Oedipus humbled, and yet it is difficult not to feel that the punishment of Oedipus is greater than he deserves. Possibly this feeling is what Aristotle meant in his observation that a tragedy arouses our pity and our fear—our compassion for Oedipus and our terror as we sense the remorselessness of a universe in which a man is doomed. Notice, however, that at the end of the play Oedipus does not curse God and die. Although such a complex play is open to many interpretations, it is probably safe to say that the play is not a bitter complaint against the universe. At last, Oedipus accepts the divine will, prays for blessings upon his children, and prepares to endure his exile—fallen from high estate but uplifted, through his newfound humility and piety, in moral dignity.

SOPHOCLES

Sophocles (496?–406 B.C.) tragic dramatist, priest, for a time one of ten Athenian generals, was one of the three great ancient Greek writers of tragedy whose work has survived. (The other two were his contemporaries: Aeschylus, his senior, and Euripides, his junior.) Sophocles won his first victory in the Athenian spring drama competition in 468 B.C., when a tragedy he had written defeated one by Aeschylus. He went on to win many prizes, writing more than 120 plays, of which only seven have survived in their entirety—Ajax, Antigone, Oedipus the King, Electra, Philoctetes, The Trachinian Women, and Oedipus at Colonus. (Of the lost plays, about a thousand fragments remain.) In his long life, Sophocles saw Greece rise to supremacy over the Persian Empire. He enjoyed the favor of the statesman Pericles, who, making peace with enemy Sparta, ruled Athens during a Golden Age (461–429 B.C.), during which the

Sophocles

Parthenon was built and music, art, drama, and philosophy flourished. The playwright lived on to see his native city-state in decline, its strength drained by the disastrous Peloponnesian War. His last play, Oedipus at Colonus, *set twenty years after the events of* Oedipus the King, *shows the former king in old age, ragged and blind, cast into exile by his sons, but still accompanied by his faithful daughter Antigone. It was written when Sophocles was nearly ninety.* Oedipus the King *is believed to have been first produced in 425 B.C., five years after the plague had broken out in Athens.*

THE ORIGINS OF *OEDIPUS THE KING*

On a Great Dionysia feast day after Athens had survived a devastating plague, the audience turned out to watch a tragedy by Sophocles, set in the city of Thebes at the moment of another terrible plague. This timely play was *Oedipus*, later given the name (in Greek) *Oedipus Tyrannos* to distinguish it from Sophocles's last Oedipus play, *Oedipus at Colonus.*

A folktale figure, Oedipus gets his name through a complex pun. *Oida* means "to know" (from the root *vid-*, "see"), pointing to the tale's contrasting themes of sight and blindness, wisdom and ignorance. *Oedipus* also means "swollen foot" or "clubfoot," pointing to the injury sustained in the title character's infancy, when his ankles were pinioned together like a goat's. Oedipus is the man who comes to knowledge of his true parentage through the evidence of his feet and his old injury. The term *tyrannos*, in the context of the play, simply means a man who comes to rule through his own intelligence and merit, though not related to the ruling family. The traditional Greek title might be translated, therefore, as *Clubfoot the Ruler*. (*Oedipus Rex*, which means "Oedipus the King," is the conventional Latin title for the play.)

Presumably the audience already knew the story portrayed in the play. They would have known that because a prophecy had foretold that Oedipus would grow up to slay his father, he had been taken out as a newborn to perish in the wilderness of Mount Cithaeron outside Thebes. (Exposure was the common fate of unwanted children in ancient Greece, though only in the most extraordinary circumstances would a royal heir be exposed.) The audience would also have known that before the baby was left to die, his feet had been pinned together. And they would have known that later, adopted by King Polybus and Queen Merope of Corinth and grown to maturity, Oedipus won both the throne and the recently widowed queen of Thebes as a reward for ridding the city of the Sphinx, a winged, woman-headed lion. All who approached the Sphinx were asked a riddle, and failure to solve it meant death. Her lethal riddle was: "What goes on four legs in the morning, two at noon, and three at evening?" Oedipus correctly answered, "Man." (As a baby he crawls on all fours, as a man he walks erect, and then as an old man he uses a cane.) Chagrined and outwitted, the Sphinx leaped from her rocky perch and dashed herself to death. Familiarity with all these events is necessary to understand *Oedipus the King*, which begins years later, after the title character has long been established as ruler of Thebes.

Laurence Olivier in *Oedipus Rex*.

Oedipus the King   425 B.C.?

Translated by David Grene

CHARACTERS

Oedipus, king of Thebes   *First Messenger*
Jocasta, his wife   *Second Messenger*
Creon, his brother-in-law   *A Herdsman*
Teiresias, an old blind prophet   *A Chorus of old men of Thebes*
A Priest

SCENE. *In front of the palace of Oedipus at Thebes. To the right of the stage near the altar stands the Priest with a crowd of children. Oedipus emerges from the central door.*

Oedipus: Children, young sons and daughters of old Cadmus,°
    why do you sit here with your suppliant crowns?°
    The town is heavy with a mingled burden
    of sounds and smells, of groans and hymns and incense;
    I did not think it fit that I should hear   5
    of this from messengers but came myself,—
    I Oedipus whom all men call the Great.

    (He turns to the Priest.)

    You're old and they are young; come, speak for them.
    What do you fear or want, that you sit here
    suppliant? Indeed I'm willing to give all   10
    that you may need; I would be very hard
    should I not pity suppliants like these.
Priest: O ruler of my country, Oedipus,
    you see our company around the altar;
    you see our ages; some of us, like these,   15
    who cannot yet fly far, and some of us
    heavy with age; these children are the chosen
    among the young, and I the priest of Zeus.
    Within the market place sit others crowned
    with suppliant garlands, at the double shrine   20
    of Pallas and the temple where Ismenus°
    gives oracles by fire.° King, you yourself
    have seen our city reeling like a wreck
    already; it can scarcely lift its prow
    out of the depths, out of the bloody surf.   25
    A blight is on the fruitful plants of the earth,

---

1 *Cadmus:* hero who, according to legend, had founded the city of Thebes, where the play takes place.
2 *suppliant crowns:* Suppliants, persons coming to beg a favor of the king, traditionally wore headbands of flowers.   20–21 *shrine of Pallas . . . Ismenus:* temples to Athena, goddess of wisdom, and Apollo, god of music, poetry, medicine, and prophecy.   22 *oracles by fire:* The ashes of fires at Ismenus were used to foretell the future. An oracle is a message from a god; it is also the name of a priestess who, while in a trance, would speak the message.

a blight is on the cattle in the fields,
a blight is on our women that no children
are born to them; a God that carries fire,
a deadly pestilence, is on our town,   30
strikes us and spares not, and the house of Cadmus
is emptied of its people while black Death
grows rich in groaning and in lamentation.
We have not come as suppliants to this altar
because we thought of you as of a God,   35
but rather judging you the first of men
in all the chances of this life and when
we mortals have to do with more than man.
You came and by your coming saved our city,
freed us from tribute which we paid of old   40
to the Sphinx, cruel singer. This you did
in virtue of no knowledge we could give you,
in virtue of no teaching; it was God
that aided you, men say, and you are held
with God's assistance to have saved our lives.   45
Now Oedipus, Greatest in all men's eyes,
here falling at your feet we all entreat you,
find us some strength for rescue.
Perhaps you'll hear a wise word from some God,
perhaps you will learn something from a man   50
(for I have seen that for the skilled of practice
the outcome of their counsels live the most).
Noblest of men, go, and raise up our city,
go,—and give heed. For now this land of ours
calls you its savior since you saved it once.   55
So, let us never speak about your reign
as of a time when first our feet were set
secure on high, but later fell to ruin.
Raise up our city, save it and raise it up.
Once you have brought us luck with happy omen;   60
be no less now in fortune.
If you will rule this land, as now you rule it,
better to rule it full of men than empty.
For neither tower nor ship is anything
when empty, and none live in it together.   65
Oedipus: I pity you, children. You have come full of longing,
but I have known the story before you told it
only too well. I know you are all sick,
yet there is not one of you, sick though you are,
that is as sick as I myself.   70
Your several sorrows each have single scope
and touch but one of you. My spirit groans
for city and myself and you at once.
You have not roused me like a man from sleep;
know that I have given many tears to this,   75

gone many ways wandering in thought,
but as I thought I found only one remedy
and that I took. I sent Menoeceus' son
Creon, Jocasta's brother, to Apollo,
to his Pythian temple,°   80
that he might learn there by what act or word
I could save this city. As I count the days,
it vexes me what ails him; he is gone
far longer than he needed for the journey.
But when he comes, then, may I prove a villain,   85
if I shall not do all the God commands.
Priest: Thanks for your gracious words. Your servants here
    signal that Creon is this moment coming.
Oedipus: His face is bright. O holy Lord Apollo,
    grant that his news too may be bright for us   90
    and bring us safety.
Priest: It is happy news,
    I think, for else his head would not be crowned
    with sprigs of fruitful laurel.
Oedipus: We will know soon,
    he's within hail. Lord Creon, my good brother,   95
    what is the word you bring us from the God?

    (Creon enters.)

Creon: A good word,—for things hard to bear themselves
    if in the final issue all is well
    I count complete good fortune.
Oedipus: What do you mean?
    What you have said so far   100
    leaves me uncertain whether to trust or fear.
Creon: If you will hear my news before these others
    I am ready to speak, or else to go within.
Oedipus: Speak it to all;
    the grief I bear, I bear it more for these   105
    than for my own heart.
Creon: I will tell you, then,
    what I heard from the God.
    King Phoebus° in plain words commanded us
    to drive out a pollution from our land,
    pollution grown ingrained within the land;   110
    drive it out, said the God, not cherish it,
    till it's past cure.
Oedipus: What is the rite
    of purification? How shall it be done?

---

80 *Pythian temple:* Oedipus has sent his brother-in-law Creon to the oracle at Delphi (or Pytho) to seek divine advice.   108 *King Phoebus:* the sun god, Phoebus Apollo. In the fifth century B.C., when Sophocles writes, the sun god and Apollo were coming to be regarded as one.

Creon: By banishing a man, or expiation
    of blood by blood, since it is murder guilt   115
    which holds our city in this destroying storm.
Oedipus: Who is this man whose fate the God pronounces?
Creon: My Lord, before you piloted the state
    we had a king called Laius.
Oedipus: I know of him by hearsay. I have not seen him.   120
Creon: The God commanded clearly: let some one
    punish with force this dead man's murderers.
Oedipus: Where are they in the world? Where would a trace
    of this old crime be found? It would be hard
    to guess where.
Creon: The clue is in this land;   125
    that which is sought is found;
    the unheeded thing escapes:
    so said the God.
Oedipus: Was it at home,
    or in the country that death came upon him,
    or in another country travelling?   130
Creon: He went, he said himself, upon an embassy,
    but never returned when he set out from home.
Oedipus: Was there no messenger, no fellow traveller
    who knew what happened? Such a one might tell
    something of use.   135
Creon: They were all killed save one. He fled in terror
    and he could tell us nothing in clear terms
    of what he knew, nothing, but one thing only.
Oedipus: What was it?
    If we could even find a slim beginning   140
    in which to hope, we might discover much.
Creon: This man said that the robbers they encountered
    were many and the hands that did the murder
    were many; it was no man's single power.
Oedipus: How could a robber dare a deed like this   145
    were he not helped with money from the city,
    money and treachery?
Creon: That indeed was thought.
    But Laius was dead and in our trouble
    there was none to help.
Oedipus: What trouble was so great to hinder you   150
    inquiring out the murder of your king?
Creon: The riddling Sphinx induced us to neglect
    mysterious crimes and rather seek solution
    of troubles at our feet.
Oedipus: I will bring this to light again. King Phoebus   155
    fittingly took this care about the dead,
    and you too fittingly.
    And justly you will see in me an ally,
    a champion of my country and the God.

For when I drive pollution from the land   160
I will not serve a distant friend's advantage,
but act in my own interest. Whoever
he was that killed the king may readily
wish to dispatch me with his murderous hand;
so helping the dead king I help myself.   165

Come, children, take your suppliant boughs and go;
up from the altars now. Call the assembly
and let it meet upon the understanding
that I'll do everything. God will decide
whether we prosper or remain in sorrow.   170
Priest: Rise, children—it was this we came to seek,
which of himself the king now offers us.
May Phoebus who gave us the oracle
come to our rescue and stay the plague.

(Exeunt all but the Chorus.)

Strophe°

Chorus: What is the sweet spoken word of God from the shrine of Pytho rich in gold   175
that has come to glorious Thebes?
I am stretched on the rack of doubt, and terror and trembling hold
my heart, O Delian Healer,° and I worship full of fears
for what doom you will bring to pass, new or renewed in the revolving years.
Speak to me, immortal voice,   180
child of golden Hope.

Antistrophe°

First I call on you, Athene, deathless daughter of Zeus,
and Artemis,° Earth Upholder,
who sits in the midst of the market place in the throne which men call Fame,
and Phoebus, the Far Shooter, three averters of Fate,   185
come to us now, if ever before, when ruin rushed upon the state,
you drove destruction's flame away
out of our land.

Strophe

Our sorrows defy number;
all the ship's timbers are rotten;   190
taking of thought is no spear for the driving away of the plague.
There are no growing children in this famous land;
there are no women bearing the pangs of childbirth.
You may see them one with another, like birds swift on the wing,

---

Strophe: according to theory, a passage sung while the chorus danced from stage right to stage left.
178 *Delian healer:* Apollo, in his capacity as god of medicine.   *Antistrophe:* a passage sung while the chorus
danced from stage left to stage right.   183 *Artemis:* twin sister of Apollo, goddess of the moon and of the
hunt.

quicker than fire unmastered, 195
speeding away to the coast of the Western God.°

Antistrophe

In the unnumbered deaths
of its people the city dies;
those children that are born lie dead on the naked earth
unpitied, spreading contagion of death; and grey haired mothers and wives 200
everywhere stand at the altar's edge, suppliant, moaning;
the hymn to the healing God rings out but with it the wailing voices are blended.
From these our sufferings grant us, O golden Daughter of Zeus,
glad-faced deliverance.

Strophe

There is no clash of brazen shields but our fight is with the War God, 205
a War God ringed with the cries of men, a savage God who burns us;
grant that he turn in racing course backwards out of our country's bounds
to the great palace of Amphitrite or where the waves of the Thracian sea
deny the stranger safe anchorage.
Whatsoever escapes the night 210
at last the light of day revisits;
so smite the War God, Father Zeus,
beneath your thunderbolt,
for you are the Lord of the lightning, the lightning that carries fire.

Antistrophe

And your unconquered arrow shafts, winged by the golden corded bow, 215
Lycean King, I beg to be at our side for help;
and the gleaming torches of Artemis with which she scours the Lycean hills,
and I call on the God with the turban of gold, who gave his name to this
country of ours,
the Bacchic God with the wind flushed face,
Evian One, who travel 220
with the Maenad company,°
combat the God that burns us
with your torch of pine;
for the God that is our enemy is a God unhonored among the Gods.

(*Oedipus returns.*)

Oedipus: For what you ask me—if you will hear my words, 225
and hearing welcome them and fight the plague,
you will find strength and lightening of your load.

Hark to me; what I say to you, I say
as one that is a stranger to the story

---

196 *Western God:* Hades, god of the underworld.   218–221 *God with the turban of gold . . . Maenad company:*
Bacchus, or Dionysus, god of wine, was said to travel with a company of Maenads, female revelers.

as stranger to the deed. For I would not   230
be far upon the track if I alone
were tracing it without a clue. But now,
since after all was finished, I became
a citizen among you, citizens—
now I proclaim to all the men of Thebes: 235
who so among you knows the murderer
by whose hand Laius, son of Labdacus,
died—I command him to tell everything
to me,—yes, though he fears himself to take the blame
on his own head; for bitter punishment   240
he shall have none, but leave this land unharmed.
Or if he knows the murderer, another,
a foreigner, still let him speak the truth.
For I will pay him and be grateful, too.
But if you shall keep silence, if perhaps   245
some one of you, to shield a guilty friend,
or for his own sake shall reject my words—
hear what I shall do then:
I forbid that man, whoever he be, my land,
my land where I hold sovereignty and throne;   250
and I forbid any to welcome him
or cry him greeting or make him a sharer
in sacrifice or offering to the Gods,
or give him water for his hands to wash.
I command all to drive him from their homes,   255
since he is our pollution, as the oracle
of Pytho's God proclaimed him now to me.
So I stand forth a champion of the God
and of the man who died.
Upon the murderer I invoke this curse—   260
whether he is one man and all unknown,
or one of many—may he wear out his life
in misery to miserable doom!
If with my knowledge he lives at my hearth
I pray that I myself may feel my curse.   265
On you I lay my charge to fulfill all this
for me, for the God, and for this land of ours
destroyed and blighted, by the God forsaken.

Even were this no matter of God's ordinance
it would not fit you so to leave it lie,   270
unpurified, since a good man is dead
and one that was a king. Search it out.
Since I am now the holder of his office,
and have his bed and wife that once was his,
and had his line not been unfortunate   275
we would have common children—(fortune leaped
upon his head)—because of all these things,

I fight in his defense as for my father,
and I shall try all means to take the murderer
of Laius the son of Labdacus   280
the son of Polydorus and before him
of Cadmus and before him of Agenor.
Those who do not obey me, may the Gods
grant no crops springing from the ground they plough
nor children to their women! May a fate   285
like this, or one still worse than this consume them!
For you whom these words please, the other Thebans,
may Justice as your ally and all the Gods
live with you, blessing you now and for ever!
Chorus: As you have held me to my oath, I speak: 290
   I neither killed the king nor can declare
   the killer; but since Phoebus set the quest
   it is his part to tell who the man is.
Oedipus: Right; but to put compulsion on the Gods
   against their will—no man can do that.   295
Chorus: May I then say what I think second best?
Oedipus: If there's a third best, too, spare not to tell it.
Chorus: I know that what the Lord Teiresias
   sees, is most often what the Lord Apollo
   sees. If you should inquire of this from him   300
   you might find out most clearly.
Oedipus: Even in this my actions have not been sluggard.
   On Creon's word I have sent two messengers
   and why the prophet is not here already
   I have been wondering.
Chorus: His skill apart   305
   there is besides only an old faint story.
Oedipus: What is it?
   I look at every story.
Chorus: It was said
   that he was killed by certain wayfarers.
Oedipus: I heard that, too, but no one saw the killer.   310
Chorus: Yet if he has a share of fear at all,
   his courage will not stand firm, hearing your curse.
Oedipus: The man who in the doing did not shrink
   will fear no word.
Chorus: Here comes his prosecutor:
   led by your men the godly prophet comes   315
   in whom alone of mankind truth is native.

(*Enter Teiresias, led by a little boy.*)

Oedipus: Teiresias, you are versed in everything,
   things teachable and things not to be spoken,
   things of the heaven and earth-creeping things.
   You have no eyes but in your mind you know   320
   with what a plague our city is afflicted.

My lord, in you alone we find a champion,
in you alone one that can rescue us.
Perhaps you have not heard the messengers,
but Phoebus sent in answer to our sending   325
an oracle declaring that our freedom
from this disease would only come when we
should learn the names of those who killed King Laius,
and kill them or expel them from our country.
Do not begrudge us oracles from birds,   330
or any other way of prophecy
within your skill; save yourself and the city,
save me; redeem the debt of our pollution
that lies on us because of this dead man.
We are in your hands; pains are most nobly taken   335
to help another when you have means and power.

Teiresias: Alas, how terrible is wisdom when
it brings no profit to the man that's wise!
This I knew well, but had forgotten it,
else I would not have come here.

Oedipus: What is this?   340
How sad you are now you have come!

Teiresias: Let me
go home. It will be easiest for us both
to bear our several destinies to the end
if you will follow my advice.

Oedipus: You'd rob us
of this your gift of prophecy? You talk   345
as one who had no care for law nor love
for Thebes who reared you.

Teiresias: Yes, but I see that even your own words
miss the mark; therefore I must fear for mine.

Oedipus: For God's sake if you know of anything,   350
do not turn from us; all of us kneel to you,
all of us here, your suppliants.

Teiresias: All of you here know nothing. I will not
bring to the light of day my troubles, mine—
rather than call them yours.

Oedipus: What do you mean?   355
You know of something but refuse to speak.
Would you betray us and destroy the city?

Teiresias: I will not bring this pain upon us both,
neither on you nor on myself. Why is it
you question me and waste your labor? I   360
will tell you nothing.

Oedipus: You would provoke a stone! Tell us, you villain,
tell us, and do not stand there quietly
unmoved and balking at the issue.

Teiresias: You blame my temper but you do not see   365
your own that lives within you; it is me
you chide.

Oedipus: Who would not feel his temper rise
    at words like these with which you shame our city?
Teiresias: Of themselves things will come, although I hide them   370
    and breathe no word of them.
Oedipus: Since they will come
    tell them to me.
Teiresias: I will say nothing further.
    Against this answer let your temper rage
    as wildly as you will.
Oedipus: Indeed I am
    so angry I shall not hold back a jot   375
    of what I think. For I would have you know
    I think you were complotter of the deed
    and doer of the deed save in so far
    as for the actual killing. Had you had eyes
    I would have said alone you murdered him.   380
Teiresias: Yes? Then I warn you faithfully to keep
    the letter of your proclamation and
    from this day forth to speak no word of greeting
    to these nor me; you are the land's pollution.
Oedipus: How shamelessly you started up this taunt!   385
    How do you think you will escape?
Teiresias: I have.
    I have escaped; the truth is what I cherish
    and that's my strength.
Oedipus: And who has taught you truth?
    Not your profession surely!
Teiresias: You have taught me,
    for you have made me speak against my will.   390
Oedipus: Speak what? Tell me again that I may learn it better.
Teiresias: Did you not understand before or would you
    provoke me into speaking?
Oedipus: I did not grasp it,
    not so to call it known. Say it again.
Teiresias: I say you are the murderer of the king   395
    whose murderer you seek.
Oedipus: Not twice you shall
    say calumnies like this and stay unpunished.
Teiresias: Shall I say more to tempt your anger more?
Oedipus: As much as you desire; it will be said
    in vain.
Teiresias: I say that with those you love best   400
    you live in foulest shame unconsciously
    and do not see where you are in calamity.
Oedipus: Do you imagine you can always talk
    like this, and live to laugh at it hereafter?
Teiresias: Yes, if the truth has anything of strength.   405

Oedipus: It has, but not for you; it has no strength
    for you because you are blind in mind and ears
    as well as in your eyes.
Teiresias: You are a poor wretch
    to taunt me with the very insults which
    every one soon will heap upon yourself.   410
Oedipus: Your life is one long night so that you cannot
    hurt me or any other who sees the light.
Teiresias: It is not fate that I should be your ruin,
    Apollo is enough; it is his care
    to work this out.
Oedipus: Was this your own design   415
    or Creon's?
Teiresias: Creon is no hurt to you,
    but you are to yourself.
Oedipus: Wealth, sovereignty and skill outmatching skill
    for the contrivance of an envied life!
    Great store of jealousy fill your treasury chests,   420
    if my friend Creon, friend from the first and loyal,
    thus secretly attacks me, secretly
    desires to drive me out and secretly
    suborns this juggling, trick devising quack,
    this wily beggar who has only eyes   425
    for his own gains, but blindness in his skill.
    For, tell me, where have you seen clear, Teiresias,
    with your prophetic eyes? When the dark singer,
    the Sphinx, was in your country, did you speak
    word of deliverance to its citizens?   430
    And yet the riddle's answer was not the province
    of a chance comer. It was a prophet's task
    and plainly you had no such gift of prophecy
    from birds nor otherwise from any God
    to glean a word of knowledge. But I came,   435
    Oedipus, who knew nothing, and I stopped her.
    I solved the riddle by my wit alone.
    Mine was no knowledge got from birds. And now
    you would expel me,
    because you think that you will find a place   440
    by Creon's throne. I think you will be sorry,
    both you and your accomplice, for your plot
    to drive me out. And did I not regard you
    as an old man, some suffering would have taught you
    that what was in your heart was treason.   445
Chorus: We look at this man's words and yours, my king,
    and we find both have spoken them in anger.
    We need no angry words but only thought
    how we may best hit the God's meaning for us.
Teiresias: If you are king, at least I have the right   450
    no less to speak in my defense against you.

Of that much I am master. I am no slave
of yours, but Loxias',° and so I shall not
enroll myself with Creon for my patron.
Since you have taunted me with being blind,   455
here is my word for you.
You have your eyes but see not where you are
in sin, nor where you live, nor whom you live with.
Do you know who your parents are? Unknowing
you are an enemy to kith and kin   460
in death, beneath the earth, and in this life.
A deadly footed, double striking curse,
from father and mother both, shall drive you forth
out of this land, with darkness on your eyes,
that now have such straight vision. Shall there be   465
a place will not be harbor to your cries,
a corner of Cithaeron° will not ring
in echo to your cries, soon, soon,—
when you shall learn the secret of your marriage,
which steered you to a haven in this house,—   470
haven no haven, after lucky voyage?
And of the multitude of other evils
establishing a grim equality
between you and your children, you know nothing.
So, muddy with contempt my words and Creon's!   475
Misery shall grind no man as it will you.
Oedipus: Is it endurable that I should hear
 such words from him? Go and a curse go with you!
 Quick, home with you! Out of my house at once!
Teiresias: I would not have come either had you not called me.   480
Oedipus: I did not know then you would talk like a fool—
 or it would have been long before I called you.
Teiresias: I am a fool then, as it seems to you—
 but to the parents who have bred you, wise.
Oedipus: What parents? Stop! Who are they of all the world?   485
Teiresias: This day will show your birth and will destroy you.
Oedipus: How needlessly your riddles darken everything.
Teiresias: But it's in riddle answering you are strongest.
Oedipus: Yes. Taunt me where you will find me great.
Teiresias: It is this very luck that has destroyed you.   490
Oedipus: I do not care, if it has saved this city.
Teiresias: Well, I will go. Come, boy, lead me away.
Oedipus: Yes, lead him off. So long as you are here,
 you'll be a stumbling block and a vexation;
 once gone, you will not trouble me again.

---

453 *Loxias'*: Apollo's.   467 *Cithaeron*: a mountain outside Thebes where the child Oedipus had been abandoned to die.

Teiresias: I have said   495
    what I came here to say not fearing your
    countenance: there is no way you can hurt me.
    I tell you, king, this man, this murderer
    (whom you have long declared you are in search of,
    indicting him in threatening proclamation   500
    as murderer of Laius)—he is here.
    In name he is a stranger among citizens
    but soon he will be shown to be a citizen
    true native Theban, and he'll have no joy
    of the discovery: blindness for sight   505
    and beggary for riches his exchange,
    he shall go journeying to a foreign country
    tapping his way before him with a stick.
    He shall be proved father and brother both
    to his own children in his house; to her   510
    that gave him birth, a son and husband both;
    a fellow sower in his father's bed
    with that same father that he murdered.
    Go within, reckon that out, and if you find me
    mistaken, say I have no skill in prophecy.   515

    (Exeunt separately Teiresias and Oedipus.)

                                   Strophe

Chorus: Who is the man proclaimed
    by Delphi's prophetic rock°
    as the bloody handed murderer,
    the doer of deeds that none dare name?
    Now is the time for him to run   520
    with a stronger foot
    than Pegasus°
    for the child of Zeus° leaps in arms upon him
    with fire and the lightning bolt,
    and terribly close on his heels   525
    are the Fates that never miss.

                                   Antistrophe

    Lately from snowy Parnassus
    clearly the voice flashed forth,
    bidding each Theban track him down,
    the unknown murderer.
    In the savage forests he lurks and in   530
    the caverns like

---

517 *Delphi's prophetic rock:* The shrine at Delphi, thought to stand at the geographical center of the world, featured a holy stone known as the Navel of the Earth.   522 *Pegasus:* in Greek mythology, the winged horse born from the neck of the dying gorgon Medusa. A blow of his hoof caused the stream Hippocrene to spring forth from Mount Helicon; its waters were thought to inspire poets to write.   523 *child of Zeus:* Apollo, armed with the thunderbolts of his father.

the mountain bull.
He is sad and lonely, and lonely his feet
that carry him far from the navel of earth;   535
but its prophecies, ever living,
flutter around his head.

Strophe

The augur has spread confusion,
terrible confusion;
I do not approve what was said   540
nor can I deny it.
I do not know what to say;
I am in a flutter of foreboding;
I never heard in the present
nor past of a quarrel between   545
the sons of Labdacus and Polybus,°
that I might bring as proof
in attacking the popular fame
of Oedipus, seeking
to take vengeance for undiscovered   550
death in the line of Labdacus.

Antistrophe

Truly Zeus and Apollo are wise
and in human things all knowing;
but amongst men there is no
distinct judgment, between the prophet   555
and me—which of us is right.
One man may pass another in wisdom
but I would never agree
with those that find fault with the king
till I should see the word   560
proved right beyond doubt. For once
in visible form the Sphinx
came on him and all of us
saw his wisdom and in that test
he saved the city. So he will not be condemned by my mind.   565

(Enter Creon.)

Creon: Citizens, I have come because I heard
deadly words spread about me, that the king
accuses me. I cannot take that from him.
If he believes that in these present troubles
he has been wronged by me in word or deed   570
I do not want to live on with the burden
of such a scandal on me. The report

---

546 *sons of Labdacus and Polybus:* The son of Labdacus was Laius, previous king of Thebes. At this moment
in the play Oedipus is assumed to be the son of Polybus, king of Corinth.

        injures me doubly and most vitally—
        for I'll be called a traitor to my city
        and traitor also to my friends and you.   575
Chorus: Perhaps it was a sudden gust of anger
        that forced that insult from him, and no judgment.
Creon: But did he say that it was in compliance
        with schemes of mine that the seer told him lies?
Chorus: Yes, he said that, but why, I do not know.   580
Creon: Were his eyes straight in his head? Was his mind right
        when he accused me in this fashion?
Chorus: I do not know; I have no eyes to see
        what princes do. Here comes the king himself.

    (Enter Oedipus.)

Oedipus: You, sir, how is it you come here? Have you so much   585
        brazen-faced daring that you venture in
        my house although you are proved manifestly
        the murderer of that man, and though you tried,
        openly, highway robbery of my crown?
        For God's sake, tell me what you saw in me,   590
        what cowardice or what stupidity,
        that made you lay a plot like this against me?
        Did you imagine I should not observe
        the crafty scheme that stole upon me or
        seeing it, take no means to counter it?   595
        Was it not stupid of you to make the attempt,
        to try to hunt down royal power without
        the people at your back or friends? For only
        with the people at your back or money can
        the hunt end in the capture of a crown.   600
Creon: Do you know what you're doing? Will you listen
        to words to answer yours, and then pass judgment?
Oedipus: You're quick to speak, but I am slow to grasp you,
        for I have found you dangerous,—and my foe.
Creon: First of all hear what I shall say to that.   605
Oedipus: At least don't tell me that you are not guilty.
Creon: If you think obstinacy without wisdom
        a valuable possession, you are wrong.
Oedipus: And you are wrong if you believe that one,
        a criminal, will not be punished only   610
        because he is my kinsman.
Creon: This is but just—
        but tell me, then, of what offense I'm guilty?
Oedipus: Did you or did you not urge me to send
        to this prophetic mumbler?
Creon: I did indeed,
        and I shall stand by what I told you.   615
Oedipus: How long ago is it since Laius. . . .
Creon: What about Laius? I don't understand.

Oedipus: Vanished—died—was murdered?

Creon: It is long,
    a long, long time to reckon.

Oedipus: Was this prophet
    in the profession then?

Creon: He was, and honored   620
    as highly as he is today.

Oedipus: At that time did he say a word about me?

Creon: Never, at least when I was near him.

Oedipus: You never made a search for the dead man?

Creon: We searched, indeed, but never learned of anything.   625

Oedipus: Why did our wise old friend not say this then?

Creon: I don't know; and when I know nothing, I
    usually hold my tongue.

Oedipus: You know this much,
    and can declare this much if you are loyal.

Creon: What is it? If I know, I'll not deny it.   630

Oedipus: That he would not have said that I killed Laius
    had he not met you first.

Creon: You know yourself
    whether he said this, but I demand that I
    should hear as much from you as you from me.

Oedipus: Then hear,—I'll not be proved a murderer.   635

Creon: Well, then. You're married to my sister.

Oedipus: Yes,
    that I am not disposed to deny.

Creon: You rule
    this country giving her an equal share
    in the government?

Oedipus: Yes, everything she wants
    she has from me.

Creon: And I, as thirdsman to you,   640
    am rated as the equal of you two?

Oedipus: Yes, and it's there you've proved yourself false friend.

Creon: Not if you will reflect on it as I do.
    Consider, first, if you think any one
    would choose to rule and fear rather than rule   645
    and sleep untroubled by a fear if power
    were equal in both cases. I, at least,
    I was not born with such a frantic yearning
    to be a king—but to do what kings do.
    And so it is with every one who has learned   650
    wisdom and self-control. As it stands now,
    the prizes are all mine—and without fear.
    But if I were the king myself, I must
    do much that went against the grain.
    How should despotic rule seem sweeter to me   655
    than painless power and an assured authority?

I am not so besotted yet that I
want other honors than those that come with profit.
Now every man's my pleasure; every man greets me;
now those who are your suitors fawn on me,—   660
success for them depends upon my favor.
Why should I let all this go to win that?
My mind would not be traitor if it's wise;
I am no treason lover, of my nature,
nor would I ever dare to join a plot.   665
Prove what I say. Go to the oracle
at Pytho and inquire about the answers,
if they are as I told you. For the rest,
if you discover I laid any plot
together with the seer, kill me, I say,   670
not only by your vote but by my own.
But do not charge me on obscure opinion
without some proof to back it. It's not just
lightly to count your knaves as honest men,
nor honest men as knaves. To throw away   675
an honest friend is, as it were, to throw
your life away, which a man loves the best.
In time you will know all with certainty;
time is the only test of honest men,
one day is space enough to know a rogue.   680
Chorus: His words are wise, king, if one fears to fall.
    Those who are quick of temper are not safe.
Oedipus: When he that plots against me secretly
    moves quickly, I must quickly counterplot.
    If I wait taking no decisive measure   685
    his business will be done, and mine be spoiled.
Creon: What do you want to do then? Banish me?
Oedipus: No, certainly; kill you, not banish you.
Creon: I do not think that you've your wits about you.
Oedipus: For my own interests, yes.
Creon: But for mine, too,   690
    you should think equally.
Oedipus: You are a rogue.
Creon: Suppose you do not understand?
Oedipus: But yet
    I must be ruler.
Creon: Not if you rule badly.
Oedipus: O, city, city!
Creon: I too have some share
    in the city; it is not yours alone.   695
Chorus: Stop, my lords! Here—and in the nick of time
    I see Jocasta coming from the house;
    with her help lay the quarrel that now stirs you.

(Enter Jocasta.)

Jocasta: For shame! Why have you raised this foolish squabbling
    brawl? Are you not ashamed to air your private   700
    griefs when the country's sick? Go in, you, Oedipus,
    and you, too, Creon, into the house. Don't magnify
    your nothing troubles.
Creon: Sister, Oedipus,
    your husband, thinks he has the right to do
    terrible wrongs—he has but to choose between   705
    two terrors: banishing or killing me.
Oedipus: He's right, Jocasta; for I find him plotting
    with knavish tricks against my person.
Creon: That God may never bless me! May I die
    accursed, if I have been guilty of   710
    one tittle of the charge you bring against me!
Jocasta: I beg you, Oedipus, trust him in this,
    spare him for the sake of this his oath to God,
    for my sake, and the sake of those who stand here.
Chorus: Be gracious, be merciful,   715
    we beg of you.
Oedipus: In what would you have me yield?
Chorus: He has been no silly child in the past.
    He is strong in his oath now.
    Spare him.   720
Oedipus: Do you know what you ask?
Chorus: Yes.
Oedipus: Tell me then.
Chorus: He has been your friend before all men's eyes; do not cast him away
    dishonored on an obscure conjecture.   725
Oedipus: I would have you know that this request of yours
    really requests my death or banishment.
Chorus: May the Sun God, king of Gods, forbid! May I die without God's blessing,
    without friends' help, if I had any such thought. But my spirit is broken by
    my unhappiness for my wasting country; and this would but add troubles 730
    amongst ourselves to the other troubles.
Oedipus: Well, let him go then—if I must die ten times for it,
    or be sent out dishonored into exile.
    It is your lips that prayed for him I pitied,
    not his; wherever he is, I shall hate him.   735
Creon: I see you sulk in yielding and you're dangerous
    when you are out of temper; natures like yours
    are justly heaviest for themselves to bear.
Oedipus: Leave me alone! Take yourself off, I tell you.
Creon: I'll go, you have not known me, but they have,   740
    and they have known my innocence.

    (Exit.)

Chorus: Won't you take him inside, lady?

Jocasta: Yes, when I've found out what was the matter.
Chorus: There was some misconceived suspicion of a story, and on the other side
    the sting of injustice. 745
Jocasta: So, on both sides?
Chorus: Yes.
Jocasta: What was the story?
Chorus: I think it best, in the interests of the country, to leave it where it ended.
Oedipus: You see where you have ended, straight of judgment 750
    although you are, by softening my anger.
Chorus: Sir, I have said before and I say again—be sure that I would have been
    proved a madman, bankrupt in sane council, if I should put you away, you
    who steered the country I love safely when she was crazed with troubles.
    God grant that now, too, you may prove a fortunate guide for us. 755
Jocasta: Tell me, my lord, I beg of you, what was it
    that roused your anger so?
Oedipus: Yes, I will tell you.
    I honor you more than I honor them.
    It was Creon and the plots he laid against me.
Jocasta: Tell me—if you can clearly tell the quarrel—
Oedipus: Creon says 760
    that I'm the murderer of Laius.
Jocasta: Of his own knowledge or on information?
Oedipus: He sent this rascal prophet to me, since
    he keeps his own mouth clean of any guilt.
Jocasta: Do not concern yourself about this matter; 765
    listen to me and learn that human beings
    have no part in the craft of prophecy.
    Of that I'll show you a short proof.
    There was an oracle once that came to Laius,—
    I will not say that it was Phoebus' own, 770
    but it was from his servants—and it told him
    that it was fate that he should die a victim
    at the hands of his own son, a son to be born
    of Laius and me. But, see now, he,
    the king, was killed by foreign highway robbers 775
    at a place where three roads meet—so goes the story;
    and for the son—before three days were out
    after his birth King Laius pierced his ankles
    and by the hands of others cast him forth
    upon a pathless hillside. So Apollo 780
    failed to fulfill his oracle to the son,
    that he should kill his father, and to Laius
    also proved false in that the thing he feared,
    death at his son's hands, never came to pass.
    So clear in this case were the oracles, 785
    so clear and false. Give them no heed, I say;
    what God discovers need of, easily
    he shows to us himself.

Oedipus: O dear Jocasta,
    as I hear this from you, there comes upon me
    a wandering of the soul—I could run mad.   790
Jocasta: What trouble is it, that you turn again
    and speak like this?
Oedipus: I thought I heard you say
    that Laius was killed at a crossroads.
Jocasta: Yes, that was how the story went and still
    that word goes round.
Oedipus: Where is this place, Jocasta,   795
    where he was murdered?
Jocasta: Phocis is the country
    and the road splits there, one of two roads from Delphi,
    another comes from Daulia.
Oedipus: How long ago is this?
Jocasta: The news came to the city just before
    you became king and all men's eyes looked to you.   800
    What is it, Oedipus, that's in your mind?
Oedipus: What have you designed, O Zeus, to do with me?
Jocasta: What is the thought that troubles your heart?
Oedipus: Don't ask me yet—tell me of Laius—
    How did he look? How old or young was he?   805
Jocasta: He was a tall man and his hair was grizzled
    already—nearly white—and in his form
    not unlike you.
Oedipus: O God, I think I have
    called curses on myself in ignorance.
Jocasta: What do you mean? I am terrified   810
    when I look at you.
Oedipus: I have a deadly fear
    that the old seer had eyes. You'll show me more
    if you can tell me one more thing.
Jocasta: I will.
    I'm frightened,—but if I can understand,
    I'll tell you all you ask.
Oedipus: How was his company?   815
    Had he few with him when he went this journey,
    or many servants, as would suit a prince?
Jocasta: In all there were but five, and among them
    a herald; and one carriage for the king.
Oedipus: It's plain—it's plain—who was it told you this?   820
Jocasta: The only servant that escaped safe home.
Oedipus: Is he at home now?
Jocasta: No, when he came home again
    and saw you king and Laius was dead,
    he came to me and touched my hand and begged

that I should send him to the fields to be   825
my shepherd and so he might see the city
as far off as he might. So I
sent him away. He was an honest man,
as slaves go, and was worthy of far more
than what he asked of me.   830
Oedipus: O, how I wish that he could come back quickly!
Jocasta: He can. Why is your heart so set on this?
Oedipus: O dear Jocasta, I am full of fears
    that I have spoken far too much; and therefore
    I wish to see this shepherd.
Jocasta: He will come;   835
    but, Oedipus, I think I'm worthy too
    to know what it is that disquiets you.
Oedipus: It shall not be kept from you, since my mind
    has gone so far with its forebodings. Whom
    should I confide in rather than you, who is there   840
    of more importance to me who have passed
    through such a fortune?
    Polybus was my father, king of Corinth,
    and Merope, the Dorian, my mother.
    I was held greatest of the citizens   845
    in Corinth till a curious chance befell me
    as I shall tell you—curious, indeed,
    but hardly worth the store I set upon it.
    There was a dinner and at it a man,
    a drunken man, accused me in his drink   850
    of being bastard. I was furious
    but held my temper under for that day.
    Next day I went and taxed my parents with it;
    they took the insult very ill from him,
    the drunken fellow who had uttered it.   855
    So I was comforted for their part, but
    still this thing rankled always, for the story
    crept about widely. And I went at last
    to Pytho, though my parents did not know.
    But Phoebus sent me home again unhonored   860
    in what I came to learn, but he foretold
    other and desperate horrors to befall me,
    that I was fated to lie with my mother,
    and show to daylight an accursed breed
    which men would not endure, and I was doomed   865
    to be murderer of the father that begot me.
    When I heard this I fled, and in the days
    that followed I would measure from the stars
    the whereabouts of Corinth—yes, I fled
    to somewhere where I should not see fulfilled   870
    the infamies told in that dreadful oracle.
    And as I journeyed I came to the place

where, as you say, this king met with his death.
Jocasta, I will tell you the whole truth.
When I was near the branching of the crossroads,   875
going on foot, I was encountered by
a herald and a carriage with a man in it,
just as you tell me. He that led the way
and the old man himself wanted to thrust me
out of the road by force. I became angry   880
and struck the coachman who was pushing me.
When the old man saw this he watched his moment,
and as I passed he struck me from his carriage,
full on the head with his two pointed goad.
But he was paid in full and presently   885
my stick had struck him backwards from the car
and he rolled out of it. And then I killed them
all. If it happened there was any tie
of kinship twixt this man and Laius,
who is then now more miserable than I,   890
what man on earth so hated by the Gods,
since neither citizen nor foreigner
may welcome me at home or even greet me,
but drive me out of doors? And it is I,
I and no other have so cursed myself.   895
And I pollute the bed of him I killed
by the hands that killed him. Was I not born evil?
Am I not utterly unclean? I had to fly
and in my banishment not even see
my kindred nor set foot in my own country,   900
or otherwise my fate was to be yoked
in marriage with my mother and kill my father,
Polybus who begot me and had reared me.
Would not one rightly judge and say that on me
these things were sent by some malignant God?   905
O no, no, no—O holy majesty
of God on high, may I not see that day!
May I be gone out of men's sight before
I see the deadly taint of this disaster
come upon me.   910
Chorus: Sir, we too fear these things. But until you see this man face to face and
hear his story, hope.
Oedipus: Yes, I have just this much of hope—to wait until the herdsman comes.
Jocasta: And when he comes, what do you want with him?
Oedipus: I'll tell you; if I find that his story is the same as yours, I at least will be   915
clear of this guilt.
Jocasta: Why, what so particularly did you learn from my story?
Oedipus: You said that he spoke of highway *robbers* who killed Laius. Now if he
uses the same number, it was not I who killed him. One man cannot be
the same as many. But if he speaks of a man travelling alone, then clearly   920
the burden of the guilt inclines towards me.

Jocasta: Be sure, at least, that this was how he told the story. He cannot unsay it now, for every one in the city heard it—not I alone. But, Oedipus, even if he diverges from what he said then, he shall never prove that the murder of Laius squares rightly with the prophecy—for Loxias declared that the king should be killed by his own 925 son. And that poor creature did not kill him surely,—for he died himself first. So as far as prophecy goes, henceforward I shall not look to the right hand or the left.

Oedipus: Right. But yet, send some one for the peasant to bring him here; do not neglect it.

Jocasta: I will send quickly. Now let me go indoors. I will do nothing except what 930 pleases you.

(*Exeunt.*)

Strophe

Chorus: May destiny ever find me
       pious in word and deed
       prescribed by the laws that live on high:
       laws begotten in the clear air of heaven,   935
       whose only father is Olympus;
       no mortal nature brought them to birth,
       no forgetfulness shall lull them to sleep;
       for God is great in them and grows not old.

Antistrophe

       Insolence breeds the tyrant, insolence   940
       if it is glutted with a surfeit, unseasonable, unprofitable,
       climbs to the roof-top and plunges
       sheer down to the ruin that must be,
       and there its feet are no service.
       But I pray that the God may never   945
       abolish the eager ambition that profits the state.
       For I shall never cease to hold the God as our protector.

Strophe

       If a man walks with haughtiness
       of hand or word and gives no heed
       to Justice and the shrines of Gods   950
       despises—may an evil doom
       smite him for his ill-starred pride of heart!—
       if he reaps gains without justice
       and will not hold from impiety
       and his fingers itch for untouchable things.   955
       When such things are done, what man shall contrive
       to shield his soul from the shafts of the God?
       When such deeds are held in honor,
       why should I honor the Gods in the dance?

Antistrophe

No longer to the holy place,   960
to the navel of earth I'll go
to worship, nor to Abae
nor to Olympia,
unless the oracles are proved to fit,
for all men's hands to point at.   965
O Zeus, if you are rightly called
the sovereign lord, all-mastering,
let this not escape you nor your ever-living power!
The oracles concerning Laius
are old and dim and men regard them not.   970
Apollo is nowhere clear in honor; God's service perishes.

(Enter Jocasta, carrying garlands.)

Jocasta: Princes of the land, I have had the thought to go
 to the Gods' temples, bringing in my hand
 garlands and gifts of incense, as you see.
 For Oedipus excites himself too much   975
 at every sort of trouble, not conjecturing,
 like a man of sense, what will be from what was,
 but he is always at the speaker's mercy,
 when he speaks terrors. I can do no good
 by my advice, and so I came as suppliant   980
 to you, Lycaean Apollo, who are nearest.
 These are the symbols of my prayer and this
 my prayer: grant us escape free of the curse.
 Now when we look to him we are all afraid;
 he's pilot of our ship and he is frightened.   985

(Enter Messenger.)

Messenger: Might I learn from you, sirs, where is the house of Oedipus? Or best of
 all, if you know, where is the king himself?
Chorus: This is his house and he is within doors. This lady is his wife and mother
 of his children.
Messenger: God bless you, lady, and God bless your household! God bless Oedipus' 990
 noble wife!
Jocasta: God bless you, sir, for your kind greeting! What do you want of us that
 you have come here? What have you to tell us?
Messenger: Good news, lady. Good for your house and for your husband.
Jocasta: What is your news? Who sent you to us?   995
Messenger: I come from Corinth and the news I bring will give you pleasure.
 Perhaps a little pain too.
Jocasta: What is this news of double meaning?
Messenger: The people of the Isthmus will choose Oedipus to be their king. That
 is the rumor there.   1000
Jocasta: But isn't their king still old Polybus?
Messenger: No. He is in his grave. Death has got him.

Jocasta: Is that the truth? Is Oedipus' father dead?

Messenger: May I die myself if it be otherwise!

Jocasta (to a servant): Be quick and run to the King with the news! O oracles of   1005
    the Gods, where are you now? It was from this man Oedipus fled, lest he
    should be his murderer! And now he is dead, in the course of nature, and
    not killed by Oedipus.

    (Enter Oedipus.)

Oedipus: Dearest Jocasta, why have you sent for me?

Jocasta: Listen to this man and when you hear reflect what is the outcome of the   1010
    holy oracles of the Gods.

Oedipus: Who is he? What is his message for me?

Jocasta: He is from Corinth and he tells us that your father Polybus is dead and gone.

Oedipus: What's this you say, sir? Tell me yourself.

Messenger: Since this is the first matter you want clearly told: Polybus has gone   1015
    down to death. You may be sure of it.

Oedipus: By treachery or sickness?

Messenger: A small thing will put old bodies asleep.

Oedipus: So he died of sickness, it seems,—poor old man!

Messenger: Yes, and of age—the long years he had measured.   1020

Oedipus: Ha! Ha! O dear Jocasta, why should one
    look to the Pythian hearth?° Why should one look
    to the birds screaming overhead? They prophesied
    that I should kill my father! But he's dead,
    and hidden deep in earth, and I stand here   1025
    who never laid a hand on spear against him,—
    unless perhaps he died of longing for me,
    and thus I am his murderer. But they,
    the oracles, as they stand—he's taken them
    away with him, they're dead as he himself is,   1030
    and worthless.

Jocasta: That I told you before now.

Oedipus: You did, but I was misled by my fear.

Jocasta: Then lay no more of them to heart, not one.

Oedipus: But surely I must fear my mother's bed?

Jocasta: Why should man fear since chance is all in all   1035
    for him, and he can clearly foreknow nothing?
    Best to live lightly, as one can, unthinkingly.
    As to your mother's marriage bed,—don't fear it.
    Before this, in dreams too, as well as oracles,
    many a man has lain with his own mother.   1040
    But he to whom such things are nothing bears
    his life most easily.

Oedipus: All that you say would be said perfectly
    if she were dead; but since she lives I must
    still fear, although you talk so well, Jocasta.   1045

1022 *Pythian hearth:* the oracle at Delphi.

Jocasta: Still in your father's death there's light of comfort?
Oedipus: Great light of comfort; but I fear the living.
Messenger: Who is the woman that makes you afraid?
Oedipus: Merope, old man, Polybus' wife.
Messenger: What about her frightens the queen and you?   1050
Oedipus: A terrible oracle, stranger, from the Gods.
Messenger: Can it be told? Or does the sacred law
    forbid another to have knowledge of it?
Oedipus: O no! Once on a time Loxias said
    that I should lie with my own mother and   1055
    take on my hands the blood of my own father.
    And so for these long years I've lived away
    from Corinth; it has been to my great happiness;
    but yet it's sweet to see the face of parents.
Messenger: This was the fear which drove you out of Corinth?   1060
Oedipus: Old man, I did not wish to kill my father.
Messenger: Why should I not free you from this fear, sir,
    since I have come to you in all goodwill?
Oedipus: You would not find me thankless if you did.
Messenger: Why, it was just for this I brought the news,—   1065
    to earn your thanks when you had come safe home.
Oedipus: No, I will never come near my parents.
Messenger: Son,
    it's very plain you don't know what you're doing.
Oedipus: What do you mean, old man? For God's sake, tell me.
Messenger: If your homecoming is checked by fears like these.   1070
Oedipus: Yes, I'm afraid that Phoebus may prove right.
Messenger: The murder and the incest?
Oedipus: Yes, old man;
    that is my constant terror.
Messenger: Do you know
    that all your fears are empty?
Oedipus: How is that,
    if they are father and mother and I their son?   1075
Messenger: Because Polybus was no kin to you in blood.
Oedipus: What, was not Polybus my father?
Messenger: No more than I but just so much.
Oedipus: How can
    my father be my father as much as one
    that's nothing to me?
Messenger: Neither he nor I   1080
    begat you.
Oedipus: Why then did he call me son?
Messenger: A gift he took you from these hands of mine.
Oedipus: Did he love so much what he took from another's hand?
Messenger: His childlessness before persuaded him.
Oedipus: Was I a child you bought or found when I   1085
    was given to him?
Messenger: On Cithaeron's slopes
    in the twisting thickets you were found.

Oedipus: And why
    were you a traveller in those parts?
Messenger: I was
    in charge of mountain flocks.
Oedipus: You were a shepherd?
    A hireling vagrant?
Messenger: Yes, but at least at that time   1090
    the man that saved your life, son.
Oedipus: What ailed me when you took me in your arms?
Messenger: In that your ankles should be witnesses.
Oedipus: Why do you speak of that old pain?
Messenger: I loosed you;
    the tendons of your feet were pierced and fettered,—   1095
Oedipus: My swaddling clothes brought me a rare disgrace.
Messenger: So that from this you're called your present name.°
Oedipus: Was this my father's doing or my mother's?
    For God's sake, tell me.
Messenger: I don't know, but he
    who gave you to me has more knowledge than I.   1100
Oedipus: You yourself did not find me then? You took me
    from someone else?
Messenger: Yes, from another shepherd.
Oedipus: Who was he? Do you know him well enough
    to tell?
Messenger: He was called Laius' man.   1105
Oedipus: You mean the king who reigned here in the old days?
Messenger: Yes, he was that man's shepherd.
Oedipus: Is he alive
    still, so that I could see him?
Messenger: You who live here
    would know that best.
Oedipus: Do any of you here
    know of this shepherd whom he speaks about   1110
    in town or in the fields? Tell me. It's time
    that this was found out once for all.
Chorus: I think he is none other than the peasant
    whom you have sought to see already; but
    Jocasta here can tell us best of that.   1115
Oedipus: Jocasta, do you know about this man
    whom we have sent for? Is he the man he mentions?
Jocasta: Why ask of whom he spoke? Don't give it heed;
    nor try to keep in mind what has been said.
    It will be wasted labor.
Oedipus: With such clues   1120
    I could not fail to bring my birth to light.
Jocasta: I beg you—do not hunt this out—I beg you,

1097 *your present name:* Oedipus's name means "swollen foot" or "clubfoot."

if you have any care for your own life.
What I am suffering is enough.

Oedipus: Keep up
your heart, Jocasta. Though I'm proved a slave,   1125
thrice slave, and though my mother is thrice slave,
you'll not be shown to be of lowly lineage.

Jocasta: O be persuaded by me, I entreat you;
do not do this.

Oedipus: I will not be persuaded to let be   1130
the chance of finding out the whole thing clearly.

Jocasta: It is because I wish you well that I
give you this counsel—and it's the best counsel.

Oedipus: Then the best counsel vexes me, and has
for some while since.

Jocasta: O Oedipus, God help you!   1135
God keep you from the knowledge of who you are!

Oedipus: Here, some one, go and fetch the shepherd for me;
and let her find her joy in her rich family!

Jocasta: O Oedipus, unhappy Oedipus!
that is all I can call you, and the last thing   1140
that I shall ever call you.

(*Exit.*)

Chorus: Why has the queen gone, Oedipus, in wild
grief rushing from us? I am afraid that trouble
will break out of this silence.

Oedipus: Break out what will! I at least shall be   1145
willing to see my ancestry, though humble.
Perhaps she is ashamed of my low birth,
for she has all a woman's high-flown pride.
But I account myself a child of Fortune,
beneficent Fortune, and I shall not be   1150
dishonored. She's the mother from whom I spring;
the months, my brothers, marked me, now as small,
and now again as mighty. Such is my breeding,
and I shall never prove so false to it,
as not to find the secret of my birth.   1155

Strophe

Chorus: If I am a prophet and wise of heart
you shall not fail, Cithaeron,
by the limitless sky, you shall not!—
to know at tomorrow's full moon
that Oedipus honors you,   1160
as native to him and mother and nurse at once;
and that you are honored in dancing by us, as finding favor in sight of our king.
Apollo, to whom we cry, find these things pleasing!

Antistrophe

Who was it bore you, child? One of
the long-lived nymphs who lay with Pan°—   1165
the father who treads the hills?
Or was she a bride of Loxias, your mother? The grassy slopes
are all of them dear to him. Or perhaps Cyllene's king°
or the Bacchants' God° that lives on the tops
of the hills received you a gift from some   1170
one of the Helicon Nymphs, with whom he mostly plays?

(Enter an old man, led by Oedipus' servants.)

Oedipus: If some one like myself who never met him
    may make a guess,—I think this is the herdsman,
    whom we were seeking. His old age is consonant
    with the other. And besides, the men who bring him   1175
    I recognize as my own servants. You
    perhaps may better me in knowledge since
    you've seen the man before.
Chorus: You can be sure
    I recognize him. For if Laius
    had ever an honest shepherd, this was he.   1180
Oedipus: You, sir, from Corinth, I must ask you first,
    is this the man you spoke of?
Messenger: This is he
    before your eyes.
Oedipus: Old man, look here at me
    and tell me what I ask you. Were you ever
    a servant of King Laius?
Herdsman: I was,—   1185
    no slave he bought but reared in his own house.
Oedipus: What did you do as work? How did you live?
Herdsman: Most of my life was spent among the flocks.
Oedipus: In what part of the country did you live?
Herdsman: Cithaeron and the places near to it.   1190
Oedipus: And somewhere there perhaps you knew this man?
Herdsman: What was his occupation? Who?
Oedipus: This man here,
    have you had any dealings with him?
Herdsman: No—
    not such that I can quickly call to mind.

1165 *nymphs who lay with Pan:* In Greek mythology, nymphs are beautiful young immortals associated with features of nature or specific places. Pan is the goat-footed god of wildlife and the flocks. In this passage the chorus speculates that Oedipus is the child of a nymph by some god. 1168 *Cyllene's king:* Hermes, messenger of the gods. 1169 *Bacchants' God:* Dionysus. Bacchants are the same as Maenads, the wine god's priestesses.

Messenger: That is no wonder, master. But I'll make him remember what he 1195
    does not know. For I know, that he well knows the country of Cithaeron,
    how he with two flocks, I with one kept company for three years—each year
    half a year—from spring till autumn time and then when winter came I drove
    my flocks to our fold home again and he to Laius' steadings. Well—am I right
    or not in what I said we did? 1200
Herdsman: You're right—although it's a long time ago.
Messenger: Do you remember giving me a child
    to bring up as my foster child?
Herdsman: What's this?
    Why do you ask this question?
Messenger: Look old man,
    here he is—here's the man who was that child! 1205
Herdsman: Death take you! Won't you hold your tongue?
Oedipus: No, no,
    do not find fault with him, old man. Your words
    are more at fault than his.
Herdsman: O best of masters,
    how do I give offense?
Oedipus: When you refuse
    to speak about the child of whom he asks you. 1210
Herdsman: He speaks out of his ignorance, without meaning.
Oedipus: If you'll not talk to gratify me, you
    will talk with pain to urge you.
Herdsman: O please, sir,
    don't hurt an old man, sir.
Oedipus (to the servants):   Here, one of you,
    twist his hands behind him.
Herdsman: Why, God help me, why? 1215
    What do you want to know?
Oedipus: You gave a child
    to him,—the child he asked you of?
Herdsman: I did.
    I wish I'd died the day I did.
Oedipus: You will
    unless you tell me truly.
Herdsman: And I'll die
    far worse if I should tell you.
Oedipus: This fellow 1220
    is bent on more delays, as it would seem.
Herdsman: O no, no! I have told you that I gave it.
Oedipus: Where did you get this child from? Was it your own
    or did you get it from another?
Herdsman: Not
    my own at all; I had it from some one. 1225
Oedipus: One of these citizens? or from what house?
Herdsman: O master, please—I beg you, master, please
    don't ask me more.

Oedipus: You're a dead man if I
    ask you again.
Herdsman: It was one of the children
    of Laius.
Oedipus: A slave? Or born in wedlock?   1230
Herdsman: O God, I am on the brink of frightful speech.
Oedipus: And I of frightful hearing. But I must hear.
Herdsman: The child was called his child; but she within,
    your wife would tell you best how all this was.
Oedipus: She gave it to you?
Herdsman: Yes, she did, my lord.   1235
Oedipus: To do what with it?
Herdsman: Make away with it.
Oedipus: She was so hard—its mother?
Herdsman: Aye, through fear
    of evil oracles.
Oedipus: Which?
Herdsman: They said that he
    should kill his parents.
Oedipus: How was it that you
    gave it away to this old man?
Herdsman: O master,   1240
    I pitied it, and thought that I could send it
    off to another country and this man
    was from another country. But he saved it
    for the most terrible troubles. If you are
    the man he says you are, you're bred to misery.   1245
Oedipus: O, O, O, they will all come,
    all come out clearly! Light of the sun, let me
    look upon you no more after today!
    I who first saw the light bred of a match
    accursed, and accursed in my living   1250
    with them I lived with, cursed in my killing.

(Exeunt all but the Chorus.)

Strophe

Chorus: O generations of men, how I
    count you as equal with those who live
    not at all!
    What man, what man on earth wins more   1255
    of happiness than a seeming
    and after that turning away?
    Oedipus, you are my pattern of this,
    Oedipus, you and your fate!
    Luckless Oedipus, whom of all men   1260
    I envy not at all.

Antistrophe

In as much as he shot his bolt
beyond the others and won the prize
of happiness complete—
O Zeus—and killed and reduced to nought   1265
the hooked taloned maid of the riddling speech,
standing a tower against death for my land:
hence he was called my king and hence
was honored the highest of all
honors; and hence he ruled   1270
in the great city of Thebes.

Strophe

But now whose tale is more miserable?
Who is there lives with a savager fate?
Whose troubles so reverse his life as his?

O Oedipus, the famous prince   1275
for whom a great haven°
the same both as father and son
sufficed for generation,
how, O how, have the furrows ploughed
by your father endured to bear you, poor wretch, 1280
and hold their peace so long?

Antistrophe

Time who sees all has found you out
against your will; judges your marriage accursed,
begetter and begot at one in it.

O child of Laius,   1285
would I had never seen you.
I weep for you and cry
a dirge of lamentation.

To speak directly, I drew my breath
from you at the first and so now I lull   1290
my mouth to sleep with your name.

(Enter a second messenger.)

Second Messenger: O Princes always honored by our country,
    what deeds you'll hear of and what horrors see,
    what grief you'll feel, if you as true born Thebans
    care for the house of Labdacus's sons.   1295
    Phasis nor Ister cannot purge this house,
    I think, with all their streams, such things
    it hides, such evils shortly will bring forth
    into the light, whether they will or not;

1276 *a great haven:* the womb of Jocasta.

and troubles hurt the most   1300
    when they prove self-inflicted.
Chorus: What we had known before did not fall short
    of bitter groaning's worth; what's more to tell?
Second Messenger: Shortest to hear and tell—our glorious queen
    Jocasta's dead.
Chorus: Unhappy woman! How?   1305
Second Messenger: By her own hand. The worst of what was done
    you cannot know. You did not see the sight.
    Yet in so far as I remember it
    you'll hear the end of our unlucky queen.
    When she came raging into the house she went   1310
    straight to her marriage bed, tearing her hair
    with both her hands, and crying upon Laius
    long dead—Do you remember, Laius,
    that night long past which bred a child for us
    to send you to your death and leave   1315
    a mother making children with her son?
    And then she groaned and cursed the bed in which
    she brought forth husband by her husband, children
    by her own child, an infamous double bond.
    How after that she died I do not know,—   1320
    for Oedipus distracted us from seeing.
    He burst upon us shouting and we looked
    to him as he paced frantically around,
    begging us always: Give me a sword, I say,
    to find this wife no wife, this mother's womb,   1325
    this field of double sowing whence I sprang
    and where I sowed my children! As he raved
    some god showed him the way—none of us there.
    Bellowing terribly and led by some
    invisible guide he rushed on the two doors,—   1330
    wrenching the hollow bolts out of their sockets,
    he charged inside. There, there, we saw his wife
    hanging, the twisted rope around her neck.
    When he saw her, he cried out fearfully
    and cut the dangling noose. Then, as she lay,   1335
    poor woman, on the ground, what happened after,
    was terrible to see. He tore the brooches—
    the gold chased brooches fastening her robe—
    away from her and lifting them up high
    dashed them on his own eyeballs, shrieking out   1340
    such things as: they will never see the crime
    I have committed or had done upon me!
    Dark eyes, now in the days to come look on
    forbidden faces, do not recognize
    those whom you long for—with such imprecations   1345
    he struck his eyes again and yet again
    with the brooches. And the bleeding eyeballs gushed
    and stained his beard—no sluggish oozing drops
    but a black rain and bloody hail poured down.

So it has broken—and not on one head   1350
but troubles mixed for husband and for wife.
The fortune of the days gone by was true
good fortune—but today groans and destruction
and death and shame—of all ills can be named
not one is missing.   1355
Chorus: Is he now in any ease from pain?
Second Messenger: He shouts
for some one to unbar the doors and show him
to all the men of Thebes, his father's killer,
his mother's—no I cannot say the word,
it is unholy—for he'll cast himself,   1360
out of the land, he says, and not remain
to bring a curse upon his house, the curse
he called upon it in his proclamation. But
he wants for strength, aye, and some one to guide him;
his sickness is too great to bear. You, too,   1365
will be shown that. The bolts are opening.
Soon you will see a sight to waken pity
even in the horror of it.

(*Enter the blinded Oedipus.*)

Chorus: This is a terrible sight for men to see!
I never found a worse!   1370
Poor wretch, what madness came upon you!
What evil spirit leaped upon your life
to your ill-luck—a leap beyond man's strength!
Indeed I pity you, but I cannot
look at you, though there's much I want to ask   1375
and much to learn and much to see.
I shudder at the sight of you.
Oedipus: O, O,
where am I going? Where is my voice
borne on the wind to and fro?   1380
Spirit, how far have you sprung?
Chorus: To a terrible place whereof men's ears
may not hear, nor their eyes behold it.
Oedipus: Darkness!
Horror of darkness enfolding, resistless, unspeakable visitant sped by an ill
   wind in haste!   1385
madness and stabbing pain and memory
of evil deeds I have done!
Chorus: In such misfortunes it's no wonder
if double weighs the burden of your grief.
Oedipus: My friend,   1390
you are the only one steadfast, the only one that attends on me;
you still stay nursing the blind man.
Your care is not unnoticed. I can know
your voice, although this darkness is my world.
Chorus: Doer of dreadful deeds, how did you dare   1395
so far to do despite to your own eyes?

what spirit urged you to it?

Oedipus: It was Apollo, friends, Apollo,
that brought this bitter bitterness, my sorrows to completion.
But the hand that struck me   1400
was none but my own.
Why should I see
whose vision showed me nothing sweet to see?

Chorus: These things are as you say.

Oedipus: What can I see to love?   1405
What greeting can touch my ears with joy?
Take me away, and haste—to a place out of the way!
Take me away, my friends, the greatly miserable,
the most accursed, whom God too hates
above all men on earth!   1410

Chorus: Unhappy in your mind and your misfortune,
would I had never known you!

Oedipus: Curse on the man who took
the cruel bonds from off my legs, as I lay in the field.
He stole me from death and saved me,   1415
no kindly service.
Had I died then
I would not be so burdensome to friends.

Chorus: I, too, could have wished it had been so.

Oedipus: Then I would not have come   1420
to kill my father and marry my mother infamously.
Now I am godless and child of impurity,
begetter in the same seed that created my wretched self.
If there is any ill worse than ill,
that is the lot of Oedipus.   1425

Chorus: I cannot say your remedy was good;
you would be better dead than blind and living.

Oedipus: What I have done here was best done—don't tell me
otherwise, do not give me further counsel.
I do not know with what eyes I could look   1430
upon my father when I die and go
under the earth, nor yet my wretched mother—
those two to whom I have done things deserving
worse punishment than hanging. Would the sight
of children, bred as mine are, gladden me?   1435
No, not these eyes, never. And my city,
its towers and sacred places of the Gods,
of these I robbed my miserable self
when I commanded all to drive *him* out,
the criminal since proved by God impure   1440
and of the race of Laius.
To this guilt I bore witness against myself—
with what eyes shall I look upon my people?
No. If there were a means to choke the fountain
of hearing I would not have stayed my hand   1445
from locking up my miserable carcase,

seeing and hearing nothing; it is sweet
to keep our thoughts out of the range of hurt.

Cithaeron, why did you receive me? Why
having received me did you not kill me straight? 1450
And so I had not shown to men my birth.

O Polybus and Corinth and the house,
the old house that I used to call my father's—
what fairness you were nurse to, and what foulness
festered beneath! Now I am found to be 1455
a sinner and a son of sinners. Crossroads,
and hidden glade, oak and the narrow way
at the crossroads, that drank my father's blood
offered you by my hands, do you remember
still what I did as you looked on, and what 1460
I did when I came here? O marriage, marriage!
you bred me and again when you had bred
bred children of your child and showed to men
brides, wives and mothers and the foulest deeds
that can be in this world of ours. 1465

Come—it's unfit to say what is unfit
to do.—I beg of you in God's name hide me
somewhere outside your country, yes, or kill me,
or throw me into the sea, to be forever
out of your sight. Approach and deign to touch me 1470
for all my wretchedness, and do not fear.
No man but I can bear my evil doom.
Chorus: Here Creon comes in fit time to perform
or give advice in what you ask of us.
Creon is left sole ruler in your stead. 1475
Oedipus: Creon! Creon! What shall I say to him?
How can I justly hope that he will trust me?
In what is past I have been proved towards him
an utter liar.

(*Enter Creon.*)

Creon: Oedipus, I've come
not so that I might laugh at you nor taunt you 1480
with evil of the past. But if you still
are without shame before the face of men
reverence at least the flame that gives all life,
our Lord the Sun, and do not show unveiled
to him pollution such that neither land 1485
nor holy rain nor light of day can welcome.

(*To a servant.*)

Be quick and take him in. It is most decent
that only kin should see and hear the troubles
of kin.

Oedipus: I beg you, since you've torn me from
  my dreadful expectations and have come   1490
  in a most noble spirit to a man
  that has used you vilely—do a thing for me.
  I shall speak for your own good, not for my own.
Creon: What do you need that you would ask of me?
Oedipus: Drive me from here with all the speed you can   1495
  to where I may not hear a human voice.
Creon: Be sure, I would have done this had not I
  wished first of all to learn from the God the course
  of action I should follow.
Oedipus: But his word
  has been quite clear to let the parricide,   1500
  the sinner, die.
Creon: Yes, that indeed was said.
  But in the present need we had best discover
  what we should do.
Oedipus: And will you ask about
  a man so wretched?
Creon: Now even you will trust
  the God.
Oedipus: So. I command you—and will beseech you— 1505
  to her that lies inside that house give burial
  as you would have it; she is yours and rightly
  you will perform the rites for her. For me—
  never let this my father's city have me
  living a dweller in it. Leave me live   1510
  in the mountains where Cithaeron is, that's called
  my mountain, which my mother and my father
  while they were living would have made my tomb.
  So I may die by their decree who sought
  indeed to kill me. Yet I know this much: 1515
  no sickness and no other thing will kill me.
  I would not have been saved from death if not
  for some strange evil fate. Well, let my fate
  go where it will.
      Creon, you need not care
  about my sons; they're men and so wherever   1520
  they are, they will not lack a livelihood.
  But my two girls—so sad and pitiful—
  whose table never stood apart from mine,
  and everything I touched they always shared—
  O Creon, have a thought for them! And most   1525
  I wish that you might suffer me to touch them
  and sorrow with them.

(Enter Antigone and Ismene, Oedipus' two daughters.)

O my lord! O true noble Creon! Can I
really be touching them, as when I saw?
What shall I say?   1530

Yes, I can hear them sobbing—my two darlings!
and Creon has had pity and has sent me
what I loved most?
Am I right?

Creon: You're right: it was I gave you this   1535
and because I knew from old days how you loved them
as I see now.

Oedipus: God bless you for it, Creon,
and may God guard you better on your road
than he did me!
                    O children,
where are you? Come here, come to my hands,   1540
a brother's hands which turned your father's eyes,
those bright eyes you knew once, to what you see,
a father seeing nothing, knowing nothing,
begetting you from his own source of life.
I weep for you—I cannot see your faces—   1545
I weep when I think of the bitterness
there will be in your lives, how you must live
before the world. At what assemblages
of citizens will you make one? to what
gay company will you go and not come home   1550
in tears instead of sharing in the holiday?
And when you're ripe for marriage, who will he be,
the man who'll risk to take such infamy
as shall cling to my children, to bring hurt
on them and those that marry with them? What   1555
curse is not there? "Your father killed his father
and sowed the seed where he had sprung himself
and begot you out of the womb that held him."
These insults you will hear. Then who will marry you?
No one, my children; clearly you are doomed   1560
to waste away in barrenness unmarried.
Son of Menoeceus, since you are all the father
left these two girls, and we, their parents, both
are dead to them—do not allow them wander
like beggars, poor and husbandless.   1565
They are of your own blood.
And do not make them equal with myself
in wretchedness; for you can see them now
so young, so utterly alone, save for you only.
Touch my hand, noble Creon, and say yes.   1570
If you were older, children, and were wiser,
there's much advice I'd give you. But as it is,
let this be what you pray: give me a life
wherever there is opportunity
to live, and better life than was my father's.   1575

Creon: Your tears have had enough of scope; now go within the house.
Oedipus: I must obey, though bitter of heart.
Creon: In season, all is good.

Oedipus: Do you know on what conditions I obey?
Creon: You tell me them,
   and I shall know them when I hear.
Oedipus: That you shall send me out   1580
   to live away from Thebes.
Creon: That gift you must ask of the God.
Oedipus: But I'm now hated by the Gods.
Creon: So quickly you'll obtain your prayer.
Oedipus: You consent then?
Creon: What I do not mean, I do not use to say.
Oedipus: Now lead me away from here.
Creon: Let go the children, then, and come.
Oedipus: Do not take them from me.
Creon: Do not seek to be master in everything,   1585
   for the things you mastered did not follow you throughout your life.

   (*As Creon and Oedipus go out.*)

Chorus: You that live in my ancestral Thebes, behold this Oedipus,—
   him who knew the famous riddles and was a man most masterful;
   not a citizen who did not look with envy on his lot—
   see him now and see the breakers of misfortune swallow him!   1590
   Look upon that last day always. Count no mortal happy till
   he has passed the final limit of his life secure from pain.

Questions

1. How explicitly does the prophet Teiresias reveal the guilt of Oedipus? Does it seem to you stupidity on the part of Oedipus or a defect in Sophocles's play that the king takes so long to recognize his guilt and to admit to it?

2. How does Oedipus exhibit weakness of character? Point to lines that reveal him as imperfectly noble in his words, deeds, or treatment of others.

3. "Oedipus is punished not for any fault in himself, but for his ignorance. Not knowing his family history, unable to recognize his parents on sight, he is blameless; and in slaying his father and marrying his mother, he behaves as any sensible person might behave in the same circumstances." Do you agree with this interpretation?

4. Besides the predictions of Teiresias, what other foreshadowings of the shepherd's revelation does the play contain?

5. Consider the character of Jocasta. Is she a "flat" character—a generalized queen figure—or an individual with distinctive traits of personality? Point to speeches or details in the play to back up your opinion.

6. What is dramatic irony? Besides the example given in Chapter 5 (Terms for Review), what other instances of dramatic irony do you find in *Oedipus the King*? What do they contribute to the effectiveness of the play?

7. In the drama of Sophocles, violence and bloodshed take place offstage; thus, the suicide of Jocasta is only reported to us. Nor do we witness Oedipus's removal of his eyes; this horror is only given in the report by the second messenger. Of what advantage or disadvantage to the play is this limitation?

8. For what reason does Oedipus blind himself? What meaning, if any, do you find in his choice of a surgical instrument?

9. What are your feelings toward him as the play ends?

10. Read the famous interpretation of this play offered by Sigmund Freud (later in this chapter). How well does Freud explain why the play moves you?

11. With what attitude toward the gods does the play leave you? By inflicting a plague on Thebes, by causing barrenness, by cursing both the people and their king, do the gods seem cruel, unjust, or tyrannical? Does the play show any reverence toward them?

12. Does this play end in total gloom?

THE BACKGROUND OF *ANTIGONE*

Although *Antigone* tells a later part of the Oedipus story, it was not part of the trilogy that originally contained *Oedipus the King* (the other plays in that trilogy have been lost). *Antigone* was written in 441 B.C., more than twenty years before the author took up the tale of Oedipus himself. In *Antigone* duties to family and duties to the state are pitted against one another in a story that has Creon, now king of Thebes many years after Oedipus's exile and death, refusing burial to the body of Oedipus's son (and brother) Polyneices, who has led an army against the city to claim the throne from his brother. His sister Antigone (Oedipus's daughter and sister) resists Creon's unjust edict in the name of family loyalty, a defiance both noble and potentially threatening to political stability in a time of crisis. Though the gods approve of her action, she dies a victim of Creon's hubris. (Or perhaps, as Patricia Lines suggests later in this chapter, Antigone's own hubris is her downfall.) Creon suffers the death (by suicide) of his son and his wife as a result. Antigone's claim is especially compelling when we imagine her played by a mature male actor who in his public life, as a citizen, must know both how to rule and how to be ruled, to submit to legitimate authority when he steps down from office.

Martha Henry in the 1971 Lincoln Center Repertory production of *Antigone*.

Antigone   441 B.C.

Translated by David Grene

CHARACTERS

Antigone	Haemon
Ismene	Teiresias
Chorus of Theban Elders	A Messenger
Creon	Eurydice
A Sentry	Second Messenger

(*The two sisters Antigone and Ismene meet in front of the palace gates in Thebes.*)

Antigone: Ismene, my dear sister,
    whose father was my father, can you think of any
    of all the evils that stem from Oedipus°
    that Zeus does not bring to pass for us, while we yet live?
    No pain, no ruin, no shame, and no dishonor   5
    but I have seen it in our mischiefs,
    yours and mine.
    And now what is the proclamation that they tell of
    made lately by the commander, publicly,
    to all the people? Do you know it? Have you heard it?   10
    Don't you notice when the evils due to enemies
    are headed towards those we love?
Ismene: Not a word, Antigone, of those we love,
    either sweet or bitter, has come to me since the moment
    when we lost our two brothers,   15
    on one day, by their hands dealing mutual death.
    Since the Argive army fled in this past night,
    I know of nothing further, nothing
    of better fortune or of more destruction.
Antigone: I knew it well; that is why I sent for you   20
    to come outside the palace gates
    to listen to me, privately.
Ismene: What is it? Certainly your words
    come of dark thoughts.

---

3 *the evils that stem from Oedipus:* As Sophocles describes in *Oedipus the King*, the King of Thebes discovered that he had lived his life under a curse. Unknowingly, he had slain his father and married his mother. On realizing this terrible truth, Oedipus put out his own eyes and departed into exile. Now, years later, as *Antigone* opens, Antigone and Ismene, daughters of Oedipus, are recalling how their two brothers died. After the abdication of their father, the brothers had ruled Thebes together. But they fell to quarreling. When Eteocles expelled Polyneices, the latter returned with an army and attacked the city. The two brothers killed each other in combat, leaving the throne to Creon. The new king of Thebes has buried Eteocles with full honors, but, calling Polyneices a traitor, has decreed that his body shall be left to the crows—an especially terrible decree, for a rotting corpse might offend Zeus; bring down plague, blight, and barrenness upon Thebes; and prevent the soul of a dead hero from entering the Elysian Fields, abode of those favored by the gods.

Antigone: Yes, indeed; for those two brothers of ours, in burial   25
    has not Creon honored the one, dishonored the other?
    Eteocles, they say he has used justly
    with lawful rites and hid him in the earth
    to have his honor among the dead men there.
    But the unhappy corpse of Polyneices   30
    he has proclaimed to all the citizens,
    they say, no man may hide
    in a grave nor mourn in funeral,
    but leave unwept, unburied, a dainty treasure
    for the birds that see him, for their feast's delight.   35
    That is what, they say, the worthy Creon
    has proclaimed for you and me—for me, I tell you—
    and he comes here to clarify to the unknowing
    his proclamation; he takes it seriously;
    for whoever breaks the edict death is prescribed,   40
    and death by stoning publicly.
    There you have it; soon you will show yourself
    as noble both in your nature and your birth,
    or yourself as base, although of noble parents.
Ismene: If things are as you say, poor sister, how   45
    can I better them? how loose or tie the knot?
Antigone: Decide if you will share the work, the deed.
Ismene: What kind of danger is there? How far have your thoughts gone?
Antigone: Here is this hand. Will you help it to lift the dead man?
Ismene: Would you bury him, when it is forbidden the city?   50
Antigone: At least he is my brother—and yours, too,
    though you deny him. *I* will not prove false to him.
Ismene: You are so headstrong. Creon has forbidden it.
Antigone: It is not for him to keep me from my own.
Ismene: O God!   55
    Consider, sister, how our father died,
    hated and infamous; how he brought to light
    his own offenses; how he himself struck out
    the sight of his two eyes;
    his own hand was their executioner.   60
    Then, mother and wife, two names in one, did shame
    violently on her life, with twisted cords.
    Third, our two brothers, on a single day,
    poor wretches, themselves worked out their mutual doom.
    Each killed the other, hand against brother's hand.   65
    Now there are only the two of us, left behind,
    and see how miserable our end shall be
    if in the teeth of law we shall transgress
    against the sovereign's decree and power.
    You ought to realize we are only women,   70
    not meant in nature to fight against men,
    and that we are ruled, by those who are stronger,
    to obedience in this and even more painful matters.

I do indeed beg those beneath the earth
to give me their forgiveness,   75
since force constrains me,
that I shall yield in this to the authorities.
Extravagant action is not sensible.

Antigone: I would not urge you now; nor if you wanted
to act would I be glad to have you with me.   80
Be as you choose to be; but for myself
I myself will bury him. It will be good
to die, so doing. I shall lie by his side,
loving him as he loved me; I shall be
a criminal—but a religious one.   85
The time in which I must please those that are dead
is longer than I must please those of this world.
For there I shall lie forever. You, if you like,
can cast dishonor on what the gods have honored.

Ismene: I will not put dishonor on them, but   90
to act in defiance of the citizenry,
my nature does not give me means for that.

Antigone: Let that be your excuse. But I will go
to heap the earth on the grave of my loved brother.

Ismene: How I fear for you, my poor sister!   95

Antigone: Do not fear for me. Make straight your own path to destiny.

Ismene: At least do not speak of this act to anyone else;
bury him in secret; I will be silent, too.

Antigone: Oh, oh, no! shout it out. I will hate you still worse
for silence—should you not proclaim it,   100
to everyone.

Ismene: You have a warm heart for such chilly deeds.

Antigone: I know I am pleasing those I should please most.

Ismene: If you can do it. But you are in love
with the impossible.   105

Antigone: No. When I can no more, then I will stop.

Ismene: It is better not to hunt the impossible
at all.

Antigone: If you will talk like this I will loathe you,
and you will be adjudged an enemy—   110
justly—by the dead's decision. Let me alone
and my folly with me, to endure this terror.
No suffering of mine will be enough
to make me die ignobly.

Ismene: Well, if you will, go on.   115
Know this; that though you are wrong to go, your friends
are right to love you.

Chorus: Sun's beam, fairest of all
that ever till now shone
on seven-gated Thebes;
O golden eye of day, you shone   120
coming over Dirce's stream;°

122 *Dirce's stream:* a river near Thebes.

You drove in headlong rout
the whiteshielded man from Argos,
complete in arms;   125
his bits rang sharper
under your urging.

Polyneices brought him here
against our land, Polyneices,
roused by contentious quarrel;   130
like an eagle he flew into our country,
with many men-at-arms,
with many a helmet crowned with horsehair.
He stood above the halls, gaping with murderous lances,
encompassing the city's   135
seven-gated mouth.
But before his jaws would be sated
with our blood, before the fire,
pine fed, should capture our crown of towers,
he went hence—   140
such clamor of war stretched behind his back,
from his dragon foe, a thing he could not overcome.

For Zeus, who hates the most
the boasts of a great tongue,
saw them coming in a great tide,   145
insolent in the clang of golden armor.
The god struck him down with hurled fire,
as he strove to raise the victory cry,
now at the very winning post.

The earth rose to strike him as he fell swinging.   150
In his frantic onslaught, possessed, he breathed upon us
with blasting winds of hate.
Sometimes the great god of war was on one side,
and sometimes he struck a staggering blow on the other;
the god was a very wheel horse on the right trace.   155

At seven gates stood seven captains,
ranged equals against equals, and there left
their brazen suits of armor
to Zeus, the god of trophies.
Only those two wretches born of one father and mother   160
set their spears to win a victory on both sides;
they worked out their share in a common death.

Now Victory, whose name is great, has come
to Thebes of many chariots
with joy to answer her joy,   165
to bring forgetfulness of these wars;
let us go to all the shrines of the gods
and dance all night long.
Let Bacchus lead the dance,
shaking Thebes to trembling.   170

But here is the king of our land,
Creon, son of Menoeceus;
in our new contingencies with the gods,
he is our new ruler.
He comes to set in motion some design—   175
what design is it? Because he has proposed
the convocation of the elders.
He sent a public summons for our discussion.

Creon: Gentlemen: as for our city's fortune,
the gods have shaken her, when the great waves broke,   180
but the gods have brought her through again to safety.
For yourselves, I chose you out of all and summoned you
to come to me, partly because I knew you
as always loyal to the throne—at first,
when Laius was king, and then again   185
when Oedipus saved our city and then again
when he died and you remained with steadfast truth
to their descendants,
until they met their double fate upon one day,
striking and stricken, defiled each by a brother's murder.   190
Now here I am, holding all authority
and the throne, in virtue of kinship with the dead.

It is impossible to know any man—
I mean his soul, intelligence, and judgment—
until he shows his skill in rule and law.   195
I think that a man supreme ruler of a whole city,
if he does not reach for the best counsel for her,
but through some fear, keeps his tongue under lock and key,
him I judge the worst of any;
I have always judged so; and anyone thinking   200
another man more a friend than his own country,
I rate him nowhere. For my part, God is my witness,
who sees all, always, I would not be silent
if I saw ruin, not safety, on the way
towards my fellow citizens. I would not count   205
any enemy of my country as a friend—
because of what I know, that she it is
which gives us our security. If she sails upright
and we sail on her, friends will be ours for the making.
In the light of rules like these, I will make her greater still.   210

In consonance with this, I here proclaim
to the citizens about Oedipus' sons.
For Eteocles, who died this city's champion,
showing his valor's supremacy everywhere,
he shall be buried in his grave with every rite   215
of sanctity given to heroes under earth.
However, his brother, Polyneices, a returned exile,

who sought to burn with fire from top to bottom
his native city, and the gods of his own people;
who sought to taste the blood he shared with us, 220
and lead the rest of us to slavery—
I here proclaim to the city that this man
shall no one honor with a grave and none shall mourn.
You shall leave him without burial; you shall watch him
chewed up by birds and dogs and violated. 225
Such is my mind in the matter; never by me
shall the wicked man have precedence in honor
over the just. But he that is loyal to the state
in death, in life alike, shall have my honor.

Chorus: Son of Menoeceus, so it is your pleasure 230
to deal with foe and friend of this our city.
To use any legal means lies in your power,
both about the dead and those of us who live.

Creon: I understand, then, you will do my bidding.

Chorus: Please lay this burden on some younger man. 235

Creon: Oh, watchers of the corpse I have already.

Chorus: What else, then, do your commands entail?

Creon: That you should not side with those who disagree.

Chorus: There is none so foolish as to love his own death.

Creon: Yes, indeed those are the wages, but often greed 240
has with its hopes brought men to ruin.

Sentry: My lord, I will never claim my shortness of breath
is due to hurrying, nor were there wings in my feet.
I stopped at many a lay-by in my thinking;
I circled myself till I met myself coming back. 245
My soul accosted me with different speeches.
"Poor fool, yourself, why are you going somewhere
when once you get there you will pay the piper?"
"Well, aren't you the daring fellow! stopping again?
and suppose Creon hears the news from someone else— 250
don't you realize that you will smart for that?"
I turned the whole matter over. I suppose I may say
"I made haste slowly" and the short road became long.
However, at last I came to a resolve:
I must go to you; even if what I say 255
is nothing, really, still I shall say it.
I come here, a man with a firm clutch on the hope
that nothing can betide him save what is fated.

Creon: What is it then that makes you so afraid?

Sentry: No, I want first of all to tell you my side of it. 260
I didn't do the thing; I never saw who did it.
It would not be fair for me to get into trouble.

Creon: You hedge, and barricade the thing itself.
Clearly you have some ugly news for me.

Sentry: Well, you know how disasters make a man 265
hesitate to be their messenger.

Creon: For God's sake, tell me and get out of here!
Sentry: Yes, I *will* tell you. Someone just now
    buried the corpse and vanished. He scattered on the skin
    some thirsty dust; he did the ritual,   270
    duly, to purge the body of desecration.
Creon: What! Now who on earth could have done that?
Sentry: I do not know. For there was there no mark
    of axe's stroke nor casting up of earth
    of any mattock; the ground was hard and dry,   275
    unbroken; there were no signs of wagon wheels.
    The doer of the deed had left no trace.
    But when the first sentry of the day pointed it out,
    there was for all of us a disagreeable
    wonder. For the body had disappeared;   280
    not in a grave, of course; but there lay upon him
    a little dust as of a hand avoiding
    the curse of violating the dead body's sanctity.
    There were no signs of any beast nor dog
    that came there; he had clearly not been torn.   285
    There was a tide of bad words at one another,
    guard taunting guard, and it might well have ended
    in blows, for there was no one there to stop it.
    Each one of us was the criminal but no one
    manifestly so; all denied knowledge of it.   290
    We were ready to take hot bars in our hands
    or walk through fire, and call on the gods with oaths
    that we had neither done it nor were privy
    to a plot with anyone, neither in planning
    nor yet in execution.   295
    At last when nothing came of all our searching,
    there was one man who spoke, made every head
    bow to the ground in fear. For we could not
    either contradict him nor yet could we see how
    if we did what he said we would come out all right.   300
    His word was that we must lay information
    about this matter to yourself; we could not cover it.
    This view prevailed and the lot of the draw chose me,
    unlucky me, to win that prize. So here
    I am. I did not want to come,   305
    and you don't want to have me. I know that.
    For no one likes the messenger of bad news.
Chorus: My lord: I wonder, could this be God's doing?
    This is the thought that keeps on haunting me.
Creon: Stop, before your words fill even me with rage,   310
    that you should be exposed as a fool, and you so old.
    For what you say is surely insupportable
    when you say the gods took forethought for this corpse.
    Is it out of excess of honor for the man,
    for the favors that he did them, they should cover him?   315

This man who came to burn their pillared temples,
their dedicated offerings—and this land
and laws he would have scattered to the winds?
Or do you see the gods as honoring
criminals? This is not so. But what I am doing 320
now, and other things before this, some men disliked,
within this very city, and muttered against me,
secretly shaking their heads; they would not bow
justly beneath the yoke to submit to me.
I am very sure that these men hired others 325
to do this thing. I tell you the worst currency
that ever grew among mankind is money. This
sacks cities, this drives people from their homes,
this teaches and corrupts the minds of the loyal
to acts of shame. This displays 330
all kinds of evil for the use of men,
instructs in the knowledge of every impious act.
Those that have done this deed have been paid to do it,
but in the end they will pay for what they have done.

It is as sure as I still reverence Zeus— 335
know this right well—and I speak under oath—
if you and your fellows do not find this man
who with his own hand did the burial
and bring him here before me face to face,
your death alone will not be enough for me. 340
You will hang alive till you open up this outrage.
That will teach you in the days to come from what
you may draw profit—safely—from your plundering.
It's not from anything and everything
you can grow rich. You will find out 345
that ill-gotten gains ruin more than they save.
Sentry: Have I your leave to say something—or should I
    just turn and go?
Creon: Don't you know your talk is painful enough already?
Sentry: Is the ache in your ears or in your mind? 350
Creon: Why do you dissect the whereabouts of my pain?
Sentry: Because it is he who did the deed who hurts
    your mind. I only hurt your ears that listen.
Creon: I am sure you have been a chatterbox since you were born.
Sentry: All the same, I did not do this thing. 355
Creon: You might have done this, too, if you sold your soul.
Sentry: It's a bad thing if one judges and judges wrongly.
Creon: You may talk as wittily as you like of judgment.
    Only, if you don't bring to light those men
    who have done this, you will yet come to say 360
    that your wretched gains have brought bad consequences.
Sentry (aside): It were best that he were found, but whether
    the criminal is taken or he isn't—

for that chance will decide—one thing is certain,
you'll never see me coming here again.   365
I never hoped to escape, never thought I could.
But now I have come off safe, I thank God heartily.

Chorus: Many are the wonders, none
     is more wonderful than what is man.
     This it is that crosses the sea   370
     with the south winds storming and the waves swelling,
     breaking around him in roaring surf.
     He it is again who wears away
     the Earth, oldest of gods, immortal, unwearied,
     as the ploughs wind across her from year to year   375
     when he works her with the breed that comes from horses.

     The tribe of the lighthearted birds he snares
     and takes prisoner the races of savage beasts
     and the brood of the fish of the sea,
     with the close-spun web of nets.   380
     A cunning fellow is man. His contrivances
     make him master of beasts of the field
     and those that move in the mountains.
     So he brings the horse with the shaggy neck
     to bend underneath the yoke;   385
     and also the untamed mountain bull;
     and speech and windswift thought
     and the tempers that go with city living
     he has taught himself, and how to avoid
     the sharp frost, when lodging is cold   390
     under the open sky
     and pelting strokes of the rain.
     He has a way against everything,
     and he faces nothing that is to come
     without contrivance.   395
     Only against death
     can he call on no means of escape;
     but escape from hopeless diseases
     he has found in the depths of his mind.
     With some sort of cunning, inventive   400
     beyond all expectation
     he reaches sometimes evil,
     and sometimes good.

     If he honors the laws of earth,
     and the justice of the gods he has confirmed by oath,   405
     high is his city; no city
     has he with whom dwells dishonor
     prompted by recklessness.
     He who is so, may he never
     share my hearth!   410
     may he never think my thoughts!

Is this a portent sent by God?
I cannot tell.
I know her. How can I say
that this is not Antigone?   415
Unhappy girl, child of unhappy Oedipus,
what is this?
Surely it is not you they bring here
as disobedient to the royal edict,
surely not you, taken in such folly.   420

Sentry: She is the one who did the deed;
  we took her burying him. But where is Creon?

Chorus: He is just coming from the house, when you most need him.

Creon: What is this? What has happened that I come
  so opportunely?   425

Sentry: My lord, there is nothing
  that a man should swear he would never do.
  Second thoughts make liars of the first resolution.
  I would have vowed it would be long enough
  before I came again, lashed hence by your threats.   430
  But since the joy that comes past hope, and against all hope,
  is like no other pleasure in extent,
  I have come here, though I break my oath in coming.
  I bring this girl here who has been captured
  giving the grace of burial to the dead man.   435
  This time no lot chose me; this was my jackpot,
  and no one else's. Now, my lord, take her
  and as you please judge her and test her; I
  am justly free and clear of all this trouble.

Creon: This girl—how did you take her and from where?   440

Sentry: She was burying the man. Now you know all.

Creon: Do you know what you are saying? Do you mean it?

Sentry: She is the one; I saw her burying
  the dead man you forbade the burial of.
  Now, do I speak plainly and clearly enough?   445

Creon: How was she seen? How was she caught in the act?

Sentry: This is how it was. When we came there,
  with those dreadful threats of yours upon us,
  we brushed off all the dust that lay upon
  the dead man's body, heedfully   450
  leaving it moist and naked.
  We sat on the brow of the hill, to windward,
  that we might shun the smell of the corpse upon us.
  Each of us wakefully urged his fellow
  with torrents of abuse, not to be careless   455
  in this work of ours. So it went on,
  until in the midst of the sky the sun's bright circle
  stood still; the heat was burning. Suddenly
  a squall lifted out of the earth a storm of dust,
  a trouble in the sky. It filled the plain,   460

ruining all the foliage of the wood
that was around it. The great empty air
was filled with it. We closed our eyes, enduring
this plague sent by the gods. When at long last
we were quit of it, why, then we saw the girl.   465

She was crying out with the shrill cry
of an embittered bird
that sees its nest robbed of its nestlings
and the bed empty. So, too, when she saw
the body stripped of its cover, she burst out in groans,   470
calling terrible curses on those that had done that deed;
and with her hands immediately
brought thirsty dust to the body; from a shapely brazen
urn, held high over it, poured a triple stream
of funeral offerings; and crowned the corpse.   475
When we saw that, we rushed upon her and
caught our quarry then and there, not a bit disturbed.
We charged her with what she had done, then and the first time.
She did not deny a word of it—to my joy,
but to my pain as well. It is most pleasant   480
to have escaped oneself out of such troubles
but painful to bring into it those whom we love.
However, it is but natural for me
to count all this less than my own escape.
Creon: You there, that turn your eyes upon the ground,   485
    do you confess or deny what you have done?
Antigone: Yes, I confess; I will not deny my deed.
Creon (to the Sentry): You take yourself off where you like.
    You are free of a heavy charge.
    Now, Antigone, tell me shortly and to the point,   490
    did you know the proclamation against your action?
Antigone: I knew it; of course I did. For it was public.
Creon: And did you dare to disobey that law?
Antigone: Yes, it was not Zeus that made the proclamation;
    nor did Justice, which lives with those below, enact   495
    such laws as that, for mankind. I did not believe
    your proclamation had such power to enable
    one who will someday die to override
    God's ordinances, unwritten and secure.
    They are not of today and yesterday;   500
    they live forever; none knows when first they were.
    These are the laws whose penalties I would not
    incur from the gods, through fear of any man's temper.

    I know that I will die—of course I do—
    even if you had not doomed me by proclamation.   505
    If I shall die before my time, I count that
    a profit. How can such as I, that live

among such troubles, not find a profit in death?
So for such as me, to face such a fate as this
is pain that does not count. But if I dared to leave   510
the dead man, my mother's son, dead and unburied,
that would have been real pain. The other is not.
Now, if you think me a fool to act like this,
perhaps it is a fool that judges so.

Chorus: The savage spirit of a savage father   515
    shows itself in this girl. She does not know
    how to yield to trouble.

Creon: I would have you know the most fanatic spirits
    fall most of all. It is the toughest iron,
    baked in the fire to hardness, you may see   520
    most shattered, twisted, shivered to fragments.
    I know hot horses are restrained
    by a small curb. For he that is his neighbor's slave cannot
    be high in spirit. This girl had learned her insolence
    before this, when she broke the established laws.   525
    But here is still another insolence
    in that she boasts of it, laughs at what she did.
    I swear I am no man and she the man
    if she can win this and not pay for it.
    No; though she were my sister's child or closer   530
    in blood than all that my hearth god acknowledges
    as mine, neither she nor her sister should escape
    the utmost sentence—death. For indeed I accuse her,
    the sister, equally of plotting the burial.
    Summon her. I saw her inside, just now,   535
    crazy, distraught. When people plot
    mischief in the dark, it is the mind which first
    is convicted of deceit. But surely I hate indeed
    the one that is caught in evil and then makes
    that evil look like good.   540

Antigone: Do you want anything
    beyond my taking and my execution?

Creon: Oh, nothing! Once I have that I have everything.

Antigone: Why do you wait, then? Nothing that you say
    pleases me; God forbid it ever should.   545
    So my words, too, naturally offend you.
    Yet how could I win a greater share of glory
    than putting my own brother in his grave?
    All that are here would surely say that's true,
    if fear did not lock their tongues up. A prince's power   550
    is blessed in many things, not least in this,
    that he can say and do whatever he likes.

Creon: You are alone among the people of Thebes
    to see things in that way.

Antigone: No, these do, too,   555
    but keep their mouths shut for the fear of you.

Creon: Are you not ashamed to think so differently
    from them?
Antigone: There is nothing shameful in honoring my brother.
Creon: Was not he that died on the other side your brother?   560
Antigone: Yes, indeed, of my own blood from father and mother.
Creon: Why then do you show a grace that must be impious
    in *his* sight?
Antigone: *That* other dead man
    would never bear you witness in what you say.   565
Creon: Yes he would, if you put him only on equality
    with one that was a desecrator.
Antigone: It was his brother, not his slave, that died.
Creon: He died destroying the country the other defended.
Antigone: The god of death demands these rites for both.   570
Creon: But the good man does not seek an *equal* share only,
    with the bad.
Antigone: Who knows
    if in that other world this is true piety?
Creon: My enemy is still my enemy, even in death.
Antigone: My nature is to join in love, not hate.   575
Creon: Go then to the world below, yourself, if you
    must love. Love *them.* When I am alive no woman shall rule.
Chorus: Here before the gates comes Ismene
    shedding tears for the love of a brother.
    A cloud over her brow casts shame
    on her flushed face, as the tears wet   580
    her fair cheeks.
Creon: You there, who lurked in my house, viper-like—
    secretly drawing its lifeblood; I never thought
    that I was raising two sources of destruction,   585
    two rebels against my throne. Come tell me now,
    will you, too, say you bore a hand in the burial
    or will you swear that you know nothing of it?
Ismene: I did it, yes—if she will say I did it
    I bear my share in it, bear the guilt, too.   590
Antigone: Justice will not allow you what you refused
    and I will have none of your partnership.
Ismene: But in your troubles I am not ashamed
    to sail with you the sea of suffering.
Antigone: Where the act was death, the dead are witnesses.   595
    I do not love a friend who loves in words.
Ismene: Sister, do not dishonor me, denying me
    a common death with you, a common honoring
    of the dead man.
Antigone: Don't die with me, nor make your own   600
    what you have never touched. I that die am enough.
Ismene: What life is there for me, once I have lost you?
Antigone: Ask Creon; all your care was on his behalf.
Ismene: Why do you hurt me, when you gain nothing by it?
Antigone: I am hurt by my own mockery—if I mock you.   605

Ismene: Even now—what can I do to help you still?
Antigone: Save yourself; I do not grudge you your escape.
Ismene: I cannot bear it! Not even to share your death!
Antigone: Life was your choice, and death was mine.
Ismene: You cannot say I accepted that choice in silence.   610
Antigone: You were right in the eyes of one party, I in the other.
Ismene: Well then, the fault is equally between us.
Antigone: Take heart; you are alive, but my life died
    long ago, to serve the dead.
Creon: Here are two girls; I think that one of them   615
    has suddenly lost her wits—the other was always so.
Ismene: Yes, for, my lord, the wits that they are born with
    do not stay firm for the unfortunate.
    They go astray.
Creon: Certainly yours do,
    when you share troubles with the troublemaker.   620
Ismene: What life can be mine alone without her?
Creon: Do not
    speak of *her. She* isn't, anymore.
Ismene: Will you kill your son's wife to be?
Creon: Yes, there are other fields for him to plough.
Ismene: Not with the mutual love of him and her.   625
Creon: I hate a bad wife for a son of mine.
Antigone: Dear Haemon, how your father dishonors you.
Creon: There is too much of you—and of your marriage!
Chorus: Will you rob your son of this girl?
Creon: Death—it is death that will stop the marriage for me.   630
Chorus: Your decision it seems is taken: she shall die.
Creon: Both you and I have decided it. No more delay.

    (*He turns to the servants.*)

    Bring her inside, you. From this time forth,
    these must be women, and not free to roam.
    For even the stout of heart shrink when they see   635
    the approach of death close to their lives.
Chorus: Lucky are those whose lives
    know no taste of sorrow.
    But for those whose house has been shaken by God
    there is never cessation of ruin;   640
    it steals on generation after generation
    within a breed. Even as the swell
    is driven over the dark deep
    by the fierce Thracian winds
    I see the ancient evils of Labdacus' house   645
    are heaped on the evils of the dead.
    No generation frees another, some god
    strikes them down; there is no deliverance.
    Here was the light of hope stretched
    over the last roots of Oedipus' house,   650
    and the bloody dust due to the gods below

has mowed it down—that and the folly of speech
and ruin's enchantment of the mind.

Your power, O Zeus, what sin of man can limit?   655
All-aging sleep does not overtake it,
nor the unwearied months of the gods; and you,
for whom time brings no age,
you hold the glowing brightness of Olympus.

For the future near and far,
and the past, this law holds good: 660
nothing very great
comes to the life of mortal man
without ruin to accompany it.
For Hope, widely wandering, comes to many of mankind
as a blessing,   665
but to many as the deceiver,
using light-minded lusts;
she comes to him that knows nothing
till he burns his foot in the glowing fire.
With wisdom has someone declared   670
a word of distinction:
that evil seems good to one whose mind
the god leads to ruin,
and but for the briefest moment of time
is his life outside of calamity.   675

    Here is Haemon, youngest of your sons.
Does he come grieving
for the fate of his bride to be,
in agony at being cheated of his marriage?
Creon: Soon we will know that better than the prophets.   680
My son, can it be that you have not heard
of my final decision on your betrothed?
Can you have come here in your fury against your father?
Or have I your love still, no matter what I do?
Haemon: Father, I am yours; with your excellent judgment   685
you lay the right before me, and I shall follow it.
No marriage will ever be so valued by me
as to override the goodness of your leadership.
Creon: Yes, my son, this should always be
in your very heart, that everything else   690
shall be second to your father's decision.
It is for this that fathers pray to have
obedient sons begotten in their halls,
that they may requite with ill their father's enemy
and honor his friend no less than he would himself.   695
If a man have sons that are no use to him,
what can one say of him but that he has bred
so many sorrows to himself, laughter to his enemies?
Do not, my son, banish your good sense
through pleasure in a woman, since you know   700

that the embrace grows cold
when an evil woman shares your bed and home.
What greater wound can there be than a false friend?
No. Spit on her, throw her out like an enemy,
this girl, to marry someone in Death's house.   705
I caught her openly in disobedience
alone out of all this city and I shall not make
myself a liar in the city's sight. No, I will kill her.
So let her cry if she will on the Zeus of kinship;
for if I rear those of my race and breeding   710
to be rebels, surely I will do so with those outside it.
For he who is in his household a good man
will be found a just man, too, in the city.
But he that breaches the law or does it violence
or thinks to dictate to those who govern him   715
shall never have my good word.
The man the city sets up in authority
must be obeyed in small things and in just
but also in their opposites.
I am confident such a man of whom I speak   720
will be a good ruler, and willing to be well ruled.
He will stand on his country's side, faithful and just,
in the storm of battle. There is nothing worse
than disobedience to authority.
It destroys cities, it demolishes homes;   725
it breaks and routs one's allies. Of successful lives
the most of them are saved by discipline.
So we must stand on the side of what is orderly;
we cannot give victory to a woman.
If we must accept defeat, let it be from a man;   730
we must not let people say that a woman beat us.
Chorus: We think, if we are not victims of Time the Thief,
    that you speak intelligently of what you speak.
Haemon: Father, the natural sense that the gods breed
    in men is surely the best of their possessions.   735
I certainly could not declare you wrong—
may I never know how to do so!—Still there might
be something useful that some other than you might think.
It is natural for me to be watchful on your behalf
concerning what all men say or do or find to blame.   740
Your face is terrible to a simple citizen;
it frightens him from words you dislike to hear.
But what I can hear, in the dark, are things like these:
the city mourns for this girl; they think she is dying
most wrongly and most undeservedly   745
of all womenkind, for the most glorious acts.
Here is one who would not leave her brother unburied,
a brother who had fallen in bloody conflict,
to meet his end by greedy dogs or by
the bird that chanced that way. Surely what she merits   750

is golden honor, isn't it? That's the dark rumor
that spreads in secret. Nothing I own
I value more highly, father, than your success.
What greater distinction can a son have than the glory
of a successful father, and for a father   755
the distinction of successful children?
Do not bear this single habit of mind, to think
that what you say and nothing else is true.
A man who thinks that he alone is right,
or what he says, or what he *is* himself,   760
unique, such men, when opened up, are seen
to be quite empty. For a man, though he be wise,
it is no shame to learn—learn many things,
and not maintain his views too rigidly.
You notice how by streams in wintertime   765
the trees that yield preserve their branches safely,
but those that fight the tempest perish utterly.
The man who keeps the sheet of his sail tight
and never slackens capsizes his boat
and makes the rest of his trip keel uppermost.   770
Yield something of your anger, give way a little.
If a much younger man, like me, may have
a judgment, I would say it were far better
to be one altogether wise by nature, but,
as things incline not to be so, then it is good   775
also to learn from those who advise well.
Chorus: My lord, if he says anything to the point,
      you should learn from him, and you, too, Haemon,
      learn from your father. Both of you
      have spoken well.   780
Creon: Should we that are my age learn wisdom
      from young men such as he is?
Haemon: Not learn injustice, certainly. If I am young,
      do not look at my years but what I do.
Creon: Is what you do to have respect for rebels?
Haemon: I   785
      would not urge you to be scrupulous
      towards the wicked.
Creon: Is *she* not tainted by the disease of wickedness?
Haemon: The entire people of Thebes says no to that.
Creon: Should the city tell me how I am to rule them?   790
Haemon: Do you see what a young man's words these are of yours?
Creon: Must I rule the land by someone else's judgment
      rather than my own?
Haemon: There is no city
      possessed by one man only.
Creon: Is not the city thought to be the ruler's?   795
Haemon: You would be a fine dictator of a desert.
Creon: It seems this boy is on the woman's side.
Haemon: If you are a woman——my care is all for you.

Creon: You villain, to bandy words with your own father!

Haemon: I see your acts as mistaken and unjust.   800

Creon: Am I mistaken, reverencing my own office?

Haemon: There is no reverence in trampling on God's honor.

Creon: Your nature is vile, in yielding to a woman.

Haemon: You will not find me yield to what is shameful.

Creon: At least, your argument is all for her.   805

Haemon: Yes, and for you and me—and for the gods below.

Creon: You will never marry her while her life lasts.

Haemon: Then she must die—and dying destroy another.

Creon: Has your daring gone so far, to threaten me?

Haemon: What threat is it to speak against empty judgments?   810

Creon: Empty of sense yourself, you will regret
　　　your schooling of me in sense.

Haemon:　　　　　　　　　　　　If you were not
　　　my father, I would say you are insane.

Creon: You woman's slave, do not try to wheedle me.

Haemon: You want to talk but never to hear and listen.   815

Creon: Is that so? By the heavens above you will not—
　　　be sure of that—get off scot-free, insulting,
　　　abusing me.

(*He speaks to the servants.*)

　　　　　　　You people bring out this creature,
　　　this hated creature, that she may die before
　　　his very eyes, right now, next her would-be husband.   820

Haemon: Not at my side! Never think that! She will not
　　　die by my side. But you will never again
　　　set eyes upon my face. Go then and rage
　　　with such of your friends as are willing to endure it.

Chorus: The man is gone, my lord, quick in his anger.   825
　　　A young man's mind is fierce when he is hurt.

Creon: Let him go, and do and think things superhuman.
　　　But these two girls he shall not save from death.

Chorus: Both of them? Do you mean to kill them both?

Creon: No, not the one that didn't do anything.   830
　　　You are quite right there.

Chorus: And by what form of death do you mean to kill her?

Creon: I will bring her where the path is loneliest,
　　　and hide her alive in a rocky cavern there.
　　　I'll give just enough of food as shall suffice   835
　　　for a bare expiation, that the city may avoid pollution.
　　　In that place she shall call on Hades, god of death,
　　　in her prayers. That god only she reveres.
　　　Perhaps she will win from him escape from death
　　　or at least in that last moment will recognize   840
　　　her honoring of the dead is labor lost.

Chorus: Love undefeated in the fight,
　　　　　Love that makes havoc of possessions,
　　　　　Love who lives at night in a young girl's soft cheeks,

Who travels over sea, or in huts in the countryside— 845
there is no god able to escape you
nor anyone of men, whose life is a day only,
and whom you possess is mad.

You wrench the minds of just men to injustice,
to their disgrace; this conflict among kinsmen 850
it is you who stirred to turmoil.
The winner is desire. She gleaming kindles
from the eyes of the girl good to bed.
Love shares the throne with the great powers that rule.
For the golden Aphrodite° holds her play there 855
and then no one can overcome her.

Here I too am borne out of the course of lawfulness
when I see these things, and I cannot control
the springs of my tears
when I see Antigone making her way 860
to her bed—but the bed
that is rest for everyone.

Antigone: You see me, you people of my country,
as I set out on my last road of all,
looking for the last time on this light of this sun— 865
never again. I am alive but Hades who gives sleep to everyone
is leading me to the shores of Acheron,°
though I have known nothing of marriage songs
nor the chant that brings the bride to bed.
My husband is to be the Lord of Death. 870

Chorus: Yes, you go to the place where the dead are hidden,
but you go with distinction and praise.
You have not been stricken by wasting sickness;
you have not earned the wages of the sword;
it was your own choice and alone among mankind 875
you will descend, alive,
to that world of death.

Antigone: But indeed I have heard of the saddest of deaths—
of the Phrygian stranger, daughter of Tantalus,°
whom the rocky growth subdued, like clinging ivy. 880
The rains never leave her, the snow never fails,
as she wastes away. That is how men tell the story.
From streaming eyes her tears wet the crags;
most like to her the god brings me to rest.

Chorus: Yes, but she was a god, and god born, 885
and you are mortal and mortal born.
Surely it is great renown
for a woman that dies, that in life and death
her lot is a lot shared with demigods.

---

855 *Aphrodite:* goddess of love and beauty.   867 *Acheron:* a river in Hades, domain of the dead.   879 *daughter of Tantalus:* Niobe, a Theban queen whose fourteen children were slain. She wept so copiously she was transformed into a stone on Mount Sipylos, and her tears became the mountain's streams.

Antigone: You mock me. In the name of our fathers' gods   890
    why do you not wait till I am gone to insult me?
    Must you do it face to face?
    My city! Rich citizens of my city!
    You springs of Dirce, you holy groves of Thebes,
    famed for its chariots! I would still have you as my witnesses,   895
    with what dry-eyed friends, under what laws
    I make my way to my prison sealed like a tomb.
    Pity me. Neither among the living nor the dead
    do I have a home in common—
    neither with the living nor the dead.   900
Chorus: You went to the extreme of daring
    and against the high throne of Justice
    you fell, my daughter, grievously.
    But perhaps it was for some ordeal of your father
    that you are paying requital.   905
Antigone: You have touched the most painful of my cares—
    the pity for my father, ever reawakened,
    and the fate of all of our race, the famous Labdacids;
    the doomed self-destruction of my mother's bed
    when she slept with her own son,   910
    my father.
    What parents I was born of, God help me!
    To them I am going to share their home,
    the curse on me, too, and unmarried.
    Brother, it was a luckless marriage you made,   915
    and dying killed my life.
Chorus: There *is* a certain reverence for piety.
    But for him in authority,
    he cannot see that authority defied;
    it is your own self-willed temper   920
    that has destroyed you.
Antigone: No tears for me, no friends, no marriage. Brokenhearted
    I am led along the road ready before me.
    I shall never again be suffered
    to look on the holy eye of the day.   925
    But my fate claims no tears—
    no friend cries for me.
Creon (to the servants): Don't you know that weeping and wailing before death
    would never stop if one is allowed to weep and wail?
    Lead her away at once. Enfold her   930
    in that rocky tomb of hers—as I told you to.
    There leave her alone, solitary,
    to die if she so wishes
    or live a buried life in such a home;
    we are guiltless in respect of her, this girl.   935
    But living above, among the rest of us, this life
    she shall certainly lose.

Antigone: Tomb, bridal chamber, prison forever
            dug in rock, it is to you I am going
            to join my people, that great number that have died,   940
            whom in their death Persephone° received.
            I am the last of them and I go down
            in the worst death of all—for I have not lived
            the due term of my life. But when I come
            to that other world my hope is strong   945
            that my coming will be welcome to my father,
            and dear to you, my mother, and dear to you,
            my brother deeply loved. For when you died,
            with my own hands I washed and dressed you all,
            and poured the lustral offerings on your graves.   950
            And now, Polyneices, it was for such care of your body
            that I have earned these wages.
            Yet those who think rightly will think I did right
            in honoring you. Had I been a mother
            of children, and my husband been dead and rotten,   955
            I would not have taken this weary task upon me
            against the will of the city. What law backs me
            when I say this? I will tell you:
            If my husband were dead, I might have had another,
            and child from another man, if I lost the first.   960
            But when father and mother both were hidden in death
            no brother's life would bloom for me again.
            That is the law under which I gave you precedence,
            my dearest brother, and that is why Creon thinks me
            wrong, even a criminal, and now takes me   965
            by the hand and leads me away,
            unbedded, without bridal, without share
            in marriage and in nurturing of children;
            as lonely as you see me; without friends;
            with fate against me I go to the vault of death   970
            while still alive. What law of God have I broken?
            Why should I still look to the gods in my misery?
            Whom should I summon as ally? For indeed
            because of piety I was called impious.
            If this proceeding is good in the gods' eyes   975
            I shall know my sin, once I have suffered.
            But if Creon and his people are the wrongdoers
            let their suffering be no worse than the injustice
            they are meting out to me.
Chorus: It is the same blasts, the tempests of the soul,   980
            possess her.
Creon: Then for this her guards,
            who are so slow, will find themselves in trouble.

---

941 *Persephone:* daughter of Zeus and Demeter whom Pluto, god of the underworld, abducted to be his queen.

Antigone (*cries out*): Oh, that word has come
    very close to death.
Creon: I will not comfort you   985
    with hope that the sentence will not be accomplished.
Antigone: O my father's city, in Theban land,
    O gods that sired my race,
    I am led away, I have no more stay.
    Look on me, princes of Thebes,   990
    the last remnant of the old royal line;
    see what I suffer and who makes me suffer
    because I gave reverence to what claims reverence.
Chorus: Danae suffered,° too, when, her beauty lost, she gave
    the light of heaven in exchange for brassbound walls,   995
    and in the tomb-like cell was she hidden and held;
    yet she was honored in her breeding, child,
    and she kept, as guardian, the seed of Zeus
    that came to her in a golden shower.
    But there is some terrible power in destiny   1000
    and neither wealth nor war
    nor tower nor black ships, beaten by the sea,
    can give escape from it.

    The hot-tempered son of Dryas,° the Edonian king,
    in fury mocked Dionysus,   1005
    who then held him in restraint
    in a rocky dungeon.
    So the terrible force and flower of his madness
    drained away. He came to know the god
    whom in frenzy he had touched with his mocking tongue,   1010
    when he would have checked the inspired women
    and the fire of Dionysus,
    when he provoked the Muses that love the lyre.

    By the black rocks, dividing the sea in two,
    are the shores of the Bosporus, Thracian Salmydessus.   1015
    There the god of war who lives near the city
    saw the terrible blinding wound
    dealt by his savage wife
    on Phineus' two sons.
    She blinded and tore with the points of her shuttle,   1020
    and her bloodied hands, those eyes
    that else would have looked on her vengefully.
    As they wasted away, they lamented

---

994 *Danae suffered*: In legend, when an oracle told Acrisius, king of Argos, that his daughter Danae would bear a son who would grow up to slay him, he locked the princess into a chamber made of bronze, lest any man impregnate her. But Zeus, father of the gods, entered Danae's prison in a shower of gold. The resultant child, the hero Perseus, was accidentally to fulfill the prophecy by killing Acrisius with an ill-aimed discus throw.   1004 *son of Dryas*: King Lycurgus of Thrace, whom Dionysus, god of wine, caused to be stricken with madness.

their unhappy fate that they were doomed
to be born of a mother cursed in her marriage. 1025
She traced her descent from the seed
of the ancient Erechtheidae.
In far-distant caves she was raised
among her father's storms, that child of Boreas,
quick as a horse, over the steep hills, 1030
a daughter of the gods.
But, my child, the long-lived Fates
bore hard upon her, too.

(Enter Teiresias, the blind prophet, led by a boy.)

Teiresias: My lords of Thebes, we have come here together,
one pair of eyes serving us both. For the blind 1035
such must be the way of going, by a guide's leading.
Creon: What is the news, my old Teiresias?
Teiresias: I will tell you; and you, listen to the prophet.
Creon: Never in the past have I turned from your advice.
Teiresias: And so you have steered well the ship of state. 1040
Creon: I have benefited and can testify to that.
Teiresias: Then realize you are on the razor edge
of danger.
Creon: What can that be? I shudder to hear those words.
Teiresias: When you learn the signs recognized by my art 1045
you will understand.
I sat at my ancient place of divination
for watching the birds, where every bird finds shelter;
and I heard an unwonted voice among them;
they were horribly distressed, and screamed unmeaningly. 1050
I knew they were tearing each other murderously;
the beating of their wings was a clear sign.
I was full of fear; at once on all the altars,
as they were fully kindled, I tasted the offerings,
but the god of fire refused to burn from the sacrifice, 1055
and from the thighbones a dark stream of moisture
oozed from the embers, smoked and sputtered.
The gall bladder burst and scattered to the air
and the streaming thighbones lay exposed
from the fat wrapped round them— 1060
so much I learned from this boy here,
the fading prophecies of a rite that failed.
This boy here is my guide, as I am others'.
This is the city's sickness—and your plans are the cause of it.
For our altars and our sacrificial hearths 1065
are filled with the carrion meat of birds and dogs,
torn from the flesh of Oedipus' poor son.
So the gods will not take our prayers or sacrifice
nor yet the flame from the thighbones, and no bird

cries shrill and clear, so glutted 1070
are they with fat of the blood of the killed man.
Reflect on these things, son. All men
can make mistakes; but, once mistaken,
a man is no longer stupid nor accursed
who, having fallen on ill, tries to cure that ill, 1075
not taking a fine undeviating stand.
It is obstinacy that convicts of folly.
Yield to the dead man; do not stab him—
now he is gone—what bravery is this,
to inflict another death upon the dead? 1080
I mean you well and speak well for your good.
It is never sweeter to learn from a good counselor
than when he counsels to your benefit.

Creon: Old man, you are all archers, and I am your mark.
I must be tried by your prophecies as well. 1085
By the breed of you I have been bought and sold
and made a merchandise, for ages now.
But I tell you: make your profit from silver-gold
from Sardis and the gold from India
if you will. But this dead man you shall not hide 1090
in a grave, not though the eagles of Zeus should bear
the carrion, snatching it to the throne of Zeus itself.
Even so, I shall not so tremble at the pollution
to let you bury him.

                No, I am certain
no human has the power to pollute the gods. 1095
They fall, you old Teiresias, those men,
—so very clever—in a bad fall whenever
they eloquently speak vile words for profit.

Teiresias: I wonder if there's a man who dares consider—

Creon: What do you mean? What sort of generalization 1100
    is this talk of yours?

Teiresias: How much the best of possessions is the ability
    to listen to wise advice.

Creon: As I should imagine that the worst
    injury must be native stupidity. 1105

Teiresias: Now that is exactly where your mind is sick.

Creon: I do not like to answer a seer with insults.

Teiresias: But you do, when you say my prophecies are lies.

Creon: Well,
    the whole breed of prophets certainly loves money. 1110

Teiresias: And the breed that comes from princes loves to take
    advantage—base advantage.

Creon: Do you realize
    you are speaking in such terms of your own prince?

Teiresias: I know. But it is through me you have saved the city.

Creon: You are a wise prophet, but what you love is wrong. 1115

Teiresias: You will force me to declare what should be hidden
    in my own heart.
Creon: Out with it—
    but only if your words are not for gain.
Teiresias: They won't be for *your* gain—that I am sure of.
Creon: But realize you will not make a merchandise   1120
    of my decisions.
Teiresias: And you must realize
    that you will not outlive many cycles more
    of this swift sun before you give in exchange
    one of your own loins bred, a corpse for a corpse,
    for you have thrust one that belongs above   1125
    below the earth, and bitterly dishonored
    a living soul by lodging her in the grave;
    while one that belonged indeed to the underworld
    gods you have kept on this earth without due share
    of rites of burial, of due funeral offerings,   1130
    a corpse unhallowed. With all of this you, Creon,
    have nothing to do, nor have the gods above.
    These acts of yours are violence, on your part.
    And in requital the avenging Spirits
    of Death itself and the gods' Furies shall   1135
    after *your* deeds, lie in ambush for you, and
    in their hands you shall be taken cruelly.
    Now, look at this and tell me I was bribed
    to say it! The delay will not be long
    before the cries of mourning in your house,   1140
    of men and women. All the cities will stir in hatred
    against you, because their sons in mangled shreds
    received their burial rites from dogs, from wild beasts
    or when some bird of the air brought a vile stink
    to each city that contained the hearths of the dead.   1145
    These are the arrows that archer-like I launched—
    you vexed me so to anger—at your heart.
    You shall not escape their sting. You, boy,
    lead me away to my house, so he may discharge
    his anger on younger men; so may he come to know   1150
    to bear a quieter tongue in his head and a better
    mind than that now he carries in him.
Chorus: That was a terrible prophecy, my lord.
    The man has gone. Since these hairs of mine grew white
    from the black they once were, he has never spoken   1155
    a word of a lie to our city.
Creon: I know, I know.
    My mind is all bewildered. To yield is terrible.
    But by opposition to destroy my very being
    with a self-destructive curse must also be reckoned   1160
    in what is terrible.
Chorus: You need good counsel, son of Menoeceus,
    and need to take it.

Creon: What must I do, then? Tell me; I shall agree.

Chorus: The girl—go now and bring her up from her cave,   1165
    and for the exposed dead man, give him his burial.

Creon: That is really your advice? You would have me yield.

Chorus: And quickly as you may, my lord. Swift harms
    sent by the gods cut off the paths of the foolish.

Creon: Oh, it is hard; I must give up what my heart   1170
    would have me do. But it is ill to fight
    against what must be.

Chorus: Go now, and do this;
    do not give the task to others.

Creon: I will go,   1175
    just as I am. Come, servants, all of you;
    take axes in your hands; away with you
    to the place you see, there.
    For my part, since my intention is so changed,
    as I bound her myself, myself will free her.   1180
    I am afraid it may be best, in the end
    of life, to have kept the old accepted laws.

Chorus: You of many names,° glory of the Cadmeian
    bride, breed of loud thundering Zeus;
    you who watch over famous Italy;   1185
    you who rule where all are welcome in Eleusis;
    in the sheltered plains of Deo—
    O Bacchus that dwells in Thebes,
    the mother city of Bacchanals,
    by the flowing stream of Ismenus,   1190
    in the ground sown by the fierce dragon's teeth.

    You are he on whom the murky gleam of torches glares,
    above the twin peaks of the crag
    where come the Corycean nymphs
    to worship you, the Bacchanals;   1195
    and the stream of Castalia° has seen you, too;
    and you are he that the ivy-clad
    slopes of Nisaean hills,
    and the green shore ivy-clustered,
    sent to watch over the roads of Thebes,   1200
    where the immortal Evoe° chant rings out.

1183 *You of many names:* Dionysus was also called Iacchos (or, by the Romans, Bacchus). He was the son of Zeus ("the Thunderer") and of Semele, daughter of Kadmos (or Cadmus), legendary founder of Thebes. "Regent of Eleusis' plain" is another name for Dionysus, honored in secret rites at Eleusis, a town northwest of Athens. "Prince of maenad Thebes" is yet another: the Maenads were women of Thebes said to worship Dionysus with wild orgiastic rites. Kadmos, so the story goes, sowed dragon's teeth in a field beside the river Ismenus. Up sprang a crop of fierce warriors who fought among themselves until only five remained. These victors became the first Thebans. 1196 *Castalia:* a spring on Mount Parnassus, named for a maiden who drowned herself in it to avoid rape by the god Apollo. She became a nymph, or nature spirit, dwelling in its waters. In the temple of Delphi, at the mountain's foot, priestesses of Dionysus (the "nymphs of Iacchos") used the spring's waters in rites of purification. 1201 *Evoe:* cry of the Maenads in supplicating Dionysus: "Come forth, come forth!"

It is Thebes which you honor most of all cities,
you and your mother both,
she who died by the blast of Zeus' thunderbolt.
And now when the city, with all its folk,   1205
is gripped by a violent plague,
come with healing foot, over the slopes of Parnassus,
over the moaning strait.
You lead the dance of the fire-breathing stars,
you are master of the voices of the night.   1210
True-born child of Zeus, appear,
my lord, with your Thyiad attendants,
who in frenzy all night long
dance in your house, Iacchus,
dispenser of gifts.   1215

Messenger: You who live by the house of Cadmus and Amphion,°
hear me. There is no condition of man's life
that stands secure. As such I would not
praise it or blame. It is chance that sets upright;
it is chance that brings down the lucky and the unlucky,   1220
each in his turn. For men, that belong to death,
there is no prophet of established things.
Once Creon was a man worthy of envy—
of my envy, at least. For he saved this city
of Thebes from her enemies, and attained   1225
the throne of the land, with all a king's power.
He guided it right. His race bloomed
with good children. But when a man forfeits joy
I do not count his life as life, but only
a life trapped in a corpse.   1230
Be rich within your house, yes greatly rich,
if so you will, and live in a prince's style.
If the gladness of these things is gone, I would not
give the shadow of smoke for the rest,
as against joy.   1235

Chorus: What is the sorrow of our princes
of which you are the messenger?

Messenger: Death; and the living are guilty of their deaths.

Chorus: But who is the murderer? Who the murdered? Tell us.

Messenger: Haemon is dead; the hand that shed his blood   1240
was his very own.

Chorus: Truly his own hand? Or his father's?

Messenger: His own hand, in his anger
against his father for a murder.

Chorus: Prophet, how truly you have made good your word!   1245

Messenger: These things are so; you may debate the rest.

1216 *Amphion:* a name for Thebes. Amphion, son of Zeus, had built a wall around the city by playing so
beautifully on his lyre that the charmed stones leaped into their slots.

Chorus: Here I see Creon's wife Eurydice
    approaching. Unhappy woman!
    Does she come from the house as hearing about her son
    or has she come by chance?   1250
Eurydice: I heard your words, all you men of Thebes, as I
    was going out to greet Pallas° with my prayers.
    I was just drawing back the bolts of the gate
    to open it when a cry struck through my ears
    telling of my household's ruin. I fell backward   1255
    in terror into the arms of my servants; I fainted.
    But tell me again, what is the story? I
    will hear it as one who is no stranger to sorrow.
Messenger: Dear mistress, I will tell you, for I was there,
    and I will leave out no word of the truth.   1260
    Why should I comfort you and then tomorrow
    be proved a liar? The truth is always best.

    I followed your husband, at his heels, to the end of the plain
    where Polyneices' body still lay unpitied,
    and torn by dogs. We prayed to Hecate, goddess   1265
    of the crossroads, and also to Pluto°
    that they might restrain their anger and turn kind.
    And him we washed with sacred lustral water
    and with fresh-cut boughs we burned what was left of him
    and raised a high mound of his native earth;   1270
    then we set out again for the hollowed rock,
    death's stone bridal chamber for the girl.
    Someone then heard a voice of bitter weeping
    while we were still far off, coming from that unblest room.
    The man came to tell our master Creon of it.   1275
    As the king drew nearer, there swarmed about him
    a cry of misery but no clear words.
    He groaned and in an anguished mourning voice
    cried "Oh, am I a true prophet? Is this the road
    that I must travel, saddest of all my wayfaring?   1280
    It is my son's voice that haunts my ear. Servants,
    get closer, quickly. Stand around the tomb
    and look. There is a gap there where the stones
    have been wrenched away; enter there, by the very mouth,
    and see whether I recognize the voice of Haemon   1285
    or if the gods deceive me." On the command
    of our despairing master we went to look.
    In the furthest part of the tomb we saw her, hanging
    by her neck. She had tied a noose of muslin on it.
    Haernon's hands were about her waist embracing her,   1290
    while he cried for the loss of his bride gone to the dead,

---

1252 *Pallas:* Pallas Athene, goddess of wisdom, and hence an excellent source of advice.   1265–1266 *Hecate . . . Pluto:* two fearful divinities—the goddess of witchcraft and sorcery and the king of Hades, underworld of the dead.

and for all his father had done, and his own sad love.
When Creon saw him he gave a bitter cry,
went in and called to him with a groan: "Poor son!
what have you done? What can you have meant?   1295
What happened to destroy you? Come out, I pray you!"
The boy glared at him with savage eyes, and then
spat in his face, without a word of answer.
He drew his double-hilted sword. As his father
ran to escape him, Haemon failed to strike him,   1300
and the poor wretch in anger at himself
leaned on his sword and drove it halfway in,
into his ribs. Then he folded the girl to him,
in his arms, while he was conscious still,
and gasping poured a sharp stream of bloody drops   1305
on her white cheeks. There they lie,
the dead upon the dead. So he has won
the pitiful fulfillment of his marriage
within death's house. In this human world he has shown
how the wrong choice in plans is for a man   1310
his greatest evil.

Chorus: What do you make of this? My lady is gone,
    without a word of good or bad.

Messenger: I, too,
    am lost in wonder. I am inclined to hope
    that hearing of her son's death she could not   1315
    open her sorrow to the city, but chose rather
    within her house to lay upon her maids
    the mourning for the household grief. Her judgment
    is good; she will not make any false step.

Chorus: I do not know. To me this over-heavy silence   1320
    seems just as dangerous as much empty wailing.

Messenger: I will go in and learn if in her passionate
    heart she keeps hidden some secret purpose.
    You are right; there is sometimes danger in too much silence.

Chorus: Here comes our king himself. He bears in his hands   1325
    a memorial all too clear;
    it is a ruin of none other's making,
    purely his own if one dare to say that.

Creon: The mistakes of a blinded man
    are themselves rigid and laden with death.   1330
    You look at us the killer and the killed
    of the one blood. Oh, the awful blindness
    of those plans of mine. My son, you were so young,
    so young to die. You were freed from the bonds of life
    through no folly of your own—only through mine.   1335

Chorus: I think you have learned justice—but too late.

Creon: Yes, I have learned it to my bitterness. At this moment
    God has sprung on my head with a vast weight
    and struck me down. He shook me in my savage ways;
    he has overturned my joy, has trampled it,   1340

underfoot. The pains men suffer
are pains indeed.
Second Messenger: My lord, you have troubles and a store besides;
some are there in your hands, but there are others
you will surely see when you come to your house.   1345
Creon: What trouble can there be beside these troubles?
Second Messenger: The queen is dead. She was indeed true mother
of the dead son. She died, poor lady,
by recent violence upon herself.
Creon: Haven of death, you can never have enough.   1350
Why, why do you destroy me?
You messenger, who have brought me bitter news,
what is this tale you tell?
It is a dead man that you kill again—
what new message of yours is this, boy?   1355
Is this new slaughter of a woman
a doom to lie on the pile of the dead?
Chorus: You can see. It is no longer
hidden in a corner.

(*By some stage device, perhaps the so-called eccyclema,° the inside of the palace is
shown, with the body of the dead Queen.*)

Creon: Here is yet another horror   1360
for my unhappy eyes to see.
What doom still waits for me?
I have but now taken in my arms my son,
and again I look upon another dead face.
Poor mother and poor son!   1365
Second Messenger: She stood at the altar, and with keen whetted knife
she suffered her darkening eyes to close.
First she cried in agony recalling the noble fate of Megareus,°
who died before all this,
and then for the fate of this son; and in the end   1370
she cursed you for the evil you had done
in killing her sons.
Creon: I am distracted with fear. Why does not someone
strike a two-edged sword right through me?
I am dissolved in an agony of misery.   1375
Second Messenger: You were indeed accused
by her that is dead
of Haemon's and of Megareus' death.
Creon: By what kind of violence did she find her end?
Second Messenger: Her own hand struck her to the entrails   1380
when she heard of her son's lamentable death.
Creon: These acts can never be made to fit another
to free me from the guilt. It was I that killed her.

1359 s.d. *eccyclema:* a platform on wheels pushed onto the stage to display an offstage scene.   1368 *Megareus:*
Son of Creon and brother of Haemon, Megareus was slain in the unsuccessful attack upon Thebes.

Poor wretch that I am, I say it is true!
Servants, lead me away, quickly, quickly.   1385
I am no more a live man than one dead.
Chorus: What you say is for the best—if there be a best
    in evil such as this. For the shortest way
    is best with troubles that lie at our feet.
Creon: O, let it come, let it come,   1390
    that best of fates that waits on my last day.
    Surely best fate of all. Let it come, let it come!
    That I may never see one more day's light!
Chorus: These things are for the future. We must deal
    with what impends. What in the future is to care for   1395
    rests with those whose duty it is
    to care for them.
Creon: At least, all that I want
    is in that prayer of mine.
Chorus: Pray for no more at all. For what is destined   1400
    for us, men mortal, there is no escape.
Creon: Lead me away, a vain silly man
    who killed you, son, and you, too, lady.
    I did not mean to, but I did.
    I do not know where to turn my eyes   1405
    to look to, for support.
    Everything in my hands is crossed. A most unwelcome fate
    has leaped upon me.
Chorus: Wisdom is far the chief element in happiness
    and, secondly, no irreverence towards the gods.   1410
    But great words of haughty men exact
    in retribution blows as great
    and in old age teach wisdom.

Questions

1. What is Creon's motivation for forbidding the burial of his own nephew Polyneices? Why would he issue an edict that runs so contrary to his family obligations?

2. What are Antigone's reasons for performing funeral rites on her brother's corpse in direct violation of Creon's edict?

3. What are the larger issues behind the conflicting positions of both Creon and Antigone? Is either person or position clearly wrong?

4. Does the chorus take a position in the argument between Creon and Antigone?

5. If Antigone is a tragic heroine, what is her tragic flaw? Does she have any particular hubris or excess of virtue that dooms her?

6. Can a modern reader discern Sophocles's own position on the debate between civic responsibility (Creon's edict) and family duty (Antigone's defiance)? Are his authorial sympathies anywhere evident in the play?

7. What is the role of Eurydice? Is her presence essential to the story? What would be the effect of removing her from the drama?

8. Can you imagine a modern setting in which a new production of *Antigone* might be staged? Describe your idea in terms of sets, costumes, and staging.

CRITICS ON SOPHOCLES

Aristotle (384–322 B.C.)

Defining Tragedy   330 B.C.?

Translated by L. J. Potts

Tragedy is an imitation of an action of high importance, complete and of some amplitude; in language enhanced by distinct and varying beauties; acted not narrated;
by means of pity and fear effecting its purgation of these emotions. By the beauties
enhancing the language I mean rhythm and melody; by "distinct and varying" I mean
that some are produced by meter alone, and others at another time by melody.

•••

What will produce the tragic effect? Since, then, tragedy, to be at its finest,
requires a complex, not a simple, structure, and its structure should also imitate fearful and pitiful events (for that is the peculiarity of this sort of imitation), it is clear:
first, that decent people must not be shown passing from good fortune to misfortune
(for that is not fearful or pitiful but disgusting); again, vicious people must not be
shown passing from misfortune to good fortune (for that is the most untragic situation possible—it has none of the requisites, it is neither humane, nor pitiful, nor fearful); nor again should an utterly evil man fall from good fortune into misfortune (for
though a plot of that kind would be humane, it would not induce pity or fear—pity
is induced by undeserved misfortune, and fear by the misfortunes of normal people,
so that this situation will be neither pitiful nor fearful). So we are left with the man
between these extremes: that is to say, the kind of man who neither is distinguished
for excellence and virtue, nor comes to grief on account of baseness and vice, but on
account of some error; a man of great reputation and prosperity, like Oedipus and
Thyestes and conspicuous people of such families as theirs. So, to be well formed, a
fable must be single rather than (as some say) double—there must be no change from
misfortune to good fortune, but only the opposite, from good fortune to misfortune;
the cause must not be vice, but a great error; and the man must be either of the type
specified or better, rather than worse. This is borne out by the practice of poets; at
first they picked a fable at random and made an inventory of its contents, but now
the finest tragedies are plotted, and concern a few families—for example, the tragedies about Alcmeon, Oedipus, Orestes, Meleager, Thyestes, Telephus, and any others
whose lives were attended by terrible experiences or doings.

   This is the plot that will produce the technically finest tragedy. Those critics are
therefore wrong who censure Euripides on this very ground—because he does this in
his tragedies, and many of them end in misfortune; for it is, as I have said, the right
thing to do. This is clearly demonstrated on the stage in the competitions, where
such plays, if they succeed, are the most tragic, and Euripides, even if he is inefficient
in every other respect, still shows himself the most tragic of our poets. The next best
plot, which is said by some people to be the best, is the tragedy with a double plot,
like the *Odyssey*, ending in one way for the better people and in the opposite way for
the worse. But it is the weakness of theatrical performances that gives priority to this
kind; when poets write what the audience would like to happen, they are in leading
strings.° This is not the pleasure proper to tragedy, but rather to comedy, where the

---

in leading strings: each is led, by a string, wherever the audience wills.

greatest enemies in the fable, say Orestes and Aegisthus, make friends and go off at the end, and nobody is killed by anybody.

•••

The pity and fear can be brought about by the *mise en scène*;° but they can also come from the mere plotting of the incidents, which is preferable, and better poetry. For, without seeing anything, the fable ought to have been so plotted that if one heard the bare facts, the chain of circumstances would make one shudder and pity. That would happen to any one who heard the fable of the *Oedipus*. To produce this effect by the *mise en scène* is less artistic and puts one at the mercy of the technician; and those who use it not to frighten but merely to startle have lost touch with tragedy altogether. We should not try to get all sorts of pleasure from tragedy, but the particular tragic pleasure. And clearly, since this pleasure coming from pity and fear has to be produced by imitation, it is by his handling of the incidents that the poet must create it.

From *Poetics, VI, XIII, XIV*

Sigmund Freud (1856–1939)

The Destiny of Oedipus   1900

Translated by James Strachey

If *Oedipus the King* moves a modern audience no less than it did the contemporary Greek one, the explanation can only be that its effect does not lie in the contrast between destiny and human will, but is to be looked for in the particular nature of the material on which that contrast is exemplified. There must be something which makes a voice within us ready to recognize the compelling force of destiny in the *Oedipus*, while we can dismiss as merely arbitrary such dispositions as are laid down in *Die Ahnfrau*° or other modern tragedies of destiny. And a factor of this kind is in fact involved in the story of King Oedipus. His destiny moves us only because it might have been ours— because the oracle laid the same curse upon us before our birth as upon him. It is the fate of all of us, perhaps, to direct our first sexual impulse towards our mother and our first hatred and our first murderous wish against our father. Our dreams convince us that that is so. King Oedipus, who slew his father Laius and married his mother Jocasta, merely shows us the fulfillment of our own childhood wishes. But, more fortunate than he, we have meanwhile succeeded, insofar as we have not become psychoneurotics, in detaching our sexual impulses from our mothers and in forgetting our jealousy of our fathers. Here is one in whom these primeval wishes of our childhood have been fulfilled, and we shrink back from him with the whole force of the repression by which those wishes have since that time been held down within us. While the poet, as he unravels the past, brings to light the guilt of Oedipus, he is at the same time compelling us to recognize our own inner minds, in which those same impulses, though suppressed, are still to be found. The contrast with which the closing Chorus leaves us confronted—

---

mise en scène: arrangement of actors and scenery.   *Die Ahnfrau: The Foremother,* a play by Franz Grillparzer (1791–1872), Austrian dramatist and poet.

look upon Oedipus.

This is the king who solved the famous riddle
And towered up, most powerful of men.
No mortal eyes but looked on him with envy,
Yet in the end ruin swept over him.

—strikes as a warning at ourselves and our pride, at us who since our childhood have grown so wise and so mighty in our own eyes. Like Oedipus, we live in ignorance of these wishes, repugnant to morality, which have been forced upon us by Nature, and after their revelation we may all of us well seek to close our eyes to the scenes of our childhood.

From The Interpretation of Dreams

A. E. Haigh   (1855–1905)

The Irony of Sophocles   1896

The use of "tragic irony," as it has been called, is a favorite device in all dramatic literature. It is mostly employed when some catastrophe is about to happen, which is known and foreseen by the spectators, but concealed either from all, or from some, of the actors in the drama. In such cases the dialogue may be couched in terms which, though perfectly harmless upon the surface, carry an ominous significance to the initiated, and point suggestively to what is about to happen; and the contrast between the outer and the inner meaning of the language produces a deep effect upon the stage. Examples of this "irony" are to be found in most tragic writers, but especially in those of Greece, who use it with far greater frequency than the moderns; the reason being that, as the subjects of Greek tragedy were taken from the old legends with which everyone was familiar, it was far easier for the ancient dramatist to indulge in those ambiguous allusions which presuppose a certain knowledge on the part of the spectators. Sophocles, however, is distinguished even among the Greek poets for his predilection for this form of speech, and his "irony" has become proverbial. It figures so prominently in his dramas, and goes so far to determine their general tone, that a detailed consideration of the matter will not be out of place.

Tragic irony may be divided into two kinds, the conscious and the unconscious. Conscious irony occurs in those cases where the speaker is not himself the victim of any illusion, but foresees the calamity that is about to fall on others, and exults in the prospect. His language, though equivocal, is easily intelligible to the audience, and to those actors who are acquainted with the facts; and its dark humor adds to the horror of the situation. This kind of irony is the one more commonly met with in the modern drama.

•••

The other kind of irony, the unconscious, is perhaps the more impressive of the two. Here the sufferer is himself the spokesman. Utterly blind as to the doom which overhangs him, he uses words which, to the mind of the audience, have an ominous suggestiveness, and without knowing it, probes his own wounds to the bottom. Such irony is not confined merely to the language, but runs through the whole situation; and the contrast between the cheerful heedlessness of the victim, and the dark shadows which surround him, produces an impression more terrible than that which any form of speech could convey. Scenes of this kind had a peculiar fascination for the ancients. The fear of a sudden reverse of fortune, and of some fatal Nemesis which waits upon pride and boastfulness, was of all ideas the one most deeply impressed upon the mind of antiquity. Hence the popularity upon the stage of those thrilling spectacles, in which confidence and presumption were seen advancing blindfold to destruction, and the bitterness of the doom was intensified by the unconscious utterances of the victim.

●●●

The greatest example of all is the *Oedipus Rex*, the masterpiece of Sophocles, and the most typical of all Greek tragedies. The irony of destiny is here exhibited with unexampled force. In the opening scene Oedipus is depicted in the height of his prosperity, renowned and venerated, and surrounded by his suppliant countrymen; and the priest addresses him as the "wisest of men in dealing with life's chances and with the visitations of heaven." To the audience who know that within a few short hours the wrath of heaven will have crushed and shattered him, the pathetic meaning of these words is indescribable. From this first scene until the final catastrophe the speeches of Oedipus are all full of the same tragic allusiveness. He can scarcely open his lips without touching unconsciously on his own approaching fate. When he insists upon the fact that his search for the assassin is "not on behalf of strangers, but in his own cause," and when he cautiously warns Jocasta that, as his mother still lives, the guilt of incest is not yet an impossibility, every word that he utters has a concealed barb. Perhaps the most tragic passage of all is that in which, while cursing the murderer of Laius, he pronounces his own doom. "As for the man who did the deed of guilt, whether alone he lurks, or in league with others, I pray that he may waste his life away in suffering, perishing vilely for his vile actions. And if he should become a dweller in my house, I knowing it, may every curse I utter fall on my own head."

From The Tragic Drama of the Greeks

David Wiles

The Chorus as Democrat
2000

Oedipus becomes a political play when we focus on the interaction of actor and chorus, and see how the chorus forms a democratic mass jury. Each sequence of dialogue takes the form of a contest for the chorus' sympathy, with Oedipus sliding from the role of prosecutor to that of defendant, and each choral dance offers a provisional verdict. After Oedipus' set-to with Teiresias the soothsayer, the chorus decides to trust Oedipus on the basis of his past record; after his argument with his brother-in-law Creon, the chorus shows their distress and urges compromise. Once Oedipus has confessed to a killing and Iocaste has declared that oracles have no force, the chorus is forced to think about political tyranny, torn between respect for divine law and trust in their rulers. In the next dance they assume that the contradiction is resolved and Oedipus has turned out to be the son of a god. Finally a slave's evidence reveals that the man most honored by society is in fact the least to be envied. The political implications are clear: there is no space in democratic society for such as Oedipus. Athenians, like the chorus of the play, must reject the temptation to believe one man can calculate the future.

From Greek Theatre Performance: An Introduction

Patricia M. Lines (b. 1938)

What Is Antigone's Tragic Flaw?
1999

Antigone does not seem to fit the Aristotelian formula. Aristotle himself did not seem to know what to make of it. In the *Poetica*'s sole reference to the play Aristotle offers *Antigone* as an example of a poor plot for a tragedy. The least tragic plot, he avers, involves a character who resolves to do a fearful deed and does not do it. His example is Haemon who seems ready to slay his father, Creon, and does not. This may be one of those rare cases where Aristotle misses the point. First, after more than two millennia of experience with drama, one can imagine a situation where delay in doing the dread deed makes the tragedy. Nor is it clear that Haemon had resolved to kill his father; his veiled threat may have been to kill himself, an action which he finally takes. Most important, the conflict between Haemon and his father does not stir our emotions as much as the conflict swirling around Antigone.

The play strikes us as a fine one—Hegel thought it was the supreme example of tragedy, prompting him to pose a different theory for the form. Hegel sees a dialectical clash between two ideals of justice. A noble and wise Antigone fights for the justice of traditional belief, while a tyrannical Creon fights for a right based on might. Irving Babbitt has suggested a more subtle variation of dialectic theory, hailing Antigone as the "perfect example of the ethical imagination" in contrast to her sister, Ismene, who knows merely "the law of the community." Both Antigone and Ismene are ethical, but Ismene lacks ethical imagination. As Babbitt sees it:

> This law, the convention of a particular place and time, is always but a very imperfect image, a mere shadow indeed of the unwritten law which being above the ordinary rational level is . . . infinite and incapable of final formulation.

While such interpretations no doubt are true—with each uncovering layers of meaning—alone they reduce *Antigone* to a morality play. Such interpretations fail to explain the play's more complex and turbulent moods.

• • •

The suggestion that Sophocles intended to present a flawed Antigone rubs against the grain. She is the paragon. The religion of the Greeks, like virtually all religions, required burial of the dead—even the enemy dead. The ancient tales in the *Iliad*, the bible to the Greeks, warn of the anger of the gods upon a failure to honor the dead. Besides, the restless shades of the unburied could cause trouble. Antigone stands for all that is right and for the opposition to tyranny. Thus, we have only a play about Creon's excessive harshness and his tragically delayed conversion. Yet, Sophocles provides a fair amount of evidence that he intended to create something more complex than a morality play.

Consider first the parallels between *Antigone* and *Oedipus Rex*. Both stories begin with a problem facing family and polis, and with the central character resolving to make things right. Antigone proceeds with unswerving resolution in her judgment of the situation. She possesses complete confidence in her ability to choose and execute a just action. She does not see the full situation; she is blind to key elements of the problem. She is like her father in most respects. Both Antigone and Oedipus claim to know justice with the certainty of a god. Oedipus believes most in his cunning and strength, Antigone in her goodness.

The flaw of hubris is easy to spot in Oedipus, but Antigone's brilliance is so dazzling that we overlook her flaw. After all, she has formulated a great and noble truth and maintains it with courage. She asserts God's law over man's law. Especially in our own time, where we formally recognize the superiority, within specified spheres, of individual right over the demands of overly broad laws, Antigone seems a genius beyond her time.

Creon, by contrast, understands the needs of the polis. Following a civil war, he has placed a premium on order. He will do whatever is necessary, including the stern enforcement of harsh rules. He faces another dilemma in his role as leader: he forbade the burial of Polyneices and decreed this harsh punishment before he was aware of Antigone's guilt. To pardon his future daughter-in-law as his first serious act as ruler of Thebes would compromise all future claims to fairness in his rule. Yet Creon listens to the chorus of old men; he listens to the blind seer. After struggling with the issue, he reconsiders his judgment; he determines to bury the body of Polyneices and to unbury Antigone with his own hands.

Antigone, on the other hand, recognizes the demands of true justice and champions it. She spurns Ismene, who initially hesitated to assist her but soon after wished to share in her sister's punishment and death. Antigone refuses the offer. When Ismene asks whether her sister has cast her aside, Antigone's answer ignores Ismene's change of heart: "Yes. For you chose to live when I chose death." Antigone seems to speak not to spare Ismene, but to wound her to the quick. Antigone leaves Haemon, her betrothed, in the cold, as she left Ismene. She never seeks him out, nor even mentions his name. Yet Haemon is ready to defy his father for Antigone's sake, and he refuses to live without her. Ironically, this may be what he must do to win her affection, for Antigone reveals no tenderness for anyone except those already dead.

• • •

The chorus, often the truth-sayer for Sophocles, provides more clues. Of Antigone, they tell us:

> The girl is bitter. She's her father's child.
> She cannot yield to trouble; nor could he.

In perhaps the most revealing exchange, the chorus turns to Antigone and tells her, plainly:

> You showed respect for the dead.
> So we for you: but power
> is not to be thwarted so.
> Your self-sufficiency has brought you down.

The last line is key: "δ' αὐτόγνωτος ὤλεσ'ὀργά." The above quotation is from Wyckoff's translation. But all translations seem to head in the same direction: "A self-determined impulse hath undone thee" (Campbell). "You were self-willed. That has been your undoing" (Townsend). "And thee, thy stubborne mood, self-chosen, layeth low" (students of the University of Notre Dame, 1983).[1] In any translation, it seems the chorus has identified Antigone's flaw. She follows a truth that springs only from her self: It is αὐτόγνωτος, or autognotos. She will not consult with others. We could call it self-certainty or, perhaps even better, self-righteousness. It is a form of hubris.

---

[1] Lines 920-21 in the Grene translation: "it is your own self-willed temper / that has destroyed you."

At another point, the chorus tells Antigone she is autonomous. Literally, this means "a law unto yourself." The English word autonomy does not convey quite the right meaning, as individual autonomy was a condition the Greeks viewed with discomfort and suspicion. The autonomous being is either beast or god, living only within the horizons of its own laws.

"Antigone's Flaw"

■ WRITING *effectively*

A. E. Haigh on Writing

The Style of Sophocles   1896

The critic Dionysius, in his treatise on the art of literary composition, divides the various kinds of diction into three classes—the "austere style," with its rough force and archaic simplicity, the "flowery style," with its soft and flowing attractiveness, and the "middle style," which comes between the two and unites the excellencies of both, combining smoothness with power, and grace with dignity. This last kind is in his opinion the most perfect of all forms of diction, and Sophocles its most distinguished exponent among tragic poets. ... Indeed, there is no Greek poet whose works exhibit in greater perfection the peculiar characteristics of the "middle style"—the combination of supreme beauty of form with strength and energy. The pre-eminence of Sophocles in these two points was universally recognized by the ancients. The grace and sweetness of his language procured for him, among his contemporaries, the title of "The Bee," and his lips were said by Aristophanes to have been "smeared with honey."

From *The Tragic Drama of the Greeks*

THINKING ABOUT GREEK TRAGEDY

Reading an ancient work of literature, such as Sophocles's *Oedipus the King* or *Antigone*, you might have two contradictory reactions. On the one hand, you are likely to note how differently people thought, spoke, and conducted themselves in the ancient world from the way they do now. On the other hand, you might notice how many facets of human nature remain constant across the ages. Though Sophocles's characters are mythic, they also are recognizably human.

■ **Stay alert to both impulses.** Be open to the play's universal appeal, but never overlook its foreignness. Take note of the basic beliefs and values that the characters hold that are different from your own. How do those elements influence their actions and motivations?

■ **Jot down something about each major character that seems odd or exotic to you.** Don't worry about being too basic; these notes are just a starting place. You might observe, for example, that Oedipus and Jocasta both believe in the power of prophecy. They also believe that Apollo and the other gods would punish the city with a plague because of an unsolved crime committed twenty years earlier. These are certainly not mainstream modern beliefs.

■ **Focus on the differences themselves.** You do not need to understand the historical origins or cultural context of the differences you note. You can safely leave those things to scholars. But observing these differences—at least a few important ones—will keep you from making inappropriate modern assumptions about the characters, and keeping the differences in mind will give you greater insight into their behavior.

CHECKLIST: Writing About Greek Drama

☐ Identify the play's major characters.

☐ In what ways do they seem alien to you?

☐ What do you notice about a character's beliefs? About his or her values? How do these differ from your own?

☐ In what ways are the play's characters like the people you know?

☐ How do these qualities—both the alien and the familiar—influence the characters' motivations and actions?

TOPICS FOR WRITING ON SOPHOCLES

1. Write a brief personality profile (two or three pages) of any major character in *Oedipus the King* or *Antigone*. Describe the character's age, social position, family background, personality, and beliefs. What is his or her major motivation in the play? In what ways does the character resemble his or her modern equivalent? In what ways do they differ?

2. Suppose you were to direct and produce a new stage production of *Oedipus the King*. How would you go about it? Would you use masks? How would you render the chorus? Would you set the play in contemporary North America? Justify your decisions by referring to the play itself.

3. Write a brief comment on the play under the title "Does Sophocles's Oedipus Have an Oedipus Complex?" Consider Sigmund Freud's famous observations (quoted earlier in this chapter). Your comment can be either serious or light.

4. Compare *Oedipus the King* to *Antigone* in terms of their characterizations of their protagonists. In what ways does Antigone resemble Oedipus, and in what ways does she differ?

5. Taking the protagonist of either play by Sophocles, write an essay explaining how he or she exemplifies or refutes Aristotle's definition of a tragic hero.

▶ TERMS FOR *review*

Stagecraft in Ancient Greece

Orchestra ▶ "The place for dancing"; a circular, level performance space at the base of a horseshoe-shaped amphitheater, where twelve, then later (in Sophocles's plays) fifteen masked young male chorus members sang and danced the odes interspersed between dramatic episodes in a play. (Today the term *orchestra* refers to the ground-floor seats in a theater or concert hall.)

Skene ▶ The canvas or wooden stage building in which actors changed masks and costumes when changing roles. Its façade, with double center doors and possibly two side doors, served as the setting for action taking place before a palace, temple, cave, or other interior space.

Deus ex machina ▶ (Latin for "god out of the machine.") Originally, the phrase referred to the Greek playwrights' frequent use of a god, mechanically lowered to the stage from the *skene* roof to resolve the human conflict. Today, *deus ex machina* refers to any forced or improbable device used to resolve a plot.

Masks ▶ (In Latin, *personae*.) Classical Greek theater masks covered an actor's entire head. Large, recognizable masks allowed far-away spectators to distinguish the conventional characters of tragedy and comedy.

Cothurni ▶ High, thick-soled elevator boots worn by tragic actors in late classical times to make them appear taller than ordinary men. (Earlier, in the fifth-century classical Athenian theater, actors wore soft shoes or boots or went barefoot.)

Elements of Classical Tragedy

Hamartia ▶ (Greek for "error.") An offense committed in ignorance of some material fact; a great mistake made as a result of an error by a morally good person.

Tragic flaw ▶ A fatal weakness or moral flaw in the protagonist that brings him or her to a bad end. Sometimes offered as an alternative understanding of *hamartia*, in contrast to the idea that the tragic hero's catastrophe is caused by an error in judgment.

Hubris ▶ Overweening pride, outrageous behavior, or the insolence that leads to ruin, the antithesis of moderation or rectitude.

Katharsis, catharsis ▶ (Often translated from Greek as *purgation* or *purification*.) The feeling of emotional release or calm the spectator feels at the end of tragedy. The term is drawn from Aristotle's definition of tragedy, relating to the final cause or purpose of tragic art. Some feel that through *katharsis*, drama taught the audience compassion for the vulnerabilities of others and schooled it in justice and other civic virtues.

Peripeteia ▶ (Anglicized as *peripety*; Greek for "sudden change.") A reversal of fortune, a sudden change of circumstance affecting the protagonist. According to Aristotle, the play's peripety occurs when a certain result is expected and instead its *opposite* effect is produced. In a tragedy, the reversal takes the protagonist from good fortune to catastrophe.

Recognition ▶ In tragic plotting, the moment of recognition occurs when ignorance gives way to knowledge, illusion to disillusion.

38 CRITICAL CASEBOOK
Shakespeare

Principum   *amicitias!*

"To be or not to be . . . " Is it Shakespeare? In 2009 the Shakespeare Birthplace Trust unveiled this newly discovered portrait they believe is William Shakespeare. If authentic—and many scholars disagree—it is the only surviving portrait of the author painted during his lifetime.

All the world's a stage.

—WILLIAM SHAKESPEARE, *AS YOU LIKE IT* (II, vii, 139)

The reconstructed Globe Theatre in today's London—built in 1997 as an exact replica of the original.

THE THEATER OF SHAKESPEARE

Compared with the technical resources of a theater of today, those of a London public theater in the time of Queen Elizabeth I seem hopelessly limited. Plays had to be performed by daylight, and scenery had to be kept simple: a table, a chair, a throne, perhaps an artificial tree or two to suggest a forest. But these limitations were, in a sense, advantages. What the theater of today can spell out for us realistically, with massive scenery and electric lighting, Elizabethan playgoers had to imagine and the playwright had to make vivid for them by means of language. Not having a lighting technician to work a panel, Shakespeare had to indicate the dawn by having Horatio, in *Hamlet*, say in a speech rich in metaphor and descriptive detail:

> But look, the morn in russet mantle clad
> Walks o'er the dew of yon high eastward hill.

And yet the theater of Shakespeare was not bare, for the playwright did have *some* valuable technical resources. Costumes could be elaborate, and apparently some costumes conveyed recognized meanings: one theater manager's inventory included "a robe for to go invisible in." There could be musical accompaniment and sound effects such as gunpowder explosions and the beating of a pan to simulate thunder.

The stage itself was remarkably versatile. At its back were doors for exits and entrances and a curtained booth or alcove useful for hiding inside. Above the stage was a higher acting area—perhaps a porch or balcony—useful for a Juliet to stand upon and for a Romeo to raise his eyes to. In the stage floor was a trapdoor leading to a "hell" or cellar, especially useful for ghosts or devils who had to appear or disappear. The stage itself was a rectangular platform that projected into a yard enclosed by three-storied galleries.

The building was round or octagonal. In *Henry V*, Shakespeare calls it a "wooden O." The audience sat in these galleries or else stood in the yard in front of the stage and at its sides. A roof or awning protected the stage and the high-priced gallery seats, but in a sudden rain, the *groundlings*, who paid a penny to stand in the yard, must have been dampened.

Built by the theatrical company to which Shakespeare belonged, the Globe, most celebrated of Elizabethan theaters, was not in the city of London itself but on the south bank of the Thames River. This location had been chosen because earlier, in 1574, public plays had been banished from the city by an ordinance that blamed them for "corruptions of youth and other enormities" (such as providing opportunities for prostitutes and pickpockets).

A playwright had to please all members of the audience, not only the mannered and educated. This obligation may help to explain the wide range of subject matter and tone in an Elizabethan play: passages of subtle poetry, of deep philosophy, of coarse bawdry; scenes of sensational violence and of quiet psychological conflict (not that most members of the audience did not enjoy all these elements). Because he was an actor as well as a playwright, Shakespeare well knew what his company could do and what his audience wanted. In devising a play, he could write a part to take advantage of some actor's specific skills, or he could avoid straining the company's resources (some of his plays have few female parts, perhaps because of a shortage of competent boy actors). The company might offer as many as thirty plays in a season, customarily changing the program daily. The actors thus had to hold many parts in their heads, which may account for Elizabethan playwrights' fondness for blank verse. Lines of fixed length were easier for actors to commit to memory.

CLASSIC MOMENTS FROM SHAKESPEARE[1]

The works of William Shakespeare helped shape and enrich the English language we know today. Phrases from his plays have become everyday expressions, such as "break the ice," "vanish into thin air," and "in a pickle." He invented words (or created fresh versions of old words) that are now also embedded in standard English, such as "bedazzled," "new-fangled," and "fashionable." Most importantly, Shakespeare's great lines and speeches have fixed themselves in the imaginations of readers across the globe. Here are five brief yet powerful moments from Shakespeare that conjure a universe of reflection, inspiration, and heartache.

"All the World's a Stage" Speech from *As You Like It* (Act II, Scene vii)

Jaques:	All the world's a stage,	138
	And all the men and women merely players.	
	They have their exits and their entrances,	140
	And one man in his time plays many parts,	
	His acts being seven ages. At first the infant,	
	Mewling° and puking in the nurse's arms.	
	Then the whining schoolboy, with his satchel	
	And shining morning face, creeping like snail	145
	Unwillingly to school. And then the lover,	

143 *Mewling* crying with a catlike noise

[1]The text of these plays is taken from David Bevington's book *The Complete Works of Shakespeare*, Updated 4th ed. (New York: Longman; 1997). For the reader's convenience, Mr. Bevington has added some indication of scenes and stage directions. Such additions are enclosed in brackets.

Sighing like furnace, with a woeful ballad
Made to his mistress' eyebrow. Then a soldier,
Full of strange oaths and bearded like the pard,°
Jealous in honor,° sudden,° and quick in quarrel,   150
Seeking the bubble reputation
Even in the cannon's mouth. And then the justice,
In fair round belly with good capon° lined,
With eyes severe and beard of formal cut,
Full of wise saws° and modern instances;°   155
And so he plays his part. The sixth age shifts
Into the lean and slippered pantaloon,°
With spectacles on nose and pouch on side,
His youthful hose, well saved, a world too wide
For his shrunk shank,° and his big manly voice,   160
Turning again toward childish treble, pipes
And whistles in his° sound. Last scene of all,
That ends this strange, eventful history,
Is second childishness and mere oblivion,°
Sans teeth, sans eyes, sans taste, sans everything.   165

Kevin Kline as Jaques in the film _As You Like It_ (2006).

149 _bearded . . . pard_ having bristling mustaches like the leopard's whiskers   150 _Jealous in honor_ quick
to anger in matters of honor.   _sudden_ rash   153 _capon_ rooster castrated to make the flesh more tender
for eating (and often presented to judges as a bribe)   155 _saws_ sayings.   _modern instances_ commonplace
illustrations   157 _pantaloon_ ridiculous, enfeebled old man. (A stock type in Italian comedy.)   160 _shank_
lower leg   162 _his_ its   164 _mere oblivion_ total forgetfulness

Claire Danes and Leonardo DiCaprio in the title roles of Baz Luhrmann's *Romeo and Juliet* (1996).

Balcony Scene from *Romeo and Juliet* (Act II, Scene ii)

[*A light appears above, as at Juliet's window.*]

Romeo: But, soft, what light through yonder window breaks?   2
    It is the east, and Juliet is the sun.
    Arise, fair sun, and kill the envious moon,
    Who is already sick and pale with grief   5
    That thou her maid° art far more fair than she.
    Be not her maid, since she is envious;
    Her vestal livery° is but sick and green°
    And none but fools do wear it. Cast it off.

[*Juliet is visible at her window.*]

    It is my lady, O, it is my love.   10
    O, that she knew she were!
    She speaks, yet she says nothing. What of that?
    Her eye discourses. I will answer it.
    I am too bold. 'Tis not to me she speaks.
    Two of the fairest stars in all the heaven,   15
    Having some business, do entreat her eyes
    To twinkle in their spheres° till they return.
    What if her eyes were there,° they in her head?
    The brightness of her cheek would shame those stars
    As daylight doth a lamp; her eyes in heaven   20

6 *maid* i.e. votary of Diana, goddess of the moon and patroness of virgins   8 *Her vestal livery* the uniform of Diana's chaste votaries.   *sick and green* (Suggesting the pallor of moonlight, as well as anemia or *greensickness*, to which teenage girls were susceptible.)   17 *spheres* transparent concentric shells supposed to carry the heavenly bodies with them in their revolution around the earth   18 *there* i.e., in the spheres

Would through the airy region stream° so bright
That birds would sing and think it were not night.
See how she leans her cheek upon her hand!
O, that I were a glove upon that hand,
That I might touch that cheek!

Juliet: Ay me!

Romeo: She speaks.   25
O, speak again, bright angel, for thou art
As glorious to this night, being o'er my head,
As is a wingèd messenger of heaven
Unto the white-upturnèd° wondering eyes
Of mortals that fall back to gaze on him   30
When he bestrides the lazy puffing clouds
And sails upon the bosom of the air.

Juliet [to herself]: O Romeo, Romeo, wherefore° art thou Romeo?
Deny thy father and refuse thy name!
Or, if thou wilt not, be but sworn my love,   35
And I'll no longer be a Capulet.

Romeo [aside]: Shall I hear more, or shall I speak at this?

Juliet: 'Tis but thy name that is my enemy;
Thou art thyself, though not a Montague.°
What's Montague? It is nor hand,° nor foot,   40
Nor arm, nor face, nor any other part
Belonging to a man. O, be some other name!
What's in a name? That which we call a rose
By any other name would smell as sweet;
So Romeo would, were he not Romeo called,   45
Retain that dear perfection which he owes°
Without that title. Romeo, doff° thy name,
And for° that name, which is no part of thee,
Take all myself.

Romeo: I take thee at thy word!
Call me but love, and I'll be new baptized;   50
Henceforth I never will be Romeo.

Juliet: What man art thou that, thus bescreened° in night,
So stumblest on my counsel?°

Romeo: By a name
I know not how to tell thee who I am.
My name, dear saint, is hateful to myself,   55
Because it is an enemy to thee;
Had I it written, I would tear the word.

Juliet: My ears have not yet drunk a hundred words
Of that tongue's uttering, yet I know the sound:
Art thou not Romeo and a Montague?   60

---

21 *stream* shine   29 *white-upturnèd* looking upward so that the whites of the eyes are visible   33 *wherefore* why   39 *though not a Montague* i.e., even if you were not a Montague   40 *nor hand* neither hand   46 *owes* owns   47 *doff* cast off   48 *for* in exchange for   52 *bescreened* concealed   53 *counsel* secret thought

Romeo: Neither, fair maid, if either thee dislike.°
Juliet: How camest thou hither, tell me, and wherefore?
    The orchard walls are high and hard to climb,
    And the place death, considering who thou art,
    If any of my kinsmen find thee here.   65
Romeo: With love's light wings did I o'erperch° these walls,
    For stony limits cannot hold love out,
    And what love can do, that dares love attempt;
    Therefore thy kinsmen are no stop to me.
Juliet: If they do see thee, they will murder thee.   70
Romeo: Alack, there lies more peril in thine eye
    Than twenty of their swords. Look thou but sweet,
    And I am proof° against their enmity.
Juliet: I would not for the world they saw thee here.
Romeo: I have night's cloak to hide me from their eyes;   75
    And but° thou love me, let them find me here.
    My life were better ended by their hate
    Than death proroguèd,° wanting° of thy love.
Juliet: By whose direction found'st thou out this place?
Romeo: By love, that first did prompt me to inquire.   80
    He lent me counsel, and I lent him eyes.
    I am no pilot; yet, wert thou as far
    As that vast shore washed with the farthest sea,
    I should adventure for such merchandise.
Juliet: Thou know'st the mask of night is on my face,   85
    Else would a maiden blush bepaint my cheek
    For that which thou hast heard me speak tonight.
    Fain° would I dwell on form° —fain, fain deny
    What I have spoke; but farewell compliment!°
    Dost thou love me? I know thou wilt say "Ay,"   90
    And I will take thy word. Yet if thou swear'st
    Thou mayst prove false. At lovers' perjuries,
    Then say, Jove laughs. O gentle Romeo,
    If thou dost love, pronounce it faithfully.
    Or if thou thinkest I am too quickly won,   95
    I'll frown and be perverse and say thee nay,
    So° thou wilt woo, but else° not for the world.
    In truth, fair Montague, I am too fond,°
    And therefore thou mayst think my havior light.°
    But trust me, gentleman, I'll prove more true   100
    Than those that have more cunning to be strange.°
    I should have been more strange, I must confess,
    But that thou overheard'st, ere I was ware,°

---

61 *thee dislike* displeases you   66 *o'erperch* fly over   73 *proof* protected   76 *but* unless   78 *proroguèd* postponed. *wanting of* lacking   88 *Fain* gladly. *dwell on form* preserve the proper formalities   89 *compliment* etiquette, convention   97 *So* as long as, if only. *else* otherwise   98 *fond* infatuated   99 *havior light* behavior frivolous   101 *strange* reserved, aloof, modest   103 *ware* aware

My true-love passion. Therefore pardon me,
And not impute this yielding to light love, 105
Which° the dark night hath so discoverèd.°
Romeo: Lady, by yonder blessèd moon I vow,
That tips with silver all these fruit-tree tops—
Juliet: O, swear not by the moon, th' inconstant moon,
That monthly changes in her circled orb,° 110
Lest that thy love prove likewise variable.
Romeo: What shall I swear by?
Juliet: Do not swear at all;
Or, if thou wilt, swear by thy gracious self,
Which is the god of my idolatry,
And I'll believe thee.
Romeo: If my heart's dear love— 115
Juliet: Well, do not swear. Although I joy in thee,
I have no joy of this contract° tonight.
It is too rash, too unadvised,° too sudden,
Too like the lightning, which doth cease to be
Ere one can say it lightens. Sweet, good night! 120
This bud of love, by summer's ripening breath,
May prove a beauteous flower when next we meet.
Good night, good night! As° sweet repose and rest
Come to thy heart as that within my breast!
Romeo: O, wilt thou leave me so unsatisfied? 125
Juliet: What satisfaction canst thou have tonight?
Romeo: Th' exchange of thy love's faithful vow for mine.
Juliet: I gave thee mine before thou didst request it;
And yet I would it were° to give again.
Romeo: Wouldst thou withdraw it? For what purpose, love? 130
Juliet: But to be frank° and give it thee again.
And yet I wish but for the thing I have.
My bounty is as boundless as the sea,
My love as deep; the more I give to thee,
The more I have, for both are infinite. 135

[*The Nurse calls within.*]

I hear some noise within. Dear love, adieu!—
Anon, good Nurse!—Sweet Montague, be true.
Stay but a little; I will come again.

[*Exit, above.*]

Romeo: O blessèd, blessèd night! I am afeard,
Being in night, all this is but a dream, 140
Too flattering-sweet to be substantial.

---

106 *Which* i.e., which yielding. *discoverèd* revealed   110 *orb* i.e., sphere; see above line 17   117 *contract* exchanging of vows   118 *unadvised* unconsidered   123 *As* may just as   129 *were* were available   131 *frank* liberal, bounteous

[*Enter Juliet, above.*]

Juliet: Three words, dear Romeo, and good night indeed.
If that thy bent° of love be honorable,
Thy purpose marriage, send me word tomorrow,
By one that I'll procure to come to thee,   145
Where and what time thou wilt perform the rite,
And all my fortunes at thy foot I'll lay
And follow thee my lord throughout the world.
Nurse [within]: Madam!

Juliet: I come, anon.—But if thou meanest not well,   150
I do beseech thee—
Nurse [within]:   Madam!
Juliet: By and by,° I come—
To cease thy strife° and leave me to my grief.
Tomorrow will I send.
Romeo: So thrive my soul—
Juliet: A thousand times good night!   155

[*Exit, above.*]

Romeo: A thousand times the worse, to want thy light.
Love goes toward love, as schoolboys from their books,
But love from love, toward school with heavy looks.

"To Be or Not to Be" Soliloquy from *Hamlet* (Act III, Scene i)

Hamlet: To be, or not to be: that is the question: 57
Whether 'tis nobler in the mind to suffer
The slings° and arrows of outrageous fortune,
Or to take arms against a sea of troubles   60
And by opposing end them. To die, to sleep—
No more—and by a sleep to say we end
The heartache and the thousand natural shocks
That flesh is heir to. 'Tis a consummation
Devoutly to be wished. To die, to sleep;   65
To sleep, perchance to dream. Ay, there's the rub,°
For in that sleep of death what dreams may come,
When we have shuffled° off this mortal coil,°
Must give us pause. There's the respect°
That makes calamity of so long life.°   70
For who would bear the whips and scorns of time,
Th' oppressor's wrong, the proud man's contumely,°
The pangs of disprized° love, the law's delay,
The insolence of office,° and the spurns°
That patient merit of th' unworthy takes,°   75

---

143 *bent* purpose, inclination   151 *By and by* immediately   152 *strife* striving   59 *slings* missiles   66 *rub* (Literally, an obstacle in the game of bowls.)   68 *shuffled* sloughed, cast. *coil* turmoil   69 *respect* consideration   70 *of . . . life* so long-lived, something we willingly endure for so long (also suggesting that long life is itself a calamity)   72 *contumely* insolent abuse   73 *disprized* unvalued   74 *office* officialdom. *spurns* insults   75 *of . . . takes* receives from unworthy persons

Kenneth Branagh starring in the 1996 film version of *Hamlet*, which he directed.

When he himself might his quietus° make
With a bare bodkin?° Who would fardels° bear,
To grunt and sweat under a weary life,
But that the dread of something after death,
The undiscovered country from whose bourn°   80
No traveler returns, puzzles the will,
And makes us rather bear those ills we have
Than fly to others that we know not of?
Thus conscience does make cowards of us all;
And thus the native hue° of resolution   85
Is sicklied o'er with the pale cast° of thought,
And enterprises of great pitch° and moment°
With this regard° their currents° turn awry
And lose the name of action.

"Quality of Mercy" Speech from *The Merchant of Venice* (Act IV, Scene i)

Portia: The quality of mercy is not strained.°   182
　　　It droppeth as the gentle rain from heaven
　　　Upon the place beneath. It is twice blest:°
　　　It blesseth him that gives and him that takes.   185
　　　'Tis mightiest in the mightiest; it becomes
　　　The thronèd monarch better than his crown.
　　　His scepter shows the force of temporal power,
　　　The attribute to° awe and majesty,
　　　Wherein doth sit the dread and fear of kings.   190
　　　But mercy is above this sceptered sway;
　　　It is enthronèd in the hearts of kings;

---

76 *quietus* acquitance; here, death 77 *a bare bodkin* a mere dagger, unsheathed. *fardels* burdens 80 *bourn* frontier, boundary 85 *native hue* natural color, complexion 86 *cast* tinge, shade of color 87 *pitch* height (as of a falcon's flight). *moment* importance 88 *regard* respect, consideration. *currents* courses 182 *strained* forced, constrained 184 *is twice blest* grants a double blessing 189 *attribute to* symbol of

**Rachel Pickup as Portia in *The
Merchant of Venice* performed at the
Globe Theater in London, 2015.**

It is an attribute to God himself;
And earthly power doth then show likest God's
When mercy seasons justice. Therefore, Jew,   195
Though justice be thy plea, consider this,
That in the course of justice none of us
Should see salvation. We do pray for mercy,
And that same prayer doth teach us all to render
The deeds of mercy. I have spoke thus much   200
To mitigate the justice of thy plea,°
Which if thou follow, this strict court of Venice
Must needs give sentence 'gainst the merchant there.

"Band of Brothers" Speech from *Henry V* (Act IV, Scene iii)
King Henry addresses his troops before battle

Westmorland: O, that we now had here   16
    But one ten thousand of those men in England
    That do no work today!
King Henry V: What's° he that wishes so?
    My cousin Westmorland? No, my fair cousin.
    If we are marked to die, we are enough   20
    To do our country loss;° and if to live,
    The fewer men, the greater share of honor.
    God's will, I pray thee, wish not one man more.

201 *To . . . plea* i.e. to moderate your plea for strict justice   18 *What's* who is   20–21 *enough . . . loss*
enough loss for our country to suffer

**Kenneth Branagh starring in the 1989 film version of *Henry V*,
which he directed.**

By Jove, I am not covetous for gold,
Nor care I who doth feed upon my cost;°   25
It yearns° me not if men my garments wear;
Such outward things dwell not in my desires.
But if it be a sin to covet honor
I am the most offending soul alive.
No, faith, my coz,° wish not a man from England.   30
God's peace, I would not lose so great an honor
As one man more, methinks, would share from me°
For the best hope I have. O, do not wish one more!
Rather proclaim it, Westmorland, through my host,°
That he which hath no stomach to° this fight,   35
Let him depart; his passport shall be made
And crowns for convoy° put into his purse.
We would not die in that man's company
That fears his fellowship to die with us.°
This day is called the Feast of Crispian.°   40
He that outlives this day, and comes safe home
Will stand a-tiptoe when the day is named
And rouse him at the name of Crispian.
He that shall see this day, and live° old age,
Will yearly on the vigil° feast his neighbors   45
And say, "Tomorrow is Saint Crispian."
Then will he strip his sleeve and show his scars,
And say, "These wounds I had on Crispin's day."
Old men forget; yet° all shall be forgot,

25 *upon my cost* at my expense   26 *yearns* grieves   30 *coz* cousin, kinsman   32 *share from me* take from
me as his share   34 *host* army   35 *stomach to* appetite for   37 *crowns for convoy* travel money   39 *That
. . . us* who is afraid to risk his life in my company   40 *Feast of Crispian* Saint Crispin's day, October 25.
(Cripinus and Crispianus were martyrs who fled from Rome in the third century: according to legend they
disguised themselves as shoemakers, and afterward became the patron saints of that craft.)   44 *live* live to
see   45 *vigil* evening before a feast day   49 *yet* in time

But he'll remember with advantages° 50
What feats he did that day. Then shall our names.
Familiar in his mouth as household words—
Harry the King, Bedford and Exeter,
Warwick and Talbot, Salisbury and Gloucester—
Be in their flowing° cups freshly remembered. 55
This story shall the good man teach his son;
And Crispin Crispian° shall ne'er go by,
From this day to the ending of the world,
But we in it shall be rememberèd—
We few, we happy few, we band of brothers. 60
For he today that sheds his blood with me
Shall be my brother; be he ne'er so vile,°
This day shall gentle his condition.°
And gentlemen in England now abed
Shall think themselves accursed they were not here, 65
And hold their manhoods cheap whiles any speaks
That fought with us upon Saint Crispin's day.

WILLIAM SHAKESPEARE

William Shakespeare (1564–1616), the supreme writer of English, was born, baptized, and buried in the market town of Stratford-on-Avon, eighty miles from London. Son of a glove maker and merchant who was high bailiff (or mayor) of the town, he probably attended grammar school and learned to read Latin authors in the original. At eighteen, he married Anne Hathaway, twenty-six, by whom he had three children, including twins. By 1592 he had become well known and envied as an actor and playwright in London. From 1594 until he retired, he belonged to the same theatrical company, the Lord Chamberlain's Men (later renamed the King's Men in honor of their patron, James I), for whom he wrote thirty-six plays—some of them, such as Hamlet *and* King Lear, *profound reworkings*

William Shakespeare

of old plays. As an actor, Shakespeare is believed to have played supporting roles, such as the ghost of Hamlet's father. The company prospered, moved into the Globe in 1599, and in 1608 bought the fashionable Blackfriars as well; Shakespeare owned an interest in both theaters. When plagues shut down the theaters from 1592 to 1594, Shakespeare turned to story poems; his great Sonnets (published only in 1609) probably also date from the 1590s. Plays were regarded as entertainments of little literary merit, like comic books today, and Shakespeare did not bother to supervise their publication. After writing The Tempest *(1611), the last play entirely from his hand, he retired to Stratford, where since 1597 he had owned*

---

50 *advantages* additions of his own   55 *flowing* overflowing   57 *Crispin Crispian* (*Editor's note:* In this speech, the King switches between two patron saints with similar names, thought to be twin brothers, whose feast day is celebrated on October 25, the date of their execution by Roman Emperor Diocletian in the year 286.)   62 *vile* lowly   63 *gentle his condition* raise him to the rank of gentleman

James Earl Jones as Othello.

the second-largest house in town. Most critics agree that when he wrote Othello, *about 1604, Shakespeare was at the height of his powers.*

A NOTE ON *OTHELLO*

Othello, the Moor of Venice, here offered for study, may be (if you are fortunate) new to you. It is seldom taught in high school, for it is ablaze with passion and violence. Even if you already know the play, we trust that you (like your instructor and these editors) still have much more to learn from it. Following his usual practice, Shakespeare based the play on a story he had appropriated—from a tale, "Of the Unfaithfulness of Husbands and Wives," by a sixteenth-century Italian writer, Giraldi Cinthio. As he could not help but do, Shakespeare freely transformed his source material. In the original tale, the heroine Disdemona (whose name Shakespeare improved) is beaten to death with a stocking full of sand—a shoddier death than the bard reimagined for her.

Surely no character in literature can touch us more than Desdemona; no character can shock and disgust us more than Iago. Between these two extremes stands Othello, a black man of courage and dignity—and yet insecure, capable of being fooled, a pushover for bad advice. Besides breathing life into these characters and a host of others, Shakespeare—as brilliant a writer as any the world has known—enables them to speak poetry. Sometimes this poetry seems splendid and rich in imagery; at other times quiet and understated. Always, it seems to grow naturally from the nature of Shakespeare's characters and from their situations. *Othello, the Moor of Venice* has never ceased to grip readers and beholders alike. It is a safe bet that it will triumphantly live as long as fathers dislike whomever their daughters marry, as long as husbands suspect their wives of cheating, as long as blacks remember slavery, and as long as the ambitious court favor and the jealous practice deceit. The play may well make sense as long as public officials connive behind smiling faces, and it may even endure as long as the world makes room for the kind, the true, the beautiful—the blessed pure in heart.

PICTURING *Othello*

▲ Desdemona's father,
Brabantio, *page 1303*

▲ Iago toasts Cassio, *page 1332*

◄ Desdemona and Othello,
page 1317

▼ Othello berates Desdemona, *page 1374*

▼ Roderigo suspects
Iago, *page 1377*

▲ Emilia prepares Desdemona
for bed, *page 1380*

▼ Iago plots to get the fateful handkerchief, *page 1352*

▲ Cassio wonders how he got the handkerchief, *page 1362*

▲ Othello despairs, *page 1372*

▼ Othello realizes his terrible mistake, *page 1395*

▲ Othello attacks Desdemona in a jealous rage, *page 1389*

PRODUCTION PHOTOS
The photos illustrating the play are from the 2008 Utah Shakespeare Festival production of *Othello*. (All photos by Karl Hugh. Copyright Utah Shakespeare Festival 2008.)

Jonathan Earl Peck *Othello*
James Newcomb *Iago*
Lindsey Wochley *Desdemona*
Justin Matthew Gordon *Cassio*
Corliss Preston *Emilia*

Will Zahrn *Brabantio*
Marcella Rose Sciotto *Bianca*
Danny Camiel *Roderigo*
Drew Shirley *Lodovico*
Bernie Balbot *Servant*

Othello, the Moor of Venice   1604?

Edited by David Bevington

THE NAMES OF THE ACTORS

Othello, the Moor
Brabantio, [a senator,] father to Desdemona
Cassio, an honorable lieutenant [to Othello]
Iago, [Othello's ancient,] a villain
Roderigo, a gulled gentleman
Duke of Venice
Senators [of Venice]
Montano, governor of Cyprus
Gentlemen of Cyprus
Lodovico and Gratiano, [kinsmen to Brabantio,] two noble Venetians
Sailors
Clown
Desdemona, [daughter to Brabantio and] wife to Othello
Emilia, wife to Iago
Bianca, a courtesan [and mistress to Cassio]
[*A Messenger*
A Herald
A Musician
Servants, Attendants, Officers, Senators, Musicians, Gentlemen

SCENE. *Venice; a seaport in Cyprus*]

ACT I

SCENE I [VENICE. A STREET.]

Enter Roderigo and Iago.

Roderigo: Tush, never tell me!° I take it much unkindly
          That thou, Iago, who hast had my purse
          As if the strings were thine, shouldst know of this.°
Iago: 'Sblood,° but you'll not hear me.
          If ever I did dream of such a matter,   5
          Abhor me.

NOTE ON THE TEXT:
This text of *Othello* is based on that of the First Folio, or large collection, of Shakespeare's plays
(1623). But there are many differences between the Folio text and that of the play's first printing in
the Quarto, or small volume, of 1621 (eighteen or nineteen years after the play's first performance).
Some readings from the Quarto are included. For the reader's convenience, some material has been
added by the editor, David Bevington (some indications of scene, some stage directions). Such
additions are enclosed in brackets. Mr. Bevington's text and notes were prepared for his book *The
Complete Works of Shakespeare*, updated 4th ed. (New York: Longman, 1997).

1 *never tell me* (An expression of incredulity, like "tell me another one.")   3 *this* i.e., Desdemona's
elopement   4 *'Sblood* by His (Christ's) blood

Roderigo: Thou toldst me thou didst hold him in thy hate.
Iago: Despise me
    If I do not. Three great ones of the city,
    In personal suit to make me his lieutenant,   10
    Off-capped to him;° and by the faith of man,
    I know my price, I am worth no worse a place.
    But he, as loving his own pride and purposes,
    Evades them with a bombast circumstance°
    Horribly stuffed with epithets of war,°   15
    And, in conclusion,
    Nonsuits° my mediators. For, "Certes,"° says he,
    "I have already chose my officer."
    And what was he?
    Forsooth, a great arithmetician,°   20
    One Michael Cassio, a Florentine,
    A fellow almost damned in a fair wife,°
    That never set a squadron in the field
    Nor the division of a battle° knows
    More than a spinster°—unless the bookish theoric,°   25
    Wherein the togaed° consuls° can propose°
    As masterly as he. Mere prattle without practice
    Is all his soldiership. But he, sir, had th' election;
    And I, of whom his° eyes had seen the proof
    At Rhodes, at Cyprus, and on other grounds   30
    Christened° and heathen, must be beleed and calmed°
    By debitor and creditor.° This countercaster,°
    He, in good time,° must his lieutenant be,
    And I—God bless the mark!°—his Moorship's ancient.°
Roderigo: By heaven, I rather would have been his hangman.°   35
Iago: Why, there's no remedy. 'Tis the curse of service;
    Preferment° goes by letter and affection,°
    And not by old gradation,° where each second
    Stood heir to th' first. Now, sir, be judge yourself
    Whether I in any just term° am affined°   40
    To love the Moor.

---

11 *him* i.e., Othello   14 *bombast circumstance* wordy evasion. (Bombast is cotton padding.)   15 *epithets of war* military expressions   17 *Nonsuits* rejects the petition of.   *Certes* certainly   20 *arithmetician* i.e., a man whose military knowledge is merely theoretical, based on books of tactics   22 *A . . . wife* (Cassio does not seem to be married, but his counterpart in Shakespeare's source does have a woman in his house. See also IV, i, 127.)   24 *division of a battle* disposition of a military unit   25 *a spinster* i.e., a housewife, one whose regular occupation is spinning.   *theoric* theory   26 *togaed* wearing the toga.   *consuls* counselors, senators.   *propose* discuss   29 *his* i.e., Othello's   31 *Christened* Christian.   *beleed and calmed* left to leeward without wind, becalmed. (A sailing metaphor.)   32 *debitor and creditor* (A name for a system of bookkeeping, here used as a contemptuous nickname for Cassio.)   *countercaster* i.e., bookkeeper, one who tallies with *counters*, or "metal disks." (Said contemptuously.)   33 *in good time* opportunely, i.e., forsooth   34 *God bless the mark* (Perhaps originally a formula to ward off evil; here an expression of impatience.)   *ancient* standard-bearer, ensign   35 *his hangman* his executioner   37 *Preferment* promotion. *letter and affection* personal influence and favoritism   38 *old gradation* step-by-step seniority, the traditional way   40 *term* respect.   *affined* bound

Roderigo: I would not follow him then.
Iago: O sir, content you.°
I follow him to serve my turn upon him.
We cannot all be masters, nor all masters   45
Cannot be truly° followed. You shall mark
Many a duteous and knee-crooking knave
That, doting on his own obsequious bondage,
Wears out his time, much like his master's ass,
For naught but provender, and when he's old, cashiered.°   50
Whip me° such honest knaves. Others there are
Who, trimmed in forms and visages of duty,°
Keep yet their hearts attending on themselves,
And, throwing but shows of service on their lords,
Do well thrive by them, and when they have lined their coats,°   55
Do themselves homage.° These fellows have some soul,
And such a one do I profess myself. For, sir,
It is as sure as you are Roderigo,
Were I the Moor I would not be Iago.°
In following him, I follow but myself—   60
Heaven is my judge, not I for love and duty,
But seeming so for my peculiar° end.
For when my outward action doth demonstrate
The native° act and figure° of my heart
In compliment extern,° 'tis not long after   65
But I will wear my heart upon my sleeve
For daws° to peck at. I am not what I am.°
Roderigo: What a full° fortune does the thick-lips° owe°
If he can carry 't thus!°
Iago: Call up her father.
Rouse him, make after him, poison his delight,   70
Proclaim him in the streets; incense her kinsmen,
And, though he in a fertile climate dwell,
Plague him with flies.° Though that his joy be joy,°
Yet throw such changes of vexation° on 't
As it may° lose some color.°   75
Roderigo: Here is her father's house. I'll call aloud.
Iago: Do, with like timorous° accent and dire yell

43 *content you* don't you worry about that   46 *truly* faithfully   50 *cashiered* dismissed from service
51 *Whip me* whip, as far as I'm concerned   52 *trimmed . . . duty* dressed up in the mere form and show
of dutifulness   55 *lined their coats* i.e., stuffed their purses   56 *Do themselves homage* i.e., attend to self-
interest solely   59 *Were . . . Iago* i.e., if I were able to assume command, I certainly would not choose to
remain a subordinate, or, I would keep a suspicious eye on a flattering subordinate   62 *peculiar* particular,
personal   64 *native* innate. *figure* shape, intent   65 *compliment extern* outward show. (Conforming in
this case to the inner workings and intention of the heart.)   67 *daws* small crowlike birds, proverbially
stupid and avaricious. *I am not what I am* i.e., I am not one who wears his heart on his sleeve   68 *full*
swelling. *thick-lips* (Elizabethans often applied the term "Moor" to blacks.)   *owe* own   69 *carry 't thus*
carry this off   72–73 *though . . . flies* though he seems prosperous and happy now, vex him with misery
73 *Though . . . be joy* although he seems fortunate and happy. (Repeats the idea of line 72.)   74 *changes
of vexation* vexing changes   75 *As it may* that may cause it to. *some color* some of its fresh gloss
77 *timorous* frightening

Brabantio asks, "What is the matter there?" (I, i, 85).

As when, by night and negligence,° the fire
Is spied in populous cities.
Roderigo: What ho, Brabantio! Signor Brabantio, ho!   80
Iago: Awake! What ho, Brabantio! Thieves, thieves, thieves!
Look to your house, your daughter, and your bags!
Thieves, thieves!

    Brabantio [enters] above [at a window].°

Brabantio: What is the reason of this terrible summons?
What is the matter° there?   85
Roderigo: Signor, is all your family within?
Iago: Are your doors locked?
Brabantio: Why, wherefore ask you this?
Iago: Zounds,° sir, you're robbed. For shame, put on your gown!
Your heart is burst; you have lost half your soul.
Even now, now, very now, an old black ram   90
Is tupping° your white ewe. Arise, arise!
Awake the snorting° citizens with the bell,
Or else the devil° will make a grandsire of you.
Arise, I say!
Brabantio: What, have you lost your wits?
Roderigo: Most reverend signor, do you know my voice?   95

78 *and negligence* i.e., by negligence. 83 s.d. *at a window* (This stage direction, from the Quarto, probably calls for an appearance on the gallery above and rearstage.) 85 *the matter* your business 88 *Zounds* by His (Christ's) wounds 91 *tupping* covering, copulating with. (Said of sheep.) 92 *snorting* snoring 93 *the devil* (The devil was conventionally pictured as black.)

Brabantio: Not I. What are you?

Roderigo: My name is Roderigo.

Brabantio: The worser welcome.
    I have charged thee not to haunt about my doors.
    In honest plainness thou hast heard me say 100
    My daughter is not for thee; and now, in madness,
    Being full of supper and distempering° drafts,
    Upon malicious bravery° dost thou come
    To start° my quiet.

Roderigo: Sir, sir, sir—

Brabantio: But thou must needs be sure 105
    My spirits and my place° have in° their power
    To make this bitter to thee.

Roderigo: Patience, good sir.

Brabantio: What tell'st thou me of robbing? This is Venice;
    My house is not a grange.°

Roderigo: Most grave Brabantio,
    In simple° and pure soul I come to you. 110

Iago: Zounds, sir, you are one of those that will not serve God if the devil bid you.
    Because we come to do you service and you think we are ruffians, you'll have
    your daughter covered with a Barbary° horse; you'll have your nephews° neigh
    to you; you'll have coursers° for cousins° and jennets° for germans.°

Brabantio: What profane wretch art thou? 115

Iago: I am one, sir, that comes to tell you your daughter and the Moor are now
    making the beast with two backs.

Brabantio: Thou art a villain.

Iago: You are—a senator.°

Brabantio: This thou shalt answer.° I know thee, Roderigo.

Roderigo: Sir, I will answer anything. But I beseech you, 120
    If't be your pleasure and most wise° consent—
    As partly I find it is—that your fair daughter,
    At this odd-even° and dull watch o' the night,
    Transported with° no worse nor better guard
    But with a knave° of common hire, a gondolier, 125
    To the gross clasps of a lascivious Moor—
    If this be known to you and your allowance°
    We then have done you bold and saucy° wrongs.
    But if you know not this, my manners tell me
    We have your wrong rebuke. Do not believe 130

---

102 *distempering* intoxicating   103 *Upon malicious bravery* with hostile intent to defy me   104 *start* startle, disrupt   106 *My spirits and my place* my temperament and my authority of office. *have in* have it in   109 *grange* isolated country house   110 *simple* sincere   113 *Barbary* from northern Africa (and hence associated with Othello). *nephews* i.e., grandsons   114 *coursers* powerful horses. *cousins* kinsmen. *jennets* small Spanish horses. *germans* near relatives   118 *a senator* (Said with mock politeness, as though the word itself were an insult.)   119 *answer* be held accountable for   121 *wise* well-informed   123 *odd-even* between one day and the next, i.e., about midnight   124 *with* by   125 *But with a knave* than by a low fellow, a servant 127 *allowance* permission   128 *saucy* insolent

That, from° the sense of all civility,°
I thus would play and trifle with your reverence.°
Your daughter, if you have not given her leave,
I say again, hath made a gross revolt,
Tying her duty, beauty, wit,° and fortunes   135
In an extravagant° and wheeling° stranger°
Of here and everywhere. Straight° satisfy yourself.
If she be in her chamber or your house,
Let loose on me the justice of the state
For thus deluding you.

Brabantio: Strike on the tinder,° ho!   140
Give me a taper! Call up all my people!
This accident° is not unlike my dream.
Belief of it oppresses me already.
Light, I say, light!   *Exit [above].*

Iago: Farewell, for I must leave you.
It seems not meet° nor wholesome to my place°   145
To be producted°—as, if I stay, I shall—
Against the Moor. For I do know the state,
However this may gall° him with some check,°
Cannot with safety cast° him, for he's embarked°
With such loud reason° to the Cyprus wars,   150
Which even now stands in act,° that, for their souls,°
Another of his fathom° they have none
To lead their business; in which regard,°
Though I do hate him as I do hell pains,
Yet for necessity of present life°   155
I must show out a flag and sign of love,
Which is indeed but sign. That you shall surely find him,
Lead to the Sagittary° the raisèd search,°
And there will I be with him. So farewell.

                                                                 Exit.

Enter [below] Brabantio [in his nightgown°] with servants and torches.

Brabantio: It is too true an evil. Gone she is;   160
And what's to come of my despisèd time°
Is naught but bitterness. Now, Roderigo,
Where didst thou see her?—O unhappy girl!—
With the Moor, sayst thou?—Who would be a father!—
How didst thou know 'twas she?—O, she deceives me   165

---

131 *from* contrary to. *civility* good manners, decency   132 *your reverence* the respect due to
you   135 *wit* intelligence   136 *extravagant* expatriate, wandering far from home. *wheeling* roving about,
vagabond. *stranger* foreigner   137 *Straight* straightway   140 *tinder* charred linen ignited by a spark from
flint and steel, used to light torches or *tapers* (lines 141, 166)   142 *accident* occurrence, event   145 *meet*
fitting. *place* position (as ensign)   146 *producted* produced (as a witness)   148 *gall* rub; oppress. *check*
rebuke   149 *cast* dismiss. *embarked* engaged   150 *loud reason* unanimous shout of confirmation (in the
Senate)   151 *stands in act* are going on. *for their souls* to save themselves   152 *fathom* i.e., ability, depth
of experience   153 *in which regard* out of regard for which   155 *life* livelihood   158 *Sagittary* (An inn or
house where Othello and Desdemona are staying, named for its sign of Sagittarius, or Centaur.) *raisèd*
search search party roused out of sleep   159 s.d. *nightgown* dressing gown. (This costuming is specified in
the Quarto text.)   161 *time* i.e., remainder of life

Past thought!—What said she to you?—Get more tapers.
Raise all my kindred.—Are they married, think you?
Roderigo: Truly, I think they are.
Brabantio: O heaven! How got she out? O treason of the blood!
Fathers, from hence trust not your daughters' minds   170
By what you see them act. Is there not charms°
By which the property° of youth and maidhood
May be abused?° Have you not read, Roderigo,
Of some such thing?
Roderigo: Yes, sir, I have indeed.
Brabantio: Call up my brother.—O, would you had had her!—   175
Some one way, some another.—Do you know
Where we may apprehend her and the Moor?
Roderigo: I think I can discover° him, if you please
To get good guard and go along with me.
Brabantio: Pray you, lead on. At every house I'll call;   180
I may command° at most.—Get weapons, ho!
And raise some special officers of night.—
On, good Roderigo. I will deserve° your pains.

Exeunt.

SCENE II [VENICE. ANOTHER STREET, BEFORE OTHELLO'S LODGINGS.]

Enter Othello, Iago, attendants with torches.

Iago: Though in the trade of war I have slain men,
Yet do I hold it very stuff ° o' the conscience
To do no contrived° murder. I lack iniquity
Sometimes to do me service. Nine or ten times
I had thought t' have yerked° him° here under the ribs.   5
Othello: 'Tis better as it is.
Iago: Nay, but he prated,
And spoke such scurvy and provoking terms
Against your honor
That, with the little godliness I have,
I did full hard forbear him.° But, I pray you, sir,   10
Are you fast married? Be assured of this,
That the magnifico° is much beloved,
And hath in his effect° a voice potential°
As double as the Duke's. He will divorce you,
Or put upon you what restraint or grievance   15
The law, with all his might to enforce it on,
Will give him cable.°

171 *charms* spells 172 *property* special quality, nature 173 *abused* deceived 178 *discover* reveal, uncover 181 *command* demand assistance 183 *deserve* show gratitude for 2 *very stuff* essence, basic material (continuing the metaphor of *trade* from line 1) 3 *contrived* premeditated 5 *yerked* stabbed. *him* i.e., Roderigo 10 *I . . . him* I restrained myself with great difficulty from assaulting him 12 *magnifico* Venetian grandee, i.e., Brabantio 13 *in his effect* at his command. *potential* powerful 17 *cable* i.e., scope

Othello: Let him do his spite.
      My services which I have done the seigniory°
      Shall out-tongue his complaints. 'Tis yet to know°—
      Which, when I know that boasting is an honor,   20
      I shall promulgate—I fetch my life and being
      From men of royal siege,° and my demerits°
      May speak unbonneted° to as proud a fortune
      As this that I have reached. For know, Iago,
      But that I love the gentle Desdemona,   25
      I would not my unhousèd° free condition
      Put into circumscription and confine°
      For the sea's worth.° But look, what lights come yond?

      Enter Cassio [and certain officers°] with torches.

Iago: Those are the raisèd father and his friends.
      You were best go in.
Othello: Not I. I must be found.   30
      My parts, my title, and my perfect soul°
      Shall manifest me rightly. Is it they?
Iago: By Janus,° I think no.
Othello: The servants of the Duke? And my lieutenant?
      The goodness of the night upon you, friends!   35
      What is the news?
Cassio: The Duke does greet you, General,
      And he requires your haste-post-haste appearance
      Even on the instant.
Othello: What is the matter,° think you?
Cassio: Something from Cyprus, as I may divine.°
      It is a business of some heat.° The galleys   40
      Have sent a dozen sequent° messengers
      This very night at one another's heels,
      And many of the consuls,° raised and met,
      Are at the Duke's already. You have been hotly called for;
      When, being not at your lodging to be found,   45
      The Senate hath sent about° three several° quests
      To search you out.
Othello: 'Tis well I am found by you.
      I will but spend a word here in the house
      And go with you.   [*Exit.*]
Cassio: Ancient, what makes° he here?

---

18 *seigniory* Venetian government   19 *yet to know* not yet widely known   22 *siege* i.e., rank. (Literally, a seat used by a person of distinction.)   *demerits* deserts   23 *unbonneted* without removing the hat, i.e., on equal terms (?) (Or "with hat off," "in all due modesty.")   26 *unhousèd* unconfined, undomesticated   27 *circumscription and confine* restriction and confinement   28 *the sea's worth* all the riches at the bottom of the sea.   s.d. *officers* (The Quarto text calls for "Cassio with lights, officers with torches.")   31 *My . . . soul* my natural gifts, my position or reputation, and my unflawed conscience   33 *Janus* Roman two-faced god of beginnings   38 *matter* business   39 *divine* guess   40 *heat* urgency   41 *sequent* successive   43 *consuls* senators   46 *about* all over the city.   *several* separate   49 *makes* does

Iago: Faith, he tonight hath boarded° a land carrack.°   50
　　If it prove lawful prize,° he's made forever.
Cassio: I do not understand.
Iago:　　　　　　　　　　He's married.
Cassio:　　　　　　　　　　　　　To who?

　　[*Enter Othello.*]

Iago: Marry,° to—Come, Captain, will you go?
Othello: Have with you.°
Cassio: Here comes another troop to seek for you.   55

　　Enter Brabantio, Roderigo, with officers and torches.°

Iago: It is Brabantio. General, be advised.°
　　He comes to bad intent.
Othello:　　　　　　　Holla! Stand there!
Roderigo: Signor, it is the Moor.
Brabantio:　　　　　　　Down with him, thief!

　　[*They draw on both sides.*]

Iago: You, Roderigo! Come, sir, I am for you.
Othello: Keep up° your bright swords, for the dew will rust them.   60
　　Good signor, you shall more command with years
　　Than with your weapons.
Brabantio: O thou foul thief, where hast thou stowed my daughter?
　　Damned as thou art, thou hast enchanted her!
　　For I'll refer me° to all things of sense,°   65
　　If she in chains of magic were not bound
　　Whether a maid so tender, fair, and happy,
　　So opposite to marriage that she shunned
　　The wealthy curlèd darlings of our nation,
　　Would ever have, t' incur a general mock,   70
　　Run from her guardage° to the sooty bosom
　　Of such a thing as thou—to fear, not to delight.
　　Judge me the world if 'tis not gross in sense°
　　That thou hast practiced on her with foul charms,
　　Abused her delicate youth with drugs or minerals°   75
　　That weaken motion.° I'll have 't disputed on;°
　　'Tis probable and palpable to thinking.
　　I therefore apprehend and do attach° thee
　　For an abuser of the world, a practicer
　　Of arts inhibited° and out of warrant.°—   80

50 *boarded* gone aboard and seized as an act of piracy (with sexual suggestion). *carrack* large merchant ship 51 *prize* booty 53 *Marry* (An oath, originally "by the Virgin Mary"; here used with wordplay on *married*.) 54 *Have with you* i.e., let's go 55 s.d. *officers and torches* (The Quarto text calls for "others with lights and weapons.") 56 *be advised* be on your guard 60 *Keep up* keep in the sheath 65 *refer me* submit my case. *things of sense* commonsense understandings, or, creatures possessing common sense 71 *her guardage* my guardianship of her 73 *gross in sense* obvious 75 *minerals* i.e., poisons 76 *weaken motion* impair the vital faculties. *disputed on* argued in court by professional counsel, debated by experts 78 *attach* arrest 80 *arts inhibited* prohibited arts, black magic. *out of warrant* illegal

Lay hold upon him! If he do resist,
Subdue him at his peril.
Othello: Hold your hands,
Both you of my inclining° and the rest.
Were it my cue to fight, I should have known it
Without a prompter.—Whither will you that I go   85
To answer this your charge?
Brabantio: To prison, till fit time
Of law and course of direct session°
Call thee to answer.
Othello: What if I do obey?
How may the Duke be therewith satisfied,   90
Whose messengers are here about my side
Upon some present business of the state
To bring me to him?
Officer: 'Tis true, most worthy signor.
The Duke's in council, and your noble self,
I am sure, is sent for.
Brabantio: How? The Duke in council?   95
In this time of the night? Bring him away.°
Mine's not an idle° cause. The Duke himself,
Or any of my brothers of the state,
Cannot but feel this wrong as 'twere their own;
For if such actions may have passage free,°   100
Bondslaves and pagans shall our statesmen be.

Exeunt.

SCENE III [VENICE. A COUNCIL CHAMBER.]

*Enter Duke [and] Senators [and sit at a table, with lights], and Officers.° [The
Duke and Senators are reading dispatches.]*

Duke: There is no composition° in these news
That gives them credit.
First Senator: Indeed, they are disproportioned.°
My letters say a hundred and seven galleys.
Duke: And mine, a hundred forty.
Second Senator: And mine, two hundred.   5
But though they jump° not on a just° account—
As in these cases, where the aim° reports
'Tis oft with difference—yet do they all confirm
A Turkish fleet, and bearing up to Cyprus.

83 *inclining* following, party   88 *course of direct session* regular or specially convened legal proceedings
96 *away* right along   97 *idle* trifling   100 *have passage free* are allowed to go unchecked   s.d. *Enter . . .*
Officers (The Quarto text calls for the Duke and senators to "sit at a table with lights and attendants.")
1 *composition* consistency   3 *disproportioned* inconsistent   6 *jump* agree.   *just* exact   7 *the aim* conjecture

Duke: Nay, it is possible enough to judgment.   10
    I do not so secure me in the error
    But the main article I do approve°
    In fearful sense.
Sailor (within):   What ho, what ho, what ho!

        Enter Sailor.

Officer: A messenger from the galleys.
Duke: Now, what's the business?   15
Sailor: The Turkish preparation° makes for Rhodes.
    So was I bid report here to the state
    By Signor Angelo.
Duke: How say you by° this change?
First Senator: This cannot be
    By no assay° of reason. 'Tis a pageant°   20
    To keep us in false gaze.° When we consider
    Th' importancy of Cyprus to the Turk,
    And let ourselves again but understand
    That, as it more concerns the Turk than Rhodes,
    So may he with more facile question bear it,°   25
    For that° it stands not in such warlike brace,°
    But altogether lacks th' abilities°
    That Rhodes is dressed in°—if we make thought of this,
    We must not think the Turk is so unskillful°
    To leave that latest° which concerns him first,   30
    Neglecting an attempt of ease and gain
    To wake° and wage° a danger profitless.
Duke: Nay, in all confidence, he's not for Rhodes.
Officer: Here is more news.

        Enter a Messenger.

Messenger: The Ottomites, reverend and gracious,   35
    Steering with due course toward the isle of Rhodes,
    Have there injointed them° with an after° fleet.
First Senator: Ay, so I thought. How many, as you guess?
Messenger: Of thirty sail; and now they do restem
    Their backward course,° bearing with frank appearance°   40
    Their purposes toward Cyprus. Signor Montano,
    Your trusty and most valiant servitor,°
    With his free duty° recommends° you thus,

11–12 *I do not . . . approve* I do not take such (false) comfort in the discrepancies that I fail to perceive the main point, i.e., that the Turkish fleet is threatening   16 *preparation* fleet prepared for battle   19 *by* about   20 *assay* test.   *pageant* mere show   21 *in false gaze* looking the wrong way   25 *So may . . . it* so also he (the Turk) can more easily capture it (Cyprus)   26 *For that* since.   *brace* state of defense   27 *abilities* means of self-defense   28 *dressed in* equipped with   29 *unskillful* deficient in judgment   30 *latest* last   32 *wake* stir up.   *wage* risk   37 *injointed them* joined themselves.   *after* second, following   39–40 *restem . . . course* retrace their original course   40 *frank appearance* undisguised intent   42 *servitor* officer under your command   43 *free duty* freely given and loyal service.   *recommends* commends himself and reports to

And prays you to believe him.
Duke: 'Tis certain then for Cyprus.   45
  Marcus Luccicos, is not he in town?
First Senator: He's now in Florence.
Duke: Write from us to him, post-post-haste. Dispatch.
First Senator: Here comes Brabantio and the valiant Moor.

  Enter Brabantio, Othello, Cassio, Iago, Roderigo, and officers.

Duke: Valiant Othello, we must straight° employ you   50
  Against the general enemy° Ottoman.
  [*To Brabantio.*] I did not see you; welcome, gentle° signor.
  We lacked your counsel and your help tonight.
Brabantio: So did I yours. Good Your Grace, pardon me;
  Neither my place° nor aught I heard of business   55
  Hath raised me from my bed, nor doth the general care
  Take hold on me, for my particular° grief
  Is of so floodgate° and o'erbearing nature
  That it engluts° and swallows other sorrows
  And it is still itself.°
Duke: Why, what's the matter?   60
Brabantio: My daughter! O, my daughter!
Duke and Senators: Dead?
Brabantio: Ay, to me.
  She is abused,° stol'n from me, and corrupted
  By spells and medicines bought of mountebanks;
  For nature so preposterously to err,
  Being not deficient,° blind, or lame of sense,°   65
  Sans° witchcraft could not.
Duke: Whoe'er he be that in this foul proceeding
  Hath thus beguiled your daughter of herself,
  And you of her, the bloody book of law
  You shall yourself read in the bitter letter   70
  After your own sense°—yea, though our proper° son
  Stood in your action.°
Brabantio: Humbly I thank Your Grace.
  Here is the man, this Moor, whom now it seems
  Your special mandate for the state affairs
  Hath hither brought.
All: We are very sorry for 't.   75
Duke [to Othello]: What, in your own part, can you say to this?
Brabantio: Nothing, but this is so.
Othello: Most potent, grave, and reverend signors,
  My very noble and approved° good masters:

---

50 *straight* straightway   51 *general enemy* universal enemy to all Christendom   52 *gentle* noble   55 *place* official position   57 *particular* personal   58 *floodgate* i.e., overwhelming (as when floodgates are opened)   59 *engluts* engulfs   60 *is still itself* remains undiminished   62 *abused* deceived   65 *deficient* defective.   *lame of sense* deficient in sensory perception   66 *Sans* without   71 *After . . . sense* according to your own interpretation.   *our proper* my own   72 *Stood . . . action* were under your accusation   79 *approved* proved, esteemed

That I have ta'en away this old man's daughter, 80
It is most true; true, I have married her.
The very head and front° of my offending
Hath this extent, no more. Rude° am I in my speech,
And little blessed with the soft phrase of peace;
For since these arms of mine had seven years' pith,° 85
Till now some nine moons wasted,° they have used
Their dearest° action in the tented field;
And little of this great world can I speak
More than pertains to feats of broils and battle,
And therefore little shall I grace my cause 90
In speaking for myself. Yet, by your gracious patience,
I will a round° unvarnished tale deliver
Of my whole course of love—what drugs, what charms,
What conjuration, and what mighty magic,
For such proceeding I am charged withal,° 95
I won his daughter.

Brabantio: A maiden never bold;
Of spirit so still and quiet that her motion
Blushed at herself;° and she, in spite of nature,
Of years,° of country, credit,° everything,
To fall in love with what she feared to look on! 100
It is a judgment maimed and most imperfect
That will confess° perfection so could err
Against all rules of nature, and must be driven
To find out practices° of cunning hell
Why this should be. I therefore vouch° again 105
That with some mixtures powerful o'er the blood,°
Or with some dram conjured to this effect,°
He wrought upon her.

Duke: To vouch this is no proof,
Without more wider° and more overt test°
Than these thin habits° and poor likelihoods° 110
Of modern seeming° do prefer° against him.

First Senator: But Othello, speak.
Did you by indirect and forcèd courses°
Subdue and poison this young maid's affections?
Or came it by request and such fair question° 115
As soul to soul affordeth?

Othello: I do beseech you,

---

82 *head and front* height and breadth, entire extent   83 *Rude* unpolished   85 *since . . . pith* i.e., since I
was seven. *pith* strength, vigor   86 *Till . . . wasted* until some nine months ago (since when Othello has
evidently not been on active duty, but in Venice)   87 *dearest* most valuable   92 *round* plain   95 *withal*
with   97–98 *her . . . herself* i.e., she blushed easily at herself. (*Motion* can suggest the impulse of the
soul or of the emotions, or physical movement.)   99 *years* i.e., difference in age.   *credit* virtuous reputation   102 *confess* concede (that)   104 *practices* plots   105 *vouch* assert   106 *blood* passions   107 *dram . . .
effect* dose made by magical spells to have this effect   109 *more wider* fuller.   *test* testimony   110 *habits*
garments, i.e., appearances.   *poor likelihoods* weak inferences   111 *modern seeming* commonplace assumption.   *prefer* bring forth   113 *forcèd courses* means used against her will   115 *question* conversation

Send for the lady to the Sagittary
And let her speak of me before her father.
If you do find me foul in her report,
The trust, the office I do hold of you   120
Not only take away, but let your sentence
Even fall upon my life.
Duke: Fetch Desdemona hither.
Othello: Ancient, conduct them. You best know the place.

   [*Exeunt Iago and attendants.*]

And, till she come, as truly as to heaven
I do confess the vices of my blood,°   125
So justly° to your grave ears I'll present
How I did thrive in this fair lady's love,
And she in mine.
Duke: Say it, Othello.
Othello: Her father loved me, oft invited me,   130
Still° questioned me the story of my life
From year to year—the battles, sieges, fortunes
That I have passed.
I ran it through, even from my boyish days
To th' very moment that he bade me tell it,   135
Wherein I spoke of most disastrous chances,
Of moving accidents° by flood and field,
Of hairbreadth scapes i' th' imminent deadly breach,°
Of being taken by the insolent foe
And sold to slavery, of my redemption thence,   140
And portance° in my travels' history,
Wherein of antres° vast and deserts idle,°
Rough quarries,° rocks, and hills whose heads touch heaven,
It was my hint° to speak—such was my process—
And of the Cannibals that each other eat,   145
The Anthropophagi,° and men whose heads
Do grow beneath their shoulders. These things to hear
Would Desdemona seriously incline;
But still the house affairs would draw her thence,
Which ever as she could with haste dispatch   150
She'd come again, and with a greedy ear
Devour up my discourse. Which I, observing,
Took once a pliant° hour, and found good means
To draw from her a prayer of earnest heart
That I would all my pilgrimage dilate,°   155

---

125 *blood* passions, human nature   126 *justly* truthfully, accurately   131 *Still* continually   137 *moving accident* stirring happenings   138 *imminent . . . breach* death-threatening gaps made in a fortification   141 *portance* conduct   142 *antres* caverns.   *idle* barren, desolate   143 *Rough quarries* rugged rock formations   144 *hint* occasion, opportunity   146 *Anthropophagi* man-eaters. (A term from Pliny's *Natural History*.)   153 *pliant* well-suiting   155 *dilate* relate in detail

Whereof by parcels° she had something heard,
But not intentively.° I did consent,
And often did beguile her of her tears,
When I did speak of some distressful stroke
That my youth suffered. My story being done,   160
She gave me for my pains a world of sighs.
She swore, in faith, 'twas strange, 'twas passing° strange,
'Twas pitiful, 'twas wondrous pitiful.
She wished she had not heard it, yet she wished
That heaven had made her° such a man. She thanked me,   165
And bade me, if I had a friend that loved her,
I should but teach him how to tell my story,
And that would woo her. Upon this hint° I spake.
She loved me for the dangers I had passed,
And I loved her that she did pity them.   170
This only is the witchcraft I have used.
Here comes the lady. Let her witness it.

Enter Desdemona, Iago, [and] attendants.

Duke: I think this tale would win my daughter too.
    Good Brabantio,
    Take up this mangled matter at the best.°   175
    Men do their broken weapons rather use
    Than their bare hands.
Brabantio: I pray you, hear her speak.
    If she confess that she was half the wooer,
    Destruction on my head if my bad blame
    Light on the man!—Come hither, gentle mistress.   180
    Do you perceive in all this noble company
    Where most you owe obedience?
Desdemona: My noble Father,
    I do perceive here a divided duty.
    To you I am bound for life and education;°
    My life and education both do learn° me   185
    How to respect you. You are the lord of duty;°
    I am hitherto your daughter. But here's my husband,
    And so much duty as my mother showed
    To you, preferring you before her father,
    So much I challenge° that I may profess   190
    Due to the Moor my lord.
Brabantio: God be with you! I have done.
    Please it Your Grace, on to the state affairs.
    I had rather to adopt a child than get° it.

---

156 *by parcels* piecemeal 157 *intentively* with full attention, continuously 162 *passing* exceedingly 165 *made her* created her to be 168 *hint* opportunity. (Othello does not mean that she was dropping hints.) 175 *Take . . . best* make the best of a bad bargain 184 *education* upbringing 185 *learn* teach 186 *of duty* to whom duty is due 190 *challenge* claim 194 *get* beget

Desdemona tells her father, "I do perceive here a divided duty" (I, iii, 183).

Come hither, Moor.   *[He joins the hands of Othello and Desdemona.]*   195
I here do give thee that with all my heart°
Which, but thou hast already, with all my heart°
I would keep from thee.—For your sake,° jewel,
I am glad at soul I have no other child,
For thy escape° would teach me tyranny,   200
To hang clogs° on them.—I have done, my lord.
Duke: Let me speak like yourself,° and lay a sentence°
  Which, as a grece° or step, may help these lovers
  Into your favor.
  When remedies° are past, the griefs are ended   205
  By seeing the worst, which late on hopes depended.°
  To mourn a mischief° that is past and gone
  Is the next° way to draw new mischief on.
  What° cannot be preserved when fortune takes,
  Patience her injury a mockery makes.°   210
  The robbed that smiles steals something from the thief;
  He robs himself that spends a bootless grief.°
Brabantio: So let the Turk of Cyprus us beguile,
  We lose it not, so long as we can smile.

196 *with all my heart* wherein my whole affection has been engaged   197 *with all my heart* willingly, gladly   198 *For your sake* on your account   200 *escape* elopement   201 *clogs* (Literally, blocks of wood fastened to the legs of criminals or convicts to inhibit escape.)   202 *like yourself* i.e., as you would, in your proper temper.   *lay a sentence* apply a maxim   203 *grece* step   205 *remedies* hopes of remedy   206 *which . . . depended* which griefs were sustained until recently by hopeful anticipation   207 *mischief* misfortune, injury   208 *next* nearest   209 *What* whatever   210 *Patience . . . makes* patience laughs at the injury inflicted by fortune (and thus eases the pain)   212 *spends a bootless grief* indulges in unavailing grief

He bears the sentence well that nothing bears   ·   215
But the free comfort which from thence he hears,
But he bears both the sentence and the sorrow
That, to pay grief, must of poor patience borrow.°
These sentences, to sugar or to gall,
Being strong on both sides, are equivocal.°   220
But words are words. I never yet did hear
That the bruisèd heart was piercèd through the ear.°
I humbly beseech you, proceed to th' affairs of state.
Duke: The Turk with a most mighty preparation makes for Cyprus. Othello, the
    fortitude° of the place is best known to you; and though we have there a   225
    substitute° of most allowed° sufficiency, yet opinion, a sovereign mistress
    of effects, throws a more safer voice on you.° You must therefore be content
    to slubber° the gloss of your new fortunes with this more stubborn° and
    boisterous expedition.
Othello: The tyrant custom, most grave senators,   230
    Hath made the flinty and steel couch of war
    My thrice-driven° bed of down. I do agnize°
    A natural and prompt alacrity
    I find in hardness,° and do undertake
    These present wars against the Ottomites.   235
    Most humbly therefore bending to your state,°
    I crave fit disposition for my wife,
    Due reference of place and exhibition,°
    With such accommodation° and besort°
    As levels° with her breeding.°   240
Duke: Why, at her father's.
Brabantio: I will not have it so.
Othello: Nor I.
Desdemona: Nor I. I would not there reside,
    To put my father in impatient thoughts
    By being in his eye. Most gracious Duke,
    To my unfolding° lend your prosperous° ear,   245
    And let me find a charter° in your voice,
    T' assist my simpleness.
Duke: What would you, Desdemona?
Desdemona: That I did love the Moor to live with him,
    My downright violence and storm of fortunes°   250

215–218 *He bears . . . borrow* a person well bears out your maxim who can enjoy its platitudinous comfort, free of all genuine sorrow, but anyone whose grief bankrupts his poor patience is left with your saying and his sorrow, too. (*Bears the sentence* also plays on the meaning, "receives judicial sentence.")   219–220 *These . . . equivocal* these fine maxims are equivocal, either sweet or bitter in their application   222 *piercèd . . . ear* i.e., surgically lanced and cured by mere words of advice   225 *fortitude* strength   226 *substitute* deputy. *allowed* acknowledged   226–227 *opinion . . . on you* general opinion, an important determiner of affairs, chooses you as the best man   228 *slubber* soil, sully. *stubborn* harsh, rough   232 *thrice-driven* thrice sifted, winnowed. *agnize* know in myself, acknowledge   234 *hardness* hardship   236 *bending . . . state* bowing or kneeling to your authority   238 *reference . . . exhibition* provision of appropriate place to live and allowance of money   239 *accommodation* suitable provision. *besort* attendance   240 *levels* equals, suits. *breeding* social position, upbringing   245 *unfolding* explanation, proposal. *prosperous* propitious   246 *charter* privilege, authorization   250 *My . . . fortunes* my plain and total breach of social custom, taking my future by storm and disrupting my whole life

Desdemona declares her loyalty to her husband Othello (I, iii, 182–301).

May trumpet to the world. My heart's subdued
Even to the very quality of my lord.°
I saw Othello's visage in his mind,
And to his honors and his valiant parts°
Did I my soul and fortunes consecrate.   255
So that, dear lords, if I be left behind
A moth° of peace, and he go to the war,
The rites° for why I love him are bereft me,
And I a heavy interim shall support
By his dear° absence. Let me go with him.   260
Othello: Let her have your voice.°
Vouch with me, heaven, I therefore beg it not
To please the palate of my appetite,
Nor to comply with heat°—the young affects°
In me defunct—and proper° satisfaction,   265
But to be free° and bounteous to her mind.
And heaven defend° your good souls that you think°
I will your serious and great business scant
When she is with me. No, when light-winged toys
Of feathered Cupid seel° with wanton dullness   270
My speculative and officed instruments,°

251–252 *My heart's . . . lord* my heart is brought wholly into accord with Othello's virtues; I love him for
his virtues   254 *parts* qualities   257 *moth* i.e., one who consumes merely   258 *rites* rites of love (with a
suggestion, too, of "rights," sharing)   260 *dear* (1) heartfelt (2) costly   261 *voice* consent   264 *heat* sexual passion. *young affects* passions of youth, desires   265 *proper* personal   266 *free* generous   267 *defend*
forbid. *think* should think   270 *seel* i.e., make blind (as in falconry, by sewing up the eyes of the hawk
during training)   271 *speculative . . . instruments* eyes and other faculties used in the performance of duty

That° my disports° corrupt and taint° my business,
Let huswives make a skillet of my helm,
And all indign° and base adversities
Make head° against my estimation!°   275
Duke: Be it as you shall privately determine,
Either for her stay or going. Th' affair cries haste,
And speed must answer it.
A Senator: You must away tonight.
Desdemona: Tonight, my lord?
Duke: This night.
Othello: With all my heart.
Duke: At nine i' the morning here we'll meet again.   280
Othello, leave some officer behind,
And he shall our commission bring to you,
With such things else of quality and respect°
As doth import° you.
Othello: So please Your Grace, my ancient;
A man he is of honesty and trust.   285
To his conveyance I assign my wife,
With what else needful Your Good Grace shall think
To be sent after me.
Duke: Let it be so.
Good night to everyone. [*To Brabantio.*] And, noble signor,
If virtue no delighted° beauty lack,   290
Your son-in-law is far more fair than black.
First Senator: Adieu, brave Moor. Use Desdemona well.
Brabantio: Look to her, Moor, if thou hast eyes to see.
She has deceived her father, and may thee.

Exeunt [Duke, Brabantio, Cassio, Senators, and officers].

Othello: My life upon her faith! Honest Iago,   295
My Desdemona must I leave to thee.
I prithee, let thy wife attend on her,
And bring them after in the best advantage.°
Come, Desdemona. I have but an hour
Of love, of worldly matters and direction,°   300
To spend with thee. We must obey the time.°

Exit [with Desdemona].

Roderigo: Iago—
Iago: What sayst thou, noble heart?
Roderigo: What will I do, think'st thou?
Iago: Why, go to bed and sleep.   305
Roderigo: I will incontinently° drown myself.

272 *That* so that. *disports* sexual pastimes. *taint* impair   274 *indign* unworthy, shameful   275 *Make head* raise an army. *estimation* reputation   283 *of quality and respect* of importance and relevance   284 *import* concern   290 *delighted* capable of delighting   298 *in . . . advantage* at the most favorable opportunity   300 *direction* instructions   301 *the time* the urgency of the present crisis   306 *incontinently* immediately, without self-restraint

Iago: If thou dost, I shall never love thee after. Why, thou silly gentleman?

Roderigo: It is silliness to live when to live is torment; and then have we a prescription° to die when death is our physician.

Iago: O villainous!° I have looked upon the world for four times seven years, and, since I could distinguish betwixt a benefit and an injury, I never found man that knew how to love himself. Ere I would say I would drown myself for the love of a guinea hen,° I would change my humanity with a baboon.   310

Roderigo: What should I do? I confess it is my shame to be so fond,° but it is not in my virtue° to amend it.   315

Iago: Virtue? A fig!° 'Tis in ourselves that we are thus or thus. Our bodies are our gardens, to the which our wills are gardeners; so that if we will plant nettles or sow lettuce, set hyssop° and weed up thyme, supply it with one gender° of herbs or distract it with° many, either to have it sterile with idleness° or manured with industry—why, the power and corrigible authority° of this lies in our wills. If the beam° of our lives had not one scale of reason to poise° another of sensuality, the blood° and baseness of our natures would conduct us to most preposterous conclusions. But we have reason to cool our raging motions,° our carnal stings, our unbitted° lusts, whereof I take this that you call love to be a sect or scion.°   320 325

Roderigo: It cannot be.

Iago: It is merely a lust of the blood and a permission of the will. Come, be a man. Drown thyself? Drown cats and blind puppies. I have professed me thy friend, and I confess me knit to thy deserving with cables of perdurable° toughness. I could never better stead° thee than now. Put money in thy purse. Follow thou the wars; defeat thy favor° with an usurped° beard. I say, put money in thy purse. It cannot be long that Desdemona should continue her love to the Moor—put money in thy purse—nor he his to her. It was a violent commencement in her, and thou shalt see an answerable sequestration°—put but money in thy purse. These Moors are changeable in their wills°—fill thy purse with money. The food that to him now is as luscious as locusts° shall be to him shortly as bitter as coloquintida.° She must change for youth; when she is sated with his body, she will find the error of her choice. She must have change, she must. Therefore put money in thy purse. If thou wilt needs damn thyself, do it a more delicate way than drowning. Make° all the money thou canst. If sanctimony° and a frail vow betwixt an erring° barbarian and a supersubtle Venetian be not too hard for my wits and all the tribe of hell, thou shalt enjoy her. Therefore make money. A pox of drowning thyself! It is clean out of the way.° Seek thou rather to be hanged in compassing° thy joy than to be drowned and go without her.   330 335 340 345

309 *prescription* (1) right based on long-established custom (2) doctor's prescription   310 *villainous* i.e., what perfect nonsense   313 *guinea hen* (A slang term for a prostitute.)   314 *fond* infatuated   315 *virtue* strength, nature   316 *fig* (To give a fig is to thrust the thumb between the first and second fingers in a vulgar and insulting gesture.)   318 *hyssop* an herb of the mint family.   *gender* kind   319 *distract it with* divide it among.   *idleness* want of cultivation   320 *corrigible authority* power to correct   321 *beam* balance.   *poise* counterbalance   322 *blood* natural passions   324 *motions* appetites.   *unbitted* unbridled, uncontrolled   325 *sect or scion* cutting or offshoot   329 *perdurable* very durable   330 *stead* assist   331 *defeat thy favor* disguise your face.   *usurped* (The suggestion is that Roderigo is not man enough to have a beard of his own.)   334 *an answerable sequestration* a corresponding separation or estrangement   335 *wills* carnal appetites   336 *locusts* fruit of the carob tree (see Matthew 3:4), or perhaps honeysuckle 337 *coloquintida* colocynth or bitter apple, a purgative   340 *Make* raise, collect   341 *sanctimony* sacred ceremony.   *erring* wandering, vagabond, unsteady   344 *clean . . . way* entirely unsuitable as a course of action 345 *compassing* encompassing, embracing

Roderigo: Wilt thou be fast° to my hopes if I depend on the issue?°

Iago: Thou art sure of me. Go, make money. I have told thee often, and I retell thee again and again, I hate the Moor. My cause is hearted;° thine hath no less reason. Let us be conjunctive° in our revenge against him. If thou canst cuckold him, thou dost thyself a pleasure, me a sport. There are many   350
events in the womb of time which will be delivered. Traverse,° go, provide thy money. We will have more of this tomorrow. Adieu.

Roderigo: Where shall we meet i' the morning?

Iago: At my lodging.

Roderigo: I'll be with thee betimes.°   [*He starts to leave.*]   355

Iago: Go to, farewell.—Do you hear, Roderigo?

Roderigo: What say you?

Iago: No more of drowning, do you hear?

Roderigo: I am changed.

Iago: Go to, farewell. Put money enough in your purse.   360

Roderigo: I'll sell all my land.   *Exit.*

Iago: Thus do I ever make my fool my purse;
    For I mine own gained knowledge should profane
    If I would time expend with such a snipe°
    But for my sport and profit. I hate the Moor;   365
    And it is thought abroad° that twixt my sheets
    He's done my office.° I know not if 't be true;
    But I, for mere suspicion in that kind,
    Will do as if for surety.° He holds me well;°
    The better shall my purpose work on him.   370
    Cassio's a proper° man. Let me see now:
    To get his place and to plume up° my will
    In double knavery—How, how?—Let's see:
    After some time, to abuse° Othello's ear
    That he° is too familiar with his wife.   375
    He hath a person and a smooth dispose°
    To be suspected, framed to make women false.
    The Moor is of a free° and open° nature,
    That thinks men honest that but seem to be so,
    And will as tenderly° be led by the nose   380
    As asses are.
    I have 't. It is engendered. Hell and night
    Must bring this monstrous birth to the world's light.

    [*Exit.*]

---

346 *fast* true. *issue* (successful) outcome   348 *hearted* fixed in the heart, heartfelt   349 *conjunctive* united   351 *Traverse* (A military marching term.)   355 *betimes* early   364 *snipe* woodcock, i.e., fool   366 *it is thought abroad* it is rumored   367 *my office* i.e., my sexual function as husband   369 *do . . . surety* act as if on certain knowledge.   *holds me well* regards me favorably   371 *proper* handsome   372 *plume up* put a feather in the cap of, i.e., glorify, gratify   374 *abuse* deceive   375 *he* i.e., Cassio   376 *dispose* disposition   378 *free* frank, generous.   *open* unsuspicious   380 *tenderly* readily

ACT II

SCENE I [A SEAPORT IN CYPRUS. AN OPEN PLACE NEAR THE QUAY.]

Enter Montano and two Gentlemen.

Montano: What from the cape can you discern at sea?
First Gentleman: Nothing at all. It is a high-wrought flood.°
    I cannot, twixt the heaven and the main,°
    Descry a sail.
Montano: Methinks the wind hath spoke aloud at land;   5
    A fuller blast ne'er shook our battlements.
    If it hath ruffianed° so upon the sea,
    What ribs of oak, when mountains° melt on them,
    Can hold the mortise? ° What shall we hear of this?
Second Gentleman: A segregation° of the Turkish fleet.   10
    For do but stand upon the foaming shore,
    The chidden° billow seems to pelt the clouds;
    The wind-shaked surge, with high and monstrous mane,°
    Seems to cast water on the burning Bear°
    And quench the guards of th' ever-fixèd pole.   15
    I never did like molestation° view
    On the enchafèd° flood.
Montano: If that° the Turkish fleet
    Be not ensheltered and embayed,° they are drowned;
    It is impossible to bear it out.°   20

Enter a [Third] Gentleman.

Third Gentleman: News, lads! Our wars are done.
    The desperate tempest hath so banged the Turks
    That their designment° halts.° A noble ship of Venice
    Hath seen a grievous wreck° and sufferance°
    On most part of their fleet.   25
Montano: How? Is this true?
Third Gentleman: The ship is here put in,
    A Veronesa;° Michael Cassio,
    Lieutenant to the warlike Moor Othello,
    Is come on shore; the Moor himself at sea,   30
    And is in full commission here for Cyprus.
Montano: I am glad on 't. 'Tis a worthy governor.

---

2 *high-wrought flood* very agitated sea   3 *main* ocean (also at line 41)   7 *ruffianed* raged   8 *mountains* i.e., of water   9 *hold the mortise* hold their joints together. (A *mortise* is the socket hollowed out in fitting timbers.)   10 *segregation* dispersal   12 *chidden* i.e., rebuked, repelled (by the shore), and thus shot into the air   13 *monstrous mane* (The surf is like the mane of a wild beast.)   14 *the burning Bear* i.e., the constellation Ursa Minor or the Little Bear, which includes the polestar (and hence regarded as the *guards of th' ever-fixèd pole* in the next line; sometimes the term *guards* is applied to the two "pointers" of the Big Bear or Dipper, which may be intended here).   16 *like molestation* comparable disturbance   17 *enchafèd* angry   18 *If that* if   19 *embayed* sheltered by a bay   20 *bear it out* survive, weather the storm   23 *designment* design, enterprise. *halts* is lame   24 *wreck* shipwreck. *sufferance* damage, disaster   28 *Veronesa* i.e., fitted out in Verona for Venetian service, or possibly *Verennessa* (the Folio spelling), i.e., *verrinessa,* a cutter (from *verrinare,* "to cut through")

Third Gentleman: But this same Cassio, though he speak of comfort
  Touching the Turkish loss, yet he looks sadly°
  And prays the Moor be safe, for they were parted   35
  With foul and violent tempest.
Montano: Pray heaven he be,
  For I have served him, and the man commands
  Like a full° soldier. Let's to the seaside, ho!
  As well to see the vessel that's come in
  As to throw out our eyes for brave Othello,   40
  Even till we make the main and th' aerial blue°
  An indistinct regard.°
Third Gentleman: Come, let's do so,
  For every minute is expectancy°
  Of more arrivance.°

  Enter Cassio.

Cassio: Thanks, you the valiant of this warlike isle,   45
  That so approve° the Moor! O, let the heavens
  Give him defense against the elements,
  For I have lost him on a dangerous sea.
Montano: Is he well shipped?
Cassio: His bark is stoutly timbered, and his pilot   50
  Of very expert and approved allowance;°
  Therefore my hopes, not surfeited to death,°
  Stand in bold cure.°

  [*A cry*] *within:*   "A sail, a sail, a sail!"

Cassio: What noise?
A Gentleman: The town is empty. On the brow o' the sea°   55
  Stand ranks of people, and they cry "A sail!"
Cassio: My hopes do shape him for° the governor.

  [*A shot within.*]

Second Gentleman: They do discharge their shot of courtesy;°
  Our friends at least.
Cassio: I pray you, sir, go forth,
  And give us truth who 'tis that is arrived.   60
Second Gentleman: I shall.   *Exit.*
Montano: But, good Lieutenant, is your general wived?
Cassio: Most fortunately. He hath achieved a maid
  That paragons° description and wild fame,°

---

34 *sadly* gravely 38 *full* perfect 41 *the main . . . blue* the sea and the sky 42 *An indistinct regard* indistinguishable in our view 43 *is expectancy* gives expectation 44 *arrivance* arrival 46 *approve* admire, honor 51 *approved allowance* tested reputation 52 *surfeited to death* i.e., overextended, worn thin through repeated application or delayed fulfillment 53 *in bold cure* in strong hopes of fulfillment 55 *brow o' the sea* cliff-edge 57 *My . . . for* I hope it is 58 *discharge . . . courtesy* fire a salute in token of respect and courtesy 64 *paragons* surpasses. *wild fame* extravagant report

One that excels the quirks° of blazoning° pens,   65
And in th' essential vesture of creation
Does tire the enginer.°

Enter [Second] Gentleman.°

                              How now? Who has put in?°
Second Gentleman: 'Tis one Iago, ancient to the General.
Cassio: He's had most favorable and happy speed.
      Tempests themselves, high seas, and howling winds,   70
      The guttered° rocks and congregated sands—
      Traitors ensteeped° to clog the guiltless keel—
      As° having sense of beauty, do omit°
      Their mortal° natures, letting go safely by
      The divine Desdemona.
Montano: What is she?   75
Cassio: She that I spake of, our great captain's captain,
      Left in the conduct of the bold Iago,
      Whose footing° here anticipates our thoughts
      A sennight's° speed. Great Jove, Othello guard,
      And swell his sail with thine own powerful breath,   80
      That he may bless this bay with his tall° ship,
      Make love's quick pants in Desdemona's arms,
      Give renewed fire to our extincted spirits,
      And bring all Cyprus comfort!

Enter Desdemona, Iago, Roderigo, and Emilia.

                              O, behold,
      The riches of the ship is come on shore!   85
      You men of Cyprus, let her have your knees.

[The gentlemen make curtsy to Desdemona.]

      Hail to thee, lady! And the grace of heaven
      Before, behind thee, and on every hand
      Enwheel thee round!
Desdemona: I thank you, valiant Cassio.
      What tidings can you tell me of my lord?   90
Cassio: He is not yet arrived, nor know I aught
      But that he's well and will be shortly here.
Desdemona: O, but I fear—How lost you company?

---

65 *quirks* witty conceits. *blazoning* setting forth as though in heraldic language 66–67 *in . . . enginer* in
her real, God-given, beauty, (she) defeats any attempt to praise her. *enginer* engineer, i.e., poet, one who
devises. s.d. *[Second] Gentleman* (So identified in the Quarto text here and in lines 58, 61, 68, and 96; the
Folio calls him a gentleman.) 67 *put in* i.e., to harbor 71 *guttered* jagged, trenched 72 *ensteeped* lying
under water 73 *As* as if. *omit* forbear to exercise 74 *mortal* deadly 78 *footing* landing 79 *sennight's*
week's 81 *tall* splendid, gallant

"I thank you, valiant Cassio. / What tidings can you tell me of my lord?" (II, i, 89–90).

Cassio: The great contention of the sea and skies
　　Parted our fellowship.
　　(Within)　　　　　　 "A sail, a sail!" [*A shot.*]
　　　　　　　　　　　　　　　　But hark. A sail!　　　　　　　　　95
Second Gentleman: They give their greeting to the citadel.
　　This likewise is a friend.
Cassio:　　　　　　　　　See for the news.

　　[*Exit Second Gentleman.*]

　　Good Ancient, you are welcome. [*Kissing Emilia.*] Welcome, mistress.
　　Let it not gall your patience, good Iago,
　　That I extend° my manners; 'tis my breeding°　　　　　　100
　　That gives me this bold show of courtesy.
Iago: Sir, would she give you so much of her lips
　　As of her tongue she oft bestows on me,
　　You would have enough.
Desdemona: Alas, she has no speech!°　　　　　　　　　105
Iago: In faith, too much.
　　I find it still,° when I have list° to sleep.
　　Marry, before your ladyship, I grant,
　　She puts her tongue a little in her heart
　　And chides with thinking.°
Emilia:　　　　　　　You have little cause to say so.　　110

---

100 *extend* give scope to.　*breeding* training in the niceties of etiquette　105 *she has no speech* i.e., she's not a chatterbox, as you allege　107 *still* always.　*list* desire　110 *with thinking* i.e., in her thoughts only

Iago: Come on, come on. You are pictures out of doors,°
    Bells° in your parlors, wildcats in your kitchens,°
    Saints° in your injuries, devils being offended,
    Players° in your huswifery,° and huswives° in your beds.
Desdemona: O, fie upon thee, slanderer!   115
Iago: Nay, it is true, or else I am a Turk.°
    You rise to play, and go to bed to work.
Emilia: You shall not write my praise.
Iago: No, let me not.
Desdemona: What wouldst thou write of me, if thou shouldst praise me?
Iago: O gentle lady, do not put me to 't,   120
    For I am nothing if not critical.°
Desdemona: Come on, essay.°—There's one gone to the harbor?
Iago: Ay, madam.
Desdemona: I am not merry, but I do beguile
    The thing I am° by seeming otherwise.   125
    Come, how wouldst thou praise me?
Iago: I am about it, but indeed my invention
    Comes from my pate as birdlime° does from frieze°—
    It plucks out brains and all. But my Muse labors,°
    And thus she is delivered: 130
    If she be fair and wise, fairness and wit,
    The one's for use, the other useth it.°
Desdemona: Well praised! How if she be black° and witty?
Iago: If she be black, and thereto have a wit,
    She'll find a white° that shall her blackness fit.°   135
Desdemona: Worse and worse.
Emilia: How if fair and foolish?
Iago: She never yet was foolish that was fair,
    For even her folly° helped her to an heir.°
Desdemona: These are old fond° paradoxes to make fools laugh i' th' alehouse.
    What miserable praise hast thou for her that's foul and foolish?   140
Iago: There's none so foul° and foolish thereunto,°
    But does foul° pranks which fair and wise ones do.
Desdemona: O heavy ignorance! Thou praisest the worst best. But what praise
    couldst thou bestow on a deserving woman indeed, one that, in the authority
    of her merit, did justly put on the vouch° of very malice itself?   145

---

111 *pictures out of doors* i.e., silent and well-behaved in public   112 *Bells* i.e., jangling, noisy, and brazen.
in your kitchens i.e., in domestic affairs. (Ladies would not do the cooking.)   113 *Saints* martyrs   114 *Players*
idlers, triflers, or deceivers. *huswifery* housekeeping. *huswives* hussies (i.e., women are "busy" in bed, or
unduly thrifty in dispensing sexual favors)   116 *a Turk* an infidel, not to be believed   121 *critical* censorious
122 *essay* try   125 *The thing I am* i.e., my anxious self   128 *birdlime* sticky substance used to catch small
birds. *frieze* coarse woolen cloth   129 *labors* (1) exerts herself (2) prepares to deliver a child (with a
following pun on *delivered* in line 130)   132 *The one's . . . it* i.e., her cleverness will make use of her
beauty   133 *black* dark-complexioned, brunette   135 *a white* a fair person (with word-play on "wight,"
a person). *fit* (with sexual suggestion of mating)   138 *folly* (with added meaning of "lechery, wantonness").
to an heir i.e., to bear a child   139 *fond* foolish   141 *foul* ugly. *thereunto* in addition   142 *foul* sluttish
145 *put . . . vouch* compel the approval

Iago: She that was ever fair, and never proud,
    Had tongue at will, and yet was never loud,
    Never lacked gold and yet went never gay,°
    Fled from her wish, and yet said, "Now I may,"°
    She that being angered, her revenge being nigh,   150
    Bade her wrong stay° and her displeasure fly,
    She that in wisdom never was so frail
    To change the cod's head for the salmon's tail,°
    She that could think and ne'er disclose her mind,
    See suitors following and not look behind,   155
    She was a wight, if ever such wight were—
Desdemona: To do what?
Iago: To suckle fools° and chronicle small beer.°
Desdemona: O most lame and impotent conclusion! Do not learn of him, Emilia,
    though he be thy husband. How say you, Cassio? Is he not a most profane°   160
    and liberal° counselor?
Cassio: He speaks home,° madam. You may relish° him more in° the soldier than
    in the scholar.

[*Cassio and Desdemona stand together, conversing intimately.*]

Iago [*aside*]: He takes her by the palm. Ay, well said,° whisper. With as little a
    web as this will I ensnare as great a fly as Cassio. Ay, smile upon her, do;   165
    I will gyve° thee in thine own courtship.° You say true;° 'tis so, indeed. If
    such tricks as these strip you out of your lieutenantry, it had been better you
    had not kissed your three fingers so oft, which now again you are most apt
    to play the sir° in. Very good; well kissed! An excellent courtesy! 'Tis so,
    indeed. Yet again your fingers to your lips? Would they were clyster pipes°   170
    for your sake! [*Trumpet within.*] The Moor! I know his trumpet.
Cassio: 'Tis truly so.
Desdemona: Let's meet him and receive him.
Cassio: Lo, where he comes!

    Enter *Othello and attendants.*

Othello: O my fair warrior!
Desdemona: My dear Othello!   175
Othello: It gives me wonder great as my content
    To see you here before me. O my soul's joy,
    If after every tempest come such calms,
    May the winds blow till they have wakened death,
    And let the laboring bark climb hills of seas   180

---

148 *gay* extravagantly clothed   149 *Fled . . . may* avoided temptation where the choice was hers   151 *Bade
. . . stay* i.e., resolved to put up with her injury patiently   153 *To . . . tail* i.e., to exchange a lacklus-
ter husband for a sexy lover (?) (*Cod's head* is slang for "penis," and *tail*, for "pudendum.")   158 *suckle
fools* breastfeed babies.   *chronicle small beer* i.e., keep petty household accounts, keep track of trivial matters   160 *profane* irreverent, ribald.   161 *liberal* licentious, free-spoken   162 *home* right to the target. (A
term from fencing.)   *relish* appreciate.   *in* in the character of   164 *well said* well done   166 *gyve* fetter,
shackle.   *courtship* courtesy, show of courtly manners.   *You say true* i.e., that's right, go ahead   169 *the sir*
i.e., the fine gentleman   170 *clyster pipes* tubes used for enemas and douches

Olympus-high, and duck again as low
As hell's from heaven! If it were now to die,
'Twere now to be most happy, for I fear
My soul hath her content so absolute
That not another comfort like to this   185
Succeeds in unknown fate.°
Desdemona: The heavens forbid
But that our loves and comforts should increase
Even as our days do grow!
Othello: Amen to that, sweet powers!
I cannot speak enough of this content.   190
It stops me here; it is too much of joy.
And this, and this, the greatest discords be

[*They kiss.*]°

That e'er our hearts shall make!
Iago [*aside*]: O, you are well tuned now!
But I'll set down° the pegs that make this music,   195
As honest as I am.°
Othello: Come, let us to the castle.
News, friends! Our wars are done, the Turks are drowned.
How does my old acquaintance of this isle?—
Honey, you shall be well desired° in Cyprus;   200
I have found great love amongst them. O my sweet,
I prattle out of fashion,° and I dote
In mine own comforts.—I prithee, good Iago,
Go to the bay and disembark my coffers.°
Bring thou the master° to the citadel;   205
He is a good one, and his worthiness
Does challenge° much respect.—Come, Desdemona.—
Once more, well met at Cyprus!

Exeunt Othello and Desdemona [and all but Iago and Roderigo].

Iago [*to an attendant*]: Do thou meet me presently at the harbor. [*To Roderigo.*]
Come hither. If thou be'st valiant—as, they say, base men° being in love 210
have then a nobility in their natures more than is native to them—list° me.
The Lieutenant tonight watches on the court of guard.° First, I must tell thee
this: Desdemona is directly in love with him.
Roderigo: With him? Why, 'tis not possible.
Iago: Lay thy finger thus,° and let thy soul be instructed. Mark me with what vio- 215
lence she first loved the Moor, but° for bragging and telling her fantastical lies.
To love him still for prating? Let not thy discreet heart think it. Her eye must

186 *Succeeds . . . fate* i.e., can follow in the unknown future   192 s.d. *They kiss* (The direction is from
the Quarto.)   195 *set down* loosen (and hence untune the instrument)   196 *As . . . I am* for all my
supposed honesty   200 *desired* welcomed   202 *out of fashion* irrelevantly, incoherently (?)   204 *coffers*
chests, baggage   205 *master* ship's captain   207 *challenge* lay claim to, deserve   210 *base men* even lowly
born men   211 *list* listen to   212 *court of guard* guardhouse. (Cassio is in charge of the watch.)   215 *thus*
i.e., on your lips   216 *but* only

be fed; and what delight shall she have to look on the devil? When the blood is made dull with the act of sport,° there should be, again to inflame it and to give satiety a fresh appetite, loveliness in favor,° sympathy° in years, man- 220 ners, and beauties—all which the Moor is defective in. Now, for want of these required conveniences,° her delicate tenderness will find itself abused,° begin to heave the gorge,° disrelish and abhor the Moor. Very nature° will instruct her in it and compel her to some second choice. Now, sir, this granted—as it is a most pregnant° and unforced position—who stands so eminent in the 225 degree of° this fortune as Cassio does? A knave very voluble,° no further con- scionable° than in putting on the mere form of civil and humane° seeming for the better compassing of his salt° and most hidden loose affection.° Why, none, why, none. A slipper° and subtle knave, a finder out of occasions, that has an eye can stamp° and counterfeit advantages,° though true advantage 230 never present itself; a devilish knave. Besides, the knave is handsome, young, and hath all those requisites in him that folly° and green° minds look after. A pestilent complete knave, and the woman hath found him° already.

Roderigo: I cannot believe that in her. She's full of most blessed condition.°

Iago: Blessed fig's end!° The wine she drinks is made of grapes. If she had been 235 blessed, she would never have loved the Moor. Blessed pudding!° Didst thou not see her paddle with the palm of his hand? Didst not mark that?

Roderigo: Yes, that I did; but that was but courtesy.

Iago: Lechery, by this hand. An index° and obscure° prologue to the history of lust and foul thoughts. They met so near with their lips that their breaths 240 embraced together. Villainous thoughts, Roderigo! When these mutualities° so marshal the way, hard at hand° comes the master and main exercise, th' incorporate° conclusion. Pish! But, sir, be you ruled by me. I have brought you from Venice. Watch you° tonight; for the command, I'll lay 't upon you.° Cassio knows you not. I'll not be far from you. Do you find some occasion to 245 anger Cassio, either by speaking too loud, or tainting° his discipline, or from what other course you please, which the time shall more favorably minister.°

Roderigo: Well.

Iago: Sir, he's rash and very sudden in choler,° and haply° may strike at you. Provoke him that he may, for even out of that will I cause these of Cyprus to mutiny,° 250 whose qualification° shall come into no true taste° again but by the displanting of Cassio. So shall you have a shorter journey to your desires by the means I shall then have to prefer° them, and the impediment most profitably removed, without the which there were no expectation of our prosperity.

Roderigo: I will do this, if you can bring it to any opportunity. 255

---

219 *the act of sport* sex 220 *favor* appearance. *sympathy* correspondence, similarity 222 *required conve- niences* things conducive to sexual compatibility. *abused* cheated, revolted 223 *heave the gorge* experience nausea. *Very nature* her very instincts 225 *pregnant* evident, cogent 225–226 *in the degree of* as next in line for. *voluble* facile, glib 226–227 *conscionable* conscientious, conscience-bound 227 *humane* polite, courteous 228 *salt* licentious. *affection* passion 229 *slipper* slippery 230 *an eye can stamp* an eye that can coin, create. *advantages* favorable opportunities 232 *folly* wantonness. *green* immature 233 *found him* sized him up, perceived his intent 234 *condition* disposition 235 *fig's end* (See Act I, Scene iii, line 316, for the vulgar gesture of the fig.) 236 *pudding* sausage 239 *index* table of contents. *obscure* (i.e., the *lust and foul thoughts* in lines 239–240 are secret, hidden from view) 241 *mutualities* exchanges, intima- cies 242 *hard at hand* closely following 243 *incorporate* carnal 244 *Watch you* stand watch. *for the command . . . you* I'll arrange for you to be appointed, given orders 246 *tainting* disparaging 247 *minister* provide 249 *choler* wrath. *haply* perhaps 250 *mutiny* riot 251 *qualification* appeasement. *true taste* i.e., acceptable state 253 *prefer* advance

Iago: I warrant° thee. Meet me by and by° at the citadel. I must fetch his
    necessaries ashore. Farewell.

Roderigo: Adieu.   *Exit.*

Iago: That Cassio loves her, I do well believe 't;
    That she loves him, 'tis apt° and of great credit.°   260
    The Moor, howbeit that I endure him not,
    Is of a constant, loving, noble nature,
    And I dare think he'll prove to Desdemona
    A most dear husband. Now, I do love her too,
    Not out of absolute lust—though peradventure   265
    I stand accountant° for as great a sin—
    But partly led to diet° my revenge
    For that I do suspect the lusty Moor
    Hath leaped into my seat, the thought whereof
    Doth, like a poisonous mineral, gnaw my innards;   270
    And nothing can or shall content my soul
    Till I am evened with him, wife for wife,
    Or failing so, yet that I put the Moor
    At least into a jealousy so strong
    That judgment cannot cure. Which thing to do,   275
    If this poor trash of Venice, whom I trace°
    For° his quick hunting, stand the putting on,°
    I'll have our Michael Cassio on the hip,°
    Abuse° him to the Moor in the rank garb°—
    For I fear Cassio with my nightcap° too—   280
    Make the Moor thank me, love me, and reward me
    For making him egregiously an ass
    And practicing upon° his peace and quiet
    Even to madness. 'Tis here, but yet confused.
    Knavery's plain face is never seen till used.   *Exit.* 285

SCENE II [CYPRUS. A STREET.]

Enter Othello's Herald with a proclamation.

Herald: It is Othello's pleasure, our noble and valiant general, that, upon certain tidings now arrived, importing the mere perdition° of the Turkish fleet,
every man put himself into triumph:° some to dance, some to make bonfires,
each man to what sport and revels his addiction° leads him. For, besides
these beneficial news, it is the celebration of his nuptial. So much was his   5
pleasure should be proclaimed. All offices° are open, and there is full liberty

---

256 *warrant* assure. *by and by* immediately   260 *apt* probable. *credit* credibility   266 *accountant*
accountable   267 *diet* feed   276 *trace* i.e., train, or follow (?), or perhaps *trash*, a hunting term, meaning
to put weights on a hunting dog in order to slow him down   277 *For* to make more eager. *stand . . . on*
respond properly when I incite him to quarrel   278 *on the hip* at my mercy, where I can throw him. (A
wrestling term.)   279 *Abuse* slander. *rank garb* coarse manner, gross fashion   280 *with my nightcap* i.e., as
a rival in my bed, as one who gives me cuckold's horns   283 *practicing upon* plotting against   2 *mere perdi-*
tion complete destruction   3 *triumph* public celebration   4 *addiction* inclination   6 *offices* rooms where
food and drink are kept

of feasting from this present hour of five till the bell have told eleven.
Heaven bless the isle of Cyprus and our noble general Othello!

Exit.

SCENE III [CYPRUS. THE CITADEL.]

Enter Othello, Desdemona, Cassio, and attendants.

Othello: Good Michael, look you to the guard tonight.
Let's teach ourselves that honorable stop°
Not to outsport° discretion.
Cassio: Iago hath direction what to do,
But notwithstanding, with my personal eye   5
Will I look to 't.
Othello: Iago is most honest.
Michael, good night. Tomorrow with your earliest°
Let me have speech with you. [*To Desdemona.*]
                              Come, my dear love,
The purchase made, the fruits are to ensue;
That profit's yet to come 'tween me and you.°—   10
Good night.

Exit [Othello, with Desdemona and attendants].

Enter Iago.

Cassio: Welcome, Iago. We must to the watch.
Iago: Not this hour,° Lieutenant; 'tis not yet ten o' the clock. Our general cast°
us thus early for the love of his Desdemona; who° let us not therefore blame.
He hath not yet made wanton the night with her, and she is sport for Jove.   15
Cassio: She's a most exquisite lady.
Iago: And, I'll warrant her, full of game.
Cassio: Indeed, she's a most fresh and delicate creature.
Iago: What an eye she has! Methinks it sounds a parley° to provocation.
Cassio: An inviting eye, and yet methinks right modest.   20
Iago: And when she speaks, is it not an alarum° to love?
Cassio: She is indeed perfection.
Iago: Well, happiness to their sheets! Come, Lieutenant, I have a stoup° of wine,
and here without° are a brace° of Cyprus gallants that would fain have a
measure° to the health of black Othello.   25
Cassio: Not tonight, good Iago. I have very poor and unhappy brains for drinking.
I could well wish courtesy would invent some other custom of entertainment.

2 *stop* restraint   3 *outsport* celebrate beyond the bounds of   7 *with your earliest* at your earliest convenience   9–10 *The purchase . . . you* i.e., though married, we haven't yet consummated our love   13 *Not
this hour* not for an hour yet.   *cast* dismissed   14 *who* i.e., Othello   19 *sounds a parley* calls for a conference, issues an invitation   21 *alarum* signal calling men to arms (continuing the military metaphor of *parley*, line 19)   23 *stoup* measure of liquor, two quarts   24 *without* outside.   *brace* pair.   *fain have a measure*
gladly drink a toast

Iago: O, they are our friends. But one cup! I'll drink for you.°

Cassio: I have drunk but one cup tonight, and that was craftily qualified° too, and behold what innovation° it makes here.° I am unfortunate in the   30
infirmity and dare not task my weakness with any more.

Iago: What, man? 'Tis a night of revels. The gallants desire it.

Cassio: Where are they?

Iago: Here at the door. I pray you, call them in.

Cassio: I'll do 't, but it dislikes me.°   *Exit.*   35

Iago: If I can fasten but one cup upon him,
With that which he hath drunk tonight already,
He'll be as full of quarrel and offense°
As my young mistress' dog. Now, my sick fool Roderigo,
Whom love hath turned almost the wrong side out,   40
To Desdemona hath tonight caroused°
Potations pottle-deep;° and he's to watch.°
Three lads of Cyprus—noble swelling° spirits,
That hold their honors in a wary distance,°
The very elements° of this warlike isle—   45
Have I tonight flustered with flowing cups,
And they watch° too. Now, 'mongst this flock of drunkards
Am I to put our Cassio in some action
That may offend the isle.—But here they come.

Enter Cassio, Montano, and gentlemen [servants following with wine].

If consequence do but approve my dream,°   50
My boat sails freely both with wind and stream.°

Cassio: 'Fore God, they have given me a rouse° already.

Montano: Good faith, a little one; not past a pint, as I am a soldier.

Iago: Some wine, ho! [*He sings.*]
              "And let me the cannikin° clink, clink,   55
              And let me the cannikin clink.
              A soldier's a man,
              O, man's life's but a span;°
              Why, then, let a soldier drink."

Some wine, boys!   60

Cassio: 'Fore God, an excellent song.

Iago: I learned it in England, where indeed they are most potent in potting.°
Your Dane, your German, and your swag-bellied Hollander—drink, ho!—
are nothing to your English.

Cassio: Is your Englishman so exquisite in his drinking?   65

28 *for you* in your place. (Iago will do the steady drinking to keep the gallants company while Cassio has only one cup.)   29 *qualified* diluted   30 *innovation* disturbance, insurrection.   *here* i.e., in my head   35 *it dislikes me* i.e., I'm reluctant   38 *offense* readiness to take offense   41 *caroused* drunk off   42 *pottle-deep* to the bottom of the tankard.   *watch* stand watch   43 *swelling* proud   44 *hold . . . distance* i.e., are extremely sensitive of their honor   45 *very elements* typical sort   47 *watch* are members of the guard   50 *If . . . dream* if subsequent events will only substantiate my scheme   51 *stream* current   52 *rouse* full draft of liquor   55 *cannikin* small drinking vessel   58 *span* brief span of time. (Compare Psalm 39:6 as rendered in the 1928 Book of Common Prayer: "Thou hast made my days as it were a span long.")   62 *potting* drinking

Iago persuades Cassio to have a drink, "To the health of our general!" (II, iii, 69).

Iago: Why, he drinks you,° with facility, your Dane° dead drunk; he sweats not°
  to overthrow your Almain;° he gives your Hollander a vomit ere the next
  pottle can be filled.
Cassio: To the health of our general!
Montano: I am for it, Lieutenant, and I'll do you justice.°   70
Iago: O sweet England! [*He sings.*]
          "King Stephen was a worthy peer,
          His breeches cost him but a crown;
          He held them sixpence all too dear,
          With that he called the tailor lown.°   75

          He was a wight of high renown,
          And thou art but of low degree.
          'Tis pride° that pulls the country down;
          Then take thy auld° cloak about thee."
    Some wine, ho!   80
Cassio: 'Fore God, this is a more exquisite song than the other.
Iago: Will you hear 't again?
Cassio: No, for I hold him to be unworthy of his place that does those things.
  Well, God's above all; and there be souls must be saved, and there be souls
  must not be saved.   85
Iago: It's true, good Lieutenant.

66 *drinks you* drinks.   *your Dane* your typical Dane.   *sweats not* i.e., need not exert himself   67 *Almain*
German   70 *I'll . . . justice* i.e., I'll drink as much as you   75 *lown* lout, rascal   78 *pride* i.e., extravagance
in dress   79 *auld* old

Cassio: For mine own part—no offense to the General, nor any man of quality°—
I hope to be saved.
Iago: And so do I too, Lieutenant.
Cassio: Ay, but, by your leave, not before me; the lieutenant is to be saved before   90
the ancient. Let's have no more of this; let's to our affairs.—God forgive us
our sins!—Gentlemen, let's look to our business. Do not think, gentlemen, I
am drunk. This is my ancient; this is my right hand, and this is my left. I am
not drunk now. I can stand well enough, and speak well enough.
Gentlemen: Excellent well.   95
Cassio: Why, very well then; you must not think then that I am drunk.   *Exit.*
Montano: To th' platform, masters. Come, let's set the watch.°

     [*Exeunt Gentlemen.*]

Iago: You see this fellow that is gone before.
     He's a soldier fit to stand by Caesar
     And give direction; and do but see his vice.   100
     'Tis to his virtue a just equinox,°
     The one as long as th' other. 'Tis pity of him.
     I fear the trust Othello puts him in,
     On some odd time of his infirmity,
     Will shake this island.
Montano: But is he often thus?   105
Iago: 'Tis evermore the prologue to his sleep.
     He'll watch the horologe a double set,°
     If drink rock not his cradle.
Montano: It were well
     The General were put in mind of it.
     Perhaps he sees it not, or his good nature   110
     Prizes the virtue that appears in Cassio
     And looks not on his evils. Is not this true?

     Enter Roderigo.

Iago [*aside to him*]: How now, Roderigo?
     I pray you, after the Lieutenant; go.   [*Exit Roderigo.*]
Montano: And 'tis great pity that the noble Moor   115
     Should hazard such a place as his own second
     With° one of an engraffed° infirmity.
     It were an honest action to say so
     To the Moor.
Iago: Not I, for this fair island.
     I do love Cassio well and would do much   120
     To cure him of this evil.   [*Cry within: "Help! Help!"*]
          But, hark! What noise?

---

87 *quality* rank   97 *set the watch* mount the guard   101 *just equinox* exact counterpart. (*Equinox* is an equal
length of days and nights.)   107 *watch . . . set* stay awake twice around the clock or *horologe*   116–117
hazard . . . With risk giving such an important position as his second in command to   117 *engraffed*
engrafted, inveterate

Enter Cassio, pursuing° Roderigo.

Cassio: Zounds, you rogue! You rascal!
Montano: What's the matter, Lieutenant?
Cassio: A knave teach me my duty?
    I'll beat the knave into a twiggen° bottle.
Roderigo: Beat me?   125
Cassio: Dost thou prate, rogue?   [*He strikes Roderigo.*]
Montano: Nay, good Lieutenant. [*Restraining him.*] I pray you, sir, hold your hand.
Cassio: Let me go, sir, or I'll knock you o'er the mazard.°
Montano: Come, come, you're drunk.
Cassio: Drunk?   [*They fight.*] 130
Iago [*aside to Roderigo*]: Away, I say. Go out and cry a mutiny.°

    [*Exit Roderigo.*]

    Nay, good Lieutenant—God's will, gentlemen—
    Help, ho!—Lieutenant—sir—Montano—sir—
    Help, masters!°—Here's a goodly watch indeed!

    [*A bell rings.*]°

    Who's that which rings the bell?—Diablo,° ho!   135
    The town will rise.° God's will, Lieutenant, hold!
    You'll be ashamed forever.

    Enter Othello and attendants [*with weapons*].

Othello: What is the matter here?
Montano: Zounds, I bleed still.
    I am hurt to th' death. He dies!   [*He thrusts at Cassio.*]
Othello: Hold, for your lives!
Iago: Hold, ho! Lieutenant—sir—Montano—gentlemen—   140
    Have you forgot all sense of place and duty?
    Hold! The General speaks to you. Hold, for shame!
Othello: Why, how now, ho! From whence ariseth this?
    Are we turned Turks, and to ourselves do that
    Which heaven hath forbid the Ottomites?°   145
    For Christian shame, put by this barbarous brawl!
    He that stirs next to carve for° his own rage
    Holds his soul light;° he dies upon his motion.°

121 s.d. *pursuing* (The Quarto text reads, "driving in.")   124 *twiggen* wicker-covered (Cassio vows to assail Roderigo until his skin resembles wickerwork or until he has driven Roderigo through the holes in a wickerwork.)   128 *mazard* i.e., head. (Literally, a drinking vessel.)   131 *mutiny* riot   134 *masters* sirs.   s.d. *A bell rings* (This direction is from the Quarto, as are *Exit Roderigo* at line 114, *They fight* at line 130, and *with weapons* at line 137.)   135 *Diablo* the devil   136 *rise* grow riotous   144–145 *to ourselves . . . Ottomites* inflict on ourselves the harm that heaven has prevented the Turks from doing (by destroying their fleet)   147 *carve for* i.e., indulge, satisfy with his sword   148 *Holds . . . light* i.e., places little value on his life.   *upon his motion* if he moves

Silence that dreadful bell. It frights the isle
From her propriety.° What is the matter, masters?   150
Honest Iago, that looks dead with grieving,
Speak. Who began this? On thy love, I charge thee.

Iago: I do not know. Friends all but now, even now,
In quarter° and in terms° like bride and groom
Devesting them° for bed; and then, but now—   155
As if some planet had unwitted men—
Swords out, and tilting one at others' breasts
In opposition bloody. I cannot speak°
Any beginning to this peevish odds;°
And would in action glorious I had lost   160
Those legs that brought me to a part of it!

Othello: How comes it, Michael, you are thus forgot?°

Cassio: I pray you, pardon me. I cannot speak.

Othello: Worthy Montano, you were wont be° civil;
The gravity and stillness° of your youth   165
The world hath noted, and your name is great
In mouths of wisest censure.° What's the matter
That you unlace° your reputation thus
And spend your rich opinion° for the name
Of a night-brawler? Give me answer to it.   170

Montano: Worthy Othello, I am hurt to danger.
Your officer, Iago, can inform you—
While I spare speech, which something° now offends° me—
Of all that I do know; nor know I aught
By me that's said or done amiss this night,   175
Unless self-charity be sometimes a vice,
And to defend ourselves it be a sin
When violence assails us.

Othello: Now, by heaven,
My blood° begins my safer guides° to rule,
And passion, having my best judgment collied,°   180
Essays° to lead the way. Zounds, if I stir,
Or do but lift this arm, the best of you
Shall sink in my rebuke. Give me to know
How this foul rout° began, who set it on;
And he that is approved in° this offense,   185
Though he had twinned with me, both at a birth,
Shall lose me. What? In a town of ° war
Yet wild, the people's hearts brim full of fear,

---

150 *propriety* proper state or condition   154 *In quarter* in friendly conduct, within bounds.   *in terms* on good terms   155 *Devesting them* undressing themselves   158 *speak* explain   159 *peevish odds* childish quarrel   162 *are thus forgot* have forgotten yourself thus   164 *wont be* accustomed to be   165 *stillness* sobriety   167 *censure* judgment   168 *unlace* undo, lay open (as one might loose the strings of a purse containing reputation)   169 *opinion* reputation   173 *something* somewhat.   *offends* pains   179 *blood* passion (of anger).   *guides* i.e., reason   180 *collied* darkened   181 *Essays* undertakes   184 *rout* riot   185 *approved in* found guilty of   187 *town of* town garrisoned for

To manage° private and domestic quarrel?
In night, and on the court and guard of safety?°   190
'Tis monstrous. Iago, who began 't?
Montano [to Iago]: If partially affined,° or leagued in office,°
Thou dost deliver more or less than truth,
Thou art no soldier.
Iago: Touch me not so near.
I had rather have this tongue cut from my mouth   195
Than it should do offense to Michael Cassio;
Yet, I persuade myself, to speak the truth
Shall nothing wrong him. Thus it is, General.
Montano and myself being in speech,
There comes a fellow crying out for help,   200
And Cassio following him with determined sword
To execute° upon him. Sir, this gentleman

[indicating Montano]

Steps in to Cassio and entreats his pause.°
Myself the crying fellow did pursue,
Lest by his clamor—as it so fell out—   205
The town might fall in fright. He, swift of foot,
Outran my purpose, and I returned, the rather°
For that I heard the clink and fall of swords
And Cassio high in oath, which till tonight
I ne'er might say before. When I came back—   210
For this was brief—I found them close together
At blow and thrust, even as again they were
When you yourself did part them.
More of this matter cannot I report.
But men are men; the best sometimes forget.°   215
Though Cassio did some little wrong to him,
As men in rage strike those that wish them best,°
Yet surely Cassio, I believe, received
From him that fled some strange indignity,
Which patience could not pass.°
Othello: I know, Iago,   220
Thy honesty and love doth mince this matter,
Making it light to Cassio. Cassio, I love thee,
But nevermore be officer of mine.

Enter Desdemona, attended.

Look if my gentle love be not raised up.
I'll make thee an example.   225

---

189 *manage* undertake   190 *on . . . safety* at the main guardhouse or headquarters and on watch
192 *partially affined* made partial by some personal relationship.   *leagued in office* in league as fellow officers
202 *execute* give effect to (his anger)   203 *his pause* him to stop   207 *rather* sooner   215 *forget* forget
themselves   217 *those . . . best* i.e., even those who are well disposed   220 *pass* pass over, overlook

Desdemona: What is the matter, dear?
Othello: All's well now, sweeting;
    Come away to bed. [*To Montano.*] Sir, for your hurts,
    Myself will be your surgeon.°—Lead him off.

[*Montano is led off.*]

    Iago, look with care about the town
    And silence those whom this vile brawl distracted.   230
    Come, Desdemona. 'Tis the soldiers' life
    To have their balmy slumbers waked with strife.

    Exit [*with all but Iago and Cassio*].

Iago: What, are you hurt, Lieutenant?
Cassio: Ay, past all surgery.
Iago: Marry, God forbid!   235
Cassio: Reputation, reputation, reputation! O, I have lost my reputation! I have
    lost the immortal part of myself, and what remains is bestial. My reputation,
    Iago, my reputation!
Iago: As I am an honest man, I thought you had received some bodily wound;
    there is more sense in that than in reputation. Reputation is an idle and 240
    most false imposition,° oft got without merit and lost without deserving.
    You have lost no reputation at all, unless you repute yourself such a loser.
    What, man, there are more ways to recover° the General again. You are but
    now cast in his mood°—a punishment more in policy° than in malice, even
    so as one would beat his offenseless dog to affright an imperious lion.° Sue° 245
    to him again and he's yours.
Cassio: I will rather sue to be despised than to deceive so good a commander
    with so slight,° so drunken, and so indiscreet an officer. Drunk? And speak
    parrot?° And squabble? Swagger? Swear? And discourse fustian with one's
    own shadow? O thou invisible spirit of wine, if thou hast no name to be 250
    known by, let us call thee devil!
Iago: What was he that you followed with your sword? What had he done to you?
Cassio: I know not.
Iago: Is 't possible?
Cassio: I remember a mass of things, but nothing distinctly; a quarrel, but noth- 255
    ing wherefore.° O God, that men should put an enemy in their mouths
    to steal away their brains! That we should, with joy, pleasance, revel, and
    applause° transform ourselves into beasts!
Iago: Why, but you are now well enough. How came you thus recovered?
Cassio: It hath pleased the devil drunkenness to give place to the devil wrath. 260
    One unperfectness shows me another, to make me frankly despise myself.

---

228 *be your surgeon* i.e., make sure you receive medical attention   241 *false imposition* thing artifi-
cially imposed and of no real value   243 *recover* regain favor with.   244 *cast in his mood* dismissed in
a moment of anger. *in policy* done for expediency's sake and as a public gesture   245 *would . . .
lion* i.e., would make an example of a minor offender in order to deter more important and dangerous
offenders. *Sue* petition   248 *slight* worthless   248–249 *speak parrot* talk nonsense, rant   256 *wherefore*
why   258 *applause* desire for applause

Iago advises Cassio to ask Desdemona to plead his cause with Othello (II, iii, 233–286).

Iago: Come, you are too severe a moraler.° As the time, the place, and the condition of this country stands, I could heartily wish this had not befallen; but since it is as it is, mend it for your own good.

Cassio: I will ask him for my place again; he shall tell me I am a drunkard. Had I   265
as many mouths as Hydra,° such an answer would stop them all. To be now a sensible man, by and by a fool, and presently a beast! O, strange! Every inordinate cup is unblessed, and the ingredient is a devil.

Iago: Come, come, good wine is a good familiar creature, if it be well used. Exclaim no more against it. And, good Lieutenant, I think you think I   270
love you.

Cassio: I have well approved° it, sir. I drunk!

Iago: You or any man living may be drunk at a time,° man. I'll tell you what you shall do. Our general's wife is now the general—I may say so in this respect, for that° he hath devoted and given up himself to the contem-   275
plation, mark, and denotement° of her parts° and graces. Confess yourself

262 *moraler* moralizer   266 *Hydra* the Lernaean Hydra, a monster with many heads and the ability to grow two heads when one was cut off, slain by Hercules as the second of his twelve labors   272 *approved* proved   273 *at a time* at one time or another   274–275 *in . . . that* in view of this fact, that   276 *mark, and denotement* (Both words mean "observation.").   *parts* qualities

freely to her; importune her help to put you in your place again. She is of so
free,° so kind, so apt, so blessed a disposition, she holds it a vice in her goodness not to do more than she is requested. This broken joint between you
and her husband entreat her to splinter;° and, my fortunes against any lay°   280
worth naming, this crack of your love shall grow stronger than it was before.
Cassio: You advise me well.
Iago: I protest,° in the sincerity of love and honest kindness.
Cassio: I think it freely;° and betimes in the morning I will beseech the virtuous Desdemona to undertake for me. I am desperate of my fortunes if they   285
check° me here.
Iago: You are in the right. Good night, Lieutenant. I must to the watch.
Cassio: Good night, honest Iago.   *Exit Cassio.*
Iago: And what's he then that says I play the villain,
    When this advice is free° I give, and honest,   290
    Probal° to thinking, and indeed the course
    To win the Moor again? For 'tis most easy
    Th' inclining° Desdemona to subdue°
    In any honest suit; she's framed as fruitful°
    As the free elements.° And then for her   295
    To win the Moor—were 't to renounce his baptism,
    All seals and symbols of redeemèd sin—
    His soul is so enfettered to her love
    That she may make, unmake, do what she list,
    Even as her appetite° shall play the god   300
    With his weak function.° How am I then a villain,
    To counsel Cassio to this parallel° course
    Directly to his good? Divinity of hell!°
    When devils will the blackest sins put on,°
    They do suggest° at first with heavenly shows,   305
    As I do now. For whiles this honest fool
    Plies Desdemona to repair his fortune,
    And she for him pleads strongly to the Moor,
    I'll pour this pestilence into his ear,
    That she repeals him° for her body's lust;   310
    And by how much she strives to do him good,
    She shall undo her credit with the Moor.
    So will I turn her virtue into pitch,°
    And out of her own goodness make the net
    That shall enmesh them all.   315

Enter Roderigo.

How now, Roderigo?

278 *free* generous   280 *splinter* bind with splints.   *lay* stake, wager   283 *protest* insist, declare   284 *freely*
unreservedly   286 *check* repulse   290 *free* (1) free from guile (2) freely given   291 *Probal* probable, reasonable
293 *inclining* favorably disposed.   *subdue* persuade   294 *framed as fruitful* created as generous   295 *free elements* i.e., earth, air, fire, and water, unrestrained and spontaneous   300 *her appetite* her desire, or, perhaps, his desire for her   301 *function* exercise of faculties (weakened by his fondness for her)   302 *parallel*
corresponding to these facts and to his best interests   303 *Divinity of hell* inverted theology of hell (which
seduces the soul to its damnation)   304 *put on* further, instigate   305 *suggest* tempt   310 *repeals him*
attempts to get him restored   313 *pitch* i.e., (1) foul blackness (2) a snaring substance

Roderigo: I do follow here in the chase, not like a hound that hunts, but one that
    fills up the cry.° My money is almost spent; I have been tonight exceedingly
    well cudgeled; and I think the issue will be I shall have so much° experience
    for my pains, and so, with no money at all and a little more wit, return again
    to Venice.   320

Iago: How poor are they that have not patience!
    What wound did ever heal but by degrees?
    Thou know'st we work by wit, and not by witchcraft,
    And wit depends on dilatory time.
    Does 't not go well? Cassio hath beaten thee,   325
    And thou, by that small hurt, hast cashiered° Cassio.
    Though other things grow fair against the sun,
    Yet fruits that blossom first will first be ripe.°
    Content thyself awhile. By the Mass, 'tis morning!
    Pleasure and action make the hours seem short.   330
    Retire thee; go where thou art billeted.
    Away, I say! Thou shalt know more hereafter.
    Nay, get thee gone.   *Exit Roderigo.*
                    Two things are to be done.
    My wife must move° for Cassio to her mistress;
    I'll set her on;   335
    Myself the while to draw the Moor apart
    And bring him jump° when he may Cassio find
    Soliciting his wife. Ay, that's the way.
    Dull not device° by coldness° and delay.   *Exit.*

ACT III

SCENE I [BEFORE THE CHAMBER OF OTHELLO AND DESDEMONA.]

Enter Cassio [and] Musicians.

Cassio: Masters, play here—I will content your pains°—
    Something that's brief, and bid "Good morrow, General."   [*They play.*]

[*Enter*] *Clown.*

Clown: Why, masters, have your instruments been in Naples, that they speak i'
    the nose° thus?
A Musician: How, sir, how?   5
Clown: Are these, I pray you, wind instruments?

---

317 *fills up the cry* merely takes part as one of the pack   318 *so much* just so much and no more   326 *cashiered*
dismissed from service   327–328 *Though . . . ripe* i.e., plans that are well prepared and set expeditiously in
motion will soonest ripen into success   334 *move* plead   337 *jump* precisely   339 *device* plot. *coldness*
lack of zeal   1 *content your pains* reward your efforts   3–4 *speak i' the nose* (1) sound nasal (2) sound like
one whose nose has been attacked by syphilis. (Naples was popularly supposed to have a high incidence of
venereal disease.)

Cassio sends a message to Desdemona's gentle-woman (III, i, 21–23).

A Musician: Ay, marry, are they, sir.

Clown: O, thereby hangs a tail.

A Musician: Whereby hangs a tale, sir?

Clown: Marry, sir, by many a wind instrument° that I know. But, masters, here's   10
money for you. [*He gives money.*] And the General so likes your music that
he desires you, for love's sake,° to make no more noise with it.

A Musician: Well, sir, we will not.

Clown: If you have any music that may not° be heard, to 't again; but, as they
say, to hear music the General does not greatly care.   15

A Musician: We have none such, sir.

Clown: Then put up your pipes in your bag, for I'll away.° Go, vanish into air,
away!

                                                            Exeunt Musicians.

Cassio: Dost thou hear, mine honest friend?

Clown: No, I hear not your honest friend; I hear you.   20

---

10 *wind instrument* (With a joke on flatulence. The *tail,* line 8, that hangs nearby the *wind instrument* suggests the penis.)   12 *for love's sake* (1) out of friendship and affection (2) for the sake of lovemaking in Othello's marriage   14 *may not* cannot   17 *I'll away* (Possibly a misprint, or a snatch of song?)

Cassio: Prithee, keep up° thy quillets.° There's a poor piece of gold for thee. [*He gives money.*] If the gentle-woman that attends the General's wife be stirring, tell her there's one Cassio entreats her a little favor of speech.° Wilt thou do this?
Clown: She is stirring, sir. If she will stir° hither, I shall seem° to notify unto her.
Cassio: Do, good my friend.   *Exit Clown.*

    Enter Iago.

                  In happy time,° Iago.   25
Iago: You have not been abed, then?
Cassio: Why, no. The day had broke
    Before we parted. I have made bold, Iago,
    To send in to your wife. My suit to her
    Is that she will to virtuous Desdemona   30
    Procure me some access.
Iago: I'll send her to you presently;
    And I'll devise a means to draw the Moor
    Out of the way, that your converse and business
    May be more free.   35
Cassio: I humbly thank you for 't.   *Exit [Iago].*
                  I never knew
    A Florentine° more kind and honest.

    Enter Emilia.

Emilia: Good morrow, good Lieutenant. I am sorry
    For your displeasure;° but all will sure be well.
    The General and his wife are talking of it,   40
    And she speaks for you stoutly.° The Moor replies
    That he you hurt is of great fame° in Cyprus
    And great affinity,° and that in wholesome wisdom
    He might not but refuse you; but he protests° he loves you
    And needs no other suitor but his likings   45
    To take the safest occasion by the front°
    To bring you in again.
Cassio: Yet I beseech you,
    If you think fit, or that it may be done,
    Give me advantage of some brief discourse
    With Desdemona alone.
Emilia: Pray you, come in.   50
    I will bestow you where you shall have time
    To speak your bosom° freely.
Cassio: I am much bound to you.   [*Exeunt.*]

---

21 *keep up* do not bring out, do not use. *quillets* quibbles, puns   23 *a little . . . speech* the favor of a brief talk   24 *stir* bestir herself (with a play on *stirring*, "rousing herself from rest").   *seem* deem it good, think fit   25 *In happy time* i.e., well met   37 *Florentine* i.e., even a fellow Florentine. (Iago is a Venetian; Cassio is a Florentine.)   39 *displeasure* fall from favor   41 *stoutly* spiritedly   42 *fame* reputation, importance   43 *affinity* kindred, family connection   44 *protests* insists   46 *occasion . . . front* opportunity by the forelock   52 *bosom* inmost thoughts

SCENE II [THE CITADEL.]

Enter Othello, Iago, and Gentlemen.

Othello [giving letters]: These letters give, Iago, to the pilot,
  And by him do my duties° to the Senate.
  That done, I will be walking on the works;°
  Repair° there to me.
Iago: Well, my good lord, I'll do 't.
Othello: This fortification, gentlemen, shall we see 't?   5
Gentlemen: We'll wait upon° your lordship.   *Exeunt.*

SCENE III [THE GARDEN OF THE CITADEL.]

Enter Desdemona, Cassio, and Emilia.

Desdemona: Be thou assured, good Cassio, I will do
  All my abilities in thy behalf.
Emilia: Good madam, do. I warrant it grieves my husband
  As if the cause were his.
Desdemona: O, that's an honest fellow. Do not doubt, Cassio,   5
  But I will have my lord and you again
  As friendly as you were.
Cassio: Bounteous madam,
  Whatever shall become of Michael Cassio,
  He's never anything but your true servant.
Desdemona: I know 't. I thank you. You do love my lord;   10
  You have known him long, and be you well assured
  He shall in strangeness° stand no farther off
  Than in a politic° distance.
Cassio: Ay, but, lady,
  That policy may either last so long,
  Or feed upon such nice and waterish diet,°   15
  Or breed itself so out of circumstance,°
  That, I being absent and my place supplied,°
  My general will forget my love and service.
Desdemona: Do not doubt° that. Before Emilia here
  I give thee warrant° of thy place. Assure thee,   20
  If I do vow a friendship I'll perform it
  To the last article. My lord shall never rest.
  I'll watch him tame° and talk him out of patience;°
  His bed shall seem a school, his board° a shrift;°

---

2 *do my duties* convey my respects   3 *works* breastworks, fortifications   4 *Repair* return, come   6 *wait upon* attend   12 *strangeness* aloofness   13 *politic* required by wise policy   15 *Or . . . diet* or sustain itself at length upon such trivial and meager technicalities   16 *breed . . . circumstance* continually renew itself so out of chance events, or yield so few chances for my being pardoned   17 *supplied* filled by another person   19 *doubt* fear   20 *warrant* guarantee   23 *watch him tame* tame him by keeping him from sleeping. (A term from falconry.)   *out of patience* past his endurance   24 *board* dining table.   *shrift* confessional

I'll intermingle everything he does   25
With Cassio's suit. Therefore be merry, Cassio,
For thy solicitor° shall rather die
Than give thy cause away.°

Enter Othello and Iago [at a distance].

Emilia: Madam, here comes my lord.
Cassio: Madam, I'll take my leave.   30
Desdemona: Why, stay, and hear me speak.
Cassio: Madam, not now. I am very ill at ease,
    Unfit for mine own purposes.
Desdemona: Well, do your discretion.°   *Exit Cassio.*
Iago: Ha? I like not that.   35
Othello: What dost thou say?
Iago: Nothing, my lord; or if—I know not what.
Othello: Was not that Cassio parted from my wife?
Iago: Cassio, my lord? No, sure, I cannot think it,
    That he would steal away so guiltylike,   40
    Seeing you coming.
Othello: I do believe 'twas he.
Desdemona: How now, my lord?
    I have been talking with a suitor here,
    A man that languishes in your displeasure.   45
Othello: Who is 't you mean?
Desdemona: Why, your lieutenant, Cassio. Good my lord,
    If I have any grace or power to move you,
    His present reconciliation take;°
    For if he be not one that truly loves you,   50
    That errs in ignorance and not in cunning,°
    I have no judgment in an honest face.
    I prithee, call him back.
Othello: Went he hence now?
Desdemona: Yes, faith, so humbled   55
    That he hath left part of his grief with me
    To suffer with him. Good love, call him back.
Othello: Not now, sweet Desdemon. Some other time.
Desdemona: But shall 't be shortly?
Othello: The sooner, sweet, for you.   60
Desdemona: Shall 't be tonight at supper?
Othello: No, not tonight.
Desdemona: Tomorrow dinner,° then?
Othello: I shall not dine at home.
    I meet the captains at the citadel.   65
Desdemona: Why, then, tomorrow night, or Tuesday morn,
    On Tuesday noon, or night, on Wednesday morn.

27 *solicitor* advocate   28 *away* up   34 *do your discretion* act according to your own discretion   49 *His . . . take*
let him be reconciled to you right away   51 *in cunning* wittingly   63 *dinner* (The noontime meal.)

I prithee, name the time, but let it not
Exceed three days. In faith, he's penitent;
And yet his trespass, in our common reason°—   70
Save that, they say, the wars must make example
Out of her best°—is not almost° a fault
T' incur a private check.° When shall he come?
Tell me, Othello. I wonder in my soul
What you would ask me that I should deny,   75
Or stand so mammering on.° What? Michael Cassio,
That came a-wooing with you, and so many a time,
When I have spoke of you dispraisingly,
Hath ta'en your part—to have so much to do
To bring him in!° By 'r Lady, I could do much—   80
Othello: Prithee, no more. Let him come when he will;
I will deny thee nothing.
Desdemona: Why, this is not a boon.
'Tis as I should entreat you wear your gloves,
Or feed on nourishing dishes, or keep you warm,   85
Or sue to you to do a peculiar° profit
To your own person. Nay, when I have a suit
Wherein I mean to touch° your love indeed,
It shall be full of poise° and difficult weight,
And fearful to be granted.   90
Othello: I will deny thee nothing.
Whereon,° I do beseech thee, grant me this,
To leave me but a little to myself.
Desdemona: Shall I deny you? No. Farewell, my lord.
Othello: Farewell, my Desdemona. I'll come to thee straight.°   95
Desdemona: Emilia, come.—Be as your fancies° teach you;
Whate'er you be, I am obedient.   *Exit [with Emilia.]*
Othello: Excellent wretch!° Perdition catch my soul
But I do love thee! And when I love thee not,
Chaos is come again.°   100
Iago: My noble lord—
Othello: What dost thou say, Iago?
Iago: Did Michael Cassio, when you wooed my lady,
Know of your love?
Othello: He did, from first to last. Why dost thou ask?   105
Iago: But for a satisfaction of my thought;
No further harm.

---

70 *common reason* everyday judgments   71–72 *Save . . . best* were it not that, as the saying goes, military discipline requires making an example of the very best men. (He refers to *wars* as a singular concept.) 72 *not almost* scarcely   73 *private check* even a private reprimand   76 *mammering on* wavering about   80 *bring him in* restore him to favor   86 *peculiar* particular, personal   88 *touch* test   89 *poise* weight, heaviness; or equipoise, delicate balance involving hard choice   92 *Whereon* in return for which   95 *straight* straightway   96 *fancies* inclinations   98 *wretch* (A term of affectionate endearment.)   99–100 *And . . . again* i.e., my love for you will last forever, until the end of time when chaos will return. (But with an unconscious, ironic suggestion that, if anything should induce Othello to cease loving Desdemona, the result would be chaos.)

Othello:　　　　　Why of thy thought, Iago?

Iago: I did not think he had been acquainted with her.

Othello: O, yes, and went between us very oft.

Iago: Indeed?　　　　　　　　　　　　　　　　　　　　110

Othello: Indeed? Ay, indeed. Discern'st thou aught in that?
　　Is he not honest?

Iago: Honest, my lord?

Othello: Honest. Ay, honest.

Iago: My lord, for aught I know.　　　　　　　　　　　115

Othello: What dost thou think?

Iago: Think, my lord?

Othello: "Think, my lord?" By heaven, thou echo'st me,
　　As if there were some monster in thy thought
　　Too hideous to be shown. Thou dost mean something.　120
　　I heard thee say even now, thou lik'st not that,
　　When Cassio left my wife. What didst not like?
　　And when I told thee he was of my counsel°
　　In my whole course of wooing, thou criedst "Indeed?"
　　And didst contract and purse° thy brow together　　125
　　As if thou then hadst shut up in thy brain
　　Some horrible conceit.° If thou dost love me,
　　Show me thy thought.

Iago: My lord, you know I love you.

Othello: I think thou dost;　　　　　　　　　　　　130
　　And, for° I know thou'rt full of love and honesty,
　　And weigh'st thy words before thou giv'st them breath,
　　Therefore these stops° of thine fright me the more;
　　For such things in a false disloyal knave
　　Are tricks of custom,° but in a man that's just　　135
　　They're close dilations,° working from the heart
　　That passion cannot rule.°

Iago:　　　　　　　　　For° Michael Cassio,
　　I dare be sworn I think that he is honest.

Othello: I think so too.

Iago:　　　　　　　Men should be what they seem;
　　Or those that be not, would they might seem none!°　140

Othello: Certain, men should be what they seem.

Iago: Why, then, I think Cassio's an honest man.

Othello: Nay, yet there's more in this.
　　I prithee, speak to me as to thy thinkings,
　　As thou dost ruminate, and give thy worst of thoughts　145
　　The worst of words.

Iago:　　　　　　　Good my lord, pardon me.
　　Though I am bound to every act of duty,

---

123 *of my counsel* in my confidence　125 *purse* knit　127 *conceit* fancy　131 *for* because　133 *stops* pauses　135 *of custom* customary　136 *close dilations* secret or involuntary expressions or delays　137 *That passion cannot rule* i.e., that are too passionately strong to be restrained (referring to the workings), or that cannot rule its own passions (referring to the heart).　*For* as for　140 *none* i.e., not to be men, or not seem to be honest

I am not bound to that° all slaves are free to.°
Utter my thoughts? Why, say they are vile and false,
As where's the palace whereinto foul things   150
Sometimes intrude not? Who has that breast so pure
But some uncleanly apprehensions
Keep leets and law days,° and in sessions sit
With° meditations lawful?°

Othello: Thou dost conspire against thy friend,° Iago,   155
If thou but think'st him wronged and mak'st his ear
A stranger to thy thoughts.

Iago: I do beseech you,
Though I perchance am vicious° in my guess—
As I confess it is my nature's plague
To spy into abuses, and oft my jealousy°   160
Shapes faults that are not—that your wisdom then,°
From one° that so imperfectly conceits,°
Would take no notice, nor build yourself a trouble
Out of his scattering° and unsure observance.
It were not for your quiet nor your good,   165
Nor for my manhood, honesty, and wisdom,
To let you know my thoughts.

Othello: What dost thou mean?

Iago: Good name in man and woman, dear my lord,
Is the immediate° jewel of their souls.
Who steals my purse steals trash; 'tis something, nothing;   170
'Twas mine, 'tis his, and has been slave to thousands;
But he that filches from me my good name
Robs me of that which not enriches him
And makes me poor indeed.

Othello: By heaven, I'll know thy thoughts.   175

Iago: You cannot, if° my heart were in your hand,
Nor shall not, whilst 'tis in my custody.

Othello: Ha?

Iago: O, beware, my lord, of jealousy.
It is the green-eyed monster which doth mock
The meat it feeds on.° That cuckold lives in bliss   180
Who, certain of his fate, loves not his wronger;°
But O, what damnèd minutes tells° he o'er
Who dotes, yet doubts, suspects, yet fondly loves!

Othello: O misery!

---

148 *that* that which. *free to* free with respect to   153 *Keep leets and law days* i.e., hold court, set up their authority in one's heart. (*Leets* are a kind of manor court; *law days* are the days courts sit in session, or those sessions.)   154 *With* along with. *lawful* innocent   155 *thy friend* i.e., Othello   158 *vicious* wrong   160 *jealousy* suspicious nature   161 *then* on that account   162 *one* i.e., myself, Iago. *conceits* judges, conjectures   164 *scattering* random   169 *immediate* essential, most precious   176 *if* even if   179–180 *doth mock . . . on* mocks and torments the heart of its victim, the man who suffers jealousy   181 *his wronger* i.e., his faithless wife. (The unsuspecting cuckold is spared the misery of loving his wife only to discover she is cheating on him.)   182 *tells* counts

Iago: Poor and content is rich, and rich enough,°   185
     But riches fineless° is as poor as winter
     To him that ever fears he shall be poor.
     Good God, the souls of all my tribe defend
     From jealousy!
Othello: Why, why is this?   190
     Think'st thou I'd make a life of jealousy,
     To follow still the changes of the moon
     With fresh suspicions?° No! To be once in doubt
     Is once° to be resolved.° Exchange me for a goat
     When I shall turn the business of my soul   195
     To such exsufflicate and blown° surmises
     Matching thy inference.° 'Tis not to make me jealous
     To say my wife is fair, feeds well, loves company,
     Is free of speech, sings, plays, and dances well;
     Where virtue is, these are more virtuous.   200
     Nor from mine own weak merits will I draw
     The smallest fear or doubt of her revolt,°
     For she had eyes, and chose me. No, Iago,
     I'll see before I doubt; when I doubt, prove;
     And on the proof, there is no more but this—   205
     Away at once with love or jealousy.
Iago: I am glad of this, for now I shall have reason
     To show the love and duty that I bear you
     With franker spirit. Therefore, as I am bound,
     Receive it from me. I speak not yet of proof.   210
     Look to your wife; observe her well with Cassio.
     Wear your eyes thus, not° jealous nor secure.°
     I would not have your free and noble nature,
     Out of self-bounty,° be abused.° Look to 't.
     I know our country disposition well;   215
     In Venice they do let God see the pranks
     They dare not show their husbands; their best conscience
     Is not to leave 't undone, but keep 't unknown.
Othello: Dost thou say so?
Iago: She did deceive her father, marrying you;   220
     And when she seemed to shake and fear your looks,
     She loved them most.
Othello: And so she did.
Iago: Why, go to,° then!

---

185 *Poor . . . enough* to be content with what little one has is the greatest wealth of all. (Proverbial.)   186 *fineless* boundless   192–193 *To follow . . . suspicions* to be constantly imagining new causes
for suspicion, changing incessantly like the moon   194 *once* once and for all.   *resolved* free of doubt, having settled the matter   196 *exsufflicate and blown* inflated and blown up, rumored about, or, spat out and
flyblown, hence, loathsome, disgusting   197 *inference* description or allegation   202 *doubt . . . revolt* fear
of her unfaithfulness   212 *not* neither.   *secure* free from uncertainty   214 *self-bounty* inherent or natural
goodness and generosity.   *abused* deceived   222 *go to* (An expression of impatience.)

She that, so young, could give out such a seeming,°
To seel° her father's eyes up close as oak,°
He thought 'twas witchcraft! But I am much to blame.   225
I humbly do beseech you of your pardon
For too much loving you.
Othello: I am bound° to thee forever.
Iago: I see this hath a little dashed your spirits.
Othello: Not a jot, not a jot.
Iago: I' faith, I fear it has.   230
I hope you will consider what is spoke
Comes from my love. But I do see you're moved.
I am to pray you not to strain my speech
To grosser issues° nor to larger reach°
Than to suspicion.   235
Othello: I will not.
Iago: Should you do so, my lord,
My speech should fall into such vile success°
Which my thoughts aimed not. Cassio's my worthy friend.
My lord, I see you're moved.
Othello: No, not much moved.   240
I do not think but Desdemona's honest.°
Iago: Long live she so! And long live you to think so!
Othello: And yet, how nature erring from itself—
Iago: Ay, there's the point! As—to be bold with you—
Not to affect° many proposèd matches   245
Of her own clime, complexion, and degree,°
Whereto we see in all things nature tends—
Foh! One may smell in such a will° most rank,
Foul disproportion,° thoughts unnatural.
But pardon me. I do not in position°   250
Distinctly speak of her, though I may fear
Her will, recoiling° to her better° judgment,
May fall to match you with her country forms°
And happily repent.°
Othello: Farewell, farewell!
If more thou dost perceive, let me know more.   255
Set on thy wife to observe. Leave me, Iago.
Iago [*going*]: My lord, I take my leave.
Othello: Why did I marry? This honest creature doubtless
Sees and knows more, much more, than he unfolds.
Iago [*returning*]: My Lord, I would I might entreat your honor   260

---

223 *seeming* false appearance   224 *seel* blind. (A term from falconry.)   *oak* (A close-grained wood.)
228 *bound* indebted (but perhaps with ironic sense of "tied")   234 *issues* significances.   *reach* meaning, scope   238 *success* effect, result   241 *honest* chaste   245 *affect* prefer, desire   246 *clime . . . degree*
country, color, and social position   248 *will* sensuality, appetite   249 *disproportion* abnormality
250 *position* argument, proposition   252 *recoiling* reverting.   *better* i.e., more natural and reconsidered
253 *fall . . . forms* undertake to compare you with Venetian norms of handsomeness   254 *happily repent*
happily repent her marriage

To scan° this thing no farther. Leave it to time.
Although 'tis fit that Cassio have his place—
For, sure, he fills it up with great ability—
Yet, if you please to hold him off awhile,
You shall by that perceive him and his means.°   265
Note if your lady strain his entertainment°
With any strong or vehement importunity;
Much will be seen in that. In the meantime,
Let me be thought too busy° in my fears—
As worthy cause I have to fear I am—   270
And hold her free,° I do beseech your honor.
Othello: Fear not my government.°
Iago: I once more take my leave.   *Exit.*
Othello: This fellow's of exceeding honesty,
And knows all qualities,° with a learnèd spirit,   275
Of human dealings. If I do prove her haggard,°
Though that her jesses° were my dear heartstrings,
I'd whistle her off and let her down the wind°
To prey at fortune.° Haply, for° I am black
And have not those soft parts of conversation°   280
That chamberers° have, or for I am declined
Into the vale of years—yet that's not much—
She's gone. I am abused,° and my relief
Must be to loathe her. O curse of marriage,
That we can call these delicate creatures ours   285
And not their appetites! I had rather be a toad
And live upon the vapor of a dungeon
Than keep a corner in the thing I love
For others' uses. Yet, 'tis the plague of great ones;
Prerogatived° are they less than the base.°   290
'Tis destiny unshunnable, like death.
Even then this forkèd° plague is fated to us
When we do quicken.° Look where she comes.

Enter Desdemona and Emilia.

If she be false, O, then heaven mocks itself!
I'll not believe 't.
Desdemona: How now, my dear Othello?   295

261 *scan* scrutinize   265 *his means* the method he uses (to regain his post)   266 *strain his entertainment* urge his reinstatement   269 *busy* interfering   271 *hold her free* regard her as innocent   272 *government* self-control, conduct   275 *qualities* natures, types   276 *haggard* wild (like a wild female hawk)   277 *jesses* straps fastened around the legs of a trained hawk   278 *I'd . . . wind* i.e., I'd let her go forever. (To release a hawk downwind was to invite it not to return.)   279 *prey at fortune* fend for herself in the wild.   *Haply, for* perhaps because   280 *soft . . . conversation* pleasing graces of social behavior   281 *chamberers* gallants   283 *abused* deceived   290 *Prerogatived* privileged (to have honest wives).   *the base* ordinary citizens. (Socially prominent men are especially prone to the unavoidable destiny of being cuckolded and to the public shame that goes with it.)   292 *forkèd* (An allusion to the horns of the cuckold.)   293 *quicken* receive life. (Quicken may also mean to swarm with maggots as the body festers, as in IV, ii, 69, in which case lines 292–293 suggest that *even then*, in death, we are cuckolded by *forkèd* worms.)

Your dinner, and the generous° islanders
By you invited, do attend° your presence.
Othello: I am to blame.
Desdemona: Why do you speak so faintly?
    Are you not well?
Othello: I have a pain upon my forehead here.   300
Desdemona: Faith, that's with watching.° 'Twill away again.

    [*She offers her handkerchief.*]

    Let me but bind it hard, within this hour
    It will be well.
Othello: Your napkin° is too little.
    Let it alone.° Come, I'll go in with you.

    [*He puts the handkerchief from him, and it drops.*]

Desdemona: I am very sorry that you are not well.   305

    Exit [with Othello].

Emilia [picking up the handkerchief]: I am glad I have found this napkin.
    This was her first remembrance from the Moor.
    My wayward° husband hath a hundred times
    Wooed me to steal it, but she so loves the token—
    For he conjured her she should ever keep it—   310
    That she reserves it evermore about her
    To kiss and talk to. I'll have the work ta'en out,°
    And give 't Iago. What he will do with it
    Heaven knows, not I;
    I nothing but to please his fantasy.°   315

    Enter Iago.

Iago: How now? What do you here alone?
Emilia: Do not you chide. I have a thing for you.
Iago: You have a thing for me? It is a common thing°—
Emilia: Ha?
Iago: To have a foolish wife.   320
Emilia: O, is that all? What will you give me now
    For that same handkerchief?
Iago: What handkerchief?
Emilia: What handkerchief?
    Why, that the Moor first gave to Desdemona;   325
    That which so often you did bid me steal.
Iago: Hast stolen it from her?

296 *generous* noble 297 *attend* await 301 *watching* too little sleep 303 *napkin* handkerchief 304 *Let it alone* i.e., never mind 308 *wayward* capricious 312 *work ta'en out* design of the embroidery copied 315 *fantasy* whim 318 *common thing* (With bawdy suggestion; *common* suggests coarseness and availability to all comers, and *thing* is a slang term for the pudendum.)

**Emilia gets the fateful handkerchief for Iago
(III, iii, 316–335).**

Emilia: No, faith. She let it drop by negligence,
   And to th' advantage° I, being here, took 't up.
   Look, here 'tis.
Iago: A good wench! Give it me.   330
Emilia: What will you do with 't, that you have been so earnest
   To have me filch it?
Iago [snatching it]:   Why, what is that to you?
Emilia: If it be not for some purpose of import,
   Give 't me again. Poor lady, she'll run mad
   When she shall lack° it.
Iago: Be not acknown on 't.°   335
   I have use for it. Go, leave me.   *Exit Emilia.*
   I will in Cassio's lodging lose° this napkin
   And let him find it. Trifles light as air
   Are to the jealous confirmations strong
   As proofs of Holy Writ. This may do something.   340

---

329 *to th' advantage* taking the opportunity   335 *lack* miss.   *Be . . . on 't* do not confess knowledge of
it   337 *lose* (The Folio spelling, *loose*, is a normal spelling for "lose," but it may also contain the idea of
"let go," "release.")

The Moor already changes with my poison.
Dangerous conceits° are in their natures poisons,
Which at the first are scarce found to distaste,°
But with a little act° upon the blood
Burn like the mines of sulfur.

Enter Othello.

                              I did say so.   345
Look where he comes! Not poppy nor mandragora°
Nor all the drowsy syrups of the world
Shall ever medicine thee to that sweet sleep
Which thou owedst° yesterday.
Othello: Ha, ha, false to me?
Iago: Why, how now, General? No more of that.   350
Othello: Avaunt! Begone! Thou hast set me on the rack.
    I swear 'tis better to be much abused
    Than but to know 't a little.
Iago: How now, my lord?
Othello: What sense had I of her stolen hours of lust?
    I saw 't not, thought it not, it harmed not me.   355
    I slept the next night well, fed well, was free° and merry;
    I found not Cassio's kisses on her lips.
    He that is robbed, not wanting° what is stolen,
    Let him not know 't and he's not robbed at all.
Iago: I am sorry to hear this.   360
Othello: I had been happy if the general camp,
    Pioners° and all, had tasted her sweet body,
    So° I had nothing known. O, now, forever
    Farewell the tranquil mind! Farewell content!
    Farewell the plumèd troops and the big° wars   365
    That makes ambition virtue! O, farewell!
    Farewell the neighing steed and the shrill trump,
    The spirit-stirring drum, th' ear-piercing fife,
    The royal banner, and all quality,°
    Pride,° pomp, and circumstance° of glorious war!   370
    And O, you mortal engines,° whose rude throats
    Th' immortal Jove's dread clamors° counterfeit,
    Farewell! Othello's occupation's gone.
Iago: Is 't possible, my lord?
Othello: Villain, be sure thou prove my love a whore!   375
    Be sure of it. Give me the ocular proof,
    Or, by the worth of mine eternal soul,
    Thou hadst been better have been born a dog
    Than answer my waked wrath!

342 *conceits* fancies, ideas   343 *distaste* be distasteful   344 *act* action, working   346 *mandragora* an opiate made of the mandrake root   349 *thou owedst* you did own   356 *free* carefree   358 *wanting* missing   362 *Pioners* diggers of mines, the lowest grade of soldiers   363 *So* provided   365 *big* stately   369 *quality* character, essential nature   370 *Pride* rich display. *circumstance* pageantry   371 *mortal engines* i.e., cannon. (*Mortal* means "deadly.")   372 *Jove's dread clamors* i.e., thunder

Iago: Is 't come to this?

Othello: Make me to see 't, or at the least so prove it   380
    That the probation° bear no hinge nor loop
    To hang a doubt on, or woe upon thy life!

Iago: My noble lord—

Othello: If thou dost slander her and torture me,
    Never pray more; abandon all remorse;°   385
    On horror's head horrors accumulate;°
    Do deeds to make heaven weep, all earth amazed;°
    For nothing canst thou to damnation add
    Greater than that.

Iago: O grace! O heaven forgive me!
    Are you a man? Have you a soul or sense?   390
    God b' wi' you; take mine office. O wretched fool,°
    That lov'st to make thine honesty a vice!°
    O monstrous world! Take note, take note, O world,
    To be direct and honest is not safe.
    I thank you for this profit,° and from hence°   395
    I'll love no friend, sith° love breeds such offense.°

Othello: Nay, stay. Thou shouldst be° honest.

Iago: I should be wise, for honesty's a fool
    And loses that° it works for.

Othello: By the world,
    I think my wife be honest and think she is not;   400
    I think that thou art just and think thou art not.
    I'll have some proof. My name, that was as fresh
    As Dian's° visage, is now begrimed and black
    As mine own face. If there be cords, or knives,
    Poison, or fire, or suffocating streams,   405
    I'll not endure it. Would I were satisfied!

Iago: I see, sir, you are eaten up with passion.
    I do repent me that I put it to you.
    You would be satisfied?

Othello: Would? Nay, and I will.

Iago: And may; but how? How satisfied, my lord?   410
    Would you, the supervisor,° grossly gape on?
    Behold her topped?

Othello: Death and damnation! O!

Iago: It were a tedious difficulty, I think,
    To bring them to that prospect. Damn them then,°
    If ever mortal eyes do see them bolster°   415

---

381 *probation* proof   385 *remorse* pity, penitent hope for salvation   386 *horrors accumulate* add still more horrors   387 *amazed* confounded with horror   391 *O wretched fool* (Iago addresses himself as a fool for having carried honesty too far.)   392 *vice* failing, something overdone   395 *profit* profitable instruction. *hence* henceforth   396 *sith* since. *offense* i.e., harm to the one who offers help and friendship   397 *Thou shouldst be* it appears that you are. (But Iago replies in the sense of "ought to be.")   399 *that* what   403 *Dian's* Diana, goddess of the moon and of chastity   411 *supervisor* onlooker   414 *Damn them then* i.e., they would have to be really incorrigible   415 *bolster* go to bed together, share a bolster

More° than their own.° What then? How then?
What shall I say? Where's satisfaction?
It is impossible you should see this,
Were they as prime° as goats, as hot as monkeys,
As salt° as wolves in pride,° and fools as gross   420
As ignorance made drunk. But yet I say,
If imputation and strong circumstances°
Which lead directly to the door of truth
Will give you satisfaction, you might have 't.
Othello: Give me a living reason she's disloyal.   425
Iago: I do not like the office.
But sith° I am entered in this cause so far,
Pricked° to 't by foolish honesty and love,
I will go on. I lay with Cassio lately,
And being troubled with a raging tooth   430
I could not sleep. There are a kind of men
So loose of soul that in their sleeps will mutter
Their affairs. One of this kind is Cassio.
In sleep I heard him say, "Sweet Desdemona,
Let us be wary, let us hide our loves!"   435
And then, sir, would he grip and wring my hand,
Cry "O sweet creature!" and then kiss me hard,
As if he plucked up kisses by the roots
That grew upon my lips; then laid his leg
Over my thigh, and sighed, and kissed, and then   440
Cried, "Cursèd fate that gave thee to the Moor!"
Othello: O monstrous! Monstrous!
Iago: Nay, this was but his dream.
Othello: But this denoted a foregone conclusion.°
'Tis a shrewd doubt,° though it be but a dream.
Iago: And this may help to thicken other proofs   445
That do demonstrate thinly.
Othello: I'll tear her all to pieces.
Iago: Nay, but be wise. Yet we see nothing done;
She may be honest yet. Tell me but this:
Have you not sometimes seen a handkerchief
Spotted with strawberries° in your wife's hand?   450
Othello: I gave her such a one. 'Twas my first gift.
Iago: I know not that; but such a handkerchief—
I am sure it was your wife's—did I today
See Cassio wipe his beard with.
Othello: If it be that—
Iago: If it be that, or any that was hers,   455
It speaks against her with the other proofs.

---

416 *More* other. *own* own eyes 419 *prime* lustful 420 *salt* wanton, sensual. *pride* heat 422 *imputa-tion . . . circumstances* strong circumstantial evidence 427 *sith* since 428 *Pricked* spurred 443 *foregone conclusion* concluded experience or action 444 *shrewd doubt* suspicious circumstance 450 *Spotted with strawberries* embroidered with a strawberry pattern

Othello: O, that the slave° had forty thousand lives!
    One is too poor, too weak for my revenge.
    Now do I see 'tis true. Look here, Iago,
    All my fond° love thus do I blow to heaven.   460
    'Tis gone.
    Arise, black vengeance, from the hollow hell!
    Yield up, O love, thy crown and hearted° throne
    To tyrannous hate! Swell, bosom, with thy freight,°
    For 'tis of aspics'° tongues!   465
Iago: Yet be content.°
Othello: O, blood, blood, blood!
Iago: Patience, I say. Your mind perhaps may change.
Othello: Never, Iago. Like to the Pontic Sea,°
    Whose icy current and compulsive course   470
    Ne'er feels retiring ebb, but keeps due on
    To the Propontic° and the Hellespont,°
    Even so my bloody thoughts with violent pace
    Shall ne'er look back, ne'er ebb to humble love,
    Till that a capable° and wide revenge   475
    Swallow them up. Now, by yond marble° heaven,
    [*Kneeling*] In the due reverence of a sacred vow
    I here engage my words.
Iago: Do not rise yet.
    [*He kneels.*°] Witness, you ever-burning lights above,
    You elements that clip° us round about,   480
    Witness that here Iago doth give up
    The execution° of his wit,° hands, heart,
    To wronged Othello's service. Let him command,
    And to obey shall be in me remorse,°
    What bloody business ever.°   [*They rise.*]
Othello: I greet thy love,   485
    Not with vain thanks, but with acceptance bounteous,
    And will upon the instant put thee to 't.°
    Within these three days let me hear thee say
    That Cassio's not alive.
Iago: My friend is dead;
    'Tis done at your request. But let her live.   490
Othello: Damn her, lewd minx!° O, damn her, damn her!
    Come, go with me apart. I will withdraw
    To furnish me with some swift means of death
    For the fair devil. Now art thou my lieutenant.
Iago: I am your own forever.   *Exeunt.* 495

---

457 *the slave* i.e., Cassio   460 *fond* foolish (but also suggesting "affectionate")   463 *hearted* fixed in the heart   464 *freight* burden   465 *aspics'* venomous serpents'   466 *content* calm   469 *Pontic Sea* Black Sea   472 *Propontic* Sea of Marmara, between the Black Sea and the Aegean.   *Hellespont* Dardanelles, straits where the Sea of Marmara joins with the Aegean   475 *capable* ample, comprehensive   476 *marble* i.e., gleaming like marble and unrelenting   479 s.d. *He kneels* (In the Quarto text, Iago kneels here after Othello has knelt at line 477.)   480 *clip* encompass   482 *execution* exercise, action.   *wit* mind   484 *remorse* pity (for Othello's wrongs)   485 *ever* soever   487 *to 't* to the proof   491 *minx* wanton

SCENE IV [BEFORE THE CITADEL.]

Enter Desdemona, Emilia, and Clown.

Desdemona: Do you know, sirrah,° where Lieutenant Cassio lies?°
Clown: I dare not say he lies anywhere.
Desdemona: Why, man?
Clown: He's a soldier, and for me to say a soldier lies, 'tis stabbing.
Desdemona: Go to. Where lodges he?   5
Clown: To tell you where he lodges is to tell you where I lie.
Desdemona: Can anything be made of this?
Clown: I know not where he lodges, and for me to devise a lodging and say he
    lies here, or he lies there, were to lie in mine own throat.°
Desdemona: Can you inquire him out, and be edified by report?   10
Clown: I will catechize the world for him; that is, make questions, and by them
    answer.
Desdemona: Seek him, bid him come hither. Tell him I have moved° my lord on
    his behalf and hope all will be well.
Clown: To do this is within the compass of man's wit, and therefore I will attempt   15
    the doing it.   *Exit Clown.*
Desdemona: Where should I lose that handkerchief, Emilia?
Emilia: I know not, madam.
Desdemona: Believe me, I had rather have lost my purse
    Full of crusadoes;° and but my noble Moor   20
    Is true of mind and made of no such baseness
    As jealous creatures are, it were enough
    To put him to ill thinking.
Emilia: Is he not jealous?
Desdemona: Who, he? I think the sun where he was born
    Drew all such humors° from him.
Emilia: Look where he comes.   25

    Enter Othello.

Desdemona: I will not leave him now till Cassio
    Be called to him.—How is 't with you, my lord?
Othello: Well, my good lady. [*Aside.*] O, hardness to dissemble!—
    How do you, Desdemona?
Desdemona: Well, my good lord.
Othello: Give me your hand. [*She gives her hand.*] This hand is moist, my lady.   30
Desdemona: It yet hath felt no age nor known no sorrow.
Othello: This argues° fruitfulness° and liberal° heart.
    Hot, hot, and moist. This hand of yours requires

---

1 *sirrah* (A form of address to an inferior.) *lies* lodges. (But the Clown makes the obvious pun.) 9 *lie . . .
throat* (1) lie egregiously and deliberately (2) use the windpipe to speak a lie 13 *moved* petitioned
20 *crusadoes* Portuguese gold coins 25 *humors* (Refers to the four bodily fluids thought to determine
temperament.) 32 *argues* gives evidence of. *fruitfulness* generosity, amorousness, and fecundity.
liberal generous and sexually free

Othello's suspicions are building: "This hand of yours requires / A sequester from liberty . . ." (III, iv, 30–41).

A sequester° from liberty, fasting and prayer,
Much castigation,° exercise devout;°   35
For here's a young and sweating devil here
That commonly rebels. 'Tis a good hand,
A frank° one.
Desdemona: You may indeed say so,
For 'twas that hand that gave away my heart.
Othello: A liberal hand. The hearts of old gave hands,°   40
But our new heraldry is hands, not hearts.°
Desdemona: I cannot speak of this. Come now, your promise.
Othello: What promise, chuck?°

34 *sequester* separation, sequestration   35 *castigation* corrective discipline.   *exercise devout* i.e., prayer, religious meditation, etc.   38 *frank* generous, open (with sexual suggestion)   40 *The hearts . . . hands* i.e., in former times, people would give their hearts when they gave their hands to something   41 *But . . . hearts* i.e., in our decadent times, the joining of hands is no longer a badge to signify the giving of hearts   43 *chuck* (A term of endearment.)

Desdemona: I have sent to bid Cassio come speak with you.
Othello: I have a salt and sorry rheum° offends me;   45
    Lend me thy handkerchief.
Desdemona: Here, my lord.   [*She offers a handkerchief.*]
Othello: That which I gave you.
Desdemona: I have it not about me.
Othello: Not?
Desdemona: No, faith, my lord.   50
Othello: That's a fault. That handkerchief
    Did an Egyptian to my mother give.
    She was a charmer,° and could almost read
    The thoughts of people. She told her, while she kept it
    'Twould make her amiable° and subdue my father   55
    Entirely to her love, but if she lost it
    Or made a gift of it, my father's eye
    Should hold her loathèd and his spirits should hunt
    After new fancies.° She, dying, gave it me,
    And bid me, when my fate would have me wived,   60
    To give it her.° I did so; and take heed on 't;
    Make it a darling like your precious eye.
    To lose 't or give 't away were such perdition°
    As nothing else could match.
Desdemona: Is 't possible?
Othello: 'Tis true. There's magic in the web° of it.   65
    A sibyl, that had numbered in the world
    The sun to course two hundred compasses,°
    In her prophetic fury° sewed the work;°
    The worms were hallowed that did breed the silk,
    And it was dyed in mummy° which the skillful   70
    Conserved of° maidens' hearts.
Desdemona: I' faith! Is 't true?
Othello: Most veritable. Therefore look to 't well.
Desdemona: Then would to God that I had never seen 't!
Othello: Ha? Wherefore?
Desdemona: Why do you speak so startingly and rash?°   75
Othello: Is 't lost? Is 't gone? Speak, is 't out o' the way?°
Desdemona: Heaven bless us!
Othello: Say you?
Desdemona: It is not lost; but what an if° it were?
Othello: How?   80
Desdemona: I say it is not lost.
Othello: Fetch 't, let me see 't.

---

45 *salt . . . rheum* distressful head cold or watering of the eyes   53 *charmer* sorceress   55 *amiable* desirable   59 *fancies* loves   61 *her* i.e., to my wife   63 *perdition* loss   65 *web* fabric, weaving   67 *compasses* annual circlings. (The *sibyl*, or prophetess, was two hundred years old.)   68 *prophetic fury* frenzy of prophetic inspiration.   *work* embroidered pattern   70 *mummy* medicinal or magical preparation drained from mummified bodies   71 *Conserved of* prepared or preserved out of   75 *startingly and rash* disjointedly and impetuously, excitedly   76 *out o' the way* lost, misplaced   79 *an if* if

Desdemona: Why, so I can, sir, but I will not now.
  This is a trick to put me from my suit.
  Pray you, let Cassio be received again.
Othello: Fetch me the handkerchief! My mind misgives.   85
Desdemona: Come, come,
  You'll never meet a more sufficient° man.
Othello: The handkerchief!
Desdemona: I pray, talk° me of Cassio.
Othello: The handkerchief!
Desdemona: A man that all his time°
  Hath founded his good fortunes on your love,   90
  Shared dangers with you—
Othello: The handkerchief!
Desdemona: I' faith, you are to blame.
Othello: Zounds!   *Exit Othello.*
Emilia: Is not this man jealous?   95
Desdemona: I ne'er saw this before.
  Sure, there's some wonder in this handkerchief.
  I am most unhappy in the loss of it.
Emilia: 'Tis not a year or two shows us a man.°
  They are all but stomachs, and we all but° food;   100
  They eat us hungerly,° and when they are full
  They belch us.

  Enter Iago and Cassio.

              Look you, Cassio and my husband.
Iago [to Cassio]: There is no other way; 'tis she must do 't.
  And, lo, the happiness!° Go and importune her.
Desdemona: How now, good Cassio? What's the news with you?   105
Cassio: Madam, my former suit. I do beseech you
  That by your virtuous° means I may again
  Exist and be a member of his love
  Whom I, with all the office° of my heart,
  Entirely honor. I would not be delayed.   110
  If my offense be of such mortal° kind
  That nor my service past, nor° present sorrows,
  Nor purposed merit in futurity
  Can ransom me into his love again,
  But to know so must be my benefit;°   115
  So shall I clothe me in a forced content,
  And shut myself up in° some other course,
  To fortune's alms.°
Desdemona: Alas, thrice-gentle Cassio,

87 *sufficient* able, complete 88 *talk* talk to 89 *all his time* throughout his career 99 *'Tis . . . man* i.e., you can't really know a man even in a year or two of experience (?), or, real men come along seldom (?) 100 *but* nothing but 101 *hungerly* hungrily 104 *the happiness* in happy time, fortunately met 107 *virtuous* efficacious 109 *office* loyal service 111 *mortal* fatal 112 *nor . . . nor* neither . . . nor 115 *But . . . benefit* merely to know that my case is hopeless will have to content me (and will be better than uncertainty) 117 *shut . . . in* confine myself to 118 *To fortune's alms* throwing myself on the mercy of fortune

My advocation° is not now in tune.
My lord is not my lord; nor should I know him,   120
Were he in favor° as in humor° altered.
So help me every spirit sanctified
As I have spoken for you all my best
And stood within the blank° of his displeasure
For my free speech! You must awhile be patient.   125
What I can do I will, and more I will
Than for myself I dare. Let that suffice you.

Iago: Is my lord angry?

Emilia: He went hence but now,
And certainly in strange unquietness.

Iago: Can he be angry? I have seen the cannon   130
When it hath blown his ranks into the air,
And like the devil from his very arm
Puffed his own brother—and is he angry?
Something of moment° then. I will go meet him.
There's matter in 't indeed, if he be angry.   135

Desdemona: I prithee, do so.   *Exit [Iago].*
                    Something, sure, of state,°
Either from Venice, or some unhatched practice°
Made demonstrable here in Cyprus to him,
Hath puddled° his clear spirit; and in such cases
Men's natures wrangle with inferior things,   140
Though great ones are their object. 'Tis even so;
For let our finger ache, and it indues°
Our other, healthful members even to a sense
Of pain. Nay, we must think men are not gods,
Nor of them look for such observancy°   145
As fits the bridal.° Beshrew me° much, Emilia,
I was, unhandsome° warrior as I am,
Arraigning his unkindness with° my soul;
But now I find I had suborned the witness,°
And he's indicted falsely.

Emilia: Pray heaven it be   150
State matters, as you think, and no conception
Nor no jealous toy° concerning you.

Desdemona: Alas the day! I never gave him cause.

Emilia: But jealous souls will not be answered so;
They are not ever jealous for the cause,   155
But jealous for° they're jealous. It is a monster
Begot upon itself,° born on itself.

---

119 *advocation* advocacy   121 *favor* appearance. *humor* mood   124 *within the blank* within point-blank range. (The *blank* is the center of the target.)   134 *of moment* of immediate importance, momentous   136 *of state* concerning state affairs   137 *unhatched practice* as yet unexecuted or undiscovered plot   139 *puddled* muddied   142 *indues* brings to the same condition   145 *observancy* attentiveness   146 *bridal* wedding (when a bridegroom is newly attentive to his bride). *Beshrew me* (A mild oath.)   147 *unhandsome* insufficient, unskillful   148 *with* before the bar of   149 *suborned the witness* induced the witness to give false testimony   152 *toy* fancy   156 *for* because   157 *Begot upon itself* generated solely from itself

Cassio explains to Bianca that he does not know how the handkerchief appeared in his room (III, iv, 171–186).

Desdemona: Heaven keep that monster from Othello's mind!
Emilia: Lady, amen.
Desdemona: I will go seek him. Cassio, walk hereabout.   160
    If I do find him fit, I'll move your suit
    And seek to effect it to my uttermost.
Cassio: I humbly thank your ladyship.

    Exit [*Desdemona with Emilia*].

    Enter *Bianca.*

Bianca: Save° you, friend Cassio!
Cassio: What make° you from home?
    How is 't with you, my most fair Bianca?   165
    I' faith, sweet love, I was coming to your house.
Bianca: And I was going to your lodging, Cassio.
    What, keep a week away? Seven days and nights?
    Eightscore-eight° hours? And lovers' absent hours
    More tedious than the dial° eightscore times?   170
    O weary reckoning!
Cassio: Pardon me, Bianca.
    I have this while with leaden thoughts been pressed;
    But I shall, in a more continuate° time,

164 *Save* God save. *make* do   169 *Eightscore-eight* one hundred sixty-eight, the number of hours in a week   170 *the dial* a complete revolution of the clock   173 *continuate* uninterrupted

Strike off this score° of absence. Sweet Bianca,

[*giving her Desdemona's handkerchief*]

Take me this work out.°

Bianca: O Cassio, whence came this?   175
This is some token from a newer friend.°
To the felt absence now I feel a cause.
Is 't come to this? Well, well.

Cassio: Go to, woman!
Throw your vile guesses in the devil's teeth,
From whence you have them. You are jealous now   180
That this is from some mistress, some remembrance.
No, by my faith, Bianca.

Bianca: Why, whose is it?

Cassio: I know not, neither. I found it in my chamber.
I like the work well. Ere it be demanded°—
As like° enough it will—I would have it copied.   185
Take it and do 't, and leave me for this time.

Bianca: Leave you? Wherefore?

Cassio: I do attend here on the General,
And think it no addition,° nor my wish,
To have him see me womaned.   190

Bianca: Why, I pray you?

Cassio: Not that I love you not.

Bianca: But that you do not love me.
I pray you, bring° me on the way a little,
And say if I shall see you soon at night.   195

Cassio: 'Tis but a little way that I can bring you,
For I attend here; but I'll see you soon.

Bianca: 'Tis very good. I must be circumstanced.°

Exeunt omnes.

ACT IV

SCENE I [BEFORE THE CITADEL.]

Enter Othello and Iago.

Iago: Will you think so?

Othello: Think so, Iago?

Iago: What,
To kiss in private?

Othello: An unauthorized kiss!

Iago: Or to be naked with her friend in bed
An hour or more, not meaning any harm?

---

174 *Strike . . . score* settle this account   175 *Take . . . out* copy this embroidery for me   176 *friend* mistress   184 *demanded* inquired for   185 *like* likely   189 *addition* i.e., addition to my reputation   194 *bring* accompany   198 *be circumstanced* be governed by circumstance, yield to your conditions

Othello: Naked in bed, Iago, and not mean harm?   5
      It is hypocrisy against the devil.
      They that mean virtuously and yet do so,
      The devil their virtue tempts, and they tempt heaven.
Iago: If they do nothing, 'tis a venial° slip.
      But if I give my wife a handkerchief—   10
Othello: What then?
Iago: Why then, 'tis hers, my lord, and being hers,
      She may, I think, bestow 't on any man.
Othello: She is protectress of her honor too.
      May she give that?   15
Iago: Her honor is an essence that's not seen;
      They have it° very oft that have it not.
      But, for the handkerchief—
Othello: By heaven, I would most gladly have forgot it.
      Thou saidst—O, it comes o'er my memory   20
      As doth the raven o'er the infectious house,°
      Boding to all—he had my handkerchief.
Iago: Ay, what of that?
Othello: That's not so good now.
Iago: What
      If I had said I had seen him do you wrong?
      Or heard him say—as knaves be such abroad,°   25
      Who having, by their own importunate suit,
      Or voluntary dotage° of some mistress,
      Convincèd or supplied° them, cannot choose
      But they must blab—
Othello: Hath he said anything?
Iago: He hath, my lord; but, be you well assured,   30
      No more than he'll unswear.
Othello: What hath he said?
Iago: Faith, that he did—I know not what he did.
Othello: What? What?
Iago: Lie—
Othello: With her?
Iago: With her, on her; what you will.
Othello: Lie with her? Lie on her? We say "lie on her" when they belie° her. Lie   35
      with her? Zounds, that's fulsome.°—Handkerchief—confessions—handker-
      chief!—To confess and be hanged for his labor—first to be hanged and then
      to confess.°—I tremble at it. Nature would not invest herself in such shad-
      owing passion without some instruction.° It is not words° that shakes me
      thus. Pish! Noses, ears, and lips.—Is't possible?—Confess—handkerchief!—   40
      O devil!

9 *venial* pardonable   17 *They have it* i.e., they enjoy a reputation for it   21 *raven . . . house* (Allusion to the belief that the raven hovered over a house of sickness or infection, such as one visited by the plague.)   25 *abroad* around about   27 *voluntary dotage* willing infatuation   28 *Convincèd or supplied* seduced or sexually gratified   35 *belie* slander   36 *fulsome* foul   37–38 *first . . . to confess* (Othello reverses the proverbial *confess* and *be hanged*; Cassio is to be given no time to confess before he dies.)   38–39 *Nature . . . instruction* i.e., without some foundation in fact, nature would not have dressed herself in such an overwhelming passion that comes over me now and fills my mind with images, or in such a lifelike fantasy as Cassio had in his dream of lying with Desdemona   39 *words* mere words

Falls in a trance.

Iago: Work on,
   My medicine, work! Thus credulous fools are caught,
   And many worthy and chaste dames even thus,
   All guiltless, meet reproach.—What, ho! My lord!   45
   My lord, I say! Othello!

   Enter Cassio.

                    How now, Cassio?
Cassio: What's the matter?
Iago: My lord is fall'n into an epilepsy.
   This is his second fit. He had one yesterday.
Cassio: Rub him about the temples.
Iago: No, forbear.   50
   The lethargy° must have his° quiet course.
   If not, he foams at mouth, and by and by
   Breaks out to savage madness. Look, he stirs.
   Do you withdraw yourself a little while.
   He will recover straight. When he is gone,   55
   I would on great occasion° speak with you.

   [*Exit Cassio.*]

   How is it, General? Have you not hurt your head?
Othello: Dost thou mock me?°
Iago: I mock you not, by heaven.
   Would you would bear your fortune like a man!
Othello: A hornèd man's a monster and a beast.   60
Iago: There's many a beast then in a populous city,
   And many a civil° monster.
Othello: Did he confess it?
Iago: Good sir, be a man.
   Think every bearded fellow that's but yoked°   65
   May draw with you.° There's millions now alive
   That nightly lie in those unproper° beds
   Which they dare swear peculiar.° Your case is better.°
   O, 'tis the spite of hell, the fiend's arch-mock,
   To lip° a wanton in a secure° couch   70
   And to suppose her chaste! No, let me know,
   And knowing what I am,° I know what she shall be.°
Othello: O, thou art wise. 'Tis certain.
Iago: Stand you awhile apart;
   Confine yourself but in a patient list.°   75

51 *lethargy* coma.   *his* its   56 *on great occasion* on a matter of great importance   58 *mock me* (Othello takes Iago's question about hurting his head to be a mocking reference to the cuckold's horns.)   62 *civil* i.e., dwelling in a city   65 *yoked* (1) married (2) put into the yoke of infamy and cuckoldry   66 *draw with you* pull as you do, like oxen who are yoked, i.e., share your fate as cuckold   67 *unproper* not exclusively their own   68 *peculiar* private, their own.   *better* i.e., because you know the truth   70 *lip* kiss.   *secure* free from suspicion   72 *what I am* i.e., a cuckold.   *she shall be* will happen to her   75 *in . . . list* within the bounds of patience

Whilst you were here o'erwhelmèd with your grief—
A passion most unsuiting such a man—
Cassio came hither. I shifted him away,°
And laid good 'scuse upon your ecstasy,°
Bade him anon return and here speak with me,   80
The which he promised. Do but encave° yourself
And mark the fleers,° the gibes, and notable° scorns
That dwell in every region of his face;
For I will make him tell the tale anew,
Where, how, how oft, how long ago, and when   85
He hath and is again to cope° your wife.
I say, but mark his gesture. Marry, patience!
Or I shall say you're all-in-all in spleen,°
And nothing of a man.
Othello: Dost thou hear, Iago?
I will be found most cunning in my patience;   90
But—dost thou hear?—most bloody.
Iago: That's not amiss;
But yet keep time° in all. Will you withdraw?

[*Othello stands apart.*]

Now will I question Cassio of Bianca,
A huswife° that by selling her desires
Buys herself bread and clothes. It is a creature   95
That dotes on Cassio—as 'tis the strumpet's plague
To beguile many and be beguiled by one.
He, when he hears of her, cannot restrain°
From the excess of laughter. Here he comes.

Enter Cassio.

As he shall smile, Othello shall go mad;   100
And his unbookish° jealousy must conster°
Poor Cassio's smiles, gestures, and light behaviors
Quite in the wrong.—How do you now, Lieutenant?
Cassio: The worser that you give me the addition°
Whose want° even kills me.   105
Iago: Ply Desdemona well and you are sure on 't.
 [*Speaking lower.*] Now, if this suit lay in Bianca's power,
 How quickly should you speed!
Cassio [*laughing*]: Alas, poor caitiff!°
Othello [*aside*]: Look how he laughs already!   110
Iago: I never knew a woman love man so.
Cassio: Alas, poor rogue! I think, i' faith, she loves me.
Othello: Now he denies it faintly, and laughs it out.

---

78 *shifted him away* used a dodge to get rid of him 79 *ecstasy* trance 81 *encave* conceal 82 *fleers* sneers. *notable* obvious 86 *cope* encounter with, have sex with 88 *all-in-all in spleen* utterly governed by passionate impulses 92 *keep time* keep yourself steady (as in music) 94 *huswife* hussy 98 *restrain* refrain 101 *unbookish* uninstructed. *conster* construe 104 *addition* title 105 *Whose want* the lack of which 109 *caitiff* wretch

Iago: Do you hear, Cassio?

Othello: Now he importunes him
    To tell it o'er. Go to!° Well said,° well said.   115

Iago: She gives it out that you shall marry her.
    Do you intend it?

Cassio: Ha, ha, ha!

Othello: Do you triumph, Roman?° Do you triumph?

Cassio: I marry her? What? A customer?° Prithee, bear some charity to my wit;°   120
    do not think it so unwholesome. Ha, ha, ha!

Othello: So, so, so, so! They laugh that win.°

Iago: Faith, the cry° goes that you shall marry her.

Cassio: Prithee, say true.

Iago: I am a very villain else.°   125

Othello: Have you scored me?° Well.

Cassio: This is the monkey's own giving out. She is persuaded I will marry her
    out of her own love and flattery,° not out of my promise.

Othello: Iago beckons° me. Now he begins the story.

Cassio: She was here even now; she haunts me in every place. I was the other   130
    day talking on the seabank° with certain Venetians, and thither comes the
    bauble,° and, by this hand,° she falls me thus about my neck—

    [*He embraces Iago.*]

Othello: Crying, "O dear Cassio!" as it were; his gesture imports it.

Cassio: So hangs and lolls and weeps upon me, so shakes and pulls me. Ha, ha, ha!

Othello: Now he tells how she plucked him to my chamber. O, I see that nose of   135
    yours, but not that dog I shall throw it to.°

Cassio: Well, I must leave her company.

Iago: Before me,° look where she comes.

    Enter Bianca [with Othello's handkerchief].

Cassio: 'Tis such another fitchew!° Marry, a perfumed one.—What do you mean
    by this haunting of me?   140

Bianca: Let the devil and his dam° haunt you! What did you mean by that same
    handkerchief you gave me even now? I was a fine fool to take it. I must
    take out the work? A likely piece of work,° that you should find it in your
    chamber and know not who left it there! This is some minx's token, and I
    must take out the work? There; give it your hobbyhorse.° [*She gives him the*   145
    handkerchief.] Wheresoever you had it, I'll take out no work on 't.

Cassio: How now, my sweet Bianca? How now? How now?

Othello: By heaven, that should be° my handkerchief!

---

115 *Go to!* (An expression of remonstrance.)   *Well said* well done   119 *Roman* (The Romans were noted
for their *triumphs* or triumphal processions.)   120 *customer* i.e., prostitute.   *bear . . . wit* be more charitable to my judgment   122 *They . . . win* i.e., they that laugh last laugh best   123 *cry* rumor   125 *I . . .
else* call me a complete rogue if I'm not telling the truth   126 *scored me* scored off me, beaten me, made
up my reckoning, branded me   128 *flattery* self-flattery, self-deception   129 *beckons* signals   131 *seabank*
seashore.   132 *bauble* plaything.   *by this hand* I make my vow   136 *not . . . to* (Othello imagines himself
cutting off Cassio's nose and throwing it to a dog.)   138 *Before me* i.e., on my soul   139 *'Tis . . . fitchew*
what a polecat she is! Just like all the others. (Polecats were often compared with prostitutes because of
their rank smell and presumed lechery.)   141 *dam* mother   143 *A likely . . . work* a fine story   145 *hobbyhorse*
harlot   148 *should be* must be

Bianca: If you'll come to supper tonight, you may; if you will not, come when you are
next prepared for.°   *Exit.*   150
Iago: After her, after her.
Cassio: Faith, I must. She'll rail in the streets else.
Iago: Will you sup there?
Cassio: Faith, I intend so.
Iago: Well, I may chance to see you, for I would very fain speak with you.   155
Cassio: Prithee, come. Will you?
Iago: Go to.° Say no more.   [*Exit Cassio.*]
Othello [*advancing*]: How shall I murder him, Iago?
Iago: Did you perceive how he laughed at his vice?
Othello: O, Iago!   160
Iago: And did you see the handkerchief?
Othello: Was that mine?
Iago: Yours, by this hand. And to see how he prizes the foolish woman your wife!
She gave it him, and he hath given it his whore.
Othello: I would have him nine years a-killing. A fine woman! A fair woman! A   165
sweet woman!
Iago: Nay, you must forget that.
Othello: Ay, let her rot and perish, and be damned tonight, for she shall not live.
No, my heart is turned to stone; I strike it, and it hurts my hand. O, the
world hath not a sweeter creature! She might lie by an emperor's side and   170
command him tasks.
Iago: Nay, that's not your way.°
Othello: Hang her! I do but say what she is. So delicate with her needle! An
admirable musician! O, she will sing the savageness out of a bear. Of so high
and plenteous wit and invention!°   175
Iago: She's the worse for all this.
Othello: O, a thousand, a thousand times! And then, of so gentle a condition!°
Iago: Ay, too gentle.°
Othello: Nay, that's certain. But yet the pity of it, Iago! O, Iago, the pity of it, Iago!
Iago: If you are so fond° over her iniquity, give her patent° to offend, for if it   180
touch not you it comes near nobody.
Othello: I will chop her into messes.° Cuckold me?
Iago: O, 'tis foul in her.
Othello: With mine officer?
Iago: That's fouler.   185
Othello: Get me some poison, Iago, this night. I'll not expostulate with her, lest
her body and beauty unprovide° my mind again. This night, Iago.
Iago: Do it not with poison. Strangle her in her bed, even the bed she hath
contaminated.
Othello: Good, good! The justice of it pleases. Very good.   190
Iago: And for Cassio, let me be his undertaker.° You shall hear more by midnight.
Othello: Excellent good. [*A trumpet within.*] What trumpet is that same?
Iago: I warrant, something from Venice.

149–150 *when . . . for* when I'm ready for you (i.e., never)   157 *Go to* (An expression of remonstrance.)   172 *your way* i.e., the way you should think of her   175 *invention* imagination   177 *gentle a*
condition wellborn and well-bred   178 *gentle* generous, yielding (to other men)   180 *fond* foolish.   *patent*
license   182 *messes* portions of meat, i.e., bits   187 *unprovide* weaken, render unfit   191 *be his undertaker*
undertake to dispatch him

Enter Lodovico, Desdemona, and attendants.

'Tis Lodovico. This comes from the Duke.
See, your wife's with him.   195
Lodovico: God save you, worthy General!
Othello: With all my heart,° sir.
Lodovico [giving him a letter]: The Duke and the senators of Venice greet you.
Othello: I kiss the instrument of their pleasures.

[*He opens the letter, and reads.*]

Desdemona: And what's the news, good cousin Lodovico?
Iago: I am very glad to see you, signor.   200
    Welcome to Cyprus.
Lodovico: I thank you. How does Lieutenant Cassio?
Iago: Lives, sir.
Desdemona: Cousin, there's fall'n between him and my lord
    An unkind° breach; but you shall make all well.   205
Othello: Are you sure of that?
Desdemona: My lord?
Othello [reads]: "This fail you not to do, as you will—"
Lodovico: He did not call; he's busy in the paper.
    Is there division twixt my lord and Cassio?   210
Desdemona: A most unhappy one. I would do much
    T' atone° them, for the love I bear to Cassio.
Othello: Fire and brimstone!
Desdemona: My lord?
Othello: Are you wise?   215
Desdemona: What, is he angry?
Lodovico: Maybe the letter moved him;
    For, as I think, they do command him home,
    Deputing Cassio in his government.°
Desdemona: By my troth, I am glad on 't.°
Othello: Indeed?   220
Desdemona: My lord?
Othello: I am glad to see you mad.°
Desdemona: Why, sweet Othello—
Othello [striking her]: Devil!
Desdemona: I have not deserved this.   225
Lodovico: My lord, this would not be believed in Venice,
    Though I should swear I saw 't. 'Tis very much.°
    Make her amends; she weeps.
Othello: O devil, devil!
    If that the earth could teem° with woman's tears,
    Each drop she falls would prove a crocodile.°   230
    Out of my sight!

196 *With all my heart* i.e., I thank you most heartily   205 *unkind* unnatural, contrary to their natures; hurt-
ful   212 *atone* reconcile   218 *government* office   219 *on 't of it*   222 *I am . . . mad* i.e., I am glad to see
that you are insane enough to rejoice in Cassio's promotion (?) (Othello bitterly plays on Desdemona's *I
am glad.*)   227 *very much* too much, outrageous   229 *teem* breed, be impregnated   230 *falls . . . crocodile*
(Crocodiles were supposed to weep hypocritical tears for their victims.)

Desdemona:　　　　　I will not stay to offend you. [*Going.*]
Lodovico: Truly, an obedient lady.
　　　I do beseech your lordship, call her back.
Othello: Mistress!
Desdemona [*returning*]: My lord?　　　　　　　　　　　　　235
Othello: What would you with her, sir?°
Lodovico: Who, I, my lord?
Othello: Ay, you did wish that I would make her turn.
　　　Sir, she can turn, and turn, and yet go on
　　　And turn again; and she can weep, sir, weep;　　　　240
　　　And she's obedient,° as you say, obedient,
　　　Very obedient.—Proceed you in your tears.—
　　　Concerning this, sir—O well-painted passion!°—
　　　I am commanded home.—Get you away;
　　　I'll send for you anon.—Sir, I obey the mandate　　　245
　　　And will return to Venice.—Hence, avaunt!

　　　[*Exit Desdemona.*]

　　　Cassio shall have my place. And, sir, tonight
　　　I do entreat that we may sup together.
　　　You are welcome, sir, to Cyprus.—Goats and monkeys!°　　*Exit.*
Lodovico: Is this the noble Moor whom our full Senate　　　250
　　　Call all in all sufficient? Is this the nature
　　　Whom passion could not shake? Whose solid virtue
　　　The shot of accident nor dart of chance
　　　Could neither graze nor pierce?
Iago:　　　　　　　　　He is much changed.
Lodovico: Are his wits safe? Is he not light of brain?　　　255
Iago: He's that he is. I may not breathe my censure
　　　What he might be. If what he might he is not,
　　　I would to heaven he were!°
Lodovico:　　　　　　　What, strike his wife?
Iago: Faith, that was not so well; yet would I knew
　　　That stroke would prove the worst!
Lodovico:　　　　　　　　Is it his use?°　　　　260
　　　Or did the letters work upon his blood°
　　　And new-create his fault?
Iago:　　　　　　　Alas, alas!
　　　It is not honesty in me to speak
　　　What I have seen and known. You shall observe him,
　　　And his own courses will denote° him so　　　　265
　　　That I may save my speech. Do but go after,
　　　And mark how he continues.
Lodovico: I am sorry that I am deceived in him.　　　　*Exeunt.*

236 *What . . . sir* (Othello implies that Desdemona is pliant and will do a *turn*, lines 238–240, for any man.)　241 *obedient* (With much the same sexual connotation as *turn* in lines 238–240.)　243 *passion* i.e., grief　249 *Goats and monkeys* (See III, iii, 419.)　256–258 *I may . . . were* i.e., I dare not venture an opinion as to whether he's of unsound mind, as you suggest, but, if he isn't, then it might be better to wish he were in fact insane, since only that could excuse his wild behavior　260 *use* custom　261 *blood* passions　265 *courses will denote* actions will reveal

SCENE II [THE CITADEL.]

Enter Othello and Emilia.

Othello: You have seen nothing then?
Emilia: Nor ever heard, nor ever did suspect.
Othello: Yes, you have seen Cassio and she together.
Emilia: But then I saw no harm, and then I heard
      Each syllable that breath that breath made up between them.   5
Othello: What, did they never whisper?
Emilia: Never, my lord.
Othello: Nor send you out o' the way?
Emilia: Never.
Othello: To fetch her fan, her gloves, her mask, nor nothing?   10
Emilia: Never, my lord.
Othello: That's strange.
Emilia: I durst, my lord, to wager she is honest,
      Lay down my soul at stake.° If you think other,
      Remove your thought; it doth abuse your bosom.°   15
      If any wretch have put this in your head,
      Let heaven requite it with the serpent's curse!°
      For if she be not honest, chaste, and true,
      There's no man happy; the purest of their wives
      Is foul as slander.
Othello: Bid her come hither. Go.   20

      Exit Emilia.

      She says enough; yet she's a simple bawd
      That cannot say as much.° This° is a subtle whore,
      A closet lock and key° of villainous secrets.
      And yet she'll kneel and pray; I have seen her do 't.

      Enter Desdemona and Emilia.

Desdemona: My lord, what is your will?   25
Othello: Pray you, chuck, come hither.
Desdemona: What is your pleasure?
Othello: Let me see your eyes.
      Look in my face.
Desdemona: What horrible fancy's this?
Othello [*to Emilia*]: Some of your function,° mistress.
      Leave procreants° alone and shut the door;   30
      Cough or cry "hem" if anybody come.
      Your mystery, your mystery!° Nay, dispatch.

      Exit Emilia.

---

14 *at stake* as the wager   15 *abuse your bosom* deceive you   17 *the serpent's curse* the curse pronounced by God on the serpent for deceiving Eve, just as some man has done to Othello and Desdemona. (See Genesis 3:14.)   21–22 *she's . . . much* i.e., any procuress or go-between who couldn't make up as plausible a story as Emilia's would have to be pretty stupid   22 *This* i.e., Desdemona   23 *closet lock and key* i.e., concealer   29 *Some . . . function* i.e., practice your chosen profession, that of bawd (by guarding the door)   30 *procreants* mating couples   32 *mystery* trade, occupation

"Ah, Desdemon! Away, away, away!" (IV, ii, 43).

Desdemona [kneeling]: Upon my knees, what doth your speech import?
    I understand a fury in your words,
    But not the words.   35
Othello: Why, what art thou?
Desdemona: Your wife, my lord, your true
    And loyal wife.
Othello: Come, swear it, damn thyself,
    Lest, being like one of heaven,° the devils themselves
    Should fear to seize thee. Therefore be double damned:
    Swear thou art honest.
Desdemona: Heaven doth truly know it.   40
Othello: Heaven truly knows that thou art false as hell.
Desdemona: To whom, my lord? With whom? How am I false?
Othello [weeping]: Ah, Desdemon! Away, away, away!
Desdemona: Alas the heavy day! Why do you weep?
    Am I the motive° of these tears, my lord?   45
    If haply you my father do suspect
    An instrument of this your calling back,
    Lay not your blame on me. If you have lost him,
    I have lost him too.
Othello: Had it pleased heaven
    To try me with affliction, had they° rained   50
    All kinds of sores and shames on my bare head,

38 being . . . heaven looking like an angel   *45 motive* cause   *50 they* i.e., heavenly powers

Steeped me in poverty to the very lips,
Given to captivity me and my utmost hopes,
I should have found in some place of my soul
A drop of patience. But, alas, to make me   55
A fixèd figure for the time of scorn°
To point his° slow and moving finger° at!
Yet could I bear that too, well, very well.
But there where I have garnered° up my heart,
Where either I must live or bear no life,   60
The fountain° from the which my current runs
Or else dries up—to be discarded thence!
Or keep it as a cistern° for foul toads
To knot° and gender° in! Turn thy complexion there,°
Patience, thou young and rose-lipped cherubin—   65
Ay, there look grim as hell!°
Desdemona: I hope my noble lord esteems me honest.°
Othello: O, ay, as summer flies are in the shambles,°
     That quicken° even with blowing.° O thou weed,
     Who art so lovely fair and smell'st so sweet   70
     That the sense aches at thee, would thou hadst ne'er been born!
Desdemona: Alas, what ignorant sin° have I committed?
Othello: Was this fair paper, this most goodly book,
     Made to write "whore" upon? What committed?
     Committed? O thou public commoner!°   75
     I should make very forges of my cheeks,
     That would to cinders burn up modesty,
     Did I but speak thy deeds. What committed?
     Heaven stops the nose at it and the moon winks;°
     The bawdy° wind, that kisses all it meets,   80
     Is hushed within the hollow mine° of earth
     And will not hear 't. What committed?
     Impudent strumpet!
Desdemona: By heaven, you do me wrong.
Othello: Are not you a strumpet?
Desdemona: No, as I am a Christian.   85
     If to preserve this vessel° for my lord
     From any other foul unlawful touch
     Be not to be a strumpet, I am none.

---

56 *time of scorn* i.e., scornful world   57 *his* its.   *slow and moving finger* i.e., hour hand of the clock, moving so slowly it seems hardly to move at all. (Othello envisages himself as being eternally pointed at by the scornful world as the numbers on a clock are pointed at by the hour hand.)   59 *garnered* stored   61 *fountain* spring   63 *cistern* cesspool   64 *knot* couple.   *gender* engender.   *Turn . . . there* change your color, grow pale, at such a sight   65–66 *Patience . . . hell* (Even Patience, that rose-lipped cherub, will look grim and pale at this spectacle.)   67 *honest* chaste   68 *shambles* slaughterhouse   69 *quicken* come to life.   *with blowing* i.e., with the puffing up of something rotten in which maggots are breeding   72 *ignorant sin* sin in ignorance   75 *commoner* prostitute   79 *winks* closes her eyes. (The moon symbolizes chastity.)   80 *bawdy* kissing one and all   81 *mine* cave (where the winds were thought to dwell)   86 *vessel* body

Othello berates Desdemona as a "strumpet" and "cunning whore" (IV, ii, 73–98).

Othello: What, not a whore?
Desdemona: No, as I shall be saved.   90
Othello: Is 't possible?
Desdemona: O, heaven forgive us!
Othello: I cry you mercy,° then.
   I took you for that cunning whore of Venice
   That married with Othello. [*Calling out.*] You, mistress,
   That have the office opposite to Saint Peter   95
   And keep the gate of hell!

   Enter Emilia.

                                     You, you, ay, you!
   We have done our course.° There's money for your pains.   [*He gives money.*]
   I pray you, turn the key and keep our counsel.
                                                                                          Exit.

Emilia: Alas, what does this gentleman conceive?°
   How do you, madam? How do you, my good lady?   100
Desdemona: Faith, half asleep.°
Emilia: Good madam, what's the matter with my lord?
Desdemona: With who?
Emilia: Why, with my lord, madam.
Desdemona: Who is thy lord?
Emilia: He that is yours, sweet lady.   105

92 *cry you mercy* beg your pardon   97 *course* business (with an indecent suggestion of "trick," turn at sex)   99 *conceive* suppose, think   101 *half asleep* i.e., dazed

Desdemona: I have none. Do not talk to me, Emilia.
    I cannot weep, nor answers have I none
    But what should go by water.° Prithee, tonight
    Lay on my bed my wedding sheets, remember;
    And call thy husband hither.   110
Emilia: Here's a change indeed!   *Exit.*
Desdemona: 'Tis meet I should be used so, very meet.°
    How have I been behaved, that he might stick°
    The small'st opinion° on my least misuse?°

    Enter Iago.

Iago: What is your pleasure, madam? How is 't with you?   115
Desdemona: I cannot tell. Those that do teach young babes
    Do it with gentle means and easy tasks.
    He might have chid me so, for, in good faith,
    I am a child to chiding.
Iago: What is the matter, lady?   120
Emilia: Alas, Iago, my lord hath so bewhored her,
    Thrown such despite and heavy terms upon her,
    That true hearts cannot bear it.
Desdemona: Am I that name, Iago?
Iago: What name, fair lady?   125
Desdemona: Such as she said my lord did say I was.
Emilia: He called her whore. A beggar in his drink
    Could not have laid such terms upon his callet.°
Iago: Why did he so?
Desdemona [weeping]: I do not know. I am sure I am none such.   130
Iago: Do not weep, do not weep. Alas the day!
Emilia: Hath she forsook so many noble matches,
    Her father and her country and her friends,
    To be called whore? Would it not make one weep?
Desdemona: It is my wretched fortune.
Iago: Beshrew° him for 't!   135
    How comes this trick° upon him?
Desdemona: Nay, heaven doth know.
Emilia: I will be hanged if some eternal° villain,
    Some busy and insinuating° rogue,
    Some cogging,° cozening° slave, to get some office,
    Have not devised this slander. I will be hanged else.   140
Iago: Fie, there is no such man. It is impossible.
Desdemona: If any such there be, heaven pardon him!
Emilia: A halter° pardon him! And hell gnaw his bones!
    Why should he call her whore? Who keeps her company?
    What place? What time? What form?° What likelihood?   145
    The Moor's abused by some most villainous knave,

---

108 *go by water* be expressed by tears   112 *meet* fitting   113 *stick* attach   114 *opinion* censure. *least misuse* slightest misconduct   128 *callet* whore   135 *Beshrew* curse   136 *trick* strange behavior, delusion   137 *eternal* inveterate   138 *insinuating* ingratiating, fawning, wheedling   139 *cogging* cheating. *cozening* defrauding   143 *halter* hangman's noose   145 *form* appearance, circumstance

Some base notorious knave, some scurvy fellow.
O heaven, that° such companions° thou'dst unfold,°
And put in every honest hand a whip
To lash the rascals naked through the world   150
Even from the east to th' west!
Iago: Speak within door.°
Emilia: O, fie upon them! Some such squire° he was
That turned your wit the seamy side without°
And made you to suspect me with the Moor.
Iago: You are a fool. Go to.°
Desdemona: Alas, Iago,   155
What shall I do to win my lord again?
Good friend, go to him; for, by this light of heaven,
I know not how I lost him. Here I kneel. [*She kneels.*]
If e'er my will did trespass 'gainst his love,
Either in discourse of thought° or actual deed,   160
Or that° mine eyes, mine ears, or any sense
Delighted them° in any other form;
Or that I do not yet,° and ever did,
And ever will—though he do shake me off
To beggarly divorcement—love him dearly,   165
Comfort forswear° me! Unkindness may do much,
And his unkindness may defeat° my life,
But never taint my love. I cannot say "whore."
It does abhor° me now I speak the word;
To do the act that might the addition° earn   170
Not the world's mass of vanity° could make me.

[*She rises.*]

Iago: I pray you, be content. 'Tis but his humor.°
The business of the state does him offense,
And he does chide with you.
Desdemona: If 'twere no other—   175
Iago: It is but so, I warrant.   [*Trumpets within.*]
Hark, how these instruments summon you to supper!
The messengers of Venice stays the meat.°
Go in, and weep not. All things shall be well.

Exeunt Desdemona and Emilia.

Enter Roderigo.

How now, Roderigo?   180
Roderigo: I do not find that thou deal'st justly with me.
Iago: What in the contrary?

148 *that* would that. *companions* fellows. *unfold* expose 151 *within door* i.e., not so loud 152 *squire* fellow 153 *seamy side without* wrong side out 155 *Go to* i.e., that's enough 160 *discourse of thought* process of thinking 161 *that* if. (Also in line 163.) 162 *Delighted them* took delight 163 *yet* still 166 *Comfort forswear* may heavenly comfort forsake 167 *defeat* destroy 169 *abhor* (1) fill me with abhorrence (2) make me whorelike 170 *addition* title 171 *vanity* showy splendor 172 *humor* mood 178 *stays the meat* are waiting to dine

Roderigo starts to suspect Iago's duplicities.

Roderigo: Every day thou daff'st me° with some device,° Iago, and rather, as it
    seems to me now, keep'st from me all conveniency° than suppliest me with
    the least advantage° of hope. I will indeed no longer endure it, nor am I yet   185
    persuaded to put up° in peace what already I have foolishly suffered.
Iago: Will you hear me, Roderigo?
Roderigo: Faith, I have heard too much, for your words and performances are no
    kin together.
Iago: You charge me most unjustly.   190
Roderigo: With naught but truth. I have wasted myself out of my means. The jewels
    you have had from me to deliver° Desdemona would half have corrupted a
    votarist.° You have told me she hath received them and returned me expecta-
    tions and comforts of sudden respect° and acquaintance, but I find none.
Iago: Well, go to, very well.   195
Roderigo: "Very well"! "Go to"! I cannot go to,° man, nor 'tis not very well. By
    this hand, I think it is scurvy, and begin to find myself fopped° in it.
Iago: Very well.
Roderigo: I tell you 'tis not very well.° I will make myself known to Desdemona.
    If she will return me my jewels, I will give over my suit and repent my unlawful   200
    solicitation; if not, assure yourself I will seek satisfaction° of you.
Iago: You have said now?°
Roderigo: Ay, and said nothing but what I protest intendment° of doing.

---

183 *thou daff'st me* you put me off. *device* excuse, trick   184 *conveniency* advantage, opportunity
185 *advantage* increase   186 *put up* submit to, tolerate   192 *deliver* deliver to   193 *votarist* nun
194 *sudden respect* immediate consideration   196 *I cannot go to* (Roderigo changes Iago's *go to,* an expression urging patience, to *I cannot go to,* "I have no opportunity for success in wooing.")   197 *fopped* fooled,
duped   199 *not very well* (Roderigo changes Iago's *very well,* "all right, then," to *not very well,* "not at all
good.")   201 *satisfaction* repayment. (The term normally means settling of accounts in a duel.)   202 *You
. . . now* have you finished?   203 *intendment* intention

Iago: Why, now I see there's mettle in thee, and even from this instant do build
     on thee a better opinion than ever before. Give me thy hand, Roderigo.   205
     Thou hast taken against me a most just exception; but yet I protest I have
     dealt most directly in thy affair.
Roderigo: It hath not appeared.
Iago: I grant indeed it hath not appeared, and your suspicion is not without wit and
     judgment. But, Roderigo, if thou hast that in thee indeed which I have greater   210
     reason to believe now than ever—I mean purpose, courage, and valor—this
     night show it. If thou the next night following enjoy not Desdemona, take me
     from this world with treachery and devise engines for° my life.
Roderigo: Well, what is it? Is it within reason and compass?
Iago: Sir, there is especial commission come from Venice to depute Cassio in   215
     Othello's place.
Roderigo: Is that true? Why, then Othello and Desdemona return again to Venice.
Iago: O, no; he goes into Mauritania and takes away with him the fair Desde-
     mona, unless his abode be lingered here by some accident; wherein none
     can be so determinate° as the removing of Cassio.   220
Roderigo: How do you mean, removing of him?
Iago: Why, by making him uncapable of Othello's place—knocking out his
     brains.
Roderigo: And that you would have me to do?
Iago: Ay, if you dare do yourself a profit and a right. He sups tonight with a   225
     harlotry,° and thither will I go to him. He knows not yet of his honorable
     fortune. If you will watch his going thence, which I will fashion to fall out°
     between twelve and one, you may take him at your pleasure. I will be near to
     second your attempt, and he shall fall between us. Come, stand not amazed
     at it, but go along with me. I will show you such a necessity in his death that   230
     you shall think yourself bound to put it on him. It is now high° suppertime,
     and the night grows to waste.° About it.
Roderigo: I will hear further reason for this.
Iago: And you shall be satisfied.   *Exeunt.*

SCENE III [THE CITADEL.]

Enter Othello, Lodovico, Desdemona, Emilia, and attendants.

Lodovico: I do beseech you, sir, trouble yourself no further.
Othello: O, pardon me; 'twill do me good to walk.
Lodovico: Madam, good night. I humbly thank your ladyship.
Desdemona: Your honor is most welcome.
Othello: Will you walk, sir?
     O, Desdemona!   5
Desdemona: My lord?
Othello: Get you to bed on th' instant. I will be returned
     forthwith. Dismiss your attendant there.
     Look 't be done.
Desdemona: I will, my lord.   10

     Exit [Othello, with Lodovico and attendants].

213 *engines for* plots against   220 *determinate* conclusive   226 *harlotry* slut   227 *fall out* occur   231 *high*
fully   232 *grows to waste* wastes away

Emilia: How goes it now? He looks gentler than he did.

Desdemona: He says he will return incontinent,°
   And hath commanded me to go to bed,
   And bid me to dismiss you.

Emilia: Dismiss me?   15

Desdemona: It was his bidding. Therefore, good Emilia,
   Give me my nightly wearing, and adieu.
   We must not now displease him.

Emilia: I would you had never seen him!

Desdemona: So would not I. My love doth so approve him   20
   That even his stubbornness,° his checks,° his frowns—
   Prithee, unpin me—have grace and favor in them.

   [*Emilia prepares Desdemona for bed.*]

Emilia: I have laid those sheets you bade me on the bed.

Desdemona: All's one.° Good faith, how foolish are our minds!
   If I do die before thee, prithee shroud me   25
   In one of these same sheets.

Emilia: Come, come, you talk.°

Desdemona: My mother had a maid called Barbary.
   She was in love, and he she loved proved mad°
   And did forsake her. She had a song of "Willow."
   An old thing 'twas, but it expressed her fortune,   30
   And she died singing it. That song tonight
   Will not go from my mind; I have much to do
   But to go hang° my head all at one side
   And sing it like poor Barbary. Prithee, dispatch.

Emilia: Shall I go fetch your nightgown?°   35

Desdemona: No, unpin me here.
   This Lodovico is a proper° man.

Emilia: A very handsome man.

Desdemona: He speaks well.

Emilia: I know a lady in Venice would have walked barefoot to Palestine for a   40
touch of his nether lip.

Desdemona [*singing*]:
             "The poor soul sat sighing by a sycamore tree,
             Sing all a green willow;°
             Her hand on her bosom, her head on her knee,
             Sing willow, willow, willow.   45
             The fresh streams ran by her and murmured her moans;
             Sing willow, willow, willow;
             Her salt tears fell from her, and softened the stones—"
   Lay by these.
             [*Singing.*] "Sing willow, willow, willow—"   50
   Prithee, hie thee.° He'll come anon.°

---

12 *incontinent* immediately   21 *stubbornness* roughness.   *checks* rebukes   24 *All's one* all right. It doesn't really matter   26 *talk* i.e., prattle   28 *mad* wild, i.e., faithless   32–33 *I . . . hang* I can scarcely keep myself from hanging   35 *nightgown* dressing gown   37 *proper* handsome   43 *willow* (A conventional emblem of disappointed love.)   51 *hie thee* hurry.   *anon* right away

Emilia prepares Desdemona for bed.

[*Singing.*] "Sing all a green willow must be my garland.
            Let nobody blame him; his scorn I approve—"
Nay, that's not next.—Hark! Who is 't that knocks?
Emilia: It's the wind.   55
Desdemona [*singing*]:
            "I called my love false love; but what said he then?
            Sing willow, willow, willow;
            If I court more women, you'll couch with more men."

So, get thee gone. Good night. Mine eyes do itch;
    Doth that bode weeping?
Emilia: 'Tis neither here nor there.   60
Desdemona: I have heard it said so. O, these men, these men!
    Dost thou in conscience think—tell me, Emilia—
    That there be women do abuse° their husbands
    In such gross kind?
Emilia: There be some such, no question.
Desdemona: Wouldst thou do such a deed for all the world?   65
Emilia: Why, would not you?
Desdemona: No, by this heavenly light!
Emilia: Nor I neither by this heavenly light;
    I might do 't as well i' the dark.
Desdemona: Wouldst thou do such a deed for all the world?
Emilia: The world's a huge thing. It is a great price   70
    For a small vice.
Desdemona: Good troth, I think thou wouldst not.
Emilia: By my troth, I think I should, and undo 't when I had done. Marry, I
    would not do such a thing for a joint ring,° nor for measures of lawn,° nor for

63 *abuse* deceive   74 *joint ring* a ring made in separate halves.   *lawn* fine linen

gowns, petticoats, nor caps, nor any petty exhibition.° But for all the whole   75
world! Uds° pity, who would not make her husband a cuckold to make him
a monarch? I should venture purgatory for 't.
Desdemona: Beshrew me if I would do such a wrong
    For the whole world.
Emilia: Why, the wrong is but a wrong i' the world, and having the world for your   80
labor, 'tis a wrong in your own world, and you might quickly make it right.
Desdemona: I do not think there is any such woman.
Emilia: Yes, a dozen, and as many
    To th' vantage° as would store° the world they played° for.
    But I do think it is their husbands' faults   85
    If wives do fall. Say that they slack their duties°
    And pour our treasures into foreign laps,°
    Or else break out in peevish jealousies,
    Throwing restraint upon us?° Or say they strike us,
    Or scant our former having in despite?°   90
    Why, we have galls,° and though we have some grace,
    Yet have we some revenge. Let husbands know
    Their wives have sense° like them. They see, and smell,
    And have their palates both for sweet and sour,
    As husbands have. What is it that they do   95
    When they change us for others? Is it sport?°
    I think it is. And doth affection° breed it?
    I think it doth. Is 't frailty that thus errs?
    It is so, too. And have not we affections,
    Desires for sport, and frailty, as men have?   100
    Then let them use us well; else let them know,
    The ills we do, their ills instruct us so.
Desdemona: Good night, good night. God me such uses° send
    Not to pick bad from bad, but by bad mend!°

    Exeunt.

ACT V

SCENE I [A STREET IN CYPRUS.]

    Enter Iago and Roderigo.

Iago: Here stand behind this bulk.° Straight will he come.
    Wear thy good rapier bare,° and put it home.

---

75 *exhibition* gift.   76 *Uds* God's   84 *To th' vantage* in addition, to boot.   *store* populate.   *played* (1) gambled (2) sported sexually   86 *duties* marital duties   87 *pour . . . laps* i.e., are unfaithful, give what is rightfully ours (semen) to other women   89 *Throwing . . . us* i.e., jealously restricting our freedom to see other men   90 *scant . . . despite* reduce our allowance to spite us   91 *have galls* i.e., are capable of resenting injury and insult   93 *sense* physical sense   96 *sport* sexual pastime   97 *affection* passion   103 *uses* habit, practice   104 *Not . . . mend* i.e., not to learn bad conduct from others' badness (as Emilia has suggested women learn from men), but to mend my ways by perceiving what badness is, making spiritual benefit out of evil and adversity   1 *bulk* framework projecting from the front of a shop   2 *bare* unsheathed

Quick, quick! Fear nothing. I'll be at thy elbow.
It makes us or it mars us. Think on that,
And fix most firm thy resolution.   5
Roderigo: Be near at hand. I may miscarry in 't.
Iago: Here, at thy hand. Be bold, and take thy stand.

[*Iago stands aside. Roderigo conceals himself.*]

Roderigo: I have no great devotion to the deed;
And yet he hath given me satisfying reasons.
'Tis but a man gone. Forth, my sword! He dies.   10

[*He draws.*]

Iago: I have rubbed this young quat° almost to the sense,°
And he grows angry. Now, whether he kill Cassio
Or Cassio him, or each do kill the other,
Every way makes my gain. Live Roderigo,°
He calls me to a restitution large   15
Of gold and jewels that I bobbed° from him
As gifts to Desdemona.
It must not be. If Cassio do remain,
He hath a daily beauty in his life
That makes me ugly; and besides, the Moor   20
May unfold° me to him; there stand I in much peril.
No, he must die. Be 't so. I hear him coming.

Enter Cassio.

Roderigo [*coming forth*]: I know his gait, 'tis he.—Villain, thou diest!

[*He attacks Cassio.*]

Cassio: That thrust had been mine enemy indeed,
But that my coat° is better than thou know'st.   25
I will make proof° of thine.

[*He draws, and wounds Roderigo.*]

Roderigo: O, I am slain!   [*He falls.*]

[*Iago, from behind, wounds Cassio in the leg, and exits.*]

Cassio: I am maimed forever. Help, ho! Murder! Murder!

Enter Othello.

Othello: The voice of Cassio! Iago keeps his word.
Roderigo: O, villain that I am!
Othello: It is even so.   30
Cassio: O, help, ho! Light! A surgeon!

---

11 *quat* pimple, pustule.   *to the sense* to the quick   14 *Live Roderigo* if Roderigo lives   16 *bobbed* swindled   21 *unfold* expose   25 *coat* (Possibly a garment of mail under the outer clothing, or simply a tougher coat than Roderigo expected.)   26 *proof* a test

Othello: 'Tis he. O brave Iago, honest and just,
    That hast such noble sense of thy friend's wrong!
    Thou teachest me. Minion,° your dear lies dead,
    And your unblest fate hies.° Strumpet, I come.   35
    Forth of ° my heart those charms, thine eyes, are blotted;
    Thy bed, lust-stained, shall with lust's blood be spotted.   *Exit Othello.*

    Enter Lodovico and Gratiano.

Cassio: What ho! No watch? No passage?° Murder! Murder!
Gratiano: 'Tis some mischance. The voice is very direful.
Cassio: O, help!   40
Lodovico: Hark!
Roderigo: O wretched villain!
Lodovico: Two or three groan. 'Tis heavy° night;
    These may be counterfeits. Let's think 't unsafe
    To come in to° the cry without more help.   45

    [They remain near the entrance.]

Roderigo: Nobody come? Then shall I bleed to death.

    Enter Iago [in his shirtsleeves, with a light].

Lodovico: Hark!
Gratiano: Here's one comes in his shirt, with light and weapons.
Iago: Who's there? Whose noise is this that cries on° murder?
Lodovico: We do not know.
Iago: Did not you hear a cry?   50
Cassio: Here, here! For heaven's sake, help me!
Iago: What's the matter?

    [He moves toward Cassio.]

Gratiano [to Lodovico]: This is Othello's ancient, as I take it.
Lodovico [to Gratiano]: The same indeed, a very valiant fellow.
Iago [to Cassio]: What° are you here that cry so grievously?
Cassio: Iago? O, I am spoiled,° undone by villains!   55
    Give me some help.
Iago: O me, Lieutenant! What villains have done this?
Cassio: I think that one of them is hereabout,
    And cannot make° away.
Iago: O treacherous villains!

    [To Lodovico and Gratiano.]

    What are you there? Come in, and give some help.   *[They advance.]* 60
Roderigo: O, help me there!
Cassio: That's one of them.

---

34 *Minion* hussy (i.e., Desdemona)   35 *hies* hastens on   36 *Forth of* from out   38 *passage* people passing by   43 *heavy* thick, dark   45 *come in to* approach   49 *cries on* cries out   54 *What* who (also at lines 60 and 66)   55 *spoiled* ruined, done for   59 *make* get

Iago: O murderous slave! O villain!

[He stabs Roderigo.]

Roderigo: O damned Iago! O inhuman dog!
Iago: Kill men i' the dark?—Where be these bloody thieves?—
      How silent is this town!—Ho! Murder, murder!—   65
      [To Lodovico and Gratiano.] What may you be? Are you of good or evil?
Lodovico: As you shall prove us, praise° us.
Iago: Signor Lodovico?
Lodovico: He, sir.
Iago: I cry you mercy.° Here's Cassio hurt by villains.   70
Gratiano: Cassio?
Iago: How is 't, brother?
Cassio: My leg is cut in two.
Iago: Marry, heaven forbid!
      Light, gentlemen! I'll bind it with my shirt.   75

[He hands them the light, and tends to Cassio's wound.]

Enter Bianca.

Bianca: What is the matter, ho? Who is 't that cried?
Iago: Who is 't that cried?
Bianca: O my dear Cassio!
      My sweet Cassio! O Cassio, Cassio, Cassio!
Iago: O notable strumpet! Cassio, may you suspect
      Who they should be that have thus mangled you?   80
Cassio: No.
Gratiano: I am sorry to find you thus. I have been to seek you.
Iago: Lend me a garter. [He applies a tourniquet.] So.—O, for a chair,°
      To bear him easily hence!
Bianca: Alas, he faints! O Cassio, Cassio, Cassio!   85
Iago: Gentlemen all, I do suspect this trash
      To be a party in this injury.—
      Patience awhile, good Cassio.—Come, come;
      Lend me a light.   [He shines the light on Roderigo.]
                         Know we this face or no?
      Alas, my friend and my dear countryman   90
      Roderigo! No.—Yes, sure.—O heaven! Roderigo!
Gratiano: What, of Venice?
Iago: Even he, sir. Did you know him?
Gratiano: Know him? Ay.
Iago: Signor Gratiano? I cry your gentle° pardon.   95
      These bloody accidents° must excuse my manners
      That so neglected you.
Gratiano: I am glad to see you.
Iago: How do you, Cassio? O, a chair, a chair!
Gratiano: Roderigo!

---

67 *praise* appraise   70 *I cry you mercy* I beg your pardon   83 *chair* litter   95 *gentle* noble   96 *accidents* sudden events

Iago: He, he, 'tis he. [*A litter is brought in.*] O, that's well said;° the chair.   100
　　Some good man bear him carefully from hence;
　　I'll fetch the General's surgeon. [*To Bianca.*] For you, mistress,
　　Save you your labor.°—He that lies slain here, Cassio,
　　Was my dear friend. What malice° was between you?
Cassio: None in the world, nor do I know the man.   105
Iago [*to Bianca*]: What, look you pale?—O, bear him out o' th' air.°

　　[*Cassio and Roderigo are borne off.*]

　　Stay you,° good gentlemen.—Look you pale, mistress?—
　　Do you perceive the gastness° of her eye?—
　　Nay, if you stare,° we shall hear more anon.—
　　Behold her well; I pray you, look upon her.   110
　　Do you see, gentlemen? Nay, guiltiness
　　Will speak, though tongues were out of use.

　　[*Enter Emilia.*]

Emilia: 'Las, what's the matter? What's the matter, husband?
Iago: Cassio hath here been set on in the dark
　　By Roderigo and fellows that are scaped.   115
　　He's almost slain, and Roderigo dead.
Emilia: Alas, good gentleman! Alas, good Cassio!
Iago: This is the fruits of whoring. Prithee, Emilia,
　　Go know° of Cassio where he supped tonight.
　　[*To Bianca.*] What, do you shake at that?   120
Bianca: He supped at my house, but I therefore shake not.
Iago: O, did he so? I charge you go with me.
Emilia: O, fie upon thee, strumpet!
Bianca: I am no strumpet, but of life as honest°
　　As you that thus abuse me.   125
Emilia: As I? Faugh! Fie upon thee!
Iago: Kind gentlemen, let's go see poor Cassio dressed.°—
　　Come, mistress, you must tell's another tale.
　　Emilia, run you to the citadel
　　And tell my lord and lady what hath happed.—   130
　　Will you go on afore? [*Aside.*] This is the night
　　That either makes me or fordoes° me quite.   *Exeunt.*

SCENE II [A BEDCHAMBER IN THE CITADEL.]

　　Enter Othello [with a light], and Desdemona in her bed.°

Othello: It is the cause,° it is the cause, my soul.

---

100 *well said* well done   103 *Save . . . labor* i.e., never you mind tending Cassio   104 *malice* enmity   106 *bear . . . air* (Fresh air was thought to be dangerous for a wound.)   107 *Stay you* (Lodovico and Gratiano are evidently about to leave.)   108 *gastness* terror   109 *stare* (Iago pretends to interpret Bianca's wild looks as an involuntary confession of guilt.)   119 *know* learn   124 *honest* chaste   127 *Cassio dressed* Cassio's wounds dressed   132 *fordoes* undoes, ruins.   s.d. *in her bed* (Either the curtains are drawn back to reveal the bed in a recessed area backstage, or the bed is "thrust out" onstage as the scene begins.)   1 *cause* i.e., cause of justice, the offense itself, which Othello must correct as an agent of justice

Let me not name it to you, you chaste stars!
It is the cause. Yet I'll not shed her blood,
Nor scar that whiter skin of hers than snow,
And smooth as monumental° alabaster. 5
Yet she must die, else she'll betray more men.
Put out the light, and then put out the light.°
If I quench thee, thou flaming minister,°
I can again thy former light restore,
Should I repent me;° but once put out thy light, 10
Thou cunning'st pattern° of excelling nature,
I know not where is that Promethean heat°
That can thy light relume.° When I have plucked thy rose,
I cannot give it vital growth again;
It needs must wither. I'll smell thee on the tree. 15

[*He kisses her.*]

O balmy breath, that dost almost persuade
Justice to break her sword! One more, one more.
Be thus when thou art dead, and I will kill thee,
And love thee after. One more, and that's the last.

[*He kisses her.*]

So sweet was ne'er so fatal. I must weep, 20
But they are cruel° tears. This sorrow's heavenly;
It strikes where it doth love.° She wakes.
Desdemona: Who's there? Othello?
Othello: Ay, Desdemona.
Desdemona: Will you come to bed, my lord? 25
Othello: Have you prayed tonight, Desdemon?
Desdemona: Ay, my lord.
Othello: If you bethink yourself of any crime°
   Unreconciled as yet to heaven and grace,
   Solicit° for it straight.° 30
Desdemona: Alack, my lord, what may you mean by that?
Othello: Well, do it, and be brief. I will walk by.
   I would not kill thy unprepareèd spirit.
   No, heaven forfend!° I would not kill thy soul.
Desdemona: Talk you of killing?
Othello: Ay, I do.
Desdemona: Then heaven 35
   Have mercy on me!
Othello: Amen, with all my heart!

---

5 *monumental* i.e., used in making tombs and funeral monuments   7 *the light . . . light* the torch or lamp . . . Desdemona's life   8 *flaming minister* torch or lamp that serves me   10 *repent me* change my mind   11 *Thou . . . pattern* you skillfully wrought perfect example   12 *Promethean heat* divine fire. (Alluding to the theft of fire from heaven by Prometheus.)   13 *relume* rekindle   21 *cruel* unrelenting   22 *It . . . love* (Compare Hebrews 12:6: "For whom the Lord loveth he chasteneth.")   28 *crime* sin   30 *Solicit* petition, pray.   *straight* immediately   34 *forfend* forbid

Othello asks if Desdemona has confessed all her crimes (V, ii, 31–55).

Desdemona: If you say so, I hope you will not kill me.
Othello: Humh!
Desdemona: And yet I fear you; for you're fatal then
    When your eyes roll so. Why I should fear I know not,   40
    Since guiltiness I know not; but yet I feel I fear.
Othello: Think on thy sins.
Desdemona: They are loves I bear to you.°
Othello: Ay, and for that thou diest.
Desdemona: That death's unnatural that kills for loving.
    Alas, why gnaw you so your nether lip?   45
    Some bloody passion shakes your very frame.
    These are portents; but yet I hope, I hope,
    They do not point on° me.
Othello: Peace, and be still!
Desdemona: I will so. What's the matter?   50
Othello: That handkerchief which I so loved and gave thee
    Thou gav'st to Cassio.
Desdemona: No, by my life and soul!
    Send for the man and ask him.
Othello: Sweet soul, take heed, take heed of perjury.
    Thou art on thy deathbed.   55
Desdemona: Ay, but not yet to die.

---

42 *They are . . . you* i.e., if I sinned, it was in loving you more than my father or more than God   48 *point on* point at, predict what is to happen to

Othello: Yes, presently.°
    Therefore confess thee freely of thy sin;
    For to deny each article with oath
    Cannot remove nor choke the strong conception°
    That I do groan withal.° Thou art to die.   60
Desdemona: Then Lord have mercy on me!
Othello: I say, amen.
Desdemona: And have you mercy too! I never did
    Offend° you in my life; never loved Cassio
    But with such general warranty° of heaven
    As I might love. I never gave him token.   65
Othello: By heaven, I saw my handkerchief in 's hand.
    O perjured woman! Thou dost stone° my heart,
    And makes me call what I intend to do
    A murder, which I thought a sacrifice.
    I saw the handkerchief.
Desdemona: He found it, then.   70
    I never gave it him. Send for him hither;
    Let him confess a truth.
Othello: He hath confessed.
Desdemona: What, my lord?
Othello: That he hath used thee.
Desdemona: How? Unlawfully?
Othello: Ay.
Desdemona: He will not say so.
Othello: No, his mouth is stopped;   75
    Honest Iago hath ta'en order° for 't.
Desdemona: O, my fear interprets. What, is he dead?
Othello: Had all his hairs been lives, my great revenge
    Had stomach for them all.
Desdemona: Alas, he is betrayed and I undone!   [*She weeps.*]   80
Othello: Out, strumpet! Weep'st thou for him to my face?
Desdemona: O, banish me, my lord, but kill me not!
Othello: Down, strumpet!
Desdemona: Kill me tomorrow; let me live tonight!
Othello: Nay, if you strive—   85
Desdemona: But half an hour!
Othello: Being done,° there is no pause.
Desdemona: But while I say one prayer!
Othello: It is too late.

    Smothers her.

Emilia [at the door]: My lord, my lord! What, ho! My lord, my lord!
Othello: What noise is this? Not dead? Not yet quite dead?
    I that am cruel am yet merciful;   90
    I would not have thee linger in thy pain.

---

56 *presently* immediately   59 *conception* (1) belief in your guilt (2) plan in my mind   60 *groan withal* (1)
groan at in sorrow (2) as in giving birth   63 *Offend* wrong   64 *warranty* sanction   67 *stone* turn to stone,
harden   76 *ta'en order* taken measures   86 *Being done* i.e., since justice has begun its relentless course

"It is too late" (V, ii, 87).

[*He dispatches her.*]

                                              So, so.

Emilia [*within*]: What, ho! My lord, my lord!
Othello: Who's there?
Emilia [*within*]: O, good my lord, I would speak a word with you!
Othello: Yes, 'tis Emilia.—By and by.—She's dead.
   'Tis like° she comes to speak of Cassio's death.—   95
   The noise was here.° Ha! No more moving?
   Still as the grave. Shall she come in? Were 't good?—
   I think she stirs again. No. What's best to do?
   If she come in, she'll sure speak to my wife.
   My wife! My wife! What wife? I have no wife.   100
   O, insupportable! O heavy hour!
   Methinks it should be now a huge eclipse
   Of sun and moon, and that th' affrighted globe
   Should yawn° at alteration.°
Emilia [*within*]:   I do beseech you
   That I may speak with you, O, good my lord!   105
Othello: I had forgot thee. O, come in, Emilia.—
   Soft,° by and by. Let me the curtains draw.—

95 *like* likely that   96 *here* (The Folio's *high* is possible, suggesting that the commotion of the attack on Cassio was loud.)   104 *yawn* gape in amazement, i.e., move in an earthquake. (According to Pliny, earthquakes often happen during eclipses.)   *at alteration* at these cataclysmic events in nature, well suited to express the horror of Desdemona's death   107 *Soft* wait a minute

[*He closes the bed-curtains and opens the door.*]

Where art thou?

Enter Emilia.

What's the matter with thee now?
Emilia: O, my good lord, yonder's foul murders done!
Othello: What, now?
Emilia: But now, my lord.   110
Othello: It is the very error° of the moon;
    She comes more nearer earth than she was wont,
    And makes men mad.
Emilia: Cassio, my lord, hath killed a young Venetian   115
    Called Roderigo.
Othello: Roderigo killed?
    And Cassio killed?
Emilia: No, Cassio is not killed.
Othello: Not Cassio killed? Then murder's out of tune,
    And sweet revenge grows harsh.
Desdemona: O, falsely, falsely murdered!   120
Emilia: O Lord, what cry is that?
Othello: That? What?
Emilia: Out° and alas, that was my lady's voice.

[*She opens the bed-curtains.*]

Help, help, ho, help! O lady, speak again!
Sweet Desdemona! O sweet mistress, speak!   125
Desdemona: A guiltless death I die.
Emilia: O, who hath done this deed?
Desdemona: Nobody; I myself. Farewell.
    Commend me to my kind lord. O, farewell!   [*She dies.*]
Othello: Why, how should she be murdered?
Emilia: Alas, who knows?   130
Othello: You heard her say herself it was not I.
Emilia: She said so. I must needs report the truth.
Othello: She's like a liar gone to burning hell!
    'Twas I that killed her.
Emilia: O, the more angel she,
    And you the blacker devil!   135
Othello: She turned to folly,° and she was a whore.
Emilia: Thou dost belie° her, and thou art a devil.
Othello: She was false as water.
Emilia: Thou art rash as fire to say
    That she was false. O, she was heavenly true!   140

---

112 *error* aberration, irregularity   123 *Out* (A cry of dismay, intensifying *alas*.)   136 *folly* i.e., wantonness, fleshly sin   137 *belie* slander

Othello: Cassio did top her. Ask thy husband else.°
    O, I were damned beneath all depth in hell
    But that I did proceed upon just grounds
    To this extremity. Thy husband knew it all.
Emilia: My husband?   145
Othello: Thy husband.
Emilia: That she was false to wedlock?
Othello: Ay, with Cassio. Nay, had she been true,
    If heaven would make me such another world
    Of one entire and perfect chrysolite,°   150
    I'd not have sold her for it.
Emilia: My husband?
Othello: Ay, 'twas he that told me on her first.
    An honest man he is, and hates the slime
    That sticks on filthy deeds.   155
Emilia: My husband?
Othello: What needs this iterance,° woman? I say thy husband.
Emilia: O mistress, villainy hath made mocks with° love!
    My husband say that she was false?
Othello: He, woman;
    I say thy husband. Dost understand the word?   160
    My friend, thy husband, honest, honest Iago.
Emilia: If he say so, may his pernicious soul
    Rot half a grain a day! He lies to th' heart.
    She was too fond of her most filthy bargain.
Othello: Ha?   [He draws.] 165
Emilia: Do thy worst!
    This deed of thine is no more worthy heaven
    Than thou wast worthy her.
Othello: Peace, you were best.°
Emilia: Thou hast not half that power to do me harm
    As I have to be hurt.° O gull!° O dolt!   170
    As ignorant as dirt! Thou hast done a deed—
    I care not for thy sword; I'll make thee known,
    Though I lost twenty lives.—Help! Help, ho, help!
    The Moor hath killed my mistress! Murder, murder!

    Enter Montano, Gratiano, and Iago.

Montano: What is the matter? How now, General?   175
Emilia: O, are you come, Iago? You have done well,
    That men must lay their murders on your neck.
Gratiano: What is the matter?
Emilia [to Iago]: Disprove this villain, if thou be'st a man.
    He says thou toldst him that his wife was false.   180

---

141 *else* i.e., if you don't believe me   150 *chrysolite* precious topaz   157 *iterance* iteration, repetition
158 *made mocks with* derided, made sport of   168 *you were best* it would be best for you   170 *to be hurt*
i.e., to endure hurt.   *gull* dupe

I know thou didst not; thou'rt not such a villain.
Speak, for my heart is full.
Iago: I told him what I thought, and told no more
Than what he found himself was apt° and true.
Emilia: But did you ever tell him she was false?   185
Iago: I did.
Emilia: You told a lie, an odious, damnèd lie!
Upon my soul, a lie, a wicked lie.
She false with Cassio? Did you say with Cassio?
Iago: With Cassio, mistress. Go to, charm° your tongue.   190
Emilia: I will not charm my tongue; I am bound to speak.
My mistress here lies murdered in her bed—
All: O heavens forfend!
Emilia: And your reports have set the murder on.
Othello: Nay, stare not, masters. It is true indeed.   195
Gratiano: 'Tis a strange truth.
Montano: O monstrous act!
Emilia: Villainy, villainy, villainy!
I think upon 't—I think I smell 't! O villainy!
I thought so then°—I'll kill myself for grief—
O villainy, villainy!   200
Iago: What, are you mad? I charge you, get you home.
Emilia: Good gentlemen, let me have leave to speak.
'Tis proper I obey him, but not now.
Perchance, Iago, I will ne'er go home.
Othello: O! O! O!   [*Othello falls on the bed.*°]   205
Emilia: Nay, lay thee down and roar,
For thou hast killed the sweetest innocent
That e'er did lift up eye.°
Othello [*rising*]:   O, she was foul!
I scarce did know you, uncle. There lies your niece,
Whose breath indeed these hands have newly stopped.
I know this act shows° horrible and grim.   210
Gratiano: Poor Desdemon! I am glad thy father's dead.
Thy match was mortal to him, and pure grief
Shore his old thread° in twain. Did he live now,
This sight would make him do a desperate turn,°
Yea, curse his better angel from his side,   215
And fall to reprobance.°
Othello: 'Tis pitiful. But yet Iago knows
That she with Cassio hath the act of shame
A thousand times committed. Cassio confessed it;
And she did gratify° his amorous works   220

---

184 *apt* plausible   190 *charm* keep silent (as though by a magic spell)   199 *then* (Perhaps at III, iii,
331–332, and IV, ii, 137–154.)   205 s.d. *Othello . . . bed* (This direction is from the Quarto, as also *He
kisses her* at line 19 and *She dies* at line 129.)   207 *lift up eye* i.e., lift her eyes to heaven   210 *shows*
looks   213 *Shore . . . thread* sheared the thread of his old age (as Atropos, one of the three Fates, was
thought to do)   214 *turn* deed   216 *reprobance* damnation, i.e., suicide   220 *gratify* reward

With that recognizance° and pledge of love
Which I first gave her. I saw it in his hand;
It was a handkerchief, an antique token
My father gave my mother.
Emilia: O God! O heavenly God!   225
Iago: Zounds, hold your peace.
Emilia: 'Twill out, 'twill out! I peace?
No, I will speak as liberal as the north.°
Let heaven and men and devils, let them all,
All, all, cry shame against me, yet I'll speak.
Iago: Be wise, and get you home.
Emilia: I will not.

[*Iago threatens Emilia.*]

Gratiano: Fie!   230
Your sword upon a woman?
Emilia: O thou dull Moor! That handkerchief thou speak'st of
I found by fortune and did give my husband;
For often, with a solemn earnestness,
More than indeed belonged° to such a trifle,   235
He begged of me to steal 't.
Iago: Villainous whore!
Emilia: She give it Cassio? No, alas! I found it,
And I did give 't my husband.
Iago: Filth, thou liest!
Emilia: By heaven, I do not, I do not, gentlemen.
O murderous coxcomb!° What should such a fool   240
Do with so good a wife?
Othello: Are there no stones° in heaven
But what serves for the thunder?—Precious° villain!

[*He runs at Iago; Montano disarms Othello. Iago, from behind, stabs Emilia.°*]

Gratiano: The woman falls! Sure he hath killed his wife.
Emilia: Ay, ay. O, lay me by my mistress' side.   245

Exit [*Iago.*]

Gratiano: He's gone, but his wife's killed.
Montano: 'Tis a notorious villain. Take you this weapon,
Which I have here recovered from the Moor.
Come, guard the door without. Let him not pass,
But kill him rather. I'll after that same villain,   250
For 'tis a damnèd slave.

Exit [*with all but Othello and Emilia, who has been laid by Desdemona's side*].

---

221 *recognizance* token   227 *liberal as the north* freely as the north wind (blows)   235 *belonged* was appropriate   240 *coxcomb* fool. (Addressed to Othello.)   242 *stones* bolts, such as those used for thunderbolts   243 *Precious* i.e., arrant, utter.   s.d. *He . . . Emilia* (The Quarto text reads, "The Moor runs at Iago. Iago kills his wife." The Quarto also specifies the exit of Iago at line 245 and the death of Emilia at line 260.)

Othello: I am not valiant neither,
    But every puny whipster° gets my sword.
    But why should honor° outlive honesty?°
    Let it go all.
Emilia: What did thy song bode, lady?   255
    Hark, canst thou hear me? I will play the swan,
    And die in music. [*She sings.*] "Willow, willow, willow."
    Moor, she was chaste. She loved thee, cruel Moor.
    So come my soul to bliss as I speak true.
    So speaking as I think, alas, I die.   [*She dies.*] 260
Othello: I have another weapon in this chamber;
    It was a sword of Spain, the ice-brook's temper°—
    O, here it is. [*He finds a sword.*] Uncle, I must come forth.
Gratiano [*within*]: If thou attempt it, it will cost thee dear.
    Thou hast no weapon, and perforce must suffer.   265
Othello: Look in upon me then and speak with me,
    Or, naked° as I am, I will assault thee.

    [*Enter Gratiano.*]

Gratiano: What is the matter?
Othello: Behold, I have a weapon;
    A better never did itself sustain
    Upon a soldier's thigh. I have seen the day   270
    That, with this little arm and this good sword,
    I have made my way through more impediments
    Than twenty times your stop.° But O, vain boast!
    Who can control his fate? 'Tis not so now.
    Be not afraid, though you do see me weaponed;   275
    Here is my journey's end, here is my butt°
    And very seamark° of my utmost sail.

    [*Gratiano steps back.*]

    Do you go back dismayed? 'Tis a lost° fear;
    Man but a rush° against Othello's breast
    And he retires. Where should Othello go?   280

    [*He turns to Desdemona.*]

    Now, how dost thou look now? O ill-starred wench!
    Pale as thy smock! When we shall meet at compt,°
    This look of thine will hurl my soul from heaven,
    And fiends will snatch at it. Cold, cold, my girl?
    Even like thy chastity. O cursèd, cursèd slave!°   285
    Whip me, ye devils,

---

253 *whipster* contemptible fellow (one who is always ready to whip out his sword)   254 *honor* i.e., the
bravery for which one enjoys a soldier's reputation.   *honesty* true integrity   262 *the ice-brook's temper* tempered in ice-cold water   267 *naked* unarmed   273 *stop* power (to stop)   276 *butt* goal, limit. (An archery
term.)   277 *seamark* beacon (marking his destination or limit)   278 *lost* wasted, unneeded   279 *Man . . .
rush* wield no more than a reed   282 *compt* account, judgment day   285 *slave* i.e., Othello himself

"O Desdemon! Dead, Desdemon! Dead! O! O!" (V, ii, 290).

From the possession of this heavenly sight!
Blow me about in winds! Roast me in sulfur!
Wash me in steep-down gulfs of liquid fire!
O Desdemon! Dead, Desdemon! Dead! O! O!   290

*Enter Lodovico, Cassio [carried in a litter°], Montano, and Iago [prisoner],
with officers.*

Lodovico: Where is this rash and most unfortunate man?
Othello: That's he that was Othello. Here I am.
Lodovico: Where is that viper? Bring the villain forth.

[*Iago is led forward.*]

Othello: I look down towards his feet;° but that's a fable.
If that thou be'st a devil, I cannot kill thee.   295

[*He wounds Iago.*]

Lodovico: Wrench his sword from him.   [*Othello is disarmed.*]
Iago: I bleed, sir, but not killed.

290 s.d. *in a litter* (The Quarto specifies that Cassio is "in a chair.")   294 *towards his feet* i.e., to see if they
are cloven, as the devil's are fabled to be

Iago is taken prisoner and his plots are exposed (V, ii, 293–347).

Othello: I am not sorry neither. I'd have thee live,
 For in my sense° 'tis happiness to die.
Lodovico: O thou Othello, that was once so good,
 Fall'n in the practice° of a cursèd slave,°   300
 What shall be said to thee?
Othello: Why, anything.
 An honorable murderer, if you will,
 For naught I did in hate, but all in honor.
Lodovico: This wretch hath part confessed his villainy.
 Did you and he consent° in Cassio's death?   305
Othello: Ay.
Cassio: Dear General, I never gave you cause.
Othello: I do believe it, and I ask your pardon.

---

298 *in my sense* to one who feels as I do   300 *in the practice* through the plotting, into the snare.
slave villain   305 *consent* agree

Will you, I pray, demand that demi-devil
Why he hath thus ensnared my soul and body?   310
Iago: Demand me nothing. What you know, you know.
From this time forth I never will speak word.
Lodovico: What, not to pray?
Gratiano: Torments° will ope your lips.
Othello: Well, thou dost best.   315
Lodovico: Sir, you shall understand what hath befall'n,
Which, as I think, you know not. Here is a letter
Found in the pocket of the slain Roderigo;
And here another. [*He produces letters.*] The one of them imports
The death of Cassio, to be undertook   320
By Roderigo.
Othello: O villain!
Cassio: Most heathenish and most gross!°
Lodovico [*showing another paper*]: Now here's another discontented° paper
Found in his pocket too. And this, it seems,
Roderigo meant t' have sent this damnèd villain;   325
But that belike° Iago in the interim
Came in and satisfied him.°
Othello: O thou pernicious caitiff!—
How came you, Cassio, by that handkerchief
That was my wife's?
Cassio: I found it in my chamber;   330
And he himself confessed but even now
That there he dropped it for a special purpose
Which wrought to his desire.°
Othello: O fool, fool, fool!
Cassio: There is besides in Roderigo's letter
How he upbraids Iago, that he made him   335
Brave° me upon the watch, whereon it came°
That I was cast;° and even but now he spake,
After long seeming dead, Iago hurt him,
Iago set him on.
Lodovico [*to Othello*]: You must forsake this room and go with us.   340
Your power and your command is taken off,°
And Cassio rules in Cyprus. For this slave,
If there be any cunning cruelty
That can torment him much and hold him long,°
It shall be his. You shall close prisoner rest°   345
Till that the nature of your fault be known
To the Venetian state.—Come, bring away.

---

314 *Torments* torture   322 *gross* monstrous   323 *discontented* full of discontent   326 *belike* most likely   327 *Came . . . him* interposed and gave him satisfactory explanation   333 *wrought . . . desire* worked out as he wished, fitted in with his plan   336 *Brave* defy.   *whereon it came* whereof it came about   337 *cast* dismissed   341 *taken off* taken away   344 *hold him long* keep him alive a long time (during his torture)   345 *rest* remain

Othello: Soft you;° a word or two before you go.
    I have done the state some service, and they know 't.
    No more of that. I pray you, in your letters,   350
    When you shall these unlucky° deeds relate,
    Speak of me as I am; nothing extenuate,
    Nor set down aught in malice. Then must you speak
    Of one that loved not wisely but too well;
    Of one not easily jealous but, being wrought,°   355
    Perplexed° in the extreme; of one whose hand,
    Like the base Indian,° threw a pearl away
    Richer than all his tribe; of one whose subdued° eyes,
    Albeit unusèd to the melting mood,
    Drop tears as fast as the Arabian trees   360
    Their medicinable gum.° Set you down this;
    And say besides that in Aleppo once,
    Where a malignant and a turbaned Turk
    Beat a Venetian and traduced the state,
    I took by th' throat the circumcisèd dog   365
    And smote him, thus.   *[He stabs himself.°]*
Lodovico: O bloody period!°
Gratiano: All that is spoke is marred.
Othello: I kissed thee ere I killed thee. No way but this,
    Killing myself, to die upon a kiss.   370

    [He kisses Desdemona and dies.]

Cassio: This did I fear, but thought he had no weapon;
    For he was great of heart.
Lodovico [to Iago]:   O Spartan dog,°
    More fell° than anguish, hunger, or the sea!
    Look on the tragic loading of this bed.
    This is thy work. The object poisons sight;   375
    Let it be hid.° Gratiano, keep° the house,

    [The bed curtains are drawn.]

    And seize upon° the fortunes of the Moor,
    For they succeed on° you. *[To Cassio.]* To you, Lord Governor,
    Remains the censure° of this hellish villain,
    The time, the place, the torture. O, enforce it!   380
    Myself will straight aboard, and to the state
    This heavy act with heavy heart relate.   *Exeunt.*

---

348 *Soft you* one moment   351 *unlucky* unfortunate   355 *wrought* worked upon, worked into a frenzy   356 *Perplexed* distraught   357 *Indian* (This reading from the Quarto pictures an ignorant savage who cannot recognize the value of a precious jewel. The Folio reading, *Iudean* or *Judean*, i.e., infidel or disbeliever, may refer to Herod, who slew Miriamne in a fit of jealousy, or to Judas Iscariot, the betrayer of Christ.)   358 *subdued* i.e., overcome by grief   361 *gum* i.e., myrr   366 s.d. *He stabs himself* (This direction is in the Quarto text.)   367 *period* termination, conclusion   372 *Spartan dog* (Spartan dogs were noted for their savagery and silence.)   373 *fell* cruel   376 *Let it be hid* i.e., draw the bed curtains. (No stage direction specifies that the dead are to be carried offstage at the end of the play.)   *keep* remain in   377 *seize upon* take legal possession of   378 *succeed on* pass as though by inheritance to   379 *censure* sentencing

Questions

ACT I

1. What is Othello's position in society? How is he regarded by those who know him? By his own words, when we first meet him in Scene ii, what traits of character does he manifest?
2. How do you account for Brabantio's dismay on learning of his daughter's marriage, despite the fact that Desdemona has married a man so generally honored and admired?
3. What is Iago's view of human nature? In his fondness for likening men to animals (as in I, i, 49–50; I, i, 90–91; and I, iii, 378–379), what does he tell us about himself?
4. What reasons does Iago give for his hatred of Othello?
5. In Othello's defense before the senators (Scene iii), how does he explain Desdemona's gradual falling in love with him?
6. Is Brabantio's warning to Othello (I, iii, 293–294) an accurate or an inaccurate prophecy?
7. By what strategy does Iago enlist Roderigo in his plot against the Moor? In what lines do we learn Iago's true feelings toward Roderigo?

ACT II

1. What do the Cypriots think of Othello? Do their words (in Scene i) make him seem to us a lesser man or a larger one?
2. What cruelty does Iago display toward Emilia? How well founded is his distrust of his wife's fidelity?
3. In II, iii, 221, Othello speaks of Iago's "honesty and love." How do you account for Othello's being so totally deceived?
4. For what major events does the merrymaking (proclaimed in Scene ii) give opportunity?

ACT III

1. Trace the steps by which Iago rouses Othello to suspicion. Is there anything in Othello's character or circumstances that renders him particularly susceptible to Iago's wiles?
2. In III, iv, 49–98, Emilia knows of Desdemona's distress over the lost handkerchief. At this moment, how do you explain her failure to relieve Desdemona's mind? Is Emilia aware of her husband's villainy?

ACT IV

1. In this act, what circumstantial evidence is added to Othello's case against Desdemona?
2. How plausible do you find Bianca's flinging the handkerchief at Cassio just when Othello is looking on? How important is the handkerchief in this play? What does it represent? What suggestions or hints do you find in it?
3. What prevents Othello from being moved by Desdemona's appeal (IV, ii, 33–92)?
4. When Roderigo grows impatient with Iago (IV, ii, 181–201), how does Iago make use of his fellow plotter's discontent?
5. What does the conversation between Emilia and Desdemona (Scene iii) tell us about the nature of each?
6. In this act, what scenes (or speeches) contain memorable dramatic irony?

ACT V

1. Summarize the events that lead to Iago's unmasking.
2. How does Othello's mistaken belief that Cassio is slain (V, i, 27–34) affect the outcome of the play?
3. What is Iago's motive in stabbing Roderigo?

4. In your interpretation of the play, exactly what impels Othello to kill Desdemona? Jealousy? Desire for revenge? Excess idealism? A wish to be a public avenger who punishes, "else she'll betray more men"?

5. What do you understand by Othello's calling himself "one that loved not wisely but too well" (V, ii, 354)?

6. In your view, does Othello's long speech in V, ii, 348–366 succeed in restoring his original dignity and nobility? Do you agree with Cassio (V, ii, 372) that Othello was "great of heart"?

General Questions

1. What motivates Iago to carry out his schemes? Do you find him a devil incarnate, a madman, or a rational human being?

2. Whom besides Othello does Iago deceive? What is Desdemona's opinion of him? Emilia's? Cassio's (before Iago is found out)? To what do you attribute Iago's success as a deceiver?

3. How essential to the play is the fact that Othello is a black man, a Moor, and not a native of Venice?

4. In the introduction to his edition of the play in *The Complete Signet Classic Shakespeare*, Alvin Kernan remarks:

> *Othello* is probably the most neatly, the most formally constructed of Shakespeare's plays. Every character is, for example, balanced by another similar or contrasting character. Desdemona is balanced by her opposite, Iago; love and concern for others at one end of the scale, hatred and concern for self at the other.

Besides Desdemona and Iago, what other pairs of characters strike balances?

5. Consider any passage of the play in which there is a shift from verse to prose, or from prose to verse. What is the effect of this shift?

6. Indicate a passage that you consider memorable for its poetry. Does the passage seem introduced for its own sake? Does it in any way advance the action of the play, express theme, or demonstrate character?

7. Does the play contain any tragic *recognition*—as discussed in Chapter 37, a moment of terrible enlightenment, a "realization of the unthinkable"?

8. Does the downfall of Othello proceed from any flaw in his nature, or is his downfall entirely the work of Iago?

THE BACKGROUND OF *A MIDSUMMER NIGHT'S DREAM*

The theme in *A Midsummer Night's Dream* of love being best fulfilled in marital union suggests that the play may have originally been written for performance at an aristocratic wedding. The work is certainly Shakespeare's most lyrical and romantic comedy, full of reflections on fantasy, dreaming, and desire, set mostly amid festive palaces and moonlit woods filled with fairies.

In the Renaissance there were two major varieties of comedy—both borrowed from Greek and Roman drama. The first was satiric comedy, which usually poked bitter fun at human folly. Shakespeare generally avoided this mode, which was very well practiced by his friend Ben Jonson. Instead, Shakespeare preferred the second type, romantic comedy, which he had discovered as a schoolboy reading the Latin plays of Terence and Plautus. Romantic comedy is less concerned with correcting misdeeds and folly than with following the delightful and embarrassing behavior of imperfect but mostly likeable characters. Always ending in the happy marriage (or marriages) of young lovers who have overcome considerable obstacles to unite, romantic comedy also encourages the viewer to accept and forgive human faults and frailties.

Kevin Kline as Bottom and Michelle Pfeiffer as Titania in a 1999 film adaptation of *A Midsummer Night's Dream*.

A Midsummer Night's Dream also demonstrates Shakespeare's particular genius for plotting, a necessary skill for comic theater. Although Shakespeare often borrowed (and usually greatly improved) the stories of his plays from various sources, the plot of *A Midsummer Night's Dream* appears to be original, though he took individual characters like Theseus and Titania from classical mythology. The comedy has a delightfully complex structure combining four different plots—all romantic in different ways, from young love to marital reconciliation.

The play presents five different sets of lovers. The general action is framed around the wedding of the first set of lovers, King Theseus and the Amazon Queen Hippolyta, whom he has conquered in war and taken as his wife. Both a personal and public union, their marriage will end the enmity between their nations. More complicated are the love affairs of the second group, the young aristocrats—Helena, Lysander, Hermia, and Demetrius. The adventures of these two passionately mismatched couples, who ultimately find happy marriages, form the main plot of the comedy. The third set of lovers is a supernatural couple, Oberon and Titania, the king and queen of the fairy realm, who are in the midst of a bitter marital dispute. Then, there is a group of rustic workmen dominated by Nick Bottom, a weaver with theatrical aspirations. While this group does not initially seem to contain any lovers, Bottom eventually becomes entangled in a series of enchantments that transforms him into Titania's ass-eared darling for a single night. Finally, at the play's end the rustics perform a burlesque of tragic love that presents a fifth, imaginary set of lovers, Pyramus and Thisbe. Their tale of "tragical mirth" subtly comments on the consequences of doomed romance. No other comedy by Shakespeare focuses so single-mindedly or happily on sexual love and marriage. No wonder *A Midsummer Night's Dream* has been popular for centuries, not only in English-speaking countries but around the world.

PICTURING *A Midsummer*

▲ Hippolyta and Theseus, *page 1406*

▲ Lysander and Hermia, *page 1409*

◀ Bottom as ass, *page 1432*

▼ Oberon enchants Titania, *page 1426*

▶ "You thief of love," *page 1443*

Night's Dream

▲ The rustics plan their play,
page 1413

▲ Demetrius to Helena:
"Let me go!"
page 1423

◄ Oberon directs Puck,
page 1420

◄ The fairies tend to Bottom,
page 1449

PRODUCTION PHOTOS
The photos illustrating the play are from the 2005 Utah Shakespeare Festival production of *A Midsummer Night's Dream*. (All photos by Karl Hugh. Copyright Utah Shakespeare Festival 2005.)

Anne Newhall *Hippolyta and Titania*
Michael Sharon *Theseus and Oberon*
Christine Williams *Hermia*
Michael Brusasco *Lysander*
Tiffany Scott *Helena*
Ashley Smith *Demetrius*

Corliss Preston *Puck*
John Tillotson *Bottom*
Aaron Galligan-Stierle *Flute*
Peter Sham *Quince*
Kevin Kiler *Snout*
Martin Swoverland *Snug*

A Midsummer Night's Dream

about 1594–1595

Edited By David Bevington

[DRAMATIS PERSONAE

Theseus, Duke of Athens
Hippolyta, Queen of the Amazons, betrothed to Theseus
Philostrate, Master of the Revels
Egeus, father of Hermia
Hermia, daughter of Egeus, in love with Lysander
Lysander, in love with Hermia
Demetrius, in love with Hermia and favored by Egeus
Helena, in love with Demetrius

Oberon, King of the Fairies
Titania, Queen of the Fairies
Puck, or Robin Goodfellow
Peaseblossom,
Cobweb,
Mote,   } fairies attending Titania
Mustardseed,
Other fairies attending

Peter Quince, a carpenter,   Prologue
Nick Bottom, a weaver,   Pyramus
Francis Flute, a bellows mender, } representing   Thisbe
Tom Snout, a tinker,   Wall
Snug, a joiner,   Lion
Robin Starveling, a tailor,   Moonshine

Lords and Attendants on Theseus and Hippolyta

SCENE. *Athens, and a wood near it*]

ACT I

SCENE I [ATHENS. THESEUS' COURT.]

Enter Theseus, Hippolyta, [and Philostrate,] with others.

Theseus: Now, fair Hippolyta, our nuptial hour
    Draws on apace. Four happy days bring in
    Another moon; but, O, methinks, how slow

NOTE ON THE TEXT:
This text of *A Midsummer Night's Dream* is taken from the First Quarto of 1600. For the reader's convenience, some material has been added by the editor, David Bevington (some indications of scenes and some stage directions). Such additions are enclosed in brackets. Mr. Bevington's text and notes were prepared for his book *The Complete Works of Shakespeare*, Updated 4th ed. (New York: Longman, 1997).

This old moon wanes! She lingers° my desires,
Like to a stepdame° or a dowager°   5
Long withering out° a young man's revenue.
Hippolyta: Four days will quickly steep themselves° in night;
Four nights will quickly dream away the time;
And then the moon, like to a silver bow
New bent in heaven, shall behold the night   10
Of our solemnities.°
Theseus: Go, Philostrate,
Stir up the Athenian youth to merriments.
Awake the pert and nimble spirit of mirth.
Turn melancholy forth to funerals;
The pale companion° is not for our pomp.°   [*Exit Philostrate.*]   15
Hippolyta, I wooed thee with my sword°
And won thy love doing thee injuries;
But I will wed thee in another key,
With pomp, with triumph,° and with reveling.

Enter Egeus and his daughter Hermia, and Lysander, and Demetrius.

Egeus: Happy be Theseus, our renownèd duke!   20
Theseus: Thanks, good Egeus. What's the news with thee?
Egeus: Full of vexation come I, with complaint
Against my child, my daughter Hermia.—
Stand forth, Demetrius.—My noble lord,
This man hath my consent to marry her.—   25
Stand forth, Lysander.—And, my gracious Duke,
This man hath bewitched the bosom of my child.
Thou, thou Lysander, thou hast given her rhymes
And interchanged love tokens with my child.
Thou hast by moonlight at her window sung   30
With feigning° voice verses of feigning° love,
And stol'n the impression of her fantasy°
With bracelets of thy hair, rings, gauds,° conceits,°
Knacks,° trifles, nosegays, sweetmeats—messengers
Of strong prevailment in° unhardened youth.   35
With cunning hast thou filched my daughter's heart,
Turned her obedience, which is due to me,
To stubborn harshness. And, my gracious Duke,
Be it so° she will not here before Your Grace
Consent to marry with Demetrius,   40

---

4 *lingers* postpones, delays the fulfillment of   5 *stepdame* stepmother.   *a dowager* i.e., a widow (whose right of inheritance from her dead husband is eating into her son's estate)   6 *withering out* causing to dwindle   7 *steep themselves* saturate themselves, be absorbed in   11 *solemnities* festive ceremonies of marriage   15 *companion* fellow.   *pomp* ceremonial magnificence   16 *with my sword* i.e., in a military engagement against the Amazons, when Hippolyta was taken captive   19 *triumph* public festivity   31 *feigning* (1) counterfeiting (2) faining, desirous   32 *And . . . fantasy* and made her fall in love with you (imprinting your image on her imagination) by stealthy and dishonest means   33 *gauds* playthings.   *conceits* fanciful trifles   34 *Knacks* knickknacks   35 *prevailment in* influence on   39 *Be it so* if

Hippolyta, Queen of the Amazons, and her betrothed, Theseus, Duke of Athens.

> I beg the ancient privilege of Athens:
> As she is mine, I may dispose of her,
> Which shall be either to this gentleman
> Or to her death, according to our law
> Immediately° provided in that case.   45
> *Theseus:* What say you, Hermia? Be advised, fair maid.
> To you your father should be as a god—
> One that composed your beauties, yea, and one
> To whom you are but as a form in wax
> By him imprinted, and within his power   50
> To leave° the figure or disfigure° it.
> Demetrius is a worthy gentleman.
> *Hermia:* So is Lysander.
> *Theseus:*   In himself he is;
> But in this kind,° wanting° your father's voice,°
> The other must be held the worthier.   55

45 *Immediately* directly, with nothing intervening   51 *leave* i.e., leave unaltered.   *disfigure* obliterate
54 *kind* respect.   *wanting* lacking.   *voice* approval

Hermia: I would my father looked but with my eyes.

Theseus: Rather your eyes must with his judgment look.

Hermia: I do entreat Your Grace to pardon me.
    I know not by what power I am made bold,
    Nor how it may concern° my modesty   60
    In such a presence here to plead my thoughts;
    But I beseech Your Grace that I may know
    The worst that may befall me in this case
    If I refuse to wed Demetrius.

Theseus: Either to die the death° or to abjure   65
    Forever the society of men.
    Therefore, fair Hermia, question your desires,
    Know of your youth, examine well your blood,°
    Whether, if you yield not to your father's choice,
    You can endure the livery° of a nun,   70
    For aye° to be in shady cloister mewed,°
    To live a barren sister all your life,
    Chanting faint hymns to the cold fruitless moon.
    Thrice blessèd they that master so their blood
    To undergo such maiden pilgrimage;   75
    But earthlier happy° is the rose distilled°
    Than that which, withering on the virgin thorn,
    Grows, lives, and dies in single blessedness.

Hermia: So will I grow, so live, so die, my lord,
    Ere I will yield my virgin patent° up   80
    Unto his lordship, whose unwishèd yoke
    My soul consents not to give sovereignty.

Theseus: Take time to pause, and by the next new moon—
    The sealing day betwixt my love and me
    For everlasting bond of fellowship—   85
    Upon that day either prepare to die
    For disobedience to your father's will,
    Or° else to wed Demetrius, as he would,
    Or on Diana's altar to protest°
    For aye austerity and single life.   90

Demetrius: Relent, sweet Hermia, and, Lysander, yield
    Thy crazèd° title to my certain right.

Lysander: You have her father's love, Demetrius;
    Let me have Hermia's. Do you marry him.

Egeus: Scornful Lysander! True, he hath my love,   95
    And what is mine my love shall render him.
    And she is mine, and all my right of her
    I do estate unto° Demetrius.

---

60 *concern* befit   65 *die the death* be executed by legal process   68 *blood* passions   70 *livery* habit, costume   71 *aye* ever. *mewed* shut in. (Said of a hawk, poultry, etc.)   76 *earthlier happy* happier as respects this world. *distilled* i.e., to make perfume   80 *patent* privilege   88 *Or* either   89 *protest* vow   92 *crazèd* cracked, unsound   98 *estate unto* settle or bestow upon

Lysander: I am, my lord, as well derived° as he,
    As well possessed;° my love is more than his;   100
    My fortunes every way as fairly° ranked,
    If not with vantage,° as Demetrius';
    And, which is more than all these boasts can be,
    I am beloved of beauteous Hermia.
    Why should not I then prosecute my right?   105
    Demetrius, I'll avouch it to his head,°
    Made love to Nedar's daughter, Helena,
    And won her soul; and she, sweet lady, dotes,
    Devoutly dotes, dotes in idolatry
    Upon this spotted° and inconstant man.   110
Theseus: I must confess that I have heard so much,
    And with Demetrius thought to have spoke thereof;
    But, being overfull of self-affairs,°
    My mind did lose it. But, Demetrius, come,
    And come, Egeus, you shall go with me;   115
    I have some private schooling° for you both.
    For you, fair Hermia, look you arm° yourself
    To fit your fancies° to your father's will,
    Or else the law of Athens yields you up—
    Which by no means we may extenuate°—   120
    To death or to a vow of single life.
    Come, my Hippolyta. What cheer, my love?
    Demetrius and Egeus, go° along.
    I must employ you in some business
    Against° our nuptial, and confer with you   125
    Of something nearly that° concerns yourselves.
Egeus: With duty and desire we follow you.

                  Exeunt [all but Lysander and Hermia].

Lysander: How now, my love, why is your cheek so pale?
    How chance the roses there do fade so fast?
Hermia: Belike° for want of rain, which I could well   130
    Beteem° them from the tempest of my eyes.
Lysander: Ay me! For aught that I could ever read,
    Could ever hear by tale or history,
    The course of true love never did run smooth;
    But either it was different in blood°—   135
Hermia: O cross!° Too high to be enthralled to low.
Lysander: Or else misgrafted° in respect of years—
Hermia: O spite! Too old to be engaged to young.
Lysander: Or else it stood upon the choice of friends°—

---

99 *as well derived* as well born and descended   100 *possessed* endowed with wealth   101 *fairly* hand-
somely   102 *vantage* superiority   106 *head* i.e., face   110 *spotted* i.e., morally stained   113 *self-affairs*
my own concerns   116 *schooling* admonition   117 *look you arm* take care you prepare   118 *fancies* lik-
ings, thoughts of love   120 *extenuate* mitigate, relax   123 *go* i.e., come   125 *Against* in preparation
for   126 *nearly that* that closely   130 *Belike* very likely   131 *Beteem* grant, afford   135 *blood* hereditary
station   136 *cross* vexation   137 *misgrafted* ill grafted, badly matched   139 *friends* relatives

The young lovers Lysander and Hermia.

Hermia: O hell, to choose love by another's eyes!   140
Lysander: Or if there were a sympathy° in choice,
        War, death, or sickness did lay siege to it,
        Making it momentany° as a sound,
        Swift as a shadow, short as any dream,
        Brief as the lightning in the collied° night   145
        That in a spleen° unfolds° both heaven and earth,
        And ere a man hath power to say "Behold!"
        The jaws of darkness do devour it up.
        So quick° bright things come to confusion.°

141 *sympathy* agreement   143 *momentany* lasting but a moment   145 *collied* blackened (as with coal
dust), darkened   146 *in a spleen* in a swift impulse, in a violent flash.   *unfolds* reveals   149 *quick* quickly;
also, living, alive.   *confusion* ruin

Hermia: If then true lovers have been ever crossed,° 150
  It stands as an edict in destiny.
  Then let us teach our trial patience,°
  Because it is a customary cross,
  As due to love as thoughts, and dreams, and sighs,
  Wishes, and tears, poor fancy's° followers. 155
Lysander: A good persuasion.° Therefore, hear me, Hermia:
  I have a widow aunt, a dowager
  Of great revenue, and she hath no child.
  From Athens is her house remote seven leagues;
  And she respects° me as her only son. 160
  There, gentle Hermia, may I marry thee,
  And to that place the sharp Athenian law
  Cannot pursue us. If thou lovest me, then,
  Steal forth thy father's house tomorrow night;
  And in the wood, a league without° the town, 165
  Where I did meet thee once with Helena
  To do observance to a morn of May,°
  There will I stay for thee.
Hermia: My good Lysander!
  I swear to thee by Cupid's strongest bow,
  By his best arrow° with the golden head, 170
  By the simplicity° of Venus' doves,°
  By that which knitteth souls and prospers loves,
  And by that fire which burned the Carthage queen°
  When the false Trojan° under sail was seen,
  By all the vows that ever men have broke, 175
  In number more than ever women spoke,
  In that same place thou hast appointed me
  Tomorrow truly will I meet with thee.
Lysander: Keep promise, love. Look, here comes Helena.

  Enter Helena.

Hermia: God speed, fair° Helena! Whither away? 180
Helena: Call you me fair? That "fair" again unsay.
  Demetrius loves your fair.° O happy fair!°
  Your eyes are lodestars,° and your tongue's sweet air°
  More tunable° than lark to shepherd's ear
  When wheat is green, when hawthorn buds appear. 185
  Sickness is catching. O, were favor° so,

150 *ever crossed* always thwarted   152 *teach . . . patience* i.e., teach ourselves patience in this trial
155 *fancy's* amorous passion's   156 *persuasion* doctrine   160 *respects* regards   165 *without* outside
167 *do . . . May* perform the ceremonies of May Day   170 *best arrow* (Cupid's best gold-pointed arrows
were supposed to induce love; his blunt leaden arrows, aversion.)   171 *simplicity* innocence.   *doves* i.e.,
those that drew Venus' chariot   173, 174 *Carthage queen, false Trojan* (Dido, Queen of Carthage, immo-
lated herself on a funeral pyre after having been deserted by the Trojan hero Aeneas.)   180 *fair* fair-
complexioned (generally regarded by the Elizabethans as more beautiful than a dark complexion)
182 *your fair* your beauty (even though Hermia is dark-complexioned).   *happy fair* lucky fair one
183 *lodestars* guiding stars.   *air* music   184 *tunable* tuneful, melodious   186 *favor* appearance, looks

Yours would I catch, fair Hermia, ere I go;
My ear should catch your voice, my eye your eye,
My tongue should catch your tongue's sweet melody.
Were the world mine, Demetrius being bated,°   190
The rest I'd give to be to you translated.°
O, teach me how you look and with what art
You sway° the motion° of Demetrius' heart.

Hermia: I frown upon him, yet he loves me still.

Helena: O, that your frowns would teach my smiles such skill!   195

Hermia: I give him curses, yet he gives me love.

Helena: O, that my prayers could such affection° move!°

Hermia: The more I hate, the more he follows me.

Helena: The more I love, the more he hateth me.

Hermia: His folly, Helena, is no fault of mine.   200

Helena: None, but your beauty. Would that fault were mine!

Hermia: Take comfort. He no more shall see my face.
Lysander and myself will fly this place.
Before the time I did Lysander see
Seemed Athens as a paradise to me.°   205
O, then, what graces in my love do dwell,
That he hath turned a heaven unto a hell?

Lysander: Helen, to you our minds we will unfold.
Tomorrow night, when Phoebe° doth behold
Her silver visage in the watery glass,°   210
Decking with liquid pearl the bladed grass,
A time that lovers' flights doth still° conceal,
Through Athens' gates have we devised to steal.

Hermia: And in the wood, where often you and I
Upon faint° primrose beds were wont to lie,   215
Emptying our bosoms of their counsel° sweet,
There my Lysander and myself shall meet,
And thence from Athens turn away our eyes
To seek new friends and stranger companies.°
Farewell, sweet playfellow. Pray thou for us,   220
And good luck grant thee thy Demetrius!
Keep word, Lysander: We must starve our sight
From lovers' food till morrow deep midnight.

Lysander: I will, my Hermia. *(Exit Hermia.)* Helena, adieu.
As you on him, Demetrius dote on you!   225

                                                Exit Lysander.

Helena: How happy some o'er other some can be!°
Through Athens I am thought as fair as she.
But what of that? Demetrius thinks not so;

---

190 *bated* excepted   191 *translated* transformed   193 *sway* control. *motion* impulse   197 *affection* passion. *move* arouse   204–205 *Before . . . to me* (Hermia seemingly means that love has led to complications and jealousies, making Athens hell for her.)   209 *Phoebe* Diana, the moon   210 *glass* mirror 212 *still* always   215 *faint* pale   216 *counsel* secret thought   219 *stranger companies* the company of strangers   226 *o'er . . . can be* can be in comparison to some others

He will not know what all but he do know.
And as he errs, doting on Hermia's eyes,   230
So I, admiring of° his qualities.
Things base and vile, holding no quantity,°
Love can transpose to form and dignity.
Love looks not with the eyes, but with the mind,
And therefore is winged Cupid painted blind.   235
Nor hath Love's mind of any judgment taste;°
Wings and no eyes figure° unheedy haste.
And therefore is Love said to be a child,
Because in choice° he is so oft beguiled.°
As waggish° boys in game° themselves forswear,   240
So the boy Love is perjured everywhere.
For ere Demetrius looked on Hermia's eyne,°
He hailed down oaths that he was only mine;
And when this hail some heat from Hermia felt,
So he dissolved, and showers of oaths did melt.   245
I will go tell him of fair Hermia's flight.
Then to the wood will he tomorrow night
Pursue her; and for this intelligence°
If I have thanks, it is a dear expense.°
But herein mean I to enrich my pain,   250
To have his sight thither and back again.

                                                        Exit.

SCENE II [ATHENS.]

*Enter Quince the carpenter, and Snug the joiner, and Bottom the weaver, and
Flute the bellows mender, and Snout the tinker, and Starveling the tailor.*

Quince: Is all our company here?
Bottom: You were best to call them generally,° man by man, according to the scrip.°
Quince: Here is the scroll of every man's name which is thought fit, through all
     Athens, to play in our interlude° before the Duke and the Duchess on his
     wedding day at night.   5
Bottom: First, good Peter Quince, say what the play treats on, then read the
     names of the actors, and so grow to° a point.
Quince: Marry,° our play is "The most lamentable comedy and most cruel death
     of Pyramus and Thisbe."
Bottom: A very good piece of work, I assure you, and a merry. Now, good Peter   10
     Quince, call forth your actors by the scroll. Masters, spread yourselves.
Quince: Answer as I call you. Nick Bottom,° the weaver.

---

231 *admiring of* wondering at   232 *holding no quantity* i.e., unsubstantial, unshapely   236 *Nor . . . taste* i.e., nor
has Love, which dwells in the fancy or imagination, any *taste* or least bit of judgment or reason   237 *figure* are
a symbol of   239 *in choice* in choosing.   *beguiled* self-deluded, making unaccountable choices   240 *waggish*
playful, mischievous.   *game* sport, jest   242 *eyne* eyes. (Old form of plural.)   248 *intelligence* information   249 *a dear expense* i.e., a trouble worth taking on my part, or a begrudging effort on his part.   *dear*
costly   2 *generally* (Bottom's blunder for "individually.")   *scrip* scrap (Bottom's error for "script.")   4 *interlude*
play   7 *grow to* come to   8 *Marry* (A mild oath; originally the name of the Virgin Mary.)   12 *Bottom* (As
a weaver's term, a *bottom* was an object around which thread was wound.)

The workers meet to plan their play, and Quince hands out the parts.

Bottom: Ready. Name what part I am for, and proceed.

Quince: You, Nick Bottom, are set down for Pyramus.

Bottom: What is Pyramus? A lover or a tyrant?   15

Quince: A lover, that kills himself most gallant for love.

Bottom: That will ask some tears in the true performing of it. If I do it, let the audience look to their eyes. I will move storms; I will condole° in some measure.
To the rest—yet my chief humor° is for a tyrant. I could play Ercles° rarely, or
a part to tear a cat° in, to make all split.°   20

    "The raging rocks
    And shivering shocks
    Shall break the locks

---

18 *condole* lament, arouse pity 19 *humor* inclination, whim. *Ercles* Hercules (The tradition of ranting
came from Seneca's *Hercules Furens.*) 20 *tear a cat* i.e., rant. *make all split* i.e., cause a stir, bring the
house down

> Of prison gates;
> And Phibbus' car°   25
> Shall shine from far
> And make and mar
> The foolish Fates."

This was lofty! Now name the rest of the players. This is Ercles' vein, a tyrant's vein. A lover is more condoling.   30

Quince: Francis Flute, the bellows mender.

Flute: Here, Peter Quince.

Quince: Flute, you must take Thisbe on you.

Flute: What is Thisbe? A wandering knight?

Quince: It is the lady that Pyramus must love.   35

Flute: Nay, faith, let not me play a woman. I have a beard coming.

Quince: That's all one.° You shall play it in a mask, and you may speak as small° as you will.

Bottom: An° I may hide my face, let me play Thisbe too. I'll speak in a monstrous little voice, "Thisne, Thisne!" "Ah Pyramus, my lover dear! Thy Thisbe   40 dear, and lady dear!"

Quince: No, no, you must play Pyramus, and Flute, you Thisbe.

Bottom: Well, proceed.

Quince: Robin Starveling, the tailor.

Starveling: Here, Peter Quince.   45

Quince: Robin Starveling, you must play Thisbe's mother. Tom Snout, the tinker.

Snout: Here, Peter Quince.

Quince: You, Pyramus' father; myself, Thisbe's father; Snug, the joiner, you, the lion's part, and I hope here is a play fitted.

Snug: Have you the lion's part written? Pray you, if it be, give it me, for I am slow   50 of study.

Quince: You may do it extempore, for it is nothing but roaring.

Bottom: Let me play the lion too. I will roar that I will do any man's heart good to hear me. I will roar that I will make the Duke say, "Let him roar again, let him roar again."   55

Quince: An you should do it too terribly, you would fright the Duchess and the ladies, that they would shriek; and that were enough to hang us all.

All: That would hang us, every mother's son.

Bottom: I grant you, friends, if you should fright the ladies out of their wits, they would have no more discretion but to hang us; but I will aggravate° my   60 voice so that I will roar you° as gently as any sucking dove;° I will roar you an 'twere° any nightingale.

Quince: You can play no part but Pyramus; for Pyramus is a sweet-faced man, a proper° man as one shall see in a summer's day, a most lovely gentlemanlike man. Therefore you must needs play Pyramus.   65

Bottom: Well, I will undertake it. What beard were I best to play it in?

Quince: Why, what you will.

---

25 *Phibbus' car* Phoebus', the sun god's, chariot   37 *That's all one* it makes no difference.   *small* high-pitched   39 *An* if (also at line 56)   60 *aggravate* (Bottom's blunder for "moderate.")   61 *roar you* i.e., roar for you.   *sucking dove* (Bottom conflates *sitting dove* and *sucking lamb*, two proverbial images of innocence.)   62 *an 'twere* as if it were   64 *proper* handsome

Bottom: I will discharge° it in either your° straw-color beard, your orange-tawny beard, your purple-in-grain° beard, or your French-crown-color° beard, your perfect yellow.   70

Quince: Some of your French crowns° have no hair at all, and then you will play barefaced. But, masters, here are your parts. [*He distributes parts.*] And I am to entreat you, request you, and desire you to con° them by tomorrow night, and meet me in the palace wood, a mile without the town, by moonlight. There will we rehearse; for if we meet in the city, we shall be dogged with   75 company, and our devices° known. In the meantime I will draw a bill° of properties, such as our play wants. I pray you, fail me not.

Bottom: We will meet, and there we may rehearse most obscenely° and courageously. Take pains, be perfect.° Adieu.

Quince: At the Duke's oak we meet.   80

Bottom: Enough. Hold, or cut bowstrings.°   *Exeunt.*

ACT II

SCENE I [A WOOD NEAR ATHENS.]

Enter a Fairy at one door, and Robin Goodfellow [Puck] at another.

Puck: How now, spirit, whither wander you?

Fairy: Over hill, over dale,
                    Thorough° bush, thorough brier,
             Over park, over pale,°
                    Thorough flood, thorough fire,   5
             I do wander everywhere,
             Swifter than the moon's sphere; °
             And I serve the Fairy Queen,
             To dew° her orbs° upon the green.
             The cowslips tall her pensioners° be.   10
             In their gold coats spots you see;
             Those be rubies, fairy favors;
             In those freckles live their savors.
        I must go seek some dewdrops here
        And hang a pearl in every cowslip's ear.   15
        Farewell, thou lob° of spirits; I'll be gone.
        Our Queen and all her elves come here anon.°

Puck: The King doth keep his revels here tonight.
        Take heed the Queen come not within his sight.

68 *discharge* perform. *your* i.e., you know the kind I mean   69 *purple-in-grain* dyed a very deep red. (From *grain*, the name applied to the dried insect used to make the dye.) *French-crown-color* i.e., color of a French crown, a gold coin   71 *crowns* heads bald from syphilis, the "French disease"   73 *con* learn by heart   76 *devices* plans. *draw a bill* draw up a list   78 *obscenely* (An unintentionally funny blunder, whatever Bottom meant to say.)   79 *perfect* i.e., letter-perfect in memorizing your parts   81 *Hold . . . bowstrings* (An archer's expression, not definitely explained, but probably meaning here "keep your promises, or give up the play.")   3 *Thorough* through   4 *pale* enclosure   7 *sphere* orbit   9 *dew* sprinkle with dew. *orbs* circles, i.e., fairy rings (circular bands of grass, darker than the surrounding area, caused by fungi enriching the soil)   10 *pensioners* retainers, members of the royal bodyguard   12 *favors* love tokens   13 *savors* sweet smells   16 *lob* country bumpkin   17 *anon* at once

For Oberon is passing fell° and wrath,°   20
Because that she as her attendant hath
A lovely boy, stolen from an Indian king;
She never had so sweet a changeling.°
And jealous Oberon would have the child
Knight of his train, to trace° the forests wild.   25
But she perforce° withholds the lovèd boy,
Crowns him with flowers, and makes him all her joy.
And now they never meet in grove or green,
By fountain° clear, or spangled starlight sheen,°
But they do square,° that all their elves for fear   30
Creep into acorn cups and hide them there.

Fairy: Either I mistake your shape and making quite,
Or else you are that shrewd° and knavish sprite°
Called Robin Goodfellow. Are not you he
That frights the maidens of the villagery,°   35
Skim milk,° and sometimes labor in the quern,°
And bootless° make the breathless huswife° churn,
And sometimes make the drink to bear no barm,°
Mislead night wanderers,° laughing at their harm?
Those that "Hobgoblin" call you, and "Sweet Puck,"°   40
You do their work, and they shall have good luck.
Are you not he?

Puck: Thou speakest aright;
I am that merry wanderer of the night.
I jest to Oberon and make him smile
When I a fat and bean-fed° horse beguile,   45
Neighing in likeness of a filly foal;
And sometimes lurk I in a gossip's° bowl
In very likeness of a roasted crab,°
And when she drinks, against her lips I bob
And on her withered dewlap° pour the ale.   50
The wisest aunt,° telling the saddest° tale,
Sometimes for three-foot stool mistaketh me;
Then slip I from her bum, down topples she,
And "Tailor"° cries, and falls into a cough;
And then the whole choir° hold their hips and laugh,   55
And waxen° in their mirth, and neeze,° and swear

---

20 *passing fell* exceedingly angry. *wrath* wrathful 23 *changeling* child exchanged for another by the fairies 25 *trace* range through 26 *perforce* forcibly 29 *fountain* spring. *starlight sheen* shining starlight 30 *square* quarrel 33 *shrewd* mischievous. *sprite* spirit 35 *villagery* village population 36 *Skim milk* i.e., steal the cream. *quern* hand mill (where Puck presumably hampers the grinding of grain) 37 *bootless* in vain (Puck prevents the cream from turning to butter.) *huswife* housewife 38 *barm* head on the ale (Puck prevents the barm or yeast from producing fermentation.) 39 *Mislead night wanderers* i.e., mislead with false fire those who walk abroad at night (hence earning Puck his other names of Jack o' Lantern and Will o' the Wisp) 40 *Those . . . Puck* i.e., those who call you by the names you favor rather than those denoting the mischief you do. 45 *bean-fed* well fed on field beans 47 *gossip's* old woman's 48 *crab* crab apple 50 *dewlap* loose skin on neck 51 *aunt* old woman. *saddest* most serious 54 *Tailor* (possibly because she ends up sitting cross-legged on the floor, looking like a tailor, or else referring to the *tail* or buttocks.) 55 *choir* company 56 *waxen* increase. *neeze* sneeze

A merrier hour was never wasted° there.
But, room,° fairy! Here comes Oberon.
Fairy: And here my mistress. Would that he were gone!

*Enter [Oberon] the King of Fairies at one door, with his train, and [Titania] the
Queen at another, with hers.*

Oberon: Ill met by moonlight, proud Titania.   60
Titania: What, jealous Oberon? Fairies, skip hence.
I have forsworn his bed and company.
Oberon: Tarry, rash wanton.° Am not I thy lord?
Titania: Then I must be thy lady; but I know
When thou hast stolen away from Fairyland   65
And in the shape of Corin° sat all day,
Playing on pipes of corn° and versing love
To amorous Phillida.° Why art thou here
Come from the farthest step° of India,
But that, forsooth, the bouncing Amazon,   70
Your buskined° mistress and your warrior love,
To Theseus must be wedded, and you come
To give their bed joy and prosperity.
Oberon: How canst thou thus for shame, Titania,
Glance at my credit with Hippolyta,°   75
Knowing I know thy love to Theseus?
Didst not thou lead him through the glimmering night
From Perigenia,° whom he ravishèd?
And make him with fair Aegles° break his faith,
With Ariadne° and Antiopa?°   80
Titania: These are the forgeries of jealousy;
And never, since the middle summer's spring,°
Met we on hill, in dale, forest, or mead,°
By pavèd° fountain or by rushy° brook,
Or in° the beachèd margent° of the sea,   85
To dance our ringlets° to° the whistling wind,
But with thy brawls thou hast disturbed our sport.
Therefore the winds, piping to us in vain,
As in revenge, have sucked up from the sea
Contagious° fogs which, falling in the land,   90
Hath every pelting° river made so proud

57 *wasted* spent 58 *room* stand aside, make room 63 *wanton* headstrong creature 66, 68 *Corin, Phillida*
(Conventional names of pastoral lovers.) 67 *corn* (Here, oat stalks.) 69 *step* farthest limit of travel, or,
perhaps, *steep,* "mountain range" 71 *buskined* wearing half-boots called *buskins* 75 *Glance . . . Hippolyta*
make insinuations about my favored relationship with Hippolyta 78 *Perigenia* i.e., Perigouna, one of
Theseus's conquests. (This and the following women are named in Thomas North's translation of Plutarch's "Life of Theseus.") 79 *Aegles* i.e., Aegle, for whom Theseus deserted Ariadne according to some
accounts 80 *Ariadne* the daughter of Minos, King of Crete, who helped Theseus to escape the labyrinth
after killing the Minotaur; later she was abandoned by Theseus. *Antiopa* Queen of the Amazons and wife
of Theseus; elsewhere identified with Hippolyta, but here thought of as a separate woman 82 *middle
summer's spring* beginning of midsummer 83 *mead* meadow 84 *pavèd* with pebbled bottom. *rushy* bordered
with rushes 85 *in* on. *margent* edge, border 86 *ringlets* dances in a ring. (See *orbs* in line 9.) *to* to the
sound of 90 *Contagious* noxious 91 *pelting* paltry

Titania and Oberon.

That they have overborne their continents.°
The ox hath therefore stretched his yoke° in vain,
The plowman lost his sweat, and the green corn°
Hath rotted ere his youth attained a beard;   95
The fold° stands empty in the drownèd field,
And crows are fatted with the murrain° flock;
The nine-men's morris° is filled up with mud,
And the quaint mazes° in the wanton° green
For lack of tread are undistinguishable.   100

92 *continents* banks that contain them   93 *stretched his yoke* i.e., pulled at his yoke in plowing   94 *corn* grain of any kind   96 *fold* pen for sheep or cattle   97 *murrain* having died of the plague   98 *nine-men's morris* i.e., portion of the village green marked out in a square for a game played with nine pebbles or pegs   99 *quaint mazes* i.e., intricate paths marked out on the village green to be followed rapidly on foot as a kind of contest.   *wanton* luxuriant

The human mortals want° their winter° here;
No night is now with hymn or carol blessed.
Therefore° the moon, the governess of floods,
Pale in her anger, washes° all the air,
That rheumatic diseases° do abound.   105
And thorough this distemperature° we see
The seasons alter: hoary-headed frosts
Fall in the fresh lap of the crimson rose,
And on old Hiems'° thin and icy crown
An odorous chaplet of sweet summer buds   110
Is, as in mockery, set. The spring, the summer,
The childing° autumn, angry winter, change
Their wonted liveries,° and the mazèd° world
By their increase° now knows not which is which.
And this same progeny of evils comes   115
From our debate,° from our dissension.
We are their parents and original.°
Oberon: Do you amend it, then. It lies in you.
Why should Titania cross her Oberon?
I do but beg a little changeling boy   120
To be my henchman.°
Titania: Set your heart at rest.
The fairy land buys not the child of me.
His mother was a vot'ress of my order,°
And in the spicèd Indian air by night
Full often hath she gossiped by my side   125
And sat with me on Neptune's yellow sands,
Marking th' embarkèd traders° on the flood,°
When we have laughed to see the sails conceive
And grow big-bellied with the wanton° wind;
Which she, with pretty and with swimming° gait,   130
Following—her womb then rich with my young squire—
Would imitate, and sail upon the land
To fetch me trifles, and return again
As from a voyage, rich with merchandise.
But she, being mortal, of that boy did die;   135
And for her sake do I rear up her boy,
And for her sake I will not part with him.
Oberon: How long within this wood intend you stay?
Titania: Perchance till after Theseus' wedding day.
If you will patiently dance in our round°   140

---

101 *want* lack. *winter* i.e., regular winter season; or, proper observances of winter, such as the *hymn or carol* in the next line (?) 103 *Therefore* i.e., as a result of our quarrel 104 *washes* saturates with moisture 105 *rheumatic diseases* colds, flu, and other respiratory infections 106 *distemperature* disturbance in nature 109 *Hiems'* the winter god's 112 *childing* fruitful, pregnant 113 *wonted liveries* usual apparel. *mazèd* bewildered 114 *their increase* their yield, what they produce 116 *debate* quarrel 117 *original* origin 121 *henchman* attendant, page 123 *was . . . order* had taken a vow to serve me 127 *traders* trading vessels. *flood* flood tide 129 *wanton* (1) playful (2) amorous 130 *swimming* smooth, gliding 140 *round* circular dance

Oberon directs Puck to fetch the magic flower.

And see our moonlight revels, go with us;
    If not, shun me, and I will spare° your haunts.
Oberon: Give me that boy, and I will go with thee.
Titania: Not for thy fairy kingdom. Fairies, away!
    We shall chide downright, if I longer stay.   145
                                        Exeunt [Titania with her train].
Oberon: Well, go thy way. Thou shalt not from° this grove
    Till I torment thee for this injury.
    My gentle Puck, come hither. Thou rememb'rest
    Since° once I sat upon a promontory,
    And heard a mermaid on a dolphin's back   150
    Uttering such dulcet° and harmonious breath°

142 *spare* shun   146 *from* go from   149 *Since* when   151 *dulcet* sweet.   *breath* voice, song

    That the rude° sea grew civil at her song,
    And certain stars shot madly from their spheres
    To hear the sea-maid's music?

Puck: I remember.

Oberon: That very time I saw, but thou couldst not,   155
    Flying between the cold moon and the earth
    Cupid, all° armed. A certain° aim he took
    At a fair vestal° thronèd by° the west,
    And loosed° his love shaft smartly from his bow
    As° it should pierce a hundred thousand hearts;   160
    But I might° see young Cupid's fiery shaft
    Quenched in the chaste beams of the watery moon,
    And the imperial vot'ress passèd on,
    In maiden meditation, fancy-free.°
    Yet marked I where the bolt° of Cupid fell: 165
    It fell upon a little western flower,
    Before milk-white, now purple with love's wound,
    And maidens call it love-in-idleness.°
    Fetch me that flower; the herb I showed thee once.
    The juice of it on sleeping eyelids laid   170
    Will make or man or° woman madly dote
    Upon the next live creature that it sees.
    Fetch me this herb, and be thou here again
    Ere the leviathan° can swim a league.

Puck: I'll put a girdle round about the earth   175
    In forty° minutes.   *[Exit.]*

Oberon: Having once this juice,
    I'll watch Titania when she is asleep
    And drop the liquor of it in her eyes.
    The next thing then she waking looks upon,
    Be it on lion, bear, or wolf, or bull,   180
    On meddling monkey, or on busy ape,
    She shall pursue it with the soul of love.
    And ere I take this charm from off her sight,
    As I can take it with another herb,
    I'll make her render up her page to me.   185
    But who comes here? I am invisible,
    And I will overhear their conference.

    Enter Demetrius, Helena following him.

Demetrius: I love thee not; therefore pursue me not.
    Where is Lysander and fair Hermia?
    The one I'll slay; the other slayeth me.   190

---

152 *rude* rough   157 *all* fully.   *certain* sure   158 *vestal* vestal virgin. (Contains a complimentary allusion to Queen Elizabeth as a votaress of Diana and probably refers to an actual entertainment in her honor at Elvetham in 1591.)   *by* in the region of   159 *loosed* released   160 *As* as if   161 *might* could   164 *fancy-free* free of love's spell   165 *bolt* arrow   168 *love-in-idleness* pansy, heartsease   171 *or . . . or* either . . . or   174 *leviathan* sea monster, whale   176 *forty* (Used indefinitely.)

Thou toldst me they were stol'n unto this wood;
And here am I, and wood° within this wood
Because I cannot meet my Hermia.
Hence, get thee gone, and follow me no more.

Helena: You draw me, you hardhearted adamant!° 195
But yet you draw not iron, for my heart
Is true as steel. Leave you° your power to draw,
And I shall have no power to follow you.

Demetrius: Do I entice you? Do I speak you fair?°
Or rather do I not in plainest truth 200
Tell you I do not nor I cannot love you?

Helena: And even for that do I love you the more.
I am your spaniel; and, Demetrius,
The more you beat me I will fawn on you.
Use me but as your spaniel, spurn me, strike me, 205
Neglect me, lose me; only give me leave,
Unworthy as I am, to follow you.
What worser place can I beg in your love—
And yet a place of high respect with me—
Than to be usèd as you use your dog? 210

Demetrius: Tempt not too much the hatred of my spirit,
For I am sick when I do look on thee.

Helena: And I am sick when I look not on you.

Demetrius: You do impeach° your modesty too much
To leave° the city and commit yourself 215
Into the hands of one that loves you not,
To trust the opportunity of night
And the ill counsel of a desert° place
With the rich worth of your virginity.

Helena: Your virtue° is my privilege.° For that° 220
It is not night when I do see your face,
Therefore I think I am not in the night;
Nor doth this wood lack worlds of company,
For you, in my respect,° are all the world.
Then how can it be said I am alone 225
When all the world is here to look on me?

Demetrius: I'll run from thee and hide me in the brakes,°
And leave thee to the mercy of wild beasts.

Helena: The wildest hath not such a heart as you.
Run when you will. The story shall be changed: 230
Apollo flies and Daphne holds the chase,°

---

192 *and wood* and mad, frantic (with an obvious word play on *wood*, meaning "woods") 195 *adamant* lodestone, magnet (with pun on *hardhearted*, since adamant was also thought to be the hardest of all stones and was confused with the diamond) 197 *Leave you* give up 199 *speak you fair* speak courteously to you 214 *impeach* call into question 215 *To leave* by leaving 218 *desert* deserted 220 *virtue* goodness or power to attract. *privilege* safeguard, warrant. *For that* because 224 *in my respect* as far as I am concerned, in my esteem 227 *brakes* thickets 231 *Apollo . . . chase* (In the ancient myth, Daphne fled from Apollo and was saved from rape by being transformed into a laurel tree; here it is the female who *holds the chase*, or pursues, instead of the male.)

"Let me go!" Demetrius tells Helena after she follows him into the woods (II, i, 235).

The dove pursues the griffin,° the mild hind°
Makes speed to catch the tiger—bootless° speed,
When cowardice pursues and valor flies!
Demetrius: I will not stay° thy questions.° Let me go!   235
    Or if thou follow me, do not believe
    But I shall do thee mischief in the wood.
Helena: Ay, in the temple, in the town, the field,
    You do me mischief. Fie, Demetrius!
    Your wrongs do set a scandal on my sex.°   240

232 *griffin* a fabulous monster with the head and wings of an eagle and the body of a lion. *hind* female
deer   233 *bootless* fruitless   235 *stay* wait for, put up with. *questions* talk or argument   240 *Your . . . sex*
i.e., the wrongs that you do me cause me to act in a manner that disgraces my sex

We cannot fight for love, as men may do;
We should be wooed and were not made to woo.

[*Exit Demetrius.*]

I'll follow thee and make a heaven of hell,
To die upon° the hand I love so well. [*Exit.*]
Oberon: Fare thee well, nymph. Ere he do leave this grove, 245
Thou shalt fly him, and he shall seek thy love.

Enter Puck.

Hast thou the flower there? Welcome, wanderer.
Puck: Ay, there it is. [*He offers the flower.*]
Oberon: I pray thee, give it me.
I know a bank where the wild thyme blows,°
Where oxlips° and the nodding violet grows, 250
Quite overcanopied with luscious woodbine,°
With sweet muskroses° and with eglantine.°
There sleeps Titania sometimes of° the night,
Lulled in these flowers with dances and delight;
And there the snake throws° her enameled skin, 255
Weed° wide enough to wrap a fairy in.
And with the juice of this I'll streak° her eyes
And make her full of hateful fantasies.
Take thou some of it, and seek through this grove.

[*He gives some love juice.*]

A sweet Athenian lady is in love 260
With a disdainful youth. Anoint his eyes,
But do it when the next thing he espies
May be the lady. Thou shalt know the man
By the Athenian garments he hath on.
Effect it with some care, that he may prove 265
More fond on° her than she upon her love;
And look thou meet me ere the first cock crow.
Puck: Fear not, my lord, your servant shall do so.

Exeunt [separately].

SCENE II [THE WOOD.]

Enter Titania, Queen of Fairies, with her train.

Titania: Come, now a roundel° and a fairy song;
Then, for the third part of a minute,° hence—
Some to kill cankers° in the muskrose buds,
Some war with reremice° for their leathern wings

---

244 *upon* by   249 *blows* blooms   250 *oxlips* flowers resembling cowslip and primrose   251 *woodbine* honeysuckle   252 *muskroses* a kind of large, sweet-scented rose.   *eglantine* sweetbrier, another kind of rose   253 *sometimes of* for part of   255 *throws* sloughs off, sheds   256 *Weed* garment   257 *streak* anoint, touch gently   266 *fond on* doting on   1 *roundel* dance in a ring   2 *the third . . . minute* (Indicative of the fairies' quickness.)   3 *cankers* cankerworms (i.e., caterpillars or grubs)   4 *reremice* bats

To make my small elves coats, and some keep back   5
The clamorous owl, that nightly hoots and wonders
At our quaint° spirits. Sing me now asleep.
Then to your offices, and let me rest.

Fairies sing.

First Fairy: You spotted snakes with double° tongue,
                Thorny hedgehogs, be not seen;   10
        Newts° and blindworms, do no wrong;
                Come not near our Fairy Queen.
Chorus [dancing]:   Philomel,° with melody
                Sing in our sweet lullaby;
        Lulla, lulla, lullaby, lulla, lulla, lullaby.   15
                Never harm
                Nor spell nor charm
        Come our lovely lady nigh.
        So good night, with lullaby.
First Fairy: Weaving spiders, come not here;   20
                Hence, you long-legged spinners, hence!
        Beetles black, approach not near;
                Worm nor snail, do no offense.°
Chorus [dancing]: Philomel, with melody
                Sing in our sweet lullaby;   25
        Lulla, lulla, lullaby, lulla, lulla, lullaby.
                Never harm
                Nor spell nor charm
        Come our lovely lady nigh.
        So good night, with lullaby.   30

                                            [Titania sleeps.]

Second Fairy: Hence, away! Now all is well.
        One aloof stand sentinel.°

                     [Exeunt Fairies, leaving one sentinel.]

Enter Oberon [and squeezes the flower on Titania's eyelids].

Oberon: What thou seest when thou dost wake,
        Do it for thy true love take;
        Love and languish for his sake.   35
        Be it ounce,° or cat, or bear,
        Pard,° or boar with bristled hair,
        In thy eye that shall appear
        When thou wak'st, it is thy dear.
        Wake when some vile thing is near.   *[Exit.]* 40

---

7 *quaint* dainty   9 *double* forked   11 *Newts* water lizards (considered poisonous, as were *blindworms*—small snakes with tiny eyes—and spiders)   13 *Philomel* the nightingale. (Philomela, daughter of King Pandion, was transformed into a nightingale, according to Ovid's *Metamorphoses* 6, after she had been raped by her sister Procne's husband, Tereus.)   23 *offense* harm   32 *sentinel* (Presumably Oberon is able to outwit or intimidate this guard.)   36 *ounce* lynx   37 *Pard* leopard

Oberon squeezes the magic flower's juice onto Titania's eyelids.

Enter Lysander and Hermia.

Lysander: Fair love, you faint with wandering in the wood;
    And to speak truth, I have forgot our way.
    We'll rest us, Hermia, if you think it good,
    And tarry for the comfort of the day.
Hermia: Be it so, Lysander. Find you out a bed,   45
    For I upon this bank will rest my head.
Lysander: One turf shall serve as pillow for us both;
    One heart, one bed, two bosoms, and one troth.°
Hermia: Nay, good Lysander, for my sake, my dear,
    Lie further off yet. Do not lie so near.   50

48 *troth* faith, trothplight

Lysander: O, take the sense, sweet, of my innocence!°
    Love takes the meaning in love's conference.°
    I mean that my heart unto yours is knit,
    So that but one heart we can make of it;
    Two bosoms interchainèd with an oath—   55
    So then two bosoms and a single troth.
    Then by your side no bed-room me deny,
    For lying so, Hermia, I do not lie.°
Hermia: Lysander riddles very prettily.
    Now much beshrew° my manners and my pride   60
    If Hermia meant to say Lysander lied.
    But, gentle friend, for love and courtesy
    Lie further off, in human° modesty.
    Such separation as may well be said
    Becomes a virtuous bachelor and a maid,   65
    So far be distant; and good night, sweet friend.
    Thy love ne'er alter till thy sweet life end!
Lysander: Amen, amen, to that fair prayer, say I,
    And then end life when I end loyalty!
    Here is my bed. Sleep give thee all his rest!   70
Hermia: With half that wish the wisher's eyes be pressed!°
                  [*They sleep, separated by a short distance.*]

    Enter Puck.

Puck: Through the forest have I gone,
        But Athenian found I none
        On whose eyes I might approve°
        This flower's force in stirring love.   75
        Night and silence.—Who is here?
        Weeds of Athens he doth wear.
        This is he, my master said,
        Despisèd the Athenian maid;
        And here the maiden, sleeping sound,   80
        On the dank and dirty ground.
        Pretty soul, she durst not lie
        Near this lack-love, this kill-courtesy.
        Churl, upon thy eyes I throw
        All the power this charm doth owe.°   85
                  [*He applies the love juice.*]
        When thou wak'st, let love forbid
        Sleep his seat on thy eyelid.
        So awake when I am gone,
        For I must now to Oberon.   *Exit.*

---

51 *take . . . innocence* i.e., interpret my intention as innocent   52 *Love . . . conference* i.e., when lovers confer, love teaches each lover to interpret the other's meaning lovingly   58 *lie* tell a falsehood (with a riddling pun on *lie,* "recline")   60 *beshrew* curse. (But mildly meant.)   63 *human* courteous (and perhaps suggesting "humane," the Quarto spelling)   71 *With . . . pressed* i.e., may we share your wish, so that your eyes too are *pressed,* closed, in sleep   74 *approve* test   85 *owe* own

Enter Demetrius and Helena, running.

Helena: Stay, though thou kill me, sweet Demetrius!   90
Demetrius: I charge thee, hence, and do not haunt me thus.
Helena: O, wilt thou darkling° leave me? Do not so.
Demetrius: Stay, on thy peril!° I alone will go.   [*Exit.*]
Helena: O, I am out of breath in this fond° chase!
    The more my prayer, the lesser is my grace.°   95
    Happy is Hermia, wheresoe'er she lies,°
    For she hath blessèd and attractive eyes.
    How came her eyes so bright? Not with salt tears;
    If so, my eyes are oftener washed than hers.
    No, no, I am as ugly as a bear,   100
    For beasts that meet me run away for fear.
    Therefore no marvel though Demetrius
    Do, as a monster, fly my presence thus.°
    What wicked and dissembling glass of mine
    Made me compare° with Hermia's sphery eyne?°   105
    But who is here? Lysander, on the ground?
    Dead, or asleep? I see no blood, no wound.
    Lysander, if you live, good sir, awake.
Lysander [*awaking*]: And run through fire I will for thy sweet sake.
    Transparent° Helena! Nature shows art,°   110
    That through thy bosom makes me see thy heart.
    Where is Demetrius? O, how fit a word
    Is that vile name to perish on my sword!
Helena: Do not say so, Lysander, say not so.
    What though he love your Hermia? Lord, what though?   115
    Yet Hermia still loves you. Then be content.
Lysander: Content with Hermia? No! I do repent
    The tedious minutes I with her have spent.
    Not Hermia but Helena I love.
    Who will not change a raven for a dove?   120
    The will° of man is by his reason swayed,
    And reason says you are the worthier maid.
    Things growing are not ripe until their season;
    So I, being young, till now ripe not° to reason.
    And, touching° now the point° of human skill,°   125
    Reason becomes the marshal to my will
    And leads me to your eyes, where I o'erlook°
    Love's stories written in love's richest book.
Helena: Wherefore° was I to this keen mockery born?
    When at your hands did I deserve this scorn?   130

---

92 *darkling* in the dark   93 *on thy peril* i.e., on pain of danger to you if you don't obey me and stay   94 *fond* doting   95 *my grace* the favor I obtain   96 *lies* dwells   102–103 *no marvel . . . thus* i.e., no wonder that Demetrius flies from me as from a monster   105 *compare* vie.   *sphery eyne* eyes as bright as stars in their spheres   110 *Transparent* (1) radiant (2) able to be seen through, lacking in deceit.   *art* skill, magic power   121 *will* desire   124 *ripe not* (am) not ripened   125 *touching* reaching.   *point* summit.   *skill* judgment   127 *o'erlook* read   129 *Wherefore* why

Is 't not enough, is 't not enough, young man,
That I did never—no, nor never can—
Deserve a sweet look from Demetrius' eye,
But you must flout my insufficiency?
Good troth, you do me wrong, good sooth,° you do, 135
In such disdainful manner me to woo.
But fare you well. Perforce I must confess
I thought you lord of° more true gentleness.°
O, that a lady, of° one man refused,
Should of another therefore be abused!°   *Exit.* 140

Lysander: She sees not Hermia. Hermia, sleep thou there,
And never mayst thou come Lysander near!
For as a surfeit of the sweetest things
The deepest loathing to the stomach brings,
Or as the heresies that men do leave 145
Are hated most of those they did deceive,°
So thou, my surfeit and my heresy,
Of all be hated, but the most of° me!
And, all my powers, address° your love and might
To honor Helen and to be her knight!   *Exit.* 150

Hermia [awaking]: Help me, Lysander, help me! Do thy best
To pluck this crawling serpent from my breast!
Ay me, for pity! What a dream was here!
Lysander, look how I do quake with fear.
Methought a serpent ate my heart away, 155
And you sat smiling at his cruel prey.°
Lysander! What, removed? Lysander! Lord!
What, out of hearing? Gone? No sound, no word?
Alack, where are you? Speak, an if° you hear;
Speak, of all loves!° I swoon almost with fear. 160
No? Then I well perceive you are not nigh.
Either death, or you, I'll find immediately.

Exit. [The sleeping Titania remains.]

ACT III

SCENE I [THE ACTION IS CONTINUOUS.]

Enter the clowns° [Quince, Snug, Bottom, Flute, Snout, and Starveling].

Bottom: Are we all met?

Quince: Pat,° pat; and here's a marvelous convenient place for our rehearsal.
This green plot shall be our stage, this hawthorn brake° our tiring-house,°
and we will do it in action as we will do it before the Duke.

135 *Good troth, good sooth* i.e., indeed, truly   138 *lord of* i.e., possessor of.   *gentleness* courtesy   139 *of*
by   140 *abused* ill treated   145–146 *as . . . deceive* as renounced heresies are hated most by those persons
who formerly were deceived by them   148 *Of . . . of* by . . . by   149 *address* direct, apply   156 *prey* act
of preying   159 *an if* if   160 *of all loves* for all love's sake   s.d. *clowns* rustics   2 *Pat* on the dot, punctu-
ally   3 *brake* thicket.   *tiring-house* attiring area, hence backstage

Bottom: Peter Quince?   5
Quince: What sayest thou, bully° Bottom?
Bottom: There are things in this comedy of Pyramus and Thisbe that will never
    please. First, Pyramus must draw a sword to kill himself, which the ladies
    cannot abide. How answer you that?
Snout: By 'r lakin,° a parlous° fear.   10
Starveling: I believe we must leave the killing out, when all is done.°
Bottom: Not a whit. I have a device to make all well. Write me° a prologue, and let
    the prologue seem to say, we will do no harm with our swords, and that Pyramus
    is not killed indeed; and for the more better assurance, tell them that I, Pyra-
    mus, am not Pyramus but Bottom the weaver. This will put them out of fear.   15
Quince: Well, we will have such a prologue, and it shall be written in eight and six.°
Bottom: No, make it two more: let it be written in eight and eight.
Snout: Will not the ladies be afeard of the lion?
Starveling: I fear it, I promise you.
Bottom: Masters, you ought to consider with yourself, to bring in—God shield   20
    us!—a lion among ladies° is a most dreadful thing. For there is not a more
    fearful° wildfowl than your lion living, and we ought to look to 't.
Snout: Therefore another prologue must tell he is not a lion.
Bottom: Nay, you must name his name, and half his face must be seen through
    the lion's neck, and he himself must speak through, saying thus or to the   25
    same defect:° "Ladies," or "Fair ladies, I would wish you," or "I would request
    you," or "I would entreat you, not to fear, not to tremble; my life for yours.°
    If you think I come hither as a lion, it were pity of my life.° No, I am no such
    thing; I am a man as other men are." And there indeed let him name his
    name, and tell them plainly he is Snug the joiner.   30
Quince: Well, it shall be so. But there is two hard things: that is, to bring the moon-
    light into a chamber; for, you know, Pyramus and Thisbe meet by moonlight.
Snout: Doth the moon shine that night we play our play?
Bottom: A calendar, a calendar! Look in the almanac. Find out moonshine, find
    out moonshine.   35
                                                                [*They consult an almanac.*]
Quince: Yes, it doth shine that night.
Bottom: Why then may you leave a casement of the great chamber window
    where we play open, and the moon may shine in at the casement.
Quince: Ay; or else one must come in with a bush of thorns° and a lantern and
    say he comes to disfigure,° or to present,° the person of Moonshine. Then   40
    there is another thing: we must have a wall in the great chamber; for Pyra-
    mus and Thisbe, says the story, did talk through the chink of a wall.

6 *bully* i.e., worthy, jolly, fine fellow   10 *By 'r lakin* by our ladykin, i.e., the Virgin Mary.   *parlous* peril-
ous, alarming   11 *when all is done* i.e., when all is said and done   12 *Write me* i.e., write at my suggestion
(*Me* is used colloquially.)   16 *eight and six* alternate lines of eight and six syllables, a common ballad
measure   21 *lion among ladies* (A contemporary pamphlet tells how, at the christening in 1594 of Prince
Henry, eldest son of King James VI of Scotland, later James I of England, a "blackamoor" instead of a
lion drew the triumphal chariot, since the lion's presence might have "brought some fear to the nearest.")   22 *fearful* fear-inspiring   26 *defect* (Bottom's blunder for "effect.")   27 *my life for yours* i.e., I
pledge my life to make your lives safe   28 *it were . . . life* i.e., I should be sorry, by my life; or, my life would
be endangered   39 *bush of thorns* bundle of thornbush faggots (part of the accoutrements of the man in
the moon, according to the popular notions of the time, along with his lantern and his dog)   40 *disfigure*
(Quince's blunder for "figure.")   *present* represent

Snout: You can never bring in a wall. What say you, Bottom?

Bottom: Some man or other must present Wall. And let him have some plaster, or some loam, or some roughcast° about him, to signify wall; or let him hold 45
his fingers thus, and through that cranny shall Pyramus and Thisbe whisper.

Quince: If that may be, then all is well. Come, sit down, every mother's son, and rehearse your parts. Pyramus, you begin. When you have spoken your speech, enter into that brake, and so everyone according to his cue.

Enter Robin [Puck].

Puck [aside]: What hempen homespuns° have we swaggering here 50
So near the cradle° of the Fairy Queen?
What, a play toward?° I'll be an auditor;
An actor, too, perhaps, if I see cause.

Quince: Speak, Pyramus. Thisbe, stand forth.

Bottom [as Pyramus]: "Thisbe, the flowers of odious savors sweet—" 55

Quince: Odors, odors.

Bottom: "—Odors savors sweet;
So hath thy breath, my dearest Thisbe dear.
But hark, a voice! Stay thou but here awhile,
And by and by I will to thee appear."   *Exit.* 60

Puck: A stranger Pyramus than e'er played here.°   *[Exit.]*

Flute: Must I speak now?

Quince: Ay, marry, must you; for you must understand he goes but to see a noise that he heard, and is to come again.

Flute [as Thisbe]: "Most radiant Pyramus, most lily-white of hue, 65
Of color like the red rose on triumphant° brier,
Most brisky juvenal° and eke° most lovely Jew,°
As true as truest horse that yet would never tire.
I'll meet thee, Pyramus, at Ninny's tomb."

Quince: "Ninus'° tomb," man. Why, you must not speak that yet. That you 70
answer to Pyramus: You speak all your part° at once, cues and all. Pyramus,
enter. Your cue is past; it is "never tire."

Flute: O—"As true as truest horse, that yet would never tire."

[Enter Puck, and Bottom as Pyramus with the ass head.°]

Bottom: "If I were fair,° Thisbe, I were° only thine."

Quince: O, monstrous! O, strange! We are haunted. Pray, masters! Fly, masters! 75
Help!

[Exeunt Quince, Snug, Flute, Snout, and Starveling.]

45 *roughcast* a mixture of lime and gravel used to plaster the outside of buildings   50 *hempen homespuns* i.e., rustics dressed in clothes woven of coarse, homespun fabric made from hemp   51 *cradle* i.e., Titania's bower   52 *toward* about to take place   61 *A stranger . . . here* (Either Puck refers to an earlier dramatic version played in the same theater, or he has conceived of a plan to present a "stranger" Pyramus than ever seen before.)   66 *triumphant* magnificent   67 *brisky juvenal* lively youth.   *eke* also.   *Jew* (An absurd repetition of the first syllable of *juvenal*, and an indication of how desperately Quince searches for his rhymes.)   70 *Ninus* mythical founder of Nineveh (whose wife, Semiramis, was supposed to have built the walls of Babylon where the story of Pyramus and Thisbe takes place)   71 *part* (An actor's *part* was a script consisting only of his speeches and their cues.)   s.d. *with the ass head* (This stage direction, taken from the Folio, presumably refers to a standard stage property.)   74 *fair* handsome.   *were* would be

Bottom is transformed into an ass.

Puck: I'll follow you, I'll lead you about a round,°
    Thorough bog, thorough bush, thorough brake, thorough brier.
  Sometimes a horse I'll be, sometimes a hound,
    A hog, a headless bear, sometimes a fire;°   80
  And neigh, and bark, and grunt, and roar, and burn,
    Like horse, hound, hog, bear, fire, at every turn.   *Exit.*
Bottom: Why do they run away? This is a knavery of them to make me afeard.

    Enter Snout.

Snout: O Bottom, thou art changed! What do I see on thee?
Bottom: What do you see? You see an ass head of your own, do you?   85
                                          [Exit Snout.]

77 *about a round* roundabout   80 *fire* will-o'-the-wisp

Enter Quince.

Quince: Bless thee, Bottom, bless thee! Thou art translated.°   *Exit.*

Bottom: I see their knavery. This is to make an ass of me, to fright me, if they
     could. But I will not stir from this place, do what they can. I will walk up
     and down here, and will sing, that they shall hear I am not afraid.

                                            [He sings.]

           The ouzel cock° so black of hue,   90
              With orange-tawny bill,
           The throstle° with his note so true,
              The wren with little quill°—

Titania [awaking]: What angel wakes me from my flowery bed?

Bottom [sings]:   The finch, the sparrow, and the lark,   95
              The plainsong° cuckoo gray,
           Whose note full many a man doth mark,
              And dares not answer nay°—

     For, indeed, who would set his wit to° so foolish a bird? Who would give a
     bird the lie,° though he cry "cuckoo" never so?°   100

Titania: I pray thee, gentle mortal, sing again.
     Mine ear is much enamored of thy note;
     So is mine eye enthrallèd to thy shape;
     And thy fair virtue's force° perforce doth move me
     On the first view to say, to swear, I love thee.   105

Bottom: Methinks, mistress, you should have little reason for that. And yet, to
     say the truth, reason and love keep little company together nowadays—the
     more the pity that some honest neighbors will not make them friends. Nay,
     I can gleek° upon occasion.

Titania: Thou art as wise as thou art beautiful.   110

Bottom: Not so, neither. But if I had wit enough to get out of this wood, I have
     enough to serve mine own turn.°

Titania: Out of this wood do not desire to go.
     Thou shalt remain here, whether thou wilt or no.
     I am a spirit of no common rate.°   115
     The summer still doth tend upon my state,°
     And I do love thee. Therefore go with me.
     I'll give thee fairies to attend on thee,
     And they shall fetch thee jewels from the deep,
     And sing while thou on pressèd flowers dost sleep.   120
     And I will purge thy mortal grossness° so
     That thou shalt like an airy spirit go.
     Peaseblossom, Cobweb, Mote,° and Mustardseed!

---

86 *translated* transformed   90 *ouzel cock* male blackbird   92 *throstle* song thrush   93 *quill* (Literally, a reed
pipe; hence, the bird's piping song.)   96 *plainsong* singing a melody without variations   98 *dares . . . nay*
i.e., cannot deny that he is a cuckold   99 *set his wit to* employ his intelligence to answer   99–100 *give . . .
lie* call the bird a liar   100 *never so* ever so much   104 *thy . . . force* the power of your unblemished excellence   109 *gleek* jest   112 *. . . turn* answer my purpose   115 *rate* rank, value   116 *still . . . state*
always waits upon me as a part of my royal retinue   121 *mortal grossness* materiality (i.e., the corporeal
nature of a mortal being)   123 *Mote* i.e., speck. (The two words *moth* and *mote* were pronounced alike,
and both meanings may be present.)

Enter four Fairies [Peaseblossom, Cobweb, Mote, and Mustardseed].

Peaseblossom: Ready.
Cobweb: And I.
Mote: And I.
Mustardseed: And I.
All: Where shall we go?   125
Titania: Be kind and courteous to this gentleman.
　Hop in his walks and gambol in his eyes;°
　Feed him with apricots and dewberries,°
　With purple grapes, green figs, and mulberries;
　The honey bags steal from the humble-bees,   130
　And for night tapers crop their waxen thighs
　And light them at the fiery glowworms' eyes,
　To have my love to bed and to arise;
　And pluck the wings from painted butterflies
　To fan the moonbeams from his sleeping eyes.   135
　Nod to him, elves, and do him courtesies.
Peaseblossom: Hail, mortal!
Cobweb: Hail!
Mote: Hail!
Mustardseed: Hail!   140
Bottom: I cry your worships mercy,° heartily. I beseech your worship's name.
Cobweb: Cobweb.
Bottom: I shall desire you of more acquaintance,° good Master Cobweb. If I cut
　my finger, I shall make bold with you.°—Your name, honest gentleman?
Peaseblossom: Peaseblossom.   145
Bottom: I pray you, commend me to Mistress Squash,° your mother, and to Master
　Peascod,° your father. Good Master Peaseblossom, I shall desire you of more
　acquaintance too.—Your name, I beseech you, sir?
Mustardseed: Mustardseed.
Bottom: Good Master Mustardseed, I know your patience° well. That same cow- 150
　ardly, giantlike ox-beef hath devoured many a gentleman of your house. I
　promise you, your kindred hath made my eyes water° ere now. I desire you of
　more acquaintance, good Master Mustardseed.
Titania: Come wait upon him; lead him to my bower.
　The moon methinks looks with a watery eye;   155
　And when she weeps,° weeps every little flower,
　Lamenting some enforcèd° chastity.
　Tie up my lover's tongue,° bring him silently.
　　　　　　　　　　　　　　　　　　　[Exeunt.]

---

127 *in his eyes* in his sight (i.e., before him)   128 *dewberries* blackberries   141 *I cry . . . mercy* I beg pardon
of your worships (for presuming to ask a question)   143 *I . . . acquaintance* I crave to be better acquainted
with you   143–144 *If . . . you* (Cobwebs were used to stanch bleeding.)   146 *Squash* unripe pea
pod   147 *Peascod* ripe pea pod   150 *your patience* what you have endured. (Mustard is eaten with beef.)
152 *water* (1) weep for sympathy (2) smart, sting   156 *she weeps* i.e., she causes dew   157 *enforcèd*
forced, violated; or, possibly, constrained (since Titania at this moment is hardly concerned about
chastity)   158 *Tie . . . tongue* (Presumably Bottom is braying like an ass.)

SCENE II [THE WOOD.]

    Enter [*Oberon,*] *King of Fairies.*

Oberon: I wonder if Titania be awaked;
    Then, what it was that next came in her eye,
    Which she must dote on in extremity.

    [*Enter*] *Robin Goodfellow* [*Puck*].

    Here comes my messenger. How now, mad spirit?
    What night-rule° now about this haunted° grove?   5
Puck: My mistress with a monster is in love.
    Near to her close° and consecrated bower,
    While she was in her dull° and sleeping hour,
    A crew of patches,° rude mechanicals,°
    That work for bread upon Athenian stalls,°   10
    Were met together to rehearse a play
    Intended for great Theseus' nuptial day.
    The shallowest thickskin of that barren sort,°
    Who Pyramus presented,° in their sport
    Forsook his scene° and entered in a brake.   15
    When I did him at this advantage take,
    An ass's noll° I fixèd on his head.
    Anon his Thisbe must be answerèd,
    And forth my mimic° comes. When they him spy,
    As wild geese that the creeping fowler° eye,   20
    Or russet-pated choughs,° many in sort,°
    Rising and cawing at the gun's report,
    Sever° themselves and madly sweep the sky,
    So, at his sight, away his fellows fly;
    And, at our stamp, here o'er and o'er one falls;   25
    He "Murder!" cries and help from Athens calls.
    Their sense thus weak, lost with their fears thus strong,
    Made senseless things begin to do them wrong,
    For briers and thorns at their apparel snatch;
    Some, sleeves—some, hats; from yielders all things catch.°   30
    I led them on in this distracted fear
    And left sweet Pyramus translated there,
    When in that moment, so it came to pass,
    Titania waked and straightway loved an ass.
Oberon: This falls out better than I could devise.   35
    But hast thou yet latched° the Athenian's eyes
    With the love juice, as I did bid thee do?

---

5 *night-rule* diversion or misrule for the night. *haunted* much frequented   7 *close* secret, private   8 *dull* drowsy   9 *patches* clowns, fools. *rude mechanicals* ignorant artisans   10 *stalls* market booths   13 *barren sort* stupid company or crew   14 *presented* acted   15 *scene* playing area   17 *noll* noddle, head   19 *mimic* burlesque actor   20 *fowler* hunter of game birds   21 *russet-pated choughs* reddish brown or gray-headed jackdaws. *in sort* in a flock   23 *Sever* i.e., scatter   30 *from . . . catch* i.e., everything preys on those who yield to fear   36 *latched* fastened, snared

Puck: I took him sleeping—that is finished too—
   And the Athenian woman by his side,
   That, when he waked, of force° she must be eyed.   40

   Enter Demetrius and Hermia.

Oberon: Stand close. This is the same Athenian.
Puck: This is the woman, but not this the man.

                                                                    [*They stand aside.*]

Demetrius: O, why rebuke you him that loves you so?
   Lay breath so bitter on your bitter foe.
Hermia: Now I but chide; but I should use thee worse,   45
   For thou, I fear, hast given me cause to curse.
   If thou hast slain Lysander in his sleep,
   Being o'er shoes° in blood, plunge in the deep,
   And kill me too.
   The sun was not so true unto the day   50
   As he to me. Would he have stolen away
   From sleeping Hermia? I'll believe as soon
   This whole° earth may be bored, and that the moon
   May through the center creep, and so displease
   Her brother's° noontide with th' Antipodes.°   55
   It cannot be but thou hast murdered him;
   So should a murderer look, so dead,° so grim.
Demetrius: So should the murdered look, and so should I,
   Pierced through the heart with your stern cruelty.
   Yet you, the murderer, look as bright, as clear   60
   As yonder Venus in her glimmering sphere.
Hermia: What's this to° my Lysander? Where is he?
   Ah, good Demetrius, wilt thou give him me?
Demetrius: I had rather give his carcass to my hounds.
Hermia: Out, dog! Out, cur! Thou driv'st me past the bounds   65
   Of maiden's patience. Hast thou slain him, then?
   Henceforth be never numbered among men.
   O, once° tell true, tell true, even for my sake:
   Durst thou have looked upon him being awake?
   And hast thou killed him sleeping? O brave touch!°   70
   Could not a worm,° an adder, do so much?
   An adder did it; for with doubler° tongue
   Than thine, thou serpent, never adder stung.
Demetrius: You spend your passion° on a misprised mood.°
   I am not guilty of Lysander's blood,   75
   Nor is he dead, for aught that I can tell.
Hermia: I pray thee, tell me then that he is well.

---

40 *of force* perforce   48 *Being o'er shoes* having waded in so far   53 *whole* solid   55 *Her brother's* i.e., the sun's.   *th' Antipodes* the people on the opposite side of the earth (where the moon is imagined bringing night to noontime)   57 *dead* deadly, or deathly pale   62 *to* to do with   68 *once* once and for all   70 *brave touch!* fine stroke! (Said ironically.)   71 *worm* serpent   72 *doubler* (1) more forked (2) more deceitful   74 *passion* violent feelings.   *misprised mood* anger based on misconception

Demetrius: And if I could, what should I get therefor?°
Hermia: A privilege never to see me more.
    And from thy hated presence part I so.
    See me no more, whether he be dead or no.   *Exit.*   80
Demetrius: There is no following her in this fierce vein.
    Here therefore for a while I will remain.
    So sorrow's heaviness doth heavier° grow
    For debt that bankrupt° sleep doth sorrow owe;   85
    Which now in some slight measure it will pay,
    If for his tender here I make some stay.°   *[He] lie[s] down [and sleeps].*
Oberon: What hast thou done? Thou hast mistaken quite
    And laid the love juice on some true love's sight.
    Of thy misprision° must perforce ensue   90
    Some true love turned, and not a false turned true.
Puck: Then fate o'errules, that, one man holding troth,°
    A million fail, confounding oath on oath.°
Oberon: About the wood go swifter than the wind,
    And Helena of Athens look° thou find.   95
    All fancy-sick° she is and pale of cheer°
    With sighs of love, that cost the fresh blood° dear.
    By some illusion see thou bring her here.
    I'll charm his eyes against she do appear.°
Puck: I go, I go, look how I go,   100
    Swifter than arrow from the Tartar's bow.°   *[Exit.]*
Oberon [applying love juice to Demetrius' eyes]:
        Flower of this purple dye,
        Hit with Cupid's archery,
        Sink in apple° of his eye.
        When his love he doth espy,   105
        Let her shine as gloriously
        As the Venus of the sky.
        When thou wak'st, if she be by,
        Beg of her for remedy.

    Enter Puck.

Puck: Captain of our fairy band,   110
        Helena is here at hand,
        And the youth, mistook by me,
        Pleading for a lover's fee.°

---

78 *therefor* in return for that   84 *heavier* (1) harder to bear (2) more drowsy   85 *bankrupt* (Demetrius is saying that his sleepiness adds to the weariness caused by sorrow.)   86–87 *Which . . . stay* i.e., to a small extent, I will be able to "pay back" and hence find some relief from sorrow, if I pause here awhile (*make some stay*) while sleep "tenders" or offers itself by way of paying the debt owed to sorrow   90 *misprision* mistake   92 *that . . . troth* in that, for each man keeping true faith in love   93 *confounding . . . oath* i.e., breaking oath after oath   95 *look* i.e., be sure   96 *fancy-sick* lovesick. *cheer* face   97 *sighs . . . blood* (An allusion to the physiological theory that each sigh costs the heart a drop of blood.)   99 *against . . . appear* in anticipation of her coming   101 *Tartar's bow* (Tartars were famed for their skill with the bow.)   104 *apple* pupil   113 *fee* privilege, reward

	Shall we their fond pageant° see?	
	Lord, what fools these mortals be!	115
Oberon:	Stand aside. The noise they make	
	Will cause Demetrius to awake.	
Puck:	Then will two at once woo one;	
	That must needs be sport alone.°	
	And those things do best please me	120
	That befall preposterously.°	

[They stand aside.]

Enter Lysander and Helena.

Lysander: Why should you think that I should woo in scorn?
  Scorn and derision never come in tears.
  Look when° I vow, I weep; and vows so born,
    In their nativity all truth appears.° 125
  How can these things in me seem scorn to you,
  Bearing the badge° of faith to prove them true?
Helena: You do advance° your cunning more and more.
  When truth kills truth,° O, devilish-holy fray!
  These vows are Hermia's. Will you give her o'er? 130
    Weigh oath with oath, and you will nothing weigh.
  Your vows to her and me, put in two scales,
  Will even weigh, and both as light as tales.°
Lysander: I had no judgment when to her I swore.
Helena: Nor none, in my mind, now you give her o'er. 135
Lysander: Demetrius loves her, and he loves not you.
Demetrius [*awaking*]: O Helen, goddess, nymph, perfect, divine!
  To what, my love, shall I compare thine eyne?
  Crystal is muddy. O, how ripe in show°
  Thy lips, those kissing cherries, tempting grow! 140
  That pure congealèd white, high Taurus'° snow,
  Fanned with the eastern wind, turns to a crow°
  When thou hold'st up thy hand. O, let me kiss
  This princess of pure white, this seal° of bliss!
Helena: O spite! O hell! I see you all are bent 145
  To set against° me for your merriment.
  If you were civil and knew courtesy,
  You would not do me thus much injury.
  Can you not hate me, as I know you do,
  But you must join in souls° to mock me too? 150
  If you were men, as men you are in show,
  You would not use a gentle lady so—

---

114 *fond pageant* foolish spectacle   119 *alone* unequaled   121 *preposterously* out of the natural order
124 *Look when* whenever   124–125 *vows . . . appears* i.e., vows made by one who is weeping give evidence thereby of their sincerity   127 *badge* identifying device such as that worn on servants' livery (here, his tears)   128 *advance* carry forward, display   129 *truth kills truth* i.e., one of Lysander's vows must invalidate the other   133 *tales* lies   139 *show* appearance   141 *Taurus* a lofty mountain range in Asia Minor   142 *turns to a crow* i.e., seems black by contrast   144 *seal* pledge   146 *set against* attack   150 *in souls* i.e., heart and soul

Helena believes the enchanted Demetrius is only pretending to love her in order to mock her.

To vow, and swear, and superpraise° my parts,°
When I am sure you hate me with your hearts.
You both are rivals, and love Hermia,   155
And now both rivals, to mock Helena.
A trim° exploit, a manly enterprise,
To conjure tears up in a poor maid's eyes
With your derision! None of noble sort°
Would so offend a virgin and extort°   160
A poor soul's patience, all to make you sport.

153 *superpraise* overpraise. *parts* qualities   157 *trim* pretty, fine (Said ironically.)   159 *sort* character, quality   160 *extort* twist, torture

Lysander: You are unkind, Demetrius. Be not so.
  For you love Hermia; this you know I know.
  And here, with all good will, with all my heart,
  In Hermia's love I yield you up my part;   165
  And yours of Helena to me bequeath,
  Whom I do love, and will do till my death.
Helena: Never did mockers waste more idle breath.
Demetrius: Lysander, keep thy Hermia; I will none.°
  If e'er I loved her, all that love is gone.   170
  My heart to her but as guestwise sojourned,°
  And now to Helen is it home returned,
  There to remain.
Lysander: Helen, it is not so.
Demetrius: Disparage not the faith thou dost not know,
  Lest, to thy peril, thou aby° it dear.   175
  Look where thy love comes; yonder is thy dear.

  Enter Hermia.

Hermia: Dark night, that from the eye his° function takes,
  The ear more quick of apprehension makes;
  Wherein it doth impair the seeing sense,
  It pays the hearing double recompense.   180
  Thou art not by mine eye, Lysander, found;
  Mine ear, I thank it, brought me to thy sound.
  But why unkindly didst thou leave me so?
Lysander: Why should he stay, whom love doth press to go?
Hermia: What love could press Lysander from my side?   185
Lysander: Lysander's love, that would not let him bide—
  Fair Helena, who more engilds° the night
  Than all yon fiery oes° and eyes of light.
  Why seek'st thou me? Could not this make thee know
  The hate I bear thee made me leave thee so?   190
Hermia: You speak not as you think. It cannot be.
Helena: Lo, she is one of this confederacy!
  Now I perceive they have conjoined all three
  To fashion this false sport in spite of me.°
  Injurious Hermia, most ungrateful maid!   195
  Have you conspired, have you with these contrived°
  To bait° me with this foul derision?
  Is all the counsel° that we two have shared—
  The sisters' vows, the hours that we have spent
  When we have chid the hasty-footed time   200
  For parting us—O, is all forgot?
  All schooldays' friendship, childhood innocence?

---

169 *will none* i.e., want no part of her 171 *to . . . sojourned* only visited with her 175 *aby* pay for 177 *his* its 187 *engilds* gilds, brightens with a golden light 188 *oes* spangles (here, stars) 194 *in spite of me* to vex me 196 *contrived* plotted 197 *bait* torment, as one sets on dogs to bait a bear 198 *counsel* confidential talk

We, Hermia, like two artificial° gods,
Have with our needles created both one flower,
Both on one sampler, sitting on one cushion,   205
Both warbling of one song, both in one key,
As if our hands, our sides, voices, and minds
Had been incorporate.° So we grew together,
Like to a double cherry, seeming parted,
But yet an union in partition,   210
Two lovely° berries molded on one stem;
So with two seeming bodies but one heart,
Two of the first, like coats in heraldry,
Due but to one and crownèd with one crest.°
And will you rend our ancient love asunder,   215
To join with men in scorning your poor friend?
It is not friendly, 'tis not maidenly.
Our sex, as well as I, may chide you for it,
Though I alone do feel the injury.
Hermia: I am amazèd at your passionate words.   220
　　I scorn you not. It seems that you scorn me.
Helena: Have you not set Lysander, as in scorn,
　　To follow me and praise my eyes and face?
　　And made your other love, Demetrius,
　　Who even but now did spurn me with his foot,   225
　　To call me goddess, nymph, divine, and rare,
　　Precious, celestial? Wherefore speaks he this
　　To her he hates? And wherefore doth Lysander
　　Deny your love, so rich within his soul,
　　And tender° me, forsooth, affection,   230
　　But by your setting on, by your consent?
　　What though I be not so in grace° as you,
　　So hung upon with love, so fortunate,
　　But miserable most, to love unloved?
　　This you should pity rather than despise.   235
Hermia: I understand not what you mean by this.
Helena: Ay, do! Persever, counterfeit sad° looks,
　　Make mouths° upon° me when I turn my back,
　　Wink each at other, hold the sweet jest up.°
　　This sport, well carried,° shall be chronicled.   240
　　If you have any pity, grace, or manners,
　　You would not make me such an argument.°
　　But fare ye well. 'Tis partly my own fault,
　　Which death, or absence, soon shall remedy.
Lysander: Stay, gentle Helena; hear my excuse,   245
　　My love, my life, my soul, fair Helena!

203 *artificial* skilled in art or creation　208 *incorporate* of one body　211 *lovely* loving　213–214 *Two . . . crest* i.e., we have two separate bodies, just as a coat of arms in heraldry can be represented twice on a shield but surmounted by a single crest　230 *tender* offer　232 *grace* favor　237 *sad* grave, serious　238 *mouths* i.e., moves, faces, grimaces.　*upon* at　239 *hold . . . up* keep up the joke　240 *carried* managed　242 *argument* subject for a jest

Helena: O excellent!

Hermia [to Lysander]: Sweet, do not scorn her so.

Demetrius [to Lysander]: If she cannot entreat,° I can compel.

Lysander: Thou canst compel no more than she entreat.
 Thy threats have no more strength than her weak prayers.   250
 Helen, I love thee, by my life I do!
 I swear by that which I will lose for thee,
 To prove him false that says I love thee not.

Demetrius [to Helena]: I say I love thee more than he can do.

Lysander: If thou say so, withdraw, and prove it too.°   255

Demetrius: Quick, come!

Hermia: Lysander, where to tends all this?

Lysander: Away, you Ethiope!°

              [*He tries to break away from Hermia.*]

Demetrius: No, no; he'll
 Seem to break loose; take on as° you would follow,
 But yet come not. You are a tame man. Go!

Lysander [to Hermia]: Hang off,° thou cat, thou burr! Vile thing, let loose,   260
 Or I will shake thee from me like a serpent!

Hermia: Why are you grown so rude? What change is this,
 Sweet love?

Lysander: Thy love? Out, tawny Tartar, out!
 Out, loathèd med'cine!° O hated potion, hence!

Hermia: Do you not jest?

Helena: Yes, sooth,° and so do you.   265

Lysander: Demetrius, I will keep my word with thee.

Demetrius: I would I had your bond, for I perceive
 A weak bond° holds you. I'll not trust your word.

Lysander: What, should I hurt her, strike her, kill her dead?
 Although I hate her, I'll not harm her so.   270

Hermia: What, can you do me greater harm than hate?
 Hate me? Wherefore? O me, what news,° my love?
 Am not I Hermia? Are not you Lysander?
 I am as fair now as I was erewhile.°
 Since night you loved me; yet since night you left me.   275
 Why, then you left me—O, the gods forbid!—
 In earnest, shall I say?

Lysander: Ay, by my life!
 And never did desire to see thee more.
 Therefore be out of hope, of question, of doubt;
 Be certain, nothing truer. 'Tis no jest   280
 That I do hate thee and love Helena.

---

248 *entreat* i.e., succeed by entreaty 255 *withdraw . . . too* i.e., withdraw with me and prove your claim in a duel. (The two gentlemen are armed.) 257 *Ethiope* (Referring to Hermia's relatively dark hair and complexion; see also *tawny Tartar* six lines later.) 258 *take on as* act as if, make a fuss as if 260 *Hang off* let go 264 *med'cine* i.e., poison 265 *sooth* truly 268 *weak bond* i.e., Hermia's arm (with a pun on *bond*, "oath," in the previous line) 272 *what news* what is the matter 274 *erewhile* just now

Hermia berates Helena, "You thief of love!" (III, ii, 283).

Hermia [to Helena]: O me! You juggler! You cankerblossom!°
    You thief of love! What, have you come by night
    And stol'n my love's heart from him?
Helena: Fine, i' faith!
    Have you no modesty, no maiden shame,   285
    No touch of bashfulness? What, will you tear
    Impatient answers from my gentle tongue?
    Fie, fie! You counterfeit, you puppet,° you!
Hermia: "Puppet"? Why, so!° Ay, that way goes the game.
    Now I perceive that she hath made compare   290
    Between our statures; she hath urged her height,
    And with her personage, her tall personage,
    Her height, forsooth, she hath prevailed with him.
    And are you grown so high in his esteem
    Because I am so dwarfish and so low?   295
    How low am I, thou painted maypole? Speak!
    How low am I? I am not yet so low
    But that my nails can reach unto thine eyes.

                             [She flails at Helena but is restrained.]

---

282 *cankerblossom* worm that destroys the flower bud, or wild rose   288 *puppet* (1) counterfeit (2) dwarfish
woman (in reference to Hermia's smaller stature)   289 *Why, so* i.e., Oh, so that's how it is

Helena: I pray you, though you mock me, gentlemen,
    Let her not hurt me. I was never curst;°   300
    I have no gift at all in shrewishness;
    I am a right° maid for my cowardice.
    Let her not strike me. You perhaps may think,
    Because she is something° lower than myself,
    That I can match her.
Hermia: Lower? Hark, again!   305
Helena: Good Hermia, do not be so bitter with me.
    I evermore did love you, Hermia,
    Did ever keep your counsels, never wronged you,
    Save that, in love unto Demetrius,
    I told him of your stealth° unto this wood.   310
    He followed you; for love I followed him.
    But he hath chid me hence° and threatened me
    To strike me, spurn me, nay, to kill me too.
    And now, so° you will let me quiet go,
    To Athens will I bear my folly back   315
    And follow you no further. Let me go.
    You see how simple and how fond° I am.
Hermia: Why, get you gone. Who is 't that hinders you?
Helena: A foolish heart, that I leave here behind.
Hermia: What, with Lysander?
Helena: With Demetrius.   320
Lysander: Be not afraid; she shall not harm thee, Helena.
Demetrius: No, sir, she shall not, though you take her part.
Helena: O, when she is angry, she is keen° and shrewd.°
    She was a vixen when she went to school;
    And though she be but little, she is fierce.   325
Hermia: "Little" again? Nothing but "low" and "little"?
    Why will you suffer her to flout me thus?
    Let me come to her.
Lysander: Get you gone, you dwarf!
    You minimus,° of hindering knotgrass° made!
    You bead, you acorn!
Demetrius: You are too officious   330
    In her behalf that scorns your services.
    Let her alone. Speak not of Helena;
    Take not her part. For, if thou dost intend°
    Never so little show of love to her,
    Thou shalt aby° it.
Lysander: Now she holds me not.   335
    Now follow, if thou dar'st, to try whose right,
    Of thine or mine, is most in Helena   *[Exit.]*

---

300 *curst* shrewish   302 *right* true   304 *something* somewhat   310 *stealth* stealing away   312 *chid me hence* driven me away with his scolding   314 *so* if only   317 *fond* foolish   323 *keen* fierce, cruel.   *shrewd* shrewish   329 *minimus* diminutive creature.   *knotgrass* a weed, an infusion of which was thought to stunt the growth   333 *intend* give sign of   335 *aby* pay for

Demetrius: Follow? Nay, I'll go with thee, cheek by jowl.°

[Exit, following Lysander.]

Hermia: You, mistress, all this coil° is 'long of° you.
Nay, go not back.°
Helena: I will not trust you, I,   340
Nor longer stay in your curst company.
Your hands than mine are quicker for a fray;
My legs are longer, though, to run away.   [*Exit.*]
Hermia: I am amazed and know not what to say.   *Exit.*

    [*Oberon and Puck come forward.*]

Oberon: This is thy negligence. Still thou mistak'st,   345
Or else committ'st thy knaveries willfully.
Puck: Believe me, king of shadows, I mistook.
Did not you tell me I should know the man
By the Athenian garments he had on?
And so far blameless proves my enterprise   350
That I have 'nointed an Athenian's eyes;
And so far° am I glad it so did sort,°
As° this their jangling I esteem a sport.
Oberon: Thou seest these lovers seek a place to fight.
Hie° therefore, Robin, overcast the night;   355
The starry welkin° cover thou anon
With drooping fog as black as Acheron,°
And lead these testy rivals so astray
As° one come not within another's way.
Like to Lysander sometimes frame thy tongue,   360
Then stir Demetrius up with bitter wrong;°
And sometimes rail thou like Demetrius.
And from each other look thou lead them thus,
Till o'er their brows death-counterfeiting sleep
With leaden legs and batty° wings doth creep.   365
Then crush this herb° into Lysander's eye,   [*giving herb.*]
Whose liquor hath this virtuous° property,
To take from thence all error with his° might
And make his eyeballs roll with wonted° sight.
When they next wake, all this derision°   370
Shall seem a dream and fruitless vision,
And back to Athens shall the lovers wend
With league whose date° till death shall never end.
Whiles I in this affair do thee employ,
I'll to my queen and beg her Indian boy;   375

---

338 *cheek by jowl* i.e., side by side **339** *coil* turmoil, dissension. *'long of* on account of **340** *go not back* i.e., don't retreat (Hermia is again proposing a fight.) **352** *so far* at least to this extent. *sort* turn out **353** *As* that **355** *Hie* hasten **356** *welkin* sky **357** *Acheron* river of Hades (here representing Hades itself) **359** *As* that **361** *wrong* insults **365** *batty* batlike **366** *this herb* i.e., the antidote (mentioned in II, i, 184) to love-in-idleness **367** *virtuous* efficacious **368** *his* its **369** *wonted* accustomed **370** *derision* laughable business **373** *date* term of existence

And then I will her charmèd eye release
From monster's view, and all things shall be peace.
Puck: My fairy lord, this must be done with haste,
For night's swift dragons° cut the clouds full fast,
And yonder shines Aurora's harbinger,°   380
At whose approach ghosts, wand'ring here and there,
Troop home to churchyards. Damnèd spirits all,
That in crossways and floods have burial,°
Already to their wormy beds are gone.
For fear lest day should look their shames upon,   385
They willfully themselves exile from light
And must for aye° consort with black-browed night.
Oberon: But we are spirits of another sort.
I with the Morning's love° have oft made sport,
And, like a forester,° the groves may tread   390
Even till the eastern gate, all fiery red,
Opening on Neptune with fair blessèd beams,
Turns into yellow gold his salt green streams.
But notwithstanding, haste, make no delay.
We may effect this business yet ere day.   [*Exit.*]   395
Puck: Up and down, up and down,
I will lead them up and down.
I am feared in field and town.
Goblin,° lead them up and down.
Here comes one.   400

Enter Lysander.

Lysander: Where art thou, proud Demetrius? Speak thou now.
Puck [*mimicking Demetrius*]: Here, villain, drawn° and ready. Where art thou?
Lysander: I will be with thee straight.°
Puck: Follow me, then,
To plainer° ground.

                        [*Lysander wanders about,° following the voice.*]

Enter Demetrius.
Demetrius: Lysander! Speak again!
Thou runaway, thou coward, art thou fled?   405
Speak! In some bush? Where dost thou hide thy head?

---

379 *dragons* (Supposed by Shakespeare to be yoked to the car of the goddess of night or the moon.)   380 *Aurora's harbinger* the morning star, precursor of dawn   383 *crossways . . . burial* (Those who had committed suicide were buried at crossways, with a stake driven through them; those who intentionally or accidentally drowned [in floods or deep water], would be condemned to wander disconsolate for lack of burial rites.)   387 *for aye* forever   389 *the Morning's love* Cephalus, a beautiful youth beloved by Aurora; or perhaps the goddess of the dawn herself   390 *forester* keeper of a royal forest   399 *Goblin* Hobgoblin. (Puck refers to himself.)   402 *drawn* with drawn sword   403 *straight* immediately   404 *plainer* more open.   s.d. *Lysander wanders about* (Lysander may exit here, but perhaps not; neither exit nor reentrance is indicated in the early texts.)

Puck [*mimicking Lysander*]:
Thou coward, art thou bragging to the stars,
Telling the bushes that thou look'st for wars,
And wilt not come? Come, recreant;° come, thou child,
I'll whip thee with a rod. He is defiled   410
That draws a sword on thee.
Demetrius: Yea, art thou there?
Puck: Follow my voice. We'll try° no manhood here.

Exeunt.

[*Lysander returns.*]

Lysander: He goes before me and still dares me on.
When I come where he calls, then he is gone.
The villain is much lighter-heeled than I.   415
I followed fast, but faster he did fly,
That fallen am I in dark uneven way,
And here will rest me. [*He lies down.*] Come, thou gentle day!
For if but once thou show me thy gray light,
I'll find Demetrius and revenge this spite.   [*He sleeps.*] 420

[*Enter*] *Robin* [*Puck*] *and Demetrius.*

Puck: Ho, ho, ho! Coward, why com'st thou not?
Demetrius: Abide° me, if thou dar'st; for well I wot°
Thou runn'st before me, shifting every place,
And dar'st not stand nor look me in the face.
Where art thou now?
Puck: Come hither. I am here.   425
Demetrius: Nay, then, thou mock'st me. Thou shalt buy° this dear,°
If ever I thy face by daylight see.
Now, go thy way. Faintness constraineth me
To measure out my length on this cold bed.
By day's approach look to be visited.   430

[*He lies down and sleeps.*]

Enter Helena.

Helena: O weary night, O long and tedious night,
Abate° thy hours! Shine comforts from the east,
That I may back to Athens by daylight
From these that my poor company detest;
And sleep, that sometimes shuts up sorrow's eye,   435
Steal me awhile from mine own company.

[*She lies down and*] *sleep*[*s*].

Puck: Yet but three? Come one more;
Two of both kinds makes up four.
Here she comes, curst° and sad.
Cupid is a knavish lad,   440
Thus to make poor females mad.

---

409 *recreant* cowardly wretch   412 *try* test   422 *Abide* confront, face.   *wot* know   426 *buy* aby, pay for.   *dear* dearly   432 *Abate* lessen, shorten   439 *curst* ill-tempered

[*Enter Hermia.*]

Hermia: Never so weary, never so in woe,
    Bedabbled with the dew and torn with briers,
I can no further crawl, no further go;
    My legs can keep no pace with my desires.   445
Here will I rest me till the break of day.
Heavens shield Lysander, if they mean a fray!

[*She lies down and sleeps.*]

Puck: On the ground
        Sleep sound.
        I'll apply   450
        To your eye,
Gentle lover, remedy.

[*He squeezes the juice on Lysander's eyes.*]

        When thou wak'st,
        Thou tak'st
        True delight   455
        In the sight
Of thy former lady's eye;
And the country proverb known,
That every man should take his own,
In your waking shall be shown: 460
        Jack shall have Jill;°
        Naught shall go ill;
The man shall have his mare again, and all shall be well.

[*Exit. The four sleeping lovers remain.*]

ACT IV

SCENE I [THE ACTION IS CONTINUOUS. THE FOUR LOVERS ARE STILL ASLEEP°
ONSTAGE.]

    Enter [*Titania,*] *Queen of Fairies, and* [*Bottom the*] *clown, and Fairies; and*
    [*Oberon,*] *the King, behind them.*

Titania: Come, sit thee down upon this flowery bed,
    While I thy amiable° cheeks do coy,°
    And stick muskroses in thy sleek smooth head,
    And kiss thy fair large ears, my gentle joy.

[*They recline.*]

Bottom: Where's Peaseblossom?   5
Peaseblossom: Ready.
Bottom: Scratch my head, Peaseblossom. Where's Monsieur Cobweb?
Cobweb: Ready.

461 *Jack shall have Jill* (Proverbial for "boy gets girl.")   s.d. *still asleep* (Compare with the Folio stage direction: "They sleep all the act.")   2 *amiable* lovely.   *coy* caress

The fairies tend to Bottom's wishes.

Bottom: Monsieur Cobweb, good monsieur, get you your weapons in your hand, and kill me a red-hipped humble-bee on the top of a thistle; and, good mon-   10
    sieur, bring me the honey bag. Do not fret yourself too much in the action, monsieur; and, good monsieur, have a care the honey bag break not. I would be loath to have you overflown with a honey bag, signor. [*Exit Cobweb.*] Where's Monsieur Mustardseed?

Mustardseed: Ready.   15

Bottom: Give me your neaf,° Monsieur Mustardseed. Pray you, leave your courtesy,° good monsieur.

Mustardseed: What's your will?

Bottom: Nothing, good monsieur, but to help Cavalery° Cobweb° to scratch. I
    must to the barber's, monsieur, for methinks I am marvelous hairy about the   20
    face; and I am such a tender ass, if my hair do but tickle me I must scratch.

Titania: What, wilt thou hear some music, my sweet love?

Bottom: I have a reasonable good ear in music. Let's have the tongs and the bones.°
                                   [*Music: tongs, rural music.*°]

Titania: Or say, sweet love, what thou desirest to eat.

Bottom: Truly, a peck of provender.° I could munch your good dry oats. Methinks   25
    I have a great desire to a bottle° of hay. Good hay, sweet hay, hath no fellow.°

16 *neaf* fist. *leave your courtesy* i.e., stop bowing, or put on your hat 19 *Cavalery* cavalier. (Form of address for a gentleman.) *Cobweb* (Seemingly an error, since Cobweb has been sent to bring honey, while Peaseblossom has been asked to scratch.) 23 *tongs . . . bones* instruments for rustic music. (The tongs were played like a triangle, whereas the bones were held between the fingers and used as clappers.) s.d. *Music . . . music* (This stage direction is added from the Folio.) 25 *peck of provender* one-quarter bushel of grain 26 *bottle* bundle. *fellow* equal

Titania: I have a venturous fairy that shall seek
　　The squirrel's hoard, and fetch thee new nuts.
Bottom: I had rather have a handful or two of dried peas. But, I pray you, let
　　none of your people stir° me. I have an exposition of° sleep come upon me.　　30
Titania: Sleep thou, and I will wind thee in my arms.
　　Fairies, begone, and be all ways° away.

[Exeunt Fairies.]

　　So doth the woodbine° the sweet honeysuckle
　　Gently entwist; the female ivy so
　　Enrings the barky fingers of the elm.　　35
　　O, how I love thee! How I dote on thee!

[They sleep.]

　　Enter Robin Goodfellow [Puck].

Oberon [coming forward]: Welcome, good Robin. Seest thou this sweet sight?
　　Her dotage now I do begin to pity.
　　For, meeting her of late behind the wood
　　Seeking sweet favors° for this hateful fool,　　40
　　I did upbraid her and fall out with her.
　　For she his hairy temples then had rounded
　　With coronet of fresh and fragrant flowers;
　　And that same dew, which sometime° on the buds
　　Was wont to swell like round and orient° pearls,　　45
　　Stood now within the pretty flowerets' eyes
　　Like tears that did their own disgrace bewail.
　　When I had at my pleasure taunted her,
　　And she in mild terms begged my patience,
　　I then did ask of her her changeling child,　　50
　　Which straight she gave me, and her fairy sent
　　To bear him to my bower in Fairyland.
　　And, now I have the boy, I will undo
　　This hateful imperfection of her eyes.
　　And, gentle Puck, take this transformèd scalp　　55
　　From off the head of this Athenian swain,
　　That he, awaking when the other° do,
　　May all to Athens back again repair,°
　　And think no more of this night's accidents
　　But as the fierce vexation of a dream.　　60
　　But first I will release the Fairy Queen.

[He squeezes an herb on her eyes.]

　　　　Be as thou wast wont to be;
　　　　See as thou wast wont to see.
　　　　Dian's bud° o'er Cupid's flower
　　　　Hath such force and blessèd power.　　65

---

30 *stir* disturb.　*exposition of* (Bottom's phrase for "disposition to.")　32 *all ways* in all directions　33 *woodbine* bindweed, a climbing plant that twines in the opposite direction from that of honeysuckle　40 *favors* i.e., gifts of flowers　44 *sometime* formerly　45 *orient pearls* i.e., the most beautiful of all pearls, those coming from the Orient　57 *other* others　58 *repair* return　64 *Dian's bud* (Perhaps the flower of the *agnus castus* or chaste-tree, supposed to preserve chastity; or perhaps referring simply to Oberon's herb by which he can undo the effects of "Cupid's flower," the love-in-idleness of II, i, 166–168.)

Now, my Titania, wake you, my sweet queen.
Titania [*waking*]: My Oberon! What visions have I seen!
    Methought I was enamored of an ass.
Oberon: There lies your love.
Titania: How came these things to pass?
    O, how mine eyes do loathe his visage now!   70
Oberon: Silence awhile. Robin, take off this head.
    Titania, music call, and strike more dead
    Than common sleep of all these five° the sense.
Titania: Music, ho! Music, such as charmeth° sleep!   [*Music.*]
Puck [*removing the ass head*]:
    Now, when thou wak'st, with thine own fool's eyes peep.   75
Oberon: Sound, music! Come, my queen, take hands with me,
    And rock the ground whereon these sleepers be.   [*They dance.*]
    Now thou and I are new in amity,
    And will tomorrow midnight solemnly°
    Dance in Duke Theseus' house triumphantly,   80
    And bless it to all fair prosperity.
    There shall the pairs of faithful lovers be
    Wedded, with Theseus, all in jollity.

Puck: Fairy King, attend, and mark:
                    I do hear the morning lark.   85
Oberon: Then, my queen, in silence sad,°
                    Trip we after night's shade.
                    We the globe can compass soon,
                    Swifter than the wandering moon.
Titania: Come, my lord, and in our flight   90
                    Tell me how it came this night
                    That I sleeping here was found
                    With these mortals on the ground.
                                Exeunt [*Oberon, Titania, and Puck*].
                                       Wind horn [*within*].

Enter Theseus and all his train; [*Hippolyta, Egeus*].

Theseus: Go, one of you, find out the forester,
    For now our observation° is performed;   95
    And since we have the vaward° of the day,
    My love shall hear the music of my hounds.
    Uncouple° in the western valley; let them go.
    Dispatch, I say, and find the forester.   [*Exit an Attendant.*]
    We will, fair queen, up to the mountain's top   100
    And mark the musical confusion
    Of hounds and echo in conjunction.

---

73 *these five* i.e., the four lovers and Bottom   74 *charmeth* brings about, as though by a charm   79 *solemnly* ceremoniously   86 *sad* sober   95 *observation* i.e., observance to a morn of May (I, i, 167)   96 *vaward* vanguard, i.e., earliest part   98 *Uncouple* set free for the hunt

Hippolyta: I was with Hercules and Cadmus° once,
　　When in a wood of Crete they bayed° the bear
　　With hounds of Sparta.° Never did I hear　　　　　　　　　　　105
　　Such gallant chiding;° for, besides the groves,
　　The skies, the fountains, every region near
　　Seemed all one mutual cry. I never heard
　　So musical a discord, such sweet thunder.
Theseus: My hounds are bred out of the Spartan kind,°　　　110
　　So flewed,° so sanded;° and their heads are hung
　　With ears that sweep away the morning dew;
　　Crook-kneed, and dewlapped° like Thessalian bulls;
　　Slow in pursuit, but matched in mouth like bells,
　　Each under each.° A cry° more tunable°　　　　　　　　　　115
　　Was never holloed to nor cheered° with horn
　　In Crete, in Sparta, nor in Thessaly.
　　Judge when you hear.　　　　　　　　　　　　　　　[*He sees the sleepers.*]
　　　　　　　　　　But soft!° What nymphs are these?
Egeus: My lord, this is my daughter here asleep,
　　And this Lysander; this Demetrius is;　　　　　　　　　　　120
　　This Helena, old Nedar's Helena.
　　I wonder of° their being here together.
Theseus: No doubt they rose up early to observe
　　The rite of May, and hearing our intent,
　　Came here in grace of our solemnity.°　　　　　　　　　　　125
　　But speak, Egeus. Is not this the day
　　That Hermia should give answer of her choice?
Egeus: It is, my lord.
Theseus: Go, bid the huntsmen wake them with their horns.

　　　　　　　　　　　　　　　　　　　　　　　　[*Exit an Attendant.*]

Shout within. Wind horns. They all start up.

　　Good morrow, friends. Saint Valentine° is past.　　　　　130
　　Begin these woodbirds but to couple now?
Lysander: Pardon, my lord.　　　　　　　　　　　　　　[*They kneel.*]
Theseus:　　　　　　　　I pray you all, stand up.　　　[*They stand.*]
　　I know you two are rival enemies;
　　How comes this gentle concord in the world,
　　That hatred is so far from jealousy°　　　　　　　　　　　135
　　To sleep by hate and fear no enmity?

103 *Cadmus* mythical founder of Thebes. (This story about him is unknown.)　104 *bayed* brought
to bay　105 *hounds of Sparta* (A breed famous in antiquity for their hunting skill.)　106 *chiding* i.e.,
yelping　110 *kind* strain, breed　111 *So flewed* similarly having large hanging chaps or fleshy covering of the jaw.　*sanded* of sandy color　113 *dewlapped* having pendulous folds of skin under the
neck　114–115 *matched . . . each* i.e., harmoniously matched in their various cries like a set of bells,
from treble down to bass　115 *cry* pack of hounds.　*tunable* well tuned, melodious　116 *cheered* encouraged　118 *soft* i.e., gently, wait a minute　122 *wonder of* wonder at　125 *in . . . solemnity* in honor of our
wedding ceremony　130 *Saint Valentine* (Birds were supposed to choose their mates on Saint Valentine's
Day.)　135 *jealousy* suspicion

Lysander: My lord, I shall reply amazedly,
    Half sleep, half waking; but as yet, I swear,
    I cannot truly say how I came here.
    But, as I think—for truly would I speak,   140
    And now I do bethink me, so it is—
    I came with Hermia hither. Our intent
    Was to be gone from Athens, where° we might,
    Without° the peril of the Athenian law—
Egeus: Enough, enough, my lord; you have enough.   145
    I beg the law, the law, upon his head.
    They would have stol'n away; they would, Demetrius,
    Thereby to have defeated° you and me,
    You of your wife and me of my consent,
    Of my consent that she should be your wife.   150
Demetrius: My lord, fair Helen told me of their stealth,
    Of this their purpose hither° to this wood,
    And I in fury hither followed them,
    Fair Helena in fancy° following me.
    But, my good lord, I wot not by what power—   155
    But by some power it is—my love to Hermia,
    Melted as the snow, seems to me now
    As the remembrance of an idle gaud°
    Which in my childhood I did dote upon;
    And all the faith, the virtue of my heart,   160
    The object and the pleasure of mine eye,
    Is only Helena. To her, my lord,
    Was I betrothed ere I saw Hermia,
    But like a sickness did I loathe this food;
    But, as in health, come to my natural taste,   165
    Now I do wish it, love it, long for it,
    And will forevermore be true to it.
Theseus: Fair lovers, you are fortunately met.
    Of this discourse we more will hear anon.
    Egeus, I will overbear your will;   170
    For in the temple, by and by, with us
    These couples shall eternally be knit.
    And, for° the morning now is something° worn,
    Our purposed hunting shall be set aside.
    Away with us to Athens. Three and three,   175
    We'll hold a feast in great solemnity.°
    Come, Hippolyta.

                  [Exeunt Theseus, Hippolyta, Egeus, and train.]
Demetrius: These things seem small and undistinguishable,
    Like far-off mountains turnèd into clouds.

---

143 *where* wherever; or, to where   144 *Without* outside of, beyond   148 *defeated* defrauded   152 *hither* in coming hither   154 *in fancy* driven by love   158 *idle gaud* worthless trinket   173 *for* since. *something* somewhat   176 *in great solemnity* with great ceremony

Hermia: Methinks I see these things with parted° eye,   180
    When everything seems double.
Helena: So methinks;
    And I have found Demetrius like a jewel,
    Mine own, and not mine own.°
Demetrius: Are you sure
    That we are awake? It seems to me
    That yet we sleep, we dream. Do not you think   185
    The Duke was here, and bid us follow him?
Hermia: Yea, and my father.
Helena: And Hippolyta.
Lysander: And he did bid us follow to the temple.
Demetrius: Why, then, we are awake. Let's follow him,
    And by the way let us recount our dreams.   [*Exeunt the lovers.*]   190
Bottom [*awaking*]: When my cue comes, call me, and I will answer. My next is,
    "Most fair Pyramus." Heigh—ho! Peter Quince! Flute, the bellows mender!
    Snout, the tinker! Starveling! God's° my life, stolen hence and left me
    asleep! I have had a most rare vision. I have had a dream, past the wit of
    man to say what dream it was. Man is but an ass if he go about° to expound   195
    this dream. Methought I was— there is no man can tell what. Methought I
    was—and methought I had— but man is but a patched° fool if he will offer°
    to say what methought I had. The eye of man hath not heard, the ear of
    man hath not seen, man's hand is not able to taste, his tongue to conceive,
    nor his heart to report,° what my dream was. I will get Peter Quince to write   200
    a ballad° of this dream. It shall be called "Bottom's Dream," because it hath
    no bottom;° and I will sing it in the latter end of a play, before the Duke.
    Peradventure, to make it the more gracious, I shall sing it at her° death.
                                                                        [*Exit.*]

SCENE II [ATHENS.]

    Enter Quince, Flute, [*Snout, and Starveling*].

Quince: Have you sent to Bottom's house? Is he come home yet?
Starveling: He cannot be heard of. Out of doubt he is transported.°
Flute: If he come not, then the play is marred. It goes not forward. Doth it?
Quince: It is not possible. You have not a man in all Athens able to discharge°
    Pyramus but he.   5
Flute: No, he hath simply the best wit° of any handicraft man in Athens.
Quince: Yea, and the best person° too, and he is a very paramour for a sweet
    voice.
Flute: You must say "paragon." A paramour is, God bless us, a thing of naught.°

    Enter Snug the joiner.

180 *parted* i.e., improperly focused   182–183 *like . . . mine own* i.e., like a jewel that one finds by chance and
therefore possesses but cannot certainly consider one's own property   193 *God's* may God save   195 *go
about* attempt   197 *patched* wearing motley, i.e., a dress of various colors.   *offer* venture   198–200 *The
eye . . . report* (Bottom garbles the terms of 1 Corinthians 2:9)   201 *ballad* (The proper medium for relating sensational stories and preposterous events.)   201–202 *hath no bottom* is unfathomable   203 *her*
Thisbe's (?)   2 *transported* carried off by fairies; or, possibly, transformed   4 *discharge* perform   6 *wit*
intellect   7 *person* appearance   9 *a . . . naught* a shameful thing

The workers celebrate the return of Bottom and prepare to put on their play.

Snug: Masters, the Duke is coming from the temple, and there is two or three   10
lords and ladies more married. If our sport had gone forward, we had all been
made men.°

Flute: O sweet bully Bottom! Thus hath he lost sixpence a day° during his life;
he could not have scaped sixpence a day. An the Duke had not given him
sixpence a day for playing Pyramus, I'll be hanged. He would have deserved   15
it. Sixpence a day in Pyramus, or nothing.

Enter Bottom.

Bottom: Where are these lads? Where are these hearts?°
Quince: Bottom! O most courageous day! O most happy hour!
Bottom: Masters, I am to discourse wonders.° But ask me not what; for if I tell
you, I am no true Athenian. I will tell you everything, right as it fell out.   20
Quince: Let us hear, sweet Bottom.
Bottom: Not a word of° me. All that I will tell you is that the Duke hath dined.
Get your apparel together, good strings° to your beards, new ribbons to your
pumps;° meet presently° at the palace; every man look o'er his part; for the
short and the long is, our play is preferred.° In any case, let Thisbe have   25
clean linen; and let not him that plays the lion pare his nails, for they shall

11–12 *we . . . men* i.e., we would have had our fortunes made   13 *sixpence a day* i.e., as a royal pension
17 *hearts* good fellows   19 *am . . . wonders* have wonders to relate   22 *of* out of   23 *strings* (to attach the
beards).   24 *pumps* light shoes or slippers.   *presently* immediately   25 *preferred* selected for consideration

hang out for the lion's claws. And, most dear actors, eat no onions nor garlic, for we are to utter sweet breath; and I do not doubt but to hear them say
it is a sweet comedy. No more words. Away! Go, away!

[*Exeunt.*]

ACT V

SCENE I [ATHENS. THE PALACE OF THESEUS.]

Enter Theseus, Hippolyta, and Philostrate, [lords, and attendants].

Hippolyta: 'Tis strange, my Theseus, that° these lovers speak of.
Theseus: More strange than true. I never may° believe
    These antique° fables nor these fairy toys.°
    Lovers and madmen have such seething brains,
    Such shaping fantasies,° that apprehend°   5
    More than cool reason ever comprehends.°
    The lunatic, the lover, and the poet
    Are of imagination all compact.°
    One sees more devils than vast hell can hold;
    That is the madman. The lover, all as frantic,   10
    Sees Helen's° beauty in a brow of Egypt.°
    The poet's eye, in a fine frenzy rolling,
    Doth glance from heaven to earth, from earth to heaven;
    And as imagination bodies forth
    The forms of things unknown, the poet's pen   15
    Turns them to shapes and gives to airy nothing
    A local habitation and a name.
    Such tricks hath strong imagination
    That, if it would but apprehend some joy,
    It comprehends some bringer° of that joy;   20
    Or in the night, imagining some fear,°
    How easy is a bush supposed a bear!
Hippolyta: But all the story of the night told over,
    And all their minds transfigured so together,
    More witnesseth than fancy's images°   25
    And grows to something of great constancy;°
    But, howsoever,° strange and admirable.°

Enter lovers: Lysander, Demetrius, Hermia, and Helena.

Theseus: Here come the lovers, full of joy and mirth.
    Joy, gentle friends! Joy and fresh days of love
    Accompany your hearts!

1 *that* that which   2 *may* can   3 *antique* old-fashioned (punning too on "antic," "strange," "grotesque").
fairy toys trifling stories about fairies   5 *fantasies* imaginations.   *apprehend* conceive, imagine   6 *comprehends*
understands   8 *compact* formed, composed   11 *Helen's* i.e., of Helen of Troy, pattern of beauty.   *brow
of Egypt* i.e., face of a gypsy   20 *bringer* i.e., source   21 *fear* object of fear   25 *More . . . images* testi-
fies to something more substantial than mere imaginings   26 *constancy* certainty   27 *howsoever* in any
case.   *admirable* a source of wonder

Lysander: More than to us   30
    Wait in your royal walks, your board, your bed!
Theseus: Come now, what masques,° what dances shall we have,
    To wear away this long age of three hours
    Between our after-supper and bedtime?
    Where is our usual manager of mirth?   35
    What revels are in hand? Is there no play
    To ease the anguish of a torturing hour?
    Call Philostrate.
Philostrate: Here, mighty Theseus.
Theseus: Say, what abridgment° have you for this evening?
    What masque? What music? How shall we beguile   40
    The lazy time, if not with some delight?
Philostrate [*giving him a paper*]: There is a brief° how many sports are ripe.
    Make choice of which Your Highness will see first.
Theseus [*He reads*]: "The battle with the Centaurs,° to be sung
    By an Athenian eunuch to the harp"?   45
    We'll none of that. That have I told my love,
    In glory of my kinsman° Hercules.
    [*He reads.*] "The riot of the tipsy Bacchanals,
    Tearing the Thracian singer in their rage"?°
    That is an old device;° and it was played   50
    When I from Thebes came last a conqueror.
    [*He reads.*] "The thrice three Muses mourning for the death
    Of Learning, late deceased in beggary"?°
    That is some satire, keen and critical,
    Not sorting with° a nuptial ceremony.   55
    [*He reads.*] "A tedious brief scene of young Pyramus
    And his love Thisbe; very tragical mirth"?
    Merry and tragical? Tedious and brief?
    That is, hot ice and wondrous strange° snow.
    How shall we find the concord of this discord?   60
Philostrate: A play there is, my lord, some ten words long,
    Which is as brief as I have known a play;
    But by ten words, my lord, it is too long,
    Which makes it tedious. For in all the play
    There is not one word apt, one player fitted.   65
    And tragical, my noble lord, it is,
    For Pyramus therein doth kill himself.

---

32 *masques* courtly entertainments   39 *abridgment* pastime (to abridge or shorten the evening)   42 *brief* short written statement, summary   44 *battle . . . Centaurs* (Probably refers to the battle of the Centaurs and the Lapithae, when the Centaurs attempted to carry off Hippodamia, bride of Theseus' friend Pirothous. The story is told in Ovid's *Metamorphoses* 12.)   47 *kinsman* (Plutarch's "Life of Theseus" states that Hercules and Theseus were near kinsmen. Theseus is referring to a version of the battle of the Centaurs in which Hercules was said to be present.)   48–49 *The riot . . . rage* (This was the story of the death of Orpheus, as told in *Metamorphoses* 11.)   50 *device* show, performance   52–53 *The thrice . . . beggary* (Possibly an allusion to Spenser's *Teares of the Muses*, 1591, though "satires" deploring the neglect of learning and the creative arts were commonplace.)   55 *sorting with* befitting   59 *strange* (Sometimes emended to an adjective that would contrast with *snow*, just as *hot* contrasts with *ice*.)

Which, when I saw rehearsed, I must confess,
Made mine eyes water; but more merry tears
The passion of loud laughter never shed.   70
Theseus: What are they that do play it?
Philostrate: Hardhanded men that work in Athens here,
Which never labored in their minds till now,
And now have toiled° their unbreathed° memories
With this same play, against° your nuptial.   75
Theseus: And we will hear it.
Philostrate: No, my noble lord,
It is not for you. I have heard it over,
And it is nothing, nothing in the world;
Unless you can find sport in their intents,
Extremely stretched° and conned° with cruel pain   80
To do you service.
Theseus: I will hear that play;
For never anything can be amiss
When simpleness° and duty tender it.
Go, bring them in; and take your places, ladies.

                              [Philostrate goes to summon the players.]

Hippolyta: I love not to see wretchedness o'ercharged,°   85
And duty in his service° perishing.
Theseus: Why, gentle sweet, you shall see no such thing.
Hippolyta: He says they can do nothing in this kind.°
Theseus: The kinder we, to give them thanks for nothing.
Our sport shall be to take what they mistake;   90
And what poor duty cannot do, noble respect°
Takes it in might, not merit.°
Where I have come, great clerks° have purposèd
To greet me with premeditated welcomes;
Where I have seen them shiver and look pale,   95
Make periods in the midst of sentences,
Throttle their practiced accent° in their fears,
And in conclusion dumbly have broke off,
Not paying me a welcome. Trust me, sweet,
Out of this silence yet I picked a welcome;   100
And in the modesty of fearful duty
I read as much as from the rattling tongue
Of saucy and audacious eloquence.
Love, therefore, and tongue-tied simplicity
In least° speak most, to my capacity.°   105

[Philostrate returns.]

74 *toiled* taxed. *unbreathed* unexercised 75 *against* in preparation for 80 *stretched* strained. *conned* memorized 83 *simpleness* simplicity 85 *wretchedness o'ercharged* social or intellectual inferiors overburdened 86 *his service* its attempt to serve 88 *kind* kind of thing 91 *respect* evaluation, consideration 92 *Takes . . . merit* values it for the effort made rather than for the excellence achieved 93 *clerks* learned men 97 *practiced accent* i.e., rehearsed speech; or, usual way of speaking 105 *least* i.e., saying least. *to my capacity* in my judgment and understanding

Philostrate: So please Your Grace, the Prologue° is addressed.°
Theseus: Let him approach.   [*A flourish of trumpets.*]

    Enter the Prologue [*Quince*].

Prologue: If we offend, it is with our good will.
    That you should think, we come not to offend,
    But with good will. To show our simple skill,   110
        That is the true beginning of our end.
    Consider, then, we come but in despite.
        We do not come, as minding° to content you,
    Our true intent is. All for your delight
        We are not here. That you should here repent you,   115
    The actors are at hand; and, by their show,
    You shall know all that you are like to know.
Theseus: This fellow doth not stand upon points.°
Lysander: He hath rid° his prologue like a rough° colt; he knows not the stop.° A
    good moral, my lord: it is not enough to speak, but to speak true.   120
Hippolyta: Indeed, he hath played on his prologue like a child on a recorder;° a
    sound, but not in government.°
Theseus: His speech was like a tangled chain: nothing° impaired, but all disordered.
    Who is next?

    Enter Pyramus [*Bottom*], *and Thisbe* [*Flute*], *and Wall* [*Snout*], *and Moonshine*
    [*Starveling*], *and Lion* [*Snug*].

Prologue: Gentles, perchance you wonder at this show;   125
    But wonder on, till truth makes all things plain.
    This man is Pyramus, if you would know;
        This beauteous lady Thisbe is, certain.
    This man with lime and roughcast doth present
        Wall, that vile wall which did these lovers sunder;   130
    And through Wall's chink, poor souls, they are content
        To whisper. At the which let no man wonder.
    This man, with lantern, dog, and bush of thorn,
        Presenteth Moonshine; for, if you will know,
    By moonshine did these lovers think no scorn°   135
        To meet at Ninus' tomb, there, there to woo.
    This grisly beast, which Lion hight° by name,
    The trusty Thisbe coming first by night
    Did scare away, or rather did affright;
    And as she fled, her mantle she did fall,°   140
        Which Lion vile with bloody mouth did stain.

---

106 *Prologue* speaker of the prologue. *addressed* ready 113 *minding* intending 118 *stand upon points*
(1) heed niceties or small points (2) pay attention to punctuation in his reading. (The humor of Quince's
speech is in the blunders of its punctuation.) 119 *rid* ridden. *rough* unbroken. *stop* (1) the stopping of
a colt by reining it in (2) punctuation mark 121 *recorder* a wind instrument like a flute 122 *government*
control 123 *nothing* not at all 135 *think no scorn* think it no disgraceful matter 137 *hight* is called
140 *fall* let fall

Anon comes Pyramus, sweet youth and tall,°
 And finds his trusty Thisbe's mantle slain;
Whereat, with blade, with bloody, blameful blade,
 He bravely broached° his boiling bloody breast.   145
And Thisbe, tarrying in mulberry shade,
 His dagger drew, and died. For all the rest,
Let Lion, Moonshine, Wall, and lovers twain
At large° discourse, while here they do remain.

> *Exeunt Lion, Thisbe, and Moonshine.*

Theseus: I wonder if the lion be to speak.   150
Demetrius: No wonder, my lord. One lion may, when many asses do.
Wall: In this same interlude° it doth befall
 That I, one Snout by name, present a wall;
 And such a wall as I would have you think
 That had in it a crannied hole or chink,   155
 Through which the lovers, Pyramus and Thisbe,
 Did whisper often, very secretly.
 This loam, this roughcast, and this stone doth show
 That I am that same wall; the truth is so.
 And this the cranny is, right and sinister,°   160
 Through which the fearful lovers are to whisper.
Theseus: Would you desire lime and hair to speak better?
Demetrius: It is the wittiest partition° that ever I heard discourse, my lord.

 [*Pyramus comes forward.*]

Theseus: Pyramus draws near the wall. Silence!
Pyramus: O grim-looked° night! O night with hue so black!   165
 O night, which ever art when day is not!
 O night, O night! Alack, alack, alack,
 I fear my Thisbe's promise is forgot.
 And thou, O wall, O sweet, O lovely wall,
 That stand'st between her father's ground and mine,   170
 Thou wall, O wall, O sweet and lovely wall,
 Show me thy chink, to blink through with mine eyne.

> [*Wall makes a chink with his fingers.*]

 Thanks, courteous wall. Jove shield thee well for this.
 But what see I? No Thisbe do I see.
 O wicked wall, through whom I see no bliss!   175
 Cursed be thy stones for thus deceiving me!
Theseus: The wall, methinks, being sensible,° should curse again.°
Pyramus: No, in truth, sir, he should not. "Deceiving me" is Thisbe's cue: she is
 to enter now, and I am to spy her through the wall. You shall see, it will fall
 pat° as I told you. Yonder she comes.   180

---

142 *tall* courageous   145 *broached* stabbed   149 *At large* in full, at length   152 *interlude* play   160 *right and sinister* i.e., the right side of it and the left; or, running from right to left, horizontally   163 *partition* (1) wall (2) section of a learned treatise or oration   165 *grim-looked* grim-looking   177 *sensible* capable of feeling.   *again* in return   180 *pat* exactly

The workers perform *Pyramus and Thisbe*.

Enter Thisbe.

Thisbe: O wall, full often hast thou heard my moans
    For parting my fair Pyramus and me.
My cherry lips have often kissed thy stones,
    Thy stones with lime and hair knit up in thee.
Pyramus: I see a voice. Now will I to the chink,   185
    To spy an° I can hear my Thisbe's face.
    Thisbe!
Thisbe: My love! Thou art my love, I think.
Pyramus: Think what thou wilt, I am thy lover's grace,°
    And like Limander° am I trusty still.
Thisbe: And I like Helen,° till the Fates me kill.   190

186 *an if*   188 *lover's grace* i.e., gracious lover   189, 190 *Limander, Helen* (Blunders for "Leander" and "Hero.")

Pyramus: Not Shafalus° to Procrus° was so true.
Thisbe: As Shafalus to Procrus, I to you.
Pyramus: O, kiss me through the hole of this vile wall!
Thisbe: I kiss the wall's hole, not your lips at all.
Pyramus: Wilt thou at Ninny's tomb meet me straightway? 195
Thisbe: 'Tide° life, 'tide death, I come without delay.

[Exeunt Pyramus and Thisbe.]

Wall: Thus have I, Wall, my part dischargèd so;
    And, being done, thus Wall away doth go.   [*Exit.*]
Theseus: Now is the mural down between the two neighbors.
Demetrius: No remedy, my lord, when walls are so willful° to hear without 200
    warning.°
Hippolyta: This is the silliest stuff that ever I heard.
Theseus: The best in this kind° are but shadows;° and the worst are no worse, if
    imagination amend them.
Hippolyta: It must be your imagination then, and not theirs. 205
Theseus: If we imagine no worse of them than they of themselves, they may pass
    for excellent men. Here come two noble beasts in, a man and a lion.

    Enter Lion and Moonshine.

Lion: You, ladies, you, whose gentle hearts do fear
    The smallest monstrous mouse that creeps on floor,
May now perchance both quake and tremble here, 210
    When lion rough in wildest rage doth roar.
Then know that I, as Snug the joiner, am
A lion fell,° nor else no lion's dam;
For, if I should as lion come in strife
Into this place, 'twere pity on my life. 215
Theseus: A very gentle beast, and of a good conscience.
Demetrius: The very best at a beast, my lord, that e'er I saw.
Lysander: This lion is a very fox for his valor.°
Theseus: True; and a goose for his discretion.°
Demetrius: Not so, my lord; for his valor cannot carry his discretion, and the fox 220
    carries the goose.
Theseus: His discretion, I am sure, cannot carry his valor; for the goose carries not
    the fox. It is well. Leave it to his discretion, and let us listen to the moon.
Moon: This lanthorn° doth the hornèd moon present—
Demetrius: He should have worn the horns on his head.° 225
Theseus: He is no crescent,° and his horns are invisible within the circumference.

191 *Shafalus, Procrus* (Blunders for "Cephalus" and "Procris," also famous lovers.)   196 *'Tide* betide, come   200 *willful* willing*   200–201 *without warning* i.e., without warning the parents (Demetrius makes a joke on the proverb "Walls have ears.")   203 *in this kind* of this sort.   *shadows* likenesses, representations   213 *lion fell* fierce lion (with a play on the idea of "lion skin")   218 *is . . . valor* i.e., his valor consists of craftiness and discretion   219 *a goose . . . discretion* i.e., as discreet as a goose, that is, more foolish than discreet   224 *lanthorn* (This original spelling, *lanthorn*, may suggest a play on the *horn* of which lanterns were made, and also on a cuckold's horns; however, the spelling *lanthorn* is not used consistently for comic effect in this play or elsewhere. At V, i, 133, for example, the word is *lantern* in the original.)   225 *on his head* (as a sign of cuckoldry)   226 *crescent* a waxing moon

Moon: This lanthorn doth the hornèd moon present;
    Myself the man i' the moon do seem to be.
Theseus: This is the greatest error of all the rest. The man should be put into the
    lanthorn. How is it else the man i' the moon?   230
Demetrius: He dares not come there for° the candle, for you see it is already in snuff.°
Hippolyta: I am aweary of this moon. Would he would change!
Theseus: It appears, by his small light of discretion, that he is in the wane; but
    yet, in courtesy, in all reason, we must stay the time.
Lysander: Proceed, Moon.   235
Moon: All that I have to say is to tell you that the lanthorn is the moon, I, the
    man i' the moon, this thornbush my thornbush, and this dog my dog.
Demetrius: Why, all these should be in the lanthorn, for all these are in the
    moon. But silence! Here comes Thisbe.

    Enter Thisbe.

Thisbe: This is old Ninny's tomb. Where is my love?   240
Lion [roaring]: O!
Demetrius: Well roared, Lion.
          [Thisbe runs off, dropping her mantle.]
Theseus: Well run, Thisbe.
Hippolyta: Well shone, Moon. Truly, the moon shines with a good grace.
          [The Lion worries Thisbe's mantle.]
Theseus: Well moused,° Lion.   245
          [Enter Pyramus; exit Lion.]

Demetrius: And then came Pyramus.
Lysander: And so the lion vanished.
Pyramus: Sweet Moon, I thank thee for thy sunny beams;
    I thank thee, Moon, for shining now so bright;
For, by thy gracious, golden, glittering gleams,   250
    I trust to take of truest Thisbe sight.
        But stay, O spite!
        But mark, poor knight,
    What dreadful dole° is here?
        Eyes, do you see?   255
        How can it be?
    O dainty duck! O dear!
        Thy mantle good,
        What, stained with blood?
    Approach, ye Furies° fell!°   260
        O Fates,° come, come,
        Cut thread and thrum;°
    Quail,° crush, conclude, and quell!°

---

231 *for* because of, for fear of. *in snuff* (1) offended (2) in need of snuffing or trimming   245 *moused*
shaken, torn, bitten   254 *dole* grievous event   260 *Furies* avenging goddesses of Greek myth. *fell*
fierce   261 *Fates* the three goddesses (Clotho, Lachesis, Atropos) of Greek myth who spun, drew, and cut
the thread of human life   262 *thread and thrum* i.e., everything—the good and bad alike; literally, the warp
in weaving and the loose end of the weft   263 *Quail* overpower. *quell* kill, destroy

Theseus: This passion, and the death of a dear friend, would go near to make a man look sad.° 265

Hippolyta: Beshrew my heart, but I pity the man.

Pyramus: O, wherefore, Nature, didst thou lions frame?
    Since lion vile hath here deflowered my dear,
    Which is—no, no, which was—the fairest dame
    That lived, that loved, that liked, that looked with cheer.° 270
        Come, tears, confound,
        Out, sword, and wound
    The pap° of Pyramus;
        Ay, that left pap,
        Where heart doth hop.   *[He stabs himself.]* 275
    Thus die I, thus, thus, thus.
        Now am I dead,
        Now am I fled;
    My soul is in the sky.
        Tongue, lose thy light; 280
        Moon, take thy flight.   *[Exit Moonshine.]*
    Now die, die, die, die, die.   *[Pyramus dies.]*

Demetrius: No die, but an ace,° for him; for he is but one.°

Lysander: Less than an ace, man; for he is dead, he is nothing.

Theseus: With the help of a surgeon he might yet recover, and yet prove an ass.° 285

Hippolyta: How chance Moonshine is gone before Thisbe comes back and finds her lover?

Theseus: She will find him by starlight.

    [Enter Thisbe.]

    Here she comes, and her passion ends the play.

Hippolyta: Methinks she should not use a long one for such a Pyramus. I hope she 290
will be brief.

Demetrius: A mote° will turn the balance, which Pyramus, which° Thisbe, is the better: he for a man, God warrant us; she for a woman, God bless us.

Lysander: She hath spied him already with those sweet eyes.

Demetrius: And thus she means,° videlicet:° 295

Thisbe: Asleep, my love?
        What, dead, my dove?
    O Pyramus, arise!
        Speak, speak. Quite dumb?
        Dead, dead? A tomb 300
    Must cover thy sweet eyes.
        These lily lips,
        This cherry nose,

264–265 *This . . . sad* i.e., if one had other reason to grieve, one might be sad, but not from this absurd portrayal of passion   270 *cheer* countenance   273 *pap* breast   283 *ace* the side of the die featuring the single pip, or spot (The pun is on *die* as a singular of *dice*; Bottom's performance is not worth a whole *die* but rather one single face of it, one small portion.)   *one* (1) an individual person (2) unique   285 *ass* (with a pun on *ace*)   292 *mote* small particle.   *which . . . which* whether . . . or   295 *means* moans, laments (with a pun on the meaning, "lodge a formal complaint").   *videlicet* to wit

These yellow cowslip cheeks,
   Are gone, are gone!   305
   Lovers, make moan.
His eyes were green as leeks.
   O Sisters Three,°
   Come, come to me,
With hands as pale as milk;   310
   Lay them in gore,
   Since you have shore°
With shears his thread of silk.
   Tongue, not a word.
   Come, trusty sword,   315
Come, blade, my breast imbrue!°   [*She stabs herself.*]
   And farewell, friends.
   Thus Thisbe ends.
   Adieu, adieu, adieu.   [*She dies.*]

Theseus: Moonshine and Lion are left to bury the dead.   320
Demetrius: Ay, and Wall too.
Bottom [*starting up, as Flute does also*]: No, I assure you, the wall is down that
   parted their fathers. Will it please you to see the epilogue, or to hear a
   Bergomask dance° between two of our company?

[*The other players enter.*]

Theseus: No epilogue, I pray you; for your play needs no excuse. Never excuse;   325
   for when the players are all dead, there need none to be blamed. Marry, if
   he that writ it had played Pyramus and hanged himself in Thisbe's garter,
   it would have been a fine tragedy; and so it is, truly, and very notably dis-
   charged. But, come, your Bergomask. Let your epilogue alone.   [*A dance.*]
The iron tongue° of midnight hath told° twelve.   330
Lovers, to bed, 'tis almost fairy time.
I fear we shall outsleep the coming morn
As much as we this night have overwatched.°
This palpable-gross° play hath well beguiled
The heavy° gait of night. Sweet friends, to bed.   335
A fortnight hold we this solemnity,
In nightly revels and new jollity.   *Exeunt.*

Enter Puck [*carrying a broom*].

Puck: Now the hungry lion roars,
      And the wolf behowls the moon,
     Whilst the heavy° plowman snores,   340
      All with weary task fordone.°
     Now the wasted brands° do glow,
      Whilst the screech owl, screeching loud,

---

308 *Sisters Three* the Fates   **312** *shore* shorn   **316** *imbrue* stain with blood   **324** *Bergomask dance* a
rustic dance named from Bergamo, a province in the state of Venice   **330** *iron tongue* i.e., of a bell.   *told*
counted, struck ("tolled")   **333** *overwatched* stayed up too late   **334** *palpable-gross* palpably gross, obviously crude   **335** *heavy* drowsy, dull   **340** *heavy* tired   **341** *fordone* exhausted   **342** *wasted brands* burned-
out logs

Puts the wretch that lies in woe
  In remembrance of a shroud.   345
Now it is the time of night
  That the graves, all gaping wide,
Every one lets forth his sprite,°
  In the church-way paths to glide.
And we fairies, that do run   350
  By the triple Hecate's° team
From the presence of the sun,
  Following darkness like a dream,
Now are frolic.° Not a mouse
Shall disturb this hallowed house.   355
I am sent with broom before,
To sweep the dust behind° the door.

Enter [Oberon and Titania,] King and Queen of Fairies, with all their train.

Oberon: Through the house give glimmering light,
            By the dead and drowsy fire;
          Every elf and fairy sprite   360
            Hop as light as bird from brier;
          And this ditty, after me,
          Sing, and dance it trippingly.
Titania: First, rehearse° your song by rote,
          To each word a warbling note.   365
          Hand in hand, with fairy grace,
          Will we sing, and bless this place.

                                             [*Song and dance.*]

Oberon: Now, until the break of day,
          Through this house each fairy stray.
          To the best bride-bed will we,   370
          Which by us shall blessèd be;
          And the issue there create°
          Ever shall be fortunate.
          So shall all the couples three
          Ever true in loving be;   375
          And the blots of Nature's hand
          Shall not in their issue stand;
          Never mole, harelip, nor scar,
          Nor mark prodigious,° such as are
          Despisèd in nativity,   380
          Shall upon their children be.
          With this field dew consecrate°

---

348 *Every . . . sprite* every grave lets forth its ghost   351 *triple Hecate's* (Hecate ruled in three capacities: as Luna or Cynthia in heaven, as Diana on earth, and as Proserpina in hell.)   354 *frolic* merry   357 *behind* from behind, or else like sweeping the dirt under the carpet. (Robin Goodfellow was a household spirit who helped good housemaids and punished lazy ones, but he could, of course, be mischievous.)   364 *rehearse* recite   372 *create* created   379 *prodigious* monstrous, unnatural   382 *consecrate* consecrated

"If we shadows have offended, / Think but this, and all is mended"
(V, i, 390–391).

Every fairy take his gait,°
And each several° chamber bless,
Through this palace, with sweet peace;   385
And the owner of it blest
Ever shall in safety rest.
Trip away; make no stay;
Meet me all by break of day.

                       Exeunt [Oberon, Titania, and train].

Puck [to the audience]: If we shadows have offended,   390
           Think but this, and all is mended,
           That you have but slumbered here°

383 *take his gait* go his way   384 *several* separate   392 *That . . . here* i.e., that it is a "midsummer night's
dream"

While these visions did appear.
And this weak and idle theme,
No more yielding but° a dream,   395
Gentles, do not reprehend.
If you pardon, we will mend.°
And, as I am an honest Puck,
If we have unearnèd luck
Now to scape the serpent's tongue,°   400
We will make amends ere long;
Else the Puck a liar call.
So, good night unto you all.
Give me your hands,° if we be friends,
And Robin shall restore amends.°   405

[*Exit.*]

Questions

1. Describe the relationship between King Theseus and Queen Hippolyta in the opening scene. How did they meet? Does their imminent marriage promise to be happy?
2. Describe the personality of each young aristocratic lover. How does Shakespeare differentiate them?
3. Characterize Nick Bottom. What aspects of his personality and behavior make him comic?
4. In what ways does Shakespeare differentiate his rustic tradesmen from the aristocrats?
5. Are the supernatural lovers, Oberon and Titania, characterized differently from their mortal counterparts? How are they similar to the aristocratic lovers and how are they different from them?
6. In what ways is Puck the unifying character of the play? How do his actions touch on every plot and subplot?
7. The main plot of *A Midsummer Night's Dream* concludes by the end of Act IV. What purpose does the final act serve in the play? Could it be omitted without significant loss?

---

395 *No . . . but* yielding no more than   397 *mend* improve   400 *serpent's tongue* i.e., hissing   404 *Give . . . hands* applaud   405 *restore amends* give satisfaction in return

CRITICS ON SHAKESPEARE

Oberon and Titania in the Ninagawa Company's 1996 production of *A Midsummer Night's Dream*.

Anthony Burgess (1917–1993)

An Asian Culture Looks at Shakespeare   1982

Is translation possible? I first found myself asking this question in the Far East, when I was given the task of translating T. S. Eliot's *The Waste Land* into Indonesian. The difficulties began with the first line: "April is the cruellest month . . ." This I rendered as "*Bulan Abril ia-lah bulan yang dzalim sa-kali . . .*" I had to take *dzalim* from Arabic, since Indonesian did not, at that time, seem to possess a word for *cruel*. The term was accepted, but not the notion that a month, as opposed to a person or institution, could be cruel. Moreover, even if a month could be cruel, how—in the tropics where all the months are the same and the concepts of spring and winter do not exist—can one month be crueller than another? When I came to *forgetful snow*—rendered as *thalji berlupa*—I had to borrow a highly poetical word from the Persian, acceptable as a useful descriptive device for the brown skin of the beloved but not known in terms of a climatic reality. And, again, how could this inanimate substance possess the faculty of forgetting? I gave up the task as hopeless. Evidently the imagery of *The Waste Land* does not relate to a universal experience but applies only to the northern hemisphere, with its temperate climate and tradition of spring and fertility rituals.

As a teacher in Malaysia, I had to consider with a mixed group of Malay, Chinese, Indian, and Eurasian students, seasoned with the odd Buginese, Achinese, and Japanese, a piece of representative postwar British fiction. Although the setting of the book is West Africa, I felt that its story was of universal import. It was a novel by Graham Greene called *The Heart of the Matter*—a tragic story about a police officer named Scobie who is a Catholic convert. He is in love with his wife but falls in love with another woman, discovers that he cannot repent of this adultery, makes a sacrilegious communion so that his very Catholic wife will not suspect that a love affair is in progress, then commits suicide in despair, trusting that God will thrust him into the outer darkness and be no longer agonized by the exploits of sinning Scobie. To us this is a tragic situation. To my Muslim students it was extremely funny. One girl said: "Why cannot this Mr. Scobie become a Muslim? Then he can have four wives and there is no problem."

The only author who seemed to have the quality of universal appeal in Malaysia was William Shakespeare. Despite the problems of translating him, there is always an intelligible residue. I remember seeing in a Borneo kampong the film of *Richard III* made by Laurence Olivier, and the illiterate tribe which surrounded me was most appreciative. They knew nothing here of literary history and nothing of the great world outside this jungle clearing. They took this film about medieval conspiracy and tyranny to be a kind of newsreel representation of contemporary England. They approved the medieval costumes because they resembled their own ceremonial dress. This story of the assassination of innocents, including children, Machiavellian massacre, and the eventual defeat of a tyrant was typical of their own history, even their contemporary experience, and they accepted Shakespeare as a great poet. Eliot would not have registered with them at all. Translation is not a matter of words only; it is a matter of making intelligible a whole culture. Evidently the Elizabethan culture was still primitive enough to survive transportation over much time and space.

From spoken remarks on the "Importance of Translation"

W. H. Auden (1907–1973)

Iago as a Triumphant Villain   1962

Any consideration of the *Tragedy of Othello* must be primarily occupied, not with its official hero but with its villain. I cannot think of any other play in which only one character performs personal actions—all the *deeds* are Iago's—and all the others without exception only exhibit behavior. In marrying each other, Othello and Desdemona have performed a deed, but this took place before the play begins. Nor can I think of another play in which the villain is so completely triumphant: everything Iago sets out to do, he accomplishes—(among his goals, I include his self-destruction). Even Cassio, who survives, is maimed for life.

If *Othello* is a tragedy—and one certainly cannot call it a comedy—it is tragic in a peculiar way. In most tragedies the fall of the hero from glory to misery and death is the work, either of the gods, or of his own freely chosen acts, or, more commonly, a mixture of both. But the fall of Othello is the work of another human being; nothing he says or does originates with himself. In consequence we feel pity for him but no respect; our aesthetic respect is reserved for Iago.

Iago is a wicked man. The wicked man, the stage villain, as a subject of serious dramatic interest does not, so far as I know, appear in the drama of western Europe before the Elizabethans. In the mystery plays, the wicked characters, like Satan or Herod, are treated comically, but the theme of the triumphant villain cannot be treated comically because the suffering he inflicts is real.

From "The Joker in the Pack"

Maud Bodkin (1875–1967)

Lucifer in Shakespeare's *Othello* 1934

If we attempt to define the devil in psychological terms, regarding him as an arche-type, a persistent or recurrent mode of apprehension, we may say that the devil is our tendency to represent in personal form the forces within and without us that threaten our supreme values. When Othello finds those values of confident love, of honor, and pride in soldiership, that made up his purposeful life, falling into ruin, his sense of the devil in all around him becomes acute. Desdemona has become "a fair devil"; he feels "a young and sweating devil" in her hand. The cry "O devil" breaks out among his incoherent words of raving. When Iago's falsehoods are disclosed, and Othello at last, too late, wrenches himself free from the spell of Iago's power over him, his sense of the devil incarnate in Iago's shape before him becomes overwhelming. If those who tell of the devil have failed to describe Iago, they have lied:

I look down towards his feet; but that's a fable.
If that thou be'st a devil, I cannot kill thee.

We also, watching or reading the play, experience the archetype. Intellectu-ally aware, as we reflect, of natural forces, within a man himself as well as in society around, that betray or shatter his ideals, we yet feel these forces aptly symbolized for the imagination by such a figure as Iago—a being though personal yet hardly human, concentrated wholly on the hunting to destruction of its destined prey, the proud figure of the hero.

From Archetypal Patterns in Poetry

Virginia Mason Vaughan (b. 1947)

Black and White in *Othello* 1994

> If virtue no delighted beauty lack,
> Your son-in-law is far more fair than black.
> —*Othello* (1.3.290–291)

Black/white oppositions permeate *Othello*. Throughout the play, Shakespeare exploits a discourse of racial difference that by 1604 had become ingrained in the English psyche. From Iago's initial racial epithets at Brabantio's window ("old black ram," "barbary horse") to Emilia's cries of outrage in the final scene ("ignorant as dirt"), Shakespeare shows that the union of a white Venetian maiden and a black Moorish

1472 Chapter 38 ■ Critical Casebook: Shakespeare

general is from at least one perspective emphatically unnatural. The union is of course a central fact of the play, and to some commentators, the spectacle of the pale-skinned woman caught in Othello's black arms has indeed seemed monstrous. Yet that spectacle is a major source of *Othello*'s emotional power. From Shakespeare's day to the present, the sight has titillated and terrified predominantly white audiences.

The effect of *Othello* depends, in other words, on the essential fact of the hero's darkness, the visual signifier of his Otherness. To Shakespeare's original audience, this chromatic sign was probably dark black, although there were other signifiers as well. Roderigo describes the Moor as having "thick lips," a term many sixteenth-century explorers employed in their descriptions of Africans. But, as historian Winthrop Jordan notes, by the late sixteenth century, "Blackness became so generally associated with Africa that every African seemed a black man[,] . . . the terms *Moor* and *Negro* used almost interchangeably." "Moor" became, G. K. Hunter observes, "a word for 'people not like us,' so signaled by color." Richard Burbage's Othello was probably black. But in any production, whether he appears as a tawny Moor (as nineteenth-century actors preferred) or as a black man of African descent, Othello bears the visual signs of his Otherness, a difference that the play's language insists can never be eradicated.

From Othello: A Contextual History

Samuel Johnson (1709–1784)

Shakespeare's Universality   1765

Shakespeare is above all writers, at least above all modern writers, the poet of nature; the poet that holds up to his readers a faithful mirrour of manners and of life. His characters are not modified by the customs of particular places, unpractised by the rest of the world; by the peculiarities of studies or professions, which can operate but upon small numbers; or by the accidents of transient fashions or temporary opinions: they are the genuine progeny of common humanity, such as the world will always supply, and observation will always find. His persons act and speak by the influence of those general passions and principles by which all minds are agitated, and the whole system of life is continued in motion. In the writings of other poets a character is too often an individual; in those of Shakespeare it is commonly a species.

From the Preface to Shakespeare

Clare Asquith (b. 1951)

Shakespeare's Language as a Hidden Political Code   2005

Shakespeare was the one sixteenth-century writer who, it appears, never fell foul of the authorities. Yet in a strangely insistent passage, the editors of the First Folio of his work, published in 1623, urge us to look beneath the surface of the great universal plays to something hidden below. Though they are sure that his wit can "no more lie hid than it could be lost," they press us to "Read him therefore, and again, and again." We must seek help from his friends if we miss his "hidden wit," and we should act as guides to others if we find it. The insistence on readers acting as guides is striking and unusual.

• • •

Whatever its impact at the time, Shakespeare's cautious artistry was so great that his hidden language remained undetectable to succeeding generations that accepted the official version of England's Reformation. Yet the subterfuge was essential if he and his work were to survive. He was writing in a climate more dangerous and oppressive than anything experienced by his predecessors. By the 1580s, the censorship laws, regularly tightened under Elizabeth, were strictly enforced. Yet he could not remain silent. He was driven to write by a different fear, to which he returns throughout his work. This was the growing concern, shared by many contemporaries, that the true history of the age would never be told. . . . Shakespeare not only needed to write; he needed to find a new method of writing, one capable of recording the whole unhappy story of the country's political and spiritual collapse against the background of a regime for whom the slightest topical reference was justification enough to imprison a playwright.

• • •

In these dramas, there would be no room for asides or explanations. Instead, Shakespeare worked out a set of simple markers, basic call-signs that would alert his audience to the entry point they needed to access the hidden story. Unlike Erasmus, Sidney and Donne, who were poets and essayists, he was a seasoned actor addressing restless spectators, so he kept his signals simple and consistent. But he was also one of a brotherhood of dissident writers, and to them his pointers would have been as readily—even wittily—recognizable as they became baffling to later readers.

The master key to the hidden level is so simple that it is easy to miss. It takes the form of twin terms that identify the polar opposites in Elizabeth's England. They are not Shakespeare's only terms, and he uses them sparingly, but with pinpoint accuracy. They are the terms "high" and "fair," which always indicate Catholicism, and "low" and "dark," which always suggest Protestantism. Shakespeare's treatment of these words is sufficiently remarkable for critics to have wondered whether he was writing for a tall blond actor and a short dark one—but the theory is untenable. Shakespeare was not a dramatist who would have deliberately created casting problems, and the references span a ten-year period.

The opposition of high and low, representing the two opposing sides of the Reformation, was commonplace at the time. The modern Christian distinction between high and low church goes back to pre-Reformation days when High Mass, high day, and high altars involved full liturgical ceremony—Low Mass and low altars were for every day.

The opposition of dark and fair was equally recognizable. The glittering, skin-deep attractions of the scarlet woman were constantly under fire from Protestant plays, sermons, and literature: the sober reformers wore plain black, and the new Prayer Book was shorn of illuminated initials and, as far as possible, red print.

• • •

His markers are morally neutral. Fair, tall characters can be corrupt, while dark, low ones are often noble—the words merely identify the religious allegiance of one or two characters, providing a key compass-bearing from which alert readers and spectators can work out the rest of the shadowed plot. In the process an enjoyable trail of punning wordplay emerges, deepening and confirming the discovery.

From *Shadowplay: The Hidden Beliefs and Coded Politics of William Shakespeare*

Linda Bamber (b. 1945)

Female Power in *A Midsummer Night's Dream*   1982

The best example of the relationship between male dominance and the status quo comes in *A Midsummer Night's Dream*, which begins with a rebellion of the feminine against the power of masculine authority. Hermia refuses the man both Egeus and Theseus order her to marry; her refusal sends us off into the forest, beyond the power of the father and the masculine state. Once in the forest, of course, we find the social situation metaphorically repeated in this world of imagination and nature. The fairy king, Oberon, rules the forest. His rule, too, is troubled by the rebellion of the feminine. Titania has refused to give him her page, the child of a human friend who died in childbirth. But by the end of the story Titania is conquered, the child relinquished, and order restored. Even here the comic upheavals, whether we see them as May games or bad dreams, are associated with an uprising of women. David P. Young, in *Something of Great Constancy*, has pointed out how firmly this play connects order with masculine dominance and the disruption of order with the rebellion of the feminine:

> It is appropriate that Theseus, as representative of daylight and right reason, should have subdued his bride-to-be to the rule of his masculine will. That is the natural order of things. It is equally appropriate that Oberon, as king of darkness and fantasy, should have lost control of his wife, and that the corresponding natural disorder described by Titania should ensue.

The natural order, the status quo, is for men to rule women. When they fail to do so, we have the exceptional situation, the festive, disruptive, disorderly moment of comedy.

● ● ●

Where are we to bestow our sympathies? On the forces that make for the disruption of the status quo and therefore for the plot? Or on the force that asserts itself against the disruption and reestablishes a workable social order? Of course we cannot choose. We can only say that in comedy we owe our holiday to such forces as the tendency of the feminine to rebel, whereas to the successful reassertion of masculine power we owe our everyday order. Shakespearean comedy endorses both sides. Holiday is, of course, the subject and the analogue of each play; but the plays always end in a return to everyday life. The optimistic reading of Shakespearean comedy says that everyday life is clarified and enriched by our holiday from it; according to the pessimistic reading the temporary subversion of the social order has revealed how much that order excludes, how high a price we pay for it. But whether our return to everyday life is a comfortable one or not, the return itself is the inevitable conclusion to the journey out.

From *Comic Women, Tragic Men*

■ WRITING *effectively*

Ben Jonson on Writing   (1573?–1637)

On His Friend and Rival William Shakespeare   1640

I remember the players have often mentioned it as an honor to Shakespeare, that in his writing (whatsoever he penned) he never blotted out a line. My answer hath been, "Would he had blotted a thousand," which they thought a malevolent speech. I had not told posterity this but for their ignorance who chose that circumstance to commend their friend by wherein he most faulted; and to justify mine own candor, for I loved the man, and do honor his memory on this side idolatry as much as any. He was, indeed, honest, and of an open and free nature; had an excellent phantasy, brave notions, and gentle expressions, wherein he flowed with that facility that sometimes it was necessary he should be stopped. "*Sufflaminandus erat*,"°

Ben Jonson

as Augustus° said of Haterius.° His wit was in his own power; would the rule of it had been so, too! Many times he fell into those things, could not escape laughter, as when he said in the person of Caesar,° one speaking to him, "Caesar, thou dost me wrong." He replied, "Caesar did never wrong but with just cause"; and such like, which were ridiculous. But he redeemed his vices with his virtues. There was ever more in him to be praised than to be pardoned.

From *Discoveries*

UNDERSTANDING SHAKESPEARE

The basic problem a modern reader faces with Shakespeare is language. Shakespeare's English is now four hundred years old, and it differs in innumerable small ways from contemporary American English. Although Shakespeare's idiom may at first seem daunting, it is easily mastered if you make the effort. To grow comfortable with his language, you must immerse yourself in it. Fortunately, doing so isn't all that hard; you might even find it pleasurable.

Sufflaminandus erat: Latin for "He ought to have been plugged up."   *Augustus*: the first emperor of Rome (63 B.C.–14 A.D.).   *Haterius*: a very verbose orator of the Augustan age.   *Caesar*: Shakespeare's tragedy *Julius Caesar*. Jonson misremembers the quotation, which (in the First Folio) actually reads "Know, Caesar doth not wrong, nor without cause will he be satisfied" (III, i, 47).

■ **Let your ears do the work.** There is no substitute for hearing Shakespeare's words in performance. After all, the plays were written to be seen, not to be read silently on the page. After reading the play, listen to or watch a recording of it. It sometimes helps to read along as you listen or watch, hitting the pause button as needed. If you can attend a live performance of any Shakespeare play, do so.

■ **But read the text first.** Watching a production is never a full substitute for reading an assigned play. Many productions abridge the play, leaving passages out. Even more important, directors and actors choose a particular interpretation of a play, and their choices might skew your understanding of events and motivation if you are unfamiliar with the original itself.

■ **Before you write a paper, read the play again.** The first time through an Elizabethan-era text, you will almost certainly miss many things. As you grow more familiar with Shakespeare's language, you will be able to read it with greater comprehension. If you choose to write about a particular episode or character, carefully study the speeches and dialogue in question (and pay special attention to the footnotes) so that you understand each word.

■ **Enjoy yourself.** From Beijing to Berlin, Buenos Aires to Oslo, Shakespeare is almost universally acknowledged as the world's greatest playwright, a master entertainer as well as a consummate artist.

CHECKLIST: Writing About Shakespeare

☐ Read closely. Work through passages with difficult language.

☐ Pay special attention to footnotes.

☐ Read the play more than once if necessary.

☐ Watch a DVD or listen to an audio recording after reading a play. Immerse yourself in Shakespeare's language until it becomes familiar.

☐ As you view or listen to a play, read along, or revisit the text afterward.

☐ Carefully study any speeches and dialogue you choose to write about.

☐ Be sure you understand each word of any passage you decide to discuss or quote.

TOPICS FOR WRITING ON SHAKESPEARE

1. Write a defense of Iago.

2. "Never was any play fraught, like this of *Othello*, with improbabilities," wrote Thomas Rymer in a famous attack (*A Short View of Tragedy*, 1692). Consider Rymer's objection to the play, either answering it or finding evidence to back it up.

3. Suppose yourself a casting director assigned to a film version of *Othello*. What well-known actors would you cast in the principal roles? Write a report justifying your choices. Don't merely discuss the stars and their qualifications; discuss (with specific reference to the play) what Shakespeare appears to call for.

4. Emilia's long speech at the end of Act IV (iii, 83–102) has been called a Renaissance plea for women's rights. Do you agree? Write a brief, close analysis of this speech. How timely is it?

5. "The downfall of Oedipus is the work of the gods; the downfall of Othello is self-inflicted." Test this comment with reference to the two plays, and report your findings.

6. Contrast the palace and the woods as settings in *A Midsummer Night's Dream*.

7. Explain the connection between the comic sketch presented by the rustic tradesmen on Pyramus and Thisbe and the events that occur elsewhere in the play.

8. Select any tragedy found in the book (*Othello*, *Oedipus the King*, or *Antigone*), and analyze it using Aristotle's definition of the form. Does the play measure up to Aristotle's requirements for a tragedy? In what ways does it meet the definition? In what ways does it depart from it? (Be sure to state clearly the Aristotelian rules by which drama is to be judged.)

SAMPLE STUDENT PAPER

Here is an example of a paper analyzing how Shakespeare's *Othello* fits Aristotle's classic definition of tragedy. It was written by Janet Housden, a student of Melinda Barth at El Camino College.

Housden 1

Janet Housden

Professor Barth

English 201

3 January 2019

Othello: Tragedy or Soap Opera?

When we hear the word "tragedy," we usually think of either a terrible real-life disaster, or a dark and serious drama filled with pain, suffering, and loss that involves the downfall of a powerful person due to some character flaw or error in judgment. William Shakespeare's *Othello* is such a drama. Set in Venice and Cyprus during the Renaissance, the play tells the story of Othello, a Moorish general in the Venetian army, who has just married Desdemona, the daughter of a Venetian nobleman. Through the plotting of a jealous villain, Iago, Othello is deceived into believing that Desdemona has been unfaithful to him. He murders her in revenge, only to discover too late how he has been tricked. Overcome by shame and grief, Othello kills himself.

Dealing as it does with jealousy, murder, and suicide, the play is certainly dark, but is *Othello* a true tragedy? In the fourth century B.C., the Greek philosopher Aristotle proposed a formal definition of tragedy (Kennedy et al., 1200–01), which only partially fits *Othello*.

The first characteristic of tragedy identified by Aristotle is that the protagonist is a person of outstanding quality and high social position. While Othello is not of royal birth as are many tragic heroes and heroines, he does occupy a sufficiently high position to satisfy this part of Aristotle's definition. Although Othello is a foreigner and a soldier by trade, he has risen to the rank of general and has married into a noble family, which is quite an accomplishment for an outsider. Furthermore,

First paragraph gives name of author and work

Key plot information avoids excessive retelling

Central question is raised

Thesis statement provides response

Topic sentence on Othello's social position

Essay systematically applies Aristotle's definition of tragedy to Othello

Othello is generally liked and respected by those around him. He is often described by others as being "noble," "brave," and "valiant." By virtue of his high rank and the respect he commands from others, Othello would appear to possess the high stature commonly given to the tragic hero in order to make his eventual fall seem all the more tragic.

Topic sentence on Othello's tragic flaw

While Othello displays the nobility and high status commonly associated with the tragic hero, he also possesses another, less admirable characteristic, the flaw or character defect shared by all heroes of classical tragedy. In Othello's case, it is a stunning gullibility, combined with a violent temper that once awakened overcomes all reason. These flaws permit Othello to be easily deceived and manipulated by the villainous Iago and make him easy prey for the "green-eyed monster" (3.3.179).

Quotes from play as evidence to support point

It is because of this tragic flaw, according to Aristotle, that the hero is at least partially to blame for his own downfall. While Othello's "free and open nature, / That thinks men honest that but seem to be so" (1.3.376–77) is not a fault in itself, it does allow Iago to convince the Moor of his wife's infidelity without one shred of concrete evidence. Furthermore, once Othello has been convinced of Desdemona's guilt, he makes up his mind to take vengeance, and says that his "bloody thoughts with violent pace / Shall ne'er look back, ne'er ebb to humble love" (3.3.473–74).

Topic sentence elaborates on idea raised in previous paragraphs

He thereby renders himself deaf to the voice of reason, and ignoring Desdemona's protestations of innocence, brutally murders her, only to discover too late that he has made a terrible mistake. Although he is goaded into his crime by Iago, who is a master at manipulating people, it is Othello's own character flaws that lead to his horrible misjudgment.

Aristotle's definition also states that the hero's misfortune is not wholly deserved, that the punishment he receives exceeds his crime. Although it is hard to sympathize with a man as cruel as Othello is to the innocent Desdemona, Othello pays an extremely high price for his sin of gullibility. Othello loses everything—his wife, his position, even his life. Even though it's partially his fault, Othello is not entirely to blame, for without Iago's interference it's highly unlikely that things would turn out as they do. Though it seems incredibly stupid on Othello's part,

Topic sentence on Othello's misfortune

that a man who has travelled the world and commanded armies should be so easily deceived, there is little evidence that Othello has had much experience with civilian society, and although he is "declined / Into the vale of years" (3.3.281–82) Othello has apparently never been married before. By his own admission, "little of this great world can I speak / More than pertains to feats of broils and battle" (1.3.88–89).

Transitional words signal argument's direction

Furthermore, Othello has no reason to suspect that "honest Iago" is anything but his loyal friend and supporter.

While it is understandable that Othello could be fooled into believing Desdemona unfaithful, the question remains whether his fate is deserved. In addition to his mistake of believing Iago's lies, Othello commits a more serious error: he lets himself be blinded by anger. Worse yet, in deciding to take vengeance, he also makes up his mind not to be swayed from his course, even by his love for Desdemona. In fact, he refuses to listen to her at all, "lest her body and beauty unprovide my mind again" (4.1.186–87), therefore denying her the right to defend herself. Because of his rage and unfairness, perhaps Othello deserves his fate more than Aristotle's ideal tragic hero. Othello's punishment does exceed his crime, but just barely.

Topic sentence elaborates on Othello's misfortune

According to Aristotle, the tragic hero's fall gives the protagonist deeper understanding and self-awareness. Othello departs from Aristotle's model in that Othello apparently learns nothing from his mistakes. He never realizes that he is partly at fault. He sees himself only as an innocent victim and blames his misfortune on fate rather than accepting responsibility for his actions. To be sure, he realizes he has been tricked and deeply regrets his mistake, but he seems to feel that he was justified under the circumstances, "For naught I did in hate, but all in honor" (5.2.303). Othello sees himself not as someone whose bad judgment and worse temper have resulted in the death of an innocent party, but as one who has "loved not wisely but too well" (5.2.354). This failure to grasp the true nature of his error indicates that Othello hasn't learned his lesson.

Topic sentence on whether Othello learns from his mistakes

Neither accepting responsibility nor learning from his mistakes, Othello fails to fulfill yet another of Aristotle's requirements. Since the protagonist usually gains some understanding along with his defeat, classical tragedy conveys a sense of human greatness and of life's unrealized potentialities—a quality totally absent from *Othello*. Not only does Othello fail to learn from his mistakes, he never really realizes what those mistakes are, and it apparently never crosses his mind that things could have turned out any differently. "Who can control his fate?" Othello asks (5.2.274), and this defeatist attitude, combined with his failure to salvage any wisdom from his defeat, separates *Othello* from the tragedy as defined by Aristotle.

Topic sentence elaborating further on whether Othello learns from his errors

The last part of Aristotle's definition states that viewing the conclusion of a tragedy should result in catharsis for the audience, and that the audience should be left with a feeling of exaltation rather than depression. Unfortunately, the feeling we are left with after viewing *Othello* is neither catharsis nor exaltation but rather a feeling of horror, pity, and disgust at the senseless waste of human lives. The deaths of Desdemona and Othello, as well as those of Emilia and Roderigo, serve no purpose whatsoever. They die not in the service of a great cause but because of lies,

Topic sentence on catharsis

treachery, jealousy, and spite. Their deaths don't even benefit Iago, who is directly or indirectly responsible for all of them. No lesson is learned, no epiphany is reached, and the audience, instead of experiencing catharsis, is left with its negative feeling unresolved.

Restatement of thesis

Since *Othello* only partially fits Aristotle's definition of tragedy, it is questionable whether or not it should be classified as one. Though it does involve a great man undone by a defect in his own character, the hero gains neither insight nor understanding from his defeat, and so there can be no inspiration or catharsis for the audience, as there would be in a "true" tragedy. *Othello* is tragic only in

Conclusion

the everyday sense of the word, the way a plane crash or fire is tragic. At least in terms of Aristotle's classic definition, *Othello* ultimately comes across as more of a melodrama or soap opera than a tragedy.

Works Cited

Kennedy, X. J., et al., editors. *Literature: An Introduction to Fiction, Poetry, Drama, and Writing*. 14th ed., Pearson, 2020, pp. 1200–01.

Shakespeare, William. *Othello: The Moor of Venice. Literature: An Introduction to Fiction, Poetry, Drama, and Writing*, edited by X. J. Kennedy et al., 14th ed., Pearson, 2020, pp. 1300–98.

THE MODERN THEATER

Speak of the moderns without contempt,
and of the ancients without idolatry.

—LORD CHESTERFIELD

What You Will Learn in This Chapter

- To identify and define *Realism* as a dramatic mode
- To describe the stagecraft developments of modern theater
- To define other major movements of modern theater, such as *Naturalism*, *Symbolism*, and *Expressionism*
- To analyze classic works of modern theater

REALISM

The ancient art of the drama experienced a revival in the Renaissance and went through a number of changes over the next several centuries. Elizabethan drama was marked by strong characterization, heightened and intense language, and crowded, sometimes sprawling plots. In the neoclassical period of the seventeenth and eighteenth centuries, greater emphasis was placed upon formality, decorum, and Aristotle's unities of time, place, and action. The early nineteenth century saw the rise of melodrama, with its florid dialogue, plots that relied heavily on often absurd coincidences, and crude stereotypes of good and evil characters. Through all these developments—from kings and generals to lords and ladies of high society to purehearted swashbucklers and craven villains—the one thing that seemed to remain constant was an absence of **realism**—the attempt to reproduce faithfully the surface appearance of life, especially that of ordinary people in everyday situations.

By the end of the nineteenth century, however, realism had become the drama's dominant mode. The writer most responsible for that shift was the Norwegian playwright Henrik Ibsen. From *Pillars of Society* (1877) to *Hedda Gabler* (1890), he wrote a series of prose dramas in which realistically portrayed middle-class characters face conflicts in their lives and relationships. They are often called "problem plays" because of their engagement of social issues, such as women's place in society (*A Doll's House*) and inherited venereal disease (*Ghosts*). In actuality, the social problems in these plays serve as a context for Ibsen's real concern, an examination of the complexities of human personality and psychology, especially those aspects of our natures that are hidden or repressed because of society's expectations.

The attempt to use the theater to present the real lives of real people was taken even further by the Russian dramatist Anton Chekhov. In Chekhov's mature plays, the dialogue seems at times to meander and there appears to be little or no action.

The Cherry Orchard (1904), his last and greatest play, presents a decayed aristocratic clan unable to deal with a threatened foreclosure on the family estate, despite advice from all quarters. The play has sparked debate for over a century: Is it a comedy or a tragedy? Are its characters foolish or sympathetic? Does it lament the passing of an old way of life or greet the dawn of a new age? The answer, of course, is *All of the above*—just like life itself.

Conventions of Realism

From Italian playhouses of the sixteenth century, the theater had inherited the **picture-frame stage**: a structure that holds the action within a **proscenium arch**, a gateway standing (as the word *proscenium* indicates) "in front of the scenery." This manner of constructing a playhouse in effect divided the actors from their audience; most commercial theaters even today are so constructed. But as the nineteenth century gave way to the twentieth, actors less often declaimed their passions in oratorical style in front of backdrops painted with waterfalls and volcanoes, while stationed exactly at the center of the stage as if to sing "duets meant to bring forth applause" (as Swedish playwright August Strindberg complained).

In the theater of Realism, a room was represented by a **box set**—three walls that joined in two corners and a ceiling that tilted as if seen in perspective—replacing drapery walls that had billowed and doors that had flapped, not slammed. Instead of posing at stage center and directly facing the audience to deliver key speeches, actors were instructed to speak from wherever the dramatic situation placed them, and now and then even to turn their backs upon the audience. They were to behave as if they were in a room with the fourth wall sliced away, unaware that they had an audience.

To encourage actors further to imitate reality, the influential director Constantin Stanislavsky of the Moscow Art Theater developed his famous system to help actors feel at home inside a playwright's characters. One of Stanislavsky's exercises was to have actors search their memories for personal experiences like those of the characters in the play; another was to have them act out things a character did *not* do in the play but might do in life. The system enabled Stanislavsky to bring authenticity to his productions of Chekhov's plays and of Maxim Gorky's *The Lower Depths* (1902), a play that showed the tenants of a sordid lodging house drinking themselves to death (and hanging themselves) in surroundings of realistic squalor. Stanislavsky's techniques are still used by stage and film actors today.

NATURALISM

Gorky's play is a masterpiece of **Naturalism**, a kind of realism in fiction and drama dealing with the more brutal or unpleasant aspects of reality. As codified by French novelist and playwright Émile Zola, who influenced Ibsen, Naturalism viewed a person as a creature whose acts are determined by heredity and environment; Zola urged writers to study their characters' behavior with the detachment of zoologists studying animals.

Another masterpiece of the naturalistic tradition is *The Hairy Ape* (1922) by the American playwright Eugene O'Neill. The title character is Yank, a brutish but good-natured engine-stoker on an ocean liner. After a rich young woman calls him a "filthy beast," he grows depressed and dislocated, trying and failing to find a comfortable place for himself in society. He ends up at the zoo, where he dies in a gorilla's embrace. (The play's enduring power was affirmed by a successful New York revival in 2006.) Universally regarded as the first true genius of the American theater, O'Neill greatly influenced several generations of American playwrights, including Arthur

Miller. In many of his plays, Miller portrayed working-class characters whose lives are shaped and constrained by powerful social and cultural forces. Miller was also influenced by Ibsen, whose *Enemy of the People* he adapted for the Broadway stage in 1950.

SYMBOLISM AND EXPRESSIONISM

The ascendance of Realism had liberated drama from some outworn styles and opened rich new areas of artistic exploration, but when it became the dominant tradition, some writers began to feel confined by its themes and theatrical conventions, and new forms of drama emerged. One of these was the **Symbolist movement** in the French theater, most influentially expressed by Belgian playwright Maurice Maeterlinck, whose work conjures up a spirit world we cannot directly perceive, as in his play *The Intruder* (1890), when a blind man sees the approach of Death.

In Ireland, poet William Butler Yeats wrote (among other plays) "plays for dancers" to be performed in drawing rooms, often in friends' homes, with simple costumes and props, a few masked actors, and a very few musicians. In Sweden, August Strindberg, who earlier had won fame as a Naturalist, reversed direction and in *The Dream Play* (1902) and *The Ghost Sonata* (1907) introduced characters who change their identities and, ignoring space and time, move across dreamlike landscapes.

In these plays Strindberg anticipated the movement in German theater after World War I called **Expressionism**. Delighting in bizarre sets and exaggerated makeup and costuming, Expressionist playwrights and producers sought to reflect intense states of emotion and, sometimes, to depict the world through lunatic eyes. A classic film example is *The Cabinet of Dr. Caligari*, made in Berlin in 1919 and 1920, in which a hypnotist sends forth a subject to murder people. Garbed in jet black, the killer sleepwalks through a town of lopsided houses, twisted streets, and railings that tilt at gravity-defying angles. A restless experimenter throughout his career, Eugene O'Neill employed Expressionist techniques in his 1926 play *The Great God Brown*, in which characters speak through masks and wear one another's clothes (and identities).

AMERICAN MODERNISM

If modern American drama first came of age with Eugene O'Neill, it soon found powerful new voices. Thornton Wilder wrote experimental plays such as *Our Town* (1938) and *The Skin of Our Teeth* (1942) that were so carefully constructed, witty, innovative, and evocative that they achieved enormous popular and critical success.

It was not until the mid-1940s that two playwrights emerged who would rival O'Neill in the depth and artistry of their work—Arthur Miller and Tennessee Williams. Miller achieved his first major success with *All My Sons* (1947), in which an idealistic young man discovers that his father was guilty of supplying defective airplane parts to the government during World War II, resulting in the deaths of American servicemen. But it was his next play, *Death of a Salesman* (1949), that established Miller's work as a permanent part of America's literary heritage. In this emotionally devastating drama, Miller once again presents a tormented young man trying to come to terms with the deeply flawed father that he loves.

Tennessee Williams had made his mark a bit earlier, with *The Glass Menagerie*, produced in Chicago in December 1944 and on Broadway the following March. From there, Williams would go on to greater triumphs, especially in *A Streetcar Named*

Desire (1947) and *Cat on a Hot Tin Roof* (1955). These two plays established the qualities most associated with Williams's name—strong but driven and sometimes brutal men who dominate their families; sensitive yet ambitious women; a kind of folk poetry grounded in vigorous speech rhythms (hinted at in the evocative titles of the plays); Southern settings in which contemporary decay embodies a nostalgia for a more refined past. But *The Glass Menagerie* is extraordinary for its tender lyricism and in the high quotient of human decency among its characters; partly for these reasons, it is still one of the most popular, if not *the* most popular, of Williams's works.

Lorraine Hansberry's *A Raisin in the Sun* (1959) came a bit later and made history as the first play by a black woman to be produced on Broadway. It explores how we are shaped by our experience in families, how our identities and achievements are influenced by our background and upbringing. First produced at the start of the civil rights movement, *A Raisin in the Sun* depicts troubled relationships between parents and children, brother and sister, husband and wife. Set against the backdrop of a specific era and society, it has a larger, lasting relevance in its portrayal of a family that ultimately holds together.

Following Hansberry's play is one of the pioneering works of Realism, Henrik Ibsen's *A Doll's House*, which also addresses family and marriage, but in a much different way. The play derives a good deal of its power from our ability to identify with its characters and the lives they live, an identification that Ibsen achieves in part by framing the action with the details of daily existence.

Lorraine Hansberry

A Raisin in the Sun   1959

Lorraine Hansberry (1930–1965) was born in Chicago. Her father was a banker and real-estate broker, her mother a former schoolteacher; both were active in the struggle for social justice. When Lorraine Hansberry was eight years old, her father bought a home in what she described as a "hellishly hostile 'white neighborhood' in which, literally, howling mobs surrounded our house. . . . My memories . . . include being spat on, cursed and pummeled in the daily trek to and from school." Hansberry's father brought a lawsuit over his right to purchase the house; the case went all the way to the U.S. Supreme Court, which ruled in his favor. Visitors to the family home when Lorraine Hansberry was young included W. E. B. Du Bois, Duke Ellington, Langston Hughes, Paul Robeson, and other prominent black artists and intellectuals. After two years of study at the University of Wisconsin, Hansberry moved to New York City in 1950. She became associate editor of the newspaper Freedom, *published by Paul Robeson, but resigned in 1953 to concentrate on her writing. A Raisin in the Sun made history in March 1959 when it became the first play by a black woman to be produced on Broadway. It ran for nineteen months, won the New York Drama Critics Circle Award as Best Play of the Year, and was made into a film in 1961. Her second full-length play,* The Sign in Sidney Brustein's Window, *opened on Broadway in October 1964. By the time of its production, Hansberry was terminally ill; she died of cancer in January 1965, at the age of thirty-four. Posthumously produced works included* To Be Young, Gifted and Black *(1969) and* Les Blancs *(1970). The text of* A Raisin in the Sun *presented here is the most complete version available; it includes two short scenes omitted for reasons of length from the Broadway production and omitted as well from the early published editions.*

CHARACTERS

Ruth Younger
Travis Younger
Walter Lee Younger (Brother)
Beneatha Younger
Lena Younger (Mama)
Joseph Asagai

George Murchison
Mrs. Johnson
Karl Lindner
Bobo
Moving Men

The action of the play is set in Chicago's Southside, sometime between World War II and the present.

ACT I
Scene 1: *Friday morning.*
Scene 2: *The following morning.*

ACT II
Scene 1: *Later, the same day.*
Scene 2: *Friday night, a few weeks later.*
Scene 3: *Moving day, one week later.*

ACT III
An hour later.

What happens to a dream deferred?
Does it dry up
Like a raisin in the sun?
Or fester like a sore—
And then run?
Does it stink like rotten meat
Or crust and sugar over—
Like a syrupy sweet?

Maybe it just sags
Like a heavy load.

Or does it explode?

—LANGSTON HUGHES

ACT I

SCENE I

The Younger living room would be a comfortable and well-ordered room if it were not for a number of indestructible contradictions to this state of being. Its furnishings are typical and undistinguished and their primary feature now is that they have clearly had to accommodate the living of too many people for too many years—and they are tired. Still, we can see that at some time, a time probably no longer remembered by the family (except perhaps for Mama), the furnishings of this room were actually selected with care and love and even hope—and brought to this apartment and arranged with taste and pride.

That was a long time ago. Now the once loved pattern of the couch upholstery has to fight to show itself from under acres of crocheted doilies and couch covers which have themselves finally come to be more important than the upholstery. And here a table or a chair has been moved to disguise the worn places in the carpet; but the carpet has fought back by showing its weariness, with depressing uniformity, elsewhere on its surface.

Weariness has, in fact, won in this room. Everything has been polished, washed, sat on, used, scrubbed too often. All pretenses but living itself have long since vanished from the very atmosphere of this room.

Moreover, a section of this room, for it is not really a room unto itself, though the landlord's lease would make it seem so, slopes backward to provide a small kitchen area, where the family prepares the meals that are eaten in the living room proper, which must also serve as dining room. The single window that has been provided for these "two" rooms is located in this kitchen area. The sole natural light the family may enjoy in the course of a day is only that which fights its way through this little window.

At left, a door leads to a bedroom which is shared by Mama and her daughter, Beneatha. At right, opposite, is a second room (which in the beginning of the life of this apartment was probably a breakfast room) which serves as a bedroom for Walter and his wife, Ruth.

TIME. *Sometime between World War II and the present.*

PLACE. *Chicago's Southside.*

Diana Sands, Ruby Dee, Claudia McNeil, and Sidney Poitier in the original 1959 Broadway production of *A Raisin in the Sun*. The play was made into a film with the same cast in 1961.

AT RISE. *It is morning dark in the living room. Travis is asleep on the make-down bed at center. An alarm clock sounds from within the bedroom at right, and presently Ruth enters from that room and closes the door behind her. She crosses sleepily toward the window. As she passes her sleeping son she reaches down and shakes him a little. At the window she raises the shade and a dusky Southside morning light comes in feebly. She fills a pot with water and puts it on to boil. She calls to the boy, between yawns, in a slightly muffled voice.*

Ruth is about thirty. We can see that she was a pretty girl, even exceptionally so, but now it is apparent that life has been little that she expected, and disappointment has already begun to hang in her face. In a few years, before thirty-five even, she will be known among her people as a "settled woman."

She crosses to her son and gives him a good, final, rousing shake.

Ruth: Come on now, boy, it's seven thirty! *(Her son sits up at last, in a stupor of sleepiness.)* I say hurry up, Travis! You ain't the only person in the world got to use a bathroom!

(The child, a sturdy, handsome little boy of ten or eleven, drags himself out of the bed and almost blindly takes his towels and "today's clothes" from drawers and a closet and goes out to the bathroom, which is in an outside hall and which is shared by another family or families on the same floor. Ruth crosses to the bedroom door at right and opens it and calls in to her husband.)

Walter Lee! . . . It's after seven thirty! Lemme see you do some waking up in there now! *(She waits.)* You better get up from there, man! It's after seven thirty

Sean Combs and Phylicia Rashad in the 2008 film of *A Raisin in the Sun.*

I tell you. (*She waits again.*) All right, you just go ahead and lay there and next thing you know Travis be finished and Mr. Johnson'll be in there and you'll be fussing and cussing round here like a madman! And be late too! (*She waits, at the end of patience.*) Walter Lee—it's time for you to GET UP!

(*She waits another second and then starts to go into the bedroom, but is apparently satisfied that her husband has begun to get up. She stops, pulls the door to, and returns to the kitchen area. She wipes her face with a moist cloth and runs her fingers through her sleep-disheveled hair in a vain effort and ties an apron around her housecoat. The bedroom door at right opens and her husband stands in the doorway in his pajamas, which are rumpled and mismated. He is a lean, intense young man in his middle thirties, inclined to quick nervous movements and erratic speech habits—and always in his voice there is a quality of indictment.*)

Walter: Is he out yet?

Ruth: What you mean *out*? He ain't hardly got in there good yet.

Walter (*wandering in, still more oriented to sleep than to a new day*): Well, what was you doing all that yelling for if I can't even get in there yet? (*Stopping and thinking.*) Check coming today?

Ruth: They *said* Saturday and this is just Friday and I hopes to God you ain't going to get up here first thing this morning and start talking to me 'bout no money— 'cause I 'bout don't want to hear it.

Walter: Something the matter with you this morning?

Ruth: No—I'm just sleepy as the devil. What kind of eggs you want?

Walter: Not scrambled. (*Ruth starts to scramble eggs.*) Paper come? (*Ruth points impatiently to the rolled up Tribune on the table, and he gets it and spreads it out and vaguely reads the front page.*) Set off another bomb yesterday.

Ruth (*maximum indifference*): Did they?

Walter (*looking up*): What's the matter with you?

Ruth: Ain't nothing the matter with me. And don't keep asking me that this morning.

Walter: Ain't nobody bothering you. (*Reading the news of the day absently again.*) Say Colonel McCormick° is sick.

Ruth (*affecting tea-party interest*): Is he now? Poor thing.

Walter (*sighing and looking at his watch*): Oh, me. (*He waits.*) Now what is that boy doing in that bathroom all this time? He just going to have to start getting up earlier. I can't be being late to work on account of him fooling around in there.

Ruth (*turning on him*): Oh, no he ain't going to be getting up no earlier no such thing! It ain't his fault that he can't get to bed no earlier nights 'cause he got a bunch of crazy good-for-nothing clowns sitting up running their mouths in what is supposed to be his bedroom after ten o'clock at night . . .

Walter: That's what you mad about, ain't it? The things I want to talk about with my friends just couldn't be important in your mind, could they?

(*He rises and finds a cigarette in her handbag on the table and crosses to the little window and looks out, smoking and deeply enjoying this first one.*)

Colonel McCormick: Robert R. McCormick (1880–1955) was an eccentric but influential newspaper publisher who founded the *Chicago Tribune* in 1914.

Ruth (almost matter of factly, a complaint too automatic to deserve emphasis): Why you always got to smoke before you eat in the morning?

Walter (at the window): Just look at 'em down there . . . Running and racing to work . . . *(He turns and faces his wife and watches her a moment at the stove, and then, suddenly)* You look young this morning, baby.

Ruth (indifferently): Yeah?

Walter: Just for a second—stirring them eggs. Just for a second it was—you looked real young again. *(He reaches for her; she crosses away. Then, drily)* It's gone now—you look like yourself again!

Ruth: Man, if you don't shut up and leave me alone.

Walter (looking out to the street again): First thing a man ought to learn in life is not to make love to no colored woman first thing in the morning. You all some eeeevil people at eight o'clock in the morning.

(Travis appears in the hall doorway, almost fully dressed and quite wide awake now, his towels and pajamas across his shoulders. He opens the door and signals for his father to make the bathroom in a hurry.)

Travis (watching the bathroom): Daddy, come on!

(Walter gets his bathroom utensils and flies out to the bathroom.)

Ruth: Sit down and have your breakfast, Travis.

Travis: Mama, this is Friday. *(Gleefully)* Check coming tomorrow, huh?

Ruth: You get your mind off money and eat your breakfast.

Travis (eating): This is the morning we supposed to bring the fifty cents to school.

Ruth: Well, I ain't got no fifty cents this morning.

Travis: Teacher say we have to.

Ruth: I don't care what teacher say. I ain't got it. Eat your breakfast, Travis.

Travis: I *am* eating.

Ruth: Hush up now and just eat!

(The boy gives her an exasperated look for her lack of understanding, and eats grudgingly.)

Travis: You think Grandmama would have it?

Ruth: No! And I want you to stop asking your grandmother for money, you hear me?

Travis (outraged): Gaaaleee! I don't ask her, she just gimme it sometimes!

Ruth: Travis Willard Younger—I got too much on me this morning to be—

Travis: Maybe Daddy—

Ruth: Travis!

(The boy hushes abruptly. They are both quiet and tense for several seconds.)

Travis (presently): Could I maybe go carry some groceries in front of the supermarket for a little while after school then?

Ruth: Just hush, I said. *(Travis jabs his spoon into his cereal bowl viciously, and rests his head in anger upon his fists.)* If you through eating, you can get over there and make up your bed.

(The boy obeys stiffly and crosses the room, almost mechanically, to the bed and more or less folds the bedding into a heap, then angrily gets his books and cap.)

Travis (sulking and standing apart from her unnaturally): I'm gone.

Ruth (looking up from the stove to inspect him automatically): Come here. *(He crosses to her and she studies his head.)* If you don't take this comb and fix this here head, you better! *(Travis puts down his books with a great sigh of oppression, and crosses to the mirror. His mother mutters under her breath about his "slubbornness.")* 'Bout to march out of here with that head looking just like chickens slept in it! I just don't know where you get your slubborn ways . . . And get your jacket, too. Looks chilly out this morning.

Travis (with conspicuously brushed hair and jacket): I'm gone.

Ruth: Get carfare and milk money—*(waving one finger)*—and not a single penny for no caps, you hear me?

Travis (with sullen politeness): Yes'm.

(He turns in outrage to leave. His mother watches after him as in his frustration he approaches the door almost comically. When she speaks to him, her voice has become a very gentle tease.)

Ruth (mocking; as she thinks he would say it): Oh, Mama makes me so mad sometimes, I don't know what to do! *(She waits and continues to his back as he stands stock-still in front of the door.)* I wouldn't kiss that woman good-bye for nothing in this world this morning!

(The boy finally turns around and rolls his eyes at her, knowing the mood has changed and he is vindicated; he does not, however, move toward her yet.)

Not for nothing in this world!

(She finally laughs aloud at him and holds out her arms to him and we see that it is a way between them, very old and practiced. He crosses to her and allows her to embrace him warmly but keeps his face fixed with masculine rigidity. She holds him back from her presently and looks at him and runs her fingers over the features of his face. With utter gentleness—)

Now—whose little old angry man are you?

Travis (the masculinity and gruffness start to fade at last): Aw gaalee—Mama . . .

Ruth (mimicking): Aw—gaaaaalleeeee, Mama! *(She pushes him, with rough playfulness and finality, toward the door.)* Get on out of here or you going to be late.

Travis (in the face of love, new aggressiveness): Mama, could I *please* go carry groceries?

Ruth: Honey, it's starting to get so cold evenings.

Walter (coming in from the bathroom and drawing a make-believe gun from a make-believe holster and shooting at his son): What is it he wants to do?

Ruth: Go carry groceries after school at the supermarket.

Walter: Well, let him go . . .

Travis (quickly, to the ally): I have to—she won't gimme the fifty cents . . .

Walter (to his wife only): Why not?

Ruth (simply, and with flavor): 'Cause we don't have it.

Walter (to Ruth only): What you tell the boy things like that for? *(Reaching down into his pants with a rather important gesture.)* Here, son—

(He hands the boy the coin, but his eyes are directed to his wife's. Travis takes the money happily.)

Travis: Thanks, Daddy.

(He starts out. Ruth watches both of them with murder in her eyes. Walter stands and stares back at her with defiance, and suddenly reaches into his pocket again on an afterthought.)

Walter *(without even looking at his son, still staring hard at his wife):* In fact, here's another fifty cents . . . Buy yourself some fruit today—or take a taxicab to school or something!

Travis: Whoopee—

(He leaps up and clasps his father around the middle with his legs, and they face each other in mutual appreciation; slowly Walter Lee peeks around the boy to catch the violent rays from his wife's eyes and draws his head back as if shot.)

Walter: You better get down now—and get to school, man.

Travis *(at the door):* O.K. Good-bye. *(He exits.)*

Walter *(after him, pointing with pride):* That's my boy. *(She looks at him in disgust and turns back to her work.)* You know what I was thinking 'bout in the bathroom this morning?

Ruth: No.

Walter: How come you always try to be so pleasant!

Ruth: What is there to be pleasant 'bout!

Walter: You want to know what I was thinking 'bout in the bathroom or not!

Ruth: I know what you thinking 'bout.

Walter *(ignoring her):* 'Bout what me and Willy Harris was talking about last night.

Ruth *(immediately—a refrain):* Willy Harris is a good-for-nothing loudmouth.

Walter: Anybody who talks to me has got to be a good-for-nothing loudmouth, ain't he? And what you know about who is just a good-for-nothing loudmouth? Charlie Atkins was just a "good-for-nothing loudmouth" too, wasn't he! When he wanted me to go in the dry-cleaning business with him. And now—he's grossing a hundred thousand a year. A hundred thousand dollars a year! You still call *him* a loudmouth!

Ruth *(bitterly):* Oh, Walter Lee . . .

(She folds her head on her arms over the table.)

Walter *(rising and coming to her and standing over her):* You tired, ain't you? Tired of everything. Me, the boy, the way we live—this beat-up hole—everything. Ain't you? *(She doesn't look up, doesn't answer.)* So tired—moaning and groaning all the time, but you wouldn't do nothing to help, would you? You couldn't be on my side that long for nothing, could you?

Ruth: Walter, please leave me alone.

Walter: A man needs for a woman to back him up . . .

Ruth: Walter—

Walter: Mama would listen to you. You know she listen to you more than she do me and Bennie. She think more of you. All you have to do is just sit down with her when you drinking your coffee one morning and talking 'bout things like you do and—*(He sits down beside her and demonstrates graphically what he thinks her methods and tone should be.)*—you just sip your coffee, see, and say easy like that you been thinking 'bout that deal Walter Lee is so interested in, 'bout the store and all, and sip some more coffee, like what you saying ain't really that important to you—And the next thing you know, she be listening good and asking you questions and when I come home—I can tell her the details. This ain't no fly-by-night proposition, baby. I mean we figured it out, me and Willy and Bobo.

Ruth (with a frown): Bobo?

Walter: Yeah. You see, this little liquor store we got in mind cost seventy-five thousand and we figured the initial investment on the place be 'bout thirty thousand, see. That be ten thousand each. Course, there's a couple of hundred you got to pay so's you don't spend your life just waiting for them clowns to let your license get approved—

Ruth: You mean graft?

Walter (frowning impatiently): Don't call it that. See there, that just goes to show you what women understand about the world. Baby, don't *nothing* happen for you in this world 'less you pay *somebody* off!

Ruth: Walter, leave me alone! *(She raises her head and stares at him vigorously—then says, more quietly.)* Eat your eggs, they gonna be cold.

Walter (straightening up from her and looking off): That's it. There you are. Man say to his woman: I got me a dream. His woman say: Eat your eggs. *(Sadly, but gaining in power.)* Man say: I got to take hold of this here world, baby! And a woman will say: Eat your eggs and go to work. *(Passionately now.)* Man say: I got to change my life, I'm choking to death, baby! And his woman say—*(In utter anguish as he brings his fists down on his thighs)*—Your eggs is getting cold!

Ruth (softly): Walter, that ain't none of our money.

Walter (not listening at all or even looking at her): This morning, I was lookin' in the mirror and thinking about it . . . I'm thirty-five years old; I been married eleven years and I got a boy who sleeps in the living room—*(very, very quietly)*—and all I got to give him is stories about how rich white people live . . .

Ruth: Eat your eggs, Walter.

Walter (slams the table and jumps up): DAMN MY EGGS—DAMN ALL THE EGGS THAT EVER WAS!

Ruth: Then go to work.

Walter (looking up at her): See—I'm trying to talk to you 'bout myself—*(Shaking his head with the repetition.)*—and all you can say is eat them eggs and go to work.

Ruth (wearily): Honey, you never say nothing new. I listen to you every day, every night and every morning, and you never say nothing new. *(Shrugging.)* So you would rather *be* Mr. Arnold than be his chauffeur. So—I would *rather* be living in Buckingham Palace.

Walter: That is just what is wrong with the colored woman in this world . . . Don't understand about building their men up and making 'em feel like they somebody. Like they can do something.

Ruth (drily, but to hurt): There *are* colored men who do things.

Walter: No thanks to the colored woman.

Ruth: Well, being a colored woman, I guess I can't help myself none.

(She rises and gets the ironing board and sets it up and attacks a huge pile of rough-dried clothes, sprinkling them in preparation for the ironing and then rolling them into tight fat balls.)

Walter (mumbling): We one group of men tied to a race of women with small minds!

(His sister Beneatha enters. She is about twenty, as slim and intense as her brother. She is not as pretty as her sister-in-law, but her lean, almost intellectual face has a

handsomeness of its own. She wears a bright-red flannel nightie, and her thick hair stands wildly about her head. Her speech is a mixture of many things; it is different from the rest of the family's insofar as education has permeated her sense of English—and perhaps the Midwest rather than the South has finally—at last—won out in her inflection; but not altogether, because over all of it is a soft slurring and transformed use of vowels which is the decided influence of the Southside. She passes through the room without looking at either Ruth or Walter and goes to the outside door and looks, a little blindly, out to the bathroom. She sees that it has been lost to the Johnsons. She closes the door with a sleepy vengeance and crosses to the table and sits down a little defeated.)*

Beneatha: I am going to start timing those people.

Walter: You should get up earlier.

Beneatha (her face in her hands. She is still fighting the urge to go back to bed): Really—would you suggest dawn? Where's the paper?

Walter (pushing the paper across the table to her as he studies her almost clinically, as though he has never seen her before): You a horrible-looking chick at this hour.

Beneatha (drily): Good morning, everybody.

Walter (senselessly): How is school coming?

Beneatha (in the same spirit): Lovely. Lovely. And you know, biology is the greatest. *(Looking up at him.)* I dissected something that looked just like you yesterday.

Walter: I just wondered if you've made up your mind and everything.

Beneatha (gaining in sharpness and impatience): And what did I answer yesterday morning—and the day before that?

Ruth (from the ironing board, like someone disinterested and old): Don't be so nasty, Bennie.

Beneatha (still to her brother): And the day before that and the day before that!

Walter (defensively): I'm interested in you. Something wrong with that? Ain't many girls who decide—

Walter and Beneatha (in unison): —"to be a doctor."

(Silence.)

Walter: Have we figured out yet just exactly how much medical school is going to cost?

Ruth: Walter Lee, why don't you leave that girl alone and get out of here to work?

Beneatha (exits to the bathroom and bangs on the door): Come on out of there, please!

(She comes back into the room.)

Walter (looking at his sister intently): You know the check is coming tomorrow.

Beneatha (turning on him with a sharpness all her own): That money belongs to Mama, Walter, and it's for her to decide how she wants to use it. I don't care if she wants to buy a house or a rocket ship or just nail it up somewhere and look at it. It's hers. Not ours—hers.

Walter (bitterly): Now ain't that fine! You just got your mother's interest at heart, ain't you, girl? You such a nice girl—but if Mama got that money she can always take a few thousand and help you through school too—can't she?

Beneatha: I have never asked anyone around here to do anything for me!

Walter: No! And the line between asking and just accepting when the time comes is big and wide—ain't it!

Beneatha (with fury): What do you want from me, Brother—that I quit school or just drop dead, which!

Walter: I don't want nothing but for you to stop acting holy 'round here. Me and Ruth done made some sacrifices for you—why can't you do something for the family?

Ruth: Walter, don't be dragging me in it.

Walter: You are in it—Don't you get up and go work in somebody's kitchen for the last three years to help put clothes on her back?

Ruth: Oh, Walter—that's not fair . . .

Walter: It ain't that nobody expects you to get on your knees and say thank you, Brother; thank you, Ruth; thank you, Mama—and thank you, Travis, for wearing the same pair of shoes for two semesters—

Beneatha (dropping to her knees): Well—I *do*—all right?—thank everybody! And forgive me for ever wanting to be anything at all! *(Pursuing him on her knees across the floor.)* FORGIVE ME, FORGIVE ME, FORGIVE ME!

Ruth: Please stop it! Your mama'll hear you.

Walter: Who the hell told you you had to be a doctor? If you so crazy 'bout messing 'round with sick people—then go be a nurse like other women—or just get married and be quiet . . .

Beneatha: Well—you finally got it said . . . It took you three years but you finally got it said. Walter, give up; leave me alone—it's Mama's money.

Walter: He was my father, too!

Beneatha: So what? He was mine, too—and Travis' grandfather—but the insurance money belongs to Mama. Picking on me is not going to make her give it to you to invest in any liquor stores—*(Underbreath, dropping into a chair.)*—and I for one say, God bless Mama for that!

Walter (to Ruth): See—did you hear? Did you hear!

Ruth: Honey, please go to work.

Walter: Nobody in this house is ever going to understand me.

Beneatha: Because you're a nut.

Walter: Who's a nut?

Beneatha: You—you are a nut. Thee is mad, boy.

Walter (looking at his wife and his sister from the door, very sadly): The world's most backward race of people, and that's a fact.

Beneatha (turning slowly in her chair): And then there are all those prophets who would lead us out of the wilderness—*(Walter slams out of the house.)*—into the swamps!

Ruth: Bennie, why you always gotta be pickin' on your brother? Can't you be a little sweeter sometimes?

(Door opens. Walter walks in. He fumbles with his cap, starts to speak, clears throat, looks everywhere but at Ruth. Finally:)

Walter (to Ruth): I need some money for carfare.

Ruth (looks at him, then warms; teasing, but tenderly): Fifty cents? *(She goes to her bag and gets money.)* Here—take a taxi!

(Walter exits. Mama enters. She is a woman in her early sixties, full-bodied and strong. She is one of those women of a certain grace and beauty who wear it so unobtrusively that it takes a while to notice. Her dark-brown face is surrounded by the total whiteness of her hair, and, being a woman who has adjusted to many things in life and overcome many more, her face is full of strength. She has, we can see, wit and faith of a kind that keep her eyes lit and full of interest and expectancy. She is, in a word, a beautiful

woman. *Her bearing is perhaps most like the noble bearing of the women of the Hereros of Southwest Africa—rather as if she imagines that as she walks she still bears a basket or a vessel upon her head. Her speech, on the other hand, is as careless as her carriage is precise—she is inclined to slur everything—but her voice is perhaps not so much quiet as simply soft.)*

Mama: Who that 'round here slamming doors at this hour?

(She crosses through the room, goes to the window, opens it, and brings in a feeble little plant growing doggedly in a small pot on the windowsill. She feels the dirt and puts it back out.)

Ruth: That was Walter Lee. He and Bennie was at it again.

Mama: My children and they tempers. Lord, if this little old plant don't get more sun than it's been getting it ain't never going to see spring again. *(She turns from the window.)* What's the matter with you this morning, Ruth? You looks right peaked. You aiming to iron all them things? Leave some for me. I'll get to 'em this afternoon. Bennie honey, it's too drafty for you to be sitting 'round half dressed. Where's your robe?

Beneatha: In the cleaners.

Mama: Well, go get mine and put it on.

Beneatha: I'm not cold, Mama, honest.

Mama: I know—but you so thin . . .

Beneatha *(irritably)*: Mama, I'm not cold.

Mama *(seeing the make-down bed as Travis has left it)*: Lord have mercy, look at that poor bed. Bless his heart—he tries, don't he? *(She moves to the bed Travis has sloppily made up.)*

Ruth: No—he don't half try at all 'cause he knows you going to come along behind him and fix everything. That's just how come he don't know how to do nothing right now—you done spoiled that boy so.

Mama *(folding bedding)*: Well—he's a little boy. Ain't supposed to know 'bout housekeeping. My baby, that's what he is. What you fix for his breakfast this morning?

Ruth *(angrily)*: I feed my son, Lena!

Mama: I ain't meddling—*(Underbreath; busy-bodyish)* I just noticed all last week he had cold cereal, and when it starts getting this chilly in the fall a child ought to have some hot grits or something when he goes out in the cold—

Ruth *(furious)*: I gave him hot oats—is that all right!

Mama: I ain't meddling. *(Pause.)* Put a lot of nice butter on it? *(Ruth shoots her an angry look and does not reply.)* He likes lots of butter.

Ruth *(exasperated)*: Lena—

Mama *(to Beneatha. Mama is inclined to wander conversationally sometimes)*: What was you and your brother fussing 'bout this morning?

Beneatha: It's not important, Mama.

(She gets up and goes to look out at the bathroom, which is apparently free, and she picks up her towels and rushes out.)

Mama: What was they fighting about?

Ruth: Now you know as well as I do.

Mama *(shaking her head)*: Brother still worrying hisself sick about that money?

Ruth: You know he is.

Mama: You had breakfast?

Ruth: Some coffee.

Mama: Girl, you better start eating and looking after yourself better. You almost thin as Travis.

Ruth: Lena—

Mama: Un-hunh?

Ruth: What are you going to do with it?

Mama: Now don't you start, child. It's too early in the morning to be talking about money. It ain't Christian.

Ruth: It's just that he got his heart set on that store—

Mama: You mean that liquor store that Willy Harris want him to invest in?

Ruth: Yes—

Mama: We ain't no business people, Ruth. We just plain working folks.

Ruth: Ain't nobody business people till they go into business. Walter Lee say colored people ain't never going to start getting ahead till they start gambling on some different kinds of things in the world—investments and things.

Mama: What done got into you, girl? Walter Lee done finally sold you on investing.

Ruth: No. Mama, something is happening between Walter and me. I don't know what it is—but he needs something—something I can't give him any more. He needs this chance, Lena.

Mama (frowning deeply): But liquor, honey—

Ruth: Well—like Walter say—I spec people going to always be drinking themselves some liquor.

Mama: Well—whether they drinks it or not ain't none of my business. But whether I go into business selling it to 'em *is*, and I don't want that on my ledger this late in life. *(Stopping suddenly and studying her daughter-in-law.)* Ruth Younger, what's the matter with you today? You look like you could fall over right there.

Ruth: I'm tired.

Mama: Then you better stay home from work today.

Ruth: I can't stay home. She'd be calling up the agency and screaming at them, "My girl didn't come in today—send me somebody! My girl didn't come in!" Oh, she just have a fit . . .

Mama: Well, let her have it. I'll just call her up and say you got the flu—

Ruth (laughing): Why the flu?

Mama: 'Cause it sounds respectable to 'em. Something white people get, too. They know 'bout the flu. Otherwise they think you been cut up or something when you tell 'em you sick.

Ruth: I got to go in. We need the money.

Mama: Somebody would of thought my children done all but starved to death the way they talk about money here late. Child, we got a great big old check coming tomorrow.

Ruth (sincerely, but also self-righteously): Now that's your money. It ain't got nothing to do with me. We all feel like that—Walter and Bennie and me—even Travis.

Mama (thoughtfully, and suddenly very far away): Ten thousand dollars—

Ruth: Sure is wonderful.

Mama: Ten thousand dollars.

Ruth: You know what you should do, Miss Lena? You should take yourself a trip somewhere. To Europe or South America or someplace—

Mama (throwing up her hands at the thought): Oh, child!

Ruth: I'm serious. Just pack up and leave! Go on away and enjoy yourself some. Forget about the family and have yourself a ball for once in your life—

Mama (drily): You sound like I'm just about ready to die. Who'd go with me? What I look like wandering 'round Europe by myself?

Ruth: Shoot—these here rich white women do it all the time. They don't think nothing of packing up they suitcases and piling on one of them big steamships and—swoosh!—they gone, child.

Mama: Something always told me I wasn't no rich white woman.

Ruth: Well—what are you going to do with it then?

Mama: I ain't rightly decided. (*Thinking. She speaks now with emphasis.*) Some of it got to be put away for Beneatha and her schoolin'—and ain't nothing going to touch that part of it. Nothing. (*She waits several seconds, trying to make up her mind about something, and looks at Ruth a little tentatively before going on.*) Been thinking that we maybe could meet the notes on a little old two-story somewhere, with a yard where Travis could play in the summertime, if we use part of the insurance for a down payment and everybody kind of pitch in. I could maybe take on a little day work again, few days a week—

Ruth (studying her mother-in-law furtively and concentrating on her ironing, anxious to encourage without seeming to): Well, Lord knows, we've put enough rent into this here rat trap to pay for four houses by now . . .

Mama (looking up at the words "rat trap" and then looking around and leaning back and sighing—in a suddenly reflective mood): "Rat trap"—yes, that's all it is. (*Smiling.*) I remember just as well the day me and Big Walter moved in here. Hadn't been married but two weeks and wasn't planning on living here no more than a year. (*She shakes her head at the dissolved dream.*) We was going to set away, little by little, don't you know, and buy a little place out in Morgan Park. We had even picked out the house. (*Chuckling a little.*) Looks right dumpy today. But Lord, child, you should know all the dreams I had 'bout buying that house and fixing it up and making me a little garden in the back—(*She waits and stops smiling.*) And didn't none of it happen. (*Dropping her hands in a futile gesture.*)

Ruth (keeps her head down, ironing): Yes, life can be a barrel of disappointments, sometimes.

Mama: Honey, Big Walter would come in here some nights back then and slump down on that couch there and just look at the rug, and look at me and look at the rug and then back at me—and I'd know he was down then . . . really down. (*After a second very long and thoughtful pause; she is seeing back to times that only she can see.*) And then, Lord, when I lost that baby—little Claude—I almost thought I was going to lose Big Walter too. Oh, that man grieved hisself! He was one man to love his children.

Ruth: Ain't nothin' can tear at you like losin' your baby.

Mama: I guess that's how come that man finally worked hisself to death like he done. Like he was fighting his own war with this here world that took his baby from him.

Ruth: He sure was a fine man, all right. I always liked Mr. Younger.

Mama: Crazy 'bout his children! God knows there was plenty wrong with Walter Younger—hard-headed, mean, kind of wild with women—plenty wrong with him. But he sure loved his children. Always wanted them to have something—be something. That's where Brother gets all these notions, I reckon. Big Walter used to say, he'd get right wet in the eyes sometimes, lean his head back with the water standing in his eyes and say, "Seem like God didn't see fit to give the black man nothing but dreams—but He did give us children to make them dreams seem worth while." *(She smiles.)* He could talk like that, don't you know.

Ruth: Yes, he sure could. He was a good man, Mr. Younger.

Mama: Yes, a fine man—just couldn't never catch up with his dreams, that's all.

(Beneatha comes in, brushing her hair and looking up to the ceiling, where the sound of a vacuum cleaner has started up.)

Beneatha: What could be so dirty on that woman's rugs that she has to vacuum them every single day?

Ruth: I wish certain young women 'round here who I could name would take inspiration about certain rugs in a certain apartment I could also mention.

Beneatha (shrugging): How much cleaning can a house need, for Christ's sakes.

Mama (not liking the Lord's name used thus): Bennie!

Ruth: Just listen to her—just listen!

Beneatha: Oh, God!

Mama: If you use the Lord's name just one more time—

Beneatha (a bit of a whine): Oh, Mama—

Ruth: Fresh—just fresh as salt, this girl!

Beneatha (drily): Well—if the salt loses its savor°—

Mama: Now that will do. I just ain't going to have you 'round here reciting the scriptures in vain—you hear me?

Beneatha: How did I manage to get on everybody's wrong side by just walking into a room?

Ruth: If you weren't so fresh—

Beneatha: Ruth, I'm twenty years old.

Mama: What time you be home from school today?

Beneatha: Kind of late. *(With enthusiasm.)* Madeline is going to start my guitar lessons today.

(Mama and Ruth look up with the same expression.)

Mama: Your *what* kind of lessons?

Beneatha: Guitar.

Ruth: Oh, Father!

Mama: How come you done taken it in your mind to learn to play the guitar?

Beneatha: I just want to, that's all.

Mama (smiling): Lord, child, don't you know what to do with yourself? How long it going to be before you get tired of this now—like you got tired of that little play-acting group you joined last year? *(Looking at Ruth.)* And what was it the year before that?

Ruth: The horseback-riding club for which she bought that fifty-five-dollar riding habit that's been hanging in the closet ever since!

Mama (to Beneatha): Why you got to flit so from one thing to another, baby?

Beneatha (sharply): I just want to learn to play the guitar. Is there anything wrong with that?

Mama: Ain't nobody trying to stop you. I just wonders sometimes why you has to flit so from one thing to another all the time. You ain't never done nothing with all that camera equipment you brought home—

---

if the salt loses its savor: Beneatha's retort is a reference to the verse from Matthew 5:13—"You are the salt of the earth: but if the salt have lost his savor, wherewith shall it be salted? It is thenceforth good for nothing, but to be cast out . . ."

Beneatha: I don't flit! I—I experiment with different forms of expression—

Ruth: Like riding a horse?

Beneatha: —People have to express themselves one way or another.

Mama: What is it you want to express?

Beneatha (angrily): Me! *(Mama and Ruth look at each other and burst into raucous laughter.)* Don't worry—I don't expect you to understand.

Mama (to change the subject): Who you going out with tomorrow night?

Beneatha (with displeasure): George Murchison again.

Mama (pleased): Oh—you getting a little sweet on him?

Ruth: You ask me, this child ain't sweet on nobody but herself—*(Underbreath.)* Express herself! *(They laugh.)*

Beneatha: Oh—I like George all right, Mama. I mean I like him enough to go out with him and stuff, but—

Ruth (for devilment): What does *and stuff* mean?

Beneatha: Mind your own business.

Mama: Stop picking at her now, Ruth. *(She chuckles. A thoughtful pause, and then a suspicious sudden look at her daughter as she turns in her chair for emphasis.)* What DOES it mean?

Beneatha (wearily): Oh, I just mean I couldn't ever really be serious about George. He's—he's so shallow.

Ruth: Shallow—what do you mean he's shallow? He's *rich!*

Mama: Hush, Ruth.

Beneatha: I know he's rich. He knows he's rich, too.

Ruth: Well—what other qualities a man got to have to satisfy you, little girl?

Beneatha: You wouldn't even begin to understand. Anybody who married Walter could not possibly understand.

Mama (outraged): What kind of way is that to talk about your brother?

Beneatha: Brother is a flip—let's face it.

Mama (to Ruth, helplessly): What's a flip?

Ruth (glad to add kindling): She's saying he's crazy.

Beneatha: Not crazy. Brother isn't really crazy yet—he—he's an elaborate neurotic.

Mama: Hush your mouth!

Beneatha: As for George. Well. George looks good—he's got a beautiful car and he takes me to nice places and, as my sister-in-law says, he is probably the richest boy I will ever get to know and I even like him sometimes—but if the Youngers are sitting around waiting to see if their little Bennie is going to tie up the family with the Murchisons, they are wasting their time.

Ruth: You mean you wouldn't marry George Murchison if he asked you someday? That pretty, rich thing? Honey, I knew you was odd—

Beneatha: No I would not marry him if all I felt for him was what I feel now. Besides, George's family wouldn't really like it.

Mama: Why not?

Beneatha: Oh, Mama—The Murchisons are honest-to-God-real-*live*-rich colored people, and the only people in the world who are more snobbish than rich white people are rich colored people. I thought everybody knew that. I've met Mrs. Murchison. She's a scene!

Mama: You must not dislike people 'cause they well off, honey.

Beneatha: Why not? It makes just as much sense as disliking people 'cause they are poor, and lots of people do that.

Ruth (*a wisdom-of-the-ages manner. To Mama*): Well, she'll get over some of this—

Beneatha: Get over it? What are you talking about, Ruth? Listen, I'm going to be a doctor. I'm not worried about who I'm going to marry yet—if I ever get married.

Mama and Ruth: If!

Mama: Now, Bennie—

Beneatha: Oh, I probably will . . . but first I'm going to be a doctor, and George, for one, still thinks that's pretty funny. I couldn't be bothered with that. I am going to be a doctor and everybody around here better understand that!

Mama (*kindly*): 'Course you going to be a doctor, honey, God willing.

Beneatha (*drily*): God hasn't got a thing to do with it.

Mama: Beneatha—that just wasn't necessary.

Beneatha: Well—neither is God. I get sick of hearing about God.

Mama: Beneatha!

Beneatha: I mean it! I'm just tired of hearing about God all the time. What has He got to do with anything? Does He pay tuition?

Mama: You 'bout to get your fresh little jaw slapped!

Ruth: That's just what she needs, all right!

Beneatha: Why? Why can't I say what I want to around here, like everybody else?

Mama: It don't sound nice for a young girl to say things like that—you wasn't brought up that way. Me and your father went to trouble to get you and Brother to church every Sunday.

Beneatha: Mama, you don't understand. It's all a matter of ideas, and God is just one idea I don't accept. It's not important. I am not going out and be immoral or commit crimes because I don't believe in God. I don't even think about it. It's just that I get tired of Him getting credit for all the things the human race achieves through its own stubborn effort. There simply is no blasted God—there is only man and it is *he* who makes miracles!

(*Mama absorbs this speech, studies her daughter and rises slowly and crosses to Beneatha and slaps her powerfully across the face. After, there is only silence and the daughter drops her eyes from her mother's face, and Mama is very tall before her.*)

Mama: Now—you say after me, in my mother's house there is still God. (*There is a long pause and Beneatha stares at the floor wordlessly. Mama repeats the phrase with precision and cool emotion.*) In my mother's house there is still God.

Beneatha: In my mother's house there is still God.

(*A long pause.*)

Mama (*walking away from Beneatha, too disturbed for triumphant posture. Stopping and turning back to her daughter*): There are some ideas we ain't going to have in this house. Not long as I am at the head of this family.

Beneatha: Yes, ma'am.

(*Mama walks out of the room.*)

Ruth (*almost gently, with profound understanding*): You think you a woman, Bennie— but you still a little girl. What you did was childish—so you got treated like a child.

Beneatha: I see. (*Quietly.*) I also see that everybody thinks it's all right for Mama to be a tyrant. But all the tyranny in the world will never put a God in the heavens!

(She picks up her books and goes out. Pause.)

Ruth (goes to Mama's door): She said she was sorry.

Mama (coming out, going to her plant): They frightens me, Ruth. My children.

Ruth: You got good children, Lena. They just a little off sometimes—but they're good.

Mama: No—there's something come down between me and them that don't let us understand each other and I don't know what it is. One done almost lost his mind thinking 'bout money all the time and the other done commence to talk about things I can't seem to understand in no form or fashion. What is it that's changing, Ruth?

Ruth (soothingly, older than her years): Now . . . you taking it all too seriously. You just got strong-willed children and it takes a strong woman like you to keep 'em in hand.

Mama (looking at her plant and sprinkling a little water on it): They spirited all right, my children. Got to admit they got spirit—Bennie and Walter. Like this little old plant that ain't never had enough sunshine or nothing—and look at it . . .

(She has her back to Ruth, who has had to stop ironing and lean against something and put the back of her hand to her forehead.)

Ruth (trying to keep Mama from noticing): You . . . sure . . . loves that little old thing, don't you? . . .

Mama: Well, I always wanted me a garden like I used to see sometimes at the back of the houses down home. This plant is close as I ever got to having one. *(She looks out of the window as she replaces the plant.)* Lord, ain't nothing as dreary as the view from this window on a dreary day, is there? Why ain't you singing this morning, Ruth? Sing that "No Ways Tired." That song always lifts me up so— *(She turns at last to see that Ruth has slipped quietly to the floor, in a state of semiconsciousness.)* Ruth! Ruth honey—what's the matter with you . . . Ruth!

ACT I

SCENE II

It is the following morning; a Saturday morning, and house cleaning is in progress at the Youngers'. Furniture has been shoved hither and yon and Mama is giving the kitchen-area walls a washing down. Beneatha, in dungrees, with a handkerchief tied around her face, is spraying insecticide into the cracks in the walls. As they work, the radio is on and a Southside disk-jockey program is inappropriately filling the house with a rather exotic saxophone blues. Travis, the sole idle one, is leaning on his arms, looking out of the window.

Travis: Grandmama, that stuff Bennie is using smells awful. Can I go downstairs, please?

Mama: Did you get all them chores done already? I ain't seen you doing much.

Travis: Yes'm—finished early. Where did Mama go this morning?

Mama (looking at Beneatha): She had to go on a little errand.

(The phone rings. Beneatha runs to answer it and reaches it before Walter, who has entered from bedroom.)

Travis: Where?

Mama: To tend to her business.

Beneatha: Haylo . . . *(Disappointed.)* Yes, he is. *(She tosses the phone to Walter, who barely catches it.)* It's Willie Harris again.

Walter (as privately as possible under Mama's gaze): Hello, Willie. Did you get the papers from the lawyer? . . . No, not yet. I told you the mailman doesn't get here till ten-thirty . . . No, I'll come there . . . Yeah! Right away. *(He hangs up and goes for his coat.)*

Beneatha: Brother, where did Ruth go?

Walter (as he exits): How should I know!

Travis: Aw come on, Grandma. Can I go outside?

Mama: Oh, I guess so. You stay right in front of the house, though, and keep a good lookout for the postman.

Travis: Yes'm. *(He darts into bedroom for stickball and bat, reenters, and sees Beneatha on her knees spraying under sofa with behind upraised. He edges closer to the target, takes aim, and lets her have it. She screams.)* Leave them poor little cockroaches alone, they ain't bothering you none! *(He runs as she swings the spraygun at him viciously and playfully.)* Grandma! Grandma!

Mama: Look out there, girl, before you be spilling some of that stuff on that child!

Travis (safely behind the bastion of Mama): That's right—look out, now! *(He exits.)*

Beneatha (drily): I can't imagine that it would hurt him—it has never hurt the roaches.

Mama: Well, little boys' hides ain't as tough as Southside roaches. You better get over there behind the bureau. I seen one marching out of there like Napoleon yesterday.

Beneatha: There's really only one way to get rid of them, Mama—

Mama: How?

Beneatha: Set fire to this building! Mama, where did Ruth go?

Mama (looking at her with meaning): To the doctor, I think.

Beneatha: The doctor? What's the matter? *(They exchange glances.)* You don't think—

Mama (with her sense of drama): Now I ain't saying what I think. But I ain't never been wrong 'bout a woman neither.

(The phone rings.)

Beneatha (at the phone): Hay-lo . . . *(pause, and a moment of recognition)* Well—when did you get back! . . . And how was it? . . . Of course I've missed you—in my way . . . This morning? No . . . house cleaning and all that and Mama hates it if I let people come over when the house is like this . . . You *have?* Well, that's different . . . What is it—Oh, what the hell, come on over . . . Right, see you then. *Arrividerci.* *(She hangs up.)*

Mama (who has listened vigorously, as is her habit): Who is that you inviting over here with this house looking like this? You ain't got the pride you was born with!

Beneatha: Asagai doesn't care how houses look, Mama—he's an intellectual.

Mama: Who?

Beneatha: Asagai—Joseph Asagai. He's an African boy I met on campus. He's been studying in Canada all summer.

Mama: What's his name?

Beneatha: Asagai, Joseph. Ah-sah-guy . . . He's from Nigeria.

Mama: Oh, that's the little country that was founded by slaves way back . . .

Beneatha: No, Mama—that's Liberia.

Mama: I don't think I never met no African before.

Beneatha: Well, do me a favor and don't ask him a whole lot of ignorant questions about Africans. I mean, do they wear clothes and all that—

Mama: Well, now, I guess if you think we so ignorant 'round here maybe you shouldn't bring your friends here—

Beneatha: It's just that people ask such crazy things. All anyone seems to know about when it comes to Africa is Tarzan—

Mama (*indignantly*): Why should I know anything about Africa?

Beneatha: Why do you give money at church for the missionary work?

Mama: Well, that's to help save people.

Beneatha: You mean save them from *heathenism*—

Mama (*innocently*): Yes.

Beneatha: I'm afraid they need more salvation from the British and the French.

> (*Ruth comes in forlornly and pulls off her coat with dejection. They both turn to look at her.*)

Ruth (*dispiritedly*): Well, I guess from all the happy faces—everybody knows.

Beneatha: You pregnant?

Mama: Lord have mercy, I sure hope it's a little old girl. Travis ought to have a sister.

> (*Beneatha and Ruth give her a hopeless look for this grandmotherly enthusiasm.*)

Beneatha: How far along are you?

Ruth: Two months.

Beneatha: Did you mean to? I mean did you plan it or was it an accident?

Mama: What do you know about planning or not planning?

Beneatha: Oh, Mama.

Ruth (*wearily*): She's twenty years old, Lena.

Beneatha: Did you plan it, Ruth?

Ruth: Mind your own business.

Beneatha: It is my business—where is he going to live, on the *roof*? (*There is silence following the remark as the three women react to the sense of it.*) Gee—I didn't mean that, Ruth, honest. Gee, I don't feel like that at all. I—I think it is wonderful.

Ruth (*dully*): Wonderful.

Beneatha: Yes—really. (*There is a sudden commotion from the street and she goes to the window to look out.*) What on earth is going on out there? These kids. (*There are, as she throws open the window, the shouts of children rising up from the street. She sticks her head out to see better and calls out.*) TRAVIS! TRAVIS! . . . WHAT ARE YOU DOING DOWN THERE? (*She sees.*) Oh Lord, they're chasing a rat!

> (*Ruth covers her face with hands and turns away.*)

Mama (*angrily*): Tell that youngun to get himself up here, at once!

Beneatha: TRAVIS . . . YOU COME UPSTAIRS . . . AT ONCE!

Ruth (*her face twisted*): Chasing a rat . . .

Mama (*looking at Ruth, worried*): Doctor say everything going to be all right?

Ruth (*far away*): Yes—she says everything is going to be fine . . .

Mama (*immediately suspicious*): "She"—What doctor you went to?

> (*Ruth just looks at Mama meaningfully and Mama opens her mouth to speak as Travis bursts in.*)

Travis (*excited and full of narrative, coming directly to his mother*): Mama, you should of seen the rat . . . Big as a cat, honest! (*He shows an exaggerated size with his hands.*)

Gaaleee, that rat was really cuttin' and Bubber caught him with his heel and the janitor, Mr. Barnett, got him with a stick—and then they got him in a corner and—BAM! BAM! BAM!—and he was still jumping around and bleeding like everything too—there's rat blood all over the street—

(*Ruth reaches out suddenly and grabs her son without even looking at him and clamps her hand over his mouth and holds him to her. Mama crosses to them rapidly and takes the boy from her.*)

Mama: You hush up now . . . talking all that terrible stuff . . .

(*Travis is staring at his mother with a stunned expression. Beneatha comes quickly and takes him away from his grandmother and ushers him to the door.*)

Beneatha: You go back outside and play . . . but not with any rats. (*She pushes him gently out the door with the boy straining to see what is wrong with his mother.*)

Mama (*worriedly hovering over Ruth*): Ruth honey—what's the matter with you—you sick?

(*Ruth has her fists clenched on her thighs and is fighting hard to suppress a scream that seems to be rising in her.*)

Beneatha: What's the matter with her, Mama?

Mama (*working her fingers in Ruth's shoulders to relax her*): She be all right. Women gets right depressed sometimes when they get her way. (*Speaking softly, expertly, rapidly.*) Now you just relax. That's right . . . just lean back, don't think 'bout nothing at all . . . nothing at all—

Ruth: I'm all right . . .

(*The glassy-eyed look melts and then she collapses into a fit of heavy sobbing. The bell rings.*)

Beneatha: Oh, my God—that must be Asagai.

Mama (*to Ruth*): Come on now, honey. You need to lie down and rest awhile . . . then have some nice hot food.

(*They exit, Ruth's weight on her mother-in-law. Beneatha, herself profoundly disturbed, opens the door to admit a rather dramatic-looking young man with a large package.*)

Asagai: Hello, Alaiyo—

Beneatha (*holding the door open and regarding him with pleasure*): Hello . . . (*Long pause.*) Well—come in. And please excuse everything. My mother was very upset about my letting anyone come here with the place like this.

Asagai (*coming into the room*): You look disturbed too . . . Is something wrong?

Beneatha (*still at the door, absently*): Yes . . . we've all got acute ghetto-itis. (*She smiles and comes toward him, finding a cigarette and sitting.*) So—sit down! No! Wait! (*She whips the spray gun off sofa where she had left it and puts the cushions back. At last perches on arm of sofa. He sits.*) So, how was Canada?

Asagai (*a sophisticate*): Canadian.

Beneatha (*looking at him*): Asagai, I'm very glad you are back.

Asagai (*looking back at her in turn*): Are you really?

Beneatha: Yes—very.

Asagai: Why?—you were quite glad when I went away. What happened?

Beneatha: You went away.

Asagai: Ahhhhhhhh.

Beneatha: Before—you wanted to be so serious before there was time.

Asagai: How much time must there be before one knows what one feels?

Beneatha (stalling this particular conversation. Her hands pressed together, in a deliberately childish gesture): What did you bring me?

Asagai (handing her the package): Open it and see.

Beneatha (eagerly opening the package and drawing out some records and the colorful robes of a Nigerian woman): Oh, Asagai! . . . You got them for me! . . . How beautiful . . . and the records too! (*She lifts out the robes and runs to the mirror with them and holds the drapery up in front of herself.*)

Asagai (coming to her at the mirror): I shall have to teach you how to drape it properly. (*He flings the material about her for the moment and stands back to look at her.*) Ah—Oh-pay-gay-day, oh-gbah-mu-shay. (*A Yoruba exclamation for admiration.*) You wear it well . . . very well . . . mutilated hair and all.

Beneatha (turning suddenly): My hair—what's wrong with my hair?

Asagai (shrugging): Were you born with it like that?

Beneatha (reaching up to touch it): No . . . of course not. (*She looks back to the mirror, disturbed.*)

Asagai (smiling): How then?

Beneatha: You know perfectly well how . . . as crinkly as yours . . . that's how.

Asagai: And it is ugly to you that way?

Beneatha (quickly): Oh, no—not ugly . . . (*More slowly, apologetically.*) But it's so hard to manage when it's, well—raw.

Asagai: And so to accommodate that—you mutilate it every week?

Beneatha: It's not mutilation!

Asagai (laughing aloud at her seriousness): Oh . . . please! I am only teasing you because you are so very serious about these things. (*He stands back from her and folds his arms across his chest as he watches her pulling at her hair and frowning in the mirror.*) Do you remember the first time you met me at school? . . . (*He laughs.*) You came up to me and you said—and I thought you were the most serious little thing I had ever seen—you said: (*He imitates her.*) "Mr. Asagai—I want very much to talk with you. About Africa. You see, Mr. Asagai, I am looking for my *identity!*"

(*He laughs.*)

Beneatha (turning to him, not laughing): Yes—(*Her face is quizzical, profoundly disturbed.*)

Asagai (still teasing and reaching out and taking her face in his hands and turning her profile to him): Well . . . it is true that this is not so much a profile of a Hollywood queen as perhaps a queen of the Nile—(*A mock dismissal of the importance of the question.*) But what does it matter? Assimilationism is so popular in your country.

Beneatha (wheeling, passionately, sharply): I am not an assimilationist!

Asagai (the protest hangs in the room for a moment and Asagai studies her, his laughter fading): Such a serious one. (*There is a pause.*) So—you like the robes? You must take excellent care of them—they are from my sister's personal wardrobe.

Beneatha (with incredulity): You—you sent all the way home—for me?

Asagai (with charm): For you—I would do much more . . . Well, that is what I came for. I must go.

Beneatha: Will you call me Monday?

Asagai: Yes . . . We have a great deal to talk about. I mean about identity and time and all that.

Beneatha: Time?

Asagai: Yes. About how much time one needs to know what one feels.

Beneatha: You see! You never understood that there is more than one kind of feeling which can exist between a man and a woman—or, at least, there should be.

Asagai (shaking his head negatively but gently): No. Between a man and a woman there need be only one kind of feeling. I have that for you . . . Now even . . . right this moment . . .

Beneatha: I know—and by itself—it won't do. I can find that anywhere.

Asagai: For a woman it should be enough.

Beneatha: I know—because that's what it says in all the novels that men write. But it isn't. Go ahead and laugh—but I'm not interested in being someone's little episode in America or—(with feminine vengeance)—one of them! (*Asagai has burst into laughter again.*) That's funny as hell, huh!

Asagai: It's just that every American girl I have known has said that to me. White—black—in this you are all the same. And the same speech, too!

Beneatha (angrily): Yuk, yuk, yuk!

Asagai: It's how you can be sure that the world's most liberated women are not liberated at all. You all talk about it too much!

(*Mama enters and is immediately all social charm because of the presence of a guest.*)

Beneatha: Oh—Mama—this is Mr. Asagai.

Mama: How do you do?

Asagai (total politeness to an elder): How do you do, Mrs. Younger. Please forgive me for coming at such an outrageous hour on a Saturday.

Mama: Well, you are quite welcome. I just hope you understand that our house don't always look like this. (*Chatterish.*) You must come again. I would love to hear all about—(*Not sure of the name.*)—your country. I think it's so sad the way our American Negroes don't know nothing about Africa 'cept Tarzan and all that. And all that money they pour into these churches when they ought to be helping you people over there drive out them French and Englishmen done taken away your land.

(*The mother flashes a slightly superior look at her daughter upon completion of the recitation.*)

Asagai (taken aback by this sudden and acutely unrelated expression of sympathy): Yes . . . yes . . .

Mama (smiling at him suddenly and relaxing and looking him over): How many miles is it from here to where you come from?

Asagai: Many thousands.

Mama (looking at him as she would Walter): I bet you don't half look after yourself, being away from your mama either. I spec you better come 'round here from time to time to get yourself some decent homecooked meals . . .

Asagai (moved): Thank you. Thank you very much. (*They are all quiet, then:*) Well . . . I must go. I will call you Monday, Alaiyo.

Mama: What's that he call you?

Asagai: Oh—"Alaiyo." I hope you don't mind. It is what you would call a nickname, I think. It is a Yoruba word. I am a Yoruba.

Mama (*looking at Beneatha*): I—I thought he was from—(*Uncertain.*)

Asagai (*understanding*): Nigeria is my country. Yoruba is my tribal origin—

Beneatha: You didn't tell us what Alaiyo means . . . for all I know, you might be calling me Little Idiot or something . . .

Asagai: Well . . . let me see . . . I do not know how just to explain it. . . . The sense of a thing can be so different when it changes languages.

Beneatha: You're evading.

Asagai: No—really it is difficult . . . (*Thinking.*) It means . . . it means One for Whom Bread—Food—Is Not Enough. (*He looks at her.*) Is that all right?

Beneatha (*understanding, softly*): Thank you.

Mama (*looking from one to the other and not understanding any of it*): Well . . . that's nice . . . You must come see us again—Mr.—

Asagai: Ah-sah-guy . . .

Mama: Yes . . . Do come again.

Asagai: Good-bye. (*He exits.*)

Mama (*after him*): Lord, that's a pretty thing just went out here!(*Insinuatingly, to her daughter.*) Yes, I guess I see why we done commence to get so interested in Africa 'round here. Missionaries my aunt Jenny! (*She exits.*)

Beneatha: Oh, Mama! . . .

(*She picks up the Nigerian dress and holds it up to her in front of the mirror again. She sets the headdress on haphazardly and then notices her hair again and clutches at it and then replaces the headdress and frowns at herself. Then she starts to wriggle in front of the mirror as she thinks a Nigerian woman might. Travis enters and stands regarding her.*)

Travis: What's the matter, girl, you cracking up?

Beneatha: Shut up.

(*She pulls the headdress off and looks at herself in the mirror and clutches at her hair again and squinches her eyes as if trying to imagine something. Then, suddenly, she gets her raincoat and kerchief and hurriedly prepares for going out.*)

Mama (*coming back into the room*): She's resting now. Travis, baby, run next door and ask Miss Johnson to please let me have a little kitchen cleanser. This here can is empty as Jacob's kettle.°

Travis: I just came in.

Mama: Do as you told. (*He exits and she looks at her daughter.*) Where you going?

Beneatha (*halting at the door*): To become a queen of the Nile!

(*She exits in a breathless blaze of glory. Ruth appears in the bedroom doorway.*)

Mama: Who told you to get up?

Ruth: Ain't nothing wrong with me to be lying in no bed for. Where did Bennie go?

Mama (*drumming her fingers*): Far as I could make out—to Egypt. (*Ruth just looks at her.*) What time is it getting to?

Ruth: Ten twenty. And the mailman going to ring that bell this morning just like he done every morning for the last umpteen years.

(*Travis comes in with the cleanser can.*)

Jacob's kettle: an allusion to Genesis 25:29-34, where the hungry Esau sells his birthright to his twin brother Jacob in return for all the stew in his pot or "kettle."

Travis: She say to tell you that she don't have much.

Mama (angrily): Lord, some people I could name sure is tight-fisted! (*Directing her grandson.*) Mark two cans of cleanser down on the list there. If she that hard up for kitchen cleanser, I sure don't want to forget to get her none!

Ruth: Lena—maybe the woman is just short on cleanser—

Mama (not listening): Much baking powder as she done borrowed from me all these years, she could of done gone into the baking business!

(*The bell sounds suddenly and sharply and all three are stunned—serious and silent—mid-speech. In spite of all the other conversations and distractions of the morning, this is what they have been waiting for, even Travis, who looks helplessly from his mother to his grandmother. Ruth is the first to come to life again.*)

Ruth (to Travis): Get down them steps, boy!

(*Travis snaps to life and flies out to get the mail.*)

Mama (her eyes wide, her hand to her breast): You mean it done really come?

Ruth (excited): Oh, Miss Lena!

Mama (collecting herself): Well . . . I don't know what we all so excited about 'round here for. We known it was coming for months.

Ruth: That's a whole lot different from having it come and being able to hold it in your hands . . . a piece of paper worth ten thousand dollars . . .

(*Travis bursts back into the room. He holds the envelope high above his head, like a little dancer, his face is radiant and he is breathless. He moves to his grandmother with sudden slow ceremony and puts the envelope into her hands. She accepts it, and then merely holds it and looks at it.*)

Come on! Open it . . . Lord have mercy, I wish Walter Lee was here!

Travis: Open it, Grandmama!

Mama (staring at it): Now you all be quiet. It's just a check.

Ruth: Open it . . .

Mama (still staring at it): Now don't act silly . . . We ain't never been no people to act silly 'bout no money—

Ruth (swiftly): We ain't never had none before—OPEN IT!

(*Mama finally makes a good strong tear and pulls out the thin blue slice of paper and inspects it closely. The boy and his mother study it raptly over Mama's shoulders.*)

Mama: Travis! (*She is counting off with doubt.*) Is that the right number of zeros?

Travis: Yes'm . . . ten thousand dollars. Gaalee, Grandmama, you rich.

Mama (she holds the check away from her, still looking at it. Slowly her face sobers into a mask of unhappiness): Ten thousand dollars. (*She hands it to Ruth.*) Put it away somewhere, Ruth. (*She does not look at Ruth; her eyes seem to be seeing something somewhere very far off.*) Ten thousand dollars they give you. Ten thousand dollars.

Travis (to his mother, sincerely): What's the matter with Grandmama—don't she want to be rich?

Ruth (distractedly): You go on out and play now, baby. (*Travis exits. Mama starts wiping dishes absently, humming intently to herself. Ruth turns to her, with kind exasperation.*) You've gone and got yourself upset.

Mama (*not looking at her*): I spec if it wasn't for you all . . . I would just put that money away or give it to the church or something.

Ruth: Now what kind of talk is that. Mr. Younger would just be plain mad if he could hear you talking foolish like that.

Mama (*stopping and staring off*): Yes . . . he sure would. (*Sighing.*) We got enough to do with that money, all right. (*She halts then, and turns and looks at her daughter-in-law hard; Ruth avoids her eyes and Mama wipes her hands with finality and starts to speak firmly to Ruth.*) Where did you go today, girl?

Ruth: To the doctor.

Mama (*impatiently*): Now, Ruth . . . you know better than that. Old Doctor Jones is strange enough in his way but there ain't nothing 'bout him make somebody slip and call him "she"—like you done this morning.

Ruth: Well, that's what happened—my tongue slipped.

Mama: You went to see that woman, didn't you?

Ruth (*defensively, giving herself away*): What woman you talking about?

Mama (*angrily*): That woman who—

(*Walter enters in great excitement.*)

Walter: Did it come?

Mama (*quietly*): Can't you give people a Christian greeting before you start asking about money?

Walter (*to Ruth*): Did it come? (*Ruth unfolds the check and lays it quietly before him, watching him intently with thoughts of her own. Walter sits down and grasps it close and counts off the zeros.*) Ten thousand dollars—(*He turns suddenly, frantically to his mother and draws some papers out of his breast pocket.*) Mama—look. Old Willy Harris put everything on paper—

Mama: Son—I think you ought to talk to your wife . . . I'll go on out and leave you alone if you want—

Walter: I can talk to her later—Mama, look—

Mama: Son—

Walter: WILL SOMEBODY PLEASE LISTEN TO ME TODAY!

Mama (*quietly*): I don't 'low no yellin' in this house, Walter Lee, and you know it— (*Walter stares at them in frustration and starts to speak several times.*) And there ain't going to be no investing in no liquor stores.

Walter: But, Mama, you ain't even looked at it.

Mama: I don't aim to have to speak on that again.

(*A long pause.*)

Walter: You ain't looked at it and you don't aim to have to speak on that again? You ain't even looked at it and *you* have decided—(*Crumpling his papers.*) Well, you tell that to my boy tonight when you put him to sleep on the living-room couch . . . (*Turning to Mama and speaking directly to her.*) Yeah—and tell it to my wife, Mama, tomorrow when she has to go out of here to look after somebody else's kids. And tell it to me, Mama, every time we need a new pair of curtains and I have to watch you go out and work in somebody's kitchen. Yeah, you tell me then! (*Walter starts out.*)

Ruth: Where you going?

Walter: I'm going out!

Ruth: Where?

Walter: Just out of this house somewhere—

Ruth (getting her coat): I'll come too.

Walter: I don't want you to come!

Ruth: I got something to talk to you about, Walter.

Walter: That's too bad.

Mama (still quietly): Walter Lee—*(She waits and he finally turns and looks at her.)* Sit down.

Walter: I'm a grown man, Mama.

Mama: Ain't nobody said you wasn't grown. But you still in my house and my presence. And as long as you are—you'll talk to your wife civil. Now sit down.

Ruth (suddenly): Oh, let him go on out and drink himself to death! He makes me sick to my stomach! *(She flings her coat against him and exits to bedroom.)*

Walter (violently flinging the coat after her): And you turn mine too, baby! *(The door slams behind her.)* That was my biggest mistake—

Mama (still quietly): Walter, what is the matter with you?

Walter: Matter with me? Ain't nothing the matter with *me!*

Mama: Yes there is. Something eating you up like a crazy man. Something more than me not giving you this money. The past few years I been watching it happen to you. You get all nervous acting and kind of wild in the eyes—*(Walter jumps up impatiently at her words.)* I said sit there now, I'm talking to you!

Walter: Mama—I don't need no nagging at me today.

Mama: Seem like you getting to a place where you always tied up in some kind of knot about something. But if anybody ask you 'bout it you just yell at 'em and bust out the house and go out and drink somewheres. Walter Lee, people can't live with that. Ruth's a good, patient girl in her way—but you getting to be too much. Boy, don't make the mistake of driving that girl away from you.

Walter: Why—what she do for me?

Mama: She loves you.

Walter: Mama—I'm going out. I want to go off somewhere and be by myself for a while.

Mama: I'm sorry 'bout your liquor store, son. It just wasn't the thing for us to do. That's what I want to tell you about—

Walter: I got to go out, Mama—*(He rises.)*

Mama: It's dangerous, son.

Walter: What's dangerous?

Mama: When a man goes outside his home to look for peace.

Walter (beseechingly): Then why can't there never be no peace in this house then?

Mama: You done found it in some other house?

Walter: No—there ain't no woman! Why do women always think there's a woman somewhere when a man gets restless. *(Picks up the check.)* Do you know what this money means to me? Do you know what this money can do for us? *(Puts it back.)* Mama—Mama—I want so many things . . .

Mama: Yes, son—

Walter: I want so many things that they are driving me kind of crazy . . . Mama—look at me.

Mama: I'm looking at you. You a good-looking boy. You got a job, a nice wife, a fine boy and—

Walter: A job. (*Looks at her.*) Mama, a job? I open and close car doors all day long. I drive a man around in his limousine and I say, "Yes, sir; no, sir; very good, sir; shall I take the Drive, sir?" Mama, that ain't no kind of job . . . that ain't nothing at all. (*Very quietly.*) Mama, I don't know if I can make you understand.

Mama: Understand what, baby?

Walter (quietly): Sometimes it's like I can see the future stretched out in front of me—just plain as day. The future, Mama. Hanging over there at the edge of my days. Just waiting for me—a big, looming blank space—full of *nothing.* Just waiting for *me.* But it don't have to be. (*Pause. Kneeling beside her chair.*) Mama—sometimes when I'm downtown and I pass them cool, quiet-looking restaurants where them white boys are sitting back and talking 'bout things . . . sitting there turning deals worth millions of dollars . . . sometimes I see guys don't look much older than me—

Mama: Son—how come you talk so much 'bout money?

Walter (with immense passion): Because it is life, Mama!

Mama (quietly): Oh—(*Very quietly.*) So now it's life. Money is life. Once upon a time freedom used to be life—now it's money. I guess the world really do change . . .

Walter: No—it was always money, Mama. We just didn't know about it.

Mama: No . . . something has changed. (*She looks at him.*) You something new, boy. In my time we was worried about not being lynched and getting to the North if we could and how to stay alive and still have a pinch of dignity too . . . Now here come you and Beneatha—talking 'bout things we ain't never even thought about hardly, me and your daddy. You ain't satisfied or proud of nothing we done. I mean that you had a home; that we kept you out of trouble till you was grown; that you don't have to ride to work on the back of nobody's streetcar—You my children—but how different we done become.

Walter (a long beat. He pats her hand and gets up): You just don't understand, Mama, you just don't understand.

Mama: Son—do you know your wife is expecting another baby? (*Walter stands, stunned, and absorbs what his mother has said.*) That's what she wanted to talk to you about. (*Walter sinks down into a chair.*) This ain't for me to be telling—but you ought to know. (*She waits.*) I think Ruth is thinking 'bout getting rid of that child.

Walter (slowly understanding): No—no—Ruth wouldn't do that.

Mama: When the world gets ugly enough—a woman will do anything for her family. The part that's already living.

Walter: You don't know Ruth, Mama, if you think she would do that.

(*Ruth opens the bedroom door and stands there a little limp.*)

Ruth (beaten): Yes I would too, Walter. (*Pause.*) I gave her a five-dollar down payment.

(*There is total silence as the man stares at his wife and the mother stares at her son.*)

Mama (presently): Well—(*Tightly.*) Well—son, I'm waiting to hear you say some-thing . . . (*She waits.*) I'm waiting to hear how you be your father's son. Be the man he was . . . (*Pause. The silence shouts.*) Your wife say she going to destroy your child. And I'm waiting to hear you talk like him and say we a people who give children life, not who destroys them—(*She rises.*) I'm waiting to see you stand up and look like your daddy and say we done give up one baby to poverty and that we ain't going to give up nary another one . . . I'm waiting.

Walter: Ruth—(*He can say nothing.*)

Mama: If you a son of mine, tell her! *(Walter picks up his keys and his coat and walks out. She continues, bitterly.)* You . . . you are a disgrace to your father's memory. Somebody get me my hat!

ACT II

SCENE I

TIME. *Later the same day*

AT RISE. *Ruth is ironing again. She has the radio going. Presently Beneatha's bedroom door opens and Ruth's mouth falls and she puts down the iron in fascination.*

Ruth: What have we got on tonight!

Beneatha *(emerging grandly from the doorway so that we can see her thoroughly robed in the costume Asagai brought)*: You are looking at what a well-dressed Nigerian woman wears—

(She parades for Ruth, her hair completely hidden by the headdress; she is coquettishly fanning herself with an ornate oriental fan, mistakenly more like Butterfly° than any Nigerian that ever was.)

Isn't it beautiful? *(She promenades to the radio and, with an arrogant flourish, turns off the good loud blues that is playing.)* Enough of this assimilationist junk!

(Ruth follows her with her eyes as she goes to the phonograph and puts on a record and turns and waits ceremoniously for the music to come up. Then, with a shout—) OCOMOGOSIAY!

(Ruth jumps. The music comes up, a lovely Nigerian melody. Beneatha listens, enraptured, her eyes far away—"back to the past." She begins to dance. Ruth is dumfounded.)

Ruth: What kind of dance is that?
Beneatha: A folk dance.
Ruth *(Pearl Bailey°)*: What kind of folks do that, honey?
Beneatha: It's from Nigeria. It's a dance of welcome.
Ruth: Who you welcoming?
Beneatha: The men back to the village.
Ruth: Where they been?
Beneatha: How should I know—out hunting or something. Anyway, they are coming back now . . .
Ruth: Well, that's good.
Beneatha *(with the record)*:

Alundi, alundi
Alundi alunya
Jop pu a jeepua
Ang gu soooooooooo

Ai yai yae . . .
Ayehaye—alundi . . .

Butterfly: the lead character of *Madama Butterfly* (1904), Giacomo Puccini's (1858–1924) famous tragic opera about a Japanese woman abandoned by her American husband.   *Pearl Bailey:* Pearl Mae Bailey (1918–1990) was an American entertainer known for her singing voice and larger-than-life personality.

(Walter comes in during this performance; he has obviously been drinking. He leans against the door heavily and watches his sister, at first with distaste. Then his eyes look off—"back to the past"—as he lifts both his fists to the roof, screaming.)

Walter: YEAH . . . AND ETHIOPIA STRETCH FORTH HER HANDS AGAIN! . . .

Ruth *(drily, looking at him)*: Yes—and Africa sure is claiming her own tonight. *(She gives them both up and starts ironing again.)*

Walter *(all in a drunken, dramatic shout)*: Shut up! . . . I'm digging them drums . . . them drums move me! . . . *(He makes his weaving way to his wife's face and leans in close to her.)* In my heart of hearts—*(He thumps his chest.)*—I am much warrior!

Ruth *(without even looking up)*: In your heart of hearts you are much drunkard.

Walter *(coming away from her and starting to wander around the room, shouting)*: Me and Jomo° . . . *(Intently, in his sister's face. She has stopped dancing to watch him in this unknown mood.)* That's my man, Kenyatta. *(Shouting and thumping his chest.)* FLAMING SPEAR! HOT DAMN! *(He is suddenly in possession of an imaginary spear and actively spearing enemies all over the room.)* OCOMOGOSIAY . . .

Beneatha *(to encourage Walter, thoroughly caught up with this side of him)*: OCOMOGOSIAY, FLAMING SPEAR!

Walter: THE LION IS WAKING . . . OWIMOWEH!° *(He pulls his shirt open and leaps up on the table and gestures with his spear.)*

Beneatha: OWIMOWEH!

Walter *(on the table, very far gone, his eyes pure glass sheets. He sees what we cannot, that he is a leader of his people, a great chief, a descendant of Chaka,° and that the hour to march has come)*: Listen, my black brothers—

Beneatha: OCOMOGOSIAY!

Walter: —Do you hear the waters rushing against the shores of the coastlands—

Beneatha: OCOMOGOSIAY!

Walter: —Do you hear the screeching of the cocks in yonder hills beyond where the chiefs meet in council for the coming of the mighty war—

Beneatha: OCOMOGOSIAY!

(And now the lighting shifts subtly to suggest the world of Walter's imagination, and the mood shifts from pure comedy. It is the inner Walter speaking: the Southside chauffeur has assumed an unexpected majesty.)

Walter: —Do you hear the beating of the wings of the birds flying low over the mountains and the low places of our land—

Beneatha: OCOMOGOSIAY!

Walter: —Do you hear the singing of the women, singing the war songs of our fathers to the babies in the great houses? Singing the sweet war songs! *(The doorbell rings.)* OH, DO YOU HEAR, MY BLACK BROTHERS!

Beneatha *(completely gone)*: We hear you, Flaming Spear—

(Ruth shuts off the phonograph and opens the door. George Murchison enters.)

Jomo: Jomo Kenyatta (1893?-1978) was a famous African political leader and the first president of Kenya (1964–1978). *THE LION IS WAKING . . . OWIMOWEH:* Walter is referring to the popular pop song "The Lion Sleeps Tonight," whose chorus keeps repeating "Owimoweh." The song, originally recorded by the South African singer Solomon Linda, has been covered by many artists, and became even more popular when used in Disney's *The Lion King. Chaka:* or Shaka (1785?-1828), was a famous Zulu warrior and chieftain.

Walter: Telling us to prepare for the GREATNESS OF THE TIME! (*Lights back to normal. He turns and sees George.*) Black Brother! (*He extends his hand for the fraternal clasp.*)

George: Black Brother, hell!

Ruth (*having had enough, and embarrassed for the family*): Beneatha, you got company— what's the matter with you? Walter Lee Younger, get down off that table and stop acting like a fool . . .

(*Walter comes down off the table suddenly and makes a quick exit to the bathroom.*)

Ruth: He's had a little to drink . . . I don't know what her excuse is.

George (*to Beneatha*): Look honey, we're going *to* the theatre—we're not going to be *in* it . . . so go change, huh?

(*Beneatha looks at him and slowly, ceremoniously, lifts her hands and pulls off the headdress. Her hair is close-cropped and unstraightened. George freezes mid-sentence and Ruth's eyes all but fall out of her head.*)

George: What in the name of—

Ruth (*touching Beneatha's hair*): Girl, you done lost your natural mind!? Look at your head!

George: What have you done to your head—I mean your hair!

Beneatha: Nothing—except cut it off.

Ruth: Now that's the truth—it's what ain't been done to it! You expect this boy to go out with you with your head all nappy like that?

Beneatha (*looking at George*): That's up to George. If he's ashamed of his heritage—

George: Oh, don't be so proud of yourself, Bennie—just because you look eccentric.

Beneatha: How can something that's natural be eccentric?

George: That's what being eccentric means—being natural. Get dressed.

Beneatha: I don't like that, George.

Ruth: Why must you and your brother make an argument out of everything people say?

Beneatha: Because I hate assimilationist Negroes!

Ruth: Will somebody please tell me what assimila-whoever means!

George: Oh, it's just a college girl's way of calling people Uncle Toms—but that isn't what it means at all.

Ruth: Well, what does it mean?

Beneatha (*cutting George off and staring at him as she replies to Ruth.*) It means someone who is willing to give up his own culture and submerge himself completely in the dominant, and in this case *oppressive,* culture!

George: Oh, dear, dear, dear! Here we go! A lecture on the African past! On our Great West African Heritage! In one second we will hear all about the great Ashanti empires; the great Songhay civilizations; and the great sculpture of Bénin—and then some poetry in the Bantu—and the whole monologue will end with the word *heritage!* (*Nastily.*) Let's face it, baby, your heritage is nothing but a bunch of raggedy-assed spirituals and some grass huts!

Beneatha: GRASS HUTS! (*Ruth crosses to her and forcibly pushes her toward the bedroom.*) See there . . . you are standing there in your splendid ignorance talking about people who were the first to smelt iron on the face of the earth! (*Ruth is pushing her through the door.*) The Ashanti were performing surgical operations when the English—(*Ruth pulls the door to, with Beneatha on the other side, and* smiles graciously at George. Beneatha opens the door and shouts the end of the sentence defiantly at George.)—were still tatooing themselves with blue dragons! *(She goes back inside.)*

Ruth: Have a seat, George. *(They both sit. Ruth folds her hands rather primly on her lap, determined to demonstrate the civilization of the family.)* Warm, ain't it? I mean for September. *(Pause.)* Just like they always say about Chicago weather: If it's too hot or cold for you, just wait a minute and it'll change. *(She smiles happily at this cliché of clichés.)* Everybody say it's got to do with them bombs and things they keep setting off. *(Pause.)* Would you like a nice cold beer?

George: No, thank you. I don't care for beer. *(He looks at his watch.)* I hope she hurries up.

Ruth: What time is the show?

George: It's an eight-thirty curtain. That's just Chicago, though. In New York standard curtain time is eight forty. *(He is rather proud of this knowledge.)*

Ruth *(properly appreciating it)*: You get to New York a lot?

George *(offhand)*: Few times a year.

Ruth: Oh—that's nice. I've never been to New York.

(Walter enters. We feel he has relieved himself, but the edge of unreality is still with him.)

Walter: New York ain't got nothing Chicago ain't. Just a bunch of hustling people all squeezed up together—being "Eastern." *(He turns his face into a screw of displeasure.)*

George: Oh—you've been?

Walter: Plenty of times.

Ruth *(shocked at the lie)*: Walter Lee Younger!

Walter *(staring her down)*: Plenty! *(Pause.)* What we got to drink in this house? Why don't you offer this man some refreshment. *(To George.)* They don't know how to entertain people in this house, man.

George: Thank you—I don't really care for anything.

Walter *(feeling his head; sobriety coming.)* Where's Mama?

Ruth: She ain't come back yet.

Walter *(looking Murchison over from head to toe, scrutinizing his carefully casual tweed sports jacket over cashmere V-neck sweater over soft eyelet shirt and tie, and soft slacks, finished off with white buckskin shoes)*: Why all you college boys wear them faggoty-looking white shoes?

Ruth: Walter Lee!

(George Murchison ignores the remark.)

Walter *(to Ruth)*: Well, they look crazy as hell—white shoes, cold as it is.

Ruth *(crushed)*: You have to excuse him—

Walter: No he don't! Excuse me for what? What you always excusing me for! I'll excuse myself when I needs to be excused! *(A pause.)* They look as funny as them black knee socks Beneatha wears out of here all the time.

Ruth: It's the college *style,* Walter.

Walter: Style, hell. She looks like she got burnt legs or something!

Ruth: Oh, Walter—

Walter *(an irritable mimic)*: Oh, Walter! Oh, Walter! *(To Murchison.)* How's your old man making out? I understand you all going to buy that big hotel on the Drive? *(He finds a beer in the refrigerator, wanders over to Murchison, sipping and wiping* his lips with the back of his hand, and straddling a chair backwards to talk to the other man.) Shrewd move. Your old man is all right, man. (Tapping his head and half winking for emphasis.) I mean he knows how to operate. I mean he thinks big, you know what I mean, I mean for a home, you know? But I think he's kind of running out of ideas now. I'd like to talk to him. Listen, man, I got some plans that could turn this city upside down. I mean think like he does. Big. Invest big, gamble big, hell, lose big if you have to, you know what I mean. It's hard to find a man on this whole Southside who understands my kind of thinking—you dig? (He scrutinizes Murchison again, drinks his beer, squints his eyes and leans in close, confidential, man to man.) Me and you ought to sit down and talk sometimes, man. Man, I got me some ideas . . .

Murchison (with boredom): Yeah—sometimes we'll have to do that, Walter.

Walter (understanding the indifference, and offended): Yeah—well, when you get the time, man. I know you a busy little boy.

Ruth: Walter, please—

Walter (bitterly, hurt): I know ain't nothing in this world as busy as you colored college boys with your fraternity pins and white shoes . . .

Ruth (covering her face with humiliation): Oh, Walter Lee—

Walter: I see you all the time—with the books tucked under your arms—going to your (British A—a mimic.) "clahsses." And for what! What the hell you learning over there? Filling up your heads—(counting off on his fingers)—with the sociology and the psychology—but they teaching you how to be a man? How to take over and run the world? They teaching you how to run a rubber plantation or a steel mill? Naw—just to talk proper and read books and wear them faggoty-looking white shoes . . .

George (looking at him with distaste, a little above it all): You're all wacked up with bitterness, man.

Walter (intently, almost quietly, between the teeth, glaring at the boy): And you—ain't you bitter, man? Ain't you just about had it yet? Don't you see no stars gleaming that you can't reach out and grab? You happy?—You contented son-of-a-bitch—you happy? You got it made? Bitter? Man, I'm a volcano. Bitter? Here I am a giant—surrounded by ants! Ants who can't even understand what it is the giant is talking about.

Ruth (passionately and suddenly): Oh, Walter—ain't you with nobody!

Walter (violently): No! 'Cause ain't nobody with me! Not even my own mother!

Ruth: Walter, that's a terrible thing to say!

(Beneatha enters, dressed for the evening in a cocktail dress and earrings, hair natural.)

George: Well—hey—(Crosses to Beneatha; thoughtful, with emphasis, since this is a reversal.) You look great!

Walter (seeing his sister's hair for the first time): What's the matter with your head?

Beneatha (tired of the jokes now): I cut it off, Brother.

Walter (coming close to inspect it and walking around her): Well, I'll be damned. So that's what they mean by the African bush . . .

Beneatha: Ha ha. Let's go, George.

George (looking at her): You know something? I like it. It's sharp. I mean it really is. (Helps her into her wrap.)

Ruth: Yes—I think so, too. (She goes to the mirror and starts to clutch at her hair.)

Walter: Oh no! You leave yours alone, baby. You might turn out to have a pin-shaped head or something!

Beneatha: See you all later.

Ruth: Have a nice time.

George: Thanks. Good night. *(Half out the door, he reopens it. To Walter.)* Good night, Prometheus!°

(Beneatha and George exit.)

Walter (to Ruth): Who is Prometheus?

Ruth: I don't know. Don't worry about it.

Walter (in fury, pointing after George): See there—they get to a point where they can't insult you man to man—they got to go talk about something ain't nobody never heard of!

Ruth: How do you know it was an insult? *(To humor him.)* Maybe Prometheus is a nice fellow.

Walter: Prometheus! I bet there ain't even no such thing! I bet that simple-minded clown—

Ruth: Walter—*(She stops what she is doing and looks at him.)*

Walter (yelling): Don't start!

Ruth: Start what?

Walter: Your nagging! Where was I? Who was I with? How much money did I spend?

Ruth (plaintively): Walter Lee—why don't we just try to talk about it . . .

Walter (not listening): I been out talking with people who understand me. People who care about the things I got on my mind.

Ruth (wearily): I guess that means people like Willy Harris.

Walter: Yes, people like Willy Harris.

Ruth (with a sudden flash of impatience): Why don't you all just hurry up and go into the banking business and stop talking about it!

Walter: Why? You want to know why? 'Cause we all tied up in a race of people that don't know how to do nothing but moan, pray and have babies!

(The line is too bitter even for him and he looks at her and sits down.)

Ruth: Oh, Walter . . . *(Softly.)* Honey, why can't you stop fighting me?

Walter (without thinking): Who's fighting you? Who even cares about you? *(This line begins the retardation of his mood.)*

Ruth: Well—*(She waits a long time, and then with resignation starts to put away her things.)* I guess I might as well go on to bed . . . *(More or less to herself.)* I don't know where we lost it . . . but we have . . . *(Then, to him.)* I—I'm sorry about this new baby, Walter. I guess maybe I better go on and do what I started . . . I guess I just didn't realize how bad things was with us . . . I guess I just didn't really realize—*(She starts out to the bedroom and stops.)* You want some hot milk?

Walter: Hot milk?

Ruth: Yes—hot milk.

Walter: Why hot milk?

Ruth: 'Cause after all that liquor you come home with you ought to have something hot in your stomach.

Walter: I don't want no milk.

Ruth: You want some coffee then?

Prometheus: in Greek legend, the god who gave the secret of fire to humanity.

Walter: No, I don't want no coffee. I don't want nothing hot to drink.(*Almost plaintively.*) Why you always trying to give me something to eat?

Ruth (*standing and looking at him helplessly*): What else can I give you, Walter Lee Younger?

(*She stands and looks at him and presently turns to go out again. He lifts his head and watches her going away from him in a new mood which began to emerge when he asked her "Who even cares about you?"*)

Walter: It's been rough, ain't it, baby? (*She hears and stops but does not turn around and he continues to her back.*) I guess between two people there ain't never as much understood as folks generally thinks there is. I mean like between me and you— (*She turns to face him.*) How we gets to the place where we scared to talk softness to each other. (*He waits, thinking hard himself.*) Why you think it got to be like that? (*He is thoughtful, almost as a child would be.*) Ruth, what is it gets into people ought to be close?

Ruth: I don't know, honey. I think about it a lot.

Walter: On account of you and me, you mean? The way things are with us. The way something done come down between us.

Ruth: There ain't so much between us, Walter . . . Not when you come to me and try to talk to me. Try to be with me . . . a little even.

Walter (*total honesty*): Sometimes . . . sometimes . . . I don't even know how to try.

Ruth: Walter—

Walter: Yes?

Ruth (*coming to him, gently and with misgiving, but coming to him*): Honey . . . life don't have to be like this. I mean sometimes people can do things so that things are better . . . You remember how we used to talk when Travis was born . . . about the way we were going to live . . . the kind of house . . . (*She is stroking his head.*) Well, it's all starting to slip away from us . . .

(*He turns her to him and they look at each other and kiss, tenderly and hungrily. The door opens and Mama enters—Walter breaks away and jumps up. A beat.*)

Walter: Mama, where have you been?

Mama: My—them steps is longer than they used to be. Whew! (*She sits down and ignores him.*) How you feeling this evening, Ruth?

(*Ruth shrugs, disturbed at having been interrupted and watching her husband knowingly.*)

Walter: Mama, where have you been all day?

Mama (*still ignoring him and leaning on the table and changing to more comfortable shoes*): Where's Travis?

Ruth: I let him go out earlier and he ain't come back yet. Boy, is he going to get it!

Walter: Mama!

Mama (*as if she has heard him for the first time*): Yes, son?

Walter: Where did you go this afternoon?

Mama: I went downtown to tend to some business that I had to tend to.

Walter: What kind of business?

Mama: You know better than to question me like a child, Brother.

Walter (*rising and bending over the table*): Where were you, Mama? (*Bringing his fists down and shouting.*) Mama, you didn't go do something with that insurance money, something crazy?

(The front door opens slowly, interrupting him, and Travis peeks his head in, less than hopefully.)

Travis *(to his mother)*: Mama, I—

Ruth: "Mama I" nothing! You're going to get it, boy! Get on in that bedroom and get yourself ready!

Travis: But I—

Mama: Why don't you all never let the child explain hisself.

Ruth: Keep out of it now, Lena.

(Mama clamps her lips together, and Ruth advances toward her son menacingly.)

Ruth: A thousand times I have told you not to go off like that—

Mama *(holding out her arms to her grandson)*: Well—at least let me tell him something. I want him to be the first one to hear . . . Come here, Travis. *(The boy obeys, gladly.)* Travis—*(She takes him by the shoulder and looks into his face.)*—you know that money we got in the mail this morning?

Travis: Yes'm—

Mama: Well—what you think your grandmama gone and done with that money?

Travis: I don't know, Grandmama.

Mama *(putting her finger on his nose for emphasis)*: She went out and she bought you a house! *(The explosion comes from Walter at the end of the revelation and he jumps up and turns away from all of them in a fury. Mama continues, to Travis.)* You glad about the house? It's going to be yours when you get to be a man.

Travis: Yeah—I always wanted to live in a house.

Mama: All right, gimme some sugar then—*(Travis puts his arms around her neck as she watches her son over the boy's shoulder. Then, to Travis, after the embrace.)* Now when you say your prayers tonight, you thank God and your grandfather—'cause it was him who give you the house—in his way.

Ruth *(taking the boy from Mama and pushing him toward the bedroom)*: Now you get out of here and get ready for your beating.

Travis: Aw, Mama—

Ruth: Get on in there—*(Closing the door behind him and turning radiantly to her mother-in-law.)* So you went and did it!

Mama *(quietly, looking at her son with pain)*: Yes, I did.

Ruth *(raising both arms classically)*: PRAISE GOD! *(Looks at Walter a moment, who says nothing. She crosses rapidly to her husband.)* Please, honey —let me be glad . . . you be glad too. *(She has laid her hands on his shoulders, but he shakes himself free of her roughly, without turning to face her.)* Oh Walter . . . a home . . . a home. *(She comes back to Mama.)* Well—where is it? How big is it? How much it going to cost?

Mama: Well—

Ruth: When we moving?

Mama *(smiling at her)*: First of the month.

Ruth *(throwing back her head with jubilance)*: Praise God!

Mama *(tentatively, still looking at her son's back turned against her and Ruth)*: It's—it's a nice house too . . . *(She cannot help speaking directly to him. An imploring quality in her voice, her manner, makes her almost like a girl now.)* Three bedrooms—nice big one for you and Ruth . . . Me and Beneatha still have to share our room, but Travis have one of his own—and *(With difficulty.)* I figure if the—new baby—is a boy, we could get one of them double-decker outfits . . . And there's a yard with a little patch of dirt where I could maybe get to grow me a few flowers . . . And a nice big basement . . .

Ruth: Walter honey, be glad—

Mama (still to his back, fingering things on the table): 'Course I don't want to make it sound fancier than it is . . . It's just a plain little old house—but it's made good and solid—and it will be *ours*. Walter Lee—it makes a difference in a man when he can walk on floors that belong to him . . .

Ruth: Where is it?

Mama (frightened at this telling): Well—well—it's out there in Clybourne Park—

(*Ruth's radiance fades abruptly, and Walter finally turns slowly to face his mother with incredulity and hostility.*)

Ruth: Where?

Mama (matter-of-factly): Four o six Clybourne Street, Clybourne Park.

Ruth: Clybourne Park? Mama, there ain't no colored people living in Clybourne Park.

Mama (almost idiotically): Well, I guess there's going to be some now.

Walter (bitterly): So that's the peace and comfort you went out and bought for us today!

Mama (raising her eyes to meet his finally): Son—I just tried to find the nicest place for the least amount of money for my family.

Ruth (trying to recover from the shock): Well—well—'course I ain't one never been 'fraid of no crackers, mind you—but—well, wasn't there no other houses nowhere?

Mama: Them houses they put up for colored in them areas way out all seem to cost twice as much as other houses. I did the best I could.

Ruth (struck senseless with the news, in its various degrees of goodness and trouble, she sits a moment, her fists propping her chin in thought, and then she starts to rise, bringing her fists down with vigor, the radiance spreading from cheek to cheek again): Well—well!— All I can say is—if this is my time in life—MY TIME—to say good-bye—(*And she builds with momentum as she starts to circle the room with an exuberant, almost tearfully happy release.*)—to these goddamned cracking walls!—(*She pounds the walls.*)—and these marching roaches!—(*She wipes at an imaginary army of marching roaches.*)— and this cramped little closet which ain't now or never was no kitchen! . . . then I say it loud and good, HALLELUJAH! AND GOOD-BYE MISERY . . . I DON'T NEVER WANT TO SEE YOUR UGLY FACE AGAIN! (*She laughs joyously, having practically destroyed the apartment, and flings her arms up and lets them come down happily, slowly, reflectively, over her abdomen, aware for the first time perhaps that the life therein pulses with happiness and not despair.*) Lena?

Mama (moved, watching her happiness): Yes, honey?

Ruth (looking off): Is there—is there a whole lot of sunlight?

Mama (understanding): Yes, child, there's a whole lot of sunlight.

(*Long pause.*)

Ruth (collecting herself and going to the door of the room Travis is in): Well—I guess I better see 'bout Travis. (*to Mama.*) Lord, I sure don't feel like whipping nobody today! (*She exits.*)

Mama (the mother and son are left alone now and the mother waits a long time, considering deeply, before she speaks): Son—you—you understand what I done, don't you? (*Walter is silent and sullen.*) I—I just seen my family falling apart today . . . just falling to pieces in front of my eyes . . . We couldn't of gone on like we was today. We was going backwards 'stead of forwards—talking 'bout killing babies and wishing each other was dead . . . When it gets like that in life—you just got to do something different, push on out and do something bigger . . . (*She waits.*) I wish you say something, son . . . I wish you'd say how deep inside you think I done the right thing—

Walter (*crossing slowly to his bedroom door and finally turning there and speaking measuredly*): What you need me to say you done right for? You the head of this family. You run our lives like you want to. It was your money and you did what you wanted with it. So what you need for me to say it was all right for? (*Bitterly, to hurt her as deeply as he knows is possible.*) So you butchered up a dream of mine— you—who always talking 'bout your children's dreams . . .

Mama: Walter Lee—

(*He just closes the door behind him. Mama sits alone, thinking heavily.*)

ACT II

SCENE II

TIME. *Friday night. A few weeks later.*

AT RISE. *Packing crates mark the intention of the family to move. Beneatha and George come in, presumably from an evening out again.*

George: O.K. . . . O.K., whatever you say . . . (*They both sit on the couch. He tries to kiss her. She moves away.*) Look, we've had a nice evening; let's not spoil it, huh? . . .

(*He again turns her head and tries to nuzzle in and she turns away from him, not with distaste but with momentary lack of interest; in a mood to pursue what they were talking about.*)

Beneatha: I'm trying to talk to you.

George: We always talk.

Beneatha: Yes—and I love to talk.

George (*exasperated; rising*): I know it and I don't mind it sometimes . . . I want you to cut it out, see—The moody stuff, I mean. I don't like it. You're a nice-looking girl . . . all over. That's all you need, honey, forget the atmosphere. Guys aren't going to go for the atmosphere—they're going to go for what they see. Be glad for that. Drop the Garbo° routine. It doesn't go with you. As for myself, I want a nice—(*groping*)—simple (*thoughtfully*)—sophisticated girl . . . not a poet—O.K.?

(*He starts to kiss her, she rebuffs him again and he jumps up.*)

Beneatha: Why are you angry, George?

George: Because this is stupid! I don't go out with you to discuss the nature of "quiet desperation"° or to hear all about your thoughts—because the world will go on thinking what it thinks regardless—

Beneatha: Then why read books? Why go to school?

Garbo: Greta Garbo (1905–1990) was a glamorous and reclusive movie star of the 1920s and 1930s. *"quiet desperation"*: quotation from Henry David Thoreau's *Walden* (1854): "The mass of men lead lives of quiet desperation."

George (with artificial patience, counting on his fingers): It's simple. You read books—to learn facts—to get grades—to pass the course—to get a degree. That's all—it has nothing to do with thoughts.

(A long pause.)

Beneatha: I see. *(He starts to sit.)* Good night, George.

(George looks at her a little oddly, and starts to exit. He meets Mama coming in.)

George: Oh—hello, Mrs. Younger.
Mama: Hello, George, how you feeling?
George: Fine—fine, how are you?
Mama: Oh, a little tired. You know them steps can get you after a day's work. You all have a nice time tonight?
George: Yes—a fine time. A fine time.
Mama: Well, good night.
George: Good night. *(He exits. Mama closes the door behind her.)*
Mama: Hello, honey. What you sitting like that for?
Beneatha: I'm just sitting.
Mama: Didn't you have a nice time?
Beneatha: No.
Mama: No? What's the matter?
Beneatha: Mama, George is a fool—honest *(She rises.)*
Mama *(hustling around unloading the packages she has entered with. She stops):* Is he, baby?
Beneatha: Yes. *(Beneatha makes up Travis' bed as she talks.)*
Mama: You sure?
Beneatha: Yes.
Mama: Well—I guess you better not waste your time with no fools.

(Beneatha looks up at her mother, watching her put groceries in the refrigerator. Finally she gathers up her things and starts into the bedroom. At the door she stops and looks back at her mother.)

Beneatha: Mama—
Mama: Yes, baby—
Beneatha: Thank you.
Mama: For what?
Beneatha: For understanding me this time.

(She exits quickly and the mother stands, smiling a little, looking at the place where Beneatha just stood. Ruth enters.)

Ruth: Now don't you fool with any of this stuff, Lena—
Mama: Oh, I just thought I'd sort a few things out. Is Brother here?
Ruth: Yes.
Mama *(with concern):* Is he—
Ruth *(reading her eyes):* Yes.

(Mama is silent and someone knocks on the door. Mama and Ruth exchange weary and knowing glances and Ruth opens it to admit the neighbor, Mrs. Johnson, who is a rather squeaky wide-eyed lady of no particular age, with a newspaper under her arm.)

Mama (changing her expression to acute delight and a ringing cheerful greeting): Oh—
hello, there, Johnson.

*Johnson (this is a woman who decided long ago to be enthusiastic about EVERYTHING
in life and she is inclined to wave her wrist vigorously at the height of her exclamatory
comments)*: Hello there, yourself! H'you this evening, Ruth?

Ruth (not much of a deceptive type): Fine, Mis' Johnson, h'you?

Johnson: Fine. *(Reaching out quickly, playfully, and patting Ruth's stomach.)* Ain't you
starting to poke out none yet! *(She mugs with delight at the overfamiliar remark and
her eyes dart around looking at the crates and packing preparation; Mama's face is a
cold sheet of endurance.)* Oh, ain't we getting ready 'round here, though! Yessir!
Lookathere! I'm telling you the Youngers is really getting ready to "move on up a
little higher!"—Bless God!

Mama (a little drily, doubting the total sincerity of the Blesser): Bless God.

Johnson: He's good, ain't He?

Mama: Oh yes, He's good.

Johnson: I mean sometimes He works in mysterious ways . . . but He works, don't He!

Mama (the same): Yes, He does.

Johnson: I'm just soooooo happy for y'all. And this here child—*(about Ruth)* looks
like she could just pop open with happiness, don't she. Where's all the rest of the
family?

Mama: Bennie's gone to bed—

Johnson: Ain't no . . . . *(The implication is pregnancy.)* sickness done hit you—
I hope . . . ?

Mama: No—she just tired. She was out this evening.

Johnson (all is a coo, an emphatic coo): Aw—ain't that lovely. She still going out with
the little Murchison boy?

Mama (drily): Ummmm huh.

Johnson: That's lovely. You sure got lovely children, Younger. Me and Isaiah talks all
the time 'bout what fine children you was blessed with. We sure do.

Mama: Ruth, give Mis' Johnson a piece of sweet potato pie and some milk.

Johnson: Oh honey, I can't stay hardly a minute—I just dropped in to see if there was
anything I could do. *(Accepting the food easily.)* I guess y'all seen the news what's
all over the colored paper this week . . .

Mama: No—didn't get mine yet this week.

Johnson (lifting her head and blinking with the spirit of catastrophe): You mean you ain't
read 'bout them colored people that was bombed out their place out there?

*(Ruth straightens with concern and takes the paper and reads it. Johnson notices her
and feeds commentary.)*

Johnson: Ain't it something how bad these here white folks is getting here in
Chicago! Lord, getting so you think you right down in Mississippi! *(With a
tremendous and rather insincere sense of melodrama.)* 'Course I thinks it's wonderful
how our folks keeps on pushing out. You hear some of these Negroes round here
talking 'bout how they don't go where they ain't wanted and all that—but not
me, honey! *(This is a lie.)* Wilhemenia Othella Johnson goes anywhere, any time
she feels like it! *(With head movement for emphasis.)* Yes I do! Why if we left it up
to these here crackers, the poor niggers wouldn't have nothing—*(She clasps her
hand over her mouth.)* Oh, I always forgets you don't 'low that word in your house.

Mama (quietly, looking at her): No—I don't 'low it.

Johnson (*vigorously again*): Me neither! I was just telling Isaiah yesterday when he come using it in front of me—I said, "Isaiah, it's just like Mis' Younger says all the time—"

Mama: Don't you want some more pie?

Johnson: No—no thank you; this was lovely. I got to get on over home and have my midnight coffee. I hear some people say it don't let them sleep but I finds I can't close my eyes right lessen I done had that laaaast cup of coffee . . . (*She waits. A beat. Undaunted.*) My Goodnight coffee, I calls it!

Mama (*with much eye-rolling and communication between herself and Ruth*): Ruth, why don't you give Mis' Johnson some coffee.

(*Ruth gives Mama an unpleasant look for her kindness.*)

Johnson (*accepting the coffee*): Where's Brother tonight?

Mama: He's lying down.

Johnson: Mmmmmm, he sure gets his beauty rest, don't he? Good-looking man. Sure is a good-looking man! (*Reaching out to pat Ruth's stomach again.*) I guess that's how come we keep on having babies around here. (*She winks at Mama.*) One thing 'bout Brother, he always know how to have a *good* time. And sooooo ambitious! I bet it was his idea y'all moving out to Clybourne Park. Lord—I bet this time next month y'all's names will have been in the papers plenty— (*Holding up her hands to mark off each word of the headline she can see in front of her.*) "NEGROES INVADE CLYBOURNE PARK—BOMBED!"

Mama (*she and Ruth look at the woman in amazement*): We ain't exactly moving out there to get bombed.

Johnson: Oh, honey—you know I'm praying to God every day that don't nothing like that happen! But you have to think of life like it is—and these here Chicago peckerwoods is some baaaad peckerwoods.

Mama (*wearily*): We done thought about all that, Mis' Johnson.

(*Beneatha comes out of the bedroom in her robe and passes through to the bathroom. Mrs. Johnson turns.*)

Johnson: Hello there, Bennie!

Beneatha (*crisply*): Hello, Mrs. Johnson.

Johnson: How is school?

Beneatha (*crisply*): Fine, thank you. (*She goes out.*)

Johnson (*insulted*): Getting so she don't have much to say to nobody.

Mama: The child was on her way to the bathroom.

Johnson: I know—but sometimes she act like ain't got time to pass the time of day with nobody ain't been to college. Oh—I ain't criticizing her none. It's just— you know how some of our young people gets when they get a little education. (*Mama and Ruth say nothing, just look at her.*) Yes—well. Well, I guess I better get on home. (*Unmoving.*) 'Course I can understand how she must be proud and everything—being the only one in the family to make something of herself. I know just being a chauffeur ain't never satisfied Brother none. He shouldn't feel like that, though. Ain't nothing wrong with being a chauffeur.

Mama: There's plenty wrong with it.

Johnson: What?

Mama: Plenty. My husband always said being any kind of a servant wasn't a fit thing for a man to have to be. He always said a man's hands was made to make things, or to turn the earth with—not to drive nobody's car for 'em—or—(*She looks at her own hands.*) carry they slop jars. And my boy is just like him—he wasn't meant to wait on nobody.

Johnson (*rising, somewhat offended*): Mmmmmmmmmm. The Youngers is too much for me! (*She looks around.*) You sure one proud-acting bunch of colored folks. Well—I always thinks like Booker T. Washington° said that time—"Education has spoiled many a good plow hand"—

Mama: Is that what old Booker T. said?

Johnson: He sure did.

Mama: Well, it sounds just like him. The fool.

Johnson (*indignantly*): Well—he was one of our great men.

Mama: Who said so?

Johnson (*nonplussed*): You know, me and you ain't never agreed about some things, Lena Younger. I guess I better be going—

Ruth (*quickly*): Good night.

Johnson: Good night. Oh—(*Thrusting it at her.*) You can keep the paper! (*With a trill.*) 'Night.

Mama: Good night, Mis' Johnson. (*Mrs. Johnson exits.*)

Ruth: If ignorance was gold . . .

Mama: Shush. Don't talk about folks behind their backs.

Ruth: You do.

Mama: I'm old and corrupted. (*Beneatha enters.*) You was rude to Mis' Johnson, Beneatha, and I don't like it at all.

Beneatha (*at her door*): Mama, if there are two things we, as a people, have got to overcome, one is the Ku Klux Klan—and the other is Mrs. Johnson. (*She exits.*)

Mama: Smart aleck.

(*The phone rings.*)

Ruth: I'll get it.

Mama: Lord, ain't this a popular place tonight.

Ruth (*at the phone*): Hello—Just a minute. (*Goes to door.*) Walter, it's Mrs. Arnold. (*Waits. Goes back to the phone. Tense.*) Hello. Yes, this is his wife speaking . . . He's lying down now. Yes . . . well, he'll be in tomorrow. He's been very sick. Yes—I know we should have called, but we were so sure he'd be able to come in today. Yes—yes, I'm very sorry. Yes . . . Thank you very much. (*She hangs up. Walter is standing in the doorway of the bedroom behind her.*) That was Mrs. Arnold.

Walter (*indifferently*): Was it?

Ruth: She said if you don't come in tomorrow that they are getting a new man . . .

Walter: Ain't that sad—ain't that crying sad.

Ruth: She said Mr. Arnold has had to take a cab for three days . . . Walter, you ain't been to work for three days! (*This is a revelation to her.*) Where you been, Walter Lee Younger? (*Walter looks at her and starts to laugh.*) You're going to lose your job.

Walter: That's right . . . (*He turns on the radio.*)

Booker T. Washington: the most influential black educator and leader of his time, Washington (1858–1915) was criticized by W. E. B. Du Bois and others for being too accepting of inequality and injustice.

Ruth: Oh, Walter, and with your mother working like a dog every day—

(A steamy, deep blues pours into the room.)

Walter: That's sad too—Everything is sad.

Mama: What you been doing for these three days, son?

Walter: Mama—you don't know all the things a man what got leisure can find to do in this city . . . What's this—Friday night? Well—Wednesday I borrowed Willy Harris' car and I went for a drive . . . just me and myself and I drove and drove . . . Way out . . . way past South Chicago, and I parked the car and I sat and looked at the steel mills all day long. I just sat in the car and looked at them big black chimneys for hours. Then I drove back and I went to the Green Hat. *(Pause.)* And Thursday—Thursday I borrowed the car again and I got in it and I pointed it the other way and I drove the other way—for hours—way, way up to Wisconsin, and I looked at the farms. I just drove and looked at the farms. Then I drove back and I went to the Green Hat. *(Pause.)* And today—today I didn't get the car. Today I just walked. All over the Southside. And I looked at the Negroes and they looked at me and finally I just sat down on the curb at Thirty-ninth and South Parkway and I just sat there and watched the Negroes go by. And then I went to the Green Hat. You all sad? You all depressed? And you know where I am going right now—

(Ruth goes out quietly.)

Mama: Oh, Big Walter, is this the harvest of our days?

Walter: You know what I like about the Green Hat? I like this little cat they got there who blows a sax . . . He blows. He talks to me. He ain't but 'bout five feet tall and he's got a conked head and his eyes is always closed and he's all music—

Mama (rising and getting some papers out of her handbag): Walter—

Walter: And there's this other guy who plays the piano . . . and they got a sound. I mean they can work on some music . . . They got the best little combo in the world in the Green Hat . . . You can just sit there and drink and listen to them three men play and you realize that don't nothing matter worth a damn, but just being there—

Mama: I've helped do it to you, haven't I, son? Walter, I been wrong.

Walter: Naw—you ain't never been wrong about nothing, Mama.

Mama: Listen to me, now. I say I been wrong, son. That I been doing to you what the rest of the world been doing to you. *(She turns off the radio.)* Walter—*(She stops and he looks up slowly at her and she meets his eyes pleadingly.)* What you ain't never understood is that I ain't got nothing, don't own nothing, ain't never really wanted nothing that wasn't for you. There ain't nothing as precious to me . . . There ain't nothing worth holding on to, money, dreams, nothing else— if it means—if it means it's going to destroy my boy. *(She takes an envelope out of her handbag and puts it in front of him and he watches her without speaking or moving.)* I paid the man thirty-five hundred dollars down on the house. That leaves sixty-five hundred dollars. Monday morning I want you to take this money and take three thousand dollars and put it in a savings account for Beneatha's medical schooling. The rest you put in a checking account—with your name on it. And from now on any penny that come out of it or that go in it is for you to look after. For you to decide. *(She drops her hands a little helplessly.)* It ain't much, but it's all I got in the world and I'm putting it in your hands. I'm telling you to be the head of this family from now on like you supposed to be.

Walter (stares at the money): You trust me like that, Mama?

Mama: I ain't never stop trusting you. Like I ain't never stop loving you.

(She goes out, and Walter sits looking at the money on the table. Finally, in a decisive gesture, he gets up, and, in mingled joy and desperation, picks up the money. At the same moment, Travis enters for bed.)

Travis: What's the matter, Daddy? You drunk?

Walter (sweetly, more sweetly than we have ever known him): No, Daddy ain't drunk. Daddy ain't going to never be drunk again . . .

Travis: Well, good night, Daddy.

(The Father has come from behind the couch and leans over, embracing his son.)

Walter: Son, I feel like talking to you tonight.

Travis: About what?

Walter: Oh, about a lot of things. About you and what kind of man you going to be when you grow up . . . Son—son, what do you want to be when you grow up?

Travis: A bus driver.

Walter (laughing a little): A what? Man, that ain't nothing to want to be!

Travis: Why not?

Walter: 'Cause, man—it ain't big enough—you know what I mean.

Travis: I don't know then. I can't make up my mind. Sometimes Mama asks me that too. And sometimes when I tell her I just want to be like you—she says she don't want me to be like that and sometimes she says she does . . .

Walter (gathering him up in his arms): You know what, Travis? In seven years you going to be seventeen years old. And things is going to be very different with us in seven years, Travis . . . One day when you are seventeen I'll come home—home from my office downtown somewhere—

Travis: You don't work in no office, Daddy.

Walter: No—but after tonight. After what your daddy gonna do tonight, there's going to be offices—a whole lot of offices . . .

Travis: What you gonna do tonight, Daddy?

Walter: You wouldn't understand yet, son, but your daddy's gonna make a transaction . . . a business transaction that's going to change our lives . . . That's how come one day when you 'bout seventeen years old I'll come home and I'll be pretty tired, you know what I mean, after a day of conferences and secretaries getting things wrong the way they do . . . 'cause an executive's life is hell, man— *(The more he talks the farther away he gets.)* And I'll pull the car up on the driveway . . . just a plain black Chrysler, I think, with white walls—no—black tires. More elegant. Rich people don't have to be flashy . . . though I'll have to get something a little sportier for Ruth—maybe a Cadillac convertible to do her shopping in . . . And I'll come up the steps to the house and the gardener will be clipping away at the hedges and he'll say, "Good evening, Mr. Younger." And I'll say, "Hello, Jefferson, how are you this evening?" And I'll go inside and Ruth will come downstairs and meet me at the door and we'll kiss each other and she'll take my arm and we'll go up to your room to see you sitting on the floor with the catalogues of all the great schools in America around you . . . All the great schools in the world! And—and I'll say, all right son—it's your seventeenth birthday, what is it you've decided? . . . Just tell me where you want to go to school and you'll go. Just tell me, what it is you want to be—and you'll be it . . . Whatever you want to be—Yessir! (*He holds his arms open for Travis.*) You just name it, son . . . (*Travis leaps into them.*) and I hand you the world!

(*Walter's voice has risen in pitch and hysterical promise and on the last line he lifts Travis high.*)

ACT II

SCENE III

TIME. *Saturday, moving day, one week later.*

Before the curtain rises, Ruth's voice, a strident, dramatic church alto, cuts through the silence.

It is, in the darkness, a triumphant surge, a penetrating statement of expectation: "Oh, Lord, I don't feel no ways tired! Children, oh, glory hallelujah!"

As the curtain rises we see that Ruth is alone in the living room, finishing up the family's packing. It is moving day. She is nailing crates and tying cartons. Beneatha enters, carrying a guitar case, and watches her exuberant sister-in-law.

Ruth: Hey!
Beneatha (putting away the case): Hi.
Ruth (pointing at a package): Honey—look in that package there and see what I found on sale this morning at the South Center. (*Ruth gets up and moves to the package and draws out some curtains.*) Lookahere—hand-turned hems!
Beneatha: How do you know the window size out there?
Ruth (who hadn't thought of that): Oh—Well, they bound to fit something in the whole house. Anyhow, they was too good a bargain to pass up. (*Ruth slaps her head, suddenly remembering something.*) Oh, Bennie—I meant to put a special note on that carton over there. That's your mama's good china and she wants 'em to be very careful with it.
Beneatha: I'll do it.

(*Beneatha finds a piece of paper and starts to draw large letters on it.*)

Ruth: You know what I'm going to do soon as I get in that new house?
Beneatha: What?
Ruth: Honey—I'm going to run me a tub of water up to here . . . (*With her fingers practically up to her nostrils.*) And I'm going to get in it—and I am going to sit . . . and sit . . . and sit in that hot water and the first person who knocks to tell me to hurry up and come out—
Beneatha: Gets shot at sunrise.
Ruth (laughing happily): You said it, sister! (*Noticing how large Beneatha is absent--mindedly making the note.*) Honey, they ain't going to read that from no airplane.
Beneatha (laughing herself): I guess I always think things have more emphasis if they are big, somehow.
Ruth (looking up at her and smiling): You and your brother seem to have that as a philosophy of life. Lord, that man—done changed so 'round here. You know—you know what we did last night? Me and Walter Lee?
Beneatha: What?

Ruth (smiling to herself): We went to the movies. (*Looking at Beneatha to see if she understands.*) We went to the movies. You know the last time me and Walter went to the movies together?

Beneatha: No.

Ruth: Me neither. That's how long it been. (*Smiling again.*) But we went last night. The picture wasn't much good, but that didn't seem to matter. We went—and we held hands.

Beneatha: Oh, Lord!

Ruth: We held hands—and you know what?

Beneatha: What?

Ruth: When we come out of the show it was late and dark and all the stores and things was closed up . . . and it was kind of chilly and there wasn't many people on the streets . . . and we was still holding hands, me and Walter.

Beneatha: You're killing me.

(*Walter enters with a large package. His happiness is deep in him; he cannot keep still with his new-found exuberance. He is singing and wiggling and snapping his fingers. He puts his package in a corner and puts a phonograph record, which he has brought in with him, on the record player. As the music, soulful and sensuous, comes up he dances over to Ruth and tries to get her to dance with him. She gives in at last to his raunchiness and in a fit of giggling allows herself to be drawn into his mood. They dip and she melts into his arms in a classic, body-melding "slow drag."*)

Beneatha (regarding them a long time as they dance, then drawing in her breath for a deeply exaggerated comment which she does not particularly mean): Talk about—olddddddddddd-fashioneddddddddd—Negroes!

Walter (stopping momentarily): What kind of Negroes? (*He says this in fun. He is not angry with her today, nor with anyone. He starts to dance with his wife again.*)

Beneatha: Old-fashioned.

Walter (as he dances with Ruth): You know, when these New Negroes have their convention—(*Pointing at his sister.*)—that is going to be the chairman of the Committee on Unending Agitation. (*He goes on dancing, then stops.*) Race, race, race! . . . Girl, I do believe you are the first person in the history of the entire human race to successfully brainwash yourself. (*Beneatha breaks up and he goes on dancing. He stops again, enjoying his tease.*) Damn, even the N double A C P takes a holiday sometimes! (*Beneatha and Ruth laugh. He dances with Ruth some more and starts to laugh and stops and pantomimes someone over an operating table.*) I can just see that chick someday looking down at some poor cat on an operating table and before she starts to slice him, she says . . . (*Pulling his sleeves back maliciously.*) "By the way, what are your views on civil rights down there? . . ."

(*He laughs at her again and starts to dance happily. The bell sounds.*)

Beneatha: Sticks and stones may break my bones but . . . words will never hurt me!

(*Beneatha goes to the door and opens it as Walter and Ruth go on with the clowning. Beneatha is somewhat surprised to see a quiet-looking middle-aged white man in a business suit holding his hat and a briefcase in his hand and consulting a small piece of paper.*)

Man: Uh—how do you do, miss. I am looking for a Mrs.—(*He looks at the slip of paper.*) Mrs. Lena Younger? (*He stops short, struck dumb at the sight of the oblivious Walter and Ruth.*)

Beneatha (smoothing her hair with slight embarrassment): Oh—yes, that's my mother. Excuse me. *(She closes the door and turns to quiet the other two.)* Ruth! Brother! *(Enunciating precisely but soundlessly:* "There's a white man at the door!" *They stop dancing, Ruth cuts off the phonograph, Beneatha opens the door. The man casts a curious quick glance at all of them.)* Uh—come in please.

Man (coming in): Thank you.

Beneatha: My mother isn't here just now. Is it business?

Man: Yes . . . well, of a sort.

Walter (freely, the Man of the House): Have a seat. I'm Mrs. Younger's son. I look after most of her business matters.

(Ruth and Beneatha exchange amused glances.)

Man (regarding Walter, and sitting): Well—My name is Karl Lindner . . .

Walter (stretching out his hand): Walter Younger. This is my wife—*(Ruth nods politely.)*—and my sister.

Lindner: How do you do.

Walter (amiably, as he sits himself easily on a chair, leaning forward on his knees with interest and looking expectantly into the newcomer's face): What can we do for you, Mr. Lindner!

Lindner (some minor shuffling of the hat and briefcase on his knees): Well—I am a representative of the Clybourne Park Improvement Association—

Walter (pointing): Why don't you sit your things on the floor?

Lindner: Oh—yes. Thank you. *(He slides the briefcase and hat under the chair.)* And as I was saying—I am from the Clybourne Park Improvement Association and we have had it brought to our attention at the last meeting that you people—or at least your mother—has bought a piece of residential property at—*(He digs for the slip of paper again.)*—four o six Clybourne Street . . .

Walter: That's right. Care for something to drink? Ruth, get Mr. Lindner a beer.

Lindner (upset for some reason): Oh—no, really. I mean thank you very much, but no thank you.

Ruth (innocently): Some coffee?

Lindner: Thank you, nothing at all. *(Beneatha is watching the man carefully.)* Well, I don't know how much you folks know about our organization. *(He is a gentle man; thoughtful and somewhat labored in his manner.)* It is one of these community organizations set up to look after—oh, you know, things like block upkeep and special projects and we also have what we call our New Neighbors Orientation Committee . . .

Beneatha (drily): Yes—and what do they do?

Lindner (turning a little to her and then returning the main force to Walter): Well—it's what you might call a sort of welcoming committee, I guess. I mean they, we— I'm the chairman of the committee—go around and see the new people who move into the neighborhood and sort of give them the lowdown on the way we do things out in Clybourne Park.

Beneatha (with appreciation of the two meanings, which escape Ruth and Walter.) Un-huh.

Lindner: And we also have the category of what the association calls—*(He looks elsewhere.)*—uh—special community problems . . .

Beneatha: Yes—and what are some of those?

Walter: Girl, let the man talk.

Lindner (with understated relief): Thank you. I would sort of like to explain this thing in my own way. I mean I want to explain to you in a certain way.

Walter: Go ahead.

Lindner: Yes. Well. I'm going to try to get right to the point. I'm sure we'll all appreciate that in the long run.

Beneatha: Yes.

Walter: Be still now!

Lindner: Well—

Ruth (still innocently): Would you like another chair—you don't look comfortable.

Lindner (more frustrated than annoyed): No, thank you very much. Please. Well—to get right to the point I—(*A great breath, and he is off at last.*) I am sure you people must be aware of some of the incidents which have happened in various parts of the city when colored people have moved into certain areas—

(*Beneatha exhales heavily and starts tossing a piece of fruit up and down in the air.*)

Well—because we have what I think is going to be a unique type of organization in American community life—not only do we deplore that kind of thing—but we are trying to do something about it.

(*Beneatha stops tossing and turns with a new and quizzical interest to the man.*)

We feel—(*Gaining confidence in his mission because of the interest in the faces of the people he is talking to.*)—we feel that most of the trouble in this world, when you come right down to it—(*He hits his knee for emphasis.*)—most of the trouble exists because people just don't sit down and talk to each other.

Ruth (nodding as she might in church, pleased with the remark): You can say that again, mister.

Lindner (more encouraged by such affirmation): That we don't try hard enough in this world to understand the other fellow's problem. The other guy's point of view.

Ruth: Now that's right.

(*Beneatha and Walter merely watch and listen with genuine interest.*)

Lindner: Yes—that's the way we feel out in Clybourne Park. And that's why I was elected to come here this afternoon and talk to you people. Friendly like, you know, the way people should talk to each other and see if we couldn't find some way to work this thing out. As I say, the whole business is a matter of *caring* about the other fellow. Anybody can see that you are a nice family of folks, hard-working and honest I'm sure.

(*Beneatha frowns slightly, quizzically, her head tilted regarding him.*)

Today everybody knows what it means to be on the outside of *something*. And of course, there is always somebody who is out to take advantage of people who don't always understand.

Walter: What do you mean?

Lindner: Well—you see our community is made up of people who've worked hard as the dickens for years to build up that little community. They're not rich and fancy people; just hard-working, honest people who don't really have much but those little homes and a dream of the kind of community they want to raise their children in. Now, I don't say we are perfect and there is a lot wrong in some of the things they want. But you've got to admit that a man, right or wrong, has the right to want to have the neighborhood he lives in a certain kind of way. And at the moment the overwhelming majority of our people out there feel that people get along better, take more of a common interest in the life of the community, when they share a common background. I want you to believe me when I tell you that race prejudice simply doesn't enter into it. It is a matter of the people of Clybourne Park believing, rightly or wrongly, as I say, that for the happiness of all concerned that our Negro families are happier when they live in their *own* communities.

Beneatha (with a grand and bitter gesture): This, friends, is the Welcoming Committee!

Walter (dumfounded, looking at Lindner): Is this what you came marching all the way over here to tell us?

Lindner: Well, now we've been having a fine conversation. I hope you'll hear me all the way through.

Walter (tightly): Go ahead, man.

Lindner: You see—in the face of all the things I have said, we are prepared to make your family a very generous offer. . . .

Beneatha: Thirty pieces and not a coin less!°

Walter: Yeah?

Lindner (putting on his glasses and drawing a form out of the briefcase): Our association is prepared, through the collective effort of our people, to buy the house from you at a financial gain to your family.

Ruth: Lord have mercy, ain't this the living gall!

Walter: All right, you through?

Lindner: Well, I want to give you the exact terms of the financial arrangement—

Walter: We don't want to hear no exact terms of no arrangements. I want to know if you got any more to tell us 'bout getting together?

Linder (taking off his glasses): Well—I don't suppose that you feel . . .

Walter: Never mind how I feel—you got any more to say 'bout how people ought to sit down and talk to each other? . . . Get out of my house, man. (*He turns his back and walks to the door.*)

Lindner (looking around at the hostile faces and reaching and assembling his hat and briefcase): Well—I don't understand why you people are reacting this way. What do you think you are going to gain by moving into a neighborhood where you just aren't wanted and where some elements—well—people can get awful worked up when they feel that their whole way of life and everything they've ever worked for is threatened.

Walter: Get out.

Lindner (at the door, holding a small card): Well—I'm sorry it went like this.

Walter: Get out.

Lindner (almost sadly regarding Walter): You just can't force people to change their hearts, son.

(*He turns and put his card on a table and exits. Walter pushes the door to with stinging hatred, and stands looking at it. Ruth just sits and Beneatha just stands. They say nothing. Mama and Travis enter.*)

Thirty pieces and not a coin less: reference to Judas's betrayal of Jesus for thirty pieces of silver (Matthew 26: 14–16).

Mama: Well—this all the packing got done since I left out of here this morning? I testify before God that my children got all the energy of the *dead!* What time the moving men due?

Beneatha: Four o'clock. You had a caller, Mama. *(She is smiling, teasingly.)*

Mama: Sure enough—who?

Beneatha (her arms folded saucily): The Welcoming Committee.

> *(Walter and Ruth giggle.)*

Mama (innocently): Who?

Beneatha: The Welcoming Committee. They said they're sure going to be glad to see you when you get there.

Walter (devilishly): Yeah, they said they can't hardly wait to see your face. *(Laughter.)*

Mama (sensing their facetiousness): What's the matter with you all?

Walter: Ain't nothing the matter with us. We just telling you 'bout the gentleman who came to see you this afternoon. From the Clybourne Park Improvement Association.

Mama: What he want?

Ruth (in the same mood as Beneatha and Walter): To welcome you, honey.

Walter: He said they can't hardly wait. He said the one thing they don't have, that they just *dying* to have out there, is a fine family of fine colored people! *(To Ruth and Beneatha.)* Ain't that right!

Ruth (mockingly): Yeah! He left his card—

Beneatha (handing card to Mama): In case—

> *(Mama reads and throws it on the floor—understanding and looking off as she draws her chair up to the table on which she has put her plant and some sticks and some cord.)*

Mama: Father, give us strength. *(Knowingly—and without fun.)* Did he threaten us?

Beneatha: Oh—Mama—they don't do it like that any more. He talked Brotherhood. He said everybody ought to learn how to sit down and hate each other with good Christian fellowship.

> *(She and Walter shake hands to ridicule the remark.)*

Mama (sadly): Lord, protect us . . .

Ruth: You should hear the money those folks raised to buy the house from us. All we paid and then some.

Beneatha: What they think we going to do—eat 'em?

Ruth: No, honey, marry 'em.

Mama (shaking her head): Lord, Lord, Lord . . .

Ruth: Well—that's the way the crackers crumble. *(A beat.)* Joke.

Beneatha (laughingly noticing what her mother is doing): Mama, what are you doing?

Mama: Fixing my plant so it won't get hurt none on the way . . .

Beneatha: Mama, you going to take *that* to the new house?

Mama: Un-huh—

Beneatha: That raggedy-looking old thing?

Mama (stopping and looking at her): It expresses ME!

Ruth (with delight, to Beneatha): So there, Miss Thing!

> *(Walter comes to Mama suddenly and bends down behind her and squeezes her in his arms with all his strength. She is overwhelmed by the suddenness of it and, though delighted, her manner is like that of Ruth and Travis.)*

Mama: Look out now, boy! You make me mess up my thing here!

Walter (his face lit, he slips down on his knees beside her, his arms still about her): Mama . . . you know what it means to climb up in the chariot?

Mama (gruffly, very happy): Get on away from me now . . .

Ruth (near the gift-wrapped package, trying to catch Walter's eye): Psst—

Walter: What the old song say, Mama . . .

Ruth: Walter—Now? *(She is pointing at the package.)*

Walter (speaking the lines, sweetly, playfully, in his mother's face):

> I got wings! . . . you got wings! . . .
> All God's Children got wings . . .

Mama: Boy—get out of my face and do some work . . .

Walter:

> When I get to heaven gonna put on my wings,
> Gonna fly all over God's heaven . . .

Beneatha (teasingly, from across the room): Everybody talking 'bout heaven ain't going there!

Walter (to Ruth, who is carrying the box across to them): I don't know, you think we ought to give her that . . . Seems to me she ain't been very appreciative around here.

Mama (eying the box, which is obviously a gift): What is that?

Walter (taking it from Ruth and putting it on the table in front of Mama): Well—what you all think? Should we give it to her?

Ruth: Oh—she was pretty good today.

Mama: I'll good you—*(She turns her eyes to the box again.)*

Beneatha: Open it, Mama.

(She stands up, looks at it, turns and looks at all of them, and then presses her hands together and does not open the package.)

Walter (sweetly): Open it, Mama. It's for you. *(Mama looks in his eyes. It is the first present in her life without its being Christmas. Slowly she opens her package and lifts out, one by one, a brand-new sparkling set of gardening tools. Walter continues, prodding.)* Ruth made up the note—read it . . .

Mama (picking up the card and adjusting her glasses): "To our own Mrs. Miniver°—Love from Brother, Ruth and Beneatha." Ain't that lovely . . .

Travis (tugging at his father's sleeve): Daddy, can I give her mine now?

Walter: All right, son. *(Travis flies to get his gift.)*

Mama: Now I don't have to use my knives and forks no more . . .

Walter: Travis didn't want to go in with the rest of us, Mama. He got his own. *(Somewhat amused.)* We don't know what it is . . .

Travis (racing back in the room with a large hatbox and putting it in front of his grandmother): Here!

Mama: Lord have mercy, baby. You done gone and bought your grandmother a hat?

Travis (very proud): Open it!

(She does and lifts out an elaborate, but very elaborate, wide gardening hat, and all the adults break up at the sight of it.)

Mrs. Miniver: As portrayed by Greer Garson in the Academy Award-winning World War II film, Mrs. Miniver is a British housewife who loves her family and gardening, and is called to show great courage, strength, and perseverance in the face of German bombardments.

Ruth: Travis, honey, what is that?

Travis (who thinks it is beautiful and appropriate): It's a gardening hat! Like the ladies always have on in the magazines when they work in their gardens.

Beneatha (giggling fiercely): Travis—we were trying to make Mama Mrs. Miniver—not Scarlett O'Hara!°

Mama (indignantly): What's the matter with you all! This here is a beautiful hat! *(Absurdly.)* I always wanted me one just like it!

(She pops it on her head to prove it to her grandson, and the hat is ludicrous and considerably oversized.)

Ruth: Hot dog! Go, Mama!

Walter (doubled over with laughter): I'm sorry, Mama—but you look like you ready to go out and chop you some cotton sure enough!

(They all laugh except Mama, out of deference to Travis' feelings.)

Mama (gathering the boy up to her): Bless your heart—this is the prettiest hat I ever owned—(Walter, Ruth, and Beneatha chime in—noisily, festively and insincerely congratulating Travis on his gift.) What are we all standing around here for? We ain't finished packin' yet. Bennie, you ain't packed one book.

(The bell rings.)

Beneatha: That couldn't be the movers . . . it's not hardly two o'clock yet—

(Beneatha goes into her room. Mama starts for door.)

Walter (turning, stiffening): Wait—wait—I'll get it. *(He stands and looks at the door.)*

Mama: You expecting company, son?

Walter (just looking at the door): Yeah—yeah . . .

(Mama looks at Ruth, and they exchange innocent and unfrightened glances.)

Mama (not understanding): Well, let them in, son.

Beneatha (from her room): We need some more string.

Mama: Travis—you run to the hardware and get me some string cord.

(Mama goes out and Walter turns and looks at Ruth. Travis goes to a dish for money.)

Ruth: Why don't you answer the door, man?

Walter (suddenly bounding across the floor to embrace her): 'Cause sometimes it hard to let the future begin! *(Stooping down in her face.)*

I got wings! You got wings!
All God's children got wings!

(He crosses to the door and throws it open. Standing there is a very slight little man in a not too prosperous business suit and with haunted frightened eyes and a hat pulled down tightly, brim up, around his forehead. Travis passes between the men and exits. Walter leans deep in the man's face, still in his jubilance.)

When I get to heaven gonna put on my wings,
Gonna fly all over God's heaven . . .

Scarlett O'Hara: the young, flamboyant, and histrionic heroine of *Gone with the Wind* (1936) by Margaret Mitchell—made into a blockbuster movie in 1939 by David O. Selznick. The Southern belle Scarlett O'Hara is a sharp contrast to the down-to-earth, sensible Mrs. Miniver.

(The little man just stares at him.)

Heaven—

(Suddenly he stops and looks past the little man into the empty hallway.)

Where's Willy, man?

Bobo: He ain't with me.

Walter (not disturbed): Oh—come on in. You know my wife.

Bobo (dumbly, taking off his hat): Yes—h'you, Miss Ruth.

Ruth (quietly, a mood apart from her husband already, seeing Bobo): Hello, Bobo.

Walter: You right on time today . . . Right on time. That's the way! *(He slaps Bobo on his back.)* Sit down . . . lemme hear.

(Ruth stands stiffly and quietly in back of them, as though somehow she senses death, her eyes fixed on her husband.)

Bobo (his frightened eyes on the floor, his hat in his hands): Could I please get a drink of water, before I tell you about it, Walter Lee?

(Walter does not take his eyes off the man. Ruth goes blindly to the tap and gets a glass of water and brings it to Bobo.)

Walter: There ain't nothing wrong, is there?

Bobo: Lemme tell you—

Walter: Man—didn't nothing go wrong?

Bobo: Lemme tell you—Walter Lee. *(Looking at Ruth and talking to her more than to Walter.)* You know how it was. I got to tell you how it was. I mean first I got to tell you how it was all the way . . . I mean about the money I put in, Walter Lee . . .

Walter (with taut agitation now): What about the money you put in?

Bobo: Well—it wasn't much as we told you—me and Willy—*(He stops.)* I'm sorry, Walter. I got a bad feeling about it. I got a real bad feeling about it . . .

Walter: Man, what you telling me about all this for? . . . Tell me what happened in Springfield . . .

Bobo: Springfield.

Ruth (like a dead woman): What was supposed to happen in Springfield?

Bobo (to her): This deal that me and Walter went into with Willy—Me and Willy was going to go down to Springfield and spread some money 'round so's we wouldn't have to wait so long for the liquor license . . . That's what we were going to do. Everybody said that was the way you had to do, you understand, Miss Ruth?

Walter: Man—what happened down there?

Bobo (a pitiful man, near tears): I'm trying to tell you, Walter.

Walter (screaming at him suddenly): THEN TELL ME, GODDAMMIT . . . WHAT'S THE MATTER WITH YOU?

Bobo: Man . . . I didn't go to no Springfield, yesterday.

Walter (halted, life hanging in the moment): Why not?

Bobo (the long way, the hard way to tell): 'Cause I didn't have no reasons to . . .

Walter: Man, what are you talking about!

Bobo: I'm talking about the fact that when I got to the train station yesterday morning—eight o'clock like we planned . . . Man—*Willy didn't never show up.*

Walter: Why . . . where was he . . . where is he?

Bobo: That's what I'm trying to tell you . . . I don't know . . . I waited six hours . . . I called his house . . . and I waited . . . six hours . . . I waited in that train station six hours . . . (*Breaking into tears.*) That was all the extra money I had in the world . . . (*Looking up at Walter with tears running down his face.*) Man, *Willy is gone.*

Walter: Gone, what you mean Willy is gone? Gone where? You mean he went by himself. You mean he went off to Springfield by himself—to take care of getting the license—(*Turns and looks anxiously at Ruth.*) You mean maybe he didn't want too many people in on the business down there? (*Looks to Ruth again, as before.*) You know Willy got his own ways. (*Looks back to Bobo.*) Maybe you was late yesterday and he just went on down there without you. Maybe—maybe—he's been callin' you at home tryin' to tell you what happened or something. Maybe— maybe—he just got sick. He's somewhere—he's got to be somewhere. We just got to find him—me and you got to find him. (*Grabs Bobo senselessly by the collar and starts to shake him.*) We got to!

Bobo (*in sudden angry, frightened agony*): What's the matter with you, Walter! *When a cat take off with your money he don't leave you no road maps!*

Walter (*turning madly, as though he is looking for Willy in every room*): Willy! . . . Willy . . . don't do it . . . Please don't do it . . . Man, not with that money . . . Man, please, not with that money . . . Oh, God . . . Don't let it be true . . . (*He is wandering around, crying out for Willy and looking for him or perhaps for help from God.*) Man . . . I trusted you . . . Man, I put my life in your hands . . .

(*He starts to crumple down on the floor as Ruth just covers her face in horror. Mama opens the door and comes into the room, with Beneatha behind her.*)

Man . . . (*He starts to pound the floor with his fists, sobbing wildly.*) THAT MONEY IS MADE OUT OF MY FATHER'S FLESH—

Bobo (*standing over him helplessly*): I'm sorry, Walter . . . (*Only Walter's sobs reply. Bobo puts on his hat.*) I had my life staked on this deal, too . . . (*He exits.*)

Mama (*to Walter*): Son—(*She goes to him, bends down to him, talks to his bent head.*) Son . . . Is it gone? Son, I gave you sixty-five hundred dollars. Is it gone? All of it? Beneatha's money too?

Walter (*lifting his head slowly*): Mama . . . I never . . . went to the bank at all . . .

Mama (*not wanting to believe him*): You mean . . . Your sister's school money . . . you used that too . . . Walter? . . .

Walter: Yessss! All of it . . . It's all gone. . . .

(*There is total silence. Ruth stands with her face covered with her hands; Beneatha leans forlornly against a wall, fingering a piece of red ribbon from the mother's gift. Mama stops and looks at her son without recognition and then, quite without thinking about it, starts to beat him senselessly in the face. Beneatha goes to them and stops it.*)

Beneatha: Mama!

(*Mama stops and looks at both of her children and rises slowly and wanders vaguely, aimlessly away from them.*)

Mama: I seen . . . him . . . night after night . . . come in . . . and look at that rug . . . and then look at me . . . the red showing in his eyes . . . the veins moving in his head . . . I seen him grow thin and old before he was forty . . . working and working and working like somebody's old horse . . . killing himself . . . and you—you give it all away in a day—(*She raises her arms to strike him again.*)

Beneatha: Mama—

Mama: Oh, God . . . (*She looks up to Him.*) Look down here—and show me the strength.

Beneatha: Mama—

Mama (folding over): Strength . . .

Beneatha (plaintively): Mama . . .

Mama: Strength!

ACT III

TIME. *An hour later*

At curtain, there is a sullen light of gloom in the living room, gray light not unlike that which began the first scene of Act One. At left we can see Walter within his room, alone with himself. He is stretched out on the bed, his shirt out and open, his arms under his head. He does not smoke, he does not cry out, he merely lies there, looking up at the ceiling, much as if he were alone in the world.

In the living room Beneatha sits at the table, still surrounded by the now almost ominous packing crates. She sits looking off. We feel that this is a mood struck perhaps an hour before, and it lingers now, full of the empty sound of profound disappointment. We see on a line from her brother's bedroom the sameness of their attitudes. Presently the bell rings and Beneatha rises without ambition or interest in answering. It is Asagai, smiling broadly, striding into the room with energy and happy expectation and conversation.

Asagai: I came over . . . I had some free time. I thought I might help with the packing. Ah, I like the look of packing crates! A household in preparation for a journey! It depresses some people . . . but for me . . . it is another feeling. Something full of the flow of life, do you understand? Movement, progress . . . It makes me think of Africa.

Beneatha: Africa!

Asagai: What kind of a mood is this? Have I told you how deeply you move me?

Beneatha: He gave away the money, Asagai . . .

Asagai: Who gave away what money?

Beneatha: The insurance money. My brother gave it away.

Asagai: Gave it away?

Beneatha: He made an investment! With a man even Travis wouldn't have trusted with his most worn-out marbles.

Asagai: And it's gone?

Beneatha: Gone!

Asagai: I'm very sorry . . . And you, now?

Beneatha: Me? . . . Me? . . . Me, I'm nothing . . . Me. When I was very small . . . we used to take our sleds out in the wintertime and the only hills we had were the ice-covered stone steps of some houses down the street. And we used to fill them in with snow and make them smooth and slide down them all day . . . and it was very dangerous, you know . . . far too steep . . . and sure enough one day a kid named Rufus came down too fast and hit the sidewalk and we saw his face just split open right there in front of us . . . And I remember standing there looking at his bloody open face thinking that was the end of Rufus. But the ambulance came and they took him to the hospital and they fixed the broken bones and they sewed it all up . . . and the next time I saw Rufus he just had a little line down the middle of his face . . . I never got over that . . .

Asagai: What?

Beneatha: That that was what one person could do for another, fix him up—sew up the problem, make him all right again. That was the most marvelous thing in the world . . . I wanted to do that. I always thought it was the one concrete thing in the world that a human being could do. Fix up the sick, you know—and make them whole again. This was truly being God . . .

Asagai: You wanted to be God?

Beneatha: No—I wanted to cure. It used to be so important to me. I wanted to cure. It used to matter. I used to care. I mean about people and how their bodies hurt . . .

Asagai: And you've stopped caring?

Beneatha: Yes—I think so.

Asagai: Why?

Beneatha (bitterly): Because it doesn't seem deep enough, close enough to what ails mankind! It was a child's way of seeing things—or an idealist's.

Asagai: Children see things very well sometimes—and idealists even better.

Beneatha: I know that's what you think. Because you are still where I left off. You with all your talk and dreams about Africa! You still think you can patch up the world. Cure the Great Sore of Colonialism—(*Loftily, mocking it.*) with the Penicillin of Independence—!

Asagai: Yes!

Beneatha: Independence *and then what?* What about all the crooks and thieves and just plain idiots who will come into power and steal and plunder the same as before—only now they will be black and do it in the name of the new Independence—WHAT ABOUT THEM?!

Asagai: That will be the problem for another time. First we must get there.

Beneatha: And where does it end?

Asagai: End? Who even spoke of an end? To life? To living?

Beneatha: An end to misery! To stupidity! Don't you see there isn't any real progress, Asagai, there is only one large circle that we march in, around and around, each of us with our own little picture in front of us—our own little mirage that we think is the future.

Asagai: That is the mistake.

Beneatha: What?

Asagai: What you just said about the circle. It isn't a circle—it is simply a long line—as in geometry, you know, one that reaches into infinity. And because we cannot see the end—we also cannot see how it changes. And it is very odd but those who see the changes—who dream, who will not give up—are called idealists . . . and those who see only the circle we call *them* the "realists"!

Beneatha: Asagai, while I was sleeping in that bed in there, people went out and took the future right out of my hands! And nobody asked me, nobody consulted me— they just went out and changed my life!

Asagai: Was it your money?

Beneatha: What?

Asagai: Was it your money he gave away?

Beneatha: It belonged to all of us.

Asagai: But did you earn it? Would you have had it at all if your father had not died?

Beneatha: No.

Asagai: Then isn't there something wrong in a house—in a world—where all dreams, good or bad, must depend on the death of a man? I never thought to see *you* like this, Alaiyo. You! Your brother made a mistake and you are grateful to him so that now you can give up the ailing human race on account of it! You talk about what good is struggle; what good is anything! Where are we all going and why are we bothering?

Beneatha: AND YOU CANNOT ANSWER IT!

Asagai (shouting over her): I LIVE THE ANSWER! *(Pause.)* In my village at home it is the exceptional man who can even read a newspaper . . . or who ever sees a book at all. I will go home and much of what I will have to say will seem strange to the people of my village. But I will teach and work and things will happen, slowly and swiftly. At times it will seem that nothing changes at all . . . and then again the sudden dramatic events which make history leap into the future. And then quiet again. Retrogression even. Guns, murder, revolution. And I even will have moments when I wonder if the quiet was not better than all that death and hatred. But I will look about my village at the illiteracy and disease and ignorance and I will not wonder long. And perhaps . . . perhaps I will be a great man . . . I mean perhaps I will hold on to the substance of truth and find my way always with the right course . . . and perhaps for it I will be butchered in my bed some night by the servants of empire . . .

Beneatha: The martyr!

Asagai (he smiles): . . . or perhaps I shall live to be a very old man, respected and esteemed in my new nation . . . And perhaps I shall hold office and this is what I'm trying to tell you, Alaiyo: Perhaps the things I believe now for my country will be wrong and outmoded, and I will not understand and do terrible things to have things my way or merely to keep my power. Don't you see that there will be young men and women—not British soldiers then, but my own black country-men—to step out of the shadows some evening and slit my then useless throat? Don't you see they have always been there . . . that they always will be. And that such a thing as my own death will be an advance? They who might kill me even . . . actually replenish all that I was.

Beneatha: Oh, Asagai, I know all that.

Asagai: Good! Then stop moaning and groaning and tell me what you plan to do.

Beneatha: Do?

Asagai: I have a bit of a suggestion.

Beneatha: What?

Asagai (rather quietly for him): That when it is all over—that you come home with me—

Beneatha (staring at him and crossing away with exasperation): Oh—Asagai—at this moment you decide to be romantic!

Asagai (quickly understanding the misunderstanding): My dear, young creature of the New World—I do not mean across the city—I mean across the ocean: home—to Africa.

Beneatha (slowly understanding and turning to him with murmured amazement): To Africa?

Asagai: Yes! . . . (*Smiling and lifting his arms playfully.*) Three hundred years later the African Prince rose up out of the seas and swept the maiden back across the middle passage over which her ancestors had come—

Beneatha (*unable to play*): To—to Nigeria?

Asagai: Nigeria. Home. (*Coming to her with genuine romantic flippancy.*) I will show you our mountains and our stars; and give you cool drinks from gourds and teach you the old songs and the ways of our people—and, in time, we will pretend that—(*Very softly.*)—you have only been away for a day. Say that you'll come—(*He swings her around and takes her full in his arms in a kiss which proceeds to passion.*)

Beneatha (*pulling away suddenly*): You're getting me all mixed up—

Asagai: Why?

Beneatha: Too many things—too many things have happened today. I must sit down and think. I don't know what I feel about anything right this minute. (*She promptly sits down and props her chin on her fist.*)

Asagai (*charmed*): All right, I shall leave you. No—don't get up. (*Touching her, gently, sweetly.*) Just sit awhile and think . . . Never be afraid to sit awhile and think. (*He goes to door and looks at her.*) How often I have looked at you and said, "Ah—so this is what the New World hath finally wrought . . ."

(*He exits. Beneatha sits on alone. Presently Walter enters from his room and starts to rummage through things, feverishly looking for something. She looks up and turns in her seat.*)

Beneatha (*hissingly*): Yes—just look at what the New World hath wrought! . . . Just look! (*She gestures with bitter disgust.*) There he is! *Monsieur le petit bourgeois noir*°—himself! There he is—Symbol of a Rising Class! Entrepreneur! Titan of the system!

(*Walter ignores her completely and continues frantically and destructively looking for something and hurling things to floor and tearing things out of their place in his search. Beneatha ignores the eccentricity of his actions and goes on with the monologue of insult.*)

Did you dream of yachts on Lake Michigan, Brother? Did you see yourself on that Great Day sitting down at the Conference Table, surrounded by all the mighty bald-headed men in America? All halted, waiting, breathless, waiting for your pronouncements on industry? Waiting for you—Chairman of the Board!

(*Walter finds what he is looking for—a small piece of white paper—and pushes it in his pocket and puts on his coat and rushes out without ever having looked at her. She shouts after him.*)

I look at you and I see the final triumph of stupidity in the world!

(*The door slams and she returns to just sitting again. Ruth comes quickly out of Mama's room.*)

Ruth: Who was that?

Beneatha: Your husband.

Ruth: Where did he go?

Beneatha: Who knows—maybe he has an appointment at U.S. Steel.

Ruth (*anxiously, with frightened eyes*): You didn't say nothing bad to him, did you?

Monsieur le petit bourgeois noir: French for "Mr. Black Middle Class."

Beneatha: Bad? Say anything bad to him? No—I told him he was a sweet boy and full of dreams and everything is strictly peachy keen, as the ofay° kids say!

(*Mama enters from her bedroom. She is lost, vague, trying to catch hold, to make some sense of her former command of the world, but it still eludes her. A sense of waste overwhelms her gait; a measure of apology rides on her shoulders. She goes to her plant, which has remained on the table, looks at it, picks it up and takes it to the windowsill and sits it outside, and she stands and looks at it a long moment. Then she closes the window, straightens her body with effort and turns around to her children.*)

Mama: Well—ain't it a mess in here, though? (*A false cheerfulness, a beginning of something.*) I guess we all better stop moping around and get some work done. All this unpacking and everything we got to do. (*Ruth raises her head slowly in response to the sense of the line; and Beneatha in similar manner turns very slowly to look at her mother.*) One of you all better call the moving people and tell 'em not to come.

Ruth: Tell 'em not to come?

Mama: Of course, baby. Ain't no need in 'em coming all the way here and having to go back. They charges for that too. (*She sits down, fingers to her brow, thinking.*) Lord, ever since I was a little girl, I always remembers people saying, "Lena—Lena Eggleston, you aims too high all the time. You needs to slow down and see life a little more like it is. Just slow down some." That's what they always used to say down home—"Lord, that Lena Eggleston is a high-minded thing. She'll get her due one day!"

Ruth: No, Lena . . .

Mama: Me and Big Walter just didn't never learn right.

Ruth: Lena, no! We gotta go. Bennie—tell her . . . (*She rises and crosses to Beneatha with her arms outstretched. Beneatha doesn't respond.*) Tell her we can still move . . . the notes ain't but a hundred and twenty-five a month. We got four grown people in this house—we can work . . .

Mama (*to herself*): Just aimed too high all the time—

Ruth (*turning and going to Mama fast—the words pouring out with urgency and desperation*): Lena—I'll work . . . I'll work twenty hours a day in all the kitchens in Chicago . . . I'll strap my baby on my back if I have to and scrub all the floors in America and wash all the sheets in America if I have to—but we got to MOVE! We got to get OUT OF HERE!!

(*Mama reaches out absently and pats Ruth's hand.*)

Mama: No—I sees things differently now. Been thinking 'bout some of the things we could do to fix this place up some. I seen a second-hand bureau over on Maxwell Street just the other day that could fit right there. (*She points to where the new furniture might go. Ruth wanders away from her.*) Would need some new handles on it and then a little varnish and it look like something brand-new. And—we can put up them new curtains in the kitchen . . . Why this place be looking fine. Cheer us all up so that we forget trouble ever come . . . (*To Ruth.*) And you could get some nice screens to put up in your room 'round the baby's bassinet . . . (*She looks at both of them, pleadingly.*) Sometimes you just got to know when to give up some things . . . and hold on to what you got . . .

---

ofay: Pig Latin for "foe."

(Walter enters from the outside, looking spent and leaning against the door, his coat hanging from him.)

Mama: Where you been, son?

Walter *(breathing hard)*: Made a call.

Mama: To who, son?

Walter: To The Man. *(He heads for his room.)*

Mama: What man, baby?

Walter *(stops in the door)*: The Man, Mama. Don't you know who The Man is?

Ruth: Walter Lee?

Walter: *The Man*. Like the guys in the streets say—The Man. Captain Boss—Mistuh Charley . . . Old Cap'n Please Mr. Bossman . . .

Beneatha *(suddenly)*: Lindner!

Walter: That's right! That's good. I told him to come right over.

Beneatha *(fiercely, understanding)*: For what? What do you want to see him for!

Walter *(looking at his sister)*: We going to do business with him.

Mama: What you talking 'bout, son?

Walter: Talking 'bout life, Mama. You all always telling me to see life like it is. Well—I laid in there on my back today . . . and I figured it out. Life just like it is. Who gets and who don't get. *(He sits down with his coat on and laughs.)* Mama, you know it's all divided up. Life is. Sure enough. Between the takers and the "tooken." *(He laughs.)* I've figured it out finally. *(He looks around at them.)* Yeah. Some of us always getting "tooken." *(He laughs.)* People like Willy Harris, they don't never get "tooken." And you know why the rest of us do? 'Cause we all mixed up. Mixed up bad. We get to looking 'round for the right and the wrong; and we worry about it and cry about it and stay up nights trying to figure out 'bout the wrong and the right of things all the time . . . And all the time, man, them takers is out there operating, just taking and taking. Willy Harris? Shoot—Willy Harris don't even count. He don't even count in the big scheme of things. But I'll say one thing for old Willy Harris . . . he's taught me something. He's taught me to keep my eye on what counts in this world. Yeah—*(Shouting out a little.)* Thanks, Willy!

Ruth: What did you call that man for, Walter Lee?

Walter: Called him to tell him to come on over to the show. Gonna put on a show for the man. Just what he wants to see. You see, Mama, the man came here today and he told us that them people out there where you want us to move—well they so upset they willing to pay us *not* to move! *(He laughs again.)* And—and oh, Mama—you would of been proud of the way me and Ruth and Bennie acted. We told him to get out . . . Lord have mercy! We told the man to get out! Oh, we was some proud folks this afternoon, yeah. *(He lights a cigarette.)* We were still full of that old-time stuff . . .

Ruth *(coming toward him slowly)*: You talking 'bout taking them people's money to keep us from moving in that house?

Walter: I ain't just talking 'bout it, baby—I'm telling you that's what's going to happen!

Beneatha: Oh, God! Where is the bottom! Where is the real honest-to-God bottom so he can't go any farther!

Walter: See—that's the old stuff. You and that boy that was here today. You all want everybody to carry a flag and a spear and sing some marching songs, huh? You wanna spend your life looking into things and trying to find the right and the wrong part, huh? Yeah. You know what's going to happen to that boy someday—he'll find himself sitting in a dungeon, locked in forever—and the takers will have the key! Forget it, baby! There ain't no causes—there ain't nothing but taking in this world, and he who takes most is smartest—and it don't make a damn bit of difference *how*.

Mama: You making something inside me cry, son. Some awful pain inside me.

Walter: Don't cry, Mama. Understand. That white man is going to walk in that door able to write checks for more money than we ever had. It's important to him and I'm going to help him . . . I'm going to put on the show, Mama.

Mama: Son—I come from five generations of people who was slaves and sharecroppers—but ain't nobody in my family never let nobody pay 'em no money that was a way of telling us we wasn't fit to walk the earth. We ain't never been that poor. (*Raising her eyes and looking at him.*) We ain't never been that—dead inside.

Beneatha: Well—we are dead now. All the talk about dreams and sunlight that goes on in this house. It's all dead now.

Walter: What's the matter with you all! I didn't make this world! It was give to me this way! Hell, yes, I want me some yachts someday! Yes, I want to hang some real pearls 'round my wife's neck. Ain't she supposed to wear no pearls? Somebody tell me—tell me, who decides which women is suppose to wear pearls in this world. I tell you I am a *man*—and I think my wife should wear some pearls in this world!

(*This last line hangs a good while and Walter begins to move about the room. The word "Man" has penetrated his consciousness; he mumbles it to himself repeatedly between strange agitated pauses as he moves about.*)

Mama: Baby, how you going to feel on the inside?

Walter: Fine! . . . Going to feel fine . . . a man . . .

Mama: You won't have nothing left then, Walter Lee.

Walter (*coming to her*): I'm going to feel fine, Mama. I'm going to look that son-of-a-bitch in the eyes and say—(*He falters.*)—and say, "All right, Mr. Lindner—(*He falters even more.*)—that's *your* neighborhood out there! You got the right to keep it like you want! You got the right to have it like you want! Just write the check and—the house is yours." And—and I am going to say—(*His voice almost breaks.*) "And you—you people just put the money in my hand and you won't have to live next to this bunch of stinking niggers! . . . " (*He straightens up and moves away from his mother, walking around the room.*) And maybe—maybe I'll just get down on my black knees . . . (*He does so; Ruth and Bennie and Mama watch him in frozen horror.*) "Captain, Mistuh, Bossman—(*Groveling and grinning and wringing his hands in profoundly anguished imitation of the slow-witted movie stereotype.*) A-hee-hee-hee! Oh, yassuh boss! Yasssssuh! Great white—(*Voice breaking, he forces himself to go on.*)— Father, just gi' ussen de money, fo' God's sake, and we's—we's ain't gwine come out deh and dirty up yo' white folks neighborhood . . ." (*He breaks down completely.*) And I'll feel fine! Fine! FINE! (*He gets up and goes into the bedroom.*)

Beneatha: That is not a man. That is nothing but a toothless rat.

Mama: Yes—death done come in this here house. (*She is nodding, slowly, reflectively.*) Done come walking in my house on the lips of my children. You what supposed to be my beginning again. You—what supposed to be my harvest. (*To Beneatha.*) You—you mourning your brother?

Beneatha: He's no brother of mine.

Mama: What you say?

Beneatha: I said that that individual in that room is no brother of mine.

Mama: That's what I thought you said. You feeling like you better than he is today? (*Beneatha does not answer.*) Yes? What you tell him a minute ago? That he wasn't a man? Yes? You give him up for me? You done wrote his epitaph too—like the rest of the world? Well, who give you the privilege?

Beneatha: Be on my side for once! You saw what he just did, Mama! You saw him— down on his knees. Wasn't it you who taught me to despise any man who would do that? Do what he's going to do?

Mama: Yes—I taught you that. Me and your daddy. But I thought I taught you something else too . . . I thought I taught you to love him.

Beneatha: Love him? There is nothing left to love.

Mama: There is *always* something left to love. And if you ain't learned that, you ain't learned nothing. (*Looking at her.*) Have you cried for that boy today? I don't mean for yourself and for the family 'cause we lost the money. I mean for him: what he been through and what it done to him. Child, when do you think is the time to love somebody the most? When they done good and made things easy for everybody? Well then, you ain't through learning—because that ain't the time at all. It's when he's at his lowest and can't believe in hisself 'cause the world done whipped him so! When you starts measuring somebody, measure him right, child, measure him right. Make sure you done taken into account what hills and valleys he come through before he got to wherever he is.

(*Travis bursts into the room at the end of the speech, leaving the door open.*)

Travis: Grandmama—the moving men are downstairs! The truck just pulled up.

Mama (*turning and looking at him*): Are they, baby? They downstairs?

(*She sighs and sits. Lindner appears in the doorway. He peers in and knocks lightly, to gain attention, and comes in. All turn to look at him.*)

Lindner (*hat and briefcase in hand*): Uh—hello . . .

(*Ruth crosses mechanically to the bedroom door and opens it and lets it swing open freely and slowly as the lights come up on Walter within, still in his coat, sitting at the far corner of the room. He looks up and out through the room to Lindner.*)

Ruth: He's here.

(*A long minute passes and Walter slowly gets up.*)

Lindner (*coming to the table with efficiency, putting his briefcase on the table and starting to unfold papers and unscrew fountain pens*): Well, I certainly was glad to hear from you people.

(*Walter has begun the trek out of the room, slowly and awkwardly, rather like a small boy, passing the back of his sleeve across his mouth from time to time.*)

Life can really be so much simpler than people let it be most of the time. Well— with whom do I negotiate? You, Mrs. Younger, or your son here?

(*Mama sits with her hands folded on her lap and her eyes closed as Walter advances. Travis goes closer to Lindner and looks at the papers curiously.*)

Just some official papers, sonny.

Ruth: Travis, you go downstairs—

Mama (*opening her eyes and looking into Walter's*): No. Travis, you stay right here. And you make him understand what you doing, Walter Lee. You teach him good. Like Willy Harris taught you. You show where our five generations done come to. (*Walter looks from her to the boy, who grins at him innocently.*) Go ahead, son— (*She folds her hands and closes her eyes.*) Go ahead.

Walter (*at last crosses to Lindner, who is reviewing the contract*): Well, Mr. Lindner. (*Beneatha turns away.*) We called you—(*There is a profound, simple groping quality in his speech.*)—because, well, me and my family (*He looks around and shifts from one foot to the other.*) Well—we are very plain people. . . .

Lindner: Yes—

Walter: I mean—I have worked as a chauffeur most of my life—and my wife here, she does domestic work in people's kitchens. So does my mother. I mean—we are plain people . . .

Lindner: Yes, Mr. Younger—

Walter (*really like a small boy, looking down at his shoes and then up at the man*): And— uh—well, my father, well, he was a laborer most of his life . . .

Lindner (*absolutely confused*): Uh, yes—yes, I understand. (*He turns back to the contract.*)

Walter (*a beat; staring at him*): And my father—(*With sudden intensity.*) My father almost *beat a man to death* once because this man called him a bad name or something, you know what I mean?

Lindner (*looking up, frozen*): No, no, I'm afraid I don't—

Walter (*a beat. The tension hangs; then Walter steps back from it*): Yeah. Well—what I mean is that we come from people who had a lot of *pride*. I mean—we are very proud people. And that's my sister over there and she's going to be a doctor— and we are very proud—

Lindner: Well—I am sure that is very nice, but—

Walter: What I am telling you is that we called you over here to tell you that we are very proud and that this—(*Signaling to Travis.*) Travis, come here. (*Travis crosses and Walter draws him before him facing the man.*) This is my son, and he makes the sixth generation of our family in this country. And we have all thought about your offer—

Lindner: Well, good . . . good—

Walter: And we have decided to move into our house because my father—my father—he earned it for us brick by brick. (*Mama has her eyes closed and is rocking back and forth as though she were in church, with her head nodding the Amen yes.*) We don't want to make no trouble for nobody or fight no causes, and we will try to be good neighbors. And that's *all* we got to say about that. (*He looks the man absolutely in the eyes.*) We don't want your money. (*He turns and walks away.*)

Lindner (*looking around at all of them*): I take it then—that you have decided to occupy . . .

Beneatha: That's what the man said.

Lindner (*to Mama in her reverie*): Then I would like to appeal to you, Mrs. Younger. You are older and wiser and understand things better I am sure . . .

Mama: I am afraid you don't understand. My son said we was going to move and there ain't nothing left for me to say. (*Briskly.*) You know how these young folks is nowadays, mister. Can't do a thing with 'em! (*As he opens his mouth, she rises.*) Good-bye.

Lindner (*folding up his materials*): Well—if you are that final about it . . . there is nothing left for me to say. (*He finishes, almost ignored by the family, who are concentrating on*

Walter Lee. At the door Lindner halts and looks around.) I sure hope you people know what you're getting into. (*He shakes his head and exits.*)

Ruth (looking around and coming to life): Well, for God's sake—if the moving men are here—LET'S GET THE HELL OUT OF HERE!

Mama (into action): Ain't it the truth! Look at all this here mess. Ruth, put Travis' good jacket on him . . . Walter Lee, fix your tie and tuck your shirt in; you look like somebody's hoodlum! Lord have mercy, where is my plant? (*She flies to get it amid the general bustling of the family, who are deliberately trying to ignore the nobility of the past moment.*) You all start on down . . . Travis child, don't go empty-handed . . . Ruth, where did I put that box with my skillets in it? I want to be in charge of it myself . . . I'm going to make us the biggest dinner we ever ate tonight . . . Beneatha, what's the matter with them stockings? Pull them things up, girl . . .

(*The family starts to file out as two moving men appear and begin to carry out the heavier pieces of furniture, bumping into the family as they move about.*)

Beneatha: Mama, Asagai asked me to marry him today and go to Africa—

Mama (in the middle of her getting-ready activity): He did? You ain't old enough to marry nobody—(*Seeing the moving men lifting one of her chairs precariously.*) Darling, that ain't no bale of cotton, please handle it so we can sit in it again! I had that chair twenty-five years . . .

(*The movers sigh with exasperation and go on with their work.*)

Beneatha (girlishly and unreasonably trying to pursue the conversation): To go to Africa, Mama—be a doctor in Africa . . .

Mama (distracted): Yes, baby—

Walter: Africa! What he want you to go to Africa for?

Beneatha: To practice there . . .

Walter: Girl, if you don't get all them silly ideas out your head! You better marry yourself a man with some loot . . .

Beneatha (angrily, precisely as in the first scene of the play): What have you got to do with who I marry!

Walter: Plenty. Now I think George Murchison—

Beneatha: George Murchison! I wouldn't marry him if he was Adam and I was Eve!

(*Walter and Beneatha go out yelling at each other vigorously and the anger is loud and real till their voices diminish. Ruth stands at the door and turns to Mama and smiles knowingly.*)

Mama (fixing her hat at last): Yeah—they something all right, my children . . .

Ruth: Yeah—they're something. Let's go, Lena.

Mama (stalling, starting to look around at the house): Yes—I'm coming. Ruth—

Ruth: Yes?

Mama (quietly, woman to woman): He finally come into his manhood today, didn't he? Kind of like a rainbow after the rain . . .

Ruth (biting her lip lest her own pride explode in front of Mama): Yes, Lena.

(*Walter's voice calls for them raucously.*)

Walter (off stage): Y'all come on! These people charges by the hour, you know!

Mama (waving Ruth out vaguely): All right, honey—go on down. I be down directly.

(Ruth hesitates, then exits. Mama stands, at last alone in the living room, her plant on the table before her as the lights start to come down. She looks around at all the walls and ceilings and suddenly, despite herself, while the children call below, a great heaving thing rises in her and she puts her fist to her mouth to stifle it, takes a final desperate look, pulls her coat about her, pats her hat and goes out. The lights dim down. The door opens and she comes back in, grabs her plant, and goes out for the last time.)

CURTAIN

Questions

1. In the opening scene of the play, what factors account for the irritation and hostility that the family members show toward one another?

2. What values do the members of the family associate with Mama's late husband? In what ways do they try to live up to those values in their own lives?

3. How would you characterize the relationship between Walter and his sister, Beneatha? Do they seem to have a genuine affection for one another?

4. Mama maintains that everything she does is for her family. Do her actions support this claim, in your opinion, or not?

5. Why does Asagai call Beneatha "Alaiyo: One for Whom Bread—Food—Is Not Enough"? (Act I, Scene II.) Why is she flattered by this description?

6. Do Walter and Ruth respect one another? Cite specific details from the play to back up your conclusions.

7. What does Mama mean when she says in Act II, Scene III, about her flower: "It expresses ME!"?

8. Even though the future of the Younger family in their new neighborhood is uncertain, to say the least, does the play have a happy ending? Explain.

Lorraine Hansberry on Writing

A Letter to My Mother

1959

Hotel Taft
New Haven, Conn.
January 19, 1959

Dear Mother,

Well—here we are. I am sitting alone in a nice hotel room in New Haven, Conn. Downstairs, next door in the Shubert Theatre, technicians are putting the finishing touches on a living room that is supposed to be a Chicago living room. Wednesday the curtain goes up at 8 P.M. The next day the New Haven papers will say what they think about our efforts. A great deal of money has been spent and a lot of people have done some hard, hard work, and it may be the beginning of many different careers.

The actors are very good and the director is a very talented man—so if it is a poor show I won't be able to blame a soul but your youngest daughter.

Lorraine Hansberry

Mama, it is a play that tells the truth about people, Negroes and life and I think it will help a lot of people to understand how we are just as complicated as they are—and just as mixed up—but above all, that we have among our miserable and downtrodden ranks—people who are the very essence of human dignity. That is what, after all the laughter and tears, the play is supposed to say. I hope it will make you very proud. See you soon. Love to all.

From *To Be Young, Gifted and Black*

Henrik Ibsen

A Doll's House

1879

Translated by R. Farquharson Sharp
Revised by Viktoria Michelsen

Henrik Ibsen (1828–1906) was born in Skien, a seaport in Norway. When he was six, his father's business losses suddenly reduced his wealthy family to poverty. After a brief attempt to study medicine, young Ibsen worked as a stage manager in provincial Bergen; then, becoming known as a playwright, he moved to Oslo as artistic director of the National Theater—practical experiences that gained him firm grounding in his craft. Discouraged when his theater failed and the king turned down his plea for a grant to enable him to write, Ibsen left Norway and for twenty-seven years lived in Italy and Germany. There, in his middle years (1879–1891), he wrote most of his famed plays about small-town life, among them A Doll's House, Ghosts, An Enemy of the People, The Wild Duck, and Hedda Gabler. Introducing social problems to the stage, these plays aroused storms of controversy. Although best known as a Realist, Ibsen early in his career wrote poetic dramas based on Norwegian history and folklore: the tragedy Brand (1866) and the powerful, wildly fantastic Peer Gynt (1867). He ended as a Symbolist in John Gabriel Borkman (1896) and When We Dead Awaken (1899), both encompassing huge mountains that heaven-assaulting heroes try to climb. Late in life Ibsen returned to Oslo, honored at last both at home and abroad.

CHARACTERS

Torvald Helmer, a lawyer
Nora, his wife
Doctor Rank
Mrs. Kristine Linde
Nils Krogstad
The Helmers' three young children
Anne Marie, their nursemaid
Helene, the maid
A Porter

The action takes place in the Helmers' apartment.

ACT I

The scene is a room furnished comfortably and tastefully, but not extravagantly. At the back wall, a door to the right leads to the entrance hall. Another to the left leads to Helmer's study. Between the doors there is a piano. In the middle of the left-hand wall is a door, and beyond it a window. Near the window are a round table, armchairs, and a small sofa. In the right-hand wall, at the farther end, is another door, and on the same side, nearer the footlights, a stove, two easy chairs and a rocking chair. Between the stove and the door there is a small table. There are engravings on the walls, a cabinet with china and other small objects, and a small bookcase with expensively bound books. The floors are carpeted, and a fire burns in the stove. It is winter.

A bell rings in the hall. A moment later, we hear the door being opened. Enter Nora, humming a tune and in high spirits. She is wearing a hat and coat and carries a number of packages, which she puts down on the table to the right. She leaves the outer door open behind her. Through the door we see a porter who is carrying a Christmas tree and a basket, which he gives to the maid, who has opened the door.

Nora: Hide the Christmas tree carefully, Helene. Make sure the children don't see it
    till it's decorated this evening. (To the Porter, taking out her purse.) How much?
Porter: Fifty ore.
Nora: Here's a krone. No, keep the change.

(The Porter thanks her and goes out. Nora shuts the door. She is laughing to herself as she takes off her hat and coat. She takes a bag of macaroons from her pocket and eats one or two, then goes cautiously to the door of her husband's study and listens.)

Yes, he's there. (Still humming, she goes to the table on the right.)

Helmer (calls out from his study): Is that my little lark twittering out there?

The 1896 production of *A Doll's House* at the Empire Theatre in New York.

Nora (busy opening some of the packages): Yes, it is!

Helmer: Is it my little squirrel bustling around?

Nora: Yes!

Helmer: When did my squirrel come home?

Nora: Just now. (*Puts the bag of macaroons into her pocket and wipes her mouth.*) Come in here, Torvald, and see what I bought.

Helmer: I'm very busy right now. (*A little later, he opens the door and looks into the room, pen in hand.*) Bought, did you say? All these things? Has my little spendthrift been wasting money again?

Nora: Yes, but, Torvald, this year we really can let ourselves go a little. This is the first Christmas that we don't have to watch every penny.

Helmer: Still, you know, we can't spend money recklessly.

Nora: Yes, Torvald, but we can be a little more reckless now, can't we? Just a tiny little bit! You're going to have a big salary and you'll be making lots and lots of money.

Helmer: Yes, after the New Year. But it'll still be a whole three months before the money starts coming in.

Nora: Pooh! We can borrow till then.

Helmer: Nora! (*Goes up to her and takes her playfully by the ear.*) The same little featherbrain! Just suppose that I borrowed a thousand kroner today, and you spent it all on Christmas, and then on New Year's Eve a roof tile fell on my head and killed me, and—

Nora (putting her hand over his mouth): Oh! Don't say such horrible things.

Helmer: Still, suppose that happened. What then?

The 2009 adaptation of *A Doll's House* at the Donmar Warehouse in London, starring Gillian Anderson and Toby Stephens.

Nora: If that happened, I don't suppose I'd care whether I owed anyone money or not.

Helmer: Yes, but what about the people who'd lent it to us?

Nora: Them? Who'd care about them? I wouldn't even know who they were.

Helmer: That's just like a woman! But seriously, Nora, you know how I feel about that. No debt, no borrowing. There can't be any freedom or beauty in a home life that depends on borrowing and debt. We two have managed to stay on the straight road so far, and we'll go on the same way for the short time that we still have to be careful.

Nora (moving towards the stove): As you wish, Torvald.

Helmer (following her): Now, now, my little skylark mustn't let her wings droop. What's the matter? Is my little squirrel sulking? *(Taking out his purse.)* Nora, what do you think I've got here?

Nora (turning round quickly): Money!

Helmer: There you are. *(Gives her some money.)* Do you think I don't know how much you need for the house at Christmastime?

Nora (counting): Ten, twenty, thirty, forty! Thank you, thank you, Torvald. That'll keep me going for a long time.

Helmer: It's going to have to.

Nora: Yes, yes, it will. But come here and let me show you what I bought. And all so cheap! Look, here's a new suit for Ivar, and a sword. And a horse and a trumpet for Bob. And a doll and doll's bed for Emmy. They're not the best, but she'll break them soon enough anyway. And here's dress material and handkerchiefs for the maids. Old Anne Marie really should have something nicer.

Helmer: And what's in this package?

Nora (crying out): No, no! You can't see that till this evening.

Helmer: If you say so. But now tell me, you extravagant little thing, what would you like for yourself?

Nora: For myself? Oh, I'm sure I don't want anything.

Helmer: But you must. Tell me something that you'd especially like to have—within reasonable limits.

Nora: No, I really can't think of anything. Unless, Torvald . . .

Helmer: Well?

Nora (playing with his coat buttons, and without raising her eyes to his): If you really want to give me something, you might . . . you might . . .

Helmer: Well, out with it!

Nora (speaking quickly): You might give me money, Torvald. Only just as much as you can afford. And then one of these days I'll buy something with it.

Helmer: But, Nora—

Nora: Oh, do! Dear Torvald, please, please do! Then I'll wrap it up in beautiful gold paper and hang it on the Christmas tree. Wouldn't that be fun?

Helmer: What do they call those little creatures that are always wasting money?

Nora: Spendthrifts. I know. Let's do as I suggest, Torvald, and then I'll have time to think about what I need most. That's a very sensible plan, isn't it?

Helmer (smiling): Yes, it is. That is, if you really did save some of the money I give you, and then really buy something for yourself. But if you spend it all on the housekeeping and all kinds of unnecessary things, then I just have to open my wallet all over again.

Nora: Oh, but, Torvald—

Helmer: You can't deny it, my dear little Nora. (*Puts his arm around her waist.*) She's a sweet little spendthrift, but she uses up a lot of money. One would hardly believe how expensive such little creatures are!

Nora: That's a terrible thing to say. I really do save all I can.

Helmer (laughing): That's true. All you can. But you can't save anything!

Nora (smiling quietly and happily): You have no idea how many bills skylarks and squirrels have, Torvald.

Helmer: You're an odd little soul. Just like your father. You always find some new way of wheedling money out of me, and, as soon as you've got it, it seems to melt in your hands. You never know where it's gone. Still, one has to take you as you are. It's in the blood. Because, you know, it's true that you can inherit these things, Nora.

Nora: Ah, I wish I'd inherited a lot of Papa's traits.

Helmer: And I wouldn't want you to be anything but just what you are, my sweet little skylark. But, you know, it seems to me that you look rather—how can I put it—rather uneasy today.

Nora: Do I?

Helmer: You do, really. Look straight at me.

Nora (looks at him): Well?

Helmer (wagging his finger at her): Has little Miss Sweet Tooth been breaking our rules in town today?

Nora: No, what makes you think that?

Helmer: Has she paid a visit to the bakery?

Nora: No, I assure you, Torvald—

Helmer: Not been nibbling pastries?

Nora: No, certainly not.

Helmer: Not even taken a bite of a macaroon or two?

Nora: No, Torvald, I assure you, really—

Helmer: Come on, you know I was only kidding.

Nora (going to the table on the right): I wouldn't dream of going against your wishes.

Helmer: No, I'm sure of that. Besides, you gave me your word. (*Going up to her.*) Keep your little Christmas secrets to yourself, my darling. They'll all be revealed tonight when the Christmas tree is lit, no doubt.

Nora: Did you remember to invite Doctor Rank?

Helmer: No. But there's no need. It goes without saying that he'll have dinner with us. All the same, I'll ask him when he comes over this morning. I've ordered some good wine. Nora, you have no idea how much I'm looking forward to this evening.

Nora: So am I! And how the children will enjoy themselves, Torvald!

Helmer: It's great to feel that you have a completely secure position and a big enough income. It's a delightful thought, isn't it?

Nora: It's wonderful!

Helmer: Do you remember last Christmas? For three whole weeks you hid yourself away every evening until long after midnight, making ornaments for the Christmas tree and all the other fine things that were going to be a surprise for us. It was the most boring three weeks I ever spent!

Nora: I wasn't bored.

Helmer (smiling): But there was precious little to show for it, Nora.

Nora: Oh, you're not going to tease me about that again. How could I help it that the cat went in and tore everything to pieces?

Helmer: Of course you couldn't, poor little girl. You had the best of intentions to make us all happy, and that's the main thing. But it's a good thing that our hard times are over.

Nora: Yes, it really is wonderful.

Helmer: This time I don't have to sit here and be bored all by myself, and you don't have to ruin your dear eyes and your pretty little hands—

Nora (clapping her hands): No, Torvald, I don't have to any more, do I! It's wonderfully lovely to hear you say so! *(Taking his arm.)* Now let me tell you how I've been thinking we should arrange things, Torvald. As soon as Christmas is over— *(A bell rings in the hall.)* There's the bell. *(She tidies the room a little.)* There's somebody at the door. What a nuisance!

Helmer: If someone's visiting, remember I'm not home.

Maid (in the doorway): A lady to see you, ma'am. A stranger.

Nora: Ask her to come in.

Maid (to Helmer): The doctor's here too, sir.

Helmer: Did he go straight into my study?

Maid: Yes, sir.

(Helmer goes into his study. The maid ushers in Mrs. Linde, who is in traveling clothes, and shuts the door.)

Mrs. Linde (in a dejected and timid voice): Hello, Nora.

Nora (doubtfully): Hello.

Mrs. Linde: You don't recognize me, I suppose.

Nora: No, I don't know . . . Yes, of course, I think so—*(Suddenly.)* Yes! Kristine! Is it really you?

Mrs. Linde: Yes, it is.

Nora: Kristine! Imagine my not recognizing you! And yet how could I—*(In a gentle voice.)* You've changed, Kristine!

Mrs. Linde: Yes, I certainly have. In nine, ten long years—

Nora: Is it that long since we've seen each other? I suppose it is. The last eight years have been a happy time for me, you know. And so now you've come to town, and you've taken this long trip in the winter. That was brave of you.

Mrs. Linde: I arrived by steamer this morning.

Nora: To have some fun at Christmastime, of course. How delightful! We'll have such fun together! But take off your things. You're not cold, I hope. *(Helps her.)* Now we'll sit down by the stove and be cozy. No, take this armchair. I'll sit here in the rocking chair. *(Takes her hands.)* Now you look like your old self again. It was only that first moment. You are a little paler, Kristine, and maybe a little thinner.

Mrs. Linde: And much, much older, Nora.

Nora: Maybe a little older. Very, very little. Surely not very much. *(Stops suddenly and speaks seriously.)* What a thoughtless thing I am, chattering away like this. My poor, dear Kristine, please forgive me.

Mrs. Linde: What do you mean, Nora?

Nora (gently): Poor Kristine, you're a widow.

Mrs. Linde: Yes. For three years now.

Nora: Yes, I knew. I saw it in the papers. I swear to you, Kristine, I kept meaning to write to you at the time, but I always put it off and something always came up.

Mrs. Linde: I understand completely, dear.

Nora: It was very bad of me, Kristine. Poor thing, how you must have suffered. And he left you nothing?

Mrs. Linde: No.

Nora: And no children?

Mrs. Linde: No.

Nora: Nothing at all, then?

Mrs. Linde: Not even any sorrow or grief to live on.

Nora (looking at her in disbelief): But, Kristine, is that possible?

Mrs. Linde (smiles sadly and strokes Nora's hair): It happens sometimes, Nora.

Nora: So you're completely alone. How terribly sad that must be. I have three beautiful children. You can't see them just now, because they're out with their nurse-maid. But now you must tell me all about it.

Mrs. Linde: No, no, I want to hear about you.

Nora: No, you go first. I mustn't be selfish today. Today I should think only about you. But there is one thing I have to tell you. Do you know we've just had a fabulous piece of good luck?

Mrs. Linde: No, what is it?

Nora: Just imagine, my husband's been appointed manager of the bank!

Mrs. Linde: Your husband? That is good luck!

Nora: Yes, it's tremendous! A lawyer's life is so uncertain, especially if he won't take any cases that are the slightest bit shady, and of course Torvald has never been willing to do that, and I completely agree with him. You can imagine how delighted we are! He starts his job in the bank at New Year's, and then he'll have a big salary and lots of commissions. From now on we can live very differently. We can do just what we want. I feel so relieved and so happy, Kristine! It'll be wonderful to have heaps of money and not have to worry about anything, won't it?

Mrs. Linde: Yes. Anyway, I think it would be delightful to have what you need.

Nora: No, not only what you need, but heaps and heaps of money.

Mrs. Linde (smiling): Nora, Nora, haven't you learned any sense yet? Back in school you were a terrible spendthrift.

Nora (laughing): Yes, that's what Torvald says now. *(Wags her finger at her.)* But "Nora, Nora" isn't as silly as you think. We haven't been in a position for me to waste money. We've both had to work.

Mrs. Linde: You too?

Nora: Oh, yes, odds and ends, needlework, crocheting, embroidery, and that kind of thing. *(Dropping her voice.)* And other things too. You know Torvald left his government job when we got married? There was no chance of promotion, and he had to try to earn more money than he was making there. But in that first year he overworked himself terribly. You see, he had to make money any way he could, and he worked all hours, but he couldn't take it, and he got very sick, and the doctors said he had to go south, to a warmer climate.

Mrs. Linde: You spent a whole year in Italy, didn't you?

Nora: Yes. It wasn't easy to get away, I can tell you that. It was just after Ivar was born, but obviously we had to go. It was a wonderful, beautiful trip, and it saved Torvald's life. But it cost a tremendous amount of money, Kristine.

Mrs. Linde: I would imagine so.

Nora: It cost about four thousand, eight hundred kroner. That's a lot, isn't it?

Mrs. Linde: Yes, it is, and when you have an emergency like that it's lucky to have the money.

Nora: Well, the fact is, we got it from Papa.

Mrs. Linde: Oh, I see. It was just about that time that he died, wasn't it?

Nora: Yes, and, just think of it, I couldn't even go and take care of him. I was expecting little Ivar any day and I had my poor sick Torvald to look after. My dear, kind father. I never saw him again, Kristine. That was the worst experience I've gone through since we got married.

Mrs. Linde: I know how fond of him you were. And then you went off to Italy?

Nora: Yes. You see, we had money then, and the doctors insisted that we go, so we left a month later.

Mrs. Linde: And your husband came back completely recovered?

Nora: The picture of health!

Mrs. Linde: But . . . the doctor?

Nora: What doctor?

Mrs. Linde: Didn't your maid say that the gentleman who arrived here with me was the doctor?

Nora: Yes, that was Doctor Rank, but he doesn't come here professionally. He's our dearest friend, and he drops in at least once every day. No, Torvald hasn't been sick for an hour since then, and our children are strong and healthy, and so am I. (*Jumps up and claps her hands.*) Kristine! Kristine! It's good to be alive and happy! But how awful of me. I'm talking about nothing but myself. (*Sits on a nearby stool and rests her arms on her knees.*) Please don't be mad at me. Tell me, is it really true that you didn't love your husband? Why did you marry him?

Mrs. Linde: My mother was still alive then, and she was bedridden and helpless, and I had to provide for my two younger brothers, so I didn't think I had any right to turn him down.

Nora: No, maybe you did the right thing. So he was rich then?

Mrs. Linde: I believe he was quite well off. But his business wasn't very solid, and when he died, it all went to pieces and there was nothing left.

Nora: And then?

Mrs. Linde: Well, I had to turn my hand to anything I could find. First a small shop, then a small school, and so on. The last three years have seemed like one long workday, with no rest. Now it's over, Nora. My poor mother's gone and doesn't need me any more, and the boys don't need me, either. They've got jobs now and can manage for themselves.

Nora: What a relief it must be if—

Mrs. Linde: No, not at all. All I feel is an unbearable emptiness. No one to live for anymore. (*Gets up restlessly.*) That's why I couldn't stand it any longer in my little backwater. I hope it'll be easier to find something here that'll keep me busy and occupy my mind. If I could be lucky enough to find some regular work, office work of some kind—

Nora: But, Kristine, that's so awfully tiring, and you look tired out now. It'd be much better for you if you could get away to a resort.

Mrs. Linde (*walking to the window*): I don't have a father to give me money for a trip, Nora.

Nora (*rising*): Oh, don't be mad at me!

Mrs. *Linde (going up to her)*: It's you who mustn't be mad at me, dear. The worst thing about a situation like mine is that it makes you so bitter. No one to work for, and yet you have to always be on the lookout for opportunities. You have to live, and so you grow selfish. When you told me about your good luck—you'll find this hard to believe—I was delighted less for you than for myself.

Nora: What do you mean? Oh, I understand. You mean that maybe Torvald could find you a job.

Mrs. *Linde*: Yes, that's what I was thinking.

Nora: He must, Kristine. Just leave it to me. I'll broach the subject very cleverly. I'll think of something that'll put him in a really good mood. It'll make me so happy to be of some use to you.

Mrs. *Linde*: How kind you are, Nora, to be so eager to help me! It's doubly kind of you, since you know so little of the burdens and troubles of life.

Nora: Me? I know so little of them?

Mrs. *Linde (smiling)*: My dear! Small household cares and that sort of thing! You're a child, Nora.

Nora *(tosses her head and crosses the stage)*: You shouldn't act so superior.

Mrs. *Linde*: No?

Nora: You're just like the others. They all think I'm incapable of anything really serious—

Mrs. *Linde*: Come on—

Nora: —that I haven't had to deal with any real problems in my life.

Mrs. *Linde*: But, my dear Nora, you've just told me all your troubles.

Nora: Pooh! That was nothing. *(Lowering her voice.)* I haven't told you the important thing.

Mrs. *Linde*: The important thing? What do you mean?

Nora: You really look down on me, Kristine, but you shouldn't. Aren't you proud of having worked so hard and so long for your mother?

Mrs. *Linde*: Believe me, I don't look down on anyone. But it's true, I'm proud and I'm glad that I had the privilege of making my mother's last days almost worry-free.

Nora: And you're proud of what you did for your brothers?

Mrs. *Linde*: I think I have the right to be.

Nora: I think so, too. But now, listen to this. I have something to be proud of and happy about too.

Mrs. *Linde*: I'm sure you do. But what do you mean?

Nora: Keep your voice down. If Torvald were to overhear! He can't find out, not under any circumstances. No one in the world must know, Kristine, except you.

Mrs. *Linde*: But what is it?

Nora: Come here. *(Pulls her down on the sofa beside her.)* Now I'll show you that I too have something to be proud and happy about. I'm the one who saved Torvald's life.

Mrs. *Linde*: Saved? How?

Nora: I told you about our trip to Italy. Torvald would never have recovered if he hadn't gone there—

Mrs. *Linde*: Yes, but your father gave you the money you needed.

Nora *(smiling)*: Yes, that's what Torvald thinks, along with everybody else, but—

Mrs. *Linde*: But—

Nora: Papa didn't give us a penny. I was the one who raised the money.

Mrs. *Linde*: You? That huge amount?

Nora: That's right, four thousand, eight hundred kroner. What do you think of that?

Mrs. Linde: But, Nora, how could you possibly? Did you win the lottery?

Nora (disdainfully): The lottery? That wouldn't have been any accomplishment.

Mrs. Linde: But where did you get it from, then?

Nora (humming and smiling with an air of mystery): Hm, hm! Ha!

Mrs. Linde: Because you couldn't have borrowed it.

Nora: Couldn't I? Why not?

Mrs. Linde: No, a wife can't borrow money without her husband's consent.

Nora (tossing her head): Oh, if it's a wife with a head for business, a wife who has the brains to be a little clever—

Mrs. Linde: I don't understand this at all, Nora.

Nora: There's no reason why you should. I never said I'd borrowed the money. Maybe I got it some other way. *(Lies back on the sofa.)* Maybe I got it from an admirer. When a woman's as pretty as I am—

Mrs. Linde: You're crazy.

Nora: Now, you know you're dying of curiosity, Kristine.

Mrs. Linde: Listen to me, Nora dear. Have you done something rash?

Nora (sits up straight): Is it rash to save your husband's life?

Mrs. Linde: I think it's rash, without his knowledge, to—

Nora: But it was absolutely necessary that he not know! My goodness, can't you understand that? It was necessary he have no idea how sick he was. The doctors came to *me* and said his life was in danger and the only thing that could save him was to live in the south. Don't you think I tried first to get him to do it as if it was for me? I told him how much I would love to travel abroad like other young wives. I tried tears and pleading with him. I told him he should remember the condition I was in, and that he should be kind and indulgent to me. I even hinted that he might take out a loan. That almost made him mad, Kristine. He said I was thoughtless, and that it was his duty as my husband not to indulge me in my "whims and caprices," as I believe he called them. All right, I thought, you need to be saved. And that was how I came to think up a way out of the mess—

Mrs. Linde: And your husband never found out from your father that the money hadn't come from him?

Nora: No, never. Papa died just then. I'd meant to let him in on the secret and beg him never to reveal it. But he was so sick. Unfortunately, there never was any need to tell him.

Mrs. Linde: And since then you've never told your secret to your husband?

Nora: Good heavens, no! How could you think I would? A man with such strong opinions about these things! Besides, how painful and humiliating it would be for Torvald, with his masculine pride, to know that he owed me anything! It would completely upset the balance of our relationship. Our beautiful happy home would never be the same.

Mrs. Linde: Are you never going to tell him about it?

Nora (meditatively, and with a half smile): Yes, someday, maybe, in many years, when I'm not as pretty as I am now. Don't laugh at me! I mean, of course, when Torvald is no longer as devoted to me as he is now, when he's grown tired of my dancing and dressing up and reciting. Then it may be a good thing to have something in reserve—*(Breaking off.)* What nonsense! That time will never come. Now, what do you think of my great secret, Kristine? Do you still think I'm useless? And the fact is, this whole situation has caused me a lot of worry. It hasn't been easy for me to make my payments on time. I can tell you that there's something in business that's called quarterly interest, and something else called installment payments, and it's always so terribly difficult to keep up with them. I've had to save a little here and there, wherever I could, you understand. I haven't been able to put much aside from my housekeeping money, because Torvald has to live well. And I couldn't let my children be shabbily dressed. I feel I have to spend everything he gives me for them, the sweet little darlings!

Mrs. Linde: So it's all had to come out of your own allowance, poor Nora?

Nora: Of course. Besides, I was the one responsible for it. Whenever Torvald has given me money for new dresses and things like that, I've never spent more than half of it. I've always bought the simplest and cheapest things. Thank heaven, any clothes look good on me, and so Torvald's never noticed anything. But it was often very hard on me, Kristine, because it is delightful to be really well dressed, isn't it?

Mrs. Linde: I suppose so.

Nora: Well, then I've found other ways of earning money. Last winter I was lucky enough to get a lot of copying to do, so I locked myself up and sat writing every evening until late into the night. A lot of the time I was desperately tired, but all the same it was a tremendous pleasure to sit there working and earning money. It was like being a man.

Mrs. Linde: How much have you been able to pay off that way?

Nora: I can't tell you exactly. You see, it's very hard to keep a strict account of a business matter like that. I only know that I've paid out every penny I could scrape together. Many a time I was at my wits' end. (*Smiles.*) Then I used to sit here and imagine that a rich old gentleman had fallen in love with me—

Mrs. Linde: What! Who was it?

Nora: Oh, be quiet! That he had died, and that when his will was opened it said, in great big letters: "The lovely Mrs. Nora Helmer is to have everything I own paid over to her immediately in cash."

Mrs. Linde: But, my dear Nora, who could the man be?

Nora: Good gracious, can't you understand? There wasn't any old gentleman. It was only something that I used to sit here and imagine, when I couldn't think of any way of getting money. But it's all right now. The tiresome old gent can stay right where he is, as far as I'm concerned. I don't care about him or his will either, because now I'm worry-free. (*Jumps up.*) My goodness, it's delightful to think of, Kristine! Worry-free! To be able to have no worries, no worries at all! To be able to play and romp with the children! To be able to keep the house beautifully and have everything just the way Torvald likes it! And, just think of it, soon the spring will come and the big blue sky! Maybe we can take a little trip. Maybe I can see the sea again! Oh, it's a wonderful thing to be alive and happy.

(*A bell rings in the hall.*)

Mrs. Linde (rising): There's the bell. Perhaps I should be going.

Nora: No, don't go. No one will come in here. It's sure to be for Torvald.

Servant (at the hall door): Excuse me, ma'am. There's a gentleman to see the master, and as the doctor is still with him—

Nora: Who is it?

Krogstad (at the door): It's me, Mrs. Helmer.

(*Mrs. Linde starts, trembles, and turns toward the window.*)

Nora (*takes a step toward him, and speaks in a strained, low voice*): You? What is it? What do you want to see my husband for?

Krogstad: Bank business, in a way. I have a small position in the bank, and I hear your husband is going to be our boss now—

Nora: Then it's—

Krogstad: Nothing but dry business matters, Mrs. Helmer, that's all.

Nora: Then please go into the study.

(*She bows indifferently to him and shuts the door into the hall, then comes back and makes up the fire in the stove.*)

Mrs. Linde: Nora, who was that man?

Nora: A lawyer. His name is Krogstad.

Mrs. Linde: Then it really was him.

Nora: Do you know the man?

Mrs. Linde: I used to, many years ago. At one time he was a law clerk in our town.

Nora: That's right, he was.

Mrs. Linde: How much he's changed.

Nora: He had a very unhappy marriage.

Mrs. Linde: He's a widower now, isn't he?

Nora: With several children. There, now it's really caught. (*Shuts the door of the stove and moves the rocking chair aside.*)

Mrs. Linde: They say he's mixed up in a lot of questionable business.

Nora: Really? Maybe he is. I don't know anything about it. But let's not talk about business. It's so tiresome.

Doctor Rank (*comes out of Helmer's study. Before he shuts the door he calls to Helmer*): No, my dear fellow, I won't disturb you. I'd rather go in and talk to your wife for a little while.

(*Shuts the door and sees Mrs. Linde.*)

I beg your pardon. I'm afraid I'm in the way here too.

Nora: No, not at all. (*Introducing him:*) Doctor Rank, Mrs. Linde.

Rank: I've often heard that name in this house. I think I passed you on the stairs when I arrived, Mrs. Linde?

Mrs. Linde: Yes, I take stairs very slowly. I can't manage them very well.

Rank: Oh, some small internal problem?

Mrs. Linde: No, it's just that I've been overworking myself.

Rank: Is that all? Then I suppose you've come to town to get some rest by sampling our social life.

Mrs. Linde: I've come to look for work.

Rank: Is that a good cure for overwork?

Mrs. Linde: One has to live, Doctor Rank.

Rank: Yes, that seems to be the general opinion.

Nora: Now, now, Doctor Rank, you know you want to live.

Rank: Of course I do. However miserable I may feel, I want to prolong the agony for as long as possible. All my patients are the same way. And so are those who are morally sick. In fact, one of them, and a bad case too, is at this very moment inside with Helmer—

Mrs. Linde (sadly): Ah!

Nora: Who are you talking about?

Rank: A lawyer by the name of Krogstad, a fellow you don't know at all. He's a completely worthless creature, Mrs. Helmer. But even he started out by saying, as if it were a matter of the utmost importance, that he has to live.

Nora: Did he? What did he want to talk to Torvald about?

Rank: I have no idea. All I heard was that it was something about the bank.

Nora: I didn't know this—what's his name—Krogstad had anything to do with the bank.

Rank: Yes, he has some kind of a position there. *(To Mrs. Linde)* I don't know whether you find the same thing in your part of the world, that there are certain people who go around zealously looking to sniff out moral corruption, and, as soon as they find some, they put the person involved in some cushy job where they can keep an eye on him. Meanwhile, the morally healthy ones are left out in the cold.

Mrs. Linde: Still, I think it's the sick who are most in need of being taken care of.

Rank (shrugging his shoulders): Well, there you have it. That's the attitude that's turning society into a hospital.

(Nora, who has been absorbed in her thoughts, breaks out into smothered laughter and claps her hands.)

Rank: Why are you laughing at that? Do you have any idea what society really is?

Nora: What do I care about your boring society? I'm laughing at something else, something very funny. Tell me, Doctor Rank, are all the people who work in the bank dependent on Torvald now?

Rank: That's what's so funny?

Nora (smiling and humming): That's my business! *(Walking around the room.)* It's just wonderful to think that we have—that Torvald has—so much power over so many people. *(Takes the bag out of her pocket.)* Doctor Rank, what do you say to a macaroon?

Rank: Macaroons? I thought they were forbidden here.

Nora: Yes, but these are some Kristine gave me.

Mrs. Linde: What! Me?

Nora: Oh, well, don't be upset! How could you know that Torvald had forbidden them? I have to tell you, he's afraid they'll ruin my teeth. But so what? Once in a while, that's all right, isn't it, Doctor Rank? With your permission! *(Puts a macaroon into his mouth.)* You have to have one too, Kristine. And I'll have one, just a little one—or no more than two. *(Walking around.)* I am tremendously happy. There's just one thing in the world now that I would dearly love to do.

Rank: Well, what is it?

Nora: It's something I would dearly love to say, if Torvald could hear me.

Rank: Well, why can't you say it?

Nora: No, I don't dare. It's too shocking.

Mrs. Linde: Shocking?

Rank: Well then, I'd advise you not to say it. Still, in front of us you might risk it. What is it you'd so much like to say if Torvald could hear you?

Nora: I would just love to say—"Well, I'll be damned!"

Rank: Are you crazy?

Mrs. Linde: Nora, dear!

Rank: Here he is. Say it!

Nora (hiding the bag): Shh, shh, shh!

(*Helmer comes out of his room, with his coat over his arm and his hat in his hand.*)

Nora: Well, Torvald dear, did you get rid of him?

Helmer: Yes, he just left.

Nora: Let me introduce you. This is Kristine. She's just arrived in town.

Helmer: Kristine? I'm sorry, but I don't know any—

Nora: Mrs. Linde, dear, Kristine Linde.

Helmer: Oh, of course. A school friend of my wife's, I believe?

Mrs. Linde: Yes, we knew each other back then.

Nora: And just think, she's come all this way in order to see you.

Helmer: What do you mean?

Mrs. Linde: No, really, I—

Nora: Kristine is extremely good at bookkeeping, and she's very eager to work for some talented man, so she can perfect her skills—

Helmer: Very sensible, Mrs. Linde.

Nora: And when she heard that you'd been named manager of the bank—the news was sent by telegraph, you know—she traveled here as quickly as she could. Torvald, I'm sure you'll be able to do something for Kristine, for my sake, won't you?

Helmer: Well, it's not completely out of the question. I expect that you're a widow, Mrs. Linde?

Mrs. Linde: Yes.

Helmer: And you've had some bookkeeping experience?

Mrs. Linde: Yes, a fair amount.

Helmer: Ah! Well, there's a very good chance that I'll be able to find something for you—

Nora (clapping her hands): What did I tell you? What did I tell you?

Helmer: You've just come at a lucky moment, Mrs. Linde.

Mrs. Linde: How can I thank you?

Helmer: There's no need. (*Puts on his coat.*) But now you must excuse me—

Rank: Wait a minute. I'll come with you. (*Brings his fur coat from the hall and warms it at the fire.*)

Nora: Don't be long, Torvald dear.

Helmer: About an hour, that's all.

Nora: Are you leaving too, Kristine?

Mrs. Linde (putting on her cloak): Yes, I have to go and look for a place to stay.

Helmer: Oh, well then, we can walk down the street together.

Nora (helping her): It's too bad we're so short of space here. I'm afraid it's impossible for us—

Mrs. Linde: Please don't even think of it! Goodbye, Nora dear, and many thanks.

Nora: Goodbye for now. Of course you'll come back this evening. And you too, Dr. Rank. What do you say? If you're feeling up to it? Oh, you have to be! Wrap yourself up warmly.

(*They go to the door all talking together. Children's voices are heard on the staircase.*)

Nora: There they are! There they are!

(*She runs to open the door. The nursemaid comes in with the children.*)

Come in! Come in! (*Stoops and kisses them.*) Oh, you sweet blessings! Look at them, Kristine! Aren't they darlings?

Rank: Let's not stand here in the draft.

Helmer: Come along, Mrs. Linde. Only a mother will be able to stand it in here now!

(*Rank, Helmer, and Mrs. Linde go downstairs. The Nursemaid comes forward with the children. Nora shuts the hall door.*)

Nora: How fresh and healthy you look! Cheeks as red as apples and roses. (*The children all talk at once while she speaks to them.*) Did you have a lot of fun? That's wonderful! What, you pulled Emmy and Bob on the sled? Both at once? That was really something. You *are* a clever boy, Ivar. Let me take her for a little, Anne Marie. My sweet little baby doll! (*Takes the baby from the maid and dances her up and down.*) Yes, yes, mother will dance with Bob too. What! Have you been throwing snowballs? I wish I'd been there too! No, no, I'll take their things off, Anne Marie, please let me do it, it's such fun. Go inside now, you look half frozen. There's some hot coffee for you on the stove.

(*The Nursemaid goes into the room on the left. Nora takes off the children's things and throws them around, while they all talk to her at once.*)

Nora: Really! Did a big dog run after you? But it didn't bite you? No, dogs don't bite nice little dolly children. You mustn't look at the packages, Ivar. What are they? Oh, I'll bet you'd like to know. No, no, it's something boring! Come on, let's play a game! What should we play? Hide and seek? Yes, we'll play hide and seek. Bob will hide first. You want me to hide? All right, I'll hide first.

(*She and the children laugh and shout, and romp in and out of the room. At last Nora hides under the table. The children rush in and out looking for her, but they don't see her. They hear her smothered laughter, run to the table, lift up the cloth and find her. Shouts of laughter. She crawls forward and pretends to scare them. More laughter. Meanwhile there has been a knock at the hall door, but none of them has noticed it. The door is opened halfway and Krogstad appears. He waits for a little while. The game goes on.*)

Krogstad: Excuse me, Mrs. Helmer.

Nora (with a stifled cry, turns round and gets up onto her knees): Oh! What do you want?

Krogstad: Excuse me, the outside door was open. I suppose someone forgot to shut it.

Nora (rising): My husband is out, Mr. Krogstad.

Krogstad: I know that.

Nora: What do you want here, then?

Krogstad: A word with you.

Nora: With me? (*To the children, gently.*) Go inside to Anne Marie. What? No, the strange man won't hurt Mother. When he's gone we'll play another game. (*She takes the children into the room on the left, and shuts the door after them.*) You want to speak to me?

Krogstad: Yes, I do.

Nora: Today? It isn't the first of the month yet.

Krogstad: No, it's Christmas Eve, and it's up to you what kind of Christmas you're going to have.

Nora: What do you mean? Today it's absolutely impossible for me—

Krogstad: We won't talk about that until later on. This is something else. I presume you can spare me a moment?

Nora: Yes, yes, I can. Although . . .

Krogstad: Good. I was in Olsen's restaurant and I saw your husband going down the street—

Nora: Yes?

Krogstad: With a lady.

Nora: So?

Krogstad: May I be so bold as to ask if it was a Mrs. Linde?

Nora: It was.

Krogstad: Just arrived in town?

Nora: Yes, today.

Krogstad: She's a very good friend of yours, isn't she?

Nora: She is. But I don't see—

Krogstad: I knew her too, once upon a time.

Nora: I'm aware of that.

Krogstad: Are you? So you know all about it. I thought so. Then I can ask you, without beating around the bush. Is Mrs. Linde going to work in the bank?

Nora: What right do you have to question me, Mr. Krogstad? You're one of my husband's employees. But since you ask, I'll tell you. Yes, Mrs. Linde is going to work in the bank. And I'm the one who spoke up for her, Mr. Krogstad. So now you know.

Krogstad: So I was right, then.

Nora (walking up and down the stage): Sometimes one has a tiny little bit of influence, I should hope. Just because I'm a woman, it doesn't necessarily follow that— You know, when somebody's in a subordinate position, Mr. Krogstad, they should really be careful to avoid offending anyone who—who—

Krogstad: Who has influence?

Nora: Exactly.

Krogstad (changing his tone): Mrs. Helmer, may I ask you to use *your* influence on my behalf?

Nora: What? What do you mean?

Krogstad: Will you be kind enough to see to it that I'm allowed to keep my subordinate position in the bank?

Nora: What do you mean by that? Who's threatening to take your job away from you?

Krogstad: Oh, there's no need to keep up the pretence of ignorance. I can understand that your friend isn't very anxious to expose herself to the chance of rubbing shoulders with me. And now I realize exactly who I have to thank for pushing me out.

Nora: But I swear to you—

Krogstad: Yes, yes. But, to get right to the point, there's still time to prevent it, and I would advise you to use your influence to do so.

Nora: But, Mr. Krogstad, I have no influence.

Krogstad: Oh no? Didn't you yourself just say—

Nora: Well, obviously, I didn't mean for you to take it that way. Me? What would make you think I have that kind of influence with my husband?

Krogstad: Oh, I've known your husband since our school days. I don't suppose he's any more unpersuadable than other husbands.

Nora: If you're going to talk disrespectfully about my husband, I'll have to ask you to leave my house.

Krogstad: Bold talk, Mrs. Helmer.

Nora: I'm not afraid of you anymore. When the New Year comes, I'll soon be free of the whole thing.

Krogstad (controlling himself): Listen to me, Mrs. Helmer. If I have to, I'm ready to fight for my little job in the bank as if I were fighting for my life.

Nora: So it seems.

Krogstad: It's not just for the sake of the money. In fact, that matters the least to me. There's another reason. Well, I might as well tell you. Here's my situation. I suppose, like everybody else, you know that many years ago I did something pretty foolish.

Nora: I think I heard something about it.

Krogstad: It never got as far as the courtroom, but every door seemed closed to me after that. So I got involved in the business that you know about. I had to do something, and, honestly, I think there are many worse than me. But now I have to get myself free of all that. My sons are growing up. For their sake I have to try to win back as much respect as I can in this town. The job in the bank was like the first step up for me, and now your husband is going to kick me downstairs back into the mud.

Nora: But you have to believe me, Mr. Krogstad, it's not in my power to help you at all.

Krogstad: Then it's because you don't want to. But I have ways of making you.

Nora: You don't mean you'll tell my husband I owe you money?

Krogstad: Hm! And what if I did tell him?

Nora: That would be a terrible thing for you to do. *(Sobbing.)* To think he would learn my secret, which has been my pride and joy, in such an ugly, clumsy way—that he would learn it from you! And it would put me in a horribly uncomfortable position—

Krogstad: Just uncomfortable?

Nora (impetuously): Well, go ahead and do it, then! And it'll be so much the worse for you. My husband will see for himself how vile you are, and then you'll lose your job for sure.

Krogstad: I asked you if it's just an uncomfortable situation at home that you're afraid of.

Nora: If my husband does find out about it, of course he'll immediately pay you what I still owe, and then we'll be through with you once and for all.

Krogstad (coming a step closer): Listen to me, Mrs. Helmer. Either you have a very bad memory or you don't know much about business. I can see I'm going to have to remind you of a few details.

Nora: What do you mean?

Krogstad: When your husband was sick, you came to me to borrow four thousand, eight hundred kroner.

Nora: I didn't know anyone else to go to.

Krogstad: I promised to get you that amount—

Nora: Yes, and you did so.

Krogstad: I promised to get you that amount, on certain conditions. You were so preoccupied with your husband's illness, and you were so anxious to get the money for your trip, that you seem to have paid no attention to the conditions of our bargain. So it won't be out of place for me to remind you of them. Now, I promised to get the money on the security of a note which I drew up.

Nora: Yes, and which I signed.

Krogstad: Good. But underneath your signature there were a few lines naming your father as a co-signer who guaranteed the repayment of the loan. Your father was supposed to sign that part.

Nora: Supposed to? He did sign it.

Krogstad: I had left the date blank. That was because your father was supposed to fill in the date when he signed the paper. Do you remember that?

Nora: Yes, I think I remember. . . .

Krogstad: Then I gave you the note to mail to your father. Isn't that so?

Nora: Yes.

Krogstad: And obviously you mailed it right away, because five or six days later you brought me the note with your father's signature. And then I gave you the money.

Nora: Well, haven't I been paying it back regularly?

Krogstad: Fairly regularly, yes. But, to get back to the point, that must have been a very difficult time for you, Mrs. Helmer.

Nora: Yes, it was.

Krogstad: Your father was very sick, wasn't he?

Nora: He was very near the end.

Krogstad: And he died soon after?

Nora: Yes.

Krogstad: Tell me, Mrs. Helmer, can you by any chance remember what day your father died? On what day of the month, I mean.

Nora: Papa died on the 29th of September.

Krogstad: That's right. I looked it up myself. And, since that is the case, there's something extremely peculiar (*taking a piece of paper from his pocket*) that I can't account for.

Nora: Peculiar in what way? I don't know—

Krogstad: The peculiar thing, Mrs. Helmer, is the fact that your father signed this note three days after he died.

Nora: What do you mean? I don't understand—

Krogstad: Your father died on the 29th of September. But, look here. Your father dated his signature the 2nd of October. It is mighty peculiar, isn't it? (*Nora is silent.*) Can you explain it to me? (*Nora is still silent.*) And what's just as peculiar is that the words "October 2," as well as the year, are not in your father's handwriting, but in someone else's, which I think I recognize. Well, of course it can all be explained. Your father might have forgotten to date his signature, and someone else might have filled in the date before they knew that he had died. There's no harm in that. It all depends on the signature, and that's genuine, isn't it, Mrs. Helmer? It was your father himself who signed his name here?

Nora (*after a short pause, lifts her head up and looks defiantly at him*): No, it wasn't. I'm the one who wrote Papa's name.

Krogstad: Are you aware that you're making a very serious confession?

Nora: How so? You'll get your money soon.

Krogstad: Let me ask you something. Why didn't you send the paper to your father?

Nora: It was out of the question. Papa was too sick. If I had asked him to sign something, I'd have had to tell him what the money was for, and when he was so sick himself I couldn't tell him that my husband's life was in danger. It was out of the question.

Krogstad: It would have been better for you if you'd given up your trip abroad.

Nora: No, that was impossible. That trip was to save my husband's life. I couldn't give that up.

Krogstad: But didn't it ever occur to you that you were committing a fraud against me?

Nora: I couldn't take that into account. I didn't trouble myself about you at all. I couldn't stand you, because you put so many heartless difficulties in my way, even though you knew how seriously ill my husband was.

Krogstad: Mrs. Helmer, you evidently don't realize clearly what you're guilty of. But, believe me, my one mistake, which cost me my whole reputation, was nothing more and nothing worse than what you did.

Nora: You? You expect me to believe that you were brave enough to take a risk to save your wife's life?

Krogstad: The law doesn't care about motives.

Nora: Then the law must be very stupid.

Krogstad: Stupid or not, it's the law that's going to judge you, if I produce this paper in court.

Nora: I don't believe it. Isn't a daughter allowed to spare her dying father anxiety and concern? Isn't a wife allowed to save her husband's life? I don't know much about the law, but I'm sure there must be provisions for things like that. Don't you know anything about such provisions? You seem like a very poor excuse for a lawyer, Mr. Krogstad.

Krogstad: That's as may be. But business, the kind of business you and I have done together—do you think I don't know about that? Fine. Do what you want. But I can assure you of this. If I lose everything all over again, this time you're going down with me. *(He bows, and goes out through the hall.)*

Nora (appears buried in thought for a short time, then tosses her head): Nonsense! He's just trying to scare me! I'm not as naïve as he thinks I am. *(Begins to busy herself putting the children's things in order.)* And yet . . . ? No, it's impossible! I did it for love.

Children (in the doorway on the left): Mother, the strange man is gone. He went out through the gate.

Nora: Yes, dears, I know. But don't tell anyone about the strange man. Do you hear me? Not even Papa.

Children: No, Mother. But will you come and play with us again?

Nora: No, no, not just now.

Children: But, Mother, you promised us.

Nora: Yes, but I can't right now. Go inside. I have too much to do. Go inside, my sweet little darlings.

(She gets them into the room bit by bit and shuts the door on them. Then she sits down on the sofa, takes up a piece of needlework and sews a few stitches, but soon stops.)

No! *(Throws down the work, gets up, goes to the hall door and calls out.)* Helene! Bring the tree in. *(Goes to the table on the left, opens a drawer, and stops again.)* No, no! It's completely impossible!

Maid (coming in with the tree): Where should I put it, ma'am?

Nora: Here, in the middle of the floor.

Maid: Do you need anything else?

Nora: No, thank you. I have everything I want.

(Exit Maid.)

Nora (begins decorating the tree): A candle here, and flowers here. That horrible man! It's all nonsense, there's nothing wrong. The tree is going to be magnificent! I'll do everything I can think of to make you happy, Torvald! I'll sing for you, dance for you—

(Helmer comes in with some papers under his arm.)

Oh! You're back already?

Helmer: Yes. Has anyone been here?

Nora: Here? No.

Helmer: That's strange. I saw Krogstad going out the gate.

Nora: You did? Oh yes, I forgot, Krogstad was here for a moment.

Helmer: Nora, I can tell from the way you're acting that he was here begging you to put in a good word for him.

Nora: Yes, he was.

Helmer: And you were supposed to pretend it was all your idea and not tell me that he'd been here to see you. Didn't he beg you to do that too?

Nora: Yes, Torvald, but—

Helmer: Nora, Nora, to think that you'd be a party to that sort of thing! To have any kind of conversation with a man like that, and promise him anything at all? And to lie to me in the bargain?

Nora: Lie?

Helmer: Didn't you tell me no one had been here? *(Shakes his finger at her.)* My little songbird must never do that again. A songbird must have a clean beak to chirp with. No false notes! *(Puts his arm round her waist.)* That's true, isn't it? Yes, I'm sure it is. *(Lets her go.)* We won't mention this again. *(Sits down by the stove.)* How warm and cozy it is here! *(Turns over his papers.)*

Nora (after a short pause, during which she busies herself with the Christmas tree): Torvald!

Helmer: Yes?

Nora: I'm really looking forward to the masquerade ball at the Stenborgs' the day after tomorrow.

Helmer: And I'm really curious to see what you're going to surprise me with.

Nora: Oh, it was very silly of me to want to do that.

Helmer: What do you mean?

Nora: I can't come up with anything good. Everything I think of seems so stupid and pointless.

Helmer: So my little Nora finally admits that?

Nora (standing behind his chair with her arms on the back of it): Are you very busy, Torvald?

Helmer: Well . . .

Nora: What are all those papers?

Helmer: Bank business.

Nora: Already?

Helmer: I've gotten the authority from the retiring manager to reorganize the work procedures and make the necessary personnel changes. I need to take care of it during Christmas week, so as to have everything in place for the new year.

Nora: Then that was why this poor Krogstad—

Helmer: Hm!

Nora (leans against the back of his chair and strokes his hair): If you weren't so busy, I would have asked you for a huge favor, Torvald.

Helmer: What favor? Tell me.

Nora: No one has such good taste as you. And I really want to look nice at the fancy-dress ball. Torvald, couldn't you take me in hand and decide what I should go as and what kind of costume I should wear?

Helmer: Aha! So my obstinate little woman has to get someone to come to her rescue?

Nora: Yes, Torvald, I can't get along at all without your help.

Helmer: All right, I'll think it over. I'm sure we'll come up with something.

Nora: That's so nice of you. *(Goes to the Christmas tree. A short pause.)* How pretty the red flowers look. But, tell me, was it really something very bad that this Krogstad was guilty of?

Helmer: He forged someone's name. Do you have any idea what that means?

Nora: Isn't it possible that he was forced to do it by necessity?

Helmer: Yes. Or, the way it is in so many cases, by foolishness. I'm not so heartless that I'd absolutely condemn a man because of one mistake like that.

Nora: No, you wouldn't, would you, Torvald?

Helmer: Many a man has been able to rehabilitate himself, if he's openly admitted his guilt and taken his punishment.

Nora: Punishment?

Helmer: But Krogstad didn't do that. He wriggled out of it with lies and trickery, and that's what completely undermined his moral character.

Nora: But do you think that that would—

Helmer: Just think how a guilty man like that has to lie and act like a hypocrite with everyone, how he has to wear a mask in front of the people closest to him, even with his own wife and children. And the children. That's the most terrible part of it all, Nora.

Nora: How so?

Helmer: Because an atmosphere of lies infects and poisons the whole life of a home. Every breath the children take in a house like that is full of the germs of moral corruption.

Nora (coming closer to him): Are you sure of that?

Helmer: My dear, I've seen it many times in my legal career. Almost everyone who's gone wrong at a young age had a dishonest mother.

Nora: Why only the mother?

Helmer: It usually seems to be the mother's influence, though naturally a bad father would have the same result. Every lawyer knows this. This Krogstad, now, has been systematically poisoning his own children with lies and deceit. That's why I say he's lost all moral character. *(Holds out his hands to her.)* And that's why my sweet little Nora must promise me not to plead his cause. Give me your hand on it. Come now, what's this? Give me your hand. There, that's settled. Believe me, it would be impossible for me to work with him. It literally makes me feel physically ill to be around people like that.

Nora (takes her hand out of his and goes to the opposite side of the Christmas tree): How hot it is in here! And I have so much to do.

Helmer (getting up and putting his papers in order): Yes, and I have to try to read through some of these before dinner. And I have to think about your costume, too. And it's just possible I'll have something wrapped in gold paper to hang up on the tree. *(Puts his hand on her head.)* My precious little songbird! *(He goes into his study and closes the door behind him.)*

Nora (after a pause, whispers): No, no, it's not true. It's impossible. It has to be impossible.

(*The nursemaid opens the door on the left.*)

Nursemaid: The little ones are begging so hard to be allowed to come in to see Mama.
Nora: No, no, no! Don't let them come in to me! You stay with them, Anne Marie.
Nursemaid: Very well, ma'am. (*Shuts the door.*)
Nora (pale with terror): Corrupt my little children? Poison my home? (*A short pause. Then she tosses her head.*) It's not true. It can't possibly be true.

ACT II

The same scene. The Christmas tree is in the corner by the piano, stripped of its ornaments and with burnt-down candle-ends on its disheveled branches. Nora's coat and hat are lying on the sofa. She is alone in the room, walking around uneasily. She stops by the sofa and picks up her coat.

Nora (drops her coat): Someone's coming! (*Goes to the door and listens.*) No, there's no one there. Of course, no one will come today. It's Christmas Day. And not tomorrow either. But maybe . . . (*opens the door and looks out*) No, nothing in the mailbox. It's empty. (*Comes forward.*) What nonsense! Of course he can't be serious about it. A thing like that couldn't happen. It's impossible. I have three little children.

(*Enter the nursemaid Anne Marie from the room on the left, carrying a big cardboard box.*)

Nursemaid: I finally found the box with the costume.
Nora: Thank you. Put it on the table.
Nursemaid (doing so): But it really needs to be mended.
Nora: I'd like to tear it into a hundred thousand pieces.
Nursemaid: What an idea! It can easily be fixed up. All you need is a little patience.
Nora: Yes, I'll go get Mrs. Linde to come and help me with it.
Nursemaid: What, going out again? In this horrible weather? You'll catch cold, Miss Nora, and make yourself sick.
Nora: Well, worse things than that might happen. How are the children?
Nursemaid: The poor little ones are playing with their Christmas presents, but—
Nora: Do they ask for me much?
Nursemaid: You see, they're so used to having their Mama with them.
Nora: Yes, but, Anne Marie, I won't be able to spend as much time with them now as I did before.
Nursemaid: Oh well, young children quickly get used to anything.
Nora: Do you think so? Do you think they'd forget their mother if she went away for good?
Nursemaid: Good heavens! Went away for good?
Nora: Anne Marie, I want you to tell me something I've often wondered about. How could you have the heart to let your own child be raised by strangers?
Nursemaid: I had to, if I wanted to be little Nora's nursemaid.
Nora: Yes, but how could you agree to it?

Nursemaid: What, when I was going to get such a good situation out of it? A poor girl who's gotten herself in trouble should be glad to. Besides, that worthless man didn't do a single thing for me.

Nora: But I suppose your daughter has completely forgotten you.

Nursemaid: No, she hasn't, not at all. She wrote to me when she was confirmed, and again when she got married.

Nora (putting her arms round her neck): Dear old Anne Marie, you were such a good mother to me when I was little.

Nursemaid: Poor little Nora, you had no other mother but me.

Nora: And if my little ones had no other mother, I'm sure that you would—What nonsense I'm talking! *(Opens the box.)* Go in and see to them. Now I have to . . . You'll see how lovely I'll look tomorrow.

Nursemaid: I'm sure there'll be no one at the ball as lovely as you, Miss Nora.

(Goes into the room on the left.)

Nora (begins to unpack the box, but soon pushes it away from her): If only I dared to go out. If only no one would come. If only I could be sure nothing would happen here in the meantime. What nonsense! No one's going to come. I just have to stop thinking about it. This muff needs to be brushed. What beautiful, beautiful gloves! Stop thinking about it, stop thinking about it! One, two, three, four, five, six—*(Screams.)* Aaah! Somebody *is* coming—*(Makes a movement towards the door, but stands in hesitation.)*

(Enter Mrs. Linde from the hall, where she has taken off her coat and hat.)

Nora: Oh, it's you, Kristine. There's no one else out in the hall, is there? How good of you to come!

Mrs. Linde: I heard you came by asking for me.

Nora: Yes, I was passing by. As a matter of fact, it's something you could help me with. Let's sit down here on the sofa. Listen, tomorrow evening there's going to be a fancy-dress ball at the Stenborgs'—they live upstairs from us—and Torvald wants me to go as a Neapolitan fisher-girl and dance the tarantella. I learned it when we were at Capri.

Mrs. Linde: I see. You're going to give them the whole show.

Nora: Yes, Torvald wants me to. Look, here's the dress. Torvald had it made for me there, but now it's all so torn, and I don't have any idea—

Mrs. Linde: We can easily fix that. Some of the trim has just come loose here and there. Do you have a needle and thread? That's all we need.

Nora: This is so nice of you.

Mrs. Linde (sewing): So you're going to be dressed up tomorrow, Nora. I'll tell you what. I'll stop by for a moment so I can see you in your finery. Oh, meanwhile I've completely forgotten to thank you for a delightful evening last night.

Nora (gets up, and crosses the stage): Well, I didn't think last night was as pleasant as usual. You should have come to town a little earlier, Kristine. Torvald really knows how to make a home pleasant and attractive.

Mrs. Linde: And so do you, if you ask me. You're not your father's daughter for nothing. But tell me, is Doctor Rank always as depressed as he was yesterday?

Nora: No, yesterday it was especially noticeable. But you have to understand that he has a very serious disease. He has tuberculosis of the spine, poor creature. His father was a horrible man who always had mistresses, and that's why his son has been sickly since childhood, if you know what I mean.

Mrs. Linde (*dropping her sewing*): But, my dear Nora, how do you know anything about such things?

Nora (*walking around the room*): Pooh! When you have three children, you get visits now and then from—from married women, who know something about medical matters, and they talk about one thing and another.

Mrs. Linde (*goes on sewing. A short silence*): Does Doctor Rank come here every day?

Nora: Every day, like clockwork. He's Torvald's best friend, and a great friend of mine too. He's just like one of the family.

Mrs. Linde: But tell me, is he really sincere? I mean, isn't he the kind of man who tends to play up to people?

Nora: No, not at all. What makes you think that?

Mrs. Linde: When you introduced him to me yesterday, he told me he'd often heard my name mentioned in this house, but later I could see that your husband didn't have the slightest idea who I was. So how could Doctor Rank—?

Nora: That's true, Kristine. Torvald is so ridiculously fond of me that he wants me completely to himself, as he says. At first he used to seem almost jealous if I even mentioned any of my friends back home, so naturally I stopped talking about them to him. But I often talk about things like that with Doctor Rank, because he likes hearing about them.

Mrs. Linde: Listen to me, Nora. You're still like a child in a lot of ways, and I'm older than you and more experienced. So pay attention. You'd better stop all this with Doctor Rank.

Nora: Stop all what?

Mrs. Linde: Two things, I think. Yesterday you talked some nonsense about a rich admirer who was going to leave you his money—

Nora: An admirer who doesn't exist, unfortunately! But so what?

Mrs. Linde: Is Doctor Rank a wealthy man?

Nora: Yes, he is.

Mrs. Linde: And he has no dependents?

Nora: No, no one. But—

Mrs. Linde: And he comes here every day?

Nora: Yes, I told you he does.

Mrs. Linde: But how can such a well-bred man be so tactless?

Nora: I don't understand what you mean.

Mrs. Linde: Don't try to play dumb, Nora. Do you think I didn't guess who lent you the four thousand, eight hundred kroner?

Nora: Are you out of your mind? How can you even think that? A friend of ours, who comes here every day! Don't you realize what an incredibly awkward position that would put me in?

Mrs. Linde: Then he's really not the one?

Nora: Absolutely not. It would never have come into my head for one second. Besides, he had nothing to lend back then. He inherited his money later on.

Mrs. Linde: Well, I think that was lucky for you, my dear Nora.

Nora: No, it would never have crossed my mind to ask Doctor Rank. Although I'm sure that if I had asked him—

Mrs. Linde: But of course you won't.

Nora: Of course not. I have no reason to think I could possibly need to. But I'm absolutely certain that if I told Doctor Rank—

Mrs. Linde: Behind your husband's back?

Nora: I have to finish up with the other one, and that'll be behind his back too. I've got to wash my hands of him.

Mrs. Linde: Yes, that's what I told you yesterday, but—

Nora (walking up and down): A man can take care of these things so much more easily than a woman.

Mrs. Linde: If he's your husband, yes.

Nora: Nonsense! *(Standing still.)* When you pay off a debt you get your note back, don't you?

Mrs. Linde: Yes, of course.

Nora: And you can tear it into a hundred thousand pieces and burn up the filthy, nasty piece of paper!

Mrs. Linde (stares at her, puts down her sewing and gets up slowly): Nora, you're hiding something from me.

Nora: You can tell by looking at me?

Mrs. Linde: Something's happened to you since yesterday morning. Nora, what is it?

Nora (going nearer to her): Kristine! *(Listens.)* Shh! I hear Torvald. He's come home. Would you mind going in to the children's room for a little while? Torvald can't stand to see all this sewing going on. You can get Anne Marie to help you.

Mrs. Linde (gathering some of the things together): All right, but I'm not leaving this house until we've talked this thing through.

(She goes into the room on the left, as Helmer comes in from the hall.)

Nora (going up to Helmer): I've missed you so much, Torvald dear.

Helmer: Was that the seamstress?

Nora: No, it was Kristine. She's helping me fix up my dress. You'll see how nice I'm going to look.

Helmer: Wasn't that a good idea of mine, now?

Nora: Wonderful! But don't you think it's nice of me, too, to do what you said?

Helmer: Nice, because you do what your husband tells you to? Go on, you silly little thing, I am sure you didn't mean it like that. But I'll stay out of your way. I imagine you'll be trying on your dress.

Nora: I suppose you're going to do some work.

Helmer: Yes. *(Shows her a stack of papers.)* Look at that. I've just been at the bank. *(Turns to go into his room.)*

Nora: Torvald.

Helmer: Yes?

Nora: If your little squirrel were to ask you for something in a very, very charming way—

Helmer: Well?

Nora: Would you do it?

Helmer: I'd have to know what it is, first.

Nora: Your squirrel would run around and do all her tricks if you would be really nice and do what she wants.

Helmer: Speak plainly.

Nora: Your skylark would chirp her beautiful song in every room—

Helmer: Well, my skylark does that anyhow.

Nora: I'd be a little elf and dance in the moonlight for you, Torvald.

Helmer: Nora, you can't be referring to what you talked about this morning.

Nora (moving close to him): Yes, Torvald, I'm really begging you—

Helmer: You really have the nerve to bring that up again?

Nora: Yes, dear, you have to do this for me. You have to let Krogstad keep his job in the bank.

Helmer: My dear Nora, his job is the one that I'm giving to Mrs. Linde.

Nora: Yes, you've been awfully sweet about that. But you could just as easily get rid of somebody else instead of Krogstad.

Helmer: This is just unbelievable stubbornness! Because you decided to foolishly promise that you'd speak up for him, you expect me to—

Nora: That's not the reason, Torvald. It's for your own sake. This man writes for the trashiest newspapers, you've told me so yourself. He can do you an incredible amount of harm. I'm scared to death of him—

Helmer: Oh, I see, it's bad memories that are making you afraid.

Nora: What do you mean?

Helmer: Obviously you're thinking about your father.

Nora: Yes. Yes, of course. You remember what those hateful creatures wrote in the papers about Papa, and how horribly they slandered him. I believe they'd have gotten him fired if the department hadn't sent you over to look into it, and if you hadn't been so kind and helpful to him.

Helmer: My little Nora, there's an important difference between your father and me. His reputation as a public official was not above suspicion. Mine is, and I hope it will continue to be for as long as I hold my office.

Nora: You never can tell what trouble these men might cause. We could be so well off, so snug and happy here in our peaceful home, without a care in the world, you and I and the children, Torvald! That's why I'm begging you to—

Helmer: And the more you plead for him, the more you make it impossible for me to keep him. They already know at the bank that I'm going to fire Krogstad. Do you think I'm going to let them all say that the new manager has changed his mind because his wife said to—

Nora: And what if they did?

Helmer: Right! What does it matter, as long as this stubborn little creature gets her own way! Do you think I'm going to make myself look ridiculous in front of my whole staff, and let people think that I can be pushed around by all sorts of outside influence? That would soon come back to haunt me, you can be sure! And besides, there's one thing that makes it totally impossible for me to have Krogstad working in the bank as long as I'm the manager.

Nora: What's that?

Helmer: I might have been able to overlook his moral failings, if need be—

Nora: Yes, you could do that, couldn't you?

Helmer: And I hear he's a good worker, too. But I knew him when we were boys. It was one of those rash friendships that so often turn out to be a millstone around the neck later on. I might as well tell you straight out, we were very close friends at one time. But he has no tact and no self-restraint, especially when other people are around. He thinks he has the right to still call me by my first name, and every minute it's Torvald this and Torvald that. I don't mind telling you, I find it extremely annoying. He would make my position at the bank intolerable.

Nora: Torvald, I can't believe you're serious.

Helmer: Oh no? Why not?

Nora: Because it's so petty.

Helmer: What do you mean, petty? You think I'm petty?

Nora: No, just the opposite, dear, and that's why I can't—

Helmer: It's the same thing. You say my attitude's petty, so I must be petty too! Petty! Fine! Well, I'll put a stop to this once and for all. (*Goes to the hall door and calls.*) Helene!

Nora: What are you going to do?

Helmer (*looking among his papers*): Settle it.

(*Enter Maid.*)

Here, take this letter downstairs right now. Find a messenger and tell him to deliver it, and to be quick about it. The address is on it, and here's the money.

Maid: Yes, sir. (*Exits with the letter.*)

Helmer (*putting his papers together*): There, Little Pigheaded Miss.

Nora (*breathlessly*): Torvald, what was that letter?

Helmer: Krogstad's notice.

Nora: Call her back, Torvald! There's still time. Oh, Torvald, call her back! Do it for my sake—for your own sake—for the children's sake! Do you hear me, Torvald? Call her back! You don't know what that letter can do to us.

Helmer: It's too late.

Nora: Yes, it's too late.

Helmer: My dear Nora, I can forgive this anxiety of yours, even though it's insulting to me. It really is. Don't you think it's insulting to suggest that I should be afraid of retaliation from a grubby pen-pusher? But I forgive you anyway, because it's such a beautiful demonstration of how much you love me. (*Takes her in his arms.*) And that is as it should be, my own darling Nora. Come what may, you can rest assured that I'll have both courage and strength if necessary. You'll see that I'm man enough to take everything on myself.

Nora (*in a horror-stricken voice*): What do you mean by that?

Helmer: Everything, I say.

Nora (*recovering herself*): You'll never have to do that.

Helmer: That's right, we'll take it on together, Nora, as man and wife. That's just how it should be. (*Caressing her.*) Are you satisfied now? There, there! Don't look at me that way, like a frightened dove! This whole thing is just your imagination running away with you. Now you should go and run through the tarantella and practice your tambourine. I'll go into my study and shut the door so I can't hear anything. You can make all the noise you want. (*Turns back at the door.*) And when Rank comes, tell him where I am.

(*Nods to her, takes his papers and goes into his room, and shuts the door behind him.*)

Nora (*bewildered with anxiety, stands as if rooted to the spot and whispers*): He's capable of doing it. He's going to do it. He'll do it in spite of everything. No, not that! Never, never! Anything but that! Oh, for somebody to help me find some way out of this! (*The doorbell rings.*) Doctor Rank! Anything but that—anything, whatever it is!

(*She puts her hands over her face, pulls herself together, goes to the door and opens it. Rank is standing in the hall, hanging up his coat. During the following dialogue it starts to grow dark.*)

Nora: Hello, Doctor Rank. I recognized your ring. But you'd better not go in and see Torvald just now. I think he's busy with something.

Rank: And you?

Nora (brings him in and shuts the door behind him): Oh, you know perfectly well I always have time for you.

Rank: Thank you. I'll make use of it for as long as I can.

Nora: What does that mean, for as long as you can?

Rank: Why, does that frighten you?

Nora: It was such a strange way of putting it. Is something going to happen?

Rank: Nothing but what I've been expecting for a long time. But I never thought it would happen so soon.

Nora (gripping him by the arm): What have you found out? Doctor Rank, you must tell me.

Rank (sitting down by the stove): I'm done for. And there's nothing I can do about it.

Nora (with a sigh of relief): Oh—you're talking about yourself?

Rank: Who else? And there's no use lying to myself. I'm the sickest patient I have, Mrs. Helmer. Lately I've been adding up my internal account. Bankrupt! In a month I'll probably be rotting in the ground.

Nora: What a horrible thing to say!

Rank: The thing itself is horrible, and the worst of it is all the horrible things I'll have to go through before it's over. I'm going to examine myself just once more. When that's done, I'll be pretty sure when I'm going to start breaking down. There's something I want to say to you. Helmer's sensitive nature makes him completely unable to deal with anything ugly. I don't want him in my sickroom.

Nora: Oh, but, Doctor Rank—

Rank: I won't have him there, period. I'll lock the door to keep him out. As soon as I'm quite sure that the worst has come, I'll send you my card with a black cross on it, and that way you'll know that the final stage of the horror has started.

Nora: You're being really absurd today. And I so much wanted you to be in a good mood.

Rank: With death stalking me? Having to pay this price for another man's sins? Where's the justice in that? In every single family, in one way or another, some such unavoidable retribution is being imposed.

Nora (putting her hands over her ears): Nonsense! Can't you talk about something cheerful?

Rank: Oh, this *is* something cheerful. In fact, it's hilarious. My poor innocent spine has to suffer for my father's youthful self-indulgence.

Nora (sitting at the table on the left): Yes, he did love asparagus and *pâté de foie gras,* didn't he?

Rank: Yes, and truffles.

Nora: Truffles, yes. And oysters too, I suppose?

Rank: Oysters, of course. That goes without saying.

Nora: And oceans of port and champagne. Isn't it sad that all those delightful things should take their revenge on our bones?

Rank: Especially that they should take their revenge on the unlucky bones of people who haven't even had the satisfaction of enjoying them.

Nora: Yes, that's the saddest part of all.

Rank (with a searching look at her): Hm!

Nora (after a short pause): Why did you smile?

Rank: No, it was you who laughed.

Nora: No, it was you who smiled, Doctor Rank!

Rank (rising): You're even more of a tease than I thought you were.

Nora: I am in a crazy mood today.

Rank: Apparently so.

Nora (putting her hands on his shoulders): Dear, dear Doctor Rank, we can't let death take you away from Torvald and me.

Rank: It's a loss that you'll easily recover from. Those who are gone are soon forgotten.

Nora (looking at him anxiously): Do you really believe that?

Rank: People make new friends, and then—

Nora: Who'll make new friends?

Rank: Both you and Helmer, when I'm gone. You yourself are already well on the way to it, I think. What was that Mrs. Linde doing here last night?

Nora: Oho! You're not telling me that you're jealous of poor Kristine, are you?

Rank: Yes, I am. She'll be my successor in this house. When I'm six feet under, this woman will—

Nora: Shh! Don't talk so loud. She's in that room.

Rank: Again today. There, you see.

Nora: She's just come to sew my dress for me. Goodness, how unreasonable you are! *(Sits down on the sofa.)* Be nice now, Doctor Rank, and tomorrow you'll see how beautifully I'll dance, and you can pretend that I'm doing it just for you—and for Torvald too, of course. *(Takes various things out of the box.)* Doctor Rank, come and sit down here, and I'll show you something.

Rank (sitting down): What is it?

Nora: Just look at these!

Rank: Silk stockings.

Nora: Flesh-colored. Aren't they lovely? It's so dark here now, but tomorrow—No, no, no! You're only supposed to look at the feet. Oh well, you have my permission to look at the legs too.

Rank: Hm!

Nora: Why do you look so critical? Don't you think they'll fit me?

Rank: I have no basis for forming an opinion on that subject.

Nora (looks at him for a moment): Shame on you! *(Hits him lightly on the ear with the stockings.)* That's your punishment. *(Folds them up again.)*

Rank: And what other pretty things do I have your permission to look at?

Nora: Not one single thing. That's what you get for being so naughty. *(She looks among the things, humming to herself.)*

Rank (after a short silence): When I'm sitting here, talking to you so intimately this way, I can't imagine for a moment what would have become of me if I'd never come into this house.

Nora (smiling): I believe you really do feel completely at home with us.

Rank (in a lower voice, looking straight in front of him): And to have to leave it all—

Nora: Nonsense, you're not going to leave it.

Rank (as before): And not to be able to leave behind the slightest token of my gratitude, hardly even a fleeting regret. Nothing but an empty place to be filled by the first person who comes along.

Nora: And if I were to ask you now for a—No, never mind!

Rank: For a what?

Nora: For a great proof of your friendship—

Rank: Yes, yes!

Nora: I mean a tremendously huge favor—

Rank: Would you really make me so happy, just this once?

Nora: But you don't know what it is yet.

Rank: No, but tell me.

Nora: I really can't, Doctor Rank. It's too much to ask. It involves advice, and help, and a favor—

Rank: So much the better. I can't imagine what you mean. Tell me what it is. You do trust me, don't you?

Nora: More than anyone. I know that you're my best and truest friend, so I'll tell you what it is. Well, Doctor Rank, it's something you have to help me prevent. You know how devoted Torvald is to me, how deeply he loves me. He wouldn't hesitate for a second to give his life for me.

Rank (leaning towards her): Nora, do you think that he's the only one—

Nora (with a slight start): The only one?

Rank: Who would gladly give his life for you.

Nora (sadly): Oh, is that it?

Rank: I'd made up my mind to tell you before I—I go away, and there'll never be a better opportunity than this. Now you know it, Nora. And now you know that you can trust me more than you can trust anyone else.

Nora (rises, deliberately and quietly): Let me by.

Rank (makes room for her to pass him, but sits still): Nora!

Nora (at the hall door): Helene, bring in the lamp. (*Goes over to the stove.*) Dear Doctor Rank, that was really horrible of you.

Rank: To love you just as much as somebody else does? Is that so horrible?

Nora: No, but to go and tell me like that. There was really no need—

Rank: What do you mean? Did you know—

(*Maid enters with lamp, puts it down on the table, and goes out.*)

Nora—Mrs. Helmer—tell me, did you have any idea I felt this way?

Nora: Oh, how do I know whether I did or I didn't? I really can't answer that. How could you be so clumsy, Doctor Rank? When we were getting along so nicely.

Rank: Well, at any rate, now you know that I'm yours to command, body and soul. So won't you tell me what it is?

Nora (looking at him): After what just happened?

Rank: I beg you to let me know what it is.

Nora: I can't tell you anything now.

Rank: Yes, yes. Please don't punish me that way. Give me permission to do anything for you that a man can do.

Nora: You can't do anything for me now. Besides, I really don't need any help at all. The whole thing is just my imagination. It really is. It has to be! (*Sits down in the rocking chair, and smiles at him.*) You're a nice man, Doctor Rank. Don't you feel ashamed of yourself, now that the lamp is lit?

Rank: Not a bit. But maybe it would be better if I left—and never came back?

Nora: No, no, you can't do that. You must keep coming here just as you always did. You know very well Torvald can't do without you.

Rank: But what about you?

Nora: Oh, I'm always extremely pleased to see you.

Rank: And that's just what gave me the wrong idea. You're a puzzle to me. I've often felt that you'd almost just as soon be in my company as in Helmer's.

Nora: Yes, you see, there are the people you love the most, and then there are the people whose company you enjoy the most.

Rank: Yes, there's something to that.

Nora: When I lived at home, of course I loved Papa best. But I always thought it was great fun to sneak down to the maids' room, because they never preached at me, and I loved listening to the way they talked to each other.

Rank: I see. So I'm their replacement.

Nora (jumping up and going to him): Oh, dear, sweet Doctor Rank, I didn't mean it that way. But surely you can understand that being with Torvald is a little like being with Papa—

(Enter Maid from the hall.)

Maid: Excuse me, ma'am. *(Whispers and hands her a card.)*

Nora (glancing at the card): Oh! *(Puts it in her pocket.)*

Rank: Is something wrong?

Nora: No, no, not at all. It's just—it's my new dress—

Rank: What? Your dress is lying right there.

Nora: Oh, yes, that one. But this is another one, one that I ordered. I don't want Torvald to find out about it—

Rank: Oh! So that was the big secret.

Nora: Yes, that's it. Why don't you just go inside and see him? He's in his study. Stay with him for as long as—

Rank: Put your mind at ease. I won't let him escape. *(Goes into Helmer's study.)*

Nora (to the maid): And he's waiting in the kitchen?

Maid: Yes, ma'am. He came up the back stairs.

Nora: Didn't you tell him no one was home?

Maid: Yes, but it didn't do any good.

Nora: He won't go away?

Maid: No, he says he won't leave until he sees you, ma'am.

Nora: Well, show him in, but quietly. Helene, I don't want you to say anything about this to anyone. It's a surprise for my husband.

Maid: Yes, ma'am. I understand. *(Exit.)*

Nora: This horrible thing is really going to happen! It's going to happen in spite of me! No, no, no, it can't happen! I can't let it happen!

(She bolts the door of Helmer's study. The maid opens the hall door for Krogstad and closes it behind him. He is wearing a fur coat, high boots, and a fur cap.)

Nora (advancing towards him): Speak quietly. My husband's home.

Krogstad: What do I care about that?

Nora: What do you want from me?

Krogstad: An explanation of something.

Nora: Be quick, then. What is it?

Krogstad: I suppose you're aware that I've been let go.

Nora: I couldn't prevent it, Mr. Krogstad. I fought for you as hard as I could, but it was no use.

Krogstad: Does your husband love you so little, then? He knows what I can expose you to, and he still goes ahead and—

Nora: How can you think that he knows any such thing?

Krogstad: I didn't think so for a moment. It wouldn't be at all like dear old Torvald
    Helmer to show that kind of courage—

Nora: Mr. Krogstad, a little respect for my husband, please.

Krogstad: Certainly—all the respect he deserves. But since you've kept everything so
    carefully to yourself, may I be bold enough to assume that you see a little more
    clearly than you did yesterday just what it is that you've done?

Nora: More than you could ever teach me.

Krogstad: Yes, such a poor excuse for a lawyer as I am.

Nora: What is it you want from me?

Krogstad: Only to see how you're doing, Mrs. Helmer. I've been thinking about you
    all day. A mere bill collector, a pen-pusher, a—well, a man like me—even he has
    a little of what people call feelings, you know.

Nora: Why don't you show some, then? Think about my little children.

Krogstad: Have you and your husband thought about mine? But never mind about
    that. I just wanted to tell you not to take this business too seriously. I won't make
    any accusations against you. Not for now, anyway.

Nora: No, of course not. I was sure you wouldn't.

Krogstad: The whole thing can be settled amicably. There's no need for anyone to
    know anything about it. It'll be our little secret, just the three of us.

Nora: My husband must never know anything about it.

Krogstad: How are you going to keep him from finding out? Are you telling me that
    you can pay off the whole balance?

Nora: No, not just yet.

Krogstad: Or that you have some other way of raising the money soon?

Nora: No way that I plan to make use of.

Krogstad: Well, in any case, it wouldn't be any use to you now even if you did. If you
    stood in front of me with a stack of bills in each hand, I still wouldn't give you
    back your note.

Nora: What are you planning to do with it?

Krogstad: I just want to hold onto it, just keep it in my possession. No one who isn't
    involved in the matter will ever know anything about it. So, if you've been
    thinking about doing something desperate—

Nora: I have.

Krogstad: If you've been thinking about running away—

Nora: I have.

Krogstad: Or doing something even worse—

Nora: How could you know that?

Krogstad: Stop thinking about it.

Nora: How did you know I'd thought of that?

Krogstad: Most of us think about that at first. I did, too. But I didn't have the courage.

Nora (faintly): Neither do I.

Krogstad (in a tone of relief): No, that's true, isn't it? You don't have the courage either?

Nora: No, I don't. I don't.

Krogstad: Besides, it would have been an incredibly stupid thing to do. Once the first
    storm at home blows over . . . I have a letter for your husband in my pocket.

Nora: Telling him everything?

Krogstad: As gently as possible.

Nora (quickly): He can't see that letter. Tear it up. I'll find some way of getting money.

Krogstad: Excuse me, Mrs. Helmer, but didn't I just tell you—

Nora: I'm not talking about what I owe you. Tell me how much you want from my husband, and I'll get the money.

Krogstad: I don't want any money from your husband.

Nora: Then what do you want?

Krogstad: I'll tell you what I want. I want a fresh start, Mrs. Helmer, and I want to move up in the world. And your husband's going to help me do it. I've steered clear of anything questionable for the last year and a half. In all that time I've been struggling along, pinching every penny. I was content to work my way up step by step. But now I've been fired, and it's not going to be enough just to get my job back, as if you people were doing me some huge favor. I want to move up, I tell you. I want to get back into the bank again, but with a promotion. Your husband's going to have to find me a position—

Nora: He'll never do it!

Krogstad: Oh yes, he will. I know him. He won't dare object. And as soon as I'm back there with him, then you'll see! Inside of a year I'll be the manager's right-hand man. It'll be Nils Krogstad, not Torvald Helmer, who's running the bank.

Nora: That's never going to happen!

Krogstad: Do you mean that you'll—

Nora: I have enough courage for it now.

Krogstad: Oh, you can't scare me. An elegant, spoiled lady like you—

Nora: You'll see, you'll see.

Krogstad: Under the ice, maybe? Down in the cold, coal-black water? And then floating up to the surface in the spring, all horrible and unrecognizable, with your hair fallen out—

Nora: You can't scare me.

Krogstad: And you can't scare me. People don't do that kind of thing, Mrs. Helmer. Besides, what good would it do? I'd still have him completely in my power.

Nora: Even then? When I'm no longer—

Krogstad: Have you forgotten that your reputation is completely in my hands? (*Nora stands speechless, looking at him.*) Well, now I've warned you. Don't do anything foolish. I'll be expecting an answer from Helmer after he reads my letter. And remember, it's your husband himself who's forced me to act this way again. I'll never forgive him for that. Goodbye, Mrs. Helmer. (*Exits through the hall.*)

Nora (*goes to the hall door, opens it slightly and listens.*): He's leaving. He isn't putting the letter in the box. Oh no, no! He couldn't! (*Opens the door little by little.*) What? He's standing out there. He's not going downstairs. He's hesitating? Is he?

(*A letter drops into the box. Then Krogstad's footsteps are heard, until they die away as he goes downstairs. Nora utters a stifled cry, and runs across the room to the table by the sofa. A short pause.*)

Nora: In the mailbox. (*Steals across to the hall door.*) It's there! Torvald, Torvald, there's no hope for us now!

(*Mrs. Linde comes in from the room on the left, carrying the dress.*)

Mrs. Linde: There, I can't find anything more to mend. Would you like to try it on?

Nora (*in a hoarse whisper*): Kristine, come here.

Mrs. Linde (*throwing the dress down on the sofa*): What's the matter with you? You look so agitated!

Nora: Come here. Do you see that letter? There, look. You can see it through the glass in the mailbox.

Mrs. Linde: Yes, I see it.

Nora: That letter is from Krogstad.

Mrs. Linde: Nora! It was Krogstad who lent you the money!

Nora: Yes, and now Torvald will know all about it.

Mrs. Linde: Believe me, Nora, that's the best thing for both of you.

Nora: You don't know the whole story. I forged a name.

Mrs. Linde: My God!

Nora: There's something I want to say to you, Kristine. I need you to be my witness.

Mrs. Linde: Your witness? What do you mean? What am I supposed to—

Nora: If I should go out of my mind—and it could easily happen—

Mrs. Linde: Nora!

Nora: Or if anything else should happen to me—anything, for instance, that might keep me from being here—

Mrs. Linde: Nora! Nora! What's the matter with you?

Nora: And if it turned out that somebody wanted to take all the responsibility, all the blame, you understand what I mean—

Mrs. Linde: Yes, yes, but how can you imagine—

Nora: Then you must be my witness that it's not true, Kristine. I'm not out of my mind at all. I'm perfectly rational right now, and I'm telling you that no one else ever knew anything about it. I did the whole thing all by myself. Remember that.

Mrs. Linde: I will. But I don't understand all this.

Nora: How could you understand it? Or the miracle that's going to happen!

Mrs. Linde: A miracle?

Nora: Yes, a miracle! But it's so terrible, Kristine. I can't let it happen, not for the whole world.

Mrs. Linde: I'll go and see Krogstad right this minute.

Nora: No, don't. He'll do something to hurt you too.

Mrs. Linde: There was a time when he would have gladly done anything for my sake.

Nora: What?

Mrs. Linde: Where does he live?

Nora: How should I know? Yes *(feeling in her pocket)*, here's his card. But the letter, the letter—

Helmer (calls from his room, knocking at the door): Nora!

Nora (cries out anxiously): What is it? What do you want?

Helmer: Don't be so afraid. We're not coming in. You've locked the door. Are you trying on your dress?

Nora: Yes, that's it. Oh, it's going to look so nice, Torvald.

Mrs. Linde (who has read the card): Look, he lives right around the corner.

Nora: But it's no use. It's all over. The letter's lying right there in the box.

Mrs. Linde: And your husband has the key?

Nora: Yes, always.

Mrs. Linde: Krogstad can ask for his letter back unread. He'll have to make up some reason—

Nora: But now is just about the time that Torvald usually—

Mrs. Linde: You have to prevent him. Go in and talk to him. I'll be back as soon as I can.

(She hurries out through the hall door.)

Nora (goes to Helmer's door, opens it and peeps in): Torvald!

Helmer (from the inner room): Well? May I finally come back into my own room? Come along, Rank, now you'll see—(*Stopping in the doorway.*) But what's this?

Nora: What's what, dear?

Helmer: Rank led me to expect an amazing transformation.

Rank (in the doorway): So I understood, but apparently I was mistaken.

Nora: Yes, nobody gets to admire me in my dress until tomorrow.

Helmer: But, my dear Nora, you look exhausted. Have you been practicing too much?

Nora: No, I haven't been practicing at all.

Helmer: But you'll have to—

Nora: Yes, of course I will, Torvald. But I can't get anywhere without you helping me. I've completely forgotten the whole thing.

Helmer: Oh, we'll soon get you back up to form again.

Nora: Yes, help me, Torvald. Promise that you will! I'm so nervous about it—all those people. I need you to devote yourself completely to me this evening. Not even the tiniest little bit of business. You can't even pick up a pen. Do you promise, Torvald dear?

Helmer: I promise. This evening I will be wholly and absolutely at your service, you helpless little creature. But first I'm just going to—(*Goes towards the hall door.*)

Nora: Just going to what?

Helmer: To see if there's any mail.

Nora: No, no! Don't do that, Torvald!

Helmer: Why not?

Nora: Torvald, please don't. There's nothing there.

Helmer: Well, let me look. (*Turns to go to the mailbox. Nora, at the piano, plays the first bars of the tarantella. Helmer stops in the doorway.*) Aha!

Nora: I can't dance tomorrow if I don't practice with you.

Helmer (going up to her): Are you really so worried about it, dear?

Nora: Yes, terribly worried about it. Let me practice right now. We have time before dinner. Sit down and play for me, Torvald dear. Criticize me and correct me, the way you always do.

Helmer: With great pleasure, if you want me to. (*Sits down at the piano.*)

Nora (takes a tambourine and a long multicolored shawl out of the box. She hastily drapes the shawl around her. Then she bounds to the front of the stage and calls out): Now play for me! I'm going to dance!

(*Helmer plays and Nora dances. Rank stands by the piano behind Helmer and watches.*)

Helmer (as he plays): Slower, slower!

Nora: I can't do it any other way.

Helmer: Not so violently, Nora!

Nora: This is the way.

Helmer (stops playing): No, no, that's not right at all.

Nora (laughing and swinging the tambourine): Didn't I tell you so?

Rank: Let me play for her.

Helmer (getting up): Good idea. I can correct her better that way.

(*Rank sits down at the piano and plays. Nora dances more and more wildly. Helmer has taken up a position beside the stove, and as she dances, he gives her frequent instructions. She doesn't seem to hear him. Her hair comes undone and falls over her shoulders. She pays no attention to it, but goes on dancing. Enter Mrs. Linde.)*

Mrs. Linde *(standing as if spellbound in the doorway)*: Oh!

Nora *(as she dances)*: What fun, Kristine!

Helmer: My dear darling Nora, you're dancing as if your life depended on it.

Nora: It does.

Helmer: Stop, Rank. This is insane! I said stop!

(Rank stops playing, and Nora suddenly stands still. Helmer goes up to her.)

I never would have believed it. You've forgotten everything I taught you.

Nora *(throwing the tambourine aside)*: There, you see.

Helmer: You're going to need a lot of coaching.

Nora: Yes, you see how much I need it. You have to coach me right up to the last minute. Promise me you will, Torvald!

Helmer: You can depend on me.

Nora: You can't think about anything but me, today or tomorrow. Don't open a single letter. Don't even open the mailbox—

Helmer: You're still afraid of that man—

Nora: Yes, yes, I am.

Helmer: Nora, I can tell from your face that there's a letter from him in the box.

Nora: I don't know. I think there is. But you can't read anything like that now. Nothing nasty must come between us until this is all over.

Rank *(whispers to Helmer)*: Don't contradict her.

Helmer *(taking her in his arms)*: The child shall have her way. But tomorrow night, after you've danced—

Nora: Then you'll be free.

(The Maid appears in the doorway to the right.)

Maid: Dinner is served, ma'am.

Nora: We'll have champagne, Helene.

Maid: Yes, ma'am. *(Exit.)*

Helmer: Oh, are we having a banquet?

Nora: Yes, a banquet. Champagne till dawn! *(Calls out.)* And a few macaroons, Helene. Lots of them, just this once!

Helmer: Come on, stop acting so wild and nervous. Be my own little skylark again.

Nora: Yes, dear, I will. But go inside now, and you too, Doctor Rank. Kristine, please help me do up my hair.

Rank *(whispers to Helmer as they go out)*: There isn't anything—she's not expecting—?

Helmer: No, nothing like that. It's just this childish nervousness I was telling you about. *(They go into the right-hand room.)*

Nora: Well?

Mrs. Linde: Out of town.

Nora: I could tell from your face.

Mrs. Linde: He'll be back tomorrow evening. I wrote him a note.

Nora: You should have left it alone. Don't try to prevent anything. After all, it's exciting to be waiting for a miracle to happen.

Mrs. Linde: What is it that you're waiting for?

Nora: Oh, you wouldn't understand. Go inside with them, I'll be there in a moment.

(*Mrs. Linde goes into the dining room. Nora stands still for a little while, as if to compose herself. Then she looks at her watch.*)

Five o'clock. Seven hours till midnight, and another twenty-four hours till the next midnight. And then the tarantella will be over. Twenty-four plus seven? Thirty-one hours to live.

Helmer (from the doorway on the right): Where's my little skylark?

Nora (going to him with her arms outstretched): Here she is!

ACT III

The same scene. The table has been placed in the middle of the stage, with chairs around it. A lamp is burning on the table. The door into the hall stands open. Dance music is heard in the room above. Mrs. Linde is sitting at the table idly turning over the pages of a book. She tries to read, but she seems unable to concentrate. Every now and then she listens intently for a sound at the outer door.

Mrs. Linde (looking at her watch): Not yet—and the time's nearly up. If only he doesn't—(*Listens again.*) Ah, there he is. (*Goes into the hall and opens the outer door carefully. Light footsteps are heard on the stairs. She whispers.*) Come in. There's no one else here.

Krogstad (in the doorway): I found a note from you at home. What does this mean?

Mrs. Linde: It's absolutely necessary that I have a talk with you.

Krogstad: Really? And is it absolutely necessary that we have it here?

Mrs. Linde: It's impossible where I live. There's no private entrance to my apartment. Come in. We're all alone. The maid's asleep, and the Helmers are upstairs at a dance.

Krogstad (coming into the room): Are the Helmers really at a dance tonight?

Mrs. Linde: Yes. Why shouldn't they be?

Krogstad: Certainly—why not?

Mrs. Linde: Now, Nils, let's have a talk.

Krogstad: What can we two have to talk about?

Mrs. Linde: Quite a lot.

Krogstad: I wouldn't have thought so.

Mrs. Linde: Of course not. You've never really understood me.

Krogstad: What was there to understand, except what the whole world could see—a heartless woman drops a man when a better catch comes along?

Mrs. Linde: Do you think I'm really that heartless? And that I broke it off with you so lightly?

Krogstad: Didn't you?

Mrs. Linde: Nils, did you really think that?

Krogstad: If not, why did you write what you did to me?

Mrs. Linde: What else could I do? Since I had to break it off with you, I had an obligation to stamp out your feelings for me.

Krogstad (wringing his hands): So that was it. And all this just for the sake of money!

Mrs. Linde: Don't forget that I had an invalid mother and two little brothers. We couldn't wait for you, Nils. Success seemed a long way off for you back then.

Krogstad: That may be so, but you had no right to cast me aside for anyone else's sake.

Mrs. Linde: I don't know if I did or not. Many times I've asked myself if I had the right.

Krogstad (more gently): When I lost you, it was as if the earth crumbled under my feet. Look at me now—a shipwrecked man clinging to a bit of wreckage.

Mrs. Linde: But help may be on the way.

Krogstad: It *was* on the way, till you came along and blocked it.

Mrs. Linde: Without knowing it, Nils. It wasn't till today that I found out I'd be taking your job.

Krogstad: I believe you, if you say so. But now that you know it, are you going to step aside?

Mrs. Linde: No, because it wouldn't do you any good.

Krogstad: Good? *I* would quit whether it did any good or not.

Mrs. Linde: I've learned to be practical. Life and hard, bitter necessity have taught me that.

Krogstad: And life has taught me not to believe in fine speeches.

Mrs. Linde: Then life has taught you something very sensible. But surely you believe in actions?

Krogstad: What do you mean by that?

Mrs. Linde: You said you were like a shipwrecked man clinging to a piece of wreckage.

Krogstad: I had good reason to say so.

Mrs. Linde: Well, I'm like a shipwrecked woman clinging to a piece of wreckage, with no one to mourn for and no one to care for.

Krogstad: That was your own choice.

Mrs. Linde: I had no other choice—then.

Krogstad: Well, what about now?

Mrs. Linde: Nils, how would it be if we two shipwrecked people could reach out to each other?

Krogstad: What are you saying?

Mrs. Linde: Two people on the same piece of wreckage would stand a better chance than each one on their own.

Krogstad: Kristine, I . . .

Mrs. Linde: Why do you think I came to town?

Krogstad: You can't mean that you were thinking about me?

Mrs. Linde: Life is unendurable without work. I've worked all my life, for as long as I can remember, and it's been my greatest and my only pleasure. But now that I'm completely alone in the world, my life is so terribly empty and I feel so abandoned. There isn't the slightest pleasure in working only for yourself. Nils, give me someone and something to work for.

Krogstad: I don't trust this. It's just some romantic female impulse, a high-minded urge for self-sacrifice.

Mrs. Linde: Have you ever known me to be like that?

Krogstad: Could you really do it? Tell me, do you know all about my past?

Mrs. Linde: Yes.

Krogstad: And you know what they think of me around here?

Mrs. Linde: Didn't you imply that with me you might have been a very different person?

Krogstad: I'm sure I would have.

Mrs. Linde: Is it too late now?

Krogstad: Kristine, are you serious about all this? Yes, I'm sure you are. I can see it in your face. Do you really have the courage, then—

Mrs. Linde: I want to be a mother to someone, and your children need a mother. We two need each other. Nils, I have faith in your true nature. I can face anything together with you.

Krogstad (grasps her hands): Thank you, thank you, Kristine! Now I can find a way to clear myself in the eyes of the world. Ah, but I forgot—

Mrs. Linde (listening): Shh! The tarantella! You have to go!

Krogstad: Why? What's the matter?

Mrs. Linde: Do you hear them up there? They'll probably come home as soon as this dance is over.

Krogstad: Yes, yes, I'll go. But it won't make any difference. You don't know what I've done about my situation with the Helmers.

Mrs. Linde: Yes, I know all about that.

Krogstad: And in spite of that you still have the courage to—

Mrs. Linde: I understand completely what despair can drive a man like you to do.

Krogstad: If only I could undo it!

Mrs. Linde: You can't. Your letter's lying in the mailbox now.

Krogstad: Are you sure?

Mrs. Linde: Quite sure, but—

Krogstad (with a searching look at her): Is that what this is all about? That you want to save your friend, no matter what you have to do? Tell me the truth. Is that it?

Mrs. Linde: Nils, when a woman has sold herself for someone else's sake, she doesn't do it a second time.

Krogstad: I'll ask for my letter back.

Mrs. Linde: No, no.

Krogstad: Yes, of course I will. I'll wait here until Helmer comes home. I'll tell him he has to give me back my letter, that it's only about my being fired, that I don't want him to read it—

Mrs. Linde: No, Nils, don't ask for it back.

Krogstad: But wasn't that the reason why you asked me to meet you here?

Mrs. Linde: In my first moment of panic, it was. But twenty-four hours have gone by since then, and in the meantime I've seen some incredible things in this house. Helmer has to know all about it. This terrible secret has to come out. They have to have a complete understanding between them. It's time for all this lying and pretending to stop.

Krogstad: All right then, if you think it's worth the risk. But there's at least one thing I can do, and do right away—

Mrs. Linde (listening): You have to leave this instant! The dance is over. They could walk in here any minute.

Krogstad: I'll wait for you downstairs.

Mrs. Linde: Yes, please do. I want you to walk me home.

Krogstad: I've never been so happy in my entire life!

(Goes out through the outer door. The door between the room and the hall remains open.)

Mrs. Linde (straightening up the room and getting her hat and coat ready): How different things will be! Someone to work for and live for, a home to bring happiness into. I'm certainly going to try. I wish they'd hurry up and come home—*(Listens.)* Ah, here they are now. I'd better put on my things.

(Picks up her hat and coat. Helmer's and Nora's voices are heard outside. A key is turned, and Helmer brings Nora into the hall almost by force. She is in an Italian peasant costume with a large black shawl wrapped around her. He is in formal wear and a black domino—a hooded cloak with an eye-mask—which is open.)

Nora *(hanging back in the doorway and struggling with him)*: No, no, no! Don't bring me inside. I want to go back upstairs. I don't want to leave so early.

Helmer: But, my dearest Nora—

Nora: Please, Torvald dear, please, please, only one more hour.

Helmer: Not one more minute, my sweet Nora. You know this is what we agreed on. Come inside. You'll catch cold standing out there.

(He brings her gently into the room, in spite of her resistance.)

Mrs. Linde: Good evening.

Nora: Kristine!

Helmer: What are you doing here so late, Mrs. Linde?

Mrs. Linde: You must excuse me. I was so anxious to see Nora in her dress.

Nora: Have you been sitting here waiting for me?

Mrs. Linde: Yes, unfortunately I came too late, you'd already gone upstairs. And I didn't want to go away again without seeing you.

Helmer *(taking off Nora's shawl)*: Yes, take a good look at her. I think she's worth looking at. Isn't she charming, Mrs. Linde?

Mrs. Linde: Yes, indeed she is.

Helmer: Doesn't she look especially pretty? Everyone thought so at the dance. But this sweet little person is extremely stubborn. What are we going to do with her? Believe it or not, I almost had to drag her away by force.

Nora: Torvald, you'll be sorry you didn't let me stay, even if only for half an hour.

Helmer: Listen to her, Mrs. Linde! She danced her tarantella and it was a huge success, as it deserved to be, though maybe her performance was a tiny bit too realistic, a little more so than it might have been by strict artistic standards. But never mind about that! The main thing is, she was a success, a tremendous success. Do you think I was going to let her stay there after that, and spoil the effect? Not a chance! I took my charming little Capri girl—my capricious little Capri girl, I should say—I took her by the arm, one quick circle around the room, a curtsey to one and all, and, as they say in novels, the beautiful vision vanished. An exit should always make an effect, Mrs. Linde, but I can't make Nora understand that. Whew, this room is hot!

(Throws his domino on a chair and opens the door to his study.)

Why is it so dark in here? Oh, of course. Excuse me.

(He goes in and lights some candles.)

Nora *(in a hurried, breathless whisper)*: Well?

Mrs. Linde *(in a low voice)*: I talked to him.

Nora: And?

Mrs. Linde: Nora, you have to tell your husband the whole story.

Nora *(in an expressionless voice)*: I knew it.

Mrs. Linde: You have nothing to fear from Krogstad, but you still have to tell him.

Nora: I'm not going to.

Mrs. Linde: Then the letter will.

Nora: Thank you, Kristine. Now I know what I have to do. Shh!

Helmer (coming in again): Well, Mrs. Linde, have you been admiring her?

Mrs. Linde: Yes, I have, and now I'll say goodnight.

Helmer: What, already? Is this your knitting?

Mrs. Linde (taking it): Yes, thank you, I'd almost forgotten it.

Helmer: So you knit?

Mrs. Linde: Yes, of course.

Helmer: You know, you ought to embroider.

Mrs. Linde: Really? Why?

Helmer: It's much more graceful-looking. Here, let me show you. You hold the embroidery this way in your left hand, and use the needle with your right, like this, with a long, easy sweep. Do you see?

Mrs. Linde: Yes, I suppose—

Helmer: But knitting, that can never be anything but awkward. Here, look. The arms close together, the knitting needles going up and down. It's sort of Chinese looking. That was really excellent champagne they gave us.

Mrs. Linde: Well, good night, Nora, and don't be stubborn anymore.

Helmer: That's right, Mrs. Linde.

Mrs. Linde: Good night, Mr. Helmer.

Helmer (seeing her to the door): Good night, good night. I hope you get home safely. I'd be very happy to—but you only have a short way to go. Good night, good night.

(*She goes out. He closes the door behind her, and comes in again.*)

Ah, rid of her at last! What a bore that woman is.

Nora: Aren't you tired, Torvald?

Helmer: No, not at all.

Nora: You're not sleepy?

Helmer: Not a bit. As a matter of fact, I feel very lively. And what about you? You really look tired *and* sleepy.

Nora: Yes, I am very tired. I want to go to sleep right away.

Helmer: So, you see how right I was not to let you stay there any longer.

Nora: You're always right, Torvald.

Helmer (kissing her on the forehead): Now my little skylark is talking sense. Did you notice what a good mood Rank was in this evening?

Nora: Really? Was he? I didn't talk to him at all.

Helmer: And I only talked to him for a little while, but it's a long time since I've seen him so cheerful. (*Looks at her for a while and then moves closer to her.*) It's delightful to be home again by ourselves, to be alone with you, you fascinating, charming little darling!

Nora: Don't look at me like that, Torvald.

Helmer: Why shouldn't I look at my dearest treasure? At all the beauty that is mine, all my very own?

Nora (going to the other side of the table): I wish you wouldn't talk that way to me tonight.

Helmer (following her): You've still got the tarantella in your blood, I see. And it makes you more captivating than ever. Listen, the guests are starting to leave now. (*In a lower voice.*) Nora, soon the whole house will be quiet.

Nora: Yes, I hope so.

Helmer: Yes, my own darling Nora. Do you know why, when we're out at a party like this, why I hardly talk to you, and keep away from you, and only steal a glance at you now and then? Do you know why I do that? It's because I'm pretending to myself that we're secretly in love, and we're secretly engaged, and no one suspects that there's anything between us.

Nora: Yes, yes, I know you're thinking about me every moment.

Helmer: And when we're leaving, and I'm putting the shawl over your beautiful young shoulders, on your lovely neck, then I imagine that you're my young bride and that we've just come from our wedding and I'm bringing you home for the first time, to be alone with you for the first time, all alone with my shy little darling! This whole night I've been longing for you alone. My blood was on fire watching you move when you danced the tarantella. I couldn't stand it any longer, and that's why I brought you home so early—

Nora: Stop it, Torvald! Let me go. I won't—

Helmer: What? You're not serious, Nora! You won't? You won't? I'm your husband—

(*There is a knock at the outer door.*)

Nora (starting): Did you hear—

Helmer (going into the hall): Who is it?

Rank (outside): It's me. May I come in for a moment?

Helmer (in an irritated whisper): What does he want now? (*Aloud.*) Wait a minute! (*Unlocks the door.*) Come in. It's good of you not to pass by our door without saying hello.

Rank: I thought I heard your voice, and I felt like dropping by. (*With a quick look around.*) Ah, yes, these dear familiar rooms. You two are very happy and cozy in here.

Helmer: You seemed to be making yourself pretty happy upstairs too.

Rank: Very much so. Why shouldn't I? Why shouldn't we enjoy everything in this world? At least as much as we can, for as long as we can. The wine was first-rate—

Helmer: Especially the champagne.

Rank: So you noticed that too? It's almost unbelievable how much of it I managed to put away!

Nora: Torvald drank a lot of champagne tonight too.

Rank: Did he?

Nora: Yes, and it always makes him so merry.

Rank: Well, why shouldn't a person have a merry evening after a well-spent day?

Helmer: Well-spent? I'm afraid I can't take credit for that.

Rank (clapping him on the back): But I can, you know!

Nora: Doctor Rank, you must have been busy with some scientific investigation today.

Rank: Exactly.

Helmer: Listen to this! Little Nora talking about scientific investigations!

Nora: And may I congratulate you on the result?

Rank: Indeed you may.

Nora: Was it favorable, then?

Rank: The best possible result, for both doctor and patient—certainty.

Nora (quickly and searchingly): Certainty?

Rank: Absolute certainty. So wasn't I entitled to make a merry evening of it after that?

Nora: Yes, you certainly were, Doctor Rank.

Helmer: I think so too, as long as you don't have to pay for it in the morning.

Rank: Oh well, you can't have anything in this life without paying for it.

Nora: Doctor Rank, are you fond of fancy-dress balls?

Rank: Yes, if there are a lot of pretty costumes.

Nora: Tell me, what should the two of us wear to the next one?

Helmer: Little featherbrain! You're thinking of the next one already?

Rank: The two of us? Yes, I can tell you. You'll go as a good-luck charm—

Helmer: Yes, but what would be the costume for that?

Rank: She just needs to dress the way she always does.

Helmer: That was very nicely put. But aren't you going to tell us what you'll be?

Rank: Yes, my dear friend, I've already made up my mind about that.

Helmer: Well?

Rank: At the next fancy-dress ball I'm going to be invisible.

Helmer: That's a good one!

Rank: There's a big black cap . . . Haven't you ever heard of the cap that makes you invisible? Once you put it on, no one can see you anymore.

Helmer (suppressing a smile): Yes, that's right.

Rank: But I'm clean forgetting what I came for. Helmer, give me a cigar. One of the dark Havanas.

Helmer: With the greatest pleasure. *(Offers him his case.)*

Rank (takes a cigar and cuts off the end): Thanks.

Nora (striking a match): Let me give you a light.

Rank: Thank you. *(She holds the match for him to light his cigar.)* And now goodbye!

Helmer: Goodbye, goodbye, my dear old friend.

Nora: Sleep well, Doctor Rank.

Rank: Thank you for that wish.

Nora: Wish me the same.

Rank: You? Well, if you want me to. Sleep well! And thanks for the light. *(He nods to them both and goes out.)*

Helmer (in a subdued voice): He's had too much to drink.

Nora (absently): Maybe.

(Helmer takes a bunch of keys out of his pocket and goes into the hall.)

Torvald! What are you going to do out there?

Helmer: Empty the mailbox. It's quite full. There won't be any room for the newspaper in the morning.

Nora: Are you going to work tonight?

Helmer: You know I'm not. What's this? Someone's been at the lock.

Nora: At the lock?

Helmer: Yes, it's been tampered with. What does this mean? I never would have thought the maid—Look, here's a broken hairpin. It's one of yours, Nora.

Nora (quickly): Then it must have been the children—

Helmer: Then you'd better break them of those habits. There, I've finally got it open.

(Empties the mailbox and calls out to the kitchen.)

Helene! Helene, put out the light over the front door.

(Comes back into the room and shuts the door into the hall. He holds out his hand full of letters.)

Look at that. Look what a pile of them there are. *(Turning them over.)* What's this?

Nora (at the window): The letter! No! Torvald, no!

Helmer: Two calling cards of Rank's.

Nora: Of Doctor Rank's?

Helmer (looking at them): Yes, Doctor Rank. They were on top. He must have put them in there when he left just now.

Nora: Is there anything written on them?

Helmer: There's a black cross over the name. Look. What a morbid thing to do! It looks as if he's announcing his own death.

Nora: That's exactly what he's doing.

Helmer: What? Do you know anything about it? Has he said anything to you?

Nora: Yes. He told me that when the cards came it would be his farewell to us. He means to close himself off and die.

Helmer: My poor old friend! Of course I knew we wouldn't have him for very long. But this soon! And he goes and hides himself away like a wounded animal.

Nora: If it has to happen, it's better that it be done without a word. Don't you think so, Torvald?

Helmer (walking up and down): He's become so much a part of our lives, I can't imagine him not being with us anymore. With his poor health and his loneliness, he was like a cloudy background to our sunlit happiness. Well, maybe it's all for the best. For him, anyway. *(Standing still.)* And maybe for us too, Nora. Now we have only each other to rely on. *(Puts his arms around her.)* My darling wife, I feel as though I can't possibly hold you tight enough. You know, Nora, I've often wished you were in some kind of serious danger, so that I could risk everything, even my own life, to save you.

Nora (disengages herself from him, and says firmly and decidedly): Now you must go and read your letters, Torvald.

Helmer: No, no, not tonight. I want to be with you, my darling wife.

Nora: With the thought of your friend's death—

Helmer: You're right, it has affected us both. Something ugly has come between us, the thought of the horrors of death. We have to try to put it out of our minds. Until we do, we'll each go to our own room.

Nora (with her arms around his neck): Good night, Torvald. Good night!

Helmer (kissing her on the forehead): Good night, my little songbird. Sleep well, Nora. Now I'll go read all my mail. *(He takes his letters and goes into his room, shutting the door behind him.)*

Nora (gropes distractedly about, picks up Helmer's domino and wraps it around her, while she says in quick, hoarse, spasmodic whispers): Never to see him again. Never! Never! *(Puts her shawl over her head.)* Never to see my children again either, never again. Never! Never! Oh, the icy, black water, the bottomless depths! If only it were over! He's got it now, now he's reading it. Goodbye, Torvald . . . children!

(She is about to rush out through the hall when Helmer opens his door hurriedly and stands with an open letter in his hand.)

Helmer: Nora!

Nora: Ah!

Helmer: What is this? Do you know what's in this letter?

Nora: Yes, I know. Let me go! Let me get out!

Helmer (holding her back): Where are you going?

Nora (trying to get free): You're not going to save me, Torvald!

Helmer (reeling): It's true? Is this true, what it says here? This is horrible! No, no, it can't possibly be true.

Nora: It is true. I've loved you more than anything else in the world.

Helmer: Don't start with your ridiculous excuses.

Nora (taking a step towards him): Torvald!

Helmer: You little fool, do you know what you've done?

Nora: Let me go. I won't let you suffer for my sake. You're not going to take it on yourself.

Helmer: Stop play-acting. *(Locks the hall door.)* You're going to stay right here and give me an explanation. Do you understand what you've done? Answer me! Do you understand what you've done?

Nora (looks steadily at him and says with a growing look of coldness in her face): Yes, I'm beginning to understand everything now.

Helmer (walking around the room): What a horrible awakening! The woman who was my pride and joy for eight years, a hypocrite, a liar, worse than that, much worse—a criminal! The unspeakable ugliness of it all! The shame of it! The shame!

(Nora is silent and looks steadily at him. He stops in front of her.)

I should have realized that something like this was bound to happen. I should have seen it coming. Your father's shifty nature—be quiet!—your father's shifty nature has come out in you. No religion, no morality, no sense of duty. This is my punishment for closing my eyes to what he did! I did it for your sake, and this is how you pay me back.

Nora: Yes, that's right.

Helmer: Now you've destroyed all my happiness. You've ruined my whole future. It's horrible to think about! I'm in the power of an unscrupulous man. He can do what he wants with me, ask me for anything he wants, give me any orders he wants, and I don't dare say no. And I have to sink to such miserable depths, all because of a feather-brained woman!

Nora: When I'm out of the way, you'll be free.

Helmer: Spare me the speeches. Your father had always plenty of those on hand, too. What good would it do me if you were out of the way, as you say? Not the slightest. He can tell everybody the whole story. And if he does, I could be wrongly suspected of having been in on it with you. People will probably think I was behind it all, that I put you up to it! And I have you to thank for all this, after I've cherished you the whole time we've been married. Do you understand what you've done to me?

Nora (coldly and quietly): Yes.

Helmer: It's so incredible that I can't take it all in. But we have to come to some understanding. Take off that shawl. Take it off, I said. I have to try to appease him some way or another. It has to be hushed up, no matter what it costs. And as for you and me, we have to make it look as if everything is just as it always was, but only for the sake of appearances, obviously. You'll stay here in my house, of course. But I won't let you bring up the children. I can't trust them to you. To think that I have to say these things to someone I've loved so dearly, and that I still—No, that's all over. From this moment on happiness is out of the question. All that matters now is to save the bits and pieces, to keep up the appearance—

(The front doorbell rings.)

Helmer *(with a start)*: What's that? At this hour! Can the worst—Can he—Go and hide yourself, Nora. Say you don't feel well. *(Nora stands motionless. Helmer goes and unlocks the hall door.)*

Maid *(half-dressed, comes to the door)*: A letter for Mrs. Helmer.

Helmer: Give it to me. *(Takes the letter, and shuts the door.)* Yes, it's from him. I'm not giving it to you. I'll read it myself.

Nora: Go ahead, read it.

Helmer *(standing by the lamp)*: I barely have the courage to. It could mean ruin for both of us. No, I have to know. *(Tears open the letter, runs his eye over a few lines, looks at a piece of paper enclosed with it, and gives a shout of joy.)* Nora! *(She looks at him questioningly.)* Nora! No, I'd better read it again. Yes, it's true! I'm saved! Nora, I'm saved!

Nora: And what about me?

Helmer: You too, of course. We're both saved, you and I. Look, he's returned your note. He says he's sorry and he apologizes—that a happy change in his life— what difference does it make what he says! We're saved, Nora! Nobody can hurt you. Oh, Nora, Nora! No, first I have to destroy these horrible things. Let me see. . . . *(Glances at the note.)* No, no, I don't want to look at it. This whole business will be nothing but a bad dream to me.

(Tears up the note and both letters, throws them all into the stove, and watches them burn.)

There, now it doesn't exist anymore. He says that you've known since Christmas Eve. These must have been a horrible three days for you, Nora.

Nora: I fought a hard fight these three days.

Helmer: And suffered agonies, and saw no way out but—No, we won't dwell on any of those horrors. We'll just shout for joy and keep saying, "It's all over! It's all over!" Listen to me, Nora. You don't seem to realize that it's all over. What's this? Such a cold, hard face! My poor little Nora, I understand. You find it hard to believe that I've really forgiven you. But I swear that it's true, Nora. I forgive you for everything. I know that you did it all out of love for me.

Nora: That's true.

Helmer: You've loved me the way a wife ought to love her husband. You just didn't have the awareness to see what was wrong with the means you used. But do you think I love you any less because you don't understand how to deal with these things? No, of course not. I want you to lean on me. I'll advise you and guide you. I wouldn't be a man if this womanly helplessness didn't make you twice as attractive to me. Don't think anymore about the hard things I said when I was so upset at first, when I thought everything was going to crush me. I forgive you, Nora. I swear to you that I forgive you.

Nora: Thank you for your forgiveness. *(She goes out through the door to the right.)*

Helmer: No, don't go—*(Looks in.)* What are you doing in there?

Nora *(from within)*: Taking off my costume.

Helmer (standing at the open door): Yes, do. Try to calm yourself, and ease your mind again, my frightened little songbird. I want you to rest and feel secure. I have wide wings for you to take shelter underneath. (*Walks up and down by the door.*) What a warm and cozy home we have, Nora: Here's a safe haven for you, and I'll protect you like a hunted dove that I've rescued from a hawk's claws. I'll calm your poor pounding heart. It will happen, little by little, Nora, believe me. In the morning you'll see it in a very different light. Soon everything will be exactly the way it was before. Before you know it, you won't need my reassurances that I've forgiven you. You'll know for certain that I have. You can't imagine that I'd ever consider rejecting you, or even blaming you? You have no idea what a man feels in his heart, Nora. A man finds it indescribably sweet and satisfying to know that he's forgiven his wife, freely and with all his heart. It's as if he's made her his own all over again. He's given her a new life, in a way, and she's become both wife and child to him. And from this moment on that's what you'll be to me, my little scared, helpless darling. Don't worry about anything, Nora. Just be honest and open with me, and I'll be your will and your conscience. What's this? You haven't gone to bed yet? Have you changed?

Nora (in everyday dress): Yes, Torvald, I've changed.

Helmer: But why—It's so late.

Nora: I'm not going to sleep tonight.

Helmer: But, my dear Nora—

Nora (looking at her watch): It's not that late. Sit down here, Torvald. You and I have a lot to talk about. (*She sits down at one side of the table.*)

Helmer: Nora, what is this? Why this cold, hard face?

Nora: Sit down. This is going to take a while. I have a lot to say to you.

Helmer (sits down at the opposite side of the table): You're making me nervous, Nora. And I don't understand you.

Nora: No, that's it exactly. You don't understand me, and I've never understood you either, until tonight. No, don't interrupt me. I want you to listen to what I have to say. Torvald, I'm settling accounts with you.

Helmer: What do you mean by that?

Nora (after a short silence): Doesn't anything strike you as odd about the way we're sitting here like this?

Helmer: No, what?

Nora: We've been married for eight years. Doesn't it occur to you that this is the first time the two of us, you and I, husband and wife, have had a serious conversation?

Helmer: What do you mean by serious?

Nora: In the whole eight years—longer than that, for the whole time we've known each other—we've never exchanged one word on any serious subject.

Helmer: Did you expect me to be constantly worrying you with problems that you weren't capable of helping me deal with?

Nora: I'm not talking about business. I mean we've never sat down together seriously to try to get to the bottom of anything.

Helmer: But, dearest Nora, what good would that have done you?

Nora: That's just it. You've never understood me. I've been treated badly, Torvald, first by Papa and then by you.

Helmer: What? The two people who've loved you more than anyone else?

Nora (shaking her head): You've never loved me. You just thought it was pleasant to be in love with me.

Helmer: Nora, what are you saying?

Nora: It's true, Torvald. When I lived at home with Papa, he gave me his opinion about everything, and so I had all the same opinions, and if I didn't, I kept my mouth shut, because he wouldn't have liked it. He used to call me his doll-child, and he played with me the way I played with my dolls. And when I came to live in your house—

Helmer: What kind of way is that to talk about our marriage?

Nora (undisturbed): I mean that I was just passed from Papa's hands to yours. You arranged everything according to your own taste, and so I had all the same tastes as you. Or else I pretended to, I'm not really sure which. Sometimes I think it's one way and sometimes the other. When I look back, it's as if I've been living here like a beggar, from hand to mouth. I've supported myself by performing tricks for you, Torvald. But that's the way you wanted it. You and Papa have committed a terrible sin against me. It's your fault that I've done nothing with my life.

Helmer: This is so unfair and ungrateful of you, Nora! Haven't you been happy here?

Nora: No, I've never really been happy. I thought I was, but it wasn't true.

Helmer: Not—not happy!

Nora: No, just cheerful. You've always been very kind to me. But our home's been nothing but a playroom. I've been your doll-wife, the same way that I was Papa's doll-child. And the children have been my dolls. I thought it was great fun when you played with me, the way they thought it was when I played with them. That's what our marriage has been, Torvald.

Helmer: There's some truth in what you're saying, even though your view of it is exaggerated and overwrought. But things will be different from now on. Playtime is over, and now it's lesson-time.

Nora: Whose lessons? Mine, or the children's?

Helmer: Both yours and the children's, my darling Nora.

Nora: I'm sorry, Torvald, but you're not the man to give me lessons on how to be a proper wife to you.

Helmer: How can you say that?

Nora: And as for me, who am I to be allowed to bring up the children?

Helmer: Nora!

Nora: Didn't you say so yourself a little while ago, that you don't dare trust them to me?

Helmer: That was in a moment of anger! Why can't you let it go?

Nora: Because you were absolutely right. I'm not fit for the job. There's another job I have to take on first. I have to try to educate myself. You're not the man to help me with that. I have to do that for myself. And that's why I'm going to leave you now.

Helmer (jumping up): What are you saying?

Nora: I have to stand completely on my own, if I'm going to understand myself and everything around me. That's why I can't stay here with you any longer.

Helmer: Nora, Nora!

Nora: I'm leaving right now. I'm sure Kristine will put me up for the night—

Helmer: You're out of your mind! I won't let you go! I forbid it!

Nora: It's no use forbidding me anything anymore. I'm taking only what belongs to me. I won't take anything from you, now or later.

Helmer: This is insanity!

Nora: Tomorrow I'm going home. Back to where I came from, I mean. It'll be easier for me to find something to do there.

Helmer: You're a blind, senseless woman!

Nora: Then I'd better try to get some sense, Torvald.

Helmer: But to desert your home, your husband, and your children! And aren't you concerned about what people will say?

Nora: I can't concern myself with that. I only know that this is what I have to do.

Helmer: This is outrageous! You're just going to walk away from your most sacred duties?

Nora: What do you consider to be my most sacred duties?

Helmer: Do you need me to tell you that? Aren't they your duties to your husband and your children?

Nora: I have other duties just as sacred.

Helmer: No, you do not. What could they be?

Nora: Duties to myself.

Helmer: First and foremost, you're a wife and a mother.

Nora: I don't believe that anymore. I believe that first and foremost I'm a human being, just as you are—or, at least, that I have to try to become one. I know very well, Torvald, that most people would agree with you, and that opinions like yours are in books, but I can't be satisfied anymore with what most people say, or with what's in books. I have to think things through for myself and come to understand them.

Helmer: Why can't you understand your place in your own home? Don't you have an infallible guide in matters like that? What about your religion?

Nora: Torvald, I'm afraid I'm not sure what religion is.

Helmer: What are you saying?

Nora: All I know is what Pastor Hansen said when I was confirmed. He told us that religion was this, that, and the other thing. When I'm away from all this and on my own, I'll look into that subject too. I'll see if what he said is true or not, or at least whether it's true for me.

Helmer: This is unheard of, coming from a young woman like you! But if religion doesn't guide you, let me appeal to your conscience. I assume you have some moral sense. Or do you have none? Answer me.

Nora: Torvald, that's not an easy question to answer. I really don't know. It's very confusing to me. I only know that you and I look at it in very different ways. I'm learning too that the law isn't at all what I thought it was, and I can't convince myself that the law is right. A woman has no right to spare her old dying father or to save her husband's life? I can't believe that.

Helmer: You talk like a child. You don't understand anything about the world you live in.

Nora: No, I don't. But I'm going to try. I'm going to see if I can figure out who's right, me or the world.

Helmer: You're sick, Nora. You're delirious. I'm half convinced that you're out of your mind.

Nora: I've never felt so clearheaded and sure of myself as I do tonight.

Helmer: Clearheaded and sure of yourself—and that's the spirit in which you forsake your husband and your children?

Nora: Yes, it is.

Helmer: Then there's only one possible explanation.

Nora: Which is?

Helmer: You don't love me anymore.

Nora: Exactly.

Helmer: Nora! How can you say that?

Nora: It's very painful for me to say it, Torvald, because you've always been so good to me, but I can't help it. I don't love you anymore.

Helmer (regaining his composure): Are you clearheaded and sure of yourself when you say that too?

Nora: Yes, totally clearheaded and sure of myself. That's why I can't stay here.

Helmer: Can you tell me what I did to make you stop loving me?

Nora: Yes, I can. It was tonight, when the miracle didn't happen. That's when I realized you're not the man I thought you were.

Helmer: Can you explain that more clearly? I don't understand you.

Nora: I've been waiting so patiently for the last eight years. Of course I knew that miracles don't happen every day. Then when I found myself in this horrible situation, I was sure that the miracle was about to happen at last. When Krogstad's letter was lying out there, never for a moment did I imagine that you would agree to his conditions. I was absolutely certain that you'd say to him: Go ahead, tell the whole world. And when he had—

Helmer: Yes, what then? After I'd exposed my wife to shame and disgrace?

Nora: When he had, I was absolutely certain you'd come forward and take the whole thing on yourself, and say: I'm the guilty one.

Helmer: Nora—!

Nora: You mean that I would never have let you make such a sacrifice for me? Of course I wouldn't. But who would have believed my word against yours? That was the miracle that I hoped for and dreaded. And it was to keep it from happening that made me want to kill myself.

Helmer: I'd gladly work night and day for you, Nora, and endure sorrow and poverty for your sake. But no man would sacrifice his honor for the one he loves.

Nora: Hundreds of thousands of women have done it.

Helmer: Oh, you think and talk like a thoughtless child.

Nora: Maybe so. But you don't think or talk like the man I want to be with for the rest of my life. As soon as your fear had passed—and it wasn't fear for what threatened me, but for what might happen to you—when the whole thing was past, as far as you were concerned it was just as if nothing at all had happened. I was still your little skylark, your doll, but now you'd handle me twice as gently and carefully as before, because I was so delicate and fragile. (*Getting up.*) Torvald, that's when it dawned on me that for eight years I'd been living here with a stranger and had borne him three children. Oh, I can't bear to think about it! I could tear myself into little pieces!

Helmer (sadly): I see, I see. An abyss has opened up between us. There's no denying it. But, Nora, can't we find some way to close it?

Nora: The way I am now, I'm no wife for you.

Helmer: I can find it in myself to become a different man.

Nora: Maybe so—if your doll is taken away from you.

Helmer: But to be apart!—to be apart from you! No, no, Nora, I can't conceive of it.

Nora (*going out to the right*): All the more reason why it has to be done.

(*She comes back with her coat and hat and a small suitcase which she puts on a chair by the table.*)

Helmer: Nora, Nora, not now! Wait till tomorrow.

Nora (*putting on her cloak*): I can't spend the night in a strange man's room.

Helmer: But couldn't we live here together like brother and sister?

Nora (*putting on her hat*): You know how long that would last. (*Puts the shawl around her.*) Goodbye, Torvald. I won't look in on the children. I know they're in better hands than mine. The way I am now, I'm no use to them.

Helmer: But someday, Nora, someday?

Nora: How can I tell? I have no idea what's going to become of me.

Helmer: But you're my wife, whatever becomes of you.

Nora: Listen, Torvald. I've heard that when a wife deserts her husband's house, the way I'm doing now, he's free of all legal obligations to her. In any event, I set you free from all your obligations. I don't want you to feel bound in the slightest, any more than I will. There has to be complete freedom on both sides. Look, here's your ring back. Give me mine.

Helmer: That too?

Nora: That too.

Helmer: Here it is.

Nora: Good. Now it's all over. I've left the keys here. The maids know all about how to run the house, much better than I do. Kristine will come by tomorrow after I leave her place and pack up my own things, the ones I brought with me from home. I'd like to have them sent to me.

Helmer: All over! All over! Nora, will you ever think about me again?

Nora: I know I'll often think about you, and the children, and this house.

Helmer: May I write to you, Nora?

Nora: No, never. You mustn't do that.

Helmer: But at least let me send you—

Nora: Nothing, nothing.

Helmer: Let me help you if you're in need.

Nora: No. I can't accept anything from a stranger.

Helmer: Nora . . . can't I ever be anything more than a stranger to you?

Nora (*picking up her bag*): Ah, Torvald, for that, the most wonderful miracle of all would have to happen.

Helmer: Tell me what that would be!

Nora: We'd both have to change so much that—Oh, Torvald, I've stopped believing in miracles.

Helmer: But I'll believe. Tell me! Change so much that . . . ?

Nora: That our life together would be a true marriage. Goodbye.

(*She goes out through the hall.*)

Helmer (*sinks down into a chair at the door and buries his face in his hands*): Nora! Nora! (*Looks around, and stands up.*) Empty. She's gone. (*A hope flashes across his mind.*) The most wonderful miracle of all . . . ?

(*The heavy sound of a closing door is heard from below.*)

Questions

ACT I

1. From the opening conversation between Helmer and Nora, what are your impressions of him? Of her? Of their marriage?
2. At what moment in the play do you understand why it is called *A Doll's House*?
3. In what ways does Mrs. Linde provide a contrast for Nora?
4. What in Krogstad's first appearance on stage, and in Dr. Rank's remarks about him, indicates that the bank clerk is a menace?
5. Of what illegal deed is Nora guilty? How does she justify it?
6. When the curtain falls on Act I, what problems now confront Nora?

ACT II

1. As Act II opens, what are your feelings on seeing the stripped, ragged Christmas tree? How is it suggestive?
2. What events that soon occur make Nora's situation even more difficult?
3. How does she try to save herself?
4. Why does Nora fling herself into the wild tarantella?

ACT III

1. For what possible reasons does Mrs. Linde pledge herself to Krogstad?
2. How does Dr. Rank's announcement of his impending death affect Nora and Helmer?
3. What is Helmer's reaction to learning the truth about Nora's misdeed? Why does he blame Nora's father? What is revealing (of Helmer's own character) in his remark, "From this moment on happiness is out of the question. All that matters now is to save the bits and pieces, to keep up the appearance—"?
4. When Helmer finds that Krogstad has sent back the note, what is his response? How do you feel toward him?
5. How does the character of Nora develop in this act?
6. How do you interpret her final slamming of the door?

General Questions

1. In what ways do you find Nora a victim? In what ways is she at fault?
2. Try to state the theme of the play. Does it involve women's rights? Self-fulfillment?
3. What dramatic question does the play embody? At what moment can this question first be stated?
4. What is the crisis? In what way is this moment or event a "turning point"? (In what new direction does the action turn?)
5. Eric Bentley, in an essay titled "Ibsen, Pro and Con" (*In Search of Theater* [New York: Knopf, 1953]), criticizes the character of Krogstad, calling him "a mere pawn of the plot." He then adds, "When convenient to Ibsen, he is a blackmailer. When inconvenient, he is converted." Do you agree or disagree?
6. Why is the play considered a work of Realism? Is there anything in it that does not seem realistic?
7. In what respects does *A Doll's House* seem to apply to life today? Is it in any way dated? Could there be a Nora in North America today?

Henrik Ibsen on Writing

Correspondence on the Final Scene of *A Doll's House*   1880, 1891

Translated by John Nilsen Laurvik and Mary Morison

Munich, 17 February 1880

To the Editor of the *Nationaltidende*

Sir,

In No. 1360 of your esteemed paper I have read a letter from Flensburg, in which it is stated that *A Doll's House* (in German *Nora*) has been acted there, and that the conclusion of the play has been changed—the alteration having been made, it is asserted, by my orders. This last statement is untrue. Immediately after the publication of *Nora*, I received from my translator, Mr. Wilhelm Lange of Berlin, the information that he had reason to fear that an "adaptation" of the play, giving it a different ending, was about to be published, and that this would probably be chosen in preference to the original by several of the North German theaters.

Henrik Ibsen

In order to prevent such a possibility, I sent to him, for use in case of absolute necessity, a draft of an altered last scene, according to which Nora does not leave the house, but is forcibly led by Helmer to the door of the children's bedroom; a short dialogue takes place, Nora sinks down at the door, and the curtain falls.

This change, I myself, in the letter to my translator, stigmatize as "barbaric violence" done to the play. Those who make use of the altered scene do so entirely against my wish. But I trust that it will not be used at very many German theaters.

. . . When my works are threatened, I prefer, taught by experience, to commit the act of violence myself, instead of leaving them to be treated and "adapted" by less careful and less skilful hands.

Yours respectfully,
Henrik Ibsen

Dear Count Proznor,   1891

Mr. Luigi Capuana° has, I regret to see, given you a great deal of trouble by his proposal to alter the last scene of *A Doll's House* for performance in the Italian theaters. . . . [T]he fact is that I cannot possibly directly authorize any change whatever in the ending of the drama. I may almost say that it was for the sake of the last scene that the whole play was written.

And, besides, I believe that Mr. Capuana is mistaken in fearing that the Italian public would not be able to understand or approve of my work if it were put on the stage in its original form. The experiment, ought, at any rate, to be tried. If it turns

---

Luigi Capuana: Italian novelist and dramatic critic who translated *A Doll's House* into Italian. It was the famous actress Eleonora Duse who wished him to alter the last scene of the play, but she finally relented and acted it in the original form.

out a failure, then let Mr. Capuana, on his own responsibility, employ your adaptation of the closing scene; for I cannot formally authorize, or approve of, such a proceeding.

I wrote to Mr. Capuana yesterday, briefly expressing my views on the subject; and I hope that he will disregard his misgivings until he has proved by experience that they are well founded.

At the time when *A Doll's House* was quite new, I was obliged to give my consent to an alteration of the last scene for Frau Hedwig Niemann-Raabe, who was to play the part of Nora in Berlin. At that time I had no choice. I was entirely unprotected by copyright law in Germany, and could, consequently prevent nothing. . . . With its altered ending it had only a short run. In its unchanged form it is still being played. . . .

> Your sincere and obliged,
>
> Henrik Ibsen

Tennessee Williams

The Glass Menagerie   1945

Tennessee Williams (1911–1983) was born Thomas Lanier Williams in Columbus, Mississippi, went to high school in St. Louis, and graduated from the University of Iowa. As an undergraduate, he saw a performance of Ibsen's Ghosts and decided to become a playwright himself. His family bore a close resemblance to the Wingfields in The Glass Menagerie: his mother came from a line of Southern blue bloods (Tennessee pioneers); his sister Rose suffered from incapacitating shyness; and as a young man, Williams himself, like Tom, worked at a job he disliked (in a shoe factory where his father worked), wrote poetry, sought refuge in moviegoing, and finally left home to wander and hold odd jobs. He worked as a bellhop in a New Orleans hotel; a teletype operator in Jacksonville, Florida; an usher and a waiter in New York. In 1945 The Glass Menagerie scored a success on Broadway, winning a Drama Critics Circle award. Two years later Williams received a Pulitzer Prize for A Streetcar Named Desire, a grim, powerful study of a woman's illusions and frustrations, set in New Orleans. In 1955 Williams was awarded another Pulitzer Prize for Cat on a Hot Tin Roof. Besides other plays, including Summer and Smoke (1948), Sweet Bird of Youth (1959), The Night of the Iguana (1961), Small Craft Warnings (1973), Clothes for a Summer Hotel (1980), and A House Not Meant to Stand (1981), Williams wrote two novels, poetry, essays, short stories, and Memoirs (1975).

CHARACTERS

Amanda Wingfield, the mother. A little woman of great but confused vitality clinging frantically to another time and place. Her characterization must be carefully created, not copied from type. She is not paranoiac, but her life is paranoia. There is much to admire in Amanda, and as much to love and pity as there is to laugh at. Certainly she has endurance and a kind of heroism, and though her foolishness makes her unwittingly cruel at times, there is tenderness in her slight person.

Laura Wingfield, her daughter. Amanda, having failed to establish contact with reality, continues to live vitally in her illusions, but Laura's situation is even graver. A childhood illness has left her crippled, one leg slightly shorter than the other, and held in a brace. This defect need not be more than suggested on the stage. Stemming from this, Laura's separation increases till she is like a piece of her own glass collection, too exquisitely fragile to move from the shelf.

Tom Wingfield, her son. And the narrator of the play. A poet with a job in a warehouse. His nature is not remorseless, but to escape from a trap he has to act without pity.

Jim O'Connor, the gentleman caller. A nice, ordinary, young man.

SCENE. *An alley in St. Louis.*

PART I. *Preparation for a Gentleman Caller.*

PART II. *The Gentleman Calls.*

TIME. *Now and the Past.*

> *Nobody, not even the rain, has such small hands.*
> —E. E. CUMMINGS

SCENE I

The Wingfield apartment is in the rear of the building, one of those vast hive-like conglomerations of cellular living-units that flower as warty growths in overcrowded urban centers of lower middle-class population and are symptomatic of the impulse of this largest and fundamentally enslaved section of American society to avoid fluidity and differentiation and to exist and function as one interfused mass of automatism.

The apartment faces an alley and is entered by a fire escape, a structure whose name is a touch of accidental poetic truth, for all of these huge buildings are always burning with the slow and implacable fires of human desperation. The fire escape is included in the set—that is, the landing of it and steps descending from it.

The scene is memory and is therefore unrealistic. Memory takes a lot of poetic license. It omits some details; others are exaggerated, according to the emotional value of the articles it touches, for memory is seated predominantly in the heart. The interior is therefore rather dim and poetic.

At the rise of the curtain, the audience is faced with the dark, grim rear wall of the Wingfield tenement. This building is flanked on both sides by dark, narrow alleys which run into murky canyons of tangled clotheslines, garbage cans, and the sinister latticework of neighboring fire escapes. It is up and down these side alleys that exterior entrances and exits are made during the play. At the end of Tom's opening commentary, the dark tenement wall slowly becomes transparent and reveals the interior of the ground-floor Wingfield apartment.

Nearest the audience is the living room, which also serves as a sleeping room for Laura, the sofa unfolding to make her bed. Just beyond, separated by a wide arch or second proscenium with transparent faded portieres (or second curtain), is the dining room. In an old-fashioned whatnot in the living room are seen scores of transparent glass animals. A blown-up photograph of the father hangs on the wall of the living room, to the left of the archway. It is the face of a very handsome young man in a doughboy's First World War cap. He is gallantly smiling, ineluctably smiling, as if to say "I will be smiling forever."

Also hanging on the wall, near the photograph, are a typewriter keyboard chart and a Gregg shorthand diagram. An upright typewriter on a small table stands beneath the charts.

Five years after *The Glass Menagerie*'s Broadway debut, a movie version was filmed starring Kirk Douglas, Jane Wyman, Gertrude Lawrence, and Arthur Kennedy.

The audience hears and sees the opening scene in the dining room through both the transparent fourth wall of the building and the transparent gauze portieres of the dining-room arch. It is during this revealing scene that the fourth wall slowly ascends, out of sight. This transparent exterior wall is not brought down again until the very end of the play, during Tom's final speech.

The narrator is an undisguised convention of the play. He takes whatever license with dramatic convention is convenient to his purposes.

Tom enters, dressed as a merchant sailor, and strolls across to the fire escape. There he stops and lights a cigarette. He addresses the audience.

Tom: Yes, I have tricks in my pocket, I have things up my sleeve. But I am the opposite of a stage magician. He gives you illusion that has the appearance of truth. I give you truth in the pleasant disguise of illusion.

To begin with, I turn back time. I reverse it to that quaint period, the thirties, when the huge middle class of America was matriculating in a school for the blind. Their eyes had failed them, or they had failed their eyes, and so they were having their fingers pressed forcibly down on the fiery Braille alphabet of a dissolving economy.

In Spain there was revolution. Here there was only shouting and confusion. In Spain there was Guernica. Here there were disturbances of labor, sometimes pretty violent, in otherwise peaceful cities such as Chicago, Cleveland, St. Louis. . . . This is the social background of the play.

Karen Allen and John Malkovich in a 1987 film of *The Glass Menagerie*, **directed by Paul Newman.**

(Music Begins To Play.)

The play is memory. Being a memory play, it is dimly lighted, it is sentimental, it is not realistic. In memory everything seems to happen to music. That explains the fiddle in the wings.

I am the narrator of the play, and also a character in it. The other characters are my mother, Amanda, my sister, Laura, and a gentleman caller who appears in the final scenes. He is the most realistic character in the play, being an emissary from a world of reality that we were somehow set apart from. But since I have a poet's weakness for symbols, I am using this character also as a symbol; he is the long-delayed but always expected something that we live for.

There is a fifth character in the play who doesn't appear except in this larger-than-life-size photograph over the mantel. This is our father who left us a long time ago. He was a telephone man who fell in love with long distances; he gave up his job with the telephone company and skipped the light fantastic out of town....

The last we heard of him was a picture postcard from Mazatlan, on the Pacific coast of Mexico, containing a message of two words: "Hello—Goodbye!" and an address. I think the rest of the play will explain itself....

Amanda's voice becomes audible through the portieres.

(Legend On Screen: "Où Sont Les Neiges.")°

"Où Son Les Nieges": A slide bearing this line is to be projected on a stage wall. The phrase is part of a famous line from French poet François Villon's *Ballad of the Dead Ladies*. The full line *"Où Sont Les Neiges D'antan?,"* meaning "But, where are the snows of yester-year?," is projected on the wall later in this scene.

Tom divides the portieres and enters the dining room. Amanda and Laura are seated at a drop-leaf table. Eating is indicated by gestures without food or utensils. Amanda faces the audience. Tom and Laura are seated in profile. The interior has lit up softly and through the scrim we see Amanda and Laura seated at the table.

Amanda *(calling)*: Tom?

Tom: Yes, Mother.

Amanda: We can't say grace until you come to the table!

Tom: Coming, Mother. *(He bows slightly and withdraws, reappearing a few moments later in his place at the table.)*

Amanda *(to her son)*: Honey, don't *push* with your *fingers*. If you have to push with something, the thing to push with is a crust of bread. And chew—chew! Animals have secretions in their stomachs which enable them to digest food without mastication, but human beings are supposed to chew their food before they swallow it down. Eat food leisurely, son, and really enjoy it. A well-cooked meal has lots of delicate flavors that have to be held in the mouth for appreciation. So chew your food and give your salivary glands a chance to function!

Tom deliberately lays his imaginary fork down and pushes his chair back from the table.

Tom: I haven't enjoyed one bite of this dinner because of your constant directions on how to eat it. It's you that make me rush through meals with your hawklike attention to every bite I take. Sickening—spoils my appetite—all this discussion of—animals' secretion—salivary glands—mastication!

Amanda *(lightly)*: Temperament like a Metropolitan star!

Tom rises and walks toward the living room.

You're not excused from the table.

Tom: I am getting a cigarette.

Amanda: You smoke too much.

Laura rises.

Laura: I'll bring in the blanc mange.

Tom remains standing with his cigarette by the portieres.

Amanda *(rising)*: No, sister, no, sister—you be the lady this time and I'll be the darky.

Laura: I'm already up.

Amanda: Resume your seat, little sister—I want you to stay fresh and pretty—for gentlemen callers!

Laura *(sitting down)*: I'm not expecting any gentlemen callers.

Amanda *(crossing out to kitchenette, airily)*: Sometimes they come when they are least expected! Why, I remember one Sunday afternoon in Blue Mountain—*(enters the kitchenette.)*

Tom: I know what's coming!

Laura: Yes. But let her tell it.

Tom: Again?

Laura: She loves to tell it.

Amanda returns with a bowl of dessert.

Amanda: One Sunday afternoon in Blue Mountain—your mother received— *seventeen!*—gentlemen callers! Why, sometimes there weren't chairs enough to accommodate them all. We had to send the nigger over to bring in folding chairs from the parish house.

Tom (remaining at the portieres): How did you entertain those gentlemen callers?

Amanda: I understood the art of conversation!

Tom: I bet you could talk.

Amanda: Girls in those days *knew* how to talk, I can tell you.

Tom: Yes?

(Image On Screen: Amanda As A Girl On A Porch, Greeting Callers.)

Amanda: They knew how to entertain their gentlemen callers. It wasn't enough for a girl to be possessed of a pretty face and a graceful figure—although I wasn't slighted in either respect. She also needed to have a nimble wit and a tongue to meet all occasions.

Tom: What did you talk about?

Amanda: Things of importance going on in the world! Never anything coarse or common or vulgar. *(She addresses Tom as though he were seated in the vacant chair at the table though he remains by the portieres. He plays this scene as though reading from a script.)* My callers were gentlemen—all! Among my callers were some of the most prominent young planters of the Mississippi Delta—planters and sons of planters!

Tom motions for music and a spot of light on Amanda. Her eyes lift, her face glows, her voice becomes rich and elegiac.

(Screen Legend: "Où Sont Les Neiges D'antan?")

There was young Champ Laughlin who later became vice-president of the Delta Planters Bank. Hadley Stevenson who was drowned in Moon Lake and left his widow one hundred and fifty thousand in Government bonds. There were the Cutrere brothers, Wesley and Bates. Bates was one of my bright particular beaux! He got in a quarrel with that wild Wainright boy. They shot it out on the floor of Moon Lake Casino. Bates was shot through the stomach. Died in the ambulance on his way to Memphis. His widow was also well provided-for, came into eight or ten thousand acres, that's all. She married him on the rebound—never loved her—carried my picture on him the night he died! And there was that boy that every girl in the Delta had set her cap for! That beautiful, brilliant young Fitzhugh boy from Greene County!

Tom: What did he leave his widow?

Amanda: He never married! Gracious, you talk as though all of my old admirers had turned up their toes to the daisies!

Tom: Isn't this the first you've mentioned that still survives?

Amanda: That Fitzhugh boy went North and made a fortune—came to be known as the Wolf of Wall Street! He had the Midas touch, whatever he touched turned to gold! And I could have been Mrs. Duncan J. Fitzhugh, mind you! But—I picked your *father*!

Laura (rising): Mother, let me clear the table.

Amanda: No, dear, you go in front and study your typewriter chart. Or practice your shorthand a little. Stay fresh and pretty!—It's almost time for our gentlemen callers to start arriving. (*She flounces girlishly toward the kitchenette.*) How many do you suppose we're going to entertain this afternoon?

Tom throws down the paper and jumps up with a groan.

Laura (*alone in the dining room*): I don't believe we're going to receive any, Mother.

Amanda (*reappearing, airily*): What? No one—not one? You must be joking! (*Laura nervously echoes her laugh. She slips in a fugitive manner through the half-open portieres and draws them gently behind her. A shaft of very clear light is thrown on her face against the faded tapestry of the curtains. Faintly the music of "The Glass Menagerie" is heard as she continues, lightly.*) Not one gentleman caller? It can't be true! There must be a flood, there must have been a tornado!

Laura: It isn't a flood, it's not a tornado, Mother. I'm just not popular like you were in Blue Mountain. . . . (*Tom utters another groan. Laura glances at him with a faint, apologetic smile. Her voice catches a little.*) Mother's afraid I'm going to be an old maid.

(The Scene Dims Out With The "Glass Menagerie" Music.)

SCENE II

On the dark stage the screen is lighted with the image of blue roses. Gradually Laura's figure becomes apparent and the screen goes out. The music subsides.

Laura is seated in the delicate ivory chair at the small clawfoot table. She wears a dress of soft violet material for a kimono—her hair is tied back from her forehead with a ribbon. She is washing and polishing her collection of glass. Amanda appears on the fire escape steps. At the sound of her ascent, Laura catches her breath, thrusts the bowl of ornaments away, and seats herself stiffly before the diagram of the typewriter keyboard as though it held her spellbound. Something has happened to Amanda. It is written in her face as she climbs to the landing: a look that is grim and hopeless and a little absurd. She has on one of those cheap or imitation velvety-looking cloth coats with imitation fur collar. Her hat is five or six years old, one of those dreadful cloche hats that were worn in the late Twenties, and she is clutching an enormous black patent-leather pocketbook with nickel clasps and initials. This is her full-dress outfit, the one she usually wears to the D.A.R. Before entering she looks through the door. She purses her lips, opens her eyes wide, rolls them upward and shakes her head. Then she slowly lets herself in the door. Seeing her mother's expression Laura touches her lips with a nervous gesture.

Laura: Hello, Mother, I was—(*She makes a nervous gesture toward the chart on the wall. Amanda leans against the shut door and stares at Laura with a martyred look.*)

Amanda: Deception? Deception? (*She slowly removes her hat and gloves, continuing the sweet suffering stare. She lets the hat and gloves fall on the floor—a bit of acting.*)

Laura (*shakily*): How was the D.A.R. meeting? (*Amanda slowly opens her purse and removes a dainty white handkerchief which she shakes out delicately and delicately touches to her lips and nostrils.*) Didn't you go to the D.A.R. meeting, Mother?

Amanda (*faintly, almost inaudibly*): —No.—No. (*Then more forcibly.*) I did not have the strength—to go to the D.A.R. In fact, I did not have the courage! I wanted to find a hole in the ground and hide myself in it forever! (*She crosses slowly to the wall and removes the diagram of the typewriter keyboard. She holds it in front of her for a second, staring at it sweetly and sorrowfully—then bites her lips and tears it in two pieces.*)

Laura (faintly): Why did you do that, Mother? (*Amanda repeats the same procedure with the chart of the Gregg Alphabet.*) Why are you—

Amanda: Why? Why? How old are you, Laura?

Laura: Mother, you know my age.

Amanda: I thought that you were an adult; it seems that I was mistaken. (*She crosses slowly to the sofa and sinks down and stares at Laura.*)

Laura: Please don't stare at me, Mother.

Amanda closes her eyes and lowers her head. There is a ten-second pause.

Amanda: What are we going to do, what is going to become of us, what is the future?

There is another pause.

Laura: Has something happened, Mother? (*Amanda draws a long breath, takes out the handkerchief again, goes through the dabbing process.*) Mother, has—something happened?

Amanda: I'll be all right in a minute, I'm just bewildered—(*She hesitates.*)—by life . . .

Laura: Mother, I wish that you would tell me what's happened.

Amanda: As you know, I was supposed to be inducted into my office at the D.A.R. this afternoon. (**Screen Image: A Swarm of Typewriters.**) But I stopped off at Rubicam's Business College to speak to your teachers about your having a cold and ask them what progress they thought you were making down there.

Laura: Oh . . .

Amanda: I went to the typing instructor and introduced myself as your mother. She didn't know who you were. "Wingfield," she said, "We don't have any such student enrolled at the school!"

I assured her she did, that you had been going to classes since early in January.

"I wonder," she said, "if you could be talking about that terribly shy little girl who dropped out of school after only a few days' attendance?"

"No," I said, "Laura, my daughter, has been going to school every day for the past six weeks!"

"Excuse me," she said. She took the attendance book out and there was your name, unmistakably printed, and all the dates you were absent until they decided that you had dropped out of school.

I still said, "No, there must have been some mistake! There must have been some mix-up in the records!"

And she said, "No—I remember her perfectly now. Her hands shook so that she couldn't hit the right keys! The first time we gave a speed test, she broke down completely—was sick at the stomach and almost had to be carried into the wash room! After that morning she never showed up any more. We phoned the house but never got any answer"—While I was working at Famous-Barr, I suppose, demonstrating those—(*She indicates a brassiere with her hands.*) Oh! I felt so weak I could barely keep on my feet! I had to sit down while they got me a glass of water! Fifty dollars' tuition, all of our plans—my hopes and ambitions for you—just gone up the spout, just gone up the spout like that. (*Laura draws a long breath and gets awkwardly to her feet. She crosses to the Victrola and winds it up.*) What are you doing?

Laura: Oh! (*She releases the handle and returns to her seat.*)

Amanda: Laura, where have you been going when you've gone out pretending that you were going to business college?

Laura: I've just been going out walking.

Amanda: That's not true.

Laura: It is. I just went walking.

Amanda: Walking? Walking? In winter? Deliberately courting pneumonia in that light coat? Where did you walk to, Laura?

Laura: All sorts of places—mostly in the park.

Amanda: Even after you'd started catching that cold?

Laura: It was the lesser of two evils, Mother. (**Screen Image: Winter Scene In Park.**) I couldn't go back there. I—threw up—on the floor!

Amanda: From half past seven till after five every day you mean to tell me you walked around in the park, because you wanted to make me think that you were still going to Rubicam's Business College?

Laura: It wasn't as bad as it sounds. I went inside places to get warmed up.

Amanda: Inside where?

Laura: I went in the art museum and the bird houses at the Zoo. I visited the penguins every day! Sometimes I did without lunch and went to the movies. Lately I've been spending most of my afternoons in the Jewel box, that big glass house where they raise the tropical flowers.

Amanda: You did all this to deceive me, just for deception? (*Laura looks down.*) Why?

Laura: Mother, when you're disappointed, you get that awful suffering look on your face, like the picture of Jesus' mother in the museum!

Amanda: Hush!

Laura: I couldn't face it.

> There is a pause. A whisper of strings is heard.

(Legend On Screen: "The Crust Of Humility.")

Amanda (hopelessly fingering the huge pocketbook): So what are we going to do the rest of our lives? Stay home and watch the parades go by? Amuse ourselves with the glass menagerie, darling? Eternally play those worn-out phonograph records your father left as a painful reminder of him? We won't have a business career—we've given that up because it gave us nervous indigestion! (*She laughs wearily.*) What is there left but dependency all our lives? I know so well what becomes of unmarried women who aren't prepared to occupy a position. I've seen such pitiful cases in the South—barely tolerated spinsters living upon the grudging patronage of sister's husband or brother's wife!—stuck away in some little mousetrap of a room—encouraged by one in-law to visit another—little birdlike women without any nest—eating the crust of humility all their life!

Is that the future that we've mapped out for ourselves? I swear it's the only alternative I can think of! (*She pauses.*) It isn't a very pleasant alternative, is it? (*She pauses again.*) Of course—some girls *do* marry. (*Laura twists her hands nervously.*) Haven't you ever liked some boy?

Laura: Yes. I liked one once. (*She rises.*) I came across his picture a while ago.

Amanda (with some interest): He gave you his picture?

Laura: No, it's in the yearbook.

Amanda (disappointed): Oh—a high school boy.

(Screen Image: Jim As A High-School Hero Bearing A Silver Cup.)

Laura: Yes. His name was Jim. (*Laura lifts the heavy annual from the claw-foot table.*) Here he is in *The Pirates of Penzance*.

Amanda (absently): The what?

Laura: The operetta the senior class put on. He had a wonderful voice and we sat across the aisle from each other Mondays, Wednesdays, and Fridays in the Aud. Here he is with the silver cup for debating! See his grin?

Amanda (absently): He must have had a jolly disposition.

Laura: He used to call me—Blue Roses.

(Image: Blue Roses.)

Amanda: Why did he call you such a name as that?

Laura: When I had that attack of pleurosis—he asked me what was the matter when I came back. I said pleurosis—he thought that I said Blue Roses! So that's what he always called me after that. Whenever he saw me, he'd holler, "Hello, Blue Roses!" I didn't care for the girl he went out with. Emily Meisenbach. Emily was the best-dressed girl at Soldan. She never struck me, though, as being sincere . . . It says in the Personal Section—they're engaged. That's—six years ago! They must be married by now.

Amanda: Girls that aren't cut out for business careers usually wind up married to some nice man. *(Gets up with a spark of revival.)* Sister, that's what you'll do!

Laura utters a startled, doubtful laugh. She reaches quickly for a piece of glass.

Laura: But, Mother—

Amanda: Yes? *(She goes over to the photograph.)*

Laura (in a tone of frightened apology): I'm—crippled!

Amanda: Nonsense! Laura, I've told you never, never to use that word. Why, you're not crippled, you just have a little defect—hardly noticeable, even! When people have some slight disadvantage like that, they cultivate other things to make up for it—develop charm—and vivacity—and—*charm!* That's all you have to do! *(She turns again to the photograph.)* One thing your father had *plenty of*—was *charm!*

(The Scene Fades Out With Music.)

SCENE III

(Legend On The Screen: "After The Fiasco—")

Tom speaks from the fire escape landing.

Tom: After the fiasco at Rubicam's Business College, the idea of getting a gentleman caller for Laura began to play a more and more important part in Mother's calculations. It became an obsession. Like some archetype of the universal unconscious, the image of the gentleman caller haunted our small apartment. . . . **(Screen Image: Young Man At The Door Of A House With Flowers.)** An evening at home rarely passed without some allusion to this image, this specter, this hope. . . . Even when he wasn't mentioned, his presence hung in Mother's preoccupied look and in my sister's frightened, apologetic manner—hung like a sentence passed upon the Wingfields!

Mother was a woman of action as well as words. She began to take logical steps in the planned direction. Late that winter and in the early spring— realizing that extra money would be needed to properly feather the nest and plume the bird—she conducted a vigorous campaign on the telephone, roping in subscribers to one of those magazines for matrons called *The Homemaker's Companion*, the type of journal that features the serialized sublimations of ladies of letters who think in terms of delicate cuplike breasts, slim, tapering waists, rich, creamy thighs, eyes like wood smoke in autumn, fingers that soothe and caress like strains of music, bodies as powerful as Etruscan sculpture.

(Screen Image: The Cover of a Glamor Magazine.)

Amanda enters with the telephone on a long extension cord. She is spotlighted in the dim stage.

Amanda: Ida Scott? This is Amanda Wingfield! We *missed* you at the D.A.R. last Monday! I said to myself: She's probably suffering with that sinus condition! How is that sinus condition?

 Horrors! Heaven have mercy!—You're a Christian martyr, yes, that's what you are, a Christian martyr!

 Well, I just now happened to notice that your subscription to the *Companion*'s about to expire! Yes, it expires with the next issue, honey!—just when that wonderful new serial by Bessie Mae Hopper is getting off to such an exciting start. Oh, honey, it's something that you can't miss! You remember how *Gone With the Wind* took everybody by storm? You simply couldn't go out if you hadn't read it. All everybody *talked* was Scarlett O'Hara. Well, this is a book that critics already compare to *Gone With the Wind*. It's the *Gone With the Wind* of the post-World-War generation!—What?—Burning?—Oh, honey, don't let them burn, go take a look in the oven and I'll hold the wire! Heavens—I think she's hung up!

(The Scene Dims Out.)
(Legend On Screen: "You Think I'm In Love With Continental Shoemakers?")

Before the lights come up again, the violent voices of Tom and Amanda are heard. They are quarreling behind the portieres. In front of them stands Laura with clenched hands and panicky expression. A clear pool of light is on her figure throughout this scene.

Tom: What in Christ's name am I—

Amanda (shrilly): Don't you use that—

Tom: —supposed to do!

Amanda: —expression! Not in my—

Tom: Ohhh!

Amanda: —presence! Have you gone out of your senses?

Tom: I have, that's true, *driven* out!

Amanda: What is the matter with you, you—big—big—IDIOT!

Tom: Look—I've got *no thing*, no single thing—

Amanda: Lower your voice!

Tom: —in my life here that I can call my OWN! Everything is—

Amanda: Stop that shouting!

Tom: Yesterday you confiscated my books! You had the nerve to—

Amanda: I took that horrible novel back to the library—yes! That hideous book by that insane Mr. Lawrence. (*Tom laughs wildly.*) I cannot control the output of diseased minds or people who cater to them—(*Tom laughs still more wildly.*) BUT I WON'T ALLOW SUCH FILTH BROUGHT INTO MY HOUSE! No, no, no, no, no!

Tom: House, house! Who pays rent on it, who makes a slave of himself to—

Amanda (fairly screeching): Don't you DARE to—

Tom: No, no, I mustn't say things! *I've* got to just—

Amanda: Let me tell you—

Tom: I don't want to hear any more!

> He tears the portieres open. The dining-room area is lit with a turgid smoky red glow. Now we see Amanda; her hair is in metal curlers and she is wearing a very old bathrobe, much too large for her slight figure, a relic of the faithless Mr. Wingfield. The upright typewriter now stands on the drop-leaf table, along with a wild disarray of manuscripts. The quarrel was probably precipitated by Amanda's interruption of Tom's creative labor. A chair lies overthrown on the floor. Their gesticulating shadows are cast on the ceiling by the fiery glow.

Amanda: You *will* hear more, you—

Tom: No, I won't hear more, I'm going out!

Amanda: You come right back in—

Tom: Out, out, out! Because I'm—

Amanda: Come back here, Tom Wingfield! I'm not through talking to you!

Tom: Oh, go—

Laura (desperately): —Tom!

Amanda: You're going to listen, and no more insolence from you! I'm at the end of my patience! *(He comes back toward her.)*

Tom: What do you think I'm at? Aren't I supposed to have any patience to reach the end of, Mother? I know, I know. It seems unimportant to you, what I'm *doing*—what I *want* to do—having a little *difference* between them! You don't think that—

Amanda: I think you've been doing things that you're ashamed of. That's why you act like this. I don't believe that you go every night to the movies. Nobody goes to the movies night after night. Nobody in their right minds goes to the movies as often as you pretend to. People don't go to the movies at nearly midnight, and movies don't let out at two A.M. Come in stumbling. Muttering to yourself like a maniac! You get three hours' sleep and then go to work. Oh, I can picture the way you're doing down there. Moping, doping, because you're in no condition.

Tom (wildly): No, I'm in no condition!

Amanda: What right have you got to jeopardize your job? Jeopardize the security of us all? How do you think we'd manage if you were—

Tom: Listen! You think I'm crazy about the *warehouse? (He bends fiercely toward her slight figure.)* You think I'm in love with the Continental Shoemakers? You think I want to spend fifty-five *years* down there in that—*celotex interior!* with— *fluorescent—tubes!* Look! I'd rather somebody picked up a crowbar and battered out my brains—than go back mornings! I *go!* Every time you come in yelling that God-damn "*Rise and Shine!*" "*Rise and Shine!*" I say to myself "How *lucky dead* people are!" But I get up. I *go!* For sixty-five dollars a month I give up all that I dream of doing and being *ever!* And you say self—*self's* all I ever think of. Why, listen, if self is what I thought of, Mother, I'd be where he is—GONE! *(He points to his father's picture.)* As far as the system of transportation reaches! *(He starts past her. She grabs his arm.)* Don't grab at me, Mother!

Amanda: Where are you going?

Tom: I'm going to the *movies!*

Amanda: I don't believe that lie!

Tom (Tom crouches toward her, overtowering her tiny figure. She backs away, gasping): I'm going to opium dens! Yes, opium dens, dens of vice and criminals' hangouts, Mother. I've joined the Hogan gang, I'm a hired assassin, I carry a tommy-gun in a violin case! I run a string of cat houses in the Valley! They call me Killer, Killer Wingfield, I'm leading a double-life, a simple, honest warehouse worker by day, by night a dynamic *czar* of the *underworld*, Mother. I go to gambling casinos, I spin away fortunes on the roulette table! I wear a patch over one eye and a false mustache, sometimes I put on green whiskers. On those occasions they call me— *El Diablo!* Oh, I could tell you many things to make you sleepless! My enemies plan to dynamite this place. They're going to blow us all sky-high some night! I'll be glad, very happy, and so will you! You'll go up, up on a broomstick, over Blue Mountain with seventeen gentlemen callers! You ugly—babbling old—*witch.* . . . *(He goes through a series of violent, clumsy movements, seizing his overcoat, lunging to the door, pulling it fiercely open. The women watch him, aghast. His arm catches in the sleeve of the coat as he struggles to pull it on. For a moment he is pinioned by the bulky garment. With an outraged groan he tears the coat off again, splitting the shoulder of it, and hurls it across the room. It strikes against the shelf of Laura's glass collection, and there is a tinkle of shattering glass. Laura cries out as if wounded.)*

(Music Legend: "The Glass Menagerie.")

Laura (shrilly): My glass!—menagerie. . . . *(She covers her face and turns away.)*

But Amanda is still stunned and stupefied by the "ugly witch" so that she barely notices this occurrence. Now she recovers her speech.

Amanda (in an awful voice): I won't speak to you—until you apologize! *(She crosses through the portieres and draws them together behind her. Tom is left with Laura. Laura clings weakly to the mantel with her face averted. Tom stares at her stupidly for a moment. Then he crosses to the shelf. He drops awkwardly on his knees to collect the fallen glass, glancing at Laura as if he would speak but couldn't.)*

("The Glass Menagerie" Music Steals In As The Scene Dims Out.)

SCENE IV

The interior of the apartment is dark. There is a faint light in the alley. A deep-voiced bell in a church is tolling the hour of five.

Tom appears at the top of the alley. After each solemn boom of the bell in the tower, he shakes a little noisemaker or rattle as if to express the tiny spasm of man in contrast to the sustained power and dignity of the Almighty. This and the unsteadiness of his advance make it evident that he has been drinking.

As he climbs the few steps to the fire escape landing light steals up inside. Laura appears in the front room in a nightdress. She notices that Tom's bed is empty.

Tom fishes in his pockets for his door key, removing a motley assortment of articles in the search, including a shower of movie ticket stubs and an empty bottle. At last he finds the key, but just as he is about to insert it, it slips from his fingers. He strikes a match and crouches below the door.

Tom (bitterly): One crack—and it falls through!

    Laura opens the door.

Laura: Tom! Tom, what are you doing?

Tom: Looking for a door key.

Laura: Where have you been all this time?

Tom: I have been to the movies.

Laura: All this time at the movies?

Tom: There was a very long program. There was a Garbo picture and a Mickey Mouse and a travelogue and a newsreel and a preview of coming attractions. And there was an organ solo and a collection for the Milk Fund—simultaneously—which ended up in a terrible fight between a fat lady and an usher!

Laura (innocently): Did you have to stay through everything?

Tom: Of course! And, oh, I forgot! There was a big stage show! The headliner on this stage show was Malvolio the Magician. He performed wonderful tricks, many of them, such as pouring water back and forth between pitchers. First it turned to wine and then it turned to beer and then it turned to whiskey. I know it was whiskey it finally turned into because he needed somebody to come up out of the audience to help him, and I came up—both shows! It was Kentucky Straight Bourbon. A very generous fellow, he gave souvenirs. *(He pulls from his back pocket a shimmering rainbow-colored scarf.)* He gave me this. This is his magic scarf. You can have it, Laura. You wave it over a canary cage and you get a bowl of goldfish. You wave it over the goldfish bowl and they fly away canaries. . . . But the wonderfullest trick of all was the coffin trick. We nailed him into a coffin and he got out of the coffin without removing one nail. *(He has come inside.)* There is a trick that would come in handy for me—get me out of this two-by-four situation! *(He flops onto the bed and starts removing his shoes.)*

Laura: Tom—shhh!

Tom: What're you shushing me for?

Laura: You'll wake up Mother.

Tom: Goody, goody! Pay 'er back for all those "Rise an' Shines." *(He lies down, groaning.)* You know it don't take much intelligence to get yourself into a nailed-up coffin, Laura. But who in hell ever got himself out of one without removing one nail?

    As if in answer, the father's grinning photograph lights up.

(The Scene Dims Out.)

Immediately following, the church bell is heard striking six. At the sixth stroke the alarm clock goes off in Amanda's room, and after a few moments we hear her calling: "Rise and Shine! Rise and Shine! Laura, go tell your brother to rise and shine!"

Tom (sitting up slowly): I'll rise—but I won't shine.

    The light increases.

Amanda: Laura, tell your brother his coffee is ready.

    Laura slips into the front room.

Laura: Tom!—It's nearly seven. Don't make Mother nervous. *(He stares at her stupidly.)* *(Beseechingly)* Tom, speak to Mother this morning. Make up with her, apologize, speak to her!

Tom: She won't to me. It's her that started not speaking.

Laura: If you just say you're sorry she'll start speaking.

Tom: Her not speaking—is that such a tragedy?

Laura: Please—please!

Amanda (calling from the kitchenette): Laura, are you going to do what I asked you to do, or do I have to get dressed and go out myself?

Laura: Going, going—soon as I get on my coat! *(She pulls on a shapeless felt hat with a nervous, jerky movement, pleadingly glancing at Tom. She rushes awkwardly for her coat. The coat is one of Amanda's, inaccurately made-over, the sleeves too short for Laura.)* Butter and what else?

Amanda (entering from the kitchenette): Just butter. Tell them to charge it.

Laura: Mother, they make such faces when I do that.

Amanda: Sticks and stones can break our bones, but the expression on Mr. Garfinkel's face won't harm us! Tell your brother his coffee is getting cold.

Laura (at the door): Do what I asked you, will you, will you, Tom?

> He looks sullenly away.

Amanda: Laura, go now or just don't go at all!

Laura (rushing out): Going—going! *(A second later she cries out. Tom springs up and crosses to the door. Tom opens the door.)*

Tom: Laura?

Laura: I'm all right. I slipped, but I'm all right.

Amanda (peering anxiously after her): If anyone breaks a leg on those fire-escape steps, the landlord ought to be sued for every cent he possesses! *(She shuts the door. Now she remembers she isn't speaking to Tom and returns to the other room.)*

> *As Tom comes listlessly for his coffee, she turns her back to him and stands rigidly facing the window on the gloomy gray vault of the areaway. Its light on her face with its aged but childish features is cruelly sharp, satirical as a Daumier print. The music of "Ave Maria," is heard softly.*

> *Tom glances sheepishly but sullenly at her averted figure and slumps at the table. The coffee is scalding hot; he sips it and gasps and spits it back in the cup. At his gasp, Amanda catches her breath and half turns. Then she catches herself and turns back to the window. Tom blows on his coffee, glancing sidewise at his mother. She clears her throat. Tom clears his. He starts to rise, sinks back down again, scratches his head, clears his throat again. Amanda coughs. Tom raises his cup in both hands to blow on it, his eyes staring over the rim of it at his mother for several moments. Then he slowly sets the cup down and awkwardly and hesitantly rises from the chair.*

Tom (hoarsely): Mother. I—I apologize. Mother. *(Amanda draws a quick, shuddering breath. Her face works grotesquely. She breaks into childlike tears.)* I'm sorry for what I said, for everything that I said, I didn't mean it.

Amanda (sobbingly): My devotion has made me a witch and so I make myself hateful to my children!

Tom: No, you *don't.*

Amanda: I worry so much, don't sleep, it makes me nervous!

Tom (gently): I understand that.

Amanda: I've had to put up a solitary battle all these years. But you're my right-hand bower!° Don't fall down, don't fail!

right-hand bower: the highest ranking and most powerful card in a card game.

Tom (gently): I try, Mother.

Amanda (with great enthusiasm): Try and you will *succeed!* (*The notion makes her breathless.*) Why, you—you're just *full* of natural endowments! Both of my children— they're *unusual* children! Don't you think I know it? I'm so—*proud!* Happy and—feel I've—so much to be thankful for but—promise me one thing, son!

Tom: What, Mother?

Amanda: Promise, son, you'll—never be a drunkard!

Tom (turns to her grinning): I will never be a drunkard, Mother.

Amanda: That's what frightened me so, that you'd be drinking! Eat a bowl of Purina!

Tom: Just coffee, Mother.

Amanda: Shredded wheat biscuit?

Tom: No. No, Mother, just coffee.

Amanda: You can't put in a day's work on an empty stomach. You've got ten minutes—don't gulp! Drinking too-hot liquids makes cancer of the stomach. . . . Put cream in.

Tom: No, thank you.

Amanda: To cool it.

Tom: No! No, thank you, I want it black.

Amanda: I know, but it's not good for you. We have to do all that we can to build ourselves up. In these trying times we live in, all that we have to cling to is—each other. . . . That's why it's so important to—Tom, I—I sent out your sister so I could discuss something with you. If you hadn't spoken I would have spoken to you. (*She sits down.*)

Tom (gently): What is it, Mother, that you want to discuss?

Amanda: Laura!

Tom puts his cup down slowly.

(Legend On Screen: "Laura.")

(Music: "The Glass Menagerie.")

Tom: —Oh.—Laura . . .

Amanda (touching his sleeve): You know how Laura is. So quiet but—still water runs deep! She notices things and I think she—broods about them. (*Tom looks up.*) A few days ago I came in and she was crying.

Tom: What about?

Amanda: You.

Tom: Me?

Amanda: She has an idea that you're not happy here.

Tom: What gave her that idea?

Amanda: What gives her any idea? However, you do act strangely. I—I'm not criticizing, understand *that!* I know your ambitions do not lie in the warehouse, that like everybody in the whole wide world—you've had to—make sacrifices, but— Tom—Tom—life's not easy, it calls for—Spartan endurance! There's so many things in my heart that I cannot describe to you! I've never told you but I—*loved* your father. . . .

Tom (gently): I know that, Mother.

Amanda: And you—when I see you taking after his ways! Staying out late—and— well, you *had* been drinking the night you were in that—terrifying condition!

Laura says that you hate the apartment and that you go out nights to get away from it! Is that true, Tom?

Tom: No. You say there's so much in your heart that you can't describe to me. That's true of me, too. There's so much in my heart that I can't describe to *you!* So let's respect each other's—

Amanda: But, why—*why,* Tom—are you always so *restless?* Where do you go to, nights?

Tom: I—go to the movies.

Amanda: Why do you go to the movies so much, Tom?

Tom: I go to the movies because—I like adventure. Adventure is something I don't have much of at work, so I go to the movies.

Amanda: But, Tom, you go to the movies *entirely* too *much!*

Tom: I like a lot of adventure.

Amanda looks baffled, then hurt. As the familiar inquisition resumes, Tom becomes hard and impatient again. Amanda slips back into her querulous attitude toward him.

(Image On Screen: Sailing Vessel With Jolly Roger.)

Amanda: Most young men find adventure in their careers.

Tom: Then most young men are not employed in a warehouse.

Amanda: The world is full of young men employed in warehouses and offices and factories.

Tom: Do all of them find adventure in their careers?

Amanda: They do or they do without it! Not everybody has a craze for adventure.

Tom: Man is by instinct a lover, a hunter, a fighter, and none of those instincts are given much play at the warehouse!

Amanda: Man is by instinct! Don't quote instinct to me! Instinct is something that people have got away from! It belongs to animals! Christian adults don't want it!

Tom: What do Christian adults want, then, Mother?

Amanda: Superior things! Things of the mind and the spirit! Only animals have to satisfy instincts! Surely your aims are somewhat higher than theirs! Than monkeys—pigs—

Tom: I reckon they're not.

Amanda: You're joking. However, that isn't what I wanted to discuss.

Tom (rising): I haven't much time.

Amanda (pushing his shoulder): Sit down.

Tom: You want me to punch in red at the warehouse, Mother?

Amanda: You have five minutes. I want to talk about Laura.

(Screen Legend: "Plans And Provisions.")

Tom: All right! What about Laura?

Amanda: We have to be making some plans and provisions for her. She's older than you, two years, and nothing has happened. She just drifts along doing nothing. It frightens me terribly how she just drifts along.

Tom: I guess she's the type that people call home girls.

Amanda: There's no such type, and if there is, it's a pity! That is unless the home is hers, with a husband!

Tom: What?

Amanda: Oh, I can see the handwriting on the wall as plain as I see the nose in front of my face! It's terrifying! More and more you remind me of your father! He was out all hours without explanation—Then *left! Goodbye!* And me with the bag to hold. I saw that letter you got from the Merchant Marine. I know what you're dreaming of. I'm not standing here blindfolded. (*She pauses.*) Very well, then. Then *do* it! But not till there's somebody to take your place.

Tom: What do you mean?

Amanda: I mean that as soon as Laura has got somebody to take care of her, married, a home of her own, independent—why, then you'll be free to go wherever you please, on land, on sea, whichever way the wind blows! But until that time you've got to look out for your sister. I don't say me because I'm old and don't matter! I say for your sister because she's young and dependent.

I put her in business college—a dismal failure! Frightened her so it made her sick at her stomach. I took her over to the Young People's League at the church. Another fiasco. She spoke to nobody, nobody spoke to her. Now all she does is fool with those pieces of glass and play those worn-out records. What kind of a life is that for a girl to lead!

Tom: What can I do about it?

Amanda: Overcome selfishness! Self, self, self is all that you ever think of! (*Tom springs up and crosses to get his coat. It is ugly and bulky. He pulls on a cap with earmuffs.*) Where is your muffler? Put your wool muffler on! (*He snatches it angrily from the closet, tosses it around his neck and pulls both ends tight.*) Tom! I haven't said what I had in mind to ask you.

Tom: I'm too late to—

Amanda (*catching his arm—very importunately; then shyly*): Down at the warehouse, aren't there some—nice young men?

Tom: No!

Amanda: There *must* be—*some . . .*

Tom: Mother—

He gestures.

Amanda: Find out one that's clean-living—doesn't drink and ask him out for sister!

Tom: What?

Amanda: For *sister!* To *meet! Get acquainted!*

Tom (*stamping to the door*): Oh, my go-osh!

Amanda: Will you? (*He opens the door, imploringly.*) Will you? (*He starts down the fire escape.*) Will you? *Will* you, dear?

Tom (*calling back*): Yes!

Amanda closes the door hesitantly and with a troubled but faintly hopeful expression.

(Screen Image: The Cover Of A Glamor Magazine.)

The spotlight picks up Amanda at the phone.

Amanda: Ella Cartwright? This is Amanda Wingfield! How are you, honey?
How is that kidney condition? (*There is a five-second pause.*) Horrors! (*There is another pause.*) You're a Christian martyr, yes, honey, that's what you are, a Christian martyr! Well, I just now happened to notice in my little red book that your subscription to the *Companion* has just run out! I knew that you wouldn't want to miss out on the wonderful serial starting in this new issue. It's by Bessie

Mae Hopper, the first thing she's written since *Honeymoon for Three*. Wasn't that a strange and interesting story? Well, this one is even lovelier, I believe. It has a sophisticated, society background. It's all about the horsey set on Long Island!

(The Light Fades Out.)

SCENE V

(Legend On The Screen: "Annunciation.")

Music is heard as the light slowly comes on.

It is early dusk of a spring evening. Supper has just been finished in the Wingfield apartment. Amanda and Laura in light-colored dresses are removing dishes from the table in the dining room, which is shadowy, their movements formalized almost as a dance or ritual, their moving forms as pale and silent as moths. Tom, in white shirt and trousers, rises from the table and crosses toward the fire escape.

Amanda (as he passes her): Son, will you do me a favor?
Tom: What?
Amanda: Comb your hair! You look so pretty when your hair is combed! (*Tom slouches on the sofa with the evening paper. Its enormous headline reads: "Franco Triumphs."*) There is only one respect in which I would like you to emulate your father.
Tom: What respect is that?
Amanda: The care he always took of his appearance. He never allowed himself to look untidy. (*He throws down the paper and crosses to fire escape.*) Where are you going?
Tom: I'm going out to smoke.
Amanda: You smoke too much. A pack a day at fifteen cents a pack. How much would that amount to in a month? Thirty times fifteen is how much, Tom? Figure it out and you will be astounded at what you could save. Enough to give you a night-school course in accounting at Washington U.! Just think what a wonderful thing that would be for you, son!

Tom is unmoved by the thought.

Tom: I'd rather smoke. (*He steps out on the landing, letting the screen door slam.*)
Amanda (sharply): I know! That's the tragedy of it. . . . (*Alone, she turns to look at her husband's picture.*)

(Dance Music: "The World Is Waiting For The Sunrise.")

Tom (to the audience): Across the alley from us was the Paradise Dance Hall. On evenings in spring the windows and doors were open and the music came outdoors. Sometimes the lights were turned out except for a large glass sphere that hung from the ceiling. It would turn slowly about and filter the dusk with delicate rainbow colors. Then the orchestra played a waltz or a tango, something that had a slow and sensuous rhythm. Couples would come outside, to the relative privacy of the alley. You could see them kissing behind ash pits and telephone poles. This was the compensation for lives that passed like mine, without any change or adventure. Adventure and change were imminent in this year. They were waiting around the corner for all these kids. Suspended in the mist over Berchtesgaden, caught in the folds of Chamberlain's umbrella. In Spain there was Guernica! But here there was only hot swing music and liquor, dance halls, bars, and movies, and sex that hung in the gloom like a chandelier and flooded the world with brief, deceptive rainbows. . . . All the world was waiting for bombardments!

Amanda turns from the picture and comes outside.

Amanda (sighing): A fire escape landing's a poor excuse for a porch. (*She spreads a newspaper on a step and sits down, gracefully and demurely as if she were settling into a swing on a Mississippi veranda.*) What are you looking at?

Tom: The moon.

Amanda: Is there a moon this evening?

Tom: It's rising over Garfinkel's Delicatessen.

Amanda: So it is! A little silver slipper of a moon. Have you made a wish on it yet?

Tom: Um-hum.

Amanda: What did you wish for?

Tom: That's a secret.

Amanda: A secret, huh? Well, I won't tell mine either. I will be just as mysterious as you.

Tom: I bet I can guess what yours is.

Amanda: Is my head so transparent?

Tom: You're not a sphinx.

Amanda: No, I don't have secrets. I'll tell you what I wished for on the moon. Success and happiness for my precious children! I wish for that whenever there's a moon, and when there isn't a moon, I wish for it, too.

Tom: I thought perhaps you wished for a gentleman caller.

Amanda: Why do you say that?

Tom: Don't you remember asking me to fetch one?

Amanda: I remember suggesting that it would be nice for your sister if you brought home some nice young man from the warehouse. I think I've made that suggestion more than once.

Tom: Yes, you have made it repeatedly.

Amanda: Well?

Tom: We are going to have one.

Amanda: What?

Tom: A gentleman caller!

(The Annunciation Is Celebrated With Music.)

Amanda rises.

(Image On Screen: A Caller With A Bouquet.)

Amanda: You mean you have asked some nice young man to come over?

Tom: Yep. I've asked him to dinner.

Amanda: You really did?

Tom: I did!

Amanda: You did, and did he—*accept?*

Tom: He did!

Amanda: Well, well—well, well! That's—lovely!

Tom: I thought that you would be pleased.

Amanda: It's definite, then?

Tom: Very definite.

Amanda: Soon?

Tom: Very soon.

Amanda: For heaven's sake, stop putting on and tell me some things, will you?

Tom: What things do you want me to tell you?

Amanda: *Naturally* I would like to know when he's *coming!*

Tom: He's coming tomorrow.

Amanda: *Tomorrow?*

Tom: Yep. Tomorrow.

Amanda: But, Tom!

Tom: Yes, Mother?

Amanda: Tomorrow gives me no time!

Tom: Time for what?

Amanda: Preparations! Why didn't you phone me at once, as soon as you asked him, the minute that he accepted? Then, don't you see, I could have been getting ready!

Tom: You don't have to make any fuss.

Amanda: Oh, Tom, Tom, Tom, of course I have to make a fuss! I want things nice, not sloppy! Not thrown together. I'll certainly have to do some fast thinking, won't I?

Tom: I don't see why you have to think at all.

Amanda: You just don't know. We can't have a gentleman caller in a pigsty! All my wedding silver has to be polished, the monogrammed table linen ought to be laundered! The windows have to be washed and fresh curtains put up. And how about clothes? We have to *wear* something, don't we?

Tom: Mother, this boy is no one to make a fuss over!

Amanda: Do you realize he's the first young man we've introduced to your sister? It's terrible, dreadful, disgraceful that poor little sister has never received a single gentleman caller! Tom, come inside! *(She opens the screen door.)*

Tom: What for?

Amanda: I want to ask you some things.

Tom: If you're going to make such a fuss, I'll call it off, I'll tell him not to come.

Amanda: You certainly won't do anything of the kind. Nothing offends people worse than broken engagements. It simply means I'll have to work like a Turk! We won't be brilliant, but we will pass inspection. Come on inside. *(Tom follows her inside, groaning.)* Sit down.

Tom: Any particular place you would like me to sit?

Amanda: Thank heavens I've got that new sofa! I'm also making payments on a floor lamp I'll have sent out! And put the chintz covers on, they'll brighten things up! Of course I'd hoped to have these walls re-papered. . . . What is the young man's name?

Tom: His name is O'Connor.

Amanda: That, of course, means fish—tomorrow is Friday! I'll have that salmon loaf—with Durkee's dressing! What does he do? He works at the warehouse?

Tom: Of course! How else would I—

Amanda: Tom, he—doesn't drink?

Tom: Why do you ask me that?

Amanda: Your father *did!*

Tom: Don't get started on that!

Amanda: He *does* drink, then?

Tom: Not that I know of!

Amanda: Make sure, be certain! The last thing I want for my daughter's a boy who drinks!

Tom: Aren't you being a little premature? Mr. O'Connor has not yet appeared on the scene!

Amanda: But will tomorrow. To meet your sister, and what do I know about his character? Nothing! Old maids are better off than wives of drunkards!

Tom: Oh, my God!

Amanda: Be still!

Tom (leaning forward to whisper): Lots of fellows meet girls whom they don't marry!

Amanda: Oh, talk sensibly, Tom—and don't be sarcastic! *(She has gotten a hairbrush.)*

Tom: What are you doing?

Amanda: I'm brushing that cowlick down! *(She attacks his hair with the brush.)* What is this young man's position at the warehouse?

Tom (submitting grimly to the brush and the interrogation): This young man's position is that of a shipping clerk, Mother.

Amanda: Sounds to me like a fairly responsible job, the sort of a job *you* would be in if you just had more *get-up*. What is his salary? Have you any idea?

Tom: I would judge it to be approximately eighty-five dollars a month.

Amanda: Well—not princely, but—

Tom: Twenty more than I make.

Amanda: Yes, how well I know! But for a family man, eighty-five dollars a month is not much more than you can just get by on. . . .

Tom: Yes, but Mr. O'Connor is not a family man.

Amanda: He might be, mightn't he? Some time in the future?

Tom: I see. Plans and provisions.

Amanda: You are the only young man that I know of who ignores the fact that the future becomes the present, the present the past, and the past turns into everlasting regret if you don't plan for it!

Tom: I will think that over and see what I can make of it!

Amanda: Don't be supercilious with your mother! Tell me some more about this— what do you call him?

Tom: James D. O'Connor. The D. is for Delaney.

Amanda: Irish on *both* sides! *Gracious!* And doesn't drink?

Tom: Shall I call him up and ask him right this minute?

Amanda: The only way to find out about those things is to make discreet inquiries at the proper moment. When I was a girl in Blue Mountain and it was suspected that a young man drank, the girl whose attentions he had been receiving, if any girl *was*, would sometimes speak to the minister of his church, or rather her father would if her father was living, and sort of feel him out on the young man's character. That is the way such things are discreetly handled to keep a young woman from making a tragic mistake!

Tom: Then how did you happen to make a tragic mistake?

Amanda: That innocent look of your father's had everyone fooled! He *smiled*—the world was *enchanted!* No girl can do worse than put herself at the mercy of a handsome appearance! I hope that Mr. O'Connor is not too good-looking.

Tom: No, he's not too good-looking. He's covered with freckles and hasn't too much of a nose.

Amanda: He's not right-down homely, though?

Tom: Not right-down homely. Just medium homely, I'd say.

Amanda: Character's what to look for in a man.

Tom: That's what I've always said, Mother.

Amanda: You've never said anything of the kind and I suspect you would never give it a thought.

Tom: Don't be suspicious of me.

Amanda: At least I hope he's the type that's up and coming.

Tom: I think he really goes in for self-improvement.

Amanda: What reason have you to think so?

Tom: He goes to night school.

Amanda (beaming): Splendid! What does he do, I mean study?

Tom: Radio engineering and public speaking!

Amanda: Then he has visions of being advanced in the world! Any young man who studies public speaking is aiming to have an executive job some day! And radio engineering? A thing for the future! Both of these facts are very illuminating. Those are the sort of things that a mother should know concerning any young man who comes to call on her daughter. Seriously or—not.

Tom: One little warning. He doesn't know about Laura. I didn't let on that we had dark ulterior motives. I just said, why don't you come and have dinner with us? He said okay and that was the whole conversation.

Amanda: I bet it was! You're eloquent as an oyster. However, he'll know about Laura when he gets here. When he sees how lovely and sweet and pretty she is, he'll thank his lucky stars he was asked to dinner.

Tom: Mother, you mustn't expect too much of Laura.

Amanda: What do you mean?

Tom: Laura seems all those things to you and me because she's ours and we love her. We don't even notice she's crippled any more.

Amanda: Don't say crippled! You know that I never allow that word to be used!

Tom: But face facts, Mother. She is and—that's not all—

Amanda: What do you mean "not all"?

Tom: Laura is very different from other girls.

Amanda: I think the difference is all to her advantage.

Tom: Not quite all—in the eyes of others—strangers—she's terribly shy and lives in a world of her own and those things make her seem a little peculiar to people outside the house.

Amanda: Don't say peculiar.

Tom: Face the facts. She is.

(The Dance Hall Music Changes To A Tango That Has A Minor And Somewhat Ominous Tone.)

Amanda: In what way is she peculiar—may I ask?

Tom (gently): She lives in a world of her own—a world of little glass ornaments, Mother.... (*He gets up. Amanda remains holding the brush, looking at him, troubled.*) She plays old phonograph records and—that's about all—(*He glances at himself in the mirror and crosses to the door.*)

Amanda (sharply): Where are you going?

Tom: I'm going to the movies. (*He goes out the screen door.*)

Amanda: Not to the movies, every night to the movies! (*She follows quickly to the screen door.*) I don't believe you always go to the movies! (*He is gone. Amanda looks worriedly after him for a moment. Then vitality and optimism return and she turns from the door, crossing to the portieres.)* Laura! Laura! *(Laura answers from the kitchenette.)*

Laura: Yes, Mother.

Amanda: Let those dishes go and come in front! *(Laura appears with a dish towel. Amanda speaks to her gaily.)* Laura, come here and make a wish on the moon!

(Screen Image: The Moon)

Laura (entering): Moon—moon?

Amanda: A little silver slipper of a moon. Look over your left shoulder, Laura, and make a wish! *(Laura looks faintly puzzled as if called out of sleep. Amanda seizes her shoulders and turns her at an angle by the door.)* Now! Now, darling, wish!

Laura: What shall I wish for, Mother?

Amanda (her voice trembling and her eyes suddenly filling with tears): Happiness! Good fortune!

The sound of the violin rises and the stage dims out.

SCENE VI

The light comes up on the fire escape landing. Tom is leaning against the grill, smoking.

(Screen Image: The High School Hero.)

Tom: And so the following evening I brought Jim home to dinner. I had known Jim slightly in high school. In high school Jim was a hero. He had tremendous Irish good nature and vitality with the scrubbed and polished look of white chinaware. He seemed to move in a continual spotlight. He was a star in basketball, captain of the debating club, president of the senior class and the glee club and he sang the male lead in the annual light operas. He was always running or bounding, never just walking. He seemed always at the point of defeating the law of gravity. He was shooting with such velocity through his adolescence that you would logically expect him to arrive at nothing short of the White House by the time he was thirty. But Jim apparently ran into more interference after his graduation from Soldan. His speed had definitely slowed. Six years after he left high school he was holding a job that wasn't much better than mine.

(Screen Image: The Clerk.)

He was the only one at the warehouse with whom I was on friendly terms. I was valuable to him as someone who could remember his former glory, who had seen him win basketball games and the silver cup in debating. He knew of my secret practice of retiring to a cabinet of the washroom to work on my poems when business was slack in the warehouse. He called me Shakespeare. And while the other boys in the warehouse regarded me with suspicious hostility, Jim took a humorous attitude toward me. Gradually his attitude affected the others, their hostility wore off and they also began to smile at me as people smile at an oddly fashioned dog who trots across their path at some distance.

I knew that Jim and Laura had known each other at Soldan, and I had heard Laura speak admiringly of his voice. I didn't know if Jim remembered her or not. In high school Laura had been as unobtrusive as Jim had been astonishing. If he did remember Laura, it was not as my sister, for when I asked him to dinner, he grinned and said, "You know, Shakespeare, I never thought of you as having folks!"

He was about to discover that I did. . . .

(Legend On Screen: "The Accent Of A Coming Foot.")

The light dims out on Tom and comes up in the Wingfield living room—a delicate, lemony light. It is about five on a Friday evening of late spring which comes "scattering poems in the sky."

Amanda has worked like a Turk in preparation for the gentleman caller. The results are astonishing. The new floor lamp with its rose silk shade is in place, a colored paper lantern conceals the broken light fixture in the ceiling, new billowing white curtains are at the windows, chintz covers are on chairs and sofa, a pair of new sofa pillows make their initial appearance. Open boxes and tissue paper are scattered on the floor.

Laura stands in the middle of the room with lifted arms while Amanda crouches before her, adjusting the hem of a new dress, devout and ritualistic. The dress is colored and designed by memory. The arrangement of Laura's hair is changed; it is softer and more becoming. A fragile, unearthly prettiness has come out in Laura: she is like a piece of translucent glass touched by light, given a momentary radiance, not actual, not lasting.

Amanda (impatiently): Why are you trembling?

Laura: Mother, you've made me so nervous!

Amanda: How have I made you nervous?

Laura: By all this fuss! You make it seem so important!

Amanda: I don't understand you, Laura. You couldn't be satisfied with just sitting home, and yet whenever I try to arrange something for you, you seem to resist it. (*She gets up.*) Now take a look at yourself. No, wait! Wait just a moment—I have an idea!

Laura: What is it now?

Amanda produces two powder puffs which she wraps in handkerchiefs and stuffs in Laura's bosom.

Laura: Mother, what are you doing?

Amanda: They call them "Gay Deceivers"!

Laura: I won't wear them!

Amanda: You will!

Laura: Why should I?

Amanda: Because, to be painfully honest, your chest is flat.

Laura: You make it seem like we were setting a trap.

Amanda: All pretty girls are a trap, a pretty trap, and men expect them to be. **(Legend On Screen: "A Pretty Trap.")** Now look at yourself, young lady. This is the prettiest you will ever be! (*She stands back to admire Laura.*) I've got to fix myself now! You're going to be surprised by your mother's appearance!

Amanda crosses through the portieres, humming gaily. Laura moves slowly to the long mirror and stares solemnly at herself. A wind blows the white curtains inward in a slow, graceful motion and with a faint, sorrowful sighing.

Amanda (from somewhere behind the portieres): It isn't dark enough yet. (*Laura turns slowly before the mirror with a troubled look.*)

(Legend On Screen: "This Is My Sister: Celebrate Her With Strings!" Music Plays.)

Amanda (laughing, still not visible): I'm going to show you something. I'm going to make a spectacular appearance!

Laura: What is it, Mother?

Amanda: Possess your soul in patience—you will see! Something I've resurrected from that old trunk! Styles haven't changed so terribly much after all. . . . (*She parts the portieres.*) Now just look at your mother! (*She wears a girlish frock of yellowed voile with a blue silk sash. She carries a bunch of jonquils—the legend of her youth is nearly revived. Now she speaks feverishly.*) This is the dress in which I led the cotillion. Won the cakewalk twice at Sunset Hill, wore one Spring to the Governor's Ball in Jackson! See how I sashayed around the ballroom, Laura? (*She raises her skirt and does a mincing step around the room.*) I wore it on Sundays for my gentlemen callers! I had it on the day I met your father . . . I had malaria fever all that Spring. The change of climate from East Tennessee to the Delta— weakened resistance—I had a little temperature all the time—not enough to be serious—just enough to make me restless and giddy! Invitations poured in— parties all over the Delta!—"Stay in bed," said Mother, "you have fever!"—but I just wouldn't. I took quinine but kept on going, going! Evenings, dances! After- noons, long, long rides! Picnics—lovely! So lovely, that country in May—all lacy with dogwood, literally flooded with jonquils! That was the spring I had the craze for jonquils. Jonquils became an absolute obsession. Mother said, "Honey, there's no more room for jonquils." And still I kept on bringing in more jonquils. Whenever, wherever I saw them, I'd say, "Stop! Stop! I see jonquils!" I made the young men help me gather the jonquils! It was a joke, Amanda and her jonquils! Finally there were no more vases to hold them, every available space was filled with jonquils. No vases to hold them? All right, I'll hold them myself! And then I—(*She stops in front of the picture.*) (**Music Plays.**) met your father! Malaria fever and jonquils and then—this—boy. . . . (*She switches on the rose-colored lamp.*) I hope they get here before it starts to rain. (*She crosses the room and places the jonquils in a bowl on the table.*) I gave your brother a little extra change so he and Mr. O'Connor could take the service car home.

Laura (with an altered look): What did you say his name was?

Amanda: O'Connor.

Laura: What is his first name?

Amanda: I don't remember. Oh, yes, I do. It was—Jim!

Laura sways slightly and catches hold of a chair.

(Legend On Screen. "Not Jim!")

Laura (faintly): Not—Jim!

Amanda: Yes, that was it, it was Jim! I've never known a Jim that wasn't nice!

(Music: The Music Becomes Ominous.)

Laura: Are you sure his name is Jim O'Connor?

Amanda: Yes. Why?

Laura: Is he the one that Tom used to know in high school?

Amanda: He didn't say so. I think he just got to know him at the warehouse.

Laura: There was a Jim O'Connor we both knew in high school—(*Then, with effort.*) If that is the one that Tom is bringing to dinner—you'll have to excuse me, I won't come to the table.

Amanda: What sort of nonsense is this?

Laura: You asked me once if I'd ever liked a boy. Don't you remember I showed you this boy's picture?

Amanda: You mean the boy you showed me in the yearbook?

Laura: Yes, that boy.

Amanda: Laura, Laura, were you in love with that boy?

Laura: I don't know, Mother. All I know is I couldn't sit at the table if it was him!

Amanda: It won't be him! It isn't the least bit likely. But whether it is or not, you will come to the table. You will not be excused.

Laura: I'll have to be, Mother.

Amanda: I don't intend to humor your silliness, Laura. I've had too much from you and your brother, both! So just sit down and compose yourself till they come. Tom has forgotten his key so you'll have to let them in, when they arrive.

Laura (panicky): Oh, Mother—*you* answer the door!

Amanda (lightly): I'll be in the kitchen—busy!

Laura: Oh, Mother, please answer the door, don't make me do it!

Amanda (crossing into the kitchenette): I've got to fix the dressing for the salmon. Fuss, fuss—silliness!—over a gentleman caller!

The door swings shut. Laura is left alone.

(Legend On Screen: "Terror!")

She utters a low moan and turns off the lamp—sits stiffly on the edge of the sofa, knotting her fingers together.

(Legend On Screen: "The Opening Of A Door!")

Tom and Jim appear on the fire escape steps and climb to the landing. Hearing their approach, Laura rises with a panicky gesture. She retreats to the portieres. The doorbell rings. Laura catches her breath and touches her throat. Low drums sound.

Amanda (calling): Laura, sweetheart! The door!

Laura stares at it without moving.

Jim: I think we just beat the rain.

Tom: Uh-huh. (*He rings again, nervously. Jim whistles and fishes for a cigarette.*)

Amanda (very, very gaily): Laura, that is your brother and Mr. O'Connor! Will you let them in, darling?

Laura crosses toward the kitchenette door.

Laura (breathlessly): Mother—you go to the door!

Amanda steps out of the kitchenette and stares furiously at Laura. She points imperiously at the door.

Laura: Please, please!

Amanda (in a fierce whisper): What is the matter with you, you silly thing?

Laura (desperately): Please, you answer it, *please!*

Amanda: I told you I wasn't going to humor you, Laura. Why have you chosen this moment to lose your mind?

Laura: Please, please, please, you go!

Amanda: You'll have to go to the door because I can't!

Laura (despairingly): I can't either!

Amanda: Why?

Laura: I'm sick!

Amanda: I'm sick, too—of your nonsense! Why can't you and your brother be normal people? Fantastic whims and behavior! (*Tom gives a long ring.*) Preposterous goings on! Can you give me one reason—(*She calls out lyrically.*) Coming! Just one second!—why should you be afraid to open a door? Now you answer it, Laura!

Laura: Oh, oh, oh . . . (*She returns through the portieres, darts to the Victrola, winds it frantically and turns it on.*)

Amanda: Laura Wingfield, you march right to that door!

Laura: Yes—yes, Mother!

> *A faraway, scratchy rendition of "Dardanella" softens the air and gives her strength to move through it. She slips to the door and draws it cautiously open. Tom enters with the caller, Jim O'Connor.*

Tom: Laura, this is Jim. Jim, this is my sister, Laura.

Jim (stepping inside): I didn't know that Shakespeare had a sister!

Laura (retreating, stiff and trembling, from the door): How—how do you do?

Jim (heartily, extending his hand): Okay!

> *Laura touches it hesitantly with hers.*

Jim: Your hand's *cold*, Laura!

Laura: Yes, well—I've been playing the Victrola. . . .

Jim: Must have been playing classical music on it! You ought to play a little hot swing music to warm you up!

Laura: Excuse me—I haven't finished playing the Victrola. . . .

> *She turns awkwardly and hurries into the front room. She pauses a second by the Victrola. Then she catches her breath and darts through the portieres like a frightened deer.*

Jim (grinning): What was the matter?

Tom: Oh—with Laura? Laura is—terribly shy.

Jim: Shy, huh? It's unusual to meet a shy girl nowadays. I don't believe you ever mentioned you had a sister.

Tom: Well, now you know. I have one. Here is the *Post Dispatch*. You want a piece of it?

Jim: Uh-huh.

Tom: What piece? The comics?

Jim: Sports! (*He glances at it.*) Ole Dizzy Dean is on his bad behavior.

Tom (uninterest): Yeah? (*He lights a cigarette and goes over to the fire-escape door.*)

Jim: Where are *you* going?

Tom: I'm going out on the terrace.

Jim (going after him): You know, Shakespeare—I'm going to sell you a bill of goods!

Tom: What goods?

Jim: A course I'm taking.

Tom: Huh?

Jim: In public speaking! You and me, we're not the warehouse type.

Tom: Thanks—that's good news. But what has public speaking got to do with it?

Jim: It fits you for—executive positions!

Tom: Awww.

Jim: I tell you it's done a helluva lot for me.

(Image On Screen: Executive At His Desk.)

Tom: In what respect?

Jim: In every! Ask yourself what is the difference between you an' me and men in the office down front? Brains?—No!—Ability?—No! Then what? Just one little thing—

Tom: What is that one little thing?

Jim: Primarily it amounts to—social poise! Being able to square up to people and hold your own on any social level!

Amanda (from the kitchenette): Tom?

Tom: Yes, Mother?

Amanda: Is that you and Mr. O'Connor?

Tom: Yes, Mother.

Amanda: Well, you just make yourselves comfortable in there.

Tom: Yes, Mother.

Amanda: Ask Mr. O'Connor if he would like to wash his hands.

Jim: Aw, no—no—thank you—I took care of that at the warehouse. Tom—

Tom: Yes?

Jim: Mr. Mendoza was speaking to me about you.

Tom: Favorably?

Jim: What do you think?

Tom: Well—

Jim: You're going to be out of a job if you don't wake up.

Tom: I am waking up—

Jim: You show no signs.

Tom: The signs are interior.

(Image On Screen: The Sailing Vessel With Jolly Roger Again.)

Tom: I'm planning to change. (*He leans over the fire-escape rail, speaking with quiet exhilaration. The incandescent marquees and signs of the first-run movie houses light his face from across the alley. He looks like a voyager.*) I'm right at the point of committing myself to a future that doesn't include the warehouse and Mr. Mendoza or even a night-school course in public speaking.

Jim: What are you gassing about?

Tom: I'm tired of the movies.

Jim: Movies!

Tom: Yes, movies! Look at them—(*A wave toward the marvels of Grand Avenue.*) All of those glamorous people—having adventures—hogging it all, gobbling the whole thing up! You know what happens? People go to the *movies* instead of *moving*! Hollywood characters are supposed to have all the adventures for everybody in America, while everybody in America sits in a dark room and watches them have them! Yes, until there's a war. That's when adventure becomes available to the masses! *Everyone's* dish, not only Gable's! Then the people in the dark room come out of the dark room to have some adventures themselves—goody, goody! It's our turn now, to go to the South Sea Island—to make a safari—to be exotic, far-off—But I'm not patient. I don't want to wait till then. I'm tired of the *movies* and I am *about* to *move*!

Jim *(incredulously)*: Move?

Tom: Yes!

Jim: When?

Tom: Soon!

Jim: Where? Where?

The music seems to answer the question, while Tom thinks it over. He searches in his pockets.

Tom: I'm starting to boil inside. I know I seem dreamy, but inside—well, I'm boiling! Whenever I pick up a shoe, I shudder a little thinking how short life is and what I am doing! Whatever that means. I know it doesn't mean shoes—except as something to wear on a traveler's feet! *(He finds what he has been searching for in his pockets and holds out a paper to Jim.)* Look—

Jim: What?

Tom: I'm a member.

Jim *(reading)*: The Union of Merchant Seamen.

Tom: I paid my dues this month, instead of the light bill.

Jim: You will regret it when they turn the lights off.

Tom: I won't be here.

Jim: How about your mother?

Tom: I'm like my father. The bastard son of a bastard! Did you notice how he's grinning in his picture in there? And he's been absent going on sixteen years!

Jim: You're just talking, you drip. How does your mother feel about it?

Tom: Shhh! Here comes Mother! Mother is not acquainted with my plans!

Amanda *(coming through the portieres)*: Where are you all?

Tom: On the terrace, Mother.

They start inside. She advances to them. Tom is distinctly shocked at her appearance. Even Jim blinks a little. He is making his first contact with girlish Southern vivacity and in spite of the night-school course in public speaking is somewhat thrown off the beam by the unexpected outlay of social charm. Certain responses are attempted by Jim but are swept aside by Amanda's gay laughter and chatter. Tom is embarrassed but after the first shock Jim reacts very warmly. He grins and chuckles, is altogether won over.

(Image On Screen: Amanda As A Girl.)

Amanda *(coyly smiling, shaking her girlish ringlets)*: Well, well, well, so this is Mr. O'Connor. Introductions entirely unnecessary. I've heard so much about you from my boy. I finally said to him, Tom—good gracious!—why don't you bring this paragon to supper? I'd like to meet this nice young man at the warehouse!—Instead of just hearing him sing your praises so much! I don't know why my son is so stand-offish—that's not Southern behavior!

Let's sit down and—I think we could stand a little more air in here! Tom, leave the door open. I felt a nice fresh breeze a moment ago. Where has it gone to? Mmm, so warm already! And not quite summer, even. We're going to burn up when summer really gets started. However, we're having—we're having a very light supper. I think light things are better fo' this time of year. The same as light clothes are. Light clothes an' light food are what warm weather calls fo'. You know our blood gets so thick during th' winter—it takes a while fo' us to *adjust* ou'selves!—when the season changes . . . It's come so quick this year. I wasn't prepared. All of a sudden—heavens! Already summer! I ran to the trunk an' pulled out this light dress—Terribly old! Historical almost! But feels so good—so good an' co-ol, y' know. . . .

Tom: Mother—

Amanda: Yes, honey?

Tom: How about—supper?

Amanda: Honey, you go ask Sister if supper is ready! You know that Sister is in full charge of supper! Tell her you hungry boys are waiting for it. *(To Jim)* Have you met Laura?

Jim: She—

Amanda: Let you in? Oh, good, you've met already! It's rare for a girl as sweet an' pretty as Laura to be domestic! But Laura is, thank heavens, not only pretty but also very domestic. I'm not at all. I never was a bit. I never could make a thing but angel-food cake. Well, in the South we had so many servants. Gone, gone, gone. All vestige of gracious living! Gone completely! I wasn't prepared for what the future brought me. All of my gentlemen callers were sons of planters and so of course I assumed that I would be married to one and raise my family on a large piece of land with plenty of servants. But man proposes—and woman accepts the proposal! To vary that old, old saying a little bit—I married no planter! I married a man who worked for the telephone company! That gallantly smiling gentleman over there! *(She points to the picture.)* A telephone man who—fell in love with long-distance! Now he travels and I don't even know where! But what am I going on for about my—tribulations? Tell me yours—I hope you don't have any! Tom?

Tom (returning): Yes, Mother?

Amanda: Is supper nearly ready?

Tom: It looks to me like supper is on the table.

Amanda: Let me look—(*She rises prettily and looks through portieres.*) Oh, lovely! But where is Sister?

Tom: Laura is not feeling well and she says that she thinks she'd better not come to the table.

Amanda: What? Nonsense! Laura? Oh, Laura!

Laura (from the kitchenette, faintly): Yes, Mother.

Amanda: You really must come to the table. We won't be seated until you come to the table! Come in, Mr. O'Connor. You sit over there, and I'll . . . Laura? Laura Wingfield! You're keeping us waiting, honey! We can't say grace until you come to the table!

The kitchenette door is pushed weakly open and Laura comes in. She is obviously quite faint, her lips trembling, her eyes wide and staring. She moves unsteadily toward the table.

(Screen Legend: "Terror!")

Outside a summer storm is coming on abruptly. The white curtains billow inward at the windows and there is a sorrowful murmur and deep blue dusk.

Laura suddenly stumbles; she catches at a chair with a faint moan.

Tom: Laura!

Amanda: Laura! *(There is a clap of thunder.)* (**Screen Legend: "Ah!"**) *(Despairingly.)* Why, Laura, you *are* ill, darling! Tom, help your sister into the living room, dear! Sit in the living room, Laura—rest on the sofa. Well! *(To Jim as Tom helps his sister to the sofa in the living room)* Standing over the hot stove made her ill! I told her that it was just too warm this evening, but—*(Tom comes back to the table.)* Is Laura all right now?

Tom: Yes.

Amanda: What *is* that? Rain? A nice cool rain has come up! *(She gives Jim a frightened look.)* I think we may—have grace—now . . . *(Tom looks at her stupidly.)* Tom, honey—you say grace!

Tom: Oh . . . "For these and all thy mercies—" *(They bow their heads, Amanda stealing a nervous glance at Jim. In the living room Laura, stretched on the sofa, clenches her hand to her lips, to hold back a shuddering sob.)* God's Holy Name be praised—

(The Scene Dims Out.)

SCENE VII

It is half an hour later. Dinner is just being finished in the dining room. Laura is still huddled upon the sofa, her feet drawn under her, her head resting on a pale blue pillow, her eyes wide and mysteriously watchful. The new floor lamp with its shade of rose-colored silk gives a soft, becoming light to her face, bringing out the fragile, unearthly prettiness which usually escapes attention. From outside there is a steady murmur of rain, but it is slackening and soon the air outside becomes pale and luminous as the moon breaks through the clouds. A moment after the curtain rises, the lights in both rooms flicker and go out.

Jim: Hey, there, Mr. Light Bulb!

Amanda laughs nervously.

(Legend On Screen: "Suspension Of A Public Service.")

Amanda: Where was Moses when the lights went out? Ha-ha. Do you know the answer to that one, Mr. O'Connor?

Jim: No, Ma'am, what's the answer?

Amanda: In the dark! *(Jim laughs appreciatively.)* Everybody sit still. I'll light the candles. Isn't it lucky we have them on the table? Where's a match? Which of you gentlemen can provide a match?

Jim: Here.

Amanda: Thank you, sir.

Jim: Not at all, Ma'am!

Amanda (as she lights the candles): I guess the fuse has burnt out. Mr. O'Connor, can you tell a burnt-out fuse? I know I can't and Tom is a total loss when it comes to mechanics. *(They rise from the table and go into the kitchenette, from where their voices are heard.)* Oh, be careful you don't bump into something. We don't want our gentleman caller to break his neck. Now wouldn't that be a fine howdy-do?

Jim: Ha-ha! Where is the fuse-box?

Amanda: Right here next to the stove. Can you see anything?

Jim: Just a minute.

Amanda: Isn't electricity a mysterious thing? Wasn't it Benjamin Franklin who tied a key to a kite? We live in such a mysterious universe, don't we? Some people say that science clears up all the mysteries for us. In my opinion it only creates more! Have you found it yet?

Jim: No, Ma'am. All these fuses look okay to me.

Amanda: Tom!

Tom: Yes, Mother?

Amanda: That light bill I gave you several days ago. The one I told you we got the notices about?

(Legend: "Ha!")

Tom: Oh—yeah.

Amanda: You didn't neglect to pay it by any chance?

Tom: Why, I—

Amanda: Didn't! I might have known it!

Jim: Shakespeare probably wrote a poem on that light bill, Mrs. Wingfield.

Amanda: I might have known better than to trust him with it! There's such a high price for negligence in this world!

Jim: Maybe the poem will win a ten-dollar prize.

Amanda: We'll just have to spend the remainder of the evening in the nineteenth century, before Mr. Edison made the Mazda lamp!

Jim: Candlelight is my favorite kind of light.

Amanda: That shows you're romantic! But that's no excuse for Tom. Well, we got through dinner. Very considerate of them to let us get through dinner before they plunged us into everlasting darkness, wasn't it, Mr. O'Connor?

Jim: Ha-ha!

Amanda: Tom, as a penalty for your carelessness you can help me with the dishes.

Jim: Let me give you a hand.

Amanda: Indeed you will not!

Jim: I ought to be good for something.

Amanda: Good for something? (*Her tone is rhapsodic.*) You? Why, Mr. O'Connor, nobody, *nobody's* given me this much entertainment in years—as you have!

Jim: Aw, now, Mrs. Wingfield!

Amanda: I'm not exaggerating, not one bit! But Sister is all by her lonesome. You go keep her company in the parlor! I'll give you this lovely old candelabrum that used to be on the altar at the church of the Heavenly Rest. It was melted a little out of shape when the church burnt down. Lightning struck it one spring. Gypsy Jones was holding a revival at the time and he intimated that the church was destroyed because the Episcopalians gave card parties.

Jim: Ha-ha.

Amanda: And how about you coaxing Sister to drink a little wine? I think it would be good for her! Can you carry both at once?

Jim: Sure. I'm Superman!

Amanda: Now, Thomas, get into this apron!

Jim comes into the dining room, carrying the candelabrum, its candles lighted, in one hand and a glass of wine in the other. The door of the kitchenette swings closed on Amanda's gay laughter; the flickering light approaches the portieres. Laura sits up nervously as Jim enters. She can hardly speak from the almost intolerable strain of being alone with a stranger.

(Screen Legend: "I Don't Suppose You Remember Me At All!")

At first, before Jim's warmth overcomes her paralyzing shyness, Laura's voice is thin and breathless, as though she had just run up a steep flight of stairs. Jim's attitude is gently humorous. While the incident is apparently unimportant, it is to Laura the climax of her secret life.

Jim: Hello there, Laura.

Laura (faintly): Hello. *(She clears her throat.)*

Jim: How are you feeling now? Better?

Laura: Yes. Yes, thank you.

Jim: This is for you. A little dandelion wine. *(He extends the glass toward her with extravagant gallantry.)*

Laura: Thank you.

Jim: Drink it—but don't get drunk! *(He laughs heartily. Laura takes the glass uncertainly; laughs shyly.)* Where shall I set the candles?

Laura: Oh—oh, anywhere...

Jim: How about here on the floor? Any objections?

Laura: No.

Jim: I'll spread a newspaper under to catch the drippings. I like to sit on the floor. Mind if I do?

Laura: Oh, no.

Jim: Give me a pillow?

Laura: What?

Jim: A pillow!

Laura: Oh . . . *(She hands him one quickly.)*

Jim: How about you? Don't you like to sit on the floor?

Laura: Oh—yes.

Jim: Why don't you, then?

Laura: I—will.

Jim: Take a pillow! *(Laura does. She sits on the floor on the other side of the candelabrum. Jim crosses his legs and smiles engagingly at her.)* I can't hardly see you sitting way over there.

Laura: I can—see you.

Jim: I know, but that's not fair, I'm in the limelight. *(Laura moves her pillow closer.)* Good! Now I can see you! Comfortable?

Laura: Yes.

Jim: So am I. Comfortable as a cow. Will you have some gum?

Laura: No, thank you.

Jim: I think that I will indulge, with your permission. *(He musingly unwraps it and holds it up.)* Think of the fortune made by the guy that invented the first piece of chewing gum. Amazing, huh? The Wrigley Building is one of the sights of Chicago—I saw it when I went up to the Century of Progress. Did you take in the Century of Progress?

Laura: No, I didn't.

Jim: Well, it was quite a wonderful exposition. What impressed me most was the Hall of Science. Gives you an idea of what the future will be in America, even more wonderful than the present time is! *(There is a pause. Jim smiles at her.)* Your brother tells me you're shy. Is that right, Laura?

Laura: I—don't know.

Jim: I judge you to be an old-fashioned type of girl. Well, I think that's a pretty good type to be. Hope you don't think I'm being too personal—do you?

Laura (hastily, out of embarrassment): I believe I *will* take a piece of gum, if you—don't mind. *(Clearing her throat.)* Mr. O'Connor, have you—kept up with your singing?

Jim: Singing? Me?

Laura: Yes. I remember what a beautiful voice you had.

Jim: When did you hear me sing?

> *Laura does not answer, and in the long pause which follows a man's voice is heard singing offstage.*

Voice:

> O blow, ye winds, heigh-ho,
> A-roving I will go!
> I'm off to my love
> With a boxing glove—
> Ten thousand miles away!

Jim: You say you've heard me sing?

Laura: Oh, yes! Yes, very often . . . I—don't suppose—you remember me—at all?

Jim (smiling doubtfully): You know I have an idea I've seen you before. I had that idea soon as you opened the door. It seemed almost like I was about to remember your name. But the name that I started to call you—wasn't a name! And so I stopped myself before I said it.

Laura: Wasn't it—Blue Roses?

Jim (springing up, grinning): Blue Roses! My gosh, yes—Blue Roses! That's what I had on my tongue when you opened the door! Isn't it funny what tricks your memory plays? I didn't connect you with high school somehow or other. But that's where it was; it was high school. I didn't even know you were Shakespeare's sister! Gosh, I'm sorry.

Laura: I didn't expect you to. You—barely knew me!

Jim: But we did have a speaking acquaintance, huh?

Laura: Yes, we—spoke to each other.

Jim: When did you recognize me?

Laura: Oh, right away!

Jim: Soon as I came in the door?

Laura: When I heard your name I thought it was probably you. I knew that Tom used to know you a little in high school. So when you came in the door—well, then I was—sure.

Jim: Why didn't you *say* something, then?

Laura (breathlessly): I didn't know what to say, I was—too surprised!

Jim: For goodness' sakes! You know, this sure is funny!

Laura: Yes! Yes, isn't it, though…

Jim: Didn't we have a class in something together?

Laura: Yes, we did.

Jim: What class was that?

Laura: It was—singing—chorus!

Jim: Aw!

Laura: I sat across the aisle from you in the Aud.

Jim: Aw.

Laura: Mondays, Wednesdays, and Fridays.

Jim: Now I remember—you always came in late.

Laura: Yes, it was so hard for me, getting upstairs. I had that brace on my leg—it clumped so loud!

Jim: I never heard any clumping.

Laura (wincing at the recollection): To me it sounded like—thunder!

Jim: Well, well, well, I never even noticed.

Laura: And everybody was seated before I came in. I had to walk in front of all those people. My seat was in the back row. I had to go clumping all the way up the aisle with everyone watching!

Jim: You shouldn't have been self-conscious.

Laura: I know, but I was. It was always such a relief when the singing started.

Jim: Aw, yes, I've placed you now! I used to call you Blue Roses. How was it that I got started calling you that?

Laura: I was out of school a little while with pleurosis. When I came back you asked me what was the matter. I said I had pleurosis—you thought I said *Blue Roses.* That's what you always called me after that!

Jim: I hope you didn't mind.

Laura: Oh, no—I liked it. You see, I wasn't acquainted with many—people. . . .

Jim: As I remember you sort of stuck by yourself.

Laura: I—I—never had much luck at—making friends.

Jim: I don't see why you wouldn't.

Laura: Well, I—started out badly.

Jim: You mean being—

Laura: Yes, it sort of—stood between me—

Jim: You shouldn't have let it!

Laura: I know, but it did, and—

Jim: You were shy with people!

Laura: I tried not to be but never could—

Jim: Overcome it?

Laura: No, I—I never could!

Jim: I guess being shy is something you have to work out of kind of gradually.

Laura (sorrowfully): Yes—I guess it—

Jim: Takes time!

Laura: Yes—

Jim: People are not so dreadful when you know them. That's what you have to remember! And everybody has problems, not just you, but practically everybody has got some problems. You think of yourself as having the only problems, as being the only one who is disappointed. But just look around you and you will see lots of people as disappointed as you are. For instance, I hoped when I was going to high school that I would be further along at this time, six years later, than I am now. You remember that wonderful write-up I had in *The Torch?*

Laura: Yes! *(She rises and crosses to the table.)*

Jim: It said I was bound to succeed in anything I went into! *(Laura returns with the high school yearbook.)* Holy Jeez! *The Torch!* *(He accepts it reverently. They smile across the book with mutual wonder. Laura crouches beside him and they begin to turn the pages. Laura's shyness is dissolving in his warmth.)*

Laura: Here you are in *The Pirates of Penzance!*

Jim (wistfully): I sang the baritone lead in that operetta.

Laura (raptly): So—*beautifully!*

Jim (protesting): Aw—

Laura: Yes, yes—beautifully—beautifully!

Jim: You heard me?

Laura: All three times!

Jim: No!

Laura: Yes!

Jim: All three performances?

Laura (looking down): Yes.

Jim: Why?

Laura: I—wanted to ask you to—autograph my program.

Jim: Why didn't you ask me to?

Laura: You were always surrounded by your own friends so much that I never had a chance to.

Jim: You should have just—

Laura: Well, I—thought you might think I was—

Jim: Thought I might think you was—what?

Laura: Oh—

Jim (with reflective relish): I was beleaguered by females in those days.

Laura: You were terribly popular!

Jim: Yeah—

Laura: You had such a—friendly way—

Jim: I was spoiled in high school.

Laura: Everybody—liked you!

Jim: Including you?

Laura: I—yes, I—did, too—(*She gently closes the book in her lap.*)

Jim: Well, well, well!—Give me that program, Laura. (*She hands it to him. He signs it with a flourish.*) There you are—better late than never!

Laura: Oh, I—what a—surprise!

Jim: My signature isn't worth very much right now. But some day—maybe—it will increase in value! Being disappointed is one thing and being discouraged is something else. I am disappointed but I'm not discouraged. I'm twenty-three years old. How old are you?

Laura: I'll be twenty-four in June.

Jim: That's not old age!

Laura: No, but—

Jim: You finished high school?

Laura (with difficulty): I didn't go back.

Jim: You mean you dropped out?

Laura: I made bad grades in my final examinations. (*She rises and replaces the book and the program on the table. Her voice is strained.*) How is—Emily Meisenbach getting along?

Jim: Oh, that kraut-head!

Laura: Why do you call her that?

Jim: That's what she was.

Laura: You're not still—going with her?

Jim: I never see her.

Laura: It said in the "Personal" section that you were—engaged!
Jim: I know, but I wasn't impressed by that—propaganda!
Laura: It wasn't—the truth?
Jim: Only in Emily's optimistic opinion!
Laura: Oh—

(Legend: "What Have You Done Since High School?")

Jim lights a cigarette and leans indolently back on his elbows smiling at Laura with a warmth and charm which lights her inwardly with altar candles. She remains by the table, picks up a piece from the glass menagerie collection, and turns it in her hands to cover her tumult.

Jim (after several reflective puffs on his cigarette): What have you done since high school? *(She seems not to hear him.)* Huh? *(Laura looks up.)* I said what have you done since high school, Laura?
Laura: Nothing much.
Jim: You must have been doing something these six long years.
Laura: Yes.
Jim: Well, then, such as what?
Laura: I took a business course at business college—
Jim: How did that work out?
Laura: Well, not very—well—I had to drop out, it gave me—indigestion—

Jim laughs gently.

Jim: What are you doing now?
Laura: I don't do anything—much. Oh, please don't think I sit around doing nothing! My glass collection takes up a good deal of time. Glass is something you have to take good care of.
Jim: What did you say—about glass?
Laura: Collection I said—I have one—*(She clears her throat and turns away again, acutely shy.)*
Jim (abruptly): You know what I judge to be the trouble with you? Inferiority complex! Know what that is? That's what they call it when someone low-rates himself! I understand it because I had it, too. Although my case was not so aggravated as yours seems to be. I had it until I took up public speaking, developed my voice, and learned that I had an aptitude for science. Before that time I never thought of myself as being outstanding in any way whatsoever! Now I've never made a regular study of it, but I have a friend who says I can analyze people better than doctors that make a profession of it. I don't claim that to be necessarily true, but I can sure guess a person's psychology, Laura! *(He takes out his gum.)* Excuse me, Laura. I always take it out when the flavor is gone. I'll use this scrap of paper to wrap it in. I know how it is to get it stuck on a shoe. *(He wraps the gum in paper and puts it in his pocket.)* Yep—that's what I judge to be your principal trouble. A lack of confidence in yourself as a person. You don't have the proper amount of faith in yourself. I'm basing that fact on a number of your remarks and also on certain observations I've made. For instance that clumping you thought was so awful in high school. You say that you even dreaded to walk into class. You see what you did? You dropped out of school, you gave up an education because of

a clump, which as far as I know was practically non-existent! A little physical defect is what you have. Hardly noticeable even! Magnified thousands of times by imagination! You know what my strong advice to you is? Think of yourself as *superior* in some way!

Laura: In what way would I think?

Jim: Why, man alive, Laura! Just look about you a little. What do you see? A world full of common people! All of 'em born and all of 'em going to die! Which of them has one-tenth of your good points! Or mine! Or anyone else's, as far as that goes—gosh! Everybody excels in some one thing. Some in many! *(He unconsciously glances at himself in the mirror.)* All you've got to do is discover in *what!* Take me, for instance. *(He adjusts his tie at the mirror.)* My interest happens to lie in electro-dynamics. I'm taking a course in radio engineering at night school, Laura, on top of a fairly responsible job at the warehouse. I'm taking that course and studying public speaking.

Laura: Ohhhh.

Jim: Because I believe in the future of television! *(Turning his back to her.)* I wish to be ready to go up right along with it. Therefore I'm planning to get in on the ground floor. In fact I've already made the right connections and all that remains is for the industry itself to get under way! Full steam—*(His eyes are starry.)* Knowledge—Zzzzzp! Money—Zzzzzp!—Power! That's the cycle democracy is built on! *(His attitude is convincingly dynamic. Laura stares at him, even her shyness eclipsed in her absolute wonder. He suddenly grins.)* I guess you think I think a lot of myself!

Laura: No—o-o-o, I—

Jim: Now how about you? Isn't there something you take more interest in than anything else?

Laura: Well, I do—as I said—have my—glass collection—

A peal of girlish laughter rings from the kitchenette.

Jim: I'm not right sure I know what you're talking about. What kind of glass is it?

Laura: Little articles of it, they're ornaments mostly! Most of them are little animals made out of glass, the tiniest little animals in the world. Mother calls them a glass menagerie! Here's an example of one, if you'd like to see it! This one is one of the oldest. It's nearly thirteen. *(He stretches out his hand.)* (**Music: "The Glass Menagerie."**) Oh, be careful—if you breathe, it breaks!

Jim: I'd better not take it. I'm pretty clumsy with things.

Laura: Go on, I trust you with him! *(She places the piece in his palm.)* There now— you're holding him gently! Hold him over the light, he loves the light! You see how the light shines through him?

Jim: It sure does shine!

Laura: I shouldn't be partial, but he is my favorite one.

Jim: What kind of a thing is this one supposed to be?

Laura: Haven't you noticed the single horn on his forehead?

Jim: A unicorn, huh?

Laura: Mmm-hmmm!

Jim: Unicorns—aren't they extinct in the modern world?

Laura: I know!

Jim: Poor little fellow, he must feel sort of lonesome.

Laura (smiling): Well, if he does, he doesn't complain about it. He stays on a shelf with some horses that don't have horns and all of them seem to get along nicely together.

Jim: How do you know?

Laura (lightly): I haven't heard any arguments among them!

Jim (grinning): No arguments, huh? Well, that's a pretty good sign! Where shall I set him?

Laura: Put him on the table. They all like a change of scenery once in a while!

Jim: Well, well, well, well—(*He places the glass piece on the table, then raises his arms and stretches.*) Look how big my shadow is when I stretch!

Laura: Oh, oh, yes—it stretches across the ceiling!

Jim (crossing to the door): I think it's stopped raining. (*He opens the fire-escape door and the background music changes to a dance tune.*) Where does the music come from?

Laura: From the Paradise Dance Hall across the alley.

Jim: How about cutting the rug a little, Miss Wingfield?

Laura: Oh, I—

Jim: Or is your program filled up? Let me have a look at it. (*He grasps an imaginary card.*) Why, every dance is taken! I'll just have to scratch some out. (**Waltz Music: "La Golondrina."**) Ahhh, a waltz! (*He executes some sweeping turns by himself, then holds his arms toward Laura.*)

Laura (breathlessly): I—can't dance!

Jim: There you go, that inferiority stuff!

Laura: I've never danced in my life!

Jim: Come on, try!

Laura: Oh, but I'd step on you!

Jim: I'm not made out of glass.

Laura: How—how—how do we start?

Jim: Just leave it to me. You hold your arms out a little.

Laura: Like this?

Jim (taking her in his arms): A little bit higher. Right. Now don't tighten up, that's the main thing about it—relax.

Laura (laughing breathlessly): It's hard not to.

Jim: Okay.

Laura: I'm afraid you can't budge me.

Jim: What do you bet I can't? (*He swings her into motion.*)

Laura: Goodness, yes, you can!

Jim: Let yourself go, now, Laura, just let yourself go.

Laura: I'm—

Jim: Come on!

Laura: —trying!

Jim: Not so stiff—easy does it!

Laura: I know but I'm—

Jim: Loosen th' backbone! There now, that's a lot better.

Laura: Am I?

Jim: Lots, lots better! (*He moves her about the room in a clumsy waltz.*)

Laura: Oh, my!

Jim: Ha-ha!

Laura: Oh, my goodness!

Jim: Ha-ha-ha! (*They suddenly bump into the table, and the glass piece on it falls to the floor. Jim stops the dance.*) What did we hit on?

Laura: Table.

Jim: Did something fall off it? I think—

Laura: Yes.

Jim: I hope that it wasn't the little glass horse with the horn!

Laura: Yes. (*She stoops to pick it up.*)

Jim: Aw, aw, aw. Is it broken?

Laura: Now it is just like all the other horses.

Jim: It's lost its—

Laura: Horn! It doesn't matter. Maybe it's a blessing in disguise.

Jim: You'll never forgive me. I bet that that was your favorite piece of glass.

Laura: I don't have favorites much. It's no tragedy, Freckles. Glass breaks so easily. No matter how careful you are. The traffic jars the shelves and things fall off them.

Jim: Still I'm awfully sorry that I was the cause.

Laura (smiling): I'll just imagine he had an operation. The horn was removed to make him feel less—freakish! (*They both laugh.*) Now he will feel more at home with the other horses, the ones that don't have horns . . .

Jim: Ha-ha, that's very funny! (*Suddenly he is serious.*) I'm glad to see that you have a sense of humor. You know—you're—well—very different! Surprisingly different from anyone else I know! (*His voice becomes soft and hesitant with a genuine feeling.*) Do you mind me telling you that? (*Laura is abashed beyond speech.*) I mean it in a nice way—(*Laura nods shyly, looking away.*) You make me feel sort of—I don't know how to put it! I'm usually pretty good at expressing things, but—this is something that I don't know how to say! (*Laura touches her throat and clears it—turns the broken unicorn in her hands. His voice becomes softer.*) Has anyone ever told you that you were pretty? (*There is a pause, and the music rises slightly. Laura looks up slowly, with wonder, and shakes her head.*) Well, you are! In a very different way from anyone else. And all the nicer because of the difference, too. (*His voice becomes low and husky. Laura turns away, nearly faint with the novelty of her emotions.*) I wish that you were my sister. I'd teach you to have some confidence in yourself. The different people are not like other people, but being different is nothing to be ashamed of. Because other people are not such wonderful people. They're one hundred times one thousand. You're one times one! They walk all over the earth. You just stay here. They're common as—weeds, but—you—well, you're—*Blue Roses!*

(Image On Screen: Blue Roses.)

(The Music Changes.)

Laura: But blue is wrong for—roses . . .

Jim: It's right for you! You're—pretty!

Laura: In what respect am I pretty?

Jim: In all respects—believe me! Your eyes—your hair—are pretty! Your hands are pretty! (*He catches hold of her hand.*) You think I'm making this up because I'm invited to dinner and have to be nice. Oh, I could do that! I could put on an act for you, Laura, and say lots of things without being very sincere. But this time I am. I'm talking to you sincerely. I happened to notice you had this inferiority complex that keeps you from feeling comfortable with people. Somebody needs to build your confidence up and make you proud instead of shy and turning away and—blushing. Somebody—ought to—*kiss* you, Laura! (*His hand slips slowly up her arm to her shoulder as the music swells tumultuously. He suddenly turns her about and kisses her on the lips. When he releases her, Laura sinks on the sofa with a bright, dazed look. Jim backs away and fishes in his pocket for a cigarette.*) (**Legend On Screen: "A Souvenir."**) Stumblejohn! (*He lights the cigarette, avoiding her look. There is a peal of girlish laughter from Amanda in the kitchenette. Laura slowly raises and opens her hand. It still contains the little broken glass animal. She looks at it with a tender, bewildered expression.*) Stumblejohn! I shouldn't have done that—That was way off the beam. You don't smoke, do you? (*She looks up, smiling, not hearing the question. He sits beside her rather gingerly. She looks at him speechlessly—waiting. He coughs decorously and moves a little farther aside as he considers the situation and senses her feelings, dimly, with perturbation. He speaks gently.*) Would you—care for a—mint? (*She doesn't seem to hear him but her look grows brighter even.*) Peppermint? Life Saver? My pocket's a regular drug store—wherever I go . . . (*He pops a mint in his mouth. Then he gulps and decides to make a clean breast of it. He speaks slowly and gingerly.*) Laura, you know, if I had a sister like you, I'd do the same thing as Tom. I'd bring out fellows and—introduce her to them. The right type of boys—of a type to—appreciate her. Only—well—he made a mistake about me. Maybe I've got no call to be saying this. That may not have been the idea in having me over. But what if it was? There's nothing wrong about that. The only trouble is that in my case—I'm not in a situation to—do the right thing. I can't take down your number and say I'll phone. I can't call up next week and—ask for a date. I thought I had better explain the situation in case you—misunderstood it and—I hurt your feelings. . . . (*There is a pause. Slowly, very slowly, Laura's look changes, her eyes returning slowly from his to the glass figure in her palm. Amanda utters another gay laugh in the kitchenette.*)

Laura (*faintly*): You—won't—call again?
Jim: No, Laura, I can't. (*He rises from the sofa.*) As I was just explaining, I've—got strings on me. Laura, I've—been going steady! I go out all the time with a girl named Betty. She's a home-girl like you, and Catholic, and Irish, and in a great many ways we—get along fine. I met her last summer on a moonlight boat trip up the river to Alton, on the *Majestic*. Well—right away from the start it was—love! (**Legend On Screen: Love!**) (*Laura sways slightly forward and grips the arm of the sofa. He fails to notice, now enrapt in his own comfortable being.*) Being in love has made a new man of me! (*Leaning stiffly forward, clutching the arm of the sofa, Laura struggles visibly with her storm. But Jim is oblivious; she is a long way off.*) The power of love is really pretty tremendous! Love is something that—changes the whole world, Laura! (*The storm abates a little and Laura leans back. He notices her again.*) It happened that Betty's aunt took sick, she got a wire and had to go to Centralia. So Tom—when he asked me to dinner—I naturally just accepted the invitation, not knowing that you—that he—that I—(*He stops awkwardly.*) Huh—I'm a stumblejohn (*He flops back on the sofa. The holy candles on the altar of Laura's face have been snuffed out. There is a look of almost infinite desolation. Jim glances at her uneasily.*) I wish that you would—say something. (*She bites her lip which was trembling and then bravely smiles. She opens her hand again on the broken glass figure. Then she gently takes his hand and raises it level with her own. She carefully places the unicorn in the palm of his hand, then pushes his fingers closed upon it.*) What are you—doing that for? You want me to have him? Laura? (*She nods.*) What for?

Laura: A—souvenir . . .

She rises unsteadily and crouches beside the Victrola to wind it up.

(Legend On Screen: "Things Have A Way Of Turning Out So Badly.")

(Or Image: "Gentleman Caller Waving Goodbye! Gaily.")

At this moment Amanda rushes brightly back into the living room. She bears a pitcher of fruit punch in an old-fashioned cut-glass pitcher, and a plate of macaroons. The plate has a gold border and poppies painted on it.

Amanda: Well, well, well! Isn't the air delightful after the shower? I've made you children a little liquid refreshment. *(She turns gaily to Jim.)* Jim, do you know that song about lemonade?

> "Lemonade, lemonade
> Made in the shade and stirred with a spade—
> Good enough for any old maid!"

Jim (uneasily): Ha-ha! No—I never heard it.

Amanda: Why, Laura! You look so serious!

Jim: We were having a serious conversation.

Amanda: Good! Now you're better acquainted!

Jim (uncertainly): Ha-ha! Yes.

Amanda: You modern young people are much more serious-minded than my generation. I was so gay as a girl!

Jim: You haven't changed, Mrs. Wingfield.

Amanda: Tonight I'm rejuvenated! The gaiety of the occasion, Mr. O'Connor! *(She tosses her head with a peal of laughter, spilling some lemonade.)* Oooo! I'm baptizing myself!

Jim: Here—let me—

Amanda (setting the pitcher down): There now. I discovered we had some maraschino cherries. I dumped them in, juice and all!

Jim: You shouldn't have gone to that trouble, Mrs. Wingfield.

Amanda: Trouble, trouble? Why, it was loads of fun! Didn't you hear me cutting up in the kitchen? I bet your ears were burning! I told Tom how outdone with him I was for keeping you to himself so long a time! He should have brought you over much, much sooner! Well, now that you've found your way, I want you to be a very frequent caller! Not just occasional but all the time. Oh, we're going to have a lot of gay times together! I see them coming! Mmm, just breathe that air! So fresh, and the moon's so pretty! I'll skip back out—I know where my place is when young folks are having a—serious conversation!

Jim: Oh, don't go out, Mrs. Wingfield. The fact of the matter is I've got to be going.

Amanda: Going, now? You're joking! Why, it's only the shank of the evening, Mr. O'Connor!

Jim: Well, you know how it is.

Amanda: You mean you're a young workingman and have to keep workingmen's hours. We'll let you off early tonight. But only on the condition that next time you stay later. What's the best night for you? Isn't Saturday night the best night for you workingmen?

Jim: I have a couple of time-clocks to punch, Mrs. Wingfield. One at morning, another one at night!

Amanda: My, but you *are* ambitious! You work at night, too?

Jim: No, Ma'am, not work but—Betty! (*He crosses deliberately to pick up his hat. The band at the Paradise Dance Hall goes into a tender waltz.*)

Amanda: Betty? Betty? Who's—Betty? (*There is an ominous cracking sound in the sky.*)

Jim: Oh, just a girl. The girl I go steady with! (*He smiles charmingly. The sky falls.*)

(Legend On Screen: "The Sky Falls.")

Amanda (*a long-drawn exhalation*): Ohhhh . . . Is it a serious romance, Mr. O'Connor?

Jim: We're going to be married the second Sunday in June.

Amanda: Ohhhh—how nice! Tom didn't mention that you were engaged to be married.

Jim: The cat's not out of the bag at the warehouse yet. You know how they are. They call you Romeo and stuff like that. (*He stops at the oval mirror to put on his hat. He carefully shapes the brim and the crown to give a discreetly dashing effect.*) It's been a wonderful evening, Mrs. Wingfield. I guess this is what they mean by Southern hospitality.

Amanda: It really wasn't anything at all.

Jim: I hope it don't seem like I'm rushing off. But I promised Betty I'd pick her up at the Wabash depot, an' by the time I get my jalopy down there her train'll be in. Some women are pretty upset if you keep 'em waiting.

Amanda: Yes, I know—The tyranny of women! (*Extends her hand.*) Goodbye, Mr. O'Connor. I wish you luck—and happiness—and success! All three of them, and so does Laura!—Don't you, Laura?

Laura: Yes!

Jim (*taking Laura's hand*): Goodbye, Laura. I'm certainly going to treasure that souvenir. And don't you forget the good advice I gave you. (*He raises his voice to a cheery shout.*) So long, Shakespeare! Thanks again, ladies. Good night!

He grins and ducks jauntily out. Still bravely grimacing, Amanda closes the door on the gentleman caller. Then she turns back to the room with a puzzled expression. She and Laura don't dare to face each other. Laura crouches beside the Victrola to wind it.

Amanda (*faintly*): Things have a way of turning out so badly. I don't believe that I would play the Victrola. Well, well—well—Our gentleman caller was engaged to be married! (*She raises her voice.*) Tom!

Tom (*from the kitchenette*): Yes, Mother?

Amanda: Come in here a minute. I want to tell you something awfully funny.

Tom (*entering with a macaroon and a glass of the lemonade*): Has the gentleman caller gotten away already?

Amanda: The gentleman caller has made an early departure. What a wonderful joke you played on us!

Tom: How do you mean?

Amanda: You didn't mention that he was engaged to be married.

Tom: Jim? Engaged?

Amanda: That's what he just informed us.

Tom: I'll be jiggered! I didn't know about that.

Amanda: That seems very peculiar.

Tom: What's peculiar about it?

Amanda: Didn't you call him your best friend down at the warehouse?

Tom: He is, but how did I know?

Amanda: It seems extremely peculiar that you wouldn't know your best friend was going to be married!

Tom: The warehouse is where I work, not where I know things about people!

Amanda: You don't know things anywhere! You live in a dream; you manufacture illusions! *(He crosses to the door.)* Where are you going?

Tom: I'm going to the movies.

Amanda: That's right, now that you've had us make such fools of ourselves. The effort, the preparations, all the expense! The new floor lamp, the rug, the clothes for Laura! All for what? To entertain some other girl's fiancé! Go to the movies, go! Don't think about us, a mother deserted, an unmarried sister who's crippled and has no job! Don't let anything interfere with your selfish pleasure! Just go, go, go—to the movies!

Tom: All right, I will! The more you shout about my selfishness to me the quicker I'll go, and I won't go to the movies!

Amanda: Go, then! Go to the moon—you selfish dreamer!

Tom smashes his glass on the floor. He plunges out on the fire escape, slamming the door. Laura screams in fright. The dance-hall music becomes louder. Tom stands on the fire escape, gripping the rail. The moon breaks through the storm clouds, illuminating his face.

(Legend On Screen: "And So Goodbye . . .")

Tom's closing speech is timed with what is happening inside the house. We see, as though through soundproof glass, that Amanda appears to be making a comforting speech to Laura, who is huddled upon the sofa. Now that we cannot hear the mother's speech, her silliness is gone and she has dignity and tragic beauty. Laura's hair hides her face until, at the end of the speech, she lifts her head to smile at her mother. Amanda's gestures are slow and graceful, almost dancelike, as she comforts her daughter. At the end of her speech she glances a moment at the father's picture— then withdraws through the portieres. At the close of Tom's speech, Laura blows out the candles, ending the play.

Tom: I didn't go to the moon, I went much further—for time is the longest distance between two places. Not long after that I was fired for writing a poem on the lid of a shoe-box. I left Saint Louis. I descended the steps of this fire escape for a last time and followed, from then on, in my father's footsteps, attempting to find in motion what was lost in space. I traveled around a great deal. The cities swept about me like dead leaves, leaves that were brightly colored but torn away from the branches. I would have stopped, but I was pursued by something. It always came upon me unawares, taking me altogether by surprise. Perhaps it was a familiar bit of music. Perhaps it was only a piece of transparent glass. Perhaps I am walking along a street at night, in some strange city, before I have found companions. I pass the lighted window of a shop where perfume is sold. The window is filled with pieces of colored glass, tiny transparent bottles in delicate colors, like bits of a shattered rainbow. Then all at once my sister touches my shoulder. I turn around and look into her eyes. Oh, Laura, Laura, I tried to leave you behind me, but I am more faithful than I intended to be! I reach for a cigarette, I cross the street, I run into the movies or a bar, I buy a drink, I speak to the nearest stranger— anything that can blow your candles out! *Laura bends over the candles.* For nowadays the world is lit by lightning! Blow out your candles, Laura—and so Goodbye. . . .

She blows the candles out.

Questions

1. How do Amanda's dreams for her daughter contrast with the realities of the Wingfields' day-to-day existence?
2. What suggestions do you find in Laura's glass menagerie? In the glass unicorn?
3. In the cast of characters, Jim O'Connor is listed as "a nice, ordinary, young man." Why does his coming to dinner have such earthshaking implications for Amanda? For Laura?
4. Try to describe Jim's feelings toward Laura during their long conversation in Scene VII. After he kisses her, how do his feelings seem to change?
5. Near the end of the play, Amanda tells Tom, "You live in a dream; you manufacture illusions!" What is ironic about her speech? Is there any truth in it?
6. Who is the main character in *The Glass Menagerie*? Tom? Laura? Amanda? (It may be helpful to review the definition of a protagonist.)
7. Has Tom, at the conclusion of the play, successfully made his escape from home? Does he appear to have fulfilled his dream?
8. How effective is the device of accompanying the action by projecting slides on a screen, bearing titles and images? Do you think most producers of the play are wise to leave it out?

Tennessee Williams on Writing

How to Stage *The Glass Menagerie* 1945

Being a "memory play," *The Glass Menagerie* can be presented with unusual freedom of convention. Because of its considerably delicate or tenuous material, atmospheric touches and subtleties of direction play a particularly important part. Expressionism and all other unconventional techniques in drama have only one valid aim, and that is a closer approach to truth. When a play employs unconventional techniques, it is not, or certainly shouldn't be, trying to escape its responsibility of dealing with reality, or interpreting experience, but is actually or should be attempting to find a closer approach, a more penetrating and vivid expression of things as they are. The straight realistic play with its genuine Frigidaire and authentic ice-cubes, its characters that speak exactly as its audience speaks,

Tennessee Williams celebrating the 20th anniversary of *The Glass Menagerie*.

corresponds to the academic landscape and has the same virtue of a photographic likeness. Everyone should know nowadays the unimportance of the photographic in art: that truth, life, or reality is an organic thing which the poetic imagination can represent or suggest, in essence, only through transformation, through changing into other forms than those which were merely present in appearance.

These remarks are not meant as a preface only to this particular play. They have to do with a conception of a new, plastic theater which must take the place of the exhausted theater of realistic conventions if the theater is to resume vitality as a part of our culture.

THE SCREEN DEVICE. There is *only one important difference between the original and acting version of the play* and that is the *omission* in the latter of the device which I tentatively included in my *original* script. This device was the use of a screen on which were projected magic-lantern slides bearing images or titles. I do not regret the omission of this device from the present Broadway production. The extraordinary power of Miss Taylor's performance° made it suitable to have the utmost simplicity in the physical production. But I think it may be interesting to some readers to see how this device was conceived. So I am putting it into the published manuscript. These images and legends, projected from behind, were cast on a section of wall between the front-room and dining-room areas, which should be indistinguishable from the rest when not in use.

The purpose of this will probably be apparent. It is to give accent to certain values in each case. Each scene contains a particular point (or several) which is structurally the most important. In an episodic play, such as this, the basic structure or narrative line may be obscured from the audience; the effect may seem fragmentary rather than architectural. This may not be the fault of the play so much as a lack of attention in the audience. The legend or image upon the screen will strengthen the effect of what is merely allusion in the writing and allow the primary point to be made more simply and lightly than if the entire responsibility were on the spoken lines. Aside from this structural value, I think the screen will have a definite emotional appeal, less definable but just as important. An imaginative producer or director may invent many other uses for this device than those indicated in the present script. In fact the possibilities of the device seem much larger to me than the instance of this play can possibly utilize.

THE MUSIC. Another extra-literary accent in this play is provided by the use of music. A single recurring tune, "The Glass Menagerie," is used to give emotional emphasis to suitable passages. This tune is like circus music, not when you are on the grounds or in the immediate vicinity of the parade, but when you are at some distance and very likely thinking of something else. It seems under those circumstances to continue almost interminably and it weaves in and out of your preoccupied consciousness; then it is the lightest, most delicate music in the world and perhaps the saddest. It expresses the surface vivacity of life with the underlying strain of immutable and inexpressible sorrow. When you look at a piece of delicately spun glass you think of two things: how beautiful it is and how easily it can be broken. Both of those ideas should be woven into the recurring tune, which dips in and out of the play as if it were carried on a wind that changes. It serves as a thread of connection and allusion between the narrator with his separate point in time and space and the subject of his story. Between each episode it returns as reference to the emotion, nostalgia, which is the first condition of the play. It is primarily Laura's music and therefore comes out most clearly when the play focuses upon her and the lovely fragility of glass which is her image.

THE LIGHTING. The lighting in the play is not realistic. In keeping with the atmosphere of memory, the stage is dim. Shafts of light are focused on selected areas or actors, sometimes in contradistinction to what is the apparent center. For instance, in

Miss Taylor's performance: In the original Broadway production of the play in 1945 the role of Amanda Wingfield, the mother, was played by veteran actress Laurette Taylor.

the quarrel scene between Tom and Amanda, in which Laura has no active part, the clearest pool of light is on her figure. This is also true of the supper scene, when her silent figure on the sofa should remain the visual center. The light upon Laura should be distinct from the others, having a peculiar pristine clarity such as light used in early religious portraits of female saints or madonnas. A certain correspondence to light in religious paintings, such as El Greco's, where the figures are radiant in atmosphere that is relatively dusky, could be effectively used throughout the play. (It will also permit a more effective use of the screen.) A free, imaginative use of light can be of enormous value in giving a mobile, plastic quality to plays of a more or less static nature.

From the author's production notes for *The Glass Menagerie*

TRAGICOMEDY AND THE ABSURD

One of the more prominent developments in mid-twentieth-century drama was the rise of **tragicomedies**, plays that stir us not only to pity and fear (echoing Aristotle's description of the effect of tragedy) but also to laughter. Although tragicomedy is a kind of drama we think distinctively modern, it is by no means new. The term was used (although jokingly) by the Roman writer of comedy Plautus in about 185 B.C.

Shakespeare's darker comedies such as *Measure for Measure* and *The Merchant of Venice* deal so forcefully with such stark themes as lust, greed, racism, revenge, and cruelty that they often seem like tragedies until their happy endings. In the tragedies of Shakespeare and others, passages of clownish humor are sometimes called **comic relief**, meaning that the section of comedy introduces a sharp contrast in mood. But such passages can do more than provide relief. In *Othello* (Chapter 38, 3.4.1–16) the clown's banter with Desdemona for a moment makes the surrounding tragedy seem, by comparison, more poignant and intense.

No one doubts that *Othello* is a tragedy, but some twentieth-century plays leave us both bemused and confused: should we laugh or cry? One of the most talked-about plays after World War II, Samuel Beckett's *Waiting for Godot* (1953) portrays two clownish tramps who mark time in a wasteland, wistfully looking for a savior who never arrives. Modern drama, by the way, has often featured such **antiheroes**: ordinary people, inglorious and inarticulate, who carry on not from bravery but from inertia. We cannot help laughing, in *Godot*, at the tramps' painful situation; but, turning the idea around, we also feel deeply moved by their ridiculous plight. Perhaps a modern tragicomedy like *Godot* does not show us great souls suffering greatly—as we observe in a classical tragedy—but Beckett's play nonetheless touches mysteriously on the universal sorrows of human existence.

Theater of the Absurd

Straddling the fence between tragedy and comedy, the plays of some modern playwrights portray people whose suffering seems ridiculous. These plays belong to the **theater of the absurd**: a general name for a type of play first staged in Paris in the 1950s and taken up by playwrights around the world, including the Czech writer and political activist Václav Havel, who later became his country's president. "For the modern critical spirit, nothing can be taken entirely seriously, nor entirely lightly," said Eugène Ionesco, one of the movement's leading playwrights. Behind the literary conventions of the theater of the absurd stands a philosophical fear that human existence has no meaning. Every person, such playwrights assume, is a helpless waif alone in a universe full of ridiculous obstacles. (*Absurd* comes from a Latin root meaning *deaf* or *out of tune.*) In Ionesco's *Rhinoceros* (1958), the human race starts turning into rhinos, except for one man, who remains human and isolated. A favorite theme in the theater of the absurd is that communication between people is impossible. Language is therefore futile. Ionesco's *The Bald Soprano* (1948) accordingly pokes fun at polite social conversation in a scene whose dialogue consists entirely of illogical strings of catchphrases.

RETURN TO REALISM

Trends in drama change along with playwrights' convictions, and during the 1970s and 1980s the theater of the absurd no longer seemed the dominant influence on new drama in America. Along with other protests of the 1960s, experimental theater seemed to have spent its force. During the later period most of the critically celebrated new plays were neither absurd nor experimental. David Mamet's *American Buffalo* (1975) realistically portrays three petty thieves in a junk shop as they plot to steal a coin collection. Albert Innaurato's *Gemini* (1977) takes a realistic (and comic) view of family life and sexual awakening in one of Philadelphia's Italian neighborhoods. Beth Henley's 1979 Pulitzer Prize–winning play *Crimes of the Heart* presents an eccentric but still believable group of sisters in a small Southern town. The dialogue in all three plays shows high fidelity to ordinary speech. Meanwhile, many of the most influential plays of **feminist theater**, which explores the lives, problems, and occasional triumphs of contemporary women, were also written in a realistic style. Notable success—with both critics and the ticket-buying public—greeted plays such as Marsha Norman's *'night, Mother* (1983), Tina Howe's *Painting Churches* (1983), and Wendy Wasserstein's *The Heidi Chronicles* (1988).

Some leading critics, among them Richard Gilman, believed that the American theater had entered an era of "new naturalism." Indeed many plays of this time subjected the lives of people, especially poor and unhappy people, to a realistic, searching light, showing the forces that shaped them. Sam Shepard in *Buried Child* (1978) explores violence and desperation in a family that dwells on the edge of poverty; while August Wilson in *Joe Turner's Come and Gone* (1988) convincingly portrays life in a Pittsburgh ghetto lodging house. But if these newly established playwrights sometimes showed life as frankly as did the earlier Naturalists, many also employed rich and suggestive symbolism.

EXPERIMENTAL DRAMA

In the latter part of the twentieth century, experimental drama, greatly influenced by the traditions of earlier Symbolist, Expressionist, and absurdist theater, continued to flourish. For example, David Henry Hwang's work combines realistic elements with ritualistic and symbolic devices drawn from Asian theater (see his one-act play, *The Sound of a Voice*, in Chapter 41). Caryl Churchill's *Top Girls* (1982) presents a dinner party in which a contemporary woman invites legendary women from history to a dinner party in a restaurant. Tony Kushner's *Angels in America* (1992) also mixes realism and fantasy to dramatize the plight of AIDS. Shel Silverstein, popular author of children's poetry, wrote a raucous one-man play, *The Devil and Billy Markham* (1991), entirely in rime, about a series of fantastic adventures in hell featuring a hard-drinking gambler and the Prince of Darkness. Silverstein's play is simultaneously experimental in form but traditional in content with its homage to American ballads and tall tales.

Experimental theater continues to exert a strong influence on contemporary drama. The following play, Milcha Sanchez-Scott's *The Cuban Swimmer*, deftly assimilates several dramatic styles—symbolism, new naturalism, ethnic drama, theater of the absurd—to create a brilliant original work. The play is simultaneously a family drama, a Latin comedy, a religious parable, and a critique of a media-obsessed American culture.

Milcha Sanchez-Scott

The Cuban Swimmer   1984

Milcha Sanchez-Scott was born in 1955 on the island of Bali. Her father was Colombian; her mother was Chinese, Indonesian, and Dutch. Her father's work as an agronomist required constant travel, so when the young Sanchez-Scott reached school age, she was sent to a convent boarding school near London where she first learned English. Colombia, however, remained the family's one permanent home. Every Christmas and summer vacation was spent on a ranch in San Marta, Colombia, where four generations of family lived together. When Sanchez-Scott was fourteen, her family moved to California. After attending the University of San Diego, where she majored in literature and philosophy, she worked at the San Diego Zoo and later at an employment agency in Los Angeles. Her first play, Latina, premiered in 1980 and won seven Drama-Logue awards. Dog Lady and The Cuban Swimmer followed in 1984. Sanchez-Scott then went to New York for a year to work with playwright Irene Fornes, in whose theater workshop she developed Roosters (1988). A feature-film version of Roosters, starring Edward James Olmos, was released in 1995. Her other plays include Evening Star (1989), El Dorado (1990), and The Old Matador (1995). Sanchez-Scott lives in Los Angeles.

CHARACTERS

Margarita Suárez, the swimmer
Eduardo Suárez, her father, the coach
Simón Suárez, her brother
Aída Suárez, her mother
Abuela, her grandmother
Voice of Mel Munson
Voice of Mary Beth White
Voice of Radio Operator

SETTING. *The Pacific Ocean between San Pedro and Catalina Island.*

TIME. *Summer.*

Live conga drums can be used to punctuate the action of the play.

SCENE I

Pacific Ocean. Midday. On the horizon, in perspective, a small boat enters upstage left, crosses to upstage right, and exits. Pause. Lower on the horizon, the same boat, in larger perspective, enters upstage right, crosses and exits upstage left. Blackout.

SCENE II

Pacific Ocean. Midday. The swimmer, Margarita Suárez, is swimming. On the boat following behind her are her father, Eduardo Suárez, holding a megaphone, and Simón, her brother, sitting on top of the cabin with his shirt off, punk sunglasses on, binoculars hanging on his chest.

Eduardo *(leaning forward, shouting in time to Margarita's swimming)*: Uno, dos, uno, dos. Y uno, dos° . . . keep your shoulders parallel to the water.
Simón: I'm gonna take these glasses off and look straight into the sun.
Eduardo *(through megaphone)*: Muy bien, muy bien° . . . but punch those arms in, baby.
Simón *(looking directly at the sun through binoculars)*: Come on, come on, zap me. Show me something. *(He looks behind at the shoreline and ahead at the sea.)* Stop! Stop, Papi! Stop!

(Aída Suárez and Abuela, the swimmer's mother and grandmother, enter running from the back of the boat.)

Aída and Abuela: Qué? Qué es?°
Aída: Es un shark?°
Eduardo: Eh?
Abuela: Que es un shark dicen?°

(Eduardo blows whistle. Margarita looks up at the boat.)

Simón: No, Papi, no shark, no shark. We've reached the halfway mark.
Abuela *(looking into the water)*: A dónde está?°
Aída: It's not in the water.
Abuela: Oh, no? Oh, no?
Aída: No! A poco do you think they're gonna have signs in the water to say you are halfway to Santa Catalina? No. It's done very scientific. A ver, hijo,° explain it to your grandma.
Simón: Well, you see, Abuela—*(He points behind.)* There's San Pedro. *(He points ahead.)* And there's Santa Catalina. Looks halfway to me.

(Abuela shakes her head and is looking back and forth, trying to make the decision, when suddenly the sound of a helicopter is heard.)

Abuela *(looking up)*: Virgencita de la Caridad del Cobre. Qué es eso?°

(Sound of helicopter gets closer. Margarita looks up.)

Margarita: Papi, Papi!

(A small commotion on the boat, with everybody pointing at the helicopter above. Shadows of the helicopter fall on the boat. Simón looks up at it through binoculars.)

Papi—qué es? What is it?

Eduardo *(through megaphone)*: Uh . . . uh . . . uh, un momentico . . . mi hija.° . . . Your papi's got everything under control, understand? Uh . . . you just keep stroking. And stay . . . uh . . . close to the boat.

Uno, dos, uno, dos. Y uno, dos: One, two, one, two. And one, two.   *Muy bien, muy bien:* Very good, very good.   *Qué? Qué es?:* What? What is it?   *Es un shark?:* Is it a shark?   *Que es un shark dicen?:* Did they say a shark?   *A dónde está?:* Where is it?   *A ver, hijo:* Look here, son.   *Virgencita de la Caridad del Cobre. Qué es eso?:* Virgin of Charity. What is that?   *un momentico . . . mi hija:* just a second, my daughter.

A 2005 production of *The Cuban Swimmer* at the People's Light and Theatre, Malvern, Pennsylvania.

Simón: Wow, *Papi!* We're on TV, man! Holy Christ, we're all over the fucking U.S.A.! It's Mel Munson and Mary Beth White!

Aída: Por Dios!° Simón, don't swear. And put on your shirt.

(*Aída fluffs her hair, puts on her sunglasses and waves to the helicopter. Simón leans over the side of the boat and yells to Margarita.*)

Simón: Yo, Margo! You're on TV, man.

Eduardo: Leave your sister alone. Turn on the radio.

Margarita: Papi! Qué está pasando?°

Abuela: Que es la televisión dicen? (*She shakes her head.*) *Porque como yo no puedo ver nada sin mis espejuelos.°*

(*Abuela rummages through the boat, looking for her glasses. Voices of Mel Munson and Mary Beth White are heard over the boat's radio.*)

Mel's Voice: As we take a closer look at the gallant crew of *La Havana* . . . and there . . . yes, there she is . . . the little Cuban swimmer from Long Beach, California, nineteen-year-old Margarita Suárez. The unknown swimmer is our Cinderella entry . . . a bundle of tenacity, battling her way through the choppy, murky waters of the cold Pacific to reach the Island of Romance . . . Santa Catalina . . . where should she be the first to arrive, two thousand dollars and a gold cup will be waiting for her.

Aída: Doesn't even cover our expenses.

Abuela: Qué dice?

Eduardo: Shhhh!

Por Dios!: For God's Sake!   *Papi! Qué está pasando?:* Dad! What's happening?   *Que es la televisión dicen? Porque como yo no puedo ver nada sin mis espejuelos:* Did they say television? Because I can't see without my glasses.

Mary Beth's Voice: This is really a family effort, Mel, and—

Mel's Voice: Indeed it is. Her trainer, her coach, her mentor, is her father, Eduardo Suárez. Not a swimmer himself, it says here, Mr. Suárez is head usher of the Holy Name Society and the owner-operator of Suárez Treasures of the Sea and Salvage Yard. I guess it's one of those places—

Mary Beth's Voice: If I might interject a fact here, Mel, assisting in this swim is Mrs. Suárez, who is a former Miss Cuba.

Mel's Voice: And a beautiful woman in her own right. Let's try and get a closer look.

(Helicopter sound gets louder. Margarita, frightened, looks up again.)

Margarita: Papi!

Eduardo (through megaphone): Mi hija, don't get nervous . . . it's the press. I'm handling it.

Aída: I see how you're handling it.

Eduardo (through megaphone): Do you hear? Everything is under control. Get back into your rhythm. Keep your elbows high and kick and kick and kick and kick . . .

Abuela (finds her glasses and puts them on): Ay sí, es la televisión° . . . *(She points to helicopter.)* Qué lindo mira° . . . *(She fluffs her hair, gives a big wave.)* Aló América! Viva mi Margarita, viva todo los Cubanos en los Estados Unidos!°

Aída: Ay por Dios, Cecilia, the man didn't come all this way in his helicopter to look at you jumping up and down, making a fool of yourself.

Abuela: I don't care. I'm proud.

Aída: He can't understand you anyway.

Abuela: Viva . . . *(She stops.)* Simón, cómo se dice viva?°

Simón: Hurray.

Abuela: Hurray for mi Margarita y for all the Cubans living en the United States, y un abrazo . . . Simón, abrazo . . .

Simón: A big hug.

Abuela: Sí, a big hug to all my friends in Miami, Long Beach, Union City, except for my son Carlos, who lives in New York in sin! He lives . . . *(She crosses herself.)* in Brooklyn with a Puerto Rican woman in sin! No decente…

Simón: Decent.

Abuela: Carlos, no decente. This family, decente.

Aída: Cecilia, por Dios.

Mel's Voice: Look at that enthusiasm. The whole family has turned out to cheer little Margarita on to victory! I hope they won't be too disappointed.

Mary Beth's Voice: She seems to be making good time, Mel.

Mel's Voice: Yes, it takes all kinds to make a race. And it's a testimonial to the all-encompassing fairness . . . the greatness of this, the Wrigley Invitational Women's Swim to Catalina, where among all the professionals there is still room for the amateurs . . . like these, the simple people we see below us on the ragtag La Havana, taking their long-shot chance to victory. Vaya con Dios!°

(Helicopter sound fading as family, including Margarita, watch silently. Static as Simón turns radio off. Eduardo walks to bow of boat, looks out on the horizon.)

Eduardo (to himself): Amateurs.

Ay sí, es la televisión: Oh yes, it is the television.   *Qué lindo mira:* Look how pretty.   *Aló América! Viva mi Margarita, viva todo los Cubanos en los Estados Unidos!:* Hello America! Hurray for my Margarita, hurray for all the Cubans in the United States!   *cómo se dice viva?:* how do you say "viva" [in English]?   *Vaya con Dios!:* Go with God! [God bless you.]

Aída: Eduardo, that person insulted us. Did you hear, Eduardo? That he called us a simple people in a ragtag boat? Did you hear . . . ?

Abuela (clenching her fist at departing helicopter): Mal-Rayo los parta!°

Simón (same gesture): Asshole!

(*Aída follows Eduardo as he goes to side of boat and stares at Margarita.*)

Aída: This person comes in his helicopter to insult your wife, your family, your daughter . . .

Margarita (pops her head out of the water): Papi?

Aída: Do you hear me, Eduardo? I am not simple.

Abuela: Sí.

Aída: I am complicated.

Abuela: Sí, demasiada complicada.

Aída: Me and my family are not so simple.

Simón: Mom, the guy's an asshole.

Abuela (shaking her fist at helicopter): Asshole!

Aída: If my daughter was simple, she would not be in that water swimming.

Margarita: Simple? Papi . . . ?

Aída: Ahora, Eduardo, this is what I want you to do. When we get to Santa Catalina, I want you to call the TV station and demand an apology.

Eduardo: Cállete mujer! Aquí mando yo.° I will decide what is to be done.

Margarita: Papi, tell me what's going on.

Eduardo: Do you understand what I am saying to you, Aída?

Simón (leaning over side of boat, to Margarita): Yo Margo! You know that Mel Munson guy on TV? He called you a simple amateur and said you didn't have a chance.

Abuela (leaning directly behind Simón): Mi hija, insultó a la familia. Desgraciado!

Aída (leaning in behind Abuela): He called us peasants! And your father is not doing anything about it. He just knows how to yell at me.

Eduardo (through megaphone): Shut up! All of you! Do you want to break her concentration? Is that what you are after? Eh?

(*Abuela, Aída and Simón shrink back. Eduardo paces before them.*)

Swimming is rhythm and concentration. You win a race aquí. (*Pointing to his head.*) Now . . . (*To Simón.*) you, take care of the boat, Aída y Mama . . . do something. Anything. Something practical.

(*Abuela and Aída get on knees and pray in Spanish.*)

Hija, give it everything, eh? . . . por la familia. Uno . . . dos. . . . You must win.

(*Simón goes into cabin. The prayers continue as lights change to indicate bright sunlight, later in the afternoon.*)

SCENE III

Tableau for a couple of beats. Eduardo on bow with timer in one hand as he counts strokes per minute. Simón is in the cabin steering, wearing his sunglasses, baseball cap on backward. Abuela and Aída are at the side of the boat, heads down, hands folded, still muttering prayers in Spanish.

Aída and Abuela (crossing themselves): En el nombre del Padre, del Hijo y del Espíritu Santo amén.°

Mal-Rayo los parta!: To hell with you!   Cállete mujer! Aquí mando yo: Quiet woman! I'm in charge here.   En el nombre del Padre, del Hijo y del Espíritu Santo amén: In the name of the Father, the Son, and the Holy Ghost, Amen.

Eduardo (through megaphone): You're stroking seventy-two!

Simón (singing): Mama's stroking, Mama's stroking seventy-two. . . .

Eduardo (through megaphone): You comfortable with it?

Simón (singing): Seventy-two, seventy-two, seventy-two for you.

Aída (looking at the heavens): Ay, Eduardo, *ven acá,*° we should be grateful that *Nuestro Señor*° gave us such a beautiful day.

Abuela (crosses herself): *Sí, gracias a Dios.*°

Eduardo: She's stroking seventy-two, with no problem. (*He throws a kiss to the sky.*) It's a beautiful day to win.

Aída: *Qué hermoso!*° So clear and bright. Not a cloud in the sky. *Mira! Mira!*° Even rainbows on the water . . . a sign from God.

Simón (singing): Rainbows on the water . . . you in my arms . . .

Abuela and Eduardo (looking the wrong way): *Dónde?*

Aída (pointing toward Margarita): There, dancing in front of Margarita, leading her on . . .

Eduardo: Rainbows on . . . Ay coño! It's an oil slick! You . . . you . . . (*To Simón.*) Stop the boat. (*Runs to bow, yelling.*) Margarita! Margarita!

(*On the next stroke, Margarita comes up all covered in black oil.*)

Margarita: Papi! Papi . . . !

(*Everybody goes to the side and stares at Margarita, who stares back. Eduardo freezes.*)

Aída: *Apúrate,* Eduardo, move . . . what's wrong with you . . . *no me oíste,*° get my daughter out of the water.

Eduardo (softly): We can't touch her. If we touch her, she's disqualified.

Aída: But I'm her mother.

Eduardo: Not even by her own mother. Especially by her own mother. . . . You always want the rules to be different for you, you always want to be the exception. (*To Simón.*) And you . . . you didn't see it, eh? You were playing again?

Simón: Papi, I was watching . . .

Aída (interrupting): *Pues,* do something Eduardo. You are the big coach, the monitor.

Simón: Mentor! Mentor!

Eduardo: How can a person think around you? (*He walks off to bow, puts head in hands.*)

Abuela (looking over side): *Mira como todos los* little birds are dead. (*She crosses herself*)

Aída: Their little wings are glued to their sides.

Simón: Christ, this is like the La Brea tar pits.

Aída: They can't move their little wings.

Abuela: *Esa niña tiene que moverse.*°

Simón: Yeah, Margo, you gotta move, man.

(*Abuela and Simón gesture for Margarita to move. Aída gestures for her to swim.*)

Abuela: *Anda niña, muévete.*°

Aída: Swim, *hija,* swim or the *aceite*° will stick to your wings.

Margarita: Papi?

Abuela (taking megaphone): Your *papi* say "move it!"

(*Margarita with difficulty starts moving.*)

ven acá: look here .*Nuestro Señor*: Our Father [God]. *Sí, gracias a Dios*: Yes, thanks be to God. *Qué hermoso!*: How beautiful! *Mira!*: look. *Apúrate . . . no me oíste*: Finish this . . . didn't you hear me? *Esa niña tiene que moverse*: That girl has to move. *Anda niña, muévete*: Come on, girl, move. *aceite*: oil.

Abuela, Aída and Simón (laboriously counting): Uno, dos . . . uno, dos . . . anda . . . uno, dos.
Eduardo (running to take megaphone from Abuela): Uno, dos . . .

    (Simón races into cabin and starts the engine. Abuela, Aída and Eduardo count together.)

Simón (looking ahead): Papi, it's over there!
Eduardo: Eh?
Simón (pointing ahead and to the right): It's getting clearer over there.
Eduardo (through megaphone): Now pay attention to me. Go to the right.

    (Simón, Abuela, Aída and Eduardo all lean over side. They point ahead and to the right, except Abuela, who points to the left.)

Family (shouting together): Para yá!° Para yá!

    (Lights go down on boat. A special light on Margarita, swimming through the oil, and on Abuela, watching her.)

Abuela: Sangre de mi sangre,° you will be another to save us. En Bolondron, where your great-grandmother Luz Suárez was born, they say one day it rained blood. All the people, they run into their houses. They cry, they pray, *pero* your great-grandmother Luz she had *cojones* like a man. She run outside. She look straight at the sky. She shake her fist. And she say to the evil one, "Mira . . . *(Beating her chest.)* coño, Diablo, aquí estoy si me quieres."° And she open her mouth, and she drunk the blood.

BLACKOUT

SCENE IV

Lights up on boat. Aída and Eduardo are on deck watching Margarita swim. We hear the gentle, rhythmic lap, lap, lap of the water, then the sound of inhaling and exhaling as Margarita's breathing becomes louder. Then Margarita's heartbeat is heard, with the lapping of the water and the breathing under it. These sounds continue beneath the dialogue to the end of the scene.

Aída: Dios mío. Look how she moves through the water. . . .
Eduardo: You see, it's very simple. It is a matter of concentration.
Aída: The first time I put her in water she came to life, she grew before my eyes. She moved, she smiled, she loved it more than me. She didn't want my breast any longer. She wanted the water.
Eduardo: And of course, the rhythm. The rhythm takes away the pain and helps the concentration.

    (Pause. Aída and Eduardo watch Margarita.)

Aída: Is that my child or a seal. . . .
Eduardo: Ah, a seal, the reason for that is that she's keeping her arms very close to her body. She cups her hands, and then she reaches and digs, reaches and digs.
Aída: To think that a daughter of mine. . . .
Eduardo: It's the training, the hours in the water. I used to tie weights around her little wrists and ankles.
Aída: A spirit, an ocean spirit, must have entered my body when I was carrying her.

Para yá: Over there. *Sangre de mi sangre:* Blood of my blood. *Mira . . . coño, Diablo, aquí estoy si me quieres:* Look . . . damn it, Devil, here I am if you want me.

Eduardo (to Margarita): Your stroke is slowing down.

(*Pause. We hear Margarita's heartbeat with the breathing under, faster now.*)

Aída: Eduardo, that night, the night on the boat. . . .

Eduardo: Ah, the night on the boat again . . . the moon was . . .

Aída: The moon was full. We were coming to America. . . . *Qué romantico.*

(*Heartbeat and breathing continue.*)

Eduardo: We were cold, afraid, with no money, and on top of everything, you were hysterical, yelling at me, tearing at me with your nails. (*Opens his shirt, points to the base of his neck.*) Look, I still bear the scars . . . telling me that I didn't know what I was doing . . . saying that we were going to die. . . .

Aída: You took me, you stole me from my home . . . you didn't give me a chance to prepare. You just said we have to go now, now! Now, you said. You didn't let me take anything. I left everything behind. . . . I left everything behind.

Eduardo: Saying that I wasn't good enough, that your father didn't raise you so that I could drown you in the sea.

Aída: You didn't let me say even a good-bye. You took me, you stole me, you tore me from my home.

Eduardo: I took you so we could be married.

Aída: That was in Miami. But that night on the boat, Eduardo. . . . We were not married, that night on the boat.

Eduardo: No pasó nada!° Once and for all get it out of your head, it was cold, you hated me, and we were afraid. . . .

Aída: Mentiroso!°

Eduardo: A man can't do it when he is afraid.

Aída: Liar! You did it very well.

Eduardo: I did?

Aída: Sí. Gentle. You were so gentle and then strong . . . my passion for you so deep. Standing next to you . . . I would ache . . . looking at your hands I would forget to breathe, you were irresistible.

Eduardo: I was?

Aída: You took me into your arms, you touched my face with your fingertips . . . you kissed my eyes . . . *la esquina de la boca y°.* . . .

Eduardo: Sí, Sí, and then. . .

Aída: I look at your face on top of mine, and I see the lights of Havana in your eyes. That's when you seduced me.

Eduardo: Shhh, they're gonna hear you.

(*Lights go down. Special on Aída.*)

Aída: That was the night. A woman doesn't forget those things . . . and later that night was the dream . . . the dream of a big country with fields of fertile land and big, giant things growing. And there by a green, slimy pond I found a giant pea pod and when I opened it, it was full of little, tiny baby frogs.

(*Aída crosses herself as she watches Margarita. We hear louder breathing and heartbeat.*)

No pasó nada!: Nothing happened!   *Mentiroso!*: Liar!   *la esquina de la boca y . . .*: the corner of the mouth and . . .

Margarita: Santa Teresa. Little Flower of God, pray for me. San Martín de Porres, pray for me. Santa Rosa de Lima, *Virgencita de la Caridad del Cobre,* pray for me. . . . Mother pray for me.

SCENE V

Loud howling of wind is heard, as lights change to indicate unstable weather, fog and mist. Family on deck, braced and huddled against the wind. Simón is at the helm.

Aída: Ay Dios mío, qué viento.°
Eduardo (through megaphone): Don't drift out . . . that wind is pushing you out. *(To Simón.)* You! Slow down. Can't you see your sister is drifting out?
Simón: It's the wind, *Papi.*
Aída: Baby, don't go so far....
Abuela (to heaven): Ay Gran Poder de Dios, quita este maldito viento.°
Simón: Margo! Margo! Stay close to the boat.
Eduardo: Dig in. Dig in hard. . . . Reach down from your guts and dig in.
Abuela (to heaven): Ay Virgen de la Caridad del Cobre, por lo más tú quieres a pararla.
Aída (putting her hand out, reaching for Margarita): Baby, don't go far.

> *(Abuela crosses herself. Action freezes. Lights get dimmer, special on Margarita. She keeps swimming, stops, starts again, stops, then, finally exhausted, stops altogether. The boat stops moving.)*

Eduardo: What's going on here? Why are we stopping?
Simón: *Papi,* she's not moving! Yo Margo!

> *(The family all run to the side.)*

Eduardo: Hija! . . . Hijita! You're tired, eh?
Aída: Por supuesto she's tired. I like to see you get in the water, waving your arms and legs from San Pedro to Santa Catalina. A person isn't a machine, a person has to rest.
Simón: Yo, Mama! Cool out, it ain't fucking brain surgery.
Eduardo (to Simón): Shut up, you. *(Louder to Margarita.)* I guess your mother's right for once, huh? . . . I guess you had to stop, eh? . . . Give your brother, the idiot . . . a chance to catch up with you.
Simón (clowning like Mortimer Snerd): Dum dee dum dee dum ooops, ah shucks...
Eduardo: I don't think he's Cuban.
Simón (like Ricky Ricardo): Oye, Lucy! I'm home! Ba ba lu!
Eduardo (joins in clowning, grabbing Simón in a headlock): What am I gonna do with this idiot, eh? I don't understand this idiot. He's not like us, Margarita. *(Laughing.)* You think if we put him into your bathing suit with a cap on his head . . . *(He laughs hysterically.)* You think anyone would know . . . huh? Do you think anyone would know? *(Laughs.)*
Simón (vamping): Ay, mi amor. Anybody looking for tits would know.

> *(Eduardo slaps Simón across the face, knocking him down. Aída runs to Simón's aid. Abuela holds Eduardo back.)*

Ay Dios mío, qué viento: Oh my God, what wind.   Ay Gran Poder de Dios, quita este maldito viento: By the great power of God, keep the cursed winds away.

Margarita: Mía culpa!° Mía culpa!

Abuela: Qué dices hija? °

Margarita: Papi, it's my fault, it's all my fault. . . . I'm so cold, I can't move. . . . I put my face in the water . . . and I hear them whispering . . . laughing at me....

Aída: Who is laughing at you?

Margarita: The fish are all biting me . . . they hate me . . . they whisper about me. She can't swim, they say. She can't glide. She has no grace. . . . Yellowtails, bonita, tuna, man-o'-war, snub-nose sharks, *los baracudas* . . . they all hate me . . . only the dolphins care . . . and sometimes I hear the whales crying . . . she is lost, she is dead. I'm so numb, I can't feel. *Papi! Papi!* Am I dead?

Eduardo: *Vamos*, baby, punch those arms in. Come on . . . do you hear me?

Margarita: Papi . . . Papi . . . forgive me....

(*All is silent on the boat. Eduardo drops his megaphone, his head bent down in dejection. Abuela, Aída, Simón, all leaning over the side of the boat. Simón slowly walks away.*)

Aída: Mi hija, qué tienes?

Simón: Oh, Christ, don't make her say it. Please don't make her say it.

Abuela: Say what? *Qué cosa?*

Simón: She wants to quit, can't you see she's had enough?

Abuela: *Mira, para eso. Esta niña* is turning blue.

Aída: *Oyeme, mi hija.* Do you want to come out of the water?

Margarita: Papi?

Simón (to Eduardo): She won't come out until *you* tell her.

Aída: Eduardo . . . answer your daughter.

Eduardo: *Le dije* to concentrate . . . concentrate on your rhythm. Then the rhythm would carry her . . . ay, it's a beautiful thing, Aída. It's like yoga, like meditation, the mind over matter . . . the mind controlling the body . . . that's how the great things in the world have been done. I wish you . . . I wish my wife could understand.

Margarita: Papi?

Simón (to Margarita): Forget him.

Aída (imploring): Eduardo, *por favor.*

Eduardo (walking in circles): Why didn't you let her concentrate? Don't you understand, the concentration, the rhythm is everything. But no, you wouldn't listen. (*Screaming to the ocean.*) Goddamn Cubans, why, God, why do you make us go everywhere with our families? (*He goes to back of boat.*)

Aída (opening her arms): Mi hija, ven, come to Mami. (*Rocking.*) Your *mami* knows.

(*Abuela has taken the training bottle, puts it in a net. She and Simón lower it to Margarita.*)

Simón: Take this. Drink it. (*As Margarita drinks, Abuela crosses herself.*)

Abuela: Sangre de mi sangre.

(*Music comes up softly. Margarita drinks, gives the bottle back, stretches out her arms, as if on a cross. Floats on her back. She begins a graceful backstroke. Lights fade on boat as special lights come up on Margarita. She stops. Slowly turns over and starts to swim, gradually picking up speed. Suddenly as if in pain she stops, tries again, then stops in pain again. She becomes disoriented and falls to the bottom of the sea. Special on Margarita at the bottom of the sea.*)

Mía culpa!: It's my fault!   *Qué dices hija?:* What do you say, daughter?

Margarita: Ya no puedo . . . I can't. . . . A person isn't a machine . . . *es mi culpa* . . . Father forgive me . . . *Papi! Papi!* One, two. *Uno, dos. (Pause.) Papi!* A dónde estás? *(Pause.)* One, two, one, two. *Papi! Ay, Papi!* Where are you . . . ? Don't leave me. . . . Why don't you answer me? *(Pause. She starts to swim, slowly.) Uno, dos, uno, dos.* Dig in, dig in. *(Stops swimming.) Por favor, Papi! (Starts to swim again.)* One, two, one, two. Kick from your hip, kick from your hip. *(Stops swimming. Starts to cry.)* Oh God, please. . . . *(Pause.)* Hail Mary, full of grace . . . dig in, dig in . . . the Lord is with thee. . . . *(She swims to the rhythm of her Hail Mary.)* Hail Mary, full of grace . . . dig in, dig in . . . the Lord is with thee . . . dig in, dig in. . . . Blessed art thou among women. . . . *Mami,* it hurts. You let go of my hand. I'm lost. . . . And blessed is the fruit of thy womb, now and at the hour of our death. Amen. I don't want to die, I don't want to die.

(Margarita is still swimming. Blackout. She is gone.)

SCENE VI

Lights up on boat, we hear radio static. There is a heavy mist. On deck we see only black outline of Abuela with shawl over her head. We hear the voices of Eduardo, Aída, and Radio Operator.

Eduardo's Voice: La Havana! Coming from San Pedro. Over.
Radio Operator's Voice: Right, DT6-6, you say you've lost a swimmer.
Aída's Voice: Our child, our only daughter . . . listen to me. Her name is Margarita Inez Suárez, she is wearing a black one-piece bathing suit cut high in the legs with a white racing stripe down the sides, a white bathing cap with goggles and her whole body covered with a . . . with a...
Eduardo's Voice: With lanolin and paraffin.
Aída's Voice: Sí . . . con lanolin and paraffin.

(More radio static. Special on Simón, on the edge of the boat.)

Simón: Margo! Yo Margo! *(Pause.)* Man don't do this. *(Pause.)* Come on. . . . Come on. . . . *(Pause.)* God, why does everything have to be so hard? *(Pause.)* Stupid. You know you're not supposed to die for this. Stupid. It's his dream and he can't even swim. *(Pause.)* Punch those arms in. Come home. Come home. I'm your little brother. Don't forget what Mama said. You're not supposed to leave me behind. *Vamos,* Margarita, take your little brother, hold his hand tight when you cross the street. He's so little. *(Pause.)* Oh Christ, give us a sign. . . . I know! I know! Margo, I'll send you a message . . . like mental telepathy. I'll hold my breath, close my eyes, and I'll bring you home. *(He takes a deep breath; a few beats.)* This time I'll beep . . . I'll send out sonar signals like a dolphin. *(He imitates dolphin sounds.)*

(The sound of real dolphins takes over from Simón, then fades into sound of Abuela saying the Hail Mary in Spanish, as full lights come up slowly.)

SCENE VII

Eduardo coming out of cabin, sobbing, Aída holding him. Simón anxiously scanning the horizon. Abuela looking calmly ahead.

Eduardo: Es mi culpa, sí, es mi culpa.° *(He hits his chest.)*

Aída: Ya, ya viejo.° . . . it was my sin . . . I left my home.

Eduardo: Forgive me, forgive me. I've lost our daughter, our sister, our granddaughter, mi carne, mi sangre, mis ilusiones.° *(To heaven.) Dios mío,* take me . . . take me, I say . . . Goddammit, take me!

Simón: I'm going in.

Aída and Eduardo: No!

Eduardo (grabbing and holding Simón, speaking to heaven): God, take me, not my children. They are my dreams, my illusions . . . and not this one, this one is my mystery . . . he has my secret dreams. In him are the parts of me I cannot see.

(Eduardo embraces Simón. Radio static becomes louder.)

Aída: I . . . I think I see her.

Simón: No, it's just a seal.

Abuela (looking out with binoculars): Mi nietacita, dónde estás? *(She feels her heart.)* I don't feel the knife in my heart . . . my little fish is not lost.

(Radio crackles with static. As lights dim on boat, Voices of Mel and Mary Beth are heard over the radio.)

Mel's Voice: Tragedy has marred the face of the Wrigley Invitational Women's Race to Catalina. The Cuban swimmer, little Margarita Suárez, has reportedly been lost at sea. Coast Guard and divers are looking for her as we speak. Yet in spite of this tragedy the race must go on because...

Mary Beth's Voice (interrupting loudly): Mel!

Mel's Voice (startled): What!

Mary Beth's Voice: Ah . . . excuse me, Mel . . . we have a winner. We've just received word from Catalina that one of the swimmers is just fifty yards from the breakers . . . it's, oh, it's . . . Margarita Suárez!

(Special on family in cabin listening to radio.)

Mel's Voice: What? I thought she died!

(Special on Margarita, taking off bathing cap, trophy in hand, walking on the water.)

Mary Beth's Voice: Ahh . . . unless . . . unless this is a tragic . . . No . . . there she is, Mel. Margarita Suárez! The only one in the race wearing a black bathing suit cut high in the legs with a racing stripe down the side.

(Family cheering, embracing.)

Simón (screaming): Way to go, Margo!

Mel's Voice: This is indeed a miracle! It's a resurrection! Margarita Suárez, with a flotilla of boats to meet her, is now walking on the waters, through the breakers . . . onto the beach, with crowds of people cheering her on. What a jubilation! This is a miracle!

(Sound of crowds cheering. Lights and cheering sounds fade.)

BLACKOUT

Es mi culpa, sí, es mi culpa: It's my fault, yes, it's my fault.   *Ya, ya viejo:* Yes, yes, old man.   *mi carne, mi sangre, mis ilusiones:* my flesh, my blood, my dreams.

Milcha Sanchez-Scott on Writing

Writing *The Cuban Swimmer* 1989

From these women [recent immigrants Sanchez-Scott met at the employment agency where she worked] I got my material for *Latina*, my first play. I'd never tried to write. I was just collecting stories—for instance, a woman told me her child had died two years previously, and that at the mortuary she had lifted her child and put it across her face to give it a last goodbye. For two years, she said, the whole side of her face and her lips were cold. And being with my cousin again reminded me of the way we say things in Colombia: "Do you remember the summer when all the birds flew into the bedroom?" I was just writing things down.

Milcha Sanchez-Scott

About this time I was hired by Susan Loewenberg of L.A. Theatre Works to act in a project at the women's prison in Chino. I saw the way Doris Baizley, the writer, had put the women's stories together. When I offered Susan my notes, hoping she could make a piece out of them, she persuaded me to write it myself.

I'd found a channel to get all sorts of things flowing out. I liked controlling my own time, and *making* things—I've always admired architects. Acting seemed very airy to me because I could never take it home and show it to anybody. I had trouble being alone for long periods, but then I would go to the airport or someplace else busy to write. Doris and I used to do things like write under blankets by flashlight, which makes you feel like a little kid with a big secret.

L.A. Theatre Works got a grant and we toured *Latina* up and down the state with ten Latin actresses who were always feuding. We had one who was illegal, and wouldn't perform any place she thought Immigration might come, so I had to go on in her place. Then Susan commissioned me to write something else, which turned out to be *Dog Lady* and *Cuban Swimmer*. I saw the long-distance swimmer Diana Nyad on TV and I saw Salazar—the Cuban runner—and started thinking. I wanted to set a play in the water. So I put a family on a boat and a swimmer in the water and said, "Now, *what*?" I happened to be in a church and saw the most beautiful Stations of the Cross. It struck me as a good outline for anybody undertaking an endeavor—there's all this tripping and falling and rising. So that's what I used.

From On New Ground

DOCUMENTARY DRAMA

Some playwrights combine experimental and naturalistic elements, creating documentary works that dramatize actual events. British dramatist Michael Frayn presented the European physicists who did the work preceding the atom bomb in *Copenhagen* (1998) and explored the career of director Max Reinhardt in Nazi-era Austria in *Afterlife* (2008). Actress-playwright Anna Deavere Smith created an extremely innovative version of documentary drama in which she performed *all* of the roles herself in bravura one-woman shows. Using the actual words of real people, she constructed performance pieces to explore complex social events such as the race riots in Crown Heights, Brooklyn, in 1991 and in Los Angeles in 1992.

Anna Deavere Smith

Scenes from Twilight: Los Angeles, 1992   1994

Anna Deavere Smith was born in Baltimore, Maryland, in 1950, the daughter of a business-man and an elementary school principal. She graduated from Beaver College in 1971 and earned a Master of Fine Arts degree from the American Conservatory Theater in 1977. She taught drama at Stanford University from 1990 to 2000 and is presently a professor at both the Tisch School of the Arts at New York University and the NYU School of Law. Over many years Smith has conducted more than two thousand interviews; from them she has fashioned a number of works of "documentary theater," each of which is a stage presentation in which a single performer speaks a series of monologues using the actual words of her interview subjects. The best-known of these are Fires in the Mirror *(1993), drawn from the 1991 race riots in Crown Heights, Brooklyn,* Twilight: Los Angeles, 1992 *(1994), derived from the 1992 riot in that city, and* Let Me Down Easy *(2009), which examines health care issues. Smith has frequently performed these pieces herself, winning rave reviews both for the works and for her extraordinary ability to bring to life characters of both sexes and many ages and races. In its review of* Twilight: Los Angeles, 1992, *the New York Times said: "Anna Deavere Smith is the ultimate impressionist: she does people's souls." As an actress, she has also made many appearances on stage and in films, including* Philadelphia *and* The American President, *and has been seen on television in* The West Wing *and* Nurse Jackie. *Included here are three scenes from the more than fifty monologues in* Twilight: Los Angeles, 1992.

CHARACTERS

Angela King, Rodney King's aunt, African American
Mrs. Young-Soon Han, former liquor store owner, Korean American, 40s, heavy accent
Twilight Bey, gang truce organizer, African American, early 30s/late 20s, Crips gang.

GENERAL PRODUCTION NOTE

> *A slide with the following language should begin the show, just after lights down and before any other visual image:*
>
> *This play is based on interviews conducted by Anna Deavere Smith soon after the race riots in Los Angeles of 1992. All words were spoken by real people and are verbatim from those interviews.*

ANGELA KING

Rodney King's Aunt

Here's a Nobody

Returning from white iron-gated doorway. To her stool. Heavy pounding rain outside. Day. On her stool, in her studio. Crying, has been crying, prior to the speech for ten minutes straight.

We weren't raised like this.
We weren't raised with no black and white thing.
We were raised with all kinds of friends.
Mexicans, Indians, blacks, whites, Chinese
Most of our friends were Spanish.
Who'd have thought this would happen to us?

Well, I guess there's a first time for everything you know.

> (*Blowing her nose, she stops crying. A sense in the rest of the speech that she is recovering from a long cry.*)

I guess you want me to tell the story
I don't know if you understand sometimes I'm just not in the mood, you know just
not in the mood.

> (*Slight pause.*)

His brother Galen called to say "Cops done beat Glen up!"
Talkin' about Rodney.
I said "What?"
"Police. They got it on tape."
And when I was just turning the channels
I saw this white car.
I heard him holler,
I recognized him layin' there on the ground
that's what got me.
And he looked just like his father too.
Galen was the one used to favor his father.
Now Rodney looks just like him, identical.
I don't know if it's when you lose a life
it comes back in somebody else.
Oh you should have seen him.
It's a hell of a look.
went through three plastic surgeons just to get Rodney to look like
Rodney again.
I tell him he's got a lot
to be thankful for.
A hell of a lot.
He couldn't talk, just der der der
I said, "Goddamn!"

> (*Angry.*)

My brother's son out there was lookin' like hell
that I saw in that bed and I was gonna fight for every bit of
our justice and fairness.
That (Officer) Koon
that's the one in the whole trial,
that man showed no-kind-of-remorse-at-all,
you know that?
He sit there like "it ain't
no big thing
and I
will do it it *again.*"
And he smile at you.
The nerve,
the audacity!
But I didn't give a damn if it was the President's
whatever it was.

(Slight pause, responding to a question.)

You see how everybody rave when something happens with the
President of the United States?
You know, 'cause he's a higher sort?
Okay, here's a nobody.
But the way they beat him.
This is the way I felt towards him.
You understand what I'm sayin' now?
You do? Alright.

(She lights a "More" cigarette, or long brown cigarette.)

MRS. YOUNG-SOON HAN

Former Liquor Store Owner

Swallowing the Bitterness

At a low coffee table. Deep voice.

When I was in Korea,
I used to watch many luxurious Hollywood lifestyle movies.
I never saw any poor man,
any black
maybe one housemaid?
Until last year
I believed America is the best.
I still believe it.
I don't deny that now.

Anna Deavere Smith as Mrs. Young-Soon Han.

Because I'm victim.
But
as
the year ends in ninety-two,
and we were still in turmoil,
and having all the financial problems,
and mental problems,
then a couple months ago,
I really realized that
Korean immigrants were left out
from this
society and we were nothing.
What is our right?
Is it because we are Korean?
Is it because we have no politicians?
Is it because we don't
speak good English?
Why? ·
Why do we have to be left out?

> (*She is hitting her hand on the coffee table.*)

We are not qualified to have medical treatment!
We are not qualified to get, uh,
food stamps!

> (*She hits the table once.*)

No GR!

> (*Hits the table once.*)

No welfare!

> (*Hits the table once.*)

Anything!
Many Afro-Americans

> (*Two quick hits.*)

who never worked

> (*One hit.*)

they get
at least minimum amount

> (*One hit.*)

of money

> (*One hit.*)

to survive!

> (*One hit.*)

We don't get any!

(*Large hit with full hand spread.*)

Because we have a *car*!

(*One hit.*)

and we have a *house*!

(*Pause six seconds.*)

And we are *high tax payers*!

(*One hit.*)

(*Pause fourteen seconds.*)

Where do I finda [sic] justice?
Okay, black people
Probably,
believe they won
by the trial?
Even some complains only half, right
justice was there?
But I watched the television
that Sunday morning
Early morning as they started
I started watch it all day.
They were having party, and then they celebrated (*Pronounced CeLEbreted.*)
all of South Central,
all the churches,
they finally found that justice exists
in this society.
Then where is the victims' rights?
They got their rights
by destroying *innocent Korean merchants* (*Louder.*)
They have a lot of respect, (*Softer.*)
as I do
for Dr. Martin King?
He is the only model for black community.
I don't care Jesse Jackson.
But,
he was the model
of non-violence
Non-violence?
They like to have hiseh [sic] spirits.
What about last year?
They destroyed innocent people!

(*Five second pause.*)

And I wonder if that is really justice, (*And a very soft "uh" after "justice" like "justicah,"
but very quick.*)
to get their rights

in this way.

(*Thirteen second pause.*)

I waseh swallowing the bitternesseh.
Sitting here alone, and watching them.
They became all hilarious.

(*Three second pause.*)

And uh,
in a way I was happy for them,
and I felt glad for them,
at least they got something back, you know.
Just lets forget Korean victims or other victims
who are destroyed by them.
They have fought
for their rights

(*One hit simultaneous with the word "rights."*)

over two centuries

(*One hit simultaneous with "centuries."*)

and I have a lot of sympathy and understanding for them.
Because of their effort, and sacrificing,
other minorities, like Hispanic
or Asians
maybe we have to suffer more
by mainstream,
you know?
That's why I understand.
And then
I like to be part of their
'joyment.
But.
That's why I had mixed feeling
as soon as I heard the verdict.
I wish I could
live together
with eh [sic] blacks
but after the riots
there were too much differences
The fire is still there
how do you call it

(*She says a Korean word asking for translation. In Korean, she says "igniting fire."*)

igni
igniting fire
It canuh
burst out any time.

TWILIGHT BEY

Organizer, Gang Truce

Limbo

Walking the full stage and around the table from the dinner party.

So a lot of times when I've brought up ideas to my homeboys,
They say
"Twilight
that's before your time
that's something you can't do now."
When I talked about the truce back in 1988,
that was something they considered before its time.
Yet
in 1992,
we made it
realistic.
So to me, it's like I'm stuck in limbo,
like the sun is stuck between night and day,
in the twilight hours,
You know?
I'm in an area not many people exist.
Night time to me
is like a lack of sun.
And I don't affiliate
darkness with anything negative.
I affiliate

Anna Deavere Smith as Twilight Bey.

darkness of what was first
because it *was first*
and then relative to my complexion,
I am a *dark* individual,
and with me stuck in limbo
I see the darkness as myself
I see the light (*he lights a candle*) as knowledge and the wisdom
of the world and understanding others.
And in order for me to be, a to be, a true human being.
I can't forever dwell in darkness.
I can't forever dwell in the idea,
just identifying with people like me, and understanding me and
mine.
So twilight
is
that time
between day and night
limbo
I call it limbo.

(He blows out the candle and walks off the stage.)

Questions

1. Angela King says of her nephew, Rodney, "I tell him he's got a lot / to be thankful for." Is she being deliberately ironic? Is there a larger irony in her comment?

2. Do you find Mrs. Young-Soon Han to be a sympathetic character? Why or why not?

3. Does the speech by Twilight Bey, which concludes the play, seem conciliatory? Does it explain why the play is called *Twilight*?

4. Taking these monologues together, what do you see as the mood that emerges from the text—despair? hopefulness? resignation? Explain.

Anna Deavere Smith on Writing

On Documentary Theater

1993

Interviewer: Are you comfortable labeling your work as "documentary"?

Smith: On the one hand, my work can be called documentary, but I started out by dealing with the idea of distorted truth. We often use the metaphor of the mirror as a metaphor for theatre. We feel that theatre will reflect society. I thought that mirror was too small and tried to broaden it. During the course of that work, I realized that I am not a mirror at all, but that I too have distortions. The challenge for myself is still to create as big a mirror as possible so that it becomes easier to see the distortions.

Anna Deavere Smith

• • •

Interviewer: In *Newsweek*, Jack Kroll wrote that watching you portray the various characters in *Fires in the Mirror* "is like seeing those events in a series of lightning bolts that illuminate the protagonists at their quintessential moments." How do you edit your material in order to find the most revealing passages from your interviews?

Smith: It actually begins during the interview. It's like a photographer saying, "That's the picture." That's basically what I'm looking for while talking with somebody. I'm not necessarily looking for the quintessential moment of that person, because the person is ultimately going to be in a community of thought, one among a lot of other people from the whole arena I need to make a show. Somebody will say something extraordinarily communicative, so I'll know I have to use that. Also, from doing so many interviews, some people really stand out. I hear someone express themselves in a unique way, and I've never heard anything like it out of anybody's mouth, so I'll know I must put that in my show.

From "Embodiment of Diversity"
An Interview by Michael Scassera in *Performing Arts*

■ WRITING *effectively*

THINKING ABOUT DRAMATIC REALISM

When critics use the word *realism* in relation to a play, are they claiming it is true to life? Not necessarily. Realism generally refers to certain dramatic conventions that emerged during the nineteenth century. A realistic play is not necessarily any truer to life than an experimental one, although the conventions of Realist drama have become so familiar to us that other kinds of drama—though no more artificial—can seem mannered and even bizarre to the casual viewer. Remember, though, that all drama—even the theater of Realism—is artifice.

■ **Notice the conventions of Realist drama.** Compare, for example, a play by Henrik Ibsen with one by Sophocles (Chapter 37). Ibsen's characters speak in prose, not verse. His settings are drawn from contemporary life, not a legendary past. His characters are ordinary middle-class citizens, not kings, queens, and aristocrats.

■ **Be aware that the inner lives, memories, and motivations of the characters play a crucial role in the dramatic action.** Ibsen, like other Realist playwrights, seeks to portray the complexity of human psychology—especially motivation—in detailed, subtle ways. In contrast, Shakespeare appears less interested in the reason for Iago's villainy than its consequences. Did Iago have an unhappy childhood or a troubled adolescence? These questions do not greatly matter in Renaissance drama, but to Ibsen they become central.

In *A Doll's House*, for example, we can infer that Nora's self-absorption and naiveté result from her father's overprotection.

- **Remember though, Realist drama does not necessarily come any closer than other dramatic styles to getting at the truths of human existence.** *A Doll's House*, for example, does not provide a more profound picture of psychological struggle than *Oedipus the King*. But Ibsen does offer a more detailed view of his protagonist's inner life and her daily routine.

CHECKLIST: Writing About a Realist Play

☐ List every detail the play gives about the protagonist's past. How does each detail affect the character's current behavior?

☐ What is the protagonist's primary motivation? What are the origins of that motivation?

☐ Do the other characters understand the protagonist's deeper motivations?

☐ How much of the plot arises from misunderstandings among characters?

☐ Do major plot events grow from characters' interactions? Or, do they occur at random?

☐ How does the protagonist's psychology determine his or her reactions to events?

TOPICS FOR WRITING ON REALISM

1. *A Raisin in the Sun* takes its title from Langston Hughes's poem "Harlem" (Chapter 32). Read the poem, then write an essay in which you discuss how its theme applies to the members of the Younger family.

2. There is a great deal of conflict among the family members in the play. Are their arguments caused more by simple differences of opinion or by a failure to understand one another's feelings and desires? Refer as specifically as possible to the words and actions of the characters to back up your conclusions.

3. How relevant is *A Doll's House* today? Do women like Nora still exist? How about men like Torvald? Build an argument, either that the concerns of *A Doll's House* are timeless and universal or that the issues addressed by the play are historical, not contemporary.

4. Placing yourself in the character of Ibsen's Torvald Helmer, write a defense of him and his attitudes as he himself might write it.

5. Who is the protagonist of *The Glass Menagerie*? Give the reasons for your choice. Is there an antagonist? If so, who is it, and why?

6. At the end of *The Glass Menagerie*, Amanda says to Tom, "You live in a dream; you manufacture illusions." Discuss the degree to which this is true of each of the characters in the play.

7. Choose a character from Milcha Sanchez-Scott's *The Cuban Swimmer* and examine his or her motivations. What makes your character act as he or she does? Present evidence from the play to back up your argument.

8. Describe some of the difficulties of staging *The Cuban Swimmer* as a play. What would be lost or gained by remaking it as a movie?

9. How effective is the technique of *Twilight: Los Angeles, 1992*? Does the lack of interplay between characters make it less dramatic, or is there sufficient drama in what the speakers say and the ways in which they present themselves?

10. Write a paper that compares and contrasts the different points of view of two characters in *Twilight: Los Angeles, 1992*.

11. Imagine you're a casting director. Choose a play from this chapter and cast it with well-known television and movie stars. Explain, in depth, what qualities in the characters you hope to emphasize by your casting choices.

12. Al Capovilla of Folsom Lake Center College has developed an ingenious assignment based on Ibsen's *A Doll's House* that asks students to combine the skills of a literary critic with those of a lawyer. See the following pages for a sample response to this assignment by Professor Capovilla:

> You are the family lawyer for Torvald and Nora Helmer. The couple comes to you with a request. They want you to listen to an account of their domestic problems and recommend whether they should pursue a divorce or try to reconcile.
>
> You listen to both sides of the argument. (You also know everything that is said by every character.)
>
> Now, it is your task to write a short decision. In stating your opinion, provide a clear and organized explanation of your reasoning. Show both sides of the argument. You may employ as evidence anything said or done in the play.
>
> Conclude your paper with your recommendation. What do you advise under the circumstances—divorce or an attempt at reconciliation?

SAMPLE STUDENT PAPER

Here is a paper written by a student of Professor Capovilla at Folsom Lake Center College.

Llarena 1

Carlota Llarena

Professor Capovilla

English 320

19 January 2019

Helmer vs. Helmer

Introduction establishes premise of essay

In reaching a determination of whether Torvald and Nora Helmer should either get divorced or attempt reconciliation, I have carefully considered the events leading to the breakdown of their marriage in order to decide on an amicable solution to their present predicament. In my belief, marriage is a sacred institution—one that should not be taken lightly. Love and happiness in a marriage should be cultivated by the parties. Obstacles are often found throughout marriage, but in order to overcome those obstacles, a husband and wife should share responsibilities, discuss whatever problems arise, and jointly work on finding solutions to those problems. Based on this belief, I recommend that Torvald and

Thesis statement

Nora Helmer attempt a reconciliation of the marriage.

Topic sentence weighing Torvald's faults

In reviewing the testimony provided by both parties, I find it true that Torvald has treated Nora in such a manner as to make her feel she was considered a child rather than an equal partner. Torvald handled all their finances and solely resolved all their problems. Torvald never discussed any of their household problems with Nora or attempted to seek her advice. In that regard, I believe that Torvald treated Nora in that fashion because he felt Nora was incapable of handling these types of situations. Nora's every need had always been looked after by her father. She grew up with nannies, never had to take responsibility for herself, and never had to work to earn money as money was always given to her.

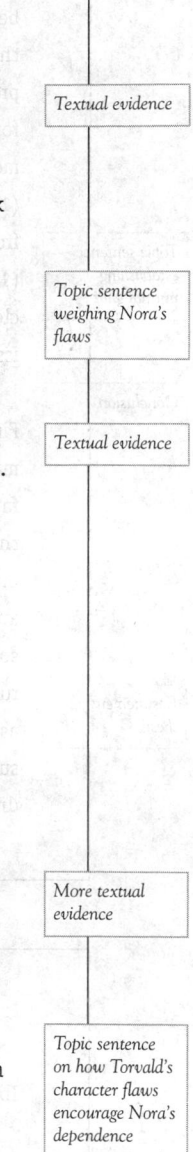

Textual evidence

I find it also true, however, that Nora has always acted like a child. She has the tendency to sulk if matters don't go her way, is happy when rewarded with gifts, hides treats (like macaroons) for herself when they are prohibited, and likes to play games. These characteristics are clearly evident in Nora. There are at least six examples of her child-like behaviors in the testimonies. First, Nora denied nibbling on a macaroon or two (1553; act 1) as a child would deny any wrongdoing. Second, Nora thought it would be "fun" to hang the money in pretty gold paper on the Christmas tree (1552; act 1) as a child would enjoy bright and colorful objects. Third, Nora considered it to be "a tremendous pleasure" to sit and work to earn money "like being a man" (1559; act 1) as a child would pretend and play-act adult roles. Fourth, Nora was excited when she received a gift of money from Torvald (1551; act 1) as a child would be excited when she receives a present. Fifth, Nora enjoyed dreaming of a rich old gentleman falling in love with her (1559; act 1) as a child would dream of getting married to a rich man who would take complete care of her. And, finally, Nora would "do everything I can think of . . . I'll sing for you, dance for you" (1568; act 1) as a child would always attempt to please her parents.

Topic sentence weighing Nora's flaws

Textual evidence

Unfortunately, Torvald reinforced Nora's child-like characteristics by calling her names such as "my little skylark" (1552; act 1), "my little squirrel" (1551; act 1), "little Miss Sweet Tooth" (1553; act 1), and "my little Nora" (1568; act 1). These nicknames seem more appropriate for a child than a grown woman. Torvald has also been very protective of Nora—just as a parent would be protective of a child. Torvald claimed that Nora had "precious eyes" and "fair little delicate hands" which indicates his belief that Nora was a fragile person, one who does not know how to take care of herself. Since Nora was treated in that same manner by her father, she has never experienced life in any other fashion other than that of a child.

More textual evidence

Topic sentence on how Torvald's character flaws encourage Nora's dependence

As a further review of the testimony presented, I opine that Torvald is not solely to be blamed for the predicament at hand. Nora has allowed Torvald to treat her in this manner during the eight years they were married. She never told Torvald that she wanted to be treated as an adult and as his equal or that she wanted to

Llarena 3

become more involved with family matters to help determine solutions to problems they may have. Nora was also guilty of not confiding in Torvald or discussing her problems with him. Did Nora discuss with Torvald the need for them to live in Italy for a year (1557; act 1)? Did she sit with her husband and discuss issues concerning money to make such a trip to Italy feasible and where the money actually came from (1558; act 1)? Did Nora ever tell Torvald the truth that she had borrowed the money from Krogstad, how she was repaying the loan and what she did to secure that loan (1558, 1565; act 1)? The answer to all these questions is no! Accordingly, it is quite clear that Nora and Torvald are both equally guilty of not discussing problems and issues with one another.

Topic sentence establishing mutual guilt

Conclusion

In summation, Nora and Torvald are equally at fault on the following issues. First, Torvald treated Nora as a child, and Nora allowed herself to be treated in that manner. Second, Torvald never confided in Nora regarding matters concerning the family or their finances. Nora, however, also did not confide in Torvald. Now that these issues and concerns are made known to the parties, the parties may work on resolving their differences, share the responsibility of handling both family and financial matters by discussing them with one another and finding amicable solutions, and cultivate the trust and judgment of one another. Accordingly, it is my ruling that Nora and Torvald attempt reconciling their marriage and forgo divorce as an immediate option. Only if the parties reach an impasse after an honest and sustained attempt at reconciliation would I suggest reconsidering the option of divorce.

Restatement of thesis

Llarena 4

Work Cited

Ibsen, Henrik. *A Doll's House*. Translated by R. Farquharson Sharp, revised by Viktoria Michelsen, *Literature: An Introduction to Fiction, Poetry, Drama, and Writing,* edited by X. J. Kennedy et al., 14th ed., Pearson, 2020, pp. 1549–99.

▶ TERMS FOR *review*

Modern Theater Movements

Realism ▶ An attempt to reproduce faithfully on the stage the surface appearance of life, especially that of ordinary people in everyday situations. In a historical sense, Realism (usually capitalized) refers to a movement in nineteenth-century European theater. Realist drama customarily focused on the middle class (and occasionally the working class) rather than the aristocracy.

Naturalism ▶ A type of drama in which the characters are presented as products or victims of environment and heredity. Naturalism, considered an extreme form of Realism, customarily depicts the social, psychological, and economic milieu of the primary characters.

Symbolist drama ▶ A style of drama that avoids direct statement and exposition for powerful evocation and suggestion. In place of realistic stage settings and actions, Symbolist drama uses lighting, music, and dialogue to create a mystical atmosphere.

Expressionism ▶ A dramatic style developed between 1910 and 1924 in Germany in reaction against Realism's focus on surface details and external reality. Expressionist style used episodic plots, distorted lines, exaggerated shapes, abnormally intense coloring, mechanical physical movement, and telegraphic speech to create a dreamlike subjective realm.

Theater of the absurd ▶ Postwar European genre depicting the grotesquely comic plight of human beings thrown by accident into an irrational and meaningless world. The critic Martin Esslin coined the term to characterize plays by writers such as Samuel Beckett, Jean Genet, and Eugène Ionesco.

Aspects of Drama

Tragicomedy ▶ A type of drama that combines elements of both tragedy and comedy. Usually it creates potentially tragic situations that bring the protagonists to the brink of disaster but then ends happily.

Comic relief ▶ The appearance of a comic situation or character, or clownish humor in the midst of a serious action, introducing a sharp contrast in mood.

Antihero ▶ A protagonist who is lacking in one or more of the conventional qualities attributed to a hero. Instead of being dignified, brave, idealistic, or purposeful, for instance, the antihero may be buffoonish, cowardly, self-interested, or weak. The antihero is often considered an essentially modern form of characterization, a satiric or realistic commentary on traditional portrayals of idealized characters.

The Stage

Proscenium arch ▶ An architectural picture frame or gateway "standing in front of the scenery" (as the name *proscenium* indicates) that separates the auditorium from the raised stage and the world of the play.

Picture-frame stage ▶ A stage that holds the action within a proscenium arch, with painted scene panels (receding into the middle distance) designed to give the illusion of three-dimensional perspective. Picture-frame stages became the norm throughout Europe and England into the twentieth century.

Box set ▶ A stage set consisting of three walls joined in two corners and a ceiling that tilts, as if seen in perspective, to provide the illusion of scenic realism for interior rooms.

40 EVALUATING A PLAY

The critic should describe, and not prescribe.

—EUGÈNE IONESCO

What You Will Learn in This Chapter

- To evaluate the qualities of a play

To **evaluate** a play is to decide whether the play is any good and, if so, how good it is in relation to other plays of its kind. In the theater, evaluation is usually the task of the drama critic, ordinarily a person who sees a new play on its first night and who then tells us, in print, online, or over the air, what the play is about, how well it is done, and whether or not we ought to go to see it. Enthroned in an excellent free seat, the drama critic apparently plies a glamorous trade. What fun it must be to whittle a nasty epigram, for example, to be able to observe, as did a critic of a faltering production of *Uncle Tom's Cabin*, that "the Siberian wolf hound was weakly supported."

The opportunities to be a drama critic today, though, are probably limited. Much more significant, for most of us, is the task of evaluating for our own satisfaction. We see a play, a film, or a television program, and then we make up our minds about it; we often have to decide whether to recommend it to someone else.

To evaluate new drama isn't easy. (For this discussion, let us define *drama* broadly as including not only plays but also anything that actors perform in the movies or on television, since most of us see more movies and television programs than plays.) By the time we see a production of any kind, at least a part of the process of evaluation has already been accomplished for us. To produce a new play, even in an amateur theater, or to produce a new drama for the movies or for television is complicated and involves large sums of money and the efforts of many people. Sifted from a mountain of submitted scripts, already subjected to long scrutiny and evaluation, a new play or film, whether or not it is of deep interest, arrives with a built-in air of professional competence. It seldom happens that a dull play written by the producer's relative or friend finds enough financial backers to reach the stage; only on the fictitious Broadway of Mel Brooks's film and hit play *The Producers* could there be a musical comedy as awful as *Springtime for Hitler*.

And so new plays—the few that we do see—are usually, like television drama, somebody's safe investment. More often than not, our powers of evaluation confront only slick, pleasant, and efficient mediocrity. We owe it to ourselves to discriminate. Life is too short and theater tickets too expensive to spend either on the agreeably second-rate. There are too many marvelous plays we might miss.

■ WRITING *effectively*

JUDGING A PLAY

To write an informed, useful evaluation of a dramatic work, consider how the play itself asks to be judged. Does it belong to a particular type of drama? It might be a farce, a comedy of manners, or a melodrama (a piece in which suspense and physical action are the prime ingredients). Remember that theaters, such as the classic Greek theater of Sophocles, impose conventions. It isn't useful to condemn *Oedipus the King* for the reason one spectator gave: "That damned chorus keeps sticking their noses in!" Nor is it useful to complain that Hamlet utters soliloquies. So, you might ask, what aspects of a play are up for critique?

- ■ **Judge how well a play fulfills its own conventions.** Ask yourself whether or not it delivers on the expectations it sets up. If a tragedy wants you to feel for the protagonist while also approving the rightness of his downfall, decide whether it has achieved those goals, and if not, why not.
- ■ **Consider whether the play's main characters are fully rounded and believable.** Ask also whether or not their actions follow naturally from their personalities. In a satisfying play, the resolution arises from the nature of the characters, and not through some *deus ex machina* or nick-of-time arrival of the Marines.
- ■ **Consider the play's theme.** How readily can you apply it to the human world beyond the play? Is it trivial, or does it seem to touch a universal chord?
- ■ **Don't be afraid to state your own honest reactions.** We cannot truthfully judge a work of art without somehow involving our own reaction—simple or complicated—to the experience of it.
- ■ **Be careful to distinguish a production from the play itself.** It is important to maintain the distinction between direction, acting, setting, and other elements of production, on the one hand, and the script, on the other.

CHECKLIST: Evaluating a Play

- ☐ What type of play are you watching or reading?
- ☐ What are the conventions of that type of play?
- ☐ How well does the play fulfill those conventions?
- ☐ Are the play's main characters fully realized?
- ☐ Do their actions follow from their personalities, or do the actions seem imposed upon them?
- ☐ Do any symbols stand out? If so, do they reveal meaning?
- ☐ Is the play sentimental? Or does it evoke honest emotion in the viewer?
- ☐ What is the play's theme? Is it of universal importance?

TOPICS FOR WRITING ON EVALUATION

1. Many of the plays in this book are available in performance online or on DVD. Choose one to watch. Pretend you are a critic attending the world premiere, and write a review. Be sure to state your criteria for judgment clearly. For tips on writing a review, see Chapter 45, "Writing About a Play."

2. Read and evaluate a work from "Plays for Further Reading." Begin with your own personal response to the text, but be sure to temper it with the considerations listed above.

3. Attend a performance of a play you haven't read and write a critical review of it. Be sure to consider both the play itself and the production. For advice on reviewing and a sample review, see Chapter 45.

4. Read a modern or contemporary play not found in this book. In an essay of 500 to 750 words, evaluate it. You might choose your subject from this list:

> *The Zoo Story* by Edward Albee
> *Disgraced* by Ayad Akhtar
> *Waiting for Godot* by Samuel Beckett
> *"Master Harold" and the Boys* by Athol Fugard
> *The Madwoman of Chaillot* by Jean Giraudoux
> *Six Degrees of Separation* by John Guare
> *Crimes of the Heart* by Beth Henley
> *Hedda Gabler, The Master Builder*, or *Peer Gynt* by Henrik Ibsen
> *The Bald Soprano* or *The Chairs* by Eugène Ionesco
> *Words, Words, Words* by David Ives
> *The Humans* by Stephen Karam
> *August: Osage County* by Tracy Letts
> *American Buffalo* by David Mamet
> *Andre's Mother* by Terrence McNally
> *'night, Mother* by Marsha Norman
> *Sweat* by Lynn Nottage
> *Long Day's Journey into Night* by Eugene O'Neill
> *Topdog/Underdog* by Suzan-Lori Parks
> *The Birthday Party* or *The Caretaker* by Harold Pinter
> *No Exit* by Jean-Paul Sartre
> *for colored girls who have considered suicide / when the rainbow is enuf*
>   by Ntozake Shange
> *Major Barbara* or *Pygmalion* by George Bernard Shaw
> *Buried Child* or *True West* by Sam Shepard
> *Rosencrantz and Guildenstern Are Dead* or *Arcadia* by Tom Stoppard
> *How I Learned to Drive* by Paula Vogel
> *The Heidi Chronicles* by Wendy Wasserstein
> *The Piano Lesson* by August Wilson

41

PLAYS FOR FURTHER READING

A play isn't a text. It's an event.

—TOM STOPPARD

David Henry Hwang

The Sound of a Voice   1983

David Henry Hwang (b. 1957) grew up in San Gabriel, California, the son of first-generation Chinese immigrants. He was born into a family of musicians: his mother was a concert pianist, his sister plays cello in a string quartet, and he studied the violin. In 1979, as a senior at Stanford University, he directed his first play, F.O.B. (an acronym for "fresh off the boat"), in a dormitory lounge. F.O.B. was later staged at the New York Shakespeare

American Repertory Theater's 2003 production of *The Sound of a Voice* in Cambridge, Massachusetts.

Festival Public Theater and won a 1981 Obie Award. The Sound of a Voice was also produced at the Public Theater as part of a double bill with another one-act play by Hwang, The House of Sleeping Beauties. *Hwang enjoyed his greatest commercial and critical success with* M. Butterfly *(1988), which won the Tony Award for best play. His other plays include* Face Value *(1993),* Golden Child *(1997), and* Yellowface *(2007). While some of his plays are realistic in their approach, Hwang has always been fascinated by the possibilities of symbolic drama. In* The Sound of a Voice, *he creates a timeless, placeless scene in which two characters named Man and Woman act out a story reminiscent of a folk legend or a traditional Japanese Nō drama (a type of symbolic aristocratic drama developed in the fourteenth century in which a ghost recounts the struggles of his or her life for a traveler). Hwang's interest in nonrealistic and experimental drama has also led him to explore opera. He has collaborated with composer Philip Glass on three works:* 1000 Airplanes on the Roof *(1988), a science-fiction music drama;* The Voyage *(1992), an allegorical grand opera commissioned by New York's Metropolitan Opera for the 500th anniversary of Christopher Columbus's arrival in America; and* The Sound of a Voice *(2003), a combined staging of the following play with* The House of Sleeping Beauties. *He has also written the books for the shows* Aida *(2000), with music by Elton John and lyrics by Tim Rice, and* Tarzan *(2006), with music and lyrics by Phil Collins. Recent works include the play* Kung Fu *(2014) and the libretto for* Dream of the Red Chamber, *an opera composed by Bright Sheng, which premiered at San Francisco Opera in 2016. Hwang lives in Brooklyn, New York.*

CHARACTERS

Man, fifties, Japanese
Woman, fifties, Japanese

SETTING. *Woman's house, in a remote corner of the forest.*

SCENE I

Woman pours tea for Man. Man rubs himself, trying to get warm.

Man: You're very kind to take me in.
Woman: This is a remote corner of the world. Guests are rare.
Man: The tea—you pour it well.
Woman: No.
Man: The sound it makes—in the cup—very soothing.
Woman: That is the tea's skill, not mine. (*She hands the cup to him.*) May I get you something else? Rice, perhaps?
Man: No.
Woman: And some vegetables?
Man: No, thank you.
Woman: Fish? (*Pause.*) It is at least two days' walk to the nearest village. I saw no horse. You must be very hungry. You would do a great honor to dine with me. Guests are rare.
Man: Thank you.
Woman (*Woman gets up, leaves. Man holds the cup in his hands, using it to warm himself. He gets up, walks around the room. It is sparsely furnished, drab, except for one shelf on which stands a vase of brightly colored flowers. The flowers stand out in sharp contrast to the starkness of the room. Slowly, he reaches out towards them. He touches*

them. *Quickly, he takes one of the flowers from the vase, hides it in his clothes. He returns to where he had sat previously. He waits. Woman re-enters. She carries a tray with food.):* Please. Eat. It will give me great pleasure.

Man: This—this is magnificent.

Woman: Eat.

Man: Thank you. *(He motions for Woman to join him.)*

Woman: No, thank you.

Man: This is wonderful. The best I've tasted.

Woman: You are reckless in your flattery. But anything you say, I will enjoy hearing. It's not even the words. It's the sound of a voice, the way it moves through the air.

Man: How long has it been since you last had a visitor? *(Pause.)*

Woman: I don't know.

Man: Oh?

Woman: I lose track. Perhaps five months ago, perhaps ten years, perhaps yesterday. I don't consider time when there is no voice in the air. It's pointless. Time begins with the entrance of a visitor, and ends with his exit.

Man: And in between? You don't keep track of the days? You can't help but notice—

Woman: Of course I notice.

Man: Oh.

Woman: I notice, but I don't keep track. *(Pause.)* May I bring out more?

Man: More? No. No. This was wonderful.

Woman: I have more.

Man: Really—the best I've had.

Woman: You must be tired. Did you sleep in the forest last night?

Man: Yes.

Woman: Or did you not sleep at all?

Man: I slept.

Woman: Where?

Man: By a waterfall. The sound of the water put me to sleep. It rumbled like the sounds of a city. You see, I can't sleep in too much silence. It scares me. It makes me feel that I have no control over what is about to happen.

Woman: I feel the same way.

Man: But you live here—alone?

Woman: Yes.

Man: It's so quiet here. How can you sleep?

Woman: Tonight, I'll sleep. I'll lie down in the next room, and hear your breathing through the wall, and fall asleep shamelessly. There will be no silence.

Man: You're very kind to let me stay here.

Woman: This is yours. *(She unrolls a mat; there is a beautiful design of a flower on the mat. The flower looks exactly like the flowers in the vase.)*

Man: Did you make it yourself?

Woman: Yes. There is a place to wash outside.

Man: Thank you.

Woman: Goodnight.

Man: Goodnight. *(Man starts to leave.)*

Woman: May I know your name?

Man: No. I mean, I would rather not say. If I gave you a name, it would only be made-up. Why should I deceive you? You are too kind for that.

Woman: Then what should I call you? Perhaps—"Man Who Fears Silence"?
Man: How about, "Man Who Fears Women"?
Woman: That name is much too common.
Man: And you?
Woman: Yokiko.
Man: That's your name?
Woman: It's what you may call me.
Man: Goodnight, Yokiko. You are very kind.
Woman: You are very smart. Goodnight.

> (*Man exits. Hanako°* goes to the mat. She tidies it, brushes it off. She goes to the vase. She picks up the flowers, studies them. She carries them out of the room with her. Man re-enters. He takes off his outer clothing. He glimpses the spot where the vase used to sit. He reaches into his clothing, pulls out the stolen flower. He studies it. He puts it underneath his head as he lies down to sleep, like a pillow. He starts to fall asleep. Suddenly, a start. He picks up his head. He listens.*)

SCENE II

Dawn. Man is getting dressed. Woman enters with food.

Woman: Good morning.
Man: Good morning, Yokiko.
Woman: You weren't planning to leave?
Man: I have quite a distance to travel today.
Woman: Please. (*She offers him food.*)
Man: Thank you.
Woman: May I ask where you're travelling to?
Man: It's far.
Woman: I know this region well.
Man: Oh? Do you leave the house often?
Woman: I used to. I used to travel a great deal. I know the region from those days.
Man: You probably wouldn't know the place I'm headed.
Woman: Why not?
Man: It's new. A new village. It didn't exist in "those days." (*Pause.*)
Woman: I thought you said you wouldn't deceive me.
Man: I didn't. You don't believe me, do you?
Woman: No.
Man: Then I didn't deceive you. I'm travelling. That much is true.
Woman: Are you in such a hurry?
Man: Travelling is a matter of timing. Catching the light. (*Woman exits; Man finishes eating, puts down his bowl. Woman re-enters with the vase of flowers.*) Where did you find those? They don't grow native around these parts, do they?

Hanako: The woman.

Woman: No; they've all been brought in. They were brought in by visitors. Such as yourself. They were left here. In my custody.

Man: But—they look so fresh, so alive.

Woman: I take care of them. They remind me of the people and places outside this house.

Man: May I touch them?

Woman: Certainly.

Man: These have just blossomed.

Woman: No; they were in bloom yesterday. If you'd noticed them before, you would know that.

Man: You must have received these very recently. I would guess—within five days.

Woman: I don't know. But I wouldn't trust your estimate. It's all in the amount of care you show to them. I create a world which is outside the realm of what you know.

Man: What do you do?

Woman: I can't explain. Words are too inefficient. It takes hundreds of words to describe a single act of caring. With hundreds of acts, words become irrelevant. (*Pause.*) But perhaps you can stay.

Man: How long?

Woman: As long as you'd like.

Man: Why?

Woman: To see how I care for them.

Man: I *am* tired.

Woman: Rest.

Man: The light?

Woman: It will return.

SCENE III

Man is carrying chopped wood. He is stripped to the waist. Woman enters.

Woman: You're very kind to do that for me.

Man: I enjoy it, you know. Chopping wood. It's clean. No questions. You take your axe, you stand up the log, you aim—pow!—you either hit it or you don't. Success or failure.

Woman: You seem to have been very successful today.

Man: Why shouldn't I be? It's a beautiful day. I can see to those hills. The trees are cool. The sun is gentle. Ideal. If a man can't be successful on a day like this, he might as well kick the dust up into his own face. (*Man notices Woman staring at him. Man pats his belly, looks at her.*) Protection from falls.

Woman: What? (*Man pinches his belly, showing some fat.*) Oh. Don't be silly. (*Man begins slapping the fat on his belly to a rhythm.*)

Man: Listen—I can make music—see?—that wasn't always possible. But now—that I've developed this—whenever I need entertainment.

Woman: You shouldn't make fun of your body.

Man: Why not? I saw you. You were staring.

Woman: I wasn't making fun. (*Man inflates his cheeks.*) I was just—stop that!

Man: Then why were you staring?

Woman: I was—

Man: Laughing?

Woman: No.

Man: Well?

Woman: I was—Your body. It's . . . strong. (Pause.)

Man: People say that. But they don't know. I've heard that age brings wisdom. That's a laugh. The years don't accumulate here. They accumulate here. (Pause; he pinches his belly.) But today is a day to be happy, right? The woods. The sun. Blue. It's a happy day. I'm going to chop wood.

Woman: There's nothing left to chop. Look.

Man: Oh. I guess . . . that's it.

Woman: Sit. Here.

Man: But—

Woman: There's nothing left. (Man sits; Woman stares at his belly.) Learn to love it.

Man: Don't be ridiculous.

Woman: Touch it.

Man: It's flabby.

Woman: It's strong.

Man: It's weak.

Woman: And smooth.

Man: Do you mind if I put on my shirt?

Woman: Of course not. Shall I get it for you?

Man: No. No. Just sit there. (Man starts to put on his shirt. He pauses, studies his body.) You think it's cute, huh?

Woman: I think you should learn to love it. (Man pats his belly, talks to it.)

Man (to belly): You're okay, sir. You hang onto my body like a great horseman.

Woman: Not like that.

Man (ibid.°): You're also faithful. You'll never leave me for another man.

Woman: No.

Man: What do you want me to say? (Woman walks over to Man. She touches his belly with her hand. They look at each other.)

SCENE IV

Night. Man is alone. Flowers are gone from stand. Mat is unrolled. Man lies on it, sleeping. Suddenly, he starts. He lifts up his head. He listens. Silence. He goes back to sleep. Another start. He lifts up his head, strains to hear. Slowly, we begin to make out the strains of a single shakuhachi° playing a haunting line. It is very soft. He strains to hear it. The instrument slowly fades out. He waits for it to return, but it does not. He takes out the stolen flower. He stares into it.

SCENE V

Day. Woman is cleaning, while Man relaxes. She is on her hands and knees, scrubbing. She is dressed in a simple outfit, for working. Her hair is tied back. Man is sweating. He has not, however, removed his shirt.

---

ibid.: an abbreviation of the Latin word ibidem, meaning "in the same place."   shakuhachi: a Japanese bamboo flute.

Man: I heard your playing last night.

Woman: My playing?

Man: Shakuhachi.

Woman: Oh.

Man: You played very softly. I had to strain to hear it. Next time, don't be afraid. Play out. Fully. Clear. It must've been very beautiful, if only I could've heard it clearly. Why don't you play for me sometime?

Woman: I'm very shy about it.

Man: Why?

Woman: I play for my own satisfaction. That's all. It's something I developed on my own. I don't know if it's at all acceptable by outside standards.

Man: Play for me. I'll tell you.

Woman: No; I'm sure you're too knowledgeable in the arts.

Man: Who? Me?

Woman: You being from the city and all.

Man: I'm ignorant, believe me.

Woman: I'd play, and you'd probably bite your cheek.

Man: Ask me a question about music. Any question. I'll answer incorrectly. I guarantee it.

Woman: Look at this.

Man: What?

Woman: A stain.

Man: Where?

Woman: Here? See? I can't get it out.

Man: Oh. I hadn't noticed it before.

Woman: I notice it every time I clean.

Man: Here. Let me try.

Woman: Thank you.

Man: Ugh. It's tough.

Woman: I know.

Man: How did it get here?

Woman: It's been there as long as I've lived here.

Man: I hardly stand a chance. *(Pause.)* But I'll try. Uh—one—two—three—four! One—two—three—four! See, you set up . . . gotta set up . . . a rhythm—two—three—four. Like fighting! Like battle! One—two—three—four! Used to practice with a rhythm . . . beat . . . battle! Yes! *(The stain starts to fade away.)* Look—it's—yes!—whoo!—there it goes—got the sides—the edges—yes!—fading quick—fading away—ooo—here we come—towards the center—to the heart—two—three—four—slow—slow death—tough—dead! *(Man rolls over in triumphant laughter.)*

Woman: Dead.

Man: I got it! I got it! Whoo! A little rhythm! All it took! Four! Four!

Woman: Thank you.

Man: I didn't think I could do it—but there—it's gone—I did it!

Woman: Yes. You did.

Man: And you—you were great.

Woman: No—I was carried away.

Man: We were a team! You and me!

Woman: I only provided encouragement.

Man: You were great! You were! (*Man grabs Woman. Pause.*)

Woman: It's gone. Thank you. Would you like to hear me play *shakuhachi*?

Man: Yes I would.

Woman: I don't usually play for visitors. It's so . . . I'm not sure. I developed it—all by myself—in times when I was alone. I heard nothing—no human voice. So I learned to play *shakuhachi*. I tried to make these sounds resemble the human voice. The *shakuhachi* became my weapon. To ward off the air. It kept me from choking on many a silent evening.

Man: I'm here. You can hear my voice.

Woman: Speak again.

Man: I will.

SCENE VI

Night. Man is sleeping. Suddenly, a start. He lifts his head up. He listens. Silence. He strains to hear. The shakuhachi melody rises up once more. This time, however, it becomes louder and more clear than before. He gets up. He cannot tell from what direction the music is coming. He walks around the room, putting his ear to different places in the wall, but he cannot locate the sound. It seems to come from all directions at once, as omnipresent as the air. Slowly, he moves towards the wall with the sliding panel through which the Woman enters and exits. He puts his ear against it, thinking the music may be coming from there. Slowly, he slides the door open just a crack, ever so carefully. He peeks through the crack. As he peeks through, the Upstage wall of the set becomes transparent, and through the scrim, we are able to see what he sees. Woman is Upstage of the scrim. She is tending a room filled with potted and vased flowers of all variety. The lushness and beauty of the room Upstage of the scrim stands out in stark contrast to the barrenness of the main set. She is also transformed. She is a young woman. She is beautiful. She wears a brightly colored kimono. Man observes this scene for a long time. He then slides the door shut. The scrim returns to opaque. The music continues. He returns to his mat. He picks up the stolen flower. It is brown and wilted, dead. He looks at it. The music slowly fades out.

SCENE VII

Morning. Man is half-dressed. He is practicing sword maneuvers. He practices with the feel of a man whose spirit is willing, but the flesh is inept. He tries to execute deft movements, but is dissatisfied with his efforts. He curses himself, and returns to basic exercises. Suddenly, he feels something buzzing around his neck—a mosquito. He slaps his neck, but misses it. He sees it flying near him. He swipes at it with his sword. He keeps missing. Finally, he thinks he's hit it. He runs over, kneels down to recover the fallen insect. He picks up two halves of a mosquito on two different fingers. Woman enters the room. She looks as she normally does. She is carrying a vase of flowers, which she places on its shelf.

Man: Look.

Woman: I'm sorry?

Man: Look.

Woman: What? (*He brings over the two halves of mosquito to show her.*)

Man: See?

Woman: Oh.

Man: I hit it—chop!

Woman: These are new forms of target practice?

Man: Huh? Well—yes—in a way.

Woman: You seem to do well at it.

Man: Thank you. For last night. I heard your *shakuhachi.* It was very loud, strong—good tone.

Woman: Did you enjoy it? I wanted you to enjoy it. If you wish, I'll play it for you every night.

Man: Every night!

Woman: If you wish.

Man: No—I don't—I don't want you to treat me like a baby.

Woman: What? I'm not.

Man: Oh, yes. Like a baby. Who you must feed in the middle of the night or he cries. Waaah! Waaah!

Woman: Stop that!

Man: You need your sleep.

Woman: I don't mind getting up for you. *(Pause.)* I would enjoy playing for you. Every night. While you sleep. It will make me feel—like I'm shaping your dreams. I go through long stretches when there is no one in my dreams. It's terrible. During those times, I avoid my bed as much as possible. I paint. I weave. I play *shakuhachi.* I sit on mats and rub powder into my face. Anything to keep from facing a bed with no dreams. It is like sleeping on ice.

Man: What do you dream of now?

Woman: Last night—I dreamt of you. I don't remember what happened. But you were very funny. Not in a mocking way. I wasn't laughing at you. But you made me laugh. And you were very warm. I remember that. *(Pause.)* What do you remember about last night?

Man: Just your playing. That's all. I got up, listened to it, and went back to sleep. *(Man gets up, resumes practicing with his sword.)*

Woman: Another mosquito bothering you?

Man: Just practicing. Ah! Weak! Too weak! I tell you, it wasn't always like this. I'm telling you, there were days when I could chop the fruit from a tree without ever taking my eyes off the ground. *(He continues practicing.)* You ever use one of these?

Woman: I've had to pick one up, yes.

Man: Oh?

Woman: You forget—I live alone—out here—there is . . . not much to sustain me but what I manage to learn myself. It wasn't really a matter of choice.

Man: I used to be very good, you know. Perhaps I can give you some pointers.

Woman: I'd really rather not.

Man: C'mon—a woman like you—you're absolutely right. You need to know how to defend yourself.

Woman: As you wish.

Man: Do you have something to practice with?

Woman: Yes. Excuse me. *(She exits. He practices more. She re-enters with two wooden sticks. He takes one of them.)* Will these do?

Man: Nice. Now, show me what you can do.

Woman: I'm sorry?

Man: Run up and hit me.

Woman: Please.

Man: Go on—I'll block it.

Woman: I feel so . . . undignified.

Man: Go on. (*She hits him playfully with stick.*) Not like that!

Woman: I'll try to be gentle.

Man: What?

Woman: I don't want to hurt you.

Man: You won't—Hit me! (*Woman charges at Man, quickly, deftly. She scores a hit.*) Oh!

Woman: Did I hurt you?

Man: No—you were—let's try that again. (*They square off again. Woman rushes forward. She appears to attempt a strike. He blocks that apparent strike, which turns out to be a feint. She scores.*) Huh?

Woman: Did I hurt you? I'm sorry.

Man: No.

Woman: I hurt you.

Man: No.

Woman: Do you wish to hit me?

Man: No.

Woman: Do you want me to try again?

Man: No.

Woman: Thank you.

Man: Just practice there—by yourself—let me see you run through some maneuvers.

Woman: Must I?

Man: Yes! Go! (*She goes to an open area.*) My greatest strength was always as a teacher. (*Woman executes a series of deft movements. Her whole manner is transformed. Man watches with increasing amazement. Her movements end. She regains her submissive manner.*)

Woman: I'm so embarrassed. My skills—they're so—inappropriate. I look like a man.

Man: Where did you learn that?

Woman: There is much time to practice here.

Man: But you—the techniques.

Woman: I don't know what's fashionable in the outside world. (*Pause.*) Are you unhappy?

Man: No.

Woman: Really?

Man: I'm just . . . surprised.

Woman: You think it's unbecoming for a woman.

Man: No, no. Not at all.

Woman: You want to leave.

Man: No!

Woman: All visitors do. I know. I've met many. They say they'll stay. And they do. For a while. Until they see too much. Or they learn something new. There are boundaries outside of which visitors do not want to see me step. Only who knows what those boundaries are? Not I. They change with every visitor. You have to be careful not to cross them, but you never know where they are. And one day, inevitably, you step outside the lines. The visitor knows. You don't. You didn't know that you'd done anything different. You thought it was just another part of you. The visitor sneaks away. The next day, you learn that you had stepped outside his heart. I'm afraid you've seen too much.

Man: There are stories.

Woman: What?

Man: People talk.

Woman: Where? We're two days from the nearest village.

Man: Word travels.

Woman: What are you talking about?

Man: There are stories about you. I heard them. They say that your visitors never leave this house.

Woman: That's what you heard?

Man: They say you imprison them.

Woman: Then you were a fool to come here.

Man: Listen.

Woman: Me? Listen? You. Look! Where are these prisoners? Have you seen any?

Man: They told me you were very beautiful.

Woman: Then they are blind as well as ignorant.

Man: You are.

Woman: What?

Man: Beautiful.

Woman: Stop that! My skin feels like seaweed.

Man: I didn't realize it at first. I must confess—I didn't. But over these few days— your face has changed for me. The shape of it. The feel of it. The color. All changed. I look at you now, and I'm no longer sure you are the same woman who had poured tea for me just a week ago. And because of that I remembered—how little I know about a face that changes in the night. (*Pause.*) Have you heard those stories?

Woman: I don't listen to old wives' tales.

Man: But have you heard them?

Woman: Yes. I've heard them. From other visitors—young—hotblooded—or old— who came here because they were told great glory was to be had by killing the witch in the woods.

Man: I was told that no man could spend time in this house without falling in love.

Woman: Oh? So why did you come? Did you wager gold that you could come out untouched? The outside world is so flattering to me. And you—are you like the rest? Passion passing through your heart so powerfully that you can't hold onto it?

Man: No! I'm afraid!

Woman: Of what?

Man: Sometimes—when I look into the flowers, I think I hear a voice—from inside—a voice beneath the petals. A human voice.

Woman: What does it say? "Let me out"?

Man: No. Listen. It hums. It hums with the peacefulness of one who is completely imprisoned.

Woman: I understand that if you listen closely enough, you can hear the ocean.

Man: No. Wait. Look at it. See the layers? Each petal—hiding the next. Try and see where they end. You can't. Follow them down, further down, around—and as you come down—faster and faster—the breeze picks up. The breeze becomes a wail. And in that rush of air—in the silent midst of it—you can hear a voice.

Woman (grabs flower from Man): So, you believe I water and prune my lovers? How can you be so foolish? (*She snaps the flower in half, at the stem. She throws it to the ground.*) Do you come only to leave again? To take a chunk of my heart, then leave with your booty on your belt, like a prize? You say that I imprison hearts in these flowers? Well, bits of my heart are trapped with travellers across this land. I can't even keep track. So kill me. If you came here to destroy a witch, kill me now. I can't stand to have it happen again.

Man: I won't leave you.

Woman: I believe you. (*She looks at the flower that she has broken, bends to pick it up. He touches her. They embrace.*)

SCENE VIII

Day. Woman wears a simple undergarment, over which she is donning a brightly colored kimono, the same one we saw her wearing Upstage of the scrim. Man stands apart.

Woman: I can't cry. I don't have the capacity. Right from birth, I didn't cry. My mother and father were shocked. They thought they'd given birth to a ghost, a demon. Sometimes I've thought myself that. When great sadness has welled up inside me, I've prayed for a means to release the pain from my body. But my prayers went unanswered. The grief remained inside me. It would sit like water, still. (*Pause; she models her kimono.*) Do you like it?

Man: Yes, it's beautiful.

Woman: I wanted to wear something special today.

Man: It's beautiful. Excuse me. I must practice.

Woman: Shall I get you something?

Man: No.

Woman: Some tea, maybe?

Man: No. (*Man resumes swordplay.*)

Woman: Perhaps later today—perhaps we can go out—just around here. We can look for flowers.

Man: Alright.

Woman: We don't have to.

Man: No. Let's.

Woman: I just thought if—

Man: Fine. Where do you want to go?

Woman: There are very few recreational activities around here, I know.

Man: Alright. We'll go this afternoon. (*Pause.*)

Woman: Can I get you something?

Man (turning around): What?

Woman: You might be—

Man: I'm not hungry or thirsty or cold or hot.

Woman: Then what are you?

Man: Practicing. (*Man resumes practicing; Woman exits. As soon as she exits, he rests. He sits down. He examines his sword. He runs his finger along the edge of it. He takes the tip, runs it against the soft skin under his chin. He places the sword on the ground with the tip pointed directly upwards. He keeps it from falling by placing the tip under his chin. He experiments with different degrees of pressure. Woman re-enters. She sees him in this precarious position. She jerks his head upward; the sword falls.*)

Woman: Don't do that!

Man: What?

Woman: You can hurt yourself!

Man: I was practicing!

Woman: You were playing!

Man: I was practicing!

Woman: It's dangerous.

Man: What do you take me for—a child?

Woman: Sometimes wise men do childish things.

Man: I knew what I was doing!

Woman: It scares me.

Man: Don't be ridiculous. (*He reaches for the sword again.*)

Woman: Don't! Don't do that!

Man: Get back! (*He places the sword back in its previous position, suspended between the floor and his chin, upright.*)

Woman: But—

Man: Sssssh!

Woman: I wish—

Man: Listen to me! The slightest shock, you know—the slightest shock—surprise—it might make me jerk or—something—and then . . . so you must be perfectly still and quiet.

Woman: But I—

Man: Sssssh! (*Silence.*) I learned this exercise from a friend—I can't even remember his name—good swordsman—many years ago. He called it his meditation position. He said, like this, he could feel the line between this world and the others because he rested on it. If he saw something in another world that he liked better, all he would have to do is let his head drop, and he'd be there. Simple. No fuss. One day, they found him with the tip of his sword run clean out the back of his neck. He was smiling. I guess he saw something he liked. Or else he'd fallen asleep.

Woman: Stop that.

Man: Stop what?

Woman: Tormenting me.

Man: I'm not.

Woman: Take it away!

Man: You don't have to watch, you know.

Woman: Do you want to die that way—an accident?

Man: I was doing this before you came in.

Woman: If you do, all you need to do is tell me.

Man: What?

Woman: I can walk right over. Lean on the back of your head.

Man: Don't try to threaten—

Woman: Or jerk your sword up.

Man: Or scare me. You can't threaten—

Woman: I'm not. But if that's what you want.

Man: You can't threaten me. You wouldn't do it.

Woman: Oh?

Man: Then I'd be gone. You wouldn't let me leave that easily.

Woman: Yes, I would.

Man: You'd be alone.

Woman: No. I'd follow you. Forever. (*Pause.*) Now, let's stop this nonsense.

Man: No! I can do what I want! Don't come any closer!

Woman: Then release your sword.

Man: Come any closer and I'll drop my head.

Woman (*Woman slowly approaches Man. She grabs the hilt of the sword. She looks into his eyes. She pulls it out from under his chin.*): There will be no more of this. (*She exits with the sword. He starts to follow her, then stops. He touches under his chin. On his finger, he finds a drop of blood.*)

SCENE IX

Night. Man is leaving the house. He is just about out, when he hears a shakuhachi *playing. He looks around, trying to locate the sound. Woman appears in the doorway to the outside.* Shakuhachi *slowly fades out.*

Woman: It's time for you to go?

Man: Yes. I'm sorry.

Woman: You're just going to sneak out? A thief in the night? A frightened child?

Man: I care about you.

Woman: You express it strangely.

Man: I leave in shame because it is proper. (*Pause.*) I came seeking glory.

Woman: To kill me? You can say it. You'll be surprised at how little I blanch. As if you'd said, "I came for a bowl of rice," or "I came seeking love" or "I came to kill you."

Man: Weakness. All weakness. Too weak to kill you. Too weak to kill myself. Too weak to do anything but sneak away in shame. (*Woman brings out Man's sword.*)

Woman: Were you even planning to leave without this? (*He takes sword.*) Why not stay here?

Man: I can't live with someone who's defeated me.

Woman: I never thought of defeating you. I only wanted to take care of you. To make you happy. Because that made me happy and I was no longer alone.

Man: You defeated me.

Woman: Why do you think that way?

Man: I came here with a purpose. The world was clear. You changed the shape of your face, the shape of my heart—rearranged everything—created a world where I could do nothing.

Woman: I only tried to care for you.

Man: I guess that was all it took. (*Pause.*)

Woman: You still think I'm a witch. Just because old women gossip. You are so cruel. Once you arrived, there were only two possibilities: I would die or you would leave. (*Pause.*) If you believe I'm a witch, then kill me. Rid the province of one more evil.

Man: I can't—

Woman: Why not? If you believe that about me, then it's the right thing to do.

Man: You know I can't.

Woman: Then stay.

Man: Don't try and force me.

Woman: I won't force you to do anything. *(Pause.)* All I wanted was an escape—for both of us. The sound of a human voice—the simplest thing to find, and the hardest to hold onto. This house—my loneliness is etched into the walls. Kill me, but don't leave. Even in death, my spirit would rest here and be comforted by your presence.

Man: Force me to stay.

Woman: I won't. *(Man starts to leave.)* Beware.

Man: What?

Woman: The ground on which you walk is weak. It could give way at any moment. The crevice beneath is dark.

Man: Are you talking about death? I'm ready to die.

Woman: Fear for what is worse than death.

Man: What?

Woman: Falling. Falling through the darkness. Waiting to hit the ground. Picking up speed. Waiting for the ground. Falling faster. Falling alone. Waiting. Falling. Waiting. Falling.

(Woman wails and runs out through the door to her room. Man stands, confused, not knowing what to do. He starts to follow her, then hesitates, and rushes out the door to the outside. Silence. Slowly, he re-enters from the outside. He looks for her in the main room. He goes slowly towards the panel to her room. He throws down his sword. He opens the panel. He goes inside. He comes out. He unrolls his mat. He sits on it, cross-legged. He looks out into space. He notices near him a shakuhachi. He picks it up. He begins to blow into it. He tries to make sounds. He continues trying through the end of the play. The Upstage scrim lights up. Upstage, we see the Woman. She is young. She is hanging from a rope suspended from the roof. She has hung herself. Around her are scores of vases with flowers in them whose blossoms have been blown off. Only the stems remain in the vases. Around her swirl the thousands of petals from the flowers. They fill the Upstage scrim area like a blizzard of color. Man continues to attempt to play. Lights fade to black.)

David Henry Hwang on Writing

Multicultural Theater 1989

Interviewer: How did you begin . . . exploring your [Chinese American] heritage?

Hwang: A lot of that happened in college. I was in college in the mid-to-late 1970s, and whereas most people seem to associate collegiate life in the seventies with John Travolta, there was at that time a third-world consciousness, a third-world power movement, in the universities, particularly among Hispanics and Asians. The blacks really started it in the late sixties and early seventies, and it took a while

From *Contemporary Authors* V 132, 0E. © 1991 Gale, a part of Cengage, Inc. Reproduced by permission. http://www.cengage.com/permissions.

David Henry Hwang

to trickle down into the other third-world communities. Asians probably picked it up last. . . . While I was never a very ardent Marxist, I studied the ideas and I was interested in the degree to which we all may have been affected by certain prejudices in the society without having realized it, and to what degree we had incorporated that into our persons by the time we'd reached our early twenties.

The other thing that I think fascinated me about exploring my Chineseness at that time was consistent with my interest in play-writing. I had become very interested in Sam Shepard, particularly in the way in which Shepard likes to create a sort of American mythology. In his case it's the cowboy mythology, but nonetheless it's something that is larger than simply our present-day, fast-food existence. In my context, creating a mythology, creating a past for myself, involved going into Chinese history and Chinese American history. I think the combination of wanting to delve into those things for artistic reasons and being exposed to an active third-world-consciousness movement was what started to get me interested in my roots when I was in college.

Interviewer: I wonder if there will come a time when the expression "ethnic theater" won't have any meaning.

Hwang: I'm hopeful that there will be a time at some point, but I think it's going to be fifty years or so down the road. The whole idea of being ethnic only applies when it's clear what the dominant culture is. Once it becomes less clear and the culture is acknowledged to be more multicultural, then the idea of what's ethnic becomes irrelevant. I think even today we're starting to see that. The monoethnic theaters—that is, the Asian theaters, the black theaters, the Hispanic theaters—are really useful; they serve a purpose. But I think, if we do our jobs correctly, we will phase out our own need for existence, and the future of theaters will be in multicultural theaters, theaters that do a black play and a Jewish play and a classic and whatever . . .

There are so many people now who can't be labeled. I know a couple in which the man is Japanese and Jewish and the woman is Haitian and Filipino. They have a child, and sociologists have told them that a child of that stock probably hasn't existed before. When someone like that becomes a writer, what do we call him? Do we say he's an Asian writer, or what? As those distinctions become increasingly muddled, the whole notion of what is ethnic as opposed to what is mainstream is going to become more and more difficult to define.

Edward Bok Lee

El Santo Americano   2001

Edward Bok Lee was born in Fargo, North Dakota, the son of Korean immigrants. He attended kindergarten in Seoul, South Korea, but grew up mostly in North Dakota and Minnesota. He received a BA in comparative literature from the University of Minnesota and an MFA from Brown University. While enrolled in a graduate program in comparative literature at the University of California, Berkeley, he wrote his first full-length play, St. Petersburg: An Exodus (2000). Lee writes plays, poetry, fiction, and memoir. His 2011 poetry collection, Whorled, won an American Book Award. A former bartender, custodian, journalist, and translator, Lee has performed his work in the United States, Europe, and Asia, as well as on public radio and on television, including MTV. His prose and poetry collection Real Karaoke People (2005) won the Asian American Literary Award and the PEN/Open Book Award. Lee currently teaches at Metropolitan State University. El Santo Americano (2001) was originally developed as part of a "ten-minute-play" project at the Guthrie Theater in Minneapolis. His other plays include Athens County (1997) and History K (2003). "Art can show you," Lee has observed, "the interior of another person's life and soul, if only just for a few minutes."

CHARACTERS

Clay, a man
Evalana, his wife

TIME. *Present*
PLACE. *The desert at night.*

Clay (driving at night, 80 mph): that's because in Mexico it's normal to wear a mask. almost everybody does. silk and satin and form-fitting lycra. it makes the whole body more aerodynamic. you ought see them flying around, doing triple flips in mid-air. they got these long flowing capes like colorful wings sprouting from their shoulders. they don't talk much, though. not the great ones. the silence is mysterious. it adds a kind of weight to them when they climb into the ring. get a guy with that much gold and glitter on him here and you know he'd have to talk shit. in Mexico they just wrestle. the masks come from thousands and thousands of years ago. fiestas. ancient rituals. slip one over your head and you could become a tiger or donkey, a bat or giant lizard. a corn spirit dancing under the clouds for rain. those were your gods if you lived back then. you'll like it there in Mexico. don't you think you'll like it there? Jesse?

(Evalana, brooding, eventually looks in the backseat then faces front again.)

Clay: he asleep back there?
a growing boy needs his sleep.
yes he does.
you hungry?
Evalana: don't talk to me.
Clay: hard to fall asleep on an empty stomach.
Evalana: i can't sleep.
Clay: you ain't tried to.

(She checks her outburst, then looks in the backseat again, perhaps adjusting their son's blanket, then faces front. they drive on for a time.)

Clay (looking in rearview mirror): hey there Jesse.
you have a nice nap?
we'll be there come morning, so you just sit back.
how you like that comic book i got you?
Jesse?
what's the matter, boy? you not feeling well?
Jesse?

Evalana: sometimes he sleeps with his eyes open.
Clay: like you.
Evalana: i do not sleep with my eyes open.
Clay: how do you know?
Evalana: i know.
Clay: how?
Evalana: 'cause someone would have said something. including you.
Clay: people do all kinds of things they're not aware of.
    my daddy used to wander through the house all night, buck naked,
    up and down the stairs. opening and closing windows.
    carrying only his briefcase chockfull of all the vending machine products he sold.
    combs. candy. chicken bouillon.
    my momma warned if we woke him up he'd have a heart attack.
    so we just let him sleepwalk.
    he didn't know.
Evalana: maybe somebody should have told him.
Clay: he didn't want to know.

    (They drive on.)

Evalana: you talk in your sleep.
    you snore.
    you drool.
    and you fart. all night.

    (They drive on awhile.)

Clay: i love you, Ev.
Evalana: jesus, Clay. listen to yourself.
    your whole life you been faking it.
    fake husband. fake father.
    fake man. that's what they ought to call you:
    Fake Man.

    (Clay drives on for a little while longer through the night, then pulls the car to a stop on the side of the road and gets out. he walks a good ways away from the car, holding a flashlight in one hand and a gun in the other—not aimed at her, but clearly present, under the starlight. Evalana hesitates, then gets out, the flashlight's beam now on her.)

Clay (directs flashlight beam to a place in the brush): there's a bush over there.

    (Evalana, hesitant at first, then grabs her purse and crosses past Clay.)

Evalana (off): i won't run!
    i promise!

    (Clay thinks, then lowers flashlight beam and switches it off. dim moonlight. sounds of desert at night.)

Clay: you should have seen me last week, Ev!

Darton, he cut me a break! he didn't have to, but he did 'cause i been loyal to him all these years! you remember when we used to work at the turkey plant together! the smell on my hands when i'd come home and try to kiss you . . .

the match was against the eleventh-ranked contender! brand new guy, from Montreal! Kid Canuck they call him! long blonde hair, tan, all bulked up in white trunks with a red maple leaf you know where! some rich producer's nephew or something! he was scheduled to wrestle the Sheik in the opening match, but the old guy had a hernia while they was warming up, so Darton, he give me a break and put me on the bill against Kid Canuck at the last minute!

we didn't have time to choreograph much action! i think he was kind of nervous! two minutes in he starts grabbing my hair! hard! for real! trying to get the audience more into it! he wasn't telegraphing his head butts neither! soon enough my nose was a cherry caught under a dumptruck! the blood all over sure got the crowd into it boy! up till then they was pretty quiet, waiting for the main headliners to come out!

raking my eyes, slapping my face. i told him to ease up, it don't work like that here, but he wasn't listening. dancing around. cursing at me in French. winding his right arm up, then smacking me hard with the left until both my ears are firebells going off.

now i can take just about anything. you know me. i've been pile-drived, figure-foured, and suplexed into losses by the best of them. but on this particular night, something happened. and one pop i took in the mouth shot my adrenaline way up, my blood running all over hell now like carbolic acid, and him twisting my arm for real, not giving a flying fuck about my bad elbow, my bad back, or my five-year-old son, who don't even like to watch wrestling no more 'cause he's ashamed, 'cause his friends call his daddy a loser, and he don't know what to say or believe in, and the next thing i knew i had that pretty boy son of a bitch Kid Canuck down hard on the mat in a scorpion leg lock!!

they had to haul him off on a stretcher!

i was a little dazed yet, and the crowd, they didn't know what to think!

then the referee threw my arm up under the hot lights and before i knew it all the noise in the arena was more like cheering! it was a chemical thing! at first some people in the upper bleachers stood up! and then all of them did! everywhere! stomping, and starting to chant my name! and not 'cause they hated the other guy! they didn't! they was cheering 'cause i beat the guy fair and square! he gave up out of pain, right there in the middle of the ring! i had him wrenched in that scorpion leg lock a good two minutes screaming like a baby, like a cut pig, like a man in real pain! and they knew it!

you can't fake that! they'd seen so much phony bullshit through the years, and they could tell this match was different! and they appreciated that! they appreciated being shown the truth, just once in their sorry-ass lives!

Darton threw a wet towel at my face in the locker room.

i went out on a limb for you! he says. six months of planning and promotion! tens of thousands of dollars! t-shirts! coffee mugs! now who the hell's gonna believe Kid Canuck is a contender for the federation championship when he lost his debut match to you!!

i told him i was sorry, and after a while he put his hand on my shoulder. asked me what i'd been thinking there in the ring. tell me the truth, he says. so i can go home and feel at least a little bad about firing your dumb ass.

and i wanted to say that i did it for you.

for my wife, Evalana, who i never gave nothing to believe in.

and i did it for my boy, Jesse, who only ever got to see his daddy get beat time and again. i wanted to tell him i did it 'cause my wife and child was out there in the audience. not living in some other town. i wanted to say you was both out there watching over me. 'cause where else would you be?

Ev? Evalana!

(Clay switches on flashlight and directs its beam onto the "bush" in the desert. Evalana has run off. he directs the flashlight all around, searching in vain.)

shit.

(Clay turns off the flashlight and sits down on a stone. in the moonlight, he pulls out from his pocket a colorful Mexican wrestler's mask and slips it over his head. he sits there in the darkness alone for a moment. he then, as a little boy might, twirls the gun on his finger, and pretends what it'd be like to shoot himself in the head. he tries it from a couple different angles, in strange fun. eventually he places the gun in his mouth, holds it there for a second or two with his hand, then lets go. it remains stuck there in his mouth from here on out. eventually, out of the darkness of the desert, Evalana reappears.)

Evalana: once, when i was about Jesse's age, we took a trip to California. Disneyland. we drove all the way cross country in Daddy's Ford Falcon. Ma said it was the honeymoon she never got. a lot of the highway had just been tarred, and you could feel it. i thought we was gonna sail on forever into the future. it was somewhere in Arizona that Daddy woke us all up so we could see this great big dam at night. we stood there looking down at the bright lights and roaring darkness. Ma moved off to one side and stared down, a thousand feet.
i knew she wanted to jump.
then suddenly, she pointed at something. look, Ev, she said. a rainbow!

Shane and Darlene came running over, climbing up on the guard-rail but they couldn't see nothing. neither could Daddy.

a few hours later, somewhere outside of Flagstaff i told them i saw that rainbow too. it wasn't just Ma who saw it. i saw it too. Shane and Darlene were asleep now. Ma didn't say nothing. we drove on deeper into the night. then Daddy looked at me. i could see his eyes in the rear view mirror. hovering there in the blackness. "there's no such thing as a rainbow at night," he said. "not a real rainbow anyway."

the next day at dusk we camped on high ground. from where i stood looking down, you could see all the layers of sediment carved in the side of the mountains they cleared away for the highways a long time ago. red, black, brown, white, and sometimes almost blue, like a human vein in the side of a mountain, running parallel to the horizon. i stood there a long time, watching all the layers of earthen rainbows darkening all around me. then slowly, i noticed something. in the far distance, a cluster of fallen stars. only, it wasn't a cluster of stars, but a town. far off the highway, down there in the middle of nowhere. you wouldn't even notice it by day. but at night you could see something. twinkling. i imagined i'd been born in that town, and that that was where we was all heading back to. not Disneyland. but that town shining with tiny stars that weren't really stars, surrounded by rainbows that weren't really rainbows. but erosion. as far as the eye could see. for thousands and thousands of years. both real and imaginary. like that town down there in the valley at night. just barely shimmering. like . . . Eden.

(We hear the sound of their car start and drive off into the night. Clay in mask with gun still in mouth and Evalana slowly turn to watch the vehicle go, converging closer together as they walk and watch. "Jesse" has driven off into the night. once the sound of the car has faded into the distance, Clay in mask with gun in mouth and Evalana slowly turn to one another. after a moment, Evalana reaches up and removes the gun from Clay's mouth and slowly points it at him.

Fade to black.)

END OF PLAY

Edward Bok Lee on Writing

On Being a Korean American Writer   2006

Interviewer: Do you think of yourself as a Korean American writer?

Lee: What I'm doing, intentionally, is trying to participate in this thing we call Asian America, this Asian American culture, which is influenced by my parents and the way that they brought me up, their philosophies and their religious beliefs, their culture—everything from the food to the song to the art form.

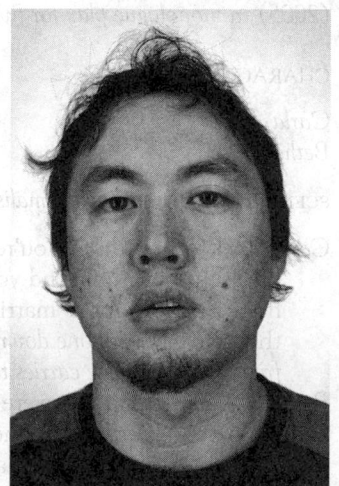

Edward Bok Lee

I believe that a given culture has a given orientation of the soul. And you can hear it in a culture's music. It's live, it's right in front of you, it's all around you. I really believe that when I hear a culture—whether it's Irish or African or English or Hawaiian—when I hear the traditional songs coming out of people, I definitely sense that there are differences of the soul. So in that way, I feel alive with some sort of Asian, and more Asian American sensibilities. I have no idea how to try and quantify those things, but I feel it.

It's sort of drenching the country when I go back to Korea—especially the countryside. It's tied to the land, it's tied to the history. It's a history, in Korea, of oppression, of colonization, and of survival. I feel, like it or not, that that ethos or whatever you want to call it, is infused in my work.

. . . I feel like a conduit between something going on in another realm. It might be something like the past, history, or something beyond memory. Voices. It's in the realm of intuition . . . and it's mysterious. And that's when I feel like I'm at my best in writing. Versus that I have things to say that I want to communicate. If that were the case, then I think I would do journalism, or write essays.

I think I'm in love with the unspeakable, the inarticulate. You're always coming up against this invisible wall, and putting a cup to it, trying to hear what's going on the other side. You're always trying to transcribe those things.

From "Thinking Souls: An Interview with Edward Bok Lee"
by Shannon Gibney

Jane Martin

Beauty   2001

The identity of Jane Martin is a closely guarded secret. No biographical details, public state-ments, or photographs of this Kentucky-based playwright have been published, nor has she given any interviews or made any public appearances. Often called "America's best known, unknown playwright," Martin first came to public notice in 1981 for Talking With, *a collection of monologues that received a number of productions worldwide and won a Best Foreign Play of the Year award in Germany. Of Martin's many plays, others include* What Mama Don't Know *(1988),* Cementville *(1991),* Keely and Du *(which was a finalist for the 1993 Pulitzer Prize),* Middle-Aged White Guys *(1995),* Jack and Jill *(1996),* Mr. Bundy *(1998),* Anton in Show Business *(2000),* Flaming Guns of the Purple Sage *(2001),* Beauty *(2001), and* Good Boys *(2002). Her most recent work is* Sez She *(2005), a monologue play for five actresses.*

CHARACTERS

Carla
Bethany

SCENE. *An apartment. Minimalist set. A young woman, Carla, on the phone.*

Carla: In love with me? You're in love with me? Could you describe yourself again? Uh-huh. Uh-huh. And you spoke to me? (*A knock at the door.*) Listen, I always hate to interrupt a marriage proposal, but . . . could you possibly hold that thought? (*Puts phone down and goes to door. Bethany, the same age as Carla and a friend, is there. She carries the sort of mid-eastern lamp we know of from Aladdin.*)

Bethany: Thank God you were home. I mean, you're not going to believe this!

Carla: Somebody on the phone. (*Goes back to it.*)

Bethany: I mean, I just had a beach urge, so I told them at work my uncle was dying . . .

Carla (motions to Bethany for quiet): And you were the one in the leather jacket with the tattoo? What was the tattoo? (*Carla again asks Bethany, who is gesturing wildly that she should hang up, to cool it.*) Look, a screaming eagle from shoulder to shoul-der, maybe. There were a lot of people in the bar.

Bethany (gesturing and mouthing): I have to get back to work.

Carla (on phone): See, the thing is, I'm probably not going to marry someone I can't remember . . . particularly when I don't drink. Sorry. Sorry. Sorry. (*She hangs up.*) Madness.

Bethany: So I ran out to the beach . . .

Carla: This was some guy I never met who apparently offered me a beer . . .

Bethany: . . . low tide and this . . . (*The lamp*) . . . was just sitting there, lying there . . .

Carla: . . . and he tracks me down . . .

Bethany: . . . on the beach, and I lift this lid thing . . .

Carla: . . . and seriously proposes marriage.

Bethany: . . . and a genie comes out.

Carla: I mean, that's twice in a . . . what?

Bethany: A genie comes out of this thing.

Carla: A genie?

Bethany: I'm not kidding, the whole Disney kind of thing, swirling smoke, and then this twenty-foot-high, see-through guy in like an Arabian outfit.

Carla: Very funny.

Bethany: Yes, funny, but twenty feet high! I look up and down the beach, I'm alone. I don't have my pepper spray or my hand alarm. You know me, when I'm petrified I joke. I say his voice is too high for Robin Williams, and he says he's a castrati. Naturally. Who else would I meet?

Carla: What's a castrati?

Bethany: You know . . .

(*The appropriate gesture.*)

Carla: Bethany, dear one, I have three modeling calls. I am meeting Ralph Lauren!

Bethany: Okay, good. Ralph Lauren. Look, I am not kidding!

Carla: You're not kidding what?!

Bethany: There is a genie in this thingamajig.

Carla: Uh-huh. I'll be back around eight.

Bethany: And he offered me wishes!

Carla: Is this some elaborate practical joke because it's my birthday?

Bethany: No, happy birthday, but I'm like crazed because I'm on this deserted beach with a twenty-foot-high, see-through genie, so like sarcastically . . . you know how I need a new car . . . I said fine, gimme 25,000 dollars . . .

Carla: On the beach with the genie?

Bethany: Yeah, right, exactly, and it rains down out of the sky.

Carla: Oh sure.

Bethany (*pulling a wad out of her purse*): Count it, those are thousands. I lost one in the surf.

(*Carla sees the top bill. Looks at Bethany, who nods encouragement. Carla thumbs through them.*)

Carla: These look real.

Bethany: Yeah.

Carla: And they rained down out of the sky?

Bethany: Yeah.

Carla: You've been really strange lately, are you dealing?

Bethany: Dealing what, I've even given up chocolate.

Carla: Let me see the genie.

Bethany: Wait, wait.

Carla: Bethany, I don't have time to screw around. Let me see the genie or let me go on my appointments.

Bethany: Wait! So I pick up the money . . . see, there's sand on the money . . . and I'm like nuts so I say, you know, "Okay, look, ummm, big guy, my uncle is in the

hospital" . . . because as you know when I said to the people at work my uncle
was dying, I was on one level telling the truth although it had nothing to do
with the beach, but he was in Intensive Care after the accident, and that's on my
mind, so I say, okay, Genie, heal my uncle . . . which is like impossible given he
was hit by two trucks, and the genie says, "Yes, Master" . . . like they're supposed
to say, and he goes into this like kind of whirlwind, kicking up sand and stuff, and
I'm like, "Oh my God!" and the air clears, and he bows, you know, and says, "It is
done, Master," and I say, "Okay, whatever-you-are, I'm calling on my cell phone,"
and I get it out and I get this doctor who is like dumbstruck who says my uncle
came to, walked out of Intensive Care and left the hospital! I'm not kidding, Carla.

Carla: On your mother's grave?

Bethany: On my mother's grave.

(They look at each other.)

Carla: Let me see the genie.

Bethany: No, no, look, that's the whole thing . . . I was just, like, reacting, you know,
responding, and that's already two wishes . . . although I'm really pleased about
my uncle, the $25,000 thing, I could have asked for $10 million, and there is
only one wish left.

Carla: So ask for $10 million.

Bethany: I don't think so. I don't think so. I mean, I gotta focus in here. Do you have
a sparkling water?

Carla: No. Bethany, I'm missing Ralph Lauren now. Very possibly my one chance
to go from catalogue model to the very, very big time, so, if you are joking, stop
joking.

Bethany: Not joking. See, see, the thing is, I know what I want. In my guts. Yes.
Underneath my entire bitch of a life is this unspoken, ferocious, all-consuming
urge . . .

Carla (trying to get her to move this along): Ferocious, all-consuming urge . . .

Bethany: I want to be like you.

Carla: Me?

Bethany: Yes.

Carla: Half the time you don't even like me.

Bethany: Jealous. The ogre of jealousy.

Carla: You're the one with the $40,000 job straight out of school. You're the one who
has published short stories. I'm the one hanging on by her fingernails in modeling. The one who has creeps calling her on the phone. The one who had to have
a nose job.

Bethany: I want to be beautiful.

Carla: You are beautiful.

Bethany: Carla, I'm not beautiful.

Carla: You have charm. You have personality. You know perfectly well you're pretty.

Bethany: "Pretty," see, that's it. Pretty is the minor leagues of beautiful. Pretty is what
people discover about you after they know you. Beautiful is what knocks them
out across the room. Pretty, you get called a couple of times a year; *beautiful* is
24 hours a day.

Carla: Yeah? So?

Bethany: So?! We're talking *beauty* here. Don't say "So?" Beauty is the real deal. You
are the center of any moment of your life. People stare. Men flock. I've seen you

get offered discounts on makeup for no reason. Parents treat beautiful children better. Studies show your income goes up. You can have sex anytime you want it. Men have to know me. That takes up to a year. I'm continually horny.

Carla: Bethany, I don't even like sex. I can't have a conversation without men coming on to me. I have no privacy. I get hassled on the street. They start pressuring me from the beginning. Half the time, it never occurs to them to start with a conversation. Smart guys like you. You've had three long-term relationships, and you're only twenty-three. I haven't had one. The good guys, the smart guys are scared to death of me. I'm surrounded by male bimbos who think a preposition is when you go to school away from home. I have no woman friends except you. I don't even want to talk about this!

Bethany: I knew you'd say something like this. See, you're "in the club" so you can say this. It's the way beauty functions as an elite. You're trying to keep it all for yourself.

Carla: I'm trying to tell you it's no picnic.

Bethany: But it's what everybody wants. It's the nasty secret at large in the world. It's the unspoken tidal desire in every room and on every street. It's the unspoken, the soundless whisper . . . millions upon millions of people longing hopelessly and forever to stop being whatever they are and be beautiful, but the difference between those ardent multitudes and me is that I have a goddamn genie and one more wish!

Carla: Well, it's not what I want. This is me, Carla. I have never read a whole book. Page 6, I can't remember page 4. The last thing I read was "The Complete Idiot's Guide to WordPerfect." I leave dinner parties right after the dessert because I'm out of conversation. You know the dumb blond joke about on the application where it says, "Sign here," she put Sagittarius? I've done that. Only beautiful guys approach me, and that's because they want to borrow my eye shadow. I barely exist outside a mirror! You don't want to *be me.*

Bethany: None of you tell the truth. That's why you have no friends. We can all see you're just trying to make us feel better because we aren't in your league. This only proves to me it should be my third wish. Money can only buy things. Beauty makes you the center of the universe.

(Bethany picks up the lamp.)

Carla: Don't do it. Bethany, don't wish it! I am telling you you'll regret it.

(Bethany lifts the lid. There is a tremendous crash, and the lights go out. Then they flicker and come back up, revealing Bethany and Carla on the floor where they have been thrown by the explosion. We don't realize it at first, but they have exchanged places.)

Carla/Bethany: Oh God.
Bethany/Carla: Oh God.
Carla/Bethany: Am I bleeding? Am I dying?
Bethany/Carla: I'm so dizzy. You're not bleeding.
Carla/Bethany: Neither are you.
Bethany/Carla: I feel so weird.
Carla/Bethany: Me too. I feel . . . *(Looking at her hands.)* Oh, my God, I'm wearing your jewelry. I'm wearing your nail polish.

Bethany/Carla: I know I'm over here, but I can see myself over there.

Carla/Bethany: I'm wearing your dress. I have your legs!!

Bethany/Carla: These aren't my shoes. I can't meet Ralph Lauren wearing these shoes!

Carla/Bethany: I wanted to be beautiful, but I didn't want to be you.

Bethany/Carla: Thanks a lot!!

Carla/Bethany: I've got to go. I want to pick someone out and get laid.

Bethany/Carla: You can't just walk out of here in my body!

Carla/Bethany: Wait a minute. Wait a minute. What's eleven eighteenths of 1,726?
    Bethany/Carla: Why?

Carla/Bethany: I'm a public accountant. I want to know if you have my brain.

Bethany/Carla: One hundred thirty-two and a half.

Carla/Bethany: You have my brain.

Bethany/Carla: What shade of Rubenstein lipstick does Cindy Crawford wear with teal blue?

Carla/Bethany: Raging Storm.

Bethany/Carla: You have my brain. You poor bastard.

Carla/Bethany: I don't care. Don't you see?

Bethany/Carla: See what?

Carla/Bethany: We both have the one thing, the one and only thing everybody wants.

Bethany/Carla: What is that?

Carla/Bethany: It's better than beauty for me; it's better than brains for you.

Bethany/Carla: What? What?!

Carla/Bethany: Different problems.

BLACKOUT

END OF PLAY

Brighde Mullins

Click   2001

Brighde Mullins (b. 1963) was born into a military family at Camp Lejeune, North Carolina, and was raised in Las Vegas, Nevada. Her plays have been developed and produced in New York, Dallas, Salt Lake City, London, Los Angeles, and San Francisco. Her full-length plays include The Bourgeois Pig; Rare Bird; Those Who Can, Do; Monkey in the Middle; Teach; Fire Eater; Topographical Eden; *and* Increase. Click, *her darkly comic one-act play, was commissioned by the Actors Theatre of Louisville for the 2001 Humana Festival. Her awards include a Guggenheim Fellowship in Playwriting, a United States Artists Fellowship in Literature, a Whiting Foundation Award, a Gold Medal from the Pinter* Review, *and an NEA Fellowship, and her book of poems,* Water Stories (2003), *was nominated for a Pushcart Prize. She has taught at Brown University and was the Director of Creative Writing at Harvard (where she was also a Briggs-Copeland Lecturer in Playwriting). Presently Mullins teaches at the University of Southern California, where she directs the Master of Professional Writing Program. She also teaches in the Theatre Department at the University of California, Santa Barbara. Mullins lives in Los Angeles.*

CHARACTERS

Man
Woman

SCENE. *Dark stage. The low hum of a bad phone connection over thousands of miles. The voices of a Man and a Woman are heard; they are in the middle of a conversation.*

Man: —what are you doing?
Woman: Doing?
Man: While you're talking to me. I hear something. What are you doing?
Woman: What does it sound like?
Man: Click—click—click
Woman (in a rush, in one breath): Oh—that click?—it's the window blind in a breeze, a slight breeze, it's me unsnapping my tortoise shell barrette, I clipped and unclipped it, it's my Italian lighter lighting up my last Blonde Gauloise, it's some cheap Christmas trash racketing its way down the street, it's my birthstone ring hitting the floor, it's a bird's beak tapping, it's Morse code, it's an urgent message we can't decipher but need to know, it's the deadbolt on the back-door, it's the heater clacking into action, it's the clock stuck on One, One, One, it's a glitch on the wires, it's the loose jawbone that clicks in my head from where I took a fall on the ice last winter. It's my nailclipper.
Man: I'm really sick of your metaphors.
Woman: You used to like my turns of phrase.
Man: That was before I started re-hab.
Woman: Recovery takes the Poetry out of Things, huh?
Man: At a nickel a minute from a payphone in a drafty corridor, yeah. I'd say so.

(slight beat)

Yeah. It's all just words.
Woman: That's all we have right now, isn't it? You're two thousand miles away and we're reduced to Words, Right?
Man: Yeah. I guess so.
Woman: So the corridor is drafty.
Man: Yeah.
Woman: What color are the walls?
Man: Green.
Woman: Make me see the green.
Man: Greenish.
Woman: A brown green or a yellow green?
Man: Cocktail olive green. Drab green. Military green.
Woman: Windows?
Man: One up high. Too small for a body to crawl through.
Woman: Describe it.
Man: High. And sideways. And there are tables, and old mouldy armchairs, they give off a smell like sweat and urine—or maybe it's like old cheese—
Woman: Brie?
Man: Cracker Barrel—sharp and sickly—and there are magazines, lots of them. Piles of old *National Geographics*. And God all of this and talking to you and "this is like" and "this is like." "Nothing" is "Like Anything" except that I could use something like a drink.

(*sound in: CLICK*)

Man: There's that click again. Are you opening a beer?

Woman (*momentary pause*): I'm opening a SODA.

Man: You're drinking beer! You're drinking beer while I'm calling you from rehab?

Woman: I understand how very difficult this is for you, and I'm talking to you and I'm trying to be supportive. I would never drink a beer while talking to you.

(*pause*)

It's a lite beer. It's practically a soda.

Man: A *lite* beer? I have to go.

Woman: Wait. That was a Metaphor—

(*SOUND IN: Click. Dead Wire*)

Hullo? Hey? Hey.

END PLAY

Brighde Mullins on Writing

Advice for Young Playwrights   2007

The word *playwright* is in the same etymological family as that of a shipwright, a cartwright, a wheelwright. The words *shipwright, cartwright, wheelwright* are descriptive: they summon up a craftsperson making a useful object—a ship, a cart, a wheel. A playwright is the maker of a script for the stage, a useful text. The second half of the word *playwright*, then, emphasizes the craft aspect of writing for the stage. Not that there isn't a good deal of artfulness, and a wealth of aesthetic complexity involved in playwrighting. But these elements are yoked to the psyche of the maker, so much so that they are idiosyncratic and unteachable. . . .

Brighde Mullins

Writing for the stage implies that you are writing words that will be spoken by actors and heard by an audience. If you are writing for actors, then actors are your vehicles, your instruments. This is the most important distinction between writing for the stage and writing for another genre. Poems and prose occur in a private space between the reader and the writer. The play, however, like a composer's score or an architect's blueprint, exists as a written text as a stop along the way. The play fully exists only in production, and therefore the single most vital element that a playwright has to shaping her craft is access to a theater.

The most important information that a playwright can have is an arsenal of experiences in the theater. By experiences I don't mean that you have to have worked on plays although that is of course extremely useful. Indeed, one playwright

I know (Paul Selig) has said that his best insights and ideas have come to him when he worked on running crew backstage and sat waiting for a cue light. There are some things that only proximity to stagecraft can transmit. If you cannot work in or on a production, the next best thing is to read and then to see plays in performance.

• • •

That is the most practical way to begin to understand the relationship between the page and the stage. A production is a somatic event, an experience that engages all of the senses. There is no substitute for witnessing live theater. It is the necessary background. The full immersion of a production is what any play is written towards. And so, seeing a play in production after reading it can help you to fill in the gaps. You can start to see and then to articulate the contributions that designers, actors and directors make in embodying the play. You start to be able to imagine your own writing as being breathed into a space where it can be met and taken up by a collaborator.

From "Writing for the Stage"

August Wilson

Fences   1985

August Wilson (1945–2005) was born in Pittsburgh, one of six children of a German American father and an African American mother. His parents separated early, and the young Wilson was raised on the Hill, an impoverished Pittsburgh neighborhood. Although he quit school in the ninth grade when a teacher wrongly accused him of submitting a ghost-written paper, Wilson continued his education in local libraries, supporting himself by working as a cook and stock clerk. In 1968 he co-founded a community troupe, the Black Horizons Theater, staging plays by politically radical writers such as LeRoi Jones (a.k.a Amiri Baraka); later Wilson moved from Pittsburgh to Saint Paul, Minnesota, where at last he saw a play of his own performed. Jitney, his first important work, won him entry to a 1982 playwrights' conference at the Eugene O'Neill Theater Center. There, Lloyd Richards, dean of Yale University School of Drama, took an interest in Wilson's work and offered to produce his plays at Yale. Ma Rainey's Black Bottom was the first to reach Broadway (in 1985), where it ran for ten months and received an award from the New York Drama Critics Circle. In 1987 Fences, starring Mary Alice and James Earl Jones, won another Critics Circle Award, as well as a Tony Award and the Pulitzer Prize for best American play of its year. It set a box office record for a Broadway nonmusical. Joc Turner's Come and Gone (1988) also received high acclaim, and The Piano Lesson (1990) won Wilson a second Pulitzer Prize. His subsequent plays were Two Trains Running (1992), Seven Guitars (1995), King Hedley II (2000), Gem of the Ocean (2003), and Radio Golf (2005). In 2016, Denzel Washington directed and starred in a film adaptation of Fences, which was widely praised by critics and received four Oscar nominations.

Wilson's ten plays, each one set in a different decade of the 1900s, constitute his "Century Cycle" that traces the black experience in America throughout the twentieth century. Seamlessly interweaving realistic and mythic approaches, filled with vivid characters, pungent dialogue, and strong dramatic scenes, it is one of the most ambitious projects in the history of the American theater and an epic achievement in our literature. Wilson died of liver cancer in October 2005, a few months after completing the final play in his cycle. Two weeks after his death the Virginia Theater on Broadway was renamed the August Wilson Theater in his honor. A published poet as well as a dramatist, Wilson once told an interviewer, "After writing poetry for twenty-one years, I approach a play the same way. The mental process is poetic: you use metaphor and condense."

For Lloyd Richards, Who Adds to Whatever He Touches

> When the sins of our fathers visit us
> We do not have to play host.
> We can banish them with forgiveness
> As God, in His Largeness and Laws.

—AUGUST WILSON

LIST OF CHARACTERS

Troy Maxson
Jim Bono, Troy's friend
Rose, Troy's wife
Lyons, Troy's oldest son by previous marriage
Gabriel, Troy's brother
Cory, Troy and Rose's son
Raynell, Troy's daughter

SETTING. *The setting is the yard which fronts the only entrance to the Maxson household, an ancient two-story brick house set back off a small alley in a big-city neighborhood. The entrance to the house is gained by two or three steps leading to a wooden porch badly in need of paint.*

A relatively recent addition to the house and running its full width, the porch lacks congruence. It is a sturdy porch with a flat roof. One or two chairs of dubious value sit at one end where the kitchen window opens onto the porch. An old-fashioned icebox stands silent guard at the opposite end.

The yard is a small dirt yard, partially fenced, except for the last scene, with a wooden saw horse, a pile of lumber, and other fence-building equipment set off to the side. Opposite is a tree from which hangs a ball made of rags. A baseball bat leans against the tree. Two oil drums serve as garbage receptacles and sit near the house at right to complete the setting.

THE PLAY. *Near the turn of the century, the destitute of Europe sprang on the city with tenacious claws and an honest and solid dream. The city devoured them. They swelled its belly until it burst into a thousand furnaces and sewing machines, a thousand butcher shops and bakers' ovens, a thousand churches and hospitals and funeral parlors and money-lenders. The city grew. It nourished itself and offered each man a partnership limited only by his talent, his guile, and his willingness and capacity for hard work. For the immigrants of Europe, a dream dared and won true.*

The descendants of African slaves were offered no such welcome or participation. They came from places called the Carolinas and the Virginias, Georgia, Alabama, Mississippi, and Tennessee. They came strong, eager, searching. The city rejected them and they fled and settled along the riverbanks and under bridges in shallow, ramshackle houses made of sticks and tarpaper. They collected rags and wood. They sold the use of their muscles and their bodies. They cleaned houses and washed clothes, they shined shoes, and in quiet desperation and vengeful pride, they stole, and lived in pursuit of their own dream. That they could breathe free, finally, and stand to meet life with the force of dignity and whatever eloquence the heart could call upon.

Mary Alice, Ray Aranha, and James Earl Jones in Yale Repertory Theatre's 1985 world premiere of *Fences.*

By 1957, the hard-won victories of the European immigrants had solidified the industrial might of America. War had been confronted and won with new energies that used loyalty and patriotism as its fuel. Life was rich, full, and flourishing. The Milwaukee Braves won the World Series, and the hot winds of change that would make the sixties a turbulent, racing, dangerous, and provocative decade had not yet begun to blow full.

ACT I

SCENE I

It is 1957. Troy and Bono enter the yard, engaged in conversation. Troy is fifty-three years old, a large man with thick, heavy hands; it is this largeness that he strives to fill out and make an accommodation with. Together with his blackness, his largeness informs his sensibilities and the choices he has made in his life.

Of the two men, Bono is obviously the follower. His commitment to their friendship of thirty-odd years is rooted in his admiration of Troy's honesty, capacity for hard work, and his strength, which Bono seeks to emulate.

It is Friday night, payday, and the one night of the week the two men engage in a ritual of talk and drink. Troy is usually the most talkative and at times he can be crude and almost vulgar, though he is capable of rising to profound heights of expression. The men carry lunch buckets and wear or carry burlap aprons and are dressed in clothes suitable to their jobs as garbage collectors.

Viola Davis and Denzel Washington in the 2010 Broadway production of *Fences.*

Bono: Troy, you ought to stop that lying!

Troy: I ain't lying! The nigger had a watermelon this big. *(He indicates with his hands.)* Talking about . . . "What watermelon, Mr. Rand?" I liked to fell out! "What watermelon, Mr. Rand?" . . . And it sitting there big as life.

Bono: What did Mr. Rand say?

Troy: Ain't said nothing. Figure if the nigger too dumb to know he carrying a watermelon, he wasn't gonna get much sense out of him. Trying to hide that great big old watermelon under his coat. Afraid to let the white man see him carry it home.

Bono: I'm like you . . . I ain't got no time for them kind of people.

Troy: Now what he look like getting mad cause he see the man from the union talking to Mr. Rand?

Bono: He come to me talking about . . . "Maxson gonna get us fired." I told him to get away from me with that. He walked away from me calling you a troublemaker. What Mr. Rand say?

Troy: Ain't said nothing. He told me to go down the Commissioner's office next Friday. They called me down there to see them.

Bono: Well, as long as you got your complaint filed, they can't fire you. That's what one of them white fellows tell me.

Troy: I ain't worried about them firing me. They gonna fire me cause I asked a question? That's all I did. I went to Mr. Rand and asked him, "Why? Why you got the white mens driving and the colored lifting?" Told him, "what's the matter, don't I count? You think only white fellows got sense enough to drive a truck. That ain't no paper job! Hell, anybody can drive a truck. How come you got all whites driving and the colored lifting?" He told me "take it to the union." Well, hell, that's what I done! Now they wanna come up with this pack of lies.

Bono: I told Brownie if the man come and ask him any questions . . . just tell the truth! It ain't nothing but something they done trumped up on you cause you filed a complaint on them.

Troy: Brownie don't understand nothing. All I want them to do is change the job description. Give everybody a chance to drive the truck. Brownie can't see that. He ain't got that much sense.

Bono: How you figure he be making out with that gal be up at Taylors' all the time . . . that Alberta gal?

Troy: Same as you and me. Getting just as much as we is. Which is to say nothing.

Bono: It is, huh? I figure you doing a little better than me . . . and I ain't saying what I'm doing.

Troy: Aw, nigger, look here . . . I know you. If you had got anywhere near that gal, twenty minutes later you be looking to tell somebody. And the first one you gonna tell . . . that you gonna want to brag to . . . is gonna be me.

Bono: I ain't saying that. I see where you be eyeing her.

Troy: I eye all the women. I don't miss nothing. Don't never let nobody tell you Troy Maxson don't eye the women.

Bono: You been doing more than eyeing her. You done bought her a drink or two.

Troy: Hell yeah, I bought her a drink! What that mean? I bought you one, too. What that mean cause I buy her a drink? I'm just being polite.

Bono: It's alright to buy her one drink. That's what you call being polite. But when you wanna be buying two or three . . . that's what you call eyeing her.

Troy: Look here, as long as you known me . . . you ever known me to chase after women?

Bono: Hell yeah! Long as I done known you. You forgetting I knew you when.

Troy: Naw, I'm talking about since I been married to Rose?

Bono: Oh, not since you been married to Rose. Now, that's the truth, there. I can say that.

Troy: Alright then! Case closed.

Bono: I see you be walking up around Alberta's house. You supposed to be at Taylors' and you be walking up around there.

Troy: What you watching where I'm walking for? I ain't watching after you.

Bono: I seen you walking around there more than once.

Troy: Hell, you liable to see me walking anywhere! That don't mean nothing cause you see me walking around there.

Bono: Where she come from anyway? She just kinda showed up one day.

Troy: Tallahassee. You can look at her and tell she one of them Florida gals. They got some big healthy women down there. Grow them right up out the ground. Got a little bit of Indian in her. Most of them niggers down in Florida got some Indian in them.

Bono: I don't know about that Indian part. But she damn sure big and healthy. Woman wear some big stockings. Got them great big old legs and hips as wide as the Mississippi River.

Troy: Legs don't mean nothing. You don't do nothing but push them out of the way. But them hips cushion the ride!

Bono: Troy, you ain't got no sense.

Troy: It's the truth! Like you riding on Goodyears!

(Rose enters from the house. She is ten years younger than Troy, her devotion to him stems from her recognition of the possibilities of her life without him: a succession of abusive men and their babies, a life of partying and running the streets, the Church, or aloneness with its attendant pain and frustration. She recognizes Troy's spirit as a fine and illuminating one and she either ignores or forgives his faults, only some of which she recognizes. Though she doesn't drink, her presence is an integral part of the Friday night rituals. She alternates between the porch and the kitchen, where supper preparations are under way.)

Rose: What you all out here getting into?

Troy: What you worried about what we getting into for? This is men talk, woman.

Rose: What I care what you all talking about? Bono, you gonna stay for supper?

Bono: No, I thank you, Rose. But Lucille say she cooking up a pot of pigfeet.

Troy: Pigfeet! Hell, I'm going home with you! Might even stay the night if you got some pigfeet. You got something in there to top them pigfeet, Rose?

Rose: I'm cooking up some chicken. I got some chicken and collard greens.

Troy: Well, go on back in the house and let me and Bono finish what we was talking about. This is men talk. I got some talk for you later. You know what kind of talk I mean. You go on and powder it up.

Rose: Troy Maxson, don't you start that now!

Troy (puts his arm around her): Aw, woman . . . come here. Look here, Bono . . . when I met this woman . . . I got out that place, say, "Hitch up my pony, saddle up my mare . . . there's a woman out there for me somewhere. I looked here. Looked there. Saw Rose and latched on to her." I latched on to her and told her—I'm gonna tell you the truth—I told her, "Baby, I don't wanna marry, I just wanna be your man." Rose told me . . . tell him what you told me, Rose.

Rose: I told him if he wasn't the marrying kind, then move out the way so the marrying kind could find me.

Troy: That's what she told me. "Nigger, you in my way. You blocking the view! Move out the way so I can find me a husband." I thought it over two or three days. Come back—

Rose: Ain't no two or three days nothing. You was back the same night.

Troy: Come back, told her . . . "Okay, baby . . . but I'm gonna buy me a banty rooster and put him out there in the backyard . . . and when he see a stranger come, he'll flap his wings and crow . . ." Look here, Bono, I could watch the front door by myself . . . it was that back door I was worried about.

Rose: Troy, you ought not talk like that. Troy ain't doing nothing but telling a lie.

Troy: Only thing is . . . when we first got married . . . forget the rooster . . . we ain't had no yard!

Bono: I hear you tell it. Me and Lucille was staying down there on Logan Street. Had two rooms with the outhouse in the back. I ain't mind the outhouse none. But when that goddamn wind blow through there in the winter . . . that's what I'm talking about! To this day I wonder why in the hell I ever stayed down there for six long years. But see, I didn't know I could do no better. I thought only white folks had inside toilets and things.

Rose: There's a lot of people don't know they can do no better than they doing now. That's just something you got to learn. A lot of folks still shop at Bella's.

Troy: Ain't nothing wrong with shopping at Bella's. She got fresh food.

Rose: I ain't said nothing about if she got fresh food. I'm talking about what she charge. She charge ten cents more than the A&P.

Troy: The A&P ain't never done nothing for me. I spends my money where I'm treated right. I go down to Bella, say, "I need a loaf of bread, I'll pay you Friday." She give it to me. What sense that make when I got money to go and spend it somewhere else and ignore the person who done right by me? That ain't in the Bible.

Rose: We ain't talking about what's in the Bible. What sense it make to shop there when she overcharge?

Troy: You shop where you want to. I'll do my shopping where the people been good to me.

Rose: Well, I don't think it's right for her to overcharge. That's all I was saying.

Bono: Look here . . . I got to get on. Lucille going be raising all kind of hell.

Troy: Where you going, nigger? We ain't finished this pint. Come here, finish this pint.

Bono: Well, hell, I am . . . if you ever turn the bottle loose.

Troy (hands him the bottle): The only thing I say about the A&P is I'm glad Cory got that job down there. Help him take care of his school clothes and things. Gabe done moved out and things getting tight around here. He got that job . . . He can start to look out for himself.

Rose: Cory done went and got recruited by a college football team.

Troy: I told that boy about that football stuff. The white man ain't gonna let him get nowhere with that football. I told him when he first come to me with it. Now you come telling me he done went and got more tied up in it. He ought to go and get recruited in how to fix cars or something where he can make a living.

Rose: He ain't talking about making no living playing football. It's just something the boys in school do. They gonna send a recruiter by to talk to you. He'll tell you he ain't talking about making no living playing football. It's a honor to be recruited.

Troy: It ain't gonna get him nowhere. Bono'll tell you that.

Bono: If he be like you in the sports . . . he's gonna be alright. Ain't but two men ever played baseball as good as you. That's Babe Ruth and Josh Gibson.° Them's the only two men ever hit more home runs than you.

Troy: What it ever get me? Ain't got a pot to piss in or a window to throw it out of.

Rose: Times have changed since you was playing baseball, Troy. That was before the war. Times have changed a lot since then.

Troy: How in hell they done changed?

Rose: They got lots of colored boys playing ball now. Baseball and football.

Bono: You right about that, Rose. Times have changed, Troy. You just come along too early.

Troy: There ought not never have been no time called too early! Now you take that fellow . . . what's that fellow they had playing right field for the Yankees back then? You know who I'm talking about, Bono. Used to play right field for the Yankees.

Rose: Selkirk?°

Troy: Selkirk! That's it! Man batting .269, understand? .269. What kind of sense that make? I was hitting .432 with thirty-seven home runs! Man batting .269 and

---

Josh Gibson: legendary catcher in the Negro Leagues whose batting average and home-run totals far outstripped Major League records; he died of a stroke at age 35 in January 1947, three months before Jackie Robinson's debut with the Brooklyn Dodgers. *Selkirk:* Andy Selkirk, Yankee outfielder who hit .269 in 118 games in 1940.

playing right field for the Yankees! I saw Josh Gibson's daughter yesterday. She walking around with raggedy shoes on her feet. Now I bet you Selkirk's daughter ain't walking around with raggedy shoes on her feet! I bet you that!

Rose: They got a lot of colored baseball players now. Jackie Robinson° was the first. Folks had to wait for Jackie Robinson.

Troy: I done seen a hundred niggers play baseball better than Jackie Robinson. Hell, I know some teams Jackie Robinson couldn't even make! What you talking about Jackie Robinson. Jackie Robinson wasn't nobody. I'm talking about if you could play ball then they ought to have let you play. Don't care what color you were. Come telling me I come along too early. If you could play . . . then they ought to have let you play.

(Troy takes a long drink from the bottle.)

Rose: You gonna drink yourself to death. You don't need to be drinking like that.

Troy: Death ain't nothing. I done seen him. Done wrassled with him. You can't tell me nothing about death. Death ain't nothing but a fastball on the outside corner. And you know what I'll do to that! Lookee here, Bono . . . am I lying? You get one of them fastballs, about waist high, over the outside corner of the plate where you can get the meat of the bat on it . . . and good god! You can kiss it goodbye. Now, am I lying?

Bono: Naw, you telling the truth there. I seen you do it.

Troy: If I'm lying . . . that 450 feet worth of lying! *(Pause.)* That's all death is to me. A fastball on the outside corner.

Rose: I don't know why you want to get on talking about death.

Troy: Ain't nothing wrong with talking about death. That's part of life. Everybody gonna die. You gonna die, I'm gonna die. Bono's gonna die. Hell, we all gonna die.

Rose: But you ain't got to talk about it. I don't like to talk about it.

Troy: You the one brought it up. Me and Bono was talking about baseball . . . you tell me I'm gonna drink myself to death. Ain't that right, Bono? You know I don't drink this but one night out of the week. That's Friday night. I'm gonna drink just enough to where I can handle it. Then I cuts it loose. I leave it alone. So don't you worry about me drinking myself to death. 'Cause I ain't worried about Death. I done seen him. I done wrestled with him.

  Look here, Bono . . . I looked up one day and Death was marching straight at me. Like Soldiers on Parade! The Army of Death was marching straight at me. The middle of July, 1941. It got real cold just like it be winter. It seem like Death himself reached out and touched me on the shoulder. He touch me just like I touch you. I got cold as ice and Death standing there grinning at me.

Rose: Troy, why don't you hush that talk.

Troy: I say . . . what you want, Mr. Death? You be wanting me? You done brought your army to be getting me? I looked him dead in the eye. I wasn't fearing nothing. I was ready to tangle. Just like I'm ready to tangle now. The Bible say be ever vigilant. That's why I don't get but so drunk. I got to keep watch.

Jackie Robinson: the first African American to play Major League Baseball, joined the Brooklyn Dodgers in 1947.

Rose: Troy was right down there in Mercy Hospital. You remember he had pneumonia? Laying there with a fever talking plumb out of his head.

Troy: Death standing there staring at me . . . carrying that sickle in his hand. Finally he say, "You want bound over for another year?" See, just like that . . . "You want bound over for another year?" I told him, "Bound over hell! Let's settle this now!"

      It seem like he kinda fell back when I said that, and all the cold went out of me. I reached down and grabbed that sickle and threw it just as far as I could throw it . . . and me and him commenced to wrestling.

      We wrestled for three days and three nights. I can't say where I found the strength from. Everytime it seemed like he was gonna get the best of me, I'd reach way down deep inside myself and find the strength to do him one better.

Rose: Every time Troy tell that story he find different ways to tell it. Different things to make up about it.

Troy: I ain't making up nothing. I'm telling you the facts of what happened. I wrestled with Death for three days and three nights and I'm standing here to tell you about it. *(Pause.)* Alright. At the end of the third night we done weakened each other to where we can't hardly move. Death stood up, throwed on his robe . . . had him a white robe with a hood on it. He throwed on that robe and went off to look for his sickle. Say, "I'll be back." Just like that. "I'll be back." I told him, say, "Yeah, but . . . you gonna have to find me!" I wasn't no fool. I wasn't going looking for him. Death ain't nothing to play with. And I know he's gonna get me. I know I got to join his army . . . his camp followers. But as long as I keep my strength and see him coming . . . as long as I keep up my vigilance . . . he's gonna have to fight to get me. I ain't going easy.

Bono: Well, look here, since you got to keep up your vigilance . . . let me have the bottle.

Troy: Aw hell, I shouldn't have told you that part. I should have left out that part.

Rose: Troy be talking that stuff and half the time don't even know what he be talking about.

Troy: Bono know me better than that.

Bono: That's right. I know you. I know you got some Uncle Remus in your blood. You got more stories than the devil got sinners.

Troy: Aw hell, I done seen him too! Done talked with the devil.

Rose: Troy, don't nobody wanna be hearing all that stuff.

      (Lyons enters the yard from the street. Thirty-four years old, Troy's son by a previous marriage, he sports a neatly trimmed goatee, sport coat, white shirt, tieless and buttoned at the collar. Though he fancies himself a musician, he is more caught up in the rituals and "idea" of being a musician than in the actual practice of the music. He has come to borrow money from Troy, and while he knows he will be successful, he is uncertain as to what extent his lifestyle will be held up to scrutiny and ridicule.)

Lyons: Hey, Pop.

Troy: What you come "Hey, Popping" me for?

Lyons: How you doing, Rose? *(He kisses her.)* Mr. Bono. How you doing?

Bono: Hey, Lyons . . . how you been?

Troy: He must have been doing alright. I ain't seen him around here last week.

Rose: Troy, leave your boy alone. He come by to see you and you wanna start all that nonsense.

Troy: I ain't bothering Lyons. *(Offers him the bottle.)* Here . . . get you a drink. We got an understanding. I know why he come by to see me and he know I know.

Lyons: Come on, Pop . . . I just stopped by to say hi . . . see how you was doing.

Troy: You ain't stopped by yesterday.

Rose: You gonna stay for supper, Lyons? I got some chicken cooking in the oven.

Lyons: No, Rose . . . thanks. I was just in the neighborhood and thought I'd stop by for a minute.

Troy: You was in the neighborhood alright, nigger. You telling the truth there. You was in the neighborhood cause it's my payday.

Lyons: Well, hell, since you mentioned it . . . let me have ten dollars.

Troy: I'll be damned! I'll die and go to hell and play blackjack with the devil before I give you ten dollars.

Bono: That's what I wanna know about . . . that devil you done seen.

Lyons: What . . . Pop done seen the devil? You too much, Pops.

Troy: Yeah, I done seen him. Talked to him too!

Rose: You ain't seen no devil. I done told you that man ain't had nothing to do with the devil. Anything you can't understand, you want to call it the devil.

Troy: Look here, Bono . . . I went down to see Hertzberger about some furniture. Got three rooms for two-ninety-eight. That what it say on the radio. "Three rooms . . . two-ninety-eight." Even made up a little song about it. Go down there . . . man tell me I can't get no credit. I'm working every day and can't get no credit. What to do? I got an empty house with some raggedy furniture in it. Cory ain't got no bed. He's sleeping on a pile of rags on the floor. Working every day and can't get no credit. Come back here—Rose'll tell you—madder than hell. Sit down . . . try to figure what I'm gonna do. Come a knock on the door. Ain't been living here but three days. Who know I'm here? Open the door . . . devil standing there bigger than life. White fellow . . . got on good clothes and everything. Standing there with a clipboard in his hand. I ain't had to say nothing. First words come out of his mouth was . . . "I understand you need some furniture and can't get no credit." I liked to fell over. He say "I'll give you all the credit you want, but you got to pay the interest on it." I told him, "Give me three rooms worth and charge whatever you want." Next day a truck pulled up here and two men unloaded them three rooms. Man what drove the truck give me a book. Say send ten dollars, first of every month to the address in the book and every thing will be alright. Say if I miss a payment the devil was coming back and it'll be hell to pay. That was fifteen years ago. To this day . . . the first of the month I send my ten dollars, Rose'll tell you.

Rose: Troy lying.

Troy: I ain't never seen that man since. Now you tell me who else that could have been but the devil? I ain't sold my soul or nothing like that, you understand. Naw, I wouldn't have truck with the devil about nothing like that. I got my furniture and pays my ten dollars the first of the month just like clockwork.

Bono: How long you say you been paying this ten dollars a month?

Troy: Fifteen years!

Bono: Hell, ain't you finished paying for it yet? How much the man done charged you?

Troy: Aw hell, I done paid for it. I done paid for it ten times over! The fact is I'm scared to stop paying it.

Rose: Troy lying. We got that furniture from Mr. Glickman. He ain't paying no ten
    dollars a month to nobody.

Troy: Aw hell, woman. Bono know I ain't that big a fool.

Lyons: I was just getting ready to say . . . I know where there's a bridge for sale.

Troy: Look here, I'll tell you this . . . it don't matter to me if he was the devil. It don't
    matter if the devil give credit. Somebody has got to give it.

Rose: It ought to matter. You going around talking about having truck with the
    devil . . . God's the one you gonna have to answer to. He's the one gonna be at
    the Judgment.

Lyons: Yeah, well, look here, Pop . . . Let me have that ten dollars. I'll give it back to
    you. Bonnie got a job working at the hospital.

Troy: What I tell you, Bono? The only time I see this nigger is when he wants some-
    thing. That's the only time I see him.

Lyons: Come on, Pop, Mr. Bono don't want to hear all that. Let me have the ten
    dollars. I told you Bonnie working.

Troy: What that mean to me? "Bonnie working." I don't care if she working. Go ask
    her for the ten dollars if she working. Talking about "Bonnie working." Why
    ain't you working?

Lyons: Aw, Pop, you know I can't find no decent job. Where am I gonna get a job at?
    You know I can't get no job.

Troy: I told you I know some people down there. I can get you on the rubbish if
    you want to work. I told you that the last time you came by here asking me for
    something.

Lyons: Naw, Pop . . . thanks. That ain't for me. I don't wanna be carrying nobody's
    rubbish. I don't wanna be punching nobody's time clock.

Troy: What's the matter, you too good to carry people's rubbish? Where you think
    that ten dollars you talking about come from? I'm just supposed to haul people's
    rubbish and give my money to you cause you too lazy to work. You too lazy to
    work and wanna know why you ain't got what I got.

Rose: What hospital Bonnie working at? Mercy?

Lyons: She's down at Passavant working in the laundry.

Troy: I ain't got nothing as it is. I give you that ten dollars and I got to eat beans the
    rest of the week. Naw . . . you ain't getting no ten dollars here.

Lyons: You ain't got to be eating no beans. I don't know why you wanna say that.

Troy: I ain't got no extra money. Gabe done moved over to Miss Pearl's paying her
    the rent and things done got tight around here. I can't afford to be giving you
    every payday.

Lyons: I ain't asked you to give me nothing. I asked you to loan me ten dollars.
    I know you got ten dollars.

Troy: Yeah, I got it. You know why I got it? Cause I don't throw my money away out
    there in the streets. You living the fast life . . . wanna be a musician . . . running
    around in them clubs and things . . . then, you learn to take care of yourself. You
    ain't gonna find me going and asking nobody for nothing. I done spent too many
    years without.

Lyons: You and me is two different people, Pop.

Troy: I done learned my mistake and learned to do what's right by it. You still trying
    to get something for nothing. Life don't owe you nothing. You owe it to yourself.
    Ask Bono. He'll tell you I'm right.

Lyons: You got your way of dealing with the world . . . I got mine. The only thing that matters to me is the music.

Troy: Yeah, I can see that! It don't matter how you gonna eat . . . where your next dollar is coming from. You telling the truth there.

Lyons: I know I got to eat. But I got to live too. I need something that gonna help me to get out of the bed in the morning. Make me feel like I belong in the world. I don't bother nobody. I just stay with my music cause that's the only way I can find to live in the world. Otherwise there ain't no telling what I might do. Now I don't come criticizing you and how you live. I just come by to ask you for ten dollars. I don't wanna hear all that about how I live.

Troy: Boy, your mama did a hell of a job raising you.

Lyons: You can't change me, Pop. I'm thirty-four years old. If you wanted to change me, you should have been there when I was growing up. I come by to see you . . . ask for ten dollars and you want to talk about how I was raised. You don't know nothing about how I was raised.

Rose: Let the boy have ten dollars, Troy.

Troy (to Lyons): What the hell you looking at me for? I ain't got no ten dollars. You know what I do with my money. *(To Rose.)* Give him ten dollars if you want him to have it.

Rose: I will. Just as soon as you turn it loose.

Troy (handing Rose the money): There it is. Seventy-six dollars and forty-two cents. You see this, Bono? Now, I ain't gonna get but six of that back.

Rose: You ought to stop telling that lie. Here, Lyons. *(She hands him the money.)*

Lyons: Thanks, Rose. Look . . . I got to run . . . I'll see you later.

Troy: Wait a minute. You gonna say, "thanks, Rose" and ain't gonna look to see where she got that ten dollars from? See how they do me, Bono?

Lyons: I know she got it from you, Pop. Thanks. I'll give it back to you.

Troy: There he go telling another lie. Time I see that ten dollars . . . he'll be owing me thirty more.

Lyons: See you, Mr. Bono.

Bono: Take care, Lyons!

Lyons: Thanks, Pop. I'll see you again.

(Lyons exits the yard.)

Troy: I don't know why he don't go and get him a decent job and take care of that woman he got.

Bono: He'll be alright, Troy. The boy is still young.

Troy: The *boy* is thirty-four years old.

Rose: Let's not get off into all that.

Bono: Look here . . . I got to be going. I got to be getting on. Lucille gonna be waiting.

Troy (puts his arm around Rose): See this woman, Bono? I love this woman. I love this woman so much it hurts. I love her so much . . . I done run out of ways of loving her. So I got to go back to basics. Don't you come by my house Monday morning talking about time to go to work . . . 'cause I'm still gonna be stroking!

Rose: Troy! Stop it now!

Bono: I ain't paying him no mind, Rose. That ain't nothing but gin-talk. Go on, Troy. I'll see you Monday.

Troy: Don't you come by my house, nigger! I done told you what I'm gonna be doing.

(*The lights go down to black.*)

SCENE II

The lights come up on Rose hanging up clothes. She hums and sings softly to herself. It is the following morning.

Rose (sings):

> Jesus, be a fence all around me every day
> Jesus, I want you to protect me as I travel on my way.
> Jesus, be a fence all around me every day.

(*Troy enters from the house.*)

> Jesus, I want you to protect me
> As I travel on my way.

(*To Troy.*) 'Morning. You ready for breakfast? I can fix it soon as I finish hanging up these clothes.

Troy: I got the coffee on. That'll be alright. I'll just drink some of that this morning.

Rose: That 651 hit yesterday. That's the second time this month. Miss Pearl hit for a dollar . . . seem like those that need the least always get lucky. Poor folks can't get nothing.

Troy: Them numbers don't know nobody. I don't know why you fool with them. You and Lyons both.

Rose: It's something to do.

Troy: You ain't doing nothing but throwing your money away.

Rose: Troy, you know I don't play foolishly. I just play a nickel here and a nickel there.

Troy: That's two nickels you done thrown away.

Rose: Now I hit sometimes . . . that makes up for it. It always comes in handy when I do hit. I don't hear you complaining then.

Troy: I ain't complaining now. I just say it's foolish. Trying to guess out of six hundred ways which way the number gonna come. If I had all the money niggers, these Negroes, throw away on numbers for one week—just one week—I'd be a rich man.

Rose: Well, you wishing and calling it foolish ain't gonna stop folks from playing numbers. That's one thing for sure. Besides . . . some good things come from playing numbers. Look where Pope done bought him that restaurant off of numbers.

Troy: I can't stand niggers like that. Man ain't had two dimes to rub together. He walking around with his shoes all run over bumming money for cigarettes. Alright. Got lucky there and hit the numbers . . .

Rose: Troy, I know all about it.

Troy: Had good sense, I'll say that for him. He ain't throwed his money away. I seen niggers hit the numbers and go through two thousand dollars in four days. Man bought him that restaurant down there . . . fixed it up real nice . . . and then didn't want nobody to come in it! A Negro go in there and can't get no kind of service. I seen a white fellow come in there and order a bowl of stew. Pope picked all the meat out of the pot for him. Man ain't had nothing but a bowl of meat! Negro come behind him and ain't got nothing but the potatoes and carrots. Talking about what numbers do for people, you picked a wrong example. Ain't done nothing but make a worser fool out of him than he was before.

Rose: Troy, you ought to stop worrying about what happened at work yesterday.

Troy: I ain't worried. Just told me to be down there at the Commissioner's office on Friday. Everybody think they gonna fire me. I ain't worried about them firing me. You ain't got to worry about that. (*Pause.*) Where's Cory? Cory in the house? (*Calls.*) Cory?

Rose: He gone out.

Troy: Out, huh? He gone out 'cause he know I want him to help me with this fence. I know how he is. That boy scared of work.

(*Gabriel enters. He comes halfway down the alley and, hearing Troy's voice, stops.*)

Troy (continues): He ain't done a lick of work in his life.

Rose: He had to go to football practice. Coach wanted them to get in a little extra practice before the season start.

Troy: I got his practice . . . running out of here before he get his chores done.

Rose: Troy, what is wrong with you this morning? Don't nothing set right with you. Go on back in there and go to bed . . . get up on the other side.

Troy: Why something got to be wrong with me? I ain't said nothing wrong with me.

Rose: You got something to say about everything. First it's the numbers . . . then it's the way the man runs his restaurant . . . then you done got on Cory. What's it gonna be next? Take a look up there and see if the weather suits you . . . or is it gonna be how you gonna put up the fence with the clothes hanging in the yard?

Troy: You hit the nail on the head then.

Rose: I know you like I know the back of my hand. Go on in there and get you some coffee . . . see if that straighten you up. 'Cause you ain't right this morning.

(*Troy starts into the house and sees Gabriel. Gabriel starts singing. Troy's brother, he is seven years younger than Troy. Injured in World War II, he has a metal plate in his head. He carries an old trumpet tied around his waist and believes with every fiber of his being that he is the Archangel Gabriel. He carries a chipped basket with an assortment of discarded fruits and vegetables he has picked up in the Strip District and which he attempts to sell.*)

Gabriel (singing):
> Yes, ma'am, I got plums
> You ask me how I sell them
> Oh ten cents apiece
> Three for a quarter
> Come and buy now
> 'Cause I'm here today
> And tomorrow I'll be gone

(*Gabriel enters.*)

> Hey, Rose!

Rose: How you doing, Gabe?

Gabriel: There's Troy . . . Hey, Troy!

Troy: Hey, Gabe.

(Exit into kitchen.)

Rose *(to Gabriel)*: What you got there?

Gabriel: You know what I got, Rose. I got fruits and vegetables.

Rose *(looking in basket)*: Where's all these plums you talking about?

Gabriel: I ain't got no plums today, Rose. I was just singing that. Have some tomorrow. Put me in a big order for plums. Have enough plums tomorrow for St. Peter and everybody.

(Troy reenters from kitchen, crosses to steps.)

(To Rose.) Troy's mad at me.

Troy: I ain't mad at you. What I got to be mad at you about? You ain't done nothing to me.

Gabriel: I just moved over to Miss Pearl's to keep out from in your way. I ain't mean no harm by it.

Troy: Who said anything about that? I ain't said anything about that.

Gabriel: You ain't mad at me, is you?

Troy: Naw . . . I ain't mad at you, Gabe. If I was mad at you I'd tell you about it.

Gabriel: Got me two rooms. In the basement. Got my own door too. Wanna see my key? *(He holds up a key.)* That's my own key! Ain't nobody else got a key like that. That's my key! My two rooms!

Troy: Well, that's good, Gabe. You got your own key . . . that's good.

Rose: You hungry, Gabe? I was just fixing to cook Troy his breakfast.

Gabriel: I'll take some biscuits. You got some biscuits? Did you know when I was in heaven . . . every morning me and St. Peter would sit down by the gate and eat some big fat biscuits? Oh, yeah! We had us a good time. We'd sit there and eat us them biscuits and then St. Peter would go off to sleep and tell me to wake him up when it's time to open the gates for the judgment.

Rose: Well, come on . . . I'll make up a batch of biscuits.

(Rose exits into the house.)

Gabriel: Troy . . . St. Peter got your name in the book. I seen it. It say . . . Troy Maxson. I say . . . I know him! He got the same name like what I got. That's my brother!

Troy: How many times you gonna tell me that, Gabe?

Gabriel: Ain't got my name in the book. Don't have to have my name. I done died and went to heaven. He got your name though. One morning St. Peter was looking at his book . . . marking it up for the judgment . . . and he let me see your name. Got it in there under M. Got Rose's name . . . I ain't seen it like I seen yours . . . but I know it's in there. He got a great big book. Got everybody's name what was ever been born. That's what he told me. But I seen your name. Seen it with my own eyes.

Troy: Go on in the house there. Rose going to fix you something to eat.

Gabriel: Oh, I ain't hungry. I done had breakfast with Aunt Jemimah. She come by and cooked me up a whole mess of flapjacks. Remember how we used to eat them flapjacks?

Troy: Go on in the house and get you something to eat now.

Gabriel: I got to sell my plums. I done sold some tomatoes. Got me two quarters. Wanna see? *(He shows Troy his quarters.)* I'm gonna save them and buy me a new horn so St. Peter can hear me when it's time to open the gates. (*Gabriel stops suddenly. Listens.*) Hear that? That's the hellhounds. I got to chase them out of here. Go on get out of here! Get out!

(*Gabriel exits singing.*)

> Better get ready for the judgment
> Better get ready for the judgment
> My Lord is coming down

(*Rose enters from the house.*)

Troy: He gone off somewhere.

Gabriel (*offstage*):

> Better get ready for the judgment
> Better get ready for the judgment morning
> Better get ready for the judgment
> My God is coming down

Rose: He ain't eating right. Miss Pearl say she can't get him to eat nothing.

Troy: What you want me to do about it, Rose? I done did everything I can for the man. I can't make him get well. Man got half his head blown away . . . what you expect?

Rose: Seem like something ought to be done to help him.

Troy: Man don't bother nobody. He just mixed up from that metal plate he got in his head. Ain't no sense for him to go back into the hospital.

Rose: Least he be eating right. They can help him take care of himself.

Troy: Don't nobody wanna be locked up, Rose. What you wanna lock him up for? Man go over there and fight the war . . . messin' around with them Japs, get half his head blown off . . . and they give him a lousy three thousand dollars. And I had to swoop down on that.

Rose: Is you fixing to go into that again?

Troy: That's the only way I got a roof over my head . . . cause of that metal plate.

Rose: Ain't no sense you blaming yourself for nothing. Gabe wasn't in no condition to manage that money. You done what was right by him. Can't nobody say you ain't done what was right by him. Look how long you took care of him . . . till he wanted to have his own place and moved over there with Miss Pearl.

Troy: That ain't what I'm saying, woman! I'm just stating the facts. If my brother didn't have that metal plate in his head . . . I wouldn't have a pot to piss in or a window to throw it out of. And I'm fifty-three years old. Now see if you can understand that!

(*Troy gets up from the porch and starts to exit the yard.*)

Rose: Where you going off to? You been running out of here every Saturday for weeks. I thought you was gonna work on this fence?

Troy: I'm gonna walk down to Taylors'. Listen to the ball game. I'll be back in a bit. I'll work on it when I get back.

(*He exits the yard. The lights go to black.*)

SCENE III

The lights come up on the yard. It is four hours later. Rose is taking down the clothes from the line. Cory enters carrying his football equipment.

Rose: Your daddy like to had a fit with you running out of here this morning without doing your chores.

Cory: I told you I had to go to practice.

Rose: He say you were supposed to help him with this fence.

Cory: He been saying that the last four or five Saturdays, and then he don't never do nothing, but go down to Taylors'. Did you tell him about the recruiter?

Rose: Yeah, I told him.

Cory: What he say?

Rose: He ain't said nothing too much. You get in there and get started on your chores before he gets back. Go on and scrub down them steps before he gets back here hollering and carrying on.

Cory: I'm hungry. What you got to eat, Mama?

Rose: Go on and get started on your chores. I got some meat loaf in there. Go on and make you a sandwich . . . and don't leave no mess in there.

(Cory exits into the house. Rose continues to take down the clothes. Troy enters the yard and sneaks up and grabs her from behind.)

Troy! Go on, now. You liked to scared me to death. What was the score of the game? Lucille had me on the phone and I couldn't keep up with it.

Troy: What I care about the game? Come here, woman. *(He tries to kiss her.)*

Rose: I thought you went down Taylors' to listen to the game. Go on, Troy! You supposed to be putting up this fence.

Troy *(attempting to kiss her again)*: I'll put it up when I finish with what is at hand.

Rose: Go on, Troy. I ain't studying you.

Troy *(chasing after her)*: I'm studying you . . . fixing to do my homework!

Rose: Troy, you better leave me alone.

Troy: Where's Cory? That boy brought his butt home yet?

Rose: He's in the house doing his chores.

Troy *(calling)*: Cory! Get your butt out here, boy!

(Rose exits into the house with the laundry. Troy goes over to the pile of wood, picks up a board, and starts sawing. Cory enters from the house.)

Troy: You just now coming in here from leaving this morning?

Cory: Yeah, I had to go to football practice.

Troy: Yeah, what?

Cory: Yessir.

Troy: I ain't but two seconds off you noway. The garbage sitting in there overflowing . . . you ain't done none of your chores . . . and you come in here talking about "Yeah."

Cory: I was just getting ready to do my chores now, Pop . . .

Troy: Your first chore is to help me with this fence on Saturday. Everything else come after that. Now get that saw and cut them boards.

(Cory takes the saw and begins cutting the boards. Troy continues working. There is a long pause.)

Cory: Hey, Pop . . . why don't you buy a TV?

Troy: What I want with a TV? What I want one of them for?

Cory: Everybody got one. Earl, Ba Bra . . . Jesse!

Troy: I ain't asked you who had one. I say what I want with one?

Cory: So you can watch it. They got lots of things on TV. Baseball games and every-thing. We could watch the World Series.

Troy: Yeah . . . and how much this TV cost?

Cory: I don't know. They got them on sale for around two hundred dollars.

Troy: Two hundred dollars, huh?

Cory: That ain't that much, Pop.

Troy: Naw, it's just two hundred dollars. See that roof you got over your head at night? Let me tell you something about that roof. It's been over ten years since that roof was last tarred. See now . . . the snow come this winter and sit up there on that roof like it is . . . and it's gonna seep inside. It's just gonna be a little bit . . . ain't gonna hardly notice it. Then the next thing you know, it's gonna be leaking all over the house. Then the wood rot from all that water and you gonna need a whole new roof. Now, how much you think it cost to get that roof tarred?

Cory: I don't know.

Troy: Two hundred and sixty-four dollars . . . cash money. While you thinking about a TV, I got to be thinking about the roof . . . and whatever else go wrong here. Now if you had two hundred dollars, what would you do . . . fix the roof or buy a TV?

Cory: I'd buy a TV. Then when the roof started to leak . . . when it needed fixing . . . I'd fix it.

Troy: Where you gonna get the money from? You done spent it for a TV. You gonna sit up and watch the water run all over your brand new TV.

Cory: Aw, Pop. You got money. I know you do.

Troy: Where I got it at, huh?

Cory: You got it in the bank.

Troy: You wanna see my bankbook? You wanna see that seventy-three dollars and twenty-two cents I got sitting up in there?

Cory: You ain't got to pay for it all at one time. You can put a down payment on it and carry it on home with you.

Troy: Not me. I ain't gonna owe nobody nothing if I can help it. Miss a payment and they come and snatch it right out of your house. Then what you got? Now, soon as I get two hundred dollars clear, then I'll buy a TV. Right now, as soon as I get two hundred and sixty-four dollars, I'm gonna have this roof tarred.

Cory: Aw . . . Pop!

Troy: You go on and get you two hundred dollars and buy one if ya want it. I got bet-ter things to do with my money.

Cory: I can't get no two hundred dollars. I ain't never seen two hundred dollars.

Troy: I'll tell you what . . . you get you a hundred dollars and I'll put the other hundred with it.

Cory: Alright, I'm gonna show you.

Troy: You gonna show me how you can cut them boards right now.

(Cory begins to cut the boards. There is a long pause.)

Cory: The Pirates won today. That makes five in a row.

Troy: I ain't thinking about the Pirates. Got an all-white team. Got that boy . . . that Puerto Rican boy . . . Clemente.° Don't even half-play him. That boy could be something if they give him a chance. Play him one day and sit him on the bench the next.

Cory: He gets a lot of chances to play.

Troy: I'm talking about playing regular. Playing every day so you can get your timing. That's what I'm talking about.

Cory: They got some white guys on the team that don't play every day. You can't play everybody at the same time.

Troy: If they got a white fellow sitting on the bench . . . you can bet your last dollar he can't play! The colored guy got to be twice as good before he get on the team. That's why I don't want you to get all tied up in them sports. Man on the team and what it get him? They got colored on the team and don't use them. Same as not having them. All them teams the same.

Cory: The Braves got Hank Aaron and Wes Covington. Hank Aaron hit two home runs today. That makes forty-three.

Troy: Hank Aaron ain't nobody. That's what you supposed to do. That's how you supposed to play the game. Ain't nothing to it. It's just a matter of timing . . . getting the right follow-through. Hell, I can hit forty-three home runs right now!

Cory: Not off no major-league pitching, you couldn't.

Troy: We had better pitching in the Negro leagues. I hit seven home runs off of Satchel Paige.° You can't get no better than that!

Cory: Sandy Koufax.° He's leading the league in strikeouts.

Troy: I ain't thinking of no Sandy Koufax.

Cory: You got Warren Spahn° and Lew Burdette.° I bet you couldn't hit no home runs off of Warren Spahn.

Troy: I'm through with it now. You go on and cut them boards. *(Pause.)* Your mama tell me you done got recruited by a college football team? Is that right?

Cory: Yeah. Coach Zellman say the recruiter gonna be coming by to talk to you. Get you to sign the permission papers.

Troy: I thought you supposed to be working down there at the A&P. Ain't you suppose to be working down there after school?

Cory: Mr. Stawicki say he gonna hold my job for me until after the football season. Say starting next week I can work weekends.

Troy: I thought we had an understanding about this football stuff? You suppose to keep up with your chores and hold that job down at the A&P. Ain't been around here all day on a Saturday. Ain't none of your chores done . . . and now you telling me you done quit your job.

Cory: I'm going to be working weekends.

Troy: You damn right you are! And ain't no need for nobody coming around here to talk to me about signing nothing.

Cory: Hey, Pop . . . you can't do that. He's coming all the way from North Carolina.

Troy: I don't care where he coming from. The white man ain't gonna let you get nowhere with that football noway. You go on and get your book-learning so you

---

Clemente: Hall of Fame outfielder Roberto Clemente, a dark-skinned Puerto Rican, played 17 seasons with the Pittsburgh Pirates.   *Satchel Paige . . . Sandy Koufax . . . Warren Spahn . . . Lew Burdette:* The great Satchel Paige pitched many years in the Negro Leagues; beginning in 1948, when he was in his forties and long past his prime, he appeared in nearly 200 games in the American League. Star pitchers Sandy Koufax of the Dodgers and Warren Spahn and Lew Burdette of the Braves were all white.

can work yourself up in that A&P or learn how to fix cars or build houses or something, get you a trade. That way you have something can't nobody take away from you. You go on and learn how to put your hands to some good use. Besides hauling people's garbage.

Cory: I get good grades, Pop. That's why the recruiter wants to talk with you. You got to keep up your grades to get recruited. This way I'll be going to college. I'll get a chance . . .

Troy: First you gonna get your butt down there to the A&P and get your job back.

Cory: Mr. Stawicki done already hired somebody else 'cause I told him I was playing football.

Troy: You a bigger fool than I thought . . . to let somebody take away your job so you can play some football. Where you gonna get your money to take out your girlfriend and whatnot? What kind of foolishness is that to let somebody take away your job?

Cory: I'm still gonna be working weekends.

Troy: Naw . . . naw. You getting your butt out of here and finding you another job.

Cory: Come on, Pop! I got to practice. I can't work after school and play football too. The team needs me. That's what Coach Zellman say . . .

Troy: I don't care what nobody else say. I'm the boss . . . you understand? I'm the boss around here. I do the only saying what counts.

Cory: Come on, Pop!

Troy: I asked you . . . did you understand?

Cory: Yeah . . .

Troy: What?!

Cory: Yessir.

Troy: You go on down there to that A&P and see if you can get your job back. If you can't do both . . . then you quit the football team. You've got to take the crookeds with the straights.

Cory: Yessir. (*Pause.*) Can I ask you a question?

Troy: What the hell you wanna ask me? Mr. Stawicki the one you got the questions for.

Cory: How come you ain't never liked me?

Troy: Liked you? Who the hell say I got to like you? What law is there say I got to like you? Wanna stand up in my face and ask a damn fool-ass question like that. Talking about liking somebody. Come here, boy, when I talk to you.

(*Cory comes over to where Troy is working. He stands slouched over and Troy shoves him on his shoulder.*)

Straighten up, goddammit! I asked you a question . . . what law is there say I got to like you?

Cory: None.

Troy: Well, alright then! Don't you eat every day? (*Pause.*) Answer me when I talk to you! Don't you eat every day?

Cory: Yeah.

Troy: Nigger, as long as you in my house, you put that sir on the end of it when you talk to me.

Cory: Yes . . . sir.

Troy: You eat every day.

Cory: Yessir!

Troy: Got a roof over your head.

Cory: Yessir!

Troy: Got clothes on your back.

Cory: Yessir.

Troy: Why you think that is?

Cory: Cause of you.

Troy: Aw, hell I know it's cause of me . . . but why do you think that is?

Cory (hesitant): 'Cause you like me.

Troy: Like you? I go out of here every morning . . . bust my butt . . . putting up with them crackers every day . . . cause I like you? You about the biggest fool I ever saw. (*Pause.*) It's my job. It's my responsibility! You understand that? A man got to take care of his family. You live in my house . . . sleep you behind on my bedclothes . . . fill you belly up with my food . . . cause you my son. You my flesh and blood. Not cause I like you! Cause it's my duty to take care of you. I owe a responsibility to you!

Let's get this straight right here . . . before it go along any further . . . I ain't got to like you. Mr. Rand don't give me my money come payday cause he likes me. He gives me cause he owe me. I done give you everything I had to give you. I gave you your life! Me and your mama worked that out between us. And liking your black ass wasn't part of the bargain. Don't you try and go through life worrying about if somebody like you or not. You best be making sure they doing right by you. You understand what I'm saying, boy?

Cory: Yessir.

Troy: Then get the hell out of my face, and get on down to that A&P.

(*Rose has been standing behind the screen door for much of the scene. She enters as Cory exits.*)

Rose: Why don't you let the boy go ahead and play football, Troy? Ain't no harm in that. He's just trying to be like you with the sports.

Troy: I don't want him to be like me! I want him to move as far away from my life as he can get. You the only decent thing that ever happened to me. I wish him that. But I don't wish him a thing else from my life. I decided seventeen years ago that boy wasn't getting involved in no sports. Not after what they did to me in the sports.

Rose: Troy, why don't you admit you was too old to play in the major leagues? For once . . . why don't you admit that?

Troy: What do you mean too old? Don't come telling me I was too old. I just wasn't the right color. Hell, I'm fifty-three years old and can do better than Selkirk's .269 right now!

Rose: How's was you gonna play ball when you were over forty? Sometimes I can't get no sense out of you.

Troy: I got good sense, woman. I got sense enough not to let my boy get hurt over playing no sports. You been mothering that boy too much. Worried about if people like him.

Rose: Everything that boy do . . . he do for you. He wants you to say "Good job, son." That's all.

Troy: Rose, I ain't got time for that. He's alive. He's healthy. He's got to make his own way. I made mine. Ain't nobody gonna hold his hand when he get out there in that world.

Rose: Times have changed from when you was young, Troy. People change. The world's changing around you and you can't even see it.

Troy (slow, methodical): Woman . . . I do the best I can do. I come in here every Friday. I carry a sack of potatoes and a bucket of lard. You all line up at the door with your hands out. I give you the lint from my pockets. I give you my sweat and my blood. I ain't got no tears. I done spent them. We go upstairs in that room at night . . . and I fall down on you and try to blast a hole into forever. I get up Monday morning . . . find my lunch on the table. I go out. Make my way. Find my strength to carry me through to the next Friday. *(Pause.)* That's all I got, Rose. That's all I got to give. I can't give nothing else.

(Troy exits into the house. The lights go down to black.)

SCENE IV

It is Friday. Two weeks later. Cory starts out of the house with his football equipment. The phone rings.

Cory (calling): I got it! *(He answers the phone and stands in the screen door talking.)* Hello? Hey, Jesse. Naw . . . I was just getting ready to leave now.

Rose (calling): Cory!

Cory: I told you, man, them spikes is all tore up. You can use them if you want, but they ain't no good. Earl got some spikes.

Rose (calling): Cory!

Cory (calling to Rose): Mam? I'm talking to Jesse. *(Into phone.)* When she say that? *(Pause.)* Aw, you lying, man. I'm gonna tell her you said that.

Rose (calling): Cory, don't you go nowhere!

Cory: I got to go to the game, Ma! *(Into the phone.)* Yeah, hey, look, I'll talk to you later. Yeah, I'll meet you over Earl's house. Later. Bye, Ma.

(Cory exits the house and starts out the yard.)

Rose: Cory, where you going off to? You got that stuff all pulled out and thrown all over your room.

Cory (in the yard): I was looking for my spikes. Jesse wanted to borrow my spikes.

Rose: Get up there and get that cleaned up before your daddy get back in here.

Cory: I got to go to the game! I'll clean it up when I get back.

(Cory exits.)

Rose: That's all he need to do is see that room all messed up.

(Rose exits into the house. Troy and Bono enter the yard. Troy is dressed in clothes other than his work clothes.)

Bono: He told him the same thing he told you. Take it to the union.

Troy: Brownie ain't got that much sense. Man wasn't thinking about nothing. He wait until I confront them on it . . . then he wanna come crying seniority. *(Calls.)* Hey, Rose!

Bono: I wish I could have seen Mr. Rand's face when he told you.

Troy: He couldn't get it out of his mouth! Liked to bit his tongue! When they called me down there to the Commissioner's office . . . he thought they was gonna fire me. Like everybody else.

Bono: I didn't think they was gonna fire you. I thought they was gonna put you on the warning paper.

Troy: Hey, Rose! (*To Bono.*) Yeah, Mr. Rand like to bit his tongue.

(*Troy breaks the seal on the bottle, takes a drink, and hands it to Bono.*)

Bono: I see you run right down to Taylors' and told that Alberta gal.

Troy (calling): Hey, Rose! (*To Bono.*) I told everybody. Hey, Rose! I went down there to cash my check.

Rose (entering from the house): Hush all that hollering, man! I know you out here. What they say down there at the Commissioner's office?

Troy: You supposed to come when I call you, woman. Bono'll tell you that. (*To Bono.*) Don't Lucille come when you call her?

Rose: Man, hush your mouth. I ain't no dog . . . talk about "come when you call me."

Troy (puts his arm around Rose): You hear this, Bono? I had me an old dog used to get uppity like that. You say, "C'mere, Blue!" . . . and he just lay there and look at you. End up getting a stick and chasing him away trying to make him come.

Rose: I ain't studying you and your dog. I remember you used to sing that old song.

Troy (he sings):
    Hear it ring! Hear it ring!
    I had a dog his name was Blue.

Rose: Don't nobody wanna hear you sing that old song.

Troy (sings):
    You know Blue was mighty true.

Rose: Used to have Cory running around here singing that song.

Bono: Hell, I remember that song myself.

Troy (sings):
    You know Blue was a good old dog.
    Blue treed a possum in a hollow log.
  That was my daddy's song. My daddy made up that song.

Rose: I don't care who made it up. Don't nobody wanna hear you sing it.

Troy (makes a song like calling a dog): Come here, woman.

Rose: You come in here carrying on, I reckon they ain't fired you. What they say down there at the Commissioner's office?

Troy: Look here, Rose . . . Mr. Rand called me into his office today when I got back from talking to them people down there . . . it come from up top . . . he called me in and told me they was making me a driver.

Rose: Troy, you kidding!

Troy: No I ain't. Ask Bono.

Rose: Well, that's great, Troy. Now you don't have to hassle them people no more.

(*Lyons enters from the street.*)

Troy: Aw hell, I wasn't looking to see you today. I thought you was in jail. Got it all over the front page of the *Courier* about them raiding Sefus's place . . . where you be hanging out with all them thugs.

Lyons: Hey, Pop . . . that ain't got nothing to do with me. I don't go down there gambling. I go down there to sit in with the band. I ain't got nothing to do with the gambling part. They got some good music down there.

Troy: They got some rogues . . . is what they got.

Lyons: How you been, Mr. Bono? Hi, Rose.

Bono: I see where you playing down at the Crawford Grill tonight.

Rose: How come you ain't brought Bonnie like I told you? You should have brought Bonnie with you, she ain't been over in a month of Sundays.

Lyons: I was just in the neighborhood . . . thought I'd stop by.

Troy: Here he come . . .

Bono: Your daddy got a promotion on the rubbish. He's gonna be the first colored driver. Ain't got to do nothing but sit up there and read the paper like them white fellows.

Lyons: Hey, Pop . . . if you knew how to read you'd be alright.

Bono: Naw . . . naw . . . you mean if the nigger knew how to *drive* he'd be alright. Been fighting with them people about driving and ain't even got a license. Mr. Rand know you ain't got no driver's license?

Troy: Driving ain't nothing. All you do is point the truck where you want it to go. Driving ain't nothing.

Bono: Do Mr. Rand know you ain't got no driver's license? That's what I'm talking about. I ain't asked if driving was easy. I asked if Mr. Rand know you ain't got no driver's license.

Troy: He ain't got to know. The man ain't got to know my business. Time he find out, I have two or three driver's licenses.

Lyons (going into his pocket): Say, look here, Pop . . .

Troy: I knew it was coming. Didn't I tell you, Bono? I know what kind of "Look here, Pop" that was. The nigger fixing to ask me for some money. It's Friday night. It's my payday. All them rogues down there on the avenue . . . the ones that ain't in jail . . . and Lyons is hopping in his shoes to get down there with them.

Lyons: See, Pop . . . if you give somebody else a chance to talk sometime, you'd see that I was fixing to pay you back your ten dollars like I told you. Here . . . I told you I'd pay you when Bonnie got paid.

Troy: Naw . . . you go ahead and keep that ten dollars. Put it in the bank. The next time you feel like you wanna come by here and ask me for something . . . you go on down there and get that.

Lyons: Here's your ten dollars, Pop. I told you I don't want you to give me nothing. I just wanted to borrow ten dollars.

Troy: Naw . . . you go on and keep that for the next time you want to ask me.

Lyons: Come on, Pop . . . here go your ten dollars.

Rose: Why don't you go on and let the boy pay you back, Troy?

Lyons: Here you go, Rose. If you don't take it I'm gonna have to hear about it for the next six months. *(He hands her the money.)*

Rose: You can hand yours over here too, Troy.

Troy: You see this, Bono. You see how they do me.

Bono: Yeah, Lucille do me the same way.

   (Gabriel is heard singing offstage. He enters.)

Gabriel: Better get ready for the Judgment! Better get ready for . . . Hey! . . . Hey! . . . There's Troy's boy!

Lyons: How are you doing, Uncle Gabe?

Gabriel: Lyons . . . The King of the Jungle! Rose . . . hey, Rose. Got a flower for you. *(He takes a rose from his pocket.)* Picked it myself. That's the same rose like you is!

Rose: That's right nice of you, Gabe.

Lyons: What you been doing, Uncle Gabe?

Gabriel: Oh, I been chasing hellhounds and waiting on the time to tell St. Peter to open the gates.

Lyons: You been chasing hellhounds, huh? Well . . . you doing the right thing, Uncle Gabe. Somebody got to chase them.

Gabriel: Oh, yeah . . . I know it. The devil's strong. The devil ain't no pushover. Hellhounds snipping at everybody's heels. But I got my trumpet waiting on the judgment time.

Lyons: Waiting on the Battle of Armageddon, huh?

Gabriel: Ain't gonna be too much of a battle when God get to waving that Judgment sword. But the people's gonna have a hell of a time trying to get into heaven if them gates ain't open.

Lyons (putting his arm around Gabriel): You hear this, Pop. Uncle Gabe, you alright!

Gabriel (laughing with Lyons): Lyons! King of the Jungle.

Rose: You gonna stay for supper, Gabe? Want me to fix you a plate?

Gabriel: I'll take a sandwich, Rose. Don't want no plate. Just wanna eat with my hands. I'll take a sandwich.

Rose: How about you, Lyons? You staying? Got some short ribs cooking.

Lyons: Naw, I won't eat nothing till after we finished playing. *(Pause.)* You ought to come down and listen to me play, Pop.

Troy: I don't like that Chinese music. All that noise.

Rose: Go on in the house and wash up, Gabe . . . I'll fix you a sandwich.

Gabriel (to Lyons, as he exits): Troy's mad at me.

Lyons: What you mad at Uncle Gabe for, Pop?

Rose: He thinks Troy's mad at him cause he moved over to Miss Pearl's.

Troy: I ain't mad at the man. He can live where he want to live at.

Lyons: What he move over there for? Miss Pearl don't like nobody.

Rose: She don't mind him none. She treats him real nice. She just don't allow all that singing.

Troy: She don't mind that rent he be paying . . . that's what she don't mind.

Rose: Troy, I ain't going through that with you no more. He's over there cause he want to have his own place. He can come and go as he please.

Troy: Hell, he could come and go as he please here. I wasn't stopping him. I ain't put no rules on him.

Rose: It ain't the same thing, Troy. And you know it.

(Gabriel comes to the door.)

Now, that's the last I wanna hear about that. I don't wanna hear nothing else about Gabe and Miss Pearl. And next week . . .

Gabriel: I'm ready for my sandwich, Rose.

Rose: And next week . . . when that recruiter come from that school . . . I want you to sign that paper and go on and let Cory play football. Then that'll be the last I have to hear about that.

Troy (to Rose as she exits into the house): I ain't thinking about Cory nothing.

Lyons: What . . . Cory got recruited? What school he going to?

Troy: That boy walking around here smelling his piss . . . thinking he's grown. Thinking he's gonna do what he want, irrespective of what I say. Look here, Bono . . . I left the Commissioner's office and went down to the A&P . . . that boy ain't working down there. He lying to me. Telling me he got his job back . . .

telling me he working weekends . . . telling me he working after school . . . Mr. Stawicki tell me he ain't working down there at all!

Lyons: Cory just growing up. He's just busting at the seams trying to fill out your shoes.

Troy: I don't care what he's doing. When he get to the point where he wanna disobey me . . . then it's time for him to move on. Bono'll tell you that. I bet he ain't never disobeyed his daddy without paying the consequences.

Bono: I ain't never had a chance. My daddy came on through . . . but I ain't never knew him to see him . . . or what he had on his mind or where he went. Just moving on through. Searching out the New Land. That's what the old folks used to call it. See a fellow moving around from place to place . . . woman to woman . . . called it searching out the New Land. I can't say if he ever found it. I come along, didn't want no kids. Didn't know if I was gonna be in one place long enough to fix on them right as their daddy. I figured I was going searching too. As it turned out I been hooked up with Lucille near about as long as your daddy been with Rose. Going on sixteen years.

Troy: Sometimes I wish I hadn't known my daddy. He ain't cared nothing about no kids. A kid to him wasn't nothing. All he wanted was for you to learn how to walk so he could start you to working. When it come time for eating . . . he ate first. If there was anything left over, that's what you got. Man would sit down and eat two chickens and give you the wing.

Lyons: You ought to stop that, Pop. Everybody feed their kids. No matter how hard times is . . . everybody care about their kids. Make sure they have something to eat.

Troy: The only thing my daddy cared about was getting them bales of cotton in to Mr. Lubin. That's the only thing that mattered to him. Sometimes I used to wonder why he was living. Wonder why the devil hadn't come and got him. "Get them bales of cotton in to Mr. Lubin" and find out he owe him money . . .

Lyons: He should have just went on and left when he saw he couldn't get nowhere. That's what I would have done.

Troy: How he gonna leave with eleven kids? And where he gonna go? He ain't knew how to do nothing but farm. No, he was trapped and I think he knew it. But I'll say this for him . . . he felt a responsibility toward us. Maybe he ain't treated us the way I felt he should have . . . but without that responsibility he could have walked off and left us . . . made his own way.

Bono: A lot of them did. Back in those days what you talking about . . . they walk out their front door and just take on down one road or another and keep on walking.

Lyons: There you go! That's what I'm talking about.

Bono: Just keep on walking till you come to something else. Ain't you never heard of nobody having the walking blues? Well, that's what you call it when you just take off like that.

Troy: My daddy ain't had them walking blues! What you talking about? He stayed right there with his family. But he was just as evil as he could be. My mama couldn't stand him. Couldn't stand that evilness. She run off when I was about eight. She sneaked off one night after he had gone to sleep. Told me she was coming back for me. I ain't never seen her no more. All his women run off and left him. He wasn't good for nobody.

When my turn come to head out, I was fourteen and got to sniffing around Joe Canewell's daughter. Had us an old mule we called Greyboy. My daddy sent me out to do some plowing and I tied up Greyboy and went to fooling around with Joe Canewell's daughter. We done found us a nice little spot, got real cozy with each other. She about thirteen and we done figured we was grown anyway . . . so we down there enjoying ourselves . . . ain't thinking about nothing. We didn't know Greyboy had got loose and wandered back to the house and my daddy was looking for me. We down there by the creek enjoying ourselves when my daddy come up on us. Surprised us. He had them leather straps off the mule and commenced to whupping me like there was no tomorrow. I jumped up, mad and embarrassed. I was scared of my daddy. When he commenced to whupping on me . . . quite naturally I run to get out of the way. *(Pause.)* Now I thought he was mad cause I ain't done my work. But I see where he was chasing me off so he could have the gal for himself. When I see what the matter of it was, I lost all fear of my daddy. Right there is where I become a man . . . at fourteen years of age. *(Pause.)* Now it was my turn to run him off. I picked up them same reins that he had used on me. I picked up them reins and commenced to whupping on him. The gal jumped up and run off . . . and when my daddy turned to face me, I could see why the devil had never come to get him . . . cause he was the devil himself. I don't know what happened. When I woke up, I was laying right there by the creek, and Blue . . . this old dog we had . . . was licking my face. I thought I was blind. I couldn't see nothing. Both my eyes were swollen shut. I layed there and cried. I didn't know what I was gonna do. The only thing I knew was the time had come for me to leave my daddy's house. And right there the world suddenly got big. And it was a long time before I could cut it down to where I could handle it.

Part of that cutting down was when I got to the place where I could feel him kicking in my blood and knew that the only thing that separated us was the matter of a few years.

(Gabriel enters from the house with a sandwich.)

Lyons: What you got there, Uncle Gabe?

Gabriel: Got me a ham sandwich. Rose gave me a ham sandwich.

Troy: I don't know what happened to him. I done lost touch with everybody except Gabriel. But I hope he's dead. I hope he found some peace.

Lyons: That's a heavy story, Pop. I didn't know you left home when you was fourteen.

Troy: And didn't know nothing. The only part of the world I knew was the forty-two acres of Mr. Lubin's land. That's all I knew about life.

Lyons: Fourteen's kinda young to be out on your own. *(Phone rings.)* I don't even think I was ready to be out on my own at fourteen. I don't know what I would have done.

Troy: I got up from the creek and walked on down to Mobile. I was through with farming. Figured I could do better in the city. So I walked the two hundred miles to Mobile.

Lyons: Wait a minute . . . you ain't walked no two hundred miles, Pop. Ain't nobody gonna walk no two hundred miles. You talking about some walking there.

Bono: That's the only way you got anywhere back in them days.

Lyons: Shhh. Damn if I wouldn't have hitched a ride with somebody!

Troy: Who you gonna hitch it with? They ain't had no cars and things like they got now. We talking about 1918.

Rose *(entering)*: What you all out here getting into?

Troy (to Rose): I'm telling Lyons how good he got it. He don't know nothing about this I'm talking.

Rose: Lyons, that was Bonnie on the phone. She say you supposed to pick her up.

Lyons: Yeah, okay, Rose.

Troy: I walked on down to Mobile and hitched up with some of them fellows that was heading this way. Got up here and found out . . . not only couldn't you get a job . . . you couldn't find no place to live. I thought I was in freedom. Shhh. Colored folks living down there on the riverbanks in whatever kind of shelter they could find for themselves. Right down there under the Brady Street Bridge. Living in shacks made of sticks and tarpaper. Messed around there and went from bad to worse. Started stealing. First it was food. Then I figured, hell, if I steal money I can buy me some food. Buy me some shoes too! One thing led to another. Met your mama. I was young and anxious to be a man. Met your mama and had you. What I do that for? Now I got to worry about feeding you and her. Got to steal three times as much. Went out one day looking for somebody to rob . . . that's what I was, a robber. I'll tell you the truth. I'm ashamed of it today. But it's the truth. Went to rob this fellow . . . pulled out my knife . . . and he pulled out a gun. Shot me in the chest. It felt just like somebody had taken a hot branding iron and laid it on me. When he shot me I jumped at him with my knife. They told me I killed him and they put me in the penitentiary and locked me up for fifteen years. That's where I met Bono. That's where I learned how to play baseball. Got out that place and your mama had taken you and went on to make life without me. Fifteen years was a long time for her to wait. But that fifteen years cured me of that robbing stuff. Rose'll tell you. She asked me when I met her if I had gotten all that foolishness out of my system. And I told her, "Baby, it's you and baseball all what count with me." You hear me, Bono? I meant it too. She say, "Which one comes first?" I told her, "Baby, ain't no doubt it's baseball . . . but you stick and get old with me and we'll both outlive this baseball." Am I right, Rose? And it's true.

Rose: Man, hush your mouth. You ain't said no such thing. Talking about, "Baby you know you'll always be number one with me." That's what you was talking.

Troy: You hear that, Bono. That's why I love her.

Bono: Rose'll keep you straight. You get off the track, she'll straighten you up.

Rose: Lyons, you better get on up and get Bonnie. She waiting on you.

Lyons (gets up to go): Hey, Pop, why don't you come on down to the Grill and hear me play?

Troy: I ain't going down there. I'm too old to be sitting around in them clubs.

Bono: You got to be good to play down at the Grill.

Lyons: Come on, Pop . . .

Troy: I got to get up in the morning.

Lyons: You ain't got to stay long.

Troy: Naw, I'm gonna get my supper and go on to bed.

Lyons: Well, I got to go. I'll see you again.

Troy: Don't you come around my house on my payday.

Rose: Pick up the phone and let somebody know you coming. And bring Bonnie with you. You know I'm always glad to see her.

Lyons: Yeah, I'll do that, Rose. You take care now. See you, Pop. See you, Mr. Bono. See you, Uncle Gabe.

Gabriel: Lyons! King of the Jungle!

(Lyons exits.)

Troy: Is supper ready, woman? Me and you got some business to take care of. I'm gonna tear it up too.

Rose: Troy, I done told you now!

Troy *(puts his arm around Bono)*: Aw hell, woman . . . this is Bono. Bono like family. I done known this nigger since . . . how long I done know you?

Bono: It's been a long time.

Troy: I done know this nigger since Skippy was a pup. Me and him done been through some times.

Bono: You sure right about that.

Troy: Hell, I done know him longer than I known you. And we still standing shoulder to shoulder. Hey, look here, Bono . . . a man can't ask for no more than that. *(Drinks to him.)* I love you, nigger.

Bono: Hell, I love you too . . . but I got to get home see my woman. You got yours in hand. I got to go get mine.

(Bono starts to exit as Cory enters the yard, dressed in his football uniform. He gives Troy a hard, uncompromising look.)

Cory: What you do that for, Pop?

(He throws his helmet down in the direction of Troy.)

Rose: What's the matter? Cory . . . what's the matter?

Cory: Papa done went up to the school and told Coach Zellman I can't play football no more. Wouldn't even let me play the game. Told him to tell the recruiter not to come.

Rose: Troy . . .

Troy: What you Troying me for. Yeah, I did it. And the boy know why I did it.

Cory: Why you wanna do that to me? That was the one chance I had.

Rose: Ain't nothing wrong with Cory playing football, Troy.

Troy: The boy lied to me. I told the nigger if he wanna play football . . . to keep up his chores and hold down that job at the A&P. That was the conditions. Stopped down there to see Mr. Stawicki . . .

Cory: I can't work after school during the football season, Pop! I tried to tell you that Mr. Stawicki's holding my job for me. You don't never want to listen to nobody. And then you wanna go and do this to me!

Troy: I ain't done nothing to you. You done it to yourself.

Cory: Just cause you didn't have a chance! You just scared I'm gonna be better than you, that's all.

Troy: Come here.

Rose: Troy . . .

(Cory reluctantly crosses over to Troy.)

Troy: Alright! See. You done made a mistake.

Cory: I didn't even do nothing!

Troy: I'm gonna tell you what your mistake was. See . . . you swung at the ball and didn't hit it. That's strike one. See, you in the batter's box now. You swung and you missed. That's strike one. Don't you strike out!

(Lights fade to black.)

ACT II

SCENE I

The following morning. Cory is at the tree hitting the ball with the bat. He tries to mimic Troy, but his swing is awkward, less sure. Rose enters from the house.

Rose: Cory, I want you to help me with this cupboard.

Cory: I ain't quitting the team. I don't care what Poppa say.

Rose: I'll talk to him when he gets back. He had to go see about your Uncle Gabe. The police done arrested him. Say he was disturbing the peace. He'll be back directly. Come on in here and help me clean out the top of this cupboard.

(Cory exits into the house. Rose sees Troy and Bono coming down the alley.)

Troy . . . what they say down there?

Troy: Ain't said nothing. I give them fifty dollars and they let him go. I'll talk to you about it. Where's Cory?

Rose: He's in there helping me clean out these cupboards.

Troy: Tell him to get his butt out here.

(Troy and Bono go over to the pile of wood. Bono picks up the saw and begins sawing.)

Troy (to Bono): All they want is the money. That makes six or seven times I done went down there and got him. See me coming they stick out their *hands.*

Bono: Yeah. I know what you mean. That's all they care about . . . that money. They don't care about what's right. *(Pause.)* Nigger, why you got to go and get some hard wood? You ain't doing nothing but building a little old fence. Get you some soft pine wood. That's all you need.

Troy: I know what I'm doing. This is outside wood. You put pine wood inside the house. Pine wood is inside wood. This here is outside wood. Now you tell me where the fence is gonna be?

Bono: You don't need this wood. You can put it up with pine wood and it'll stand as long as you gonna be here looking at it.

Troy: How you know how long I'm gonna be here, nigger? Hell, I might just live forever. Live longer than old man Horsely.

Bono: That's what Magee used to say.

Troy: Magee's a damn fool. Now you tell me who you ever heard of gonna pull their own teeth with a pair of rusty pliers.

Bono: The old folks . . . my granddaddy used to pull his teeth with pliers. They ain't had no dentists for the colored folks back then.

Troy: Get clean pliers! You understand? Clean pliers! Sterilize them! Besides we ain't living back then. All Magee had to do was walk over to Doc Goldblum's.

Bono: I see where you and that Tallahassee gal . . . that Alberta . . . I see where you all done got tight.

Troy: What you mean "got tight"?

Bono: I see where you be laughing and joking with her all the time.

Troy: I laughs and jokes with all of them, Bono. You know me.

Bono: That ain't the kind of laughing and joking I'm talking about.

(Cory enters from the house.)

Cory: How you doing, Mr. Bono?

Troy: Cory? Get that saw from Bono and cut some wood. He talking about the wood's too hard to cut. Stand back there, Jim, and let that young boy show you how it's done.

Bono: He's sure welcome to it.

(*Cory takes the saw and begins to cut the wood.*)

Whew-e-e! Look at that. Big old strong boy. Look like Joe Louis. Hell, must be getting old the way I'm watching that boy whip through that wood.

Cory: I don't see why Mama want a fence around the yard noways.

Troy: Damn if I know either. What the hell she keeping out with it? She ain't got nothing nobody want.

Bono: Some people build fences to keep people out . . . and other people build fences to keep people in. Rose wants to hold on to you all. She loves you.

Troy: Hell, nigger, I don't need nobody to tell me my wife loves me. Cory . . . go on in the house and see if you can find that other saw.

Cory: Where's it at?

Troy: I said find it! Look for it till you find it!

(*Cory exits into the house.*)

What's that supposed to mean? Wanna keep us in?

Bono: Troy . . . I done known you seem like damn near my whole life. You and Rose both. I done know both of you all for a long time. I remember when you met Rose. When you was hitting them baseball out the park. A lot of them old gals was after you then. You had the pick of the litter. When you picked Rose, I was happy for you. That was the first time I knew you had any sense. I said . . . My man Troy knows what he's doing . . . I'm gonna follow this nigger . . . he might take me somewhere. I been following you too. I done learned a whole heap of things about life watching you. I done learned how to tell where the shit lies. How to tell it from the alfalfa. You done learned me a lot of things. You showed me how to not make the same mistakes . . . to take life as it comes along and keep putting one foot in front of the other. (*Pause.*) Rose a good woman, Troy.

Troy: Hell, nigger, I know she a good woman. I been married to her for eighteen years. What you got on your mind, Bono?

Bono: I just say she a good woman. Just like I say anything. I ain't got to have nothing on my mind.

Troy: You just gonna say she a good woman and leave it hanging out there like that? Why you telling me she a good woman?

Bono: She loves you, Troy. Rose loves you.

Troy: You saying I don't measure up. That's what you trying to say. I don't measure up cause I'm seeing this other gal. I know what you trying to say.

Bono: I know what Rose means to you, Troy. I'm just trying to say I don't want to see you mess up.

Troy: Yeah, I appreciate that, Bono. If you was messing around on Lucille I'd be telling you the same thing.

Bono: Well, that's all I got to say. I just say that because I love you both.

Troy: Hell, you know me . . . I wasn't out there looking for nothing. You can't find a better woman than Rose. I know that. But seems like this woman just stuck onto me where I can't shake her loose. I done wrestled with it, tried to throw her off me . . . but she just stuck on tighter. Now she's stuck on for good.

Bono: You's in control . . . that's what you tell me all the time. You responsible for what you do.

Troy: I ain't ducking the responsibility of it. As long as it sets right in my heart . . . then I'm okay. Cause that's all I listen to. It'll tell me right from wrong every time. And I ain't talking about doing Rose no bad turn. I love Rose. She done carried me a long ways and I love and respect her for that.

Bono: I know you do. That's why I don't want to see you hurt her. But what you gonna do when she find out? What you got then? If you try and juggle both of them . . . sooner or later you gonna drop one of them. That's common sense.

Troy: Yeah, I hear what you saying, Bono. I been trying to figure a way to work it out.

Bono: Work it out right, Troy. I don't want to be getting all up between you and Rose's business . . . but work it so it come out right.

Troy: Aw hell, I get all up between you and Lucille's business. When you gonna get that woman that refrigerator she been wanting? Don't tell me you ain't got no money now. I know who your banker is. Mellon° don't need that money bad as Lucille want that refrigerator. I'll tell you that.

Bono: Tell you what I'll do . . . when you finish building this fence for Rose . . . I'll buy Lucille that refrigerator.

Troy: You done stuck your foot in your mouth now!

(Troy grabs up a board and begins to saw. Bono starts to walk out the yard.)

Hey, nigger . . . where you going?

Bono: I'm going home. I know you don't expect me to help you now. I'm protecting my money. I wanna see you put that fence up by yourself. That's what I want to see. You'll be here another six months without me.

Troy: Nigger, you ain't right.

Bono: When it comes to my money . . . I'm right as fireworks on the Fourth of July.

Troy: Alright, we gonna see now. You better get out your bankbook.

(Bono exits, and Troy continues to work. Rose enters from the house.)

Rose: What they say down there? What's happening with Gabe?

Troy: I went down there and got him out. Cost me fifty dollars. Say he was disturbing the peace. Judge set up a hearing for him in three weeks. Say to show cause why he shouldn't be re-committed.

Rose: What was he doing that cause them to arrest him?

Troy: Some kids was teasing him and he run them off home. Say he was howling and carrying on. Some folks seen him and called the police. That's all it was.

Rose: Well, what's you say? What'd you tell the judge?

Troy: Told him I'd look after him. It didn't make no sense to recommit the man. He stuck out his big greasy palm and told me to give him fifty dollars and take him on home.

Rose: Where's he at now? Where'd he go off to?

Troy: He's gone on about his business. He don't need nobody to hold his hand.

Mellon: banker and industrialist Andrew Mellon (1855–1937), U.S. Treasury Secretary 1921–32, was active in philanthropic enterprises, especially in his native Pittsburgh.

Rose: Well, I don't know. Seem like that would be the best place for him if they did put him into the hospital. I know what you're gonna say. But that's what I think would be best.

Troy: The man done had his life ruined fighting for what? And they wanna take and lock him up. Let him be free. He don't bother nobody.

Rose: Well, everybody got their own way of looking at it I guess. Come on and get your lunch. I got a bowl of lima beans and some cornbread in the oven. Come on get something to eat. Ain't no sense you fretting over Gabe.

(Rose turns to go into the house.)

Troy: Rose . . . got something to tell you.

Rose: Well, come on . . . wait till I get this food on the table.

Troy: Rose!

(She stops and turns around.)

I don't know how to say this. *(Pause.)* I can't explain it none. It just sort of grows on you till it gets out of hand. It starts out like a little bush . . . and the next thing you know it's a whole forest.

Rose: Troy . . . what is you talking about?

Troy: I'm talking, woman, let me talk. I'm trying to find a way to tell you . . . I'm gonna be a daddy. I'm gonna be somebody's daddy.

Rose: Troy . . . you're not telling me this? You're gonna be . . . what?

Troy: Rose . . . now . . . see . . .

Rose: You telling me you gonna be somebody's daddy? You telling your *wife* this?

(Gabriel enters from the street. He carries a rose in his hand.)

Gabriel: Hey, Troy! Hey, Rose!

Rose: I have to wait eighteen years to hear something like this.

Gabriel: Hey, Rose . . . I got a flower for you. *(He hands it to her.)* That's a rose. Same rose like you is.

Rose: Thanks, Gabe.

Gabriel: Troy, you ain't mad at me is you? Them bad mens come and put me away. You ain't mad at me is you?

Troy: Naw, Gabe, I ain't mad at you.

Rose: Eighteen years and you wanna come with this.

Gabriel (takes a quarter out of his pocket): See what I got? Got a brand new quarter.

Troy: Rose . . . it's just . . .

Rose: Ain't nothing you can say, Troy. Ain't no way of explaining that.

Gabriel: Fellow that give me this quarter had a whole mess of them. I'm gonna keep this quarter till it stop shining.

Rose: Gabe, go on in the house there. I got some watermelon in the Frigidaire. Go on and get you a piece.

Gabriel: Say, Rose . . . you know I was chasing hellhounds and them bad mens come and get me and take me away. Troy helped me. He come down there and told them they better let me go before he beat them up. Yeah, he did!

Rose: You go on and get you a piece of watermelon, Gabe. Them bad mens is gone now.

Gabriel: Okay, Rose . . . gonna get me some watermelon. The kind with the stripes on it.

(Gabriel exits into the house.)

Rose: Why, Troy? Why? After all these years to come dragging this in to me now. It don't make no sense at your age. I could have expected this ten or fifteen years ago, but not now.

Troy: Age ain't got nothing to do with it, Rose.

Rose: I done tried to be everything a wife should be. Everything a wife could be. Been married eighteen years and I got to live to see the day you tell me you been seeing another woman and done fathered a child by her. And you know I ain't never wanted no half nothing in my family. My whole family is half. Everybody got different fathers and mothers . . . my two sisters and my brother. Can't hardly tell who's who. Can't never sit down and talk about Papa and Mama. It's your papa and your mama and my papa and my mama . . .

Troy: Rose . . . stop it now.

Rose: I ain't never wanted that for none of my children. And now you wanna drag your behind in here and tell me something like this.

Troy: You ought to know. It's time for you to know.

Rose: Well, I don't want to know, goddamn it!

Troy: I can't just make it go away. It's done now. I can't wish the circumstance of the thing away.

Rose: And you don't want to either. Maybe you want to wish me and my boy away. Maybe that's what you want? Well, you can't wish us away. I've got eighteen years of my life invested in you. You ought to have stayed upstairs in my bed where you belong.

Troy: Rose . . . now listen to me . . . we can get a handle on this thing. We can talk this out . . . come to an understanding.

Rose: All of a sudden it's "we." Where was "we" at when you was down there rolling around with some godforsaken woman? "We" should have come to an understanding before you started making a damn fool of yourself. You're a day late and a dollar short when it comes to an understanding with me.

Troy: It's just . . . She gives me a different idea . . . a different understanding about myself. I can step out of this house and get away from the pressures and problems . . . be a different man. I ain't got to wonder how I'm gonna pay the bills or get the roof fixed. I can just be a part of myself that I ain't never been.

Rose: What I want to know . . . is do you plan to continue seeing her. That's all you can say to me.

Troy: I can sit up in her house and laugh. Do you understand what I'm saying. I can laugh out loud . . . and it feels good. It reaches all the way down to the bottom of my shoes. *(Pause.)* Rose, I can't give that up.

Rose: Maybe you ought to go on and stay down there with her . . . if she's a better woman than me.

Troy: It ain't about nobody being a better woman or nothing. Rose, you ain't the blame. A man couldn't ask for no woman to be a better wife than you've been. I'm responsible for it. I done locked myself into a pattern trying to take care of you all that I forgot about myself.

Rose: What the hell was I there for? That was my job, not somebody else's.

Troy: Rose, I done tried all my life to live decent . . . to live a clean . . . hard . . . useful life. I tried to be a good husband to you. In every way I knew how. Maybe I come into the world backwards, I don't know. But . . . you born with two strikes on you before you come to the plate. You got to guard it closely . . . always looking for the curve-ball on the inside corner. You can't afford to let none get past you. You can't afford a call strike. If you going down . . . you going down swinging. Everything lined up against you. What you gonna do. I fooled them, Rose. I bunted. When I found you and Cory and a halfway decent job . . . . I was safe. Couldn't nothing touch me. I wasn't gonna strike out no more. I wasn't going back to the penitentiary. I wasn't gonna lay in the streets with a bottle of wine. I was safe. I had me a family. A job. I wasn't gonna get that last strike. I was on first looking for one of them boys to knock me in. To get me home.

Rose: You should have stayed in my bed, Troy.

Troy: Then when I saw that gal . . . she firmed up my backbone. And I got to thinking that if I tried . . . I just might be able to steal second. Do you understand after eighteen years I wanted to steal second.

Rose: You should have held me tight. You should have grabbed me and held on.

Troy: I stood on first base for eighteen years and I thought . . . well, goddamn it . . . go on for it!

Rose: We're not talking about baseball! We're talking about you going off to lay in bed with another woman . . . and then bring it home to me. That's what we're talking about. We ain't talking about no baseball.

Troy: Rose, you're not listening to me. I'm trying the best I can to explain it to you. It's not easy for me to admit that I been standing in the same place for eighteen years.

Rose: I been standing with you! I been right here with you, Troy. I got a life too. I gave eighteen years of my life to stand in the same spot with you. Don't you think I ever wanted other things? Don't you think I had dreams and hopes? What about my life? What about me. Don't you think it ever crossed my mind to want to know other men? That I wanted to lay up somewhere and forget about my responsibilities? That I wanted someone to make me laugh so I could feel good? You not the only one who's got wants and needs. But I held on to you, Troy. I took all my feelings, my wants and needs, my dreams . . . and I buried them inside you. I planted a seed and watched and prayed over it. I planted myself inside you and waited to bloom. And it didn't take me no eighteen years to find out the soil was hard and rocky and it wasn't never gonna bloom.

But I held on to you, Troy. I held you tighter. You was my husband. I owed you everything I had. Every part of me I could find to give you. And upstairs in that room . . . with the darkness falling in on me . . . I gave everything I had to try and erase the doubt that you wasn't the finest man in the world. And wherever you was going . . . I wanted to be there with you. Cause you was my husband. Cause that's the only way I was gonna survive as your wife. You always talking about what you give . . . and what you don't have to give. But you take too. You take . . . and don't even know nobody's giving!

(Rose turns to exit into the house; Troy grabs her arm.)

Troy: You say I take and don't give!

Rose: Troy! You're hurting me!

Troy: You say I take and don't give.

Rose: Troy . . . you're hurting my arm! Let go!

Troy: I done give you everything I got. Don't you tell that lie on me.

Rose: Troy!

Troy: Don't you tell that lie on me!

(*Cory enters from the house.*)

Cory: Mama!
Rose: Troy. You're hurting me.
Troy: Don't you tell me about no taking and giving.

(*Cory comes up behind Troy and grabs him. Troy, surprised, is thrown off balance just as Cory throws a glancing blow that catches him on the chest and knocks him down. Troy is stunned, as is Cory.*)

Rose: Troy. Troy. No!

(*Troy gets to his feet and starts at Cory.*)

Troy . . . no. Please! Troy!

(*Rose pulls on Troy to hold him back. Troy stops himself.*)

Troy (to Cory): Alright. That's strike two. You stay away from around me, boy. Don't you strike out. You living with a full count. Don't you strike out.

(*Troy exits out the yard as the lights go down.*)

SCENE II

It is six months later, early afternoon. Troy enters from the house and starts to exit the yard. Rose enters from the house.

Rose: Troy, I want to talk to you.
Troy: All of a sudden, after all this time, you want to talk to me, huh? You ain't wanted to talk to me for months. You ain't wanted to talk to me last night. You ain't wanted no part of me then. What you wanna talk to me about now?
Rose: Tomorrow's Friday.
Troy: I know what day tomorrow is. You think I don't know tomorrow's Friday? My whole life I ain't done nothing but look to see Friday coming and you got to tell me it's Friday.
Rose: I want to know if you're coming home.
Troy: I always come home, Rose. You know that. There ain't never been a night I ain't come home.
Rose: That ain't what I mean . . . and you know it. I want to know if you're coming straight home after work.
Troy: I figure I'd cash my check . . . hang out at Taylors' with the boys . . . maybe play a game of checkers . . .
Rose: Troy, I can't live like this. I won't live like this. You livin' on borrowed time with me. It's been going on six months now you ain't been coming home.
Troy: I be here every night. Every night of the year. That's 365 days.
Rose: I want you to come home tomorrow after work.
Troy: Rose . . . I don't mess up my pay. You know that now. I take my pay and I give it to you. I don't have no money but what you give me back. I just want to have a little time to myself . . . a little time to enjoy life.
Rose: What about me? When's my time to enjoy life?

Troy: I don't know what to tell you, Rose. I'm doing the best I can.

Rose: You ain't been home from work but time enough to change your clothes and run out . . . and you wanna call that the best you can do?

Troy: I'm going over to the hospital to see Alberta. She went into the hospital this afternoon. Look like she might have the baby early. I won't be gone long.

Rose: Well, you ought to know. They went over to Miss Pearl's and got Gabe today. She said you told them to go ahead and lock him up.

Troy: I ain't said no such thing. Whoever told you that is telling a lie. Pearl ain't doing nothing but telling a big fat lie.

Rose: She ain't had to tell me. I read it on the papers.

Troy: I ain't told them nothing of the kind.

Rose: I saw it right there on the papers.

Troy: What it say, huh?

Rose: It said you told them to take him.

Troy: Then they screwed that up, just the way they screw up everything. I ain't worried about what they got on the paper.

Rose: Say the government send part of his check to the hospital and the other part to you.

Troy: I ain't got nothing to do with that if that's the way it works. I ain't made up the rules about how it work.

Rose: You did Gabe just like you did Cory. You wouldn't sign the paper for Cory . . . but you signed for Gabe. You signed that paper.

(The telephone is heard ringing inside the house.)

Troy: I told you I ain't signed nothing, woman! The only thing I signed was the release form. Hell, I can't read, I don't know what they had on that paper! I ain't signed nothing about sending Gabe away.

Rose: I said send him to the hospital . . . you said let him be free . . . now you done went down there and signed him to the hospital for half his money. You went back on yourself, Troy. You gonna have to answer for that.

Troy: See now . . . you been over there talking to Miss Pearl. She done got mad cause she ain't getting Gabe's rent money. That's all it is. She's liable to say anything.

Rose: Troy, I seen where you signed the paper.

Troy: You ain't seen nothing I signed. What she doing got papers on my brother anyway? Miss Pearl telling a big fat lie. And I'm gonna tell her about it too! You ain't seen nothing I signed. Say . . . you ain't seen nothing I signed.

(Rose exits into the house to answer the telephone. Presently she returns.)

Rose: Troy . . . that was the hospital. Alberta had the baby.

Troy: What she have? What is it?

Rose: It's a girl.

Troy: I better get on down to the hospital to see her.

Rose: Troy . . .

Troy: Rose . . . I got to go see her now. That's only right . . . what's the matter . . . the baby's alright, ain't it?

Rose: Alberta died having the baby.

Troy: Died . . . you say she's dead? Alberta's dead?

Rose: They said they done all they could. They couldn't do nothing for her.

Troy: The baby? How's the baby?

Rose: They say it's healthy. I wonder who's gonna bury her.

Troy: She had family, Rose. She wasn't living in the world by herself.

Rose: I know she wasn't living in the world by herself.

Troy: Next thing you gonna want to know if she had any insurance.

Rose: Troy, you ain't got to talk like that.

Troy: That's the first thing that jumped out your mouth. "Who's gonna bury her?" Like I'm fixing to take on that task for myself.

Rose: I am your wife. Don't push me away.

Troy: I ain't pushing nobody away. Just give me some space. That's all. Just give me some room to breathe.

(*Rose exits into the house. Troy walks about the yard.*)

Troy (*with a quiet rage that threatens to consume him*): Alright . . . Mr. Death. See now . . . I'm gonna tell you what I'm gonna do. I'm gonna take and build me a fence around this yard. See? I'm gonna build me a fence around what belongs to me. And then I want you to stay on the other side. See? You stay over there until you're ready for me. Then you come on. Bring your army. Bring your sickle. Bring your wrestling clothes. I ain't gonna fall down on my vigilance this time. You ain't gonna sneak up on me no more. When you ready for me . . . when the top of your list say Troy Maxson . . . that's when you come around here. You come up and knock on the front door. Ain't nobody else got nothing to do with this. This is between you and me. Man to man. You stay on the other side of that fence until you ready for me. Then you come up and knock on the front door. Anytime you want. I'll be ready for you.

(*The lights go down to black.*)

SCENE III

The lights come up on the porch. It is late evening three days later. Rose sits listening to the ball game waiting for Troy. The final out of the game is made and Rose switches off the radio. Troy enters the yard carrying an infant wrapped in blankets. He stands back from the house and calls.

Rose enters and stands on the porch. There is a long, awkward silence, the weight of which grows heavier with each passing second.

Troy: Rose . . . I'm standing here with my daughter in my arms. She ain't but a wee bittie little old thing. She don't know nothing about grownups' business. She innocent . . . and she ain't got no mama.

Rose: What you telling me for, Troy?

(*She turns and exits into the house.*)

Troy: Well . . . I guess we'll just sit out here on the porch.

(*He sits down on the porch. There is an awkward indelicateness about the way he handles the baby. His largeness engulfs and seems to swallow it. He speaks loud enough for Rose to hear.*)

A man's got to do what's right for him. I ain't sorry for nothing I done. It felt right in my heart. (*To the baby.*) What you smiling at? Your daddy's a big man.

Got these great big old hands. But sometimes he's scared. And right now your daddy's scared cause we sitting out here and ain't got no home. Oh, I been homeless before. I ain't had no little baby with me. But I been homeless. You just be out on the road by your lonesome and you see one of them trains coming and you just kinda go like this . . .

(He sings as a lullaby.)

> Please, Mr. Engineer let a man ride the line
> Please, Mr. Engineer let a man ride the line
> I ain't got no ticket please let me ride the blinds

(Rose enters from the house. Troy, hearing her steps behind him, stands and faces her.)

She's my daughter, Rose. My own flesh and blood. I can't deny her no more than I can deny them boys. *(Pause.)* You and them boys is my family. You and them and this child is all I got in the world. So I guess what I'm saying is . . . I'd appreciate it if you'd help me take care of her.

Rose: Okay, Troy . . . you're right. I'll take care of your baby for you . . . cause . . . like you say . . . she's innocent . . . and you can't visit the sins of the father upon the child. A motherless child has got a hard time. *(She takes the baby from him.)* From right now . . . this child got a mother. But you a womanless man.

(Rose turns and exits into the house with the baby. Lights go down to black.)

SCENE IV

It is two months later. Lyons enters the street. He knocks on the door and calls.

Lyons: Hey, Rose! *(Pause.)* Rose!

Rose (from inside the house): Stop that yelling. You gonna wake up Raynell. I just got her to sleep.

Lyons: I just stopped by to pay Papa this twenty dollars I owe him. Where's Papa at?

Rose: He should be here in a minute. I'm getting ready to go down to the church. Sit down and wait on him.

Lyons: I got to go pick up Bonnie over her mother's house.

Rose: Well, sit it down there on the table. He'll get it.

Lyons (enters the house and sets the money on the table): Tell Papa I said thanks. I'll see you again.

Rose: Alright, Lyons. We'll see you.

(Lyons starts to exit as Cory enters.)

Cory: Hey, Lyons.

Lyons: What's happening, Cory? Say man, I'm sorry I missed your graduation. You know I had a gig and couldn't get away. Otherwise, I would have been there, man. So what you doing?

Cory: I'm trying to find a job.

Lyons: Yeah I know how that go, man. It's rough out here. Jobs are scarce.

Cory: Yeah, I know.

Lyons: Look here, I got to run. Talk to Papa . . . he know some people. He'll be able to help get you a job. Talk to him . . . see what he say.

Cory: Yeah . . . alright, Lyons.

Lyons: You take care. I'll talk to you soon. We'll find some time to talk.

(*Lyons exits the yard. Cory wanders over to the tree, picks up the bat, and assumes a batting stance. He studies an imaginary pitcher and swings. Dissatisfied with the result, he tries again. Troy enters. They eye each other for a beat. Cory puts the bat down and exits the yard. Troy starts into the house as Rose exits with Raynell. She is carrying a cake.*)

Troy: I'm coming in and everybody's going out.

Rose: I'm taking this cake down to the church for the bake sale. Lyons was by to see you. He stopped by to pay you your twenty dollars. It's laying in there on the table.

Troy (going into his pocket): Well . . . here go this money.

Rose: Put it in there on the table, Troy. I'll get it.

Troy: What time you coming back?

Rose: Ain't no use in you studying me. It don't matter what time I come back.

Troy: I just asked you a question, woman. What's the matter . . . can't I ask you a question?

Rose: Troy, I don't want to go into it. Your dinner's in there on the stove. All you got to do is heat it up. And don't you be eating the rest of them cakes in there. I'm coming back for them. We having a bake sale at the church tomorrow.

(*Rose exits the yard. Troy sits down on the steps, takes a pint bottle from his pocket, opens it and drinks. He begins to sing.*)

Troy:

>Hear it ring! Hear it ring!
>Had an old dog his name was Blue
>You know Blue was mighty true
>You know Blue was a good old dog
>Blue treed a possum in a hollow log
>You know from that he was a good old dog

(*Bono enters the yard.*)

Bono: Hey, Troy.

Troy: Hey, what's happening, Bono?

Bono: I just thought I'd stop by to see you.

Troy: What you stop by and see me for? You ain't stopped by in a month of Sundays. Hell, I must owe you money or something.

Bono: Since you got your promotion I can't keep up with you. Used to see you every day. Now I don't even know what route you working.

Troy: They keep switching me around. Got me out in Greentree now . . . hauling white folks' garbage.

Bono: Greentree, huh? You lucky, at least you ain't got to be lifting them barrels. Damn if they ain't getting heavier. I'm gonna put in my two years and call it quits.

Troy: I'm thinking about retiring myself.

Bono: You got it easy. You can *drive* for another five years.

Troy: It ain't the same, Bono. It ain't like working the back of the truck. Ain't got nobody to talk to . . . feel like you working by yourself. Naw, I'm thinking about retiring. How's Lucille?

Bono: She alright. Her arthritis get to acting up on her sometime. Saw Rose on my way in. She going down to the church, huh?

Troy: Yeah, she took up going down there. All them preachers looking for somebody to fatten their pockets. *(Pause.)* Got some gin here.

Bono: Naw, thanks. I just stopped by to say hello.

Troy: Hell, nigger . . . you can take a drink. I ain't never known you to say no to a drink. You ain't got to work tomorrow.

Bono: I just stopped by. I'm fixing to go over to Skinner's. We got us a domino game going over his house every Friday.

Troy: Nigger, you can't play no dominoes. I used to whup you four games out of five.

Bono: Well, that learned me. I'm getting better.

Troy: Yeah? Well, that's alright.

Bono: Look here . . . I got to be getting on. Stop by sometime, huh?

Troy: Yeah, I'll do that, Bono. Lucille told Rose you bought her a new refrigerator.

Bono: Yeah, Rose told Lucille you had finally built your fence . . . so I figured we'd call it even.

Troy: I knew you would.

Bono: Yeah . . . okay. I'll be talking to you.

Troy: Yeah, take care, Bono. Good to see you. I'm gonna stop over.

Bono: Yeah. Okay, Troy.

(Bono exits. Troy drinks from the bottle.)

Troy:

    Old Blue died and I dug his grave
    Let him down with a golden chain
    Every night when I hear old Blue bark
    I know Blue treed a possum in Noah's Ark.
    Hear it ring! Hear it ring!

(Cory enters the yard. They eye each other for a beat. Troy is sitting in the middle of the steps. Cory walks over.)

Cory: I got to get by.

Troy: Say what? What's you say?

Cory: You in my way. I got to get by.

Troy: You got to get by where? This is my house. Bought and paid for. In full. Took me fifteen years. And if you wanna go in my house and I'm sitting on the steps . . . you say excuse me. Like your mama taught you.

Cory: Come on, Pop . . . I got to get by.

(Cory starts to maneuver his way past Troy. Troy grabs his leg and shoves him back.)

Troy: You just gonna walk over top of me?

Cory: I live here too!

Troy (advancing toward him): You just gonna walk over top of me in my own house?

Cory: I ain't scared of you.

Troy: I ain't asked if you was scared of me. I asked you if you was fixing to walk over top of me in my own house? That's the question. You ain't gonna say excuse me? You just gonna walk over top of me?

Cory: If you wanna put it like that.

Troy: How else am I gonna put it?

Cory: I was walking by you to go into the house cause you sitting on the steps drunk, singing to yourself. You can put it like that.

Troy: Without saying excuse me???

(Cory doesn't respond.)

I asked you a question. Without saying excuse me???

Cory: I ain't got to say excuse me to you. You don't count around here no more.

Troy: Oh, I see . . . I don't count around here no more. You ain't got to say excuse me to your daddy. All of a sudden you done got so grown that your daddy don't count around here no more . . . Around here in his own house and yard that he done paid for with the sweat of his brow. You done got so grown to where you gonna take over. You gonna take over my house. Is that right? You gonna wear my pants. You gonna go in there and stretch out on my bed. You ain't got to say excuse me cause I don't count around here no more. Is that right?

Cory: That's right. You always talking this dumb stuff. Now, why don't you just get out my way?

Troy: I guess you got someplace to sleep and something to put in your belly. You got that, huh? You got that? That's what you need. You got that, huh?

Cory: You don't know what I got. You ain't got to worry about what I got.

Troy: You right! You one hundred percent right! I done spent the last seventeen years worrying about what you got. Now it's your turn, see? I'll tell you what to do. You grown . . . we done established that. You a man. Now, let's see you act like one. Turn your behind around and walk out this yard. And when you get out there in the alley . . . you can forget about this house. See? Cause this is my house. You go on and be a man and get your own house. You can forget about this. Cause this is mine. You go on and get yours cause I'm through with doing for you.

Cory: You talking about what you did for me . . . what'd you ever give me?

Troy: Them feet and bones! That pumping heart, nigger! I give you more than anybody else is ever gonna give you.

Cory: You ain't never gave me nothing! You ain't never done nothing but hold me back. Afraid I was gonna be better than you. All you ever did was try and make me scared of you. I used to tremble every time you called my name. Every time I heard your footsteps in the house. Wondering all the time . . . what's Papa gonna say if I do this? . . . What's he gonna say if I do that? . . . What's Papa gonna say if I turn on the radio? And Mama, too . . . she tries . . . but she's scared of you.

Troy: You leave your mama out of this. She ain't got nothing to do with this.

Cory: I don't know how she stand you . . . after what you did to her.

Troy: I told you to leave your mama out of this!

(He advances toward Cory.)

Cory: What you gonna do . . . give me a whupping? You can't whup me no more. You're too old. You just an old man.

Troy (shoves him on his shoulder): Nigger! That's what you are. You just another nigger on the street to me!

Cory: You crazy! You know that?

Troy: Go on now! You got the devil in you. Get on away from me!

Cory: You just a crazy old man . . . talking about I got the devil in me.

Troy: Yeah, I'm crazy! If you don't get on the other side of that yard . . . I'm gonna show you how crazy I am! Go on . . . get the hell out of my yard.

Cory: It ain't your yard. You took Uncle Gabe's money he got from the army to buy this house and then you put him out.

Troy (advances on Cory): Get your black ass out of my yard!

(Troy's advance backs Cory up against the tree. Cory grabs up the bat.)

Cory: I ain't going nowhere! Come on . . . put me out! I ain't scared of you.

Troy: That's my bat!

Cory: Come on!

Troy: Put my bat down!

Cory: Come on, put me out.

(Cory swings at Troy, who backs across the yard.)

What's the matter? You so bad . . . put me out!

(Troy advances toward Cory.)

Cory (backing up): Come on! Come on!

Troy: You're gonna have to use it! You wanna draw that bat back on me . . . you're gonna have to use it.

Cory: Come on! . . . Come on!

(Cory swings the bat at Troy a second time. He misses. Troy continues to advance toward him.)

Troy: You're gonna have to kill me! You wanna draw that bat back on me. You're gonna have to kill me.

(Cory, backed up against the tree, can go no farther. Troy taunts him. He sticks out his head and offers him a target.)

Come on! Come on!

(Cory is unable to swing the bat. Troy grabs it.)

Troy: Then I'll show you.

(Cory and Troy struggle over the bat. The struggle is fierce and fully engaged. Troy ultimately is the stronger, and takes the bat from Cory and stands over him ready to swing. He stops himself.)

Go on and get away from around my house.

(Cory, stung by his defeat, picks himself up, walks slowly out of the yard and up the alley.)

Cory: Tell Mama I'll be back for my things.

Troy: They'll be on the other side of that fence.

(Cory exits.)

Troy: I can't taste nothing. Helluljah! I can't taste nothing no more. (*Troy assumes a batting posture and begins to taunt Death, the fastball on the outside corner.*) Come on! It's between you and me now! Come on! Anytime you want! Come on! I be ready for you . . . but I ain't gonna be easy.

(*The lights go down on the scene.*)

SCENE V

The time is 1965. The lights come up in the yard. It is the morning of Troy's funeral. A funeral plaque with a light hangs beside the door. There is a small garden plot off to the side. There is noise and activity in the house as Rose, Lyons, and Bono have gathered. The door opens and Raynell, seven years old, enters dressed in a flannel nightgown. She crosses to the garden and pokes around with a stick. Rose calls from the house.

Rose: Raynell!
Raynell: Mam?
Rose: What you doing out there?
Raynell: Nothing.

(*Rose comes to the door.*)

Rose: Girl, get in here and get dressed. What you doing?
Raynell: Seeing if my garden growed.
Rose: I told you it ain't gonna grow overnight. You got to wait.
Raynell: It don't look like it never gonna grow. Dag!
Rose: I told you a watched pot never boils. Get in here and get dressed.
Raynell: This ain't even no pot, Mama.
Rose: You just have to give it a chance. It'll grow. Now you come on and do what I told you. We got to be getting ready. This ain't no morning to be playing around. You hear me?
Raynell: Yes, Mam.

(*Rose exits into the house. Raynell continues to poke at her garden with a stick. Cory enters. He is dressed in a Marine corporal's uniform, and carries a duffelbag. His posture is that of a military man, and his speech has a clipped sternness.*)

Cory (to Raynell): Hi. (*Pause.*) I bet your name is Raynell.
Raynell: Uh huh.
Cory: Is your mama home?

(*Raynell runs up on the porch and calls through the screen door.*)

Raynell: Mama . . . there's some man out here. Mama?

(*Rose comes to the door.*)

Rose: Cory? Lord have mercy! Look here, you all!

(*Rose and Cory embrace in a tearful reunion as Bono and Lyons enter from the house dressed in funeral clothes.*)

Bono: Aw, looka here . . .
Rose: Done got all grown up!

Cory: Don't cry, Mama. What you crying about?

Rose: I'm just so glad you made it.

Cory: Hey Lyons. How you doing, Mr. Bono.

(*Lyons goes to embrace Cory.*)

Lyons: Look at you, man. Look at you. Don't he look good, Rose. Got them Corporal stripes.

Rose: What took you so long?

Cory: You know how the Marines are, Mama. They got to get all their paperwork straight before they let you do anything.

Rose: Well, I'm sure glad you made it. They let Lyons come. Your Uncle Gabe's still in the hospital. They don't know if they gonna let him out or not. I just talked to them a little while ago.

Lyons: A Corporal in the United States Marines.

Bono: Your daddy knew you had it in you. He used to tell me all the time.

Lyons: Don't he look good, Mr. Bono?

Bono: Yeah, he remind me of Troy when I first met him. (*Pause.*) Say, Rose, Lucille's down at the church with the choir. I'm gonna go down and get the pallbearers lined up. I'll be back to get you all.

Rose: Thanks, Jim.

Cory: See you, Mr. Bono.

Lyons (*with his arm around Raynell*): Cory . . . look at Raynell. Ain't she precious? She gonna break a whole lot of hearts.

Rose: Raynell, come and say hello to your brother. This is your brother, Cory. You remember Cory.

Raynell: No, Mam.

Cory: She don't remember me, Mama.

Rose: Well, we talk about you. She heard us talk about you. (*To Raynell.*) This is your brother, Cory. Come on and say hello.

Raynell: Hi.

Cory: Hi. So you're Raynell. Mama told me a lot about you.

Rose: You all come on into the house and let me fix you some breakfast. Keep up your strength.

Cory: I ain't hungry, Mama.

Lyons: You can fix me something, Rose. I'll be in there in a minute.

Rose: Cory, you sure you don't want nothing? I know they ain't feeding you right.

Cory: No, Mama . . . thanks. I don't feel like eating. I'll get something later.

Rose: Raynell . . . get on upstairs and get that dress on like I told you.

(*Rose and Raynell exit into the house.*)

Lyons: So . . . I hear you thinking about getting married.

Cory: Yeah, I done found the right one, Lyons. It's about time.

Lyons: Me and Bonnie been split up about four years now. About the time Papa retired. I guess she just got tired of all them changes I was putting her through. (*Pause.*) I always knew you was gonna make something out yourself. Your head was always in the right direction. So . . . you gonna stay in . . . make it a career . . . put in your twenty years?

Cory: I don't know. I got six already, I think that's enough.

Lyons: Stick with Uncle Sam and retire early. Ain't nothing out here. I guess Rose told you what happened with me. They got me down the workhouse. I thought I was being slick cashing other people's checks.

Cory: How much time you doing?

Lyons: They give me three years. I got that beat now. I ain't got but nine more months. It ain't so bad. You learn to deal with it like anything else. You got to take the crookeds with the straights. That's what Papa used to say. He used to say that when he struck out. I seen him strike out three times in a row . . . and the next time up he hit the ball over the grandstand. Right out there in Homestead Field. He wasn't satisfied hitting in the seats . . . he want to hit it over everything! After the game he had two hundred people standing around waiting to shake his hand. You got to take the crookeds with the straights. Yeah, Papa was something else.

Cory: You still playing?

Lyons: Cory . . . you know I'm gonna do that. There's some fellows down there we got us a band . . . we gonna try and stay together when we get out . . . but yeah, I'm still playing. It still helps me to get out of bed in the morning. As long as it do that I'm gonna be right there playing and trying to make some sense out of it.

Rose (calling): Lyons, I got these eggs in the pan.

Lyons: Let me go on and get these eggs, man. Get ready to go bury Papa. *(Pause.)* How you doing? You doing alright?

(Cory nods. Lyons touches him on the shoulder and they share a moment of silent grief. Lyons exits into the house. Cory wanders about the yard. Raynell enters.)

Raynell: Hi.

Cory: Hi.

Raynell: Did you used to sleep in my room?

Cory: Yeah . . . that used to be my room.

Raynell: That's what Papa call it. "Cory's room." It got your football in the closet.

(Rose comes to the door.)

Rose: Raynell, get in there and get them good shoes on.

Raynell: Mama, can't I wear these? Them other one hurt my feet.

Rose: Well, they just gonna have to hurt your feet for a while. You ain't said they hurt your feet when you went down to the store and got them.

Raynell: They didn't hurt then. My feet done got bigger.

Rose: Don't you give me no backtalk now. You get in there and get them shoes on.

(Raynell exits into the house.)

Ain't too much changed. He still got that piece of rag tied to that tree. He was out here swinging that bat. I was just ready to go back in the house. He swung that bat and then he just fell over. Seem like he swung it and stood there with this grin on his face . . . and then he just fell over. They carried him on down to the hospital, but I knew there wasn't no need . . . why don't you come on in the house?

Cory: Mama . . . I got something to tell you. I don't know how to tell you this . . . but I've got to tell you . . . I'm not going to Papa's funeral.

Rose: Boy, hush your mouth. That's your daddy you talking about. I don't want hear that kind of talk this morning. I done raised you to come to this? You standing there all healthy and grown talking about you ain't going to your daddy's funeral?

Cory: Mama . . . listen . . .

Rose: I don't want to hear it, Cory. You just get that thought out of your head.

Cory: I can't drag Papa with me everywhere I go. I've got to say no to him. One time in my life I've got to say no.

Rose: Don't nobody have to listen to nothing like that. I know you and your daddy ain't seen eye to eye, but I ain't got to listen to that kind of talk this morning. Whatever was between you and your daddy . . . the time has come to put it aside. Just take it and set it over there on the shelf and forget about it. Disrespecting your daddy ain't gonna make you a man, Cory. You got to find a way to come to that on your own. Not going to your daddy's funeral ain't gonna make you a man.

Cory: The whole time I was growing up . . . living in his house . . . Papa was like a shadow that followed you everywhere. It weighed on you and sunk into your flesh. It would wrap around you and lay there until you couldn't tell which one was you anymore. That shadow digging in your flesh. Trying to crawl in. Trying to live through you. Everywhere I looked, Troy Maxson was staring back at me . . . hiding under the bed . . . in the closet. I'm just saying I've got to find a way to get rid of that shadow, Mama.

Rose: You just like him. You got him in you good.

Cory: Don't tell me that, Mama.

Rose: You Troy Maxson all over again.

Cory: I don't want to be Troy Maxson. I want to be me.

Rose: You can't be nobody but who you are, Cory. That shadow wasn't nothing but you growing into yourself. You either got to grow into it or cut it down to fit you. But that's all you got to make life with. That's all you got to measure yourself against that world out there. Your daddy wanted you to be everything he wasn't . . . and at the same time he tried to make you into everything he was. I don't know if he was right or wrong . . . but I do know he meant to do more good than he meant to do harm. He wasn't always right. Sometimes when he touched he bruised. And sometimes when he took me in his arms he cut.

    When I first met your daddy I thought . . . Here is a man I can lay down with and make a baby. That's the first thing I thought when I seen him. I was thirty years old and had done seen my share of men. But when he walked up to me and said, "I can dance a waltz that'll make you dizzy," I thought, Rose Lee, here is a man that you can open yourself up to and be filled to bursting. Here is a man that can fill all them empty spaces you been tipping around the edges of. One of them empty spaces was being somebody's mother.

    I married your daddy and settled down to cooking his supper and keeping clean sheets on the bed. When your daddy walked through the house he was so big he filled it up. That was my first mistake. Not to make him leave some room for me. For my part in the matter. But at that time I wanted that. I wanted a house that I could sing in. And that's what your daddy gave me. I didn't know to keep up his strength I had to give up little pieces of mine. I did that. I took on his life as mine and mixed up the pieces so that you couldn't hardly tell which was which anymore. It was my choice. It was my life and I didn't have to live it like that. But that's what life offered me in the way of being a woman and I took it. I grabbed hold of it with both hands.

    By the time Raynell came into the house, me and your daddy had done lost touch with one another. I didn't want to make my blessing off of nobody's misfortune . . . but I took on to Raynell like she was all them babies I had wanted and never had.

(The phone rings.)

Like I'd been blessed to relive a part of my life. And if the Lord see fit to keep up my strength . . . I'm gonna do her just like your daddy did you . . . I'm gonna give her the best of what's in me.

Raynell (entering, still with her old shoes): Mama . . . Reverend Tolliver on the phone.

(Rose exits into the house.)

Raynell: Hi.
Cory: Hi.
Raynell: You in the Army or the Marines?
Cory: Marines.
Raynell: Papa said it was the Army. Did you know Blue?
Cory: Blue? Who's Blue?
Raynell: Papa's dog what he sing about all the time.
Cory (singing):

> Hear it ring! Hear it ring!
> I had a dog his name was Blue
> You know Blue was mighty true
> You know Blue was a good old dog
> Blue treed a possum in a hollow log
> You know from that he was a good old dog.
> Hear it ring! Hear it ring!

(Raynell joins in singing.)

Cory and Raynell:

> Blue treed a possum out on a limb
> Blue looked at me and I looked at him
> Grabbed that possum and put him in a sack
> Blue stayed there till I came back
> Old Blue's feets was big and round
> Never allowed a possum to touch the ground.
>
> Old Blue died and I dug his grave
> I dug his grave with a silver spade
> Let him down with a golden chain
> And every night I call his name
> Go on Blue, you good dog you
> Go on Blue, you good dog you.

Raynell:

> Blue laid down and died like a man
> Blue laid down and died . . .

Both:

> Blue laid down and died like a man
> Now he's treeing possums in the Promised Land
> I'm gonna tell you this to let you know
> Blue's gone where the good dogs go
> When I hear old Blue bark
> When I hear old Blue bark

Blue treed a possum in Noah's Ark
Blue treed a possum in Noah's Ark.

(Rose comes to the screen door.)

Rose: Cory, we gonna be ready to go in a minute.

Cory (to Raynell): You go on in the house and change them shoes like Mama told you so we can go to Papa's funeral.

Raynell: Okay, I'll be back.

(Raynell exits into the house. Cory gets up and crosses over to the tree. Rose stands in the screen door watching him. Gabriel enters from the alley.)

Gabriel (calling): Hey, Rose!

Rose: Gabe?

Gabriel: I'm here, Rose. Hey, Rose, I'm here!

(Rose enters from the house.)

Rose: Lord . . . Look here, Lyons!

Lyons: See, I told you, Rose . . . I told you they'd let him come.

Cory: How you doing, Uncle Gabe?

Lyons: How you doing, Uncle Gabe?

Gabriel: Hey, Rose. It's time. It's time to tell St. Peter to open the gates. Troy, you ready? You ready, Troy. I'm gonna tell St. Peter to open the gates. You get ready now.

(Gabriel, with great fanfare, braces himself to blow. The trumpet is without a mouthpiece. He puts the end of it into his mouth and blows with great force, like a man who has been waiting some twenty-odd years for this single moment. No sound comes out of the trumpet. He braces himself and blows again with the same result. A third time he blows. There is a weight of impossible description that falls away and leaves him bare and exposed to a frightful realization. It is a trauma that a sane and normal mind would be unable to withstand. He begins to dance. A slow, strange dance, eerie and life-giving. A dance of atavistic signature and ritual. Lyons attempts to embrace him. Gabriel pushes Lyons away. He begins to howl in what is an attempt at song, or perhaps a song turning back into itself in an attempt at speech. He finishes his dance and the gates of heaven stand open as wide as God's closet.)

That's the way that go!

BLACKOUT

August Wilson on Writing

A Look into Black America   1999

Interviewer: Is it a concern to effect social change with your plays?

Wilson: I don't write primarily to effect social change. I believe writing can do that, but that's not why I write. I work as an artist. However, all art is political in the sense that it serves the politics of someone. Here in America whites have a particular view of blacks, and I think my plays offer them a different and new way to look at black Americans. For instance, in *Fences* they see a garbageman, a person they really don't look at, although they may see a garbageman every day. By looking at Troy's life, white people find out that the content of this black garbageman's life is very similar to their own,

August Wilson

that he is affected by the same things—love, honor, beauty, betrayal, duty. Recognizing that these things are as much a part of his life as of theirs can be revolutionary and can affect how they think about and deal with black people in their lives.

Interviewer: How would that same play, *Fences*, affect a black audience?

Wilson: Blacks see the content of their lives being elevated into art. They don't always know that it is possible, and it's important to know that.

From "Interview with August Wilson"
by Bonnie Lyons and George Plimpton

Gabriel Garcia Márquez at work, c. 1970s.

WRITING

42

WRITING ABOUT LITERATURE

If one waits for the right time to come before writing, the right time never comes.

——JAMES RUSSELL LOWELL

What You Will Learn in This Chapter

- To read actively
- To plan, draft, and revise a literary argument
- To document your sources

Assigned to write an essay on *Hamlet*, a student might well wonder, "What can I say that hasn't been said a thousand times before?" Often the most difficult aspect of writing about a story, poem, or play is the feeling that we have nothing of interest to contribute to the ongoing conversation about some celebrated literary work. There's always room, though, for a reader's fresh take on an old standby.

Remember that, in the study of literature, common sense is never out of place. For most of a class hour, a professor once rhapsodized about the arrangement of the contents of W. H. Auden's *Collected Poems*. Auden, he claimed, was a master of thematic continuity, who had brilliantly placed the poems in the order that they best complemented each other. Near the end of the hour, his theories were punctured—with a great inaudible pop—when a student, timidly raising a hand, pointed out that Auden had arranged the poems in the book not by theme but in alphabetical order according to the first word of each poem. The professor's jaw dropped: "Why didn't you say that sooner?" The student was apologetic: "I—I was afraid I'd sound too *ordinary*."

Don't be afraid to state a conviction, though it seems obvious. Does it matter that you may be repeating something that, once upon a time or even just the other day, has been said before? What matters more is that you are actively engaged in thinking about literature. There are excellent old ideas as well as new ones. You have something to say.

READ ACTIVELY

Most people read in a relaxed, almost passive way. They let the story or poem carry them along without asking too many questions. To write about literature well, however, you need to *read actively*, paying special attention to various aspects of the text. This special sort of attention will not only deepen your enjoyment of the story, poem, or play but will also help generate the information and ideas that will become your final paper. How do you become an active reader? Here are some steps to get you started:

- ▪ **Preview the text.** To get acquainted with a work of literature before you settle in for a closer reading, skim it for an overview of its content and organization. Take a quick look at all parts of the work. Even a book's cover, preface, introduction, footnotes, and biographical notes about the author can provide you with some context for reading the work itself.

- ▪ **Take notes. Annotate the text.** Read with a highlighter and pencil at hand, making appropriate annotations to the text. Later, you'll easily be able to review these highlights, and, when you write your paper, quickly refer to supporting evidence.

  - Underline words, phrases, or sentences that seem interesting or important, or that raise questions.
  - Jot down brief notes in the margin ("*key symbol—this foreshadows the ending,*" for example, or "*dramatic irony*").
  - Use lines or arrows to indicate passages that seem to speak to each other—for instance, all the places in which you find the same theme or related symbols.

Robert Frost

Nothing Gold Can Stay

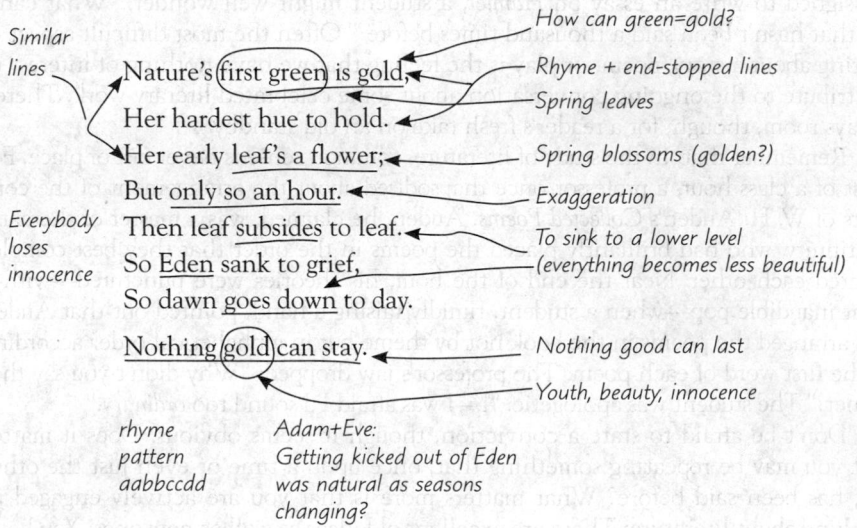

Similar lines

Nature's first green is gold,
Her hardest hue to hold.
Her early leaf's a flower;
But only so an hour.

Everybody loses innocence

Then leaf subsides to leaf.
So Eden sank to grief,
So dawn goes down to day.

Nothing gold can stay.

How can green=gold?
Rhyme + end-stopped lines
Spring leaves
Spring blossoms (golden?)
Exaggeration
To sink to a lower level
(everything becomes less beautiful)
Nothing good can last
Youth, beauty, innocence

rhyme pattern aabbccdd

Adam+Eve:
Getting kicked out of Eden was natural as seasons changing?

- ▪ **Read closely.** Once you have begun reading in earnest, don't skim or skip over words you don't recognize; sometimes, looking up those very words will unlock a piece's meaning.

- ▪ **Reread as needed.** If a piece is short, read it several times. Often, knowing the ending of a poem or short story will allow you to extract new meaning from its beginning and middle. If the piece is longer, reread the passages you thought important enough to highlight.

PLAN YOUR ESSAY

If you have actively reread the work you plan to write about and have made notes or annotations, you are already well on your way to writing your paper. Your mind has already begun to work through some initial impressions and ideas. Now you need to arrange those early notions into an organized and logical essay. Here is some advice on how to manage the writing process:

- **Leave yourself time.** Good writing involves thought and revision. Anyone who has ever been a student knows what it's like to pull an all-nighter, churning out a term paper hours before it is due. Still, the best writing takes time. Your ideas need to marinate. For the sake of your writing—not to mention your sanity—it's far better to get the job started well before your deadline.

- **Choose a subject you care about.** If you have been given a choice of literary works to write about, always choose the play, story, or poem that evokes the strongest emotional response. Your writing will be liveliest if you feel engaged by your subject.

- **Know your purpose.** As you write, keep the assignment in mind. You may have been asked to write a response, in which you describe your reactions to a literary work. Perhaps your purpose is to interpret a work, analyzing how one or more of its elements contribute to its meaning. You may have been instructed to write an evaluation, in which you judge a work's merits. Whatever the assignment, how you approach your essay will depend in large part on your purpose.

- **Think about your audience.** When you write journal entries or rough drafts, you may be composing for your own eyes only. More often, though, you are likely to be writing for an audience, even if it is an audience of one: your professor. Whenever you write for others, you need to be conscious of your readers. Your task is to convince them that your take on a work of literature is a plausible one. To do so, you need to keep your audience's needs and expectations in mind.

- **Define your topic narrowly.** Worried about having enough to say, students sometimes frame their topic so broadly that they can't do justice to it in the allotted number of pages. Your paper will be stronger if you go more deeply into a well-focused subject than if you choose a gigantic subject and touch on most aspects of it only superficially. A thorough explication of a short story is hardly possible in a 250-word paper, but an explication of a paragraph or two could work in that space. A profound topic ("The Character of Hamlet") might overflow a book, but a more focused one ("Hamlet's View of Acting" or "Hamlet's Puns") could result in a manageable paper.

PREWRITING: GENERATE IDEAS AND ISSUES

Topic in hand, you can begin to get your ideas on the page. To generate new ideas and clarify the thoughts you already have, try one or more of the following useful prewriting techniques:

- **Brainstorm.** Writing quickly, list everything that comes into your mind about your subject. Set a time limit—ten or fifteen minutes—and force yourself to keep adding items to the list, even when you think you have run out of things to say. Sometimes, if you press onward past the point where you feel you are finished, you will surprise yourself with new and fresh ideas.

> gold = early leaves/blossoms
> or gold = something precious (both?)
> early leaf = flower (yellow blossoms)
> spring (lasts an hour)
> leaves subside (sink to lower level)
> Eden = paradise = perfection = beauty
> Loss of innocence?
> What about original sin?
> dawn becomes day (dawn is more precious?)
> Adam and Eve had to fall? Part of natural order.
> seasons/days/people's lives
> title = last line: perfection can't last
> spring/summer/autumn
> dawn/day
> innocence can't last

■ **Cluster.** This prewriting technique works especially well for visual thinkers. In clustering, you build a diagram to help you explore the relationships among your ideas. To get started, write your subject at the center of a sheet of paper. Circle it. Then jot down ideas, linking each to the central circle with lines. As you write down each new idea, draw lines to link it to related old ideas. The result will look something like the following web.

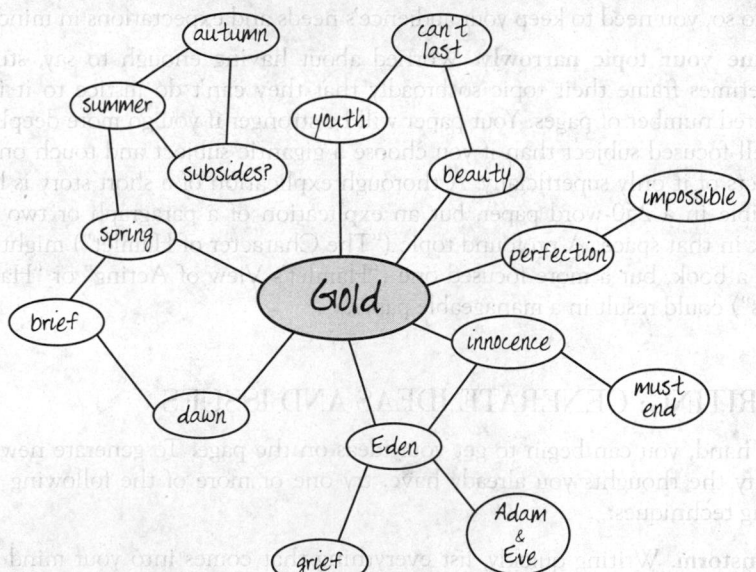

- **List.** Look over the notes and annotations that you made in your active reading of the work. You have probably already underlined or noted more information than you can possibly use. One way to sort through your material to find the most useful information is to make a list of the important items. It helps to make several short lists under different headings. Here are some lists you might make after rereading Frost's "Nothing Gold Can Stay." Don't be afraid to add more comments or questions on the lists to help your thought process.

Images	Colors
leaf ("early leaf")	green
flower	gold ("hardest hue to hold")
dawn	
day	
Eden	
gold	

Key Actions
gold is hard to hold
early leaf lasts only an hour
leaf subsides to leaf (what does this mean?)
Eden sinks to grief (paradise is lost)
dawn goes down to day
gold can't stay (perfection is impossible?)

- **Freewrite.** Most writers have snarky little voices in their heads, telling them that the words they're committing to paper aren't interesting or deep or elegant enough. To drown out those little voices, try freewriting. Give yourself a set amount of time (say, ten minutes) and write, nonstop, on your topic. Force your pen to keep moving or your fingers to keep typing, even if you have run out of things to say. If all you can think of to write is "I'm stuck" or "This is dumb," so be it. Keep writing and something else will most likely occur to you. Don't worry, yet, about grammar or spelling. When your time is up, read what you have written, highlighting the best ideas for later use.

> How can green be gold? By nature's first green, I guess he means the first
> leaves in spring. Are those leaves gold? They're more delicate and yellow
> than summer leaves . . . so maybe in a sense they look gold. Or maybe
> he means spring blossoms. Sometimes they're yellow. Also the first line
> seems to connect with the third one, where he comes right out and says
> that flowers are like early leaves. Still, I think he also means that the first
> leaves are the most precious ones, like gold. I don't think the poem wants
> me to take all of these statements literally. Flowers on trees last more than
> an hour, but that really beautiful moment in spring when blossoms are
> everywhere always ends too quickly, so maybe that's what he means by "only
> so an hour." I had to look up "subsides." It means to sink to a lower level . . . as
> if the later leaves will be less perfect than the first ones. I don't know if

I agree. Aren't fall leaves precious? Then he says, "So Eden sank to grief" which seems to be saying that Adam and Eve's fall would have happened no matter what they did, because everything that seems perfect falls apart . . . nothing gold can stay. Is he saying Adam and Eve didn't really have a choice? No matter what, everything gets older, less beautiful, less innocent . . . even people.

■ **Journal.** Your instructor might ask you to keep a journal in which you jot down your ideas, feelings, and impressions before they are fully formulated. Sometimes a journal is meant for your eyes only; in other instances your instructor might read it. Either way, it is meant to be informal and immediate, and to provide raw material that you may later choose to refine into a formal essay. Here are some tips for keeping a useful journal:

- Get your ideas down as soon as they occur to you.
- Write quickly.
- Jot down your feelings about and first impressions of the story, poem, or play you are reading.
- Don't worry about grammar, spelling, or punctuation.
- Don't worry about sounding academic.
- Don't worry about whether your ideas are good or bad ones; you can sort that out later.
- Try out invention strategies such as freewriting, clustering, and outlining.
- Keep writing, even after you think you have run out of things to say. You might surprise yourself.
- Write about what interests you most.
- Write in your journal on a regular basis.

For a more detailed explanation of how to approach journal writing, read Chapter 47, "Writing as Discovery: Keeping a Journal."

■ **Outline.** Some topics by their very nature suggest obvious ways to organize a paper. "An Explication of a Sonnet by Wordsworth" might mean simply working through the poem line by line. If this isn't the case, some kind of outline will probably prove helpful. Your outline needn't be elaborate to be useful. While a long research paper on several literary works might call for a detailed outline, a 500-word analysis of a short story's figures of speech might call for just a simple list of points in the order that makes the most logical sense—not necessarily the order in which those thoughts first came to mind.

1. Passage of time = fall from innocence
   blossoms
   gold
   dawn
   grief

2. Innocence = perfection
   Adam and Eve
   loss of innocence = inevitable
   real original sin = passing of time
   paradise sinks to grief

3. Grief = knowledge
        experience of sin & suffering
        unavoidable as grow older

DEVELOP YOUR ARGUMENT

Once you have finished a rough outline of your ideas, you need to refine it into a clear and logical shape. You need to state your thesis—your paper's main claim—clearly and then support it with logical and accurate evidence. Here is a practical approach to this crucial stage of the writing process:

- **Consider your purpose.** As you develop your argument, be sure to refer back to the specific assignment; let it guide you. Your instructor might request one of the following kinds of papers:

  - *Response,* in which you explore your reaction to a work of literature.
  - *Evaluation,* in which you assess the literary merits of a work.
  - *Interpretation,* in which you discuss a work's meaning. If your instructor has assigned an interpretation, he or she may have more specifically asked for an *analysis, explication,* or *comparison/contrast* essay, among other possibilities.

- **Remember your audience.** Practically speaking, your professor (and sometimes your classmates) will be your paper's primary audience. Some assignments may specify a particular audience beyond your professor and classmates. Keep your readers in mind. Be sure to adapt your writing to meet their needs and interests. If, for example, the audience has presumably already read a story under discussion, you won't need to relate the plot in its entirety. Instead, you will be free to bring up only those plot points that serve as evidence for your thesis.

- **Narrow your topic to fit the assignment.** Though you may be tempted to choose a broad topic so that you will have no shortage of things to say, remember that a good paper needs focus. Your choice should be narrow enough for you to do it justice in the space and time allotted.

- **Decide on a thesis: clearly state the paper's claim.** Just as you need to know your destination before you set out on a trip, you need to decide what point you're traveling toward before you begin your first draft. Start by writing a provisional thesis sentence: a summing up of the main idea or argument your paper will explore. While your thesis doesn't need to be outrageous or deliberately provocative, it does need to take a stand. A clear, decisive statement gives you something to prove and lends vigor to your essay.

  WORKING THESIS

  The poem argues that, like Adam and Eve, we all lose our innocence, and the passage of time is inevitable.

This first stab at a thesis sentence gave its author a sense of purpose and direction that allowed him to finish his first draft. Later, as he revised his essay, he found he needed to refine his thesis to make more specific and focused assertions.

STRENGTHEN YOUR ARGUMENT: RHETORICAL APPEALS

An argumentative essay states its thesis—its main claim—and tries to influence the reader's opinion. Argumentative essays have something in common with opinion pieces and editorials, as well as with most political speeches. All of these forms are used to try to convince people of something.

After you've formulated a thesis, your task is clear: you need to convince your audience that your thesis is correct. It will help to have an understanding of some key elements of argument as you write to persuade your reader. Effective argumentation requires you to combine logical reasoning with emotional appeals. Remember that you need to speak to both the reader's heart and mind. Additionally, you need to recognize that in any piece you write, your own credibility will be on display through your tone and manner.

Common approaches to effective argumentation—also called **rhetorical appeals**—are traditionally divided into three basic types:

■ *Logos* **(logical argumentation).** This approach persuades an audience through logic or reason. *Logos* is the part of an argument that appeals to the head, not the heart. Is the claim of your essay clear? Is the argumentation logical? Is the evidence you offer reasonable? *Logos* is the aspect of the argument a reader can most easily define and analyze. It is essential to get your logical argumentation right in order to convince a reader of your thesis.

■ *Pathos* **(emotional persuasion).** This approach evokes emotion or empathy. *Pathos* is the aspect of an argument that appeals to the heart. An argument that uses *pathos* creates an emotional response rather than an intellectual one. Logic alone is often not enough to convince a reader. If you can also make the reader respond with emotion, he or she is more likely to be convinced by your argument.

■ *Ethos* **(credibility).** This approach establishes the credibility or character of the writer or speaker. Obviously, readers are more likely to believe the argument of someone who is an established expert on the topic being discussed or someone they believe to be honorable and trustworthy. Credibility can be established through the tone and style of the essay itself, or independently, through the known reputation of the writer.

Logical Argumentation: Evidence and Organization

Logos or logical argumentation requires clear and compelling evidence in support of claims. Here are some pointers on building the logical structure of your argument:

■ **State your claims.** Your essay's main claim is your thesis—the central point of your paper. It should be clear, focused, and convincing. Your paper will be more interesting, though, if its main claim is not something entirely obvious. What is a claim? Any time you make a statement you intend to be taken as true, you have made a claim. Some claims are unlikely to be contradicted ("the sky is blue" or "today is Tuesday"), but others are debatable ("every college sophomore dreams of running off to see the world"). The process of supporting your claims will help you clarify and refine your ideas.

■ **Offer evidence.** When you offer a debatable claim, you should support it with evidence. When you write about a work of literature, the most convincing evidence generally comes from the text itself. Direct quotations from the poem, play, or story under discussion can provide particularly convincing support for your claims. Be sure to introduce any quotation by putting it in the context of the larger work. It is even more important to follow up each quotation with your own analysis of what it shows about the work.

- **Evaluate how well your evidence supports your claim.** If you were to make the claim that today's weather is absolutely perfect and offer as your evidence the blue sky, your logic would include an unspoken **assumption,** or **warrant**: sunny weather is perfect weather. Not everyone will agree with your example, though. Some folks (perhaps farmers) might prefer rain. In making any argument, including one about literature, you may find that you sometimes need to explain why your evidence is sound. This is especially true when the evidence you provide can lead to conclusions other than the one you are hoping to prove.

- **Refine your thesis as necessary.** If you find the evidence doesn't support certain aspects of your thesis, then refine the thesis. Remember: until you turn in your essay, it is a work in progress. Anything can and should be changed if it doesn't further the development of your paper's main idea.

- **Organize your argument.** Unless you are writing an explication that works its way line by line through an entire literary work, you will need to make crucial decisions about how to shape your essay. Its order should be driven by the logic of your argument, not by the structure of the story, play, or poem you're discussing. In other words, you need not work your way mechanically from start to finish through your source material, touching on every point. Instead, choose only the major points needed to prove your thesis, and present them in whatever order best supports your claim. A rough outline can help you to determine the best order.

Emotional Argumentation

Pathos, or emotional argumentation, requires you to go beyond simply presenting the logical elements of your argument. You also need to create an emotional connection and response in the reader that will lead him or her to support your point of view. Here are some pointers on building the emotional framework for your argument.

- **Create a human connection.** Don't let your entire essay consist of abstract argumentation and support. What emotions can you describe or invoke that will earn the reader's attention and endorsement? How do you use that emotion to support your point of view? Always remember that you are writing for your fellow human beings, not for a computer.

- **Observe and describe emotion.** When you write about a short story, poem, or play, there is almost always emotional content in the text. (Sometimes the emotions are explicit; sometimes they are mostly implied.) Observe how the author evokes and uses that *pathos* to express his or her meaning. Find an emotional element in the work you are discussing and describe it in a way that invites the reader to respond in a manner appropriate to your argument. Don't hesitate to communicate your own emotions, if they are relevant to your argument. Give an example or anecdote that conveys that emotion.

- **Review the role of emotion in your argumentation.** Once you have drafted your essay, review its emotional content. Do you use *pathos* to support any of your points? If so, do you use it effectively? (Unfocused emotion may actually undermine your logical arguments and credibility.) Revise your essay accordingly to strengthen its emotional connection to the reader. Find those points in your essay where you can make an emotional connection to support your reasoning. Find the right example to create emotional support for your argument.

Credibility: Tone and Balance

Ethos, or credibility, is the reader's sense of the author's character and reliability—how trustworthy does the author seem? When weighing the merits of any claim, you probably take into account the credibility of the person making the case. Often this happens almost automatically. An expert on any given topic has a certain brand of authority not available to most of us. Fortunately, there are other ways to establish your own credibility. To strengthen the credibility of your argument, you should also consider the following principles:

- **Keep your tone thoughtful.** Your reader will develop a sense of who you are through your words. If you come across as belligerent, flippant, or disrespectful to those inclined to disagree with your views, you may lose your reader's goodwill. If you seem to exaggerate your evidence, the reader will discount your credibility. Therefore, express your ideas calmly and thoughtfully. A level tone demonstrates that you are interested in thinking through an issue or idea, not in bullying your reader into submission.

- **Take opposing arguments into account.** To make an argument more convincing, demonstrate familiarity with other possible points of view. Doing so indicates that you have taken other claims into account before arriving at your thesis; it reveals your fairness as well as your understanding of your subject matter. In laying out other points of view, though, be sure to represent them fairly but also to respectfully make clear why your thesis is the soundest claim; you don't want your reader to doubt where you stand.

- **Demonstrate your knowledge.** To gain your reader's trust, it helps to demonstrate a solid understanding of your subject matter. Always check your facts; factual errors can call your knowledge into doubt. It also helps to have a command of the conventions of writing. Errors in punctuation, spelling, or grammar can undermine your credibility.

CHECKLIST: Developing an Argument

- ☐ What is your essay's purpose?
- ☐ Who is your audience?
- ☐ Is your topic narrow enough?
- ☐ Is your thesis interesting and thought-provoking?
- ☐ Is your thesis reasonable? Can you support it with logical evidence?
- ☐ Are there emotional elements or examples you can use to support your thesis?
- ☐ Does everything in your essay support your thesis?
- ☐ Have you considered and refuted alternative views?

☐ Is your tone thoughtful?
☐ Is your argument sensibly organized? Are similar ideas grouped together? Does one point lead logically to the next?

DRAFT YOUR ARGUMENT

Seated at last, you prepare to write, only to find yourself besieged with petty distractions. All of a sudden you remember a friend you had promised to call, some double-A batteries you were supposed to pick up, a neglected cup of coffee (in another room) growing colder by the minute. If your paper is to be written, you have only one course of action: collar these thoughts and for the moment banish them. Here are a few tips for writing your rough draft:

- **Review your argument.** The shape of your argument, its support, and the evidence you have collected will form the basis of your rough draft.

- **Get your thoughts down.** The best way to draft a paper is to get your ideas down quickly. At this stage, don't fuss over details. The critical, analytical side of your mind can worry about spelling, grammar, and punctuation later. For now, let your creative mind take charge. This part of yourself has the good ideas, insight, and confidence. Forge ahead. Believe in yourself and in your ideas.

- **Write the part you feel most comfortable with first.** There's no need to start at the paper's beginning and work your way methodically through to the end. Instead, plunge right into the parts of the paper you feel most prepared to write. You can always go back later and fill in the blanks.

- **Leave yourself plenty of space.** As you compose, leave plenty of space between lines and set wide margins. When you print out your draft, you will easily be able to go back and squeeze other thoughts in.

- **Focus on the argument.** As you jot down your first draft, you might not want to look at the notes you have compiled. When you come to a place where a note will fit, just insert a reminder to yourself such as "See card 19" or "See Aristotle on comedy." Also, whenever you bring up a new point, it's good to tie it back to your thesis. If you can't find a way to connect a point to your thesis, it's probably better to leave it out of your paper and come up with a point that advances your central claim.

- **Does your thesis hold up?** If, as you write, you find that most of the evidence you uncover is not helping you prove your paper's thesis, it may be that the thesis needs honing. Adjust it as needed.

- **Be open to new ideas.** Writing rarely proceeds in a straight line. Even after you outline your paper and begin to write and revise, expect to discover new thoughts—perhaps the best thoughts of all. If you do, be sure to invite them in.

SAMPLE STUDENT ROUGH DRAFT: ARGUMENT PAPER

Here is a student's rough draft for an argument essay on "Nothing Gold Can Stay."

On Robert Frost's "Nothing Gold Can Stay"

Most of the lines in the poem "Nothing Gold Can Stay" by Robert Frost focus on the changing of the seasons. The poem's first line says that the first leaves of spring are actually blossoms, and the actual leaves that follow are less precious. Those first blossoms only last a little while. The reader realizes that nature is a metaphor for a person's state of mind. People start off perfectly innocent, but as time passes, they can't help but lose that innocence. The poem argues that, like Adam and Eve, we all lose our innocence, and the passage of time is inevitable.

The poem's first image is of the color found in nature. The early gold of spring blossoms is nature's "hardest hue to hold." The color gold is associated with the mineral gold, a precious commodity. There's a hint that early spring is nature in its perfect state, and perfection is impossible to hold on to. To the poem's speaker, the colors of early spring seem to last only an hour. If you blink, they are gone. Like early spring, innocence can't last.

The line "leaf subsides to leaf" brings us from early spring through summer and fall. The golden blossoms and delicate leaves of spring subside, or sink to a lower level, meaning they become less special and beautiful. There's nothing more special and beautiful than a baby, so people are the same way. In literature, summer often means the prime of your life, and autumn often means the declining years. These times are less beautiful ones. "So dawn goes down to day" is a similar kind of image. Dawns are unbelievably colorful and beautiful but they don't last very long. Day is nice, but not as special as dawn.

The most surprising line in the poem is the one that isn't about nature. Instead it's about human beings. Eden may have been a garden (a part of nature), but it also represents a state of mind. The traditional religious view is that Adam and Eve chose to disobey God and eat from the tree of knowledge. They could have stayed in paradise forever if they had followed God's orders. So it's surprising that Frost writes "So Eden sank to grief" in a poem that is all about how inevitable change is. It seems like he's saying that no matter what Adam and Eve had done, the Garden of Eden wouldn't stay the paradise it started out being. When Adam and Eve ate the apple, they lost their innocence. The apple is supposed to represent knowledge, so they became wiser but less perfect. But the poem implies that no matter what Adam and Eve had done, they would have grown sadder and wiser. That's true for all people. We can't stay young and innocent.

It's almost as if Frost is defying the Bible, suggesting that there is no such thing as sin. We can't help getting older and wiser. It's a natural process. Suffering happens not because we choose to do bad things but because passing time takes our innocence. The real original sin is that time has to pass and we all have to grow wiser and less innocent.

The poem "Nothing Gold Can Stay" makes the point that people can't stay innocent forever. Suffering is the inevitable result of the aging process. Like the first leaves of spring, we are at the best at the very beginning, and it's all downhill from there.

REVISE YOUR ARGUMENT

A writer rarely—if ever—achieves perfection on the first try. For most of us, good writing is largely a matter of revision. Once your first draft is done, you can—and should—turn on your analytical mind. Painstaking revision is more than just tidying up grammar and spelling. It might mean expanding your ideas or sharpening the focus by cutting out any unnecessary thoughts. To achieve effective writing, you must have the courage to be merciless. Tear your rough drafts apart and reassemble their pieces into a stronger order. As you revise, consider the following:

- **Be sure your thesis—your argument's main claim—is clear, decisive, and thought-provoking.** The most basic ingredient in a good essay is a strong thesis—the sentence in which you summarize the claim you are making. Your thesis should say something more than just the obvious; it should be clear and decisive and make a point that requires evidence to persuade your reader to agree. A sharp, bold thesis lends energy to your argument. A revision of the working thesis used in the rough draft above provides a good example.

WORKING THESIS

The poem argues that, like Adam and Eve, we all lose our innocence, and the passage of time is inevitable.

This thesis may not be bold or specific enough to make for an interesting argument. A careful reader would be hard pressed to disagree with the observation that Frost's poem depicts the passage of time or the loss of innocence. In a revision of his thesis, however, the essay's author pushes the claim further, going beyond the obvious to its implications.

REVISED THESIS

In "Nothing Gold Can Stay," Frost makes a bold claim: sin, suffering, and loss are inevitable because the passage of time causes everyone to fall from grace.

Instead of simply asserting that the poem looks with sorrow on the passage of time, the revised thesis raises the issue of why this is so. It makes a more thought-provoking claim about the poem. An arguable thesis can result in a more energetic, purposeful essay. A thesis that is obvious to everyone, on the other hand, leads to a static, dull paper.

▪ **Ascertain whether the evidence you provide supports your argument.** Does everything within your paper work to support its thesis sentence? While a solid paper might be written about the poetic form of "Nothing Gold Can Stay," the student paper above would not be well served by bringing the subject up unless the author could show how the poem's form contributes to its message that time causes everyone to lose his or her innocence. If you find yourself including information that doesn't serve your argument, consider going back into the poem, story, or play for more useful evidence. On the other hand, if you're beginning to have a sneaking feeling that your thesis itself is shaky, consider reworking *it* so that it more accurately reflects the evidence in the text.

▪ **Check whether your argument is logical.** Does one point lead naturally to the next? Reread the paper, looking for logical fallacies, moments in which the claims you make are not sufficiently supported by evidence, or the connection between one thought and the next seems less than rational. Classic logical fallacies include making hasty generalizations, confusing cause and effect, or using a non sequitur, a statement that doesn't follow from the statement that precedes it. An example of two seemingly unconnected thoughts may be found in the second paragraph of the draft above:

> To the poem's speaker, the colors of early spring seem to last only an hour. If you blink, they are gone. Like early spring, innocence can't last.

Though there may well be a logical connection between the first two sentences and the third one, the paper doesn't spell that connection out. Asked to clarify the warrant, or assumption, that makes possible the leap from the subject of spring to the subject of innocence, the author revised the passage this way:

> To the poem's speaker, the colors of early spring seem to last only an hour. When poets write of seasons, they often also are commenting on the life cycle. To make a statement that spring can't last more than an hour implies that a person's youth (often symbolically associated with spring) is all too short. Therefore, the poem implies that innocent youth, like spring, lasts for only the briefest time.

The revised version spells out the author's thought process, helping the reader to follow the argument.

▪ **Supply transitional words and phrases.** To ensure that your reader's journey from one idea to the next is a smooth one, insert transitional words and phrases at the start of new paragraphs or sentences. Phrases such as "in contrast" and "however" signal a U-turn in logic, while those such as "in addition" and "similarly" alert the reader that you are continuing in the same direction you have been traveling. Seemingly inconsequential words and phrases such as "also" and "as well" or "as mentioned above" can smooth the reader's path from one thought to the next, as in the example that follows.

DRAFT

Though Frost is writing about nature, his real subject is humanity. In literature, spring often represents youth. Summer symbolizes young adulthood, autumn stands for middle age, and winter represents old age. The adult stages of life are, for Frost, less precious than childhood, which passes very quickly. The innocence of childhood is, like those spring leaves, precious as gold.

ADDING TRANSITIONAL WORDS AND PHRASES

Though Frost is writing about nature, his real subject is humanity. As mentioned above, in literature, spring often represents youth. Similarly, summer symbolizes young adulthood, autumn stands for middle age, and winter represents old age. The adult stages of life are, for Frost, less precious than childhood, which passes very quickly. Also, the innocence of childhood is, like those spring leaves, precious as gold.

- **Make sure each paragraph contains a topic sentence.** Each paragraph in your essay should develop a single idea; this idea should be conveyed in a topic sentence. As astute readers often expect to get a sense of a paragraph's purpose from its first few sentences, a topic sentence is often well placed at or near a paragraph's start.

- **Make a good first impression.** Your introductory paragraph may have seemed just fine as you began the writing process. Be sure to reconsider it in light of the entire paper. Does the introduction draw readers in and prepare them for what follows? If not, be sure to rework it, as the author of the rough draft above did. Look at his first paragraph again:

DRAFT OF OPENING PARAGRAPH

Most of the lines in the poem "Nothing Gold Can Stay" by Robert Frost focus on the changing of the seasons. The poem's first line says that the first leaves of spring are actually blossoms, and the actual leaves that follow are less precious. Those first blossoms only last a little while. The reader realizes that nature is a metaphor for a person's state of mind. People start off perfectly innocent, but as time passes, they can't help but lose that happy innocence. The poem argues that like Adam and Eve we all lose our innocence and the passage of time is inevitable.

While serviceable, this paragraph could be more compelling. Its author improved it by adding specifics to bring his ideas to more vivid life. For example, the rather pedestrian sentence "People start off perfectly innocent, but as time passes, they can't help but lose that innocence" became this livelier one: "As babies we are all perfectly innocent, but as time passes, we can't help but lose that innocence." By adding a specific image—the baby—the author gave the reader a visual picture to illustrate the abstract idea of innocence. He also sharpened his thesis sentence, making it less general and more thought-provoking. By varying the length of his sentences, he made the paragraph less monotonous.

REVISED OPENING PARAGRAPH

Most of the lines in Robert Frost's brief poem "Nothing Gold Can Stay" focus on nature: the changing of the seasons and the fading of dawn into day. The poem's opening line asserts that the first blossoms of spring are more precious than the leaves that follow. Likewise, dawn is more special than day. Though Frost's subject seems to be nature, the reader soon realizes that his real subject is human nature. As babies we are all perfectly innocent, but as time passes, we can't help but lose that happy innocence. In "Nothing Gold Can Stay," Frost makes a bold claim: sin, suffering, and loss are inevitable because the passage of time causes everyone to fall from grace.

■ **Remember that last impressions count too.** Your paper's conclusion should give the reader some closure, tying up the paper's loose ends without simply (and boringly) restating all that has come before. The author of the rough draft above initially ended his paper with a paragraph that repeated the paper's main ideas without pushing those ideas any further:

DRAFT OF CONCLUSION

The poem "Nothing Gold Can Stay" makes the point that people can't stay innocent forever. Grief is the inevitable result of the aging process. Like the first leaves of spring, we are at the best at the very beginning, and it's all downhill from there.

While revising his paper, the author realized that the ideas in his next-to-last paragraph would serve to sum up the paper. The new final paragraph doesn't simply restate the thesis; it pushes the idea further, in its last two sentences, by exploring the poem's implications.

REVISED CONCLUSION

Some people might view Frost's poem as sacrilegious because it seems to say that Adam and Eve had no choice; everything in life is doomed to fall. Growing less innocent and more knowing seems less a choice in Frost's view than a natural process like the changing of golden blossoms to green leaves. "Eden sank to grief" not because we choose to do evil things but because time takes away our innocence as we encounter the suffering and loss of human existence. Frost suggests that the real original sin is that time has to pass and we all must grow wiser and less innocent.

■ **Give your paper a compelling title.** Like the introduction, a title should be inviting to readers, giving them a sense of what's coming. "On Robert Frost's 'Nothing Gold Can Stay'" is a duller, less informative title than "Lost Innocence in Robert Frost's 'Nothing Gold Can Stay,'" which may spark the reader's interest and prepare him or her for what is to come.

CHECKLIST: Revising Your Argument

☐ Is your thesis clear? Can it be sharpened?

☐ Does all your evidence serve to advance the argument put forth in your thesis?

☐ Is your argument logical?

☐ Have you made an emotional connection with the reader?

☐ Does your presentation seem credible?

☐ Do transitional words and phrases signal movement from one idea to the next?

☐ Does each paragraph contain a topic sentence?

☐ Does your introduction draw the reader in? Does it prepare the reader for what follows?

☐ Does your conclusion tie up the paper's loose ends? Does it avoid merely restating what has come before?

☐ Is your title compelling?

FINAL ADVICE ON REWRITING

■ **Whenever possible, get feedback from a trusted reader.** In every project there comes a time when the writer has gotten so close to the work that he or she can't see it clearly. A talented roommate or a tutor in the campus writing center can tell you what isn't yet clear on the page, what questions still need answering, or what line of argument isn't yet as persuasive as it could be.

■ **Be willing to refine your thesis.** Once you have fleshed out your whole paper, you may find that your original thesis is not borne out by the rest of your argument. If so, you will need to rewrite your thesis so that it more precisely fits the evidence at hand.

■ **Be prepared to question your whole approach to a work of literature.** On occasion, you may even need to entertain the notion of throwing everything you have written into the wastebasket and starting over again. Occasionally having to start from scratch is the lot of any writer.

■ **Rework troublesome passages.** Look for skimpy paragraphs of one or two sentences—evidence that your ideas might need more fleshing out. Can you supply more evidence, more explanation, more examples or illustrations?

■ **Cut out any unnecessary information.** Everything in your paper should serve to further its thesis. Delete any sentences or paragraphs that detract from your focus.

■ **Aim for intelligent clarity when you use literary terminology.** Critical terms can help sharpen your thoughts and make them easier to handle. Nothing is less sophisticated or more opaque, however, than too many technical terms thrown together for grandiose effect: "The mythic *symbolism* of this *archetype* is the *antithesis* of the *dramatic situation*." Choose plain words you're already at ease with. When you use specialized terms, do so to smooth the way for your reader—to make your meaning more precise. It is less cumbersome, for example, to refer to the *tone* of a story than to say, "the way the author makes you feel what she is talking about."

■ **Set your paper aside for a while.** Even an hour or two away from your essay can help you see it with fresh eyes. Remember that the literal meaning of "revision" is "seeing again."

■ **Finally, carefully read your paper one last time to edit it.** Now it's time to sweat the small stuff. Check any uncertain spellings, scan for run-on sentences and fragments, pull out a weak word and send in a stronger one. Like soup stains on a job interviewee's tie, finicky errors distract from the overall impression and prejudice your reader against your essay.

SAMPLE STUDENT ARGUMENT PAPER

Here is the revised version of the student paper we have been examining.

Gabriel 1

Noah Gabriel
Professor James
English 2171
7 December 2019

Lost Innocence in
Robert Frost's "Nothing Gold Can Stay"

Most of the lines in Robert Frost's brief poem "Nothing Gold Can Stay" focus on nature: the changing of the seasons and the fading of dawn into day. The poem's opening line asserts that the first blossoms of spring are more precious than the leaves that follow. Likewise, dawn is more special than day. Though Frost's subject seems to be nature, the reader soon realizes that his real subject is human nature. As babies we are all perfectly innocent, but as time passes, we can't help but lose that happy innocence. In "Nothing Gold Can Stay," Frost makes a bold claim: sin, suffering, and loss are inevitable because the passage of time causes everyone to fall from grace.

Thesis sentence states the main claim

The poem begins with a deceptively simple sentence: "Nature's first green is gold." The subject seems to be the first, delicate leaves of spring which are less green and more golden than summer leaves. However, the poem goes on to say, "Her early leaf's a flower" (line 3), indicating that Frost is describing the first blossoms of spring. In fact, he's describing both the new leaves and blossoms. Both are as rare and precious as the mineral gold. They are precious because they don't last long; the early gold of spring blossoms is nature's "hardest hue to hold" (2). Early spring is an example of nature in its perfect state, and

Logos: Textual evidence backs up thesis

Gabriel 2

perfection is impossible to hold on to. To the poem's speaker, in fact, the colors of early spring seem to last only an hour. When poets write of seasons, they often also are commenting on the life cycle. To make a statement that spring can't last more than an hour implies that a person's youth (often symbolically associated with spring) is all too short. Therefore, the poem implies that innocent youth, like spring, lasts for only the briefest time.

While Frost takes four lines to describe the decline of the spring blossoms, he picks up the pace when he describes what happens next. The line "Then leaf subsides to leaf" (5) brings us from early spring through summer and fall, compressing three seasons into a single line. Just as time seems to pass slowly when we are children, and then much more quickly when we grow up, the poem moves quickly once the first golden moment is past. The word "subsides" feels important. The golden blossoms and delicate leaves of spring subside, or sink to a lower level, meaning they become less special and beautiful.

Though Frost is writing about nature, his real subject is humanity. As mentioned above, in literature, spring often represents youth. Similarly, summer symbolizes young adulthood, autumn stands for middle age, and winter represents old age. The adult stages of life are, for Frost, less precious than childhood, which passes very quickly, as we later realize. Also, the innocence of childhood is, like those spring leaves, precious as gold.

Frost shifts his view from the cycle of the seasons to the cycle of a single day to make a similar point. Just as spring turns to summer, "So dawn goes down to day" (7). Like spring, dawn is unbelievably colorful and beautiful but doesn't last very long. Like "subsides," the phrase "goes down" implies that full daylight is actually a falling off from dawn. As beautiful as daylight is, it's ordinary, while dawn is special because it is more fleeting.

Among these natural images, one line stands out: "So Eden sank to grief" (6). This line is the only one in the poem that deals directly with human beings. Eden may have been a garden (a part of nature) but it represents a state of mind—perfect innocence. In the traditional religious view, Adam and Eve chose to disobey God by eating an apple from the tree of knowledge. They were presented with a choice: to be obedient and remain in paradise forever, or to disobey God's order. People often speak of that first choice as "original sin." In this religious view, "Eden sank to grief" because the first humans chose to sin.

Frost, however, takes a different view. He compares the Fall of Man to the changing of spring to summer, as though it was as inevitable as the passage

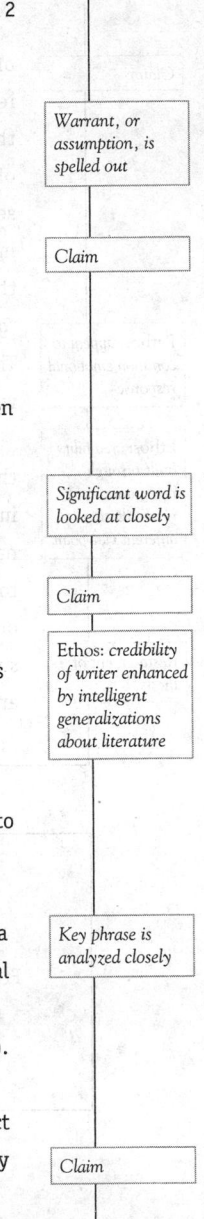

Warrant, or assumption, is spelled out

Claim

Significant word is looked at closely

Claim

Ethos: credibility of writer enhanced by intelligent generalizations about literature

Key phrase is analyzed closely

Claim

Gabriel 3

Claim

of time. The poem implies that no matter what Adam and Eve did, they couldn't remain in paradise. Original sin in Frost's view seems less a voluntary moral action than a natural, if unhappy sort of maturation. The innocent perfection of the garden of Eden couldn't possibly last. The apple represents knowledge, so in a symbolic sense God wanted Adam and Eve to stay unknowing, or innocent. But the poem implies that it was inevitable that Adam and Eve would gain knowledge and lose their innocence, becoming wiser but less perfect. They lost Eden and encountered "grief," the knowledge of suffering and loss associated with the human condition.

Pathos: appeal to common emotional response

This is certainly true for the rest of us human beings. As much as we might like to, we can't stay young or innocent forever.

Ethos: credibility built through recognition and reconciliation of different viewpoint

Some people might view Frost's poem as sacrilegious because it seems to say that Adam and Eve had no choice; everything in life is doomed to fall. Growing less innocent and more knowing seems less a choice, however, in Frost's view than a natural process like the changing of golden blossoms to green leaves. "Eden sank to grief" not because we choose to do evil things but because time takes away

Restatement of thesis

our innocence as we encounter the suffering and loss of human existence. Frost suggests that the real original sin is that time has to pass and we all must grow wiser and less innocent.

Gabriel 4

Works Cited

Frost, Robert. "Nothing Gold Can Stay." *Literature: An Introduction to Fiction, Poetry, Drama, and Writing*, edited by X. J. Kennedy et al., 14th ed., Pearson, 2020, p. 1762.

DOCUMENT SOURCES TO AVOID PLAGIARISM

Certain literary works, because they offer intriguing difficulties, have attracted professional critics by the score. On library shelves, great phalanxes of critical books now stand at the side of James Joyce's *Ulysses* and T. S. Eliot's allusive poem *The Waste Land*. The student who undertakes to study such works seriously is well advised to profit from the critics' labors. Chances are, too, that even in discussing a relatively uncomplicated work, you will want to seek the aid of some critics.

If you do so, you may find yourself wanting to borrow quotations for your own papers. This is a fine thing to do—provided you give credit for those words to their rightful author. To do otherwise is plagiarism—a serious offense—and most English instructors are likely to recognize it when they see it. In any but the most superlative student paper, a brilliant (or even not so brilliant) phrase from a renowned critic is likely to stand out like a golf ball in a garter snake's midriff.

To avoid plagiarism, you must reproduce the text you are using with quotation marks around it, and give credit where it is due. Even if you summarize a critic's idea in your own words, rather than quoting his or her exact words, you have to give credit to your source. Chapter 46, "Writing a Research Paper," will discuss the topic of properly citing your sources in greater depth. For now, students should simply remember that claiming another's work as one's own is the worst offense of the learning community. It negates the very purpose of education, which is to learn to think for oneself.

THE FORM OF YOUR FINISHED PAPER

If your instructor has not specified the form of your finished paper, follow these commonly accepted guidelines:

- Choose standard letter-size ($8\frac{1}{2} \times 11$) white paper.
- Use standard, easy-to-read type fonts, such as Times New Roman or Garamond. Be sure the italic type style contrasts with the regular style.
- Give your name, your instructor's name, the course number, and the date at the top left-hand corner of your first page, starting one inch from the top.
- On all pages, insert a header—your last name and the page number—in the upper right-hand corner, one-half inch from the top.
- Remember to give your paper a title that reflects your thesis.
- Leave one inch of margin on all four sides of each page.
- If you include a works-cited section, begin it on a new page.
- Double-space all your text, including quotations, notes, and the works-cited page.
- Italicize the titles of longer works—books, plays, periodicals, and book-length poems such as *The Odyssey*. The titles of shorter works—poems, articles, or short stories—should appear in quotation marks.

SPELL-CHECK AND GRAMMAR-CHECK PROGRAMS

Most computer software includes a program to automatically check spelling. While such programs make proofreading easier, there are certain kinds of errors they won't catch. Words that are perfectly acceptable in other contexts but not the ones you intended ("is" where you meant "in," or "he" where you meant "the") will slip by undetected, making it clear to your instructor that your computer—and not you—did the proofreading. This is why it's still crucial that you proofread and correct your papers the old-fashioned way—read them yourself.

Another common problem is that the names of most authors, places, and special literary terms won't be in many standard spell-check memories. Unfamiliar words will be identified during the spell-check process, but you still must check all proper nouns carefully, so that Robert Forst, Gwendolyn Broks, or Emily Dickensen doesn't make an unauthorized appearance midway in your otherwise exemplary paper. As the well-known authors Dina Gioia, Dan Goia, Dana Glola, Dona Diora, and Dana Gioia advise, always check the spelling of names.

As an example of the kinds of mistakes your spell-checker won't catch, here are some cautionary verses that have circulated on the Internet. (Based on a charming piece of light verse by Jerrold H. Zar, "Candidate for a Pullet Surprise," this version reflects additions and revisions by numerous anonymous Internet collaborators.)

A Little Poem Regarding Computer Spell-Checkers

2000?

Eye halve a spelling checker
    It came with my pea sea
It plainly marques four my revue
    Miss steaks eye kin knot sea.

Eye strike a key and type a word   5
    And weight four it two say
Weather eye am wrong oar write
    It shows me strait a weigh.

As soon as a mist ache is made
    It nose bee fore two long   10
And eye can put the error rite
    Its rare lea ever wrong.

Eye have run this poem threw it
    I am shore your pleased two no
Its letter perfect awl the weigh   15
    My checker tolled me sew.

Another mixed blessing is the grammar-check program that highlights sentences containing obvious grammatical mistakes. Unfortunately, if you don't know what is wrong with your sentence in the first place, the grammar program won't always tell you. You can try reworking the sentence until the highlighting disappears (indicating that it's now grammatically correct). Better still, you can take steps to ensure that you have a good grasp of grammar already. Most colleges offer brief refresher courses in grammar, and, of course, writers' handbooks with grammar rules are readily available. Still, the best way to improve your grammar, your spelling, and your general command of language is to read widely and well.

To that end, we urge you to read the works of literature collected in this book beyond those texts assigned to you by your teacher. A well-furnished mind is a great place to live, an address you'll want to have forever.

43

WRITING ABOUT
A STORY

Don't write merely to be understood.
Write so that you cannot possibly be misunderstood.

—ROBERT LOUIS STEVENSON

What You Will Learn in This Chapter

- To read a story actively
- To plan, draft, and revise a literary argument about fiction
- To write a fiction analysis, explication, comparison and contrast, and response paper

Writing about fiction presents its own set of challenges and rewards. Because a well-wrought work of fiction can catch us up in the twists and turns of its plot, we may be tempted to read it in a trance, passively letting its plot wash over us, as we might watch an entertaining film. Or, because stories, even short ones, unfold over time, there is often so much to say about them that narrowing down and organizing your thoughts can seem daunting.

To write compellingly about fiction, you need to read actively, identify a meaningful topic, and focus on making a point about which you feel strongly. (For pointers on finding a topic, organizing, writing, and revising your paper, see the previous chapter, "Writing About Literature." Some methods especially useful for writing about stories are described in the present chapter.)

In this chapter much of the discussions and many of the examples refer to Edgar Allan Poe's short story "The Tell-Tale Heart" (Chapter 12). If you haven't already read it, you can do so in only a few minutes, so that the rest of this chapter will make more sense to you.

READ ACTIVELY

Unlike a brief poem or a painting that you can take in with one long glance, a work of fiction—even a short story—may be too complicated to hold all at once in the mind's eye. Before you can write about it, you may need to give it two or more careful readings, and even then, as you begin to think further about it, you will probably have to thumb through it to reread passages. The first time through, it is best just to read attentively, open to whatever pleasure and wisdom the story may afford. The second time, you will find it useful to read with pencil in hand, either to mark your text or to take notes to jog your memory. To work out the design and meaning of a story need not be a boring chore, any more than it is to land a fighting fish and to study it with admiration.

- **Read the story at least twice.** The first time through, allow yourself just to enjoy the story—to experience surprise and emotion. Once you know how the tale ends, you'll find it easier to reread with some detachment, noticing details you may have glossed over the first time.

- **Annotate the text.** Reread the story, taking notes in the margins or highlighting key passages as you go. When you sit down to write, you probably will have to skim the story to refresh your memory, and those notes and highlighted passages should prove useful. Here is a sample of an annotated passage, from paragraph 3 of Edgar Allan Poe's "The Tell-Tale Heart."

Who is his listener?

    Now this is the point. You fancy me mad. Madmen know nothing. *Is this true?*

But you should have seen *me*. You should have seen how wisely I proceeded—with what caution—with what foresight—with what dissimulation I went to work! I was never kinder to the old man than during the whole week before I killed him. And every night, about midnight, I turned the latch of his door and opened it—oh, so gently! And then, *He's not so mad he doesn't know what he's doing*

when I had made an opening sufficient for my head, I put in a dark lantern, all closed, closed, so that no light shone out, and then I thrust in my head. Oh, you would have laughed to see how cunningly I thrust it in! I moved it slowly—very, very slowly, so that I might not disturb *He's strangely happy/ excited*

the old man's sleep. It took me an hour to place my whole head within the opening so far that I could see him as he lay upon his bed. Ha!—would a

Careful planning madman have been so wise as this? And then, when my head was well in the room, I undid the lantern cautiously—oh, so cautiously—cautiously

(for the hinges creaked)—I undid it just so much that a single thin ray *Creepy image. Who is the vulture here?*

fell upon the vulture eye. And this I did for seven long nights—every

What did he expect?! night just at midnight—but I found the eye always closed; and so it was

impossible to do the work; for it was not the old man who vexed me, but

his Evil Eye *Peculiar obsession*

THINK ABOUT THE STORY

Once you have reread the story, you can begin to process your ideas about it. To get started, try the following steps:

- **Identify the protagonist and the conflict.** Whose story is being told? What does that character desire more than anything else? What stands in the way of that character's achievement of his or her goal? The answers to these questions can give you a better handle on the story's plot.

- **Consider the story's point of view.** What does it contribute to the story? How might the tale change if told from another point of view?

- **Think about the setting.** Does it play a significant role in the plot? How does setting affect the story's tone?

- **Notice key symbols.** If any symbols catch your attention as you go, be sure to highlight each place in which they appear in the text. What do these symbols contribute to the story's meaning? (Remember, not every image is a symbol—only those important recurrent persons, places, or things that seem to suggest more than their literal meaning.)

- **Look for the theme.** Is the story's central meaning stated directly? If not, how does it reveal itself?

- **Think about tone and style.** How would you characterize the style in which the story is written? Consider elements such as diction, sentence structure, tone, and organization. How does the story's style contribute to its tone?

PREWRITING: GENERATE IDEAS AND ISSUES

Once you have given the story some preliminary thought, it is time to write as a means of discovering what it is you have to say. Brainstorming, clustering, listing, freewriting, keeping a journal, and outlining all can help you clarify your thoughts about the story and, in doing so, generate ideas for your paper. While you don't need to use *all* these techniques, try them to find the one or two that work best for you.

- **Brainstorm.** If you aren't sure what, exactly, to say about a story, try jotting down everything you can think of about it. Work quickly, without pausing to judge what you have written. Set yourself a time limit of ten or fifteen minutes and keep writing even if you think you have said it all. A list that results from brainstorming on "The Tell-Tale Heart" might look something like this:

> madness? seems crazy
> unreliable narrator
> Could story be a dream?
> Could heartbeat be supernatural?
> heartbeat = speaker's paranoia
> tone: dramatic, intense, quick mood changes
> glee/terror
> lots of exclamation points
> telling his story to listener
> old man = father? boss? friend?

old man's gold/treasures
old man's eye = motive
vulture eye = symbolic
calls plotting murder "work"
careful/patient
chops up body
perfect crime
policemen don't hear heartbeat
guilt makes him confess

■ **Cluster.** Clustering involves generating ideas by diagramming the relationship among your many ideas. First, write your subject at the center of a sheet of paper and circle it. Then, jot down ideas as they occur to you, drawing lines to link each idea to related ones. Here is an example of how you might cluster your ideas about "The Tell-Tale Heart."

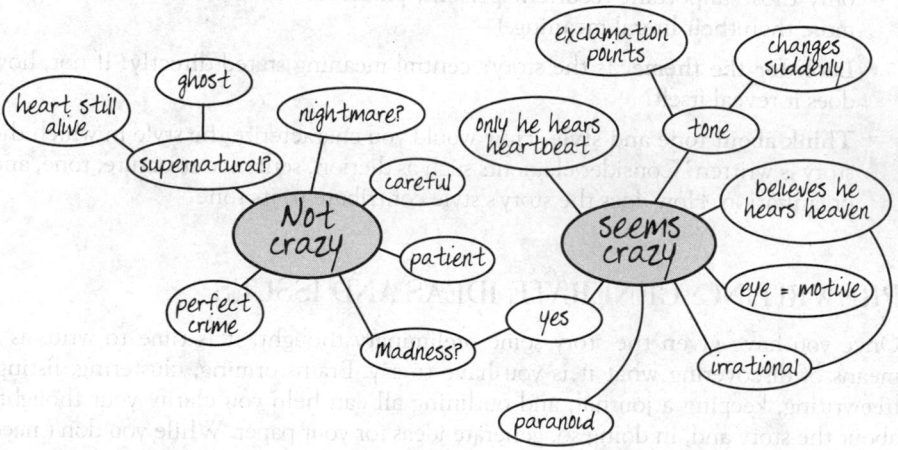

■ **List.** Using your notes and annotations as a guide, list information that seems useful, adding any notes that help you to keep track of your thought process. Use different headings to organize related concepts. Your lists might look something like this:

<u>Unreliable Narrator</u>
mood swings
insists too much on being sane
confusion
disease
sharpened senses
loved old man
murder
patience
guilt
hearing things

<u>Other Possibilities</u>
nightmare
supernatural
heart still alive?
ghost's heartbeat?

- **Freewrite.** Before you try to write a coherent first draft of your essay, take time to write freely, exploring your ideas as they occur to you. Writing quickly, without thinking too hard about grammar or spelling, can call forth surprising new ideas that wouldn't arrive if you were composing in a more reflective, cautious manner. To freewrite, give yourself a set amount of time—fifteen or twenty minutes. Put your pen to paper (or your fingers to the keyboard) and write without pausing to think. Keep going even if you run out of things to say. A freewrite on "The Tell-Tale Heart" might look like this:

> The guy seems crazy. He keeps insisting he's sane, so maybe others have accused him of being insane. He's speaking to someone—a judge? a fellow inmate? The story feels spoken out loud, like a dramatic monologue. His mood changes really quickly. One minute he's gleeful, and then impatient, then terrified. The story is full of dashes and exclamation points. He says he can hear everything in heaven and earth and even some things in hell. That seems crazy. His disease has sharpened his senses. Is he the old man's son, or his employee? I don't think the story says. It does say he loves the old man but he's obsessed with the vulture eye. He describes it in detail. It sounds like a blind eye, but it makes him more paranoid than the old man's other eye which probably can see. The things that freak the narrator out are little things—body parts, an eye and a heart. He's really careful in planning the murder. This is supposed to mean he is sane, but don't mentally ill people sometimes hatch careful plots and pay attention to detail? He says his senses are sharp but maybe he's hearing things that aren't there?

- **Journal.** If your instructor has asked you to keep a reading journal, don't forget to look back at it for your first responses to the story. Doing so may jog your memory and provide raw material for your essay.

- **Outline.** Some writers organize their papers by trial and error, writing them and going back in, cutting out useless material and filling in what seems to be missing. For a more efficient approach to organization, though, try making an outline—a simple list of points arranged in an order that makes logical sense. Such an outline might look like this:

1. Point of view is ironic (speaker is mad/unreliable)
    hears things in heaven/hell
    excited tone
    focus on strange detail
2. Can we trust story really happened?
    nightmare?
    more interesting if actual
3. Supernatural elements?
    ghost heartbeat?
    heart still alive?
4. More interesting/believable if speaker is mad

DRAFT YOUR ARGUMENT

Once your prewriting exercises have sparked an idea or two, you will be ready to begin shaping your thoughts into a rough draft. Refer to the section "Develop Your Argument" in Chapter 42 for help getting started. You can still keep your approach loose and informal; don't worry yet about phrasing things perfectly or pinning down the ideal word. For now, your goal is to begin finding a shape for your argument.

- **Remember your purpose.** Before you begin work on your first draft, be sure to check the assignment you have been given. There is no sense in writing even the most elegant *analysis* (in which you focus on one particular element of a story) if you have been told to write an *explication* (a detailed, line-by-line interpretation of a passage).

- **Consider your audience.** Though your professor and classmates will likely be your paper's actual audience, the assignment might specify hypothetical readers. Whoever your audience may be, keep their needs in mind as you write.

- **Formulate your thesis: clearly state your paper's claim.** Before you get going on your rough draft, you will need a thesis sentence summing up your paper's main claim. Begin with a provisional thesis to give your argument direction. As you write, be sure to keep your provisional thesis in mind; doing so will help you stay on track. Here is a working thesis for a paper on "The Tell-Tale Heart":

    WORKING THESIS

    The story contains many hints that the narrator of "The Tell-Tale Heart" is crazy.

    While this thesis gives its author something to work toward, it isn't yet as sharp as it could be. Most readers would agree that the story's narrator shows obvious signs of insanity. A more compelling thesis would go into the specifics of what, exactly, gives away the narrator's madness, or it might spell out the implications of this madness for the story. The following reworked version of this thesis sentence does both:

    REVISED THESIS

    The narrator's tenuous hold on reality and his wild shifts in mood indicate that he is insane and, therefore, that his point of view is untrustworthy.

    Like this statement, your thesis should be decisive and specific. As you write a rough draft, your task is to persuade readers of the wisdom of your thesis.

- **Support your argument with evidence.** The bulk of your essay should be spent providing evidence that proves your thesis. Because the most persuasive evidence tends to be that which comes from the story itself, be sure to quote as needed. As you flesh out your argument, check back frequently to make sure your thesis continues to hold up to the evidence. If you find that the facts of the story don't bear out your thesis, the problem may be with the evidence or with the thesis itself. Could your point be better proved by presenting different evidence? If so, exchange what you have for more convincing information. If not, go back in and refine your thesis sentence. Then make sure that the rest of the evidence bears out your new and improved thesis.

- **Organize your argument.** Choose the points you need to prove your thesis and present them, along with supporting evidence, in whatever order best makes your case. A rough outline is often a useful tool.

- **Identify and address possible objections to your argument.** What are the possible objections to your argument? Consider opposing points of view and refute them to support your argument.

CHECKLIST: Drafting Your Argument

- ☐ What is your essay's purpose?
- ☐ Who is your audience? What do they need to know?
- ☐ What is your main claim? Is it arguable?
- ☐ Does everything in your essay support your thesis?
- ☐ Is your argument sensibly organized?
- ☐ Do you identify and address possible objections to your argument?

REVISE YOUR DRAFT

Once your first draft has been committed to paper, you will need to begin revising—going back in and reworking it to make the argument as persuasive and the prose as seamless as can be. First, though, it is an excellent idea to get feedback on your draft from a trusted reader—a classmate, a roommate, a tutor in your school's writing center, or even your instructor—who can tell you which ideas are, and are not, coming across clearly, or where your argument is persuasive and where it could be more convincing. For writers at all levels of expertise, there simply is no substitute for constructive criticism from a thoughtful reader. If, however, you find readers are in short supply, put your rough draft away for at least an hour or two, and reread it with fresh eyes before you begin revising.

   The following is an example of how one student used his instructor's comments to improve his paper's opening paragraph. (The final paper appears later in the chapter.)

DRAFT OF OPENING PARAGRAPH

The narrator of Edgar Allan Poe's "The Tell-Tale Heart"   *Provide specifics.*

is a very mysterious and murderous character. The reader

Tell me more! doesn't know much about him, except for how he speaks   *Why is this important?*

and what he has to say for himself. There is one (important fact)

What are some of these? revealed by evidence in the story. The story contains

many hints that the narrator of "The Tell-Tale Heart" is crazy.

REVISED OPENING PARAGRAPH

Although there are many things we do not know about the narrator of Edgar Allan Poe's story "The Tell-Tale Heart"—is he a son? a servant? a companion?—there is one thing we are sure of from the start. He is mad. In the opening paragraph, Poe makes the narrator's condition unmistakable, not only from his excited and worked-up speech (full of dashes and exclamation points), but also from his wild claims. He says it is merely some disease which has sharpened his senses that has made people call him crazy. Who but a madman, however, would say, "I heard all things in the heaven and in the earth," and brag how his ear is a kind of radio, listening in on hell? The narrator's tenuous hold on reality and his wild shifts in mood indicate that he is mad and, therefore, that his point of view is untrustworthy.

Remember that revision means more than just cleaning up typos and doing away with stray semicolons. Revision might mean fleshing out your ideas with new paragraphs, rearranging material, or paring away passages that detract from your focus. As you rewrite, make sure every paragraph has a topic sentence that announces its main idea. Feel free to link your ideas with transitional words and phrases such as "moreover," "in addition," or "in contrast" to help your reader understand how each new idea relates to the one that precedes it.

CHECKLIST: Revising Your Argument

- ☐ Is your thesis clear? Does it say something significant but not entirely obvious about the story?
- ☐ Does all your evidence serve to advance the argument put forth in your thesis?
- ☐ Is your argument clear and logical?
- ☐ Have you made an emotional connection with the reader?
- ☐ Does your presentation seem credible?
- ☐ Do transitional words and phrases help signal movement from one idea to the next?
- ☐ Does your introduction draw the reader in? Does it prepare the reader for what follows?
- ☐ Does your conclusion tie up the paper's loose ends? Does it avoid merely restating what has come before?
- ☐ Does each paragraph contain a topic sentence?
- ☐ Does the paper have an interesting and compelling title?

WHAT'S YOUR PURPOSE? COMMON APPROACHES TO WRITING ABOUT FICTION

It is crucial to keep your paper's purpose in mind. When you write an academic paper, you are likely to have been given a specific set of marching orders. Maybe you have been asked to write for a particular audience besides the obvious one (your professor, that is). Perhaps you have been asked to describe your personal reaction to a literary work. Maybe your purpose is to interpret a work, analyzing how one or more of its elements contribute to its meaning. You may have been instructed to write an evaluation in which you judge a work's merits. Let the assignment dictate your paper's tone and content. Below are several commonly used approaches to writing about fiction.

Explication Paper

Explication is the patient unfolding of meanings in a work of literature. An explication proceeds carefully through a story, usually interpreting it line by line— perhaps even word by word—dwelling on details a casual reader might miss and illustrating how a story's smaller parts contribute to the whole. Alert and willing to take pains, the writer of such an essay notices anything meaningful that isn't obvious, whether it is a colossal theme suggested by a symbol or a little hint contained in a single word.

To write an honest explication of an entire story takes time and space, and it is a better assignment for a term paper, an honors thesis, or a dissertation than a short essay. A thorough explication of Nathaniel Hawthorne's "Young Goodman Brown," for example, would likely run much longer than the rich and intriguing short story itself. Ordinarily, explication is best suited to a short passage or section of a story: a key scene, a critical conversation, a statement of theme, or an opening or closing paragraph. In a long critical essay that doesn't adhere to one method all the way through, the method of explication may appear from time to time, as when the critic, in discussing a story, stops to unravel a particularly knotty passage. Here are tips for writing a successful explication of your own:

- **Focus on the details that strike you as most meaningful.** Do not try to cover everything.

- **Try working through the original passage sentence by sentence.** If you choose this method, be sure to vary your transitions from one point to the next, to avoid the danger of falling into a boring singsong: "In the first sentence I noticed . . .," "In the next sentence . . .," "Now in the third sentence . . .," and "Finally, in the last sentence. . . ."

- **Consider working from a simple outline.** In writing the explication that follows of a passage from "The Tell-Tale Heart," the student began with a list of points she wanted to express:

  1. Speaker's extreme care and exactness—typical of some mental illnesses.
  2. Speaker doesn't act by usual logic but by a crazy logic.
  3. Dreamlike connection between latch and lantern and old man's eye.

Storytellers who are especially fond of language invite closer attention to their words than others might. Edgar Allan Poe, for one, was a poet sensitive to the rhythms of his sentences and a symbolist whose stories abound in potent suggestions. Here is a student's explication of a short but essential passage in "The Tell-Tale Heart." The passage occurs in the third paragraph of the story, and to help us follow the explication, the student quotes the passage in full at the paper's beginning.

Kim 1

Susan Kim

Professor A. M. Lundy

English 100

20 March 2019

By Lantern Light: An Explication

of a Passage in Poe's "The Tell-Tale Heart"

Quotes passage to be explicated

And every night, about midnight, I turned the latch of his door and opened it—oh, so gently! And then, when I had made an opening sufficient for my head, I put in a dark lantern, all closed, closed, so that no light shone out, and then I thrust in my head. Oh, you would have laughed to see how cunningly I thrust it in! I moved it slowly—very, very slowly, so that I might not disturb the old man's sleep. It took me an hour to place my whole head within the opening so far that I could see him as he lay upon his bed. Ha!—would a madman have been so wise as this? And then, when my head was well in the room, I undid the lantern cautiously—oh, so cautiously—cautiously (for the hinges creaked)—I undid it just so much that a single thin ray fell upon the vulture eye. And this I did for seven long nights—every night just at midnight—but I found the eye always closed; and so it was impossible to do the work; for it was not the old man who vexed me, but his Evil Eye. (par. 3)

Thesis sentence—statement of paper's main claim

Although Edgar Allan Poe has suggested in the first lines of his story "The Tell-Tale Heart" that the person who addresses us is insane, it is only when we come to the speaker's account of his preparations for murdering the old man that we find his madness fully revealed. Even more convincingly than his earlier words (for we might possibly think that someone who claims to hear things in heaven and hell is a religious mystic), these preparations reveal him to be mad. What strikes us is that they are so elaborate and meticulous. A significant detail is the exactness of his schedule for spying: "every night just at midnight."

Textual evidence supports claim

The words with which he describes his motions also convey the most extreme care (and I will indicate them by italics): "how wisely I proceeded—with *what caution*," "I turned the latch of his door and opened it—oh, so *gently*!" "how *cunningly* I thrust it [my head] in! I moved it slowly—*very, very slowly*," "I undid the lantern *cautiously*—oh, *so cautiously*—*cautiously*." Taking a whole hour to intrude his head into the room, he asks, "Ha!—would a madman have been so wise as this?" But of course the word *wise* is unconsciously ironic, for clearly it is not wisdom the speaker displays, but an absurd degree of care, an almost fiendish ingenuity. Such behavior, I understand, is typical of certain mental illnesses. All his careful preparations that he thinks prove him sane only convince us instead that he is mad.

Obviously his behavior is self-defeating. He wants to catch the "vulture eye" open, and yet he takes all these pains not to disturb the old man's sleep. If he behaved logically, he might go barging into the bedroom with his lantern ablaze, shouting at the top of his voice. And yet, if we can see things his way, there *is* a strange logic to his reasoning. He regards the eye as a creature in itself, quite apart from its possessor. "It was not," he says, "the old man who vexed me, but his Evil Eye." Apparently, to be inspired to do his deed, the madman needs to behold the eye—at least, this is my understanding of his remark, "I found the eye always closed; and so it was impossible to do the work." Poe's choice of the word *work*, by the way, is also revealing. Murder is made to seem a duty or a job; and anyone who so regards murder is either extremely cold-blooded, like a hired killer for a gangland assassination, or else deranged. Besides, the word suggests again the curious sense of detachment that the speaker feels toward the owner of the eye.

> *Topic sentence on narrator's mad logic*

In still another of his assumptions, the speaker shows that he is madly logical, or operating on the logic of a dream. There seems a dreamlike relationship between his dark lantern "all closed, closed, so that no light shone out," and the sleeping victim. When the madman opens his lantern so that it emits a single ray, he is hoping that the eye in the old man's head will be open too, letting out its corresponding gleam. The latch that he turns so gently, too, seems like the eye, whose lid needs to be opened in order for the murderer to go ahead. It is as though the speaker is *trying* to get the eyelid to lift. By taking such great pains and by going through all this nightly ritual, he is practicing some kind of magic, whose rules are laid down not by our logic, but by the logic of dreams.

> *Conclusion pushes thesis further, making it more specific*

Work Cited

Poe, Edgar Allan. "The Tell-Tale Heart." *Literature: An Introduction to Fiction, Poetry, Drama, and Writing*, edited by X. J. Kennedy et al., 14th ed., Pearson, 2020, pp. 449–52.

An unusually well written essay, "By Lantern Light" cost its author two or three careful revisions. Rather than attempting to say something about *everything* in the passage from Poe, she selects only the details that strike her as most meaningful. In her very first sentence, she briefly shows us how the passage functions in the context of Poe's story: how it clinches our suspicions that the narrator is mad. Notice too that the student who wrote the essay doesn't inch through the passage sentence by sentence, but freely takes up its details in an order that seems appropriate to her argument.

Analysis Paper

Examining a single component of a story can afford us a better understanding of the entire work. This is perhaps why in most literature classes students are asked to write at least one **analysis** (from the Greek: "breaking up"), an essay that breaks a story or novel into its elements and, usually, studies one part closely. One likely topic for an analysis might be "The Character of James Baldwin's Sonny," in which the writer would concentrate on showing us Sonny's highly individual features and traits of personality. Other topics for an analysis might be "Irony in ZZ Packer's 'Brownies,'" or "Setting in Kate Chopin's 'The Storm,'" or "The Unidentified Narrator in 'A Rose for Emily.'"

To be sure, no element of a story dwells in isolation from the story's other elements. In "The Tell-Tale Heart," the madness of the leading character apparently makes it necessary to tell the story from a special point of view and probably helps determine the author's choice of theme, setting, symbolism, tone, style, and ironies. But it would be mind-boggling to try to study all those elements simultaneously. For this reason, when we write an analysis, we generally study just one element, though we may suggest—probably at the start of the essay—its relation to the whole story. Here are two points to keep in mind when writing an analysis:

- **Decide upon a thesis, and include only relevant insights.** As tempting as it might be to include your every idea, stick to those that will help to prove your point.

- **Support your contentions with specific references to the story you are analyzing.** Quotations can be particularly convincing.

The following paper is an example of a solid, brief analysis. Written by a student, it focuses on just one element of "The Tell-Tale Heart"—the story's point of view.

Frederick 1

Mike Frederick

Professor Trudeau

English 110

18 January 2019

The Hearer of the Tell-Tale Heart

States author and work

Although there are many things we do not know about the narrator of Edgar Allan Poe's story "The Tell-Tale Heart"—is he a son? a servant? a companion?—there is one thing we are sure of from the start. He is mad. In the

Frederick 2

opening paragraph, Poe makes the narrator's condition unmistakable, not only from his excited and worked-up speech (full of dashes and exclamation points), but also from his wild claims. He says it is merely some disease which has sharpened his senses that has made people call him crazy. Who but a madman, however, would say, "I heard all things in the heaven and in the earth," and brag how his ear is a kind of radio, listening in on hell? The narrator's tenuous hold on reality and his wild shifts in mood indicate that he is insane and, therefore, that his point of view is untrustworthy.

> *Thesis statement —paper's main claim*

Because the participant narrator is telling his story in the first person, some details in the story stand out more than others. When the narrator goes on to tell how he watches the old man sleeping, he rivets his attention on the old man's "vulture eye." When a ray from his lantern finds the Evil Eye open, he says, "I could see nothing else of the old man's face or person" (par. 9). Actually, the reader can see almost nothing else about the old man anywhere in the rest of the story. All we are told is that the old man treated the younger man well, and we gather that the old man was rich, because his house is full of treasures. We do not have a clear idea of what the old man looks like, though, nor do we know how he talks, for we are not given any of his words. Our knowledge of him is mainly confined to his eye and its effect on the narrator. This confinement gives that symbolic eye a lot of importance in the story. The narrator tells us all we know and directs our attention to parts of it.

> *Topic sentence— how point of view determines emphasis*

This point of view raises an interesting question. Since we are dependent on the narrator for all our information, how do we know the whole story isn't just a nightmare in his demented mind? We have really no way to be sure it isn't, as far as I can see. I assume, however, that there really is a dark shuttered house and an old man and real policemen who start snooping around when screams are heard in the neighborhood because it is a more memorable story if it is a crazy man's view of reality than if it is all just a terrible dream. But we can't rely on the madman's interpretation of what happens. Poe keeps putting distances between what the narrator says and what we are apparently supposed to think. For instance: the narrator has boasted that he is calm and clear in the head, but as soon as he starts trying to explain why he killed the old man, we gather that he is confused, to say the least. "I think it was his eye!" the narrator exclaims, as if not quite sure (par. 2). As he goes on to explain how he conducted the murder, we realize that he is a man with a fixed idea working with a patience that is certainly mad, almost diabolical.

> *Raises question, then explores answer*

> *Topic sentence on how narrator's madness is revealed*

Frederick 3

Raises question, then explores answer

Some readers might wonder if "The Tell-Tale Heart" is a story of the supernatural. Is the heartbeat that the narrator hears a ghost come back to haunt him? Here, I think, the point of view is our best guide to what to believe. The simple explanation for the heartbeat is this: it is all in the madman's mind. Perhaps he feels such guilt that he starts hearing things. Another explanation

Secondary source paraphrase

is possible, one suggested by Daniel Hoffman, a critic who has discussed the story: the killer hears the sound of his *own* heart (227). Hoffman's explanation (which I don't like as well as mine) also is a natural one, and it fits the story as a whole. Back when the narrator first entered the old man's bedroom to kill him, the heartbeat sounded so loud to him that he was afraid the neighbors would hear it too. Evidently they didn't, and so Hoffman may be right in thinking that the sound was only that of his own heart pounding in his ears. Whichever explanation you take, it is a more down-to-earth and reasonable explanation than (as the narrator believes) that the heart is still alive, even though its owner has been cut to pieces. Then, too, the police keep chatting. If they heard the heartbeat, wouldn't they leap to their feet, draw their guns, and look all around the room? As the author keeps showing us in the rest of the story, the narrator's view of things is untrustworthy. You don't kill someone just because you dislike the look in his eye. You don't think that such a murder is funny. For all its Gothic atmosphere of the old dark house with a secret hidden inside, "The Tell-Tale

Restatement of thesis

Heart" is not a ghost story. We have only to see its point of view to know it is a study in abnormal psychology.

Frederick 4

Works Cited

Hoffman, Daniel. *Poe Poe Poe Poe Poe Poe Poe*. Doubleday, 1972.

Poe, Edgar Allan. "The Tell-Tale Heart." *Literature: An Introduction to Fiction, Poetry, Drama, and Writing*, edited by X. J. Kennedy et al., 14th ed., Pearson, 2020, pp. 449–52.

The temptation in writing an analysis is to include all sorts of insights that the writer proudly wishes to display, even though they aren't related to the main idea. In the preceding essay, the student resists this temptation admirably. In fairly plump and ample paragraphs, he works out his ideas and supports his contentions with specific references to Poe's story. Although his paper is not brilliantly written and contains no insight so fresh as the suggestion (by the writer of the first paper) that the madman's lantern is like the old man's head, still, it is a good brief analysis. By sticking faithfully to his purpose and by confronting the problems he raises ("How do we know the whole story isn't just a nightmare?"), the writer persuades us that he understands not only the story's point of view but also the story in its entirety.

Card Report Analysis

Another form of analysis, a **card report** breaks down a story into its various elements. Though card reports tend to include only as much information as can fit on both sides of a single 5- by 8-inch index card, they are at least as challenging to write as full-fledged essays. The author of a successful card report can dissect a story into its elements and describe them succinctly and accurately. A typical card report on "The Tell-Tale Heart" follows. In this assignment, the student was asked to include the following items:

1. The story's title and the date of its original publication.
2. The author's name and dates of birth and death.
3. The name (if any) of the main character, along with a description of that character's dominant traits or features.
4. Similar information for other characters.
5. A short description of the setting.
6. The point of view from which the story is told.
7. A terse summary of the story's main events in chronological order.
8. A description of the general tone, or, in other words, the author's feelings toward the central character or the main event.
9. Some comments on the style in which the story is written. Brief illustrative quotations are helpful if space allows.
10. Whatever kinds of irony the story contains and what they contribute to the story.
11. The story's main theme, in a sentence.
12. Key symbols (if the story has any), with an educated guess at what each symbol suggests.
13. Finally, an evaluation of the story as a whole, concisely setting forth the student's opinion of it. (Some instructors consider this the most important part of the report, and most students find that, by the time they have so painstakingly separated the ingredients of the story, they have arrived at a definite opinion of its merits.)

Front of Card

Carly Grace   English 101

<u>Story</u>: "The Tell-Tale Heart," 1850

<u>Author</u>: Edgar Allan Poe (1809-1849)

    <u>Central character</u>: An unnamed younger man whom people call mad, who claims that a nervous disease has greatly sharpened his sense perceptions. He is proud of his own cleverness.

    <u>Other characters</u>: The old man, whose leading feature is one pale blue, filmed eye; said to be rich, kind, and lovable. Also three policemen, not individually described.

    <u>Setting</u>: A shuttered house full of wind, mice, and treasures; pitch dark even in the afternoon.

    <u>Narrator</u>: The madman himself.

    <u>Events in summary</u>: (1) Dreading one vulture-like eye of the old man he shares a house with, a madman determines to kill its owner. (2) Each night he spies on the sleeping old man, but finding the eye shut, he stays his hand. (3) On the eighth night, finding the eye open, he suffocates its owner beneath the mattress and conceals the dismembered body under the floor of the bedchamber. (4) Entertaining some inquiring police officers in the very room where the body lies hidden, the killer again hears (or thinks he hears) the beat of the victim's heart. (5) Terrified, convinced that the police also hear the heartbeat growing louder, the killer confesses.

    <u>Tone</u>: Horror at the events described, skepticism toward the narrator's claims to be sane, detachment from his gaiety and laughter.

    As you might expect, fitting so much information on one card is like trying to engrave the Declaration of Independence on the head of a pin. The student who wrote this report had to spoil a few trial cards before she was able to complete the assignment. The card report is an extreme exercise in making every word count, a worthwhile discipline in almost any kind of writing. Some students enjoy the challenge, and most are surprised at how thoroughly they come to understand the story. A longer story, even a novel, may be analyzed in the same way, but insist on taking a second card if you are asked to analyze an especially hefty and complicated novel.

Back of Card

<u>Style:</u> Written as if told aloud by a deranged man eager to be believed, the story is punctuated by laughter, interjections ("Hearken!"), nervous halts, and fresh beginnings—indicated by dashes that grow more frequent as the story goes on and the narrator becomes more excited. Poe often relies on general adjectives ("mournful," "hideous" "hellish") to convey atmosphere; also on exact details (the lantern that emits "a single dim ray, like the thread of a spider").

<u>Irony:</u> The whole story is ironic in its point of view. Presumably the author is not mad, nor does he share the madman's self-admiration. Many of the narrator's statements therefore seem verbal ironies: his account of taking an hour to move his head through the bedroom door.

<u>Theme:</u> Possibly "Murder will out," but I really don't find any theme either stated or clearly implied.

<u>Symbols:</u> The vulture eye, called an Evil Eye (in superstition, one that can implant a curse), perhaps suggesting too the all-seeing eye of God the Father, from whom no guilt can be concealed. The ghostly heartbeat, sound of the victim's coming back to be avenged (or the God who cannot be slain?). Death watches: beetles said to be death omens, whose ticking sound foreshadows the sound of the tell-tale heart *as a watch makes when enveloped in cotton.*

<u>Evaluation:</u> Despite the overwrought style (to me slightly comic-bookish), a powerful story, admirable for its conclusion and for its memorable portrait of a deranged killer. Poe knows how it is to be mad.

Comparison and Contrast Paper

If you were to write on "The Humor of Alice Walker's 'Everyday Use' and John Updike's 'A & P,'" you would probably employ one or two methods. You might use **comparison**, placing the two stories side by side and pointing out their similarities, or **contrast**, pointing out their differences. Most of the time, in dealing with a pair of stories, you will find them similar in some ways and different in others, and you'll use both methods. Keep the following points in mind when writing a comparison-contrast paper:

- **Choose stories with something significant in common.** This will simplify your task and help ensure that your paper hangs together. Before you start writing, ask yourself if the two stories you've selected throw some light on each other. If the answer is no, rethink your story selection.

- **Choose a focus.** Simply ticking off every similarity and difference between two stories would make for a slack and rambling essay. More compelling writing would result from better-focused topics such as "The Experience of Coming of Age in James Joyce's 'Araby' and William Faulkner's 'Barn Burning'" or "Mother-Daughter Relationships in Alice Walker's 'Everyday Use' and Jamaica Kincaid's 'Girl.'"

- **Don't feel you need to spend equal amounts of time on comparing and contrasting.** If your chosen stories are more similar than different, you naturally will spend more space on comparison, and vice versa.

- **Don't devote the first half of your paper to one story and the second half to the other.** Such a paper wouldn't be a comparison or contrast so much as a pair of analyses yoked together. To reap the full benefits of the assignment, let the two stories mingle.

- **Before you start writing, draw up a brief list of points you would like to touch on.** Then address each point, first in one story and then in the other. A sample outline follows for a paper on William Faulkner's "A Rose for Emily" and Katherine Mansfield's "Miss Brill." The essay's topic is "Adapting to Change: The Characters of Emily Grierson and Miss Brill."

    1. Adapting to change (both women)
        Miss Brill more successful
    2. Portrait of women
        Miss Emily—unflattering
        Miss Brill—empathetic
    3. Imagery
        Miss Emily—morbid
        Miss Brill—cheerful
    4. Plot
        Miss Emily
        – loses sanity
        – refuses to adapt
        Miss Brill
        – finds place in society
        – adapts
    5. Summary: Miss Brill is more successful

- **Emphasize the points that interest you the most.** This strategy will help keep you from following your outline in a plodding fashion ("Well, now it's time to whip over to Miss Brill again . . .").

- **If the assignment allows, consider applying comparison and contrast in an essay on a single story.** You might, for example, analyze the attitudes of the younger and older waiters in Hemingway's "A Clean, Well-Lighted Place." Or you might contrast Mrs. Turpin's smug view of herself with the young Mary Grace's merciless view of her in Flannery O'Connor's "Revelation."

The following student-written paper compares and contrasts the main characters in "A Rose for Emily" and "Miss Brill." Notice how the author focuses the discussion on a single aspect of each woman's personality—the ability to adapt to change and the passage of time. By looking through the lens of three different elements of the short story—diction, imagery, and plot—this clear and systematic essay convincingly argues its thesis.

Ortiz 1

Michelle Ortiz
Professor Gregg
English 200
25 February 2019

Successful Adaptation in
"A Rose for Emily" and "Miss Brill"

In William Faulkner's "A Rose for Emily" and Katherine Mansfield's "Miss Brill," the reader is given a glimpse into the lives of two old women living in different worlds but sharing many similar characteristics. Both Miss Emily and Miss Brill attempt to adapt to a changing environment as they grow older. Through the authors' use of language, imagery, and plot, it becomes clear to the reader that Miss Brill is more successful at adapting to the world around her and finding happiness.

Clear statement of thesis—paper's main claim

In "A Rose for Emily," Faulkner's use of language paints an unflattering picture of Miss Emily. His tone evokes pity and disgust rather than sympathy. The reader identifies with the narrator of the story and shares the townspeople's opinion that Miss Emily is somehow "perverse" (par. 51). In "Miss Brill," however, the reader can identify with the title character and feel sympathy for her because of the lonely life she leads. Mansfield's attitude toward the young couple at the end makes the reader hate them for ruining the happiness that Miss Brill has found, however small it may be.

Textual evidence on language supports thesis

The imagery in "A Rose for Emily" keeps the reader from further identifying with Miss Emily by creating several morbid images of her. For example, there are several images of decay throughout the story. The house she lived in is falling apart and described as "filled with dust and shadows" (par. 52), "an eyesore among eyesores" (par. 2). Emily herself is described as looking "bloated, like a body long submerged in motionless water" (par. 6). Faulkner also uses words like "skeleton," "dank," "decay," and "cold" to reinforce these morbid, deathly images (par. 6, 5, 2, 8).

Imagery in Faulkner's story supports argument

Ortiz 2

Contrasting imagery in Mansfield's story supports argument

In "Miss Brill," however, Mansfield uses more cheerful imagery. The music and the lively action in the park make Miss Brill feel alive inside. She notices the other old people in the park are "still as statues," "odd," and "silent" (par. 5). She says they "looked as though they'd just come from dark little rooms or even—even cupboards!" (par. 5). In the final paragraph, her own room is described as "like a cupboard," but during the action of the story she does not include herself among those other old people. She still feels alive.

Characters contrasted with examples drawn from plots

Through the plots of both stories the reader can also see that Miss Brill is more successful in adapting to her environment. Miss Emily loses her sanity and ends up committing a crime in order to control her environment. Throughout the story, she refuses to adapt to any of the changes going on in the town, such as the taxes or the mailboxes. Miss Brill is able to find her own special place in society where she can be happy and remain sane.

The final conclusion is stated and the thesis is restated

In "A Rose for Emily" and "Miss Brill" the authors' use of language and the plots of the stories illustrate that Miss Brill is more successful in her story. Instead of hiding herself away she emerges from the "cupboard" to participate in life. She adapts to the world that is changing as she grows older, without losing her sanity or committing crimes, as Miss Emily does. The language of "Miss Brill" allows the reader to sympathize with the main character. The imagery in the story is lighter and less morbid than in "A Rose for Emily." The resulting portrait is of an aging woman who has found creative ways to adjust to her lonely life.

Ortiz 3

Works Cited

Faulkner, William. "A Rose for Emily." *Literature: An Introduction to Fiction, Poetry, Drama, and Writing*, edited by X. J. Kennedy et al., 14th ed., Pearson, 2020, pp. 30–36.

Mansfield, Katherine. "Miss Brill." *Literature: An Introduction to Fiction, Poetry, Drama, and Writing*, edited by X. J. Kennedy et al., 14th ed., Pearson, 2020, pp. 648–51.

Response Paper

One popular form of writing assignment is the **response paper**, a short essay that expresses your personal reaction to a work of literature. Both instructors and students often find the response paper an ideal introductory writing assignment. It provides you with an opportunity to craft a focused essay about a literary work, but it does not usually require any outside research. What it does require is careful reading, clear thinking, and honest writing.

The purpose of a response paper is to convey your thoughts and feelings about an aspect of a particular literary work. It isn't a book report (summarizing the work's content) or a book review (evaluating the quality of a work). A response paper expresses what you experienced in reading and thinking about the assigned text. Your reaction should reflect your background, values, and attitudes in response to the work, not what the instructor thinks about it. You might even consider your response paper a conversation with the work you have just read. What questions does it seem to ask you? What reactions does it elicit? You might also regard your paper as a personal message to your instructor telling him or her what you really think about one of the reading assignments.

Of course, you can't say everything you thought and felt about your reading in a short paper. Focus on an important aspect (such as a main character, setting, or theme) and discuss your reaction to it. Don't gush or meander. Personal writing doesn't mean disorganized writing. Identify your main ideas and present your point of view in a clear and organized way. Once you get started you might surprise yourself by discovering that it's fun to explore your own responses. Stranger things have happened.

Here are tips for writing a successful response paper of your own:

- **Make quick notes as you read or reread the work.** Don't worry about writing anything organized at this point. Just write a word or two in the margin noting your reactions as you read (e.g., "very interesting" or "reminds me of my sister"). These little notes will jog your memory when you go back to write your paper.

- **Consider which aspect of the work affected you the most.** That aspect will probably be a good starting point for your response.

- **Be candid in your writing.** Remember that the literary work is only half of the subject matter of your paper. The other half is your reaction.

- **Try to understand and explain why you have reacted the way you did.** It's not enough just to state your responses. You also want to justify or explain them.

- **Refer to the text in your paper.** Demonstrate to the reader that your response is based on the text. Provide specific textual details and quotations wherever relevant.

The following paper is one student's response to Tim O'Brien's story "The Things They Carried" (Chapter 14).

Martin 1

Ethan Martin

English 99

Professor Merrill

31 March 2019

"Perfect Balance and Perfect Posture":

Reflecting on "The Things They Carried"

Reading Tim O'Brien's short story "The Things They Carried" became a very personal experience. It reminded me of my father, who is a Vietnam veteran, and the stories he used to tell me. Growing up, I regularly asked my dad to share stories from his past, especially about his service in the United States Marine Corps. He would rarely talk about his tour during the Vietnam War for more than a few minutes, and what he shared was usually the same: the monsoon rain could chill to the bone, the mosquitoes would never stop biting, and the M-16 rifles often jammed in a moment of crisis. He dug a new foxhole where he slept every night, he traded the cigarettes from his C-rations for food, and—since he was the radio man of his platoon—the combination of his backpack and radio was very heavy during the long, daily walks through rice paddies and jungles. For these reasons, "The Things They Carried" powerfully affected me.

While reading the story, I felt as if I was "humping" (par. 4) through Vietnam with Lieutenant Jimmy Cross, Rat Kiley, Ted Lavender, and especially Mitchell Sanders—who carries the 26-pound radio and battery. Every day, we carry our backpacks to school. Inside are some objects that we need to use in class: books, paper, and pens. But most of us probably include "unnecessary" items that reveal something about who we are or what we value—photographs, perfume, or good-luck charms. O'Brien uses this device to tell his story. At times he lists the things that the soldiers literally carried, such as weapons, medicine, and flak jackets. These military items weigh between 30 and 70 pounds, depending on one's rank or function in the platoon. The narrator says, "They carried all they could bear, and then some, including a silent awe for the terrible power of the things they carried" (par. 12).

Some of this "terrible power" comes from the sentimental objects the men keep. Although these are relatively light, they weigh down the hearts of the soldiers. Lt. Jimmy Cross carries 10-ounce letters and a pebble from Martha, a girl in his hometown who doesn't love him back. Rat Kiley carries comic books, and Norman Bowker carries a diary. I now own the small, water-logged Bible that my

Martin 2

father carried through his tour in Vietnam, which was a gift from his mother. When I open its pages, I can almost hear his voice praying to survive the war.

The price of such survival is costly. O'Brien's platoon carries ghosts, memories, and "the land itself" (par. 39). Their intangible burdens are heavier than what they carry in their backpacks. My father has always said that, while he was in Vietnam, an inexpressible feeling of death hung heavy in the air, which he could not escape. O'Brien notes that an emotional weight of fear and cowardice "could never be put down, it required perfect balance and perfect posture" (par. 77), and I wonder if this may be part of what my father meant.

Both Tim O'Brien and my father were wounded by shrapnel, and now they both carry a Purple Heart. They carry the weight of survival. They carry memories that I will never know. "The Things They Carried" is not a war story about glory and honor. It is a portrait of the psychological damage that war can bring. It is a story about storytelling and how hard it can be to find the truth. And it is a beautiful account of what the human heart can endure.

Martin 3

Work Cited

O'Brien, Tim. "The Things They Carried." *Literature: An Introduction to Fiction, Poetry, Drama, and Writing,* edited by X. J. Kennedy et al., 14th ed., Pearson, 2020, pp. 652–63.

TOPICS FOR WRITING BRIEF PAPERS (250–500 WORDS)

1. Explicate the opening paragraph or first few lines of a story. Show how the opening prepares the reader for what will follow. In an essay of this length, you will need to limit your discussion to the most important elements of the passage you explicate; there won't be room to deal with everything. Or, as thoroughly as the word count allows, explicate the final paragraph of a story. What does the ending imply about the fates of the story's characters, and about the story's take on its central theme?

2. Select a story that features a first-person narrator. Write a concise yet thorough analysis of how that character's point of view colors the story.

3. Following the directions in this chapter, write a card report on any short story in this book.

4. Consider a short story in which the central character has to make a decision or must take some decisive step that will alter the rest of his or her life. Faulkner's "Barn Burning" (Chapter 5) is one such story; another is Updike's "A & P" (Chapter 1). As concisely and as thoroughly as you can, explain the nature of the character's decision, the reasons for it, and its probable consequences (as suggested by what the author tells us).

5. Choose two stories that might be interesting to compare and contrast. Write a brief defense of your choice. How might these two stories illuminate each other?

6. Choose a key passage from a story you admire. As closely as the word count allows, explicate that passage and explain why it strikes you as an important moment in the story. Concentrate on the aspects of the passage that seem most essential.

7. Write a new ending to a story of your choice. Try to imitate the author's writing style. Add a paragraph explaining how this exercise illuminates the author's choices in the original.

8. Drawing on your own experience, make the case that a character in any short story behaves (or doesn't behave) as people do in real life. Your audience for this assignment is your classmates; tailor your tone and argument accordingly.

TOPICS FOR WRITING MORE EXTENDED PAPERS (600–1,000 WORDS)

1. Write an analysis of a short story, focusing on a single element, such as point of view, theme, symbolism, character, or the author's voice (tone, style, irony). For a sample paper in response to this assignment, see "The Hearer of the Tell-Tale Heart" (earlier in this chapter).

2. Compare and contrast two stories with protagonists who share an important personality trait. Make character the focus of your essay.

3. Write a thorough explication of a short passage (preferably not more than four sentences) in a story you admire. Pick a crucial moment in the plot, or a passage that reveals the story's theme. You might look to the paper "By Lantern Light" (earlier in this chapter) as a model.

4. Write an analysis of a story in which the protagonist experiences an epiphany or revelation of some sort. Describe the nature of this change of heart. How is the reader prepared for it? What are its repercussions in the character's life? Some possible story choices are Alice Walker's "Everyday Use" (Chapter 12), William Faulkner's "Barn Burning (Chapter 5)," Raymond Carver's "Cathedral" (Chapter 3), James Baldwin's "Sonny's Blues" (Chapter 2), and, not surprisingly, Flannery O'Connor's "Revelation" (Chapter 11).

5. Imagine you are given the task of teaching a story to your class. Write an explanation of how you would address this challenge.

6. Imagine a reluctant reader, one who would rather play video games than crack a book. Which story in this book would you recommend to him or her? Write an essay to that imagined reader, describing the story's merits.

TOPICS FOR WRITING LONG PAPERS (1,500 WORDS OR MORE)

1. Write an analysis of a longer work of fiction. Concentrate on a single element of the story, quoting as necessary to make your point.

2. Read three or four short stories by an author whose work you admire. Concentrating on a single element treated similarly in all of the stories, write an analysis of the author's work as exemplified by your chosen stories.

3. Adapt a short story in this book into a one-act play. This may prove harder than it sounds; be sure to choose a story in which most of the action takes place in the physical world and not in the protagonist's mind. Don't forget to include stage directions.

4. Describe the process of reading a story for the first time and gradually learning to understand and appreciate it. First, choose a story you haven't yet read. As you read it for the first time, take notes on aspects of the story you find difficult or puzzling. Read the story a second time. Now write about the experience. What uncertainties were resolved when you read the story the second time? What, if any, uncertainties remain? What has this experience taught you about reading fiction?

5. Choose two stories that treat a similar theme. Compare and contrast the stance each story takes toward that theme, marshalling quotations and specifics as necessary to back up your argument.

6. Browse through newspapers and magazines for a story with the elements of good fiction. Now rewrite the story *as* fiction. Then write a one-page accompanying essay explaining the challenges of the task. What did it teach you about the relative natures of journalism and fiction?

44

WRITING ABOUT A POEM

I love being a writer.
What I can't stand is the paperwork.

—PETER DE VRIES

What You Will Learn in This Chapter

- To read a poem actively
- To plan, draft, and revise a literary argument about poetry
- To write a poetry explication, analysis, and comparison and contrast paper
- To quote a poem

Many readers—even some enthusiastic ones—are wary of poems. "I don't know anything about poetry," some people say, if the subject arises. While poems aren't booby traps designed to trip up careless readers, it is true that poetry demands a special level of concentration. Poetry is language at its most intense and condensed, and in a good poem, every word counts. With practice, though, anyone can become a more confident reader—and critic—of poetry. Remember that the purpose of poetry isn't intimidation but wisdom and pleasure. Even writing a paper on poetry can occasion a certain enjoyment. Here are some tips.

- **Choose a poem that speaks to you.** Let pleasure be your guide in choosing the poem you write about. The act of writing is easier if your feelings are engaged. Write about something you dislike and don't understand, and your essay will be as dismal to read as it was for you to write. But write about something that interests you, and your essay will communicate that interest and enthusiasm.

- **Allow yourself time to get comfortable with your subject.** As most professors will tell you, when students try to fudge their way through a paper on a topic they don't fully understand, the lack of comfort shows, making for muddled, directionless prose. The more familiar you become with a poem, however, the easier and more pleasurable it will be to write about it. Expect to read the poem several times over before its meaning becomes clear. Better still, reread it over the course of several days.

READ ACTIVELY

A poem differs from most prose in that it should be read slowly, carefully, and attentively. Good poems yield more if read twice, and the best poems—after ten, twenty, or even thirty readings—keep on yielding. Here are some suggestions to enhance your reading of a poem you plan to write about.

- **Read the poem aloud.** There is no better way to understand a poem than to effectively read it aloud. Read slowly, paying attention to punctuation cues. Listen for the auditory effects.
- **Read closely and painstakingly, annotating as you go.** Keep your mind (and your pencil) sharp and ready. The subtleties of language are essential to a poem. Pay attention to the connotations or suggestions of words, and to the rhythm of phrases and lines. Underline words and images that jump out at you. Use arrows to link phrases that seem connected. Highlight key passages or take notes in the margins as ideas or questions occur to you.

Robert Frost (1874–1963)

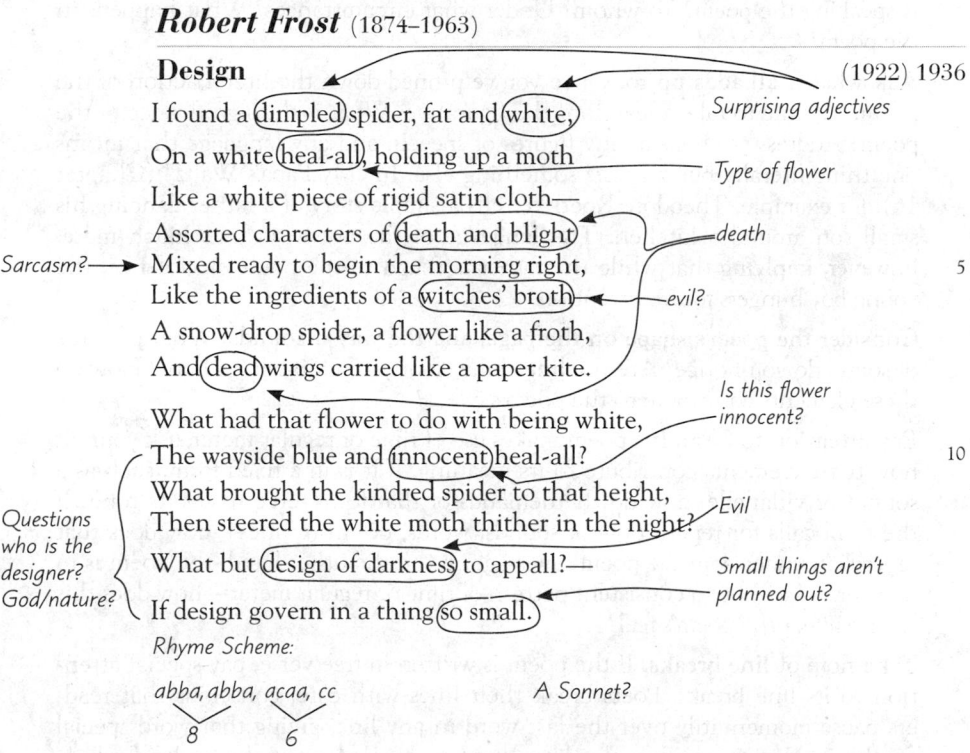

Design   (1922) 1936

I found a dimpled spider, fat and white,   *Surprising adjectives*
On a white heal-all, holding up a moth   *— Type of flower*
Like a white piece of rigid satin cloth—
Assorted characters of death and blight   *=death*
Sarcasm? → Mixed ready to begin the morning right,   5
Like the ingredients of a witches' broth—   *—evil?*
A snow-drop spider, a flower like a froth,
And dead wings carried like a paper kite.
                                                                                       Is this flower
What had that flower to do with being white,   *innocent?*
The wayside blue and innocent heal-all?   10
What brought the kindred spider to that height,   *Evil*
Questions who is the Then steered the white moth thither in the night?
designer? God/nature? What but design of darkness to appall?—   *Small things aren't*
If design govern in a thing so small.   *planned out?*

Rhyme Scheme:

abba, abba, acaa, cc   *A Sonnet?*
   ⌣   ⌣
   8   6

- **Look up any unfamiliar words, allusions, or references.** Often the very words you may be tempted to skim over will provide the key to a poem's meaning. Thomas Hardy's "The Ruined Maid" (Chapter 17) will remain elusive to a reader unfamiliar with the archaic meaning of the word "ruin"—a woman's loss of virginity to a man other than her husband. Similarly, be sure to acquaint yourself with any references or allusions that appear in a poem. H.D.'s poem "Helen" (Chapter 27) will make sense only to readers who are familiar with the story of Helen of Troy.

THINK ABOUT THE POEM

Before you begin writing, take some time to collect your thoughts. The following steps can be useful in thinking about a poem.

- **Let your emotions guide you into the poem.** Do any images or phrases call up a strong emotional response? If so, try to puzzle out why those passages seem so emotionally loaded. In a word or two, describe the poem's tone.

- **Determine what's literally happening in the poem.** Separating literal language from figurative or symbolic language can be one of the trickiest—and most essential—tasks in poetic interpretation. Begin by working out the literal. Who is speaking the poem? To whom? Under what circumstances? What happens in the poem?

- **Ask what it all adds up to.** Once you've pinned down the literal action of the poem, it's time to take a leap into the figurative. What is the significance of the poem? Address symbolism, any figures of speech, and any language that means one thing literally but suggests something else. In "My Papa's Waltz" (Chapter 16), for example, Theodore Roethke tells a simple story of a father dancing his small son around a kitchen. The language of the poem suggests much more, however, implying that while the father is rough to the point of violence, the young boy hungers for his attention.

- **Consider the poem's shape on the page, and the way it sounds.** What patterns of sound do you notice? Are the lines long, short, or a mixture of both? How do these elements contribute to the poem's effect?

- **Pay attention to form.** If a poem makes use of rime or regular meter, ask yourself how those elements contribute to its meaning. If it is in a fixed form, such as a sonnet or villanelle, how do the demands of that form serve to set its tone? If the form calls for repetition—of sounds, words, or entire lines—how does that repetition underscore the poem's message? If, on the other hand, the poem is in free verse—without a consistent pattern of rime or regular meter—how does this choice affect the poem's feel?

- **Take note of line breaks.** If the poem is written in free verse, pay special attention to its line breaks. Poets break their lines with care, conscious that readers pause momentarily over the last word in any line, giving that word special emphasis. Notice whether the lines tend to be broken at the ends of whole phrases and sentences or in the middle of phrases. Then ask yourself what effect is created by the poet's choice of line breaks. How does that effect contribute to the poem's meaning?

PREWRITING: GENERATE IDEAS AND ISSUES

Now that you have thought the poem through, it's time to let your ideas crystallize on the page (or screen). Try one or more of the following prewriting techniques.

- **Brainstorm.** With the poem in front of you, jot down every single thing you can think of about it. Write quickly, without worrying about the value of your thoughts; you can sort that out later. Brainstorming works best if you set a time limit of ten or fifteen minutes and force yourself to keep working until the time is up. A list that results from brainstorming on "Design" might look something like this:

white spider	white = strangeness
heal-all/flower	heal-all usually blue
dead moth like a kite	flower doesn't heal all
white = innocence?	design = God or nature
death/blight	design of darkness = the devil?
begin the morning right = oddly cheerful	maybe no design (no God?)
irony	God doesn't govern small things
witches' broth/scary	

- **Cluster.** If you are a visual thinker, you might find yourself drawn to clustering as a way to explore the relationships among your ideas. Begin by writing your subject at the center of a sheet of paper. Circle it. Then write ideas as they occur to you, drawing lines linking each new idea to ones that seem related. Here is an example of clustering on "Design."

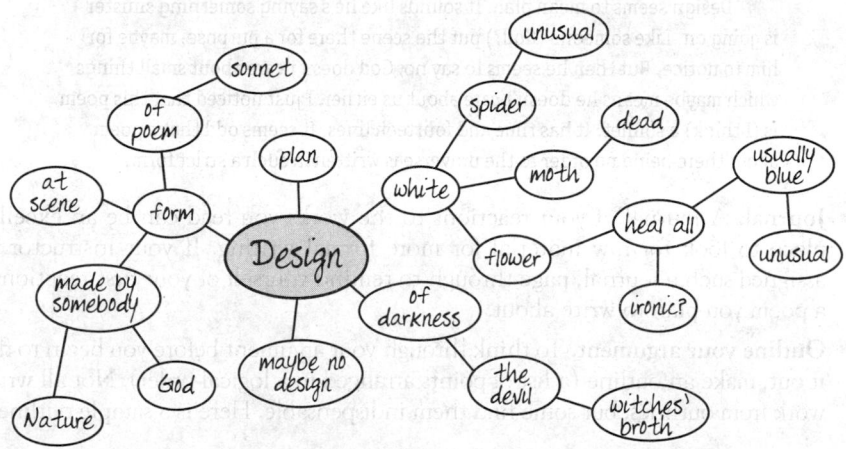

- **List.** Make a list of information that seems useful. Feel free to add notes that will help you to remember what you meant by each item. Headings can help you to organize related concepts. A list might look like this:

Odd Coincidence	Questions
white spider	Accidental or by design?
white flower (not blue, innocent)	Whose design?
white moth (stiff, dead)	Nature or God?
characters of death/blight	Does God care?
morning (hopeful) = ironic	
witches' broth	Form of Poem
	sonnet (strict, orderly)
	form of universe = not so orderly?

■ **Freewrite.** Another approach to generating ideas is to let your thoughts pour out onto the page. To freewrite, give yourself a time limit: fifteen or twenty minutes will work well. Then write, without stopping to think, for that whole time. Keep writing. Don't worry about grammar or spelling or even logic; your task is to come up with fresh ideas that might evade you if you were writing more cautiously. Keep writing even (or especially) if you run out of ideas. New and surprising thoughts sometimes arrive when we least expect them. Here is a sample of freewriting on "Design."

> The scene seems strange. Spiders aren't usually white, and heal-alls are supposed to be blue. Moths are white, but this one is described as being like a rigid satin cloth or a paper kite. It's dead, which is why it is rigid, but the images seem to focus on its stiffness—its deadness—in a creepy way. The poet seems surprised at all this whiteness. Whiteness usually represents innocence, but here he says the flower would ordinarily be blue and innocent, so maybe it's not innocent now? I think he's saying this is a kind of deathly pageant; he calls the three things assorted characters though a flower can't be a character. The second part of the poem is all questions, no answers. What does he mean by "design of darkness"?
>
> Design seems to mean plan. It sounds like he's saying something sinister is going on. Like someone (God?) put the scene there for a purpose, maybe for him to notice. But then he seems to say no, God doesn't care about small things which maybe means he doesn't care about us either. I just noticed that this poem is (I think) a sonnet. It has rime and fourteen lines. It seems odd that a poem about there being no order to the universe is written in such a strict form.

■ **Journal.** A journal of your reactions to the works you read can be an excellent place to look for raw material for more formal writing. If your instructor has assigned such a journal, page through to remind yourself of your first reactions to a poem you plan to write about.

■ **Outline your argument.** To think through your argument before you begin to flesh it out, make an outline (a list of points arranged in a logical order). Not all writers work from outlines, but some find them indispensable. Here is a sample outline.

1. Italian sonnet (define)
   - two parts
   - octave draws picture
   - sestet asks questions

2. Rime
   - "ite" sound stresses whiteness

3. Sonnet form = order
   - poem's subject = order
   - irony/no order in universe

4. Design of poem is unpredictable
   - looks orderly but isn't

5. Design of universe is unpredictable

DRAFT YOUR ARGUMENT

When your prewriting work has given you a sense of direction, you will be ready to begin forming your thoughts and writing a first draft of your essay. Refer to the section "Develop Your Argument" in Chapter 42 "Writing About Literature," for help getting started.

- **Review your purpose and audience.** Begin by referring back to the exact assignment you have been given. No matter how crystal clear your prose or intriguing your ideas, an essay that fails to respond to the assignment is likely to fall flat. As you begin your first draft, consider how best to focus your essay to fulfill the instructor's requirements. Whatever the assignment, you need to keep your purpose in mind as you write. You also need to consider your audience's needs, whether that audience is your professor, your fellow students, or some hypothetical set of readers.

- **Define your thesis: clearly state your paper's claim.** To keep you focused on the task at hand, and to signal your intentions to your reader, you will need, first of all, to come up with a thesis—a claim you are going to argue and defend. Like the rest of your first draft, that thesis sentence can be rough around the edges; you can refine it later in the process. For now, though, the thesis gives you something to work toward. You need to make a decisive statement that offers an insight that isn't entirely obvious about the work under discussion. In the final paper your task will be to convince readers that your thesis is sound. Here is a working thesis sentence for an analytical essay on Frost's poem "Design."

  WORKING THESIS

  The poem "Design" both is and isn't formal.

  This rough thesis defines the essay's focus—the poem's form. But the statement is still very vague. A later, sharper version will clarify the idea and show what the author means by the claim that the poem both is and isn't formal. The revision also will push this idea further by connecting the poem's form to its meaning.

  REVISED THESIS

  Although Frost's sonnet "Design" is a well-designed formal poem, the conclusions it presents are not predictable but both surprising and disturbing.

  In its revised form, this thesis makes a stronger and more specific claim. Because the revision says something specific about how the poem works, it is more compelling than the vaguer original.

- **Support your argument with evidence that proves your point.** Once you've settled on a working thesis, your next task is to decide what evidence will best prove your point. Be sure to quote from the poem to back up each point you make; there is no evidence more convincing than the words of the poem itself.

■ **Organize your argument.** You will need to make clear what each bit of evidence illustrates. Connect your argument back to the thesis as often as it takes to clarify your line of reasoning for the reader.

■ **Concentrate on getting your ideas onto the page.** Later you will go back and revise, making your prose clearer and more elegant. At that point, you can add information that seems to be missing and discard passages that seem beside the point. For now, though, the goal is to spell out your argument while it is clear in your mind.

CHECKLIST: Drafting Your Argument

☐ What is your assignment? Does the essay fulfill it?

☐ Who is your audience?

☐ What is your thesis—your paper's main claim?

☐ Is your thesis thought-provoking rather than a statement of the obvious?

☐ Have you provided evidence to support your thesis?

☐ Does anything in your essay undercut your thesis?

☐ Have you quoted from the poem? Would more quotations strengthen your argument?

☐ Is your argument organized in a logical way?

REVISE YOUR DRAFT

■ **Have a reader review your paper.** Once you have completed your rough draft, consider enlisting the aid of a reader, professional (a writing center tutor) or otherwise (a trusted friend). The author of the paragraph below used her instructor's comments to improve her paper's introduction.

DRAFT OF OPENING PARAGRAPH

Robert Frost's poem "Design" is an Italian sonnet, a form that divides its argument into two parts, an octave and a sestet. The octave, or first part of the poem, concentrates on telling the reader about a peculiar scene the poet has noticed: a white spider holding a dead moth on a white flower. The sestet, or second part of the poem, asks what the scene means. It doesn't really provide any answers.

Good start. I'm glad you're thinking about the poem's form. How does the form suit the content?

Add a little more. Is the scene significant? How so?

Does it hint at answers? Be more specific.

REVISED OPENING PARAGRAPH

For Robert Frost's poem "Design," the sonnet form has at least two advantages. As in most Italian sonnets, the poem's

argument falls into two parts. In the octave Frost's persona draws
a still life of a spider, a flower, and a moth; then in the sestet he
contemplates the meaning of his still life. The sestet focuses on a
universal: the possible existence of a vindictive deity who causes the
spider to catch the moth and, no doubt, also causes—when viewed
anthropomorphically—other suffering.

This essay appears in its entirety later in this chapter under the title "The Design in Robert Frost's 'Design.'" (It's worth noting that while the thesis sentence often appears in an essay's first paragraph, this paper takes a different tack. The first paragraph introduces the essay's focus—the benefits of the sonnet form for this particular poem—then builds carefully toward its thesis, which appears in the last paragraph.)

- **Make your argument more specific.** Use specifics instead of generalities in describing the poem. Writing imprecisely or vaguely, favoring the abstract over the concrete, is a common problem for student writers. When discussing ideas or principles, you can communicate more fully to your reader by supplying specific examples of those ideas or principles in action, as this student did when she reworked the ending of the paragraph above.

- **Make your language fresh and accurate.** It is easy to depend on habitual expressions and to overuse a few convenient words. Mechanical language may tempt you to think of the poem in mechanical terms. Here, for instance is a plodding discussion of Frost's "Design":

DRAFT

The symbols Frost uses in "Design" are very successful. Frost makes the spider
stand for Nature. He wants us to see nature as blind and cruel. He also employs
good sounds. He uses a lot of *i*'s because he is trying to make you think of
falling rain.

What's wrong with this "analysis"? The underscored words are worth questioning here. While understandable, the words *employs* and *uses* seem to lead the writer to see Frost only as a conscious tool-manipulator. To be sure, Frost in a sense "uses" symbols, but did he grab hold of them and lay them into his poem? For all we know, perhaps the symbols arrived quite unbidden and used the poet. To write a good poem, Frost maintained, the poet himself has to be surprised. (How, by the way, can we hope to know what a poet wants to do? And there isn't much point in saying that the poet is *trying* to do something. He has already done it, if he has written a good poem.) At least it is likely that Frost didn't plan to fulfill a certain quota of *i*-sounds. Writing his poem, not by following a blueprint but probably by bringing it slowly to the surface of his mind, Frost no doubt had enough to do without trying to engineer the reactions of his possible audience. Like all true symbols, Frost's spider doesn't *stand for* anything. The writer would be closer to the truth in saying that the spider *suggests* or *reminds us* of nature or of certain forces in the natural world. (Symbols just hint; they don't indicate.)

After the student discussed the paper with her instructor, she rewrote her sentences:

REVISION

The symbols in Frost's "Design" are highly effective. The spider, for instance, suggests the blindness and cruelty of Nature. Frost's word-sounds, too, are part of the meaning of his poem, for the *i*'s remind the reader of falling rain.

Not every reader of "Design" will hear rain falling, but the student's revision probably comes closer to describing the experience of the poem most of us have.

■ **Be clear and precise.** Another very real pitfall of writing literary criticism is the temptation to write in official-sounding Critic Speak. Writers who aren't quite sure about what to say may try to compensate for this uncertainty with unnecessarily ornate sentences that don't say much of anything. Other times, they will begin a sentence and find themselves completely entangled in its structure, unable to make a perfectly sound idea clear to the reader. Should you feel yourself being tugged out to sea by an undertow of fancy language, here is a trick for getting back ashore: speak your ideas aloud, in the simplest terms possible, to a friend, or a tape recorder, or your mirror. When you've formulated your ideas simply and clearly, write down your exact words. Most likely, your instructor will be grateful for the resulting clarity of expression.

CHECKLIST: Revising Your Draft

☐ Is your thesis clear and decisive?
☐ Does all your evidence advance your argument?
☐ Is information presented in the most logical order?
☐ Have you made an emotional connection with the reader?
☐ Does your presentation seem credible?
☐ Could your prose be clearer? More precise? More specific?
☐ Do transitional words and phrases signal movement from one idea to the next?
☐ Does your introduction draw the reader in? Does it prepare him or her for what follows?
☐ Does your conclusion tie up the essay's loose ends?
☐ Does each paragraph include a topic sentence?
☐ Does your title give a sense of the essay's subject?

COMMON APPROACHES TO WRITING ABOUT POETRY

Explication Paper

In an **explication** (literally, "an unfolding"), a writer explains an entire poem in detail, unraveling its complexities. An explication, however, should not be confused with a paraphrase, which puts the poem's literal meaning into plain prose. While an explication might include some paraphrasing, it does more than simply restate. It explains a poem, in great detail, showing how each part contributes to the whole. In writing an explication, keep the following tips in mind:

- **Start with the poem's first line, and keep working straight through to the end.** As needed, though, you can take up points out of order.

- **Read closely, addressing the poem's details.** You may choose to include allusions, the denotations or connotations of words, the possible meanings of symbols, the effects of certain sounds and rhythms and formal elements (rime schemes, for instance), the sense of any statements that contain irony, and other particulars.

- **Show how each part of the poem contributes to the meaning of the whole.** Your explication should go beyond dissecting the pieces of a poem; it should also bring them together in a way that casts light on the poem in its entirety.

Here is a successful student-authored explication of Frost's "Design." The assignment was to explain, in no more than 750 words, whatever in the poem seemed most essential.

Jasper 1

Ted Jasper

Professor Koss

English 130

21 November 2019

An Unfolding of Robert Frost's "Design"

"I always wanted to be very observing," Robert Frost once told an audience, after reading aloud his poem "Design." Then he added, "But I have always been afraid of my own observations" (qtd. in Cook 126–27). What could Frost have observed that could scare him? Let's examine the poem in question and see what we discover.

Starting with the title, "Design," any reader of this poem will find it full of meaning. As the *Merriam-Webster Dictionary* defines *design*, the word can denote among other things a plan, purpose, or intention ("Design"). Some arguments for the existence of God (I remember from Sunday School) are based on the "argument from design": that because the world shows a systematic order, there must be a Designer who made it. But the word *design* can also mean "a deliberate undercover project or scheme" such as we attribute to a "designing person" ("Design"). As we shall see, Frost's poem incorporates all of these meanings. His poem raises the old philosophic question of whether there is a Designer, an evil Designer, or no Designer at all.

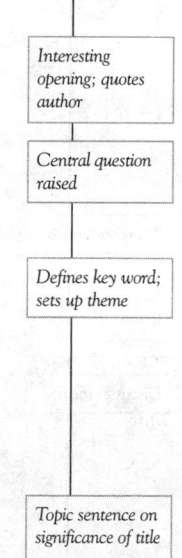

Interesting opening; quotes author

Central question raised

Defines key word; sets up theme

Topic sentence on significance of title

Jasper 2

Begins line-by-line unfolding of meaning

Discusses images

Explores language

Refers to sound

Transition words

Quotes secondary source

Discusses theme

Like many other sonnets, "Design" is divided into two parts. The first eight lines draw a picture centering on the spider, who at first seems almost jolly. It is *dimpled* and *fat* like a baby, or Santa Claus. The spider stands on a wildflower whose name, *heal-all*, seems ironic: a heal-all is supposed to cure any disease, but this flower has no power to restore life to the dead moth. (Later, in line 10, we learn that the heal-all used to be blue. Presumably, it has died and become bleached-looking.) In the second line we discover, too, that the spider has hold of another creature, a dead moth. We then see the moth described with an odd simile in line 3: "Like a white piece of rigid satin cloth." Suddenly, the moth becomes not a creature but a piece of fabric—lifeless and dead—and yet *satin* has connotations of beauty. Satin is a luxurious material used in rich formal clothing, such as coronation gowns and brides' dresses. Additionally, there is great accuracy in the word: the smooth and slightly plush surface of satin is like the powder-smooth surface of moths' wings. But this "cloth," rigid and white, could be the lining to Dracula's coffin.

In the fifth line an invisible hand enters. The characters are "mixed" like ingredients in an evil potion. Some force doing the mixing is behind the scene. The characters in themselves are innocent enough, but when brought together, their whiteness and look of *rigor mortis* are overwhelming. There is something diabolical in the spider's feast. The "morning right" echoes the word *rite*, a ritual—in this case apparently a Black Mass or a Witches' Sabbath. The simile in line 7 ("a flower like a froth") is more ambiguous and harder to describe. Froth is white, foamy, and delicate—something found on a brook in the woods or on a beach after a wave recedes. However, in the natural world, froth also can be ugly: the foam on a polluted stream or a rabid dog's mouth. The dualism in nature—its beauty and its horror—is there in that one simile.

So far, the poem has portrayed a small, frozen scene, with the dimpled killer holding its victim as innocently as a boy holds a kite. Already, Frost has hinted that Nature may be, as Radcliffe Squires suggests, "Nothing but an ash-white plain without love or faith or hope, where ignorant appetites cross by chance" (87). Now, in the last six lines of the sonnet, Frost comes out and directly states his theme. What else could bring these deathly pale, stiff things together "but design of darkness to appall"? The question is clearly rhetorical; we are meant to answer, "Yes, there does seem to be an evil design at work here!" I take the next-to-last line to mean, "What except a design so dark and sinister that we're appalled by it?" "Appall," by the way, is the second pun in

Jasper 3

the poem: it sounds like a pall or shroud. (The derivation of *appall*, according to *Merriam-Webster*, is ultimately from a Latin word meaning "to be pale"—an interesting word choice for a poem full of pale white images ["Appall"].) *Steered* carries the suggestion of a steering-wheel or rudder that some pilot had to control. Like the word *brought*, it implies that some invisible force charted the paths of spider, heal-all, and moth, so that they arrived together.

> *Defines key word*

Having suggested that the universe is in the hands of that sinister force (an indifferent God? Fate? the Devil?), Frost adds a note of doubt. The Bible tells us that "His eye is on the sparrow," but at the moment the poet doesn't seem sure. Maybe, he hints, when things in the universe drop below a certain size, they pass completely out of the Designer's notice. When creatures are this little, maybe God doesn't bother to govern them but just lets them run wild. And possibly the same mindless chance is all that governs human lives. And because this is even more senseless than having an angry God intent on punishing us, it is, Frost suggests, the worst suspicion of all.

> *Answers question raised in introduction*

> *Conclusion*

Jasper 4

Works Cited

"Appall." *Merriam-Webster.com*, 2019, www.merriam-webster.com/dictionary/appall.

Cook, Reginald. *Robert Frost: A Living Voice.* U of Massachusetts P, 1974.

"Design." *Merriam-Webster.com*, 2019, www.merriam-webster.com/dictionary/design.

Frost, Robert. "Design." *Collected Poems, Prose and Plays*, Library of America, 1995, p. 275.

Squires, Radcliffe. *The Major Themes of Robert Frost.* U of Michigan P, 1963.

This excellent paper finds something worth unfolding in every line of Frost's poem, without seeming mechanical. Although the student proceeds sequentially through the poem from the title to the last line, he takes up some points out of order when it serves his purpose. In paragraph 2, for example, he looks ahead to the poem's ending and briefly states its main theme in order to relate it to the poem's title. In the third paragraph, he explicates the poem's later image of the heal-all, relating it to the first image. He also comments on the poem's form ("Like many other sonnets"), on its similes and puns, and on its denotations and connotations.

This paper also demonstrates good use of manuscript form, following the *MLA Handbook*, 8th ed. Brief references (in parentheses) tell us where the writer found Frost's remarks and give the page number for his quotation from the book by Radcliffe Squires. At the end of the paper, a list of works cited uses abbreviations that the *MLA Handbook* recommends.

A Critic's Explication of Frost's "Design"

It might seem that to work through a poem line by line is a mechanical task, and yet there can be genuine excitement in doing so. Randall Jarrell once wrote an explication of "Design" in which he managed to convey just such excitement. See if you can sense Jarrell's joy in writing about the poem.

> Frost's details are so diabolically good that it seems criminal to leave some unremarked; but notice how *dimpled, fat,* and *white* (all but one; all but one) come from our regular description of any baby; notice how the *heal-all,* because of its name, is the one flower in all the world picked to be the altar for this Devil's Mass; notice how *holding up* the moth brings something ritual and hieratic, a ghostly, ghastly formality, to this priest and its sacrificial victim; notice how terrible to the fingers, how full of the stilling rigor of death, that *white piece of rigid satin cloth* is. And *assorted characters of death and blight* is, like so many things in this poem, sharply ambiguous: *a mixed bunch of actors* or *diverse representative signs.* The tone of the phrase *assorted characters of death and blight* is beautifully developed in the ironic Breakfast-Club-calisthenics, Radio-Kitchen heartiness of *mixed ready to begin the morning right* (which assures us, so unreassuringly, that this isn't any sort of Strindberg *Spook Sonata,* but hard fact), and concludes in the *ingredients* of the witches' broth, giving the soup a sort of cuddly shimmer that the cauldron in *Macbeth* never had; the *broth,* even, is brought to life—we realize that witches' broth *is* broth, to be supped with a long spoon.[1]

Evidently, Jarrell's cultural interests are broad: ranging from August Strindberg's ground-breaking modern play down to *The Breakfast Club* (a once-popular radio program that cheerfully exhorted its listeners to march around their tables). And yet breadth of knowledge, however much it deepens and enriches Jarrell's writing, isn't all that he brings to the reading of poetry. For him an explication isn't a dull plod, but a voyage of discovery. His prose—full of figures of speech (*diabolically good, cuddly shimmer*)—conveys the apparent delight he takes in showing off his findings. Such a joy, of course, can't be acquired deliberately. But it can grow, the more you read and study poetry.

Analysis Paper

Like a news commentator's parsing of a crisis in the Middle East or a chemist's study of an unknown fluid, an **analysis** separates a poem into elements as a means to understanding that subject. Usually, the writer of an analysis focuses on one particular element: "Imagery of Light and Darkness in Frost's 'Design'" or "The Character of Satan

---

[1] *Poetry and the Age* (New York: Knopf, 1953), 42–43.

in Milton's *Paradise Lost.*" In this book, you probably already have encountered a few brief analyses: the discussion of connotations in William Blake's "London" (Chapter 18), for instance, or the examination of symbols in T. S. Eliot's "The *Boston Evening Transcript*" (Chapter 26). In fact, most of the discussions in this book are analyses. To write an analysis, remember two key points:

- **Focus on a single, manageable element of a poem.** Some possible choices are tone, irony, literal meaning, imagery, figures of speech, sound, rhythm, theme, and symbolism.

- **Show how this element of the poem contributes to the meaning of the whole.** While no element of a poem exists apart from all the others, by taking a closer look at one particular aspect of the poem, you can see the whole more clearly.

The paper that follows analyzes a particularly tricky subject—the formal and technical elements of Frost's "Design." Long analyses of metrical feet, rime schemes, and indentations can make for ponderous reading, but this paper shows how formal analysis can be interesting and can cast light on a poem.

Lopez 1

Guadalupe Lopez

Professor Faber

English 210

16 November 2019

The Design of Robert Frost's "Design"

For Robert Frost's poem "Design," the sonnet form has at least two advantages. As in most Italian sonnets, the poem's argument falls into two parts. In the octave Frost's persona draws a still life of a spider, a flower, and a moth; then in the sestet he contemplates the meaning of his still life. Although the poem is perfectly formal in its shape, the ideas it presents are not predictable, but are instead both surprising and disturbing. The sestet focuses on a universal: the possible existence of a vindictive deity who causes the spider to catch the moth and, no doubt, also causes—when viewed anthropomorphically—other suffering.

Introduction gives overview of poem's form

Thesis sentence states paper's main claim

Frost's persona weaves his own little web. The unwary audience is led through the poem's argument from its opening "story" to a point at which something must be made of the story's symbolic significance. Even the rhyme scheme contributes to the poem's successful leading of the audience toward the sestet's theological questioning. The word *white* ends the first line of the sestet, and the same vowel sound is echoed in the lines that follow. All in all, half of the sonnet's lines end in the "ite" sound, as if to render significant the wh*ite*ness—the symbolic innocence—of nature's representation of a greater truth.

Topic sentence on how poem subtly makes its point

Lopez 2

Topic sentence on how form relates to theme

A sonnet has a familiar design, and the poem's classical form points to the thematic concern that there seems to be an order to the universe that might be perceived by looking at even seemingly insignificant natural events. The sonnet must follow certain conventions, and nature, though not as readily apprehensible as a poetic form, is apparently governed by a set of laws. There is a ready-made irony in Frost's choosing such an order-driven form to meditate on whether or not there is any order in the universe. However, whether or not his questioning sestet is actually approaching an answer or, indeed, the answer, Frost has approached an order that seems to echo a larger order in his using the sonnet form. An approach through poetic form and substance is itself significant in Frost's own estimation, for he argues that what a poet achieves in writing poetry is "a momentary stay against confusion" ("Figure" 777).

Conclusion

Although design clearly governs in this poem—in this "thing so small"—the design is not entirely predictable. The poem does start out in the form of an Italian sonnet, relying on only two rhyming sounds. However, unlike an Italian sonnet, one of the octave's rhyming sounds—the "ite"—continues into the sestet. And additionally, "Design" ends in a couplet, much in the manner of the Shakespearean sonnet, which frequently offers, in the final couplet, a summing up of the sonnet's argument. Perhaps not only nature's "story" of the spider, the flower, and the moth but also Frost's poem itself echoes the larger universe. It looks perfectly orderly until the details are given their due.

Lopez 3

Works Cited

Frost, Robert. "Design." *Collected Poems, Prose and Plays*, Library of America, 1995, p. 275.

---. "The Figure a Poem Makes." *Collected Poems, Prose and Plays*, Library of America, 1995, pp. 776-78.

Comparison and Contrast Paper

The process of **comparison** and **contrast** places two poems side by side and studies their differences and similarities in order to shed light on both works. Writing an effective comparison-contrast paper involves the following steps:

- **Pair two poems with much in common.** Comparing two poems with surface similarities—for example, Dorothy Parker's caustic "Résumé" (Chapter 23) and Ben Jonson's profoundly elegiac "On My First Son" (Chapter 34)—can be a futile endeavor. Though both poems are about death, the two seem hopelessly removed from each other in diction, tone, complexity, and scope. Instead, choose two poems with enough in common that their differences take on interesting weight.

- **Point to further, unsuspected resemblances.** Steer clear of the obvious ("'Design' and 'Wing-Spread' are both about bugs"). The interesting resemblances take some thought to discover.

- **Show noteworthy differences.** Avoid those your reader will see without any help.

- **Carefully consider your essay's organization.** While you may be tempted to discuss first one poem and then the other, this simple structure may weaken your essay if it leads you to keep the two poems in total isolation from each other. After all, the point is to see what can be learned by comparison. There is nothing wrong in discussing all of poem A first and then discussing poem B—if in discussing B you keep referring back to A. Another strategy is to do a point-by-point comparison of the two poems all the way through your paper, dealing first, perhaps, with their themes, then with their central metaphors, and finally with their respective merits.

A comparison-contrast essay is often a kind of analysis—a study of a theme common to two poems, perhaps, or of two poets' similar fondness for the myth of Eden. In some cases, though, a comparison can also involve evaluation—a judgment on the relative worth of two poems.

Here, for example, is a poem by Abbie Huston Evans, followed by a paper that considers the merits of that poem and Frost's "Design." Through comparison and contrast, this student makes a case for his view of which poet deserves the brighter laurels.

Abbie Huston Evans (1881–1983)

Wing-Spread   1938

The midge spins out to safety
Through the spider's rope;
But the moth, less lucky,
Has to grope.

Mired in glue-like cable   5
See him foundered swing
By the gap he opened
With his wing,

Dusty web enlacing
All that blue and beryl.   10
In a netted universe
Wing-spread is peril.

1824 Chapter 44 ■ Writing About a Poem

Tom Munjee

Professor Mickey

English 110

21 February 2019

"Wing-Spread" Does a Dip

Thesis sentence states paper's main claim

Abbie Huston Evans's "Wing-Spread" is an effective short poem, but it lacks the complexity and depth of Robert Frost's "Design." These two poems were published only two years apart, and both present a murderous spider and an unlucky moth, but Frost's treatment differs from Evans's approach in at least

Outlines the argument

two important ways. First, Frost uses poetic language more evocatively than Evans. Second, "Design" digs more deeply into the situation to uncover a more memorable theme.

If we compare the language of the two poems, we find "Design" is full of words and phrases rich with suggestions. The language of "Wing-Spread," by comparison, seems thinner. Frost's "dimpled spider, fat and white," for example,

Textual evidence— contrasts diction of two poems

is certainly a more suggestive description. Actually, Evans does not describe her spider; she just says, "the spider's rope." (Evans does vividly show the spider and moth in action. In Frost's poem, they are already dead and petrified.) In "Design," the spider's dimples show that it is like a chubby little baby. This seems an odd way to look at a spider, but it is more original than Evans's conventional view (although I like her word *cable*, suggesting that the spider's web is a kind of high-tech food trap). Frost's word choice—his repetition of *white*—paints a more striking scene than Evans's slightly vague "All that blue and beryl." Except for her brief personification of the moth in the second stanza, Evans hardly uses any figures of speech, and even this one is not a clear personification—she simply gives the moth a sex by referring to it as "him." Frost's striking metaphors, similes, and even puns (*right*, *appall*) show him, as usual, to be a master of figures of speech. He calls the moth's wings "satin cloth" and "a paper kite"; Evans just refers in line 8 to a moth's wing. As far as the language of the two poems goes, we might as well compare a vase brimming with flowers and a single flower stuck in a vase. In fairness to Evans, I would say that her poem, while lacking complexity, still makes its point effectively. Her poem has powerful sounds: short lines with the riming words coming at us again and again.

Contrasts thematic approach

In theme, however, "Wing-Spread" seems much more narrow than "Design." The first time I read Evans's poem, all I felt was: Ho hum, the moth's wings were too wide and got stuck. The second time I read it, I realized that she was saying

Munjee 2

something with a universal application. This message comes out in line 11, in "a netted universe." That metaphorical phrase is the most interesting part of her poem. *Netted* makes me imagine the universe as being full of nets rigged by someone who is fishing for us. Maybe, like Frost, Evans sees an evil plan operating. She does not, though, investigate it. She says that the midge escapes because it is tiny. On the other hand, things with wide wing-spreads get stuck. Her theme as I read it is, "Be small and inconspicuous if you want to survive," or maybe, "Isn't it too bad that in this world the big beautiful types crack up and die, while the little puny punks keep sailing?" Now, this is a valuable idea. I have often thought that very same thing myself. But Frost's closing note ("If design govern in a thing so small") is really devastating because it raises a huge uncertainty. "Wing-Spread" leaves us with not much besides a moth stuck in a web and a moral. In both language and theme, "Design" climbs to a higher altitude.

Conclusion restates thesis

Munjee 3

Works Cited

Evans, Abbie Huston. "Wing-Spread." *Literature: An Introduction to Fiction,*
    Poetry, Drama, and Writing, edited by X. J. Kennedy et al., 14th ed., Pearson,
    2020, p. 1823.
Frost, Robert. "Design." *Collected Poems, Prose and Plays*, Library of America, 1995,
    p. 275.

HOW TO QUOTE A POEM

Quoted to illustrate some point, memorable lines can enliven your paper. Carefully chosen quotations can serve to back up your thesis, or to alert your readers to a phrase or passage they may have neglected. Quoting poetry accurately, however, raises certain difficulties you don't face in quoting prose. Poets choose their line breaks with deliberation, and part of a critic's job is to take those breaks into account. Here are guidelines for respecting a poet's line breaks and for making your essay more polished in the bargain.

- **Quoting a few lines.** If you are quoting fewer than four lines of poetry, transform the passage into prose form, separating each line by a space, a diagonal (/), and another space. The diagonal (/) indicates where the poet's lines begin and end. Two diagonals (//) signal a new stanza. Do not change the poet's capitalization or punctuation. Be sure to identify the line numbers you are quoting, as follows:

> The color white preoccupies Frost. The spider is "fat and white, / On a white heal-all" (1–2), and even the victim moth is pale, too.

■ **Quoting four or more lines.** If you are quoting four or more lines of verse, set them off from your text, and arrange them just as they occur on the page, white space and all. Be sure to identify the lines you are quoting. In general, follow these rules:

- Indent the quotation one inch from the left-hand margin.
- Double-space between the quoted lines.
- Type the poem exactly as it appears in the original. You do not need to use quotation marks.
- If you begin the quotation in the middle of a line of verse, position the starting word about where it occurs in the poem—not at the left-hand margin.
- If a line you are quoting runs too long to fit on one line, indent the return one-quarter inch.
- Cite the line numbers you are quoting in parentheses.

> At the end of the poem, the poet asks what deity or fate cursed this particular
>
> mutant flower
>
>   with being white,
>
> The wayside blue and innocent heal-all?
>
> What brought the kindred spider to that height,
>
> Then steered the white moth thither in the night? (9–12)

■ **Omitting words.** If you omit words from the lines you quote, indicate the omission with an ellipsis (. . .), as in the following example:

> The color white preoccupies Frost in his description of the spider "fat and white, / On a white heal-all . . . / Like a white piece of rigid satin cloth" (1–3).

■ **Quoting only a brief phrase.** There's no need for an ellipsis if it is obvious that only a phrase is being quoted.

> The speaker says that he "found a dimpled spider," and he goes on to portray it as a kite-flying boy.

■ **Omitting full lines of verse.** If you leave out lines of verse, indicate the omission by spaced periods about the length of a line of the poem you are quoting.

Maybe, she hints, when things in the universe drop below a certain size, they

pass completely out of the Designer's notice:

> The midge spins out to safety
>
> Through the spider's rope;
>
> . . . .
>
> In a netted universe
>
> Wing-spread is peril. (1–2, 11–12)

One last note: often a paper on a short poem will include the whole text of the poem at its beginning, with the lines numbered so that your reader can refer to it with ease. Ask your instructor whether he or she prefers the full text to be quoted this way.

TOPICS FOR WRITING BRIEF PAPERS (250–500 WORDS)

1. Write a concise *explication* of a short poem of your choice. Concentrate on those facets of the poem that you think most need explaining.

2. Write an *analysis* of a short poem, focusing on how a single key element shapes its meaning. Here are some possible topics to consider:

    - Tone in Edna St. Vincent Millay's "Recuerdo" (Chapter 34)
    - Imagery in Wallace Stevens's "The Emperor of Ice-Cream" (Chapter 34)
    - Kinds of irony in Thomas Hardy's "The Workbox" (Chapter 16)
    - Theme in W. H. Auden's "Musée des Beaux Arts" (Chapter 34)
    - Extended metaphor in Langston Hughes's "The Negro Speaks of Rivers" (Chapter 32). (Explain the one main comparison that the poem makes and show how the whole poem makes it. Other poems that would lend themselves to a paper on extended metaphor include: Emily Dickinson's "Because I could not stop for Death" (Chapter 32), Robert Lowell's "Skunk Hour" (Chapter 34), Adrienne Rich's "Aunt Jennifer's Tigers" (Chapter 15).)

3. Select a poem in which the main speaker is a character who for any reason interests you. You might consider, for instance, Robert Browning's "Soliloquy of the Spanish Cloister" (Chapter 34), T. S. Eliot's "The Love Song of J. Alfred Prufrock" (Chapter 33), or Rhina Espaillat's "Bilingual/*Bilingüe*" (Chapter 16). Then write a brief profile of this character, drawing only on what the poem tells you (or reveals). What is the character's age? Situation in life? Attitude toward self? Attitude toward others? General personality? Do you find this character admirable?

4. Choose a brief poem that you find difficult. Write an essay in which you begin by listing the points in the poem that strike you as most impenetrable. Next, reread the poem at least twice. In the essay's second half, describe how further readings changed your experience of the poem.

5. Although each of these poems tells a story, what happens in the poem isn't necessarily obvious: E. E. Cummings's "anyone lived in a pretty how town" (Chapter 17) T. S. Eliot's "The Love Song of J. Alfred Prufrock," Edwin Arlington Robinson's "Luke Havergal" (Chapter 16). Choose one of these poems, and in a paragraph sum up what you think happens in it. Then in a second paragraph, ask yourself: what, *besides* the element of story, did you consider in order to understand the poem?

6. Imagine a reader who categorically dislikes poetry. Choose a poem for that person to read, and, addressing your skeptical reader, explain the ways in which this particular poem rewards a careful reader.

TOPICS FOR WRITING MORE EXTENDED PAPERS (600–1,000 WORDS)

1. Perform a line-by-line explication of a brief poem of your choice. Imagine that your audience is unfamiliar with the poem and needs your assistance in interpreting it.

2. Explicate a passage from a longer poem. Choose a passage that is, in your opinion, central to the poem's meaning.

3. Compare and contrast any two poems that treat a similar theme. Let your comparison bring you to an evaluation of the poems. Which is the stronger, more satisfying one?

4. Write a comparison-contrast essay on any two or more poems by a single poet. Look for two poems that share a characteristic thematic concern. (This book contains multiple selections by Auden, Blake, Cummings, Dickinson, Donne, Eliot, Frost, Hardy, Hopkins, Hughes, Keats, Shakespeare, Stevens, Tennyson, Whitman, Williams, Wordsworth, Yeats, and many others.) Here are some possible topics:

   - Mortality in the work of John Keats
   - Nature in the poems of William Wordsworth
   - How Emily Dickinson's lyric poems resemble hymns
   - E. E. Cummings's approach to the free-verse line
   - Gerard Manley Hopkins's sonic effects

5. Evaluate by the method of comparison two versions of a poem, one an early draft and one a late draft, or perhaps two translations of the same poem from another language.

6. If the previous topic appeals to you, consider this. In 1912, ten years before he published "Design," Robert Frost sent a correspondent this early version:

In White

A dented spider like a snow drop white
On a white Heal-all, holding up a moth
Like a white piece of lifeless satin cloth—
Saw ever curious eye so strange a sight?
Portent in little, assorted death and blight
Like the ingredients of a witches' broth?
The beady spider, the flower like a froth,

And the moth carried like a paper kite.
What had that flower to do with being white,
The blue Brunella every child's delight.
What brought the kindred spider to that height?
(Make we no thesis of the miller's plight.)
What but design of darkness and of night?
Design, design! Do I use the word aright?

Compare "In White" with "Design." In what respects is the finished poem superior?

TOPICS FOR WRITING LONG PAPERS (1,500 WORDS OR MORE)

1. Review an entire poetry collection by a poet featured in this book. You will need to communicate to your reader a sense of the work's style and thematic preoccupations. Finally, make a value judgment about the work's quality.

2. Read five or six poems by a single author. Start with a poet featured in this book, and then find additional poems at the library or on the Internet. Write an analysis of a single element of that poet's work—for example, theme, imagery, diction, or form.

3. Write a line-by-line explication of a poem rich in matters to explain or of a longer poem that offers ample difficulty. While relatively short, John Donne's "A Valediction: Forbidding Mourning" and Gerard Manley Hopkins's "The Windhover" (both in Chapter 34) are poems that will take a good bit of time to explicate. Even a short, apparently simple poem such as Robert Frost's "Stopping by Woods on a Snowy Evening" (Chapter 32) can provide more than enough material to explicate thoughtfully in a longer paper.

4. Write an analysis of a certain theme (or other element) that you find in the work of two or more poets. It is probable that in your conclusion you will want to set the poets' works side by side, comparing or contrasting them, and perhaps making some evaluation. Here are some sample topics to consider:

   • Langston Hughes, Gwendolyn Brooks, and Dudley Randall as Prophets of Social Change
   • What It Is to Be a Woman: The Special Knowledge of Sylvia Plath, Anne Sexton, and Adrienne Rich
   • The Complex Relations Between Fathers and Children in the Poetry of Robert Hayden, Rhina Espaillat, and Theodore Roethke
   • Making Up New Words for New Meanings: Neologisms in Lewis Carroll and Kay Ryan

5. Apply the ideas in one of the critical excerpts in the "Writing Effectively" section found at the end of most chapters to a poem by the same author. Formulate a thesis about whether or not the prose excerpt sheds any light on the poetry. How do T. S. Eliot's thoughts on the music of poetry, or William Butler Yeats's observations on poetic symbolism, help you to better understand their poems? Quote as needed to back up your argument.

45

WRITING ABOUT A PLAY

*The play was a great success,
but the audience was a total failure.*

—OSCAR WILDE

What You Will Learn in This Chapter

- To read a play critically
- To write a review of a play
- To quote a play

Writing about a play you've read is similar, in many ways, to writing about poetry or fiction. If your subject is a play you have actually seen performed, however, some differences will quickly become apparent. Although, like a story or a poem, a play in print is usually the work of a single author, a play on stage may be the joint effort of seventy or eighty people—actors, director, costumers, set designers, and technicians. Though a play on the page stays fixed and changeless, a play in performance changes in many details from season to season—and even from night to night.

Later in this chapter you will find advice on reviewing a performance of a play, as you might do for a class assignment or for publication in a campus newspaper. In a literature course, though, you will probably write about the plays you quietly read and behold only in the theater of your mind.

READ CRITICALLY

- **Read the whole play—not just the dialogue, but also everything in italics, including stage directions and descriptions of settings.** The meaning of a scene, or even of an entire play, may depend on the tone of voice in which an actor is supposed to deliver a significant line. At the end of *A Doll's House* (Chapter 39), for example, we need to pay attention to *how* Helmer's last line is spoken—"A hope flashes across his mind"—if we are to understand that Nora ignores his last desperate hope for reconciliation when she closes the door. The meaning of a line may depend upon the actions described in the stage directions. If Nora did not leave the house or close the door, but hesitated at Helmer's last line, the meaning of the play would be slightly different.

- **Highlight key passages and take notes as you read.** Later you will want to quote or refer to important moments in the play, and marking those moments will simplify your job. Following is an example of a student's notes on a key scene in Susan Glaspell's *Trifles* (Chapter 35).

Mrs. Peters (*to the other woman*): Oh, her fruit; it did freeze. (*To the County Attorney*) She worried about that when it turned so cold. She said the fire'd go out and her jars would break.

Sheriff: Well, can you beat the women! Held for murder and worryin' about her preserves.

Both men are insulting toward Mrs. Wright.

County Attorney: I guess before we're through she may have something more serious than preserves to worry about.

He thinks he's being kind.

Hale: Well, women are used to worrying over trifles.

Is housework really insignificant?

(*The two women move a little closer together.*)

The women side with each other.

County Attorney (*with the gallantry of a young politician*): And yet, for all their worries, what would we do without the ladies? (*The women do not unbend. He goes to the sink, takes a dipperful of water from the pail and pouring it into a basin, washes his hands. Starts to wipe them on the roller towel, turns it for a cleaner place.*) Dirty towels! (*Kicks his foot against the pans under the sink.*) Not much of a housekeeper, would you say, ladies?

Courtesy toward women, but condescending

Mrs. Hale (*stiffly*): There's a great deal of work to be done on a farm.

The two women aren't buying it.

She holds back, but she's mad.

Small, insignificant things or not?

I don't like this guy!

Play's title. Significant word? The men miss the "clues"—too trifling.

- If your subject is a play in verse—such as those by Sophocles and Shakespeare—keep track of act, scene, and line numbers as you take notes. This will help you to easily relocate any text you want to refer to or quote.

> Iago's hypocrisy is apparent in his speech defending his good name (3.3.168–74).

COMMON APPROACHES TO WRITING ABOUT DRAMA

The methods commonly used to write about fiction and poetry—for example, explication, analysis, or comparison and contrast—are all well suited to writing about drama. These methods are discussed in depth in earlier chapters. Here are a few suggestions for using these methods to write about plays in particular.

Explication Paper

A whole play is too much to cover in an ordinary **explication**, a line-by-line unfolding of meaning in a literary work. In drama, explication is best suited to brief passages—a key soliloquy, for example, or a moment of dialogue that lays bare the play's theme. Closely examining a critical moment in a play can shed light on the play in its entirety. To be successful, an explication needs to concentrate on a passage probably not much more than 20 lines long.

Analysis Paper

A separation of a literary work into elements, **analysis** is a very useful method for writing about drama. To write an analysis, choose a single element in a play—for example, animal imagery in some speeches from *Othello* (Chapter 38), or the theme of fragility in *The Glass Menagerie* (Chapter 39). Plays certainly offer many choices of elements for analysis: characters, themes, tone, irony, imagery, figures of speech, and symbols, for example. Keep in mind, though, that not all plays contain the same elements you would find in poetry or fiction. Few plays have a narrator, and in most cases the point of view is that of the audience, which perceives the events not through a narrator's eyes but through its own. And while we might analyze a short story's all-pervading style, a play might contain as many styles as there are speaking characters. (Noteworthy exceptions do exist, though: you might argue that in Susan Glaspell's *Trifles*, both main characters speak the same language.) As for traditional poetic devices such as metaphor and metrical pattern, they may be found in plays such as *Othello*, but not in most contemporary plays, in which the dialogue tends to sound like ordinary conversation.

Comparison and Contrast Analysis

The method of **comparison** and **contrast** involves setting two plays side by side and pointing out their similarities and differences. Because plays are complicated entities, you need to choose a narrow focus, or you will find yourself overwhelmed. A profound topic—"The Self-Deception of Othello and Oedipus"—might do for a three-hundred-page dissertation, but an essay of a mere thousand words could never do it justice. A large but finite topic—say, attitudes toward marriage in *A Doll's House* and *Trifles*—would best suit a long term paper. To apply this method to a shorter term paper, you might compare and contrast a certain aspect of personality in two characters within the same play—for example, Troy's and Cory's ambitions in *Fences* (Chapter 41).

Card Report

In place of an essay, some instructors like to assign a **card report**, a succinct but thorough method of analyzing the components of a play. For more information on this kind of assignment, see "The Card Report" in Chapter 43. Keep in mind, though, that when dealing with a play, you will find some elements that differ from those in a short story. Specifying the work's narrator may not be relevant to a play, for example. Also, for a full-length play, you may need to write on both sides of two 5- × 8-inch index cards instead of on one card, as you might for a short story. Still, in order to write a good card report, you have to be both brief and specific. Before you start, sort out your impressions of the play and try to decide which characters, scenes, and lines of dialogue are the most memorable and important. Reducing your scattered impressions to essentials, you will have to reexamine what you have read. When you finish, you will know the play much more thoroughly.

Here is an example: a card report on Susan Glaspell's one-act play *Trifles*. By including only the elements that seemed most important, the writer managed to analyze the brief play on the front and back of one card. Still, he managed to work in a few pertinent quotations to give a sense of the play's remarkable language. Although the report does not say everything about Glaspell's little masterpiece, an adequate criticism of the play could hardly be much briefer. For this report, the writer was assigned to include the following:

1. The playwright's name, nationality, and dates.
2. The title of the play and the date of its first performance.
3. The central character or characters, with a brief description that includes leading traits.
4. Other characters, also described.
5. The scene or scenes and, if the play does not take place in the present, the time of its action.
6. The dramatic question. This question is whatever the play leads us to ask ourselves: some conflict whose outcome we wonder about, some uncertainty whose resolution we look forward to.
7. A brief summary of the play's principal events, in the order in which the playwright presents them. If you are reporting on a play longer than *Trifles*, you may find it simplest to sum up what happens in each act, perhaps in each scene.
8. The tone of the play, as best you can detect it. Try to describe the playwright's apparent feelings toward the characters or what happens to them.
9. The language spoken in the play. Try to describe it. Does any character speak with a choice of words or with figures of speech that strike you as unusual, distinctive, poetic—or maybe dull and drab? Does language indicate a character's background or place of birth? Brief quotations, in what space you have, will be valuable.
10. A one-sentence summary of the play's central theme. If you find none, say so. Plays often contain more than one theme. Which of them seems most clearly borne out by the main events?
11. Any symbols you notice and believe to be important. Try to state in a few words what each suggests.
12. A concise evaluation of the play. What did you think of it? (For more suggestions on being a drama critic, see Chapter 40, "Evaluating a Play.")

Here is a card report on *Trifles*.

Front of Card

Ben Nelson English 101

Susan Glaspell, American, 1876–1948

Trifles, 1916

Central characters: Mrs. Peters, the sheriff's nervous wife, dutiful but independent, not "married to the law"—whose sorrows make her able to sympathize with a woman accused of murder. Mrs. Hale, who knows the accused; more decisive.

Other characters: The County Attorney, self-important but short-sighted. The Sheriff, a man of only middling intelligence, another sexist. Hale, a farmer, a cautious man. Not seen on stage, two others are central: Minnie (Foster) Wright, the accused, a music lover reduced to near despair by years of grim marriage and isolation; and John Wright, the victim, known for his cruelty.

Scene: The kitchen of a gloomy farmhouse after the arrest of a wife on suspicion of murder; little things left in disarray.

Major dramatic question: Why did Minnie Wright kill her husband? When this question is answered, a new major dramatic question is raised: Will Mrs. Peters and Mrs. Hale cover up incriminating evidence?

Events: In the exposition, Sheriff and C.A., investigating the death of Wright, hear Hale tell how he found the body and a distracted Mrs. Wright. Then (1) C.A. starts looking for a motive. (2) His jeering at Mrs. Wright (and all women) for their concern with "trifles" causes Mrs. Peters and Mrs. Hale to rally to the woman's defense. (3) When the two women find evidence that Mrs. Wright had panicked (a patch of wild sewing in a quilt), Mrs. Hale destroys it. (4) Mrs. Peters finds more evidence: a wrecked birdcage. (5) The women find a canary with its neck wrung and realize that Minnie killed her husband in a similar way. (6) The women align themselves with Minnie when Mrs. Peters recalls her own sorrows, and Mrs. Hale decides her own failure to visit Minnie was "a crime." (7) The C.A. unwittingly provides Mrs. Peters with a means to smuggle out the canary. (8) The two women unite to seize the evidence.

[continued on back of card]

Back of Card

> Tone: Made clear in the women's dialogue: mingled horror and sadness at what has happened, compassion for a fellow woman, smoldering resentment toward men who crush women.
>
> Language: The plain speech of farm people, with a dash of rural Midwestern slang (*red-up* for tidy; Hale's remark that the accused was "kind of done up"). Unschooled speech: Mrs. Hale says *ain't*—and yet her speech rises at moments to simple poetry: "She used to sing. He killed that too." Glaspell hints at the self-importance of the County Attorney by his heavy reliance on the first person.
>
> Central theme: Women, in their supposed concern for trifles, see more deeply than men do.
>
> Symbols: The broken birdcage and the dead canary, both suggesting the music and the joy that John Wright stifled in Minnie.
>
> Evaluation: A powerful, successful, realistic play that conveys its theme with great economy—in its views, more than fifty years ahead of its time.

A Drama Review

Writing a **play review**, a brief critical account of an actual performance, involves going out on a limb and making an evaluation. It also can mean assessing various aspects of the production, including the acting, direction, sets, costumes, lighting, and possibly even the play itself. While reviews can be challenging to write, many students find them more stimulating—even more fun—than most writing assignments. There is no better way to understand—and appreciate—drama than by seeing live theater. Here are some tips for writing a review.

- **Clarify what you are evaluating.** Is it the play's script, or the performance? If the latter, are you concentrating on the performance in its entirety, or on certain elements, such as the acting or the direction? If the play is a classic one, the more urgent task for the reviewer will be not to evaluate the playwright's work but to comment on the success of the actors', director's, and production crew's particular interpretation of it. If the play is newer and less well established, you may profitably evaluate the script itself.

- **If the play itself is your subject, be aware of the conventions within which the playwright is working.** For a list of considerations see "Judging a Play" in Chapter 40.

- **Don't simply sneer or gush; give reasons for your opinions.** Ground your praise or criticism of a production in specifics. Incidentally, harsh evaluations can tempt a reviewer to flashes of wit. One celebrated flash was writer Eugene Field's observation of an actor in a production of *King Lear*, that "he played the king as though he were in constant fear that someone else was about to play the ace." The comment isn't merely nasty; it implies that Field had closely watched the actor's performance and had discerned what was wrong with it.

- **Early in the review, provide the basic facts.** Give the play's title and author, the theatrical company producing it, and the theater in which it is performed.

- **Give the names of actors in lead roles, and evaluate their performances.** How well cast do the leads seem? If an actor stands out—for good or ill—in a supporting role, he or she may deserve a mention as well.

- **Provide a brief plot summary.** Your reader may be unacquainted with the play, and will certainly want a general sense of what it is about. Out of consideration to the reader, however, it is best not to reveal any plot surprises, unless the play is a classic one with an ending likely to be common knowledge.

- **If the play is unfamiliar, summarize its theme.** This exercise will not only help your reader understand your review but probably sharpen your analysis.

- **For a well-known play, evaluate the director's approach to familiar material.** Is the production exactly what you'd expect, or are there any fresh and apparently original innovations? If a production is unusual, does it achieve newness by violating the play? The director of one college production of *Othello* emphasized the play's being partly set in Venice by staging it in the campus swimming pool, with actors floating on barges and a homemade gondola—a fresh, but not entirely successful, innovation.

- **Comment on the director's work.** Can you discern the director's approach to the play? Do the actors hurry their lines or speak too slowly? Do they speak and gesture naturally, or in an awkward, stylized manner? Are these touches effective or distracting?

- **Pay attention to costumes, sets, and lighting.** Though such matters may seem small, they have an effect on the play's overall tone.

- **Finally, to prepare yourself, read a few professional play reviews.** Reviews appear regularly in magazines such as the *New Yorker*, *Time*, the *New Criterion*, and *American Theatre*, and also on the entertainment pages of most metropolitan newspapers. Newspaper reviews can often be accessed online; for example, *New York Times* reviews may be found at theater.nytimes.com.

Here is a good, concise review of an amateur production of *Trifles*, as it might be written for a college newspaper or as a course assignment.

Trifles Scores Mixed Success in
Monday Players' Production

Women have come a long way since 1916. At least, that impression was conveyed yesterday when the Monday Players presented Susan Glaspell's classic one-act play *Trifles* in Alpaugh Theater.

Opening paragraph gives information on play and production

At first, in Glaspell's taut story of two subjugated farm women who figure out why a fellow farm woman strangled her husband, actors Lloyd Fox and Cal Federicci get to strut around. As a small-town sheriff and a county attorney, they lord it over the womenfolk, making sexist remarks about women in general. Fox and Federicci obviously enjoy themselves as the pompous types that Glaspell means them to be.

But of course it is the women with their keen eyes for small details who prove the superior detectives. In the demanding roles of the two Nebraska Miss Marples, Kathy Betts and Ruth Fine cope as best they can with what is asked of them. Fine is especially convincing. As Mrs. Hale, a friend of the wife accused of the murder, she projects a growing sense of independence. Visibly smarting under the verbal lashes of the menfolk, she seems to straighten her spine inch by inch as the play goes on.

Evaluates performances

Unluckily for Betts, director Alvin Klein seems determined to view Mrs. Peters as a comedian. Though Glaspell's stage directions call the woman "nervous," I doubt she is supposed to be quite so fidgety as Betts makes her. Betts vibrates like a tuning fork every time a new clue turns up, and when she is obliged to smell a dead canary bird (another clue), you would think she was whiffing a dead hippopotamus. Mrs. Peters, whose sad past includes a lost baby and a kitten some maniac chopped up with a hatchet, is no figure of fun to my mind. Played for laughs, her character fails to grow visibly on stage, as Fine makes Mrs. Hale grow.

Analyzes direction

Klein, be it said in his favor, makes the quiet action proceed at a brisk pace. Feminists in the audience must have been a little embarrassed, though, by his having Betts and Fine deliver every speech defending women in an extra-loud voice. After all, Glaspell makes her points clearly enough just by showing us what she shows. Not everything is overstated, however. As a farmer who found the murder victim, Ron Valdez acts his part with quiet authority.

Further elaborates on stage direction

Despite flaws in its direction, this powerful play still spellbinds an audience. Anna Winterbright's set, seen last week as a background for *Dracula* and just slightly touched up, provides appropriate gloom.

Overall evaluation

HOW TO QUOTE A PLAY

The guidelines for quoting prose or poetry generally apply to quoting from a play. Plays present certain challenges of their own, however. When you quote an extended section of a play or dialogue that involves more than one character, use the following MLA format to set the passage off from the body of your paper:

- Indent half an inch.
- Type the character's name in all capitals, followed by a period.
- If a speech runs for more than a single line, indent any additional lines one-quarter inch.
- Provide a citation reference:

    If the play is written in prose, provide a page number and scene or act number.

    If the play is written in verse, provide the act, scene, and line numbers.

Here is an example of that format:

> The men never find a motive for the murder because, ironically, they consider all the real clues "trifles" that don't warrant their attention:
>
> > SHERIFF. Well, can you beat the women! Held for murder and worryin'
> > about her preserves.
> > COUNTY ATTORNEY. I guess before we're through she may have
> > something more serious than preserves to worry about.
> > HALE. Well, women are used to worrying over trifles. (1145; act 1)

When you are quoting a verse play, be careful to respect the line breaks. For citation references, you should provide the act, scene, and line numbers, so that your reader will be able to find the quotation in any edition of the play. A quotation from a verse play should look like this:

> Even before her death, Othello will not confront Desdemona with his specific suspicions:
>
> > OTHELLO. Think on thy sins.
> > DESDEMONA.   They are loves I bear to you.
> > OTHELLO. Ay, and for that thou diest.
> > DESDEMONA. That death's unnatural that kills for loving.
> > > Alas, why gnaw you so your nether lip?
> > > Some bloody passion shakes your very frame.
> > > These are portents; but yet I hope, I hope,
> > > They do not point on me. (5.2.42–48)

TOPICS FOR WRITING BRIEF PAPERS (250–500 WORDS)

1. Analyze a key character from any play in this book. Some choices might be Tom Wingfield in *The Glass Menagerie*, Torvald Helmer in *A Doll's House*, or Troy Maxson in *Fences*. What motivates that character? Point to specific moments in the play to make your case.

2. When the curtain comes down on the conclusion of some plays, the audience is left to decide exactly what finally happened. In a short informal essay, state your interpretation of the conclusion of one of these plays: *The Sound of a Voice* (Chapter 41), *El Santo Americano* (Chapter 41), *The Glass Menagerie*. Don't just give a plot summary; tell what you think the conclusion means.

3. Sum up the main suggestions you find in one of these meaningful objects (or actions): the handkerchief in *Othello*; the Christmas tree in *A Doll's House* (or Nora's doing a wild tarantella); Troy's work on the fence in *Fences*; Laura's collection of figurines in *The Glass Menagerie*.

4. Here is an exercise in being terse. Write a card report on a short, one-scene play (other than *Trifles*), and confine your remarks to both sides of one 5- × 8-inch card. Possible subjects include *The Sound of a Voice*, *Beauty* (Chapter 41), and *Sure Thing* (Chapter 36).

5. Attend a play and write a review. In an assignment this brief, you will need to concentrate your remarks on either the performance or the script itself. Be sure to back up your opinions with specific observations.

TOPICS FOR WRITING MORE EXTENDED PAPERS (600–1,000 WORDS)

1. From a play you have enjoyed, choose a passage that strikes you as difficult, worth reading closely. Try to pick a passage not longer than about 20 lines. Explicate it—give it a close, sentence-by-sentence reading—and explain how this small part of the play relates to the whole. For instance, any of the following passages might be considered memorable (and essential to their plays):

   • Othello's soliloquy beginning "It is the cause, it is the cause, my soul" (*Othello*, 5.2.1–22).
   • Oedipus to Teiresias, speech beginning "Wealth, sovereignty and skill" (*Oedipus the King*, 418–45).
   • Nora to Mrs. Linde, speech beginning "Yes, someday, maybe, in many years when I am not as pretty as I am now" (*A Doll's House*, pages 1559–60).

2. Analyze the complexities and contradictions to be found in a well-rounded character from a play of your choice. Some good subjects might be Hamlet, Othello, Nora Helmer (in *A Doll's House*), or Tom Wingfield (in *The Glass Menagerie*).

3. Take just a single line or sentence from a play, one that stands out for some reason as greatly important. Perhaps it states a theme, reveals a character, or serves as a crisis (or turning point). Write an essay demonstrating its importance—how it functions, why it is necessary. Some possible lines include:

   • Iago to Roderigo: "I am not what I am" (*Othello*, 1.1.67).
   • Amanda to Tom: "You live in a dream; you manufacture illusions!" (*The Glass Menagerie*, Scene vii).
   • Bono to Cory and Troy: "Some people build fences to keep people out . . . and other people build fences to keep people in" (*Fences*, Act II, Scene i).

4. Write an analysis essay in which you single out an element of a play for examination—character, plot, setting, theme, dramatic irony, tone, language, symbolism, conventions, or any other element. Try to relate this element to the play as a whole. Sample topics: "The Function of Teiresias in *Oedipus the King*" (Chapter 37), "Imagery of Poison in *Othello*," "Irony in *Antigone*" (Chapter 37) "Williams's Use of Magic-Lantern Slides in *The Glass Menagerie*," "The Theme of Masculinity in *Fences*."

5. How would you stage an updated production of a play by Shakespeare, Sophocles, or Ibsen, transplanting it to our time? Choose a play, and describe the challenges and difficulties of this endeavor. How would you overcome them—or, if they cannot be overcome, why not?

6. Louis Phillips, of the School of Visual Arts in New York City, developed the following assignment. Read this statement from Woody Allen:

> Sports to me is like music. It's completely satisfying. There were times I would sit at a game with the old Knicks and think to myself in the fourth quarter, this is everything the theatre should be and isn't. There's an outcome that's unpredictable. The audience is not ahead of the dramatists. The drama is ahead of the audience.

What does Allen mean by the notion of the audience being ahead of (or behind) the dramatist? Apply that to a play you have read. If Woody Allen feels that sports is more satisfying than drama, why does he continue to make movies?

TOPICS FOR WRITING LONG PAPERS (1,500 WORDS OR MORE)

1. Choose a play you admire from this book, and read a second play by the same author. Compare and contrast the two plays with attention to a single element—a theme they have in common, or a particular kind of imagery, for example.

2. Read *Othello* and view a movie version of the play. You might choose Oliver Parker's 1995 take on the play with Laurence Fishburne and Kenneth Branagh, or even O (2001), an updated version that has a prep school as its setting and a basketball star as its protagonist. Review the movie. What does it manage to convey of the original? What gets lost in the translation?

3. Choosing any of the works in "Plays for Further Reading" (Chapter 41) or taking some other play your instructor suggests, report any difficulties you encountered in reading and responding to it. Explicate any troublesome passages for the benefit of other readers.

4. Attend a play and write an in-depth review, taking into account many elements of the drama: acting, direction, staging, costumes, lighting, and—if the work is relatively new and not a classic—the play itself.

5. Have you ever taken part in a dramatic production, either as an actor or a member of the crew? What did the experience teach you about the nature of drama and about what makes a play effective?

6. Write a one-act play of your own, featuring a minor character from one of the plays you have read for class. Think about what motivates that character, and let the play's central conflict grow from his or her preoccupations.

46

WRITING A
RESEARCH PAPER

*A writer is a person for whom writing is
more difficult than it is for other people.*

—THOMAS MANN

What You Will Learn in This Chapter

- To choose a topic for your research paper
- To find and evaluate sources
- To organize, write, and revise your research paper
- To cite and document your sources using MLA style

Oh no! You've been assigned a research paper, and every time you even think about starting it, your spirits sink and your blood pressure rises. You remember that Emily Dickinson was fun to talk about in class, but when you Google her name, the search engine states that there are millions of entries. Time to switch authors, you decide. How about Ernest Hemingway? You really liked that one story from the assigned readings, but when you entered his name in a search of the college library catalog it listed 135 books about him. What should you do? The paper is due in two weeks, not twenty years. Why would an otherwise very nice instructor put you through this mental trauma?

Why is it worthwhile to write a research paper? (Apart from the fact that you want a passing grade in the class, that is.) While you can learn much by exploring your own responses to a literary work, there is no substitute for entering into a conversation with others who have studied and thought about your topic. Literary criticism is that conversation. Your reading will expose you to the ideas of others who can shed light on a story, poem, or play. It will introduce you to the wide range of informed opinions that exist about literature, as about almost any subject. Sometimes, too, your research will uncover information about an author's life that leads you to new insights into a literary work. Undertaking a research paper gives you a chance to test your ideas against those of others, and in doing so to clarify your own opinions.

BROWSE THE RESEARCH

The most daunting aspect of the research paper may well be the mountains of information available on almost any literary subject. It can be hard to know where to begin. Sifting through books and articles is part of the research process. Unfortunately, the first material you uncover in the library or on the Internet is rarely the evidence you need to develop or support your thesis. Keep looking until you uncover helpful sources.

Another common pitfall in the process is the creeping feeling that your idea has already been examined a dozen times over. But take heart: like Odysseus, tie yourself to the mast so that when you hear the siren voices of published professors, you can listen without abandoning your own point of view. Your idea may have been treated, but not yet by you. Your particular take on a topic is bound to be different from someone else's. After all, thousands of books have been written on Shakespeare's plays, but people still find new things to say about them.

CHOOSE A TOPIC: FORMULATE YOUR ARGUMENT

- **Find a topic that interests you.** A crucial first step in writing a research paper is coming up with a topic that interests you. If you start with a topic that bores you, the process will be a chore and yield dull results. But if you begin with a topic that intrigues you, developing a compelling research question becomes easier, and seeking its answer will prove to be a more engaging process. The paper that results will inevitably be stronger and more interesting.

- **Find a way to get started.** Browsing through online journal articles and blogs, or skimming through books of literary criticism in the library, can help to spark an idea or two. Prewriting techniques such as brainstorming, freewriting, listing, and clustering can also help you to generate ideas on a specific work of literature. If you take notes and jot down ideas as they occur to you, when you start the formal writing process you will discover you have already begun.

- **Keep your purpose and audience in mind.** Refer often to the assignment, and approach your essay accordingly. Think of your audience as well—is it your professor, your classmates, or some hypothetical reader? As you plan your essay, keep your audience's expectations and needs in mind.

- **Identify an argument—your thesis—that you hope to support with research, and look for material that will help you demonstrate its plausibility.** Your thesis is a work in progress. Do not be afraid to let it evolve as you research your topic and reflect on your findings. Remember: the ideal research paper is based on your own observations and interpretations of a literary text.

BEGIN YOUR RESEARCH

Writing a research paper on literature calls for two kinds of sources. First, there are your primary sources—the literary works that are the central subject of your paper. Then there are your secondary sources—the critical or biographical books, articles, web and database resources that discuss the author or work you are examining. In writing a research paper, your task is to use both kinds of sources to develop a sustained and logical discussion of a specific topic.

Reliable Web Sources

As you begin your research, your first impulse may be to search online for websites and blogs that discuss your topic. If so, proceed with care. Websites may be written and published by anybody for any purpose, with no oversight. Even the online reference site *Wikipedia*, for example, is an amalgamation of voluntary contributors and is rife with small factual errors and contributor biases. Carefully analyze any material you gather from a general online search and compare it with other reputable sources of information. To garner the best sources possible, take these steps:

- **Begin your search at a reliable website.** To avoid sloppy and inaccurate sites, begin your search with one of the following excellent guides through cyberspace:

  - *Library of Congress's Alcove 9.* Fortunately, you don't have to trek to Washington to visit this venerable institution's annotated collection of reference websites in the humanities and social sciences. For your purpose—writing a literary research paper—access the Subject Index, click on "Literatures in English," and then click "Literary Criticism." This will take you to a list of metapages and websites with collections of reliable critical and biographical materials on authors and their works. (A metapage provides links to other websites.)

  - *ipl2.* The aggregation of two popular research websites, *Internet Public Library* and *Librarians' Internet Index, ipl2* is hosted and maintained by Drexel University's College of Science and Technology and a consortium of other universities. This site lets you search for literary criticism by author, work, country of origin, or literary period.

  - *Library Spot.* This is a portal to more than 5,000 libraries around the world, and to periodicals, online texts, reference works, and links to metapages and websites on any topic including literary criticism. This carefully maintained site is published by StartSpot Mediaworks, Inc., in the Northwestern University/Evanston Research Park in Evanston, Illinois.

  - *Voice of the Shuttle.* Research links in more than twenty-five categories in the humanities and social sciences, including online texts, libraries, academic websites, and metapages, may be found at this site. It was developed and is maintained by Dr. Alan Liu in the English Department of the University of California, Santa Barbara.

Print Resources

Don't overlook books and print journals. Until quite recently, most literary material existed solely in print—and only some of these resources have been transferred into digital formats. When you are hunting down secondary sources, a good place to begin is your campus library. Plan to spend some time thumbing through scholarly books and journals, looking for passages that you find particularly interesting or that pertain to your topic. Begin your search with the online catalog to get a sense of where you might find the books and journals you need.

To choose from the many books available on your library's shelves and through interlibrary loan, you might turn to book reviews for a sense of which volumes would best suit your purpose. *Book Review Digest* contains the full texts of many book reviews and excerpts of others. The *Digest* may be found in printed form in the reference section of your campus library, which may also provide access to the online version. Whether you are using the online or print version, you will need the author's name, title, and date of first publication of any book for which you hope to find a review.

Also helpful is the multivolume *Dictionary of Literary Biography.* This useful series of more than 360 volumes has entries on most well-known authors and presents excerpts of the best scholarship with complete citations. You may be able to research your entire paper from this comprehensive source alone. Many schools have either a print version of this reference work or subscribe to its online database.

Scholarly journals are another excellent resource for articles on your topic. Indexes to magazines and journals may be found in your library's reference section or on your library's website.

Online Databases

Most college libraries subscribe to specialized online database services covering all academic subjects—treasure troves of reliable sources. If you find yourself unsure of how to use your library's database system, ask the reference librarian to help you get started. Or explore the section on databases or research tools on your library's website to see what your school has available on literature. Many college library home pages provide students with access to subscription databases, which means that if you really can't bear to leave your comfy desk at home, you can still pay a virtual visit. The following databases are particularly useful for literary research:

- *Literature Resource Center* (Thomson Gale) provides biographies, bibliographies, and critical analyses of more than 120,000 authors and their work. This information is culled from journal articles and reference works.
- MLA *International Bibliography*, the Modern Language Association's database, is an excellent way to search for books and full-text articles on literary topics.
- *Google Scholar* provides one of the simplest ways to broadly search for a topic across a vast array of publicly available scholarly articles, theses, books, and other research documents. Some documents may require a university login to access.
- *JSTOR*, a nonprofit organization, indexes articles or abstracts from an archive of journals in more than fifty disciplines.
- *Literature Online (LION)* provides a vast searchable database of critical articles and reference works as well as full texts of more than 300,000 works of prose, poetry, and drama.
- *Project Muse*, a collaboration between publishers and libraries, offers access to more than 400 journals in the humanities, arts, and social sciences.
- *EBSCO*, a multisubject resource, covers literature and the humanities, as well as the social sciences, the medical sciences, linguistics, and other fields.

CHECKLIST: Finding Reliable Sources

☐ Locate reputable websites by starting at a reputable website designed for that purpose.

☐ Visit your campus library. Ask the reference librarian for advice.

☐ Check the library catalog for books and journals on your topic.

☐ Look into the online databases subscribed to by your library.

Visual Images

The web is an excellent source of visual images. If a picture, chart, or graph will enhance your argument, you may find the perfect one via an image search on Google,

PicSearch, or other search engines. The digital collections at the Library of Congress website offer a wealth of images documenting American political, social, and cultural history—including portraits, prints, photographs, letters, and original manuscripts. Remember, though, that not all images are available for use by the general public. If there is an image you want to use, check for a copyright notice to see if its originator allows it to be reproduced. If so, you may include the photograph, provided you credit your source as you would if you were quoting text.

Lombardo 4

Fig. 1. *Landscape with the Fall of Icarus* by **Pieter Brueghel the Elder** (c. 1558, Musées Royaux des Beaux-Arts de Belgique, Brussels)

W. H. Auden's poem "Musée des Beaux Arts" refers to a specific painting to prove its point that the most honest depictions of death take into account the way life simply goes on even after the most tragic of events. In line 14, Auden turns specifically to Pieter Brueghel the Elder's masterwork *The Fall of Icarus* (see Fig. 1), pointing to the painting's understated depiction of tragedy. In this painting, the death of Icarus does not take place on center stage. A plowman and his horse take up the painting's foreground, while the leg of Icarus falling into the sea takes up a tiny portion of the painting's lower-right corner. A viewer who fails to take the painting's title into account might not even notice Icarus at all.

One note on images: use them carefully. Choose visuals that provide supporting evidence for the point you are trying to make or that enhance your reader's understanding of the work. Label your images with captions. Your goal should be to make your argument more convincing. In the example on the previous page, a reproduction of Brueghel's painting helps to advance the author's argument and provide insight into Auden's poem.

CHECKLIST: Using Visual Images

- ☐ Use images as evidence to support your argument.
- ☐ Use images to enhance communication and understanding.
- ☐ Refer to the images in your text.
- ☐ Label each image with a figure number—"Fig. 1" in the example above—and provide a title or caption.
- ☐ Check copyrights.
- ☐ Include sources in a works-cited list.

EVALUATE YOUR SOURCES

Trustworthy Resources Build Your Paper's Credibility

It's an old saying, but a useful one: don't believe everything you read. The fact that a book or an article is printed and published doesn't necessarily mean it is accurate or unbiased. Likewise, the highest-ranking results of your web search may not be the most reliable or credible. Resources fall into two categories: scholarly and popular. Scholarly articles and books are written by and for faculty, scholars, and researchers and they feature original research, scholarly or academic language, and full citations for sources. Popular articles and books are written by journalists or professional writers for a general audience. These articles tend to be shorter, use simpler language, and rarely provide full citations of their sources. How can you ensure that the resource you are considering is a scholarly one?

Begin your search in a place that has taken some of the work out of quality control—your school library. Books and articles you find there are regarded by librarians as having some obvious merit. If your search takes you beyond the library and online, though, you will need to be discerning when choosing resources. As you weigh the value of each document, take the following into account:

- **Look closely at information provided about the author.** Is he or she known for expertise in the field? What are the author's academic or association credentials? Is there any reason to believe that the author is biased in any way? For example, a biography of an author written by that author's son or daughter might not be as unbiased as one written by a scholar with no personal connections. If the document appears online, is the web entry unsigned and anonymous? If the website is sponsored by an organization, is it a reputable one?

- **Determine the publisher's reliability.** Books, articles, and blogs published by an advocacy group might be expected to take a particular—possibly biased—slant on an issue. Be aware also that some books are published by vanity presses, companies that are paid by an author to publish his or her books. As a result, vanity press-published books generally aren't subject to the same rigorous quality control as those put out by more reputable publishing houses.

A word of warning: individual student pages posted on university sites have not necessarily been reviewed by that university and are not reliable sources of information. Also, postings on *Wikipedia* are not subject to a scholarly review process and have been found to contain inaccuracies. It's safer to use a published encyclopedia.

- **Always check for a publication date.** If a document lists an edition number, check to see whether you are using the latest edition of the material. If the article appears on a website or blog, when was it last updated? In some cases you may want to base your essay on the most current information or theories, so you will want to steer toward the most recently published material.

- **For periodicals, decide whether a publication is an academic journal or a popular magazine.** What type of reputation does it have? Obviously, you do not want to use a magazine that periodically reports on Elvis sightings and alien births. And even articles on writers in magazines such as *Time* and *People* are likely to be too brief and superficial for purposes of serious research. Instead, choose scholarly journals designed to enhance the study of literature.

- **Consult experts.** Cornell University Library has two good online documents with guidance for analyzing sources, titled "Critically Analyzing Information Sources" and "Distinguishing Scholarly from Non-Scholarly Periodicals." Your school's research librarian or library website may have similar resources.

CHECKLIST: Evaluating Your Sources

- ☐ Who wrote it? What are the author's credentials?
- ☐ Is he or she an expert in the field?
- ☐ Does he or she appear to be unbiased toward the subject matter?
- ☐ Does the content seem consistent with demonstrated scholarship?
- ☐ Is the publisher reputable? Is it an advocacy group or a vanity press?
- ☐ Is the source an online journal or magazine? Is it scholarly or popular?
- ☐ When was the source published? Do later editions exist? If so, would a later edition be more useful?

ORGANIZE YOUR RESEARCH

- **Get your thoughts down on note cards or the equivalent on your laptop.** Once you have amassed your secondary sources, it will be time to begin reading in earnest. As you do so, be sure to take notes on any passage that pertains to your topic. A convenient way to organize your many thoughts is to write them down on index cards, which are easy to shuffle and rearrange. If you prefer to use your computer to take notes, you might consider using digital note-card software like *SimpleNote* or *EverNote*. For longer papers, it may be worthwhile to look into more sophisticated programs like *Scrivener*, which give you additional tools for planning and structuring your research and writing. Whatever approach you use, keep to a single fact or opinion on each card. This will make it easier for you to shuffle the deck and re-envision the order in which you deliver information to your reader.

■ **Keep careful track of the sources of quotations and paraphrases.** As you take notes, make it unmistakably clear which thoughts and phrases are yours and which derive from others. (Remember, *quotation* means using the exact words of your source and placing the entire passage in quotation marks and citing the author. *Paraphrase* means expressing the ideas of your source in your own words, again citing the author.) Bear in mind the cautionary tale of a well-known historian, Doris Kearns Goodwin. She was charged with plagiarizing sections of two of her famous books when her words were found to be jarringly similar to those published in other books. Because she had not clearly indicated on her note cards which ideas and passages were hers and which came from other sources, Goodwin was forced to admit to plagiarism. Her reputation suffered enormously from these charges, but you can learn from her mistakes and save your own reputation—and your grades.

■ **Keep track of the sources of ideas and concepts.** When an idea is inspired by or directly taken from someone else's writing, be sure to jot down the source on that same card or in your computer file. Your deck of cards or computer list will function as a working bibliography, which later will help you put together a works-cited list. To save yourself work, keep a separate list of the sources you're using. Then, as you make the note, you need write only the material's author or title and page reference on the card in order to identify your source. It's also useful to classify the note in a way that will help you to organize your material, making it easy, for example, to separate cards that deal with a story's theme from cards that deal with point of view or symbolism. Another helpful tip is to use an online bibliography manager like *EasyBib*, *Mendeley*, *RefWorks*, or *Zotero*. Many of these services will let you create an account to store your list of sources online and will also generate correctly formatted bibliographies for free.

■ **Make notes of your own thoughts and reactions to your research.** When a critical article sparks your own original idea, be sure to capture that thought in your notes and mark it as your own. As you plan your paper, these notes may form the outline for your arguments.

■ **Make photocopies or printouts to simplify the process and ensure accuracy.** Scholars once had to spend long hours copying out prose passages by hand. Luckily, for a small investment you can simply photocopy or print your sources to ensure accuracy in quoting and citing your sources. If you do photocopy material from a source, you should make it a habit to copy the publication page from the front of the book. This will ensure you always have the full title and citation information for your bibliography. Some instructors will require you to hand in photocopies of your original sources with the final paper, along with printouts of articles downloaded from an Internet database. Even if this is not the case, photocopying your sources and holding onto your printouts can help you to reproduce quotations accurately in your essay—and accuracy is crucial.

CREATE AN ANNOTATED BIBLIOGRAPHY

As you research and prepare to write your essay, you should make a list of the books, articles, websites, and other sources you have referred to along the way. If your instructor requires an annotated bibliography, you can simply add an annotation—a brief descriptive paragraph—after each citation.

You may be asked to write a **summary annotation**, which briefly describes your source, or an **evaluative annotation**, which provides a description as well as comments on relevance, accuracy, and quality. This paragraph is also a good place to mention any specific examples or quotes from the text that you are thinking of using in your essay. A good annotation might include several items:

- A summary of the theme and scope of the book or article
- An evaluation of the authority or background of the writer
- Comments on the intended audience
- A comparison with another source on your list
- An explanation of how this source helps you understand the topic better

As you write your essay, refer often to your annotated bibliography, and it will help you locate support for your claims and new connections between the ideas and commentary of others.

EXAMPLE SUMMARY ANNOTATION

Heller, Peter. "Kafka: The Futility of Striving." *Dialectics and Nihilism,* U of Massachusetts P, 1966. pp. 227–306. This collection of critical essays contains thorough analyses of the selected works of four German poet-philosophers: Lessing, Mann, Nietzsche, and Kafka. Heller examines each writer in turn to form a broader argument about the role of dialectics in the rise of nihilism.

EXAMPLE EVALUATIVE ANNOTATION

Heller, Peter. "Kafka: The Futility of Striving." *Dialectics and Nihilism,* U of Massachusetts P, 1966, pp. 227–306. This collection of critical essays contains thorough analyses of the selected works of four German poet-philosophers: Lessing, Mann, Nietzsche, and Kafka. Heller examines each writer in turn to form a broader argument about the role of dialectics in the rise of nihilism. Heller notes that Kafka represented the "mainstream of German literary and intellectual tradition," a nihilistic tradition which extends from Goethe and Lessing to the present (289). Perhaps the most interesting of Heller's points revolves around the idea that Kafka's style creates works that cannot be explained with a single interpretation. Heller describes Kafka using his style to separate himself from his characters, a technique that develops a contrast between the calmness of his style and the nervous desperation of his characters (237). Because Kafka allows his pictures to "speak for themselves," "Kafka's texts have been subject to a variety of widely divergent approaches" (236). Whether one is reading on a social, moral, psychological, metaphysical, theological, or existential level, Kafka "tends to suspend all distinction and thus to revert to total ambiguity" (285). According to Heller, this characteristic mysteriousness becomes "the epitome of his art" (230).

REFINE YOUR THESIS

As you read secondary sources and take notes, you should begin to refine your essay's thesis, or main claim. This, in turn, will help you to winnow your stacks of source material down to the secondary sources that will best help you to make and support your argument. Even your revised thesis doesn't have to be etched in stone. It should simply give you a sense of direction as you start to plan your essay.

- **Be willing to fine-tune your thesis or even rework it completely.** Your research may reveal that you have misinterpreted an idea, or that there is not much evidence to support your thesis. Of course, it is annoying to find that you may be wrong about something, but don't let these discoveries put you off. Use your research to refine your thoughts.

- **Let your initial idea be the jumping-off point to other, better ideas.** Say, for example, that you plan to write about the peculiar physical description of Arnold Friend in Joyce Carol Oates's story "Where Are You Going, Where Have You Been?" (Chapter 3) You may have noticed he has trouble standing in his shoes, and you want to explore that odd detail. If you research this character, you may find Arnold Friend likened to the devil (whose cloven hooves might give him similar problems with standard-issue cowboy boots), or to the wolf in "Little Red Riding Hood" (also a character who would have a hard time managing human clothes). Use your research to sharpen your focus. Can you think of other stories that deal with potentially supernatural, possibly even evil, characters? What about Nathaniel Hawthorne's "Young Goodman Brown" (Chapter 14)? Or Flannery O'Connor's "A Good Man Is Hard to Find" (Chapter 11)? How might you compare Arnold Friend with Hawthorne's devil or O'Connor's Misfit?

ORGANIZE YOUR PAPER

With your thesis in mind and your notes spread before you, draw up an outline—a rough map of how best to argue your thesis and present your material. Determine what main points you need to make, and look for quotations that support those points. Even if you generally prefer to navigate the paper-writing process without a map, you will find that an outline makes the research-paper writing process considerably smoother. When organizing information from many different sources, it pays to plan ahead.

WRITE AND REVISE

As with any other kind of essay, a research paper rarely, if ever, reaches its full potential in a single draft. Leave yourself time to rewrite. The knowledge that your first draft won't be your final one can free you up to take chances and to jot down your ideas as quickly as they occur to you. If your phrasing is less than elegant, it hardly matters in a first draft; the object is to work out your ideas on paper. Dash off the paper, working as quickly as you can. Later you can rearrange paragraphs and smooth out any rough patches.

Once you've got the first draft down, it's an excellent idea to run it by a friend, a writing center tutor, or even your instructor. A writer can't know how clear or persuasive his or her argument is without a trusted reader to give feedback.

When you do revise, be open to making both large and small changes. Sometimes revising means adding needed paragraphs, or even refining the thesis a bit further. Be willing to start from scratch if you need to, but even as you take the whole picture into account, remember that details are important too. Before you hand in that final draft, be sure to proofread for small errors that could detract from the finished product.

MAINTAIN ACADEMIC INTEGRITY

What Is Plagiarism?

Simply put, plagiarism is the use of another person's words, ideas, research, or arguments without giving proper credit to their source. In Western academic settings, plagiarism is viewed as a serious type of theft or forgery. By claiming someone else's ideas and language as your own, you rob them of the rightful recognition of their intellectual labor. On the other hand, if you responsibly recognize and respond to the scholarly work of others with proper citations, your own writing will convey more authority and competence.

Papers for Sale Are Papers That "F"ail

Do not be seduced by the apparent ease of cheating by computer. Your Internet searches may turn up several sites that offer term papers to download. Most of these sites charge money for what they offer, but a few do not, happy to strike a blow against the "oppressive" insistence of English teachers that students learn to think and write.

Plagiarized term papers are an old game: the fraternity file and the "research assistance" service have been around far longer than the computer. It may seem easy enough to download a paper, put your name at the head of it, and turn it in for an easy grade. As any writing instructor can tell you, though, such papers usually stick out like a sore thumb. The style will be wrong, the work will not be consistent with other work by the same student in any number of ways, and the teacher will sometimes even have seen the same phony paper before. The ease with which electronic texts are reproduced makes this last possibility increasingly likely.

The odds of being caught and facing the unpleasant consequences are reasonably high. It is far better to take the grade you have earned for your own effort, no matter how mediocre, than to try to pass off someone else's work as your own. Even if, somehow, your instructor does not recognize your submission as a plagiarized paper, you have diminished your character through dishonesty and lost an opportunity to learn something on your own.

A Warning Against Internet Plagiarism

Plagiarism detection services are often a professor's ally in the battle against academic dishonesty. Questionable research papers can be sent to these services (such as Turnitin.com and EVE2), which perform complex searches of the Internet and of a growing database of purchased term papers. The research paper will be returned to the professor with plagiarized sections annotated and the sources documented. The end result will certainly be a failing grade on the essay, possibly a failing grade for the course, and, depending on the policies of your university, expulsion.

ACKNOWLEDGE ALL SOURCES

The brand of straight-out dishonesty described above is one type of plagiarism. There is, however, another, subtler kind: when students incorporate somebody else's words *or* ideas into their papers without giving proper credit. To avoid this second—sometimes quite accidental—variety of plagiarism, familiarize yourself with the conventions for acknowledging sources. First and foremost, remember to give credit to any writer who supplies you with ideas, information, or specific words and phrases.

Using Quotations

■ **Acknowledge your source when you quote a writer's words or phrases.** When you use someone else's words or phrases, you should reproduce his or her exact words in quotation marks, and be sure to properly credit the source.

> Already, Frost has hinted that Nature may be, as Radcliffe Squires suggests, "Nothing but an ash-white plain without love or faith or hope, where ignorant appetites cross by chance" (87).

■ **If you quote more than four lines, set your quotation off from the body of the paper.** Start a new line; indent one inch and type the quotation, double-spaced. (You do not need to use quotation marks, as the format tells the reader the passage is a quotation.)

> Samuel Maio made an astute observation about the nature of Weldon Kees's distinctive tone:
>> Kees has therefore combined a personal subject matter with an impersonal voice—that is, one that is consistent in its tone evenly recording the speaker's thoughts without showing any emotional intensity which might lie behind those thoughts. (136)

Citing Ideas

■ **Acknowledge your source when you mention a critic's ideas.** Even if you are not quoting exact words or phrases, be sure to acknowledge the source of any original ideas or concepts you have used.

> Another explanation is suggested by Daniel Hoffman, a critic who has discussed the story: the killer hears the sound of his *own* heart (227).

■ **Acknowledge your source when you paraphrase a writer's words.** To paraphrase a critic, you should do more than just rearrange his or her words: you should translate them into your own original sentences—again, always being sure to credit the original source. As an example, suppose you wish to refer to an insight of Randall Jarrell, who commented as follows on the images of spider, flower, and moth in Robert Frost's poem "Design":

RANDALL JARRELL'S ORIGINAL TEXT

Notice how the *heal-all*, because of its name, is the one flower in all the world picked to be the altar for this Devil's Mass; notice how *holding up* the moth brings something ritual and hieratic, a ghostly, ghastly formality, to this priest and its sacrificial victim.[1]

It would be too close to the original to write, without quotation marks, these sentences:

PLAGIARIZED REWORDING

Frost picks the *heal-all* as the one flower in all the world to be the altar for this Devil's Mass. There is a ghostly, ghastly formality to the spider *holding up* the moth, like a priest holding a sacrificial victim.

This rewording, although not exactly in Jarrell's language, manages to steal his memorable phrases without giving him credit. Nor is it sufficient just to include Jarrell's essay in the works-cited list at the end of your paper. If you do, you are still a crook; you merely point to the scene of the crime. Instead, think through Jarrell's words to the point he is making, so that it can be restated in your own original way. If you want to keep any of his striking phrases (and why not?), put them exactly as he wrote them in quotation marks:

APPROPRIATE PARAPHRASE, ACKNOWLEDGES SOURCE

As Randall Jarrell points out, Frost portrays the spider as a kind of priest in a Mass, or Black Mass, elevating the moth like an object for sacrifice, with "a ghostly, ghastly formality" (42).

Note also that this improved passage gives Jarrell the credit not just for his words but for his insight into the poem. Both the idea and the words in which it was originally expressed are the properties of their originator. Finally, notice the page reference that follows the quotation (this system of documenting your sources is detailed in the next section).

DOCUMENT SOURCES USING MLA STYLE

You must document everything you take from a source. When you quote from other writers, when you borrow their information, when you summarize or paraphrase their ideas, make sure you give them proper credit. Identify the writer by name and cite the book, magazine, newspaper, pamphlet, website, or other source you have used.

The conventions that govern the proper way to document sources are available in the *MLA Handbook*, 8th ed. (2016). The following brief list of pointers is not meant to take the place of the *MLA Handbook* itself, but to give you a basic sense of the rules for documentation.

[1] *Poetry and the Age* (Alfred A. Knopf, 1953) p. 42.

Keep a List of Sources

Keep a working list of your research sources—all the references from which you might quote, summarize, paraphrase, or take information. When your paper is in finished form, it will end with a neat copy of the works you actually used (once called a "Bibliography," now titled "Works Cited").

Use Parenthetical References

In the body of your paper, every time you refer to a source, you need to provide information to help a reader locate it in your works-cited list. You can usually give just the author's name and a page citation in parentheses. For example, if you are writing a paper on Weldon Kees's sonnet "For My Daughter" (Chapter 16) and want to include an observation you found on page 136 of Samuel Maio's book *Creating Another Self*, write:

> One critic has observed that the distinctive tone of "For My Daughter" depends on Kees's combination of "personal subject matter with an impersonal voice" (Maio 136).

If you mention the author's name in your sentence, you need give only the page number in your reference:

> As Samuel Maio has observed, Kees creates a distinctive tone in this sonnet by combining a "personal subject with an impersonal voice" (136).

If you have two books or magazine articles by Samuel Maio in your works-cited list, how will the reader tell them apart? In your text, refer to the title of each book or article by condensing it into a word or two. Condensed book titles are italicized, and condensed article titles are still placed within quotation marks.

> One critic has observed that the distinctive tone of "For My Daughter" depends on Kees's combination of "personal subject matter with an impersonal voice" (Maio, *Creating* 136).

Create a Works-Cited List

Provide a full citation for each source on your works-cited page. At the end of your paper, in your list of works cited, your reader will find a full description of your source—for the above examples, a critical book:

> Maio, Samuel. *Creating Another Self: Voices in Modern American Personal Poetry*. 2nd ed., Thomas Jefferson UP, 2005.

Put your works-cited list in proper form. The *MLA Handbook* provides detailed instructions for citing a myriad of different types of sources, from books to *YouTube* videos. To format your list:

1. Start a new page for the works-cited list, and continue the page numbering from the body of your paper.
2. Center the title, "Works Cited," one inch from the top of the page.

3. Double-space between all lines (including after title and between entries).

4. Type each entry beginning at the left-hand margin. If an entry runs longer than a single line, indent the following lines one-half inch from the left-hand margin.

5. Alphabetize each entry according to the author's last name, or if there is no author, the first word of the entry.

Cite Sources in MLA Style

Each entry in your list should contain all relevant information, as available, that helps your reader locate your source.

Core Elements of Each Entry

1. **Author's full name** as it appears on the title page or section of the work, last name first, followed by a period.

   (a) If the author has a different role than writing the work, identity that role (e.g. "editor" or "translator").

   (b) If the work is published without the author's name, skip this element.

2. **Title of source** (include the subtitle, if there is one, separated from the title by a colon), followed by a period.

   (a) Italicize titles of major works such as books, plays, websites, paintings, photographs, television shows, albums.

   (b) Use quotation marks for titles of shorter works such as poems, short stories, newspaper or journal articles, episodes in television series, song titles.

3. **Title of container,** italicized, and followed by comma. The MLA has coined the term "container" as a descriptor for the place where your source is "held." Some examples include the following:

   - magazine or newspaper that published source article
   - website that published source article
   - television series of which source episode is part
   - dictionary that contains source definition
   - anthology that printed source poem
   - website that published source blog or comment

4. **Other contributors,** followed by a comma. These are individuals involved in creating the source or its container, if relevant. Precede the names of contributors with a description of their role:

   - translated by
   - performance by
   - edited by

5. **Version,** followed by a comma. Oftentimes works are updated or published in different forms. Be sure to identify the specific version you used. Some examples:

   - Book editions are cited as 2nd ed, rev. ed., updated ed., or expanded ed.
   - Film versions might be cited as uncut version or director's cut version.

6. **Number,** followed by comma. If your source's container uses a numbering system, be sure to cite the numbers. Some examples:

- Academic journals often use volumes and numbers: vol. 7, no. 2.
- Television series often number episodes: season 4, episode 7.
- Books can be issued in multivolume sets: vol. 3.

7. **Publisher,** followed by comma. Publishers are generally found on the copyright section of your book or website, but there are circumstances in which publisher information is unavailable.

   (a) **Use the full name of the publisher.** Eliminate articles (*A, An, The*) and business abbreviations (*Co., Corp., Inc., Ltd.*). Abbreviate the names of university presses, by using the letters *U* (for University) and *P* (for Press).

Publisher's Name	Proper Citation
Harvard University Press	Harvard UP
University of Chicago Press	U of Chicago P
Alfred A. Knopf, Inc.	Alfred A. Knopf

   (b) **You can omit the publisher's name in circumstances where it does not add additional information):**

   - periodical or newspaper
   - work published by the author
   - website whose name is the same as the publisher

8. **Publication date,** followed by comma. Many sources have more than one publication date, particularly when works are published in multiple media. The *MLA Handbook* suggests citing the date that is most relevant to your use of the source.

9. **Location,** followed by period. MLA uses the word "location" to designate whatever specific information will help your reader pinpoint your source most easily, e.g.:

   - page numbers (abbreviated as *p.* for a single page or *pp.* for a range of pages)
   - web addresses such as URLs, DOIs (digital object identifiers), or permalinks
   - disc numbers
   - physical locations—such as the name of the museum where you viewed a piece of art, or the location where you heard an author give a speech.

Each of your entries should end with a period, no matter what element it concludes with. Remember, if the information is not available, you can safely leave it out of your citation. You should focus on providing all the relevant information in a clear manner. Don't worry if you are unsure exactly how properly to cite your source: the 8th edition of the *MLA Handbook* reassures us "there is often more than one correct way to document a source" (4).

Example Citations

Using the practice template created by the MLA, let's consider how the citation for a standard book entry is developed:

Maio, Samuel. *Creating Another Self: Voice in Modern American Personal Poetry.* 2nd ed., Thomas *Jefferson* UP, 2005.

AUTHOR / TITLE

1. Author.	Maio, Samuel.
2. Title of source.	*Creating Another Self: Voice in Modern American Personal Poetry.*

CONTAINER 1

3. Title of container,	
4. Other contributors,	
5. Version,	2nd ed.,
6. Number,	
7. Publisher,	Thomas Jefferson UP,
8. Publication date,	2005,
9. Location.	

Here is the development of a citation for an article found on the web:

> "The Poet at Work." *Emily Dickinson Museum,* Trustees of Amherst College, www.emilydickinsonmuseum.org/poet_at_work.

AUTHOR / TITLE

1. Author.	(No author cited)
2. Title of source.	"The Poet at Work."

CONTAINER 1

3. Title of container,	*Emily Dickinson Museum,*
4. Other contributors,	
5. Version,	
6. Number,	
7. Publisher,	Trustees of Amherst College,
8. Publication date,	
9. Location.	www.emilydickinsonmuseum.org/poet_at_work.

Two "Containers"

Sometimes you will find a source (e.g. a journal article) that is included in a "container" (the journal), which you accessed from a second, larger "container" (e.g. an online database). As another example, your source might be a TV episode, which is part of a TV series (the first container), which you streamed from *Netflix* (the second, larger container). When you have multiple containers, use the same procedures to provide complete information for each one. Study the MLA's template below to work through the citation for a print article that was accessed in an online database.

> Nelson, Raymond. "The Fitful Life of Weldon Kees." *American Literary History,* vol. 1, no. 4, Winter 1989, pp. 816–52. *JSTOR,* www.jstor.org/stable/489775.

AUTHOR / TITLE

1. Author.	Nelson, Raymond.
2. Title of source.	"The Fitful Life of Weldon Kees."

CONTAINER 1

3. Title of container,	*American Literary History,*
4. Other contributors,	
5. Version,	
6. Number,	vol. 1, no. 4,
7. Publisher,	
8. Publication date,	Winter 1989,
9. Location.	pp. 816–52.

CONTAINER 2

3. Title of container,	*JSTOR,*
4. Other contributors,	
5. Version,	
6. Number,	
7. Publisher,	
8. Publication date,	
9. Location.	www.jstor.org/stable/489775.

Optional Elements

You may include any additional elements in your entry you think relevant to your use of the source. Place them with the core elements they relate to so the inclusion makes sense for the reader. Some optional elements commonly added include the following:

- **Date of original publication,** or prior publication dates
- **City of publication,** particularly if the book was published in many countries
- **Other facts about the source**—for example, whether it is part of a unique series
- **Added descriptor for an unexpected type of source** (such as a personal meeting with an author or an unpublished letter)
- **Date you accessed online resource** will be relevant in some cases

Sample List of Works Cited

For a paper on Weldon Kees's "For My Daughter," a student's works-cited list might look as follows:

Works Cited

Grosholz, Emily. "The Poetry of Memory." *Weldon Kees: A Critical Introduction*,
 edited by Jim Elledge, Scarecrow Press, 1985, pp. 46–47.

Kees, Weldon. *The Collected Poems of Weldon Kees*. Edited by Donald Justice,
 U of Nebraska P, 1975.

---. "Hotel Apex Kinesis Films 1952 by Weldon Kees." *YouTube*,
 posted by James Reidel, 27 June 2015, www.youtube.com/
 watch?v=vqV2MGmvDJU.

Lane, Anthony. "The Disappearing Poet: What Ever Happened to
 Weldon Kees?" *The New Yorker*, 4 July 2005, www.newyorker.com/
 magazine/2005/07/04/the-disappearing-poet.

Maio, Samuel. *Creating Another Self: Voice in Modern American Personal
 Poetry*. 2nd ed., Thomas Jefferson UP, 2005.

Nelson, Raymond. "The Fitful Life of Weldon Kees." *American Literary
 History*, vol. 1, no. 4, Winter 1989, pp. 816–52. JSTOR, www.jstor.org/
 stable/489775.

Reidel, James. *Vanished Act: The Life and Art of Weldon Kees*. U of Nebraska
 P, 2003.

---, editor. "Weldon Kees." *Nebraska Center for Writers*, Creighton University,
 www.mockingbird.creighton.edu/NCW/kees.htm.

Ross, William T. *Weldon Kees*. Twayne Publishing, 1985. Twayne's US Authors
 Series, 484.

"Weldon Kees." *Poetry Out Loud*, National Endowment for the Arts/Poetry
 Foundation, www.poetryoutloud.org/poet/weldon-kees.

Additional Resources on MLA Style

As you put together your works-cited list, keep in mind that the little things—page numbers, quotation marks—count. Documentation may seem tedious, but it has an important purpose: it's for the reader of your paper who wants to pursue a topic you have researched. Luckily, you don't have to know the rules by heart. You can refer as necessary to the *MLA Handbook* or to the "Reference Guide for Citations" examples in this book. The MLA also has a website with tips and advice—*style.mla.org*—or you may find it helpful to use an online citation manager such as *EasyBib* or *Zotero* to generate the citation for a source automatically.

ENDNOTES AND FOOTNOTES

Citations and quotations in the text of your essay should be brief and snappy, lest they bog down your prose. You may, however, wish to provide your reader with passages of less important (yet possibly valuable) information, or make qualifying statements

("On the other hand, not every expert agrees. John Binks finds poets are often a little magazine's only cash customers, while Molly MacGuire maintains that . . ."). To insert such information without awkwardly interrupting your paper, put it into an **endnote** (placed at the end of a paper) or a **footnote** (placed at the bottom of the page). Footnotes and endnotes are now used mainly for such asides, but they are also a time-honored way to document sources.

Adding Footnotes

When an aside seems appropriate, insert a number in the text of your essay to send your reader to the corresponding note. Use the "Insert Footnote" option in your word processing program, or create a superscript number from the font menu. This will lift the number slightly above the level of your prose, so that it stands out.

> as many observers have claimed.[2]

Once you insert the number of your footnote into the text, your word processing program will cleverly take care of the formatting and placement of the footnote, automatically sending it to the bottom of the page.

> [2]On the other hand, not every expert agrees. John Binks, to name only
> one such observer, finds that poets are often a little magazine's only cash
> customers . . .

CONCLUDING THOUGHTS

A well-crafted research essay is a wondrous thing—as delightful, in its own way, as a well-crafted poem or short story or play. Good essays prompt thought and add to knowledge. Writing a research paper sharpens your own mind and exposes you to the honed insights of other thinkers. Think of anything you write as a piece that could be published for the benefit of other people interested in your topic. After all, such a goal is not as far-fetched as it seems: this textbook, for example, features a number of papers written by students. Why shouldn't yours number among them? Aim high.

SAMPLE STUDENT RESEARCH PAPER

This challenging assignment for a research paper comes from Professor Michael Cass of Mercer University. He asked his students to select the fiction writer on their reading list whose work impressed them most. Each student had to write a paper defending that author's claim to literary greatness and research the author using at least five critical sources. The student had to present clear reasons why the author was a major writer and to support the argument with both examples from the writer's work and statements from critics. Here is a short research paper by a student in Professor Cass's class, Stephanie Crowe, who discussed why she believed that Franz Kafka was a great writer.

Stephanie Crowe

Professor Cass

English 120

21 November 2019

Kafka's Greatness

Although most of his major works remained unfinished and unpublished at his untimely death in 1924, Franz Kafka was still one of the great writers of the twentieth century. By 1977, well over ten thousand works of commentary had appeared on Kafka, and many more have been written since then (Goodden 2). According to critic Peter Heller, Kafka represents the "mainstream of German literary and intellectual tradition," a nihilistic tradition which extends from Goethe and Lessing to the present (289).

Not only is Kafka generally considered one of the greatest fiction writers of the modern era, he is also indisputably one of the most influential. In his 1989 study, *After Kafka*, Shimon Sandbank discusses Kafka's influence on a dozen modern writers, including Jean Paul Sartre, Albert Camus, Samuel Beckett, Jorge Luis Borges, and Eugene Ionesco. His effects on these writers differ. Some borrow his understated, almost passive prose style while others adopt his recurrent images and themes. Whatever the specific elements they use, however, Kafka's ability to influence these writers is another measure of his stature.

Great literature often gives us the stories and images to understand our own age, a process that necessarily includes understanding our deepest problems. The twentieth century, to borrow a phrase from W. H. Auden, was mostly an "Age of Anxiety." Most modern people are no longer bound to follow the occupations, behaviors, and beliefs of their parents, but they gain this newfound freedom at the expense of a constant, difficult search for identity. The personal quest for meaningful identity often leads to despair. This "existential crisis" is the basis for many contemporary problems including the decline of religion, the rise of totalitarianism, the breakdown of social identity, and the decay of traditional family structure.

Kafka's works dramatize these problems memorably because they provide us with myths, images, stories, and situations that describe the particular crises of the early twentieth century. When faced with the modern challenge of not having a predetermined social or religious identity, Kafka's characters desperately attempt to

Introduction of essay's main claim

Builds creditability for claim with 2 citations of secondary sources

Support point #1 for argument: Kafka's widespread influence

Assumption stated about what determines great literature

Support point #2: Kafka's memorable dramatization of important 20th century concerns

Crowe 2

find certainty. The problem, however, is that they are usually afraid to do anything decisive because everything is uncertain. Auden observed:

Long quotation
from secondary
source, set off
from text

> Far from being confident of success, the Kafka hero is convinced from the start that he is doomed to fail, as he is also doomed, being who he is, to make prodigious and unending efforts to reach it [the goal]. Indeed, the mere desire to reach the goal is itself a proof, not that he is one of the elect, but that he is under a special curse. (162)

Elaborates support
point about Kafka's
memorable
dramatizations

One way that Kafka memorably dramatizes the modern struggle for identity is by reversing the traditional quest narrative. In a quest story, the hero knows the goal that he wants to achieve and has some confidence that he will be able to achieve it. As he tries to reach the goal, he must overcome various enemies and obstacles. "In a typical Kafka story, on the other hand, the goal is peculiar to the hero himself: he has no competitors" (Auden 162). His question then becomes not a practical "Can I succeed?" but instead a vague and problematic "What should I do?" Unable to answer this question satisfactorily, the hero becomes increasingly alienated from his own surroundings. This alienation is yet another symptom of "the inhumanity of modern society" that Kafka so memorably portrayed (Kuna 62).

Quotation from
secondary source

Support point #3:
Kafka's distinctive
style

Kafka also distinguishes himself as a great writer because he created a distinctive style that effectively dramatizes modern problems. Although Kafka's fiction often describes extreme situations, his prose usually seems strangely calm and detached. He uses "clear and simple language" that paints "concrete pictures of human beings, pictures that, in a sense, have to speak for themselves" (Cooper 19). These haunting images (the unreachable castle, the unknown laws, the unspecified trial) dramatize the mysterious struggles of the characters.

Elaborates support
point on style

Kafka also uses his style to separate himself from his characters, a technique that develops a contrast between the calmness of his style and the nervous desperation of his characters (Heller 237). For example, the opening of Kafka's novella *The Metamorphosis*, which is perhaps the most famous first sentence in modern fiction, describes an outrageous event—a young man who wakes up transformed into a giant bug—in a strangely matter-of-fact tone. This contrast is important because it reminds us of the desperation of modern man imprisoned in a world he can neither understand nor control.

Support point #4:
importance of
Kafka's deliberate
ambiguity

Perhaps the most interesting and influential feature of Kafka's style is his ability to create works that cannot be explained by a single interpretation. Because he allows his pictures to "speak for themselves," "Kafka's texts have been subject to a variety of widely divergent approaches" (Heller 236). Another critic, speaking directly of *The Metamorphosis*, agrees: "Gregor's transformation has a double meaning: it is both an escape from his oppressive life and a representation or even an intensification of it" (Goldfarb). Therefore, no single interpretation can adequately explain an entire work of Kafka's. Most interpretations may illuminate particular moments in a work, but inevitably they lead to a dead end when pressed to explain the whole narrative. Whether one is reading on a social, moral, psychological, metaphysical, theological, or existential level, Kafka "tends to suspend all distinction and thus to revert to total ambiguity" (Heller 285). According to Heller, this characteristic mysteriousness becomes "the epitome of his art" (230).

Auden believed that the impossibility of interpreting Kafka's work is essential in defining him as an important and influential writer. He says that "Kafka is a great, perhaps the greatest, master of the pure parable, a literary genre about which a critic can say very little worth saying" (159). Since the meaning of a parable is different for each individual, critics cannot explain them without revealing their own visions and values. Kafka develops stories with important symbols that are easily identified; attempting to interpret these symbols, however, only leads to frustration.

The frustration that comes from trying to interpret Kafka's works exemplifies his recurrent, and particularly twentieth-century, theme, which Peter Heller has described as man's "ever frustrated, ever defeated striving for self-realization in an inhuman human universe in which he is alienated from himself and from the world he lives in" (305). Kafka uses his characteristic difficult symbolism and ambiguity, along with his theme of hopelessness and despair, as a common thread that binds all of his works together.

Kafka's book *The Great Wall of China* contains several short pieces which have a slightly less desperate tone than that of *The Metamorphosis*. Many of the stories in *The Great Wall of China*, however, still present the theme of hopelessness. In the reflection entitled "The Problem of Our Laws," Kafka examines the origins and legitimacy of law. This parable begins with the narrator stating, "Our laws are not generally known; they are kept secret by the small group of nobles who rule us" (147). Next, the narrator goes through a laborious process of rationally questioning why only the nobility knows the laws, whether the laws really exist, and whether it will ever be possible for common men to know the laws. He finally concludes that the only way to know the law would be a quiet revolution that ends nobility. But even this solution, he realizes, is futile. The nobility cannot be eliminated because

Elaborates support point on Kafka's use of ambiguity and complexity

Support point #5: Kafka's exemplary 20th century themes of despair and alienation

Elaborates discussion on theme with examples from texts

Quotation from primary source

they provide the only order that exists. While this parable makes several interesting points, its structure is essentially static. The narrator ends where he began—trapped in an unknowable world.

Additional examples from texts

One of Kafka's unfinished novels, *The Trial*, also concentrates on the unknown symbol of the Law. In the novel, Joseph K. is arrested for a crime that no one ever knows. Joseph, like most of Kafka's characters, is a common man with an uneventful life who admits that he knows little of the Law. The drama of the novel is the protagonist's hopeless attempts to master an unknown and impossible situation. Joseph K.'s life itself becomes a trial, although he is never sentenced. Finally, one year after his arrest, two men come and murder him. Instead of trying to understand the Law, "In the end he appears to accept the verdict as a release from the condition of despair," and "dies like an animal, without comprehending the rationale of the Law which condemns him" (Heller 280-81). Like many men, before his death K. is struggling to discover his identity in relation to the Law that governs him; however, K.'s hopeless life ends with a pointless murder.

Another example from text

Kafka's other great, unfinished novel, *The Castle*, also concentrates on the theme of unknowability and despair. Instead of trying to understand the Law, K. in *The Castle* has another impossible quest, his attempt to enter the castle of the local ruler to report for duty as a land surveyor. His constant efforts, however, prove futile. As in *The Trial*, the protagonist is at the mercy of an arbitrary and unknowable Law:

> In many ways the castle functions like a secret court system: the officials
> decide and carry out policies that are conceived as stipulations of law; they
> lean on their law books, try to serve the law, and know the clandestine ways
> of law. Many decisions are arrived at arbitrarily and remain secret; even legal
> actions such as an official indictment can be kept hidden for some time.
> (Heidsieck 3)

Only when K. lies on his deathbed does a call from the castle come, giving him permission to live in the town. Once again, the protagonist suffers hopelessly and dies in despair.

Summarizes textual examples of Kafka's themes

While *The Trial* emphasizes political and psychological themes characteristic of the twentieth century, *The Castle* focuses on the religious identity crisis. *The Metamorphosis* examines similar themes of identity on a personal and family level. All of these works focus on modern humanity's difficult struggle to define its place in existence.

Kafka, through his works, accurately describes the modern condition of many by using memorable images and a distinctive style. This characteristic style influenced many twentieth-century writers and readers. While difficult and somewhat bleak, Kafka's often ambiguous, yet understated dramatizations of man's condition, along with his lasting influence, form the foundation of his greatness.

> Conclusion sums up paper's argument

Works Cited

Auden, W. H. "The I Without a Self." *The Dyer's Hand,* Random House, 1989, pp. 159–70.

Cooper, Gabriele von Natzmer. *Kafka and Language: In the Stream of Thoughts and Life.* Ariadne Press, 1991.

Goldfarb, Sheldon. "Critical Essay on *The Metamorphosis.*" *Short Stories for Students,* edited by Jennifer Smith, vol. 12, Gale Group, 2001. *Literature Resource Center,* Gale Group, doi: H1420035801.

Goodden, Christina. "Points of Departure." *The Kafka Debate: New Perspectives for Our Time,* edited by Angel Flores, Gordian Press, 1988, pp. 2–9.

Heidsieck, Arnold. "Community, Delusion and Anti-Semitism in Kafka's *The Castle.*" *German Studies Program,* German Dept., U of Southern California, usc.edu/dept/LAS/german/track/heidsiec/KafkaAntisemitism/ KafkaAntisemitism.pdf.

Heller, Peter. "Kafka: The Futility of Striving." *Dialectics and Nihilism,* U of Massachusetts P, 1966, pp. 227–306.

Kafka, Franz. "The Problem of Our Laws." *The Great Wall of China,* Schocken Books, 1946, pp. 147–49.

Kuna, Franz. *Franz Kafka: Literature as Corrective Punishment.* Indiana UP, 1974.

Sandbank, Shimon. *After Kafka: The Influence of Kafka's Fiction.* U of Georgia P, 1989.

REFERENCE GUIDE FOR MLA CITATIONS

Here are examples of the types of citations you are likely to need for most student papers. The formats follow current MLA style for works-cited lists.

PRINT PUBLICATIONS

Books

No Author Listed

The Chicago Manual of Style. 17th ed., U of Chicago P, 2017.

One Author or Editor

Middlebrook, Diane Wood. *Anne Sexton: A Biography.* Houghton Mifflin, 1991.

Monteiro, George, editor. *Conversations with Elizabeth Bishop.* UP of Mississippi, 1996.

Two Authors or Editors

Jarman, Mark, and Robert McDowell. *The Reaper: Essays.* Story Line Press, 1996.

Craig, David, and Janet McCann, editors. *Odd Angles of Heaven: Contemporary Poetry by People of Faith.* Harold Shaw Publishing, 1994.

Three or More Authors

Phillips, Rodney, et al. *The Hand of the Poet.* Rizzoli International Publications, 1997.

Multiple Works by the Same Author

Bawer, Bruce. *The Aspect of Eternity.* Graywolf Press, 1993.

---. "Civilized Pleasures." *The Hudson Review,* vol. 59, no. 1, Spring 2006. *JSTOR,* www.jstor.org/stable/i20464510.

---. *Diminishing Fictions: Essays on the Modern American Novel and Its Critics.* Graywolf Press, 1988.

Corporate Author and Publisher

Reading at Risk: A Survey of Literary Reading in America. National Endowment for the Arts, June 2004.

Author and Editor

Shakespeare, William. *The Sonnets.* Edited by G. Blakemore Evans, Cambridge UP, 1996.

Translator

Dante Alighieri. *Inferno: A New Verse Translation*. Translated by Michael Palma,
    W. W. Norton, 2002.

Introduction, Preface, Foreword, or Afterword

Lapham, Lewis. Introduction. *Understanding Media: The Extensions of Man*, by Marshall
    McLuhan, MIT P, 1994, pp. vi–x.

Thwaite, Anthony. Preface. *Contemporary Poets*, edited by Thomas Riggs, 6th ed.,
    St. James Press, 1996, pp. vii–viii.

Work in an Anthology

Rodriguez, Richard. "Aria: A Memoir of a Bilingual Childhood." *The Best American Essays
    of the Century,* edited by Robert Atwan and Joyce Carol Oates, Houghton Mifflin,
    2001, pp. 447–66. Best American Series.

Translation in an Anthology

Neruda, Pablo. "We Are Many." Translated by Alastair Reid. *Literature: An Introduction
    to Fiction, Poetry, Drama, and Writing*, edited by X. J. Kennedy et al., 14th ed.,
    Pearson, 2020, pp. 963–64.

Revised or Subsequent Edition

Janouch, Gustav. *Conversations with Kafka*. Translated by Goronwy Rees, rev. ed., New
    Directions Publishing, 1971.

Republished Book

Ellison, Ralph. *Invisible Man*. 1952. Vintage Books, 1995.

Multivolume Work

Wellek, René. *A History of Modern Criticism, 1750–1950*. 8 vols., Yale UP, 1955–92.

One Volume of a Multivolume Work

Wellek, René. *A History of Modern Criticism, 1750–1950*. Vol. 7, Yale UP, 1991. 8 vols.

Book in a Series

Ross, William T. *Weldon Kees*. Twayne Publishing, 1985. Twayne's United States Authors
    Series, 484.

Signed Article in a Reference Book

Cavoto, Janice E. "Harper Lee's *To Kill a Mockingbird." The Oxford Encyclopedia of American Literature,* edited by Jay Parini, vol. 2, Oxford UP, 2004, pp. 418–21.

Unsigned Encyclopedia Article—Standard Reference Book

"James Dickey." *The New Encyclopaedia Britannica: Micropaedia.* 15th ed., 1987.

Dictionary Entry

"Design." *Merriam-Webster's Collegiate Dictionary.* 11th ed., 2003.

Periodicals

Journal

Salter, Mary Jo. "The Heart Is Slow to Learn." *The New Criterion,* vol. 10, no. 8, Apr. 1992, pp. 23–29.

Signed Magazine Article

Gioia, Dana. "Studying with Miss Bishop." *The New Yorker,* 5 Sept. 1986, pp. 90–101.

Unsigned Magazine Article

"The Real Test." *New Republic,* 5 Feb. 2001, p. 7.

Newspaper Article

Lyall, Sarah. "In Poetry, Ted Hughes Breaks His Silence on Sylvia Plath." *The New York Times,* 19 Jan. 1998, natl. ed., pp. A1+.

Signed Book Review

Fugard, Lisa. "Divided We Love," Review of *Unaccustomed Earth,* by Jhumpa Lahiri. *The Los Angeles Times,* 30 Mar. 2008, p. R1.

Unsigned, Untitled Book Review

Review of *Otherwise: New and Selected Poems,* by Jane Kenyon. *Virginia Quarterly Review,* vol. 72, no. 1, Winter 1996, p. 136.

WEB RESOURCES

Website

Liu, Alan, director. *Voice of the Shuttle.* English Dept., U of California Santa Barbara,
     vos.ucsb.edu.

Document on a Website

"A Hughes Timeline." *PBS,* Public Broadcasting Service, www.pbs.org.wgbh/
     masterpiece/americancollection/cora/hughes_timeline.html.
"Wallace Stevens." *Poets.org.,* Academy of American Poets, www.poets.org/poetsorg/
     poet/wallace-stevens.

Online Reference Database

"Brooks, Gwendolyn." *Encyclopaedia Britannica,* www.britannica.com/biography/
     Gwendolyn-Brooks.

Entire Online Book, Previously Appeared in Print

Jewett, Sarah Orne. *The Country of the Pointed Firs.* 1896. *Project Gutenberg,* 11 July
     2008, www.gutenberg.org/files/367/367-h/367-h.htm. Ebook 367.

Article in an Online Newspaper

Atwood, Margaret. "The Writer: A New Canadian Life-Form." *The New York Times on
     the Web,* 18 May 1997, www.nytimes.com/books/97/05/18/bookend/
     bookend.html.

Article in an Online Magazine

Garner, Dwight. "Jamaica Kincaid." *Salon,* 13 Jan. 1996, www.salon.com/1996/01/13/
     kincaid_2/.

Article in an Online Scholarly Journal

Carter, Sarah. "From the Ridiculous to the Sublime: Ovidian and Neoplatonic Registers
     in *A Midsummer Night's Dream." Early Modern Literary Studies,* vol 12, no. 1, May
     2006, pp. 1–31, purl.oclc.org/emls/12-1/cartmnd.htm.

Article from a Scholarly Journal, Part of an Archival Online Database

Finch, Annie. "My Father Dickinson: On Poetic Influence." *The Emily Dickinson Journal,*
      vol. 17, no. 2, 2008, pp. 24–38. *Project Muse,* www.muse.jhu.edu/journals/
      emily_dickinson_journal/v017/17.2.finch.html.

Article Accessed via a Library Subscription Service

Seitler, Dana. "Unnatural Selection: Mothers, Eugenic Feminism, and Charlotte Perkins
      Gilman's Regeneration Narratives." *American Quarterly,* vol. 55, no. 1, Mar. 2003,
      pp. 61–87. *ProQuest,* search.proquest.com.libproxy1.usc.edu/ docview/
      223310934/5B0B8A7854AE4085PQ/1?accountid=14789

Online Blog

Gioia, Ted. *"White Teeth* by Zadie Smith.*" The New Canon: The Best in Fiction Since 1985,*
      www.thenewcanon.com/white_teeth.html.

Vellala, Rob. "Gilman: No Trouble to Anyone." *The American Literary Blog,* 17 Aug. 2010,
      americanliteraryblog.blogspot.com/search/label/Charlotte%20Perkins%20Gilman.

Twitter

Tan, Amy (AmyTan). "#TenThingsNotToSayToAWriter My life would make a great story.
      If you write it, we can split royalties 50–50." *Twitter,* 30 July 2015, 9:19 p.m.,
      twitter.com/AmyTan/status/626970316087132161.

Photograph or Painting Accessed Online

Langston Hughes in 1936. Wikimedia Commons, Wikimedia Foundation, commons.
      wikimedia.org/wiki/Langston_Hughes#/media/File: Langston_Hughes_1936.jpg.

Bruegel, Pieter, *Landscape with the Fall of Icarus.* c.1558. Musées Royaux des Beaux-
      Arts de Belgique, Brussels. *Ibiblio,* U of North Carolina-Chapel Hill/Center for the
      Public Domain, www.ibiblio.org/wm/paint/auth/bruegel.

Video Accessed Online

"Ozymandias: Percy Bysshe Shelley." *YouTube,* E-Verse Radio, 13 Mar. 2007,
      www.youtube.com/watch?v=6xGa-fNSHaM.

Podcast

Fox, Curtis. "The Poet's Revenge." *Poetry Off the Shelf,* Poetry Foundation, 27 Feb. 2018,
      www.poetryfoundation.org/podcasts/146086/the-poet39s-revenge.

OTHER MEDIA

Compact Disc (CD)

Shakespeare, William. *The Complete Arkangel Shakespeare: 38 Fully-Dramatized Plays.*
    Narrated by Eileen Atkins and John Gielgud, read by Imogen Stubbs, Joseph
    Fiennes, et al., Audio Partners, 2003.

DVD

Hamlet. By William Shakespeare, performance by Laurence Olivier, Eileen Herlie, and
    Basil Sydney, 1948. Criterion Collection, 2010.

Film

Hamlet. By William Shakespeare, directed by Franco Zeffirelli, performances by Mel Gibson,
    Glenn Close, Helena Bonham Carter, Alan Bates, and Paul Scofield, Warner Bros., 1991.

Television or Radio Program

Moby Dick. By Herman Melville, directed by Franc Roddam, performances by Patrick
    Stewart and Gregory Peck, 2 episodes, USA Network, 16-17 Mar. 1998.

Television Series

The Wire. By David Simon, Blown Deadline / HBO, 2002-2008.

Episode of a Television Series

"Old Cases." *The Wire,* by David Simon, season 1, episode 4, Blown Deadline / HBO,
    23 June 2002.

Episode of a Television Series Seen on DVD

"Old Cases." *The Wire: The Complete First Season,* by David Simon, episode 4, HBO Video, 2004.

Episode of a Television Series Streamed Online

"Old Cases." *The Wire: The Complete First Season,* by David Simon, episode 4. *Amazon Prime,*
    www.amazon.com/The-Detail/dp/B00BSEJR9C/ref=sr_1_1?s=instantvideo&ie=
    UTF8&qid=1459816276&sr=1-1&keywords=the+wire.

Live Performance

Heartbreak House. By George Bernard Shaw, directed by Robin Lefevre, performances
    by Philip Bosco and Swoosie Kurtz, Roundabout Theater Company, 1 Oct. 2006,
    New York.

47 WRITING AS DISCOVERY: KEEPING A JOURNAL

*I have all my life regretted
that I did not keep a regular journal.*

—SIR WALTER SCOTT

What You Will Learn in This Chapter

- To keep a journal

The novelist E. M. Forster once remarked, "How do I know what I think until I see what I say?" Few writers know precisely what they are going to say before they begin. Writing isn't simply a way to communicate ideas; it is also a way to formulate them, to try out new thoughts and hash them through. It is also a wonderful way to explore ideas that may eventually grow into longer pieces of formal writing.

THE REWARDS OF KEEPING A JOURNAL

Many instructors ask students to respond to reading in a journal—a day-to-day account of what they read and how they react to it. One great advantage of a journal is that it allows you to express your thoughts and feelings immediately, in your own words, before they grow cold. You can set down all your miscellaneous reactions to the reading, whether or not they fit into a paper topic. (If you have to write a paper later on, your journal just might suggest topics galore.) Journals are a useful place for collecting impressions, working through your ideas, and trying out false starts until you find the one that leads to someplace interesting for both you and your reader.

Journals can be useful study tools, too. If your course includes a midterm or final examination, you may well find that rereading your journal will help you to remember details of the works you read earlier in the term.

While some instructors give directives for journal entries, assigning essay questions or particular topics to address, others will give a more open-ended assignment, asking only that students respond in a way that shows they are interacting with the material. Either way, to get the most out of the experience, you might consider a few tips:

- **Capture your first reaction.** Read with pen in hand, jotting down anything you wish to remember. Write about anything that catches your attention or defies your interpretation. Does a line of dialogue surprise you? Make a note of it. Does a particular sentence seem significant? Comment on it. Does something in the story not make sense? Record your bewilderment. Better still, try to push past it into understanding. If you're at first puzzled by a character's motivation or by a line of poetry that resists interpretation, try to work through your puzzlement. A snippet from a journal entry on Denise Levertov's poem "Ancient Stairway" (see Chapter 25) might be as unprocessed as this:

> What does this poem mean? I'm on the first line, and I'm already confused. What does she mean by the line "Footsteps like water hollow?" How can water be hollow? Oh, wait . . . maybe hollow really goes with the line after it . . . so the footsteps hollow the "broad curves of stone" which I guess means the steps. But why didn't she break the lines to make the poem easier to read, I wonder. Why not break the line after water instead of hollow? But I like how the next line is just two words "ascending, descending." I guess this means the stairs go both ways like all stairs.

Writing as you read can help you to begin to get a handle on difficult passages. It can also focus your mind. If your thoughts tend to meander away from the pages before you, or if you find yourself tempted to skim instead of paying close attention, writing in your journal can keep you involved and alert.

- **Just get it down.** In keeping a journal, you are writing primarily for yourself. You aren't obliged to polish your prose. It isn't necessary to develop your ideas. Just jot them down. Your aim is to store information without delay, to record your observations and impressions. Although your instructor may read your journal, he or she is unlikely to be looking there for fully processed ideas; those will come in more formal pieces of writing. Your teacher will most likely be reading your journal to ascertain that you are thinking your way through the work and the issues it raises. To be safe, though, ask your professor how formal or informal the journal needs to be.

- **Get personal.** Your journal is a place in which to sound off and express gut reactions. Don't just copy your class notes into it. Don't simply record plot details: first X happened, then Y happened, then Z. Instead, note your own emotional responses to a piece of literature, and consider what about the work is causing you to react. Your first reactions can provide a jumping-off point for further exploration.

- **Keep writing after you've said it all.** You may think you've said everything you have to say after you've written for five minutes or covered half a page. Keep writing, working quickly, without agonizing over where your words are taking you. Sometimes when we write beyond the point where we'd rather stop, we surprise ourselves with new ideas and insights. This is why many instructors will assign a certain length to journal entries or ask students to write for a particular amount of time.

- **Read closely.** It can be tempting to paint your journal entries with a broad brush, writing about a poem's central theme or a story's plot. Don't forget the value of reading closely. Examine a paragraph, or a sentence, or even a particularly significant word. Like our DNA, which encodes genetic information about our whole selves, sometimes a small part of a poem, story, or play can reveal much about the work as a whole.

- **Stick with the text.** A moment in a story might remind you of something in your own past. Connie's encounter with Arnold Friend in "Where Are You Going, Where Have You Been?" (Chapter 3), for example, may cause you to hearken back to your own brush with a creepy character. It might be tempting to leave the story behind and write about your own experience, but doing so won't teach you much about the story. You will learn more by giving the literary work itself your full attention.

- **Try out risky ideas.** A journal is no place to play it safe. Try for new insights—go out on a limb. You can try on new ideas and discard the ones that don't fit. By taking some risks, you may come up with a more provocative thesis than you otherwise would have, one that eventually will lead you to write a more dynamic term paper.

- **Follow your interests.** If you aren't given a specific topic to treat in your journal, attack the aspects of a literary work that most intrigue you. This will make your journaling more interesting—both for you and for your reader. If you should find yourself stumped, you can always turn to any of the "Topics for Writing" that appear at the end of the chapter in which your subject appears. These can provide a good starting point for a journal entry.

- **Write often.** Journals are useful only if you keep them up to date. Jot down your insights while you still have a story, poem, or play freshly in mind. Fall weeks behind, and you will have to grind out a journal from scratch, the night before it is due, and the whole project will decay into meaningless drudgery. Instead, if you faithfully do a little reading and writing every day or so, you will find yourself keeping track of the life of your mind. You will have a lively record not only of the literature you have read, but also of your personal involvement with it.

SAMPLE JOURNAL ENTRY

The following journal entry was written by Virginia Andros, a student at Saint Joseph's University in Philadelphia. Her subject was the opening of T. S. Eliot's "The Love Song of J. Alfred Prufrock," which can be found in Chapter 33. She wrote these entries in longhand, in a notebook. (Some instructors will accept journals composed on and printed out from a computer; if unsure, have your professor clarify his or her preference.)

"Prufrock" Reflections

This poem begins with six lines written in a language I don't speak, Spanish, maybe, or Italian. I'm going to ignore those lines for now—they don't seem to be part of the poem itself. For now I'll worry about the actual poem. I like the first line: "Let us go then, you and I" because it feels like an invitation—like the lines are being spoken directly to me. I can picture the speaker stretching out his hand for me. The next lines are strange, though: "When the evening is spread out against the sky / Like a patient etherized upon a table." The part about the sky is beautiful, but the image that follows it is creepy. Already I'm wondering what kind of trip this is going to be, and if I should trust my guide.

So where are we going? We're traveling "through certain half-deserted streets" to get to "one-night cheap hotels / And sawdust restaurants with oyster-shells." What's a sawdust restaurant? Maybe the food tastes like sawdust? Or maybe the place is messy, with sawdust on the floor. It's interesting that the poem mentions "oyster shells" and not the oysters themselves. It's like we're concentrating on the garbage left over after the meal is done. The phrase "muttering retreats" is odd too . . . again, it sounds pretty negative. What's muttering? A crowd of people in the hotel lobby or the restaurant? They're not laughing or having pleasant conversation. The word "muttering" even sounds nasty . . . as though the people are complaining under their breath about the bad décor and lousy service.

Here's the next two lines. "Streets that follow like a tedious argument / Of insidious intent." How can streets be like a tedious argument? Confusion! But I picture cramped streets, in the center of a city. Maybe one leads to the next, which leads to the next, and the next . . . the way in a tedious argument one line of reasoning leads you to the next and pretty soon you've forgotten what you were arguing about in the first place, because you're bickering about something else entirely. I had to look up "insidious": it means slowly destructive. Is it the streets that have insidious intent, or the argument? I think maybe it's the argument . . . but maybe the streets do too in some way. The streets are slowly destructive? To whom? Okay, my head's starting to hurt. Maybe the streets are destructive to me, the person the speaker is speaking to.

Now the speaker talks to me (or at least to someone) directly again: "Oh, do not ask, 'What is it?' / Let us go and make our visit." I like these lines! I notice that they rhyme, so now I'm looking back to see if the other lines I've already read do too. Some do, but I hadn't noticed. Anyway, these lines make me wonder, who is the speaker? Is it J. Alfred Prufrock? And how is this a love poem? Maybe the "you" in the poem is a girlfriend? If so, this isn't much of a date.

New stanza: "In the room the women come and go / Talking of Michelangelo." Maybe we're in a museum?

Here comes more description of a sad, dirty city. The fog is "yellow" and there's chimney soot. If I'm right, and the speaker is taking his girlfriend around the city, he's sort of a loser. Why isn't he taking her someplace beautiful . . . to a nice restaurant, or out dancing? Why is he making her walk down a dirty street? Why is this poem so unromantic? If I were the girlfriend, there wouldn't be a second date.

This journal entry examines its subject closely, using key words and phrases to begin to get at the poem's meaning. Its author freely admits her confusion over certain challenging lines, but isn't content to rest on first impressions. By puzzling her way line by line through part of the poem, she begins to get at issues central to the entire poem: its speaker, its tone, its form, and its literal meaning. Doing your thinking on the page can be a crucial step in the writing—and reading—process. Even if keeping a journal isn't one of your course assignments, you might profitably apply these techniques to taking notes as you read through a poem, short story, or play. When it comes time to write a more formal paper, you're likely to be glad you've been actively thinking the material through all along.

48

WRITING AN
ESSAY EXAM

The test of literature is, I suppose,
whether we ourselves live more intensely for the reading of it.

—ELIZABETH DREW

What You Will Learn in This Chapter

- To prepare for and take an essay exam

Why might an instructor choose to give an essay examination? It may sometimes seem like sheer sadism, but there are good reasons for using essays to test your knowledge of a subject. Longer, more involved answers can reveal not just how well you have memorized course material but also how thoroughly you have processed it. An essay exam allows you to demonstrate that you can think critically about the literature you have read and the issues your reading has raised. It lets you show how well you can marshal evidence to support your assertions. It also gives you a chance to draw connections between the literary works you have read and the main themes of the course.

Whether your exam is take-home or in-class, open-book or closed, the following strategies will help you to show off what you know:

- **Be prepared.** Before you take the exam, review the readings. If you have been highlighting and annotating all semester, you will find yourself well rewarded for that extra bit of effort. A glance at highlighted portions of text can help refresh your memory about passages in a text that struck you as particularly important; your marginalia can help you to recall why that was the case.

- **Review your notes.** It is also a good idea to review any notes you have taken for the course. If you kept a reading journal, go back and reread it. (You will be surprised how many specific memories rereading your journal will trigger.) Even if you are permitted to use your books during the exam, reacquainting yourself with the material beforehand can help you better recall what it is you are looking for in those open books.

    As you review, be sure to think about the big picture. How do the literary works you have read relate to each other? If you have been reading theory and criticism, how might it apply to the course's content? If you have been given historical background about the period in which a work was written, how does the work embody its author's time? Sometimes it might help just to write down a few of the central ideas the course has explored on a separate sheet of paper—to summarize a few of the major insights the course has offered.

■ **Think it through.** Once you have been given the exam, be sure to read it all the way through before you begin writing. Figure out how much time you can afford to spend per section. Pay attention to how many points each question is worth; you may well want to budget your time accordingly. Leave yourself time to proofread your responses and add any missing information.

When you are ready to start, you might find it helpful first to attack questions about which you feel more confident. Go ahead, but save enough time to tackle the tougher ones as well.

■ **Read the questions carefully.** To ensure that you are answering the actual questions you have been asked, pay special attention to words in the directions that seem important. Verbs such as "analyze," "summarize," "explicate," "compare," "contrast," "evaluate," "interpret," and "explain" give clues to what your focus should be. Highlight or underline these action words so that you can more readily keep them in mind as you write. Understanding what you are being asked to do is crucial. Failing to follow directions might lose you precious points, no matter how brilliantly you write on your subject.

Careful reading and highlighting can also help you remember to address all parts of any given question. Don't get so caught up in answering one part of a question that you neglect the other parts.

■ **Understand your purpose.** Whenever you write, it pays to consider your audience and your purpose. Inevitably, the audience for an essay exam response will be your instructor. It's likely that he or she will be looking to see whether you have understood the material on which you are being tested. As you consider the questions you are about to answer, think back to concepts stressed by the instructor during in-class discussions. Try to touch on these concepts as you write, as long as you can do so without losing your focus. Also, since your instructor is familiar with the literary work under discussion, there's no need to relate the whole story in your exam response. Unless you are specifically asked to summarize, don't give any more plot details than are needed to accomplish the assigned task.

For clues about what your purpose should be, pay attention to those action words you have highlighted in the directions. Here are some common ones:

Analyze	Consider how a single element of the text contributes to its full meaning or effect.
Compare	Explore how two or more things resemble each other.
Contrast	Explore how two or more things differ from each other.
Evaluate	Examine a work with the purpose of determining its quality or importance.
Explain	Clarify a concept.
Explicate	Explain a brief work or a passage from a longer work in detail to show how its parts contribute to the work as a whole.
Interpret	Express a literary work's meaning in your own words.
Paraphrase	Restate a passage in your own words.
Prove	Provide evidence of the truth of a claim, drawing on information from the literary work under study.
Relate	Show a connection between two or more items.
Summarize	Give a shortened version of a literary work, touching on key points.

▪ **Plan before you write. Start with a clear thesis that accurately addresses the exam question.** A critical step in writing a good essay exam is creating a thesis sentence that succinctly expresses your main point. Using the exam question to provide direction for your thesis, come up with a statement that is both decisive and specific.

For example, if you have been asked to describe the grandmother's transformation in Flannery O'Connor's "A Good Man Is Hard to Find" (Chapter 11), your thesis should say something specific about *how* or *why* she gains insight in her last moments of life. The first thesis below does not address the assignment—it describes the grandmother, not the grandmother's transformation. It is accurate but incomplete since it does not lead anywhere useful.

IRRELEVANT THESIS

The grandmother in "A Good Man Is Hard to Find" is self-centered and silly.

The rough thesis that follows sticks with the merely obvious.

ROUGH THESIS

The grandmother in "A Good Man Is Hard to Find" is a silly, self-centered woman who undergoes a transformation at the end of the story.

The revised thesis makes a more decisive statement, providing specifics about what happens at the story's climax.

REVISED THESIS

In "A Good Man Is Hard to Find," the grandmother is transformed from a silly, self-centered woman into a wiser, more caring one.

A final revision goes further, venturing to say not only what happens in the story but why it happens. It provides a good road map for writing an essay exam.

FINAL THESIS

In "A Good Man Is Hard to Find," the grandmother is transformed by her proximity to death from a silly, self-centered woman into a wiser, more caring one.

▪ **Create a rough outline.** Though an essay question might seem like an occasion for off-the-cuff writing, it's a good idea to sketch a rough outline before you plunge in. As you write, follow the outline point by point. An outline for an essay response based on the final thesis above might look something like this:

1. Grandmother transformed by closeness to death
2. Starts out silly
   Lives in the past
   Gets directions wrong
3. Becomes wiser
   Sees her mistakes
   Sees her connection to the Misfit

    4. Starts out self-centered
       Smuggles cat on trip
       Makes family drive out of way
    5. Becomes caring
       Reaches out to Misfit
       Sees him as her own child
    6. Nearness to death
       Hears her son get shot
       Misfit's quotation

- **Make your essay shapely.** Like a more formal piece of writing, your answer will need an introduction that establishes the point you will be making. It also should include a conclusion that summarizes your argument (preferably without too much bald-faced restatement) and reinforces your thesis. The paragraphs in between should be used to flesh out your argument.

- **Give evidence.** Back up your thesis, and any assertion you make along the way, with proof from the story, poem, or play you are discussing. Direct quotations generally make the most convincing evidence, but if you are working from memory, you can do the job with references to the text. To make your argument more convincing and establish how familiar you are with the material, be as specific as you can manage.

- **Keep your focus.** As you write, refer frequently to your outline. Be sure to keep your argument on track. Don't ramble or repeat yourself to fill up space; to do so will give the impression that you are uncertain about your response or the material.

- **Make smooth transitions.** Use transitional words and phrases to connect each new idea to the one that precedes it. These handy tools can signal your intentions. If your argument is changing directions, you might signal as much with words and phrases such as "in contrast," "on the other hand," "however," "yet," or "conversely." If you are continuing along the same track you've been traveling, try "in addition," "similarly," "furthermore," or "moreover." To indicate cause and effect, you might use "because," "therefore," "as a result," or "consequently." If you make it easy for your reader to follow your train of thought, the end result is likely to be a grateful reader.

- **Pay attention to detail.** Be sure to proofread your essay before handing it in. Nothing undermines a writer's authority faster than spelling mistakes and grammatical errors. Even illegible handwriting can try a reader's patience—never a good idea when a grade is involved.

CHECKLIST: Taking an Essay Exam

Exam Preparation

- ☐ Skim the literary works that will be on the exam.
- ☐ Reread all your notes and, if you have kept one, your reader's journal.
- ☐ Consider how the literary works on the exam relate to each other.
- ☐ Consider possible relationships between the literary works and any literary criticism, theory, or historical background you have been given in the course.

Taking the Exam

☐ When you are given the exam, quickly read it all the way through.

☐ Calculate how much time you can spend per question.

☐ Read each essay question carefully, underlining key words. Take note of multipart questions.

☐ Understand your purpose before you begin.

☐ Write a thesis sentence that accurately answers the exam question.

☐ Sketch an outline for the essay response.

☐ Include an introductory paragraph and a conclusion.

☐ Back up each point you make with evidence from the text.

☐ Don't give plot summaries unless asked to.

☐ Use transitional phrases to link paragraphs and ideas.

☐ Proofread your exam before handing it in.

49

CRITICAL APPROACHES TO LITERATURE

Literary criticism should arise out of a debt of love.

—GEORGE STEINER

What You Will Learn in This Chapter

■ To define and describe the major schools of literary criticism

Literary criticism is not an abstract, intellectual exercise; it is a natural human response to literature. If a friend informs you she is reading a book you have just finished, it would be odd indeed if you did not begin swapping opinions. Literary criticism is nothing more than discourse—spoken or written—about literature. A student who sits quietly in a morning English class, intimidated by the notion of literary criticism, might spend an hour that evening talking animatedly about the meaning of rock lyrics or comparing the relative merits of the *Star Wars* trilogies. It is inevitable that people will ponder, discuss, and analyze the works of art that interest them.

The informal criticism of friends talking about literature tends to be casual, unorganized, and subjective. Since Aristotle, however, philosophers, scholars, and writers have tried to create more precise and disciplined ways of discussing literature. Literary critics have borrowed concepts from other disciplines—such as philosophy, history, linguistics, psychology, and anthropology—to analyze imaginative literature more perceptively. Some critics have found it useful to work in the abstract area of **literary theory**, criticism that tries to formulate general principles rather than discuss specific texts. Mass media critics, such as newspaper reviewers, usually spend their time evaluating works—telling us which books are worth reading, which plays not to bother seeing. But most serious literary criticism is not primarily evaluative; it assumes we know that *Othello* or *The Metamorphosis* is worth reading. Instead, such criticism is analytic; it tries to help us better understand a literary work.

In the following pages you will find overviews of nine critical approaches to literature. While these nine methods do not exhaust the total possibilities of literary criticism, they represent the most widely used contemporary approaches. Although presented separately, the approaches are not necessarily mutually exclusive; many critics mix methods to suit their needs and interests. For example, a historical critic may use formalist techniques to analyze a poem; a biographical critic will frequently use psychological theories to analyze an author. The summaries try neither to provide a history of each approach nor to present the latest trends in each school. Their purpose is to give you a practical introduction to each critical method and then provide representative examples of it. If one of these critical methods interests you, why not try to write a class paper using the approach?

FORMALIST CRITICISM

Formalist criticism regards literature as a unique form of human knowledge that needs to be examined on its own terms. "The natural and sensible starting point for work in literary scholarship," René Wellek and Austin Warren wrote in their influential *Theory of Literature*, "is the interpretation and analysis of the works of literature themselves." To a formalist, a poem or story is not primarily a social, historical, or biographical document; it is a literary work that can be understood only by reference to its intrinsic literary features—that is, those elements found in the text itself. To analyze a poem or story, therefore, the formalist critic focuses on the words of the text rather than facts about the author's life or the historical milieu in which the text was written. The critic pays special attention to the formal features of the text—the style, structure, imagery, tone, and genre. These features, however, are usually not examined in isolation, because formalist critics believe that what gives a literary text its special status as art is how all its elements work together to create the reader's total experience. As Robert Penn Warren commented, "Poetry does not inhere in any particular element but depends upon the set of relationships, the structure, which we call the poem."

A key method that formalists use to explore the intense relationships within a poem is **close reading**, a careful step-by-step analysis and explication of a text. The purpose of close reading is to understand how various elements in a literary text work together to shape its effects on the reader. Since formalists believe that the various stylistic and thematic elements of a literary work influence each other, these critics insist that form and content cannot be meaningfully separated. The complete interdependence of form and content is what makes a text literary. When we extract a work's theme or paraphrase its meaning, we destroy the aesthetic experience of the work.

Cleanth Brooks (1906–1994)

The Formalist Critic   1951

Here are some articles of faith I could subscribe to:

> That literary criticism is a description and an evaluation of its object.
>
> That the primary concern of criticism is with the problem of unity—the kind of whole which the literary work forms or fails to form, and the relation of the various parts to each other in building up this whole.
>
> That the formal relations in a work of literature may include, but certainly exceed, those of logic.
>
> That in a successful work, form and content cannot be separated.
>
> That form is meaning.
>
> That literature is ultimately metaphorical and symbolic.
>
> That the general and the universal are not seized upon by abstraction, but got at through the concrete and the particular.
>
> That literature is not a surrogate for religion.
>
> That, as Allen Tate says, "specific moral problems" are the subject matter of literature, but that the purpose of literature is not to point a moral.
>
> That the principles of criticism define the area relevant to literary criticism; they do not constitute a method for carrying out the criticism.

• • •

The formalist critic knows as well as anyone that poems and plays and novels are written by men—that they do not somehow happen—and that they are written as expressions of particular personalities and are written from all sorts of motives— for money, from a desire to express oneself, for the sake of a cause, etc. Moreover, the formalist critic knows as well as anyone that literary works are merely potential until they are read—that is, that they are recreated in the minds of actual readers, who vary enormously in their capabilities, their interests, their prejudices, their ideas. But the formalist critic is concerned primarily with the work itself. Speculation on the mental processes of the author takes the critic away from the work into biography and psychology. There is no reason, of course, why he should not turn away into biography and psychology. Such explorations are very much worth making. But they should not be confused with an account of the work. Such studies describe the process of composition, not the structure of the thing composed, and they may be performed quite as validly for the poor work as for the good one. They may be validly performed for any kind of expression—non-literary as well as literary.

From "The Formalist Critic"

Michael Clark (b. 1946)

Light and Darkness in "Sonny's Blues" 1985

"Sonny's Blues" by James Baldwin is a sensitive story about the reconciliation of two brothers, but it is much more than that. It is, in addition, an examination of the importance of the black heritage and of the central importance of music in that heritage. Finally, the story probes the central role that art must play in human existence. To examine all of these facets of human existence is a rather formidable undertaking in a short story, even in a longish short story such as this one. Baldwin not only undertakes this task, but he does it superbly. One of the central ways that Baldwin fuses all of these complex elements is by using a metaphor of childhood, which is supported by ancillary images of light and darkness. He does the job so well that the story is a *tour de force*, a penetrating study of American culture.

• • •

Sonny's quest is best described by himself when he writes to the narrator: "I feel like a man who's been trying to climb up out of some deep, real deep and funky hole and just saw the sun up there, outside. I got to get outside." Sonny is a person who finds his life a living hell, but he knows enough to strive for the "light." As it is chronicled in this story, his quest is for regaining something from the past—from his own childhood and from the pasts of all who have come before him. The means for doing this is his music, which is consistently portrayed in terms of light imagery. When Sonny has a discussion with the narrator about the future, the narrator describes Sonny's face as a mixture of concern and hope: "[T]he worry, the thoughtfulness, played on it still, the way shadows play on a face which is staring into the fire." This fire image is reinforced shortly afterward when the narrator describes Sonny's aspirations once more in terms of light: "[I]t was as though he were all wrapped up in some cloud, some fire, some vision all his own." To the narrator and to Isabel's family, the music that Sonny plays is simply "weird and disordered," but to Sonny, the music is seen in starkly positive terms: his failure to master the music will mean "death," while success will mean "life."

The light and dark imagery culminates in the final scene, where the narrator, apparently for the first time, listens to Sonny play the piano. The location is a Greenwich Village club. Appropriately enough, the narrator is seated "in a dark corner." In contrast, the stage is dominated by light, which Baldwin reiterates with a succession of images: "light . . . circle of light . . . light . . . flame . . . light." Although Sonny has a false start, he gradually settles into his playing and ends the first set with some intensity: "Everything had been burned out of [Sonny's face], and at the same time, things usually hidden were being burned in, by the fire and fury of the battle which was occurring in him up there."

The culmination of the set occurs when Creole, the leader of the players, begins to play "Am I Blue?" At this point, "something began to happen." Apparently, the narrator at this time realizes that this music *is* important. The music is central to the experience of the black experience, and it is described in terms of light imagery:

> Creole began to tell us what the blues were all about. They were not about anything very new. He and his boys up there were keeping it new, at the risk of ruin, destruction, madness, and death, in order to find new ways to make us listen. For, while the tale of how we suffer, and how we are delighted, and how we may triumph is never new, it always must be heard. There isn't any other tale to tell, it's the only light we've got in all this darkness.

From "James Baldwin's 'Sonny's Blues': Childhood, Light, and Art"

BIOGRAPHICAL CRITICISM

Biographical criticism begins with the simple but central insight that literature is written by actual people and that understanding an author's life can help readers more thoroughly comprehend the work. Anyone who reads the biography of a writer quickly sees how much an author's experience shapes—both directly and indirectly—what he or she creates. Reading that biography will also change (and usually deepen) our response to the work. Sometimes even knowing a single important fact illuminates our reading of a poem or story. Learning, for example, that poet Josephine Miles was confined to a wheelchair or that Weldon Kees committed suicide at forty-one will certainly make us pay attention to certain aspects of their poems we might otherwise have missed or considered unimportant. A formalist critic might complain that we would also have noticed those things through careful textual analysis, but biographical information provides the practical assistance of underscoring subtle but important meanings in the poems. Though many literary theorists have assailed biographical criticism on philosophical grounds, the biographical approach to literature has never disappeared because of its obvious practical advantage in illuminating literary texts.

It may be helpful here to make a distinction between biography and biographical criticism. Biography is, strictly speaking, a branch of history; it provides a written account of a person's life. To establish and interpret the facts of a poet's life, for instance, a biographer would use all the available information—not just personal documents such as letters and diaries but also the poems—for the possible light they might shed on the subject's life. A biographical *critic*, however, is not concerned with re-creating the record of an author's life. Biographical criticism focuses on explicating the literary work by using the insight provided by knowledge of the author's life. Quite often, biographical critics, such as Brett C. Millier in her discussion of

Elizabeth Bishop's "One Art" (Chapter 30), will examine the drafts of a poem or story to see both how the work came into being and how it might have been changed from its autobiographical origins.

A reader, however, must use biographical interpretations cautiously. Writers are notorious for revising the facts of their own lives; they often delete embarrassments and invent accomplishments while changing the details of real episodes to improve their literary impact. John Cheever, for example, frequently told reporters about his sunny, privileged youth; after the author's death, his biographer Scott Donaldson discovered a childhood scarred by a distant mother; a failed, alcoholic father; and nagging economic uncertainty. Likewise, Cheever's outwardly successful adulthood was plagued by alcoholism, sexual promiscuity, and family tension. The unsettling facts of Cheever's life significantly changed the way critics read his stories. The danger in the case of a famous writer (Sylvia Plath and F. Scott Fitzgerald are two modern examples) is that the life story can overwhelm and eventually distort the work. A shrewd biographical critic always remembers to base an interpretation on what is in the text itself; biographical data should amplify the meaning of the text, not drown it out with irrelevant material.

Brett C. Millier (b. 1958)

On Elizabeth Bishop's "One Art"   1993

Elizabeth Bishop left seventeen drafts of the poem "One Art" among her papers. In the first draft, she lists all the things she's lost in her life—keys, pens, glasses, cities—and then she writes "One might think this would have prepared me / for losing one average-sized not exceptionally / beautiful or dazzlingly intelligent person . . . / But it doesn't seem to have at all. . . ." By the seventeenth draft, nearly every word has been transformed, but most importantly, Bishop discovered along the way that there might be a way to master this loss.

One way to read Bishop's modulation between the first and last drafts from "the loss of you is impossible to master" to something like "I am still the master of losing even though losing you looks like a disaster" is that in the writing of such a disciplined, demanding poem as this villanelle ("[*Write* it!]") lies the potential mastery of the loss. Working through each of her losses—from the bold, painful catalog of the first draft to the finely-honed and privately meaningful final version—is the way to overcome them or, if not to overcome them, then to see the way in which she might possibly master herself in the face of loss. It is all, perhaps "one art"—writing elegy, mastering loss, mastering grief, self-mastery. Bishop had a precocious familiarity with loss. Her father died before her first birthday, and four years later her mother disappeared into a sanitarium, never to be seen by her daughter again. The losses in the poem are real: time in the form of the "hour badly spent" and, more tellingly for the orphaned Bishop, "my mother's watch": the lost houses, in Key West, Petrópolis, and Ouro Prêto, Brazil. The city of Rio de Janeiro and the whole South American continent (where she had lived for nearly two decades) were lost to her with the suicide of her Brazilian companion. And currently, in the fall of 1975, she seemed to have lost her dearest friend and lover, who was trying to end their relationship. But each version of the poem distanced the pain a little more, depersonalized it, moved it away from the tawdry self-pity and "confession" that Bishop disliked in so many of her contemporaries.

Bishop's friends remained for a long time protective of her personal reputation, and unwilling to have her grouped among lesbian poets or even among the other great poets of her generation—Robert Lowell, John Berryman, Theodore Roethke—as they seemed to self-destruct before their readers' eyes. Bishop herself taught them this reticence by keeping her private life to herself, and by investing what "confession" there was in her poems deeply in objects and places, thus deflecting biographical inquiry. In the development of this poem, discretion is both a poetic method and a part of a process of self-understanding, the seeing of a pattern in her own life.

Adapted by the author from *Elizabeth Bishop: Life and the Memory of It*

Emily Toth (b. 1944)

The Source for Alcée Laballière in "The Storm"   1990

In January 1898, right after Kate Chopin had finished writing her controversial novel *The Awakening*, about one woman's quest for love (and sexual fulfillment) outside of marriage, a St. Louis newspaper asked her to answer the question, "Is Love Divine?"

Chopin's response was telling. She wrote, "I am inclined to think that love springs from animal instinct, and therefore is, in a measure, divine. One can never resolve to love this man, this woman or child, and then carry out the resolution unless one feels irresistibly drawn by an indefinable current of magnetism."

In that case, it was no doubt magnetism that led Kate Chopin to the handsome, wealthy Creole planter Albert Sampité (pronounced "Al-bear Sam-pi-TAY") after the death of her husband Oscar. This may also be why Kate Chopin's widowhood stories emphasize hope, not bereavement; spring, not winter; possibility, not loss. After Oscar died, Kate—who had grown up in a house full of widows who managed their own lives and their own money—decided to run Oscar's businesses herself.

She became an accomplished entrepreneur, a brisk businesswoman during the day who nevertheless kept the dark night as her own, with its prospects for silence and mystery and sin. Men flocked to aid the handsome widow in 1883, but when villagers gossiped generations later about who was "sweet on Kate," one name kept recurring. It was no secret to anyone—including his wife—that Albert Sampité was pursuing Kate Chopin. An examination of Chopin's stories show that the male characters who kindle desire and who devote themselves to sexual pleasure are named Alcée, an abbreviated form of Albert Sampité. Al. S——é and Alcée are both pronounced "Al-say."

It was not unseemly, or even odd, for Monsieur Sampite (his family dropped the accent mark, though they continued to use French pronunciation) to meet with Madame Chopin at the point where their lands intersected. When merchandise arrived for Kate's store, by boat from New Orleans, she had to go down to the landing to get her goods. It was not uncommon for a local planter like Albert Sampite to be at the landing at the same time. Somehow, too, Albert Sampite became involved in Kate Chopin's money matters. Papers that he saved show that Albert was apparently helping Kate to collect money owed her—and he also valued her financial records enough to keep them with his own personal papers.

There were still other ways in which a willing couple could make connections. And in a sudden storm, it was not impossible for two people to take refuge alone together in a house—a sensual scenario Kate Chopin sketched out, years later, in her most explicit short story, "The Storm."

Kate and Albert were discreet about their romance, by the standards of a century later. If anyone wrote down dates and places and eyewitness descriptions, none of those survive—although Cloutierville residents would certainly have been able to recognize him in her writings. But an affair in the 1880s was not simply a matter of physical consummation. Much less than that could be called "making love": flirting, significant glances, stolen kisses, secret silences.

Kate Chopin, in her diary eleven years after the first spring of her widowhood, suggested that more than flirting had gone on in her life: "I had loved—lovers who were not divine," she wrote, and "And then, there are so many ways of saying good night!" And even in her published writings, Kate left proof that her relationship with Albert Sampite was much more than a casual friendship. It shaped what she wrote about women and men, and love and lust and forbidden desires.

Adapted from *Kate Chopin*

HISTORICAL CRITICISM

Historical criticism seeks to understand a literary work by investigating the social, cultural, and intellectual context that produced it—a context that necessarily includes the artist's biography and milieu. Historical critics are less concerned with explaining a work's literary significance for today's readers than with helping us understand the work by recreating, as nearly as possible, the exact meaning and impact it had for its original audience. A historical reading of a literary work begins by exploring the possible ways in which the meaning of the text has changed over time. An analysis of William Blake's poem "London" (Chapter 18), for instance, carefully examines how certain words had different connotations for the poem's original readers than they do today. It also explores the probable associations an eighteenth-century English reader would have made with certain images and characters, like the poem's persona, the chimney sweep—a type of exploited child laborer who, fortunately, no longer exists in our society.

No one doubts the value of historical criticism in reading ancient literature. There have been so many social, cultural, and linguistic changes that some older texts are incomprehensible without scholarly assistance. But historical criticism can even help one better understand modern texts. To return to Weldon Kees's "For My Daughter" (Chapter 16), for example, one learns a great deal by considering two rudimentary historical facts—the year in which the poem was first published (1940) and the nationality of its author (American)—and then asking how this information has shaped the meaning of the poem. In 1940 war had already broken out in Europe, and most Americans realized that their country, still recovering from the Depression, would soon be drawn into it. For a young man like Kees, the future seemed bleak, uncertain, and personally dangerous. Even this simple historical analysis helps explain at least part of the bitter pessimism of Kees's poem, though a psychological critic would rightly insist that Kees's dark personality also played a crucial role. In writing a paper on a poem, you might explore how the time and place of its creation affect its meaning. For a splendid example of how to recreate the historical context of a poem's genesis, read the following account by Hugh Kenner of Ezra Pound's imagistic "In a Station of the Metro."

Hugh Kenner (1923–2003)

Imagism   1971

For it was English post-Symbolist verse that Pound's Imagism set out to reform, by deleting its self-indulgences, intensifying its virtues, and elevating the glimpse into the vision. The most famous of all Imagist poems commenced, like any poem by Arthur Symons,° with an accidental glimpse. Ezra Pound, on a visit to Paris in 1911, got out of the Metro at La Concorde, and "saw suddenly a beautiful face, and then another and another, and then a beautiful child's face, and then another beautiful woman, and I tried all that day to find words for what they had meant to me, and I could not find any words that seemed to me worthy, or as lovely as that sudden emotion."

The oft-told story is worth one more retelling. This was just such an experience as Arthur Symons cultivated, bright unexpected glimpses in a dark setting, instantly to melt into the crowd's kaleidoscope. And a poem would not have given Symons any trouble. But Pound by 1911 was already unwilling to write a Symons poem.

He tells us that he first satisfied his mind when he hit on a wholly abstract vision of colors, splotches on darkness like some canvas of Kandinsky's (whose work he had not then seen). This is a most important fact. Satisfaction lay not in preserving the vision, but in devising with mental effort an abstract equivalent for it, reduced, intensified. He next wrote a 30-line poem and destroyed it; after six months he wrote a shorter poem, also destroyed; and after another year, with, as he tells us, the Japanese *hokku* in mind, he arrived at a poem which needs every one of its 20 words, including the six words of its title:

In a Station of the Metro

> The apparition of these faces in the crowd;
> Petals on a wet, black bough.

We need the title so that we can savor that vegetal contrast with the world of machines: this is not any crowd, moreover, but a crowd seen underground, as Odysseus and Orpheus and Koré saw crowds in Hades. And carrying forward the suggestion of wraiths, the word "apparition" detaches these faces from all the crowded faces, and presides over the image that conveys the quality of their separation:

> Petals on a wet, black bough.

Flowers, underground; flowers, out of the sun; flowers seen as if against a natural gleam, the bough's wetness gleaming on its darkness, in this place where wheels turn and nothing grows. The mind is touched, it may be, with a memory of Persephone, as we read of her in the 106th Canto,

> Dis' bride, Queen over Phlegethon,
>   girls faint as mist about her.

—the faces of those girls likewise "apparitions."

What is achieved, though it works by way of the visible, is no picture of the thing glimpsed, in the manner of

> The light of our cigarettes
> Went and came in the gloom.

Arthur Symons: Symons (1865–1945) was a British poet who helped introduce French symbolist verse into English. His own verse was often florid and impressionistic.

It is a simile with "like" suppressed: Pound called it an equation, meaning not a redundancy, *a* equals *a*, but a generalization of unexpected exactness. The statements of analytic geometry, he said, "are 'lords' over fact. They are the thrones and dominations that rule over form and recurrence. And in like manner are great works of art lords over fact, over race-long recurrent moods, and over tomorrow." So this tiny poem, drawing on Gauguin and on Japan, on ghosts and on Persephone, on the Underworld and on the Underground, the Metro of Mallarmé's capital and a phrase that names a station of the Metro as it might a station of the Cross, concentrates far more than it need ever specify, and indicates the means of delivering post-Symbolist poetry from its pictorialist impasse. "An 'Image' is that which presents an intellectual and emotional complex in an instant of time": that is the elusive Doctrine of the Image. And, just 20 months later, "The image . . . is a radiant node or cluster; it is what I can, and must perforce, call a VORTEX, from which, and through which, and into which, ideas are constantly rushing." And: "An *image* . . . is real because we know it directly."

From The Pound Era

Seamus Deane (b. 1940)

Joyce's Vision of Dublin   1990

Although Joyce was opposed to the folkish, even folksy, elements of the Irish Revival, he is himself a dominant figure in that movement. Officially, he stands apart, as ever. Yeats, George Moore, Edward Martyn, Lady Gregory, Synge, Padraic Colum and their supporters seemed to him to be dangerously close to committing themselves to a version of the pseudo-Irishness which had once been the preserve of the stage-Irishman of nineteenth-century England and was, by the last decade of the century, becoming the property of the Celtic Irishman of the day. Yet, despite his difference, Joyce had much in common with these writers. In the work of all of them, Ireland, or an idea of Ireland, played a special role. For the revivalists, who were intent on turning nationalist political energies into cultural channels, the idea of Ireland was an invigorating and positive force. It embodied vitality and the possibility of a new kind of community, radically different from the aggregate crowds of the industrialized democracies. The distinction was enhanced by the predominantly rural character of Irish society, transformed by the writers into something very different from its harsh reality.

• • •

Joyce made it clear that, in his opinion, the Revival was conceding to public pressure by allowing the caricatured, but popular, version of Ireland to become the abiding image of the Abbey Theatre. This was wrong on a number of grounds. It deprived the artist of his independence; it nurtured provincialism; and it did this in the guise of a return to the "natural." Exile safe-guarded independence; cosmopolitanism helped to avoid provincialism; and the return to the natural was to be achieved, not by a romanticizing of rural and peasant life, or of the idea of the Celt and his lost language, but by an unflinching realism which, like that of Ibsen, stripped the mask from the pharisaic middle-class society of urban Europe and exposed its spiritual hypocrisy and impoverishment. In that respect, Ireland was indeed a special country. It lived under the political domination of England and the religious domination of Rome while it espoused a rhetoric of freedom, uniqueness, especial privilege. Ireland was, in fact, especially underprivileged and was, on that account, more susceptible to and more in need of an exemplary art than any other European country. It was in Joyce's art that the interior history of his country could be, for the first time, written.

• • •

Joyce's civilization was not, therefore, that of Myles Joyce, of Yeats and Lady Gregory and the Abbey Theatre, or of Mangan. Equally, it was not that of the comic dramatists, Sheridan, Goldsmith, Wilde, and Shaw, all of whom performed the role of "court jester to the English." It was the civilization of Catholic Dublin, related to but distinct from that of Catholic Ireland. Joyce tried to persuade the publisher, Grant Richards, that his collection of stories, *Dubliners*, was about a city that still had not been presented, or represented, to the world. He insists, on many occasions, on the emptiness that preceded his own writings about that city. It is an historical but not yet an imaginative reality. Although Dublin has been a capital for thousands of years and is said to be the second city of the British Empire, Joyce claims that no writer has yet "presented Dublin to the world." Furthermore, "the expression 'Dubliner' seems to me to have some meaning and I doubt that the same can be said for such words as 'Londoner' and 'Parisian.'" In the following year, 1906, the same publisher received from Joyce a sequence of famous letters, defending his text from charges of indecency and suggestions for changes, and declaring the importance of this "chapter of moral history" as "the first step towards the spiritual liberation of my country." Richards is asked to "Reflect for a moment on the history of the literature of Ireland as it stands at present written in the English language before you condemn this genial illusion of mine . . . ." "It is not my fault," he writes a month later, "that the odor of ashpits and old weeds and offal hangs round my stories. I seriously believe that you will retard the course of civilization in Ireland by preventing the Irish people from having one good look at themselves in my nicely polished looking-glass." The mirror held up to Culture was going to reflect a reality no one had presented before. Dublin would find it an unwelcome sight, but Dublin and Ireland would be liberated by it. Joyce is an author without native predecessors; he is an artist who intends to have the effect of a missionary.

By insisting that Dublin had not been represented before in literature, Joyce was intensifying the problem of representation for himself. He abjured the possibility of being influenced by any other Irish writer, because there was, in effect, none who belonged to his specific and peculiar version of his civilization. He was bound, therefore, to find a mode of representation that was, as far as Irish literature was concerned, unique. But the literature of Europe did offer possible models, and Joyce repeatedly spoke of Dublin—as in the letter to Grant Richards—as a European city. Indeed, he saw it as a city that inhabited three spheres of civilization. The first was that of the British Empire; the second that of Roman Catholicism; the third that of the ancient Europe to which Ireland had made such an important contribution. All three of these co-existed in Dublin, the only major European city which had not yet been commemorated in art.

From "Joyce the Irishman"

PSYCHOLOGICAL CRITICISM

Modern psychology has had an immense effect on both literature and literary criticism. The psychoanalytic theories of the Austrian neurologist Sigmund Freud changed our notions of human behavior by exploring new or controversial areas such as wish fulfillment, sexuality, the unconscious, and repression. Perhaps Freud's greatest contribution to literary study was his elaborate demonstration of how much human mental process was unconscious. He analyzed language, often in the form of jokes and conversational slips of the tongue (now often called "Freudian slips"), to show how it reflected the speaker's unconscious fears and desires. He also examined symbols, not only in art and literature but also in dreams, to study how the unconscious mind expressed itself in coded form to avoid the censorship of the conscious mind. His theory of human cognition asserted that much of what we apparently forget is actually stored deep in the unconscious mind, including painful traumatic memories from childhood that have been repressed.

Freud admitted that he himself had learned a great deal about psychology from studying literature. Sophocles, Shakespeare, Goethe, and Dostoyevsky were as important to the development of his ideas as were his clinical studies. Some of Freud's most influential writing was, in a broad sense, literary criticism, such as his psychoanalytic examination of Sophocles's Oedipus in *The Interpretation of Dreams* (1900). In analyzing Sophocles's tragedy *Oedipus the King* (Chapter 37), Freud paid the classical Greek dramatist the considerable compliment that the playwright had such profound insight into human nature that his characters display the depth and complexity of real people. In focusing on literature, Freud and his disciples such as Carl Jung, Ernest Jones, Marie Bonaparte, and Bruno Bettelheim endorsed the belief that great literature truthfully reflects life.

Psychological criticism is a diverse category, but it often employs three approaches. First, it investigates the creative process of the arts: what is the nature of literary genius, and how does it relate to normal mental functions? Such analysis may also focus on literature's effects on the reader. How does a particular work register its impact on the reader's mental and sensory faculties? The second approach involves the psychological study of a particular artist. Most modern literary biographers employ psychology to understand their subject's motivations and behavior. One book, Diane Middlebrook's controversial *Anne Sexton: A Biography* (1991), actually used tapes of the poet's sessions with her psychiatrist as material for the study. The third common approach is the analysis of fictional characters. Freud's study of Oedipus is the prototype for this approach, which tries to bring modern insights about human behavior into the study of how fictional people act. While psychological criticism carefully examines the surface of the literary work, it customarily speculates on what lies underneath the text—the unspoken or perhaps even unspeakable memories, motives, and fears that covertly shape the work, especially in fictional characterizations.

Sigmund Freud (1856–1939)

The Nature of Dreams
1933

Let us go back once more to the latent dream-thoughts. Their dominating element is the repressed impulse, which has obtained some kind of expression, toned down and disguised though it may be, by associating itself with stimuli which happen to be there and by tacking itself on the residue of the day before. Just like any other impulse this one presses forward toward satisfaction in action, but the path to motor discharge is closed to it on account of the physiological characteristics of the state of sleep, and so it is forced to travel in the retrograde direction to perception, and content itself with an hallucinatory satisfaction. The latent dream-thoughts are therefore turned into a collection of sensory images and visual scenes. As they are travelling in this direction something happens to them which seems to us new and bewildering. All the verbal apparatus by means of which the more subtle thought-relations are expressed, the conjunctions and prepositions, the variations of declension and conjugation, are lacking, because the means of portraying them are absent: just as in primitive, grammarless speech, only the raw material of thought can be expressed, and the abstract is merged again in the concrete from which it sprang. What is left over may very well seem to lack coherence. It is as much the result of the archaic regression in the mental apparatus as of the demands of the censorship that so much use is made of the representation of certain objects and processes by means of symbols which have become strange to conscious thought. But of more far-reaching import are the other alterations to which the elements comprising the dream-thoughts are subjected. Such of them as have any point of contact are *condensed* into new unities. When the thoughts are translated into pictures those forms are indubitably preferred which allow this kind of telescoping, or condensation; it is as though a force were at work which subjected the material to a process of pressure or squeezing together. As a result of condensation one element in a manifest dream may correspond to a number of elements of the dream-thoughts; but conversely one of the elements from among the dream-thoughts may be represented by a number of pictures in the dream.

From *New Introductory Lectures on Psychoanalysis*

Harold Bloom (b. 1930)

Poetic Influence   1975

Let me reduce my argument to the hopelessly simplistic; poems, I am saying, are neither about "subjects" nor about "themselves." They are necessarily about *other poems*; a poem is a response to a poem, as a poet is a response to a poet, or a person to his parent. Trying to write a poem takes the poet back to the origins of what a poem *first was* for him, and so takes the poet back beyond the pleasure principle to the decisive initial encounter and response that began him. We do not think of W. C. Williams as a Keatsian poet, yet he *began and ended as one*, and his late celebration of his Greeny Flower is another response to Keats's odes. *Only a poet challenges a poet as poet*, and so only a poet makes a poet. To the poet-in-a-poet, a poem is always *the other man*, the precursor, and so a poem is always a person, always the father of one's Second Birth. To live, the poet must *misinterpret* the father, by the crucial act of misprision, which is the rewriting of the father.

But who, what is the poetic father? The voice of the other, of the *daimon*, is always speaking in one; the voice that cannot die because already it has survived death—*the dead poet lives in one*. In the last phase of strong poets, they attempt to join the undying *by living in the dead poets* who are already alive in them. This late Return of the Dead recalls us, as readers, to a recognition of the original motive for the catastrophe of poetic incarnation. Vico, who identified the origins of poetry with the impulse towards divination (to foretell, but also to become a god by foretelling), implicitly understood (as did Emerson, and Wordsworth) that a poem is written to escape dying. Literally, poems are refusals of mortality. Every poem therefore has two makers: the precursor, and the ephebe's rejected mortality.

A poet, I argue in consequence, is not so much a man speaking to men as a man rebelling against being spoken to by a dead man (the precursor) outrageously more alive than himself.

From *A Map of Misreading*

MYTHOLOGICAL CRITICISM

Mythological critics look for the recurrent universal patterns underlying most literary works. **Mythological criticism** is an interdisciplinary approach that combines the insights of anthropology, psychology, history, and comparative religion. If psychological criticism examines the artist as an individual, mythological criticism explores the artist's common humanity by tracing how the individual imagination uses symbols and situations—consciously or unconsciously—in ways that transcend its own historical milieu and resemble the mythology of other cultures or epochs.

A central concept in mythological criticism is the **archetype**, a symbol, character, situation, or image that evokes a deep universal response. The idea of the archetype came into literary criticism from the Swiss psychologist Carl Jung, a lifetime student of myth and religion. Jung believed that all individuals share a "collective unconscious," a set of primal memories common to the human race, existing below each person's conscious mind. Archetypal images (which often relate to experiencing primordial phenomena like the sun, moon, fire, night, and blood), Jung believed, trigger the collective unconscious. We do not need to accept the literal truth of the collective unconscious, however, to endorse the archetype as a helpful critical concept. Northrop Frye defined the archetype in considerably less occult terms as "a symbol, usually an image, which recurs often enough in literature to be recognizable as an element of one's literary experience as a whole."

Identifying archetypal symbols and situations in literary works, mythological critics almost inevitably link the individual text under discussion to a broader context of works that share an underlying pattern. In discussing Shakespeare's *Hamlet*, for instance, a mythological critic might relate Shakespeare's Danish prince to other mythic sons avenging the deaths of their fathers, like Orestes from Greek myth or Sigmund of Norse legend; or, in discussing *Othello* (Chapter 38), relate the sinister figure of Iago to the devil in traditional Christian belief. Critic Joseph Campbell took such comparisons even further; his compendious study *The Hero with a Thousand Faces* demonstrates how similar mythic characters appear in virtually every culture on every continent.

Carl Jung (1875–1961)

The Collective Unconscious and Archetypes   1931
Translated by R. F. C. Hull

A more or less superficial layer of the unconscious is undoubtedly personal. I call it the *personal unconscious*. But this personal unconscious rests upon a deeper layer, which does not derive from personal experience and is not a personal acquisition but is inborn. This deeper layer I call the *collective unconscious*. I have chosen the term "collective" because this part of the unconscious is not individual but universal; in contrast to the personal psyche, it has contents and modes of behavior that are more or less the same everywhere and in all individuals. It is, in other words, identical in all men and thus constitutes a common psyche substrate of a suprapersonal nature which is present in every one of us.

Psychic existence can be recognized only by the presence of contents that are *capable of consciousness*. We can therefore speak of an unconscious only in so far as we are able to demonstrate its contents. The contents of the personal unconscious are chiefly the *feeling-toned complexes*, as they are called; they constitute the personal and private side of psychic life. The contents of the collective unconscious, on the other hand, are known as *archetypes*. . . .

For our purposes this term is apposite and helpful, because it tells us that so far as the collective unconscious contents are concerned we are dealing with archaic or—I would say—primordial types, that is, with universal images that have existed since the remotest times. The term "representations collectives," used by Lévy-Bruhl to denote the symbolic figures in the primitive view of the world, could easily be applied to unconscious contents as well, since it means practically the same thing. Primitive tribal lore is concerned with archetypes that have been modified in a special way. They are no longer contents of the unconscious, but have already been changed into conscious formulae taught according to tradition, generally in the form of esoteric teaching. This last is a typical means of expression for the transmission of collective contents originally derived from the unconscious.

Another well-known expression of the archetypes is myth and fairy tale. But here too we are dealing with forms that have received a specific stamp and have been handed down through long periods of time. The term "archetype" thus applies only indirectly to the "representations collectives," since it designates only those psychic contents which have not yet been submitted to conscious elaboration and are therefore an immediate datum of psychic experience. In this sense there is a considerable difference between the archetype and the historical formula that has evolved. Especially on the higher levels of esoteric teaching the archetypes appear in a form that reveals quite unmistakably the critical and evaluating influence of conscious elaboration. Their immediate manifestation, as we encounter it in dreams and visions, is much more individual, less understandable, and more naïve than in myths, for example. The archetype is essentially an unconscious content that is altered by becoming conscious and by being perceived, and it takes its color from the individual consciousness in which it happens to appear.

From *The Collected Works of C. G. Jung*, Volume 9

Edmond Volpe (1922–2007)

Myth in Faulkner's "Barn Burning"   1964

"Barn Burning" however is not really concerned with class conflict. The story is centered upon Sarty's emotional dilemma. His conflict would not have been altered in any way if the person whose barn Ab burns had been a simple poor farmer, rather than an aristocratic plantation owner. The child's tension, in fact, begins to surface during the hearing in which a simple farmer accuses Ab of burning his barn. The moral antagonists mirrored in Sarty's conflict are not sharecropper and aristocrat. They are the father, Ab Snopes, versus the rest of mankind. Major De Spain is not developed as a character; his house is important to Sarty because it represents a totally new and totally different social and moral entity. Within the context of the society Faulkner is dealing with, the gap between the rich aristocrat and the poor sharecropper provides a viable metaphor for dramatizing the crisis Sarty is undergoing. Ab Snopes is by no means a social crusader. The De Spain manor is Sarty's first contact with a rich man's house, though he can recall, in the short span of his life, at least a dozen times the family had to move because Ab burned barns. Ab does not discriminate between rich and poor. For him there are only two categories: blood kin and "they," into which he lumps all the rest of mankind. Ab's division relates to Sarty's crisis and only by defining precisely the nature of the conflict the boy is undergoing can we determine the moral significance Faulkner sees in it. The clue to Sarty's conflict rests in its resolution.

• • •

The boy's anxiety is created by his awakening sense of his own individuality. Torn between strong emotional attachment to the parent and his growing need to assert his own identity, Sarty's crisis is psychological and his battle is being waged far below the level of his intellectual and moral awareness.

Faulkner makes this clear in the opening scene with imagery that might be described as synesthesia. The real smell of cheese is linked with the smell of the hermetic meat in the tin cans with the scarlet devils on the label that his "intestines believed he smelled coming in intermittent gusts momentary and brief between the other constant one, the smell and sense just a little of fear because mostly of despair and grief, the old fierce pull of blood." The smells below the level of the olfactory sense link the devil image and the blood image to identify the anxiety the father creates in the child's psyche. Tension is created by the blood demanding identification with his father against "*our enemy* he thought in that despair; *ourn! mine and hisn both! He's my father!*" Sarty's conflict is played out in terms of identification, not in moral terms. He does not think of his father as bad, his father's enemies as good.

Ab unjustly accuses Sarty of intending to betray him at the hearing, but he correctly recognizes that his son is moving out of childhood, developing a mind and will of his own and is no longer blindly loyal. In instructing the boy that everyone is the enemy and his loyalty belongs to his blood, Ab's phrasing is revealing: "'Don't you know all they wanted was a chance to get at me because they knew I had them beat?'" Ab does not use the plural "us." It is "I" and "they." Blood loyalty means total identification with Ab, and in the ensuing scenes, Snopes attempts to make his son an extension of himself by taking him to the De Spain house, having him rise up before dawn to be with Ab when he returns the rug, having him accompany Ab to the hearing against De Spain and finally making him an accomplice in the burning of De Spain's barn.

The moral import of Ab's insistence on blood loyalty is fully developed by the satanic imagery Faulkner introduces in the scene at the mansion. As they go up the drive, Sarty follows his father, seeing the stiff black form against the white plantation house. Traditionally the devil casts no shadow, and Ab's figure appears to the child as having "that impervious quality of something cut ruthlessly from tin, depthless, as though sidewise to the sun it would cast no shadow." The cloven hoof of the devil is suggested by Ab's limp upon which the boy's eyes are fixed as the foot unwaveringly comes down into the manure. Sarty's increasing tension resounds in the magnified echo of the limping foot on the porch boards, "a sound out of all proportion to the displacement of the body it bore, as though it had attained to a sort of vicious and ravening minimum not to be dwarfed by anything." At first Sarty thought the house was impervious to his father, but his burgeoning fear of the threat the father poses is reflected in his vision of Ab becoming magnified and monstrous as the black arm reaches up the white door and Sarty sees "the lifted hand like a curled claw."

The satanic images are projected out of the son's nightmarish vision of his father, but they are reinforced by the comments of the adult narrator. Sarty believes Snopes fought bravely in the Civil War, but Ab, we are told, wore no uniform, gave his fealty to no cause, admitted the authority of no man. He went to war for booty. Ab's ego is so great it creates a centripetal force into which everything must flow or be destroyed. The will-less, abject creature who is his wife symbolizes the power of his will. What Ab had done to his wife, he sets out to do to the emerging will of his son. Ab cannot tolerate any entity that challenges the dominance of his will. By allowing his hog to forage in the farmer's corn and by dirtying and ruining De Spain's rug, he deliberately creates a conflict that requires the assertion of primacy. Fire, the element of the devil, is the weapon for the preservation of his dominance. Ab's rage is not fired by social injustice. It is fired by a pride, like Lucifer's, so absolute it can accept no order beyond its own. In the satanic myth, Lucifer asserts his will against the divine order and is cast out of heaven. The angels who fall with Lucifer become extensions of his will. In the same way, Ab is an outcast and pariah among men. He accepts no order that is not of his blood.

From "'Barn Burning': A Definition of Evil"

SOCIOLOGICAL CRITICISM

Sociological criticism examines literature in the cultural, economic, and political context in which it is written or received. "Art is not created in a vacuum," critic Wilbur Scott observed, "it is the work not simply of a person, but of an author fixed in time and space, answering a community of which he is an important, because articulate part." Sociological criticism explores the relationships between the artist and society. Sometimes it looks at the sociological status of the author to evaluate how the profession of the writer in a particular milieu affected what was written. Sociological criticism also analyzes the social content of literary works—what cultural, economic, or political values a particular text implicitly or explicitly promotes. Finally, sociological criticism examines the role the audience has in shaping literature. A sociological view of Shakespeare, for example, might look at the economic position of Elizabethan playwrights and actors; it might also study the political ideas expressed in the plays or discuss how the nature of an Elizabethan theatrical audience (which was usually all male unless the play was produced at court) helped determine the subject, tone, and language of the plays.

An influential type of sociological criticism has been Marxist criticism, which focuses on the economic and political elements of art. Marxist criticism, as in the work of the Hungarian philosopher Georg Lukacs, often explores the ideological content of literature. Whereas a formalist critic would maintain that form and content are inextricably blended, Lukacs believed that content determines form and that, therefore, all art is political. Even if a work of art ignores political issues, it makes a political statement, Marxist critics believe, because it endorses the economic and political status quo. Consequently, Marxist criticism is frequently evaluative and judges some literary work better than others on an ideological basis; this tendency can lead to reductive judgment, as when Soviet critics rated Jack London a novelist superior to William Faulkner, Ernest Hemingway, Edith Wharton, and Henry James, because he illustrated the principles of class struggle more clearly. London was America's first major working-class writer. To examine the political ideas and observations found in his fiction can be illuminating, but to fault other authors for lacking his instincts and ideas is not necessarily helpful in understanding their particular qualities. There is always a danger in sociological criticism—Marxist or otherwise—of imposing the critic's personal politics on the work in question and then evaluating it according to how closely it endorses that ideology. As an analytical tool, however, Marxist criticism and sociological methods can illuminate political and economic dimensions of literature that other approaches overlook.

Georg Lukacs (1885–1971)
Content Determines Form   1962

What determines the style of a given work of art? How does the intention determine the form? (We are concerned here, of course, with the intention realized in the work; it need not coincide with the writer's conscious intention.) The distinctions that concern us are not those between stylistic "techniques" in the formalistic sense. It is the view of the world, the ideology or *Weltanschauung*° underlying a writer's work, that counts. And it is the writer's attempt to reproduce this view of the world which constitutes his "intention" and is the formative principle underlying the style of a given piece of writing. Looked at in this way, style ceases to be a formalistic category. Rather, it is rooted in content; it is the specific form of a specific content.

Content determines form. But there is no content of which Man himself is not the focal point. However various the *données*° of literature (a particular experience, a didactic purpose), the basic question is, and will remain: what is Man?

Here is a point of division: if we put the question in abstract, philosophical terms, leaving aside all formal considerations, we arrive—for the realist school—at the traditional Aristotelian dictum (which was also reached by other than purely aesthetic considerations): Man is *zoon politikon*,° a social animal. The Aristotelian dictum is applicable to all great realistic literature. Achilles and Werther, Oedipus and Tom Jones, Antigone and Anna Karenina: their individual existence—their *Sein an sich*,° in the Hegelian terminology; their "ontological being," as a more fashionable terminology has it—cannot be distinguished from their social and historical environment. Their human significance, their specific individuality cannot be separated from the context in which they were created.

From Realism in Our Time

Weltanschauung: German for "world view," an outlook on life. *données:* French for "given"; it means the materials a writer uses to create his or her work or the subject or purpose of a literary work. *zoon politikon:* Greek for "political animal." *Sein an sich:* the German philosopher G. W. F. Hegel's term for "pure existence."

Alfred Kazin (1915–1998)

Walt Whitman and Abraham Lincoln   1984

In Lincoln's lifetime Whitman was the only major writer to describe him with love. Whitman identified Lincoln with himself in the worshipful fashion that became standard after Lincoln's death. That Lincoln was a class issue says a good deal about the prejudices of American society in the East. A leading New Yorker, George Templeton Strong, noted in his diary that while he never disavowed the "lank and hard featured man," Lincoln was "despised and rejected by a third of the community, and only tolerated by the other two-thirds." Whitman the professional man of the people had complicated reasons for loving Lincoln. The uneasiness about him among America's elite was based on the fear that this unknown, untried man, elected without administrative experience (and without a majority) might not be up to his "fearful task."

• • •

Whitman related himself to the popular passion released by war and gave himself to this passion as a political cause. He understood popular opinion in a way that Emerson, Thoreau, and Hawthorne did not attempt to understand it. Emerson said, like any conventional New England clergyman, that the war was holy. He could not speak for the masses who bore the brunt of the war. Whitman was able to get so much out of the war, to create a lasting image of it, because he knew what people were feeling. He was not above the battle like Thoreau and Hawthorne, not suspicious of the majority like his fellow New Yorker Herman Melville, who in "The House-top," the most personal poem in *Battle-Pieces*, denounced the "ship-rats" who had taken over the city in the anti-draft riots of 1863.

Despite Whitman's elusiveness—he made a career out of longings it would have ended that career to fulfill—he genuinely felt at home with soldiers and other "ordinary" people who were inarticulate by the standards of men "from the schools." He was always present, if far from available, presenting the picture of a nobly accessible and social creature. He certainly got on better with omnibus drivers, workingmen, and now "simple" soldiers (especially when they were wounded and open to his ministrations) than he did with "scribblers." By the time Whitman went down after Fredericksburg to look for brother George, the war was becoming a revolution of sorts and Whitman's old radical politics were becoming "the nation." This made him adore Lincoln as the symbol of the nation's unity. An essential quality of Whitman's Civil War "memoranda" is Whitman's libidinous urge to associate himself with the great, growing, ever more powerful federal cause. Whitman's characteristic lifelong urge to join, to combine, to see life as movement, unity, totality, became during the Civil War an actively loving association with the broad masses of the people and *their* war. In his cult of the Civil War, Whitman allies himself with a heroic and creative energy which sees itself spreading out from the people and their representative men, Lincoln and Whitman.

Hawthorne's and Thoreau's horror of America as the Big State did not reflect Whitman's image of the Union. His passion for the "cause" reflected his intense faith in democracy at a juncture when the United States at war represented the revolutionary principle to Marx, the young Ibsen, Mill, Browning, Tolstoy. Whitman's deepest feeling was that his own rise from the city streets, his future as a poet of democracy, was tied up with the Northern armies.

From An American Procession

GENDER CRITICISM

Gender criticism examines how sexual identity influences the creation and reception of literary works. Gender studies began with the feminist movement and was influenced by such works as Simone de Beauvoir's *The Second Sex* (1949) and Kate Millett's *Sexual Politics* (1970) as well as sociology, psychology, and anthropology. Feminist critics believe that culture has been so completely dominated by men that literature is full of unexamined "male-produced" assumptions. Their criticism sought to correct this imbalance by analyzing and combating patriarchal attitudes. Feminist criticism has explored how an author's gender influences—consciously or unconsciously—his or her writing. While a formalist critic such as Allen Tate emphasized the universality of Emily Dickinson's poetry by demonstrating how the language, imagery, and mythmaking of her poems combine to affect a generalized reader, Sandra M. Gilbert, a pioneering feminist critic, identified attitudes and assumptions in Dickinson's poetry that she maintained were essentially female. Another important theme in feminist criticism is analyzing how sexual identity influences the reader of a text. If Tate's hypothetical reader was deliberately sexless, Gilbert's reader sees a text through the eyes of his or her sex. Finally, feminist critics examine how the images of men and women in imaginative literature reflect or reject the social forces that have historically kept the sexes from achieving total equality.

Later gender criticism expanded beyond its original feminist perspective. Critics have developed the field of gay and lesbian studies—some of whom describe their discipline as "queer theory"—to explore the impact of different sexual orientations on literary creation and reception. Seeking to establish a canon of classic gay and lesbian authors, these critics argue that sexual identity is so central a component of human personality that to ignore it in connection with such writers amounts to a fundamental misreading and misunderstanding of their work. A men's movement also emerged in response to feminism, seeking not to reject feminism but to rediscover masculine identity in a contemporary context.

The most important recent development in gender studies has been a critique of binary sexual identity. Theorists have argued that traditional male and female identities are cultural constructions, not biological imperatives. Gender is more fluid, they postulate, than binary options. Individuals are capable of constructing new identities beyond binary oppositions.

Nina Pelikan Straus (b. 1942)

Transformations in *The Metamorphosis*   1989

Traditionally, critics of *Metamorphosis* have underplayed the fact that the story is about not only Gregor's but also his family's and, especially, Grete's metamorphosis. Yet it is mainly Grete, woman, daughter, sister, on whom the social and psychoanalytic resonances of the text depend. It is she who will ironically "blossom" as her brother deteriorates; it is she whose mirror reflects women's present situations as we attempt to critique patriarchal dominance in order to create new lives that avoid the replication of invalidation. . . .

If Grete is a symbol of anything, it is the irony of self-liberation in relation to the indeterminacy of gender roles. Grete's role as a woman unfolds as Gregor's life as a man collapses. It is no accident that this gender scrolling takes place in the literature of a writer who had curious experiences in his life with women—experiences of his own weakness and of women's strengths. Traditionally, the text has been read not as revealing brother-sister or gender-based relationships, however, but as revealing a father-son conflict or Oedipus complex.

• • •

The word "shame" is central to both Grete and Gregor's experiences. It is a shame that Gregor cannot get out of bed, that he cannot get up to go to work, that his voice fails him, that he cannot open the door of his room with his insect pincers, that he must be fed, that he stinks and must hide his body that is a shame to others. Shame comes from seeing oneself through another's eyes, from Gregor's seeing himself through Grete's eyes, and from the reader's seeing Grete through the narrator's eyes. The text graphically mirrors how we see each other in various shameful (and comic) conditions. Through Gregor's condition, ultimately shameful because he is reduced to the dependency of an ugly baby, Kafka imagines what it is like to be dependent on the care of women. And Kafka is impressed with women's efforts to keep their households and bodies clean and alive. This impression is enlarged with every detail that humiliates and weakens Gregor while simultaneously empowering Grete, who cares for Gregor, ironically, at his own—and perhaps at Kafka's—expense.

The change or metamorphosis is in this sense a literary experiment that plays with problems the story's title barely suggests. For Kafka there can be no change without an exchange, no flourishing of Grete without Gregor's withering; nor can the meaning of transformation entail a final closure that prevents further transformations. The metamorphosis occurs both in the first sentence of the text—"When Gregor Samsa awoke one morning from unsettling dreams, he found himself changed in his bed into a monstrous vermin"—and in the last paragraph of the story, which describes Grete's transformation into a woman "blossoming" and "stretching" toward the family's "new dreams" once Gregor has been transformed into garbage. Grete's final transformation, rendered in concrete bodily terms, is foreshadowed in Gregor's initial transformation from human into vermin. This deliberately reflective textual pattern implies that only when the distorting mirrors of the sexist fun house are dismantled can the sons of the patriarchs recognize themselves as dehumanized and dehumanizing. Only when Grete blooms into an eligible young woman, ripe for the job and marriage markets, can we recognize that her empowerment is also an ironic reification. She has been transformed at another's expense, and she will carry within her the marketplace value that has ultimately destroyed Gregor.

From "Transforming Franz Kafka's *Metamorphosis*"

Elaine Showalter (b. 1941)

Toward a Feminist Poetics   1979

Feminist criticism can be divided into two distinct varieties. The first type is concerned with *woman as reader* —with woman as the consumer of male-produced literature, and with the way in which the hypothesis of a female reader changes our apprehension of a given text, awakening us to the significance of its sexual codes. I shall call this kind of analysis the *feminist critique*, and like other kinds of critique it is a historically grounded inquiry which probes the ideological assumptions of literary phenomena. Its subjects include the images and stereotypes of women in literature, the omissions of and misconceptions about women in criticism, and the fissures in male-constructed literary history. It is also concerned with the exploitation and manipulation of the female audience, especially in popular culture and film; and with the analysis of woman-as-sign in semiotic systems. The second type of feminist criticism is concerned with *woman as writer*—with woman as the producer of textual meaning, with the history, themes, genres, and structures of literature by women. Its subjects include the psychodynamics of female creativity; linguistics and the problem of a female language; the trajectory of the individual or collective female literary career; literary history; and, of course, studies of particular writers and works. No term exists in English for such a specialized discourse, and so I have adapted the French term *la gynocritique*: "gynocritics" (although the significance of the male pseudonym in the history of women's writing also suggested the term "georgics").

The feminist critique is essentially political and polemical, with theoretical affiliations to Marxist sociology and aesthetics; gynocritics is more self-contained and experimental, with connections to other modes of new feminist research. In a dialogue between these two positions, Carolyn Heilbrun, the writer, and Catharine Stimpson, editor of the journal *Signs: Women in Culture and Society*, compare the feminist critique to the Old Testament, "looking for the sins and errors of the past," and gynocritics to the New Testament, seeking "the grace of imagination." Both kinds are necessary, they explain, for only the Jeremiahs of the feminist critique can lead us out of the "Egypt of female servitude" to the promised land of the feminist vision. That the discussion makes use of these Biblical metaphors points to the connections between feminist consciousness and conversion narratives which often appear in women's literature; Carolyn Heilbrun comments on her own text, "When I talk about feminist criticism, I am amazed at how high a moral tone I take."

From "Toward a Feminist Poetics"

READER-RESPONSE CRITICISM

Reader-response criticism attempts to describe what happens in the reader's mind while interpreting a text. If traditional criticism assumes that imaginative writing is a creative act, reader-response theory recognizes that reading is also a creative process. Reader-response critics believe that no text provides self-contained meaning; literary texts do not exist independently of readers' interpretations. A text, according to this critical school, is not finished until it is read and interpreted. As Oscar Wilde remarked in the preface to his novel *The Picture of Dorian Gray* (1891), "It is the spectator, and not life, that art really mirrors." The practical problem then arises, however, that no two individuals necessarily read a text in exactly the same way. Rather than declare one interpretation correct and the other mistaken, reader-response criticism recognizes the inevitable plurality of readings. Instead of trying to ignore or reconcile the contradictions inherent in this situation, it explores them.

The easiest way to explain reader-response criticism is to relate it to the common experience of rereading a favorite book after many years. Rereading a novel as an adult, for example, that "changed your life" as an adolescent, is often a shocking experience. The book may seem substantially different. The character you remembered liking most now seems less admirable, and another character you disliked now seems more sympathetic. Has the book changed? Very unlikely, but *you* certainly have in the intervening years. Reader-response criticism explores how different individuals (or classes of individuals) see the same text differently. It emphasizes how religious, cultural, and social values affect readings; it also overlaps with gender criticism in exploring how men and women read the same text with different assumptions.

While reader-response criticism rejects the notion that there can be a single correct reading for a literary text, it doesn't consider all readings permissible. Each text creates limits to its possible interpretations. As Stanley Fish admits in the following critical selection, we cannot arbitrarily place an Eskimo in William Faulkner's story "A Rose for Emily" (Chapter 2), (though Professor Fish does ingeniously imagine a hypothetical situation where this bizarre interpretation might actually be possible).

Stanley Fish (b. 1938)

An Eskimo "A Rose for Emily"   1980

The fact that it remains easy to think of a reading that most of us would dismiss out of hand does not mean that the text excludes it but that there is as yet no elaborated interpretive procedure for producing that text. . . . Norman Holland's analysis of Faulkner's "A Rose for Emily" is a case in point. Holland is arguing for a kind of psychoanalytic pluralism. The text, he declares, is "at most a matrix of psychological possibilities for its readers," but, he insists, "only some possibilities . . . truly fit the matrix": "One would not say, for example, that a reader of . . . 'A Rose for Emily' who thought the 'tableau' [of Emily and her father in the doorway] described an Eskimo was really responding to the story at all—only pursuing some mysterious inner exploration."

Holland is making two arguments: first, that anyone who proposes an Eskimo reading of "A Rose for Emily" will not find a hearing in the literary community. And that, I think, is right. ("We are right to rule out at least some readings.") His second argument is that the unacceptability of the Eskimo reading is a function of the text, of what he calls its "sharable promptuary," the public "store of structured language" that sets limits to the interpretations the words can accommodate. And that, I think, is wrong. The Eskimo reading is unacceptable because there is at present no interpretive strategy for producing it, no way of "looking" or reading (and remember, all acts of looking or reading are "ways") that would result in the emergence of obviously Eskimo meanings. This does not mean, however, that no such strategy could ever come into play, and it is not difficult to imagine the circumstances under which it would establish itself. One such circumstance would be the discovery of a letter in which Faulkner confides that he has always believed himself to be an Eskimo changeling. (The example is absurd only if one forgets Yeats's *Vision* or Blake's Swedenborgianism° or James Miller's recent elaboration of a homosexual reading of *The Waste Land*.) Immediately the workers in the Faulkner industry would begin to reinterpret the canon in the light of this newly revealed "belief" and the work of reinterpretation would involve the elaboration of a symbolic or allusive system (not unlike mythological or typological criticism) whose application would immediately transform the text into one informed everywhere by Eskimo meanings. It might seem that I am admitting that there is a text to be transformed, but the object of transformation would be the text (or texts) given by whatever interpretive strategies the Eskimo strategy was in the process of dislodging or expanding. The result would be that whereas we now have a Freudian

Yeats's Vision *or Blake's Swedenborgianism:* Irish poet William Butler Yeats and Swedish mystical writer Emanuel Swedenborg both claimed to have received revelations from the spirit world; some of Swedenborg's ideas are embodied in the long poems of William Blake.

"A Rose for Emily," a mythological "A Rose for Emily," a Christological "A Rose for Emily," a regional "A Rose for Emily," a sociological "A Rose for Emily," a linguistic "A Rose for Emily," we would in addition have an Eskimo "A Rose for Emily," existing in some relation of compatibility or incompatibility with the others.

Again the point is that while there are always mechanisms for ruling out readings, their source is not the text but the presently recognized interpretive strategies for producing the text. It follows, then, that no reading, however outlandish it might appear, is inherently an impossible one.

From Is There a Text in This Class?

Robert Scholes (1929–2016)

"How Do We Make a Poem?"   1982

Let us begin with one of the shortest poetic texts in the English language, "Elegy" by W. S. Merwin:

> Who would I show it to

One line, one sentence, unpunctuated, but proclaimed an interrogative by its grammar and syntax—what makes it a poem? Certainly without its title it would not be a poem; but neither would the title alone constitute a poetic text. Nor do the two together simply make a poem by themselves. Given the title and the text, the *reader* is encouraged to make a poem. He is not forced to do so, but there is not much else he can do with this material, and certainly nothing else so rewarding. (I will use the masculine pronoun here to refer to the reader, not because all readers are male but because I am, and my hypothetical reader is not a pure construct but an idealized version of myself.)

How do we make a poem out of this text? There are only two things to work on, the title and the question posed by the single, colloquial line. The line is not simply colloquial, it is prosaic; with no words of more than one syllable, concluded by a preposition, it is within the utterance range of every speaker of English. It is, in a sense, completely intelligible. But in another sense it is opaque, mysterious. Its three pronouns—who, I, it—pose problems of reference. Its conditional verb phrase— would . . . show to—poses a problem of situation. The context that would supply the information required to make that simple sentence meaningful as well as intelligible is not there. It must be supplied by the reader.

To make a poem of this text the reader must not only know English, he must know a poetic code as well: the code of the funeral elegy, as practiced in English from the Renaissance to the present time. The "words on the page" do not constitute a poetic "work," complete and self-sufficient, but a "text," a sketch or outline that must be completed by the active participation of a reader equipped with the right sort of information. In this case part of that information consists of an acquaintance with the elegiac tradition: its procedures, assumptions, devices, and values. One needs to know works like Milton's "Lycidas," Shelley's "Adonais," Tennyson's *In Memoriam*, Whitman's "When Lilacs Last in the Dooryard Bloom'd," Thomas's "Refusal to Mourn the Death, by Fire, of a Child in London," and so on, in order to "read" this simple poem properly. In fact, it could be argued that the more elegies one can bring to bear on a reading of this one, the better, richer poem this one becomes. I would go even further, suggesting that a knowledge of the critical tradition—of Dr. Johnson's objections to "Lycidas," for instance, or Wordsworth's critique of poetic diction—will also enhance one's reading of this poem. For the poem is, of course, an anti-elegy, a refusal not simply to mourn, but to write a sonorous, eloquent, mournful, but finally acquiescent, accepting—in a word, "elegiac"—poem at all.

Reading the poem involves, then, a special knowledge of its tradition. It also involves a special interpretive skill. The forms of the short, written poem as they have developed in English over the past few centuries can be usefully seen as compressed, truncated, or fragmented imitations of other verbal forms, especially the play, story, public oration, and personal essay. The reasons for this are too complicated for consideration here, but the fact will be apparent to all who reflect upon the matter. Our short poems are almost always elliptical versions of what can easily be conceived of as dramatic, narrative, oratorical, or meditative texts. Often, they are combinations of these and other modes of address. To take an obvious example, the dramatic monologue in the hands of Robert Browning is like a speech from a play (though usually more elongated than most such speeches). But to "read" such a monologue we must imagine the setting, the situation, the context, and so on. The dramatic monologue is "like" a play but gives us less information of certain sorts than a play would, requiring us to provide that information by decoding the clues in the monologue itself in the light of our understanding of the generic model. Most short poems work this way. They require both special knowledge and special skills to be "read."

To understand "Elegy" we must construct a situation out of the clues provided. The "it" in "Who would I show it to" is of course the elegy itself. The "I" is the potential writer of the elegy. The "Who" is the audience for the poem. But the verb phrase "would . . . show to" indicates a condition contrary to fact. Who would I show it to *if* I were to write it? This implies in turn that for the potential elegiac poet there is one person whose appreciation means more than that of all the rest of the potential audience for the poem he might write, and it further implies that the death of this particular person is the one imagined in the poem. If this person were dead, the poet suggests, so would his inspiration be dead. With no one to write for, no poem would be forthcoming. This poem is not only a "refusal to mourn," like that of Dylan Thomas, it is a refusal to elegize. The whole elegiac tradition, like its cousin the funeral oration, turns finally away from mourning toward acceptance, revival, renewal, a return to the concerns of life, symbolized by the very writing of the poem. Life goes on; there *is* an audience; and the mourned person will live through accomplishments, influence, descendants, and also (not least) in the elegiac poem itself. Merwin rejects all that. *If* I wrote an elegy for X, the person for whom I have always written, X would not be alive to read it; therefore, there is no reason to write an elegy for the one person in my life who most deserves one; therefore, there is no reason to write any elegy, anymore, ever. Finally, and of course, this poem called "Elegy" is not an elegy.

From *Semiotics and Interpretation*

CULTURAL STUDIES

Unlike the other critical approaches discussed in this chapter, cultural criticism (or **cultural studies**) does not offer a single way of analyzing literature. No central methodology is associated with cultural studies. Nor is cultural criticism solely, or even mainly, concerned with literary texts in the conventional sense. Instead, the term *cultural studies* refers to a relatively recent interdisciplinary field of academic inquiry. This field borrows methodologies from other approaches to analyze a wide range of cultural products and practices.

To understand cultural studies, it helps to know a bit about its origins. In the English-speaking world, the field was first defined at the Centre for Contemporary Cultural Studies of Birmingham University in Britain. Founded in 1964, this graduate program tried to expand the range of literary study beyond traditional approaches to canonic literature in order to explore a broader spectrum of historical, cultural, and political issues. The most influential teacher at the Birmingham Centre was Raymond Williams (1921–1983), a Welsh socialist with wide intellectual interests. Williams argued that scholars should not study culture as a canon of great works by individual artists but rather examine it as an evolutionary process that involves the entire society. "We cannot separate literature and art," Williams said, "from other kinds of social practice." The cultural critic, therefore, does not study fixed aesthetic objects so much as dynamic social processes. The critic's challenge is to identify and understand the complex forms and effects of the process of culture.

A Marxist intellectual, Williams called his approach cultural materialism (a reference to the Marxist doctrine of dialectical materialism), but later scholars soon discarded that name for two broader and more neutral terms, cultural criticism and cultural studies. From the start, this interdisciplinary field relied heavily on literary theory, especially Marxist and feminist criticism. It also employed the documentary techniques of historical criticism combined with political analysis focused on issues of social class, race, and gender. (This approach flourished in the United States, where it is called New Historicism.) Cultural studies is also deeply antiformalist, since the field concerns itself with investigating the complex relationships among history, politics, and literature. Cultural studies rejects the notion that literature exists in an aesthetic realm separate from ethical and political categories.

A chief goal of cultural studies is to understand the nature of social power as reflected in "texts." For example, if the object of analysis were a sonnet by Shakespeare, the cultural studies adherent might investigate the moral, psychological, and political assumptions reflected in the poem and then deconstruct them to see what individuals, social classes, or gender might benefit from having those assumptions perceived as true. The relevant mission of cultural studies is to identify both the overt and covert values reflected in a cultural practice. The cultural studies critic also tries to trace out and understand the structures of meaning that hold those assumptions in place and give them the appearance of objective representation. Any analytical technique that helps illuminate these issues is employed.

In theory, a cultural studies critic might employ any methodology. In practice, however, he or she will most often borrow concepts from Marxist analysis, gender criticism, race theory, and psychology. Each of these earlier methodologies provides particular analytical tools that cultural critics find useful. Cultural studies also borrows from **deconstructionist criticism**—which rejects the traditional assumption that language can accurately represent reality—in its emphasis on uncovering conflict, dissent, and contradiction in the works under analysis. Whereas traditional critical approaches often sought to demonstrate the unity of a literary work, cultural studies often seeks to portray social, political, and psychological conflicts that the work masks. What cultural studies borrows from Marxist analysis is an attention to the ongoing struggle between social classes, each seeking economic (and therefore political) advantage. Cultural studies often asks questions about what social class created a work of art and what class (or classes) served as its audience. Among the many things that cultural studies borrowed from gender criticism and race theory is a concern with social inequality between the sexes and races. It seeks to investigate how these inequities have been reflected in the texts of a historical period or a society. Cultural studies is, above all, a political enterprise that views literary analysis as a means of furthering social justice.

Since cultural studies does not adhere to any single methodology (or even a consistent set of methodologies), it is impossible to characterize the field briefly, because there are exceptions to every generalization offered. What one sees most clearly are characteristic tendencies, especially the commitment to examining issues of class, race, and gender. There is also the insistence on expanding the focus of critical inquiry beyond traditional high literary culture. British cultural studies guru Anthony Easthope can, for example, analyze with equal aplomb Gerard Manley Hopkins's "The Windhover," Edgar Rice Burroughs's *Tarzan of the Apes*, a Benson and Hedges cigarette advertisement, and Sean Connery's eyebrows. Cultural studies is infamous—even among its practitioners—for its habitual use of literary jargon. It is also notorious for its complex intellectual analysis of mundane materials, such as Easthope's analysis of a cigarette ad, which may be interesting in its own right but remote from most readers' literary experience. Some scholars, such as Camille Paglia, however, use the principles of cultural studies to provide new social, political, and historical insights into canonic texts such as William Blake's "The Chimney Sweeper" (Chapter 16). Omnivorous, iconoclastic, and relentlessly analytic, cultural criticism has become a major presence in contemporary literary studies.

Camille Paglia (b. 1947)

A Reading of William Blake's "The Chimney Sweeper"   2005

Romantic writers glorified childhood as a state of innocence. Blake's "The Chimney Sweeper," written in the same year as the French Revolution, combines the Romantic cult of the child with the new radical politics, which can both be traced to social thinker Jean-Jacques Rousseau. It is the boy sweep, rather than Blake, who speaks: he acts as the poet's dramatic persona or mask. There is no anger in his tale. On the contrary, the sweep's gentle acceptance of his miserable life makes his exploitation seem all the more atrocious. Blake shifts responsibility for protest onto us.

The poem begins as autobiography, a favorite Romantic genre. Having lost his mother, his natural protector, the small child was "sold" into slavery by his father (1–2). That is, he was apprenticed to a chimney-sweeping firm whose young teams would probably have worked simply for food, lodging, and clothing—basics that the boy's widowed working-class father might well have been unable to provide for his family. Children, soberly garbed in practical black, were used for chimney sweeping because they could wriggle into narrow, cramped spaces. The health risks of this filthy job were many—deformation of a boy's growing skeleton as well as long-term toxic effects from coal dust, now known to be carcinogenic. Chronic throat and lung problems as well as skin irritation must have been common. (Among the specimens floating in formaldehyde at Philadelphia's Mütter Museum, a nineteenth-century medical collection, is a chimney sweep's foot deformed by a bulbous tumor on the instep.)

Blake's sweep was so young when indentured into service that, he admits, he still lisped (2–3). The hawking of products and services by itinerant street vendors was once a lively, raucous feature of urban life. "Sweep, sweep, sweep!" cried the wandering crews seeking a day's employment. But this tiny boy couldn't even form the word: "Weep weep weep weep!" is how it came out—inadvertently sending a damning message to the oblivious world. It's really the thundering indictment of Blake as poet-prophet: Weep, you callous society that enslaves and murders its young; weep for yourself and your defenseless victims.

"So your chimneys I sweep and in soot I sleep": this singsong, matter-of-fact line implicates the reader in the poem's crimes—a confrontational device ordinarily associated with ironically self-conscious writers like Baudelaire (4). The boy may be peacefully resigned to the horror of his everyday reality, but we, locked in our own routines and distanced by genteel book reading, are forced to face our collective indifference. The boy represents the invisible army of manual laborers, charwomen, and janitors who do our dirty work. Scrubbing the infernal warren of brick and stone tunnels, he absorbs soot (symbolizing social sin) into his own skin and clothes, while we stay neat and clean.

The anonymous sweep—made faceless by his role—chatters cheerfully away about his friend "little Tom Dacre," whom he has taken under his wing (5). In this moral vacuum, where parents and caretakers are absent or negligent, the children must nurture each other. When the newcomer's curly hair was shaved off (to keep it from catching fire from live coals), he cried at his disfigurement, experienced as loss of self. Head shaving is a familiar initiatory practice in military and religious settings to reduce individuality and enforce group norms. To soothe little Tom, the solicitous sweep resorts to consolation of pitiful illogic: "when your head's bare / You know that the soot cannot spoil your white hair" (7–8). That's like saying, "Good thing you lost your leg—now you'll never stub your toe!" Tom's white (that is, blond) "lamb's back" hair represents the innocence of the Christlike sacrificial lamb: children, according to Blake, have become scapegoats for society's amorality and greed (6). Their white hair seems unnatural, as if the boys have been vaulted forward to old age without enjoying the freedoms and satisfactions of virile adulthood. For modern readers, the bald children's caged sameness is disturbingly reminiscent of that of emaciated survivors of Nazi concentration camps, where liberation was met with blank stoicism.

Amazingly, the sweep's desperate reassurance works: Tom goes "quiet," and for the next three stanzas, the whole center of the text, we enter his dreams (9–20). The poem seems to crack open in an ecstatic allegory of rebirth: the children of industrial London escape by the "thousands" from a living death, the locked "coffins of black" that are their soot-stained bodies as well as the chimneys where they spend their days (11–12). Alas, Tom's vision of paradise is nothing more than a simple, playful childhood—the birthright that was robbed from them. The poem overflows with the boys' repressed energy and vitality, as "leaping, laughing, they run" across the "green plain" of nature, then plunge into the purifying "river." Bathed "white," they "shine" with their own inner light, bright as the "sun" (15–18).

But something goes terribly wrong. The "Angel" with the "bright key" who was their liberator inexplicably turns oppressor (13, 19). As the sweeps "rise upon clouds" toward heaven and "sport in the wind" like prankish cherubs casting off their burdens (the "bags" of brushes and collected soot), an officiously moralistic voice cuts into the dream and terminates it: "And the Angel told Tom, if he'd be a good boy, / He'd have

God for his father, and never want joy" (17–20). That Tom wakes right up suggests that the voice actually belongs to the boss or overseer, briskly rousing his charges before dawn. The angel's homily, heavy with conventional piety, stops the children's fun and free motion dead: If you'll be good boys—that is, do what we say—you'll win God's approval and find your reward in heaven. (In British English, to "never want joy" means never to *lack* it.) But God is another false father in this poem.

The trusting, optimistic children grab their bags and brushes and get right to work in the "cold" and "dark" (21–23). They want to do right, and their spirit is unquenched. But they've been brainwashed into pliability by manipulative maxims such as the one recited by our first sweep in the ominous last line: "So if all do their duty they need not fear harm" (24). This bromide is an outrageous lie. If the children were to rebel, to run away to the green paradise lying just outside the city, they would be safe. Their naive goodwill leads straight to their ruin—a short, limited life of sickliness and toil. The final stanza's off rhymes ("dark"/"work," "warm"/"harm") subtly unbalance us and make us sense the fractures in the sweep's world. The poem shows him betrayed by an ascending row of duplicitous male authority figures—his father, the profiteering boss, the turncoat angel, and God himself, who tacitly endorses or tolerates an unjust social system. As Tom's dream suggests, the only deliverance for the sweep and his friends will be death.

From *Break, Blow, Burn*

Vincent B. Leitch (b. 1944)

Poststructuralist Cultural Critique   1992

Whereas a major goal of New Criticism and much other modern formalistic criticism is aesthetic evaluation of freestanding texts, a primary objective of cultural criticism is cultural critique, which entails investigation and assessment of ruling and oppositional beliefs, categories, practices, and representations, inquiring into the causes, constitutions, and consequences as well as the modes of circulation and consumption of linguistic, social, economic, political, historical, ethical, religious, legal, scientific, philosophical, educational, familial, and aesthetic discourses and institutions. In rendering a judgment on an aesthetic artifact, a New Critic privileges such key things as textual coherence and unity, intricacy and complexity, ambiguity and irony, tension and balance, economy and autonomy, literariness and spatial form. In mounting a critique of a cultural "text," an advocate of poststructuralist cultural criticism evaluates such things as degrees of exclusion and inclusion, of complicity and resistance, of domination and letting-be, of abstraction and situatedness, of violence and tolerance, of monologue and polylogue, of quietism and activism, of sameness and otherness, of oppression and emancipation, of centralization and decentralization. Just as the aforementioned system of evaluative criteria underlies the exegetical and judgmental labor of New Criticism, so too does the above named set of commitments undergird the work of poststructuralist cultural critique.

Given its commitments, poststructuralist cultural criticism is, as I have suggested, suspicious of literary formalism. Specifically, the trouble with New Criticism is its inclination to advocate a combination of quietism and asceticism, connoisseurship and exclusiveness, aestheticism and apoliticism. . . . The monotonous practical effect of New Critical reading is to illustrate the subservience of each textual element to a higher, overarching, economical poetic structure without remainders.

What should be evident here is that the project of poststructuralist cultural criticism possesses a set of commitments and criteria that enable it to engage in the enterprise of cultural critique. It should also be evident that the cultural ethicopolitics of this enterprise is best characterized, using current terminology, as "liberal" or "leftist," meaning congruent with certain socialist, anarchist, and libertarian ideals, none of which, incidentally, are necessarily Marxian. Such congruence, derived from extrapolating a generalized stance for poststructuralism, constitutes neither a party platform nor an observable course of practical action; avowed tendencies often account for little in the unfolding of practical engagements.

From *Cultural Criticism, Literary Theory, Poststructuralism*

▶ TERMS FOR *review*

Formalist criticism ▶ A school of criticism that focuses on the *form* of a literary work. A key method that formalists use is close reading, a step-by-step analysis of the elements in a text.

Biographical criticism ▶ The practice of analyzing a literary work by using knowledge of the author's life to gain insight. Although the work is understood as an independent creation, the biography of the author provides the practical assistance of underscoring subtle but important meanings.

Historical criticism ▶ The practice of analyzing a literary work by investigating the social, cultural, and intellectual context that produced it, including the author's biography and milieu.

Psychological criticism ▶ The application of the analytical tools of psychology and psychoanalysis to authors and/or fictional characters in order to understand the underlying motivations and meanings of a literary work.

Mythological criticism ▶ The practice of analyzing a literary work by looking for recurrent universal patterns. It explores the ways in which an individual imagination uses myths and symbols shared by different cultures and epochs.

Sociological criticism ▶ The practice of analyzing a literary work by examining the cultural, economic, and political context in which it was written or received. It primarily explores the relationship between the artist and society.

Gender criticism ▶ The examination of the ways in which sexual identity influences the creation, interpretation, and evaluation of literary works. Feminism, gay culture, and the men's movement all play key roles in gender criticism.

Reader-response criticism ▶ The practice of analyzing a literary work by describing what happens in the reader's mind while interpreting the text, on the assumption that no literary text exists independently of readers' interpretations and that there is no single fixed interpretation of any literary work.

Cultural studies ▶ A contemporary interdisciplinary field of academic study that focuses on understanding the social power encoded in "texts"—which may include any analyzable phenomenon from a traditional poem to an advertising image or actor's face.

Deconstructionist criticism ▶ A school of criticism that rejects the traditional assumption that language can accurately represent reality. Deconstructionists believe that literary texts can have no single meaning; therefore, they concentrate their attention on *how* language is being used in a text, rather than what is being said.

GLOSSARY
OF LITERARY TERMS

Abstract diction *See* **Diction**.

Accent An emphasis or stress placed on a syllable in speech. Clear pronunciation of polysyllabic words almost always depends on correct placement of their accents (e.g., *de*-sert and de-*sert* are two different words and parts of speech, depending on their accent). Accent or speech stress is the basis of most meters in English. (*See also* **Accentual meter, Meter**.)

Accentual meter A meter that uses a consistent number of strong speech stresses per line. The number of unstressed syllables may vary, as long as the accented syllables do not. Much popular poetry, such as rap and nursery rimes, is written in accentual meter.

Acrostic A poem in which the initial letters of each line, when read downward, spell out a hidden word or words (often the name of a beloved person). Acrostics date back as far as the Hebrew Bible and classical Greek poetry.

Allegory A narrative in verse or prose in which the literal events (persons, places, and things) consistently point to a parallel sequence of symbolic ideas. This narrative strategy is often used to dramatize abstract ideas, historical events, religious systems, or political issues. An allegory has two levels of meaning: a literal level that tells a surface story and a symbolic level in which the abstract ideas unfold. The names of allegorical characters often hint at their symbolic roles. For example, in Nathaniel Hawthorne's "Young Goodman Brown," Faith is not only the name of the protagonist's wife but also a symbol of the protagonist's religious faith.

Alliteration The repetition of two or more consonant sounds in successive words in a line of verse or prose. Alliteration can be used at the beginning of words ("cool cats"—**initial alliteration**) or internally on stressed syllables ("In kitchen cups concupiscent curds"—which combines initial and **internal alliteration**). Alliteration was a central feature of Anglo-Saxon poetry and is still used by contemporary writers.

All-knowing narrator *See* **Omniscient narrator**.

Allusion A brief (and sometimes indirect) reference in a text to a person, place, or thing—fictitious or actual. An allusion may appear in a literary work as an initial quotation, a passing mention of a name, or a phrase borrowed from another writer—often carrying the meanings and implications of the original. Allusions imply a common set of knowledge between reader and writer and operate as a literary shorthand to enrich the meaning of a text.

Analysis The examination of a piece of literature as a means of understanding its subject or structure. An effective analysis often clarifies a work by focusing on a single element such as tone, irony, symbolism, imagery, or rhythm in a way that enhances the reader's understanding of the whole. *Analysis* comes from the Greek word meaning to "undo," to "loosen."

Anapest A metrical foot in verse in which two unstressed syllables are followed by a stressed syllable, as in "on a *boat*" or "in a *slump*" (˘ ˘ ´). (*See also* **Meter**.)

Antagonist The most significant character or force that opposes the protagonist in a narrative or drama. The antagonist may be another character, society itself, a force of nature, or even—in modern literature—conflicting impulses within the protagonist.

Anticlimax An unsatisfying and trivial turn of events in a literary work that occurs in place of a genuine climax. An anticlimax often involves a surprising shift in tone from the lofty or serious into the petty or ridiculous. The term is often used negatively to denote a feeble moment in a plot in which an author fails to create an intended effect. Anticlimax, however, can also be a strong dramatic device when a writer uses it for humorous or ironic effect.

Antihero A protagonist who is lacking in one or more of the conventional qualities attributed to a hero. Instead of being dignified, brave, idealistic, or purposeful, for instance, the antihero may be buffoonish, cowardly, self-interested, or weak. The antihero is often considered an essentially modern form of characterization, a satiric or frankly realistic commentary on traditional portrayals of idealized heroes or heroines. Modern examples range from Kafka's many protagonists to Beckett's tramps in *Waiting for Godot*.

Antithesis Words, phrases, clauses, or sentences set in deliberate contrast to one another. Antithesis balances opposing ideas, tones, or structures, usually to heighten the effect of a statement.

Apostrophe A direct address to someone or something. In poetry an apostrophe often addresses something not ordinarily spoken to (e.g., "O mountain!"). In an apostrophe, a speaker may address an inanimate object, a dead or absent person, an abstract thing, or a spirit. Apostrophe is often used to provide a speaker with means to articulate thoughts aloud.

Apprenticeship novel *See* **Bildungsroman**.

Archetype A recurring symbol, character, landscape, or event found in myth and literature across different cultures and eras. The idea of the archetype came into literary criticism from the Swiss psychologist Carl Jung, who believed that all individuals share a "collective unconscious," a set of primal memories common to the human race that exists in our subconscious. An example of an archetypal character is the devil who may appear in pure mythic form (as in John Milton's *Paradise Lost*) but occurs more often in a disguised form like Fagin in Charles Dickens's *Oliver Twist* or Abner Snopes in William Faulkner's "Barn Burning."

Aside In drama a few words or short passage spoken in an undertone or to the audience. By convention, other characters onstage are deaf to the aside.

Assonance The repetition of two or more vowel sounds in successive words, which creates a kind of rime. Like alliteration, the assonance may occur initially ("*all* the *awful auguries*") or internally ("wh*i*te l*i*lacs"). Assonance may be used to focus attention on key words or concepts. Assonance also helps make a phrase or line more memorable.

Atmosphere The dominant mood or feeling that pervades all or part of a literary work. Atmosphere is the total effect conveyed by the author's use of language, images, and physical setting. Atmosphere is often used to foreshadow the ultimate climax in a narrative.

Auditory imagery A word or sequence of words that refers to the sense of hearing. (*See also* **Imagery**.)

Ballad Traditionally, a song that tells a story. The ballad was originally an oral verse form—sung or recited and transmitted from performer to performer without being written down. Ballads are characteristically compressed, dramatic, and objective in their narrative style. There are many variations to the ballad form, most consisting of quatrains (made up of lines of three or four metrical feet) in a simple rime scheme. (*See also* **Ballad stanza**.)

Ballad stanza The most common pattern of ballad makers, consisting of four lines rimed *a b c b*, in which the first and third lines have four metrical feet and the second and fourth lines have three feet (4, 3, 4, 3).

Bathos In poetry, an unintentional lapse from the sublime to the ridiculous or trivial. Bathos differs from anticlimax, in that the latter is a deliberate effect, often for the purpose of humor or contrast, whereas bathos occurs through failure.

Bildungsroman German for "novel of growth and development." Sometimes called an **apprenticeship novel**, this genre depicts a youth who struggles toward maturity, forming a worldview or philosophy of life. Dickens's *David Copperfield* and Joyce's *Portrait of the Artist as a Young Man* are classic examples of the genre.

Biographical criticism The practice of analyzing a literary work by using knowledge of the author's life to gain insight.

Biography A factual account of a person's life, examining all available information or texts relevant to the subject.

Blank verse The most common and well-known meter of unrimed poetry in English. Blank verse contains five iambic feet per line and is never rimed. (*Blank* means "unrimed.") Many literary works have been written in blank verse, including Tennyson's "Ulysses" and Frost's "Mending Wall." Shakespeare's plays are written primarily in blank verse. (*See also* **Iambic pentameter**.)

Blues A type of folk music originally developed by African Americans in the South, often about some pain or loss. Blues lyrics traditionally consist of three-line stanzas in which the first two identical lines are followed by a third concluding, rhyming line. The influence of the blues is fundamental in virtually all styles of contemporary pop—jazz, rap, rock, gospel, country, and rhythm and blues.

Box set The illusion of scenic realism for interior rooms was achieved in the early nineteenth century with the development of the box set, consisting of three walls that joined in two corners and a ceiling that tilted as if seen in perspective. The "fourth wall," invisible, ran parallel to the proscenium arch. By the middle of the nineteenth century, the addition of realistic props and furnishings made it possible for actors to behave onstage as if they inhabited private space, oblivious to the presence of an audience, even turning their backs to the audience if the dramatic situation required it.

Broadside ballads Poems printed on a single sheet of paper, often set to traditional tunes. Most broadside ballads, which originated in the late sixteenth century, were an early form of verse journalism, cheap to print, and widely circulated. Often they were humorous or pathetic accounts of sensational news events.

Burlesque Incongruous imitation of either the style or subject matter of a serious genre, humorous because of the disparity between the treatment and the subject. On the nineteenth-century English stage, the burlesque was a broad caricature, parody, travesty, or take-off of popular plays, opera, or current events. Gilbert and Sullivan's Victorian operettas, for example, burlesqued grand opera.

Cacophony A harsh, discordant sound often mirroring the meaning of the context in which it is used. For example, "Grate on the scrannel pipes of wretched straw" (Milton's "Lycidas"). The opposite of cacophony is **euphony**.

Carpe diem Latin for "seize the day." Originally used in Horace's famous "Odes I (11)," this phrase has been applied to characterize much lyric poetry concerned with human mortality and the passing of time.

Central intelligence The character through whose sensibility and mind a story is told. Henry James developed this term to describe a narrator—not the author—whose perceptions shape the way a story is presented. (*See also* **Narrator**.)

Cesura, caesura A pause within a line of verse. Traditionally, cesuras appear near the middle of a line, but their placement may be varied to create expressive rhythmic effects. A cesura will usually occur at a mark of punctuation, but there can be a cesura even if no punctuation is present.

Character An imagined figure inhabiting a narrative or drama. By convention, the reader or spectator endows the fictional character with moral, dispositional, and emotional qualities expressed in what the character says—the dialogue—and by what he or she does—the action. What a character says and does in any particular situation is motivated by his or her desires, temperament, and moral nature. (*See also* **Dynamic character** and **Flat character**.)

Character development The process in which a character is introduced, advanced, and possibly transformed in a story. This development can prove to be either static (the character's personality is unchanging throughout the narrative) or dynamic (the character's personality undergoes some meaningful change during the course of the narrative). (*See also* **Dynamic character**.)

Characterization The techniques a writer uses to create, reveal, or develop the characters in a narrative. (*See also* **Character**.)

Child ballads American scholar Francis J. Child compiled a collection of over three hundred authentic ballads in his book *The English and Scottish Popular Ballads* (1882–1898). He demonstrated that these ballads were the creations of oral folk culture. These works have come to be called Child ballads.

Clerihew A comic verse form named for its inventor, Edmund Clerihew Bentley. A clerihew begins with the name of a person and consists of two metrically awkward, rimed couplets. Humorous and often insulting, clerihews serve as ridiculous biographies, usually of famous people.

Climax The moment of greatest intensity in a story, which almost inevitably occurs toward the end of the work. The climax often takes the form of a decisive confrontation between the protagonist and antagonist. In a conventional story, the climax is followed by the **resolution** or **dénouement** in which the effects and results of the climactic action are presented. (*See also* **Falling action, Rising action**.)

Closed couplet Two rimed lines that contain an independent and complete thought or statement. The closed couplet usually pauses lightly at the end of the first line; the second is more heavily end-stopped, or "closed." When such couplets are written in rimed iambic pentameter, they are called **heroic couplets**. (*See also* **Couplet**.)

Closed dénouement One of two types of conventional dénouement or resolution in a narrative. In closed dénouement, the author ties everything up at the end of the story so that little is left unresolved. (*See also* **Open dénouement**.)

Closed form A generic term that describes poetry written in some preexisting pattern of meter, rime, line, or stanza. A closed form produces a prescribed structure, as in the triolet, with a set rime scheme and line length. Closed forms include the sonnet, sestina, villanelle, ballade, and rondeau.

Close reading A method of analysis involving careful step-by-step explication of a poem in order to understand how various elements work together. Close reading is a common practice of formalist critics in the study of a text.

Colloquial English The casual or informal but correct language of ordinary native speakers, which may include contractions, slang, and shifts in grammar, vocabulary, and diction. Wordsworth helped introduce colloquialism into English poetry, challenging the past constraints of highly formal language in verse and calling for the poet to become "a man speaking to men." Conversational in tone, *colloquial* is derived from the Latin *colloquium*, "speaking together." (*See also* **Diction**, **Levels of diction**.)

Comedy A literary work aimed at amusing an audience. Comedy is one of the basic modes of storytelling and can be adapted to most literary forms—from poetry to film. In traditional comic plotting, the action often involves the adventures of young lovers, who face obstacles and complications that threaten disaster but are overturned at the last moment to produce a happy ending. Comic situations or comic characters can provide humor in tragicomedy and even in tragedies (the gravediggers in *Hamlet*).

Comedy of manners A realistic form of comic drama that flourished with seventeenth-century playwrights such as Molière and English Restoration dramatists. It deals with the social relations and sexual intrigues of sophisticated, intelligent, upper-class men and women, whose verbal fencing and witty repartee produce the principal comic effects. Stereotyped characters from contemporary life, such as would-be wits, jealous husbands, conniving rivals, country bumpkins, and foppish dandies, reveal by their deviations from the norm the decorum and conventional behaviors expected in polite society. Modern examples include G. B. Shaw (*Arms and the Man*), Noel Coward (*Private Lives*), and Tom Stoppard (*Arcadia*).

Comic relief The appearance of a comic situation, character, or clownish humor in the midst of a serious action that introduces a sharp contrast in mood. The drunken porter in *Macbeth*, who imagines himself the doorkeeper of Hell, not only provides comic relief but intensifies the horror of Macbeth's murder of King Duncan.

Coming-of-age story *See* **Initiation story**.

Commedia dell'arte A form of comic drama developed by guilds of professional Italian actors in the mid-sixteenth century. Playing stock characters, masked *commedia* players improvised dialogue around a given scenario (a brief outline marking entrances of characters and the main course of action). In a typical play a pair of young lovers (played without masks), aided by a clever servant (Harlequin), outwit older masked characters.

Common meter A highly regular form of ballad meter with two sets of rimes—*a b a b*. "Amazing Grace" and many other hymns are in common meter. (*See also* **Ballad stanza**.)

Comparison In the analysis or criticism of literature, one may place two works side by side to point out their similarities. The product of this, a comparison, may be more meaningful when paired with its counterpart, a **contrast**.

Complication The introduction of a significant development in the central conflict in a drama or narrative between characters (or between a character and his or her situation). Traditionally, a complication begins the rising action of a story's plot. Dramatic conflict (motivation versus obstacle) during the complication is the force that drives a literary work from action to action. Complications may be *external* or *internal* or a combination of the two. A fateful blow such as an illness or an accident that affects a character is a typical example of an *external* complication—a problem the characters cannot turn away from. An *internal* complication, in contrast, might not be immediately apparent, such as the result of some important aspect of a character's values or personality.

Conceit A poetic device using elaborate comparisons, such as equating a loved one with the graces and beauties of the world. Most notably used by the Italian poet Petrarch in praise of his beloved Laura, *conceit* comes from the Italian *concetto*, "concept" or "idea."

Conclusion In plotting, the logical end or outcome of a unified plot, shortly following the climax. Also called **resolution** or **dénouement** ("the untying of the knot"), as in resolving or untying the knots created by plot complications during the rising action. The action or intrigue ends in success or failure for the protagonist, the mystery is solved, or misunderstandings are dispelled. Sometimes a conclusion is ambiguous; at the climax of the story the characters are changed, but the conclusion suggests different possibilities for what that change is or means.

Concrete diction *See* **Diction**.

Concrete poetry A visual poetry composed exclusively for the page in which a picture or image is made of printed letters and words. Concrete poetry attempts to blur the line between language and visual art. Concrete poetry was especially popular as an experimental movement in the 1960s.

Confessional poetry A poetic genre emerging in the 1950s and 1960s primarily concerned with autobiography and the unexpurgated exposure of the poet's personal life. Notable practitioners included Robert Lowell, W. D. Snodgrass, and Anne Sexton.

Conflict In Greek, *agon*, or contest. The central struggle between two or more forces in a plot. Conflict generally occurs when some person or thing prevents the protagonist from achieving his or her intended goal. Opposition can arise from another character, external events, preexisting situations, fate, or even some aspect of the main character's own personality. Conflict is the basic material out of which most plots are made. (*See also* **Antagonist**, **Character**, **Complication**, **Rising action**.)

Connotation An association or additional meaning that a word, image, or phrase may carry, apart from its literal denotation or dictionary definition. A word picks up connotations from all the uses to which it has been put in the past. For example, an owl in literature is not merely the literal bird. It also carries the many associations (connotations, that is) attached to it.

Consonance Also called **Slant rime**. A kind of rime in which the linked words share similar consonant sounds but different vowel sounds, as in *reason* and *raisin*, *mink* and *monk*. Sometimes only the final consonant sound is identical, as in *fame* and *room*, *crack* and *truck*. Used mostly by modern poets, consonance often registers more subtly than exact rime, lending itself to special poetic effects.

Contrast A contrast of two works of literature is developed by placing them side by side to point out their differences. This method of analysis works well with its opposite, a **comparison**, which focuses on likenesses.

Convention Any established feature or technique in literature that is commonly understood by both authors and readers. A convention is something generally agreed on to be appropriate for its customary uses, such as the sonnet form for a love poem or the opening "Once upon a time" for a fairy tale.

Conventional symbols Literary symbols that have a conventional or customary effect on most readers. We would respond similarly to a black cat crossing our path or a young bride in a white dress. These are conventional symbols because they carry recognizable connotations and suggestions.

Cosmic irony Also called **irony of fate**, it is the irony that exists between a character's aspiration and the treatment he or she receives at the hands of fate. Oedipus's ill-destined relationship with his parents is an example of cosmic irony.

Cothurni High thick-soled boots worn by Greek and Roman tragic actors in late classical times to make them appear taller than ordinary men. (Earlier, in the fifth-century classical Athenian theater, actors wore soft shoes or boots or went barefoot.)

Couplet A two-line stanza in poetry, usually rimed, which tends to have lines of equal length. Shakespeare's sonnets were famous for ending with a summarizing, rimed couplet: "Give my love fame faster than Time wastes life; / So thou prevent'st his scythe and crookèd knife." (*See also* **Closed couplet.**)

Cowboy poetry A contemporary genre of folk poetry written by people with first-hand experience in the life of horse, trail, and ranch. Plainspoken and often humorous, cowboy poetry is usually composed in rimed ballad stanzas and meant to be recited aloud.

Crisis The point in a drama when the crucial action, decision, or realization must occur, marking the turning point or reversal of the protagonist's fortunes. From the Greek word *krisis*, meaning "decision." For example, Hamlet's decision to refrain from killing Claudius while the guilty king is praying is a crisis that leads directly to his accidental murder of Polonius, pointing forward to the catastrophe of Act V. Typically, the crisis inaugurates the falling action (after Hamlet's murder of Polonius, Claudius controls the events) until the catastrophe (or conclusion), which is decided by the death of the hero, King Claudius, Queen Gertrude, and Laertes. In *Oedipus*, the crisis occurs as the hero presses forward to the horrible truth, to realize he is an incestuous parricide and to take responsibility by blinding himself.

Cultural studies A contemporary interdisciplinary field of academic study that focuses on understanding the social power encoded in "texts." Cultural studies defines "texts" more broadly than literary works; they include any analyzable phenomenon from a traditional poem to an advertising image or an actor's face. Cultural studies has no central critical methodology but uses whatever intellectual tools are appropriate to the analysis at hand.

Dactyl A metrical foot of verse in which one stressed syllable is followed by two unstressed syllables ($'\smile\smile$, as in *bat*-ter-y or *par*-a-mour). The dactylic meter is less common to English than it was to classical Greek and Latin verse. Longfellow's *Evangeline* is the most famous English-language long dactylic poem.

Deconstructionist criticism A school of criticism that rejects the traditional assumption that language can accurately represent reality. Deconstructionists believe that literary texts can have no single meaning; therefore, they concentrate their attention on *how* language is being used in a text, rather than on *what* is being said.

Decorum Propriety or appropriateness. In poetry, decorum usually refers to a level of diction that is proper to use in a certain occasion. Decorum can also apply to characters, setting, and the harmony that exists between the elements in a poem. For example, aged nuns speaking inner-city jive might violate decorum.

Denotation The literal, dictionary meaning of a word. (*See also* **Connotation.**)

Dénouement The resolution or conclusion of a literary work as plot complications are unraveled after the climax. In French, *dénouement* means "unknotting" or "untying." (*See also* **Closed dénouement, Conclusion, Open dénouement.**)

Detective fiction Also called *crime fiction* and *mystery*. A narrative that presents a protagonist who solves a puzzling crime (most often a murder) by using observation, deduction, and intuition to find the culprit.

Deus ex machina Latin for "a god from a machine." The phrase refers to the Greek playwrights' frequent use of a god, mechanically lowered to the stage from the *skene* roof, to resolve human conflict with judgments and commands. Conventionally, the phrase now refers to any forced or improbable device in plot resolution.

Dialect A particular variety of language spoken by an identifiable regional group or social class of persons. Dialects are often used in literature in an attempt to present a character more realistically and to express significant differences in class or background.

Dialogue The direct representation of the conversation between two or more characters. (*See also* **Monologue**.)

Diction Word choice or vocabulary. Diction refers to the class of words that an author decides is appropriate to use in a particular work. Literary history is the story of diction being challenged, upheld, and reinvented. **Concrete diction** involves a highly specific word choice in the naming of something or someone. **Abstract diction** contains words that express more general ideas or concepts. More concrete diction would offer *boxer puppy* rather than *young canine*, *Lake Ontario* rather than *body of fresh water*. Concrete words refer to what we can immediately perceive with our senses. (*See also* **Levels of diction**.)

Didactic fiction A narrative that intends to teach a specific moral lesson or provide a model for proper behavior. This term is now often used pejoratively to describe a story in which the events seem manipulated in order to convey an uplifting idea, but much classic fiction has been written in the didactic mode—Aesop's *Fables*, John Bunyan's *The Pilgrim's Progress*, and Harriet Beecher Stowe's *Uncle Tom's Cabin*.

Didactic poetry A kind of poetry intended to teach the reader a moral lesson or impart a body of knowledge. Poetry that aims for education over art.

Dimeter A verse meter consisting of two metrical feet, or two primary stresses, per line.

Doggerel Verse full of irregularities often due to the poet's incompetence. Doggerel is crude verse that brims with cliché, obvious rime, and inept rhythm.

Double plot Also called **subplot**. Familiar in Elizabethan drama, a second story or plotline that is complete and interesting in its own right, often doubling or inverting the main plot. By analogy or counterpoint, a skillful subplot broadens perspective on the main plot to enhance rather than dilute its effect. In Shakespeare's *Othello*, for instance, Iago's duping of Roderigo reflects the main plot of Iago's treachery to Othello.

Drama Derived from the Greek *dran*, "to do," *drama* means "action" or "deed." Drama is the form of literary composition designed for performance in the theater, in which actors take the roles of the characters, perform the indicated action, and speak the written dialogue. In the *Poetics*, Aristotle described tragedy or dramatic enactment as the most fully evolved form of the impulse to imitate or make works of art.

Dramatic irony A special kind of suspenseful expectation, when the audience or reader understands the implication and meaning of a situation onstage and foresees the oncoming disaster (in tragedy) or triumph (in comedy) but the character does not. The irony forms between the contrasting levels of knowledge of the character and the audience. Dramatic irony is pervasive throughout Sophocles's *Oedipus the King*, for example, because we know from the beginning what Oedipus does not. We watch with dread and fascination the spectacle of a morally good man, committed to the salvation of his city, unwittingly preparing undeserved suffering for himself.

Dramatic monologue A poem written as a speech made by a character at some decisive moment. The speaker is usually addressing a silent listener as in T. S. Eliot's "The Love Song of J. Alfred Prufrock" or Robert Browning's "My Last Duchess."

Dramatic poetry Any verse written for the stage, as in the plays of classical Greece, the Renaissance (Shakespeare), and the neoclassical period (Molière, Racine). Also a kind of poetry that presents the voice of an imaginary character (or characters) speaking directly, without any additional narration by the author. In poetry, the term usually refers to the dramatic monologue, a lyric poem written as a speech made by a character at some decisive moment, such as Alfred, Lord Tennyson's "Ulysses." (*See also* **Dramatic monologue**.)

Dramatic point of view A point of view in which the narrator merely reports dialogue and action with minimal interpretation or access to the characters' minds. The dramatic point of view, as the name implies, uses prose fiction to approximate the method of plays (where readers are provided only with set descriptions, stage directions, and dialogue, and thus must supply motivations based solely on this external evidence).

Dramatic question The primary unresolved issue in a drama as it unfolds. The dramatic question is the result of artful plotting, raising suspense and expectation in a play's action as it moves toward its outcome. Will the Prince in *Hamlet*, for example, achieve what he has been instructed to do and what he intends to do?

Dramatic situation The basic conflict that initiates a work or establishes a scene. It usually describes both a protagonist's motivation and the forces that oppose its realization. (*See also* **Antagonist, Character, Complication, Plot, Rising action**.)

Dumb show In Renaissance theater, a mimed dramatic performance whose purpose is to prepare the audience for the main action of the play to follow. Jacobean playwrights like John Webster used it to show violent events that occur some distance from the play's locale. The most famous Renaissance example is the dumb show preceding the presentation of "The Murder of Gonzago" in *Hamlet*.

Dynamic character A character who, during the course of the narrative, grows or changes in some significant way. (*See also* **Character development**.)

Echo verse A poetic form in which the final syllables of the lines are repeated back as a reply or commentary, often using puns. Echo verse dates back to late classical Greek poetry.

Editorial omniscience When an omniscient narrator goes beyond reporting the thoughts of his or her characters to make a critical judgment or commentary, making explicit the narrator's own thoughts or philosophies.

Editorial point of view The effect that occurs when a third-person narrator adds his or her own comments (which presumably represent the ideas and opinions of the author) into the narrative.

Elegy A lament or a sadly meditative poem, often written on the occasion of a death or other solemn theme. An elegy is usually a sustained poem in a formal style.

Endnote An additional piece of information that the author includes in a note at the end of a paper or chapter. Endnotes usually contain information that the author feels is important to convey but not appropriate to fit into the main body of text. (*See also* **Footnote**.)

End rime Rime that occurs at the ends of lines, rather than within them (as internal rhyme does). End rime is the most common kind of rime in English-language poetry.

End-stopped line A line of verse that ends in a full pause, usually indicated by a mark of punctuation.

English sonnet Also called **Shakespearean sonnet**. The English sonnet has a rime scheme organized into three quatrains with a final couplet: *a b a b c d c d e f e f g g*. The poem may turn—that is, shift in mood or tone—between any of the quatrains (although it usually occurs on the ninth line). (*See also* **Sonnet**.)

Envoy A short, often summarizing stanza that appears at the end of certain poetic forms (most notably the sestina, chant royal, and French ballade). The envoy contains the poet's parting words. The word comes from the French *envoi*, meaning "sending forth."

Epic A long narrative poem usually composed in an elevated style tracing the adventures of a legendary or mythic hero. Epics are usually written in a consistent form and meter throughout. Famous epics include Homer's *Iliad* and *Odyssey*, Virgil's *Aeneid*, and Milton's *Paradise Lost*.

Epigram A very short poem, often comic, usually ending with some sharp turn of wit or meaning.

Epigraph A brief quotation preceding a story or other literary work. An epigraph usually suggests the subject, theme, or atmosphere the work will explore.

Epiphany A moment of insight, discovery, or revelation by which a character's life is greatly altered. An epiphany generally occurs near the end of a story. The term, which means "showing forth" in Greek, was first used in Christian theology to signify the manifestation of God's presence in the world. This theological idea was first borrowed by James Joyce to refer to a heightened moment of secular revelation.

Episode An incident in a large narrative that has unity in itself. An episode may bear close relation to the central narrative, but it can also be a digression.

Episodic plot, episodic structure A form of plotting where the individual scenes and events are presented chronologically without any profound sense of cause-and-effect relationship. In an episodic narrative the placement of many scenes could be changed without greatly altering the overall effect of the work.

Epistolary novel A novel in which the story is told by way of letters written by one or more of the characters. This form often lends an authenticity to the story, a sense that the author may have discovered these letters; but in fact they are a product of the author's invention.

Euphony The harmonious effect when the sounds of the words connect with the meaning in a way pleasing to the ear and mind. An example is found in Tennyson's lines, "The moan of doves in immemorial elms, / And murmuring of innumerable bees." The opposite of euphony is **cacophony**.

Exact rime A full rime in which the sounds following the initial letters of the words are identical in sound, as in *follow* and *hollow*, *go* and *slow*, *disband* and *this hand*.

Explication Literally, an "unfolding." In an explication an entire poem is explained in detail, addressing every element and unraveling any complexities as a means of analysis.

Exposition The opening portion of a narrative or drama. In the exposition, the scene is set, the protagonist is introduced, and the author discloses any other background information necessary to allow the reader to understand and relate to the events that are to follow.

Expressionism A dramatic style developed between 1910 and 1924 in Germany in reaction against realism's focus on surface details and external reality. To draw an audience into a dreamlike subjective realm, expressionistic artistic styles used episodic plots, distorted lines, exaggerated shapes, abnormally intense coloring, mechanical physical movement, and telegraphic speech (the broken syntax of a disordered psyche). Staging the contents of the unconscious, expressionist plays ranged from utopian visions of a fallen, materialistic world redeemed by the spirituality of "new men" to pessimistic nightmare visions of universal catastrophe.

Eye rime Rime in which the spelling of the words appears alike, but the pronunciations differ, as in *laughter* and *daughter*, *idea* and *flea*.

Fable A brief, often humorous narrative told to illustrate a moral. The characters in fables are traditionally animals whose personality traits symbolize human traits. Particular animals have conventionally come to represent specific human qualities or values. For example, the ant represents industry, the fox craftiness, and the lion nobility. A fable often concludes by summarizing its moral message in abstract terms. For example, Aesop's fable "The North Wind and the Sun" concludes with the moral "Persuasion is better than force." (*See also* **Allegory**.)

Fairy tale A traditional form of short narrative folklore, originally transmitted orally, that features supernatural characters such as witches, giants, fairies, or animals with human personality traits. Fairy tales often feature a hero or heroine who seems destined to achieve some desirable fate—such as marrying a prince or princess, becoming wealthy, or destroying an enemy.

Falling action The events in a narrative that follow the climax and bring the story to its conclusion, or dénouement.

Falling meter Trochaic and dactylic meters are called falling meters because their first syllable is accented, followed by one or more unaccented syllables. A foot of falling meter falls in its level of stress, as in the words *co*-medy or *aw*-ful.

Fantasy A narrative that depicts events, characters, or places that do not exist in the real world. The oldest form of romance, fantasy expresses the fears and desires of the human imagination without being required to explain them in logical terms.

Farce A type of comedy featuring exaggerated character types in ludicrous and improbable situations, provoking belly laughs with sexual mix-ups, crude verbal jokes, pratfalls, and knockabout horseplay (like the comic violence of the Punch and Judy show).

Feminine rime A rime of two or more syllables with a stress on a syllable other than the last, as in *tur*-tle and *fer*-tile. (*See also* **Masculine rime**, **Rime**.)

Feminist criticism *See* **Gender criticism**.

Fiction From the Latin *ficio*, "act of fashioning, a shaping, a making." Fiction refers to any literary work that—although it might contain factual information—is not bound by factual accuracy, but creates a narrative shaped or made up by the author's imagination. Drama and poetry (especially narrative poetry) can be considered works of fiction, but the term now usually refers more specifically to prose stories and novels. Historical and other factual writing also requires shaping and making, but it is distinct from fiction because it is not free to invent people, places, and events; forays from documented fact must identify themselves as conjecture or hypothesis. Nonfiction, as the name suggests, is a category conventionally separate from fiction. Certainly an essay or work of literary journalism is "a made thing," and writers of nonfiction routinely employ the techniques used by fiction writers (moving forward and backward in time, reporting the inner thoughts of characters, etc.), but works of nonfiction must be not only true but factual. The truth of a work of fiction depends not on facts, but on how convincingly the writer creates the world of the story.

Figure of speech An expression or comparison that relies not on its literal meaning, but rather on its connotations and suggestions. For example, "He's dumber than dirt" is not literally true; it is a figure of speech. Major figures of speech include **metaphor**, **metonymy**, **simile**, and **synecdoche**.

First-person narrator A narrator who is a participant in the action of a story. Such a narrator refers to himself or herself as "I" and may be a major or minor character in the story. His or her attitude and understanding of characters and events shapes the reader's perception of the story being told.

Fixed form A traditional verse form requiring certain predetermined elements of structure, for example, a stanza pattern, set meter, or predetermined line length. A sonnet, for instance, must have no more nor less than fourteen lines, rimed according to certain conventional patterns. (*See also* **Closed form**.)

Flashback A scene relived in a character's memory. Flashbacks may be related by the narrator in a summary or they may be experienced by the characters themselves. Flashbacks allow the author to include events that occurred before the opening of the story, which may show the reader something significant that happened in the character's past or give an indication of what kind of person the character used to be.

Flat character A term coined by English novelist E. M. Forster to describe a character with only one outstanding trait. Flat characters are rarely the central characters in a narrative and are often based on **stock characters**. Flat characters stay the same throughout a story. (*See also* **Dynamic character**.)

Folk ballads Anonymous narrative songs, usually in ballad meter, that were originally transmitted orally. Although most well-known ballads have been transcribed and published in order to protect them from being lost, they were originally created for oral performance, often resulting in many versions of a single ballad.

Folk epic Also called **Traditional epic**. A long narrative poem that traces the adventures of a tribe or nation's popular heroes. Some examples of epics are the *Iliad* and the *Odyssey* (Greek), *The Song of Roland* (French), and *The Cid* (Spanish). A folk epic originates in an oral tradition as opposed to a literary epic, which is written by an individual author consciously emulating earlier epic poetry.

Folklore The body of traditional wisdom and customs—including songs, stories, myths, and proverbs—of a people as collected and continued through oral tradition.

Folktale A short narrative drawn from folklore that has been passed down through an oral tradition. (*See also* **Fairy tale**, **Legend**.)

Foot The unit of measurement in metrical poetry. Different meters are identified by the pattern and order of stressed and unstressed syllables in their foot, usually containing two or three syllables, with one syllable accented.

Footnote An additional piece of information that the author includes at the bottom of a page, usually noted by a small reference number in the main text. A footnote might supply the reader with brief facts about a related historical figure or event, the definition of a foreign word or phrase, or any other relevant information that may help in understanding the text. (*See also* **Endnote**.)

Foreshadowing In plot construction, the technique of arranging events and information in such a way that later events are prepared for, or shadowed, beforehand. The author may introduce specific words, images, or actions in order to suggest significant later events. The effective use of foreshadowing by an author may prevent a story's outcome from seeming haphazard or contrived.

Form The means by which a literary work conveys its meaning. Traditionally, form refers to the way in which an artist expresses meaning rather than the content of that meaning, but it is now commonplace to note that form and content are inextricably related. Form, therefore, is more than the external framework of a literary work. It includes the totality of ways in which it unfolds and coheres as a structure of meaning and expression.

Formal English *See* **High diction**.

Formalist criticism A school of criticism which argues that literature may only be discussed on its own terms—that is, without outside influences or information. A key method that formalists use is close reading, a step-by-step analysis of the elements in a text.

Found poetry Poetry constructed by arranging bits of "found" prose. A found poem is a literary work made up of nonliterary language arranged for expressive effect.

Free verse From the French *vers libre*. Free verse describes poetry that organizes its lines without meter. It may be rimed (as in some poems by H.D.), but it usually is not. There is no one means of organizing free verse, and different authors have used irreconcilable systems. What unites the two approaches is a freedom from metrical regularity. (*See also* **Open form**.)

Gender criticism Gender criticism examines how sexual identity influences the creation, interpretation, and evaluation of literary works. This critical approach began with feminist criticism in the 1960s and 1970s which stated that literary study had been so dominated by men that it contained many unexamined "male-produced" assumptions. Feminist criticism sought to address this imbalance in two ways: first, by insisting that sexless interpretation was impossible, and second, by articulating responses to the texts that were explicitly male or female. More recently, gender criticism has focused on gay and lesbian literary identity as interpretive strategies.

General English *See* **Middle diction**.

Genre A conventional combination of literary form and subject matter, usually aimed at creating certain effects. A genre implies a preexisting understanding between the artist and the reader about the purpose and rules of the work. A horror story, for example, combines the form of the short story with certain conventional subjects, styles, and themes with the expectation of frightening the reader. Major short story genres include science fiction, gothic, horror, and detective tales.

Genre fiction A general category of fiction that encompasses a variety of romantic narrative forms, including **science fiction**, **fantasy**, **horror**, **detective**, **mystery**, and many other varieties of popular literature.

Gothic fiction A genre that creates terror and suspense, usually set in an isolated castle, mansion, or monastery populated by mysterious or threatening individuals. The Gothic form, invented by Horace Walpole in *The Castle of Otranto* (1764), has flourished in one form or another ever since. The term *Gothic* is also applied to medieval architecture, and Gothic fiction almost inevitably exploits claustrophobic interior architecture in its plotting—often featuring dungeons, crypts, torture chambers, locked rooms, and secret passageways. In the nineteenth century, writers such as Nathaniel Hawthorne, Edgar Allan Poe, and Charlotte Perkins Gilman brought the genre into the mainstream of American fiction.

Haiku A Japanese verse form that has three unrimed lines of five, seven, and five syllables. Traditional haiku is often serious and spiritual in tone, relying mostly on imagery, and usually set in one of the four seasons.

Hamartia Greek for "error." An offense committed in ignorance of some material fact (without deliberate criminal intent) and therefore free of blameworthiness. A great mistake unintentionally made as a result of an intellectual error (not vice or criminal wickedness) by a morally good person, usually involving the identity of a blood relation. The *hamartia* of Oedipus, quite simply, is based on his ignorance of his true parentage; inadvertently and unwittingly, then, he commits the *hamartia* of patricide and incest. (*See also* **Recognition**.)

Heptameter A verse meter consisting of seven metrical feet, or seven primary stresses, per line.

Hero The central character in a narrative. The term is derived from the Greek epic tradition, in which *heroes* were the leading warriors among the princes. By extension, *hero* and *heroine* have come to mean the principal male and female figures in a narrative or dramatic literary work, although many today call protagonists of either sex *heroes*. When a critic terms the protagonist a *hero*, the choice of words often implies a positive moral assessment of the character. (*See also* **Antihero**.)

Heroic couplet *See* **Closed couplet**.

Hexameter A verse meter consisting of six metrical feet, or six primary stresses, per line.

High comedy A comic genre evoking so-called intellectual or thoughtful laughter from an audience that remains emotionally detached from the play's depiction of the folly, pretense, and incongruity of human behavior. The French playwright Molière and the English dramatists of the Restoration period developed a special form of high comedy in the **comedy of manners**, focused on the social relations and amorous intrigues of sophisticated upper-class men and women, conducted through witty repartee and verbal combat.

High diction Also called **formal English**. The heightened, impersonal language of educated persons, usually only written, although possibly spoken on dignified occasions. (*See also* **Levels of diction**.)

Historical criticism The practice of analyzing a literary work by investigating the social, cultural, and intellectual context that produced it—a context that necessarily includes the artist's biography and milieu. Historical critics strive to recreate the exact meaning and impact a work had on its original audience.

Historical fiction A type of fiction in which the narrative is set in another time or place. In historical fiction, the author usually attempts to recreate a faithful picture of daily life during the period. For example, Robert Graves's *I, Claudius* depicts the lives of the ancient Roman ruling class in the early Imperial age. Historical fiction sometimes introduces well-known figures from the past. More often it places imaginary characters in a carefully reconstructed version of a particular historical era.

Horror A literary genre that attempts to frighten the reader by use of suspense, shock, and fear. It often places its protagonist in a mysteriously uncomfortable situation that gradually becomes more terrifying as the story progresses.

Hubris Overweening pride, outrageous behavior, or the insolence that leads to ruin, hubris was in the Greek moral vocabulary the antithesis of moderation or rectitude. Creon, in Sophocles's *Antigone*, is a good example of a character brought down by his hubris.

Hyperbole *See* **Overstatement**.

Iamb A metrical foot in verse in which an unaccented syllable is followed by an accented one, as in "ca-*ress*" or "a *cat*" ($\smile\,'$). The iambic measure is the most common meter used in English poetry.

Iambic meter A verse meter consisting of a specific recurring number of iambic feet per line. (*See also* **Iamb, Iambic pentameter**.)

Iambic pentameter The most common meter in English verse—five iambic feet per line. Many fixed forms, such as the sonnet and heroic couplets, are written in iambic pentameter. Unrimed iambic pentameter is called **blank verse**.

Identity poetics An approach to writing poetry that scrutinizes the forces that help shape the poet's identity, which may include ethnic background, family, race, gender, sexual orientation, religion, economic status, and age.

Image A word or series of words that refers to any sensory experience (usually sight, although also sound, smell, touch, or taste). An image is a direct or literal recreation of physical experience and adds immediacy to literary language.

Imagery The collective set of images in a poem or other literary work.

Impartial omniscience Refers to an omniscient narrator who, although he or she presents the thoughts and actions of the characters, does not judge them or comment on them. (Contrasts with **Editorial omniscience**.)

Implied metaphor A metaphor that uses neither connectives nor the verb *to be*. If we say, "John crowed over his victory," we imply metaphorically that John is a rooster but do not say so specifically. (*See also* **Metaphor**.)

In medias res A Latin phrase meaning "in the midst of things" that refers to a narrative device of beginning a story midway in the events it depicts (usually at an exciting or significant moment) before explaining the context or preceding actions. Epic poems such as Virgil's *Aeneid* or John Milton's *Paradise Lost* commonly begin *in medias res*, but the technique is also found in modern fiction.

Initial alliteration *See* **Alliteration**.

Initiation story Also called **Coming-of-age story**. A narrative in which the main character, usually a child or adolescent, undergoes an important experience or rite of passage—often a difficult or disillusioning one—that prepares him or her for adulthood. James Joyce's "Araby" is a classic example of an initiation story.

Innocent narrator Also called **naive narrator**. A character who fails to understand all the implications of the story he or she tells. Of course, virtually any narrator has some degree of innocence or naiveté, but the innocent narrator—often a child or childlike adult—is used by an author trying to generate irony, sympathy, or pity by creating a gap between what the narrator knows and what the reader knows. Mark Twain's Huckleberry Finn—despite his mischievous nature—is an example of an innocent narrator.

Interior monologue An extended presentation of a character's thoughts in a narrative. Usually written in the present tense and printed without quotation marks, an interior monologue reads as if the character were speaking aloud to himself or herself, for the reader to overhear. A famous example of interior monologue comes at the end of *Ulysses* when James Joyce gives us the rambling memories and reflections of Molly Bloom.

Internal alliteration *See* **Alliteration**.

Internal refrain A refrain that appears within a stanza, generally in a position that stays fixed throughout a poem. (*See also* **Refrain**.)

Internal rime Rime that occurs within a line of poetry, as opposed to **end rime**. Read aloud, these Wallace Stevens lines are rich in internal rime: "Chieftain Iffucan of Azcan in caftan / Of tan with henna hackles, halt!" (from "Bantams in Pine-Woods").

Ironic point of view The perspective of a character or narrator whose voice or position is rich in ironic contradictions. (*See also* **Irony**.)

Irony A literary device in which a discrepancy of meaning is masked beneath the surface of the language. Irony is present when a writer says one thing but means something quite the opposite. There are many kinds of irony, but the two major varieties are **verbal irony** (in which the discrepancy is contained in words) and **situational irony** (in which the discrepancy exists when something is about to happen to a character or characters who expect the opposite outcome). (*See also* **Cosmic irony, Irony of fate, Sarcasm, Verbal irony**.)

Irony of fate A type of situational irony that can be used for either tragic or comic purposes. Irony of fate is the discrepancy between actions and their results, between what characters deserve and what they get, between appearance and reality. In Sophocles's tragedy, for instance, Oedipus unwittingly fulfills the prophecy even as he takes the actions a morally good man would take to avoid it. (*See also* **Cosmic irony**.)

Italian sonnet Also called **Petrarchan sonnet**, a sonnet with the following rime pattern for the first eight lines (the **octave**): *a b b a a b b a*; the final six lines (the **sestet**) may follow any pattern of rimes, as long as it does not end in a couplet. The poem traditionally turns, or shifts in mood or tone, after the octave. (*See also* **Sonnet**.)

Katharsis, **catharsis** Often translated as "purgation" or "purification," the term is drawn from the last element of Aristotle's definition of tragedy, relating to the final cause or purpose of tragic art. Catharsis generally refers to the feeling of emotional release or calm the spectator feels at the end of tragedy. In Aristotle *katharsis* is the final effect of the playwright's skillful use of plotting, character, and poetry to elicit pity and fear from the audience. Through *katharsis*, drama taught the audience compassion for the vulnerabilities of others and schooled it in justice and other civic virtues.

Legend A traditional narrative handed down through popular oral tradition to illustrate and celebrate a remarkable character or an important event, or to explain the unexplainable. Legends, unlike other folktales, claim to be true and usually take place in real locations, often with genuine historical figures.

Levels of diction In English, there are conventionally four basic levels of formality in word choice, or four levels of diction. From the least formal to the most elevated they are **low diction, colloquial English, middle diction**, and **high diction**. (*See also* **Diction**.)

Limerick A short and usually comic verse form of five anapestic lines usually rhyming *a a b b a*. The first, second, and fifth lines traditionally have three stressed syllables each; the third and fourth have two stresses each (3, 3, 2, 2, 3).

Limited omniscience Also called *third-person limited point of view*. A type of point of view in which the narrator sees into the minds of some but not all of the characters. Most typically, limited omniscience sees through the eyes of one major or minor character. In limited omniscience, the author can compromise between the immediacy of first-person narration and the flexibility of third person.

Literary ballad Ballad not meant for singing, written for literate readers by sophisticated poets rather than arising from the anonymous oral tradition. (*See also* **Ballad**.)

Literary epic A crafted imitation of the oral folk epic written by an author living in a society where writing has been invented. Examples of the literary epic are *The Aeneid* by Virgil and *The Divine Comedy* by Dante Alighieri. (*See also* **Folk epic**.)

Literary genre *See* **Genre**.

Literary theory Literary criticism that tries to formulate general principles rather than discuss specific texts. Theory operates at a high level of abstraction and often focuses on understanding basic issues of language, communication, art, interpretation, culture, and ideological content.

Local color The use of specific regional material—unique customs, dress, habits, and speech patterns of ordinary people—to create atmosphere or realism in a literary work.

Locale The location where a story takes place.

Low comedy A comic style arousing laughter through jokes, slapstick humor, sight gags, and boisterous clowning. Unlike **high comedy**, it has little intellectual appeal. (*See also* **Comedy**.)

Low diction The language of the common people. Not necessarily containing foul or inappropriate language, it refers simply to unschooled, everyday speech. It is also called **vulgate**, a term that comes from the Latin word *vulgus*, "mob" or "common people." (*See also* **Levels of diction**.)

Lyric A short poem expressing the thoughts and feelings of a single speaker. Often written in the first person, lyric poetry traditionally has a songlike immediacy and emotional force.

Madrigal A short secular song for three or more voices arranged in counterpoint. The madrigal is often about love or pastoral themes. It originated in Italy in the fourteenth century and enjoyed great success during the Elizabethan Age.

Magic realism Also called **magical realism**. A type of contemporary narrative in which the magical and the mundane are mixed in an overall context of realistic storytelling. The term was coined by Cuban novelist Alejo Carpentier in 1949 to describe the matter-of-fact combination of the fantastic and everyday in Latin American fiction. Magic realism has become the standard name for an international trend in contemporary fiction such as Gabriel García Márquez's *One Hundred Years of Solitude*.

Masculine rime Either a rime of one-syllable words (as in *fox* and *socks*) or—in polysyllabic words—a rime on the stressed final syllables: con-*trive* and sur-*vive*. (*See also* **Feminine rime**.)

Masks In Latin, *personae*. In classical Greek theater, full facial masks made of leather, linen, or light wood, with headdress, allowed male actors to embody the conventionalized characters (or *dramatis personae*) of the tragic and comic stage. Later, in the seventeenth and eighteenth centuries, stock characters of the *commedia dell' arte* wore characteristic half masks made of leather. (*See also* **Persona**.)

Melodrama Originally a stage play featuring background music and sometimes songs to underscore the emotional mood of each scene. Melodramas were notoriously weak in characterization and motivation but famously strong on action, suspense, and passion. Melodramatic characters were stereotyped villains, heroes, and young lovers. When the term *melodrama* is applied to fiction, it is almost inevitably a negative criticism implying that the author has sacrificed psychological depth and credibility for emotional excitement and adventurous plotting.

Metafiction Fiction that consciously explores its own nature as a literary creation. The Greek word *meta* means "upon"; metafiction consequently is a mode of narrative that does not try to create the illusion of verisimilitude but delights in its own fictional nature, often by speculating on the story it is telling. The term is usually associated with late-twentieth-century writers like John Barth, Italo Calvino, and Jorge Luis Borges.

Metaphor A statement that one thing *is* something else, which, in a literal sense, it is not. By asserting that a thing is something else, a metaphor creates a close association between the two entities and usually underscores some important similarity between them. An example of metaphor is "Richard is a pig."

Meter A recurrent, regular, rhythmic pattern in verse. When stresses recur at fixed intervals, the result is meter. Traditionally, meter has been the basic organizational device of world poetry. There are many existing meters, each identified by the different patterns of recurring sounds. In English most common meters involve the arrangement of stressed and unstressed syllables.

Metonymy Figure of speech in which the name of a thing is substituted for that of another closely associated with it. For instance, in saying "The White House decided," one could mean that the president decided.

Middle diction Also called **general English**. The ordinary speech of educated native speakers. Most literate speech and writing is middle diction. Its diction is more educated than **colloquial English**, yet not as elevated as **high diction**. (*See also* **Levels of diction**.)

Minimalist fiction Contemporary fiction written in a deliberately flat, unemotional tone and an appropriately unadorned style. Minimalist fiction often relies more on dramatic action, scene, and dialogue than complex narration or authorial summary. Examples of minimalist fiction can be found in the short stories of Raymond Carver and Bobbie Ann Mason.

Mixed metaphor A metaphor that—usually unconsciously—trips over another metaphor already in the statement. Mixed metaphors are the result of combining two or more incompatible metaphors, resulting in ridiculousness or nonsense. For example, "Mary was such a tower of strength that she breezed her way through all the work" ("towers" do not "breeze").

Monologue An extended speech by a single character. The term originated in drama, where it describes a solo speech that has listeners (as opposed to a **soliloquy**, where the character speaks only to himself or herself). A short story or even a novel can be written in monologue form if it is an unbroken speech by one character to another silent character or characters.

Monometer A verse meter consisting of one metrical foot, or one primary stress, per line.

Monosyllabic foot A foot, or unit of meter, that contains only one syllable.

Moral A paraphrasable message or lesson implied or directly stated in a literary work. Commonly, a moral is stated at the end of a fable.

Motif An element that recurs significantly throughout a narrative. A motif can be an image, idea, theme, situation, or action (and was first commonly used as a musical term for a recurring melody or melodic fragment). A motif can also refer to an element that recurs across many literary works, like a beautiful lady in medieval romances who turns out to be an evil fairy or three questions that are asked a protagonist to test his or her wisdom.

Motivation What a character in a story or drama wants; the reasons an author provides for a character's actions. Motivation can be either *explicit* (in which reasons are specifically stated in a story) or *implicit* (in which reasons are only hinted at or partially revealed).

Myth A traditional narrative of anonymous authorship that arises out of a culture's oral tradition. The characters in traditional myths are usually gods or heroic figures. Myths characteristically explain the origins of things—gods, people, places, plants, animals, and natural events—usually from a cosmic view. A culture's values and belief systems are traditionally passed from generation to generation in myth. In literature, myth may also refer to boldly imagined narratives that embody primal truths about life. Myth is usually differentiated from legend, which has a specific historical base.

Mythological criticism The practice of analyzing a literary work by looking for recurrent universal patterns. Mythological criticism explores the artist's common humanity by tracing how the individual imagination uses myths and symbols that are shared by different cultures and epochs.

Mythology The body of myths belonging to a particular culture.

Naive narrator *See* **Innocent narrator**.

Narrative poem A poem that tells a story. Narrative is one of the four traditional modes of poetry, along with lyric, dramatic, and didactic. **Ballads** and **epics** are two common forms of narrative poetry.

Narrator A voice or character that provides the reader with information and insight about the characters and incidents in a narrative. A narrator's perspective and personality can greatly affect how a story is told. (*See also* **Omniscient narrator**, **Point of view**.)

Naturalism A type of fiction or drama in which the characters are presented as products or victims of environment and heredity. Naturalism, considered an extreme form of realism, customarily depicts the social, psychological, and economic milieu of the primary characters. Naturalism was first formally developed by French novelist Émile Zola in the 1870s. In promoting naturalism as a theory of animal behavior, Zola urged the modeling of naturalist literature and drama on the scientific case study. The writer, like the scientist, was to record objective reality with detachment; events onstage should be reproduced with sufficient exactness to demonstrate the strict laws of material causality. Important American Naturalists include Jack London, Theodore Dreiser, and Stephen Crane. (*See also* **Realism**.)

New Formalism A term for a contemporary literary movement (begun around 1980) in which young poets began using rime, meter, and narrative again. New Formalists attempt to write poetry that appeals to an audience beyond academia. Timothy Steele, Vikram Seth, R. S. Gwynn, David Mason, A. E. Stallings, and Marilyn Nelson are poets commonly associated with the movement.

New naturalism A term describing some American plays of the 1970s and 1980s, frankly showing the internal and external forces that shape the lives of unhappy, alienated, dehumanized, and often impoverished characters. Examples include the plays of Sam Shepard, August Wilson, and David Mamet.

Nonfiction novel A genre in which actual events are presented as a novel-length story, using the techniques of fiction (flashback, interior monologues, etc.). Truman Capote's *In Cold Blood* (1966), which depicts a multiple murder and subsequent trial in Kansas, is a classic example of this modern genre.

Nonparticipant narrator A narrator who does not appear in the story as a character but is capable of revealing the thoughts and motives of one or more characters. A nonparticipant narrator is also capable of moving from place to place in order to describe action and report dialogue. (*See also* **Omniscient narrator**.)

Novel An extended work of fictional prose narrative. The term *novel* usually implies a book-length narrative (as compared to more compact forms of prose fiction such as the short story). Because of its extended length, a novel usually has more characters, more varied scenes, and a broader coverage of time than a short story.

Novella In modern terms, a prose narrative longer than a short story but shorter than a novel (approximately 30,000 to 50,000 words). Unlike a short story, a novella is long enough to be published independently as a brief book. Classic modern novellas include Franz Kafka's *The Metamorphosis*, Joseph Conrad's *Heart of Darkness*, and Thomas Mann's *Death in Venice*. During the Renaissance, however, the term *novella* originally referred to short prose narratives such as those found in Giovanni Boccaccio's *Decameron*.

Objective point of view *See* **Dramatic point of view**.

Observer A type of first-person narrator who is relatively detached from or plays only a minor role in the events described.

Octameter A verse meter consisting of eight metrical feet, or eight primary stresses, per line.

Octave A stanza of eight lines. *Octave* is a term usually used when speaking of sonnets to indicate the first eight-line section of the poem, as distinct from the *sestet* (the final six lines). Some poets also use octaves as separate stanzas as in W. B. Yeats's "Sailing to Byzantium," which employs the *ottava rima* ("eighth rime") stanza—*a b a b a b c c*.

Off rime *See* **Slant rime**.

Omniscient narrator Also called **all-knowing narrator**. A narrator who has the ability to move freely through the consciousness of any character. The omniscient narrator also has complete knowledge of all of the external events in a story. (*See also* **Nonparticipant narrator**.)

Onomatopoeia A literary device that attempts to represent a thing or action by a word that imitates the sound associated with it (e.g., *crash, bang, pitter-patter*).

Open dénouement One of the two conventional types of dénouement or resolution. In open dénouement, the author ends a narrative with a few loose ends, or unresolved matters, on which the reader is left to speculate. (*See also* **Closed dénouement**.)

Open form Verse that has no set formal scheme—no meter, rime, or even set stanzaic pattern. Open form is always in free verse. (*See also* **Free verse**.)

Oral tradition The tradition within a culture that transmits narratives by word of mouth from one generation to another. Fables, folktales, ballads, and songs are examples of some types of narratives found originally in an oral tradition.

Orchestra In classical Greek theater architecture, "the place for dancing," a circular, level performance space at the base of a horseshoe-shaped amphitheater, where twelve, then later (in Sophocles's plays) fifteen, young, masked, male chorus members sang and danced the odes interspersed between dramatic episodes making up the classical Greek play. Today the orchestra refers to the ground floor seats in a theater or concert hall.

Overstatement Also called **hyperbole**. Exaggeration used to emphasize a point.

Parable A brief, usually allegorical narrative that teaches a moral. The parables found in Christian literature, such as "The Parable of the Prodigal Son" (Luke 15:11–32), are classic examples of the form. In parables, unlike fables (where the moral is explicitly stated within the narrative), the moral themes are implicit and can often be interpreted in several ways. Modern parables can be found in the works of Franz Kafka and Jorge Luis Borges.

Paradox A statement that at first strikes one as self-contradictory, but that on reflection reveals some deeper sense. Paradox is often achieved by a play on words.

Parallelism An arrangement of words, phrases, clauses, or sentences side by side in a similar grammatical or structural way. Parallelism organizes ideas in a way that demonstrates their coordination to the reader.

Paraphrase The restatement in one's own words of what we understand a literary work to say. A paraphrase is similar to a summary, although not as brief or simple.

Parody A mocking imitation of a literary work or individual author's style, usually for comic effect. A parody typically exaggerates distinctive features of the original for humorous purposes.

Participant narrator A narrator who participates as a character within a story. (*See also* **First-person narrator**.)

Pentameter A verse meter consisting of five metrical feet, or five primary stresses, per line. In English, the most common form of pentameter is iambic.

Peripeteia Anglicized as *peripety*, Greek for "sudden change." A reversal of fortune; in a play's plotting, a sudden change of circumstance affecting the protagonist, often also including a reversal of intent on the protagonist's part. The play's peripety occurs usually when a certain result is expected and instead its opposite effect is produced. For example, at the beginning of *Oedipus*, the protagonist expects to discover the identity of the murderer of Laius. However, after the Corinthian messenger informs Oedipus that he was adopted, the hero's intent changes to encompass the search for his true parentage. A comedy's peripety restores a character to good fortune, when a moment in which the worst can happen is suddenly turned into happy circumstance.

Persona Latin for "mask." A fictitious character created by an author to be the speaker of a poem, story, or novel. A persona is always the narrator of the work and not merely a character in it.

Personification A figure of speech in which a thing, an animal, or an abstract term is endowed with human characteristics. Personification allows an author to dramatize the nonhuman world in tangibly human terms.

Petrarchan sonnet *See* **Italian sonnet**.

Picaresque A type of narrative, usually a novel, that presents the life of a likable scoundrel who is at odds with respectable society. The narrator of a picaresque was originally a *picaro* (Spanish for "rascal" or "rogue") who recounts his adventures tricking the rich and gullible. This type of narrative rarely has a tight plot, and the episodes or adventures follow in a loose chronological order.

Picture-frame stage Developed in sixteenth-century Italian playhouses, the picture-frame stage held the action within a proscenium arch, a gateway standing "in front of the scenery" (as the word *proscenium* indicates). The proscenium framed painted scene panels (receding into the middle distance) designed to give the illusion of three-dimensional perspective. Only one seat in the auditorium, reserved for the theater's royal patron or sponsor, enjoyed the complete perspectivist illusion. The raised and framed stage separated actors from the audience and the world of the play from the real world of the auditorium. Picture-frame stages became the norm throughout Europe and England up into the twentieth century.

Play review A critical account of a performance, providing the basic facts of the production, a brief plot summary, and an evaluation (with adequate rationale) of the chief elements of performance, including the acting, the direction, scene and light design, and the script, especially if the play is new or unfamiliar.

Plot The particular arrangement of actions, events, and situations that unfold in a narrative. A plot is not merely the general story of a narrative but the author's artistic pattern made from the parts of the narrative, including the exposition, complications, climax, and dénouement. How an author chooses to construct the plot determines the way the reader experiences the story. Manipulating a plot, therefore, can be the author's most important expressive device when writing a story. More than just a story made up of episodes or a bare synopsis of the temporal order of events, the plotting is the particular embodiment of an action that allows the audience to see the causal relationship between the parts of the action. (*See also* **Climax**, **Falling action**, **Rising action**.)

Poetic diction Strictly speaking, any language deemed suitable for verse, but the term generally refers to elevated language intended for poetry rather than common use. Poetic diction often refers to the ornate language used in literary periods such as the Augustan age, when authors employed a highly specialized vocabulary for their verse. (*See also* **Diction**.)

Point of view The perspective from which a story is told. There are many types of point of view, including first-person narrator (a story in which the narrator is a participant in the action) and third-person narrator (a type of narration in which the narrator is a nonparticipant).

Portmanteau word An artificial word that combines parts of other words to express some combination of their qualities. Sometimes portmanteau words prove so useful that they become part of the standard language. For example, *smog* from *smoke* and *fog*; or *brunch* from *breakfast* and *lunch*.

Print culture A culture that depends primarily on the printed word—in books, magazines, and newspapers—to distribute and preserve information. In recent decades the electronic media have taken over much of this role from print.

Projective verse Charles Olson's theory that poets compose by listening to their own breathing and using it as a rhythmic guide rather than poetic meter or form. (*See also* **Open form**.)

Proscenium arch Separating the auditorium from the raised stage and the world of the play, the architectural picture frame or gateway "standing in front of the scenery" (as the word *proscenium* indicates) in traditional European theaters from the sixteenth century on.

Prose poem Poetic language printed in prose paragraphs but displaying the careful attention to sound, imagery, and figurative language characteristic of poetry.

Prosody The study of metrical structures in poetry. (*See also* **Scansion**.)

Protagonist The central character in a literary work. The protagonist usually initiates the main action of the story, often in conflict with the antagonist. (*See also* **Antagonist**.)

Psalms Sacred songs, usually referring to the 150 Hebrew poems collected in the Old Testament.

Psychological criticism The practice of analyzing a literary work through investigating three major areas: the nature of literary genius, the psychological study of a particular artist, and the analysis of fictional characters. This methodology uses the analytical tools of psychology and psychoanalysis to understand the underlying motivations and meanings of a literary work.

Pulp fiction A type of formulaic and quickly written fiction originally produced for cheap mass circulation magazines. The term *pulp* refers to the inexpensive wood-pulp paper developed in the mid-nineteenth century on which these magazines were printed. Most pulp fiction journals printed only melodramatic genre work—westerns, science fiction, romance, horror, adventure tales, or crime stories.

Pun A play on words in which one word is substituted for another of similar or identical sound but of very different meaning.

Purgation See *Katharsis*.

Quantitative meter A meter constructed on the principle of vowel length. Because such quantities are difficult to hear in English, this meter remains slightly foreign to our language. Classical Greek and Latin poetry were written in quantitative meters.

Quatrain A stanza consisting of four lines. Quatrains are the most common stanzas used in English-language poetry.

Rap A popular style of music that emerged in the 1980s in which lyrics are spoken or chanted over a steady beat, usually sampled or prerecorded. Rap lyrics are almost always rimed and very rhythmic—syncopating a heavy metrical beat in a manner similar to jazz. Originally an African American form, rap is now international. In that way, rap can be seen as a form of popular poetry.

Reader-response criticism The practice of analyzing a literary work by describing what happens in the reader's mind while interpreting the text. Reader-response critics believe that no literary text exists independently of readers' interpretations and that there is no single fixed interpretation of any literary work.

Realism An attempt to reproduce faithfully the surface appearance of life, especially that of ordinary people in everyday situations. As a literary term, *realism* has two meanings—one general, the other historical. In a general sense, realism refers to the representation of characters, events, and settings in ways that the spectator will consider plausible, based on consistency and likeness to type. This sort of realism does not necessarily depend on elaborate factual description or documentation but more on the author's ability to draft plots and characters within a conventional framework of social, economic, and psychological reality. In a historical sense, Realism (usually capitalized) refers to a movement in nineteenth-century European literature and theater that rejected the idealism, elitism, and romanticism of earlier verse dramas and prose fiction in an attempt to represent life truthfully. Realist literature customarily focused on the middle class (and occasionally the working class) rather than the aristocracy, and it used social and economic detail to create an accurate account of human behavior. Realism began in France with Honoré de Balzac, Gustave Flaubert, and Guy de Maupassant and then moved internationally. Other major Realists include Leo Tolstoy, Henry James, Anton Chekhov, and Edith Wharton.

Recognition In tragic plotting, the moment that occurs when ignorance gives way to knowledge, illusion to disillusion. In Aristotle's *Poetics*, this is usually a recognition of blood ties or kinship between the persons involved in grave actions involving suffering. According to Aristotle, the ideal moment of recognition coincides with *peripeteia* or reversal of fortune. The classic example occurs in *Oedipus* when Oedipus discovers that he had unwittingly killed his own father when defending himself at the crossroads and later married his own mother when assuming the Theban throne. (*See also* **Hamartia**, **Katharsis**, **Peripeteia**.)

Refrain A word, phrase, line, or stanza repeated at intervals in a song or poem. The repeated chorus of a song is a refrain.

Regionalism The literary representation of a specific locale that consciously uses the particulars of geography, custom, history, folklore, or speech. In regional narratives, the locale plays a crucial role in the presentation and progression of a story that could not be moved to another setting without artistic loss. Usually, regional narratives take place at some distance from the literary capital of a culture, often in small towns or rural areas. Examples of American regionalism can be found in the writing of Willa Cather, Kate Chopin, William Faulkner, and Eudora Welty.

Resolution The final part of a narrative, the concluding action or actions that follow the climax. (*See also* **Conclusion**, **Dénouement**.)

Retrospect *See* **Flashback**.

Reversal *See* **Peripeteia**.

Rhythm The pattern of stresses and pauses in a poem. A fixed and recurring rhythm in a poem is called **meter**.

Rime, Rhyme Two or more words that contain an identical or similar vowel sound, usually accented, with following consonant sounds (if any) identical as well: *queue* and *stew*, *prairie schooner* and *piano tuner*. (*See also* **Consonance**, **Exact rime**.)

Rime scheme, Rhyme scheme Any recurrent pattern of rime within an individual poem or fixed form. A rime scheme is usually described by using small letters to represent each end rime—*a* for the first rime, *b* for the second, and so on. The rime scheme of a stanza of **common meter** or hymn meter, for example, would be notated as *a b a b*.

Rising action That part of the play or narrative, including the exposition, in which events start moving toward a climax. In the rising action the protagonist usually faces the complications of the plot to reach his or her goal. In *Hamlet*, the rising action develops the conflict between Hamlet and Claudius, with Hamlet succeeding in controlling the course of events. Because the mainspring of the play's first half is the mystery of Claudius's guilt, the rising action reaches a climax when Hamlet proves the king's guilt by the device of the play within a play (3.2—the "mousetrap" scene), when Hamlet as heroic avenger has positive proof of Claudius's guilt.

Rising meter A meter whose movement rises from an unstressed syllable (or syllables) to a stressed syllable (for-*get*, De-*troit*). Iambic and anapestic are examples of rising meter.

Romance In general terms, romance is a narrative mode that employs exotic adventure, surprise, and wish fulfillment, in contrast to the more realistic depictions of character and action that we associate with the traditional definition of a *novel*. Most popular fiction genres—such as **detective, horror, fantasy,** and **science fiction**—develop from this mode.

Romantic comedy A form of comic drama in which the plot focuses on one or more pairs of young lovers who overcome difficulties to achieve a happy ending (usually marriage). Shakespeare's *A Midsummer Night's Dream* is a classic example of the genre.

Rondel A thirteen-line English verse form consisting of three rimed stanzas with a refrain.

Round character A term coined by English novelist E. M. Forster to describe a complex character who is presented in depth and detail in a narrative. Round characters are those who change significantly during the course of a narrative. Most often, round characters are the central characters in a narrative. (*See also* **Flat character.**)

Rubai An ancient Persian stanza form (*rubaiyat* is the plural) consisting of four lines, usually rimed *a a b a*. The most famous classical writer of *rubaiyat* was Omar Khayyam, whose verses were translated into English by Edward FitzGerald and remain internationally popular.

Run-on line A line of verse that does not end in punctuation, but carries on grammatically to the next line. Such lines are read aloud with only a slight pause at the end. A run-on line is also called *enjambment*.

Sarcasm A conspicuously bitter form of irony in which the ironic statement is designed to hurt or mock its target. (*See also* **Irony.**)

Satiric comedy A genre using derisive humor to ridicule human weakness and folly or attack political injustices and incompetence. Satiric comedy often focuses on ridiculing characters or killjoys, who resist the festive mood of comedy. Such characters, called humors, are often characterized by one dominant personality trait or ruling obsession.

Satiric poetry Poetry that blends criticism with humor to convey a message. Satire characteristically uses irony to make its points. Usually, its tone is one of detached amusement, withering contempt, and implied superiority.

Satyr play A type of Greek comic play that was performed after the tragedies at the City Dionysia, the principal civic and religious festival of Athens. The playwrights winning the right to perform their works in the festival wrote three tragedies and one satyr play to form the traditional tetralogy, or group of four. The structure of a satyr play was similar to tragedy's. Its subject matter, treated in burlesque, was drawn from myth or the epic cycles. Its chorus was composed of satyrs (half human and half horse or goat) under the leadership of Silenus, the adoptive father of Dionysius. Rascals and revelers, satyrs represented wild versions of humanity, opposing the values of civilized men. Euripides's *Cyclops* is the only complete surviving example of the genre.

Scansion A practice used to describe rhythmic patterns in a poem by separating the metrical feet, counting the syllables, marking the accents, and indicating the pauses. Scansion can be very useful in analyzing the sound of a poem and how it should be read aloud.

Scene In drama, the scene is a division of the action in an act of the play. There is no universal convention as to what constitutes a scene, and the practice differs by playwright and period. Usually, a scene represents a single dramatic action that builds to a climax (often ending in the entrance or exit of a major character). In this last sense of a vivid and unified action, the term can be applied to fiction.

Science fiction A popular genre that presents a technological innovation (such as time travel) or scientific assumption (alien races) and then logically develops a story from that imaginary premise.

Selective omniscience The point of view that sees the events of a narrative through the eyes of a single character. The selectively omniscient narrator is usually a non-participant narrator.

Sentimentality A usually pejorative description of the quality of a literary work that tries to convey great emotion but fails to give the reader sufficient grounds for sharing it.

Sestet A poem or stanza of six lines. *Sestet* is a term usually used when speaking of sonnets, to indicate the final six-line section of the poem, as distinct from the octave (the first eight lines). (*See also* **Sonnet.**)

Sestina A complex verse form ("song of sixes") in which six end words are repeated in a prescribed order through six stanzas. A sestina ends with an **envoy** of three lines in which all six words appear—for a total of thirty-nine lines. Originally used by French and Italian poets, the sestina has become a popular modern form in English.

Setting The time and place of a literary work. The setting may also include the climate and even the social, psychological, or spiritual state of the participants.

Shakespearean sonnet *See* **English sonnet.**

Short Story A prose narrative too brief to be published as a separate volume—as novellas and novels frequently are. The short story is usually a focused narrative that presents one or two main characters involved in a single compelling action.

Simile A comparison of two things, indicated by some connective, usually *like, as, than,* or a verb such as *resembles.* A simile usually compares two things that initially seem unlike but are shown to have a significant resemblance. "Cool as a cucumber" and "My love is like a red, red rose" are examples of similes.

Situational Irony *See* **Irony.**

Skene In classical Greek staging of the fifth century B.C., the temporary wooden stage building in which actors changed masks and costumes when changing roles.

Its facade, with double center doors and possibly two side doors, served as the setting for action taking place before a palace, temple, cave, or other interior space.

Slack syllable An unstressed syllable in a line of verse.

Slant rime A rime in which the final consonant sounds are the same but the vowel sounds are different, as in letter and litter, bone and bean. Slant rime may also be called *near rime, off rime,* or *imperfect rime.* (*See also* **Consonance.**)

Slapstick comedy A kind of farce, featuring pratfalls, pie-throwing, fisticuffs, and other violent action. It takes its name originally from the slapstick carried by the *commedia dell'arte*'s main servant type, Harlequin.

Sociological criticism The practice of analyzing a literary work by examining the cultural, economic, and political context in which it was written or received. Sociological criticism primarily explores the relationship between the artist and society.

Soliloquy In drama, a speech by a character alone onstage in which he or she utters his or her thoughts aloud. The soliloquy is important in drama because it gives the audience insight into a character's inner life, private motivations, and uncertainties.

Sonnet From the Italian *sonnetto*: "little song." A traditional and widely used verse form, especially popular for love poetry. The sonnet is a fixed form of fourteen lines, traditionally written in iambic pentameter, usually made up of an **octave** (the first eight lines) and a concluding **sestet** (six lines). There are, however, several variations, most conspicuously the Shakespearean, or English, sonnet, which consists of three quatrains and a concluding couplet. Most sonnets turn, or shift in tone or focus, after the first eight lines, although the placement may vary. (*See also* **English sonnet, Italian sonnet.**)

Spondee A metrical foot of verse containing two stressed syllables (′ ′) often substituted into a meter to create extra emphasis.

Stage business Nonverbal action that engages the attention of an audience. Expressing what cannot be said, stage business became a particularly important means of revealing the inner thoughts and feelings of a character in the development of Realism.

Stanza From the Italian, meaning "stopping-place" or "room." A recurring pattern of two or more lines of verse, poetry's equivalent to the paragraph in prose. The stanza is the basic organizational principle of most formal poetry.

Static character *See* **Flat character**.

Stock character A common or stereotypical character that occurs frequently in literature. Examples of stock characters are the mad scientist, the battle-scarred veteran, or the strong-but-silent cowboy. (*See also* **Archetype.**)

Stream of consciousness Not a specific technique, but a type of modern narration that uses various literary devices, especially interior monologue, in an attempt to duplicate the subjective and associative nature of human consciousness. Stream of consciousness often focuses on imagistic perception in order to capture the preverbal level of consciousness.

Stress An emphasis or accent placed on a syllable in speech. Clear pronunciation of polysyllabic words almost always depends on correct placement of their stress. (For instance, *de*-sert and de-*sert* are two different words and parts of speech, depending on their stress.) Stress is the basic principle of most English-language meter.

Style All the distinctive ways in which an author, genre, movement, or historical period uses language to create a literary work. An author's style depends on his or her characteristic use of diction, imagery, tone, syntax, and figurative language. Even sentence structure and punctuation can play a role in an author's style.

Subject The main topic of a poem, story, or play.

Subplot *See* **Double plot**.

Suggestion The power of a word to imply unspoken associations, in addition to its literal meaning.

Summary A brief condensation of the main idea or plot of a literary work. A summary is similar to a paraphrase, but less detailed.

Surrealism A modernist movement in art and literature that tries to organize art according to the irrational dictates of the unconscious mind. Founded by the French poet André Breton, Surrealism sought to reach a higher plane of reality by abandoning logic for the seemingly absurd connections made in dreams and other unconscious mental activities.

Suspense Enjoyable anxiety created in the reader by the author's handling of plot. When the outcome of events is unclear, the author's suspension of resolution intensifies the reader's interest—particularly if the plot involves characters to whom the reader or audience is sympathetic. Suspense is also created when the fate of a character is clear to the audience, but not to the character. The suspense results from the audience's anticipation of how and when the character will meet his or her inevitable fate.

Syllabic verse A verse form in which the poet establishes a pattern of a certain number of syllables to a line. Syllabic verse is the most common meter in most Romance languages such as Italian, French, and Spanish; it is less common in English because it is difficult to hear syllable count. Syllabic verse was used by several Modernist poets, most conspicuously Marianne Moore.

Symbol A person, place, or thing in a poem or narrative that suggests meanings beyond its literal sense. Symbol is related to allegory, but it works more complexly. In an allegory an object has a single additional significance. By contrast, a symbol usually contains multiple meanings and associations. In Herman Melville's *Moby-Dick*, for example, the great white whale does not have just a single significance but accrues powerful associations as the narrative progresses.

Symbolic act An action whose significance goes well beyond its literal meaning. In literature, symbolic acts usually involve some conscious or unconscious ritual element like rebirth, purification, forgiveness, vengeance, or initiation.

Symbolist movement An international literary movement that originated with nineteenth-century French poets such as Charles Baudelaire, Arthur Rimbaud, and Paul Verlaine. Symbolists aspired to make literature resemble music. They avoided direct statement and exposition for powerful evocation and suggestion. Symbolists also considered the poet as a seer who could look beyond the mundane aspects of the everyday world to capture visions of a higher reality.

Symbolists Members of the Symbolist movement.

Synecdoche The use of a significant part of a thing to stand for the whole of it or vice versa. To say *wheels* for *car* or *rime* for *poetry* are examples of synecdoche. (*See also* **Metonymy**.)

Synopsis A brief summary or outline of a story or dramatic work.

Tactile imagery A word or sequence of words that refers to the sense of touch. (*See also* **Imagery**.)

Tale A short narrative without a complex plot, the word originating from the Old English *talu*, or "speech." Tales are an ancient form of narrative found in folklore, and traditional tales often contain supernatural elements. A tale differs from a short story by its tendency toward less developed characters and linear plotting. British writer A. E. Coppard characterized the underlying difference by claiming that a story is something that is written and a tale is something that is told. The ambition of a tale is usually similar to that of a yarn: revelation of the marvelous rather than illumination of the everyday world.

Tall tale A humorous short narrative that provides a wildly exaggerated version of events. Originally an oral form, the tall tale assumes that its audience knows the narrator is distorting the events. The form is often associated with the American frontier.

Tercet A group of three lines of verse, usually all ending in the same rime. (*See also Terza rima.*)

Terminal refrain A refrain that appears at the end of each stanza in a song or poem. (*See also* **Refrain**.)

Terza rima A verse form made up of three-line stanzas that are connected by an overlapping rime scheme (*a b a, b c b, c d c, d c d*, etc.). Dante employs *terza rima* in *The Divine Comedy*.

Tetrameter A verse meter consisting of four metrical feet, or four primary stresses, per line.

Theater of the absurd Post–World War II European genre depicting the grotesquely comic plight of human beings thrown by accident into an irrational and meaningless world. The critic Martin Esslin coined the term to characterize plays by writers such as Samuel Beckett, Jean Genet, and Eugene Ionesco. Beckett's *Waiting for Godot* (1955), considered to be the greatest example of theater of the absurd, features in two nearly identical acts two tramps waiting almost without hope on a country road for an unidentified person, Godot. "Nothing happens, nobody comes, nobody goes, it's awful," one of them cries, perhaps echoing the unspoken thoughts of an audience confronted by a play that seemingly refuses to do anything.

Theme A generally recurring subject or idea conspicuously evident in a literary work. A short didactic work such as a fable may have a single obvious theme, but longer works can contain multiple themes. Not all subjects in a work can be considered themes, only the central subject or subjects.

Thesis sentence A summing up of the one main idea or argument that an essay or critical paper will embody.

Third-person narrator A type of narrator who is not a participant in the action of the story. In a third-person narrative the characters are referred to as "he," "she," or "they." Third-person narrators are most commonly omniscient, but the level of their knowledge may vary from total omniscience (the narrator knows everything about the characters and their lives) to limited omniscience (the narrator is limited to the perceptions of a single character).

Tone The attitude toward a subject conveyed in a literary work. No single stylistic device creates tone; it is the net result of the various elements an author brings to creating the work's feeling and manner. Tone may be playful, sarcastic, ironic, sad, solemn, or any other possible attitude. A writer's tone plays an important role in establishing the reader's relationship to the characters or ideas presented in a literary work.

Total omniscience A type of point of view in which the narrator knows everything about all of the characters and events in a story. A narrator with total omniscience can also move freely from one character to another. Generally, a totally omniscient narrative is written in the third person.

Traditional epic *See* **Folk epic**.

Tragedy The representation of serious and important actions that lead to a disastrous end for the protagonist. The final purpose of tragedy in Aristotle's formulation is to evoke *katharsis* by means of events involving pity and fear. A unified tragic action, from beginning to end, brings a morally good but not perfect tragic hero from happiness to unhappiness because of a mistaken act, to which he or she is led by a *hamartia*, an error in judgment. Tragic heroes move us to pity because their misfortunes are greater than they deserve, because they are not evil, having committed the fateful deed or deeds unwittingly and involuntarily. They also move us to fear, because we recognize in ourselves similar possibilities of error. We share with the tragic hero a common world of mischance. (*See also* **Tragic flaw**.)

Tragic flaw A fatal weakness or moral flaw in the protagonist that brings him or her to a bad end. Sometimes offered as an alternative translation of *hamartia*, in contrast to the idea that the tragic hero's catastrophe is caused by an error in judgment, the idea of a protagonist ruined by a tragic flaw makes more sense in relation to the Greek idea of *hubris*, commonly translated as "outrageous behavior," involving deliberate transgressions against moral or divine law.

Tragic irony A form of **dramatic irony** that ultimately arrives at some tragedy.

Tragicomedy A type of drama that combines elements of both tragedy and comedy. Usually, it creates potentially tragic situations that bring the protagonists to the brink of disaster but then ends happily. Tragicomedy can be traced as far back as the Renaissance (in plays such as Shakespeare's *Measure for Measure*), but it also refers to modern plays such as Chekhov's *Cherry Orchard* and Beckett's *Waiting for Godot*.

Transferred epithet A figure of speech in which the poet attributes some characteristic of a thing to another thing closely associated with it. Transferred epithet is a kind of metonymy. It usually places an adjective next to a noun in which the connection is not strictly logical (Milton's phrase "blind mouths" or Hart Crane's "nimble blue plateaus") but has expressive power.

Trick ending A surprising climax that depends on a quick reversal of the situation from an unexpected source. The success of a trick ending is relative to the degree in which the reader is surprised but not left incredulous when it occurs. The American writer O. Henry popularized this type of ending.

Trimeter A verse meter consisting of three metrical feet, or three primary stresses, per line.

Triolet A short lyric form of eight rimed lines borrowed from the French. The two opening lines are repeated according to a set pattern. Triolets are often playful, but dark lyric poems like Robert Bridge's "Triolet" demonstrate the form's flexibility.

Trochaic, trochee A metrical foot in which a stressed syllable is followed by an unstressed syllable ($'\smile$) as in the words *sum*-mer and *chor*-us. The trochaic meter is often associated with songs, chants, and magic spells in English.

Troubadours The minstrels of the late Middle Ages. Originally, troubadours were lyric poets living in southern France and northern Italy who sang to aristocratic audiences mostly of chivalry and love.

Understatement An ironic figure of speech that deliberately describes something in a way that is less than the true case.

Unities The three formal qualities recommended by Italian Renaissance literary critics to unify a plot in order to give it a cohesive and complete integrity. Traditionally, good plots honored the three unities—of action, time, and place. The action in neoclassical drama, therefore, was patterned by cause and effect to occur within a 24-hour period. The setting took place in one unchanging locale. In the *Poetics*, Aristotle urged only the requirement of unity of plot, with events patterned in a cause-and-effect relationship from beginning through middle to the end of the single action imitated.

Unreliable narrator A narrator who—intentionally or unintentionally—relates events in a subjective or distorted manner. The author usually provides some indication early on in such stories that the narrator is not to be completely trusted.

Verbal irony A statement in which the speaker or writer says the opposite of what is really meant. For example, a friend might comment, "How graceful you are!" after you trip clumsily on a stair.

Verisimilitude The quality in a literary work of appearing true to life. In fiction, verisimilitude is usually achieved by careful use of realistic detail in description, characterization, and dialogue. (*See also* **Realism**.)

Verse From the Latin *versum*, "to turn." Verse has two major meanings. First, it refers to any single line of poetry. Second, it refers to any composition in lines of more or less regular rhythm—in contrast to prose.

Vers libre *See* **Free verse**.

Villanelle A fixed form developed by French courtly poets of the Middle Ages in imitation of Italian folk song. A villanelle consists of six rimed stanzas in which two lines are repeated in a prescribed pattern.

Visual imagery A word or sequence of words that refers to the sense of sight or presents something one may see.

Vulgate *See* **Low diction**.

LITERARY CREDITS

FICTION

Achebe, Chinua. "Dead Men's Path," copyright © 1972, 1973 by Chinua Achebe; from GIRLS AT WAR: AND OTHER STORIES by Chinua Achebe. Used by permission of Doubleday, an imprint of the Knopf Doubleday Publishing Group, a division of Random House LLC. All rights reserved.

Alexie, Sherman. "This is What it Means to Say Phoenix, Arizona." Excerpt from THE LONE RANGER AND TONTO FISTFIGHT IN HEAVEN, copyright © 1993, 2005 by Sherman Alexie. Used by permission of Grove/Atlantic, Inc. Any third party use of this material, outside of this publication, is prohibited.

Allende, Isabel. "An Act of Vengeance" by Isabel Allende is reprinted with permission from the publisher of "SHORT STORIES BY LATIN AMERICAN WOMEN" by Cecilia Correa Zapata (©1990 Arte Publico Press—University of Houston).

Ammons, Elizabeth. "Biographical Echoes in 'The Yellow Wallpaper.'" Republished with permission of Oxford University Press, from CONFLICTING STORIES: AMERICAN WOMEN AT THE TURN OF THE CENTURY, by Elizabeth Ammons © 1991; permission conveyed through Copyright Clearance Center, Inc.

Anam, Tahmima. "Garments" by Tahmima Anam. Copyright © 2015 Tahmima Anam, used by permission of The Wylie Agency LLC.

Atwood, Margaret. "Happy Endings" from GOOD BONES AND SIMPLE MURDERS by Margaret Atwood, copyright © 1983, 1992, 1994, by O.W. Toad Ltd. Used by permission of Nan A. Talese, an imprint of the Knopf Doubleday Publishing Group, a division of Random House LLC. All rights reserved.

Baker, Houston A. "Patches: Quilts and Community in Alice Walker's 'Everyday Use,'" *Southern Review*, Vol. 21, Issue 3, pg 706. Copyright © 1985. Reprinted by permission.

Baldwin, James. "Sonny's Blues," © 1957 by James Baldwin was originally published in *Partisan Review*. Copyright renewed. Collected in GOING TO MEET THE MAN, published by Vintage Books. Used by arrangement with the James Baldwin Estate.

Baldwin, James. From "Notes of a Native Son" by James Baldwin, Copyright © 1955, renewed 1983, by James Baldwin. Reprinted by permission of Beacon Press, Boston.

Baudelaire, Charles. "Poe's Characters." Translated from preface "Histoires Extraordinaires" by Edgar Allan Poe. Paris A. Quantin, 1884.

Bidpai. "The Camel and His Friends." Retold in English by Arundhati Khanwalkar from the PANVHATANTRA. Used by permission.

Boyle, T. Corraghessan. "Greasy Lake," copyright © 1982 by T. Corraghessan Boyle; from GREASY LAKE AND OTHER STORIES by T. Coraghessan Boyle. Used by permission of Viking Books, an imprint of Penguin Publishing Group, a division of Penguin Random House LLC. All rights reserved.

Bradbury, Ray. "A Sound of Thunder." Reprinted by permission of Don Congdon Associates, Inc. Copyright © 1952 by the Crowell Collier Publishing Company, renewed 1980 by Ray Bradbury.

Bradbury, Ray. Quote from ZEN IN THE ART OF WRITING: ESSAYS ON CREATIVITY. Capra Press, 1990.

Camus, Albert. "The Guest" from EXILE AND THE KINGDOM by Albert Camus, translated by Justin O'Brien, copyright © 1957, 1958 by Alfred A. Knopf, a division of Penguin Random House LLC. Used by permission of Alfred A. Knopf, an imprint of the Knopf Doubleday Publishing Group, a division of Penguin Random House LLC. All rights reserved.

Carlson, Ron. "At the Jim Bridger" from AT THE JIM BRIDGER: STORIES by Ron Carlson. Copyright © 2002 by Ron Carlson. Reprinted by permission of Picador.

Carver, Raymond. "A Small, Good Thing— Church Little Rock" from CATHEDRAL. Knopf, 1983.

Carver, Raymond. "Cathedral" from CATHEDRAL by Raymond Carver, copyright © 1981, 1982, 1983 by Tess Gallagher. Used by permission of Alfred A. Knopf, an imprint of the Knopf Doubleday Publishing Group, a division of Penguin Random House LLC. All rights reserved.

Carver, Raymond. "On Writing" from FIRES: ESSAYS, POEMS, STORIES by Raymond Carver. Copyright 1968, 1969, 1970, 1971, 1972, 1973, 1974, 1975, 1976, 1977, 1978, 1979, 1980, 1981, 1982, 1983 by Raymond Carver. Copyright 1983, 1984 by the Estate of

Raymond Carver, used by permission of The Wylie Agency LLC.

Cather, Willa. "Paul's Case." Originally Published in *McClure's Magazine*, 1905.

Chopin, Kate. "The Story of an Hour." Originally published in *Vogue*, December 6, 1894.

Chopin, Kate. From "The Storm" by Kate Chopin from THE COMPLETE WORKS OF KATE CHOPIN. Copyright © 1969, Louisiana State University Press. Used by permission of Louisiana State University Press.

Christian, Barbara. Excerpt from EVERYDAY USE AND THE BLACK POWER MOVEMENT by Barbara Christian. Copyright © by Rutgers University Press. Used by permission of Rutgers University Press.

Cisneros, Sandra. "Barbie-Q," From WOMAN HOLLERING CREEK. Copyright © 1991 by Sandra Cisneros. Published by Vintage Books, a division of Penguin Random House, New York and originally in hardcover by Random House. By permission of Susan Bergholz Literary Services, New York, NY and Lamy, NM. All rights reserved.

Cowan, Louise S. Prose excerpt from "The Character of Mrs. Turpin in 'Revelation'" by Louise S. Cowan, copyright The Trinity Forum, Inc. Reprinted by permission.

Crane, Stephen "The Open Boat." 1897.

Defoe, Daniel. "Moll Flanders." Published by William Rufus Chetwood, 1722.

Dowling, Brendan. "I Graduated from the Library: An Interview with Ray Bradbury," by Brendan Dowling. Originally published Nov/Dec 2002 issue of *Public Libraries, Magazine of the American Library Association*.

Faulkner, William. "A Rose for Emily," copyright © 1930 and renewed 1958 by William Faulkner from COLLECTED STORIES OF WILLIAM FAULKNER by William Faulkner. Used by permission of Random House, an imprint and division of Random House LLC. All rights reserved.

Faulkner, William. "Barn Burning," copyright © 1950 by Random House, Inc. Copyright renewed 1977 by Jill Faulkner Summers; from COLLECTED STORIES OF WILLIAM FAULKNER by William Faulkner. Used by permission of Random House, an imprint and division of Random House LLC. All rights reserved.

Ference, (Fr.) Damian, "No Vague Believer (excerpt)" in *Dappled Things*, Pentecost 2012, Vol. 7, Issue 2, pp. 53–55, from "No Vague Believer: The Specificity of the Person of Christ According to Flannery O'Connor and Benedict XVI." Used by permission.

Fleenor, Juliann. Excerpt from "The Gothic Prism: Charlotte Perkins Gilman's Gothic Stories and Her Autobiography" in THE FEMALE GOTHIC by Juliann Fleenor (Montreal: Eden Press, 1983). Reprinted by permission.

Gaiman, Neil. "How to Talk to Girls at Parties" from FRAGILE THINGS: SHORT FICTIONS AND WONDERS by Neil Gaiman. Copyright © 2006 by Neil Gaiman. Reprinted by permission of Writers House LLC acting as agent for the author/illustrator.

Gilbert, Sandra M. and Gubar, Susan. "Imprisonment and Escape: The Psychology of Confinement" from THE MADWOMAN IN THE ATTIC: The Woman Writer and the Nineteenth-Century Literary Imagination. Published by Yale University Press. Copyright 1979 Yale University Press. All rights reserved. Reprinted with permission.

Gilman, Charlotte Perkins. "The Nervous Breakdown of Women." Originally published in *The Forerunner, 1916.*

Gilman, Charlotte Perkins. "The Yellow Wallpaper," "Why I Wrote the Yellow Wallpaper." Originally published in *The Forerunner*, October 1913.

Gioia, Dana; Tan, Amy. Excerpted from an interview with Amy Tan conducted by NEA for "The Big Read," August 7, 2006.

Gordimer, Nadine. "The Defeated." Reprinted by the permission of Russell & Volkening as agents for the author's estate. Copyright © 1952 by Nadine Gordimer.

Grimm, Jacob and Wilhelm Grimm. "Godfather Death," 1812. Translated by Dana Gioia.

Grimm, Wilhelm. "On the Nature of Fairy Tales," 1819. Translated by Dana Gioia.

Hammet, Dashiell. "One Hour." Originally published in *The Black Mask Magazine*, April 1, 1924.

Hammett, Dashiell. "The Maltese Falcon." Knopf, 1930.

Hawthorne, Nathaniel. "Young Goodman Brown," from "YOUNG GOODMAN BROWN, AND OTHER SHORT STORIES," Courier Corporation, 1992. Originally Published 1835.

Hemingway, Ernest. "A Clean Well-Lighted Place." Reprinted with the permission of Scribner Publishing Group, a division of Simon & Schuster, Inc. from THE SHORT STORIES OF ERNEST HEMINGWAY by Earnest Hemingway. Copyright 1933 by Charles Scribner's Sons. Copyright renewed 1961 by Mary Hemingway. All rights reserved.

Hoffman, Daniel. Excerpt from "The Father Figure in 'The Tell-Tale Heart'" from POE POE POE POE POE POE POE, copyright © 1972 by Louisiana State University Press. Reprinted by permission of the author.

Hurston, Zora Neale. "Sweat." Originally published in 1926.

Ishiguro, Kazuo. "A Family Supper" Published by Penguin, 1983. Copyright © Kazuo Ishiguro. Reproduced by permission of the author c/o Rogers, Coleridge & White Ltd, 20 Powis Mews. London W11 1JN.

Jackson, Shirley. "Biography of a Story," copyright © 1968 by Stanley Edgar Hyman; from COME ALONG WITH ME by Shirley Jackson, edited by Stanley Edgar Hyman. Used by permission of Viking Books, an imprint of Penguin Publishing Group, a division of Penguin Random House LLC. All rights reserved.

Jackson, Shirley. Reprinted by permission of Farrar, Straus and Giroux: "The Lottery" from THE LOTTERY by Shirley Jackson. Copyright © 1948, 1949 by Shirley Jackson. Copyright renewed 1976, 1977 by Laurence Hyman, Barry Hyman, Mrs. Sarah Webster and Mrs. Joanne Schnurer.

Janouch, Gustav. By Gustav Janouch, translated by Goronwy Rees, from CONVERSATIONS WITH KAFKA, copyright ©1968 by S. Fischer Verlag GMBH, translation copyright ©1971 S. Fischer Verlag GMBH. Reprinted by permission of New Directions Publishing Corp.

Jin, Ha. "Saboteur" from THE BRIDEGROOM: STORIES by Ha Jin, copyright © 2000 by Ha Jin. Used by permission of Pantheon Books, an imprint of the Knopf Doubleday Publishing Group, a division of Penguin Random House LLC. All rights reserved.

Joyce, James. "Araby." Originally Published in DUBLINERS, Grant Richards Ltd. London, 1914.

Kincaid, Jamaica. Reprinted by permission of Farrar, Straus and Giroux: "Girl" from AT THE BOTTOM OF THE RIVER by Jamaica Kincaid. Copyright © 1983 by Jamaica Kincaid.

Kodama, Maria. "The Gospel According to Mark," copyright © 1998 by Maria Kodama; translation copyright © 1998 by Penguin Random House LLC.; from COLLECTED FICTIONS: VOLUME 3 by Jorge Luis Borges, translated by Andrew Hurley. Used by permission of Viking Books, an imprint of Penguin Publishing Group, a division of Penguin Random House LLC. All rights reserved.

Lahiri, Jhumpa. "Interpreter of Maladies" from INTERPRETER OF MALADIES by Jhumpa Lahiri. Copyright © 1999 by Jhumpa Lahiri. Reprinted by permission of Houghton Mifflin Harcourt Publishing Company. All rights reserved.

Lawrence, D. H. "Why the Novel Matters," from PHOENIX: THE POSTHUMOUS PAPERS OF D. H. LAWRENCE. 1936.

Le Guin, Ursula K. "The Ones Who Walk Away from Omelas." Copyright © 1973 by Ursula K. Le Guin. First appeared in "New Dimension 3" in 1973, and then in THE WIND'S TWELVE QUARTERS, published by Harper Collins in 1975. Reprinted by permission of Curtis Brown, Ltd.

Link, Kelly. "The Faery Handbag" copyright © 2004 by Kelly Link. Originally published in THE FAERY REEL: TALES FROM THE TWILIGHT REALM, edited by Ellen Datlow and Terry Windlng (Viking) and reprinted in Kelly Link's MAGIC FOR BEGINNERS (Random House).

London, Jack. "To Build a Fire" by Jack London, *The Century Magazine*, v.76, August, 1908, 525–534.

Lovecraft, H. P. "The Outsider" from WEIRD TALES. Copyright 1926.

Mahfouz, Naguib. "The Lawsuit" from THE TIME AND THE PLACE by Naguib Mahfouz, copyright © 1991 by the American University in Cairo Press. Used by permission of Doubleday, an imprint of the Knopf Doubleday Publishing Group, a division of Penguin Random House LLC. All rights reserved.

Manguel, Alberto. "Arrendondo, Inés: 'The Shunammite.'" Translation by Alberto Manguel. © Alberto Manguel c/o Guillermo Schavelzon & Asociados, Agencia Literaria www.schavelzon.com.

Mansfield, Katherine. "Miss Brill." Originally published in *The Athenaeum*. November, 1920.

Marquez, Gabriel Garcia. All pages from "The Handsomest Drowned Man in the World" from LEAF STORM AND OTHER STORIES by Gabriel Garcia Marquez. © 1971 by Gabriel Garcia Marquez. Reprinted by permission of HarperCollins Publishers.

McInerney, Jay. "Bright Lights, Big City." Vintage Books: 1984.

Morrison, Toni "Recitatif." Copyright © 1983 by Toni Morrison Reprinted by permission of ICM Partners.

Mukherjee, Bharati. "Saints." Copyright © 1985 by Bharati Mukherjee. Originally published in *The Three Penny Review*. Reprinted by permission of the author.

Munro, Alice. "Wild Swans." Copyright © 1978 by Alice Munro.

O'Brien, John. Excerpt from INTERVIEWS WITH BLACK WRITERS, edited by John O'Brien, first published by Liveright Publishing Corp, © 1973 by Alice Walker. Reprinted by permission of The Joy Harris Literary Agency, Inc.

Oates, Joyce Carol. "Where Are You Going, Where Have You Been?" from HIGH LONESOME: NEW AND SELECTED STORIES 1955–2006 by Joyce Carol Oates. Copyright © 2006 by the Ontario Review, Inc. Reprinted by permission of HarperCollins Publishers.

O'Brien, Tim. "The Things They Carried" from THE THINGS THEY CARRIED by Tim O'Brien. Copyright 1990 by Tim O'Brien. Reprinted by permission of Houghton Mifflin Harcourt Publishing Company. All rights reserved.

O'Connor, Flannery. "A Good Man Is Hard to Find" from A GOOD MAN IS HARD TO FIND AND OTHER STORIES by Flannery O'Connor. Copyright © 1953 by Flannery O'Connor; renewed 1981 by Regina O'Connor. Reprinted by permission of Houghton

Mifflin Harcourt Publishing Company. All rights reserved.

O'Connor, Flannery. Reprinted by permission of Farrar, Straus and Giroux, LLC: "Revelation" and "Parker's Back" from EVERYTHING THAT RISES MUST CONVERGE by Flannery O'Connor. Copyright © 1965 by the Estate of Mary Flannery O'Connor. Copyright renewed 1993 by Regina O'Connor.

O'Connor, Flannery. "On Her Own Work." Reprinted by permission of Farrar, Straus and Giroux, LLC: excerpt from "On Her Own Work" from MYSTERY AND MANNERS by Flannery O'Connor, edited by Sally and Robert Fitzgerald. Copyright © 1969 by the Estate of Mary Flannery O'Connor.

O'Connor, Flannery. excerpt, "On Her Catholic Faith" from 7/20/55 letter in THE HABIT OF BEING.

Orozco, Daniel. Reprinted by permission of Farrar, Straus and Giroux: "Orientation" from ORIENTATION AND OTHER STORIES by Daniel Orozco. Copyright © 2011 by Daniel Orozco.

Percy, Benjamin. "There Will Be Blood: Writing Violence" from THRILL ME: ESSAYS ON FICTION. Copyright © 2016 by Benjamin Percy. Reprinted with the permission of The Permissions Company, Inc., on behalf of Graywolf Press, Minneapolis, Minnesota, www .graywolfpress.org.

Poe, Edgar Allan. "On Imagination." Published in the *Southern Literary Messenger* in May 1849.

Poe, Edgar Allan. "The Philosophy of Composition." Originally published in *Graham's American Monthly Magazine of Literature and Art*. April, 1846, Philadelphia.

Poe, Edgar Allan. "The Tell-Tale Heart," 1843. *The Pioneer*, Vol. I, No. I, Drew and Scammell, Philadelphia, January, 1843

Porter, William Sydney (O Henry). "The Gift of the Magi." 1905.

Pritchett, V. S. as quoted by Francine Prose. "What Makes a Short Story?" from ON WRITING SHORT STORIES by Francine Prose, et al; edited by Tom Bailey. New York: Oxford University Press, 2000.

Rulfo, Juan. "Tell Them Not to Kill Me" from pp. 60–66 from THE PLAIN IN FLAMES by Juan Rulfo, translated from the Spanish by Ilan Stavans with Harold Augenbraum, copyright © 2012. Reprinted with permission from University of Texas Press.

Satrapi, Marjane. "Kim Wilde" from PERSEPOLIS: THE STORY OF A CHILDHOOD by Marjane Satrapi, translation copyright © 2003 by L'Association, Paris, France. Used by permission of Pantheon Books, an imprint of the Knopf Doubleday Publishing Group, a division of Penguin Random House LLC. All rights reserved.

Saunders, George. "Puppy" from TENTH OF DECEMBER: STORIES by George Saunders, copyright © 2013 by George Saunders. Used by permission of Random House, an imprint and division of Penguin Random House LLC. All rights reserved.

Seneca, "Epistle 114.13."

Siscoe, John. "The Metamorphosis" by Franz Kafka, translated by John Siscoe. Reprinted by permission of John Siscoe.

Siscoe, John: "The Necklace" by Guy de Maupassant, translated by John Siscoe. Used with permission

Spark, Muriel. "The First Year of My Life." From OPEN TO THE PUBLIC, copyright © 1953, 1957, 1958, 1961, 1964, 1967,1985, 1987, 1989, 1994, 1995, 1996, 1997 by Muriel Spark. Copyright © 1985 by Copyright Administration Limited. Reprinted by permission of New Directions Publishing Corp.

Springsteen, Bruce. "Spirit In The Night." Copyright © 1972 Bruce Springsteen, renewed © 2000 Bruce Springsteen (ASCAP). Reprinted by permission. International copyright secured. All rights reserved.

Stafford, Edward. From "An Afternoon with Hemingway." *Writer's Digest*, March 11, 2008.

Steinbeck, John. "The Chrysanthemums" from THE LONG VALLEY by John Steinbeck, copyright © 1938, copyright © renewed 1966 by John Steinbeck. Used by permission of Viking Books, an imprint of Penguin Publishing Group, a division of Penguin Random House LLC. All rights reserved

Tan, Amy. "A Pair of Tickets" from THE JOY LUCK CLUB by Amy Tan, copyright © 1989 by Amy Tan. Used by permission of G. P. Putnam's Sons, an imprint of Penguin Publishing Group, a division of Penguin Random House LLC. All rights reserved.

Tan, Amy. Excerpted from an interview conducted by National Endowment for the Arts for "The Big Read."

Tate, J. O. Excerpt from "A Good Source Is Not So Hard to Find" by J. O. Tate, *The Flannery O'Connor Bulletin* 9 (1980): 98–103. Reprinted by permission of *The Flannery O'Connor Review*, Georgia College.

"The Parable of the Prodigal Son." The Bible. Authorized King James Version, Oxford UP, 1998 15:11.

Tolstoy, Leo. "The Death of Ivan Ilych." Translated by Constance Garnett. Originally published in THE DEATH OF IVAN ILYICH AND OTHER STORIES, 1915.

Tower, Wells. Reprinted by permission of Farrar, Straus and Giroux: "Everything Ravaged, Everything Burned" from EVERYTHING RAVAGED, EVERYTHING BURNED: STORIES by Wells Tower. Copyright © 2009 by Wells Tower.

Tzu, Chuang. "Independence" (4th cen. BCE). Translated by Herbert Giles.

Updike, John. "A & P" from PIGEON FEATHERS AND OTHER STORIES by John Updike, copyright © 1962, copyright renewed 1900 by John Updike. Used by permission of Alfred A. Knopf, an imprint of the Knopf Doubleday Publishing Group, a division of Random House LLC. All rights reserved.

Vonnegut Jr., Kurt. "Harrison Bergeron," © 1961 by Kurt Vonnegut Jr.; from WELCOME TO THE MONKEY HOUSE by Kurt Vonnegut. Used by permission of Dell Publishing, an imprint of Random House, a division of Random House LLC. All rights reserved.

Vonnegut Jr., Kurt. Prose excerpt from "Themes of Science Fiction," interview with Kurt Vonnegut, Jr. from the *Meanjin Quarterly*, 30, Autumn, 1971. Reprinted with permission from Donald C. Farber, Esq.

Walker, Alice and William Ferris. Interview of Alice Walker by William Ferris. From *Southern Cultures*. Copyright © 2004. Used by permission of the author.

Walker, Alice. "Everyday Use" from IN LOVE & TROUBLE: Stories of Black Women by Alice Walker. Copyright 1973, and renewed 2001 by Alice Walker. Reprinted by permission of Houghton Mifflin Harcourt Publishing Company. All rights reserved.

Welty, Eudora. "A Worn Path" from A CURTAIN OF GREEN AND OTHER STORIES by Eudora Welty. Copyright 1941 and renewed 1969 by Eudora Welty. Reprinted by permission of Houghton Mifflin Harcourt Publishing Company. All rights reserved.

Williams, Lucinda. Excerpt from "Where the Spirit Meets the Bone" by Lucinda Williams from RADIO SILENCE, Volume III. Copyright 2014. Used by permission.

Wolff, Tobias. "Bullet in the Brain" from THE NIGHT IN QUESTION: STORIES by Tobias Wolff, copyright © 1996 by Tobias Wolff. Used by permission of Alfred A. Knopf, an imprint of the Knopf Doubleday Publishing Group, a division of Penguin Random House LLC. All rights reserved.

Woolf, Virginia. "A Haunted House." From MONDAY OR TUESDAY, Originally Published by Harcourt Brace, 1921.

Yates, Donald. "On Storytelling" from "A Colloquy with Jorge Luis Borges" *Gypsy Scholar* 3, 1976. Reprinted by permission of the author.

POETRY

Abeyta, Aaron. "Thirteen ways of looking at a tortilla," by Aaron A. Abeyta, in COLCHA (Boulder: University Press of Colorado, 2011), Editor: Aaron A. Abeyta, 2001. Reprinted with permission.

Acker, Tristan. "Hope for the City." Used by permission.

Addonizio, Kim. "First Poem for You" by Kim Addonizio from THE PHILOSOPHER'S CLUB. Reprinted by permission of BOA Editions.

Aiken, Conrad. "Divers Realists," from *The Dial*, November 1917.

Alarcón, Francisco X. "The X in My Name," from NO GOLDEN GATE FOR US. (Pennywhistle Press, Tesuque, NM, 1993). Copyright 1993. Used by permission of the author.

Alarcón, Francisco X.: "Frontera/Border" by Francisco X. Alarcón. Copyright 2003. Used by permission of the author.

Alexie, Sherman. "The Powwow at the end of the World." Reprinted from "The Summer of Black Widows." © 1996 by Sherman Alexie, by permission of Hanging Loose Press.

Alexie, Sherman. "The Facebook Sonnet." Copyright © 2011 Sherman Alexie. All rights reserved. Used by permission of Nancy Stauffer Associates.

Alvarez, Julia. "By Accident." From THE WOMAN I KEPT TO MYSELF. Copyright © 2004 by Julia Alvarez. Published by Algonquin Books of Chapel Hill in 2004. First published in A POEM OF HER OWN: VOICES OF AMERICAN WOMEN YESTERDAY AND TODAY (Harry N. Abrams, 2003). By permission of Susan Bergholz Literary Services, New York, NY and Lamy, NM. All rights reserved.

An-hwei Lee, Karen. "Rainfall" from "GOD'S ONE HUNDRED PROMISES," originally published by Swan Scythe Press in 2002. Copyright © 2002. Used with permission.

Anonymous, "Unsigned Review" from *Literary World*.

Anthony, Joseph: "Robert Frost, Realist and Symbolist" first published July 4, 1920 in *The New York Times*.

Arnold, Matthew. "Dover Beach," from THE NEW POEMS, 1867.

Ashbery, John. "At North Farm" (14 lines) from A WAVE. Copyright ©1981, 1982, 1983, 1984 by John Ashbery. Reprinted by permission of Georges Borchardt, Inc., on behalf of the author.

Auden, W. H. "As I Walked Out One Evening," "Musée des Beaux Arts," "The Unknown Citizen," copyright © 1940 and renewed 1968; from W. H. AUDEN COLLECTED POEMS by W. H. Auden. Used by permission of Random House, an imprint and division of Penguin Random House LLC. All rights reserved.

Baca, Jimmy. "Spliced Wire" by Jimmy Baca, ©1982, from "What's Happening." Reprinted by permission of the author.

Barber, David. "Aria," from POETRY, March 2013. Copyright © 2013. Used by permission.

Behn, Aphra. "When maidens are young," 1687.

Belloc, Hilaire. "Fatigue." From SONNETS AND VERSE, Duckworth, London (1923)

Belloc, Hilaire. "The Hippopotamus" from THE BAD CHILD'S BOOK OF BEASTS, 1896.

Bishop, Elizabeth. Reprinted by permission of Farrar, Straus and Giroux, LLC. "The Fish," "Filling Station," "One Art," "Sestina," from POEMS by Elizabeth Bishop. Copyright ©2011 by The Alice H. Methfessel Trust. Publisher's note and compilation copyright © 2011 by Farrar, Straus and Giroux.

Blake, William. "Auguries of Innocence" from THE PICKERING MANUSCRIPT. Originally published 1863.

Blake, William. "London," "The Garden of Love," originally published in SONGS OF EXPERIENCE, 1794.

Blake, William. "The Chimney Sweeper." Originally published in two parts in SONGS OF INNOCENCE, 1789 and SONGS OF EXPERIENCE, 1794.

Blake, William. "The Sick Rose," from SONGS OF EXPERIENCE, 1794.

Blake, William. "The Tyger," from SONGS OF INNOCENCE AND EXPERIENCE, 1789.

Blake, William. "To H—" from the Blake manuscript—Notebook 1808–39.

Bloch, Chana. "Tired Sex." MRS. DUMPTY. Winner of the 1998 Felix Pollack Prize in Poetry. © 1998 by the Board of Rights of the University of Wisconsin System. Reproduced by the permission of the University of Wisconsin Press.

Bly, Robert. "Driving to Town Late to Mail a Letter" from SILENCE IN THE SNOWY FIELDS copyright 1962 by Robert Bly. Reprinted by permission of Wesleyan University Press.

Bogan, Louise. "Medusa" from BODY OF THIS DEATH, 1923.

Borges, Jorge Luis. "On his Blindness." Reprinted by permission of Robert Meezey, translator.

Borges, Jorge Luis. From "A Profession of Literary Faith," 1926.

Bradstreet, Anne (1612–1672), "The Author to Her Book."

Bridges, Robert. "Triolet" From POEMS, 1873.

Brontë, Emily. "Love and Friendship" from POEMS. Currer, Ellis, and Acton Bell. London, England: Aylott and Jones. 1846.

Brooks, Gwendolyn. From "Gwendolyn Brooks: 'Poetry Is Life Distilled'" by Christine M. Hill. Enslow Pub Inc, June 8, 2005.

Brooks, Gwendolyn: "Speech to the Young. Speech to the Progress-Toward," "the mother," "the rite for Cousin Vit," "We Real Cool," "Hearing 'We Real Cool.'" Reprinted By Consent of Brooks Permissions.

Browning, Elizabeth Barrett. "How Do I Love Thee? (Sonnet 43)" from SONNETS FROM THE PORTUGUESE, 1850.

Browning, Robert. "My Last Duchess." Originally published in 1842.

Browning, Robert. "Soliloquy of the Spanish Cloister." DRAMATIC LYRICS, 1842.

Browning, Robert. "My Last Duchess." From DRAMATIC LYRICS, originally published 1842.

Brutschy, Jennifer. "Born Again" by Jennifer Brutschy from THE SAN FRANCISCO HAIKU ANTHOLOGY. Reprinted by permission of the author.

Bukowski, Charles. "Dostoevsky" from BONE PALACE BATTLE. Copyright © 1997 by Linda Lee Bukowski. Reprinted by permission of HarperCollins Publishers.

Burns, Robert. "The Kirk's Alarm," 1801.

Carlos Williams, William. "Queen-Anne's-Lace," from SOUR GRAPES, 1921.

Carroll, Lewis. [Charles Lutwidge Dodgson]. "Jaberwocky" and "Humpty Dumpty Explicates 'Jabberwocky'" from THROUGH THE LOOKING-GLASS, and WHAT ALICE FOUND THERE. Macmillan, 1871.

Charles, Dorthi. "Concrete Cat" by Dorthi Charles. From KNOCK AT A STAR: A CHILD'S INTRODUCTION TO POETRY (Little, Brown & Co.). Copyright 1999 by X. J. Kennedy and Dorothy M. Kennedy. Used with permission.

Chaucer, Geoffrey (c.1343–1400). "Rondel of Merciless Beauty."

Chesterton, G. K. "The Donkey." from *John O'London's Weekly*, November 10, 1923.

Chesterton, G. K. from "The Defendant" (1901).

Chief Joseph. "Thunder Traveling to the Loftier Mountain Heights," October 5, 1877.

Choi, Francis. "Choi Jeong Min," originally appearing in *Poetry Magazine*, February 2016. Copyright © 2016. Used with permission of the author.

Chu-i, Po, "The Cranes." From 170 CHINESE POEMS, translated by Arthur Waley, 1918.

Ciardi, John. "Most Like an Arch This Marriage" from I MARRY YOU (New Brunswick, NJ: Rutgers University Press, 1958). Reprinted with permission from John L. Ciardi, Trustee, Ciardi Publishing Trust.

Ciardi, John. From his article in *Saturday Review*, April 12, 1958.

Clark, Annie. "Severed Crossed Fingers" Written by Annie Clark ©2013 Songs of Big Deal (ASCAP)/Nail Polish Manifesto (ASCAP) All Rights Reserved. Used by Permission. International Copyright Secured.

Cleghorn, Sarah N. "The Golf Links," in *The New York Tribune*, 1914.

Cole, William: "On my boat on Lake Cayuga" by William Cole. Reprinted with permission from the Estate of William Rossa Cole.

Coleridge, Samuel Taylor. "Christabel," 1816.

Coleridge, Samuel Taylor. "Kubla Khan," 1816.

Collins, Billy. "Embrace" by Billy Collins. Permission by Chris Calhoun Agency, © Billy Collins.

Collins, Billy. "Introduction to Poetry" from THE APPLE THAT ASTONISHED PARIS. Copyright © 1988, 1996 by Billy Collins. Reprinted with the permission of The Permissions Company, Inc., on behalf of the University of Arkansas Press, www.uapress.com.

Cope, Wendy. "Variation on Belloc's Fatigue" by Wendy Cope from SERIOUS CONCERNS (© Wendy Cope, 1992) is printed by permission of United Agents (www.unitedagents.co.uk) on behalf of Wendy Cope.

Cope, Wendy. "Lonely Hearts." Reprinted by permission of United Agents on behalf of Wendy Cope.

Cornford, Frances. "The Watch" from POEMS, 1910.

Cortez, Sarah. "Adam" from VANISHING POINTS: POEMS AND PHOTOGRAPHS OF TEXAS ROADSIDE MEMORIALS. *Texas Review Press*, 2016. Copyright 2016. Used by Permission.

Crabbe, George. "The Parish Register," 1807.

Crane, Hart. "My Grandmother's Love Letters," from WHITE BUILDINGS. New York: Boni and Livewright, 1926.

Crane, Stephen. "In the Desert," from THE BLACK RIDERS AND OTHER LINES, 1895.

Crane, Stephen. "The Wayfarer" from WAR IS KIND AND OTHER LINES, published May 20, 1899.

Creeley, Robert. "Oh, no." Republished with permission of University of California Press, from Robert Creeley, THE COLLECTED POEMS OF ROBERT CREELEY, 1945–1975; permission conveyed through Copyright Clearance Center, Inc.

Cummings, E. E. "anyone lived in a pretty how town." Copyright 1940, © 1968, 1991 by the Trustees for the E. E. Cummings Trust. Used by permission of Liveright Publishing Corporation.

Cummings, E. E. "Buffalo Bill 's." Copyright 1923, 1951, © 1991 by the Trustees for the E. E. Cummings Trust. Copyright © 1976 by George James Firmage, from COMPLETE POEMS:1904–1962 by E. E. Cummings, edited by George J. Firmage. Used by permission of Liveright Publishing Corporation.

Cummings, E. E. "if (touched by love's own secret)," from XAIPE, Liveright, 1950.

Cummings, E. E. "in Just—." Copyright 1923, 1951, © 1991 by the Trustees for the E. E. Cummings Trust. Copyright © 1976 by George James Firmage. Used by permission of Liveright Publishing Corporation.

Cummings, E. E. "next to of course god america i." Copyright 1926, 1954, © 1991 by the Trustees for the E. E. Cummings Trust. Used by permission of Liveright Publishing Corporation.

Cummings, E. E. Copyright 1923, 1951, © 1991 by the Trustees for the E. E. Cummings Trust. Copyright © 1976 by George James Firmage, "somewhere i have never travelled,gladly beyond." Used by permission of Liveright Publishing Corporation.

Cunningham, J. V. "Friend, on this scaffold Thomas More lies dead" J. V. Cunningham. Reprinted with permission.

Davidson, John. "Thirty Bob a Week." From SELECTED POEMS. London & New York: John Lane, The Bodley Head, 1905.

de la Cruz, Sor Juana Inés (1648–1695). "Presente en que el Cariño Hace Regalo la Llaneza."

de los Santos, Marisa. "Perfect Dress" from FROM THE BONES OUT. Used with permission.

Deutsch, Babette. "The Falling Flower" by Arakida Moritake, translated by Babette Deutsch. Copyright 1957. Reprinted by permission of Benjamin Yarmolinsky and the Estate of Babette Deutsch.

Deutsch, Babette. "Another Impressionist," in *The New Republic*. February 1918.

Dickinson, Emily. Excerpt from "'Hope' is the thing with feathers." POEMS, SECOND SERIES, edited by T. W. Higginson and Mabel Loomis Todd, Roberts Brothers, 1891.

Dickinson, Emily. "A Route of Evanescence." From *Atlantic Monthly*, 68, October 1891.

Dickinson, Emily. "Because I could not stop for Death," "I dwell in possibility," "I heard a Fly buzz – when I died," "I started Early – Took my Dog," "My Life had stood – a Loaded Gun," "Tell all the Truth but tell it slant," "The Lightning is a yellow Fork." THE POEMS OF EMILY DICKINSON: VARIORUM EDITION, edited by Ralph W. Franklin, Cambridge, Mass.: The Belknap Press of Harvard University Press, Copyright © 1998 by the President and Fellows of Harvard College. Copyright © 1951, 1955 by the President and Fellows of Harvard College. Copyright © renewed 1979, 1983 by the President and Fellows of Harvard College. Copyright © 1914, 1918, 1919, 1924, 1929, 1930, 1932, 1935, 1937, 1942 by Martha Dickinson Bianchi. Copyright © 1952, 1957, 1958, 1963, 1965 by Mary L. Hampson.

Dickinson, Emily. "It dropped so low—in my Regard," "I felt a Funeral, in my Brain," "I'm Nobody! Who are you?," "The Soul selects her own Society," "Much Madness is divinest Sense," "This is my letter to the World." THE POEMS OF EMILY DICKINSON, edited by Thomas H. Johnson, The Belknap Press of Harvard University Press, 1955.

Dickinson, Emily. "Safe in their Alabaster Chambers," "Wild Nights – Wild Nights!," "Some keep the Sabbath going to Church." THE POEMS OF EMILY DICKINSON, edited by Thomas H. Johnson, Cambridge, Mass.: The Belknap Press of Harvard University Press, Copyright © 1951, 1955, 1979, 1983 by the President and Fellows of Harvard College.

Dickinson, Emily. THE LETTERS OF EMILY DICKINSON, edited by Thomas H. Johnson with Theodora van Wagenen Ward, The Belknap Press of Harvard University Press, 1958. Letter to Thomas Wentworth Higginson, 25 April 1862.

Dickinson, Emily. The Discovery of Emily Dickinson's Manuscripts excerpted from Introduction. Reprinted by permission of the publishers and the Trustees of Amherst College from THE POEMS OF EMILY DICKINSON, edited by Thomas H. Johnson, pp. xviii–xix; xxxix–xl, Cambridge, Mass.: The Belknap Press of Harvard University Press, Copyright © 1951, 1955 by the President and Fellows of Harvard College. Copyright © renewed 1979, 1983 by the President and Fellows of Harvard College. Copyright © 1914, 1918, 1919, 1924, 1929, 1930, 1932, 1935, 1937, 1942, by Martha Dickinson Bianchi. Copyright © 1952, 1957, 1958, 1963, 1965, by Mary L. Hampson.

Dickinson, Emily. LETTERS OF EMILY DICKINSON, edited by Mabel Loomis Todd, Roberts Brothers, 1894. From an April 25, 1862 letter written to Thomas Wentworth Higginson.

Dickinson, Emily. THE LETTERS OF EMILY DICKINSON 1845-1886, edited by Mabel Loomis Todd, Little, Brown and Company, 1906. Excerpt from a letter Thomas Wentworth Higginson wrote to his wife, dated 1870, about a conversation he had with Emily Dickinson.

Dinesen, Isak (Karen Blixen). Excerpt from OUT OF AFRICA. Putnam, 1937.

Disch, Thomas: "Zewhyexary" by Tom Disch from YES, LET'S: NEW AND SELECTED POEMS. Copyright 1989 by Tom Disch. Reprinted with permission of Estate of Thomas Disch.

Donne, John. "A Valediction: Forbidding Mourning," "Batter my heart, three-personed God, for You," "Death be not proud, "The Flea," from SONGS AND SONNETS, 1633.

Donne, John. "Song," 1633

Doolittle, H. (Hilda Doolittle). "Helen," from COLLECTED POEMS, 1912–1944, copyright ©1982 by The Estate of Hilda Doolittle. Reprinted by permission of New Directions Publishing Corp.

Doolittle, Hilda. "Heat." Originally published in Poetry, 1915.

Doolittle, Hilda. "Sea Rose", from SEA GARDEN. St. Martin's Press. New York, 1916.

Dove, Rita and Marilyn Nelson. "A Black Rainbow: Modern Afro-American Poetry" from POETRY AFTER MODERNISM, edited by Robert McDowell. Published by Story Line Press. Copyright 1998. Used with permission.

Dowson, Ernest C.: "Days of Wine and Rose" from VITAE SUMMA BREVIS. Published in 1896.

Drayton, Michael. "Idea 61: Since there's no help, come let us kiss and part" 1622.

Dryden, John. "Mac Flecknoe," 1682.

Dunbar, Paul Laurence. "We Wear the Mask." from LYRICS OF LOWLY LIFE. Dodd, Mead, and Company, 1896.

Dyer, John. "Grongar Hill," 1726.

Dylan, Bob. "The Times They Are a-Changin" by Bob Dylan. Reprinted by permission of Special Rider Music.

Eberhart, Richard. "The Fury of Aerial Bombardment" from COLLECTED POEMS 1930–1986 by Richard Eberhart (1988). Copyright © 1960, 1976, 1987 by Richard Eberhart. Used by permission.

Edgar Allan Poe, "Annabel Lee" published in Sartain's Union Magazine, 1849.

Eisler, Rachel. "Marilyn's Nocturne." Used by permission.

Eliot, T. S. "The Boston Evening Transcript," published in Poetry, 1915.

Eliot, T. S. "The Love Song of J. Alfred Prufrock" from PRUFROCK AND OTHER OBSERVATIONS. The Egoist Ltd, 1917.

Eliot, T. S. "Tradition and the Individual Talent," from THE SACRED WOOD, 1920.

Eliot, T. S. Excerpt from "Hamlet and His Problems," from THE SACRED WOOD: ESSAYS ON POETRY AND CRITICISM, 1920.

Eliot, T. S. "Preludes" originally published in PRUFROCK AND OTHER OBSERVATIONS, 1917.

Eliot, T. S. "The Journey of the Magi," "Virginia" from COLLECTED POEMS 1909–1962 by T. S. Eliot. Copyright 1936 by Houghton Mifflin Harcourt Publishing Company. Copyright © renewed 1964 by Thomas Stearns Eliot. Reprinted by permission of Houghton Mifflin Harcourt Publishing Company. All rights reserved.

Eliot, T. S. Excerpt from "Reflections on Vers Libre" published in The New Statesman, March 3, 1917.

Eliot, T. S. Reprinted by permission of Farrar, Straus and Giroux: Excerpt from "The Music of Poetry" from ON POETRY AND POETS by T. S. Eliot. Copyright © 1957 by T. S. Eliot. Copyright renewed © 1985 by Valerie Eliot.

Ellmann, Maud. "Will There be Time?" by Maud Ellmann from THE POETICS OF IMPERSONALITY: T. S. ELIOT AND EZRA POUND. Copyright 1988. Published by Edinburgh University Press www.eupublishing.com. Used by permission.

Espaillat, Rhina P. "Bilingual/Bilingüe" from WHERE HORIZONS GO by Rhina Espaillat, published by Truman State University Press Copyright ©1998. Reprinted by permission of the author.

Espaillat, Rhina P. "Bra." Republished with permission of Truman State University Press, from WHERE HORIZONS GO, Rhina P. Espaillat © 1999. Permission conveyed through Copyright Clearance Center, Inc.

Espaillat, Rhina P. "Translating Frost into Spanish." Copyright © 2014 by Rhina P. Espaillat. Printed by permission of the author.

Espaillat, Rhina P. Afterword on Being a Bilingual Writer: "Bilingual/Bilingüe" by Rhina Espaillat from WHERE HORIZONS GO, published by Truman State University Press, © 1999.

Essbaum, Jill. "The Heart" by Jill Alexander Essbaum from HARLOT. Reprinted by permission of Jill Essbaum.

Factor, Jenny. "Rubyfruit" (from "Extramarital...") from UNRAVELING AT

THE NAME. Copyright © 2002 by Jenny Factor. Reprinted with the permission of The Permissions Company, Inc., on behalf of Copper Canyon Press, www.coppercanyonpress.org.

Foley, Adelle. "Learning to Shave (Father teaching son)" by Adelle Foley. Reprinted with permission from Adelle Foley.

Foust, Rebecca. "What You Work For." From ALL THAT GORGEOUS PITILESS SONG, Copyright © 2010. Many Mountains Moving Press. Used by permission of the author.

Fowles, John. From THE FRENCH LIEUTENANT'S WOMAN. Jonathan Cape, 1969.

Frost, Robert. "Birches," "The Road Not Taken," from MOUNTAIN INTERVAL. Henry Holt and Company, 1916.

Frost, Robert. "Fire and Ice," from NEW HAMPSHIRE. Henry Holt and Company, 1923.

Frost, Robert. "A Patch of Old Snow," From MOUNTAIN INTERVAL, 1920.

Frost, Robert. "After Apple Picking," "Home Burial," "Mending Wall," from NORTH OF BOSTON. David Nutt, 1914.

Frost, Robert. "Design" from AMERICAN POETRY: A MISCELLANY. Copyright 1922. First published by Harcourt Brace.

Frost, Robert. "Mowing" from A BOY'S WILL, "My November Guest," Henry Holt and Company, 1915.

Frost, Robert. "Out, Out—." Originally published in *McClure's*, July 1916.

Frost, Robert. "The Figure a Poem Makes" from the book THE SELECTED PROSE OF ROBERT FROST edited by Hyde Cox and Edward Connery Lathem. Copyright © 1923, 1929, 1969 by Henry Holt and Company. Copyright © 1936, 1951, 1956 by Robert Frost. © 1964 by Lesley Frost Ballantine. Reprinted by permission of Henry Holt and Company, LLC. All rights reserved.

Frost, Robert. "The Sound of Sense" from a Letter to John Bartlett. July, 4 1913.

Frost, Robert. "Desert Places" from the book THE POETRY OF ROBERT FROST edited by Edward Connery Lathem. Copyright © 1923, 1928, 1969 by Henry Holt and Company, copyright © 1936 1942, 1951, 1956 by Robert Frost, copyright © 1964, 1970 by Lesley Frost Ballantine. Reprinted by permission of Henry Holt and Company, LLC.

Frost, Robert. "Nothing Gold Can Stay" from the book THE POETRY OF ROBERT FROST edited Edward Connery Lathem. Copyright © 1923, 1928, 1969 by Henry Holt and Company, LLC, copyright © 1936 1942, 1951, 1956 by Robert Frost, copyright © 1964, 1970 by Lesley Frost Ballantine.

Frost, Robert. "Acquainted with the Night," "Stopping by Woods on a Snowy Evening" from the book THE POETRY OF ROBERT FROST edited by Edward Connery Lathem. Copyright © 1923, 1928, 1969 by Henry Holt and Company, LLC, copyright © 1936, 1951, 1956 by Robert Frost, copyright © 1964 by Lesley Frost Ballantine. Reprinted by permission of Henry Holt and Company, LLC. All Rights Reserved.

Frost, Robert: "The Importance of Poetic Metaphor" from Education by Poetry. Address at Amherst College, 1930.

Gay, Garry. "Hole in the Ozone" by Garry Gay. Reprinted by permission of the author.

Ginsberg, Allen. All lines from "A Supermarket in California" from COLLECTED POEMS 1947–1980 by Allen Ginsberg. Copyright © 1955 by Allen Ginsberg. Reprinted by permission of HarperCollins Publishers.

Gioia, Dana. "Frost's Dramatic Narratives." Virginia Quarterly Review, Spring 2013. Used by permission of the author.

Gioia, Dana. "Money" from THE GODS OF WINTER. Copyright © 1991 by Dana Gioia. Reprinted with the permission of The Permissions Company, Inc., on behalf of Graywolf Press, www.graywolfpress.org.

Gooden, Kimberly. "Anger." Translation of César Vallejo poem. Used by permission.

Gordon, George (Lord Byron). "Childe Harold's Pilgrimage," 1812.

Gordon, George (Lord Byron). "The Destruction of Sennacherib," published in HEBREW MELODIES, 1815.

Gordon, George [Lord Byron]. "So, We'll Go No More ing a-Roving" from LETTERS AND JOURNALS OF LORD BYRON. Thomas Moore, 1830.

Graves, Robert. "Down, Wanton, Down" by Robert Graves from ROBERT GRAVES: THE COMPLETE POEMS IN ONE VOLUME, copyright 2001. Reprinted by permission of Carcanet Press Limited.

Gray, Thomas. "Elegy Written in a Country Churchyard," 1751.

Guest, Edgar A. "The Crucible of Life," 1917.

Guiterman, Arthur. "On the Vanity of Earthly Greatness" from GAILY THE TROUBADOUR. Reprinted with the permission of Richard E. Sclove.

Gwynn, R. S. "Shakespearean Sonnet" Copyright © by R. S. Gwynn. Used by permission of R. S. Gwynn.

Gylys, Beth. "Briefly" from BODIES THAT HUM, Silverfish Review Press, 1999.

Haaland, Tami. "Lipstick" from BREATH IN EVERY ROOM by Tami Haaland. Copyright 2001 by Tami Haaland. Reprinted by permission of the author.

Hadas, Rachel. "The Three Silences." Used by permission.

Hakuro, Wada. "Even the Croaking of Frogs," by Wada Hakuro, translated by Violet Kazue de Cristoro in MAY SKY: THERE IS ALWAYS TOMORROW. Reprinted by permission of Kimiko de Cristoforo.

Hardy, Thomas. "Hap" WESSEX POEMS AND OTHER VERSES, 1898.

Hardy, Thomas. "Neutral Tones," from WESSEX POEMS AND OTHER VERSES, 1898.

Hardy, Thomas. "The Abbey Mason." Originally published in *Harper's Magazine*, 1912.

Hardy, Thomas. "The Convergence of the Twain," SATIRES OF CIRCUMSTANCE, LYRICS AND REVERIES WITH MISCELLANEOUS PIECES. London: Macmillan, 1915.

Hardy, Thomas. "The Ruined Maid." Written in 1866, first published in POEMS OF THE PAST AND PRESENT, 1901.

Hardy, Thomas. "The Workbox" From SATIRES OF CIRCUMSTANCE, 1914.

Harrington, Sir John. "Of Treason," 1618.

Harter, Penny: "Broken Bowl" by Penny Harter from IN THE BROKEN CURVE. Used by permission. Burnt Lake Press, 1984.

Hayden, Robert. "Frederick Douglass," "Those Winter Sundays," Copyright © 1966 by Robert Hayden, from COLLECTED POEMS OF ROBERT HAYDEN by Robert Hayden, edited by Frederick Glaysher. Used by permission of Liveright Publishing Corporation.

Heaney, Seamus. Reprinted by permission of Farrar, Straus and Giroux: "Digging" from OPENED GROUND: SELECTED POEMS 1966–1996 by Seamus Heaney. Copyright © 1998 by Seamus Heaney.

Henley, William Ernest. "Invictus," from BOOK OF VERSES, 1888.

Herbert, George. "Easter Wings," "Redemption," from THE TEMPLE, 1633.

Herbert, George. "Love."

Herbert, George. "The Pulley," 1633

Herrera, Juan Felipe. "El ángel de la guarda" from LOTERÍA CARDS AND FORTUNE POEMS: A BOOK OF LIVES, with linocuts by Artemil Rodrígues. Copyright © 1999 by Juan Felipe Herrera. Reprinted with the permission of The Permissions Company, Inc., on behalf of City Lights Books, www.citylights.com

Herrick, Robert. "Corinna's going a Maying," "To Oenone," "To the Virgins, to Make Much of Time," "Upon Julia's Clothes," from HESPERIDES, 1648.

Higginson, Thomas Wentworth. "Meeting Emily Dickinson" published in *The Atlantic Magazine*, 1891.

Holden, Karen. "Bats in a Box" first appeared in CONFLUENCE 2010. Copyright © 2010, 2016. Used with permission of the author. All rights reserved.

Hollander, John. "Swan and Shadow" by John Hollander from TYPES OF SHAPE. Copyright © 1969 by John Hollander. Used by permission.

Hood, Thomas. "Faithless Nelly Gray," 1826.

Hood, Thomas. "The Bridge of Sighs," 1844.

Hopkins, Gerard Manley. "God's Grandeur." Written in 1877, published posthumously in POEMS OF GERARD MANLEY HOPKINS, 1918.

Hopkins, Gerard Manley. "Pied Beauty," "The Windhover," from POEMS OF GERARD MANLEY HOPKINS, 1918.

Hopkins. Gerard Manley. "Spring and Fall." (1844–1889)

Housman, A. E. "Loveliest of trees, the cherry now," "To an Athlete Dying Young," "When I was one-and-twenty," from A SHROPSHIRE LAD. Kegan Paul, Trench, Treubner & Company, 1896.

Hughes, Langston. "Cross," "Homecoming," "Song for a Dark Girl," "Prayer [2]," "Theme for English B," "Dream Boogie," "I, Too," "Harlem (2)," "Two Somewhat Different Epigrams" from THE COLLECTED POEMS OF LANGSTON HUGHES by Langston Hughes, edited by Arnold Rampersad with David Roessel, Associate Editor, copyright 1994 by the Estate of Langston Hughes. Used by permission of Alfred A. Knopf, an imprint of the Knopf Doubleday Publishing Group, a division of Random House LLC. All rights reserved.

Hughes, Langston. "Mother to Son" published in *The Crisis*, Dec. 1922.

Hughes, Langston. "My People" published in *The Crisis*, June 1922.

Hughes, Langston. "Song for a Banjo Dancer" from *The Crisis*, October, 1922.

Hughes, Langston. "The Negro Artist and the Racial Mountain." Reprinted by permission of Harold Ober Associates Incorporated. First published in *The Nation*. Copyright © 1926 by Langston Hughes.

Hughes, Langston. "The Negro Speaks of Rivers" published in *The Crisis*, June 1921.

Hughes, Langston. "The Negro" from *The Crisis*, January 1922.

Hughes, Langston. Reprinted by permission of Hill and Wang, a division of Farrar, Straus and Giroux: excerpt from "When the Negro Was in Vogue" from THE BIG SEA by Langston Hughes. Copyright © 1940 by Langston Hughes. Copyright renewed 1968 by Arna Bontemps and George Houston Bass.

Hummel, Maria. "The Tree" by Hummel Maria from HOUSE AND FIRE , 2013. Used by permission of Maria Hummel.

Hunter, Alberta and Lovie Austin. "Downhearted Blues." Paramount, 1922.

Jarrell, Randall. Reprinted by permission of Farrar, Straus and Giroux, LLC. "The Death of the Ball Turret Gunner" from THE COMPLETE POEMS by Randall Jarrell. Copyright © 1969, renewed 1997 by Mary von S. Jarrell.

Jeffers, Robinson. Poems from THE COLLECTED POETRY OF ROBINSON JEFFERS, edited by Tim Hunt, Volume 2, 1928–1938. Published by Stanford University Press. Copyright 1938, renewed by Donnan Jeffers and Garth Jeffers. All rights reserved. Used with the permission of Stanford University Press, www.sup.org

Jin, Ha. "Missed Time," from *Poetry Magazine*, July 2000. Used with permission.

Johnson, James Weldon. "Sence You Went Away." From FIFTY YEARS AND OTHER POEMS. The Cornhill Company, Boston: 1917

Johnson, Samuel. From LIVES OF ENGLISH POETS, 3 vols. (Oxford: Clarendon Press, 1905)

Jonson, Ben. "To Celia," 1616, "On My First Son," 1616.

Joyce, James. "All Day I Hear" from CHAMBER MUSIC, 1907.

Justice, Donald. "On the Death of Friends in Childhood" from COLLECTED POEMS, copyright © 2004 by Donald Justice. Used by permission of Alfred A. Knopf, an imprint of the Knopf Doubleday Publishing Group, a division of Penguin Random House LLC. All rights reserved

Kaufman, Bob. "No More Jazz at Alcatraz" from CRANIAL GUITAR: SELECTED POEMS. Copyright © 1996 by Eileen Kaufman. Reprinted with the permission of The Permissions Company, Inc. on behalf of Coffee House Press, www.coffeehousepress.org.

Kearns, Katherine. "On Mending Wall," excerpt from "Frost on the Doorstep and Lyricism at the Millennium," in ROADS NOT TAKEN: REREADING ROBERT FROST," Earl J. Wilcox and Jonathan N. Barron eds., by Permission of the University of Missouri Press. Copyright © 2000 by the Curators of the University of Missouri.

Keats, John. "Bright star, would I were steadfast as thou art." Originally Published in *The Plymouth and Devonport Weekly Journal*, 1838.

Keats, John. "La Belle Dame sans Merci," 1819.

Keats, John. "Ode on a Grecian Urn," "Ode to a Nightingale" from *Annals of the Fine Arts*, Number 15, January 1820.

Keats, John. "The Eve of St. Agnes," 1820.

Keats, John. "When I have fears that I may cease to be" from LIFE, LETTERS, AND LITERARY REMAINS OF JOHN KEATS, 1848.

Keeler, Gregory. "There ain't no such thing as a Montana Cowboy." Used by permission.

Kees, Weldon. "For My Daughter." Reprinted from THE COLLECTED POEMS OF WELDON KEES edited by Donald Justice by permission of the University of Nebraska Press. Copyright renewed 2003 by the University of Nebraska Press.

Kenyon, Jane. "The Suitor" by Jane Kenyon from ROOM TO ROOM. Copyright © 1978 by Alice James Books. Used by permission of Alice James Books.

Khayaam, Omar. "A Book of Verses underneath the Bough," from RUBAIYAT, 1120. Translated by Edward FitzGerald.

Khayyam, Omar (1048–1131). "Rubaiyat LXXI (The Moving Finger writes)," translated by Edward FitzGerald.

Khayyam, Omar (1048–1131). "Rubaiyat VII (Come fill the Cup)," translated by Edward FitzGerald.

Khayyam, Omar (1048–1131). "Rubaiyat XCIX (Ah Love! Could you and I with Him conspire)," translated by Edward FitzGerald.

Khayyam, Omar (1048–1131). "Rubaiyat," translated by Edward FitzGerald.

Khayyam, Omar. "Rubaiyat 19," translated by Edward FitzGerald, 1859.

Kim, Suji Kwock. "Occupation." From NOTES FROM THE DIVIDED COUNTRY: POEMS by Suji Kwock Kim. Copyright © 2003, Louisiana State University Press. Used by permission of Louisiana State University Press.

King James Bible. "Psalm 150." Authorized King James Version, Oxford UP, 1998.

Kipling, Rudyard. "The Law of Jungle," from THE JUNGLE BOOK. Macmillan, 1894.

Kipling, Rudyard. "Harp Song of the Dane Women," from PUCK OF POOK'S HILL, 1906.

Kobayashi, Issa. "Cricket" by Kobayashi Issa, trans. Robert Bly. Reprinted by permission of Robert Bly.

Kobayashi, Issa. Cid Corman's translation of the Issa poem, 'Only one guy' is reprinted from ONE MAN'S MOON by permission of Gnomon Press.

Komunyakaa, Yusef. "Facing It" from PLEASURE DOME: NEW AND COLLECTED POEMS © 2001 by Yusef Komunyakaa. Reprinted with permission of Wesleyan University Press.

Kooser, Ted. "Abandoned Farmhouse," "Carrie," from SURE SIGNS: NEW AND SELECTED POEMS, 1980. Reprinted by permission of the University of Pittsburgh Press.

Langland, William. "Piers plowman," Written 1370–1390.

Larios, Julie. "What Bee Did." Originally appeared in *The Cortland Review*. Copyright © 2006. Used with permission of the author.

Larkin, Philip. Reprinted by permission of Farrar, Straus and Giroux: "Poetry of Departures," "Aubade," "Home is so Sad," from THE COMPLETE POEMS OF PHILIP LARKIN by Philip Larkin, edited by Archie Burnett. Copyright © 2012 by The Estate of Philip Larkin.

Lawrence, D. H. "Piano," from NEW POEMS, 1918.

Lazarus, Emma. "The New Colossus," 1883. Posted on the Statue of Liberty, 1903.

Lear, Edward. "The Jumblies" from A VICTORIAN ANTHOLOGY, 1837–1895. Edmund Clarence Stedman, ed. 1895.

Lee, Li-Young. "Night Mirror" from BOOK OF MY NIGHTS. Copyright © 2001 by Li-Young Lee. Reprinted with the permission of The Permissions Company, Inc., on behalf of BOA Editions, Ltd., www.boaeditions.org.

Lessing, Doris. From AFRICAN LAUGHTER: FOUR VISITS TO ZIMBABWE. HarperCollins, 1992.

Levertov, Denise. "Ancient Stairway" from THIS GREAT UNKNOWING, copyright © 1999 by The Denise Levertov Literary Trust, Paul A. Lacey and Valerie Trueblood Rapport, Co-Trustees. Reprinted by permission of New Directions Publishing Corp.

Levertov, Denise. "O Taste and See." By Denise Levertov, from POEMS 1960–1967, copyright © 1964 by Denise Levertov. Reprinted by permission of New Directions Publishing Corp.

Lim, Shirley Geok-lin. "Riding into California," "Learning to love America," from WHAT THE FORTUNE TELLER DIDN'T SAY. Copyright © 1998 by Shirley Geok-lin Lim. Reprinted with the permission of The Permissions Company, Inc., on behalf of West End Press, Albuquerque, New Mexico, http://www.westendpress.org.

Longfellow, Henry Wadsworth. "A Psalm of Life." Originally published in *The Knickerbocker*, October 1838.

Longfellow, Henry Wadsworth. "Aftermath," from AFTERMATH, 1873.

Longfellow, Henry Wadsworth. "Evangeline, A Tale of Acadie," 1847.

Lovelace, Richard. "To Lucasta, Going to the Warres," from LUCASTA, 1649.

Lowell, Robert. Reprinted by permission of Farrar, Straus & Giroux, LLC: "Skunk Hour" from COLLECTED POEMS by Robert Lowell. Copyright © 2003 by Harriet Lowell and Sheridan Lowell.

Machado, Antonio. "The Traveler" by Antonio Machado in CAMPOS DE CASTILLA, 1922, translated by Michael Ortiz 2011. Used by permission.

Majmudar, Amit. "Rites to Allay the Dead." © 2009 by Amit Majmudar. Published 2009 by TriQuarterly Books/Northwestern University Press. All rights reserved.

Mali, Taylor. "Totally like whatever, you know?" Used by permission.

Mallarmé, Stéphane. From Jules Huret: ENQUETE SUR L'ÉVOLUTION LITTÉRAIRE. Paris: Fasquelle, 1913, pp 55–65.

Markham, Edwin. "Outwitted" from THE SHOES OF HAPPINESS AND OTHER POEMS, Doubleday, Page & Company, 1915.

Marlowe, Christopher. "The Tragical History of the Life and Death of Doctor Faustus," 1592.

Marvell, Andrew. "To His Coy Mistress," 1681.

Masefield, John. "Cargoes." From BALLADS. Elkin Mathews, Vigo Street. London, 1903.

Mason, David. "Song of the Powers" from THE COUNTRY I REMEMBER. Story Line Press, 1996. Reprinted by permission of the author.

Matsou, Basho. "Heat-lightning streak," "In the old stone pool," translated by X. J. Kennedy.

Matsushita, Suiko. "Cosmos in Bloom," "Rain Shower from Mountain," by Suiko Matsushita, translated by Violet Kazue de Cristoro in MAY SKY: THERE IS ALWAYS TOMORROW. Reprinted by permission of Kimiko de Cristoforo.

Matthews, Washington. "Last Words of the Prophet," from THE MOUNTAIN CHANT: A NAVAJO CEREMONY. Government Printing Office, Washington, 1887.

McKay, Claude. "If We Must Die." Originally published in *The Liberator*, July 1919.

McKay, Claude. "America." Originally published in *The Liberator*, December 1921.

Menashe, Samuel. "Bread," from COLLECTED POEMS by Samuel Menashe. Copyright 1986 by Samuel Menashe. Reprinted by permission of the author.

Merwin, W. S. "For the Anniversary of My Death," by W. S. Merwin. Originally published in THE LICE and currently collected in "THE SECOND FOUR BOOK OF POEMS." Copyright 1967, 1968, 1969, 1970, 1971, 1972, 1973, 1993 by W. S. Merwin, used by permission of The Wylie Agency LLC.

Millay, Edna St. Vincent. "Recuerdo," from A FEW FIGS FROM THISTLES: POEMS AND SONNETS. New York and London: Harper, 1922.

Millay, Edna St. Vincent. "Second Fig," from A FEW FIGS FROM THISTLES. Harper and Brothers Publishers. London, 1920.

Millay, Edna St. Vincent. "What lips my lips have kissed, and where, and why," from THE HARP-WEAVER AND OTHER POEMS, 1923.

Millay, Edna St. Vincent. "Counting-out Rhyme," from COLLECTED POEMS. Copyright 1928, © 1955 by Edna St. Vincent Millay and Norma Millay Ellis. Reprinted with the permission of The Permissions Company, Inc., on behalf of Holly Peppe, Literary Executor, The Millay Society, www.millay.org.

Milton, John. "Paradise Lost," Samuel Simmons, 1667.

Milton, John. "When I consider how my light is spent," from POEMS, 1673.

Milton, John. From "Paradise Lost." Published by Samuel Simmons, 1674 (second edition).

Momaday, N. Scott. "Simile" from ANGLE OF GESE AND OTHER POEMS. Copyright 1974. Used by permission of the author.

Moore, Marianne. "Poetry," 1915.

Moore, Marianne. "A Note on T. S. Eliot's Book," in *Poetry* 12, pp 36–37, 1918.

Morgan, Emanuel (Witter Bynner). "Opus 6" from SPECTRA: A BOOK OF POETIC EXPERIMENTS, 1916.

Moss, Howard. "Shall I Compare Thee to a Summer's Day," from A SWIM OFF THE ROCKS: LIGHT VERSE by Howard Moss. Reprinted by permission of the Estate of Howard Moss.

Mother Goose. "Pussy Cat, Pussy Cat," published by James William Elliott in NATIONAL NURSERY RHYMES AND NURSERY SONGS, 1870.

Neiji, Ozawa. "The War—This Year" by Ozawa Neiji, translated by Violet Kazue de Cristoro in MAY SKY: THERE IS ALWAYS TOMORROW. Reprinted by permission of Kimiko de Cristoforo.

Nelson, Marilyn. "A Strange Beautiful Woman" from THE FIELDS OF PRAISE, 1997 Louisiana State University Press. Used by permission of Louisiana State University Press.

Neruda, Pablo. Reprinted by permission of Farrar, Straus and Giroux: "We Are Many," from EXTRAVAGARIA, translated by Alastair Reid. Translation copyright © 1974 by Alastair Reid.

Newton, John. "Amazing Grace," from OLNEY HYMNS, 1779.

Nezhukumatathil, Aimee. "What I Learned from the Incredible Hulk" from MIRACLE FRUIT. Copyright © 2003 by Aimee Nezhukumatathil. Published by Tupelo Press. Reprinted by permission of the author.

Nguyen, Hieu Minh. "Arranged." Copyright © 2014. Used by permission.

Nguyen, Thao. "Meticulous Bird," licensed courtesy of Domino Publishing Company Ltd.

Niedecker, Lorine. "Sorrow Moves in Wide Waves" from COLLECTED WORKS, edited by Jenny Penberthy, Copyright © 2002 Regents of the University of California. Published by University of California Press. Permission conveyed through Copyright Clearance Center, Inc.

Niedecker, Lorine: "Popcorn-can cover" from LORINE NIEDECKER: COLLECTED WORKS, edited by Jenny Penberthy, Copyright © 2002 Regents of the University of California. Permission conveyed through Copyright Clearance Center, Inc.

Nims, Frederick. "Contemplation" by Frederick Nims, first appeared under the Title "A Thought for Tristam" in *The New Yorker Magazine*, 1967. Republished in SELECTED POEMS, © 1982 by the University of Chicago Press. Reprinted by permission of the University of Chicago Press.

Noguchi, Yone. "Oh, How Cool."

Noguchi, Yone. Japanese Hokku.

O'Donnell, Angela Alaimo. "Tattoo," from MOVING HOUSE © 2009 WordTech Communications LLC. Cincinnati, Ohio, USA.

O'Hara, Frank. "To the Harbormaster." Excerpts from MEDITATIONS IN AN EMERGENCY, copyright © 1957 by Frank O'Hara. Used by permission of Grove/Atlantic, Inc. Any third party use of this material, outside of this publication, is prohibited.

Olds, Sharon. "Rite of Passage" from THE DEATH AND THE LIVING by Sharon Olds, copyright © 1975, 1978, 1979, 1980, 1981, 1982, 1983 by Sharon Olds. Used by permission of Alfred A. Knopf, a division of Penguin Random House LLC. All rights reserved.

Oliver, Mary. "Wild Geese." Excerpts from DREAM WORK, copyright © 1986 by Mary Oliver. Used by permission of Grove/Atlantic, Inc. Any third party use of this material, outside of this publication, is prohibited.

Ortiz Cofer, Judith. "Quinceañera" is reprinted with permission from the publisher of SILENT DANCING by Judith Ortiz Cofer (© 1991 Arte Publico Press—University of Houston).

Owen, Wilfred. On Writing, "War Poetry," 1917.

Owen, Wilfred. "Anthem for Doomed Youth," 1817.

Owen, Wilfred. "Dulce et Decorum Est." Originally published in POEMS, 1920.

Owen, Wilfred. "Strange Meeting," 1919.

Pacheco, Jose Emilio. "Alta Traición," ("High Treason") from DON'T ASK ME HOW THE TIME GOES BY by Jose Emilio Pacheco, translated by Alastair Reid. Copyright © 1978 Columbia University Press. Reprinted with permission of the publisher.

Parker, Dorothy. "Resume," copyright 1926, 1928, renewed 1954, © 1956 by Dorothy Parker; from THE PORTABLE DOROTHY PARKER by Dorothy Parker, edited by Marion Meade. Used by permission of Viking Books, an imprint of Penguin Publishing Group, a division of Penguin Random House LLC. All rights reserved.

Paz, Octavio. "Con los ojos cerrados" and "With eyes closed" Octavio Paz, translated by Eliot Weinberger, from THE COLLECTED POEMS 1957–1987, copyright © 1986 by Octavio Paz and Eliot Weinberger. Reprinted by permission of New Directions Publishing Corp.

Paz, Octavio. From "The Bow and the Lyre The Poem, The Poetic Revelation, Poetry and History." © 1956 by the Fondo de Cultura Economica, Mexico, D.F.

Pinckney, Darryl. "Black Identity in Langston Hughes," excerpt from "Suitcase in Harlem" by Darryl Pinckney from *The New York Review of Books*, Feb. 16, 1989. Reprinted by permission of The New York Review of Books.

Plath, Sylvia. "Lady Lazarus," all lines from "Daddy," from THE COLLECTED POEMS OF SYLVIA PLATH, edited by Ted Hughes. Copyright © 1960, 1965, 1971, 1981 by the Estate of Sylvia Plath. Reprint by Permission of HarperCollins Publishers.

Plath, Sylvia. "Metaphors" from "CROSSING THE WATER by Sylvia Plath. Copyright © 1960 by Ted Hughes. Reprinted by the permission of HarperCollins Publishers.

Po, Li (701–762). "Drinking Alone by Moonlight."

Poe, Edgar Allan. "A Long Poem Does Not Exist," from THE POETIC PRINCIPLE, 1850.

Poe, Edgar Allan. "Annabel Lee," from The Obituary of Edgar Allen Poe in *The New York Daily Tribune*, October 9, 1849.

Poe, Edgar Allan. "To Helen," from POEMS OF EDGAR A. POE, 1831.

Poe, Edgar Allan. From "The Poetic Principle," published in *Home Journal*, no. 36, August 31, 1850.

Poe, Edgar Allen: "Ulalume." Originally Published in the *American Whig Review*. December, 1847.

Pope, Alexander. "A little Learning is a dang'rous Thing," "True Ease in Writing Comes from Art, Not Chance," from "An Essay on Criticism," 1711.

Pound, Ezra. "In a station of Metro." Originally published in *Poetry*, 1913.

Pound, Ezra. "Letter from Pound to Monroe," January 1915, November 1914, September 1914.

Pound, Ezra. "Review: Modern Georgics," "A review of 'North of Boston'" by Robert Frost. From *Poetry*, Vol. 5, No. 3 (Dec., 1914), pp. 127–130.

Pound, Ezra. "Salutation" from LUSTRA OF EZRA POUND, 1916.

Pound, Ezra. "The Image" from "A Retrospect"— Including "A Few Don'ts." Originally published in PAVANNES AND DIVAGATIONS, 1918.

Pound, Ezra. "The River-Merchant's Wife: A Letter," original by Rihaku, from PERSONAE, copyright 1926 by Ezra Pound. Reprinted by permission of New Directions Publishing Corp.

Pound, Ezra. From "A Few Don'ts" (1913)

Raffel, Burton. "Indeterminancy in Eliot's Poetry," from T. S. ELIOT. Reprinted by the permission of the Burton Nathan Raffel Estate.

Raine, Craig. "A Martian Sends a Postcard Home," by Craig Raine. Reprinted by permission of David Godwin Associates.

Rampersad, Arnold. "Hughes as an Experimentalist," from AFRICAN AMERICAN WRITERS. Reprinted with permission of the author.

Randall, Dudley. "Ballad of Birmingham," from CITIES BURNING with permission of the Dudley Randall Estate.

Randall, Dudley. Reprinted by permission of the Dudley Randall Literary Estate. "Ballad of Birmingham," in ROSES AND REVOLUTIONS: THE SELECTED WRITINGS OF DUDLEY RANDALL.

Reed, Henry. "Naming of Parts." Reprinted with permission from John Tydeman, literary executor of the Estate of Henry Reed.

Reed, Ishmael. "Oakland Blues." Excerpted from the book, NEW AND COLLECTED POEMS, 1964–2006. Copyright © 2006 by Ishmael Reed. Permission granted by Lowenstein Associates, Inc.

Reid, Alastair. "On Writing Translating Neruda" from NERUDA AND BORGES.

Rich, Adrienne. "Aunt Jennifer's Tigers." Copyright © 2002, 1951 by Adrienne Rich, from THE FACT OF A DOORFRAME: SELECTED POEMS 1950–2001 by Adrienne Rich. Used by permission of W. W. Norton & Company, Inc.

Rich, Adrienne. "Living in Sin." Copyright © 2002, 1955 by Adrienne Rich, from THE FACT OF A DOORFRAME: SELECTED POEMS 1950–2001 by Adrienne Rich. Used by permission of W. W. Norton & Company, Inc.

Rich, Adrienne. "Women." Copyright © 1993 by Adrienne Rich. Copyright © 1969 by W. W. Norton & Company, Inc, from COLLECTED EARLY POEMS: 1950–1970 Adrienne Rich. Used by permission of W. W. Norton & Company, Inc.

Rich, Adrienne. Excerpt from "'When We Dead Awaken': Writing as Re-Vision," from ARTS OF THE POSSIBLE: ESSAYS AND CONVERSATIONS by Adrienne Rich. Copyright © 2001 by Adrienne Rich. Used by permission of W. W. Norton & Company, Inc.

Richard, Wilbur. "Concerning 'Love Calls Us to the Things of This World'" by Richard Wilbur from ON MY OWN WORK, © 1983. Reprinted by permission of the author.

Ricks, Christopher. "What's in a Name?" T. S. Eliot and Prejudice, © 1988 by Christopher Ricks. Published by the University of California Press. Reprinted with permission.

Robinson, Edwin Arlington. "Luke Havergal." Originally published in THE TORRENT AND THE NIGHT BEFORE, 1896.

Robinson, Edwin Arlington. "Miniver Cheevy," from THE TOWN DOWN THE RIVER, 1910.

Robinson, Edwin Arlington. "Richard Cory," from THE CHILDREN OF THE NIGHT, 1897.

Robinson, Jeffers. "The Collected Poetry of Robinson Jeffers," edited by Tim Hunt, Volume 2 1928–1938 by Robinson Jeffers. Copyright © 1938 renewed 1966 by Donna Jeffers and Garth Jeffers. All rights reserved. Used with the permission of Stanford University Press, www.sup.org.

Rodriguez, Luis J. "Praise to Shoes." Reprinted by permission of Luis J. Rodriguez.

Roethke, Theodore. "My Papa's Waltz," copyright © 1942 by Hearst Magazines, Inc., copyright © 1966 and renewed 1994 by Beatrice Lushington; "Root Cellar," copyright © 1943 by Modern Poetry Association, Inc; from COLLECTED POEMS by Theodore Roethke. Used by permission of Doubleday, an imprint of the Knopf Doubleday Publishing Group, a division of Penguin Random House LLC. All rights reserved.

Rossetti, Christina. "Song." Originally published GOBLIN MARKET AND OTHER POEMS, 1862.

Rossetti, Christina. "Up-Hill," from GOBLIN MARKET AND OTHER POEMS. Macmillan, 1862.

Ryan, Kay, "Turtle" from FLAMINGO WATCHING, copyright © 1994 by Kay Ryan. Used by permission of Copper Beech Press.

Ryan, Kay. "A Conversation with Kay Ryan" conducted by Dana Gioia.

Ryan, Kay. "That Will to Divest," "Blandeur." Excerpt from SAY UNCLE, copyright © 1991 by Kay Ryan. Used by permission of Grove/Atlantic, Inc. Any third party use of this material, outside of this publication, is prohibited.

Saltus, Francis. "Dolce Far Niente."

Sandburg, Carl. "Grass" from CORNHUSKERS, Originally published by Henry Holt and Company, 1918.

Sandburg, Carl. "Fog," from CHICAGO POEMS, 1916.

Satyamurti, Carole. "I Shall Paint my Nails Red" by Carole Satyamurti from STITCHING IN THE DARK: NEW AND SELECTED POEMS, copyright 2005 by Bloodaxe Books. Reprinted by permission of Bloodaxe Books.

Service, Robert. "The Shooting of Dan McGrew," from THE SONGS OF A SOURDOUGH, 1907.

Sexton, Anne. "Cinderella" from TRANSFORMATIONS by Anne Sexton. Copyright © 1971 by Anne Sexton, renewed 1989 by Linda G. Sexton. Reprinted by permission of Houghton Mifflin Harcourt Publishing Company. All rights reserved.

Shakespeare, William. "When daisies pied and violets blue," from "Love Labour's Lost, Act V, Scene II"; "Balcony Scene," from "Romeo and Juliet," Act II, Scene 2; "My mistress' eyes are nothing like the sun (Sonnet 130)," from SONNETS, 1609; "O mistress mine," from "Twelfth Night," Act II, Scene III; "Sonnet 116," from SONNETS, 1609; "Sonnet 18" from SONNETS, 1609; "Sonnet 65," from SONNETS, 1609; "When to the sessions of sweet silent thought (Sonnet 30)," from SONNETS, 1609; "When, in disgrace with Fortune and men's eyes (Sonnet 29)," from SONNETS, 1609.

Shelley, Percy Bysshe. "Adonais: An Elegy on the Death of John Keats, Author of Endymion, Hyperion, etc." 1821.

Shelley, Percy Bysshe. "Ode to the West Wind," from PROMETHEUS UNBOUND, A LYRICAL DRAMA IN FOUR ACTS, WITH OTHER POEMS, 1820.

Shelley, Percy Bysshe. "Ozymandias" from ROSALIND AND HELEN, A MODERN ECLOGUE; WITH OTHER POEMS, 1819.

Shihab Nye, Naomi. "The Traveling Onion." Reprinted by permission of the author, Naomi Shihab Nye, 2014.

Simic, Charles. "The Magic Study of Happiness" by Charles Simic from DIME-STORE ALCHEMY: THE ART OF JOSEPH CORNELL, published by Ecco Press, © 1992. Reprinted by permission of the author.

Simic, Charles. "Butcher Shop," from Selected Early Poems. Copyright © 1971 by Charles Simic. Reprinted with the permission of The Permissions Company, Inc., on behalf of George Braziller, Inc., www.georgebraziller.com. All rights reserved.

Simon, Paul. "Richard Cory." Copyright © 1966 Paul Simon. Used by permission of the publisher: Paul Simon Music.

Sitwell, Edith. "Mariner Man," originally published in WHEELS, 1918.

Smart, Christopher. "Jubilate Agno, Fragment B, [For I will consider my Cat Jeoffry]." Written between 1759 and 1763, published 1939 in REJOICE IN THE LAMB: A SONG FROM BEDLAM, edited by W. F. Stead.

Smith, Bessie. "Jailhouse Blues." Brooks/Rust, 1923.

Smith, Patricia. "Hip-Hop Ghazal" from SHOULDA BEEN JIMI SAVANNAH. Copyright © 2012 by Patricia Smith. Reprinted with the permission of The Permissions Company, Inc., on behalf of Coffee House Press, www.coffeehousepress.org.

Smith, Stevie. "Not Waving but Drowning" by Stevie Smith, from COLLECTED POEMS OF STEVIE SMITH, copyright ©1957 by Stevie Smith. Reprinted by permission of New Directions Publishing Corp.

Snyder, Gary. "Mid-August at Sourdough Mountain" by Gary Snyder, from EARTH HOUSE HOLD, copyright ©1969 by Gary Snyder. Reprinted by permission of New Directions Publishing Corp.

Song, Cathy. "Stamp Collecting", from FRAMELESS WINDOWS, SQUARES OF LIGHT: POEMS by Cathy Song. Copyright © 1988 by Cathy Song. Used by permission of W. W. Norton & Company, Inc.

Spenser, Edmund. "Epithalamion" from AMORETTI AND EPITHALAMION. Printed by William Ponsonby, 1595.

Stafford, William. "Ask Me" from ASK ME: 100 ESSENTIAL POEMS. Copyright 1977, 2014 by William Stafford and the Estate of William Stafford. Reprinted with the permission of The Permissions Company, Inc. on behalf of Graywolf Press, www.graywolfpress.org.

Stallings, A. E. "Sine Qua Non," from HAPAX: POEMS. © 2006 by A. E. Stallings. Published 2006 by TriQuarterly Books/Northwestern University Press. All rights reserved.

Stallings, A. E. "First Love: A Quiz." Copyright © 2006 by A. E. Stallings. Published 2006 by Northwestern University Press. All rights reserved.

Stallings, A. E. "On Form and Artifice" by A. E. Stallings from "Crooked Roads Without Improvement: Some Thoughts on Formal Verse." Copyright by A. E. Stallings. Used by permission.

Steele, Timothy: "Epitaph," from "An Interlude of Epigrams," from SAPPHICS AND UNCERTAINTIES: POEMS 1970–1986. Copyright © 1986, 1995 by Timothy Steele. Reprinted with the permission of The Permissions Company, Inc., on behalf of the University of Arkansas Press, www.uapress.com.

Stein, Gertrude. "Nothing Elegant," from TENDER BUTTONS, 1914

Stephens, James. "The Wind." From COLLECTED POEMS, 1926.

Stevens, Wallace. "Anecdote of the Jar," "The Snow Man," "Thirteen Ways of Looking at a Blackbird," from HARMONIUM. Knopf, 1923.

Stevens, Wallace. "Disillusionment of Ten O'Clock," From HARMONIUM, 1915.

Stevens, Wallace. "Sunday Morning." Originally Published in *Poetry*, VII No. 2, 1915.

Stevens, Wallace. "The Emperor of Ice-Cream," from HARMONIUM. Knopf, 1922.

Stevens, Wallace. From "Adagia," in OPUS POSTHUMOUS. Knopf, 1957.

Stevenson, Anne. "The Victory," by Anne Stevenson from POEMS 1955–2005, copyright 2005 by Bloodaxe Books. Reprinted by permission of Bloodaxe Books.

Stewart, Aurora. "word play." Used by permission.

Stillman, Michael. Reprinted by permission from Michael Stillman, "In Memoriam John Coltrane." Published by Occident, Fall 1971. Copyright © 1971 by Michael Stillman.

Swift, Jonathan. "A Description of the Morning," originally published in The Tatler, October 1710.

Swinburne, Algernon Charles. "Atalanta in Calydon," 1865.

Taniguchi, Benson. "That Piercing Chill I Feel," from INTRODUCTION TO HAIKU by Harold Gould Henderson, copyright © 1958 by Harold G. Henderson. Used by permission of Doubleday, an imprint of the Knopf Doubleday Publishing Group, a division of Random House LLC. All rights reserved.

Taniguchi, Buson. "Moonrise on mudflats," by Buson Taniguchi, translated by Michael Stillman. Reprinted by permission of Michael Stillman.

Taniguchi, Buson. "On the one-ton temple bell," translated by X. J. Kennedy.

Tennyson, Lord Alfred. "Break, Break, Break," 1834

Tennyson, Lord Alfred. "In Memoriam," 1850

Tennyson, Lord Alfred. "Tears, Idle Tears," "Come Down, O Maid." From THE PRINCESS, 1847.

Tennyson, Lord Alfred. "The Eagle," 1851.

Tennyson, Lord Alfred. "The Splendor Falls on Castle Walls," 1847.

Tennyson, Lord Alfred. "Ulysses," 1842.

Tennyson, Lord Alfred. "Flower in the Crannied Wall," 1863.

The Bible. "The Parable of the Good Seed," Matthew 13:24–30.

Thiel, Diane. "Map of Myth," by Diane Thiel. Copyright © 2014, by Diane Thiel. Used by permission of Diane Thiel.

Thiel, Diane. "Memento Mori," "The Minefield," by Diane Thiel from ECHOLOCATIONS, Story Line Press, November 1, 2000, edited by Diane Thiel. Copyright © 2000, by Diane Thiel. Used by permission of Diane Thiel.

Thiel, Diane. Translation of "Presente en que el Carino Hace Regalo la Llaneza," by Sor Juana. Translated as "A Simple Gift Made Rich by Affection." Used with permission of Diane Thiel.

Thomas, Dylan. "Do not go gentle into that good night," from THE POEMS OF DYLAN THOMAS, copyright © 1952 by Dylan Thomas. Reprinted by permission of New Directions Publishing Corp.

Thomas, Dylan. "Fern Hill," from THE POEMS OF DYLAN THOMAS, copyright ©1945 by The Trustees for the Copyrights of Dylan Thomas. Reprinted by permission of New Directions Publishing Corp.

Thomas, Dylan. "Under Milk Wood," 1954.

Thompson, Anne-Marie. "Audiation," from AUDIATION. Published by Story Line Press. Copyright 2013. Used with permission.

Tillman, Joshua. "Bored in the U.S.A." Written by Joshua Tillman. Published by Kobalt Music Services Ltd (KMS) obo Cripple Creek Ferries.

Toomer, Jean. "Reapers," from CANE by Jean Toomer. Copyright 1923 by Boni & Liveright, renewed 1951 by Jean Toomer. Used by permission of Liveright Publishing Corporation.

Townsend, Peter. JAZZ IN AMERICAN CULTURE (Jackson: University Press of Mississippi, 2000), 126–128.

Trethewey, Natasha. "White Lies," from DOMESTIC WORK. Copyright © 1998, 2000 by Natasha Trethewey. Reprinted with the permission of The Permissions Company, Inc., on behalf of Graywolf Press, www.graywolfpress.org.

Turner, Brian. "The Hurt Locker," from HERE, BULLET published Alice James Books. Copyright 2005. Reprinted with permission of The Permissions Company, Inc. on behalf of Alice James Books.

Twain, Mark. From his "Fulton Day, Jamestown," speech of September 23, 1907.

Uyematsu, Amy. "Deliberate," 30 MILES FROM J-TOWN (1992, Story Line Press). Copyright by Amy Uyematsu. Reprinted by permission of the author.

Valdés, Gina. "English con Salsa." Published by The Americas Review, Houston, Texas. Reprinted by permission of the author.

Vallejo, César. "La cólera que quiebra al hombre en niños." POEMAS HUMANOS, 1937.

Videlock, Wendy. "If Not for the Dark," from THE DARK GNU AND OTHER POEMS, Able Muse Press. Copyright © 2013. Used by permission of the author.

Virgilio, Nick. "The Old Neighborhood," by Nick Virgilio from NICK VIRGILIO: A LIFE IN HAIKU, copyright © 2012. Reprinted by permission of Anthony Virgilio.

Walcott, Derek. "Sea Grapes," from COLLECTED POEMS 1948–1984. Copyright © 1986 by Derek Walcott. Reprinted by permission of Farrar, Straus and Giroux, LLC.

Walker, Cody. "I'm like," from Able Muse: A Review of Poetry, Prose, and Art, Number 22, Winter 2016. Used by permission.

Waller, Edmund. "Go, Lovely Rose," 1645.

Webster, John. "The Duchess of Malfi," 1623.

Whitman, Walt. "Beat! Beat! Drums!" Originally Published in Harper's Weekly, 1861.

Whitman, Walt. "I Hear America Singing," "O Captain! My Captain," "The Runner," "To A Stranger," "When I Heard the Learn'd Astronomer," from LEAVES OF GRASS, 1867.

Whitman, Walt. "Song of Myself" from LEAVES OF GRASS, 1892.

Whitman, Walt. "Song of the Open Road," from LEAVES OF GRASS, 1856.

Whitman, Walt. "The Poetry of the Future." From the *North American Review,* February 12, 1881.

Whitman, Walt. "When Lilacs Last in the Door-yard Bloom'd," from SEQUEL TO DRUM-TAPS, 1865

Wilbur, Richard. "Love Calls Us To The Things Of This World," from THINGS OF THIS WORLD by Richard Wilbur. Copyright 1956 and renewed 1984 by Richard Wilbur. Reprinted by permission of Houghton Mifflin Harcourt Publishing Company. All rights reserved.

Wilbur, Richard. From "Sumptuous Destitution," from RESPONSES: PROSE PIECES, 1953–1976 by Richard Wilbur. Reprinted with permission from the author.

William, Stafford. A paraphrase of "Ask Me," excerpted from FIFTY CONTEMPORARY POETS: THE CREATIVE PROCESS, edited by Alberta T. Turner (David McKay Company, Inc., 1977), as shown.

Williams, Miller. As quoted by Mike Holtzclaw in "One reporter's fond memory of a chat with the great poet Miller Williams." *The Daily Press,* January 5, 2015.

Williams, William Carlos. "El hombre." Originally published in AL QUE QUIERE!, 1917.

Williams, William Carlos. "Smell!" originally published in *Poetry Magazine,* July 1917.

Williams, William Carlos. "Queen-Anne's-Lace," "The Widow's Lament in Springtime," "Winter Trees," from SOUR GRAPES. Boston: The Four Seas Company, 1921.

Williams, William Carlos. "The Red Wheelbar-row," "This is Just to Say," by William Carlos Williams, from THE COLLECTED POEMS: VOLUME I, 1909–1939, copyright ©1938 by New Directions Publishing Corp. Reprinted by permission of New Directions Publishing Corp.

Williams, William Carlos. "The Dance (In Brueghel's)," by William Carlos Williams, from THE COLLECTED POEMS: VOLUME II, 1939–1962, copyright ©1944 by William Carlos Williams. Reprinted by permission of New Directions Publishing Corp.

Wolff, Cynthia Griffin. "Dickinson and Death" (A Reading of "Because I could not stop for Death") from THE COLUMBIA HISTORY OF AMERICAN POETRY by Jay Parini & Brett Miller. Copyright Columbia University Press. Reprinted with permission of the publisher.

Woodworth, Samuel. "The Old Oaken Bucket," from THE WORLD'S BEST POETRY. Volume I. Of Home: of Friendship. 1904.

Wordsworth, Dorothy. "Journal Entry," 1802.

Wordsworth, William. "Resolution and Independence," "Composed upon Westminster Bridge, September 3, 1802," "My Heart Leaps Up" also known as "The Rainbow," "The world is too much with us," "I Wandered Lonely as a Cloud," from POEMS IN TWO VOLUMES, 1807.

Wordsworth, William. "A Slumber Did My Spirit Seal," Originally published in LYRICAL BAL-LADS, 1800

Wordsworth, William. "Mutability." From ECCLESIASTICAL SKETCHES, 1822.

Wordsworth, William. From the Preface to LYRI-CAL BALLADS WITH A FEW OTHER PIECES OF POETRY, 1798.

Wright, Franz. "Alcohol," from ILL LIT: SELECTED AND NEW POEMS. Copyright © 1989 by Franz Wright. Reprinted with the per-mission of Oberlin College Press.

Wright, James. "Autumn Begins at Martin's Ferry, Ohio," from COLLECTED POEMS © 1962 by James Wright. Reprinted by permission of Wes-leyan University Press.

Wroth, Mary Sidney. (1587–1651/1653) "In this strange labyrinth."

Wyatt, Sir Thomas. (1503–1542) "They flee from me that sometime did me sekë."

Yeats, W. B. Reprinted with the permission of Scribner Publishing Group, a division of Simon & Schuster, Inc. from THE COLLECTED WORKS OF W. B. YEATS, VOLUME I: THE POEMS, REVISED by W. B. Yeats, edited by Richard J. Finneran. Copyright © 1928 by The Macmillan Company, renewed © 1956 by Georgie Yeats. All rights reserved. Yeats, Wil-liam Butler. "A Prayer for Old Age," from PAR-NELL'S FUNERAL AND OTHER POEMS, 1935.

Yeats, William Butler. "He Wishes for the Cloths of Heaven," from THE WIND AMONG THE REEDS, 1899.

Yeats, William Butler. "Poetic Symbols," from THE PHILOSOPHY OF SHELLEY'S POETRY. The Sign of the Unicorn, 1900.

Yeats, William Butler. "The Lake Isle of Innisfree." Originally published in *National Observer,* 1890.

Yeats, William Butler. "The Magi," from *Poetry,* vol. IV no. 11, May 1914.

Yeats, William Butler. "The Second Coming," from MICHAEL ROBARTES AND THE DANCER, 1921.

Yeats, William Butler. "When You Are Old," from THE COUNTLESS KATHLEEN AND VARI-OUS LEGENDS AND LYRICS, 1892.

Yeats, William Butler. "Who Goes with Fergus?" from THE ROSE, 1892.

Zollo, Paul. Reprinted with permission of Paul Zollo, from "Bob Dylan," SONGWRITERS ON SONGWRITING. Copyright Paul Zollo 1991, 1997.

DRAMA

Aristotle; Potts, L. J. Excerpt from "Aristotle on the Art of Fiction," by Aristotle, trans. by L. J. Potts. Copyright ©1953 Cambridge University Press. Reprinted with the permission of Cam-bridge University Press.

Asquith, Clare. SHADOWPLAY: THE HIDDEN BELIEFS AND CODED POLITICS OF WILLIAM SHAKESPEARE, © 2005 Clare Asquith (PublicAffairs, New York, NY). Reprinted by permission of the author.

Auden, W. H. "Iago as a Triumphant Villain," from "The Joker in the Pack" in THE DYERS HAND AND OTHER ESSAYS. Random House, 1962.

Bamber, Linda. Excerpt from COMIC WOMEN, TRAGIC MEN by Linda Bamber. Copyright © 1982 by the Board of Trustees of the Leland Stanford Jr. University. All rights reserved. Reprinted with permission of Stanford University Press, www.sup.org

Bevington, David. "Othello," and "A Midsummer Night's Dream," from THE COMPLETE WORKS OF SHAKESPEARE, 7th ed., © 2014. Reprinted by permission of Pearson Education, Inc., Upper Saddle River, New Jersey.

Bodkin, Maud. "Lucifer in Shakespeare's Othello." From ARCHETYPAL PATTERNS IN POETRY, 1934.

Bok Lee, Edward. "On Being a Korean American Writer." Copyright © 2006 by Edward Bok Lee. Reprinted by permission of the author.

Bok Lee, Edward. Excerpt from "El Santo Americano," by Edward Bok Lee. Reprinted by permission of the author.

Burgess, Anthony. "An Asian Culture Looks at Shakespeare," from "The Importance of Translation" by Anthony Burgess. Reprinted by permission of David Higham Associates Limited.

Cooper, Sharon, E. "Mistaken Identity," Originally published in published in LAUGH LINES: SHORT COMIC PLAYS, edited by Eric Lane and Nina Shengold, Vintage, 2007. Used by permission. For inquiries regarding production, please contact the playwright directly. secooper1@yahoo.com. www.sharonecooper.com.

Freud, Sigmund. "The Destiny of Oedipus," from THE INTERPRETATION OF DREAMS. Macmillan, 1913.

Glaspell, Susan "On Creating 'Trifles.'" From *Dramatist*; Sep/Oct 2009, Vol. 12 Issue 1, p 76,

Glaspell, Susan "Trifles." First performed at the Wharf Theatre in Provincetown, MA. August 8, 1916.

Grene, David. "Antigonê," "Oedipus the King," by Sophocles, translated by David Grene from Sophocles I, 3rd edition Copyright © 2013. University of Chicago Press. Used with permission.

Haigh, A. E. "The Irony of Sophocles," from THE TRAGIC DRAMA OF THE GREEKS. Clarendon Press: 1896.

Haigh, Arthur Elam. From "The Tragic Drama of the Greeks," Dover Publications 1896.

Hansberry, Lorraine. Entire play from "A Raisin in the Sun" by Lorraine Hansberry, copyright © 1958 by Robert Nemiroff, as an unpublished work. Copyright © 1959, 1966, 1984 by Robert Nemiroff. Copyright renewed 1986, 1987 by Robert Nemiroff. Used by permission of Random House, an imprint and division of Penguin Random House LLC. All rights reserved.

Hansberry, Lorraine. From TO BE YOUNG, GIFTED AND BLACK: LORRAINE HANSBERRY IN HER OWN WORDS by Lorraine Hansberry, adapted by Robert Nemiroff. Copyright © 1969 by Robert Nemiroff and Robert Nemiroff as Executor of the Estate of Lorraine Hansberry. Reprinted with the permission of Simon & Schuster, Inc. All rights reserved.

Hwang, David Henry. "The Sound of a Voice," from FOB AND OTHER PLAYS by David Henry Hwang. Reproduced with permission from the Steven Barclay Agency.

Ibsen, Henrik. Correspondence on the final scene of "A Doll's House." LETTERS OF HENRIK IBSEN. Fox, Duffield, and Company, 1905

Isben, Henrik. "A Doll's House," translated by R. Farquharson Sharp and Eleanor Marx-Aveling, revised 2008 by Viktoria Michelsen. Copyright © 2008 by Viktoria Michelsen. Reprinted by permission.

Ives, David. "An Interview with David Ives." Reprinted with permission.

Ives, David. "Sure Thing," from ALL IN THE TIMING: FOURTEEN PLAYS BY DAVID IVES, copyright © 1989, 1990, 1992 by David Ives. Used by permission of Vintage Books, an imprint of the Knopf Doubleday Publishing Group, a division of Penguin Random House LLC. All rights reserved.

Ives, David. Prose, "On the One-Act Play," (excerpt from "The Exploding Rose." *The Dramatist* (2006)). Reprinted with permission of the author.

Johnson, Samuel. "Shakespeare's Universality," from PREFACE TO SHAKESPEARE, 1765.

Jonson, Ben. "On His Friend and Rival William Shakespeare," 1640.

Lines, Patricia M. Excerpt from "What Is Antigonê's Tragic Flaw?" by Patricia M. Lines. Reprinted by permission of the author.

Marlowe, Christopher. Scene from "Doctor Faustus," (about 1588). Edited by Sylvan Barnet.

Martin, Jane. "Beauty." Used by permission.

Mullins, Brighde. "Click." Humana Festival, Louisville, KY, 2000. Used by permission.

Mullins, Brighde. Excerpt from STAGE by Brighde Mullins. Copyright by Brighde Mullins. Used with permission from Brighde Mullins.

Sanchez Scott, Milcha. "On Writing The Cuban Swimmer," by Milcha Sanchez Scott from ON NEW GROUND: CONTEMPORARY HISPANIC AMERICAN PLAYS. Copyright © 1993 by Milcha Sanchez Scott. used by permission of William Morris Agency.

Sanchez Scott, Milcha. "The Cuban Swimmer," by Milcha Sanchez Scott from The Cuban Swimmer. Copyright © 1984, 1988 by Milcha Sanchez

Scott. Used by permission of the William Morris Agency.

Scasserra, Michael: Excerpt selections from interview between Michael Scasserra and Anna Deavere Smith from *Performing Arts, Greater Los Angeles Edition*, July 1993, Vol. 27, No. 7, Pages 40, 41. Copyright © 1993, by Michael Scasserra. Used by permission of the author and the consent of the Centre Theatre Group.

Shakespeare, William. "All the World's a Stage," speech from "As You Like It," Act II, Scene 7; "Balcony Scene," from "Romeo and Juliet," Act II, Scene 2; "Band of brothers," speech from "Henry V," Act IV, Scene 3; "Quality of Mercy," speech from "The Merchant of Venice," Act IV, Scene 1; "To Be or Not to Be," speech from "Hamlet," Act III, Scene 1.

Smith, Anna Deveare. Scenes from the play "Twilight: Los Angeles 1992" (Dramatist's Play Service Edition). Reprinted by permission of Anna Deavere Smith and the Watkins/Loomis Agency.

Vaughn, Virginia Mason. "Black and White in Othello," from OTHELLO: A CONTEXTUAL HISTORY. Cambridge University Press 1994.

Wilde, Oscar. Scene, "Lady Bracknell Interviews Her Daughter's Suitor," from "The Importance of Being Earnest." St James's Theatre, London, February 14, 1895.

Wiles, David. "The Chorus as Democrat" from GREEK THEATRE PERFORMANCE: AN INTRODUCTION

Williams, Tennessee. "The Glass Menagerie." Copyright © 1945, renewed 1973 The University of the South. Reprinted by permission of Georges Borchardt, Inc. for the Estate of Tennessee Williams.

Wilson, August. Entire play from "Fences" copyright © 1986 by August Wilson. Used by permission of New American Library, an imprint of Penguin Publishing Group, a division of Penguin Random House LLC. All rights reserved

Wilson, August. Excerpt from an interview with August Wilson from "The Art of Theater No. 14," interviewed by Bonnie Lyons and George Plimpton, originally published in *The Paris Review*.

WRITING

Bloom, Harold. Excerpt from "Poetic Influence," from A MAP OF MISREADING by Harold Bloom. © 1975 by Oxford University Press. Used by permission of Oxford University Press, Inc., CCC Republication.

Brooks, Cleanth. Excerpts from "The Formalist Critic," copyright 1951 by Cleanth Brooks. Originally appeared in *The Kenyon Review*. Reprinted by permission of the publisher.

Clark, Michael. "James Baldwin's 'Sonny's Blues': Childhood, Light and Art," by Michael Clark. *College Language Association Journal* 29,

December 1985. Copyright 1985. Used with permission.

Deane, Seamus. "Joyce the Irishman," by Seamus Deane from THE CAMBRIDGE COMPANION TO JAMES JOYCE, 2nd edition, edited by Derek Attridge. Copyright © 1990, 2004 by Cambridge University Press. Reprinted by permission of Cambridge University Press.

Evans, Abbie Huston. "Wing-spread," from COLLECTED POEMS, by Abbie Huston Evans, Copyright 1950, 1952, 1953, 1956, 1960, 1961, 1966, 1970. Reprinted by permission of the University of Pittsburg Press.

Fish, Stanley. Reprinted by permission of the publisher from IS THERE A TEXT IN THIS CLASS?: THE AUTHORITY OF INTERPRETIVE COMMUNITIES by Stanley Fish, pp. 345–347, Cambridge, Mass.: Harvard University Press, Copyright © 1980 by the President and Fellows of Harvard College.

Freud, Sigmund. "The Nature of Dreams," from NEW INTRODUCTORY LECTURES ON PSYCHOANALYSIS. W. W. Norton & Company, Inc.

Frost, Robert. "Design," from AMERICAN POETRY: A MISCELLANY. First published by Harcourt Brace, 1922.

Jung, Carl. Republished with permission of Princeton University Press, from THE COLLECTIVE UNCONSCIOUS AND ARCHETYPES by Carl Jung Translated by R. F. C. Hull, 2nd edition © 2014; permission conveyed through Copyright Clearance Center, Inc.

Kazin, Alfred. Excerpt(s) from AN AMERICAN PROCESSION by Alfred Kazin, copyright © 1984 by Alfred Kazin. Used by permission of Alfred A. Knopf, an imprint of the Knopf Doubleday Publishing Group, a division of Penguin Random House LLC. All rights reserved

Kenner, Hugh. "Imagism," by Hugh Kenner from THE POUND ERA. University of California Press. Copyright © 1973. Reprinted by permission of University of California Press books provided by Copyright Clearance Center.

Leitch, Vincent B. From CULTURAL CRITICISM, LITERARY THEORY, by Vincent B. Leitch. Copyright © 1992 Columbia University Press. Reprinted with permission of the publisher."

Lukacs, Georg. "Content Determines Form," from REALISM IN OUR TIME. Harper & Row, 1964.

Millier, Brett Candlish. Excerpt from "Elusive Mastery: The Drafts of Elizabeth Bishop's 'One Art,'" by Brett Candlish Millier, © 1990 *New England Review*, Winter Edition.

Pagila, Camille. Excerpt(s) from BREAK, BLOW, BURN: CAMILLE PAGLIA READS FORTY-THREE OF THE WORLD'S BEST POEMS by Camille Paglia, copyright © 2005 by Camille Paglia. Used by permission of Pantheon Books, an imprint of the Knopf Doubleday Publishing

Group, a division of Random House LLC. All rights reserved.

Scholes, Robert. "How Do we Make a Poem?" from SEMIOTICS AND INTERPRETATION. Copyright 1982. Published by Yale University Press. All rights reserved. Used with permission of Yale University Press.

Scott, Sir Walter. From MEMOIRS OF THE LIFE OF SIR WALTER SCOTT vol. 1, p. 1. By John Gibson Lockhart. Houghton Mifflin and Co, 1901.

Showalter, Elaine. "Toward a Feminist Poetics," from WOMEN'S WRITING AND WRITING ABOUT WOMEN, edited by Mary Jacobus. Croon Helm, 1979. Used by permission of the author.

Straus, Nina Pelikan. Excerpt from "Transformations in 'The Metamorphosis,'" by Nina Pelikan Straus from *Journal Of Women in Culture and Society* 1./3. Copyright © 1989, by Nina Pelikan Straus. Used by permission of Nina Pelikan Straus.

Toth, Emily. Reprinted with permission of Toth, Emily. "The Source for Alcée Laballiere in 'The Storm,'" from KATE CHOPIN: A LIFE OF THE AUTHOR OF AWAKENING (William Morrow, 1990).

Volpe, Edmond. "Myth in Faulkner's 'Barn Burning,'" by Edmond Volpe from FAULKNER, THE UNAPPEASED IMAGINATION: A COLLECTION OF CRITICAL ESSAYS edited by Glen O. Carey (Whitston Publishing, 1980). Reprinted by permission of the author.

PHOTO CREDITS

Fiction

1: Jim McHugh/Los Angeles; 2: Jim McHugh/Los Angeles; 3: Sara Krulwich/The New York Times/Redux Pictures; 8: Chronicle/Alamy Stock Photo; 9: Ms 680/1389 f.24 The Lion, the King of the Animals, from "The Fables of Bidpai," c.1480 (vellum), German School, (15th century)/Musee Conde, Chantilly, France/Bridgeman Images; 12: Ian Woolcock/SuperStock; 17: Art Archive, The aa525683/Superstock; 29: Library of Congress Prints and Photographs Division [LC-USZC4-4907]; 36: PA Images/Alamy Stock Photo; 42: AP Images; 69: Everett Collection Historical/Alamy Stock Photo; 75: BALTEL/SIPA/Newscom; 79: Bernard Gotfryd/Premium Archive/Getty Images; 91: CSU Archives/Everett Collection Inc/Alamy Stock Photo; 115: Agence Opale/Alamy Stock Photo; 121: J. A. Scholten/Missouri History Museum, St. Louis; 125: CSU Archives/Everett Collection Inc/Alamy Stock Photo; 135: MICHAEL GOULDING/MCT/Newscom; 160: WENN Ltd/Alamy Stock Photo; 183: Pictorial Press Ltd/Alamy Stock Photo; 187: Shaun Higson/Portraits/Alamy Stock Photo; 190: World History Archive/Alamy Stock Photo; 195: Lebrecht Music & Arts/Alamy Stock Photo; 212: INTERFOTO/Alamy Stock Photo; 214: World History Archive/Alamy Stock Photo; 220: Jack Mitchell/Archive Photos/Getty Images; 226: Pictorial Press Ltd/Alamy Stock Photo; 233: Pictorial Press Ltd/Alamy Stock Photo; 239: Photo provided by the Oregon Historical Society. Courtesy of The Oregon Journal, Reprinted by permission from Barcroft Media; 250: AP Images; 259: Everett Collections; 260: Courtesy of Mary Hiecke; 269: Beth Gwinn/Writer Pictures/AP Images; 283: Everett Collections; 287: SNAP/ZUMAPRESS/Newscom; 296: CSU Archives/Everett Collection Inc/Alamy Stock Photo; 303: Library of Congress Prints and Photographs Division [LC-USZ62-67518]; 341: Chronicle/Alamy Stock Photo; 381: Everett Collection Historical/Alamy Stock Photo; 385: INTERFOTO/Alamy Stock Photo; 391: AP Images; 396: Everett Collection Inc/Alamy Stock Photo; 398: Apic/RETIRED/Hulton Archive/Getty Images; 437: © Joe McTyre/AJC/Associated Press; 439: © Floyd Jillson/Atlanta Journal-Constitution via AP; 440: Everett Collection Inc/Alamy Stock Photo; 448: Courtesy of American Bookmen. From Dodd, Mead and Co., NY. 1898; 450: Everett Collection, Inc./Alamy Stock Photo; 453: John Sherffius/National Endowment for the Arts; 455: Library of Congress Prints and Photographs Division [LC-USZ62-62310]; 457: Library of Congress Prints and Photographs Division [LC-USZ62-49035]; 469: Stanford University Press; 471: Ascent Releasing; 475: CSU Archives/Everett Collection Inc/Alamy Stock Photo; 482: NOAH BERGER/AP Images; 486: Photo by Suzanne England@2003; 489: Quilted coverlet (cotton), American School, (19th century)/Private Collection/Photo © Christie's Images/Bridgeman Images; 492: Oleksandr Molotkovych/Shutterstock; 493: Carlo Bavagnoli/The LIFE Picture Collection/Getty Images; 495: Agence Opale/Alamy Stock Photo; 503: Ana Segovia; 510: Everett Collection Historical/Alamy Stock Photo; 519: Heritage Image Partnership Ltd/Alamy Stock Photo; 529: INTERFOTO/Alamy Stock Photo; 536: Steven Senne/AP images; 543: Neal Boenzi/New York Times Co./Hulton Archive/Getty Images; 545: Chris Steele-Perkins/Magnum Photos; 548: Marty Lederhandler/AP Photo; 555: Reg Innell/Toronto Star/Getty Images; 562: Agence Opale/Alamy Stock Photo; 572: Anthony Pidgeon/Redferns/Getty Images; 581: Jamieson Fry; 588: Edward Steichen/Conde Nast Collection/Getty Images; 603: Dpa picture alliance/Alamy Stock Photo; 611: Art Collection 3/Alamy Stock Photo; 621: Everett Collection Historical/Alamy Stock Photo; 629: Photo 12/Archives Snark/Alamy Stock Photo; 634: Adrian Mueller/Aurora Photos/Alamy Stock Photo; 648: World History Archive/Alamy Stock Photo; 651: David Pickoff/AP Images; 663: @ Krysta Ficca; 667: Beowulf Sheehan/ZUMA Press/Newscom; 673: Ulf Andersen/Getty Images Entertainment/Getty Images; 684: Ian Dagnall Computing/Alamy Stock Photo.

Poetry

687: Martin Klimek (CC-BY-4.0). Courtesy of the John D. and Catherine T. MacArthur Foundation; 688: Steve Yeater/AP Images; 689: Thomas W. Roster; 703: Everett Collection; 726: Fotosearch/Stringer/Archive Photos/Getty Images; 744: Dan Streck Photography; 748: Oleg Golovnev/Shutterstock; 749: Library of Congress Prints and Photographs Division [LC-USZ62-70064]; 763: AP Images; 779: David Lees/Corbis Historical/Getty Images; 801: Everett Collection; 824: Everett Collection; 842: AP Images; 859:

Everett Collection Inc. /Alamy Stock Photo; 879: John Psaropoulos; 889: Erich Lessing/Art Resource, NY; 900: Library of Congress Prints and Photographs Division [LC-USZ62-89948] 913: Art Collection 4/Alamy Stock Photo; 915: Library of Congress Prints and Photographs Division [LC-USZ62-87604]; 935: Diane Thiel; 956: Rhina P. Espaillat; 961: Art Collection 3/Alamy Stock Photo; 962: RDA/Archive Photos/Getty Images; 964: Everett Collection Inc/Alamy Stock Photo; 965: Mary Kent/AP Images; 967: Everett Collection Historical/Alamy Stock Photo; 986: Courtesy of American Bookmen. From Dodd, Mead and Co., NY. 1898; 992: Amherst College; 992: Everett Collection Historical/Alamy Stock Photo; 992: Everett Collection; 998: Caricature by John Sherffius, Courtesy of the National Endowment for the Arts; 999: Lebrecht Authors/Lebrecht Music & Arts/Alamy Stock Photo; 1006: MPI/Archive Photos/Getty Images; 1013: Hulton Archive/ Archive Photos/Getty Images; 1015: Michael Ochs Archives/Getty Images; 1020: Fred Stein Archive/Archive Photos/Getty Images; 1023: Eric Schaal/The LIFE Picture Collection/Getty Images; 1033: Eric Schaal/The LIFE Picture Collection/Getty Images; 1036: B. Anthony Stewart/ National Geographic/Getty Images; 1039: Randy Duchaine/Alamy Stock Photo; 1042: MS Am 2560 (179a) by Permission of the Harvard Library, Houghton University; 1043: Chronicle/Alamy Stock Photo; 1049: National Poetry Foundation; 1051: TopFoto/The Image Works; 1054: Pictorial Press Ltd/Alamy Stock Photo; 1060: Aaron A. Abeyta; 1062: Ramon Espinosa/AP Images; 1066: Lebrecht Authors/Lebrecht Music & Arts/Alamy Stock Photo; 1068: Scala/Art Resource, NY; 1069: Everett Collection; 1072: Everett Collection Inc./ Alamy Stock Photo; 1075: MAGNOLIA PICTURES/MONTFORT, MICHAEL/Album/Newscom; 1079: Lorenzo Dalberto/Alamy Stock Photo; 1080: Library of Congress Prints and Photographs Division [LC-USZ62-116342]; 1081: Luigi Ciuffetelli; 1086: CSU Archives/Everett Collection Inc/ Alamy Stock Photo; 1090: Juan Felipe Herrera, "El ángel de la guarda" from LOTERÍA CARDS AND FORTUNE POEMS: A BOOK OF LIVES, with linocuts by Artemil Rodrígues. Copyright © 1999 by Juan Felipe Herrera. Reprinted with the permission of The Permissions Company, Inc., on behalf of City Lights Books, www.citylights.com; 1092: Popperfoto/Getty Images; 1095: Hulton Archive/ Getty Images; 1097: GL Archive/Alamy Stock Photo; 1099: TopFoto/The Image Works; 1101: Steven Lewis; 1103: Copyright Shirley Geok-Lin Lim; 1107: Photo Researchers/Science History Images/Alamy Stock Photo; 1108: Pictorial Press Ltd/Alamy Stock Photo; 1110: Beowulf Sheehan/ ZUMAPRESS.com/Newscom; 1111: Bygone Collection/Alamy Stock Photo; 1112: Science History Images/Alamy Stock Photo; 1117: Everett Collection; 1121: Philip Simic/Newscom; 1124: John Eddy. From School Figures, by Cathy Song,

© 1994. Reprinted by permission of the University of Pittsburgh Press; 1125: AP Image; 1126: Sueddeutsche Zeitung Photo/The Image Works; 1127: Photo by Raul C. Contreras/Amy Uyematsu; 1130: Library of Congress Prints and Photographs Division [LC-USZ62-82784]; 1131: Fine Art Images/Heritage Image Partnership Ltd/Alamy Stock Photo; 1134: Pictorial Press Ltd/Alamy Stock Photo.

Drama

1137: Joseph Marzullo/WENN.com/Newscom; 1138: Frank Franklin II/AP Images; 1139: Timothy Hiatt/Getty Images Entertainment/Getty Images; 1145: TRIFLES by Susan Glaspell. Original 1916 Performance; Wharf Theater, Provincetown, Massachusetts; 1158: AP Images; 1168: Doctor Faustus, from the Utah Shakespeare Festival's 2005 production; 1173: Elnur/Shutterstock; 1176: Geraint Lewis/Alamy Stock Photo; 1180: James Leynse Photography; 1188: Kevin Watkins Photography; 1193: Janette Pellegrini/WireImage/ Getty Images; 1196: The Granger, NYC; 1198: R. C. Flickinger; 1199: V J Matthew/Shutterstock; 1202: Antiqueimagesdotnet/123RF; 1203: Merlyn Severn/Picture Post/Getty Images; 1243: Swope, Martha/New York Public Library; 1284: Oli Scarff/Getty Images News/Getty Images; 1285: Andrea Pistolesi/The Image Bank/Getty Images; 1287: Moviestore Collection Ltd/Alamy Stock Photo; 1288: Entertainment Pictures/ Alamy Stock Photo; 1293: Moviestore collection Ltd/Alamy Stock Photo; 1294: Bettina Strenske/Vibrant Pictures/Alamy Stock Photo; 1295: AF archive/Alamy Stock Photo; 1296: Georgios Kollidas/Alamy Stock Photo; 1297: Martha Swope/The New York Public Library; 1303: Photo by Karl Hugh. Copyright Utah Shakespeare Festival, 2008; 1315: Photo by Karl Hugh. Copyright Utah Shakespeare Festival, 2008; 1317: Photo by Karl Hugh. Copyright Utah Shakespeare Festival, 2008; 1324: Photo by Karl Hugh. Copyright Utah Shakespeare Festival, 2008; 1332: Photo by Karl Hugh. Copyright Utah Shakespeare Festival, 2008; 1338: Photo by Karl Hugh. Copyright Utah Shakespeare Festival, 2008; 1341: Photo by Karl Hugh. Copyright Utah Shakespeare Festival, 2008; 1352: Photo by Karl Hugh. Copyright Utah Shakespeare Festival, 2008; 1358: Photo by Karl Hugh. Copyright Utah Shakespeare Festival, 2008; 1362: Photo by Karl Hugh. Copyright Utah Shakespeare Festival, 2008; 1372: Photo by Karl Hugh. Copyright Utah Shakespeare Festival, 2008. 1374: Photo by Karl Hugh. Copyright Utah Shakespeare Festival, 2008; 1377: Photo by Karl Hugh. Copyright Utah Shakespeare Festival, 2008; 1380: Photo by Karl Hugh. Copyright Utah Shakespeare Festival, 2008; 1387: Photo by Karl Hugh. Copyright Utah Shakespeare Festival, 2008; 1389: Photo by Karl Hugh. Copyright

Utah Shakespeare Festival, 2008; 1395: Photo by Karl Hugh. Copyright Utah Shakespeare Festival, 2008; 1396: Photo by Karl Hugh. Copyright Utah Shakespeare Festival, 2008; 1401: Photofest; 1406: Utah Shakespeare Festival; 1409: Utah Shakespeare Festival; 1413: Utah Shakespeare Festival; 1418: Utah Shakespeare Festival; 1420: Utah Shakespeare Festival; 1423: Utah Shakespeare Festival; 1426: Utah Shakespeare Festival; 1432: Utah Shakespeare Festival; 1439: Utah Shakespeare Festival; 1443: Utah Shakespeare Festival; 1449: Utah Shakespeare Festival; 1455: Utah Shakespeare Festival; 1461: Utah Shakespeare Festival; 1467: Utah Shakespeare Festival; 1469: Donald Cooper/Photostage; 1475: Classic Image/Alamy Stock Photo; 1486: Everett Collection; 1487: AF archive/Alamy Stock Photo; 1548: Everett Collection Historical/Alamy Stock Photo; 1550: Harvard Theatre Collection; 1551: Geraint Lewis/Alamy Stock Photo; 1601: Fine Art Images/Heritage Image Partnership Ltd/Alamy Stock Photo; 1604: Everett Collection; 1605: Cineplex-Odeon Pictures/courtesy Everett Collection; 1647: Library of Congress Prints and Photographs Division [LC-USZ62-128957]; 1653: Mark Garvin; 1663: Courtesy of Milcha Sanchez-Scott; 1666: Jay Thompson Archives/Center Theatre Group; 1670: Jay Thompson Archives/Center Theatre Group; 1671: Joe Kohen/WireImage/Getty Images; 1681: Suzan Hanson and Herbert Perry in the American Repertory Theater's 2003 world premiere production of the "The Sound of a Voice" in Cambridge, Massachusetts. Photo by Richard Feldman; 1695: Adam Rountree/Getty Images News/Getty Images; 1701: Jeff Wheeler/Minneapolis Star T/ZUMA Press/Alamy Stock Photo; 1708: Cam Sanders/Brighde Mullins; 1711: 1987 Ron Scherl/StageImage/The Image Works; 1712: JM11 WENN/Newscom; 1758: RICH SUGG/KRT/Newscom.

Writing

1759: CSU Archives/Everett Collection/Alamy Stock Photo; 1845: Scala/Art Resource, New York.

INDEX OF MAJOR THEMES

If you prefer to study by theme or want to research possible subjects for an essay, here is a listing of stories, poems, and plays arranged into sixteen major themes.

Comedy and Satire

Death

Faith, Doubt, and Religious Vision

Families/Parents and Children

Loneliness and Alienation

Love and Desire

Men and Women

Nature

Race, Class, and Culture

War, Murder, and Violence

Woman's Identity

INDEX OF FIRST LINES OF POETRY

INDEX OF AUTHORS AND TITLES

Every page number immediately following a writer's name indicates a quotation from or reference to that writer. A number in **bold** refers you to the page on which you will find the author's biography.

INDEX OF LITERARY TERMS

Page numbers indicate discussion of terms in anthology. A page number in **bold** indicates entry in the **Glossary of Literary Terms**. The letter "n" following a page number indicates entry in a note.